Oxford Dictionary of National Biography

IN ASSOCIATION WITH

The British Academy

From the earliest times to the year 2000

Edited by

H. C. G. Matthew

and

Brian Harrison

Volume 40

Murrell–Nooth

OXFORD

UNIVERSITY PRESS

OXFORD
UNIVERSITY PRESS

Great Clarendon Street, Oxford OX2 6DP

Oxford University Press is a department of the University of Oxford.
It furthers the University's objective of excellence in research, scholarship,
and education by publishing worldwide in

Oxford New York

Auckland Bangkok Buenos Aires Cape Town
Chennai Dar es Salaam Delhi Hong Kong Istanbul Karachi
Kolkata Kuala Lumpur Madrid Melbourne Mexico City Mumbai Nairobi
São Paulo Shanghai Taipei Tokyo Toronto

Oxford is a registered trade mark of Oxford University Press
in the UK and in certain other countries

Published in the United States
by Oxford University Press Inc., New York

© Oxford University Press 2004

Illustrations © individual copyright holders as listed in
'Picture credits', and reproduced with permission

Database right Oxford University Press (maker)

First published 2004

All rights reserved. No part of this material may be reproduced,
stored in a retrieval system, or transmitted, in any form or by any means,
without the prior permission in writing of Oxford University Press,
or as expressly permitted by law, or under terms agreed with the appropriate
reprographics rights organization. Enquiries concerning reproduction
outside the scope of the above should be sent to the Rights Department,
Oxford University Press, at the address above

You must not circulate this book in any other binding or cover
and you must impose this same condition on any acquirer

British Library Cataloguing in Publication Data
Data available

Library of Congress Cataloging in Publication Data
Data available: for details see volume 1, p. iv

ISBN 0-19-861390-3 (this volume)
ISBN 0-19-861411-X (set of sixty volumes)

Text captured by Alliance Phototypesetters, Pondicherry
Illustrations reproduced and archived by
Alliance Graphics Ltd, UK
Typeset in OUP Swift by Interactive Sciences Limited, Gloucester
Printed in Great Britain on acid-free paper by
Butler and Tanner Ltd,
Frome, Somerset

LIST OF ABBREVIATIONS

1 General abbreviations

AB	bachelor of arts
ABC	Australian Broadcasting Corporation
ABC TV	ABC Television
act.	active
A$	Australian dollar
AD	*anno domini*
AFC	Air Force Cross
AIDS	acquired immune deficiency syndrome
AK	Alaska
AL	Alabama
A level	advanced level [examination]
ALS	associate of the Linnean Society
AM	master of arts
AMICE	associate member of the Institution of Civil Engineers
ANZAC	Australian and New Zealand Army Corps
appx *pl.* appxs	appendix(es)
AR	Arkansas
ARA	associate of the Royal Academy
ARCA	associate of the Royal College of Art
ARCM	associate of the Royal College of Music
ARCO	associate of the Royal College of Organists
ARIBA	associate of the Royal Institute of British Architects
ARP	air-raid precautions
ARRC	associate of the Royal Red Cross
ARSA	associate of the Royal Scottish Academy
art.	article / item
ASC	Army Service Corps
Asch	Austrian Schilling
ASDIC	Antisubmarine Detection Investigation Committee
ATS	Auxiliary Territorial Service
ATV	Associated Television
Aug	August
AZ	Arizona
b.	born
BA	bachelor of arts
BA (Admin.)	bachelor of arts (administration)
BAFTA	British Academy of Film and Television Arts
BAO	bachelor of arts in obstetrics
bap.	baptized
BBC	British Broadcasting Corporation / Company
BC	before Christ
BCE	before the common (*or* Christian) era
BCE	bachelor of civil engineering
BCG	bacillus of Calmette and Guérin [inoculation against tuberculosis]
BCh	bachelor of surgery
BChir	bachelor of surgery
BCL	bachelor of civil law

BCnL	bachelor of canon law
BCom	bachelor of commerce
BD	bachelor of divinity
BEd	bachelor of education
BEng	bachelor of engineering
bk *pl.* bks	book(s)
BL	bachelor of law / letters / literature
BLitt	bachelor of letters
BM	bachelor of medicine
BMus	bachelor of music
BP	before present
BP	British Petroleum
Bros.	Brothers
BS	(1) bachelor of science; (2) bachelor of surgery; (3) British standard
BSc	bachelor of science
BSc (Econ.)	bachelor of science (economics)
BSc (Eng.)	bachelor of science (engineering)
bt	baronet
BTh	bachelor of theology
bur.	buried
C.	command [identifier for published parliamentary papers]
c.	*circa*
c.	*capitulum pl. capitula*: chapter(s)
CA	California
Cantab.	Cantabrigiensis
cap.	*capitulum pl. capitula*: chapter(s)
CB	companion of the Bath
CBE	commander of the Order of the British Empire
CBS	Columbia Broadcasting System
cc	cubic centimetres
C$	Canadian dollar
CD	compact disc
Cd	command [identifier for published parliamentary papers]
CE	Common (*or* Christian) Era
cent.	century
cf.	compare
CH	Companion of Honour
chap.	chapter
ChB	bachelor of surgery
CI	Imperial Order of the Crown of India
CIA	Central Intelligence Agency
CID	Criminal Investigation Department
CIE	companion of the Order of the Indian Empire
Cie	Compagnie
CLit	companion of literature
CM	master of surgery
cm	centimetre(s)

Cmd	command [identifier for published parliamentary papers]		edn	edition
CMG	companion of the Order of St Michael and St George		EEC	European Economic Community
			EFTA	European Free Trade Association
Cmnd	command [identifier for published parliamentary papers]		EICS	East India Company Service
			EMI	Electrical and Musical Industries (Ltd)
CO	Colorado		Eng.	English
Co.	company		enl.	enlarged
co.	county		ENSA	Entertainments National Service Association
col. *pl.* cols.	column(s)		ep. *pl.* epp.	*epistola(e)*
Corp.	corporation		ESP	extra-sensory perception
CSE	certificate of secondary education		esp.	especially
CSI	companion of the Order of the Star of India		esq.	esquire
CT	Connecticut		est.	estimate / estimated
CVO	commander of the Royal Victorian Order		EU	European Union
cwt	hundredweight		ex	sold by (*lit.* out of)
$	(American) dollar		excl.	excludes / excluding
d.	(1) penny (pence); (2) died		exh.	exhibited
DBE	dame commander of the Order of the British Empire		exh. cat.	exhibition catalogue
			f. *pl.* ff.	following [pages]
DCH	diploma in child health		FA	Football Association
DCh	doctor of surgery		FACP	fellow of the American College of Physicians
DCL	doctor of civil law		facs.	facsimile
DCnL	doctor of canon law		FANY	First Aid Nursing Yeomanry
DCVO	dame commander of the Royal Victorian Order		FBA	fellow of the British Academy
DD	doctor of divinity		FBI	Federation of British Industries
DE	Delaware		FCS	fellow of the Chemical Society
Dec	December		Feb	February
dem.	demolished		FEng	fellow of the Fellowship of Engineering
DEng	doctor of engineering		FFCM	fellow of the Faculty of Community Medicine
des.	destroyed		FGS	fellow of the Geological Society
DFC	Distinguished Flying Cross		fig.	figure
DipEd	diploma in education		FIMechE	fellow of the Institution of Mechanical Engineers
DipPsych	diploma in psychiatry			
diss.	dissertation		FL	Florida
DL	deputy lieutenant		*fl.*	*floruit*
DLitt	doctor of letters		FLS	fellow of the Linnean Society
DLittCelt	doctor of Celtic letters		FM	frequency modulation
DM	(1) Deutschmark; (2) doctor of medicine; (3) doctor of musical arts		fol. *pl.* fols.	folio(s)
			Fr	French francs
DMus	doctor of music		Fr.	French
DNA	dioxyribonucleic acid		FRAeS	fellow of the Royal Aeronautical Society
doc.	document		FRAI	fellow of the Royal Anthropological Institute
DOL	doctor of oriental learning		FRAM	fellow of the Royal Academy of Music
DPH	diploma in public health		FRAS	(1) fellow of the Royal Asiatic Society; (2) fellow of the Royal Astronomical Society
DPhil	doctor of philosophy			
DPM	diploma in psychological medicine		FRCM	fellow of the Royal College of Music
DSC	Distinguished Service Cross		FRCO	fellow of the Royal College of Organists
DSc	doctor of science		FRCOG	fellow of the Royal College of Obstetricians and Gynaecologists
DSc (Econ.)	doctor of science (economics)			
DSc (Eng.)	doctor of science (engineering)		FRCP(C)	fellow of the Royal College of Physicians of Canada
DSM	Distinguished Service Medal			
DSO	companion of the Distinguished Service Order		FRCP (Edin.)	fellow of the Royal College of Physicians of Edinburgh
DSocSc	doctor of social science		FRCP (Lond.)	fellow of the Royal College of Physicians of London
DTech	doctor of technology			
DTh	doctor of theology		FRCPath	fellow of the Royal College of Pathologists
DTM	diploma in tropical medicine		FRCPsych	fellow of the Royal College of Psychiatrists
DTMH	diploma in tropical medicine and hygiene		FRCS	fellow of the Royal College of Surgeons
DU	doctor of the university		FRGS	fellow of the Royal Geographical Society
DUniv	doctor of the university		FRIBA	fellow of the Royal Institute of British Architects
dwt	pennyweight		FRICS	fellow of the Royal Institute of Chartered Surveyors
EC	European Community			
ed. *pl.* eds.	edited / edited by / editor(s)		FRS	fellow of the Royal Society
Edin.	Edinburgh		FRSA	fellow of the Royal Society of Arts

FRSCM	fellow of the Royal School of Church Music	ISO	companion of the Imperial Service Order
FRSE	fellow of the Royal Society of Edinburgh	It.	Italian
FRSL	fellow of the Royal Society of Literature	ITA	Independent Television Authority
FSA	fellow of the Society of Antiquaries	ITV	Independent Television
ft	foot *pl.* feet	Jan	January
FTCL	fellow of Trinity College of Music, London	JP	justice of the peace
ft-lb per min.	foot-pounds per minute [unit of horsepower]	jun.	junior
FZS	fellow of the Zoological Society	KB	knight of the Order of the Bath
GA	Georgia	KBE	knight commander of the Order of the British Empire
GBE	knight or dame grand cross of the Order of the British Empire	KC	king's counsel
GCB	knight grand cross of the Order of the Bath	kcal	kilocalorie
GCE	general certificate of education	KCB	knight commander of the Order of the Bath
GCH	knight grand cross of the Royal Guelphic Order	KCH	knight commander of the Royal Guelphic Order
GCHQ	government communications headquarters	KCIE	knight commander of the Order of the Indian Empire
GCIE	knight grand commander of the Order of the Indian Empire	KCMG	knight commander of the Order of St Michael and St George
GCMG	knight or dame grand cross of the Order of St Michael and St George	KCSI	knight commander of the Order of the Star of India
GCSE	general certificate of secondary education	KCVO	knight commander of the Royal Victorian Order
GCSI	knight grand commander of the Order of the Star of India	keV	kilo-electron-volt
GCStJ	bailiff or dame grand cross of the order of St John of Jerusalem	KG	knight of the Order of the Garter
		KGB	[Soviet committee of state security]
GCVO	knight or dame grand cross of the Royal Victorian Order	KH	knight of the Royal Guelphic Order
GEC	General Electric Company	KLM	Koninklijke Luchtvaart Maatschappij (Royal Dutch Air Lines)
Ger.	German	km	kilometre(s)
GI	government (*or* general) issue	KP	knight of the Order of St Patrick
GMT	Greenwich mean time	KS	Kansas
GP	general practitioner	KT	knight of the Order of the Thistle
GPU	[Soviet special police unit]	kt	knight
GSO	general staff officer	KY	Kentucky
Heb.	Hebrew	£	pound(s) sterling
HEICS	Honourable East India Company Service	£E	Egyptian pound
HI	Hawaii	L	lira *pl.* lire
HIV	human immunodeficiency virus	l. *pl.* ll.	line(s)
HK$	Hong Kong dollar	LA	Lousiana
HM	his / her majesty('s)	LAA	light anti-aircraft
HMAS	his / her majesty's Australian ship	LAH	licentiate of the Apothecaries' Hall, Dublin
HMNZS	his / her majesty's New Zealand ship	Lat.	Latin
HMS	his / her majesty's ship	lb	pound(s), unit of weight
HMSO	His / Her Majesty's Stationery Office	LDS	licence in dental surgery
HMV	His Master's Voice	*lit.*	literally
Hon.	Honourable	LittB	bachelor of letters
hp	horsepower	LittD	doctor of letters
hr	hour(s)	LKQCPI	licentiate of the King and Queen's College of Physicians, Ireland
HRH	his / her royal highness	LLA	lady literate in arts
HTV	Harlech Television	LLB	bachelor of laws
IA	Iowa	LLD	doctor of laws
ibid.	*ibidem*: in the same place	LLM	master of laws
ICI	Imperial Chemical Industries (Ltd)	LM	licentiate in midwifery
ID	Idaho	LP	long-playing record
IL	Illinois	LRAM	licentiate of the Royal Academy of Music
illus.	illustration	LRCP	licentiate of the Royal College of Physicians
illustr.	illustrated	LRCPS (Glasgow)	licentiate of the Royal College of Physicians and Surgeons of Glasgow
IN	Indiana	LRCS	licentiate of the Royal College of Surgeons
in.	inch(es)	LSA	licentiate of the Society of Apothecaries
Inc.	Incorporated	LSD	lysergic acid diethylamide
incl.	includes / including	LVO	lieutenant of the Royal Victorian Order
IOU	I owe you	M. *pl.* MM.	Monsieur *pl.* Messieurs
IQ	intelligence quotient	m	metre(s)
Ir£	Irish pound		
IRA	Irish Republican Army		

m. *pl.* mm.	membrane(s)
MA	(1) Massachusetts; (2) master of arts
MAI	master of engineering
MB	bachelor of medicine
MBA	master of business administration
MBE	member of the Order of the British Empire
MC	Military Cross
MCC	Marylebone Cricket Club
MCh	master of surgery
MChir	master of surgery
MCom	master of commerce
MD	(1) doctor of medicine; (2) Maryland
MDMA	methylenedioxymethamphetamine
ME	Maine
MEd	master of education
MEng	master of engineering
MEP	member of the European parliament
MG	Morris Garages
MGM	Metro-Goldwyn-Mayer
Mgr	Monsignor
MI	(1) Michigan; (2) military intelligence
MI1c	[secret intelligence department]
MI5	[military intelligence department]
MI6	[secret intelligence department]
MI9	[secret escape service]
MICE	member of the Institution of Civil Engineers
MIEE	member of the Institution of Electrical Engineers
min.	minute(s)
Mk	mark
ML	(1) licentiate of medicine; (2) master of laws
MLitt	master of letters
Mlle	Mademoiselle
mm	millimetre(s)
Mme	Madame
MN	Minnesota
MO	Missouri
MOH	medical officer of health
MP	member of parliament
m.p.h.	miles per hour
MPhil	master of philosophy
MRCP	member of the Royal College of Physicians
MRCS	member of the Royal College of Surgeons
MRCVS	member of the Royal College of Veterinary Surgeons
MRIA	member of the Royal Irish Academy
MS	(1) master of science; (2) Mississippi
MS *pl.* MSS	manuscript(s)
MSc	master of science
MSc (Econ.)	master of science (economics)
MT	Montana
MusB	bachelor of music
MusBac	bachelor of music
MusD	doctor of music
MV	motor vessel
MVO	member of the Royal Victorian Order
n. *pl.* nn.	note(s)
NAAFI	Navy, Army, and Air Force Institutes
NASA	National Aeronautics and Space Administration
NATO	North Atlantic Treaty Organization
NBC	National Broadcasting Corporation
NC	North Carolina
NCO	non-commissioned officer
ND	North Dakota
n.d.	no date
NE	Nebraska
nem. con.	*nemine contradicente*: unanimously
new ser.	new series
NH	New Hampshire
NHS	National Health Service
NJ	New Jersey
NKVD	[Soviet people's commissariat for internal affairs]
NM	New Mexico
nm	nanometre(s)
no. *pl.* nos.	number(s)
Nov	November
n.p.	no place [of publication]
NS	new style
NV	Nevada
NY	New York
NZBS	New Zealand Broadcasting Service
OBE	officer of the Order of the British Empire
obit.	obituary
Oct	October
OCTU	officer cadets training unit
OECD	Organization for Economic Co-operation and Development
OEEC	Organization for European Economic Co-operation
OFM	order of Friars Minor [Franciscans]
OFMCap	Ordine Frati Minori Cappucini: member of the Capuchin order
OH	Ohio
OK	Oklahoma
O level	ordinary level [examination]
OM	Order of Merit
OP	order of Preachers [Dominicans]
op. *pl.* opp.	opus *pl.* opera
OPEC	Organization of Petroleum Exporting Countries
OR	Oregon
orig.	original
OS	old style
OSB	Order of St Benedict
OTC	Officers' Training Corps
OWS	Old Watercolour Society
Oxon.	Oxoniensis
p. *pl.* pp.	page(s)
PA	Pennsylvania
p.a.	per annum
para.	paragraph
PAYE	pay as you earn
pbk *pl.* pbks	paperback(s)
per.	[during the] period
PhD	doctor of philosophy
pl.	(1) plate(s); (2) plural
priv. coll.	private collection
pt *pl.* pts	part(s)
pubd	published
PVC	polyvinyl chloride
q. *pl.* qq.	(1) question(s); (2) quire(s)
QC	queen's counsel
R	rand
R.	Rex / Regina
r	recto
r.	reigned / ruled
RA	Royal Academy / Royal Academician

RAC	Royal Automobile Club		Skr	Swedish krona
RAF	Royal Air Force		Span.	Spanish
RAFVR	Royal Air Force Volunteer Reserve		SPCK	Society for Promoting Christian Knowledge
RAM	[member of the] Royal Academy of Music		SS	(1) Santissimi; (2) Schutzstaffel; (3) steam ship
RAMC	Royal Army Medical Corps		STB	bachelor of theology
RCA	Royal College of Art		STD	doctor of theology
RCNC	Royal Corps of Naval Constructors		STM	master of theology
RCOG	Royal College of Obstetricians and Gynaecologists		STP	doctor of theology
RDI	royal designer for industry		*supp.*	supposedly
RE	Royal Engineers		suppl. *pl.* suppls.	supplement(s)
repr. *pl.* reprs.	reprint(s) / reprinted		s.v.	*sub verbo* / *sub voce*: under the word / heading
repro.	reproduced		SY	steam yacht
rev.	revised / revised by / reviser / revision		TA	Territorial Army
Revd	Reverend		TASS	[Soviet news agency]
RHA	Royal Hibernian Academy		TB	tuberculosis (*lit.* tubercle bacillus)
RI	(1) Rhode Island; (2) Royal Institute of Painters in Water-Colours		TD	(1) *teachtaí dála* (member of the Dáil); (2) territorial decoration
RIBA	Royal Institute of British Architects		TN	Tennessee
RIN	Royal Indian Navy		TNT	trinitrotoluene
RM	Reichsmark		trans.	translated / translated by / translation / translator
RMS	Royal Mail steamer		TT	tourist trophy
RN	Royal Navy		TUC	Trades Union Congress
RNA	ribonucleic acid		TX	Texas
RNAS	Royal Naval Air Service		U-boat	*Unterseeboot*: submarine
RNR	Royal Naval Reserve		Ufa	Universum-Film AG
RNVR	Royal Naval Volunteer Reserve		UMIST	University of Manchester Institute of Science and Technology
RO	Record Office		UN	United Nations
r.p.m.	revolutions per minute		UNESCO	United Nations Educational, Scientific, and Cultural Organization
RRS	royal research ship		UNICEF	United Nations International Children's Emergency Fund
Rs	rupees		unpubd	unpublished
RSA	(1) Royal Scottish Academician; (2) Royal Society of Arts		USS	United States ship
RSPCA	Royal Society for the Prevention of Cruelty to Animals		UT	Utah
Rt Hon.	Right Honourable		*v*	verso
Rt Revd	Right Reverend		v.	versus
RUC	Royal Ulster Constabulary		VA	Virginia
Russ.	Russian		VAD	Voluntary Aid Detachment
RWS	Royal Watercolour Society		VC	Victoria Cross
S4C	Sianel Pedwar Cymru		VE-day	victory in Europe day
s.	shilling(s)		Ven.	Venerable
s.a.	*sub anno*: under the year		VJ-day	victory over Japan day
SABC	South African Broadcasting Corporation		vol. *pl.* vols.	volume(s)
SAS	Special Air Service		VT	Vermont
SC	South Carolina		WA	Washington [state]
ScD	doctor of science		WAAC	Women's Auxiliary Army Corps
S$	Singapore dollar		WAAF	Women's Auxiliary Air Force
SD	South Dakota		WEA	Workers' Educational Association
sec.	second(s)		WHO	World Health Organization
sel.	selected		WI	Wisconsin
sen.	senior		WRAF	Women's Royal Air Force
Sept	September		WRNS	Women's Royal Naval Service
ser.	series		WV	West Virginia
SHAPE	supreme headquarters allied powers, Europe		WVS	Women's Voluntary Service
SIDRO	Société Internationale d'Énergie Hydro-Électrique		WY	Wyoming
sig. *pl.* sigs.	signature(s)		¥	yen
sing.	singular		YMCA	Young Men's Christian Association
SIS	Secret Intelligence Service		YWCA	Young Women's Christian Association
SJ	Society of Jesus			

2 Institution abbreviations

All Souls Oxf.	All Souls College, Oxford	Garr. Club	Garrick Club, London
AM Oxf.	Ashmolean Museum, Oxford	Girton Cam.	Girton College, Cambridge
Balliol Oxf.	Balliol College, Oxford	GL	Guildhall Library, London
BBC WAC	BBC Written Archives Centre, Reading	Glos. RO	Gloucestershire Record Office, Gloucester
Beds. & Luton ARS	Bedfordshire and Luton Archives and Record Service, Bedford	Gon. & Caius Cam.	Gonville and Caius College, Cambridge
		Gov. Art Coll.	Government Art Collection
Berks. RO	Berkshire Record Office, Reading	GS Lond.	Geological Society of London
BFI	British Film Institute, London	Hants. RO	Hampshire Record Office, Winchester
BFI NFTVA	British Film Institute, London, National Film and Television Archive	Harris Man. Oxf.	Harris Manchester College, Oxford
		Harvard TC	Harvard Theatre Collection, Harvard University, Cambridge, Massachusetts, Nathan Marsh Pusey Library
BGS	British Geological Survey, Keyworth, Nottingham		
Birm. CA	Birmingham Central Library, Birmingham City Archives	Harvard U.	Harvard University, Cambridge, Massachusetts
		Harvard U., Houghton L.	Harvard University, Cambridge, Massachusetts, Houghton Library
Birm. CL	Birmingham Central Library		
BL	British Library, London	Herefs. RO	Herefordshire Record Office, Hereford
BL NSA	British Library, London, National Sound Archive	Herts. ALS	Hertfordshire Archives and Local Studies, Hertford
BL OIOC	British Library, London, Oriental and India Office Collections	Hist. Soc. Penn.	Historical Society of Pennsylvania, Philadelphia
BLPES	London School of Economics and Political Science, British Library of Political and Economic Science	HLRO	House of Lords Record Office, London
		Hult. Arch.	Hulton Archive, London and New York
		Hunt. L.	Huntington Library, San Marino, California
BM	British Museum, London	ICL	Imperial College, London
Bodl. Oxf.	Bodleian Library, Oxford	Inst. CE	Institution of Civil Engineers, London
Bodl. RH	Bodleian Library of Commonwealth and African Studies at Rhodes House, Oxford	Inst. EE	Institution of Electrical Engineers, London
		IWM	Imperial War Museum, London
Borth. Inst.	Borthwick Institute of Historical Research, University of York	IWM FVA	Imperial War Museum, London, Film and Video Archive
Boston PL	Boston Public Library, Massachusetts	IWM SA	Imperial War Museum, London, Sound Archive
Bristol RO	Bristol Record Office		
Bucks. RLSS	Buckinghamshire Records and Local Studies Service, Aylesbury	JRL	John Rylands University Library of Manchester
		King's AC Cam.	King's College Archives Centre, Cambridge
CAC Cam.	Churchill College, Cambridge, Churchill Archives Centre	King's Cam.	King's College, Cambridge
		King's Lond.	King's College, London
Cambs. AS	Cambridgeshire Archive Service	King's Lond., Liddell Hart C.	King's College, London, Liddell Hart Centre for Military Archives
CCC Cam.	Corpus Christi College, Cambridge		
CCC Oxf.	Corpus Christi College, Oxford	Lancs. RO	Lancashire Record Office, Preston
Ches. & Chester ALSS	Cheshire and Chester Archives and Local Studies Service	L. Cong.	Library of Congress, Washington, DC
		Leics. RO	Leicestershire, Leicester, and Rutland Record Office, Leicester
Christ Church Oxf.	Christ Church, Oxford		
Christies	Christies, London	Lincs. Arch.	Lincolnshire Archives, Lincoln
City Westm. AC	City of Westminster Archives Centre, London	Linn. Soc.	Linnean Society of London
CKS	Centre for Kentish Studies, Maidstone	LMA	London Metropolitan Archives
CLRO	Corporation of London Records Office	LPL	Lambeth Palace, London
Coll. Arms	College of Arms, London	Lpool RO	Liverpool Record Office and Local Studies Service
Col. U.	Columbia University, New York		
Cornwall RO	Cornwall Record Office, Truro	LUL	London University Library
Courtauld Inst.	Courtauld Institute of Art, London	Magd. Cam.	Magdalene College, Cambridge
CUL	Cambridge University Library	Magd. Oxf.	Magdalen College, Oxford
Cumbria AS	Cumbria Archive Service	Man. City Gall.	Manchester City Galleries
Derbys. RO	Derbyshire Record Office, Matlock	Man. CL	Manchester Central Library
Devon RO	Devon Record Office, Exeter	Mass. Hist. Soc.	Massachusetts Historical Society, Boston
Dorset RO	Dorset Record Office, Dorchester	Merton Oxf.	Merton College, Oxford
Duke U.	Duke University, Durham, North Carolina	MHS Oxf.	Museum of the History of Science, Oxford
Duke U., Perkins L.	Duke University, Durham, North Carolina, William R. Perkins Library	Mitchell L., Glas.	Mitchell Library, Glasgow
		Mitchell L., NSW	State Library of New South Wales, Sydney, Mitchell Library
Durham Cath. CL	Durham Cathedral, chapter library		
Durham RO	Durham Record Office	Morgan L.	Pierpont Morgan Library, New York
DWL	Dr Williams's Library, London	NA Canada	National Archives of Canada, Ottawa
Essex RO	Essex Record Office	NA Ire.	National Archives of Ireland, Dublin
E. Sussex RO	East Sussex Record Office, Lewes	NAM	National Army Museum, London
Eton	Eton College, Berkshire	NA Scot.	National Archives of Scotland, Edinburgh
FM Cam.	Fitzwilliam Museum, Cambridge	News Int. RO	News International Record Office, London
Folger	Folger Shakespeare Library, Washington, DC	NG Ire.	National Gallery of Ireland, Dublin

NG Scot.	National Gallery of Scotland, Edinburgh		Suffolk RO	Suffolk Record Office
NHM	Natural History Museum, London		Surrey HC	Surrey History Centre, Woking
NL Aus.	National Library of Australia, Canberra		TCD	Trinity College, Dublin
NL Ire.	National Library of Ireland, Dublin		Trinity Cam.	Trinity College, Cambridge
NL NZ	National Library of New Zealand, Wellington		U. Aberdeen	University of Aberdeen
NL NZ, Turnbull L.	National Library of New Zealand, Wellington, Alexander Turnbull Library		U. Birm.	University of Birmingham
			U. Birm. L.	University of Birmingham Library
NL Scot.	National Library of Scotland, Edinburgh		U. Cal.	University of California
NL Wales	National Library of Wales, Aberystwyth		U. Cam.	University of Cambridge
NMG Wales	National Museum and Gallery of Wales, Cardiff		UCL	University College, London
NMM	National Maritime Museum, London		U. Durham	University of Durham
Norfolk RO	Norfolk Record Office, Norwich		U. Durham L.	University of Durham Library
Northants. RO	Northamptonshire Record Office, Northampton		U. Edin.	University of Edinburgh
			U. Edin., New Coll.	University of Edinburgh, New College
Northumbd RO	Northumberland Record Office		U. Edin., New Coll. L.	University of Edinburgh, New College Library
Notts. Arch.	Nottinghamshire Archives, Nottingham			
NPG	National Portrait Gallery, London		U. Edin. L.	University of Edinburgh Library
NRA	National Archives, London, Historical Manuscripts Commission, National Register of Archives		U. Glas.	University of Glasgow
			U. Glas. L.	University of Glasgow Library
			U. Hull	University of Hull
Nuffield Oxf.	Nuffield College, Oxford		U. Hull, Brynmor Jones L.	University of Hull, Brynmor Jones Library
N. Yorks. CRO	North Yorkshire County Record Office, Northallerton			
			U. Leeds	University of Leeds
NYPL	New York Public Library		U. Leeds, Brotherton L.	University of Leeds, Brotherton Library
Oxf. UA	Oxford University Archives			
Oxf. U. Mus. NH	Oxford University Museum of Natural History		U. Lond.	University of London
Oxon. RO	Oxfordshire Record Office, Oxford		U. Lpool	University of Liverpool
Pembroke Cam.	Pembroke College, Cambridge		U. Lpool L.	University of Liverpool Library
PRO	National Archives, London, Public Record Office		U. Mich.	University of Michigan, Ann Arbor
			U. Mich., Clements L.	University of Michigan, Ann Arbor, William L. Clements Library
PRO NIre.	Public Record Office for Northern Ireland, Belfast			
			U. Newcastle	University of Newcastle upon Tyne
Pusey Oxf.	Pusey House, Oxford		U. Newcastle, Robinson L.	University of Newcastle upon Tyne, Robinson Library
RA	Royal Academy of Arts, London			
Ransom HRC	Harry Ransom Humanities Research Center, University of Texas, Austin		U. Nott.	University of Nottingham
			U. Nott. L.	University of Nottingham Library
RAS	Royal Astronomical Society, London		U. Oxf.	University of Oxford
RBG Kew	Royal Botanic Gardens, Kew, London		U. Reading	University of Reading
RCP Lond.	Royal College of Physicians of London		U. Reading L.	University of Reading Library
RCS Eng.	Royal College of Surgeons of England, London		U. St Andr.	University of St Andrews
RGS	Royal Geographical Society, London		U. St Andr. L.	University of St Andrews Library
RIBA	Royal Institute of British Architects, London		U. Southampton	University of Southampton
RIBA BAL	Royal Institute of British Architects, London, British Architectural Library		U. Southampton L.	University of Southampton Library
			U. Sussex	University of Sussex, Brighton
Royal Arch.	Royal Archives, Windsor Castle, Berkshire [by gracious permission of her majesty the queen]		U. Texas	University of Texas, Austin
			U. Wales	University of Wales
Royal Irish Acad.	Royal Irish Academy, Dublin		U. Warwick Mod. RC	University of Warwick, Coventry, Modern Records Centre
Royal Scot. Acad.	Royal Scottish Academy, Edinburgh			
RS	Royal Society, London		V&A	Victoria and Albert Museum, London
RSA	Royal Society of Arts, London		V&A NAL	Victoria and Albert Museum, London, National Art Library
RS Friends, Lond.	Religious Society of Friends, London			
St Ant. Oxf.	St Antony's College, Oxford		Warks. CRO	Warwickshire County Record Office, Warwick
St John Cam.	St John's College, Cambridge		Wellcome L.	Wellcome Library for the History and Understanding of Medicine, London
S. Antiquaries, Lond.	Society of Antiquaries of London			
			Westm. DA	Westminster Diocesan Archives, London
Sci. Mus.	Science Museum, London		Wilts. & Swindon RO	Wiltshire and Swindon Record Office, Trowbridge
Scot. NPG	Scottish National Portrait Gallery, Edinburgh			
Scott Polar RI	University of Cambridge, Scott Polar Research Institute		Worcs. RO	Worcestershire Record Office, Worcester
			W. Sussex RO	West Sussex Record Office, Chichester
Sheff. Arch.	Sheffield Archives		W. Yorks. AS	West Yorkshire Archive Service
Shrops. RRC	Shropshire Records and Research Centre, Shrewsbury		Yale U.	Yale University, New Haven, Connecticut
			Yale U., Beinecke L.	Yale University, New Haven, Connecticut, Beinecke Rare Book and Manuscript Library
SOAS	School of Oriental and African Studies, London			
Som. ARS	Somerset Archive and Record Service, Taunton		Yale U. CBA	Yale University, New Haven, Connecticut, Yale Center for British Art
Staffs. RO	Staffordshire Record Office, Stafford			

3 Bibliographic abbreviations

Adams, *Drama* — W. D. Adams, *A dictionary of the drama*, 1: *A–G* (1904); 2: *H–Z* (1956) [vol. 2 microfilm only]

AFM — J O'Donovan, ed. and trans., *Annala rioghachta Eireann / Annals of the kingdom of Ireland by the four masters*, 7 vols. (1848–51); 2nd edn (1856); 3rd edn (1990)

Allibone, *Dict.* — S. A. Allibone, *A critical dictionary of English literature and British and American authors*, 3 vols. (1859–71); suppl. by J. F. Kirk, 2 vols. (1891)

ANB — J. A. Garraty and M. C. Carnes, eds., *American national biography*, 24 vols. (1999)

Anderson, *Scot. nat.* — W. Anderson, *The Scottish nation, or, The surnames, families, literature, honours, and biographical history of the people of Scotland*, 3 vols. (1859–63)

Ann. mon. — H. R. Luard, ed., *Annales monastici*, 5 vols., Rolls Series, 36 (1864–9)

Ann. Ulster — S. Mac Airt and G. Mac Niocaill, eds., *Annals of Ulster (to AD 1131)* (1983)

APC — *Acts of the privy council of England*, new ser., 46 vols. (1890–1964)

APS — *The acts of the parliaments of Scotland*, 12 vols. in 13 (1814–75)

Arber, *Regs. Stationers* — F. Arber, ed., *A transcript of the registers of the Company of Stationers of London, 1554–1640 AD*, 5 vols. (1875–94)

ArchR — *Architectural Review*

ASC — D. Whitelock, D. C. Douglas, and S. I. Tucker, ed. and trans., *The Anglo-Saxon Chronicle: a revised translation* (1961)

AS chart. — P. H. Sawyer, *Anglo-Saxon charters: an annotated list and bibliography*, Royal Historical Society Guides and Handbooks (1968)

AusDB — D. Pike and others, eds., *Australian dictionary of biography*, 16 vols. (1966–2002)

Baker, *Serjeants* — J. H. Baker, *The order of serjeants at law*, SeldS, suppl. ser., 5 (1984)

Bale, *Cat.* — J. Bale, *Scriptorum illustrium Maioris Brytannie, quam nunc Angliam et Scotiam vocant: catalogus*, 2 vols. in 1 (Basel, 1557–9); facs. edn (1971)

Bale, *Index* — J. Bale, *Index Britanniae scriptorum*, ed. R. L. Poole and M. Bateson (1902); facs. edn (1990)

BBCS — *Bulletin of the Board of Celtic Studies*

BDMBR — J. O. Baylen and N. J. Gossman, eds., *Biographical dictionary of modern British radicals*, 3 vols. in 4 (1979–88)

Bede, *Hist. eccl.* — *Bede's Ecclesiastical history of the English people*, ed. and trans. B. Colgrave and R. A. B. Mynors, OMT (1969); repr. (1991)

Bénézit, *Dict.* — E. Bénézit, *Dictionnaire critique et documentaire des peintres, sculpteurs, dessinateurs et graveurs*, 3 vols. (Paris, 1911–23); new edn, 8 vols. (1948–66), repr. (1966); 3rd edn, rev. and enl., 10 vols. (1976); 4th edn, 14 vols. (1999)

BIHR — *Bulletin of the Institute of Historical Research*

Birch, *Seals* — W. de Birch, *Catalogue of seals in the department of manuscripts in the British Museum*, 6 vols. (1887–1900)

Bishop Burnet's History — *Bishop Burnet's History of his own time*, ed. M. J. Routh, 2nd edn, 6 vols. (1833)

Blackwood — *Blackwood's [Edinburgh] Magazine*, 328 vols. (1817–1980)

Blain, Clements & Grundy, *Feminist comp.* — V. Blain, P. Clements, and I. Grundy, eds., *The feminist companion to literature in English* (1990)

BL cat. — *The British Library general catalogue of printed books* [in 360 vols. with suppls., also CD-ROM and online]

BMJ — *British Medical Journal*

Boase & Courtney, *Bibl. Corn.* — G. C. Boase and W. P. Courtney, *Bibliotheca Cornubiensis: a catalogue of the writings … of Cornishmen*, 3 vols. (1874–82)

Boase, *Mod. Eng. biog.* — F. Boase, *Modern English biography: containing many thousand concise memoirs of persons who have died since the year 1850*, 6 vols. (privately printed, Truro, 1892–1921); repr. (1965)

Boswell, *Life* — *Boswell's Life of Johnson: together with Journal of a tour to the Hebrides and Johnson's Diary of a journey into north Wales*, ed. G. B. Hill, enl. edn, rev. L. F. Powell, 6 vols. (1934–50); 2nd edn (1964); repr. (1971)

Brown & Stratton, *Brit. mus.* — J. D. Brown and S. S. Stratton, *British musical biography* (1897)

Bryan, *Painters* — M. Bryan, *A biographical and critical dictionary of painters and engravers*, 2 vols. (1816); new edn, ed. G. Stanley (1849); new edn, ed. R. E. Graves and W. Armstrong, 2 vols. (1886–9); [4th edn], ed. G. C. Williamson, 5 vols. (1903–5) [various reprs.]

Burke, *Gen. GB* — J. Burke, *A genealogical and heraldic history of the commoners of Great Britain and Ireland*, 4 vols. (1833–8); new edn as *A genealogical and heraldic dictionary of the landed gentry of Great Britain and Ireland*, 3 vols. [1843–9] [many later edns]

Burke, *Gen. Ire.* — J. B. Burke, *A genealogical and heraldic history of the landed gentry of Ireland* (1899); 2nd edn (1904); 3rd edn (1912); 4th edn (1958); 5th edn as *Burke's Irish family records* (1976)

Burke, *Peerage* — J. Burke, *A general [later edns A genealogical] and heraldic dictionary of the peerage and baronetage of the United Kingdom* [later edns *the British empire*] (1829–)

Burney, *Hist. mus.* — C. Burney, *A general history of music, from the earliest ages to the present period*, 4 vols. (1776–89)

Burtchaell & Sadleir, *Alum. Dubl.* — G. D. Burtchaell and T. U. Sadleir, *Alumni Dublinenses: a register of the students, graduates, and provosts of Trinity College* (1924); [2nd edn], with suppl., in 2 pts (1935)

Calamy rev. — A. G. Matthews, *Calamy revised* (1934); repr. (1988)

CCI — *Calendar of confirmations and inventories granted and given up in the several commissariots of Scotland* (1876–)

CClR — *Calendar of the close rolls preserved in the Public Record Office*, 47 vols. (1892–1963)

CDS — J. Bain, ed., *Calendar of documents relating to Scotland*, 4 vols., PRO (1881–8); suppl. vol. 5, ed. G. G. Simpson and J. D. Galbraith [1986]

CEPR letters — W. H. Bliss, C. Johnson, and J. Twemlow, eds., *Calendar of entries in the papal registers relating to Great Britain and Ireland: papal letters* (1893–)

CGPLA — *Calendars of the grants of probate and letters of administration* [in 4 ser.: England & Wales, Northern Ireland, Ireland, and Éire]

Chambers, *Scots.* — R. Chambers, ed., *A biographical dictionary of eminent Scotsmen*, 4 vols. (1832–5)

Chancery records — chancery records pubd by the PRO

Chancery records (RC) — chancery records pubd by the Record Commissions

CIPM	*Calendar of inquisitions post mortem*, [20 vols.], PRO (1904–); also *Henry VII*, 3 vols. (1898–1955)
Clarendon, *Hist. rebellion*	E. Hyde, earl of Clarendon, *The history of the rebellion and civil wars in England*, 6 vols. (1888); repr. (1958) and (1992)
Cobbett, *Parl. hist.*	W. Cobbett and J. Wright, eds., *Cobbett's Parliamentary history of England*, 36 vols. (1806–1820)
Colvin, *Archs.*	H. Colvin, *A biographical dictionary of British architects, 1600–1840*, 3rd edn (1995)
Cooper, *Ath. Cantab.*	C. H. Cooper and T. Cooper, *Athenae Cantabrigienses*, 3 vols. (1858–1913); repr. (1967)
CPR	*Calendar of the patent rolls preserved in the Public Record Office* (1891–)
Crockford	*Crockford's Clerical Directory*
CS	Camden Society
CSP	*Calendar of state papers* [in 11 ser.: domestic, Scotland, Scottish series, Ireland, colonial, Commonwealth, foreign, Spain [at Simancas], Rome, Milan, and Venice]
CYS	Canterbury and York Society
DAB	*Dictionary of American biography*, 21 vols. (1928–36), repr. in 11 vols. (1964); 10 suppls. (1944–96)
DBB	D. J. Jeremy, ed., *Dictionary of business biography*, 5 vols. (1984–6)
DCB	G. W. Brown and others, *Dictionary of Canadian biography*, [14 vols.] (1966–)
Debrett's Peerage	*Debrett's Peerage* (1803–) [sometimes *Debrett's Illustrated peerage*]
Desmond, *Botanists*	R. Desmond, *Dictionary of British and Irish botanists and horticulturists* (1977); rev. edn (1994)
Dir. Brit. archs.	A. Felstead, J. Franklin, and L. Pinfield, eds., *Directory of British architects, 1834–1900* (1993); 2nd edn, ed. A. Brodie and others, 2 vols. (2001)
DLB	J. M. Bellamy and J. Saville, eds., *Dictionary of labour biography*, [10 vols.] (1972–)
DLitB	Dictionary of Literary Biography
DNB	*Dictionary of national biography*, 63 vols. (1885–1900), suppl., 3 vols. (1901); repr. in 22 vols. (1908–9); 10 further suppls. (1912–96); *Missing persons* (1993)
DNZB	W. H. Oliver and C. Orange, eds., *The dictionary of New Zealand biography*, 5 vols. (1990–2000)
DSAB	W. J. de Kock and others, eds., *Dictionary of South African biography*, 5 vols. (1968–87)
DSB	C. C. Gillispie and F. L. Holmes, eds., *Dictionary of scientific biography*, 16 vols. (1970–80); repr. in 8 vols. (1981); 2 vol. suppl. (1990)
DSBB	A. Slaven and S. Checkland, eds., *Dictionary of Scottish business biography, 1860–1960*, 2 vols. (1986–90)
DSCHT	N. M. de S. Cameron and others, eds., *Dictionary of Scottish church history and theology* (1993)
Dugdale, *Monasticon*	W. Dugdale, *Monasticon Anglicanum*, 3 vols. (1655–72); 2nd edn, 3 vols. (1661–82); new edn, ed. J. Caley, J. Ellis, and B. Bandinel, 6 vols. in 8 pts (1817–30); repr. (1846) and (1970)
DWB	J. E. Lloyd and others, eds., *Dictionary of Welsh biography down to 1940* (1959) [Eng. trans. of *Y bywgraffiadur Cymreig hyd 1940*, 2nd edn (1954)]
EdinR	*Edinburgh Review, or, Critical Journal*
EETS	Early English Text Society
Emden, *Cam.*	A. B. Emden, *A biographical register of the University of Cambridge to 1500* (1963)
Emden, *Oxf.*	A. B. Emden, *A biographical register of the University of Oxford to AD 1500*, 3 vols. (1957–9); also *A biographical register of the University of Oxford, AD 1501 to 1540* (1974)
EngHR	*English Historical Review*
Engraved Brit. ports.	F. M. O'Donoghue and H. M. Hake, *Catalogue of engraved British portraits preserved in the department of prints and drawings in the British Museum*, 6 vols. (1908–25)
ER	*The English Reports*, 178 vols. (1900–32)
ESTC	*English short title catalogue, 1475–1800* [CD-ROM and online]
Evelyn, *Diary*	*The diary of John Evelyn*, ed. E. S. De Beer, 6 vols. (1955); repr. (2000)
Farington, *Diary*	*The diary of Joseph Farington*, ed. K. Garlick and others, 17 vols. (1978–98)
Fasti Angl. (Hardy)	J. Le Neve, *Fasti ecclesiae Anglicanae*, ed. T. D. Hardy, 3 vols. (1854)
Fasti Angl., 1066–1300	[J. Le Neve], *Fasti ecclesiae Anglicanae, 1066–1300*, ed. D. E. Greenway and J. S. Barrow, [8 vols.] (1968–)
Fasti Angl., 1300–1541	[J. Le Neve], *Fasti ecclesiae Anglicanae, 1300–1541*, 12 vols. (1962–7)
Fasti Angl., 1541–1857	[J. Le Neve], *Fasti ecclesiae Anglicanae, 1541–1857*, ed. J. M. Horn, D. M. Smith, and D. S. Bailey, [9 vols.] (1969–)
Fasti Scot.	H. Scott, *Fasti ecclesiae Scoticanae*, 3 vols. in 6 (1871); new edn, [11 vols.] (1915–)
FO List	*Foreign Office List*
Fortescue, *Brit. army*	J. W. Fortescue, *A history of the British army*, 13 vols. (1899–1930)
Foss, *Judges*	E. Foss, *The judges of England*, 9 vols. (1848–64); repr. (1966)
Foster, *Alum. Oxon.*	J. Foster, ed., *Alumni Oxonienses: the members of the University of Oxford, 1715–1886*, 4 vols. (1887–8); later edn (1891); also *Alumni Oxonienses … 1500–1714*, 4 vols. (1891–2); 8 vol. repr. (1968) and (2000)
Fuller, *Worthies*	T. Fuller, *The history of the worthies of England*, 4 pts (1662); new edn, 2 vols., ed. J. Nichols (1811); new edn, 3 vols., ed. P. A. Nuttall (1840); repr. (1965)
GEC, *Baronetage*	G. E. Cokayne, *Complete baronetage*, 6 vols. (1900–09); repr. (1983) [microprint]
GEC, *Peerage*	G. E. C. [G. E. Cokayne], *The complete peerage of England, Scotland, Ireland, Great Britain, and the United Kingdom*, 8 vols. (1887–98); new edn, ed. V. Gibbs and others, 14 vols. in 15 (1910–98); microprint repr. (1982) and (1987)
Genest, *Eng. stage*	J. Genest, *Some account of the English stage from the Restoration in 1660 to 1830*, 10 vols. (1832); repr. [New York, 1965]
Gillow, *Lit. biog. hist.*	J. Gillow, *A literary and biographical history or bibliographical dictionary of the English Catholics, from the breach with Rome, in 1534, to the present time*, 5 vols. [1885–1902]; repr. (1961); repr. with preface by C. Gillow (1999)
Gir. Camb. opera	*Giraldi Cambrensis opera*, ed. J. S. Brewer, J. F. Dimock, and G. F. Warner, 8 vols., Rolls Series, 21 (1861–91)
GJ	*Geographical Journal*

Gladstone, *Diaries* — *The Gladstone diaries: with cabinet minutes and prime-ministerial correspondence*, ed. M. R. D. Foot and H. C. G. Matthew, 14 vols. (1968–94)

GM — *Gentleman's Magazine*

Graves, *Artists* — A. Graves, ed., *A dictionary of artists who have exhibited works in the principal London exhibitions of oil paintings from 1760 to 1880* (1884); new edn (1895); 3rd edn (1901); facs. edn (1969); repr. [1970], (1973), and (1984)

Graves, *Brit. Inst.* — A. Graves, *The British Institution, 1806–1867: a complete dictionary of contributors and their work from the foundation of the institution* (1875); facs. edn (1908); repr. (1969)

Graves, *RA exhibitors* — A. Graves, *The Royal Academy of Arts: a complete dictionary of contributors and their work from its foundation in 1769 to 1904*, 8 vols. (1905–6); repr. in 4 vols. (1970) and (1972)

Graves, *Soc. Artists* — A. Graves, *The Society of Artists of Great Britain, 1760–1791, the Free Society of Artists, 1761–1783: a complete dictionary* (1907); facs. edn (1969)

Greaves & Zaller, *BDBR* — R. L. Greaves and R. Zaller, eds., *Biographical dictionary of British radicals in the seventeenth century*, 3 vols. (1982–4)

Grove, *Dict. mus.* — G. Grove, ed., *A dictionary of music and musicians*, 5 vols. (1878–90); 2nd edn, ed. J. A. Fuller Maitland (1904–10); 3rd edn, ed. H. C. Colles (1927); 4th edn with suppl. (1940); 5th edn, ed. E. Blom, 9 vols. (1954); suppl. (1961) [see also *New Grove*]

Hall, *Dramatic ports.* — L. A. Hall, *Catalogue of dramatic portraits in the theatre collection of the Harvard College library*, 4 vols. (1930–34)

Hansard — *Hansard's parliamentary debates*, ser. 1–5 (1803–)

Highfill, Burnim & Langhans, *BDA* — P. H. Highfill, K. A. Burnim, and E. A. Langhans, *A biographical dictionary of actors, actresses, musicians, dancers, managers, and other stage personnel in London, 1660–1800*, 16 vols. (1973–93)

Hist. U. Oxf. — T. H. Aston, ed., *The history of the University of Oxford*, 8 vols. (1984–2000) [1: *The early Oxford schools*, ed. J. I. Catto (1984); 2: *Late medieval Oxford*, ed. J. I. Catto and R. Evans (1992); 3: *The collegiate university*, ed. J. McConica (1986); 4: *Seventeenth-century Oxford*, ed. N. Tyacke (1997); 5: *The eighteenth century*, ed. L. S. Sutherland and L. G. Mitchell (1986); 6–7: *Nineteenth-century Oxford*, ed. M. G. Brock and M. C. Curthoys (1997–2000); 8: *The twentieth century*, ed. B. Harrison (2000)]

HJ — *Historical Journal*

HMC — Historical Manuscripts Commission

Holdsworth, *Eng. law* — W. S. Holdsworth, *A history of English law*, ed. A. L. Goodhart and H. L. Hanbury, 17 vols. (1903–72)

HoP, *Commons* — *The history of parliament: the House of Commons* [1386–1421, ed. J. S. Roskell, L. Clark, and C. Rawcliffe, 4 vols. (1992); 1509–1558, ed. S. T. Bindoff, 3 vols. (1982); 1558–1603, ed. P. W. Hasler, 3 vols. (1981); 1660–1690, ed. B. D. Henning, 3 vols. (1983); 1690–1715, ed. D. W. Hayton, E. Cruickshanks, and S. Handley, 5 vols. (2002); 1715–1754, ed. R. Sedgwick, 2 vols. (1970); 1754–1790, ed. L. Namier and J. Brooke, 3 vols. (1964), repr. (1985); 1790–1820, ed. R. G. Thorne, 5 vols. (1986); in draft (used with permission): 1422–1504, 1604–1629, 1640–1660, and 1820–1832]

IGI — *International Genealogical Index*, Church of Jesus Christ of the Latterday Saints

ILN — *Illustrated London News*

IMC — Irish Manuscripts Commission

Irving, *Scots.* — J. Irving, ed., *The book of Scotsmen eminent for achievements in arms and arts, church and state, law, legislation and literature, commerce, science, travel and philanthropy* (1881)

JCS — *Journal of the Chemical Society*

JHC — *Journals of the House of Commons*

JHL — *Journals of the House of Lords*

John of Worcester, *Chron.* — *The chronicle of John of Worcester*, ed. R. R. Darlington and P. McGurk, trans. J. Bray and P. McGurk, 3 vols., OMT (1995–) [vol. 1 forthcoming]

Keeler, *Long Parliament* — M. F. Keeler, *The Long Parliament, 1640–1641: a biographical study of its members* (1954)

Kelly, *Handbk* — *The upper ten thousand: an alphabetical list of all members of noble families*, 3 vols. (1875–7); continued as *Kelly's handbook of the upper ten thousand for 1878* [1879], 2 vols. (1878–9); continued as *Kelly's handbook to the titled, landed and official classes*, 94 vols. (1880–1973)

LondG — *London Gazette*

LP Henry VIII — J. S. Brewer, J. Gairdner, and R. H. Brodie, eds., *Letters and papers, foreign and domestic, of the reign of Henry VIII*, 23 vols. in 38 (1862–1932); repr. (1965)

Mallalieu, *Watercolour artists* — H. L. Mallalieu, *The dictionary of British watercolour artists up to 1820*, 3 vols. (1976–90); vol. 1, 2nd edn (1986)

Memoirs FRS — *Biographical Memoirs of Fellows of the Royal Society*

MGH — Monumenta Germaniae Historica

MT — *Musical Times*

Munk, *Roll* — W. Munk, *The roll of the Royal College of Physicians of London*, 2 vols. (1861); 2nd edn, 3 vols. (1878)

N&Q — *Notes and Queries*

New Grove — S. Sadie, ed., *The new Grove dictionary of music and musicians*, 20 vols. (1980); 2nd edn, 29 vols. (2001) [also online edn; see also Grove, *Dict. mus.*]

Nichols, *Illustrations* — J. Nichols and J. B. Nichols, *Illustrations of the literary history of the eighteenth century*, 8 vols. (1817–58)

Nichols, *Lit. anecdotes* — J. Nichols, *Literary anecdotes of the eighteenth century*, 9 vols. (1812–16); facs. edn (1966)

Obits. FRS — *Obituary Notices of Fellows of the Royal Society*

O'Byrne, *Naval biog. dict.* — W. R. O'Byrne, *A naval biographical dictionary* (1849); repr. (1990); [2nd edn], 2 vols. (1861)

OHS — Oxford Historical Society

Old Westminsters — *The record of Old Westminsters*, 1–2, ed. G. F. R. Barker and A. H. Stenning (1928); suppl. 1, ed. J. B. Whitmore and G. R. Y. Radcliffe [1938]; 3, ed. J. B. Whitmore, G. R. Y. Radcliffe, and D. C. Simpson (1963); suppl. 2, ed. F. E. Pagan (1978); 4, ed. F. E. Pagan and H. E. Pagan (1992)

OMT — Oxford Medieval Texts

Ordericus Vitalis, *Eccl. hist.* — *The ecclesiastical history of Orderic Vitalis*, ed. and trans. M. Chibnall, 6 vols., OMT (1969–80); repr. (1990)

Paris, *Chron.* — *Matthaei Parisiensis, monachi sancti Albani, chronica majora*, ed. H. R. Luard, Rolls Series, 7 vols. (1872–83)

Parl. papers — *Parliamentary papers* (1801–)

PBA — *Proceedings of the British Academy*

Pepys, *Diary*	*The diary of Samuel Pepys*, ed. R. Latham and W. Matthews, 11 vols. (1970–83); repr. (1995) and (2000)
Pevsner	N. Pevsner and others, Buildings of England series
PICE	*Proceedings of the Institution of Civil Engineers*
Pipe rolls	*The great roll of the pipe for . . .*, PRSoc. (1884–)
PRO	Public Record Office
PRS	*Proceedings of the Royal Society of London*
PRSoc.	Pipe Roll Society
PTRS	*Philosophical Transactions of the Royal Society*
QR	*Quarterly Review*
RC	Record Commissions
Redgrave, *Artists*	S. Redgrave, *A dictionary of artists of the English school* (1874); rev. edn (1878); repr. (1970)
Reg. Oxf.	C. W. Boase and A. Clark, eds., *Register of the University of Oxford*, 5 vols., OHS, 1, 10–12, 14 (1885–9)
Reg. PCS	J. H. Burton and others, eds., *The register of the privy council of Scotland*, 1st ser., 14 vols. (1877–98); 2nd ser., 8 vols. (1899–1908); 3rd ser., [16 vols.] (1908–70)
Reg. RAN	H. W. C. Davis and others, eds., *Regesta regum Anglo-Normannorum, 1066–1154*, 4 vols. (1913–69)
RIBA Journal	*Journal of the Royal Institute of British Architects* [later *RIBA Journal*]
RotP	J. Strachey, ed., *Rotuli parliamentorum ut et petitiones, et placita in parliamento*, 6 vols. (1767–77)
RotS	D. Macpherson, J. Caley, and W. Illingworth, eds., *Rotuli Scotiae in Turri Londinensi et in domo capitulari Westmonasteriensi asservati*, 2 vols., RC, 14 (1814–19)
RS	Record(s) Society
Rymer, *Foedera*	T. Rymer and R. Sanderson, eds., *Foedera, conventiones, literae et cuiuscunque generis acta publica inter reges Angliae et alios quosvis imperatores, reges, pontifices, principes, vel communitates*, 20 vols. (1704–35); 2nd edn, 20 vols. (1726–35); 3rd edn, 10 vols. (1739–45), facs. edn (1967); new edn, ed. A. Clarke, J. Caley, and F. Holbrooke, 4 vols., RC, 50 (1816–30)
Sainty, *Judges*	J. Sainty, ed., *The judges of England, 1272–1990*, SeldS, suppl. ser., 10 (1993)
Sainty, *King's counsel*	J. Sainty, ed., *A list of English law officers and king's counsel*, SeldS, suppl. ser., 7 (1987)
SCH	Studies in Church History
Scots peerage	J. B. Paul, ed. *The Scots peerage, founded on Wood's edition of Sir Robert Douglas's Peerage of Scotland, containing an historical and genealogical account of the nobility of that kingdom*, 9 vols. (1904–14)
SeldS	Selden Society
SHR	*Scottish Historical Review*
State trials	T. B. Howell and T. J. Howell, eds., *Cobbett's Complete collection of state trials*, 34 vols. (1809–28)
STC, 1475–1640	A. W. Pollard, G. R. Redgrave, and others, eds., *A short-title catalogue of . . . English books . . . 1475–1640* (1926); 2nd edn, ed. W. A. Jackson, F. S. Ferguson, and K. F. Pantzer, 3 vols. (1976–91) [see also Wing, *STC*]
STS	Scottish Text Society
SurtS	Surtees Society
Symeon of Durham, *Opera*	*Symeonis monachi opera omnia*, ed. T. Arnold, 2 vols., Rolls Series, 75 (1882–5); repr. (1965)
Tanner, *Bibl. Brit.-Hib.*	T. Tanner, *Bibliotheca Britannico-Hibernica*, ed. D. Wilkins (1748); repr. (1963)
Thieme & Becker, *Allgemeines Lexikon*	U. Thieme, F. Becker, and H. Vollmer, eds., *Allgemeines Lexikon der bildenden Künstler von der Antike bis zur Gegenwart*, 37 vols. (Leipzig, 1907–50); repr. (1961–5), (1983), and (1992)
Thurloe, *State papers*	*A collection of the state papers of John Thurloe*, ed. T. Birch, 7 vols. (1742)
TLS	*Times Literary Supplement*
Tout, *Admin. hist.*	T. F. Tout, *Chapters in the administrative history of mediaeval England: the wardrobe, the chamber, and the small seals*, 6 vols. (1920–33); repr. (1967)
TRHS	*Transactions of the Royal Historical Society*
VCH	H. A. Doubleday and others, eds., *The Victoria history of the counties of England*, [88 vols.] (1900–)
Venn, *Alum. Cant.*	J. Venn and J. A. Venn, *Alumni Cantabrigienses: a biographical list of all known students, graduates, and holders of office at the University of Cambridge, from the earliest times to 1900*, 10 vols. (1922–54); repr. in 2 vols. (1974–8)
Vertue, *Note books*	[G. Vertue], *Note books*, ed. K. Esdaile, earl of Ilchester, and H. M. Hake, 6 vols., Walpole Society, 18, 20, 22, 24, 26, 30 (1930–55)
VF	*Vanity Fair*
Walford, *County families*	E. Walford, *The county families of the United Kingdom, or, Royal manual of the titled and untitled aristocracy of Great Britain and Ireland* (1860)
Walker rev.	A. G. Matthews, *Walker revised: being a revision of John Walker's Sufferings of the clergy during the grand rebellion, 1642–60* (1948); repr. (1988)
Walpole, *Corr.*	*The Yale edition of Horace Walpole's correspondence*, ed. W. S. Lewis, 48 vols. (1937–83)
Ward, *Men of the reign*	T. H. Ward, ed., *Men of the reign: a biographical dictionary of eminent persons of British and colonial birth who have died during the reign of Queen Victoria* (1885); repr. (Graz, 1968)
Waterhouse, *18c painters*	E. Waterhouse, *The dictionary of 18th century painters in oils and crayons* (1981); repr. as *British 18th century painters in oils and crayons* (1991), vol. 2 of *Dictionary of British art*
Watt, *Bibl. Brit.*	R. Watt, *Bibliotheca Britannica, or, A general index to British and foreign literature*, 4 vols. (1824) [many reprs.]
Wellesley index	W. E. Houghton, ed., *The Wellesley index to Victorian periodicals, 1824–1900*, 5 vols. (1966–89); new edn (1999) [CD-ROM]
Wing, *STC*	D. Wing, ed., *Short-title catalogue of . . . English books . . . 1641–1700*, 3 vols. (1945–51); 2nd edn (1972–88); rev. and enl. edn, ed. J. J. Morrison, C. W. Nelson, and M. Seccombe, 4 vols. (1994–8) [see also *STC, 1475–1640*]
Wisden	*John Wisden's Cricketer's Almanack*
Wood, *Ath. Oxon.*	A. Wood, *Athenae Oxonienses . . . to which are added the Fasti*, 2 vols. (1691–2); 2nd edn (1721); new edn, 4 vols., ed. P. Bliss (1813–20); repr. (1967) and (1969)
Wood, *Vic. painters*	C. Wood, *Dictionary of Victorian painters* (1971); 2nd edn (1978); 3rd edn as *Victorian painters*, 2 vols. (1995), vol. 4 of *Dictionary of British art*
WW	*Who's who* (1849–)
WWBMP	M. Stenton and S. Lees, eds., *Who's who of British members of parliament*, 4 vols. (1976–81)
WWW	*Who was who* (1929–)

Murrell, Christine Mary (1874–1933), physician, was born on 18 October 1874 at 1 Jeffrey's Road, Clapham Road, London, the only child of Charles Murrell, a coal merchant, and his wife, Alice Elizabeth Rains. Being both the only child and the only grandchild of a well-to-do family, she grew up enjoying plenty of affection and attention from family members, who later seem to have been willing to help her to pursue a professional career. In 1894 she entered the London School of Medicine for Women; she received the degrees of MB BS at the University of London in 1899. During the early part of her career she held various posts, including locum tenens at Morpeth, resident clinical assistant at the Northumberland County Asylum, medical officer at the Victoria settlement in Liverpool, and house physician and medical registrar at the Royal Free Hospital, London. In 1903, with financial support from her grandfather John Rains, she set up a private practice in Bayswater, London, with her lifelong partner and friend Dr (Elizabeth) Honor Bone. After experiencing some initial difficulty, they became established in practice by 1908. Meanwhile Murrell had completed an MD in psychology and mental diseases at the University of London (1905). Like many doctors at that time she was also interested in the problem of infant welfare. In 1907 she took charge of the St Marylebone Health Society's 'Infant Consultation' on Lisson Grove, one of the earliest infant welfare clinics. There she provided medical examinations for infants and advice to mothers for the following eighteen years.

Murrell's most significant achievement was her fight for equal opportunities for women. She believed that it was women's lack of knowledge about their own physiology and health that led them to the erroneous idea that their 'disabilities' were natural. Thus, for about twenty years she gave a series of evening lectures at the London county council, directed mainly at working-class women and covering various health-related subjects, including first aid, home nursing, infant care, and the physiology of adolescence. The lecture series on physiology was published in 1923 as *Womanhood and Health*. Another important contribution in this area was her study of menstruation. In 1925, under the auspices of the London Association of the Medical Women's Federation, Murrell and Letitia Fairfield initiated a survey on menstrual experience among girls in an attempt to eliminate negative associations with it. A larger-scale survey was launched in 1926 and the results appeared in *The Lancet* in 1930. Murrell's opposition to the proposed restrictive legislation for women in industry can be understood as an extension of this research, because such legislation was based on the assumption that women were physically inferior and therefore unsuitable for certain types of work. She argued that instead of this kind of legislation there should be 'an improvement in the general conditions of labour, good pay, reasonable hours, and healthy conditions under which to work' (*BMJ*, 1932, 106).

Before the First World War, Murrell's fight for equality also extended to the women's suffrage movement. As her biographer recounted, Murrell

Christine Mary Murrell (1874–1933), by Dorothy Wilding, 1926

helped to manage one of the suffrage propaganda shops, addressed meetings, went on the deputations …, marched in the processions … and put her medical skill at the service of the hunger-strikers, when, near death, they were released from prison under the 'Cat and Mouse Act'.   (St John, 57)

During the war, she worked as one of the medical officers, and was later chair, of the Women's Emergency Corps. She also served as a medical officer to the Metropolitan Special Constabulary. After the passage of the Sex Disqualification Removal Bill in 1918, she joined the women's election committee which sought the adoption of women candidates for election to the House of Commons.

Murrell did a great deal of public work and achieved many distinctions. She was an active member of the Medical Women's Federation, serving as its fifth president (1926–8), and was a member of the International Medical Women's Association. Although she was a prominent medical woman, her professional activities were not limited to women's issues. She served on various committees and high offices of the British Medical Association, which culminated in her being elected the first female member of the council in 1924. In September 1933 she was elected as the first female representative to the General Medical Council, the governing body of the medical profession, but before she could take the seat she died of cancer at her home, 21 North Gate, London, on 18 October 1933. She never married.   YOUNGRAN JO

Sources C. St John, *Christine Murrell, M.D.: her life and her work* (1935) · C. M. Murrell, *Womanhood and health* (1923) · *BMJ* (28 Oct

1933), 801–3 • *The Lancet* (28 Oct 1933) • *Medical Women's Federation Newsletter* (Nov 1933) • C. M. Murrell, 'International Medical Women's Association', *Medical Women's Federation Newsletter* (Nov 1922), 18–21 • C. M. Murrell, 'Presidential address', *Medical Women's Federation Newsletter* (Nov 1926), 18–26 • b. cert. • d. cert.
Archives Wellcome L., Medical Women's Federation Archive
Likenesses D. Wilding, photograph, 1926, NPG [*see illus.*] • D. Wilding, photograph, repro. in *BMJ*, 801 • D. Wilding, photograph, repro. in St John, *Christine Murrell*, frontispiece
Wealth at death £27,954 2*s.* 1*d.*: resworn probate, 24 Jan 1934, *CGPLA Eng. & Wales*

Hilda Murrell (1906–1984), by unknown photographer, *c.*1980

Murrell, Hilda (1906–1984), environmentalist and peace campaigner, was born on 3 February 1906 at Shrewsbury, the elder daughter of Owen Charles Murrell, nurseryman, and his wife, Lily Maria Lowe. She was educated at Shrewsbury High School for Girls (1918–23), winning a scholarship to Newnham College, Cambridge, where she read English and French (1924–7), gaining a 2:1 in both the English tripos and French. She joined the firm of rose growers founded by her father and uncle, and there developed her knowledge of business and of horticulture. In 1943 she became an associate of the Chartered Institute of Secretaries. From 1930 to 1970 she was a director, and later the proprietor and sole manager, of the family firm, Portland Nurseries, Shrewsbury, until she sold the business to Percy Thrower. She was an internationally acknowledged authority on rose species, old varieties, and miniature roses, regularly winning gold awards at Chelsea, and her rose catalogues were masterpieces of evocative yet scientifically accurate description. A new (David Austin) rose was named after her, following her death. During and after the Second World War, Hilda Murrell was actively concerned with the care and resettlement of wartime refugees, working with the Jewish Refugee Children's Society. She raised money for the cause by organizing concerts by such artists as Jelly d'Aranyi and Myra Hess and also took immense trouble herself to help desperate individuals.

Hilda Murrell was a devoted hillwalker and fell climber with a special love of both sides of the Welsh marches— 'sheer bliss [to] be greeted by perfection—to be able to look *over* some hill-tops' (*Hilda Murrell's Nature Diaries*, 198), she recorded in her posthumously published *Nature Diaries* (1987). In 1962 she became a founder member of the Shropshire Conservation Trust and she also worked vigorously for the Shropshire branch of the Council for the Protection of Rural England. She took a naturalist's interest in the varied habitats in Anglesey and the marches, as attested in her *Nature Diaries*, illustrated by her own meticulous botanical line drawings and colour photography. After her retirement in 1970 she built her retreat, The Shack, Maes Uchaf, on a plot of land at Fron Goch, near Llanymynech Hill, Oswestry. The Shack was mysteriously damaged in an arson attack on 26 January 1985.

Increasingly, Hilda Murrell became deeply concerned by the threat of mass extermination posed by the uncontrolled nuclear weapons race and by the irreversible damage to the environment risked by the nuclear power industry. She was a member of the European Nuclear Disarmament Movement founded by E. P. Thompson in 1981, a member of the Shropshire Peace Alliance, a supporter of the women demonstrators against cruise missiles at the American airbase at Greenham Common, a founder member of the nuclear freeze movement in Britain, and, finally, a private researcher seeking to understand and argue against the implications of building another nuclear reactor at Sizewell B in Suffolk. At the age of seventy-eight she completed her paper criticizing the government white paper (*Parl. papers*, 1981–2, Cmnd 8607) on radioactive waste management. The paper was accepted and eventually read to the public inquiry on Sizewell in September 1984.

On 21 March 1984 Hilda Murrell returned home from shopping and was surprised by one or more intruders who had systematically searched her house and papers and disconnected her telephone (in such a way that she could not ring out but anyone ringing in would believe the line was still working). There was a struggle; she was apparently abducted in her own car and driven out 6 miles into the countryside, where she was taken from the car, attacked with a breadknife, and left to die of her wounds and exposure. Three days later her body was discovered. At the end of the century West Mercia police reported that the murder file on Hilda Murrell was still open.

There are composite and conflicting theories, including both conspiracy and incompetence, for Hilda Murrell's terrible end. The most anodyne explanation is that a little old lady was surprised by a psychotic burglar who panicked. But Hilda Murrell was no ordinary little old lady. Sizewell objectors were being kept under surveillance by a detective agency for a private client, and Hilda Murrell had told several people before her death that she had fears for her personal safety. Two possible motives emerged for the systematic search of her house—a wish to check out her case against Sizewell B and/or a wish to find any possibly 'sensitive' documents concerning the Falklands War that might have been left in her safe keeping by her nephew Commander Rob Green. Green had resigned from the navy after the Falklands War, during which he had been one of the two officers who at Northwood naval headquarters had interpreted the signals emanating from the Argentinian ship the *Belgrano* when she was sunk by the British in May 1982 with the loss of 368 lives. Green categorically denied having left naval documents of any kind with his aunt. At the time of writing it is still not known whether Hilda Murrell was in fact under surveillance by MI5.

Hilda Murrell's murder roused intense speculation in the press, as well as many attempts to pay her adequate tribute. A fictional variation on her character, her beliefs, and her fate is detectable in Maggie Gee's eponymous *Grace* (1988). Also in 1988 a 'Summer forum to celebrate the countryside interests of Hilda Murrell' was inaugurated in Shropshire, and was held there every June until the tenth anniversary of her death.

Shy, tough-minded, humorous, kind, and possessing an exceptional responsiveness to nature, Hilda Murrell was enjoyed and admired by her friends for her many gifts, for her intellectual and moral courage, and for her refusal to be handicapped either by her arthritis or by the fact that she had lost the use of her right eye in infancy. Her life as a rose grower, plantswoman, writer, and environmental activist was a constructive and creative one; she deserves to be remembered for that life quite apart from the unsolved mystery of its brutal end. Her ashes were scattered on 25 August 1984 near the standing stone in Bwlch Maengwynedd—the open roof of Wales.

SYBIL OLDFIELD

Sources Hilda Murrell's nature diaries, 1961–1983, ed. C. Sinker (1987) · J. Cook, Who killed Hilda Murrell? (1985) · J. Cook, Unlawful killing (1994) · The Times (6 April 1984) · C. Sinker and K. M. B., 'Hilda Murrell, 1906–1984 (Newnham, 1924–1927)', Newnham College Roll Letter (1985), 62–3 · A. Tucker, 'Murder victim's Sizewell scorn', The Guardian (18 Aug 1984) · R. Green, 'Who killed Hilda Murrell and why?', New Reporter in a New World, 4 (March–April 1994) · 'Stalker investigates the death of Hilda Murrell', Network First, 1 Nov 1994 [television transmission, Central Independent Television] · [A. B. White], ed., Newnham College register, 2: 1924–1950 (1964), 413–4 · private information (2004)
Archives Shrops. RRC, nature diaries | FILM BFI NFTVA, World in action, Granada, 4 March 1985 · BFI NFTVA, Network first, Central Independent Television, 1 Nov 1994
Likenesses group photographs, 1925–7, repro. in New College Albums · photograph, 1975, repro. in Sinker, ed., Hilda Murrell's nature diaries, frontispiece · photograph, c.1980, repro. in Cook, Unlawful killing [see illus.]
Wealth at death £152,560: probate, 18 May 1984, CGPLA Eng. & Wales

Murrell, John (*fl.* 1614–1630), writer on cookery, has left little record other than his books, in which he claims to have extended his knowledge of cookery by travels in France, the Low Countries, Italy, and 'divers other places'; he gives no indication of the situation which occasioned these travels. Most of his books include dedicatory addresses giving a succession of employers and/or patrons associated with his career. McKerrow in his *Dictionary of Printers and Booksellers* of 1910 cites *A Booke of Cookery* published by John Browne in 1614 for which there is an entry in the Stationers' registers dated 14 October 1614. No copy is known and in view of the late entry date it is possible that this is the same work as *A New Booke of Cookerie, Set Forthe by the Observations of a Traveller I. M.* (1615), for which there is no specific entry in the registers. Another edition, with additions, in 1617 was 'By John Murrell'. Both were published by Browne and dedicated to Mistress Francis Herbert. *The Ladies Practice* was entered to John Browne, April 1617, and stated by McKerrow to have been published in the same year. No copy is known.

A Daily Exercise for Ladies and Gentlewomen was published by the Widow Helme in 1617. It was dedicated to Elizabeth Bingham, wife of Nicholas Bingham. The scope of the book is given on the title page as 'Whereby they may learn and practice the whole Art of making Pastes, Preserves, Marmalades, Conserves, Tartstuffes, Gellies, Breads, Sucket Candies, Cordiall waters, Conceits in Sugar-workes of severall kinds as also to dry Limmonds, Oranges or other Fruits'. *A Delightful Daily Exercise for Ladies and Gentlewomen*, published by Thomas Dewe in 1621, had no personal dedicatory address. It is a compilation of similar recipes, which include some rather curious methods for preserving potatoes. These entail boiling mashed potatoes in sugar syrup, forming the paste into 'round cakes', drying, and storing them, or boiling quartered potatoes in sugar syrup, again storing them after drying. A third method appears to involve boiling them with sugar and storing them in the syrup but the instructions are rather vague. A selection of plain cookery recipes is appended as a separate section. These two books are similar in format and partly in content to the contemporary works *Delightes for Ladies* and *A Closet for Ladies and Gentlewomen*, but differ from them in dealing solely with foodstuffs.

Murrell's books of cookery are of unorthodox type, intended for the kitchen rather than the lady's still room. The first or 'new' book of cookery consists of recipes for 'Boyled' and 'Baked Meates', a number of which are described as being in the French fashion, together with a section on puddings. There is, in addition, a section entitled 'English Cookerie'. Recipes for 'boyled meats' in this section and their counterparts in the French fashion make such common use of ingredients including almonds, sugar, eggs, dates, grapes, gooseberries, barberries, and lemons that any distinction between the two styles of cookery is negligible. It is also very strange that of the thirty-five recipes which he selects as specifically English, there is not a single example of a broiled, baked, or roast dish.

In the general collection of recipes Murrell includes an unusual one for 'Buds of Hoppes', in which the tender tips of the stalks are boiled and served with melted butter. Doubtless workers in the hop gardens would have early discovered that the tender shoots cut during the course of cultivation could be a useful addition to their stewpots; certainly Thomas Muffet in his *Healths Improvement*, first published in 1655 but originating, and very possibly written, in the sixteenth century, includes hop-shoots among the nourishing herbs and comments on their resemblance to asparagus. Their very restricted availability must have precluded their general recognition for culinary use.

There is nothing of particular interest in the *Second Booke*, which is shorter than the first, and in which a large proportion of the recipes are merely variants of those in the first book. To the two books of cooking is appended a third book entitled *A New Booke of Carving and Sewing*. This is actually a transcript of a book first published in 1508 and reprinted in various forms during the sixteenth century. It contains instructions for carving, rules for the duties of a chamberlain, vintner, and pantler, *inter alia*, and protocol for serving meals in a royal household.

Unlike most of the authors of cookery books of the period Murrell does not include sections devoted to medical recipes in any of his books. He has, however, in his *Two Bookes* 'an excellent and much approved receit for a long Consumption' incorporating snails. This is an early record of such a remedy, which became commonplace in the medical sections of the cookery books of the later years of the seventeenth century and the first half of the eighteenth century. The circumstances of his death are not known. PETER TARGETT

Sources Arber, *Regs. Stationers* · A. W. Oxford, *Notes from a collector's catalogue, with a bibliography of English cookery books up to 1699* (1909) · H. G. Aldis and others, *A dictionary of printers and booksellers in England, Scotland and Ireland, and of foreign printers of English books, 1557–1640*, ed. R. B. McKerrow (1910) · *Messrs Sotheby's book sale catalogue, London* (30 May 77), lot 119 · *STC, 1475–1640* · *BL cat.* · *National Union catalogue* · A. W. Oxford, *English cookery books to the year 1850* (1913) · W. C. Hazlitt, *Old cookery books and ancient cuisine* (1902) · Watt, *Bibl. Brit.*

Murrie, Sir William Stuart (1903–1994), civil servant, was born on 19 December 1903 at 125 Perth Road, Dundee, the elder of the two sons of Thomas Murrie (1877–1908), commercial traveller, of Broughty Ferry, Dundee, and his wife, Catherine Stuart Burgh (1873–1942), daughter of William Burgh, of 21 Jamaica Street, Dundee. Thomas Murrie died while his sons were still young, and his widow emigrated to Valparaiso, Chile, where in 1912 she married Thomas Heggie, bookseller, also originally from Dundee. Murrie attended the German school in Valparaiso, and thus became fluent in German as well as Spanish. Subsequently he attended the Liceo de Aplicación in Santiago before returning in 1919 to Dundee to prepare himself at the Harris Academy for university education in Britain. He graduated with first-class honours in classics from Edinburgh University—in three years instead of the usual four for an honours course—and then, having won a Craven scholarship, attended Balliol College, Oxford, to continue with his study of the classics. He received a second-class degree in *literae humaniores* in 1928.

Having passed third in the civil service examination, Murrie entered the Scottish Office in 1927. In his early years there he served as private secretary, first to Noel Skelton (the parliamentary under-secretary) and then to the secretary of state, Sir Godfrey Collins. On 29 July 1932 he married an American, Eleanore Boswell (d. 1966), who was six years his senior, a university lecturer and Shakespearian scholar, the daughter of Arthur Boswell, of Philadelphia. From 1935 Murrie held senior positions in the Department of Health for Scotland and was the driving force behind the comprehensive arrangements for the evacuation of Scottish children from centres of population at the start of the Second World War. In 1944 he moved as an under-secretary to the war cabinet, and in 1947 was promoted to be deputy secretary to the cabinet. Between 1948 and 1952 he was deputy under-secretary of state at the Home Office, but in 1952 (the year in which he was appointed KBE) he returned to the Scottish Office as head of the Scottish education department, a post he held until 1957, when he became head of the Scottish home department. In 1959 he was promoted to be the permanent under-secretary of state at the Scottish Office. During his time as head of the Scottish Office he reorganized the functions of the various component departments into a more efficient and logically coherent structure.

The high standards that Murrie achieved as an outstanding administrator derived from his powerful analytic mind, formidable memory, and capacity for hard work. He could, and did, show anger towards colleagues who were not, in his view, 'putting their backs into' their work, so that he was feared as well as respected as a departmental head. Fortunately, Murrie had the knack of relaxing completely away from work and the office. He was an excellent companion walking the Scottish hills, an entertaining host serving meals he had expertly cooked, and always the stimulator of good discussions on a wide range of issues. His tall, strong physique equipped him well for hill walking. His extensive knowledge of the arts, music, literature, and the countryside meant that what he had to say was always worth listening to—but he wore his learning lightly, and his interest was in eliciting the views of others rather than in demonstrating his own grasp of a subject. This characteristic may have led to the confidence he inspired in children, who responded with grave friendship to someone who treated them as equals. Although he respected the beliefs of others and conformed where necessary and appropriate to the observances of the church, the rational rigour of his mind made him uncomfortable with any form of theism. An unexpected and attractive trait of this formidable intellect and forceful manager of large numbers of staff was his readiness to take pains to perform some (often quite trivial or menial) task which he had detected would be of service to a friend.

Murrie retired in 1964, and in the same year he was appointed GCB. He then undertook several important public appointments: chairman of the board of trustees of the National Galleries of Scotland, member of the Council on Tribunals, member of the General Practice Finance Corporation, general council assessor of Edinburgh University court, chairman of the governors of Edinburgh College of Art, and member (and latterly chairman) of the advisory committee on Rhodesian travel restrictions. After his wife's death he lived alone for twenty-seven years until the physical handicaps of his great age, and in particular osteoporosis, forced him into St Raphael's Nursing Home, South Oswald Road, Edinburgh. His mind and memory remained as sharp as ever until his death there on 6 June 1994. He was cremated four days later at Mortonhall crematorium, Edinburgh.

J. F. McCLELLAN

Sources WW (1982) · *Who's who in Scotland* (1992–3) · D. Williamson and P. Ellis, eds., *Debrett's distinguished people of today*, 2nd edn (1989) · C. Cunningham, 'Sir William Stuart Murrie: an appreciation', *The Scotsman* (9 June 1994), 12 · *The Times* (20 June 1994) · *The Independent* (10 June 1994) · private information (2004) · personal knowledge (2004) · J. S. Gibson, *The thistle and the crown: a history of the Scottish office* (1985) · G. Pottinger, *The secretaries of state for Scotland, 1926–1976* (1979) · I. Levitt, ed., *The Scottish office: depression and reconstruction, 1919–59*, Scottish History Society, 5th ser., 5 (1992) · M. Macdonald and A. Redpath, 'The Scottish office, 1954 to 1979', *Scottish Government Year Book 1980* [ed., H. M. Drucker] · b. cert.
Archives U. Edin. L., letters to M. M. Swann, Baron Swann
Likenesses photograph, repro. in *The Times* · photograph, repro. in *The Independent*
Wealth at death £555,425.51: confirmation, 29 Sept 1994, *CCI*

Murrow, Edward Roscoe [Ed; *formerly* Egbert Roscoe] (**1908–1965**), radio and television broadcaster, was born on 25 April 1908 at Polecat Creek, near Greensboro, North Carolina, USA, the youngest of the four sons (one of whom died in infancy) of Roscoe C. Murrow (*c.*1879–1955), farmer, and his wife, Ethel (1876–1961), schoolteacher, daughter of George Van Buren Lamb, farmer. His parents were both Quakers. In 1913 the family moved west to Blanchard, Washington, where his father worked as an engine driver for a timber company. Murrow was educated at Edison High School, and in 1926, after a year working as a compassman on a survey gang in the timber camps of the Olympic peninsula, he enrolled at Washington State College, Pullman. It was at this time that he became Edward, and shortened his name to Ed. At college he took a course in radio broadcasting, the first such course in the United States, and graduated in 1930 with a BA in speech.

In 1930 Murrow was elected president of the National Student Federation of America, based in New York city. From 1932 to 1935 he was assistant director of the Institute of International Education, and through this he became assistant secretary to the emergency committee in aid of displaced German scholars, formed in 1933 to place exiled German professors in American universities. On 27 October 1934 he married Janet Huntington Brewster (*b.* 1910), daughter of Charles Huntington Brewster, car dealer, of Middletown, Connecticut: they had one son. She was a cousin of Kingman Brewster, later president of Yale University and American ambassador in London from 1977 to 1981.

Murrow joined Columbia Broadcasting System (CBS) in 1935 as director of talks and education, and in 1937 was appointed European director, based in London. At first he had no staff, but as war approached he built up a team of reporters. In Warsaw at the time of the *Anschluss*, he chartered a plane and flew to Vienna, where he made his first broadcast on 13 March 1938, the day before Hitler entered the city. After war was declared, Murrow and the other American correspondents in London were given every

Edward Roscoe Murrow (1908–1965), by Sir Cecil Beaton

facility by the BBC: the American liaison unit helped to arrange visits to enable them to see as much as possible of the British war effort, as the government realized the propaganda value of these broadcasts in influencing American public opinion. Murrow remained in London throughout the blitz, and managed to get permission from the Air Ministry to send live reports from rooftops during air raids, refusing to go into an air-raid shelter except as a reporter. In his daily broadcasts to America, which always began 'This is London', he described in detail, in a calm, deliberate style, what he saw happening in London, against a background of air-raid sirens and falling bombs. He saw his role as that of a reporter, not a commentator, but the effect was to bring the reality of war and the extent of British suffering to the American public, and to help the British cause in the United States. At a dinner in honour of Murrow in New York in December 1941, the poet Archibald MacLeish said:

> You burned the city of London in our houses and we felt the flames that burned it. You laid the dead of London at our doors and we knew the dead were our dead—were all men's dead—were mankind's dead—and ours.   (Friendly, xvi)

He flew on over twenty-five bombing missions: many thought his best report was from the plane 'D-for-Dog', returning from a bombing raid on Berlin on 3 December 1943. He was the first allied war correspondent at Buchenwald, reporting on its liberation on 15 April 1945. Many of his broadcasts to America were repeated by the BBC, and he also appeared on BBC programmes: he was a frequent panellist on *Freedom Forum*, and he introduced *Meet Uncle Sam* in 1941. A close associate of the prime minister, Winston Churchill, and a frequent visitor to Chartwell, Murrow greatly admired Britain for maintaining parliamentary democracy throughout the war. In his last broadcast before leaving London he said,

> I am persuaded that the most important thing that happened in Britain was that this nation chose to win or lose

this war under the established rules of parliamentary procedure … I have been privileged to see an entire people give the reply to tyranny that their history demanded of them. (10 March 1946)

Murrow returned to New York in 1946 as vice-president and director of public affairs at CBS, but he hated administration, and returned to radio broadcasting in 1947, when he was also appointed to the CBS board of directors. For the next twelve years he delivered a nightly radio news broadcast. With Fred Friendly, later president of CBS News, he established the CBS documentary unit, and launched the radio documentary series *Hear it now* in 1948, which became the television series *See it now* in 1951. In *See it now* Murrow tackled the most controversial and important subjects of the day. His programmes on McCarthyism, including an attack on Senator Joseph McCarthy himself on 9 March 1954, helped to discredit McCarthy, who was condemned by the senate in 1955. He interviewed J. Robert Oppenheimer, the nuclear physicist accused of disloyalty, and in 'The lost class of 1959' reported on the closed schools of Norfolk, Virginia. Continuing his wartime tradition of eyewitness reports, he flew on bombing missions during the Korean War, reported in September 1957 from Little Rock, Arkansas, on the desegregation of schools, and flew into the eye of Hurricane Edna with the air weather service. *See it now* came to be regarded as the most important television show on the air, but it was dropped in 1958, and Murrow, worried by the replacement of serious programmes with popular entertainment during peak viewing hours, took a year's sabbatical in 1959. *CBS Reports* replaced *See it now*, but Murrow had less control over the content. One of the last programmes he narrated was *Harvest of Shame*, put out at Thanksgiving 1960, an exposé of the exploitation of migrant farm labourers, described as a 1960 *Grapes of Wrath*. In a lighter vein, from 1953 to 1959 Murrow presented *Person to Person*, in which he went into the homes of famous people. During these years he continued to visit Britain and to take part in BBC discussions, and he covered the coronation in 1953 for CBS.

Murrow left CBS in 1961 on his appointment by President Kennedy as director of the United States Information Agency (USIA) in Washington, with a seat on the National Security Council. Kennedy wanted the USIA to play a more active role in promoting a good image of the United States abroad, and Murrow concentrated on improving the Voice of America broadcasts, establishing the principle that all the facts should be broadcast, including those embarrassing to the government, believing that such objectivity could only enhance the prestige and credibility of the Voice of America. He felt that the director should take part in making policy, or at least be informed in advance, but one of his first tasks was to explain the Bay of Pigs invasion of Cuba in April 1961, an invasion he disapproved of, and had not known about. Murrow was suggested as a possible Democrat senator in 1962, but he collapsed with pneumonia, and in 1963 was operated on for lung cancer. He resigned from the USIA in January 1964.

Murrow was awarded the medal of freedom, the highest American civil honour, in 1964, and was appointed an honorary KBE in March 1965. He died of lung cancer on 27 April 1965 at his home, Glen Arden Farm, Quaker Hill, Pawling, New York.   ANNE PIMLOTT BAKER

Sources E. Barnouw, *A history of broadcasting in the United States*, 2: *The golden web, 1933 to 1953* (1968) · A. Kendrick, *Prime time: the life of Edward R. Murrow* (1969) · E. Bliss, ed., *In search of light: the broadcasts of Edward R. Murrow, 1938–1961* (1968) · *DAB* · A. M. Sperber, *Murrow: his life and times* (1987) · J. E. Persico, *Edward R. Murrow* (1988) · F. W. Friendly, *Due to circumstances beyond our control* (1967) · BBC WAC · *The Times* (28 Feb 1965) · *New York Times* (28 April 1965) · *WW*
Archives Tufts University, Medford, Massachusetts, Fletcher School of Law and Diplomacy, Edward R. Murrow Center, papers |SOUND BBC Sound Archives
Likenesses photographs, *c*.1945–1958, Hult. Arch. · photograph, 1953, repro. in Sperber, *Murrow*, following p. 588 · C. Beaton, photograph, Sothebys, London, Cecil Beaton archive [*see illus.*] · photograph, repro. in Bliss, ed., *In search of light*, facing p. 145

Murry, John Middleton (1889–1957), writer and journal editor, was born on 6 August 1889 in Peckham, London, the elder of the two sons of John Murry (1860/61–1947), a clerk in the Inland Revenue, and his wife, Emily (1869/70–1951), *née* Wheeler. John Murry was a determined man from an impoverished and illiterate background who taught himself to write. Poor but ambitious, he saw education as the sole means to fulfil his aspirations for his son. Subjected to intense pressure to learn from the time he could speak, John Middleton Murry could read by the age of two. He won one of the first six scholarships to Christ's Hospital, where he attended school (1901–8), and then won an exhibition and a scholarship to study classics at Brasenose College, Oxford, where he took a first in honour moderations (1910) and a second class in his finals (1912).

By this time Murry had abandoned Oxford to live with the writer Kathleen Beauchamp (Katherine Mansfield) [see Murry, Kathleen (1888–1923)]; they married on 3 May 1918. He had also begun his distinguished editorial career as founder of the avant-garde magazine *Rhythm* (1911–13). His friendship with D. H. Lawrence further secured his passionate commitment to modernism in the arts. He and Katherine Mansfield were the witnesses for the Lawrences' wedding in 1914 and the two couples were intimate until their estrangement in 1918. Murry's early career as a journalist demonstrated his exceptional promise and his lifelong capacity for hard work. As well as reviewing literature and art for the *Westminster Gazette* (1912–14), and writing for the *Times Literary Supplement* (1914–18), Murry worked in the War Office in the political intelligence department from 1916 to 1919, first as a translator and then as editor of the confidential *Daily Review of the Foreign Press*. In 1919 he was made chief censor, for which he was made OBE in 1920. As editor of the ailing but still prestigious *Athenaeum* from 1919 to 1921, he championed modernism in literature and provided a platform for the work of writers as diverse as George Santayana, Paul-Ambrose Valéry, Lawrence, Aldous Huxley, T. S. Eliot, and Virginia Woolf. His own first significant critical work, *Dostoevsky*

John Middleton Murry (1889–1957), by Howard Coster, 1934

(1916), and his most frequently reprinted book, *The Problem of Style* (1922), further secured his reputation with his contemporaries.

Katherine Mansfield's death from tuberculosis in 1923 marked a watershed for Murry, whose subsequent life was shadowed by his devotion to her memory, as well as by his embattled engagement with D. H. Lawrence's ideas. Indeed, despite publishing over forty books and pamphlets, Murry now is remembered chiefly for his relationships with these two central figures of his youth. His controversial, often mystical, criticism and journalism returned obsessively to the ideas of the sanctity of art and the need for a new order of pseudo-religious brotherhood, although the forms these ideas took changed through his life. He designed his journal, *The Adelphi*, which he edited from 1923 to 1948, specifically to promote his often fluctuating, but always passionately held principles.

Murry's personal life remained as turbulent as his intellectual affiliations. On 24 April 1924 he married Violet Le Maistre (*c.*1901–1931). They had two children: a daughter, Katherine Middleton, in 1925, and a son, John Middleton, in 1926. Preoccupied by his grief for his first wife, Murry was shocked to discover that Violet, who cultivated her uncanny resemblance to Katherine Mansfield, welcomed the tuberculosis that killed her in 1931 as a Romantic disease. His third marriage, to Ada Elizabeth Cockbayne (1896–1954), housekeeper, on 23 May 1931, proved even more difficult. Although the couple produced two children, a daughter, Mary (born 27 January 1932), and a son, David (born 25 May 1938), the marriage was disastrous. Murry left in October 1941 to live with the author and political activist Mary Gamble (1897–1983). They married on

10 March 1954, after Elizabeth's death in the previous month. Murry's final marriage was his happiest.

Throughout his writing career, Murry remained preoccupied by a semi-mystical Romantic humanism which showed itself to best advantage in his books *Keats and Shakespeare* (1925), *William Blake* (1933), and *Jonathan Swift* (1954). His book on D. H. Lawrence, *Son of Woman* (1931), is still read for its argumentative fidelity in the presentation of Lawrence's life and ideas. Murry's autobiography, *Between Two Worlds* (1935), stands as one of the classic memoirs of the modernist period. Finally, his many essays on Katherine Mansfield, as well as his editions of her stories, journals, and letters, provide invaluable documentary sources for the rise of literary modernism in England.

From the early 1930s through to the end of the 1940s, Murry dedicated himself to socialist and pacifist causes. His writing of this period, such as *The Necessity of Communism* (1932) and *The Necessity of Pacifism* (1937), reflect these commitments. In demand as a lecturer, in both Great Britain and America, he was the editor of the pacifist publication *Peace News* from 1940 to 1946, and suffered a great shock when he learned of Hitler's and Stalin's death camps in 1945. Unsurprisingly, his political views further diminished his already faded reputation during the war. His brief experiment in communal living on his farm, Lower Lodge, Thelnetham, on the Norfolk–Suffolk border, in the 1940s ended with the dozen young men and women he recruited to the project all drifting away. But if the commune foundered, the farm was a success, and Murry ended his life as a well-off gentleman farmer, a Conservative voter, and an integral member of the Thelnetham village community. Murry died of a heart attack on 13 March 1957 in the West Suffolk Hospital, Bury St Edmunds. He was buried three days later in Thelnetham churchyard.

KATE FULLBROOK

Sources F. A. Lea, *The life of John Middleton Murry* (1959) · K. M. Murry, *Beloved Quixote: the unknown life of John Middleton Murry* (1986) · J. M. Murry, *Between two worlds: an autobiography* (1935) · *The letters of John Middleton Murry to Katherine Mansfield*, ed. C. A. Hankin (1983) · P. Mairet, *John Middleton Murry* (1958) · WWW · A. Alpers, *The life of Katherine Mansfield* (1980) · C. Tomalin, *Katherine Mansfield: a secret life* (1987) · I. Ousby, ed., *The Cambridge guide to literature in English* (1988) · M. Drabble, ed., *The Oxford companion to English literature*, 5th edn (1985) · *The Times* (14 March 1957), 15 · *The Times* (6 July 1983), 12 · *DNB* · *CGPLA Eng. & Wales* (1957)

Archives BL, corresp. with the Society of Authors, Add. MSS 63308–63310 · Ransom HRC, MSS and letters · U. Edin. L., corresp., papers, and literary MSS · U. Lond., Institute of Education, letters and MSS relating to the Moot · U. Reading L., corresp. · University of Calgary Library, corresp. · University of Cincinnati, papers | BL, letters to Sydney Schiff and Violet Schiff, Add. MS 52951 · CAC Cam., corresp. with Monty Belgion · U. Newcastle, Robinson L., letters to Jack Common and Mary Common · U. Nott. L., department of manuscripts and special collections, MS biography of D. H. Lawrence · UCL, letters to Sir Richard Rees

Likenesses H. Coster, photograph, 1934, NPG [*see illus.*] · photograph, 1948, Hult. Arch. · B. Hardy, photograph, 5 Aug 1950, Hult. Arch. · H. Coster, photographs, NPG · W. Rothenstein, drawing, repro. in W. Rothenstein, *Twenty-four portraits*, 2nd ser. (1923)

Wealth at death £31,758 1s. 8d.: probate, 25 Sept 1957, *CGPLA Eng. & Wales*

Murry [*née* Beauchamp; *other married name* Bowden], **Kathleen** [*known as* Katherine Mansfield] (1888–1923), writer, was born Kathleen Mansfield Beauchamp at 11 Tinakori Road, Wellington, New Zealand, on 14 October 1888. She was the third child and daughter of Harold Beauchamp (1858–1938) and his wife, Anne Burnell (Annie) Dyer (1864–1918), both born in Australia of parents who had left England in the mid-nineteenth century. Harold Beauchamp had a hard start in life and scant education, but he was ambitious and able, and he prospered greatly as a businessman in the expanding economy of New Zealand; his wife shared his financial and social aspirations. They made the first of many voyages to England in the year after Kathleen's birth, leaving the children in the care of Mrs Beauchamp's mother. There were two more daughters, one dying in infancy, and a cherished son, Leslie. Kathleen, never a favourite, felt herself to be 'the odd man out of the family—the ugly duckling' (*Turnbull Library Record*, 8).

Education and early life In 1893 the Beauchamps moved out of Wellington to a country house at Karori, where Kathleen attended primary school (some of her best-known stories, including 'Prelude' and 'At the Bay', draw on memories of this time). They returned to the city in 1898, and the girls went to the high school and then to the more exclusive Miss Swainson's school. By now Kathleen was a keen reader and beginning to write stories.

In 1903 Beauchamp, eager for his three elder daughters to be 'finished' in Europe, took them to London and left them at Queen's College, the remarkable school founded by F. D. Maurice. They remained for three years in this liberal environment; teaching was by visiting professors, and pupils were free to walk about London unchaperoned. They were also allowed to choose their own course of studies, in Kathleen's case music, German, French, and English. Under the influence of an enthusiastic teacher, Walter Rippmann, she read Ibsen, Tolstoy, Shaw, and Wilde, and edited the school magazine, for which she wrote stories. She also made a friendship that lasted throughout her life with Ida Baker, who gave her an intense and unwavering devotion, and although Kathleen was an imperious and sometimes cruel friend, she thereafter called on Ida whenever she needed help.

Kathleen and her sisters were given holidays in Paris and Brussels, where two young New Zealand musicians, the Trowell brothers, gave her a glimpse of the *vie de bohème* which impressed her. She went reluctantly home to New Zealand in 1906, determined to persuade her parents to allow her to return to London. As she saw it, they stood for trade, she for art. She continued to read voraciously—Maupassant, Bashkirtseff, Balzac—and placed some stories in a New Zealand magazine, the *Native Companion*. She made a trip through the northern wilderness of New Zealand, and also conducted a love affair with a young woman artist, Edith Bendall. This may have persuaded her parents to let her go, and she sailed for England in July 1908. She never returned to New Zealand, and spent the rest of her life on the move.

Arriving in London, Kathleen had an allowance of £100 a year and a room booked in a hostel for young women in Warwick Crescent, Paddington. Ida Baker met the boat train, and became her principal support through the chaotic events of the next year, during which Kathleen joined a touring opera company to be with the young musician Garnet Trowell. She became pregnant by him, but soon parted from him, and made a hasty marriage to a respectable singing teacher, George Bowden (1877–1975), on 2 March 1909. She left him after the ceremony to take refuge with Ida. Hearing of the marriage, Mrs Beauchamp crossed the world to investigate, warning Ida's family about lesbianism and taking Kathleen straight off to a Bavarian spa, Bad Wörishofen. Here she abandoned Kathleen and returned to Wellington, where she disinherited her. Her father, however, continued to pay her allowance, and over the years increased it to £300 per annum.

Kathleen meanwhile had a miscarriage and acquired a

Kathleen Murry [Katherine Mansfield] (**1888–1923**), by Ida Baker, 1920 [at her work table at the Villa Isola, Menton, France]

Polish lover, Floryan Sobienowski. She was very short of money and only when Ida sent her the fare was she able to return to London. She was planning to join Sobienowski in Paris and marry him, once divorced; but early in 1910 she became seriously ill with the effects of untreated gonorrhoea. An operation left her unable to have children, with her health permanently undermined. Sobienowski was dropped.

'A writer first' While in the spa Kathleen set down her impressions of it in a set of bold stories, some humorous and cynical, some with a strongly feminist slant. Her husband, whom she now saw again, introduced her to A. R. Orage, editor of the *New Age*, a fine radical weekly supported by Bernard Shaw. Orage was delighted with Kathleen, and her stories began to appear in the *New Age*, which led to the publication in 1911 of her first collection: *In a German Pension*, under the name Katherine Mansfield. One story, 'The Child-who-was-Tired', was an unacknowledged adaptation of a Chekhov story, an act of plagiarism which haunted her later; but the book was clever and original, and made its mark in the literary world.

Mansfield was leading a peripatetic life, borrowing flats from friends, sometimes sharing with Ida, sometimes staying with Orage, and involved with a series of male lovers. She was strikingly attractive, small and slender, her dark hair now cut short with a fringe. Her eyes, according to Virginia Woolf, were 'beautiful eyes—rather doglike, brown, very wide apart, with a steady slow rather faithful & sad expression. Her nose was sharp … Her lips thin & hard' (*Diary of Virginia Woolf*, 225–7). Others described her face as like a mask, and the painter Anne Estelle Rice, who became a close friend, noticed how she enjoyed changing her appearance dramatically from day to day. There was a Russian Mansfield, a Japanese one, a French one, and so on: she was a natural performer. She often spoke her stories to herself before she wrote them down, and said she would like to act them out before an audience as Dickens had done.

Soon after *In a German Pension* appeared Mansfield met John Middleton *Murry (1889–1957), an Oxford undergraduate who was also running an avant-garde magazine, *Rhythm*. He became first her lodger in her flat in Clovelly Mansions in the Gray's Inn Road, London, then her lover, at which point he abandoned his formal studies and his Oxford scholarship. They called themselves 'the two tigers', and worked together as editors on *Rhythm* (later the *Blue Review*), living on her allowance and what small sums they could earn, and always on the move, in Sussex, in London, and in Paris. They ran up debts but they attracted exceptional talents, including D. H. Lawrence and the French artist Henri Gaudier-Brzeska. Rupert Brooke was asked for a poem, and introduced them to Edward Marsh, who gave them some financial support. On a trip to Paris, Murry introduced Mansfield to a minor French writer, Francis Carco, and she discovered and greatly admired the work of Colette. In 1913 Lawrence and Frieda Weekley returned to England, and the two unmarried couples became close friends. Their circle expanded to include the writer Gilbert Canaan, the painter Mark Gertler, and S. S.

Koteliansky, a Ukrainian political exile whose affections became fixed on Mansfield and D. H. Lawrence.

After the outbreak of war in August 1914, first the Lawrences and then Murry and Mansfield established themselves in two uncomfortable cottages near Chesham in Buckinghamshire; they dined together twice a week, and Frieda found Mansfield 'gay and gallant and wonderful' (*Memoirs and Correspondence*, 425). Her reminiscences of New Zealand probably inspired Lawrence with the lesbian episode in *The Rainbow* (written in winter 1914–15), and she was certainly the model for Gudrun in *Women in Love*.

Mansfield was, however, doing little effective writing herself at this period, and she was dissatisfied with Murry. Early in 1915 she went to France and began a love affair with Carco, making a daring visit to him at the front which she described in 'An Indiscreet Journey'. She then borrowed his flat on the Quai aux Fleurs in Paris, and began to write the story that became *Prelude*. In May she was back in London, living with Murry again in Acacia Road, St John's Wood, helping to edit a new magazine, *Signature*, with Lawrence, and seeing her brother, Leslie, who had volunteered for the army. In October, when Leslie was killed accidentally while giving grenade instruction in France, she insisted on leaving for the south of France in her grief. January 1916 saw her installed with Murry in the Villa Pauline in Bandol: a short period of stability and happiness followed, as they worked side by side.

Then, summoned by the Lawrences, Murry and Mansfield joined them in Cornwall, at Higher Tregerthen, near Zennor, in an attempt at communal living. It was a failure. Mansfield wrote a memorable description of a quarrel between Lawrence and Frieda, and the quarrels extended to involve them all. Within weeks she and Murry moved on; but her loyalty to Lawrence remained, and later in the year she famously defended him in the Café Royal, where two undergraduates at another table were laughing at Lawrence's newly published poems. She went up to them, asked politely for the book, took it, and walked out into the street with it, leaving an admiring Gertler and Koteliansky to report the scene to Lawrence, who immediately wrote it into *Women in Love*.

During the summer of 1916 Mansfield invited herself to Garsington Manor, where Murry was already a frequent guest of the Morrells. She made a conquest of Lady Ottoline Morrell and friends of two women painters she met there, Dorothy Brett and (Dora) Carrington; later in the year she shared a house with them in London at 3 Gower Street. There was a flirtation with Bertrand Russell, and Lytton Strachey was impressed by her. Through him she met Virginia Woolf in 1917; the friendship was important to both aspiring writers, each of whom had so far published one book, and Virginia encouraged her to finish *Prelude*, which she was eager to publish with the Hogarth Press, the small publishing firm Woolf ran with her husband Leonard. He also thought highly of Mansfield, describing her as 'a very serious writer' with the gifts of 'an intense realist, with a superb sense of ironic humour' (*Autobiography of Leonard Woolf*, 204). Both the Woolfs deplored the influence of Murry who encouraged her, they believed, in a 'sickly sentimentality', which does indeed spoil some of her work. There were tensions and jealousies between the two women, but Virginia Woolf entertained her and visited her, and in her diaries showed the value she placed on their meetings: 'to no one else can I talk in the same disembodied way about writing; without altering my thought more than I alter it in writing here' (*Diary of Virginia Woolf*, 45). Again, Woolf wrote that she got 'the queerest sense of an echo coming back to me from her mind the second after I've spoken' (ibid., 61).

Before *Prelude* could appear, Mansfield, currently sharing a studio flat in London with Ida at 141A Old Church Street, Kensington, became seriously ill again. In December 1917 tuberculosis was diagnosed, and she was told she must go south. She travelled alone through wartime France to Bandol in January 1918, and there she suffered her first haemorrhage. Like Lawrence, she would not consider treatment in a sanatorium. Part of her understood the seriousness of her condition, but another part sought to deny the reality of her illness altogether.

Ida Baker, by pleading with the authorities against the wartime prohibition on travel, managed to join Mansfield in France, only to find her insistent on returning to England in March. One reason for this was that her divorce from Bowden was about to come through, and she and Murry could be married. On the way the two women were trapped in Paris during a prolonged German bombardment, and when she arrived back in London at last she was so exhausted and emaciated that Murry was aghast, and fearful of catching tuberculosis himself; instead of embracing her, he turned aside and put a handkerchief to his lips. They were nevertheless married on 3 May 1918 at Kensington register office. Almost at once she developed pleurisy and had to go to Cornwall to recover. Murry took a house, 2 Portland Villas, overlooking Hampstead Heath, and Mansfield persuaded Ida to give up her job and become their housekeeper.

In October Mansfield was warned that she had only four years to live unless she went into a sanatorium. From now on her life was a series of increasingly desperate journeys between London, France, and Switzerland, while her condition grew steadily worse. The four summer months could be spent in Hampstead, then she had to leave England again. She resented Murry's absorption in his work as editor of *The Athenaeum*, and found the separations from him hard to bear. She also resented her dependence on Ida, who accompanied her when she went abroad; but it was Ida's care that allowed her to go on writing, and to produce some of her best work. This she acknowledged in the end, when she wrote to Ida, 'the truth is I can't really work unless I know you are there', and called her 'wife', in acknowledgement of the role she had played (Baker, 203).

Lawrence, also denying his tuberculosis, and penniless, was angry with Murry for refusing to print his work, and transferred the anger to Mansfield in a furious letter (now lost) early in 1920: 'You revolt me, stewing in your consumption' (*Letters between Katherine Mansfield and John Middleton Murry*, 274). After an angry reply she forgave

him, continued to think of him with affection to the end, and left him a book in her will.

Murry gave Mansfield work reviewing fiction for *The Athenaeum*, and he negotiated the publication of her second collection, *Bliss and other Stories*, with Constable, in December 1920. Her £40 advance was lost when Floryan Sobienowski blackmailed her with her old letters. *Bliss* was a success in both London and New York, and that winter she wrote 'The Daughters of the Late Colonel', praised by Thomas Hardy.

In May 1921 Mansfield and Ida moved to the Châlet des Sapins, high up in Montana-Sierre in Switzerland. Murry joined them and they lived quietly for six months, during which Mansfield wrote 'At the Bay', 'The Voyage', and 'The Garden Party' and began 'A Married Man's Story', a brilliant and sinister fragment (published in *The Dial* and *The Dove's Nest*). The publication of her third collection, *The Garden Party and other Stories*, in February 1922 brought her great and deserved acclaim. In the same month she decided to go to Paris, where a Russian doctor was offering a new treatment for tuberculosis by irradiating the spleen with X-rays. It was useless and unpleasant. 'If I were a proper martyr I should begin to have that awful smile that martyrs in the flames put on when they begin to sizzle', she wrote to Brett, but she persisted (*Letters of Katherine Mansfield*, 2.199). While she was in Paris she refused her agent Pinker permission for a reissue of *In a German Pension*, the most likely reason being her fear that the Chekhov plagiarism would be noticed.

Last years In August 1921 Mansfield was in London without Murry, staying at Dorothy Brett's house at 6 Pond Street, Hampstead. She saw her father, who had been widowed and was remarried and about to be knighted, and Koteliansky, who urged her to work as a way of facing pain and suffering. Orage told her he was giving up his editorship in order to follow the teachings of Gurdjieff, a Greek-Armenian guru with a new establishment, Le Prieuré, financed by Lady Rothermere, at Fontainebleau, outside Paris. Gurdjieff preached that civilization had thrown the physical, mental, and emotional aspects of humanity out of balance; Orage was impressed, and so was Mansfield.

Mansfield knew that she was dying. About the time of her thirty-fourth birthday she wrote, 'My spirit is nearly dead. My spring of life is so starved that it's just not dry. Nearly all my improved health is pretence—acting' (*Journal of Katherine Mansfield*, 248). Still she set out her hope that she might yet live to enjoy 'a garden, a small house, grass, animals, books, pictures, music'—and life (ibid., 251). In spite of her growing reputation, she was dismissive of the stories she had written so far, and wanted to do better work.

In mid-October 1922 Ida accompanied Mansfield to Fontainebleau, only to have Mansfield send her away, for the last time. She had a few weeks to live, but started to learn Russian, since most of Gurdjieff's disciples were Russian speakers. At first she was given a comfortable room, then moved to one without a fire until her suffering was obviously and she was restored to the better room at Christmas.

Gurdjieff allowed her to invite Murry to visit. He came on 9 January 1923 and found her 'very pale, but radiant' (*Katherine Mansfield's Letters to John Middleton Murry*, 700). That evening as she went up the stairs she began to cough, a haemorrhage started, she said 'I believe … I'm going to die', and within minutes she was dead (ibid., 701). On 12 January Mansfield was buried in the nearby cemetery at Avon, with Murry, Ida, Brett, and two of her sisters present. Murry inherited her manuscripts and over the next two decades he edited and published almost all her remaining stories and fragments, her journals, her poems, her reviews, and her letters. In doing so he presented to the world an image of a saintly young woman and suppressed the darker aspects of her character and experience, perhaps understandably, given the conventions of the time. He also made a good income out of her considerable royalties. Not a penny went to Ida Baker.

Mansfield's journal, with its vivid impressions of travel, of landscape and weather, gardens, and animals, and of her ever-fluctuating moods, has made her into a cult figure among young women especially. Her stories have found many distinguished admirers including, in addition to those already mentioned, Walter de la Mare, Elizabeth Bowen, V. S. Pritchett, Brigid Brophy, Christopher Isherwood, Angus Wilson, and Alice Munro. She is praised for her economy and speed in assembling and dissolving a scene; for her wit, and touch of the surreal; for her divination of the hatred and cruelties beneath the sweet surfaces of family life; and for her sympathy with the vulnerable, the displaced, and the lonely. She fails chiefly where she falls into sentimentality, and succeeds best when her touch is lightest. She has also had detractors—Aldous Huxley (who portrayed her as Gilray in *Point Counter Point*) was one—and even among her friends both Lawrence and Virginia Woolf regretted that so much inferior work was published by Murry. By the end of the twentieth century her reputation lagged far behind that of the more prolific Woolf, but it is still secure, and not only in English-speaking countries, for she is particularly admired in France and Germany.

For many years there was no likeness of Mansfield in the National Portrait Gallery (at the time of her death a rule forbade the acquisition of any portrait until ten years after the death of a subject). In 1932 Theodora Bosanquet offered the gallery a portrait painted by Anne Estelle Rice in Cornwall in 1918, and letters of support were sent to the trustees by, among others, Leonard and Virginia Woolf, G. K. Chesterton, Rose Macaulay, H. G. Wells, Rebecca West, Walter de la Mare, Edward Garnett, Winifred Holtby, Viola Meynell, and J. C. Squire. Despite this, and despite receiving expert advice that the portrait was a good one, the trustees rejected it and for many years took no further steps to acquire even a photograph (in 1940 the portrait was bought by the National Art Gallery of New Zealand). In 1999 a photograph of Katherine Mansfield was finally hung in the National Portrait Gallery.

CLAIRE TOMALIN

Sources C. Tomalin, *Katherine Mansfield: a secret life* (1987) • *Journal of Katherine Mansfield*, ed. J. M. Murry (1927) • *The letters of Katherine Mansfield*, ed. J. M. Murry, 2 vols. (1928) • *Katherine Mansfield's letters to John Middleton Murry, 1913–1922*, ed. J. M. Murry (1951) • *Letters between Katherine Mansfield and John Middleton Murry*, ed. J. M. Murry and C. A. Hankin (1988) • *The letters and journals of Katherine Mansfield: a selection*, ed. C. K. Stead (1977) • *The collected letters of Katherine Mansfield*, ed. M. Scott and V. O'Sullivan (1984–) • K. Mansfield, MS notes transcribed by M. Scott, *Turnbull Library Record* (March 1970) • I. Gordon, *The Urewera notebook* (1980) • A. Alpers, *Katherine Mansfield: a biography* (1953) • H. Beauchamp, *Reminiscences and recollections* (1937) • I. Baker, *Katherine Mansfield: the memories of L. M.* (1971) • *The diary of Virginia Woolf*, ed. A. O. Bell and A. McNeillie, 2 (1978) • *The memoirs and correspondence of Frieda Lawrence*, ed. E. W. Tedlock (1961) • *The autobiography of Leonard Woolf*, 3 (1964)

Archives NL NZ, Turnbull L., notebooks and letters to husband John Middleton Murry • NRA, corresp. and literary papers • Queen's College, London, notebooks and papers while a student at Queen's College, London • Ransom HRC, letters, literary MSS, photographs • University of Windsor, Ontario | BL, letters to Ida Constance Baker, Add. MS 49064 • BL, letters to S. S. Koteliansky, Add. MSS 48969–48970 • BL, letters to Elizabeth Russell, Add. MS 50844 • BL, letters to Sydney and Violet Schiff, Add. MS 52919 • CUL, letters to W. A. Gerhardie [mostly copies] • Hunt. L., letters to Mary Annette, Countess Russell • McMaster University Library, Hamilton, Ontario, letters to Bertrand Russell • NL NZ, Turnbull L., corresp. with John Galsworthy and William Gerhardi • U. Sussex Library, letters to Virginia Woolf

Likenesses A. E. Rice, portrait, 1918, National Gallery of New Zealand • I. Baker, photograph, 1920, NL NZ, Turnbull L. [*see illus.*] • photograph, NPG

Wealth at death £266 6s. 4d.: probate, 5 April 1923, *CGPLA Eng. & Wales*

Muru mac Feradaig (*fl. c.*600–*c.*650). See under Ulster, saints of (*act. c.*400–*c.*650).

Musard family (*per. c.*1070–*c.*1330), gentry, with land in Gloucestershire and Derbyshire, was of Breton origin, probably from the seigneuries of Dol-Combour and Fougères in north-east Brittany. In 1086 three Musards, perhaps brothers, held land in England. **Hascoit Musard** (*fl.* 1086–*c.*1100), probably the eldest, was a tenant-in-chief holding a little under 89 hides across six counties, of which just over 67 hides were retained in demesne and valued at £75. The most significant collection of manors lay in Gloucestershire, but there were also demesne manors in Derbyshire (where his acquisitions probably began *c.*1070), Warwickshire, Berkshire, and Oxfordshire; principal residences emerged at Greenhampstead (or 'la Musarder', now Miserden), Gloucestershire, where by 1146 there was a motte and bailey castle, ruinous in 1289, and at Staveley in Derbyshire; both of these were referred to as the *caput* of the Musard barony. Few details survive of Hascoit's life and career, but he appears to have lived into the early years of Henry I's reign. The *Liber Eliensis* records a tradition of his devotion to St Etheldreda and the monks of Ely, whose community he entered as a monk, and to whom he granted a manor named 'Estona', probably Aston Somerville, Gloucestershire.

Hascoit was succeeded by his son, **Robert [i] Musard** (*fl. c.*1100–1146), who by the 1140s appears to have been a supporter of the Empress Matilda against King Stephen. In 1146 he was captured and, threatened with hanging, surrendered his castle, presumably Miserden, to Philip, son of the earl of Gloucester. Robert endowed the church of St

Mary, Monmouth, and either he or his father granted tithes to Tewkesbury Abbey. There are references to a Richard Musard, but it is not clear if he was Robert's son or brother; however, it was to Richard's son, **Hascuil Musard** (d. 1185/6), that the family estate descended in 1161/2. In 1166 Hascuil held twelve fees of the old enfeoffment, to which had been added since 1135 a half fee, a one-fifteenth fee, and two fees held in dower by the widow of Richard Musard. He made several religious endowments, including grants to the Premonstratensian abbey at Welbeck in Nottinghamshire, to the Cistercian house of Louth Park in Lincolnshire, and for a community at Birley in Derbyshire, while, in celebration of their marriage, Hascuil and his wife, Joan, between 1162 and 1182 gave half the advowson of Staveley church to the knights hospitallers and their Derbyshire preceptory at Yeaveley. Hascuil seems to have had a particular affection for the hospitallers, making further grants to them which included a part of the Miserden estate, given to the preceptory at Quenington, Gloucestershire. This interest in the military orders was maintained by several Musard tenants in the late twelfth and thirteenth centuries, and by Hascuil's grandson Robert.

Hascuil Musard left a widow and young heir in the custody of the sheriff of Nottinghamshire and Derbyshire, who in 1185-6 accounted for £60 for the farm of Hascuil's lands. In 1190 Hascuil's son, **Sir Ralph** [i] **Musard** (d. 1230), owed £100 for his lands, and for the right to marry as he wished. Recorded as holding fifteen fees in 1205, by 1216 he was a member of the affinity of William (I) Marshal, earl of Pembroke, and as one of his household knights is reported to have encouraged him to accept charge of the kingdom during the minority of Henry III. Sheriff of Gloucestershire between 1215 and 1225, Sir Ralph served regularly as a justice itinerant during the 1220s. He must have married at least twice, for his sons, Robert [ii] and Ralph [ii], were born at least thirteen years before his marriage c.1220 to Isabel, the widow of John de Neville. She died in 1228, Sir Ralph being allowed access to her inheritance except where this was lands that she had held in chief. Sir Ralph himself died in late June 1230. Like his father, he supported Welbeck Abbey with grants from Staveley and their other Derbyshire lands. He, and later his son Ralph [ii], also endowed Welbeck's daughter house at Beauchief, where Sir Ralph joined the community shortly before his death, and where he was buried. Isabel, however, left her body to St Nicholas, Exeter.

Shortly before Sir Ralph's death there appears to have been a family quarrel in which his eldest son, **Robert** [ii] **Musard** (d. 1239), seized the castle of Miserden. The sheriff restored the castle to Sir Ralph, but he died soon afterwards, and in September 1230 Robert took possession of his inheritance, although the castle was temporarily retained in royal custody. His family's links with the earls of Pembroke remained important, and when Richard Marshal rebelled in 1233, abortive orders were given to raze Musard's castle, while his lands were taken into royal hands. But a promise of faithful service soon led to their restoration; they included lands in Lincolnshire and Yorkshire, part of the dower rights of Robert's wife, Juliana (whose former married name was Vavassur).

Robert [ii] died in 1239, his son and heir, Ralph [iii], c.1247, when his inheritance passed to his uncle, **Ralph** [ii] **Musard** (d. 1264). At the time of his death, this Ralph had lands valued at £74, and was survived by several children and a widow, Christiana, who was still alive in 1296-7. His eldest son, **Ralph** [iv] **Musard** (c.1234-1272), was among those who joined the Montfortian faction in the barons' war. He was admitted to the king's peace in December 1266, on condition of future good behaviour, though he temporarily lost some of his lands to the royalist Alan (II), or perhaps Adam, de Plugenet, regaining them by payments under the dictum of Kenilworth. In 1272 Henry III pardoned him £75 owed for the redemption of lands in Berkshire, not wanting any harm to come to Ralph. When he died his estate was valued at a little over £52, of which his widow, Matilda, received interests in Saintbury, and the manor of Siddington. She later married Thomas Trailli, c.1301.

By the mid- and late thirteenth century the financial position of the Musards had become increasingly difficult. The Domesday demesne had become significantly reduced, largely as a result of subinfeudation, concentrating the demesne manors in Derbyshire and Gloucestershire. Here too there was some subinfeudation, and to this was added the pressure of dower settlements. By 1230 Ralph [i] had run up numerous debts, for which his executors were being held responsible in 1231-3, and by 1266 Ralph [iv] owed money to the Jewish financiers of Worcester. The demands made under the dictum cannot have eased matters, and it is possible that the Gloucestershire manor of Eyford, which seems to disappear from the Musard estate by 1273, was sold as a result. It was certainly the case that in 1269 Ralph [iv] Musard agreed to demise the important manor of Staveley to Peter of Chester for a term of seventeen years, in return for which Peter acquitted Ralph of all his debts to the Jewish moneylenders of London, Worcester, and elsewhere, and paid a further £40 in addition. Ralph [iv]'s heir, **John Musard** (c.1267-1289), a minor when his father died, became a ward of the king, who exploited his rights to the full. John was finally given seisin of his lands in December 1287, but had died by 7 February 1289. His three demesne manors of Saintbury, Miserden, and Staveley were together valued around £53, of which Staveley was by far the most valuable, at a little under £38. By the late thirteenth century there had been a shift in the relative values of the demesnes, the role of the Gloucestershire manors diminishing in value by comparison with the key Derbyshire manor of Staveley.

John was succeeded by his uncle, **Nicholas Musard** (c.1240-1300), a clerk in orders, who was granted his lands in April 1289, and was the last in the legitimate Musard line. He had at least three sons and two daughters, but as he was rector of Staveley these children were illegitimate and thereby discounted from the inheritance, which at the time of his death, by December 1300, had been further reduced to the manor of Staveley, valued at a little under

£35. This was divided between his three sisters or their offspring. Nevertheless, Nicholas made provision for his children. In 1298/9 he gave lands in Staveley to his daughter Christiana and he conveyed Miserden to his son **Malcolm Musard** (*fl. c.*1296–*c.*1330), who in turn granted the manor in 1296/7 to Hugh Despenser the elder, a grant which Nicholas confirmed in 1297/8. Similarly, Nicholas enfeoffed Malcolm with Saintbury, which in April 1300 Malcolm was pardoned for having entered without licence, and allowed to retain. However, in 1303 Malcolm obtained a licence to alienate this manor in mortmain to Evesham Abbey.

Neither of these grants by Malcolm stands in isolation. He perhaps saw ties with Hugh Despenser as a means of securing his future. By 1302/3 he had assigned the reversion of the manor of Siddington, held for life by Thomas Trailli and his wife, Matilda Musard, to Hugh, and he also granted to him various other lands and rents. He was a member of Hugh's retinue in 1305, owed him 100 marks in 1306, and as an adherent of Despenser was to have his lands confiscated in 1327. In 1311 Evesham Abbey was pardoned for having acquired a knight's fee in Aston Somerville from Malcolm in mortmain, without royal licence, while in 1316 the abbey also received lands in Warwickshire from him.

Malcolm Musard illustrates well the propensity for some early fourteenth-century gentry to further their prospects and careers by violence. He can be linked with offences of poaching, theft, assault, intimidation, and extortion, sometimes leading in person the gang of associates that did his bidding. He became chief forester of Feckenham, where he had scope to continue his activities, and he fulfilled a number of royal commissions, including keeper of Hanley Castle in 1321. Last recorded in 1330, he was probably dead by 1333.

The Musard family's arms are listed as gules three roundels argent.   JOHN HUNT

Sources *Chancery records* · *Pipe rolls* · *chancery inquisitions post mortem*, PRO, C132/31, no. 16; C132/40, no. 17; C133/2, no. 4; C133/53, no. 6; C133/99, no. 18 · J. Morris, ed., *Domesday Book: a survey of the counties of England*, 38 vols. (1983–92), vols. 5, 13, 14–15, 23, 27 [Berkshire, Buckinghamshire, Oxfordshire, Gloucestershire, Warwickshire, Derbyshire] · F. Madden, 'Pedigree of the Frecheville and Musard families, lords of Crich and Staveley, in Derbyshire', *Collectanea Topographica et Genealogica*, 4 (1837), 1–28 · H. Hall, ed., *The Red Book of the Exchequer*, 3 vols., Rolls Series, 99 (1896) · Dugdale, *Monasticon*, new edn · *Reg. RAN*, vol. 1 · E. O. Blake, ed., *Liber Eliensis*, CS, 3rd ser., 92 (1962) · F. Palgrave, ed., *The parliamentary writs and writs of military summons*, 2 vols. in 4 (1827–34) · J. H. Round, ed., *Calendar of documents preserved in France, illustrative of the history of Great Britain and Ireland* (1899) · K. R. Potter and R. H. C. Davis, eds., *Gesta Stephani*, OMT (1976) · *Paris, Chron.*, vol. 2 · R. H. Hilton, *A medieval society: the west midlands at the end of the thirteenth century* (1983) · D. A. Carpenter, *The minority of Henry III* (1990) · D. Crouch, *William Marshal* (1990) · J. Hudson, *Land, law, and lordship in Anglo-Norman England* (1994) · M. Curtis, 'Sparsholt', *VCH Berkshire*, 4.312–13 · W. J. Sheils, 'Miserden', *VCH Gloucestershire*, 11.47–54 · C. R. Elrington and H. O'Neil, 'Eyford', *VCH Gloucestershire*, 6.72–6 · W. O. Hassall, 'Horspath', *VCH Oxfordshire*, 5.177–89, esp. 177–8 · J. C. Cox, 'The Abbey of Beauchief', *VCH Derbyshire*, 2.63–8 · W. Dugdale, *The baronage of England*, 2 vols. (1675–6) · W. Dugdale, *The antiquities of Warwickshire illustrated* (1656) · K. S. B. Keats-Rohan, 'The Bretons and Normans in England, 1066–1154: the family, the fief and the feudal monarchy', *Nottingham Medieval Studies*, 36 (1992), 42–78
Wealth at death £75; Hascoit Musard: Morris, ed., *Domesday book* · £74; Ralph [ii] Musard: inquisition post mortem, 1264 · £52 15s. 11d.; Ralph [iv] Musard: inquisition post mortem, 1272 · £53 9s. 7d.; John Musard: inquisition post mortem, 1289 · £34 15s. 10 ¾d.; Nicholas Musard: inquisition post mortem, 1300

Musard, Hascoit (*fl.* 1086–*c.*1100). *See under* Musard family (*per. c.*1070–*c.*1330).

Musard, Hascuil (*d.* 1185/6). *See under* Musard family (*per. c.*1070–*c.*1330).

Musard, John (*c.*1267–1289). *See under* Musard family (*per. c.*1070–*c.*1330).

Musard, Malcolm (*fl. c.*1296–*c.*1330). *See under* Musard family (*per. c.*1070–*c.*1330).

Musard, Nicholas (*c.*1240–1300). *See under* Musard family (*per. c.*1070–*c.*1330).

Musard, Sir Ralph (*d.* 1230). *See under* Musard family (*per. c.*1070–*c.*1330).

Musard, Ralph (*d.* 1264). *See under* Musard family (*per. c.*1070–*c.*1330).

Musard, Ralph (*c.*1234–1272). *See under* Musard family (*per. c.*1070–*c.*1330).

Musard, Robert (*fl. c.*1100–1146). *See under* Musard family (*per. c.*1070–*c.*1330).

Musard, Robert (*d.* 1239). *See under* Musard family (*per. c.*1070–*c.*1330).

Muschamp, Geoffrey de (*d.* 1208), bishop of Coventry, began his career as a protégé of Geoffrey (*d.* 1212), illegitimate son of Henry II and archbishop of York. According to the chronicler Roger Howden, the latter, who had been his father's chancellor, while still in possession of the great seal after Henry's death in 1189 fraudulently used it to present Muschamp to the archdeaconry of Cleveland, as well as two other men to canonries at York. This apparently emerged in 1194, when Archbishop Geoffrey made his peace with Richard I, at a cost to himself of 2000 marks, and confessed to his fault of five years earlier. Archdeacon Geoffrey was deprived of his office, though a payment of £100 for the king's grace which he made with two others seems to have secured its restitution, since in the following year he attended a legatine council at York as archdeacon of Cleveland. The truth of the matter is hard to establish, but it seems more likely that in 1189 the archbishop had been acting on the late king's orders, while by 1194 patron and protégé had fallen out, with Muschamp siding with the York chapter in its dispute with the archbishop. He was one of the three members of the delegation that had gone to Rome in that year on the chapter's behalf, and successfully sought papal letters nullifying the sentences of excommunication and sequestration imposed by the archbishop. And his opposition to Archbishop Geoffrey and his representatives thereafter remained implacable; Howden tells a story of his throwing chrism that had been consecrated by Bishop John of Whithorn—at the time the archbishop's only suffragan—onto a dunghill.

In 1198 Muschamp was elected bishop of Coventry, apparently by the monks without reference to the cathedral's secular canons, but in reality by virtue of royal power. He was consecrated by Archbishop Hubert Walter (d. 1205) at Canterbury on 21 June 1198, and was present at King John's coronation on 27 May of the following year. Little can be said of his episcopate, though as a diocesan he seems to have been assiduous enough. He attended a provincial council at Westminster in September 1200, and a legatine council at Reading in October 1206. In 1205 he had been one of the English bishops who composed a letter to the pope, in defence of episcopal involvement in the election of archbishops of Canterbury. As bishop his usual style was 'dei gratia Coventrensis ecclesie minister', and, unlike many of his contemporaries, he does not appear to have adopted the practice of dating his *acta* by either pontifical or incarnational year. He died on 6 October 1208, and, according to Lichfield custom, was buried in the cathedral there.

M. J. FRANKLIN

Sources M. J. Franklin, 'The bishops of Coventry and Lichfield, c.1072–1208', *Coventry's first cathedral: the cathedral and priory of St Mary* [Coventry 1993], ed. G. Demidowicz (1994), 118–38 · *Chronica magistri Rogeri de Hovedene*, ed. W. Stubbs, 4 vols., Rolls Series, 51 (1868–71) · M. Richter, ed., *Canterbury professions*, CYS, 67 (1973) · Dugdale, *Monasticon*, new edn · S. Painter, *The reign of King John* (1949) · D. Whitelock, M. Brett, and C. N. L. Brooke, eds., *Councils and synods with other documents relating to the English church, 871–1204*, 2 (1981) · F. M. Powicke and C. R. Cheney, eds., *Councils and synods with other documents relating to the English church, 1205–1313*, 1 (1964) · *Pipe rolls*, 7 Richard I · M. J. Franklin, ed., *Coventry and Lichfield, 1183–1208*, English Episcopal Acta, 17 (1998)

Musgrave, Sir Anthony (1828–1888), colonial governor, was born at St John's, Antigua, on 17 November 1828, the son of Dr Anthony Musgrave (1793–1852), treasurer of Antigua from 1824 to 1852, and his wife, Mary, *née* Sheriff. He was educated in the British West Indies, and served as private secretary to the governor of Antigua from September 1850 to April 1851. His father sent him to the Inner Temple in London in 1851, but he returned to Antigua as colonial secretary in January 1854 and that same year married Christine Elizabeth Byam; they had a son who died young and a daughter. His wife died in 1858, and in 1860–61 Musgrave was in Nevis as acting president. From April 1861 to May 1862 he was administrator, and then to August 1864 lieutenant-governor, of St Vincent. As governor of Newfoundland from September 1864 he skilfully defused the sectarian issue and zealously advocated federation with the new dominion of Canada, but in mid-1869 he was transferred to British Columbia, and a pro-federation ministry was decisively defeated a few months later. *En route* for the new post he travelled overland across the United States, and in San Francisco married Jeannie Lucinda Field; the couple had three sons.

Musgrave reached British Columbia in August 1869. This time his advocacy of federation was rewarded. British Columbia entered on excellent terms, including

Sir Anthony Musgrave (1828–1888), by Lionel Grimston Fawkes

the assumption of the colonial debt and a firm commitment to a transcontinental railway. Musgrave also reformed the province's rudimentary public service and prepared the introduction of responsible government before leaving in July 1871. He was created CMG in February 1871 and was governor of Natal in 1872–3 and of South Australia from 9 June 1873 to 21 January 1877. South Australia was booming but politically unstable: Musgrave presided over three changes of government, and in his 1877 valedictory address he criticized the system and urged stability. He encouraged several expeditions into the desert country between South and Western Australia, and the Musgrave range in the Northern Territory commemorates him. He was promoted to KCMG on 30 August 1875 and GCMG on 6 June 1885. He published *Studies in Political Economy* in 1875, in which he explored the concept of money as a store of value and drew largely on his colonial experience. As governor of Jamaica from 1877 to 1883 he encouraged bilateral trade relations with Canada, contrary to the policy of the Colonial Office, which viewed him as 'notoriously unsound in his opinion on these matters'. He returned to Australia as governor of Queensland on 6 November 1883. The Musgraves developed a strong sympathy with the liberal premier Samuel Griffith, with whom they shared cultured tastes, concern for reform in the Pacific island labour trade, and the creation of a federal council as a first step towards a closer union of the Australian colonies. Musgrave ridiculed Australian fears of the German threat to New Guinea, but the Germans seized much of it in 1884; that same year he accepted the belated establishment of a British protectorate over southern New Guinea. He also found time for more economic pamphleteering and in 1886 published *The Future of Money: Bimetallism*. First published in the *Westminster Review*, of which he was a shareholder, this work supported W. S. Jevons against Henry Sidgwick. Musgrave also published other economic articles in London journals. At the elections of April 1888 Sir Thomas McIlwraith, whom he detested, returned to power, and was soon at odds with the governor over the exercise of the prerogative of mercy in a test case widely regarded as setting a precedent affecting labour recruiters imprisoned for atrocities against Pacific islanders. On reference to the Colonial Office the McIlwraith government was supported against Musgrave, who was distressed by the outcome and died suddenly, probably of angina pectoris, at Government House, Brisbane, Queensland, on 3 October 1888. He was buried in Toowong cemetery, Brisbane. His second wife survived him with two of their three sons.　　　GEOFFREY BOLTON

Sources *DCB*, vol. 11 · *AusDB* · I. D. McNaughten, 'The case of Benjamin Kidd', *Journal of the Royal Historical Society of Queensland*, 4 (1951) · W. L. Morton, *The critical years: the union of British North America, 1857–1873* (1964) · D. M. L. Farr, *The colonial office and Canada, 1867–1887* (1955) · K. M. Haworth, 'Governor Anthony Musgrave, confederation, and the challenge of responsible government', MA diss., University of Victoria, 1975 · B. Scott, 'The governorship of Sir Anthony Musgrave, 1883–1888', BA diss., University of Queensland, 1956 · R. J. Cain, 'The administrative career of Sir Anthony Musgrave', MA diss., Duke U., 1965 · W. P. Morrell, *British colonial policy in the mid-Victorian age* (1969) · R. B. Joyce, *Sir Samuel Walker Griffith* (1984) · A. Musgrave, *Studies in political economy* (1875) · A. Musgrave, *The future of money: bimetallism* (1886) · Boase, *Mod. Eng. biog.* · R. Hyam, *Britain's imperial century, 1815–1914: a study of empire and expansion*, 2nd edn (1993) · *CGPLA Eng. & Wales* (1889)
Archives Duke U., Perkins L., corresp. and papers · NL Aus., MSS | Bodl. Oxf., corresp. with Lord Kimberley · NA Scot., letters to Sir H. B. Loch
Likenesses L. G. Fawkes, watercolour drawing, Gov. Art Coll. [*see illus.*]
Wealth at death £6020 18s. 8d.: probate, 7 Feb 1889, *CGPLA Eng. & Wales*

Musgrave, Sir Christopher, fourth baronet (*c.*1631–1704), politician, was the third son of Sir Philip *Musgrave, second baronet (1607–1678), of Edenhall, Cumberland, and Julian (*c.*1607–1660), daughter of Sir Richard Hutton of Goldsborough, Yorkshire. Musgrave entered Queen's College, Oxford, on 10 May 1651, graduating BA the same day, and three years later was admitted to Gray's Inn, London, but was never called to the bar.

Musgrave's political sympathies first became apparent with his involvement in the royalist conspiracies of 1655 and 1659, the first of which led to a spell in the Tower. Shortly before the restoration of Charles II, Musgrave travelled to the Netherlands in the hope of coming to the notice of the Stuart court, and succeeded in being appointed deputy governor of Carlisle Castle in 1660 and in gaining commissions in the castle's garrison, first as lieutenant and then as captain. On 31 May 1660 Musgrave married

Sir Christopher Musgrave, fourth baronet (*c.*1631–1704), by John Riley

Mary, daughter of the London merchant Sir Andrew Cogan, first baronet, with whom he had two sons and one daughter before her death on 8 July 1664. Musgrave first secured his return to the Commons in 1661, for the borough of Carlisle, and he was returned to every subsequent parliament until his death. During the 1660s Musgrave also gained a number of minor government and court offices, including an appointment in 1663 as clerk of the robes to Queen Catherine of Braganza, and on 26 May 1671 he was knighted. About this time Musgrave married, by a licence dated 15 May 1671, Elizabeth, the daughter of Sir John Franklin of Willesden, Middlesex, with whom he had six sons and six daughters before her death on 11 April 1701.

Musgrave's political and administrative careers were unremarkable until the late 1670s, when the political crisis occasioned by the revelations of the Popish Plot and the attempts to exclude James, duke of York, from the succession placed a premium on loyalty to the Stuarts. Musgrave became a leading advocate of the court's case, and his endeavours brought both personal advancement, in the form of an appointment as master-general of the ordnance in 1679, and the personal gratitude of the duke of York. That Musgrave was in high favour for the remainder of Charles II's reign is clear from his promotion to lord lieutenant of the ordnance in 1682, and he proved himself an ardent supporter of royal policy at this time, most notably in his support for the surrender of the Appleby and Carlisle charters in 1684.

Musgrave retained his offices following the accession of James II, and in the 1685 parliament was a prominent proponent of a generous financial settlement for the new king. In March 1687, however, it became apparent that loyalty to the crown was not his sole concern. When questioned by the king as to whether he would support the repeal of the penal laws and the Test Acts, Musgrave responded in the negative, though assuring James that 'his Majesty might strip him to his shirt, if he pleased, but that he w[oul]d sell that shirt, if he had nothing else, for a sword to fight for his Majesty' ('Memoirs of Lord Crewe'). Musgrave was consequently stripped of his offices. Later in the same year, on 27 December, he succeeded his brother as the fourth baronet of Edenhall. Though he had been unwilling to support the attempt to dismantle the Anglican monopoly of civil office, he played no part in the plans for the northern rising that accompanied William of Orange's invasion of 1688. Following William's landing he secured the surrender of the Catholic troops based in the garrison at Carlisle, but his actions stemmed from a desire to preserve order rather than support for William's actions.

During the Convention Parliament, called following the flight of James II, Musgrave became a leading tory spokesman, opposing the resolution that the throne be declared vacant and advocating that a regency be established. Bishop Gilbert Burnet claimed that following the revolution Musgrave was 'alienated from the King' by William III's refusal to grant him any mark of official favour (*Bishop Burnet's History*, 4.195–6), and it is certainly the case that immediately after the revolution he aspired to a return to office. He was, however, overlooked for the post of governor of Carlisle Castle and was refused a place on the privy council. His hopes of high office dashed, Musgrave became one of the leading tory and opposition spokesmen in the Commons into the early years of the reign of Queen Anne, a position he owed to his ability to articulate the concerns and prejudices of the typical back-bench tory MP. His defence of the rights of the established church, advocacy of concentrating on naval supremacy in the wars against France, and wariness of foreign allies all struck a chord with country tory back-benchers, as did his concern to scrutinize supply legislation and minimize the financial impact of the Nine Years' War. Hostility towards the granting of supply in the 1690s led him into fierce parliamentary confrontations with Sir John Lowther of Lowther, one of the leading government spokesmen in the Commons, but Musgrave's determination carefully to examine supply legislation was consistent throughout the 1690s irrespective of the leading figures at the Treasury. Burnet subsequently alleged that 'upon many critical occasions, he [Musgrave] gave up some important points, for which the king found it necessary to pay him very liberally', most notably in 1697 when Musgrave was reported to have supported the settlement of the civil list at £700,000 p.a. in return for personal financial benefits (*Bishop Burnet's History*, 4.195–6). The truth of this claim is difficult to assess. A contemporary account of the 1697 debate indicates that Musgrave in fact opposed this settlement of the civil list, but Burnet was not the only contemporary to make such allegations.

Musgrave's opposition to successive ministries was not limited to matters of finance, and he became an ardent supporter of measures, such as triennial and place bills, intended to place limits upon the royal prerogative. His political opponents were quick to highlight the contrast between Musgrave's opposition to William's administrations and his support for the court during the reigns of Charles II and James II, and such reflections fuelled speculation concerning Musgrave's loyalty to the revolution settlement. These concerns were heightened by Musgrave's consistent opposition to the imposition of oaths abjuring James II, most notably in 1696 when he was among those who initially refused to sign the Association, and Musgrave did little to dampen such rumours by his association in Cumberland and Westmorland politics with non-jurors and Jacobite conspirators. Such actions, and his consistent harrying in parliament of ministerial proposals, led to Jacobite agents expressing the hope that he could be brought into measures to restore James II, but there is little evidence of any direct involvement in Jacobite intrigue.

Following the accession of Queen Anne in 1702, and the consequent establishment of a predominantly tory ministry, Musgrave returned to government office, accepting the lucrative post of teller of the exchequer. He nevertheless found the habits of opposition hard to break. He opposed government policy on a number of occasions in the parliamentary session of 1702–3, and it was not until the following session that he began to temper his partisan ardour. On 25 July 1704 he was 'seized with an apoplexy', a fit brought on, according to his close friend William Nicolson, bishop of Carlisle, by falling from 'a diligent attendance in Parliament all winter … into too plentiful and indulgent a way of living' (Gray and Birley, 201). Musgrave died four days later at his town house in Swallow Street, and was buried at Holy Trinity Minories, London. Succeeded in his baronetcy by his grandson, Musgrave left to his heir and younger sons an estate estimated by contemporaries to be worth over £30,000, a large enough sum to give rise to speculation as to whether he had received secret payments from William III or even Louis XIV of France. However, even a political enemy and propagator of these claims such as Burnet was prepared to concede Musgrave's contribution to post-revolution politics, describing him as 'the wisest man of the party' and claiming that following his death the tories 'wanted his direction' (*Bishop Burnet's History*, 4.196).

RICHARD D. HARRISON

Sources 'Musgrave, Sir Christopher, 4th bt', HoP, *Commons, 1690–1715* [draft] · E. Cruickshanks, 'Musgrave, Christopher', HoP, *Commons, 1660–90* · will, PRO, PROB 11/477, sig. 167 · Foster, *Alum. Oxon.* · *Bishop Burnet's History*, 4.195–6 · *The manuscripts of the earl of Dartmouth*, 3 vols., HMC, 20 (1887–96), vol. 1, p. 53 · [J. Smith], 'Memoirs of Nathaniel, Lord Crewe', ed. A. Clark, *Camden miscellany, IX*, CS, new ser., 53 (1895), esp. 30 · *CSP dom.*, 1697, 523 · BL, Add. MS 30000 A, fols. 409–10 · Sir William Simpson to John Methuen, 3 Oct 1704, University of Kansas, Lawrence, Kenneth Spencer Research Library, Simpson–Methuen correspondence, MS C163 · T. Gray and E. Birley, eds., 'Bishop Nicolson's diary', *Transactions of*

the Cumberland and Westmorland Antiquarian and Archaeological Society, new ser., 46 (1947), 191–222
Archives Cumbria AS, Carlisle, corresp. | BL, letters to Robert Harley, loan 29 · BL, letters to Lord Oxford, Add. MS 70289 · Cumbria AS, Carlisle, corresp., mainly with Sir Daniel Fleming
Likenesses J. Riley, portrait, priv. coll. [*see illus.*]
Wealth at death approx. £30,000; left estates in Cumberland and Westmorland, and mines in co. Durham: Sir William Simpson to John Methuen, 3 Oct 1704, University of Kansas, Lawrence, Kenneth Spencer Research Library, Simpson–Methuen correspondence, MS C163; will, PRO, PROB 11/477, sig. 167

Musgrave, George Musgrave (1798–1883), Church of England clergyman and travel writer, was born in the parish of St Marylebone, Middlesex, on 1 July 1798, the eldest son of George Musgrave (1769–1861) of Marylebone and of Shillington Manor, Bedfordshire, married on 19 August 1790 to Margaret (*d.* 1859), only daughter of Edmund Kennedy. He was one of the earliest pupils of the Revd Charles Parr Burney, archdeacon of St Albans and then of Colchester, who in 1813 had taken over his father's school in Greenwich. On 17 February 1816 Musgrave matriculated from Brasenose College, Oxford. He graduated BA in 1819, when he took a second class in classics. Having made his first trip to the continent, he proceeded MA in 1822, and he was ordained deacon in 1822 and priest in 1823. In 1824 he held the curacy of All Souls, Marylebone, and from 1826 to 1829 he served in the same position at Marylebone parish church. While serving there he married, on 4 July 1827, Charlotte Emily (*d.* in or before 1877), youngest daughter of Thomas Oakes, formerly senior member of council and president of the board of revenue, Madras; they had two sons and three daughters.

During the years 1835–8 Musgrave was rector of Bexwell, near Downham, Norfolk, and he was vicar of Borden, Kent, from 1838 until 1854, when he resigned in favour of his son-in-law. Musgrave was lord of the manor of Borden and one of its chief landowners: during his time as vicar he filled the east and west windows of the church with stained glass to the memory of his relations. After 1854 he lived in retirement, first at Withycombe Raleigh, near Exmouth, Devon; then near Hyde Park, London, and lastly in Bath. It was probably during his residence at Bath that he married, on 24 July 1877, Charlotte Matilda, elder daughter of the Revd William Stamer, rector of St Saviour's, Bath, and widow of Richard Hall Appleyard, barrister.

During the years of his retirement Musgrave travelled much. He knew France particularly well and also travelled in Sicily, the Apennines, and the Alps, and along the Elbe and the Danube. He frequently lectured at local institutions about his tours or his antiquarian studies. In 1863 he issued under the name of Viator Verax MA a pamphlet entitled *Continental Excursions: Cautions for the First Tour*, whose exaggerated account of the difficulties of continental travelling proved popular. These difficulties did not dissuade him from travel, however, and he published seven quite well-received books narrating his leisurely and gossiping rambles in his favourite country of France between 1848 and 1870. Earlier, while at Borden, Musgrave had published several educational and devotional works for the

benefit of his parishioners, both children and adults. He also published three works of translation and verse, of which his translation of Homer's *Odyssey* into English blank verse won him enrolment in the Institut de France. He was an honorary exhibitor at the Royal Academy.

Two prizes were founded by Musgrave at the Clergy Orphan Corporation School for Boys, St Thomas's Mount, Canterbury, and three at its girls' school at St John's Wood, London. Musgrave died at 13 Grosvenor Place, Bath, on 26 December 1883. His eldest son, Horace, had predeceased him. His second wife died at Paignton on 20 April 1893 and was buried at Bath.

W. P. COURTNEY, *rev.* ELIZABETH BAIGENT

Sources Foster, *Alum. Oxon.* · Burke, *Gen. GB* (1886) · Crockford (1882) · *GM*, 3rd ser., 11 (1861), 215 · *Men of the time* (1875) · Allibone, *Dict.*, suppl. · Boase, *Mod. Eng. biog.* · *CGPLA Eng. & Wales* (1884) · *The Academy* (5 Jan 1884), 9
Wealth at death £4190 9s. 8d.: probate, 21 Aug 1884, *CGPLA Eng. & Wales*

Musgrave, Sir James, baronet (1826–1904), industrialist and philanthropist, was born at Lisburn, co. Antrim, Ireland, on 30 December 1826, the seventh of nine sons (and one of the twelve children) of Dr Samuel Musgrave (1770–1836), a leading physician of Lisburn, and his wife, Mary (*d.* 1862), daughter of William Riddel, of Comber, co. Down. The Musgrave family had come to Ulster from Cumberland in the seventeenth century. Musgrave's father, who sympathized with the United Irishmen, was arrested on 16 September 1796 on a charge of high treason and imprisoned in the new gaol, Dublin. Released in 1798, he resumed professional work in Lisburn; but in 1803 he was again arrested and imprisoned for a time on a similar charge.

After attending local schools and receiving private tuition, Musgrave began early a business career in Belfast, and ultimately, with two of his brothers, John Riddel and Robert, he established the important firm of Musgrave Brothers, iron founders and engineers. Taking part in the public life of Belfast, he was in 1876 elected one of the Belfast harbour commissioners, and was subsequently regularly re-elected, serving as a chairman of the commission from 1887 to 1903. Under Musgrave's direction the harbour was greatly improved, and new docks, quays, and deep water channels constructed for the increasing trade, one of these being named the Musgrave Channel in his honour.

In 1877 Musgrave was elected president of the Belfast chamber of commerce. The moving spirit in the establishment of the Belfast Technical School, he helped greatly in the erection of the Royal Victoria Hospital in Belfast, in commemoration of the jubilee of Queen Victoria, and founded in 1901 the Musgrave chair of pathology in Queen's College, Belfast. Musgrave worked hard as a member of the Recess Committee, formed in 1895 by Sir Horace Plunkett to devise means for the improvement of the agricultural and economic condition of Ireland, and whose proposals were embodied in 1899 in an act of parliament.

In 1866 Musgrave and his brother John purchased an

Sir James Musgrave, baronet (1826–1904), by Walter Frederick Osborne, 1898

estate of some 60,000 acres in co. Donegal. During part of every year he resided on the estate at Carrick Lodge, Glencolumbkille, taking a personal interest in the welfare of the tenants. He was appointed JP and deputy lieutenant of co. Donegal, and served as high sheriff in 1885–6. He was chairman of the Donegal Railway Company, in the establishment of which he had a large share. In 1897 he was created a baronet of the United Kingdom. Musgrave, who was unmarried, died at his home, Drumglass House, Belfast, on 22 February 1904, and was buried in the cathedral churchyard, Lisburn. A stained-glass window to his memory, and to that of other members of the family, was put up in the First Lisburn Presbyterian Church, to which his ancestors belonged.

THOMAS HAMILTON, rev. IAN ST JOHN

Sources Belfast News-Letter (23 Feb 1904) · WWW, 1897–1915 · Belfast News-Letter (19 Sept 1796) · personal knowledge (1912) [H. Musgrave DL] · private information (1912) [H. Musgrave DL] · CGPLA Eng. & Wales (1904)
Likenesses W. F. Osborne, oils, 1898, Belfast Harbour Commissioners' collection [see illus.] · A. McF. Shannan, marble bust; formerly in Belfast Harbour Office, 1912
Wealth at death £37,475 19s. 3d.—effects in England: Irish probate sealed in London, 18 April 1904, CGPLA Eng. & Wales

Musgrave, John (fl. 1642–1654), pamphleteer, was the younger son of John Musgrave (d. in or before 1654) and Isabel, daughter of Thomas Musgrave of Hayton, Cumberland; he may have been the John Musgrave baptized as the son of Isabel and John Musgrave on 2 October 1608 at Newton Reigny, Cumberland. A grandson, through his father, of Sir Simon Musgrave of Edenhall, Musgrave appears to have been a cousin of the royalist army officer Sir Philip Musgrave. The Dictionary of National Biography claims that he lived at Milnerigg in Cumberland at some point, but it has not been possible to identify such a place.

Musgrave's early years are obscure. Samuel Chidley, defending Musgrave in a pamphlet of 1652, claimed he had been 'bred up in the law from his youth and also is versed in the Scripture' (Chidley, 6–7); there is no evidence that he attended Oxford or Cambridge, or any of the inns of court, but he apparently became an attorney with a practice in London. In 1642 he joined the parliamentarian forces and attained the rank of captain. The justices and commissioners of array for royalist-controlled Cumberland, however, ordered him to be imprisoned in Carlisle gaol for six months. He was later moved, with a fellow prisoner Captain Richard Crackenthorpe, to London by habeas corpus; following a petition to the Commons, they were both released on 13 December 1642. He spent most of the next two years in Scotland, and on his return to Cumberland in 1644 found the county still under royalist control. This prompted him, along with another parliamentary exile, John Osmotherley, to go to London to petition parliament on behalf of the 'well affected' of Cumberland and Westmorland. He particularly complained that Richard Barwis, member for Carlisle, had betrayed his trust by placing disaffected persons in office.

The Commons referred the matter to a committee and, following Musgrave's refusal to answer certain interrogatories, imprisoned him in the Fleet for contempt on 28 October 1645. Over the following year he published three works protesting against his imprisonment: A word to the wise, displaying great augmented grievances and heavie pressures of dangerous consequence (1646), Another Word to the Wise, Shewing that the Delay of Justice is Great Injustice (1646), and Yet another word to the wise, shewing that the grievances … in Cumberland and Westmoreland … are so far yet from being redressed (1646). He repeatedly denounced 'the not redressing of our countries grievances', and complained that 'they are now under far more heavy pressures, then formerly they were, under the King's party' (Yet another word to the wise, 33). Musgrave's case became a cause célèbre for those who could identify with his rhetoric of first royalist and then parliamentary tyranny, in particular those in the rising Leveller movement: John Lilburne took up Musgrave's plight in Englands Birth-Right Justified (1645), William Larner described Musgrave as one who 'suffereth for the Freedom of the Nation' (Larner, 16), and Richard Overton recommended Musgrave's writings in his own work.

Musgrave was released in January 1647, whereupon he petitioned the Lords complaining of the losses he had suffered 'for adhering to the Parliament' (JHL, 9.670). He justified himself in A Fourth Word to the Wise, or, A Plaine Discovery of Englands Misery (1647), addressed to Henry Ireton, which appeared in May. This denounced the 'professed enemies and known delinquents' who controlled Cumberland, and complained that 'some corrupted members [of the Commons] falsyfie and betray their trust, and as much as in them lies, seek the destruction of that House and their countrey' (pp. 5, 9). That summer Musgrave also published an extract, attributed to François Balduin, from Edward

Grimstone's history of the Netherlands, under the title *Good Counsel in Bad Times* (1647). He had read Grimstone's work while in prison and added a characteristic epistle lambasting 'the arbitrary and tyrannicall government of our corrupt magistracy and ministery' in Cumberland (sig. A2r). In the meantime the Lords referred Musgrave's petition to the Commons, which declined to grant any compensation and in July ordered him to be imprisoned once again for publishing 'scurrilous and scandalous pamphlets' (*JHC*, 5.245). In the same month the New Model Army and its agitators called for his release, listing him alongside the leaders of the Levellers as a sufferer of parliamentary tyranny.

In September 1647 Musgrave convened a meeting of London apprentices at the Guildhall in a bid to force parliament to redress his alleged grievances. This resulted in some bloodshed, and, though Musgrave later denied having been present, on 25 September the Commons resolved to indict him in king's bench for high treason and ordered him to be imprisoned in Newgate. This prompted Musgrave to write another pamphlet, entitled *A declaration of Captaine John Musgrave … vindicating him against the misprisians and imputed reasons of his sad imprisonment for high treason against the state* (1647), in which he demanded satisfaction against 'all the traductions that ayme at my life' (Musgrave, 5). Proceedings against him were later dropped, and on 3 June 1648 the Commons allowed him to be released on bail.

Musgrave thereafter devoted himself to uncovering delinquents and seeing that they compounded for their estates to the highest value. He later claimed that his activities generated revenue worth £13,000 a year. Leveller petitions were still citing his case in 1649, for example in *The Young Men, and Apprentices Outcry*. On 27 August he was among those who submitted a remonstrance to the council of state calling for the militia of Cumberland and Westmorland to be placed in trusty hands. Charles Howard, later first earl of Carlisle, challenged him to substantiate his claims. Musgrave then objected to the persons nominated by Sir Arthur Hesilrige to be militia commissioners for the northern counties. He was ordered to formulate his accusations, and Hesilrige reported them to be groundless. Musgrave responded with *A true and exact relation of the great and heavy pressures and grievances the well-affected of the northern bordering counties lye under by Sir Arthur Haslerigs misgovernment* (1650), in which he attacked 'the great and heavy oppressions we lay under, by the disorder and misgovernment of those placed in authority, by Sir Arthur Haslerigs procurement, and recommendation' (p. 3). The council of state ordered this pamphlet to be seized on 19 December 1650. A reply, entitled *Musgrave Muzl'd*, appeared in 1651, which Musgrave answered in *Musgraves musle broken … wherein is discovered how the Commonwealth is abused by sub-commissioners for sequestrations* (1651). Here he reiterated his charges against Hesilrige and his commissioners, complaining that they 'now more tyrannize, oppose and squeeze the countery, cozen the state, and inrich themselves out of the ruines of poor plundered people, then any ever did, or durst attempt under a King

and prelates' (sig. *2r). In January 1651 the council of state declared Musgrave's charges against Howard and Hesilrige to be 'false and scandalous' (*CSP dom.*, 1651, 21, 23), and recommended Hesilrige to begin legal proceedings against him.

By this time Musgrave was widely mistrusted on all sides. On 3 February 1651 the committee for advance of money compelled him to enter into a bond of £1000 to prosecute several Cumberland men for alleged under-valuations in their compositions. Musgrave published one further pamphlet, entitled *A Cry of Bloud of an Innocent Abel Against Two Bloudy Cains* (1654). This grew out of a violent family dispute over some property, following his mother's second marriage to John Vaux, and in the pamphlet Musgrave cast himself as 'Innocent Abel'. The dispute was eventually settled in chancery.   DAVID L. SMITH

Sources state papers domestic, Charles I, PRO, SP 16 · state papers domestic, interregnum, PRO, SP 18 · M. A. E. Green, ed., *Calendar of the proceedings of the committee for advance of money, 1642–1656*, 3 vols., PRO (1888) · M. A. E. Green, ed., *Calendar of the proceedings of the committee for compounding … 1643–1660*, 5 vols., PRO (1889–92) · JHC, 2–5 (1640–48) · JHL, 9 (1646–7) · J. Musgrave, *A declaration of Captaine John Musgrave … vindicating him against the misprisians and imputed reasons of his sad imprisonment for high treason against the state* (1647) · IGI · DNB · W. Hutchinson, *The history of the county of Cumberland* (1794–7), vol. 2, p. 289 · S. Jefferson, *The history and antiquities of Cumberland*, 1 (1840), 415–16 · S. Chidley, *The dissembling Scot* (1652) · [J. Lilburne], *England's birth-right justified* (1645) · [W. Larner], *A true relation of all the remarkable passages, and illegall proceedings, of some sathannicall or doeg-like accusers of their brethren* (1646) · private information (2004) [P. Baker]

Musgrave, Sir Philip, second baronet (1607–1678), royalist army officer and local politician, was born on 21 May 1607 at Edenhall, Cumberland, the son of Sir Richard Musgrave, first baronet (1584/5–1615), of Hartley, Westmorland, and his wife, Frances Wharton (c.1590–1629), daughter of Philip, third Baron Wharton. While Musgrave was still a child his father, who had been MP for Westmorland in the parliament of 1604–11, abandoned his estates only to die a Catholic in Naples while on the grand tour. Musgrave was left in the care of his mother, 'a lady of great virtue, witt and spirit' and her father (*Life*, 2). After three years with them, about 1618 he went to live in the household of the judge Sir Richard *Hutton, where he was privately educated until going to Cambridge. He was admitted as a fellow-commoner to Peterhouse on 17 October 1622. However, as his earliest biographer noted, Musgrave's 'sickly body was an hindrance to his learning', and he continued at Cambridge 'scarcely a yeare, the air not agreeing with him' (*Life*, 3). Oxford seems to have suited him little better: he attended Trinity College there for nine months, a period ended by his being called back north by the death of his grandfather in March 1625.

Late in 1625 or early in 1626 Musgrave married Julian Hutton (c.1607–1660), the youngest daughter of Sir Richard, and upon marriage moved back into his father-in-law's household, where he lived for the next three years. On 15 May 1626 he was admitted to Gray's Inn, which he attended for a year (he was readmitted on 2 February 1630). With the birth of their first son, in 1628 or 1629,

Musgrave and his wife moved back to the family seat at Hartley Castle. The couple had six sons and one daughter, not all of whom survived into adulthood. Musgrave's main seat remained Hartley in the 1630s. By the mid-1650s he had moved his residence to Edenhall; perhaps initially a means of retrenchment after the civil war, the move was permanent by the Restoration, leaving Hartley as the residence for his heir's household.

Musgrave initially returned home to a very 'tangled and disordered Estate' and he took great care to revive the condition and income of his inheritance in the years before the civil wars (*Life*, 4). He was a staunch supporter of the crown and became a local politician of some note. Otherwise he had a 'melancholly disposition and Weak body not much addicted to those pleasures which young gentlemen commonly accustom themselves to' (ibid., 5). He was made young a justice of the peace and a deputy lieutenant in Cumberland and Westmorland; his biographer suggests that he was appointed JP in 1629 or 1630, but the firmest dates for his holding both posts come somewhat later, as JP from 1638 and deputy lieutenant from 1639; these dates match with the mounting crisis with Scotland, during which Musgrave was appointed captain of the trained bands and secured Carlisle. He was elected MP for Westmorland in both the Short and Long parliaments.

With the outbreak of civil war Musgrave acted swiftly to defend the king's rights. He was appointed commander-in-chief of the royalist forces in Cumberland and Westmorland and, attempting to transform the local militia into a royalist army, was never neutral, unlike some of his neighbours. His factious temper and overbearing manner caused many difficulties for them and there was some resentment at his elevation. The result was that Musgrave was barely able to use the troops outside his own county. Major disagreements between Musgrave and his officers were also frequent and his orders were often challenged or affronted. He did not serve at Marston Moor in 1644, but in the aftermath of the battle was forced to retreat into Carlisle. While the city was besieged for some nine months his lands and home were seized and plundered. After the surrender of Carlisle Musgrave went to join the king's forces at Cardiff; his forces were among those scattered at Rowton Heath in 1646, while he himself was wounded and taken prisoner. Having been imprisoned at York for five weeks he was then moved to Pontefract Castle and eventually released. He then went to King Charles at Newcastle until the Scots handed the king over to parliament. After that he remained in the north country and the borders for some months, although he did pay a visit to Charles I while the latter was at Hampton Court, once more returning north when the king fled to the Isle of Wight.

In the meanwhile Musgrave's eldest son had died in Paris. He took this death very hard, but he was willing to involve himself in the intrigues that led to the second civil war. His forces captured Carlisle on 29 April 1648 and he also went to Edinburgh to negotiate with the Scots. Scottish forces relieved the subsequently besieged city, but Musgrave was not present at the battle of Preston.

Instead in the aftermath of that defeat he threw himself and his forces into Appleby and was finally forced to capitulate on 9 October 1648. In 1649 following the death of Charles I he left England and was part of the exiled royalist community, serving Charles II in Scotland in 1650 until the Scots tried to have him removed from the king's entourage. Musgrave subsequently moved to the Isle of Man to join the earl of Derby. He returned to England to take part in the Worcester campaign, but missed the king and was nearly captured. After this he returned to Man and was made governor there until its surrender.

Musgrave returned to England only under the protectorate, although much of his landed estate and valuables had been seized from him as a proscribed royalist and he was subject to frequent arrest and harassment in 1653 and 1655 and was summoned before the council of state in 1659. He came back into his own again at the Restoration, being present once more in the monarchical retinue at the king's entrance into London in May 1660. For his past services Musgrave was subsequently offered a peerage, but he refused; the poverty of his estate, he claimed, could not bear the honour.

As an important local officer in the north of Restoration England, Sir Philip Musgrave once more came into constant conflict with his fellow magistrates throughout the early 1660s. Civil war animosities were still rife at the local level in Cumberland and Westmorland and one of his colleagues, evidently resentful at Musgrave's manner, described him as acting as though he were a 'Grand Vizar and Bashawes Begg of Westmorland' (Fleming papers, MS WD/Ry 34, fol. 59). His obvious loyalty to the crown, however, saw Musgrave return as both a reliable governor of Carlisle and as a member of parliament for Westmorland. In the Cavalier Parliament he was moderately active, serving at home in the local government of Cumberland and Westmorland during the various recesses.

Musgrave remained violently opposed to religious dissent and the 'dregs of schism' as he called them throughout his life (HoP, *Commons, 1660–90*, 2.121). He fiercely imposed the penal laws and was a self-proclaimed state physician in his area, purging, punishing, and fining all those nonconformists, particularly Quakers, unfortunate enough to cross his path. George Fox merely noted of both Musgrave and his son Christopher *Musgrave that they were 'wicked' men (*Journal of George Fox*, 454). In the early 1660s Musgrave was also keen to gather any intelligence on the activities of the nonconformists, which he saw as simple plotting, and on the movements of ex-republican and Cromwellian officers located in the north-west. As such he was in constant contact with central government and used spies and informers to keep Lord Arlington's office acquainted with all of the activities of such men. In 1663 he was thus well placed to assist in the destruction of those involved in the Kaber Rigg plot.

Musgrave's later years were well rewarded and his hold on the area under his control, as well as his inclination for conflict with his neighbours, began to slacken only as old age and increasing infirmities crept upon him. He died aged seventy on 7 February 1678 and was buried in the parish church of St Cuthbert at Edenhall. He was succeeded by two of his sons in turn—first Richard, and after his death in December 1687, Christopher. A staunch and uncompromising royalist throughout his active life, Musgrave's loyalty to the crown was never in doubt. Experienced in both military affairs and plotting in the 1640s and 1650s, he was well placed at the Restoration to keep the two counties of Cumberland and Westmorland firmly under royal control. The image of Musgrave from his public life remains very much that of an 'Orlando Furioso' in local politics. In his private life he was less self-assured, being subject to melancholy, and in a letter written to his wife when he was imprisoned in 1655 he bitterly regretted his imprisonment, noting that 'Yo[u]rself and my Children are the nearest relations, [and] the Greatest comforts I have upon earth' (*Life*, 53).   ALAN MARSHALL

Sources *The life of Sir Philip Musgrave bart. … now published from an original MS. by the Rev. Gilbert Burton* (1840) · letters bundle, Cumbria AS, Musgrave papers, D Mus, 5–6 · HoP, *Commons, 1660–90* · *The journal of George Fox*, rev. edn, ed. J. L. Nickalls (1952) · GEC, *Baronetage*, 1.31 · C. B. Phillips, 'The royalist north: the Cumberland and Westmorland gentry, 1642–1660', *Northern History*, 14 (1978), 169–92 · C. H. Firth, ed., 'The relation of Sir Philip Musgrave', *Miscellany … II*, Scottish History Society, 44 (1904), 302–11 · *The manuscripts of S. H. Le Fleming*, HMC, 25 (1890), 1250–1322 · *CSP dom.*, 1660–78 · A. Marshall, *Intelligence and espionage in the reign of Charles II, 1660–1685* (1994) · Venn, *Alum. Cant.* · J. Foster, *The register of admissions to Gray's Inn, 1521–1889, together with the register of marriages in Gray's Inn chapel, 1695–1754* (privately printed, London, 1889) · Cumbria AS, Fleming papers, MS WD/Ry 34 · Keeler, *Long Parliament*

Archives Cumbria AS, Carlisle, corresp. and papers | Cumbria AS, Kendal, memoirs and corresp. with Sir Daniel Fleming · PRO, state papers Charles II, SP 29

Musgrave, Sir Richard, first baronet (*c.*1755–1818), political writer and politician, was the eldest son of Christopher Musgrave of Tourin, co. Waterford, and Susannah, daughter of James Usher of Ballintaylor in the same county. Musgrave's father was a man of very strong protestant ascendancy convictions who married into the west Waterford protestant gentry. Little is known about the early life and education of Richard Musgrave. Apart from an unquestioned acceptance of his father's extreme view of Irish Catholic threats to the country's protestant interest, he became proficient in the French language and familiar with classical authors. He completed whatever formal education he received in Ireland at the inns of court, London.

On 10 November 1780 Musgrave married Deborah, daughter of Sir Henry Cavendish, receiver-general and later deputy vice-treasurer of Ireland. The marriage was followed immediately by a grant of a baronetcy to Musgrave. The marriage produced no children and was an unhappy one ending in estrangement by about 1799.

Musgrave's public career began in 1778 when he was returned for the borough of Lismore (controlled by his father-in-law's relation the fifth duke of Devonshire) in the Irish House of Commons. Initially he allied himself with the Ponsonby connection but broke with them over Catholic relief issues. Becoming increasingly conservative, he insisted that vigorous law enforcement was the only practical remedy for the periodic outbreaks of violence in rural Ireland. As high sheriff of co. Waterford in 1786 Musgrave personally flogged convicted rioters when no one else could be found to do so.

After the outbreak of war with France in 1793 Musgrave warned repeatedly of a possible French-inspired rebellion in Ireland, claiming to have written more against treason and sedition in 1797 and 1798 than any other person in Ireland. Even before the rising of 1798 had been fully suppressed, Musgrave began collecting massive amounts of information relating to it. In 1798 and 1799, under the pseudonyms Camillus and Veridicus, he published pamphlets defending the army's use of free quarters and pre-emptive disarming, absolving the Dublin government from allegations of provoking the population and causing the uprising.

Musgrave completed and published his two-volume *magnum opus*, *Memoirs of the different rebellions in Ireland from the arrival of the English, with particular detail of that which broke out the 23rd of May, 1798; the history of the conspiracy which preceded it, and the characters of the principal actors in it*, in 1801. For Musgrave the events of 1798 had a single cause: papist aggression against protestants. Not surprisingly the account of the rising is filled with frightening examples of Irish Catholic brutality and perfidy intended to illustrate their total unfitness for political liberty. For Musgrave the great lesson to be learned from 1798 was the impossibility of political compromise with Irish Catholics.

Initially Musgrave's *Memoirs* succeeded commercially, running through three editions in two years. Yet the strident sectarianism of the work also invited many critical responses. One from James Caulfield, Roman Catholic bishop of Ferns, prompted a response from Musgrave in 1802. In time the book gradually lost credibility and readership, coming to be seen as a historically worthless sectarian diatribe. However, changing historiographical perspectives altered part of that extremely negative judgement. Two centuries after the work first appeared, Musgrave was again praised for his conscientious collection of evidence and his insight into the organizational sophistication of Roman Catholic rebel groups.

As for Musgrave himself, he was appointed in 1800 to the collectorship of excise for Dublin, a post worth £420 per annum; in the same year he dutifully voted for the Act of Union. Musgrave wrote very little after the *Memoirs*, publishing only one pamphlet critical of Catholic affairs in 1814. He died at his residence in Holles Street, Dublin, on 7 April 1818. Musgrave's baronetcy devolved upon his brother, Sir Christopher Frederick Musgrave, and then descended, ironically, to a nephew who joined the Catholic Association in 1826 and later was elected as repeal MP for co. Waterford.   ROBERT E. BURNS

Sources DNB · D. Dickson, foreword, in R. Musgrave, *Memoirs of the different rebellions in Ireland*, ed. S. W. Myers and D. E. McKnight, 4th edn (1995) · R. Musgrave, *Considerations on the present state of England and France* (1796) · R. Musgrave, *A letter on the present situation of public affairs* (1794) · Camillus [R. Musgrave], *To the magistrates, the military, and the yeomanry of Ireland* (1798) · Veridicus [R. Musgrave], *A concise account of the material events and atrocities which occurred in the* *late rebellion* (1799) • R. Musgrave, *Observations on Dr. Drumgoole's speech to the Catholic board* (1814) • T. Bartlett, *The fall and rise of the Irish nation: the Catholic question, 1690–1830* (1992) • D. Keogh and N. Furlong, eds., *The mighty wave: the 1798 rebellion in Wexford* (1996) **Archives** BL, letters to Lord Hardwicke and others, Add. MSS 35729–35757, *passim* • BL, corresp. with Sir Robert Peel, Add. MSS 40222–40267, *passim* • NL Ire., Percy MSS, MS 4157 • PRO NIre., Grandison MSS, T3131 • TCD, Perceval MSS, MS 10047

Musgrave, Samuel (1732–1780), physician and classical scholar, was born at Washfield, Devon, on 29 September 1732, eldest son of the three children of Richard Musgrave (*c*.1693–1739), physician, of Washfield, and Elizabeth (*b*. *c*.1704), daughter of the Revd Samuel Burges. He was educated at Barnstaple grammar school and matriculated from Queen's College, Oxford, on 11 May 1749. After attaining a scholarship from Corpus Christi College, Oxford, on 27 February 1750, he graduated BA on 27 February 1754 and MA on 5 March 1756. About 1754 he was elected Radcliffe travelling fellow of University College, and spent many years on the continent, chiefly in Holland and France. In 1756 he returned to London for the publication of his edition of *Hippolytus* by Euripides. On 6 February 1758 he married Mary Townsend (*b*. *c*.1738) of Bath. They had a son, Richard, who died young, and two daughters, Mary and Elizabeth.

In 1759, though not then a medical student, Musgrave made his first contribution to medicine with *Remarks on Dr Boerhaave's Theory of the Attrition of the Blood in the Lungs*. This caused some consternation, marking him out as a dissenter, even before taking up medicine as a university study. Though Boerhaave had died in 1738, and the Leiden medical school was in decline, his successors Gaub and B. S. Albinus evidently regarded Musgrave's work as illfounded, and it made little impact. On 12 July 1760 he was elected a fellow of the Royal Society. In 1762 in the preface to his *Exercitationes duae in Euripidem* he confessed to his sponsors his desire to become a physician. Pursuing this course, he graduated MD at Leiden in 1763. His inaugural dissertation was typically controversial—a defence of empirical medicine, entitled *Dissertatio medica inauguralis, sive, Apologia pro medicina empirica*. His main purpose was to demonstrate that medicine, despite its many theories, held no single theory which guaranteed absolute truth about the human body and its ailments. He praised Albinus, to whom he dedicated his dissertation, but criticized at length the animistic theories of Stahl, and here he was in alliance with Haller. If there was some value in Musgrave's thesis it was that he stirred the pot and that he emphasized the unreliability of current medical doctrines.

Musgrave was resident in Paris in 1763 when he was elected a corresponding member of the Royal Academy of Inscriptions and Belles-Lettres. Still resident in Paris in 1764, he afterwards alleged his discovery of a piece of political chicanery in which the peace treaty signed the previous year, which had ended the Seven Years' War, had been sold to the French by persons of high rank—the princess dowager, Lord Bute, and Lord Holland. In May 1765, on his return to England, he reported this to the secretary of state, Lord Halifax, and in the absence of an adequate

response, to the speaker of the Commons, again with no response. His tenure of the Radcliffe fellowship had now expired and he settled in Exeter in 1766, after having been elected physician to the Devon and Exeter Hospital. His expectations of practice, however, were not realized and in 1768 he moved to Plymouth. He continued to express his political opinions about the late peace and on 12 August 1769 he had printed an *Address to the Gentlemen, Clergy, and Freeholders of Devon*, as a preliminary to a meeting called at Exeter Castle the following October, which caused general astonishment. Admitting his own inability to prove the charges, he branded Halifax's action as 'a wilful obstruction of national justice' (*DNB*). He further published *An account of the Chevalier d'Eon's overtures to impeach three persons, by name, of selling the peace to the French*. D'Eon, French plenipotentiary in England in 1763, was alleged to have been silenced by the accused parties. Many pamphlets appeared for and against Musgrave, including one from d'Eon who denied all knowledge of Musgrave and his allegations. Cartoons, articles, and letters sympathetic to Musgrave appeared in the *Oxford Magazine* and elsewhere in the press. After a full hearing in the House of Commons the accusations were voted to be 'frivolous and unworthy of credit' (*GM*, 40, 1770, 93) on 2 January 1770. Musgrave insisted that he had acted on purely patriotic grounds. Support was accorded him by Junius: 'Dr Musgrave, with no other support but truth, and his own firmness, resisted and overcame the whole House of Commons' (Junius, 1.297n.).

Musgrave's hopes of professional success at Plymouth were blighted by these events and he moved to London. He took his degree of MD at Oxford on 8 December 1775 and settled at Hart Street, Bloomsbury. In 1776 he republished a work of his great-uncle William Musgrave (1655–1721), *De arthritide primigenia et regulari*, previously published at Oxford in 1726, and two short booklets, *Speculations and Conjectures on the Qualities of the Nerves* and an *Essay on the Nature and Cure of Worm Fever*. The first of these marked him out as an early proponent of psychosomatic medicine, some 200 years in advance of Speransky: 'We must attribute to this 18th century English doctor the merit of having understood at that time that one is better able to restore the patient's personality by taking into account a factor which cannot be measured—the psychological one' (Ceccarelli, 302, 304). Hitherto Musgrave's contribution in this area has been ignored. He was elected a fellow of the Royal College of Physicians on 30 September 1777 and was appointed Goulstonian lecturer and censor in 1779, his lectures being on 'Pleurisy and pulmonary consumption'. Pecuniary difficulties plagued him, and in default of professional success he was forced to eke out a living by his pen.

As a Greek scholar Musgrave had few superiors, and his great delight was the study and annotation of the works of Euripides. He himself was unable through want to publish a comprehensive edition of that author, but his extensive notes and collections, designed to form the basis of such a work, were published in four volumes in 1778 as *Euripidis quae extant omnia*; this edition continued to be embodied in numerous later editions after his death and is still respected as a contribution. His notes on Sophocles were bought by the Clarendon Press after his death for £200 and were used for an edition of the tragedies in 1800. He died in very reduced circumstances at his home in Hart Street, Bloomsbury, on 4 July 1780, and was buried in the burial-ground of St George's, Bloomsbury. His library was sold in 1780, and Thomas Tyrwhitt surrendered to his widow a bond for several hundred pounds advanced by him to Musgrave. As a benefaction to Mary Musgrave, Tyrwhitt also arranged in 1781 for the posthumous publication of Musgrave's *Two dissertations: On the Grecian mythology; An examination of Sir Isaac Newton's objections to the chronology of the Olympiads.* ALICK CAMERON

Sources *DNB* · Munk, *Roll* · A. Cameron, *Thomas Glass, MD: physician of Georgian Exeter* (1996), 101–4 · A. M. Luyendijk-Elshout, 'Samuel Musgrave's attack upon Stahl's and Boerhaave's doctrines in 1763', *Janus*, 67 (1980), 141–56 · U. Ceccarelli, *Rivista di storia della medicina*, 6 (1962), 295–304 · *Oxford Magazine* (Sept–Oct 1769), 95–100, 108–10, 184–7 · Nichols, *Lit. anecdotes*, 3.49–50, 663; 4.285, 288; 6.387; 8.119; 9.685 · *GM*, 1st ser., 39 (1769), 429–31, 453, 502 · *GM*, 1st ser., 40 (1770), 93 · *GM*, 1st ser., 50 (1780), 347 · *GM*, 1st ser., 56 (1786), 654, 718 · *GM*, 1st ser., 95/1 (1825), 389 · *The letters of Junius*, ed. J. Wade, another edn, 2 vols. (1904), vol. 1, p. 297
Archives Bodl. Oxf., notes on the plays of Sophocles with annotated proofs, and transcript of the lexicon of Photius, MS Clar. Press e. 34 | BL, Aeschylus Gr. and Latin. MS notes, shelf mark C. 45. c.21, 22
Wealth at death insolvent: *DNB*; Munk, *Roll* (1878); Nichols, *Lit. anecdotes*

Musgrave, Thomas, Lord Musgrave (*b.* in or before 1307, *d. c.*1385), soldier, was the son of Thomas Musgrave (*d.* in or before 1328), of Musgrave, Westmorland, and Sarah Harcla. In wardship in 1314, Musgrave was of age by 1328, when he succeeded to lands in Westmorland, Cumberland, and Lancashire. Although he was imprisoned in Carlisle Castle in 1334 for a forest offence, by the following year he had embarked on a career of nearly continuous official employment. Having been joint commissioner of array in Westmorland, he also served as deputy sheriff of the county under Robert, Lord Clifford, from 1339, as knight of the shire in parliament from 1340 to 1344, and as warden of Appleby Castle between 1343 and 1345.

Anglo-Scottish hostilities brought Musgrave additional military duties, and by 1345 he had become warden of the west march, a position which led to his participation in the battle of Nevilles Cross on 17 October 1346. According to the *Anonimalle Chronicle* Musgrave was knighted on the day and fought in the vanguard alongside his fellow march wardens. Shortly afterwards he became keeper of Berwick. His stewardship of the town, from 1347 until 1349, was followed by a host of new commissions in the north of England and on the Anglo-Scottish marches, and he was also one of the English ambassadors at the sealing of the treaty of Berwick on 3 October 1357. Musgrave undertook further peace negotiations with the Scots in 1360 and 1362. His experience in the marches led to his attending the council at Westminster in 1350, and again in 1353 and 1358, to discuss the Scottish threat. He was also periodically summoned to parliament as a peer from November 1350 to October 1373.

Musgrave's first wife was Margaret, daughter and coheir of William Roos, of Youlton, Yorkshire. Their son and heir, Thomas, was born about 1338. After Margaret's death Musgrave married Isabel, widow of Robert, Lord Clifford, and daughter of Maurice, Lord Berkeley, between May 1344 and June 1345. On her death in 1362, he sought to exclude his stepson Roger de Clifford from Isabel's Yorkshire estates at Skipton. Clifford's attempts to recover these through litigation in 1366 led to disorder in Westmorland. Musgrave and his followers broke into and poached from Clifford's park at Murton in 1368. Clifford responded by besieging Musgrave's manor house at Hartley in 1370, which Musgrave had been given licence to crenellate in 1353 due to repeated Scottish attacks.

Musgrave was ordered to prepare to resist Scottish invasion in 1365, recalled as west march warden and arrayer from 1369 to 1374, and was reappointed keeper of Berwick in 1373. He was granted a life annuity of 100 marks in 1370. However, on 27 August 1377 he and his grandson Thomas were captured during a raid into Scottish territory. According to Froissart, Musgrave's detachment of 600 lances and archers was ambushed and overwhelmed by a force of 2700 Scottish troops near Melrose. His failure to fulfil his conditions of ransom led to a summons for his arrest in 1379 and the threat of retaliation by his captor, the Scottish earl of March, against the English east march. Musgrave was further threatened in 1382 with the distraint of his estates to reimburse his ransomer, John, Lord Neville. He died about 1385, having outlived Thomas, his son, who died in 1372. Although his grandson continued in a number of his offices, he did not attain Lord Musgrave's martial pre-eminence. R. R. BAXTER

Sources GEC, *Peerage*, new edn, vol. 9 · *Chancery records* · *RotS* · PRO, Exchequer, Queen's Remembrancer, Accounts Various, E 101 · 'Return of the names of members of the lower house of parliament', *Parl. papers* (1878), vol. 62, nos. 69, 69-I, 69-II · V. H. Galbraith, ed., *The Anonimalle chronicle, 1333 to 1381* (1927) · *Sir J. Froissart's Chronicles of England, France … and the adjoining countries*, trans. T. Johnes, 4 vols. (1814–16) · V. J. C. Rees, 'The Clifford family in the later middle ages, 1259–1461', MLitt diss., University of Lancaster, 1973 · C. Rawcliffe, 'Musgrave, Sir Thomas', HoP, *Commons, 1386–1421*
Archives PRO, military indentures and warden's accounts, E 101

Musgrave, Sir Thomas, seventh baronet (1738–1812), army officer, was born on 26 November 1738, the youngest of the six sons of Sir Richard Musgrave, fourth baronet (1701–1739), of Hayton Castle, Cumberland, and his wife, Anne Hylton (1697–1766), the daughter of John Hylton of Hylton Castle, co. Durham. He entered the army as an ensign in the 3rd foot on 31 December 1754, was promoted lieutenant on 21 June 1756, and served at the capture of Guadeloupe in May 1759. On 20 August 1759 he became a captain in the 64th regiment and on 22 July 1772 brevet major. After the battle of Long Island he succeeded to the lieutenant-colonelcy of the 40th foot (28 August 1776), and in September 1777 he led the regiment to Philadelphia. On the morning of 4 October 1777, when a large force of Americans attacked the British outpost at Germantown, it was Musgrave who, by throwing himself and 200 of his men into a large building called Chew House, held up the

Sir Thomas Musgrave, seventh baronet (1738–1812), by Lemuel Francis Abbott, 1786

Madras. Here Musgrave chafed: denied permission to rejoin the field army, in October 1791 he sought leave to return to England. Cornwallis, who considered Musgrave troublesome, did not attempt to dissuade him.

In 1796 Musgrave was appointed governor of Gravesend and Tilbury forts; he was made a lieutenant-general on 26 January 1797 and for a time commanded the northern district. In 1800 he inherited a baronetcy from his brother, and on 29 April 1802 he became a full general. He died, unmarried, at his London home, 21 Bolton Street, Piccadilly, on 31 December 1812 and was interred on 8 January 1813 in the burial-ground of St George's, Hanover Square. His cousins Mrs Jane Clay and James Musgrave (who inherited the baronetcy) were the main beneficiaries of his will, by which he left an estate liable for duty valued at £45,000.   ALASTAIR W. MASSIE

Sources PRO, Cornwallis MSS, PRO 30/11/28–46, 174, 176 · Glos. RO, Wykeham-Musgrave MSS, D2383, C5, F6 · 'Military biography: the late general Sir Thomas Musgrave', *Military Panorama*, 2 (1813), 493–500 · GEC, *Peerage* · *Army List* · PRO, CO 5/5–6 · PRO, IR 26/583 (26) · *GM*, 1st ser., 82/2 (1812), 674 · PRO, PROB 11/1540 (34) · parish register, St George's, Hanover Square, City Westm. AC [burial] · E. C. Joslin, A. R. Litherland, B. T. Simpkin, and others, eds., *British battles and medals*, 6th edn (1988) · *DNB*
Archives Glos. RO, family and biographical notes, D2383 C5
Likenesses L. F. Abbott, portrait, 1786; Christies, 18 Oct 1985, lot 156 [*see illus.*] · G. S. Facius, stipple, 1797 (after L. F. Abbott, 1786), BM
Wealth at death £45,000—personal estate: PRO, death duty registers, IR 26/583, 26

enemy assault until reinforcements arrived. To commemorate this repulse of the Americans, Musgrave ordered a silver medal to be struck depicting the defence of Chew House. The following year the 40th foot sailed from New York as part of the expedition to the Caribbean; Musgrave took command of the garrison on Antigua in July 1779 and in February 1780 was appointed quartermaster-general of the army in the West Indies. Having fallen ill, he then sailed home and was made deputy governor of Stirling Castle. However, he returned to America as a colonel (breveted on 18 April 1782) and local brigadier-general. In August 1783 he became the last British commandant of New York.

On 12 October 1787 Musgrave was named colonel of the new 76th (Hindoostan) regiment. Raised for service in India, the regiment drew many of its recruits from the Musgrave family estates. Upon arrival with his men in India, however, Musgrave was rash enough to dispute the authority of the governor-general, Lord Cornwallis, to order him to Madras. Although he eventually obeyed, Musgrave did so with bad grace, complaining that the civil authorities at Madras failed to liaise with him. He was still there in February 1790 when General William Medows, newly arrived to take command of the war with Mysore, decided to adopt a plan devised by Musgrave to invade Tipu Sultan's domains from the south; Musgrave took the field under Medows and was promoted major-general on 28 April 1790. But Medows's campaign miscarried, and Lord Cornwallis, who preferred an alternative strategy, took command in person and sent Musgrave back to

Musgrave, Thomas (1788–1860), archbishop of York, was the eldest of the three sons of W. Peete Musgrave, a wealthy whig tailor and woollen draper of Cambridge, and his wife, Sarah. He was born on 30 March 1788 in Slaughter House Lane, Cambridge, and baptized at the parish church of Great St Mary's on 25 April. Educated at Richmond grammar school, Yorkshire, under the well-known master James Tate, he was admitted pensioner of Trinity College, Cambridge, on 6 July 1804, and was made a scholar in 1807. He graduated BA in 1810 as fourteenth wrangler, was member's prizeman in 1811, and proceeded MA in 1813, BD and DD in 1837. He held a variety of offices at Trinity. As college bursar his sound business acumen made a valuable contribution to advancing Trinity's not inconsiderable finances. He also held a number of offices in the university, including (despite his limited knowledge of the subject) Lord Almoner's professor of Arabic (1821–37) and senior proctor (1831–2). Moreover, during 1834 he became one of the leaders in the campaign to abolish religious tests at Cambridge. In civil affairs he was an active and judicious county magistrate. Between June and October 1815 Musgrave (with two companions) made the grand tour of Europe; references appear in his journal to the battle of Waterloo, which occurred during their stay at Brussels and Antwerp, as does a description of the battlefield itself, which they later visited. In 1839 he married Catherine (d. 16 May 1863), daughter of Richard Cavendish, second Lord Waterpark; the marriage produced no children.

Musgrave was ordained deacon by William Lort Mansel,

bishop of Bristol, on 25 May 1816, and priest by Richard Beadon, bishop of Bath and Wells, on 21 December 1817. He afterwards occupied a number of college livings, including Over, Cambridgeshire (1823–5), Great St Mary's, Cambridge (1825–33), Orwell, Cambridgeshire (1835), and Bottisham, Cambridgeshire (1837). His university distinctions and liberal politics soon marked him out for preferment from the whig government of Lord Melbourne, and he was appointed dean of Bristol on 27 March 1837, holding the position only briefly before, on 5 August, being nominated (also by Melbourne) to fill the see of Hereford, recently vacated by the death of Edward Grey, brother to Earl Grey.

Musgrave was consecrated by Archbishop Howley at Lambeth Palace on 1 October 1837. His episcopate at Hereford was energetic and reform-minded, its numerous undertakings being summarized in his diocesan charge of 1845: he revived the office of rural dean; he established the Diocesan Church Building Society, through which at least twenty-two new churches were built and many older ones enlarged; he increased the number of second services on Sundays, and the frequency with which holy communion was celebrated in parish churches; he curtailed pluralism, and almost completely eliminated non-residence; parish and diocesan boundaries were reorganized; he began the restoration of the cathedral, then in a perilous state; and he expanded the educational resources of the diocese, building more than thirty new schools and enlarging a number of existing ones. Musgrave also endeavoured to counter the attempts of a growing number of his clergy to (as he complained) '"unprotestantize" our Church, and bring us into nearer conformity with Rome' (Charge, 1845, 26).

On 15 November 1847 Musgrave was nominated by Lord John Russell as the next archbishop of York, in succession to Vernon Harcourt. His enthronement in York Minster took place on 15 January 1848. Musgrave's elevation was regarded as something of a surprise, The Record newspaper drily commenting: 'what has caused him to be preferred to many other older and equally respectable prelates no one can imagine'. The Morning Post was even less restrained. Musgrave has, it remarked, 'abilities of a certain kind which it is understood were found useful to the Whigs in electioneering affairs'. His elevation over senior church figures such as Maltby of Durham, Whatley of Dublin, Kaye of Lincoln, and Blomfield of London may have been due to the influence of the third Earl Grey, then chief secretary to the colonies. On the other hand, Musgrave had acquired considerable local knowledge of Yorkshire while serving as bursar of Trinity, the college possessing extensive estates in the county. No doubt it was thought that his energetic and reforming episcopate at Hereford, if repeated, would at York be a welcome contrast to the rather old-fashioned and conservative policies of his predecessor.

It was therefore perhaps something of a surprise that Musgrave's archiepiscopate was characterized by no great initiatives or improvements. Although he encouraged a number of practical reforms, such as the building of new churches (and the rebuilding of a number of existing ones), the expansion of local education, and the appointment (in 1850) of a royal commission of inquiry into the state of the ancient universities, he assiduously opposed any suggestion of doctrinal or administrative 'innovation'; his motto was Quieta non movere (roughly 'let sleeping dogs lie'). Nor did Musgrave exhibit much interest in pastoral affairs, preferring, when necessary, 'personal communication' from his clergy to visitation or written correspondence (Charge, 1853). Most emphatic was his opposition to the revival of convocation in the northern province. Musgrave's liberal outlook led him to stand firm against what he regarded as the rise of religious dogmatism in the church, most especially Tractarian rhetoric, which appeared to him likely to dominate the proceedings of a revived convocation. Consequently, while the convocation of Canterbury gained almost complete freedom of debate between 1847 and 1855, that of York remained inert until Musgrave's death in 1860.

When a storm of protest erupted over the nomination of R. D. Hampden as bishop of Hereford in late 1847, Musgrave refused to join the majority of his fellow bishops in remonstrating with the prime minister. He willingly became involved in the public debate over the celebrated Gorham case, however, commending (Charge, 1849) the evangelical William Goode's The Effects of Infant Baptism (1849) and arguing that regeneration could not be insisted upon as a 'ruled doctrine of our Church', but must be regarded as conditional. When the case reached the judicial committee of the privy council in March 1850, Musgrave (together with Archbishop Sumner) voted with the majority to reverse the decision of the court of arches and uphold Gorham's right to be instituted as vicar of Brampford Speke.

In 1854 Musgrave suffered a severe attack of ill health which prevented him from attending to the affairs of office for some time. He died on 4 May 1860, at his London home, 41 Belgrave Square, and was buried at Kensal Green cemetery. Although described occasionally as an evangelical, he was by inclination closely aligned with the liberal or broad-church party. Increasingly conservative over time, Musgrave yet remained committed to the ideal of an anti-dogmatic and inclusive Anglicanism. Despite the controversy surrounding his opposition to the revival of convocation, he was held in some affection by local people, the Yorkshire Gazette in its obituary (12 May 1860) recalling his 'kindness of heart, gentleness of rule, Christian liberality and unostentatious piety'.

GRAYSON CARTER

Sources GM, 3rd ser., 8 (1860), 625–6 · D. A. Jennings, The revival of the Convocation of York, 1837–1861, Borthwick Papers, 47 (1975) · D. M. Lewis, ed., The Blackwell dictionary of evangelical biography, 1730–1860, 2 vols. (1995) · Venn, Alum. Cant. · Crockford (1860), 687 · W. H. Phillott, Diocesan histories: Hereford (1888) · J. C. S. Nias, Gorham and the bishop of Exeter (1951) · J. Foster, ed., Index ecclesiasticus, or, Alphabetical lists of all ecclesiastical dignitaries in England and Wales since the Reformation (1890), 128 · D. A. Winstanley, Early Victorian Cambridge (1940), 89, 92 n.3, 220 · A. de Morgan, A budget of paradoxes (1872), 196–7 · J. Ingamells, Catalogue of portraits at Bishopthorpe Palace (1972)

86154

Archives Borth Inst., corresp., travel journals (Waterloo battle-field), and family papers · LPL, corresp. · Notts. Arch., corresp. and papers · Trinity Cam., letters · York Minster Library, MSS | Bristol RO, subscription book, 1816 · Som. ARS, diocesan records, Ordination MSS
Likenesses C. Lucy, portrait, 1838 · T. Butler, portrait, 1839 · W. C. Cross, miniature, exh. RA 1842, Bishopthorpe Palace, York · F. R. Saye, oils, 1850, bishop's palace, Hereford · F. R. Saye, oils, 1850, Bishopthorpe Palace, York · F. R. Saye, oils, 1850, Trinity Cam. · M. Noble, effigy, 1864, York Minster
Wealth at death under £70,000: resworn probate, April 1861, *CGPLA Eng. & Wales* (1860)

Musgrave, Sir William (*b.* in or before **1506**, *d.* **1544**), landowner and administrator, was the eldest son of Sir Edward Musgrave (*d.* 1542), of Hartley, near Kirkby Stephen, Westmorland, and of Edenhall, near Penrith, Cumberland, and his wife, Jane, daughter of Sir Christopher Ward. Knighted at Jedburgh in Scotland in 1523, he served as Sir Edward's under-sheriff in Cumberland in 1527–8. In 1529–30 he appears as a household officer of William, third Baron Dacre. He sat as a member for Westmorland in the Reformation Parliament (1529–36) and may have held the same seat subsequently. His public career was based on royal service. By 1529 he was a knight of the body to Henry VIII: he was appointed marshal of Berwick-on-Tweed in the same year, and made constable or keeper of the border castle of Bewcastle in 1531. He was also steward of the Cumberland estates of the duchy of Lancaster, an office perhaps attached to the constableship of Bewcastle. He was sheriff in Cumberland in 1532–3 and 1541–2.

Musgrave owes his reputation to the role he played in the complicated and imperfectly understood politics of the western Anglo-Scottish borders during the early 1530s. As with others of his contemporaries, he has been interpreted as a 'new man', a royal servant given an office in the north to undermine the standing of the established noble families. In fact the constableship of Bewcastle, although Dacre had secured a grant in reversion in 1527, had been held by a cadet of the Musgrave family for most of the previous half century. His appointment to the constableship of Bewcastle did bring Musgrave into conflict with Dacre, but as he had served in the Dacre household, it is none too certain that Dacre was fundamentally opposed to Musgrave's appointment. Although Musgrave was later a partisan of the first earl of Cumberland, there is no evidence that his appointment to Bewcastle should be read as a move against Dacre and may best be seen as a continuation of the early Tudor policy of dividing responsibilities on the borders. Following Musgrave's appointment, friction developed fairly quickly. A dispute over the collection of rents in Bewcastledale prompted a council decree in 1531 but was still unresolved as late as 1538. Nevertheless, a letter of May 1532 in which Dacre refers to Musgrave in friendly terms does not suggest that there was at that stage any irreconcilable breach.

Musgrave seems to have turned against Dacre out of the realization that in the Anglo-Scottish war of 1532–3 Dacre had negotiated private truces with his corresponding number in Scotland and had diverted Scottish raids onto Bewcastle. Dacre's inactivity was a matter of comment as the war progressed, but it is clear enough that it was Musgrave who supplied the information about Dacre's conduct on which he was indicted in June 1534. Dacre, however, was acquitted at his trial before the House of Lords, but heavily fined, deprived of his offices, and for a period forbidden to leave the environs of London. Musgrave increasingly became attached to the earl of Cumberland, who followed Dacre as warden. When Richard Dacre tried to assassinate Cumberland's son Henry, Lord Clifford, in Carlisle on 9 December 1536, Musgrave was in his company, and in his one extant letter to the earl he speaks of his faithfulness to him.

Lord Dacre's trial and Musgrave's opposition to the Commons on the Cumberland rebellion of 1536 seem to have destroyed the latter's reputation within the north-west and made it impossible for the crown to continue to use him there. It is noticeable that he was passed over in the reorganization of the government of the north in the spring of 1537, when it was his neighbour from Westmorland Sir Thomas Wharton who was selected to exercise the office of warden. However, he remained captain of Bewcastle to his death. After 1537 Musgrave mostly abandoned Cumberland and moved to his house in London. His second wife's correspondence with Cromwell suggests that the last years of his life were marked by an acute awareness of his unpopularity on the borders and by financial problems arising from his dependence on his father (who died in 1542, only some seventeen months before Sir William himself). Yet he was active in the early stages of the Anglo-Scottish war after 1542 and was among those at the English victory at Solway Moss. He died (it is not clear where) on 18 October 1544.

Musgrave was married at least twice; first, by 1524, to Elizabeth, daughter of Sir Thomas Curwen of Workington, Cumberland, and second, some time after 1533, to Elizabeth, daughter of Philip Denkaring and widow of Thomas Tamworth of Essex. In 1540 he contemplated, and may have entered into, a third marriage, with a daughter of Thomas, third Baron Burgh of Gainsborough. His son and heir from his first marriage, Sir Richard Musgrave, married Agnes, daughter of Thomas, first Baron Wharton, and was MP for Cumberland in 1547 and 1553, but died prematurely in 1555.   R. W. HOYLE

Sources HoP, *Commons, 1509–58*, 2.646–8 · *LP Henry VIII*, vols. 3–19 · R. W. Hoyle, ed., 'Letters of the Cliffords, lords Clifford and earls of Cumberland, *c*.1500–1565', Camden miscellany, XXXI, CS, 4th ser., 44 (1993), 1–189 · S. G. Ellis, *Tudor frontiers and noble power: the making of the British state* (1995)

Musgrave, William (1655–1721), physician and antiquary, was born on 4 November 1655, in Nettlecombe, Somerset, the third son of Richard Musgrave (*d.* 1686) of Nettlecombe, and Mary (1629–1683), daughter of George Bond. He was educated at Winchester College, being elected to a scholarship in 1669, and at New College, Oxford, where he was admitted as scholar on 7 August 1675, holding a fellowship from 7 August 1677 to September 1692. He passed one session at the University of Leiden, his name being recorded there on 28 March 1680; but soon returning to

Oxford, he graduated BCL on 14 June 1682. For his distinction in natural philosophy and physic he was elected FRS on 19 March 1684. The same year he was elected second secretary of the Royal Society, a post from which he resigned after a year, but during which he edited the *Philosophical Transactions*, numbers 167 to 178. On his retirement he was presented with a service of plate weighing 60 ounces.

Musgrave graduated MB at Oxford, by decree of convocation, on 8 December 1685, and proceeded MD on 6 July 1689. He was one of a small group who in the autumn of 1685 formed the Philosophical Society of Oxford, and for some years he practised in that city. On 30 September 1691 he married Phillippa (1660–1715), daughter of William Speke of Jordans. They had a son, William (1696–1724), and a daughter, Phillippa (Mrs Browne).

On 30 September 1692 Musgrave was elected a fellow of the Royal College of Physicians. In the previous year he had settled at Exeter, where he practised with distinction. His house was in St Lawrence parish, Trinity Lane, later called Musgrave Alley in recognition of his restoration of the chapel of Holy Trinity. Thomas Hearne recalled how, some years earlier, the ill-natured Anthony Wood had been reprimanded for a sly attempt to ruin the 'Reputation of Dr Musgrave the Physitian, by writing Letters without any Name into the Country where the Doctor was' (*Remarks*, 1.266).

Musgrave himself made many contributions to *Philosophical Transactions*. He had carried out experiments on digestion at Oxford, and wrote *inter alia* on the lacteals, palsy, and respiration, in which he quoted his Exeter colleague (and later patient), Dr Malachi Thruston. His important medical works were on arthritis, and its many associated effects: *De arthritide symptomatica* in 1703, and *De arthritide anomala* in 1707, an updated version of each appearing in 1715. His view of arthritis ranged over a huge clinical spectrum; *De arthritide symptomatica* (2nd edn, 1715, 65), for example, gives the first scientific description of the 'Devonshire colic', referred to later by John Huxham and George Baker. In the same work, dealing with melancholic complications, he describes with sensitivity and respect his distinguished patient, Dr Malachi Thruston, who died insane in 1701. The manuscript of an earlier treatise was found after Musgrave's death and sent to the Clarendon press by his son, who did not live to see it in print. This was *De arthritide primogenia et regulari*, published at Oxford in 1726, and reissued by Samuel Musgrave, Musgrave's great-nephew, at London in 1776. That it had been written before the two main works is confirmed by William Stukeley (Stukeley, 1.157), when he visited Musgrave's son at Exeter in 1723.

Musgrave's other major field of activity was in the detailed study of Roman Britain, in particular, the area formerly inhabited by the Belgae, extending from Hampshire through Wiltshire to Somerset. He wrote several short works on antiquarian matters, the most important of which were incorporated into his large three-volume work, *Antiquitates Britanno-Belgicae*, published in 1711, 1716, 1719, and, with a final supplementary volume, in 1720.

These volumes describe numerous Roman remains found in this territory. For this work George I presented Musgrave with a diamond ring, which the College of Arms allowed him to incorporate into his family crest in 1720. When Stukeley visited Musgrave's son, he saw in his garden the colossal head of the empress Julia Domna (consort to Lucius Septimius Severus, who died at York AD 211), previously excavated at Bath, and still visible in Exeter in 1853. A number of letters on antiquarian topics passed between Musgrave and Walter Moyle. There are several collections of manuscript letters in the Bodleian and British libraries. For many years a laudatory Latin verse by Musgrave was attached to William Gandy's portrait of John Patch (1691–1743), the Exeter surgeon; it was quoted in full by Delpratt Harris (*History of the Devon and Exeter Hospital*).

Musgrave died in Trinity Lane, St Lawrence parish, Exeter on 16 December 1721 and was buried alongside his wife in St Leonard's churchyard, outside the city, on 23 December 1721; the tomb was embellished with richly ornate panels. Musgrave considered that burial within the city was unwholesome for the living. It seems that both father and son may have lived beyond their means. There are accounts of debts in the Devon Record Office (Moger suppl. I, PR 514/40). The only substantial property mentioned in Musgrave's will was his farm and barton at Pallesland, valued at £1500, which was left to his daughter. The residue was left to his son, who died insolvent three years later. His grandson, Richard, records that he was still receiving demands from creditors in 1753.

ALICK CAMERON

Sources Munk, *Roll* · *DNB* · H. W. Holman, *Devon and Cornwall Notes and Queries*, 12 (1918), 193–7 · J. F. Chanter, *Devon and Cornwall Notes and Queries*, 12 (1918), 264–5 · T. N. Brushfield, 'Dr. William Musgrave', *Notes and Queries for Somerset and Dorset*, 2 (1891), 223–4 · W. Stukeley, *Itinerarium curiosum, or, An account of the antiquitys and remarkable curiositys in nature or art* (1724), 157 · *Remarks and collections of Thomas Hearne*, ed. C. E. Doble and others, 1, OHS, 2 (1885), 266 · H. Lyons, *The Royal Society, 1660–1940: a history of its administration under its charters* (1944), 100–01 · *The record of the Royal Society of London*, 4th edn (1940), 342 · will, PRO, PROB 11/583 · Wood, *Ath. Oxon.* · R. Dymond, *History of the suburban parish church of St Leonard, Exeter* (1873), 29–30 · J. D. Harris, *The Royal Devon and Exeter hospital* (1922), 26

Archives BL · Bodl. Oxf., corresp. and papers relating to Oxford Philosophical Society · Queens College, Oxford, annotated copy of *Pharmacopoeia Bateana* · RS, letters and papers · Trinity Cam., corresp. | BL, letters to Sir Hans Sloane

Likenesses T. Hawker, oils, 1718, Royal Albert Memorial Museum, Exeter · M. Vandergucht, engraving (after W. Gandy), Wellcome L.; repro. in W. Musgrave, *Antiquitates Britanno-Belgicae*, 1 (1719)

Wealth at death both father and son probably lived beyond means; many debts: Devon RO, Moger suppl. 1, PR 514/40 · son, William, died insolvent; wife paid off many debts

Mush [*alias* Ratcliffe], **John** (1552–1612), Roman Catholic priest and author, was born in the diocese of Chester, probably in that part of Yorkshire between York and Ripon. Tradition suggests that, in 1572, he was in the household of the religiously conservative medical doctor Thomas Vavasour, in the parish of Holy Trinity, King's Court, within the city of York, before he set off for the seminary at Douai, where he arrived on 9 March 1576. He was sent to Rome in October of that year as one of the first students at the new college for English students established there. In 1581 he was appointed deacon of chapel at the college, and by his own account was one of three students ordained at St John Lateran by Pope Gregory XIII in person. The date of this ordination is uncertain, but in September 1583 he left Rome with three companions to return to England and the mission.

Mush's reputation for scholarship brought him to the attention of Cardinal Allen, who considered appointing him vice-president of Douai, but he returned to the north of England where his qualities soon secured him a leading role among the northern clergy. In 1584–5 he combined with the Jesuit Richard Holtby, another northerner, in the ordering of the northern mission, dividing it into circuits shared by two or three priests. Mush took responsibility for the circuit based at York, sharing it first with Thomas Bell and later with Francis Ingleby. While on the mission Mush regularly adopted the alias of Ratcliffe, and some time in 1584 he made contact with Margaret *Clitherow, the Catholic wife of a leading York butcher, whose confessor he became. Margaret Clitherow was a devout and convinced Catholic who had taught herself enough Latin to follow the liturgy and simple devotional works, and who was a key figure in a small Catholic congregation worshipping in the Shambles, in the centre of York, where there was a safe house with a priest's hiding hole. She was accused of harbouring Mush and Ingleby in 1586 and, refusing to plead before the court, was tried before the council of the north and sentenced to be pressed to death. Shortly before her death Margaret, constant in her beliefs, is alleged to have smuggled a note from prison to Mush stating that she did not want a reprieve. Margaret died on 25 March 1586, and in the following months Mush compiled an account of her life, trial, and martyrdom as an example to her fellow Catholics. Much of the information he acquired from his own knowledge or from friends of Margaret, and the account of her final days was probably provided by the widowed Mistress Vavasour; the *True Relation of the Life and Death of Mistress Margaret Clitherow* circulated in manuscript in a number of versions until a short account was published in 1619. This concentrated principally on the trial and martyrdom and was dedicated to Margaret's daughter Anne, at that time a nun in the Augustinian convent at Louvain. A longer text, incorporating the virtues of Margaret's life, was published in 1849 and another version, edited by John Morris, appeared in 1877 in volume 3 of his collection *The Troubles of our Catholic Forefathers*. This was based on the manuscript owned by the Middleton family of Stockeld Park, who were related to Margaret, and in his transcription Morris removed the more virulent anti-protestant passages of the original.

Soon after Margaret's death Mush was himself captured at the York house of Richard Langley, who was executed on 1 December 1586; but Mush escaped and was said to be at Mitcham, Surrey, in 1587 and in London the following year. Mush went to Rome in 1593, returning via Flanders, and became involved in the Wisbech stirs, siding generally with the anti-Jesuit faction. In response to the Jesuit Thomas Lister's vigorous pamphlet of 1598 against the seculars' position, *Contra factiosos in ecclesia*, Mush produced a collection of documents in defence of the secular clergy, including the text of their original appeal to the pope in 1598, from which their designation as appellants derives, and this was published as *Declaratio motuum ac turbationem* in 1601. In the same year he also published, again anonymously, an English defence of the seculars' position aimed at a lay audience entitled *A Dialogue between a Secular Priest and a Lay Gentleman*. He was an uncompromising opponent of George Blackwell, the arch-priest, and was suspended for a time, leaving his congregation of prisoners at York Castle desolate. In 1602 he was chosen to represent the appellants' case at Rome, and left an account of his visit there. He signed the oath of allegiance to Queen Elizabeth in January 1603 and the memorial to the pope from Paris later that year. He returned to the north of England and was one of the assistants to Blackwell's successor as arch-priest, George Birkhead. He remained opposed to the Jesuits, writing to Cardinal Farnese in Rome with his views. He supported the appointment of a bishop for the English Catholics and was a senior figure in clerical circles, acting as an arbitrator between the Benedictines and the secular clergy in the north in their dispute over the legality of the oath of allegiance of 1606, about which the seculars accused the Benedictines of being too lax. Mush is said to have written an account of the sufferings of Catholics in the north during his time there, and also a response to his former colleague Thomas Bell, who had turned apostate and was a vigorous anti-Catholic polemicist in the service of Tobie Matthew, archbishop of York. No versions of these manuscripts can be identified with certainty, but Morris speculated that the former might be the Oscott manuscript which he also published in his collection as 'A Yorkshire recusant's relation'. After a short illness Mush died on 22 November 1612, leaving books and asking that £50 be given for prayers for his soul.

WILLIAM JOSEPH SHEILS

Sources J. Morris, ed., *The troubles of our Catholic forefathers related by themselves*, 3 (1877) · G. Anstruther, *The seminary priests*, 1 (1969) · M. C. Questier, *Newsletters from the archpresbyterate of George Birkhead*, CS, 5th ser., 12 (1998) · J. C. H. Aveling, *Catholic recusancy in the city of York, 1558–1791*, Catholic RS, monograph ser., 2 (1970) · M. Claridge, *Margaret Clitherow, 1556?–1586* (1966) · M. C. Cross, 'The religious life of women in sixteenth-century Yorkshire', *Women in the church on the eve of the dissolution*, ed. W. J. Sheils and D. Wood, SCH, 27 (1990), 307–24 · R. Rex, 'Thomas Vavasour', *Recusant History*, 20 (1990–91), 436–54

Mushaver Pasha. *See* Slade, Sir Adolphus (1804–1877).

Mushet, David (1772–1847), ironmaster and metallurgist, was born on 2 October 1772 at Dalkeith, near Edinburgh, the eldest son of William Mushet, foundry owner, and his wife, Margaret Cochrane. He had two younger sisters and five brothers, including William and George who together eventually ran the family foundry, and Robert *Mushet (1782–1828) who became chief melter and clerk at the

Royal Mint in London. David Mushet was educated at Dalkeith grammar school. His first post was as accountant at the Clyde ironworks, near Glasgow, in 1792. Here, outside working hours, he began his scientific investigation into the smelting of iron ores and the metallurgy of iron and steel. Later he was encouraged by his employers, and the works laboratory and assay furnace were made available to him for a while. These privileges were later withdrawn and his research forbidden. In 1794 he nevertheless built his own assay furnace away from the works and contributed papers to the *Philosophical Magazine*. In 1798 he married Agnes Wilson of Edinburgh; they had three daughters and three sons.

In 1800 Mushet became a partner in the Calder ironworks near Airdrie and took up its management. In 1801 he discovered the black band ironstone in Monklands parish and proved its value as an iron ore. This act contributed greatly to the subsequent wealth of Scottish ironmasters. His reputation spread among the scientific circles of Edinburgh and Glasgow and his advice was often sought. In 1805 he left the Calder partnership to take up a new managership and partnership in the Riddings ironworks, near Alfreton in Derbyshire, and he and his family resided at The Hermitage (subsequently Hermitage Farm) nearby. His brother George acted as an assistant for six months. On 14 February 1805 Mushet read a paper to the Royal Society on the smelting of the Wootz ores of India (*PTRS*, 95, 1805, 163–75). In 1807 he contributed the article on iron to the *Encyclopaedia Britannica* which appeared in the supplement of 1824 edited by M. Napier, and articles on the blast furnace and the blowing machine to *The Cyclopaedia …* (1819), edited by Abraham Rees.

In March 1808 the engraver Wilson Lowry introduced Mushet to Thomas Halford, a London stockbroker, who owned a major share in an ironworks in the Forest of Dean. The following month Mushet and Halford visited these works at Whitecliff, near Coleford, Gloucestershire, and also examined the associated collieries and iron-ore sources. After supervising their rebuilding he became in 1810 a partner at the Whitecliff concern and left Alfreton for Coleford, where he lived at Tump House (subsequently Forest House). Despite much experimentation Whitecliff ironworks proved unprofitable and he withdrew. With Halford he also developed collieries and promoted tram roads, particularly the Monmouth Railway and the Severn and Wye Railway and Canal Company.

Mushet's researches continued at Coleford, where he built a laboratory on Cinder Hill, and in 1818 he built a small furnace at Darkhill. In 1822 he provided a stratigraphy of the Dean coalfield for an investigation of the geology of south-west England by William Buckland and W. D. Conybeare. In 1825 he opened iron-ore mines and constructed a tram road in the Oakwood valley. By 1841 he owned the collieries of Old Furnace Level, Howlers Slade, Protection Level, Bixslade levels, Darkhill, and Shutcastle in the Forest of Dean. At Darkhill he also owned a blast furnace and a brickworks. Mushet gave valuable evidence in the case tried at Edinburgh in 1843 in which J. B. Neilson sought to prove infringements of his hot blast furnace

patent by Baird & Co. This trial was one of the great *causes célèbres* of the early industrial age, and judgment was eventually given in Neilson's favour.

Mushet's major inventions concern direct steel making in crucibles (patent no. 2447, 1800) and improvements to the puddling process (patent no. 6908, 1835). He was also a pioneer of technical writing in an industry that had been very slow to generate a technical literature. His many communications to the *Philosophical Magazine* were in 1840 published in a single volume entitled *Papers on Iron and Steel, Practical and Experimental*, which included analytical data on many coals and their coking properties. He also wrote *The Wrongs of the Animal World* (1839).

About 1843 Mushet removed from Coleford to Monmouth, where he died in St James's Street on 7 June 1847. He was buried at Staunton, near Coleford. His son Robert Forester *Mushet (1811–1891) also became a metallurgist and contributed some major advances to steel making, including an adaptation of the Bessemer process developed by Sir Henry Bessemer.   IAN J. STANDING

Sources F. M. Osborn, *The story of the Mushets* (1952) · C. E. Hart, 'The coke iron industry', *The industrial history of Dean* (1971) · *The diary of George Mushet, 1805–1813*, ed. R. M. Healey (1982) · I. J. Standing, 'The Whitecliff Ironworks in the Forest of Dean, pt 1: 1798–1808', *Gloucestershire Society for Industrial Archaeology Journal* (1980), 18–28 · I. J. Standing, '"Dear Mushet": a history of the Whitecliff Ironworks, pt 2: 1808–1810', *Gloucestershire Society for Industrial Archaeology Journal* (1981), 32–71 · I. J. Standing, 'The Whitecliff Ironworks in the Forest of Dean', *Gloucestershire Society for Industrial Archaeology Journal* (1986), 2–20 · D. Bick, 'Darkhill Ironworks and the Mushet family', *Gloucestershire Historical Studies*, 4 (1970), 60–64 · K. C. Barraclough, *Steelmaking before Bessemer*, 2 (1984), 63, 85–86 · J. Percy, *Metallurgy: iron and steel*, 2 (1864), 203, 652, 776 · d. cert.
Archives Glos. RO, corresp. relating to iron industry, D2646 · Glos. RO, legal and family corresp. and papers, D637 II 7 B1
Likenesses portrait, Aurora plc; repro. in Osborn, *Story of the Mushets*

Mushet, Robert (1782–1828), official of the Royal Mint, was born at Dalkeith on 10 November 1782, the sixth son of William Mushet and his wife, Margaret Cochrane. He was a brother of David *Mushet. He married Henrietta, daughter of John *Hunter (1745–1837) of St Andrews.

Mushet entered the service of the mint about 1804 and was listed in the *Royal Kalendar* for 1808 as third clerk to the master. Subsequently he held the posts of first clerk to the master, melter (1815), and refiner. In collaboration with Sir James William Morrison (1774–1856), deputy master of the mint, he made significant innovations in the casting process, which were described in his article 'Coinage', published in the supplement to the fourth and fifth editions of the *Encyclopaedia Britannica* (1818). In 1823 he took out a patent (no. 4802) for preparing copper for sheathing ships by alloying it with small quantities of zinc, tin, antimony, and arsenic.

Mushet was cited as an authority in contemporary debates on currency questions. His work *An enquiry into the effect produced on the national currency and rates of exchange by the Bank Restriction Bill* (3rd edn, 1811) was noticed by Thomas Malthus in the *Edinburgh Review*, 17 (1810–11). He gave evidence on 19 March 1819 to the House of Commons committee on the resumption of cash payments, chaired by Robert Peel, and on 29 March and 7 April 1819 to the House of Lords committee on the same subject. He stated that he had compiled tables of the exchanges and prices of gold from 1760 to 1810. In 1821 he published *Tables exhibiting the gain and loss to the fundholder arising from the fluctuations of the value of the currency from 1800 to 1821* (2nd edn, corrected, 1821), which traced the history of the variation between the value of the gold coin and paper in circulation. One of the founder members of the Political Economy Club in April 1821, he published in 1826 an investigation into the causes of the financial panic of 1825, which he attributed to the excess issue of bank notes. This was noticed in the *Quarterly Review*, 39 (1829).

Mushet died at Millfield House, Edmonton, on 1 February 1828, leaving a widow and children.

R. B. PROSSER, rev. M. C. CURTHOYS

Sources GM, 1st ser., 98/1 (1828), 275 · R. H. I. Palgrave, ed., *Dictionary of political economy*, 3 vols. (1894–9) · C. E. Challis, ed., *A new history of the royal mint* (1992) · *The works and correspondence of David Ricardo*, ed. P. Sraffa and M. H. Dobb, 11 vols. (1951–73) · private information (1894)

Mushet, Robert (1811–1871), official of the Royal Mint, born at Dalkeith, was the second son of Richard Mushet—a brother of David *Mushet and of Robert *Mushet (1782–1828). His mother was Marion Walker. He matriculated at St Catharine's College, Cambridge, in 1827, and was admitted to Gonville and Caius College in the following year, but did not graduate. He was subsequently the author of two works on ancient mythology, *The Trinities of the Ancients* (1837) and *The Book of Symbols* (1844; 2nd edn, 1847).

Mushet went to London to assist his uncle Robert Mushet in the mint, and in 1833 his name appears for the first time in the *Royal Kalendar* as 'second clerk and probationer melter'. On the reorganization of the mint in 1851, when the 'moneyers' were abolished, Mushet was appointed senior clerk and melter with a residence at the mint. He held that office until his death. His technical expertise and long service gave him strong claims to succeed William Barton as deputy master of the mint. But on the latter's death in 1868 the position was given to a young civil servant from the Treasury, Sir Charles William Fremantle (1834–1914), who had been Disraeli's private secretary. The appointment was criticized in the House of Commons (2 April 1869). Mushet was elected FGS in 1863. He wrote the article 'Coinage' in the eighth edition of *Encyclopaedia Britannica*. He died on 4 September 1871 at Belair House, Haywards Heath, Sussex, and was buried at Haywards Heath. He left a widow, Mary Anne. Their eldest son, Robert Smith Mushet (b. 1859), was called to the bar in 1883.

R. B. PROSSER, rev. M. C. CURTHOYS

Sources private information (1894) · Boase, *Mod. Eng. biog.* · Venn, *Alum. Cant.* · CGPLA Eng. & Wales (1871)

Wealth at death under £14,000: probate, 1 Dec 1871, CGPLA Eng. & Wales

Mushet, Robert Forester (1811–1891), metallurgist, was born at Coleford in the Forest of Dean on 8 April 1811. He was the youngest of the six children of David *Mushet

(1772–1847), metallurgist, and Agnes Wilson; his middle name, Forester, came, it is said, from his birthplace, though he rarely used it and was always known as Robert Mushet. Mushet's early years seem to have been spent at Coleford, assisting his father in his metallurgical researches and experiments. He thus became familiar with the value of manganese in steelmaking. Mushet married Mary Ann Thomas (1819–1914) in 1841: they had a daughter and two sons. In 1848 his attention was accidentally directed to a sample of 'spiegeleisen', an alloy of iron, carbon, and manganese, manufactured in Rhenish Prussia from a double carbonate of iron and manganese known as spathose iron ore. Mushet immediately commenced making experiments with this metal, and although the results were of no immediate practical value, they ultimately became of great importance in connection with the invention of the pneumatic steelmaking process by Sir Henry *Bessemer (1813–1898).

Bessemer announced his invention at Cheltenham in 1856, but his celebrated process of refining iron by blowing air through it immediately ran into problems. Early trials produced steel that was 'rotten', due partly to a little understood problem that would now be termed overoxidation, whereby the iron had become wholly decarburized. It is reliably reported that a manager of the Ebbw Vale Iron Company visited Mushet almost immediately after Bessemer's announcement, bringing with him samples of Bessemer metal. Mushet immediately recognized the problem with the 'burnt' wrought iron and corrected it with the addition of molten spiegeleisen. 'I saw then', said Mushet, 'that the Bessemer process was perfected, and that, with fair play, untold wealth would reward Mr Bessemer and myself' (Mushet, 11).

Mushet was mistaken in his financial hopes. He patented the use of his 'triple compound' of iron-carbon-manganese only a month after the Cheltenham meeting, but he allowed himself to be persuaded to couple this with the use of a worthless steelmaking patent in the name of Martien; this was held by the Ebbw Vale Company, with whom Mushet was then collaborating. It is reported that Bessemer journeyed to Coleford to discuss his problems with Mushet, but the latter was bound to the Welsh company and felt unable to help him. This was unfortunate, since when the Ebbw Vale Company failed to pay the stamp duty on the patent it became public property from early 1859 onwards.

When Bessemer's process revolutionized world steel manufacture in the 1860s, depending for its success on additions of spiegeleisen very much along the lines suggested by Mushet, the stage was set for a celebrated controversy as to whether Bessemer or Mushet had priority concerning the use of spiegeleisen. Bessemer declined to credit Mushet or to pay him any royalties. He was supported by well-known ironmasters, such as J. S. Jeans, who stated that, 'as a matter of fact, Bessemer had actually gone so far with his experiments on manganese that he had virtually solved the problem before the Mushet patents were published' (*Engineering Review*, 20 July 1893,

7). Mushet stated his own case in 1883 in a pamphlet titled, pointedly, *The Bessemer–Mushet Process*. In it he argued that although Bessemer may have discovered the spiegeleisen process eventually, 'I, however, was fortunate to anticipate him' (Mushet, preface). Historians have mostly agreed with him and have emphasized Bessemer's reliance on both Mushet and Swedish ironmasters for the eventual success of his invention. Bessemer himself, it seems, also softened his attitude once the triumph of his process was assured. In 1867 Bessemer, 'though [he] did not then care to give … reasons for doing so' (Bessemer, 294), granted Mushet an annual pension of £300—a belated recognition of his crucial contribution.

Meanwhile, between 1859 and 1861 Mushet took out about twenty patents for the manufacture of alloys of iron and steel with titanium, tungsten, and chromium. In 1868 he found that the addition of finely powdered wolfram ore (tungsten) produced a steel which did not require anything but cooling in the open air to give it a cutting edge hard enough for lathe and other similar tools. This self-hardening steel—the first specialized tool steel for engineers' tools—contained about 7 per cent tungsten and made possible a 50 per cent faster cutting speed. After an abortive attempt to manufacture this steel through his Titanic Steel and Iron Company of Coleford, Mushet (who decided not to patent tungsten tool steel, but kept the formula secret) licensed the product to Samuel Osborn & Co. of Sheffield. Osborns acquired the sole right to manufacture R. Mushet's Special Steel (RMS), as it came to be known, which it did with great success. Mushet received a royalty on every ton: alongside his income from Bessemer, this gave him financial security in his later years.

Mushet was of a very self-contained and reliant disposition, well able to defend himself even against so flinty a character as Bessemer. As he admitted, he had never been inside a steel works except his own; nor did he ever visit Sheffield, the centre of the steel industry. Yet although 'he shunned the limelight of personal contact [he] revelled in paper disputations. He would dodge Bessemer behind his umbrella but sharpen his pen like a rapier before writing a letter to him, or to the technical press' (Osborn, 103). From about 1848 onwards he was a regular correspondent of the *Mining Journal*. In 1857–8 he wrote a series of letters on the Bessemer process to that publication under the sobriquet Sideros, while also carrying on a correspondence under his own name. He was also frequently in touch by letter with Samuel Osborn, concerning the manufacture of RMS. Mushet's two sons, Edward Maxwell Tom (1842–1908) and Henry Charles Brooklyn (1845–1923), joined Samuel Osborn's company in 1870 to supervise the manufacture of Mushet tool steel.

Despite his apparent isolation, Mushet's work was of fundamental importance to the emerging steel industry. This was recognized at the time to a certain extent—the Iron and Steel Institute awarded him in 1876 its Bessemer gold medal, supported by no less a person than Bessemer himself—but since then Mushet's reputation has grown even more. He is usually regarded as the first important

pioneer of alloy steels. After many years of enfeebled health, Mushet died on 29 January 1891 at 10 Sydenham Villas, Cheltenham; he was buried at Cheltenham.

R. B. PROSSER, *rev.* GEOFFREY TWEEDALE

Sources F. M. Osborn, *The story of the Mushets* (1952) • R. F. Mushet, *The Bessemer–Mushet process, or, manufacture of cheap steel* (1883) • H. Bessemer, *Sir Henry Bessemer, FRS: an autobiography* (1905) • E. F. Lange, 'Bessemer, Göransson and Mushet: a contribution to technical history', *Memoirs of the Literary and Philosophical Society of Manchester*, 57/17 (1912–13), 1–44 • T. A. Seed, *Pioneers for a century, 1852–1952: the growth and achievement of Samuel Osborn & Co. Ltd, Sheffield* (1952) • K. C. Barraclough, *Steelmaking before Bessemer*, 2 (1984) • G. Tweedale, *Sheffield steel and America: a century of commercial and technological interdependence, 1830–1930* (1987) • d. cert.
Archives Sheff. Arch., Hadfield MSS • Sheff. Arch., Samuel Osborn & Co. records
Likenesses photograph, Iron and Steel Institute • portrait, repro. in Osborn, *Story of the Mushets* • portrait (after photograph), repro. in *Engineering Review* (20 July 1893), 7
Wealth at death £1677 15*s.*: probate, 25 Feb 1891, *CGPLA Eng. & Wales*

Mushet, William (1715/16–1792), physician, was born in Dublin, the son of William Mushet, a Jacobite who had fled to Dublin from Stirling. He was admitted to Trinity College, Dublin, in 1730, and entered Leiden University on 26 August 1745, 'aged 29' (Venn, *Alum. Cant.*). Mushet later became a member of King's College, Cambridge, and there proceeded MA (incorporated from Dublin) and MD in 1746. He became a candidate of the Royal College of Physicians on 4 April 1748, and a fellow on 20 March 1749. In 1751 he delivered the Goulstonian lectures. He was then made physician-in-chief to the forces, and served at the battle of Minden (1759). For unknown reasons he declined an offer of a baronetcy for his services in that campaign.

Mushet was closely associated with the duke of Rutland and for eleven years had apartments at Belvoir Castle, Leicestershire. He died at York on 11 December 1792. On the monument erected to his memory by his daughter Mary in the church of St Mary Castlegate, York, where he was buried, Sir Robert Sinclair's tribute recalls Mushet's 'cheerful disposition and lively imagination' (Munk, 170).

L. M. M. SCOTT, *rev.* JEFFREY S. REZNICK

Sources Munk, *Roll* • E. Peacock, *Index to English speaking students who have graduated at Leyden University* (1883) • Venn, *Alum. Cant.*
Likenesses monument, 1792–9, church of St Mary Castlegate, York

Musker, Harold (1897–1970), banker, was born in Bootle, Lancashire, on 10 March 1897, to Charles Musker, a civil and mechanical engineer, and his wife, Lizzie Ethel. He was educated at Merchant Taylors' School until the age of seventeen, when he joined London County and Westminster Bank in December 1914. He was married twice: first to Julia Agnes Draddy in 1927, from whom he was divorced, and then, on 26 December 1946, to Bertha Keith, *née* Strachan, a widow with two young sons. He had at least a daughter.

Between November 1915 and May 1919, Musker served in the Royal Artillery, winning the Military Cross in France. He then spent a year working in London, studying shorthand, and working in Greece for the United States shipping board.

In December 1920 Musker joined the Imperial Bank of Persia, later called the British Bank of the Middle East (BBME), and he was soon posted to Bombay. When he left in 1923, he worked for nearly two years in the bank's London office, before becoming manager of the small Barforush branch in Persia in March 1925. Reputedly one of the brightest of the bank's juniors, he rose rapidly in its service, despite an apparently abrasive and argumentative manner.

After experience in Duzdab, Basrah, Khorramshahr, Kermanshah, Shiraz, and Tehran, where he was assistant and later travelling inspector, Musker became acting deputy chief manager in April 1939. Confirmed in this post in July 1939, he spent the war years in London, serving as acting chief manager between May and October of 1945. In June 1946 he requested a transfer from the bank's foreign service to the London office for personal reasons. Normally this would have blighted his career prospects, but he was by then an experienced member of staff, and was within reach of the chief managership. As a result, Musker joined the London office in April 1947, becoming sub-manager in October of that year. The manager-secretary was a sick man, and over the next few years Musker's influence grew. In January 1951, he was appointed acting London manager and secretary, being confirmed as such in October of that year. He became the bank's first general manager and secretary in July 1952.

Musker has been described as a 'short, plump and introspective man, who was both decisive and dictatorial' (Jones, 38). He exerted great influence over the affairs of the bank, because of his autocratic inclinations and the fact that the average age of the board was relatively high. He was not a great innovator, however. His banking and political judgements were no different from those of most men of his time. Nor did he move in overseas banking circles. His significance lay rather in the fact that he supported and continued the expansion of the bank, which had already started, and which transformed it from a purely Persian into a Middle Eastern institution following the discovery of oil. He was prepared to take the risks of expansion in spite of the political uncertainties of the Middle East, a policy which reaped its reward when the bank was forced out of Iran in 1952. During his time as general manager, thirteen new branches were opened, and the bank went back in to Iran with a joint-venture subsidiary.

Musker quickly established his authority over the bank's board. Members were told only enough for them to come to the decision that he wanted, and he usually got his own way. Indeed, when the then chairman espoused the cause of amalgamation with Chartered Bank, and Musker, finding out at the last minute, objected, it was the chairman who resigned, and Musker who orchestrated the failure of the plan. Musker was furious, C. F. Warr thought, 'chiefly because he had not been consulted and second because he did not like the Chartered Bank' (Jones, 76).

Musker was, however, as enthusiastic about merger with the Hongkong and Shanghai Bank as he was obstructive over that with Chartered. He considered that Chartered, on merger with BBME, would get rid of him and other senior staff, whereas the Hong Kong Bank had had close links with BBME since the 1890s (Jones, 78). Musker's preferred option materialized and, circulating the staff the day before the merger was announced, he assured them that the BBME would keep its identity and nobody would lose their job. Musker's own position was secure, and indeed he was elected to the BBME's board in July 1960.

Musker retired as general manager in December 1961, and from BBME's board in 1966, settling at Riverlea, Newtown Road, Warwash, Fareham, Hampshire. He died on 30 July 1970 at the General Hospital, Southampton; he was survived by his second wife.   FRANCES BOSTOCK

Sources G. Jones, *The history of the British Bank of the Middle East*, 2: *Banking and oil* (1987), 38 · m. cert. [second marriage] · b. cert. · d. cert. · HSBC Group Archives, London, BBME archive · will, 20 Aug 1963, proved London, 16 Oct 1970 · *CGPLA Eng. & Wales* (1970)
Archives HSBC Group Archives, London, BBME archive
Likenesses photographs, HSBC Group Archives, London, Midland Bank archives, BBME archive · photographs, repro. in Jones, *Banking & oil*
Wealth at death £32,649: probate, 16 Oct 1970, *CGPLA Eng. & Wales*

Muskerry. For this title name *see* MacCarthy, Cormac Oge Laidhir, lord of Muskerry (d. 1536).

Musket, George. *See* Fisher, George (c.1580–1645).

Muspratt, Edmund Knowles (1833–1923), industrial chemist, was born on 6 November 1833 in Linacre, near Bootle, the youngest in the family of four sons and six daughters of James *Muspratt (1793–1886), founder of the alkali industry in Lancashire, and his wife, Julia Josephine Connor of Dublin. He was educated at the Pestalozzian Institute, Worksop, after which, in 1850, his father sent him to study chemistry under his close friend Justus von Liebig at the University of Giessen in Hesse. When Liebig moved to the University of Munich in 1852 Muspratt followed him to study medicine. In 1856 he returned to Liverpool to join his father's rapidly expanding chemical company, largely concerned with the manufacture of soda by the Leblanc process. The demands of the business prevented his following his original intention of becoming a professional chemist. He was, however, always keenly interested in industrial chemistry and was a founder member of the Society of Chemical Industry (1881) and its president (1885–6). In 1861 he married Frances Jane, daughter of Thomas *Baines, a former editor of the *Liverpool Times*; they had five sons (one of whom died as a child) and four daughters, including Nessie Stewart *Brown who became a notable local politician.

In 1890 James Muspratt & Sons, with many other Leblanc soda manufacturers, amalgamated to form the United Alkali Company, of which Muspratt became a director and later honorary president. The object was to resist increasing competition from the intrinsically superior ammonia-soda process, developed by the Solvay

Muspratts and the British chemical industry', *Endeavour*, 14 (1955), 29–33 · *Journal of the Society of Chemical Industry* (July 1931), 54 [jubilee number]

Likenesses A. John, portrait, 1906, University of Liverpool [see illus.]

Wealth at death £438,466 1s. 5d.: probate, 19 Nov 1923, *CGPLA Eng. & Wales*

Muspratt, James (1793–1886), chemical manufacturer, was born in Dublin on 12 August 1793, the youngest of three children of Evan Muspratt (d. 1810) and his wife, Sarah. It is believed that his father had emigrated from southern England; his mother was a member of the Mainwaring family of Cheshire. After local schooling he was apprenticed to a wholesale chemist. In 1810 his father died and his mother soon afterwards married John Corley of Dublin, but herself died only a few months later. Probably because of the unsettling effect of these events, Muspratt left Dublin to seek his fortune in the Peninsular War. After the abandonment of Madrid in 1812 he walked 100 miles to Lisbon, despite illness, and there enlisted in the navy. Finding the harsh discipline intolerable, he deserted, swimming ashore while his ship was anchored in Swansea Bay, and made his way back to Dublin. There he came into an inheritance, much diminished by chancery proceedings, and in 1818 set up a chemical works in partnership with Thomas Abbot, an established drug and general merchant. The venture was probably prompted partly by his previous apprenticeship and partly by his friendship with the family of Robert Kane, who were acid manufacturers. In the same year he married Julia Josephine Connor. While applying himself to his business, he enjoyed a very active social life, especially among people associated with the Irish stage. His close friends included the dramatist James Sheridan Knowles, the talented actress Eliza O'Neill, and the painter and songwriter Samuel Lover.

Dublin and Liverpool had long-standing trading connections and, as a chemical manufacturer, Muspratt would have been familiar with the soap-making industry on Merseyside. This was then dependent on imported natural alkali, but in 1823 an alternative began to become available. In that year the government abolished the £30 per ton duty on salt and this made it economically attractive to exploit in Britain the soda manufacturing process patented in France in 1791 by Nicolas Leblanc. The basic raw materials were salt, sulphuric acid, and coal—all readily available in the Liverpool area, with its excellent port facilities.

There Muspratt set up, in an old glass factory, a small chemical works in 1823. The Leblanc process had already been worked on a small scale on the Tyne (1814) and the Clyde (1816) but the salt tax had proved severely limiting. Initially the soap boilers, used to vegetable alkali, distrusted the synthetic product, but demand grew quickly. In 1828 Muspratt, who had been forced out of Liverpool for polluting the atmosphere, built a new works at St Helens, for a time in partnership with another Irish chemist, Josias Gamble. They parted after two years and he moved again, to Newton on the St Helens Canal.

Edmund Knowles Muspratt (1833–1923), by Augustus John, 1906

brothers in Belgium, and operated under licence by Brunner, Mond & Co. Ltd at Winnington since 1873. It was, however, a losing battle: by the turn of the century the Solvay process was producing six times as much soda as the Leblanc. In 1926 both United Alkali and Brunner Mond were absorbed into the newly created Imperial Chemical Industries, of which Muspratt's son Sir Max *Muspratt [see under Muspratt, James] became a director.

Despite his business commitments Muspratt found time to develop many other interests—in politics, education, foreign travel, and (like his father) in music and the theatre. Politically he was a radical, keenly interested in free trade and home rule. He unsuccessfully contested the Widnes division in 1885. Interest in local politics led him to become a member of Liverpool town council and Lancashire county council; he also served as chairman of Liverpool chamber of commerce. His interest in education was reflected in his active role in founding University College, Liverpool, in 1881; when it became the University of Liverpool in 1903 he was elected pro-chancellor. Later, in 1910, he helped to establish the Liverpool repertory theatre. Those who knew him described Muspratt as energetic, public-spirited, accomplished, and generous.

Muspratt died on 1 September 1923 at Seaforth Hall, Seaforth, near Liverpool, which his father had built when he settled on Merseyside.   TREVOR I. WILLIAMS, *rev.*

Sources E. K. Muspratt, *My life and work* (1917) · D. Reilly, 'The Muspratts and the Gambles—pioneers in England's alkali industry', *Journal of Chemical Education*, 28 (1951), 650–53 · D. W. F. Hardie, 'The

Although chemically efficient, and necessary to a product for which there was a growing demand, the Leblanc process had a serious intrinsic defect. It produced clouds of noxious hydrochloric acid in direct proportion to the amount of soda made. Inevitably, local landowners, as well as Liverpool corporation, objected strongly. From 1832 until 1850 Muspratt was continually involved in litigation, which in the end forced him to close both his works. He largely withdrew from the business but subsequently his sons, Richard and Frederic, with his support, opened successful new works at Flint and Widnes. Around 1837 Muspratt experimented for two or three years with the more environmentally acceptable ammonia-soda process, but it was beyond the technology of the day. The difficulties were not finally overcome until 1863, by Ernest Solvay in Belgium: Muspratt's experiment cost him £8000.

Despite his legal problems, Muspratt prospered and built a splendid house, Seaforth Hall, on the dunes near Bootle, where he raised a family of ten children. From this base he indulged his taste for social life and travel, the latter for both business and pleasure. In 1837 the British Association for the Advancement of Science held its annual meeting in Liverpool, and Muspratt met Justus von Liebig, one of the leading chemists of the day. This led to a long friendship—marred only by a brief dispute over an unsuccessful venture in synthetic fertilizers in the 1840s—and frequent visits to Giessen, where Muspratt sent one of his sons to study chemistry, and later Munich. In the 1840s he opened offices in New York and Philadelphia and in 1842 he visited America, where one of his daughters was married to an American. He also travelled frequently in Italy and, with the Glasgow chemical industrialist, Charles Tennant, invested unsuccessfully in sulphur mines in Sicily.

As in Dublin, Muspratt continued to enjoy the company of people associated with art, literature, and the stage. He had a deep love of English poetry and was gifted with a remarkable memory: even in his eighties he could repeat long passages from his favourite poems. In 1847 the famous American Cushman sisters, Charlotte and Susan, attended a fancy-dress ball at Seaforth Hall. Muspratt's son, Sheridan, named after his Dublin friend James Sheridan Knowles, was attracted by Susan and married her in the following year. The match was blessed by Charles Dickens, also a visitor at Seaforth Hall when his theatrical touring company visited Liverpool at the same time.

In his later years Muspratt took a keen interest in education and in 1825 helped to found the Liverpool Institute, successor to an earlier mechanics' institute. In 1848 he assisted his son Sheridan in establishing—with the blessing of Liebig and the patronage of the prince consort—the Liverpool College of Practical Chemistry. Muspratt died at Seaforth Hall on 4 May 1886 and was buried in the nearby parish churchyard at Walton.

Three of Muspratt's sons, James Sheridan *Muspratt, Richard, and Frederic, were actively engaged in the chemical industry. So, too, was a fourth, Edmund Knowles *Muspratt, who was largely responsible for the merger of some fifty firms that led to the formation of the United Alkali Company in 1890, an ultimately unsuccessful attempt to make the Leblanc process competitive with Solvay's ammonia-soda process. From 1873 the process was worked under licence by Brunner, Mond & Co. at Winnington. In 1926 this company and the United Alkali Company were absorbed into the newly formed Imperial Chemical Industries, of which Edmund's son Max was appointed a director.

Sir Max Muspratt, baronet (1872–1934) was born at Seaforth Hall on 3 February 1872. In 1896 he married Helena Agnes Dalrymple Ainsworth of Blackburn. They had two sons, of whom one died in childhood, and two daughters. After studying industrial chemistry at Zürich Polytechnic he became a director of United Alkali in 1890 and chairman in 1914. During the First World War he advised the Ministry of Munitions on industrial chemical matters, particularly the supply of critically important sulphuric acid. He was created a baronet in 1922; his son Rudolph died in 1929, so the title became extinct on his own death on 20 April 1934. He was active in local and national politics in the Liberal interest (until 1926) and was elected MP in 1910, representing Liverpool Exchange division for a short time.

TREVOR I. WILLIAMS

Sources DNB · D. W. F. Hardie, 'The Muspratts and the British chemical industry', *Endeavour*, 14 (1955), 29–33 · J. Fenwick Allen, *Some founders of the chemical industry: men to be remembered*, 2nd edn (1907) · E. K. Muspratt, 'President's address, fifth annual meeting of the society', *Journal of the Society of Chemical Industry*, 5 (1886), 401–14 · Horace Muspratt (grandson) in centenary of the alkali industry, 1823–1923, 1923, United Alkali Company, Widnes · K. Warren, *Chemical foundations: the alkali industry in Britain to 1926* (1980) · D. Reilly, 'The Muspratts and the Gambles—pioneers in England's alkali industry', *Journal of Chemical Education*, 28 (1951), 650–53 · P. N. Reed, 'Muspratt, Sir Max', *DBB* · D. W. F. Hardie, *A history of the chemical industry in Widnes* (1950) · M. D. Stephens and G. W. Roderick, 'The Muspratts of Liverpool', *Annals of Science*, 29 (1972), 287–311 · *The Times* (21 April 1934) [Max Muspratt] · *Chemistry and Industry* (27 April 1934) [Max Muspratt] · WWW
Archives Lpool RO, corresp. and papers
Likenesses portrait, repro. in *Endeavour*, 25
Wealth at death £12,358 8s. 3d.: resworn probate, Dec 1887, CGPLA Eng. & Wales · £208,044 14s. 4d.—Max Muspratt: probate, 5 July 1934, CGPLA Eng. & Wales

Muspratt, James Sheridan (1821–1871), chemist, was born on 8 March 1821, in Dublin, the eldest son in the family of four sons and six daughters of James *Muspratt (1793–1886), chemical manufacturer, and his wife, Julia Josephine Connor. He and three of his brothers, including Edmund Knowles *Muspratt, were active in the alkali industry on Merseyside and in north Wales, as was his nephew Sir Max Muspratt. He was thus a member of a chemical dynasty spanning the years 1793–1934. This, coupled with a strong family interest in music, drama, and literature, greatly influenced his life. The name Sheridan was assumed, not given, prompted by his admiration for the actor and dramatist James Sheridan Knowles. Although he was a very capable chemist, his talent proved to lie in research (he published more than forty papers) and teaching rather than in industry. His commercial ventures were mostly disastrous.

By the time Muspratt, who attended private schools in

Bootle, was thirteen his father was a wealthy man, and he was sent with tutors to travel on the continent. In 1836 he went to study chemistry at Anderson's University, Glasgow, under Thomas Graham, with whom his father was acquainted through the Tennants of St Rollox. In 1837 Graham was appointed to the chair of chemistry in University College, London, and Muspratt followed him there. He became involved in a project to make alkali by a novel (ammonia-soda) process and persuaded his father to invest in it. It was unsuccessful and cost his father £8000. Ironically, this technically difficult process was successfully launched on Merseyside by Brunner, Mond & Co. in 1872 and eventually displaced the Leblanc process on which the Muspratt fortunes had been built. Undismayed, his father sent him to Philadelphia in 1841 to manage the growing Muspratt business interests there but his optimistic forecasts of sales were far from fulfilled and he was called home after a year. Again, it was an expensive failure.

In 1837 the British Association for the Advancement of Science held its annual meeting in Liverpool, and the elder Muspratt met the great German chemist Justus von Liebig; the two became close friends. Muspratt was then sent to work with Liebig at Giessen. He acquitted himself well in the laboratory, earning a prestigious doctorate in 1844, but much less satisfactorily in promoting Liebig's interest in synthetic fertilizers for which his father had taken out a patent on Liebig's behalf in 1845. Back on Merseyside Muspratt tried to work the process but without success. Worse, in a foolish indiscretion he disclosed the formula to an outsider, leading to a furious quarrel with Liebig. Between 1845 and 1848 he also worked with A. W. Hofmann at the Royal College of Chemistry. Together they published important papers on toluidine and nitraniline.

Alongside his erratic industrial life, Muspratt took a keen interest in local theatre and in 1847 acted as organizing secretary for the visit of Charles Dickens's amateur company. It was the first appearance in Liverpool of the celebrated American actresses the Cushman sisters, Charlotte (1816–1876) and Susan (1822–1859), and they were invited to the Muspratt mansion, Seaforth Hall, where his father entertained lavishly. Muspratt and Susan, a widow, were mutually attracted and were married on 22 March 1848; they had three daughters.

After this, Muspratt found his true vocation. In the same year he established the successful Liverpool College of Practical Chemistry, endorsed by Liebig and with the prince consort as patron. During his time at Giessen he had translated a German work on the use of the blowpipe in chemistry. This was well received and he was invited in 1848 to compile an encyclopaedic work, *Chemistry … as Applied to the Arts and Manufacture*, to appear in monthly parts. It was completed in 1860 and then appeared in book form and was highly successful. It was translated into several foreign languages, including Russian and German. Harvard University conferred an honorary MD on Muspratt.

Sadly, Muspratt's young wife did not live to share his success. She died on 10 May 1859 and in the following year he married Ann Neale, of Rainhill, near Liverpool, who survived him. They had no children. He died on 3 February 1871 at his home, The Hollies, West Derby, near Liverpool. P. J. HARTOG, *rev.* TREVOR I. WILLIAMS

Sources D. W. F. Hardie, 'The Muspratts and the British chemical industry', *Endeavour*, 14 (1955), 29–33 · M. D. Stephens and G. W. Roderick, 'The Muspratts of Liverpool', *Annals of Science*, 29 (1972), 287–311 · *JCS*, 24 (1871), 620–21 · P. J. T. Morris and C. A. Russell, *Archives of the British chemical industry, 1750–1914: a handlist* (1988)
Archives Lpool RO, corresp. and papers
Likenesses W. Holl, stipple (after photograph), BM, NPG · J. Le Conte, stipple and line engraving (after photograph by Foard & Beard), NPG · portrait, repro. in Hardie, 'The Muspratts and the British chemical industry'
Wealth at death under £50,000: probate, 17 March 1871, *CGPLA Eng. & Wales*

Muspratt, Sir Max, baronet (1872–1934). *See under* Muspratt, James (1793–1886).

Muss, Charles (1779–1824), enamel and glass painter, was born probably in Newcastle upon Tyne, the son of Bonificio Musso, an Italian artist practising in Newcastle who was one of the exhibitors at the Society of Artists in 1790. Charles Muss is thought to have moved to London shortly after 1800 and appears at first to have been engaged in work as a painter on porcelain at the Caughley factory, while another tradition links him with work as a colourer of prints. Subsequently he developed into a glass painter and found employment with William Collins at the latter's glass works in the Strand, near Temple Bar. He obtained the title 'Enamel painter to the King'. Muss executed a number of enamels after old masters, among them the *Assumption of the Virgin Mary* after Guido Reni and a *Holy Family* after Parmegiano, for George IV. His enamel works were on both glass and copper, and his mature style has been likened to the smoothness of ivory. He first exhibited at the Royal Academy in 1802, showing two miniature portraits.

Muss executed a number of windows, including a *Descent from the Cross* after Rubens for St Bride's, Fleet Street, a window for St Mary Redcliffe, Bristol, armorial glass for the oriel of the hall of Queens' College, Cambridge (removed 1854), and panels for the marquess of Westminster's Eaton Hall. Fragments of his three-light west window of the baron's hall, Brancepeth Castle, Northumberland, showing the battle of Nevilles Cross, after Thomas Stothard RA, appear to survive.

Muss was the teacher and collaborator of the painter John Martin, who finished several of Muss's commissions after the latter's death, which had occurred by 30 June 1824. On 30 June administration of his estate was granted to his widow, Mary, and his address recorded as Warren Street, Fitzroy Square, Middlesex. Inventory records indicate that at the time of his death he was insolvent. His remaining works and drawings were auctioned for the benefit of his widow on 29 and 30 November 1824. L. H. CUST, *rev.* ALEXANDER KOLLER

Sources *Journal of the British Society of Master Glass-Painters*, 13 (1960–61), 403–4 · Redgrave, *Artists* · S. F. Baylis, 'Glass-painting in Britain, *c.*1760–*c.*1840: a revolution in taste', PhD diss., U. Cam.,

1990 · P. Cowen, *A guide to stained glass in Britain* (1985), 73 · J. A. Forrest, 'Stained glass', *Proceedings of the Liverpool Architectural and Archaeological Society*, 1 (1852), 90 · G. Godwin, *The churches of London*, 2 vols. (1838) · *GM*, 1st ser., 94/2 (1824), 186 · C. H. Grinling, 'Ancient stained glass in Oxford', *Proceedings of the Oxford Architectural and Historical Society*, new ser., 4 (1883), 111–89 · will, PRO, PROB 6/200, fol. 204r · estate duties, PRO, IR/26/219, fols. 239v–240r

Archives Queens' College, Cambridge, MSS

Wealth at death 'insolvent': PRO, death duty registers, IR 26/219, fols. 239v–240r; will, PRO, PROB 6/200, fol. 204r

Mussabini, Scipio Africanus [*formerly* Scipio Arnaud Godolphin] (1867–1927), athletics coach and author, was born at 6 Collyer Buildings, Blackheath Hill, Lewisham, London, on 11 March 1867, the fourth of six children of Neocles Gaspard Mussabini (1827–1915), a journalist and war correspondent, and his wife, Aline *née* Farçat (*c*.1840–*c*.1911) of Grenoble, France. His name was registered at birth as Scipio Arnaud Godolphin Mussabini, but he later used the forenames Scipio Africanus. His great-grandfather was a Syrian merchant from Damascus who italianized his name to Mussabini. His father was born in Smyrna, Turkey, of an Italian mother and became a naturalized British subject on 17 April 1857. Mussabini attended school in France, probably at a private establishment in Grenoble. From about the age of sixteen he was apprenticed as a journalist. On 14 September 1885, giving his age as twenty-one, he married Emma Nicholls (1866–1961), the daughter of Samuel Nicholls, a farmer, of Hove, Sussex; she was expecting the first of their seven children (three sons and four daughters).

During the 1880s Mussabini became involved with the professional running circuit, and in the following decade he coached athletes and cyclists, and was a freelance writer on athletics and billiards for the *Sporting Life*, *Referee*, and *Westminster Gazette*. In the early 1890s he trained members of the Polytechnic cycling club and in 1894 was appointed trainer to the Dunlop pacing team, based at the Herne Hill track, which set many world cycling records. He had meanwhile become a respected writer on billiards, and in collaboration with Sydenham Dixon founded in 1900 a monthly journal, *World of Billiards*, of which he was assistant editor. He became proprietor and editor of the journal in 1910, but it proved a commercial failure. With J. P. Mannock, a leading player, he wrote *Billiards Expounded to All Degrees of Amateur Players* (1904). When he encountered financial difficulties during the First World War he became a fee-earning billiards referee.

From about 1900, as professional athletics and cycling went into decline, Mussabini turned to training amateur athletes. Adopting the contemporary usage of the public schools and American colleges, he styled himself a 'coach', as opposed to a 'trainer', and by 1913 was employed by Polytechnic Harriers at the Herne Hill track. He thus became the first coach in British athletics. His advanced methods of preparing athletes were described in his book *The Complete Athletic Trainer* (1913), written in collaboration with Charles Ranson; it was notable for his emphasis on the detail of running movement, such as stride-length and arm-swing. After the First World War Mussabini used cine-cameras in order to analyse runners'

techniques, and he became famous for his lectures illustrated by cine-films. Six of his athletes won a total of five gold, two silver, and four bronze medals in track events at the 1920, 1924, and 1928 Olympic games. In 1923 he was a member of the British Olympic commission which made preparations for the British team at the 1924 games and also coached Vera Palmer-Searle, who set three women's world sprinting records in 1923 and 1924.

Nicknamed SAM, from his initials, Mussabini was dedicated to his work, and stood at an old-fashioned writing-desk to prepare his copy. A good listener, he could also be stubborn when he believed that he was right, and would not stand humbug from anyone. In his final years he suffered from diabetes. Returning from convalescence at Nice he died near Calais, France, on 25 March 1927 and was buried in the family grave at Hampstead cemetery on 31 March. In the film *Chariots of Fire* (1981) Mussabini was portrayed as Harold Abrahams's coach. On 4 December 1998 the National Coaches' Foundation struck the Mussabini medal for outstanding British coaches. The first award was made posthumously to Ron Pickering (1930–1991).

DAVID TERRY

Sources D. Terry, 'An athletic coach ahead of his time', *British Society of Sports History Newsletter*, 11 (spring 2000), 34–8 · *Billiard Player* (April–May 1927) · G. Moon, 'Old Sam and the Poly', in G. Moon, *Albert Hill: a proper perspective* (1992) · private information (2004) [K. Kelley] · m. cert. · d. cert.

Archives FILM BFI NFTVA, sports footage

Likenesses photograph, 1912, repro. in S. A. Mussabini, *The complete athletic trainer* (1913), facing p. 134 · double portrait, photograph, 1923–4 (with Harold Abrahams), repro. in C. Krümnel, *Athletik*, 207 · double portrait, photograph, 1923–4 (with Harold Abrahams), repro. in H. M. Abrahams, *Athletics* (1926), facing p. 38 · double portrait, photograph (with Reggie Walker), repro. in R. E. Walker, *Text book of sprinting, health and strength* (1910), 17 · photograph, repro. in S. A. Mussabini, *Running, walking and jumping* (1926), art supplement

Wealth at death £373 15s. 8d.: probate, 13 June 1927, CGPLA Eng. & Wales

Mussel-Mou'd Charlie. *See* Leslie, Charles (1676/7–1782).

Musson, Dame Ellen Mary (1867–1960), nurse, was born on 11 August 1867 at The Castle, Clitheroe, Lancashire, one of the six children of William Edward Musson (1831–1917), surgeon, and his wife, Susanna Catherine Robinson (1839–1911). Musson received a good education at home (1870–85), travelled in France and Germany, and worked as a governess before deciding at the age of twenty-seven to become a nurse. She undertook a three-year training (1895–8) at St Bartholomew's Hospital, London, where she was the gold medallist in her final year. The matron at that time was Isla Stewart, a leading personality in nursing politics and education, and Musson spent eight years working with her as night superintendent, sister, and assistant matron. In 1906 she moved to Swansea to become the matron of the Swansea General and Eye Hospital, and two years later was appointed matron of the General Hospital, Birmingham.

As a matron of a large provincial hospital from 1909 until 1923, Musson was very aware of the needs of the emerging profession of nursing, and she worked to

Dame Ellen Mary Musson (1867–1960), by unknown photographer

improve the nurses' working conditions and salaries. She also understood the need for proper professional education for nurses and developed the training syllabus, post-certificate courses in radiography, and the treatment of venereal disease, and established an important school of massage. Before leaving Birmingham she fulfilled one of her dreams, to open a club for nurses and professional women, with the financial support of Mrs Cadbury, the lady mayoress of Birmingham, and the local branch of the College of Nursing.

Musson joined the Territorial Force Nursing Service when it was established in 1908, and at the start of the First World War was appointed a principal matron. She was responsible for recruiting a large number of nurses for service at home and overseas, as well as for the supervision of the nursing in the 1st Southern General Hospital, based at Birmingham. This hospital started the war with 520 beds and finished it with over 6000. She was awarded the Royal Red Cross, first class, for her services.

Musson shared the view of the leaders of the campaign for the state registration of nurses, believing that nurses required professional independence. She took an active part in the various societies campaigning for state registration, and was a member of the influential League of St Bartholomew's Nurses and president of the General Hospital Birmingham Nurses' League. In 1916 she became one of the first supporters of the College of Nursing, despite the opposition of the leaders of the state registration campaign: she believed that the college offered a chance for unity within the profession. Her decision was a turning point for the party of moderation in the battle for control of the nursing profession, and through her influence and active support she contributed to the college's success. She was involved with the college for the rest of her life, as a member of the council until 1939, as honorary treasurer from 1938 to 1950, and as vice-president from 1950 to 1960. One of her main concerns was the poor economic position of nurses and she worked hard to improve this: one of her finest achievements was the establishment of the federated superannuation scheme for nurses in 1928.

Apart from her work for the College of Nursing, Musson had a distinguished career with the General Nursing Council for England and Wales (GNC). In 1923, when she was elected to this new statutory body responsible for registration under the 1919 Nurses' Act, she retired from full-time work in Birmingham and moved to Pevensey Bay, Sussex. In 1926 she became the first elected chairman of the GNC; she held this position until she stood down in 1943. As the first nurse chairman of the GNC she had a difficult task: not only was the profession divided ideologically but it was also at odds with the Ministry of Health. The government was more concerned with recruitment levels and the cost of running the hospitals than with raising the standard of nurses' professional education and status.

In the inter-war years the biggest concern for the profession was the shortage of nurses and the large number of untrained 'assistant nurses' who made up the shortfall. In 1937 Musson was one of the four nurses to be appointed to the interdepartmental committee on nursing services, chaired by the earl of Athlone. This government committee made many recommendations concerning the conditions, discipline, and social life of nurses, but its report was overshadowed by the start of the Second World War. The recommendations were taken up by the Royal College of Nursing, which appointed a special committee in 1941 to consider how they could be implemented. Musson was also a member of this committee, chaired by Lord Horder, which published several influential reports concerning the assistant nurse, recruitment, education and training, and the social and economic conditions of nurses. After the war, when the National Health Service was being organized, many of the ideas of the Athlone and Horder committees became the foundation of future policy, including the recognition of the assistant nurse.

In 1925 Musson attended the first post-war congress of the International Council of Nurses (ICN), held in Helsinki, as a representative of the College of Nursing, which had been invited by the president of the Finnish Nurses' Association to send an observer. (The college was not affiliated to the national association in Britain, the National Council of Nurses, because of the opposition of Mrs Bedford Fenwick, the founder of the latter and of the ICN.) Musson was very surprised to find herself elected honorary treasurer of the ICN at the meeting. This manoeuvre on the part of the organizers of the ICN illustrates Musson's status as a bridge between the two parties in British nursing. She was a very successful and popular treasurer of the ICN, and was persuaded to remain in office until 1947, when, at the age of eighty, she insisted on retiring. She contributed to the work of the ICN in many fields, including in 1934 the establishment of the Florence Nightingale International Foundation to provide funds for postgraduate study for nurses, as a memorial to Miss Nightingale. On Musson's retirement she was granted honorary membership of the ICN, and at the age of eighty-two she was persuaded to attend its fiftieth anniversary congress, held in Stockholm, when she was made an honorary member of the Swedish Nurses' Association.

Musson's many tributes included appointment as CBE (1928) and DBE (1939), an honorary LLD degree from the University of Leeds (1932), and the international Florence Nightingale medal (1939), and she held many distinguished offices, including the presidency of the National Council of Nurses of Great Britain and Ireland (1945). She devoted her life to the profession of nursing, and to everything she did she brought a first-class brain and integrity. Despite the very real divisions within the nursing profession in Britain, she was accepted by all parties as fair. She was good-looking, with a kind face, and described her hobbies as motoring and travelling. She spent the last fourteen years of her long life, which stretched from the days of Florence Nightingale's nursing reforms to those of the National Health Service, with her brother and sister at their home in Eastbourne. Musson died at the age of ninety-three on 7 November 1960, at her home, Badlesmere, 10 Trinity Trees, Eastbourne, and was cremated in the town on 11 November. SUSAN McGANN

Sources Royal College of Nursing Archives, Edinburgh, MSS · S. McGann, 'Ellen Musson: a wise chairman', *The battle of the nurses: a study of eight women who influenced the development of professional nursing, 1880–1930* (1992), 190–216 · annual reports, 1909–23, General Hospital, Birmingham, archives · house committee minutes, 1906–13, General Hospital, Birmingham, archives · *International Nursing Review*, 6/3 · *The Times* (9 Nov 1960) · b. cert. · d. cert. · CGPLA Eng. & Wales (1961) · *Clitheroe Advertiser & Times* (1 June 1917)

Archives General Hospital, Birmingham, archives · PRO, General Nursing Council records · Royal College of Nursing Archives, Edinburgh, MSS · St Bartholomew's Hospital, London, archives

Likenesses Elliott & Fry, photograph, 1945, Royal College of Nursing Archives, Edinburgh · L. Knight, oils, exh. RA 1955, United Kingdom Central Council for Nursing, London · photograph, repro. in *Nursing Times* (10 Feb 1923), 125 · photograph, repro. in *Nursing Times* (7 Jan 1939), 4 · photograph, repro. in *Nursing Times* (5 Feb 1944), 92 · photograph, repro. in *Nursing Times* (16 Aug 1957), 908 · photograph, Royal College of Nursing Archives, Edinburgh [see illus.]

Wealth at death £12,339 8s. 6d.: probate, 20 March 1961, CGPLA Eng. & Wales

Mustapha, Ernst August (d. 1738), royal servant, was probably born in the Ottoman empire. As a young man he was captured in battle by a Swedish officer during the war between the Habsburg and Ottoman empires in the 1680s, and not, as is traditionally stated, by Prince Georg Ludwig of Hanover, later George I of Great Britain. He served this Swedish officer for a few years, and transferred to Georg Ludwig's entourage about 1686. Unlike his more elevated colleague Mehemet, he remained a *Leibdiener*, or body servant, throughout his career.

Otherwise Mustapha's career followed a similar pattern

to Mehemet's. He continued in Georg Ludwig's service when the latter became elector of Hanover in 1698, and at some point converted to Christianity, taking the forenames Ernst August at his baptism. On 4 January 1708 he married Magdalena Catharina Homeyer (*bap.* 1686, *d.* 1756), the daughter of a Hanoverian burgher and *Ratsschmied* (presumably the civic blacksmith); the couple had one son.

Following the accession of Georg Ludwig to the British throne as George I in 1714, Mustapha travelled to London as part of the approximately seventy-strong Hanoverian entourage. He was one of the select twenty-five 'Hanoverians' who remained in Britain after 1716. He lived in apartments near the king's, and served George I into the final hours of his life. George I's recourse to his confidential Turkish-Hanoverian bodyservants greatly reduced the presence and influence of the British bedchamber staff and court ritual, and probably incurred nativist jealousies against the foreignness of the Hanoverian court in England. The level of interest shown in his presence in Britain was similar to that directed towards other allegedly exotic or unusual people. The secretive and private nature of the first George's court made public projection of anxieties about Turks and Germans onto Mustapha all the more easy. Again, like Mehemet, he was painted by William Kent in the grand staircase hall mural at Kensington Palace, depicting him at an age from his mid-fifties to his mid-sixties, and clothed in a quasi-Turkish style. Following Mehemet's death in 1726, Mustapha took his place, and was with the king in his last days of life in June 1727. He was able to inform George's doctors that the king had risen from his bed several times the night before his fatal stroke, and so had no need to be purged. Mustapha survived George I by over a decade. He returned to Hanover, where he died in 1738, and was buried in the Marktkirche, Hanover, on 18 May that year. His widow died on 1 December 1756. J. J. CAUDLE

Sources H. Funke, ed., *Schloss-Kirchenbuch Hannover, 1680–1812*, 2 vols. (Hanover, 1992) · R. Hatton, *George I: elector and king* (1978) · J. M. Beattie, *The English court in the reign of George I* (1967) · J. Marlow, *The life and times of George I* (1973) · O. Millar, *The Tudor, Stuart and early Georgian pictures in the collection of her majesty the queen*, 2 vols. (1963)

Likenesses Göhrde, portrait, 1725, Royal Collection; repro. in J. Prüser, *Die Göhrde: ein Beträg zur Geschichte des Jaged - und Forstwesens in Niedersachsen* (Hildesheim, 1969) · W. Kent, mural, 1725–7, Kensington Palace, London

Musters, George Chaworth (1841–1879), sailor and explorer, was the younger son of John George Musters of Wiverton Hall, Nottinghamshire, formerly of the 10th Royal Hussars, and his wife, Emily, daughter of Philip Hamond, of Westacre, Norfolk. His grandmother, Mary Ann Musters *née* Chaworth of Annesley, Nottinghamshire, was a cousin of Byron and the Mary of his poem 'The Dream'.

Musters was born at Naples, while his parents were travelling, on 13 February 1841; he was one of three children. His father died in 1842, and his mother in 1845, and he was brought up chiefly by his mother's brothers. He was educated in the Isle of Wight, and in Kent, and then at Dr Burney's academy at Gosport in preparation for the navy. He joined HMS *Algiers* in 1854, and served with distinction in the Crimean War, receiving the English and Turkish Crimean medals by the time he was fifteen. He served in several other vessels between 1856 and 1861, before joining the royal yacht *Victoria and Albert* as mate in 1861. He was promoted to lieutenant on 4 September 1861, and joined HMS *Stromboli*, serving on the coast of South America from December 1861 until she was paid off in June 1866. When at Rio in 1862, he and a midshipman of the *Stromboli*, in a youthful prank, climbed Sugar Loaf Mountain, and planted the British ensign on the summit. While serving in South America he bought land, and started sheep farming at Montevideo.

After Musters was placed on half pay, in 1869–70 he carried out a long-cherished ambition to travel in southern South America. He was one of the first Europeans to document the region, living with Patagonian Indians, and travelling with one of their bands from the Strait of Magellan to the River Negro, and then crossing northern Patagonia from east to west, a journey of almost 1400 miles, half of which was unknown to Europeans. His acute powers of observation provided the first comprehensive account of the eastern foothills of the Andes, and of the lifestyle of the Tehuelche, Pampas, and Araucanian Indians. The journey is described in his *At home with the Patagonians: a year's wanderings over untrodden ground from the Straits of Magellan to the Rio Negro*, (1871; 2nd edn, 1873). The book was published in German in Jena (1877), and Spanish in Buenos Aires (1911 and 1964). In 1872 the Royal Geographical Society presented him with a gold watch 'for his route maps and contribution to knowledge of the Patagonian people'. His travels earned him the nickname 'the king of Patagonia', and he came to be regarded as one of the most distinguished nineteenth-century explorers of southern Argentina.

Also in 1872 Musters visited Vancouver Island, but a promised account of his adventures with the Native Americans of British Columbia was never published. He went back to South America and set out to cross Chile and Patagonia from west to east, but was obliged to return to Valparaiso. He went home to England in June 1873, and married Herminia Williams, daughter of an Englishman resident in Sucre, Bolivia. They returned to South America and from February 1874 to September 1876 Musters travelled extensively in Bolivia, gathering a large amount of geographical information. This was published, together with detailed maps of the areas around Lake Titicaca and La Paz (by J. B. Minchin), in the *Journal of the Royal Geographical Society* in 1877. After his return home Musters resided mainly with his brother at Wiverton, seat of the Chaworth family. In October 1878 he moved to London in order to prepare to take up an appointment as consul in Mozambique, but he died on 25 January 1879 at Bailey's Hotel, Queen's Gate, London.

H. M. CHICHESTER, *rev.* JOHN DICKENSON

Sources *Proceedings* [Royal Geographical Society], new ser., 1 (1879), 397–8 · 'George Chaworth Musters', *GJ*, 48 (1916), 513–14 · Burke, *Gen. GB* · G. C. Musters, *At home with the Patagonians: a year's wanderings over untrodden ground from the Straits of Magellan to the Rio Negro* (1871) · G. C. Musters, 'Notes on Bolivia, to accompany original maps', *Journal of the Royal Geographical Society*, 47 (1877), 210–16
Likenesses photograph, RGS
Wealth at death under £5000: probate, 7 April 1879, *CGPLA Eng. & Wales*

Mutesa II (1924–1969), king of Buganda, was born Edward Frederick William David Walugembe Mutebi Luwangula Mutesa on 19 November 1924 in Kampala, Uganda, the only son of Kabaka Daudi Chwa II (*d.* 1939) and his wife, Irene Namaganda. Mutesa was the thirty-fifth *kabaka* (king) of the kingdom of Buganda in Uganda, in a line of kings dating back to the sixteenth century. In an eventful career he suffered exile to Britain twice, first by the Uganda protectorate government in 1953 and second by President Obote of Uganda in 1966. In Britain he was popularly known as King Freddie of Buganda.

Mutesa was sent to King's College, Budo, at the age of five, where he soon showed his prowess at sport and was captain of football. Later he went to Makerere College in Kampala, and in 1945 to Magdalene College, Cambridge, though he did not complete a degree. He became an honorary lieutenant-colonel of the Grenadier Guards, and through his education he acquired the style and bearing of 'a perfect English gentleman' which he retained to the end of his life. During his reign as *kabaka* he frequently appeared in his guards' uniform and he was always immaculately dressed. For his people, the Baganda, he was the symbol of their historic prestige and power as a centrally organized monarchical state, and his court retained the elaborate ritual of former times. His chiefs knelt before him, while commoners had to prostrate themselves on the ground. Relations with the British protectorate government of Uganda had been firmly established in the Buganda agreement of 1900, which the Baganda maintained was not a document imposing colonial rule but a treaty between two allies. As the British preferred to develop Uganda as a unitary state with a strong central government, this traditional view of the agreement was bound to cause tension.

Mutesa's father died in 1939, when Mutesa was a youth of fifteen, so he was guided by three regents until he reached the age of eighteen, when he was crowned as *kabaka*. In 1948 he married Damali Kisosonkole. In this period he had to face the first serious demonstrations of political and economic unrest, in the riots of 1945 and 1949 in Buganda. These were symptomatic of the growing pressures in the process of modernization, in Buganda and in the protectorate as a whole. The process was to be carried forward at a much faster pace by the new governor of Uganda, Sir Andrew Cohen, who arrived in 1952. A brilliant and ambitious administrator, Cohen soon showed through his reforms that he wished to build up a strong central government with a rapidly expanding and increasingly elective central legislative council (the embryo parliament). To the Baganda, it looked as if the semi-autonomy and privileged position of the kingdom safe-guarded by the 1900 agreement would be in jeopardy. The other three smaller monarchies in Uganda shared the same fears. Mutesa faced a fundamental dilemma in that he wished to defend the monarchy and the powers of his government, while at the same time he was obliged by the agreement to co-operate with the protectorate govern-ment. For the enlarged legislative council, the Buganda *lukiko* (consultative council) was called on to nominate three representatives to it, or, if they refused, as seemed likely, the *kabaka* was to nominate them instead. If he complied, he would undermine his own position as their *kabaka*. At the same time, the Baganda feared British inten-tions to form a federation of east Africa, in which Kenya, with its settler-dominated government, would inevitably play the major role and the kingdom of Buganda would lose its powers. Instead, the *lukiko* was pressing for a time-table for independence for Buganda alone. Cohen insisted that Mutesa must comply and nominate the three repre-sentatives. Mutesa considered that in a contest of loyalty he owed his allegiance to his own people, so he refused. Cohen then declared he was in breach of the 1900 agree-ment: he was no longer recognized as *kabaka*, and he was peremptorily deported in great secrecy to Britain. This was a staggering blow to the Baganda, and in the following two years they were very hostile to the protectorate gov-ernment. However, Cohen's action was by no means uni-versally approved by the British, and it was recognized that the *kabaka* must return. Long negotiations ended in the second agreement of 1955, with the *kabaka* this time as a constitutional monarch, that is with limited powers. Mutesa returned in October, to a tremendous welcome in Buganda. If he was not always popular before, now he was a martyr and a hero. In 1962 he was made a KBE.

As independence for Uganda loomed in 1962, Buganda again showed strong separatist ambitions, but it was won over by the promise of a federal status within the inde-pendent state, partly through the moderating counsels of Mutesa. Milton Obote's party was temporarily allied to the *kabaka yekka* party of Baganda royalists, in order to win his victory. He duly became prime minister and Mutesa was elected president of independent Uganda, but after Obote discarded the alliance with the *kabaka yekka* party there was little co-operation between the two men and Mutesa's position as president looked dangerous. The final crisis came in 1966 when Obote arrested five cabinet ministers, including the leading minister from Buganda. In a period of desperate plotting by Obote to overthrow his political adversaries, who included Mutesa among them in their counter-plotting, Mutesa requested foreign governments, including the British, to send in troops. Obote replied by suspending the constitution and dismissing Mutesa as president; he then ordered the army to storm the palace in May 1966, and Mutesa had to flee to Britain, an exile for the second time and lucky to escape with his life. He described this in his book *The Desecration of my Kingdom* (1967).

Mutesa arrived penniless in Britain and had to borrow clothes from friends among the guards officers. The British government, which had provided him with a sti-pend during his first exile, this time failed to give him sup-port or due recognition as a former friend and ally but chose to continue their support of Obote. Mutesa lived in poor circumstances until his death, at 28 Orchard House, Rotherhithe, London, on 21 November 1969, aged forty-five. President Amin ordered his body to be brought back to Uganda for a state funeral, and he was buried at the Kasubi royal tombs in April 1971. Mutesa had been torn between conflicting loyalties to his people, the kingdom of Buganda, and the state of Uganda; he was ever a man of two worlds, Western, urbane, debonair, yet the staunch head of an African traditional monarchy. He was survived by his wife and several children, one of whom, Ronald Mutebi, was crowned as the next *kabaka* in 1993.

OLIVER FURLEY

Sources S. Cooper, 'Educating the kabaka: Magdalene, Buganda and the empire, 1945–1948', *Magdalene College Magazine and Record*, new ser., 34 (1989–90), 39–44 · E. F. Mutesa, *The desecration of my kingdom* (1967) · D. A. Low and R. C. Pratt, *Buganda and British overrule* (1970) · P. Mutibwa, *Uganda since independence* (1992) · D. Brown and M. V. Brown, eds., *Looking back at the Uganda protectorate* (1996) · P. Kavuma, *Crisis in Buganda, 1953–55* (1979) · L. Brown, *Three worlds: one word* (1981) · 'When Mutesa II "ate" Obuganda', *The Monitor* (13–16 April 1993) · *The Times* (26 Nov 1969) · *The Times* (29 Nov 1969) · D. Foot, letter, *The Times* (3 Dec 1969) · R. Hunt, *Daily Telegraph* (6 April 1999) · R. Hunt, *The Times* (29 April 1999) · P. H. Cordle, 'Lieu-tenant Colonel His Highness Sir Edward Mutesa', *Guards Magazine*, summer (1999) · Kabaka Ronald Mutebi II, 'The 1966 crisis', www.buganda.com/crisis66.htm, 2000 · private information (2004) [D. N. McMaster, M. Macpherson, Andrew Stuart, Alice Walusimbi] · d. cert. · *WWW* · *The People* (6 April 1971) [special issue, 'In memory of Sir Edward']
Archives CUL, letter of Sir R. Bennett, MS 45 | FILM BFI NFTVA, news footage · IWM FVA, documentary footage · IWM FVA, news footage
Likenesses portrait, repro. in Mutesa, *Desecration of my kingdom*

Mutford, John (*b.* in or before **1258**, *d.* **1329**), justice, took his name from the north Suffolk village of Mutford, where he and his wife, Katherine (whom he married before 1286), held and acquired property. Mutford is the next vil-lage to the Gisleham from which William of Gisleham, a prominent serjeant and royal justice of the preceding gen-eration, came. John is first found acting as an attorney of the common bench in 1279. By 1286 he was a serjeant on the Norfolk eyre. The earliest evidence of Mutford as a ser-jeant of the common bench comes from 1290, the year Gisleham was appointed a justice of that court. Between 1290 and 1308 Mutford appears regularly in reports and final concord authorizations as a serjeant of the common bench, though he left the court to serve as the king's ser-jeant on the southern eyre circuit (a position previously held by Gisleham) for the Kent and Middlesex eyres of 1293 and 1293–4 respectively, and later for the Cambridge-shire and Ely eyres of 1299, and the Cornwall eyre of 1302. On all these eyres he was active on behalf of private cli-ents as well. His other clients included the city of Nor-wich, which paid him an annual pension.

Mutford represented the king in the exchequer on a number of occasions from 1294 onwards. His first admin-istrative commission was to inquire into the levying of the king's debts in Bedfordshire and Buckinghamshire in 1297. In February 1307 he was appointed a junior justice on the south-western trailbaston circuit led by William Martin, and by November in the same year he had joined William Howard and Robert Retford as a justice of the south midland assize circuit. In August 1310 he was reassigned to an assize and gaol-delivery circuit in the north midlands with Roger Scotere and Nicholas Bolingbroke. In Easter term 1316 he became a justice of the common bench in place of William Inge, who had been appointed chief justice of king's bench, and served continuously as a justice of that court until Hilary term 1329. Mutford was still alive on 20 March 1329 but dead by 29 May of that year. He was buried in Norwich Cathedral.   PAUL BRAND

Sources *Chancery records* · P. A. Brand, *The origins of the English legal profession* (1992) · P. A. Brand, ed., *The earliest English law reports*, 2, SeldS, 112 (1996) · A. J. Horwood, ed. and trans., *Year books of the reign of King Edward the First*, 5 vols., Rolls Series, 31 (1863–79) · F. M. Maitland and others, eds., *Year books of Edward II*, 26 vols. in 28, SeldS (1903–69) · unpublished law reports of the reigns of Edward I and Edward II · assize rolls, PRO, JUST 1 · court of common pleas, PRO, CP 40 · exchequer of pleas, PRO, E 13

Mutrie, Annie Feray (1826–1893). *See under* Mutrie, Martha Darley (1824–1885).

Mutrie, Martha Darley (1824–1885), still-life painter, elder daughter of Robert and Sarah Mutrie, was born at Ardwick, then a suburb of Manchester, and baptized on 14 May 1824 at Manchester Cathedral. Her father was a native of Rothesay in Bute, who had settled in Manchester in the cotton trade. She studied from 1844 to 1846 in the private classes of the Manchester School of Design, then under the direction of George Wallis, and afterwards in his private art school. She exhibited from 1845 at the Royal Manchester Institution, and in 1853 sent her first contribution, *Fruit*, to the Royal Academy, where she afterwards exhibited annually until 1878. From 1854 she lived in London. Her pictures of *Geraniums* and *Primulas* in the Royal Academy exhibition of 1856 attracted the notice of John Ruskin, who praised them in his *Notes on some of the Principal Pictures in the Royal Academy*. She also exhibited over many years in the annual exhibitions of Liverpool, Edinburgh, Glasgow, Bristol, and Birmingham. She was represented in the Art Treasures Exhibition (Manchester) in 1857, the International Exhibition (London) in 1862, and in several international exhibitions abroad (Philadelphia, 1876). Her works were bought by fellow artists such as Augustus Egg, Thomas Creswick, F. R. Lee, and James Baker Pyne and acquired by most of the leading collectors of contemporary art including the Lloyd brothers, W. H. Herbert, Theophilus Burnard, Elhanan and Henry Bicknell, Henry McConnell, and R. A. Cosier. Her importance in the Victorian art world as a successful female artist was reflected in the invitation to judge the awards at the Female School of Art in 1867. She died at 36 Palace Gardens Terrace, Kensington, where she had lived with her sister since 1874, on 30 December 1885, and was buried in Brompton cemetery. Her work is represented in the Victoria and Albert Museum, London, and the Russell-Cotes Museum and Art Gallery, Bournemouth.

Martha Mutrie's younger sister **Annie Feray Mutrie** (1826–1893), still-life painter, was born at Ardwick on 6 March 1826. Her career was remarkably similar to her sister's. She also studied at the Manchester School of Design and under George Wallis. She exhibited at the Royal Manchester Institution from 1845, and first appeared at the Royal Academy in 1851, with *Fruit*. She moved with her sister to London in 1854, and in 1855 her exhibits at the Royal Academy were highly praised by John Ruskin in his *Notes on some of the Principal Pictures* for their 'very lovely, pure, and yet unobtrusive colour' (E. T. Cook and A. Wedderburn, eds., The works of John Ruskin 1903–12, 14.7). She continued to exhibit almost annually, she and her sister becoming the leading British painters in oils of flowers. She also exhibited at the British Institution and the annual exhibitions in Birmingham, Edinburgh, Glasgow, at the Art Treasures Exhibition (Manchester) in 1857, the International Exhibition (London) in 1862, and elsewhere (including Philadelphia, 1876) until 1887, when she and her sister were represented in the Manchester Jubilee Exhibition. Like her sister's paintings, her work was bought by fellow artists such as Egg and Creswick and by most leading collectors of contemporary art. She travelled in Italy in 1869 and 1881. Her importance to her contemporaries is reflected in her nomination for associateship of the Royal Academy in 1870, an honour that was effectively though not technically impossible since the academy controversially practised a ban on female membership though its rules did not demand it. She died at 26 Lower Rock Gardens, Brighton, on 28 September 1893, and was buried in Brompton cemetery. Her work is represented in the Victoria and Albert Museum, London; the Harris Museum and Art Gallery, Preston; the Russell-Cotes Museum and Art Gallery, Bournemouth; and the Tunbridge Wells Museum and Art Gallery. Neither of the Mutrie sisters married.

R. E. GRAVES, rev. PAMELA GERRISH NUNN

Sources *DNB* · *The Athenaeum* (9 Jan 1886), 75 · *The Athenaeum* (7 Oct 1893), 496 · *Manchester Guardian* (11 Oct 1893), 7 · C. E. Clement and L. Hutton, *Artists of the nineteenth century and their works: a handbook containing two thousand and fifty biographical sketches*, rev. edn, 2 vols. in 1 (Boston, MA, 1884), 140 · P. G. Nunn, *Victorian women artists* (1987) · P. G. Nunn, 'Ruskin's patronage of women artists', *Women's Art Journal*, 2 (1981–2), 8–13 · *The exhibition of the Royal Academy* (1851–82) [exhibition catalogues] · *IGI* · d. cert. [Annie Feray Mutrie] · *CGPLA Eng. & Wales* (1893)
Likenesses Maull & Co., carte-de-visite, NPG
Wealth at death £8418 6s. 6d.: probate, 3 Feb 1886, *CGPLA Eng. & Wales* · £9828 14s. 9d. (in UK)—Annie Feray Mutrie: probate, 25 Oct 1893, *CGPLA Eng. & Wales*

Muybridge, Eadweard James [*formerly* Edward James Muggeridge] (**1830–1904**), developer of motion photography, was born on 9 April 1830 at Kingston upon Thames, Surrey, the second of four sons of John Muggeridge (1797–1843), corn chandler, of Kingston, and his wife, Susannah (1807/8–1874), daughter of the Smith barge-owning family of Hampton Wick. Nothing is known of his education and upbringing. By the time he emigrated to New York in the early 1850s, he had changed his name to

Eadweard James Muybridge (1830–1904), by London Stereoscopic Co., c.1895

Eadweard Muybridge (probably inspired by the recent discovery in Kingston of a Saxon coronation stone memorializing two King Eadweards). He soon prospered in the business of importing English books, and by 1855 his befriending of the New York daguerreotypist Silas T. Selleck brought him into contact with the emerging art of photography. In his later *Animals in Motion* Muybridge recalled studying with interest during this period the flight of seabirds.

Following Selleck and the gold rush to California, Muybridge moved to the burgeoning city of San Francisco in 1855, establishing a bookstore at 113 Montgomery Street. He became an active member of the literary community, serving on the board of the Mercantile Library Association and also selling photographs in his bookshop. His ingenuity in mechanical devices was demonstrated by his taking out a patent in 1860 for improvements to printing and another in 1861 for machinery for washing cloth. A younger brother George (1833–1858) joined him in business, but George's early death from tuberculosis brought in another brother, Thomas (1835–1923). An 1860 business and vacation trip to Europe was cut short by a stagecoach accident in Texas, in which Muybridge was so seriously injured that his doctor, Sir William Gull, recommended an active outdoor life for recovery.

Between 1860 and 1866 Muybridge travelled between England, New York, and the continent. Some time during this period a Kingston friend, Arthur Brown, taught him wet plate photography, and about 1866 he returned to San Francisco where he joined Silas Selleck in his photography business. By 1868 he offered splendid views of Yosemite under the name of 'Helios'.

Muybridge emerged as a highly talented and ingenious photographer, building an extensive catalogue of views of the American west, recording the emerging San Francisco, and accepting various positions as photographer for government boards and expeditions. His reputation as a leading photographer led to an 1872 commission that changed his professional life. Former governor Leland Stanford, the wealthy president of the Central Pacific Railroad and an avid horse racer, hired him to provide scientific evidence whether a horse could ever have all four feet off the ground at once. By contriving a high speed shutter and speeding up his exposure by recording only a silhouette of the horse against white sheets, in May 1872 Muybridge made several negatives of Occident, Stanford's celebrated horse, as it trotted laterally in front of his camera at the speed of 38 feet per second. These experiments, which showed that the horse's four feet were at times all off the ground, were further developed in 1873. In the same year he photographed the Modoc Indian war, and continued his western views.

In 1871 Muybridge married Flora Shallcross Stone (1851–1875), a divorcée half his age. The birth of a son in 1874 led to his discovering that the true father was Harry Larkyns, an English drama critic and adventurer. Enraged, he shot and killed his rival. He was acquitted of the charge of murder in an emotional trial, and quickly escaped to Central America, photographing for the Pacific Mail Steamship Company. He was formally divorced in the same year. One of his first efforts on his return to San Francisco early in 1876 was an enormous panoramic view of the city. In 1877 he proposed photographing on a reduced scale the official records of San Jose (an approach directly akin to modern microfilming). He again took up photographing horses in motion, now under Stanford's sponsorship at his stud farm in Palo Alto, California.

The photographs for Muybridge's earliest experiments had been made with a single camera, and required a separate trotting for each exposure. His 1877 experiments carried out a suggestion first made by Oscar Gustav Rejdlander, of employing a number of cameras placed in a line, thus obtaining a succession of exposures at regulated intervals of time. Twelve electrically tripped cameras were arranged in a line, pointing at a measured backdrop. Six views were published in 1878 under the title of *The Horse in Motion*. In his analysis of the quadrupedal walk, Muybridge's investigations led to much modification of the treatment of animal movements in the works of painters and sculptors. In 1878 Muybridge patented his 'method and apparatus for photographing objects in motion'. His battery of cameras was expanded to twenty-four and his subject matter extended, first to animals other than the horse, and by 1879 to the study of the human figure in motion (the latter possibly inspired by correspondence with the painter, Thomas Eakins). By then Stanford had spent more than $42,000 on supporting Muybridge's studies. Muybridge's work had captured the attention of the French scientist and photographer Étienne Jules Marey, professor at the Collège de France, and his active promotion of Muybridge's pioneering efforts did much to establish him in the scientific world.

In 1878 the editor of the *Scientific American* suggested mounting Muybridge's sequence photographs in a zoetrope, a popular children's toy based on the phenakistoscope, that utilized slits to give an illusion of continuous movement to the images inside. In 1869 Sir John Herschel (in the same article in which he coined the term 'snapshot'), had prophesied that photographs might one day be used in the phenakistoscope to show continuous motion. A decade later Muybridge, using a device he called the Zoöpraxiscope, became the first to exhibit photographic motion pictures taken from life. It was a direct step towards modern film making, and was a popular device. By its means horse races were reproduced on a screen with such fidelity as to show the individual characteristics of the motion of each animal, flocks of birds flew with every movement of their wings clearly perceptible, two gladiators contended for victory, athletes turned somersaults, and the like. At Marey's home in Paris in September 1881 Muybridge lectured before the assembled men of science with his newly animated illustrations for the first time in Europe. He then lectured in London, before the Royal Institution, the Royal Academy of Arts, the Royal Society of Arts, and the Royal Society.

With such enthusiastic reception, Muybridge was on the verge of transferring his base of operations to his native England. He was invited to prepare a paper on animal locomotion for the Royal Society. Just days before this was to be published, he was summoned to its rooms and confronted with Dr J. B. Stillman's just released book, *The Horse in Motion*, which illustrated Muybridge's photographs through drawings. Published by Muybridge's patron, Leland Stanford, the book made absolutely no mention of Muybridge's contribution, and it is understandable that the society viewed him as a plagiarist. Francis Galton, acting as referee, diplomatically referred to concern about photographs to which Muybridge had 'no sure legal claim', but the immediate damage was done. Muybridge's standing in Britain was destroyed. Stanford's actions were never satisfactorily explained, and legal actions instituted by Muybridge failed to redress the situation.

During a lecture tour of American cities in 1883 Muybridge circulated a prospectus for a massive reference work of animal locomotion. Numerous backers were found in Philadelphia, and the University of Pennsylvania became his scientific home. Specially constructed apparatus allowed the photographing of a living, moving subject from several angles simultaneously. Improved photographic materials finally enabled him to give these photographs full tones, rather than work with the silhouettes he had previously been restricted to. In 1884–5 more than a hundred thousand photographic plates were obtained and embodied in a work published at Philadelphia in 1887 as *Animal locomotion, an electrophotographic investigation of consecutive phases of animal movement, 1872–1885*. The work contains over two thousand figures of moving men, women, children, beasts, and birds, in 781 photoengravings, bound in eleven folio volumes. The great cost of preparing and printing this work restricted its sale to a very few complete sets, and a selection of the most important plates on a reduced scale was published in London in 1899 as *Animals in Motion*.

For several years Muybridge, now more respected than ever, alternated between England and America. In 1892 he lectured on animal locomotion in a specially built hall at the World's Columbian Exposition in Chicago. Legal problems continued to plague him, but from 1894, apart from a visit to America in 1897, he lived in his native Kingston, residing with a cousin at Park View, 2 Liverpool Road and actively corresponding with publications. He died on 8 May 1904, while digging a miniature scale reproduction of the Great Lakes in his garden. His cremated remains were buried at Woking. He left £300 to Kingston Public Library, together with his lantern slides, Zoöpraxiscope, and a selection from the plates of *Animal Locomotion*.

LARRY J. SCHAAF

Sources R. B. Haas, *Muybridge: man in motion* (1976) · G. Hendricks, *Eadweard Muybridge: the father of the motion picture* (1975) · D. Harris and E. Sandweiss, *Eadweard Muybridge and the photographic panorama of San Francisco, 1850–1880* (1993) · A. V. Mozley, *Eadweard Muybridge, the Stanford years, 1872–1882* (1972) · E. B. Burns, *Eadweard Muybridge in Guatemala, 1875* (1986) · K. MacDonnell, *Eadweard Muybridge, the man who invented the moving picture* (1972) · H. Hecht, *Pre-cinema history* (1993) · *DNB*

Archives George Eastman House, Rochester, New York · Kingston upon Thames Museum and Art Gallery, scrapbooks and notebooks [microfilm] · Stanford University, California · U. Cal., Berkeley, Bancroft Library · University of Pennsylvania, Philadelphia

Likenesses London Stereoscopic Co., photograph, c.1895, Hult. Arch. [*see illus.*] · R. Taylor, wood-engraving (after W. Wilson), NPG; repro. in *ILN* (25 May 1889)

Wealth at death £2919 3s. 7d.: probate, 30 Sept 1904, *CGPLA Eng. & Wales*

Mwanga, Basamula Danieri (*c.*1866–1903), king of Buganda, born in the royal capital at Nakawa, Kyadondo, Buganda, was the son of King Mutesa I (*c.*1838–1884) and Bagalayaza Abisagi of the otter clan, one of his many wives. Shortly after Mutesa's death on 10 October 1884, Mwanga was selected as successor from among dozens of older eligible princes. An immature and easily influenced teenager, Mwanga was used to perpetuate the inordinate power exercised by Katikiro ('chief minister') Mukasa during Mutesa's long illness.

When Mwanga became *kabaka* ('king') he inherited a militarily powerful state of perhaps 3 million people. He also inherited a potential instability caused by divisive new religious loyalties. Young Muslims converted by Arab traders from Zanzibar, together with adherents of the British protestant Church Missionary Society and French Roman Catholic missionaries—who arrived in 1877 and 1879 respectively—posed a challenge to traditional (Lubare) religion. Mwanga himself had attended both Christian missions, leading to exaggerated hopes for a royal conversion. But *Katikiro* Mukasa staunchly defended the old order. It was his influence on the insecure young king that led to two atrocities for which Mwanga gained infamy: the execution of the first British bishop, James Hannington, on 29 October 1885, and the martyrdom in June 1886 of young Catholic and protestant converts—the 'Uganda martyrs'—of whom twenty-two Catholics were canonized in 1964. These extreme measures were instigated by the *katikiro* to protect Buganda from foreign religions and secure his own position of power behind the throne.

Seeking to free himself from the overbearing Mukasa and the older chiefs, Mwanga quickly pardoned the surviving Christians and formed them, together with the Muslims, into four gun-armed regiments under his own control. These he sent to harass and intimidate the old guard chiefs. But Mwanga was still unsure of himself and was persuaded by the wily *katikiro* that the regiments were more loyal to their foreign religious teachers than to their king, and might one day use their guns to depose him. Mwanga attempted to disarm the converts in September 1888; fearing another persecution they used their guns to overthrow both Mwanga and Mukasa, who was subsequently killed. Mwanga fled by canoe into exile across Lake Victoria.

Unable to agree on a replacement for Mwanga, Muslims and Christians turned their firearms on each other in a bloody civil war that devastated the country. The Christian combatants then recalled Mwanga in order to rally the general population. In October 1889 Muslim forces were defeated and Mwanga resumed the kingship, but with severely reduced powers. The arrival in 1890 of Captain Frederick Lugard of the Imperial British East Africa Company with a small force of askaris shifted the balance of power. On 26 December Mwanga reluctantly signed an agreement whereby Buganda came under the company's protection, further reducing his prerogatives. Fighting broke out in January 1892 between protestants and Catholics, whom Mwanga at that time favoured. Lugard at Kampala intervened decisively with his askaris and Maxim gun (which repeatedly jammed) in support of the protestants, led by Apolo Kagwa. Mwanga fled to Bulingugwe Island in Lake Victoria, and then to German East Africa, but returned in March and signed a further agreement with Lugard. In 1894 Buganda was declared a British protectorate.

Mwanga, however, still held the allegiance of many of the Ganda, who had never welcomed alien rule. The last straw for the king came when British authorities told him to pay export tax on his own consignments of ivory to the coast—or be charged with 'smuggling'. A popular song of the time declared 'Woe to the son of Mutesa—the foreigner is bullying him, but he is not afraid'. In fact Mwanga had a well deserved reputation for timidity, but in July 1897 he risked everything and proclaimed rebellion—shortly after accepting a medal for loyalty to the empire. Leading protestant and Catholic chiefs did not support him, but were in the minority. Maxim guns, however, proved decisive; his uprising collapsed and he was deposed by the British acting commissioner, Colonel Trevor Ternan. An infant son, Daudi *Chwa, became king under the guardianship of three Christian regents, the senior of whom was Apolo Kagwa. Mwanga sought refuge with his former enemy Kabarega of Bunyoro, who was engaged in a five-year war of resistance against the British. Both were eventually captured in 1899 and exiled to the Seychelles Islands, where Mwanga died on 8 May 1903. His body was returned for reburial in Kampala, Buganda in 1910.

Mwanga's reign saw major changes in Buganda: a shift of power and wealth away from the *kabaka* to the chiefs, divisive civil war which depopulated much of the country, the ascendancy of Christianity, and a new dominant protestant establishment in partnership with British colonial rule. Mwanga's inexperience, weak character, and indecisiveness contributed to his loss of power, but even a stronger monarch like Kabarega of Bunyoro was unable to prevent British conquest. An unintended result of Mwanga's misrule, however, was the alliance of protestant chiefs with Lugard and the British, which led to Buganda's dominance within the larger Uganda protectorate.   JOHN A. ROWE

Sources A. Kagwa, *Basekabaka be Buganda* (1927) ['The former kings of Buganda'] · H. Mukasa, *Simuda Nyuma: ebya Mwanga* (1942) ['Do not turn back: the reign of Mwanga'] · H. Mukasa, 'Simuda Nyuma: ebya Mwanga n'ebya Daudi Chwa' ['Do not turn back: the reigns of Mwanga and Daudi Chwa'] · A. Kagwa, *The clans of the Baganda*, trans. B. Kirwan (Mengo, Uganda, 1949) [Ganda orig. *Ekitabo kye bika bya Baganda*] · T. B. Fletcher, 'Mwanga: the man and his times', *Uganda Journal*, 4 (1936–7), 162–7 · M. S. M. Kiwanuka, *A history of Buganda* (1972) · J. Rowe, *Lugard at Kampala* (1969) · J. Rowe, 'The purge of Christians at Mwanga's court', *Journal of African History*, 5 (1964), 55–71 · M. Twaddle, *Kakungulu and the creation of Uganda* (1993) · M. Perham, *Lugard*, 1: *The years of adventure, 1858–1898* (1956) · K. Ingham, *A history of East Africa*, 3rd edn (1965) · M. S. M. Kiwanuka, *Background to the martyrs* (1969) · E. Millar to Baylis, 15 May 1899, Church Missionary Society Archives, G3A7/01 · E. Kintu, *Sulutani anatoloka* ['The king has escaped'] · A. Cook, *Uganda memories* (1945), 278
Likenesses photograph (as Kabaka of Buganda, 1893), repro. in G. Portal, *The mission to Uganda* (1894), 210

Myddelton [Middleton], **Sir Hugh**, baronet (1556×60?–1631), goldsmith and entrepreneur, was born probably between 1555 and 1560 at Galch Hill in the parish of Henllan, Denbighshire, north Wales. He was the sixth son of the nine sons and seven daughters of Richard Myddelton (*d. c.*1578), MP and governor of Denbigh, and his wife, Jane (*d.* 1565), daughter of Hugh Dryhurst, an alderman of Denbigh, and his wife, Lucy. Sir Thomas *Myddelton (1549×56–1631) was his elder brother.

A practising goldsmith In 1576 Myddelton went to London, where he was apprenticed to Thomas Hartop, a goldsmith. He was still an apprentice at the time of Hartop's death in 1582, but in his will the goldsmith granted him 'all the reste of his yeares that he hathe to serve by his Indenture both beyond the Seas, and here' (PRO, PROB 11/64/45), and promised that his wife would make him free provided that Myddelton helped her for six months. He was indeed made free of the Goldsmiths' Company, and entered the livery in 1592. He practised as a high-class

Sir Hugh Myddelton, baronet (1556×60?–1631), by Cornelius Johnson, 1628

goldsmith in Cheapside, London, among other things making pieces of jewellery for members of the nobility and for royalty, and presumably established contacts at court which sustained his later career. He served as warden of the Goldsmiths' Company between Christmas 1604 and Christmas 1606, and as prime warden in 1610 and 1624. On a number of occasions he was one of the goldsmiths deputed to test the coinage for weight and purity, in the ceremony known as 'the trial of the pyx', and he also acted on their behalf in repulsing attempts by courtiers to extract money from the company.

Like many of his trade, Myddelton lent out money on the security of jewellery and plate; some of his clients claimed that he broke the usury laws and that he indulged in underhand deals by which he initially exaggerated the value of gems which he took as security and then pursued his creditors for land in order to recover the 'true' value of the loan. Whether or not such allegations were true, Myddelton certainly prospered, and in a law suit of April 1592 was styled a 'man of great welthe & ability' (PRO, STAC 5/M56/13). In 1585 he married Anne, the daughter of Richard Collins of Lichfield. She was the widow of Richard Edwards of London and was considerably older than him. The marriage was childless; she died at the age of fifty-three, and was buried on 11 January 1597. The following year Myddelton married Elizabeth Olmstead, the daughter of John Olmstead of Ingatestone, Essex, and Jane Danvers of London. By the time of the match John Olmstead was dead and Jane had married Thomas Myddelton, Hugh's brother (he thus married his brother's stepdaughter). The couple had fifteen children, of whom only three

sons and four daughters seem to have outlived their father.

As Myddelton's choice of wife might suggest, he co-operated closely with his kin. At least three of his brothers were also merchants in the capital. Bound by common nationality and language as well as by blood (there were few Welshmen in Elizabethan and Jacobean London), they regularly assisted each other and often invested in the same schemes. In 1589, for instance, Hugh and two of his brothers invested in a privateering venture against the Spanish. Although Myddelton was resident in London for most of his adult life, he maintained extensive contacts with his native north Wales and with his relatives there. In 1596 he assisted Denbigh to gain a new charter. The following year he was made an alderman of the borough, and on 20 September 1597 he personally signed the new corporation by-laws, inscribing expressions of good wishes in Welsh into the borough minute book; he also later presented the town with silver plate as a token of his esteem. He was MP for Denbigh in 1603, 1614, 1620, 1624, 1625, and 1628. As there were several Myddeltons in each of these parliaments, it is difficult to establish exactly how active he was in the chamber, but he does not seem to have been a frequent speaker or an assiduous committee man. Nineteenth-century commentators were almost certainly mistaken when they suggested that he was the Myddelton who spoke against the Cockayne project in the parliament of 1614.

The New River Company Myddelton's historical reputation is based on his sponsorship of projects rather than on his political role and his mercantile activities. His first attempt—prospecting for coal near Denbigh—was apparently unsuccessful, but early in the seventeenth century he became involved in the ultimately successful endeavour to bring a supply of water to London. This supply, and the company which he established, known as the New River Company, remained the most important source of piped water in the metropolis well into the nineteenth century.

By about 1600 the great growth in the capital's population was placing a considerable strain on its sources of water, and through the 1590s and the first decade of the seventeenth century the aldermen entertained a number of proposals to generate additional supplies. A number of projectors, notably the engineer William Inglebert and one Edward Colthurst, proposed that these should be brought to the City by digging canals or aqueducts between London and springs in Hertfordshire; on 18 April 1604 Colthurst was granted a licence by letter patent to dig such channels and to employ them to cleanse the noxious city ditches and supply the capital. However, although he began work on the project, he soon ran into financial difficulties and appealed to Viscount Cranborne, the privy council, and, through them, the City for financial assistance. In 1605 the City sponsored and obtained an act of parliament which permitted them to bring a stream of running water from the springs of Amwell and Chadwell near Hertford to the north side of the City (3 James I c. 18), and obtained a second to clarify their rights to do this the following year (4 James I c. 12).

Despite the initiative of Colthurst and others, it was Myddelton who brought this scheme to fruition. He was a member of the Commons committee which considered the 1605 statute, but his involvement did not become apparent for some time. Indeed, a number of contemporary commentators, including John Aubrey, reckoned that he did not deserve all the credit which he gained for establishing the New River. Whether or not these judgements are warranted, the first public record of Myddelton's interest in the scheme is when the journal of the common council of London noted on 28 March 1609 that Hugh Myddelton had offered to start work on the project within two months and promised to bring the stream to Islington within four years, and that, 'after longe and deliberate consultacon and advisement', the common council had indeed decided to make him their deputy in this matter, granting him the statutory powers which the City had been granted in 1605 (Corporation of London RO, journal of the common council, 27, fols. 377v–378).

Work on the New River began with an initial survey in March 1609; construction was under way by early May that year. In order to further his scheme Myddelton employed many of the most talented surveyors and mathematicians available in London, including Colthurst, the mathematician and almanac writer Edward Pond, and Edward Wright, who translated Napier's work on logarithms into English. Despite all this technical expertise, the scheme did not go smoothly. A group of Hertfordshire landowners, notably a minor royal official named William Purvey, opposed the enterprise, claiming that it was technologically impossible and that it would drown their lands. In the parliament of 1610 they called for the repeal of the statute by which Myddelton was advancing the New River. The City of London vigorously supported Myddelton, writing to the privy council and petitioning parliament in November of that year for them to end the 'great hinderaunce of the undertaker and greife of the whole Citye' (Corporation of London RO, journal of the common council, 29, fol. 89; letter-book DD fol. 223). The protesters were ultimately unsuccessful, but they delayed the enterprise for two years, causing Myddelton considerable financial difficulty and what he termed 'many affrontes & dysgraces' (Berks. RO, D/EN 024(4)).

Myddelton was thus obliged to spread the financial load of the undertaking and commenced negotiations with James I. On 2 May 1612 he and the king entered into a partnership for the completion of the project. By this bond James agreed to pay half the costs of the enterprise and in return was granted half the profits in perpetuity. In addition, Myddelton divided his half-share of the enterprise into thirty-two shares, some of which he distributed to his financial backers and to Edward Colthurst.

Work recommenced despite these problems, and on Michaelmas day 1613 the New River was ceremoniously opened by the lord mayor, Sir John Swinnerton, the lord mayor elect (Myddelton's brother Thomas), and the aldermen of London. The high point of the ceremony was a pageant composed for the occasion by the playwright Thomas Middleton (1570–1627). It was a great technical achievement, as the water was led in a winding canal 10 feet wide and 4 feet deep following the contours to London, a distance of 38¾ miles, to form a head of water near Islington. From there wooden water mains were laid through London streets, and householders paid for a supply to be laid on to their dwellings. However, the business grew only gradually and after a good deal of prompting from the City fathers and the crown. It was not until Michaelmas 1618 that the company was supplying more than 1000 houses within the capital.

For the remainder of his life Myddelton was actively involved in the running of the company, which was granted a royal charter on 21 June 1619. Its earliest leases were made out as agreements between the customer and Myddelton personally and were signed by him. The company held its meetings at his house in the City of London, first in Little Wood Street, then in Great Wood Street, and finally in Bassishaw Street. He signed every page of the company's accounts and was re-elected as governor of the company less than a month before he died. In 1630 it regained overall control of the business, for Charles I returned the crown's half-share in return for a remission of royal debts to the company and an annual payment of £500, no doubt because at this point the company was not profitable (it only issued its first dividends in 1633, after Myddelton had died). Thereafter the business grew impressively; by 1638 the company was serving 2154 customers, each paying on average 26s. 8d. a year. Its business and its dividend increased throughout the seventeenth and eighteenth centuries.

Mining and land draining projects Although the establishment of the New River is Myddelton's main claim to fame, contemporaries also remarked on his sponsorship of other commercial ventures based on technical innovation. When James I granted him a baronetcy with an exemption from the usual fee on 19 October 1622, the grant stated that it was in recognition of his work on the New River and a reward for his discovery of silver in mines in north Wales. As this indicates, Myddelton had extensive and profitable interests in developing mines in the principality. In 1617 he obtained a fourteen-year lease from the Mines Royal for the extraction of copper, gold, silver, and quicksilver from mines in north Wales. This lease was extended in 1625 and apparently provided Myddelton with healthy profits, for he (or more likely his technical advisers) seems to have overcome some of the drainage problems which dogged such operations. One mine in particular, Cwmsymlog, near Aberystwyth, was said in the second half of the seventeenth century to have yielded him a profit of £2000 a month. Although this figure is almost certainly an exaggeration, Myddelton does seem to have recouped many of his losses on the New River from these mines. He had, however, regularly to protect his schemes from competitors who claimed to be able to extract metal more effectively from the ore, or to have invented superior machines for the draining of mines, and thus sought royal grants which would have removed or eroded his privileges.

Myddelton was also involved in draining land on the Isle of Wight. As with the New River, he became involved in this project in a circuitous fashion. In 1616 Henry Gibb, one of the gentlemen of James I's bedchamber, obtained a grant of land at Brading harbour on the east coast of the island with permission to reclaim salt marsh there from the sea. Two years later Sir Bevis Thelwall (brother of Eubele Thelwall), another gentleman of the bedchamber and a kinsman and business associate of Myddelton's, gained this grant from Gibb, promising to pay him somewhere between £200 and £2000 for it—there are several conflicting versions of the story (PRO, C2/CHAS I/M63/60; Sir John Oglander's diary and accounts, Isle of Wight RO, i 110). Thelwall then apparently approached Myddelton for assistance. Although the latter may initially have been reluctant to become involved, by the summer of 1620 he had entered into a partnership with both Bevis and Eubele Thelwall to drain the land. The three partners apparently brought in Dutch experts to superintend the work, which had started by December of that year. However, their activities provoked a good deal of local opposition from other inhabitants, who felt that their property rights were being infringed and who sued Myddelton and his partners in exchequer and Star Chamber. The Dutchmen imported a pile-driving engine from Emden, and by 1622 they had succeeded in draining an area of land and (according to Sir John Oglander) making the whole area considerably healthier. Myddelton apparently tried out a variety of crops on this reclaimed land, but in September 1624 sold his interest in the venture to Thelwall. Subsequent events showed that he had acted wisely, or as one Isle of Wight gentleman reckoned, 'lyke a craftie Fox and subtel cytison' (J. Oglander, *The Oglander Memoirs*, ed. W. H. Long, 1888, 113). For in 1630 the sea wall at Brading gave way and all the reclaimed land was drowned. Thelwall and Myddelton were still locked in legal conflict over the allocation of financial responsibility when Myddelton died on 7 December 1631 in London. He was interred three days later in St Matthew's, Friday Street, London, where he had served as churchwarden and where a number of his children were buried.

Myddelton's fame lasted long after his death. When London's water supply became politically contentious in the early nineteenth century, competing political groups sought to associate Myddelton with their points of view about the most just and efficient means of providing the capital with piped water, a task made easier by the lack of evidence about his character and motivations. Some celebrated him as a public-spirited and generous provider of public water supplies; others portrayed his legacy as epitomizing the general benefits of private enterprise in water supply. In 1862 a statue was erected to his honour on Islington Green, and Samuel Smiles influentially celebrated his achievements in his *Lives of the Engineers*, developing Robert Stephenson's opinion that Myddelton was 'the first English Engineer'. As a result of this later celebrity many colourful but almost certainly unfounded stories grew up around him, such as that he customarily smoked tobacco with Sir Walter Ralegh.

One of these stories was that he exhausted his private fortune in the public service of the New River. Although the company paid no dividends during Myddelton's lifetime, he does not seem to have been reduced to penury when he died. His will reveals that he had already transferred some of his property to his children but also made generous bequests to relatives and left land in Islington and Denbigh. The Goldsmiths' Company was left one share in the New River in order to relieve his own poor relatives and impecunious goldsmiths (J. G. Nichols and J. Bruce, eds., *Wills from Doctors Commons*, CS, 83, 1862, 92–8). However, he clearly also left behind some financial problems. His widow had difficulties repaying a £3000 loan which he had received from the City of London in order to expedite the New River. Moreover, his estate never managed to pay the £500 which he left to his daughter Anne (PRO, PROB 11/170/33). When his widow made her will in January 1640, it was largely concerned with clearing the remainder of her spouse's debts. She appears, however, to have been a woman of considerable drive, for even though she retired to their country house near Edmonton, Middlesex, she briefly took over the collection of the New River Company rents after her husband's death and pursued her claims to profits from the north Wales mines with energy, if not always success. She died on 19 July 1643 and was buried in Edmonton parish church.

MARK S. R. JENNER

Sources J. W. Gough, *Sir Hugh Myddelton: entrepreneur and engineer* (1964) · B. Rudden, *The New River: a legal history* (1985) · G. C. Berry, 'Sir Hugh Myddelton and the New River', *Transactions of the Honourable Society of Cymmrodorion* (1957), 17–46 · PRO, PROB 11/160, sig. 137 · PRO, PROB 10 · PRO, SP 16 · PRO, SP 38/11, 38/12 · PRO, STAC 5 · PRO, STAC 8 · PRO, C2 / CHAS I · PRO, C3 · PRO, C24 · PRO, E178 · PRO, REQ 2 · letters and receipts about New River, Berks. RO, Neville and Aldworth MSS, D/EN/024 · LMA, Acc. 2558, NR 13/7, 13/8 [typed notes of fire-damaged and unavailable New River Company minutes] · journals, CLRO, court of common council · repertories of the court of aldermen, CLRO · letter-books, CLRO · churchwardens' accounts, St Matthew's, Friday Street, GL, MS 1016/1 · A. M. B. Bannerman, ed., *The register of St Matthew, Friday Street, London, 1538–1812, and the united parishes of St Matthew and St Peter Cheap*, Harleian Society, register section, 63 (1933) · minutes, Goldsmiths' Hall, London, vols. O–S · BL, Add. Ch. 56224 · BL, Egerton MSS, MS 2882, fol. 123v · Sir John Oglander's diary and accounts, Isle of Wight RO · S. L. Adams, 'Office-holders of the borough of Denbigh and the stewards of the lordship of Denbighshire in the reign of Elizabeth I', *Transactions of the Denbighshire Historical Society*, 25 (1976), 92–113 · *The parish register and tithing book of Thomas Hassall of Amwell*, ed. S. G. Doree, Hertfordshire Record Society, 5 (1989) · J. P. Malcolm, *Londinium redivivum, or, An antient history and modern description of London*, 4 vols. (1802–7) · J. Wright, *The dolphin* (1827) · P. Cunningham, *A handbook for London: past and present*, 2 vols. (1849) · 'Drinking fountain and statue of Myddelton on Islington Green', *The Builder*, 20 (1862), 262 · A. H. Dodd, 'The north Wales coal industry during the industrial revolution', *Archaeologia Cambrensis*, 84 (1929), 197–228 · H. A. Lloyd, *The gentry of south-west Wales, 1540–1640* (1968) · R. G. Lang, ed., *Two Tudor subsidy assessment rolls for the city of London, 1541 and 1581*, London RS, 29 (1993) · *The obituary of Richard Smyth … being a catalogue of all such persons as he knew in their life*, ed. H. Ellis, CS, 44 (1849)

Archives NL Wales, Wynn of Gwydir MSS · PRO, accounts of New River, LR2/27–35
Likenesses C. Johnson, oils, 1628, Goldsmiths' Hall, London · C. Johnson, oils, 1628, NPG · C. Johnson, oils, 1628, Baltimore Museum of Art [*see illus.*] · statue, 1862, Islington Green · G. Vertue, engraving (after C. Janssen) · engraving (after C. Johnson), repro. in W. Matthews, *Hydraulia: an historical and descriptive account of the water works of London* (1835), frontispiece · engraving (after statue, 1862), repro. in 'Drinking fountain and statue'

Myddelton [*née* Needham], **Jane** (*bap.* 1646, *d.* 1692×1703), beauty, was baptized on 23 January 1646 at St Mary's, Lambeth, Surrey, the eldest daughter of Sir Robert Needham (*d.* 1661), and his second wife, Jane (1619–1666), daughter and heir of Sir William Cockayne of Clapham, and widow of John Worfield of Barking. The Needhams were Welsh gentry, Sir Robert's father being Thomas Needham, esquire of Clocaenog, Denbighshire, the brother of Robert Needham, first Viscount Kilmorey in the peerage of Ireland. Jane Myddelton was probably born in the Lambeth house of her paternal grandmother Eleanor, Lady Salisbery, and was brought up in Lambeth and Clapham, one of a numerous family. She was married at the age of fourteen, on 18 October 1660 at St Mary's, Lambeth, as his second wife, to a man some ten years older than herself, Charles Myddelton (1635–1690×91), sixth son of Sir Thomas *Myddelton, of Chirk Castle and Cefn-y-wern, Ruabon, Denbighshire.

At first the Myddeltons lived in Lambeth, where their daughter Jane was baptized on 21 November 1661 in the parish church, and Charles's brother visited them in 1662–3. Sir Thomas Myddelton rebuilt a house called Plas Badi, afterwards New Hall, in Ruabon, Denbighshire, for the young couple to live in, but although they may have spent some time in Wales they appear to have preferred London. According to the courtier and writer Anthony Hamilton's ironic pen-portrait, Mrs Myddelton's beauty soon attracted many admirers, but she had an air of 'indolent langour' which not everyone found appealing, and her efforts to appear brilliant succeeded only in putting her audience to sleep (Hamilton, 109–10, 115). His acerbic comments may owe something to the failure of his friend the comte de Gramont to seduce her. Gramont, who arrived in London in January 1663, instantly pursued Jane Myddelton, as did Richard Jones, Viscount Ranelagh. Gramont soon desisted, the French ambassador reporting in August 1663 that Mrs Myddelton had ordered him to stop as it was both useless and disagreeable. Colonel William Russell, son of the Hon. Edward Russell, and grandson of Francis, fourth earl of Bedford, sent her presents and owned her portrait but only one of the admirers mentioned by Hamilton certainly became her lover—Ralph *Montagu (*bap.* 1638, *d.* 1709), master of the horse to the duchess of York and then the queen. Mrs Myddelton was painted by Sir Peter Lely in the early 1660s as one of a series of portraits of beautiful women to hang in St James's Palace. The portrait indicates she was blonde, with the fashionably full face, heavy-lidded eyes, 'bee-stung' lips, and rounded figure of the Restoration. In 1665 the diarist Samuel Pepys saw Jane twice: on 22 March at Gresham College, when he called her 'a very great beauty I never knew

Jane Myddelton (*bap.* 1646, *d.* 1692×1703), by Sir Peter Lely, *c.*1663–5

or heard of before', and on 10 April in Hyde Park, where she was the only 'beauty' he saw that day. The writer John Evelyn, who was distantly related to Sir Robert Needham by marriage, told Pepys that Mrs Myddelton was a proficient painter (Pepys, 6.64, 77, 243). On 3 October Pepys was troubled to hear that she was 'noted for carrying about her body a continued soure base smell that is very offensive especially, if she be a little hot' (ibid., 6.251), a problem referred to in two later satires 'Colin' (1679) and 'The Ladies March' (1681):

Middleton, where'er she goes,
confirms the scandal of her toes.
(Wilson, 24, 57)

About 1665 the Myddeltons had a second daughter, baptized Althamia, probably after Jane's friend the nonconformist Elizabeth, countess of Anglesey, whose maiden name was Altham. In the winter of 1665–6 Mrs Myddelton was staying with the Angleseys, at their country house at Bletchingdon, Oxfordshire. Sir Richard Browne reported from Oxford (where the court had moved to avoid the plague) that Mrs Myddelton came sometimes to town with the countess and received visits from courtiers, and that he himself had kissed her hand. Rumours circulated that Jane was to be appointed a dresser to the queen but, Browne wrote, 'the conditions have not yett a mutuall consent and I am told hir last indisposition hath a little impaired hir *esclat*' (Browne to John Evelyn, 19 Nov 1665, BL, Evelyn papers, JE A8, unfol.). Nothing seems to have come of the negotiations. Pepys saw Mrs Myddelton on 5 February 1667 at the King's Theatre in Drury Lane, and on 23 June that year he wrote that a previous rumour he had heard, that Mrs Myddelton was now a mistress of the duke of York, was untrue. Robert, second earl of Sunderland, commissioned her picture from Lely in 1666, Lorenzo Magalotti visiting England in 1668 included her in his list of English beauties, and the following year the French ambassador reported that the king was pursuing her, but again she seems to have avoided becoming a royal mistress.

Mrs Myddelton's mother and father-in-law had died in 1666, each leaving the couple £100; although never rich, the Myddeltons could afford to move to a fashionable address in Charles Street in the parish of St Martin-in-the-Fields in 1668-9. By 1672 the undistinguished Charles Myddelton had bought a captain's commission in the army and he went on the expedition to Virginia in the autumn of 1676. Jane Myddelton's younger sister, Eleanor Needham, became the mistress of the king's son James, duke of Monmouth, about 1674 and had four children with him. Mrs Myddelton became friendly with both the king's mistress, the duchess of Portsmouth, and her rival the duchess of Mazarin, in 1676. In the summer of that year the French ambassador, Courtin, reported that Mrs Myddelton was the most beautiful woman in the kingdom and that the aged poet and philosopher M. de Saint-Evremond had fallen hopelessly in love with her, but that Ralph Montagu, who had been her lover for a long time, had now fallen for the duchess of Mazarin. Courtin was greatly attracted to Mrs Myddelton, who he claimed was not only a great beauty but most amiable. It was, however, difficult to get near her as she was surrounded by admirers and, moreover, Courtin did not think she could be seduced by money, having once refused a significant present from Gramont. Courtin's praise was such that the French minister Louvois requested her portrait. In the autumn and winter of 1676-7 she attended a series of dinner parties in the duchess of Portsmouth's company, but she was also friendly with Elizabeth, Lady Harvey, an enemy of Portsmouth, and in 1678 she fell out with Portsmouth, who accused her (and Lady Harvey) of trying to interest the king in Jane's eldest daughter.

Laurence *Hyde, later earl of Rochester (*bap.* 1642, *d.* 1711), was Mrs Myddelton's lover about 1676-80, while the elderly poet and MP Edmund *Waller claimed her as his mistress in a platonic sense. Letters from Waller to Jane, dated 1675-83, reveal that she had a dwelling at Greenwich (she may have been the Mrs Myddelton with an apartment in the king's house at Greenwich in 1684), and was a friend of the duke and duchess of Buckingham, whom she sometimes visited at their country house at Cliveden, Buckinghamshire. Dorothy, dowager countess of Sunderland, wrote on 8 July 1680 that she and Mrs Myddelton had 'lost old Waller—he has gone away frightened', perhaps referring to Waller's withdrawing from politics at this time (Chernaik, 38). In 1680 there were five copies of Mrs Myddelton's picture in Sir Peter Lely's studio. Evelyn recorded a visit by her, 'that famous and indeede incomparable beautiful Lady' to his house, Sayes Court, Deptford, in the company of Colonel John Russell in August 1683 (Evelyn, 4.334), and she continued to be

part of the Angleseys' circle, the earl of Anglesey's diary recording several occasions in the 1680s when she dined with them. Some court wits and poets evidently preferred to gaze upon Mrs Myddelton uninterrupted by her conversation: her reputation for affectation was referred to by the wit Sir George Etherege in 1686 (*Letters of Sir George Etherege*, ed. F. Bracher, 1974, 60-61) and in Saint-Evremond's 'Scene de Bassette', in which Jane irritates the duchess of Mazarin by talking continually and pretentiously while playing cards.

The 'Mrs Middleton' paid £500 a year by James II in 1687-8 was probably Jane, although the reason for the pension remains unclear. Charles Myddelton was a commissioner in the alienations office from 1679 until at least 1686; then in 1689-90 he held a place in the prize office, said to be worth some £400 a year. He died insolvent between June 1690, when he was reported to be dying, and July 1691, when administration of his estate was granted in to a creditor. He was buried at Lambeth. Jane Myddelton herself died between 1692, after which she was no longer mentioned in the ratebooks as living in Charles Street, and September 1703, when Saint-Evremond, who wrote a poem and epitaph on her death, himself died. She was survived by her two daughters. The eldest lived with her aunt Frances Needham in St Albans and was involved in looking after the daughters of Sarah, duchess of Marlborough, in the 1690s before marrying Charles May, nephew of Baptist May, of Frant, Sussex. When she died in 1740, her will revealed that her sister had married a Mr Boden.

From a protestant Welsh gentry background and married young into a similar family, not wealthy and with nonconformist friends such as the Angleseys, Jane Myddelton's image as a 'beauty', which she no doubt cultivated, gave her an entrée to court circles and gained her many male admirers, although she in fact seems to have been attracted to relatively few of them. 'Illustre entre les belles' ('Illustrious among beauties'; Steinman, 60), 'handsomely made, all white and golden' (Hamilton, 109), for her own and subsequent generations Jane Myddelton was the epitome of the Restoration beauty, never mentioned without the epithet 'fair' or 'beautiful'. Such indeed was the exclusive interest in her looks that she seems almost wholly defined by them and the person remains rather less accessible than the famous image.   S. M. WYNNE

Sources G. S. Steinman, *Some particulars contributed towards a memoir of Mrs. Myddelton, the great beauty of the time of Charles II* (privately printed, 1864) · French diplomatic correspondence, 1660–85, PRO, 31/3/121, 133 [Croissy to Lionne, 8 April 1669, PRO, 31/3/121, fol. 90; Courtin to Pomponne, 2 July 1676, PRO, 31/3/133, fols. 3–6] · French diplomatic correspondence, 1663–85, Archives du Ministère des Affaires Étrangères, Paris, Correspondance Politique, Angleterre (CPA), vols. 119–29 [Comminges to de Lionne [15] Aug 1663, CPA, vol. 80, fol. 69; Courtin to Pomponne, 21 Sept 1676, CPA, vol. 119, fols. 264–5; Courtin to Louvois, 24 Sept 1676, CPA, vol. 120c, fol. 150; Courtin to Pomponne, 15 Oct 1676, CPA, vol. 120, fol. 107v; Courtin to Louvois, 29 Oct 1676, CPA, vol. 120c, fol. 188v; Courtin to Pomponne, 4 Feb 1677, 11 March 1677, CPA, vol. 122, fols. 137–8, 245v–246; Barrillon to Pomponne, 25 July 1678, CPA, vol. 129, fols. 148–9] · H. Fornéron, *The court of Charles II*, trans. G. M. Crawford, 5th edn (1897) · A. Hamilton, *Memoirs of the comte de Gramont*, trans. P. Quennell (1930) · Pepys, *Diary*, vols. 6–8 · Evelyn, *Diary*, vols. 3–

4 · letter of Sir Richard Browne to Mary Evelyn, [12 Nov 1665], BL, Evelyn papers, ME2, unfol. · letter of Sir Richard Browne to Mary Evelyn, 17 Dec 1665, BL, Evelyn papers, ME2, unfol. · letter of Sir Richard Browne to Mary Evelyn, 8 Jan 1666, BL, Evelyn papers, ME2, unfol. · letter of Sir Richard Browne to John Evelyn, 19 Nov 1665, BL, Evelyn papers, JE A8, unfol. · parish register, St Mary-at-Lambeth, LMA · G. de F. Lord and others, eds., *Poems on affairs of state: Augustan satirical verse, 1660–1714*, 7 vols. (1963–75), vol. 2 · W. L. Chernaik, *The poetry of limitation: a study of Edmund Waller* (1968) · A. Annesley, earl of Anglesey, diary, BL, Add. MS 18730, fols. 84, 111*v*, 112, 113 · accounts of Robert, 2nd earl of Sunderland, BL, Add. MS 61489, fol. 62 · will of Sir Thomas Myddelton, 1667, PRO, PROB 11/323, sig. 39 · letters of Jane Middleton (the younger) and Frances Needham, BL, Add. MS 61455, fols. 105–37 · letters of Elizabeth Annesley, countess of Anglesey, BL, Add. MS 61453, fols. 21–2 · W. M. Myddelton, ed., *Chirk Castle accounts, AD 1605–1666* (privately printed, St Albans, 1908) · W. M. Myddelton, ed., *Chirk Castle accounts, AD 1666–1753* (1931) · W. A. Shaw, ed., *Calendar of treasury books*, 5–8, PRO (1911–23) · *CSP dom., 1683–4* · J. H. Wilson, *Court satires of the Restoration* (1976) · *Lorenzo Magalotti at the court of Charles II: his Relazione d'Inghilterra of 1668*, ed. and trans. W. E. K. Middleton (1980) · *Report on the manuscripts of Allan George Finch*, 5 vols., HMC, 71 (1913–2003), vol. 2 · *The manuscripts of the House of Lords*, new ser., 12 vols. (1900–77), vol. 5 · 'Sir Peter Lely's collection', *Burlington Magazine*, 83 (1943), 185–91 · GEC, *Peerage* · F. P. Verney and M. M. Verney, *Memoirs of the Verney family during the seventeenth century*, 2nd edn, 4 vols. in 2 (1907), vol. 2, p. 244

Likenesses P. Lely, oils, *c.*1663–1665, Royal Collection [*see illus.*] · P. Lely, oils, *c.*1665, Althorp, Northamptonshire · P. Lely, oils, *c.*1670, Goodwood House, West Sussex · studio of P. Lely, oils, Althorp, Northamptonshire · P. Lely, portrait, Hampton Court · R. Tompson, mezzotint (after P. Lely), BM, NPG

Sir Thomas Myddelton (1549x56–1631), by unknown artist

Myddelton [Middleton], **Sir Thomas** (1549x56–1631), merchant and politician, was the fourth son and one of the sixteen children of Richard Myddelton (*d. c.*1578), MP and governor of Denbigh, who in that capacity served the earl of Leicester as a lieutenant in Denbighshire, and his wife, Jane Dryhurst (*d.* 1565). Sir Hugh *Myddelton (1556x60?–1631) was his younger brother. In 1575, he was apprenticed in London to a member of the Grocers' Company, Fernandino Poyntz, whom he served in the sugar trade at Flushing and Antwerp. He completed his apprenticeship by January 1582, when he was admitted to the Grocers' Company. Probably within the year he established a household in the parish of St Mary Aldermanbury with the first of his four wives, Hester, the daughter of Richard Saltonstall, MP for London in 1586 and lord mayor in 1597. Thereafter Myddelton embarked on a many-sided career, first as a merchant and manufacturer, then as a surveyor of the customs, an investor in privateering voyages, a financier, and finally as a landowner in Denbighshire and Essex.

The enterprising merchant Between 1583 and 1588 Myddelton developed his specialized knowledge of the sugar trade into manufacturing enterprises in England and Wales, and into a wider commercial network in northern Europe. Using his younger brother Robert as a commission agent in Middelburg, he exported kerseys produced in Hampshire and Surrey and imported mercery items made in Italy, as well as flax, dyestuffs, and brazilwood. He also exported broadcloth and kerseys to Caen, exported fish from Plymouth to the Mediterranean, and, in 1588, established a depot in Stade, evidence of his long-standing commitment to commerce through that port. His manufacturing activities were similarly diverse. With two partners, he bought and operated a sugar refinery in Mincing Lane, London, and also invested in and directed the manufacture of copper in Neath in Wales and the processing of calamine in Lambeth. No specific figures for his accumulation of capital in this early period have survived, but his retrospective impression was that the trade in commodities had produced 'a very small profit considering what long time I have foreborne my money, and the great hazard of adventure at the sea' (Dodd, 252). With Myddelton's growing connections to the political world, moreover, he gave increasing priority to financial activities and investments in land.

In the decade after he turned thirty (one source gives his age as thirty-one in 1587) Myddelton's wealth and political influence expanded rapidly. Sir Francis Walsingham appointed him to be a collector of the customs in 1587, and five years later he became one of four surveyors of the outports with an income of £450 per annum. Customs officers conventionally had use of the money collected before the end of the fiscal period when the balance was due to be paid. With whatever commercial and manufacturing wealth he had accrued, this additional liquidity from the customs enabled Myddelton, as the most significant of his new projects, to buy shares in numerous privateering voyages directed against Spain and her colonial possessions.

After the defeat of the Spanish armada, Myddelton took positions of financial and administrative responsibility in organizing some well-known voyages. He invested at least twice in those of Richard Hawkins, and he made a small investment in the syndicate which succeeded in capturing the *Madre de Dios* with one of the most valuable cargoes of the period. In other voyages he divided shares in a syndicate with his partners from the sugar refinery and with his brothers Hugh and Foulk. Myddelton served as treasurer for two syndicates, one that in 1592 financed the expedition of Martin Frobisher and Sir Walter Ralegh to the West Indies, and one that, two years later, funded the expedition of Hawkins and Sir Francis Drake to the Azores. Often of greater importance than the investments Myddelton made in the voyages themselves was his purchase and resale of prize commodities. He sold the iron which Ralegh seized from ships in the Bay of Biscay, for instance, and was part of a syndicate which bought pepper for £4600 from Queen Elizabeth, her share from the *Madre de Dios*. These speculations were on the whole highly profitable, but not invariably so. On the second of the Hawkins voyages, in which Myddelton ventured £1500, he obtained a good return of 30 per cent; but he lost entire investments in some voyages when commanders were unable to seize valuable commodities, such as when he staked £300 in the voyage of the *Rosalyn*.

After 1593 Myddelton diversified and secured his wealth by loaning substantial sums of money to prominent government officials and to the landed élite. Among his more significant loans were to the Lord Keeper Egerton for £1000, Chief Justice Popham for £1700, and the earl of Shrewsbury for £1000. His borrowers used a variety of assets for collateral, most commonly gold, jewels, or, most significantly for his later career, land; and they paid 10 per cent interest, the maximum allowable rate by law.

It was also in 1593 that Myddelton began in earnest his acquisition of land in Denbighshire by purchase and through defaults on loans. Although he was the fourth son, he inherited his father's estate in Galch Hill after the latter's death about 1578 because the eldest two sons had died and the third son, William, had become an ardent Catholic who lived in Ghent on a Spanish pension. In 1593 Thomas bought land around Galch Hill from the earl of Leicester's heir, Lady Warwick, in 1595 he bought the lordship and estate of Chirk Castle for £4800 from Lord St John of Bletso, and in 1599 he bought the lordship of Henllan for £500. While expending at least an additional £5000 on further purchases around Chirk and in Merioneth over the seven years between 1595 and 1602, he also acquired land when members of the local gentry defaulted on loans made by him. Richard Rogers lost his lands in Kellowen in 1598, in debt to Myddelton by several hundred pounds; Robert Salesbury of Rug lost land in Segrwyd in Denbighshire for the same reason. Myddelton's earnings on these lands he secured was generally between 5 and 7 per cent; and, as the size of these holdings grew and the complexity of business connected to them increased, he hired his brother Foulk as a full-time overseer.

Political and puritan interests Myddelton's quick ascent to prominence created divisions of opinion about his political and economic aims in the county. On some occasions he could be very generous in his financial dealings. When

he bought the land of Roger Kyttie, he reportedly paid £230 over the value of the mortgage, which was £650, in order to help Kyttie out of indebtedness. He made a number of small loans to local landowners, 'so much', as he noted in his account book, 'as I have no delight to set it particularly in my book hier' (Dodd, 274). With the ties of finance came common political interests, and, despite defaulting on a mortgage to Myddelton, Robert Salesbury, the son-in-law of Henry Bagwell, maintained a political alliance with him, together with Griffith Nanney of Nannau. Salesbury had served as MP for Denbighshire in 1586 and for Merioneth in 1589, which seat Nanney had secured in the succeeding election in 1593. Whatever his generosity and the alliances he was able to form, however, Myddelton's sudden prominence in the county was not unopposed. In 1594 he began his service in Wales as a commissioner for the peace in Denbighshire; but when he sought the parliamentary seat for Merioneth in 1597, a rival faction led by John Lewis Owen and Cadwaladr Price, who had served as MP for Merioneth in 1572 and 1584 respectively, supported the unsuccessful candidacy of John Vaughn of Caer Gai. Opposition to Myddelton in that year was not limited to a contested election, but extended to the use of local land. The neighbouring Edwards family of Plas Newydd brought a suit against him in Star Chamber, charging him with enclosure on lands around Chirk Castle, and identifying him as a 'usurer' from London. The suit did not result in any action being taken, and did not hinder his continued political service. Myddelton was appointed constable of Denbigh Castle in 1597, and in parliament he served on committees touching on important Welsh issues, such as the building of a bridge at Newport, and national issues, such as the poor law and, despite the charges made against him, enclosure. He completed his political career in north Wales in 1599, when he was appointed lord lieutenant and *custos rotulorum* of Merioneth.

While he did not openly dissent on religious topics during his political career in Wales or in London, Myddelton worked in many subtle ways to further puritanism. Recorded among his accounts, for instance, was the payment of 10s. in wages to a Dutch minister for three months; in 1621 he was reported to have given 'a very religious speech and exhortation' at a gathering of the Grocers' Company. His financial support for translations of religious texts into Welsh was to be of greater significance still. Myddelton first took an active role when he paid £10 to a London stationer, who was a nephew of the translator Henry Salisbury, to print a translation of a tract, *The Sickman's Salve*, by the militant author Thomas Becon; in 1602 he provided an interest-free sum of £30 for a translation of the psalms into Welsh verse by his cousin William Myddelton; and after Salisbury translated the Bible into Welsh in 1620 and published it in folio, Myddelton was one of the financial backers (who also included Rowland Heylyn) of a portable edition, which was to be of enduring popularity and which, in ensuing centuries, promoted an active use of the language. His religious convictions were none the less neither dogmatic nor extreme, at least where his heterodox family were concerned: reportedly his Catholic brother William was a welcome visitor to Thomas's home in London.

Despite the attention he devoted to the affairs of Wales, Myddelton was also in the 1590s to strengthen his ties to London. In 1592 he was admitted to the livery of the Grocers' Company, and in 1595 he moved with his second wife, Elizabeth, and his children from his first residence in St Mary Aldermanbury to a new house, The Bear, in Tower Street. Other London property he bought for purposes of investment included houses in the parishes of St Bartholomew by the Exchange in 1589 and St Paul in 1595, as well as Barnard's Castle in 1602.

Under the Jacobean regime Myddelton relinquished his political interests in Wales and took a position of leadership in the government of the City, albeit reluctantly in the first instance. In May 1603 he was elected alderman for Queenhithe ward, and when he claimed an exemption, on the grounds that he was a surveyor of the customs, the lord mayor and aldermen committed him to Newgate gaol. He was sworn in eleven days after his initial imprisonment despite the intercession of James, who supported the principle of exemption for servants of the state. Myddelton was elected sheriff three days later, and in the following July James knighted him.

Having been co-opted in this way, Myddelton became active in civic government for the next ten years. At Michaelmas 1613, at the age of fifty-seven, he was elected lord mayor. His inaugural pageant, *The Triumphs of Truth*, was written by the dramatist who shared his name, Thomas Middleton. The Grocers' Company took pride of place among the livery companies in a procession from Guildhall to the Thames and back to Guildhall by way of St Paul's Cathedral and Cheapside, which culminated on Leadenhall with fireworks and, in the accompanying morality play, with the defeat by Truth of Ignorance, Envy, Barbarism, and other evils. In a preface addressed to the new lord mayor the dramatist judged the office to have crowned 'the perfection of your days and the gravity of your life with power, respect and reverence' (Middleton, 217).

Myddelton continued to hold one or more offices until the end of his life. During his mayoral tenure he was elected president of Bridewell and Bethlem hospitals, and he transferred his aldermanic seat, by prerogative of office, to Coleman Street ward, where he served seventeen further years, many of them as senior alderman, or father of the City. He held the commission of colonel in the City militia and, most significantly, returned to national politics as one of four MPs for London to the parliaments of 1624–5, 1625, and 1626.

Later years In his later years Myddelton was part of several entrepreneurial projects, but none of them was as demanding as his roles in privateering, commerce, or manufacturing. He invested in the first trading voyage to Asia in 1599 and in the following year was a founder member of the East India Company. He was one of a prominent merchant group that petitioned James in December 1603 not to sell his allotment of pepper from the first voyage, which would cause the price to fall precipitously and threaten investment in the second voyage, a venture headed by his kinsman Henry Middleton, and one in which Sir Thomas invested capital. In 1609 he supported the first attempts to colonize North America by buying a share in the Virginia Company. He also invested in the ambitious project by his brother Hugh to pipe water for a fee to London residents under the aegis of the New River Company; the opening ceremony for the project took place on the day of Sir Thomas's election to the mayoralty.

Myddelton was a widower three times. His first wife, the 'beloved' Hester, died in 1587, less than five years after their marriage, and he was left to bring up his son Thomas *Myddelton; another son, Richard, died shortly after his mother. Myddelton remarried the following year; his new wife was Elizabeth Olmstead, herself a widow and the stepdaughter of an alderman and business associate, Richard Tailor. The couple had four children—Henry, who died young, Timothy, Hester, who married Henry Salisbury, later a baronet, and Mary, who married Sir John Maynard. Of Elizabeth's death, Sir Thomas's subsequent marriage, to the twice-widowed Elizabeth Hobart, and the latter's death, nothing is known. But when, towards the end of his life, Myddelton married for the fourth time, this time the young Flemish widow of a London brewer, Anne Wittewronge (*d.* 1646), her supposed infidelity was the source of a popular song, 'Room for cuckolds, here comes my lord mayor'.

Just before he became lord mayor, in 1612, Myddelton began reorganization of his landholdings, settling Chirk Castle on his son Thomas. In 1615 he bought an estate at Stansted Mountfitchet in Essex. After his death, on 12 August 1631 (at which time he was said to be eighty-one), it was at the church there, in the south side of the chancel, that he was buried on 8 September, a place marked by a full-size effigy within a marble monument 20 feet high and 10 feet wide. Among the inscriptions on the monument is one which extolled the 'support and refuge' he offered to his relations. 'Some he advanced to honour; all to riches.'

By the provisions of his will, Myddelton divided his estate according to the custom of London, even though, as he noted, he had already made substantial provision for his children. One-third of the estate went to his wife, Anne, one-third to the surviving children, Thomas, Timothy, and Mary, and one-third was divided between the four once specific bequests to others had been made. His principal charitable donation was £100 to Bridewell Hospital for the purpose of securing apprenticeships for poor children; and he gave sums of either £10 or £20 for the poor of Christ's Hospital and to the poor of the parishes of St Mary Aldermanbury, Stansted Mountfitchet, Denbigh, Henllan, and Chirk. There was a four-part division of land. Myddelton bequeathed much of his London landholdings, including property on Thomas Street and Barnard's Castle, to the Grocers' Company. His son Thomas was to be given, after twenty years, additional lands in Wales, in

Montgomeryshire; Timothy inherited Stansted Mount-fitchet and all other lands in Essex; and Sir John and Mary Maynard inherited an assortment of land in Somerset and Worcestershire, as well as a parsonage in Bradford, Yorkshire.   CHARLES WELCH, rev. TREVOR DICKIE

Sources A. H. Dodd, 'Mr Myddelton, the merchant of Tower Street', *Elizabethan government and society: essays presented to Sir John Neale*, ed. S. T. Bindoff, J. Hurstfield, and C. H. Williams (1961), 249–81 · HoP, *Commons* · PRO, PROB 11/160, sig. 94 · *Analytical index, to the series of records known as Remembrancia, preserved among the archives of the City of London*, Corporation of London, ed. [W. H. Overall and H. C. Overall] (1878) · T. Middleton, *Works*, 5 (1890) · [P. Muilman], *A new and complete history of Essex, by a gentleman*, 6 vols. (1769–72) · W. D. Pink, *Notes on the Middleton family of Denbighshire and London* (1891) · G. Birdwood, ed., *The register of letters … of the governour and company of merchants of London trading into the East Indies, 1600–1619* (1893) · T. K. Rabb, *Enterprise and empire: merchant and gentry investment in the expansion of England, 1575–1630* (1967) · B. Rudden, *The New River: a legal history* (1985)
Archives Chirk Castle, Denbighshire, principal account book of Thomas Myddelton
Likenesses group portrait, monumental effigy, 1588 (with family), parish church, Galch Hill, Denbighshire · marble monumental effigy, 1631, parish church, Stansted Mountfitchet, Essex · oils, Guildhall Art Gallery, London [see illus.]
Wealth at death exact sum unknown, but wealthy; estate at Stansted Mountfitchet, Essex; property in London, Somerset, Worcestershire, and Yorkshire: will, PRO, PROB 11/160, fols. 197–202

Myddelton, Sir Thomas (1586–1666), parliamentarian army officer, was born in Mincing Lane, London, in July 1586 and baptized at St Dunstan-in-the-East on 10 July. He was the only son of Sir Thomas *Myddelton (1549×56–1631), merchant, of Tower Street, London, and his wife, Hester Saltonstall (d. 1587), daughter of Sir Richard Saltonstall (d. 1601) of London and South Ockenden, Essex, lord mayor of London in 1597–8, and his wife, Susan, daughter of Thomas Poyntz of North Ockendon. Myddelton's mother died shortly after his birth and he was brought up by his stepmother, Elizabeth Olmstead, whom his father married in 1587, and upon her death by his second stepmother, Elizabeth Hobart. Nothing is known of Myddelton's pre-university schooling. On 22 February 1605 he matriculated at Queen's College, Oxford, but did not graduate. On 4 February 1607 he entered Gray's Inn. On 29 July 1612 Myddelton married Margaret Savile, daughter of George Savile of Wakefield, who died in childbirth in November 1613. On 10 February 1617 he was knighted and on 18 February he married Mary Napier (1598–1675), eldest daughter of Sir Robert Napier, first baronet, of Luton Hoo, Bedfordshire, and his wife, Mary Robinson. Myddelton and his second wife had seven sons (of whom Thomas, who became first baronet, was the eldest) and six daughters.

In 1612 Myddelton's father settled his Chirk Castle estate in Denbighshire on him. In 1624 Myddelton was elected MP for Weymouth and Melcombe Regis, Dorset, and in 1625 for Denbighshire. After the dissolution of this short-lived parliament he did not again seek re-election until November 1640. He soon became disenchanted with the turn of events (such as the execution of Strafford) and withdrew from parliament in July 1641 before most royalist members. The outbreak of the Irish uprising and its

consequences, however, caused him to question the motives of the king. In June 1643 parliament appointed him sergeant-major-general of all horse and foot raised in north Wales. Apart from Gloucester the royalists were in the ascendant along a line extending from Chester to Bristol. Furthermore the truce (or 'cessation') with the Irish insurgents in September 1643 freed seasoned soldiers to join the king's forces on the mainland. Well-founded surmise that they would land in ports in north Wales prompted Sir William Brereton and Myddelton to attempt to intercept them. The crossing of the Dee at Holt in November after a fierce engagement led to the capture of Wrexham and to the unfulfilled expectation that Chirk Castle (in enemy hands since 1643) would speedily be returned to him. Myddelton proceeded to Denbigh Castle but could not prevail upon the governor to surrender. The landing of 'Irish' forces at Mostyn, Flintshire, demoralized the parliamentarian troops who precipitately retreated to Cheshire.

In December, Myddelton subscribed to the solemn league and covenant and requested the Commons to provide reinforcements. In March 1644 he and Brereton were 'ordered to be immediately sent down into their countries' (*CSP dom.*, *1644*, 73). Myddelton's troops, sometimes mutinous, raised the siege of Oswestry on 2 July, the fateful day that Rupert was routed at Marston Moor. The ensuing conflict centred upon Montgomeryshire. In September Myddelton took Montgomery Castle, but only temporarily, for it was soon attacked by royalists who recognized its strategic significance. To Myddelton's aid came Brereton, Sir John Meldrum, and cavalry from Yorkshire under Sir William Fairfax, who was slain in this, the biggest battle fought in Wales during the first civil war. Parliament's victory on 2 September drove a wedge between north and south Wales. Rupert considered the loss of Montgomery Castle to be greater than that of York, for the lines of communication between the recruiting areas of north and central Wales and the training ground at Shrewsbury were gravely imperilled. Myddelton's command ended in June 1645, already extended forty days after the self-denying ordinance came into force.

Once home, now restored to him, Myddelton attended to the work of county committees within his sphere of influence in north Wales. For a time he regularly attended parliament. During the second civil war he headed the list of parliamentarian negotiators who signed the treaty whereby Anglesey royalists surrendered in October 1648. His ardour, however, was waning. In December Pride's Purge ended his membership of the Long Parliament. Suspicions concerning his loyalty prompted the council of state to place in Chirk Castle a garrison which was not removed until he publicly undertook not to oppose the Commonwealth. He did not insulate himself entirely from affairs of state. He was critical of the commissioners under the Act for the Propagation of the Gospel in Wales (1650–53), mainly because of their failure to appoint suitable ministers in place of those ejected for insufficiency. He declared himself openly in the early summer of 1659 when he participated in the presbyterian–royalist uprising led by Sir George Booth. Before joining Booth at Chester he declared Charles king at Wrexham. In August the rebels were soundly defeated at Winnington Bridge. His estates were ordered to be sequestered and his house demolished. Meanwhile he sought sanctuary with London royalists and planned a further insurrection in the Welsh marches. The exiled Charles appointed him commander-in-chief for north Wales and on 12 May 1660 Myddelton again declared him king at Wrexham. Later he publicly announced his acceptance of the declaration of Breda and thus of the general pardon which it proffered. Talk of a viscountcy came to nothing. However, it is said that he received from Charles II a painted inlaid cabinet chased with silver, attributed to Rubens and then worth about £10,000.

Myddelton was elected to represent Denbighshire in the Convention Parliament. He served on a few committees before returning to Wales where he contributed to a voluntary gift presented to Charles by the gentry of north Wales. Chirk Castle, though not demolished, was so damaged that it was not fully habitable until 1672. Myddelton lived in a nearby manor house, Cefn-y-wern, which he extended for the benefit of his household.

Portraits of Myddelton suggest a man suffused with melancholy. He was occasionally impetuous. There are signs that he was kind-hearted and his dispatches from the field reveal human touches. Apart from his large family his main passions were his garden and his library. Cards, bowls, and shuffleboard he found relaxing and also horse-racing. But withal he remains colourless and elusive. The Chirk Castle papers were carefully kept, but Myddelton's correspondence, both here and in other collections, is exceedingly sparse. In quieter times, except for attendance at parliament, he would seldom have stirred from north-east Wales. Rural pursuits meant more to him than metropolitan delights. What then prompted a man of fifty-six without visible appetite for power to leave home, surrounded and soon occupied by royalists, to endanger life and fortune as an untried soldier? The notion, sometimes floated, that he was a presbyterian cannot survive scrutiny. At most it was a convenient political label. In his private chapel there was a crucifix and Richard Baxter rightly declared that Myddelton was 'conformable to Episcopacy and Parochial Worship' (R. Baxter, *Richard Baxter's Penitent Confession*, 1691, 30). In short, he was a moderate, loyal Anglican, and so remained. The mainspring of his actions was the fear of militant Catholicism on the continent and of developments in Ireland, allied to uneasiness concerning Charles's affiliations at home and abroad. As a constitutional royalist he became increasingly mistrustful of the republican government so that at the age of seventy-one he again took to the field. Circumstances, not his basic principles, had changed. Moderation was to him a virtue. He would have been happier in the eighteenth century.

The responsibilities of local government rested lightly upon Myddelton. He held many offices, for example, those of deputy lieutenant for Denbighshire (1614–42 and 1660–

66) and *custos rotulorum* from 1631, with one brief interruption, until 1666. But he did not attend a single quarter sessions. The consolidation and extension of his estate, however, was a prime concern. Within thirty years he doubled its size to over 60,000 acres, increasing his rental by 50 per cent to more than £5000. Additional income from the sale of cattle, the lending of money, and the exploitation of coal and iron resources in Denbighshire and Shropshire cannot be reliably estimated. When he died Myddelton was wealthier than many peers, despite the severe demands of war upon his capital and the settling of lands upon his sons and of substantial portions upon his daughters. Lady Sussex, wife of the sixth earl, remarked that marriage to his heir was 'on of the best maches in inglande that is to be hade' (Verney and Verney, 1.151). To have established the Myddeltons among the leading landed families of Britain was the achievement for which he is chiefly to be remembered.

Late in 1666 Myddelton was plagued with exceedingly painful ulcers upon his body. He died on 11 December at Cefn-y-wern surrounded by his family. Funeral expenses were almost £1100. The herald Randle Holme directed a funeral procession 1 mile long to Chirk parish church where Myddelton was buried on 22 January 1667.

J. GWYNN WILLIAMS

Sources G. R. Thomas, 'Sir Thomas Myddelton, 1586–1666', MA diss., U. Wales, 1964 · NL Wales, Chirk Castle papers · W. M. Myddelton, ed., *Chirk Castle accounts, 1605–1666* (privately printed, 1908) · W. M. Myddelton, ed., *Chirk Castle accounts AD[sic] 1666–1673* (1931) · A. H. Dodd, 'The civil war in East Denbighshire', *Transactions of the Denbighshire Historical Society*, 3 (1954), 41–89 · M. W. Helmes and A. M. Mimardière, 'Myddelton, Thomas', HoP, *Commons, 1660–90* · F. P. Verney and M. M. Verney, *Memoirs of the Verney family during the seventeenth century*, 3rd edn, 2 vols. (1925) · R. N. Dore, 'Sir Thomas Myddelton's attempted conquest of Powys, 1664–1665', *Montgomeryshire Collections*, 57 (1961–2), 91–118 · I. Edwards, 'The early ironworks of north-west Shropshire', *Transactions of the Shropshire Archaeological Society*, 56 (1957–60), 185–202 · N. R. F. Tucker, *North Wales in the civil war* (1958); new edn (1992) · A. W. Hughes Clarke, ed., *The register of St Dunstan in the East, London*, 1, Harleian Society, register section, 69 (1939), 25 · Foster, *Alum. Oxon.* · *The letter books of Sir William Brereton*, ed. R. N. Dore, 2 vols., Lancashire and Cheshire RS, 123, 128 (1984–90) · A. H. Dodd, 'Myddelton, Thomas', HoP, *Commons, 1558–1603*

Archives Denbighshire RO, Ruthin, papers relating to dispute between Myddelton and Sir Edward Trevor · NL Wales, Chirk Castle collection

Likenesses attrib. R. Walker, oils, c.1650–1660, Chirk Castle, Denbighshire · W. Bond, stipple (after R. Walker, c.1650–1660), BM; repro. in Yorke, *Royal Tribes of Wales* (1799) · J. Bushnell, memorial sculpture, Chirk parish church, Denbighshire · line engraving, BM, NPG; repro. in Vicar, *England's worthies* (1647) · pen-and-ink drawing, NPG · print, NL Wales

Myddelton, William. See Midleton, Wiliam (c.1550–1596?).

Myers, Arthur Thomas (1851–1894), physician, was born on 16 April 1851 at St John's parsonage, Keswick, Cumberland. He was the third and youngest child of the Revd Frederic *Myers (1811–1851), perpetual curate of St John's, Keswick, and his wife, Susan Harriet, née Marshall (1811–1896). In July 1851 his father died, and his mother, who came from a wealthy family, moved with her three sons first to Blackheath and then to Cheltenham, where all three were sent as day boys to Cheltenham College. Arthur was a good all-rounder, who played cricket and rackets for the school. He entered Trinity College, Cambridge, in 1869, became a scholar of the college in 1872, and in 1873 obtained a first class in the classical tripos and a second class in the natural sciences tripos. He also won the Winchester reading prize. He was captain of the college cricket eleven, and gained a half blue at real tennis. After graduating Myers turned to medicine, studying at Cambridge and at St George's Hospital, London. He obtained his LSA in 1879, a Cambridge MD in 1881, and his MRCP in 1882. He settled in London, becoming house physician and medical registrar at St George's and physician to the Belgrave Hospital for Children. He also practised privately, and he published several rather routine medical papers.

Myers's interests lay particularly in mental disorders and their treatment by hypnotism. Hypnotism, little known in Britain, was attracting considerable attention in France. In and after 1881 he paid a number of visits to Charcot, Bernheim, and other leading French authorities, with many of whom he established friendly personal relations. His own publications on the subject, though neither numerous nor lengthy, are moderate in judgement and exceptionally well informed. No British medical man knew more about contemporary European hypnotism, or about the history of mesmerism and hypnotism; he wrote the article on James Esdaile for the *Dictionary of National Biography*.

Related to his interest in hypnotism was his involvement in the Society for Psychical Research (founded in 1882), of which his eldest brother, Frederic William Henry *Myers, to whom he was very close, was a leading member. A well-established tradition held that the hypnotic, or mesmeric state is especially conducive to telepathy and clairvoyance, and Arthur Myers was involved as participant or adviser in various of the society's early hypnotic experiments. His activities were mocked, though not unkindly, in J. K. Stephen's poem 'To A.T.M.', a clever parody of Frederic Myers's *St Paul*. He was also often consulted on the psychopathological issues which can arise in psychical investigations. On behalf of the society he and his brother assembled an outstanding collection, still extant, of rare books, periodicals, and pamphlets on mesmerism and hypnosis.

Myers's hypnotic studies and his interests in psychical research came fruitfully together in a long, thoughtful, and frequently cited paper, 'Mind-cure, faith-cure, and the miracles of Lourdes', which he and Frederic published in the *Proceedings of the Society for Psychical Research* in 1893. The paper discussed the kind of evidence that reports of allegedly miraculous cures ought to offer, presented a selection of the most striking and better attested cures, and showed that very similar cures had been obtained without any hint of the miraculous. In the great majority of the 'miraculous' cases there was inadequate testimony or the likelihood of misdiagnosis, sometimes combined with a strong element of suggestion.

Various photographs of Arthur Myers survive, but no description of him. Although a bachelor, he was a kindly and sociable if occasionally brusque individual, an enthusiastic cricket and tennis player, and a keen walker, skater, and climber. His many friends included several of his most eminent contemporaries. His undoubted abilities as a physician (he became an FRCP in 1893) could have led to a distinguished medical career. But, despite valiant endeavours to remain cheerful and positive, his life was increasingly overshadowed by a then hopeless malady. His first slight attacks of what was diagnosed as *petit mal* epilepsy took place in 1871. At first they amounted to no more than a brief but overwhelming absorption 'in a vivid and unexpected recollection'. He also had a few *grand mal* attacks. However it was the so-called *petit mal* which gradually disabled him. It steadily progressed into more frequent episodes of what would now be termed psycho-motor epilepsy, involving superficially intelligent but really disordered sequences of actions for which he had afterwards no recollection. On rare occasions these seem to have resulted in anti-social behaviour. He gave up medical practice in October 1893. In 1877 and subsequently he consulted J. Hughlings Jackson, the celebrated neurologist. Jackson published two papers (Jackson, 1889; Jackson and Colman, 1898) largely about Myers's case. He made extensive use of Myers's own notes. These papers are still regarded as milestones in the development of modern ideas about temporal lobe epilepsy.

On the morning of Tuesday, 9 January 1894 Myers was found at his London home, 2 Manchester Square, in a coma apparently induced by some narcotic medicine. He died the following day, and was cremated at Woking five days later. At the inquest the possibility of suicide was clearly in the air. But testimony was heard that he had been in unusually good spirits on the Monday afternoon and evening; he was known to have regularly taken narcotics, and there was no suggestion of financial worries (his estate was later valued at £28,056). His death was attributed to asphyxia during epileptic coma, accelerated by a dose of narcotic medicine while suffering from incipient Bright's disease. Hughlings Jackson (who chanced to be Myers's neighbour) assisted at the post-mortem, seeking the temporal lobe lesion which he anticipated. He was rewarded by the discovery of a very small cavity in the left mesial temporal lobe—a tiny thing (if indeed it underlay Myers's epilepsy) to have ruined the career of a sensitive, brave, and intelligent man.   ALAN GAULD

Sources D. C. Taylor and S. M. Marsh, 'Hughlings Jackson's Dr Z: the paradigm of temporal lobe epilepsy revealed', *Journal of Neurology, Neurosurgery, and Psychiatry*, 43 (1980), 758–67 · *BMJ* (27 Jan 1894), 223 · *Journal of the Society for Psychical Research*, 6 (1893–4), 195–97 · J. H. Jackson and W. S. Colman, 'Case of epilepsy with tasting movements and "dreamy" state–very small patch of softening in the left uncinate gyrus', *Brain*, 21 (1898), 580–90 · J. H. Jackson, 'On a particular variety of epilepsy ("intellectual aura"), one case with symptoms of organic brain disease', *Brain*, 11 (1889), 179–207 · *The Times* (15 Jan 1894) [inquest report] · A. Gauld, *A history of hypnotism*

(1992), 336, 337, 390 · Venn, *Alum. Cant.* · Munk, *Roll*, 4.365–6 · W. Jerrold and R. M. Leonard, *A century of parody and imitation* (1913), 419–20 · d. cert. · F. W. H. Myers, diaries, Trinity Cam.
Archives Trinity Cam., F. W. H. Myers MSS, corresp.
Likenesses E. Myers, photograph, NPG, Eveleen Myers Albums · photograph (as a boy), Trinity Cam., F. W. H. Myers MSS
Wealth at death £28,056 3s. 7d.: resworn probate, June 1894, *CGPLA Eng. & Wales*

Myers, Charles Samuel (1873–1946), psychologist, was born in London on 13 March 1873, the eldest son of Wolf Myers, merchant, and his wife, Esther Eugenie Moses. His father's family was principally interested in commerce. From his mother and her family came powerful social, musical, and philosophical influences. As a boy at the City of London School, Myers turned towards science, and later at Gonville and Caius College, Cambridge, he gained first-class honours in both parts of the natural sciences tripos (1893, 1895) and was Arnold Gerstenberg student in 1896. He proceeded MB at St Bartholomew's Hospital, London, in 1898, but disinclined to medical practice, in that year he went with the Cambridge anthropological expedition to the Torres Strait. He joined W. H. R. Rivers and William McDougall in experimental studies of the sensory reactions of the inhabitants of that area, and he became profoundly interested in ethnic music.

In 1902 Myers returned to Cambridge to help Rivers teach the physiology of the special senses. In 1904 Myers married Edith Babette, youngest daughter of Isaac Seligman, merchant, of London; they had three daughters and two sons. Myers remained in Cambridge to become, in succession, demonstrator, lecturer, and, in 1921, reader in experimental psychology. From 1906 to 1909 he was also professor in experimental psychology at King's College, London. At about the time of the First World War he did much to develop scientific psychology in Britain, for example, by using his enthusiasm and ability to raise funds to establish the first English experimental laboratory especially designed for psychology at Cambridge in 1912.

In 1915 Myers was given a commission in the Royal Army Medical Corps and in 1916 he was appointed consultant psychologist to the British armies in France. Frustrated with opposition to his view that shell-shock was a treatable condition, after the war he returned to his Cambridge position. But here too he was deeply dissatisfied, wanting wider opportunities for the development of his more practical interests, and feeling that official and academic circles showed little genuine interest in psychology. In 1922 he left Cambridge for London, thereafter devoting himself to the development of the National Institute of Industrial Psychology which he had founded with Henry John Welch in 1921. He was also involved in what became the industrial health research board and was the first president of the British Psychological Society.

Myers's *Text-Book of Experimental Psychology* (1909) was for long the best work of its kind in any language. His *Introduction to Experimental Psychology* (1911) went through several editions. *Mind and Work* (1920), *Industrial Psychology in Great*

Charles Samuel Myers (1873–1946), by unknown photographer, 1920s

Britain (1926), and *Ten Years of Industrial Psychology* (with H. J. Welch, 1932) all dealt with the later interests of his life. He also published two volumes of essays: *A Psychologist's Point of View* (1933) and *In the Realm of Mind* (1937). His many contributions in the field of ethnic music won him an international reputation in anthropology.

In 1915 Myers was elected FRS; he was appointed CBE in 1919, and received honorary degrees from the universities of Manchester (DSc, 1927), Calcutta (LLD), and Pennsylvania (DSc). He was a fellow (1919) and later an honorary fellow (1935) of Gonville and Caius College, Cambridge, a foreign associate of the French Société de Psychologie, twice president of the psychology section of the British Association (1922, 1931), president of the International Congress of Psychology in 1923, and editor of the *British Journal of Psychology* (1911–24).

Myers was rather above medium height, well built, and remembered for his smile. He made friends readily, but had a tendency to imagine enemies. He enjoyed mountain climbing and lawn tennis, and was a talented violinist. He combined freemasonry with philanthropic activity for the Jewish community. Students and visitors from every part of the world were always welcome at his home. Myers died at his home at Winsford Glebe, near Minehead, Somerset, on 12 October 1946. He was survived by his wife.

Myers undertook more laboratory experimental work

than his publications would suggest, but his greatest contributions to the emergent science of psychology in Britain were in establishing many of its pioneering institutions, and promoting it internationally.

F. C. BARTLETT, *rev.* HUGH SERIES

Sources F. C. Bartlett, *Obits. FRS*, 5 (1945–8), 767–77 · *WWW* · S. Bakewell, 'The life and times of the Myers collection', *Medical History*, 37 (1993), 197–200 · 'C. S. Myers', *A history of psychology in autobiography*, ed. C. Murchison, 3 (1936) · private information (1954) · personal knowledge (1954) · *CGPLA Eng. & Wales* (1946)
Archives CUL, diary of the Torres Strait expeditions · Royal Anthropological Institute, London, anthropometric measurements of Egyptians · Wellcome L., the Myers collection | University of Bristol Library, corresp. with Conwy Lloyd Morgan
Likenesses photograph, 1920–29, NPG [*see illus.*] · W. Stoneman, photograph, 1933, NPG · photograph, repro. in Bartlett, *Obits. FRS*
Wealth at death £2577 4s. 6d.: probate, 29 Nov 1946, *CGPLA Eng. & Wales*

Myers, Edmund Charles Wolf (1906–1997), intelligence officer and engineer, was born on 12 October 1906 at 17 Kensington Palace Gardens, Kensington, London, the elder son among the five children of Dr Charles Samuel *Myers (1873–1946), consultant psychologist to the British expeditionary force during the First World War and reader in experimental psychology at the University of Cambridge, and his wife, Edith Babette Seligman, daughter of Isaac Seligman, a successful Jewish banker.

Educated at Chelverton Elms in Devon, Haileybury College, and the Royal Military Academy, Woolwich, Myers was commissioned into the Royal Engineers in August 1926. In October 1927 he went up to Gonville and Caius College, Cambridge, where his father had been a fellow, and he completed a BA degree in mechanical science before returning full-time to the army in 1929. It was at Woolwich, during his cadet days, that he was first called Eddie, the name by which he was known for the rest of his life, after Eddie Myers, a famous footballer. A talented sportsman himself, Myers was an accomplished horseman and keen pilot and was the first ever secretary of the Royal Engineers Flying Club from 1934 to 1935.

In 1935 Myers was posted to Palestine, where he saw active service during the Arab revolt and was mentioned in dispatches. Still in the Middle East when war broke out, he served in the 7th armoured division as commander of the 2nd (Cheshire) field company, during General Wavell's offensive against the Italians in Cyrenaica in 1941. He then attended the Middle East Staff College, Haifa, from 1939 to 1940, and was later a senior instructor at a combined operations school on the Suez Canal, when he completed a course in parachuting at a neighbouring SAS camp.

In Cairo in September 1942, while an acting brigadier in the combined operations branch of general headquarters (military) Middle East, Myers was approached by the Special Operations Executive (SOE) and was asked to lead a demolition team on a special mission to occupied Greece. The task, Myers was told, would be to sever the Thessaloniki–Athens railway line, Germany's main supply route to Rommel's Afrika Korps. Despite the short notice, and though within a fortnight of qualifying for a posting home by completing seven years' service in the Middle East, he agreed to go and promptly assembled what SOE's official historian called 'one of the strongest teams which SOE ever sent out' (Mackenzie, 450). At the end of the month, with his second in command, Major C. M. Woodhouse (1917–2001), and the rest of the twelve-strong mission (code-named Harling), Myers parachuted into Greece.

After selecting the Gorgopotamos railway viaduct as a suitable target and securing the combined support of local communist-led ELAS and non-communist EDES guerrillas, the attack went in on the night of 25–6 November 1942. It was a spectacular success, cutting for six weeks Rommel's supply line during his retreat from El Alamein, convincing the allied command of the value and potential of the Greek resistance forces, and winning Myers a DSO. Indeed, so impressive was their achievement that Harling received orders to remain in Greece, under Myers's command, to be the nucleus of the official British military mission to the Greek resistance.

Harling had gone into Greece on the understanding that the whole party would be evacuated once the demolition was done, and Myers, who had been recruited on the strength of his engineering and parachute experience, now had to show skills as a politician and diplomat. Over the following months he worked hard to persuade the rival guerrilla groups to fight the Germans instead of each other and eventually negotiated the 'national bands' agreement, by which ELAS and EDES agreed to co-ordinate their actions with the plans of Britain's Middle East headquarters. Myers also succeeded in organizing an intensified guerrilla campaign as part of the allied deception plan to divert German attention from the allied invasion of Sicily, and helped plan the destruction, in June 1943, of the Asopos railway viaduct that closed the Lamia–Athens line for over ten weeks. For these successes he was appointed CBE in 1944. His recommendation for the award remarked on the effect of 'his efforts, personal contacts, long marches all over Greece and extraordinary personality' and that he was seen by the Greeks almost 'as a possible future Byron' (private information).

In August 1943, with a representative guerrilla delegation, Myers left Greece for Cairo. There the delegates demanded, among other things, that the Greek king, George II, should not return to Greece until a plebiscite had been held. This was not what the king or the British authorities wished to hear. The delegation was sent back to Greece and Myers made a scapegoat by the Foreign Office, which unjustly accused him of being too 'pro-ELAS' and having dreamt up the plebiscite idea. Myers was forbidden from returning to Greece, though not before he had visited London and nearly persuaded Churchill to tone down his support of the Greek monarchy. A sensitive, loyal man, who in Greece had remained tightly focused on carrying out his brief, Myers was hurt and disappointed not to be going back. Instead, he watched from the sidelines as Greece slipped further into the civil conflict he had predicted.

Remaining in London, Myers worked for SOE in the months up to the invasion of Europe, running a training school for 300 allied officers and wireless operators assigned to the missions code-named Jedburgh, then acting as SOE London's liaison officer with the Supreme Headquarters Allied Expeditionary Force. In July he left SOE and, as a lieutenant-colonel, was appointed commander Royal Engineers with Major-General Roy Urquhart's 1st airborne division. There, admiringly but incongruously, Myers would be known as Tito Myers after his record in the Balkans. After dropping at Arnhem in September 1944, Myers effectively abandoned his job as Urquhart's chief engineer to play important roles in liaising with Major-General Stanislaw Sosabowski's Poles and organizing the evacuation of survivors across the lower Rhine. Later he took part in the division's liberation of Norway.

On 12 October 1943, in Cairo, Myers married Louisa Mary Hay (Lutie) (1908/9–1995), elder daughter of Aldred Bickham Sweet-Escott, a marine engineer, of Newport and Bristol, and his wife, Mary Amy, daughter of Michael Waistall Cowan. Lutie was then working for SOE in Cairo, having been recruited by her brother, Bickham Aldred Cowan Sweet-Escott, who served in SOE's London headquarters throughout the war. They had one daughter, Thalia, born in April 1945.

At the war's end Myers was appointed Mountbatten's deputy director of intelligence in the Far East, subsequently becoming senior military representative to the joint intelligence bureau in London. During the Korean War he served as commander Royal Engineers, 1st Commonwealth division, receiving a mention in dispatches and the American Legion of Merit. Later he was senior army instructor at the RAF Staff College, Bracknell, 1952–5; chief engineer, British troops, Egypt, 1955–6; and deputy director of personnel administration at the War Office, 1957–9. After retiring from the army in 1959, Myers pursued a successful career in civil engineering. He was chief civil engineer with Cleveland Bridge and Engineering Company Ltd from 1959 to 1964 and construction manager with Power Gas Corporation Ltd from 1964 to 1967.

'Eddie' Myers was tall and fair with a long face and long nose, heavily lidded eyes, and a high, broad forehead. Noted for his courage and resourcefulness, his drive and determination, he was a well-liked, articulate, and intelligent man who led from the front and could impress his views on a diverse range of personalities. He found time in the army to write *Greek Entanglement*, a memoir of his SOE work in Greece, published in 1955, and, in 1973, at a conference on wartime guerrilla movements, contributed a detailed paper on a particular aspect of that work, later published in 1975 as 'The Andarte delegation to Cairo' (in P. Auty and R. Clogg, eds., *British Policy towards Wartime Resistance in Yugoslavia and Greece*, pp. 147–66).

In full retirement, Myers settled with his wife in the Cotswolds. There he played an active role in local affairs, becoming a parish councillor, and maintained his lifelong interest in country sports of all kinds, serving for a time as a regional secretary of the British Field Sports Society.

Myers died on 6 December 1997 in the Moore Cottage Hospital, Bourton on the Water, Gloucestershire.

RODERICK BAILEY

Sources E. Myers, *Greek entanglement* (1955) · E. Myers, 'The Andarte delegation to Cairo', *British policy towards wartime resistance in Yugoslavia and Greece*, ed. P. Auty and R. Clogg (1975) · *The Times* (10 Dec 1997) · *The Guardian* (24 Dec 1997) · W. J. M. Mackenzie, *The secret history of SOE* (2000) · M. Middlebrook, *Arnhem, 1944* (1994) · C. Woodhouse, *Apple of discord* (1948) · N. Hammond, *Venture into Greece* (1983) · private information (2004) [special operations executive adviser] · *WWW, 1996–2000* · *DNB* · *CGPLA Eng. & Wales* (1998) · b. cert. · m. cert. · d. cert.
Archives King's Lond., Liddell Hart C., papers, incl. some relating to destruction of Asopos viaduct, Greece
Wealth at death £219,864: probate, 5 June 1998, *CGPLA Eng. & Wales*

Myers, Ernest James (1844–1921), poet and translator, was born at Keswick on 13 October 1844, the second son of Frederic *Myers (1811–1851), perpetual curate of St John's, Keswick, and his second wife, Susan Harriet (1811–1896), the youngest daughter of John Marshall of Hallsteads, on Ullswater. His elder brother was Frederic William Henry *Myers (1843–1901). Ernest Myers, who spent many of his summer holidays in the fell country, retained throughout his life an ardent love for the region.

From Cheltenham College, where he was head of the school, Myers went in 1863 as an exhibitioner to Balliol College, Oxford. He enjoyed college life to the full, rowing in the college eight and playing rackets and tennis. He was also academically successful, obtaining a first class in classical moderations (1865) and the Gaisford prize for Greek verse (1865), but he narrowly missed the Hertford scholarship and a first class in *literae humaniores*. In 1868 he was elected a fellow of Wadham College, where he remained for three years as a lecturer. While at Wadham, he wrote and published his first poem, *The Puritans* (1869), a short drama intentionally reminiscent of the *Persae* of Aeschylus.

From 1871 to 1891 Myers lived in London, where he was called to the bar (1874) but never practised. During these years he published his prose translations of Pindar's *Odes* (1874) and of the last eight books of the *Iliad* (with Andrew Lang and Walter Leaf, 1882), as well as some essays in magazines, and one, on Aeschylus, in the collection entitled *Hellenica*, edited by Evelyn Abbott (1880). Myers's enthusiasm for Greece was the most striking characteristic of his writing, although he also compiled a selection of prose passages by Milton (*Parchment Series*, 1884); a short biography of Viscount Althorp (1890), whose services in connection with the Reform Act of 1832 he thought to be insufficiently recognized; and three volumes of verse, *Poems* (1877), *The Defence of Rome* (1880), and *The Judgement of Prometheus* (1886).

Myers's activities during his life in London were not confined to literature. From 1876, for nearly six years, he acted as secretary to the London Society for the Extension of University Teaching. He was on the council of the Hellenic

Society from its foundation in 1879. Later, after abandoning the idea of parliamentary life, he worked for the Charity Organization Society, serving on its central administrative committee until he left London.

On 1 February 1883 Myers married Nora Margaret, daughter of Samuel Lodge, rector of Scrivelsby, Lincolnshire; they had two sons and three daughters. In 1891 the family moved to a house at Chislehurst on the edge of Paul's Cray Common, which was to feature in his poem 'A Common', in his *Gathered Poems*. Here Myers remained for the rest of his life, abandoning the habit of continental travel to which some of his poems bear witness, but paying a weekly visit to London in order to see friends and to attend the council meetings of the Society for the Protection of Women and Children. Most of the verse composed in these years is included in *Gathered Poems* (1904), a collection which also contained what he thought best in the volumes previously published. Myers died of pneumonia at Fontridge, Burwash, Sussex, on 25 November 1921. He was survived by his wife, one son, and two daughters; one daughter had died in infancy, and his elder son was killed while serving in France in 1918.

A. C. BELL, rev. MEGAN A. STEPHAN

Sources Foster, *Alum. Oxon.* · J. Foster, *Men-at-the-bar: a biographical hand-list of the members of the various inns of court*, 2nd edn (1885), 333 · Allibone, *Dict.* · J. Foster, *Oxford men and their colleges* (1893), 532 · m. cert. · d. cert. · IGI
Wealth at death £73,870 8s. 7d.: probate, 6 Jan 1922, CGPLA Eng. & Wales

Myers, Frederic (1811–1851), Church of England clergyman and author, was born at Blackheath, Kent, on 20 September 1811, the son of Thomas *Myers (1774–1834), mathematician and geographer, and his wife, Anna Maria, *née* Hale. After being carefully educated by his father, who was then on the staff of the Royal Military Academy at Woolwich, Myers entered Clare College, Cambridge, as a scholar in 1829. The following year he gained the Hulsean essay prize, and he became in 1833 Crosse scholar and graduated BA. Shortly afterwards he was elected a fellow of his college, and in 1836 gained the Tyrwhitt Hebrew scholarship. He was ordained in 1835 to the curacy of Ancaster in Lincolnshire. In 1838 he was appointed perpetual curate of the newly formed district parish of St John's, Keswick, and in this, his sole preferment, he remained until his death. On 9 October 1839 he married Fanny, youngest daughter of J. C. Lucas Calcraft. In January 1840 she died, and on 30 March 1842 he married Susan Harriet (1811–1896), youngest daughter of John Marshall of Hallsteads, Cumberland, MP for Yorkshire before 1832. They had several children, among them Frederic William Henry *Myers, a pioneer of psychical research, Arthur Thomas *Myers, a London physician, and Ernest James *Myers, poet and translator.

Besides the charm of scenery and the attraction of congenial neighbours—Wordsworth was still living at Rydal Mount—the new incumbent of St John's found satisfaction in being able, in a recently constituted parish, to develop his own pattern of pastoral care. The level of his commitment was evidenced by the fact that his *Lectures on*

Great Men, which went through many editions, began life as simple parish lectures.

The most important of Myers's published works was *Catholic Thoughts on the Bible and Theology*, a four-part work on the church of Christ, the Church of England, the Bible, and theology. The first part was privately printed in 1834, and the whole, after being reprinted at intervals in 1841 and 1848, still for private circulation, was published in a collected form in 1873, with the author's name, in the series of Latter-Day Papers edited by Bishop Alexander Ewing; it was again issued in 1883, with an introduction by the author's son F. W. H. Myers. The work is of some interest, for while on the one hand its specific rejection of what Myers called a 'priestly Caste' placed it firmly in the mainstream of English protestant writing, on the other its attitude to the Bible illustrated an early attempt to reconcile traditional views with the newer liberal and critical ideas. To this end Myers made a distinction between revelation and the actual text of the Bible, seeing the latter as an imperfect and inaccurate vehicle of revelation; in his own words the significance of the Bible was 'of a character intermediate between the Literal and the Rational'. Myers's advanced theological views, similar to those of F. W. Robertson and F. D. Maurice, would have attracted more attention had *Catholic Thoughts* been more widely available when first printed. In addition to this work Myers also published a number of sermons and lectures.

In the spring of 1850 Myers became ill; he died at Clifton, Cumberland, on 20 July 1851. He was buried in Keswick churchyard on 26 July.

J. H. LUPTON, rev. GEORGE HERRING

Sources F. W. H. Myers, 'Introduction', in F. Myers, *Catholic thoughts on the Bible and theology* (1883) · T. D. H. Battersby and H. V. Elliott, *Two sermons preached in St John's Church, Keswick … on the death of its first minister, the Reverend Frederic Myers* (1851) · B. M. G. Reardon, *From Coleridge to Gore: a century of religious thought in Britain* (1971), 216–19 · GM, 2nd ser., 36 (1851), 327 · Boase, *Mod. Eng. biog.* · Venn, *Alum. Cant.*

Myers, Frederic William Henry (1843–1901), psychical researcher and essayist, was born on 6 February 1843 at St John's parsonage, Keswick, Cumberland, the eldest son of Frederic *Myers (1811–1851), perpetual curate of St John's, and his second wife, Susan Harriet Marshall (1811–1896). The mathematician Thomas *Myers was his grandfather, and the poet Ernest James *Myers a younger brother.

The classical scholar On his father's death Myers's mother moved with her three sons to Blackheath, Kent, where Frederic attended a preparatory school. Mrs Myers was a daughter of John *Marshall (1765–1845), owner of large estates in the Lake District, whose considerable fortune came from his Leeds flax mills. Money was not a serious problem, and in 1856 she took a substantial house in Cheltenham, sending her sons as day boys to Cheltenham College. There Myers's love of poetry and taste for classical literature were recognized and fostered. An early admiration for Virgil (instilled by his father) was followed by enthusiasms for other Greek and Latin authors. The reading of Plato's *Phaedo* at the age of sixteen occasioned a

Frederic William
Henry Myers
(1843–1901), by
Eveleen Myers

kind of religious conversion, which profoundly influenced his later thought. Before he left school he had learned the whole of Virgil by heart. These early enthusiasms were matched by a remarkable precocity in the use of language. At fourteen two of his poems were placed first and second for the college's English verse prize (the subject was 'Belisarius'), and in the same year he won the prize for a Latin lyric. In 1859 he came second in a national competition for a Robert Burns centenary poem. At the end of that year he left school to study privately, but in 1860 won the English verse prize (for which he was still eligible) with a striking poem on 'The Death of Socrates'.

That October, Myers went up to Trinity College, Cambridge, as a minor scholar. His university career was outstandingly successful. He won two university classical scholarships (the Bell and the Craven), the chancellor's medal for English verse twice, the Camden medal for Latin verse once, and the members' prize for a Latin essay three times. In 1864 he was second in the first classes of both the classical and the moral sciences triposes. Despite these achievements, Myers was not popular. Many thought him an eccentric and a poseur. The fervent and emotionally intense Hellenism which consumed him might easily have seemed like an affectation, but it was not. Thirty years later he wrote: 'That tone of thought came to me naturally; the classics were but intensifications of my own being' (Myers, 10). However, he added: 'They drew from me and fostered evil as well as good; they might aid imaginative impulse and detachment from sordid interests, but they had no check for lust or pride' (ibid.).

It was more than anything overweening conceit which led Myers into a piece of folly that seriously damaged his reputation. He had won the Camden medal for Latin verse in 1862. Into his entry for the following year he packed (mostly without acknowledgement) a considerable number of what he considered the best lines from past Oxford prize poems. He was following what he believed to have been Virgil's practice, and to his friends would disdainfully quote Virgil's remark *Aurum colligo e stercore Ennii* ('I

am collecting gold from Ennius's dunghill'). He was awarded the prize, but when the borrowings were discovered was forced to resign it.

The outward events of Myers's life over the next few years are easily told. He took his BA in 1864 and his MA in 1867, was a fellow of Trinity from 1865 until 1874, and a college lecturer in classics from 1865 to 1869. Feeling himself unsuited for teaching, he resigned his lectureship to work on behalf of the movement for the higher education of women. In 1872 he became an inspector of schools, an occupation which he followed until not long before his death without much impeding his other activities, and in 1875 was appointed to the Cambridge district.

The inward events were more interesting and a great deal more complex. A tour in the summer of 1864 of classical sites in Italy, Greece and Asia Minor had somewhat cooled Myers's Hellenic ardour by showing him how unattainable was that vanished ideal world. A tour of Canada and the United States the following summer found him for the first and last time in a state of religious apathy which was brought home to him when, about to swim the river below Niagara Falls, he asked himself, 'What if I die?' and found the answer void of emotion. To a man of Myers's eager temperament sustained indifference was not possible. Christianity had for many years been displaced in his mind by Platonism, but now he was converted to Christianity by Mrs Josephine Butler, wife of the vice-principal of Cheltenham College, a lady for whom niceties of dogma were subordinate to the lived experience of Christian verities. Under her influence Myers for several years passed much of his life in prayer, self-discipline, and inner rapture. His best-known poem, 'St Paul' (1867), which was dedicated to Mrs Butler, reflects the feelings of this period.

Moving towards spiritualism By 1869 disillusion had set in. It came, Myers said, 'from increased knowledge of history and science, from a wider outlook on the world … insensibly the celestial vision faded' (Myers, 13). The years of religious doubt that followed were exceedingly painful. Though for a while he moved much in the society of Mary Ann Evans (George Eliot) and other earnest disbelievers, he could derive no satisfaction from their attempts to find meaning in a life bereft of God and the prospect of immortality.

Myers now turned, with the collaboration and cautious encouragement of his Trinity colleague and mentor, Henry Sidgwick, to an investigation of spiritualistic and kindred phenomena, which were then attracting a fair amount of interest. Between 1873 and 1878 Myers, Sidgwick, and a group of Trinity fellows and friends, including Edmund Gurney, Walter Leaf, Lord Rayleigh, and Arthur Balfour, together with Balfour's sisters, Eleanor (who was to marry Henry Sidgwick) and Evelyn (Lady Rayleigh), sat in various permutations and combinations with a good many mediums. Most proved in the end disappointing but Myers felt that he had witnessed occasional phenomena which justified continued hope that such investigations might eventually open an escape route from the prison of materialism.

These investigations coincided with other events which were to have a profound influence on the rest of Myers's life. His first cousin, Walter James Marshall, had married in 1866 Annie Eliza Hill, but Walter's increasingly frequent manic-depressive episodes and eccentric behaviour put great strains on the marriage. Myers and Annie were often in each other's company, partly because of family attempts to cope with the problem of Walter, and from about 1873 a deep, though unconsummated, affection developed between them. In May 1876 Walter was certified insane and taken to a private asylum at Ticehurst in Sussex where he was (wrongly) pronounced incurable (Beer, chap. 4). His anger and recriminations distressed Annie and, overwhelmed by these and other problems, she drowned herself in Ullswater on 29 August 1876. Myers, who had gone abroad, was devastated. Annie had shared his religious doubts and his interest in spiritualism and was already associated in his mind with his quest for evidence of survival of death; proof of her survival now became a principal object of that quest.

In the years following 1876 Myers threw himself into literary work, publishing (mostly in the *Fortnightly Review* and the *Nineteenth Century*) the essays later collected as *Essays Modern* (1883) and *Essays Classical* (1883). In several of these essays are passages—most notably the end of his essay on Ernest Renan, and the section on the neoplatonists in the essay on Greek Oracles—which foreshadow much of his subsequent thought. To this period also belong a further volume of poems, *The Renewal of Youth* (1882), and 'Wordsworth' (1880), a brief sketch for the English Men of Letters series. The latter was frequently reprinted—Myers's love for and intimate knowledge of the Lake District, together with his own poetic gifts and strong sense of a spiritual reality behind and interpenetrating the sensible world, fitted him particularly well to be a biographer and interpreter of Wordsworth.

On 13 March 1880, after a whirlwind courtship, Myers married Eveleen Tennant, the youngest daughter of Charles Tennant, of Cadoxton Lodge, Neath, Glamorgan. In most ways they were exceedingly different. Eveleen's interests were social and artistic—she was a gifted photographer—and not in the least intellectual, still less otherworldly. The bond between them was emotional and passionate. Eveleen was a devoted if somewhat possessive wife and mother—they had three children, Leopold Hamilton *Myers (1881–1944), Silvia (b. 1883) and Harold (b. 1886)—and the marriage was on the whole happy, despite the fact that Myers's inmost affections remained secretly fixed on the idealized Annie Marshall.

Myers and his wife both came from wealthy families (at his death his estate was valued at £37,370) and they were able to enjoy a settled and comfortable lifestyle. In 1881 he built as their home the substantial Leckhampton House, set in 4 acres of grounds just to the west of Grange Road, Cambridge. From then on his outward life—the activities for which the world at large most particularly knew him—and his inward life came together more fully than they had previously done. The result was twenty years of sustained endeavour and impressive productivity.

The Society for Psychical Research Early in 1882 Myers joined Sir William Barrett, the physicist, certain prominent spiritualists, notably E. Dawson Rogers and W. Stainton Moses, his own Trinity friends, Henry Sidgwick and Edmund Gurney, and various others, in setting up the Society for Psychical Research (the SPR). The aim of this society was to investigate psychic phenomena in a scientific spirit and without presuppositions as to outcome or explanations. Sidgwick became its first president and, more than anyone, set its tone, but it was above all Myers whose enthusiasm drove it on. His own motivation was of course broadly religious, but it would be unjust to accuse him of wholesale credulity. His experience of spiritualistic frauds was considerable, and his tendency towards belief was restrained by his sense that momentous issues were at stake. His contribution to the SPR and to psychical research in general was fourfold. He was centrally involved in organizing the society and in promoting its image, which he did by recruiting distinguished members, speaking at international psychological conferences and placing informative articles in leading reviews. He devoted a great deal of time and energy to the investigation of cases of apparitions (he was co-author with Edmund Gurney and Frank Podmore of the monumental *Phantasms of the Living*, 2 vols., 1886) and of automatic writing, trance mediumship, and so forth, and travelled widely in Britain and abroad to obtain first-hand testimony and sit with mediums. (Sittings with the American trance medium Mrs Leonora Piper and with the English Mrs Rosina Thompson eventually convinced him that he had made contact with Annie Marshall.) He used his classical learning to coin a specialist vocabulary for psychical research, the term 'telepathy' being one of his inventions. And he developed a theory to unite the findings of psychical research with the latest discoveries in psychopathology, abnormal psychology, and hypnotism.

The reading with which he supported this theory was prodigious. He probably knew more than any man in England (except perhaps his own youngest brother and close collaborator, the physician Arthur Thomas *Myers (1851–1894)) about current continental work on hypnosis, dissociation, and secondary personality, and had met many of the leading French authorities. He was the first to describe in English the early work of Pierre Janet and Freud. The development of his theory of the subliminal self can be traced through numerous lengthy articles in the *Proceedings* of the SPR, and a more popular book, *Science and a Future Life* (1893), to its fullest, though still incomplete, expression in his posthumous *Human Personality and its Survival of Bodily Death* (2 vols., 1903). Myers regards each human personality as consisting of a number of distinct streams of consciousness, which he sometimes compares to geological strata. These are in some sense modifications of the same soul, and have the potential for unification. But normally they remain separate, and one, the ordinary 'supraliminal' stream of consciousness, has evolved to cope with the problems of everyday living. Others, however, may possess faculties, for instance telepathy, of less immediate practical relevance. Waking telepathic experiences may be regarded as leaks or messages from these 'subliminal' streams of consciousness, and telepathy is most likely to occur when such streams are tapped, as in dreams or hypnosis, or become to an extent detached and autonomous, as in automatic writing or secondary personality. This theory had for a while great influence within psychical research, and some outside it. Whether it could be made credible or even wholly coherent might be doubted. None the less *Human Personality*—despite the rhapsodical style in which some passages are written—remains an impressive attempt to systematize a vast quantity of interesting materials.

Character and appearance As a person the later Myers was admired by many but also disliked by not a few. The self-conceit of his earlier days had been replaced by a chastened insight into his own shortcomings, and the snobbery and excessive respect for titles, which had irritated his American friend, William James, was substantially moderated. But lingering memories of the Camden medal affair, together with his unconventional religious views, made some doubt his sincerity, a doubt not allayed by the sonorous fluency with which he would talk or lecture on his favourite themes. His prose was liable to similar excesses; they represented, however, not insincerity but a brief lifting of the curtain on his intense inner life. A sentence from the manuscript of his autobiography runs: 'I cannot feel that I am entirely candid unless I write in this emotional, over-decorated style which corresponds in some subtle way to the idiosyncrasy of the soul within.' His ordinary bearing was serene and reserved, and he had great social gifts; he had, however, few close friends, and these—Edmund Gurney, Henry Sidgwick and his wife, Oliver Lodge, the French physiologist Charles Richet, William James—were mostly individuals whom he thought of as fellow workers in the great endeavour.

Myers was about 5 feet 10 inches in height, tending somewhat to stoutness, with brown eyes, dark hair, later thinning and becoming grizzled, and a short beard. According to members of his family he was almost tone deaf and had little appreciation of music, a failing which is perhaps reflected in his poetry. In 1898, 1899, and 1900 Myers had severe attacks of influenza. He developed Bright's disease, with enlargement of the heart. Towards the end of 1900 he went abroad for his health. He died of pneumonia in a clinic in Rome on 17 January 1901. A memorial tablet was erected in the city's protestant cemetery. Myers was buried in the graveyard of St John's Church, Keswick, between his father's (more substantial) grave and a gateway into the garden of the house where he was born. He was survived by his wife.

ALAN GAULD

Sources A. Gauld, *The founders of psychical research* (1968) · A. C. Benson, *The leaves of the tree: studies in biography* (1911), 163–86 · F. W. H. Myers, *Fragments of inner life* (1961) · F. M. Turner, *Between science and religion: the reaction to scientific naturalism in late Victorian England* (1974), 104–33 · C. D. Broad, 'The life and work of F. W. H. Myers', *c*.1965, CUL, Society for Psychical Research archives · J. Oppenheim, *The other world: spiritualism and psychical research in England, 1850–1914* (1985) · E. W. Cook, 'The subliminal consciousness: F. W. H. Myers's approach to the problem of survival', *Journal of Parapsychology*, 58 (1994), 39–58 · W. James, 'Frederic Myers' services to psychology', *Proceedings of the Society for Psychical Research*, 17 (1901–3), 13–23 · C. Richet, 'In memoriam F. W. H. Myers', *Proceedings of the Society for Psychical Research*, 17 (1901–3), 24–8 · W. Leaf, 'F. W. H. Myers as man of letters', *Proceedings of the Society for Psychical Research*, 17 (1901–3), 33–6 · J. Beer, *Providence and love: studies in Wordsworth, Channing, Myers, George Eliot, and Ruskin* (1998) · b. cert. · *CGPLA Eng. & Wales* (1901) · private information (2004)

Archives NRA, corresp. and papers · Trinity Cam., corresp. and papers | BL, letters to T. H. S. Escott, Add. MS 58787 · BL, letters to Macmillans, Add. MS 55006 · CUL, Society for Psychical Research archives, corresp. with Sir Oliver Lodge · King's Cam., letters to Oscar Browning · priv. coll. · U. St Andr. L., letters to Wilfred Ward

Likenesses E. Myers, photographs, 1890–99, NPG · C. H. Wontner, oils, 1896, NPG · E. Myers, photograph, NPG [*see illus.*] · H. A. Prothero, sculpture, Cheltenham College Chapel

Wealth at death £37,370 10s. 9d.: probate, 1 March 1901, *CGPLA Eng. & Wales*

Myers, George (1803–1875), builder and craftsman, known as 'Pugin's builder', was born in Kingston upon Hull, Yorkshire, the son of George Myers, whitesmith, (*d. c.*1823), and of his second wife, Mary Benson (*d.* 1845). Family details are vague, including the religious affiliation of his parents at the time of his birth. Myers certainly died a Roman Catholic. Only one brother and one half-sister have been traced. As a boy Myers was apprenticed to William Comins, the master mason at Beverley Minster. He continued working there until 1829, and it was there, in 1827, that he first met A. W. N. Pugin, who had gone there to draw; they were not to meet again for ten years.

In 1829 Myers returned to Hull and set up in business as a stonemason and builder. Expanding towns and cities, together with Catholic emancipation and the religious revival, created a need for more churches, and new wealth created a desire for new buildings of every kind. In Hull, Myers built the Wilberforce memorial (1834) as well as public baths, houses, mills, and churches. In 1837 he met Pugin again when he tendered to build St Mary's Church in Derby, not realizing that the architect was the young boy he had helped in Beverley Minster a decade earlier. Pugin, according to his biographer, Benjamin Ferrey, is said to have flung his arms round his neck and promised that he should execute all his buildings, a promise which he kept to the best of his ability. It has been said that Myers was the rock on which Pugin built the Gothic revival. Pugin described Myers as 'a rough diamond, but a real diamond' (Spencer-Silver, 61). It would have been difficult, if not impossible, for him to have found another builder with Myers's knowledge of medieval Gothic who was also capable of working from Pugin's sketchy drawings. They became true friends and collaborators, yet no evidence has come to light to show that Myers had any hand in the decorating or furnishing of the houses of parliament. Myers carried out about forty major contracts for Pugin. The grand finale of their work together was the medieval court at the Great Exhibition of 1851. Myers was awarded a medal for his sculpture. Pugin died the next year and it

George Myers
(1803–1875), by
unknown artist,
c.1860

was Myers himself who carved the full length effigy on his tomb in St Augustine's Church, Ramsgate.

In 1842 Myers had moved to London. In 1845 he took on the lease of Ordnance Wharf, Lambeth, just downstream from Westminster Bridge. Here he established workshops where his craftsmen carved, sculpted, made furniture and also made the patterns for some of the metalwork produced by John Hardman (1811–1867) of Birmingham. With his yards on the bank of the river and Waterloo Station nearby, transport was no problem and he was well equipped to take a leading part in the great building boom of the 1850s and 1860s.

Myers's most spectacular works were carried out for architects other than Pugin—in all, 240 of his contracts have been traced. He was involved in many government contracts. He built the first barracks at Aldershot, where the red-bearded, frock-coated contractor with his stove-pipe hat, driving his high-wheeled gig, was remembered for many years. He enlarged the Royal Military Academy at Woolwich, and built Netley Hospital on Southampton Water, the Herbert Hospital at Woolwich, and the Staff College at Camberley. He restored the Tower of London using stone from his own quarries, and also the Guildhall in the City; and he worked at Windsor Castle. He built asylums, including Colney Hatch and Broadmoor and he enlarged and modernized Bedlam (the Bethlem Hospital). In the City of London he built banks, offices and warehouses. He also constructed a number of small railways, in addition to building stately homes.

Myers was the Rothschilds' favourite builder and built Mentmore in Buckinghamshire and Ferrière near Paris, as well as many of their other houses, both in London and in the country. He built nearly a hundred churches for all denominations, and one synagogue. His craftsmen's work travelled far: an altar table and lectern went to Newfoundland, a Pugin-designed tombstone for two babies was dispatched to New Orleans, and three model churches, which took to pieces, as well as church furniture in stone and tombstones, were sent to Tasmania. It is impossible to go far in London without coming across an example of Myers's work, and most counties in England can boast at least one of his buildings.

On 10 May 1829 Myers married Isabella, daughter of William Patterson of Beverley, Yorkshire; they had two sons and his wife died in 1834 giving birth to a third son, who died soon after. On 18 March 1841 Myers married Judith, daughter of David Ruddock of Horbury, Yorkshire, who gave birth to three sons and three daughters. The youngest girl married her cousin Sir John Jackson in 1876. In June 1873 Myers retired and handed over the business to David and Joseph, the two sons of his first marriage. In the spring of 1874, he had a stroke; he died of 'exhaustion' at his home, Thanet House, Montague Place, Lambeth, London, on 25 January 1875. He was buried in Norwood cemetery. The lease of Ordnance Wharf came to an end that year, and was not renewed. Judith Myers survived for another sixteen years.   PATRICIA SPENCER-SILVER

Sources P. Spencer-Silver, *Pugin's builder: the life and work of George Myers*, pbk edn (1993) · Magd. Oxf., Pugin MSS · application to be admitted to the freedom of the City of London, 27 May 1873, CLRO · census returns · d. cert. · *Creating a Gothic paradise: Pugin at the Antipodes* (2002) [exhibition catalogue, Hobart, Canberra, Sydney, Bendigo, 2002–3]
Archives priv. coll., family trust
Likenesses portrait, *c.*1860, repro. in Spencer-Silver, *Pugin's builder* [*see illus.*]
Wealth at death under £40,000: probate, 16 Feb 1875, *CGPLA Eng. & Wales*

Myers, Leopold Hamilton (1881–1944), novelist, was born at Leckhampton, Grange Road, Cambridge, on 6 September 1881, the eldest of the three children (two sons and a daughter) of Frederic William Henry *Myers (1843–1901), writer and founder member of the Society for Psychical Research, and his wife, Eveleen Tennant, a renowned intellectual hostess and an experimenter with the early technology of photography. Myers was educated at Eton College, spent a year in Germany, and was then briefly at Trinity College, Cambridge, before his father's death in January 1901. He then accompanied his mother on a trip to the United States, where she was to have a pre-arranged 'after-death' meeting with her husband. The meeting failed to materialize. Myers met and proposed to Elsie (1873–1955), daughter of General William Jackson Palmer, founder of the city of Colorado Springs, Colorado. Elsie Palmer was nine years older than Myers, and he had to wait seven years before she agreed to marry him in 1908. The couple had two daughters and lived in Marlow in Buckinghamshire.

Myers came to literature comparatively late and wrote slowly. His first published work was *Arvat* (1908), a play in verse. During the First World War he worked in the trade department of the Foreign Office. His first novel, *The Orissers* (1922), is an account of the relations between a poor aristocratic family and a family involved in the City. In 1925 he published *The Clio* about the tensions among the passengers of a luxury yacht travelling up the Amazon. Myers's great work, however, is a sequence of novels set in India in the reign of Akbar. Focusing on a young prince's life and spiritual quest at the corrupt political centre of an empire, the series included *The Near and the Far*, *Prince Jali*, *The Root and the Flower*, *Rajah Amar*, and *The Pool of Vishnu*. *The Root and the Flower* won the Femina Vie Heureuse and James Tait Black prizes after its publication in 1935. The novels were collected in Britain in 1943 as *The Near and the Far* and in the United States in 1945 as *The Root and the Flower*. Although the series is set in sixteenth-century India, Myers was cavalier with historical facts and stressed that he was using a historical setting to address contemporary issues:

It has certainly not been my intention to set aside the social and ethical problems that force themselves upon us at the present time. On the contrary, my hope has been that we might view them better from the distant vantage ground of an imaginary world.

Myers paid a great deal of attention to his public image; his manners and grooming were meticulous and his clothes expensively tailored. His character, however, was often painfully contradictory. A contemplative searcher for spiritual truths, he was nevertheless extremely sociable and active first in the Bloomsbury group (E. M. Forster found him 'chilly'), and then among the left-wing intelligentsia of the thirties (a friend of Orwell and J. D. Bernal). He could be a vicious snob and became very angry with his daughter for not marrying a peer. Myers read a great deal of philosophy while maintaining a strong prejudice against 'dry' academics. While he suffered from depression, he could, particularly as a young man, be gregarious and playful. He visited Egypt, Italy, Ceylon, and other countries, raced at Brooklands, flew in a balloon, and idled at social gatherings and fashionable restaurants funded by an inheritance he received from a godfather in 1906 which left him wealthy enough not to have to work.

Myers's writing is often concerned with spirituality and religious philosophy. After the death of his father he had a mystical experience in a hotel bedroom in Chicago, and as he became older this became proof to him that experiences beyond the rational did occur. Yet he could never submit himself to the discipline of any specific religious faith. Instead he trawled widely through writings on Christianity, Hinduism, and Buddhism and on Freudian, Adlerian, and especially Jungian psychology. In later life he became a communist and, although he never visited Russia, he looked on it as a spiritual utopia, commenting in one letter, 'Stalin's birthday: God bless him' and in another, in reference to the Red Army general, 'our hearts are with Timoschenko, and our attitude: who dies if Russia lives?' Myers tried to express his new faith in a semi-sociological work that was abandoned before it was finished. Following this failure he managed to complete a class-conscious autobiography. Almost as soon as he had finished, he turned against it and rounded up all the copies he had distributed to his friends and publishers before destroying every one.

During the Second World War, Leopold Myers became increasingly isolated and depressed. On the night of 7 April 1944 he committed suicide by taking an overdose of a commercial sedative, Veronal. He was found dead on the morning of the 8th at his home, Tylecotes, Oxford Road, Marlow-on-Thames, and was cremated without a ceremony on Saturday 15 April in Reading.

SOPHIA CRESWELL

Sources G. H. Bantock, *L. H. Myers—a critical study* (1956) • *The Times* (10 April 1944) • T. W. Earp, 'L. H. Myers', *New Statesman and Nation* (29 April 1944) • P. Parker and F. Kermode, eds., *The reader's companion to twentieth-century writers* (1995) • S. J. Kunitz and H. Haycraft, eds., *Twentieth century authors: a biographical dictionary of modern literature* (1942) • *DNB* • b. cert.
Likenesses E. Myers, double portrait, photograph, c.1892 (with his father), NPG • E. Myers, photograph, 1892, NPG • H. Coster, photographs, 1930–39, NPG • W. Rothenstein, chalk drawing, c.1936, NPG; repro. in Bantock, *L. H. Myers*
Wealth at death £32,434 16s. 6d.: probate, 30 Sept 1944, CGPLA Eng. & Wales

Myers, Thomas (1774–1834), mathematician and geographer, was born on 13 February 1774 at Hovingham, near York, of a family long settled in the county. In October 1806 he was appointed one of the mathematics masters at the Royal Military Academy, Woolwich. The following year he married Anna Maria, youngest daughter of John Hale; one of their children, Frederic *Myers, was a notable theological writer.

Myers's own works included *A Compendious System of Modern Geography* (1st edn, 1812), *A Statistical Chart of Europe* (1813), and *A Practical Treatise on Finding the Latitude and Longitude at Sea, with Tables* (1815). He also wrote *An Essay on Improving the Condition of the Poor* (1814) and *Remarks on a course of education designed to prepare the youthful mind for a career of honour, patriotism, and philanthropy* (1818). In the second of these the author, described as honorary member of the Philosophical Society of London, emphasizes the moral benefits of the study of mathematics, and especially of geometry. The work was reprinted in the twelfth volume of the *Pamphleteer*. Myers also wrote essays, chiefly on astronomical subjects, in various of the annual numbers of *Time's Telescope* from 1811 onwards. The memoir of Captain William Edward Parry in one of these, and an 'Essay on man' are praised in the *Gentleman's Magazine* for 1823 and 1825. Myers was the founder of a minor literary dynasty: several of his descendants were popular writers in their time. He died on 21 April 1834, at his home in Lee Terrace, Lee Park, Blackheath, Kent.

J. H. LUPTON, *rev.* ADRIAN RICE

Sources private information (1894) • T. Myers, *Remarks on a course of education …* (1818) • *GM*, 2nd ser., 2 (1834), 108 • *GM*, 1st ser., 93/2 (1823), 524–8 • *GM*, 1st ser., 95/2 (1825), 541–2 • H. D. Buchanan-Dunlop, ed., *Records of the Royal Military Academy, 1741–1892* (1895)

Myers, William Joseph (1858–1899), army officer and collector of antiquities, was born near Primrose Hill, London, on 4 August 1858, the eldest son of Thomas Borron Myers (1826–1882) of Porters Park, near Shenley, south Hertfordshire, and his wife, Margaret Storie, daughter of Henry *Melvill, canon of St Paul's Cathedral. In November 1858 Myers's father inherited the family property in Hertfordshire, and Myers spent his boyhood there. He attended private schools at Brighton and Great Malvern, and Eton College (1872–75). He went to a coach at Ehrenbreitstein on the Rhine, and after a short preparation passed into the Royal Military College, Sandhurst, in 1877.

Myers was commissioned second lieutenant in the 16th foot on 1 May 1878; he became second lieutenant in the King's Royal Rifle Corps (KRRC) on 19 February 1880, lieutenant on 10 November 1880, and captain on 14 March 1888. He served with the 3rd battalion in the Anglo-Zulu War from April to September 1879. From 1882 to 1887 he served in Egypt, acting as aide-de-camp to Sir Frederick Stephenson in operations of the Sudan frontier field force in 1885–6, and taking part in the battle of Giniss (30 December 1885); he was awarded the Mejidiye, fourth class. He also served in Gibraltar, Cyprus, and India. He was on the north-west frontier in 1891 with the 1st battalion, KRRC in the Hazara and Miranzai expeditions—which included the engagements at Sangar and Mastan—and served on the 1892 Isazai expedition. He left the regular army in 1894 and joined the KRRC 7th (militia) battalion in February 1897; he was promoted major in February 1899. He was devoted to, and a generous donor to, Eton College, and from February 1898 was adjutant of the Eton College rifle volunteers. In May they formed a guard of honour at Gladstone's funeral.

Myers had strong artistic and musical tastes and was a keen collector. From his schooldays he collected stamps, in South Africa Zulu weapons and trophies (and the pen with which the treaty of Ulundi was signed), in Egypt oriental fabrics and carpets, and later old prints and furniture. His most important collection was of Egyptian antiquities, purchased during his service in Egypt and on private visits there. At a time when extensive excavations were flooding the market with antiquities, Myers, with the advice and assistance of the German Egyptologist Emile Brugsch of the Bulaq Museum, purchased much from dealers and villagers. Among his friends was Percy Edward Newberry (later professor of ancient history and archaeology at Cairo University) who was to catalogue Myers's collection. It was wide-ranging and idiosyncratic: Myers bought what he considered aesthetically pleasing rather than archaeologically significant. He was especially fond of faience, 'Egyptian blue', glazed steatite, and glass. His collection was among the finest in England, and in 1895 he was one of the principal contributors to the Burlington Fine Arts Club 'Exhibition of the art of ancient Egypt'. In 1898 he was elected FSA. He travelled extensively in Europe, Asia, the West Indies, and South America—he rode across the Andes—and attended music festivals, operatic productions, and the Oberammergau passion play. Apparently a confirmed bachelor, he was devoted to his widowed mother, and 'it has been said by those who know him best, that after his mother's death, Eton seemed in some sort to supply her place in his heart' (Eton College Chronicle, 19 Dec 1899, 763).

In 1899 Myers went to South Africa to fight in the Second South African War. He wrote back, 'Eton is never out of my thoughts … we shall all remember Floreat Etona' (Eton College Chronicle, 19 Dec 1899, 763). He served with the 1st battalion, KRRC in Sir George White's force based at Ladysmith, Natal. Within three days of reaching the front he took part in White's unsuccessful offensive (variously named the battle of Ladysmith, Farquhar's Farm, Lombard's Kop, and Modder Spruit) on 'Mournful Monday', 30 October 1899. British officers were conspicuous and were targeted by Boer marksmen. Myers was killed, shot in the head, near Farquhar's Farm, near and east of Ladysmith, Natal. The Eton College Chronicle stated, 'We cannot but believe that it was the death of all others that he would have chosen' (ibid.). He is thought to have been buried at or near Ladysmith. Myers was commemorated by a memorial window in the lower chapel at Eton. He bequeathed his collection to Eton College, to form part of Eton's education and to inspire future generations. It is still held there, in the Myers Museum, together with his diary in thirty-six volumes.   ROGER T. STEARN

Sources Eton College Chronicle (11 June 1898), 516 · Eton College Chronicle (19 Dec 1899), 759–64 · Eton College Chronicle (29 Oct 1936), 243 · The Eton register, 4 (privately printed, Eton, 1907) · Hart's Army List (1891) · Hart's Army List (1899) · Burke, Gen. GB (1914) · Burke, Gen. GB (1937) · W. R. Dawson and E. P. Uphill, Who was who in Egyptology, 3rd edn, rev. M. L. Bierbrier (1995) · N. Reeves, 'Egyptian antiquities from Eton', Burlington Magazine, 130 (1988), 482–3 · H. C. Maxwell Lyte, A history of Eton College, 1440–1910, 4th edn (1911) · Boase, Mod. Eng. biog. · L. S. Amery, ed., The Times history of the war in South Africa, 2 (1902) · H. M. Jones and M. G. M. Jones, A gazetteer of the second Anglo-Boer War, 1899–1902 (1999) · B. Nasson, The South African War, 1899–1902 (1999) · S. Spurr, N. Reeves, and S. Quirke, Egyptian art at Eton College: selections from the Myers Museum (1999) · CGPLA Eng. & Wales (1900)

Archives Eton, diaries

Likenesses photograph, c.1898, repro. in Eton College Chronicle (19 Dec 1899), p. 762 · photograph, repro. in Navy & Army Illustrated (25 Nov 1899), p. 242 · photograph, repro. in Dawson and Uphill, Who was who in Egyptology, p. 305

Wealth at death £40,190 3s. 2d.: probate, 16 Feb 1900, CGPLA Eng. & Wales

Myersbach, Theodor (c.1730–1798), uroscopist, was probably born in Bavaria. Virtually all the particulars of his life were discovered initially by Dr John Coakley Lettsom, who pertinaciously investigated Myersbach's background and exposed his dubious practices. As Lettsom was a Quaker of the highest personal and professional integrity, who used as evidence Myersbach's letters and prescriptions that he had openly acquired, his account can be taken as essentially reliable.

Myersbach is said to have begun his working life in Germany as a postboy, delivering letters; he then rose to a clerkship in a Post Office. He married a sister of Joseph Brenner of Schweinfurt, near Würzburg, possibly in 1755; they were to have two sons, Alexander and Polycarp. However, owing to 'misdemeanours'—not specified by Lettsom—Myersbach had to leave Germany. After residing for a while in Amsterdam he moved to England, about 1772, but was very poor as he was unable to find work.

Myersbach first tried for a post with a starch manufacturer in Essex. Then, while lodging over a chandler's shop in Soho, London, he and his son Alexander developed 'the itch'. Not knowing how to treat this affliction he consulted a Dr Griffenberg, who lived nearby. Griffenberg directed him towards a job in a local riding school, but Myersbach failed as his figure was not imposing enough. Once cured of his affliction, however, he moved in with the doctor and soon acquired some expertise and much jargon. Griffenberg died not long afterwards, and in gratitude Myersbach undertook to pay a pension of 6s. a week to his widow.

In December 1773 Myersbach produced an advertisement which proclaimed, with some stretching of the truth, that 'Dr von Mayersbach' was newly arrived from Prague; he set himself up in Berwick Street, Soho. The practice of diagnosing ills from the scrutiny of a sufferer's urine went back fifteen centuries, the title of 'piss prophet' perhaps reflecting some lay contempt for this vocation. However, as Myersbach had such a slender grasp of medicine he chose this profession cannily, as no bodily examination was needed. He disguised his insignificant figure with very expensive apparel; that, and his elegant coach and horses, put people in awe of him. So did his pronouncements in very broken English. He would wave his hands some inches above the recumbent victim to discover the seat of the problem, and over some spot exclaim, 'It is here, it is here', moving on if the patient disagreed. Sometimes he knew precisely, because his employees had initiated or overheard conversations in the waiting room.

Lettsom asserted that Myersbach often made two hundred consultations daily, which would have meant treating one patient every three or four minutes during a twelve-hour day. More realistically he was supposed to earn 1000 guineas a month, equivalent to the income of a small German principality. He charged half a guinea per consultation and also received one-third of the income from the medicines he prescribed, each of which cost 7s.–10s. Lettsom bought and analysed some hundreds of Myersbach's prescriptions: a red powder contained saltpetre; green drops were a tincture of tansy; sweet drops consisted mostly of sugar; and black pills were made from a hallucinogenic mixture of brandy and opium.

Early in 1776 Myersbach moved from Soho to Hatton Garden in the City of London. That April, David Garrick, the actor, consulted him for the gout and the stone that had plagued him for many years, and found relief. Among other patients were Charles Lennox, the third duke of Richmond, and his wife, the first Baron Hawke, the second Baron Archer, and a Lady Harrington. However, at the beginning of 1777 Myersbach left Britain; perhaps the Royal College of Physicians had been asking awkward questions over his improperly describing himself as a doctor. At about this time Myersbach purchased a doctorate of medicine from the University of Erfurt in Thuringia, and within twelve months he was back in London, building up as extensive a following as before.

Lettsom for his part had learnt that unfortunately his relentless pillorying of Myersbach had entirely failed to break him. He in his turn had to face not only anonymous counter-attacks in the press and through pamphlets, but also some hostility from eminent colleagues, aware that Myersbach did cure cases that had baffled orthodox medicine. Myersbach continued his practice until he died in

London early in February 1798, after only a few hours' illness; he was described as a 'water-doctor'. Although clearly a wealthy man, no will under his name was sworn at the prerogative court of Canterbury. However, on 19 February of that year, the will of Alexander von Myersbach (no occupation being given), of Savile Row, London, was proved there. This rare substantive information gave the wife's name as Sarah. She may possibly have been Myersbach's second wife, as the two older sons were mentioned separately from two daughters Penelope and Caroline and a son Henry Ferdinand, then minors. Regrettably, Lettsom's sleuthing instincts were never brought to bear on the riddle of this final identification.

T. A. B. Corley

Sources J. C. Lettsom, 'Fugitive Pieces', Wellcome L., vols. 1–3 · J. C. Lettsom, *Observations preparatory to the use of Dr. Myersbach's medicines* (1776) · *GM*, 1st ser., 46 (1776), 520–21 · *GM*, 1st ser., 68 (1798), 175 · *The Times* (14 Feb 1798) · R. Porter, 'The controversy between Dr Theodor Myersbach and Dr. John Coakley Lettsom', *Medical fringe and medical orthodoxy, 1750–1850*, ed. W. F. Bynum and R. Porter (1987), 56–78 · R. Porter, *Health for sale: quackery in England, 1660–1850* (1989) · will, PRO, PROB 11/1302
Wealth at death see will, PRO, PROB 11/1302

Mykelfeld, William. *See* Macclesfield, William of (d. 1303).

Mylchreest, Joseph (1836/7–1896), diamond miner, was born at Shore Road, Peel, Isle of Man, the sixth of the ten children of John Mylchreest (1805–1862), mariner, and his wife, Christian Moore (1805–1867). He was baptized in the parish of German, Isle of Man on 15 September 1839. His father owned the Peel-built 71 ton sailing ship *Peveril* which traded around the British coast. Joe attended the Clothworkers' School in Peel before being apprenticed as a joiner in the shipyard of Henry Graves in Peel. On 14 November 1857, while still a minor, he married Catharine Skelly (1833/4–1858), daughter of a lead miner from Foxdale. His wife died the following March, following the birth of a daughter, who survived.

After his wife's death, Mylchreest worked his passage to Australia, and there joined his brothers Thomas and John, who had sailed the *Peveril* there, arriving in Melbourne in 1860. The brothers went to Ballarat in search of gold, but their efforts proved unrewarding, and they split up. Joe continued to pursue gold, travelling to New Zealand and on to British Columbia, the Yukon, California, Paraguay, Chile, and Peru. While working in a lead mine in Peru in 1872 he heard that diamonds had been found in southern Africa, and determined to go there next. He made his way via Australia, and arrived in Port Elizabeth in July 1876. He took a bullock wagon train to Kimberley, pitched his tent, and spent his last two shillings on tobacco and a drink.

Thousands of diamond prospectors were already at work in the Kimberley diamond fields, and Mylchreest began by panning in the Vaal River. Results were poor, and in 1878 he moved to the Dutoitspan mine, where he found work as a carpenter. In 1882 he married Phoebe Hannah Bishop (1862–1942), the daughter of a miner from Burford in Oxfordshire; they had five sons and a daughter. Soon after his marriage Joe noticed a small group of unworked claims in the Dutoitspan mine. They belonged to the

Royal Mining Company, and were available for lease at £300 a month. He borrowed the money for the first month's rent, and went to work. It was the turning point in his life. By hard work and personal leadership, Mylchreest became one of the most successful 'diamond diggers' in the Kimberley area: by 1885 he owned 115 claims in the mine. At one stage his hundreds of employees were moving the diamond-bearing 'blue ground' at the rate of one ton every thirty seconds. The claims were on a rich seam of diamonds; one, found in 1885, was 199 carats in weight. Split into two perfect stones, valued at £100,000, the 'Mylchreest diamond' was displayed at exhibitions in London and Chicago.

In 1886 Mylchreest took his family to visit the Isle of Man, where he was greeted with great enthusiasm and dubbed 'the Diamond King'. He returned to Kimberley (taking with him a group of miners from the depressed Manx mines), determined to sell out on the best possible terms and retire to his homeland. He approached Cecil Rhodes, whom he had known for some years and who was hoping to consolidate the control of his De Beers company over the diamond mines. In October 1887 Rhodes bought out Mylchreest for £115,000, but Mylchreest retained the right to work the claims for six months longer, and was allowed a further six months' 'washing up time'. He took full advantage of this time, working the mines twenty-four hours a day to extract as much as possible of the 'blue ground', which could then be 'washed up' to produce the diamonds at greater leisure. It was thought that he made more money in these last months than from the original sale.

Mylchreest and his family returned to the Isle of Man in November 1888. He was accorded a hero's welcome by the people of Peel, who were very proud of their returned native son. He purchased the White House Farm estate in Kirk Michael and stocked its 500 acres with pedigree animals. He lived there in the grand style of the Victorian self-made man, but retained his common touch. He was elected member of the House of Keys for Peel in 1891, and was a justice of the peace. He invested heavily in the island, both in agriculture and tourism, having a special interest in the development of Peel as a holiday resort. At the peak of his retirement, still full of energy and ideas, with a family of six young children (the youngest only a year old), Joseph Mylchreest died suddenly at the White House on 28 December 1896, at the age of fifty-nine. He was buried in the Peel new cemetery on new year's eve. Mylchreest was a huge man, 6 feet 4 inches tall, and weighing up to 20 stones, with black hair and a booming voice. A friend and neighbour, the popular novelist Sir Hall Caine (who drew on Mylchreest for several of his fictional creations), wrote of his:

> sterling manliness, which truckled to the rank and place of no man; of his generous humanity …; his generous heart … and of all the other qualities which made him in truth a man, and in the best and highest sense a nobleman. (Mylchreest, 51)

BRIAN MYLCHREEST

Sources A.W. Moore, *Manx worthies* (1901) • B. Mylchreest, *The Diamond King* (1994) • private information (2004) [Brian Mylchreest] • *Rand Daily Mail* (1880–89) • *Daily Telegraph* (29 Dec 1896) • *Isle of Man Times and General Advertiser* (2 Jan 1897) • *Peel City Guardian* (14 Dec 1888) • *Mona's Herald* (24 Nov 1886) • parish register, German, Isle of Man, 15 Sept 1839 [baptism] • m. cert. [Catharine Skelly]
Archives priv. coll.
Likenesses G. B. Cowin, photograph, 1893–7, priv. coll. • photographs, repro. in Mylchreest, *The Diamond King*
Wealth at death £200,000: probate and valuation documents

Myles, John. *See* Miles, John (1620/21–1683).

Myles [*née* Findlay], **Margaret Fraser** [Maggie] (1892–1988), midwife, was born at 52 Spital, Aberdeen, on 30 December 1892, the daughter of Robert Fraser Findlay, journeyman house painter, and his wife, Mary, *née* McDougall. Her father was a native of Aberdeen; her mother, who had been brought up in Selkirk in the Scottish borders, is believed to have been in domestic service before her marriage. Margaret Findlay spent her childhood in Aberdeen but emigrated from Scotland to Canada soon after leaving school and became engaged to a Canadian farmer, Charles James Myles (d. 1920). He was an officer in the Canadian army during the First World War, and while he was in France she trained as a nurse at Yorktown, Saskatchewan. They were married in 1919 and their son Ian was born in the following year. In that same year Charles Myles died and Margaret was left a widow with an infant son.

Myles returned to her parental home in Aberdeen and decided to train as a midwife and then to practise as a district nurse in and around the Aberdeenshire village of Alford. In 1924 her son died of pneumonia and she left Alford and went to repeat her nursing training at Edinburgh Royal Infirmary. She then returned to Canada, undertook an education course at McGill University, and subsequently worked in Philadelphia and Detroit as director of midwifery education. Around 1935 she had heard that a new maternity hospital was being built in Edinburgh and she decided this was where she would like to practise as a midwifery tutor. She therefore returned to the UK and took a midwifery teacher's diploma in London and in 1939, when the Simpson Memorial Maternity Pavilion was opened in Edinburgh, she was appointed midwifery tutor, a post she held for seventeen years.

Myles retired in 1954, the year after the publication of the first edition of her *Textbook for Midwives*. Before that she had contributed articles to professional journals in the UK, Canada, and the USA on midwifery and education, and had written a book on the care of babies for schoolchildren. Aware of the limited range of books available for midwifery education, she was commissioned by an altruistic Edinburgh publisher to write a textbook that would fill the gap. It quickly became a best-seller for the author and for Churchill Livingstone, the publishing house. As midwifery tutor she was always known as Mrs Myles, but through her textbook she became a household name, at least in maternity hospitals, as Maggie Myles, the author of the book that for some thirty years informed maternity practice and was used by midwives and medical students alike. In her lifetime ten different editions of the textbook were published, there were twenty reprints, and it was translated into five different languages, including Japanese. In 1985 it was said that the book was on sale in every country of the world except Russia, and at that time sixty per cent of the sales were in America. As part of the seventy-fifth anniversary celebrations of the *American Journal of Nursing*, Myles's *Textbook for Midwives* was identified as its book of the year.

Though Myles gave up her teaching and clinical responsibilities on her retirement, she remained very involved in midwifery and obstetric education and practice for many years. She did not hold sentimental links with past practices; she could remember the era when there was little or no antenatal care for pregnant women, and when maternal and infant mortality rates were so high that they represented a significant social problem. She was aware that well-trained and educated midwives were crucially important in lowering these mortality rates, and to this end she worked tirelessly, long into her retirement, ensuring that the information included in her textbook reflected current knowledge and developments. In Scotland she was a revered presence, but she travelled the world to promote the formal training of midwives and as a result became internationally known and respected as an authoritative lecturer on her chosen profession.

Myles was not seriously interested or involved in the politics of her profession or in those of the National Health Service, and she turned down many offers of honours and honorary appointments. An exception was in 1978 when she was made an honorary fellow of the Edinburgh Obstetrical Society, an award she felt was appropriate to her career and professional interests, and one which very few midwives achieved. Myles was a strong personality and a memorable teacher. In retirement, while she pursued interests in pottery, painting, and writing romantic fiction, her real and abiding interest remained midwifery. She died on 15 February 1988 at the Hillside Nursing Home, Banchory, Kincardineshire, not far from the village of Alford where she had lived with her infant son and where she first practised as a midwife. She was cremated the same month at Aberdeen crematorium. E. J. C. SCOTT

Sources S. Bramley and M. Turner, 'Mrs. Margaret Fraser Myles, 1892–1988', *Midwifery* (1988), 93-4 · L. Dobson, 'Gospel according to Myles', *Nursing Times* (18 July 1985) · 'The gospel according to Myles' [n.d.] [article in Longman's house magazine] · private information (2004) · b. cert. · d. cert.

Wealth at death £288,301.32: confirmation, 2 June 1988, *CCI*

Mylius, Hermann (1603–1657), diplomat, was born on 10 November 1603 in Berne, in the German principality of Oldenburg, perhaps the second of at least two sons of the miller Ocko Müller (*d*. 1625) and his first wife, who died in 1615. His humanist schooling began in that Lutheran town under Albertus Essenius, and continued at the *Gymnasium* in Hamburg and in 1616 at the University of Helmstedt. Mylius surfaces again in 1625–6 at the university in Rostock, where among his friends and contemporaries he could count the poet Johannes Rist. His legal studies then took him to the universities of Strasbourg (1627),

Hermann Mylius (1603–1657), by P. Aubry

Tübingen (1628), and Basel, where in 1632 he graduated with a licence in canon and civil law. In 1634 he matriculated as a student of law at Leiden, from where, however, he soon returned without a degree to Oldenburg. There he was appointed in July 1634 as a secretary in the chancellery of Graf (Count) Anton Günther (1583–1667), ruler of Oldenburg, and thus began a career as a diplomat.

Caught between the northern European great powers of the seventeenth century, the protestant principality of Oldenburg depended on skilful diplomacy to sustain its independence and neutrality, and also to keep secure its lucrative tolls on shipping on the River Weser. This was a formidable challenge during the Thirty Years' War, especially as Danish–Swedish conflict intensified. It was a challenge well met, to which Mylius made a major contribution. In 1636 his diplomacy led to the successful negotiation in Wismar with the Swedish chancellor Axel Oxenstierna, who accepted Oldenburg's neutrality despite its Danish connections. In late August 1637 the threat from Hessian forces led to Mylius's deputation to the Netherlands. That year he married Katharina Mausolius (1613–1655), daughter of Johannes Mausolius, treasurer of Oldenburg. In 1638 he went on a mission to England to persuade Charles I to press his nephew Karl Ludwig, the exiled elector palatine, not to embroil Oldenburg in the quest to retrieve his electorate. After arriving in England on 24 April, Mylius met Sir John Coke and had audiences with Charles I and his ministers. He befriended Georg Rudolph Weckherlin, the German poet who assisted the

English government as secretary for foreign correspondence; three years later he wrote to Weckherlin to congratulate him on his *Gaistliche und weltliche Gedichte*. The successful outcome of Mylius's audiences with the crown and its ministers allowed his departure by the end of May.

In the following years Mylius's tireless work on behalf of Oldenburg included representations in the treaties of Brömsebro (1645) and Osnabrück (1648), as the contest between Denmark and Sweden late in the Thirty Years' War continued to put his native principality under heavy diplomatic and economic pressure. With the conclusion of that long conflict, there was the further matter of withstanding Bremen's claims to the Weser tolls. Mylius's successes derived from his seasoned powers as a most persistent diplomat; his dispatches also mention many gifts—not least of horses from the famous Oldenburg stud—to be used in support of negotiations. His effectiveness found recognition from Graf Anton Günther. In 1646 he was made a regional justice of the peace (*Landrichter*) in Kniphausen, near the city of Oldenburg; in 1648 he was given the substantial estate of Gnadenfeld in the lowlands nearby; he also acquired through his wife a substantial house in Oldenburg, still standing in the twenty-first century. As Oldenburg's premier diplomat Mylius had frequent errands to run even after the peace of Westphalia (1648), especially as the complexities of international demobilization and war reparations required much negotiation, lest new instabilities follow or Oldenburg incur too much of the cost of settlement.

In the months preceding the outbreak of the First Anglo-Dutch War (1652–4), further diplomacy was required to maintain the neutrality of the Oldenburg flag. Mylius set out on 24 July 1651 on missions that led to an extended visit to England. His errand took him first to the Low Countries. Then, after a stormy crossing, he arrived at Margate on 26 August 1651 and went to London two days later. His diplomatic work toward gaining a safeguard (*salvaguardia*) for Oldenburg then encountered repeated setbacks. Delays in accreditation were not unusual in the Commonwealth, but in Mylius's case they were compounded in the aftermath of the battle of Worcester on 3 September by Commonwealth suspicions that Oldenburg might be sympathetic to the vanquished house of Stuart, and by a powerful mercantile interest stirred up by the Bremen agent in its resentment of the Weser tolls. Although Mylius renewed his acquaintance with Weckherlin and soon gained access to Sir Oliver Fleming, master of ceremonies, diplomatic business was languishing at this date, as major matters of state took precedence and there was much suspicion of foreign interference. To rewrite the safeguard and translate it into English, Mylius needed some well-placed English assistance, but he encountered much frustration on this front. His hopes of Henry Neville were dashed when that politician adhered to the council of state's decree against council members having any contact with foreigners. John Milton too did not at first respond to Mylius's approaches. However, on 20 October 1651 Fleming escorted Mylius to a meeting

with the lords commissioners Bulstrode Whitelocke, Henry Vane, Sir Henry Mildmay, and Sir John Trevor, with 'the great Milton' (*magnus Miltonius*) attending and serving as translator. Mylius proposed to work with Milton on successive drafts of the safeguard, though Milton's obligations to the council seemed at first to require frequent postponements of any personal visit. In November, Mylius came to believe that Milton would play no great role in promoting his business and instead turned his attentions to John Bradshaw, president of the council. Progress remained slow, however, and in December Mylius was still canvassing support at Whitehall in London, especially from Fleming, but also now from Hugh Peter, John Dury, and Milton again. Nevertheless, restrictions were still in place, and the arrival of a grand Dutch embassy in London on 17 December once more delayed progress on Oldenburg business. Only by the end of the month had a committee (comprising Neville, Thomas Challoner, John Lisle, and Whitelocke) been established to deal with it.

New year 1652 saw new developments. Mylius secured a private interview with Milton, who supplied the visitor with encouragement, co-operation on the Oldenburg safeguard, and books from his famous controversy with Salmasius. Milton later reminded Mylius that in doing so he had incurred suspicion for overstepping the limits on contact with foreigners. The outcome of the many successive drafts of the Oldenburg safeguard, the final version of which had been translated, met with initial review by the council of state on 20 January. Some concern about the Bremen interest prevented any ready assent to it, and the matter was postponed for further report by Neville and Challoner to the council—Neville, Mylius knew, was less of a friend to Oldenburg than Milton supposed and instead, like the mercantile interest in council and parliament, more sympathetic to Bremen's needs. Dutch and other negotiations then compounded this further delay. Mylius again reminded the English councillors of the terms of the treaty of Westphalia that had secured the Weser tolls for Oldenburg. In the meanwhile his legal training allowed him to prepare for the reforming Hugh Peter a summary of the Roman law on inheritance and succession.

Eventually Mylius's persistence led to the council of state referring a much revised safeguard to the standing committee on foreign affairs on 10 February. A week later the House of Commons voted on the safeguard and granted it. But nothing came of the provision that had been sought to extend its terms to cover the count of Oldenburgh's heirs and successors, because the Danish coolness to the new English republic occasioned fears that Oldenburg too might come to prove less neutral. On 20 February, Mylius learned from Fleming of this outcome, achieved just as the appearance on the scene of Hanseatic representatives threatened to undo his long efforts. Shortly after, a charge of bribery was made against Fleming by way of impugning his efforts on Oldenburg's behalf, but it was unsuccessful, and soon Mylius was free to leave. Having given a valedictory address to representatives of the council of state, and presented £25 to Milton and Frost, and £50 to Dury, in acknowledgement of their assistance, he departed London for the continent on 12 March 1652.

In his manuscript 'Relatio von der Gesandschaft nach London', and in his weekly letters to his friend Matthias Wolzogen von Missingdorff, Mylius left a record of his visit to England and acquaintance with Milton. Particularly notable in his accounts are the evident frustrations attendant on working with a young republic and his later verdict on Oliver Cromwell as a skilled actor (*histrio*). As an international humanist, learned circles in England were open to him: he was said to be a good poet, and the style of his letters lends some plausibility to this claim, but there may be some confusion with a contemporary namesake who was a poet in Cologne.

In the next few years Mylius engaged in further diplomatic activity, in missions to the electors in which he masterfully overcame fresh challenges from Bremen for the Weser tolls and also sought the legitimation of the son of Graf Anton Günther. In 1652 his services led to his elevation to the nobility, as Baron Mylius of Gnadenfeld. He happened to be at home in April 1654, when he suffered his first stroke. Despite sulphur baths and other cures of the day, he made only a partial recovery in the following months, though in 1656 he was appointed to the privy council of Graf Anton Günther. Mylius's wife died in 1655, and two years later he sustained a second and fatal stroke. He was buried in 1657 in St Lamberti Church in Oldenburg, but his monument there was lost when the church collapsed in 1791. His only son died childless.

NICHOLAS VON MALTZAHN

Sources Acta Grafsch, Oldenburg, Niedersächsisches Staatsarchiv, Oldenburg, Bestand 20, Titel 38, fasc. 1–14 [Mylius's journals and correspondence] · Acta Grafsch, Oldenburg, Niedersächsisches Staatsarchiv, Oldenburg, Bestand 20, Titel 42B, no. 4 [Mylius's record of his 1638 mission] · H. Mylius, *Kurzer, jedoch gründlicher Bericht was in der hochgräflich oldenburgischen Weser-Zoll-Sache von der Zeit der münsterischen Friedens-Tractates bis auf Ostern 1653 vorgegangen, mit angefügten 85 Beilagen zu jedmänniglicher Information* (1653) · H. Lübbing, 'Hermann Mylius (1603–1657): oldenburgische Rat, Landrichter und Diplomat', *Oldenburgische Familienkunde*, 9 (1967), 538–57 · L. Miller, *John Milton and the Oldenburg safeguard* (1985) · *The works of John Milton*, ed. F. A. Patterson, 18 vols. (1931–8), vol. 12, pp. 337–79; vol. 18, pp. 484–92 · *Complete prose works of John Milton*, ed. D. Wolfe, 8 vols. in 10 (1953–82), vol. 4, pp. 828–51 · H. Friedl, 'Mylius von Gnadenfeld (Müller)', in H. Friedl and others, *Biographisches Handbuch zur Geschichte des Landes Oldenburg* (1992), 509–10 · H. Friedl, 'Mylius, Hermann', *Neue deutsche Biographie*, 18 (Berlin, 1996), 669–70 · K. Düssmann, 'Graf Anton Günther von Oldenburg und der westfälische Friede', *Oldenburgische Forschungen*, 1 (1935) · G. Rüthning, *Oldenburgische Geschichte* (1937)
Likenesses A. van Hulle, engraving, 1649, repro. in *Celeberrimi ad pacificandum christiani nominis orbem legati* (Antwerp, 1648–56) · P. Aubry, engraving, AM Oxf. [see illus.]

Myllar [Millar], **Andrew** (*fl.* 1503–1508), printer, may have been born in Fife if identifiable with the Andreas Myllar who was incorporated at St Andrews University in 1492 but did not complete his studies. The first firm evidence of Myllar's career dates from 29 March 1503 when he was paid £10 for delivering a number of works on canon law and theology to James IV, 'viz. Decretum Magnum, Decretales Sextus cum Clementinis, Scotus super quatuor libris sententiarum, Quartum Scoti, Opera Gersonis in tribus voluminibus' (Dickson and Edmond, 25). Myllar's name appears in the colophon of *Multorum vocabulorum equivocorum interpretatio* printed by Pierre Violette in Rouen in 1505 while another work, *Expositio sequentiarum, seu prosarum*, printed by Violette a year later, bears Myllar's device, suggesting that the Scot was probably in France at that time. Both works were evidently aimed at the English market: the interpretation of the *Multorum* was in English and the *Expositio* was according to the use of Sarum. These works may explain his absence and the consequent involvement of his wife in the delivery of 50s. worth of books to the king on 22 December 1507.

On 15 September 1507 Myllar and Walter *Chepman (1471?–1528), both described as burgesses of Edinburgh, were granted a patent by James IV to set up the first printing house in Scotland:

> to furnis and bring hame ane prent, with all stuff belangand tharto, and expert men to use the samyne, for imprinting within our Realme of the bukis of our Lawis, actis of parliament, croniclis, mess bukis, and portuus efter the use of our Realme, with addicions and legendis of Scottis sanctis, now gaderit to be ekit tharto, and al utheris bukis that salbe sene necessar, and to sel the sammyn for competent pricis. (Dickson and Edmond, 8)

Bishop William Elphinstone—'whose *Breviarium Aberdonense* of 1510 was the press's *magnum opus*'—seems to have been instrumental in securing this grant (Mann, 7–8). With Chepman providing the capital and court connections and Myllar the printing experience, the two men set up their shop in the Southgait (or Cowgate) of Edinburgh.

What seems to be the first print from their press—and hence the first book printed in Scotland—was *The Maying or Disport of Chaucer* (actually a work by John Lydgate) which appeared on 4 April 1508. It includes the devices of both Myllar and Chepman; Myllar's device (involving a pun on his name, portraying a miller climbing a ladder into a windmill) also appears in *The Knightly Tale of Golagros and Gawane*, *The Porteous of Noblenes*, William Dunbar's *The Golden Targe*, and *The Ballade of Lord Barnard Stewart*, *The Flyting of Dunbar and Kennedy*, and Robert Henryson's *The Tale of Orpheus and Eurydice*. In two items, his name appears in the imprint as 'Millar'. Chepman went on to print Elphinstone's *Breviarium Aberdonense* in two volumes (1509–10), but by this time Myllar was no longer his partner. If Myllar was indeed the Andreas Myllar at St Andrews in 1492, it seems likely he was the Andreas Millar who reappeared there in 1509 and once again failed to continue his graduate studies. There is otherwise no further information about his subsequent career. JOHN DURKAN

Sources R. Dickson and J. P. Edmond, *Annals of Scottish printing* (1890) · J. M. Anderson, ed., *Early records of the University of St Andrews*, Scottish History Society, 3rd ser., 8 (1926), 190, 204 · M. Livingstone, D. Hay Fleming, and others, eds., *Registrum secreti sigilli regum Scotorum / The register of the privy seal of Scotland*, 2 (1921), 1346 · W. K. Sessions and E. M. Sessions, eds., *Printing in York from the 1490s to the present day* (1976), 10–11 · *The protocol book of John Foular*, ed. M. Wood, 2, Scottish RS, 72 (1941) · J. B. Paul, ed., *Compota thesaurariorum regum Scotorum / Accounts of the lord high treasurer of Scotland*, 2

(1900); 4 (1902) · *STC, 1475–1640* · E. G. Duff, *A century of the English book trade* (1905) · A. J. Mann, *The Scottish book trade, 1500–1720* (2000)

Mylne, Alexander (*c.*1470–1548), abbot of Cambuskenneth and historian, who about 1534 was said to be in his sixty-fourth year, was born in Angus (Forfarshire) and may have been the son of John Mylne, master mason to James III and James IV. Having graduated BA at St Andrews University in 1494, he acted as clerk and archivist to the official of Dunkeld for three years, and by 1500 he was notary public by apostolic authority. On 19 October 1501 he is recorded as scribe to George Brown, bishop of Dunkeld. In 1505 he became dean of the Christianity of Angus (rural dean), and in the same year parson of Lundeiff. By 7 April 1506 he had become a canon of Dunkeld Cathedral. In 1512 he is recorded as holding the prebend of Moneydie (and also that of Philorth in the diocese of Aberdeen), and in 1513 he became official of Dunkeld. In 1516 he was presented to the Augustinian abbey of Cambuskenneth; papal provision followed in 1519. Mylne had already showed himself a man of practical talents, being appointed in 1510 as master of the works at the bridge of Dunkeld; as abbot he oversaw substantial building works, leading to the rededication of the church, buildings, and cemetery, on 11 June 1521.

His abilities had also caused Mylne to become involved in secular government. In the years after the battle of Flodden he gave his support to the duke of Albany as governor, and with the bishops of Dunkeld and Ross acted to secure French support for the defence of Scotland against further English attacks, while also investigating the possibility of a marriage treaty between the French and Scottish crowns. It was Albany who petitioned the papacy for Mylne's appointment to Cambuskenneth. Mylne subsequently became master mason to the young James V. In 1524 he went on embassy to England, and in the following year he was appointed one of the guardians of the king, who was still a minor. In 1528 he was present at the execution of Patrick Hamilton for heresy. A regular attendant at parliament, notably as a lord of the articles between 1532 and 1542, in the former year he was appointed first president of the newly established college of justice, an office he retained until his death. In 1539, moreover, he was appointed to be coadjutor to, and administrator for, two of the king's illegitimate sons, Robert Stewart, who was commendator of Holyrood Abbey, and James Stewart, the commendator of St Andrews Priory.

In spite of these secular employments Mylne was clearly a conscientious abbot, who showed himself aware of contemporary calls for improved standards in Scotland's monasteries. Writing to the abbot of St Victor in Paris in a letter dated 15 June 1522, he asked for aid in reviving the observance of the rule of St Augustine at Cambuskenneth, and declared his intention that novices from his own house should be trained and educated at St Victor, both to enable them to set an example to their brethren at Cambuskenneth, and to equip them better for the performance of the divine offices. In his efforts to protect monastic interests, Mylne was prepared to oppose the king himself, when James tried to exploit the revenues of Holyrood and St Andrews after granting them to his sons. In an indignant letter sent to Pope Paul III on 5 June 1540, the king revealed that Mylne had refused to allow lands belonging to these monasteries to be leased out in the names of the two commendators, who were little more than boys. Mylne's services to his own monastery included the preservation of its records, which he found in a confused and dilapidated condition, and which he caused to be transcribed; the result of his activities was a new abbey register, completed in 1535.

Mylne was a historian as well as an abbot who was aware of the importance of his house's archive. His only certain work is his *Vitae Dunkeldensis ecclesiae episcoporum*, consisting of the lives of the bishops of Dunkeld from 1127 to 1515. Probably completed by 1517 it is largely valueless for the early bishops, but it becomes a useful and sometimes important source as it comes closer to its author's own time, in spite of a predominantly eulogistic tone. Thus it contains valuable information on the episcopate of George Brown, from 1484 to 1515, for instance on the manoeuvrings whereby he obtained his see. It is probable that Mylne was also the author of the historical text known as *Extracta e variis cronicis Scocie*, a work heavily dependent on Bower but making use of material from Cambuskenneth as well, and with many close parallels in Mylne's *Vitae*. Like the latter work it is demonstrably incorrect on some points, while also containing information not found elsewhere. Mylne's death, in July 1548, deprived the Scottish crown and church alike of a versatile, intelligent, and principled servant.   J. A. GOULD

Sources W. Fraser, ed., *Registrum monasterii S. Marie de Cambuskenneth*, Grampian Club, 4 (1872), lxxxviii–xcvi · J. M. Thomson and others, eds., *Registrum magni sigilli regum Scotorum / The register of the great seal of Scotland*, 11 vols. (1882–1914), vol. 2, nos. 2608, 2955, 3098, 3151, 3482; vol. 3, nos. 113, 138, 233, 354, 484, 492, 605, 607, 615, 627, 1758, 1844, 2232, 2262, 2611 · H. M. Paton, ed., *Accounts of the masters of works for building and repairing royal palaces and castles* (1957), vol. 1 (1529–1615), 55, 114, 195, 196, 197, 234, 310 · M. Livingstone, D. Hay Fleming, and others, eds., *Registrum secreti sigilli regum Scotorum / The register of the privy seal of Scotland*, 8 vols. (1908–82), vol. 1, no. 2681; vol. 2, nos. 3096–7 · APS, 1424–1567, 291–2, 295–6, 300, 304, 321, 334–7, 339–401, 352–41, 383–4, 404 · *The letters of James V*, ed. R. K. Hannay and D. Hay (1954), 32, 42–5, 90–91, 399–400 · D. E. R. Watt, ed., *Fasti ecclesiae Scoticanae medii aevi ad annum 1638*, [2nd edn], Scottish RS, new ser., 1 (1969), 125 · J. Dowden, *The bishops of Scotland … prior to the Reformation*, ed. J. M. Thomson (1912), 44, 77, 81, 86, 266 · G. G. Coulton, ed., *Commentary on the rule of St Augustine by Robert Richardinus*, Scottish History Society, 3rd ser., 26 (1935), 3, 92, 127 · M. G. J. Kinloch, *A history of Scotland* (1888), vol. 1, p. 328 · R. S. Mylne, *The master masons to the crown of Scotland and their works* (1893), 17–35 · G. Brunton and D. Haig, *An historical account of the senators of the college of justice, from its institution in MDXXXII* (1832), 5–10 · *DSCHT*, 616 · C. McGladdery, *James II* (1990)

Mylne, Alexander (1613–1643). *See under* Mylne, John (1611–1667).

Mylne, Andrew (1776–1856), schoolmaster and Church of Scotland minister, born at Haddington, East Lothian, Scotland, was the son of Andrew M. Mylne, fuller, and his wife, Jean Harkis. Educated at the local grammar school, Mylne (pronounced Mill) later ran an English school in Edinburgh, at the same time composing textbooks and contributing articles to David Brewster's *Edinburgh Encyclopaedia*. He also tutored the children of the Edinburgh lawyer and Clackmannanshire landowner, Craufurd Tait, then in dispute with the minister of the tiny parish of Dollar in Clackmannanshire over a legacy for a poor school left in 1802 by a London shipowner, Captain John McNabb. Tait and other parishioners preferred a free day school for the parish to the session's plan for an elementary charity boarding-school. Tait bought the advowson of the living of Dollar in 1805 and commenced to block the kirk session's plan.

In 1807, probably with Tait's assistance, Mylne attended Edinburgh University, graduating MA in 1810, and thereafter commencing to study for the ministry, becoming a probationer in the Church of Scotland in 1812. On the death of the incumbent minister of Dollar in 1815, Tait immediately appointed Mylne in his place. Mylne, as chief trustee, transferred control over the disputed bequest, amounting to the then vast sum of £92,345, from chancery to the Scottish Court of Session. He proceeded to set up a school, commissioning the architect, William Playfair, to design a splendid building, and appointing staff, including a surgeon and midwife for the poor. A man of great erudition and energy, Mylne was set on creating what he called 'a Great Academy or Seminary of Education', in which the poor would receive free education as a 'right', while the richer pupils would have the 'privilege' of sharing it by paying fees on a sliding scale. A boarding element was also to be included to 'improve the manners and effect a new stimulus to exertion'.

Pupils attended only the subjects of their choice from an extensive curriculum offering: English grammar, writing, arithmetic, book-keeping, history, mathematics, astronomy, navigation, science, geography, Latin, Greek, Hebrew, Persic, French, Italian, German, drawing (artistic and technical), sewing, and botany. The grounds were planned as 'Oeconomic and Botanic Gardens' to train a small number of garden apprentices, eventually producing head gardeners for Windsor, Kew, and Canada. Later, an infant school for three- to five-year-olds and evening classes for adults were instituted. This remarkable concept of a school for both rich and poor, which was, in modern terms, both co-educational and comprehensive, soon proved successful and its blend of parish children and boarders lasted, with the later co-operation of the county council, until local government reform in 1975.

Mylne was awarded a DD by Glasgow University in 1821 and was elected to the Royal Physical Society and the Society of Scottish Antiquaries. As minister he was also responsible for the erection of a new parish church in 1841 (designed by William Tite, architect of the London Royal Exchange) and for the learned parish entry in the second statistical account of 1841. In 1844, aged sixty-eight and in failing health, Mylne married Barbara (*d.* 1879), daughter of Captain Macaulay, RM. He retired as principal of Dollar Academy in 1849 and died at his home, St Columba's Manse, Dollar, on 27 October 1856. He was buried in Dollar cemetery, on the site of his pulpit within the ruin of the old parish church. B. E. BAILLIE

Sources E. G. Taylor, 'Dr Andrew Mylne', *Dollar Magazine*, 54 (1956), 219 · J. M. C. Wilson, *A history of Dollar Academy* (*c.*1930) · J. Tait, *Dollar past and present* (1885) · Dollar Academy, Clackmannanshire, archives · *Fasti Scot.*, new edn, 4.307 · Dollar parish register

Likenesses death mask, 1856, Dollar Academy, Clackmannanshire · G. H. Paulin, statuette, *c.*1940, Dollar Academy, Clackmannanshire · I. A. Campbell, oils, 1965 (after portrait by unknown artist destroyed 1961), Dollar Academy, Clackmannanshire

Wealth at death £1420: Dollar Academy, Clackmannanshire, archives

Mylne, James (1738/9–1788), poet and tenant farmer, was the son of George Mylne (*d.* 1744), farmer, of Barns, Haddingtonshire. A precocious poet, Mylne seems to have inked a small collection of juvenile verse while attending the grammar school of Dalkeith. Many of these early odes, epistles, fables, and songs touch on the sensitive nerve of class. The favourite target of his sense of position when young was Henry Dundas of Arniston (later the first Viscount Melville). Dundas played the role of 'the oak'—'So straight so vigorous while so young'—to Mylne's 'ivy' who, 'deny'd' by 'Fate', would never 'rise' along with the oak like a 'crown of laurel', but was destined to 'creep contented' in some 'poor shrub'ry'. This last was, in fact, a most pleasant farm cottage situated on a gentle slope rising up towards the Garleton Hills, and known throughout the region as 'Lochhill' (sometimes 'Lochill').

Mylne married Marion Rannie who died in 1809, aged sixty-three. Their sons George and James were baptized at the parish church in Aberlady in November 1762 and August 1766. Mylne died of an 'inflammatory fever' at Lochhill on 9 December 1788, aged forty-nine, and was buried in the family plot at Aberlady parish church. Lochhill remained in the Mylne family, through James and Marion's numerous grandchildren, until at least the end of the next century.

Mylne's overtures to Burns, like himself a farmer–poet, have brought him a notoriety that his writing might not otherwise have warranted. His poem 'To Mr Burns, On his Poems', an invitation to Burns to visit him on his farm, was a late composition, and was delivered to Burns only after Mylne's death, in January 1789. Burns's response came in March, when he wrote that 'my success has encouraged such a shoal of ill-spawned monsters to crawl into public notice, under the title of Scottish poets' (letter to Mrs Dunlop, 4 March 1789). Burns expressed the wish that Mylne had never desecrated the Scots tongue, but did think that Mylne's English pieces should be published, and not just for 'pity to that family'.

In 1790 Mylne's son George published his father's works in *Poems, Consisting of Miscellaneous Pieces and Two Tragedies*. He dedicated the volume to his father's youthful friend Henry Dundas, and alluded to Dundas's fidelity to the memory of that friendship of his 'early youth', and to his exertions 'in favour of merit and virtue' and for those who prove 'an advantage and ornament to their country'. Clearly, George saw his father as such an 'ornament', a 'man of virtue' known among his friends for his 'unaffected modesty, warm and generous feelings, an amiable simplicity of manners, and uncorrupted integrity of heart'.   J. C. STEWART-ROBERTSON

Sources D. E. Baker, *The companion to the play-house*, 1 (1764); new edn pubd as *Biographia dramatica, or, A companion to the playhouse*, rev. I. Reed (1782); new edn, rev. S. Jones (1812), 537 • T. Tobin, *Plays by Scots, 1660–1800* (1974), 222 • T. Grieder, 'Annotated checklist of the British drama, 1789–99', *Restoration and Eighteenth-Century Theatre Research*, 4/1 (1965), 21–47 • *The works of Robert Burns*, another edn, ed. C. Annandale, 4 (1888), 129–31 • M. Lindsay, *The Burns encyclopedia*, 3rd edn (1980), 69, 253–4 • [Clarke], *The Georgian era: memoirs of the most eminent persons*, 4 vols. (1832–4) • *Memorials of his time, by Henry Cockburn*, another edn, ed. H. A. Cockburn (1910) • *Scots Magazine*, 50 (1788), 623 • J. Stone, *Illustrated maps of Scotland from Blaeu's 'Atlas novus' of the 17th century* (1991), pl. no. 5 • *Scottish church records* (1995) [parish church of Aberlady, East Lothian] • monumental inscription, Aberlady parish church, East Lothian
Wealth at death Lochhill was a not insubstantial legacy: General Register Office for Scotland, Edinburgh

Mylne, James (1757–1839), philosopher and political reformer, was born on 3 September 1757, probably at the manse at Kinnaird in Gowrie, Perthshire, the seventh of nine children of the Revd James Mylne (d. 1783), Church of Scotland minister of that parish, and Janet, *née* Faichney (d. 1790). Between 1770 and 1772 he was educated at the University of St Andrews, to where he returned as a divinity student in 1774–5 and 1778–9, before being licensed and ordained by the presbytery of Dundee in his final year of study.

In 1783, after serving as a deputy chaplain in the 83rd regiment of foot, Mylne was presented by the earl of Abercorn to the congregation of Paisley Abbey, where he was admitted minister of the second charge on 27 March. On 24 August 1789 he married Grizel Davidson (d. 1790). Mylne held his post at Paisley until August 1797 when, on the death of Archibald Arthur, he was unanimously elected to the chair of moral philosophy at Glasgow University. On 26 June of the following year he married Agnes (d. 1827), daughter of John Millar, professor of civil law at the university.

As a philosopher Mylne's thinking was heavily influenced by the French sensationalist school of Condillac, whose teaching he adopted in his critique of the recent work of his eminent Edinburgh counterpart, Dugald Stewart. From four sets of extant student lecture notes taken over his long career, Mylne's preference for the sensationalist approach over the teaching of Stewart, as well as over the common-sense philosophy of Thomas Reid and Humean scepticism, emerges clearly. Sensationalism brought with it the charge of philosophical radicalism from students such as David Murray. Mylne was accused of undermining certain fundamental or instinctive principles of belief which governed relations to external reality, to memory, and even to the self.

Such elemental radicalism went hand in hand with Mylne's political activities and affiliations during his long teaching career at Glasgow. During the 1790s he showed an open avowal of liberal, reformist, and at times radical principles. Soon after taking up his chair at Glasgow, Mylne was appointed clerk of the senate and clerk of the

faculty of the university (1799–1802). Later he served as vice-rector (1805–7) and, two years on, as college chaplain (1809–19). It was in this capacity that he achieved notoriety as a political radical. In March 1815 he was accused of treason after purportedly offering prayers for Napoleon. Mylne vigorously defended himself and claimed that lawyers, academics, and clergymen were now in danger of prosecution when Biblical readings 'may be converted into "subject matter of a precognition"' (U. Glas., Archives and Business Records Centre, pamphlet 30383, 57). Subsequent to the ill-fated chapel prayers of 1815, Mylne's meeting with the Irish political reformer Daniel O'Connell, and with William Cobbett during his visit to Glasgow in 1832, confirms his place as a member of the 'old steady Whig faction' that made up the city's reform-minded Crow Club (Strang, 548).

Among Mylne's more distinguished pupils, James McCosh—later the president of Princeton University—left a rather unflattering picture of his ability as a teacher, no doubt owing in part to McCosh's preference for the work of Reid and Stewart. Nevertheless, if Mylne's account of the mind and its ideas was adjudged 'cool' and his sermons 'cold', his lectures offered a 'searching' examination of every subject. In this respect the 'radical' equal of Thomas Brown at Edinburgh or the utilitarian James Mill, it was McCosh's view that Mylne's 'liberalism' so infected his tone that he was regarded by many as 'secretly a rationalist or a Socinian' (McCosh, *Scottish Philosophy*).

Following the death of his second wife, Agnes, in 1827, Mylne remained active in organizations such as the College Club, and in the welfare of students past and present. He died in Glasgow on 21 September 1839, and was survived by four sons.   J. C. STEWART-ROBERTSON

Sources *University of Glasgow* (1837), vol. 2 of *Evidence, oral and documentary, taken and received by the commissioners … for visiting the universities of Scotland* • *Fasti Scot.*, new edn, 3.169; 5.346 • J. McCosh, 'Scottish metaphysicians', *North British Review*, 27 (1857), 402–34 • J. McCosh, *The Scottish philosophy: biographical, expository, critical, from Hutcheson to Hamilton* (1875), article 48 • D. Murray, *Memories of the old college of Glasgow: some chapters in the history of the university* (1927) • J. Strang, *Glasgow and its clubs* (1856) • G. Gilfillan, *The history of a man* (1856), 87ff. • J. Coutts, *A history of the University of Glasgow* (1909) • W. C. Lehmann, *John Millar of Glasgow, 1735–1801* (1960) • J. Young, *Lectures on intellectual philosophy*, ed. W. Cairns (1835) • testament dative of James Mylne, NA Scot., no. 8921/4
Wealth at death £673 6s. 3d.: will, NA Scot., 8921/4

Mylne, John (d. 1621), mason, was the son of the mason Thomas Mylne (*fl.* 1561–1593), possibly identifiable with the Thomas Mylne buried in Elgin in 1605. Masons from the Mylne family were active in Dundee in the sixteenth century, supplying stone for royal works and other projects from the quarries at Kingudie, near Dundee. Although neither John nor his father was appointed royal master mason by privy seal, family tradition held that he was the fourth in a direct line to fill that office. A pedigree of royal masons is also claimed in a document drawn up in 1658 by the lodge of Scone at Perth, of which John Mylne was probably master.

According to a seventeenth-century Somerville family

chronicle, which describes him as the king's master mason, in 1584–5 Mylne was engaged in building Drum House, Edinburgh, subsequently to be remodelled by William Adam. He was afterwards employed on several public works at Dundee, and was on 12 September 1587 admitted a burgess, 'for service done and to be done' (Mylne, 66) to the burgh, in particular rebuilding the harbour works. In 1586 he erected the market cross in the High Street, which was subsequently removed in 1777; the shaft was re-erected in 1874 in the grounds of the town's church. In 1589, with another Dundee mason, George Thomson, he contracted with Thomas Bannatyne, senator of the college of justice, to build a gallery and other additions to his house at Kirktoun of Newtyle, Forfarshire, long known as Bannatyne House.

In 1599 fund-raising began for the erection of the bridge over the Tay at Perth; on 17 July 1605 John Mylne and his men started work. In consequence of his connection with the project he was admitted 'frelie' a burgess in 1607. After considerable delay, the bridge appears to have been completed about 1617. It was destroyed by a flood on 4 October 1621, and was not replaced; the present bridge, erected in 1766–71, is built over a broader part of the river. The lodge of Scone claimed in 1658 that, under his mastership, Mylne had entered James VI as 'frieman Meason and fellow craft'. Mylne died in 1621, probably in Perth, and was buried in the town's Greyfriars churchyard, where there is a stone, originally the top stone of a table monument, with a verse epitaph. Robert Mylne (1734–1811) placed a mural tablet near the tomb in 1774.

John Mylne (d. 1657), son of John Mylne and his wife, Helen Kennereis, assisted his father as mason on the bridge at Perth; he was called to Edinburgh in 1616 by the town council to complete a statue of James I at the Netherbow port, and in acknowledgement of this and other works in the town was made a burgess of Edinburgh on 4 June 1617. On 19 January 1620 he was commissioned by David, lord of Scone, to erect Falkland church (rebuilt 1849–50). From 1619 to 1623 he supplied dressed stone from Kingudie for the steeple of the tolbooth at Aberdeen, and was in consequence made a burgess of the city ex gratia on 12 May 1622. He was admitted as a burgess of Dundee on 24 March 1627. Assisted by his sons, he made alterations at Drummond Castle, Perthshire, in 1629–30 and carved the garden sundial. He constructed a water-pond by the palace of Holyroodhouse for the king in 1629. With the help of his sons John *Mylne (1611–1667) and Alexander *Mylne (1613–1643) [see under Mylne, John (1611–1667)] he carved the polyhedron sundial at the palace of Holyroodhouse in 1633. He was appointed principal master mason of all Scotland to Charles I on 17 December 1631, but resigned in favour of his son John in 1636. He was engaged on the church steeple, tolbooth, and fortifications at Dundee from 1643 to 1651. Mylne was made fellow of craft in the lodge of Edinburgh in October 1633, and was master of the lodge at Scone from 1621 to 1657. On 23 March 1643 he was admitted gratis as a burgess of Kirkcaldy, where he repaired and enlarged the burgh church. He married Isobel Wilson of Perth in January 1610, and

died between September and December 1657. His daughter Barbara, born in Edinburgh in 1617, is frequently mentioned in the Canongate and Edinburgh burgh records as being accused of witchcraft.

BERTHA PORTER, rev. DEBORAH HOWARD

Sources NA Scot., Mylne family MSS, GD1/51 · RIBA BAL, Mylne family MSS · R. S. Mylne, *The master masons to the crown of Scotland and their works* (1893) · Colvin, *Archs.* · J. Maidment, ed., *The Chronicle of Perth from the year 1210–1668* (1831) · M. Wood, ed., *Extracts from the records of the burgh of Edinburgh, 1604–1626*, [7] (1931) · J. Imrie and J. G. Dunbar, eds., *Accounts of the masters of works for building and repairing royal palaces and castles*, 2 (1982) · J. Somerville, *Memorie of the Somervilles: being a history of the baronial house of Somerville*, ed. W. Scott, 2 vols. (1815), vol. 1, pp. 459–61 · H. Adamson, *The muse's threnodie*, ed. J. Cant, 2 vols. (1774), vol. 1, pp. 79–82 · D. MacGibbon and T. Ross, *The castellated and domestic architecture of Scotland*, 5 vols. (1887–92), vol. 5, pp. 417–18, 441–3 · T. H. Marshall, *The history of Perth from the earliest period to the present time* (1849), 461, 467–8 · Dunelm, 'Robert Mylne, etc.', *N&Q*, 2nd ser., 12 (1861), 223 · *Tolbooths and town houses: civic architecture in Scotland to 1833*, Royal Commission on the Ancient and Historical Monuments of Scotland (1996), 13, 30 · A. Maxwell, *The history of old Dundee* (1884)
Archives NA Scot., family MSS, GD1/51 · RIBA BAL, family MSS
Likenesses oils (John Mylne), Scot. NPG · pencil drawing (John Mylne), Scot. NPG

Mylne, John (d. 1657). See under Mylne, John (d. 1621).

Mylne, John (1611–1667), master mason, son of John *Mylne (d. 1657) [see under Mylne, John (d. 1621)] and his wife, Isobel Wilson, was probably born in Perth. He served an apprenticeship with his father, and before 1634 he married Agnes (Ann) Fraser of Edinburgh; after her death (after 1642) he married, on 11 February 1647, Janet Primrose, who died soon after, for on 27 April 1648 he married Janet Fowlis.

On 9 October 1633 Mylne was admitted a burgess of Edinburgh, by right of descent, and on the same day was made fellow of craft in the Edinburgh masonic lodge. He succeeded his father as principal master mason to the crown of Scotland on 1 February 1636, and in the same year, as deacon of the masons of Edinburgh, was for the first time elected their representative on the town council. In 1637 he was appointed master mason to the town of Edinburgh. He designed the Tron Church in Edinburgh, begun in 1637 and opened in 1647; the roof was not completed until 1663. The church was truncated in 1788, and the spire was burnt in 1824, when it was rebuilt in its present form.

In August 1637 Mylne restored the great east window of St Giles's Church, Edinburgh. He designed Cowane's Hospital, Stirling, erected in 1637–48, carving the statue of the benefactor himself. He was employed in strengthening Edinburgh Castle in 1639–40. In 1642 he surveyed and reported on the condition of the abbey church at Jedburgh, and was appointed a burgess of Jedburgh. He was appointed master mason to Heriot's Hospital, Edinburgh, in 1643 and continued the works there until their completion in 1659. At the college of Edinburgh he designed and carved the monument to its benefactor Bartholomew Somervell (d. 1640), later moved to Craighall Rattray, Blairgowrie, Perthshire. In 1646 he repaired the crown steeple of St Giles's Church, Edinburgh. In 1649–50 he was busy on the fortifications of both Leith and Edinburgh. He proposed works to Newbattle Abbey, Edinburghshire (1650), Coldingham church, Berwickshire, and Addiston House, Ratho (both 1661).

In 1656 Mylne contracted to build a house for the professor of divinity and lodgings for six students at the college of Edinburgh; four years later he reconstructed the dam on the Water of Leith, and in the same year, together with his son-in-law the wright John Smith, began to rebuild Edinburgh's weigh-house. He made a survey of the palace of Holyroodhouse with proposed new additions, dated 1663, now in the Bodleian Library, Oxford. In 1666 he began Panmure House, Forfarshire, demolished in 1955; and in the same year he added a staircase to Balgonie Castle, Fife. In November 1667 he made a design for the town hall or tolbooth at Linlithgow, erected to another design by John Smith after his death. At the time of his death late in 1667 Mylne was engaged in the remodelling of Leslie House, Fife.

Mylne's activity was not confined to his professional work. He was also an expert in fortification, a politician, and a pioneer freemason. On 4 September 1646 Charles I appointed him captain of pioneers and principal master gunner of all Scotland, confirmed by Charles II on 31 December 1664, together with the post of royal master mason. In August 1652 he was chosen to represent the convention of royal burghs at the English parliament in London. He returned to Edinburgh in July 1653, and either he or his father was present at Perth on 12 May 1654 on the proclamation of Cromwell as lord protector. In November 1655, when a member of the Edinburgh town council, he was asked to advise the burgh over the economical subdivision of parish churches, but was accused in the diary of John Nicoll of having led the town into much expense by constant alteration of its churches. From 1655 to 1659 he represented the city of Edinburgh at the convention of royal burghs. In 1662 he was elected MP for Edinburgh in the parliament of Scotland, and attended the first and second sessions of Charles II's first parliament in Edinburgh. Late in 1667 he was invited by the town council of Perth to erect a market cross in that town, but died in Edinburgh on 24 December. He was buried on 28 December in Greyfriars churchyard, where a handsome monument was erected by his nephew Robert *Mylne (1633–1710). The epitaphs describe him as 'Great Artisan, Grave Senator' and most expert in architecture ('artis architectonicae eximie perito'). In 1668 his portrait and a commemorative inscription were placed over the door of Mary's Chapel, Edinburgh's masonic lodge, where he had served ten times as deacon.

Alexander Mylne (1613–1643), probably born in Perth and brother of John, was a sculptor who worked on many of his brother's buildings, on the parliament house (1635–7) and other public buildings in Edinburgh. His statues of Justice and Mercy remained at the parliament house, although not in their original position. He was made fellow of craft in the lodge of Edinburgh on 2 January 1635. About 1632 he married Anna Vegilman, with whom he had two sons and one daughter. Robert Mylne (1633–1710)

was the elder son. He died at Canongate, Edinburgh, on 20 February 1643, apparently of the plague, and was buried in Holyrood Abbey, where a monument, with Latin and English inscriptions to his memory, is fixed against the north-east buttress of the abbey church.

BERTHA PORTER, *rev.* DEBORAH HOWARD

Sources NA Scot., Mylne family MSS, GD1/51 • RIBA BAL, Mylne family MSS • R. S. Mylne, *The master masons to the crown of Scotland and their works* (1893) • Colvin, *Archs.* • M. Wood, ed., *Extracts from the records of the burgh of Edinburgh, 1626–1641*, [8] (1936) • M. Wood, ed., *Extracts from the records of the burgh of Edinburgh, 1642–1655*, [9] (1938) • M. Wood, ed., *Extracts from the records of the burgh of Edinburgh, 1655–1665*, [10] (1940) • *An inventory of the ancient and historical monuments of the city of Edinburgh, with the thirteenth report of the commission*, Royal Commission on the Ancient and Historical Monuments in Scotland (1951) • D. M. Lyon, *History of the lodge of Edinburgh (Mary's Chapel no. 1)* (1900) • *Edinburgh*, Pevsner (1984) • M. Wood, 'The Tron Kirk', *Book of the Old Edinburgh Club*, 29 (1956), 93–110 • J. Imrie and J. G. Dunbar, eds., *Accounts of the masters of works for building and repairing royal palaces and castles*, 2 (1982) • T. Ross, 'An old Edinburgh monument now in Perthshire', *Book of the Old Edinburgh Club*, 4 (1911), 145–52 • J. Nicoll, *A diary of public transactions and other occurrences, chiefly in Scotland, from January 1650 to June 1667*, ed. D. Laing, Bannatyne Club, 52 (1836) • *Tolbooths and town houses: civic architecture in Scotland to 1833*, Royal Commission on the Ancient and Historical Monuments of Scotland (1996), 136–7 • *An inventory of the ancient and historical monuments of the city of Edinburgh, with the thirteenth report of the commission*, Royal Commission on the Ancient and Historical Monuments in Scotland (1951), 2.289–92 • W. Adam, *Vitruvius Scoticus*, ed. J. Simpson (1980), 29, 32, pl. 66–8, 129–31 • *Members of parliament: return to two orders of the honorable the House of Commons*, House of Commons, 2 (1878), 573 • H. Paton, ed., *The register of marriages for the parish of Edinburgh, 1595–1700*, Scottish RS, old ser., 27 (1905)

Archives NA Scot., GD1/51 • RIBA BAL

Likenesses oils, Scot. NPG • oils on copper, Scot. NPG • pencil drawing, Scot. NPG

Wealth at death £25,000 Scots—moveable estate: Imrie and Dunbar, eds., *Accounts of the masters of works*, 2, lxi

Mylne, Robert (1633–1710), master mason, eldest son of Alexander *Mylne (1613–1643), a sculptor [see under Mylne, John (1611–1667)], and of his wife, Anna Vegilman, was born in Edinburgh. In 1653 he was apprenticed to his uncle John Mylne (1611–1667). In 1660 he was made a burgess of Edinburgh, and later that year was admitted as a fellow-craft of Mary's Chapel, Edinburgh's masonic lodge. He was elected warden of the lodge in 1663 and 1664; although his election as deacon in 1674 proved controversial, he again served as deacon five times in the 1680s. On 11 April 1661 he married Elizabeth Meikle of Cramond.

In 1665 Mylne erected John Wood's Hospital at Largo in Fife (rebuilt in 1870); in the same year he built a fort and barracks at Lerwick in Shetland, only to oversee its dismantling in 1668. Also in 1668, on 28 February, he succeeded his uncle as master mason to Charles II by privy seal. In 1668–9 he executed the market cross at Perth (des. 1765). In 1669–72 he built an addition to the house of the earl of Wemyss at West Wemyss in Fife, still largely extant at the end of the twentieth century.

Several of Mylne's early works were executed to designs of William Bruce. After the death of his uncle, with advice from Bruce, he continued Leslie House (1667–72) for the duke of Rothes; it was largely destroyed by fire in 1763. In

1670–72 he was employed on Bruce's remodelling of Thirlestane Castle, Lauder. Also for the earl of Lauderdale, and again with Bruce's advice, in 1671 and 1675 he made a series of stone gateposts which were shipped to London for Ham House. As royal master mason, Mylne reconstructed the palace of Holyroodhouse to Bruce's designs between 1671 and 1680; one of the piers in the courtyard is inscribed 'FVN. BE. R. MYLNE IVL 1671'. A series of drawings in his hand is now in the British Library.

Meanwhile Mylne set about establishing his own social standing, as well as that of his forebears. In 1672 he matriculated the family coat of arms at the Lyon office. In 1674 he acquired a country estate of about 200 acres at Balfargie in Fife; henceforth he was known as Robert Mylne of Balfargie. In the same year, he obtained permission from the burgh of Edinburgh to erect a tomb in Greyfriars churchyard in memory of his uncle.

During his career Mylne executed numerous works in Edinburgh: in 1674–6, for instance, he was employed by the burgh to build five cisterns and fountains for the capital's new water supply. His Doric pedestals for the pumpheads, made to Bruce's designs, may still be seen in Edinburgh's High Street. In 1687–8, with Thomas Sandilands, he rebuilt in stone the wooden guardhouse in the High Street (later removed). In 1689 he built a battery at Edinburgh Castle, still known as Mylne's Mound. In 1693 he contracted to build the steeple at Heriot's Hospital, Edinburgh.

Mylne's most significant contribution to the townscape of Edinburgh was the rebuilding of stone tenements, in line with the legislation enacted after the 1674 fire. These included buildings in Parliament Close, as well as Writer's Court on the north side of the High Street. In 1684, in partnership with the wright Andrew Paterson, he began Milne's Square opposite his uncle's Tron Church. This spacious development, occupying two feu-widths (each feu being a long thin plot with a street frontage of about 20 feet), was dated 1689; its east side having been demolished in 1787, the remainder disappeared in the 1890s. Off the Lawnmarket, with Paterson, he built Milne's Court, again opening up two closes. Three sides survive, though much restored, the entrance pend being dated 1690. Mylne's tenements were characterized by large sash-windows, scale-and-platt stairs, and polished ashlar masonry on the street frontages. In 1701 he was fined 500 merks for the excessive height of his new buildings in Parliament Close, and ordered to reduce their height; in 1703 he was fined again, for encroaching on the street near St Giles's.

During the same period Mylne was heavily involved in developments at Leith, where he inherited from his uncle the responsibility for maintaining the quay. In 1677 he acquired a site at Leith between The Shore and the Timber Bush (a wood depot). In 1678 work on his own house was delaying his repairs to the quay. In 1685 he acquired more land from the city, with the Hopes of Hopetoun taking over as feudal superiors in 1686. By 1691 a windmill, tenements, and offices already existed on the site, while other houses were still to be built. The ground floor of one of his tenements at 18–22 The Shore, Leith, dated 1678, still

remains, although the neighbouring tenement to the north, which formerly bore a pedimented entrance with his monogram and the date 1678, has been largely reconstructed. The windmill has survived, though much altered.

Mylne's last work was the monument to the Trotters of Mortonhall at Greyfriars churchyard, Edinburgh, begun in 1709 and finished after his death by his son William; also in Greyfriars may be seen his tomb of Alexander Beaton (d. 1672). Mylne died at his house at Inveresk on 10 December 1710 and may have been buried in Greyfriars churchyard. His epitaph on the family monument at Greyfriars declares that he left eight sons and six daughters. His daughter Janet married the architect James Smith, who had assisted Robert at Holyrood.

William Mylne (bap. 1665, d. 1728), his son, was baptized in Edinburgh on 8 July 1665. He resided mainly in Leith where a door inscribed 'William Mylne 1715' existed until 1773. He was admitted to the lodge of Edinburgh in 1681, where he passed as fellow-craft in 1685 and played an active role in the lodge's affairs from 1692 to 1723, serving as warden in 1695–7. Like his father, he was active in tenement building in Edinburgh. A tenement at Halkerston's Wynd was inscribed on the lintel: 'BVILT BY WILLIAM MYLNE MASON 1715'. A family chronicle asserts that 'He seems not to have been possessed of the abilities and industry of his father' (Mylne family MS 1/1, British Architecture Library, RIBA). He incurred various debts, and in 1711 he sold his father's estate at Balfargie. He married Elizabeth Thomson; their offspring included twin boys, born in 1701. William Mylne died on 9 March 1728 at Leith, and was buried two days later in South Leith parish church.

DEBORAH HOWARD

Sources NA Scot., Mylne family MSS, GD1/51 · RIBA BAL, Mylne family MSS · R. S. Mylne, *The master masons to the crown of Scotland and their works* (1893) · Colvin, *Archs.* · M. Wood, ed., *Extracts from the records of the burgh of Edinburgh, 1665–1680*, [11] (1950) · M. Wood and H. Armet, eds., *Extracts from the records of the burgh of Edinburgh, 1680–1689*, [12] (1954) · H. Armet, ed., *Extracts from the records of the burgh of Edinburgh, 1689–1701*, [13] (1962) · H. Armet, ed., *Extracts from the records of the burgh of Edinburgh, 1701–1718*, [14] (1967) · *An inventory of the ancient and historical monuments of the city of Edinburgh, with the thirteenth report of the commission*, Royal Commission on the Ancient and Historical Monuments in Scotland (1951) · *Edinburgh*, Pevsner (1984) · D. M. Lyon, *History of the lodge of Edinburgh (Mary's Chapel no. 1)* (1900) · R. M. Pinkerton and W. J. Windram, *Mylne's Court: three hundred years of Lawnmarket heritage* (1983) · J. G. Dunbar and K. Davies, eds., 'Some late 17th-century building contracts', *Miscellany … XI*, Scottish History Society, 5th ser., 3 (1990), 316–21 · H. Armet, 'Notes on the rebuilding in Edinburgh in the last quarter of the 17th century', *Book of the Old Edinburgh Club*, 29 (1956), 111–37 · I. A. Stirling, 'Mylne Square', *Book of the Old Edinburgh Club*, 14 (1925), 45–8 · J. Dunbar, *Sir William Bruce, 1630–1710* (1970) · *Fife*, Pevsner (1988) · R. G. Ball, 'The Shetland garrison, 1665–1668', *Journal of the Society for Army Historical Research*, 43 (1965), 5–26 · D. Wilson, *Memorials of Edinburgh in the olden time*, 2 vols. (1848) · J. G. Fyfe, ed., *Scottish diaries and memoirs, 1530–1746*, 1 (1928), 129–30 · J. Grant, *Cassell's old and new Edinburgh*, 3 vols. [1880–83], vol. 1 · *The diary of Mr John Lamont of Newton, 1649–1671*, ed. G. R. Kinloch, Maitland Club, 7 (1830), 177–8 · W. Fraser, *Memorials of the family of Wemyss of Wemyss*, 3 vols. (1888), vol. 1, p. 284 · W. Adam, *Vitruvius Scoticus*, ed. J. Simpson (1980), 29, pl. 66–8 · J. G. Dunbar, 'The building-

activities of the duke and duchess of Lauderdale, 1670–82', *Archaeological Journal*, 132 (1975), 202–30 • T. H. Marshall, *The history of Perth from the earliest period to the present time* (1849), 475 • NA Scot., Mylne family MSS, GD1/51/69 • H. Paton, ed., *The register of marriages for the parish of Edinburgh, 1595–1700*, Scottish RS, old ser., 27 (1905), 476 • RIBA BAL, Mylne family MS 1/1
Archives NA Scot., family MSS, GD1/51 • RIBA BAL, family MSS

Mylne, Robert (1643?–1747), antiquary, was born in Edinburgh, probably late in December 1643. On 29 August 1678 he married Barbara (1653–1725), second daughter of the Revd John Govean of Muckhart, Perthshire. The Mylnes had twelve children, of whom six died in infancy, with only one, Margaret (wife of John McLeod of Edinburgh), still alive at her father's death.

Mylne was a 'writer' by profession, that is, an attorney or law agent (a poem addressed to him suggests that he might have held the position of writer to the signet, a position in the Scottish legal profession with certain specific responsibilities). He was celebrated in his own day as 'a person well known to be indefatigable in the study of Scots antiquities', compiling 'vast collections from the public records', which he made freely available to historians and genealogists (Crawfurd, vi). According to Maidment's memoir, he 'lost no opportunity of copying with his own hand, such manuscripts as he deemed worthy of transcription', and 'his innumerable notebooks, written both carefully and closely', testify to his 'industry' (Maidment, ix).

Many of Mylne's antiquarian manuscripts can be found in the National Library of Scotland and the Edinburgh University Library. These include a history of the kings of Scotland, an inventory of early Scottish royal charters, a collection of various charters and acts of parliament, transcripts of letters and other documents, and miscellaneous notes on historical and religious matters. The National Library of Scotland manuscripts also include a detailed genealogical account of the 'descent probative' of Barbara Mylne, compiled by her son Robert in 1728 and corrected by her husband (NL Scot., Adv. MS 2094) and 'Ane catalogue of the Books Manuscripts and pamphlets Belonging to Robert Mylne writer in Edr. 1709', largely in the hand of Mylne's son John (*d.* 1710), with notes and additions by Mylne from 1709 to 1743 (NL Scot., Adv. MS 23.6.17).

Mylne was an ardent Jacobite, and his papers include a large collection of political satires and lampoons of the late seventeenth and early eighteenth centuries, transcribed and annotated by Mylne. The opening lines of the 'Epitaph on William of Orange, Usurper' (1702), possibly by Mylne himself, is typical of their political stance:

> Howl, howl, ye fiends, your sables deeper dye,
> For here interr'd your greatest friend doth lye.
> (Maidment, 75)

The satiric manuscripts include 'The mysterie of iniquitie, or, The revolution, deduced from the time of K. J. his being forced … to retire from England', several satires by Mylne's friend and fellow Jacobite Archibald Pitcairne, lampoons on the sexual exploits of the Revd David Williamson or 'Dainty Davie', an extended 'Satyre on the Familie of Stairs', and a number of satiric epigrams which may be by Mylne himself. Many of the Jacobite satires and lampoons collected by Mylne were published by James Maidment in *A Book of Scottish Pasquils* (1827), which includes an extensive memoir, and in *A Second Book* and *Third Book of Scottish Pasquils* (1828).

Despite his strong political prejudices, Mylne was described as an 'amiable man' who formed 'habits of intimacy with many persons of a different way of thinking' (Maidment, viii). He died in Edinburgh on 21 December 1747 at the age of 103. According to his obituary notice 'he enjoyed his Sight and the Exercise of his Understanding till a little before his Death, and was buried on his Birthday'.   WARREN CHERNAIK

Sources J. Maidment, ed., *A book of Scottish pasquils* (1827) • G. Crawfurd, *The history of the shire of Renfrew* (1782) • *DNB* • NL Scot., Adv. MSS 2094, 23.6.17 • O. Geddes, correspondence, NL Scot. • *British Magazine, or, The London and Edinburgh Intelligencer* (Dec 1747) • [A. Pitcairne], *Babell: a satirical poem on the proceedings of the general assembly* (1830)
Archives NL Scot., catalogue of library, Advocates MS 23.6.17 • NL Scot., MSS, Advocates MSS 1987–2091, 2094, 2804 • NL Scot., MS satires and lampoons, Advocates MSS 2092–2093 • NL Scot., transcripts and collections, Advocates MSS 6/2/2, 6/2/18, 12/2/1–2, 15/2/22–24, 15/2/29, 16/1/1, 23/3/24, 25/3/4, 31/6/1, 32/3/10, 32/6/6, 34/2/9, 34/3/12, 34/3/15, 34/6/2, 34/6/9–12, 73/1/17 • U. Edin. L., heraldic and historical collections, MSS Dc 4 32, La iii 231, 287, 289, 297, 302, 324, 518, 662

Mylne, Robert (1733–1811), architect and engineer, was born on 4 January 1733 in Edinburgh. His father, **Thomas Mylne** (*d.* 1763), master mason of Edinburgh, was a descendant of the distinguished family of masons to the Scottish crown. Virtually all his work was located in or near Edinburgh and he is notable mainly as a leading figure in freemasonry in the city. He was master of the lodge (1735–6) and treasurer of its successor, the grand lodge, a wholly 'speculative' society (1737–55). Chiefly a building contractor rather than an architect, he nevertheless sometimes provided designs for execution by others, including some houses at Musselburgh, and the Edinburgh Infirmary has been attributed to him. He died on 5 March 1763 in Edinburgh and was buried in Greyfriars churchyard there. He married Elizabeth Duncan (*d.* 1778), with whom he had seven children.

After education at Edinburgh high school, in 1747 Robert Mylne was apprenticed to Daniel Wright, a carpenter, and he subsequently worked in that capacity at Blair Atholl. In 1754 he decided to join his brother William [*see below*], who had left for France to seek architectural training, and the brothers then travelled to Rome, mostly on foot. They arrived in early 1755 and became part of the community of artists associated with young British aristocrats on the grand tour. An important architectural influence in Rome was Piranesi, who also encouraged Mylne's interest in ancient water systems. In addition, Mylne established contact with several future patrons, and sometimes gave them architectural lessons. In 1758 he visited Naples and Sicily and made drawings of the Greek temples, of which use was made by Winckelmann. Later in the same year he became the first Briton to win the silver medal at the Concorso Clementino of the Accademia di San Luca, submitting designs for a large public building to house monuments of famous men. The drawings show the influence of the French academic tradition, tempered with the more austere idioms of neo-classicism.

In 1759 Mylne travelled through the Netherlands to London, where publicity of his success had preceded him and no doubt contributed to the second triumph with which he met. The competition for a new bridge over the Thames at Blackfriars was to close in October, allowing just enough time for Mylne to enter. His design showed influences both from Italian historical precedent and Piranesi's contemporary engravings, and was among the eleven short-listed. Its elliptical arches were controversial, and became the subject of a lively correspondence in the press, to which Samuel Johnson contributed on behalf of another short-listed entrant, his friend John Gwynn. There were also entries from William Chambers and John Smeaton, the engineer. The debate was fuelled by the publication of a pamphlet, *Observations on Bridge-Building* (1760), by one Publicus, who, if not Mylne himself, must certainly have worked with his close collaboration. The pamphlet condemned every entry except Mylne's, which it praised extravagantly. In February 1760 the committee decided in favour of Mylne's design, a remarkable achievement then confirmed by his appointment as surveyor to oversee the construction.

Blackfriars Bridge, opened in 1769, became one of London's major landmarks. Its nine arches stretched from the former mouth of the River Fleet, which was at the same time covered over, to undeveloped land on the south bank. The piers were adorned with twin Ionic columns supporting recesses from the carriageway above, crowned by a continuous balustrade. The curvature formed the arc of a circle. The grand new approach roads widened out at the bridge entrances to form quadrants with stairs bending down to the river.

Mylne's bridge, which was replaced in the 1860s, remained his masterpiece. Its prominence generated other commissions, both for architecture and engineering. From 1762 he kept an office diary from which the course of his subsequent career can be studied. It seems that his chief aspiration at this time was to succeed as an architect. In 1760 he sent to Edinburgh the designs for St Cecilia's Hall, a concert room, and over the next few years was responsible for Almack's Club in St James's, London, for important alterations to King's Weston, near Bristol, and Cally, in Galloway. He was also consulted on several bridges, and was involved in the design or reconstruction of many others, including those at Newcastle and Glasgow.

In the later 1760s Mylne was appointed to significant permanent posts, including those of surveyor to St Paul's Cathedral—which called for an annual survey of the fabric and the management of repairs and accounts—and the engineering roles of assistant surveyor (1767) and surveyor (1771) at the New River Company. His commitment

to the company lasted until 1810, entailing regular inspections and repairs, pursuing the company's interests in disputes, and maintaining and extending the water supply to London. In turn, the appointment led both to new architectural opportunities (including the building of Wormleybury, Hertfordshire, for Sir Abraham Hume, and new offices for the company in Dorset Street, following a fire), and to other work in water engineering, such as river surveys on the Thames and the Lee.

In 1767 Mylne was elected a fellow of the Royal Society; he was by then working on Tusmore, Oxfordshire, for William Fermor. When Blackfriars Bridge was finished, the City commissioned from him new premises for its lying-in hospital. Despite visits to Edinburgh, his relations with his family had become distant and it was only after the event that they were informed of his marriage on 10 September 1770 to Maria (May) Home (1748–1797), sister of Anne, poet and wife of Dr John Hunter. In 1769 he had been obliged to act as guarantor for part of the costs incurred by the collapse of William Mylne's bridge in Edinburgh (see below). He took over from William work at Inveraray Castle for the duke of Argyll, a fruitful relationship which generated fine interiors in the castle, bridges and landscaping in the park, as well as a church and town planning. Bridge work also continued elsewhere, and, although Mylne's engineering output generally was less prominent in the 1770s, his commitment to the new profession was demonstrated by his founding, with John Smeaton, the Society of Civil Engineers.

In 1773–4 Mylne made extended visits to Shropshire, where, through John Mytton of Halston, he was introduced to several local landowners who commissioned both alterations and new work. In the latter category was Woodhouse, a distinguished design reflecting Mylne's simplified idiom. Its severe formality can be contrasted with the softer, more domestic mode to be seen in The Wick (1775), at Richmond, Surrey, for Lady St Aubyn. In London a difficulty arose that seems to have affected the wisdom of Mylne's career choices. With a growing family, his need for income besides his permanent posts encouraged him to press the City for payment of the remaining 5 per cent commission on the cost of Blackfriars, which they refused to do until 1776, and then only under the pressure of counsel's opinion. Meanwhile, in addition to his other posts, Mylne had unwisely accepted the subordinate role of clerk of works at Greenwich Hospital, where the surveyor was James Stuart. This relationship was not a success and the many disputes over the rebuilding of the hospital chapel after a fire led in 1782 to Mylne's dismissal.

In the 1780s Mylne's separate architectural commissions became somewhat less frequent. Work continued at Inveraray, and his family continued to expand with the birth of two sons, Robert Mylne and William Chadwell *Mylne (1781–1863), who was to succeed him in several appointments. But towards the end of the decade, with the renewal of interest in improving waterways, several engineering commissions occurred, bringing a substantial workload. Besides needing to travel, he was in regular demand as a representative at Westminster parliamentary committees on specific canal or river navigation proposals. He planned the Eau Brinck Cut to facilitate drainage into King's Lynn harbour, a project finally completed by John Rennie from 1817. He became the chief engineer to the Gloucester and Berkeley Canal, which involved frequent and often contentious meetings in Gloucester, but this venture too resulted in his dismissal in 1798, causing great bitterness. The canal was not completed until the 1820s, under the supervision of Thomas Telford. Many of Mylne's professional reports on engineering projects were published, in his distinctively concise and trenchant prose.

Little time remained for architecture, but Mylne's qualifications in that field ensured his inclusion as a founder member of the Architects' Club (1791). Towards the end of the 1790s the frustrations of the water engineering projects were made worse by a series of family tragedies, including the deaths of his wife, two eldest daughters, and son Robert. The family lived mainly at Amwell, Hertfordshire, in a villa Mylne had designed, and in 1800 he erected a mausoleum for them in the churchyard there. At the same time, on an island in the New River at Amwell, he placed a memorial urn to its chief initiator, Sir Hugh Myddelton, drafting suitable inscriptions and publishing an explanatory pamphlet.

The final ten years of Mylne's life were spent mostly as a property and land consultant. He assisted the duke of Northumberland in disputes over his river in Middlesex, and designed the boathouse by the Thames at Sion. He acted as general surveyor to the Stationers' Company, overseeing their properties in the City, including the hall, which he refaced in 1800. Addington, Surrey, one of his earlier houses, was refurbished for the archbishop of Canterbury, and several London properties were renovated for the marquess of Bute and his father-in-law—and school-fellow of Mylne's—Thomas Coutts, the banker. He continued as surveyor to Blackfriars Bridge and St Paul's, where he installed Wren's monument, as well as working as consultant on the new docks, especially the West India and the London. The year 1810 is the last one covered in his diary. He died at his home, New River Head, Clerkenwell, on 6 May 1811, and was buried in St Paul's Cathedral on 13 May.

Mylne was never able to repeat the peak experience of Blackfriars Bridge. But his work in both architecture and engineering, as well as much involvement in property management and surveying, continued successfully and with equal commitment of time and energy to each category. This makes him unusual, if not unique: his contemporaries, even if they initially practised both building design and engineering projects, generally specialized in one or the other. Mylne's contributions towards the development of engineering and architecture as professions were also important. Mylne was a meticulous practitioner, and impatiently expected similar behaviour from others. The prominent chin, roman nose, and determined expression in the three surviving profiles, drawn at different points in time, convey his temperament. He was to

some 'a man of austere manners and violent temper' (Elmes, 339–40), but to others, less formidably, a man 'much disposed towards conversation, & drank wine at & after his meals freely' (Farington, *Diary*, 3931). Standards of integrity and professionalism were never compromised by this forceful personality.

William Mylne (1734–1790), architect and engineer, Robert's brother, was less assertive. Also born in Edinburgh, he was apprenticed as a mason and took over his father's business in Edinburgh on his return from Italy in 1758. He shared with Robert the design for the Jamaica Bridge in Glasgow (1768–72) and preceded him in the work at Inveraray Castle. His main achievement would have been the North Bridge in Edinburgh, but in August 1769, during its construction, an arch collapsed, killing five people. He was held financially responsible for this disaster and, in 1773 in some distress, migrated to North America, where he worked as a planter in South Carolina and attempted unsuccessfully to become an architect in New York. In 1774 he returned to settle in Ireland, where he became engineer to the Dublin waterworks, in which capacity he was responsible for extensive improvements. He died there in March 1790 and was buried in the churchyard of St Catherine's, Dublin. His brother Robert erected a plaque to his memory in the church. William Mylne never married, but he left an illegitimate son.

ROGER WOODLEY

Sources Mylne family MSS, inc. diaries and letters [listed under archives, below] · R. S. Mylne, *The master masons to the crown of Scotland and their works* (1893) · Colvin, *Archs.* · T. Ruddock, *Arch bridges and their builders, 1735–1835* (1979) · R. J. Woodley, 'Robert Mylne', PhD diss., U. Lond., 1998 · R. Woodley, 'Professionals: early episodes amongst architects and engineers', *Construction History*, 15 (1999), 15–22 · R. Woodley, '"A very mortifying situation": Robert Mylne's struggle to get paid for Blackfriars Bridge', *Architectural History*, 43 (2000), 172–86 · C. Gotch, 'The life and work of Robert Mylne', diss., RIBA, 1953 · A. E. Richardson, *Robert Mylne* (1955) · *GM*, 1st ser., 81/1 (1811), 499 · I. G. Lindsay and M. Cosh, *Inveraray and the dukes of Argyll* (1973) · E. Ruddock, *Travels in the colonies, 1773–1775* (1993) · J. Elmes, 'A history of architecture in Great Britain', *Civil Engineers and Architects Journal*, 10 (1847), 339–40 · Farington, *Diary*, vol. 11

Archives CLRO · Inst. CE · LPL, letters and MSS as surveyor to St Paul's Cathedral · NA Scot., family MSS, GD 1/51 · RIBA BAL, family MSS, MYFAM | Birm. CA, letters to Boulton family · LMA, New River Company records · U. Nott. L., corresp. with the third duke of Portland

Likenesses oils, *c*.1760 (William Mylne), priv. coll. · Vangeliste, line engraving, pubd 1783 (after R. Brompton), NPG · G. Dance the younger, pencil drawing, 1795, NPG · R. Brompton, drawing (aged twenty-four), repro. in Mylne, *Master masons* · M. Mylne, miniature (aged about fifty-five), repro. in Mylne, *Master masons* · J. F. Skill, J. Gilbert, W. and E. Walker, group portrait, pencil and wash (*Men of science living in 1807–08*), NPG · two caricatures, BM

Wealth at death property at Great Amwell: will, proved 1 June 1811; *GM* (1811)

Mylne, Robert William (1817–1890). *See under* Mylne, William Chadwell (1781–1863).

Mylne, Thomas (*d.* 1763). *See under* Mylne, Robert (1733–1811).

Mylne, Walter (*c*.1476–1558), protestant martyr, was a priest at Lunan, Forfarshire, for more than forty years.

After he had ceased to say mass on the grounds that he regarded it as idolatrous, he was accused of heresy by David Beaton, abbot of Arbroath. Before he could be apprehended he fled in the late 1530s to the German states, where he fully embraced protestant tenets. He returned to Scotland in 1556, though he had to maintain a low profile when John Hamilton, archbishop of St Andrews, sought his apprehension, partly because of his theology, and partly because he had married. He subsequently explained that he wed to avoid fornication and to have a helpmeet. He and his wife had two children. When the parish priest at Dysart, Fife, learned in April 1558 that Mylne was providing religious instruction to a widow and her children, he had him arrested and sent to St Andrews.

Although offered a monk's portion in Dunfermline Abbey, Mylne would not recant and so was summoned before a group of bishops, abbots, doctors of theology, and Dominican and Franciscan friars in the abbey church at St Andrews on 20 April. His trial was preceded by a sermon from the Observantine Franciscan, Symon Maltman of Legerwood. Despite physical infirmity resulting from age and the effects of incarceration in the castle, Mylne offered a spirited apologia, defending clerical marriage, insisting on only two sacraments, and denying transubstantiation. He derisorily likened the mass to a supper in an aristocratic house where a bell summoned people to eat. Bishops were castigated for living sensually and for not performing their spiritual responsibilities, and pilgrimages were satirized as the occasion for more whoredom than anywhere except brothels. When Mylne again declined to recant, he was pronounced guilty of heresy. However, the provost of St Andrews refused to carry out the sentence unless Mylne was first convicted in a civil court, and he rejected Archbishop Hamilton's request to convene such a trial. Finally, one of Hamilton's retainers held the requisite hearing on 25 April, at which Mylne again refused to recant. Hostile to the burning of the 82-year-old cleric, the townsfolk declined to provide timber, rope, and tar, thereby delaying the execution. On 28 April armed men escorted Mylne to a site in front of the priory of St Andrews, and there he gave his final speech, denouncing Catholicism as the sect of Antichrist.

Mylne's was the last execution for heresy by the pre-Reformation church in Scotland, and the only one since Adam Wallace's death in 1550. The bishops of Caithness, Dunblane, Dunkeld, and Moray were present for the occasion. Although the lords of the congregation protested against Mylne's fate to Mary of Guise, she disclaimed responsibility, casting blame on the prelates. The townsfolk piled stones in Mylne's memory on the site of his burning, repeating their action after the stones were removed, only to have them taken away a second time. But the memory lingered in the popular imagination, and when John Knox preached in St Andrews in June 1559 on Christ's cleansing of the temple, a bonfire of images was made at the place where Mylne suffered. Mylne's widow was still living in 1573, when she received £6 13s. 4d. from the thirds of benefices.   RICHARD L. GREAVES

Sources *The acts and monuments of John Foxe*, new edn, ed. G. Townsend, 8 vols. (1843–9); facs. edn (1965), vol. 5, pp. 644–7 · *John Knox's History of the Reformation in Scotland*, ed. W. C. Dickinson, 2 vols. (1949) · *The history of Scotland. Written in Latin by George Buchanan* (1690), 16.123 · J. Ridley, *John Knox* (1968) · D. Calderwood, *The true history of the Church of Scotland, from the beginning of the Reformation, unto the end of the reigne of King James VI* (1678) · *The works of John Knox*, ed. D. Laing, 6 vols., Bannatyne Club, 112 (1846–64), vol. 1, p. 550 · *Fasti Scot.*, new edn, 5.445 · W. M. Bryce, *The Scottish Grey friars*, 1 (1909), 291 · J. Kirk, *Patterns of reform: continuity and change in the Reformation kirk* (1989) · A. Petrie, *A compendious history of the Catholick church, from the year 600 untill the year 1600*, 2 vols. (1662) · *The historie and cronicles of Scotland … by Robert Lindesay of Pitscottie*, ed. A. J. G. Mackay, 2, STS, 43 (1899), 130–36

Mylne, William (*bap.* 1665, *d.* 1728). *See under* Mylne, Robert (1633–1710).

Mylne, William (1734–1790). *See under* Mylne, Robert (1733–1811).

Mylne, William Chadwell (1781–1863), engineer and architect, was born on 5 or 6 April 1781 in London, the second son in the family of ten children of Robert *Mylne (1733–1811), engineer, and architect of Blackfriars Bridge, and his wife, Maria (May; 1748–1797), daughter of Robert Boyne Home, surgeon. Mylne came from a long line of Scottish master masons. He probably exhibited two works at the Royal Academy, *A Temple at Tivoli* in 1797, 'made out and restored from actual measurements', and *A View in Hertfordshire* in 1802.

In 1797 Mylne was already helping his father to stake out the lands for the Eau Brinck Cut, a fens drainage scheme near King's Lynn, and he also worked on the Gloucester and Berkeley Ship Canal. In 1804 he was appointed assistant engineer to the New River Company, the precursor of the Metropolitan Water Board, and in 1811 he succeeded his father as chief engineer, a position he held until 1861. Among the works he undertook for the New River Company were the conversion of the old wooden mains and service pipes between Charing Cross and Bishopsgate Street into cast iron, and the construction of settling reservoirs at Stoke Newington in order to improve the water supply of the area north of London. Following the Metropolis Waterworks Act of 1852 Mylne embarked on extensive improvements in the works of the New River Company.

Mylne undertook other engineering projects concerned with water supply and drainage, especially in the fens, and made improvements in the River Ouse between Littleport and Ely in 1826, in the River Cam in 1829, and in the drainage of the district of Burnt Fen. He constructed the intercepting drain at Bristol, thus removing the sewage from the floating harbour. He designed the Garret Hostel Bridge over the River Cam at Cambridge (1835–7; dem. 1960), a single iron arch, with Gothic detailing. In 1827 he was one of the unsuccessful competitors for Clifton Bridge, Bristol.

Mylne also practised as an architect and from 1819, as surveyor to the New River Company, he laid out 50 acres of its property near Islington for streets and buildings, including Myddelton Square and other buildings in Clerkenwell, and designed St Mark's Church, Myddelton Square (1826–8), in the Gothic style. He also designed Harpole rectory, Northamptonshire (1816).

In 1840 Mylne gave evidence before committees of the House of Lords on the supply of water to London, and again in 1850 before the sanitary commission of the Board of Health, and (with Sir John Rennie) on the embanking of the River Thames. With H. B. Gunning he was employed as surveyor under the act for making preliminary inquiries in certain cases of application for local acts in 1847, at Leeds, Rochdale, and elsewhere. His many printed reports include one (with J. Walker) on the intended Eau Brinck Cut (1825), and one addressed to the New River Company on the supply of water to the sewers of London (1854). In 1831 he described some Roman remains discovered at Ware in Hertfordshire in a report to the Society of Antiquaries. He became surveyor of the Stationers' Company on the death of his father in 1811, and held the post until 1861; he designed an octagonal card room at Stationers' Hall for the company in 1825.

Mylne was elected fellow of the Astronomical Society in 1821, FRS on 16 March 1826, fellow of the Institute of British Architects in 1834, member of the Institution of Civil Engineers on 28 June 1842 (on the council from 1844 to 1848), and was treasurer to the Smeatonian Society of Engineers for forty-two years.

Mylne married Mary Smith (1791–1874), daughter of George S. Coxhead, and they had three sons and three daughters. He retired in 1861, and died at Amwell in Hertfordshire, where he had lived since 1844, on 25 December 1863.

William Mylne's son **Robert William Mylne** (1817–1890), engineer and geologist, was born on 14 June 1817, the last of twelve generations of the family to practise in the field of architecture. He worked with Sir Richard Gibney in the construction of a new pier (1836) on the northern side of the River Wear. After visiting Paris with James Watt in 1839 he travelled in Italy and Sicily in 1841–2. In 1852 he married Hannah (1826–1885), daughter of George Scott JP, of Ravenscourt Park, Middlesex. He worked with his father in London for about twenty years, and became an authority on questions of water supply and drainage, but he failed to win the competition to rebuild Blackfriars Bridge, which had been built by his grandfather Robert Mylne in 1759. He held the post of engineer to the Limerick Water Company for some time. His most noticeable work was the providing of a good supply of water for one of the sunk forts in the sea at Spithead, Hampshire. He succeeded his father in 1861 as surveyor to the Stationers' Company, and held the post until his death. He designed and rebuilt houses in Ave Maria Lane and Amen Corner, London (1887), and was responsible for drawing attention to the fact that one of the powder stores in Edinburgh Castle had been the chapel of Queen Margaret, the redesigning of which was subsequently entrusted to Hippolyte Blanc. He was an associate of the Institute of British Architects in 1839, a fellow of the institute (1849–89), and a member of the Geological

Society from 1848: he served on the society's council from 1854 to 1868, and again in 1879, and was one of the secretaries in 1856–7. He was also a fellow of the Geological Society of France in recognition of his advice over the construction of the Canal du Midi. He was elected FRS in 1860. He was also a member and treasurer of the Smeatonian Society of Civil Engineers, and belonged to both the London and the Edinburgh societies of antiquaries. His publications included: *On the Supply of Water from Artesian Wells in the London Basin* (1840), for which he was awarded the Telford bronze medal by the Institution of Civil Engineers; *An Account of the Ancient Basilica of San Clemente at Rome* (1845); *Sections of the London Strata* (1850); *A Topographical Map of London and its Environs* (1851); *A Map of the Geology and Contours of London and its Environs* (1856), a work which was used officially until superseded by the Ordnance Survey; and *A Map of London, Geological—Waterworks and Sewers* (1858). He was preparing a work on the architectural antiquities of eastern Scotland at the time of his death, at Home Lodge, Great Amwell, on 2 July 1890.

BERTHA PORTER, *rev.* ANNE PIMLOTT BAKER

Sources R. S. Mylne, *The master masons to the crown of Scotland and their works* (1893), chap. 14 · Colvin, *Archs.* · *Dir. Brit. archs.* · Boase, *Mod. Eng. biog.* · C. Hussey, 'Georgian London: the lesser known squares, 1—Clerkenwell', *Country Life*, 85 (1939), 90–94 · *The Builder*, 22 (1864), 7–8 · *PRS*, 14 (1865), xii–xiii · A. Geikie, *Quarterly Journal of the Geological Society*, 47 (1891), 59–61 [obit. of Robert William Mylne] · P. J. M. McEwan, *Dictionary of Scottish art and architecture* (1994) · Graves, *RA exhibitors*
Archives RIBA, nomination papers · RIBA BAL, wills and papers relating to succession to his estates | UCL, corresp. with E. Chadwick
Likenesses H. W. Phillips, portrait, 1856, repro. in Mylne, *Master masons to the crown of Scotland*, facing p. 284 · H. Adlard, stipple and line engraving, pubd 1860 (after H. W. Phillips), BM · portraits, RIBA BAL
Wealth at death under £20,000: will, 12 Feb 1864, CGPLA Eng. & Wales · £3649 12s. 4d.—Robert William Mylne: resworn probate, June 1892, CGPLA Eng. & Wales (1890)

Myngs, Sir Christopher (*bap.* 1625, *d.* 1666), naval officer, was baptized at Salthouse, Norfolk, on 22 November 1625, the son of John Myngs, shoemaker, originally of the neighbouring village of Cockthorpe but then living in London, and his wife, Katherine, daughter of Christopher Parr. In later life Myngs freely acknowledged his father to be a shoemaker, as indeed he was, and said his mother was a hoyman's daughter. In fact both his parents were from landowning families, and Myngs himself inherited property at Salthouse which he passed to his own son. Possibly his political radicalism inclined him to stress, indeed exaggerate, the simpler aspects of his origins. Doubtless it helped him to associate more easily with the seafaring men whose company he had known from his early years in the coastal trade. His friend the puritan divine Thomas Brooks had served with Myngs before 1648, and, since Brooks had been a chaplain in the parliamentary fleet, Myngs must have seen service in or soon after the civil war. In 1648 he signed a petition urging parliament to pursue the revolted fleet and joined the royalists; his fellow signatories included William Goodson and Richard Badiley, with both of whom he would serve.

In northern waters Myngs sailed to the Mediterranean in December 1651 with Badiley's convoy, serving as a reformado (supernumerary officer) on the flagship *Paragon*. He was second in command of the *Elizabeth* at the start of the First Dutch War, and on 28 August 1652 participated in the action off Elba in which four English warships fought off ten Dutchmen; the *Elizabeth* was heavily engaged but suffered little loss. On the return voyage in May 1653 her captain was killed and Myngs was advanced to his first command. He took his ship into action before Katwijk and Scheveningen on 29–31 July, the last major engagement of the war.

In October Myngs took the vice-chancellor of Poland to Dieppe, arriving on the 3rd. On the following day he met a Dutch convoy escorted by two men-of-war. He drove off the escorts and brought about twenty captured merchantmen into the Downs; his own master was killed. This incident cannot, as has been supposed (Firth, 'Sailors', 257–8) be that related by Richard Gibson in which Myngs, as captain of the *Elizabeth*, is said to have captured three Dutch men-of-war homeward bound, and to have brought them back for Blake's admiration, only to receive a rebuke from the general for risking his own ship against such odds: 'I do not love a foolhardy captain' (Gardiner, 1.13). Since this story is set in 1652, off the Isles of Scilly, when the *Elizabeth* was in the Mediterranean and Myngs not yet her captain, it cannot be verified.

In November Myngs, in the *Elizabeth*, was part of the squadron which took Bulstrode Whitelocke to Sweden as ambassador. Having arrived at Göteborg on the 15th, the crews were much weakened by disease and on the return had to decline engaging a Dutch convoy they met. Myngs returned to Portsmouth, and was active in patrolling the channel.

In January 1655 Myngs's career was promoted by Brooks, now preacher at St Margaret's, New Fish Street Hill, London, who praised Myngs's 'blameless life and conversation' and the valour he had shown in several engagements, to which Goodson and Badiley could witness (PRO, SP 18/103, no. 128).

Spanish main These credentials were put to the test in October when Myngs was appointed to take the *Marston Moor* back to the Caribbean from which she had only just returned. Cromwell was keen to confirm his acquisition of Jamaica, the only achievement of the 1655 expedition of Penn and Venables. But the crew of the *Marston Moor*, who had been denied pay on return to Portsmouth, mutinied. When Myngs (after some delay for which Brooks had to apologize to the admiralty) arrived to take up his command, he saw that he had no chance of persuading the crew to serve again, so he dismissed them and looked for volunteers among the other returned ships. With about thirty of an intended complement of 280, he stood to Spithead and asked that payment be made there and then to such men as he had. The navy agent, Josiah Childs, was reluctant to accede to so irregular a request. But Myngs

insisted, denying that he had already bribed those he had with him. He somehow put together a crew, at least thirty of whom were under suspension for striking an officer on another ship, and sailed on 10 November.

Myngs reached Jamaica on 15 January 1656, there joining Goodson who commanded the station. Cromwell's orders were that the Jamaica squadron should scour the Spanish main for such Spanish plate ships as they might find. On 4 May an attack to this purpose was made on Rio del Hacha (in modern Colombia), at which Myngs was present in the *Marston Moor*. The English took so much time negotiating the shoals that the Spanish shipping there was able to escape. Back on Jamaica Myngs did much to foster the new English colony, bringing 1400 settlers from the island of Nevis.

Myngs returned to England in July 1657. During the refit of his ship he went off to be married; it is uncertain if this was to his first wife, Mary, or to his second, Rebecca Stone (d. 1678/9). In August he was still about his private concerns when he was called to London, and again Brooks had to explain his absence to the Admiralty. He sailed back in December, carrying over £2500 with which to fortify Jamaica. He arrived there on 2 March, having taken three victuallers and six Dutchmen off Barbados, alleging they were trading in contravention of English regulations (deriving from a 1650 act of parliament intended to deny supplies to the royalist fleet, since departed). To Myngs's annoyance the admiralty court in Jamaica did not immediately condemn his acquisitions as prize, but instead began a prolonged investigation. The matter was referred back to London (while, as Myngs pointed out sourly, the ships and their cargoes rotted) and was not resolved until 1659, when only one of the ships was declared prize.

Meanwhile Myngs, as senior captain on the station, conducted operations to disrupt Spanish trade wherever he could, and to counter Spain's intermittent attempts to recover Jamaica. In 1659 the governor, Edward D'Oyley, instructed him to make a sweep of the Spanish main, for which he took three frigates and 300 or more soldiers. After attacks on Cumaná and Puerto Cabello he moved further west along the coast (of modern Venezuela) to Coro. Here he seized twenty-two chests of bullion, estimated at £200,000 to £300,000, and £50,000 more in specie. When the ships returned to Jamaica the treasure chests were empty. Myngs was clearly in collusion with his crew, if not personally involved in the share-out. Direct accusations against him were made by the steward-general of the colony, Cornelius Burrough, and Colonel William Dalyson, one of the planters. It was suggested that Myngs had been 'unhinged' by frustration over his Dutch prizes. D'Oyley sent Myngs home in the *Marston Moor* (on which he alleged there had been 'a constant market … without any controule'), claiming that Myngs's conduct made him 'so distasteful to the other officers of the fleet' that he would not have a fair hearing in Jamaica (Dyer, 182). But it is doubtful if the war council, before which Myngs was summoned on 1 June, was much disposed to condemn the most popular man in the navy and an officer of undoubted gallantry. That he was among friends in London is evident from his signature to the officers' letter to Monck of 4 November supporting the dissolution of the Rump Parliament. By this time Myngs, the charges against him (which he denied) having been quietly dropped, was about to return to Jamaica, where he arrived in January 1660. He retained his command after the Restoration. In 1662 the new governor, Lord Windsor, was instructed by the government of Charles II to exert pressure on the Spanish to accept the English presence in the West Indies, and on 20 September Myngs was formally commissioned to take the frigate *Griffith* and such volunteers as he could assemble to attack Spanish shipping, towns, and fortifications, whereby they 'may be better inclyned to receive the settlement of a trade' (Marsden, 42). On 22 September Myngs sailed, and on 5 October stood off Cuba. His purpose was not so much to do business at gunpoint as to deter further attempts to retake Jamaica, which had chiefly been directed from Santiago on Cuba's southern coast. This port he duly took, having to deter his men from firing the churches in retaliation for Spanish atrocities in Jamaica, and spent ten days rounding up the garrison and demolishing the forts. By 24 October he was back in Jamaica and was sworn of the island council. His mission had been well conducted and, within its limited objectives, successful: no conquest of Cuba was in prospect, but England's hold on Jamaica was the more secure. In 1663 he led a further assault on Cuba, at Compeachey (Campechuela), where he was badly wounded. On 21 August he was back in the Downs.

Home station During 1664 Myngs commanded the *Gloucester*, the *Portland*, and the *Royal Oak*, in the last of which he hoisted his flag as vice-admiral in the channel. At the battle of Lowestoft on 3 June 1665 he commanded the *Triumph* and served as vice-admiral of the white. He fired the first shots, before dawn, and in the course of the action was wounded in the leg. On 27 June he was knighted. Following the reorganization of the fleet under Sandwich's command, on 2 July Myngs became vice-admiral of the blue, Allin's squadron. In July and August he took part in the mission to Bergen, and would later join in the criticism of Sandwich for breaking bulk in contravention of prize law during this voyage. Sir William Coventry suggested that Myngs should then lead an expedition to Guinea, but this was not feasible; Myngs remained in home waters, in command of the *Fairfax*, during the winter of 1665–6.

In March 1666 Myngs convoyed the Hamburg fleet; rumours that he had taken fourteen Dutchmen proved incorrect and he returned with nothing more than supplies on 15 March. On the following day, still in the *Fairfax*, he was made vice-admiral of the red. On 29 May, having already shifted his flag to the *Victory*, he was chosen to be vice-admiral of Rupert's detached squadron, searching for the French in the channel while from 1 June Monck engaged the Dutch off the North Foreland. When the English forces reassembled on the evening of 3 June Myngs was at the flag officers' meeting which took the decision to re-engage on the following day. On the morning of 4 June Myngs led the van, engaging De Liefde in broadsides and failing to burn him with a fireship. 'Stout Lawson and Minn … emptied their guns in their enemies hearts' (C. H. Firth, ed., *Naval Songs and Ballads*, Navy Records Society, 33, 1908, 61). During this very close fighting Myngs received successive wounds to the throat and shoulder; he first remained on deck, refusing treatment, but was finally obliged to yield command to his protégé John Narbrough. Myngs was brought back to his London house at Goodman's Fields in Whitechapel; at first it was thought he would recover, but on 10 June his death was reported. He was buried in St Mary's, Whitechapel, on the 13th. Pepys noted that Coventry was the only 'person of quality' present. As Pepys and Coventry were leaving they were approached by a dozen of Myngs's long-serving comrades, who asked to be recommended to crew a fireship in the hope of performing some service 'that shall show our memory of our dead commander and our revenge'. It seems that this fine offer was accepted. To Pepys it was the 'most Romantique' case he had ever known, and while all concerned were no doubt affected by the emotion of the occasion, it was a striking instance of the 'following', that bonding of seamen with a cherished commander which would be of considerable significance in the next century (Pepys, *Diary*, 7.165).

Myngs left a son, Christopher, who was later a distinguished officer and a commissioner of the navy, and (from his first marriage) a daughter, Mary. His widow, who was carrying another child, received a state pension. Pepys thought it particularly tragic that Myngs had died before he could establish his family in prosperity, and supposed that in consequence he would be 'quite forgot in a few months, as if he had never been'. Pepys's own tribute has done much to defeat this prediction. He characterized Myngs as 'a very stout man, and a man of great parts', one who was proud of his 'ordinary friends', and who loved to join in 'sports' with his men on deck (Pepys, *Diary*, 6.279, 7.165–6; *Samuel Pepys and the Second Dutch War*, 202). Not everyone was impressed by this easy nature and Coventry criticized the 'indulgence and popularity' of Myngs for allegedly saving a runaway from execution (R. L. Ollard, *Man of War*, 1969, 215 n. 25).

Myngs was, perhaps not undesignedly, a figure in the Elizabethan buccaneering tradition, impatient with red tape and gold braid; but he was also accounted a 'rational man' (Thurloe, 6.235), and in his courage and his unremitting concern for the welfare of his men, one displaying the highest attributes of his profession.

C. S. KNIGHTON

Sources F. E. Dyer, 'Captain Christopher Myngs in the West Indies', *Mariner's Mirror*, 18 (1932), 168–87 · C. H. Firth, 'The capture of Santiago, in Cuba, by Captain Myngs, 1662', *EngHR*, 14 (1899), 536–40 · R. G. Marsden, ed., *Documents relating to law and custom of the sea*, 2: *AD 1649–1767*, Navy RS, 50 (1916), 41–5 · *CSP dom.*, 1652–66 · *CSP col.*, vols. 1, 5 · *LondG* (11–15 Jan 1665) · *LondG* (26–9 March 1666) · B. Capp, *Cromwell's navy: the fleet and the English revolution, 1648–1660* (1989), 31, 96, 105, 178, 182, 240, 263, 282, 285 (n. 125), 344, 386 · J. D. Davies, *Gentlemen and tarpaulins: the officers and men of the Restoration navy* (1991), 24, 129, 141 · R. Ollard, *Cromwell's earl: a life of Edward Mountagu, 1st earl of Sandwich* (1994), 143 · *The journals of Sir Thomas Allin, 1660–1678*, ed. R. C. Anderson, 1, Navy RS, 79 (1939), 114, 125, 234, 270 · *The journal of Edward Mountagu, first earl of Sandwich, admiral and general at sea, 1659–1665*, ed. R. C. Anderson, Navy RS, 64

(1929), 215, 273 • Pepys, *Diary*, 3.63; 6.147, 230, 278–9; 7.71, 76, 150, 155, 158, 165–6; 8.461 • *Samuel Pepys and the Second Dutch War: Pepys's navy white book and Brooke House papers*, ed. R. Latham, Navy RS, 133 (1995), 207 [transcribed by W. Matthews and C. Knighton] • S. R. Gardiner and C. T. Atkinson, eds., *Letters and papers relating to the First Dutch War, 1652–1654*, 1, Navy RS, 13 (1899), 12–13 • J. R. Powell and E. K. Timings, eds., *The Rupert and Monck letter book, 1666*, Navy RS, 112 (1969), 16, 19, 20, 196, 202, 240, 245 • C. H. Firth, 'Sailors of the civil war, the Commonwealth and the protectorate', *Mariner's Mirror*, 12 (1926), 237–59, esp. 257–8 • Thurloe, *State papers* • PRO, SP 18/103, no. 128 • will, PRO, PROB 11/322, fol. 225*v* • parish register, Salthouse, 22 Nov 1625, Norfolk RO [baptism] • *DNB* • G. W. Marshall, 'Additions to Le Neve's *Pedigrees of the knights* [pt 1]', *The Genealogist*, 1 (1877), 37–54, esp. 38–9

Archives Bodl. Oxf., account of capture of Santiago | PRO, SP various

Likenesses P. Lely, oils, 1666, NMM; repro. in F. Fox, *Great ships* (1980), 78 • R. Dunkarton, mezzotint, pubd 1813 (after J. R. Bullfinch), BM, NPG • pen-and-ink drawing (after J. Brand), NPG

Wealth at death small landholding in Norfolk: will, PRO, PROB 11/322, fol. 225*v*

Mynn, Alfred (1807–1861), cricketer, born at Twysden Lodge, Goudhurst, Kent, on 19 January 1807, was the fourth son of William Mynn (*bap.* 1763, *d.* 1837), a gentleman farmer, whose family had lived in Kent for at least two generations, and his wife, Ann, *née* Clark (*d.* 1837). He probably had little formal education. In 1825 he moved with his family to Harrietsham in Kent, and soon he was playing for nearby Leeds Park, one of the strongest village sides in the county. Here he was coached by John Willes in round-arm bowling, which Willes himself had pioneered (1807) despite considerable opposition.

On 15 December 1828 Mynn married Sarah (*d.* 1881), daughter of Dr James Powell of Lenham. They had seven children, of whom only the five daughters survived to adulthood. Until 1829 he was styled in parish records as 'a farmer' and thereafter as 'a gentleman', playing his cricket as such. Despite both patronage and the reimbursement of expenses, this brought some financial distress and in 1845 he had brief spells of imprisonment because of bankruptcy. In the last few years of his life he was a hop merchant.

Mynn made his first appearance at Lord's in 1832, for the Gentlemen against the Players, and took part in almost every such match for twenty years. Without him the Gentlemen could not have met the Players on equal terms, and their victories in 1842, 1843, and 1848 were mainly due to him. It was also largely due to him that Kent cricket was for twenty years pre-eminent. He was a member of the touring All England eleven, formed by William Clarke of Nottingham, from 1846 to 1854. His most remarkable performance as a batsman was in scoring a total of 283 runs in four consecutive innings, two of them not out, in 1836. After making 45 and 92 for the MCC against Sussex in Brighton he played his first match for the North against the South at Leicester. An ankle injury before the game led to his leg swelling, but despite this he scored 21 not out and 125 not out. The subsequent journey to London, strapped on the top of a stagecoach, so exacerbated the injury that Mynn might have suffered the amputation of the leg and even risked death. He was fortunate, however, to make a full recovery. His last appearances

were at Lord's for Kent against the MCC in 1854, at the Oval in the Veterans' match against England in 1858, and for Kent against Middlesex in 1860.

Like his ancestors, who were renowned for their great stature and physical strength, Mynn was a very powerful man; he was 6 feet 1 inch in height and at his peak weighed from 18 to 19 stone. He was a hard-hitting batsman, and was especially good against fast bowling. He had a strong defence. It was as a bowler, however, that Mynn made his reputation. He was the first important fast round-arm bowler. He achieved great pace and late movement with a command of line and length off a short run. Before him the chief round-arm bowlers, such as Frederick William Lillywhite, had been slow and had depended for their success on accuracy and the ability to turn the ball. It was Mynn who added pace to accuracy. He was also a great single-wicket player, beating James Dearman, the champion of the north, in 1838, and Felix (Nicholas Wanostrocht), his former Kent colleague, in 1846.

In his later years Mynn lived in Thurnham, near Maidstone, Kent. He died from diabetes at his brother's home, 22 Merrick Square, London, on 1 November 1861. He was buried five days later at Thurnham parish church with military honours, the Leeds and Hillingbourne volunteer rifle corps, of which he was a member, following his coffin to the grave. On his death, *Bell's Life in London* printed W. J. Prowse's stanzas 'In Memoriam', ending with the oft-quoted epitaph 'Lightly lie the turf upon thee, kind and manly Alfred Mynn!'

J. W. ALLEN, *rev.* GERALD M. D. HOWAT

Sources P. Morrah, *Alfred Mynn* (1963) • *Bell's Life in London* (10 Nov 1861) • A. Haygarth, *Arthur Haygarth's cricket scores and biographies*, 15 vols. (1862–1925), vols. 2–4 • W. Denison, *Sketches of the players* (1846) • Lord Harris, ed., *The history of Kent county cricket* (1907) • J. Pycroft, *The cricket field, or, The history and the science of cricket* (1851) • H. S. Altham, *A history of cricket* (1926)

Likenesses G. F. Watts, pencil drawing, 1837, Marylebone Cricket Club, Lord's, London • W. Bromley, oils, *c.*1840, Marylebone Cricket Club, Lord's, London • C. Cousins, lithograph, 1846 • N. Plosczynski, group portrait, chromolithograph, pubd 1847 (*The Eleven of England*), Marylebone Cricket Club, Lord's, London • N. Wanostrocht, group portrait, watercolour, 1847, Marylebone Cricket Club, Lord's, London • G. H. Phillips, group portrait, chromolithograph, pubd 1849 (after W. Drummond and C. J. Basebe; *A cricket match between Sussex and Kent*), Marylebone Cricket Club, Lord's, London • J. C. Anderson, lithograph, 1851, Marylebone Cricket Club, Lord's, London • W. Nicholson, coloured woodcut, 1898, repro. in W. N. P. Nicholson, *An almanac of twelve sports* (1898) • N. Wanostrocht, coloured lithograph (after G. F. Watt, 1848), Marylebone Cricket Club, Lord's, London • G. F. Watts, lithograph, BM

Wealth at death died in straitened circumstances: Morrah, *Alfred Mynn*, 201

Mynne, George (*d.* 1648), ironmaster and politician, was of obscure origins, but is not to be confused with his Herefordshire relative and namesake, who was the father-in-law of George Calvert, later first Baron Baltimore. He seems to have had family and property connections in Shropshire and Surrey.

Initially described as a woollen draper and/or clothier, Mynne's main commercial interests came to be in the metal industries, notably in the smelting of iron. His first recorded entry into royal service was as deputy paymaster of the forces in Ireland in 1614. He was deputy governor of the Mineral and Battery Company, a quasi-monopolistic body, for twenty-five years (from about 1621 to 1646), and a partner in various ventures to produce iron, chiefly in the Forest of Dean, together with Sir Basil Brooke of Madeley, Coalbrookdale. In the 1630s the two were convicted of breaking the newly enforced forest laws, by the alleged theft of wood (to make charcoal), and were fined the huge sum of £59,000, eventually reduced to £12,000. Mynne was also charged with waste of timber in Carmarthenshire, presumably for his lesser ironworks in the neighbouring county of Pembrokeshire. Given the dependence of the industry on charcoal, it was difficult if not impossible for ironmasters to avoid putting themselves at risk, certainly in England, perhaps less so in Ireland.

Mynne was MP for Old Sarum in 1621 and West Looe in 1624, both being closed boroughs under royal patronage. His purchases of the clerkship of the hanaper in chancery (for £2400 in 1620) may help to explain this. In the former (and better recorded) of these two parliaments he spoke as a kind of expert witness about the problems connected with English cloth exports to the Netherlands, in favour of free speech (in the context of puritan attempts to silence pro-Catholics), and for measures being proposed against the taking of fees by office-holders being extended to lawyers in private practice. Charles I's commission on exacted fees and innovated offices was investigating Mynne and the hanaper (in effect the treasury of the great seal) in 1630; he got off then but was finally brought to trial for extortion in 1634. Some of his judges in Star Chamber waxed eloquent about Mynne's misuse of his position, distinguishing this from his legitimate attempt to improve his status and rise in the social hierarchy. He was sentenced to pay a large fine, and to surrender his office to trustees (one of whom was his own brother-in-law), although the intricacies of the case were not settled until at least 1636. Meanwhile he continued also to operate as a moneylender, advancing large sums on bond during these same decades, and was appointed to a royal commission on the cloth trade in the late 1630s.

The ambivalence of Mynne's relations with the crown is epitomized by the repeated accusations of delinquency (that is, royalism) brought against him by one of the parliamentarian committees in charge of penal taxation during the years 1643–7. There seems little doubt that he supplied the king's war effort with raw iron, if not with actual munitions, and his fine was finally set at just under £5000, although, after he died intestate early in 1648, his executors alleged that he and his estate had paid out over £13,000 in all. Mynne's son and heir, also George, who died three or four years later, left cash legacies largely in the form of sums still owing by his father's debtors.

Mynne married Ann, daughter of Sir Robert Parkhurst (d. 1636), lord mayor of London, and sister of Sir Robert Parkhurst MP (d. 1651). Their two daughters married, respectively, Richard, brother of John Evelyn, the diarist, and Sir John Lewkenor MP. Marriage here would seem to have been both cause and effect of upward social mobility.

It might appear that Mynne and his family had been ruined by a combination of the forest laws, the drive against exacted fees, and finally by backing the losing side in the civil war: yet their liquid assets must have been very considerable. If George Mynne or his son had survived until the Restoration, with male heirs to succeed them, the family's history might have been very different.

G. E. AYLMER, *rev.*

Sources G. E. Aylmer, *The king's servants: the civil service of Charles I, 1625–1642* (1961); rev. edn (1974) · G. E. Aylmer, 'Charles I's commission on fees, 1627–40', *BIHR*, 31 (1958), 58–67 · G. Hammersley, 'The revival of the forest laws under Charles I', *History*, new ser., 45 (1960) · Evelyn, *Diary* · W. Notestein, F. H. Relf, and H. Simpson, eds., *Commons debates, 1621*, 7 (1935) · *VCH Surrey*, 274 · PRO, PROB 11/PCC, 24 Pile · BL Loan MS 16/2 · private information (1993)

Mynors, Robert (1739–1806), surgeon, born at Eccleshall, Staffordshire, on 29 August 1739, was the fourth son of John Mynors (b. 1696) and his wife, Catherine James, of High Offley, Staffordshire. His family were substantial landowners across the midlands. On 1 June 1756 he was the first of four apprentices bound to Thomas Kirkland, surgeon, of Ashby-de-la-Zouch, Leicestershire; Mynors was to serve for seven years with a premium of £50. At the end of his apprenticeship he moved to Birmingham, where he practised for the rest of his life. In 1765 he was both a benefactor and subscriber to the new general hospital there, which opened in 1779 and to which he continued to give 2 guineas a year until his death. By 1767 Mynors lived at 14 The Square, which had had medical occupants before, and again after he left in 1780. Mynors practised in Birmingham as a surgeon and man midwife, also undertaking poor law work for adjacent parishes. He acted as a consulting surgeon at the general hospital for 'extraordinary Occasions in Surgery' (general hospital governors' minutes, Birm. CA) during its first decade.

In 1783 Mynors's *Practical Observations on Amputation* appeared, one of many eighteenth-century volumes on the topic, on which Percivall Pott also published in that year. Mynors published *A History of the Practice of Trepanning* in 1785, an account of a prehistoric surgical technique that, as late as 1806, was still used for treating epilepsy. The latter book was dedicated to William Withering, his neighbour at 15 The Square. Mynors invented a many tailed bandage for dressing amputation stumps. During the 1780s and 1790s Mynors took five boys as apprentices, each for seven years and with the substantial premium of £157. In the period 1792–1801 he indentured another four youths jointly with a fellow Birmingham surgeon, Thomas James Vickers, on the same terms. Mynors seems to have known the important Birmingham citizens in the late eighteenth century, including Matthew Boulton, while Dr Edward Johnstone was to be one of his executors.

About 1780 Mynors moved to Snow Hill, a newly developed residential area. He married Susanna Eden (1755–1823), a gentleman's daughter of Broad Marston, Gloucestershire, at Ilmington, Warwickshire, on 24 September 1787. They had three children, all born at Snow Hill: Robert Edward Eden (1789–1842), John (1793–1797), and Henry

(1794–1860). In 1797 the family moved to an estate of some 600 acres at Weatheroak Hall, near Alvechurch, Worcestershire, which was virtually rebuilt for Mynors, as shown in a portrait of the family that year by James Millar, who had been their neighbour in The Square, Birmingham.

Robert Mynors died from 'a short but violent attack of the gout' (*Birmingham Commercial Herald*, 6 Oct 1806) in Birmingham on 5 October 1806 aged sixty-seven; his obituary notices commented that he had been an eminent surgeon of Birmingham for forty-five years, noting the success of his practice, 'his maturated judgment, his skill, and his capacity' (*Aris's Birmingham Gazette*, 6 Oct 1806). His wife died on 26 May 1823 at Keynsham, near Bristol, where their youngest son, Henry, lived. Mynors's descendants lived on at Weatheroak Hall (later Kings Norton Golf Club) until 1935, when the family died out. Mynors died a wealthy man and in his will, made on 31 August 1805, apart from small charitable bequests, his widow and two surviving sons were the main beneficiaries.

JOAN LANE

Sources J. Hill and R. K. Dent, *Memorials of the Old Square* (1897) · Birm. CA, Mynors estate MSS, MSS 442356–442976 · Birm. CA, MSS 1356, 1561 · general hospital governors' minutes and annual reports, Birm. CA · P. J. Wallis and R. V. Wallis, *Eighteenth century medics*, 2nd edn (1988) · Burke, *Gen. GB* · *Birmingham Commercial Herald* (6 Oct 1806) · *Aris's Birmingham Gazette* (6 Oct 1806) · *Aris's Birmingham Gazette* (2 June 1823) · *Worcester Journal* (9 Oct 1806) · IGI · will, PRO, PROB 11/1457 · *The Birmingham school* (1990) [Birmingham Museum and Art Gallery catalogue] · P. Ricketts, *The road to Weatheroak* (1992)

Archives Birm. CA

Likenesses J. Millar, group portrait, oils, 1797, Soho House, Birmingham; repro. in *The Birmingham school*

Wealth at death wealthy: will, PRO, PROB 11/1457

Mynors, Sir Roger Aubrey Baskerville (1903–1989), classical scholar, was born on 28 July 1903, probably at Langley Burrell, Wiltshire, the eldest of four sons and second of five children of the Revd Aubrey Baskerville Mynors, rector of Langley Burrell, and his wife, Margery Musgrave, daughter of the Revd Charles Musgrave Harvey, prebendary of St Paul's Cathedral. His younger twin, Humphrey Charles Baskerville (1903–1989), later first baronet, to whom he bore a confusing resemblance in earlier years, was to become deputy governor of the Bank of England, a position that had been held by his mother's brother, Sir Ernest Musgrave Harvey, first baronet. He was educated at Eton College (scholar, 1916) and Balliol College, Oxford (exhibitioner, 1922), where he obtained firsts in classical honour moderations (1924) and *literae humaniores* (1926), as well as the Hertford (1924), Craven (1924), and Derby (1926) scholarships.

Mynors was elected a fellow of Balliol in 1926; pupils remember how he introduced them to authors remote from the syllabus. In 1940 he went to the exchange control department of the Treasury as a temporary principal. In 1944 he was elected to the Kennedy chair of Latin at Cambridge, where he became a fellow of Pembroke College, but he never seemed to settle. On 12 December 1945 he married Lavinia Sybil (*d.* 1994), daughter of the Very Revd

Cyril Argentine *Alington, dean of Durham and formerly his headmaster at Eton, and his wife, Hester Margaret, a daughter of the fourth Baron Lyttelton; it was to prove an ideally happy union. There were no children. His sister-in-law Elizabeth was married to Lord Home of the Hirsel. Lavinia Mynors was a medical researcher and a diarist.

In 1949 Mynors was disappointed not to become master of Balliol, when Sir David Keir was preferred. In 1953 he returned to Oxford as Corpus Christi professor of Latin in succession to Eduard Fraenkel, and he remained at Corpus Christi College until his retirement in 1970.

Mynors's contribution to learning for most of his life centred on Latin manuscripts. He saw them as part of the cultural history of Europe; for him the scribes were not anonymous symbols at the foot of the page, but human beings and friends, who could be placed and dated and sometimes identified. He was a rapid and meticulous collator from an age without microfilms; his apparatus criticus was always elegant and unfussy, like everything else including his handwriting, but he was not assertive enough to offer many conjectures of his own. He edited the *Institutiones* of Cassiodorus (1937), Catullus (1958), Pliny's letters (1963), the *Panegyrici Latini* (1964), and Virgil (1969). He was a medievalist at least as much as a classical scholar, and he did much to promote Nelson's Medieval Texts, where he was generous with unobtrusive help to others. He produced catalogues of the manuscripts of Durham Cathedral before 1200, a sumptuous book (1939), and of Balliol College, a conspicuously professional performance (1963). He was a precise and economical translator who contributed much to the Toronto translation of Erasmus (from 1974) and took part in the final revision of the *New English Bible*.

Mynors was a fascinating lecturer whom undergraduates flocked to hear, not because he helped them for their examinations but because they found him so interesting. He supervised graduate students by describing his own researches and inspiring them to do likewise. He was a courteous chairman, yet with something in his manner that discouraged time-wasters. He was a delightful letter-writer to his friends, with great sympathy for the young, but did not hurry to reply on matters of business. He was not easy to find, but was there to help when it mattered most. His charm was memorable, but there was a touch of astringency towards the incompetent and self-important, and in spite of his urbanity he showed a diffidence that was not entirely assumed. Though the least didactic of teachers, he could throw off a remark that changed one's approach to the subject, and sensible people followed up his most tentative suggestions.

For many years Mynors occupied himself with a commentary on Virgil's *Georgics* that appeared posthumously in 1990. It paid no particular regard to recent periodical articles, or to the fads and fancies of a younger generation of scholars. Instead it showed an expert knowledge of ancient and modern agriculture, a flair for integrating interesting things from a wide range of reading, and a sensitive ear for what the poet is actually saying. Above all it was directed by the author's feeling for the countryside, and particularly for Treago, the estate he inherited near St Weonards in Herefordshire. Anybody who wishes to know what Mynors was like should read this book.

He became a fellow of the British Academy in 1944 and was knighted in 1963. He was an honorary fellow of Balliol (1963) and Corpus Christi (1970) colleges, Oxford, of Pembroke College, Cambridge (1965), and of the Warburg Institute. He was an honorary member of the American Academy of Arts and Sciences, the American Philosophical Society, and the Istituto di Studi Romani. He held honorary degrees from the universities of Cambridge, Durham, Edinburgh, Sheffield, and Toronto.

Mynors died on 17 October 1989 as the result of a road accident outside Hereford; he was driving back to Treago after working on his catalogue of the manuscripts in Hereford Cathedral Library. As he left the cathedral he was heard to say that he had had a good day. He was buried at St Weonards. R. G. M. NISBET, rev.

Sources R. G. M. Nisbet, *Gnomon*, 62 (1990) · M. Winterbottom, 'Roger Aubrey Baskerville Mynors, 1903–1989', *PBA*, 80 (1993), 371–402 · A. Hayter, ed., *A wise woman: a memoir of Lavinia Mynors from her diaries and letters* (1996) · *The Times* (19 Oct 1989) · *The Guardian* (23 Oct 1989) · personal knowledge (1996) · *CGPLA Eng. & Wales* (1990) Archives Bodl. Oxf., corresp. relating to Society for Protection of Science and Learning · Tate collection, corresp. with Lord Clark Likenesses photograph (as a young man), repro. in Winterbottom, *PBA*, 372 · photograph, repro. in Hayter, ed., *Wise woman*, 94 Wealth at death £594,190: administration with will, 5 April 1990, *CGPLA Eng. & Wales*

Mynyddog Mwynfawr (*supp. fl.* **6th cent.**), king in Britain, is traditionally thought to have been lord of Din Eidyn (Edinburgh) when it was the principal stronghold of the king of the Gododdin. The Gododdin were the Votadini of the Roman period (Gododdin is a later form of the name Votadini), whose territory appears to have extended from around Stirling down the eastern side of the country as far as Hadrian's Wall. It was Mynyddog Mwynfawr, so the traditional interpretation goes, who sent a cavalry expedition to fight against the Deirans at Catraeth, the former Roman fort of Catterick in north Yorkshire. The heroic deaths of the three hundred or so horsemen, first feasted for a year and then sent southwards by Mynyddog, were commemorated in the poem to which the name of the people was attached, *Y Gododdin*. Presumably after the Gododdin had all been brought under Bernician (Northumbrian) rule—Din Eidyn itself may have been taken by siege in 638—the poem became the memorial, not just of the horsemen of Mynyddog, but of the entire people. As the Bernicians came to be, for a millennium, the traditional enemies of the Britons, so the *Gododdin* became a classic celebration of heroic defeat. Unfortunately, the transmission of the poem to the thirteenth-century Book of Aneirin was such as to make it exceedingly difficult to prove that any particular section of text is a faithful representative of a sixth- or early seventh-century original.

There are also historical difficulties that make this traditional account problematic. First, Mynyddog is not an attested name (Mynyddog Mwynfawr means 'Mountainous of Great Wealth'). There is no record of his pedigree or his descendants and he is not even celebrated within the poem as having led the expedition. Instead another warrior, Urfai or Yrfai, is described as lord of Eidyn (Din Eidyn); and yet another, Gwlyged (perhaps Gwlgod or Gwlygod) has, as his epithet, the name of the people, Gododdin, suggesting that he might have been their ruler. For these reasons it has been proposed that Mynyddog is not the name of a person at all, but rather a description of the court on the *mynydd* ('mountain' or 'mount') at Din Eidyn, probably the site of the present Edinburgh Castle. Mynyddog Mwynfawr would then mean something like 'Mountain Court of Great Wealth'. An intermediate position would allow that Mynyddog is not a proper name, but would still interpret it as a description of a person rather than a court.

Leaving aside for a moment the problem of the name, there is a further difficulty over the date and purpose of the expedition. The situation of Catraeth, by *c.*630 within the Anglian kingdom of Deira, suggests that the expedition was mounted before Bernicia, with its original core around Bamburgh, Lindisfarne, and Yeavering, became the principal threat to the Gododdin—that is, before the reign of Æthelfrith (*r.* 592–*c.*616). On the other hand, the British kingdoms most closely concerned with Catraeth were Rheged, probably lying west, across Stainmore, and Elmet (near present-day Leeds). Elmet was not conquered until the reign of Eadwine (*r. c.*616–633). Rheged, if it included Carlisle, had become part of Northumbria at the latest by 685. While, therefore, the traditional view is inclined to place the expedition *c.*590–600, and therefore just before or within the reign of Æthelfrith, a more recent proposal is that the expedition took place considerably earlier, *c.*540, before the foundation of the Anglian kingdom of Bernicia (placed by Bede in 547). More recently still it has been argued that the battle of Catraeth was not between Britons and Angles, but between two armies both of which included Britons and Angles; it has also been queried whether the evidence demonstrates that the expedition, however glorious in the eyes of the poet, was any more than a cattle raid. For medieval Welsh tradition Mynyddog was a person but significant solely because of the fate of his war-band.

T. M. CHARLES-EDWARDS

Sources *Llyfr Aneirin*, ed. D. Huws (1989) [facs. of the Book of Aneirin] · I. Williams, ed., *Canu Aneirin* (1938) · Aneirin, *'Y Gododdin': Britain's oldest heroic poem*, trans. A. O. H. Jarman (1988) · *The 'Gododdin' of Aneirin: text and context from dark-age north Britain*, ed. and trans. J. T. Koch (1997) · K. H. Jackson, *The 'Gododdin': the oldest Scottish poem* (1969) · Bede, *Hist. eccl.* · Nennius, 'British history' and 'The Welsh annals', ed. and trans. J. Morris (1980) · P. H. Blair, 'The Moore memoranda on Northumbrian history', *The early cultures of north-west Europe: H. M. Chadwick memorial studies*, ed. C. Fox and B. Dickins (1950), 245–57 · P. H. Blair, 'The origins of Northumbria', *Archaeologia Aeliana*, 4th ser., 25 (1947), 1–51 · D. N. Dumville, 'The origins of Northumbria', *The origins of Anglo-Saxon kingdoms*, ed. S. Bassett (1989), 213–22 · J. Rowland, 'Warfare and horses in the *Gododdin* and the problem of Catraeth', *Cambrian Medieval Celtic Studies*, 30 (1995), 13–40

Myrddin Wyllt. *See* Merlin (*supp. fl.* 6th cent.).

Myres, Sir John Linton (1869–1954), archaeologist and historian, was born on 3 July 1869 at Preston, Lancashire, the

Sir John Linton Myres (1869–1954), by Lafayette, 1929

only son of the Revd William Miles Myres (*d*. 1901), vicar of St Paul's, Preston, and his first wife, Jane, daughter of the Revd Henry Linton. He won scholarships to Winchester College, thence to New College, Oxford, where he took first classes in honour moderations (1890) and *literae humaniores* (1892). He had already shown a lively interest in antiquities and local history as an undergraduate, publishing articles, digging at Alchester, and organizing the local history museum at Aylesbury. As a fellow of Magdalen (1892–5) and Craven fellow (1892) he was able to visit the Mediterranean, travelling in the Greek islands, exploring Caria and the Dodecanese, and working with Arthur Evans. He travelled widely in Crete, collecting minor antiquities and copying inscriptions. These were the early days of excavation in the island and of the discovery of Minoan civilization, although Knossos itself had yet to be dug. By comparing Cretan vases with some vase fragments found by Flinders Petrie in Egypt, at Kahun, he found the first important link and correlation to be observed between the two ancient civilizations. He did not join Evans in the excavations at Knossos, but dug with the British School at Palaikastro, and, notably, at the hilltop shrine of Petsofa, the finds from which he soon published.

It was to Cyprus and to Cypriot antiquities that much of his archaeological work was at first devoted, and he several times returned to the problems of its archaeology in his writings. He had conducted excavations in the island in 1894, at Kition; he wrote a catalogue of the Cyprus Museum (1899, with M. Ohnefalsch-Richter); and in 1914 published an exemplary catalogue of the rich Cesnola collection in New York. In these years he had been a student of Christ Church (1895–1907) and university lecturer in classical archaeology, and he went to Liverpool as professor of Greek and lecturer in ancient geography (1907–10). In his early teaching and writing his knowledge of the geography of the Aegean was put to good account and he had the happy gift of being able to elucidate problems of antiquity by modern analogies. Quite apart from his Greek studies, he wrote a schools' *History of Rome* which was published in 1902.

The creation of the new Wykeham professorship in ancient history took Myres back to Oxford in 1910 and he held this chair until his retirement in 1939. The title of his inaugural lecture—'Greek lands and the Greek people'—set the theme of his future interests and these years saw the publication of several books on the various aspects of ancient history which his wide experience encompassed. *The Dawn of History* (1911) was a semi-popular exposition of fundamental principles about the study of early civilizations and approach to ancient history. It displayed already the easy style of writing which informed all his work. To the *Cambridge Ancient History* he contributed several chapters. *Who Were the Greeks?* (1930) was his most brilliant and provocative work, based on the Sather lectures which he had been again invited to deliver in California in 1927 (the first time had been in 1914). On Sir Arthur Evans's death in 1941 he took on the task of editing the Linear B tablets from Knossos which, half a century after their discovery, were finally published (as *Scripta Minoa II*) in 1952, and he lived to applaud the decipherment by Michael Ventris of their language as Greek. Myres continued writing until his death—a vivid and highly personal account, *Herodotus: Father of History* (1953), and essays on *Homer and his Critics*, edited after his death by Dorothea Gray in 1958. To his collection of essays *Geographical History in Greek Lands* (1953), he appended a select bibliography of his writings. The most valuable aspect of his work was probably not so much the new material or solutions which he presented—although these were numerous—but the challenging approach to the more conventional problems of ancient history which a scholar versed in geography, anthropology, and the classics could take. His services to scholarship were recognized by honorary degrees from Wales, Manchester, Witwatersrand, and Athens, and the Victoria medal of the Royal Geographical Society (1953). He was elected FBA in 1923 and knighted in 1943.

Myres's interests were not confined to any narrow field of research in antiquity. When he went to Greece in 1892 one of his awards was the Burdett-Coutts geological scholarship. As an anthropologist he served the Royal Anthropological Institute as its honorary secretary, then president (1928–31); and in 1901 he had inaugurated its new monthly periodical, *Man*, which he edited in 1901–3, and again in 1931–46, and to which he regularly contributed on subjects often far removed from classical studies. As a Hellenist and archaeologist he was vice-president of the Society of Antiquaries (1924–9) and its gold medallist in

1942; president of the Hellenic Society (1935–8); chairman of the British School at Athens (1934–47), and organizer of its jubilee exhibition in Burlington House in 1936. He was librarian of New College, Oxford, up to 1946. He was general secretary of the British Association from 1919 to 1932, following its conferences to many parts of the world. His range in scholarship was matched by the variety and vigour of his other activities. As well as his concern for the administration and welfare of the various societies which he served, he was active in Oxford politics, in the establishment of new graduate degrees, and the promotion of new subjects, notably geography and anthropology. In the First World War he commanded small craft in raiding operations on the Turkish coast on the tug *Syros* and then the former royal yacht *Aulis*. In this his ingenuity and buccaneering spirit served him no less than his detailed knowledge of the geography and people of the Asia Minor coast. He ended the war as acting commander of the Royal Naval Volunteer Reserve and was made OBE and appointed to the Greek order of George I. In the Second World War he used his great experience of the geography of Greece in editing handbooks for naval intelligence.

Through most of his life Myres was troubled by his eyesight and at the end, although still writing, was quite blind. In appearance he was a handsome man, bearded and blue-eyed. In his dealings with younger scholars he was generous and kindly, and his work must be judged not only by what he wrote but also by what he inspired in others, by example or casual precept. He founded no school. In his lifetime he saw classical archaeology grow from a dilettante study to a discipline which has much to contribute to all departments of classical scholarship. His part in this development was to show how historian, archaeologist, anthropologist, and geographer should combine their skills in the study of antiquity.

In 1895 Myres married Sophia Florence (d. 1960), daughter of Charles Ballance, with whom he had two sons and one daughter. The younger son, John Nowell Linton *Myres, was Bodley's librarian at Oxford (1948–65). Myres died in Oxford on 6 March 1954.

JOHN BOARDMAN, rev.

Sources T. J. Dunbabin, 'Sir John Myres, 1869–1954', *PBA*, 41 (1955), 349–65 • T. J. Dunbabin, obituary and supplementary bibliography, *Annual of British School at Athens*, 49 (1954), 311–14 • J. N. L. Myres, *Commander J. L. Myres, RNVR: the Blackbeard of the Aegean* (1980) • J. L. Myres, 'Praeterita', unpublished autobiography transcribed by Dr M. T. Myres, priv. coll.
Archives AM Oxf., corresp., notes, etc. • Bodl. Oxf., corresp. and MSS • Bodl. Oxf., topographical collections for Buckinghamshire parishes • S. Antiquaries, Lond., corresp. relating to Scripta Minoa | BL, corresp. with Society of Authors, Add. MSS 63311 • Bodl. Oxf., letters to O. G. S. Crawford • Bodl. Oxf., corresp. with Gilbert Murray • Bodl. Oxf., letters to Sir Alfred Zimmero
Likenesses W. Stoneman, photograph, 1923, NPG • Lafayette, photograph, 1929, NPG [see illus.] • W. Stoneman, photograph, 1930, NPG • A. Rutherston, pencil drawing, New College, Oxford • A. Rutherston, pencil drawing, U. Oxf., school of geography and the environment
Wealth at death £20,441 2s. 2d.: probate, 24 May 1954, *CGPLA Eng. & Wales*

Myres, (John) Nowell Linton (1902–1989), archaeologist and librarian, was born at 1 Wellington Place, Oxford, on 27 December 1902, the younger son and second of three children of Sir John Linton *Myres (1869–1954), archaeologist and historian, and his wife, Sophia Florence, *née* Ballance (d. 1960), who was of Huguenot descent. Books brought over by her forebears in 1685, as well as sixteenth-century *incunabula* bought with his own pocket money, contributed to the boyhood inheritance of the future custodian of Bodley. From his preparatory school on the Surrey–Sussex border he won a scholarship to Winchester College. Deeply influenced by the college architecture and the inspired history teaching of A. T. P. Williams, later bishop of Durham and of Winchester, he went to New College, Oxford, in 1921 determined to make history his subject; substituting the history preliminary examination for classical honour moderations, he took a first in *literae humaniores* (1924) in three years and another in modern history (1926) in two.

After appointment as a college lecturer in modern history in 1926 Myres was elected a student of Christ Church in 1928. In 1929 he married a teacher, Joan Mary Lovell (d. 1991), sister of Charles Stevens, his school friend and fellow excavator of St Catharine's Hill, Winchester, and daughter of George Lovell Stevens, farmer in southern Africa. They had two sons, the elder, Timothy, associate professor of zoology in the University of Calgary, the younger, Rear-Admiral John Myres, hydrographer of the Royal Navy.

From 1928, apart from wartime civil service (1940–45), in which Myres rose to be head of the fruit and vegetable products division of the Ministry of Food (he was a keen vegetable gardener), tutoring and lecturing were his formal occupation for the next twenty years.

They were also years of strenuous extra-collegial activity. Earlier excavations at St Catharine's Hill and at Caerleon amphitheatre were now followed by others at Colchester, Butley Priory in Suffolk, and Aldborough in Yorkshire. In 1931 Myres was invited to contribute a section on the English settlements, based on archaeological as well as historical sources, to the first volume (*Roman Britain and the English Settlements*, 1936) of the *Oxford History of England*. R. G. Collingwood was his fellow author.

Librarian of Christ Church from 1938, Myres, with his versatile scholarship and proven ability as an administrator, was a natural choice in 1948 as successor to Sir H. H. Edmund Craster as Bodley's librarian, after a brief tenure by H. R. Creswick. His own tenure lasted for eighteen years and involved integrating the 1939 extension with the parent institution, the major repair and internal reordering of the buildings round the schools quadrangle, and supervision of a total structural overhaul of the fabric of Duke Humfrey, the fifteenth-century reading room above the vault of the divinity school. He also presided over the establishment of the new law library in St Cross Road. He widened the Bodleian's status and repute by setting up and hosting the copyright libraries conference and establishing the standing conference of national and university libraries; also he founded the Society of Bodley's

(John) Nowell Linton Myres (1902–1989), by unknown photographer

1972. He was a fellow (1951–77) and sub-warden of Winchester, honorary fellow of New College (1973), and successively research, emeritus, and honorary student (1971) of Christ Church. He received honorary doctorates from the universities of Toronto (1954), Reading (1964), Belfast (1965), and Durham (1983). Myres died at his home, the Manor House, Kennington, near Oxford, on 25 July 1989.

ARNOLD TAYLOR, rev.

Sources Oxford Times (24 Jan 1986) · The Times (26 July 1989) · J. N. L. Myres, 'Recent discoveries in the Bodleian Library', Archaeologia, 101 (1967), 151–68 · A. Taylor, 'John Nowell Linton Myres, 1902–1989', PBA, 76 (1990), 513–28 [incl. bibliography] · [V. I. Evison], 'The published works of John Nowell Linton Myres', Angles, Saxons, and Jutes: essays presented to J. N. L. Myres, ed. V. I. Evison (1981), xvii–xxx · unpublished autobiography, priv. coll. · personal knowledge (1996)
Archives priv. coll. | Bodl. Oxf., letter to O. G. S. Crawford
Likenesses photograph, Hult. Arch. [see illus.]
Wealth at death £229,210: probate, 17 Oct 1989, CGPLA Eng. & Wales

American Friends. Though a non-professional, in 1963 he was elected president of the Library Association. Bitter disagreement with the university authorities over their refusal to accept his defence of the Bodleian's claim to the premises of the Indian Institute led to his resignation after a dramatic debate in congregation in 1965. (As Bodley's librarian he invariably wore a dark coat and striped trousers, even when riding a bicycle, and in later life grew a huge beard like his father's.)

From now on Myres gave his whole mind to archaeology and the pursuit of the course he had set himself in 1931. His Rhind lectures of 1964–5 appeared in 1969 as Anglo-Saxon Pottery and the Settlement of England; in 1973 came The Anglo-Saxon Cemeteries of Caistor-by-Norwich and Markshall (jointly with Barbara Green); 1977 saw the achievement of the long-envisaged A Corpus of Anglo-Saxon Pottery of the Pagan Period; finally, in 1986, he was able to bring out a revision and reassessment, as an independent volume of the Oxford History, of his English Settlements of fifty years earlier.

Many societies benefited from Myres's unremitting involvement in their affairs, notably the Oxford University Archaeological Society, the Council for British Archaeology (of which he was a joint originator), the Sachsensymposium, and the Society for Medieval Archaeology. The Society of Antiquaries of London, whose president he was in 1970–75, awarded him their gold medal in 1976 for services to archaeology. He was a valued member of many official bodies including the Royal Commission on Historical Monuments in 1969–74 and the Ancient Monuments Board in 1959–76. He was especially noted for his friendliness and sense of fun, as also for his helpfulness to younger scholars. Totally without pomposity, he brightened his later bedridden days with the use of one of his doctoral robes as a dressing-gown. Quick to apply modern terms to ancient situations, he chuckled a lot when giving the title 'Charlemagne on Miniskirts' to a learned but light-hearted note in Antiquity (42, 1968, p. 125).

Myres was elected FBA in 1966 and appointed CBE in

Myrtle, Mrs Harriet. See Miller, Lydia Mackenzie Falconer (bap. 1812, d. 1876).

Mysore, Sir Krishnaraja Wadiyar Bahadur. See Wodeyar, Krishnaraja (1884–1940).

Mytens [Mijtens], **Daniel** (c.1590–1647), painter, was born at Delft in the northern Netherlands, one of four sons of Maerten Mytens (b. 1551/2) and his wife, Anneke Pieters. He probably spent part of his childhood at The Hague in a house belonging to his father, a coachbuilder and saddler who supplied the royal court. Details of Mytens's early artistic training are unknown. He may well have studied initially with a relative, as he belonged to an artistic dynasty extending from Aert Mytens (1541–1602) to members of the Van Loo family in the eighteenth century. In early seventeenth-century Holland the Mytens family was socially well-established and included burgomasters, notaries, and advocates. Mytens perhaps studied subsequently at The Hague with Jan Anthonisz van Ravesteyn, or at Delft with Michiel van Mierevelt (d. 1641), who influenced Mytens's own portraits. The works Mytens painted during his youth in the Netherlands remain unidentified. In 1610 he joined the Guild of St Luke, the professional association of painters at The Hague. He married Gratia Cletcher, sister of the international jeweller Thomas Cletcher the younger, in 1612.

Move to London In the mid-1610s Mytens travelled to London, where he joined a community of Dutch and Flemish artists. Their interrelated families lived in the same area of the city and worshipped at the same Dutch Reformed church. Possibly Mytens assisted his relative, the royal painter Paul van Somer, who could have encountered Mytens while visiting The Hague in 1615.

Mytens probably came to the notice of his first major English patron through Dudley Carleton, English ambassador at The Hague. Carleton's correspondence with Thomas Howard, second earl of Arundel, refers to Mytens as 'Your Lordship's painter' (W. Hookham Carpenter, Pictorial Notices, 1844, 176–7). The earliest evidence of

Daniel Mytens (c.1590–1647), self-portrait, c.1630

Mytens's presence in England is his letter of 18 August 1618 to Carleton, referring to an earlier visit to London (PRO, state papers foreign, Holland, vols. 84–5, fol. 176), and to his portraits of the earl and countess of Arundel, including large portraits which particularly pleased the earl. These were probably the two full lengths, each measuring 207 cm by 127 cm, *Thomas Howard, Earl of Arundel* and *Alatheia, Countess of Arundel*, now at Arundel Castle (on loan from NPG). Mytens's portrait of the earl depicts him richly but soberly clad in his customary black, sitting before a sculpture gallery: an idealized reference to the celebrated collection of antiquities at Arundel's London house. Arundel holds the official staff of earl marshal (a post traditionally granted to members of his family, although until 1621 Arundel was merely a commissioner in the earl marshal's office). The companion portrait of Lady Arundel (Howard had married the heiress Alatheia Talbot in 1806) shows her sitting before a gallery of painted portraits, and wearing magnificent lace and jewellery.

In these portraits the essence of Mytens's mature style is already evident in the strong sense which they convey of their sitters' physical presence, achieved through naturalistic drawing and the sensitive handling of the fall of light upon textiles and flesh. Mytens's impeccable Netherlandish drawing technique brought a new sense of weightiness and three-dimensionality to Jacobean portraiture, previously dominated by flattened images of sitters posing stiffly in a uniform and artificial light. While doing justice to the magnificence of contemporary court dress (long a dominant feature of English court portraiture), Mytens strongly emphasized the faces of his sitters, an emphasis in keeping with Mierevelt's influence on northern Netherlandish portraiture. Above all, Mytens gave his sitters a sober dignity. His finest portraits suggest considerable insight into human character.

Royal patronage Mytens soon found more patrons at the English court. William Herbert, third earl of Pembroke, a relative of the Arundels, commissioned many portraits from Mytens between 1623 and 1631. His career as a royal portraitist benefited from the departure from England in 1621 of the Flemish artist Anthony Van Dyck, engaged by James I as royal painter. Van Dyck's temporary absence stretched into years and with the death of Paul van Somer the field was open for Mytens. His earliest recorded payment from the crown was that of May 1620, for an imposing full length, *The Earl of Nottingham, Lord High Admiral* (NMM). Records begin in 1623 for portraits by Mytens, probably painted in 1622, of King James himself and of Charles, prince of Wales. These include a *James I* for the ambassador of the government of the Spanish Netherlands, and *Charles, Prince of Wales* for the Spanish ambassador.

James I perhaps recognized in Mytens's dignified art a modern approach to royal portraiture, which, like his new Banqueting House, would give a favourable impression of the British court, and support the king's efforts to secure a marriage between the prince of Wales and the infanta of Spain (the 'Spanish match'). Mytens's portraits, while naturalistic, probably flattered his royal sitters, as was required in court portraiture. His *King James I and VI* (1621; NPG) tactfully presents the king, an ageing heavy drinker averse to washing, as a dignified monarch, in keeping with his reputation as the 'British Solomon'.

On 19 July 1624 the king granted Mytens a life pension of £50 a year, conditional on Mytens's binding agreement to serve James and his heirs 'faithfullie and diligently' (PRO, state papers domestic, vol. 39/16, nos. 46, 47). The artist was forbidden to leave England without royal leave (ibid., Interregnum, warrant 46, App. V). In August, Mytens was made an English denizen on the order of the prince of Wales. On 30 December 1624, he enrolled the lease of a house in St Martin's Lane, London, through the prince's chancellor Sir Henry Hobart, who sat to Mytens for a portrait now at Blickling Hall, Norfolk.

After the death of James I, the new king appointed Mytens one of his picture-drawers of his chamber in ordinary on 4 June 1625, citing Mytens's previous good service: 'we having experience of the faculty and skill of Daniel Mitens in the art of picture drawing' (PRO, patent rolls, 66 2371. M. 19; exchequer of receipt issues, enrolments, registers, 403/2518, fol. 5). This was a lifetime appointment, although at a lower salary than Mytens had received from James I: only £20 per year.

Mytens's art continued to develop. Charles I's commissions for copies of paintings in the Royal Collection (at higher fees than portraits) allowed Mytens to study Titian's *Pardo Venus* and, in 1629, Palma Vecchio's *Virgin and Child with SS. Catherine of Alexandria and S. John the Baptist* (the latter remains in the Royal Collection). Mytens revisited the Netherlands on a travel pass issued for six months on 18 August 1626, doubtless encountering contemporary Dutch (and perhaps Flemish) portraiture. His portrait of Charles I's sister, living in exile at The Hague, *Queen Elizabeth of Bohemia* (Royal Collection), was probably painted during this trip.

Further commissions In England many payments are recorded between 1626 and 1632 for Mytens's increasingly elegant portraits. His *George Calvert, First Baron Baltimore* (1627; formerly Wentworth Woodhouse, Yorkshire) is one of his finest. He surpassed it with *James, First Duke of Hamilton* (1629; Scot. NPG), presenting his sitter as a confident man rather than the diffident youth portrayed in his earlier *James Hamilton when Earl of Arran* (1623; Tate collection). The 1629 portrait of Hamilton shows some French influence, perhaps because Mytens or his sitter had seen French prints. (Londoners had followed closely the progress of the recent struggle for the protestant stronghold of La Rochelle in France, in which English forces participated.) Its unconventional colour scheme demonstrates Mytens's gifts as a colourist: Hamilton's sun-bronzed face contrasts with his silver-grey clothing, and the powder blue curtain behind him. At the same time Mytens's portrayal characteristically conveys a firm impression of Hamilton's personality.

Portraits of Charles I Mytens's letter of 1618 to Carleton had mentioned an unsuccessful attempt to obtain a sitting from Charles, prince of Wales, frustrated by the prince's departure for the hunt. From 1621, however, Mytens painted a remarkable series of portraits tracing the maturing of the prince from hesitant heir to the throne to self-assured monarch. These dominated his output as royal portraitist. Surviving accounts (PRO, lord chamberlain's dept, miscellanea, vol. 5/132) record some fifteen portraits of Charles supplied by Mytens or his studio between 1628 and 1631. He probably painted many more. (The relevant volume of warrants, covering payments to Mytens during his period of service from c.1619 to 1628, is missing from state papers.)

Most of these portraits of Charles were traditionally posed full lengths, dependent upon changes in dress and background for variety. The conventions of royal portraiture required Mytens to produce acceptable autograph prototypes. Each was disseminated for several years through studio replicas and copies, produced with the aid of assistants, until a new pattern was deemed necessary.

The initial portraits of Charles as prince of Wales in various poses culminate in *Charles I when Prince of Wales* (1624; National Gallery of Canada, Ottawa), for which a replica survives (Royal Museum of Fine Arts, Copenhagen), as well as a closely related head-and-shoulders portrait (Weiss Gallery, London) and an engraving by the Dutch engraver Willem Delff (1580–1638). In these images the awkwardness of the young heir to the throne is evident, despite his rich clothing. From 1625 Mytens adapted Charles's poses to give the young monarch an increasingly commanding appearance, enhanced by lighting effects. On Mytens's return from the Netherlands in 1627

he added an image of Charles to an architectural background painted a year earlier by Hendrick Steenwyck, a specialist in architectural painting. The resulting *Charles I with Architectural Background* (Pinacoteca Sabauda, Turin) is a large version of a type of portrait fashionable at The Hague during the 1620s. Mytens repeated the king's figure in *Charles I with Balustrade* (1628; Royal Collection). In 1629, when Charles I began to rule without parliament, Mytens's *Charles I* (Metropolitan Museum of Art, New York) represented him as a more robust figure, standing confidently with his face to the light: a monarch fit for the new era of personal rule. The Salomonic column in the background is a detail derived from the Raphael tapestry cartoons in the Royal Collection, already incorporated by Van Dyck and Rubens in paintings for British courtiers. Mytens may have used it here to represent the wisdom and judgment of King Solomon, already associated with Charles's father, James I.

Family life On 2 September 1628 the widowed Mytens remarried at the Dutch church in Austin Friars, London. His new wife was Johanna Drossaert. The registers of marriages and baptisms for the Dutch church and the French protestant church in Threadneedle Street indicate that Mytens now moved in a circle of prosperous city merchants, deacons, and elders of Dutch or French protestant descent. His twin daughters Elizabeth and Susanna were baptized at the Dutch Reformed church, Austin Friars, in July 1629.

Artistic rivals Mytens's career survived the brief visit to London in 1628 of the Netherlandish painter Gerrit van Honthorst, who demonstrated his range as a royal portraitist with his intimate *Charles I Reading* (NPG), and an enormous *Apollo and Diana* (Royal Collection), a Dutch Arcadian evocation of contemporary court masques incorporating portraits of Charles I, Queen Henrietta Maria, and leading Stuart courtiers. Mytens's career also weathered the visit of Peter Paul Rubens to London in 1629. Only Van Dyck's return to settle in London in 1632 blighted Mytens's prospects. A more imaginative artist, Van Dyck surpassed Mytens in depicting the human figure in motion, a valuable talent at this time, when the essentially static poses of Jacobean and early Carolean court portraiture were giving way to full-length images depicting the royal family interacting with one another. The choreographed elegance of Van Dyck's portraits made him a perfect portraitist for Charles I in the 1630s. The king demonstrated his desire for a carefully controlled presentation of the Stuart monarchy by insisting on increased formality in court etiquette. Van Dyck quickly assumed the position of 'principall Painter in Ordinary to their Majesties', and was knighted on 5 July 1632. In 1633 he was awarded an annual pension of £200, far more than Mytens. Although Charles offered to continue Mytens's pension and find work for him, Mytens retired to the Netherlands. His decision to retire, according to an anecdote recorded in two versions by the eighteenth-century British antiquarian George Vertue, was prompted by his recognition that 'now his Majesty had got a much better

Artist and had made him his principal painter' (Vertue, *Note Books*, 1.55 and 2.145). Significantly, it was a portrait of Henrietta Maria by Van Dyck which Charles showed to Mytens at the interview referred to by Vertue. The queen's importance at court had increased, following the death of the royal favourite George Villiers, first duke of Buckingham, and the birth of the new prince of Wales. In the 1630s court festivities celebrated the royal marriage as a love match, its harmony a model for the British state. Satisfactory portraits of the queen were now more important than ever. Van Dyck's enchanting interpretations of the somewhat plain Henrietta Maria delighted Charles I, now in love with his wife. Mytens's portraits of Henrietta Maria, painted repeatedly since 1625, the year of her marriage, were far less attractive, although considered acceptable in the absence of Van Dyck. (He made two replicas of his portrait *Henrietta Maria with Jeffrey Hudson*, 1628.) Dudley Carleton had previously criticized Mytens's portraits of the countess of Arundel as unflattering; his full-length double portrait of *Charles I and Henrietta Maria Departing for the Chase* (1630–32; Royal Collection), painted with assistants, must have seemed clumsy beside Van Dyck's representations. Dissatisfaction with Mytens's interpretation of the queen's appearance is evident in Mytens's half-length double portrait *Charles I and Henrietta Maria* (c.1630–32; Royal Collection), in which her face was repainted to resemble more closely Van Dyck's image of *Henrietta Maria* (Royal Collection). Mytens's portrait was then superseded by Van Dyck's own more graceful double portrait, of *Charles I and Henrietta Maria* (c.1632; archbishop's palace, Kremsier, Austria).

Mytens evidently recognized Van Dyck's superiority in portrait compositions. He borrowed ideas from the Flemish artist. However, Van Dyck himself borrowed from Mytens, adopting for his own *Portrait of Charles I in Robes of State* (Royal Collection) a pose used by Mytens in 1633 for his *Charles I in Garter Robes* (priv. coll.). As Sir Oliver Millar has pointed out, the Chatsworth version of the Mytens design, painted in 1631 by Cornelius Jonson (apparently Mytens's assistant at this date) incorporates a dog modelled on that in Van Dyck's *Children of Charles I* (Royal Collection).

Mytens's portraits continued to be prominently displayed at Whitehall, dominating the collection of royal and court portraits inventoried in the Bear Gallery in 1659. However, in the king's bedchamber, where Charles assembled favourite images of his relatives by Van Dyck and Honthorst, the only Mytens portrait was *Henry, Prince of Wales*, copied from a portrait miniature of Charles's late brother by Isaac Oliver.

Return to the Netherlands In September 1630 a pass was issued to Mytens permitting him to travel to the Low Countries 'with his trunckes' (PRO, Privy Council Office, registers 2/40, 104). On 11 May 1631 a further pass permitted Mytens's wife to depart with their three children, two maids, and 'truncks of apparel' (ibid., 495). A final payment to Mytens for a royal portrait (£100 for two portraits of Charles) was recorded in May 1634. Mytens's pension continued to be paid to him at The Hague. He worked

there as an art-collecting agent for British courtiers, including Arundel, for whom in 1637 he assessed the authenticity of works by Holbein, Dürer, Raphael, Andrea del Sarto, and Titian, and haggled over the prices of books. He produced a few minor portraits, including one of his former brother-in-law the jeweller Thomas Cletcher (Gemeentemuseum, The Hague), and remained active in his church, serving as deacon in 1638 and elder in 1647. On 22 June 1647, a local document referred to Mytens as 'deceased' (Bredius and Moes, 95).

Daniel Mytens's self-portrait remained at Whitehall, hanging in the same room as self-portraits by Van Dyck and Rubens, the other major painters who had served Charles I. For modern art historians Mytens remains overshadowed by Van Dyck, as Van Dyck is perhaps by Rubens. Mytens's portrait *James, First Duke of Hamilton*, one of the finest seventeenth-century portraits, is a reminder that his artistic career was a distinguished one, and that his premature retirement curtailed the development of an artist already capable of greatness.   ANNE THACKRAY

Sources A. Bredius and E. W. Moes, 'De Schildefamilie Mytens', *Oud Holland*, 24 (1906), 1ff.; 25 (1907), 84–96 • K. Garas, 'Mijtens (1): Daniel Mijtens I', *The dictionary of art*, ed. J. Turner (1996) • B. Haak, *The golden age Dutch painters of the seventeenth century* (1984) • F. M. Kelly, 'Mytens and his portraits of Charles I', *Burlington Magazine*, 37 (1920), 84–9 • O. Millar, *The Tudor, Stuart and early Georgian pictures in the collection of her majesty the queen*, 2 vols. (1963), vol. 1, pp. 84–5. • O. Millar, 'An attribution to Cornelius Johnson reinstated', *Burlington Magazine*, 90 (1948), 322 • O. Millar, *The age of Charles I: painting in England, 1620–1649* (1972), 12–13, 24–8 [exhibition catalogue, Tate Gallery, London, 15 Nov 1972 – 14 Jan 1973] • W. J. C. Moens, ed., *The marriage, baptismal and burial registers, 1571 to 1874, and monumental inscriptions of the Dutch Reformed church, Austin Friars, London* (privately printed, Lymington, 1884), 122–51 • C. C. Stopes, 'Daniel Mytens in England', *Burlington Magazine*, 17 (1910), 160–61 • O. Ter Kuile, 'Daniel Mijtens, "His Majesties picture-drawer"', *Nederlands Kunsthistorisch Jaarboek*, 20 (1969), 1–106 [incl. catalogue raisonné, appx of documents, and family tree] • Thieme & Becker, *Allgemeines Lexikon* • D. Thomson, 'Two Hamilton portraits', *National Art Collections Fund Review* (1988), 112–13 • E. Waterhouse, *Painting in Britain, 1530–1790*, 4th edn (1978)

Likenesses D. Mytens, self-portrait, oils, c.1625, Brukenthal Museum, Sibiu, Romania • D. Mytens, self-portrait, oils, c.1630, Royal Collection [*see illus.*] • D. Mytens, self-portrait, oils, c.1630, Kilkerran House, Strathclyde

Mytton, John [Jack] (1796–1834), sportsman and eccentric, born at Halston, Shropshire, on 30 September 1796 and baptized there on 3 October that year, was the only son of John Mytton (1768–1798), landowner, of Halston, and his wife, Sarah Harriet (1774–1853), a younger daughter of William Mostyn Owen, of nearby Woodhouse. He was brought up, perhaps indulgently, by his mother, taught by the chaplain at Halston, and nicknamed Mango, the King of the Pickles by a neighbour. At Westminster School (from 1807) he spent twice his £400 yearly allowance and was expelled in 1811, as he is said to have been from Harrow in 1813. He was later placed with a private tutor, whom he knocked down, and thereafter avoided the universities and education: always impervious to advice, he read only the *Racing Calendar* and *Stud Book*. At the age of eighteen he toured the continent, and on 30 May 1816 he became a cornet in the 7th hussars, part of the army of occupation in France. He left the army the following year but continued in the North Shropshire yeomanry cavalry (captain 1812, major 1822) until his death. He was sheriff of Merioneth in 1821 and of Shropshire in 1823.

On 21 May 1818 Mytton married Harriet Emma, the eldest daughter of Sir Thomas Jones bt, of Stanley Hall, Shropshire. They had a daughter, Harriet Emma Charlotte (1819–1885), who married, on 26 June 1841, Clement Delves, the fifth son of Colonel John Hill of Hawkstone. Following the death of his first wife on 2 July 1820 Mytton married (on 29 October 1821) Caroline Mallet, sixth daughter of Thomas Giffard, of Chillington, Staffordshire.

As master of foxhounds from 1818 to 1821 Jack Mytton, as he was known, hunted a vast country extending from Halston into Staffordshire and including what was later the country of the Albrighton hunt. Both then and later in the 1820s, when he hunted around Halston with new hounds and harriers, he flouted many established hunting conventions. He was on the turf from 1817 to 1830 but, though he kept a large racing stable, he never bred a good horse. Mytton (who was painted with his celebrated horse Euphrates by W. Webb in 1825) had a pleasing countenance rather than a handsome face. He was a man of great physical strength and foolhardy courage, with a strong taste for practical jokes. He was a splendid shot and a daring horseman, and there are numberless stories of his recklessness. He is said to have galloped at full speed over a rabbit warren just to see if his horse would fall, which it did and rolled over him. Again, for a wager he drove a tandem at night across country, surmounting a sunk fence 3 yards wide, a broad deep drain, and two stiff quickset hedges. He would sometimes strip to his shirt to follow

wildfowl in hard weather, and is said once to have stripped naked to follow some duck over the ice. One night he even set fire to his nightshirt to frighten away the hiccups. Inordinately convivial, Mytton drank from four to six bottles of port a day, beginning in the morning while shaving, and he eventually lived in a 'nearly constant state of intoxication'.

Unable to manage money, Mytton was open-handed and generous, as the Shrewsbury voters found when they elected him their tory MP at a by-election in 1819. He failed to stand at the 1820 general election, perhaps owing to financial troubles. His Shropshire and Montgomeryshire estates yielded almost £5000 a year, but he scorned his agent's advice to save his estate by living on £6000. By 1819 all his lands were heavily mortgaged and loans on his personal security were hard to find; sales of Shrewsbury properties began in 1820. In May 1831 he stood for Shropshire as a supporter of the Grey ministry's reform bill at the general election, but his popularity was waning among the independent freeholders, who disliked 'seeing a gentleman sink in the social scale', and he came bottom of the poll. Six months later, in November, he fled from his creditors to Calais. He had lost his entire fortune, and in 1832 his effects at Halston were sold up. He crossed the channel thrice more before his death and in England was committed to gaol more than once, before dying (accessible to religious consolation) of delirium tremens in the king's bench prison, Southwark, on 29 March 1834, aged thirty-eight. His death revived public affection for him, and on 9 April a half-mile procession of tenants, friends, and yeomanry troops escorted his body the last five miles to Halston chapel, where, in the presence of perhaps 2000

John Mytton (1796–1834), by John Frederick Herring senior, 1828

onlookers, he was buried in the family vault. Mytton's eldest son by his second wife, John Fox Fitz-Giffard Mytton (1823–1875), the only one of their five children to pass the age of fifty, inherited many paternal traits; he sold Habberley in 1846 and Halston—the family seat and its last landed estate—the following year.

G. F. R. BARKER, rev. GEORGE C. BAUGH

Sources Nimrod [C. J. Apperley], *Memoirs of the life of the late John Mytton* (1851) · J. Rice, *History of the British turf* (1879), 1.179–81 · Cecil, *Records of the chase and memoirs of celebrated sportsmen* (1877), 218–21 · Thormanby [W. W. Dixon], *Men of the turf: anecdotes of their career, and notes on many famous races* [1887], 55–63 · J. B. Burke, *Vicissitudes of families* (1869), 1.330–44 · Burke, *Gen. GB* (1879) · *GM*, 2nd ser., 1 (1834), 657 · *Shrewsbury Chronicle* (4 April 1834) · *Shrewsbury Chronicle* (11 April 1834) · *N&Q*, 5th ser., 7 (1877), 108, 197, 236 · *Army List* (1817) · R. G. Thorne, 'Mytton, John', *HoP, Commons, 1790–1820*, 4.651–2 · *Old Westminsters* · M. G. Dauglish and P. K. Stephenson, eds., *The Harrow School register, 1800–1911*, 3rd edn (1911)
Likenesses photogravure, 1818 (after W. Webb), NPG · J. F. Herring senior, oils, 1828, Ackerman and Johnson, London [*see illus.*] · W. Giller, engraving (after W. Webb) · W. Webb, portrait

Mytton, Thomas (1596/7–1656), parliamentarian army officer, was the son of Richard Mytton and his wife, Margaret Owen. His father came of a family whose members had been citizens of Shrewsbury for 400 years. The Myttons had prospered through contracting marriage alliances with Shropshire gentry families. The family had held Dinas Mawddwy, Merioneth, in the early fifteenth century, and Thomas Mytton's great-grandfather exchanged that manor for that of Halston, a hamlet just over 3 miles from Oswestry, Shropshire. Thomas's mother, Margaret, was the daughter of Thomas *Owen of Condover, near Shrewsbury, a judge of common pleas and member of the council in the marches of Wales. Mytton matriculated at Balliol College, Oxford, aged eighteen, on 11 May 1615, and entered Lincoln's Inn, London, on 27 February 1616. In 1629 he married Magdalen (d. 1648), daughter of Sir Robert *Napier [*see under* Napier, Richard] of Luton, Bedfordshire, and sister-in-law of Sir Thomas *Myddelton. This marriage alliance with a leading London Welsh puritan family, the history of puritan opposition to the government of James I by members of his mother's family, and the embryonic puritanism of the Oswestry area together account for his siding with parliament at the outbreak of the civil war, when most of Shropshire was for the king. He seems not to have rushed to join in the conflict, however. From London in mid-July 1642, when pursuing a private legal dispute, Mytton reported home in a rather detached tone on the composition of the king's commission of array for Shropshire. He posted home with approval a skit on puritans by John Taylor, the 'Water Poet', hardly suggesting that he was at this point a committed enthusiast for godly reform.

On 24 February 1643 Mytton was named to the first parliamentarian tax commission for Shropshire, and on the following 10 April he was named as a member of the committee for that county in the newly created military association with Warwickshire and Staffordshire. At the end of May he received commissions from the earl of Essex to raise horse, foot, and dragoons in Shropshire, and subsequently appointed three of his fellow committee men as junior officers in his regiment. On 12 June his brother-in-law Myddelton was by parliamentary ordinance created major-general (commander-in-chief under the earl of Essex) of the six counties of north Wales. On 4 July Sir John Corbet, colonel-general in Shropshire, was instructed by the Commons to abandon his military command to attend to his parliamentary duties, leaving Colonel Mytton as *de facto* commander in that county. Family ties with Myddelton gave Mytton the potential for a pivotal role in relations between the earl of Denbigh's Warwickshire and Staffordshire association and Myddelton's army, and Mytton availed himself of the opportunity. On 4 September Myddelton and Sir William Brereton mustered Staffordshire, and Mytton was successful in bringing enough troops to garrison Wem, of which he became governor. On 17 October, with 300 men, Mytton successfully defended Wem against a much larger force of royalists under Lord Capel, in retreat from Nantwich. He was named sheriff of Shropshire twice, for 1643–4 and for 1645–6, and in March 1644 let it be known that he was willing to serve as an MP, but no seat was found for him. He was less than happy about his military post, and expressed a wish that he had taken a captaincy in the army of the earl of Essex, as Myddelton's men were proving reluctant to accept his orders.

On 12 January 1644, under cover of darkness, Mytton left Wem to attack Lord Byron's force at Ellesmere, 8 miles away, and took a number of important prisoners. He went to London in April to report to parliament on military affairs in Shropshire and Cheshire, and by doing so sowed the seeds of resentment among the Shropshire committee men, who felt abandoned by the military and thought that Mytton was ingratiating himself with the earl of Denbigh at their expense. On 18 April the Commons awarded Mytton £100 out of royal revenues, in appreciation of his services at Wem. In May a number of his colleagues on the Shropshire committee procured an ordinance that supported their attempts to exercise authority over Mytton, and poisoned relations between the soldier and the civilians. On 15 June, from Stourbridge in Worcestershire, Mytton wrote with other commissioners of Denbigh's army to urge a combination of the forces of Denbigh, Myddelton, and Sir William Waller to disperse the dangerous concentration of royalists near Shrewsbury. Four days later Mytton intercepted a royalist ammunition train at Dudleston Heath, then joined with Denbigh to besiege Oswestry, of which he became governor when it fell to them on 22 June. By this time, his decisive and intelligent conduct in the field had earned him a reputation as 'heroic conqueror' (Phillips, 2.172, quoting *Two Great Victories*, 1644), and other victories soon followed after Myddelton took Welshpool on 3 August. Mytton took Montgomery Castle and town in September, then High Ercall, and besieged Shrawardine. With the help of his colleagues on the Shropshire committee, and with Colonel Reinking, he organized an effective night raid on Shrewsbury on 22 February 1645 and easily took this strategically important regional capital. He and Reinking disputed the honours for taking Shrewsbury, but neither was appointed governor. Instead Mytton was on 12 May 1645 appointed major-general of the counties of north Wales in succession to Myddelton, who had been obliged to surrender his commission under the terms of the self-denying ordinance.

Under Mytton's generalship the royalist strongholds in north Wales began to fall to parliament after he had beaten the king's forces out of Ruthin town on 24 January 1646. A dispute between the Shropshire committee and Mytton had developed as early as January 1645 over the boundaries of their authority in Oswestry garrison and elsewhere, fuelled by what they suspected was his personal ambition to be commander-in-chief in the county. His critics on the committee noted his slowness to leave Shropshire to reduce north Wales, but he reminded them of his continuing commission to be governor of Oswestry. In the House of Commons on 8 April 1646 he was voted 100 horse and 100 dragoons for north Wales, with the title of major-general under Sir Thomas Fairfax, apparently after moves in the house to appoint another commander were scotched. An ally of his advised Mytton that a parliamentary seat would help him, but as in 1644 he did not press for a place in the Shropshire 'recruiter' election of 1646. Indeed, as a serving sheriff, he was barred from standing, but instead promoted his favoured candidate: his relative Humphrey Edwards. His enemies alleged that he changed the venue and time of the contest at Oswestry on 27 August 1646, denied a poll several times, and declared the election complete against the wishes of his opponents. Only thus, they alleged, could Mytton secure Edwards's victory and the defeat of the more popular Andrew Lloyd. As both candidates were Shropshire committee men, the contest probably drew its heat from the persistent feud between Mytton and a section of the committee. After Ruthin Castle fell on 12 April, in succession Flint, Caernarfon, Anglesey, Conwy, Denbigh, Holt, and finally Harlech surrendered, the last not until 13 March 1647. In the wake of these victories, Mytton became more deeply involved in civil authority, becoming an important member of the north Wales county committees. He had persuaded John Williams, archbishop of York, to throw himself on the mercies of parliament at the time of Conwy's surrender. In October 1647 Archbishop Williams considered Mytton to be much more acceptable as a local ruler than Colonel John Jones, his radical subordinate and a future regicide. Even so, Mytton, under the influence of the presbyterian and conservative MP and lawyer John Glynne, had already been imposing the solemn league and covenant on the populace and ejecting Anglican ministers. This activity and his choice of the orthodox puritan Robert Fogg as chaplain, together with his later omission from the Independent-dominated commission for the propagation of the gospel in Wales in 1650, suggest that his religious leanings were towards a conservative, 'presbyterian' puritanism.

Mytton was appointed vice-admiral of north Wales on 30 December 1647. He seems to have striven to treat the north Wales counties equitably in regard to their tax burden. His command, before 1646 independent of the New Model Army, was untouched by the attempt to disband that force in 1647, but, because of its former association with conservatives like Glynne, was a natural target in the 'great disbandment' of February and March 1648. Mytton's political vulnerability and isolation at that time is suggested by the involvement of Archbishop Williams, towards whom Oliver Cromwell was sympathetic, in the disbanding process: a few months later, parliament's committee of both houses was suspicious of Williams's motives, and urged Mytton to enforce discipline among his remaining troops. Mytton's final military action was on 5 June 1648, to help suppress the revolt of Sir John Owen during the second civil war. Membership of the bodies established to impose penal taxation and sequestration on the region in August 1649 inevitably followed.

Mytton retained his adherence to the parliamentarian cause despite the execution of the king, and was a member of the court martial to try the earl of Derby in September 1651. Nevertheless, his relations with the regicide John Jones, a key figure in north Wales before he became a member of the council of state, were cool and somewhat distrustful. Mytton was willing to serve both the Commonwealth and the protectorate as a local assessment commissioner, in Shropshire and north Wales, and finally secured a seat in the House of Commons, for Shropshire, in the parliament of 1654–5. He made no mark on its proceedings, however. His last local appointment was as a commissioner for securing the peace of the Commonwealth during the period of rule by major-generals in 1655–6. Thomas Mytton died in November 1656 in London, and was buried at St Chad's Church, Shrewsbury, on 29 November. He left properties in nine counties, and £1500 each to three unmarried daughters.

STEPHEN K. ROBERTS

Sources The letter books of Sir William Brereton, ed. R. N. Dore, 2 vols., Lancashire and Cheshire RS, 123, 128 (1984–90) · J. R. Phillips, Memoirs of the civil war in Wales and the marches, 1642–1649, 2 vols. (1874) · Calendar of Wynn (of Gwydir) papers (1926) · DWB · 'Mytton manuscripts: letters and papers of Thomas Mytton of Halston (1642–1655)', ed. S. Leighton, Montgomeryshire Collections, 7 (1874), 353–76; 8 (1875), 293–311 · H. Owen and J. B. Blakeway, A history of Shrewsbury, 2 vols. (1825) · C. H. Firth and R. S. Rait, eds., Acts and ordinances of the interregnum, 1642–1660, 3 vols. (1911) · CSP dom., 1644; 1648–9 · A. Hughes, List of sheriffs for England and Wales: from the earliest times to AD 1831, PRO (1898); repr. (New York, 1963) · JHC, 3 (1642–4) · JHL, 7 (1644–5) · Bodl. Oxf., MSS Tanner 57–60 · T. Pennant, Tours in Wales, ed. J. Rhys, 3 vols. (1883) · Calamy rev. · Foster, Alum. Oxon. · will, Shrops. RRC, 2171/143 · J. E. Auden, '"My case with the committee of Salop": Colonel Mytton versus the parliamentarian committee', Transactions of the Shropshire Archaeological Society, 48 (1934–5), 49–60 · S. Leighton, 'Records of the corporation of Oswestry', Transactions of the Shropshire Archaeological and Natural History Society, 3 (1880), 141–6 · T. Mytton, settlement, 1654, Shrops. RRC, 2171/95 · W. W. E. W, 'Correspondence during the great rebellion', Archaeologia Cambrensis, 4th ser., 6 (1875), 201–10 · W. J. Farrow, The great civil war in Shropshire (1642–49) (1926) · H. T. Weyman, Shropshire members of parliament (1926–8), 134–5 · I. Gentles, The New Model Army in England, Ireland, and Scotland, 1645–1653 (1992) · W. P. W. Phillimore and others, eds., Diocese of Lichfield: St

Chad's, Shrewsbury parish registers, 3 vols., Shropshire Parish Registers, 29–31 (1913) [burial, Magdalen Mytton, 20 Aug. 1648]
Archives Bodl. Oxf., Tanner MSS, corresp. · Bodl. Oxf., biographical papers · NAM, papers · NL Wales, papers · Shrops. RRC, papers · U. Wales, Bangor
Likenesses S. Harding, stipple and line engraving, pubd 1796 (after unknown artist), NPG · line engraving, BM, NPG; repro. in J. Vicars, *England's worthies* (1647), 105 · pen-and-ink drawing, NPG
Wealth at death £1500 each for three daughters; lands in Shropshire, Merioneth, Denbighshire, Flintshire, Caernarvonshire, Anglesey, Gloucestershire, Devon, and Middlesex: settlement, 1654, Shrops. RRC, 2171/95

Mytton, William (1693–1746). *See under* Lloyd, Edward (*bap.* 1666, *d.* 1715).

Nabakrishna [Nobkissen], **maharaja** (*c.*1718–1797), political agent and adventurer, rendered major services to the British in their rise to power in Bengal and reaped rich rewards as a consequence. His father was a minor official in the government of the nawabs, the Mughal rulers of Bengal, and lived in a village in the district of Murshidabad; he is believed to have taught Persian to Warren Hastings, who arrived in Calcutta in 1750, and to other servants of the East India Company.

Nabakrishna was appointed a *munshi*, or Persian writer, by Governor Drake in 1756. Stories abound of how he supplied the company's servants with food and information at Falta, after the sack of Calcutta by the nawab of Bengal in June of that year. He followed Colonel Robert Clive and saw the recovery of Calcutta, the capture by the British of the French settlement at Chandernagore, and the defeat and overthrow of the nawab at the battle of Plassey in 1757. After the battle the victors, led by Clive, moved to loot the nawab's treasury for the British. A Persian history records, however, that gold, silver, and jewels worth, it was rumoured, Rs 80 million (about £8 million) were hidden in the harem. Nabakrishna got a substantial share of this. He was able to buy land in and around Calcutta and to win influence with the East India Company so as to become a most important citizen, building his beautiful palace at Sobha Bazar in the north of the city.

Nabakrishna impressed Clive with his ability and became 'political banyan', that is Indian political agent, during Clive's second administration from 1765 to 1767 and during the administration of Harry Verelst that followed. In 1765 he obtained the title of raja and in 1766 that of maharaja from the Mughal emperor Shah Alam. He appeared as part of Clive's entourage in 1767 in the list of those whom the East India Company honoured by awarding *khelats* (ceremonial dresses). He realized that distributing patronage was necessary if he was to assume the headship of the Indian community in Bengal, and gave grants of land to important pandits and to Brahman legal scholars, who left their native places in return for lucrative stipends and grants of land which enabled them to reside close to the city. One such luminary who received Nabakrishna's patronage was the great pandit Mahamahopadhyaya Baneswar Vidyalankar.

Maharaja Nandakumar was Maharaja Nabakrishna's competitor for the leadership of the Indian community.

Their rivalry was both bitter and all pervasive. Nandakumar was discredited after being exposed for trying unsuccessfully to induce a Brahman's wife to accuse Nabakrishna of raping her. When Nandakumar was being tried for his life in 1775 on a charge of forgery, he had the misfortune of having Nabakrishna appointed as the expert to give his opinion about the signature on a Persian document alleged to be forged.

Through acquiring land Nabakrishna became the *zamindar*, loosely translatable as the lord of the manor, of the Sutanati domain, which comprised the larger part of Calcutta. This brought him even closer to the British. He regularly entertained company officials at his house and gave a large piece of land for the founding of the new St John's Church in 1786. His relations with Hastings ended in a dispute about a sum of over £30,000 which he claimed was a loan due for repayment, but which Hastings insisted had been a free gift. Much was made of this at Hastings's impeachment, and Nabakrishna later filed a bill in the English court of chancery, which was dismissed in 1804.

Adventurers like Nabakrishna made their fortunes not by trade but by taking presents, by perquisites, and by commissions on the collection of the revenue. In Nabakrishna's case, the plunder after Plassey helped to make him the richest Indian who made money out of associating with the East India Company. Like others, he spent his money on building up his position in society. He is supposed to have spent Rs 900,000 (about £90,000) on his mother's funeral rites. Little is known about his personal life and character. Not having a son in spite of several marriages, he adopted his immediate brother's son, who later became Raja Gopee Mohan Deb Bahadur. Then, in the last years of his life, a son, Rajakrisna, was born to him. He died at Sobha Bazar on 22 November 1797 and was cremated. After his death a long-drawn-out lawsuit about his succession ensued.   SOMENDRA C. NANDY

Sources N. N. Ghose, *Memoirs of Maharaja Nubkissen Bahadur* (1901) · P. J. Marshall, 'Nobkisen versus Hastings', *Bulletin of the School of Oriental and African Studies*, 27 (1964), 382–96 · *Further report from the committee of secrecy appointed to enquire into the state of East India Company* (1793), appx 60 (6) · S. C. Nandy, 'Citra Campu of Mahamahopadhyaya Banesvara Vidyalankara', *Bengal Past and Present*, 102 (1983), 55–9
Archives BL, Hastings MSS · BL OIOC, East India Company MSS · West Bengal Archives, Kolkata (Calcutta), East India Company MSS
Likenesses portrait, priv. coll.
Wealth at death left Rs 10 million, plus income from properties; undoubtedly the richest of the adventurers of eighteenth-century Bengal: Ghose, *Memoirs*

Nabarro, Sir Gerald David Nunes (1913–1973), politician, was born in London on 29 June 1913, the eldest surviving son of Solomon Nunes Nabarro, a Sephardic Jew—the name Nabarro was derived from Navarre, where the family originated—and his wife, Lena Drucquer (*d.* 1921). His father was a retail tobacconist who went bankrupt in 1921. Educated at elementary schools, he left at the age of fourteen to go briefly to sea, then 'entered industry as labourer in sawmills … worked as a machine-hand, charge-hand, foreman, cost clerk, Works Manager, General Manager

Sir Gerald David Nunes Nabarro (1913–1973), by Elliott & Fry, 1953

and Managing Director' (*WW*, 1954). Nabarro was proud of being a self-made man who became rich, a knight of the shire with a country house, and all this in a frequently antisemitic party.

The army made the man. From 1930 to 1937 Nabarro was a regular soldier, finishing as a staff sergeant instructor, and thereafter served in the territorials until 1946; he was commissioned lieutenant in the Royal Artillery at the outbreak of the Second World War. On 1 June 1943 he married Joan Maud Violet im Thurn, elder daughter of Colonel Bernhardt Basil von Brumsey im Thurn DSO, of Winchester. They had two sons and two daughters. Having become an officer and gentleman, albeit in the Terry-Thomas manner of contemporary films, and cheerfully confessing himself a 'bounder', Nabarro worked after 1943 in industry, and eventually put down his roots in Worcestershire.

A staunch anti-socialist, Nabarro moved naturally to the Conservative right. Though beaten at West Bromwich in 1945, he threw himself into the Conservatives' organization by becoming chairman of the West Midlands Young Conservatives and, in 1950, MP for Kidderminster. He remained Kidderminster's MP until ill health enforced retirement in 1964—'Better to be a live vegetable than a dead politician' (*Daily Telegraph*, 19 Nov 1973)—but quickly regretted the decision and returned to the Commons for South Worcestershire in 1966. Though Nabarro entered the house in the vintage tory 'class of 1950', he did not prosper in a generation that included Heath, Maudling,

and Macleod. This encouraged him to develop more outrageously his tendency to the eccentric and the outsize. His clipped military moustache grew into a giant handlebar, making him instantly recognizable in political cartoons. His tall figure, booming voice, silk top hat on budget day, trenchant views, and the panache with which he defended them, made him popular with broadcasters and audiences on radio's *Any Questions*. Readiness to provide journalists with printable quotations on any issue reinforced his public exposure. In time he added two racy autobiographies, a fleet of cars (each with personalized registration plates—the favourite Daimler was labelled NAB 1), and support for the Severn Valley Steam Railway and Elgar Birthplace trusts. By the late 1950s he was one of Britain's most recognizable politicians. Tory leaders regretted tactless Commons interventions, but regarded him as harmless—a Falstaff rather than a Hotspur. When agreeing in 1963 that the equally moustachioed comedian Jimmy Edwards could continue to perform if elected an MP, the party chairman reflected, 'after all, we have Nabarro!' (Ramsden, 145).

Nabarro himself, like any comedian wanting to play Hamlet, saw himself as a serious politician, and could fairly claim unusual achievements for a back-bencher. While admitting 'the preposterous hamminess of the style', the experienced parliamentary commentator Norman Shrapnel in 1969 pointed out that 'inside the overripe Victoria plum there is usually a hard stone of relevance. In short, Nabarro is often really on to something' (Shrapnel, 11). The most visible among his achievements was his campaign against taxation, especially purchase tax and its anomalous application to different goods. His constant harrying helped produce a more rational system. He was less successful in holding down motor taxation, though brazenly and with some truth he claimed that increases would have been steeper without his efforts. In demanding lower taxes and in opposing British involvement with the EEC, he was well ahead of partisan trends within Conservatism, though in supporting Enoch Powell over race and in opposing sanctions against Rhodesia he was more conventionally right-wing. But Nabarro defied categorization: he was the parliamentary sponsor of the innovative Clean Air Act (1955) and of compulsory health warnings on cigarette packets (1971), while simultaneously articulating motorists' right to cheap petrol. He was also a consistent supporter of Tony Benn's campaign to renounce his peerage, a cross-party populist alliance that belied his usual partisanship.

Nabarro was never more than a hyperactive backbencher. Although the whips dangled preferment before him to persuade him to behave, and found him useful when the Conservatives were the opposition, he was too unpredictable for ministerial duties. In time he accepted that there was more distinction—and far more fun—in being the country's most famous back-bencher than in being a gagged junior minister. His buccaneering style did occasionally produce real trouble: he lost a libel case to Randolph Churchill in 1958, and his claims of a budget leak were scathingly dismissed by a parliamentary inquiry in 1969. Disarmingly, he explained that 'when one is propagating views and ideas, one does not determine too closely what is fact and what is supposition' (*The Times*, 19 Nov 1973). Nabarro was impossible to squash. In 1972 he was convicted of 'deliberate and outrageous' dangerous driving, including navigating a roundabout anti-clockwise, a serious humiliation for the motorists' member, but took the case to appeal, found six extra witnesses, and was unanimously acquitted by an (all-male) jury at a retrial.

Nabarro's early death on 18 November 1973, at his home, Orchard House, Broadway, Worcestershire, still an MP, deprived the political world of a one-off character, and one whose golf club bar instincts were those with which ordinary tory voters could so easily identify. He was buried on 21 November at St Michael's Church, Broadway. His wife survived him. *The Times* concluded that 'those who laughed at his faddish views forgot that his pursuit of the seemingly ridiculous did help bring about real reforms' (*The Times*, 19 Nov 1973). In 1972 Nabarro had himself responded enthusiastically when asked by the *Daily Telegraph* magazine to draft his own obituary:

> A splendid moustache, a deep resonant voice, a remarkable memory were among the characteristics of this notorious man … He tried hard, always, but never quite made it. He failed to reach the top in the Army; he failed to become a Captain of Industry; he never reached ministerial rank in politics. But he was a kind man, and the world will be the poorer without his whoopee. (*Daily Telegraph*, 19 Nov 1973)

Few men have the gift to see themselves with such clarity.   JOHN RAMSDEN

Sources *WW* (1952); (1954); (1960); (1972) · *The Times* (19 Nov 1973) · *Daily Telegraph* (19 Nov 1973) · J. Ramsden, *The winds of change: Macmillan to Heath, 1957–1975* (1996) · G. Nabarro, *NAB 1: portrait of a politician* (1969) · G. Nabarro, *Exploits of a politician* (1973) · *DNB* · N. Shrapnel, 'Nabarro: villain and ham', *The Guardian* (4 Feb 1969), 11
Archives NRA, papers | U. Birm. L., corresp. with Lord Avon
Likenesses Elliott & Fry, photograph, 1953, NPG [*see illus.*]
Wealth at death £164,904: probate, 11 Jan 1974, *CGPLA Eng. & Wales*

Nabbes, Thomas (1604/5–1641), playwright, matriculated from Exeter College, Oxford, on 3 May 1621 as Thomas Nabbes 'of co. Worcester, pleb. … aged 16', but there is no evidence that he earned a degree. He may have been associated informally with the inns of court, since he dedicated his comedy *The Bride* to his 'noble friends' there, and Bullen suggested that he spent some time in the service of a nobleman on the basis of his poem 'Upon the Losing of his Way in a Forest'.

By the early 1630s Nabbes had settled in London and started to write plays for the professional theatre. He is generally considered one of the 'sons of Ben', and while there is no evidence that he knew Ben Jonson personally his work shows Jonson's strong influence. This is especially evident in his first two plays, *Covent Garden* and *Tottenham Court*. Both were first performed in 1633, at the Cockpit and Salisbury Court theatres respectively, as part of a brief vogue for city comedies centred around specific locations in London. Both are also filled with characters who satirize broad types in the manner of Jonson's comedies of humours, and both contrast a virtuous, Neoplatonic hero with a more sensuous, libertine counterpart, a theme that would recur throughout Nabbes's career.

The main plot of *Covent Garden* concerns the attempts of the courtly gentleman Artlove to woo Dorothy Worthy, and of Artlove's critic, the libertine Hugh Jerker, to woo Dorothy's young stepmother, Lady Worthy. It was printed in 1638 with a dedication to Sir John Suckling and a prologue that repeatedly alludes to Richard Brome's *The Weeding of Covent Garden*, to which Nabbes's play is a response. *Tottenham Court* concerns the adventures of the poor but virtuous gentleman Worthgood and his beloved, the witty heiress Bellamie, who are separated while fleeing Bellamie's disapproving uncle. Bellamie encounters a series of wild and sensuous wooers before finally being reunited with Worthgood. The play was also printed in 1638 with a dedication to William Mills, esquire.

In 1635 Nabbes switched direction with a tragedy, *Hannibal and Scipio*, produced by Queen Henrietta's Men at the Cockpit. His account of the two ancient generals of the title is drawn primarily from Livy and from North's translation of Plutarch (but not, despite the assertion of Lee in the *Dictionary of National Biography*, from Marston's play *Sophonisba*). As in Nabbes's earlier comedies there is a contrast between the brave and temperate Scipio and the conflicted Hannibal, whose initial virtue is ultimately undermined by sins of the flesh. The play was printed in 1637 with a full cast list and two prefatory poems by Nabbes. The second of these refers to the author's

> thinne cheeke, hollow eye,
> And ghostlike colour

and implies that he was in financial straits.

Hannibal and Scipio had differed from Nabbes's early comedies not just in its subject matter but in its probable use of perspective scenery and its increased use of song and dance. These trends continued in his next effort, *Microcosmus: a Morall Maske*. This work combines elements of the medieval morality play with those of court masques, following the lead of similar hybrids such as Ford's and Dekker's *The Sun's Darling*, also labelled by its authors 'a moral masque'. Nabbes chronicles the temptations of an Everyman figure, Physander, who is led astray by Sensuality and the personified five senses before being rescued by Temperance. In the climactic trial scene Physander acquits himself against Sensuality and Malus Genius, who are banished to hell. The play was written in 1636 and first performed at Salisbury Court in 1637, after a long plague closure. It was printed the same year with commendatory verses by Richard Brome and William Cufaude.

In 1638, emboldened by the apparent success of *Microcosmus*, Nabbes came out with a volume containing two short masques and ten brief non-dramatic poems, two of which mention his home county of Worcestershire. The first masque, 'The Spring's Glorie', revisits some of Nabbes's favourite themes. It depicts a debate between Platonic love based in the soul, represented by

Venus and Cupid, and sensual delights, represented by Ceres and Bacchus. The merits of the two sides are debated by Christmas and Shrovetide, who initially rule for Ceres before Lent enters to rule in favour of Venus. The second masque in the volume is 'A Presentation Intended for the Prince his Highness on his Birth-Day the 29 of May, 1638', which ends with dancing masquers representing eight princes of Wales. It was written for eight-year-old Prince Charles, in an obvious bid for court favour, but was apparently never performed, as the title implies. Two separate issues of the volume exist, dedicated to Benedict Roberts and William Ball respectively.

His desire for royal patronage rebuffed, Nabbes reverted to comedy with his next work, *The Bride*, produced at the Cockpit by Beeston's Boys in the summer of 1638. This play is less didactic than his earlier works and aimed at an audience of merchants and citizens rather than the Cockpit's normal upper-crust clientele. The bride of the title (who is never named) is engaged to Goodlove, but instead elopes with her fiancé's stepson Theophilus. The runaway couple is separated by Theophilus's cousin, the villainous Raven, whose armed thugs nearly rape the bride. In the end, however, the lovers are reunited and Raven repents. The play was printed in 1640 with a dedication to the author's 'noble friends' at the inns of court.

For his next play, which turned out to be his last, Nabbes tried his hand at an Italian revenge tragedy that observes the unities of time and place. *The Unfortunate Mother* depicts the intrigues of Corvino, prime minister of the court of Ferrara, as he uses his family and friends in his bloody quest for political power. Typically for this genre Corvino's plans fail and most of the main characters die by the end. The play was apparently rejected by the acting companies but Nabbes published it anyway, in a 1640 quarto, declaring it 'never acted'. He dedicated the volume to Richard Brathwaite, added a 'proeme' declaring his intentions for the piece, and persuaded three friends to write commendatory verses.

In addition to his dramatic works Nabbes wrote numerous commendatory verses for his literary friends. He wrote verses for *Cupid and Psyche* (1637), by his 'true friend' Shakerley Marmion; for Robert Chamberlain's *Nocturnall Lucubrations* (1638); Thomas Jordan's *Poetical Varieties* (1640); John Tatham's *Fancies Theater* (1640); Humphrey Mills's *A Nights Search* (1640); and for Thomas Beedome's *Poems Divine and Humane* (1641). He also wrote a prose 'Continuation of the Turkish historie, from the yeare of Our Lord 1628, to the end of the yeare 1637', which appeared in the fifth edition of Richard Knolles's *General Historie of the Turkes* (1638), with a dedicatory epistle to Sir Thomas Rowe.

At some point Nabbes married a woman named Bridget and settled in St Giles-in-the-Fields in London, the parish of the Cockpit theatre. The couple's daughter Bridget was baptized there on 27 May 1638 and buried on 30 June 1642; a son named William was buried on 29 August 1643. Nabbes himself was buried in St Giles on 6 April 1641, and the following year the parish granted 1s. for poor relief to

'Mrs. Mabbs, a poet's wife, her husband being dead' (Bentley, 929). Samuel Sheppard praised Nabbes in *The Times Displayed* (1646) and John Cotgrave included thirty-eight quotations from his plays in *The English Treasury of Wit and Language* (1655). DAVID KATHMAN

Sources N. Sanders, 'Thomas Nabbes', *Jacobean and Caroline dramatists*, ed. F. Bowers, DLitB, 58 (1987), 223–30 · G. E. Bentley, *The Jacobean and Caroline stage*, 7 vols. (1941–68), vol. 4, pp. 927–9 · C. Moore, *The dramatic works of Thomas Nabbes* (Menasha, WI, 1918) · A. H. Bullen, *The works of Thomas Nabbes* (1887) · Foster, *Alum. Oxon., 1500–1714* · *DNB* · R. W. Vince, 'Thomas Nabbes's *Hannibal and Scipio*: sources and theme', *Studies in English Literature*, 11 (1971), 327–43

Wealth at death probably died poor: Bentley, *Jacobean and Caroline stage*, 928–9

Nabob (*fl.* **1780**). *See under* Indian visitors (*act. c.*1720–*c.*1810).

Nadel, Siegfried Ferdinand Stephan (1903–1956), social anthropologist and musicologist, was born on 24 April 1903 at Lemberg (Lwów), Galicia, Austria, the only son of the two children of Dr Moritz Nadel (*b.* 1871), a lawyer, and his wife, Adele Hirschsprung (1880–1955). His parents were both born at Lemberg and of Jewish descent. From 1912 the family was registered in Vienna, Austria, where Nadel attended secondary school. In 1920 he began to study piano and composition at the Academy of Music, and from 1921 to 1925 musicology, psychology, and philosophy at the University of Vienna with the teachers Moritz Schlick (the founder of the Vienna circle of philosophy) and the Gestalt psychologist Karl Bühler. He graduated with the degree of doctor of philosophy with honours in 1925. The Düsseldorf opera house in Germany engaged him for a period as a temporary assistant conductor, despite his being only twenty-two. On 3 July 1926 he married Dr Lisbeth Braun (*b.* 30 Nov 1900), also a musicologist.

Nadel demonstrated an interest in comparative musicology from early in his career. In 1926–7 he devised a number of radio programmes for Radio Vienna dealing with African, Caucasian, Javanese, and black American music. A participant at the International Congress of Folk Music in Prague in 1928, two years later he presented a treatise on marimba music to the Phonogrammarchivkommission of the Vienna Academy of Science. During the early 1930s Nadel began to research the musicology of primitive peoples at the Phonogrammarchiv in Berlin. He also began the study of African languages at the University of Berlin. A meeting with a representative of the Rockefeller Foundation gave Nadel the opportunity to escape the increasing antisemitic pressure: he was awarded a Rockefeller fellowship to train as a social anthropologist, for which his earlier studies had been an excellent preparation. In October 1932 he became a postgraduate student at the London School of Economics with Charles Gabriel Seligman and Bronislaw Malinowski. Nadel soon took a leading role in Malinowski's seminar, 'with the zest for constructive theoretical argument which was characteristic of him till the end of his days' (Firth, 118). His capacity for mastering languages proved to be of advantage in Britain, as well as during his fieldwork.

On Christmas eve 1933 Nadel, accompanied by his wife, started his research among the Nupe in Northern Nigeria. Returning to the London School of Economics in 1935 he was awarded a PhD degree for his thesis entitled 'Political and religious structure of Nupe society (Northern Nigeria)'. With a group of other psychologists, anthropologists, and sociologists he participated in discussions that led to the publication of *The Science of Society* (1939). From October 1935 to November 1936 he spent a further period investigating the Nupe. The fruits of his work were summarized in a number of articles and in two books, *A Black Byzantium* (1942) and *Nupe Religion* (1954).

In 1937 Sir Douglas Newbold, governor of the Kordofan province, invited Nadel to prepare a survey of the hill tribes scattered over the Nuba Mountains with whose administration the official governmental authorities had frequently experienced difficulties. Nadel worked among different tribes of the district for a year, having been appointed government anthropologist by the government of Anglo-Egyptian Sudan. His analysis and suggestions were later published in his book *The Nuba* (1947), and in a number of articles. During the Second World War Nadel, by now a British citizen, joined the Sudan defence force and later the east African command of the British army. Holding the rank of major and then of lieutenant-colonel, he was appointed secretary of native affairs in the British military administration of Eritrea and Tripolitania. Service in the administration enabled him to put his experiences as anthropologist into practice. Through reforms he tried to improve the administrative system which the government authorities applied to tribal groups. In 1945 he was transferred to the home establishment, and received a gazetted commendation for outstanding services. In June 1946 he was released from military service and returned to London, to his wife and a daughter born during the war.

Nadel started his academic teaching career as a lecturer at the London School of Economics in 1946. Two years later he became reader in anthropology at King's College, Newcastle upon Tyne (then part of Durham University). He had long-standing interests in the theoretical side of his field, and especially in its status as a science; this led in 1951 to the publication of his *Foundations of Social Anthropology*. His stated intention was to examine the logical premises that underlay knowledge of all societies, primitive or otherwise. 'It was a bold enterprise', Raymond Firth later wrote, but 'in some respects, it was only partly successful' (Firth, 121). 'A magnificent teacher', he influenced several generations of students; and with his strong methodological bent 'he moved more than his colleagues, towards a new synthesis of social disciplines' (ibid., 122).

In 1950 Nadel was appointed to the first chair in anthropology at the new Australian National University in Canberra. As well as setting up the new department, he became dean of the research school of Pacific studies. On 14 July 1956 Nadel died unexpectedly, in Canberra, of a coronary thrombosis, not yet fifty-three years old. Seven days earlier he had completed the manuscript of *The Theory of Social Structure* (1957), which became a standard work; his wife survived him.   JANA SALAT

Sources J. Salat, *Reasoning as enterprise: the anthropology of S. F. Nadel* (1983) • R. Firth, 'Siegfried F. Nadel', *American Anthropologist*, 59/1 (1957), 117–24 • J. D. Freeman, 'Siegfried F. Nadel', *Oceania*, 27/1 (1956), 1–11 • A. Kuper, *Anthropology and anthropologists: the modern British school*, 3rd edn (1996) • J. C. Faris, 'Pax Britannica and the Sudan: S. F. Nadel', *Anthropology and the colonial encounter*, ed. T. Asad (1973) • *The Times* (27 Jan 1956) • Central Registering Bureau of the National Police Directory, Vienna, no. III/Rh/728/M/74/Sot

Archives BLPES, field notebooks, diaries, and papers | CUL, corresp. with Meyer Forbes

Naden, Constance Caroline Woodhill (1858–1889), poet and philosopher, born on 24 January 1858 at 15 Francis Road, Edgbaston, Birmingham, was the only child of Thomas Naden, afterwards president of the Birmingham Architectural Association, and his wife, Caroline Anne, daughter of J. C. Woodhill of Pakenham House, Charlotte Road, Edgbaston. Her mother died within a fortnight of the child's birth, and Constance was brought up by her maternal grandparents. Her maternal grandfather was a retired jeweller, an elder of a Baptist church, and a man of some literary taste.

From the age of eight until sixteen or seventeen Constance Naden attended a private day school in Frederick Road, Edgbaston, run by two Unitarian women, the Misses Martin. There she learned French, German, Latin, and some Greek, and was much attracted to the writings of James Hinton, and to R. A. Vaughan's *Hours with the Mystics*. After leaving school she remained with her grandparents; she travelled widely in Europe, and worked at odd moments on *Songs and Sonnets of Springtime*, published in 1881. In 1879–80 and 1880–81 she attended botany classes at the Birmingham and Midland Institute and acquired an interest in science. In the autumn of 1881 she became a student at Mason College, studying physics, chemistry, botany, zoology, physiology, and geology. She took a very lively part in debating societies, and she presented several papers on evolution and sociology to the sociological section of the Birmingham Natural History Society, begun in 1883 in order to study the principles put forth by Herbert Spencer. She became a very eager and sympathetic student of Spencer's philosophy. In 1885 she won the Paxton prize for an essay on the geology of the district; and in 1887 she won the Heslop gold medal with an essay, 'Induction and deduction'. She also contributed pieces to the *Journal of Science*, *Knowledge*, the *Agnostic Annual*, and other periodicals, some of them under the name Constance Arden.

In 1887 Constance Naden published her second volume of poems, *'A Modern Apostle'; 'The Elixir of Life'; 'The Story of Clarice'; and other Poems*. Her grandfather died on 27 December 1881, and she inherited a fortune on the death of her grandmother on 21 June 1887. In that year she became good friends with Madelene Daniell (1832–1906), a philanthropist and promoter of women's education. In the autumn she and Daniell made a tour to Constantinople and through Palestine, Egypt, and India, where Naden met Lord Dufferin, the governor-general, and,

Constance Caroline Woodhill Naden (1858–1889), by George J. Stodart, pubd 1890

equipped with an introduction from the German orientalist and language scholar Max Müller, several Indian reformers who, she was pleased to observe, were well acquainted with Spencer's writings. On her return to England in June 1888, she and Daniell lived together in Naden's home near Grosvenor Square, and she became much involved in philosophical and philanthropic circles in London. She was affiliated with the Indian National Association, where she was able to further her crusade against the marriage of infants and child widows in India. She also campaigned in support of Dr Garrett Anderson's work to supply medical aid to Indian women. Naden was active in the Working Ladies' Guild, and before her death was at the point of taking charge of the Campden Houses, accommodation for indigent women; she was also planning the New Hospital for Women. A public advocate for women's suffrage, and a vigorous Liberal and home-ruler, Naden was slight and tall, with a delicate face and 'clear blue-grey eyes' (Hughes, 59). She was a spirited and amusing conversationalist and was thoroughly self-possessed in public speaking. She joined the Aristotelian Society in 1888, where she 'at once attracted attention by her clear and striking contributions to [the] discussions' (*Proceedings of the Aristotelian Society*, 160). She died a month before she was to present to the society a paper on rational and empiricist ethics; neither were her plans to establish an association to study social evolution realized.

Constance Naden's poems had attracted little notice until W. E. Gladstone called attention to them in an 1890 article in *The Speaker* on British poetry, in which he named her, along with Christina Rossetti and Elizabeth Barrett Browning, as one of the eight best women poets. Gladstone was especially impressed by the poem 'Solomon redivivus', which caricatured the reunion of the queen of Sheba and King Solomon after their evolutionary descent from the first amoeba. Many of her poems incorporated her interest in the biological sciences; they also reflected her growing scepticism in the nonconformist faith of her childhood. Her verse was imaginative and often witty, as in the poem 'Natural Selection' (appearing in *A Modern Apostle*), which imagines an earnest young scholar losing his suit to a more brawny admirer: 'And I watch, scientific though sad, the Law of Selection at work' (*'A Modern Apostle'*, 143). *'A Modern Apostle'* was favourably reviewed in the London press, including the assessment in the Oscar Wilde-edited *Woman's World* that it displayed 'both culture and courage—culture in its use of language, courage in its choice of subject matter' (*Woman's World*, 81–2). Nevertheless, Naden came to regard poetry as mere amusement and stopped writing in 1887. This decision was influenced by a retired army doctor, Robert Lewins, whom she had met in 1876 and with whom she had corresponded. He advanced an idiosyncratic medley of idealism and materialism which he termed 'hylo-idealism'. Thomas Carlyle dismissed Lewins's speculations as 'the shallower side of English spiritualism' and complained that they occasioned sentiments of 'pain, of ghastly disgust and loathing pity' (cited in Hughes, 86). Naden's friends were only marginally more sympathetic; they regretted Lewins's influence, particularly over her decision to abandon poetry. Naden's first philosophical essays reproduced aspects of Lewins's system. *Induction and Deduction* was published posthumously in 1890, edited by Lewins, and had a fond 'Memoir' by Daniell. In this work Naden maintained that all knowledge is relative and therefore purely subjective, and concluded from this that anything beyond sensation is unknowable. This marriage of a Protagorean subjectivism with a dogmatic materialism made the individual the only measure of all things; her argument that our senses are necessary to distinguish phenomena led to some confusion about whether an external universe or an objective world beyond subjective experience did exist. Yet Naden rejected absolute idealism because she maintained that it was insufficiently interested in the material world. Her writings exhibit the influence of Herbert Spencer, for, like Spencer, she married a belief in an Unknowable with a positivist form of naturalism and she appealed to an evolutionary utilitarianism in which the evolutionary process engendered a character which spontaneously pursues the common good. She also found persuasive Leslie Stephen's treatment of sympathy in *The Science of Ethics* (1882). While her interest in evolutionary ethics coincided with a widespread engagement with similar issues among such diverse theorists as T. H. Huxley, Stephen, and D. G. Ritchie, her work followed too closely that of Spencer and she failed to establish a distinctive position before her death. Spencer admired her intelligence and cited her early death as evidence that 'the mental powers so highly developed in a woman are in some measure abnormal, and involve a physiological cost which the feminine organisation will not bear without injury more or less profound' (ibid., 90). Symptoms of a fatal disease began to appear in the summer of 1889; on 5 December Naden underwent surgery from which she never recovered. She died on 23 December of that year at her home, 114 Park Street, near Grosvenor Square, Mayfair, London, and was buried beside her mother in the old cemetery in Warstone Lane, Birmingham.   S. M. DEN OTTER

Sources W. R. Hughes, *Constance Naden: a memoir* (1890) · M. Daniell, 'Memoir', in C. Naden, *Induction and deduction and other essays*, ed. R. Lewins (1890) · *Further reliques of Constance Naden*, ed. G. M. McCrie (1891) · P. E. Smith and S. M. Smith, 'Constance Naden: late Victorian feminist poet and philosopher', *Victorian Poetry*, 15 (1977), 367–70 · *Selections from the philosophical and poetical works of Constance C. W. Naden*, ed. E. Hughes and E. Hughes (1893) · *Proceedings of the Aristotelian Society*, 1/3 (1890), 160 · review of *Induction and deduction and other essays*, *Mind*, 15 (1890), 570–71 · review of *Induction and deduction and other essays*, *Monist*, 1 (1890), 292–4 · W. E. Gladstone, 'British poetry of the nineteenth century', *The Speaker* (11 Jan 1890), 35 · review of 'A modern apostle'; 'The elixir of life'; 'The story of Clarice'; *and other poems*, *Woman's World*, 1 (1887), 81–2 · *DNB* · *CGPLA Eng. & Wales* (1890)
Likenesses G. J. Stodart (after portrait by Whitlock), repro. in Naden, *Induction and deduction* [*see illus.*] · W. Tyler, marble bust, Mason College, Birmingham
Wealth at death £34,379 11s. 3d.: resworn probate, April 1891, *CGPLA Eng. & Wales* (1890)

Nadin, Joseph (1765–1848), police officer, son of Joseph Nadin, farmer, was born at Fairfield, near Buxton, Derbyshire. At the age of twelve he began work at Stockport, Cheshire, and was subsequently successful in business as a master spinner. He married Mary Rowlinson in 1792 and they had several children. In 1802 Nadin was appointed Manchester's deputy constable, the principal executive agent of the local authorities, responsible for the town's beadles and special constables; his appointment was due to the recommendation of the Society for the Prosecution of Felons (founded in Manchester in 1787) and the reputation he had already acquired as a 'thief taker'. Manchester was still governed by parish and manorial institutions, and Nadin's services were highly regarded by his employers (the court leet), who later added the night watch and the town's firemen to his responsibilities. He was also entrusted with several important market offices. Nadin's appointments gave him ample opportunity for feathering his own nest, as was the general custom of the day. He was said to have gained considerably from the perquisites of the office of deputy constable, responsibility for prosecutions resting with officials who could draw a profit from them. However, Nadin was an effective official, who tempered petty corruption with crime control and never lost the confidence of the authorities. His thief catching owed as much to intrigue as detection, and benefited from his use of spies and informers.

Nadin earned the enmity of political radicals when his skills of information gathering and arrest were used by the magistrates and military in the persecution of Luddites and reformers in Lancashire and Yorkshire in the decade following 1812. Trials ensued, in which Nadin's spies gave crucial, although sometimes far from reliable, testimony. His reputation in reforming circles was sealed by the fateful events of 16 August 1819. As deputy constable, Nadin was instructed by the magistrates to serve a warrant for the arrest of Henry Hunt and others at a reform meeting on St Peter's Field, Manchester. Unable to do so, he requested the aid of the military and was accompanied by the yeomanry who cut a path through the crowd to reach the hustings. From this resulted the violent dispersal of the meeting, much injury and loss of life, and dispute ever since over the day's events. Nadin's role at Peterloo, as elsewhere in the attempts of the authorities to resist the tide of political radicalism, was as an executor of the decisions of others, rather than as a political force in his own right.

Nadin's sombre reputation endured throughout the nineteenth century. He appears in two of Mrs Linnaeus Banks's novels, once as a sort of Jonathan Wild character in *God's Providence House* and again as himself in *The Manchester Man*. Nadin's physical appearance and personal demeanour are described by Samuel Bamford, who was arrested by him. Nadin was:

> about 6 feet 1 inch in height, with an uncommon breadth and solidity of frame [and] … strongly built; [he was] upright in gait and active in motion. … his features were broad and non-intellectual, his voice loud, his language coarse and illiterate, and his manner rude and overbearing to equals or inferiors. (Bamford, 1.82)

Nadin amassed a considerable fortune and after his retirement from office in 1821 farmed an estate at Cheadle in Cheshire. He died there on 4 March 1848, aged eighty-three, and was buried at St James's Church, Manchester.

ALAN J. KIDD

Sources S. Bamford, *Passages in the life of a radical*, 2 vols. (1841) · A. Prentice, *Historical sketches and personal recollections of Manchester intended to illustrate the progress of public opinion from 1792 to 1832*, 2nd edn (1851) · *Transactions of the Lancashire and Cheshire Antiquarian Society*, 11 (1893), 138–39 · *Manchester Notes and Queries*, 1 (1878), 283, 291–99, 310, 328–29 [letters] · D. Read, *Peterloo: the massacre and its background* (1958) · J. P. Earwaker, ed., *The constables' accounts of the manor of Manchester*, 3 vols. (1891–2) · private information (1894)
Likenesses W. Bradley, engraving, Chetham's Library, Manchester

Naesmyth [Nasmyth], **Sir James**, **second baronet** (d. **1779**), arboriculturist, was the eldest son of Sir James *Nasmyth, first baronet (d. 1720), lawyer, and his third wife, Barbara (d. 1768), daughter of Andrew Pringle of Clifton. Naesmyth was said to have studied with Linnaeus and was among the first in Scotland to plant larch (inexplicably 'birch' in many sources)—at Dawyck, Peebles, his estate on the south bank of upper Tweeddale, bought in 1691 by his father from the impoverished John Veitch, last of the original Dawyck lairds. He made the grand tour to Italy in 1724–5 with his tutor, Patrick Wood; they are alleged to have been in touch with Jacobites in Rome. On his return from the Italian Tyrol, Naesmyth established the larch in 1725, the first recorded planting in Scotland after that in the Edinburgh Physic Garden in 1683: nine of the original trees were still there in 1838, one was felled in 1897 and its timber used to panel a room at Dawyck, and five survived until at least 1933, one reaching 98 feet by 1982. In 1730 he planted a lime avenue for three-quarters of a mile, to the east of the house. In 1740 Naesmyth created an extensive plantation of Scots pine and later planted other trees including, for the first time in Scotland, balsam firs (in 1743, raising new trees from their seed in 1761) and Lombardy poplars (1765). However, it was his grandson, the fourth baronet, Sir John Murray Naesmyth (1803–1876), who was to enlarge the conifer collection, making it the important arboretum it eventually became, and who also brought into cultivation from the woods nearby the familiar fastigiate beech, a cultivar now called 'Dawyck'. The estate, set in one of the coldest parts of Britain, remained in the family until 1897 and came to the Royal Botanic Garden, Edinburgh in 1978.

Naesmyth was MP for Peeblesshire in 1732–41 and in 1767 was elected FRS. He married Jean, daughter of Thomas Keith, grandson of the Earl Marischal, and had two sons and a daughter. He died at Philiphaugh, Selkirkshire, on 4 February 1779. His eldest son, James, the third baronet, was grandfather of the fifth baronet through his marriage in 1785 to Eleanor Murray (d. 1807), and to the sixth through his 1828 marriage to Harriet Jones.

It is held that William Hudson (1734–1793) commemorated Naesmyth in his Latin name for the pipewort, an aquatic plant first collected in 1768 by Sir John Macpherson on Skye and of great interest at the time, *Nasmythia articulata*, now *Eriocaulon aquaticum*. Hudson did not explicitly mention James Naesmyth, a truly minor figure of the eighteenth century, one who seems to have written nothing at all on plants, so that it is perhaps more likely that Hudson intended to honour James's kinsman, John Nasmith (Naysmith or Nasmyth; d. 1619?), a notable botanist who was surgeon to James VI of Scotland and a friend of Matthias de l'Obel, who wrote highly of John's talents.

D. J. MABBERLEY

Sources J. W. Buchan and H. Paton, eds., *A history of Peeblesshire*, 3 vols. (1925–7) · W. Chambers, *A history of Peeblesshire* (1864) · W. Balfour Gourlay, 'Dawyck', *Journal of the Royal Horticultural Society*, 72 (1947), 5–12 · F. R. S. Balfour, 'Conifers at Dawyck', *Country Life*, 74 (1933), 156–8 · J. C. Loudon, *Arboretum et fruticetum Britannicum, or, The trees and shrubs of Britain*, 1 (1838), 93–4 · W. J. Bean, *Trees and shrubs hardy in the British Isles*, 8th edn, 2 (1973) · D. L. Clarke, *Bean's trees & shrubs hardy in the British Isles: supplement* (1988) · election certificate, RS · J. Ingamells, ed., *A dictionary of British and Irish travellers in Italy, 1701–1800* (1997), 698 · D. Bown, *4 gardens in one: the Royal Botanic Garden Edinburgh* (1992), chap. 6

Likenesses oils, repro. in Buchan and Paton, *History of Peeblesshire*, vol. 3, facing p. 568

Naftel, Isabel (bap. 1832, d. 1912). *See under* Naftel, Paul Jacob (1817–1891).

Naftel, Maud (1856–1890). *See under* Naftel, Paul Jacob (1817–1891).

Naftel, Paul Jacob (1817–1891), watercolour painter and art teacher, was born in Guernsey on 13 October 1817, the second of the eleven children of Paul Naftel (1795–1870) and his wife, Sophia Bird. The family name, meaning 'little turnip', was said to be reflected in their features. His father was a clockmaker and watchmaker who also kept a shop selling artists' materials and prints. Neither parent showed any aptitude for art, but from his earliest years Naftel delighted in drawing and painting. He gave up business to follow his vocation and earned a living by giving

lessons in art at various schools on Guernsey. After several years of dedicated hard work he was appointed drawing-master at Elizabeth College (1847–70), the chief college on the island. His subjects in his early years were to be found in the scenery of the Channel Islands. He made 'graceful studies of the tangled water-lanes and embowered stone-built springs' characteristic of the region (Roget, 2.353). These drawings were remarkable for 'an extremely lavish use of body colour' which was less prevalent in his later work, but which enabled him to capture 'the bright contrasts of colour' afforded by the coastline, where 'gay vegetation … crowns the sea-cliffs which rise pink and grey above clear blue waves' (ibid.). The artistic quality of his work did not lie in his use of colour alone, and a series of effective woodcuts from his paintings was used to illustrate D. T. Ansted's and R. G. Latham's elaborate volume *The Channel Islands* (1862). Naftel married, first, Elizabeth Robilliard (1810–1849) of Alderney and second, in 1853, Isabel [see below], the youngest daughter of the watercolour painter Octavius *Oakley (1800–1867), who visited Guernsey in 1844. Isabel Naftel was herself an accomplished artist, and their daughter, Maud [see below], inherited the artistic talent of both her parents. Paul and Isabel Naftel also had two sons, Cecil Oakley (b. 1845) and Percy Hartley (b. 1859). With Octavius Oakley, Naftel visited north Wales in the late 1840s and was influenced by the work of David Cox. Naftel commissioned a studio at his house, Millmount, St Peter Port, where he held private views of his work that were very popular.

Paul Naftel's watercolours gained wide renown; he was elected an associate of the Society of Painters in Water Colours on 11 February 1856 and became a full member on 13 June 1859. He was a prolific contributor to the exhibitions of the society, and between 1850 and 1891 exhibited 689 works at Pall Mall East as well as a handful at other galleries. He did not settle in England until the latter part of 1870, when he moved to 4 St Stephen's Square, Westbourne Park, his home for the next thirteen years. In London he continued his highly successful work as a teacher of drawing and watercolour painting, and among his pupils was the landscape painter Kate Prentice. He continued this work until his death, but gradually devoted less time to it as the demand for his paintings increased. About 1883–4 he moved to 76 Elm Park Road, Fulham Road, Chelsea, and later he moved to a house at 1 Walpole Gardens, Strawberry Hill, Twickenham, where he died on 13 September 1891. He was buried in Twickenham on 16 September 1891.

While the Channel Islands were his speciality, Naftel also travelled widely throughout Britain, visiting Scotland several times, Wales, and Ireland at least once. He also made studies abroad, first in Switzerland in 1851, where he produced three paintings, and in Italy between 1860 and 1866, where he produced a number of views of the bays of Salerno and Naples, as well as nine or ten drawings of the ruins at Paestum. In December 1870 he visited Spain to paint the total solar eclipse at Cadiz for the Royal Astronomical Society in London. His studio sale was held at Christies on 6 April 1892.

Isabel Naftel (*bap.* 1832, *d.* 1912), who was baptized in Derby on 20 July 1832, was the youngest of the three daughters of Octavius Oakley and his wife, Maria Moseley. She became the second wife of Paul Jacob Naftel, whom she married in Dorking, Surrey, in 1853. Isabel Naftel painted portraits, genre, and flowers, as well as views of the Channel Islands and the south coast. She exhibited fifty-four works between 1857 and 1891, among them nine at the New Watercolour Society, ten at the Royal Academy, and thirteen at the Society of British Artists in Suffolk Street. Her works at the academy included *A Little Red Riding Hood* (1862), *Musing* (1869), and *A Sark Cottage* (1885). She died in London in 1912.

Maud Naftel (1856–1890), painter, was born on 1 June 1856, the daughter of Paul and Isabel Naftel. At first a pupil of her father, she afterwards studied at the Slade School of Fine Art, London, and in Paris under M. Carolus Duran. A 'charming flower painter and a very competent landscapist' (Mallalieu, *Watercolour artists*, 186), she attained distinction in watercolours and was especially noted for her paintings of flowers. She sent eight drawings, mostly of landscapes but with some flowers, to the general watercolour exhibitions at the Dudley Gallery (1877–82), and she was a subscribing member of the supplementary Dudley Gallery Art Society, to which she sent two drawings in 1883 and another in 1885. In addition she exhibited in London at the Grosvenor Gallery, the New Gallery, and the Royal Academy, where her studies were mostly flower subjects such as *An Autumn Garden*, but to which she also sent *Sand Dunes Near Boulogne*. She was elected an associate of the Royal Society of Painters in Water Colours in March 1887. She had shown sixteen drawings there, almost all of flowers, when her promising career was cut short by a painful illness which soon resulted in death. She died at her father's house at Elm Park Road on 18 February 1890. She was a member of the Crematorium Society and one of the first to be cremated at Woking crematorium; her ashes were buried in the grave of her grandfather Octavius Oakley at Highgate cemetery, London. Her book *Flowers and How to Paint Them* (1886; new edn, 1906), illustrated with colour plates and wood-engravings, became a standard work on the subject. A posthumous work was exhibited in the Lady Artists' Exhibition in the spring of 1890, entitled *Unwillingly to School*.

Isabel Naftel (*fl.* 1870–1873), painter, is presumed by some authorities to have been the daughter of Paul Jacob Naftel and his second wife, Isabel, even though Roget's *History of the 'Old Water-Colour' Society* describes Maud Naftel as their 'only daughter' (Roget, 2.352). While it is possible that she may have been a sister of Paul Naftel, it is more likely that these references are to his wife Isabel. Isabel Naftel lived in Guernsey and exhibited four works at the Royal Academy, including a portrait of the dowager duchess of St Albans and works entitled *The Letter* and *The Little Model*.   MARK POTTLE

Sources S. Furniss, *Paul Jacob Naftel, 1817–1891* (1991) [exhibition catalogue, Guernsey Museum and Art Gallery, 1991] · J. L. Roget, *A history of the 'Old Water-Colour' Society*, 2 vols. (1891) · B. Stewart and M. Cutten, *The dictionary of portrait painters in Britain up to 1920* (1997) · Bryan, *Painters* (1903–5) · Mallalieu, *Watercolour artists* · Wood, *Vic. painters*, 2nd edn · J. Ruskin, *Notes on some of the principal pictures exhibited in the rooms of the Royal Academy, and the Society of Painters in Water Colours: no. II, 1856* (1856) · J. Ruskin, *Notes on some of the principal pictures…: no. III, 1857* (1857) · J. Ruskin, *Notes on some of the principal pictures…: no. IV, 1858* (1858) · J. Ruskin, *Notes on some of the principal pictures…: no. V, 1859* (1859) · *Art Journal*, new ser., 11 (1891) · S. W. Fisher, *A dictionary of watercolour painters, 1750–1900* (1972) · H. M. Cundall, *A history of British watercolour painting* (1929) · M. Naftel, *Flowers and how to paint them* (1886); new edn (1906) · private information (1894) · *CGPLA Eng. & Wales* (1891) · *DNB*
Likenesses J. & C. Watkins, carte-de-visite, *c.*1862, NPG · T. Mogford, watercolour drawing, Guernsey Museum
Wealth at death £4695 18*s.* 0*d.*: resworn probate, 1892, *CGPLA Eng. & Wales* (1891)

Nagle, Sir Edmund (1757–1830), naval officer, was born at Bloomfield, co. Cork, probably the only son of Edmund Nagle (*d.* 1763) and his wife. After Edmund Nagle senior's death, his brother Garret and his first cousin Edmund *Burke looked after the young Edmund. Burke aided him in his later career and continued to offer him a home when he was in London. After a voyage in the East India Company's service he entered the navy in 1770, under the care of Captain John Stott, on the frigate *Juno*, in which he went to the Falkland Islands on the occasion of their being surrendered by Spain in 1771. He passed his examination on 7 May 1777 and on 25 October he was promoted lieutenant of the storeship *Greenwich*, on the North American station. In 1779 he was in the *Syren*, in the North Sea, and from 1780 to 1782 he was again on the coast of North America, this time in the *Warwick*, with Captain George Elphinstone. On 1 August 1782 he was promoted to the command of the brig *Racoon*, which was shortly afterwards captured off the mouth of the Delaware by the French frigate *Aigle*.

Nagle regained his liberty on 11 September after the *Aigle* was herself captured by the *Warwick*. He was then appointed to the sloop *Hound*, and on 27 January 1783 he was promoted captain of the *Grana*, which he brought home and paid off. In 1793 he commissioned the frigate *Active*, and early in 1794 he was moved into the *Artois* (44 guns), in which for the next three years he was actively employed, first under the command of Sir Edward Pellew (afterwards Viscount Exmouth) and later Sir John Borlase Warren. On 21 October 1794, off Ushant, the little squadron, then commanded by Pellew, sighted the French frigate *Révolutionnaire* (44 guns), which the *Artois* chased and brought to action. On the other frigates' coming up the *Révolutionnaire* surrendered. Nagle was knighted for this action. The *Artois* was with Warren in the expedition to Quiberon in 1795, and, continuing on the French coast, was lost on a sandbank off Rochelle on 31 July 1797, when in chase of a French frigate.

In August 1798 Nagle married Mary, a wealthy woman, the widow of John Lucie Blackman of Craven Street, London, after which he had little service at sea. Between 1801 and 1802 he commanded the *Majestic*; afterwards he was in charge of the *Juste* for a few months, and in 1803 he was appointed to command the sea fencibles of the Sussex coast, nearly 1000 men and 50 boats, making his headquarters at Brighton. He was introduced to the prince of Wales, and as a result of his conviviality became a great favourite. He was promoted rear-admiral on 9 November 1805, and for a short time hoisted his flag on the *Inconstant* at Guernsey. He became vice-admiral on 31 July 1810, and, again for a short time, was commander-in-chief at Leith. In 1813 he was governor of Newfoundland, and in the following year he was nominated aide-de-camp to the prince at the review of the fleet at Spithead. On 2 January 1815 he was made a KCB, and on 12 August 1819 promoted admiral.

During all this time, however, with these few intermissions, Nagle was in attendance on the prince, and in 1820, on the prince's accession as George IV, he was appointed groom of the bedchamber. Nagle was said to have been a man of great good nature and a simplicity of mind that made him the butt for some coarse practical jokes. After his marriage he resided at 25 Craven Street, but later occupied quarters in various royal residences, and had a house at East Molesey, Surrey, where he died on 14 March 1830. He and his wife had no children and he left his estate to his wife and to his sister Mary. Although his family had property in co. Cork, he did not share in it.

Nagle is referred to in his early years as having 'a spirited and pleasing simplicity in his manner' (*Correspondence of Edmund Burke*, 2.19) and, although this eventually led to his being referred to as 'the court buffoon' (*Letters and Papers of … Thos. Byam Martin*, 1.19), he was evidently an effective captain and was thought worthy of higher posts. He is said once to have dived overboard to save a life.

J. K. LAUGHTON, *rev.* A. W. H. PEARSALL

Sources *Private papers of George, second Earl Spencer*, ed. J. S. Corbett and H. W. Richmond, 1, Navy RS, 46 (1913), 100, 275 · *Letters and papers of Admiral of the Fleet Sir Thos. Byam Martin, GCB*, ed. R. V. Hamilton, 3 vols., Navy RS, 12, 19, 24 (1898–1903) · *The correspondence of Edmund Burke*, ed. T. W. Copeland and others, 10 vols. (1958–78) · J. Marshall, *Royal naval biography*, 1/1 (1823), 277–8 · *GM*, 1st ser., 100/1 (1830), 469 · PRO, Adm 1/2230, 36/7429, 107/6, p. 387
Likenesses E. Scriven, stipple and aquatint, pubd 1826 (after P. Stephanoff), BM, NG Ire.; repro. in G. Nayler, *History of the coronation of George IV* (1839) · W. J. Ward, mezzotint, pubd 1830 (after W. Corden), BM, NPG · H. Turner, watercolour drawing, NPG

Nagle [*née* Watson], **Florence** (1894–1988), racehorse trainer, was born at Woodleigh, Wilbraham Road, Fallowfield, Manchester, on 26 October 1894, the daughter and eldest child of William George Watson (1861–1930), a merchant for Manchester goods who was created a baronet in 1912 and settled at Sulhampstead, Berkshire, and his second wife, Bessie (*d.* 1942), daughter of Thomas Atkinson of Workington, Cumberland. She had two brothers. On 1 July 1916 she married James Nagle, an Irishman who had returned from Toronto to serve in the King's Royal Rifle Corps during the First World War. In 1920 she began a racing partnership with him. Their first winner, trained by Harry Powney, was Fernley in the River handicap at Kempton Park. Unhappily her husband's heavy and unsuccessful gambling forced a withdrawal from turf activities. They were divorced in 1928; he died in 1933. She resumed in 1934, using an inheritance from her father to finance a stud at Sulhampstead and a small training establishment at Savile House, Newmarket, with Hugh Powney, a brother of Harry. From here emerged

Florence Nagle (1894–1988), by unknown photographer, 1948

Sandsprite, who ran second in the 1937 Derby. During the Second World War Nagle moved her stud to Westerlands, formerly part of Lord Woolavington's stud, and purchased Rose of England, the 1930 Oaks winner, as her foundation mare.

In due course Nagle also began to train there—and later at Petworth in Sussex—and in 1947 saddled her first winner, Thoroughwort, at Lingfield. However, it was not her name that appeared as trainer on the race card, but that of her head lad. The Jockey Club in Britain had constantly refused to grant licences to women to train and hence the subterfuge of using a male nominee had to be resorted to. This prohibition on women training racehorses had more to do with authority structures in the sport than the perceived physical demands of the job. During times of emergency, such as illness and accident, many women had run their husband's stables, but racing propriety demanded that where a widow took over the licence be held by her head lad. Similarly when Norah Wilmot inherited her father's training enterprise in 1931 she was not allowed to hold the licence, this despite having been his assistant for twenty years. Not all racing authorities were as rigid. In correspondence to the Jockey Club Nagle pointed out that women had been granted training licences in the United States, Australia, Germany, Kenya, several Scandinavian countries, and Belgium, from where Madame du Bois had

had entries accepted for races at Ascot. She added that the situation was hypocritical, as everyone in the industry knew that she and Norah Wilmot were trainers in all but name. Even the queen had sent the occasional horse to the Wilmot stables. She never received any statement from the Jockey Club giving reasons for their stance.

Finally, after two decades of fruitless campaigning, Florence Nagle took the club to court in 1966. She was seventy-one at the time with hardly a career to look forward to, but argued 'there was a principle involved in my fight. I am a feminist and believe that things should be decided on ability and not sex' (*Daily Telegraph*). The Jockey Club initially resisted, but threatened with High Court action capitulated, accepting legal advice that they had no case, as there was nothing in their rules to justify their action. They immediately said that they were prepared to grant her a licence provided that she acknowledged that it was given at the absolute and unfettered discretion of the stewards. This was no different to what was accepted by any trainer. In July they stated that they would be prepared to grant training licences to 'suitable women' and on 3 August Florence and Norah Wilmot received their permits. Wilmot, at the age of seventy-seven, had the honour of saddling the first flat-race winner by a recognized female trainer when Scobie Breasley rode Pat to victory in the South Coast Stakes at Brighton that same day. By 1973 seventeen women held licences and between them they had trained over 300 winners since 1966.

Florence Nagle died at her home, Little Mayfield, Lordings Lane, West Chiltington, Pulborough, Sussex, on 30 October 1988. Her training record was moderate, though she won eight races with Elf Arrow, including the Liverpool St Leger. Nevertheless her action, as she put it, 'in dragging the Jockey Club into the twentieth century' (Ramsden, 117) paved the way for Jenny Pitman, Venetia Williams, Mary Reveley, and others who have competed with—and beaten—male trainers.   WRAY VAMPLEW

Sources C. Ramsden, *Ladies in racing: sixteenth century to the present day* (1973) · *Daily Telegraph* (28 July 1966) · J. Randall and T. Mewis, *A century of champions* (1999) · b. cert. · d. cert. · Burke, *Peerage* (1967) [Watson of Sulhampstead]
Likenesses photograph, 1948, Empics Sports Photo Agency, Nottingham [*see illus.*] · photograph, repro. in Randall and Mewis, *Century of champions*, 24
Wealth at death £885,739: probate, 14 March 1989, *CGPLA Eng. & Wales*

Nagle, Honora [Nano] (**1718–1784**), educationist and founder of the Presentation order, was born at Ballygriffin, near Mallow, co. Cork, the eldest of seven children of Garret Nagle (*d. c.*1746), landowner and merchant, and his wife, Ann (*d.* 1748), daughter of George and Martha Mathew of Thurles, co. Tipperary. As members of the Catholic gentry the Nagles were disadvantaged by the penal legislation of the late seventeenth and early eighteenth centuries, and Garret Nagle himself was suspected of involvement in the Jacobite cause. Nevertheless Nano's upbringing was a relatively privileged one. Having received her earliest schooling at home she completed her

Honora Nagle (1718–1784), by Charles Turner, pubd 1809

education in France and subsequently lived for a number of years in Paris.

Following the death of her father about 1746, Nano returned to Ireland and lived in Dublin with her mother and her sister Ann, whose 'uncommon piety' and early death she cited as influencing her own choice of career (Walsh, 382). Encountering the widespread destitution which characterized eighteenth-century Ireland she was as shocked by the ignorance of religion among the poor as by their miserable living conditions. Discouraged by the difficulties involved in addressing these problems she decided to enter a convent in France but, unable to dispel the conviction that her vocation lay in Ireland, she left the convent before taking her final vows, in order to return home.

In Cork, where she settled with her brother and sister-in-law, Nano established a school for poor girls. In doing so she was flouting the legislation which banned Catholic education and felt it necessary to act with discretion. She described this period thus:

> When I arrived I kept my design a profound secret, as I knew, if it were spoken of, I should meet with opposition on every side, particularly from my immediate family as in all appearance they would suffer from it. My confessor was the only person I told of it; and as I could not appear in the affair, I sent my maid to get a good mistress and to take in thirty poor girls ... In about nine months I had 200 children. (Walsh, 345)

In fact the penal legislation was never activated against Nano's work and her family suffered no repercussions as a result of her activities; indeed a legacy from her wealthy uncle Joseph Nagle permitted her to expand her efforts. By

1769 she had seven schools in various parts of Cork, providing poor children with basic academic, vocational, and, above all, religious instruction.

Anxious to safeguard the future of her schools, Nano was convinced that this could best be done by placing them in the hands of a religious order. In 1767, in association with her friend and spiritual adviser Dr Francis Moylan, she began negotiations with the Ursulines in Paris, and in 1771 four Irish-born novices and a mother superior arrived in Cork to establish the first Ursuline foundation in Ireland in a convent which Nagle had built for them in Cove Lane. Six months later, in January 1772, the Ursulines opened a fee-paying school there.

However, the rule of enclosure to which the Ursulines were subject prevented them from taking over the running of the poor schools and the other charitable projects, such as the visitation and care of the old and sick, that Nano had established. She therefore determined to create a new type of sisterhood, whose members would be unenclosed and 'devoted solely to works of charity among the poor' (Walsh, 99). In December 1775 she and three companions began their noviciate, and on 24 June 1776 they took vows as sisters of the Charitable Instruction of the Sacred Heart of Jesus. On Christmas day 1777 the sisters inaugurated a longstanding tradition by entertaining fifty beggars to dinner, and in 1780 they moved into a new convent which Nano had built in Cove Lane.

Despite her age and worsening health, and the austerities and penances to which she subjected herself, Nano continued to participate fully in the work of her foundation. In 1783 she reported to her friend Teresa Mulally that she was building an almshouse for elderly women, and at the time of her death she was planning to establish an asylum 'for unhappy females' (Coppinger, 26). On the day before the onset of her final illness 'she went as usual to all her schools, and was penetrated with rain, as of late she walked so slow' (Walsh, 368). She died a few days later, on 26 April 1784, at the convent, and was buried in the graveyard of the Ursuline convent adjoining her own convent at Cove Lane.

In the years immediately following Nano's death the survival of her congregation was threatened by financial difficulties and a shortage of new recruits. In 1793, however, a second foundation was established in Killarney; by the end of the century the society also had houses in Dublin and in Waterford, and a second foundation in Cork, and in 1805 Pope Pius VII raised the congregation to the status of a religious order. During the nineteenth century, as the Presentation order, Nagle's foundation established itself in Britain, North America, Australasia, and India, as well as in Ireland, where it pioneered the active social role assumed by nuns in the post-famine period.

ROSEMARY RAUGHTER

Sources W. Coppinger, *The life of Miss Nano Nagle, as sketched … in a funeral sermon preached in Cork on the anniversary of her death* (1794) • T. J. Walsh, *Nano Nagle and the Presentation sisters* (1959) • R. Raughter, 'A discreet benevolence: female philanthropy and the Catholic resurgence in 18th-century Ireland', *Women's History Review*, 6 (1997), 465–84 • C. Clear, *Nuns in 19th-century Ireland* (1987) • P. J. Corish, *The Irish Catholic experience* (1985) • R. Liebowitz, 'Virgins in the service of Christ: the dispute over an active apostolate for women during the Counter Reformation', *Women of spirit*, ed. E. McLaughlin and R. Reuther (1979), 131–52 • *DNB*

Archives South Presentation convent, Cork, archives | Presentation convent, Dublin, archives

Likenesses oils, 18th cent., Crawford Gallery, Cork • J. Barry, oils, 1770?, South Presentation convent, Cork • C. Turner, stipple engraving, pubd 1809, BM, NPG [*see illus.*]

Wealth at death see will and misappropriation of legacies detailed in Walsh, *Nano Nagle*, 142–3

Nagle, Jacob (1761–1841), sailor and diarist, was born in Reading, Pennsylvania, on 15 September 1761, the son of George Nagel (1735–1789), a German immigrant, and Rebecca Rogers (*d*. 1793). On the outbreak of the American War of Independence George Nagel assumed command of a series of Pennsylvania regiments. Jacob joined him in August 1777. He served in George Washington's artillery, saw action at the battle of Brandywine, and then wintered at Valley Forge. Upon his father's abrupt resignation of his commission in June 1778, Nagle also left the revolutionary army. Early in 1780 he joined the *Saratoga*, a 16-gun sloop then being built at Philadelphia for the navy. With the launch of this ship delayed, Nagle changed to the *Fair American*, a 16-gun privateer. In company with the *Holker*, this captured more than twenty ships in six months' cruising. In 1781 Nagle went on two cruises on the 20-gun *Rising Sun*. In October he was shipwrecked on the Virginia coast, after which he joined the *Trojan*, only for it to be disabled in a storm, then captured by HMS *Royal Oak*. This led to Nagle's serving in another navy.

Still a prisoner of war, Nagle went down to St Kitts in the *Royal Oak*, and regained his liberty when French forces took the island in January 1782. This respite was brief, for in early March he was imprisoned at Fort Royal, Martinique, for aiding a British sailor. In May 1782, after the battle of the Saints, he was among prisoners of war exchanged for French ones. On and off Nagle was to serve in the Royal Navy for twenty years. On 25 May he joined the *St Lucia* as able seaman. The following April, upon the ending of the war, he transferred to the *Ardent*, in which he sailed from Antigua to Plymouth, where he was paid off in August 1783. Rather than return home, he first joined the *Ganges*, which went down to Gibraltar, and then one of the guardships at Portsmouth.

In March 1787 Nagle was one of the young seamen selected for service on the *Sirius*, the frigate escorting the first fleet to New South Wales. He experienced the long voyage down the Atlantic and across the Indian Oceans, with stops at Tenerife, Rio de Janeiro, and Cape Town, before arriving at Botany Bay in January 1788. In October Nagle went in the *Sirius* to Cape Town, returning to Sydney in May 1789. In March 1790 he was in this ship when it was wrecked at Norfolk Island, and distinguished himself by twice swimming between ship and shore as the crew struggled to save its precious supplies.

After twelve months on Norfolk Island Nagle returned to England in April 1792 in the *Waaksamheyd*. For some months he lived in London's East End, experiencing its life to the full. In August he was pressed into the *Hector*, where he stayed for seven months, which included the time when the *Bounty* mutineers were held onboard. He next went into the *Brunswick*, from which he deserted in April 1794 to enter the East Indiaman *Rose*, in which he voyaged to Madras and Calcutta, where he met two convict women from Sydney who had established a brothel.

The *Rose* returned to England in July 1795, whereupon Nagle entered HMS *Gorgon*. At this time he married a Miss Pitmans (*d.* 1802)—'a lively hansome girl in my eye' (*Nagle Journal*, 186)—and the pair had several children in the next years. In November 1795 the *Gorgon* sailed to Gibraltar and into the Mediterranean. At Corsica in April 1796 Nagle transferred to the *Blanche*, so that he then saw action under the general command of Horatio Nelson and John Jervis. He returned to Portsmouth at the end of June 1798. In July he entered the *Netley*, which cruised most along the coasts of Portugal. Appointed prize-master, he prospered from the ship's success. In June 1801 he transferred to the *Gorgon*, which sailed to Alexandria, and from which he was discharged at Woolwich in April 1802, as the peace of Amiens briefly held.

Nagle now decided to return to America. After visiting family members he went to sea again in the merchant navy, sometimes American, sometimes British, where he continued for twenty-two years. During this long period he voyaged to the West Indies, to Central America, to China in the *Neptune* (1806–8), and to Canada, Florida, and South America. In 1811 he sailed to Brazil, where he stayed until 1821. After several more trading voyages, in mid-1824 he retired from the sea. Thereafter Nagle had a somewhat restless life, sometimes working, sometimes living with relatives or friends until their patience ran out. He died in Canton, Ohio, on 17 February 1841 and was buried there on 18 February.

Jacob Nagle prided himself on being the most skilful of sailors. He also took pride in his personal appearance, being given to wearing waistcoats and silk jackets. He frequented prostitutes, towards whom he acted charitably when he thought their case merited it. He did not gather worldly possessions about him. However, late in life he wrote a long and surprisingly accurate reminiscence, which is full of details of and insights into the life of an ordinary seaman in the eighteenth-century royal and merchant navies.

As the form will for seamen put it so eloquently, Nagle knew all 'the Perils and Dangers of the Seas, and other Uncertainties of this transitory Life'. He suffered severely from scurvy, felt the lash on his back, saw men killed in battle and executed. He was robbed and cheated of his money. He lost his wife and children to yellow fever at Lisbon in 1802. In twenty years he did not see his family; and by the time he returned to the United States his parents were dead. When in the throes of illness in Brazil, he wrote feelingly:

> though I had traveled a good many years through the four quarters of the globe, been a prisoner twice, cast a way three times, and the ship foundering under me, two days and a night in an open boat on the wide ocion without anything to eat or water to norish us, and numbers of times in want of water or victuals, at other time in action, men slain along side of me, and with all, at this minute it apeared to me that I

was in greater distress and missery than I ever had been in any country during my life. I fell on my nees, and never did I pray with a sincerer hart than I did at that presentime. (*Nagle Journal*, 312–13)

Jacob Nagle was an ordinary man who lived an extraordinary life. It is for this life, so richly recorded in his journal, that he deserves the remembrance of posterity.

ALAN FROST

Sources *The Nagle journal: a diary of the life of Jacob Nagle, sailor, from the year 1775 to 1841*, ed. J. C. Dann (1988) · **Archives** U. Mich., Clements L., library, personal memoirs of time in Royal Navy

Nagle, Sir Richard (1635/6–1699), lawyer and Jacobite politician, was born in co. Cork, the second of at least five sons of James Nagle (*d.* 1678) of Clenor, co. Cork, and his wife, Honora, daughter of Maurice Nugent of Aghanagh, co. Cork. The Nagles (sometimes rendered Nangle or Neagle) were a Roman Catholic family descended from Anglo-Norman settlers who had lived in the Blackwater valley in north co. Cork since the early fourteenth century. James Nagle had forfeited his estate in the Cromwellian confiscation, but was living at Annakissy, co. Cork, in Charles II's reign.

Details of Richard Nagle's early career are sketchy, though it appears that he was intended for the priesthood, probably the Jesuits, before turning to the law; he was admitted by Gray's Inn in 1663, at the comparatively late age of twenty-seven, a delay explicable by the vicissitudes of the Cromwellian 1650s. In 1669 he married Joan Kearney of Rathcool, Fethard, co. Tipperary, whose sister married his elder brother Pierce in 1675. They lived at Carrigacunna, a Nagle property in co. Cork, and, from 1684, in Dublin. Called to the Irish bar in November 1668 he appeared for both protestant and Roman Catholic clients. As his legal practice expanded he acquired more land in north Cork and Waterford. The extent of his earned wealth is clear from substantial loans, recorded in the Dublin statute staple, which he made in 1683 (£1800) and 1686 (£2000). The earl of Clarendon, the lord lieutenant, reported in 1686 Nagle's view that no chief justice's place 'would equal his present gains which he must consider because of his great charge of children' (*CSP dom.*, 1686–7, 153), which in fact amounted to seven sons and six daughters.

Nagle's involvement in politics began in 1686, a year after James II's accession. Initially he appeared a reluctant participant. In June 1686 he declined nomination to the Irish privy council on the grounds, according to Clarendon, that 'to appear at the bar after he is a councillor will be very indecent' (*Correspondence of Henry Hyde*, 1.417). But his refusal of a council seat could not disguise a growing engagement with politics over the summer of 1686. When Tyrconnell visited Ireland to inspect the army Nagle acted as his principal legal adviser, and an increasingly hostile tone becomes apparent in Lord Clarendon's references to a lawyer whom he had at first regarded as 'a very learned and an honest man' (ibid.). At a bad-tempered but inconclusive meeting in mid-August 1686, attended by Clarendon and Tyrconnell, both Nagle and Sir Stephen Rice, the

Sir Richard Nagle (1635/6–1699), by unknown artist

newly appointed Roman Catholic chief baron of the exchequer, argued that it was only in an Irish parliament that the land question should be determined. A week later Nagle accompanied Tyrconnell on his return to Whitehall, news which alarmed those Irish protestants who took it as a sign that Tyrconnell's aim was to have the king agree to an Irish parliament 'in order to the breaking of the acts of settlement and explanation' (earl of Longford to duke of Ormond, 31 Aug 1686 in *Ormonde MSS*, 7.449–50).

But opinion at Whitehall was not yet ready for so radical a departure in policy. The prevailing view at Whitehall, argued by Sunderland, the secretary of state, was that a royal declaration confirming the acts of settlement and explanation would be needed to reassure Irish protestants in the event of Tyrconnell's appointment as viceroy. The means devised by Tyrconnell and Nagle to thwart Sunderland's plan was the Coventry letter. In what was in effect a manuscript pamphlet, Nagle argued robustly against any royal declaration confirming the existing land settlement; what was needed was a new Irish land act which would restore many 'innocent' Roman Catholics whose cases had not been heard in the 1660s. For Catholics in Ireland the unique opportunity offered by a co-religionist on the throne must not be lost: 'nothing can support catholic religion in that kingdom, but to make catholics there considerable in their fortunes' (*Ormonde MSS*, 7.464–7). Ostensibly written by Nagle on 26 October during an insomniac night in Coventry on his return journey to Ireland, the letter had all the appearances of having been carefully drafted while Nagle was still in London. In the short term

it achieved its immediate objective and put paid to Sunderland's plans for a royal declaration to accompany the now inevitable announcement of Tyrconnell's appointment as viceroy. Despite this limited success Nagle allegedly disowned authorship, letting it be known in Dublin that 'he would arrest any man in an action of ten thousand pound, who should father it on him' (*A Full and Impartial Account of All the Secret Consults*, 55).

Appointed attorney-general and knighted in February 1686 Nagle was from the start a member of the new lord deputy's 'cabinet' (T. Sheridan, 'Narrative' in *Stuart Papers*, 1.18). On 12 February, the day Tyrconnell was sworn in, he lodged an information against the city of Dublin concerning their claims to certain liberties and franchises. It was an early indication of what would occupy his attention in the coming months. The *quo warranto* challenges to borough charters, which Nagle as attorney-general orchestrated throughout Ireland, where necessary bringing recalcitrant boroughs to court, were designed to restore local government to the ousted Roman Catholic élite while at the same time ensuring that borough representation in the anticipated parliament would be predominantly Catholic. Closely linked with these proceedings was the appointment of Catholic sheriffs to the counties.

When Tyrconnell travelled to Chester to meet the king in August 1687 he took Nagle with him. This was the crucial meeting from which Tyrconnell returned with the king's permission to prepare bills to modify the land settlement. The extent of Nagle's involvement in the subsequent drafting of alternative bills can be inferred from both the office he now held and the role he had played in 1686 in providing the main intellectual justification for new legislation. He did not, however, take the draft bills to London in March 1688; that was left to Sir Stephen Rice and Chief Justice Nugent, though both Nagle and Rice were alleged to have advised against the unimpressive Nugent's appointment as an emissary of the Dublin government.

Nagle continued as attorney-general after James II's arrival in Ireland in March 1689. When James summoned a parliament Nagle was returned for co. Cork (of which his brother Pierce was by now sheriff), and his younger brother David was returned for Mallow. Another brother, James, was appointed serjeant-at-arms to the Commons (and later clerk and engrosser of chancery writs). When parliament met on 7 May, Richard was elected speaker. In the absence of primary sources his role as speaker is difficult to reconstruct, but it is reasonable to assume that the author of the Coventry letter approved of legislation which, by repealing the Restoration Land Acts and attainting more than 2000 substantial protestants, laid the basis for a full-scale restoration of the Catholic élite.

With the prorogation of parliament in July, Nagle's role in the Jacobite administration became increasingly significant. In August, when the earl of Melfort was effectively forced to resign as secretary for war, D'Avaux, the French ambassador, was astonished that the militarily inexperienced Nagle, 'un habile homme pour les affaires de droit, mais qui est si neuf dans celle de la guerre qu'il n'en a pas les premiers elements' ('a clever man in legal affairs, but who is so new in those of war that he has not the first elements of them'; *Négociations de M. le Comte d'Avaux en Irlande*, 445), should be his replacement, a decision the king weakly defended on the grounds that he could not withstand the continual importuning of the Irish. Nagle threw himself with enthusiasm into his new duties, preparing army lists and equipping the Jacobite forces for imminent war. Notwithstanding his initial doubts about Nagle's suitability for military administration in February 1690 D'Avaux could tell Louis XIV of 'une grande union entre le duc de Tirconnel, le chevalier Negle et moy' ('a great union between the duke of Tyrconnell, Sir Richard Nagle, and myself'; ibid., 623).

Despite defeat at the Boyne (July 1690) and James II's immediate departure for France, the war was not yet over, as William III's subsequent failure at the first siege of Limerick showed. In September, when Tyrconnell travelled to France for consultations with James and the French government, Nagle either accompanied him or followed on soon after. They returned together in January 1691, landing at Galway and travelling on to Limerick. Nagle resumed his duties as secretary of state for war and attorney-general, but little is known of his role or influence over the succeeding months when Jacobite politics in Ireland was deeply divided between the followers of Sarsfield and Tyrconnell. On Tyrconnell's death in August 1691, which Nagle described as 'a fatal stroke to this poor country in this nick of time', a sealed commission from James II came into effect, appointing Nagle, Alexander Fitton, the Jacobite lord chancellor, and Francis Plowden, commissioner of the revenue, as lords justices. They seem, however, to have had no significant part in the treaty negotiations of late September and early October, and by November Nagle was on his way into permanent exile in France. Outlawed since October 1689 by the court of king's bench in London, Nagle forfeited his estate, which was granted in 1693 to Viscount Sydney, William III's viceroy.

Throughout the 1690s Nagle remained in James II's service at St Germain-en-Laye. He continued as Jacobite secretary for war and attorney-general of Ireland up to his death in 1699, though his duties were not confined to Irish business. He enjoyed the king's confidence to the extent that James appointed him a commissioner of the royal household in 1698 and nominated him in his will as member of a council to advise the queen on the guardianship of the prince of Wales. In fact Nagle predeceased the king by two years and died at St Germain on 4 April 1699. The cause of his death is unknown.   JAMES McGUIRE

Sources CSP dom., 1685–9 • *The correspondence of Henry Hyde, earl of Clarendon, and of his brother Laurence Hyde, earl of Rochester*, ed. S. W. Singer, 2 vols. (1828) • *Calendar of the Stuart papers belonging to his majesty the king, preserved at Windsor Castle*, 7 vols., HMC, 56 (1902–23), vols. 1–2, 6 • *Calendar of the manuscripts of the marquess of Ormonde*, new ser., 8 vols., HMC, 36 (1902–20), vols. 7–8 • *Négociations de M. le Comte d'Avaux en Irlande, 1689–90*, ed. J. Hogan, 2 vols., IMC (1934–58) • E. Keane, P. Beryl Phair, and T. U. Sadleir, eds., *King's Inns admission papers, 1607–1867*, IMC (1982), 360 • D. Ó Murchadha, *Family names of co. Cork* (1985), 258–9 • B. O'Connell, 'The Nagles of Garnavilla', *Irish Genealogist*, 3/1 (1956), 17–24 • B. O'Connell, 'The Nagles of Mount Nagle', *Irish Genealogist*, 2/12 (1955), 377–89 • B. O'Connell, 'The Nagles of Annakissy', *Irish Genealogist*, 2 (1954), 337–48 • R. Hayes, 'Biographical dictionary of Irishmen in France', *Studies*, 34 (1945), 109 • J. Ohlmeyer and É. Ó Ciardha, eds., *The Irish statute staple books, 1596–1687* (1998), 127 • J. L. J. Hughes, ed., *Patentee officers in Ireland, 1173–1826, including high sheriffs, 1661–1684 and 1761–1816*, IMC (1960) • J. Foster, *The register of admissions to Gray's Inn, 1521–1889, together with the register of marriages in Gray's Inn chapel, 1695–1754* (privately printed, London, 1889) • W. King, *The state of the protestants of Ireland under the late King James's government* (1691) • *A full and impartial account of all the secret consults … of the Romish party in Ireland* (1690), 55 • T. C. Croker, ed., *Narratives illustrative of the contests in Ireland in 1641 and 1690* (1841), 132 • J. G. Simms, *Jacobite Ireland, 1685–91* (1969) • J. G. Simms, *The Williamite confiscation in Ireland, 1690–1703* (1956) • J. Miller, 'The earl of Tyrconnell and James II's Irish policy, 1685–1688', *HJ*, 20 (1977), 803–23 • R. Bagwell, *Ireland under the Stuarts*, 3 (1916)
Archives Bodl. Oxf., Clarendon MSS, 'Coventry letter' [copy] • NL Ire., Drummond MSS, 'Coventry letter' [copy]
Likenesses W. Dobson, oils, NG Ire. • portrait, NG Ire. [*see illus.*]
Wealth at death outlawed by Williamite authorities and lost his properties in Ireland: Simms, *Williamite confiscation*

Naidu [*née* Chattopadhyay], **Sarojini** (1879–1949), politician and poet, born on 13 February 1879 in Hyderabad, was the second child and eldest daughter of Aghorenath and Baradasundari Chattopadhyay (Chatterji). Her father, a DSc of Edinburgh University, came from a family of Sanskrit scholars of east Bengal and was a bon viveur with a wide range of interests which included literature (Western and Indian) and alchemy. As principal of Nizam's College, Hyderabad, he developed an empathy with Indo-Islamic culture, and his ardent patriotism at times got him into trouble with the authorities. His wife was a skilled musician and dancer. Between them they created a joyous home imbued with high culture. Sarojini was deeply influenced by her father and the environment at home. Educated more at home than at school, she became a celebrity when at the age of twelve she stood first in the matriculation examination of Madras University. The following year she wrote a long poem in English modelled on Tennyson's *Lady of the Lake*. A volume of her poems was published in 1895. She had been sent to England in 1895 on a scholarship granted by the *nizam* and spent three years at King's College, London, and Girton College, Cambridge. Always opposed to structured education, she did not take any degree but acquired two important literary friends, Edmund Gosse and Arthur Symons. The former advised her to give up imitating English romantic poetry and try instead 'to be a genuinely Indian poet'. Sarojini took this advice to heart and began to write verses with an exclusively Indian background. The very lush poems which resulted were first published in a volume entitled *The Golden Threshold* (1905). In his introduction to the volume Gosse described her as India's most accomplished poet, at least among those writing in English.

Following her return to India Sarojini married Dr Govindarajulu Naidu in December 1898, with whom she had fallen in love as a teenager. The marriage, registered

Sarojini Naidu (1879–1949), by unknown photographer, 1930 [right, with Mahatma Gandhi during the salt march]

under the Act III of 1872, was a civil marriage and 'progressive' on several counts—a marriage of love, between individuals belonging to different castes and linguistic cultures. The couple had two sons and two daughters. Their Hyderabad home was described by a friend as an expression of perfect artistic taste.

From 1903 Sarojini Naidu entered the public phase of her career without abjuring her poetic pursuits. Between that year and 1917, she came into close contact with some of the most illustrious figures of India's political and cultural life—Gokhale, Tagore, Mrs Besant, Gandhi, and Jawaharlal Nehru. In 1904 she attended the Bombay session of the Indian National Congress and by 1909 she had emerged as a political leader of the first rank, thanks to Gokhale's patronage and her prominent role in the 1907 Calcutta meeting condemning the partition of Bengal. Besides, she had participated in the Madras conference on widow remarriage in 1908, beginning thereby to play a prominent role in the women's movement. She was awarded the kaisar-i-Hind medal by the government for her services during a plague epidemic. Her socially radical views were given a practical expression when she participated in the All-India Depressed Classes conference. Her concern for Hindu–Muslim unity made her a great admirer of M. A. Jinnah, whom she first met in 1919.

But the one encounter which changed Naidu's life was her meeting with Gandhi in 1915. Nationalist politics rather than poetry now became her dominant concern. In 1925 she presided over the Cawnpore session of the Indian National Congress. In 1928 she went to the USA as an unofficial ambassador of the nationalist movement and pleaded the cause of Indian independence in a very effective lecture tour from coast to coast. In 1930 she was arrested for her participation in the civil disobedience movement. She was also one of the hand-picked group of followers who accompanied Gandhi on the famous Dandi march to violate the British government's salt laws. In 1931 she participated in the round-table conference in London. She was appointed governor of United Provinces, India's largest state, in 1947, and died there while she was still holding that office on 1 February 1949. She was cremated three days later.

Sarojini Naidu was an outstanding example of India's pioneering women who achieved a high level of education, championed the rights of women, participated in the struggle for independence, and contributed to many areas of national life. She was a person of great charm, with a strong sense of humour. Her opposition to colonial rule notwithstanding, she, like Nehru, was deeply influenced by English culture, and English was in effect her mother tongue. The cosmopolitan ambiance of her paternal home had given her a sense of empathy with the grand tradition of Indo-Islamic culture, and one of her dominant concerns in public life was the achievement of Hindu–Muslim unity. The partition of India and the communal violence which accompanied it tarnished for her, as for many others in her generation, the sense of fulfilment when India became free.   TAPAN RAYCHAUDHURI

Sources P. Sengupta, *Sarojini Naidu: a biography* (1966) · M. E. Cousins, *The awakening of Asian womanhood* (1922) · T. Zinkin, *Reporting India* (1962) · S. Naidu, *The golden threshold* (1905)
Archives BL OIOC, letters and papers, MS Eur. A 95 · Nehru Museum, New Delhi | National Archives of India, New Delhi, Home Department files | FILM IWM FVA, documentary footage · Ministry of Information and Broadcasting, New Delhi, films division, documentary footage | SOUND IWM SA, oral history interviews
Likenesses photograph, 1930, Hult. Arch. [*see illus.*] · portrait, Indian Parliament Building, New Delhi, India · portrait, Raj Bhavan, Lucknow, India

Naipaul, Shivadhar Srinivasa [Shiva] (1945–1985), writer, was born on 25 February 1945 at a kinsman's house in Woodbrook, a quarter of Port of Spain, Trinidad, but was soon taken to Nepaul Street in the neighbouring quarter of St James, where he grew up. He was the sixth of the seven children, two of them sons, of Seepersad Naipaul (1906–1952), journalist, and his wife, Droapatie Capildeo; his elder brother by more than twelve years was the novelist V. S. Naipaul. The family belonged to the Indian community which had originally migrated to Trinidad as indentured labourers in the nineteenth century.

Family life was close and essentially feminine after the death of his father when Shiva was seven and his brother's departure to England. Naipaul himself wrote that he enjoyed the company of women and was 'responsive to the tidal motions of their moods—their curious gaieties and darknesses; and without consciously intending it, I see that they have had a major role in my fiction'.

He was educated at Queen's Royal and St Mary's colleges in Port of Spain whence he won an Island scholarship to Oxford. Naipaul later wrote that he never revisited Port of Spain without a sense of panic 'that, having arrived there, I may never be able to get out again'. But he never truly felt at home anywhere; and so began a rootless and dislocated existence starting in Britain in 1964 where not 'being straightforwardly Indian or straightforwardly West Indian' was a confusion that the rest of the world could not deal with (Naipaul, *Beyond the Dragon's Mouth*).

Naipaul went up to University College, Oxford, where he read psychology, philosophy, and physiology before changing capriciously to Chinese; he took a third class in 1968. Naipaul was a striking figure at Oxford—he wore long black boots and long black hair in those days—with an affectionate and bibulous circle of friends. As an undergraduate he met Virginia Margaret, daughter of Douglas Stuart, a BBC journalist; Jenny, as she was known, was his helpmeet for eighteen years. They were married in Oxford on 17 June 1967 and their son Tarun was born in 1973.

Before he left university, Naipaul had begun a novel. He said later, in an essay in which he wrote of comparisons with his brother, that he 'never made a decision to become a "writer"' and became one not because of 'doppelgänger absolutism which had so marred and scarred my childhood' but because 'there is nothing else I can do' (Naipaul, *An Unfinished Journey*, 27–9). The novel was continued in a bedsitter off Ladbroke Grove in London, the first of several modest homes before he found a flat in Warrington Crescent in 1975. The result was *Fireflies*, published in 1970 and recognized as a work of very high talent. It was set in Indian Port of Spain and told the story of Ram Lutchman, his long-suffering wife, and their two sons in limpid prose, with a crystal ear for dialogue and comedy. Through the human story of struggle it strikes at the heart of the functioning of the Hindu community in Trinidad. The book won three awards, the John Llewellyn Rhys memorial prize, the Jock Campbell *New Statesman* award, and the Winifred Holtby memorial prize of the Royal Society of Literature. Its few detractors, however, read *Fireflies* as a misanthropic work which 'displayed a memorable contempt for the weak and the stupid' (*The Times*). It was followed in 1973 by *The Chip-Chip Gatherers*, also set in Trinidad, tragicomic again though palpably more sombre and oppressive in tone. It described in Darwinian terms the triumph of the ruthless over the quiescent. It was nevertheless enthusiastically received and won the Whitbread award.

The enthusiasts were perplexed that no novel followed for ten years. During those years Naipaul turned to the short story with *The Adventures of Guru Deva* (1976). He also travelled and wrote a good deal of outstanding journalism, much of it collected in *Beyond the Dragon's Mouth* (1984), an anthology of articles and short stories. He also published two works of non-fiction. *North of South* (1978) was a bleak account of a journey through Kenya, Tanzania, and Zambia. It was too bleak for those *bien pensants* who wanted to see only the best and the most hopeful in independent Africa. Naipaul was in fact a painfully honest observer, reacting with savage indignation to this 'hopeless, doomed continent ... swaddled in lies—the lies of an aborted European civilisation; the lies of liberation. Nothing but lies.'

Naipaul had a specific advantage over the *bien pensants* as a non-European quite free from 'white liberal' hang-ups of colonial and racial guilt. This advantage was put to further use. In 1979–80 the Naipauls spent more than a year intermittently in San Francisco and Connecticut as he worked on a bleaker subject still. *Black and White* (1980) recounted the background to a ghastly story, the mass suicide at a jungle camp in Guyana by the deluded followers of a Californian heresiarch called Jim Jones. If *North of South* had been called 'anti-African', the unflinchingly sharp-eyed *Black and White* was called 'anti-American'; again unjustly: it was another cry of rage at folly and cruelty. Naipaul's third novel appeared at last in 1983. He had evidently had some block or inhibition, but at the same time *A Hot Country* is a tribute to his fastidiousness and perfectionism, which were always as much a blessing to his readers as they were a trial to his publishers and editors: he was a writer who could spend a morning working on one sentence, to delete it in the afternoon. Direct and intense, his style is now pared down to a minimum. Maybe for that reason the book was underrated at the time. Its dark vision and satire of 'radical Third world black nationalist assertion' may not have been palatable to new readers.

In 1984 Naipaul visited Australia to write a book about the country. His work in progress on that book was included in his posthumous collection *An Unfinished Journey* (1986). He had just moved to an airy flat at 79A Belsize Park Gardens, London, where in a small workroom he wrote in longhand standing at an old-fashioned lectern.

Naipaul was above medium height but stooping and thickly built. He was bear-like in looks and also in manner. Prickly, acutely sensitive, difficult at times, he provoked hostility without trying; or perhaps without trying much. Some found him arrogant or truculent, and by his own hilarious account his visit to Australia ended in a succession of socially disastrous evenings. Others relished his company. A group of friends, a number of them writers associated with *The Spectator*, where his wife was the editor's secretary, regarded him with amused affection and awed respect. Sardonic and world-weary, over a long wine-fuelled lunch or a long whisky-fuelled evening he was the most engaging and rewarding of companions.

He celebrated his fortieth birthday at home in February 1985. He had always been afraid of death. In that sense alone it came to him mercifully six months later when he was struck by a thrombosis at his flat on 13 August 1985 and died instantly. He was cremated by Hindu rites at Golders Green crematorium, London. *The Spectator* established the Shiva Naipaul prize for young travel writers in his memory. GEOFFREY WHEATCROFT, *rev.*

Sources S. Naipaul, *Beyond the dragon's mouth* (1984) · S. Naipaul, *An unfinished journey* (1986) · *The Times* (16 Aug 1985) · *The Times* (21 Aug 1985) · personal knowledge (1990) · private information (1990) · B. King, 'The new internationalism: Shiva Naipaul, Salman

Rushdie, Buchi Emecheta, Timothy Mo and Kazuo Ishiguro', *The British and Irish novel since 1960*, ed. J. Acheson (1991)
Wealth at death £8818: probate, 14 Jan 1986, *CGPLA Eng. & Wales*

Nair, Sir Chettur Sankaran (1857–1934), judge and politician in India, was born on 11 July 1857 at the small village of Mankara on the Bhorata River about 16 miles west of Palghat in south Malabar, India, into the Hindu matrilineal Nair community, the son of Ramunni Panickar, a tahsildar (revenue collector) in the Madras government service—who according to his son's autobiography 'lived in great state' and 'had belted peons carrying swords before him' (Nair, 8)—and his wife, Chettur Parvathy Amma.

Dumb until his fifth year, Sankaran Nair was educated at home, then at schools in Angadipuram, Cannanore, and Calicut, partly by British masters whom he liked, and from about 1875 at the Presidency College, Madras, gaining his BA (1877) with distinction and winning the history and English essay prizes. He joined the Law College and gained his BL (1879). For a year he was apprenticed to Horatio Shepherd, who took a friendly personal interest in him. In March 1880 he was enrolled as a vakil at the Madras high court. His practice prospered. In 1885 he married Kunhammalu Amma (*d.* 1926) of the Palat family; they had one son, R. M. Palat, barrister and Madras minister, and five daughters.

Fortunate in his personal contacts with British men in India, Nair was predisposed in favour of Britain. In 1893 he visited England to instruct counsel in an appeal before the privy council. He joined the National Liberal Club and met Liberal politicians. He much admired Gladstone, 'a great friend of freedom' (Nair, 40), called him his guru, and considered that John Morley's *Gladstone* showed Morley was incapable of reading Gladstone's character. Nair recorded in his autobiography how kind and helpful London policemen were to his wife. He favoured English-language education as crucial to progress, opposing Curzon's vernacular policy. He praised British achievement in suppressing 'loathsome, horrible practices' (ibid., 44), and he was instrumental in the erecting in Madras of a statue of Lord Ripon. However, he criticized some aspects of the raj and demanded further reform.

In 1899 Nair was appointed government pleader and public prosecutor. In 1900, responding to an official circular from Curzon, Nair offered his services in the Second South African War; the government thanked him but declined his services. On occasion in 1904 and 1905 he officiated as a high court judge. In 1907 he was appointed advocate-general, and later that year was appointed by Morley (secretary of state for India) a judge of the Madras high court. He asserted judicial independence of the executive and opposed any Indian Civil Service interference. Reportedly his independence of outlook and expert knowledge of west coast legal systems enabled him to contribute some valuable judgments. He was made a CIE in 1904 and knighted in 1912.

A social reformer, concerned with the position of Hindu women, Nair was active in public life through various

Sir Chettur Sankaran Nair (1857–1934), by Lafayette, 1929

organizations. In 1893 he was nominated a member of the Madras legislative council. In 1897 he was the youngest president yet of the Indian National Congress—then not a mass party, and with little activity beyond its annual conference—at Amraoti, and there criticized Indian military expenditure. In 1899 he became a fellow of Madras University, and in 1902 Curzon appointed him to the Raleigh university commission. He was sometime president of the Madras Social Reform Association, Madras Cosmopolitan Club, the Society for the Prevention of Cruelty to Animals, the Pinjrapole Society for Disabled Animals, and the Depressed Classes Mission, and was an influential member of the Hindu Mahasabha. He was the founder editor of the *Madras Review* and co-editor of the *Madras Law Journal*, and contributed to the *Contemporary Review*.

In 1915 Nair was the third Indian appointed to the viceroy's executive council, and he became responsible for education and health: Ramsay MacDonald commented it was significant as the 'appointment of an Indian to a Department of constructive policy' (MacDonald, 65). Nair's tenure was rather uneasy, but he liked the Liberal Lord Hardinge (viceroy from 1910 to 1916). He found the Conservative Lord Chelmsford (viceroy from 1916 to 1921) 'cold and distant' (Nair, 83). In 1916 he told Chelmsford that at present self-government was incompatible with Indian caste and class feeling and the low status of women. From 1916 at least he had the reputation with his colleagues of being influenced by politicians. In 1919 he wrote two minutes of dissent criticizing aspects of British rule and suggesting reforms. After the suppression of the Punjab revolt he resigned in 1919, in protest at the delay in withdrawing martial law.

Nair was among those whom Edwin Samuel Montagu (secretary of state for India from 1917 to 1922) consulted on his visit to India in 1917–18. Montagu found Nair unpleasant, untruthful, disloyal, unreliable, and negative. He wrote in his diary that Nair was 'really an impossible person ... he shouts at the top of his voice, refuses to listen to anything when one argues, and is absolutely uncompromising ... frightfully quarrelsome, vilely mannered, and obviously out to wreck' (Montagu, 31, 180). Nevertheless in 1919 Montagu appointed Nair to the secretary of state's council in London. In 1921 Nair resigned and returned to India as adviser to the Indore state.

A moderate and constitutionalist—his biographer called him 'in many ways, an eminent Victorian' (Menon, 127)—Nair disagreed with Gandhi's non-co-operation. Shocked by the 1921 Moplah rising atrocities against his own people, triggered by Gandhi's campaign, Nair published *Gandhi and Anarchy* (1922), intended to stop Gandhi's activities. It claimed Gandhi's non-co-operation led to violence, and demanded drastic action against the Moplahs. It argued that Gandhi was opposed 'to any government in any form' (Nanda, 203), was undermining respect for laws and protection to persons and property, and was unleashing forces of disorder he was unable to control. It was translated into Urdu and Hindi and distributed by government as propaganda. However, in it Nair criticized Sir Michael O'Dwyer for alleged 'atrocities' in the suppression of the Punjab revolt. O'Dwyer sued Nair for libel. The case was tried in 1924 in the King's Bench Division in London before Mr Justice McCardie and resulted in Nair's paying damages and costs; the case was criticized by Ramsay MacDonald and other Labour politicians. Nair became a member of the council of state, in 1927 proposing the abolition of communal electorates, and resigning in 1932. He wanted dominion status for India. In 1928 he became chairman of the Indian central committee appointed to co-operate with the Simon statutory commission. The committee failed to agree and Nair's chairmanship has been severely criticized, but the task of reconciling its discordant elements was difficult. Nair was invited to the three round-table conferences but declined. He wrote his autobiography, which was published in 1966 by his eldest daughter K. P. Parvathi Amma, Lady Madhavan Nair.

Exceptionally able, Nair was proud—according to his biographer he was 'a man of intense self-respect' who 'would not brook any affront to his dignity' (Menon, 123, 52)—and sometimes courteous, sometimes rude. His official colleagues found him combative and lacking in reticence. He was almost 6 feet tall, well built, relatively fair, and 'looked an Aryan of Aryans in the Dravidian south' (ibid., 119). He was abstemious and practised yoga. A devout Hindu and a student of Hindu religious classics, he worshipped Lord Subramanya as his personal deity.

In March 1934 Nair was in a motor accident and suffered a head injury from which he never recovered. He died on 24 April 1934 at his eldest daughter's house, Spring Gardens, Madras. His body was cremated at his native village Mankara, on the bank of the Bharatu Puzha, and his son erected a small memorial there. Though latterly, like other liberal moderates of his generation, overshadowed by Gandhi, since 1947 Nair has been praised as an architect of independence and builder of modern India.

ROGER T. STEARN

Sources C. S. Nair, *Autobiography of Sir C. Sankaran Nair* (1966) • K. P. S. Menon, *C. Sankaran Nair* (1967) • *Dictionary of national biography*, 3 (1974) [Calcutta] • *The Times* (25 April 1934) • *WWW, 1929–40* • *Debrett's Peerage* (1924) • private information (1949) • E. S. Montagu, *An Indian diary*, ed. V. Montagu (1930) • P. G. Robb, *The government of India and reform: policies towards politics and the constitution, 1916–1921* (1976) • M. O'Dwyer, *India as I knew it, 1885–1925* (1925) • B. R. Nanda, *Mahatma Gandhi: a biography* (1996) • I. Colvin, *The life of General Dyer* (1931) • J. R. MacDonald, *The government of India* (1919) • S. Reed, *The India I knew, 1897–1947* (1952) • P. Spear, *The Oxford history of modern India, 1740–1947* (1965) • J. M. Brown, *Modern India: the origins of an Asian democracy*, 2nd edn (1994) • B. R. Nanda, *Gokhale: the Indian moderates and the British raj* (1977) • J. M. Brown, *Gandhi's rise to power: Indian politics, 1915–1922* (1972)
Likenesses photograph, *c.*1920, repro. in Nair, *Autobiography*, facing p. 241 • Lafayette, photograph, 1929, NPG [*see illus.*]

Nairac, Robert Laurence (1948–1977), army officer, was born in Mauritius on 31 August 1948, the youngest of four children (two daughters and two sons) of Maurice Nairac, an ophthalmic surgeon, and his wife, Barbara Dykes (*d.* 1999). His brother David, who was five years older, predeceased him at the age of nineteen. He was educated at Gilling Castle preparatory school and Ampleforth College, both in the North Riding of Yorkshire, before going up in 1968 to Lincoln College, Oxford, where he gained a third in modern history in 1972. He also won a boxing blue.

Nairac joined the army while still at Oxford, trained at Sandhurst, and was commissioned into the Grenadier Guards before being sent to Belfast in 1973. Instructed in survival, intelligence gathering, and psychological operations, he was attached to '4 field survey troop', a cover name for the unit that became known as 14th intelligence company or 14 Int. The exact nature of his duties remains obscure but his unit was responsible for gathering information about republican and loyalist terrorist suspects through covert surveillance and the recruitment of informers. While in Belfast, he wrote in an army report that the Provisional IRA in south Armagh was exporting its expertise to the rest of Northern Ireland. He concluded that an army intelligence officer with qualities of imagination, determination, and adaptability should be sent there. 'I would put his chances of surviving his tour at less than 50 per cent' (Hamill, 214).

In 1976 Nairac was sent to south Armagh to fill the role he had himself described, with the title of SAS liaison officer. His task was to co-ordinate the work of the SAS, regular army units, and the Royal Ulster Constabulary's special branch in countering the terrorist threat. An SAS major interviewed after his death said that Nairac exceeded his brief:

Basically he was doubling up as an undercover man and a source [informer] handler ... It was all pretty amateurish and you just can't combine an undercover role with an overt role. As an operator with 14 Int he had done a good job but he couldn't let go. He was trying to do everything. (Harnden, 214)

South Armagh, dubbed in 1974 'bandit country' by Merlyn Rees, the then Northern Ireland Secretary, was the most dangerous posting in the world for a British soldier. Despite the deadly proficiency of the local IRA unit, Nairac sang rebel songs in pubs and sought to make contacts. A devout Roman Catholic, he was learning the Irish language, and there is some evidence that he was sympathetic to the plight of Irish nationalists. But in an army paper entitled 'Talking to people in south Armagh' Nairac said that all Catholics in the area had some sympathy for the IRA and it was 'important to regard any local as a possible source of information' (Harnden, 367).

The most likely explanation for Nairac's death just after midnight on 14/15 May 1977 is that he was trying to recruit an informer. At 9 p.m. on 14 May he had driven from his base at Bessbrook Mill to the Three Steps inn, a known IRA haunt in the village of Drumintee. Dispensing with normal procedure, he failed to arrange for army back-up to protect him and did not return at the appointed time of 11.30 p.m. After singing some rebel songs and telling people he was Danny McErlaine from Belfast, Nairac was challenged by some local men, at least one of whom was an IRA member. A fight ensued in the car park outside and Nairac was dragged into a car and driven across the border, less than a mile away, into the Irish republic. He was taken to a bridge, badly beaten and shot dead. Liam Townson, an IRA member who was convicted of his murder, said in a statement to detectives: 'I shot the British captain. He never told us anything. He was a great soldier' (Dillon, 174). Four others were convicted of offences linked to the killing.

Robert Nairac's body was never found. It is thought to have been destroyed at a local meat processing plant. In February 1979 it was announced he was to be awarded a posthumous George Cross, the highest honour for gallantry in peacetime.

In death, Nairac has become a hugely controversial figure. To some in the security forces who served in Northern Ireland he was a brave and unorthodox officer who paid the ultimate price for his attempts to help quell terrorism. To others he was an eccentric who misguidedly put his own and others' lives at risk to fulfil a romantic and unattainable notion of being a spy. A third group views him as a murderous agent of an oppressive state acting illegally in Ulster. In his maiden speech to the House of Commons in July 1987 Ken Livingstone said that Nairac was suspected of killing three members of the Miami Showband pop group and John Francis Green, an IRA member, in 1975. Nairac has subsequently been accused of taking part in the 1974 bombing in co. Monaghan in which five people died. Some extreme loyalists have claimed that he helped the IRA to murder protestant members of the Ulster Defence Regiment in south Armagh. Despite the widespread repetition of some of the allegations against him, particularly by Irish republicans and their supporters, no convincing evidence of Nairac's involvement in any of these events has ever emerged.

TOBY HARNDEN

Sources T. Harnden, '*Bandit country': the IRA and south Armagh* (1999) · M. Dillon, *The dirty war* (1990) · J. Parker, *Death of a hero: Captain Robert Nairac, GC and the undercover war in Northern Ireland* (1999) · D. Hamill, *Pig in the middle: the army in Northern Ireland, 1969–1984* (1985) · A. Bradley, *Requiem for a spy: the killing of Robert Nairac* (1993) · *The register of the George cross*, 2nd edn (1990)
Wealth at death £4394: administration, 21 Feb 1979, *CGPLA Eng. & Wales*

Nairn, Gerald (1897–1980). *See under* Nairn, Norman (1894–1968).

Nairn, Ian Douglas (1930–1983), architectural writer, was born at 4 Milton Road, Bedford, on 24 August 1930, the son of John Nairn, an airship draughtsman at the royal airship works at Cardington, and his wife, Margaret Moor. Two months after his birth the R101 left Cardington on its last, fatal flight and with the consequent collapse of the British airship industry Nairn's father moved from what his son later described as 'the most characterless county town in England' (*Architects' Journal*) to Frimley, to become a civil servant. Nairn was brought up in a part of west Surrey 'that produced a deep hatred of characterless buildings and places' (Pevsner, *Surrey*, dustjacket) as well as of suburban attitudes; he always felt that his real roots were in Jarrow, as his family had come from the north-east of England.

'Appalling local secondary schooling' (*Architects' Journal*) encouraged the development of Nairn's awkward and iconoclastic nature, but his first passion was for aeroplanes rather than architecture. He first made what he later described as two false starts. He read mathematics at Birmingham University (1947–50) and then, having joined the University Air Squadron, entered the RAF as a pilot officer. He later claimed that his ability as a fighter pilot was poor, but the aerial photographs which illustrated some of his later publications were taken by William J. Toomey from an aircraft which Nairn piloted.

On 22 March 1952 Nairn married Joan Elisabeth Parsons (b. 1931/2), a librarian, in Sutton Coldfield; although he later wrote that he was 'tremendously happy' with 'two hearts and incomes beating as one' (*Architects' Journal*, 87), this ended in divorce. Frustrated with service life, Nairn resigned his commission in 1953 and determined to write about architecture. He once claimed that he had no interest in the subject until he came round after being knocked unconscious in a bicycle accident when in the RAF, but this seems unlikely; elsewhere he recorded that he was looking at Georgian churches when at university and that, when stationed with his squadron at Horsham St Faith, near Norwich, in 1952–3, he navigated by Perpendicular church towers. Nairn joined the *Architectural Review* in July 1954; Colin Boyne recalled that,

The editors … had little choice in the matter. Calling at Queen Anne's Gate almost daily, still wearing a dyed RAF overcoat and constantly submitting articles, he demanded a job and in the face of such conviction an intrigued H. de C. Hastings gave it him. (*ArchR*)

The editor's decision was soon justified by the special number of the journal published in June 1955. Entitled *Outrage* and written by Nairn, with drawings by Gordon Cullen, this was an influential and devastating assault on the planning and bureaucratic attitudes which were spoiling both urban and rural Britain. Nairn identified the evil as 'Subtopia', which he defined as 'the annihilation of the site, the steamrollering of all individuality of place to one uniform and mediocre pattern' (*ArchR*, June 1955, 371) and the accompanying photographs suggested how 'the end of Southampton will look like the beginning of Carlisle; the parts in between will look like the end of Carlisle or the beginning of Southampton' (ibid., 365). Nairn continued the argument with 'Counter-attack against Subtopia' in the *Architectural Review* for December 1956 and these passionate, entertaining tracts helped inspire the foundation of the Civic Trust the following year.

Nairn parted company with the Architectural Press in 1962 and, during the sadly few creative years that followed before he was overwhelmed by depression, he became a prolific journalist and broadcaster. He made several series of television programmes for the BBC including *Nairn's Travels* (1970). His radio programmes printed in *The Listener* were published in 1967 by the BBC as *Britain's Changing Towns*, with each chapter accompanied by a postscript excoriating the damage being done by comprehensive redevelopment or official indifference to architectural quality. *Your England Revisited* of 1964 developed the theme that 'every bit of the visible world can be exciting, expressive and individual', while 'Every time that somebody hurts a landscape or a townscape he is being loveless and stupid and arrogant' (p. 9). The following year Nairn published *A Study of the American Landscape*. His guide to *Modern Buildings in London*, which appeared in 1964, reflected a short-lived optimism about modern architecture.

Nairn's increasing anger at the arrogance of architects and planners 'stamping over the landscape in jackboots' culminated in 1966 in a long article in *The Observer* (13 February 1966). Entitled 'Stop the architects now', this marked a significant step in the growing challenge to the urban policies of the Modern Movement in architecture which resulted in a change in direction the following decade. Nairn's assertion that 'The outstanding and appalling fact about modern British architecture is that it is just not good enough. It is not standing up to use or climate, either in single buildings or the whole environment', provoked a response from the Royal Institute of British Architects in defence of its members, to which Nairn perceptively replied that

> My intention was not, in Lord Esher's phrase, to shoot the pianist, but to suggest that the piano is waiting to be played in another room altogether. It is too big to be moved, so it is the pianist that must shift—even if it means moving altogether out of the door marked architect or planner. (*The Observer*, 6 March 1966)

Nairn became best-known as the author of several distinctive and compelling architectural guides. He was the first to be invited by Nikolaus Pevsner to collaborate on *The Buildings of England*, and the resulting volume on *Surrey* (1962) was largely his work. Nairn was then entrusted with the whole of *Sussex* but, as Pevsner complained, 'when he had completed West Sussex, he found that he could no longer bear to write the detailed descriptions which are essential ... His decision filled me with sadness' (Pevsner, *Sussex*, 11). Nairn met his second wife, Janette Geraldine (Judy) Perry (1931–1991), when working for *The Buildings of England*, where she was the editorial assistant responsible for publication and 'found that the only way she could ensure the volume's appearance on time was to marry him', which she did on 21 August 1961 (Pevsner, *Surrey*, dustjacket). Nairn went on to publish a few more guidebooks on his own. In *Nairn's London* (1966) 'the thinly veiled subjectivity which colours so many of the entries in West Sussex has been allowed to erupt' (Pevsner, *Sussex*, dustjacket) and as well as dealing with famous buildings he celebrated the obscure as well as the ordinary and eccentric, such as Sydenham Hill Station or the Salisbury pub in St Martin's Lane, London. *Nairn's Paris* was published in 1968; future Nairn's guides to *London's Countryside*, *The Industrial North*, and *Rome and Florence* were promised but never appeared. Nairn's much vaunted affection for public houses combined with his connoisseurship of beer soon proved to be his nemesis, and he only published some short travel guides for the *Sunday Times* before collapsing into inarticulate melancholia. Eventually paid off by the newspaper, Nairn spent much of his last years drinking and betting in the St George's Tavern in Belgrave Road, near his flat at 3 Eccleston Square. He died in the Cromwell Hospital, Kensington, of cirrhosis of the liver and chronic alcoholism on 14 August 1983 (just a few days before Pevsner's death) and was buried in September 1983 in Kensington Hanwell cemetery, a fulfilment of his wish to lie under the flight path into Heathrow airport.

Nairn's colleague at the Architectural Press Colin Boyne recalled that 'In his prime he was a big, fat, sociable fellow, delighting in pub architecture' (*ArchR*). Nairn described himself as 'a person who drinks a lot and can't bear either pretensions or possessiveness' (*Nairn's Paris*, 13). 'Difficult and intolerant he may have been', Christopher Hurst concluded, 'but his heart was warm. This fact shaped his whole world view—his anger was compassionate, on behalf of people and against the impersonal' (*ArchR*). During his short, furious, productive career, Ian Nairn had a more beneficial effect on the face of Britain than any other architectural writer of his generation.

GAVIN STAMP

Sources *ArchR*, 174 (1983), 4 · 'Ian Nairn', *Architects' Journal* (19 Jan 1956), 87 · biography file, RIBA BAL · private information (2004) [Elizabeth Williamson] · private information (2004) [Jonathan Meades] · b. cert. · m. cert. [Joan Parsons] · m. cert. [Judy Perry] · d. cert. · *Surrey*, Pevsner (1962) · I. Nairn, *Nairn's London* (1966) · I. Nairn, *Nairn's Paris* (1968)
Likenesses photographs, repro. in *Architects' Journal*

Wealth at death under £40,000: administration, 1983, *CGPLA Eng. & Wales*

Nairn, James (1629–1678), Church of Scotland minister and book collector, was born in Edinburgh early in 1629, the son of James Nairn (*c*.1585–*c*.1656), a prosperous merchant, and his wife, Elizabeth Tod. He entered Edinburgh University in 1646 and graduated MA in 1650. After theological study, combined with a period as librarian of Edinburgh University, 1652–3, and then as chaplain to the countess of Wemyss, he was elected in 1655 to the second charge of the Canongate parish, Edinburgh. He moved to the first charge in 1656.

Conforming to episcopacy after 1660, but influenced by anti-episcopal feeling in his parish, and uneasy about being too near the centre of political life, Nairn, a shy and retiring man, became minister of Bolton, Haddingtonshire, in 1662. He transferred to Wemyss in Fife in 1665. In 1670 he preached in south-west Scotland with five colleagues in an attempt to stem disaffection with episcopacy. This mission was instituted by Robert Leighton, archbishop of Glasgow, an influence on Nairn since the 1650s, when Leighton had been principal of Edinburgh University.

Nominated bishop of Dunblane in succession to Leighton in May 1672 Nairn declined the appointment. Poor health was one reason for his decision (he was in Paris having bladder stones excised at this time), but dislike of government ecclesiastical policy was undoubtedly another. However, he did become a king's chaplain-in-ordinary in Scotland in 1675. His health, never robust, continued to decline and he left Wemyss for Edinburgh in April 1678. He died of a urinary infection at a house in the university precincts on 18 July 1678 and was buried on 21 July. He never married.

Nairn made two bequests to Edinburgh University: £4000 Scots for divinity bursaries, and, more important, his book collection, numbering more than 1900 titles. This was a very large library in Scottish terms for the period. With a well-structured and wide content range, and collected over a relatively short period of time, it is a unique source for the study of the intellectual climate of Scotland in the Restoration period. A detailed catalogue, prefaced by a biography in Latin, was printed in the year of its bequest. It shows that Nairn was responsive to current European thought, as the collection contained works by Descartes and his followers and even Spinoza, as well as by Jansenist, Anglican, and mainstream Catholic scholars. Robert Boyle was particularly well represented and there were several contemporary works on natural history, medicine, and mineralogy. The library was also strong on Latin classics and works of history, geography, and political theory, but sadly weak on vernacular English literature.

Nairn was admired by contemporaries as an eloquent preacher, and was an influence on several clerical colleagues, notably Gilbert Burnet, later bishop of Salisbury. He declared Nairn to be 'the brightest man I ever knew among all our Scotish divines' (*Bishop Burnet's History*, ed. Burnet and Burnet, 1.215). Another friend was the theologian Lawrence Charteris. No literary remains by Nairn survive, except notes taken by others of some sermons, always delivered extempore. MURRAY C. T. SIMPSON

Sources *Catalogus librorum quibus Bibliothecam Academiae Jacobi Regis Edinburgenae adauxit R. D. Jacobus Narnius* (1678) • M. C. T. Simpson, 'The library of the Reverend James Nairn (1629–1678): scholarly book collecting in Restoration Scotland', PhD diss., U. Edin., 1987 • M. C. T. Simpson, *A catalogue of the library of the Revd James Nairn (1629–1678) bequeathed by him to Edinburgh University Library* (1990) • *Bishop Burnet's History of his own time*, 1, ed. G. Burnet and T. Burnet (1724) • Testament of James Nairn, 7 May 1656, NA Scot., 8/8/68, fols. 278r–279r • *Fasti Scot.* • Lord Wemyss's diary, priv. coll. • matriculation albums, U. Edin. L., special collections division, university archives
Archives Bodl. Oxf., sermon, MS 14260, fols. 99–104
Wealth at death over 6000 merks [£4000 Scots] to found two divinity bursaries: *Catalogus librorum*

Nairn, Michael (1804–1858). *See under* Nairn, Sir Michael Barker, first baronet (1838–1915).

Nairn, Sir Michael, second baronet (1874–1952). *See under* Nairn, Sir Michael Barker, first baronet (1838–1915).

Nairn, Sir Michael Barker, first baronet (1838–1915), floorcloth and linoleum manufacturer, was born on 29 May 1838, probably in Kirkcaldy, the second son in the family of six sons and two daughters of Michael Nairn and his wife, Catharine (*c*.1815–*c*.1891), daughter of Alexander Ingram of Kirkcaldy, Fife, owner of a bleaching yard.

Michael Nairn (1804–1858), floorcloth manufacturer, was born on 4 April 1804, probably in Kirkcaldy, the son of James Nairn and his wife, Isabel, *née* Barker. He returned to Kirkcaldy after serving an apprenticeship to a weaver in Dundee. He set up in business at Coal Wynd, Kirkcaldy, in 1828, weaving sailmakers' canvas, and was soon exporting canvas all over the world. By the early 1840s he was supplying canvas backing material to many English floorcloth manufacturers, and in 1848 he opened his own floorcloth factory, the Scottish Floorcloth Manufactory. In the 1850s Nairn introduced a new method of printing designs on floorcloth, moving one reviewer of the floorcloth exhibits at the 1861 International Exhibition to write that floorcloth could now be produced with 'all the richness, the minuteness, and the finish of a velvet-pile carpet' (*Art Journal*, 1 Dec 1862). He died suddenly on 18 January 1858, leaving his widow as sole owner of the business, and she created the new firm of Michael Nairn & Co.

Michael Barker Nairn was educated at the burgh school, Kirkcaldy, and apprenticed to a lawyer and writer to the signet in 1855, but on his father's death he joined the business, entering the partnership in 1861. In 1866 he married Emily Frances (*d*. 1939), daughter of Alfred Rimington Spencer of Weybridge, Surrey. They had three sons and eight daughters: two of these children died in childhood. He quickly became the dominant force in the business, overshadowing his elder brother, Robert. A great innovator, he was responsible for the rapid expansion in the 1860s. With the help of John Wright, a Glasgow engineer, he speeded up the drying process for the floorcloth by installing steam power, and in 1869 he opened St Mary's canvas factory, installing power looms. He commissioned the interior decorator and author of *The Grammar of Ornament* (1856), Owen Jones, to design an exhibit for the Paris Universal Exhibition in 1867, where Nairns' floorcloths were regarded as the most magnificent work of the kind ever produced. By then Nairns was supplying floorcloth to most of the royal families of Europe. The firm manufactured other goods, including waterproofed carriage roofing, staircloths, and bath mats, and in 1868 began to make table baize. A London warehouse was opened in 1873, followed by warehouses in Paris, Manchester, and Glasgow.

When Frederick Walton's patents for linoleum expired in 1877, Nairn built a new linoleum manufacturing factory in Kirkcaldy, the first in Scotland, and made several improvements. From 1881 Nairns was able to make seamless linoleum 4 yards wide, and in 1895 began to manufacture inlaid linoleum. World sales grew: 'I have seen our floorcloth and linoleum beyond the first cataract of the Nile … and in the mosques of Constantinople', Nairn recorded (Muir, 96). To avoid high import tariffs, Nairn began to manufacture linoleum abroad, opening an American subsidiary at Kearny, New Jersey, in 1888, and factories in Choisy-le-Roi, near Paris, and Bietigheim, near Stuttgart, in the 1890s. The directors of these subsidiaries always included Nairn or members of his family, and Scots from the Kirkcaldy firm. In 1893 the business became a limited liability company with Michael Barker Nairn as chairman and joint managing director; he retired as managing director in 1909, but remained chairman until his death.

Nairn left the Liberal Party over home rule, standing unsuccessfully as Unionist candidate for Kirkcaldy in the 1900 parliamentary election. He was created a baronet in 1904. A great benefactor of the town of Kirkcaldy, he built its hospital in 1890, financed the building of the new high school in 1894, and donated the sites for the YMCA building, opened in 1895, and for the Queen's Nurses' Home in 1897. He was a member of Kirkcaldy Free Church, and contributed to the cost of building St Brycedale Free Church, completed in 1881; he was an elder of the church from 1881 to 1910. He died on 24 November 1915 in Kirkcaldy, leaving Michael Nairn & Co. the largest linoleum and floorcloth manufacturing concern in Scotland. He was buried at Monimail churchyard on 27 November.

His eldest surviving son, **Sir Michael Nairn**, second baronet (1874–1952), was born on 19 February 1874 in Kirkcaldy. He was educated at Edinburgh Academy, Sherborne School, and Marburg University before joining the firm in 1895. He became a director in 1899, and married Mildred Margaret (*d.* 1953), daughter of George Watson Neish, in 1901. They had one son and four daughters. He became managing director of the company in 1909.

In 1922 Nairns took over Walton's firm in Greenwich, forming a holding company, Michael Nairn and Greenwich Ltd, to manufacture inlaid linoleum. Nairn became chairman of this company in 1924, and on the death of his uncle, John Nairn, in 1928, became chairman of Michael Nairn & Co. Ltd Kirkcaldy. Foreign production continued to grow with the formation of Michael Nairn & Co. (Australia) in 1927, and the first congoleum factory in Britain opened in Kirkcaldy in 1927. During the 1930s the warehouses were expanded, and new ones opened in Birmingham and Bristol. During the Second World War the Nairn factories made war materials, including clothing impervious to mustard gas for the armed forces, and fuel tanks for Halifax bombers.

Like his father, Nairn was a benefactor, giving the grounds of Dysart House, including the ruins of Ravenscraig Castle, to the town of Kirkcaldy as a public park in 1929, and donating generously to Kirkcaldy General Hospital. He retired as chairman of both companies in January 1952, and died at his home, Elie House, Elie, Fife, on 24 September 1952.   ANNE PIMLOTT BAKER

Sources A. Muir, *Nairns of Kirkcaldy* (1956) · *DSBB*, 1.377–383 · C. Edwards, 'Floorcloth and linoleum: aspects of the history of oil-coated materials for floors', *Textile History*, 27 (1996), 148–71 · P. K. Livingstone, *A history of Kirkcaldy, 1843–1949* (1955) · P. K. Livingstone, *St Brycedale church, Kirkcaldy* (1957) · P. J. Gooderson, *Lord Linoleum: Lord Ashton, Lancaster, and the rise of the British oilcloth and linoleum industry* (1996) · *Art Journal*, 24 (1862), 238–9 · *The Times* (25 Nov 1915) · *The Times* (25 Sept 1952) · Burke, *Peerage* · *WWW* · *The Times* (30 Sept 1952) · bap. reg. Scot.
Likenesses O. Birley, portrait, 1907–9 (*Sir Michael Nairn*), repro. in Muir, *Nairns of Kirkcaldy*, 110 · D. Alison, oils (*Sir Michael Barker Nairn*), St Brycedale Church, Kirkcaldy, Fife; repro. in Livingstone, *St Brycedale Church*, 86 · bust, Kirkcaldy High School · photograph, repro. in Muir, *Nairns of Kirkcaldy*, facing p. 46 · portrait (*Michael Nairn*), repro. in Gooderson, *Lord Linoleum*, 63
Wealth at death £1,034,738 10s. 9d.: *DSBB* · £339,670 12s. 8d.— Michael Nairn (1874–1952): *DSBB*

Nairn, Norman (1894–1968), managing director of a transport company in the Middle East, was born on 19 November 1894 in Blenheim, South Island, New Zealand, the eldest of the four sons of David Mathieson Nairn (1863–1924), a local doctor, and his second wife, Hannah Maria Farmar (1869/70–1949). David Nairn had four daughters from his first marriage, and after his wife's death he married her sister. Their second son, **Gerald Nairn** (1897–1980), was also born in Blenheim, on 1 February 1897.

Dr Nairn was one of the first people in New Zealand to own a motor car, and Nairn and his brother Gerald learned to be skilled mechanics and were given the responsibility of keeping their father's cars in good repair. In 1908 Norman went to Marlborough high school (later Marlborough College), Blenheim, where he excelled at sport; he left in 1910 to set up a cycle business in Blenheim, with financial help from his father. Gerald attended the same school from 1911 to 1915, before joining his brother's business. They branched out into motor cycles, and became the agents for makes including Royal Enfield and Harley-Davidson. Norman concentrated on the managerial side of the business, while Gerald was in charge of the technical side. Norman Nairn was in Europe when war broke out in 1914, and joined the British army, serving with Allenby in Palestine, while Gerald enlisted in the Canterbury mounted rifles in New Zealand, and was posted to Beirut in 1918.

The brothers became interested in the idea of starting a business in the Middle East after the war, and in 1919 they were able to raise the capital to start a garage in Beirut, selling cars. When the business failed in 1920, they used their three remaining cars to start a taxi service between Beirut and Haifa, undertaking to do the 70 mile journey down the coast in less than a day, instead of the three days it took horse-drawn vehicles. With the help of new American cars, and excellent mechanics, the Nairns gained a reputation for reliability, and were soon winning contracts to carry mail. In 1923 they were asked by the British consul in Damascus to look into the feasibility of establishing a regular mail service across the Syrian desert, from Damascus to Baghdad. On 5 June 1923 Norman Nairn married Elsie MacDonald (b. 1897/8), daughter of John Mathewson Barclay, a timber merchant; they had one son and one daughter. His brother Gerald married Rea Foley (d. 1966) in 1925, and they had two sons.

By the beginning of the twentieth century the old overland caravan routes across the desert were hardly used, and most mail and travellers to Baghdad went by the sea route from Port Said through the Suez Canal, down the Red Sea, and up the Persian Gulf to Basrah. Although there was an airmail service by 1921, it was irregular and expensive. Nairn made many trial runs to determine the quickest and most reliable route across the desert, where roads hardly existed, and where there was a danger of attack from nomadic Bedouins. He created a new track, avoiding most of the hazards apart from a section of road in the mud flats which tended to flood when there was heavy rain during the wet season, and for the first few years he had to make deals with local leaders in order to guarantee safe passage for his cars. The route was 603 miles long, including a desert section of 425 miles, and the average journey took twenty-eight hours, although Nairn did it in a record time of sixteen and a quarter hours of continuous driving for a bet, watching the sun rise in Baghdad and set in Damascus.

A regular weekly mail service began in October 1923, after Nairn had signed a five-year contract with the Baghdad post office for a service to connect with the European mail boats at Port Said, bringing Baghdad within ten days of London, in contrast to the ocean route, which took three times as long. In his publicity Nairn claimed that the introduction of his motorized service meant that in future Iraq would turn her face to the West instead of towards the East. Once the mail service was established, Nairn went to Detroit and bought four seven-seater Cadillacs, and began advertising for passengers, increasing his run to two journeys a week. After arranging with Thomas Cook & Son to include the Nairn desert crossing in their London–Baghdad itinerary, famous travellers including St John Philby, Freya Stark, and Gertrude Bell used the Nairn service. Nairn was appointed OBE in 1926 for his pioneering role in desert transport in the Middle East.

In 1926 the Nairns sold their company in order to form the Nairn Eastern Transport Company, a public company with shareholders including the Anglo-Persian Oil Company, the Ottoman Bank, and the Imperial Bank of Persia. Norman and Gerald Nairn were joint managing directors,

with their headquarters in Damascus, where they built a large new garage, and branches in Beirut and Baghdad. They had already introduced buses, and in 1926 invested in a fifteen-passenger American Safeway bus, later adding air-conditioning. They were no longer alone in running a bus service across the desert, and had to keep thinking of ways to keep ahead of their competitors in providing a fast, reliable, and comfortable service. With the development of the oil industry in Iraq, business increased dramatically, and the Nairns carried the employees of the Anglo-Persian Oil Company, who were laying the oil pipeline from Kirkuk to the Mediterranean. In 1930 Nairn introduced trailer buses, and in 1931 a 24-passenger coach. The 1933 Marmon-Herrington, advertised as the biggest bus in the world, seated thirty-eight and had reclining seats, a lavatory, and a buffet serving packed lunches. When the board refused to raise the capital to build a new, eighteen-passenger bus capable of speeds up to 65 m.p.h., designed by Nairn himself, in 1936 he bought back a controlling interest in the company, which became the Nairn Transport Company. He had two of his stainless steel tractor-buses built in the United States, and they remained in continuous service for twenty years. Another innovation was the rest house, built at Rutbah, halfway between Damascus and Baghdad, where the passengers could have a bath, drink English beer, and eat English food. By 1939 the Nairn Transport Company employed fifty people.

The Nairns suspended the overland service between Damascus and Baghdad in April 1941, but later in that year they were asked to organize a new service to transport allied troops, equipment, and supplies across the desert from India, and they were given access to oil and fuel, previously unavailable. They reduced the time of the journey for the convoys from five days to twenty-four hours. Nairn was appointed CBE in 1948 for his services. After the war, relations between the brothers became difficult, and in 1946 Gerald retired to New Zealand. His wife died, in 1966, and in October 1969 he married a widow, Mrs Nellie Coker of Blenheim, New Zealand. Gerald Nairn died on 28 July 1980 at Wairau Hospital, Blenheim.

With the situation in the Middle East likely to remain unstable, and growing competition from the airlines, Norman Nairn decided to retire, and in 1950 he handed the company over to his employees as a going concern. It went out of business in 1960. In his retirement he lived for a time in Bermuda, and then in France, before returning to the Lebanon to build a villa on the coast at Fidar, north of Beirut. Nairn was married three times. After his first divorce he married Mrs Varina Stone of Alabama, USA, in 1945. That marriage also failed, and in 1960 he married his third wife, Muriel. Nairn died on 20 September 1968 at Mount Alvernia, Guildford, Surrey, and was cremated on 25 September at Guildford.   ANNE PIMLOTT BAKER

Sources J. M. Munro, *The Nairn way: desert bus and Baghdad* (1980) · *The Times* (23 Sept 1968) · *The Times* (25 Sept 1968) · *The Times* (31 May 1923) · *The Times* (22 Jan 1925) · private information (2004) [archivist, Marlborough College, Blenheim, New Zealand] · m. cert. [Elsie MacDonald Barclay] · b. cert. · b. cert. [Gerald Nairn, 75613]

Likenesses M. Farrouk, drawing, 1935, repro. in Munro, *The Nairn way*, 101 · photograph, repro. in Munro, *The Nairn way*, 89

Nairn, Robert, of Strathord, first Lord Nairne (*c.*1600–1683), judge, was the eldest son of Robert Nairn (*d.* 1652) of Muckersie and later Strathord, both in Perthshire, an advocate, and his wife, Catherine, daughter of Sir John *Preston of Penicuik, lord president of the court of session. Like his father, Robert became a lawyer, and was admitted to the Faculty of Advocates on 20 February 1644. He was captured at Alyth with leading members of the Scottish regime on 28 August 1651 and imprisoned in the Tower of London, where he remained until the Restoration.

In 1661 Charles II knighted Nairn and appointed him a senator of the college of justice (13 February). He became a lord of session on 1 June 1661, as Lord Strathord, and one of the lords commissioners of justiciary in January 1671. Ten years after that, in January 1681, the king made him a Scottish peer with the title Lord Nairne. After 10 January 1657 he married Margaret Graham (*d.* 1704), daughter of Patrick Graham of Inchbrackie; their only son died, and so it was arranged that on Nairne's death his title should pass to the husband of his daughter, Margaret, Lord William Murray, who changed his name to William *Nairne.

According to Robert Wodrow, by the time Nairne took part in the treason trial of Archibald, ninth earl of Argyll, in 1681 he was 'an old infirm man', so far decayed that he had been unable for some time to carry out his judicial duties. However, when the judges at the trial were equally divided as to the relevance of the charges, he was 'wakned out of his sleep' in the middle of the night, 'roused out of his bed and brought into the court' (Wodrow, 2.211–12). As he had not been present at most of the earlier proceedings, the clerk was ordered to read out the record of what had happened, whereupon Nairne fell asleep again. When he was wakened once more, he voted for the relevance of the indictment. On 10 April 1683 the king decided to excuse Nairne on account of his infirmity and old age, and he was replaced as one of the criminal lords by Lord Castlehill. At this he commented wryly that when he himself had been a prisoner in the Tower because of his support of the royalist cause, Castlehill had been one of Oliver Cromwell's pages and servants. Six weeks later, on 30 May, Nairne died; he was buried in an aisle in the church of Auchtergaven, near Dunkeld, in June.

T. F. Henderson, *rev.* Rosalind K. Marshall

Sources NRA Scotland, 3698 · *Scots peerage*, 6.393 · R. Wodrow, *The history of the sufferings of the Church of Scotland from the Restoration to the revolution*, 2 (1722), 211–12 · *Historical notices of Scotish affairs, selected from the manuscripts of Sir John Lauder of Fountainhall*, ed. D. Laing, 1, Bannatyne Club, 87 (1848), 193, 226, 275, 342; 2, Bannatyne Club, 87 (1848), 435, 457 · R. Douglas, *The peerage of Scotland*, 2nd edn, ed. J. P. Wood, 2 (1813), 193, 226, 342, 373, 435, 457 · F. J. Grant, ed., *The Faculty of Advocates in Scotland, 1532–1943*, Scottish RS, 145 (1944) · G. Brunton and D. Haig, *An historical account of the senators of the college of justice, from its institution in MDXXXII* (1832), 372

Likenesses oils, *c.*1700–1799 (after D. Scougall); black and white negative, Scot. NPG

Nairne. For this title name *see* individual entries under Nairne; *see also* Nairn, Robert, of Strathord, first Lord Nairne (*c.*1600–1683); Oliphant, Carolina, Lady Nairne (1766–1845); Flahault de la Billardrie, Margaret de, *suo jure* Lady Nairne and *suo jure* Baroness Keith, and Countess de Flahault de la Billardrie in the French nobility (1788–1867).

Nairne, Alexander (1863–1936), theologian and biblical scholar, was born at Hunsdon, Hertfordshire, on 17 January 1863, the eldest child of Spencer Nairne, rector of Hunsdon, and his wife, Marion Walker, daughter of John *Marshall, first Lord Curriehill, and sister of John Marshall, second Lord Curriehill, both Scottish judges. His ancestors for several generations were Scottish ministers.

Nairne was educated at Haileybury School and at Jesus College, Cambridge, where he was a scholar. He obtained first classes in the classical (1884) and theological (1886) triposes, two university prizes, and a university scholarship. He was a fellow of Jesus from 1887 to 1893 and again from 1917 to 1932, in which year he was elected an honorary fellow. He was ordained deacon in 1887 and priest in 1888, and was curate of Great St Mary's and vice-principal of the Clergy Training School at Cambridge from 1887 to 1889. In 1889 he married Ethel (*d.* 1921), daughter of Lambert Campbell Edwards, vicar of Kingsbury, Middlesex. They had no children, and Nairne was celibate for at least some, and perhaps all, of his married life. After his marriage, Nairne worked successively as an assistant master at Harrow School (1890–92), curate of Hadleigh, Suffolk (1892–4), and rector of Tewin, Hertfordshire (1894–1912).

From 1900 to 1917 Nairne was professor of Hebrew and Old Testament exegesis at King's College, London, where he was able to demonstrate his real talents for the first time. His lectures, which combined information with poetic and mystical insights, were very popular. He also helped to gain for the 'higher criticism' of the Old Testament, already well established on the continent, a popular hearing in England. This 'higher' criticism, which sought to apply form, source, and redaction criticism to the Bible in the hope of establishing a historically accurate description of its composition and authorship, had long been treated with suspicion in English universities. But Nairne was able to convey its message in a way which did not appear to harm the religious faith of his students.

From 1914 to 1922 Nairne was a canon of Chester Cathedral, where the stimulating effect of his scholarship and his personality was warmly welcomed. In 1917 he returned to Cambridge as fellow and dean of Jesus College; he was vicar of All Saints' Church until 1919, and was made Hulsean lecturer at the University of Cambridge in 1919–20, and regius professor of divinity from 1922, a year after his wife's death, to 1932.

Nairne ignored university politics and the business of the theology faculty, finding them of no interest; but he had a wide personal influence upon undergraduates and dons alike. His lectures were found stimulating and inspiring by many, though those who sought easy answers

Alexander Nairne (1863–1936), by Francis Dodd, 1933

to examination questions were apt to be disappointed. His scholarship, love of literature, and his interest in artists, poets, as well as men of science, made his influence wide. He treated all undergraduates as his intellectual equals, and was generous in his assessments of supposed infidels such as the poet Shelley, the philosopher J. M. E. McTaggart, and James Frazer, author of *The Golden Bough*, who he thought were in touch with spiritual realities and therefore almost good Christians. He formed a society for undergraduates called the Clouds, which met once a week in his own rooms to read Plato. These sessions were crowded and, after some years, a book to which all had contributed and which was inscribed to *Nephelēgereta* (as used by Homer of Zeus, namely, 'cloudgatherer') was presented to him by the members of the Clouds.

Nairne's books were not written for specialists but contained much fine scholarship and insight. Pedants were apt to be a touch scornful of his popular and accessible style, Hebraists saying that he did not know his grammar, and the 'higher' critics that he made no contribution to their studies. It was true that Nairne was suspicious of the work of the higher critics, but his scholarly instincts, poetic sense, and religious piety made his opinions valued by many. His intellectual honesty meant that he saw more deeply than most. His book on the epistle to the Hebrews, *The Epistle of Priesthood* (1913), his Hulsean lectures, *The Faith of the New Testament* (1920), and *The Life Eternal: Here and Now* in particular represent his characteristic style.

Nairne was a canon of St George's Chapel, Windsor, from 1921 until his death, which took place at his home,

The Cloisters, Windsor Castle, on 15 March 1936. In 1931 the University of St Andrews had conferred upon him the honorary degree of DD.

Uninterested in worldly affairs, Nairne was a man of radiant charm and kindness, of alertness, of sympathy, of a goodness which compelled almost all who met him not only to like him but to love him. He gave away every penny earned from his canonry, though he left effects to the value of over £6000 after his death. An etching by Francis Dodd of 1933, the only known portrait of Nairne, was left to Jesus College, Cambridge.

A. C. HEADLAM, *rev.* GERALD LAW

Sources F. J. F. Jackson, *Cambridge Review* (1 May 1936), 346 · *The Times* (16 March 1936) · *CGPLA Eng. & Wales* (1936)

Archives LPL, letters to *Church Quarterly Review* · LPL, corresp. with Arthur Headlam

Likenesses F. Dodd, etching, 1933, Jesus College, Cambridge [*see illus.*]

Wealth at death £6310 13s. 9d.: probate, 28 July 1936, *CGPLA Eng. & Wales*

Nairne, Carolina. *See* Oliphant, Carolina, Lady Nairne (1766–1845).

Nairne, Sir Charles Edward (1836–1899), army officer, born in London on 30 June 1836, was son of Captain Alexander Nairne of the East India Company's service. He was educated privately and at Addiscombe College (1854–5), and commissioned as second-lieutenant in the Bengal artillery on 7 December 1855. He became lieutenant on 27 April 1858. In 1860 he married Sophie, daughter of the Revd John Dupré Addison, vicar of Fleet, Dorset. Nairne served in the Indian mutiny and in the Yusufzai expedition of 1863. He was promoted second-captain in the Royal Artillery on 24 March 1865, and major on 2 November 1872. From 1875 to 1880 he commanded a battery of horse artillery, and served with it in the Second Afghan War as part of the Peshawar field force.

Nairne became regimental lieutenant-colonel on 1 May 1880, and in the Egyptian expedition of 1882 he commanded the horse artillery at Qassasin and Tell al-Kebir. He was mentioned in dispatches, was made CB on 18 November 1882, and received the Mejidiye (third class). He became colonel in the army on 1 May 1884. He was colonel of the depot staff of the horse artillery from 1882 to 1885, and commandant of the School of Gunnery at Shoeburyness for the next two years. On 1 April 1887 he was appointed inspector-general of artillery in India, with the local rank of brigadier-general. He held this post for five years, and brought about much improvement in the shooting of the field artillery.

Nairne was promoted major-general on 6 November 1890, and commanded a district in Bengal from 28 March 1892 to 4 September 1893, when he was appointed to the chief command in Bombay. There he carried out with tact and ability the reorganization scheme by which the three presidential armies were merged. He became lieutenant-general on 17 November 1895 and was made KCB on 22 June 1897. From 20 March to 4 November 1898 he was acting commander-in-chief in India. He left that country with a high reputation as an administrator, and had just been appointed president of the ordnance committee when he died at the Windsor Hotel, Victoria Street, London, on 19 February 1899, survived by his wife. He was buried on 22 February at Charlton cemetery, London, with military honours.   E. M. LLOYD, *rev.* JAMES FALKNER

Sources Army List · Hart's Army List · The Times (21 Feb 1899) · Lord Roberts [F. S. Roberts], *Forty-one years in India*, 30th edn (1898) · *LondG* (2 Nov 1882) · WWW
Archives NL Wales, letters to Sir James Hill-Johnes
Likenesses Bourne and Shepherd, photograph, 1899, repro. in *Black and White Magazine* · C. W. Furse, oils, Royal Artillery Mess, Woolwich · W. Strang, mezzotint (after C. W. Furse), BM
Wealth at death £13,043 10s. 1d.: probate, 23 May 1899, *CGPLA Eng. & Wales*

Nairne, David [Jacobite Sir David Nairne, first baronet] (**1655–1740**), Jacobite courtier, was born in August 1655 at Sandford, Fife, and baptized on 7 September 1655 at St Phillins Church in St Andrews. He was the second of the four sons of Thomas Nairne (*d.* before 1672), laird of Sandford, and Margaret (*d.* 1716), daughter of Sir David Barclay of Collarnie. After graduating from St Andrews University in 1673 he studied law at the universities of Leiden, Francker, and Utrecht from 1674 to 1676. He visited Paris at the end of 1676 to learn French and decided to settle there permanently. He was converted to Catholicism in 1680.

It is not known how Nairne occupied himself during his early years in France, as he failed to secure any permanent employment. In March 1686 he obtained a small annual pension from Louis XIV, and on 17 September of that year he married Marie-Elisabeth de Compigny (1659/60–1715). He was still unemployed in the winter of 1688–9, when James II was forced into exile at St Germain by William of Orange. On the recommendation of Lewis Innes, the principal of the Collège des Écossais in Paris, Nairne was recruited by James II's secretary of state, Lord Melfort, to be his under-secretary, and he accompanied Melfort to Ireland in 1689 and then on his Rome embassy from 1689 to 1691.

At the end of 1691 Melfort returned to St Germain and for the next year and a half Nairne was kept very busy there as his under-secretary, but the arrival of Lord Middleton as joint secretary of state in 1693, with his own under-secretary, greatly reduced the correspondence which passed through Nairne's hands. He had, however, established a reputation for efficiency and honesty, so when Melfort was forced to resign in 1694 Nairne was retained as under-secretary by his successor, John Caryll.

By 1696 Nairne had succeeded in winning the complete confidence of James II and Mary of Modena, who entrusted to him their most secret correspondence. In February of that year the queen appointed Nairne to be clerk of her council, and in March and April he spent nine weeks with the king at Calais while James was preparing to invade England. The two men were drawn together by their strong religious faith, and when James II established the Confraternity for a Happy Death (Bona Morte) in the chapel at St Germain Nairne joined it in April 1698. Two days later Nairne was confirmed at Notre Dame de Paris.

About the same time James II gave Nairne a secret additional pension.

The treaty of Ryswick greatly reduced the political work of the secretariat at St Germain, and from 1697 to 1703 Nairne was largely employed in helping Caryll translate parts of the Bible into English for use at the Jacobite court. In 1697 they translated the book of Psalms and from 1697 to 1702 the entire New Testament, but only the psalms were ever published (under Caryll's name in 1700) and their other translations have not survived. From 1699 to 1701 Nairne and Caryll also wrote *The Life of James II* up to the year 1677 (published in 1816), and when the king died in 1701 Nairne arranged and copied his papers and helped supervise the writing and publication of Père Bretonneau's *Abrégé de la vie de Jacques II* in 1703.

These literary activities came to an end in June 1703 when Lord Middleton's under-secretary returned to Scotland and Nairne was entrusted with his duties. He played an increasingly important role in advising Lord Middleton, and thus Mary of Modena and the young James III (James Francis Edward Stuart). He was appointed clerk of the king's council in June 1706 and accompanied James during his attempted invasion of Scotland in 1708 and then during his campaigns in Flanders in 1708 and 1709.

Nairne continued to work for Caryll until the latter's death in 1711, after which Lord Middleton took over all the Jacobite political correspondence. When James III left St Germain in 1712 to take up residence in Lorraine he was accompanied by both Middleton and Nairne, but the former increasingly delegated his work to Nairne, who mainly corresponded with the Jacobites in Great Britain before and after the treaty of Utrecht. When Middleton resigned in December 1713 Nairne began to work directly for James III rather than the new secretary of state. He was given the title of secretary of the closet for the king's private letters and dispatches, and was entrusted with the correspondence with the court of Rome. He also continued to handle the most secret correspondence with the Jacobites in England, and played an important role in advising James III during the negotiations for a possible restoration in 1714.

Nairne remained James III's most trusted adviser for the next four years and accompanied him to Scotland at the end of 1715. After the failure of the Scottish rising, when James was obliged to live at Avignon (1716–17) and then in the Papal States, Nairne's responsibility for all the Jacobite correspondence with the court of Rome gave him a particularly important role. He worked successfully with Gualterio, the cardinal protector of England, and this greatly helped the Jacobites, most of them protestant, when they first took refuge in papal territory.

Nairne was with James III when he visited Rome from May to July 1717 and he then accompanied him to Urbino, where the Jacobite court was established from July 1717 until the end of 1718. While he was at Urbino Nairne's position was weakened, as James III came completely under the influence of his new secretary of state (the Jacobite duke of Mar) and his relations and friends. They turned James against his old advisers and persuaded him to reject his entire St Germain background. As a result the other old servants gradually left the court and Nairne became an isolated figure, but he remained indispensable because he was the only Jacobite who could correspond and negotiate in both Italian and French.

In the autumn of 1718, when Maria Clementina Sobieska, princess of Poland, was arrested by the emperor to stop her marrying James, Nairne was sent to Rome, where he obtained the diplomatic support of the pope. He also negotiated the transfer of the Jacobite court from Urbino to the papal capital, which resulted in the acquisition for the Stuarts of the Palazzo Muti.

In February 1719 James III left Rome secretly to join the planned Spanish invasion of England. Nairne was created a baronet by James and left behind to break the news to the pope and look after Jacobite interests at Rome, in conjunction with Cardinal Gualterio. But Nairne lost his independence when he was placed under the authority of James III's new favourite, James Murray, a much younger man with whom his relations were already strained. By the time James III returned from Spain Nairne was very discontented and keen to retire to France. He was not invited to James's wedding with Maria Clementina Sobieska at Montefiascone in August, and when he joined them shortly afterwards he was informed that thenceforth Murray would replace him as the liaison with Cardinal Gualterio. He was retained as secretary of the closet because he was still the only Jacobite who was fluent in French and Italian, and partly also because, as a Catholic, he was trusted at the papal court.

For the next few years Nairne continued to carry out general secretarial duties for James III, but he no longer dealt with political questions. Although he repeatedly asked to retire, he was not allowed to do so, and he accompanied James to Bologna in 1726 following the separation from Maria Clementina. He remained there until James's return to Rome in 1729, when he finally retired, but was not allowed to return to Paris until the end of 1733.

Nairne and his wife had nine children, of whom only one son and two daughters survived. His wife had died in March 1715, while he was in Lorraine, and his son had joined the Spanish army. His elder daughter became a Benedictine nun in Paris in 1731 and his younger married in June 1735 the chevalier Andrew Ramsay, who was created a baronet by James III at Nairne's request. Nairne and Ramsay were in very close contact and perhaps even lodging together when the latter wrote his celebrated masonic *Discours* in 1737. It is probable that Nairne was one of the first freemasons at St Germain and that he had introduced Ramsay to freemasonry when they had first met at Rome in 1724.

Nairne was of small stature and had a scar on the left side of his chin, the result of a student duel in 1675. He was modest and unassuming to a fault and would have had and retained much more influence with James III if he had been a better courtier. He was a man of wide culture and a talented musician. Nairne is best known because he assembled an important collection of papers and brought them with him when he returned to Paris. After his death

there in January 1740 they were left in the Collège des Écossais, whence they were stolen by Thomas Carte in 1742, published in Macpherson's *Original Papers* in 1775, and given to the Bodleian Library in 1778. As the archives of the Stuart court at St Germain were virtually all destroyed during the French Revolution, historians of the politics of that court are still obliged to rely heavily on Nairne's papers.

EDWARD CORP

Sources E. Corp, 'The musical manuscripts of "Copiste Z": David Nairne, François Couperin, and the Stuart court at Saint-Germain-en-Laye', *Revue de Musicologie*, 84/1 (June 1998), 37–62 · E. Corp, 'An inventory of the archives of the Stuart court at Saint-Germain-en-Laye, 1689–1718', *Archives*, 23 (1998), 118–46 · E. T. Corp, 'The exiled court of James II and James III: a centre of Italian music in France, 1689–1712', *Journal of the Royal Musical Association*, 120 (1995), 216–31 · E. Corp, 'Music at the Stuart court at Urbino, 1717–1718', *Music and Letters*, 81 (2000), 351–63 · E. Corp, 'Lord Burlington's clandestine support for the Stuart court at Saint-Germain-en-Laye', *Lord Burlington: the man and his politics*, ed. E. Corp (1998), 7–26 · *Calendar of the Stuart papers belonging to his majesty the king, preserved at Windsor Castle*, 7 vols., HMC, 56 (1902–23) · [E. T. Corp and J. Sanson], eds., *La cour des Stuarts* (Paris, 1992) [exhibition catalogue, Musée des Antiquités Nationales de Saint-Germain-en-Laye, 13 Feb – 27 April 1992] · Nairne MSS, Bodl. Oxf., MSS Carte · D. Nairne, journal, NL Scot., MS 14266 · Scottish Catholic Archives, Blairs MSS · BL, Gualterio MSS, Add MSS 20298–20302 · Royal Arch., Stuart papers · 'Birth brieve of Mr David Nairne, 1687', *Scottish Antiquary, or, Northern Notes and Queries*, 9 (1894–5), 118–24 · A. de Compigny des Bordes de Villiers de l'Isle Adam, G. Gleize, and A. Prénat, *Fénelon et le chevalier de Ramsay: les entretiens de Cambrai* (Paris, 1929) · A. de Compigny des Bordes de Villiers de l'Isle Adam, *Au déclin de l'ancien régime: personnages francais, écossais, et canadie du XVIIIe siecle* (Paris, 1924)

Archives Bodl. Oxf., MSS · NL Scot., journal | BL, corresp. with Cardinal Gualterio, Add. 20298, 31259–31261 · Royal Arch., Stuart MSS · Scottish Catholic Archives, Edinburgh, Blairs MSS

Likenesses A.-S. Belle, oils, 1714, repro. in Corp and Sanson, eds., *La cour des Stuarts*, 166; priv. coll.

Nairne, Edward (1726–1806), instrument maker and natural philosopher, was the son of Edward Nairne, and perhaps a native of Sandwich, Kent. In 1741 he was apprenticed to the London optical instrument maker Matthew Loft, to whose business he succeeded, becoming free of the Spectaclemakers' Company in 1748 and its master in 1768. At his shop in 20 Cornhill, London, he employed many workmen, including the eminent Jesse Ramsden and Thomas Blunt; the latter was apprenticed to Nairne in 1760, became his partner in 1774, and set up on his own in 1793. Nairne collaborated with natural philosophers such as Benjamin Franklin, for whom he made magnets in 1758 and a short achromatic telescope in 1765; and Joseph Priestley, to whom he supplied microscopes and who advertised Nairne's novel pencil erasers in his perspective textbook in 1770.

The Royal Society, of which Nairne was elected fellow in June 1776, provided him with publicity for his devices and colleagues to use them. He made a range of optical instruments, some for the Royal Observatory, and described an equatorial telescope adapted from James Short's design at the Royal Society in 1771. He devised wooden telescope tubes which could withstand warping and wheel arrangements to switch between a range of lenses in refractors.

He maintained a very close relationship with Henry Cavendish, who purchased and commissioned many instruments from him. Cavendish used Nairne's shop for trials on electrometers, and in 1775 got him to test shocks from leather and pewter models of electric fish, linked to Nairne's batteries and glass plates, to show sceptics that such fish might well be electrical even though they generated no sparks. In 1782 Nairne supplied Cavendish with air collected at the Theatre Royal, Drury Lane, London, for trials on the goodness of various airs, and the following year the two men tested Nairne's mercury thermometers for use in the extreme cold of Hudson Bay. Nairne became one of the most famous English instrument makers, issuing his trade card in French as well as English, supplying Harvard University in 1764 with drawing and magnetic instruments on Franklin's recommendation, and winning royal patronage in 1785. On 13 September 1788 he married a widow, Elizabeth Lawson, who already had several children. One of these, Henry *Lawson (1774–1855), was apprenticed to Nairne.

Navigational interests stimulated Nairne's schemes. In the spring of 1772 he demonstrated large and almost frictionless magnetic dipping needles for the board of longitude with the astronomer William Wales, who then took them on James Cook's second voyage to the Pacific. Nairne also worked with Cavendish on improvements to variation compasses. In 1773 the naval commander Constantine Phipps took to Spitsbergen Nairne's dipping needles and a marine barometer. This Nairne designed with a very thin bore to prevent the mercury from pumping in the tube and so breaking it, and it was set on gimbals, so that its level could be read even with the ship under way. In early 1776 he told the Royal Society about ways of desalinating sea water obtained from a mineral water warehouse.

Nairne made a range of optical instruments, some for the Royal Greenwich Observatory, and in 1771 described to the Royal Society an equatorial telescope adapted from James Short's design. He marketed a wide range of other mathematical and philosophical instruments, such as James Lind's portable wind gauge, advertised in 1775, and accurate scale dividers advertised in a pamphlet of 1778. He claimed to have introduced a new kind of compound microscope with a mirror mounted on a secure post below the stage, which could be folded away into a small box when not in use. He also produced a range of air-pumps, the best costing as much as £60. In 1777 he conducted tests with Cavendish on pear gauges used by the engineer John Smeaton to calibrate air-pumps, judged them defective, and touted his own as producing a vacuum of less than one-three-hundredth of an atmosphere in six minutes. With these pumps he employed acid as a drying agent, a process later widely emulated.

Nairne performed considerable work on the design and improvement of electrical machines. In the 1760s he supplied natural philosophy lecturers with small portable spinning globe machines costing about £7, advertised by Priestley in his History of Electricity (1767). At the end of that decade, with Priestley's backing, Nairne began making larger machines, replacing the sphere with a turning cylinder, which allowed a greater area of glass to be rubbed with less leakage of the charge and more power. One of these devices, which could cost over £150, was commissioned for the Tuscan court. In late 1773 Nairne demonstrated the cylindrical machine for the Royal Society, showing 14 inch sparks and the fatal effects of electricity on animals and plants. Such demonstrations formed part of the campaign on behalf of Franklin's electrical theories and the use of pointed rods as defence against lightning. In 1772 a Royal Society committee chaired by Cavendish advised the Ordnance office that such pointed conductors should be used to protect the Purfleet arsenal in Essex. With other electrical philosophers Nairne reported on the effects of lightning strikes on George Whitfield's Tottenham Court Road Chapel in March 1772 and at Ratcliffe Highway, in the East End of London, in July 1775, coming out for Franklin and the superiority of pointed rods over the metal balls promoted by the natural philosopher Benjamin Wilson. In 1777, however, the arsenal was damaged by lightning. The following year Nairne published an analysis of such strikes. Using his cylindrical machine, he tried to prove that high points were better than balls, because if well earthed they could slowly discharge all electrical clouds in the vicinity. Though Nairne's paper was then attacked by Wilson's allies, it was an important contribution to Franklinist orthodoxy. In January 1782 Nairne was again sent by the Royal Society to report on a destructive lightning strike on an apparently well-defended poorhouse in Norfolk, where, it emerged, damage had been caused because the pointed rods there were not well earthed.

In the early 1780s Nairne also showed the society's fellows, including Cavendish and Smeaton, that iron wires would markedly shorten in length when electricity was discharged through them from a battery or by lightning strikes. He followed up with a new medical electrical machine, patented in February 1782 and described in a pamphlet of 1783. His description was translated into French in 1784 and German in 1786. The device involved a cylinder insulated on glass pillars and allowed for the first time the generation of both positive and negative electricity. Compact and portable, it was popular for the treatment of ailments such as nervous disorders, toothache, deafness, and lockjaw, and was common well into the nineteenth century. One was used by Humphry Davy at the new Royal Institution, of which Nairne became a founder proprietor in 1800. In 1801 he gave up his Cornhill business and moved to Lindsay Row, Chelsea, where he died on 1 September 1806 at the age of eighty.

The electrician must not be confused with a contemporary, **Edward Nairne** (c.1742–1799), lawyer and customs official, who was supervisor of customs at Sandwich, where he was born. From his light verse he was known as the Sandwich Bard. He died at Sandwich on 5 July 1799.

SIMON SCHAFFER

Sources G. Clifton, *Directory of British scientific instrument makers, 1550–1851*, ed. G. L'E. Turner (1995) · E. G. R. Taylor, *The mathematical practitioners of Hanoverian England, 1714–1840* (1966) · W. D.

Hackmann, *Electricity from glass: the history of the frictional electrical machine, 1600–1850* (1978) • E. Nairne, *Description and use of Nairne's patent electrical machine*, 8th edn (1796) • E. Nairne, 'Experiments on electricity', *PTRS*, 68 (1778), 823–60 • E. Nairne, 'Electrical experiments', *PTRS*, 64 (1774), 79–89 • *GM*, 1st ser., 76 (1806), 880 • *A scientific autobiography of Joseph Priestley*, ed. R. E. Schofield (1966) • D. P. Wheatland, *Tha apparatus of science at Harvard, 1765–1800* (1968) • P. Fara, *Sympathetic attractions: magnetic practices, beliefs, and symbolism in eighteenth-century England* (1996) • J. L. Heilbron, *Electricity in the 17th and 18th centuries: a study of early modern physics* (1979) • J. Clerk Maxwell, *Electrical researches of Henry Cavendish* (1879) • *GM*, 1st ser., 69 (1799), 626 • D. J. Warner, 'Edward Nairne: scientist and instrument-maker', *Rittenhouse*, 12 (1998), 244–55

Archives Harvard U. • Istituto e Museo di Storia della Scienca, Florence • Meteorological Office, Bracknell, Berkshire, National Meteorological Library and Archive, meteorological journal relating to Cornhill • MHS Oxf. • Sci. Mus. • Smithsonian Institution, Washington, DC • Whipple Museum, Cambridge

Wealth at death under £20,000: PRO, death duty registers, IR 26/115

Nairne, Edward (*c*.1742–1799). *See under* Nairne, Edward (1726–1806).

Nairne, John, styled third Lord Nairne and Jacobite second earl of Nairne (1690/91–1770), Jacobite army officer, was the eldest son of William *Nairne (formerly Murray), styled second Lord Nairne and Jacobite first earl of Nairne (1664–1726), and his wife, Margaret (1669–1747), the only child of Sir Robert Nairne, first Lord Nairne. John was brought up in the nonjuring episcopalian tradition at the family's seat (rebuilt between 1709 and 1712), near Loak, close to Perth and Dunkeld. In November 1712 he married his cousin Lady Catherine (1692–1754), the youngest daughter of Charles *Murray, first earl of Dunmore, and Catherine, *née* Watts; the couple had eight sons and five daughters, five of their children dying in infancy.

Both sides of Nairne's family were staunch supporters of the Jacobite cause, and in 1715 he accompanied his father in Mar's rising, serving as a lieutenant-colonel in Lord Charles Murray's regiment in which he performed with great determination 'and always went with them [the highlanders] on foot through the worst and deepest ways, and in highland dress' (Patten, 44). Following the Jacobites' defeat at Preston in November he and his father were arrested and taken to London. Lord Nairne was twice saved from imminent execution, before in August 1717 he and John were released and pardoned in return for his forfeiture of the peerage and any interest in Lady Nairne's estate. Lord Nairne returned to his Jacobite activities until his death in February 1726, when his attainted lordship and the Jacobite earldom of Nairne passed to his eldest son. The third Lord Nairne also retained his association with the Stuart cause, though the attainder prevented the sale of the family's Perthshire estate, sinking him into insolvency. In August 1732 he was offered, but unable to accept, 19,000 guineas for the house of Nairne and some of its land, which would have removed his debt and provided him with £400 pa. Four years later he was able to secure assurances from his creditors 'that they wont molest him for a yr by such time he hopes to gett an act … to sell the estate' (Atholl, 2.421). In 1738 parliament granted him permission to carry out lawsuits and to inherit property.

As in 1715 Nairne and his family played an active part in the Jacobite rising of 1745. His daughter, Mrs Robertson of Lude, prepared Blair Castle for the arrival of Charles Edward Stuart, the Young Pretender, where Nairne joined him. With Donald Cameron of Lochiel, he then led his Athollmen in the capture of Dunkeld and Perth in early September 1745. Nairne was again with the prince at Holyrood on 18 September 1745, and at the battle of Prestonpans (21 September) he led between 250 and 450 Athollmen. During the battle he commanded the second line consisting of Athollmen, Robertsons, MacLachlans, and Drummonds and proved a popular leader in the field. Present at all of the major battles of the 'Forty-Five, Nairne was among those who gathered at Ruthven prepared to carry on the rising after the defeat at Culloden. The Young Pretender's decision to abandon military operations prompted Nairne to escape to France. In June 1746 he was sentenced to death in the first act of attainder, but remained in exile and died, aged seventy-nine, at Sancerre on 11 July 1770.

Due to the attainder the peerage failed to pass to Nairne's eldest surviving son, John (his second), a lieutenant-colonel in the British army. However, in June 1824 the title was restored and inherited by John's son William Murray Nairne (1757–1830), the husband of the Jacobite poet Carolina *Oliphant, Lady Nairne, daughter of Laurence Oliphant of Gask. Of the third lord's remaining children, Charles and Henry served as officers of the United Provinces and France respectively, while Thomas fought with the Jacobites under Lord John Drummond, was captured while entering Scotland on board the French ship *L'Esperance* in October 1745, and died at Sancerre in April 1777.   KRISTEN ROBINSON

Sources DNB • J. J. H. H. Stewart-Murray, seventh duke of Atholl, *Chronicles of the Atholl and Tullibardine families*, 5 vols. (privately printed, Edinburgh, 1908) • W. MacLeod, ed., *A list of persons concerned in the rebellion*, Publications of the Scottish History Society, 8 (1890) • B. G. Seton and J. G. Arnot, eds., *The prisoners of the '45*, Scottish History Society, 3rd ser., 13–15 (1928–9) • A. M. Smith, *Jacobite estates of the Forty-Five* (1982) • GEC, *Peerage* • W. B. Blaikie, ed., *Origins of the 'Forty-Five and other papers relating to that rising*, Scottish History Society, 2nd ser., 2 (1916); facs. repr. (1975) • R. Patten, *The history of the rebellion in the year 1715*, 3rd edn (1745) • *Scots peerage*

Nairne [*formerly* Murray], **William**, styled second Lord Nairne and Jacobite first earl of Nairne (1664–1726), Jacobite army officer, fourth son among the twelve children of John *Murray, first marquess of Atholl (1631–1703), and his wife, Lady Amelia Sophia (1633–1703), daughter of James *Stanley, seventh earl of Derby, was born on 10 December 1664. Known as Lord William Murray from birth, he was educated in England, perhaps at Eton College. He entered the English navy about January 1683 and served bravely. He commanded a troop of Perthshire gentry under his father against Argyll's rising in 1685; they suffered casualties in a mistaken night attack by Sir Ewen Cameron of Lochiel. One of several officers favoured with simultaneous army and naval commissions, Lord William was made lieutenant in Major-General Worden's English cavalry regiment on 15 February 1687, and lieutenant on the *Tiger* on 23 May 1688. Always considering himself more seaman than soldier, he served on the *Tiger* during the English fleet's feeble campaign against William of Orange's invasion, leaving her on 28 November. On quitting his posts, he returned to Scotland.

In 1676 Sir Robert Nairne, first Lord Nairne, had contracted his only child, Margaret Nairne (1669–1747), to Atholl's youngest son, George; his peerage contained a remainder to George or any other younger son of Atholl she should wed. George's failing health led to her marrying William instead, by contracts of 18 January and 28 February 1690. William took the surname Nairne on his marriage and inherited the title, which had been suspended since Robert Nairne's death in May 1683.

As Lord Nairne, William claimed his parliamentary seat as a peer on 22 April 1690, after long-debated government objections, as one of the Jacobites taking the oaths in order to support Sir James Montgomery's plot to restore James II through parliament. After that failed, he did not again attend in William's or Anne's reigns, despite relatives' exhortations. In 1697 he and his brothers went north to rescue their sister the Dowager Lady Lovat from Simon Fraser. While the Act of Union was being passed, he was one of a committee who, though not themselves sitting, advised its parliamentary opponents.

During the 1707 preparations for a French invasion and Scottish rising, and as the French fleet approached in 1708, Nairne was an intermediary between his brother John *Murray, first duke of Atholl, and the French agents; and in 1708 he rode to inform Anne, dowager duchess of Hamilton, of the expedition's approach. A warrant for him was issued on 8 March 1708. He was among the prisoners carried to London afterwards, but his wife's solicitations helped secure his early release.

The costs of imprisonment increased Nairne's financial difficulties, caused by inherited debt, a large family (twelve children), and a costly rebuilding of his seat, the house of Nairne, near Loak, between Perth and Dunkeld, during 1709–1712. The Nairnes were nonjuring episcopalians, and in 1713 helped establish a meeting-house in Dunkeld, the seat of the first duke of Atholl, a presbyterian. The families were nevertheless on close terms, which enabled Lady Nairne, a far stronger character and Jacobite than her husband, to influence decisively his nephews, William Murray, marquess of Tullibardine, and lords Charles Murray and George Murray. During the rising of 1715 she spied.

Nairne himself joined the earl of Mar in September 1715 when he occupied Atholl, and his three nephews and he became colonels of the four regiments raised there. Nairne's eldest son, John *Nairne, later styled third Lord Nairne, was lieutenant-colonel in Lord Charles Murray's regiment. Both regiments were selected for the expedition across the Forth under Brigadier William Mackintosh of Borlum. Nairne, distrusting the expedition and, increasingly, his commander, claimed to have urged his dependants not to accompany him. After the surrender at Preston on 13 November, many of the Atholl officers and men, tried locally, were hanged or transported; and Lord Nairne and his son were carried prisoners to London.

Nairne, with six other peers, was impeached for treason before the House of Lords and, like all but one, pleaded guilty on 19 January 1716, threw himself on George I's mercy, and was sentenced to death on 9 February. He was twice ordered for execution the next day, and wrote his scaffold speech, but was reprieved through last-minute solicitations by his cousin James, tenth earl of Derby, his brother the duke of Atholl, and his wife, Lady Margaret. He also laid out £1500 among 'Lawiers and B[itche]s [royal mistresses?]' (Oliphant, 61). The legend that James, Earl Stanhope, saved him as a former Eton schoolfellow seems groundless. Nairne was imprisoned in the Tower until August 1717 when, under the general indemnity, he and his son were pardoned as to life and liberty. He forfeited the peerage, but only his life interest in his wife's estate: a 1717 private act of parliament enabled the king to provide support for her and her children, and on 28 August 1718 he regranted the estate to her.

On his return home in 1718, Nairne resumed Jacobite activity. During the 1719 Glenshiel affair he was one of the leading lowlanders prepared to rise, once the duke of Ormond's main invasion army reached England, and join Earl Marischal's highland force. Credulous Jacobites' reports of Ormond's arrival nearly made him attempt it, but George Lockhart of Carnwath warned him in time, and he remained quiet. On 24 June 1721 James III (James Francis Edward Stuart) created him Jacobite earl of Nairne and Viscount Stanley; and he later wrote to him to be ready to join proposed risings in 1723 and 1725, both abortive. Nairne died on 3 February 1726 at the house of Nairne, and was buried at Auchtergaven.

Nairne was survived by his wife, who remained important as probably the most determined Jacobite in Perthshire, and the marriages of five of her eight daughters strengthened the Jacobitism of their husbands' families. During the Jacobite rising of 1745 she laboured vigorously in support of Prince Charles Edward, whom she entertained at the house of Nairne in September 1745. She died on 14 November 1747.

PAUL HOPKINS

Sources J. J. H. H. Stewart-Murray, seventh duke of Atholl, *Chronicles of the Atholl and Tullibardine families*, 5 vols. (privately printed, Edinburgh, 1908) · Blair Castle, Perthshire, Atholl MSS · T. L. Kington-Oliphant, *The Jacobite lairds of Gask* (1870) · *Scots peerage* · NL Scot., Oliphant of Gask MSS, Adv. MSS 82.1.1, 82.9.2 · GEC, *Peerage*, vol. 9 · *State trials*, vol. 15 · N. Hooke, *The secret history of Colonel Hooke's negotiations in Scotland in favour of the Pretender, in 1707* (1760) · *Correspondence of Colonel N. Hooke*, ed. W. D. Macray, 2 vols., Roxburghe Club, 92, 95 (1870–71) · G. Lockhart, *The Lockhart papers*, ed. A. Aufrere, 2 vols. (1817) · catalogue of the Mercer Nairne Petty-Fitzmaurice, marquess of Lansdowne, archive at Meikleour House, Perthshire, NRA Scotland, NRA (S) 3698 · Royal Arch., Stuart MSS, vols. 83/10, 100/11, miscellaneous vol. 20, p. 112 · R. Patten, *The history of the late rebellion: with original papers, and the characters of the principal noblemen and gentlemen concern'd in it*, 2nd edn (1717) · J. R. Tanner, ed., *A descriptive catalogue of the naval manuscripts in the Pepysian Library at Magdalene College, Cambridge*, 4 vols. (1903–22), vol. 1 · muster book HMS *Tiger*, 1688, PRO, ADM 36/4317 · J. Sinclair, *Memoirs of the insurrection in Scotland in 1715*, ed. W. Scott (1858), vols. 1–2 · K. Thomson, *Memoirs of the Jacobites of 1715 and 1745*, 3 vols. (1845–6), vols. 1–2 · letters of Lord and Lady Nairne to the duke and duchess of Marlborough, etc., 1708–18, BL, Add. MS 61136, fols. 188–9; Add. MS 61624, fols. 41–2; Add MS 61632, fols. 178–81 ·

H. Fenwick, *Architect royal: the life and works of Sir William Bruce* (1970) · W. A. Shaw, ed., *Calendar of treasury books*, 32, PRO (1957) **Archives** BL, Blenheim MSS · Blair Castle, Perthshire, Atholl MSS · Meikleour House, Perthshire, Lansdowne MSS · NA Scot., Maxtone Graham of Cultoquhey MSS, GD 155 · NL Scot., Oliphant of Gask MSS, Advocates' MSS **Likenesses** A.-S. Belle?, oils, priv. coll. · oils (as young man; after A. S. Belle), priv. coll.

Nairne, Sir William, fifth baronet, Lord Dunsinane (*bap.* 1731, *d.* 1811), judge, was baptized on 21 May 1731 at Dundee, the younger son of Sir William Nairne, baronet (*d.* 1754), of Dunsinane, Perthshire, and his second wife, the widow Emelia Hunter, formerly Graham (*d.* 1767), of Fintry, Forfarshire. He was admitted an advocate on 11 March 1755, with the publication of his *Disputatio juridica*, and in 1758 was appointed joint commissary clerk of Edinburgh with Alexander Nairne. He was uncle to the notorious Katharine Nairne or Ogilvie, tried with her brother-in-law for the murder of her husband in August 1765, and was supposed to have connived at her subsequent escape from the Tolbooth. He assisted in the collection of the *Decisions of the Court of Session from the End of the Year 1756 to the End of the Year 1760* (1765). In 1783 Nairne was elected a fellow of the Royal Society of Edinburgh. He succeeded Robert Bruce of Kennet as an ordinary lord of session, and took his seat on the bench, with the title Lord Dunsinane, on 9 March 1786.

Nairne succeeded to the baronetcy on the death of his nephew William, the fourth baronet, in January 1790, and at the same time purchased the estate of Dunsinane from another nephew for £16,000. Nairne was not a rich man, and in order to clear off the purchase money of Dunsinane he had to adopt the most rigid economy. To save the expense of entertaining visitors he is said to have kept only one bed at Dunsinane, and upon one occasion, after trying every expedient to get rid of his friend George Dempster, he exclaimed in despair, 'George, if you stay, you will go to bed at ten and rise at three, and then I shall get the bed after you' (Kay, 1.217–18).

Nairne impressed Dr Johnson and accompanied him and Boswell on part of their long Scottish tour. According to Johnson he was 'A gentleman who could stay with us only long enough to make us know how much we lost by his leaving us' (Boswell, *Life*, 5.53). Boswell described him as 'a heaven-born judge' (ibid., 475), and he once paid for a poor man to appeal in a higher court—successfully—against one of his own erroneous judgments.

On the resignation of John Campbell of Stonefield, Nairne was appointed a lord of justiciary on 24 December 1792. He resigned his seat in the court of justiciary in 1808, and his seat in the court of session in 1809. He died, unmarried, at Dunsinane House, on 23 March 1811. The baronetcy became extinct upon his death, while his estates devolved upon his nephew John Mellis, who subsequently assumed the surname of Nairne.

G. F. R. BARKER, *rev.* ANITA MCCONNELL

Sources J. Kay, *A series of original portraits and caricature etchings … with biographical sketches and illustrative anecdotes*, ed. [H. Paton and others], new edn [3rd edn], 1 (1877), 217–19, 307, 392; 2 (1877), facing p. 380 · G. Brunton and D. Haig, *An historical account of the senators of*

the college of justice, from its institution in MDXXXII (1832), 538 · C. E. Adam, ed., *View of the political state of Scotland in the last century* (1887), 262 · Anderson, *Scot. nat.* · Irving, *Scots.* · Burke, *Gen. GB* · *Scots Magazine*, 20 (1758), 613 · *Scots Magazine*, 52 (1790), 51 · *Scots Magazine and Edinburgh Literary Miscellany*, 73 (1811), 320 · F. J. Grant, ed., *The Faculty of Advocates in Scotland, 1532–1943*, Scottish RS, 145 (1944) · J. L. Smith-Dampier, *Who's who in Boswell* (1935) · Boswell, *Life* · GEC, *Baronetage* **Archives** NL Scot., letters to Sir William Forbes **Likenesses** J. Kay, caricature, etching, 1799, BM, NPG · H. Raeburn, oils, Faculty of Advocates, Edinburgh

Naish, John (1842–1890), judge and politician, was born at Limerick on 10 July 1842, the second son of Carrol Naish of Ballycullen, co. Limerick, and first son of Anne Margaret O'Carroll, his second wife. He was educated at Tullabeg College and at the Jesuit school of Clongowes Wood in Kildare, and then entered Trinity College, Dublin. There he was double gold medallist in mathematics and in experimental science, and he obtained a non-foundation scholarship in science (1861), the Lloyd exhibition for proficiency in mathematics and physics (1862), a university studentship (1862), and a senior moderatorship both in mathematical science and in experimental and natural science (1862). After graduating BA, he entered the law school of the university, and was first prizeman in civil law in 1863, and in feudal and English law in 1864; he also won the single competitive studentship then given by the London inns of court.

Naish entered Lincoln's Inn in 1864. He was called to the Irish bar in Michaelmas term of 1865 and joined the Munster circuit. His industry and knowledge soon brought him a good practice, and in 1870 he was retained in the important case of *O'Keefe v. Cullen*. In 1871, in conjunction with Edmund Bewley, he published *A Treatise on the Common Law Procedure Acts*, which was to become a standard text. In 1880 he took silk, and became law adviser to Dublin Castle, an arduous post in troubled times, and served in the case of *R. v. Parnell* (1880). At this time, he was credited with having unearthed the statute of Edward III, which was put in force against the supporters of the Land League.

Gladstone appointed Naish successor to William Moore Johnson as solicitor-general for Ireland in January 1883; he was therefore in office during the trial of the Phoenix Park murderers. In the same year Naish stood as a Liberal for Mallow, where he was defeated by William O'Brien, the nationalist candidate. In December of the same year he was promoted to be attorney-general, succeeding Andrew Marshall Porter, and was co-opted a bencher of King's Inn. Naish was sworn of the Irish privy council in January 1884. In May 1885, at the early age of forty-two, Gladstone made him lord chancellor of Ireland, in succession to Sir Edward Sullivan; he was the second Roman Catholic chancellor since the Reformation, but held the seals only until July, in which month the Liberal government resigned office. He was appointed a permanent lord justice of appeal in August of the same year, and became again lord chancellor when Gladstone returned to office in February 1886. In June the government again resigned, and Naish with them. He thereupon resumed the duties of lord justice of appeal.

Naish had married, on 15 April 1884, Maud Mary (*d.* 1920), daughter of James Arthur Dease DL, of Turbotston, co. Westmeath. They had three children. In the summer of 1890 Naish went to Ems in Germany for his health, and he died there, of Bright's disease, on 17 August 1890. He was buried at Ems.

Clearly a man of very great intelligence, Naish was rather retiring and did not gain for himself a reputation for advocacy. He was, however, a sound and sagacious legal practitioner and, on the bench, a deliverer of 'terse, pithy and logical' judgments (*Irish Law Times*, 23 Aug 1890). He was certainly one of the most eminent Irish lawyers of his day. P. L. NOLAN, *rev.* NATHAN WELLS

Sources *Irish Law Times and Solicitors' Journal* (23 Aug 1890), 46–7 • *The Times* (19 Aug 1890) • *Thom's directory* (1890) • E. Keane, P. Beryl Phair, and T. U. Sadleir, eds., *King's Inns admission papers, 1607–1867*, IMC (1982) • Boase, *Mod. Eng. biog.* • Burke, *Gen. Ire.* (1912) [Dease] • Burtchaell & Sadleir, *Alum. Dubl.*
Likenesses portrait, repro. in Rhadamanthus, *Our judges* (1890)
Wealth at death £649 2*s.* 9*d.* in England: Irish probate sealed in England, 23 Oct 1890, *CGPLA Eng. & Wales* • £7899 12*s.* 10*d.*: probate, 6 Oct 1890, *CGPLA Ire.*

Naish, William (1766/7–1800), miniature painter, was born at Axbridge, Somerset. He entered the Royal Academy Schools on 28 November 1788, when his age was recorded as twenty-one, and practised with success in London. He exhibited at the Royal Academy almost continuously from 1786 until his death. His portraits of Thomas Morton, the dramatist, and of the actresses Mrs Twisleton and Mrs Wells were engraved by Ridley for the *Monthly Mirror* (1 July 1796). A portrait of the actor William Thomas Lewis as Vapid in F. Reynolds's *The Dramatist*, attributed to Naish, is reproduced in G. Ashton's *Pictures in the Garrick Club* (p. 236).

Naish was in Bristol for a time, and a miniature of him by H. W. Wymann was signed and dated on the reverse '"Naish, 97/H. W. Wymann. 27 College Green, Bristol"' (Foskett, 606). Foskett notes that 'he is said to have died in his house in Leicester Square, late in 1800' (ibid.). An example of Naish's work is in the Victoria and Albert Museum, London, and the department of prints and drawings at the British Museum has engravings after portraits by Naish. John Naish, a sporting and miniature painter who entered the Royal Academy Schools on 18 February 1791, aged twenty, who exhibited miniatures at the Royal Academy (1790–95), and who also worked in Bristol was Naish's younger brother. In 1792 both John and William Naish exhibited from the same address, 492 Strand, London. F. M. O'DONOGHUE, *rev.* ANNETTE PEACH

Sources D. Foskett, *Miniatures: dictionary and guide* (1987) • S. C. Hutchison, 'The Royal Academy Schools, 1768–1830', *Walpole Society*, 38 (1960–62), 123–91, esp. 150, 152 • R. Walker, *National Portrait Gallery: Regency portraits*, 1 (1985), 349 • G. Ashton, *Pictures in the Garrick Club*, ed. K. A. Burnim and A. Wilton (1997) • *Engraved Brit. ports.* • B. S. Long, *British miniaturists* (1929) • G. C. Williamson, *The history of portrait miniatures*, 1 (1904), facing 190

Naish, William (1785–1860), slavery abolitionist, son of Francis Naish, a silversmith, and Susanna, his wife, was born in High Street, Bath, on 9 March 1785. After moving to London, he opened a haberdasher's shop in Gracechurch Street, which he ran from 1823 to 1834.

Naish was a staunch Quaker, and interested himself in the anti-slavery movement, in support of which he published a large number of tracts and pamphlets (nearly all undated). These included prose descriptions of the condition of slavery, such as *The Negro's Remembrancer*, *The Negro's Friend*, *A Brief Description of the Toil and Sufferings of Slaves*, *Biographical Anecdotes*, and *Sketch of the African Slave Trade*. Other works highlighted the contrast between free and enslaved black people, such as *A Comparison between Distressed English Labourers and the Coloured People and Slaves* and *The Advantages of Free Labour over the Labour of Slaves*, and emphasized the need to boycott slave-produced sugar, such as *Reasons for Using East Indian Sugar* (1828). *A Short History of the Poor Black Slaves* was directed at children, and *The Negro Mother's Appeal* was in verse. Other works not directly related to slavery included *Plead the Cause of the Poor and Needy*, *Sketches from the History of Pennsylvania* (1845), *The Fulfilment of the Prophecy of Isaiah* (1853), and *George Fox and his Friends as Leaders in the Peace Cause* (1859). During 1829 and 1830 he opened a depository at his shop in Gracechurch Street for the sale of these and other publications. He afterwards lived at Maidstone and at Bath. He married Frances, daughter of Jasper Capper, and sister of Samuel Capper, author of *The Acknowledged Doctrines of the Church of Rome* (1849).

Naish died at his home, 6 Great Stanhope Street, Walcot, Bath, on 4 March 1860. He was buried in the Quaker burial-ground at Widcombe Hill, near Bath. His wife survived him. His son Arthur John Naish (1816–1889) was co-founder with Paul Bevan of the 'Bevan–Naish Library' of Friends' books.

CHARLOTTE FELL-SMITH, *rev.* PETER SPENCE

Sources Boase, *Mod. Eng. biog.* • registers, 1894, Devonshire House • private information (1894) • *CGPLA Eng. & Wales* (1860)
Wealth at death under £4000: probate, 1860, *CGPLA Eng. & Wales*

Naismith, William Wilson (1856–1935), mountaineer, was born on 28 February 1856 at 26 Muir Street, Hamilton, the elder of the two children of William Naismith, physician, and his wife, Mary Anne Murray. As someone who always yearned for the outdoors, he was encouraged to explore the local countryside at an early age. At his father's instigation, at the age of four he was carried on high to look down on the hills of Scotland. He climbed Ben Lomond only five years later. While still a teenager he completed a hike of 56 miles, walking from the family home at Auchincampbell to the top of Tinto Hill and then back again. Slight of stature and slim in build, Naismith's obvious talent for mountaineering came to the fore during a series of trips to the Alps and Norway in the 1880s. He and his near-constant climbing companion Gilbert Thomson honed their technical skills on rock, snow, and ice. Naismith's careful record of all his successful ascents (now in the National Library of Scotland) attests to the

William Wilson Naismith (1856–1935), by unknown photographer

importance of these formative summer trips. Having sated a desire for continental mountaineering, he spent the following two decades exploring the climbing possibilities offered by Scotland's peaks.

Naismith was the founding figure of the Scottish Mountaineering Club. His open letter, dated 10 January 1889 and published in the *Glasgow Herald*, suggested how an organization separate from the already well-established Alpine Club might direct climbers' attention to the then little-frequented hills of home. This proposal was warmly received by the cosily exclusive, all-male group of academics, businessmen, and landowners who went on to dominate Scotland's new sport of mountaineering. Naismith, himself a chartered accountant and insurance manager, served on the club committee as honorary treasurer and vice-president, and was soon one of its most respected members.

It was through his exploits in pioneering new routes on the Cuillin mountains of Skye, in Glencoe, Arran, and on Ben Nevis that Naismith secured a reputation as the foremost Scottish climber of his generation. He was not without rivals, and enjoyed provoking gentlemanly and patriotic competition with John Norman Collie, his gifted English counterpart. On discovering that Collie had managed surreptitiously to 'pick off' a number of much admired but unclimbed Scottish routes, Naismith proposed a revenge raid taking in the houses of parliament by the clock tower or alternatively a traverse of Beachy Head. The skills and expertise of the two men were combined on

one occasion during a climbing trip to their beloved Cuillin. A notable chimney route on this rocky ridge of mountains still bears Naismith's name.

At the peak of his abilities Naismith was a role model for experienced rock gymnasts and tentative beginners alike. Despite a necessarily adventurous streak he consistently stressed the importance of prudence in ambition and safety in technique. Willie was also renowned for an unfailing modesty about his personal contribution to the sport and a reluctance to make public speeches. This humility is apparent in the many published accounts of expeditions which appear in the *Scottish Mountaineering Club Journal*, although these also reveal a wryly witty and imaginative character.

Naismith also found divine inspiration in the mountains, his rockbound experiences firing a lifelong devotion to the Church of Scotland. Such were his religious convictions that he would not climb on a Sunday, although this never led him to cast judgement on those who spent their sabbath on the hill. He was an elder in Kelvinside (Botanic Gardens) church, Glasgow, for twenty-seven years and held the western treasurership of the National Bible Society for much the same period. Aside from these commitments, his enthusiasm for outdoor activity knew few bounds: his interests took in photography, skiing, fishing, ice-skating, canoeing, boxing, horse-riding, and hot-air ballooning. At the age of seventy, Naismith surprised many friends who considered him a confirmed bachelor when he married, in 1926, Edith Agnes Margaret Barron, the daughter of an Aberdeenshire minister. William and Edith shared a common commitment to the work of the church and a love of hill-walking. He died suddenly from heart failure on 27 September 1935, while the couple were attending a conference at Holly Lodge, Strathpeffer, Ross and Cromarty, on the deepening of spiritual life. He was buried at Bent cemetery, Hamilton, on 1 October 1935.

It would undoubtedly have appealed to a man who maintained that caution should always be combined with courage, that Naismith's lasting contribution to modern mountaineering would be of both practical and seemingly modest bent. A short explanation of what hill-walkers commonly refer to as 'Naismith's rule' first appeared in the 'Notes and queries' pages of the *Scottish Mountaineering Club Journal* following an outing over Stobinian. A formula allowing reliable estimations of ascent times on foot, his rule allowed 1 hour to cover every 3 miles on the map and an added hour for every 2000 feet of ascent. This has become a time-honoured rule of thumb used, with the odd modification, by many who ascend the same peaks that Naismith once scrambled over.

HAYDEN LORIMER

Sources G. Thomson, 'In memoriam: William Wilson Naismith, 1856–1935', *Scottish Mountaineering Club Journal*, 21/121 (1936), 40–44 · *Hamilton Advertiser* (5 Oct 1935) · A. E. M. [A. E. Maylard], *Alpine Journal*, 48 (1936), 164–5 · H. MacRobert, 'A short history of Scottish climbing, 1880–1914', *Scottish Mountaineering Club Journal*, 22 (1939) · b. cert. · d. cert. · Bent cemetery records, Hamilton **Archives** NL Scot., Scottish Mountaineering Club holdings **Likenesses** photograph, repro. in Thomson, 'In memoriam', 41 · photograph, Alpine Club, London [*see illus.*]

Nalson, John (*bap.* **1637**, *d.* **1686**), Church of England clergyman and author, was baptized on 2 August 1637 at Holbeck Chapel, Leeds, where his father, John Nalson (*d.* 1667), was curate. His mother was Sarah, daughter of Thomas Sharp of Little Horton near Bradford. He entered St John's College, Cambridge, in 1654, graduated BA in 1658 and proceeded MA in 1662 and LLD in 1678. He became rector of Doddington in the Isle of Ely in 1668, a living which was increasing in prosperity as a consequence of the draining of the fens, and prebendary of Ely in 1684.

Nalson exemplifies many of the characteristics of the Anglican church of his day, not least the way its structure was underpinned by patronage and place-seeking, clerical dynasties, and extended networks. On 10 October 1667 he married Alice, daughter of the Revd Algernon Peyton, his predecessor in the rectory of Doddington. Their son Valentine (*d.* 1713) graduated BA from St John's College, Cambridge, in 1703 (MA 1711) and served as vicar of St Martin's, York, from 1707 and as prebendary of Ripon from 1713. In 1687 their daughter Elizabeth married Philip Williams (*d.* 1719), Nalson's successor as rector of Doddington and also a graduate of St John's.

Nalson's clerical career also exemplifies the ecclesiastical rivalries of his day, the deeply ingrained prejudices against nonconformists and Roman Catholics, the inseparable connections between religion and politics in the age of party, and the enduring legacy of the impact of the civil wars. Nalson was a prolific writer as well as a country clergyman and his platform, in his own words, was consistently that of a 'true Church of England King's Protestant' (J. Nalson, *The True Protestant's Appeal*, 1681, 1). 'I do perfectly hate and abhor all Popery, superstition and innovation in the church', he declared. 'I do no less detest and abhor all other schismatical practices and persuasions, treacherous and disloyal doctrines and actions of Commonwealth Protestants' (ibid.). Nalson unswervingly indulged these convictions in a stream of publications which gushed forth in the unsettled years 1677 to 1685; some of them, like *The Countermine* (1677) and *Foxes and Firebrands, or, A Specimen of the Danger of Harmony and Separation* (1680), went through three editions. His style was trenchant, hard-hitting, polemical, vivid, and vitriolic. Although he frequently used the term loosely as a convenient holdall, presbyterianism was a recurring target for attack by Nalson and in *The Common Interest of King and People* (1677) was roundly denounced as 'that revived hydra of the lake of Geneva, with its many headed progeny, Anabaptists, Quakers, Levellers etc' (p. 201). He devoted twenty chapters of *The Countermine* to exposing the errors, hypocrisy, and guile of the presbyterians. He even linked presbyterians with Roman Catholics. Religious toleration to Nalson was anathema:

> I confess I think a Papist hath as fair a right to toleration as the rest of the pretenders and that is just none at all … An unregulated, promiscuous toleration of all errors [he trumpeted] for the sake of some truths which all pretend to

hold and believe [is] impious, sinful and damnable. (J. Nalson, *Toleration of Liberty of Conscience Considered*, 1685, 40)

Nalson threw himself into polemical pamphleteering, engaged with the insistent, controversial issues of his day, and was sometimes in trouble for his pains. His *Letter from a Jesuit in Paris* (1678), a clumsy diatribe, led to a reprimand and brief imprisonment (*JHC*, 9.572, 576, 592, 608). Quite clearly Nalson's uncompromising views on the contemporary scene were moulded by his reading of the horrors of the civil wars of the 1640s. He drew comparisons between the mid-century upheavals and the crises of the 1670s and 1680s. He bemoaned the fact that too little had been learned from the recent past; another disintegration, as he saw it, was about to happen. Nalson, therefore, wrote history with a present purpose and looked to the past for guidance and warnings. No period of English history, he was confident, had more lessons to teach than that of the civil wars if the country was to be saved from another disaster. He wrote, therefore, so that:

> by the fatal example of their ancestors the generous English may learn that necessary caution to be wise at the expense of their unhappy progenitors; and being enabled so easily to discover the cheat of those factious mariners who pretend to save the vessel by throwing the captain and pilots overboard they may prevent and avoid a second shipwreck. (J. Nalson, *An Impartial Collection*, 1682–3, 1.iii)

Nalson published in 1683 *A True Copy of the Journal of the High Court of Justice for the Tryal of King Charles I*, prefaced by a lengthy commentary, and dedicated it to James, duke of York. Nalson's book depicted 'the horrible tragedy' of the 'dismal, bloody, wicked and outrageous rebellion' of the mid century, 'the insolent wickedness' of those who endeavoured 'to consecrate murder, treason, sacrilege [and] perjury'. 'The Devil's trapdoors of rebellion and damnation' were opened wide in the 1640s as the 'guilty miscreants' committed 'the most barbarous and inhumane outrages'. Charles I was fulsomely celebrated in this account as 'the best and most illustrious sovereign of the christian world'. Cromwell, by contrast, was pilloried as 'that infamous usurper … that sorceror' (pp. ii, iii, xvi, viii, xviii, lxiii, lxiv). In *The Project of Peace* (1678) further insults were hurled at Cromwell, this 'original of pride, hypocrisy and ambition' (Nalson, 46) who, even as a soldier, 'owed most of his successes rather to his cunning than his valour' (ibid., 52). The pictorial frontispiece of *A True Copy* shows the Devil at the reins of a chariot riding roughshod over justice, liberty, and an executed monarch. An opening poem—whether Nalson's own work or another's is not clear—further underlines the message for 'unhappy Albion' by displaying 'the sad trophies of our Civil Wars' and denouncing 'the Black Old Cause'.

Nalson's major work, *An Impartial Collection of the Great Affairs of State* (2 vols., 1682–3), was informed by the same convictions and couched in the same kind of language. Its title-page boasted that it was 'published by his Majesty's special command'. Nalson sought in this work to discredit, and indeed to demolish, the *Historical Collections* of John Rushworth (1612?–1690), published in 1659 and dedicated to 'the short-lived meteor' Richard Cromwell. Nalson, presenting himself as an unbiased 'votary of truth', lambasted Rushworth for his partiality and prejudices and catalogued his numerous errors. That Charles I was made to shoulder the blame for the civil wars was denounced as a monstrous perversion of the truth. What else, Nalson insisted, could have been expected from this parliamentarian civil servant but a crude, one-sided account designed 'to justify the actions of the late rebels' and 'to palliate the horrid sin of rebellion'. Nalson set out, therefore, to put the record straight about Pym ('the great engineer of the faction'), Bastwick ('a notorious incendiary and mover of sedition'), and all the rest of those 'barbarous pretenders to religion and reformation', 'factious spirits', 'seditious sectaries', and 'vultures and harpies' (J. Nalson, *Impartial Collection*, 1.vi, 809, iii, 440, 665, 779; 2.887). Woe to England, declared Nalson, that the rebels triumphed and 'erected upon the ruins of this glorious, ancient and imperial monarchy, a democratic slavery under the title of the Commonwealth of England' (ibid., 1.lxxvii). In stark contrast he defended Strafford, 'the noble earl', for 'his great wisdom, learning, courage and loyalty' and heaped praise on Charles I, 'this excellent prince [always] willing and desirous to oblige his people and to take off whatever was burdensome, though to his own detriment and disadvantage' (ibid., 1.785).

Nalson's two hefty volumes published by 1683 still left his intended project remarkably incomplete; at the end of the second he had not even reached the outbreak of civil war, let alone the king's trial and execution. The many surviving volumes of his working papers in the duke of Portland's library at Welbeck Abbey and in the Bodleian Library and British Library attest to Nalson's industry as a researcher. (The collections, it should be noted, contain unreturned original state papers as well as the author's own transcripts.) Nalson clearly intended to publish more volumes and sought recognition and preferment to make this worthwhile. 'A little oil will make the wheels go easy', he wrote to Archbishop Sancroft on 14 July 1683, 'which hitherto, without complaining, I have found a very heavy draught' (Bodl. Oxf., MSS Tanner 34, 80). Full of self-importance, he was angling for a sinecure, an ambition that can hardly have been amply gratified by the prebend at Ely which came his way in 1684. He died at Doddington, Isle of Ely, on 24 March 1686 without publishing any further volumes of his *Impartial Collection*. His wife survived him.

Nalson's reputation among modern historians has been variable, to say the least. He features in R. C. Richardson's *The Debate on the English Revolution* (1977, 3rd edn 1998) not on account of his scholarly merits but owing to his historiographical significance. R. MacGillivray's *Restoration Historians and the English Civil War* (1974) contains the longest modern account, but depicts him as a rather pathetic figure, 'almost a caricature of the frenzied Tory clergyman of Charles II' (p. 109). It is significant, however, that Kevin Sharpe's attempted rehabilitation of *The Personal Rule of Charles I* (1992) values Nalson, one of the original and noisiest defenders of Charles's reputation, as an authority.

R. C. RICHARDSON

Sources J. Nalson, *The project of peace* (1678) • Venn, *Alum. Cant.* • G. D. Lumb, ed., *The registers of the parish church of Leeds, from 1612 to 1639*, Thoresby Society, 3 (1895) • *JHC*, 9 (1667–87) • R. Macgillivray, *Restoration historians and the English civil war* (1974) • R. C. Richardson, *The debate on the English revolution*, 3rd edn (1998) • K. Sharpe, *The personal rule of Charles I* (1992)
Archives BL, papers relating to plundered and scandalous ministers, Add. MSS 15669–15672 • Bodl. Oxf., historical collections • CUL, historical collections | Bodl. Oxf., Tanner MSS, letters to Archbishop Sancroft

Nalton, James (*c*.1600–1662), Church of England clergyman and ejected minister, was the son of Francis Nalton, a cleric of Walkington, near Beverley, in Yorkshire. He matriculated at Trinity College, Cambridge, in 1616, and graduated BA in 1620 and MA in 1623. He served as an assistant to Richard Conder at St Mary Colechurch, London, where his puritan principles resulted in his suspension, later removed after his submission on 14 July 1629. He was appointed rector of Rugby, Warwickshire, on 22 December 1632. There he married Jane (*d*. 1641), and together they had three children: James, Daniel, and Naomi. His wife was buried on 23 July 1641. On 31 July 1642, in Rugby, a group of armed men unsuccessfully attempted to force Nalton to read publicly *The King's Answer to the Parliament's Petition*. After spending a short time as an army chaplain to Colonel Grantham's regiment, on 13 April 1643, at the nomination of the Lords, Nalton was appointed clerk at St Leonard's, Foster Lane, London.

Nalton delivered one of the solemn fast sermons preached before the House of Commons at St Margaret's, Westminster, on 29 April 1646. Robert Jenner and Sir Peter Wentworth thanked him, and the house requested the prompt publication of the sermon, which appeared as *Delay of Reformation Provoking God's Further Indignation*. Taking as his text Leviticus 26: 23–4, Nalton exhorted his hearers to advance swiftly the reformation of the Church of England. With typical temerity he told them, 'Beware, lest out of cowardice or carnal fears, out of sinful compliance or conformity to the wills of men, ye tolerate what God would not have tolerated' (J. Nalton, *Delay of Reformation*, 1646, 4–5). Together with the other London presbyterian ministers Nalton protested against the collapse of royal government by signing the vindication and the representation of the London ministers to the army in 1649. In 1651 he was implicated in Christopher Love's plot to restore Charles II to the throne, and fled to the Netherlands. On finding refuge in Rotterdam, he became joint pastor of the English church with Thomas Cawton, and during the six months he spent there he was instrumental in that church's casting off its independent stance and becoming presbyterian.

On his return to St Leonard's in 1652, Nalton soon became embroiled in a dispute concerning the payment of tithes when he published a tract expounding the spiritual dangers of withholding such payments. In 1654 he revealed a capacity for catholicity by editing a work by a leading Independent divine, Jeremiah Burroughes, *The*

Saint's Treasury. Nalton's religious convictions undoubtedly predisposed him to favour the presbyterian cause, as did many of his colleagues in London. Sir Robert Harley, one of the leading patrons of the presbyterian party, was often upheld from the puritan pulpit as a promoter of vital godliness within the realm, from whom puritan ministers drew encouragement and practical assistance in the years before the civil war. In 1654 Sir Robert's son, Edward, wrote to his father that 'This day the monthly fast was kept at Mr. Nalton's church very sweetly, where you were affectionately remembered' (BL, Add. MS 70007, fols. 2–3). In 1660 Nalton was appointed as a commissioner for the approbation of ministers. On 17 August 1662 he was ejected for nonconformity from his living at St Leonard's. He died in London in December of that year, and was buried at St Leonard's on 1 January 1663. His funeral sermon was preached by Thomas Horton, and subsequently published as *Rich Treasure in Earthen Vessels*. A collection of twenty sermons by Nalton was published posthumously in 1664.

Nalton was known to his contemporaries as 'the Weeping Prophet'; according to Horton he was 'a man of a very yeilding and melting forme of spirit, soon dissolved into tears' (Horton, 17). This was due to his gravity of demeanour, which gave way on occasion to tears while preaching. Richard Baxter considered him an excellent and zealous preacher, as well as an able linguist. Nalton was a deeply humble divine, whose faith in Christ proved unshakeable throughout difficult times. He was a man of resolute character and deep devotion in both his public and private life. His preaching was highly regarded in the City of London, and his reputation and influence spread far through his brief spell in Rotterdam and through the dissemination of his writings in New England. The cause of his death is unknown. In the administration of his estate in January 1663 mention is made of a second wife, Mary, and a son, Samuel. Samuel Nalton followed his father into the ministry, though he did so as a conformist, and was appointed as a perpetual curate at St Mary, Hampstead, in Middlesex, on 4 May 1678.   ROGER N. McDERMOTT

Sources *Calamy rev.*, 360–61 · T. Horton, *Rich treasure in earthen vessels* (1663) · Venn, *Alum. Cant.*, 1/3.232 · G. Hennessy, *Novum repertorium ecclesiasticum parochiale Londinense, or, London diocesan clergy succession from the earliest time to the year 1898* (1898) · [W. Orme], *The practical works of the late reverend and pious Mr Richard Baxter*, 1 (1707), 243–4 · BL, Add. MS 70007, fols. 2–3 · administration, PRO, PROB 6/38
Likenesses J. Chantry, line engraving, BM, NPG; repro. in J. Nalton, *Twenty sermons preached upon several texts* (1677)

Namatjira, Albert [*formerly* Elea] (**1902–1959**), Aboriginal artist, was born on 28 July 1902 at the Lutheran mission of Hermannsburg (later Ntaria), Northern Territory, Australia, the second of the three children of Namatjira (1880–1956) and his wife, Ljukuta (1881–1934), and given the name Elea. His parents, both Western Arrernte Aboriginal people, arrived at the mission in 1902 seeking refuge from the devastating impact of European colonization. In 1905 they were received into the church: Albert and his father (who took the name Jonathon) were baptized, and his mother was blessed and received the name Emilie.

Albert Namatjira attended the Hermannsburg mission school, living separately from his parents in a boys' dormitory in accordance with mission practice. At the age of thirteen he spent six months in the bush, during which time he underwent initiation. He left the mission again when he was eighteen to marry Ilkalita, a Kukatja woman. The family returned to Hermannsburg in 1923 and Ilkalita (1903–1974) was baptized Rubina. Eight of their children survived infancy: three daughters, Maisie, Hazel, and Martha, and five sons, Enos, Oscar, Ewald, Keith, and Maurice—all of whom became painters.

An enterprising and creative individual who took advantage of every available opportunity, Namatjira trained as a blacksmith and carpenter and worked as a stockman and cameleer at Hermannsburg and on nearby pastoral stations. From the late 1920s his finely crafted mulga wood plaques and boomerangs decorated in poker-work, black ink, and paint sold in the mission shop. Among the many visitors to Hermannsburg were two artists from Victoria, Rex Battarbee and John Gardner. Fascinated by an exhibition of their work in the schoolroom at Hermannsburg in 1934, Namatjira expressed interest in learning to paint, announcing 'I can do that too' (Henson, 75). With tuition from Battarbee acquired during two month-long excursions in 1936, Namatjira began to paint—as an expression of his Aboriginal identity and a means of achieving economic independence. In 1935 his watercolours were displayed at a Lutheran conference at Nuriootpa, South Australia, and in 1938 Namatjira held his first solo exhibition at the Fine Art Society Gallery in Melbourne. In the post-war period he exhibited regularly and with great success throughout Australia in solo exhibitions and with other members of the Hermannsburg school he founded. Through his pioneering efforts Namatjira forged a new, contemporary expression for Aboriginal art, while he himself became an important role model for a future generation of Aboriginal artists.

In the following decades Namatjira achieved national and international prominence. In 1944 he became the first Aboriginal person included in *Who's who in Australia* and the subject of the first monograph devoted to an Aboriginal artist. He subsequently starred in the film *Namatjira the Painter* (1947). During successive royal visits he was presented to the duke and duchess of Gloucester (1946) and Queen Elizabeth (1954). Honours accrued: Namatjira was awarded Queen Elizabeth II's Coronation Medal (1953) and elected an honorary member of the Royal Art Society of New South Wales (1955). William Dargie's striking portrait, which won the Archibald prize in 1956, conveys both Namatjira's powerful physical presence and his proud and dignified manner.

Namatjira's watercolour landscapes achieved widespread popularity among white Australians, for whom the landscape represented an important symbol of national identity, but they were overlooked or denigrated by art institutions. To many, his use of Western techniques and the pictorial conventions of the landscape genre appeared derivative and conservative. In effect his work was misinterpreted as a symbol of assimilation and a sign of colonial domination. More recently his reputation has undergone considerable revision: his watercolours are now generally viewed as reaffirming and reclaiming his ancestral connections to country. In the words of the Yirrkala elder and political leader Galarrwuy Yunupingu, Namatjira 'showed to the rest of the world the living title held by his people to the lands they had been on for thousands of years' (Yunupingu, 66). Redressing earlier neglect, Namatjira is now represented in the collection of the National Gallery of Australia in Canberra and in all state galleries.

Namatjira's achievements highlighted the gap between the reality and rhetoric of assimilation policies. Controversies surrounded his financial situation and attempts by the mission and government agencies to maintain control over the sale and marketing of his work and that of other members of the Hermannsburg school. In 1951 he was prevented from building a house on land he had purchased in Alice Springs. The citizenship granted to him in 1957 heightened growing tension and directly impacted on the tragic events surrounding his death. Exemption from the restrictions imposed on other 'full blood' Aborigines gave Namatjira access to alcohol, which he shared with members of his family in accordance with customary law. In 1958 he was charged with supplying alcohol to the artist Henoch Raberaba and sentenced to six months' imprisonment with labour. A nationwide protest resulted in two appeals, which reduced his sentence to three months. Eventually Namatjira served two months in open detention at Papunya settlement from March to May 1959. Taken ill while living at Papunya, he died of heart failure at the Alice Springs Hospital on 8 August 1959. He was buried with a Lutheran service on 9 August at the Alice Springs cemetery. As a gesture of respect, in 1994 his granddaughter Elaine, working in collaboration with women from the Hermannsburg Potters, produced a terracotta mural for his gravestone.

SYLVIA KLEINERT

Sources J. Hardy, J. V. S. Megaw, and M. R. Megaw, eds., *The heritage of Namatjira: the watercolourists of central Australia* (1992) · B. Henson, *A straight-out man: F. W. Albrecht and the central Australian Aborigines* (1994) · C. P. Mountford, *The art of Albert Namatjira* (1944) · G. Yunupingu, 'The black/white conflict', *Aratjara: art of the first Australians*, ed. B. Lüthi and G. Lee (1987), 64–6 · R. Battarbee, *Modern Australian Aboriginal art* (1951) · *The heritage of Namatjira* (1991) [Australian Exhibitions Touring Agency] · J. D. Batty, *Namatjira: wanderer between two worlds* (1963) · Lutheran Archives, North Adelaide, South Australia · J. Morton, 'Country, people, art', *The heritage of Namatjira*, ed. J. Hardy, J. V. S. Megaw, and M. R. Megaw (1992), 23–62 · Northern Territory Archives, Darwin · Finke River Mission, Alice Springs, Northern Territory

Archives FILM ScreenSound Archives, Canberra, Australia

Likenesses A. Poignant, double portrait, photograph, 1946 (with his wife Rubina), Axel Poignant Archives · A. H. Cook, oils, 1954, repro. in N. Amadio, ed., *Albert Namatjira* (1986) · W. Dargie, oils, 1956, Queensland Art Gallery, Brisbane, Australia · R. Campbell, portrait, repro. in Batty, *Namatjira*

Namier, Sir Lewis Bernstein (1888–1960), historian, was born on 27 June 1888 at Wola Okrzejska in Russian Poland. According to family testimony the baby was presumed

Sir Lewis Bernstein Namier (1888–1960), by Bassano

dead and revived only at the last minute. His antecedents and life were complex. His parents had just moved from Warsaw to a family estate at Wola Okrzejska; when he was two they moved again, to Kobylowloki in Austrian Poland, and when he was six to Nowosiolka Skalacka. Of gentry stock, his family were Polonized Jews, who had embraced Catholicism. His father, Joseph Bernsztajn vel Niemirowski (d. 1922), was a lawyer, descended from distinguished Talmudic scholars; his mother was Anne, daughter of Maurice Theodor Sommersztajn, owner of several Galician estates. The peasantry in Galicia, for whom Namier developed great respect, were Ruthenian or Ukrainian, and adhered to the Orthodox church. As Jews, his family had been forced to change their name, and Namier subsequently changed his twice more. Many commentators have seen in Namier 'a search for identity' (Winkler, 2). The biography by his second wife gives a vivid account of his childhood, much of it dictated to her in his last months. Namier grew up with two powerful antipathies—towards the Austrian (German) authorities, and towards Jews who tried to hide their origins by assimilating with the countries in which they found themselves.

Education It took Namier time to find a congenial habitat. He was soon on bad terms with his father, yet Namier could expect to inherit the country estate purchased at Koszylowce, south of Lwów (Lemberg), in 1906. In that year he began to study law at Lwów University, but was driven away by antisemitic jeers. He transferred to Lausanne, where he could get help for the medical problems which plagued him all his life, but he soon pined for wider horizons. With Paris vetoed by his father, Namier arrived in London in 1907, enlisted at the London School of Economics to study economics, joined the Fabian Society, and was soon persuaded that Oxford was his natural home and history his proper study. In October 1908 he arrived at Balliol, an exotic young man, unmistakably Jewish, with a heavy accent, but with a reputation for brilliance.

At Balliol Namier, known as Bernstein, did well and decided that England would be his country. In 1910 he changed his name by deed poll to Naymier, and in 1913, to Anglicize it more, to Namier. He gained a first in modern history in 1911, but in November 1911 failed to obtain a fellowship at All Souls. A. F. Pollard, an examiner, wrote that

Namier had been 'the best man by far in sheer intellect', but that 'the Warden and majority of Fellows shied at his race' (Namier, 101). To augment the allowance from his father he began writing for newspapers, drawing on his knowledge of eastern Europe. Fearing lest his son should become a perpetual student, Namier's father urged him to move to America and join Louis Hammerling, a fellow Galician Jew, president of the Foreign Language Press. Namier sailed for New York in May 1913 and used the opportunity to read and consult manuscripts in the United States. According to Berlin, Hammerling found Namier's increasingly outspoken dislike of Germany unacceptable, and the arrangement was terminated (Berlin, 224). Namier thought once more of taking up law, but returned to England in just under a year.

The First World War and after: European nationalities and Zionism Soon after his return, war broke out; Namier volunteered at once for the Royal Flying Corps but was rejected for poor eyesight. He then managed to join the Royal Fusiliers but within five months was transferred to help the war effort more profitably as an expert adviser in the Foreign Office. He began a small book, *Germany and Eastern Europe*, published in 1915, with a friendly preface by H. A. L. Fisher. Namier's influence in the political intelligence department was exerted in favour of the subject nations of the Austro-Hungarian empire. In 1917 he published two short pamphlets, *The Case of Bohemia* and *The Czecho-Slovaks: an Oppressed Nationality*. He felt great sympathy for the Ukrainian nationalists. His support for the Poles was more guarded, since he suspected that, finding themselves for once on the winning side, they were likely to embrace wild expansionism. To Isaiah Berlin Namier subsequently, with characteristic extravagance, claimed to have been personally responsible for the breakup of the Habsburg empire in 1918: 'I may say', he confided, 'that I pulled it to pieces with my own hands' (Berlin, 224).

The year 1919 found Namier, like many other young men, trying to rebuild his life. The estate at Koszylowce had been looted and though restored to his family was now part of Poland: worse, when his father died in 1922 Namier discovered that he had been disinherited in favour of his sister: he never saw his mother or sister again. To add to his problems, he had embarked in January 1917 on marriage with Clara Edeleff-Poniatowska (*d.* 1945), a widow who seemed curiously vague about her former life, and proved highly strung and depressive. Balliol found Namier a temporary lectureship in April 1920. He contributed a chapter on the downfall of the Austro-Hungarian empire to Harold Temperley's official *Peace Conference in Paris* (1921), subsequently reprinted in *Vanished Supremacies* (1958). But though he flung himself into tutorial work, there was little time for his book on the origins of the American War of Independence and the lectureship was not renewed in 1921. Instead, Namier took up an offer of a well-paid job in Vienna and Prague representing a Lancashire cotton firm, with the advantage that he could send articles to the *Manchester Guardian* and other papers. He hoped to save enough to support his own historical research. The first outcome was that Clara left him,

ostensibly to go off with another man. A. J. P. Taylor, a young colleague of Namier's at Manchester in the 1930s, met her towards the end of her life, and thought her 'a bewitching character', but was not surprised that she had found Namier heavy and that he had found her exasperating (Taylor, 167–8). Namier supplied Clara's place by forming an attachment to another difficult woman, Marie Beer, whom he had first met when he was sixteen.

It is not clear whether the cotton firm benefited much from Namier's services in Prague, nor, indeed, what those services were. He made many acquaintances, including Beneš, sent dispatches home and, through playing the stock exchange, amassed a modest competence. His stay on the continent revived an interest in Zionism, first kindled by meeting Chaim Weizmann, president of the World Zionist Organization from 1920. Namier's attitude towards the Jewish question was almost purely political, and derived from his understanding of nationhood. If Czechs and Poles could have their own nation state, why could not Jews? They would then not have to submit to the servility of assimilation. He had little interest in any religion, and scant respect for priests or rabbis. The task of Zionists was to hold successive British governments to the pledge given in the Balfour declaration of 1917 for a national home in Palestine. Namier greatly valued his friendship with Blanche Dugdale (Baffy), a niece of Balfour, which not only gave him entrée to country houses, but offered a link, however tenuous, with Balfour himself, still with some influence as president of the council.

Eighteenth-century politics After three years Namier returned to London, engaged a secretary, and resumed work on his American book. He existed partly on capital, partly on loans from friends, and partly on grants from the Rhodes trustees. Baffy arranged for him to meet Harold Macmillan, another Balliol man, Conservative MP, and partner in the publishing house which agreed to take his book. *The Structure of Politics at the Accession of George III* came out in January 1929 and was followed in 1930 by *England in the Age of the American Revolution*.

The reception of these books was not unanimous. Sir Richard Lodge in *History* was dismissive. The Newcastle papers had long been known as a 'dust-heap', from which Namier had rescued some interesting details, but the title of the first book was misleading and over-ambitious (*History*, 14, 1930, 269); of the second, Lodge noted that much time had been employed 'clearing the site' and that the story had only reached December 1762: 'it is not easy to forecast—probably Mr Namier himself cannot do so— what will be the ultimate proportions of this model' (*History*, 16, 1930, 173). But D. H. Winstanley wrote that 'no previous writer has ever made so thorough and gallant an attempt to discover the actual workings of the political system of the eighteenth century' (*EngHR*, 44, 1929, 657). The review which had the most dramatic consequences was by G. M. Trevelyan, doyen of those whig historians for whom Namier had so little respect. Trevelyan wrote of the 'Namier way': 'Mr. Namier is a new factor in the historical world' (Trevelyan, 238). Reading the review at tea, Professor Jacob at Manchester telegraphed at once to offer

Namier the vacant chair of modern history. He was always grateful to Trevelyan and, characteristically, claimed to have repaid his debt by refusing ever to review Trevelyan's books.

Manchester professor Manchester rescued Namier from several predicaments. In spring 1929 he had written that he expected to devote the rest of his life to the Zionist cause, and Weizmann had persuaded him to take on the political secretaryship of the Zionist Organization. But the movement was convulsed by political and financial problems, Namier was disliked by Orthodox Jews, and the salary proposed was inadequate. Manchester, when he took up post in October 1931, treated him with great consideration. Though he took teaching and examining seriously, he did little administration. He retained his house in London, returning there most weekends, and during the week stayed outside Manchester. Nevertheless, the promised continuation of his investigation into the origins of the American War of Independence did not appear. Different explanations have been offered. Taylor thought that Namier became easily bored. John Brooke, a disciple after the war, believed that his work was inhibited by nihilistic gloom. Structural analysis, as Lodge had hinted, made extremely heavy demands on the practitioner. Namier was far from inactive, continuing his work for Zionism, reviewing widely (and selling the copies), and submitting articles. His way of life, including so much travelling and personal secretarial assistance, was expensive, and he continued to give financial help to both Marie and Clara. Scholarly work, as he frequently complained, did not pay well. The Ford lectures, delivered at Oxford on the cabinet in 1933–4, were not published. The only scholarly publication before the Second World War was a very slim volume in 1937 correcting the errors in Sir John Fortescue's first volume of the correspondence of George III. Even that was based on a review in the *Nation and Athenaeum* in 1927 (Namier, 199). Yet it was, in some ways, his most important service to historical scholarship, helping to raise the standard of editing throughout the profession, even if many people thought Namier's strictures severe.

The outbreak of war found Namier preparing for a sabbatical year. Instead he was released by the university to act as liaison officer between the Jewish Agency and the government and spent the rest of the war in London. Much of his energy was devoted to attempting to persuade the government to authorize an independent Jewish fighting force: many ministers were afraid that it would be used to seize power in Palestine after the war, and demurred. Zionists quarrelled among themselves, and Isaiah Berlin's bleak judgement was that politically Namier was 'as great a liability as an asset' (Berlin, 223).

Peak of career: honours, second marriage, and *History of Parliament* The eight years between the end of the war and Namier's retirement from Manchester in 1953 saw his reputation at its height. His two eighteenth-century books were being taken on board by his fellow historians, rather than walked round as in pre-war days, and a stream of books of essays made his name known to a far wider public, as both sage and historian—*Conflicts* (1942), *Facing East* (1947), *Diplomatic Prelude* (1948), *Europe in Decay* (1950), *In the Nazi Era* (1952), and *Avenues of History* (1952). The post-war world, recovering from fascism yet still afflicted by communism, was peculiarly receptive to his distaste for ideology: 'what shams and disasters political ideologies are apt to be' ('Human nature in politics', *Personalities and Powers*, 1955, 7). Recognition came at last and in abundance. The British Academy elected him a fellow in 1944. His Raleigh lecture, '1848: the revolution of the intellectuals' (1944), was followed by the Waynflete lectures on the German problem (1946–7); the Creighton lecture, 'Basic factors in nineteenth-century European history' (1952); the Romanes lecture, 'Monarchy and the party system' (1952); the Royal Academy of Arts lecture, 'George III: a study in personality' (1953); and the Enid Muir lecture at Newcastle, 'Country gentlemen in politics' (1954). Balliol elected him an honorary fellow in 1948 and he was knighted in 1952. Durham's honorary DLitt in 1952 was followed by honorary degrees from Oxford and Cambridge.

Namier brooded that he had been passed over for chairs at Oxford, Cambridge, or London but even his private life took a turn for the better. Clara had died in 1945, and in 1947 he married a Russian émigrée, Julia de Beausobre, *née* Kazarina (1893–1977), a widow, who devoted herself to his welfare and offered unstinted admiration. His conversion to Anglicanism, undertaken for his marriage, caused a painful breach with Weizmann who regarded it as an act of flagrant apostasy.

As soon as he retired, Namier plunged into editing the modern volumes of the *History of Parliament*, taking particular responsibility for the period 1754–90. The project had got off to a false start in the 1930s when Josiah Wedgwood's volumes on the fifteenth century had been badly received (*EngHR*, 53, 1938, 503–6). It was revived in 1951 and Namier settled down at the Institute of Historical Research with a small band of assistants to prepare the 1964 biographies and 314 accounts of the constituencies, grinding work cheered by tea-time reminiscing with his friend and fellow editor Romney Sedgwick. His zeal exposed him to further rebuffs when visits to Oxford and Cambridge revealed among fellow historians a marked lack of enthusiasm to join his great collective endeavour. He remained at his desk, conscious that his energy was ebbing fast, until the night before his death at St Mary's Hospital, London, on 19 August 1960. He was cremated at Golders Green on 24 August.

Reputation and assessment Namier's achievements were greatly praised during his lifetime and unduly disparaged subsequently. On his chosen ground, the accession of George III, he made important and probably irreversible corrections to the traditional whiggish account. The king was cleared of the charge that he was a tyrant presiding over an orgy of corruption, though at the cost of portraying him as a naïve and immature youth. Later on Namier was not so much repudiated as outflanked, by critics who pointed to the narrowness of his concerns, and his lack of interest in anything but political history. The technique of structural analysis, with which his name was inextricably linked as 'Namierism', offered, in his view, an escape from voluminous narrative. Though the attacks upon it, particularly by Herbert Butterfield in *George III and the Historians* (1957), may seem hysterical, its limitations are very evident. There are great swathes of history where, for lack of evidence, structural analysis can hardly be applied. Even where it can, there is no guarantee that it will, in itself, generate interesting and important questions. It is by no means apparent how much the 135 pages devoted by Namier in *England* to the relationship between Newcastle and Bute illuminate the problem of the American War of Independence.

As Brooke pointed out, Namier's output was but 'a mere fragment' of what he had planned. His investigation of America was abandoned. The essays on modern European diplomacy, though historical journalism of a high order, were no substitute for the volume of European history he hoped to write. Both the *History of Parliament* (1964) and the biography *Charles Townshend* (1968) were left to Brooke to finish. Even in his best work, such as the *Revolution of the Intellectuals*, one is conscious of a lack of control. Explanations are not hard to find. Namier suffered from chronic ill health, including bad eyesight, increasing deafness, a damaged right hand, breathing difficulties, debilitating insomnia, and, at times, fear of insanity. In the face of these afflictions, his resilience was heroic.

To the world Namier was a hard, combative man; yet he was vulnerable and saw himself ringed by enemies. There are innumerable testimonies, of which those by Berlin and Toynbee are the most charitable, to his awesome loquacity, which could empty any common room. He found life hard. His childhood, he told Lady Namier, had been 'a mental register of unforgettable rebuffs', and in old age an encounter at Manchester with a surly ticket-inspector was enough to set him brooding on the collapse of civilized values (Namier, 16, 300–01). Taylor found him 'a strange mixture of greatness and helplessness' (Taylor, 112), and Trevelyan, who had helped him to his chair, muttered, in his terse way, 'Great research worker, no historian' (Plumb, 18).   JOHN CANNON

Sources L. Colley, *Namier* (1989) · J. A. Cannon, ed., *The historian at work* (1980) · J. A. Cannon and others, eds., *The Blackwell dictionary of historians* (1988) · J. Namier, *Lewis Namier: a biography* (1971) · I. Berlin, *A century of conflict: essays for A. J. P. Taylor*, ed. M. Gilbert (1966) · A. J. P. Taylor, *A personal history* (1983) · P. B. M. Blaas, *Continuity and anachronism: parliamentary and constitutional development in whig historiography and the anti-whig reaction between 1890 and 1930* (1978) · H. Butterfield, *George III and the historians* (1957) · A. J. Toynbee, *Acquaintances* (1967) · J. T. Talmon, *The unique and the universal* (1965), 296–311 · J. H. Plumb, *The making of an historian* (1988) · J. R. Hale, *The evolution of British historiography: from Bacon to Namier* (1967) · W. Laqueur, *A history of Zionism* (1972) · J. Brooke, 'Namier and Namierism', *Studies in the philosophy of history*, ed. G. H. Nadel (1965) · N. Rose, *Lewis Namier and Zionism* (1980) · J. P. Kenyon, *The history men* (1983) · A. J. Toynbee, 'Lewis Namier, historian', *Encounter*, 16/1 (1961), 39–43 · J. Brooke, 'Namier and his critics', *Encounter*, 24/2 (1965), 47–9 · I. R. Christie, 'George III and the historians: thirty years on', *History*, new ser., 71 (1986), 205–21 · J. M. Price, 'Party, purpose and pattern: Sir Lewis Namier and his critics', *Journal of British Studies*, 1/1 (1961–2), 71–93 · H. C. Mansfield, 'Sir Lewis Namier considered', *Journal of British Studies*, 2/1 (1962–3), 28–55 · R. Walcott, '"Sir Lewis Namier considered" considered', *Journal of British Studies*, 3/2 (1963–4), 85–108 · H. C. Mansfield, 'Sir Lewis Namier again considered', *Journal of British Studies*, 3/2 (1963–4), 109–19 · L. S. Sutherland, 'Sir Lewis Namier', *PBA*, 48 (1962), 371–85 · H. R. Winkler, 'Sir Lewis Namier', *Journal of Modern History*, 35 (1963), 1–19 · W. R. Fryer, 'King George III, his political character and conduct: a new whig interpretation', *Renaissance and Modern Studies*, 6 (1962) · J. B. Owen, 'Professor Butterfield and the Namier school', *Cambridge Review*, 79/1932 (10 May 1958), 528–31 · H. Butterfield, 'George III and the Namier school', *Encounter*, 8/4 (1957), 70–76 · J. L. Cooper, 'Recollections and Namier', 'Lewis Namier: a biography', *Land, men and beliefs: studies in early-modern history* (1983), 251–5 · H. Butterfield, 'George III and the constitution', *History*, new ser., 43 (1958), 14–33 · C. Babington-Smith, *Julia de Beausobre: a Russian Christian in the West* (1983) · G. M. Trevelyan, 'Mr. Namier and the mid-eighteenth century', *Nation and the Athenaeum* (15 Nov 1930), 238 · D. Cannadine, *G. M. Trevelyan: a life in history* (1992) · *The Times* (22 Aug 1960) · *The Times* (21 Dec 1977)

Archives Bodl. Oxf., papers · Central Zionist Archives, Jerusalem, papers relating to Zionism · JRL, corresp. and papers, incl. material relating to the history of parliament and to his biography of Charles Townshend · Yale U., Farmington, Lewis Walpole Library, corresp. and papers | BL, corresp. with Society of Authors, Add. MS 63311 · Bodl. Oxf., corresp. with Society for Protection of Science and Learning · Bodl. Oxf., Sutherland papers · Central Zionist Archives, Jerusalem, political MSS, Babington–Smith papers · JRL, letters to the *Manchester Guardian* · King's Lond., Liddell Hart C., corresp. of him and his wife with Sir B. H. Liddell Hart | SOUND BL NSA, 'Not a place for happiness at all', T49299R TR2

Likenesses photograph, 1947, repro. in Sutherland, 'Sir Lewis Namier' · Bassano, photograph, NPG [*see illus.*] · photograph, repro. in Namier, *Lewis Namier* · photograph, repro. in *The Times* (22 Aug 1960)

Wealth at death £29,497 15*s.* 8*d.*: probate, 15 Dec 1960, *CGPLA Eng. & Wales*

Nance, Robert Morton (1873–1959), Cornish-language scholar, was born on 10 April 1873 at Clevedon Villa, The Walk, Tredegarville, Cardiff, the third of four children of William Edwin Nance (1857/8–1932), coal agent and colliery manager, of Padstow, and his wife, Jane Morton of St Ives. He trained at Cardiff Art School and under Hubert Herkomer in Bushey, Hertfordshire. He married Beatrice (b. 1871/2), an artist, the daughter of Bolton Michell, gentleman, on 3 December 1895, and set up an art school in Wales. They had a daughter, but Beatrice died in 1900. On 27 March 1906 Nance married another artist, (Annie) Maud (1872–1961), daughter of Richard Garnont Cawker, accountant, and moved to Nancledra in Cornwall, then, in 1914, to St Ives; they had two sons and another daughter.

Nance had a special interest in maritime subjects, earned a sound reputation in nautical history, illustrated books, and was a skilled model maker, with examples in various museums. He was a founder member of the Society for Nautical Research, and contributed over forty articles to the *Mariner's Mirror*. However, his principal claim to fame is his work in reviving Cornish, a native Celtic tongue not used as a spoken community language since the middle ages. The attempt was nostalgic and occasionally philologically questionable, but it was pursued with passion and meticulous attention to detail.

In Nancledra Nance wrote dialect plays, but, having begun to collect Cornish sea-words (his glossary was published posthumously), he took up Cornish proper. After the First World War, during which he was a volunteer, he set up, with the older scholar Henry Jenner (1848–1934), the first Old Cornwall Society in St Ives in 1920. By 1924 there were enough societies to constitute a federation, with Jenner as president, succeeded by Nance. Although Jenner was never really as convinced about reviving spoken Cornish, the two established in 1928 the Gorseth Kernow, a version of the bardic gathering attached to the eisteddfod. The gorsedd is of dubious historicity, but its harmless eighteenth-century Romanticism helped raise the profile of Cornish. Jenner was the first grand bard, and Nance, who took the bardic name 'Mordon' ('Sea-wave'), succeeded him in 1934, serving for twenty-five years. Nance was president of the Royal Institution of Cornwall in 1951–5 and held other such positions, but most publicly available images show him in old age in bardic robes, angular and visionary.

Jenner had published a grammar, but Nance reconstructed Cornish for revival purposes. Feeling that there was insufficient material in late Cornish in the eighteenth century, he returned to the (still somewhat limited) medieval literature, standardizing spellings and calling his language 'unified Cornish'. Deficient lexicon was remedied via Welsh and Breton, or with loans from Middle English or modern languages. The procedure was consistent enough, provided one accepted Nance's leap-frogging over late Cornish; not everyone did, sometimes dubbing his language 'Cornic' or 'Mordonnek' to distinguish it from genuine survivals. Nance's pronunciation system, based on phonetic representations of late Cornish and on the dialect of west Cornwall, was also criticized. But Nance was a popularizer and a pragmatist, providing a form in which the language *could* be learnt. In 1929 he produced *Cornish for All*, and in 1934 his first dictionary, with his close collaborator, A. S. D. Smith (1883–1950); the two provided unified Cornish versions of the medieval texts with translations, as well as original material.

One aim of the Old Cornwall societies was to 'gather the fragments'. Nance published more than two hundred articles in the journal *Old Cornwall* and elsewhere, many about Cornish domestic history, others linguistic, sometimes salvaging a coherent sentence of Cornish from a half-remembered scrap of apparent gibberish. In an original playlet (*An Balores*) written in 1932, Nance took the chough as emblem of the Cornish past, merging the bird with the spirit of King Arthur; a closing song contained the archetypally Romantic motto 'nyns-yu marow Myghtern Arthur' ('King Arthur is not dead').

The revival enjoyed success under Nance and Smith; unified Cornish was taught and examined, and works were written in it. After Nance's death its fortunes varied. School certificate examinations were abandoned in 1991 through shortage of numbers, although language boards in Cornwall maintain interest, as do groups in Australia and North America, and in 1999 parliament debated the status of the language within Europe. Against this, a proliferation of philologically more acceptable (but different) versions of unified Cornish, plus alternatives from different starting-points, led to severe linguistic schisms.

Nance translated some of the Book of Common Prayer for a service in 1933, but in a sense this was too late; the lack of a Cornish prayer book and Bible had contributed to the decline of spoken Cornish in Tudor times. Nor was the revived language strictly necessary, as in the case of modern Hebrew. However, contact with the past is always worthwhile; Nance was perhaps the last of the great Cornish antiquaries, and the continued awareness of the Cornish language is his legacy. Vigorous until the end (he was a non-smoking teetotaller and a vegetarian by conviction), Nance died in St Michael's Hospital, Hayle, on 27 May 1959, and was buried in Zennor church on 3 June; his memorial has a Cornish inscription.

BRIAN MURDOCH

Sources R. M. Nance, *A glossary of Cornish sea-words*, ed. P. A. S. Pool (Federation of Old Cornish Societies, 1963) [with Fuller's portrait and examples of his art-work, plus memoir and appreciation, pp. 9–23, and complete bibliography on maritime history and Cornish, pp. 195–204] · D. Williams, *An Baner Kernewek / The Cornish Banner*, 88 (May 1997), 3, 14–18 [incl. photographs; see also vol. 94 (1998), p. 11 for further photographs] · C. M. Raymont, *The early life of Robert Morton Nance* (1962) [with photographs] · R. M. Nance, 'Cornish beginnings', *Old Cornwall*, 5/9 (1958–61), 368–9 · P. A. S. Pool, 'Mordon remembered', *An Baner Kernewek / The Cornish Banner*, 64 (May 1991), 10–11 [incl. photograph] · A. S. D. Smith, *The story of the Cornish language*, (1947); 2nd rev. edn (1969), 13–14 · P. B. Ellis, *The Cornish language and its literature* (1974), 154–76, 193–202 [with photographs] · H. Miners, *Gorseth Kernow — the first 50 years* (1978) · K. J. George, 'The reforms of Cornish — revival of a Celtic language', *Language Reform*, 4 (1989), 355–75 [with photograph] · A. Hale, 'The Old Cornwall societies and the Cornish–Celtic revival', *Celtic History and Literature Review*, 2 (autumn 1998), 42–7 · G. Price, 'Modern Cornish in context', *Cornish Studies*, 2nd ser., 6 (1998), 187–93 · *The Times* (28 May 1959) · *The Times* (1 June 1959) · J. H. M. [J. H. Martin], *West Briton* (28 May 1959) · private information (2004) [Royal Institution of Cornwall; St Ives Museum; Institute of Cornish Studies; colleagues] · b. cert. · m. cert. (1 and 2)
Archives NMM, ship models · Royal Institution of Cornwall, Truro, Courtney Library · Sci. Mus., ship models
Likenesses L. J. Fuller, oils, 1960–61 (posthumous; after photographs), St Ives Museum, Wheal Dream, St Ives · photograph, repro. in K. George, ''The reforms of Cornish'' · photographs
Wealth at death £2757 4s. 10d.: probate, 8 July 1959, *CGPLA Eng. & Wales*

Nandakumar [Nuncomar], **maharaja** (1705?–1775), contender for office in Bengal, was born at Bhadravpur in Birbhum district in western Bengal, probably in 1705. He was the eldest son of a Brahman, Padmanav Roy (*d.* 1759), who had been an official under the nawab of Bengal, and his first wife. Nandakumar's career was an object lesson of the opportunities and the dangers for ambitious Indians in the new conditions brought about by British dominance in Bengal. He succeeded in rising to the highest office, but the savage political rivalries of the time were to cost him his life.

Nandakumar rose through the nawab's service to the office of *faujdar* or governor of the port of Hooghly. In 1757 he tacitly consented to the British attack on the French settlement at Chandernagore, which was within his jurisdiction. Then, or shortly afterwards, he formed a connection with Robert Clive, serving him as *munshi* or Persian secretary and coming to be known as the Black Colonel. In 1758 he was given the task of realizing the taxation from certain districts that had been assigned to the East India Company by Mir Jafar Ali Khan, who had been made nawab after Clive's victory at Plassey in 1757. In 1760, however, a change of nawab and a new British governor brought a sharp reverse for Nandakumar. He was accused of treasonable correspondence with the company's enemies and confined. From that time a lifelong enmity developed between him and Warren Hastings. Although other accusations were brought against him, when Mir Jafar was restored as nawab in 1763, he chose Nandakumar as his *diwan*, or administrator of his finances, and on the nawab's death in early 1765 entrusted his young son and successor to his care. The title of maharaja and the rank of a *mansabdar*, or commander of 5000 horse in the Mughal empire, were obtained for him. This was the highest point of Nandakumar's career. But from the British point of view he was far too independent and therefore too dangerous a figure to be tolerated in such a position. Further accusations were pressed against him and he was dismissed. From 1765 to 1772 Nandakumar was out of official countenance with the British.

Nandakumar was given the chance for a last comeback by the reappearance in Bengal in 1772 of his old enemy Warren Hastings, now the governor. Hastings came with orders to dismiss Muhammad Reza Khan, the man who had triumphed on Nandakumar's removal. In order to collect evidence against the khan, Hastings was permitted to use Nandakumar, which he did with misgivings. Relations remained distant and Nandakumar, feeling himself rebuffed, turned to the new councillors who arrived from Britain in 1774. As quarrels developed between them and Hastings, Nandakumar took the desperately hazardous step of giving Hastings's opponents evidence against the governor, in particular accusing him of receiving presents from the court at Murshidabad. In so doing he exposed himself to counter-attacks by his Indian and British enemies, including Hastings. The weapon that they used against him was an accusation of forgery going back to 1769. He was brought to trial before the British judges in the newly constituted supreme court at Calcutta on 8 June 1775 and found guilty. Under the terms of a British statute that made forgery a capital offence, he was sentenced to death and hanged at Cooly Bazaar, Calcutta, on 5 August 1775. He left his widow, the Rani Kshemankar, a son, and two daughters.

In his last petition Nandakumar wrote: 'They put me to death out of Enmity and Partiality to the Gentlemen who have betrayed their Trust' (Lambert, 63.127). The conclusion that he was the victim of a judicial murder is frequently drawn. There can be no doubt that the accusation was promoted by Nandakumar's enemies, and there is also clear evidence that Hastings was aware of it, if not actively involved. Sir Elijah Impey, the chief justice, was an old friend and later political ally of Hastings and this seems to support the possibility that the judges were also complicit. While few doubt that Nandakumar had committed a technical forgery, whether the British statute actually applied to India was questionable, and there

seemed to be good reasons for allowing an appeal to Britain rather than ordering an immediate execution. Impey felt that he could not do that. He later explained that the evidence of perjury during the trial and of pressure on Nandakumar's behalf was so glaring that a reprieve would have compromised the authority of the court. It is possible to accept his sincerity while rejecting his judgement.

Nandakumar aroused an unusual degree of distrust and fear among his contemporaries, both European and Indian. He has been much vilified in British historiography with little justification. In a harsh and dangerous world he took bold risks against enemies who showed as few scruples as he did, and he lost.   P. J. MARSHALL

Sources B.K. Roy, *The career and achievements of Maharaja Nanda Kumar, dewan of Bengal (1705–75)* (1969) · H. Beveridge, *The trial of Maharaja Nanda Kumar: narrative of a judicial murder* (1886) · L. S. Sutherland, 'New evidence on the Nandakuma trial', *EngHR*, 72 (1957), 438–65 · J. D. M. Derrett, 'Nandakumar's forgery', *EngHR*, 75 (1960), 223–38 · S. Lambert, ed., 'Minutes of evidence taken before a committee of the whole house', *House of Commons sessional papers of the eighteenth century*, 63 (1975) · *Calendar of Persian correspondence: being letters, referring mainly to affairs in Bengal, which passed between some of the company's servants and Indian rulers and notables*, 11 vols. (1911–69) · G. H. Khan, *A translation of the Sëir mutaqherin, or, View of modern times, being an history of India*, trans. M. Raymond, 3 vols. (1789) · A. M. Khan, *The transition in Bengal, 1756–1775: a study of Saiyid Muhammad Reza Khan* (1969) · H. E. Busteed, *Echoes from old Calcutta*, 4th edn (1908) · J. F. Stephen, *The story of Nuncomar and the impeachment of Sir Elijah Impey*, 2 vols. (1885) · N. K. Sinha, 'The trial of Maharaja Nandakumar', *Bengal Past and Present*, 78 (1959), 134–45

Archives National Archives of India, New Delhi, Persian corresp., calendar of Persian corresp.

Wealth at death 52 lakhs of rupees [£520,000] 'and full as much more in effects and other property in his possession': G. H. Khan, *Sëir mutaqherin*, 3.79

Nanfan, John (*d.* 1716), colonial governor, was the son of Bridges Nanfan (1632–1704) of Birtsmorton, Worcestershire, and his wife, Katherine Hastings (1619–1702). Nothing is known of his early years or education, but by 1697 he was resident in the colony of New York. There he found preference as a kinsman of Richard Coote, first earl of Bellomont, who was married to Nanfan's sister Catherine. Bellomont served as governor of the colony between 1698 and his death in 1701, upon which Nanfan became governor and commander-in-chief of New York.

As governor, Nanfan's principal goal was to maintain England's authority over New York. His most important contribution to the colony's security came with the Nanfan treaty of 1701, which he negotiated with the Five Nations of the Iroquois confederacy. In the treaty the Native Americans agreed to place their beaver-hunting grounds under the crown's protection, a move which Nanfan encouraged because it signified a shift in Iroquois allegiance to England and away from the French, who threatened the security of New York's borders. The English and the French competed for the friendship of the Five Nations and their valuable fur trade, and the treaty symbolized a growing rapprochement between the English and the Native Americans. Nanfan's determination to uphold England's interests is also apparent in his treatment of the Scottish colonists of Darien, who had defied England by attempting to found a Scots colony on the coast of Panama. The settlement failed spectacularly, and the colonists sailed north in great distress. When their ships arrived in New York harbour, Nanfan refused to grant them any supplies which might facilitate their return to Scotland, although he did give them sufficient provisions to fend off starvation.

Nanfan's brief tenure as governor came at a difficult time in New York politics, as the colony remained sharply polarized in the wake of the revolution of 1688 and the rebellion of the colonist Jacob Leisler and his supporters against royal authority. Although Leisler had been executed in 1691, his adherents and opponents continued to quarrel, and even in 1701 the colony's government was, in the words of prominent settler Robert Livingston, 'much out of frame, our parties being more divided I think than eleven years ago … the Councell, Assembly & indeed the whole Province [are] divided & in a foment' (Kierner, 37). As a newly appointed governor who seemed to have gained his place through connections rather than merit, Nanfan was unable to impose order upon the colony, and in 1702 he was recalled in favour of Lord Cornbury. Nanfan and his wife, Elizabeth, of whom nothing more is known, returned to England, where he died in 1716.

NATALIE ZACEK

Sources *History of Montgomery and Fulton counties, New York* (1878) · C. A. Kierner, *Traders and gentlefolk: the Livingstons of NY* (1992) · J. D. Goodfriend, *Before the melting pot* (1992) · P. U. Bonomi, *The Lord Cornbury scandal* (1996) · www.maximilian.f9.co.uk, 2 Sept 2002 **Archives** Hunt. L., letters to William Blathwayt · Pennsylvania State Archives, Harrisburg, corresp. with W. Penn

Nanfan, Sir Richard (1445–1507), diplomat and administrator, was the son of John Nanfan of Trethewell, Cornwall, and Birts Morton, Worcestershire, and of Jane, widow of Sir Renfrey Arundell of Lanherne, Cornwall. John Nanfan was a Beauchamp retainer who was appointed an esquire of the king's body and governor of the Channel Islands, and acted as a guardian of the lands of the earldom of Warwick (1436–50); the geographical context of his career—Cornwall, the midlands, service abroad—was later matched by his son's. However, although he was sheriff of Cornwall in 1479, Richard Nanfan's trajectory was redirected in 1483, perhaps under the influence of his Arundell in-laws, when he rebelled against Richard III. Following the battle of Bosworth he became under-sheriff—effectively sheriff—of Worcestershire, an important post, since his predecessor had been Sir Humphrey Stafford of Grafton, a die-hard Yorkist who rebelled in 1486. Almost all his appointments between 1485 and 1493 were to offices in the midlands. He was appointed steward of Tewkesbury for life, and also of Elmley Castle, Worcestershire; both these positions, and other offices and grants, linked him with people and places associated with Beauchamp and Neville power in the region. By 1493 he was working alongside members of the prince of Wales's council, based at Ludlow. Trusted by the Tudor regime, he continued to be appointed to sensitive areas. In Cornwall, for instance, he was granted former Warwick lands, and in 1503 became receiver-general for the duchy. He sat in the king's council in 1486, and in 1488 went to Spain to negotiate the marriage of Prince Arthur to Katherine of Aragon. Before he left, he was knighted by Henry VII in person.

Following the French campaign of 1492 Nanfan was appointed to a position of crucial importance to the security of the regime, that of deputy lieutenant of Calais under Giles, Lord Daubeney. In 1503 he served as lieutenant during a prolonged absence by Daubeney, a post he held with honour, notwithstanding the sort of temperament that brought criticism from Henry VII and a rancorous dispute with his son-in-law John Flamank and John's younger brother Bartholomew, garrison members, which led to scurrilous accusations of treason. Treason was, indeed, out of the question, and during his exchanges with his adversaries Nanfan said he would rather suffer death than surrender Calais. His period in Calais was extremely busy, and he became well known to officials in the Burgundian Netherlands and French Picardy. In 1499 he exchanged ratifications of an anti-Yorkist treaty with Riga, and in 1505 negotiated with the duke of Saxony a treaty whose implicit aim was the destruction of Richard de la Pole, the so-called 'White Rose'. He was an early patron of Thomas Wolsey (d. 1530), who became Nanfan's chaplain; Wolsey's biographer, George Cavendish, describes Nanfan in 1506 as old, worn out, and wishing only to retire to England. He may have gone back to Birts Morton, where he is commemorated on his mother's tomb, but his will ordered that he be buried in St Bartholomew's, Smithfield. He died on 1 January 1507. By his marriage to Margaret (d. 1510), daughter of John Baucombe of Barcombe, Sussex, he had at least two daughters, one of whom, Jocosa, or Joyce, married John Flamank. Sir Richard also fathered two bastards, John and William; John inherited his Birts Morton lands. His Cornish lands, lacking legitimate heirs, passed to James Erisey who, with Wolsey, was co-executor of Nanfan's will—in the eighteenth century this was interpreted as an act of gratitude by Sir Richard to the family that his father had followed to war, to the making of the Nanfans. The final word on Sir Richard is the exaggeration of an earlier generation. Considering Cornish military worthies in his *Survey of Cornwall* of 1602, Richard Carew placed Nanfan third, conceding precedence only to King Arthur and Sir Tristram.

IAN ARTHURSON

Sources *CPR, 1476–1509* · *A descriptive catalogue of ancient deeds in the Public Record Office*, 6 vols. (1890–1915) · J. C. Wedgwood and A. D. Holt, *History of parliament, 1: Biographies of the members of the Commons house, 1439–1509* (1936) · J. Gairdner, ed., *Letters and papers illustrative of the reigns of Richard III and Henry VII*, 2 vols., Rolls Series, 24 (1861–3) · C. G. Bayne and W. H. Dunham, eds., *Select cases in the council of Henry VII*, SeldS, 75 (1958) · *VCH Worcestershire*, vol. 3 · A. L. Rowse, *Tudor Cornwall: portrait of a society*, new edn (1969) · J. Polsue, *A complete parochial history of the county of Cornwall*, 4 vols. (1867–72) · G. Cavendish, *Life of Wolsey*, Folio Society (1962) · R. Carew, *The survey of Cornwall*, ed. F. E. Halliday (1953) · W. Busch, *King Henry VII,*

1485–1509, trans. A. M. Todd (1895) · B. André, *Historia regis Henrici septimi*, ed. J. Gairdner, Rolls Series, 10 (1858)
Archives Berks. RO, papers | BL, Talbot MSS, Add. MS 46455 · Cornwall RO, receiver general's accounts, 1503
Wealth at death £95 p.a. from eight manors and lands: *CIPM, Henry VII*, vol. 3, pp. 226–8

Nangle, Richard (*d.* 1541?), Church of Ireland bishop of Clonfert, is of undocumented background, but his early career was focused on Galway city and the adjoining lordship of Clanricarde. He first appears in the historical record in 1500 when, as an Augustinian friar, he persuaded Margaret (*née* Athy), wife of Stephen Lynch, several times mayor of Galway, to found a friary in Galway for his order. Nangle became a senior member of the friary and was identified as a professor of theology in 1517, an indication that he had been awarded a doctorate by then. He subsequently became the vicar provincial of the Augustinian order in Ireland, a promotion which reflects the very high regard in which he was held.

In 1536 Henry VIII appointed Nangle as the bishop of Clonfert, a diocese not far distant from Galway city, on the recommendation of Archbishop Browne of Dublin, who praised him as a well-learned man who could preach the word of God in the Irish language. Nangle was consecrated on 13 June 1537. Yet he failed to take possession of the see from Roland Burke, who had already been provided to Clonfert by Rome in 1534. The king's appointee was obliged to remain confined within Galway's city walls for fear of Bishop Burke and his accomplices. Henry VIII directed his viceroy, Lord Grey, to prosecute the papal bishop under the Statute of Provisors. However, Bishop Burke was the brother of the lord of Clanricarde and Grey decided that Clonfert was not worth the political cost of challenging one of Ireland's leading magnates. He is even alleged to have promised Burke a royal confirmation for the diocese.

Nangle abandoned the fruitless struggle for Clonfert and by early 1539 he was, in effect, the suffragan of George Browne, the first Reformation archbishop of Dublin. While the archbishop intended to preach wherever English was understood Nangle was to preach to Irish speakers. After Nangle's death, probably in 1541, Roland Burke was recognized as the bishop of Clonfert by Henry VIII.

HENRY A. JEFFERIES

Sources state papers of Ireland, Henry VIII, PRO · BL, Add. MS 4799, fol. 27v · J. Hardiman, *The history of the town and county of the town of Galway* (1820); repr. (1958) · *The whole works of Sir James Ware concerning Ireland*, ed. and trans. W. Harris, rev. edn, 1 (1764) · W. M. Brady, *The episcopal succession in England, Scotland, and Ireland, AD 1400 to 1875*, 1 (1876) · *The Irish fiants of the Tudor sovereigns*, 4 vols. (1994), vol. 1 · F. X. Martin, 'The Irish Augustinian reform movement in the fifteenth century', *Medieval studies presented to Aubrey Gwynn*, ed. J. A. Watt, J. B. Morrall, and F. X. Martin (1961), 230–64

Nanmor, Dafydd (*fl.* 1445–1490), poet, who came from Nanmor near Beddgelert in Snowdonia, is thought to have been a bardic pupil of Rhys Goch Eryri. He was exiled from his native region about 1453 on account of erotic poems which he addressed to a married woman known as Gwen o'r Ddôl; some of them have survived (although perhaps not the ones which prompted her husband to take legal action against the poet). The rest of his life seems to have been spent in south-west Wales, where his principal patrons were the Tywyn family from near Cardigan, for whom he composed poems over three generations, culminating, in his old age, with the famous poem of advice to the young Rhys ap Rhydderch. His eulogies are a melliffluous celebration of the civilization of the Welsh noble houses. One of his most popular poems is an elaborately metaphorical description of a girl's hair. Addressed to Llio Rhydderch, probably of the Gogerddan family of Cardiganshire, this is a clear example of the conventions of love poetry used for the purpose of eulogy. Dafydd was a virtuoso exponent of the bardic metres (his work includes an exemplary *awdl* using all twenty-four metres), and also displays considerable Latin learning. Fifty-three of his poems survive; the group in Peniarth MS 52 is thought to be in his own hand, though this is unproven.

Dafydd was a supporter of the Lancastrian cause, and addressed several poems of a prophetic nature to the Tudor family, beginning with one to the brothers Jasper and Edmund in 1453. He composed an elegy on Edmund's death in 1456, and sang to the infant Henry Tudor soon after his birth in January 1457, rightly seeing in him a future Lancastrian king. Given that Dafydd's latest poem can be dated *c.*1490, it is surprising that there is no reference in his work to the accession of Henry VII in 1485. Hywel Rheinallt composed an elegy on the death of Dafydd Nanmor, which he saw as *darfod y myfyrdod mawr* ('the end of the great meditation'), a comment that has been taken to refer to the profundity of Dafydd's social vision. Dafydd is said to have been buried at the Cistercian monastery at Whitland.

The poet **Rhys Nanmor** (*fl.* 1485–1513), once thought to have been Dafydd's son, was in fact probably his bardic pupil. Among his poems are a complex prophecy to Henry VII and an elegy on the death of his eldest son, Arthur, in 1502. The Dafydd Nanmor who was once thought to have flourished *c.*1400 is a figment of Iolo Morganwg's imagination.

DAFYDD JOHNSTON

Sources G. E. Ruddock, *Dafydd Nanmor* (1992) · *The poetical works of Dafydd Nanmor*, ed. T. Roberts and I. Williams (1923)
Archives NL Wales, Peniarth MS 52

Nanmor, Rhys (*fl.* 1485–1513). *See under* Nanmor, Dafydd (*fl.* 1445–1490).

Nantz, Frederic Coleman (*c.*1810–1844), actor and playwright, was born, according to his obituary in *The Era*, in Chester about 1810. As a young man he worked as a law clerk in London for a solicitor named Booth at Lincoln's Inn, where he and his fellow clerk David Prince Miller idled away the hours ranting in theatrical roles. In *The Life of a Showman* Miller recalls that Nantz 'was a very fine young man at this time, and although a great fop, had an excellent heart. Poor Fred and I, when our masters were from chambers, frequently *murdered* Brutus and Cassius, Young Norval, Glenalvon, etc.' (Miller, 1–2). In 1828 Nantz made his début as an actor at the Olympic Theatre, where his name appeared occasionally in the playbills until 1830, in roles such as Barnstaple in *The Pilot* and Justino in *The*

Gambler of Florence. He also wrote his first play, *The Brown Devil, or, Chi Chue Ali, the Charmed Pirate*, a nautical burletta founded on the ballad 'Poor Jack' by Charles Dibdin and performed at the Olympic in January 1830 and at the Garrick in 1831, and revived at the Standard in 1851. According to a colourful anecdote recorded in the Eyre manuscripts, in 1830 Nantz was acting with Brunton's company in Exeter when Edmund Kean suddenly appeared and offered to act that night as King Lear. Ordered by his manager to undertake the role of Gloucester, Nantz coolly picked up his hat and left the theatre, rather than play in support of the great Romantic actor at such short notice. During these same years a writer, presumably Nantz, contributed doggerel poems and a gothic tale under the byline F. C. N. to *The Censor*, an ebullient but short-lived theatrical journal edited by Gilbert Abbot à Beckett.

In 1832 Nantz's career got fully under way when R. W. Elliston secured him a position as a regular member of T. W. Manly's company on the Nottingham circuit, where his acting attracted occasional but uniformly favourable notice in the press. He played a wide repertory of melodramatic roles, such as Clifford in *The Hunchback* and the eponymous hero of *Pizarro*, and some classical roles as well, including Orlando to Ellen Tree's Rosalind in *As You Like It*. He wrote plays which were well received on the circuit, including *Dennis, or, The Gibbet Law of Halifax* (1833), which dramatized the life of a local folk hero who escaped execution for a crime of which he was falsely accused, and *St Ann's Well, or, 'Tis Ninety Years Since* (1833), based on the career of a celebrated Nottingham poacher. He remained with Manly until December 1835, when he moved to the Norwich circuit. There he became a popular favourite as the company's walking gentleman, noted for his exuberant performances and for the flamboyant scarlet playbills with which he advertised his benefit nights. In addition to dramatic roles, he displayed vocal talents as Count Almaviva in *The Barber of Seville* and as Massaroni in *The Brigand*, in which he sang 'Love's Ritornella'.

While with the Norwich company in 1837 Nantz published a ringing defence of the theatre, *An Actor's Vindication of his Profession*, written in response to an attack on the stage by the Revd John McCrea from the pulpit in King's Lynn. He also wrote *Pickwick, or, The Sayings and Doings of Sam Weller* (1837), one of the many imitations of Dickens's first novel, in which he once more exploited local colour by highlighting scenes set in Ipswich; acting in his own play, he delighted audiences with his impersonation of Alfred Jingle. For the rest of his career he made something of a speciality of Dickensian roles: he appeared as Mantalini in an adaptation of *Nicholas Nickleby* and Sikes in *Oliver Twist*, and offered *Barnaby Rudge* on his benefit night in Birmingham on 1 November 1841.

After Nantz's success on the Norwich circuit, his career stagnated for the next five years. In 1838–9 he acted for a season at the Theatre Royal, Bath, but the management of Woulds there ended in insolvency. He followed Woulds in 1839 to Swansea, where he danced a hornpipe on his benefit night, 7 October, as well as performing as Clifford in *The Hunchback*, as Merton in *The Silent Woman*, and as Henry

Styles, in love with Mary, in his own play, *Blue Eyed Mary*. He then joined the Birmingham company, but the routine importing of visiting stars there relegated him to supporting parts, an indignity which worsened in 1842 in Liverpool, where he not only found himself being cast in minor roles but also received poor notices in the press and had his salary reduced to half pay as Hammond, the manager, tried unsuccessfully to stave off bankruptcy. In June 1843 Nantz retreated to Birmingham, where he continued to perform until October of that year.

Finally, on 23 October 1843, Nantz reached the summit of his fame, when he secured a position at the Victoria Theatre, then managed by D. W. Osbaldiston and Eliza Vincent. He was given top billing, alongside Charles Freer, in playbills which were magniloquent, celebrating his 'immense' success in the 'great and glorious' production of *Alice Aukland, or, The Heart of an English Girl*. Later he received credit in the press for his part in introducing Shakespearian productions at the Victoria, and he played for two months to full houses in the role of Frank Danvers in *The Cross Roads of Life, or, The Scamps of London*. The *Theatrical Journal* praised him as 'a clever actor, [who] studies close, and cannot play any part, without deserving a due meed of praise' (11 May 1844), and noted that he was highly respected 'as well in his capacity as an actor as in private life' (28 Oct 1843). But no sooner had he attracted notice before a metropolitan audience than he was stricken with scarlet fever. He died suddenly in London on 6 May 1844, leaving a widowed mother who had been dependent on his income for support. He was unmarried. None of his plays was published, although handwritten copies of three of them—*The Brown Devil*, *Dennis*, and *Pickwick*—survive. Nantz was an actor of recognized ability, a playwright with a shrewd eye for audience appeal, and a colourful personality whose career epitomized the life of an actor in the heyday of melodrama.

PAUL SCHLICKE

Sources P. Schlicke, 'The life of a strolling player: Frederic Coleman Nantz, 1810–1844', *Theatre Annual*, 34 (1979), 5–24 • *The Era* (12 May 1844) • *Theatrical Journal* (18 May 1844) • *Norfolk Chronicle* (18 May 1844) • D. P. Miller, *The life of a showman* (1849)
Archives Birmingham Public Library | Suffolk RO, Ipswich, Eyre MSS

Naoroji, Dadabhai (1825–1917), politician, was born in Khadak, near Bombay, on 4 September 1825, the only son of Naoroji Palanji Dordi, a poor Parsi priest, and his wife, Manekbai. He was educated in Bombay at Elphinstone College, where he remained as a teacher and, with his appointment to the chair of mathematics and natural philosophy (1854), became the first Indian professor. He established a newspaper, *Rast Goftar*, in 1851; he was active in reform societies, being a founding member of the Bombay Association (1852).

A partner in Cama & Co., Naoroji opened an English branch in 1855, the first Indian firm to be established in England, and combined commerce with politics until 1881. He was professor of Gujarati at University College, London (1856–65). He persuaded Indian princes to fund

Dadabhai Naoroji (1825–1917), by unknown photographer

the East India Association (1866), which gave him a platform for his campaign to open the Indian Civil Service to Indians and for publicizing his 'drain theory', which presented British rule as a drain on the financial resources of India. The fullest account of this theory is in his *Poverty and Un-British Rule in India* (1901). The Maharaja Gaikwar of Baroda made him diwan in 1873 but Naoroji left after thirteen unhappy months. He served on the Bombay corporation (1875–6, 1881–5) and accepted nomination as Indian representative on the Bombay legislative council (1885–6). He was one of the founders of the Indian National Congress in 1885 and presided at the 1886 and 1893 sessions. He was also a member of its British committee.

An unsuccessful Liberal candidate for Holborn in 1886, Naoroji was adopted for Central Finsbury after a struggle within the constituency party (1888). He gained public sympathy after Lord Salisbury, the prime minister, doubted that 'a British constituency would elect a black man'. He was elected to the Commons by 2961 votes to 2956 in 1892, which brought him great popularity in India. Also in 1888, he established the Indian Political Agency—together with W. C. Bonnerjee and others—as a pressure group in Britain.

In the Commons he devoted himself to Indian affairs with an emphasis on finance and on opening the Indian Civil Service to Indians. He was assiduous, if rarely successful, in using questions to obtain information on Indian affairs. He lost his seat by 800 votes in the Conservative landslide of 1895. He served as a member of the Welby royal commission on Indian expenditure (1895–1900) but

he made an error in appearing as a witness before the other commissioners. He signed a minority report. In 1906 he stood for North Lambeth, where he split the Liberal vote and came third, standing as the candidate of the London Liberal and Radical Union. Naoroji was president of the twenty-second session of the Indian National Congress in 1906 when he tried, without great success, to heal the split between extremists and moderates. He retired in 1907 to Versova, near Bombay. Bombay University belatedly awarded him an honorary LLD in 1916.

At the age of eleven Naoroji married Gulbai, the seven-year-old daughter of Sorabji Shroff, a Parsi priest. She died in 1910. They had one son, who died in 1893, and two daughters. Naoroji died in Bombay on 30 June 1917.

DAVID LEWIS JONES, *rev.*

Sources A. M. Zaidi, ed., *The grand little man of India*, 2 vols. (1985–8) · R. P. Masani, *Dadabhai Naoroji* (1939) · R. P. Patwardhan, ed., *Dadabhai Naoroji correspondence* (1977–) · 'Royal commission on the administration of the expenditure of India', *Parl. papers* (1896), vol. 15, C. 8258; vol. 16, C. 8259 [first report]; (1900), 29.1, Cd 130; 29.553, Cd 131 [final report] · A. P. Kaminsky, *The India Office, 1880–1910* (1986)
Archives National Archives of India, New Delhi, corresp. and papers · Shastri Indo-Canadian Institute, Montreal, microfilm | BL OIOC, letters to William Digby, MS Eur. D 767 · CUL, corresp. with Lord Hardinge
Likenesses photograph, Hult. Arch. [*see illus.*]

Naorozji Rastamji (*fl.* 1724–1725). *See under* Indian visitors (*act. c.*1720–*c.*1810).

Napier, Sir Albert Edward Alexander (1881–1973), civil servant, was born in Kensington, London, on 4 September 1881, the youngest son of Robert Cornelius *Napier, first Baron Napier (1810–1890) of Magdala and Caryngton, field marshal, and his second wife, Mary Cecelia Smythe Scott CI (*d.* 1930). His career was inevitably overshadowed by that of his father, although the latter died when Albert was only eight. Albert pursued a different career path, marked by academic distinction. He was a king's scholar at Eton College and an exhibitioner at New College, Oxford, where he took a first in Greats (1904) and became Eldon law scholar (1906). He was called to the bar by the Inner Temple in 1909 but his practice did not flourish. By 1915 he was private secretary to the lord chancellor, and in the following year became deputy serjeant-at-arms in the House of Lords. On 29 August 1917 he married (Amy) Gladys (*d.* 1978), daughter of Field Marshal Sir George Stuart White; they had a daughter and a son (who was killed on war service in 1942).

Napier was assistant secretary in the Lord Chancellor's Office and deputy clerk of the crown in Chancery from 1919 until 1944 when he became permanent secretary to the lord chancellor and clerk of the crown in Chancery. He held both posts until 1954. Coming as he did between those powerful mandarins Claud Schuster and George Coldstream, Napier's contributions as permanent secretary have tended to be overlooked. To ignore his contributions is, however, unfair. Napier's period of office was one of dramatic change, which inevitably affected the courts and the judges. The Second World War itself put stress on all legal institutions. The landslide victory of Labour in the 1945 general election had a dual impact. The Rushcliffe report, produced by a committee of which Napier was secretary, and the ensuing legal aid scheme, meant that he was the midwife to civil legal aid. Meanwhile the government moved rapidly to reform the compensation system, including abolishing common employment and modifying contributory negligence. Napier had to act as intermediary between the competing interests.

At this period, the chief role of the Lord Chancellor's Office was regarded as protecting the judges from political attack. The left of the Labour Party distrusted the judges, a distrust which went back to the *Taff Vale* case and the general strike. The health minister, Aneurin Bevan, for instance, refused to have the judges involved in the National Health Service for fear of 'judicial sabotage' (Stevens, 78n.). Napier played an important part in keeping the judges 'out of politics' by emphasizing the objective nature of legal rules and the relatively narrow role played by the appeal courts. It was an attitude which was publicly underlined by the Labour lord chancellor, Lord Jowitt. When the Conservatives returned under Churchill in 1951, the same cover was provided by Lord Simonds. Indeed, Churchill's preference for Simonds over Somerville—in some ways a more obvious candidate—was attributed to Napier: Simonds had been a contemporary of Napier's at New College.

At the same time, in both administrations, Napier compensated for a defensive position in law and the courts by promoting the use of judges for the chairmanship of commissions and committees. The Labour government made extensive use of the judiciary not only to chair commissions into divorce, procedure, tax, and company law, but to investigate what was later to be called 'sleaze' and to arbitrate salaries in the new social services. While judges had been used in that way before, during Napier's time as permanent secretary, their use was significantly increased. It was also on Napier's watch that the size of the higher courts was increased, while a new Law Reform Committee was established. With the return of the Conservatives, Napier was thrust into the issue of how far the judges might be used in an effort to make the Monopolies and Restrictive Practices Commission more regulated by legal norms. Almost equally sensitive was the role Napier had to play as Churchill sought to increase judicial salaries, something the judges had sought unsuccessfully from the Attlee administration.

Napier was not himself, like Muir Mackenzie, an instigator of reform, although over the years he made the county court his especial responsibility. There was much of the Victorian about him; he was open to ideas, no matter how radical. Yet his was more of the responsive than a proactive frame of mind. Napier became a CB in 1922, KCB in 1945, a QC in 1947, and KCVO in 1954. He became a bencher of the Inner Temple in 1949. He died on 18 July 1973.   ROBERT STEVENS

Sources R. F. V. Heuston, *Lives of the lord chancellors, 1940–1970* (1987) · R. Stevens, *The independence of the judiciary: the view from the lord chancellor's office* (1993) · PRO, lord chancellor's office MSS · *The Times* (20 July 1973) · *WWW, 1971–80* · Burke, *Peerage* (1999)
Wealth at death £34,124: probate, 29 Aug 1973, *CGPLA Eng. & Wales*

Napier, Sir Alexander, of Merchiston (d. 1473/4), administrator and diplomat, was the eldest son of Alexander Napier, provost of Edinburgh in 1438. His father acquired the lands of Nether Merchiston, Edinburghshire, as security for a loan to James I. This was never repaid and the Napiers retained Merchiston until 1647. Alexander Napier the elder was one of the Scottish commissioners who went to Newcastle in August 1451 to arrange a truce with England and thereafter had a safe conduct to visit Canterbury. He died *c*.1454.

Alexander Napier the younger acquired a rent charge on property in Edinburgh in 1432. By 1439 he was in the service of Queen Joan, widow of James I, being wounded when she and her second husband were seized by Sir Alexander Livingston and his accomplices at Stirling Castle. On 7 March 1450, after the fall of the Livingstons, James II rewarded Napier with the lands of Philde, Perthshire, forfeited by Livingston's son. In 1456 Napier acquired Over Merchiston, where he may have built the existing tower house; his other acquisitions included the Poultrylands in Dean, near Edinburgh. On 24 September 1449 James II appointed him to the office of comptroller, previously occupied by Robert Livingston. He held it until August 1450, and again for short periods in 1450–51, 1453, and 1456. As comptroller he received the revenues from the crown lands and customs, which were applied to financing the royal household. Napier had to cover any shortfall in these revenues. In 1452 crown lands in Fife were pledged to him for £1000 Scots owing by the king, but these were redeemed by 1454. During the earl of Douglas's rebellion in 1452 Napier was the king's master of work at the siege of Hatton, Edinburghshire. He was provost of Edinburgh in 1453–5 and 1457 and custumar of its port between 1450 and 1457. At the parliament of March 1458 he was appointed to the session and to the committee 'to commone and provyde upon the mater of the mone' (Thomson, 2.48). While in England in May 1459 he received a safe conduct from Henry VI to go to Scotland and return at pleasure. He became comptroller again in June 1460, shortly before James II's death.

Napier was knighted in 1460 or 1461, possibly at James III's coronation. He ceased to be comptroller on 7 July 1461, when he owed money to the king for which an annuity was still chargeable on his property in Edinburgh as late as 1503. Thereafter his official career was divided mainly between diplomacy and parliament. On 24 September 1461, as admiral-depute of Scotland, he was granted a safe conduct to go to the English court with other Scottish ambassadors, and he returned to England in 1464. A commission of 24 February 1465 appointed him one of the searchers of the port of Leith to prevent the export of gold and silver. He represented Edinburgh in five parliaments (1463, 1464, 1469, 1471, and 1473) and was provost again from 1469 to 1471. In January 1468 he was chosen by parliament to retour (value) the rents of barons in the shire of Edinburgh and to modify and receive a tax. Although it has been said that he was sent to Denmark to negotiate James III's marriage, he was not in fact one of the ambassadors named by James on 28 July 1468. But he served on the committee of the articles in the parliaments of 1469 and 1471, when he was among the commissioners given power to determine all matters for the welfare of the king and the common good of the realm. In 1472 he was in Bruges, taking up 'finance' and making purchases for the king. Following the birth of an heir to the throne (the future James IV) on 17 March 1473, Napier was involved, in the absence of the treasurer, in making arrangements for James III and his queen to go on a pilgrimage to the shrine of St Ninian at Whithorn. In May 1473 James sent him on a special embassy to the duke of Burgundy with secret instructions relating to the king's claim, through his mother, to the duchy of Gueldres. On his return parliament appointed him to a committee for 'searching the money'. He also held the office of master of the king's household, being so designated in a document signed by James III on 24 October 1473. Napier was still alive on 16 November 1473, but died some time before 15 February 1474, when his son was infeft as his heir in Poultrylands. He was probably buried in St Giles's Church, Edinburgh.

Napier married Elizabeth Lauder before 9 March 1451 and they had four children: John, Henry, Alexander, and Janet. The eldest son was known as John Napier of Rusky following his marriage about 1455 to Elizabeth Menteith, sister and coheir of Patrick Menteith and daughter of Murdoch Menteith of Rusky. In November 1473 Elizabeth was served as heir of her great-grandfather, Duncan Stewart, earl of Lennox (d. 1425), in one fourth of the earldom of Lennox, which she renounced in 1490 in favour of John Stewart (d. 1495). On 26 August 1461 Henry VI of England, then in exile in Edinburgh, granted John Napier a pension for his past and future services. He was provost of Edinburgh (1471, 1484) and its commissioner to parliament (1471, 1483, and 1484). He died in or about December 1487 and his wife died between 1507 and January 1510. They were the ancestors of John Napier (d. 1617), the inventor of logarithms.   ATHOL MURRAY

Sources Scots peerage, vol. 6 · M. Napier, Memoirs of John Napier of Merchiston, his lineage, life, and times, with a history of the invention of logarithms (1834) · M. D. Young, ed., The parliaments of Scotland: burgh and shire commissioners, 2 (1993) · G. Burnett and others, eds., The exchequer rolls of Scotland, 5–8 (1882–5) · J. M. Thomson and others, eds., Registrum magni sigilli regum Scotorum / The register of the great seal of Scotland, 11 vols. (1882–1914), vol. 2 · A. L. Murray, 'The comptroller, 1425–1488', SHR, 52 (1973), 1–29 · CDS, vol. 4 · H. Armet, 'The tower of Merchiston', Book of the Old Edinburgh Club, 31 (1962), 1–12 · T. Dickson, ed., Compota thesaurariorum regum Scotorum / Accounts of the lord high treasurer of Scotland, 1 (1877) · A. B. Calderwood, ed., Acts of the lords of council, 1501–1503, 3 (1993) · Rymer, Foedera, 1st edn, vol. 11 · APS, 1424–1567 · A history of the Napiers of Merchiston (1921) · NA Scot., GD 430/16, 97

Archives NA Scot., GD 430/16, 97 · NL Scot., advocates' charters

Napier, Alexander (1814–1887). *See under* Napier, Macvey (1776–1847).

Napier, Sir Archibald, of Merchiston (1534–1608), administrator, was the eldest son of Alexander Napier of Merchiston (d. 1547) and his wife, Annabella, daughter of Sir Duncan Campbell of Glenorchy. He was a minor when he succeeded his father, who was killed at the battle of Pinkie, and his lands were divided between the barony of Merchiston near Edinburgh and a group of estates in upland Dunbartonshire and Stirlingshire, which were united as the barony of Edinbellie. Napier usually styled himself 'of Edinbellie', but Merchiston was a more ancient possession of his family, and a charter of 1572 destined his lands to his male heirs 'of the surname and arms of the place of Merchiston' (Paul and Thomson, 4.2101). Others seem more often to have referred to him as laird of Merchiston.

Napier's first marriage, to Janet (d. 1563), daughter of Sir Francis Bothwell, a lord of session, took place before 1550. Early in 1560 she complained to her brother Adam, bishop of Orkney, as his reply put it, 'that thair is sume variance betwix you and your housband, and that ye ar not sua luiffet of him as ye war wont' (Napier, 65). Later that year Adam Bothwell advised Napier about the education of his eldest son, John *Napier (1550–1617): 'I pray you, schir, to send your sone Jhone to the schuyllis; other to France or Flandaris; for he can leyr no guid at hame' (ibid., 67). John Napier later won renown as a scholar of the book of Revelation and as the inventor of logarithms.

On 16 March 1561 Napier was appointed a justice-depute by the fifth earl of Argyll, justice-general, to whom he was perhaps connected through his Campbell mother. He presided in a few cases in the justiciary court but seems rarely if ever to have acted after 1562. He was knighted in 1564 or 1565. In 1568–9 he was linked with the Lyon king of arms, Sir William Stewart of Luthrie, in the latter's spectacular trial for treason and witchcraft. Stewart and Napier had invoked and worshipped a spirit called Obirion at Merchiston and elsewhere, using Italian incantations, with the aim of divining the future for political advantage. Gilbert Balfour, Janet Bothwell's Orcadian brother-in-law, was also involved. Stewart had prophesied the downfall of Regent Moray and the return to power of the queen, married to himself; for this he was executed in 1569. Napier seems to have escaped unpunished, though at the outset of the affair, on 12 August 1568, he was bound over to remain within 2 miles of Edinburgh and to answer before the council when summoned.

Merchiston was a strategic castle near Edinburgh at the time of the civil wars which were renewed in 1570. Napier was not among the committed and prominent members of either party, but his initial sympathies, as in 1568, seem to have been for the queen. He was taken on 18 July 1571 and brought to Edinburgh Castle by Sir John Stewart of Minto and his company. It is hard to interpret this, since the captain of the castle, Sir William Kirkcaldy of Grange, was a stalwart of the queen's party, whereas Stewart of Minto appears to have been a king's man, being forfeited by the queen's party in August.

The king's party on 1 May 1572 ordered Napier to deliver

Merchiston Castle, and occupied it with their troops. On 10 May forces of the queen's party came from Edinburgh to Merchiston 'with ane cannoune and ane double mynioun, with the quhilk thai peircit the wallis thairof' (Thomson, *Diurnal*, 299–300). In a skirmish they were beaten back, but there was periodic fighting around the castle for the next few weeks and at one point it was nearly captured. On 3 July, Napier was summoned to compear four days later before the queen's lieutenants and council, on pain of rebellion. This suggests that his basic allegiance was by now to the king's party, and that he was probably resident at Merchiston.

On 8 October 1572, at the time of his son John's marriage, Napier resigned his lands to him, retaining a liferent. The charter contained an unusual provision that should he be made captive, he should be allowed to sell lands in order to raise a ransom. This may indicate that Napier actually was a captive, but probably his civil-war experiences simply left him feeling that he should take no chances.

Napier's interest in coinage and bullion first surfaces on 18 February 1576, when he witnessed a contract between Regent Morton and Abraham Peterson, a Flemish mining entrepreneur, on the development of metal mines. He became general of the mint on 31 March 1577, and in that capacity worked closely with the master of the mint, initially John Acheson. The general had day-to-day managerial responsibility for the mint's operations, while the master bore overall financial and policy-making responsibility. As general, Napier's annual fee was £150 Scots, plus the right to coin three stones of silver which was worth almost as much again. Napier's duties probably involved frequent personal attendance at the mint, near Holyrood, though he could appoint a deputy. From 1578 onwards he found work in the mint for his second son, Francis, who on 14 April 1581 was appointed assayer of the mint. Napier's continued tenure of office throughout rapid changes of regime indicates that he was important for his technical expertise rather than his political loyalties.

Although he did not normally make policy on the coinage, Napier sometimes exercised influence. Morton's regime had been coining base half-merk pieces since 1572, but according to Acheson this work was 'dischargit be the laird of Merchinstoun' on 21 March 1578 (Cochran-Patrick, 1.102). However, the mint then started overstamping older coins at a higher face value, a highly profitable operation for the crown. Napier about this time proposed the alternative of a completely new coinage, which was not adopted but 'quhairout of as is supponit sprang the inventioun of the xvis. pece' (ibid., 103). The 16s. piece was introduced as part of a tack (i.e. lease) of the mint in 1581 which proved unpopular. Throughout Napier's period of office the coinage was frequently manipulated for fiscal purposes, causing rapid inflation and complaints from the poor.

In February 1580 Napier prepared to undertake an embassy to England, but it was cancelled; he was to have received £800 Scots in compensation for the expenses of his preparations, but this was cancelled too. He had English connections since his uncles James and John, followed by his younger brothers Mungo and Alexander, had emigrated to England and established themselves in Dorset. From 1582 until at least 1593 he was from time to time a member of the general assembly and served occasionally on its commissions. In March 1590 he was commissioned to arrest Jesuits. In March 1591 he disputed with the royal almoner, Peter Young, the right to the assays (test-coins); Young was successful and the coins were distributed to the poor. In February 1603 the poor were still receiving the coins, but this was regarded as a concession by Napier. Between 1587 and 1605 he served on numerous parliamentary and council commissions on coinage, weights and measures, customs, and bullion.

On 6 August 1591 a convention of estates adopted a major project on the coinage, 'craveit and devysit be Marchingstoun' (Cochran-Patrick, 1.259). All the older gold, silver, and silver alloy coins were to be recalled and converted to a new coinage. The silver was to be 10½ deniers fineness (less than the standard 11 deniers), and the ounce thereof to be 44s. On 5 September the king entered a four-year contract with Napier's son Francis to implement the act. However, this contract was cancelled in favour of one to the goldsmith Thomas Foulis and his partners, who arranged their own lease of the mint, proposing to import English and other experts to carry out the recoinage using a new technical process. Foulis was also one of Napier's colleagues, as sinker of the irons in the mint.

The Foulis contract was proclaimed on 17 January 1592, whereupon Napier took instruments at the Edinburgh market cross demanding that the partnership should be obliged to recoin the silver alloy coins as well as other coins, and that if they did not they should be replaced by Francis Napier 'quha offeris himself yit as of befoir' (Cochran-Patrick, 1.256). Father and son then submitted two memoranda attacking Foulis and outlining a new, alternative project for revaluing older coins by overstamping them at a higher face value rather than recoining. Foulis replied with his own criticisms of the Napiers' projects, old and new. The upshot was that all the projects were dropped. This negative success for Napier was not repeated in 1592, when a statute adopted the policy of feuing the country's metal mines and made Foulis responsible for refining the ores; Napier was reduced to entering a formal protest against the act.

On 17 January 1594 Foulis persuaded a convention of estates to pass an act for a new currency, with the silver to be raised to 50s. per ounce of 11 deniers fine. Initially Foulis was himself to have taken on a tack of the mint, and the burgh of Edinburgh agreed to be his surety for this. On 21 January Napier was 'desirit' by the privy council to 'gif his opinioun anent the cunyie'; his opinion was 'that the strykeing of cunyie of xi d. fyne is verie gude, bot it is over deir and ower gude chaip to be sett for the sowme that presentlie is offerit for the same' (*Reg. PCS*, 5.118). On 26 January the mint was leased not to Foulis but to the burgh of Edinburgh, where one of the burgh's cautioners was

Francis Napier, a burgess of Edinburgh as well as a mint official. The burgh's executive officer, however, was Foulis.

Janet Napier had died in 1563, and some time before 1572 her husband married Elizabeth (*d*. 1605), daughter of Robert Mowbray of Barnbougle. His children from this marriage, Alexander, Archibald, Elizabeth, Helen, and William, were contemporaries of his grandsons through John, and referred to them as brothers. William and Francis were conjoined with their father in a commission on bullion prices in 1597. Napier bought various lands near Edinburgh for Alexander, the eldest son of his second marriage: Kingsmeadow in 1588, and Lauriston in 1593. There were later disputes between John and his half-brothers and -sisters over the teinds of Merchiston. Possession of Kingsmeadow was disputed by David Preston of Craigmillar, and between 1588 and 1590 there was a minor feud between Preston and Napier. Archibald the younger was killed by the Scotts of Buccleuch in November 1600, in the High Street of Edinburgh while parliament was sitting. Alexander and William sought revenge, while their father and half-brother John tried to restrain them.

At a convention of estates of February 1602, Napier complained that the mint tacksmen were not employing him, and that his deputy had discovered that the tacksmen had 'got' the excessive sum of £40,000 Scots in the past three months. 'But the credit of the treasurer, comptroller and other partners bare it [the complaint] down' (*CSP Scot.*, *1597–1603*, 939–40). This seems to have been a criticism of a temporary tack of the mint made on 22 September 1601 to benefit the master of Elphinstone, who resigned on that day as treasurer. In July 1601 Napier's son Alexander had been in trouble for assaulting Elphinstone's servant. The complaint may also have been directed against one of the longer-term mint tacksmen, Napier's *bête noire* Foulis.

The union of the crowns in 1603 had important implications for the coinage. Between September and December 1604 Napier visited London to negotiate with his English counterparts about the standardization of the coinages of the two realms. The issues were complex because the coinages differed not just in fineness but in gold:silver ratios. 'To the grate amazement of the Englishe', he 'caried hes bussines with a grate deall of dexteritey and skill' (Balfour, 2.2). Thereafter Napier liaised regularly with Sir Thomas Knyvett, warden of the English mint. In January 1608 he was commissioned to supervise the taking of samples of silver ore from the new mine at Hilderstone in West Lothian. Napier died at Merchiston on 15 May 1608. His estate was valued at £12,940 15*s.* 6*d.* Scots.

JULIAN GOODARE

Sources *CSP Scot.*, *1547–1603* · Reg. PCS, 1st ser., vols. 1–8 · J. M. Thomson and others, eds., *Registrum magni sigilli regum Scotorum / The register of the great seal of Scotland*, 11 vols. (1882–1914), vols. 3–6 · M. Livingstone and others, eds., *Registrum secreti sigilli regum Scotorum / The register of the privy seal of Scotland*, 3–8 (1936–82) · J. B. Paul and C. T. McInnes, eds., *Compota thesaurariorum regum Scotorum / Accounts of the lord high treasurer of Scotland*, 9–13 (1911–78) · APS, *1424–1625* · M. Napier, *Memoirs of John Napier of Merchiston* (1834) · R. W. Cochran-Patrick, ed., *Records of the coinage of Scotland*, 2 vols. (1876) · I. H. Stewart, *The Scottish coinage*, 2nd edn (1967) · J. E. L. Murray, 'The organisation and work of the Scottish mint, 1358–1603', *Coinage in medieval Scotland, 1100–1600: Second Symposium on Coinage and Monetary History* [Oxford 1977], ed. D. M. Metcalf (1977) · P. G. Maxwell-Stuart, *Satan's conspiracy: magic and witchcraft in sixteenth-century Scotland* (2001) · Scots peerage, 6.412–17 · G. Donaldson, *Reformed by bishops: Galloway, Orkney and Caithness* (1987) · M. Lynch, *Edinburgh and the Reformation* (1981) · T. Thomson, ed., *A diurnal of remarkable occurrents that have passed within the country of Scotland*, Bannatyne Club, 43 (1833) · J. D. Marwick, ed., *Extracts from the records of the burgh of Edinburgh, AD 1528–1589*, [2–4], Scottish Burgh RS, 3–5 (1871–82) · *The historical works of Sir James Balfour*, ed. J. Haig, 4 vols. (1824–5) · T. Thomson, ed., *Acts and proceedings of the general assemblies of the Kirk of Scotland*, 3 pts, Bannatyne Club, 1 (1839–45) · R. Pitcairn, ed., *Ancient criminal trials in Scotland*, 7 pts in 3, Bannatyne Club, 42 (1833) · Edinburgh testaments, 17 Feb 1609, NA Scot., CC8/8/45

Wealth at death £12,940 15*s.* 6*d.* Scots: 17 Feb 1609, NA Scot., Edinburgh testaments, CC8/8/45

Napier, Archibald, first Lord Napier of Merchistoun (*c.*1575–1645), politician, was the eldest son of the mathematician John *Napier (1550–1617) of Merchiston and his wife, Elizabeth (*d*. 1579), daughter of Sir James Stirling of Keir. Napier matriculated at the University of Glasgow in 1593, and about 1595 published a pamphlet (of which no copies survive) on a new method of manuring ground with salt rather than dung, guaranteed to increase production. A grant under the privy seal of Scotland on 22 June 1598 gave him a monopoly of this invention for twenty-nine years, but nothing more was heard of it, and it is suspected that the scheme was largely the work of his inventive father, designed to provide young Napier with an income by charging fees. Appointment as a gentleman of the king's privy chamber provided an alternative means of support, and on the union of the crowns in 1603 Napier moved to England with King James. His father was unhappy with his absence, and in 1608 urged him to come home to help settle family disputes, and then to settle his affairs in England and make his 'constant residens' in Scotland (M. Napier, *John Napier*, 316). However, Napier continued his life as a courtier for nearly another decade before conforming to his father's wishes, and even then he returned to Scotland only because he saw no future at court. He was a supporter of his fellow Scot Robert Carr, earl of Somerset, the king's favourite, but in 1614–15 George Villiers, later duke of Buckingham, replaced Somerset in royal favour. As Villiers was 'no good Friend of myne' (A. Napier, 6), Napier resolved to withdraw from court. The timing of this development is probably indicated by Napier's being knighted on 20 July 1616, and admitted to the privy council of Scotland on 20 August 1617. Past services had been rewarded, and a new career in administration in Scotland opened up. His succession to his father's estates in 1617 and his marriage (contract dated 15 April 1619) to Lady Margaret (*d*. before 1631), daughter of John Graham, fourth earl of Montrose, further anchored him in Scotland.

Napier was very active in the council's work, and his zeal was rewarded by several appointments in 1622: justice clerk and master of ceremonies, treasurer-depute, and

Archibald Napier, first Lord Napier of Merchistoun (*c.*1575–1645), by George Jamesone, 1637

ordinary lord of session. He was to resign the first two of these offices in August 1624, as had probably been intended when he became treasurer-depute. The earl of Mar, the treasurer, had managed to persuade King James to leave the office of treasurer-depute vacant for over a year, arguing that he could do both jobs himself, and the appointment of Napier came as an unpleasant surprise to Mar and his supporters. James wrote to Mar to try to reconcile him to the appointment (21 October 1622); Napier was his 'olde servant', a man free from factious humour, and directly dependent on James himself, 'with whom he hath beene bred ever from his youth'. He was a man Mar should cherish and encourage (*Mar and Kellie MSS*, 117). But Mar's supporters at court were horrified. The earl of Kellie wrote to Mar 'I must confes treulye to you that I did not dreame' of Napier getting the post (*Supplementary Mar and Kellie MSS*, 140), and suggested that Mar's rival the marquess of Hamilton was responsible for the appointment. This rumour Hamilton himself exploited, claiming Napier's promotion was a deliberate 'poynt of revenge' on Mar (A. Napier, 6). Thus Napier was faced from the first with Mar's hostility to a deputy 'thrust upon him' (A. Napier, 10–11), but, by his own account, his position was tolerable until after the death of James VI in 1625. With a new king on the throne whose favour had to be gained, stability collapsed. 'Then there was nothing but factions and factious consultations,—of the one, to hold that power and place they possessed before,—of the other, to wrest it out of their hands, and to invest themselves' (M. Napier, *Memoirs of Montrose*, 1.110). Amid the scurrying to and from court to curry favour and denounce others, Napier at first enjoyed continued favour. On 2 May 1627 he was made a baronet of

Nova Scotia, and on 4 May created Lord Napier of Merchistoun. A lucrative lease of the crown lands of Orkney followed. But these appointments offended 'the cheefe Statesmen' of Scotland (A. Napier, 12). In his subsequent 'A true relation of the unjust persute against the Lord Napier' (published in 1793 as *Memoirs of … Lord Napier*) he not surprisingly presents a picture of himself as a loyal servant beset by unscrupulous and greedy enemies. Accusations were made against him, and the king was faced with charges and counter-charges, with Napier caught up in undignified manoeuvres. In October 1628, for example, he rushed secretly to court to get in his version of events before a representative of his enemies, sent in hot pursuit, could arrive. Sir George Hay, the chancellor of Scotland, concluded judiciously of the episode, that Napier 'deserved hanging' (*Supplementary Mar and Kellie MSS*, 247).

Though Charles had considerable trust in Napier he became exasperated by the dispute, and by Napier's long stays at court to try to protect his interests, while Mar cunningly complained that he, aged and infirm, needed Napier's help in Scotland. In February 1629 enemies were delighted to report that an angry king had ordered Napier to leave, 'desiring him to goe home in the devels name' (*Supplementary Mar and Kellie MSS*, 249). In 1630 Charles acknowledged Napier's good service and integrity, but told him that because he could not work peacefully with his other leading Scottish officials royal 'service was hindered' (A. Napier, 87–8). By this time Napier realized he would have to resign, but as his grant was for life and he had committed no crime, he held out for compensation. He had no future, for his office 'could never be profitable to a man that had resolved faire and direct dealing', and he 'could never fashion' himself to the ways business was done in the Scottish council and session (A. Napier, 74). Moreover, the early death of his wife had dulled his taste for public life: 'after my wyfe dyed, a woman religious, chast, and beautifull, and my chief joy in this world, I had no pleasur to remaine in Scotland' (A. Napier, 74). In March 1631 a deal was agreed whereby he resigned as treasurer-depute and surrendered his lease of Orkney for £4000 sterling. Three years later the embittered Napier noted with satisfaction that all but one of the leaders of the 'combination' against him were dead, ruined, 'farre on the way to ruine', or had lost royal favour. Only one remained in power, and without a doubt divine punishment awaited him (A. Napier, 99). The surviving enemy referred to was Lord Traquair, his successor as treasurer-depute.

When open resistance to Charles I's policies began in Scotland in 1637 the regime was dominated by Traquair, now an earl and treasurer. None the less, Napier at first gave his support to the king, and on 22 September 1638 he and other privy councillors signed the king's covenant, Charles's abortive attempt to replace the national covenant of his enemies. However, Napier had a good deal of sympathy with the grievances of the covenanters. His own experience led him to believe the king's Scottish advisers incompetent and corrupt, and he saw Charles's policy of increasing the wealth of bishops and giving them high office in the state as destroying the primitive simplicity of the Reformation church and bound to lead to conflict. Tragedy followed 'in all places where churchmen were great' (M. Napier, *Memoirs of Montrose*, 1.104). Napier therefore drifted for a time towards co-operation with the opposition. In December 1639 he was one of the commissioners appointed by the Scottish parliament to await the report of representatives sent to the king, and in June 1640 he was elected a member of the covenanters' committee of estates, which had effectively replaced king and council as Scotland's executive. The report that late in 1640 he signed the Cumbernauld bond, obscure in wording but supported by nobles worried that the leader of the covenanters, the marquess of Argyll, was ambitious for personal power, suggests that though he had for a time identified with the covenanters he was now worried about the direction the movement was taking. By the end of the year he was meeting with the earl of Montrose (his brother-in-law, whose guardian he had been in the latter's childhood), planning to persuade the king to come to Scotland and reach a settlement. In 1640–41 a number of papers Napier drafted—and probably hoped Montrose would accept as statements of political principle—reached the conclusion that strong 'sovereign power' centred on the monarchy was necessary to prevent anarchy. That the papers in fact represent Napier's thoughts was obscured by their editor, Mark Napier, who insisted that they were really the thoughts of Montrose dictated to Napier. But the ideas expressed have little originality, being derived largely from the writings (and even copying the phrasing) of the French political theorist Jean Bodin.

When news of the correspondence with the king leaked out, Montrose, Napier, and their colleagues were imprisoned in Edinburgh Castle by the covenanters as 'Plotters' in June 1641. After interrogating Napier on 23 June the committee of estates ordered his release, but he refused to accept this, on the grounds that it would dishonour him, as people would think he had betrayed his friends. When told that he had been judged less guilty than the others he indignantly replied 'I wes as guilty as any of the rest' (M. Napier, *Memorials of Montrose*, 1.294). Eventually, after hours of argument, the stubborn old man got his way, and was sent back to the castle. On 28 August he was brought before parliament, in which Charles I was present, and indignantly (if rather unreasonably) complained about his imprisonment, demanding trial as he and his friends had only sought to serve king and kingdom. 'His Majesty noded to me, and seimed to be weill pleased' (M. Napier, *Memorials of Montrose*, 1.316). On 16 November, the covenanters having reached a settlement with the king, Napier and the other 'Plotters' were released.

In January 1643 Napier was one of the signatories of the royalist 'cross petition' to the privy council, 'crossing' the covenanters' demands that Scotland side with the English parliament in the civil war in that kingdom by urging (in the guise of covenanting rhetoric) that maintaining peace

should be the highest priority, and in 1643–4 he continued to discuss the political situation with Montrose. After Montrose began his royalist rising in Scotland in 1644 Napier came under suspicion, and on 8 October 1644 he and family were ordered to confine themselves within a mile of the palace of Holyroodhouse, where Napier still had apartments, on pain of a fine of £10,000 Scots (about £830 sterling). When his son, also Archibald *Napier, fled in 1645 the fine was exacted, and Napier, his daughter and daughter-in-law were sent to close confinement in Edinburgh Castle. He petitioned for his release in July 1645 as his life was in danger through plague, six people having already died in the castle, and because while he was a prisoner he could not raise the money to pay his fine. Parliament agreed to his release on 30 July on condition that he confine himself within a mile of either Merchiston or the burgh of Haddington—under threat of a 40,000 merks fine (about £2200 sterling). His daughter and daughter-in-law were also ordered to be freed. Thus the story that he was freed from imprisonment by his own son in Linlithgow after the battle of Kilsyth (15 August) appears to be inaccurate. However, after the battle he joined Montrose's victorious army, only to share in its disastrous defeat at Philiphaugh (13 September). He fled with Montrose back to the highlands, but had to be left behind at Fincastle, near Pitlochry, through illness. 'In respect of his great wisdom and experience, it was said, he might have been a useful concillor to Montrose' but 'That nobleman was so very old, that he could not have marched with them' (*Memoirs of Henry Guthry*, 208–9). He died at Fincastle in November, and Montrose arranged his burial in Blair Atholl.

George Wishart's eulogy presents Napier as equalling his father in philosophic and mathematical genius, and far excelling him in jurisprudence. Montrose in his childhood 'had revered him as a most indulgent parent, in his youth as his wisest counsellor, in his manhood as his truest friend' (Wishart, 156). A more balanced judgement would be that Napier was an able, hard-working, and conscientious courtier and administrator, whose grievances against Charles I's regime, as well as his underlying loyalty, had a good deal of influence on Montrose. He possessed a streak of obstinacy based on principle that could make him awkward to deal with—whether as servant, colleague, or prisoner.   DAVID STEVENSON

Sources DNB · GEC, *Peerage* · *Scots peerage* · G. Brunton and D. Haig, *An historical account of the senators of the college of justice, from its institution in MDXXXII* (1832) · Archibald, Lord Napier, *Memoirs of Archibald, first Lord Napier* (1793) · M. Napier, *Memoirs of John Napier of Merchiston, his lineage, life, and times, with a history of the invention of logarithms* (1834) · M. Napier, *Memoirs of the marquis of Montrose*, 2 vols. (1856) · M. Napier, ed., *Memorials of Montrose and his times*, 2 vols., Maitland Club, 66 (1848–50) · D. Stevenson, 'The "Letter on sovereign power" and the influence of Jean Bodin on political thought in Scotland', *SHR*, 61 (1982), 25–43 · *Report on the manuscripts of the earl of Mar and Kellie*, HMC, 60 (1904); suppl. (1930) · NA Scot., PA11/3, 4 · *The memoirs of Henry Guthry, late bishop*, ed. G. Crawford, 2nd edn (1748) · G. Wishart, *The memoirs of James, marquis of Montrose, 1639–1650*, ed. and trans. A. D. Murdoch and H. F. M. Simpson (1893) · *APS* · *Reg. PCS*, 1st ser. · *Reg. PCS*, 2nd ser. · W. A. Shaw, *The knights of England*, 2 vols. (1906)

Archives NRA, priv. coll.

Likenesses G. Jamesone, oils, 1637, Scot. NPG [*see illus.*] · oils (after G. Jamesone), Parliament Hall, Edinburgh · portrait (after G. Jamesone), priv. coll.; repro. in D. Thompson, *The life and art of George Jamesone* (1974)

Napier, Archibald, second Lord Napier of Merchistoun (*c*.1624–1658), royalist nobleman, was the second, but eldest surviving, son of Archibald *Napier, first Lord Napier (*c*.1575–1645), and Lady Margaret (*d*. before 1631), daughter of John *Graham, fourth earl of Montrose (1573–1626). He married in 1641, it is said at the age of seventeen, Lady Elizabeth (*d*. 1683), daughter of John *Erskine, earl of Mar (*c*.1585–1653). On 8 October 1644 he and his father were ordered to confine themselves within a mile of Edinburgh and live in the latter's lodging in the palace of Holyroodhouse, on pain of a fine of £10,000 Scots each, since his uncle James *Graham, marquess of Montrose, was leading a royalist rising against the covenanting regime. However, in March 1645 he fled, and joined Montrose on 21 April. In retaliation his father and wife were imprisoned in Edinburgh Castle.

Napier took part in the battles of Auldearn (9 May 1645), Alford (2 July), and Kilsyth (15 August), and on 20 August was sent to proclaim, in Linlithgow, Montrose's summons for parliament to meet. There he is said to have liberated his father and other royalist prisoners. On defeat at Philiphaugh (13 September) he withdrew with Montrose to the highlands, and on his father's death in November inherited his title. In March 1646 he withstood a two-week siege in Montrose's castle of Kincardine, escaping just before its surrender. After Montrose agreed to disband and go into exile in July 1646 Napier remained for a time in Scotland, and was heavily fined for his flight from Holyroodhouse. He gave an undertaking not to act against the covenanting regime and, having decided to go abroad, obtained agreement on 23 October that if he accidentally met Montrose this would not break his undertaking 'provided he converse not' with him (M. Napier, 2.646). He commissioned his wife and others to manage his estates in his absence, and (by one report) was 'robbed of all his money on the way' to Paris (Scot, 67). In May 1648 his uncle Robert Napier of Culcreuch begged him to return to Scotland and abandon his 'evil course', accurately predicting that if he did not the covenanters would forfeit his estates and 'your lady and children shall be reduced to extreme want, whereof they already feel the beginnings' (A. S. Napier, 141–2). However, Napier was determined to serve the royalist cause, and not only broke his undertaking not to converse with Montrose, but became so close to him that 'it was ever said that Montrose and his nephew were like the Pope and the Church, who would be inseparable' as Napier proudly reported to his wife in June 1648. When Montrose decided to leave France and visit the emperor Ferdinand III he feared he might be detained, so he left Napier in Paris as a decoy, his continued presence lending plausibility to assurances that Montrose was still in France. As instructed, Napier continued at 'his exercises [studies]' and 'to go often to court, make visits, and ever [be] in public places, at comedies, and such things' (M. Napier, 2.666–7). But in spite of this open commitment

to royalism, in defiance of the undertakings he had given before leaving Scotland, some scruple led Napier to avoid being included in a plan for Charles, prince of Wales, to go to Scotland, fearing this would jeopardize his financial position there.

Travelling from Paris to Brussels, Napier was rejoined by Montrose late in 1648, and was with him at The Hague in March 1649. In late 1649 and early 1650 he acted as Montrose's agent at The Hague in his efforts to raise support for a new royalist expedition. Napier got the consent of Charles II in April 1650 to join Montrose in Scotland: the king was 'well pleased with your repair to him' (M. Napier, 2.276). However, news of Montrose's defeat and execution led to the cancellation of Napier's plans, and when Charles himself went to Scotland in 1650 Napier had to remain behind, as the covenanters had banned him from the country.

Early in 1654 Napier landed in the north of Scotland with General John Middleton to join royalists resisting the English conquest of the country, but the rising soon collapsed in confusion. Napier, described as 'my constant great friend' by his fellow royalist-in-arms John Gwyn (*Military Memoirs*, 81), returned to the continent at the beginning of 1655, being thanked by the king for his loyalty to Middleton 'in this time of so general defection' (Firth, 224). Napier now experienced severe financial problems. During his exile his wife and five children had at first remained in Scotland, but by 1656 some at least of his children had joined him. In April 1656 he was in Cologne with the exiled court, and Edward Hyde urged that help be given to 'Lord Napper, who is, with his children, in a very sad condition' (*Clarendon State Papers*, 3.108). His wife evidently remained in Scotland, for she was granted a pension from his forfeited estates on 2 September 1656. By June 1657 Napier had become a captain in a regiment of Scottish exiles raised by Charles II, but soon lost the post, for in April 1658 he was a 'reformado'—an officer without pay or command. As the king could not support him, Napier obtained a licence from him to enlist in foreign service. In June 1658 he was planning to go to Germany to seek a military career 'if I cannot obtaine any charge in these countrys' (*Nicholas Papers*, 4.47). However, he died at Middelburg in the Netherlands on 4 September 1658. Reporting his death 'in the flower of his youth', to Sir Edward Nicholas, Sir Alexander Hume (chamberlain to the princess of Orange) stated that 'the losse of him is very deplorable, especially in the manner it is related, whereof I doute not but you will receiue information' (ibid., 4.68–9).

Napier was an ardent young royalist, eager to emulate his uncle Montrose in service to the crown. His achievements were limited, his life short, but he was remembered for his unswerving loyalty and his close association with his famous uncle. His widow (who had secretly removed and preserved Montrose's heart after his execution in 1650) was rewarded with a pension of £500 sterling per annum after the Restoration of 1660, and died in 1683.   DAVID STEVENSON

Sources DNB · M. Napier, *Memoirs of the marquis of Montrose*, 2 vols. (1856) · *Scots peerage* · GEC, *Peerage* · *Calendar of the Clarendon state papers preserved in the Bodleian Library*, ed. O. Ogle and others, 5 vols. (1869–1970) · C. H. Firth, ed., *Scotland and the protectorate: letters and papers relating to the military government of Scotland from January 1654 to June 1659*, Scottish History Society, 31 (1899) · *The Nicholas papers*, ed. G. F. Warner, 4 vols., CS, new ser., 40, 50, 57, 3rd ser., 31 (1886–1920) · A. S. Napier, *A history of the Napiers of Merchiston* (1921) · J. Scot, *The staggering state of Scottish statesmen from 1550 to 1650*, ed. C. Rogers (1872) · *Letters and papers of Patrick Ruthven … and of his family, 1615–1662*, ed. W. D. Macray, Roxburgh Club, 90 (1868) · *CSP dom., 1657–8*, 346, 376 · *Military memoirs of John Gwyn*, ed. N. Tucker (1967) · NA Scot., PA 11/3, fol. 69v; PA 11/4, fol. 54r–v · survey 156/4/50, NRA Scotland

Likenesses G. Jamesone, oils, 1640?, priv. coll. · R. C. Bell, engraving (after G. Jamesone, 1640?), repro. in Napier, *Memoirs*

Napier, Barbara (*c.*1554–1592×1600). *See under* North Berwick witches (*act.* 1590–1592).

Napier, Sir Charles (1786–1860), naval officer and politician, was born at Merchistoun Hall, Stirlingshire, on 6 March 1786, the second son of Captain the Hon. Charles Napier (1731–1807) of Merchistoun Hall and his second wife, Christian (*d.* 1814), daughter of Gabriel Hamilton of West Burn, Lanarkshire. He was the grandson of Francis Scott Napier, fifth Lord Napier; his cousins included General Sir Charles James Napier, Captain Henry Edward Napier RN, General Sir William Francis Patrick Napier, and William, eighth Lord Napier.

The French wars, 1799–1814 Educated at the high school, Edinburgh (1793–9), Napier entered the Royal Navy in 1799 under the patronage of Henry Dundas, treasurer of the navy. In 1800 he joined the *Renown*, flagship of Sir John Borlase Warren, serving in the channel and the Mediterranean. In November 1802 he joined the *Greyhound* (Captain William Hoste). After a voyage to St Helena aboard the *Egyptienne* he served with distinction in attacks on the Boulogne flotilla in 1804–5 aboard the *Mediator* and *Renommée*. On 24 April 1805 he commanded the gunbrig *Starling* at the capture of seven heavily armed coasters off Cap Gris Nez. On 30 November 1805 he was promoted lieutenant and posted to the *Courageux*, once again serving under Admiral Warren at the capture of the French warships *Marengo* and *Belle Poule* on 13 March 1806. He was then sent to the West Indies. His political and naval patrons, Dundas and the station commander, Admiral Sir Alexander Cochrane, agreed to secure his promotion to commander. Moved into the brig *Pultusk* as acting commander, his promotion was confirmed on 30 November 1807. The following month he was present at the capture of the Danish islands of St Thomas and Santa Cruz. In April 1808 he moved to the brig *Recruit*, and on 6 September engaged the French sloop *Diligente*. Although he suffered a compound fracture of the thigh Napier refused to leave the deck until the *Recruit* was disabled by the loss of her mainmast. After recuperating ashore Napier rejoined his ship in time to play a distinguished role in the capture of Martinique in February 1809. On 17 April he secured his promotion to post captain with a display of rare seamanship and bravery. While off Guadeloupe the *Recruit* pursued and engaged a fleeing French 74 gun battleship, delaying her

Sir Charles Napier (1786–1860), by Thomas Musgrove Joy, 1853

until the squadron could come up and capture her. Admiral Cochrane immediately promoted Napier into the prize. This was confirmed by the Admiralty on receipt of Cochrane's dispatch on 22 May 1809. He was then moved to the frigate *Jason* and sent home in charge of a convoy.

For the next two years Napier was unemployed, a common fate for new captains, spending the first year in Edinburgh, where he attended language classes. In the summer of 1810 he went to Portugal to visit his brother and three cousins who were all serving under Wellington in the Peninsula. At the battle of Busaco he was slightly wounded in the leg, and later caught his cousin Charles James as he fell grievously wounded. He accompanied the army back to the lines of Torres Vedras and in November moved on to Cadiz, where his younger brother, Thomas Erskine *Napier was serving.

In early 1811 Napier returned to Britain and was appointed to the small frigate *Thames* in the Mediterranean. For the next two years he served on the west coast of Naples, stopping the coasting trade, intercepting Neapolitan shipbuilding supplies and capturing islands. Such coastal and amphibious service would be the hallmark of his career. During this time he captured over eighty enemy vessels. On 21 July 1811 the *Thames* led the *Cephalus* into Porto Infreschi, capturing shipbuilding supplies, eleven gunboats and fifteen coasters. The highlight of this service came on 26 February 1812, when the *Thames* and the *Furieuse* carried the 2nd battalion of the 10th regiment into the harbour of the island of Ponza, exchanged fire with the batteries, anchored across the mole head, landed the troops, and captured the island without the loss of a single man. The following month he was transferred into the large frigate *Euryalus*, then active on the French riviera. Here he continued to harass the enemy's coastal shipping, much of which was carrying shipbuilding supplies into Toulon. Napier drove all the shipping from Toulon to the east into Cavaliere Bay, where it was covered by a warship and several batteries. On 16 May the boats of the *Euryalus* and the *Berwick* carried the batteries and brought out as prizes the warship and twenty-two trading vessels for the loss of two men.

The Anglo-American War, 1814 In June 1814 the *Euryalus* formed part of a squadron that convoyed a large fleet of transports to North America. Here Napier once again came under the command of Sir Alexander Cochrane, ensuring that he would have opportunities both to distinguish and enrich himself. During the campaign that led to the capture of Washington, Cochrane detached two frigates, under Captain James Alexander Gordon and Napier, with mortar and rocket vessels to enter the Potomac River as a diversion. Starting on 17 August 1814, and in spite of the difficulties of the navigation, the squadron reached Alexandria on the 28th. Here they received the surrender of the town and demanded that the shipping, recently scuttled, should be salvaged and reloaded as prizes of war. On the 31st the squadron began the return journey, and despite strenuous opposition from batteries and fire rafts they carried their prizes into Chesapeake Bay on 9 September. During the return voyage Napier was wounded in the neck by a rifle bullet. As a feat of seamanship and an operation of war this raid had no equal in the Anglo-American War of 1812–14. Within a week Napier was in action again. He commanded the rocket boats that bombarded Baltimore, providing both the 'bombs bursting in air' and 'the rocket's red glare' of Francis Scott Key's American national anthem. He also volunteered to take the *Euryalus* alongside Fort McHenry, the key to the defences of the city, a role his father had carried out at Havana in 1762. During the winter Napier blockaded the USS *Constellation* in Norfolk, Virginia, and issued a challenge to her captain. This was accepted, but the treaty of Ghent intervened. Needing a major repair the *Euryalus* was sent back to Britain, but Napoleon's 'hundred days' provided one last chance for glory. Napier was selected by Dundas's son, the second Lord Melville, to command a naval detachment to build pontoon bridges for Wellington's army in Belgium. Unfortunately Napier outranked the army's chief engineer and Wellington refused his assistance.

Peacetime and steam, 1815–1833 Coming ashore in 1815 Napier travelled to Scotland. His elder brother Francis having died at Madras in 1798, Napier had inherited Merchistoun Hall on the death of his mother, which he decided to sell. In 1815, pausing only to marry Frances Elizabeth, widow of Lieutenant Edward Elers RN, and daughter of his father's subordinate on the impress service, Lieutenant Younghusband, he returned to Hampshire, which would be his home for much of his life. He acquired four young stepchildren who took the name of Napier. He already had a considerable fortune in prize money. Following the final defeat of Napoleon, Napier and his wife went to live in Versailles, and later, joined by the children, travelled to Naples, where they spent most of 1816. In 1817 they wandered north through Venice and to Switzerland, reaching Paris in late 1818. Here the family lived in considerable style. There were two additions to the family, a boy and a girl. Tragically his son Charles died in 1821 after falling from a haystack. Napier became involved in a project to employ steamships on the River Seine. The first of these ships, the *Aaron Manby*, was built in sections at Tipton, Staffordshire, disassembled, and then re-erected in London. She was shown to the Admiralty before Napier steamed from London to Paris, where she arrived on 11 June 1822. A technical success, the iron steamer, and her sisters, were ahead of their time but failed financially. Napier, the major shareholder, kept the project going until 1827. When it failed he was ruined. The family then ended their peripatetic lifestyle, settling in a small cottage at Rowland's Castle in Hampshire.

Napier was now anxious for employment. Despite his expertise in steam, and repeated applications to the lord high admiral, the duke of Clarence, later William IV, he was finally appointed to the sailing frigate *Galatea* in January 1829. Napier already understood how steamships would affect the conduct of war at sea. Recognizing that contemporary steam engines were not yet ready to be fitted into warships he developed a system by which the crew of the *Galatea* used winches to drive a pair of collapsible paddle wheels. These propelled the ship at up to 3 knots, and could tow a battleship at half that speed. Although the system was commended by all who witnessed the performance the navy was already committed to steam, and elected not to pursue the winch. Napier was sent to the West Indies, where he used his rank to deprive a junior captain of a valuable freight, and in August 1830 to Lisbon, where he began a long-running connection with Portugal by demanding the restitution of impounded merchant ships. The following year he was sent to the Azores to protect British interests. Portugal was convulsed by a bitter civil war between the absolutist party of Dom Miguel and the constitutionalists under his elder brother, Dom Pedro. The *Galatea* paid off in late 1831. The following year Napier stood for parliament in Portsmouth as a radical Liberal, but was defeated by the sitting candidates. By this time he was in close contact with another Hampshire resident, the foreign secretary, Lord Palmerston. Through Palmerston's support he was offered the command of the Portuguese constitutionalist fleet in February 1833.

The Miguelite War, 1833–1834 After securing an advance on his pay, and a large life insurance policy, Napier relieved Admiral Sir George Sartorious and, to avoid making too explicit a breach of the Foreign Enlistment Act, adopted the *nom de guerre* of Dom Carlos de Ponza. Arriving in Oporto, Dom Pedro's only foothold in Portugal, in June 1833 he took command of a motley fleet of old warships, converted Indiamen and hired steamers. The crews, fewer than a thousand men, were mostly British, and commanded by officers chosen by Napier, including his stepson Lieutenant Charles Elers Napier RN. On the 20th Napier embarked a small army under Count Villa Flor, later the duke of Terceira. Napier landed the troops in the south-east corner of Portugal and accompanied them along the coast to Lagos, whence the army moved overland to Lisbon.

On 3 July Napier encountered the absolutist fleet off Cape St Vincent. He planned to use his steamers to tow the heavy ships into battle, but the engineers refused to go under fire without a heavy bonus. Because Napier could not meet their demand he had to wait two days for a reasonable wind. The absolutist fleet included two 74 gun battleships and two 50 gun frigates, while Napier had two 40 gun frigates, but he boarded and captured the four largest absolutist ships after little more than nominal resistance. Experienced fighting seamen, together with his determination and leadership, secured a decisive victory. Napier reorganized his forces at Lagos and put to sea again on the 13th, being promoted admiral and receiving Portuguese ennoblement as Visount Cape St Vincent the following day. After shaking off an outbreak of cholera the fleet arrived off the Tagus on the 24th, the day after Lisbon surrendered to Terceira. When he reached the city the following day he was gratified that Rear-Admiral Sir William Parker, commanding the British squadron in the Tagus, accorded him the honours due to a Portuguese admiral.

Feted and rewarded by the Portuguese, Napier's had been a very British triumph. It cut the Gordian knot of Iberian civil strife, destroyed the absolutist cause and discomfited the ambitions of Russia, Austria, and Prussia. Palmerston, the architect, was delighted. He had secured British interests without the direct use of British force at a time when resources were overstretched. Although the British government refused Napier any public recognition the naval lords and other senior officers appeared at public meetings to support him. Napier had been struck off the navy list in 1833 and would not be restored until 1836.

After a brief, frustrating attempt to reform the Portuguese navy and dockyards Napier returned to his true vocation. In March 1834 he sailed north, landed with one thousand seamen and marines, and launched a dynamic campaign that cleared the absolutists from northern Portugal and relieved Oporto. Raised to the dignity of count, a title he altered to Count Napier St Vincent, he went on another expedition which ended with the surrender of Ourem. The war was over, and with it Napier's usefulness. Temperamentally unsuited to the compromises of peacetime reform he submitted another ambitious plan to reorganize the Portuguese navy in September. He was relieved on 15 October 1834 and returned home the following month.

In 1835 he stood, again unsuccessfully, for Portsmouth in opposition to the sitting Liberal members, who included Sir Francis Baring. He also wrote a book, *An Account of the War in Portugal between Don Pedro and Don Miguel*, which appeared in 1836. In this he anticipated the twentieth-century practice of senior officers writing their own account of events for the public. As a history of the war it reflected Napier's limited awareness of the wider picture, but as a memoir it had few faults. He used the proceeds from his Portuguese service to purchase a 100 acre estate near Horndean in Hampshire, which he renamed Merchistoun. Henceforth he would delight in advanced farming methods when he was at home. In 1837 Napier went to Portugal, looking to play a part in Terceira's attempt to overthrow the constitution. He had not formed a very high opinion of the Portuguese, and had already offered to settle the problem with a few British warships. Palmerston decided that, on this occasion, such methods were not necessary, but he would have need of Napier again. Napier pressed the Admiralty for employment by standing as a Liberal at Greenwich. This cost him £300, and he was narrowly defeated. He turned down the resulting offer of a sea command in favour of a promotion for his stepson.

Syria, 1840–1841 In January 1839 Napier accepted command of the battleship *Powerful*, and, as senior captain in a small fleet he could expect to act as a commodore. His commander-in-chief, Admiral Sir Robert Stopford, was an elderly tory, entirely out of sympathy with the whig government and its policy, when he understood it. Palmerston and his close friend Lord Minto, the first lord of the Admiralty, selected Napier to inject a little vigour into Stopford. This was a stroke of genius, for in the following year Palmerston would have need of a covert means of making war. The cabinet included many who opposed his policy of resisting France and working with Russia to uphold Turkey against Egypt. Until the death of Lord Holland in October 1840 he could not afford to risk a war, and his private correspondence with Napier became critical to the development of strategy.

In June 1840 Napier hoisted his pendant as commodore and took a small squadron to watch events in Syria (which then included modern Syria, Lebanon, and Israel). Palmerston sought a new four or five power guarantee of the Turkish straits, and the removal of Mehmet Ali's Egyptian forces from the province. In early September Napier was joined by the admiral with the rest of the fleet and General Sir Charles Smith, who had been sent with a small force of engineers and artillerymen to command the Turkish forces ashore. Palmerston had decided to force the Egyptians out of the province before the winter by cutting their sea communications. When Smith fell ill Stopford directed a delighted Napier to take command ashore. He had always reckoned soldier's work was simple and proceeded, not without a good deal of posturing, to prove his point. When a squadron was detached to capture Sidon he insisted on taking command over the head of Captain Maurice Berkeley, who would later have a chance to pay him back. The operation was a complete success, relying on a short naval bombardment and assault by the embarked marines. When he returned Napier found that Stopford was planning a land and sea attack on Beirut. Napier led the Turkish army into the mountains, to engage the Egyptians who were positioned south of the Dog River. At this point he received orders to hand over command to Smith, who had just returned from Constantinople. Reasoning that to hand over command on the day of battle would be disastrous Napier, not for the first time, ignored orders and launched his attack. With Napier driving them on the Turks stormed up hill and defeated the Egyptians, the first time they had done so in more than a decade. The results of the battle of Boharsef, one of the Royal Navy's most unlikely victories, were immediate. The Egyptians evacuated Beirut. Napier returned to his camp, handed over to Smith and returned to the *Powerful*.

Palmerston had become thoroughly dissatisfied with Stopford's procrastination. Aware that it was vital to complete the campaign before mid-November, when the weather would become too severe for large sailing ships to operate on the Syrian coast, and anxious to preclude French intervention, Palmerston ordered Stopford to capture Acre, the last Egyptian stronghold on the coast. On 2 November the fleet attacked. The plan was for the southern watergate to be breached by naval gunfire, allowing Turkish marines to storm the fortress. Napier requested command of this operation, but instead had to be content with leading the diversionary attack on the west face of the fort, as his flagship drew too much water. On the day of battle Napier, displaying his usual initiative, led his squadron in from the north, rather than the south as ordered. He anchored expecting his followers to pass on his disengaged side and continue the line; instead, relying on Stopford's order they all anchored astern, as if they had run in from the south. Stopford was able to rectify their lack of thought by ordering in the reserve ship, but the confusion caused a good deal of ill feeling. The attack was a great success, a shell detonated the main Egyptian magazine, killing over a thousand men. The Egyptians evacuated the city before the allies could land.

When Stopford criticized his conduct Napier publicly demanded a court martial. Stopford then retracted his complaint. Many saw Napier's conduct as wilful disobedience, but it was in the best traditions of the service to employ such initiative. The post-war navy had forgotten Nelson at St Vincent and Copenhagen, a new generation preferred unthinking obedience to skill and initiative. Stopford detached Napier, now a first-class commodore, to command the blockade of Alexandria. Arriving on 21 November he understood Palmerston's policy, unlike Stopford, whom the foreign secretary wanted to sack. Consequently he offered Mehmet Ali peace and the hereditary pashalic of Egypt if he surrendered the Turkish fleet, evacuated Syria, and accepted the formal authority of the sultan. Defeated and deserted by the French, Mehmet Ali accepted. Thus pre-empted, Stopford, the British ambassador, Lord Ponsonby, and other diplomats in Constantinople attempted to repudiate the convention. Palmerston was delighted. He had secured his greatest diplomatic triumph through the daring, initiative, and enterprise of Napier. A few days later two ships were wrecked by the storms Napier and Palmerston had been anxious to avoid. Whatever the protocol, Napier had once again cut a Gordian knot for British diplomacy. His reward was limited to a KCB. Palmerston had wanted to give him a

baronetcy or a peerage, but this would have required an ever higher award for Stopford, a pill too bitter to swallow. He also received a diamond hilted sword and the order of the Mejidiye from the sultan, along with Austrian, Russian, and Prussian orders. After overseeing the implementation of the convention Napier returned home in March 1841 to a hero's welcome. He was now the most popular naval officer in the country, and would remain so until his death. After receiving the freedom of the City of London he was elected to parliament for the popular constituency of Marylebone on 19 August 1841, and published his *History of the War in Syria*.

Peacetime and steam, 1841–1849 In parliament Napier supported Palmerston, which did him little good as the whigs were then out of office. He spoke regularly on naval issues, notably the conditions of service and the treatment of warrant and petty officers, called for the abolition of corporal punishment and impressment, and on the need to maintain a large navy against France and Russia. He promoted his own ideas on ship design, and in 1845 the Admiralty authorized him to design a first-class steam frigate. This ship, the *Sidon*, reflected the pivotal role of coastal offensive operations in his career. Built with shallow draught, heavy armament, and the capacity to embark 1000 troops, she was a dedicated amphibious assault ship. He also placed her machinery below the waterline for safety.

On 9 November 1846 Napier finally reached the rank of rear-admiral. He had spent forty years as a captain because of the strict adherence to seniority and the congested state of the navy list. In May 1847 he took command of the western squadron, having agreed not to stand at the forthcoming election. The whig first lord, Lord Auckland, respected his abilities and was prepared to work round his faults. The squadron operated between Portsmouth, Gibraltar, and Lisbon; it provided opportunities for ships on passage to foreign stations to work up, for sailing and steam trials, and to support British interest in Portugal, which remained in turmoil. Napier's trials convinced Auckland to adopt screw propulsion for all future warships. On 20 December 1847 his stepson Charles was drowned when his steam frigate, the *Avenger*, was wrecked on the Sorelli rocks. This was a shattering blow. Napier had invested much political and service capital in his stepson's career, and the loss of a talented and loyal supporter among the younger generation would be sorely felt in his final command. He had for some time been estranged from his wife (she died on 19 December 1857) and he had only recently re-established close ties with his stepson. Some believed that he was never the same again. The squadron spent most of 1848 on the coast of Ireland, supporting the civil power, and in December went down to Gibraltar, in response to piracy on the Riff coast of Morocco. In April 1849 Napier returned to Spithead and hauled down his flag, the squadron being broken up.

In January 1849 Lord Auckland had died suddenly and was replaced by Sir Francis Baring. Napier's strongest supporter had been replaced by an old political enemy. As Europe had become more peaceful Lord John Russell's ministry brought Napier ashore. They rejected his application for the Mediterranean command; the alternative, a shore command at Cork, was little more than a means of keeping him out of parliament. He stood for Lambeth in August 1850, but was defeated. Angry that the Mediterranean was given to Admiral Sir James Dundas, the whig first sea lord who was more at home behind a desk and better known for partisan politics than command experience, Napier conducted an ill-advised and ill-tempered debate with Baring and Russell in the columns of *The Times*. Russell, in his usual style, managed to combine an explanation with an insult. Napier, he concluded, was distinguished for his bravery, but not his discretion. This coined one of Napier's more appropriate sobriquets, 'the Indiscreet Admiral'. The correspondence, and other letters dating back to the 1820s, suitably edited by General Sir William Napier, were published in *The Navy, its Past and Present State* in 1851. This revealed that while Napier lacked tact and discretion, he had promoted many of the reforms that had improved the condition of the service. In 1852 Napier was invited to stand for Great Yarmouth, a notoriously corrupt borough. In defeat he was shocked to find that his popularity and pledges of support had vanished in the face of the local Conservative brewing interest, and its more tangible rewards.

The Crimean War, 1854–1855 On 28 May 1853 Napier was promoted vice-admiral, and when awarded a good service pension made a point of offering his services should the 'Holy Places' crisis lead to war. Sir James Graham, the first lord, had known him since 1814, and was in office in 1833–4; he agreed with Palmerston, now home secretary, that Napier was the right man to lead a fleet should a war break out with Russia. However, Graham was reluctant to make such an overt signal of hostile intent, denying Napier any influence over the selection of captains and junior admirals for the fleet. Only on 22 February 1854, when the Crimean War had become inevitable, did Graham appoint Napier to command a Baltic fleet that existed largely on paper, being short of ships, seamen, officers, intelligence, and even basic geographical knowledge. He was fêted at the Reform Club on 7 March, and then sent to sea in haste. Graham wanted Napier to administer the Nelson touch, attacking Reval harbour and destroying the Russian fleet that normally wintered there. This would encourage Sweden to join the war. In the event Reval was empty, and Napier spent much of the short campaigning season working his fleet up into some semblance of order. He imposed an effective blockade and pinned the Russian fleet in harbour, cruising off St Petersburg in full view of the tsar. Hampered by the allied French squadron, which was in even worse order than his own, and especially by the lack of craft suitable for coastal operations, it was not until early August, when 10,000 French troops arrived, that he was able to begin offensive operations, capturing the Aland Islands with light losses. Without mortar vessels, gunboats, or rockets he could do nothing at Sveaborg and Kronstadt, the main Russian bases. He had asked for

this equipment even before he was appointed, but Graham, over sanguine of Swedish help, and reluctant to spend any money, rejected the appeal.

When rumours reached London, in late September, that Sevastopol had fallen to an assault, Graham sent Napier a private letter inviting him to use his battlefleet to attack Sveaborg. Napier very properly refused to take such a rash step. When Graham discovered that Sevastopol had not fallen he decided to sacrifice Napier to the inevitable popular clamour for results. To this end he undermined Napier's standing with his main supporters, Palmerston, and the editor of *The Times*, John Thaddeus Delane. For evidence he used the correspondence of the captains in the fleet, accusing Napier of irresolution. Their accusations were coloured by the inexperience of the post-war generation of captains, and the increasingly aristocratic character of the officer corps. They were entirely out of sympathy with Napier's views, and his brusque methods. That he was correct in every significant decision he took throughout the campaign did not matter. His critics ignored his experience and genius for war. Instead they advocated suicidal attacks, although their ships were incapable of avoiding collisions, with each other and the shore.

Thus Napier was made a scapegoat for the failure of the ministers to devise a policy for the Baltic theatre, let alone a coherent strategy. Realizing which way the wind was blowing, Napier tried to come home in time to fight a by-election at Marylebone in December. Graham knew what was planned, and demanded that he resign, which Napier refused. He was ordered to haul down his flag on reaching Spithead, and had no further employment.

Last years, 1855–1860 In July 1855 Napier was offered the GCB by the first lord, Sir Charles Wood, but he refused and demanded an enquiry into his conduct. In November he was returned unopposed at a by-election in Southwark. When Palmerston, now prime minister, spoke of the navy's role in the victory over the Russians, Napier's was the one name that he mentioned, for Napier had secured the first allied victory. As his last chance of a peerage had passed, and his services were not required for a dockyard command, Napier settled down to his parliamentary duties. He published his correspondence in G. Butler Earp's *Sir Charles Napier's Campaign in the Baltic* (1857). Politically radical—favouring franchise extension, the ballot, short parliaments, the abolition of church rates, and the exclusion of bishops from the House of Lords—his main concerns in parliament were defence and the navy. He spoke regularly on the danger from France, the needs of the navy, in favour of ironclad warships, against the construction of forts, and more generally in support of Palmerston. He waged a bitter battle with Graham and Admiral Berkeley in 1856, in which Graham raked up old gossip about Acre. Despite the general dislike of anyone who attempted to work out a personal animus in the house, Napier persuaded the majority that he had been ill-used. His conduct in parliament was frequently out of order and he paid little attention to its protocol. His politics remained radical–big navy to the end. Re-elected in

1857 and 1859 he spent much of the year at Merchistoun, still pursuing advanced farming methods. On 6 March 1860 he became a full admiral. He died at home on 6 November 1860 and was buried in Catherington churchyard, Horndean, almost within sight of Portsmouth harbour.

Assessment Napier was a remarkable man in an age not starved of such men. His radical politics, professional skill, bravery, and ambition marked him out, and left him increasingly at odds with the service after 1815. Although personally well connected, and the beneficiary of political and naval patronage on a grand scale, he affected a common touch, and claimed to have risen entirely on merit. Despite having passed hardly a year in Scotland after 1799, he affected a heavy, drawling accent to the end of his life, and was frequently incomprehensible to refined English ears. In action, he was uncommonly cool; this cold calculating courage, more than anything else, set him apart. In contrast to the majority of his contemporaries he was in full control of his faculties, and especially his intellect, at the height of battle. In every action he fought these faculties were deployed in the single-minded pursuit of victory. Only in battle could all his nervous energy be focused and employed. Ashore and in peacetime he could be unbearable, unable to settle to anything, a restless spirit constantly in search of action, glory, and advancement. His restlessness revealed itself in his personal life, with endless quarrels and disputes over money, promotion, rewards, honour, and reputation. Although personally sensitive to slights, he gave many, and suffered accordingly. His fast friends were few; most regarded him as a species of wild beast to be let loose in time of war, but too dangerous to serve in time of peace. Those who trusted him, Palmerston and Auckland, found him reliable and highly effective. He was a braggart and a self-publicist, attributes that only reinforced the Victorian consensus on his vulgarity. His ambition, both social and financial, knew no bounds, and he was frequently less than generous to colleagues and superiors. However, he was worshipped by the warrant and petty officers, and especially the seamen. After he died they erected a monument to him in Victoria Park, Portsmouth. He was the common man's naval hero. His popularity with the electors of Southwark, then a very large constituency, was a sure sign of this. His personal habits were as remarkable as his conduct. As a young man his dark complexion and black hair earned him the nickname Black Charley. In later life he was stout, lame, and invariably filthy. His clothes were shabby, faded, and stained red-brown by his copious consumption of snuff. His only surviving child, Frances, married the Revd Henry Jodrell of Gisleham in Suffolk; his elder stepson, Edward Delaval Hungerford Elers *Napier, composed his tombstone biography. Together they kept his name before the public after his death. Frances proved to be as ill-tempered and vindictive as her father. She lived to criticize the entry in the *Dictionary of National Biography* and caused a second biography to be written.

Misunderstood and maligned in an age that valued form above function, Napier, more than any other naval figure

of the era, represented the spirit that made the Royal Navy the greatest fighting service in the world. He was professional, brave, intelligent, and above all thoroughly at home in any sea or river. He did not win any great sea battles, his St Vincent was rather one-sided, but his understanding of naval power projection and amphibious, littoral warfare was unrivalled. He was invariably abreast or ahead of the latest technology, realized that men and not ships win wars, and cared enough for his country to ignore orders and break rules to advance its cause.

ANDREW LAMBERT

Sources BL, Napier MSS · PRO, Napier MSS · NMM, Napier MSS · U. Southampton L., Palmerston MSS · E. D. H. E. Napier, *The life and correspondence of Admiral Sir Charles Napier*, 2 vols. (1862) · K. Bourne, *Palmerston: the early years, 1784–1841* (1982) · A. D. Lambert, *The Crimean War: British grand strategy, 1853–56* (1990) · *Dod's Peerage* (1858) · *WWBMP*, vol. 1 · *CGPLA Eng. & Wales* (1860)

Archives BL, corresp. and papers, Add. MSS 40018–40055 · L. Cong., narrative of the operations in the Potomac by the squadron under Sir J. A. Gordon · PRO, letters and papers, PRO 30/16 | BL, corresp. with Lord Aberdeen, Add. MSS 43237–43255 · BL OIOC, Hay MSS, letters to Lord Tweeddale, MS Eur. F 96 · Bodl. Oxf., letters to Sir William Napier · Cumbria AS, Carlisle, Graham MSS · JRL, letters to Edward Davies Davenport · NMM, corresp. with Lord Minto · NRA Scotland, priv. coll., letters to Henry Duncan · NRA, priv. coll., corresp. with Admiral MFF Berkeley and Admiralty · PRO, Admiralty MSS · U. Durham L., letters to Viscount Ponsonby · U. Nott. L., letters to Sir Andrew Buchanan · U. Southampton L., corresp. with Lord Palmerston

Likenesses plaster medallion, 1811 (after J. Henning), Scot. NPG · J. Simpson, oils, c.1835, Scot. NPG · T. M. Joy, oils, 1841?, NMM · T. M. Joy, oils, 1853, Naval and Military Club, London [*see illus.*] · C. Baugniet, lithograph, pubd 1854, BM, NPG · E. W. Gill, oils, 1854, NPG · Skelton, lithograph, pubd 1854 (after A. H. Taylor), BM, NPG · G. G. Adams, bust, 1868, St Paul's Cathedral · memorial, Victoria Park, Portsmouth · memorial column, Victoria Park, Portsmouth · Staffordshire figure

Wealth at death under £30,000: probate, 12 Dec 1860, *CGPLA Eng. & Wales*

Napier, Sir **Charles James** (1782–1853), army officer, was born on 10 August 1782 in Whitehall, London, and the family moved to Celbridge, 10 miles from Dublin, in 1785. He was the eldest of the eight children of Colonel the Hon. George *Napier (1751–1804), son of the sixth Lord Napier of Merchistoun, and his second wife, Lady Sarah Bunbury, *née* Lennox (1745–1826), daughter of the second duke of Richmond. Charles had a half-sister, Louisa, from his father's first marriage. Three of his brothers became well known: George Thomas *Napier (1784–1855), Henry Edward *Napier (1789–1853), and William Francis Patrick *Napier (1785–1860), who as Charles's biographer assiduously promoted his brother's fame. The opening of his *Life and Opinions of Sir Charles Napier* (1857) claimed:

> This shall be the story of one who never tarnished his reputation by a shameful deed: of one who subdued distant nations by his valour and governed them so wisely that English rule was reverenced and loved where before it had been feared and execrated. (Napier, *Life*, 1.1)

The book went on to allege that Napier's enemies had sought to besmirch his reputation with stories of insubordination to authorities, harsh treatment of the people under his own authority, bad temper, and dishonesty. The records suggest that those enemies, a number of them

Sir Charles James Napier (1782–1853), by George Jones, 1851

much respected people, had some justification for their judgements.

Early life, 1782–1808 In his diaries and other writings Charles Napier pictured himself as a poor soldier struggling alone to advance himself against the enmity of lesser men; but though he was poor, his family connections—many of the great names of the time, including the cousin after whom he was named, Charles James Fox—were essential to his career. That his father had been tutored by David Hume in Edinburgh may explain some of the freethinking ideas of both father and son. Colonel Napier had served in America during the revolutionary war, where his first wife had died. Charles Napier greatly admired his handsome, dashing father, but his mother was apparently dominant in his affections and, at times, in shaping his career. Her beauty had led George III to propose to her, but she married Sir Charles Bunbury. She left him to live with Lord William Gordon, but after Bunbury divorced her in 1776 she married Colonel Napier in 1781. Little of this appears in the nineteenth-century accounts, but Napier's own tempestuous, unconventional career was presumably coloured by this remarkable woman. With such dramatic parents, the fact that as a child he was sickly, short-sighted, and stunted in his growth, because, according to his brother, of maltreatment by a brutal nursemaid, may partly explain his driving ambition to excel as a soldier and his lasting sense of being badly used by those in authority.

Ireland was decisive in shaping Napier's opinions and actions: repeatedly his yardstick for bad government and the misery of subject populations was Ireland. While his sympathy for the oppressed seemed genuine all his life, when he held civil and military power, as in the Ionian Islands and India, he was accused by his detractors of arbitrary cruelty. His Irish connection began in 1785 when his family moved to Celbridge, close to his mother's aristocratic Lennox relatives, including her sister, the duchess of Leinster. His military career started formally when he was commissioned ensign on 31 January 1794, aged twelve, in the 33rd regiment, transferring a few months later to the 89th, in which his father was assistant quartermaster-general. When it was sent to Ostend Napier was transferred to the 4th, but instead of joining it he was sent to the grammar school at Celbridge, where he was one of the few protestant pupils. In the Irish uprising of 1798 he helped his father defend their estate against the rioting peasants, but even then he was conscious of the oppression that had at last led them to rebel. As he put it later, the starving Irish were 'obedient to the laws of man, instead of adopting God's law of self-preservation' (Napier, *Life*, 1.438). In 1799 he became aide-de-camp to Sir James Duff, the commander of the Limerick district, where he saw what he described as 'the intolerable system of ruling', that led on both sides to 'half-hangings, floggings, cutting of throats' (ibid., 1.76). The following year he transferred to the 95th regiment, a new rifle corps being formed in Blatchington, Sussex, and for the next two years was with it in Weymouth, Hythe, and Shorncliffe. He lived the life reflected in contemporary novels: he sent challenges—that came to nothing—to fellow officers, if he felt insulted, and, as he told his sister, 'being in love with four misses at once' (ibid., 1.22) he frequently danced to daybreak. But he also read military history five hours a day, or so he told his mother. In 1803 he was back in Ireland as aide-de-camp to his cousin General Edward Fox, fighting the insurgents led by Robert Emmett, and in the same year he went back to London when Fox was transferred there. He was promoted to captain in the staff corps, a new body organized to assist the Royal Engineers, under Sir John Moore, who recognized his ability. Then in 1806 Napier's mother persuaded her cousin Charles James Fox, who had just come to power, to promote him to major in the Cape Colonial corps; however, he transferred to the 50th regiment.

Peninsular and Anglo-American wars, 1808–1814 In 1808 Napier was sent to Lisbon to join the division under Moore's command. Thirty-five years later he looked back on what he regarded as years of frustrations and disappointed hopes, and saw this appointment as the first of six crucial phases on his 'wheel of fortune' (Napier, *Life*, 2.290).

Because of the absence of its commanding officer, Moore put Napier in charge of the 50th regiment, part of the army he led into Spain. In the great battle of Corunna in 1809 Moore was killed, and Napier, after being very badly wounded, was captured by the French. His long relation of the incident, written in his vigorous, dramatic style, is, like many of his later battle accounts, a curious amalgam—a celebration of the courage of the soldiers, both his own and the enemy's, and at the same time an expression of his horror at the senseless cruelty that soldiers and officers often displayed. He was freed in an exchange of prisoners when Marshal Ney heard that his blind old mother was mourning him as dead. He rejoined the army, and after having fought in July 1810 at the battle of Coa he characteristically listed in his diary the mistakes that his commanding officer, General Crauford, had made—proving Crauford's incompetence. Even Wellington, the commander-in-chief, who later became his supporter, did not escape Napier's criticism. After the battle of Talavera he wrote that Wellington was 'rash and imprudent ... his errors seem to be more of inexperience and vanity than want of talent' (Napier, *Life*, 1.127). Shortly afterwards he joined Wellington's staff, and at the battle of Busaco on 27 September 1810 was again severely wounded. He fought in the battle of Fuentes d'Oñoro in May 1811, and returned to England in August 1811, when he was promoted lieutenant-colonel.

Napier's diaries and letters are full of complaints about his enemies in England, especially the duke of York, whom he blamed for his non-promotion. But when promotion came he was little pleased, because it was to the 102nd regiment which, according to his brother, was engaged in 'dreary, obscure, and soul-sickening service' (Napier, *Life*, 1.175). His financial problems were lightened for a time by the sinecure of non-resident governor of the Virgin Islands, but when a pension for his wounds in the Peninsular War was granted he returned to the army. In 1812, during the Anglo-American War, he was in Bermuda, commanding a brigade to harass the American coasts. He devised a plan for defeating the Americans by raising an army of slaves, who outnumbered the white inhabitants in the south, with British officers, and himself at the head. This army would march on Washington, dictate peace, and free the slaves. He alleged his superiors ignored his plan because of the effect the liberation of the American slaves would have on those in the British West Indies. His regiment was sent to Nova Scotia, but hoping for action again in the Peninsula he transferred back in September 1813 to the 50th. By the time he reached England the war with France was over.

From 1814 to 1817 Napier was at the military college at Farnham, reading not only military history but also general literature, agriculture, building construction, and political economy. Considering his limited formal schooling, this period must account for the wide knowledge shown in his writings on such diverse subjects as colonization, the poor laws, William the Conqueror, and the defects of British rule in India. This period of study was broken by his participation in 1815 in the defeat of Napoleon on his return from Elba. Years later Napier remarked that at the time he had accepted the common English view that Napoleon was a monster, threatening European civilization, but he had come to realize his greatness as a preserver of civil order and national discipline. Like Thomas Carlyle, who became his admirer, Napier believed in the merits of the strong man who sought to use power to reshape the world. This led him to be critical of the politics of the duke of Wellington: though a strong man, he had, Napier thought, opposed the just feeling of the age and tried to stem the tides of history.

Ionian Islands and after, 1819–1838 Napier's belief that he himself understood the needs of the time, and that if he were free to use military and civil power he could advance the common good, was first demonstrated at Cephalonia, one of the larger Ionian Islands, then a British protectorate. After much searching for employment, he was appointed an inspecting field officer in the Ionian Islands in 1819. He discovered the post required little work, but it gave him an opportunity to visit the Greek mainland, which was the beginning of his passionate interest in Greek independence. The insurrection of 1821 broke out a few days after he left, and he began to dream of becoming a leader of the Greeks in a war against the Turks. When he got back to England he published a pamphlet, *The War in Greece*, which vividly denounced the horrors of Turkish rule and claimed that the Greeks needed, and would welcome, foreign military intervention.

In 1821 Napier was appointed to a new post in the Ionian Islands—military resident in Cephalonia. He was, as he put it, 'the despotic lieutenant of a lord high commissioner' (Napier, *Life*, 1.304), who had charge of all the islands. Napier later referred to these years from 1822 to 1830 as the happiest in his life. He had a mistress, Anastasia, reportedly a fiery Greek patriot, and they had two daughters, Sarah Susan and Emily Cephalonia. He was devoted to them and brought them back to England, although Anastasia refused to accompany him. He took much interest in their education, believing that the way to bring up children was to reason with them, so that they would learn self-control. As for their future, he hoped they would not marry 'brutes or fools, but that is their affair' (ibid., 1.449). Sarah married Sir William Montagu McMurdo, who served under Napier in his Indian campaigns, and Emily married her first cousin, William C. E. Napier. When he was a young man Napier had written, without explanation, that he would 'never marry any but a widow' (ibid., 1.435), and after his mother died in 1826 he married the following year Elizabeth, *née* Oakeley, widow of Francis John Kelly, fifteen years older than himself, and took her to Cephalonia to look after his children. It was apparently a happy marriage. She died in 1833, and in 1835, in search of 'a protectress for his daughters and a companion for himself' (ibid., 1.457), he married an old friend, Frances, *née* Philips, widow of Captain Richard Alcock RN; she died in 1872.

The Greeks of Cephalonia were, Napier thought, like the Irish, in a state of wretched barbarism because of oppressive rulers. Given a free hand, without interference from incompetent civil superiors, Napier believed he could use his combination of military and civil authority to bring order and prosperity to Cephalonia and perhaps to all of Greece. He was later to make the same judgement about India. During this period his great friend was Lord Byron, and they spent much time together devising schemes for freeing Greece. Byron thought Napier was the man to lead the army of liberation, and perhaps to govern

Greece, but the Greek Committee in London baulked at the cost of such an endeavour.

In his diary for this period Napier analysed his religious beliefs. He took part in Anglican services, but he denied that there was any fixed and immutable religion, and rejected the divinity of Jesus, though affirming his faith in a creator. He believed in a future life but did not, he said, presume to judge what that state would be. 'My faith is made up from feelings, the result of accidents, reflections, dangers, joys, a hotch-potch of things, many of which I can't remember' (Napier, *Life*, 1.387).

Napier often enumerated his achievements in Cephalonia: harsh but fair justice; roads built to end isolation and to make trade possible; docks and other public works constructed; the weak protected against the strong. According to the enthusiastic biography by his brother, he changed the deplorable morality of the people by 'inducing industry, honesty, and useful knowledge' (Napier, *Life*, 1.417). Then, as often happened in Napier's career, his superior, the high commissioner Sir Frederick Adam, began to criticize his work, charging him with misuse of funds on unauthorized projects, disobedience to his superiors, and the use of forced labour to build his roads, including priests made to work on them in their ecclesiastical robes. Napier, despite appeals to London and fierce denunciations of Adam, was removed from his command in 1830.

Napier felt that his enemies in London had driven him from public life, intending, as his brother put it, that he 'should languish in poverty, obscurity and insignificance for the rest of his life' (Napier, *Life*, 1.435), and for the next ten years he had no official employment. He was occasionally offered postings abroad, such as an offer of 'something in Canada', but he fiercely refused to accept anything from the whigs, who, he said, were 'all that is infamous and stupid in politics' (ibid., 1.446). He was busy, however, with various schemes, such as a plan to set up a new colony in South Australia with himself as governor. To publicize his ideas, in 1835 he wrote a pamphlet, *Colonisation, Particularly in Southern Australia*, in which he said that the usual Anglo-Saxon method of colonization would be avoided, namely 'robbery, oppression, murder and extermination of natives' (ibid., 1.435). Such writing pleased the radicals, but not the government or the colonists. He also wrote a novel, *Harald*, which was subsequently lost, and the Napiers made a thinly veiled charge that Bulwer Lytton plagiarized it.

Chartism, 1839–1841 In 1838, after many bitter disappointments when people he regarded as unworthy were honoured, Napier was made a KCB, as was his brother George. In April 1839 he took command of the vast, densely populated northern district, which included Yorkshire and Lancashire, where physical-force Chartism was strong and the army's primary role was internal security in support of the civil power. He accepted the post with some misgiving. He considered himself a radical and agreed with the Chartists' six points and hostility to the new poor law. Nevertheless he opposed the use of violence to obtain reform, and was determined to preserve law and order

and prevent bloodshed: his strategy was essentially preventive. With the local civil authorities fragmented and often unreliable, and the civil police inadequate, Napier and his troops had a crucial function. He had an executive, co-ordinating role as *de facto* controller of operations against the Chartists. He made plans to defend Manchester, to intercept a Chartist army marching from Derbyshire to London, and to defeat a Chartist insurrection. He conferred with the magistrates to concert action, and gave advice to the government and the Horse Guards on political questions affecting his district. He was given authority to call out the yeomanry. He requested Irish troops, as less likely to be influenced by the Chartists, and, remembering 1798, concentrated his troops instead of dispersing them in vulnerable detachments. To deter the Chartists and prevent bloodshed he made great display of his troops and sent personal messages to the Chartist leaders at Manchester. He also used his influence with the magistrates to dissuade them from breaking up the great Chartist meeting on Kersal Moor in May 1839.

Typically Napier quarrelled with the local civil authorities and with the government, insisting that his troops would be used to maintain general order, not to crush peaceful protests. The tory magistrates were, he said, 'bad, violent, uncompromising', the whigs were 'sneaking and base' (Napier, *Life*, 2.153), and many Chartist leaders were self-seeking demagogues. Whether, as his supporters claimed, Napier saved England from a civil war is not, of course, provable, but when in September 1841 he relinquished his command the worst seemed to be over, justifying his comment that 'some service to the state I did there without bloodshed' (ibid., 2.290).

India, 1841–1850 In 1841 Napier was appointed to a Bombay command, at Poona. He wrote in 1840 that:

> Our object in conquering India, the object of all our cruelties, was money. … Every shilling of this has been picked out of blood, wiped and put into the murder's pocket. … We shall yet suffer for the crime as sure as there is a God in heaven. (Lambrick, 33)

Despite this, he said that he accepted the Indian command only 'to catch the rupees for my girls' (ibid., 36), who would be left penniless unless he got prize money from conquests in India. He also stated that his desire to try his hand with an army 'is a longing not to be described' (Napier, *Life*, 2.161). He arrived in Bombay in December 1841.

In August 1842 Napier was appointed commander of the British army in Sind. This was directly related to the disaster in Afghanistan. Napier's views on the Anglo-Afghan War, coloured by his conviction of the stupidity and incompetence of the British rulers in India, influenced his subsequent actions in Sind. He expressed his views in the margins of his copy of Vincent Eyre's book on the war. Where Eyre wrote of the officers' bravery, Napier wrote 'you were all a set of sons of bitches' (copy of V. Eyre, *The Military Operations in Cabul*, 1843, 227, BL OIOC). Eyre wrote, 'It seemed as if we were under the ban of Heaven'; Napier crossed it out, writing, 'Nonsense. These matters depend upon particular circumstances' (ibid., 127). In his accounts of his own victories in Sind, Napier always made clear that they depended upon generalship in control of circumstances. Napier was put in command not just of the military forces in Sind but also of the political officers. Of these, the two best-known were James Outram and John Jacob, who, while still army officers, were seconded to civil posts. The distinction between civil and military authority was essential in British rule in India, but throughout his career Napier argued that the only way to bring order to a disturbed area was through a leader who combined military and civil power.

Sind did not have a single ruler, but about eighteen chiefs, or amirs, mainly descendants of chieftains who had seized power as the Mughal empire declined in the eighteenth century. The British had paid little attention to the area until early in the nineteenth century, when circumstances combined to awaken their interest. One factor, as Napier emphasized, was the desire of the East India Company and British merchants in general to increase trade, and it was still widely believed that the Indus could become a great channel of commerce into the heart of Asia. The amirs opposed this, knowing what had happened elsewhere in India where British traders came. Furthermore, it was in their interest to impose tolls on any commerce in the region. Then there was the question of the security of British India, and by the 1830s the threat of a Russian advance through Afghanistan loomed large in the minds of officials. Finally the personal ambition of British soldiers and officials in India could not be disregarded. Napier and his assistants, James Outram and John Jacob, both of whom, especially Outram, became his great opponents, were undoubtedly motivated by their realization that a time of exceptional opportunity had come.

By treaties with the British, unwillingly signed in 1832 and 1839, the leading amirs had agreed that relations with other powers would be under British control, they would not collect tolls on the Indus, they would cede control of the port area of Karachi and the Lower Sind to the British, they would accept British officers as residents in their courts, and they would pay for the upkeep of a British force. Many British officials, including Napier, were convinced that the amirs were using the Afghan situation to escape from some of the more onerous terms of the treaties, and there was evidence that the amirs were gathering their armies to oppose the British. Very little was known about the internal politics of the amirs' domains, and movements of men and arms that were sometimes interpreted as anti-British were often internecine. Convinced, however, by such intelligence as he could gather, Napier concluded that not only should the existing treaties be rigorously enforced but that the amirs should sign a new one limiting their powers even more, cede new territory, redistribute the revenues, and that, as a symbol of sovereignty, the queen's head should appear on their coinage. Napier was aware how unjust these demands seemed, but he was convinced that an extension of British power over all the subcontinent was inevitable. What especially angered the amirs was that one of them, Ali Murad, whom they distrusted, had gained Napier's confidence and was

to get a disproportionate share of the revenues: 802,250 rupees while the others would divide 625,750 rupees among them. Napier said he knew that Ali Murad could not be trusted, but believed he could be manipulated into being useful for a time at least. Outram was convinced that the amirs would never agree to such an arrangement and that Napier was driving them to open rebellion.

Open antagonism was growing between the two men, partly perhaps because Outram had lost his independent status and been brought under Napier's control, but within it there was also a fairly clear policy dispute over the nature of British rule in India and the place of former rulers, such as the amirs of Sind. Napier believed that the amirs were feudal relics, oppressors of the poor, and were opposed to all change that would bring prosperity at the loss of their power. While he may not have deliberately goaded the amirs into making war against the British, he certainly did not regret that their actions gave him an excuse for abolishing their power. Since the British were unjust in being in India at all, he wrote, 'at least let the people and ourselves draw from that injustice the benefit of civilization' (Huttenback, 96). It was the argument he had used in Ireland and in the Ionian Islands. Another element in his quarrel with Outram was Napier's impatience with the argument of old Indian hands that they had a special understanding of India, whereas in fact they had worn out their minds and bodies in sensual indulgence, 'while enjoying large salaries and the adulation of black clerks' (Napier, *Administration of Scinde*, 7). Furthermore, Napier dismissed their claim of the importance of experience in a country, since all people everywhere were alike. Outram, like many British officials who had served in the princely states, had a high regard for the patriarchal, if despotic, rule of the amirs. It was true that Napier was carrying out the orders of Lord Ellenborough, the governor-general, but what they were doing, Outram told Napier, was tyrannical and would lead to great bloodshed, since the amirs' armies were undisciplined, inadequately armed, and poorly provisioned. 'Every life which may hereafter be lost in consequence will be murder' (Lambrick, 121), he wrote to Napier.

Napier made full acceptance of the new treaty an ultimatum, and when there were outbreaks of violence in Hyderabad, the main city of Sind, in December 1842 Napier began to move his troops up the Indus towards the city. In a dramatic move on 5 January 1843 he took a force of 350 men to seize the great desert fortress of Imamgarh, only to find it deserted. While Napier permitted Outram to continue negotiations at Hyderabad with the amirs, when the British residency was attacked Napier moved swiftly and met the enemy on 17 February on the Fuleli River at Miani. Victory established Napier's almost mythic reputation, for he had only 2200 men, mostly sepoys, while the enemy had about 20,000. His losses, the dead and the wounded, amounted to fewer than 300, and he estimated that the amirs had lost 6000. Afterwards it was alleged that the bloodshed could have been avoided: the amirs had in fact signed the treaty, but Napier had not informed the governor-general. If Napier had indeed deliberately withheld the fact of the treaty's being signed, it was probably because he had already decided the amirs' fate.

Napier continued his drive against them, and with reinforcements from Bombay he continued to attack those still undefeated, notably the amir of Mirpur. They met in a great battle on 24 March at Dabo, 8 miles from Hyderabad, Napier with 5000 men, the amir with 25,000, but this large force was a gathering of his men, rather than an army. Napier lost 270 men, the amir 5000. One of the few accounts by an Indian says that before this battle Napier treated 500 of his soldiers 'with copious drinks of liquor and then ordered them to attack the magazine' ('Memoir of Munshi Awatrai', BL OIOC, MS Eur. F.208.150). The amir himself escaped, but after his defeat on 14 June all organized opposition to British power was over, and in August 1843 the annexation of Sind was announced. Napier had already received £70,000 in prize money after the fall of Hyderabad; he felt, however, that he had not been justly treated and later quarrelled with the directors of the East India Company about his share.

While many praised the annexation of Sind, for which Napier was made a GCB in November 1843, some criticized the action. According to Gladstone the whole cabinet was against it, questioning both its morality and its wisdom. Members of the East India Company board of directors, ever since Wellesley's great conquests, had been critical of the conquests made in their name. The Sind war and annexation were impolitic and unjust, some of them argued, and so far from increasing the revenues of India, they showed how Sind was a drain on government finances. There was, however, no disposition on the part of the authorities in India or Great Britain to return the kingdoms to the amirs.

Napier was appointed governor of Sind and ordered to create a new administration. He made large claims for his achievements in the four and a half years he held office, but the difficulties were immense. Neither he nor his small staff, mainly army officers, were familiar with the people of the area, but they had the self-confidence characteristic of the age. Napier had a fixed idea of Asians in general, and of the Sind people in particular, and he was convinced that he knew how to govern without recourse to specialized knowledge. He was both army commander and civil administrator, functions combined nowhere else, and despite ill health he involved himself in minutiae, undoubtedly to the detriment of his ability to oversee planning as a whole. An increase in trade had been one of the aims of the treaties that had led to the conquest, and Napier encouraged the development of Karachi as a port. He organized the military occupation of the country, using John Jacob, who, though very critical of many aspects of his administration, particularly his treatment of the amirs, succeeded in stabilizing the peoples in the neighbouring hill country. He created a police force, acknowledged by other administrators to be the best in India, which became the model for others. His most difficult task, and one that could only be partially realized, was the creation of a viable civil administration, including a revenue settlement, tax collection, and a judicial system. He thought many of the amirs' taxes unjust, but when he proposed replacing them with a more rational system he discovered that this 'gave umbrage to these wild people; they would rather bear a heavy unjust one that "had always been" than a light one if it is new' (Napier, *Life*, 3.193). He took a special interest in criminal cases, often hearing them himself, as he believed the people regarded him as their saviour and approved his harsh punishments for wrongdoing. His sympathy for the poor and oppressed, he admitted, sometimes led to injustice. 'Even against the evidence, I decide in favour of the poor. My formula is this: Punish the government servants first, and inquire about the right and wrong when there is time' (ibid., 3.184). Slavery was common in certain areas of Sind, but Napier dismissed the argument that it had been part of the social fabric since time immemorial, and that when they took over the country the British had promised not to interfere in old customs. 'I listen to nothing,' he said, 'and make prisoners of all accused, condemn without proof, punish without mercy' (ibid., 3.189). His attitude was the same towards those who claimed that a man by custom had the right to kill an unfaithful wife. 'Woe be to their husbands,' he proclaimed; 'The English government will not be insulted by such felons' (Lambrick, 338). He applied the same rule to any Hindus who permitted the practice of suttee.

Napier often complained that the authorities in London did not appreciate him, but when the Anglo-Sikh War broke out in December 1845 he was ordered to take his forces to the Punjab. He marched his army to Lahore, but when they arrived the war was over.

Criticism of his administration continued in London, and in July 1847 Napier resigned and left India for Europe. He visited Ireland, but then settled in Cheltenham. In 1849, however, he was back in India to take command of the army in the Second Anglo-Sikh War, for, while the directors of the East India Company opposed his selection, he had the advocacy of Wellington. By the time he reached Calcutta in May the Sikhs had been decisively defeated. He did, however, get embroiled again in dispute. A regulation had been passed by the government depriving the sepoys of a food allowance. Napier, like many officers, had become aware that the sepoys were increasingly resentful, and that great care should be exercised with their privileges. Napier rescinded the regulation without consulting Lord Dalhousie, the governor-general, who was no admirer of Napier and who severely reprimanded him for exceeding his powers. Napier thought Dalhousie 'a poor, petulant man, cunning and sly' (Holmes, 144). Napier resigned in 1850 and returned to England in 1851, retiring to Oaklands, near Portsmouth.

Final years, appearance, and publications In retirement Napier continued controversial. When a writer in the *Quarterly Review* (vol. 182, 1852) alleged his conquest of Sind had been a 'harsh and barbarous aggression' he tried, unsuccessfully, to sue for libel, but the chief justice said that while he accepted Napier's version, the author had the right to express his opinion. Commenting on the case,

The Times claimed Napier was oversensitive to criticism, since 'the united voice of his countrymen acclaim [him] as the greatest military genius now in the Army List' (*The Times*, 24 Nov 1854). Napier died on 29 August 1853 from a cold caught when a pallbearer at Wellington's funeral, but he had suffered from a liver infection since his march to Lahore in 1846. At the time of his death he was working on a book, *Defects, Civil and Military, of the Indian Government*, published in 1853.

Napier was buried in the churchyard of the garrison chapel at Portsmouth, which was crowded with common soldiers who had come at their own expense. Napier had indeed been their friend, opposing flogging in peacetime, providing quarters for married soldiers, and mentioning for the first time, it is said, the names of common soldiers in dispatches. He was also the first to permit Roman Catholic soldiers their own church parades. His statue in Trafalgar Square was inscribed 'Erected by public subscription, the most numerous subscribers being private soldiers'. His former regiment, the 22nd Cheshire, adopted as its marching song 'Wha wadna Fecht for Charlie' (*The Times*, 29 Aug 1853). In October 2000 the statue became the subject of public controversy when Ken Livingstone, the new mayor of London, demanded its removal from the square as he 'hasn't a clue' (*The Times*, 20 Oct 2000, 6) who Napier was. This aroused strong protest in defence of the statue.

There are many descriptions of Napier, ranging from the nickname his junior officers used, Old Fagin, because of his great hooked nose, to one by Dalhousie when Napier was commander-in-chief in India. Dalhousie's description matches the many surviving portraits and sketches: 'Under his bushy eyebrows gleam a pair of piercing and brilliant eyes. He is so short-sighted as to wear spectacles constantly.' With large grey mustaches, 'he allows his beard to descend to his belt'. Although Dalhousie loathed Napier, he noted that he was 'full of fun and cleverness' (Holmes, 135). Yet the story that when he had conquered Sind he sent a telegram, 'Peccavi', was apocryphal: it originated with an 1844 *Punch* cartoon.

Napier wrote many books and pamphlets, including: *The Colonies, Treating of their Value Generally, of the Ionian Islands Particularly and Including Strictures on the Administration of Sir Frederick Adam* (1833); *Remarks on Military Law and the Punishment of Flogging* (1837); *A Dialogue on the Poor Laws* (1838); *A Letter to the Right Hon Sir J. Hobhouse, on the Baggage of the Indian Army* (1849); *A Letter on the Defence of England by Corps of Volunteers and Militia* (1852); and *William the Conqueror, a Historical Romance* (edited by Sir William Napier, 1858).   AINSLIE T. EMBREE

Sources W. F. P. Napier, *The life and opinions of General Sir Charles James Napier*, 4 vols. (1857) • J. Mawson, ed., *Records of the Indian command of General Sir Charles James Napier* (1851) • H. T. Lambrick, *Sir Charles Napier and Sind* (1952) • BL OIOC, MSS Eur. B.114, B.199, F.208 • T. R. Holmes, *Sir Charles Napier* (1925) • R. Huttenback, *British relations with Sind, 1799–1843* (1962) • W. F. P. Napier, *The conquest of Scinde: with some introductory passages in the life of Major-General Sir Charles James Napier*, 2 vols. (1845) • W. F. P. Napier, *History of … Sir Charles Napier's administration of Scinde, and campaign in the Cutchee Hills* (1851) • J. Outram, *The conquest of Scinde: a commentary* (1846) • P. Napier, *Raven Castle: Charles Napier in India, 1844–1851* (1991) • BL, Ellenborough MSS, Add. MSS 40522, 40864 • G. Buist, *Corrections of a few of the errors contained in Sir William Napier's life of his brother* (1857) • F. C. Mather, 'The government and the chartists', *Chartist studies*, ed. A. Briggs (1959), 372–405 • F. C. Mather, *Public order in the age of the Chartists* (1959) • Boase, *Mod. Eng. biog.*

Archives BL, corresp. and papers, Add. MSS 41063, 49105–49147, 54510–54563 • BL OIOC, corresp. and papers relating to India, MS Eur. C 123 • BL OIOC, memorandum relating to Sind, MS Eur. F 87–89 • Bodl. Oxf., family and Indian corresp. and papers • PRO, corresp. and papers, PRO 30/64 • Suffolk RO, Bury St Edmunds, Bunbury MSS, letters and papers relating to blockade of the Morcea and Greece | BL, corresp. with Lord Ripon, Add. MSS 40865–40877 • BL OIOC, corresp. with Sir George Clerk, MSS Eur. D 538 • BL OIOC, Elphinstone MSS • BL OIOC, letters to Robert Fitzgerald, MS Eur. D 1171 • BL OIOC, letters to H. W. Preddy, MS Eur. D 987 • Duke U., Perkins L., letters to Henry Napier • NA Scot., corresp. relating to Thomas Cochrane • NAM, corresp. with Sir James Outram • NL Scot., corresp. mainly with Lord Rutherford • PRO, corresp. with Lord Ellenborough, PRO 30/12 • W. Sussex RO, letters to duke of Richmond

Likenesses S. Gambardella, oils, *c*.1827, Wellington Museum, London • R. J. Lane, lithograph, pubd 1849 (after Count Pierlas), NPG • E. Williams, oils, 1849, NPG • G. Jones, oils, 1851, NPG [*see illus.*] • G. G. Adams, bronze bust, 1853, Scot. NPG; plaster cast of bust, 1853, NPG • J. Faed, ink drawing, 1854 (after bust by P. Park), Scot. NPG • G. G. Adams, bronze statue, 1856, Trafalgar Square, London • G. G. Adams, marble statue, St Paul's Cathedral, London • J. Doyle, caricature drawings, BM • T. W. Hunt, stipple (after photograph by Kilburn), NPG • attrib. S. P. Smart, oils, NPG • cartoon (*Peccavi: I have Sind*), repro. in *Punch* (1844) • eleven portraits, BL OIOC

Napier, David (1788–1873). *See under* Napier, David (1790–1869).

Napier, David (1790–1869), shipbuilder and engineer, was born at Dumbarton on 29 October 1790, the son of John Napier (*d.* July 1813), an engineer in Dumbarton, and his second wife, Ann McAlister. He was a cousin of Robert *Napier (1791–1876), the celebrated shipbuilder, whose younger brother was **David Napier** (1799–1850), the fifth son of James Napier, John's partner in the Dumbarton engineering business, and Jean Ewing, his wife. A third **David Napier** (1788–1873), also a cousin, was the son of Robert Napier, blacksmith to the duke of Argyll at Inveraray. All three Davids, who are often confused and sometimes taken for the same person, were trained in the Dumbarton business, which was one of the largest engineering works on the Clyde at the time, and engaged throughout their early years in boring cannons cast by the Clyde Iron Works for the war with revolutionary France. While they remained in the west of Scotland all three continued to work in one of the family's various engineering and iron-working enterprises.

The least successful was the youngest of the three. He became a partner in Napier Bros., which took over the Camlachie works from Robert in the 1830s, and in 1837 he purchased the Parkhead forge from the Reoch brothers for £2800. He almost certainly made this investment to secure a steady supply of forgings to the family's engineering businesses. He appointed William Rigby, the future son-in-law of the shipbuilder Robert Napier, as works manager. By 1847 his enterprises were in difficulties and he became bankrupt, 'being unable by reason of misfortune of business to meet any of my engagements' (Titles of

Parkhead Forge, Glasgow, Biggart Bailie, and Gifford, solicitors). He married Helen, sister of the oldest David Napier, and died at Glasgow in 1850.

The eldest cousin David Napier, born in 1788, a gifted and original mechanical engineer, left Glasgow for London about 1810. After working briefly for Henry Maudslay he became in 1815 foreman of an engineering shop in Nevil's Court, Fetter Lane, where he specialized in printing machinery. He devoted his spare time to designing new instruments. His first inventions were a folding pocket compass and the Universal Perspective Graph for copying maps and plans. Neither was successful. In 1818 he went into partnership with Francis Baisler, a London stationer, and opened a machine shop in Lloyd's Court, St Giles, repairing and later building printing machines, winning orders from the *Morning Chronicle* and a number of provincial newspapers. He developed a variety of improvements, most of which were over-elaborate and difficult to operate. Baisler left the partnership in 1822 and Napier continued in business on his own account. In 1825 T. C. Hansard, the parliamentary printer, commissioned him to make a cylindrical press of novel design named the 'Nay-peer'. Sales were slow and did not improve even when steam drive was added in 1832. When Robert Napier visited London in 1827 to promote his marine engines he stayed with David. In 1831 David joined with two of Robert's sons, James and William, in improving a steam carriage designed by David Napier (1790–1869) which had been tested near Dunoon. This second experiment also failed.

The eldest David Napier married Isabella Murdoch in 1820. The couple had seven children, the second of whom was James Murdoch Napier (father of Montague Stanley Napier), who joined the business in 1834. Two years later larger works were built in York Road, Lambeth, equipped with excellent machine tools. Father and son developed a bullet stamping machine in 1838 (patented in 1840), which was quickly ordered by Woolwich arsenal and later foreign governments. William Cotton, the deputy governor of the Bank of England, invented a machine for weighing and sorting gold coins in 1843 and invited Napier to manufacture them. Thereafter Napier developed a range of other equipment for minting and sorting coins. During the 1840s he also constructed several large hydraulic presses and lifts for Isambard Kingdom Brunel's Great Western Railway. His last invention, in 1848 in collaboration with his cousin Robert, was a registering compass to trace the course and distance covered; these were installed in vessels for the Royal Mail Steam Packet Company and P. & O. as well as those built at his cousin's Govan yard. James Murdoch Napier became a partner in 1847, when the firm became known as David Napier & Son. David moved to Surbiton in 1866; he died at 68 York Road, Lambeth, London, on 17 June 1873.

The David Napier who is the subject of this article was one of the most inventive of the pioneering Clyde engineers. After working in his father's engine shop, which moved to Glasgow in 1802, he was apprenticed to Duncan McArthur at his Greenhead foundry at Camlachie near Glasgow and in the early 1810s became his partner. At Greenhead he familiarized himself with building land engines and in 1812 made the boiler and produced the castings for the engines for the first steamboat, the *Comet*. Recognizing the potential of steam navigation, he decided to start his own engine works at Camlachie in partnership with his father, who died in July 1813 before it opened. In 1814 he married Marion Smith; they had fifteen children. While construction of his works was in progress, he continued to work at Greenhead designing the engines for the *Britannia* and *Dumbarton Castle* in 1815. Backed by his family's reputation for engineering on the Clyde, his new works (completed early in 1815) were an immediate success. His first marine engine, for the *Marion*, was delivered in 1816 and the following year he began operating her on his own account on Loch Lomond. In 1818 he was contemplating starting his own fleet of ocean-going steamers. After conducting the first experiments using a model and observations of a steamer in heavy seas to achieve an optimum hull design, he built the *Rob Roy* to provide services between Greenock and Liverpool, and Holyhead and Howth. Napier was accompanied on her maiden voyage by Charles McIntosh, the inventor of rubberized waterproof clothing, who, when they encountered a storm in the Irish Sea, was convinced they would be drowned. McIntosh was proved wrong, and Napier went on to establish a regular service between Holyhead and Howth with three ships each more powerful than the last. In 1820 he began a parallel service to his Loch Lomond steamers down Loch Eck with a steam carriage connection to the Holy Loch, where he built a hotel and holiday villas. Although technically viable, the steam carriage was too heavy and sank into the road.

Napier leased his Camlachie works to his cousin Robert in 1821 and built a new works at Lancefield, conveniently situated on the banks of the Clyde with its own wet dock. His managers were David Tod and John Macgregor, who later pioneered iron shipbuilding on the Clyde. At Lancefield, Napier introduced a raft of innovations in the design of both marine engines and propelling machinery, including improved surface condensers, feathering paddles, and twin screws. In 1826 he engined the *United Kingdom*, built for the service between Leith and London, in which he was also an investor, and the following year commissioned the *Aglaia*, the first iron steamship to be built on the Clyde for his Loch Eck service. Writing in 1841 John Scott Russell commented: 'We believe that from the year 1818 until about 1830 David Napier effected more for the improvement of steam navigation than any other man…. It is to Mr David Napier that Great Britain owes the establishment of deep-sea communication by steam vessels and of Post Office Steam Packets' (Napier, 31). However, his reputation was dealt a cruel blow on 28 July 1835 when the boiler of his steamer *Earl Grey* exploded at the quayside at Greenock, killing six people and injuring several more.

Deeply distressed by the incident Napier in 1836 decided to leave Glasgow and join his elder cousin David in London, both to exploit the potential of investing in shipping in the Thames and the south coast and to begin iron ship-building. He leased his Lancefield works to his cousin Robert and at the end of 1837 he purchased an open site on the Isle of Dogs, alongside William Fairbairn's yard. This new enterprise was managed by his sons John and Francis and later a third son, Robert Dehane, leaving their father time to concentrate on innovative designs and to investigate the market. Their first experimental iron steamer, the *Eclipse*, was launched in 1839 for service between Blackwall and Margate. The firm constructed a succession of vessels, some incorporating novel features, notably a rotary engine, developed by David Napier. The yard closed in 1852 as it was no longer possible to compete on price with the Clyde. After spending some time in Australia the three brothers returned to Glasgow to establish the engineering firm of Napier Bros. Their father remained in London, continuing his experiments until his death at home, 8 Upper Phillimore Gardens, Kensington, on 23 November 1869.

That three cousins of the same name should have made such a contribution to engineering in the first half of the nineteenth century is testimony to the Napier family's long tradition of excellent craftsmanship in metal in the west of Scotland. There were many other families with trade or craft pedigrees as long, but none with so many distinguished members as the Napiers.

MICHAEL S. MOSS

Sources D. D. Napier, *David Napier, engineer, 1790–1869: an autobiographical sketch with notes*, ed. D. Bell (1912) · C. H. Wilson and W. Reader, *Men and machines: a history of D. Napier and Son, Engineers, Ltd, 1808–1958* (1958) · J. R. Hume and M. S. Moss, *Beardmore: the history of a Scottish industrial giant* (1979) · private information (2004) · U. Glas., Archives and Business Records Centre, Napier MSS · d. cert. · *CGPLA Eng. & Wales* (1873) [David Napier]
Archives GEC plc, Essex, Napier Bros records · U. Glas., Archives and Business Records Centre
Likenesses M. Noble, plaster bust, 1870, Scot. NPG · photograph, repro. in Napier, *David Napier, engineer* · photograph (David Napier), repro. in Wilson and Reader, *Men and machines*
Wealth at death under £40,000 in the United Kingdom: probate, 7 Dec 1869, *CGPLA Eng. & Wales* · under £300—David Napier: probate, 23 Aug 1873, *CGPLA Eng. & Wales*

Napier, David (1799–1850). *See under* Napier, David (1790–1869).

Napier, Edward Delaval Hungerford Elers (1808–1870), army officer and author, was the elder son of Edward Elers (d. 1814), a lieutenant in the Royal Navy, who was the grandson of Paul Elers. His mother, Frances Elizabeth, daughter of Lieutenant George Younghusband RN, married in 1815—after the death of Edward's father—Captain Charles *Napier; he adopted her four children, who took the name of Napier in addition to Elers.

Edward Napier was educated at the Royal Military College, Sandhurst, and on 11 August 1825 was appointed ensign in the 46th regiment, in which he became lieutenant on 11 October 1826 and captain on 21 June 1831. He served with his regiment in India, and was present with the nizam's subsidiary force at the siege of Hyderabad in 1830. The regiment returned home in 1833, and in 1836

Napier entered the senior department of the Royal Military College, but left in 1837, before passing his examination, on the regiment being ordered to Gibraltar. He commanded the light company for several years. While at Gibraltar he frequently visited Spain and north Africa for field sports, and also took a cruise in his stepfather's ship, HMS *Powerful* (84 guns), in which he visited Constantinople and Asia Minor, and acquired a knowledge of the Levant, which led to his subsequent employment on special service there. He published *Remarks on the Troad*, which attracted attention, and presented a map of the locality, from his own surveys, to the Royal Geographical Society. He obtained his majority on 11 October 1839.

When the British fleet was engaged on the coast of Syria in 1840, Napier was sent out with the local rank of lieutenant-colonel and assistant adjutant-general, and was dispatched to the Nablus Mountains to keep the Druse and Maronite chiefs firm in their allegiance to the sultan. In the depth of winter, which was very severe in the mountains, he collected a force of 1500 irregular cavalry, whom he declared to be 'as ruffianly a lot of cutthroats as ever a Christian gentleman had command of'. With his irregulars he watched Ibrahim Pasha (the commander of the Egyptians, who had opened hostilities with the Turks) so closely that Ibrahim retreated through the desert east and south of Palestine instead of occupying Jerusalem and ravaging the settled country round about as he had intended. However, when Napier's force came suddenly upon an outpost of Ibrahim's cavalry, they fled, leaving Napier and three other Europeans to themselves. Napier retired to the Turkish headquarters, where he acted as military commissioner until the convention of Alexandria put an end to the war. In January 1841 Napier was dispatched to bring back the chiefs of Lebanon, whom Ibrahim Pasha had sent to work in the goldmines of Sennar, a service he successfully completed.

Napier had not long rejoined the 46th at Gibraltar when he was sent to Egypt by the Foreign Office to demand the release of the Syrian troops detained by Mahomet Ali and to take them to Beirut; in this he was successful. It occupied him from May to September 1841, during which time the plague was raging in Alexandria. He escaped it, but contracted ophthalmia, which caused him much suffering in later years. For his services in Syria and Egypt he was made brevet lieutenant-colonel from 31 December 1841, and received a gold medal from the sultan. Being reported medically unfit to accompany his regiment to the West Indies, he retired on half pay unattached in 1843, residing for some time in Portugal. Napier married in 1844 Ellen Louisa, heir of Thomas Daniel of the Madras civil service; they had two children and she survived him.

In 1846 Napier was sent to the Cape with other special service field officers to organize the indigenous levies, and ably commanded bodies of irregulars during the Cape Frontier War of 1846–7. He became brevet colonel, while still on half pay, on 20 June 1854. Admiral Sir Charles Napier, then in command of the Baltic fleet, applied to Lord Hardinge for the services of his stepson as British military commissioner with the French force in the Baltic under General Baraguay d'Hilliers, but the letter was inexplicably never answered, and Napier's applications for employment in the Crimea were unsuccessful. With characteristic energy he did good work during the first winter in the Crimea in collecting funds for warm clothing for the troops, and personally superintending its shipment. He became a major-general on 26 October 1858, was appointed colonel of the 61st (South Gloucestershire) regiment in 1864, was promoted lieutenant-general on 3 October 1864, and was transferred to the colonelcy of his former regiment, the 46th, on 22 February 1870.

Napier was a man of literary and artistic ability, who contributed to a number of magazines, chiefly *Bailey's* and the *United Service Magazine*, for over twenty years. He published several books on places he had visited, and the *Life and Correspondence of Admiral Sir Charles Napier* (1862). He died at Westhill, Shanklin, Isle of Wight, on 19 June 1870.

H. M. CHICHESTER, rev. JAMES FALKNER

Sources *Army List* · *Hart's Army List* · *Colburn's United Service Magazine*, 2 (1870), 484–92
Wealth at death under £2000: probate, 17 Aug 1870, *CGPLA Eng. & Wales*

Napier, Francis, eighth Lord Napier of Merchistoun (1758–1823), army officer, was born at Ipswich on 23 February 1758, the only son of William, seventh Lord Napier (1730–1775), army officer, and Mary Anne Cathcart (1727–1774), fourth daughter of Charles, eighth Lord Cathcart, and Marion Schaw. Nothing is known of Napier's early education. On his father's death on 2 January 1775 he became eighth Lord Napier of Merchistoun. By this time, he had joined the army; having entered as an ensign in the 31st infantry regiment on 3 December 1774, he rose to the rank of lieutenant on 21 March 1776.

After serving in Canada under General Burgoyne, Napier fought in the American War of Independence, and was one of those who surrendered at Saratoga on 16 October 1777. He was imprisoned at Cambridge, Massachusetts, for six months before being allowed to return to Europe. On 7 November 1779 he purchased a captain's commission in the 35th infantry regiment, which was reduced to half pay in 1783. On 31 May 1784, with the help of Henry Dundas, and in return for political support at Scots peerage elections, he became a full-pay captain of the 4th infantry regiment, and on 29 December purchased a major's commission, which he held until 1789.

On 13 April 1784 Napier married Maria Margaret Clavering (1756?–1821), daughter of Lieutenant-General Sir John Clavering and Lady Diana West, at St George's, Hanover Square, London. The marriage produced nine children, four sons and five daughters.

Between 1788 and 1790 Napier was Scottish grand master of the freemasons. It was in this capacity that, in the autumn of 1789, he laid the foundation-stone of the new buildings of Edinburgh University, for which he was rewarded with the degree of LLD on 11 November.

Napier's right to a peerage was questioned in July 1790 following confusion over the original charter. The matter was resolved on 25 February 1793 in his favour by the lord chancellor, and confirmed by the House of Lords on 4 July.

In the same year he was appointed lord-colonel of the Hopetoun fencibles, a position he held until the regiment was disbanded in 1799. In 1796, and again in 1802 and 1807, he was chosen as a representative peer. He became lord lieutenant of Selkirkshire on 12 November 1797.

From 1802 until his death Napier was, with Henry Dundas's help, annually nominated as lord high commissioner to the general assembly of the Church of Scotland. A member of the Society in Scotland for Propagating Christian Knowledge from November 1803, he became its president on 3 January 1805. In July of the following year he joined the board of trustees for the encouragement of Scottish fisheries and manufactures.

Both Napier and his wife died at their home, Dacre Lodge, Enfield, Middlesex, she on 29 December 1821 and he on 1 August 1823; they were buried at Enfield. On Napier's death, the title passed to his eldest son, William John *Napier. ROBERT CLYDE

Sources *DNB* · GEC, *Peerage*, new edn · B. Lenman, *Integration and enlightenment: Scotland, 1746–1832* (1992) · D. Stevenson, *The first freemasons: Scotland's early lodges and thier members* (1988) · *GM*, 1st ser., 93/2 (1823)
Archives NA Scot. · U. Edin. L., corresp. and papers · Wilts. & Swindon RO, trust papers | BL, letters to W. Adey, Add. MS 58209 · NRA, priv. coll., letters to Thomas Yorke
Likenesses J. Kay, etching, c.1793 (*Three officers of the Hopetoun fencibles*), NL Scot. · J. Kay, caricature etching, 1795, BM, NPG · W. S. Watson, group portrait, oils (*The inauguration of Robert Burns as poet laureate of the lodge Canongate, Kilwinning, 1787*), Scot. NPG

Napier, Francis, tenth Lord Napier of Merchistoun and first Baron Ettrick (1819–1898), diplomatist and administrator in India, born on 15 September 1819 at Thirlestane Castle in Selkirkshire, was the eldest son of William John *Napier, ninth Lord Napier of Merchistoun (1786–1834), and his wife, Elizabeth, *née* Cochrane-Johnstone. On his father's death on 11 October 1834 he succeeded to his titles.

Education and diplomatic career Napier was educated partly by private tutors at Thirlstane and at school at Saxe-Meiningen, and afterwards at Trinity College, Cambridge, which he entered in 1835. He left Cambridge without a degree, and passed some time at Geneva under the guardianship of the Revd Walter Patterson, and there acquired a command of foreign languages which later proved to be most useful to him. On 2 September 1845 he married Anne Jane Charlotte (1824–1911), only daughter of Robert Manners Lockwood of Dan-y-craig, Glamorgan. They had four sons. Lady Napier, who was recalled by one of her husband's diplomatic colleagues as 'the type of what an ambassadress should be' (Redesdale, 1.206), was one of the first members of the Imperial Order of the Crown of India.

In 1840 Napier had been appointed to the diplomatic service; after serving as an attaché at Vienna and at Constantinople, and subsequently as secretary of legation at Naples, and to the embassies at St Petersburg and Constantinople, he was sent as envoy to the United States of America, and from there was transferred to The Hague.

Francis Napier, tenth Lord Napier of Merchistoun and first Baron Ettrick (1819–1898), by George Frederic Watts, 1866

From December 1860 to September 1864 he was ambassador at St Petersburg, and from September 1864 to January 1866 at Berlin. In these various diplomatic posts Napier established a high reputation. When secretary of legation at Naples in 1848 and 1849 he was chargé d'affaires for eighteen months, including the critical period of the Sicilian insurrection. On that occasion the judgement and tact with which he discharged his duties were highly appreciated by Lord Palmerston, then secretary of state for foreign affairs, who judged that Napier's talents, as manifested in the higher diplomatic appointments which he subsequently held, would allow him to rise to the highest offices in the state. In the United States he was considered to have been the most acceptable envoy they had up to that time received from Britain. As ambassador at St Petersburg he was *persona grata* to the emperor, Alexander II, and an intimate of the circle surrounding Madame Olga Novikov which worked for peace between England and Russia at a time of difficulties. Alexander II wished to confer on Napier the highest Russian order, that of St Andrew, but, as no British envoy could accept a foreign order, the emperor presented him with a portrait instead. A similar compliment was afterwards paid to him by the king of Prussia.

Governor of Madras In January 1866 Napier's glittering diplomatic career was abruptly terminated and he was appointed governor of Madras. This office he held for six years, having been invited by the secretary of state for India to prolong his tenure of the office beyond the usual time. His background was very unusual for an Indian governor and he brought a fresh perspective to the duties of

administration. A few months after taking charge of the government he found himself confronted by a serious famine in Ganjam, the northern district of the presidency. He at once visited the affected tracts, instituting measures to meet the calamity. There was no branch of the administration to which he did not devote time and attention; but the business to which he devoted special attention was that connected with public health. As secretary to the embassy at Constantinople he had made the acquaintance and had acquired the friendship of Florence Nightingale, to whom his official position had enabled him to render valuable assistance in carrying out her work. Throughout his residence in India he kept up a correspondence with her on subjects connected with public health in that country. He also from the first took a great and practical interest in developing public works, and especially works of irrigation. He fully recognized the great value of the irrigation works carried out or devised by Sir Arthur Cotton. He visited them all at an early period after assuming the government, and during the six years that he remained in India he gave steady encouragement to the completion and development of the various irrigation systems then in operation. It was while Napier was governor of Madras that the Penner anicut was built, and some progress made with the distributing canals. During that time also the Rushikulya anicut in Ganjam was projected and planned, and the great work of diverting the Periyar River in Travancore from its natural channel, leading down to the western coast, where the water was not required, into the River Vaigai on the eastern side of the Peninsula, was brought by Napier before the government of India and the secretary of state. This remarkable work was successfully completed some years later.

Very shortly after Napier's arrival at Madras he visited Calcutta and made the acquaintance of Sir John Lawrence, with whom he established friendly relations, as he afterwards did with the earl of Mayo. Relations between the government of India and provincial governments, such as that of Madras, were notoriously strained, especially over questions of finance. Napier used his diplomatic skills to repair the damage and to secure much closer bases of co-operation. In February 1872, in consequence of the assassination of the earl of Mayo, Napier assumed temporarily the office of viceroy of India. During the time, a little short of three months, that the temporary viceroyalty lasted, no business of very great importance arose, and Napier, on being relieved by Lord Northbrook, returned to England. For his Indian services, in 1872 he was created Baron Ettrick of Ettrick in the peerage of the United Kingdom, becoming known as Lord Napier and Ettrick. His public career then foundered, like that of many an ex-Indian servant.

Other activities, crofters, death, and reputation In 1872 Napier took the chair at the meeting of the social science congress which was held at Plymouth. The address which he delivered on that occasion called forth some comment at the time as being unduly socialistic, but several of the measures which he suggested were later embodied in the County Councils and Parish Councils Acts. In this address, as in many of his utterances, he evinced the greatest sympathy with the condition of the poor, both in the rural and in the urban districts. While he continued to live in London he served for some time on the London school board and took an active part in its proceedings. He also served as chairman of the dwellings committee of the Charity Organization Society.

Napier subsequently took up residence at Thirlestane Castle on his estate in Selkirkshire, Scotland, and in 1883 he presided over a royal commission which was appointed by Gladstone's Liberal government to inquire into the condition of the crofters and cottars in the highlands and islands of Scotland. The inquiry was one of the fullest ever made on Scotland and it remains a central source for highland history. Though sympathic to the crofters, Napier, who wrote the report himself, regarded their claims to a historical right of occupancy as impractical and recommended a revival of highland townships as the chief focus of progress. The commission made its report in 1884 (Napier vigorously defended it in the *Nineteenth Century* against the duke of Argyll's predictable onslaught). The Liberal government, however, favoured land reform recognizing crofters' rights and, on returning to office in 1886, passed the Crofters' Holdings Act, a milestone piece of legislation stimulated by if not wholly consequent on Napier's recommendations. The report was followed by the appointment of a permanent commission, which still deals with questions concerning the crofters and cottars.

During the latter years of his life Napier lived almost entirely in Scotland, acting as convener of his county, and interesting himself generally in local affairs. He was a LLD of Edinburgh, Glasgow, and Harvard. He died very suddenly, on 19 December 1898, on the via San Gallo at Florence, where he and his wife had spent their honeymoon fifty-three years before, and where they had gone to pass the winter, and was subsequently buried at Thirlestane on 8 February 1899. He was succeeded by his eldest son, William George.

Napier's career was undoubtedly a very brilliant one up to a certain point. As the representative of the government at two of the most important courts in Europe and at Washington, he had discharged his important functions with admirable judgement and tact. His government of Madras had been so successful that he was invited to retain it beyond the usual time. His long official experience and dignified bearing would have seemed to point him out as the most fitting successor to Lord Mayo. He certainly had shown himself to be possessed of qualifications which few governors-general or viceroys of India had displayed before being appointed to that high post. But he was passed over. After his return to England he might have been expected to follow with eminent success a political career. But he was without the financial means of meeting the expenses of parliamentary life and his commitment to the causes of the poor lost him friends in high places. His many talents never came ultimately to be fulfilled, but his name will always be remembered in the Scottish highlands.   A. J. ARBUTHNOT, rev. DAVID WASHBROOK

Sources W. T. Stead, ed., *The M.P. for Russia* (1909) · W. Mosse, *The European powers and the German question* (1958) · *FO List* (1898) · C. Dewey, 'Celtic agrarian legislation and the Celtic revival: historicist implications of Gladstone's Irish and Scottish Land Acts, 1870–1886', *Past and Present*, 64 (1974), 30–70 · Gladstone, *Diaries* · *Nineteenth Century*, 16 (1884) · Lord Napier, 'The highland crofters: a vindication of the report of the Crofters' Commission', *Nineteenth Century*, 17 (1885), 437–63 · *Longman's Magazine* (Feb 1899) · GEC, *Peerage* · Lord Redesdale [A. B. Freeman-Mitford], *Memories*, 2 vols. (1915) · Burke, *Peerage*

Archives CUL, corresp. with Lord Mayo · NL Scot., corresp. relating to Edinburgh Castle · NRA Scotland, priv. coll., corresp. and papers | BL, corresp. with Lord Aberdeen, Add. MSS 43239–43251, *passim* · BL, corresp. with Sir Austen Layard, Add. MSS 38997–39117, *passim* · BL, corresp. with Florence Nightingale, Add. MS 45779 · BL, letters to Sir Stafford Northcote, Add. MS 50027 · BL OIOC, letters to Sir Owen Tudor, MS Eur. D 951 · BL OIOC, letters to Sir Mountstuart Grant Duff, MS Eur. F 234 · Bodl. Oxf., letters to Sir William Harcourt · Hants. RO, corresp. with Lord Malmesbury · NMM, letters to Sir William Parker · Notts. Arch., letters to John Savile · NRA, priv. coll., letters to Sir Edward Clive Bayley · PRO, corresp. with Lord John Russell, PRO 30/22 · PRO, corresp. with Odo Russell, FO 918 · PRO, letters to Sir William White, FO 364/1–11 · U. Nott. L., letters to Sir Andrew Buchanan · U. Southampton L., Broadlands MSS

Likenesses G. F. Watts, oils, 1866, Scot. NPG [*see illus.*]

Wealth at death £11,018 3s. 8d.: confirmation, 11 July 1899, *CCI*

Napier, George (1751–1804), army officer, was the eldest son of Francis Scott (afterwards Napier), sixth Lord Napier of Merchistoun (1705–1773), and his second wife, Henrietta Maria (1732/3–1795), daughter of George Johnston of Dublin. He was born in Edinburgh on 11 March 1751, and educated like his brothers under the supervision of David Hume, the philosopher and historian. An impoverished younger son, on 8 October 1767 he was appointed ensign in the 25th foot, then called the Edinburgh regiment. It was in Minorca and commanded by Lord George Lennox. Napier became a lieutenant in the regiment on 4 March 1771. He married on 22 January 1775 Elizabeth (d. 1780), daughter of Captain Robert Pollock, and they had children. He obtained a company in the old 80th Royal Edinburgh volunteers, raised in 1778, which was posted to America. In 1779 he went there, accompanied by his family, arriving in late August, and he served on the staff of Sir Henry Clinton. Napier, 6 feet 2 inches tall, with a fine figure, Roman-nosed but short-sighted, was reputedly 'the most active and handsome officer in the British Army in America' (Tillyard, 335). He was brave, conscientious, and methodical. He was at the 1780 siege of Charles Town, South Carolina, and, when Major John André was captured in September 1780, offered to continue his role: Clinton refused the offer. Napier's wife and young children—except one daughter—died of yellow fever; he himself was put on board ship unconscious and, it was thought, dying. Clinton undertook to sell his commission for the benefit of the surviving infant, Louisa Mary (d. 1856), but Napier recovered on the voyage. On 27 August 1781, at Goodwood parish church, Sussex, Napier married Lady Sarah Bunbury [see Napier, Lady Sarah (1745–1826)], fourth daughter of Charles *Lennox, second duke of Richmond and Lennox (1701–1750), descendant of one of Charles II's bastards by a French woman. At seventeen she captivated the young George III and, it was thought, might become queen. Horace Walpole wrote of her as by far the most charming of the ten noble maidens who bore the bride's train at the king's marriage to Charlotte of Mecklenburg in September 1761. She married on 2 June 1762 Sir Charles Thomas Bunbury (1740–1821), the well-known racing baronet and member of parliament, who, after she left him in 1769 for her paramour Lord William Gordon, in 1776 divorced her for desertion. That year she and Napier first met. Their marriage was happy; they had five sons and three daughters (two of whom died young), the former including the distinguished soldiers Charles James *Napier (1782–1853), George Thomas *Napier (1784–1855), and William Francis Patrick *Napier (1785–1860), and the historian Henry Edward *Napier (1789–1853). By his wife's aristocratic standard they were poor. She had £500 per annum from her divorce settlement; he had sold his commission in the 80th foot and had only what he earned. She pressed her relatives and friends for posts and sinecures for him.

On 30 October 1782 Napier re-entered the army as ensign in the 1st foot guards, of which he became adjutant. His brother-in-law Charles *Lennox, third duke of Richmond and Lennox (1735–1806), as master-general of the ordnance, gave Napier the post of comptroller of the Royal Laboratory, Woolwich (salary £200 per annum), which he held from 31 May 1782 to 8 April 1783. In 1788 Napier communicated to the Royal Irish Academy, of which he was a member, a paper on the 'composition of gunpowder'. Sir William Congreve, appointed comptroller of the laboratory in 1783, probably had a considerable share in the experiments. The paper was published in the *Royal Institute of Artillery Transactions* (1788, 2.97–118), and was translated into Italian and, reportedly, other languages. In 1783 Napier resigned his Royal Laboratory post when his wife, through her connections, procured him a captaincy in the 100th foot. It was disbanded so he was a captain on half pay. In 1785 he and his family moved to Celbridge, co. Kildare, 10 miles from Dublin and near some of his wife's relatives. He taught his sons swordsmanship and military engineering, and imbued them with military values. In 1793, Napier, still a half-pay captain, was appointed deputy quartermaster-general, with the rank of major, in the force assembled under Francis Rawdon Hastings, second earl of Moira (1754–1826), to assist the French royalists in the Vendée, which eventually joined the duke of York's army at Malines in July 1794. Napier was appointed lieutenant-colonel of the newly raised Londonderry regiment on 25 August 1794, and worked hard to discipline it at Macclesfield; but it was drafted to the West Indies in 1795, to Napier's disgust and contrary to the men's engagements. A place was then created for Napier as 'chief field engineer' on the staff of Lord Carhampton, the Irish commander-in-chief. When the troubles broke out in 1798, Napier did not flee like many of the gentry, but fortified his house at Celbridge and armed his sons and servants. Eventually he moved his family to Castletown. During the rebellion he commanded a yeomanry corps. In 1799 Charles, first Marquess Cornwallis

(1738–1805), the viceroy, appointed Napier the first comptroller of army accounts in Ireland, telling him, 'I want an honest man' (Moody and others, 698). Napier, who held the post until his death, renounced all fees, thus reducing his own income, and set to work loyally to reduce to order the military accounts, which were in disgraceful confusion. He became brevet colonel on 1 January 1800. For years his health had been poor, and in June 1804 he went for his health to Clifton, Bristol, where he died of consumption on 13 October 1804. A memorial slab was placed in Redlands Chapel, Clifton. His widow inherited his debts. She appealed to George III, who in 1805 granted a pension of £1000 a year to her and her children. Lady Sarah, who had long been totally blind, died in London on 20 August 1826, aged eighty-one, reportedly the last surviving great-granddaughter of Charles II.

ROGER T. STEARN

Sources Burke, *Peerage* (1967) · GEC, *Peerage* · W. Napier, *The life and opinions of Sir Charles James Napier*, 4 vols. (1857) · *Passages in the early military life of General Sir G. T. Napier*, ed. W. C. E. Napier (1884) · *Army List* · *The letters of Horace Walpole, fourth earl of Orford*, ed. P. Toynbee, 16 vols. (1903–5); suppl., 3 vols. (1918–25) · S. Tillyard, *Aristocrats: Caroline, Emily, Louisa and Sarah Lennox, 1740–1832* (1994) · O. F. G. Hogg, *The royal arsenal: its background, origin and subsequent history*, 1–2 (1963) · *GM*, 1st ser., 74 (1804), 986 · *GM*, 1st ser., 96/2 (1826), 188 · T. W. Moody and others, eds., *A new history of Ireland*, 4: *Eighteenth-century Ireland, 1691–1800* (1986) · P. Napier, *A difficult country: the Napiers in Scotland* (1972) · T. Pakenham, *The year of liberty: the history of the great Irish rebellion of 1798* (1969) · HoP, *Commons, 1754–90* · L. Stone, *Road to divorce: England, 1530–1987* (1990)
Archives BL, corresp., notebooks, journals, letter-books, Add. MSS 49086–49104 · Bodl. Oxf., family corresp. and papers | BL, letters to Lord Hardwicke and Colonel Littlehales, Add. MSS 35646–35768 · PRO, corresp. with Lord Moira and his mother, PRO30/64 · PRO NIre., letters to Thomas Staples, etc.
Likenesses Walker and Cockerell, photogravure, BM

Napier, Sir George Thomas (1784–1855), army officer and governor of the Cape of Good Hope, second son of Colonel George *Napier (1751–1804), and his second wife, Lady Sarah Bunbury, *née* Lennox [see Napier, Lady Sarah (1745–1826)], was born at Whitehall, London, on 30 June 1784. Unlike his elder brother Charles James *Napier he was a poor student. On 25 January 1800 he was appointed cornet in the 24th light dragoons, an Irish corps whose motto was 'Death or glory', in which he learned such dissipated habits that his father speedily had him transferred to a foot regiment. He became lieutenant on 18 June 1800, and was placed on half pay of the 46th foot in 1802. He was brought into the 52nd light infantry in 1803, became captain in 1804, and served with the regiment under Sir John Moore at Shorncliffe, and in Sicily, Sweden, and Portugal. He was a favourite with Moore from the first, and was one of his aides-de-camp at Corunna. The report in the *Army List* of Napier receiving a gold medal in February 1809 for the capture of Martinique is mistaken: he was not present at that action. He served with the 52nd in the Peninsular campaigns of 1809–11. At Busaco he was wounded slightly while striking with his sword at a French grenadier at the head of an opposing column. He and his brother William were two of the eleven officers promoted in honour of Masséna's retreat.

Napier became an effective major in the 52nd foot in 1811, and volunteered for the command of the stormers of the light division at the assault on Ciudad Rodrigo on 19 January 1812. John Gurwood of the 52nd led the forlorn hope. Napier on this occasion lost his right arm, which had been broken by a fragment of shell at Casal Novo three days earlier. He received a brevet lieutenant-colonelcy and a gold medal, went home, and was appointed deputy adjutant-general of the York district. He married, on 28 October 1812, Margaret (d. 1819), daughter of John Craig of Glasgow; they had two daughters and three sons before her early death.

At the beginning of 1814 Napier rejoined the 52nd as major at St Jean de Luz, and was present with it at Orthez, Tarbes, and Toulouse. Immediately after the last battle he was appointed lieutenant-colonel of the 71st Highland light infantry, which he brought home to Scotland. On 25 July the same year he was appointed captain and lieutenant-colonel in the 3rd foot guards (Scots guards), in which he served until 1821, when he retired on half pay of the Sicilian regiment. He was made CB on 4 June 1815, became a brevet colonel in 1825, and major-general in 1837, was made KCB on 10 July 1838, and became colonel 1st West India regiment on 29 February 1844, lieutenant-general in 1846, and general in 1854. He had the Peninsular gold medal for Ciudad Rodrigo, and the silver medal and four clasps.

Napier was governor and commander-in-chief at the Cape of Good Hope from 4 October 1837 to 12 December 1843. He enforced the abolition of slavery, abolished inland taxation, depending for colonial revenue on the customs duties, and ruled the colony for nearly seven years without any frontier war. He sent a detachment of troops to Port Natal, and the Boers were driven out of that territory during his government.

After his return to Europe, in 1844, Napier lived mainly at Nice. King Charles Albert offered him the command of the Sardinian army, which he declined. After Chillian-walla, Napier was proposed for the chief command in India, 'but thought, in common with the people of England, that it belonged by right to his brother Charles'. He had married in 1839, as his second wife, Frances Dorothea (d. 1881), eldest daughter of R. W. Blencowe and widow of William Peere Williams-Freeman of Fawley Court, Oxfordshire. He died at Geneva on 16 September 1855.

Napier wrote for his children *Passages in the Early Military Life of General Sir G. T. Napier*, which was published in 1885 by his youngest son, General William Craig Emilius Napier (1818–1903).

H. M. CHICHESTER, rev. LYNN MILNE

Sources Burke, *Peerage* (1939) · G. T. Napier, *Passages in the early military life of General Sir George T. Napier: written by himself*, ed. W. C. E. Napier (1884) · *GM*, 2nd ser., 44 (1855), 429 · *DSAB* · T. R. H. Davenport, *South Africa: a modern history*, 4th edn (1991)
Archives BL, corresp., Add. MSS 49167–49168 · Bodl. Oxf., family corresp. · National Archives of Zimbabwe, Harare, corresp. | BL OIOC, letters to marquess of Tweeddale, MS Eur. F 96 · Duke U., Perkins L., letters to Lord Seaton · Lpool RO, letters to fourteenth earl of Derby · PRO, letters to Lady Bunbury, PRO 30/86 · W. Sussex RO, letters to duke of Richmond
Likenesses F. J. J. Sieurac, miniature, 1814, V&A · portraits, Africana Museum, Johannesburg · portraits, Cory Library, Grahamstown · portraits, National Library of South Africa, Cape Town

Napier, Sir Gerard, first baronet (*bap.* 1606, *d.* 1673), politician, was baptized at Steeple, Dorset, on 19 October 1606, the eldest son of Sir Nathaniel Napier, of More Crichel, and his wife, Elizabeth, daughter and heir of John Gerard of Hyde, in the Isle of Purbeck; he was a grandson of Sir Robert *Napier (d. 1615) and brother of Robert *Napier (1610/11–1686). He appears not to have attended university, but on 8 November 1627 was admitted as a student of the Middle Temple. Until the death of his father in 1635 he lived at Middlemarsh Hall, near Sherborne, Dorset. By about 1636 he had married Margaret (d. 1660), daughter and coheir of John Colles of Barton, Somerset, gaining thereby connections with John Coventry, son of lord keeper Thomas Coventry, and Sir William Portman, both of whom had married daughters of Colles.

Napier's public career began unpromisingly. In March 1637 the 'presumptuous conduct' of Dorset men avoiding the press for navy service was blamed on neglect of the magistrates; Napier, the deputy vice-admiral, was 'timorous to do anything without good grounds' and wrote asking for clarification of his powers (*CSP dom.*, 1636–7, 533). Perhaps this may have reflected doubts about government policy, for in April 1639 he returned no answer to the request for a contribution to the costs of the expedition to Scotland. In April 1640 Theophilus Howard, second earl of Suffolk and lord lieutenant of Dorset, complained that his deputies, Napier and Sir George Hastings, had been lax in pressing men for the expedition to Scotland, though it now seems that their efforts in the county had been strongly resisted. It was ordered that Napier be examined by the attorney-general, and by the House of Lords. On 16 October 1640 he was made freeman of Weymouth and Melcombe Regis, and he was elected as senior MP for Melcombe on 21 October. He was created a baronet on 25 June 1641 and knighted at Whitehall four days later.

During the civil war Napier inclined to the royalist side from the first. After a summons on 22 July, the House of Commons ordered on 12 October 1642 that Sir Gerard and others be 'summoned forthwith to attend the service of the House; all delays and excuses whatsoever laid aside'; a month later it was ineffectually decreed that he be sent for as a delinquent (*JHC*, 2.845). On 5 January 1643 Napier was required to lend £500 for the service of parliament, and on 10 April, following his failure to comply, an order was issued for his arrest. On 26 May, however, a letter from two Dorset members, Sir Walter Erle (Weymouth) and John Brown, a knight of the shire, was read in the house; it declared his readiness to contribute and on this basis he was excused attendance in the Commons. On 3 August 1643, however, as a commissioner of the king, Napier wrote to the mayor and corporation of Dorchester, summoning them to surrender the town. On 22 January 1644, the opening day of the Oxford parliament, the Commons disbarred him. Later in the year, however, the military tide turned, and Napier found it advisable to make his submission to the parliament, taking the covenant on 20 September

1644 and advancing over the next months some £1200 in loans to the parliamentarian forces in Dorset. He later claimed that his estate had been sequestered by the king's party, and had sustained much damage at its hands; Napier, it was recognized, 'being a person of quality, has much furthered the parliament's service' and this told in his favour (Green, *Committee for Compounding*, 1062). On 19 December 1646 his fine was set at one tenth, £3514, against which allowance was made of £1250 in respect of his earlier loans.

During the Commonwealth period Napier is said to have entrusted £500 for Charles Stuart to Sir Gilbert Taylor, who appropriated the money. After the Restoration Napier ordered his arrest, but the king is said to have intervened personally in the dispute, persuading Sir Gerard to forgo his suit and to forgive his opponent, and arranging for an annual gift of New Forest deer to be supplied to the aggrieved party by way of recompense. It was in keeping with his moderate royalism that Gerard Napier signed the *Declaration of the Knights and Gentry of Dorset* of 16 April 1660, which recommended in a spirit of reconciliation that the future shape of politics should be left to parliament's decision. Early in 1662 Napier arranged for the bailing of John Westley (grandfather of John Wesley, the Methodist leader), whose preaching he had informed against in 1658 but who had recently been imprisoned at Blandford. In December 1662 Napier was appointed one of twelve commissioners for locating waste lands belonging to the crown in twenty-three parishes in Dorset. He entertained the king and queen at More Crichel when the court moved to Salisbury on account of the plague in 1665. His wife having predeceased him in 1660, Napier died at More Crichel on 14 May 1673, and was buried in the church of Minterne Magna, Dorset. He was succeeded as second baronet by his eldest son, Nathaniel *Napier (1636/7–1709), for whose four sons, Gerard, Windham, Lenox, and Nathaniel, he had made generous provision in his will.

STEPHEN WRIGHT

Sources Keeler, *Long Parliament* · A. R. Bayley, *The great civil war in Dorset, 1642–1660* (1910) · J. Hutchins, *The history and antiquities of the county of Dorset*, 3rd edn, ed. W. Shipp and J. W. Hodson, 4 vols. (1861–74) · GEC, *Baronetage* · [E. Bysshe], *The visitation of Dorset, 1677, made by Sir Edward Bysshe*, ed. G. D. Squibb, Harleian Society, 117 (1977) · J. Rylands, ed., *Visitation of Dorset … 1623*, Harleian Society, 20 (1885) · C. T. Martin, ed., *Minutes of parliament of the Middle Temple*, 4 vols. (1904–5), vols. 1–2 · C. H. Hopwood, ed., *Middle Temple records*, 4 vols. (1904–5), vols. 3–4 · *CSP dom.*, 1636–7; 1640; 1663–4 · M. A. E. Green, ed., *Calendar of the proceedings of the committee for compounding … 1643–1660*, 5 vols., PRO (1889–92) · M. A. E. Green, ed., *Calendar of the proceedings of the committee for advance of money, 1642–1656*, 3 vols., PRO (1888) · *JHC*, 2–3 (1640–44) · will, PRO, PROB 11/343, sig. 128
Wealth at death see will, PRO, PROB 11/343, sig. 128

Napier, Henry Edward (1789–1853), naval officer and historian, born at Celbridge, co. Kildare, Ireland, on 5 March 1789, was the son of Colonel George *Napier (1751–1804) and his wife, Lady Sarah *Napier (1745–1826), the seventh daughter of Charles *Lennox, second duke of Richmond. He was the younger brother of Sir Charles James *Napier, conqueror of Sind, Sir George Thomas *Napier, governor of the Cape of Good Hope, and Sir William Francis Patrick *Napier, historian and general, and also a first cousin of Admiral Sir Charles Napier. He entered the Royal Naval Academy, Portsmouth, on 5 May 1803, and, having joined the *Spencer* (74 guns) on 20 September 1806, was present in the expedition against Copenhagen in 1807 and assisted at the destruction of Fleckeröe Castle on the coast of Norway. Between 1808 and 1811 he served in the East Indies, and on 4 May 1810 he received his commission as lieutenant. On 7 June 1814 he was promoted to command the *Goree* (18 guns), and, soon after moving to the brig-sloop *Rifleman* (18 guns), was for a considerable time entrusted with the charge of the trade in the Bay of Fundy. In August 1815 he went on half pay, having previously declined a piece of plate which had been voted to him for his care in the conduct of convoys between the port of Saint John, New Brunswick, and Castine. His journal of this period has been published. On 18 May 1820 he was elected a fellow of the Royal Society following his work on naval reform. He married on 17 November 1823 Caroline Bennet (d. 1836), the illegitimate daughter of Charles *Lennox, third duke of Richmond, and his first cousin; they had eight children, three of whom survived infancy. On 31 December 1830 he was gazetted by the incoming whig government to the rank of captain but remained on half pay. Napier's chief claim to notice was that he was the author of *Florentine history from the earliest authentic records to the accession of Ferdinand the Third, Grandduke of Tuscany* (6 vols., 1846–7), a work showing independent judgement and a vivacious style, though it was marred by prolixity. A man of charm, intelligence, and ability, he was always in the shadow of his three military brothers, while his later years were blighted by the death of his wife, in Florence on 5 September 1836. It was on her account that he completed his Florentine history. He died at 62 Cadogan Place, London, on 13 October 1853.

G. C. BOASE, *rev.* ANDREW LAMBERT

Sources P. Napier, *The sword dance* (1971) · P. H. Napier, *Revolution and the Napier brothers, 1820–1840* (1973) · H. E. Napier, *New England blockaded in 1814* (1939) · O'Byrne, *Naval biog. dict.* · *GM*, 2nd ser., 40 (1853), 90
Archives Bodl. Oxf., family corresp. · Duke U., Perkins L., family corresp. · NMM, letter-book · RS, journal

Napier, James (1810–1884), industrial chemist, was born at Partick, Glasgow, the son of James Napier, jobbing gardener, and his wife Margaret, *née* Buchanan, a seamstress. At the age of seven he was sent to the village school where he learned to read, but after eleven months the family's poverty required that he be sent to work to contribute his few pennies to the budget. When he was twelve he started work as a hand-loom weaver, and, by hard work, was able to pay for two years' night schooling. As the weaving trade slackened, he found employment at Gilchrists, the local dye works, where his aptitude and competence earned him the position of foreman by the time he was eighteen. At twenty-one he married Christina McIndoe (d. 1881) and in his own home gathered kindred spirits for discussion and education.

By 1833 declining business at Gilchrists led the workforce to seek unionization. Napier, who took his men's part, was dismissed, and moved to a nearby bleach works. After four years his health was suffering and under medical advice he left the industry. He set up a lending library but this was not a success and he returned to Gilchrists as clerk and general manager. He had earlier written an essay on dyeing which came to the notice of John James Griffin, a scientific publisher and dealer in chemicals and chemical apparatus. During the following years Napier seems to have oscillated between Gilchrists and Griffin as work prospects allowed. With Griffin he learned a good deal of practical chemistry and met knowledgeable people, among them Dr James Young FRS, with whom he struck up an enduring friendship. In 1839 there was great interest in the new science of electrometallurgy and Griffin set Napier to explore the possibilities of using electrotyping to reproduce illustrations and artwork. This led in 1842 to his being hired by the London works of Elkington and Mason where he became one of the most experienced craftsmen in this developing field. While he was with Elkingtons, he was visited by a representative from the copper mine at Parys in Anglesey, to see if electrometallurgy could solve certain problems being encountered in extracting and refining copper. Napier thereupon devised and patented an extraction process and departed, first to Swansea, headquarters of the copper smelting industry, then to Holywell in Flintshire, where copper was worked, to try his process on a large scale. Over the next few years he experienced both success and failure, the latter often due to sabotage by workmen convinced that the new processes threatened their livelihoods.

Napier returned to Glasgow in 1849 and moved to Partick in 1852. His earlier texts on dyeing were reprinted and he contributed a volume on electrometallurgy to Griffin's scientific manual series in 1857, these works going through several editions. Partick was by that time a populous Glasgow suburb; Napier interested himself in its sanitary condition, served as a police commissioner and subsequently as burgh bailie, while earning his living as an investigating and consulting chemist and teacher. During this period he wrote numerous papers reflecting his diverse interests. In 1860 he was engaged on a survey of Lord Breadalbane's copper mine at Killin. In late 1861 he again operated as a consulting chemist, at Miller Street, Glasgow, until 1864 when he erected a small vitriol works at Camlachie. This business prospered and six years later he handed over to his eldest son and devoted himself to antiquarian and local history pursuits.

Napier joined the Philosophical Society of Glasgow in 1849 and many of his thirty-two scientific papers appeared in its proceedings. He was a fellow of the Chemical Society, a member of the Natural History and Archaeological societies of Glasgow, and was elected FRSE in 1876. He took a keen interest in the management of Anderson's College and was a trustee of the chair of technical chemistry instituted there by Young. The death of Napier's wife in 1881 was a blow from which he never recovered. For his last year he was confined to bed, and he died at his home, Maryfield, Bothwell, Lanarkshire, on 1 December 1884.   ANITA McCONNELL

Sources *Proceedings of the Philosophical Society of Glasgow*, 16 (1885), 172–84 · *The Athenaeum* (20 Dec 1884), 810 · *Proceedings of the Chemical Society*, 1 (1885), 333–6 · R. R. Tatlock, *Proceedings of the Royal Society of Edinburgh*, 14 (1886–7), 105–9 · d. cert.
Wealth at death £17,084 6s. 8d.: confirmation, 13 Feb 1885, *CCI*

Napier, John, of Merchiston (1550–1617), mathematician, was born at Merchiston Castle, the first child of Sir Archibald Napier of Merchiston (d. 1608), who was only sixteen or less, and his first wife, Janet Bothwell. On his father's side he came from a line of minor Scottish nobles, who for over a hundred years had been lairds of Merchiston (on the outskirts of Edinburgh). His mother came from a notable Edinburgh family, many of whom held burghal positions. In 1559 her brother Adam became bishop of Orkney, favouring in general whichever party he perceived to be in the ascendant. In the year following his appointment he recommended a foreign education for his nephew John, either in France or Flanders, 'for he can leyr na guid at hame, nor get na proffeit in this meist perullus worlde' (M. Napier, *Memoirs*, 67). In 1563 John enrolled at St Andrews University, but probably spent only a short time there, and then proceeded abroad in accord with his uncle's advice. The place (or places) of his foreign education is again conjectural: some have suggested Paris, but K. R. Firth has also made an interesting case for the Collège de Guyenne in Bordeaux (Firth, 135–8).

Family matters, technology, and magic Back in Scotland, in 1572 Napier married Elizabeth Stirling (d. 1579), the daughter of a prominent lawyer of noble family, and the couple took up residence at Gartness in Stirlingshire, not far from the banks of Loch Lomond. There he built a much admired castle (now a ruin), which remained his principal place of abode until his father's death in 1608, when he moved to Merchiston Castle. His first wife died in 1579 after bearing two children, Archibald *Napier and Jane, and a few years later he married Agnes, daughter of Sir James Chisholm of Cromlix in Perthshire, with whom he had five sons and five daughters. Embarrassingly for Napier, his second father-in-law was of strongly Catholic inclinations, and in 1592 he was involved in the so-called Spanish blanks affair, in which purportedly he was in collusion with the earls of Huntly, Angus, and Erroll in a plot to encourage a Spanish invasion of Scotland and England. The king was disposed to be lenient, but, although the evidence is a little ambiguous between himself and his father, it seems that John Napier, who had become a commissioner to the general assembly of the Church of Scotland in 1588, was one of a group of delegates appointed to urge stronger measures against the supposed conspirators.

Involvement in public affairs was almost inevitable at the time for someone of Napier's status, but, perhaps because of his multifarious intellectual interests, he did not allow it to occupy too much of his energy. One of his main concerns during his time at Gartness was the management of his own and his father's numerous estates.

John Napier of Merchiston (1550–1617), by unknown artist, 1616

This sometimes involved him in legal disputes about land rights, but more importantly he experimented with ways of improving the fertility of the fields, and in 1598 a patent was taken out in the name of his oldest son Archibald (who by this time was attached to the court of James VI) for a method that involved manuring land with common salt. Napier's practical philosophy, which puts him in a tradition represented earlier by Archimedes, Roger Bacon, and Leonard and Thomas Digges, and later by Cornelius Drebbel, Athanasius Kircher, and John Wilkins, also characteristically projected machines that might be useful in warfare. In a document of 1596 (transcript with facsimile, M. Napier, *Memoirs*, 247–8), when the Spanish threat could still seem real, he mentioned four such. The first two were burning mirrors, which might be of service for burning enemy ships, but the others were less traditional. One was:

> a piece of artillery, which, shott, passeth not linallie through the enemie, destroying onlie those that stand on the randon thereof, and fra them forth flying idly, as utheris do; but passeth superficially, ranging abrode within the whole appointed place, and not departing furth of the place till it hath executed his whole strength, by destroying those that be within the boundes of the said place.

Of this, the eccentric Sir Thomas Urquhart said:

> he gave proof upon a large plaine in Scotland to the destruction of a great many herds of cattel and flocks of sheep, whereof some were distant from other half a mile on all sides and some a whole mile.   (Urquhart, 100)

The final invention was:

> a round chariot of mettle made of the proofe of dooble muskett, which motion shall be by those that be within the same, more easie, more light, and more spedie by much then

so manie armed men would be otherwayes. The use hereof as well, in moving, serveth to break the array of the enemies battle and to make passage, as also in staying and abiding within the enemies battle, it serveth to destroy the environed enemy by continuall charge and shott of harquebush through small hoalles.

On a more mundane (actually sub-mundane) level he had patented at about the same time a device involving a revolving screw and axle for the draining of mines. This had at least a family resemblance—the word cochlea is even used in its description—to the *cochlias* sometimes ascribed to Archimedes, and said by Diodorus Siculus to have been used in antiquity for removing water from Spanish mines.

In his own time the projection and production of such devices resonantly evoked images of magical practices and, even if ill-founded legends are discounted, it cannot be asserted that Napier was a stranger to the occult, in at least some senses of that term. There is extant a manuscript record of a consultation between him and the German adept Daniel Müller about esoteric alchemy, and his son Robert (who became his literary executor) left behind him a work on the subject, in which he strongly emphasized the need for secrecy with regard to such a sacred science. These familial interests may have been encouraged by the fact that in 1582 John Napier's father became 'General of his Majesty's Cunzie House' (or what south of the border would be called master of the mint), with implications of an interest in gold-making, and had the 'spirit of divination' attributed to him. Also, John's uncle, the bishop of Orkney, was described as a 'sorcerer and execrable magician', and his cousin Richard Napier gained in England a very strong magical reputation. Another incident involving both valuables and probably divinatory practices was the strange contract that John Napier entered into in 1594 with a very dubious character called Robert Logan of Restalrig, to find hidden treasure at the latter's seaside property of Fastcastle, near Berwick. The venture seems to have come to a bad end, for in a somewhat later document Napier explicitly discriminated against people with the name of Logan.

Theology Napier's most widely diffused work was his *Plaine Discovery of the Whole Revelation of Saint Iohn*. This was first published in 1593, and, besides numerous editions in English, was also published several times in Dutch, French, and German. Its stance is vehemently anti-papal and in the dedication to James VI the king is urged to purge his house 'of all suspicion of Papists, and Atheists or Newtrals, wherof this Revelation foretelleth, that the number shall greatly increase in these latter daies' (J. Napier, *Plaine Discovery of the Whole Revelation of Saint Iohn*, 1593, sig. A3v). The text of the first part is presented in quasi-mathematical form as a series of propositions, starting with the manner of equating Biblical days with mundane time. Proposition 26 maintains that 'The Pope is that only Antichrist, prophecied of, in particular' (ibid., 41), and Proposition 32 that 'Gog is the Pope, and Magog is the Turkes and Mahometanes' (ibid., 59). Proposition 34 moves to more historical considerations, for the beginning of Satan's bondage was about the year AD 300, but in 1300, being freed:

> He passeth foorth to stirre up and seduce, these *Papistical* and *Mahometike* armies of *Gog* and *Magog*, to strife and warrefare. But in that 1300, yeare, began (by *Sathans* instigation) that proude strife betwixt them for supremacie, both of them chalenging to themselves the Empire of the whole earth: for Pope *Boniface* the eight, instituted the first Iubelee, that yeare, and clothed himselfe the one day in the Pontificals of a Bishop, and the other day in the robe-royall, of an Emperour, and having borne before him two swords, proclaimed these words, *Ecce duo gladii hic*: meaning thereby he was ful Monarch and more than Monarch: For, thereby he usurped to himselfe universallie both spirituall and temporall power. (ibid., 62–3)

The troubles continued until about 1560 in the time of the Reformation, when the Antichrist's 1260-year universal reign became abrogated; the way was even now being prepared for the final and utter destruction of Rome, and the Last Judgement, according to Napier, was due to occur between 1688 and 1700.

At first glance, and especially to modern eyes, Napier's account is bigotedly anti-Catholic, but not only the normally virulent theological rhetoric of the age but also special circumstances may mitigate this judgement. In an oft-quoted passage from one of the prefaces to the work, Napier wrote:

> In my tender yeares, and barneage in Sanct-Androis at the Schooles, having on the one parte contracted a loving familiaritie with a certaine Gentleman, &c. a Papist: And on the other part, being attentive to the Sermons of that worthie man of God, *Maister Christopher Goodman* [a close associate of John Knox], teaching upon the Apocalyps, I was so mooved in admiration, against the blindnes of Papists, that could not most evidently see their seven hilled citie Rome, painted out there so lively by Saint Iohn, as the mother of all spirituall whoredome, that not only bursted I out in continual reasoning against my said familiar, but also from thenceforth, I determined with my selfe (by the assistance of Gods spirit) to employ my studie and diligence to search out the remanent mysteries of that holy book: as to this houre (praised be the Lorde) I have bin doing at al such times, as conveniently I might have occasion.

This points to the origin of the work in intelligent undergraduate, or (given the age of the participants) schoolboy, debating: as such, untempered gusto should come as no surprise, and this was, at least later, combined with the rigorously systematic approach of a mathematician. The passage also shows how Napier could have very close friendships with papists, and indeed he dedicated a work published in the year of his death (the *Rabdologia*) to the crypto-Catholic Alexander Seton, earl of Dunfermline. Again, the *Plaine Discovery* was published just after his father-in-law's implication in the Spanish blanks affair, and as such it served to demonstrate a clear theological-cum-political divide between the men. In short, nuance, if not confusion, abounded.

Mathematics Besides exciting great interest among his contemporaries Napier's apocalypticism has also occupied the attention of several modern scholars. But, although by no means as 'popular', it is his mathematics

that displayed the greatest originality and provoked the greatest admiration, both with the *cognoscenti* of his time and with subsequent specialist historians. What is extant of this all centres on the subject of complicated numerical calculations. In the sixteenth century such calculations were largely at the service of trigonometry, which itself served astronomy, and it is therefore almost certain that a principal motivation for Napier's mathematical work was astronomical; although there is little evidence of his own astronomical doings, the whole family was famous for its penchant for astrology, which depended heavily upon mathematical astronomy.

Napier's extant mathematical writings may be divided into three classes: relatively traditional arithmetical (logistical) and algebraic treatises; concrete aids to calculations; and logarithms. Although there would have been overlap, the order of development was probably the arithmetic, followed by logarithms and then concrete aids to calculation. The papers relating to the arithmetical and algebraic treatises were not published until the nineteenth century, and have not been much studied. Further work may indicate whether they contain significant new approaches, and in particular whether they may be seen as inviting the idea of logarithms. It may also be significant for such a study that, at least in his earlier days, Napier had evinced considerable interest in Indian mathematics.

Rods and other artefacts Napier's concrete aids to calculation lie in the tradition of finger reckoning, the abacus or counting board, and so on. His treatise *Rabdologiae … libri duo* was first published in 1617 (the year of his death), and included appendices on the *promptuarium* and on *arithmetica localis*. In the preface he refers to logarithms, but says that he has worked out these three methods for those who prefer instead to work with 'natural numbers' as they present themselves. The main body of the text, the rabdology, deals with what became popularly known as 'Napier's rods' or 'Napier's bones'. This must be seen against the background of the ancient gelosia or lattice method for multiplication of large numbers (which probably derived initially from India). In this a large square was divided into a grid of smaller squares and then these squares divided by parallel diagonal lines, so that, for instance, in a four-by-four square there were thirty-two triangular spaces. It was then possible, by entering single digits into these spaces, to reduce the multiplication of two four-digit numbers to a series of simple multiplications (up to 9 x 9) and additions, without, it was sometimes said, too much thought. In this method the triangles were filled in as the process of multiplication proceeded, but Napier's bones present them as already supplied with digits. The basic set consists of ten quadrilateral columns with square bases: on each lateral face of each there are ten squares, each bisected diagonally, with digits being inscribed in the triangles according to prescribed rules. By placing rods side by side large numbers could be represented (up to ten digits in some cases), and their multiples up to 9 x easily read off. To multiply two numbers together, one of them is set up on the rods, its multiples by the digits of the other written down on paper with appropriate placement, and the results added together to achieve the result. Arguably this is rather more complicated than the gelosia method, but the rods had the great advantage that long divisions could be performed on them, and (with a small addition of equipment) extraction of roots. They were also adaptable to geometrical and other mensurational purposes.

The promptuary was a more complicated device also related to the gelosia method of multiplication. For it Napier prescribed 200 strips of ivory or similar material, each patterned with diagonally divided squares, which were stored in order in a box. To multiply large numbers some of the strips (most of whose triangles contained digits) were placed on top of the box and regarded as pointing towards the operator; other strips were placed on top of these and perpendicular to them. These upper strips were perforated by triangular holes, through which (with the aid of some simple addition) the multiple could be read off.

Local arithmetic was something rather different. In it numbers were translated into a binary system: that is, they were represented as sums of powers of two, rather than as sums of powers of ten, as in decimal numeration. In the full development of the method a sort of chessboard was formed (Napier describes one of 24 x 24 squares), and each square assigned a simple binary value according to rule. Multiplications, divisions, and extractions of square roots were then performed by moving counters around on the board.

Logarithms Napier's greatest achievement is universally and rightly regarded as the invention of logarithms. This was first made public in his *Mirifici logarithmorum canonis descriptio* (1614), but before this was written he had composed another work, published posthumously by his son Robert as *Mirifici logarithmorum canonis constructio* (1619). (These easily become confused in library catalogues.) The *Descriptio* swiftly appeared in English in a translation by Edward Wright (1616), and other editions, translations, and adaptations of both works followed.

The basic idea is quite simple, and depends on the difference between arithmetical and geometrical progression, or simple and proportional increase and decrease. Manifestations of it could earlier be found in musical theory, in medieval ratio theory, in Archimedes' representation of large numbers in his *Sand-Reckoner*, and perhaps most significantly in the very principles of place-value numeration, upon which Napier clearly reflected deeply, a meditation which probably facilitated his introduction of the decimal point in a manner that later became standard. Napier imagined two straight lines, one indefinitely extended from point A, and the other of finite length *az*, on each of which a point is conceived to move, a process which again has Archimedean echoes. On the second line point *b* starts from *a* and moves in such a way that the length *bz* loses equal ratios in equal times, while on the first line point B starts from point A at the same time and moves uniformly at the same speed as that which *b* had initially. Then at any time the number representing the

length *AB* is the logarithm (number of the ratio) of that representing *bz*. The crucial advantage of this conception is that it allows complex multiplications and divisions to be performed by far simpler additions and subtractions of the corresponding logarithms, a process which until very recently led to tables of logarithms being the constant companion of every school pupil with anything more than a very modest claim to mathematical competence.

But thereby comes the rub. Napier's conception may have been essentially simple, although directed to an end with the boldness of genius, but constructing tables demanded a huge amount of more mundane labour, as well as virtuosity in the framing of techniques. The *Descriptio*, which gave the principles and the actual tables, did not say how they were made. This was the central burden of the earlier *Constructio*, in the text of which what were later referred to as logarithms are called *numeri artificiales* ('artful numbers'). Because of the astronomical connection, Napier uses trigonometrical terminology in his exposition. The finite line (called *az* above) is the whole sine (*sinus totus*) or radius of a circle—sines were then seen as lines rather than as ratios—and Napier assigns the length 10,000,000 to it, which is the sine of 90°; Napier's table proceeds by intervals of 1′, but, as it includes in each line the complementary angle with respect to 90°, it does not have to go on beyond forty-five parts. Napier's method was to form three auxiliary tables of numbers decreasing by small proportional intervals from 10,000,000. By means of these, and a number of rules for assigning upper and lower bounds to logarithms, he was able to form his final table. As has often been noted, it does include a small replicated error, but not one that radically mars the outcome.

Publication of the *Descriptio* was received rapturously in certain quarters, and by two men in particular. The first reaction of the great German astronomer Johannes Kepler was somewhat muted: early in 1618 he spoke of the work of a certain Scottish baron whose name escaped him, and which he clearly did not think would be of much use to him, but quite soon, spurred on by the publication in that year of his sometime associate Benjamin Ursinus's *Cursus mathematici practici* which, as the title explained, contained a version of Napier's *trigonometria logarithmica*, his reaction became ecstatic. In his *Ephemeris* for 1620 Kepler included a eulogistic dedicatory letter to Napier dated July 1619, in which he clearly did not realize that the addressee had long been dead. Kepler also composed his own treatise on logarithms, published in 1624 complete with tables.

In England the most noteworthy respondent to the *Descriptio* was Henry Briggs, then professor of geometry at Gresham College, London, who very soon travelled to Scotland to visit Napier. In a charming if somewhat implausible account of their first meeting the astrologer William Lilly wrote that 'almost one quarter of an hour was spent, each beholding other with admiration, before one word was spoken' (M. Napier, *Memoirs*, 409). It must be noted that Napier's logarithms were not even what are now often called Naperian logarithms, but (translated into modern notation) the logarithm of x was $10^7 \log_e 10^7 - 10^7 \log_e x$. However, it seems that even before the publication of the *Descriptio* Napier had been thinking of an improved system, in which the logarithm of unity was zero, and in which the number ten occupied a special position, so that the logarithm either of ten itself, or of one tenth, or of the whole sine was 10,000,000,000. Napier was by then in ill health; he died on 4 April 1617, and was probably buried at St Cuthbert's Church, Edinburgh. It was left to Briggs to develop decimal logarithms as the direct ancestor of most later logarithmic tables.

Napier's work in retrospect At roughly the same time as Napier's work a form of logarithmic tables was being developed by the Swiss instrument maker Jost Bürgi, but there is no suggestion of influence in either direction. Bürgi did not publish on the subject until 1620; he was apparently very secretive, and even his friend Kepler did not know his work in this direction until later on.

An intriguing and oft-quoted story was propagated by the none too reliable annalist Anthony Wood, who wrote:

> It must be now known, that one Dr. Craig a Scotchman … coming out of Denmark into his own country, called upon Joh. Neper baron of Marcheston near Edinburgh, and told him among other discourses of a new invention in Denmark (by Longomontanus as 'tis said) to save the tedious multiplication and division in astronomical calculations. Neper being solicitous to know farther of him concerning this matter, he could give no other account of it, than that it was by proportionable numbers. Which hint Neper taking, he desired him at his return to call on him again. Craig, after some weeks had passed, did so, and Neper then shew'd him a rude draught of what he called *Canon mirabilis Logarithmorum*. (Wood, *Ath. Oxon.*, 2.491–2)

The informant referred to is clearly John Craig, brother to the famous jurist Thomas Craig. John had taught medicine in Germany before returning to Scotland about 1582, and O. Gingerich and R. S. Westman have recently shown that while abroad Craig copied out specimens of the so-called method of prosthaphaeresis as developed by Paul Wittich (not Longomontanus), and, despite Wood's probably proleptic reference to 'proportionable numbers', it has usually been assumed that prosthaphaeresis was the subject of his remarks. This made use of equalities such as (in modern notation) $\sin A \sin B = \frac{1}{2} \cos(A - B) - \frac{1}{2} \cos(A + B)$, and was used for easing certain trigonometrical calculations. It clearly has little resemblance to Napier's more universal method, except for the general idea of replacing multiplications and divisions by additions and subtractions, but it could be that discussions with Craig spurred Napier to intensive work along his own lines. In 1592 Craig informed Tycho Brahe that a *canon mirificus* was being constructed by a certain noble compatriot of his (*a generoso quodam consanguineo nostro*; *Opera omnia*, 7.335), and so, even if the conception did not occur much before this date, the pre-publication process of maturation was clearly long.

Early in the nineteenth century numerous papers relating to John Napier and the Napier family were lost by fire and by shipwreck. Historiographically this was grievous,

for with them a far richer and better rounded picture of this early modern Scottish Archimedes might well have been achieved.   GEORGE MOLLAND

Sources M. Napier, *Memoirs of John Napier of Merchiston, his lineage, life, and times, with a history of the invention of logarithms* (1834) · M. E. Baron, 'Napier, John', *DSB* · C. G. Knott, ed., *Napier tercentenary memorial volume* (1915) · J. Napier, *The construction of the wonderful canon of logarithms*, trans. W. R. Maconald (1889) [incl. bibliography of Napier's works] · J. Small, 'Sketches of later Scottish alchemists: John Napier of Merchiston, Robert Napier, Sir David Lindsay, first earl of Balcarres, Patrick Ruthven, Alexander Seton, and Patrick Scot', *Proceedings of the Society of Antiquaries of Scotland*, 11 (1874–6), 410–38 · K. R. Firth, *The apocalyptic tradition in Reformation Britain, 1530–1645* (1979) · A. Keller, 'The physical nature of man: science, medicine, mathematics', *Humanism in Renaissance Scotland*, ed. J. MacQueen (1990), 97–122 · W. F. Hawkins, 'The mathematical work of John Napier, 1550–1617', *Bulletin of the Australian Mathematical Society*, 26 (1982), 455–68 · J. Napier, *Rabdology*, trans. W. F. Richardson with introduction by R. E. Rider (1990) · W. F. Hawkins, 'The first calculating machine (John Napier, 1617)', *New Zealand Mathematical Society, supplement to newsletter number 16* (Dec 1979), 1–23 · K. W. Menninger, *Number words and number symbols: a cultural history of numbers*, trans. P. Broneer (1969) · C. Naux, *Histoire des logarithmes de Neper à Euler*, 2 vols. (1966) · W. Kaunzer, 'Logarithms', *Companion encyclopaedia of the history and philosophy of the mathematical sciences*, ed. I. Grattan-Guinness (1994), 1.210–28 · F. Maseres, *Scriptores logarithmici* (1791–1807) · J. M. Thomson and others, eds., *Registrum magni sigilli regum Scotorum / The register of the great seal of Scotland*, 11 vols. (1882–1914), vol. 6 · T. Urquhart, *The jewel*, ed. R. D. S. Jack and R. J. Lyall (1983) · Wood, *Ath. Oxon.* · O. Gingerich and R. S. Westman, *The Wittich connection: conflict and priority in late sixteenth-century cosmology* (1988) · *Tycho Brahe: opera omnia*, ed. J. L. E. Dreyer, 15 vols. in 7 (1913–29); repr. (Amsterdam, 1972) · *Johannes Kepler: Gesammelte Werke*, ed. W. von Dyck and M. Caspar (München, 1938–) · H. S. Carslaw, 'The discovery of logarithms by Napier of Merchistoun', *Journal of Proceedings of the Royal Society of New South Wales*, 48 (1914), 42–72

Archives LPL, papers

Likenesses portrait, 1616, U. Edin. [*see illus.*]

Wealth at death considerable: will, repr. in Napier, *Memoirs of John Napier*, 427–31

Napier, Sir Joseph, first baronet (1804–1882), judge, was born in Belfast on 26 December 1804 the youngest son of William Napier, a merchant of Belfast descended from the Napiers of Merchiston, Scotland, and Rosetta Macnaghten of Ballyreagh House, co. Antrim. His only sister, Rosetta, married James Whiteside, chief justice of Ireland. He was educated in the Belfast Academical Institution under James Sheridan Knowles, and in November 1820 he entered Trinity College, Dublin. In 1828 he married Charity, the second daughter of John Grace of Dublin, a descendant of the ancient family of the Graces of Courtstown, Kilkenny. They had two sons and three daughters.

Napier had a long association with Trinity College and the University of Dublin. He had a lifelong interest in the college historical society, of which he was the president from 1854 until his death. He was a member of parliament for the university between 1848 and 1858, and he held the office of vice-chancellor from 1867 to 1880. He was influential in mustering opposition to a proposal made by Henry Fawcett MP in 1867, which ultimately succeeded in 1873, to remove the restriction on fellowships and foundation scholarships of the college to members of the established church.

From the beginning of his career Napier adopted tory principles. His religious views were those of the protestant evangelical party, and he actively opposed the movement for Catholic emancipation. In 1826 he entered King's Inns, and in 1828 Gray's Inn, and became a pupil at the law school of the London University, where he attended the lectures of Mr Amos. He worked in the chambers of John Patteson, then the leading practitioner in common law, and in 1830 successfully practised for a term as a pleader in London.

Called to the Irish bar in the Easter term of 1831, Napier attached himself to the north-eastern circuit, and soon had an extensive practice in Dublin. He published in 1831 *A Manual of Precedents of Forms and Declarations on Bills of Exchange and Promissory Notes* and *A Treatise on the Practice of the Civil Bill Courts and Courts of Appeal*, and he edited the law reports known as *Albeck and Napier's Reports of Cases Argued in the King's Bench* in 1832–4. He lent assistance to the project of Tristram Kennedy to establish a law institute for legal education in Dublin. At the Lent assizes of 1843, held in Monaghan, he was engaged for the defence in the criminal trial of *R. v. Samuel Gray*, when he was refused permission to challenge one of the jurors. A verdict of guilty was returned, but Napier sued out a writ of error to the House of Lords, on the grounds that the jury had been illegally constituted, and his contention was upheld. In 1844 he was engaged as counsel for the crown in a second case of writ of error, following the conviction of Daniel O'Connell and others for seditious conspiracy arising out of the Clontarf meeting. A brief was sent by O'Connell; but the crown had sent theirs a few hours sooner, a fact publicly regretted by O'Connell. In November 1844 Napier received a silk gown from Sir Edward Sugden, lord chancellor of Ireland, and thenceforth there was scarcely a trial of note in which he was not retained, including appeals before the House of Lords.

In 1847 Napier unsuccessfully contested the representation of his university in parliament, but in 1848 he was returned without a contest. He was thought to be one of the first Irish lawyers who was willing to give priority to political reputation over professional emolument. He sat on the opposition benches, initially not identifying himself either with Peelites or protectionists. In his maiden speech, on 14 March 1848, he argued in favour of capital punishment. He opposed the extension of income tax to Ireland. The efforts of Lord John Russell in the cause of Jewish emancipation Napier strenuously opposed, and he disapproved of opening diplomatic relations with the Vatican. He attacked the withdrawal of a grant called 'ministers' money'—a tax for the support of protestant clergy levied upon the Roman Catholics living in certain corporate towns in the south of Ireland. A select committee was appointed, largely owing to his action and of which committee he was a member, to inquire into the state of the Irish poor law. Napier was opposed to making the solvent poor-law unions bear the defalcations of the insolvent, and he censured the government for its persistence in temporary expedients. In 1849 he revised and criticized the various acts to facilitate the sale of encumbered

estates in Ireland. He prepared and carried through the house an ecclesiastical code for the Church of Ireland. He opposed Lord John Russell's suggestion that the office of lord lieutenant of Ireland should be abolished, and in 1850 he took part in the agitation against the assumption by Catholic bishops in England of the titles of their sees, stating his case in a pamphlet entitled *England or Rome: which Shall Govern Ireland?*. He opposed the Sunday opening of museums. In representing evangelical protestant views he was hostile to the growing influence of the Catholic church and its members in public affairs, in both Ireland and Britain.

In March 1852 Napier was appointed Irish attorney-general in the administration of Lord Derby, and was made a privy councillor. He held office until December that year. In November he introduced four bills for the reframing of the land laws of Ireland, the Land Improvement Bill, the Leasing Power Bill, the Tenant's Improvement Compensation Bill, and the Landlord and Tenant Law Amendment Bill. None of his measures became law at the time, though most of his suggestions were adopted by later administrations. He had proceeded LLB and LLD at Dublin in 1851, and on the installation of Lord Derby as chancellor of Oxford University on 7 June 1853 he was created DCL there. He supported reforms in legal education, and proposed the appointment of a minister of justice for the United Kingdom.

When Lord Derby formed his second administration in February 1858, Napier became lord chancellor of Ireland, though his practice in Chancery had been small, and held that office until June 1859. It was then proposed to transfer him to the judicial committee of the privy council in London, but it was found that the act of parliament under which the committee was constituted did not then provide for the admission of ex-judges of Ireland or Scotland. Napier, who was thus left without professional employment, travelled on the continent, spending the autumn and winter of 1860 in the Tyrol and Italy.

On his return Napier mainly devoted himself to evangelical religious work. He was vice-president and an eloquent advocate of the Church Missionary Society, and urged the admission of the Bible into the government schools of India. He had a strong interest in the Church of Ireland Young Men's Christian Association. When the Social Science Association met at Liverpool in 1858, and at Dublin in 1861, he was on each occasion chosen president of the section of jurisprudence. He was a constant attendant at the church congress until 1868, when the title of his paper was 'How to increase the efficiency of church service'. In 1864 he was appointed a member of a royal commission for considering the forms of certain subscriptions and declarations required from the clergy of the churches of England and Ireland. The commissioners issued their report in February of the following year. The 'declaration of assent' then adopted was substantially the one which he had drafted.

In the summer of 1866 Lord Derby formed his third administration and Francis Blackburne resumed the office of lord chancellor of Ireland which he had held in

Derby's first government in 1852. Napier accepted Lord Derby's offer of the lord justiceship of appeal, rendered vacant by Blackburne's promotion. However, the appointment excited hostile comment owing to allegations that Napier's deafness would make it difficult for him to perform judicial functions, and three weeks later he retired so as not to embarrass the government. Personal relations among the senior Irish Conservative lawyers and judiciary at the time were strained. On 26 March 1867 he received the dignity of a baronetcy.

Napier was a champion of the Irish church, and both by speaking and writing he endeavoured to avert its disestablishment. In 1867 he was appointed one of the twenty-six members of the ritual commission. Upon the disestablishment of the church, Napier took an active part in its reconstruction. He helped largely in the revision of the prayer book, opposing the introduction of any material alterations.

In March 1868 Napier was recalled by Disraeli to professional life by his nomination to a vacancy in the judicial committee of the privy council (sitting at Westminster). For six years he was frequent in his attendance. In 1870 Disraeli consulted him on Gladstone's Irish land legislation. In 1874, when Disraeli once more became prime minister, the great seal of Ireland was put in commission for a period of nine months, with Sir Joseph as chief commissioner, since Disraeli required the services of the intended new lord chancellor, J. T. Ball, as attorney-general in the House of Commons. The shock of the death of Napier's elder son, William, aged only thirty-seven, in December 1874 impaired Napier's health, and at the close of 1878 he was attacked by paralysis. In January 1881 he resigned his seat on the judicial committee of the privy council. From Merrion Square, Dublin, where he had long dwelt, he had moved after 1874 to South Kensington in London. In 1880 he retired to St Leonards in Sussex, where his daughter lived; he died there on 9 December 1882 and was buried in Mount Jerome cemetery, Dublin, on 15 December.

DAIRE HOGAN

Sources A. C. Ewald, *The life and letters of Sir Joseph Napier* (1892) · *The lectures, essays, and letters of … Sir Joseph Napier*, ed. [G. Gardiner] (1888), introduction · D. Hogan, '"Vacancies for their friends": judicial appointments in Ireland, 1866–1867', *Brehons, serjeants, and attorneys: studies in the history of the Irish legal profession*, ed. D. Hogan and W. N. Osborough (1990), 211–29 · F. E. Ball, *The judges in Ireland, 1221–1921*, 2 vols. (1926)
Archives BL, corresp. with W. E. Gladstone, Add. MSS 44355–44408 · Bodl. Oxf., letters to Benjamin Disraeli · NRA, priv. coll., letters to S. H. Walpole · PRO, letters to Lord Cairns, PRO30/51 · PRO NIre., letters to James Emerson Tennent
Likenesses etching, 1853 (after G. Grey), NPG · S. C. Smith the elder, oils, 1860, TCD · T. Bridgford, oils, exh. 1884, King's Inns, Dublin · stipple, NPG · wood-engraving, NPG; repro. in *ILN* (23 Oct 1858)

Napier, Macvey (1776–1847), journal editor, was born on 11 April 1776 at Kirkintilloch, Dunbartonshire. His father was John Macvey, a merchant of Kirkintilloch, and his mother an illegitimate daughter of John Napier of Craigannet, Stirlingshire. He was christened Napier but later reversed his name to Macvey Napier in deference to the wish of his grandfather. He was educated at the village school in Kirkintilloch, and in 1789 went to Glasgow University and later to Edinburgh, where he read law. He was admitted to the Society of Writers to the Signet in 1799 and in 1805 became its librarian. On 2 December 1797 he married Catharine Skene (*d.* 1826), the daughter of an army officer, with whom he had ten children, seven sons and three daughters.

As was the case with many Scottish lawyers of his generation Napier's preference was for literature rather than the law. His friendship with the publisher Archibald Constable extended his connections with the Edinburgh literary scene, and in 1805 he contributed his first article to the recently established *Edinburgh Review*. In 1814, at Constable's invitation, he undertook the editorship of a supplement to the sixth edition of the *Encyclopaedia Britannica*, which he completed in six volumes in 1824. He kept up his academic interests as well as his contacts, and in 1820 Dugald Stewart proposed him as successor to Thomas Brown in the chair of moral philosophy at Edinburgh; although flattered, Napier declined. In 1824 he was appointed the first professor of conveyancing at the university, having lectured on the subject since 1816.

Napier's editorial activities meanwhile were running in tandem with his university teaching. Constable proposed that he edit the seventh edition of the *Encyclopaedia*, a project which faltered momentarily on the latter's bankruptcy and death in 1827. Adam Black acquired the project and Napier continued as editor, completing the edition in twenty-two volumes in 1842. But the primary focus of his energies from 1829 onward was the editorship of the *Edinburgh Review*, which he undertook in succession to its legendary founding editor, Francis Jeffrey. Jeffrey's appointment as dean of the Faculty of Advocates, and later lord advocate, came at a crucial point in the fortunes of the *Review*. Napier was very much a compromise candidate as his successor. According to his sister, the post was offered to the young Macaulay, who made it a condition that the *Review* be moved to London. Henry Brougham supposedly objected, the first indication of what was to become an intense rivalry between the two, and the post was offered to Napier.

Napier lacked the status and the charisma of his predecessor and he lacked also his prodigious talents, both intellectual and managerial. His personality and instincts were neither those of a political lobbyist nor a man of affairs. He was an academic with a retiring disposition and inclined to be self-effacing. Yet ironically it fell to him to translate the *Edinburgh* from its long-time role as an opposition journal to that of a government organ, following the appointment of the whig-led Grey ministry in 1830. What he did possess, through his work on the *Encyclopaedia* and his position in the university, was a substantial number of contacts. He also had the goodwill of most of the *Review*'s regular contributors, particularly that of William Empson, who became an unofficial sub-editor, keeping his finger on both the pulse of metropolitan literary life and on political developments. Jeffrey channelled political gossip through from the Lords and acted as a kind of editor emeritus. Napier made annual visits to London in the spring, combining professional duties with medical consultations about an increasing list of ailments.

Napier was an activist editor, whose first decision was to reduce the length of individual articles, much to the consternation of many regular contributors. He also revised articles without compunction, again to the irritation of many experienced writers. With some of Jeffrey's prized recruits he had little success, notably Carlyle, whose style and personality baffled him. He pronounced his essay 'Characteristics', published in the December 1831 number, as 'inscrutable', while its author feared it might be 'too scrutable'. Carlyle smarted over unexpected cuts and delayed payments, and referred to Napier behind his back as 'Naso the blockhead', an unkind reference to his prominent nose (*Collected Letters*, 5.297 n. 2, 5.355). To his mother, Carlyle pronounced him 'a dry, faint-hearted wooden kind of man whom I think I shall not get far with', which proved an accurate prediction (ibid., 6.301).

Other long-standing contributors were even more problematical, notably Brougham, who in the early 1830s sought to turn the *Edinburgh* into a personal organ in his war with the whig ministry. He behaved peremptorily, holding up publication at the eleventh hour to accommodate new material in his articles, complained of supposed insults, and became increasingly obsessed by Macaulay's eminence in the *Review*. The strain of dealing with Brougham took its toll on Napier's health to the extent that Empson at one point predicted it would end fatally. Macaulay, on the other hand, was generous and supportive in his role as the rising star of the *Review*. It was alleged by one supporter that the sales of any issue were directly determined by whether it contained an article by him. By 1840 Brougham's and Macaulay's roles in the *Review* were reversed, and Macaulay became the effective link to government circles.

Ultimately Napier steered the *Edinburgh* into the calmer waters of the 1840s, but with the calm came the gradual waning of the influence of the quarterlies. His editorship was solid but not spectacular, and the *Review*'s expected role as a government organ was short-lived. Harriet Martineau reported that Empson had been known to shake his head over the misfortunes of the *Review* under Napier, alleging that he had 'no literary faculty or cultivation whatever' (*Harriet Martineau's Autobiography*, 1.213). His other colleagues would not have agreed. But it was undoubtedly true that by the end of the 1830s the *Edinburgh*, like its old rival the *Quarterly*, had ceased to be at the cutting edge of political debate.

The penalty of prolonged editorial labours was nicely articulated by Henry Cockburn in his tribute to Napier: 'Without absolute learning or talent in the higher senses, he was intelligent and sensible, well read in morals and metaphysics, very industrious, and he had a good, plain, clear style of composition'. He went on:

The 'Encyclopaedia' and the 'Review' connected him with the whole science and literature of the country. No such stream can pass through the soil of a good mind without enriching it by its depositions. The misfortune of the

process is that the habit of merely delivering others is apt to impair or at least to supersede, the power of one's own creation. If Napier had not given his best years to the editing of these works, he would probably have produced something worthy of his own. (*Journal of Henry Cockburn*, 2.167–8)

It was a melancholy but wholly appropriate reflection on the demands of editorship as it had evolved under Jeffrey and continued under Napier. Napier's own literary output was modest: a memoir of Bacon, published posthumously with a life of Raleigh in 1853, and a handful of articles in the *Edinburgh*, mainly written before he assumed control. He was appointed one of the principal clerks of session in Edinburgh in 1837 and was elected a fellow of the Royal Society of both London and Edinburgh. He died in Edinburgh on 11 February 1847. A selection of Napier's correspondence was collected for publication (1879) by his son Macvey Napier (d. July 1893).

Another son, **Alexander Napier** (1814–1887), translator and editor, was born at Edinburgh in 1814, matriculated at Trinity College, Cambridge, in 1834, and was vicar of Holkham, Norfolk, from 1847 until his death there on 24 August 1887. Among his works was a nine-volume edition of the theological works of Isaac Barrow (1859). He also collaborated with his wife, Robina (*née* Cotterill), whom he had married in 1850, on an edition of Boswell's *Life of Dr Johnson* (1884). Her literary output included translations published as *Field Marshal Count Moltke's Letters from Russia* (1878) and the *Memoirs of Prince Metternich* (5 vols., 1880–82). JOANNE SHATTOCK

Sources J. Shattock, *Politics and reviewers: The Edinburgh and The Quarterly in the early Victorian age* (1989) · *Selections from the correspondence of … Macvey Napier*, ed. M. Napier (1879) · *The letters of Thomas Babington Macaulay*, ed. T. Pinney, 6 vols. (1974–81) · *The collected letters of Thomas and Jane Welsh Carlyle*, ed. C. R. Sanders, K. J. Fielding, and others, [30 vols.] (1970–) · *Journal of Henry Cockburn: being a continuation of the 'Memorials of his time', 1831–1854*, 2 vols. (1874) · *Harriet Martineau's autobiography*, ed. M. W. Chapman, 3 vols. (1877) · *GM*, 2nd ser., 27 (1847), 436–7 · *Wellesley index* · Boase, *Mod. Eng. biog.* · Venn, *Alum. Cant.* · *DNB*

Archives BL, corresp. and MSS, Add. MSS 34611–34631 · U. Edin. L., lecture notes · U. St Andr. L., lecture notes | BL, corresp. with John Allen, Add. MS 52182 · Glos. RO, letters to Daniel Ellis, D1501, 2227 · Herts. ALS, letters to Lord Lytton · NL Scot., corresp. with James Browne · NL Scot., letters to Thomas Carlyle · NL Scot., corresp. with George Combe · NL Scot., corresp. with Archibald Constable · NL Scot., letters to Lord Mounteagle · NL Scot., letters to William Mure · NL Scot., corresp. mainly with Lord Rutherford · NL Wales, corresp. with Nassau Senior · U. Edin. L., letters to David Laing · U. Edin., New Coll. L., letters to Thomas Chalmers · U. St Andr. L., corresp. with James David Forbes · UCL, corresp. with Edwin Chadwick

Likenesses P. Sclater, ink and wash drawing, Scot. NPG

Napier, Mark (1798–1879), lawyer and historian, born on 24 July 1798, was descended from the Napiers of Merchiston, near Edinburgh. His father was Francis Napier, a writer to the signet in Edinburgh, and his mother was Mary Elizabeth Jane Douglas, eldest daughter of Colonel Archibald Hamilton of Innerwick, East Lothian. He was educated at the high school, Edinburgh, and at Edinburgh University, and passed advocate at the Scottish bar in 1820. In 1844 he was appointed sheriff-depute of Dumfriesshire, to which Galloway was subsequently added, and he held office until his death. Although a learned lawyer in all branches of Scottish law, his reputation was literary rather than legal. His only strictly legal works are *The Law of Prescription in Scotland* (1839; 2nd edn, 1854), a standard work, and *Letters to the commissioners of supply of the county of Dumfries, in reply to a report of a committee of their number on the subject of sheriff courts* (1852; 2nd edn, 1852). In 1835 he published a *History of the Partition of Lennox*, with which earldom the Napiers had historical connection. In 1834 he published his useful *Memoirs of John Napier of Merchiston*; and in 1839 he edited John Napier's unpublished manuscripts with an introduction.

Napier researched extensively on James Graham, marquess of Montrose and on John Graham of Claverhouse; he published on them *Montrose and the Covenanters* (1838), *Life and Times of Montrose* (1840), *Memorials of Montrose and his Times* for the Maitland Club (2 vols., 1856), and *Memorials of Graham of Claverhouse* (2 vols., 1859–62). T. F. Henderson wrote of them:

> as historical guides their value is much impaired by their controversial tone and violent language. His jacobitism was of the old-fashioned fanatical type, and although in many cases his representations are substantially founded on fact, his exaggeration necessarily awakens distrust, even when he has a good case. (*DNB*)

Napier's book on Claverhouse led to a keen controversy in regard to the drowning of the two women, Margaret Maclachlan and Margaret Wilson, known as the Wigtown martyrs. Napier had questioned whether the execution took place; and he replied to his objectors in the *Case for the crown in re the Wigtown martyrs proved to be myths versus Wodrow and Lord Macaulay, Patrick the Pedlar and Principal Tulloch* (1863) and in a further work in 1870. He also edited volumes 2 and 3 of Spotiswood's *History of the Church of Scotland* for the Bannatyne Club in 1847. *The Lennox of Auld, an Epistolary Review of 'The Lennox' by William Fraser*, was published posthumously in 1880, edited by his son Francis. He occasionally wrote 'very touching as well as very spirited' verse (*The Athenaeum*, 29 Nov 1879), and possessed a valuable collection of paintings and china.

Napier married his cousin Charlotte, daughter of Alexander Ogilvie, and widow of William Dick Macfarlane, and with her had a son, Francis John, and a daughter, Frances Anne.

> Though a keen controversialist and most unsparing in epithets of abuse, Mark Napier was in person and address a genial polished gentleman of the old school—a really beautiful old man, worn to a shadow, but with a never failing kindly smile, and a lively, pleasant, intellectual face, in which the pallid cheek of age was always relieved by a little trace of seemingly hectic or of youthful colour. (*Scotsman*)

He died at his town house, 6 Ainslie Place, Edinburgh, on 23 November 1879. H. C. G. MATTHEW

Sources *The Scotsman* (24 Nov 1879) · *Journal of Jurisprudence*, 23 (1879), 652–5 · Boase, *Mod. Eng. biog.* · *DNB*
Archives NL Scot., genealogical coresp. and collections · NRA Scotland, priv. coll., letters | NRA, priv. coll., letters to Sir Charles Dalrymple Fergusson · U. Edin. L., letters to D. Laing
Likenesses C. Smith, oils, 1867, Scot. NPG

Napier, Montague Stanley (1870–1931), motor car and aero-engine manufacturer, was born on 14 April 1870 at 68 York Road, Lambeth, London, the youngest of the four sons of James Murdoch Napier, mechanical engineer, and his wife, Fanny Jemima, *née* Mackenzie. His Scottish grandfather moved from Scotland and had founded a business in York Road, Lambeth, by 1836, specializing in making printing machinery for the newspaper industry. Under James Murdoch Napier the firm made coin-weighing machines for the Royal Mint, but by his death in 1895 the business of D. Napier & Son was in decline. Nothing is known about Napier's education, but although he started working for his father at an early age, he was not doing so at the time of his father's death. He bought the family business from the executors and expanded into making machine tools for the cycle industry.

Napier turned to making motor cars in 1899, after Selwyn Edge, like Napier a keen racing cyclist and former member of the Bath Road Club, asked him to modify the Panhard et Levassor car which he had bought after it came second in the 1896 Paris–Marseilles race. Edge was so impressed with the new two-cylinder engine that Napier designed that he contracted to buy six cars from him, setting up the Motor Vehicle Company, with a showroom in Regent Street, to sell them. The first cars, ready in 1900, were so successful that Napier moved his works to larger premises in Acton in 1903, and in 1904 produced the first commercially successful six-cylinder car. While Napier concentrated on the technical side, Edge was attracting publicity for Napier cars with spectacular successes in races and competitions, winning the Gordon Bennett international trophy in 1902. Thanks to the marketing skills of Edge, Napier cars dominated the luxury car trade in Britain until challenged by Rolls-Royce Ltd after 1906.

Unlike Rolls and Royce, who formed a single company to make and market Rolls-Royce cars, Napier and Edge converted their private firms into public companies, D. Napier & Son Ltd in 1906, followed by S. F. Edge (1907) Ltd in 1907, and Edge's company agreed to buy £120,000 worth of Napier cars every year until 1921. In 1912, Napier and Edge parted company, and S. F. Edge Ltd was wound up. Napier's health began to break down in 1915, and following an operation for the removal of a kidney he moved permanently to Cannes, in the south of France, in 1917. He set up a design office there, however, remaining managing director of the firm, and, from 1924, joint managing director. He realized that his firm could not compete with the large manufacturers of mass-produced cheap cars, and although he designed one new car, which came on the market in 1920, there was little demand, and the last Napier car was sold in 1924.

Napier began to make aeroplane engines in response to the Air Ministry's need at the beginning of the First World War, and he started work on his own water-cooled engine in 1916. This engine, the 450 hp Lion, was in use by the end of the war, and in 1918 the government placed an order worth £2.5 million. The Lion became the most widely used British engine, with a larger share of the aircraft business than its rivals Rolls-Royce, Armstrong Siddeley, and Bristol, and it built up a reputation for reliability over long distances. By 1926 Imperial Airways had flown over 2 million miles with the engines, and in 1926 a Lion-powered flying boat made the first non-stop flight across the south Atlantic, from Spain to Argentina. As early as 1919 Napier realized the need to have a new design ready to replace the Lion, and began work on the 1000 hp Cub, which was eventually rejected by the government, in 1925. But throughout the 1920s the Lion continued to be successful: in 1927 Napier employed 1600 men, making fifty engines a month. After the failure of the Cub, he worked on a 250 hp engine, but the Air Ministry and Imperial Airways were more interested in the new large radial engines being developed by his rivals. By the end of 1929 Napier was producing only twelve engines a month. An attempt to take over Bentley in 1931 was thwarted by Rolls-Royce, but D. Napier & Son survived until 1942, when it was taken over by the English Electric Company. Napier's great successes had been the pre-war six-cylinder luxury cars, and the Lion aeroplane engine, but in both instances he was overtaken by Rolls-Royce.

Napier was a tall, bearded, quiet man, 'with a face not unlike an apostle' (Edge, 263), with none of the flamboyance of racing drivers such as Edge. He was not a keen motorist himself, and never drove a racing car. In 1903 he married Alice Caroline Mary, née Paterson, a school governess. They had two sons and two daughters. Napier and his wife were legally separated in 1922. He died at his home, Villa des Cistes, Cannes, France, on 22 January 1931, leaving over £1 million. The chief beneficiary of the will was Norah Mary Fryer (wife of Dr Edwin Fryer), with whom he had lived since 1915.   ANNE PIMLOTT BAKER

Sources C. H. Wilson and W. Reader, *Men and machines: a history of D. Napier and Son, Engineers, Ltd, 1808–1958* (1958) · W. J. Reader, 'Edge, Selwyn Francis', *DBB* · W. J. Reader, 'Napier, Montague Stanley', *DBB* · St J. C. Nixon, *The antique automobile* (1956), 72–7 · S. B. Saul, 'The motor industry in Britain to 1914', *Business History*, 5 (1962–3), 22–44 · R. Church, 'Markets and marketing in the British motor industry before 1914', *Journal of Transport History*, 3rd ser., 3 (1982), 1–20 · S. F. Edge, *My motoring reminiscences* (1934); repr. (1972) · G. N. Georgano, ed., *The complete encyclopedia of motorcars* (1969) · *The Times* (28 Jan 1931) · *The Times* (19 March 1931) · *The Times* (22 April 1931) · *The Times* (16 Feb 1932) · *The Times* (28–30 June 1932) [Napier will suit in the high court]
Archives Sci. Mus., specimens of Napier aero-engines and models of aircraft powered by them
Likenesses photograph, repro. in Nixon, *Antique automobile*, facing p. 109 · photographs, repro. in Wilson and Reader, *Men and machines*, 12–13, 84–5
Wealth at death £1,243,578 7s. 1d.: administration, 23 May 1931, CGPLA Eng. & Wales

Napier, Sir Nathaniel, second baronet (1636/7–1709), traveller and politician, was the first son of Sir Gerard *Napier, first baronet (*bap.* 1606, *d.* 1673), of More Crichel, Dorset, and his wife, Margaret (*d.* 1660), daughter and coheir of John Colles of Barton Grange, Pitminster, Somerset. On 16 March 1654 he matriculated from Oriel College, Oxford. He married, on 30 December 1657, Blanche (1641/2–1695), daughter and (later) coheir of Sir Hugh *Wyndham (1602/3–1684), a judge of common pleas. They

had five sons (four of whom predeceased their father), and four daughters. Napier was knighted on 16 January 1662. After spending nearly a decade resident at Edmondsham, near More Crichel, in 1667 he was made attaché to his uncle Henry Coventry, a diplomat posted to The Hague to attend the peace talks at Breda. He wrote up his experiences in a 'Particular tract'. In 1671 he visited France, again committing his thoughts on his journey to paper in another tract.

On 14 May 1673 Napier succeeded his father as second baronet, and in 1675 seemed set to cement his position in Dorset when a county seat became available in parliament. In the event he supported the candidature of his brother-in-law, John Digby, Lord Digby. When Digby succeeded as third earl of Bristol in 1677 Napier did stand but the election on 30 April was subject to a double return, and was declared void on 28 January 1678. Napier was eventually returned to parliament in 1679 for Corfe Castle. He sat in all three exclusion parliaments, but voted for the Exclusion Bill in only the third, the Oxford parliament. He quickly reversed his position, signing the Dorset address against it later in the year, and thereby earning some opprobrium in print in *A Letter from a Person of Quality*. Napier was re-elected to parliament in 1685. He opposed the repeal of the penal laws and Test Acts, but he was still seen as worthy of support by James II's electoral agents in 1688. Napier preferred to stand for Poole, however, and following the Dutch invasion he pursued the king to Salisbury to secure the restoration of the town's old charter, and also served as sheriff of Dorset for three weeks in November 1688. He was returned to the Convention Parliament for Poole, but only after a double return had been decided in his favour on 9 February 1689.

Napier was elected again in 1690 and 1695. He signed the Association in February 1696, and in the summer of that year one of his daughters married Sir John Guise, third baronet, who described Napier as 'a man of extreme levity'. Guise was even less pleased when Napier (a widower following the death of his wife on 1 April 1695) married, on 9 March 1697, Susanna Guise (1675/6–1709x11), a relative. Following Napier's inability to win a seat at the 1698 election, he travelled to France and Italy with his new wife, earning the reputation of 'a great beau' (*Rutland MSS*, 2.164). In France the couple aroused the suspicions of the English ambassador, the earl of Manchester, for 'going 'ere the late King and Queen and p[retended] Prince of Wales have appeared' (Montagu, 2.116), and they were suspected of carrying letters back with them when they returned, probably in late 1700. Napier stood unsuccessfully at Poole in both February and November 1701, but he had one final spell in parliament, winning a by-election at Dorchester on 4 February 1702 and continuing to sit for that borough until 1705. In Queen Anne's reign he served as a gentleman of the privy chamber. In July 1705 Daniel Defoe described him as 'warm' (*Portland MSS*, 4.213) in his politics. He appears to have travelled to the Netherlands in April 1704, but his trip was cut short by illness. In March 1706 he was at Spa for his health, returning to England in September 1707. Napier died on 21 January 1709, aged seventy-two and was buried 'in the dormitory of my ancestors' at Great Minterne, Dorset. He was succeeded as third baronet by his son Nathaniel.   STUART HANDLEY

Sources J. P. Ferris, 'Napier, Sir Nathaniel', HoP, *Commons, 1660–90* · GEC, *Baronetage* · Wotton, *The English baronetage*, 3 vols. (1741), vol. 2, 161–4 · Foster, *Alum. Oxon.* · J. Hutchins, *The history and antiquities of the county of Dorset*, 3rd edn, ed. W. Shipp and J. W. Hodson, 3 (1868), 125; 4 (1874), 483–4 · will, PRO, PROB 11/509, sig. 151 · [J. Guise], *Autobiography of Thomas Raymond, and Memoirs of the family of Guise of Elmore, Gloucestershire*, ed. G. Davies, CS, 3rd ser., 28 (1917), 140–41 · W. D. Montagu, seventh duke of Manchester, *Court and society from Elizabeth to Anne*, 2 vols. (1864), vol. 2, 116–19 · J. Sydenham, *The history of the town and county of Poole* (1839), 281 · *The manuscripts of his grace the duke of Rutland*, 4 vols., HMC, 24 (1888–1905), vol. 2, p. 164 · *The manuscripts of his grace the duke of Portland*, 10 vols., HMC, 29 (1891–1931), vol. 4, p. 213 · M. Knights, *Politics and opinion in crisis, 1678–1681* (1994), 86n., 338 · G. Duckett, ed., *Penal laws and Test Act*, 2 (1883), 36

Napier, Richard (1559–1634), astrological physician and Church of England clergyman, was born in Exeter on 4 May 1559, the third son of Alexander Napier and his wife, Ann (Agnes) Burchley. Napier's family pedigree involved direct descent from the Scottish Napiers, lairds of Merchiston, his father being the elder son, by a third wife, of Sir Archibald Napier (*d.* 1522), fourth laird of Merchiston. Matriculating aged eighteen at Exeter College as a commoner on 20 December 1577, Napier enjoyed an extensive education in theology at Oxford University, receiving his BA in 1584 and his MA in 1586. He was elected a fellow of Exeter College in 1580, holding the post until 1590, but maintaining his links thereafter—symbolically reaffirmed with a donation for the building of the college kitchen in 1624. He left Oxford in 1590, was ordained, and installed as rector of Great Linford, north Buckinghamshire, where he was to live and work for the next forty-four years until his death. However, an uncomfortable, highly anxious preacher at the best of times, he is said (Lilly, 53) to have broken down in the pulpit early on in his ministry. Feeling obliged to abandon this public part of his offices thenceforth, he employed a curate to substitute, whom he supported with a salary and lodging in his own house.

The practice of medicine and magic Napier devoted most of his time at Linford to the pursuit of theology, alchemy, and (more especially) astrological medicine. He had acquired a formal licence to practice from Erasmus Webb, archdeacon of Buckingham. His interest in astrology seems to have originated in a period of study with the industrious astrologer Simon Forman, after 1597. While the latter initially lampooned Napier affectionately, calling him 'a dunce', Napier's eventual talent for astrology and other personal qualities won Forman over. Such was their friendship that Forman quickly became an avuncular friend, and bequeathed Napier all his manuscripts on his death in 1611. Both men additionally knew and were strongly influenced by John Dee, the sixteenth-century astrologer, alchemist, and conjuror *par excellence*.

Despite the contested status of such arcane arts at this time, the combination of astrology and medicine clearly

Richard Napier (1559–1634), by unknown artist, *c.*1630

helped Napier to build up a prodigious and popular practice, tending to the bodily and mental ills of tens of thousands of patients. The afflicted came to him from all social ranks, although the majority of his clients were derived (and remained) from the lower middling, artisan, farming, and labouring classes. Even the poorer folk sought Napier out, no doubt encouraged by the fact that his fees were on the modest side, and that he would often forgo charging the poor, although the extent of his charity may have been exaggerated by some of his hagiographical biographers. About one-quarter of his clients were drawn from the nobility, aristocracy, and higher gentry, in part recruited initially through his brother, Sir Robert Napier [*see below*], whose success as a Levant trader made him wealthy, and who moved in the duke of Buckingham's circle. Yet this clientele, which included earls and lords (such as those of Cleveland, Northampton, and Rutland), was also some reflection of Napier's growing status as a practitioner. Eventually he was to number Sir Kenelm Digby, Sir Thomas Myddleton and other knights, baronets, and their families among his own personal friends. Perhaps the most notorious (and among the best documented) consultations recorded in Napier's notes were with those close to the duke of Buckingham, most especially the duke's brother, the adulterous and 'lunatic' Viscount Purbeck, John Villiers.

Napier produced no medical publications, but this did not disadvantage his reputation as a healer, which spread rapidly by word of mouth. The majority of his patients always came from the immediate neighbourhood, although towards the end of his life he was attracting small, but growing, numbers of patients from all over England (Devon and Cornwall only excepted), a few even coming from as far afield as Yorkshire, Lincolnshire, Shropshire, Dorset, and Somerset. Napier was assisted in his medical practice by two of his curates, who themselves adopted his methods and likewise became astrological physicians.

Most historical attention (thus far) has been accorded to Napier's mentally and psychically affected patients, who actually comprised less than 5 per cent (about 2000) of his enormous clientele. Yet his notes permit a unique and remarkable window into the mental afflictions and thought worlds of a wide range of mentally troubled and sick individuals and their families, and what they meant to a contemporary practitioner. Napier's empathy for the mental travails and ills of some of his patients may have been enhanced by the fact that he himself was evidently 'afflicted with mopish melancholy' (Bodl. Oxf., MS Ashmole 213, fol. 110). He also shared, to some extent, their anxieties about the spirit world, and offered them the kind of eclectic medical aid that they generally found highly palatable. Although reliant mainly on standard, conventional evacuative and antiphlogistic remedies, his extant medical notes show him dispensing a mixture of orthodox medicinal remedies, religio-moral counsel, and astrological, quasi-magical intervention—from purgation and bleeding, to mutual prayer, horoscope casting, the provision of amulets and charms, and ritual exorcism. Astrology informed Napier's entire practice, from the content and style of consultation and diagnosis to record-keeping and the timing and nature of treatments. Yet the stars were not his only otherworldly guides for, allegedly (according to Lilly and Aubrey), he also discoursed regularly with the spirit world, calling upon the angel Raphael for advice about his patients. However, there are (perhaps deliberately) scant signs of such angelic consultations in his notes, while even astrology remained merely a tool in his medical practice. It was a more earthly and more regularly medical assessment of signs and symptoms on which Napier relied most.

Astrology and Anglicanism Practices which smacked of magic carried a serious threat in this period, conjuring, or necromancy, being a capital crime. Yet, while Napier was attacked publicly by puritans, and was even abused by some as a conjuror or witch, he was able to chart a relatively safe course socially and professionally through a steady assertion of moderate, conforming Anglicanism. No doubt this was assisted by his occasional assaults on Catholic doctrines, his staunch championing of unity in the church, and his upbraiding of nonconformists and schismatics (although this also encouraged sporadic conflicts with leading and local puritans). Alongside his repute as a physician and astrologer, Napier was also a magnet for the hungry minds of many scholarly churchmen. They visited him, not only to engage in discussion and to use his enormous theological library, but also to consult his many astrological works, and to be personally inducted in the art by Napier. This submerging and diffusing of more esoteric arts within a thorough grounding in mainstream Anglican theology, as well as the right kind of classical and medieval learning, must have further contributed towards Napier's avoidance of hazardous controversy. Importantly, too, he declined to broadcast openly his magical interests and practices.

For these and other reasons Napier has been portrayed, somewhat antithetically, as one of the last of the Renaissance magi but also as a crusader for orthodox Anglicanism. He has been seen as a significant figure in a world in gradual, uneven transition, when astrological and magical traditions—once permissible (if suspect) even for orthodox, learned Anglicans—were losing credibility and legitimacy. Napier is also especially worthy of note in that his medico-astrological practice can be (and has been) reconstructed by historians (most notably, Macdonald and Sawyer) in remarkable detail from the prodigious amount of his private manuscripts that have survived. His medical notes (whose meticulous format seems to have been encouraged by astrological methodologies) on their own comprise sixty volumes, quite apart from his numerous correspondence, and unpublished tracts and treatises.

Napier died at Great Linford on 1 April 1634, collapsing, appropriately, while on his knees in prayer; he was buried there two weeks later. The epitaph his curate recorded in the parish register stated with fitting simplicity that he was 'the most renowned physician of both body and soul'. He bequeathed virtually his entire estate to his nephew and pupil, Richard Napier [*see below*], the second son of his elder brother, Robert. This property included the parsonage (which Napier purchased for £200 in 1610 and substantially remodelled during his lifetime) and the advowson of Great Linford, as well as his large collection of manuscripts and books (most of which are now in the Bodleian Library, Oxford). An imposing portrait in oils, showing Napier in black clerical garb and painted (anonymously) about 1630, hangs currently at the Ashmolean Museum, Oxford.

Sir Robert Napier, first baronet (1560–1637), the astrologer's brother, established himself at Bishopsgate Street, London, as a successful Turkey merchant and a member of the Grocers' Company. He purchased an estate at Luton Hoo, Bedfordshire, was knighted in 1611, and was created baronet in 1612. Elected sheriff in 1613, he declined the office and was duly fined; the following year he sought to persuade the common council that he could serve the City better if he was not called on to stand as alderman or sheriff. He married three times, and at his death in April 1637 was succeeded as second baronet by Robert, the eldest son of his third marriage.

Sir Richard Napier (1607–1676), physician, the second son of Sir Robert Napier, was born in London. He was enrolled at Gray's Inn in 1622 before entering Wadham College, Oxford, as a fellow-commoner in 1624. He graduated BA on 4 December 1624 and a year later was created MA by virtue of letters of the chancellor, which described him as a kinsman of the duchess of Richmond. This kinship was somewhat remote, depending on the descent of the duchess's husband from the Stuarts, earls of Lennox. Richard Napier was elected a fellow of All Souls, Oxford, in

1627 and proceeded BCL in July 1630. He had already been treating some of his uncle's patients at Great Linford before obtaining from John Williams, bishop of Lincoln, a licence to practise medicine. At his uncle's death he inherited all his property and manuscripts, and settled at Great Linford, the manor of which his father had purchased for him.

Napier continued to accumulate academic honours; in November 1642 he took the degree of MD at Oxford, he was knighted on 4 July 1647, he was incorporated MD at Cambridge in 1663, and in December 1664 he became an honorary fellow of the College of Physicians in London. He had previously given to the college library in 1652 thirteen finely bound volumes of the Greek commentators on Aristotle. Wood errs in describing him as an early member of the Royal Society, probably having confused him with William Napier, who was a member. Richard Napier married, first, Ann, youngest daughter of Sir Thomas Tyringham. Their eldest son, Robert (d. 1670), graduated MD at Padua. Thomas (b. 1646), the eldest son of Napier's second marriage (in 1645, to Mary, daughter of Sir Thomas Vyner, later lord mayor of London), inherited Linford and his father's medical books, papers, and correspondence.

On his way to visit Sir John Lenthall at Bessels Leigh, near Abingdon, Berkshire, in January 1676, Sir Richard rested at an inn where, according to Aubrey, on entering his chamber he saw a dead man lying upon the bed, whom on closer inspection he recognized as himself. He died shortly after his arrival at Lenthall's house on 17 January 1676 and was buried at Great Linford church. In 1769 Thomas Napier sold the estate, making over Sir Richard's manuscripts to Elias Ashmole. They are now in the Bodleian Library.   JONATHAN ANDREWS

Sources M. MacDonald, *Mystical Bedlam: madness, anxiety and healing in seventeenth century England* (1981) · M. MacDonald, 'The career of astrological medicine in England', *Religio medici: medicine and religion in seventeenth-century England*, ed. O. P. Grell and A. Cunningham (1996), 62–90 · R. C. Sawyer, 'Patients, healers, and disease in the southeast midlands, 1597–1634', PhD diss., University of Wisconsin, Madison, 1986 · DNB · W. Lilly, *Mr William Lilly's history of his life and times* (1715), 52–4 · *Aubrey's Brief lives*, ed. O. L. Dick (1949); repr. (1972), 78, 378–9 · J. Aubrey, 'Miscellanies', *Three prose works*, ed. J. Buchanan-Brown (1972), 86, 101–2 · Munk, *Roll* · Wood, *Ath. Oxon.*, new edn, 2.103–4 · will of Sir Robert Napier, PRO, PROB 11/175, sig. 342 · E. Ashmole, *The lives of … Elias Ashmole … & Mr. William Lilly, written by themselves …* (1774), 77–80 · H. R. Rollin, 'Magic and mountebanks in the development of psychiatric thought', *Journal of the Royal Society of Medicine*, 85 (1992), 381–5 · M. Macdonald, 'Popular beliefs about mental disorder in early modern England', *Münstersche Beiträge zur Geschichte und Theorie der Medizin*, ed. W. Eckhart and J. Geyer-Kordesch (Munster, 1982), 148–73 · M. Macdonald, 'Religion, social change and psychological healing in England, 1600–1800', *The church and healing*, ed. W. J. Shiels, SCH, 19 (1982), 101–25 · M. Macdonald and T. R. Murphy, *Sleepless souls: suicide in early modern England* (1990)

Archives Bucks. RLSS, financial records | BL, Sloane papers · Bodl. Oxf., Ashmole MSS

Likenesses oils, *c*.1630, AM Oxf. [*see illus.*]

Wealth at death no value given—Sir Robert Napier: will, PRO, PROB 11/175, sig. 342

Napier, Sir Richard (1607–1676). *See under* Napier, Richard (1559–1634).

Napier, Sir Robert (d. 1615), judge, was the third son of James Napier of Swyre, Dorset, and his wife, a daughter of the Hilliard family, also of Dorset. He was an undergraduate at Exeter College, Oxford, from 1559 to 1561, graduated BA in 1562, and entered the Middle Temple in London in 1566. He married twice. His first wife was Katherine, daughter of John Wareham; they had one daughter, Anne. His second wife was Magdalen (d. 1635), daughter of Sir Anthony Denton of Oxfordshire; their son and heir was Sir Nathaniel Napier.

From the 1570s onwards Napier's name appears in connection with his professional work as a lawyer. In 1574–5 he was involved in land transactions for the second earl of Bedford, to whom he may have been related through his grandmother Anne Russell. In 1591 he went to Jersey to investigate complaints against the Paulet family. He arbitrated against Anthony Paulet in 1592, and together with Tertullian Pyne produced a code of ordinances for the island. He was a trustee for Dorchester School, Dorset, and in 1592 he bought Middlemarsh Hall, Dorset. In 1586 Napier was returned a member of parliament for Dorchester. Records suggest that he may have been nominated for the seat by a patron, possibly the earl of Warwick, guardian of the third earl of Bedford. In 1593 Napier was knighted by Elizabeth I and appointed chief baron of the exchequer in Ireland.

On his arrival in Dublin in August 1593 Napier found many faults in the exchequer. He also severely criticized the sheriffs who, he said, went about in 'great companies' which terrified people and led to violence. He acquired a reputation as a conscientious and honest judge, and in October 1595 the earl of Ormond recommended he be encouraged by some reasonable reward. But Napier was initially disappointed in this respect. He hoped for a grant of land, and complained constantly that he had not received 1 acre in Ireland. He attached himself to Richard Boyle, an Englishman who was at the time deeply involved in a scheme to establish the queen's title to 'concealed' land. It was a process which involved much corruption and which was explicitly criticized by the undertreasurer, Sir Henry Wallop, and the lord chief justice, Sir Robert Gardiner, who believed it stirred up resentment, particularly in Munster. In 1594 Boyle was thrown into prison by Lord Deputy Russell but Napier protested to Lord Burghley and offered to vouch for his good character. In 1595 Napier joined with Wallop and Gardiner on a commission to investigate how far the Munster undertakers had fulfilled their obligations. Perhaps significantly Napier soon fell out with them, since they wished to delay the investigation until Sir Thomas Norris returned from Ulster while he preferred to proceed immediately. He wrote a letter to Burghley complaining that they had combined to overrule his opinions. In 1599 Napier was finally rewarded with considerable grants of land in the counties of Dublin, Meath, Kilkenny, Tipperary, and Kildare.

Napier served on two ecclesiastical commissions and between 1594 and 1601 on commissions in Connaught, Munster, and the pale as a justice of the peace. In August 1597 he was unsuccessfully recommended for the office of chief justice of the common pleas. In late 1598 he went to England and by March 1599 there were complaints that his absence was a great hindrance to the courts. He returned to Ireland but visited England again in the winter of 1599 and on this occasion was nearly shipwrecked at Holyhead. By September 1600 it was rumoured he was vacating his post, and after further complaints in February 1601 that his absence was causing serious problems in the exchequer Napier retired to Dorset. Sir Edmund Pelham was appointed in his place. Napier sat in the parliament of 1601 for Bridport, Dorset, and in that of 1603–4 for Wareham. He was appointed sheriff of Dorset in 1606. In Dorchester he erected an almshouse for ten persons called Napier's Mite, which was to be supported by the rent and profits of the manor of Little Puddle, Dorset.

Napier died on 20 September 1615 and was buried in Minterne Magna church, Dorset. The preamble to his will expresses the hope that his sins will be forgiven and that his soul be 'made clean and as white as snow by the blood, death and passion of my Lord and only Saviour'. His religious position is unclear and he may have had Roman Catholic connections through both his mother's family and his second wife. Magdalen Napier was buried beside her husband in Minterne Magna church.

JUDITH HUDSON BARRY

Sources CSP Ire., 1592–1601 · DNB · J. S. Brewer and W. Bullen, eds., Calendar of the Carew manuscripts, 3: 1589–1600, PRO (1869) · will of Sir Robert Napier, PRO, PROB 11/126, sig. 108 · J. Morrin, ed., Calendar of the patent and close rolls of chancery in Ireland, of the reigns of Henry VIII, Edward VI, Mary, and Elizabeth, 2 (1862) · E. Burke, ed., Fiants, Elizabeth I, 3 (1994) · F. E. Ball, The judges in Ireland, 1221–1921, 1 (1926), 225 · HoP, Commons, 1558–1603, 2.30–31, 315–16; 3.118–19 · H. A. C. Sturgess, ed., Register of admissions to the Honourable Society of the Middle Temple, from the fifteenth century to the year 1944, 1 (1949), 30 · R. Lascelles, ed., Liber munerum publicorum Hiberniae … or, The establishments of Ireland, later edn, 2 vols. in 7 pts (1852), vol. 1, p. 49 · J. Burke and J. B. Burke, A genealogical and heraldic history of the extinct and dormant baronetcies of England, Ireland, and Scotland (1838), 379 · Foster, Alum. Oxon., 1500–1714 [Sir Robert Napper] · M. MacCarthy-Morrogh, The Munster plantation: English migration to southern Ireland, 1583–1641 (1986), 116 · T. O. Ranger, 'Richard Boyle and the making of an Irish fortune, 1588–1614', Irish Historical Studies, 10 (1956–7), 257–97

Napier, Sir Robert, first baronet (1560–1637). See under Napier, Richard (1559–1634).

Napier, Robert (1610/11–1686), lawyer and office-holder, was the second son of Sir Nathaniel Napier (d. 1635) of More Crichel, Dorset, and Elizabeth, daughter and heir of John Gerard of Hyde, in the Isle of Purbeck; he was a grandson of Sir Robert *Napier (d. 1615) and the younger brother of Sir Gerard *Napier (bap. 1606, d. 1673). On 26 May 1628, aged seventeen, he was admitted as a student of the Middle Temple, but does not appear to have been very studious. On 21 November 1628 he matriculated from Queen's College, Oxford, but took no degree. Also on that date Napier was fined for allowing his father and others to use his chamber at the inn, where they were reported to have created noise and disorder. On 27 November 1629, after it was discovered that the chamber, in the Vine Court, was still being abused in this way the parliament of

the inn issued an order that it be seized. However, Napier seems to have avoided further trouble. On 10 February 1638, when he was called to the bar, it was noted, among his other qualifications, that 'he has been at great charge in being a rider in the last great masque performed by the four Inns of Court before the King' (Martin, 2.852–3). He married, by a licence dated 12 July 1637, Anne, daughter of Allen Corrance, merchant tailor of London and Wimbish Hall, Essex. Although not the eldest son Napier enjoyed substantial estates bought from a namesake descended from William Napier (brother of his grandfather the chief justice in Ireland) at Puncknowle and nearby Bexington or Bessingtone in Dorset.

Napier was a committed royalist during the civil war. He was appointed receiver-general and auditor of the duchy of Cornwall, resident first at Exeter, and then Truro. In 1645 he was head of the council of the prince of Wales and duke of Cornwall, and was actively involved in Sir Edward Hyde's efforts to collect the revenues in Cornwall. He was at Truro at its surrender; soon afterwards Sir Thomas Fairfax, in a letter of 20 March 1646 to Speaker William Lenthall, recommended Napier as 'a gentleman of whom I hear a very good report' who 'hath not at any time borne arms' (CSP dom., 1645–7, 381). He was removed from the office of receiver-general, however, which passed to Arthur Upton. Having taken the covenant and the negative oath, pledging not to take up arms against parliament, Napier was allowed to compound at one tenth, a figure set on 12 February 1649 at the low sum of £505 11s.; a week later the county committee of Dorset was ordered to return to him his sequestrated estates.

In 1660 Napier was a signatory to the moderate The Declaration of the Knights and Gentry of Dorset of 16 April. In February 1663 King Charles restored him to the office of receiver-general and auditor of the duchy of Cornwall. He is also reported to have acted as master of the hanaper office. At an unknown date his wife, Anne, died and he married Catherine, daughter of Sir Henry Hawley of Wivelscombe, Somerset, and sister of Francis Hawley (1608–1684), created in 1645 Baron Hawley. Napier, by licence dated 15 March 1668, married a third wife, Mary, widow of Edmund Ironside of Rickmansworth, Hertfordshire, and daughter of Sir Thomas Evelyn. Having made his will on 13 January 1686 Napier died at Puncknowle later that year; probate was granted to his widow, Mary, on 4 December.

Napier's son, **Sir Robert Napier**, first baronet (c.1640–1700), politician, was a child of Napier's first marriage, to Anne Corrance. Having entered the Middle Temple on 21 November 1655 he matriculated from Trinity College, Oxford, on 1 April 1656, but did not graduate. Though listed as a student at Padua in 1659 he must have spent some time at the inn as on 9 February 1660 he was called to the bar. By a licence dated 25 October 1667 he married Sophia, daughter of Charles Evelyn of Long Ditton, Surrey; they had one son, Charles, and three daughters, Sophia, Anna, and Theodosia.

Napier was made high sheriff for Dorset in 1680–81,

knighted on 27 January 1681, created baronet on 25 February 1682, and served as a deputy lieutenant in 1688, but there were limits to his loyalty, for in November he signed the warrants for collecting money for the forces of Prince William of Orange. He was elected for Weymouth in the Convention Parliament of January 1689, and voted to support the Lords' view that the throne was not vacant. A vocal but moderate tory Napier was named to an impressive total of forty-nine parliamentary committees, notably those on the suspension of habeas corpus, during which he is reported to have remarked 'This mistress of ours, the Habeas Corpus Act, if we part with it twice, it will become quite a common whore' (Ferris, 3.128). He also worked on the first Mutiny Bill, and on the new oaths of allegiance and supremacy. He helped frame an address of thanks for the issue by the new king of a general pardon, and in April 1689 was involved in a conference on the removal of papists from the capital. He was interested in the investigation of various abuses which had developed in the south-west, notably that of the illegal and damaging extension of aulnage to stocking manufacture and in the provision of food and beer for the fleet at Plymouth. On 15 September 1693 Napier was appointed to succeed Hugh Hodges as recorder of Dorchester. He was returned for Dorchester in the parliament of 1698 and represented the town until his death on 31 October 1700. He was buried at Puncknowle, Dorset. His wife survived him.

STEPHEN WRIGHT

Sources M. Coate, *Cornwall in the great civil war and interregnum, 1642–1660* (1933) · C. T. Martin, *Middle Temple records*, 4 vols. (1904–5), vol. 2 · C. H. Hopwood, *Middle Temple records*, 4 vols. (1904–5), vol. 3 · C. Mayo, ed., *The minute books of the Dorset standing committee* (1902) · CSP dom., 1645–7 · J. Hutchins, *The history and antiquities of the county of Dorset*, ed. W. Ship and J. W. Hodson, 3rd edn, 4 vols. (1861–73) · GEC, *Baronetage* · [E. Bysshe], *The visitation of Dorset, 1677, made by Sir Edward Bysshe*, ed. G. D. Squibb, Harleian Society, 117 (1977) · J. Rylands, ed., *Visitation of Dorset … 1623*, Harleian Society, 20 (1885) · J. P. Ferris, 'Napier, Sir Robert, 1st bt', HoP, *Commons, 1660–90* · Foster, *Alum. Oxon.* · C. Mayo, ed., *The municipal records of the borough of Dorchester* (1908) · will, PRO, PROB 11/385, sig. 170 [Robert Napier, 1686]

Napier, Sir Robert, first baronet (*c*.1640–1700). *See under* Napier, Robert (1610/11–1686).

Napier, Robert (1791–1876), marine engineer, was born at Dumbarton on 18 June 1791, the eldest surviving son of James Napier, an iron-founder and engineer, and Jean Ewing. He had five younger brothers and a sister. Educated in Dumbarton, and destined for the ministry of the Church of Scotland, he chose to be an apprentice in his father's works, where he became skilled in ornamental metalwork and millwrighting. He completed his time in 1812, and went to work in Edinburgh for Robert Stevenson, the lighthouse builder. After moving to the Glasgow works of William Lang in 1814, he set up on his own as a smith, the following year. He married, in 1818, his cousin Isabella, daughter of John Napier, his father's brother, and half-sister of David Napier, an established marine engineer with a works at Camlachie to the east of Glasgow. They raised six children including James Robert Napier (*b.* 1821) who also became a noted marine engineer.

Robert Napier (1791–1876), by unknown photographer, 1850s

When David Napier moved his business to Lancefield beside the Clyde on the other side of the city in 1821, Robert took over the Camlachie works, and appointed David Elder as his works manager. His first contract was for water pipes for Glasgow corporation, followed by a stationary steam engine for a mill in Dundee. Wishing to build marine engines like his cousin, he won an order in 1823 for the paddle steamer *Leven* from the Dumbarton shipbuilder James (A'thing) Lang, who had previously purchased his engines from Duncan McArthur, the leading engine builder in Glasgow at the time. The engines, which incorporated several novel features, outlasted three hulls. Further orders were quickly placed with the firm. In the spring of 1827 he spent time promoting his skill as an engine builder in London, which was confirmed later in the year, when two steamers fitted with his engines won a race sponsored by the Northern yacht club. The race attracted the attention of Thomas Assheton Smith, who over the next twenty years ordered a series of innovative steam yachts from Napier. Smith was well connected, and gave Napier access to those with influence in London society, and in government. Following this success Napier purchased the Camlachie works, and the Vulcan Foundry, previously Duncan McArthur's machine shop, which was not far from his cousin's Lancefield works.

In 1830 Napier handed over the Camlachie works to one of his brothers, and with Elder's help re-equipped the Vulcan Foundry to build large marine engines. Although one of the first contracts of the new shop for the Dundee and Leith Steam Packet Company was beset with difficulty and delay, the engines, when finally delivered, performed so well that they greatly enhanced Napier's reputation. To secure supplies of iron and coal, Napier took a fourth share in the Muirkirk Iron Company, and acquired the Barrowfield coal works. By now a prosperous man, he built a magnificent country house down the Clyde at West Shandon overlooking the Gareloch, as much to entertain important customers as a retreat. While his new home was being completed he won orders from the East India Company, and the Admiralty. In 1835 he leased the Lancefield works from his cousin David, who moved to London following a tragic accident to one of his steamers, and purchased them in 1841.

From the early 1830s Robert Napier had been interested in the possibility of establishing a regular and profitable steamship service across the north Atlantic. It was not until the foundation of Samuel Cunard's British and North American Steam-Packet Company in 1839 that he received contracts for Atlantic steamers, and then only after investing in the new company. Over the next twenty years Napiers built a series of larger and larger liners for Cunard. In later life Cunard attributed his line's achievement to the quality, and reliability, of Napier's first engines. In 1842 Napier began building his own iron ships at a yard in Govan on the other side of the Clyde from his Lancefield works; previously all his hulls had been of wood, and constructed by John Wood of Port Glasgow. Among his early hull contracts were the first three iron steamers for the Admiralty. In 1848 he took over the bankrupt Parkhead Forge in the east end of Glasgow to supply wrought iron plates and forgings for his works. Orders from Cunard and the Admiralty brought a steady flow of contracts from other passenger shipping companies, including Donald Currie's Castle Line, and the Pacific Steam Navigation Company, and foreign countries such as Turkey, Holland, and France.

By the early 1850s Robert Napier dominated the fast-expanding Clyde marine engineering and shipbuilding industry, attracting a galaxy of able young managers and apprentices, many of whom went on to found or control their own businesses. In 1852 he moved permanently to West Shandon, which he had much enlarged, partly to house his large collection of old masters, porcelain, sculptures and other curios. Renamed Robert Napier & Sons in 1852, the business was left in the day-to-day management of his sons, James R. Napier, one of the most distinguished marine engineers of his generation, and John Napier. Although orders continued to flow, Napiers began to lose its technical advantage to competitors such as Denny and Elder. There were also problems, not least in the construction of the first ironclad ship, *Black Prince*, in 1859–60, which lost money because of the difficulty of manufacturing wrought iron armour plate to the Admiralty specification. With Napiers on the verge of bankruptcy, William Beardmore senior was recruited to Parkhead, and solved the problem. However, Napier's financial problems persisted, exacerbated by an open disagreement between Robert and his sons about the future direction of the enterprise. By 1871 the Bank of Scotland was unwilling to advance any further money to help win new custom, and Napiers were forced to sell their interest in the Parkhead

Forge. The firm recovered largely because Robert Napier was persuaded finally to retire. His wife died on 23 October 1875, and he died at West Shandon, Dunbartonshire, on 23 June 1876. He undoubtedly deserved the accolade as father of Clyde shipbuilding, laying down the river's reputation for quality and reliability. MICHAEL S. MOSS

Sources J. Napier, *Life of Robert Napier of West Shandon* (1904) • J. R. Hume and M. S. Moss, *Beardmore: the history of a Scottish industrial giant* (1979) • D. D. Napier, *David Napier, engineer, 1790–1869: an autobiographical sketch with notes*, ed. D. Bell (1912) • G. Jackson, 'Operational problems of the transfer to steam: Dundee ports and London shipping, 1820–1945', *Scotland and the sea* [St Andrews 1991], ed. T. C. Smout (1992), 154–81 • U. Glas., Archives and Business Records Centre, Napier MSS • *CCI* (1876) • *CCI* (1877)
Archives U. Glas., Archives and Business Records Centre, corresp. and papers | U. Lpool L., Cunard collection
Likenesses A. Edouart, silhouette, 1832, Scot. NPG • E. Burton, mezzotint, 1847 (after J. G. Gilbert), BM • photograph, 1850–59, Sci. Mus. [*see illus.*] • photographs, U. Glas. • portrait, repro. in Napier, *Life of Robert Napier*
Wealth at death £45,941 19*s.* 6*d.*: confirmation, 29 Nov 1876, *CCI* • £57,229 4*s.* 11*d.*: additional estate, 22 July 1878, *CCI*

Napier, Robert Cornelis, first Baron Napier of Magdala (1810–1890), army officer, son of Major Charles Frederick Napier, Royal Artillery, and his wife, Catherine, daughter of Mr Codrington Carrington of Barbados, West Indies, was born at Colombo, Ceylon, on 6 December 1810. He was baptized in December 1811, with his second name given in commemoration of the assault on Fort Cornelis in Java on 26 August 1810, during which his father had been in command of the artillery. It was during this campaign that his father was wounded, and he died from his injuries and illness on his way to England in March 1812.

Education, early career, and marriage Napier was educated by private tutors in London and Woolwich, and at school at Hall Place. He obtained a cadetship in the Bengal Engineers and entered Addiscombe College on 4 February 1825, where he studied for two years. He was commissioned as a second-lieutenant on 15 December 1826, at the age of sixteen, and underwent a course of instruction at the Royal Engineer Establishment at Chatham, where he was promoted lieutenant on 27 September 1827 following an increase in the size of the corps.

Napier sailed for India and landed at Calcutta on 8 November 1828. He served briefly at Aligarh, the headquarters of the Bengal Sappers and Miners, before being sent to command a company at Delhi, where he took a keen interest in the local language, culture, and Mughal architecture. Illness, however, compelled him in April 1830 to take sick leave in Mussooree, where he made an extensive collection of plants that he later donated to the museum at Saharanpur. In March 1831 he was given employment as assistant on the Great Eastern Jumna Canal project, in the prestigious irrigation branch of the public works department, with Captain Proby Thomas Cautley. Napier was almost constantly employed in work maintaining the canal, which was in a poor state of repair, and other similar projects, but he found time to acquaint himself with the local population, study geology, and to indulge his favourite hobbies of reading, and landscape

Robert Cornelis Napier, first Baron Napier of Magdala (1810–1890), by unknown photographer

and portrait painting. In 1835 he suffered another serious illness caused by overwork and exposure, and in April 1836 was given three years' furlough. He returned to England and visited various civil and military engineering projects, making the acquaintance of Stephenson and Brunel. He also toured Belgium, Germany, and Italy, gaining further valuable knowledge of engineering, industry, and irrigation.

Early in 1838 Napier returned to India and, after touring the country, was appointed acting executive engineer in the Barisal division of eastern Bengal. He was sent to Darjeeling, in the Himalayas, as assistant to the superintendent to clear a site for a new settlement and build roads through dense virgin forest to connect it with the plains. He also completed organizing the local corps of Sebundy sappers, who provided the civil authorities with a body of trained and armed labourers accustomed to working in mountainous terrain. In 1840 he was appointed executive engineer of the Sirhind division, although he remained temporarily at Darjeeling to complete his work and was promoted second-captain on 25 January 1841. In September 1842 he finally proceeded to Karnal where he began laying out a new cantonment (as troops living in the existing barracks suffered a high sickness and mortality rate) intended to provide healthy accommodation for men returning from service in Afghanistan. He chose a stretch of ground several miles south of Ambala, where sufficient land existed to lay out the buildings in echelon on the slopes, thus allowing a sufficient free circulation of air,

intended as a preventive measure against disease. This arrangement, known as Napier's system, was later adopted by government elsewhere in India for other cantonments.

Napier married Anne Sarah, eldest daughter of George Pearse MD, inspector-general of hospitals at Madras, on 3 September 1840, and they had three sons, including Sir Albert Edward Alexander *Napier, and three daughters. His wife died in childbirth on 30 December 1849 and the children were brought up by Napier's mother in Europe.

The Anglo-Sikh wars and the Indian mutiny When the First Anglo-Sikh War broke out Napier was ordered on 15 December 1845 to join the army of the Sutlej, under the command of Sir Hugh Gough. He covered 150 miles in three days on horseback, arriving in the nick of time to take command of the engineers at the battle of Mudki, where his horse was killed under him during the fighting. Another mount was killed during the battle of Ferozeshahr on 21 December where, accompanying the 31st foot, he was severely wounded while storming the entrenched Sikh encampment. Although no longer in command of the engineers, now that more senior officers had arrived, he was present at the battle of Sobraon on 10 February 1846 and, as brigade major of engineers, accompanied the force advancing on Lahore. He was mentioned in dispatches, and on 3 April 1846 was promoted brevet major.

Napier briefly returned to work on the construction of Ambala cantonment and was also given responsibility for laying out new hill stations at Kasauli and Sabathu, at which he met Henry Lawrence, Herbert Edwardes, John Becher, and William Hodson. In May 1846 Napier served as chief engineer in a force under Brigadier-General Sir Hugh Wheeler sent to capture the hill fort of Kot Kangra, 130 miles east of Lahore, occupied by discontented Sikh soldiers. He distinguished himself both by moving a siege-train, consisting of thirty-three pieces of artillery and mortars, over difficult hill paths and tracks and during other engineering work that led to the surrender of the fort, for which he was mentioned in dispatches and received the special thanks of government. After surveying the local area and contracting fever he returned to Ambala. He was given the appointment of consulting engineer to the resident and council of regency of the Punjab by Henry Lawrence, following the establishment of the Lahore regency, and he began work on building new roads and supervising various public works.

Following the outbreak of the Second Anglo-Sikh War Lieutenant Herbert Edwardes requested that Napier be sent to conduct the siege of Multan, held by Diwan Mulraj. As chief engineer Napier directed the siege operations, taking part in the assault on the entrenched position on 9 and 12 September, when his leg was grazed by a cannon ball. Sher Singh and a large body of troops reinforced Multan, however, making it more difficult to prosecute the operations without further British reinforcements. Despite forcefully advocating an immediate assault, Napier's opinion was overruled and it was decided to await more troops. Colonel John Cheape took over as senior engineer when they arrived, but Napier remained and participated in the engagement at Suraj Kund, the capture of the suburbs, assault on the city, and the surrender of the fortress on 22 or 23 January 1849. He was also present when the fort at Chiniot surrendered. General Whish's division then joined Lord Gough, and Napier took part in the battle of Gujrat on 21 February 1849 as commanding engineer of the right wing, reconnoitring both the ground and the enemy position. Following this engagement he accompanied Sir Walter Raleigh Gilbert as commanding engineer during the pursuit of the defeated Sikhs and their Afghan allies to Peshawar and was present when the Jhelum was crossed and the Sikh army surrendered. He was mentioned in dispatches, and on 7 June 1849 was promoted brevet lieutenant-colonel.

Napier was appointed civil engineer to the newly appointed board of administration of the Punjab following the cessation of hostilities. He immediately began work on a comprehensive scheme of public works, including the 275 mile Grand Trunk Road between Peshawar and Lahore, the Bari Doab Canal, and other irrigation projects, roads, public buildings, new cantonments, frontier defences, and bridges throughout the area. The board of administration praised his commitment and achievements. In December 1852 he volunteered and was given command of the right column during the punitive expedition against the Hasanzais in the mountains of Hazara, for which services he was highly commended by government. He was employed in a similar expedition in November 1853, under Colonel S. B. Boileau, against the Jowaki Afridis of the Bori valley, for which he again received the special thanks of government. He became chief engineer to the chief commissioner when the board of administration was abolished, and continued engineering work in the Punjab. The rapidly escalating costs incurred during the construction of the various public works in progress, however, were a source of friction between Napier and Sir John Lawrence. Napier was promoted a brevet colonel in the army on 28 November 1854, in recognition of his work on the frontier, and a regimental lieutenant-colonel on 15 April 1856. He went on furlough in the autumn of 1856 to England, relinquishing his post after seven years as head of the public works department of the Punjab.

Napier had left England in May 1857 before news of the outbreak of the mutiny had been received, with the intention of retiring after a further three years' service in India. When he arrived at Calcutta he was briefly made officiating chief engineer of Bengal. He was soon reappointed military secretary and chief of the adjutant-general's department to General Sir James Outram, who had just been recalled to India from Persia and had been made chief commissioner in Oudh and given command of the two divisions occupying the country between Calcutta and Cawnpore. They both reached Cawnpore on 15 September 1856, where Outram waived his military rank and relinquished military command to Sir Henry Havelock, who was awaiting reinforcements before advancing to relieve Lucknow. Outram accompanied him in his civil capacity and as a volunteer with Napier at his side. Napier participated in fighting at Mangalwar, Alambagh, and

Charbagh before Lucknow was entered on 25 September, acting as de facto chief engineer and chief of staff. During the advance, however, the rear-guard, with the wounded and siege artillery, became separated from the main body and a further 250 men who were sent to find them on the 26th, in turn, became isolated, unable either to find the rear-guard or return to Lucknow. Napier volunteered to rescue them and under cover of night successfully brought the whole of the baggage, siege-train, and rear-guard to the safety of the residency.

The combined strength of the garrison and relieving force, however, was unable to break the siege of Lucknow or to safely evacuate the women and children to Cawnpore. During the continuing siege Napier participated in several small sorties from the beleaguered garrison and directed engineering work to strengthen its defensive positions and counter enemy attacks. A second British force commanded by General Sir Colin Campbell relieved Lucknow on 17 November 1857, but Napier was severely wounded while accompanying Outram and Havelock to meet Campbell and the relieving force when it reached within half a mile of their position. Napier was hospitalized for several weeks before rejoining Outram as chief of staff at the Alambagh, outside the recently evacuated city of Lucknow. He carefully prepared plans for its capture which Campbell carried out on the east side of the city on 4 March 1858. Napier commanded a brigade of engineers during the successful assault on Lucknow, which finally fell on 21 March. After its capture he drew up plans for its military occupation which released large numbers of British troops for further operations. He was mentioned in dispatches and made a CB on 24 March 1858.

Napier was instructed to take command of the Central India field force from Sir Hugh Rose in June 1858, who had resigned after being incapacitated by sickness. Tantia Topi and the rani of Jhansi suddenly attacked, however, and defeated Sindhia at Morar and took possession of the fortress of Gwalior. Rose decided to remain, and immediately advanced on Gwalior with Napier now joining him as second in command. Napier assumed control of the 2nd brigade at Bahadurpur on 16 June and the same day participated in an attack on Morar cantonment. His brigade was left behind in reserve to guard the captured cantonment, however, when Rose left for the city of Gwalior. Napier pursued the retreating enemy after the city was captured on the 20th, with orders to closely chase them as far and as fast as possible. Napier and 700 cavalry and horse-artillery attacked Tantia Topi's 12,000 men and 25 guns on the plains of Jaora Alipur on 22 June, taking them completely by surprise and capturing all their guns, ammunition, and baggage.

Napier took command of the Gwalior division on 29 June when Rose finally departed from India, continuing operations against the remaining small parties of rebels still at large in central India. A series of flying columns were sent to search the country, while a large body of troops remained in reserve at Gwalior resting and preparing for further operations. During August Napier led a force of 600 men and artillery to reinforce Brigadier-

General Smith for an attack on the fortified town of Pauri, recently captured and garrisoned by Raja Man Singh of Narwar. The attack began on 20 August with a thirty-hour bombardment by 18-pounders and mortars, but before the final assault began the town was evacuated. After demolishing its fortifications Napier returned to Gwalior, leaving a column to pursue the enemy. In December he deployed three columns to intercept a rebel force led by Ferozepore, who had joined Tantia Topi, which was finally routed at Ranod with heavy casualties after a long pursuit. Tantia Topi and Man Singh proved more elusive opponents, taking refuge in the inaccessible jungle-covered hills near Parone, which Napier endeavoured to control by destroying the local forts and cutting clearings and roads through the dense vegetation. Napier captured the remaining rebel leaders, Man Singh and Tantia Topi, who were tried and executed, after which the rebellion in central India virtually collapsed. For his services during the mutiny Napier was made a GCB, and received the thanks of parliament and of the Indian government.

The 1860 China campaign   In January 1860 Napier was given command of the 2nd division of the China expeditionary force under the overall command of General Sir Hope Grant. He supervised the equipment and embarkation of the Indian contingent at Calcutta, which arrived in good order at Hong Kong. Napier landed with his division on the right bank of the Pehtang-ho (Beitang he) between 5 and 7 August and successfully attacked across the mud flats the village of Sinho, held in strength by the enemy. Napier's division and French troops, supported by all the available artillery, led the assault on 21 August on the north Taku (Dagu) Fort on the left bank of the Peiho (Beihe), which was captured, and the remaining forts surrendered without any further resistance. Napier was made responsible for the line of communications following this engagement until after the battle of Changkiawan (Zhangjiawan). During the last stages of the campaign he supervised in October the construction of the batteries outside the Anting (Anding) gate of Peking (Beijing), to ensure entry into the city if fighting resumed. He and his staff finally embarked for Hong Kong on 19 November *en route* for India. He received the thanks of parliament for his services in China, and on 15 February 1861 was promoted major-general.

Second marriage   On 2 April 1861 Napier married Mary Cecilia, daughter of Major-General E. W. Smythe Scott, Royal Artillery, inspector-general of ordnance in India; they had six sons and three daughters. She died on 18 December 1930.

High command in India   Napier held the post of the military member of the council of the viceroy of India from January 1861 in succession to Sir James Outram. He helped arrange the amalgamation of the East India Company's European regiments with the British army, and the reduction and reorganization of the Indian army. During the administrations of lords Canning, Elgin, and Lawrence he helped to improve living conditions for British soldiers by authorizing the construction of two-storied barracks,

housing for families, and an increase in accommodation in the hills, as well as extending road and rail communications, and improving the defences and the armament of the army in India. As military member and president of the council of India from the beginning of 1863 Napier dealt not only with military affairs but also with a range of public works, and with political and financial matters. Between 21 November and 2 December 1863 he briefly acted as viceroy and governor-general, following the sudden death of Lord Elgin, until Sir William Denison arrived from Madras.

In January 1865 Napier was appointed commander-in-chief at Bombay, but before taking up his post he briefly returned to England on leave, where he met and established a lifelong friendship with the duke of Cambridge. During his period of command at Bombay he worked in close association with the governor, Sir Bartle Frere, dealing with such questions as barrack accommodation and discipline, and on 1 March 1867 was promoted lieutenant-general.

The Abyssinian expedition, 1867–1868   Through the personal influence of the duke of Cambridge and Sir Stafford Northcote, Napier was nominated to command the Abyssinian expedition on 30 August 1867, mounted to compel the release of British captives being held by King Theodore. The campaign required elaborate administrative and logistical planning, given the distance the expedition had to quickly traverse in an inhospitable climate over difficult, trackless mountainous terrain to reach Theodore's stronghold at Magdala before the rainy season commenced. Napier selected his troops primarily from the Bombay army with a comparatively small British contingent.

An advance brigade landed at Zula, in Annesley Bay, on 30 October 1867, where a large base was established, linked by a railway to the coast, where two piers were constructed to allow troops and stores to be disembarked from waiting shipping. It took some time to provide an adequate supply of water, food, fodder, and warm clothing, as well as organizing a transport corps capable of supporting operations in the mountains. The advance began on 25 January 1868, and by 10 April the force had covered 420 miles and reached the Magdala plateau, where it defeated the Abyssinian army at Arogee. The fortress of Magdala was stormed on 13 April, Theodore was found dead, and the captives were released. After destroying the stronghold the force withdrew, and by 18 June all the troops had completed the return march to the coast and departed from Africa.

Napier returned to England at the end of June, where he was fêted by the queen and nation for his brilliant leadership during such a difficult operation. He was thanked by parliament and raised to the peerage as Lord Napier of Magdala and Caryngton on 17 July 1868, with a pension of £2000 a year for himself and his next surviving male heir. He was made a GCSI, given the freedom of the City of London, and made a citizen of Edinburgh. He was also appointed honorary colonel-commandant of the 3rd London rifle corps on 22 July 1868 and awarded a DCL by Oxford University. In December 1869 he was elected FRS. He remained in England for only a few months before returning to India, where he resumed his duties as commander-in-chief at Bombay.

Commander-in-chief in India, 1870–1876 Napier was appointed commander-in-chief in India in January 1870, and in May was also made fifth ordinary member of the governor-general's council. Between April 1870 and April 1876 he endeavoured to improve living conditions for both British and Indian troops, introduced new systems of drill, tactics, and training into the Bengal army, as well as improving defensive fortifications in light of growing perceptions of a Russian threat. He also instituted a weekly holiday for all ranks on Thursday, dubbed St Napier's day. Napier helped improve military efficiency by initiating camps of exercise in India and carrying out frequent military inspections throughout the subcontinent. Throughout his tenure of command, however, he had to resist growing pressure for reductions in the army in India to cut expenditure, under the guise of army reform, believing that it was essential to maintain British rule. On 1 April 1874 he was promoted general and appointed colonel-commandant of the corps of Royal Engineers. On 10 April 1876 he finally left India after forty-eight years' service. He was present at the German manoeuvres in 1876 as the guest of the crown prince and was entertained by the emperor William.

Later career and death Napier held the post of governor and commander-in-chief at Gibraltar, in succession to Sir Fenwick Williams of Kars, between 1876 and 1883. In February 1878, however, he was recalled to London to consult with the government and was appointed to command an expeditionary force, with Major-General Sir Garnet Wolseley as chief of staff, being prepared in anticipation of a war with Russia. When war did not break out he returned to his normal duties at Gibraltar, where he took a keen interest in events in South Africa and Afghanistan. In November he was sent to Madrid as ambassador-extraordinary to represent the queen at the second marriage of the king of Spain, where he was presented with the grand cordon of Charles III. Later that year he was appointed a member of the royal commission on army reorganization, sitting in London.

Napier was promoted field marshal on 1 January 1883 after he left Gibraltar. Although nominally remaining on the active list he was not employed again on military service. He maintained a keen interest in art, and frequently participated in House of Lords debates on military topics such as the relief of Gordon, and often accompanied the duke of Cambridge during military inspections. In January 1887 he was appointed constable of the Tower of London and lieutenant and *custos rotulorum* for Tower Hamlets.

Napier died of influenza, after a few days' illness, at his London residence, 63 Eaton Square, on 14 January 1890. He had a state funeral on Tuesday 21 January 1890, and was buried in the crypt of St Paul's Cathedral. He was commemorated by an equestrian statue by Boehm at Waterloo Place, London. He was succeeded as baron by his eldest son, Robert William (1845–1921).

Napier enjoyed a distinguished and varied military career in India, in which he displayed considerable professional skill as a soldier, engineer, and administrator. Although he never conducted a campaign against a European power, in India and Abyssinia he showed himself a master of logistics and military administration, both vital in colonial warfare.   T. R. MOREMAN

Sources H. D. Napier, *Field-Marshal Lord Napier of Magdala … a memoir by his son* (1927) · *Letters of Field-Marshal Lord Napier of Magdala concerning Abyssinia, Egypt, India, South Africa etc*, ed. H. D. Napier (1936) · *Lord Napier of Magdala* (reprinted from the *Times of India*) (1876) · W. Porter, *History of the corps of royal engineers*, 2 (1889) · E. T. Thackeray, *Biographical notes of officers of the royal (Bengal) engineers* (1900) · H. M. Vibart, *Addiscombe: its heroes and men of note* (1894) · *Royal Engineers Journal*, 20 (1890), 27–30 · W. W. Knollys, 'Field Marshal Lord Napier of Magdala', *Fortnightly Review*, 53 (1890), 397–403 · *Army List* · *Despatches of Major-General Sir R. Napier reporting the operations of the second division of the China force in the expedition of 1860* [1873] · R. Napier, *Personal narrative written shortly after the actions of Moodkee and Feroze-Shuhur* (1873) · *Report on the engineering operations at the siege of Lucknow in March 1858: by the chief engineer (now Brigadier General Sir R. Napier)* (1859) · BL OIOC, Napier of Magdala MSS, MS Eur. F 114 · C. E. Buckland, *Dictionary of Indian biography* (1906) · T. A. Heathcote, *The military in British India: the development of British land forces in south Asia, 1600–1947* (1995) · Lord Roberts [F. S. Roberts], *Forty-one years in India*, 2 vols. (1897) · H. L. Nevill, *Campaigns on the north-west frontier* (1912) · *DNB* · T. J. Holland and H. Hozier, *Record of the expedition to Abyssinia*, 2 vols. (1870) · GEC, *Peerage*

Archives BL OIOC, corresp. and papers, MS Eur. F 114 | BL, letters to Sir Stafford Northcote, Add. MS 50029 · BL OIOC, letters to H. M. Durand and J. Rivett-Carnac, MS Eur. C 265 · BL OIOC, letters to Lord Elgin, MS Eur. F 83 · BL OIOC, corresp. with George Hutchinson, MS Eur. E 241 · BL OIOC, letters to Sir Richard Temple, MS Eur. F 86 · Bodl. Oxf., letters to Benjamin Disraeli · Bodl. Oxf., letters to Lord Kimberley · CUL, corresp. with Lord Mayo · Hove Central Library, letters to Viscount Wolseley · NAM, letters to Lord Roberts · NRA, priv. coll., letters to duke of Argyll

Likenesses photograph, 1860, BL OIOC, photo 353 · photograph, 1861, BL OIOC, MS Eur. D 661 · photograph, 1864–5, BL OIOC, MS Eur. F 38/2 (LXIIIb) · F. Grant, oils, 1868, Royal Engineers, Chatham, Kent, Gordon barracks · M. A. Pittatore, oils, 1869, Scot. NPG · group portrait, photograph, 1869, BL OIOC, photo 139/2 (7) · group portrait, photograph, c.1869, BL OIOC, photo 139/2 (46) · photograph, c.1870 (with Lord Mayo and his staff), BL OIOC, photo 132 (45) · group portrait, photograph, 1874, BL OIOC, photo 303/2 (13) · Lock & Whitfield, woodburytype photograph, 1878, NPG · J. E. Boehm, statue, 1880, Calcutta · L. Dickinson, oils, c.1885, Royal Engineers, Chatham, Kent, Gordon barracks · T. B. Wirgman, pencil drawing, 1886, Scot. NPG · Maull & Fox, photograph, 1887, BL OIOC, MS Eur. D 502 (186) · J. E. Boehm, plaster bust, NPG · J. E. Boehm, statue, Waterloo Place, London · Elliott & Fry, photograph, NPG · C. Mottram, mixed engraving, mezzotint (after F. Grant), BL OIOC, P2374 · W. Roffe, line and stipple engraving (after photograph), repro. in Roberts, *Forty-one years in India* · Spy [L. Ward], caricature, chromolithograph, NPG; repro. in *VF* (20 April 1878) · C. J. Tomkins, mezzotint (after C. Mercier), BL OIOC, P1558 (F204) · cartes-de-visite, NPG · photograph, repro. in Napier, *Field-Marshal Lord Napier of Magdala*, frontispiece · woodburytype photograph, NPG [*see illus.*]

Wealth at death £8988 18s. 3d.: resworn probate, Feb 1891, CGPLA Eng. & Wales (1890)

Napier [*née* Lennox; *other married name* Bunbury], **Lady Sarah** (1745–1826), noblewoman and society beauty, was born on 14 February 1745, the sixth of the seven surviving children of Charles *Lennox, second duke of Richmond and Lennox (1701–1750), and Sarah (1706–1751), daughter of William Cadogan, Earl Cadogan. She spent her early years at Goodwood, Sussex, with occasional visits to London, where she was a favoured plaything of George II. The king's interest in Sarah had commenced when he met the little girl on the Broad Walk at Kensington. She had approached him and asked, 'Comment vous portez vous, Monsiour le Roi? Vous avez une grande et belle maison ici, n'est-ce-pas?' (Fitzgerald, *Emily, Duchess of Leinster*, 77). On one of her visits the king placed Sarah in a tall Chinese jar and closed the lid. Showing no fear the child sat inside and sang 'Marlborough s'en va-t-en guerre'. However, Sarah's father died on 8 August 1750, when she was still only five, and a year later, on 25 August 1751, her mother also succumbed to a fatal illness. Thereafter Sarah was sent to live with her older sister Emilia Mary *Fitzgerald, countess of Kildare (later duchess of Leinster), at Carton, co. Kildare, before returning to England, under the terms of her father's will, to reside with her eldest sister, Lady (Georgiana) Caroline *Fox.

On her return to London in November 1759 Sarah quickly gained a reputation as a great beauty, causing the hyper-critical Horace Walpole to exclaim, 'No Magdalene by Correggio was half so lovely or expressive' (Tillyard, 122), and was presented at court. The experience was overwhelming, and her shyness pushed the king to proclaim, 'Pooh she has grown quite stupid' (Fitzgerald, *Emily, Duchess of Leinster*, 71); but she caught the eye of the prince of Wales, later George III, who felt that she was 'everything I can form to myself lovely' (Tillyard, 125). The connection was encouraged by Sarah's brother-in-law Henry Fox, and it was rumoured that he ordered Sarah to dress up each morning in country dress and rake hay in the park at Holland House so that the prince would see her as he rode by. George encouraged Fox's hopes by reportedly telling Lady Susan Strangways, after his grandfather's death, that there would be no coronation without a queen and that he thought 'Your friend the fittest person for it' (Fitzgerald, *Lady Louisa Conolly*, 52), and by hinting to Sarah that he wished to connect the grounds of Holland House to Kensington Gardens. However, Sarah herself seemed unmoved by his attentions, and the king's confidant John Stuart, third earl of Bute, and his mother, Augusta, dowager princess of Wales, strenuously opposed the match. The king capitulated and married Princess Charlotte of Mecklenburg-Strelitz in 1761. Sarah was chief bridesmaid or, as Walpole described her, 'chief angel' (ibid., 54) at the wedding, and maintained in later life that she was glad that she had never become queen, although during his illness in 1788 the king spoke of her as his first love, and in 1805, following the death of Sarah's second husband, granted her a pension of £800 p.a.

Soon after the royal wedding Sarah became secretly engaged to William John Kerr, Lord Newbattle (later fifth marquess of Lothian), but broke off the arrangement to

Lady Sarah Napier [Lennox] (1745–1826), by Sir Joshua Reynolds, 1762

marry (Thomas) Charles *Bunbury (1740–1821), MP for Suffolk, who succeeded his father as sixth baronet in 1764 and owned the horse that won the first Derby run at Epsom, in 1780. The marriage, which took place at Holland House on 2 June 1762, was not happy, as Bunbury was reputed to be cold and reserved. By 1767 Sarah was seeking consolation elsewhere. While in Paris she engaged in intrigues with Frederick Howard, fifth earl of Carlisle (1748–1825), and Armand-Louis de Gontaut, duc de Lauzun (1747–1793), but it was by her cousin Lord William Gordon (*d.* 1823), second son of Cosmo, third duke of Gordon, that she became pregnant. Bunbury offered to bring the child up as his own, but on 19 February 1768 Sarah left the marital home, never to return. Her exploits were widely reported in contemporary broadsheets, owing to her royal blood (she was a great-grandchild of Charles II) and her earlier association with the king. For a time Sarah and Gordon lived together as man and wife, and this was the basis for her divorce from Bunbury, by act of parliament, on 14 May 1776. Long before then she had renounced Gordon and returned to Goodwood to live on the estate with her daughter from the liaison, Louisa Bunbury, for the subsequent twelve years. Sarah's conduct was at first closely supervised by her family but she was gradually allowed to play a greater part in society. During this period she visited her sister Lady Louisa *Conolly and assisted her with the refurbishment of Castletown, co. Kildare, as well as appearing in fashionable company in London and Bath.

About 1776, through her brother Lord George *Lennox, Sarah met the Hon. George *Napier (1751–1804), officer of the 25th foot and second son of Francis, sixth Lord Napier, an impecunious army officer and a married man. Her family were concerned at this friendship and Napier was persuaded to transfer to the 80th foot, which was embarking for America, but when Napier's wife died in 1780 he proposed to Sarah, and they married at Goodwood on 27 August 1781. She later said that she had never known true happiness before this date. Between 1782 and 1791 the Napiers had eight children, five sons and three daughters. Three sons became generals and were knighted: Sir Charles *Napier (1782–1853), conqueror of Sind; Sir George Thomas *Napier (1784–1855); and Sir William Francis Patrick *Napier (1785–1860), military historian. Sarah's daughter Emily (1783–1863) was adopted by her sister Louisa about 1785, and in 1830 married Sir Henry Edward Bunbury (1778–1860), nephew and heir to Sarah's first husband.

To support her increasing family Sarah, who had only £500 p.a. (the interest on her fortune that she was allowed as part of her divorce settlement), exerted her influence with her relatives and friends to grant commissions to her husband. In 1782 her brother Charles *Lennox, third duke of Richmond, made Napier superintendent of the Woolwich laboratory on £300 p.a. but he lost the position in 1783. The Napiers made frequent visits to Ireland and finally settled at Celbridge, near Lady Louisa Conolly's estate, in 1787. On 13 October 1804 Napier died, and in 1806 Sarah moved to Cadogan Place, London. Soon afterwards her sight began to fail. Two of her daughters, Cecelia and Caroline, died of consumption in 1808 and 1810 respectively, while all three of her soldier sons were badly injured in the battle of Corunna, in January 1809. Gradually her mind began to fail, and she died at Cadogan Place on 26 August 1826, surrounded by her surviving children.   ROSEMARY RICHEY

Sources S. Tillyard, *Aristocrats: Caroline, Emily, Louisa and Sarah Lennox, 1740–1832*, new edn (1995) · *The life and letters of Lady Sarah Lennox*, ed. M. E. A. Dawson, countess of Ilchester and Lord Stavordale, 2 vols. (1901) · B. Fitzgerald, *Lady Louisa Conolly, 1743–1821: an Anglo-Irish biography* (1950) · B. Fitzgerald, *Emily, duchess of Leinster, 1731–1814: a study of her life and times* (1949)
Archives BL · Bodl. Oxf. · Irish Georgian Society, Dublin, Bunbury letter-book · Suffolk RO, transcripts of Bunbury's letter-book | BL, Holland House MSS · LMA, testimonies of Bunbury servants, records of consistory court, bishops of London, depositions book · NL Ire., Leinster MSS
Likenesses F. Cotes, oils, 1760, repro. in Tillyard, *Aristocrats*; priv. coll. · J. Reynolds, group portrait, oils, 1762, repro. in Tillyard, *Aristocrats*; priv. coll. · J. Reynolds, oils, 1762, Art Institute of Chicago [*see illus.*] · portrait, 1790?–1799, repro. in Tillyard, *Aristocrats*; priv. coll.
Wealth at death £2000: will, PRO, PROB 6/203, fol. 233*v*

Napier, Sir Thomas Erskine (1790–1863), army officer, second son of Captain Charles Napier (d. 19 Dec 1807) of Merchiston, Stirlingshire, and his second wife, Christian, *née* Hamilton, and brother of Admiral Sir Charles *Napier, was born on 10 May 1790. On 3 July 1805 he was appointed ensign in the 52nd regiment, and on 1 May 1806 became lieutenant. He served with the 52nd at Copenhagen in 1807, was aide-de-camp to Sir John Hope in the expedition to Sweden in 1808, and afterwards served at Corunna and in Portugal. On 27 October 1809 he was promoted captain in the *chasseurs britanniques*, a foreign corps in British pay, with which he served in Sicily, at Fuentes d'Oñoro, at the defence of Cadiz, and in Spain in 1812–13. When Hope joined the Peninsular army in 1813, Napier was again his aide-de-camp; in the battles on the Nive he was twice wounded, losing his left arm on 11 December 1813. The *chasseurs britanniques* were disbanded at the peace of 1814, and Napier was placed on half pay. He received a brevet majority on 26 December 1813, becoming brevet lieutenant-colonel on 21 June 1817 and colonel on 16 January 1837. He was for some years assistant adjutant-general at Belfast. He became a major-general in 1846, and was general officer commanding the troops in Scotland and governor of Edinburgh Castle from May 1852 until promotion to lieutenant-general on 20 June 1854. He was appointed full general on 20 September 1861, became colonel 16th regiment in 1854, and transferred to the 71st Highland light infantry on the death of Sir James Macdonell in 1857. He was made a CB in July 1838 and KCB in May 1860.

Napier married Margaret, daughter and coheir of Mr Falconer of Woodcot, Oxfordshire, and they had one daughter, Matilda (d. 1849); his wife survived him. He died at his home, Polton House, Lasswade, near Edinburgh, on 5 July 1863.   H. M. CHICHESTER, *rev.* JAMES FALKNER

Sources *Army List* · Burke, *Peerage* · *Hart's Army List* · E. D. H. E. Napier, *The life and correspondence of Admiral Sir Charles Napier*, 2 vols. (1862) · *GM*, 3rd ser., 15 (1863), 240 · *Colburn's United Service Magazine*, 2 (1849) · Boase, *Mod. Eng. biog.*
Archives NL Scot., letters to Sir George Brown
Wealth at death £7696 5s. 11d.: 2 Oct 1863, NA Scot., SC70/1/118, 12

Napier, William (*c.*1741–1812), musician and music publisher, was possibly born in Edinburgh. It has been suggested (Highfill, Burnim & Langhans, *BDA*) that he may have been related to Dr Archibald Napier, whose daughter Mary Ann married the musician Samuel Arnold in 1771. His early career included a position as violinist in Edinburgh's Canongate Theatre from 1758. Perhaps inevitably, by 1765 he was in London, joining the Royal Society of Musicians in September of that year. On 8 January of the following year, while resident at St Martin-in-the-Fields, he married Jane Stewart (*fl.* 1745–1791) at St Paul's, Covent Garden. Relatively high-profile appointments came his way, including posts as violinist in the private band of George III and the Professional Concert, as leader of the Ranelagh Gardens band in the 1780s, and as principal viola at the Handel commemoration concerts in 1784. He also played in the concerts of the Academy of Ancient Music, receiving 13 guineas in 1787–8.

In addition to his performing activities Napier forged a career as a publisher, establishing himself in 1772 at 474 the Strand, at the corner of Lancaster Court. He created a circulating music library in 1784 and served the royal family as music publisher. His employees included the musician George Smart and the caricaturist James Gillray, and strong associations with composers such as J. C. Bach and William Shield helped to create a wide-ranging catalogue of publications, from dance collections to popular ballad operas such as *Rosina* and *The Maid of the Mill*. He was also concerned with publishing repertory that was within the capabilities of the growing number of amateur instrumentalists. This did not, however, prevent financial difficulties for Napier in the harsh commercial climate of the time. About 1785 he sold copyrights, plates, and stock to Joseph Dale, raising £450. With eleven surviving children (five under the age of fourteen) to support, Napier was the beneficiary of a concert staged by Wilhelm Cramer to raise funds on 11 June 1788, followed by another one a year later at the Pantheon, and the governors of the Royal Society of Musicians offered some additional financial support. Nevertheless, bankruptcy and poor health followed in 1790–91, confining him to the king's bench and to bed.

Napier's fortunes and health improved in 1791 and were further rejuvenated as a result of Joseph Haydn's first appearance in London during the same year. Haydn provided accompaniments (for piano, violin, and cello) to a second volume of Napier's already popular collection *Scots Songs* which appeared in 1792 (with a Bartolozzi frontispiece). This successful collaboration was repeated with a third volume (1795), which, along with the other two, was reissued several times. His business was based at 49 Great Queen Street from March 1791 until about 1800, when it moved to 8 Lisle Street, Leicester Square.

Napier had long suffered from gout, and severe symptoms in his hands ended his playing career about 1795, at which time he was playing the viola in the Covent Garden oratorio series. His health and business were in decline once again from 1808, when his annual income of £37 was supplemented by the Royal Society of Musicians. His publishing business survived until 1809, when it was located at Princes Street, Leicester Square. Napier continued to receive similar grants until his death, at 'Somerston' (probably Somers Town, London) on 31 July 1812. The Royal Society of Musicians settled his medical expenses and funeral costs. One of his children may have been 'William Napier, late of Southampton and 1st Lieutenant on H.M.S. *St George*', who died in 1811 or 1812 (Highfill, Burnim & Langhans, *BDA*, 10.412). DAVID J. GOLBY

Sources Highfill, Burnim & Langhans, *BDA* · F. Kidson, H. G. Farmer, and P. W. Jones, 'Napier, William', *New Grove*, 2nd edn · H. D. Johnstone and R. Fiske, eds., *Music in Britain: the eighteenth century* (1990), 333 · C. Humphries and W. C. Smith, *Music publishing in the British Isles*, 2nd edn (1970), 241 · Brown & Stratton, *Brit. mus.*, 293 · *Scots Magazine*, 74 (Aug 1812)

Wealth at death bankrupt in 1791; received financial assistance from Royal Society of Musicians from 1808 until death; medical and funeral expenses settled

Napier, Sir William Francis Patrick (1785–1860), army officer and writer, born at Celbridge, co. Kildare, on 17 December 1785 was third son of Colonel the Hon. George

Sir William Francis Patrick Napier (1785–1860), by George Frederic Watts

*Napier (1751–1804) and his second wife, Sarah (1745–1826), *née* Lennox, formerly married to Sir Thomas Bunbury. He had four brothers—General Charles James *Napier (1782–1853), Lieutenant-General George Thomas *Napier (1784–1855), Captain Henry Edward *Napier RN (1789–1853), and Richard, QC—as well as a half-sister, Louisa (*d.* 1854), from his father's first marriage, and three sisters (Emily, Cecilia, and Caroline). The Napiers claimed descent from Scott of Thirlestane and John Napier, the inventor of logarithms; William's mother, daughter of the second duke of Richmond, from Charles II.

Early life, 1785–1804 Napier spent his youth at Celbridge House, according to his sister Emily attending 'the village school' but spending 'much of his time with a vagabond called Scully … [who was] something of a poacher' (Bruce, 1.7). From an early age Napier showed pugnacious self-reliance, once effectively wielding a large bag of marbles against a troublesome bully, and, during the 1798 Irish rising, the five Napier boys were armed to defend the family home. William Napier was commissioned second-lieutenant in the Royal Irish Artillery on 14 June 1800, became a lieutenant in the 62nd foot on 18 April 1801, and went on half pay after the peace of Amiens in March 1802. Through its colonel and his uncle, the duke of Richmond, on 22 August 1803 Napier acquired a cornetcy in the Horse Guards, moving as lieutenant on 28 December 1803 to the 52nd light infantry, part of Major-General John Moore's light brigade at Shorncliffe. Impressed by Napier, Moore thereafter took a close interest in his career. Napier nominally secured a company in a West India regiment on 2 June 1804, and shortly afterwards a battalion of reserve.

On 11 August he became a captain in the 43rd light infantry at Shorncliffe, when the 43rd had a poor professional reputation. In the words of a fellow officer, showing an aptitude for 'leaping, running, swimming &c' and displaying 'naturally polished, pleasing, gay manners' (ibid., 1.24), Napier soon transformed his company.

War service, 1804–1815 Two months after Napier's father died, in December 1804 Captain Charles Stanhope of the 52nd introduced him to his uncle, William Pitt, though the association had no political effect on Napier. In 1806 Napier went to Ireland to recruit militia volunteers for line regiments. The following year, he and the 43rd sailed with the British expedition to Denmark and fought at Kjöge, before the 43rd returned to Maldon and then Colchester. The 43rd embarked for Corunna on 13 September 1808, on arrival marching inland to Villafranca, where it formed part of the rear-guard covering Moore's retreat to Corunna; Napier spent two days and nights under attack at the Esla River, while his men demolished the Castro Gonzalo bridge. Rejoining the main force, he led a convoy of sick and wounded over the mountains to Vigo, marching for several days with bare feet, clad only in a jacket and pair of trousers. Not surprisingly, he suffered debilitating fever. Back home, in February 1809 he became aide-de-camp to the duke of Richmond, lord lieutenant of Ireland, but four months later went back to his regiment in Portugal. *En route* for Talavera, he was left at Placencia, suffering from pleurisy. When only partially recovered, he reputedly walked 48 miles to Oropesa and took post-horses for Talavera, where he promptly collapsed.

Fit again, Napier saw action on the Coa, 23 July 1810, and was shot in the left thigh as his company covered the light division's withdrawal. Still in discomfort, he fought at Busaco on 17 September 1810, as Wellington retired towards the lines of Torres Vedras. When the French retreated into Spain the following year, Napier saw action at Pombal, Redinha, and Casal Novo where, on 14 March 1811, a musket ball (never removed) lodged near his spine: paralysed below the waist, 'I escaped death by dragging myself by my hands … towards a small heap of stones which was in the midst of the field, and thus covering my head and shoulders' (Bruce, 1.55). His wound had not fully healed when Napier acted as brigade major at Fuentes d'Oñoro on 5 May 1811. He received a brevet majority on 30 May, but fell ill in June; he was sent to Lisbon, and in the autumn to England. In February 1812 Napier married Caroline Amelia (1790–1860), younger daughter of General the Hon. Henry *Fox and niece of the politician Charles James Fox. Learning that Wellington was besieging Badajoz, three weeks after his wedding Napier once more set off for active service. Arriving after the fortress had fallen he found that Lieutenant-Colonel Charles Macleod had been killed, and took command of the 43rd as the senior officer present. On 14 May 1812 Napier advanced to regimental major and led the regiment at the battle of Salamanca on 23 July in a steady 3 mile advance under heavy fire to seize the ford at Huerta, and entered Madrid with Wellington on 12 August. When the 43rd subsequently withdraw into Portugal, he went to England on leave from January to August 1813, rejoining the regiment at Vera, in the Pyrenees. On 21 September, disturbingly he informed his wife that his wound was painful and 'the doctor' thought 'a small part of the ball or backbone [was] coming away' (ibid., 1.150).

When its commanding officer became unwell, during the battle of the Nivelle, Napier took over the 43rd again, and at its head, on 10 November 1813, stormed a strong, entrenched enemy position on a steep, rocky hill, Le Petit Rhune. After Wellington forced the Nive River, the French commander Soult suddenly attacked the light division on the left bank on 10 December. For three days Napier successfully defended the church at Arcangues, being wounded in the right hip and, less seriously, when a shell splinter drove his telescope into his face. Promoted brevet lieutenant-colonel on 22 November 1813, he fought at Orthez on 27 February 1814, but, laid low with fever and dysentery, he returned to England on sick leave in late spring. He briefly attended the senior department of the Royal Military Academy, Farnham (25 February – 10 June 1815), before hastening to his regiment on news of Napoleon's escape from Elba. He missed the battle of Waterloo, but marched with the 43rd to Paris and took part in the victory parade. Napier served with the 43rd in the army of occupation until late 1818, when the 43rd moved to Belfast, where he had the opportunity to purchase its command. For financial reasons he declined, and on 17 June 1819 went on half pay. From the officers of the 43rd he received a sword 'as a testimony of their sincere regard for him and their high admiration of the gallantry and conduct he ever displayed during his exemplary career' (Bruce, 1.217). He was made CB on 4 June 1815, and received a gold medal with two clasps for the battles of Salamanca, the Nivelle, and Nive, and a silver medal with three clasps for Busaco, Fuentes d'Oñoro, and Orthez.

History of the Peninsular War, politics, and controversy, 1815–1860 In retirement, at a rented house in Sloane Terrace, London, Napier pursued 'rather a desultory though never an idle life, without any absorbing aim' (Bruce, 1.224) until he reviewed Baron Jomini's *Principes de la guerre* for the *Edinburgh Review* in 1821, and, afterwards, met Marshal Soult in Paris. Encouraged by Henry Bickersteth (later Lord Langdale), despite lack of literary experience, Napier determined to write a history of the Peninsular War. Wellington refused use of his private papers, but gave Napier Joseph Bonaparte's correspondence with Napoleon, senior military figures, and politicians captured at Vitoria, and answered copious questions. For some months in 1824 Napier lived in a cottage at Stratfield Saye, but the duchess banned him from the house, because of his 'commonplace opinions in politics' (Longford, 113). Sir George Murray, quartermaster-general in the Peninsula, denied him access to documents and maps in his possession, though Soult proved more accommodating when Napier returned to Paris, where he met other Napoleonic commanders, Ney's widow, and Jomini. Wearied through copying copious documents, he complained to his wife that 'my health is bad, my spirits worse, and my expenses very great', longing for the time when 'we will paint and walk, and read and write history' (Bruce, 1.243, 244). Indeed, Caroline (Caro to Napier) was closely involved in Napier's work, especially in deciphering the codes in Joseph Bonaparte's correspondence. Back in England Napier used journals and other printed sources, and corresponded at length with many British and French officers. For many years blind and frail, Napier's mother died on 20 August 1826. Shortly afterwards the family moved to Battle House, Bromham, near Devizes, where Napier read the works of William Cobbett, copied his system of cultivating Indian corn, and, as his daughters observed, frequently dug the kitchen garden 'wearing a labourer's white smock frock' (ibid., 1.297). He developed, too, a lasting friendship with the poet Thomas Moore, who lived close by.

Relying on a major's half pay of 9s. 6d. a day, Napier worried incessantly about money. He wrote to Lord FitzRoy Somerset (later Lord Raglan), military secretary at the Horse Guards, on 30 November 1826 seeking emolument for his third wound suffered at Arcangues, which he had not listed for fear of alarming his pregnant wife. John Murray paid Napier 1000 guineas for the copyright of the first volume of his history, published in 1828, and secured an option on the next three volumes, which he did not exercise due to financial loss on the first. So Napier raised subscriptions from individuals for Thomas and William Boone to bring out the last five volumes. The history provoked wide-ranging reaction. Soult considered it 'perfect', Sir Robert Peel 'eloquent and faithful', the Spanish general Alava felt it too pro-French, and a British officer in India demanded satisfaction on his return for a 'most unfounded calumny' about his conduct at Barossa. General Lord Beresford expressed fury at the account of Albuera, and, fourteen years after publication of the relevant volume, Colonel John Gurwood would challenge Napier's assertion that a howitzer captured at Sabugal fell to the 43rd, not 52nd, regiment. Napier thus faced a carillon of malcontents and critics, and he believed that his adverse comments about the Spaniards prevented him from commanding British troops in the Carlist wars. The work was, however, translated into French, Spanish, Italian, and German, with plans to produce a Persian version also discussed.

Napier advanced to colonel on 22 July 1830, and towards the close of 1831 moved the family to Freshford, near Bath, where he became politically outspoken, pronouncing the Reform Act too mild, the corn laws defensible (opposing their repeal), and the Poor Law Amendment Act unacceptable; in 1841 he published Essay on the Poor Laws and Observations on the Corn Laws. He spoke in favour of universal suffrage, the secret ballot, and annual parliaments without joining the Chartists, and he espoused the anti-slavery cause. However, he vigorously defended flogging in the army and opposed the abolition of purchase. A long-standing friend, James Shaw (later General Sir James Shaw Kennedy), believed him in 1805 to be 'nothing more than a complete whig of the school of Charles Fox' (Bruce, 1.346), but thirty years later he had drifted from the whigs and become a confidant of the radical MP J. A. Roebuck. In 1831

enthusiasts vainly urged Napier to head a national guard and, in 1848, to lead a march on London to demand reform. Napier declined invitations to stand for parliament in Bath, Nottingham, Glasgow, Devizes, Westminster, Oldham, and Kendal, citing inability to meet the costs involved and maintain his large family, to which he was devoted. He and his wife had one boy and nine girls (John Moore and Henrietta both being born deaf and mute); four of the girls predeceased their parents. 'How I do love my girls' (ibid., 1.196), he declared, and he worried particularly about the security of his son's clerical post in the quartermaster-general's office in Dublin. In 1833 his eldest surviving daughter, Fanny, died of consumption. Napier spent hours alone with his brother Charles during his last illness in September 1853, but, a month later, his brother Henry died before he could reach his sickbed. His half-sister, Louisa, passed away in 1854; a year later his brother George died in Geneva. These two depressing years had been prefaced by the death in September 1852 of Wellington, whom Napier so fervently admired and to whom he had dedicated his history. Grief-stricken, he carried a bannerol at the funeral on 18 November, and watched, with a select few, as the duke's coffin was lowered into its vault at St Paul's Cathedral.

Worries about finance were ever present. In 1833 Napier fleetingly considered leaving the army: his annual salary amounted to a mere £171 and, should he die, the value of his commission would be lost to the family, whereas it could be sold for £3200. Four years later he applied for 'additional pay for meritorious services', and secured £150 a year. In 1846 Napier was delighted when Lieutenant-General James Shortall, his commanding officer in the Royal Irish Artillery, bequeathed him £100. Nevertheless, money rarely motivated his extensive writing, as he sought to redress perceived injustice, promote national security, and debate historical issues in numerous publications and private correspondence. Occasionally he adopted the nom de plume Elian. He attacked Louis Thiers, the French statesman, for dismissive comments on Wellington and Moore. Thiers retorted that he would not waste time in refuting 'the assertions of ignorant or interested critics', and Napier acidly returned that he should write 'in a manner to avoid the just censures of honest and well-informed critics' (ibid., 1.555). When his brother Charles was attacked for his conduct as a military commander and civilian administrator, Napier leapt to his defence in a two-volume History of the Conquest of Scinde. It attracted fierce criticism, and his son-in-law admitted that, in this work, 'the calmness of the historian is too often wanting' (ibid., 2.193). After Charles's death, Napier completed his brother's Defects, Civil and Military, of the Indian Government. He then wrote a biography of Charles, which ignited yet more acrimonious public exchanges.

Napier displayed a keen interest in imperial and foreign affairs. During disturbances in Canada in 1838 he argued that 'Lower Canadians have been infamously used, and were driven into armed rebellion' (Bruce, 1.473). As cross-border relations with the United States deteriorated, he devised a plan for attacking over the Niagara River. With

France on the verge of anarchy in 1848, he saw Louis Napoleon as its saviour: 'Vive Napoleon ... Will he be Napoleon the Third, or Dictator, or Consul, or President?' (ibid., 2.255). As Britain became embroiled in the Crimean War, he stoutly defended his cousin, Vice-Admiral Sir Charles Napier, who was vilified for an ineffective foray into the Baltic, mused as to whether Sevastopol would ever fall to the allies, condemned the use of 'hirelings of Germany and Switzerland' (ibid., 2.363) in a British foreign legion, felt that issue of the Minié rifle to all infantry would stifle attack on the battlefield, and minutely analysed reports of the major land actions. He retained, too, his fascination for the Napoleonic era. When Soult visited Britain in 1838, he accompanied him to Manchester, Liverpool, and Birmingham, and they spoke at length about political and military figures of the First Empire. In February 1842 Napier was appointed lieutenant-governor of Guernsey, where he condemned the 'wretched state' of the island's defences, the dismal condition of the militia, and harsh, biased application of the law by the judiciary. When he left office in January 1848 he had achieved little in the face of entrenched, powerful families and a hostile press, except the appointment of one royal commission to examine the administration of criminal law, the promise of a second to look into civil law, and the recommendation from a military commission to strengthen coastal defences of Guernsey and Alderney.

Napier's chief publications were: *History of the war in the Peninsula and in the south of France from the year 1807 to the year 1814* (6 vols., 1828–40), *Reply to Various Opponents, together with Observations Illustrating Sir John Moore's Campaign* (3 vols., 1832–3), *The conquest of Scinde, with some introductory passages in the life of Major-General Sir Charles James Napier* (2 vols., 1845), *History of Sir Charles Napier's Administration of Scinde and Campaign in the Cutchee Hills* (1851), *English Battles and Sieges in the Peninsula* (1852), and *The Life and Opinions of General Sir C. J. Napier* (4 vols., 1857). He also wrote innumerable reviews, articles, pamphlets, and letters to the press, many of them contentious and polemical, and he contributed 'An explanation of the battle of Meanee' to the *Professional Papers of the Royal Engineers* (1844).

Promoted major-general on 3 November 1841, Napier was appointed colonel of the 27th foot on 5 February 1848 and created KCB on 29 April. The following year he and his family moved to Scinde House, Clapham Park, where he stayed for the rest of his life. He advanced to lieutenant-general on 11 November 1851, and succeeded Charles as colonel of the 22nd foot on 19 September 1853. However, his health noticeably declined during the winter 1857–8, and, in October 1858, he narrowly survived a severe paroxysm. In March 1859 he wrote of 'being on my death-bed' and, from April, dictated letters to his daughter Caroline. None the less, his mind remained alert. He reflected extensively on the defences of the British Isles and the military capability of European countries. His last paper, dictated in December 1859, contained comprehensive guidance to Bruce on raising a force of volunteers. Napier was promoted general on 17 October 1859, but by then his wife had developed severe dropsy, which deeply

depressed him. During the morning of Sunday 12 February 1860, she was briefly wheeled into her unconscious husband's room. At 4 p.m., in the presence of his children, grandchildren, sons-in-law, and daughter-in-law, Napier passed away 'so gently that it was impossible to say when the breathing ceased' (Bruce, 2.483). The funeral at Norwood was private, although light division veterans from the Peninsula attended. Napier's wife survived him by six weeks; of his brothers, only Richard outlived him.

Appearance, character, and conclusion Napier stood 6 feet tall, with black curly hair, fierce moustachios, shortsighted blue-grey eyes, an aquiline nose, firm mouth, and square jaw. In later years, he had flowing white hair and a full beard. According to his son-in-law, he could be 'so terrible in anger, so melting in tenderness, so sparkling in fun' (Bruce, 1.27). Napier reacted swiftly and often savagely when he believed himself, his family, or friends unfairly treated. He admitted undertaking his work on the Peninsular War principally because he considered Robert Southey's account unfair on Moore and the French army. A century afterwards, in his *History of the British Army*, J. M. Fortescue questioned the reliability of Napier's information and figures from unidentified sources, and C. W. C. Oman justifiably deemed the history 'magnificent (if somewhat prejudiced and biased)' (Oman, *Wellington's Army*, 18). Military historians now treat it with considerable caution.

If Napier was not the 'genius' which Bruce and Shaw Kennedy claimed, he had many creative attributes. Lacking detached and balanced judgement, he was nevertheless a prodigious writer of history, biography, and social and political treatises. He painted, mainly for recreation, though George Jones RA, held that his 'talent in drawing was very considerable, and if he had studied for the profession of painting I believe he would have been very successful' (Bruce, 2.490). Napier wrote poetry (notably the seven-verse 'Ode to Love') and sculpted competently; for his statuette of Alcibiades he became an honorary member of the Royal Academy. He was also elected to the Athenaeum and the Swedish Academy of Military Sciences. A statue of Napier by G. G. Adams, inscribed 'Historian of the Peninsular War', was installed in St Paul's Cathedral.   JOHN SWEETMAN

Sources *Army List* · W. F. P. Napier, *Life of General Sir William Napier*, ed. H. A. Bruce, 2 vols. (1864) · R. G. A. Levinge, *Historical records of the forty-third regiment, Monmouthshire light infantry* (1868) · R. B. Crosse, *A short history of the Oxfordshire and Buckinghamshire light infantry* (1923) · H. Newbolt, *The story of the Oxfordshire and Buckinghamshire light infantry* (1915) · E. Longford, *The years of the sword* (1971) · Fortescue, *Brit. army*, vols. 6–8 · C. W. C. Oman, *Wellington's army, 1809–1814* (1912) · G. C. Moore Smith, *The life of John Colborne, Field-Marshal Lord Seaton* (1903) · C. Oman, *Sir John Moore* (1953)

Archives BL, corresp., Add. MSS 54525–54526 · BL, papers, Add. MS 49170 · Bodl. Oxf., corresp. and papers | NL Scot., corresp. with Sir George Brown · NL Scot., corresp. with Lord Rutherfurd · NL Scot., letters to Sir John Wilson · PRO, corresp. with Lord Ellenborough, 30/12 · U. Southampton, letters to Wellington · W. Sussex RO, letters to duke of Richmond

Likenesses S. Gambardella, oils, *c*.1845, Wellington Museum · oils, *c*.1845, Wellington Museum · F. Bromley, group portrait, engraving, pubd 1847 (after *The Peninsular heroes* by J. P. Knight),

BM • G. G. Adams, marble bust, 1855, NPG • G. G. Adams, statue, 1863, St Paul's Cathedral • stipple and line engraving, 1864 (after G. F. Watts), NPG • W. H. Egleton, stipple (after W. F. P. Napier), NPG • G. F. Watts, drawing, NPG [see illus.] • portrait, repro. in Bruce, Life of Sir William Napier • portrait, repro. in The Royal Inniskilling fusiliers (1928), facing p. 312 • portrait, repro. in Newbolt, Story of the Oxfordshire and Buckinghamshire light infantry, facing p. 68 • stipple (after E. Jones), NPG • wood-engraving (after photograph by Kilburn), NPG; repro. in ILN (1860)

Wealth at death under £40,000: probate, 2 March 1860, CGPLA Eng. & Wales

Napier, William John, ninth Lord Napier of Merchistoun

Napier, William John, ninth Lord Napier of Merchistoun (1786–1834), naval officer and trade envoy, the eldest son of Francis *Napier, eighth Lord Napier of Merchistoun (1758–1823), and his wife, Maria Margaret, née Clavering (1756?–1821), was born at Kinsale in Ireland on 13 October 1786. He entered the navy in 1803 on board the Chiffonne, with Captain Charles Adam. During 1804 and 1805 he was with Captain George Hope in the Defence, and was present at Trafalgar. He was then for a year in the Foudroyant, the flagship of Sir John Borlase Warren, and was at the capture of Linois's squadron on 13 March 1806. From November 1806 to September 1809 he was in the Imperieuse with Lord Cochrane during his remarkable service on the coasts of France and Spain and in the attack on the French fleet in Aix Roads. Napier was a man of great physical power, and aboard the Imperieuse he earned a reputation as an outstanding seaman and navigator as well as a brave leader in boarding actions. He was greatly admired by his shipmate Frederick Marryat. He was promoted lieutenant on 6 October 1809, and for the next two years served in the Kent on the Mediterranean station. He was afterwards with Captain Pringle in the Sparrowhawk on the coast of Catalonia, and after being promoted, on 1 June 1812, to command the Goshawk, continued on the same service until September 1813. He then went out to the coast of North America in the Erne, and, though promoted to post rank on 4 June 1814, remained in the same command until September 1815, when the Erne returned to England and was paid off.

On 28 March 1816 Napier married Elizabeth, the only daughter of the disgraced Hon. Andrew James Cochrane-*Johnstone and the cousin of his old captain Lord Cochrane; they had two sons and five daughters. He settled down in Selkirkshire and applied himself vigorously to sheep farming. In January 1818 he was elected a fellow of the Royal Society of Edinburgh. With great personal labour, and against much opposition and ignorant prejudice, he opened out the country by new roads, in the survey of which he himself took part. He drained the land, built shelters for the sheep, and largely contributed to bringing in white-faced Cheviot sheep, a more profitable breed than the local black-faced sheep; he also published A treatise on practical store-farming as applicable to the mountainous region of Etterick forest and the pastoral district of Scotland in general (1822).

On 1 August 1823, by the death of his father, Napier succeeded to the peerage, and from 1824 to 1826 he commanded the frigate Diamond on the South American station. In December 1833 he became chief superintendent of trade in China, with instructions to protect trade at Canton (Guangzhou) and to see if it could be extended to other Chinese ports. He was appointed by the foreign secretary, Lord Palmerston, who held the family in high regard—especially his cousin Captain Charles Napier. Napier arrived at Macau (Macao) on 15 July 1834, and after organizing the British commercial community there went up to Canton, which he reached on 25 July. This measure was contrary to and in defiance of the wishes of the viceroy, who refused to have any correspondence with him, as by custom all communications regarding trade passed through the hong merchants. It was Napier's object to break down this custom and open direct communication with the government. However, he lacked the diplomatic and commercial experience to make a success of such a complex task, one which was not soluble by hard work or hard words. He ignored efforts at conciliation by the British merchants and took affront at every slight offered by the Chinese. Having failed to secure access to the viceroy, he soon began to favour military action, including the seizure of Hong Kong. He was the first British representative to recommend this particular act. Two frigates sailed upriver towards Canton on 8 September, easily passing the Chinese forts. The salutary effect of this success was then lost when the ships were left below Canton, and on the 15th Napier admitted defeat. He left Canton for Macau under Chinese escort on the 21st.

Napier reached Macau on 26 September 1834 and died there of 'fever' on 11 October; he was buried there. A brave and determined man, he had been sent out to do a job that required a degree of skill and experience he had never had the opportunity to acquire, purely on account of his name and rank. His death was a personal tragedy, but the lessons of his mission were taken to heart in London. The next time Britain had business to discuss at Canton adequate naval and military forces were sent. The career in the diplomatic service of Napier's eldest son, Francis *Napier, was promoted by Palmerston for the rest of his life.

J. K. LAUGHTON, rev. ANDREW LAMBERT

Sources G. S. Graham, The China station: war and diplomacy, 1830–1860 (1978) • J. B. Williams, British commercial policy and trade expansion, 1750–1850 (1972) • BL, Napier MSS • A. Cochrane, The fighting Cochranes (1983) • D. Thomas, Cochrane (1978) • O. Warner, Captain Marryat: a rediscovery [1953] • Burke, Peerage • GM, 2nd ser., 3 (1835), 267–9, 429

Archives NL Scot., corresp. with Mark Napier • NMM, letters to James Guttrie

Naples, Joseph

Naples, Joseph (bap. 1773), grave robber, son of Joseph Naples, stationer and bookbinder, and his wife, Mary, was baptized at St Paul's, Deptford, in London, on 24 October 1773. It is known that he served for some time aboard the Excellent and saw action off Cape Vincent, after which he returned to England before joining a vessel which cruised the English Channel. Naples then abandoned the sea and returned to London, where he became a gravedigger at the Spa Fields burial-ground. It was here that he found his way into the body-snatching business that supplied the corpses demanded by the medical profession for the teaching of anatomy.

It appears that Naples was persuaded to enter the trade by a man named White. When White was apprehended while transporting a body taken from Spa Fields, Naples was arrested and sentenced to two years' imprisonment. Naples managed to escape, however, from the house of correction but was recaptured after information was received from Ben Crouch, a fellow resurrectionist. Naples was saved from further punishment by the intervention of the eminent surgeon Sir Astley Cooper, one of the body-snatchers' most regular customers.

On his release Naples continued in his work of providing corpses for London's anatomy schools. He became a member of the city's main gang of resurrectionists, led by Ben Crouch, and is probably the author of a diary that details their activities from 28 November 1811 until 5 December 1812. The manuscript, which is held at the library of the Royal College of Surgeons, provides unique evidence of the early nineteenth-century body-snatching business. The diary records that bodies were sent to Joshua Brookes, Henry Cline, Joseph Carpue, and Algernon Frampton—all proprietors of anatomy schools—and to St Thomas's Hospital, as well as to Edinburgh; teeth, foetuses, and the bodies of children were also sold. The gang frequently removed corpses from the burial-grounds of St Bartholomew's, Guy's, and St Thomas's hospitals; some bodies were even taken before a funeral could take place. The diary records the risks the gang took—avoiding patrols and guard dogs, digging up diseased corpses—and the problems caused by a bright moon. Naples earned about 11 guineas a week for his work during the period covered in the diary.

Naples was described as 'a civil and well conducted man, slight in person, with a pleasing countenance, and of respectful manners' (Naples, 156). The passing of the Anatomy Act in 1832, which increased the supply of corpses available for dissection, led to the decline of the resurrection gangs. Naples found employment as a servant in the dissecting room of St Thomas's Hospital, after which nothing more is known of him.   IAN LYLE

Sources [J. Naples], *The diary of a resurrectionist*, ed. J. B. Bailey (1896) • R. Richardson, *Death, dissection and the destitute* (1987) • IGI **Archives** RCS Eng.

Napleton, John (1738/9–1817), Church of England clergyman and educational reformer, was the son of the Revd John Napleton of Pembridge, Herefordshire. He matriculated at Brasenose College, Oxford, on 22 March 1755, at the age of sixteen, and graduated BA in 1758, MA in 1761, and BD and DD in 1789. On 13 December 1760 he was elected to a fellowship at his college, and he remained in residence as a tutor until the close of 1777. He became vice-principal in 1769/70 and served as senior bursar in 1771/2, 1773/4, and 1775/6. He proved to be a congenial colleague, appreciated for his fund of anecdotes, but some of his pupils found him 'uncommonly strict'. He contributed a set of Greek verses to the Oxford *Epithalamia* in celebration of the marriage of George III in 1761, and in 1770 published a textbook on logic, *Elementa logicae; subjicitur appendix de usu logicae et conspectus Organi Aristotelis*, reprinted in

1776 and 1785, which was a work of some originality, taking into account modern authors, among them John Locke.

Napleton's main claim to fame came from his support of the cause of university reform. In his pamphlet *Considerations on the Residence Usually Required for Degrees in the University of Oxford* (1772) he drew attention to current abuses. His *Considerations on the Public Exercises for the First and Second Degrees*, published anonymously in 1773, was a strong indictment of the existing system. He demonstrated how the exercises had become 'totally neglected', the questions for disputation either 'trite and unimportant' or 'long and tedious', the whole business 'languid, uninstructive and uninteresting', and 'performed in so negligent a manner, that it is equally impossible they should contribute to the advancement of learning, to the improvement or reputation of the Candidates, or honour of the University' (Napleton, 1).

Napleton's recommendations for reform were comparatively modest. In the belief that the 'academical Exercises have become too private', he advised that they should be held in the presence of a full congregation, probably meeting in the Sheldonian. The examiners should range the candidates in three classes. Napleton did not tamper with the existing curriculum, which he held to be 'so well conceived, as to be capable of little, if any improvement' (Napleton, 19), believing that a logical disputation formed a good intellectual training; but he advocated greater proficiency in mathematics, and better fluency in Latin, though he suggested that at least one of the declamations should be in English rather than in Latin. Conservative as were Napleton's proposals for reform, they gave some encouragement to liberals in the university, though no major reform was to take place until 1800.

Napleton was inducted as vicar of Tarrington, Herefordshire, on 27 September 1777, and as rector of Wold, Northamptonshire, a college living, on 24 October 1777; he resigned his fellowship on 20 September 1778. When John Butler, previously bishop of Oxford, was translated to the see of Hereford, he called to his aid the services of Napleton, who became the golden prebendary in Hereford Cathedral on 8 May 1789, and the bishop's chaplain. He now endeavoured to effect an exchange of benefices, but his college ultimately refused its consent, and he was compelled to vacate the living of Wold on 28 November 1789. In the diocese of Hereford he was soon rewarded with ample preferment. He was made chancellor of the diocese (1796), master of the hospital at Ledbury, rector of Stoke Edith, vicar of Lugwardine, in the gift of the dean and chapter (1810), and was nominated by Bishop Luxmoore as praelector of divinity at Hereford Cathedral (1810); he retained most of these appointments until his death. Napleton married on 4 December 1793 Elizabeth, the only daughter of Thomas Daniell of Truro, and the sister of Ralph Allen Daniell, MP for West Looe, Cornwall. There were no children.

Napleton was the author of a number of pamphlets, including *Advice to a student in the university concerning the qualifications and duties of a minister of the gospel in the Church of England* (1795) and *The Duty of Churchwardens Respecting the Church* (1799). Many of his sermons were printed, among them *A Sermon on the Meeting of the Three Choirs at Hereford* (1789) and *A sermon preached at St. Mary's Church at the anniversary meeting of the governors of the Radcliffe Infirmary, June 19, 1792*.

Napleton died at Hereford on 9 December 1817, and was buried in a vault in the centre of the cathedral choir. A small white tablet, formerly over his grave, was later removed to the eighth bay of the bishop's cloister. A more elaborate inscription on a similar tablet was erected over the door, on the south side of the nave, which leads to the same cloister. He bequeathed £50 to the principal and fellows of Brasenose for the use of the rector of Wold, for the purchase of books or otherwise for the spiritual benefit of the inhabitants of the parish.

W. P. COURTNEY, rev. VIVIAN H. H. GREEN

Sources [J. Napleton], *Considerations on the public exercises for the first and second degrees in the University of Oxford* (1773) · *Hist. U. Oxf.* 5: *18th-cent. Oxf.* · [C. B. Heberden], ed., *Brasenose College register, 1509–1909*, 2 vols., OHS, 55 (1909) · Foster, *Alum. Oxon.* · *GM*, 1st ser., 87/2 (1817), 630 · R. Polwhele, *Reminiscences in prose and verse*, 3 vols. (1836) · Nichols, *Illustrations*
Likenesses C. Picart, stipple, 1814 (after T. Leeming), BM, NPG · Opie, portrait

Napley [*formerly* Naphtali], **Sir David** (1915–1994), solicitor, was born on 25 July 1915 at 31 Sach Road, Upper Clapton, London, the son of Joseph Naphtali, insurance broker, and his wife, Rachel (Raie), *née* Burchell, both of Jewish descent. He was educated at Burlington College rather than at a public school followed by a university, something he regretted. He was then articled as a solicitor's clerk to Philip Emmanuel of the firm of W. R. Bennett & Co. of Great Russell Street, Bloomsbury. He was admitted to the rolls in July 1937, having passed the solicitors' final examination with honours. On his admission he was invited by his contemporary Sidney Kingsley to join him in practice on a salary and profit-sharing arrangement. In 1940 he joined the Queen's Royal (West Surrey) regiment. On 8 September in the same year he married Leah Rose Saturley (*b.* 1918/19), the daughter of Thomas Reginald Saturley, company director, of London. They had two daughters.

After being commissioned in 1942 Napley served in the Indian army, where he attained the rank of captain before being invalided out in 1945 suffering from an enlarged spleen, when he was sent back to Britain to die. He recovered, however, and opened an office in New Court, Carey Street, behind the law courts, with a loan of £500, recommencing practice with Kingsley. He had been advised not to go to the bar, then very much a rich man's profession. It was advice he regretted for the rest of his life. By now, fearing the antisemitism of the time, he had Anglicized his name.

Initially attracted to the law of estate agency, the first of a number of textbooks Napley wrote was *Law on the Remuneration of Auctioneers and Estate Agents* (1947). In 1954 he edited *Bateman's Law of Auctions*. It was, however, the criminal defence side of the practice which developed and for which Napley became best-known. His most celebrated cases included the successful defence of the Liberal Party leader Jeremy Thorpe on a charge of conspiracy to murder, and that of Ian Ball, convicted of shooting at Princess Anne in the Mall. Other clients included the family of the banker Roberto Calvi, who was found hanged from Blackfriars Bridge. He also represented the family of Helen Smith, a nurse who died in mysterious circumstances in Saudi Arabia. He was one of the finest solicitor-advocates of his day.

The 1960s was a time when many members of the bar maintained a superior attitude towards solicitors and Napley was instrumental in forming the London Criminal Courts' Solicitors' Association, designed to improve the standing of what was regarded as the junior branch of the profession in criminal cases. He held the presidency from 1960 to 1963 and became president of the City of Westminster Law Society in 1967. He was elected a member of the council of the Law Society in 1962 and was its president in 1976–7. Much of his presidency was spent in preparing the society's submissions to the Benson commission on legal services, which at the time were subject to much public criticism. Throughout his career he championed the rights of audience for solicitors in higher courts and his work was recognized with the Courts and Legal Services Act 1990. He served on the Home Office Law Revision Committee from 1971 until his death.

As his practice diversified in the 1970s, Napley became involved with a chain of popular Italian trattorias and was chairman of Mario and Franco Restaurants Ltd between 1968 and 1977, and later of Burton-Race Restaurants plc. Fittingly, since his offices had moved to that area, he was a director of the Covent Garden festival from 1989 also until his death. He was a trustee of the West Ham Boys' Club, and became the club's president in 1981. Politically, he was perhaps unfortunate in his preferences. In 1951 he was the unsuccessful Conservative candidate for Rowley Regis and Tipton, and he was again defeated when standing for Gloucester in 1955. Had he followed the Labour line he might well have achieved the ennoblement he wished and so joined the two other outstanding solicitors of his era, lords Goodman and Mishcon.

Until his voice broke Napley had been a boy soprano, appearing in concerts in his youth, and he was later an accomplished painter of what might be called the representational school. For each retiring president of the Law Society he would compose and recite a poem. In later life he wrote his memoirs, *Not without Prejudice* (1982), and a number of novels based on celebrated criminal cases of the twentieth century. Perhaps the best of these was *The Camden Town Murder* (1987), based on a defence by Edward Marshall Hall, but the books enjoyed only a modest success and, in truth, the clarity of his writing never matched that of his speech. He died at Thames Valley Nuffield Hospital, Wexham Street, Wexham, Buckinghamshire, on 24 September 1994 of carcinoma of the gall bladder, and was survived by his wife and their two daughters. A memorial service was held at St Clement Danes, Strand, on 30 November 1994. A portrait by Michael Noakes hangs in the Law Society's hall in Chancery Lane, London.

JAMES MORTON

Sources *The Times* (27 Sept 1994) · *The Guardian* (27 Sept 1994) · *The Independent* (28 Sept 1994) · D. Napley, *Not without prejudice* (1982) · *Law List* (1937–40) · *Law List* (1947–) · *WWW* · private information (2004) · personal knowledge (2004) · b. cert. · m. cert. · d. cert.
Likenesses photograph, 1973, repro. in *The Independent* · M. Noakes, oils, 1977, Law Society, London · photograph, repro. in *The Times* · photograph, repro. in *The Guardian*
Wealth at death £218,357: probate, 2 Dec 1994, *CGPLA Eng. & Wales*

Narayan, Jayaprakash (1902–1979), political activist and social worker, was born on 11 October 1902 in the village of Shitab Diara, Bihar, in an upper caste (Kayastha) family of modest means, the fourth of six children of Harsu Dayal, a government official, and his wife, Phul Rani Devi. He had two brothers and three sisters. He married Prabhavati Devi (*d*. 1973) in October 1920 when he was eighteen and she fourteen. Although the marriage was never physically consummated, Prabhavati having been persuaded by Mahatma Gandhi to take a vow of lifelong celibacy, they lived in all other respects throughout their mature lives together in close companionship. Aside from his association with a 'Communist Free Lovers' Club' during his time at the University of Wisconsin, there is no other indication of an active sexual life, and he left no descendants. Jayaprakash, or J. P. as he was often called, was a tall, lean, and handsome man, somewhat austere and aloof in appearance, though in fact gentle and agreeable in his personal relationships.

Narayan's early education in Patna, at the Patna collegiate school and Patna College, was disrupted by his participation in the non-co-operation movement of 1921. Although he enrolled briefly thereafter in a new nationalist institution, Bihar Vidyapith, he completed his education in the United States, where he lived between 1922 and 1929. He took courses at the University of California at Berkeley, Iowa University, the University of Wisconsin at Madison, and Ohio State University, where he received BA and MA degrees in 1928 and 1929 respectively, supporting himself throughout by taking various odd jobs. Although his early interests were in science subjects, he came under the influence of communist and socialist teachers and students at the University of Wisconsin, leading to a change towards sociology, in which he received his MA degree.

Narayan was prevented from studying for a PhD by news of his mother's illness, which brought him back to India, where vigorous nationalist activities were under way. Through his wife, whose father was a very important Bihar politician, and who herself was ensconced in Gandhi's *ashram* at Ahmadabad, Narayan soon found himself at the centre of nationalist politics and in personal contact with both Gandhi and Nehru. Although he came close to and worked with Nehru at first, he immediately carved out a singular position for himself as the leading exponent of the position that the Indian National Congress must articulate a social and economic programme that went beyond the mere demand for independence from British rule. In 1934 he was one of a small group who formed the Congress Socialist Party, of which he became general secretary, to work within the Indian National Congress, seeking to influence the social and economic policies of the parent organization.

Narayan participated actively in most of the major movements against British rule after his return to India, and was imprisoned in 1932, in 1940, and again in 1943, emerging from gaol only in April 1946. He was one of the leading socialist figures in the Quit India movement of 1942, having escaped from prison in September of that year.

After the achievement of Indian independence in 1947 Narayan and several of his colleagues in the Congress Socialist Party severed their ties with the parent body to form a party of opposition initially called the Socialist Party, but renamed the Praja Socialist Party (PSP) after a merger with another party in 1953. In 1954 he announced his retirement from politics to join the Sarvodaya movement for social reconstruction in the countryside, emphasizing voluntary land redistribution, communal land ownership, small-scale production, and self-sufficient, self-governing village communities, but he did not finally sever his relations with the PSP until 1957. These shifts in his principal activities in Indian public life were all marked by major breaks in his political thought: from Marxism and sympathy with Soviet communism to disenchantment with the latter as well as with Indian communist practices and a shift to democratic socialism, followed by disenchantment with party politics and a shift to constructive social work and moral criticism of political authority and, finally, disillusionment with the pace and effectiveness of Sarvodaya and a call for total revolution in the moral, economic, and social bases of society through struggle, including mass movements when necessary.

During his years of retirement from active politics J. P. sought nevertheless to influence government policy and public opinion through his prolific writings on contemporary political issues, domestic and international; through public speeches and exhortations to the country's political leaders; and by offering his services as an impartial negotiator. He was also active in organizing relief activities in times of disaster and catastrophe, such as during the 1966–7 Bihar famine.

However, Narayan's most important and dramatic single contribution to his country's history occurred between 1974 and 1977, when he emerged from political retirement to lead the developing movement of opposition in different parts of the country to what he considered to be the dictatorial leadership of the prime minister, Indira Gandhi, and the debasement of politics which had occurred during the previous decade as the Indian National Congress became increasingly corrupted and its members sycophantically dependent upon Mrs Gandhi, her family, and her political entourage. It was at this time also that he gave his new call for a 'total revolution'. He was detained along with most other opposition leaders and many thousands of activists during the two-year emergency authoritarian regime imposed by Mrs Gandhi between 1975 and 1977. Despite broken health from confinement, he lived long enough to play a central role in forging the opposition unity which made possible the defeat of Mrs Gandhi and the Indian National Congress in the 1977 parliamentary elections, and the restoration of the basic features of the previous parliamentary system by the Janata government which succeeded hers. Jayaprakash Narayan survived, melancholy at the disintegration of the Janata Party and government in July 1979, in ill health and on dialysis, until his death, in Patna, on 8 October 1979.　　　　　　　　　　　　　　　　PAUL R. BRASS

Sources J. Narayan, *Towards total revolution*, 4 vols. (1978) · A. Scarfe and W. Scarfe, *J. P.: his biography* (1975) · B. Prasad, *Jayaprakash Narayan: quest and legacy* (1992) · J. Narayan, *Towards a new society* (1958) · *Prison diary: Jayaprakash Narayan*, ed. A. B. Shah (1977) · *A revolutionary's quest: selected writings of Jayaprakash Narayan*, ed. B. Prasad (1980) · *J. P.'s jail life (a collection of personal letters)* (1977) · N. Prasad, ed., *JP and social change* (1992) · J. Narayan, *Why socialism?* (1936)

Archives Nehru Museum, New Delhi | Nehru Museum, New Delhi, Brahmanand MSS

Narayan, Rahasya Rudra [Rudy] (1938–1998), barrister and civil rights activist, was born on 11 May 1938 in British Guiana, the ninth of ten children of Sase Narayan, landowner, and his wife, Taijbertie. He came from a politically active Indo-Guyanese family, engaged mainly in trading. He arrived in Britain in 1953 and after a series of menial jobs (including washing dishes at a Lyons' Corner House and working night shifts at a soap factory) joined the Royal Army Ordnance Corps. He left the army in 1965, after seven years' service, with the rank of sergeant. He then read for the bar, at Lincoln's Inn. There he helped to found the bar students' union; he became its first president and also captained the inns of court cricket club—a passion which never left him. He was called to the bar in 1968. On 5 September 1969 he married Dr Naseem Akbar (*b.* 1942/3), medical practitioner, and daughter of Mohamed Akbar, diplomat. They had two daughters, Sharmeen and Yasmeen.

In advocacy Narayan found his métier. He was a fluent, powerful, and persuasive speaker and, when he needed to be, a sound lawyer. He defended with remarkable success in a series of high-profile trials arising out of confrontations between black people and the police. But he encountered, like other black and ethnic minority barristers, the glass panel beyond which lay the steadier work and heavier briefs which were his due. After learning finally that clients who asked solicitors to brief him were being told he was not available, and angered at the apparent oversentencing of black defendants, Narayan went public. It is improbable that a more temperate assault on the legal establishment would even have been noticed; but Narayan's protest, loud and uncompromising, was not only noticed—it resulted in the first of the three disciplinary adjudications which finally drove him from the bar. This one, in 1974, for bringing the administration of justice into disrepute (by alleging that Birmingham solicitors, counsel, and judges were racist), was followed in 1980 by a reprimand for discourtesy to a judge. In 1982 he was

Rahasya Rudra [Rudy] **Narayan** (1938–1998), by Harry Kerr, 1983 [centre, with a group of his supporters in front of the High Court]

acquitted by the bar council of professional misconduct in issuing an extravagant press statement about the attorney-general and the director of public prosecutions (accusing them of 'collusion with the national front and fanning the flames of racial hatred'), though his accusations were found 'scandalous and contemptuous' and he was suspended for six weeks after being found guilty of four other, unrelated charges (*Daily Telegraph*, 30 June 1998). By then he had become an over-heavy drinker and was lashing out at the nearest target.

Narayan achieved high-profile successes in the trials arising out of the Bristol riots of 1980 and the Bradford petrol bomb case of 1982. Nevertheless in 1984 he was expelled from his chambers in the Inner Temple after assaulting the chambers' head, Sibghat Kadri, at a conference. He announced his intention of qualifying as a solicitor, but failed the Law Society examinations. Then, back at the bar, in 1988 he put himself in the wrong by accepting briefs in two contemporaneous trials. Although he attacked the all-white disciplinary tribunal which heard his case, he was suspended for two years (a fate, he asserted, which did not invariably await counsel who got themselves overbooked). In the following year he polled 177 votes standing as an independent in the Vauxhall by-election, in protest at the Labour Party's 'outrageous and blatant exclusion of black candidates for a constituency made safe for Labour by black votes' (*Daily Telegraph*, 30 June 1998).

His first marriage having ended in divorce, on 26 March 1988 Narayan married Saeeda Begum Shah (*b.* 1948/9), property dealer, and daughter of Fazal Karim Asif, advocate. This marriage, too, ended in divorce. In 1991 Narayan returned to Guyana, where little went his way. He returned to Britain three years later, an activist now without roots, an advocate turned demagogue, an anti-racialist stained with antisemitism, and now a terminal drinker. The series of disciplinary adjudications culminated in 1994 in his disbarment, for professional misconduct. In 1995 a minor riot followed his speech outside Brixton police station, following the death of a black man in custody. Narayan himself died at King's College Hospital,

Lambeth, London, on 28 June 1998, of cirrhosis of the liver. He was survived by the two daughters of his first marriage.

Narayan left behind him far more than a trail of failures. The Society of Black Lawyers, which he played a leading part in founding in 1973, remained as a necessary voice for an important professional minority. His books *Black Community on Trial* (1976), *Black England* (1977), *Barrister for the Defence* (1985), and *When Judges Conspire* (1989) may one day be revisited as more than memorials to his self-regard, though they are certainly that. The Lambeth Law Centre, of which he was the first chairman and where he held regular surgeries, survived him in a pivotal role in the south London community.

Above all, it was the waves made by a man who was too volatile and too intransigent ever to coast to success on them himself which in Narayan's lifetime began to erode the bar's and the legal system's self-assurance about racial discrimination. The setting up of the bar council's race relations committee in 1984, and the continued concern which produced an amendment of the Race Relations Act to outlaw race discrimination in the legal profession, and then, in 1995, the bar's own equality code, all owed something—possibly a good deal—to the attention which Narayan had drawn to a legal profession which had much to be embarrassed about. That he had done so extravagantly and intemperately, alienating many other ethnic minority lawyers on the way, may be less a criticism of him than an illustration of the fact that it tends to be only when an angry member of a disadvantaged group exposes him- or herself to fire that things begin to change. In his assault on the English legal system Narayan sacrificed his reputation, his practice, his bearings, and his health; but through the breach he made, younger black advocates have since passed.   STEPHEN SEDLEY

Sources *The Times* (30 June 1998) · *The Guardian* (30 June 1998) · *Daily Telegraph* (30 June 1998) · *The Independent* (6 July 1998) · private information (2004) · personal knowledge (2004) · m. certs. · d. cert. · *CGPLA Eng. & Wales* (1999)
Likenesses photograph, 1980, repro. in *Daily Telegraph* · H. Kerr, photograph, 1983, News International Syndication, London [*see illus.*] · photograph, repro. in *The Guardian* · photograph, repro. in *The Independent*
Wealth at death £2627—gross: administration with will, 27 Jan 1999, *CGPLA Eng. & Wales* · £0—net: administration with will, 27 Jan 1999, *CGPLA Eng. & Wales*

Narbeth, John Harper (1863–1944), naval architect, was born at Pembroke Dock, Wales, on 26 May 1863, the son of John Harper Narbeth and his wife, Anne Griffiths. He was the fourth child in a family of eight children. His father, after serving at Pembroke dockyard as a shipwright apprentice and writer, became a timber merchant.

Narbeth's interest in the sea began at an early age, and his pastimes of boating and yachting led him to study the behaviour and designs of ships and small craft. He was indentured as shipwright apprentice at the dockyard in 1877, and in 1882, after a competitive examination, took a course of higher training at the Royal Naval College, Greenwich. Three years later he was appointed to the

Royal Corps of Naval Constructors, and became an assistant constructor at Portsmouth Dockyard. In 1888 he married Aquila Elizabeth (*d.* 1931), daughter of W. J. Anstey, foreman shipwright, of Portsmouth. They had two sons, one of whom, John Harper Narbeth, also became a chief constructor at the Admiralty.

In 1887 Narbeth was transferred to the staff of William H. White, director of naval construction at the Admiralty. After demonstrating his skill at design work he was eventually entrusted with the preparation of warship designs of gradually increasing size and importance, ultimately resulting in three types of battleship: *King Edward VII* class (of which eight ships were built), *Lord Nelson* class, and, most famous of all, the *Dreadnought*. These ships were described by him in a paper read in 1922 before the Institution of Naval Architects. All were larger and more powerful than their forerunners. The *Dreadnought* also embodied revolutionary changes recommended by a powerful committee over which Sir John Fisher had presided. They included an armament of all big guns, higher speed, turbine propulsion, and underwater protection. Sir Philip Watts, who had succeeded White at the Admiralty and was a member of the committee, prepared, with Narbeth's assistance, a number of alternative designs; the Board of Admiralty selected one which became the *Dreadnought*. Narbeth completed the detailed design, finding solutions to the many problems encountered with such an innovative vessel.

On promotion in 1912 to be a chief constructor, health reasons prompted Narbeth to request a change of duties, and he was made directly responsible to the director for the design and construction of minor war vessels; these included high-speed motor boats, oil-carrying ships, mine-sweepers, and sloops. He made improvements in the design of each of these widely differing types of vessel. He became joint secretary to the royal commission on fuel and engines under the chairmanship of Fisher. During the First World War Narbeth designed the *Flower*-class sloops, with special design measures and procedures to allow for these vessels and mine-sweepers to be built in large numbers in small shipyards in record time.

Improvements in aircraft during and after the war and their widening use in warfare led to demands from the navy for special ships to carry them. Sir Eustace Tennyson-D'Eyncourt, who had succeeded Watts as director, arranged for Narbeth, who from 1919 was assistant director, to deal with the new designs involved. A few seaplane carriers were first obtained by modifying merchant ships: then, by converting warships, notably the fast battle cruisers of *Courageous* class, carriers were produced with a deck suitable for landing or launching aircraft. Narbeth again contributed many innovative ideas to these projects, and worked closely with a joint Admiralty and Air Ministry technical committee over which he presided (1918–23), resulting in ships which when completed were satisfactory to pilots and naval officers alike.

Narbeth retired in 1923. He was remembered for having an absolute fearlessness in confronting authority on matters of principle and a complete stubbornness if he believed he was right. In later years he became regarded as the 'father' of the Institution of Naval Architects. His services were recognized by appointment as MVO (1906), CBE (1920), and CB (1923). During his retirement he qualified as a Methodist local preacher. He died at 63 Elmbridge Road, Gloucester, on 19 May 1944 and was cremated on 23 May.

L. WOOLLARD, rev. MARC BRODIE

Sources *The Times* (23 May 1944) • L. Woolard, *Shipbuilder and Marine Engine-Builder*, 51 (1944), 274–5 • *Shipbuilder and Marine Engine-Builder*, 51 (1944), 258 • J. T. Sumida, *In defence of naval supremacy: finance, technology and British naval policy, 1889–1914* (1989) • *CGPLA Eng. & Wales* (1944) • personal knowledge (1959)

Likenesses photograph, repro. in Woolard, *Shipbuilder and Marine Engine-Builder*, 274

Wealth at death £2441 10s. 1d.: probate, 8 Nov 1944, *CGPLA Eng. & Wales*

Narbonne, Pierre-Rémi (1806–1839), Canadian *patriote* and rebel, was born at St Rémi, Lower Canada, of an old French-Canadian family. A painter and later a county bailiff, he took an active part in the events leading to the uprising in Lower Canada in 1837 and, despite having lost an arm in childhood, became one of the military leaders of the rebellion. He was among the *patriotes* defeated at St Charles-sur-Richelieu on 23 November 1837, but managed to escape to the United States, where he joined a band of *patriotes* in exile. He helped recruit volunteers for the Association des Frères-Chasseurs, a secret *patriote* army with lodges throughout Lower Canada, making his recruits solemnly swear that they would slit the throat of magistrate François Languedoc, who had arrested him on 7 November 1837. He crossed into Canada with a band of *patriotes* in 1838, but was driven back by loyalists at Moore's Corner (St Armand Station) on 28 February 1838. With other *patriotes* he made another attack on Canada in March 1838 and was taken prisoner at St Eustache, 19 miles from Montreal, and brought a captive to St Jean-sur-Richelieu.

Narbonne was released from prison in July under the amnesty by which Lord Durham, the high commissioner, hoped to pacify the region, but found his wife dead and his old employment as a county bailiff closed to him as a rebel, leaving him and his three children destitute. He joined the *patriote* army being organized from the United States by Robert Nelson and Cyrille-Hector-Octave Côté in the autumn of 1838 and took part in a number of raids on Canadian territory, but was captured at the defeat of the *patriotes* at Odelltown on 9 November 1838. He was taken to Montreal and sentenced to death for high treason. On 15 February 1839 he was hanged at Montreal gaol, together with the *patriotes* Chevalier de Lorimer, Amable Dumais, François Nicolas, and Charles Hindenlang. Narbonne's hanging was bungled; he was dropped three times before he died.

ELIZABETH BAIGENT

Sources *DCB*, vol. 7 • J. Schull, *Rebellion: the rising in French Canada, 1837* (1970) • H. Taft Manning, *The revolt of French Canada* (1962) • *DNB*

Wealth at death destitute in 1837: Schull, *Rebellion*, 185

Narbrough, Sir John (*bap.* 1640, *d.* 1688), naval officer, was baptized at Cockthorpe, Norfolk, on 11 October 1640, the fifth child of Gregory Narbrough. Nothing is known of his

early life, but tradition suggests that the family was related to that of Sir Christopher Myngs (*bap.* 1625, *d.* 1666) and that Narbrough began his seagoing career as Myngs's cabin-boy. Narbrough served in merchant ships in the 1650s and early 1660s, taking two voyages to St Helena and one to Guinea, as well as spending two years in the Mediterranean. He served under Myngs in the West Indies in 1657–61. His first commission was as lieutenant of Myngs's *Portland* from October 1664 to January 1665, and his career then largely mirrored that of Myngs through the 1665 campaign, with lieutenancies successively in the *Royal Oak*, the *Triumph* (in which he fought at the battle of Lowestoft on 3 June 1665), the *Royal James*, the *Old James*, and the *Fairfax*. On 10 April 1666 he became lieutenant of the *Victory*, in which Myngs was flying his flag as vice-admiral of the Red squadron. Narbrough fought in her during the Four Days' Battle (1–4 June), taking command when Myngs was mortally wounded. His skilful manoeuvring of the *Victory* and her seconds, effectively occupying a large proportion of the Dutch fleet, brought him to the attention of the joint admirals, Prince Rupert and the duke of Albemarle. He was given his first captain's commission, for the *Assurance*, on 9 June 1666, commanding her at the St James's day fight on 25 June. Narbrough remained in command of the *Assurance* in 1667, taking her to the West Indies as part of the squadron under Sir John Harman which was intended to counter the Franco-Dutch forces in that area. Narbrough fought in the engagement at Martinique in June 1667 and was wounded in the thigh during the attack on Surinam (7 October). Harman gave him a new command, the *Bonadventure*, on 29 October 1667 and he remained in command of her until October 1668.

On 15 May 1669 Narbrough was commissioned captain of the *Sweepstakes*, intended for a voyage to establish English trading links in South America and the Pacific. His journal for the voyage bears witness to his high degree of technical competence, his concern for his crew's welfare, and his genuine interest in the lands and peoples he saw: he sympathized with the native inhabitants of Peru, observing that 'the poor miserable Indians groans under their heavy burden' (Centre for Kentish Studies, MS U.1515/O.3, 17 Dec 1670). At Valdivia in Peru he was forced by the governor to leave behind his lieutenant and three others as hostages, an action for which he was subsequently criticized. The *Sweepstakes* returned to England in June 1671. When the Third Anglo-Dutch War began in 1672 Narbrough was lieutenant of the duke of York's flagship, the *Royal Prince*, becoming captain on 28 May during the battle of Sole Bay, when her original captain, Sir John Cox, was killed. Narbrough commanded the *Fairfax* over the winter of 1672–3, convoying trade to and from the Mediterranean; his delayed return cost him the post of rear-admiral of the blue, which had been intended for him but was given instead to Thomas Butler, earl of Ossory. Narbrough was Ossory's flag captain in the *Saint Michael* from July to September 1673, and played a prominent part in the battle of the Texel (11 August). Narbrough finally obtained his flag on 17 September 1673, when he became rear-admiral of the red with the *Henrietta* as his flagship; he was knighted at Whitehall on the 30th of the same month.

Attacks on English shipping by north African corsairs forced the government of Charles II to send large squadrons into the Mediterranean on a regular basis, and on 18 October 1674 Narbrough was commissioned to command such a force, still flying his flag in the *Henrietta*. His objective was to obtain a peace with Tripoli, and he maintained a blockade of that port throughout 1675. Narbrough moved to the *Harwich* in December 1675, employing her as his flagship on 14 January 1676 during a bold attack on four ships in Tripoli harbour itself (an attack commanded by his lieutenant and Norfolk protégé Cloudesley Shovell), and subsequently during a successful engagement at sea with another four major Tripolitine warships. Narbrough signed a treaty with Tripoli on 5 March 1676 and returned to England in September. He then married on 9 April 1677 Elizabeth Calmady (*d.* 1678), having courted her in 1676 by correspondence from the Mediterranean. Hostilities with Algiers resumed almost immediately and Narbrough received another commission to command in the Mediterranean on 30 June 1677, this time with the *Plymouth* as his flagship, and was given the title of admiral by a commission of 15 February 1678. The change in status reflected the expansion of his fleet from eight vessels to thirty-five, but despite these numbers Narbrough had little success. The strength of the Algerine forces, and his own difficulties with supplying and refitting his ships, made it difficult to pursue an effective strategy, and Narbrough's decision to place his fleet before Algiers in impressive shows of force has been criticized for diverting ships from more directly useful defence of convoys. Narbrough's fleet returned to England in the summer of 1679 and was paid off.

His first wife having died on 1 January 1678, Narbrough married on 20 June 1681 Elizabeth Hill (*d.* 1732), whose father was later a commissioner of the navy. Narbrough moved to the estate at Knowlton, Kent, which he bought with his second wife's dowry, the proceeds of prize money, and his income from 'good voyages' (the practice of carrying bullion in warships, which earned the commanders one per cent of the value). Narbrough held no further major seagoing post, serving instead as a commissioner of the navy, a position which he had obtained in 1676 and retained until his death.

From 1682 onwards Narbrough's life was taken up primarily with plans for an expedition to the West Indies to salvage the allegedly vast cargo of treasure in the wreck of the *Nuestra Senora de la Concepçion*, lost in 1641, of which he had first learned when serving with Myngs in the area in the 1650s. Narbrough promoted and partly financed a salvage project put forward by the New Englander William Phips, and after gaining £21,766 from Phips's first successful visit to the wreck in January 1687, Narbrough himself took command of a far larger expedition, for which the king provided the royal warship *Foresight*. Narbrough sailed in September 1687 and reached the wreck site in mid-December. However, others had already been plundering the site and the returns were disappointing. By April 1688 the divers were barely bringing up a pound of silver a day, and by the start of May sickness had set in aboard the *Foresight*. Narbrough himself caught the fever on the 18th and died in the morning of the 27th. He was buried at sea, but his bowels were brought back to Knowlton and buried there.

By his will, dated 26 August 1687, Narbrough made over his four estates in Kent, including Knowlton, to his elder son, John, and cash bequests totalling £25,000 to his three children, John, James, and Elizabeth. After Narbrough's death, the four-year-old John Narbrough was created a baronet, while Cloudesley Shovell married Narbrough's widow, Elizabeth, and took Sir John's sons into the navy under his command. All of them perished when Shovell's flagship, the *Association*, was wrecked on the Isles of Scilly in 1707.

Narbrough was one of the most popular senior officers of his day. His genuine concern for his men's well-being, both in terms of their health and securing the pay to which they were entitled, made many enthusiastic to serve him. His extensive surviving journals and letters also reveal him to have been a highly competent navigator, a deeply religious individual, a resourceful commander of a ship in battle, but also a man always searching for opportunities to enrich himself, and in that sense the manner of his death seems highly appropriate.

J. D. DAVIES

Sources F. E. Dyer, *The life of Admiral Sir John Narbrough* (1931) · CKS, Romney of the Mote MS U.1515 [relating to Narbrough and Sir Cloudesley Shovell] · P. Earle, *The wreck of the 'Almiranta': Sir William Phips and the search for the Hispaniola treasure* (1979) · R. C. Anderson, ed., *Journals and narratives of the Third Dutch War*, Navy RS, 86 (1946) · S. R. Hornstein, *The Restoration navy and English foreign trade, 1674–1688: a study in the peacetime use of sea power* (1991) · PRO, PROB 11/392, fols. 321–4 · J. Narbrough, letter-book, 1687–8, NMM, LBK/1 · copies of letters by Narbrough, NMM, CLU/7–8 · J. D. Davies, *Gentlemen and tarpaulins: the officers and men of the Restoration navy* (1991) · notes on genealogies of Narbrough and Shovell, NMM, MAT, Marsham-Townshend MSS · Narbrough's letters to Sir Henry Sheres, BL, Add. MS 19872 · J. S. Corbett, *England in the Mediterranean: a study of the rise and influence of British power within the straits, 1603–1713*, 2 vols. (1904) · F. L. Fox, *A distant storm: the Four Days battle of 1666* (1996) · G. E. Aylmer, 'Slavery under Charles II: the Mediterranean and Tangier', *EngHR*, 114 (1999), 378–88 · R. Marsham, 'The death of Sir John Narbrough', *N&Q*, 7th ser., 6 (1888), 502–3 · parish register, Cockthorpe, Norfolk, 11 Oct 1640 [baptism]

Archives CKS, corresp., journals, and MSS, U.1515 · NMM, letter-book, LBK/1 · NMM, naval journals, JOD/3 · BL, Add. MS 19872 · Magd. Cam., Pepys MSS · NMM, CLU/7,8 · PRO, ADM MSS

Likenesses P. Lely?, portrait, priv. coll.; repro. in Fox, *Distant storm*, 298

Wealth at death left £5000 and four manors in Kent (Knowlton, Northcote, Southcote, and Sandown) to eldest son; £10,000 to second son; £10,000 to daughter; £100 to only surviving sister; £50 to each of her children and to those of two deceased sisters; 'jewels' to wife: will, PRO, PROB 11/392, fols. 321–4; Dyer, *Life*, 241–2

Nares, Edward (1762–1841), historian and writer, was born in London on 26 March 1762, the third and youngest son of Sir George *Nares (1716–1786) of Warbrook House, Eversley, Hampshire, a justice of the court of common pleas, and his wife, Mary (1726–1782), daughter of Sir John *Strange, master of the rolls.

Nares was admitted on 9 July 1770 to Westminster School, which he left in 1779. He matriculated at Christ Church, Oxford, on 22 March 1779, and graduated BA in 1783, and MA in 1789. Nares took some time to decide on a career, travelled at home and abroad, and wrote light verse such as 'The Ballooniad', a 1000-line mock epic of 1784. He also enjoyed a varied social life, taking part in amateur theatricals at Blenheim Palace and becoming a favourite of the fourth duke of Marlborough's daughters. On 2 August 1788 he was elected a fellow of Merton College, Oxford, acting as sub-warden in 1793 and bursar in 1794. He eventually took holy orders, being ordained deacon (June 1792) and priest (30 December) by Bishop Smallwell of Oxford; Merton presented him to the college living of St Peter-in-the-East, Oxford, in November 1793.

Nares married into the Marlborough family on 16 April 1797. His bride was Lady Georgina Charlotte Spencer-Churchill (1770–1802), the duke's third daughter. Her parents were opposed to the match. None of the bride's relatives was present at the service in Henley-on-Thames, and Nares and his wife were never invited to Blenheim again. Having given up his fellowship Nares was nominated by the archbishop of Canterbury to the valuable rectory of Biddenden, Kent, in 1798, which he held until death. He was mainly resident there, and took his pastoral duties seriously; he increased communicant numbers and preached without condescension to his flock (see his *Sermons Composed for Country Congregations* of 1803). Lady Georgina Nares died after less than six years of marriage, at Bath on 15 January 1802, and was buried in the Marlborough family vault at Ardley, Oxfordshire. Nares married again on 30 June 1803; his second wife was Cordelia, second daughter of Thomas Adams (*d.* 1807), of Swift's Place, Cranbrook, Kent. Nares had children from both his marriages.

Nares was an accomplished scholar with expertise in several areas. In theology he issued anonymously *An attempt to show how far the notion of the plurality of worlds is consistent with the scriptures* in July 1801. He was Bampton lecturer in 1805, publishing his lectures as *View of the Evidences of Christianity at the Close of the Pretended Age of Reason* (1805), a text at once prescribed for ordination candidates by Bishop Porteus of London. Nares was select preacher to the University of Oxford in 1807, 1814, and 1825. He had a wide-ranging fund of geological knowledge and was a friend and regular correspondent of Jean André Deluc, one of the most important proponents of physico-theology at the end of the eighteenth century and resident at Windsor. Nares's interest was reflected in *Man as Known to Us Theologically and Geologically* (1834); it includes his thinking on Hutton's *Theory of the Earth*. 'I dispute none of their [geologists'] discoveries', he wrote, 'but I question many of the conclusions they are disposed to draw from them, and think them mistaken in a variety of ways' (p. 274). Nares was not afraid to become involved in theological controversy, and defended Athanasian orthodoxy

vigorously in his many published single sermons, as his *A letter to the Rev. Francis Stone, M.A. … in reply to his sermon preached at the visitation at Danbury on 8 July 1806* (1807). There were more extensive discussions in *Remarks on the Version of the New Testament Lately Edited by the Unitarians* (1810), and *Discourses on the Three Creeds and on the Homage Offered to our Saviour* (1819). He also reviewed widely, mainly in the *British Critic* and the *Theological Review*. Nares acted as editor of the former from 1793 to 1814.

With support from Dean Cyril Jackson, Lord Liverpool recommended Nares as regius professor of modern history in 1813, and he filled the post conscientiously for more than a decade until poor student attendance and his own disappointed ambition got the better of him. The duties were, by contemporary standards, quite onerous. He was required to deliver at least twenty lectures in either the Michaelmas (autumn) or Hilary (spring) terms, give an annual public lecture, and pay for two teachers of modern languages from his salary. His publications took a suitably historical turn in the 1820s, and they reflected his intelligent conservatism. In 1822 he added a third volume to Lord Woodhouselee's *Elements of General History, Ancient and Modern*, bringing the compilation down to 1820. He supplied in 1824 a series of historical prefaces for an issue of the Bible, 'embellished by the most eminent British artists' (3 vols.), and he contributed a preface to an edition of Burnet's *History of the Reformation* (1829). His best-known work was his monumental three-volume *Memoirs of the Life and Administration of the Right Honourable William Cecil, Lord Burghley*, published between 1828 and 1831. They were famously and caustically reviewed by Macaulay in the April 1832 number of the *Edinburgh Review*.

Nares was a gifted humorist as well as an academic. He produced anonymously *Thinks-I-to myself: a Serio-Ludicro, Tragico-Comico Tale, Written by Thinks-I-to myself who?* (2 vols., 1811) and, encouraged by nine reprints within twelve months, followed it with *I Says, Says I: a Novel, by Thinks-I-to myself* (2 vols., 1812). Both texts were appreciated for their wry account of domestic life of the well-off in the early nineteenth century. Equally quirky was *Heraldic Anomalies, by it Matters Not Who* (2 vols., 1823), published anonymously and erroneously ascribed to Archdeacon Wrangham in the British Library catalogue. In his lifetime, his titles were often attributed to his cousin Archdeacon Nares.

Edward Nares tried hard after he was sixty to relinquish his professorship, and was asking Liverpool for alternative preferment from 1821 onwards. He was no more successful in a bid for the wardenship of Merton in 1826 than in securing the Lady Margaret professorship of divinity in 1827, but received the additional living of Newchurch, Kent, the same year. As he told Peel ruefully in 1834, he felt he had been overlooked because, unlike other professors, he lived in a 'country living, out of sight' (BL, Add. MS 40407, fol. 150, 23 Dec). Peel was unmoved, and Nares gave his last lecture the following year. Nares also acted as proctor in convocation from 1812 to 1841. He died at Biddenden on 23 July 1841 and was buried at Biddenden parish church. Nares was a vivacious and likeable individual, who loved society but never overcame his diffidence in it, and whose scholarship and wit were inadequately recognized both in his lifetime and posthumously. His harsh verdict on himself in the 1820s was, 'I had never much worldly wisdom, or worldly prudence' (manuscript autobiography). NIGEL ASTON

Sources GM, 1st ser., 67 (1797), 349 · GM, 1st ser., 72 (1802), 93 · GM, 1st ser., 73 (1803), 689 · GM, 1st ser., 77 (1807) · GM, 2nd ser., 16 (1841), 435–6 · J. Welch, A list of scholars of St Peter's College, Westminster (1788), 405 · Foster, Alum. Oxon. · Fasti Angl., 1541–1857, [Canterbury], 530 · Nichols, Illustrations, 7.614, 634–5 · N&Q, 2nd ser., 9 (1860), 230 · N&Q, 5th ser., 9 (1878), 53–4, 275 · N&Q, 8th ser., 2 (1892), 91–2 · N&Q, 12th ser., 1 (1916), 69, 117 · G. C. White, A versatile professor: reminiscences of the Rev. Edward Nares, D. D. (1903) · G. V. Cox, Recollections of Oxford, 2nd edn (1870), 9, 152 · M. Soames, The profligate duke: George Spencer-Churchill, fifth duke of Marlborough, and his duchess (1987) · T. Besterman, ed., The publishing firm of Cadell & Davies (1938) · J. Black, 'A Georgian fellow of Merton: the historian Edward Nares', Postmaster (1987), 53–9 · J. Black, 'A Regency regius: the historian Edward Nares', Oxoniensia, 52 (1987), 173–8 · J. Black, 'A Williamite reprobate? Edward Nares and the investigation of his failure in 1832 to deliver his lectures', Oxoniensia, 53 (1988), 337–40 · autobiography, 2 vols., Merton Oxf., MS E.2.42 · d. cert. · BL, Add. MS 40407, fol. 150
Archives Bodl. Oxf., notebook · GS Lond., geological MSS · Merton Oxf., autobiography, MS E.2.42 · Merton Oxf., corresp., MS F.2.7 · Wellcome L., commonplace book | BL, corresp. with Sir Robert Peel, Add. MSS 40367, 40380, 40407 · BL, G. C. White MSS, Add. MS 31022, fols. 94, 96, 98 · BL, G. C. White MSS, Add. MS 40407, fols. 150, 152, 280 · BL, G. C. White MSS, Add. MS 50261, fols. 71–159b · LPL, corresp. with Cadell and Davies, MS 1801
Likenesses silhouette, c.1790, Merton Oxf., MS E.2.39

Nares, Sir George (1716–1786), judge, was born at Hanwell, Middlesex, the younger son of George Nares of Albury, Oxfordshire, steward to the second and third earls of Abingdon and brother of James *Nares, the composer. He was educated at Magdalen College School, Oxford, and at New College, Oxford. He was admitted to the Inner Temple on 19 October 1738, and was called to the bar on 12 June 1741. He practised mainly in the criminal courts, and defended at the Old Bailey Timothy Murphy, convicted of forgery in 1753, and Elizabeth Canning, convicted of perjury in 1754. In 1751 Nares married Mary (1726/7–1782), daughter of Sir John Strange, master of the rolls. They had three sons and four daughters: their youngest son, Edward *Nares, was regius professor of modern history at Oxford from 1813 to 1841.

Nares was created a serjeant-at-law in 1759, and was a king's serjeant from 1759 to 1771. Between 1763 and 1770 he was one of the counsel for the crown in several of the cases arising out of the warrant issued against the author, publisher, and printers of no. 45 of the North Briton. At the general election in March 1768 he was elected MP for the city of Oxford, with the support of the duke of Marlborough, and soon afterwards he was appointed recorder of Oxford. He supported the government over the expulsion of Wilkes on 3 February 1769, for which he was caricatured as Serjeant Circuit in Samuel Foote's comedy The Lame Lover (1770).

In 1771 Nares was appointed a justice of the common pleas, and was knighted in the same year. Oxford University awarded him a DCL in 1773. Nares died at Ramsgate on 20 July 1786, and was buried at Eversley, Hampshire, where there is a monument to his memory.

G. F. R. BARKER, rev. ANNE PIMLOTT BAKER

Sources Foss, Judges, 8.348–9 · A. W. B. Simpson, ed., Biographical dictionary of the common law (1984) · Baker, Serjeants, 528 · HoP, Commons · GM, 1st ser., 56 (1786), 622 · Foster, Alum. Oxon.
Archives Free Library of Philadelphia, cases and opinions
Likenesses W. Dickinson, mezzotint, pubd 1776 (after H. Hone), BM, NPG

Nares, Sir George Strong (bap. 1831, d. 1915), Arctic explorer, was born at Clytha, Monmouthshire, and baptized on 22 May 1831 at the nearby church of St Bridget, Llansanffraid, the third son and sixth child of Commander William Henry Nares RN (1788/9–1867) and his first wife, Elizabeth Rebecca Gould (1796/7–1836), daughter of John Dodd, of Redbourn, Hertfordshire. He entered the navy in 1845 from the Royal Naval School, New Cross, as prize cadet. After serving as a midshipman in HMS Canopus, Nares joined the Havannah on the Australian station, 1848–51. He showed courage in the attempted rescue of a man overboard. The future hydrographer G. H. Richards, a passenger in the Havannah on her return voyage, suggested, when Nares was looking for work after passing the lieutenant's examination early in 1852, that he apply to join the Franklin search expedition preparing to sail under Sir Edward Belcher. Nares was appointed mate on HMS Resolute. From winter quarters at Dealy Island, to the south of Melville Island, he took part in several sledge journeys.

After returning to England in 1854 Nares was promoted lieutenant and specialized in gunnery. He served for two years in the Mediterranean in the Conqueror before joining the staff of the training ship Illustrious in 1858. On 22 June in the same year he married Mary (d. 1905), eldest daughter of William Grant, banker of Portsmouth. They had four sons and six daughters. The Illustrious was succeeded by the larger Britannia in 1859. Nares wrote The Naval Cadet's Guide (1860) which, under the title Seamanship, ran to several editions and was regarded as the best such manual of its day. In 1862 he was promoted to commander and in September 1863 took command of the training ship Boscawen.

In July 1865, Nares's seagoing career took a further turn with his appointment to the paddle steamer Salamander on the east coast of Australia. His duties there included surveying. In 1868 he took command of the Newport for hydrographical work in the Mediterranean, which included a survey of the Gulf of Suez via the Suez Canal (opened November 1869). He was promoted to captain in December 1869. In the Shearwater (1871–2) he did similar work, including oceanographic research on the Gibraltar currents in collaboration with W. B. Carpenter. It was this work that led to Nares's appointment as captain of HMS Challenger, a steam-assisted corvette of 2306 tons dispatched by the government in December 1872 on a three-year voyage of circumnavigation devoted to oceanographic exploration.

Sir George Strong Nares (*bap.* 1831, *d.* 1915), by Stephen Pearce, 1877

Nares commanded this influential expedition, the first to undertake systematic investigation of the deep ocean for scientific purposes, for two years. His officers were all naval surveyors, and there was also a team of civilian scientists, led by Charles Wyville Thomson, on board. The methods employed to sample the life and conditions of the deep sea owed much to surveying techniques recently developed in connection with submarine telegraphy, and the expedition's work had practical as well as scientific objectives. The first year was spent in the Atlantic. Early in 1874, between Cape Town and Australia, the *Challenger* made a southerly detour, calling at Marion, Kerguelen, and Heard islands, and continuing to 66°40′ S, 78°22′ E, before being turned back by ice—being the first steam vessel to cross the Antarctic circle. The dredging of glaciated rock fragments in the deep-sea muds helped in the revival of interest in geographical exploration of Antarctic regions towards the end of the century.

Nares's leadership was an important factor in the expedition's success. The arduous and repetitive nature of the deep-sea operations, and the potential conflicts of interest between the different sections of the shipboard community on such a voyage, could have led to friction but he was perceived as a fair as well as a firm commander. The smooth running of the project made it possible for the new Conservative government to recall him in November 1874, when the expedition still had 18 months to run, to lead the British Arctic expedition of 1875–6, in the vessels *Alert* and *Discovery*, the chief aim of which was to reach the north pole. Reports of the American expeditions of Isaac Israel Hayes, 1860–61, and C. F. Hall, 1870–73, had revived

the belief in an open polar sea and suggested that land extended far to the north, west of Robeson Channel. Both these theories proved to be wrong, but at the time they indicated the Smith Sound route as the best line of advance to the pole. The vessels sailed on 29 May 1875 and reached winter quarters on the coast of Grinnell Land (Ellesmere Island), the *Discovery* in latitude 81°44′ N., and the *Alert*, with Nares, in latitude 82°27′ N 'the most northerly point hitherto reached in the Canadian Arctic' (Levere, 281). The following spring sledge parties were sent out. That led by Lieutenant Pelham Aldrich of the *Alert* explored the north coast of Ellesmere Island westwards. They reached its most northerly point (Cape Columbia) and continued to Cape Alfred Ernest (Alert Point) before turning back, having charted some 400 km of new coastline (Hattersley-Smith, 121). Lieutenant Lewis A. Beaumont of the *Discovery* followed the coast of Greenland northwards to Sherard Osborn Fjord. Meanwhile, a party led by Commander A. H. Markham of the *Alert* struck out over the ice in an attempt to get to the pole. They reached 83°20′ N, a heroic achievement considering that the pack ice was extremely rough, and also drifting south almost as fast as they were travelling northwards. Their experience and an outbreak of scurvy affecting both ships led Nares to call off the entire expedition and return home early, in the late summer of 1876.

This was a morally courageous action which undoubtedly prevented further loss of life. Nares was a humane man, but acting within the rigid structures of the Victorian navy. When one of the sub-lieutenants shot a seal (a vital source of fresh food for the scurvy sufferers) he 'was reprimanded by Nares for disturbing the ship's company at divine service. However, he was later congratulated in the wardroom by the captain on his marksmanship' (Hattersley-Smith, 124). It would be unfair to blame Nares alone for mistakes in planning the expedition, though he was responsible for the low priority given to scientific work (perhaps a reflection of his experiences in the *Challenger*.) In spite of this, valuable scientific as well as geographical results had been obtained. Nares wrote a narrative of the expedition, *A Voyage to the Polar Sea* (1878).

An Admiralty committee of inquiry subsequently blamed Nares for the outbreak of scurvy, on the grounds that the sledging parties had not been carrying lime juice. That this was due to the logistical difficulties involved was in their eyes no excuse. In spite of this slur on his competence, which was unfair in that the expedition's experience did not bear out this over-simplistic conclusion, Nares, who had been elected FRS in 1875, was created KCB in 1876, and received the founder's medal of the Royal Geographical Society in 1877 and a gold medal from the Geographical Society of Paris in 1879. In 1878 he was again in command of the *Alert* during the survey of the Strait of Magellan. From 1879 to 1896 he was employed in the harbour department of the Board of Trade, having retired from active service in 1886. From 1896 to 1910 he was a conservator of the River Mersey. He was promoted rear-admiral in 1887 and vice-admiral in 1892.

Nares was an able and conscientious naval officer who

wished to rise in the service. His search for promising openings, rather than great personal enthusiasm for science and exploration, explains the several changes in direction taken by his naval career, but he contributed to both, especially through his competent leadership of the *Challenger* expedition, whose findings presented the first substantial body of scientific information on the interior of the ocean. As a young officer he had dark hair and beard, but began to go bald in his twenties. He was described as quiet and reserved, with an equable disposition, but also as a man of action, backed by 'sound sense and good judgment' (*GJ*, 257). Nares died at his home, 10 Uxbridge Road, Kingston upon Thames, Surrey, on 15 January 1915 and was buried in Long Ditton churchyard on 19 January. His name was given to Nares harbour in the Admiralty Islands, the Nares deep in the north Atlantic, Nares Land in northern Greenland, two capes in the Canadian Arctic, and Mount Nares in Victoria Land (Antarctica). The seaway dividing Ellesmere Island from Greenland is now called Nares Strait.

Two of Nares's sons entered the navy: Lieutenant George Edward Nares died in 1905; Vice-Admiral John Dodd Nares (1877–1957) became assistant hydrographer of the navy and director of the International Hydrographic Bureau at Monaco.

R. N. RUDMOSE BROWN, *rev.* MARGARET DEACON

Sources M. Deacon and A. Savours, 'Sir George Strong Nares (1831–1915)', *Polar Record*, 18 (1976–7), 127–41 · G. Hattersley-Smith, 'The British Arctic expedition, 1875–76', *Polar Record*, 18 (1976–7), 117–26 · [C. Markham], 'Vice-Admiral Sir George Strong Nares', *GJ*, 45 (1915), 255–7 · C. R. M. [C. Markham], *PRS*, 91A (1915), lii–liii · L. S. Dawson, *Memoirs of hydrography*, 2 vols. (1885), vol. 2, pp. 170–71 · O'Byrne, *Naval biog. dict.* · *The Times* (16 Jan 1915) · *Surbiton Times* (Jan 1915) · A. Savours and M. Deacon, 'Nutritional aspects of the British Arctic (Nares) expedition and its predecessors', *Starving sailors*, ed. J. Watt, E. J. Freeman, and W. F. Bynum (1981), 131–162 · T. H. Levere, *Science and the Canadian Arctic: a century of exploration, 1818–1918* (1993) · *H.M.S. Challenger, Reports of Capt G. S. Nares, Nos. 1–3* (1873–4) · G. S. Nares, *Report of the Arctic expedition of 1875–76* (1876) · T. H. Tizard, H. N. Moseley, J. Y. Buchanan, and J. Murray, 'Narrative of the cruise of H.M.S. *Challenger*', *Report on the scientific results of the voyage of H.M.S. Challenger during the years 1872–76*, 2 vols. (1885) · private information (2004) · parish register of St Bridget, Llansanffraid, Gwent RO · *IGI* · *CGPLA Eng. & Wales* (1915)
Archives NA Canada, MG 29 B12 · NMM, journal · NMM, log book, NA S/1 · Scott Polar RI, family corresp., MS 876 · Scott Polar RI, journal and notebooks, MS 554
Likenesses E. Whymper, woodcut, 1876, BM; repro. in T. Cooper, *Men of mark: a gallery of contemporary portraits* (1878) · S. Pearce, oils, 1877, NPG [*see illus.*] · Lock & Whitfield, woodburytype photograph, 1878, NPG · photographs, priv. coll.; copies, NMM · woodengraving, NPG; repro. in *ILN* (29 May 1875) · wood-engraving, NPG; repro. in *ILN* (20 May 1875) · wood-engraving, NPG; repro. in *ILN* (5 June 1875)
Wealth at death £581 14s. 9d.: probate, 29 April 1915, *CGPLA Eng. & Wales*

Nares, James (*bap.* 1715, *d.* 1783), composer and organist, was born at Stanwell, Middlesex, and baptized there on 19 April 1715, the elder son of George Nares and brother of Sir George *Nares, judge. The family moved to Albury, Oxfordshire, and he became a chorister in the Chapel Royal under William Croft and Bernard Gates, and later studied with John Christopher Pepusch. He was deputy

James Nares (*bap.* 1715, *d.* 1783), by William Ward, pubd 1788 (after John Hoppner and George Engleheart)

organist at St George's Chapel, Windsor, for a short time, and in 1734 was appointed organist of York Cathedral, which position he retained until he was appointed, through the influence of John Fountayne, dean of York, one of the organists and composers of the Chapel Royal in 1756. In 1757 he graduated MusD at Cambridge, and in the same year succeeded Bernard Gates as master of the children of the Chapel Royal. He retained that post until ill health compelled him to resign in 1780. He married, first Jane Pease (*b.* 1727?) in 1748. His second wife was Jane Bacon of York, with whom he had four children; the eldest, Robert *Nares, became a noted philologist.

Nares composed a considerable body of church music, little of it of any particular merit, but popular in its day and exhibiting a style that Watkins Shaw described as 'mellifluous, … if neither arresting nor individual' (*New Grove*). He made great use of the solo voice, and is perhaps best represented by his most famous anthem, 'The Souls of the Righteous'. He also wrote three sets of largely undistinguished harpsichord lessons, an ambitious but unsuccessful ode, *The Royal Pastoral* (*c.*1769), two treatises on singing, and one on playing the harpsichord or organ. Several secular works by Nares appear in E. T. Warren's *Collection of Catches, Canons and Glees* (1763–94). Nares died on 10 February 1783 in Great James Street, Westminster, and was buried in St Margaret's, Westminster. His widow survived him by forty years. J. C. HADDEN, *rev.* K. D. REYNOLDS

Sources W. Shaw, 'Nares, James', *New Grove* · *GM*, 1st ser., 53 (1783), 182 · R. Nares, 'Preface', in J. Nares, *Morning and evening service and six anthems* (1788) · Venn, *Alum. Cant.* · www.nares.net/james_nares_1715.htm, 10 June 2003 [website]

Likenesses T. Hardy, stipple, BM, NPG; repro. in *European Magazine* (1795) · W. Ward, stipple (after J. Hoppner and G. Engleheart), NPG; repro. in Nares, *Morning and evening service* [*see illus.*]

Nares, Robert (1753–1829), philologist and clergyman, was born on 9 June 1753 at York, one of the four children of James *Nares (*bap.* 1715, *d.* 1783), organist of York Minster, and his second wife, Jane Bacon of York. He was the nephew of Sir George Nares (1716–1786), the judge, and a cousin of Edward Nares (1762–1841), regius professor of modern history at Oxford University. The grandson of one of his cousins was Sir George Strong Nares (1831–1915), the Arctic explorer.

Nares was educated at Westminster School, and was made a king's scholar in 1767. In 1771 he was elected to a studentship at Christ Church, Oxford, where he graduated BA in 1775 and MA in 1778. His early career was that of tutor and writer. From 1779 to 1783 he acted as tutor to Watkin and Charles Williams Wynn, the young sons of Sir Watkins Williams Wynn and Lady Charlotte Wynn. He lived with them in London and at Wynnstay, their country house in Wrexham. At Wynnstay he was called upon to write various prologues and epilogues to the dramatic entertainments that were performed there. Having taken holy orders he was presented by his college to the living of Easton Maudit, Northamptonshire, in 1782, a position he held until 1805. From 1784 he embarked on a series of other clerical appointments (some sequential, some simultaneous), while engaging in tutoring and scholarly work.

In 1784 the lord chancellor granted Nares the living of Great Doddington, a few miles north of Easton Maudit; he remained there until 1796. In 1790 Nares assisted in the compilation of the first complete edition of John Bridges' *History and Antiquities of Northamptonshire*. From 1786 to 1788 he was usher at Westminster School, where he continued his tutoring of the Wynn boys, who had by now entered the school. In 1787 he was appointed chaplain to the duke of York, and from 1788 to 1803 he acted as assistant preacher at the Honourable Society of Lincoln's Inn. In 1796 he became vicar of Dalby, Leicestershire, and from 1798 to 1799 he was rector of Sharnford, Leicestershire. From 1798 until his death in 1829 he served as a canon residentiary of Lichfield Cathedral. In 1798 he was also made a prebendary of St Paul's Cathedral, London. From April 1801 until his death he was archdeacon of Stafford, an appointment for which he was best remembered by his contemporaries. From 1805 until 1818 he was vicar of St Mary's, Reading, and, from January 1818 until 1829, rector of All Hallows, London Wall.

Nares was married three times. His first wife, Elizabeth Bayley (1762?–1785), youngest daughter of Thomas Bayley of Chelmsford, died in childbirth. So too did his second wife, Frances Maria Fleetwood (1770–1794), daughter of Charles Fleetwood and Mary Fleetwood (*née* Herdes), of London. His third wife, the younger daughter of the Revd Dr Samuel Smith, headmaster of Westminster School, and his wife, Anna Jackson, survived him. There were no children of this marriage.

Several theological publications emanated from Nares's profession as clergyman. Noteworthy are the *Sermons* that he preached at Lincoln's Inn (1794), and the *Veracity of the Evangelists* (1816). He also edited William Vincent's *Sermons* (1817) and Richard Purdy's *Lectures on the Church Catechism* (1817). A separate interest was political science, particularly the events of the French Revolution. His *Principles of Government* (1792) is a contrastive evaluation of the British and French systems.

Nares became a member of the Natural History Society of London in 1791, and was elected a fellow of the Society of Antiquaries in 1795 and a fellow of the Royal Society in 1804. He was a founder of the Royal Society of Literature, and served as its vice-president in 1823. A major undertaking, in 1793, was his establishment of the periodical the *British Critic*; for twenty years he acted as its editor. In 1798, together with William Beloe and William Tooke, he revised the *General Biographical Dictionary*, being responsible for five of the volumes. Scholarly periodicals to which he contributed items on a variety of subjects included the *Gentleman's Magazine*, the *Classical Journal*, and the *Archaeologia*.

In 1795 Nares was appointed assistant librarian in the department of manuscripts at the British Museum in London, and was promoted to keeper of manuscripts in 1799. He edited the third volume of the *Catalogue of the Harleian Manuscripts in the British Museum*, which appeared in 1808, shortly after his demitting office as keeper in 1807.

Of Nares's numerous publications two have retained the significance which his contemporaries attributed to them. Both deal with linguistic matters. His *Glossary* (1822) is a vade-mecum for readers of Elizabethan literature, the aim being to provide explanations of particular 'words, phrases, names and allusions to customs, proverbs, etc' that might be encountered, especially in the writings of Shakespeare. Nares's work proved to be extremely valuable to the average reader, and it was reprinted several times during the course of the nineteenth century. His *Elements of Orthoepy*, the origins of which may owe something to his father's interest in the teaching of singing (about 1780 his father published *A Treatise on Singing*), was published in 1784. It was one of a number of works published during the last quarter of the eighteenth century (and later) which aimed to provide speakers, especially the linguistically insecure and those aspiring to middle-class status, with clear guidance on how certain words were to be pronounced. He drew particular attention to words in which the stress pattern was susceptible of variation, designating this area of vocabulary 'the most unstable part of the English language'. His list included such words as 'abdomen', 'aristocrat', 'balcony', 'controversy', 'illustrate', 'research', and 'vibrate'. The work was popular, but, inevitably, controversial. James Boswell, nevertheless, thought highly of it, considering it a 'work of uncommon merit and great utility', and claiming that he knew of no work which contained 'in the same compass, more learning, polite literature, sound sense, accuracy of arrangement, and perspicuity of expression' (Boswell, *Life*, 4.389 n. 6).

Nares died at his house, 22 Hart Street, Bloomsbury, London, on 23 March 1829. A monument, with a verse by William L. Bowles, was erected to his memory in St Stephen's Chapel in Lichfield Cathedral. It praises his 'unaffected piety and profound learning', his 'suavity of manners', 'kindness of heart', and 'every social virtue'.

W. W. Wroth, rev. M. K. C. MacMahon

Sources R. Nares, *A glossary or collection of words*, ed. J. O. Halliwell and T. Wright (1876) · P. D. Andersen, 'The life and works of James Nares', PhD diss., Washington University, 1968 · W. Jerdan, 'The Venerable Archdeacon Nares', *National portrait gallery of illustrious and eminent personages*, 2 (1831) · R. Nares, *Elements of orthoepy* (1784) · R. Nares, *A glossary, or, Collection of words* (1822) · M. K. C. MacMahon, 'Phonology', *The Cambridge history of the English language*, ed. R. M. Hogg, 4: 1776–1997, ed. S. Romaine (1998), 373–535 · R. Nares, *Principles of government* (1792) · R. Nares, *Sermons preached before the Honourable Society of Lincoln's Inn* (1794) · *A new biographical dictionary of 3000 cotemporary [sic] public characters, British and foreign, of all ranks and professions*, 2nd edn, 3 vols. in 6 pts (1825) · 'Memoir of James Nares', *The Harmonicon*, 7 (1829), 235–6 · W. Beloe, *The sexagenarian, or, The recollections of a literary life*, ed. [T. Rennell], 2nd edn, 2 vols. (1818) · W. Bendix, *Englische Lautlehre nach Nares* (1784) (1921) · J. Eadie and others, eds., *The imperial dictionary of universal biography* [n.d.] · Foster, *Alum. Oxon.* · Boswell, *Life* · E. L. de Montluzin, 'Attributions of authorship in the *Gentleman's Magazine*, 1849–1868, and addenda, 1733–1838', *Studies in Bibliography*, 50 (1997), 322–58 · E. L. de Montluzin, 'Attributions of authorship in the *British Critic* during the editorial regime of Robert Nares, 1793–1813', *Studies in Bibliography*, 51 (1998), 241–58 · Nichols, *Illustrations* · C. Pollner, *Robert Nares: 'Elements of orthoepy'* (1784) (1976) · J. Sargeaunt, *Annals of Westminster School* (1898) · Watt, *Bibl. Brit.* · IGI · www.nares.net/james_nares_1715.htm, 10 June 2003
Archives BL, printed works with MS additions by him · Staffs. RO, papers | Bodl. Oxf., corresp. with Sir James Burges
Likenesses S. Freeman, stipple (after J. Hoppner), BM, NPG; repro. in Jerdan, 'The venerable archdeacon Nares'

Narford, Robert. *See* Nerford, Robert (*d.* 1225).

Narkov, Andrey Konstantinovich (1680?–1756). *See under* Industrial spies (*act. c.*1700–*c.*1800).

Narrien, John (1782–1860), astronomical writer, the son of a stonemason, was born at Chertsey, Surrey. From about 1811 to 1825 he kept an optician's shop in St James's Street, Westminster. On 10 December 1814 he married Elizabeth Porter (*d. c.*1852). Helped by friends and patrons, he was appointed in 1814 to the teaching staff of the Royal Military College at Sandhurst. Having been promoted in 1820 to be professor of mathematics and fortifications in the senior department, he was the virtual head of the establishment until failing eyesight obliged him to resign in 1858.

Narrien published in 1833 *An Historical Account of the Origin and Progress of Astronomy*, a work of considerable merit and research; he also compiled a series of mathematical textbooks for use at Sandhurst. He observed the partial solar eclipse of 6 May 1845 at the observatory of the college. In 1840 he was elected a fellow of the Royal Society and in 1858 he retired from the Royal Astronomical Society. He died at his home in Clarendon Road, Kensington, on 30 March 1860.

A. M. Clerke, rev. Anita McConnell

Sources *Monthly Notices of the Royal Astronomical Society*, 18 (1857–8), 100 · *Annual Register* (1860), 475 · W. T. Lynn, 'Narrien and the observations of Eudoxus of Cnidus', *The Observatory*, 11 (1888), 300–01 · *Monthly Notices of the Royal Astronomical Society*, 21 (1860–61), 102–3 · *CGPLA Eng. & Wales* (1860)
Archives Auckland Public Library, letters to Sir George Grey
Wealth at death under £7000: probate, 2 June 1860, *CGPLA Eng. & Wales*

Nary, Cornelius (1658–1738), Roman Catholic priest and religious controversialist, is believed to have been born at Tipper, near Naas, co. Kildare. The names of his father and mother are unknown, although it seems likely that his father was a substantial tenant farmer. Two brothers and three sisters are named in his will but there probably were others. He received his early education in Naas and, following ordination to the priesthood in Kilkenny, he was sent to the Irish College in Paris in 1683 for further studies. He was thus afforded the opportunity of attending the University of Paris and over the next ten years took degrees there in arts and law.

Equipped with a doctorate in canon and civil law from the University of Paris, Nary went to London in 1695 as tutor to the son of the earl of Antrim. This was something of a sinecure and gave him the opportunity to produce his first work of controversy, *A modest and true account of the chief points in controversy between Roman Catholics and protestants* (1696), in which he challenged the views expressed by the archbishop of Canterbury, the recently deceased John Tillotson. Nary arrived back in Dublin in 1698 or 1699, and was appointed parish priest of St Michan's parish in that city shortly afterwards. His new-found fame as a controversialist had apparently preceded him, for he was to find the local Anglican rector, John Clayton, spoiling for a fight, and keen to engage him in a face-to-face disputation on religious topics. His first task, however, was to collect funds for the building of a chapel, which he duly opened to his parishioners in 1704.

From 1705 to 1715 Nary was engaged on his translation into English of the New Testament. Although he regarded this as his *magnum opus* it earned him few plaudits from the critics and got him into deep trouble with Rome because of its alleged Jansenist tendencies. It was eventually condemned by the Vatican in 1722. In 1720 was published his mammoth *A New History of the World*, which, despite its title, covered only the period up to the time of Christ.

A pamphlet, *The Case of the Roman Catholics of Ireland*, which Nary wrote in 1724 against a stringent anti-Catholic bill promoted by the Irish parliament, marked the beginning of his involvement in the political scene. The Anglican archbishop of Tuam, Edward Synge, together with his son of the same name, had been advocating a special oath acceptable to Catholics for a few years. Nary was also in favour of such an oath, and when a bill for the registration of Catholic priests was before the Irish parliament in 1731, he, with some other Catholic clergy, submitted for inclusion in the bill a form of oath thought to be acceptable to Catholics. This oath rejected papal pretensions to depose princes, but there was no abjuration of the Stuarts and this apparently rendered it unacceptable to the promoters of the bill. In any event, following intensive lobbying by other Catholics opposed to any form of oath, the bill was rejected by the English privy council. Long after his death Nary's oath was to enjoy a new lease of life when the earl of Clanbrassill included it in two unsuccessful bills in 1756 and 1757 for the registration of priests.

From 1727 until his death Nary was engaged in a great public controversy on religious questions with Archbishop Synge. Although these two pulled no punches when disputing with each other points at issue, it appears that privately they were good friends. The controversy took the form of a succession of books and pamphlets written in reply to each other, totalling over a thousand pages.

As a Gallican, supposedly with Jansenist tendencies, Nary was openly critical of the pope's claim to have power to depose monarchs and to dispense their subjects from allegiance, and thus had little chance of being considered for promotion to bishop or archbishop, despite his great learning, qualifications, and ability. Nevertheless, he clearly coveted such advancement and on two occasions during the 1720s, when the archbishopric of Dublin was vacant, he found himself at the centre of unseemly wrangles among the Dublin clergy as to who should be postulated to Rome for the position.

As a registered priest Nary enjoyed a degree of immunity which he fully exploited in dangerous times, while his outstanding honesty, integrity, and great learning earned him the esteem of many protestants as well as Catholics. He lived in some comfort with his manservant in his lodgings in Bull Lane, following a very civilized lifestyle as a biblical scholar, historian, controversialist, and something of a public man, and emerging ultimately as by far the most considerable Catholic figure in Ireland in the first half of the eighteenth century. He was essentially what was known in later times as a 'Castle Catholic' (that is, Dublin Castle). More than once he protested his loyalty to the crown and his admiration for the British constitution, although he fell short of abjuring the Pretender. This accounts for the considerable latitude he was allowed in his writings, in which he was often measuredly defiant, sometimes abusive, of church and state.

Nary died, aged seventy-nine, on 3 March 1738 in Bull Lane, Dublin. The cause of his death was probably apoplexy. It is presumed that he was buried, as he had directed in his will, in Tipper graveyard near Naas.

PATRICK FAGAN

Sources P. Fagan, *Dublin's turbulent priest: Cornelius Nary (1658–1738)* (1991) · N. Donnelly, *Short histories of Dublin parishes*, pt 11 (1909) · C. Giblin, 'Catalogue of material of Irish interest in the collection *Nunziatura di Fiandra*, Vatican archives', *Collectanea Hibernica*, 1 (1958), 7–134; 3 (1960), 7–144; 4 (1961), 7–137; 5 (1962), 7–130; 9 (1966), 7–70; 10 (1967), 72–138; 11 (1968), 53–90; 12 (1969), 62–101; 13 (1970), 61–99; 14 (1971), 36–81; 15 (1972), 7–55 · P. Fagan, ed., *Ireland in the Stuart papers*, 2 vols. (1995) · P. Boyle, *The Irish College in Paris from 1578 to 1901* (1901) · annals of the Poor Clares, Poor Clares convent, Dublin · C. Nary, letters to Sir Richard Bellings, Donhead St Andrew church, Wiltshire, collection of Lord Talbot of Malahide · parish records, St Michan's, Dublin · *The whole works of Sir James Ware concerning Ireland*, ed. and trans. W. Harris, 2/2 (1746) [incl. bibliography] · [R. Clayton], *A few plain matters of fact, humbly recommended to the consideration of the Roman-Catholicks of Ireland* (1756)

Archives Donhead St Andrew church, Wiltshire, collection of Lord Talbot of Malahide, letters to Sir Richard Bellings

Likenesses J. Brooks, engraving, *c*.1729 (after unknown portrait), BM, NL Ire.; repro. in Fagan, *Dublin's turbulent priest* · A. Millar, engraving (after unknown portrait), BM, NL Ire.; repro. in Fagan, *Dublin's turbulent priest*

Wealth at death approximately £40; incl. clothes, and a few pieces of church plate and other plate; house in Chapel Street, Dublin, apparently disposed of to his successor prior to making his will: will, Fagan, *Dublin's turbulent priest*, 43–4

Nash, Frederick (1782–1856), watercolour painter and architectural draughtsman, was born in Lambeth on 28 March 1782, the youngest of five children. His father was a builder. As a child, Nash is said to have drawn on 'every available piece of paper' (Royal Watercolour Society, MS J64/11). Despite inducements offered to him by a wealthy relative to become a lawyer, Nash insisted on following art as a profession. 'I have often heard him say he did not know his own interest for he thought to be an artist was to be greater than to be king', his wife recalled after his death (ibid.). He studied architectural drawing and perspective with Thomas Malton the younger, and subsequently entered the Royal Academy Schools where, at eighteen, his first exhibited picture, *North Entrance of Westminster Abbey*, was highly praised by Benjamin West. Nash drew the abbey throughout his life: Martin Hardie commented that he must have known the place better than Ruskin knew the stones of Venice.

Although occasionally employed by architects such as Sir Robert Smirke, for some years Nash drew many designs for engravers. Examples can be found in John Britton's *Architectural Antiquities* (1807) and Britton and E. W. Brayley's *The Beauties of England and Wales* (1801–9). From 1807 Nash was employed as both an architectural draughtsman and lithographer by the Society of Antiquaries, who still own a number of his drawings. In a letter to the society of 24 December 1826, Nash wrote that 'Lithography has a much higher aim [than imitation of line engraving], that of imitating *drawings*, and drawings in fact they are' (S. Antiquaries, Lond., 1N2). In December 1846 Nash exhibited seventeen drawings of Cowdray House in Sussex to the society.

In 1808 Nash exhibited with the Associated Artists; in 1810 he was elected to the Society of Painters in Water Colours with whom he went on to exhibit some 474 pictures. A highly finished and accomplished artist, he was well paid for his work: in 1818 he was able to reject an offer of 100 guineas from Rudolph Ackermann for a drawing of Westminster Abbey, which he later sold for £125. Turner is said to have regarded Nash as the finest architectural artist of the day. The Victoria and Albert Museum owns fifteen watercolours by Nash, mostly signed either 'Nash' or 'F. Nash'. Nash also painted in oils. In 1819 he began a series of sketches of Paris which mark a change of style. J. L. Roget commented:

> These Paris views belong more to the category of modern landscape. They are light in touch, pleasant and even gay in colour, convey an impression of luminous summer air, and

Frederick Nash (1782–1856), by Jules Noguès, 1839

are treated in a manner altogether appropriate to the more lively nature of their subjects.   (Roget, 2.250–51)

Nash received 500 guineas for these works, which were published in 1823 as *Nash's Views of Paris*; he then sold the original drawings to Sir Thomas Lawrence for £250. Lawrence—both a friend and a patron of Nash—invited him in 1825 to assist with a portrait of Louis XIII and the French royal family.

Nash's greatest pleasure was to sketch from nature: in 1822 he built a small house at 1 Robert Street off the Hampstead Road with a studio on top, open on all four sides, to allow him to study the skies. He rose early and was generally out sketching between five and six in the morning, often sitting in the rain while a boy held an umbrella over him. His usual practice was to make three drawings from the same scene during the early morning, mid day, and the evening; the pictures were coloured on the spot and finished later. Peter DeWint was a frequent sketching companion. Nash made several trips abroad to sketch; in Calais and later in Caen he was apprehended by guards for drawing fortifications. He also made trips to the Lake District, the Moselle, and the Rhine.

Nash's neighbour in Robert Street was W. J. or W. T. Bennett, who, following a financial fraud, fled to America, becoming president of the New York Academy. Nash married Bennett's sister Eliza on 17 April 1824 at St Pancras Old Church; there were no children from the marriage. In his obituary in the *Art Journal*, Joseph Jenkins described Nash as 'a good husband, amiable and upright in all relations of life'. In 1834 the Nashes moved to Brighton where, in 1837,

Frederick was nearly killed during 'a violent hurricane' when a chimney stack fell through his studio ceiling. His first anxiety was for a drawing of the lady chapel at Arundel which he had recently sold but 'it had received only a slight scratch, which was easily repaired by him after a clean cambric handk. had been passed over it' (MS J64/11).

Later in life Nash turned to landscape drawing, particularly of Sussex, but the quality of his work deteriorated and his pictures rarely sold for more than £20. His income was further reduced when ill health confined him to his house, making it impossible for him to teach. In the delirium before his death, Nash imagined he was working so hard at a picture that he 'begged that it might be taken out of his sight as "if he worked at it any more it might injure his reputation as an Artist"' (MS J64/11). He died from bronchitis at his home, 44 Montpellier Road, Brighton, on 5 December 1856, and was buried in Brighton cemetery. The remainder of Nash's pictures were auctioned at his house in Brighton on 21 March 1857: the sale included a *Liber Studiorum* and fifteen engravings after Turner, as well as the palette of Sir Thomas Lawrence.

SIMON FENWICK

Sources Bankside Gallery, London, Royal Watercolour Society, MS J64/11 • J. L. Roget, *A history of the 'Old Water-Colour' Society*, 2 vols. (1891) • M. Hardie, *Water-colour painting in Britain*, ed. D. Snelgrove, J. Mayne, and B. Taylor, 3 vols. (1966–8) • papers, S. Antiquaries, Lond. • J. J. Jenkins, *Art Journal*, 19 (1857), 61 • *ILN* (29 Dec 1856) • *Brighton Gazette* (12 March 1857) • *Brighton Gazette* (18 March 1857)
Archives Bankside Gallery, London, Royal Watercolour Society archives • S. Antiquaries, Lond., MSS
Likenesses J. Noguès, watercolour drawing, 1839, NPG [*see illus.*]

Nash, Gawen [Gawin] (1605/6–1658), Church of England clergyman, was the son of Thomas Nash of Eltisley, Cambridgeshire, who was butler of Pembroke College, Cambridge. Admitted as a sizar to Pembroke in the Lent term of 1621, aged fifteen, he graduated BA early in 1625, became a fellow in 1627, and proceeded MA in 1628. He was ordained priest at Peterborough on 23 September 1632. With Alexander Gil the younger and others he contributed a prefatory verse to *Corolla varia* (1634), a collection of poems by William Hawkins, schoolmaster of Hadleigh, Suffolk. In 1635 he proceeded BD.

Three years later Nash became rector of St Matthew, Ipswich, Suffolk, and curate of nearby St Mary at the Tower. Here, if not before, he revealed himself as an ardent clericalist and ceremonialist. In 1640 the House of Commons considered accusations from his parishioners that he was 'abusive & contentious'; he had 'denied the King was supreme head of the church' and 'would not pray for him as such', saying that 'the crown stood not upon his head but by the bishops' (*Walker rev.*, 339). Simonds D'Ewes recorded that he was also suspected of belief in transubstantiation, having preached 'that Christ was corporally present in the sacrament; that hee was soe humble as to dwell under a crumme of bread' (Milton, 205). In the short term he seems to have kept his livings, and by 1643 until about 1646 he was also vicar of Waresley, Huntingdonshire, previously held by the prominent Laudian John

Pocklington. Although by 29 November 1645, when a successor was admitted, he had been sequestered from Ipswich, in May 1647 his arrest was ordered for preaching there. Uncowed, he was still officiating in 1650, but according to John Walker was finally imprisoned for refusing to take the engagement to the Commonwealth. It is possible that he was later rector of Kingsley, Staffordshire, only to be ejected by the commission of triers in the mid-1650s, or of Little Melton, Suffolk. He died in 1658; nothing is known of his wife.

Nash was survived by a son, Gawin (d. 1706). He was admitted to Trinity College, Cambridge, in 1667, graduated BA in 1672 and proceeded MA in 1675. Ordained priest at Norwich in 1674, he became a minor canon and vicar of Little Melton, but was deprived for refusing the oath to William III. VIVIENNE LARMINIE

Sources Walker rev. · Venn, *Alum. Cant.* · A. Milton, *Catholic and Reformed: the Roman and protestant churches in English protestant thought, 1600–1640* (1995)

Nash, (William) Heddle (1894–1961), singer, was born on 14 June 1894 at 62 Amersham Vale, Greenwich, London, the son of William Nash, master builder, and his wife, Harriet Emma Carr. His father was also a talented singer. After studying at Blackheath Conservatory he served with the 20th London regiment during the First World War in France, Salonika, and Palestine. After the war he got a job singing in the pit for a marionette company giving puppet performances of opera. On 7 April 1923 he married Florence Emily Violet, daughter of Henry James Pearce, a sign manufacturer. Nash subsequently went to Milan to study with Giuseppe Borgatti. He made his début in Milan in 1924, singing Almaviva in Rossini's *The Barber of Seville*, and sang in the opera houses of Genoa, Bologna, and Turin, developing an Italianate style of singing that remained with him: it was said of him that he sang everything as though it were by Verdi. He returned to London in 1925, and was engaged by Lilian Baylis to perform with the Old Vic Company, appearing as the Duke of Mantua in Verdi's *Rigoletto*, Tonio in Donizetti's *The Daughter of the Regiment*, and Tamino in Mozart's *The Magic Flute*. He toured with the British National Opera Company in a number of roles until its collapse in 1929, when he made his début at the Royal Opera House, Covent Garden, as Don Ottavio in Mozart's *Don Giovanni*.

As well as singing the leading tenor roles in Italian and French operas at Covent Garden until the Second World War, Nash was also noted for his David in Wagner's *Die Meistersinger*. He sang in the first Glyndebourne season, in 1934, taking the role of Don Basilio in Mozart's *The Marriage of Figaro* at the inaugural performance of the Glyndebourne Festival Opera, and Pedrillo in Mozart's *Die Entführung aus dem Serail*. He also sang Ferrando in Mozart's *Così fan tutte*, although, as was usual at the time, the company performed a cut version, leaving Nash with only one aria. He sang these three roles every year until 1938, and Don Ottavio in 1937.

During the Second World War Nash toured with the Carl Rosa Opera Company, often singing opposite the Australian soprano Joan Hammond, in roles including Faust in Gounod's *Faust*, Pinkerton in Puccini's *Madama Butterfly*, and Rodolfo in Puccini's *La Bohème*. After the war he sang Des Grieux in Massenet's *Manon* in the first post-war season at Covent Garden (1947–8), and continued to appear on stage until 1957, when he created the minor character Dr Manette in Arthur Benjamin's *A Tale of Two Cities* with the New Opera Company at Sadler's Wells.

Heddle Nash was also much in demand as a singer of oratorio. Asked by Elgar to sing the part of Gerontius in *The Dream of Gerontius* at the Worcester festival in 1932, he sang the part for many years—singing it at every Three Choirs festival from 1934 to 1950; and he appeared with Kathleen Ferrier (who sang the role of the Angel) and Sir John Barbirolli and the Hallé Orchestra from 1948. He took part in the first complete recording in 1945, with Gladys Ripley as the Angel, conducted by Malcolm Sargent. His song recitals often included songs by Liszt, and Handel arias. Nash performed in some of the recitals of English song given at the Wigmore Hall in May and June 1951 as part of the Festival of Britain, with pieces including Edmund Rubbra's 'Amoretti', and settings of sonnets by Edmund Spenser, with the New London Quartet. He made many recordings, the most famous of which was the serenade 'A la voix d'un amant fidèle' from Bizet's *The Fair Maid of Perth*, recorded in 1932. His first recording was in Gounod's *Faust*, conducted by Sir Thomas Beecham in 1929, and other early recordings include arias from Handel's *Jephtha*, recorded in 1931; act IV of Puccini's *La Bohème*, recorded with Beecham in 1935; and Beethoven's *Missa solemnis*, live from the Leeds festival in 1937. He sang in the Glyndebourne recordings of *The Marriage of Figaro* in 1934, and *Così fan tutte* in 1935, conducted by Fritz Busch. He also made a famous BBC broadcast in 1938 with Maggie Teyte in excerpts from *Manon*.

Nash was the leading British lyric tenor in the period from the late 1920s until the early 1950s. With his sweetness and beauty of tone, the naturalness of his diction, and his charm, he had the power to move his audiences. A cheerful and direct person, he never lost his south London accent, and according to the accompanist Gerald Moore (1899–1987) in his autobiography *Am I Too Loud?* (1962), there were as many Heddle Nash stories as there were stories about Beecham. Heddle Nash died on 13 August 1961 in Brook Hospital, Greenwich. He was survived by his wife, Violet, and two sons, one of them the baritone John Heddle Nash. ANNE PIMLOTT BAKER

Sources A. Blyth, 'Heddle Nash: a centenary note', *Opera* (June 1994), 670–73 · S. Hughes, *Glyndebourne: a history of the festival opera* (1965) · *New Grove* · *The Times* (15 Aug 1961) · b. cert. · m. cert. · d. cert.

Likenesses photograph, 1947, repro. in Blythe, 'Heddle Nash' · photograph, repro. in *The Times*

Nash, John (1752–1835), architect, was born in September 1752, possibly in London or Neath, Glamorgan, to Welsh parents. His origins are obscure; his father (possibly called Robert or John), who died about 1758, was said to have been an 'engineer and millwright in Lambeth' (Knight, 430). Nash's cousin John Edwards (d. 1818), another engineer in Lambeth, came from Neath, and his son John

John Nash (1752–1835), by Sir Thomas Lawrence, exh. RA 1827

Edwards (1772–1833), a lawyer, was later described by Nash as 'my only relative'. A 'wild, irregular youth', as he later described himself to the architect William Porden (William Porden, MS diary, 3 July 1812, quoted in Summerson, *Life*, 4), Nash entered the office of the architect Robert Taylor as an indentured pupil, probably in 1766 or 1767, and was employed first in a 'subordinate capacity' and later as a draughtsman. On 28 April 1775, having left Taylor's office, he married Jane Elizabeth, daughter of Hugh Kerr, a surgeon who practised in Walworth but owned property in Dorking; by the end of that year they were living in a house in Royal Row, Lambeth.

By 1777 Nash had established himself as a speculative builder and surveyor, latterly in partnership with Richard Heaviside, timber merchant and carpenter to the Board of Ordnance. In 1777–8 he built a pair of handsome houses on the north-western side of Bloomsbury Square and a plainer block on an adjacent site in Great Russell Street; they were among the first houses in London to be clad in stucco, a material of which Nash later made extensive use. In 1778 he took the lease of one of the houses in Great Russell Street, but in the same year his wife was sent to stay with his cousin Ann Morgan in Aberafan, Glamorgan, 'to work a reformation in her' (*Nash v. Nash*, LMA, DL/C/179/fol. 335) after she had run up large debts and had allegedly attempted to impose two spurious children on him. While there, she conducted an affair with one of Nash's childhood friends, Charles Charles, a coalyard clerk from Neath, and after she had a child by Charles in 1779 Nash instituted legal proceedings against her for adultery and against Charles for criminal conversation. The case was

tried in 1782 and Charles was imprisoned after failing to pay the costs. Nash meanwhile moved out of his house, and in 1783, all but one of the neighbouring houses having failed to sell, he was declared bankrupt.

The years in Wales   In or about 1785 Nash moved to Carmarthen, where he may already have been employed during his pupillage on the building of a new guildhall to Taylor's design. Here he set up a partnership with Samuel Saxon, a pupil of Sir William Chambers, the first product of which was the building of a new roof and ceiling in the parish church (1785). Two years later, in 1787, he successfully obtained a divorce in the London consistory court, only to suffer the rejection of the private bill which would have legalized it in the House of Lords. Meanwhile, as he later told Porden, he maintained 'the character of a Gentleman keeping the best company of *Bon Vivants* and hunting with the most desperate sportsmen' (Porden diary, 3 July 1812, quoted in Summerson, *Life*, 5). Nash resumed the practice of architecture after the collapse of his divorce case, designing a cold bath (which may never have been built) for John Vaughan, lord lieutenant of Carmarthenshire, at his country seat, Golden Grove, about 1787, and going on to gain the commission for the county gaol at Carmarthen in 1789–92. By 1793 he was employing the French royalist émigré Auguste Charles Pugin as a draughtsman, as well as an assistant, Robert George, who left him in 1796.

Nash subsequently designed other public buildings in Wales and the Welsh borders, including the gaols at Cardigan (1792–3) and Hereford (1793–6) and a market hall in Abergavenny (1794–5), all of them in the severe neoclassical style often used for this type of building at the time. He was also responsible for rebuilding the west front of St David's Cathedral (1791–3; replaced 1862)—his first excursion into Gothic architecture—and he designed a stone bridge over the River Rheidol at Aberystwyth (*c*.1797–1800) and a single-arched cast-iron bridge at Stanford-on-Teme, Worcestershire (1797): the first indication of his interest in iron as a structural material. But the largest, and architecturally the most interesting, part of his practice was domestic. The gentry of south-west Wales were eager to replace or at least remodel their unfashionable and often dilapidated houses in the early 1790s, and Nash succeeded in rehousing several of them in a dignified and unpretentious manner. Houses such as Ffynone, Pembrokeshire (1792–6), Llanerch Aeron, Cardiganshire (*c*.1794), and Llys Newydd, Cardiganshire (*c*.1795), were ingeniously planned: their plain classical elevations and comfortable interiors successfully reflect the relatively modest aspirations of their owners. A more adventurous patron was Uvedale Price of Foxley, Herefordshire, for whom Nash designed a triangular castellated villa (1791–4; dem.) on the seafront at Aberystwyth, its bay windows carefully arranged to command the view. Through Price, Nash became aware of the picturesque aesthetic—perhaps the most influential movement in English taste at the close of the eighteenth century—and at Emlyn Cottage, Newcastle Emlyn (1792), and also at Hafod, near Aberystwyth, where he designed an octagonal library for Thomas Johnes, another enthusiast for the picturesque, in 1794 (des. 1807), he showed himself capable of exploiting those scenic and evocative qualities of architecture which appealed to a growing number of clients.

By 1796 Nash had become an important figure in Carmarthen society. He lived in a substantial house, which he designed for himself, in Spilman Street (later the Ivy Bush Hotel), and he owned property which included a playhouse in which he acted (in *The School for Scandal*) in 1796. He was on close terms with the whig interest in the town and county, but his litigious temperament made him enemies, and in 1798 he was threatening to sue the Carmarthenshire bench for the non-payment of fees. In the same year Uvedale Price warned Sir George Beaumont not to trust his estimates and to 'get some other person to execute his designs' (Coleorton MSS, Pierpont Morgan Library, New York, MA 1581 (Price) 15, 8 March 1798). But by then he had already begun to spend an increasing amount of time in London, and he finally quitted Carmarthen in 1797.

Private practice in London The successful launch of Nash's career as a fashionable London architect owed much to his partnership with Humphry Repton, the best-known English landscape gardener of his time. The two men first met in 1792 at Stoke Edith, Herefordshire, where Nash designed a new parlour (1793–6; dem.) in the Etruscan style—his first substantial scheme of interior decoration—but the partnership did not come into existence until 1795, when he took Repton's son John Adey Repton into his office as an assistant. Their first joint commission was for Corsham Court, Wiltshire (1797–8), where Nash (superseding James Wyatt) remodelled and enlarged the existing house in the Tudor-Gothic style, incorporating a long ground-floor gallery with iron balconies: the first of many such rooms in his houses. More significantly, Repton and Nash quickly built up a reputation as designers of rural and suburban villas set in carefully landscaped settings on relatively small estates. In these engaging buildings Nash made a major contribution to the development of English domestic architecture, experimenting with asymmetrical plans so as to make the most of the views from the house, and, prompted by Repton and the clients, employing a wide variety of styles skilfully adapted to extract the maximum picturesque effect. The first of the villas, all of them close to London, were classical in character, though unconventional in planning and layout: Point Pleasant, or Bank Farm, Kingston upon Thames (1797; dem.), Southgate Grove (1797), Casina, Dulwich (1797; dem.), and Sundridge Park, Bromley (1799). At Luscombe, near Dawlish, Devon (1800–04), Nash employed a domesticated version of the castellated style pioneered twenty years before by Richard Payne Knight at Downton Castle, Shropshire. And at Cronkhill (c.1802), on the Attingham estate in Shropshire, he designed the first of the many irregular Italianate villas which were later to proliferate both in the English countryside and in suburbs on both sides of the Atlantic; it was inspired by the Italian vernacular houses depicted in the paintings of Claude Lorrain and praised for their picturesqueness by Payne Knight in his *Analytical Inquiry into the Principles of Taste* (1805). Both at

Cronkhill and at Luscombe Nash made use of towers the sole purpose of which was to form part of a memorable skyline: a recurrent feature in English architecture ever since the middle ages.

When Nash first returned to London he lived at 28 Duke Street, St James's, but in 1797–8, at the age of forty-six, he built himself a handsome stuccoed house at 29 Dover Street, north of Piccadilly, and on 17 December 1798, with his first wife presumably dead, he entered into a second marriage, to the 25-year-old Mary Anne (d. 1851), younger daughter of John or Robert Bradley, coal merchants and contractors of Abingdon Street, Westminster, from whom he had borrowed money twenty years before. This marriage coincided with a considerable increase in his fortune, which enabled him to buy an estate of 30 acres on a prominent coastal site overlooking the Solent at East Cowes on the Isle of Wight. Here he built a castellated villa known as East Cowes Castle (1798–1802), irregularly planned, like the slightly later Luscombe, with towers emerging romantically from the surrounding trees. Enlarged about 1810–11 and again in the 1820s, the house was used by Nash and his wife as a weekend and holiday retreat; when the diarist Joseph Farington went there in 1817, he was told that they were seldom without company. Nash's connection with the Isle of Wight was strengthened in 1802 when he purchased the core of the Hamstead estate, 5 miles from Cowes. He enlarged and remodelled an existing house on the estate as a *cottage orné*, drew an income from the surrounding farmland and from brick- and lime-kilns, and, on his occasional visits, played the country squire. Later work on the Isle of Wight included the Isle of Wight institution (1811) and the guildhall (1814–16), both at Newport, the chief town, and both designed in a restrained Palladian manner, and the austere neo-classical tower of St Mary, West Cowes (1816).

Nash's partnership with Repton ended acrimoniously in 1800, with Nash having failed, according to Repton, to pay him his share of the seven per cent fees charged to their joint clients. John Adey Repton had by then left the office, but his place was taken about 1802 by his younger brother George Stanley Repton, who remained with Nash until about 1820. By 1800 Nash was on his way to becoming one of the most successful domestic architects in England, and in the first decade of the nineteenth century he succeeded, despite the distractions of the Napoleonic wars, in building up a large and lucrative country house practice among the English and Irish gentry and minor nobility. Joseph Farington recorded him saying in 1821 that he had travelled 11,000 miles a year in England, Scotland, and Ireland, spending £1500 in chaise hire.

With universally accepted standards of architectural taste collapsing, Nash succeeded in giving his clients—both long-established gentry and *nouveaux riches* industrialists and financiers—the comfort and visual stimulation they demanded. He excelled at adapting widely divergent styles to the needs of his clients: the irregular Italianate villa, pioneered at Cronkhill, reappeared at Sandridge Park, Devon (c.1805); 'castles' sprang up at Caerhayes, Cornwall (c.1808), Knepp, Sussex (c.1808), Ravensworth, co. Durham (begun 1808; dem.), and elsewhere; a form of rococo Gothic was employed at Aqualate Hall, Staffordshire (1806–9; dem.); and at Longner Hall, Shropshire (c.1803–5), he turned to the 'old English' or neo-Tudor manner, uncannily anticipating the design of the typical early Victorian parsonage in the process. The old English manner was also used in the remodelling of older houses such as Helmingham Hall, Suffolk (1800), and Parnham, Dorset (1807–11). In his additions to eighteenth-century houses Nash sometimes opted for a rich classical style, as in the library at Barnsley Park, Gloucestershire (1806–10). His picture gallery at Attingham, Shropshire (1805–7) was a landmark in the use of iron and glass roofing in a domestic context, and his iron-roofed conservatory at Barnsley anticipated those later erected at Buckingham Palace (one of which now serves as the aroid house at Kew Gardens).

Some of Nash's most ambitious houses were in Ireland, where there was extensive building by the landed élite after the union of 1801. Arguably his finest classical country house was Rockingham, co. Roscommon (1809–10; dem.), and some of his best interiors were at Caledon, co. Tyrone (1808–10). He also employed the castle manner in houses such as Killymoon Castle, co. Tyrone (c.1801–3), and Lough Coutra, co. Galway (1811): its quasi-feudal overtones may have had a special significance in the Irish context.

A minor but important part of Nash's domestic practice took the form of gate lodges, cottages, and other estate buildings. This aspect of his work reached its apogee in the building of Blaise Hamlet, near Bristol (1810–11), an exquisite 'village' of thatched stone cottages for the pensioners of the banker J. S. Harford, set irregularly around a communal green in a wooded setting. Here, with the assistance of George Stanley Repton, Nash employed the architectural vocabulary of the picturesque in an original and totally convincing manner, appealing to the fashionable rural nostalgia of a rapidly urbanizing society and anticipating the estate villages, garden suburbs, and even the local authority housing estates, of more modern times.

Work for the prince regent In 1806, while his domestic practice was in full spate, Nash acquired his first official position, as salaried architect in the Office of Woods and Forests, the government department responsible for managing the crown estate. This post, which he may have obtained through the patronage of Lord Robert Spencer, a Foxite whig, brought him a regular, though not very substantial, income from surveying work, as well as a retainer of £200, which he shared with his assistant James Morgan, who had followed him from Wales to London. In 1811 he produced his first plans for the long-anticipated development of the crown land in Marylebone Park, but by then he had been introduced, possibly by his neighbour in the Isle of Wight Lord Henry Seymour of Norris Castle, into the circle of the prince of Wales (from 1811 prince regent and from 1820 George IV). In 1798, while still in partnership with Repton, Nash had designed a conservatory for the prince, presumably for his marine pavilion at Brighton, a drawing of which was exhibited at the Royal Academy in 1798, but there is no evidence that the two

men met at the time, and it is uncertain whether or not the conservatory was ever built. Nor is there any evidence to confirm later rumours—most explicitly articulated in a ballad and cartoon of 1822—that Nash's second wife was one of the prince's discarded mistresses, although such a liaison could, if proved, explain the rapid increase in Nash's fortune in the year of his marriage and possibly also his sudden rise to fame as the prince's architect in the years after he assumed the Regency. For whatever reasons, by 1813 Nash was said to be 'in great favour with the Prince' (S. Romilly, *Memoirs*, 3, 1840, 86), acting as an intermediary in his dealings with his former allies the Foxite whigs, and with the lord chancellor, Sir Samuel Romilly, in his negotiations with the estranged princess of Wales, and vainly aspiring to a seat in parliament.

Nash's first architectural commission from the prince was for a thatched *cottage orné* built around the nucleus of the former lower lodge in Windsor Great Park and known since the 1820s as Royal Lodge. 'At once royal and rustic', in the words of Princess Lieven (Morshead, 30), the lodge was built in 1813 and extended in 1822 and again, to the designs of Sir Jeffry Wyatville, in 1830; it was demolished, except for Wyatville's dining-room, by William IV and subsequently rebuilt in a very different style. It was in 1814 that Nash first attracted notice—some of it unfavourable—as the prince's private architect. He was employed in that year to design a series of temporary structures to celebrate the visit to London by the allied sovereigns after the treaty of Paris, including a tent-like rotunda (re-erected at Woolwich in 1820 and now the Royal Artillery Museum) in the grounds of Carlton House, the prince's main London residence, and a bridge incongruously surmounted by a pagoda—which perished in a fireworks display—in St James's Park. He also designed a series of rooms at Carlton House itself, including a spectacular gothic dining-room at basement level, facing the Mall. When James Wyatt died in 1813, Nash was given temporary responsibility for maintaining the royal palaces, and in 1815, when the office of works was reorganized, he was made one of the three 'attached architects', along with John Soane and Robert Smirke. From then on he virtually gave up taking private commissions.

Nash's most memorable commission for the prince was for the rebuilding of the Royal Pavilion at Brighton (1815–23) in what he called an 'Eastern' style, chosen by the prince to match the recently erected stable block (now the Dome) by William Porden. Drawing on the Mughal architecture illustrated by Thomas and William Daniell, and on an abortive scheme for the pavilion drawn up by Humphry Repton in 1808, Nash transformed the exterior of the existing low, sprawling building into a sensational extravaganza of Indian-inspired domes and turrets with two new reception rooms (the music room and the banqueting room) decorated with unparalleled lavishness by Frederick Crace and Robert Jones, a new gallery or corridor, and a new suite of royal apartments. Nash's exterior masks some ingenious and innovative cast-iron construction, notably in the domes, the staircases, and the internal supports. But it was in his assured handling of an exotic and little-known style in the exterior of the building that he showed his creative flair its most exuberant form, and in so doing he captured for posterity the hedonistic spirit of the age.

A more orthodox but no less lavish spirit reigns at Buckingham Palace (the former Buckingham House), rebuilt to Nash's designs after the king, as he now was, decided to abandon Carlton House as his main London residence. At the king's insistence Nash, as his 'private architect', was given the commission to remodel the existing house in 1822 despite the claims of John Soane, who had already prepared a design for a palace in Green Park; work began in 1825, when Carlton House was pulled down. In the following year the king decided to hold his courts at Buckingham Palace, and what had started as a relatively modest project, or *pied-à-terre* in the king's words, became one of the major architectural enterprises of its time. Nash's task was to add a suite of staterooms to the garden front of the existing house, reached by a new internal staircase, and to create an open entrance courtyard facing the Mall, flanked by projecting wings and entered through a Roman-inspired triumphal arch (Marble Arch, moved to Cumberland Gate, Hyde Park, in 1851). The designs, like much of Nash's work in the 1820s, were influenced by the French eighteenth-century architecture which he had seen on his visits to Paris (his only known foreign excursions) in 1814 and 1818, and the French-inspired staterooms, which survive largely intact, are among the finest interiors of the time. But the rebuilding was planned and executed with impetuous haste and the external elevations, clad in Bath stone, failed in the opinion of many critics to measure up to the dignity and gravity expected of the chief London residence of the monarch.

Nash himself admitted that the single-storeyed wings were unsuccessful as first built, and agreed to a proposal in 1828 to reconstruct them on two floors. Matters were made worse by his failure to keep the expenditure within the estimates approved by parliament: something which was virtually inevitable in view of the king's frequent changes of mind and his refusal to accept financial constraint from his ministers. In the severe political climate of the late 1820s a remote, extravagant king was bound to court unpopularity, and his death in 1830, with the palace still unfinished, led directly to Nash's own downfall.

Metropolitan improvements Nash's greatest achievements stemmed from the decision by the Office of Woods and Forests in 1810 to implement long-matured proposals for the profitable development of Marylebone Park, on the north-western fringe of London. Backed by the prince regent, who was anxious to lend his name to the improvement of London, Nash's plan for Regent's Park—as it became known—was prepared and approved in 1811–12. Drawing on earlier plans by the duke of Portland's surveyor John White, the main feature was to be a large open space laid out on picturesque, Reptonian, lines with clumps of trees, an irregular lake, and villas scattered among the plantations: a totally original concept in contemporary urban planning. Terraces of middle-class housing would line the periphery, overlooking the park, with

the Regent's Canal, of which Nash was the leading promoter and largest shareholder, running along the northern perimeter *en route* from Paddington for the River Thames at Limehouse; a branch of the canal was to lead south to Cumberland basin, serving an area of artisan housing on the eastern fringe of the development, outside the park. A *guinguette*, or pavilion, for the prince regent was proposed on a site facing the present Cumberland Terrace but, like most of the villas, this was never built. The drives and plantations were largely completed in 1812, but because of the lack of investors the canal did not fully open until 1820 (it did not pay its first dividend until 1829), and the building of the terraces, on which the profitability of the whole scheme depended, was delayed until the economy revived in the post-Waterloo years. These palatial-looking structures (including Sussex Place, 1822; Chester Terrace, 1825; and, grandest of all, Cumberland Terrace, 1825) disguise ordinary brick construction behind Nash's gleaming stuccoed façades, but as urban scenery they are second to none, justifying contemporary pride in London as an imperial capital worthy of comparison with Rome. Finally in 1825, on the north-eastern fringe of the site, spanning the Regent's Canal, Nash laid out the park village, 'more', as he said himself, 'for amusement than profit' (Report of the select committee on crown leases, 118). Inspired to some extent by his earlier essay in village planning at Blaise Hamlet, this attractive group of stuccoed villas is one of the main prototypes of the Victorian middle-class suburb.

Nash's influence on London culminated in the creation of Regent Street, linking Regent's Park with St James's Park, Whitehall, and the Strand. Here too he brought to fruition long-matured schemes, this time for a north–south thoroughfare through the West End. His first design was produced for the commissioners of Woods and Forests, who managed the project, in 1811, and work began after the passing of an act of parliament in 1813. In its final form the plan was modified to avoid some of the expensive land purchases originally envisaged, and the resulting curves, inspired by the sinuous High Street in Oxford, gave Nash the opportunity to introduce some of the picturesque groupings at which he excelled. He was responsible not only for framing the plan but also for valuing and purchasing property on behalf of the commissioners, raising funds for the construction of the street and sewers, making bargains with developers and builders, the most important of whom was James Burton, and supervising—and in some cases designing—the elevations of the new buildings. To ensure the rapid completion of the project he sometimes acted as developer himself, most notably in the design and building of the colonnaded Quadrant (1818–20; dem.), to the north of Piccadilly Circus, architecturally the most striking ensemble in the street, and the rebuilding of Suffolk Street, formerly a shabby thoroughfare to the east of Haymarket: the only part of the scheme to survive in a relatively intact form today. Among the individual buildings he designed were the Royal Opera House, Haymarket (1816–18; dem.), with its adjacent Royal Opera Arcade (London's first shopping arcade) and the Haymarket Theatre (1821), the portico of which closes one of the vistas from Lower Regent Street. He was also responsible for the church of All Souls, Langham Place (1822), the circular peristyle of which surmounted by a meagre spike by way of a spire—not one of his happiest achievements—terminates the view northward from Oxford Circus; a similar spire appears in one of the ten designs he supplied to the church commissioners under the New Churches Act of 1818. Both in its layout and in its architecture Regent Street displayed Nash's mastery of the picturesque approach to design: variety, surprise, changes of texture and style, and the artful management of vistas. By the time of its completion, in the mid-1820s, the street had transformed the face of the West End, demarcating the smart streets between Piccadilly and Oxford Street from the poorer districts to the east, supplying residents and visitors to London with a focus for fashionable shopping, and creating open spaces such as Piccadilly Circus, without which the London of today is inconceivable.

With Regent Street completed, Nash supplied designs in 1826 for a second phase of improvements at the southern end of the crown estate. Carlton House was demolished after the king's decision to move to Buckingham Palace, and the site was laid out for two magnificent blocks of housing (Carlton House Terrace) overlooking the Mall. St James's Park, between Buckingham Palace and Whitehall, was landscaped on picturesque lines, the contours of the lake softened into their present form, and clumps of trees planted in place of the earlier formal layout. Nash also initiated the development of the crown land on the southern side of Pall Mall for gentlemen's clubs by designing the United Services Club (1826–8; now the Institute of Directors) in the astylar Italian Renaissance manner which was to become fashionable in the ensuing decades. Further east, he created Trafalgar Square on ground facing the site of the Royal Mews, and he also designed a block of houses and shops on a triangular plot of crown land at the western end of the Strand (completed 1831). But the layout of Trafalgar Square and the design of the surrounding buildings was left to others, and the rest of Nash's proposals for street improvements fell victim to economies enforced by the governments of the 1830s.

Last years Nash's career reached its climax between 1811, when he produced his first designs for Regent Street and Regent's Park, and 1830, when his greatest patron, George IV, died. Portraits of the mid-1820s by Sir Thomas Lawrence and his pupil Richard Evans show him in his early seventies, at the height of his fame, as a round-faced alert-looking man, short in stature and almost bald. Seemingly lacking in vanity, he described himself to Soane in 1822 as a 'thick, squat, dwarf figure, with round head, snub nose and little eyes' (A. T. Bolton, *The Portrait of John Soane RA*, 1927, 351–5); Mrs Arbuthnot, the wife of the first commissioner of woods and forests, described him in 1824 as 'a very clever, odd, amusing man, with a face like a monkey's but civil and good-humoured to the greatest degree' (F. Bamford, ed., *The Journal of Mrs Arbuthnot, 1820–32*, 1950, 1.334). His somewhat unprepossessing features and his

shortness, captured in a sketch by Edwin Landseer of about 1830, made him easy to caricature, and he appears in several more or less scurrilous cartoons of the 1820s.

Though he considered himself badly paid for his work on Regent Street, and was allegedly 'at a stand in money matters' in 1821, Nash enjoyed a 'hospitable and expensive manner of living'; but he told Benjamin West, perhaps with his tongue in his cheek, that this was dictated by his wife and that he 'could live happily in a single room with his books about him' (*Farington Diary*, ed. Greig, 8.268–75). He flourished in the company of artists, actors, and *nouveaux riches* financiers and entrepreneurs; visitors to East Cowes Castle included the prince regent, who came to lunch in 1817, and J. M. W. Turner, who painted several views of the surroundings, as well as some impressionistic pictures of the interior. Describing Nash in company, the younger architect C. R. Cockerell wrote in November 1822 that he was 'always [the] same, merry, amusing, naive, but making the same quotations, telling the same stories' (D. Watkin, *The Life and Work of Charles Robert Cockerell*, 1974, 68). According to the Oxford clergyman Robert Finch in 1817, he was 'very fond of women' and even 'attempted' his sister-in-law, the wife of a tax inspector (Bodl. Oxf., MS Finch d.19, fol. 19*v*). His former partner Humphry Repton said in his unpublished autobiography that Nash possessed 'one of the most able heads I have ever known—he had powers of *fascination* beyond any one I have met with' (BL, Add. MS 62112, fol. 87). He was a good businessman and an excellent courtier, but John Soane told him in 1822 that there were 'few persons more anxious of fame, and who would make more sacrifices at the altar of public approbation, than yourself' (A. T. Bolton, *The Portrait of John Soane RA*, 1927, 351–5)—a comment which has a ring of truth about it.

Nash's close circle included the Ward family, neighbours in the Isle of Wight, and his cousin and business partner John Edwards, a lawyer who was involved in some of his speculative ventures. He rebuilt Edwards's country house, Rheola, near Neath, in the fashionable cottage manner in 1814–18, and in 1822–3 he built a pair of town houses, 14–16 Regent Street (dem.), for himself and Edwards at a cost of £30,000. He and his wife moved from Dover Street to 14 Regent Street, in 1823, and here, in the words of the German architect Karl Friedrich Schinkel, who visited him in 1826, he lived 'like a prince' (D. Bindman and G. Riemann, eds., *The English Journey*, 1993, 89–91). The most impressive room was a long gallery or library, with pilasters decorated after the manner of Raphael's loggia at the Vatican in Rome, casts after the antique, and a collection of architectural models made for him in Paris. The house served also as an office for his assistants and pupils, each of whom had his own private desk or compartment; they later remembered him for his 'constant gentlemanly and considerate demeanour' (*The Builder*, 13, 1855, 586).

Nash had no children by his second marriage, but from about 1813 he and his wife began to take an interest in her second cousins, the children of Thomas Pennethorne, a Worcester hop merchant, and his wife, Elizabeth. Their eldest son, Thomas, began to visit East Cowes about 1813, and later showed considerable skill at landscape drawing, but he died in 1819 at the age of twenty-one. Nash then took his younger brother James Pennethorne into his office as an assistant in place of George Stanley Repton, sending him to the drawing school run by Auguste Charles Pugin and subsequently, in 1824–6, on a two-year-long programme of foreign study and travel clearly intended to groom him as his successor. James Pennethorne's sister Ann, meanwhile, became Mrs Nash's companion, and his younger brother John followed him into Nash's office, and embarked in 1830–35 on an even more protracted foreign tour.

Nash told Farington in 1821, when he was in his seventieth year, that 'if it were not for the King he would quit his profession. … He felt indifferent to what might be his estate. He could live or die. He could fall to low estate without repining' (*Farington Diary*, ed. Greig, 8.302). In the event his career lasted for another nine years before being all but wrecked by political animosity and the death of the king. With the escalating costs of Buckingham Palace causing consternation in the Treasury, he was hauled before a Commons select committee investigating expenditure on public buildings in 1828, and in the following year, following attacks by Colonel Davies, MP for Worcester, on his financial involvement in the building of Suffolk Street and the Regent's Canal, he was questioned by another select committee on crown leases. In both cases he was exonerated from blame, but the 1829 select committee declared that it was 'undesirable for official architects to acquire a financial interest in property for which they might be called upon to give a valuation' (Report of the select committee on crown leases, 4) and the king's proposal in 1829 to reward him with a baronetcy on the grounds that he had been 'most infamously used' was vetoed by the prime minister, the duke of Wellington (*Despatches, Correspondence, and Memoranda of Field Marshal Duke of Wellington, K.G.*, new ser., 8 vols., 1867–80, 5.616). When George IV died in 1830, Nash was stripped by the whig government of his official position in the office of works. Worse followed in 1831: following a series of attacks in the press and in parliament, he was deprived of the Buckingham Palace commission. Though vindicated in his handling of the structural ironwork, criticized as faulty by some of his critics, he was condemned by a new Commons select committee for 'inexcusable irregularity and great negligence' in framing the building contracts and accounts ('Select committee on expenses of Windsor Castle and Buckingham Palace', 6). The garden front of the palace was completed to the slightly modified designs of Edward Blore in 1832–7, and Nash's façade to the Mall was hidden from view by Blore's new east range of 1847–50, itself remodelled in its present form by Sir Aston Webb in 1913.

Nash told Farington in 1821 that his health was generally good, save for a recurrent pain in his right side which his doctor called a 'dumb colic'. He had a stroke in 1830 and retired to the Isle of Wight, leaving James Pennethorne to manage what remained of his practice in London, by now

limited to the completion of projects such as Carlton House Terrace and the park village. In 1834 he formally made the practice over to Pennethorne, recommending him to the commissioners of woods and forests for future employment. By now he was in his eighties and was suffering acute financial difficulties from the failure of some of his financial dealings with the Ward family. He therefore sold his house in Regent Street and re-erected the gallery as a conservatory at East Cowes, where it survived until the whole house was demolished in 1958–63. He died at East Cowes Castle, on 13 May 1835 and was buried on 20 May at the church of St James, East Cowes, built to his own designs (but subsequently completely rebuilt, except for the tower) in 1831–3; an austere Grecian monument next to the tower marks the grave. His original intention had been to leave the bulk of his property to Nash Vaughan Edwards Vaughan, the son of John Edwards, but in a new will of 1833, the year of John Edwards's death, he left it to his wife, who inherited a debt of some £15,000, along with the houses and estates at East Cowes and Hamstead. The contents of East Cowes Castle were sold in July 1835, and the house itself was sold to the earl of Shannon; the debts were repaid by 1841. Nash's widow moved, along with Ann Pennethorne, to Hamstead, where she died in 1851; she was buried next to her husband in the same year. The Hamstead property remained in the hands of Ann Pennethorne and her brother John, from whom it has since passed by descent, though the house no longer exists.

Few English architects have had a greater influence on their surroundings than John Nash, and few have understood better than him the capacity of architecture to give pleasure, both on the grand scale of London's West End or in miniature, as in his early villas or at Blaise Hamlet. His buildings appeal more to the eye than to the intellect, and this is both his strength and his weakness as an architect. Born when Georgian classicism was all but omnipresent, during his Welsh 'exile' he developed an understanding of the picturesque matched by few of his contemporaries, and he soon developed the ability to translate his visions and those of his clients into stylistically varied forms which satisfied the widespread desire for comfort, individual expression, and conformity to the *genius loci*. He thus responded with panache to the impulses of a burgeoning consumer society deeply affected by the Romantic movement. During the Regency and the reign of George IV he had the opportunity not only to redesign the Brighton Pavilion and to create Buckingham Palace, two of the most lavish buildings of the era; he was also able, through the design of Regent's Park, Regent Street, and the associated improvements in the West End of London, to make a greater and more beneficial impact on the capital than any other single architect since Christopher Wren. Here he demonstrated an ability to compose and group buildings for their scenic effect, and to conceive and carry out large urban planning enterprises, which has rarely been matched before or since. No account of the development of the villa, the suburb, the urban park or of nineteenth-century street improvements can be written without reference to his work. He also rose to the opportunities presented by technology, and was a pioneer in the use of iron in the construction, and stucco and cement in the cladding, of buildings. He was nevertheless much criticized by the Victorians for the alleged shoddiness, slapdash detailing, and structural 'dishonesty' of his work, and the low reputation in which he was held for more than a century after his death accounts for the unfortunate demolition of many of his buildings, including all three of the houses he built for his own occupation in London and the Isle of Wight. He also suffered in the eyes of posterity from his close identification with George IV and from the financial and sexual scandals with which he was, however unjustifiably, associated. But, largely through the efforts of John Summerson, his reputation recovered in the second half of the twentieth century, and today Nash is widely recognized as one of the most creative and influential of all British architects.

GEOFFREY TYACK

Sources J. Summerson, *The life and work of John Nash, architect* (1980) · Colvin, *Archs.* · M. Mansbridge, *John Nash: a complete catalogue* (1991) · R. Suggett, *John Nash, architect in Wales* (1995) · D. Whitehead, 'John Nash and Humphry Repton: an encounter in Herefordshire, 1785–98', *Transactions of the Woolhope Naturalists' Field Club*, 47 (1991–3), 210–36 · D. Stroud, *Humphry Repton* (1962) · E. Carter, P. Goode, and K. Laurie, *Humphry Repton, landscape gardener, 1752–1818* (1982) [exhibition catalogue, Sainsbury Centre for Visual Arts, Norwich, and V&A, 21 Sept 1982 – 20 Feb 1983] · C. Musgrave, *Royal Pavilion* (1959) · J. Morley, *The making of the Royal Pavilion, Brighton* (1984) · D. Morshead, *George IV and Royal Lodge* (1965) · A. Saunders, *Regent's Park: a study of the development of the area from 1086 to the present day*, 2nd edn (1981) · H. Hobhouse, *A history of Regent Street* (1975) · H. Spencer, *London's canal* (1961) · J. M. Crook and M. H. Port, eds., *The history of the king's works*, 6 (1973) · H. C. Smith, *Buckingham Palace* (1931) · N. Temple, *John Nash and the village picturesque* (1979) · T. Davis, *John Nash: the prince regent's architect* (1973) · *The Farington diary*, ed. J. Greig, 8 (1928) · C. Knight, ed., *The English cyclopaedia: biography*, 3 (1856), 430–31 · 'Select committee on … the office of works and public buildings', *Parl. papers* (1828), 4.315, no. 446 · 'Select committee on … granting leases of, or sale of, crown lands in Pall Mall and Regent Street', *Parl. papers* (1829), 3.37, no. 343 · 'Select committee on expenses of Windsor Castle and Buckingham Palace', *Parl. papers* (1831), vol. 4, nos. 272, 329 · G. Tyack, 'John Nash and the park village', *Georgian Group Journal*, [3] (1993), 68–74 · J. Summerson, 'John Nash's "Statement", 1829', *Architectural History*, 34 (1991), 196–205 · E. Dale-Jones, 'John Nash: his place of residence in Carmarthen', *Carmarthenshire Antiquary*, 28 (1992), 117–18 · I. Sherfield, *East Cowes Castle* (1994) · *The diaries of John Nash, architect*, ed. M. Pinhorn, 2 vols. (2000) · J. M. Crook, *London's Arcadia: John Nash and the planning of Regent's Park* (2000)
Archives Northumbd RO, Newcastle upon Tyne, plans and builder's payments · priv. coll., diaries and 'statement' · RIBA, ledger and MSS relating to Regent's Canal | Carmarthenshire RO, Carmarthen, articles and agreement relating to rebuilding roof of St Peter's Church, Carmarthen · Carmarthenshire RO, Carmarthen, Cwmgwili MSS, corresp. · East Kent Archives Centre, Dover, corresp., plans, and elevations for St Alban's Street house of fifth earl of Guilford · PRO · PRO NIre., letters and accounts to second earl of Caledon · Royal Arch. · Shrops. RRC, letters to second Lord Berwick · William Salt Library, Stafford, corresp. and bills sent to J. F. Boughey · Wilts. & Swindon RO, letters relating to Corsham Court
Likenesses miniature, *c*.1798, priv. coll. · J. A. Couriguer, sculpture, *c*.1820, NPG · R. Evans, oils, *c*.1826, priv. coll. · T. Lawrence, oils, exh. RA 1827, Jesus College, Oxford [*see illus.*] · W. Behnes, marble bust, 1830, RIBA · E. Lambert, pen-and-ink sketch, *c*.1830, NPG · W. Behnes, marble bust, 1831, priv. coll.; repro. in Summerson, 'John Nash's "Statement", 1829' · E. Landseer, pen-and-ink drawing, NPG · T. Lawrence, oils, RIBA
Wealth at death under £70,000; incl. pictures and books worth £1484; East Cowes Castle and land approx. £20,000; Hamstead, Isle of Wight and land unknown; debts of approx. £15,000: will, Summerson, *Life and work*, 188

Nash, John Northcote (1893–1977), painter and printmaker, was born on 11 April 1893 at Ghuznee Lodge, Kensington, London, the younger son and second of the three children of William Harry Nash, barrister and recorder, of Abingdon, Berkshire, and his first wife, Caroline Maude, daughter of Captain Milbourne Jackson RN. He was the brother of the artist Paul *Nash (1889–1946) and of Barbara Nash, a remarkable gardener. In 1901 the family returned to its native Buckinghamshire, where the garden of Wood Lane House at Iver Heath, and the countryside of the Chiltern hills, with its sculptural beeches and chalky contours, were early influences on the development of the three children. Their lives were overshadowed by their mother's mental illness and Nash himself was greatly helped by his nurse who, with some elderly neighbours, introduced him to the universe of plants. Like his friend Cedric Morris, he would eventually describe himself as 'artist-plantsman'. He was educated at Langley Place in Slough, Buckinghamshire, and at Wellington College, Berkshire, which he hated but where he was awarded the botany prize. His mother died in 1910, when he was seventeen. Undecided on a career, he apprenticed himself to the *Middlesex and Berkshire Gazette* as a trainee journalist, but his future was in effect all laid out when, that same year, his brother Paul enrolled at the Slade School of Fine Art in London and brought home to Iver Heath two fellow students whose friendship with Nash would transform his life. They were Claughton Pellew, who, while on a walking holiday in Norfolk, was able to persuade him that he was an artist, and Dora Carrington, who introduced him to (Dorothy) Christine Kühlenthal (1895–1976), the daughter of Wilhelm Heinrich Kühlenthal, a German merchant chemist, and his wife, Ada Bustin, a Scot. (He and Christine eventually married, on 30 May 1918).

'The brothers Nash', as they were dubbed, to their lasting irritation, held a two-man exhibition at the Dorien Leigh Gallery in Pelham Street, Kensington, London, in November 1913. Nash had been advised by his brother to avoid art school training because it would ruin an exciting originality in his vision of landscape. Due to the enthusiasm of Michael Sadler and William Rothenstein, the exhibition, though modestly hung on the walls of a lampshade shop and announced by a home-made poster, was a success. Nash was now increasingly attracted to Carrington. An exchange of brilliantly illustrated letters between 1912 and 1916, the year in which he became engaged to her friend Christine, reveals their mutual delight in painting and landscape, but none on Carrington's part for the relationship he longed for. Regarding

Christine, she told him, 'She's the girl for you'. And she proved right.

Nash was unable to enlist due to health reasons until the autumn of 1916, when he joined the Artists' Rifles. He fought on the western front for nearly two years before returning home to join his brother as an official war artist. They hired a seed-shed at Chalfont St Peter, Buckinghamshire, and worked side by side on their superb war pictures, Nash's *Over the Top* (Imperial War Museum, London) providing an unforgettable image of the First World War. They were paid 30s. a day by the government, who acquired the pictures. In September 1918 Nash painted his classic *The Cornfield* (Tate collection) as a thank-you, he said, for having survived the trenches. From 1919 onwards he lived at Whiteleaf, Buckinghamshire, where, in addition to painting in oils and watercolour, he became part of the renaissance of English book illustration. His drawings and woodcuts of this period reveal his knowledge of literature and botany, the latter especially in his *Poisonous Plants* (1927). It was also at this time that he showed his sardonic wit in many comic drawings inspired by Edward Lear, whose work he had seen in the home of his Aunt Gussie, who had been one of Lear's 'freed' girlfriends.

During the 1920s Nash taught at the Ruskin School of Art, Oxford, and continued to teach until the end of his life. As with painting, botany, and music—he was an excellent pianist—he lacked any kind of formal training as a teacher, but those who attended his flower-painting classes in particular, including some of the best Kew artists, saw him as a true master. For most of the inter-war years he lived at Meadle, a hamlet near Princes Risborough, Buckinghamshire, and it was from this base that his wife organized working holidays all over Britain. His method was to fill up sketchbooks with pen, pencil, and wash studies and then develop them in oil and watercolour in the studio. The sketches were covered with notes on the weather and information on natural history, and some even noted the mood of a particular day in Cornwall or Skye. Nash liked the marks on the countryside made by farming and other rural industries, especially such features as ponds, cuttings, and quarries, and as the years passed his work became an unconscious, or unplanned, record of the agricultural depression, and its recovery during the 1950s. His wife, after showing striking promise with her painting during her years at the Slade School, was forced to give up because of glaucoma, a misfortune which halted her own career but which enabled her to give Nash the exacting regime of caring which he needed. She came to possess an amused kind of common sense which prevented her husband's self-interest and drive from overwhelming her own creativity. The single major disaster which befell them during fifty-nine years of marriage was the death of their four-year-old son William in a car accident in 1935.

In 1940 Nash was commissioned in the Royal Marines as an official war artist to the Admiralty. Although he produced a considerable body of paintings of the war, he confessed that his heart was not in this type of work as it had been in 1918. He was in his fifties when the war ended and his longing was to live and paint deep in the English countryside. Since 1929 he had painted in the summer at Wormingford in the Stour valley in Essex, where he had seen an ancient and dilapidated farmhouse down a long track. In 1944 he bought it for £750, its great attraction being the variety of soils around it which could be used for the making of his garden. His life there followed the same pattern as it had done in Buckinghamshire, though his painting holidays were now shared with other artists, particularly Carel Weight and Edward Bawden. Usually he sketched alone in the Stour valley fields or on the Suffolk coast. There was a fusion of an almost practical reality and an intense personal vision in the work of this period.

Nash was made ARA in 1940, RA in 1951, and appointed CBE in 1964, and in 1967 he was given the first ever retrospective exhibition at the Royal Academy by a living painter. He continued to teach into old age, memorably at the Flatford Mill field studies centre in Suffolk. He had said that he loved plants above all else, with music coming second, but one would only need to be with him in the countryside to recognize the priority that landscape had. Whether working solitarily in the studio or outdoors, or being gregarious in the evenings, an underlying melancholy was often present in his character—'the Nash blackness', as he called it. During his last years he suffered severely from arthritis but continued to paint until his death at St Mary's Hospital in Colchester on 23 September 1977. Christine, his wife, had died less than a year earlier. They were buried in the churchyard of St Andrew's parish church at Wormingford, Essex.   RONALD BLYTHE

Sources P. Nash and H. Read, *Outline: an autobiography and other writings* (1949) · Tate collection, Nash MSS · J. Rothenstein, *Modern English painters*, 3 vols. (1952–74) · R. Blythe, *A painter in the country*, BBC 2, 1968 [film] · R. Blythe, *John Nash at Wormingford* (1992) · R. Blythe, *First friends: Paul and Bunty, John and Christine—and Carrington* (1998) · J. Lewis, *The painter as illustrator* (1978) · S. Schiff, introduction, in J. Nash, *John Nash*, ed. S. Schiff (1925) · S. Schiff, 'John Nash', *Fleuron* (1925) · personal knowledge (2004) · private information (2004) · m. cert.

Archives AM Oxf. · Minories Gallery, Colchester · Tate collection, corresp., papers, and sketchbooks · Tate collection, John Nash Illustrated Books · Tate collection, printed material with MS annotations by him | Tate collection, corresp. with Nora Meninsky · Tate collection, corresp. with Barbara Nash | FILM BBC Archive, R. Blythe, *A painter in the country*, directed by John Read, 1968 | SOUND IWM

Likenesses P. Nash, watercolour and pencil, c.1913, NPG · J. N. Nash, self-portrait, ink and wash, c.1950, priv. coll. · E. Morgan, photographs, 1970, NPG · G. Spencer, pencil, c.1970, priv. coll. · P. Coker, pencil and chalk drawing, NPG · L. Hutchinson, bronze bust, probably NPG · S. S. Walia, photograph, NPG · photographs, Tate collection

Wealth at death £67,488: probate, 23 Jan 1978, CGPLA Eng. & Wales

Nash, Joseph (1809–1878), architectural painter and lithographer, was born on 17 December 1809 at Great Marlow, Buckinghamshire, the eldest son of the Revd Okey Nash (1779?–1862), proprietor of the Manor House School in Croydon. He was educated at his father's school and then about 1827 apprenticed to Auguste Pugin, under whose guidance he learned the art of architectural drawing and experimented with lithography. He travelled with Pugin's atelier to France to draw for *Paris and its Environs* (1830) and made lithographs of Pugin drawings published as *Views Illustrative of the Examples of Gothic Architecture* (1830). He may also have derived from Pugin his mature style of recreating the original state of old buildings and peopling them with picturesque tableaux. This style, and a preference for the later, more opulent Gothic period, was already evident in work he did for Pugin, depicting *en fête* the grander secular buildings of the fifteenth century such as Eltham and Croydon palaces. On 10 February 1831 Nash married a lady of property, Rebecca Dorothy Elwin, at Camberwell, Surrey, with whom he had two children, Joseph (b. 1835) and Mary Dorothy (b. 1838).

Nash's interests, once he was launched on his own career, shifted from ecclesiastical to secular buildings, from the Gothic to the Tudor period, and from purely architectural to more picturesque compositions. He was also attracted to lithography, and particularly to C. Hullmandel's innovations with the stump to apply tints and the brush to apply graded washes of ink (lithotinting), which gave a less precise but more lush and atmospheric effect approaching that of watercolour. His *Architecture of the Middle Ages: drawn from nature and on stone* (1838)—which belies its title by declaring a special affection for the 'richness of Fancy' evident in English and French Renaissance architecture—demonstrates his changing concerns. Nash's masterpiece, however, was the four-volume *Mansions of England in the Olden Time* (1839–49). To prepare these 100 lithographs of surviving country houses of the fifteenth to seventeenth centuries, many of them little known, Nash roamed the country and sketched each one thoroughly on site. He confined himself strictly to reproducing architectural details, exterior and interior, but enlivened them romantically with scenes of Tudor domestic life, feasting, and revels that he researched carefully in the antiquarian works of Joseph Strutt. His goal was to revive interest in these old English buildings by presenting them as the natural setting for some very modern sentiments, combining hearty feasting and drinking with class conciliation, domestic comfort, and virtue.

The *Mansions'* combination of architectural and antiquarian accuracy with contemporary values was devastatingly effective. Nash's plates were immediately engraved for mass circulation in the *Saturday Magazine* and widely copied and plagiarized in the popular illustrated press. They served as a sourcebook for architects but also as advertising placards for tourist sites around the country that became more accessible as the railway network developed. Already in 1841 Nash's work was cited before a parliamentary select committee as a factor in the growing popular taste for visiting historic buildings. The very romantic traits that made Nash's *Mansions* so popular also made them an object of suspicion. Thackeray dismissed Nash as 'a miniature scene-painter' and compared him unfavourably to the painter George Cattermole, who also favoured atmospheric historical scenes (*Fraser's Magazine*, 19, 1839, 749). Both C. L. Eastlake, in *A History of the Gothic*

Revival (1872), and Reginald Blomfield, in his preface to the 1906 edition of *Mansions*, criticized it as too facile and architecturally and morally lax. But its popularity persisted well into the twentieth century.

In his own day the *Mansions* won Nash little profit, but some esteem and further commissions. He was elected a full member of the Old Watercolour Society in 1842. He lithographed some drawings on oriental subjects by the late Sir David Wilkie, which appeared in two volumes in 1843 and 1846, and a series of views of Windsor Castle 'illustrative of the state and ceremony which distinguish the Royal hospitality' (Nash, *Views*), published under royal patronage in 1848. All of this work accounts for the delayed appearance of the final volume of the *Mansions* in 1849. After this date Nash withdrew progressively from the public eye. He was said to have suffered an attack of 'brain fever' in 1854, and the contents of his studio were sold at the end of that year. He became an irascible critic of the Old Watercolour Society which he accused of neglecting him and his son, a minor painter known for marine subjects. But he continued to produce drawings and sketches for exhibitions until shortly before his death on 19 December 1878, at his home, 84 Hereford Road, Kensington. His wife had predeceased him, perhaps in the 1840s.

PETER MANDLER

Sources J. L. Roget, *A history of the 'Old Water-Colour' Society*, 2 vols. (1891) · *DNB* · P. Mandler, *The fall and rise of the stately home* (1997) · J. Nash, *Descriptions of the plates of the mansions of England in the olden time* (1849) · J. Steegman, *Consort of taste, 1830–1870* (1950) · R. Strong, *And when did you last see your father? The Victorian painter and British history* (1978) · private information (2004) · C. L. Eastlake, *A history of the Gothic revival* (1872) · [W. M. Thackeray], 'A second lecture on the fine arts, by Michael Angelo Titmarsh, esq.: the exhibitions', *Fraser's Magazine*, 19 (1839), 743–50 · d. cert. · b. cert. [Mary Dorothy Nash] · M. Twyman, *Lithography, 1800–1850* (1970) · J. Nash, *Views of the interior and exterior of Windsor Castle* (1848) · IGI

Likenesses J. Watkins, photograph, NPG · wood-engraving, NPG; repro. in *ILN* (4 Jan 1879)

Wealth at death under £1500: probate, 18 Jan 1879, CGPLA Eng. & Wales

Nash, Michael (*fl.* 1791–1798), protestant controversialist, may have been of illegitimate birth. He is conjecturally credited with the authorship of *Stenography, or, The most Easy and Concise Method of Writing Short-Hand on an Entire New Plan* (1783).

Although often described as a Methodist, Nash was a member of the Church of England who, in December 1791, was appointed a collector of subscriptions or canvasser for the Societas Evangelica, a society for the maintenance of itinerant preachers. In the following year, in his capacity as secretary of the Society for the Promotion of the French Protestant Bible, he failed to induce the eminent evangelical clergyman, William Romaine, to preach on behalf of the society, but later discovered that Romaine had preached in his own church in aid of French Catholic refugee clergy. In consequence he published a pamphlet entitled *Gideon's Cake of Barley Meal* (1793) attacking Romaine, which produced several critical responses, including *A Charitable Morsel of Unleavened Bread* (1793) by

D. Parker, a committee member of the Societas Evangelica.

After the society dismissed Nash from his post in January 1794, he retaliated in *The Windmill Overturned by the Barley Cake* (1794). He was the author of other polemical works, including *Paine's Age of Reason Measured by the Standard of Truth* (1794) and—his last known pamphlet—*The Ignis fatuus, or, Will o' the Wisp at Providence Chapel, Detected and Exposed* (1798), a denunciation of the eccentric Calvinist preacher William Huntington. An obscure and enigmatic figure, little of his life, and nothing of his death, is known.   STEPHEN GREGORY

Sources [J. Watkins and F. Shoberl], *A biographical dictionary of the living authors of Great Britain and Ireland* (1816) · J. D. Reuss, *Alphabetical register of all the authors actually living in Great-Britain, Ireland, and in the United Provinces of North-America*, 2 vols. (1804) · J. Westby-Gibson, *The bibliography of shorthand* (1887)

Nash, Paul (1889–1946), painter, was born in London on 11 May 1889, the elder son of William Harry Nash (*d.* 1929), barrister and recorder of Abingdon, and his first wife, Caroline Maude (*d.* 1910), daughter of Captain Milbourne Jackson RN. His father's family came from Buckinghamshire farming stock, his mother's belonged to the navy, for which he was at first intended. But, with the capacity of any artist to fail where his heart is not engaged, Nash did not pass the entrance examination and so returned to finish his schooling at St Paul's School, London, which he left at seventeen. He avoided the alternative careers of architecture and banking, and pursued his interests in black and white illustration. After a short time at Chelsea Polytechnic school of art (1906–8) and then at night school at Bolt Court (the London County Council School of Photo-Engraving and Lithography), Nash went, with the encouragement of William Rothenstein, to the Slade School of Fine Art in 1910. He learned little there and left after a year. His earliest work was from his imagination, stimulated by the art and poetry of William Blake and Dante Gabriel Rossetti, the work of later Pre-Raphaelites, the early W. B. Yeats, and the plays of Gordon Bottomley, who encouraged him and became his friend. Nash earned modest fees from designing bookplates in a late arts and crafts style, and tried his hand, without obvious success, as a poet.

Unlike some of his contemporaries at the Slade School—Mark Gertler, C. R. W. Nevinson, William Roberts, and Edward Wadsworth—Nash remained uninfluenced by the two post-impressionist exhibitions organized by Roger Fry in 1910 and 1912. One day the painter Sir William Richmond said to him, 'My boy, you should go in for Nature' (Nash, 105). He did, looking at it more directly, and drawing it on the spot. The 'nature' that he went in for, although usually without human beings, was always peopled, if not by the 'star-inwrought' visions of his youth, then by what Nash himself many years later called the *genius loci*: something which was not at first formal, but evanescent, a quality of light and imagination, and which later developed a fantastic, tangible personality expressed most fully by the monoliths and monster trees of his later work.

Paul Nash (1889–1946), by Helen Muspratt, 1932

Nash had his first one-man show, of ink and wash drawings, at the prestigious Carfax Gallery, London, in 1912, and in 1913 shared an exhibition at the Dorien Leigh Gallery with his brother, John Northcote *Nash. In 1914 Nash married Margaret Theodosia (*d.* 1960), daughter of Naser Odeh, formerly priest in charge of St Mary's mission and the pro-cathedral, Cairo; there were no children. At the outbreak of war he enlisted in the Artists' Rifles; in 1916 he was commissioned in the Hampshire regiment and by March 1917 was in the Ypres salient. After four months he was invalided home as the result of an accident, but during those months he had spent all his time making drawings which were shown at the Goupil Gallery. Strongly recommended by supporters including William Rothenstein and Edward Marsh, Nash was appointed an official war artist under the newly initiated scheme run by the department of information under John Buchan (later Lord Tweedsmuir). Nash returned to the front as an official artist in November 1917 in the immediate aftermath of the battle of Passchendaele. The drawings he made then, of shorn trees in ruined and flooded landscapes, were the works that made Nash's reputation. They were shown at the Leicester Galleries in 1918 together with his first efforts at oil painting, in which he was self-taught and quickly successful, though his drawings made in the field had more immediate public impact. From April of that year until early in 1919 Nash was engaged on paintings commissioned by the department of information for the newly established Imperial War Museum, of which the largest and most famous is *The Menin Road*. Nash, who had also worked alongside the Canadian forces at Vimy Ridge, was among the select group of artists which was also commissioned to make a large painting for the Canadian war records (*A Night Bombardment*, National Gallery of Canada). His poetic imagination, instead of being crushed by the terrible circumstances of war, had expanded to produce terrible images—terrible because of their combination of detached, almost abstract, appreciation and their truth to appearance.

Nash's first note for his autobiography for the years following 1918 was 'Struggles of a war artist without a war' (Nash, 218). Disoriented, at first, and uncertain how to capitalize on success gained as a result of events people wanted to put behind them, Nash, over the following years, illustrated books, designed costumes and scenery for Sir James Barrie's *The Truth about the Russian Dancers*, was for a short time an instructor in design at the Royal College of Art, and became a leader of the revival of wood-engraving. Two important British illustrated books of the decade were Nash's *Places* (1922), landscape wood-engravings accompanied by brief prose poems, and his *Genesis* (1924) for the Nonesuch Press. It was in this decade that Nash evolved his characteristic watercolour style, his debts to Cézanne in no way concealing the depth of his kinship with the British watercolour tradition back to the eighteenth century. As an oil painter Nash developed differently, assimilating now the lessons of post-impressionism that had passed him by earlier on, as well as more recent achievements of the Paris school. But his sharp and often high-keyed colours are his own, and though Nash felt now the need to broaden his understanding of contemporary painting, he never permitted his own personality to become obscured.

In 1919 Nash moved to Dymchurch in Kent, beginning his well-known series of pictures of the sea, the breakwaters, and the long wall that prevents the sea from flooding Romney Marsh. Dymchurch wall and the marsh extending as far behind as the eye could see, with its dykes, culverts, and sheep pens, made an indelible impression on him, and he returned as late as 1937 to rework major Dymchurch designs such as *Winter Sea* (York City Art Gallery) and *Dymchurch Steps* (National Gallery of Canada). Nash also continued to paint the friendlier landscapes of his native territory, the Chilterns. He developed the flower-like forms that distinguish his later pictures, and also the study of trees, especially beechwoods, whose sun-crossed verticals inspired the structure of his near-abstract work, then just begun but in the next decade to be explored further. A second exhibition at the Leicester Galleries in 1924 confirmed Nash among the two or three leaders of British painting, while a third and particularly successful show at the same gallery in 1928 stimulated this increasingly self-critical artist to recognize that the formulae developed since 1918 would become a handicap unless he took greater risks, set himself new tasks, and explored areas of modern continental art that had bypassed England in the atmosphere of post-war cultural retrenchment.

From 1929 changes were evident in Nash's painting that were to lead him further towards abstraction, a direction Nash ultimately admitted he was unsuited to. He also explored the metaphysical art of the Italian Giorgio de Chirico, a highly productive encounter which was to lead him towards his own personal version of surrealism. His understanding of modern art in Paris was greatly stimulated by incursions into art criticism, writing in the early thirties for the *Listener* and the *Week-End Review*. Though he soon tired of regular criticism, Nash became a distinguished essayist, writing for the *Architectural Review*, *Country Life*, and other journals up to the outbreak of the Second World War. His eye for the quirky character of out-of-the-way places, and the expression in his articles of feeling for the severe classicism of the best British design, connecting Adam and Chippendale with the modern movement, reflect his keen perception of the character of British taste. Nash's *Dorset Shell Guide*, one of the first to be commissioned by John Betjeman for the series he edited for Shell-Mex, showed Nash's skill in reading the past through architectural survivals and the lineaments of the landscape.

The ten years from 1929 to the Second World War brought a new freedom in the different areas of Nash's many activities. He travelled to America (as British representative on the jury of the Carnegie International Exhibition, 1931) and in Europe (though his English roots seem to have left him always a little uneasy abroad). In 1933 Nash founded Unit One, the group of experimental painters, sculptors, and architects which included Henry Moore, Ben Nicholson, Barbara Hepworth, and Wells Coates among others. He was president of the Society of Industrial Artists, 1932–4, on the committee of the first International Surrealist Exhibition (London, New Burlington Galleries, 1936), had exhibitions at the Redfern and Leicester galleries, and showed at the Venice Biennale in 1938. During all this time he designed fabrics, posters (notably for Shell-Mex), book jackets, endpapers, and so on, the execution of which he always supervised with scrupulous care. Nash began using a camera in 1931 both as a way of recording ideas for possible pictures and as images and compositions that gave pleasure in themselves. During this time he struggled with increasingly serious ill health due to asthma, for which he tried living at Rye, Swanage in Dorset, and in Hampstead, where he stayed until the outbreak of war. In 1930 he had begun his illustrations for Sir Thomas Browne's *Urne Buriall* and *The Garden of Cyrus*. Sir Herbert Read has stressed how much Browne and Nash were akin in spirit. It was Nash's metaphysical wit combined with his odd, rather bookish sense of visual incongruities that led him to adopt his highly personal attitude to surrealism. For him, surrealism was less an international movement than a licence to paint as he chose within the terms of modern practice. Because he was neither mordant nor rebellious his work had none of the shock tactics of continental surrealism but retained the sweetness of the English landscape, the uncertainties of the English weather, and the whimsicalities of a cultivated English mind. His excursions into abstract painting had the same personal characteristics.

Nash was fascinated by evidence of prehistory, stones

and mounds in fields, and in the personalities of natural stones and flowers and twisted tree roots, and dwelt upon them both in his painting and in his writing. He started in 1937 an autobiography which was published posthumously, in 1949, as *Outline*. It traces the course of his life only to 1914; it is much concerned with the magic of childhood, and the travails as well as the excitements of growing up and facing the world. He saw 1914 and the war as a caesura, the close of an era. *Outline* is a perfect vignette and it is not perhaps surprising that Nash never took the story further. He wrote with elegance and heart; his observations of himself and others were shrewd, humorous, and searching. He was a witty man who could also inspire wit in others since his rapturous reception of remarks sharpened people's intelligence when talking to him. No nuance was lost.

When war broke out in 1939 Nash, though already a very sick man, was unwilling to forgo the kind of public role he had had in the First World War, or to retreat from positions of leadership which he felt it the duty of the experienced and successful to offer to younger men. He moved to Oxford, living at 106 Banbury Road, opened a bureau to help artists find the least wasteful kinds of work for their capabilities, and became a war artist to the Air Ministry, later transferring to the Ministry of Information. This war disturbed Nash but did not change his art as the last one had. His style and his habits were formed, and in the new war he treated his new subjects as he had treated those he had been thinking about for so long. His late paintings, both oils and watercolours, are alternately brilliant and sombre in colour with the light of setting suns and rising moons spreading over wooded and hilly landscapes. Not many of his new war paintings bear any relation to the desolate wastes of 1917, among the few being *Totes Meer* (Tate collection), a sea of broken, twisted German aeroplane wrecks on a dump outside Oxford. The disparity was partly due to the different nature of the wars, but much more to the fact that in 1917 the whole of his outraged inexperience was at the service of the war, whereas in 1940 the war was made to serve his experience. Aeroplanes were domesticated to his canvas as tree trunks or stones had been between the wars. Such an attitude was by then an artist's only remedy, his only chance of survival. On the whole, his official patrons were disappointed by his poetical aeroplanes. His last works were of flowers, in particular sunflowers, and landscapes, and giant flowers dominating landscapes.

Nash had a noteworthy sense of order and of the niceties of presentation; his pictures were beautifully framed, drawings mounted, his studio precisely and decoratively tidy, and oddments which he collected were worked up into compositions (found objects). In his life his sense of fitness extended, even on the most ordinary occasions, to his clothes. His scarf and dressing gown in the morning would be fit for a play; his suits and his ties, matched, brushed, and pressed as though by a valet. All this with his black hair, brilliant blue eyes, and fine profile made him seem a very exquisite person. But his features

never stayed put, to be admired; they were mobile, sensitive to atmosphere and—this was his saving grace—ironical. Nash died at 35 Boscombe Spa Road, Bournemouth, on 11 July 1946 and was buried on 17 July in Langley church, Buckinghamshire.

Myfanwy Piper, *rev.* Andrew Causey

Sources *DNB* · P. Nash and H. Read, *Outline: an autobiography and other writings*, another edn (1988) · A. Causey, *Paul Nash* (1980) · A. Bertram, *Paul Nash: the portrait of an artist* (1955) · C. C. Abbott and A. Bertram, eds., *Poet and painter: being the correspondence between Gordon Bottomley and Paul Nash, 1910–1946* (1955); rev. edn (1990) · A. Causey, *Paul Nash's photographs: document and image* (1973) [exhibition catalogue, Tate] · M. Eates, *Paul Nash: the master of the image, 1889–1946* (1973) · *Paul Nash: paintings and watercolours* (1975) [Tate Gallery] · A. Causey, *Paul Nash* (1980) [incl. *catalogue raisonné*] · *CGPLA Eng. & Wales* (1947) · C. Neve, *Unquiet landscape: places and ideas in twentieth century English painting* (1990)

Archives Tate collection, artwork, corresp., and MSS | Tate collection, letters to Gordon Bottomley · Tate collection, corresp. with Kenneth Clark · Tate collection, letters to John Nash · Tate collection, letters to Mercia Oakley · Tate collection, corresp. with Sir Michael Sadler · Tate collection, corresp. relating to Unit One · Tate collection, letters to R. H. Wilenski [photocopies]

Likenesses R. Lee, pencil drawing, 1913, NPG · P. Nash, self-portrait, watercolour and pencil, *c.*1913, NPG · H. Muspratt, photographs, *c.*1932, NPG [*see illus.*] · F. Man, photographs, 1943, NPG · photograph, 1944, Hult. Arch. · P. Nash, self-portraits, wood-engravings, BM · P. Nash, self-portraits, wood-engravings, V&A · Ramsey & Muspratt, photographs, Tate collection · Ramsey & Muspratt, two photographs, NPG · L. Sieveling, photograph, NPG

Wealth at death £1731 14*s.* 5*d.*: probate, 18 Jan 1947, *CGPLA Eng. & Wales*

Nash, Richard [*known as* Beau Nash] (1674–1761), master of ceremonies and social celebrity, was born on 18 October 1674 at St Mary's Street, Swansea, the son of Richard Nash, a glass maker of modest means, and his wife, the niece of the royalist army officer Colonel John *Poyer. From about the age of twelve Nash was educated at Carmarthen grammar school, and in March 1692 he matriculated from Jesus College, Oxford. His father intended that this costly education result in a legal career. However, for Richard, Oxford's attractions were social not intellectual. By the age of seventeen he had been involved in an 'intrigue' with a local woman to whom he proposed. The affair, becoming known to his college, led to Nash's dismissal from the university and the start of a brief period as a would-be womanizer.

In order to enhance his appeal Nash persuaded his father to purchase him a commission in the army, whose uniforms he sported and embellished 'to the very edge of his finances' (Goldsmith, 3.293). But military coats and brocade also brought excessive regimentation. On quitting the army, Nash enrolled as a legal student at the Inner Temple and began publicizing himself as a man about town. His finances were still very limited and he endured private hardships to present a continuously elegant and refined public image. Nash was now discovering that his talent was for self-promotion, and his desire for celebrity and social elevation. At this time he was also linked with a series of fanciful, amusing, and much recycled anecdotes which, just as much as the facts, helped identify extravagance as one of Nash's defining characteristics. Thus these

Richard Nash (1674–1761), by Nathaniel Hone, 1750

years saw him dressed both lavishly in metropolitan high society and as a beggar outside York Minster, accidentally going to sea on a British warship, and riding naked on a cow for a wager. Extravagance was also manifest in his many acts of generosity, another lifelong personality trait. In *The Spectator* (no. 248, 14 December 1711), Richard Steele described how a Temple student (identified as Nash by Oliver Goldsmith) claimed £10 from his college 'for making one man happy'; questioned by his masters, Nash explained that he had been obliged to act having overheard a man lament his misery for the want of this sum. Tales of his generosity also began to bring fame beyond the inns of court. In 1696 Nash courted a Miss Verdun who, against her father's wishes, refused him and claimed she was to marry another. Nash's request to meet his rival and offer his congratulations was developed by John Vanbrugh in his play *Aesop* (1697), in which the eponymous hero was styled the 'Count of the Inner Temple'. Miss Verdun eventually eloped with a footman.

Making of a monarch, 1695–1716 The story of Nash's emergence as an arbiter of taste and manners likewise centres on several set-piece events at which he combined self-publicity with opportunism and a definite skill for social organization and management. In 1695 he supervised a pageant held at the inns of court in honour of William III, the success of which displayed 'proofs of that spirit of regularity' and 'an attention to those little circumstances' (Goldsmith, 3.295) which, within a decade, Nash was bringing to the attention of the corporation at the spa town of Bath. The rise of Bath as a place worthy of Nash's attention was due in part to William's heir, Queen Anne, who visited the town in 1702 and 1703. The queen's stay at

what was then a relatively minor resort prompted the arrival of increasingly well-to-do and fashionable guests, the gradual development of an improved infrastructure, and the organization of diversionary entertainments under the supervision of the then master of ceremonies, Captain Thomas Webster.

Nash was no doubt drawn to Bath in 1705 for the same reasons as many other gamblers and philanderers. Yet it appears to have been Nash's talent for showmanship, for gauging the popular mood, and for understanding the economic realities facing the town's corporation that prompted him to transform an outing into a lifelong career. Shortly after Nash's arrival, the physician John Radcliffe is said to have threatened to publish against the efficacy of the spa, likening his proposal to casting a toad into the spring. Nash's response—to establish a company of musicians 'against the poison of the Doctor's reptile' (Goldsmith, 3.300)—has since become a popular element of his mythology and a key moment in the establishment of his hold over the spa's embryonic 'company'. Briefly employed as an assistant to the master of ceremonies, Nash was elected by the resort's visitors to the full post following Webster's death in a duel late in 1705. Whatever the reality of his rise to office (both of Nash's best eighteenth-century memoirists, Goldsmith and John Wood, offer the same colourful story), it appears that he displayed qualities by which he subsequently developed his control: firm but innovative leadership sweetened by charisma, the provision of quality social diversions, and the promise of commercial success.

Among his biographers it has been common to identify Nash's appointment as heralding Bath's transformation from a place of convalescence to one which combined health with a successful dedication to fashionable entertainment. In fact Nash's presence and influence need to be seen in context. His arrival coincided with a period of change as the corporation sought, through local legislation, to respond to the demands of an increasingly prosperous visiting public. Further initiatives came from citizens who currently enjoyed greater standing than the new master of ceremonies, among them the physician William Oliver (d. 1716), whose writings on spa water prompted the building of a pump room in 1705–6. Popular claims that Nash was involved in renting the new room and in employing the pumper (an office in existence since the 1680s) have also been questioned by urban historians (for example, Macintyre).

None the less it is reasonable to see Nash's early consolidation of his position both with the corporation, but more importantly with his principal object, the company, as benefiting from his contribution to this trend for enhanced civic facilities. On gaining office he fulfilled his promise to introduce a band of London musicians paid for by subscription, and appears to have supported—though not, as some state, initiated—legislation in 1707 which improved the quality of communications around Bath and of the walkways within the town. At this time he also gave his backing for Thomas Harrison's new assembly room for dancing, refreshments, and card games, which was similarly financed by weekly subscription and profits from gambling. Later satires highlight Nash's importance to the success of Harrison's rooms to which he drew customers by his reputation for fashion and gaming: 'to look out sharp, and bring Persons down to the place', so that Harrison 'grew very rich' and Nash 'very great' (*An Essay Against too much Reading*, 1728, 20–22).

Nash's growing reputation among the visiting company also owed much to a series of pronouncements by which he shaped the emerging culture of Bath fashionable society. On his arrival, élite visitors 'still preserved a tincture of *Gothic* haughtiness' (Goldsmith, 3.300), while they, and others, maintained an often boorish culture through unregulated hours. Nash's central aim was the creation of a community in which rank and background, if never discounted, were at least attuned to his general principles of accommodation and assimilation. Through promotion of these qualities Nash put into practice aspects of the current theory of social conduct which equated politeness less with an adherence to manners than with an easy and enjoyable sociability. Mindful of his predecessor's fate, he banned the carrying of swords to reduce the risk of disputes ending in violence. Anti-social customs such as smoking and drinking were also regulated, as was the duration of evening dances, at which he presided and promptly called time at 11 p.m. Nash codified these principles in a series of 'Rules to be observ'd at Bath' which, though humorous, indicate his attachment to civilized co-existence: ladies, for example, were told to depart from balls in a manner which prevented 'disturbance and inconvenience to themselves and others'; gentlemen were to show 'breeding and respect' by never appearing underdressed in female company; and no one was to spread gossip or feel snubbed when an invitation was refused. For devising and propagating his regulations he earned the sobriquet 'Arbiter Elegantiae'.

On a day-to-day basis Nash's reforms were largely successful, and while instances of duelling or drunkenness continued, they did so to a lesser extent. Yet, notwithstanding his reputation as a social organizer, Nash and his methods were often at odds with the image of the archetypal modern polite gentleman. Visitors were sometimes surprised by the contrast between Nash's reputation and his actual deportment: 'Where is that well-bred ease and affable politeness we expect? … Heavens! how grim he looks [with] … a kind of ill tempered vacancy coupled with a coarse jocularity' (J. Burton, *Epistolae altera peregrinantis*, 1748, 23). Moreover, in enforcing his rules Nash at times behaved rudely, even cruelly, to individuals whom he publicly criticized for lapses in dress code or etiquette as a lesson to the watching assembly. For Nash to upbraid a gauche tradesman or country squire might be expected. That he was able to criticize the duchess of Queensberry for wearing an apron to the assembly, or to forbid Princess Amelia to continue dancing after 11 p.m., indicates the extent of his authority. That recipients of such rebukes accepted them as coming from the reigning 'monarch', as he was often described, highlights a readiness among the company to accept the singularity of

Nash's vision for the resort. The corporation, aware of the cultural and commercial benefits he brought, granted Nash honorary freedom of the city in October 1716.

King of Bath, 1716–1738 The next twenty years saw the apogee of Nash's influence and celebrity among a company routinely numbering 8000–12,000 at the height of the season. Writing in May 1716 the future lord chief justice Dudley Ryder, then a law student visiting the spa, spoke of 'Gnash' as 'the life and soul of all … diversions. Without him there is no play or assembly nor ball' (*Diary of Dudley Ryder*, 240). In the following decade the poet Robert Whatley dedicated his latest collection to Nash, whom he described as enjoying 'a Power that is wholly despotick … Your Word is your Law; and whatever Mr N pleases to order, every one submits to with the same Pleasure and Resignation' (Whatley, vi–vii). The poet also provides a description of Nash's appearance: standing 5 feet 8 inches tall, he was of good build and proportion, of 'black brown' complexion with a physiognomy strong enough to earn the respect of men while not offending the women (ibid., xv). Others not seeking patronage were less gracious in their description of 'a very ugly man' (*Diary of Dudley Ryder*, 240) or 'a batter'd old Beau … not at all handsome' (*Diary of a Tour of Three Students from Cambridge*, 1725, quoted in Fawcett, *Voices*, 185).

At the time of this last comment Nash, though fifty, still had over thirty-five years to serve as Bath's master of ceremonies. Such longevity in office was a remarkable achievement in a society prone to celebrate the fashionable and the contemporary. He was, in his own words, 'a beau of three generations', and his hold on power has been much commented on by eighteenth-century and later observers, though its mechanics seldom analysed.

Several factors may be identified. First, despite his at best average looks, Nash appreciated the importance of establishing and maintaining a strong physical presence. Dress was central to developing a distinctive appearance by which he underpinned his career as a self-publicist. Well into old age Nash retained his youthful attachment to fine and fashionable clothes complemented by a cane and a white beaver hat which became symbolic of his position, commanding, as Lady Luxborough put it, 'more respect and non-resistance than the crowns of some kings' (Girouard, 78). To this he added appropriately majesterial trappings. Journeys between Bath and Tunbridge Wells, where he additionally became master of ceremonies in 1735, were made by a post-chaise drawn by six grey horses and attended by an Irish running footman and horn-playing outriders. On occasions such as the visit in October 1738 of Frederick and Augusta, the prince and princess of Wales, the symbolism of the king of Bath and the would-be king of Britain combined as Nash rode out 'in his Chariot and Six, to meet the Royal Pair' before entering the city in procession (*Gloucester Journal*, 24 Oct 1738, quoted in Fawcett, *Voices*, 187).

Nash was similarly conspicuous in his daily routine. Such visibility served not only to signal his diligence as the town's steward—prestigious new guests, for example, received a personal visit on arrival—but also to emphasize his absences, which left many visitors with a sense of loss and expectation for his return. From 1735 until his death he spent Bath's close season (July and August) as master at Tunbridge Wells where, as before, he introduced regulations on conduct, improved the facilities, and brought in new entertainments. Nash's presence had a rapid effect, and his second season, which attracted 900 visitors, was the best for six years. Society watchers in Bath eagerly awaited his return on 1 October, and even short delays, as in 1752 and 1754, gave cause for concern. That resort life was not fully complete during Nash's absence offers a second explanation for his hold on power. To its visitors Bath was promoted as a centre of enjoyment and diversion. Yet it could also be an unfamiliar and lonely place where the ranks were expected to socialize but to which many, especially middling types such as Dudley Ryder, brought a diffidence born of external social hierarchies. For these people Nash served as a common link to the in-crowd, someone all knew of and about whom one might either express genuine regard or feign interest to pass time with strangers. 'His sayings', wrote Ryder, 'seem to make a great part of the conversation of others and the repeating of what he does or says helps to fill up the conversation very much' (*Diary of Dudley Ryder*, 240).

To many memoirists Nash's principal achievement was his creation of a society in which established class structures gave way to the common pleasures of sociability. There is something to be said for this, given his enforcement of regulations independent of the deference which attended metropolitan entertainments. Nash's rule, moreover, could be severe. Many contemporary and later commentators have likened early eighteenth-century Bath to an autocracy and its master to a despot whose powers appeared most conspicuous when confronting social lapses among the upper classes. But equally Nash was no social leveller, and Bath no haven from the realities of class division. Oliver Goldsmith well understood that Nash's hold on power owed much to a third quality: his diverse appeal to competing interest groups. Among the nobility, therefore, he was 'an inoffensive, useful companion', while the growing numbers of middle-class visitors, aware of his background, considered him one of their own and admired him as someone with sufficient drive to become 'a person of fine sense, and great good breeding' (Goldsmith, 3.302). Nash undoubtedly played up to these groups. Ticking off a duchess at the morning assembly was followed during the evening ball by an acknowledgement of social precedence at the opening French dances, which later gave way, on Nash's orders, to their less formal English equivalents. Nash was similarly alert to the power conveyed by an association with royalty or those with access to the court. To forbid a princess to dance after 11 p.m. was an acceptable inversion of hierarchy in the exceptional context of Bath society. Yet Nash also understood the personal benefit of a more conventional relationship, as in his welcome to the duke and duchess of Marlborough in August 1714, and the visits by the prince of Orange in 1734 and the prince and princess of Wales in October 1738. Nash commemorated the latter visits with a

typically disingenuous act of marketing. Ostensibly the two obelisks that were erected near the abbey and at Queen's Square celebrated the prince of Orange's return to health, and the 'honours bestow'd' and the 'benefits conferred in this city' by Prince Frederick and Princess Augusta. But by making it known that the monuments had been put up on his initiative and at his expense, Nash used the royal visits to advertise his elevated connections and his own comparative generosity to the city. It was Goldsmith's view that the royal visit of 1738 marked the high point of Nash's mastership when he achieved 'such a pitch of authority, that I really believe *Alexander* was not greater at *Persepolis*' (Goldsmith, 3.344). It was a sign of his standing that his two sets of royal guests presented gifts—in both instances, of snuff-boxes—to their host. Keen to demonstrate their own intimacy with Nash, many visitors followed suit until he was said to possess enough boxes 'to have furnished a good toy-shop' (ibid.).

Nash's effort to promote himself as a loyal civic servant provides a final explanation for the longevity of his appeal. To many his presence had considerably improved the town's material and cultural life. This influence was particularly noticeable in the changing experience of women at the resort. A small-time philanderer in his youth, Nash by his own account renounced womanizing in adulthood. Certainly he remained popular in female company, where he gained favour for his fame, fine dress, and wit. And just as he might censure members of the élite, so his celebrity allowed him to exceed the normal boundaries of permissible polite conversation: 'He has the privilege of saying what he pleases and talking to the ladies as his fancy leads him and no affront is taken, though he sometimes puts modest women to the blush' (*Diary of Dudley Ryder*, 240). However, there is little evidence that he used his position to secure sexual favours. Indeed Nash was better known for protecting women against rakish male visitors and for reforms, such as the banning of swords which, as well as reducing duelling, also allowed for easier and more intimate socializing between the sexes.

Nash's private life consisted of two known relationships, both of which appear to have taken place during the early 1740s. The first was with Frances (Fanny) *Murray, *née* Rudman (1729–1778), a former child lover of Jack Spencer, grandson of the first duke of Marlborough. According to her colourful and often unreliable memoirs, Murray met Nash ('Mr Easy') and moved into his house on St John's Close, where Nash had lived from 1720, when she was fourteen and he in his late sixties. Young and beautiful, Murray attracted a number of suitors, with one of whom Nash is said to have duelled. However, according to Murray, Nash also grew to resent her rival celebrity and ended the affair. He had a second relationship with **Juliana Popjoy** (*bap.* 1714, *d.* 1777), the daughter of an innkeeper from Bishopstrow, near Warminster, whom he may have met while travelling to London. A former dressmaker, in Bath she was known for her grey horse propelled by a many-thonged whip for which she gained the name Lady Betty Besom. Popjoy appears to have been with

Nash at the time of the visit by George II's daughter Princess Mary, and her niece Princess Caroline, in 1740. The couple separated, possibly in the mid-1740s, and contrary to several biographies there is no evidence to suggest that she returned to care for Nash in his final years. The correspondence of Nash's executor, George Scott (1719–1780), also suggests a further association with a Mrs Hill, a difficult 'termagant Woman', with whom Scott claimed Nash lived during the 1740s and 1750s, though Hill's identity and the nature of the relationship remains unclear (BL, Egerton MS 3736, fol. 139).

It did not take too much to develop the image of Nash as a considerate defender of women into that of a generous benefactor of individual visitors and, in time, the town at large. This potential for civic responsibility had long been recognized. According to *The Original Bath Guide* (1811), the corporation's decision to elect Nash as Captain Webster's replacement had owed as much to his 'goodness of heart' as his 'polite behaviour' (*The Original Bath Guide*, 89). Likewise Goldsmith and others recorded numerous instances of Nash's personal generosity to failed gamblers or innocents snared by corrupt elders. By applying his considerable charisma and commercial sense to fundraising he further developed a reputation as one of the spa's leading benefactors. This said, Nash's attitude to charity, like his enactment of politeness, was seldom pious. He was, as Goldsmith put it, 'rude enough to make a jest of poverty' but also of 'sensibility enough to relieve it' (Goldsmith, 3.334). And, as with the enforcement of social regulations, Nash was also conspicuous and enterprising in his fundraising. He used his fame to force otherwise indifferent visitors to make sizeable donations, as in the case of an episode in the assembly room while collecting for a new general hospital. Dismissed by a duchess who professed sympathy but an empty purse, Nash is said to have produced a handful of coins and begun counting them into his hat as evidence of her pledge, producing a 30 guinea donation before she was able to escape. Such encounters, which according to one source raised an estimated £2000 in six years (see Falconer), came to fruition in 1742 with the opening of the town's infirmary, for which he acted as treasurer in 1739; thereafter he served as a moderately diligent governor during the 1740s and early 1750s. It was evidence of the importance attached to his reputation as a civic servant that Prince Hoare's statue of Nash, commissioned by the corporation in 1751 (and now in the rebuilt Pump Room), shows him holding the hospital's building plans in his right hand.

A tarnished crown, 1739–1761 Notwithstanding his popularity Nash was seldom without critics, many of whom resented the authority of a man dedicated to pleasure and the practice of triviality. Lord Chesterfield, on seeing Hoare's life-size statue placed between smaller busts of Pope and Newton, had mocked an inversion of true worth which had 'Wisdom and Wit … little seen, But Folly at full length'. However, such jibes were slight compared with what was to come, much of it of Nash's own making. As age impinged on his talent for self-promotion he found himself involved in a series of scandals, the number and

volume of complaints becoming a dominant characteristic of his old age. Observers had long been aware, and accepted, that his interest in Harrison's, and other, assembly rooms brought him financial reward through a share of the entertainment receipts. But there was less tolerance for Nash's additional income from the assembly's gaming tables, which he managed and promoted among the company. Involvement in gambling was of particular concern to the religious groups who gathered to censure Bath's diversions and its master of ceremonies. Responding to a rebuke from Lady Jerningham about 1730, for example, Nash confessed himself 'a bad Christian' and asked for her forgiveness after 'engaging att deep play' (quoted in Fawcett, *Voices*, 186). He was rather less repentant in June 1739 during a confrontation with the Methodist leader John Wesley, whom he attempted to stop preaching on the sinfulness of the town's entertainments. On this occasion Nash, expecting a pious rebuke, had been disarmed by Wesley's charitable refusal to judge the master of ceremonies at their first meeting. Yet to many his reputation as a sinner, or at least a prodigious gambler, was already well established. Cards and dice had been an important part of Nash's life since his youth, and became central at Bath and Tunbridge Wells, where gaming was a principal source of entertainment. To Goldsmith, Nash was an experienced, persistent, but ultimately unsuccessful gambler because of his natural generosity and openness. But losses at the table were slight compared with the damage done to Nash's reputation following revelations about his clandestine involvement in gambling schools at Tunbridge Wells and Bath.

Parliamentary legislation in 1739–40 and 1745 considerably reduced the number of permitted games involving cards and dice. In response new means of gambling were devised, the most successful being a form of roulette, E.O. (evens and odds), invented by Humphry Cleak and first tested at the Tunbridge assembly room. Popular with the company, the game was also lucrative for its organizers, Cleak and Metcalfe Ashe, the room's manager, who formed a syndicate to maximize their income. Nash became involved after settling a dispute over the division of profits and was, for a cut, charged with tempting players to participate while appearing to outsiders to have no interest other than as a fellow gambler. The success of E.O. led to the establishment of a rival table at Tunbridge under Thomas Joye, whom Nash persuaded to join the original syndicate with the master of ceremonies receiving a quarter share. Nash subsequently introduced the game to Bath and, for a fifth of the profits, set up a similar network with John, Walter, and William Wiltshire, owners of Wiltshire's assembly room.

The game's popularity promised an easy route to considerable wealth. Nash's mistake, however, was to leave the accounting to his partners. By the early 1750s he was convinced that he had been cheated of his share at Tunbridge to a sum, by his own calculation, of 2000 guineas. In 1754 he brought a suit in chancery against Ashe and Joye, and he repeated the action against the Wiltshires three years later. Depositions show that in 1746 Nash had received £80 from Ashe and Joye, with subsequent annual payments falling to £20 in 1750. Nash's former partners maintained that these sums were not, as he maintained, reduced profits from their gaming school but one-off gifts to their friend. In Bath, John Simpson offered a similar defence, claiming that a bequest of £50 had been made on account of Nash's increasing age and his having been 'a great friend to Bath' (Ferguson, 381).

Crucially, by arguing for the syndicate's existence, Nash revealed that he had misled visitors for personal gain. Via his own testimony the public servant and ally of the company became an example of the artifice and corruption that many saw as endemic to resorts such as Bath and Tunbridge Wells. The exposure, which followed allegations in 1748 concerning Nash's profiteering from public subscriptions, led to a severe loss of faith in a man whose purpose had previously seemed dedicated to regulating society for visitors' benefit and entertainment. In so doing, the scandal undercut two of the principal foundations—civic responsibility and personal generosity—on which he had successfully based his authority. That Nash was prepared to pursue his money through the courts, regardless of the public consequences of the lawsuit, also exposed the limited funds of someone who had hitherto presented an image of effortless affluence. A possibly truer picture of his finances, as suggested by Fanny Murray, was Nash's ongoing struggle to maintain an appearance of wealth through fine dress and trappings. Such efforts were, ironically, familiar to many of the spa's visitors and might, in differing circumstances, have brought Nash into closer contact with those he supervised. However, for a role dependent on the acceptance of natural superiority and in a society, like Bath, dedicated to show and secrets, this proximity became increasingly difficult to re-establish. From the early 1750s Goldsmith described a 'man involved in continual disputes, everyday calumniated with some new slander' (Goldsmith, 3.317), whose financial insecurity forced a move to more modest lodgings on the town's Saw Close.

Though his reputation suffered greatly Nash was never abandoned by the town's political leaders in his final decade. In 1754 the corporation began a subscription for his proposed, but never written, *History of Bath and Tunbridge*, of which it requested twenty-five copies. Other subscribers included Augusta, dowager princess of Wales, who sent a donation of £100. Despite these and other gifts, by the late 1750s Nash had been forced to sell many of his personal effects to placate his creditors, and in February 1760 the corporation granted him a monthly pension of 10 guineas. Nevertheless George Scott estimated that he still owed upwards of £1200 at his death. Throughout this period Nash also retained the office of master of ceremonies, though Goldsmith's moving description is of a man bereft of ideas and increasingly denied the goodwill of a disillusioned company. And yet, despite his reduced personal and financial status, Nash does appear to have continued to wield some authority, though its enforcement was now by his assistant (and successor), Jacques Colet. Writing in October 1760, for example, Mrs Delany

explained that Colet's ballroom arbitration was '*by Mr Nash's direction*', though the 'poor wretch is now wheeled into the Rooms' (letter to Mrs Dewes, *Autobiography ... Mrs Delany*, 3.607). By now, having suffered with apoplexy and gout for a decade, he was also subject to seizures such as that on 8 February 1761 from which, aged eighty-six, he died four days later at Saw Close. He was survived by his former companion, Juliana Popjoy, who following their separation had left Bath and, resolving 'never more to lie in a bed' (*GM*, 1st ser., 47, 1777, 195), spent the next thirty years living in a hollow tree near Warminster until her death in March 1777.

Efforts to rehabilitate Nash's reputation began almost immediately. On 14 February the corporation voted 'a sum not exceeding 50 guineas' for a 'state' funeral befitting their faithful impresario. The resulting procession, which left Saw Close for Bath Abbey on the 17th, offered a carefully chosen assembly of clergy, musicians, aldermen, and owners of the assembly rooms—led by children from the charity school and concluded by the hospital's beadles and patients—who, 'shedding unfeigned tears', provided an eloquent statement of the corporation's wish to remember Nash as much as the town's benefactor as its premier man of fashion. Nash was buried in the abbey on the same day.

A beau reviewed Nash's death also prompted a series of literary tributes. 'A faint sketch of the life' by William Oliver (d. 1764) described a 'great' public character, 'self-built and self-maintained' who in private was 'amiable, grateful, beneficent, and generous'. William King spoke of his candour, prudence, and just use of power, while an anonymous poem, 'On the death of R. Nash esq.', returned to the theme of the master of ceremonies both as defender of female liberties and innocent pleasures:

> Their sure protector and their friend
> He bid them to his laws attend
> Their happiness—his chiefest end.

and as the town's principal benefactor:

> Go ask the aged and the blind
> They'll tell you He was wondr'rous kind;
> See orphans, widows, beat their breast,
> Can sorrow better be expressed?

Not all responses were favourable, of course. Writing in the *Christian's Magazine* for February 1761, the popular preacher William Dodd criticized the 'extremely *prejudicial ... fatal* and *destructive*' nature of Nash's 'example, and your project' (Dodd, 133). A similar coolness is evident in parts of the first full-length memoir, Oliver Goldsmith's *Life of Richard Nash*, published in October 1762. Like Dodd, Goldsmith warned readers not to emulate Nash's example: 'To set him up, as some do, for a pattern of imitation, is wrong, since all his virtues received a tincture from the neighbouring folly' (Goldsmith, 3.378). At first even his successes appeared belittled: if a sovereign he was a 'weak man governing weaker subjects, and may be considered as resembling a monarch of *Cappadocia ... the little king of a little people*' (ibid., 3.289). Yet Goldsmith's is also a more subtle and, consequently, useful assessment. His challenge was to write at a time when the biography was expected to serve didactic ends by exposing either great character and heroism or moral shortcomings. Yet, as Goldsmith appreciated, Nash failed to meet either standard, being rather a new breed of biographical subject—a social celebrity ('a person so much talked of, and yet so little known'; ibid., 3.288)—in whom it was possible to detect good and bad qualities, and whose legacy could be variously appropriated to promote competing agendas.

Much has been written on Goldsmith's *Life*, partly in terms of its historical accuracy, but more particularly in an attempt to determine its dominant tone. For some Goldsmith's criticism prevails. And yet, notwithstanding the biography's reservations regarding Nash's character, it seems reasonable to see the *Life* as generally apprecia-tive of an ambiguous subject who, as Goldsmith realized, was flawed because of his humanity in a town given to temptation, and was rendered complex by the matter-of-fact approach taken by his biographer: as he explained in the preface, 'I chose to describe the man as he was' (Goldsmith, 3.289). Thus Goldsmith's account ultimately develops themes identified in more ostentatious com-memorations by William Oliver and William King: Nash as innovative reformer of social conduct and as benefac-tor, even a man of feeling—'None felt pity more strongly, and none made greater efforts to relieve distress' (ibid., 3.333). But as an early celebrity biographer, Gold-smith also appreciated the dangers of such exposure. Con-sequently the lasting theme of this, still the most valuable account of Nash's personality, is sympathy for a subject who sacrificed happiness, integrity, and independence for immediate fame and popularity within a community of which he was equally master and servant.

Such insights were rare among Bath writers, whose positive image of Nash sought to enhance the reputation of a town which quickly became synonymous with its for-mer master. Later eighteenth-century guide books rou-tinely included a complimentary sketch of Nash's life and work to introduce visitors to a resort of which, with town and master in tandem, they were expected to approve and enjoy. Regardless of Nash's failings, and his declining authority towards the end of his life, there was also by the mid-1760s a growing nostalgia for the glory days of his civic management. Nash soon came to embody a former age of more civilized manners, though in truth his had always been a pragmatic and idiosyncratic system com-pared with metropolitan theories of conduct. By contrast Nash's successors, Jacques Colet and Samuel Derrick, were judged poor substitutes for Nash in his prime. Mat-ters came to a head with the 'Bath contest' of March 1769 which ended in the heated, sometimes violent, quarrel between rival camps for Derrick's successor. The antith-esis of the measured social cohesion preached and moulded by Nash, the contest further enhanced the repu-tation of the former master of ceremonies as an effective and trusted lawmaker:

O spirit of King Nash arise!
This mighty diff'rence compromise

Arise with olive branches crown'd,
And strew them thick oe'r Bladud's ground …
(*The Bath Contest*, 1769, 46)

Innovation, good management, benevolence, and civic duty were the qualities most likely to feature in late eighteenth- and early nineteenth-century accounts of Nash. This is not to say that commentators ignored his vices, rather that, like Goldsmith, few saw Nash's gaming as an impediment to his ability to fulfil his role. 'Let the delightful annals of *King* NASH declare!', claimed a con-tributor to the *Bath Chronicle*, 'I do not urge this in support of the libertinism of the Master of the Ceremonies,—but to prove that the office does not require a total seclusion from the pleasures and enjoyments of the world' (25 Sept 1777). Vain and showy he may have been but, for *Bentley's Miscellany* (1837), Nash was still the 'social character of his age' whose principal legacy, 'greater than … generally supposed', had been to promote 'ease of address, among a people notorious for their anti-gregarious habits' (*Bentley's Miscellany*, 425).

Later nineteenth-century commentators, by contrast, found it harder to ignore Nash's moral shortcomings. Bath historians such as R. E. M. Peach corrected what they saw as a misconceived equation between the city's growth and popularity and its best-known master of ceremonies. Efforts to marginalize Nash's role ran alongside exposure of his faults; unlike eighteenth-century biographers, late Victorian critics refused to reconcile the complexity of a man who combined charity with gambling, and chose to play up the latter. To Peach, one of his most intemperate detractors, Nash was the 'great protoplasm of evil' for whom entertainment was 'the pretext for the grossest vices' (Peach, 251). Though lacking this moral agenda, later urban historians have likewise contextualized Nash's contribution to the town, if not its visiting com-pany, by means of mild rebuke. He was, to R. S. Neale, a 'large vain man', as much 'a symptom as a cause of his times' whose contribution was 'merely one of many' (Neale, 26–7).

Twentieth-century characterizations have been simi-larly coloured by the prevailing tone of the moment. Sketches from the 1930s likened Nash's hold on power to that of a benevolent dictator—'a local Mussolini', as one put it. Post-war, a less deferential, and market-orientated, society has seen a return to Goldsmith's favourable image of Nash as innovator and self-made man. For some, retell-ing the story, with all its characteristic eighteenth-century colour, has proved sufficient, making Nash a like-able, popular, and unproblematic subject for local histor-ies and a gentleman's club school of biography. However, more recent studies of eighteenth-century leisure and social conduct have started to subject Nash to closer aca-demic scrutiny, either placing his career, and its enduring myths, within broader histories of tourism, or using it to understand better the practice and enactment of man-ners. It is this—the maintenance of a role of his own cre-ation in which he made himself indispensable and, at least during the 1760s, irreplaceable—which remains one of Nash's most considerable and interesting achievements. Rightly he should be treated as one of many influences in the development of the eighteenth-century town under way on his arrival and which—with the Circus, Crescent, and New Assembly room—reached its height only after his death. Moreover, Nash's reputation for leadership was certainly enhanced when set against a somewhat cautious town corporation. And yet in the management of its visiting population over several generations he was also an unsurpassed master. Furthermore, it was a role achieved and maintained less by money or patronage than by inventiveness and force of personality. Nash was certainly vain, self-promoting, controversial, and at times below board, but he was also charismatic, entrepreneurial, talented, and successful. It is a blend, and a career path, which is not dissimilar from that of Nash's close contemporary Sir Robert Walpole.

Writing in 1724, the poet Robert Whatley had claimed that Georgian Bath would soon decline as future generations grew less dissipated and found little use for the town's fashionable diversions. In 300 years' time, he predicted, visitors would come to inspect a few preserved ruins of Hanoverian amusement. Along with the town would go its arbiter, Richard Nash, for whom the poet also saw an obscure future which would end, Whatley speculated, when a twenty-first-century scholar discovered his dedication in a long-lost book of poems. In truth, the potential for such revelation now seems unlikely. Many recent visitors to Bath, overwhelmed by the enduring richness of the eighteenth-century city, have ambled up Beau and Nash streets, ridden the Beau Nash tour bus, supped a cup of 'Beau Nash's gambler's brew', perused at the Beau Nash Gallery, and dined at Popjoy's (Nash's Saw Close house), before a late-night show at the ABC (Beau Nash), or a flutter at a nearby 'Beau's Casino'. Yet, to an extent, Whatley's prediction does ring true. Fully co-opted into the modern heritage city, Nash remains a shadowy figure—less visible than his Hanoverian peers Sally Lunn or Jane Austen—about whom, aside from his evident 'importance' and restored good name, few details are provided. In Goldsmith's phrase, a person still 'much talked of' yet 'so little known': a celebrity lacking a proper history of that fame. PHILIP CARTER

Sources O. Goldsmith, *The life of Richard Nash of Bath, esq.* (1762); repr. in *The complete works of Oliver Goldsmith*, ed. A. Friedman, 3 (1965) • O. W. Ferguson, 'The materials of history: Goldsmith's *Life of Nash*', *Proceedings of the Modern Language Association of America*, 80 (1965), 372–86 • P. Borsay, *The image of Georgian Bath, 1700–2000* (2000) • W. Connely, *Beau Nash, monarch of Bath and Tunbridge Wells* (1955) • R. Wendorf, *The elements of life: biography and portrait-painting in Stuart and Georgian England* (1990) • P. Hembry, *The English spa, 1560–1815* (1990) • T. Fawcett, *Voices of eighteenth-century Bath* (1995) • T. Fawcett, *Bath entertain'd* (1998) • A. Borsay, *Medicine and charity in Georgian Bath: a social history of the General Infirmary, c.1739–1830* (1999) • S. Macintyre, 'Bath: the rise of a resort town, 1660–1800', *County towns in pre-industrial England* (1981), 197–242 • *Diary of Dudley Ryder, 1715–16*, ed. W. Matthews (1932) • R. Whatley, *Characters at the Hot-Well, Bristol, in September, and at Bath in October 1723* (1724) • *The original Bath guide* (1811) • R. Warner, *The history of Bath* (1801) • *Memoirs of the celebrated Miss Fanny M—*, 2nd edn (1759) • R. S. Neale, *Bath: a social history, 1680–1850* (1981) • J. Walters, *Splendour and scandal: the reign of Beau Nash* (1968) • W. Dodd, *Reflections on death* (1763) • C. Gerrold, *The beaux and the dandies: Nash, Brummell, and D'Orsay* (1910) • M. Girouard, *The English town* (1990) • L. S. Benjamin, *Bath under Beau Nash* (1926) • W. H. Ainsworth, *Beau Nash, or, Bath in the eighteenth century* (1879) • J. Wilson, *Wonderful characters: comprising memoirs and anecdotes of the most remarkable persons*, 3 vols. (1821) • 'Memoir of Beau Nash', *Bentley's Miscellany*, 2 (1837), 414–25 • R. E. M. Peach, *Bath, old and new* (1888) • M. Williams, *Lady Luxborough goes to Bath* (1945) • *The letters of the Rev. John Wesley*, ed. J. Telford, 8 vols. (1931), vol. 1, pp. 310, 318 • *The new Bath guide or useful pocket companion*, 3rd edn (1764) • 'On the death of Nash, esq', Bath Reference Library, Bath Miscellaneous Plates and Text, acc. no. E8065511, class B942.38BAT • 'On Mr Nash's going from the *Bath'*, *The Bath miscellany* (1740) • *The jests of Beau Nash, late master of ceremonies at Bath* (1763) • *The autobiography and correspondence of Mary Granville, Mrs Delany*, ed. Lady Llanover, 1st ser., 3 vols. (1861) • P. Wharton and G. Wharton, *The wits and beaux of society*, 2 vols. (1860) • R. W. Falconer, *The baths and mineral water of Bath*, 6th edn (1880) • will, PRO, PROB 6/137, fol. 136v

Archives BL, George Scott letter-books, Egerton MSS 3725–3758

Likenesses T. Worlidge, drawing, 1736, Royal Collection • J. Faber jun., mezzotint, 1740 (after a portrait by Thomas Hudson), NPG • N. Hone, miniature, 1750, Holburne Museum of Art, Bath [*see illus.*] • P. Hoare, statue (marble), 1751, Pump Room, Bath • W. Hoare, portrait, oils, *c.*1761, NPG

Wealth at death debts of *c.*£1200 at death; personal possessions, incl. paintings, books, and gifts sold at auction in March 1761, and thereafter at public sale: Ferguson, 'The materials of history', 374–6

Nash, Thomas. *See* Nashe, Thomas (*bap.* 1567, *d. c.*1601).

Nash, Thomas (1587/8–1648), author and lawyer, was the second son of Thomas Nash of Tapenhall, Worcestershire. After matriculating at St Edmund Hall, Oxford, on 22 March 1605, aged seventeen, he entered the Inner Temple in November 1607. He had property at Mildenham Mills, Claines, Worcestershire, but unlike most of his family he was a royalist during the civil war; the victors deprived him of his possessions. It is said that grief at the king's defeat speeded his death in London on 25 August 1648, although to die at sixty was not, in those days, to die young. He was buried in the Temple Church.

In 1633 Nash published *Quaternio, or, A fourefold way to a happie life, set forth in a dialogue betweene a countryman and a citizen, a divine and a lawyer* by 'Tho: Nash Philopolites', which was dedicated to Thomas, Lord Coventry, keeper of the great seal. There was a second edition in 1636, and in 1639 came a third. This last bears a new title, *Miscelanea, or, A Fourefold Way*, and a refurbished title-page but is otherwise little changed. The title-pages of the first and third editions sport a cheerful epigraph from an epigram by Martial, slightly misquoted, on the legitimacy of harmless wit: 'Innocuos permitte sales, cur ludere nobis / Non liceat?' ('Permit harmless jests, why should we not be allowed to joke?'). Indeed, while the dialogue bristles with opinions on such topics as the obedience due to superiors, the dangers of religious separatism, worldly vanity, the book of nature, and the splendours of the legal profession, it also offers, especially in its packed margins, a playful—and on occasion even scatological—humour and a multitude of entertaining passages from such works as Thomas More's epigrams and Chaucer's *Canterbury Tales*.

In 1633 Nash also produced, under the name of T. N. Phil-onomon, a prefatory epistle to *Strange and dangerous voyage of Captain Thomas James, in his intended discovery of the north-west passage* by his friend Captain Thomas James. Then, in 1648, came *Gymnasiarchon, or, The schoole of potentates, wherein is shewn, the mutabilitie of worldly honour*. This trans-lates a Latin work by the German humanist Georgius Acacius Evenkellius (Ennenckel), but a majority of the vol-ume's pages are given to Nash's own thoughts on matters ranging from wetnursing to the value of knowing one's place, from Cardinal Wolsey as an aspiring magnate to debates over the role of women (a topic on which Nash is, for his time, quite reasonable). Historical examples of mis-guided potentates, he says, inculcate wisdom in the great better than does political theory so he adds many of these, together with telling quotations from classical and con-temporary writers. Nor does Nash hesitate to join urbane humour to serious commentary on overmighty subjects and careless rulers; he even includes a not unimaginative translation from Rabelais. Although loyal to the old hier-archies, Nash was not naïve, citing Machiavelli without the horror that gripped so many at that thinker's mere name. Nash died disappointed by history, but it is hard to believe that he died astonished.

SIDNEY LEE, *rev.* ANNE LAKE PRESCOTT

Sources *Reg. Oxf.*, 2/2.281 • *Members of Inner Temple, 1571–1625*, 109 • T. Nash, *Collections for the history of Worcestershire*, 1 (1781), 327 • [T. Nash], *Supplement to the 'Collections for the history of Worcestershire'* (1799), 24–5 • J. Hunter, *Chorus vatum*, BL, Add. MS 24487, fol. 85 • A. L. Prescott, 'Thomas Nash (1588–1648) and Thomas More', *Moreana*, 59–60 (1978), 35–41 • A. L. Prescott, *Imagining Rabelais in Renaissance England* (1998)

Nash, Thomas (*bap.* 1593, *d.* 1647), lawyer and land agent, was baptized on 20 June 1593 at Stratford upon Avon, the eldest son and second of three children of Anthony Nash (*d.* 1622), gentleman, of Welcombe and Old Stratford, War-wickshire, and Mary (*d.* after 1622), second daughter of Rowland Baugh of Twining, Gloucestershire. His father, although not formally entered at any of the four major inns of court, seems to have been the man of business to his kinsman Sir John Hubaud and probably also to Wil-liam Shakespeare, by whom he was left money for the pur-chase of a mourning ring. Nash was admitted to Lincoln's Inn on 15 May 1616 and called to the bar on 25 November 1623. There is no evidence of his ever having practised as a lawyer but he seems to have taken over his father's role as agent for Hubaud, being described in interrogatories as 'sometime servant to said Sir John Hubaud' (records of corporation of Stratford upon Avon, BRU 15/5/159).

On his father's death, in 1622, Nash inherited 'the little land that I have' in 'Newe Stratford' which comprised an inn called The Beare, another messuage, and a small close called the Burnt Close (typed transcript of original will, on 20 Aug 1622, DR 194/5). On 22 April 1626 he married Eliza-beth Hall (*bap.* 1608, *d.* 1670), daughter of Dr John Hall and his wife, Susanna, the elder daughter of William Shake-speare, of whom she was heir in tail. After the death of John Hall in 1635 the Nashes lived with Susanna at New

Place, Shakespeare's home, where they entertained Hen-rietta Maria in July 1643, and in the period before Edgehill no fewer than fourteen prominent parliamentarian lead-ers, including Lord Brooke, Nathaniel Fiennes, and Col-onel John Hutchinson, who stayed '9 or 10 nights and dayes'. They suffered from the depredations of the troops, who took, in addition to cattle, horses, and fodder, 'a scar-let Peticoat of my wifes' and 'a silver spoone' (records of corporation of Stratford upon Avon, BRU 15/17/3). On 24 September 1642 Nash headed the list of those 'within the Burrough of Stratford upon Avon who by way of loan have sent in money and plate to the king and parliament'; he contributed in plate and money £100, by far the largest individual contribution (ibid., 15/17/2).

Nash was never active in civic affairs; he served neither as burgess nor as churchwarden though he is five times noted as having attended the parish vestry, signing an agreement to prosecute a suit against the inhabitants of Luddington in February 1641. In a dispute with the bailiff and burgesses of Stratford upon Avon in 1635, concerning the right to a pew in Holy Trinity Church, claimed by the former for their wives, John Hall and Thomas Nash stated that they had contributed 'deeply' to the repairs of the church (Shakespeare Birthplace Trust RO, ER 1/1, fol. 123). Although Shakespeare's real estate had been entailed on Susanna and her issue, and further settled in 1639 on Elizabeth and her issue, Nash, by his will, dated 25 August 1642, devised New Place, four yardlands in the fields of Old Stratford and Welcombe, and the London property to his cousin Edward Nash, after the death of Elizabeth. Eliza-beth declined to fulfil this part of the will, resettling it after Nash's death to the use of her mother, herself, and the heirs of her body. Nash's other property included the parsonage and glebe at Haselor, various properties in Stratford, including the house adjacent to New Place, now known as Nash's House (although he never occupied it), and the property in High Street, formerly leased to Thomas Quiney, husband of Shakespeare's younger daughter, Judith, and vested in Nash and John Hall as trustees. A nuncupative codicil, dated 4 April 1647, bequeathed £50 to Susanna Hall and increased other pecu-niary legacies to relatives and servants. Nash died the same day, at New Place, and was buried in the chancel of Holy Trinity Church, Stratford upon Avon, on 5 April as 'Thomas Nash, Gent'.

M. R. MACDONALD

Sources J. O. Halliwell, *An historical account of the New Place, Stratford-upon-Avon* (1864) • R. Bearman, *Shakespeare in the Stratford records* (1994) • R. Savage, ed., *The registers of Stratford-on-Avon*, 1–2 (1897–8) [baptisms, marriages] • R. Savage, ed., *The registers of Stratford-on-Avon*, 3 (1905) [burials] • W. P. Baildon, ed., *The records of the Honorable Society of Lincoln's Inn: admissions*, 1 (1896) • W. P. Baildon, ed., *The records of the Honorable Society of Lincoln's Inn: the black books*, 2 (1898) • Records of the corporation of Stratford upon Avon, miscellaneous documents, vol. 5, Shakespeare Birthplace Trust RO, Stratford upon Avon • Records of the corporation of Stratford upon Avon, miscellaneous documents, vol. 17, Shake-speare Birthplace Trust RO, Stratford upon Avon, BRU 15/7 • vestry minute book, 1617–1909, Shakespeare Birthplace Trust RO, Strat-ford upon Avon, BRT 8/1 • copies of miscellaneous Nash and related family wills, Shakespeare Birthplace Trust RO, Stratford upon Avon, Christopher Whitfield papers, DR 194 • settlement of the estates of William Shakespeare, 27 May 1639, Shakespeare Birthplace Trust RO, Stratford upon Avon, TTD II/8 · W. Camden, *The visitation of the county of Warwick in the year 1619*, ed. J. Fetherston, Harleian Society, 12 (1877) · W. H. Turner, ed., *The visitations of the county of Oxford … 1566 … 1574 … and in 1634*, Harleian Society, 5 (1871) · J. Maclean and W. C. Heane, eds., *The visitation of the county of Gloucester taken in the year 1623*, Harleian Society, 21 (1885) · J. H. Bloom, *Shakespeare's church, otherwise the collegiate church of the Holy Trinity of Stratford-upon-Avon* (1902) · Red Book I, 40 Elizabeth, 1691, Lincoln's Inn, London, E1a1

Wealth at death land and houses in Warwickshire; £628 pecuniary bequests: will

Nash, Thomas Arthur Manly (1905–1993), entomologist, was born on 18 June 1905 at 22 Lennox Road South, Southsea, the younger of the two children of Llewellyn Thomas Manly Nash, a colonel in the Royal Army Medical Corps, and his wife, Editha Gertrude, *née* Sloggett. Tam (the nickname by which he was universally known) spent much of his early childhood in India, returning to England for his schooling at Wellington College. He obtained a BSc in entomology at the Royal College of Science (later Imperial College). In 1927 he was employed by the Colonial Office to work in the department of tsetse research and reclamation, Tanganyika Territory. There he undertook investigations on aspects of the biology of tsetse flies, the vectors of the trypanosomes which cause sleeping sickness in humans, and a related disease of domestic livestock in much of tropical Africa. After returning briefly to England he married Marjorie Wenda (1907–1988), daughter of Walter Alexander Wayte, dental surgeon, at Wadworth parish church, Yorkshire, on 22 February 1930.

Nash continued working in east Africa until 1932 by which time he had been awarded a London PhD and DSc. The following year he moved to Nigeria as medical entomologist in the sleeping sickness service of the Ministry of Health. From 1937 to 1944 he was in charge of the Anchau rural development and settlement scheme, where he was able to put to practical use his research findings on the effectiveness of partial clearing of vegetation forming the flies' habitat as a method of tsetse control. He demonstrated that tsetse control, combined with development of the rural economy, could result in freedom from human and animal trypanosomiasis and an improvement in general health and living conditions. In 1948 the Colonial Office established the West African Institute for Trypanosomiasis Research, located in Nigeria with the mandate to conduct research on the medical, veterinary, entomological, and parasitological aspects of trypanosomiasis relevant to the then four British colonies in west Africa: Ghana, Nigeria, Sierra Leone, and The Gambia. Nash transferred from the sleeping sickness service to the new institute, taking up the post of chief entomologist. Following the resignation of the founder director he became director of the institute in 1954 and remained in that position until his retirement in 1959. His achievements in Africa were acknowledged by appointment as OBE (1948) and CMG (1959).

In 1962 Nash came out of retirement and founded, with funds from the department of technical co-operation, the Tsetse Research Laboratory located on the Langford site of the veterinary school of the University of Bristol. He was a research fellow of the university and director of the laboratory. He retired for the second time in 1971, having demonstrated the feasibility of maintaining colonies of the slow breeding tsetse fly in the laboratory, an achievement on which was based subsequent extensive research programmes at Langford and elsewhere on the insect and on the diseases that it transmits.

Nash's publications included *Tsetse Flies in British West Africa* (1948), *Africa's Bane: the Tsetse Fly* (1969), *A Zoo without Bars* (1984)—a lighthearted look at his life in the wilds of east Africa in 1927–32—and numerous papers on tsetse flies and trypanosomiasis in scientific journals. He died, predeceased by his wife and only son, in the General Hospital, Weston-super-Mare, on 14 January 1993 of cerebral infarction and was cremated on the 22nd; his ashes were scattered in his much loved garden at Spring Head Farm, Upper Langford.   A. M. JORDAN

Sources personal knowledge (2004) · T. A. M. Nash, *A zoo without bars* (1984) · WWW · b. cert. · m. cert. · d. cert.

Wealth at death £481,340: probate, 2 July 1993, *CGPLA Eng. & Wales*

Nash, Treadway Russell (1725–1811), Church of England clergyman and antiquary, was born at Clerkenleap, Kempsey, Worcestershire, on 24 June 1725, youngest of the seven children of Richard Nash (*c.*1676–1740) and his wife, Elizabeth (*bap.* 1691, *d.* 1741), daughter of George Treadway. He was educated at the King's School, Worcester, and Worcester College, Oxford (BA, 1744; MA, 1747) before going in 1749 on the grand tour with his eldest brother Richard. After returning to Oxford in 1751 he was ordained priest, resumed his fellowship at Worcester College, later serving as bursar and dean, and was presented on 2 June to the vicarage of Eynsham by John Martin of Overbury, Worcestershire, banker and father of his friend John Martin.

In 1756–7 both Nash's brothers died childless, and he unexpectedly inherited the family's estates at Droitwich and Kempsey. He swiftly adapted himself as 'a mere provincial man' (T. Nash, *Collections for the History of Worcestershire*, 2 vols., 1781–2, 1.i). In 1758 he took the degrees of BD and DD, leased a house at Bevere near Worcester and on 19 October married Margaret (*bap.* 1734, *d.* 1811), youngest daughter of John Martin of Overbury. He soon acquired a larger house, rebuilt as Bevere House by Anthony Keck. In 1761 he resigned Eynsham and, as patron, presented himself on 11 and 12 May to the family vicarages of St Peter's, Droitwich, and Warndon. He was a vigorous member of the committee of Worcester Royal Infirmary from 1758, especially during its rebuilding in 1770–71, and of the county bench from 1761 to 1808. He supervised his estates carefully and, by living in style while refraining from the expensive social activities of his fellow gentry, he acquired a reputation for parsimony.

Charles Lyttelton's bequest to the Society of Antiquaries of the manuscripts of Thomas Habington and William Thomas aroused Nash's interest in Worcestershire's history. He offered £300 or £400 to open a subscription for their publication, but was persuaded by Richard Gough to undertake that task himself. He was elected FSA on 18 February 1773 and agreed to prepare the manuscripts for press, bring them up to date, and submit them for the society's approval for publication at his expense. He emphasized that he aimed only to publish *Collections for a History of Worcestershire*, but despite Gough's guidance even this was more troublesome and expensive than he had anticipated. He was demanding of his collaborators, who included John Brooke, Thomas Percy, and George Rose, keeper of the exchequer records, and was impatient at the slow progress and cost of printing by John Nichols. The *Collections*, published in two folio volumes in 1781 and 1782, was unusual in containing a facsimile of Domesday Book entries and many engravings, mostly by James Ross (1745–1821) of Worcester. The work's limitations drew lukewarm reviews, but its merits have since been increasingly appreciated. Nash suffered financial loss and even by 1799, when he published a long-promised supplement, at least 288 of the original 750 copies remained unsold. An *Index* was published by the Worcestershire Historical Society in 1894–5.

In 1785 Nash's only child, Margaret, married John Sommers Cocks of Eastnor, Herefordshire, later second Baron Sommers (1806), and Earl Sommers (1821). On 23 August 1792, having previously resigned the vicarages of St Peter's, Droitwich and Warndon, Nash was presented by Charles, first Baron Sommers, to the rectory of Leigh, near Worcester, which he held until his death. When in 1794 the widow of his brother Richard died, he inherited her Russell family estate at Strensham, took Russell as his second name from about the end of 1795 and on 23 November 1797 presented himself to its rectory, which he held in plurality with Leigh until 1807. He was also one of the proctors in convocation for Worcester diocese from 1784 to 1807.

The connection with Strensham, birthplace of Samuel Butler, led Nash to prepare a new anonymous edition of *Hudibras*. This edition, containing little new editorial material, was published in 1793 in three handsome volumes, with engravings by Ross based on earlier designs by William Hogarth and John Skipp of Ledbury (1742–1811) and republished in 1835–40 and 1847. He also contributed two papers read to the Society of Antiquaries in 1787 and 1803. Nash's annual pocket books end abruptly in August 1810. He died at Bevere House, North Claines, on 26 January 1811 and was buried at St Peter's, Droitwich, on 4 February, leaving about £60,000, excluding real estate, divided between his wife, who died on 24 May 1811, and his daughter, though probate was not obtained until 10 June 1815. He bequeathed paintings and engravings, collected on his grand tour, to Worcester College, where they remain, and his personal papers survive at Eastnor Castle, except for eight grangerized volumes of the *Collections*, sold in 1901 and destroyed in a house fire in 1979. His old friend James Ross wrote his obituary in the *Gentleman's Magazine*. BRIAN S. SMITH

Sources D. C. Cox, 'This foolish business': Dr Nash and the Worcestershire collections, Worcestershire Historical Society, 7 (1993) • J. Amphlett, *An index to Dr Nash's Collections for a history of Worcestershire*, 2 pts, Worcestershire Historical Society (1894–5) • G. W. Beard, 'Nash, historian of Worcestershire', *Transactions of the Worcestershire Archaeological Society*, new ser., 33 (1956), 14–22 • *DNB* • J. Chambers, *Biographical illustrations of Worcestershire* (1820), 459–68 • Nichols, *Illustrations*, vol. 6 • E. A. B. Barnard, 'Treadway Russell Nash', *Transactions of the Worcestershire Archaeological Society*, new ser., 24 (1947), 1–3 • *GM*, 1st ser., 81/1 (1811), 190, 393–4 • Nichols, *Lit. anecdotes*, 8.103–5 • *GM*, 1st ser., 51 (1781), 372–4 • S. Butler, *Hudibras*, ed. J. Wilders (1967) • J. Lane, *Worcester infirmary in the eighteenth century* (1992) • W. H. McMenemy, *A history of the Worcester Royal Infirmary* (1947)
Archives BL, corresp., Add. MSS 29174, 32329, 34731, 35624 • Eastnor Castle, Herefordshire, pocket books, accounts, personal and family papers | Bodl. Oxf., corresp. of Richard Gough
Likenesses J. Blackburn, oils, 1770, Eastnor Castle, Herefordshire; repro. in *Transactions of the Worcestershire Archaeological Society*, new ser., 33 (1956) • J. Caldwall, engraving (after watercolour by D. Gardener, *c*.1775), BM, NPG; repro. in Cox, 'This foolish business'
Wealth at death approx. £60,000—excl. real estate: Nash MSS, Eastnor Castle; Amphlett, *An index*; Cox, 'This foolish business', 6

Nash, Sir Walter (1882–1968), prime minister of New Zealand, was born at 93 Mill Street, Kidderminster, Worcestershire, on 12 February 1882, the son of Arthur Alfred Nash (*d*. 1913), a wool weaver and dyer, and later a clerk, and his wife, Amelia Randle (*d*. 1919), also a weaver. He had four elder brothers and one younger sister. Nash was educated at St John's church school in Kidderminster, beginning at the age of three. He soon revealed an exceptional memory and won a scholarship to King Charles I Grammar School, but the family could not afford the required uniform, so he left school when he was eleven. Thereafter he had a variety of jobs, from messenger boy to an analysis clerk in the Ariel bicycle works in Birmingham, where the family had moved about 1896. Then he opened two sweet and tobacco shops in Selly Oak, where on 16 June 1906 he married Lotty May (1880?–1961), head assistant at the Selly Oak post office and the daughter of Thomas Eaton, a plumber. They had three sons.

Apart from helping his father, a Conservative Party agent, on election days, and showing a keen interest in land taxation, Nash revealed little concern for politics in England. He began, however, the very extensive reading which assisted his later political career.

His wife wanted to travel, and in 1909 Nash sold his business and sailed for New Zealand with about £800. He settled in Wellington and entered a partnership in a firm of tailors. One of his partners misled him about the firm's debts and Nash lost what money remained after furnishing a house. Then he became a commercial traveller in cloths for suits, and proved a very successful salesman.

In Wellington, Nash became very active as a fund-raiser for the Church of England Men's Society, until the bishop discovered that he thought usury a sin and had refused to deposit the funds at interest. Through a radical parson he met the leaders of the political labour movement, Harry Holland and Peter Fraser. He was angry at the brutal actions of special police (mounted farmers) during the 1913 strike, and he joined the New Zealand Labour Party, formed in 1916. His socialism was not Marxist. He was, rather, a Christian socialist, whose thought was chiefly influenced by reading John Ruskin, William Morris, F. D.

Maurice, and Lev Tolstoy. In 1916 he became a partner (and accountant) in a firm of tailors in New Plymouth, where he started the first Labour Party branch, and where in 1919 he stood with other Labour candidates unsuccessfully in the municipal elections. His introduction of profit sharing in his firm led to trouble with the chief partner (and suggested that he was not perhaps born to make profits).

Nash set off for England, where he acquired the New Zealand agencies for several publishers. He represented the New Zealand Labour Party at the Second Socialist International in Geneva in 1920. There he met Sidney Webb, F. W. Jowett, and other famous socialists. He spoke once only, criticizing Webb's report on socialization as disguised capitalism.

After returning to New Zealand, Nash opened a bookshop and publisher's agency in Wellington—work more to his taste than selling cloths or suits. But in 1922 he was elected secretary of the Labour Party, and by the mid-1920s this took up all his time. Nash was a near perfect secretary. He (and Fraser) made the Labour Party into a national organization. Nash introduced efficient office methods, raised funds, and opened branches. He remembered every detail—indeed his memory for facts, figures, and names of people was extraordinary. Most of the other Labour leaders had trade-union, and some of them revolutionary, socialist backgrounds. Nash brought an element of middle-class and Christian respectability.

As well as working for the party Nash helped start the Institute of International Affairs and the Institute of Pacific Affairs. He represented New Zealand at conferences of the latter in Hawaii and in Canada, where he met many leading figures and gained in confidence. His knowledge of world affairs was exceeded by only a handful of people in New Zealand.

After two unsuccessful attempts, in a by-election in 1929 Nash was elected to parliament as the member for Hutt in Wellington, though he also continued as party secretary until 1932. While neither was the leader (Holland and then M. J. Savage held the official position), Fraser and Nash played the biggest part in formulating the policies which, in time of depression, led to the election of the first Labour government in 1935. Nash wrote the election manifesto. He became minister of finance, customs, and later marketing in Savage's ministry (1935–40) and minister of finance and deputy prime minister under Peter Fraser (1940–49). He and Fraser (whose intelligence and political shrewdness Nash greatly admired) made an outstanding team. Nash's contribution to the extensive reforms of 1935–8 was very great. He introduced a system of guaranteed prices for dairy produce. Although caucus rejected his own income-related contributory scheme of pensions, he played a major role in formulating and (as minister of social security) piloting through parliament in 1938 the great system of pensions, child allowances, and free medicine which was the most extensive system of social security in the world at that time.

In 1936–7 Nash spent months in England unsuccessfully trying to negotiate a new trade agreement whereby Britain would buy virtually all New Zealand's exports at agreed prices and New Zealand would import an equivalent value of British goods. In 1939 he again visited London trying to raise funds to redeem a maturing loan. New Zealand was suffering from over-importing as a result of local inflation, and Nash reacted rather belatedly by introducing import licensing. To this British leaders objected. Nash was given a rough time and succeeded in raising funds only on most arduous terms. Ironically, within a few months New Zealand was at war on Britain's side and Britain was taking New Zealand exports under a bulk purchase agreement.

By 1940 it was clear that the British could not defend New Zealand against attack. In November 1941, just before Pearl Harbor, Nash was appointed minister to Washington—New Zealand's first diplomatic representative in a foreign country. In the United States he was an outstanding success at his chief task, getting New Zealand known. He was a member of the Pacific war council and, for a time, of the war cabinet in London. He retained his cabinet rank in New Zealand and returned temporarily to present his 1943 budget.

Much of Nash's time was taken up with post-war planning. In 1944 he chaired a meeting of the International Labour Organization; he attended the international meetings at Bretton Woods, Geneva, and Havana at which the General Agreement on Tariffs and Trade and the International Monetary Fund (IMF) were created. At these meetings he took an active part. Their aim was to improve post-war economic conditions and to decrease the risk of future depression and war. The Labour caucus refused to agree to New Zealand joining the IMF—and opposition leaders such as Sidney Holland agreed with the Labour majority. The IMF was criticized, among other reasons, for involving restrictions on New Zealand's independence.

In 1949 the Fraser government lost office. Peter Fraser died in 1950 and Nash became leader of the opposition, to be confronted almost immediately with one of the greatest crises in his career. A wage dispute involving the partly communist-led Waterside Workers' Union in January 1951 encouraged the National Party government to declare a state of emergency and take a range of draconian actions against the unionists and their families. Nash spoke in support of the rights of the workers, but he was much criticized by an anti-union (and cold war) public for saying that his party was 'neither for nor against' the strikers. Labour was defeated in a snap election in 1951 and again in 1954, when many voters cast protest votes for Social Credit, not Labour.

At last, in 1957, at the age of seventy-five, Nash became prime minister, elected on a policy which included increased family benefits and pensions, easier access to housing loans, and a tax rebate of up to £100 when the pay-as-you-earn method of tax collection was introduced. On the day he took office he was informed that overseas funds had dropped disastrously because of over-importing. It seemed like 1939 all over again. This time the government probably overreacted with its severe 'black budget' and import controls. In the circumstances of economic severity, and with a parliamentary majority of only one, the government's scope was restricted. It did abolish compulsory military training, introduce equal pay in the civil service, and carry out the reforms mentioned above. It also promoted industrial development. But the public recalled with disappointment the contrast between Labour's promises and the financial stringency which followed. The party was defeated in the 1960 election.

Nash was less impressive as prime minister than as minister of finance. Although he was quite extraordinarily energetic, he was almost equally dilatory in making decisions. He attended endless petty functions from which a prime minister could have been excused for more exacting duties. He seemed too absorbed in details rather than in broad policy decisions. He was, as always, in some respects, inconsiderate of his assistants. He himself needed only four or so hours' sleep (plus catnaps) and he expected others to be available as required at almost all times. Increasing fame was paralleled by vanity. He amassed the largest private collection of papers in New Zealand, which filled his garage and, after culling, weighed 10 tons. Every scrap referring to his career—even air tickets—was filed away.

While prime minister Nash travelled abroad constantly, talking to Khrushchov, de Gaulle, Macmillan, Eisenhower. The British high commissioner in New Zealand, Sir George Mallaby, wrote that he was the only New Zealand politician with 'some pretensions to being a world figure' and that 'other world statesmen were ready to listen' (Mallaby, 78). Nash led New Zealand delegations to every conceivable conference. He continued as leader of the opposition until 1963 and was an MP until his death. His active sympathy for the underdog remained undiminished to the end, as did his hatred of militarism. In 1965 he spoke vehemently at the first two teach-ins against the Vietnam War.

Nash was sworn of the privy council in 1946 and was appointed CH in 1959 and GCMG in 1965. He received honorary doctorates from Cambridge, Victoria University of Wellington, Tufts College, and Temple University. He entered Hutt Hospital, Wellington, after a heart attack on 21 May 1968 and died there on 4 June. His remains were cremated at Karori crematorium, Wellington, on 7 June.

KEITH SINCLAIR, rev.

Sources K. Sinclair, *Walter Nash* (1976) · *New Zealand Herald* (6 June 1968) · *The Times* (5 June 1968) · A. H. McLintock, ed., *An encyclopaedia of New Zealand*, 3 vols. (1966), vol. 2 · G. Mallaby, *From my level: unwritten minutes* (1965) · *Who's who in New Zealand* (1964) · B. Gustafson, 'Nash, Walter', *DNZB*, vol. 2 · New Zealand Archives, Wellington, Nash MSS

Archives New Zealand Archives, Wellington, MSS | Bodl. Oxf., corresp. with L. G. Curtis · U. Leeds, Brotherton L., corresp. with Henry Drummond-Wolff | FILM BFI NFTVA, documentary footage · BFI NFTVA, news footage

Nashe [Nash], **Thomas** (*bap.* 1567, *d. c.*1601), writer, was born in Lowestoft, Suffolk, and baptized there at St Margaret's in November 1567, the third of the seven children of William Nashe (*d.* 1587), clergyman, and his second wife, Margaret, *née* Witchingham (*d.* 1589). The entry of his baptism in the Lowestoft parish register does not specify the day. Nashe says his father 'sprang from the Nashes

of Herefordshire' (*Lenten Stuffe*, *Works*, 3.205), and was of a family with 'larger petigrees than patrimonies' (*Strange Newes*, ibid., 1.311)—well-bred but no longer well-off, in other words. Nothing else is known of William Nashe before 1562, when he is recorded as 'minister' of St Margaret's, Lowestoft; he perhaps had the status of curate, as the living of St Margaret's was held by an absentee, John Blomvyle. The latter was related by marriage to a John Nash of Swainsthorpe, Norfolk (*d.* 1548), who may represent an earlier generation of the family in East Anglia. The vicarage of St Margaret's, presumably the author's birthplace, was destroyed by fire in the early seventeenth century; it stood in the south-western corner of the present churchyard.

Early years and education On 8 October 1573 William Nashe was presented to the living of West Harling, Norfolk (Blomefield, 1.312). Margaret Nashe, pregnant, remained in Lowestoft—a daughter, Rebecca, was baptized there in December—so it was perhaps early in 1574, when Thomas was six, that the family was established at the rectory of West Harling. Here, as far as is known, Nashe passed his childhood, together with a half-sister, Mary (*b.* 1562), from his father's first marriage; an elder brother, Israel (*b.* 1565); and a succession of younger sisters who died in infancy. Of his early education nothing is known; though boastful of his university career, Nashe makes no mention of his schooling. There was a grammar school at Thetford, but his reference to the town (*Lenten Stuffe*, *Works*, 3.156) gives no hint of personal association. It is probable his father was his chief schoolmaster.

Memories of rural childhood surface in Nashe's writings, often tinged with darkness and superstition—'I have heard aged mumping beldams as they sat warming their knees over a coale … When I was a little childe I was a great auditor of theirs, and had all their witchcrafts at my fingers endes, as perfit as good morrow and good even' (*Terrors of the Night*, *Works*, 1.369). Religion, too, casts a long shadow: for all the raciness of his pamphlets, there is a vein of troubled religiosity in him, as expressed in *Christs Teares Over Jerusalem* (1593). These oscillations between the picaresque and the penitent have been characterized as manic-depressive (Lewis, 414). None the less, Nashe speaks admiringly of his father, and there is no reason to assume an unhappy childhood. His last work, *Lenten Stuffe* (1599), is in part a celebration, written with great warmth and eloquence, of his native East Anglia.

On 13 October 1582 Nashe matriculated as a sizar scholar (one who performed menial tasks in return for free 'sizes' or rations) at St John's College, Cambridge. He was probably in residence some while before matriculating, as was fairly common. He later stated, 'I took up my inne [at St John's] for seven yere together lacking a quarter' (*Lenten Stuffe*, *Works*, 3.181), and as he was in London by the late summer of 1588, his residence must have begun about the end of 1581. He was probably intended for holy orders, but found this regimen uncongenial: 'if at the first peeping out of the shell a young student sets not a grave face on it, or seemes not mortifiedly religious ... he is cast of and discouraged' (*Christs Teares*, *Works*, 2.122–3). His academic career proceeded smoothly. In 1584 'Thomas Nashe Suffolciensis' was elected to a Lady Margaret scholarship (St John's College register; the entry is the earliest example of his handwriting). The following year he contributed to a manuscript copy of Latin verses by Lady Margaret scholars (PRO, SP 15.29, fol. 167). He graduated BA in March 1586. The latest reference to him at Cambridge is in a list of students attending philosophy lectures, dated 1588 (BL, Lansdowne MS 57.92).

Though he claimed, 'I might have been a Fellow if I had would' (*Have with You to Saffron Walden*, *Works*, 3.127), Nashe left without taking his MA degree. This curtailment may have been due to the death of his father in January 1587. In his earliest work, *The Anatomie of Absurdity*, written about 1587–8, he speaks of young 'wits' abruptly 'withdrawne from theyr studies', and asks: 'where should they finde a friend to be unto them in steed of a father, or one to perfit that which their deceased parents begun?' (*Works*, 1.37). A rather different account appears in *The Trimming of Thomas Nashe* (1597) by the Cambridge barber–surgeon Richard Lichfield. After claiming that Nashe had 'florished in all impudencie toward schollers' during his 'freshtime', Lichfield continues:

> then being Bachelor of Arte, which by great labour he got, to shew afterward he was not unworthie of it, [he] had a hand in a show called *Terminus & non terminus*, for which his partener in it was expelled the Colledge ... Then suspecting himselfe that he should be stayed for *egregie dunsus*, and not attain to the next Degree [MA], said he had commenst enough, and so forsooke Cambridge, being Batchelor of the third yere. (sig. G3)

Though highly circumstantial, this places Nashe, plausibly enough, in the raucous context of the college *comediae*: these performances, with their scholarly trappings and vigorous *ad hominem* satire, are a strong early influence on him. Another Cambridge commentator, William Covell, says the university was 'unkinde' to 'weane him before his time' (*Polimanteia*, 1595, sig. Q4); the phrasing seems to suggest Nashe's expulsion, but if this were really true, Nashe's many enemies would surely have mentioned it.

The importance of Cambridge to Nashe's career as a writer cannot be overstressed. It furnished him with the classical scholarship which seasons his more populist prose style, and with an undying dislike of puritanism. More practically, it gave him an entrée into that loose group of university-educated writers then established in London, generally called the 'university wits'. Two of its leading figures, Robert Greene and Christopher Marlowe, were also at Cambridge, and it is likely Nashe knew them there. His name appears with Marlowe's on the title-page of Marlowe's early drama, *Dido Queene of Carthage*, published posthumously in 1594; this could imply their collaboration on it at Cambridge, though more likely signals editorial work by Nashe prior to publication. Another who loomed large in Nashe's later career was Dr Gabriel Harvey, fellow of Trinity Hall, university praelector in rhetoric, and friend of the poet Spenser. Their public enmity

belongs to the 1590s, and arises from specific circumstances, but Harvey was already a controversial figure at Cambridge. He was the butt of a college comedy, *Pedantius*, first performed at Trinity College in 1581; Nashe was apparently present at a later performance, and delighted in its caricature of Harvey's 'finicaldo fine' mannerisms (*Have with You*, *Works*, 3.80).

First publications, 1588–1591 According to Lichfield, Nashe left Cambridge when he was 'Batchelor of the third yere' (that is, after March 1588), and went to London, where he 'troubled the presse' with 'sundrie workes & volumes'. His earliest work, *The Anatomie of Absurdity*, was licensed to the publisher Thomas Hackett on 19 September 1588, strongly suggesting his presence in London by that date. The *Anatomie* is a student work: clever, shallow, and tritely 'Euphuistic' (after John Lyly's *Euphues*, 1578); as Nashe later remarked, '*Euphues* I readd when I was a little ape in Cambridge, and then I thought it was *ipse ille*' (*Strange Newes*, *Works*, 1.319). The ploy of lightly coded satire, one of the trade marks of his topical pamphlets, is already in evidence; thus 'those who anatomize abuses and stubbe up sin by the rootes' (*Works*, 1.20) refers to the puritan controversialist Philip Stubbes, author of *The Anatomie of Abuses* (1583).

For whatever reason Nashe's *Anatomie* was not actually published until late 1589 or early 1590, and so it was a short and combative preface, 'To the Gentleman Students of both Universities', which announced his arrival on the literary scene. It was placed, prestigiously, at the front of Robert Greene's *Menaphon*, the latest romance by the bestselling author of the day. This was registered on 23 August 1589 and was probably on the bookstalls for the Michaelmas law term. Nashe's preface delivers an acerbic review of contemporary English writing. Among the authors praised are George Peele, Matthew Roydon, and Thomas Watson, all members of that fraternity of 'wits' to which Nashe aspired. Marlowe is not named, and may be among the theatrical 'alcumists of eloquence' whose overblown 'decasyllabons' (iambic pentameters) are criticized. This would be a case of Nashe nailing his colours to Greene's mast—Greene had already sounded off against Marlowe in another preface (*Perimedes the Blacke-Smith*, 1588)—and should not be taken as personal antagonism. These rivalries were skin-deep, anyway, and mainly served the purpose of publicity. Nashe also hits at Thomas Kyd, via a reference to the kid in Aesop's fables; and possibly at Shakespeare, though this interpretation depends on Shakespeare having written an early version of *Hamlet* by 1589, a point of view plausible but controversial (E. Sams, *The Real Shakespeare*, 1995, 121–35).

Thus entering the literary fray in the late 1580s, Nashe soon became embroiled in the 'Marprelate controversy'. In 1588–9 a series of militant puritan tracts appeared under the alias Martin Marprelate; secretly printed, and written with comic verve, they attacked the Anglican hierarchy (hence 'mar-prelate'). Official ripostes falling flat, the authorities turned to more popular writers who might 'stop Martin & his fellows mouths' by answering them 'after their own vein of writing' (Archbishop Whitgift, quoted in A. Peel, *Tracts Ascribed to Richard Bancroft*, 1953, xviii). A number of 'anti-Martinist' pamphlets and shows were produced, pseudonymously; their authorship and sequence are by no means clear. John Lyly was avowedly the author of *Pappe with an Hatchet* (1589), and the writer-spy Anthony Munday was doubtless involved. Nashe's involvement is often mentioned, by Harvey and others, and is implied by Nashe himself when he refers to the broils 'twixt Martin and us' (*Strange Newes*, *Works*, 1.270), but there is no consensus as to his contribution. The three 'Pasquill' tracts (*A Countercuffe Given to Martin Junior*, 1589; *The Return of Pasquill*, 1589; *Pasquils Apologie*, 1590) were attributed to him by McKerrow, but may just as well be by Greene (who is also included in Nashe's 'us') or Munday, or by either of them in loose collaboration with Nashe.

Stylistically, the most likely product of Nashe's pen is the bristling invective of *An Almond for a Parrat*, written in late 1589 under the alias Cutbert Curry-knave, and probably published in early 1590. It is dedicated to the comic actor Will Kemp. McKerrow included it among Nashe's 'doubtful works', largely because some remarks in it seem to suggest an Oxford-educated writer; this seems over-scrupulous, given the circumstances of the pamphlet, and the attribution to Nashe is now generally accepted (McGinn, 952–84; Nicholl, 75–9). Many were offended by the scurrilous tone of the anti-Martinists, among them the astrologer and parson Richard Harvey, younger brother of Gabriel. In his *Lamb of God* (1590; sig. a3), Harvey singles Nashe out as a 'piperly makeplay or makebate' no better than Martin himself. It is certainly true, and ironic, that the development of Nashe's comic style is indebted to Martin, and thus to puritan extremists like John Penry and Job Throckmorton, thought to be the chief authors of the Marprelate tracts.

A humorous pamphlet of 1591, *A Wonderfull … Astrologicall Prognostication* by 'Adam Fouleweather', has been unconvincingly attributed to Nashe. It was one of a trio of mock prognostications of which the others, by 'Francis Fairweather' and 'Simon Smellknave', are lost. The idea that it was a parody of Richard Harvey's *Astrological Discourse* is not borne out by the text, and with a writer as distinctive as Nashe, 'not to be convinced that it is his is almost to be certain that it is not' (F. P. Wilson, *Shakespearian and other Studies*, 1970, 265). The only certain work by him in 1591 is a short address, 'Somewhat to read for them that list', prefixed to the first edition of Sir Philip Sidney's sonnet sequence *Astrophil and Stella*. This seems another prestigious placement, but the edition, published by Thomas Newman, was unauthorized. On 18 September 1591 it was called in by order of Lord Burghley (Arber, *Regs. Stationers*, 1.555), doubtless at the request of Sidney's sister and executor, the countess of Pembroke, and when a second edition was published, also by Newman, Nashe's preface was not in it.

Some knowledge exists of Nashe's personal circumstances at this time. His panegyric to 'thrice noble Amyntas' (*Pierce Penilesse*, *Works*, 1.243–5), written in mid-1592, is taken to refer to Ferdinando Stanley, Lord Strange. The phrasing—'private experience', 'benefits received', and so on—suggests he had already enjoyed the favours of this popular nobleman, as did many writers, among them Marlowe and Kyd, who were 'writing for his plaiers' about 1591 (BL, Harley MS 6849, fol. 218). Nashe saw a performance of Shakespeare's *Henry VI* given by Strange's Men at the Rose Theatre in early 1592, and records a vivid impression of it (*Pierce Penilesse*, *Works*, 1.212). It was also for Lord Strange ('Lord S') that Nashe wrote the mildly obscene verses known as 'The Choise of Valentines' or 'Nash his Dildo' (*Works*, 3.403–16), described by Gabriel Harvey in early 1593 as 'thy unprinted packet of bawdye and filthy rimes' (*Works of Gabriel Harvey*, 2.91). The poem survives in various seventeenth-century copies (for example, Bodl. Oxf., MS Rawl. poet. 216, fols. 94–106; Inner Temple, Petyt MS 538.43, fols. 295–8; the latter was used by McKerrow for his copy text). It was not the only such piece Nashe wrote: he speaks elsewhere of 'prostituting' his pen to supply 'amorous Villanellas and Quipassas … in hope of gaine' (*Have with You*, *Works*, 3.30–31). Another early benefactor was William Beeston, probably a lawyer (see Nashe's dedication to 'Maister Apis lapis', that is, Beestone, in *Strange Newes*, *Works*, 1.255–8).

Among Nashe's literary friends was the poet Thomas Watson, who died in September 1592. Nashe recalled drinking with him at the Nag's Head in Cheapside, and said of him: 'a man he was that I dearely lov'd and honour'd, and for all things hath left few his equalls in England' (*Have with You*, *Works*, 3.126–7). Marlowe too, stabbed to death in 1593, would be remembered as one 'of my frends that usde me like a frend' (ibid., 131).

Pamphlets and quarrels, 1592–1593 The days of the flamboyant Robert Greene, described by Nashe as having a long red beard 'like the spire of a steeple' (*Strange Newes*, *Works*, 1.287), were also numbered. In the summer of 1592 he and Nashe, with an otherwise unknown companion, Will Monox, dined together on 'Rhenish wine and pickled herring'. Harvey (*Foure Letters*, *Works of Gabriel Harvey*, 1.170) claimed Greene's last illness was from a surfeit at this 'fatall banquet'; Nashe confirmed the occasion but not its consequences (*Strange Newes*, *Works*, 1.288). Greene died on 3 September 1592; his last fraught writings were published a few weeks later as *Greenes Groatsworth of Wit*, best known for its snipings at a certain 'shake-scene' or Shakespeare. Rumours that Nashe himself had written this 'scald, trivial, lying pamphlet' (as he calls it) are hotly denied in his 'epistle' to the printer Abel Jeffes, prefixed to the second edition of *Pierce Penilesse* (*Works*, 1.154). Henry Chettle, who had edited it from Greene's 'foul papers', concurred: 'it was all Greenes, not mine nor Maister Nashes, as some unjustly have affirmed' (*Kind Harts Dream*, 1592, sig. A4).

In the *Groatsworth* Greene admonishes three unnamed colleagues, his 'fellow schollers about this Cittie', not to waste their talents writing plays (sig. F1r–v). One of these (the others are Marlowe and Peele) is addressed as 'yong Juvenall, that byting satyrist, that lastly with mee together writ a Comedie'. This is almost certainly Nashe, who is also described as 'young Juvenall' by Francis Meres (*Palladis tamia*, 1598, sig. Oo6), but the recent comedy on which he and Greene had collaborated is problematic. Suggestions include *A Knack to Know a Knave*, performed by Strange's Men in June 1592 (R. Simpson, *School of Shakespeare*, 1878, 2.382–3); the anti-Harvey portion of Greene's *Quip for an Upstart Courtier*, published about July 1592 (D. McGinn, in *Studies in the English Renaissance Drama*, ed. J. A. W. Bennet, 1959, 172–88); and the spoof *Defence of Conny-Catching*, published about April 1592 as part of Greene's series of pamphlets about 'conny-catchers' or confidence tricksters (Nicholl, 125–30). The latter appeared under the alias Cuthbert Cunny-catcher, which might be thought to recall the Cutbert Curry-knave of the *Almond for a Parrat*, and was published by Abel Jeffes, with whom Nashe had connections in 1592. It is sometimes argued that 'Juvenall' is Thomas Lodge, who did indeed collaborate with Greene on a comedy, *A Looking Glasse for London* (published 1594), but Lodge had been absent on a sea voyage since mid-1591, and being older than Greene is unlikely to have been addressed as 'young' or, in the same passage, as 'sweet boy'.

Youthfulness was an almost invariable association with Nashe. Chettle also addressed him as 'boy' (*Kind Harts Dream*, sig. E2), while Harvey variously called him 'puppy', 'baby', 'brat'. The Nashe-like author Ingenioso in the Cambridge comedy *The Returne from Parnassus* (pt 2, 1601, l. 120) is likened to a 'schole-boy giving the world a bloudy nose'. Nashe even calls himself a 'stripling' in a passage written when he was about thirty years old (*Lenten Stuffe*, *Works*, 3.213). These communicate a physical impression: a small or slight man, tending to shrillness. This perceived boyishness was also due to his lack of a beard, unusual among Elizabethans. He speaks of 'my beardlesse yeeres' and the 'minoritie of my beard'; he did not wish 'to have my cheeks muffled up in furre like a Muscovian' (*Works*, 1.195, 3.129, 1.292). In *The Trimming of Thomas Nashe*, the barber Lichfield ponders 'why thou hast so much haire on thy head, and so thinne or rather almost none at all on thy face' (sig. D4); he concludes it is because Nashe is 'too effeminate, and so becomst like a woman', an imputation somewhat contradicted by his earlier suggestion (sig. D2v) that Nashe has 'lost' his beard 'by chacing after whores' (that is, as a symptom of syphilis). The *Trimming* contains the only contemporary portrait of Nashe (a later portrait in the anonymous *Tom Nash his Ghost*, 1642, is merely fanciful). This rough woodcut cannot be claimed as an authentic likeness, but the look it gives him is corroborated by the verbal descriptions: youthful, beardless, scruffy, longhaired. In Harvey's *Pierces Supererogation* (1593) Nashe is twice described as 'gag-toothed' (*Works of Gabriel Harvey*, 2.18, 225). An Elizabethan dictionary (J. Higgins, *The Nomenclator*, 1585) defines gag teeth as 'teeth standing out'. Whether this is depicted in the woodcut is a moot point; a wispy moustache may be intended.

Shortly after Greene's demise, one of Nashe's most popular and characteristic works, *Pierce Penilesse his Supplication to the Divell*, was published. Entered at Stationers' Hall on 8 August 1592, it was on sale a month later (see the third of Harvey's *Foure Letters*, 8–9 September, *Works of Gabriel Harvey*, 1.193–4). It offers a brashly witty survey of contemporary London types—the 'counterfeit politician', the 'prodigal yoong master', the merchant's wife with her 'puling' accent, the sonneteer who fills 'a whole quire of paper in praise of Lady Swin-snout, his yeolow-fac'd mistres' (*Works*, 1.169). This is framed in a semi-autobiographical narrative featuring a hard-up scribbler (Pierce puns on 'purse') in search of a patron. Having 'tost his imagination like a dogge in a blanket' (ibid., 306), he resolves to seek the Devil's patronage; his eponymous 'supplication' takes the form of a florid dedication. There are thematic connections with Marlowe's *Dr Faustus*. Fragmentary allusions to that play—'divynitie adieu', 'Faustus studie in indian silke'—are found, in Nashe's hand, in his copy of John Leland's *Principum in Anglia virorum encomia* (1589), now in the Folger Shakespeare Library (Kocher, 17–18).

Pierce Penilesse was an instant success, and went through five editions in three years. Nashe was henceforth nicknamed Pierce, in which guise—for his admirers, at least—he seemed to catch the intellectual pulse of the 1590s: quick-witted, satirical, urban, freewheeling (or indeed 'freelancing', in the journalistic sense of which Greene and Nashe were early pioneers.) A note of official disapproval was voiced by Robert Beale, clerk of the privy council, who complained of its anti-Danish sentiments: 'the realm had otherwise enemies enough, without making any more by such contumelious pamphlets' (letter to Lord Burghley, 17 March 1593; J. Strype, *Life of Whitgift*, 1822, 2.140–41).

In his 'epistle' to Jeffes, Nashe says he was 'in the country' when *Pierce Penilesse* appeared, and at the time of writing was still a 'prisoner' there. He was in fact at Croydon Palace, the summer home of the archbishop of Canterbury. The connection between Nashe and Archbishop Whitgift, temperamentally unlikely, is doubtless a ramification of Nashe's involvement in the anti-Martinist programme. A glimpse of him is offered in a letter by the biblical controversialist Hugh Broughton (*c*.1594, but referring to past events): complaining of ill treatment in Whitgift's household, Broughton recalls 'how his Nash gentleman scoffed my Ebrew studies' (BL, Lansdowne MS 107.30). At Croydon, in early October 1592, Nashe's play *Summers Last Will and Testament* was performed. It was first published in 1600, but internal references make the date and place certain; the panelled hall where it had its première is now part of the Old Palace School for Girls. This is Nashe's only extant dramatic work; he calls it a 'shewe'. Its conventional format, a masque-like presentation of seasonal themes, is enlivened by the unruly chorus, Will Summers (based on the historical Tudor jester Will Sommers (*d.* 1569)), who remains on stage to 'flout the actors' and to act as mouthpiece for Nashe's comic prose. The play includes the much anthologized lyric, 'Adieu, farewell earths blisse', sung to a lute accompaniment; it has been uncharitably suggested that one of its loveliest lines, 'brightnesse falls from the ayre', derives from a printer's error ('air' for 'hair') in the 1600 edition.

Nashe next set to work on *Strange Newes*, licensed to John

Danter on 12 January 1593, but probably published before the end of 1592. This is the first full broadside in his battle with Gabriel Harvey, though there had been various anticipatory skirmishes. In 1590, as noted, Richard Harvey had criticized Nashe and others of the 'anti-Martinist' camp. Nashe retorted belatedly in *Pierce Penilesse*, ridiculing this 'pigmy braggart' and his 'dorbellicall and lumpish' books (*Works*, 1.195–9); Greene's warning to Nashe ('yong Juvenall') about 'schollers vexed with sharpe lines' probably refers to this passage. Greene himself had tangled with the Harveys in his *Quip for an Upstart Courtier*, and Gabriel came up to London early in September 1592 with a view to taking Greene to court for 'defamation', a satisfaction denied him by Greene's death. Harvey was in London when *Pierce* was published, and rose quickly to his brother's defence in the third of his *Foure Letters and Certaine Sonnets*, published at the end of September. It was this book that Nashe now determined to answer with his new pamphlet, fully titled *Strange newes of the intercepting certaine letters and a convoy of verses* [Harvey's book] *as they were going privilie to victuall the Low Countries* (to be used as toilet paper). Harvey's reaction to *Pierce* had been haughty but surprisingly moderate, and it was primarily for his gloating account of Greene's death, in the second of the *Foure Letters*, that Nashe attacked him in *Strange Newes*— 'out upon thee for an arrant dog-killer, strike a man when he is dead?' (*Works*, 1.271). His defence of Greene is eloquent, his attacks on Harvey—'this indigested Chaos of Doctourship and greedy pot hunter after applause' (ibid., 302)—unerring or unedifying, according to taste. His array of nicknames for Harvey is well known: Gaffer Jobbernoule (a version of 'Hobbinol', Spenser's pastoral name for Harvey), Gregory Habberdine, Timothy Tiptoes, Gibraltar, Braggadocchio Glorioso. Harvey, meanwhile, took lodgings in St Paul's with the publisher John Wolfe, and there matured a lengthy riposte, *Pierces Supererogation*. This was completed by July 1593, and was published by Wolfe in October, with contributions by a trio of minor authors—Barnabe Barnes, Anthony Chute, and John Thorius—who also worked for Wolfe.

In February 1593 Nashe was 'in the countrey some threescore myle off from London', in a 'low, marish' terrain with mists 'as thicke as mould butter' (*Terrors of the Night*, *Works*, 1.378, 382). This has been convincingly identified (Harlow, 7–23) as Conington, Huntingdonshire, home of the antiquary and bibliophile Robert Cotton, three years Nashe's junior but already of formidable scholarly reputation. Their acquaintance was perhaps made in the ambit of the inns of court, where Cotton shared rooms with the poet John Davies; the latter's poem *Nosce teipsum*, published in 1599, was known to Nashe in manuscript in 1592 (*Strange Newes*, *Works*, 1.258). At Conington, Nashe wrote an early version of his gloomy 'discourse of apparitions', *The Terrors of the Night*. This was licensed to John Danter on 30 June 1593 but was not published until late 1594, altered and enlarged, and with the precaution of a separate licensing entry (25 October 1594). A conjectural explanation of this hiatus (Harlow, 7–23) is that the original version contained material about a local witchcraft trial, that

of the Samuel family, executed at Huntingdon in April 1593. An account of this, *The … Admirable Discovery of the Three Witches of Warboys*, was also licensed on 30 June; in its preface, the anonymous author thanks a certain Judge Fenner for his 'crossing' of other works which reported 'the matter partly or confusedly'. It is possible the early version of the *Terrors* was one of these suppressed books; the extant version has much about witchcraft.

Early in 1593 Nashe was also at work on his most enduringly popular book, *The Unfortunate Traveller*. The text is dated at the end 27 June 1593, and it was registered on 17 September, but publication was again delayed. With its fast-paced narrative, its Italian setting, and its waggish hero, the page-boy and dice-sharp Jack Wilton, it is often hailed as a prototypical English novel, though Nashe's description of it as a 'chronicle' is perhaps more accurate. He wrote it, he said, because certain 'frends' had urged him to try a 'cleane different vaine from other my former courses of writing' (*Works*, 2.201). It is full of clever pastiche, baroque metaphors, and razor-sharp observation of dress and gesture. It was published in 1594 with a dedication to the earl of Southampton, but there is no evidence of reciprocal favours. This was the time of Shakespeare's connection with Southampton; his *Rape of Lucrece* was also dedicated to the earl in 1594. In *Love's Labour's Lost*, a comedy abounding in riddles and in-jokes, and generally associated with the Southampton circle, Shakespeare introduces an impudent, diminutive page-boy, Moth—a 'halfepennie purse [*cf.* Pierce] of wit' (V.i.60)—who is thought to be a caricature of Nashe. There are many possible clues to the identification (*Love's Labour's Lost*, ed. R. David, 1955, xli) but that this is truly a Shakespearian sketch of Nashe remains unverifiable.

Imprisonment and silence, 1593–1596 With both *The Terrors* and *The Unfortunate Traveller* substantially written but unpublished, Nashe turned to a work which really was in a 'clean different vaine' from his previous writings: his apocalyptic religious lament, *Christs Teares Over Jerusalem*, entered on 8 September 1593 and published with a dedication to Elizabeth Carey, wife of Sir George Carey and sister-in-law of Lord Strange. Its feverishly religious tone may be in part a reaction to the arrests of Kyd and Marlowe in May 1593, and to the charges of heresy and atheism hanging over them; if so, it is ironic that Nashe's jeremiad resulted in his own arrest and imprisonment. He was no stranger to debtors' prison (*Strange Newes*, *Works*, 1.310), but this was more serious. In a letter dated 13 November 1593, Sir George Carey wrote to his wife:

> Nashe hath dedicated a booke unto you, with promis of a better. Will Cotton will disburs v li [£5] or xx nobles [£6 13s. 4d.] in yowr rewarde to him, and he shall not finde my purs shutt to relieve him out of prison, there presently in great missery, malicied for writinge against the Londoners. (Berkeley Castle, General Series Letters, bundle 4; Duncan-Jones, 15)

The offending passage begins: 'London, thou art the seeded garden of sinne, the sea that sucks in all the scumy chanels of the realm' (*Works*, 2.158–9); it was substituted with a toned-down version in the second edition (1594).

Carey's comment about Nashe being 'malicied' may refer to the activities of Gabriel Harvey, whom Nashe later describes as 'incensing my L. Mayor ... to persecute mee' (*Have with You*, *Works*, 3.95). He was probably held in Newgate, for on 20 November 'Thomas Nash *generosus*' was bound over to 'appeare at the next sessions of Gaiole delyvery of Newgate ... to make answere to all such matters as shalbe objected against him on her Majesties behalf' (Repertory for the court of aldermen, 23, fol. 125; Hutson, 199–200). Carey apparently managed to 'relieve him out of prison', and Nashe was a guest of the family at Carisbrooke Castle, Isle of Wight, over Christmas 1593 'and a great while after' (*Have with You*, *Works*, 3.96). His revamped *Terrors of the Night* is full of gratitude for Carey's help in 'my most forsaken extremities', and is dedicated to Carey's teenage daughter Elizabeth.

Christs Teares brings to a close a period of intense and exhausting literary activity. There is a tone of breakdown in it: 'I that have ... well-nie spit out al my braine at my tongues end this morning, am dumpish, drousy and wish my selfe dead' (*Works*, 2.89). It is 'woe-infirmed', haunted by death and sin, and then by the terrifying aftermath of Newgate. Nashe published no new work for three years. His final sally against Harvey, *Have with You to Saffron Walden*, published in autumn 1596, provides almost the only knowledge of his circumstances in the intervening period. For part of the time he was lodging with the printer John Danter, in Hosier Lane, Holborn; he was perhaps employed as editor and literary adviser, as Harvey had been for his publisher John Wolfe. Also mentioned in *Have with You*, as part of his circle of acquaintance, are the authors Lyly and Chettle; the soldier Sir Roger Williams, to whom he was 'excessively beholding' in mid-1594; and a certain 'young Knight' living on the Strand, who may be Sir Robert Carey, younger brother of Sir George (ibid., 3.138, 131, 108). In 1595 Nashe visited Lincolnshire, for reasons unknown, and stayed at The Dolphin inn in Cambridge on his way back to London. His claim that Harvey was staying in the next room, 'parted but by a wainscot doore', is probably apocryphal, but it may be true that Nashe had had, and refused, an opportunity to meet him at Cambridge. *Have with You* is dedicated to another Cambridge character, Richard Lichfield, but the tone of the dedication is ambiguous, and Lichfield replied with the rabidly hostile *Trimming* in 1597.

In August or September 1596 Nashe wrote from London to William Cotton, the servant of the Careys who had disbursed cash to him in Newgate three years earlier. It is his only surviving autograph letter, a single closely written page cluttered with deletions (BL, Cotton MS Jul. Caes. 3, fol. 280). It contains an extremely coarse tirade against Sir John Harington, whose *Metamorphosis of Ajax* had recently appeared. Nashe, who had recently been 'writing for the stage', also comments on the state of the theatres:

> the players, as if they had writt another *Christs Tears*, ar piteously persecuted by the L. Maior & the aldermen, and however in there old Lords tyme they thought their state setled, it is now so uncertayne they cannot build upon it.

This refers to Shakespeare's company, the Chamberlain's Men, and to the death of their patron, Lord Hunsdon, in July; his son, Sir George Carey, had inherited the company but not yet the office of lord chamberlain. Nashe may have had, or hoped for, some connection with this company, now under Carey's protection. An unauthorized quarto of *Romeo and Juliet*, 'as it was played by the Lord of Hunsdon his servants', was published by John Danter in early 1597; given his association with Danter, Nashe might be suspected of some involvement in this.

Last works, 1597–1599 Nashe's perception of unsettled relations between the players and the civic authorities proved accurate. In July 1597 a comedy called *The Isle of Dogs* was performed at one of the theatres on the Bankside. Nashe was part-author; his collaborator was a young actor, Ben Jonson, now venturing into authorship for (as far as is known) the first time. The play is lost, but whatever was in it stung the authorities into immediate action. It was denounced by the privy council as 'lewd ... seditious and sclanderous'; three of the actors, including Jonson, were imprisoned in the Marshalsea; and on 28 July a general closure of the theatres was ordered (PRO, privy council register, Eliz. 12, fol. 346; *Henslowe's Diary*, ed. W. W. Greg, 1904, 1.203). A council directive of 15 August ordered the notorious interrogator Richard Topcliffe to 'peruse soch papers as were fownd in Nash his lodgings, which Ferrys, a Messenger of the Chamber, will deliver' (PRO, privy council register, Eliz. 12, fol. 346). There is no evidence he was arrested; he had probably already left London. A document alleging his imprisonment in the Fleet is a nineteenth-century forgery by J. P. Collier. Lichfield describes Nashe as a prisoner (*Trimming*, sigs. C3v, E2), but this part of the book was written early in 1597, before the *Isle of Dogs* affair, and may anyway be wishful rather than factual; the later section (sigs. E4v–G1v) refers to Nashe as a 'fugitive', and this is broadly confirmed by Nashe's own comment that he had given birth to a 'monster' and 'it was no sooner borne but I was glad to run from it' (*Lenten Stuffe*, *Works*, 3.154).

By whatever route, Nashe arrived in Great Yarmouth, Norfolk, 'in the latter end of autumn' 1597, and found it 'a predestinate fit place for Pierse Pennilesse to set up his staffe in' (*Lenten Stuffe*, *Works*, 3.154). He stayed there some weeks, gratefully gathering material for a descriptive history of the town; this was incorporated into his last and most idiosyncratic work, *Nashes Lenten Stuffe*, or 'The Prayse of the Red Herring' (that is, the kipper, a staple of Yarmouth's economy, though the metaphorical sense is also intended.) One of his sources was a manuscript owned by a prominent Yarmouth citizen, Henry Manshyp jun., who later wrote: 'Here by way of merriment let me remember to you an odd conceit of a late pleasant-pated poet, who ... termeth Red Herring to be the titular God of Yarmouth' (*History of Great Yarmouth*, 1619, ed. C. Palmer, 1854, 120). Nashe remained 'in the country' for most, if not all, of 1598. He describes himself as 'sequestered', and 'in irksome discontented abandonment', and complains of the lack of his notebooks, presumably among the 'papers' seized at his London lodgings. His brother Israel and half-sister Mary, both now married and living in Lowestoft, may have sheltered him. In *Palladis Tamia*, licensed on 7 September 1598, Francis Meres speaks of Nashe's continued 'banishment', and encourages him: 'comfort thy selfe, sweete Tom, with Ciceros glorious return to Rome' (sig. Oo6).

Lenten Stuffe was entered to the publisher Cuthbert Burby on 11 January 1599; the entry was made 'upon condicon that he [Burby] gett yt laufully aucthorized', suggesting Nashe's position was still parlous. He was presumably back in London by then; he was certainly there when he wrote the prefatory address, 'To his Readers, hee Cares not what they be'. He bids them 'stay till Ester terme' for his next pamphlet, so was expecting *Lenten Stuffe* to be on sale, appropriately, during the Lent law term. The promised pamphlet, his 'answere to the *Trim Tram*' (the *Trimming*), never appeared. *Lenten Stuffe* was dedicated to Humfrey King, minor poet and 'King of the Tobacconists [smokers] *hic & ubique*' (*Works*, 3.148); an unsigned sonnet prefixed to King's *Hermit's Tale* (1613; sig. B2) refers to 'famous Nash, so deere unto us both'.

Lenten Stuffe has the feel of a swansong, and so it proved. On 1 June 1599 a series of 'commaundments' was issued by Archbishop Whitgift, in his capacity as chief censor. He ordered the immediate suppression of certain 'unsemely Satyres & Epigrams', among them works by Marlowe, Marston, and John Davies; and further decreed that 'all Nasshes bookes and Dr Harveyes bookes be taken wheresoever they maye be founde, and that none of theire books bee ever printed hereafter' (Arber, *Regs. Stationers*, 3.677). On 4 June various books 'thereupon were burnte' at Stationers' Hall, some of Nashe's probably among them. The finality of this edict is faintly contested by the publication, in late 1600, of *Summers Last Will and Testament* (licensed 28 October), but essentially this marks the end of Nashe's professional career. It is possible he contributed, anonymously, to *The Hospitall of Incurable Fooles*, a translation from the Italian of Tommaso Garzoni, published in 1600 by Edward Blount, a former friend and publisher of Marlowe. In a copy of this (Sothebys catalogue, 1 April 1882, no. 702; *Works*, 5.140) a certain 'P. W.' wrote, in an early seventeenth-century hand: 'Tho. Nashe had some hand in this translation and it was the last he did as I heare'. The prefatory address, 'Not to the wise reader' (sigs. a1–a2v), is signed '*Il Pazzissimo*'; it is original to Blount's edition, and is written in a lively vein, with 'a flurt of lightnesse and ostentation' (sig. a2) which is either someone sounding very like Nashe, or Nashe himself.

Nashe died about 1601, in his early thirties, in circumstances unknown. His death is announced in a Latin epitaph, 'Thomae Nashe', in *Affaniae* (Oxford, 1601, sig. N3) by Charles Fitzgeffrey. Another epitaph is in *The Returne from Parnassus* (pt 2, 314–23), performed at St John's, Cambridge, at Christmas 1601:

> His stile was wittie though it had some gall,
> Somethings he might have mended, so may all.

A more personal note is struck by Ben Jonson's elegy, preserved in a manuscript at Berkeley Castle (General Series Miscellaneous MSS 31R; K. Duncan-Jones, *TLS*, 7 July 1995): he speaks warmly of Nashe as his 'deare freind', and a

'greate spirite', and fears his passing will provoke 'a generall dearthe of witt throughout this land'. Jonson's statement that Nashe died 'a Christian faithfull penitent / Inspir'd with happie thoughts & confident' suggests that his death was not entirely sudden. Nashe's younger admirers also paid tribute: Thomas Middleton championed him in *Father Hubburds Tales* (1604, sig. B3v); and Thomas Dekker invoked the ghost of this 'sharpest satyre, luculent poet, elegant orator' (*News from Hell*, 1606, sig. 2v). If Nashe is a 'minor' author, or at any rate a flawed one, his stylistic influence was none the less major. His richly textured language is discernible in the comedies of Jonson and the journalism of Dekker, and is more subtly present in Shakespeare: in the Falstaff scenes, in the bitter clowning of *Twelfth Night*, and even in Hamlet. The inclusiveness of his pamphlets, their gossip and bric-à-brac, have made them a 'granary for commentators' (Brydges, *Restituta*, 1815, 2.359). They have, in the words of his great editor Ronald B. McKerrow (*Works*, 5.1), 'a vividness of presentation which makes them more surely and entirely of their own time and country, more representative of the England of Elizabeth, than almost any others'. Their irrepressible humour stands out sharply against the backdrop of circumstances—poverty, censorship, imprisonment—in which they were written. CHARLES NICHOLL

Sources The works of Thomas Nashe, ed. R. B. McKerrow, 5 vols. (1904–10); repr. with corrections and notes by F. P. Wilson (1958) · *The works of Gabriel Harvey*, ed. A. B. Grosart, 3 vols. (1884–5) · R. Lichfield, *The trimming of Thomas Nashe* (1597) · C. Nicholl, *A cup of news: the life of Thomas Nashe* (1984) · Arber, *Regs. Stationers*, vols. 1–3 · C. S. Lewis, *English literature in the sixteenth century excluding drama* (1954), vol. 3 of *Oxford history of English literature* · C. G. Harlow, 'Thomas Nashe, Robert Cotton the antiquary, and *The terrors of the night*', *Review of English Studies*, new ser., 12 (1961), 7–23 · K. Duncan-Jones, 'Nashe in Newgate', *TLS* (22 March 1996) · L. Hutson, 'Thomas Nashe's "persecution" by the aldermen in 1593', *N&Q*, 232 (1987), 199 · P. Kocher, 'Some Nashe marginalia concerning Marlowe', *Modern Language Notes*, 57 (1942), 17–18 · D. McGinn, 'Nashe's share in the Marprelate controversy', *Publications of the Modern Language Association of America*, 59 (1944), 952–84 · F. Blomefield and C. Parkin, *An essay towards a topographical history of the county of Norfolk*, [2nd edn], 11 vols. (1805–10) · parish register, Lowestoft, St Margaret, Nov 1567 [baptism]

Archives BL, autograph letter, Cotton MS Jul. Caes. 3, fol. 280

Likenesses line engraving, NPG · line engraving, facsimile of rough woodcut, BM, NPG; repro. in Lichfield, *Trimming of Thomas Nashe*

Nasmith, David (1799–1839), founder of town and city missions, was born at Glasgow on 21 March 1799. He attended sabbath school and the city's grammar school, with a view to the university, but, as he made no progress he was apprenticed about 1811 to a manufacturer there. In June 1813 he became secretary to the newly established Glasgow Youths' Bible Association, and devoted all his leisure to religious work in Glasgow. From 1821 until 1828 he acted as assistant secretary to twenty-three religious and charitable societies connected with the Institution Rooms in Glassford Street. Chiefly through his efforts the Glasgow City Mission was founded on 1 January 1826. In March 1828 he married Frances, daughter of Francis Hartridge of East Farleigh, Kent. He ceased working for the

Institution Rooms and in 1828 set up the Dublin City Mission. He also formed the Local Missionary Society for Ireland, in connection with which he visited various places in the country.

In July 1830 Nasmith sailed from Greenock to New York and visited between forty and fifty towns in the United States and Canada, forming in all thirty-one missions and various benevolent associations. In June 1832 he went to France and founded missions at Paris and Le Havre. In August 1834 he was rebaptized in Ireland (Lewis). In 1835 he accepted the secretaryship of the Continental Society in London. There he organized the London City Mission, with the assistance of Sir Thomas Fowell Buxton as treasurer, the Philanthropic Institution House, the Young Men's Society, the Adult School Society, the Metropolitan Monthly Tract Society, and finally the London Female Mission. Co-operation between Anglican and nonconformist evangelicals in the London City Mission was always fraught and, faced with the likelihood of Anglican withdrawal, Nasmith on 17 March 1837 resigned his office as honorary secretary of the mission. He had the previous day with a few friends formed the British and Foreign Mission, for the purposes of corresponding with the city and town missions already in existence and of founding new ones. While furthering this work Nasmith died at Guildford, Surrey, on 17 November 1839, and was buried on the 25th in Bunhill Fields, London. He died poor, and £2420 was collected by subscription and invested on behalf of his widow and five children. Nasmith was an important figure in British evangelicalism, for the city mission movement spread throughout the empire and the USA.

GORDON GOODWIN, rev. H. C. G. MATTHEW

Sources J. Campbell, *Memoir of David Nasmith* (1844) · D. M. Lewis, ed., *The Blackwell dictionary of evangelical biography, 1730–1860*, 2 vols. (1995) · *GM*, 2nd ser., 12 (1839), 665 · Chambers, *Scots.* (1835)
Likenesses J. C. Armytage, stipple, NPG; repro. in Campbell, *Memoir*

Nasmith, James (*bap.* 1740, *d.* 1808), antiquary, son of James and Susan Nasmith of Norwich, was probably baptized twice, firstly at the Presbyterian Octagon Chapel on 7 April 1740 and secondly at St George's, Colegate, in Norwich, on 7 April 1741. According to the Cambridge antiquary William Cole, who knew him well and is usually correct in such matters, his father was originally a Presbyterian of Scottish descent and 'a considerable carrier from Norwich to London' who 'sent him for about a year to a school at Amsterdam' before entering him as a pensioner at Corpus Christi College, Cambridge, in 1760 (Lamb, 406–7). He graduated BA (sixth wrangler) in 1764, and proceeded MA in 1767, and DD in 1797. He was ordained deacon in December 1763 and admitted to the curacy of Yaxham in Norfolk, elected a fellow of his college in 1765, and ordained priest at Norwich on 8 June in the following year. From about 1763 to 1773 he was minister of the sequestrated parish of Hinxton, Cambridgeshire, and from 1773 to 1796 rector of Snailwell in the same county. Nasmith married in 1774 Susanna Salmon (1738/9–1814), daughter of John Salmon, rector of Shelton, Norfolk, and sister of Benjamin Salmon, fellow of Corpus Christi.

On the approaching death of Dr Barnardiston in 1778 it was proposed to elect Nasmith to the mastership of Corpus 'as a decent Man, a good Scholar, of a good Temper, greatly beloved in the College' (Cole MSS, BL, Add. MS 5886, 44), but he made it known that he would not accept as he was busy improving his living of Snailwell and farming. He thought also that the honour would involve him in an expensive style of life to which he did not aspire. 'He was much respected. His person and manners and habits were plain', according to Sir Egerton Brydges, who met him about 1795 (Brydges, 221). He was for some time chaplain to the earl of Buckinghamshire, of Blickling Hall, Norfolk, and from 1796 rector of the rich living of Leverington, Cambridgeshire.

Nasmith was that not uncommon type the clergyman–antiquary and he was elected FSA in 1769. Cole, for whom he copied the Snailwell church inscriptions, and with whom he exchanged other antiquarian courtesies, mentions him approvingly, and his help is acknowledged in the preface to Henry Swinden's *History and Antiquities of Great Yarmouth* (1772). While a fellow of Corpus he compiled a catalogue of Archbishop Matthew Parker's manuscripts and

> when we recollect the inconvenience of the room, over the old ante-chapel, in which these manuscripts were deposited, and likewise the strictness of the rules under which they are necessarily kept by the Will of the donor, we must admire the diligence and perseverance of Mr. Nasmyth in accomplishing his undertaking. (Lamb, 406)

After five years' steady work he presented the catalogue in 1775 to the college, which had it printed at his direction at its own expense. Many years later he turned his attention to the manuscripts in the Cambridge University Library and was paid to compile an official catalogue, which, while it was done in only three years (1794–6) and was a great improvement on anything that then existed, had several obvious weaknesses besides a frank neglect of non-literary and oriental material, and it appears to have been a disappointment. It remained unpublished but was known about, and was described as 'valuable' (G. Dyer, *History of the University and Colleges*, 2, 1814, 129). His other principal works were a fresh edition of Thomas Tanner's *Notitia monastica* (1787) with additions and corrections (the remaining stock was lost by fire in 1808) and an edition from unique Corpus manuscripts of the medieval *Itineraria* of Symon son of Symeon and of William of Worcester, of which 250 copies were published by subscription (1778). A recent editor of William of Worcester observes that Nasmith's edition 'is a remarkably good one, considering the state of local studies and medieval palaeography at the time' (*Itineraries*, ed. Harvey, xxii).

For many years Nasmith was chairman of the county sessions and had strong local influence. *The Duties of Overseers of the Poor … a Charge Delivered to the Grand Jury* (1799) was written to counter the views of Robert Saunders, an overseer in the parish of Lewisham, who argued for a permanent national board of control. Saunders replied to Nasmith's remarks in a pamphlet in 1802. Nasmith's *Duties* was followed by a tract on the assize of bread in

1800. Nasmith did not share fears about undue pampering of the poor and argued that the Tudor poor laws needed not to be changed but to be administered properly and in a Christian spirit. He believed parish surgeons should prescribe diet as well as medicine and that was accepted at Ely. 'Not only sound policy, but a far superior authority teaches us, that the abundance of some should supply the wants of others' (*Duties of Overseers*, 12).

Nasmith died at Leverington after a long illness on 16 October 1808 and was buried in the church, where there is a monumental inscription. His widow died in Norwich on 11 November 1814, aged seventy-five, and bequeathed 'considerable sums for the use of public and private charities' (*DNB*). JOHN D. PICKLES

Sources Nichols, *Lit. anecdotes* · *Masters' History of the college of Corpus Christi and the Blessed Virgin Mary in the University of Cambridge*, ed. J. Lamb (1831), 406–7 · BL, Cole MSS · D. McKitterick, *Cambridge University Library, a history: the eighteenth and nineteenth centuries* (1986), 344–8 · *GM*, 1st ser., 78 (1808), 958 · E. Brydges, *Restituta, or, Titles, extracts, and characters of old books in English literature*, 4 vols. (1814–16), vol. 3, p. 221 · M. R. James, *A descriptive catalogue of the manuscripts in the library of Corpus Christi College, Cambridge*, 1 (1912), xxxi · *Itineraries [of] William Worcestre*, ed. J. H. Harvey, OMT (1969), v, xi, xxii · *DNB*
Archives Bodl. Oxf., corresp.

Nasmith, John. *See* Nasmyth, John (1556/7–1613).

Nasmyth family (*per.* 1788–1884), were active as painters and art teachers. The painter Alexander *Nasmyth (1758–1840) and his wife, Barbara Foulis (*d.* 1847), had eleven children of whom at least eight were gifted artists. The eldest, Patrick *Nasmyth (1787–1831), is noticed separately, as is their second son, the mechanical engineer James Hall *Nasmyth (1808–1890).

Alexander Nasmyth's six daughters—Jane, Barbara, Margaret, Elizabeth, Anne, and Charlotte—were all painters who assisted their father with his art classes. He was insistent that all his children should be able to be independent, and accordingly taught them to draw and paint. Because they were unable to travel to the continent during the Napoleonic wars many middle-class Scottish families spent more time in Edinburgh than had been customary. Nasmyth therefore had a constant supply of young ladies to teach, as well as would-be professional artists requiring instruction. His classes were conducted in the large studio at the top of his house in York Place, and until he died in 1840 these were managed by his eldest daughter, Jane, with the help of her sisters. Their brother James recorded that

> My sisters all possessed, in a greater or lesser degree, an innate love of art, and by their diligent application they acquired the practice of painting landscapes in oils. My father's admirable system and method of teaching rendered them expert in making accurate sketches from nature … which they turned to good account … My father sedulously kept up the attention of his daughters to fine art. By this means he enabled them to assist in the maintenance of the family while at home, and afterwards to maintain themselves … To accomplish this object … he set on foot drawing classes which were managed by his six daughters, superintended by himself. (*James Nasmyth*, 54–5)

In addition to formal tuition in the studio the girls took sketching parties to the picturesque spots in and around Edinburgh such as Arthur's Seat, Rosslyn Chapel, Hawthornden, and Calton Hill. The girls probably also assisted with the large amount of scene painting taken on by their father for most of the Scottish theatres. From 1815 onwards there is evidence that all the girls went with their father on some of his annual visits to the Royal Academy exhibitions in London. Apart from Elizabeth and Anne, who left home when they married, little is known of their daily lives. The four other girls had some independence and occasionally took lodgings in London. In 1815, the year in which Elizabeth's marriage took place in London, they lived with their mother at 4 Leicester Square, then the centre of London's art world. Between 1836 and 1840 Jane, Anne, and Charlotte occupied from time to time an apartment at 326 Regent Street, London. All the girls exhibited widely; from 1826 to 1866 they sent works variously to the Water Colour Exhibition in Spring Gardens, London, the Carlisle Exhibition, the Birmingham Society of Artists, the Royal Manchester Institution, the Liverpool Academy, the British Institution, the Society of Artists in Suffolk Street, London, and the Royal Academy (for details see Johnson and Money, 55–7). They all kept a number of finished works to send to exhibitions, working in oil and occasionally watercolour. The most prolific were Jane, Charlotte, and Margaret—with 43, 44, 41 works respectively—followed by Barbara (33) and Elizabeth (23), and then Anne (16). Except for occasional sketches of each other they engaged in landscape painting. Almost all their works were landscapes of a small size (up to 18 inches by 24 inches), and remain in private collections. Their signed and dated works come on to the market infrequently and have not yet been catalogued. More recently examples of their finely detailed landscapes were exhibited at the Saltire Society, Edinburgh (1948); 'The Nasmyth Family' (Oscar and Peter Johnson, London, 1964); 'Alexander Nasmyth and his Family' (Monks Hall Museum, Eccles, Manchester, 1973); and 'Alexander Nasmyth' (St Andrews, 1979).

Following Alexander Nasmyth's death in May 1840 his studio sale in Edinburgh of 155 Nasmyth canvases included work by every artist member of the family (except James, who, though an engineer, also painted). Mrs Nasmyth, Jane, Barbara, and Charlotte went to live with James (who had married Anne Hartop in June 1840), George, and Margaret at Green Lane House in Patricroft, Manchester. When George left in 1843 Mrs Nasmyth, Jane, Barbara, Margaret, and Charlotte moved to Richmond Terrace, Pendleton, to be near Anne and her husband, William Bennett, in Leaf Square, Salford. Mrs Nasmyth suffered a stroke and died in 1847, and by 1852 the four Nasmyth girls had followed the Bennetts to Putney. They lived around the corner from Charlwood Road at 17 Stratford Grove, remaining there until 1860, when they moved next door to the Bennetts at 1 Stanhope Villas. At one point Elizabeth and Charles Richardson lived at no. 2.

Andrew Geddes, whose Scottish home was a few doors away from the Nasmyths in York Place, painted a half-length portrait of Charlotte (NG Scot.) which shows a pretty, dark-haired girl in a frilly organdie dress, holding a flower. William Nicholson painted watercolours of Jane, Anne, Barbara, and Margaret showing them with light brown hair and the pronounced Nasmyth nose (Scot. NPG). Geddes also painted a domestic scene entitled *Dull Readings* featuring Daniel and Elizabeth Terry at home by the fire (all portraits repro. in Cooksey, 155–6, 158).

In their brother James's opinion his sisters' styles of painting were distinct from one another. However, with several members of the family painting together and occasionally adding touches to each other's work, unless the work is signed, attribution is problematic. In addition, many other artists learned to paint in the Nasmyth style— as a *View of St Bernard's Well* (Royal Scottish Academy), by Mrs Ann Cummyng, demonstrates—and this makes for more complex questions of attribution. In a letter of 1826 to his framer, William Cribb, Alexander Nasmyth describes a box of pictures for exhibition in London in which he refers to his 'View of Greenoch with some catle Painted by Miss Jane', and a woody scene in Dumfriesshire: 'this Picture is likewise by Miss Jane with some of my own painting on it as is the case with all of them' (Cooksey, 126).

Jane Nasmyth (1788–1867) was born in the parish of St Andrew Kirk, Edinburgh, on 29 March 1788. The parish register records her first name as Jean but she signed her work Jane, the name by which she was known. Nicknamed 'Old Solid' by the family, she assisted with the raising of her younger brothers and sisters before helping with the running of the school. Her brother James recorded that 'My father consulted her in every course of importance in reference to business and financial affairs' (*James Nasmyth*, 54). She sometimes accompanied her father on working trips and became his trusted confidante. The titles of her exhibited works suggest that she travelled a good deal, painting views of Windermere, Cumberland, Derbyshire, Richmond, Windsor, and Putney, as well as many others in various parts of Scotland. She also painted one scene of Geneva (exh. Royal Manchester Institution, 1851) and another of Lake Lausanne (priv. coll.). There is no evidence, however, that she went abroad, and for these two landscapes probably made use of her father's drawings. She favoured lake and mountain scenes, old trees, and sometimes her landscapes included towns such as *A View of Perth* (exh. Royal Manchester Institution, 1845), or *The Village of Swanston* (1826). Her work closely resembles that of her father, particularly in the painting of trees, rocks, and paths, and foreground details. Her figures are not so lifelike, however, and are often colourfully attired. Sometimes her foreground areas resemble water in their flat treatment, for example, *Loch Katrine* (repr. in Johnson and Money). Some of her later works are closer to those of her sister Charlotte, the tree trunks and dead branches in the trees particularly. She often bathed her distances in a pinkish evening light, so common in Scottish skies and beloved by her father. She signed her work 'Jane Nasmyth' with the date, sometimes only on the exhibition label attached to the frame or stretcher, and favoured a Glasgow framer, Brand & Co. She

died on 11 May 1867 and was buried in Putney Lower Common cemetery, in a grave to the right of the chapel. In due course her sisters Margaret, Barbara, and Charlotte were buried in the same plot.

Barbara Nasmyth (1790–1870) was born in St James's Square, St Cuthbert's parish, Edinburgh, on 15 April 1790. She accompanied her sisters Charlotte and Margaret on a visit to London in 1816, but the titles of her works suggest that, in general, though she went to Patricroft in 1840 and later settled in London, she painted mostly Scottish subjects in the vicinity of Edinburgh and in the lowlands. These included loch scenes, castles, river views, and townscapes in Edinburgh, Kenmore, and Comrie. Evidence of expeditions south of the border includes views of Westmorland, Derbyshire, and Essex. She was the last of the sisters to exhibit her work, beginning in 1845. She excelled in woodland scenery, cottages, and loch scenes, for example *Highland Landscape with Loch* (priv. coll.), in which the trees are closer to Charlotte's than her father's in their roughness of bark and lighter colouring. Her figures are finely detailed, and she loved painting sailing boats as in *Scottish Landscape* (repro. in Johnson and Money). She signed her work 'Barbara Nasmyth' neatly with a fine brush, sometimes adding the date. She died on 2 February 1870 at her home, Stanhope Villas, Charlwood Road, Putney.

Margaret Nasmyth (1791–1869) was born on 11 April 1791 in Hill Street, St Andrew's parish, Edinburgh. She followed her father in style, but like Barbara she preferred the more detailed and minute brushwork of her brother Patrick. Margaret left home in 1836 to live with her brothers James and George, at Green Lane House, Patricroft, Manchester. She did not exhibit until 1841 at the age of fifty, by which time the whole family had come to live with James, when presumably she had more time to herself. She travelled much, drawing subjects from all over Scotland as well as Cumberland, Lancashire, north Wales, Shropshire, Westmorland, and Cheshire, and further afield, in Blackford Heath and Chigwell, Essex. Her technique is fine and detailed, and she lavished much care on all parts of her paintings. Good examples are *Lake Scene* and *View of Kinfauns Castle Perthshire* (both repro. in Johnson and Money). She signed her work 'Margaret Nasmyth' in the bottom left-hand corner in a large, clear hand, though sometimes 'MN' with the date, in the bottom right-hand corner. She died at Stanhope Villas on 3 November 1869.

Elizabeth Wemyss Nasmyth (1793–1862) was born on 26 August 1793 in Hill Street, St Andrew's parish, Edinburgh. On 25 June 1815 she married the actor Daniel *Terry (1789–1829). The marriage possibly took place rather suddenly, for in Nasmyth's letter to his children in Edinburgh of a few weeks earlier he makes no mention of it. Elizabeth was a talented designer and through Daniel Terry's association with Sir Walter Scott over the building of Abbotsford prepared designs for Scott's armoury. On 15 July 1815 Terry wrote to Scott:

> Mrs Terry is at length returned to her easel our visitors are departed & quite singular labour is again embarked upon we have upon the frames three transparencies the designs of

two are already outlined & are armour clad men in
appropriate landscapes   (Wainwright, 174)

Wainwright notes that 'these transparencies could refer
to cartoons for stained glass, but they more probably refer
to transparent painted roller blinds of a type popular at
the time' (ibid., 174–5). On 11 May 1816 Terry wrote again to
Scott: '… nor the window blinds for Abbotsford are forgotten with the restored health of the artist [Mrs Terry] they
will be proceded with' (ibid.). In September 1818 Terry
advised Scott: 'I think you will like your windows with
your arms, old abbots, knights and the Stirling heads with
their coloured borders and ornaments' (ibid.). The following month Scott wrote to a friend that 'Naesmythe and his
daughter Mrs Terry have arrived here unexpectedly', presumably to see how work was progressing on the house
(ibid.).

Elizabeth continued with her painting, sending works
to the British Institution from 1816 to 1829. Her style is perhaps the coldest and least painterly of the sisters, a rare
signed example being *Driving Cattle by a Loch* (priv. coll.).
Though identifiable as of the 'Nasmyth school', and competently finished, her work is stylistically less romantic.
This is partly due to her use of bright colours, which distinguishes her work from that of her sisters. Her works
tend to be inscribed on the stretcher 'Elizabeth Nasmyth'.

The Terrys lived in London at 9 Devonshire Street, Portland Place. A letter of 1832 from Alexander Nasmyth to
T. W. Winstanley indicates that Elizabeth stored unsold
paintings and helped her father to organize his London
life. She also ran art classes with her sister Anne from this
address. Correspondence between Daniel Terry and Scott
records Elizabeth's difficulty in having children. The
couple had three children, Walter Scott Terry (*b.* 1816),
Jane Terry (*b.* 1821), and Elizabeth Terry (*b.* 1822). Daniel
Terry died after a long struggle with illness and financial
difficulty on 12 June 1829. Elizabeth then married the lexicographer Charles *Richardson (1775–1865) on 23 May
1835. They had no children. She died at 9 Charlwood Road,
Putney, Surrey, on 10 July 1862 and was buried with her
husband in Putney Lower Common cemetery. A lengthy
epitaph on her tombstone erected by her broken-hearted
husband testifies to a long and happy marriage.

Anne Gibson Nasmyth (1798–1874) was born on 13
November 1798 in Princes Street, St Andrew's parish,
Edinburgh. She assisted her sister Elizabeth with classes
in her London home and between 1829 and 1838 exhibited
sixteen works in the London galleries, including one at
the Royal Academy. Her work demonstrates her fondness
for highland and sometimes stormy scenery. Her paintings vary from close emulation of her father's style to
others reminiscent of Charlotte's (for example, *Windsor*,
repro. in Johnson and Money). She also produced some
precise pictures of small gardens, their conservatories,
and plantings, such as *Garden Scene* (repro. in Johnson and
Money). She signed her work Anne Nasmyth or 'A Nasmyth'. When they first set up as engineers in 1831 Anne
spent time with her brothers James and George in Manchester. There she met an engineer, William Bennett,
whom she married in London at the parish church of St
Pancras on 13 August 1838. She was the only one of Alexander Nasmyth's children to follow him to Italy, and spent
her honeymoon in Rome. The Bennetts lived first in Leaf
Square, Salford, Lancashire, and afterwards moved, in
1851, to Charlwood Road, Putney, where their home
became a pivotal point for the Nasmyth daughters and
granddaughters. She died on 28 January 1874, having been
widowed in 1866, and was buried with her husband beside
her four sisters.

Charlotte Nasmyth (1804–1884) was born on 17 February 1804 in York Place, St Andrew's parish, Edinburgh.
Apart from her portrait by Andrew Geddes and the titles
of her works, there is little trace of her life. A letter home
from her brother Patrick records that she first went to
London in 1816 with Margaret and Barbara to visit the
exhibitions and the theatre and to see the shops and Napoleon's carriage. Of all the sisters her style is the most recognizable: wilder, more rugged and flamboyant, and less
picturesque. Sometimes her work is close to that of her
father, for example in *Highland Pass* (repro. in Johnson and
Money), but she developed her own unique style, and
worked with a greater freedom and panache than her sisters. Her colouring is natural. She loved painting whitish
gnarled tree trunks with an array of broken branches and
large-leaved foreground plants, and she depicted wide
open spaces without framing trees to either side. She was
skilled at figures, animals, and boats, and she painted
glorious windy skies. Her own personality comes through
in *Hampstead Heath* and *Musselburgh* (both repro. in Johnson and Money). Her exhibited work shows that she also
travelled afield, painting views in Cumberland, the Lake
District, Yorkshire, north Wales, Essex, and Surrey, and
she painted one foreign view, *The Bay of Naples* (exh. Royal
Manchester Institution, 1848). She painted a wide variety
of subjects including cottages and castles, mountain
views and landscapes that appealed to her. She signed her
work 'Charlotte Nasmyth' or 'C Nasmyth' with the date in
a tidy copperplate hand. She died on 26 July 1884 at Wood
Hall, Putney, Surrey, and was buried in the family plot in
Putney Lower Common cemetery.

Their wills indicate that the Nasmyth girls lived comfortably. A few exhibition catalogues from the 1850s
which include prices record that most of the sisters
received 8 or 10 guineas for their pictures. This would have
given them ample income. They were also provided for by
their father in his will, dated 1839. James Nasmyth
amassed a large fortune and by 1856 had made his unmarried sisters completely independent. As part of a closely
knit artistic family, the Nasmyth daughters were a gifted
group of women artists. Though they lived, worked,
exhibited, and prospered in England, they continued to
draw inspiration from their Scottish origins and the landscape of Scotland.   J. C. B. COOKSEY

Sources J. C. B. Cooksey, *Alexander Nasmyth HRSA, 1758–1840: a man
of the Scottish Renaissance* (1991) · *James Nasmyth, engineer: an autobiography*, ed. S. Smiles (1883) · M. H. Grant, *A chronological history of the
old English landscape painters*, 8 vols. (1926); repr. (1957–61), vol. 4 ·
J. L. Caw, 'Alexander Nasmyth, 1758–1840', *Scots Magazine* (Feb

1940), 325-35 · D. Irwin and F. Irwin, *Scottish painters at home and abroad, 1700-1900* (1975) · F. Irwin, 'Lady amateurs and their masters in Scott's Edinburgh', *The Connoisseur*, 185 (Dec 1974), 229-37 · P. Johnson and E. Money, *The Nasmyth family of painters* (1977) [contains a list of works exhibited by Nasmyth daughters] · C. Wainwright, *The romantic interior* (1989) · parish register of births and baptisms, 6 June 1806, General Register Office for Scotland, Edinburgh · bap. reg. Scot. [Jane Nasmyth] · d. cert. [Charlotte Nasmyth] · d. cert. [Barbara Nasmyth] · bap. reg. Scot. [Margaret Nasmyth] · d. cert. [Margaret Nasmyth] · d. cert. [Elizabeth Wemyss Nasmyth] · d. cert. [Anne Gibson Nasmyth] · M. Patry, *Alexander Nasmyth and his family* (1973) [exhibition catalogue, Monks Hall Museum, Manchester] · D. Macmillan, *Painting in Scotland: the golden age* (1986) [exhibition catalogue, U. Edin., Talbot Rice Gallery, and Tate Gallery, London, 1986] · O. Johnson and P. Johnson, *The Nasmyth family of painters* (1974) [exhibition catalogue, Lowndes Lodge Gallery, London] · *The works of the Nasmyth family (1719–1890)*, Saltire Society (1948) [exhibition catalogue, Saltire Society, Edinburgh]

Archives NL Scot., letters | Scot. NPG, Madeleine Patry papers
Likenesses A. Geddes, oils, exh. RSA 1820 (Charlotte Nasmyth), repro. in Cooksey, *Alexander Nasmyth*, 157 · oils, *c*.1825 (Elizabeth Wemyss Nasmyth), repro. in Cooksey, *Alexander Nasmyth*, 158; priv. coll. · D. O. Hill, ink and wash sketch, 1829 (*Nasmyth family at home*), Scot. NPG · W. Nicholson, group portrait, watercolour drawing, exh. RSA 1842 (Anne & Jane, and Barbara & Margaret), repro. in Cooksey, *Alexander Nasmyth*, 155, 156
Wealth at death under £300—Jane Nasmyth: probate, 7 June 1867, *CGPLA Eng. & Wales* · under £800—Barbara Nasmyth: resworn probate, Nov 1871, *CGPLA Eng. & Wales* (1870) · under £14,000—Anne Gibson Nasmyth: probate, 20 Feb 1874, *CGPLA Eng. & Wales* · £16,154 8s. 3d.—Charlotte Nasmyth: probate, 3 Sept 1884, *CGPLA Eng. & Wales*

Alexander Nasmyth (1758–1840), by Andrew Geddes, *c*.1820–25

Nasmyth, Alexander (1758–1840), artist and engineer, was born on 9 September 1758 at his father's house at Anderson's Land in the Grassmarket, Edinburgh, the second of two children of Michael Naesmyth (1719–1803), an architect and builder, and his wife, Lillias Anderson, known as Mary, widow of Robert Naesmyth. Alexander's great-grandfather, grandfather, and father, all named Michael Naesmyth, worked for the government, the gentry and nobility, and the professional classes in the rapidly growing city of Edinburgh, building new houses such as those in St George's Square and St Andrew Square, and modernizing old castles and tower houses.

Nasmyth was educated at home, before attending 'Mammy' Smith's school in the Grassmarket. He studied at the high school, and was then taught arithmetic, mensuration, and geometry by his father, to prepare him for the family business. However, his elder brother Michael (1754–1819) had already opted for a life at sea and Alexander was determined to develop his artistic skills. He was apprenticed in 1773 to James Cummyng, a tradesman house-painter, and in 1774 he enrolled briefly for the drawing classes run by Alexander Runciman at the Trustees' Academy. While painting a coat of arms on a carriage for the coach-builder Alexander Crighton, Nasmyth caught the attention of Allan Ramsay, principal painter in ordinary to George III. Ramsay persuaded Cummyng to release the sixteen-year-old Nasmyth, and returned with him to his London studio. Here he joined the other apprentices producing replicas of Ramsay's portraits of the king and queen.

At the end of 1778 Nasmyth returned to Edinburgh and began his career as a portrait painter. His early works were small and tentative, for example *John Scott of Malleny* (1781; Malleny House, Midlothian), and followed Ramsay's practice of placing the sitter's head and shoulders against a plain background. However, he gradually evolved his own style and, gaining confidence and mastery of his subject, was soon placing his sitters in their own landscape settings. The backgrounds became as important as the portraits, with equal care lavished on both. He painted *Patrick Miller and his Children at Dalswinton* (1782; priv. coll.), with the theme of a shooting party, and set in the family's own parkland. This commission proved of great significance, for Miller, a retired banker, discovered the painter's scientific capabilities when the young artist drew up plans for a proposed paddle-boat (shortly to become the first steamboat), and in recognition of his services lent him £500 to broaden his artistic education on the continent.

Nasmyth left Edinburgh on 30 December 1782, painted some portraits in London *en route*, and arrived in Rome in April 1783. Views produced by him in later life from sketches suggest that he also visited the Bay of Naples, Bolsena, Ancona, and Tivoli. His homeward route may be traced through pictures of Lake Lucerne, Lake Lausanne, Lake Geneva, and Haarlem. He returned to Edinburgh at the end of 1784, gaining ample employment as a portrait painter, as there was little competition in the city. He is best-known for his small portrait *Robert Burns* (1787; NG Scot.), while the large-scale *Gordon Family at Braid* (*c*.1790; priv. coll.) handsomely represents his mature style, with its fine handling of the faces, dresses, and background details.

By 1788 Nasmyth described himself in the Edinburgh directories as a portrait and landscape painter. He loved walking around his native city, often in the company of Robert Burns, who lived close by. He joined the Edinburgh freemasons in 1777 and the Cape Club in 1791. His liberal politics and outspokenness on the perceived abuses of the tory government embarrassed some of his aristocratic patrons; but, despite warnings that commissions would cease, he persisted with his beliefs. By 1790 Raeburn's dominance of portrait painting in Edinburgh further encouraged Nasmyth to concentrate on landscapes.

On 3 January 1786 Nasmyth married his distant cousin Barbara Foulis (c.1758–1847), sister of Sir James Foulis of Colinton. They had four sons and eight daughters, of whom Patrick *Nasmyth (1787–1831), Jane *Nasmyth (1788–1867), Barbara *Nasmyth (1790–1870), Margaret *Nasmyth (1791–1869), Elizabeth Wemyss *Nasmyth (1793–1862), Anne Gibson *Nasmyth (1798–1874), and Charlotte *Nasmyth (1804–1884) all became painters [see under Nasmyth family]. The tenth child, James Hall *Nasmyth, became a mechanical engineer. After an unsettled start, they moved into their own property at 47 York Place, Edinburgh, in 1799. Nasmyth was a popular man with a wide circle of friends and the household always attracted visitors in the evenings. He was described by contemporaries as tall and handsome with a rosy complexion, and as a brilliant raconteur whose company and friendship was greatly valued. Wilkie wrote that Nasmyth's 'society and conversation was perhaps the most agreeable that I ever met with' (Smiles, 232).

While occasionally painting storm-lashed seas, moonlight, or hunting scenes, Nasmyth took as his predominant theme the Scottish landscape of a summer's evening. The distance was typically bathed in mist, and the subject matter suggested to the spectator feelings of tranquillity and romance. Fine examples are *Lugar Water* (Aberdeen Art Gallery), or the large-scale *Suspension Bridge over the Tweed near Berwick* (Royal Scottish Academy). In the 1820s he turned his attention to Edinburgh street scenes, in which he recorded fashions, daily activity, and architecture such as *Princes Street with the Royal Institution Building under Construction* (1825; NG Scot.). *Edinburgh with the High Street and Lawnmarket* (exh. RA, 1824; Royal Collection) and its companion, *Shipping at Leith* (exh. RA, 1824; City Chambers, Edinburgh) were probably painted to mark the visit of George IV to Edinburgh in 1822.

Nasmyth's style appears to have been inspired principally by that of Claude Lorrain in composition, colour, and mood, and by Jacob van Ruisdael in the handling of water, trees, and foreground detail. He painted in the studio, working from small pencil sketches that were firmly and rapidly executed and often made many years earlier. The paintings were worked up with several layers of pigment and glazing to achieve a feeling of depth, and the top layers of leaves and other vegetation were finished with great attention to detail. His style and palette, once formulated to his satisfaction, displayed a remarkable consistency in both vision and technique throughout his career,

making undated works difficult to arrange chronologically. From 1832 he began to suffer spasmodically from gout and rheumatism, and the effects of old age rendered his later works somewhat less precise.

Admired during his lifetime as 'the founder of landscape painting' (Sir David Wilkie to Mrs Barbara Nasmyth, 18 April 1840, Smiles, 232) in Scotland, Nasmyth was occasionally accused of mannerism. He was frequently asked to paint the same view several times, only varying the details such as the positioning of the figures. Few of his works are signed, and because many 'Nasmyths' contain the work of one or more of his artistic children, care must be exercised in attributing lesser works to Alexander. He sent his most ambitious pictures to London, and also exhibited in Edinburgh, Manchester, Carlisle, and Glasgow.

Nasmyth was also an extremely successful teacher of both professional and amateur artists. Some regular pupils bought courses of lessons, but many of his students attended in a less formal way, including the artists David Wilkie, David Roberts, Clarkson Stanfield, William Allan, Andrew Robertson, Andrew Geddes, Hugh William Williams, and John Thomson. Nasmyth's teaching methods involved short instructive talks at the easel combined with copying objects thrown down at random, and sometimes involving the camera obscura. Pupils were set to copy paintings, and also were taken on sketching parties in and around Edinburgh. Nasmyth did not take on apprentices in the conventional sense, because his daughters helped with both teaching and painting.

When visiting clients in the country, Nasmyth was often called upon to paint a large house or castle in its landscape, to show how the grounds might be improved, as for example at Dalmeny, where he painted a number of views (priv. coll.). At times he was employed to help his clients improve the landscape of their estates by making the garden or park resemble his pictures of them. Curiously, the very same tory aristocracy—the Roseberys, the Forbeses, the Argylls, the Atholls, the Elgins—and others who purportedly deplored his liberal politics were those who found his architectural and landscape services indispensable. Among his clients was his great friend the geologist Sir James Hall, for whom he designed Dunglass, a vast and splendid Italianate castle which literally cascaded down the hillside. He also made sketches and models to show how vistas might be opened up by selective pruning, emphasizing the importance of preserving mature trees. He was often asked to assist in the selection of a suitable site for a new house, as at Rosneath, Dunbartonshire (built c.1805–6), or to modernize or build onto an old castle. He personified the contemporary Italian idea of the *architetto-pittore*. Between 1800 and 1810 he provided designs for follies, bridges, a lighthouse, a stable complex, and some very grand mansions—including Taymouth Castle (Perthshire), Dunglass House (East Lothian), Loudoun Castle (Ayrshire), Dreghorn Castle (Midlothian), and Rosneath. These were all crowned with a tower from which to view the landscape and planting. Architects were then employed to take the projects forward but when they could not be found Nasmyth undertook the work himself.

In 1792 Patrick Millar invited Nasmyth to make designs for the Dumfries Theatre and from this time he produced stock scenery for the principal Scottish theatres, and later that in Drury Lane, London. His efforts were eulogized in the Scottish press, and the *Times* correspondent described his work as 'uncommonly beautiful' (*The Times*, 6 Jan 1823). His vast stock scenery for Glasgow, which consisted of streets, houses, cottages, palaces, interiors, and landscapes, 'excited universal admiration' (J. Ballantine, *The Life of David Roberts*, 1866, 13–14) according to David Roberts. Such was the prestige of his name on the programme, he was able to charge £125 for four scenes, while Clarkson Stanfield received only £20 for three. In addition, he also painted at least one vast panorama of Edinburgh, exhibited in special buildings in London and Glasgow. Possibly as a result of the success in 1818 of the scenery he painted for *The Heart of Midlothian* (sketches NG Scot.), Nasmyth was commissioned by Sir Walter Scott, through his publisher Archibald Constable, to provide vignettes for the 1821 edition of the Waverley novels. He went on to become a prolific illustrator of Scott's works, contributing over sixty drawings.

Nasmyth also displayed considerable talents as an engineer. He had a workshop at home where he made and kept his tools and models. He designed a tunnel to run under the Forth and made designs for bridges and bridge building (NG Scot.). In 1794 he invented the bow and string bridge and arch, used for spanning rivers or the roofs of factories and railway stations, and in 1816 compression riveting. However, he never sought to patent his inventions.

Nasmyth's life coincided with Edinburgh's major expansion, and he continued his family's tradition of embellishing the city. Nasmyth designed St Bernard's Well, the small temple over the Water of Leith, and provided the original designs for the Dean Bridge nearby and the Nelson Monument on Calton Hill. He was keenly interested in the progress of the New Town, frequently making suggestions and models and discussing his ideas with architects and builders, *Princes Street from Hanover Street* and *Edinburgh from the Calton Hill* (exh. RA, 1826; priv. coll.) show the progress of the city's development, while *Edinburgh from St Anthony's Chapel* (1832; priv. coll.) depicts in great detail the Old and New towns side by side. He was one of three prize-winning designers for the layout of the second new town—the Calton Hill scheme.

Nasmyth enjoyed a long and busy life. He successfully wove his varying strands of art, architecture, and engineering together; however, his liberal views probably prevented wider recognition. After a short illness he died at his home, 47 York Place, on 10 April 1840, and was buried beside his son Alex (who died in early youth) in St Cuthbert's churchyard, Edinburgh.   J. C. B. COOKSEY

Sources J. C. B. Cooksey, *Alexander Nasmyth HRSA, 1758–1840: a man of the Scottish Renaissance* (1991) · *James Nasmyth, engineer: an autobiography*, ed. S. Smiles (1883) · M. H. Grant, *A chronological history of the*

old English landscape painters (1926); repr. 8 vols. (1957–61), vol. 4 · J. L. Caw, 'Alexander Nasmyth, 1758–1840', *Scots Magazine* (Feb 1940), 325–35 · D. Irwin and F. Irwin, *Scottish painters at home and abroad, 1700–1900* (1975) · F. Irwin, 'Lady amateurs and their masters in Scott's Edinburgh', *The Connoisseur*, 185 (Dec 1974), 229–37 · P. Johnson and E. Money, *The Nasmyth family of painters* (1977) [incl. lists of works exhibited by Nasmyth daughters] · M. Kemp, 'Alexander Nasmyth and the style of graphic eloquence', *The Connoisseur* (Feb 1970), 93–100 · B. Skinner, 'Nasmyth revalued', *Scottish Art Review*, 10/3 (1966), 10–13 · J. C. B. Cooksey, *Alexander Nasmyth, 1758–1840* (1979) [exhibition catalogue, Balcarres Gallery, Crawford Centre for the Arts, St Andrews, 9 Feb – 11 March 1979] · M. Patry, *Alexander Nasmyth and his family* (1973) [exhibition catalogue, Monkshall Museum] · D. Macmillan, *Painting in Scotland: the golden age* (1986) [exhibition catalogue, U. Edin., Talbot Rice Gallery, and Tate Gallery, London, 1986] · O. Johnson and P. Johnson, *The Nasmyth family of painters* (1974) [exhibition catalogue, Lowndes Lodge Gallery, London] · *The works of the Nasmyth family (1719–1890)*, Saltire Society (1948) [exhibition catalogue, Edinburgh] · parish register, St Cuthbert's, Edinburgh [death] · NA Scot., SC 70/1/62/698–704

Archives NL Scot., corresp. · Royal Scot. Acad., letters | Inveraray Castle, Argyll and Bute, letters and accounts with duke of Argyll · Man. CL, letters to T. W. Winstanley

Likenesses P. Reinagle, oil sketch, *c.*1774, repro. in Smiles, ed., *James Nasmyth*, 26 · P. Nasmyth, pencil sketch, 1812, NG Scot. · W. Nicholson, oils, 1818; J. Nasmyth, copy 1884, Aberdeen Art Gallery · A. Geddes, oils, *c.*1820–1825, Royal Scot. Acad. [see illus.] · W. Berwick, oils, *c.*1823, Scot. NPG · D. O. Hill, double portrait, pen and wash sketch, 1829 (with Barbara Nasmyth), repro. in Cooksey, *Alexander Nasmyth*, pl. 6 · D. O. Hill, group portrait, pen and wash sketch, 1829 (*Nasmyth family at home*), repro. in Cooksey, *Alexander Nasmyth*, pl. 5 · J. F. Skill, J. Gilbert, W. & E. Walker, group portrait, pencil and wash, 1855–8 (*Men of science living in 1807–08*), NPG · J. Nasmyth, pencil, 1929, NL Scot. · A. Geddes, etching (after his portrait), BM; repro. in D. Laing, *Etchings by Sir David Wilkie and by Andrew Geddes* (1875), pl. 10 · Paterson, engraving (after portrait by S. Joseph, *c.*1820–1824), repro. in Smiles, ed., *James Nasmyth*, 230

Wealth at death £586 2s. 6d.: confirmation, 31 Aug 1842, NA Scot., SC 70/1/62/698–704

Nasmyth, Anne Gibson (1798–1874). *See under* Nasmyth family (*per.* 1788–1884).

Nasmyth, Barbara (1790–1870). *See under* Nasmyth family (*per.* 1788–1884).

Nasmyth, Charles (1825–1861), army officer, eldest son of Robert Nasmyth, fellow of the Royal College of Surgeons, Edinburgh, of Charlotte Square, Edinburgh, was born in Edinburgh in September 1825. He attended Addiscombe College (1843–4) and was appointed direct to the Bombay artillery, becoming second-lieutenant on 12 December 1845 and first-lieutenant on 4 February 1850. Having lost his health in Gujarat, he went on sick leave to Europe in 1853. He visited Constantinople, where Captain Twopenny, the *Times* correspondent there, engaged him as a *Times* correspondent and sent him to Omar Pasha's camp at Shumla. He visited the Dobruscha after it had been vacated by the Turks, and supplied valuable information to Lord Stratford de Redcliffe. His reports in *The Times* attracted much notice, and the paper sent him to Silistria, which he reached before it was besieged by the Russians, on 28 March 1854. Nasmyth—while continuing to report for *The Times*—and another brave, lighthearted young

British officer, Captain James Armar Butler, gained notable ascendancy over the Turkish garrison, and were crucial to the defence, which ended with the Russians being compelled to raise the siege on 22 June 1854. The defence gave the first check to the Russians, and possibly saved the allies from a campaign amid the marshes of the Danube. Nasmyth received the thanks of the British and Turkish governments and Turkish gold medals for the Danube campaign and the defence of Silistria, and the freedom of Edinburgh (March 1855).

Nasmyth returned to Constantinople in broken health and having lost all his belongings. He was transferred from the East India Company's to the queen's army, on 15 September 1854 being appointed captain unattached and brevet major for his distinguished services at the defence of Silistria. He was with the headquarters staff at the Alma and the siege of Sevastopol. In 1855 he was appointed assistant adjutant-general of the Kilkenny district, and was afterwards brigade major at the Curragh camp (1856–7), and brigade major and deputy assistant adjutant-general in Dublin (1857–8). His infirm health suggested a change to a warmer climate, and he was transferred to New South Wales as brigade major at Sydney (1858–9). He was invalided to Europe at the end of 1859, sold out on 25 May 1860, and, after long suffering, died at Pau, Basses-Pyrénées, France, on 2 June 1861, aged thirty-five. Kinglake, who knew him in the Crimea, described him as 'a man of quiet and gentle manners and so free from vanity—so free from all idea of self-gratulation' (2.245).

H. M. CHICHESTER, *rev.* ROGER T. STEARN

Sources A. W. Kinglake, *The invasion of the Crimea*, [new edn], 2 (1877), 245 · *The Times* (April–June 1854) · *Annual Register* (1854) · *Fraser's Magazine*, 50 (1854) · *Hart's Army List* (1860) · *GM*, 3rd ser., 11 (1861) · H. M. Vibart, *Addiscombe: its heroes and men of note* (1894) · [S. Morison and others], *The history of The Times*, 2 (1939) · A. D. Lambert, *The Crimean War: British grand strategy, 1853–56* (1990) · T. A. Heathcote, *The military in British India: the development of British land forces in south Asia, 1600–1947* (1995) · Boase, *Mod. Eng. biog.* · DNB
Likenesses wood-engraving (after photograph by Lock & Whitfield), NPG; repro. in *ILN* (13 July 1861)
Wealth at death £300: probate, 7 Dec 1861, *CGPLA Eng. & Wales*

Nasmyth, Charlotte (1804–1884). *See under* Nasmyth family (*per.* 1788–1884).

Nasmyth, Elizabeth Wemyss (1793–1862). *See under* Nasmyth family (*per.* 1788–1884).

Nasmyth [Naesmith], **Sir James**, **first baronet** (1654?–1720), lawyer, probably born in Peeblesshire, was the son of John Nasmyth and his wife, Isabella, daughter of Sir James Murray of Philiphaugh. He was admitted advocate in 1684, and became a successful lawyer, known by the sobriquet of the De'il o' Dawick. He had acquired the estate of Dawick (or Dawyck) from the last of the Veitch family, and rebuilt the house and garden. He had a crown charter of the barony of Dawick (or Dawyck) in 1703, ratified in parliament in 1705. He was created a baronet of Scotland on 31 July 1706. Nasmyth was married three times: first, to Jane Stewart, widow of Sir Ludovic Gordon,

of Gordonstoun, Elgin, baronet; second, to Janet, daughter of Sir William Murray of Stanhope, Peeblesshire; and, third, to Barbara (*d.* 1768), daughter of Andrew Pringle of Clifton, Roxburghshire. He died in July 1720 and was succeeded by James *Naesmyth, eldest son of his third marriage, a botanist.

B. B. WOODWARD, *rev.* ANITA MCCONNELL

Sources W. Chambers, *A history of Peeblesshire* (1864), 417–19 · IGI · J. W. Buchan and H. Paton, eds., *A history of Peeblesshire*, 3 vols. (1925–7) · W. Balfour Gourlay, 'Dawyck', *Journal of the Royal Horticultural Society*, 72 (1947), 5–12
Archives NL Scot., legal corresp. and MSS

Nasmyth, James. *See* Naesmyth, Sir James, second baronet (*d.* 1779).

Nasmyth, James Hall (1808–1890), mechanical engineer, was born on 19 August 1808, at 47 York Place, Edinburgh, the son of Alexander *Nasmyth (1758–1840), an artist and portrait painter well established in Edinburgh society, and his wife, Barbara Foulis (*d.* 1847), daughter of William Foulis of Woodhall and Colinton. He was the tenth of eleven children, several of whom demonstrated considerable artistic talent, including the eldest son, Patrick *Nasmyth, who became a professional artist like his father. Of the three sons who survived to maturity, the other two, George and James, both showed mechanical skills and became engineers. Six of Alexander and Barbara's eight daughters also became painters [*see* Nasmyth family].

Education and early career According to the account in his *Autobiography*, the education of James Nasmyth appears to have been rather disjointed. After a short time with a private tutor he was sent to the Edinburgh high school but left in 1820 to pursue his studies in private classes. His father taught him drawing, and he spent much of his spare time in a large iron foundry owned by the father of one of his friends. He quickly became very proficient in handling tools and applied this skill in making small steam engines and other machines. The sale of such models enabled him to attend classes at Edinburgh University, where he was encouraged by Professor Leslie to attend his lectures on natural philosophy. He was still only nineteen when the Scottish Society of Arts commissioned him to build a steam carriage capable of carrying half a dozen people, which was successfully put into operation on roads around Edinburgh in 1827–8.

Nasmyth went to London in 1829, attracted by the reputation of Henry Maudslay (1771–1831) as the leading engineering toolmaker of the period, and in May of that year he became an assistant to Maudslay in the latter's Lambeth workshop. Maudslay seems to have formed a high esteem for the abilities of the young man and to have given him much personal encouragement, for which Nasmyth always remained very grateful, speaking of Maudslay as his 'dear old master'. When Maudslay died in February 1831, Nasmyth passed into the service of his partner, Joshua Field, but in August of that year he returned to Scotland and spent the next two years preparing a stock of crucial machine tools with which to set up an engineering

James Hall Nasmyth (1808–1890), by David Octavius Hill and Robert Adamson, c.1844

business on his own account. He felt able to do this in 1834, and after examining the possibilities of various locations decided upon Manchester, which was then rapidly developing as a centre of engineering, and acquired a small workshop in Dale Street. One advantage of Manchester was the presence of a vigorous group of Scottish industrialists, who were very supportive in these critical years when Nasmyth was short of capital. Among those who assisted him at this time was his brother George, a couple of years older than himself. Although George's services received scant recognition in the *Autobiography*, he remained in the partnership until 1843, when he withdrew and moved to London, but continued to act as an agent for the company. Nasmyth married Anne Elizabeth Hartop (d. in or after 1890), the daughter of the manager of Earl Fitzwilliam's ironworks near Barnsley, on 16 June 1840, but there were no children of the union.

The business prospered, and in 1836 Nasmyth was able to take a lease of 6 acres of land at Patricroft, then on the edge of Manchester, and there he established the foundations of what became the Bridgewater foundry, because it was adjacent to the Bridgewater Canal. He entered into partnership with a local entrepreneur, Holbrook Gaskell, to develop his business, and it quickly acquired a very high reputation for the construction of all kinds of machinery, and especially locomotive steam engines and machine tools. To these products was added, in the 1840s, the machine tool with which the name of Nasmyth is most intimately associated, the steam hammer.

Nasmyth's steam hammer The steam hammer was invented by Nasmyth in 1839 in order to fulfil an order for a forging of exceptional size. This was the paddle shaft for the steamship *Great Britain*, then being designed by I. K. Brunel for the Great Western Steamship Company. On being presented with this problem, Nasmyth claims that he immediately applied his mind to it and 'in little more than half an hour … I had the whole contrivance in all its executant details before me in a page of my Scheme Book' (*James Nasmyth*, 231). The sketch, dated 24 November 1839, has frequently been reproduced, but it seems probable that of the two vertical steam hammers depicted on the page, the second and more complete drawing was added after that date (Cantrell, 135–7). The point of this subterfuge, if such it was, was to confirm Nasmyth's claim to priority in the invention. The trouble, from Nasmyth's point of view, was that he was not the first person to build a steam hammer. His original scheme had not been fulfilled, because Brunel persuaded the proprietors of the steamship company to change the projected paddle wheels to screw propulsion, and the need for a paddle shaft disappeared. Nasmyth accordingly put the design aside until April 1842, when, in the course of visiting the Schneider ironworks at Le Creusot in France, he was shown a specimen of his own hammer at work there. It transpired that François Bourdon, the manager at Le Creusot, had visited Patricroft in July 1840 and had been shown Nasmyth's drawings by Gaskell, or possibly by George Nasmyth. It seems likely that Bourdon, who was an accomplished engineer, had already been working on a similar design of his own, but unlike Nasmyth he had pursued the idea and had produced a working steam hammer by 1842, securing a French patent for his firm in April of that year. Nasmyth was spurred into acting immediately on his return home to secure a British patent for himself (no. 9382, 9 June 1842), and within a few months he had erected the first steam hammer in Britain at Patricroft.

Despite this element of confusion about the origins of the steam hammer, Nasmyth certainly deserves the credit both for the first drawing of such a hammer and for exploiting its enormous potential as a machine tool. The fact was that the engineering industry needed an instrument capable of forging large pieces of metal which were beyond the capabilities of traditional tilt or helve hammers. By attaching the heavy hammer head to the lower end of a piston rod from a vertical steam cylinder, it allowed the hammer to be raised well clear of the anvil and thus to accommodate any conceivable size of forging. There were several tricky technical problems which had to be overcome before the hammer could be made to work smoothly, such as protecting the piston rod from the shock of the hammer-blow, and securing a sequence of valve controls which would make it self-acting. These refinements were quickly achieved by Nasmyth, with the help of his manager, Robert Wilson, who devised the successful self-acting gear (patent no. 9850, in Nasmyth's name). From 1843 to 1856 the steam hammer became the source of enormous prosperity to the company, especially when the derivative ideas of the steam piledriver and the inverted vertical steam engine, which became very successful in marine applications, were added to it. This success allowed Nasmyth to withdraw from the company with a substantial personal fortune in 1856, and to spend the rest of his long life pursuing other interests.

The fame of the steam hammer has tended to obscure Nasmyth's other achievements as an entrepreneurial engineer, but these deserve to be recalled. As well as manufacturing superlative machine tools of all sorts, Nasmyth made important improvements in self-acting controls; he invented a nut-shaping machine while he was in Maudslay's employment; he invented a flexible shaft for driving small drills such as those used by dentists, consisting of a closely coiled spiral of wire; he suggested the use of a submerged chain for towing boats; he proposed the use of chilled cast-iron shot; and he developed a hydraulic punching machine capable of punching a hole through a block of iron 5 inches thick.

Astronomy One of the long-standing hobbies to which Nasmyth was able to devote much of his time after his retirement from industry in 1856 was astronomy. He became a very accomplished amateur astronomer, designing and building his own telescopes and using them for systematic observations of the moon and the sun. He made an effective 6 inch reflecting telescope as early as 1827, and the instrument with which he made most of his observations was a 20 inch reflector mounted on a turntable devised by himself. The eyepiece of this telescope was mounted in one of the trunnions holding the instrument, so that the observer was able to sit and view the object from the side, and this distinctive arrangement is responsible for the fact that the trunnion platform of some large telescopes is still called the Nasmyth platform.

Nasmyth's first astronomical publication was in 1843, when he contributed a paper on the great comet of that year to the *Monthly Notices* of the Royal Astronomical Society. He subsequently devoted his attention to the telescopic appearance of the surface of the moon, publishing a paper on this subject in 1846 (*Memoirs of the Royal Astronomical Society*, 15, 147), and receiving a medal from the Great Exhibition of 1851 for his series of careful drawings of the lunar surface. The culmination of his work on the moon was the publication in 1874, in conjunction with James Carpenter, of a detailed study entitled *The Moon Considered as a Planet, a World, and a Satellite*. The illustrations to this book consisted of a series of photographs, but as the direct photography of telescopic objects was still in its infancy, Nasmyth developed a technique of preparing meticulous models, which were then photographed in strong sunlight against a black backdrop to produce quite striking pictures. In his observations of the sun Nasmyth was the first astronomer to record the strangely mottled appearance of the sun's surface, to which he gave the name of 'willow leaves', and presented an account to the Manchester Literary and Philosophical Society in 1861 (*Memoirs of the Manchester Literary and Philosophical Society* 3rd ser., 1.407–11). Photography was another interest to which Nasmyth gave attention in his retirement, and he

took particular pleasure in sharing this and his astronomical interests with his friend Sir John Herschel (*James Nasmyth*, 369).

Retirement and death When he retired from his engineering business in 1856, Nasmyth did so with careful consideration. He had come to feel that his work was taking virtually the whole of his time, and that there were other things that he wanted to do with the remainder of his life. It is possible that strained relationships with his labour force might have contributed to his decision, because his introduction of self-acting machines posed a threat to many of his skilled workmen, and he had taken an orthodox anti-trade union attitude in the engineering trade lock-out of 1852, which had generated particularly bad feelings in Manchester. But having decided to make a break, he withdrew from the scene of his business successes and bought a house at Penshurst in Kent, which he named Hammerfield.

Nasmyth died at Bailey's Hotel, Gloucester Road, South Kensington, on 7 May 1890: his body was cremated according to his directions, and the ashes interred at Dean cemetery, Edinburgh. Nasmyth's estate was valued at almost £244,000, which, after providing for his widow, was divided among various charities, including a fund for 'decayed' Scottish artists to be named after Alexander Nasmyth.   R. ANGUS BUCHANAN

Sources *James Nasmyth, engineer: an autobiography*, ed. S. Smiles, new edn (1885) · J. A. Cantrell, *James Nasmyth and the Bridgewater foundry* (1984) · *The Engineer* (16 May 1890) · *The Engineer* (23 May 1890) · T. S. Rowlandson, *History of the steam hammer* (1864) · A. E. Musson, 'James Nasmyth and the early growth of mechanical engineering', *Economic History Review*, 2nd ser., 10 (1957–8) · H. W. Dickinson, 'James Nasmyth as a toolmaker', *The Engineer* (23 May 1941) · d. cert. · CGPLA Eng. & Wales (1890)
Archives BL, corresp. · Eccles Central Library, collection of business records · Edinburgh Central Reference Library, corresp. and papers · Institution of Mechanical Engineers, London, corresp. · NL Scot., sketches and letters · Salford Museum and Art Gallery, Salford City Archives, corresp. | Aberdeen Central Library, letters to Sir John Anderson · NL Scot., letters to Henry Bicknell · RS, letters to Sir John Herschel
Likenesses D. O. Hill and R. Adamson, photograph, c.1844, NPG [see illus.] · G. B. O'Neill, oils, 1874, NPG · Lock & Whitfield, woodburytype photograph, 1877, NPG · J. H. Nasmyth, self-portrait, pastel drawing, Scot. NPG · C. Roberts, engraving, repro. in Smiles, ed., *James Nasmyth, engineer*, frontispiece · photograph, repro. in Cantrell, *James Nasmyth and the Bridgewater foundry*, frontispiece · photograph, Manchester Public Libraries
Wealth at death £243,805 16s. 11d.: probate, 6 Aug 1890, CGPLA Eng. & Wales

Nasmyth, Jane (1788–1867). *See under* Nasmyth family (*per.* 1788–1884).

Nasmyth [Nasmith], **John** (1556/7–1613), surgeon, was the second son of Sir Michael Nasmyth of Posso, Peeblesshire, and Elizabeth Baird, daughter of John Baird. Sir Michael, chamberlain to John Hamilton, archbishop of St Andrews, acquired the lands of Posso and Posso Craig on his marriage. The elder Nasmyth was a supporter of Mary, queen of Scots, and fought for her at Langside in 1567. John may have attended St Mary's College, St Andrews, and was apprenticed to Gilbert Primrose, a leading Edinburgh surgeon. He was admitted burgess and guild brother of Edinburgh on 21 February 1588, and in June of that year was examined and admitted as a master of the Incorporation of Surgeons. In 1589 and 1590 he served as boxmaster (treasurer) of the incorporation and then he served as deacon for the year 1595-6. During his year of office he was forced to pay £45 6s. 8d. to the incorporation as the craft's box, which had been in his keeping, had been 'broken be some wicket persone' and the money 'theftuously stolen' (Comrie, 1.242; Dingwall, 49). He is last mentioned in the incorporation records as one of the four quartermasters in 1602; thereafter he appears to have followed a career as royal surgeon.

Nasmyth had royal connections even before he trained as a surgeon. In 1575 he travelled south in the retinue of Lord Seton, charged with the dangerous task of smuggling letters to the queen from the regent, James Douglas, earl of Morton. The letters reached their destination, but Nasmyth was forced to return north expeditiously, after which he presumably undertook his surgical apprenticeship, at the same time increasing his favour with James VI. Following his qualification as a master surgeon, he was again embroiled in the dangerous world of Jacobean politics, being involved in the attempt made by Francis Stewart, earl of Bothwell, to capture the king in December 1591. He may indeed have been one of the prime conspirators, as it was claimed that he was found 'to have been the special plotter and deviser of that business', although this is difficult to prove (Moysie, 87-8). He was subsequently imprisoned in Edinburgh Castle, then taken to Glasgow where he was threatened with torture 'to confess that the Earl of Murray was with Bothwell that night', but stated that he 'would not damn his own soul with speaking an untruth for any bodily pain' (Calderwood, 5.147). Nasmyth was then confined in Dumbarton Castle, and eventually ordered by the privy council to go abroad under caution of 1000 merks (£666 Scots). The caution was deleted by warrant of the king on 1 August 1593. Nasmyth travelled to France and treated the armed forces there until his return to Scotland in 1599. Nasmyth was riding with the king while he was hunting at Falkland on 5 August 1600, the day of the Gowrie conspiracy, and served as his emissary, confirming his close connections with the royal house. He was also one of a group to whom the funding of the recoinage was farmed in 1601. He married Helen Makmath on 26 March 1600.

Nasmyth accompanied King James to London on his accession to the English throne in 1603 and was given the appointment of royal herbalist with life tenure, his work attracting the approval of the botanist Matthias de Lobel. His royal medical service included attendance on Prince Henry during his fatal illness. He remained in England, but acquired further lands in Scotland when in 1612 the lands of Earlston in Berwickshire were sold to him by Home of Cowdenknowes, the sale being confirmed by the king on 17 June 1613.

Nasmyth died in London on 16 September 1613. His body was transported back to Edinburgh and buried in Greyfriars churchyard, where his gravestone bears the now eroded inscription:

> Here lies John Nasmyth, of the family of Posso, an honourable family of Tweeddale, a citizen of Edinburgh, chief surgeon to his most Serene Majesty, and to the King of France's troop of guards from Scotland—having excellently performed all the duties of a godly life; who dying at London, to the greif of both nations, in the exercise of office with his Majesty, ordered his body to be conveyed hither to be buried in this dormitory; acquitting himself to his King, his country, and his friends to the utmost of his power and duty. He died in the 57th year of his age, the 16th September, 1613. (Comrie, 1.177)

His testament refers to James, Anna, and Elizabeth as his children, although he apparently had another son, Henry, to whom the king conceded the lands of Cowdenknowes in 1620. In November 1626, King Charles I directed the president of the court of session (the highest law court of Scotland) to 'take special notice of the business of the children of John Nasmyth' (Balfour, 2.151). Nasmyth's testament also gives good indication of his surgical and other activities. He was owed some £9300 Scots, partly in lent money, such as the £600 Scots lent to Alexander Hay, clerk register, and partly from outstanding professional fees, including £552 Scots for the 'imbalming of a corps' at the request of Lord Roxburghe.   HELEN M. DINGWALL

Sources J. D. Comrie, *History of Scottish medicine*, 2 vols. (1932) · minute books, Royal College of Surgeons of Edinburgh · *Reg. PCS*, 1st ser., vol. 4 · J. M. Thomson and others, eds., *Registrum magni sigilli regum Scotorum / The register of the great seal of Scotland*, 11 vols. (1882–1914) · H. M. Dingwall, *Physicians, surgeons and apothecaries: medical practice in seventeenth century Edinburgh* (1995) · D. Calderwood, *The history of the Kirk of Scotland*, ed. T. Thomson and D. Laing, 8 vols., Wodrow Society, 7 (1842–9) · *The historical works of Sir James Balfour*, ed. J. Haig, 4 vols. (1824–5) · D. Hamilton, *The healers: a history of medicine in Scotland* (1981) · R. T. Gunther, *Early British botanists and their gardens* (1922) · D. Moysie, *Memoirs of the affairs of Scotland, 1577–1603*, ed. J. Dennistoun, Bannatyne Club, 39 (1830) · *DNB*
Wealth at death £9392 Scots (approx. £780 sterling), excl. bequests and debts: testament dative, NA Scot., Edinburgh commissary court, CC 8/8/19 January 1614

Nasmyth, Margaret (1791–1869). *See under* Nasmyth family (*per.* 1788–1884).

Nasmyth, Patrick (1787–1831), landscape painter, was born in Edinburgh on 7 January 1787, the eldest son of Alexander *Nasmyth (1758–1840), painter, and his wife, Barbara Foulis (*d.* 1847), daughter of William Foulis of Woodhall and Colinton. Nasmyth was part of a large and talented family: his brother, James Hall *Nasmyth, was a prominent mechanical engineer and six of his eight sisters were gifted artists [*see* Nasmyth family]. He was apparently named after his father's patron and friend Patrick Miller, an Edinburgh banker and inventor. He is described in his brother James's autobiography as showing a particularly early interest in art, frequently playing truant from school in order that he might wander in the fields and sketch the scenes and objects that surrounded him. His father was a major influence as a teacher, not only of practical techniques, but also stylistically; Patrick is recorded as having toured London with his father in 1810, looking particularly at Dutch pictures in private collections. He was forced to learn to paint with his left hand after his right had been incapacitated by an injury received while on a sketching expedition and he also suffered from deafness, the result of an illness caused by sleeping in a damp bed when he was about seventeen. From 1808 to 1813 he exhibited his works at the Associated Artists in Edinburgh; he also contributed to the exhibitions of the Royal Institution from 1821 to 1828 and to the Scottish Academy in 1830 and 1831. In 1810 he moved to London, exhibiting at the Royal Academy for the first time in 1811, when he was represented by *View of Loch Katrine*, and he afterwards contributed at intervals until 1830. In 1824 he became a foundation member of the Society of British Artists, with whom, as also in the British Institution, he exhibited during the rest of his life.

Nasmyth's work was rarely dated. After moving to London—where, as noted above, he had access to great collections of seventeenth-century Dutch landscape paintings—the work of Hobbema and Jacob van Ruisdael proved to be a particularly strong influence. He continued to paint the Scottish landscape long after he had moved south, and frequently with the Italianate glow which was such a feature of his father's work; his *View on the River Tweed in the Neighbourhood of Melrose Abbey* (NG Scot.) is probably that exhibited as late as 1819 at the Royal Academy. His meticulous drawings, again closely modelled on the methods taught by his father, delighted in recording the details of hedgerow subjects and knotted trees. The *View of Leigh Woods* (1830; FM Cam.) is one of his finest pictures, closely echoing Ruisdael.

Nasmyth is described by his brother James as being particularly careless in all his personal affairs. While recovering from an attack of influenza he caught a chill as he was sketching a group of pollard willows on the Thames; and he died, unmarried, at Lambeth, London, on 17 August 1831, propped up in bed at his own request, that he might witness a thunderstorm that was then raging. He was buried in St Mary's Church, Lambeth, where the Scottish artists in London erected a stone over his grave. A cutting from an unidentified newspaper carrying his obituary in 1831 described him as 'the English Hobbima'. Despite its distinct limitations, his work was highly popular with collectors throughout the nineteenth century. Patrick Nasmyth is one of the characters 'brought upon the scene as sketches from the life' in *Progress of the Painter*, the fictionalized account of a group of young Scottish painters in London by the painter and engraver John Burnet (London, 1854).

Nasmyth is represented in the Tate Collection by five paintings, and in the National Gallery of Scotland, Edinburgh, by seven. A chalk portrait drawing by William Bewick dates from c.1830 (NPG).

J. M. GRAY, *rev.* MUNGO CAMPBELL

Sources *James Nasmyth, engineer: an autobiography*, ed. S. Smiles (1883) · D. Irwin and F. Irwin, *Scottish painters at home and abroad,* *1700–1900* (1975) · J. C. B. Cooksey, *Alexander Nasmyth, HRSA, 1758–1840: a man of the Scottish renaissance* (1991) · J. Holloway and L. Errington, *The discovery of Scotland* (1978) · catalogues of the Associated Artists, Edinburgh, 1808–16, NG Scot. [appears occasionally as Peter Nasmyth] · file notes, NG Scot. · catalogues of the Royal Institution, Edinburgh, 1821–30, NG Scot. · *Catalogue of paintings and sculpture*, National Gallery of Scotland, 51st edn (1957) · C. Thompson and H. Brigstocke, *Shorter catalogue: National Gallery of Scotland*, 2nd edn (1978)
Likenesses W. Bewick, pencil and chalk drawing, c.1830, NPG

Nassau, George Richard Savage (1756–1823), book collector, was born at Easton Park, near Wickham Market, Suffolk, on 5 September 1756 and baptized at Easton church on 25 September, the second son of the Hon. Richard Savage Nassau (1723–1780), clerk of the board of green cloth, and Anne (1716–1771), only daughter and heir of Edward Spencer of Rendlesham, Suffolk, and widow of James Hamilton, fifth duke of Hamilton and third duke of Brandon. His grandfather was Frederick van *Nassau van Zuylestein, third earl of Rochford (1682/3–1738) [*see under* Nassau van Zuylestein, William van, second earl of Rochford]. In 1766 he inherited large estates around Trimley St Martin, Suffolk—including Grimston Hall, home of the Tudor circumnavigator Thomas Cavendish—from Sir John Fitch Barker, seventh baronet. He may have been tutored at home, as he did not attend university, but the catalogue of his large library demonstrates the breadth of his cultural interests. He lived mainly at Easton Park and never married; though sociable, he was essentially a rather private person, but he did serve the county as high sheriff in 1805.

Nassau's fine library was rich in emblem books, early English poetry, drama, history, and topography, mostly large-paper copies finely bound. Many books were grangerized, or embellished, with extra illustrative material and bound-in rare tracts. His tracts included many with humorous and sensational titles: witchcraft, murder, 'extraordinary occurrences' (*Catalogue*, pt 1, 69), and scandal fascinated him. His first love, however, was the history of Suffolk, for which he made extensive collections, both printed and manuscript, greatly enriched with engravings of people and places. He commissioned drawings and watercolours for them from Rooker, Hearne, and Byrne, and from such Suffolk artists as Gainsborough, George Frost, and Isaac Johnson. His books bore no mark of his ownership, and he published nothing himself.

In later life Nassau spent time at his London house in Charles Street, Berkeley Square, occasionally visiting his closest Suffolk friend, Charles Berners, at Woolverstone Park. He died at his London home on 18 August 1823, a few days after a stroke which paralysed him. As he left instructions in a codicil to his will 'to preclude all possibility of a premature interment', he was not buried in the Rochford vault at Easton until 26 August. His elder brother, William Henry Nassau, fifth earl of Rochford, who was his executor and principal beneficiary, ignored instructions about 'the greatest economy' (will, codicil) and put up an impressive mural monument in Easton church, which was engraved with his own customarily lame verses, beginning:

Here lies a Nassau—Honour owns the name,
And George prefixed awakens friendship's claim.
(monument, Easton church, Suffolk)

The bulk of Nassau's library, including prints, drawings, and paintings, was sold by Evans of Pall Mall in three parts spread over twenty-three days in early 1824. Almost 5000 lots realized nearly £10,000.   J. M. BLATCHLY

Sources *Catalogue of the choice, curious and extensive library of the late George Nassau* (1824) [sale catalogue, Mr Evans, Pall Mall, London, April 1824] · will, PRO, PROB 11/1683, sig. 170, fols. 152r–153r · J. Glyde, 'Suffolk worthies, no. 72', *Suffolk Chronicle* (26 Nov 1859) · *DNB* · GEC, *Baronetage* · hatchment, Trimley St Martin church, Suffolk

Wealth at death £10,000 library, plus Trimley estates and Easton Park: will, PRO, PROB 11/1683, sig. 170

Nassau van Ouwerkerk, Hendrik van (1640–1708), army officer, was born in The Hague on 12 December 1640, the third son of Lodewijk van Nassau, heer van Beverweerd (1600–1665), an illegitimate son of Prince Maurice of Orange-Nassau, grand-uncle of the future King William III, and his wife, Elisabeth, daughter of Count Hornes. Ouwerkerk was thus a cousin of William III and, brought up at the court of the stadholders, became a member of his small coterie of intimate companions. First appointed equerry to William in 1666, he accompanied him on the visit to Oxford University in 1670, receiving the degree of DCL on 20 December. In 1667 he married Françoise Isabella van Aerssen (1642–1720), daughter of Cornelis van Aerssen, heer van Sommelsdijk, and his wife, Lucia van Walta. During the *Rampjaar*, or 'disaster year' of 1672, marked by French military success against the Dutch, Ouwerkerk was colonel of the Dutch horse guards. At the battle of Seneffe (1 August 1674) he was wounded in the head. When William was struck down by smallpox in 1675, he was one of the four confidants permitted to nurse the sick prince. Ouwerkerk himself was dangerously ill during July and August 1677. At the battle of St Denis, near Mons (3 August 1678), he shot dead a French officer who was presenting his pistol at William's head: it was an act typical of Ouwerkerk, who, although somewhat passionate and impetuous, was wholly devoted to his master. The prince rewarded him with a pair of gold-chased pistols, a gold-hilted sword, and a pair of gold horse-buckles. He accompanied William on a tour of German courts during 1680 and was promoted major-general in the Dutch army in 1683. In 1685 he went to England as William's envoy to congratulate James II on his accession.

Ouwerkerk commanded the prince's life guards during the invasion of England in November–December 1688 and was made master of the horse in time for the coronation in 1689. In addition, he was naturalized by act of parliament in 1689. Created a lieutenant-general in the English army (12 September 1690), he achieved the same rank in the Dutch army in the following year. He fought at the battle of the Boyne (1 July 1690) and afterwards occupied Dublin with nine troops of horse. Later that year he saw service at the abortive siege of Limerick. At the battle of

Hendrik van Nassau van Ouwerkerk (1640–1708), by John Smith, 1706 (after Sir Godfrey Kneller, *c*.1700–05)

Steenkerke (24 July 1692) he distinguished himself by covering the withdrawal of the duke of Württemberg's defeated vanguard. He fought at Landen on 19 July 1693 and commanded the right wing of the prince de Vaudémont's corps in Flanders during 1695, seeing action at Aarsele (2–5 July 1695). He was promoted to full general in the English army during the summer of 1697, and in the Dutch army in 1701. From his deathbed William thanked him for his long and faithful service. On the death of Godard van Reede, earl of Athlone, in February 1703 Ouwerkerk was appointed to command the Dutch field army on the Meuse on 19 March 1703 and promoted to field marshal on 31 March 1704. He co-operated effectively with Marlborough, whose confidence he enjoyed, and commanded Dutch forces during the crossing of the lines of Brabant in 1705 and in the victories at Ramillies (1706) and Oudenarde (1708). Neither a noted strategist nor an inspirational battlefield commander, he was a notably loyal subordinate who was content to follow Marlborough's lead. By the time of Oudenarde he was terminally ill and, too weak to ride, had to command from a coach. He died in his tent in the camp at Rousselaere on 7 October 1708 during the siege of Lille and was buried at Ouwerkerk in Zeeland. At the time of his death he was in straitened circumstances and unable to pass any substantial financial inheritance to his children. Marlborough asked his wife to approach Queen Anne with a view to granting the pension of £1000 p.a. previously paid to Ouwerkerk's elder son, the earl of Grantham, to his younger son, Cornelis.

Ouwerkerk's widow died in January 1720. Of their five sons and three daughters their first son predeceased his father but the second, Hendrik (1672–1754), created earl of

Grantham in 1698, was keeper of the privy purse to William III between 1700 and 1702, chamberlain to the princess of Wales from 1716 to 1727, and sworn of the privy council by George II in 1727. He married Henrietta, daughter of Thomas Butler, styled earl of Ossory, the eldest son of James Butler, first duke of Ormond. They had two sons, who died childless, and three daughters, the youngest of whom, Henrietta, married, on 27 June 1732, William, second Earl Cowper. Ouwerkerk's third son, Cornelis van Nassau, heer van Woudenberg (1675–1712), became a brigadier-general in the Dutch army in 1704 and a major-general in 1709. He was killed at the battle of Denain in 1712. According to Marlborough, he was 'as virtuous and as brave a man as lives' (*Marlborough–Godolphin Correspondence*, 2.1126). The fourth son, Willem Maurits van Nassau, heer van Ouwerkerk (1679–1753), was commissioned colonel of the Dutch horse guards in 1705. Wounded at Ath and promoted to brigadier-general of the cavalry in the following year, he was elevated to major-general in 1709 and was governor of Ypres from 1713 to 1717. He ended his career as a field marshal in the Dutch army. The fifth and youngest son, Frans van Nassau (1682–1710), rose to become a brigadier-general in the English army but was killed at the battle of Almanar in Catalonia on 16 July 1710. Ouwerkerk's eldest daughter, Isabella, married in 1691 Charles Grenville, Lord Lansdowne, afterwards second earl of Bath. The others daughters were Elisabeth and Anne.   JOHN CHILDS

Sources The *Marlborough–Godolphin correspondence*, ed. H. L. Snyder, 3 vols. (1975) · C. Dalton, ed., *English army lists and commission registers, 1661–1714*, 6 vols. (1892–1904) · A. W. E. Dek, *Genealogie van het vorstenhuis Nassau* (1970) · F. J. G. ten Raa, F. de Bas, and J. W. Wijn, eds., *Het staatsche leger, 1568–1795*, 8 vols. in 10 (Breda, 1911–64) · P. C. Molhuysen and P. J. Blok, eds., *Nieuw Nederlandsch biografisch woordenboek*, 10 vols. (Leiden, 1911–37) · *Letters of William III and Louis XIV*, ed. P. Grimblot, 2 vols. (1848) · *The letters and dispatches of John Churchill, first duke of Marlborough, from 1702 to 1712*, ed. G. Murray, 5 vols. (1845)
Archives BL, corresp., Add. MSS 5130–5136 · Herts. ALS, MSS
Likenesses G. Kneller, oils, c.1700–1705, Oranje–Nassau Museum, Delft, The Hague · J. Smith, mezzotint, 1706 (after G. Kneller, c.1700–1705), BM, NPG [*see illus.*]

Nassau van Zuylestein, Frederick van, third earl of Rochford (1682/3–1738). *See under* Nassau van Zuylestein, William van, second earl of Rochford (1681?–1710).

Nassau van Zuylestein, Frederik van (1624–1672). *See under* Nassau van Zuylestein, William Frederick van, first earl of Rochford (1649–1708).

Nassau van Zuylestein, William van, second earl of Rochford (1681?–1710), army officer, was born in Zuylestein, near Utrecht, probably in late 1681, the eldest son of William Frederick van *Nassau van Zuylestein, first earl of Rochford (1649–1708), army officer, and his wife, Jane (*bap.* 1659), daughter of Sir Henry Wroth of Durrants, Enfield, Middlesex. Following his father's elevation to the peerage as earl of Rochford, he was styled Lord Tunbridge. In 1696, when still aged under sixteen, he was naturalized by act of parliament. He embarked on a military career, and served as a volunteer in the campaign in the duke of Ormond's

expedition against Cadiz in 1702 and in Flanders in 1703; he was made a brevet colonel on the Irish establishment a year on. However, the campaign of 1704 saw him in Flanders as an aide-de-camp to the duke of Marlborough, his father having 'hurried me into this field' (*Ormonde MSS*, 8.74). In August 1704 he carried the official report of the battle of Blenheim to Queen Anne, and rather than join Ormond in Ireland he seems to have tarried in London during the winter of 1704–5 and then travelled to Flanders in the following summer.

In 1705 Tunbridge was elected a member of the Irish parliament for Kilkenny owing to Ormond's influence. Ormond also helped to procure him the lieutenant-colonelcy of a newly raised regiment of foot guards in December 1705. In April 1706 he obtained the colonelcy of a regiment of foot, and in 1707 a regiment of dragoons. At the general election of 1708 Tunbridge was returned for Steyning, but his tenure of the seat was cut short by the death of his father on 30 June, before the parliament met. On the day following his father's death, Rochford wrote from Zuylestein to Marlborough hoping for the duke's support in the continuation of his father's pension of £1000 out of the Post Office revenues. Rochford took his seat in the Lords on 16 November 1708, but did not get the pension he craved. On 1 January 1710 he was promoted brigadier-general, and went via Italy to Spain, where he was killed at the battle of Almenara on 27 July 1710. As he was unmarried, the earldom devolved upon his brother.

Frederick van Nassau van Zuylestein, third earl of Rochford (1682/3–1738), landowner, was the second son of William Frederick van Nassau van Zuylestein and his wife, Jane Wroth. Like his brother he was naturalized by act of parliament in 1696. He succeeded his brother as third earl on 27 July 1710, and an early assessment by Robert Harley judged him as 'doubtful' in his attitude to the whig ministry in the House of Lords. He does not seem to have attended in the 1713 session of parliament.

Rochford married, on 3 August 1714, Elizabeth (Bessy) Savage (1698/9–1746), illegitimate daughter of Richard *Savage, fourth Earl Rivers, and Elizabeth Colleton, who brought him a country residence at St Osyth Priory, Essex. They had two sons and three daughters. He seems to have been interested in politics only intermittently, as in May 1717 Harley (now earl of Oxford) was uncertain how he would stand on his impeachment 'if in England', but in the event Rochford supported Oxford's acquittal. Perhaps in order to retain his support the whig ministry then gave him a pension of £600 p.a. in July 1717. Rochford died on 14 June 1738 at his London house in Great Queen Street, Lincoln's Inn Fields, and was buried at Easton, Suffolk, the seat of his younger brother, Henry (d. 1741). His wife married the Revd Philip Carter and died on 23 June 1746, by which a reputed £4000 p.a. devolved upon her eldest son, William Henry van *Nassau van Zuylestein, fourth earl of Rochford.   STUART HANDLEY

Sources GEC, *Peerage* · *Collins peerage of England: genealogical, biographical and historical*, ed. E. Brydges, 9 vols. (1812) · C. Dalton, ed., *English army lists and commission registers, 1661–1714*, 5 (1902), 5–6, 199, 276; 6 (1904), 228 · *Calendar of the manuscripts of the marquess of*

Ormonde, new ser., 8 vols., HMC, 36 (1902–20), vol. 8 · W. A. Shaw, ed., *Letters of denization and acts of naturalization for aliens in England and Ireland, 1603–1700*, Huguenot Society of London, 18 (1911), 241 · P. Watson, 'Zuylestein, William de', HoP, *Commons, 1690–1715* [draft] · BL, Add. MS 61292, fol. 112 · W. A. Shaw, ed., *Calendar of treasury books*, 31/2, PRO (1957), 466 · GM, 1st ser., 16 (1746), 329 · A. Page, *A topographical and genealogical history of the county of Suffolk* (1847), 98–9 · C. Jones, 'The impeachment of the earl of Oxford and the whig schism of 1717: four new lists', *BIHR*, 55 (1982), 66–87, esp. 75, 84 · C. Jones, '"The scheme lords, the necessitous lords, and the Scots lords": the earl of Oxford's management and the "party of the crown" in the House of Lords, 1711–14', *Party and management in parliament, 1660–1784*, ed. C. Jones (1984), 123–44

Likenesses B. Dandridge, oils, 1735? (Frederick van Nassau van Zuylestein), Brodick Castle, Isle of Arran · G. Kneller, oils (William van Nassau van Zuylestein?), Brodick Castle, Isle of Arran

Nassau van Zuylestein, William Frederick [Willem Frederik] **van, first earl of Rochford** (1649–1708), soldier and diplomat, was born at Zuylestein near Utrecht and baptized on 7 October 1649 at The Hague, the elder son of Frederik van Nassau van Zuylestein and his wife, Mary Killigrew (*b.* 1627), daughter of Sir William *Killigrew (*bap.* 1606, *d.* 1695) and maid of honour to Mary Stuart, princess royal of England and princess of Orange.

William Frederick's father, **Frederik van Nassau van Zuylestein** (1624–1672), soldier and courtier, was the illegitimate son of Prince William III of Orange's grandfather, Frederik Hendrik van Nassau, prince of Orange, and (it is thought) Margareta Katharina Bruyns, daughter of a burgomaster of Emmerik. Frederik Hendrik had him educated at court, giving him the title jonker van Buren and in May 1640 presenting him with the lordship of Zuylestein and Leersum. Entering the army of the states general he was appointed lieutenant-colonel of an infantry regiment in 1645, colonel three years later, and took part in Prince William II's abortive siege of Amsterdam in 1650. His marriage to Mary Killigrew on 18 October 1648 had meanwhile brought him into the English entourage of Mary Stuart, princess of Orange, who in 1659 appointed him as a suitably Anglophile governor to her eight-year-old son, the future William III. For the next seven years, first at Leiden and then at The Hague, he supervised every aspect of the prince's upbringing, from religious observance and language tuition to diet and outdoor exercise. A close bond of affection developed between them, and William was devastated when in April 1666 Zuylestein was replaced in his post by a nominee of the grand pensionary John de Witt, following the decision of the states of Holland to adopt the prince as a ward of state.

Zuylestein continued, however, to receive an official salary and he remained close to Orange. He accompanied him on his first visit to England in November 1670; and, according to Bishop Gilbert Burnet, he was the one person in whom the prince confided following a remarkable private conversation with his uncle Charles II, in which the king revealed his 'papist' beliefs (*Bishop Burnet's History*, 1.501–2). About this time Zuylestein also resumed his career in the army. Promoted lieutenant-general in January 1688 he was made military governor of Breda in April 1670 and general of foot in February 1672. From Breda in May the same year he reported the movements of invading

William Frederick van Nassau van Zuylestein, first earl of Rochford (1649–1708), by unknown artist

French forces along the Maas, and during the period of panic and disorder that followed the invasion he returned to The Hague where he witnessed the murder of the de Witt brothers by the mob on 20 August. (Whether he was personally involved in planning the murder, or in encouraging those who committed it, cannot be established with certainty, though as a prominent Orangist he was inevitably suspected of complicity.) He fought two months later in Orange's attempt to recapture Woerden on the border between Holland and Utrecht and he was killed at Grevenbrugge on 12 October 1672 by French forces under the duc de Luxembourg coming to relieve the town. Buried in the Kloosterkerk at The Hague on 17 January 1673, his remains were subsequently removed to Leersum.

With Zuylestein's death the lordship passed to his elder son, William Frederick, who was already serving in a cavalry regiment of the Dutch army. Good-looking and assured, he was close in age to the prince of Orange and had become one of his favourite companions, sharing his enthusiasm for hunting. The prince was less approving when Zuylestein seduced and was forced to marry Jane (*bap.* 1659, *d.* 1703), daughter of Sir Henry *Wroth (*d.* 1671) [*see under* Wroth, Sir Robert] and Anne Maynard, a maid of honour to the princess of Orange. The marriage ceremony was performed secretly on 28 January 1681 in the princess's chapel at The Hague and shortly afterwards a son was born, the first of six children. But Zuylestein was quickly restored to favour and in August 1687 was sent as a special envoy to London, ostensibly to offer Orange's condolences on the death of Queen Mary of Modena's mother. The real purpose of the mission was to gauge James II's intentions towards parliament and to canvass opinion among his opponents; its result was the establishment of an extensive correspondence network providing William with intelligence of English affairs. By the following spring the prince had made his decision to mount an invasion of England, provided he could be sure of support there; and it was to obtain that assurance that Zuylestein was sent on a second English mission late in June 1688. The pretext now was to convey William's congratulations to the king and queen on the birth of their son—a birth which Zuylestein found was widely considered a fraud. And he had further meetings with the king's leading opponents, approving the so-called 'invitation' in which they pledged their support for Orange and agreeing their responsibilities in the final preparations for the invasion. By early August he was back in The Hague, reporting to William on the Association of Protestant Officers in James's army. He appears to have made a brief final reconnaissance visit to England early in November. As William's armada set sail from the Maas estuary on 2/12 November he joined the prince on board the *Brill*, reporting on the strength and movements of James II's army and recommending that the fleet should land in Dorset or Devon.

Zuylestein was now a major-general in the Dutch army and his cavalry regiment was one of the fifteen which disembarked with the rest of Orange's forces at Torbay on 5/15 November to begin their six weeks' advance on London. A month later he was with the prince at Windsor when a letter was received from James II (detained at Rochester after his first attempt to flee the country) proposing a meeting with Orange in London. Zuylestein was immediately dispatched with a reply whose effect was both to evade the meeting (as William intended) and to force James out of the capital for good. Delivering his message to the king at St James's Palace on 16 December he insisted that Orange would not enter London while it contained forces under James's command. The following day those forces were withdrawn as Dutch guards occupied Whitehall, and on 18 December James himself was escorted back to Rochester. From there, four days later, he left for France.

Zuylestein was duly rewarded for his part in preparing and carrying through the revolution. He was naturalized on 11 May 1689—a month after William and Mary's coronation—and on 23 May was appointed master of the robes. Yet for all the skill and shrewdness of judgement that he had displayed in his missions of 1687 and 1688 he was reluctant to involve himself further in English political life—less perhaps out of laziness, as some alleged, than from fear of parliamentary attack. As he explained to William's private secretary, Constantijn Huygens, 'he had no pretensions to be part of the grand deliberations' since 'in England it was customary for favourites and counsellors to be accused and punished if the king had done wrong' (Huygens, *Journaal*, 1.70). Instead, his services to William III during the 1690s were principally military. He accompanied him to Ireland in June 1690, fighting at the Boyne on 1 July and returning to London in August to bring news of the campaign to the queen; and in September he was promoted lieutenant-general in the English army. Subsequent years took him to the war against France in the Low Countries, where he fought with distinction at the battle of Landen (29 July 1693), rescuing the king from danger; he was wounded and taken prisoner to Namur, though he was later exchanged.

Further honours were given to Zuylestein. On 10 May 1695 he was created Baron Enfield, Viscount Tunbridge, and earl of Rochford, while his office as master of the robes passed to William's favourite, Arnold Joost van Keppel. He took his seat in the House of Lords on 29 February 1696. From 25 December 1695 he received an annual pension from the crown of £1000; and on 26 April 1696 William granted him the confiscated estates of the marquess of Powis in Montgomeryshire, followed in July 1698 by more than 30,000 acres of forfeited Irish lands. It is unlikely, however, that he ever lived at Powis Castle; and his Irish property had to be handed over to public trustees following an Act of Resumption passed by parliament in April 1700. About this time he acquired an English country house at Easton, Suffolk, but he returned frequently to his family estates at Zuylestein, where he developed the gardens first laid out by Frederik Hendrik and experimented with afforestation. Following the death of William III in March 1702 he remained briefly in Suffolk before going back to the Netherlands, where his last years were spent. He died at Zuylestein on 12 July 1708, and was succeeded as second earl of Rochford by his eldest son William van *Nassau van Zuylestein.   HUGH DUNTHORNE

Sources P. C. Molhuysen and P. J. Blok, eds., *Nieuw Nederlandsch biografisch woordenboek*, 10 vols. (Leiden, 1911–37), vol. 1, pp. 1358–9, 1367–8 · *Collins peerage of England: genealogical, biographical and historical*, ed. E. Brydges, 9 vols. (1812), vol. 3, pp. 712-17 · F. J. G. ten Raa and F. de Bas, eds., *Het staatsche leger, 1568–1795*, 4–7 (Breda, 1918–50) · M. Bowen, *William prince of Orange* (1928) · *DNB* · P. Geyl, *Orange and Stuart, 1641–72* (1979) · S. B. Baxter, *William III* (1966) · C. Huygens, *Mémoires*, ed. T. Jorissen (The Hague, 1873), 163–75 · H. H. Rowen, *John de Witt, grand pensionary of Holland, 1625–1672* (1978) · *Bishop Burnet's History* · J. R. Jones, *The revolution of 1688 in England* (1972) · J. Carswell, *The descent on England: a study of the English revolution of 1688 and its European background* (1969) · J. Dalrymple, *Memoirs of Great Britain and Ireland*, 2 (1773), appx, pt 1, 200-10, 224-39, 293–4 · N. Luttrell, *A brief historical relation of state affairs from September 1678 to April 1714*, 6 vols. (1857), vol. 1, p. 488; vol. 2, pp. 165, 199, 230, 318, 369; vol. 3, pp. 146, 150–51, 157, 225, 467; vol. 4, pp. 20, 305, 320 · H. van der Zee and B. van der Zee, *1688: revolution in the family* (1988) · C. Huygens, *Journaal … van 21 October 1688 tot 2 September 1696*, 2 vols. (1876) · F. J. L. Krämer, ed., 'Mémoires des Monsieur de B.', *Bijdragen en Mededelingen van het Historisch Genootschap*, 19 (1898), 95–6 · 'Grant of the estates of the marquis of Powys to the earl of Rochford by William III', *Archaeologia Cambrensis*, 3rd ser., 5 (1859), 269–86 · J. D. Hunt and E. de Jong, eds., *The Anglo-Dutch garden in the age of William and Mary*, *Journal of Garden History* [special double issue], 8/ii–iii (1988), 184–6 · D. Schwennicke, ed., *Europäische Stammtafeln*, 6 (Marburg, 1978), table 59

Likenesses attrib. (separately) P. Nason, J. de Baen, oils, 1665 (Frederik van Nassau van Zuylestein), Amerongen; repro. in Bowen, *William, prince of Orange*, 262, 323 · G. Kneller, oils, *c*.1695, Brodick Castle, Arran · oils, unknown collection; copyprint, NPG [*see illus.*]

Wealth at death lands in Suffolk, Montgomeryshire, and province of Utrecht: Molhuysen and Blok, eds., *Nieuw nederlandsch biografisch woordenboek*; GEC; Collins, *Peerage*, 3.712–17

Nassau van Zuylestein, William Henry van, **fourth earl of Rochford** (1717–1781), diplomatist and politician, was born on 17 September 1717 at St Osyth Priory, Essex, the elder son of Frederick van *Nassau van Zuylestein, third earl of Rochford (1682/3–1738) [see under Nassau van Zuylestein, William van], courtier and landowner, and his wife, Elizabeth (Bessy) Savage (1698/9–1746), illegitimate daughter and heir of Richard *Savage, fourth Earl Rivers. Rochford was the first English-born son of a Dutch court family ennobled by William III in 1695. His childhood was spent at St Osyth, with occasional visits to the family's estates in Holland. He was educated at Eton College (1725–32), then spent several years in Switzerland, from where he returned fluent in French.

Rochford succeeded to the earldom in June 1738 and was appointed a gentleman of the bedchamber to George II on £1000 a year. In 1741 he inherited Easton in Suffolk from his uncle Henry Nassau, and in May 1742 he married Lucy (c.1723–1773), daughter of Edward Younge of Durnford, Wiltshire. They had no children. As a young courtier in London, Rochford lived at 48 Berkeley Square. He formed a lifelong friendship with the actor David Garrick, and their correspondence reveals Rochford as a cheerful optimist with a lively sense of humour and a passionate devotion to the theatre, music, and dancing. Rochford had no interest in political intrigue, and decided that he could best serve his king by becoming an ambassador. Thanks to the patronage of the duke of Cumberland, Rochford was duly appointed envoy-extraordinary and minister-plenipotentiary to the court of Turin, the highest rank in the service short of ambassador. He and Lucy arrived at Turin on 9 September 1749.

Envoy to Turin Savoy-Sardinia was the most important of the Italian states for British foreign policy in the eighteenth century, yet Turin was not an easy post for a novice diplomat, as France and Austria did their utmost to counteract British influence over Charles-Emmanuel III. Rochford went to great lengths to gain the king's ear, often riding out to hunt with him before breakfast. He was popular at the court of Turin, where he fostered the fashion for English country dances. His early advocacy of English interests in Savoy was successful, and he maintained close links with British consuls in the region. He played a useful role in negotiations leading to the treaty of Aranjuez (1752), and the neutrality of Savoy-Sardinia during the Seven Years' War must be credited in part to his careful cultivation of friendship between Turin and London.

Rochford went on a tour of Italy in 1753, and employed a secret agent in Rome to report on the movements of the Young Pretender. Confessing himself 'excessively curious' for plants and herbs, he made several expeditions into the Alps from Turin, sending seedlings back to St Osyth. On his return home on leave in 1754 he brought with him a Lombardy poplar sapling, tied to the centre-pole of his carriage. The poplars at St Osyth were long regarded as the earliest in England.

Rochford was recalled from Turin to replace Albemarle as groom of the stole on 2 March 1755. A week later he was sworn of the privy council. In April 1756 he was appointed

William Henry van Nassau van Zuylestein, fourth earl of Rochford (1717–1781), by Valentine Green, 1770 (after Jean Baptiste Peronneau, c.1768)

lord lieutenant of Essex, and in November 1759 colonel of the Essex militia. Much of his time during the Seven Years' War was spent on militia exercises and Essex elections. In London he renewed his friendship with Garrick and cultivated new ones with Richard Rigby, the earl of Sandwich, Viscount Barrington, and the earl of Holdernesse. In 1758 Rochford and Lucy nearly separated after quarrelling over his affair with an expensive Italian opera dancer and her affair with Lord Thanet. They were reconciled, and Rochford chose a less expensive mistress in Martha Harrison of the parish of St George's, Hanover Square, with whom he had a daughter, Maria Nassau, soon after. When George II died on 24 October 1760, Rochford as groom of the stole was entitled to the contents of the king's bedroom, but settled for £3000 in cash, a breeches Bible, and a bed quilt which long served as an altar cloth in the church at St Osyth. He yielded office with such good grace that he won George III's favour and an Irish pension of £2000 a year. Rochford fell seriously ill in April 1763 and was still convalescing when he was named ambassador to Spain on 18 June 1763.

Ambassador to Madrid Rochford reached Madrid on 6 December 1763. As at Turin, he had to deal with a widower king, but Charles III was not friendly towards Britain, and most of his ministers were strongly Francophile. Madrid was a key post in 1763, as British ministers feared a war of retaliation by the powers of the Family Compact, to recover their losses in the Seven Years' War. A major task of Rochford's embassy was to obtain naval and military intelligence, which he addressed with his customary diligence. He wrote over 400 dispatches from Madrid, and his figures for Spanish naval expansion were more accurate than those sent to Choiseul by the French ambassador. Rochford worked closely with the British consul-general in Spain, Stanier Porten, uncle of the historian Edward Gibbon, and made 'Frequent applications ... for His Majesty's trading Subjects' (Rice, 'Diplomatic career', 319). His success in an early dispute over British logwood cutters in Honduras gave him a reputation as a tough anti-Bourbon. This did not help his major negotiation over the Manila Ransom, which remained unresolved when he left Madrid. At Madrid Rochford befriended the playwright Beaumarchais, and recommended his plays to Garrick. After witnessing the Madrid riots of March 1766 which brought down Squilace, Rochford was named ambassador to Paris on 1 July 1766. It is said that he had to pawn his plate and jewels for £6000 to settle his debts before leaving Madrid on 15 May 1766.

Rochford insisted on taking Porten with him to Paris as his secretary of embassy, the start of a close working relationship which lasted until Rochford's retirement. At Paris from 28 October 1766 to 1 September 1768, Rochford was dean of the British diplomatic service, and kept in regular touch with other senior diplomats across Europe as well as leading politicians at home. While he could claim success in several minor negotiations over Dunkirk, the Canada bills, and the English East India Company, the two major crises of his Paris embassy were humiliating failures. The French foreign minister, Choiseul, regarded Rochford as evasive and anti-French after a proposal to resolve the first Falkland Islands dispute of 1766 by linking it to the Manila Ransom was bungled by the British secretary of state, Lord Shelburne. Much more serious was France's secret annexation of Corsica in 1768, about which Rochford had given only general warnings. The British cabinet was too weak and divided to support his strong stand at Paris. He also had the bad luck to fall seriously ill for two weeks at the most critical phase of the crisis. Feeling angry and betrayed, he returned to England to demand a cabinet post. The duke of Newcastle described Rochford as 'the fittest for it of any man in England'. Rochford was finally named secretary of state for the northern department on 21 October 1768.

Secretary of state for the north This appointment puzzled contemporaries, for Rochford's diplomatic experience lay in the southern department's sphere: some saw it as deference to Choiseul, but in fact it was because Viscount Weymouth wanted the more important of the two secretaryships. Foreign diplomats in London found Rochford more accessible and better informed than his predecessors, while British diplomats abroad were relieved and delighted to be instructed by an experienced former ambassador. As northern secretary (1768–70) Rochford was particularly scrupulous in his conduct of the routine correspondence and gave more coherence to British foreign policy than had been evident during the Chatham administration. The top priority at this time was the pursuit of a Russian alliance. As Michael Roberts has shown (*British Diplomacy*), the key post for this campaign was Stockholm, where Rochford sent large sums of money to Sir John Goodricke to help Russian attempts to influence the Swedish Diet. Britain could have had the Russian alliance for the price of a large subsidy, but Rochford finally decided it was not worth the money. This decision was a realistic one in 1770, but it left Britain without a continental ally on the eve of the American war.

While Rochford was busy with northern Europe, Weymouth gave Choiseul the clear impression that Britain would do anything to avoid another war at sea, and France therefore supported Spain in a much more serious dispute with Britain in 1770, that over the Falkland Islands. Weymouth's stance suddenly changed to one of inflexible belligerence. As military preparations quickened and the diplomatic situation remained deadlocked, the risk of war between Britain and the Bourbon powers came closer to flashpoint than at any time since the Seven Years' War. Indeed, historians suspect that Weymouth and his ambitious under-secretary Wood wanted to provoke war in order to collapse North's ministry and reinstate Chatham. George III and North now took personal control of the crisis, assisted by Rochford. North proposed that, in return for Spain's apology and reinstatement of the British garrison on the Falklands, Britain would give a secret verbal promise to abandon the islands some time in the near future. While the rest of the cabinet endorsed this solution, Weymouth rejected it and resigned. Rochford replaced him as southern secretary (19 December 1770) and took charge of the diplomatic negotiations. The crisis was resolved when Louis XV dismissed Choiseul, and Charles III realized that Spain could not fight Britain alone. It was Rochford's idea that the three powers disarm simultaneously. The formal agreement ending the crisis was signed on 22 January 1771, just one hour before parliament reassembled, but rumours of the secret promise made North and Rochford extremely unpopular with a jingoistic opposition and their London supporters.

Secretary of state for the south As southern secretary (1770–75) Rochford's workload increased considerably. Besides maintaining an extensive correspondence with British diplomats in Portugal, Spain, France, Switzerland, the Italian states, and elsewhere, this department had many domestic responsibilities (before the 1782 rationalization into Home and Foreign offices) as well as oversight of Ireland and the East India Company. Rochford's name appears on nearly every page of volumes 3 and 4 of the massive *Calendar of Home Office Papers of the Reign of George III*. He was now part of the inner core of North's cabinet, where he got on well with Gower and Sandwich, but disliked Suffolk and Dartmouth. Rochford was the foreign policy expert, but was too nervous a speaker to be an effective spokesman in the House of Lords. Sandwich once described one of his cabinet papers on the current situation in Europe as the best he had seen in all his years in office.

George III was clearly fond of Rochford for his 'many amiable qualities', but he was also aware of his limitations, his extravagance, and occasional indiscretions. The king once remarked to North that Rochford's 'Zeal makes him rather in a hurry', and to Suffolk that Rochford was at times 'not very prudent' (*Correspondence of George III*,

2.369–72). Yet in 1771 the king told Porten that Rochford, despite poor health, was 'more active and had more Spirit' than anyone else in the cabinet (Porten MSS, 'Notes of interview with the king', 23 June 1771) which is perhaps why he relied on Rochford as his go-between in the painful negotiations with his brother, the duke of Gloucester, after the Royal Marriages Act of 1772. This episode gave Rochford a bitter and influential enemy in the diarist Horace Walpole, for the duke's wife was Walpole's niece. In his memoirs, Walpole deliberately belittled Rochford as 'a man of no abilities and of as little knowledge, except in the routine of office' (Walpole, 3.168), a spiteful remark which too many historians have accepted uncritically.

Despite his anti-Bourbon reputation, Rochford saw that the balance of power in Europe had changed with the emergence of Russia as a major power, as shown by the 1772 partition of Poland, and warned that this 'changed absolutely the System of Europe'. He therefore initiated secret negotiations for friendlier relations with France, a bold, imaginative, but risky policy which stalled in the aftermath of the Swedish Revolution of 1772. In public, of course, he had to maintain a resolutely anti-Bourbon stance, to placate the parliamentary opposition. Rochford wrote to Gower in characteristic vein on 10 October 1772:

> We are determined to let France know that we will not be bamboozled; I hope we shall not shew our teeth without biting, though I believe it will not be necessary, for I am sure if we are *firm and temperate* we may yet keep all quiet. (Rochford to Gower, PRO 30/29/1/14)

George III shared Rochford's broader view of British diplomacy, and respected his experience and judgement, but Rochford's volatile temperament and verbal vivacity often led him into indiscreet conversations with foreign diplomats.

Final years By the spring of 1775 it was clear that Britain faced a serious colonial rebellion in North America. News of the Bunker Hill engagement reached London in late July, and forced North's government to recognize that Britain would have to fight a costly war at a great distance to keep control of her colonies. Rochford's policy of friendlier relations with the Bourbon powers now paid dividends, at least for a short time, by helping to keep France and Spain out of the conflict. Peace in Europe was vital for British success in America. The eventual American victory was mainly because Britain's resources were diverted after 1778 to the larger conflict at sea with France and Spain.

Rochford himself favoured a negotiated solution to Britain's problems in the American colonies, but this brought him into conflict with his brother-secretary Suffolk, who favoured a hardline military solution. They clashed over Suffolk's scheme to hire troops from Russia, and over a minor *faux pas* by the British chargé d'affaires in Paris; Rochford's claim that he knew more about diplomacy than Suffolk was confirmed by no less a person than the Spanish ambassador, Masserano. But Rochford's failing health and increasing isolation in cabinet led him to offer his resignation in October 1775. As he left office, Rochford

urged a treaty of guarantee among the European powers, to deprive the colonists of foreign aid: such a guarantee 'would conquer America sooner than 20,000 soldiers'. Britain's foreign policy towards the Bourbons in the first years of the war followed the lines set by Rochford, and certainly helped delay the involvement of France and Spain in the American war. At his retirement Rochford was granted a pension of £2500 a year, later increased to £3320. His departure from office was clouded by a blunder in drawing up a warrant for the arrest of an opposition pamphleteer, Stephen Sayre, who brought a successful action against Rochford in June 1776.

Lady Rochford died on 9 January 1773 and was buried at St Osyth. Rochford's daughter Maria Nassau had lived with them in Paris in 1767 and since at St Osyth. Rochford by then had two children with Anne Labbée Johnstone, who now came to live with him at St Osyth. In 1776 Rochford was made master of Trinity House, and visited his estates in Holland. He was elected a KG on 3 June 1778. George III twice visited St Osyth, and presented Rochford with portraits of himself and Queen Charlotte by Allan Ramsay. In his last years Rochford was involved as lord lieutenant in preparations to defend the coast against a threatened French invasion. Commanding a camp of militia at Fingringhoe in 1781 he caught a fever, and returned to St Osyth where he lay ill for three weeks until his death on 28 September aged sixty-four. His will disposed of landed property yielding an income of £2000 a year. The earldom passed to his bachelor nephew, at whose death in 1830 the title became extinct.

Rochford was certainly no Walpole, much less a Chatham, but he has suffered undeserved neglect as a member of the most reviled British cabinet of the eighteenth century. Nicholas Tracy has described Rochford as 'one of the stronger men of the period, ranking with Sandwich in his professionalism within his department' (N. Tracy, *Navies, Deterrence and American Independence*, 1988, 43). In his chosen profession Rochford proved himself an exceptionally diligent and effective diplomat, outwitting his French counterpart at Madrid and earning the grudging respect of Choiseul for his spirited opposition to Bourbon rearmament. Of the nine secretaries of state who controlled British foreign policy between 1763 and 1775, Rochford was the only career diplomat and former ambassador. Recent research has shown that as secretary of state he achieved as much as anyone could reasonably expect in a period of unusually difficult circumstances for Britain in Europe. He restored unity and direction to a foreign policy which had virtually collapsed in 1768, and pursued the Russian alliance as far as it was realistic to do so. It may be argued that without Rochford's skill and experience British foreign policy might have suffered worse humiliations in the period 1763–75. His more conciliatory policy towards Spain after 1771 drove a wedge into the Family Compact which delayed Spanish involvement in the American war. Hamish Scott's judgement that Rochford was 'the ablest man to control foreign policy in the first decade of peace [after 1763], a statesman of intelligence, perception and considerable application, though perhaps lacking patience and tact' remains a fair and accurate assessment (Scott, 'Anglo-Austrian relations', 9).

GEOFFREY W. RICE

Sources *DNB* · A. Collins, *The peerage of England*, ed. B. Longmate, 5th edn, 8 vols. (1779) · Rochford diplomatic letters, Bodl. Oxf., MSS Eng. lett. c. 336–30 · G. W. Rice, 'Archival sources for the life and career of the fourth earl of Rochford (1717–81), British diplomat and statesman', *Archives*, 20 (1992), 254–68 · V&A, Garrick MSS, vol. 35 · H. Walpole, *Memoirs of the reign of King George the Third*, ed. G. F. R. Barker, 3 (1894) · J. Redington and R. A. Roberts, eds., *Calendar of home office papers of the reign of George III*, 3: *1770–1772*, PRO (1881); 4: *1773–1775*, PRO (1899) · *The correspondence of King George the Third from 1760 to December 1783*, ed. J. Fortescue, 2 (1927) · *The private papers of John, earl of Sandwich*, ed. G. R. Barnes and J. H. Owen, 1, Navy RS, 69 (1932) · priv. coll., Porten MSS · G. W. Rice, 'The diplomatic career of the fourth earl of Rochford at Turin, Madrid and Paris, 1749–1768', PhD diss., University of Canterbury, NZ, 1973 · H. M. Scott, 'Anglo-Austrian relations after the Seven Years' War: Lord Stormont in Vienna, 1763–1772', PhD diss., U. Lond., 1977 · H. M. Scott, *British foreign policy in the age of the American revolution* (1990) · M. Roberts, *British diplomacy and Swedish politics, 1758–1773* (1980) · G. W. Rice, 'Lord Rochford at Turin, 1749–55', *Knights errant and true Englishmen*, ed. J. Black (1989), 92–112 · G. W. Rice, 'Great Britain, the Manila Ransom and the first Falkland Islands dispute with Spain, 1766', *International History Review*, 2/3 (July 1980), 386–409 · marriage settlement, Essex RO, D/DC, 27/729–30 · R. A. Austen-Leigh, ed., *The Eton College register, 1698–1752* (1927), 345–6

Archives BL OIOC, notebook as ambassador to Madrid, MS ZyellEmpt 37 · BL OIOC, corresp. and papers relating to India · Bodl. Oxf., corresp. relating to Turin, MSS Eng. Lett. C. 336–340 · Yale U., Farmington, Lewis Walpole Library, letters | Beds. & Luton ARS, letters to Lord Grantham · BL, corresp. with Lord Grantham, Add. MSS 24157–24161, 24174–24176 · BL, corresp. with R. Gunning, Egerton MSS 2697–2700 · BL, corresp. with Lord Holdernesse, Egerton MSS 3419–3464 · BL, corresp. with R. Keith, Lord Stormont, Lord Hardwicke, Add. MSS 35438–35611 · BL, corresp. with duke of Newcastle, Add. MSS 32724–33071 · BL, corresp. with General Rainsford, Add. MSS 23653–23654 · BL, corresp. with Lord Shelburne and Sir Andrew Mitchell, Add. MSS 6810, 6822, 6830, 9242 · BL, corresp. with Sir F. Willes, Add. MS 45519 · NRA, priv. coll., letters to Lord Cathcart · NRA, priv. coll., letters to Lord Shelburne · PRO, state papers, foreign · PRO, corresp. with Lord Stafford, PRO30/29 · U. Mich., Clements L., Shelburne MSS, vols. 22–31 · U. Nott. L., letters to duke of Newcastle · V&A, Garrick MSS, Forster 13466, vol. 35 · Warks. CRO, letters to Lord Denbigh and Lady Denbigh

Likenesses G. Jervas, oils, 1738, Brodick Castle, Isle of Arran · T. Bardwell, oils, 1741, Brodick Castle, Isle of Arran · R. Houston, mezzotint, *c.*1768 (after D. Dupra), BM, NPG · V. Green, mezzotint, 1770 (after J. B. Peronneau, *c.*1768), BM, NPG [*see illus.*] · watercolour, *c.*1780, NPG · J. Lodge, engraving (after V. Green), repro. in *London Museum* (April 1771)

Wealth at death £2000—income p.a. from landed property: *DNB*

Nassington [Nassyngton], **William** (*d.* 1354), poet and ecclesiastical administrator, was a member of a distinguished family of ecclesiastical administrators from Nassington, Northamptonshire. He enjoyed a successful, varied, and influential clerical career culminating in the composition of the *Speculum vitae*, a 16,000 line Middle English commentary on the Lord's prayer incorporating analysis of the commandments, the creed, the divine and cardinal virtues, the gifts of the Holy Ghost, the deadly sins, the beatitudes, and the heavenly rewards. While much of this poem derives directly from the French prose *Somme le roi*

(dated 1279), the *Speculum* is none the less a monument of scholastic erudition and a breathtaking synthesis of moral philosophy. The poet was clearly highly educated: he was a master of law (by 1327–8) closely associated with John Grandison, bishop of Exeter, holding various important appointments at the see (for example chancellor and auditor of causes in 1332) throughout his life. During the latter stages of his career Nassington also benefited from an association with William Zouche, archbishop of York, and held a number of major posts at York (again, chancellor and auditor of causes in 1346). He was an establishment figure *par excellence*, and his poem, which was approved by the masters of Cambridge University, circulated especially well among the Cambridge and clerical intelligentsia, despite having been written ostensibly for the ordinary laity. The *Speculum vitae* survives in numerous manuscripts, but this fact alone is not indicative of general popularity, since Nassington's readership, being institutional and intellectual, would have been inclined to preserve their books for posterity. Nassington was without doubt, however, an eminent clerical and literary figure during the first half of the fourteenth century. He died, probably of plague, in 1354.

MATTHEW SULLIVAN

Sources M. Sullivan, 'The role of the Nassington family in the medieval English church', *Nottingham Medieval Studies*, 37 (1993), 53–64 · F. C. Hingeston-Randolph, ed., *The register of John de Grandisson, bishop of Exeter*, 3 vols. (1894–9), vol. 1, pp. 118, 160, 167, 332, 510, 590; vol. 2, pp. 650, 662, 814; vol. 3, pp. 1265, 1269, 1274, 1279, 1283, 1285, 1376, 1380–81 · R. Brentano, 'Late medieval changes in the administration of vacant suffragan dioceses: province of York', *Yorkshire Archaeological Journal*, 38 (1952–5), 496–503, esp. 500–02 · Emden, *Oxf.*, 2.1339 · A. H. Thompson, 'Some letters from the register of William Zouche, archbishop of York', *Historical essays in honour of James Tait*, ed. J. G. Edwards, V. H. Galbraith, and E. F. Jacobs (1933), 328, 344n. · J. Caley and J. Bayley, eds., *Calendarium inquisitionum post mortem sive escaetarum*, 2, RC (1808), 190 · *Fasti Angl., 1300–1541*, [Salisbury], 21 · *CEPR letters*, 2.362 · *CPR, 1343–5*, 477; *1350–54*, 374 · R. M. Haines, *A calendar of the register of Wolstan de Bransford, Bishop of Worcester, 1339–49*, HMC, JP 9 (1966), 152 · S. F. Hockey, ed., *The register of William Edington, bishop of Winchester, 1346–1366*, 1, Hampshire RS, 7 (1986), 70 · J. Raine, ed., *The inventories and account rolls of the Benedictine houses or cells of Jarrow and Monk-Wearmouth*, SurtS, 29 (1854), 147 · S. J. Chadwick, 'The Dewsbury moot hall', *Yorkshire Archaeological Journal*, 21 (1910–11), 345–478, esp. 381 · *Select cases concerning the law merchant*, 1, ed. C. Gross, SeldS, 23 (1908), 96 · *The register of William Melton, archbishop of York, 1317–1340*, 1, ed. R. M. T. Hill, CYS, 70 (1970), 77

Nastyface, Jack. *See* Robinson, William (*bap.* 1787, *d.* in or after 1836).

Natares, Edmund (*d.* 1549?), college head, was born in Richmond, Yorkshire. He was admitted to St Catharine's College, Cambridge, probably about 1496, graduated BA in 1500, MA by special grace in 1502, BTh in 1509, and DTh in 1516. He became a fellow of St Catharine's about 1498 and in 1506 was keeper of the Trinity chest. In 1507 he was senior proctor of the university.

On 20 October 1514 Natares was elected master of Clare College; he held that post until his resignation in 1530. In October 1521, on the night of the election of the proctors, the master's chamber and the college treasury of Clare burned down, the former being rebuilt four years later at Natares's expense. He was four times vice-chancellor of the university, in March 1518, 1521, and 1525–7. In his capacity as vice-chancellor complaint was made to him about the preaching of Robert Barnes in St Edward's Church on 24 December 1525. Natares examined Barnes, first in the common schools and then in Clare College, and urged him to recant, for which he was styled by Foxe 'a rank enemy to Christ' (*Acts and Monuments*, 5.415). He is noted by Foxe as being among the 'swarms of friars and doctors' (ibid., 7.451) who took part in the disputations with Latimer in King's College, Cambridge in 1530.

Natares held several preferments: in 1517 he was presented to the rectory of Weston Colville, Cambridgeshire, by the prior and convent of St Pancras, Lewes, and on 26 June 1522 was presented at Winchester to the rectory of Middleton in Teesdale, co. Durham. In August that year he was included in a list of twenty people appointed to be surveyors in survivorship of mines in Devon and Cornwall. In 1532 he was executor of the will of Sir William Fynderne and in 1537 was warden of Staindrop College, co. Durham. Natares died before July 1549, when William Bell was instituted as his successor in the rectory of Middleton. He gave an estate or money to Clare College for an annual sermon at Weston Colville. JUDITH FORD

Sources Emden, *Cam.*, 419 · Cooper, *Ath. Cantab.*, 1.97 · R. Willis, *The architectural history of the University of Cambridge, and of the colleges of Cambridge and Eton*, ed. J. W. Clark, 1 (1886), 79 · *The acts and monuments of John Foxe*, ed. S. R. Cattley, 8 vols. (1837–41), vol. 5, p. 415; vol. 7, p. 451 · Venn, *Alum. Cant.*, 1/3.234 · *LP Henry VIII*, 3/2, nos. 2356, 2482; 5, no. 1617 · C. H. Cooper, *Annals of Cambridge*, 1 (1842), 314 · *Sermons and remains of Hugh Latimer*, ed. G. E. Corrie, Parker Society, 20 (1845), xii · *The letters of Stephen Gardiner*, ed. J. A. Muller (1933), 166, 175

Nath Í mac Fiachrach [Dathí mac Fiachrach] (*supp. d.* 445?), high-king of Ireland, flourished during the murky period just beyond the living memory of those who set down the first historical sources. He was also known as Dathí mac Fiachrach. Since there is good evidence for the existence of one of his sons, *Ailill Molt (d. c.*482), it is a fair presumption that Nath Í existed too. His father, Fiachra Foltsnáithech mac Echach Mugmedóin, was the eponymous ancestor of the Uí Fhiachrach dynasties of Connacht, among whom the kindreds descended from Nath Í were the most successful in the early middle ages.

Nath Í is held in many king-lists to have been king of Tara, the title of the high-kings of Ireland (after Niall Noígiallach and before Lóegaire mac Néill), although the earliest such list, *Baile Chuinn Chétchathaig*, omits him. Some scholars have suggested that he was never king of Tara, partly on the grounds that he is neglected by *Baile Chuinn*, and partly because of chronological discrepancies in the dating of Níall Noígiallach which can be partially alleviated by disposing of Nath Í. However, so confused is fifth-century chronology, encrusted with the errors and ideologies of subsequent centuries, that it is hard to say even where the balance of probability lies.

Much of the information about Nath Í comes in the form of legend. A list of his battles says that, in addition to fighting in Ireland, he frequently fought in Britain. His death-tale takes him further afield. He is said to have gone to the Alps and destroyed a tower, the religious retreat of the king of Thrace. The king besought God that the reign of Nath Í be shortened and that Nath Í's grave not be famous. Nath Í was then killed by a thunderbolt; his body was carried back to Ireland by his son and buried in the cemetery at Rathcroghan, Roscommon, the seat of the kings of Connacht.

It does not seem likely that Nath Í would have journeyed as far as the Alps. However, it is not out of the question that he fought battles in Britain. Between the departure of Roman troops and the arrival of the Anglo-Saxons, the Britons were famously afflicted by warlike Picts and Irishmen, and perhaps Nath Í was a leader of some of these. The Irish name for Britain (Albu) is very similar to the Irish name for the Alps and so even the strange story of his death could contain an element of truth.

In the best chronicle, the annals of Ulster, Nath Í has but one entry, and that incomplete. Under the year 445 there appears his name and nothing more; this was probably meant to be a notice of his death. A later hand has understood it thus and has added some details from the death-tale. Another chronicle says that Nath Í had possessed the sovereignty not only of Ireland but of the world—an excessive claim even by annalists' standards. It is possible that at some point in the transmission of the chronicle there was confusion between his obituary and an *anno mundi*, 'year of the world', date, and this error elevated him into the kingship of the world.

Nath Í's wives were said to be Fial ingen Echach, Ethne ingen Chonrach Cais, and Ruad ingen Airtig; and his sons were Ailill Molt, Amalgaid, Eochu, Cobthach, and Fiachra (or Fiachna). PHILIP IRWIN

Sources F. J. Byrne, *Irish kings and high-kings* (1973), 77–82 · T. F. O'Rahilly, *Early Irish history and mythology* (1946), 211–15 · V. Banateanu, 'Die Legende von König Dathí', *Zeitschrift für Celtische Philologie*, 18 (1929–30), 160–88 · *Ann. Ulster* · W. M. Hennessy, ed. and trans., *Chronicum Scotorum: a chronicle of Irish affairs*, Rolls Series, 46 (1866) · M. A. O'Brien, ed., *Corpus genealogiarum Hiberniae* (Dublin, 1962) · M. C. Dobbs, ed. and trans., 'The Ban-shenchus [pt 2]', *Revue Celtique*, 48 (1931), 163–234, esp. 179

Nathalan [St Nathalan, Nechtan] (*supp. d.* 452), holy man, is localized at Deeside in Aberdeenshire. His feast day is celebrated on 8 January. There are no trustworthy early traditions that can be associated with Nathalan, although this has not inhibited the development of much later traditions that provide him with a noble background and a birthplace in Tullich. He is supposed to have died in 452, an unlikely date, and been buried in Tullich. The notions that he visited Rome and returned as a bishop to Scotland in old age are worthless. Onomastic evidence might be of more value, but while he is linked with churches at Tullich, Cowie, and Bothelney, none of these preserves his name. However, Kilnaughlan on Islay may do so, although the foundation is far from his major cult associations in Aberdeenshire.

The lack of evidence for the origins of this local cult

inspired Skene, Forbes, and O'Hanlon to look beyond the shores of Scotland to neighbouring Ireland, with dubious results. All three identify Nathalan with a St Nechtan who shares the feast day of 8 January and is commemorated in *Félire Óengusso* ('The martyrology of Oengus') as Nechtan from Alba (Scotland). This Nechtan is almost as little known as Nathalan. The later notes to *Félire Óengusso* put forward the idea that his kindred were from Scotland, but bizarrely suggest the place name of Dún Geimin (Dungiven) in Ciannachta, which is in modern co. Londonderry, not Scotland. Alternatively, they offer the information that his cult is located in Scotland. Clearly, the *Félire's* glossators had no certain knowledge and were confused by the various Nechtans that proliferate in hagiographical documents. The probably twelfth-century Drummond missal provides a synchronistic solution, by suggesting that an Irish Nechtan from Dún Geimin left Ireland for the sake of Christ and journeyed to the island of Britain. Skene further identified this Nechtan with the Nechtan Ner (*d.* 679) whose death is noticed in the annals of Ulster. Nevertheless, there is simply no convincing reason to identify Nechtan Ner and the Nechtan of the *Félire Óengusso* with Nathalan of Aberdeenshire. The coincidence of feast day might be telling but cannot prove the case on its own. Unfortunately, Nathalan's cult seems to be destined for obscurity.   ELVA JOHNSTON

Sources *Félire Óengusso Céli Dé* / *The martyrology of Oengus the Culdee*, ed. and trans. W. Stokes, HBS, 29 (1905) · *Félire húi Gormáin* / *The martyrology of Gorman*, ed. and trans. W. Stokes, HBS, 9 (1895) · *The Drummond Missal*, ed. A. P. Forbes, *Kalendars of Scottish saints* (1872) · *Ann. Ulster* · W. F. Skene, *Celtic Scotland: a history of ancient Alban*, 2nd edn, 2 (1887) · A. O. Anderson, ed. and trans., *Early sources of Scottish history, AD 500 to 1286*, 2 vols. (1922)

Nathan, Alec (1872–1954), industrialist, was born on 24 September 1872 in Wellington, New Zealand, the seventh of eight sons (there were four daughters) of Joseph Edward Nathan (1835–1912) and his wife, Dinah Marks (1838–1893). The family was Jewish. Nathan was educated at Wellington College and Lincoln Agricultural College in New Zealand. His father had founded a merchant house based in Wellington and London called Joseph Nathan & Co., in which the five eldest Nathan sons became partners. Alec Nathan and his brother Frederick (1871–1938), were dairy farming at Palmerston North in New Zealand when in 1903 the family firm bought the rights to a new process for making dried milk powder. The two brothers were enlisted in its commercial development, with Alec taking responsibility for running the new plant at Bunnythorpe which processed the milk into dried powder. This factory began operations in 1904, although it was not until 1906 that the Nathans registered a new trade name of Glaxo for their product.

Nathan emigrated to England in 1907 and was thenceforth increasingly involved in the promotion of Glaxo milk powder. He was convinced that it should be marketed as a superior baby food; in 1908 he launched the annual *Glaxo Babybook* as a promotional device, and in 1908–13 he superintended an energetic mail order campaign. He also controlled its press advertising, always

writing copy himself: his slogan 'Glaxo builds bonnie babies' became a household phrase. He gave meticulous attention to selling to the health departments of municipal authorities. This branch of the business developed considerably during the First World War. He was also keenly involved in expanding sales in Australasia, and in many other foreign markets. The Glaxo milk department was only a small part of the Nathans' mercantile business, and relations between the partners were sometimes volatile.

In 1919 Nathan recruited a young pharmacist, Harry *Jephcott, to the Glaxo department to monitor product quality. He subsequently supported Jephcott in the commercial and scientific strategy of diversifying into vitamin foods in the 1920s. This culminated in the formation in 1935 of a pharmaceutical subsidiary of the Nathan business, Glaxo Laboratories Ltd, with a new factory at Greenford. Nathan was the first chairman of this concern, which during the Second World War became the earliest British pharmaceutical company to produce penicillin. He retired from business in June 1946. Six months later Glaxo Laboratories acquired the assets of its parent company, Joseph Nathan, and began a new phase of its development into the world's largest pharmaceutical multinational.

On 15 April 1909 Nathan married Muriel (1881/2–1961), daughter of Wilfred Marks, formerly proprietor of the general store at Tumut in the Snowy Mountains. They had two sons and a daughter. Nathan died of cancer on 18 October 1954 at the London Clinic, and was cremated at Golders Green. He was an intelligent, benevolent man with a strong ethical sense and an aloof but unassuming manner. Many of his family were rough and quarrelsome, but he was gentle and almost innocent. He was a patriarchial employer given to many private kindnesses and charities. Methodical, determined, and a steady strategist, he believed that business life should be a form of public service, and recoiled from both sharp practice and ostentation. At British general elections he voted Liberal or Labour, but less often Conservative. He thought that nothing was too good for the British and Australasian working class but was indifferent to foreigners. In his domestic life he seemed overshadowed by his socially and culturally ambitious wife. He was awarded the Bledisloe gold medal for New Zealand agriculturalists in 1941, but declined a knighthood.   RICHARD DAVENPORT-HINES

Sources private information (2004) · R. P. T. Davenport-Hines and J. Slinn, *Glaxo: a history to 1962* (1992) · H. Jephcott, *The first fifty years* (1969) · *The Times* (20 Oct 1954) · M. S. P. [M. S. Pitt], 'Nathan, Joseph Edward', *Encyclopaedia Judaica*, ed. C. Roth (Jerusalem, 1971–2) · d. cert.
Archives Glaxo Archives, Greenford, Middlesex, letters, memoranda, and family papers
Likenesses J. Gunn, oils, *c.*1946, Glaxo; repro. in Davenport-Hines and Slinn, *Glaxo* · photographs, Glaxo Archives, Greenford, Middlesex · photographs, priv. coll.
Wealth at death £106,387 12s. 4d.: probate, 15 Jan 1955, CGPLA Eng. & Wales

Nathan, Harry Louis, first Baron Nathan (1889–1963), lawyer and public servant, was born at 36 Bassett Road,

North Kensington, London, on 2 February 1889, the elder son of Michael Henry Nathan (*b.* 1852) and his wife, Constance (*d.* 1949), daughter of Louis Beaver, jeweller and silversmith, of Manchester. For reasons of health his father retired from his business as a fine art publisher when he was about fifty but continued his activities as a justice of the peace and as a keen Liberal in politics.

Nathan was educated at St Paul's School, London, where he was a cadet lieutenant in the corps, of which the future Field Marshal Viscount Montgomery of Alamein was a member, and vice-president and treasurer of the Union Debating Society. It was perhaps due to his numerous extra-curricular activities that he failed to obtain a scholarship at Balliol, and he decided not to go up to Oxford as a commoner, a decision he often regretted later. Instead, he became an articled clerk, was admitted a solicitor in 1913, and became junior partner to Herbert Oppenheimer, a brilliant lawyer with a good commercial practice.

As an original territorial officer Nathan reported for duty with the Royal Fusiliers when war broke out in August 1914. He served in Malta and then in Gallipoli, and was promoted captain, then major, and as lieutenant-colonel commanded his battalion, a unit of the 29th division, during the evacuations at both Suvla Bay and Helles. Subsequently the battalion was sent to France in time for the first battle of the Somme in July 1916. Shot through the back of the head by a sniper, Nathan was in hospital for eighteen months but made a remarkable recovery, although the after-effects lasted for many years.

After returning to his firm Nathan was introduced to Sir Alfred Mond, who became a client. This opened up a new field of interest as Mond was an enthusiastic supporter of the Zionist movement. Nathan became legal adviser to the Zionist Organization, to the economic board of Palestine, and later to Pinhas Rutenberg who founded the Palestine Electric Company and to Moses Novomeyski who formed the Palestine Potash Company in 1930 to extract potash from the Dead Sea. During the Second World War it supplied half the potash needed by Great Britain.

As a power in the Liberal Party, Mond was helpful to Nathan in his political career also. Unsuccessful as the Liberal candidate for Whitechapel and St George's in 1924, Nathan won North-East Bethnal Green in 1929. In his maiden speech he attacked the government proposal to authorize the Treasury to guarantee loans of £25 million without stating the precise nature of the public utility schemes to be aided. He was soon recognized by the house as an expert on economic and financial matters.

When Ramsay MacDonald formed his National Government in the summer of 1931 Nathan followed Sir Herbert Samuel, the leader of what was left of the Liberal Party, in supporting the new government on the ground that its immediate function was to put the national finances on a proper basis. After the general election in October in which the Conservatives gained an overwhelming majority, Nathan was disappointed by the course taken by the new government, stating that it was a fraud under a false alias. He crossed the floor of the house in February 1933

and sat as an independent Liberal for eighteen months before joining the Labour Party. He was bitterly attacked for betraying the Liberal Party but his action was a courageous one, both from the political standpoint and from that of his private interest, because a Labour solicitor might not be popular with the business people who were his clients.

At the general election of 1935 Nathan fought South Cardiff in the Labour interest, but did no more than reduce his opponent's majority—a failure due in part to a libel published by the *Western Mail* on the morning of the election for which the newspaper subsequently made a public apology to Nathan in court and paid a substantial sum by way of agreed damages. In April 1937 at a by-election Nathan was returned to the house as Labour member for Central Wandsworth. He became chairman of a committee known first as the territorial army public interest committee and later as the national defence public interest committee, formed to encourage recruiting first for the territorials, then also for the Auxiliary Air Force, and finally also for civil defence. Before war broke out Nathan had realized that soldiers would need help with their home problems and with the agreement of the authorities the Army Welfare Service was built up in the early days of the war. Nathan became command welfare officer of eastern command and of London district, relinquishing the former in 1941. When in 1943 the Army Council put welfare in London under an assistant adjutant-general it thanked him for his 'outstanding part in welfare work', of which he was the pioneer.

While Neville Chamberlain was still prime minister Attlee asked him to recommend Nathan for a peerage so as to strengthen Labour representation in the Lords. Before this could be done Churchill had succeeded Chamberlain. Nathan was created a baron in June 1940 and Ernest Bevin was elected member of parliament for Central Wandsworth. The suggestion that Nathan's peerage was used to make a place for Bevin was not correct. Nathan chose as his motto in his heraldic arms the words *Labor nobilitat.*

When Attlee became prime minister in 1945 Nathan went to the War Office as under-secretary of state and therefore vice-president of the Army Council. In October 1946 he was promoted to be minister of civil aviation and sworn of the privy council. This was an entirely new field: he had many problems to tackle, notably the development of the state corporations set up under the Civil Aviation Act of 1946.

In May 1948 Nathan was obliged to resign from the government owing to the advanced age of his senior partner. He continued active in public affairs and in 1950 became chairman of the charitable trusts committee whose report in 1952 on necessary changes in the law became the foundation of the Charities Act of 1960. In 1957, in collaboration with A. R. Barrowclough, he published *Medical Negligence.* He had served as crown representative on the British Medical Council, was for many years chairman of the governors of the Westminster Hospital group, and chairman of the executive of the British Empire Cancer

Campaign. He was also chairman of the Wolfson Foundation, president of the Royal Geographical Society, and chairman of the Royal Society of Arts.

As a young man Nathan had been one of the managers of the Brady Street Club in Whitechapel, the oldest of the London Jewish boys' clubs. Throughout his life he continued his interest in training for the young, such as the Maccabian associations which stressed the importance of rendering Jewish youth capable of self-defence. In 1950 he was president of the European organizing committee when the third Maccabiah games were held at Tel Aviv. It was then that he inspected the Israeli defence forces, noting that they were 'the most formidable, the best trained and the most resolute in the Middle East'.

Nathan's especial qualities have been summed up as loyalty, warm-hearted humanity, and creative imagination. To these might be added enthusiasm and capacity for hard work in regard to anything he undertook to do.

Nathan married on 27 March 1919 Eleanor Joan Clara (1892–1972), daughter of Carl Stettauer, leather merchant. She was of notable assistance to her husband in his political life. A Cambridge graduate and a governor of Girton College, she was for many years a member of the London county council and in 1947–8 its second woman chairman. They had one daughter, who married Bernard Waley-Cohen, and one son, Roger Carol Michael (b. 1922), who also became a solicitor and who succeeded to the title when his father died in Westminster Hospital, London, on 23 October 1963.   A. L. GOODHART, rev.

Sources *The Times* (25 Oct 1963) · H. M. Hyde, *Strong for service: the life of Lord Nathan of Churt* (1968) · personal knowledge (1981) · Burke, *Peerage* (1999) · *CGPLA Eng. & Wales* (1964)
Archives BLPES, papers · NRA, corresp. and papers | Bodl. Oxf., corresp. with Lord Woolton · HLRO, letters to David Lloyd George · Wellcome L., corresp. with Sir Ernst Chain
Likenesses W. Stoneman, photograph, 1943, NPG · W. Bird, photograph, 1959, NPG · H. Carr, portrait, priv. coll.
Wealth at death £85,351: probate, 15 Jan 1964, *CGPLA Eng. & Wales*

Nathan, Isaac (1790–1864), composer, was born in Canterbury, Kent, of Polish–Jewish descent. His parents intended him to become a rabbi, and consequently he was sent in 1805 to Cambridge to study Hebrew, German, and Chaldean, with Solomon Lyon, a teacher of Hebrew in the university. He made rapid progress in all his subjects, but he also diligently practised the violin, and showed such exceptional aptitude for music that his parents were persuaded to allow him to abandon theology for music. In 1809 Nathan was apprenticed by his father, cantor Menehem Mona, to Domenico Corri in London to learn singing and composition. Under Corri's guidance Nathan advanced rapidly, and eight months after the apprenticeship began the young composer wrote and published his first song, 'Infant Love'. More works in the same style followed in quick succession, the best of which was judged to be 'The Sorrows of Absence'. In 1812 he eloped with a pupil, Rosetta Worthington; they had two sons and four daughters before her death in 1824.

Nathan was introduced by Douglas Kinnaird to Lord Byron in 1814, which led to a friendship that lasted until the poet's death. In response to Kinnaird's suggestion, Byron wrote the *Hebrew Melodies* for Nathan to set to music, and subsequently Nathan bought the copyright of the work. He intended to publish the *Melodies* by subscription, and John Braham, on putting his name down for two copies, suggested that he should aid in their arrangement, and sing them in public. Accordingly the title-page of the first edition, published in 1815, stated that the music was newly arranged, harmonized, and revised by I. Nathan and J. Braham. But Braham's engagements did not allow him to share actively in the undertaking, and in later editions his name was withdrawn. The melodies were adaptations of ancient Jewish chants, and the songs were indeed first sung in London by Braham. Their success meant that they remained in print until 1861 and became the foundation and highlight of Nathan's English career. Other associates included Lady Caroline Lamb, who wrote verses for him to set to music, his pupil Princess Charlotte, and the court circles of George IV, to whom he was music librarian and possibly secret agent (*New Grove*). To support himself he not only wrote and taught, but also ran a music warehouse and publishing business, and even made a not entirely successful stage appearance as Bertram in Henry Bishop's *Guy Mannering* (1816) at Covent Garden.

In 1829 Nathan edited and published *Fugitive pieces and reminiscences of Lord Byron … together with his lordship's autograph, also some original poetry, letters, and recollections of Lady Caroline Lamb*. This publication brought him a wide reputation, but its success was not sufficient to keep him out of financial difficulties. He had previously been compelled, on account of large debts, to leave London and reputedly spent some time in the west of England and in Wales. After returning to London he concentrated on writing and publishing comic operas and burlettas with the librettist James Kenney. Among these was *Sweethearts and Wives*, which had a long run after its production at the Haymarket Theatre on 7 July 1823. It also included two of Nathan's most popular songs, 'Why are you wand'ring here, I pray?', which was still in print in 1883, and 'I'll not be a maiden forsaken'. The comic opera *The Alcaid, or, The Secrets of Office* was produced at the Haymarket on 14 July 1824, and the operatic farce *The Illustrious Stranger, or, Married and Buried* was first given at Drury Lane on 1 October 1827.

In 1823 Nathan published *An essay on the history and theory of music, and on the qualities, capabilities, and management of the human voice, with an appendix on Hebrew music*, which he dedicated to George IV. An enlarged edition was begun in 1836, but it appears that only the first volume materialized, entitled *Musurgia vocalis*. This was reviewed favourably, and Nathan followed it with *Memoirs of Madame Malibran de Bériot* (1836). However, he was eventually ruined financially by 'some unspecified services to William IV' (*New Grove*) and his failure to claim £2000 in expenses, and he emigrated to Australia in 1841. He had married in 1826 Henrietta Buckley (d. 1890). Three of their six children were born in Australia.

Nathan arrived in Melbourne in February 1841, and gave

several concerts there before moving on in April to Sydney, where he lived first at 105 Hunter Street and then in the suburb of Randwick. He did a great deal there to promote church music and choral societies, and very soon after his arrival established a singing academy, became choral director of St Mary's Cathedral, and organized an inaugural concert of classical sacred works. He enhanced his reputation by the publication of patriotic odes, including *Australia the Wide and Free* (1842), for the first municipal council of Sydney, and *Loyalty, a National Paean*. Other colonial works include *Currency Lasses* (1846), for the fifty-eighth anniversary of the founding of Sydney, *Leichardt's Grave* (1846), an ode to mark the presumed death of the explorer Luding Leichardt, and its sequel, *Thy Greeting Home Again*, for his unexpected return. His last composition, *A Song to Freedom* (1863), was written as a gift to Queen Victoria. Nathan also experimented with transcribing Aboriginal music, which resulted in *Koorinda braia* (1842) and the series of Australian melodies included in *The Southern Euphrosyne* (1846–9). He frequently lectured in Sydney on the theory and practice of music, and the first, second, and third of a series of lectures, given at Sydney College between 1844 and 1846, were published in 1846. He set up his own musical type and publishing business, and was actively involved in the early cultivation of opera and madrigals in Sydney. It was Nathan, in fact, who wrote the first Australian operas. These were *Merry Freaks in Troublous Times*, a comic opera on the life of Charles II (1843), never fully staged, and *Don John of Austria*, a historical Spanish romance (1846), first performed at the Victoria Theatre, Sydney, on 3 May 1847. Both are in the style of contemporary English ballad operas, and neither was a success financially or artistically, but three of Nathan's London operas were performed with some degree of success in Sydney in the 1840s.

It is reported that, while resident in Randwick, where he named his house after Byron, Nathan took great interest in the Asylum for Destitute Children, and arranged a concert in 1859 at the Prince of Wales's Theatre in Sydney to raise funds. He later resided at 442 Pitt Street in the city. He was killed while descending from a tramcar in Pitt Street on 15 January 1864, and was buried in Camperdown cemetery on 17 January 1864. Of his children, one son, Charles, was a fellow of the Royal College of Surgeons and died in September 1872. Another son, Robert, was an officer in the New South Wales regular artillery, and aide-de-camp to the governor, Lord Augustus Loftus. Others among his descendants have contributed to music in Australia, including Harry Nathan, claimant to the music of 'Waltzing Matilda', and the conductor Charles Mackerras.   R. H. LEGGE, *rev.* DAVID J. GOLBY

Sources E. Wood, 'Nathan, Isaac', *New Grove* · J. Warrack and E. West, *The Oxford dictionary of opera* (1992), 498 · C. B. Mackerras, *The Hebrew melodist* (1963) · *AusDB*
Archives Mitchell L., NSW
Likenesses portrait (aged twenty-five), priv. coll.

Nathan, Sir Matthew (1862–1939), civil servant and colonial governor, was born in Paddington, London, on 3 January 1862, the second son of Jonah Nathan and his second

Sir Matthew Nathan (1862–1939), by Walter Stoneman, 1920

wife, Miriam, daughter of Lewis Jacobs. His father descended from Jewish immigrants from Dessau and was a partner in a firm manufacturing paper goods. Nathan was brought up in west London and educated by private tutors. Encouraged by his mother he competed successfully in examinations and entered the Royal Military Academy, Woolwich, in 1878, graduating first in his class with prizes, and was commissioned as a subaltern in 1880 at the School of Military Engineering, Chatham, passing out as a lieutenant of the Royal Engineers. He was selected by his former commandant, Colonel Andrew Clarke, an inspector-general at the War Office, to prepare plans for colonial fortifications. His Whitehall base and influential contacts with members of the colonial defence committee resulted in a tour of Sierra Leone in 1883 to prepare defences; secondment to General Wolseley's Sudan expedition in 1884–5; three years as a fortification specialist in India and Burma; and a posting on a punitive expedition on the north-east frontier which earned him a service medal and promotion to captain. In 1895 he was appointed secretary to the colonial defence committee.

In 1898 with the rank of major Nathan was sent by the Colonial Office as interim administrator to Sierra Leone, following a 'hut tax' rebellion. He upheld direct taxation in the colony and protectorate, put down a riot in Freetown, and pushed through building and health regulations. At the end of 1899 he was back in the War Office with a sound reputation. Accordingly, Joseph Chamberlain offered him the governorship of the Gold Coast in July 1900 with orders to re-establish control over Asante. He refrained from extracting tribute from the reconquered states, but he did not restore the exiled Asantehene. He restructured Asante and the southern colony into provinces and districts under commissioners and stipended chiefs, as a measure of decentralization, and kept to direct military rule in the northern protectorate. Relations with commercial and mining representatives were improved by gold claims registration and completion of a railway to Kumasi, but Nathan encountered Aborigines' Rights Protection Society opposition to land purchases and destooling chiefs.

By 1904 his good standing earned Nathan the first-class governorship of Hong Kong, where he moved with caution, avoiding offence to Peking (Beijing) from the local press and supporting a concession for the Kowloon–Canton (Guangzhou) railway construction in the face of foreign competition. Despite this success, he was transferred in 1907 to Natal where he was caught between liberal policies and pressures from responsible government politicians for extension of martial law and the execution of Zulu rebels. Agreeing under protest to Natal ministers' demands, he kept his reputation for coolness under political fire and came to agree with settler views concerning racial segregation and the Indian franchise. Nathan can be counted as one of the midwives of the South African Act of Union by encouraging Natal's inclusion and by his support for entrenched clauses safeguarding the South African protectorates.

Unable to secure another governorship, Nathan became secretary to the General Post Office in 1909 and chairman of the Board of Inland Revenue in 1911. A lifelong Liberal, he was introduced to Herbert and Margot Asquith and their circle. Asquith and Lloyd George picked him as under-secretary for Ireland in July 1914, where he played a dutiful second to the secretary, Augustine Birrell, and reluctant confidant to Lord Lieutenant Wimborne. He supported the Liberal policy of conciliating Irish parliamentary nationalists and opposed Irish military conscription. But he failed to foresee the Easter rising of 1916, a responsibility he shared with Birrell and Wimborne. Resigning along with his superiors he returned briefly to the Royal Engineers and then acted as secretary of the Ministry of Pensions in 1919. From there he was sent by Lord Milner as governor to Queensland in 1920–25, to conciliate a Labor government which swamped the legislative council with its nominees, moved to abolish it in 1921, and threatened the independence of the judiciary. Nathan reported on this spectacle, but refrained from urging disallowance of government bills, sponsoring instead research on the Great Barrier Reef and serving as chancellor of the University of Queensland from 1922 to 1926.

In retirement Nathan served on the special commission on the constitution of Ceylon in 1927–8, and he was chairman of the colonial secretary's advisory committee on rubber from 1926 to 1928. He was appointed CMG in 1899, KCMG in 1902, and GCMG in 1908. Settling in West Coker he was high sheriff of Somerset in 1934 and devoted himself to the study of local history. He died at his home, the Manor House, West Coker, on 18 April 1939 and was buried in the Jewish cemetery of Willesden, London. A careful imperial broker rather than an innovator, Nathan survived the change from civil service promotion by patronage to selection by examination, as an outsider who became a professional administrator. Not averse to the companionship and affection of women, he remained a confirmed bachelor.   COLIN NEWBURY

Sources A. P. Haydon, *Sir Matthew Nathan. British colonial governor and civil servant* (1972) • Bodl. RH • PRO, CO 96, 129, 179, 267; HO 45 • *DNB* • *CGPLA Eng. & Wales* (1939)
Archives Bodl. Oxf., corresp. and papers, diaries, notebooks • Bodl. RH • CUL, Royal Commonwealth Society Library, papers relating to Queensland • PRO, CO 26, 96, 129, 179 | Bodl. Oxf., corresp. with Herbert Asquith • Bodl. Oxf., corresp. with Lord Selborne • HLRO, letters to David Lloyd George • Plunkett Foundation, Long Hanborough, Oxfordshire, corresp. with Sir Horace Plunkett • TCD, corresp. with John Dillon
Likenesses W. Stoneman, photographs, 1920–43, NPG [*see illus.*] • W. Bird, photograph, 1959, NPG
Wealth at death £19,692 10s. 10d.: probate, 5 June 1939, *CGPLA Eng. & Wales*

Nathan [*née* Levi], **Sarina** (1819–1882), supporter of Italian independence, was born on 7 December 1819 at Pesaro on the Adriatic coast of Italy. Her father, Angelo Levi (*d.* 1859), was a merchant in the Papal States. Her mother, *née* Ricca Rosselli, came from another family of Jewish merchants established in Livorno and London. After her mother's early death, Sarina Levi was sent to be brought up by her cousins at Livorno, where Jews were much less in danger of persecution and forcible conversion than in papal territory. Before her seventeenth birthday she was married at Livorno to Meyer Moses Nathan, who was a German from Frankfurt, and the couple in 1836 or 1837 moved to London, where they took British citizenship. Before his death in 1859 Meyer had made a modest fortune as an agent on the stock exchange. All twelve of their children were born in London.

Giuseppe Mazzini, the Italian nationalist, met Sarina Nathan through his friendship with her London cousin Michelangelo Rosselli, since the two men used to play duets at musical evenings to which she was invited. Meeting Mazzini, as she later explained, was the most important event in her life and she became his devoted disciple, helping to finance his conspiracies. In January 1848 he first sought her help in promoting a penny subscription for Italy, and her husband at once found 200 subscribers among his colleagues in the City. One of Meyer's friends, Dr Henri Conneau, was a trusted collaborator of the French emperor, Napoleon III, and not impossibly was a source for Mazzini's astonishing knowledge about the secrets of European diplomacy.

Sarina Nathan returned to Italy in 1859 following her husband's death, since her eldest daughter, Janet, needed a milder climate. At Cornigliano she barely escaped arrest when the Italian police, who saw her as a dangerous revolutionary, forced entry to her house to seize books and papers, but she escaped to Switzerland. For ten years she mainly lived at Lugano, where her house, La Tanzina, became famous as a convenient centre for planning republican revolution. Mazzini was soon referring to her and Janet as his two greatest friends. In 1872 Sarina and three of her children were present when Mazzini died at Pisa in the house of Janet's husband, Pellegrino Rosselli. For the remaining ten years of her life Sarina Nathan devoted herself to the publication of Mazzini's voluminous writings, after purchasing the copyright from his sister and publisher. Living now in Rome, helped by subscriptions from Benjamin Jowett and other English friends, she also started a free school for poor girls to propagate Mazzini's ideas on education. In this initiative she was assisted by Ernesto, the only one of her nine sons to take Italian citizenship (in 1888) and who in 1907–12 became a famous mayor of Rome. Another son, Joseph, after fighting as a volunteer in Garibaldi's army, collaborated actively with Josephine Butler in the campaigns against the state regulation of prostitution, a cause which his mother also supported.

Sarina Nathan died at 13 Portsdown Road, Kensington, London, on 19 February 1882, after surgery for what was probably cancer. Her express wish was that the funeral should be without religious ceremony, and she was buried in the campo Verano, near porta San Lorenzo, in Rome.

DENIS MACK SMITH

Sources *Scritti editi ed inediti di Giuseppe Mazzini*, 94 vols. (Imola, 1906–43) · *Mazzini's letters to an English family*, ed. E. F. Richards, 3 vols. (1920–22) · R. Ugolini, 'L'educazione popolare di orientamento mazziniano a Roma: la famiglia Nathan e la scuola "Giuseppe Mazzini" in Trastevere', *L'Associazionismo Mazziniano* (1979), 121–41 · A. Levi, 'Amici israeliti di Giuseppe Mazzini', *La Rassegna Mensile di Israel*, 2nd ser., 5 (1931), 587–612 · A. Levi, 'Amici israeliti di Giuseppe Mazzini', *Scritti minori storici e politici*, 3 (1957), 191–214 · S. Pallunto, *Sara Levi Nathan* (1903) · *Englishwoman's Review*, 13 (1882), 138–9 · d. cert. · O. Roux, *Memorie giovanili autobiografiche* (1908) · A. Levi, *Ricordi della vita e dei tempi di Ernesto Nathan* (1945)
Archives Biblioteca Archignnasio, Bologna · Domus Mazziniana, Pisa, Fondo B. Omnis · Vittoriano, Piazza Venezia, Rome, Fondo Jessie White Mario · Vittoriano, Piazza Venezia, Rome, Fondo Nathan
Likenesses engraving, repro. in G. Sacerdote, *La vita di Giuseppe Garibaldi* (1933), 10
Wealth at death considerable

Nation, Terence Joseph [Terry] **(1930–1997)**, writer for television, was born on 8 August 1930 at 284 Cowbridge Road, Cardiff, the only child of Gilbert Joseph Nation, of 113 Fairwater Grove West, Llandaff, described on Nation's birth certificate as an upholsterer journeyman, but later the owner of a furniture business and then a poultry farmer, and Susan, née Harris. He was educated in Cardiff.

At eighteen Nation began work as a commercial traveller for his father's furniture business, but he moved to London in 1955. He intended to make a career as a comedian, but was poorly received by audiences. He was rescued by the comic writer and performer Spike Milligan, then starring in and co-writing *The Goon Show*. He was taken on by Associated London Scripts, an agency and writers' co-operative of which Milligan was a founder member, and rapidly became a prolific writer for several radio comedians, including Peter Sellers, Ted Ray, Jimmy Logan, and Elsie and Doris Waters. On 29 March 1958—at St Mary the Boltons, West Brompton, London—he married Kathleen Gaunt (*b.* 1935/6), a classical pianist from

Doncaster in Yorkshire, daughter of Thomas Mitchell Gaunt, a miner.

In 1962 Nation contributed three plays to the ITV science fiction strand *Out of the Unknown* and as a consequence Nation was included on the list of possible writers for the BBC's science-fiction adventure series *Doctor Who* (originated principally by Sydney Newman). Nation later recounted to interviewers how he initially refused the commission to write seven episodes of *Doctor Who*, as he was busy writing material for the comedian Tony Hancock and was accompanying him on tour. When Hancock sacked Nation after a quarrel, Nation changed his mind and accepted the commission, regarding it as 'the sort of thing where you take the money and fly off like a bat out of hell' (*Daily Mirror*, 11 Dec 1964).

The resulting serial, broadcast between December 1963 and February 1964, made Nation famous, but his fame was dwarfed by the success of the fictional extraterrestrials his story introduced. The Daleks, natives of the planet Skaro, were unable to survive outside the metal casings they had devised in an unsuccessful attempt to limit their physical mutation following an atomic war. The appearance of the Daleks was realized by a BBC staff designer, Raymond Cusick, who modelled the casings after salt-cellars, with the attachments of an eye stalk, an extendible 'arm', and a ray gun. With Nation's dialogue—including the electronically processed Dalek battle-cry of 'Exterminate!'—and Cusick's design, the Daleks drew upon post-war Britain's fears of totalitarianism, mechanization, and nuclear war. Their robotic speech patterns somehow proved ideally suited to school playgrounds, combining with their pepper-pot shapes to make them iconic figures in late twentieth-century popular culture. Although the Daleks were destroyed at the end of Nation's story, public demand led the BBC to commission a second segment. For this story, 'The Dalek Invasion of Earth', Nation revised the creatures' motivation: originally their priority was survival as a species, but subsequently they became obsessed with the total domination of other life forms. The Daleks were now heavily influenced by the Nazis; Nation said that they were his revenge for the nights he had spent on his own in an air raid shelter in Cardiff during the Second World War, when his father was away in the army and his mother was on patrol as an air raid warden. The Daleks were the principal villains in another twelve serials over *Doctor Who*'s twenty-six years on BBC television, seven of which were written or co-written by Nation. As Nation retained co-ownership of his creations with the BBC, he became very wealthy through the sale of merchandising rights. Nation was unable to explain where the name came from: in an interview for *Radio Times* in 1971 he said that he had seen 'DAL to LEK' on the spine of an encyclopaedia, but later admitted that this was a fiction to satisfy enquirers. The success of the Daleks led many to credit Nation as the creator of *Doctor Who* itself, a mistake that he eventually gave up trying to correct.

In June 1964 Nation and his wife were able to move from their flat in Hampstead to a manor house, Lynsted Park, near Sittingbourne, Kent, where he continued to write for television. He came to specialize in episodes of filmed thriller series for ITV intended to appeal to audiences in Britain and America, including ten episodes of *The Saint*, inspired by the books by Leslie Charteris. In 1968 he became script editor on the final series of the fantasy espionage series *The Avengers*, and in 1971 was associate producer on *The Persuaders*, a highly expensive star vehicle for Tony Curtis and Roger Moore. In the 1970s he wrote again for the BBC, where he was responsible for two well-remembered science fiction series, aimed at an older audience than was *Doctor Who. Survivors*, made between 1975 and 1977, dramatized the attempts of human beings to rebuild society after a plague had decimated the population. Nation's outlook, envisaging a grim struggle for resources by individuals and small groups, conflicted with the producer's communitarian approach and he left the project after the first series. The television series was also overshadowed by a legal dispute with his former colleague on *The Avengers*, Brian Clemens, who claimed to have originated the format. Nation's novel, *Survivors* (1976), bore only a slight resemblance to the BBC's version.

Nation retained closer ties with *Blake's Seven*, of which fifty-two episodes were screened by BBC 1 between 1978 and 1981. He wrote the first fourteen instalments and several later episodes. Described as 'Robin Hood in space' (Peel, 22), this saga of a group of criminals led by a political dissident fighting an oppressive regime in the far future established a cult following among British fantasy television enthusiasts second only to that of *Doctor Who*. It was the most effective dramatization of Nation's concern that individuals should co-operate for their own interests and not for those of a faceless bureaucracy. During the 1970s he also wrote a children's novel with an ecological theme, *Rebecca's World: Journey to the Forbidden Planet* (1975), whose protagonist was based on his own daughter, and he returned to *Doctor Who* and the Daleks. In a 1975 serial, 'Genesis of the Daleks', he revised their origins to depict them as the products of genetic engineering, and introduced their fictional creator, Davros. Emotionally and physically distorted by nuclear war and confined to a Dalek-like chariot, Davros was convinced of his own moral and intellectual superiority and that of his Daleks over all other creatures, and was perhaps Nation's favourite creation.

Nation had become typecast as a writer of escapist adventure stories and, with interest in the genre waning in Britain, emigrated to the United States in September 1980. Much of his work on films and television within the Hollywood studio system went uncredited, and none of his American projects enjoyed the success or recognition of his British work. From California, he continued closely to protect his rights in the Daleks which had become part of everyday culture. This sometimes brought him criticism from *Doctor Who* enthusiasts, many of whom were quick to point out that Raymond Cusick, not Nation, had designed the Daleks. An example that illustrated the Daleks' continuing force as symbols of unfeeling bureaucracy, perhaps, was the comparison of the then BBC

director-general, John Birt, to a 'croak-voiced Dalek' by the television writer Dennis Potter, at the Edinburgh television festival in 1993. Admirers familiar with Nation's aggressive defence of his rights in the Daleks would be surprised by his generosity and his willingness to advise new writers. Nation died of emphysema at his home in Pacific Palisades, Los Angeles, California, on 9 March 1997, and was survived by his wife, Kate, and their two children, Rebecca and Joel.   MATTHEW KILBURN

Sources M. Wiggins, *Doctor Who Magazine*, 252 (4 June 1997), 6–11 · BBC WAC · biographical files, BFI [microfiche] · 'The Starburst interview: Terry Nation', *Starburst*, 1/6 (1979), 4–11 · J. Peel, 'Terry Nation remembered', *TV Zone*, 90 (1997), 20–23 · K. Newman, 'The castor way', *The Independent* (12 March 1997) · H. Jenkins, 'Nation, Terry', *Museum of Broadcast Communications encyclopedia of television*, ed. H. Newcomb, 3 vols. (1997) · C. Dunkley, 'Could you survive the end of the world?', *Radio Times* (10 April 1975) · M. Brown, 'Seven up', *Radio Times* (12 Jan 1979) · b. cert. · m. cert. · *Daily Telegraph* (12 March 1997) · *The Times* (13 March 1997) · *The Independent* (13 March 1997) · *The Scotsman* (13 March 1997?)

Archives BBC WAC, corresp. · priv. coll., MSS | FILM BBC Film & Television Library, interview for *Whicker's World*, 1968

Likenesses A. Sidey, photograph, 1964, repro. in *Daily Mirror* (11 Dec 1964) · two photographs, 1965–73, BBC; repro. in Wiggins, *Doctor Who Magazine*, 6, 8 · F. Martin, photograph, 1966, repro. in *The Guardian* (31 Jan 1966) · R. Evans, photograph, 1975, repro. in Dunkley, 'Could you survive' · double portrait, photograph, 1975 (with his daughter Rebecca), repro. in *Belfast Telegraph* (1 Sept 1975) · photograph, *c*.1979, BBC; repro. in 'The Starburst interview', *Starburst*, 8 · photograph, *c*.1979, repro. in Brown, 'Seven up' · photographs, BBC

Natter, Johann Lorenz (1705–1763), gem-engraver and medallist, was born on 21 March 1705 at Biberach-an-der-Riss, Germany, the second son of Johann Ulrich Natter, a dyer (*Garnsieder*). He first trained alongside his elder brother, Johann Georg, as a jeweller in Biberach, but in 1724 he left the town for Switzerland, where his family originated, and trained in Bern as a seal and gem-engraver, working at least for a time with the goldsmith and engraver Johannes Hug.

After six years in Switzerland Natter moved to Venice, where he worked mainly at engraving armorial seals. In 1732 he was invited to Florence by Philipp, Baron von Stosch (1691–1757), a noted antiquary, connoisseur, and agent of the British government. Von Stosch, who had established himself as an authority on ancient engraved gems with the publication of his *Gemmae antiquae caelatae* (1724), commissioned Natter to copy ancient gems in his collection. In Florence, and from 1734 in Rome, Natter developed considerable expertise in copying ancient gems, and much of his own original work, depicting figures from classical mythology and Roman portraits, also closely imitated ancient forms; he frequently used Greek signatures on his work: *NATTER* or *NATTĒR*, and *HYDROS* or *HYDROU* (a Greek translation of the German *Natter*, a snake). He was subsequently accused of profiting from the lucrative trade in forged ancient gems, but denied that he personally had mis-sold any of his work in this way.

At the same time Natter was developing a particular talent as a portraitist, and he was an early exponent of the neo-classical manner in both portrait gems and portrait medals; works from this time include a celebrated intaglio of Cardinal Alessandro Albani (c.1730–40), which helped to bring him recognition in the Roman art world, a cameo of John, Lord Hervey (c.1730–40; priv. coll.), apparently derived from Edme Bouchardon's 1729 bust of the same subject, and a medal of Charles Sackville, earl of Middlesex (1733, signed 'L. NATTER F.'; BM).

In Italy Natter began to establish a reputation not merely as a craftsman, but also as an authority on and a collector of gems in his own right, and through von Stosch and his circle he began to build a network of contacts and customers in Italy, England, and across Europe. He may also have become a freemason. In 1739 or 1740 he moved to London, but was disappointed to find that there was less demand than he expected for modern engraved gems, and for a time he worked mainly as a medallist, producing, for example, *Tribute to George II* (1741; BM) and the portrait *Sir Robert Walpole* (1741; BM), modelled on Rysbrack's terracotta bust of 1726. In 1743 he travelled with the painter, engraver, and architect Marcus Tuscher, a fellow German and protégé of von Stosch, to Copenhagen, where for nearly a year he was accommodated at the royal palace while he worked on a number of gem commissions, including a portrait of his patron, *Christian VI of Denmark* (1744; Rosenborg Palace, Copenhagen). From there he went to Stockholm and St Petersburg, but in 1747 settled in The Hague, where he found a willing patron in William IV of Orange-Nassau, who commissioned a number of royal portrait cameos, intaglios, and medals. The most remarkable of these, in Natter's own opinion, was a full-face cameo of William's wife, Anna (1748; Bibliothèque Nationale, Paris).

In 1750, while Natter was in the Netherlands, Pierre-Jean Mariette published his *Traité des pierres gravées* (1750), in which he disparaged Natter's work and accused him of deliberate forgery. Following William IV's death, Natter returned in 1751 to England, where he wrote his own *A Treatise on the Ancient Method of Engraving on Precious Stones, Compared with the Modern* (1754; French edition of the same date). The introduction contained a rebuttal of Mariette and some autobiographical passages, but the core of the work was a discussion of engraving technique, illustrated with plates of gems in British collections, including that of his friend and patron Thomas Hollis. Natter intended this to be the first part of a substantial catalogue of ancient gems in British collections, among them his own, to be called the *Museum Britannicum*. Although the *Treatise* helped Natter achieve intellectual recognition—he was made fellow of both the Society of Antiquaries (1755) and the Royal Society (1757)—it was not a commercial success, and he was forced to sell his own gem collection to finance further work. He was finally able to publish only a fraction of his researches, in *Catalogue des pierres graveés … de Mylord Comte de Bessborough* (1761). His manuscripts of the intended *Museum Britannicum*, containing drawings of more than 500 gems, survive at the Hermitage Library and Archives in St Petersburg.

In the later 1750s and early 1760s Natter lived mainly in London and The Hague, but he also revisited Copenhagen, Stockholm (where he worked as an art dealer), and St Petersburg. For a short time in 1756–7 he served as chief engraver at the mint in Utrecht, but found that he was both badly remunerated and left little time to devote to gem-engraving. In London in 1761 he was commissioned to produce George III's Coronation Medals, not for the London mint, but rather in opposition to it, since the king had rejected the mint's designs. His output of gems must still have been prolific. For example, the Bessborough collection, when sold to the duke of Marlborough about 1762, included forty heads of Roman emperors by Natter, and the duke of Marlborough himself commissioned Natter to engrave copies of a number of gems. He still excelled as a portraitist, and a number of fine gems survive from this period, mainly in the rococo style which he had first adopted in the late 1740s. Among them are a large intaglio of Frederick V of Denmark (1757; Rosenborg Palace, Copenhagen), and a cameo of Ferdinand of Brunswick (c.1760; V&A). His portrait intaglio of Thomas Hollis (1758?) is known only through casts.

Natter's family life is almost undocumented, but at his death he left a son and daughter from his first marriage, both aged under twenty-one, and a second wife, or possibly mistress, Elizabeth van Dorssen (*bap.* 1732, *d.* 1799), who was born in Utrecht. One of their two daughters was baptized in The Hague in 1758. His nephews Johann Ulrich and Georg Christoph worked with him in London, and the latter was with him at his death, which occurred in St Petersburg as the result of asthma and a heart condition on 27 October 1763. He was buried in St Petersburg on 29 October.   CHRISTOPHER MARSDEN

Sources E. Nau, *Lorenz Natter, 1705–1763, Gemmenschneider und Medailleur* (1966) · L. Natter, *A treatise on the ancient method of engraving on precious stones, compared with the modern* (1754) · L. Forrer, *Biographical dictionary of medallists*, 8 vols. (1902–30), vol. 4, pp. 225–33; vol. 8, p. 90 · J. Kagan and O. Neverov, 'Lorenz Natter's *Museum Britannicum*: gem collecting in mid-eighteenth-century England', *Apollo*, 120 (1984), 114–21, 162–8 · G. Seidmann, 'An eighteenth-century collector as patron: the 4th duke of Marlborough and the London engravers', *Engraved gems: survivals and revivals*, ed. C. M. Brown (1997), 263–79 · will, PRO, PROB 11/894, fols. 214–15 · M. Baker, C. Harrison, and A. Laing, 'Bouchardon's British sitters: sculptural portraiture in Rome and the classicising bust around 1730', *Burlington Magazine*, 142 (2000), 752–62

Archives Hermitage, St Petersburg, MSS

Likenesses F. Bartolozzi, line engraving (after self-portrait), BM; repro. in T. Hollis, *Memoirs of Thomas Hollis*, 2 vols. (1780), vol. 2, p. 586

Nattes, John Claude (c.1765–1839), topographical draughtsman and watercolour artist, lived in London for many years and also travelled widely throughout the British Isles and the continent. An engraved label on a watercolour exhibited at the Royal Academy in 1781 advertised his services as a teacher of drawing and perspective to the nobility and gentry. It also confirmed that Nattes had been a pupil of the Irish artist Hugh Primrose Dean (1746–1784?). Joseph Farington recorded in his diary in 1787 that Nattes was a Frenchman and that he had been a servant of Dean's in Rome. On 30 March 1793 Nattes married Sarah Barber (c.1756–1845) at St Botolph without Bishopsgate. Their first child, Charles Claude, was born the following year and their second son, John William, in 1795.

As with many of his contemporaries, topographical work became the mainstay of Nattes's repertory. In 1786 his first prints were published by W. Watts in *Seats of the Nobility and Gentry* and in 1789 he was commissioned by Sir Joseph Banks to record the buildings of Lincolnshire: this undertaking resulted in more than 700 drawings and watercolours, now preserved in the central library in Lincoln. A description of one of his tours is given in John Stoddart's *Scenery and Manners in Scotland*, published in 1801; this was followed by the series of drawings *Scotia depicta* published in 1804. Watercolours of Dublin exhibited at the Royal Academy in 1801 indicate the first of three known trips to Ireland and in that same year Nattes was invited with other prominent artists to take part in the first experiment in England with the new process of lithography.

Nattes and a group of friends had been meeting regularly during the winter months to sketch and converse upon art: it is no surprise, then, to find that he was among the ten artists who came together in November 1804 as founder members of the Society of Painters in Water Colours. The society's first exhibition proved a great success, with more than 12,000 people paying their shilling for admission. This proved to be the most productive period of Nattes's career. He had published *Microcosm* (1803) by his friend W. H. Pyne, a teaching manual entitled *Practical Geometry* (1805), and views of Lincoln, Bath, and Oxford, many of them collaborations with Augustus Pugin. He also completed a series of drawings of Stowe House commissioned by the marquess of Buckingham, and further series of aquatints of Versailles, Paris, and St Denis appeared in 1810.

The event for which Nattes is most often remembered—and which has undoubtedly coloured his reputation—was his expulsion in 1807 from the Old Watercolour Society for exhibiting other people's works as his own. Surprisingly, there does not appear to be any contemporary account of the incident and it does not seem to have affected his subsequent career. His two sons, both in the engineer corps of the East India Company, tragically died within six months of each other in 1818. Sketchbooks in the Victoria and Albert Museum, London, show that from 1819 to 1822 Nattes was travelling in France and Italy. At the end of 1822 he left England and almost certainly settled in France, where a number of collections of his drawings are located; his last known address was in St Germain. From surviving sketches it is evident that he made some visits back to England. He died, apparently of natural causes, on 7 September 1839 in the City of London inn, Dover, where he was buried in Cowgate cemetery on 14 September. On his death certificate his age was given as 'about 75 years'.

As an artist, Nattes never developed his style beyond a certain limited range and his surviving work is, as one would expect from a drawing master, of variable quality. It does, however, provide a vast source of material of great value to the researcher of pre-Victorian topography and social history. The main collections of his work are in the British Museum, the Victoria and Albert Museum, and the Guildhall Library, London; the print room at Windsor Castle; the Bodleian Library, Oxford; and the National Library of Scotland.   AIDAN FLOOD

Sources A. Flood, 'John Claude Nattes: unravelling the thread', MS, 1999, Camden Local Studies and Archives · Farington, *Diary* · minutes, Society of Painters in Water-Colours, 1804–7, Bankside Gallery, London · J. L. Roget, *A history of the 'Old Water-Colour' Society*, 2 vols. (1891) · d. cert.
Archives Bodl. Oxf., sketchbook · Northants. RO, sketchbooks, mainly of Castle Ashby | Bankside Gallery, London, Society of Painters in Water-Colours, archive · Lincs. Arch., accounts with Sir Joseph Banks for drawings of Lincolnshire buildings

Nau, Stephen [Étienne] (*d.* **1647**), violinist and composer, was probably born in Orléans, France. A manuscript now in Berlin describes him as the dancing-master of the princess of Heidelberg. He was a violinist at the English court from Michaelmas 1626 at the unprecedented fee of £200 p.a. and replaced Thomas Lupo senior as composer for the violins from the latter's death early in 1628. He seems to have spent a brief period at Leiden University, where a document of 11 June 1627 calls him 'Gallus Aureliensis' ('Frenchman from Orléans'). Nau apparently acted as director of Charles I's violins, receiving payment for provision of instruments and music books. He assisted in the rehearsal and composition of dances for the inns of court masque *The Triumph of Peace* and played in it on 3 and 13 February 1634. Similar duties accompanied a performance of William Cartwright's play *The Royal Slave* at Hampton Court on 12 January 1637. Nau was among those who reconstituted the Corporation of Musick of Westminster in 1635.

Relatively few compositions by Nau are known, but they are highly regarded. Apart from a virtuoso solo violin 'fantasia', most are dances. Full five-part versions show the composer exploiting skilled use of cross-rhythms and intricate counterpoint, transcending routine dance idioms.

Nau remained in England after the court was disbanded in 1642. He was ill in 1644 and was examined by the famous court physician Sir Theodore Turquet de Mayerne; the case notes survive (BL, Sloane MS 1991). Nau died on 13 March 1647 and was buried at St Giles-in-the-Fields, London, on the 16th, having requested a ceremony according to the usage of the Reformed church. A wife, Cornelia, and nine children were named in his will. On 14 July 1660 his son Stephen was sworn as lutenist at court, but did not receive a salaried place.   ANDREW ASHBEE

Sources M. Jurgens, ed., *Documents du minutier central concernant l'histoire de la musique (1600–1650)*, 2 vols. (Paris, 1967–74) · G. Dodd, *Thematic index of music for viols* (1980–) · A. Ashbee, ed., *Records of English court music*, 3 (1988); 5 (1991); 8 (1995) · P. Holman, *Four and twenty fiddlers: the violin at the English court, 1540–1690*, new edn (1993) · L. Hulse, 'Apollo's Whirligig: William Cavendish, duke of Newcastle and his music collection', *Seventeenth Century*, 9 (1994), 213–46 · P. Walls, *Music in the English courtly masque, 1604–1640* (1996) · A. Ashbee and D. Lasocki, eds., *A biographical dictionary of English court musicians, 1485–1714*, 2 vols. (1998)

Archives Deutsche Akademie der Künste, Berlin | BL, Sir Theodore Turquet de Mayerne case notes, Sloane MS 1991, fols. 232v–233r

Wealth at death £310—bequests: will

Nau de la Boissellière, Claude (*fl.* 1574–1605), administrator and courtier, was born in France, but precise details of his birth and parentage are not known. His family was originally from Touraine, but had settled in Paris. He was trained as a lawyer and gained a position as a secretary to Charles de Guise, cardinal of Lorraine, uncle to Mary, queen of Scots, and then entered the royal bureaucracy as an *auditeur ordinaire* in the *chambre des comptes* of Paris.

In 1574 Raullet, Queen Mary's secretary, died, and Nau was recommended to Mary as his successor by the cardinal of Lorraine. He entered into his duties early in 1575, travelling to Sheffield Castle where Mary was prisoner. He acted as her secretary, political adviser, and ambassador on occasion, and also advised her on financial affairs, which involved attempting to manage her considerable dower lands in France. He established himself as the most important figure in Mary's household, well known in England and abroad to the statesmen interested in her affairs. In 1577 he was used by Mary to write a long account of her life, in which she defended herself from the various charges made against her.

Nau complained in 1577 to his brother that 'I am losing in this prison my best years, and the reward of my services, and all hopes of advancement' (Leader, 397). He was still a young man, and his career in France and also prospects of marriage were interrupted by being imprisoned with perhaps a rather difficult mistress. It is generally thought, however, that he was able to enrich himself and his family while administering Mary's funds. In 1586 he made an unsuccessful attempt to find himself an English wife by paying court to Bessie Pierrepoint, a granddaughter of the countess of Shrewsbury (Bess of Hardwick) and a lady-in-waiting to Mary.

Nau was allowed by the English government to undertake an embassy to Scotland on behalf of Mary. He was sent in June 1579 to open up communications between Mary and her son, James VI, in the hope that he might agree to a plan for her restoration, in partnership with himself, to the throne of Scotland. Nothing came of this, since Nau was refused access to the young king. Mary hoped to send him again to Scotland in 1581, but did not do so. Nau was also sent on an embassy to Queen Elizabeth in late 1584; he went ostensibly to defend Mary from rumours spread by the countess of Shrewsbury that her husband, Mary's gaoler, had been too familiar in his dealings with her. This visit to court perhaps also allowed the government to take the measure of Nau, and to establish links with him which may have been useful in the months ahead.

Nau was accused by Mary herself, and by some of her sympathizers, of having played an important role in her downfall in 1586–7. The chief charge against Mary was that she had corresponded with Anthony Babington, who was plotting to release Mary and to raise rebellion with foreign support against Queen Elizabeth I. Walsingham had intercepted the letters between Mary and Babington, and was therefore aware of what was being plotted from the beginning. When the plot was revealed Nau was arrested, although lodged for most of the time in Walsingham's own house. Nau was threatened with being implicated himself in the plot, and as a result he confessed that Mary had dictated an incriminating letter to Babington. This confession formed an important part of the prosecution's case against Mary; it was good evidence because Babington had burnt the original of the letter. Mary was bitterly incensed at what she saw as her betrayal by her secretary, although what he had confessed was no more than the truth. 'Nau is the cause of my death; I suffer that he may go scathless', she is reported to have said (Nau, xlviii). Mary also felt that Nau had been instrumental in persuading Gilbert Curle, her Scottish secretary, to turn traitor too. Nau was released from custody as a result of giving his evidence, and was allowed to return to France ahead of Mary's other servants, so that he could give his side of the story first. He seems to have left England with a considerable quantity of money and clothing. There is extant a letter from Nau to Walsingham in which he gives a list of the extensive wardrobe he asked the latter to provide him with for his journey to France.

According to his enemies Nau's character was something like Malvolio's—vain, pompous, and presumptuous. When he arrived in France he wrote a spirited defence of his conduct; and he continued to profess his innocence, sending a memorial on the subject to James I as late as 1605. He managed to secure a statement from the duc de Guise in 1587 that he was innocent of the charges made against him of being complicit in Mary's execution; but this means little since the house of Guise, after its alliance with Spain in 1584, had a strong interest in seeing Mary dead. While Nau's behaviour was clearly unheroic, in historical terms it was hardly decisive; the evidence against Mary was very black, especially considering the standards of proof required in Tudor treason trials. What Nau might perhaps be accused of with more justice is not warning Mary clearly enough that it was not in her interests to correspond with hotheads like Babington.

Nau prospered after his return to France. He married Anne du Jardin, and they had a son, Jacques, and three daughters, Claire, Marthe, and Marie. He rallied successfully, like other former adherents of the house of Guise, to Henri IV. On 1 July 1600 he once more secured a position in the *chambre des comptes*, and in May 1605 he was ennobled by royal letters patent. The date of his death is not known.

PETER HOLMES

Sources DNB · F.-A. A. de La Chenaye-Desbois, *Dictionnaire de la noblesse: contenant les généalogies, l'histoire et la chronologie des familles nobles de la France*, 3rd edn, 14 (Paris, 1869) · *CSP Scot. ser., 1589–1603*, index · C. Nau, *The history of Mary Stewart*, ed. J. Stevenson (1883), chap. 1 · J. H. Pollen, *Mary queen of Scots and the Babington plot*, Scottish History Society, 3rd ser., 3 (1922) · *Lettres, instructions et mémoires de Marie Stuart, reine d'Écosse*, ed. A. Labanoff, 7 vols. (1852), vol. 4, p. 260; vol. 5, p. 95; vol. 6, pp. 28, 33, 42; vol. 7, pp. 194–209 · *CSP Scot., 1574–85* · A. Fraser, *Mary, queen of Scots* (1972), 522, 570, 573 · M. Lynch, ed., *Mary Stewart, queen in three kingdoms* (1988), 177, 180, 189, 214 · *Miscellanea, II*, Catholic RS, 2 (1906), 184 · *Miscellanea,*

IV, Catholic RS, 4 (1907), 64, 65 · J. D. Leader, *Mary queen of Scots in captivity* (1880), index · D. Moysie, *Memoirs of the affairs of Scotland, 1577–1603*, ed. J. Dennistoun, Bannatyne Club, 39 (1830), 23 · *The state papers and letters of Sir Ralph Sadler*, ed. A. Clifford, 2 vols. (1809), index · earl of Hardwicke, *State papers*, 1 (1778), 224–50

Naughton, Charles John (1886–1976). *See under* Crazy Gang (*act.* 1931–1962).

Naughton, John. *See* Ó Neachtain, Seán (1645x50?–1729).

Naughton, Thady. *See* Ó Neachtain, Tadhg (*c.*1670–*c.*1752).

Naughton, William John Francis (1910–1992), writer, was born on 12 June 1910 in Devlis, Ballyhaunis, co. Mayo, Ireland, the fourth of six children of Thomas Naughton (1873–1957), a shopkeeper and railway worker, and then coalminer in England, and his wife, Maria, *née* Fleming (1875–1949). The family emigrated to Bolton, Lancashire, in 1914, when Bill was four years old. He was educated at St Peter and St Paul School in Bolton, which is vividly recreated in fictionalized form in his novel *One Small Boy* (1957).

Leaving school at fourteen, Naughton first worked in a weaving shed, then in various labouring jobs between periods of unemployment. In 1930 he married Anne Wilcock (1905–1985), a cotton mill worker, with whom he had three children, Marie, Larry, and Sean (who died in infancy). At this time he was working as a coal-bagger and driver for the Co-operative Society in Bolton. In 1938 Naughton, who was always keen on recording events, had the chance to develop his literary skills with the Mass-Observation study of Bolton (Worktown, as it was called), under the poet and sociologist Charles Madge. However, when Naughton became a conscientious objector in the war, the Co-op felt compelled to lay him off, and his marriage broke up soon afterwards (though the couple were not divorced until 1950). After a brief spell in Manchester he finally settled in London in 1941, where he became a civil defence corps driver. He also took to writing, publishing his first stories in 1943, in the *London Evening News*. Subsequent stories were published in *Lilliput* and broadcast on BBC radio, leading Madge to commission a book from him, the result being the very successful *A Roof Over your Head* (1945), Naughton's first volume of autobiography. This led to other commissions, including an article called 'The spiv', which brought the then obscure word into popular usage.

Though he published two novels in the 1940s, *Pony Boy* (1946) and *Rafe Granite* (1947), it was in the 1950s, as a playwright, that Naughton became well known, on both radio and television. He always claimed that *Coronation Street* drew on his radio play about a Lancashire street, *June Evening* (1958), which had been adapted for television just nine months before the soap opera began (1960). Many of his most celebrated works began on radio, going through television and theatre adaptations (with Bernard Miles, at the Mermaid Theatre), thence to film. Thus the radio play *My Flesh, my Blood* (1957) subsequently became *Spring and Port Wine* (filmed in 1970); *All in Good Time* (1961) became the film *The Family Way* (1966); and, most famously, *Alfie Elkins and his Little Life* (1962) was to become the internationally successful film (and novel) *Alfie* (1966), making a star of Michael Caine in the process. This won a Screenwriters Guild award (as did *The Family Way*), and was nominated for an Academy award of merit. His more experimental radio play *The Mystery* won the Prix Italia in 1974.

Among Naughton's last works are three highly evocative volumes of autobiography, *On the Pig's Back* (1987), *Saintly Billy* (1988), and *Neither Use nor Ornament* (1995), taking us back to life in Bolton during and after the First World War. These episodic memoirs also reveal the origins of some of his short stories, of which he wrote more than 200. The best-known are collected in *Late Night on Watling Street* (1959), although arguably his best, the much anthologized 'Spit Nolan', is to be found in his collection for children, *The Goalkeeper's Revenge* (1961), which won the Other award in 1978.

Naughton, a man of medium build, described himself as having a 'big head, blue eyes, and a round face' (Naughton, *On the Pig's Back*, 69), and in later life he had a distinctive moustache. He was a private man, refusing an entry in *Who's Who*, and also something of an outsider: first as an Irish Catholic living in Bolton, then as a northerner living in London, and finally as a self-educated, working-class writer among the literati of the time. But in 1968, after living in London from the 1940s to the 1960s at 64 St George's Square, Pimlico, he moved to Ballasalla on the Isle of Man with his second wife, the Austrian Ernestine (Erna) Pirolt (b. 1929), a nurse, whom he had married on 9 September 1952. He was heavily influenced by mystical writers, especially Thomas à Kempis—after whom he named his house in Ballasalla, Kempis. Naughton was certainly driven to be honest in his observations of life, dismissing his own 'hack' work as 'a sin against the Holy Spirit—from which source all literature springs' (ibid., 33). He strove to capture actual speech patterns and rhythms, giving his writing a vibrancy and poignancy that only occasionally falls into sentimentality. (Five trunkfuls of his diaries, stretching from the 1930s to the 1990s, and running to several million words, are deposited at Bolton Library but will have to wait until 2015 before being opened to the public.) His overall contribution to the cultural ferment of the 1950s and 1960s has still to be properly assessed. Undoubtedly he was one of the first post-war writers to recreate, for the world, the authenticity of working-class life in the north of England. But his range was wider, as his London work, his contributions to popular television series (such as *Nathaniel Titlark*, *Starr and Company*, *Yorky*), his children's stories, and his more experimental, Pinteresque drama *The Mystery* show.

Towards the end of his life Naughton was consolidating his long-term interest in dreams, in an as-yet-unpublished volume, 'The Dream Mind', which he considered one of his most important works. He died at his home on the Isle of Man on 9 January 1992, shortly after a stroke, and was cremated on 14 January, to be interred at Rushen cemetery on the Isle of Man. His wife survived him.

DAVID RUDD

Sources B. Naughton, *On the pig's back: an autobiographical excursion* (1987) · B. Naughton, *Saintly Billy: a Catholic boyhood* (1988) ·

B. Naughton, *Neither use nor ornament: a memoir of Bolton, 1920s* (1995) • B. Naughton, *A roof over your head* (1945) • B. Naughton, 'The spiv', *Pilot papers: social essays and documents*, ed. C. Madge (1945), 99–108 • B. Naughton, *One small boy* (1957) • private information (2004) [Erna Naughton; Larry Naughton]

Archives BFI • Bolton Central Library, MSS | U. Sussex, Mass-Observation archive • University of Delaware, Newark, BBC Third Programme radio scripts

Likenesses I. Kar, photograph, 1957, repro. in Naughton, *One small boy*

Naunton, Sir Robert (1563–1635), politician, was born in Alderton, Suffolk, the son of Henry Naunton of Alderton and his wife, Elizabeth Asheby of Hornsby, Leicestershire.

Background and early career. The Nauntons were considered established members of the county gentry and had been so for well over two centuries. Henry Naunton was master of horse to the dowager duchess of Suffolk, while Elizabeth Asheby had a brother who became a valued member of the diplomatic corps that served Elizabeth I. But it was William Naunton, Sir Robert's grandfather, who increased the family's prestige to that point. He was a lawyer who became one of the chief servants of the duke and then the dowager duchess of Suffolk. He then married a daughter of Sir Anthony Wingfield KG, a leading servant of Henry VIII. William Naunton was also the first member of the family to serve in parliament, which he did in Edward VI's initial parliament. Yet there is no escaping the fact that by the end of the sixteenth century no member of the family had achieved anything resembling national prestige. It took lifelong efforts, but Sir Robert Naunton managed to play a role on that larger stage. He was not blessed with a flamboyant personality or great wealth. Surviving pictures from his middle age do not show a handsome individual, but rather a small, bald man whose head seems too large for his body. He was conscientious rather than creative, so his achievements came through persistence, patronage, and luck.

In the 1580s Naunton began his career at Cambridge University. Starting as a fellow-commoner at Trinity College, in November 1582 he was elected a scholar and graduated BA that same year. A minor fellow in October 1585, in March 1586 he became a major fellow, shortly before proceeding MA. Then approaching thirty, he looked for political advancement outside the university. He thought he had found it with his uncle Sir William Asheby, the English ambassador to Scotland, only to discover that his first mission was to help arrange the diplomat's retirement. The success of that venture meant another five years at Cambridge.

In the mid-1590s Naunton tried his luck once again. In hopes of impressing a patron who would advance his career, he worked on the continent as a political agent for the earl of Essex. Under the pretence of acting as a private tutor of a rich young gentleman named Vernon who was travelling abroad for his education, he spied on the French and the Spanish. He fooled no one with his cover story and had to endure a constant stream of barbed remarks from those who resented his undertaking. Yet, thanks to a series of Frenchmen and Spaniards who could not resist bragging about their nations' plans and to his gift for observing detail, for three years he managed to pass along highly praised intelligence to his patron. Unfortunately neither the earl nor the queen had any more satisfying or lucrative way of using his talents. As a result, by 1598 once again he had returned to the university. He then transferred his fellowship from Trinity College to Trinity Hall and became university orator. In April 1603 it was in this role that he greeted James I as he made his way toward London. With the new reign he launched one final, sustained effort to seek effective patronage and achieve high national office. It would take him another fifteen years of playing the courtier to achieve his goal.

Naunton began his efforts under Sir Robert Cecil's patronage and in 1604 began modestly enough as the public orator on the earl of Rutland's embassy to the court of King Christian IV of Denmark. Naunton was not a success. None the less, the following year Cecil found him a seat in the Commons for the Cornish borough of Helston. In 1612 he did become one of a small group of private secretaries employed by Cecil (now earl of Salisbury), only to have his patron die within six months.

Naunton spent the next four years fruitlessly seeking another patron. He tried his cousin Sir Ralph Winwood, the ambassador to the Dutch republic, who eventually became one of the secretaries of state. He also tried King James's favourite, Sir Robert Carr, apparently relying on John Packer, Carr's secretary, as a contact. Neither effort elicited a permanent political appointment. About all he had to show for these years was a knighthood that he received in September 1614 and a seat in the government borough of Camelford in the so-called Addled Parliament of 1614. However, in July 1616 his luck began to change. In that month he became a master of requests and in November he was appointed surveyor of the court of wards. With Carr's disgrace, Packer became secretary to another distant cousin of Naunton, George Villiers, who eventually became the duke of Buckingham. The two posts for Naunton came through Villiers's influence, and only two years later, in January 1618, James I made Naunton secretary of state and a member of the privy council in succession to Sir Ralph Winwood, who had died the previous year.

Secretary of state Shortly after Naunton became secretary of state he married Penelope Lowther (*née* Perrot), a widow with two children. As a result of this marriage he found he was closely related to several noblemen including his brother-in-law James Hay, the earl of Carlisle, one of the king's leading diplomats. Naunton and his wife had only one child, a daughter, Penelope (*bap.* 1620, *d.* in or before 1647), who survived to adulthood. She would later marry Paul, second Viscount Bayning, and then Philip Herbert, later fifth earl of Pembroke.

Through all of Naunton's frustrations both in and out of office he maintained a deep and public commitment to the protestant cause. The mainstays of his faith were the fostering of an educated, preaching clergy and a profound suspicion of papal influence in England and elsewhere.

His approach to religion had political implications. He was convinced that his brand of protestantism would never be secure as long as the Habsburg rulers of Spain and their allies remained the chief powers on the continent. Although he was far from pro-French, the weakness of the French monarchy during most of his lifetime made him willing to accept an Anglo-French alliance, if that was the best way to limit imperial Spain and its papist designs. As the Thirty Years' War got underway, in his new role as secretary of state his commitment to the protestant cause saw him very active in trying to forward the interest of King James's daughter and son-in-law, Elizabeth and Frederick, the erstwhile queen and king of Bohemia.

As secretary Naunton was jointly responsible with his colleagues, first Sir Thomas Lake and then Sir George Calvert, for taking care of the king's correspondence, both foreign and domestic, managing the affairs of the privy council, supervising the English diplomatic corps, and directing secret service operations. One secretary usually remained in attendance on the ever-wandering James I, while the second looked after matters in Whitehall. By general consensus Naunton was effective enough as secretary to provoke dangerous enemies. As a result, although officially he occupied this office until January 1623, beginning in January 1621 he was suspended from his post and placed under house arrest. The author of his disgrace was the Spanish ambassador, Count Gondomar, who forced James to repudiate both Naunton and an exploratory enquiry about a French bride for Prince Charles. Naunton was the instrument as well as the victim of a scheme that his king had initiated. James wanted to make the Spanish nervous about the outcome of the long-drawn-out marriage negotiations for Charles to obtain the hand of a Habsburg princess. When Gondomar heard the story of Naunton's secret approach to the French he called the English king's bluff and threatened to break off all discussion of a Spanish match. As a condition for continuing negotiations, the ambassador then demanded that James provide some evidence of good faith. Even though Naunton had been no more than the willing royal agent in this affair, his suspension was the gesture the Spaniard was willing to accept on behalf of his government and king.

Judging by the fate of other disgraced officials during James I's reign, Naunton should have been forced from the national political scene. But he had one last piece of good fortune. In 1624, when continuing difficulties in arranging the marriage between Charles and the Infanta Maria at last compelled James to abandon his pro-Spanish stance, some of the highest officials at court were either dismissed or demoted. Thanks to his image as a martyr for the anti-Spanish cause and his cousin Buckingham's patronage, Naunton regained favour. First, in the 1624 parliament, he was elected to the Commons for Cambridge University, the seat he had held in 1621. While he served for the university again in 1625, in 1626 he went on to hold the prestigious seat of county member for Suffolk. Part of the reason for his success stemmed from 1624 when he became master of the court of wards, a position both profitable and potentially influential. The master was the chief judicial officer in a court that disposed of the wardships of upwards of 100 rich orphans each year. Naunton remained and prospered in the post for just about a decade, only leaving it weeks before his death.

Final years Although as master of the court of wards Naunton may have been one of the crown's highest officials, by the 1630s his political views were so far out of the mainstream of the royal court that he had virtually no influence with the chief policy-makers of the government. Beginning in 1625, when Charles I succeeded his father, but especially after 1628, the year in which the duke of Buckingham was assassinated, Naunton found himself without a sympathetic listener among the royal ministers who had the king's ear. After the duke's assassination only the earl of Carlisle, now the first gentleman of the bedchamber, had anything like the same degree of access to the monarch that Buckingham had possessed and therefore the potential to provide patronage and protection. Of equal importance to Naunton, the earl's protestantism was unassailable. Carlisle, however, refused to establish a patronage network, even for his relations, leaving Naunton with no secure political connections.

In this era when few people lived beyond their fifties, Naunton was fortunate enough to have reached his seventy-first year before declining health made him vulnerable. By summer 1634 he was no longer attending to business at the court of wards and was obviously quite ill, and at this point an effort to oust him began in earnest. After clearing the field of potential competitors, Lord Cottington approached Charles I with the novel idea of forming a royal commission to investigate whether Naunton's poor health was hindering the operations of the court.

All the evidence points to these final months of his life, with the threat of an investigation hanging over him, as the time when Naunton wrote the final version of his one and only book, *Fragmenta regalia*. Under the guise of presenting a series of character sketches and observations of Elizabeth I and her court, he offered advice on a wide variety of governmental matters in this manuscript which he planned to present to the king. While ostensibly the work was designed to offer Charles I solutions to practical problems, in all likelihood its real aim was to demonstrate to the king that his current master of the court of wards still had a functioning mind, regardless of the state of his body.

In the absence of dated drafts it is difficult to tell when Naunton began his work. Even so, the evidence points toward the last six months of 1634 as the period in which it took on its final form. In discussing the earl of Essex, he mentioned Sir Henry Wotton's views on the man which were put forth in his 'Parallel of the duke of Buckingham and the earl of Essex'. Although Wotton had planned to have the work published in 1633, it did not appear in print in his lifetime. Instead it was widely circulated in manuscript during summer 1634 (*Earl of Strafforde's Letters and Dispatches*, 1.265). Naunton and Wotton were acquainted, but were never close friends. Thus it seems unlikely that Naunton could have obtained an early look at the work. Most probably he acquired a manuscript copy in the general distribution. If summer 1634 is the earliest possible date of the final composition for *Fragmenta regalia*, December 1634 is almost certainly the latest. On the 24th of that month the aged countess of Leicester finally died. In discussing the earl, Naunton described his countess as yet living.

In the end Naunton did not achieve his purpose in writing the book. Charles I revoked his patent of office in mid-March 1635 and Naunton died before the end of the month and was buried at the church near his principal manor of Leatheringham, Suffolk. His wife outlived him.

Evaluation During an era when government servants were often noted for their ability to drain the royal coffers to serve their own interests, Naunton was something of an exception. Starting as early as 1601, when a couple of people managed to swindle him out of over £1000, he showed a weakness in personal finance. In 1632, at the very end of his career, despite the fact that he was master of the court of wards, he lost the valuable wardship of his stepson to a royal favourite. In his will he indicated that he had left over £7000 owed him in the form of an uncollected government pension. He was also the only long-serving master of the court of wards who did not receive a peerage or did not have one when entering the office. Yet his wealth was by no means insubstantial. When his daughter married Paul, Viscount Bayning, she received a dowry of £4000.

Leaving money to one side, in one form or another Naunton was a royal servant for over two decades. It is difficult to argue that he deserved to play a more major role than he did. His perspective was too narrow, his methods too slow, to permit him to become a policy-maker. Yet in the final analysis he was a royal servant worth having. He was an able administrator with a particular talent for co-ordinating other people's activities and for acting as an intermediary. The field of foreign affairs was one of his particular strengths. His problem was that whereas James I found a way to fit him into his government, without the duke of Buckingham's protection, Charles I never did.

ROY E. SCHREIBER

Sources R. Schreiber, *The political career of Sir Robert Naunton* (1981) • R. Naunton, *Fragmenta regalia* (1641) • *The letters of John Chamberlain*, ed. N. E. McClure, 2 vols. (1939) • G. E. Aylmer, *The king's servants: the civil service of Charles I, 1625–1642* (1961) • T. M. Hofmann, 'Naunton, William', HoP, *Commons, 1509–58*, 3.2–3 • Venn, *Alum. Cant.*, 1/3 • BL, Egerton MSS 2592, 2593, 2598 • LPL, Bacon MS 654 • J. Howell, *Epistolae Ho-elianae*, ed. J. Jacobs, 2 vols. (1890–92) • *Members of parliament: return to two orders of the honorable the House of Commons*, House of Commons, 1 (1878) • *CSP dom.*, 1611–18 • J. Nichols, *The progresses, processions, and magnificent festivities of King James I, his royal consort, family and court*, 3 (1828) • T. L. Moir, *The Addled Parliament of 1614* (1958) • M. B. Rex, *University representation in England, 1604–1690* (1954) • D. H. Willson, *Privy councillors in the House of Commons, 1604–1629* (1940) • PRO, SP 14/70 • PRO, SP 16/121 • G. Radcliffe, *The earl of Strafforde's letters and dispatches, with an essay towards his life*, ed. W. Knowler, 2 vols. (1739) • Hunt. L., MS EL 6055 • PRO, Wards 9/98 • *DNB*

Archives Folger, 'Fragmenta regalia' | BL, letters to Lord Doncaster and others, Egerton MSS 1589, 2592–2593, 2594, 2598 • BL, Harley MSS 1580, 1581 • Boughton House, Northamptonshire, Winwood's original state papers, vol. 8, WARDS 9/93, 95, 98–100, 162, 163, 207, 275, 417, 422, 426, 535, 543–46 • LPL, letters to Anthony Bacon • PRO, E 403/1711–1716, 1723–1728 • PRO, 30/53/1–4 • PRO, 31/3/53 and 54 • PRO, SP 14/99, 111, 118, 119, 139, 146, 158, 164, 168, 169, 171, 172, 181 • PRO, SP 16/104, 166, 121, 126, 192, 284 • PRO, SP 81/14–16, 19, 20 • PRO, SP 84/73, 79, 82–89, 91–99, 106

Likenesses R. Cooper, stipple (aged fifty-two), BM, NPG; repro. in J. Caulfield, ed., *Memoirs of Sir Robert Naunton* (1814) • S. de Passe, line engraving, BM, NPG

Wealth at death bequeathed £2749 cash, not necessarily supported by estate; chain of gold and diamonds; manors in four counties; two houses; gardens and stables in Westminster; debts totalling £7200 owing to him, incl. from court of wards and exchequer: will, 3 March 1635

Navanagar. *See* Ranjitsinhji Vibhaji, maharaja jam sahib of Navanagar (1872–1933).

Nawanagar, Ranjitsinhji Vibhaji. *See* Ranjitsinhji Vibhaji, maharaja jam sahib of Navanagar (1872–1933).

Nayler, Sir George (*bap.* 1764, *d.* 1831), herald, was baptized on 29 June 1764 at Stonehouse, Gloucestershire, the fifth of six sons and seventh of nine children of George Nayler (1721/2–1780) of Stonehouse and subsequently of Stroud, Gloucestershire, surgeon, one of the coroners of the county, and his wife, Sarah (1723/4–1802), daughter of John Park of Clitheroe, Lancashire, schoolmaster. The text of the patent granting arms to Nayler when York herald in 1808 states that his family bore the same arms as the Nailours of Offord Darcy, Huntingdonshire. No descent has been proved from that county and it is possible that Nayler's paternal ancestors came from Winwick in Lancashire.

Originally a miniature painter, Nayler began his heraldic career in 1792, the year he married, on 18 September at St Leonard, Shoreditch, London, Charlotte Wilkes Williams, illegitimate daughter of Sir John Guise (1733–1794) of Highnam Court, Gloucestershire, first baronet. A loan from a clergyman named Fielding enabled him to purchase for £1300 the resignation of John Suffield Brown from the office of genealogist of the Order of the Bath, with which went the position of Blanc Coursier herald, and Nayler was appointed on 15 June 1792. In 1793 by payment of £60 he acquired a place in the College of Arms by the resignation of Lancaster herald, becoming Bluemantle pursuivant on 29 November. The accidental deaths of Somerset and York heralds on 3 February 1794 in the Haymarket Theatre led to his appointment as York herald on 13 March 1794.

The statutes of the Order of the Bath gave Nayler as its genealogist the power to examine and enter pedigrees and arms of knights and esquires. Previous genealogists had not exercised this right but in September 1793, being sure of his appointment, Nayler had written to Sir Isaac Heard (1730–1822), Garter, stating that he intended to do so. In June 1794 the letter was read at a chapter meeting in his presence: the other officers of arms wrongly thought that he was claiming the sole right to record Bath pedigrees in the College of Arms, but Nayler opened his own, separate vellum registers. He sought to strengthen his position in 1795 with a warrant from Frederick, duke of York, grand master of the Order of the Bath, setting down the fees which he might claim. In 1799 he put forward to

Sir George Nayler (*bap.* 1764, *d.* 1831), by Joseph Lee, 1833 (after Sir William Beechey, exh. RA 1826)

the secretary of state for the Home department a draft royal warrant which would command him as genealogist to enter all arms and pedigrees of members of the order since its creation in 1725. The other officers of arms opposed this and the opinion of the law officers of the crown was sought on Nayler's right to maintain separate Bath records. This they acknowledged, while insisting that all his evidence must come from the records of the College of Arms. A compromise was supposedly agreed in the attorney-general's chambers in 1804, but Nayler continued to make entries without reference to the College of Arms. On 4 June 1806 he was appointed inspector of regimental colours with responsibility for producing regimental badges.

On 25 November 1813 Nayler's standing was enhanced by a knighthood bestowed at Carlton House by the prince regent, possibly as a consolation for failing to be appointed Garter's deputy to invest the tsar with the Order of the Garter. In 1814 he brought proceedings against Sir Isaac Heard, Garter, for invading his rights by soliciting business from knights of the Bath. He was initially awarded £1000 damages, but this was reduced to 1*s*. by Mr Serjeant Bosanquet, who confirmed that Garter could not interfere with cases where Nayler was already employed. Each side bore its own costs of the referral.

Nayler's suggestion of an enlargement of the Order of the Bath was achieved by a royal warrant in 1815. This confirmed Nayler in his offices, and he was appointed officer of arms attendant upon the knights commanders and companions. Further disputes with the other heralds ensued. His interest in orders of chivalry is reflected in his

creation as king of arms of two newly created orders, the Royal Guelphic Order on 12 August 1815, of which he was made a knight on 22 March 1816, and the Order of St Michael and St George on 17 November 1818. On 30 May 1820 he was promoted over three senior heralds to be Clarenceux king of arms and officiated in place of the ninety-year-old Garter as his deputy at the coronation of George IV on 19 July 1821, the last to include the full ceremony of the banquet in Westminster Hall. Nayler succeeded Heard as Garter on 11 May 1822 and as Garter went on missions to Denmark (1822), Portugal (1823), France (1825), and Russia (1827), to invest the sovereigns of those countries with the Order of the Garter. The king of Portugal created Nayler a knight commander of the royal Portuguese order of the Tower and Sword, and by a royal licence from George IV dated 28 May 1824 he was permitted to wear the insignia. He attended the abridged coronation of King William IV and Queen Adelaide on 8 September 1831 and died suddenly in the night of 28 October 1831 at his house at 17 Hanover Square. He was survived by his wife (*d.* 5 July 1835) and four daughters. He was buried on 9 November 1831 in his family vault at St John the Baptist, Gloucester.

Nayler's extensive library was sold by Sothebys on 16–18 April 1832. In 1833 the College of Arms bought over seventy volumes of his collections from Lady Nayler for £600. 'A history of the sovereigns of the most honourable military order of the Bath', a sumptuous manuscript executed under Naylor's direction in 1803 at a cost of over £2000—for which George III had refused to pay—was eventually presented to the College of Arms by a family connection, Robert Laurie, Clarenceux. In 1861 the prince consort, as grand master of the Order of the Bath, instructed the registrar and secretary of the order to deposit the forty-seven red morocco-bound volumes compiled by Nayler in the library of the College of Arms, where they remain. Nayler's collections also included thirty-six volumes of private acts of parliament (destroyed by enemy action in 1940) and forty-five volumes of cases before the House of Lords with pedigrees added by Nayler, now in the Guildhall Library, London. Fourteen large folio volumes of impressions from English coffin plates, 1727–1831, are now in the British Library (Add. MSS 22292–22305).

Nayler wrote little, though he contributed a paper to the Society of Antiquaries in 1795 following his election as a fellow on 27 March 1794. His most splendid printed work, *A History of the Coronation of King George IV* (4 vols.), for which he employed F. P. Stephanoff and a number of other distinguished artists, was completed after his death.

Ambitious and energetic, with the eye to produce magnificent manuscripts and ceremonial that were appreciated by George IV both as prince regent and king, Nayler possessed ability and a character that inspired widely different reactions. The Revd Mark Noble in his *History of the College of Arms* (1804) eulogized him, whereas his successor as Garter, Sir Ralph Bigland (1757–1838), wrote in 1832 that 'no man ever went out of the world with so bad a Public or Private Character' (Wagner, *Heralds of England*, 495).

THOMAS WOODCOCK

Sources W. H. Godfrey, A. Wagner, and H. Stanford London, *The College of Arms, Queen Victoria Street* (1963), 63–5 · A. Wagner, *Heralds of England: a history of the office and College of Arms* (1967), 432–49 · A. R. Wagner, *The records and collections of the College of Arms* (1952), 27–8, 39–40, 45 · *Herald and Genealogist*, 7 (1873), 72–80 · *GM*, 1st ser., 101/2 (1831), 567; 102/1 (1832), 191, 443 · grants of arms, Coll. Arms, vol. 25, pp. 54–6; vol. 33, p. 199 · patents of officers of arms, Coll. Arms, Chivalry collections · M. Noble, *A history of the College of Arms* (1804), 426, 449 · *The life and letters of … Richard Harris Barham, author of the 'Ingoldsby legends'*, 1 (1870), 184
Archives BL, impressions from coffin plates, Add. MSS 22292–22305 · Coll. Arms, collections · JRL, MSS relating to precedency and notes relating to military order of the Bath · NL Wales, MS on princes of Wales | GL · U. Nott., corresp. with fourth duke of Newcastle
Likenesses E. Scriven, stipple, in or after 1824–in or before 1831 (after W. Beechey), BM · J. Lee, miniature, 1833 (after W. Beechey, exh. RA 1826); Christies, 28 Nov 1978, lot 57 [*see illus.*] · W. Beechey, oils, Coll. Arms
Wealth at death under £18,000—personal estate: PRO, death duty registers, IR 26/1299

Nayler, James (1618–1660), Quaker preacher and writer, was born at West Ardsley, near Wakefield, in the West Riding of Yorkshire. His father seems to have been an independent farmer of some means, but nothing is known of the extent of his holdings or of the family's religious opinions. Nayler must have received some education in the local schools, since one of his opponents later mentioned meeting a former schoolfellow who had become a lawyer at Gray's Inn (Deacon, *Exact History*, 3); by whatever means, he became an able writer and lucid reasoner. He married his wife, Anne, in 1639 and settled in Wakefield, where three daughters were born during the next four years, but when the civil war broke out he left the farm in his wife's care and in 1643 enlisted in the parliamentary army.

Military service and religious conversion Little is known of Nayler's nine years of military service, first as a foot soldier under Fairfax and later, for two years, as a quartermaster in John Lambert's cavalry. Lambert afterwards described him as 'a very useful person' and 'a man of a very unblameable life and conversation, a member of a very sweet society of an independent church' (*Diary of Thomas Burton*, 1.33). Nayler is known to have been present at the Cromwellian victory at Dunbar in 1650 and to have begun by then to preach. A former officer long afterwards recalled that as he rode away from the battle,

> I found it was James Nayler preaching to the people, but with such power and reaching energy as I had not till then been witness of … I was struck with more terror before the preaching of James Nayler than I was before the battle of Dunbar, when we had nothing else to expect but to fall a prey to the swords of our enemies. (J. Gough, *A History of the People called Quakers*, 4 vols., 1789–90, 1.56)

In the following year ill health (probably consumption) forced Nayler to leave the army and return home, where he resumed farming and joined the Independent congregation of Christopher Marshall at Woodchurch. Soon afterward he encountered George Fox, who was visiting one of the groups known as Seekers who were disillusioned with the organized sects, but there is no evidence to support Fox's later suggestion that this meeting was the cause of Nayler's conversion, or 'convincement', as the Quakers preferred to call it. Certainly radical religious ideas had been widely discussed in the New Model Army, and it may be more than coincidental that Anthony Nutter, whom Fox's family had known in Leicestershire, was the minister at West Ardsley when Nayler was growing up. Nayler's own account, during an interrogation in 1652, was that while ploughing he heard a voice commanding 'Get thee out from thy kindred, and from thy father's house', and after a brief hesitation, during which he fell seriously ill, he left home on impulse for a life of itinerant preaching:

> Going gateward with a friend from my own house, having on an old suit, without any money, having neither taken leave of wife or children, not thinking then of any journey, I was commanded to go into the west not knowing whither I should go nor what I was to do there. (J. Nayler, *Saul's Errand to Damascus*, 1654, 30)

At the same interrogation he was asked whether he had been among the Leveller-inspired mutineers who were put down in 1649 at Burford in Oxfordshire, and he replied, 'I was then in the north, and was never taxed for any mutiny, or any other thing while I served the parliament' (ibid.). He was expelled from communion by Marshall's congregation, which regarded him as having removed himself, and he soon became a leading figure in the nascent movement that first called itself the Children of the Light and later became the Society of Friends, known to their detractors, as Nayler observed, as 'the Quakers as thou scornfully calls us' (J. Nayler, *The Railer Rebuked*, 1655, 7).

Proselytizing and conflict with the authorities From 1652 to 1656 Nayler was increasingly prominent as an eloquent preacher and charismatic leader in a movement that explicitly repudiated hierarchy. It also repudiated formal theology, holding that orthodox Calvinism made a fetish of the scriptures and subjected believers to the moral and intellectual authority of a professional ministry. The Quaker view was that modern individuals of either sex could receive the same prophetic inspiration that the biblical writers had and, guided by the inner light, could express the Word with full authority. 'The true ministry', Nayler wrote, 'is the gift of Jesus Christ, and needs no addition of human help and learning … and therefore he chused herdsmen, fishermen, and plowmen, and such like; and he gave them an immediate call, without the leave of man' (*Saul's Errand*, 18). He himself had been a ploughman, and commented pointedly that when the apostles proclaimed the gospel 'they were counted fools and madmen by the learned generation' (Whitehead, 43).

As the puritan establishment consolidated its position, radical sects were increasingly regarded as transgressive. Marginal groups such as the Levellers, the Diggers, and the shadowy Ranters were efficiently suppressed. Harder to control were the Quakers, who began to spread their message widely throughout the north, acquiring a valuable protector in Margaret Fell of Swarthmoor Hall in Lancashire, who soon took on the role of unofficial co-ordinator of the movement. Nayler and Fox stayed together at Swarthmoor in 1652 and succeeded in persuading Margaret Fell's husband, Judge Thomas Fell, though he did not become a convert, to extend his protection. The established ministers were less welcoming. Francis Higginson of Kirkby Stephen, Westmorland, whose *Brief Relation of the Irreligion of the Northern Quakers* (1653) is a valuable source of information on their early activities, singled out Nayler as one of 'Satan's seeds-men' (p. 1) who were engaged in sowing the tares of wickedness in northern fields. The travelling evangelists were particularly repugnant to the ministers because they made a habit of interrupting religious services to proclaim their message, and demanded abolition of the benefices and tithes that supported the 'hireling priests', as they called them. It was a fixed Quaker principle to accept no payment for preaching and to address any who might listen, often speaking in the open air, rather than to form settled congregations. When the Westmorland ministers complained that unauthorized preachers were invading their territory, Nayler replied, 'It is true, our habitation is with the Lord, and our country is not of this world' (J. Nayler, *Several Petitions Answered*, 1653, 5). Some three dozen Lancashire ministers appeared at Lancaster quarter sessions to lodge a complaint against Fox and Nayler, but Judge Fell interceded on their behalf and they were released.

Hostilities continued as local people were encouraged to harass the unwelcome visitors, sometimes stoning and beating them in unruly mobs, and soon Nayler and Fox were arrested at Kirkby Stephen and imprisoned at Appleby, Westmorland, until April of 1653. For the rest of that year and throughout 1654 Nayler travelled and preached extensively in the north, winning admiration for the power and cogency of his speaking; Fox remembered an occasion when he conducted a disputation with some ministers and the crowd cried 'A Nayler, a Nayler hath confuted them all' (*Journal of George Fox*, 223). For the most part the Quakers managed during this time to stay out of trouble with the law. In a typical incident at Chesterfield the local minister tried to provoke a debate inside the church, Nayler refused to enter in order to avoid charges of disrupting the service, and the mayor agreed that he had done nothing wrong.

Nayler's writings The early Quakers insisted on the primacy of the spoken word, which was expected to be spontaneous rather than to follow a set text, and as a result were reluctant to present their beliefs in discursive form. Their critics, however, were given to frequent and angry publication, and it was soon apparent that their charges needed to be answered. Accordingly, scores of controversial works began to flow from Quaker pens, and Nayler became the most prolific and persuasive writer in the movement. Most of his nearly fifty publications were short pamphlets, but at various times he produced longer works, notably *A True Discovery of Faith* (1655) and *Love to the Lost* (1656). In 1716 George Whitehead, who had known Nayler during his last years, published an extensive selection of his writings as *A collection of sundry books, epistles and papers, written by James Nayler … with an impartial relation of the most remarkable transactions relating to his life*. Modern

scholars commonly refer to this volume as Nayler's *Works*, but misleadingly so, since Whitehead omitted many pieces that seemed dated or excessively controversial from the perspective of half a century later, and silently emended Nayler's texts at many points.

Identifying himself as 'one of England's prophets' (Whitehead, 99), Nayler sought not only to defend the socially disruptive behaviour of his colleagues but also to expound an antinomian theological position that stood in explicit opposition to the Calvinist doctrines of predestination and sin. He and his colleagues found unacceptable the orthodox view that Christ had vicariously paid the penalty for original sin and was now far away in heaven while the human race continued to grovel in enslavement to sin, from which only a few of the elect would be set free through unmerited grace. The Quaker position was that Christ was fully and immediately present in all true believers, who were admittedly a small minority of the population, and that in consequence they were literally without sin, or at least were well established on the road to perfection. 'It is true', Nayler conceded, 'the light is but manifest in the creatures by degrees, but the least degree is perfect in its measure' (Whitehead, 117). To the puritan ministers this suggestion of sinlessness was blasphemous, and they alleged further that some Quakers claimed to be personally identified with Christ. The issue was of more than theoretical significance, since the *cause célèbre* that would make Nayler notorious was to hinge on it. Nayler himself always asserted that 'flesh and blood is an enemy' (ibid., 730), and that in so far as he and others did embody the spirit of Christ, they were dead to individual selfhood and participated in an impersonal condition of divine enlightenment. But he was reluctant to define his views in formal terms, which made them hard to pin down and easy to misrepresent or travesty. When an admirer once expected to hear him refute some theological objections, he told her, 'Feed not on knowledge, it is as truly forbidden to thee as ever it was to Eve … for who feeds on knowledge dies to the innocent life' (J. Whiting, *Persecution Expos'd*, 1715, 177).

It should be emphasized that Nayler's chief influence was in speaking, not in writing, and that unlike puritans, who collected and published their sermons, Quakers considered it important never to write them down. Occasionally, however, in Nayler's usually sober prose, one can catch a hint of what his prophetic manner must have been like:

> The thing that was seen concerning Newcastle: all his pillars to be dry, and his trees to be bare, and much nakedness … for it's a stony ground, and there is much briars and thorns about her, and many trees have grown wild long, and have scarce earth to cover their roots, but their roots are seen, and how they stand in the stones, and these trees bears no fruit, but bears moss, and much wind pierces through, and clatters them together, and makes the trees shake, but still the roots are held among the stones, and are bald and naked.
> (J. Nayler, *A Discovery of the Man of Sin*, 1655, 51)

An impressive tribute to Nayler's oral powers survives

from an unexpected source: his furious opponent John Deacon conceded that he was 'a man of exceeding quick wit and sharp apprehension, enriched with that commendable gift of good oratory with a very delightful melody in his utterance' (Deacon, *Exact History*, 4).

London and Bristol As the Quaker movement spread to the west and south, Bristol proved to be a fertile ground for proselytizing, but London remained an intimidating stronghold. Nayler arrived there in June of 1655 and reported to Margaret Fell that he found it 'a great and wicked place' (Swarthmore MSS, 3.81), but he quickly proved to be the most effective Quaker proselytizer in London. Soon his colleagues were reporting that 'his fame begins to spread in the city, seeing that he hath had public disputes with many', and that 'a great love is begotten in many towards him' (Barclay, 335–6). A devout Baptist named Rebecca Travers was converted when three Baptist ministers debated with Nayler and 'were so far from getting the victory that she could feel his words smote them' (J. Whiting, *Persecution Expos'd*, 1715, 176). During this period Fox came infrequently to London, preferring to continue his travels in the countryside, and by 1656 many outsiders regarded Nayler as the movement's leader. He gave up travelling for the most part, though at least one visit to Yorkshire is recorded, during which he presumably saw his wife and family, from whom he had been separated for four years.

By the summer of 1656 tensions among the London Quakers unexpectedly surfaced, a development that caused confusion and alarm since there was no established system of organization or discipline. A group of women gathered around Nayler, led by Martha Simmonds, wife of Thomas Simmonds and sister of Giles Calvert, the two leading Quaker publishers. Women enjoyed an unusual degree of freedom in the Quaker movement, and Martha Simmonds was an intelligent and independent person, author of several moving pamphlets about spiritual seeking and apocalyptic hopes. This group now began to disrupt Quaker meetings, just as Quakers had been accustomed to disrupting the meetings of others, and to promote Nayler as *de facto* leader in preference to Edward Burrough and Francis Howgill, who had originally developed the work in London. The nature of the dispute that followed is difficult to reconstruct today, but it appears that the 'turbulent' women, as Whitehead later described them (Whitehead, vi), demanded that Nayler deliver a 'judgment' against Burrough and Howgill, and that when he refused to comply he suffered a psychological collapse, lying trembling on a table for several nights. Trembling, of course, was an accepted indication of spiritual experience, and Nayler himself had discussed at some length the scriptural passages in which 'the holy men of God do witness quaking and trembling, and roaring, and weeping, and fasting, and tears; but the world knows not the saints' conditions' (ibid., 57). Some of his colleagues concluded that Martha Simmonds and her friends were exerting a dangerous hold over him, and at the end of July

they attempted to extricate him by taking him to a meeting in Bristol. When Simmonds followed she was prevented from seeing him, and he was encouraged to go on to Launceston in Cornwall to visit Fox, who had been in prison there for six months, his trial on various charges being indefinitely postponed because, like all Quakers, he refused to swear an oath or to remove his hat in deference to the magistrate. Nayler's companions on the journey observed that he seemed seriously depressed and uncommunicative, and they never reached Launceston, since they were arrested on the road and confined in Exeter gaol under the terms of an act for the suppression of rogues and vagabonds.

Fasting as an expression of spiritual purity was a common practice among Quakers, and Nayler now undertook an extended fast of several weeks which greatly weakened him. At this time Martha Simmonds travelled to Launceston to intercede with Fox, or rather to accuse him; Fox wrote Nayler an indignant letter reporting that 'she came singing in my face, inventing words' and informing him that his heart was rotten (Swarthmore MS 3.193). In September Fox was at last released from prison and proceeded to Exeter, where he demanded that Nayler acknowledge subservience, and when Nayler refused to kiss his hand told him insultingly to kiss his foot instead. They parted bitterly, and Fox wrote Nayler a strong letter of reproof: 'James, thou separates thyself from Friends and draws a company after thee, and separated from the power of the Lord God' (RS Friends, Lond., Portfolio 24, no. 36). Long afterward Fox remembered this episode as a critical threat to the movement: 'So that after I had been warring with the world, now there was a wicked spirit risen up amongst Friends to war against' (*Journal of George Fox*, 268).

Martha Simmonds meanwhile took employment as nurse to the wife of Major-General Desborough, who interceded with her brother Oliver Cromwell to secure the release of the Quakers from Exeter gaol, which took place on 20 October. Four days later Nayler and a small party of companions, four men and three women, entered Bristol in a pelting deluge of rain and enacted the symbolic 'sign' that made him immediately notorious. Nayler was mounted on a horse, and his companions cast garments before him while singing 'Holy, holy, holy, Lord God of Sabbaoth' (Deacon, *Grand Impostor*, 1–2). This was unmistakably an imitation of Christ's entry into Jerusalem on Palm Sunday, and the group, from which the Bristol Quakers quickly dissociated themselves, were arrested and charged with blasphemy. It was noticed that in spite of the downpour Nayler's followers went bareheaded, although Quakers normally refused to doff their hats to anyone except when praying to God. And two letters from one of Nayler's companions, Hannah Stranger, were discovered that addressed him in extravagant language drawn from the Song of Solomon and seemed to suggest that his followers regarded him as divine. In an especially damaging postscript Hannah's husband John had written, 'Thy name is no more to be called James but Jesus' (ibid., 11). Fox's letter to Nayler was also found and served to exonerate him from any suspicion of complicity with the Nayler group.

A group of Bristol ministers interrogated Nayler and left a full record of the proceedings. In their opinion he consistently evaded the questioners when pressed to declare whether or not he considered himself the actual Son of God. But in fact what he consistently maintained, just as he had in print, was that all of the saints were sons of God, and that although he himself might enjoy an unusual measure of divine inspiration, he was not personally divine. His followers, however, were less cautious. Martha Simmonds testified that she had been quite right to kneel to Nayler as 'the Son of Righteousness', and Dorcas Erbury not only identified him as 'the only begotten Son of God' but startlingly asserted that she had died in Exeter gaol and been raised from the dead by Nayler (Deacon, *Grand Impostor*, 26, 34). The Quakers were accustomed to celebrate miracles of healing, in defiance of the puritans, who held that miracles had ceased after the early years of the church, and Nayler did not exactly deny this claim. It was also alleged that he had deliberately grown his hair and beard to resemble traditional portraits of Christ, which may possibly have been true, although no reliable portraits survive and the few contemporary descriptions of his appearance are not only bland and unremarkable, but usually fail to mention the beard:

> He is a man of a ruddy complexion, brown hair, and slank [lank], hanging a little below his jaw-bones; of an indifferent height; not very long visaged, nor very round; close shaven; a sad downlook, and melancholy countenance; a little band, close to his collar, with no bandstrings; his hat hanging over his brows; his nose neither high nor low, but rising a little in the middle.   (ibid., 44)

It was also alleged that at various times he had had improper relations with women, a charge which he indignantly denied, and for which no persuasive evidence was ever brought forward.

A careful reading of Nayler's responses makes clear that he meant to enact a symbolic representation, a 'prophetical act', as the presbyterian Richard Baxter disapprovingly called the public exhibitions that many Quakers performed from time to time. Baxter accurately grasped that on this occasion 'their chief leader James Nayler acted the part of Christ at Bristol, according to much of the history of the Gospel' (*Reliquiae Baxterianae*, ed. M. Sylvester, 1696, 77). Undoubtedly Nayler did believe that he had been charged with a special prophetic mission; in a pamphlet co-authored with Martha Simmonds he had recently written, 'A sign and wonder thou hast made me' (*O England, thy Time is Come*, 1656, 12). His intention seems to have been to testify to the ongoing presence of Christ in all believers, by contrast with puritans, who were content to wait for a second coming at some possibly remote date, and it seems clear that he did not think that he was personally the Messiah. There were many in positions of authority, however, who had been looking for an opportunity to repress the increasingly subversive Quakers, and Nayler furnished them with the test case they were waiting for. Instead of being tried locally at Bristol, therefore, he and several of his companions were summoned to London to face an investigation by parliament.

Trial Just seven days after the incident in Bristol, the recently elected second protectorate parliament appointed a large investigating committee of fifty-five members, which began its examination of Nayler and the more intransgent of his followers on 15 November. His responses to questioning in London were essentially the same as they had been at Bristol, and certainly did not indicate that he thought he was Christ. 'Being asked, if any prayed to Christ in him, whether he did disown it? [he] answered, "As a creature I do disown it"' (Rich and Tomlinson, 19). He stated unequivocally that in Bristol 'I was commanded by the Lord to suffer such things to be done by me, as to the outward, as a sign, not as I am a creature' (ibid., 11). Nevertheless, the committee's report concluded that he was guilty on two counts, of impersonating Christ and of claiming divine status. 'First, James Nayler did assume the gesture, words, honour, worship, and miracles of our blessed Saviour. Secondly, the names and incommunicable attributes and titles of our blessed Saviour' (ibid., 3–4).

Under the 1653 'Instrument of government' it was far from clear that parliament had the authority to conduct a trial, and the proceeding that followed reflected a constitutional struggle among various factions, but in practice—if not in principle—it was indeed a trial. The debate occupied the attention of the entire body for ten days and was conducted in secrecy, so that outsiders found it hard to learn what was going on, but fortunately for later historians an obscure MP named Thomas Burton recorded an unusually full account of it in a diary that came to light in the nineteenth century. The seldom enforced Blasphemy Act of 1650 seemed to fit the case, prescribing punishment for anyone claiming 'to be very God', and Nayler accordingly was indicted for 'horrid blasphemy'. The act, however, provided an inconveniently mild punishment of a mere six months in prison, and most MPs wanted a harsher one, which meant that they would in effect be legislating new rules to which Nayler would be subjected *post facto*. 'I conceive the judgment of parliament is so sovereign', Robert Beake said, 'that it may declare that to be an offence which never was an offence before' (*Diary of Thomas Burton*, 1.58).

Given the nature of the charges, the debate frequently turned on fine points of theology, and a number of speakers invoked laws and penalties from the Old Testament rather than from England, but it was clear throughout that the fundamental issue was political. Philip Skippon, a staunch presbyterian and the major-general in charge of the London area, spoke for many when he complained that Cromwell's policy of toleration had fostered a Quaker threat:

> Their great growth and increase is too notorious, both in England and Ireland; their principles strike at both ministry and magistracy. Many opinions are in this nation (all contrary to the government) which would join in one to destroy you, if it should please God to deliver the sword into their hands   (*Diary of Thomas Burton*, 1.24–5)

It would be wrong, however, to conclude as some historians have done that religious arguments were always political ones in disguise. For most MPs they were both at once, and even Nayler's old commander Lambert, while recalling his good behaviour in military service, took the charges very seriously:

> How he comes (by pride or otherwise) to be puffed up with this opinion I cannot determine. But this may be a warning to us all, to work out our salvation with fear and trembling. I shall be as ready to give my testimony against him as any body, if it appear to be blasphemy.   (ibid., 1.33)

Nayler was called in to testify yet again, and again declared that he had enacted a 'sign' without mistaking himself for Christ. He also rejected the imputation of political subversion: 'I am one that daily prays that magistracy may be established in this nation. I do not, nor dare affront authority' (*Diary of Thomas Burton*, 1.48). A few members were prepared to accept his account, but the majority were determined on punishment and disagreed only as to its extent. The house voted in the affirmative on two resolutions, 'That James Nayler upon the whole matter in fact, is guilty of horrid blasphemy; that James Nayler is a grand impostor, and seducer of the people' (Rich and Tomlinson, 30). By the narrow margin of 96 to 82, a motion to put him to death was defeated, and after further debate it was resolved on 16 December that Nayler be whipped through the streets by the hangman, exposed in the pillory, have his tongue bored through with a red-hot iron, and have the letter B (for blasphemy) branded on his forehead. He was then to be returned to Bristol and compelled to repeat his ride in reverse while facing the rear of his horse, and finally he was to be committed to solitary confinement in Bridewell for an indefinite period. Nayler was brought back to hear the sentence but was not permitted to speak. While he was being led away, however, he made a short and moving statement that was reported in the Quaker *True Narrative* (and in similar words in Burton's *Diary*): 'He that hath prepared the body will enable me to suffer, and I pray that he may not lay it to your charge' (Rich and Tomlinson, 57).

Nayler's punishment was carried out in every detail, including 300 lashes that tore all the skin off his back, and the concluding scene at the pillory was witnessed by a large crowd that included the diarist Burton, who approved of what was done but admired Nayler's stoicism:

> He put out his tongue very willingly, but shrinked a little when the iron came upon his forehead. He was pale when he came out of the pillory, but high-coloured after tongue-boring … Nayler embraced his executioner, and behaved himself very handsomely and patiently.   (*Diary of Thomas Burton*, 1.266)

Nayler's old enemy Deacon added that when his forehead was branded it 'gave a little flash of smoke' (Deacon, *Exact History*, 37), and a Quaker eyewitness emphasized his saintly demeanour: 'James never so much as winced, but bore it with astonishing and heart-melting patience' (*Memoirs of … James Nayler*, 69). Curiously, his companions

were permitted to join him at the pillory. Martha Simmonds, Hannah Stranger, and Dorcas Erbury took up positions that observers saw as alluding to the women at the cross, and the eccentric merchant Robert Rich licked his wounds and put up a notice that read 'This is the King of the Jews'. In the opinion of his supporters Nayler's prophetic sign had now produced its logical conclusion, a symbolic crucifixion.

Final years Nearly all Quakers hastened to repudiate Nayler, whose story was to become a regrettable 'fall' in accounts by later historians, though a few of his allies continued to visit him in prison when the solitary confinement was occasionally relaxed, and his wife journeyed from Yorkshire in an unsuccessful attempt to secure his release. For most of his imprisonment he was kept at hard labour picking hemp, but he managed to continue to write on spiritual topics with his customary clarity and energy, and a number of his pamphlets were smuggled out of prison and published. In a few places he referred allusively to the events in which he had taken part and expressed regret for any damage the movement had suffered; later writers misleadingly but understandably interpreted his reaction as a wholesale 'repentance'. If anything he seems to have felt that his symbolic gesture had been cruelly misunderstood by those who ought to have appreciated it, 'when all relations, friends and acquaintance are become farther off than strangers, and whatever thing the creature seeks to for comfort turns against him and adds to his grief' (Whitehead, 541). In September of 1659, nearly three years after Nayler entered Bridewell, the Rump Parliament declared an amnesty for Quaker prisoners and he was set free. He was reconciled at last with Fox and resumed preaching. In October of 1660 he set out on a journey to his Yorkshire home, but he never arrived. In prison he had repeatedly required medical treatment; his health was now deteriorating badly, and near Huntingdon he was robbed and beaten. Rescuers took him to the nearby home of a Quaker, where he died, uttering some moving last words that were often quoted afterward (in a suspiciously polished form):

> There is a spirit which I feel that delights to do no evil, nor to revenge any wrong, but delights to endure all things … I found it alone, being forsaken; I have fellowship therein with them who lived in dens and desolate places in the earth, who through death obtained this resurrection and eternal holy life.   (Whitehead, 696)

Nayler was buried at King's Ripton, Huntingdonshire, on 21 October.

In the decades immediately following, Nayler was largely erased from the official memory of the Quaker movement, which underwent sustained persecution during the Restoration and had good reason to minimize its radical origins. Memoirs written at that time usually referred to him obliquely as an unnamed 'other person', and his story was never publicly retold until Whitehead's biographical preface to his 1716 edition of Nayler's *Sundry Books*. Whitehead too, however, passed elliptically over the details of what happened during Nayler's time of troubles, and his marginalization was confirmed by

Willem Sewel's massive *History of the Rise, Increase, and Progress of the Christian People called Quakers* (1722), which was heavily indebted to Fox's *Journal* and implied that Fox had been the sole fountainhead of the movement. Later Quaker writers, when they mentioned Nayler at all, tended to assume that he suffered from a lamentable delusion that provoked his 'fall', and preferred to emphasize his supposed repentance afterward. Only when secular historians, notably Christopher Hill, began to see Nayler in a larger social and political context was his significance fully recognized.   LEO DAMROSCH

Sources G. Whitehead, ed., *A collection of sundry books, epistles and papers, written by James Nayler … with an impartial relation of the most remarkable transactions relating to his life* (1716) · *Diary of Thomas Burton*, ed. J. T. Rutt, 4 vols. (1828), vol. 1 · RS Friends, Lond., Swarthmore papers · J. Deacon, *The grand impostor examined, or, The life, tryal, and examination of James Nayler, the seduced and seducing Quaker with the manner of his riding into Bristol* (1656) · J. Deacon, *An exact history of the life of James Nayler* (1657) · R. Rich and W. Tomlinson, *A true narrative of the examination, tryall and sufferings of James Nayler* (1656) · *Memoirs of the life, ministry, tryal and sufferings of that very eminent person James Nayler* (1719) · A. R. Barclay, ed., *Letters, &c. of early Friends* (1841) · *The journal of George Fox*, rev. edn, ed. J. L. Nickalls (1952) · W. G. Bittle, *James Nayler, 1618–1660: the Quaker indicted by parliament* (1986) · L. Damrosch, *The sorrows of the Quaker Jesus: James Nayler and the puritan crackdown on the free spirit* (1996) · E. Fogelklou, *James Nayler, the rebel saint, 1618–1660*, trans. L. Yapp (1931) · M. R. Brailsford, *A Quaker from Cromwell's army: James Nayler* (1927) · W. C. Braithwaite, *The beginnings of Quakerism*, ed. H. J. Cadbury, 2nd edn (1955) · W. C. Braithwaite, *The second period of Quakerism*, ed. H. J. Cadbury, 2nd edn (1961) · C. Hill, *The world turned upside down: radical ideas during the English revolution* (1972); repr. (1975) · G. F. Nuttall, 'The letters of James Nayler', *The Lamb's war: Quaker essays to honor High Barbour*, ed. M. L. Birkel and J. W. Newman (1992), 38–75

Archives RS Friends, Lond., corresp. and papers | RS Friends, Lond., A. R. Barclay, Caton, Gibson, Markey, and Swarthmore MSS

Likenesses etchings, NPG · line engraving, BM, NPG; repro. in E. Pagit, *Heresiography*

Wealth at death £40 after deduction of outstanding debts: executor's account, quoted in Brailsford, *Quaker from Cromwell's army*, 197–8

Naylor, Francis Hare- (1753–1815), historian, was the grandson of Francis *Hare, bishop of Chichester, and the eldest son of Robert Hare-Naylor (d. 1797) of Herstmonceaux, Sussex, canon of Winchester, and his first wife, Sarah, daughter of Lister Selman of Chalfont St Peter, Buckinghamshire. His mother died when he was a child, and his father then married Henrietta Henckell, who sold the family properties in Norfolk, Suffolk, and Hampshire, and eventually persuaded her husband to consent to the demolition of Herstmonceux Castle, so that a modern house could be built, and settled upon her own children. Francis Hare-Naylor had a small inheritance from his mother and, being unhappy at home, lived almost entirely in London, where he made friends with Charles James Fox and became one of the circle that gathered round Georgiana Cavendish, duchess of Devonshire, at Chiswick. He was introduced by the duchess to her cousin **Georgiana Shipley** (c.1755–1806), painter, fourth daughter of Jonathan *Shipley (1713–1788), bishop of St Asaph, and his wife, Anna Maria Mordaunt (1716/17–1803), niece of the earl of Peterborough. Georgiana was described as 'tall, handsome, and self-sufficient, a scholar, and a

painter' (Leslie and Taylor, 376). She was a friend and pupil of Sir Joshua Reynolds and 'exhibited with applause' (ibid.) at the Royal Academy in 1781, where she showed a portrait of a lady and two children. The duchess took every opportunity to bring her cousin and Hare-Naylor together, and Bishop Shipley was at last persuaded to invite him to his residence at Twyford, Hampshire. The following day he was arrested for debt while driving in the episcopal coach with Georgiana and her parents. Banned from the house, he disguised himself as a beggar, and met her while driving with her family. Her recognition of him produced a crisis. The bishop refused to assist Hare-Naylor, but the duchess of Devonshire gave him and Georgiana an annuity of £200; they were married on 14 November 1784.

The couple then travelled to Karlsruhe, and afterwards to the north of Italy. Here they had four sons and a daughter, including Augustus William *Hare and Julius Charles *Hare. The family eventually settled at Bologna where Georgiana devoted herself to painting and formed a friendship with Clotilda Tambroni, the eminent professor of Greek.

In 1797 Hare-Naylor's father died. It was found that his intention of leaving everything to his second wife was frustrated by her having built her new house of Herstmonceux Place upon entailed land. The Hare-Naylors therefore departed for England, leaving three of their children in the care of Clotilda Tambroni and Father Emmanuele Aponte, an old Spanish priest, and appointing the famous Mezzofanti as tutor of their eldest son.

The Hare-Naylors settled at Herstmonceaux, but were plagued by financial problems. Hare-Naylor's democratic principles made enemies and lost friends. He indignantly rejected the offer of a baronetcy. From 1799 (when the Hare-Naylors returned to Italy to fetch their children) life became an increasing struggle with the requirements of an impoverished estate. Hare-Naylor turned to writing as a source of income. However, his plays *The Mirror* and *The Age of Chivalry* were rejected at Drury Lane. In 1801 he published his *History of the Helvetic Republics*, which was also a disappointment, although it passed into a second enlarged edition in 1809. The family was only saved from severe financial trouble by the intervention and help of Georgiana's sister, Anna Maria, widow of the orientalist Sir William Jones.

In 1804 Hare-Naylor and his family left Herstmonceaux for ever, and moved to Weimar, attracted partly by its famous literary society, but more by the friendship of the reigning duchess, who paid daily visits to Georgiana. While at Weimar, Hare-Naylor published the novel *Theodore, or, The Enthusiast*, for which John Flaxman made a series of illustrations. On 6 April 1806 (Easter Sunday) Georgiana Hare-Naylor, blind from the age of forty-eight, died at Lausanne. In the following year Hare-Naylor sold the family estate at Herstmonceaux. In the same year he married a relative of his first wife; the couple had two sons and a daughter, Georgina, who later married the theologian Frederick Denison Maurice. In September 1814 Hare-Naylor left England for the continent and in 1815 he died, after a lingering illness, at Tours. He was buried beneath the altar of Herstmonceaux church. His best-known work, *The Civil and Military History of Germany*, was published posthumously in 1816.   ALEXANDER DU TOIT

Sources *DNB* · F. Hare-Naylor, *The civil and military history of Germany from the landing of Gustavus to the conclusion of the treaty of Westphalia*, 2 vols. (1816), 1.v–vi · B. Stewart and M. Cutten, *The dictionary of portrait painters in Britain up to 1920* (1997) · C. R. Leslie and T. Taylor, *Life and times of Sir Joshua Reynolds*, 2 (1865)
Likenesses portrait (Georgiana Shipley), repro. in *Sussex County Magazine*, 6 (Nov 1932), 673

Neade, William (*fl.* 1624–1637), archer, first came to notice with his attempts to revive the use of the bow in warfare by devising a combined weapon consisting of a bow attached to a movable pivot in the middle of the pike shaft. His object was to enable the pikeman to defend himself and to fight while the enemy were still at a distance, rather than having to wait until they came within reach of his pike. In 1624 he demonstrated this weapon before the king in St James's Park, Westminster, and the Honourable Artillery Company subsequently tested it in the Artillery Garden north of the City. A manuscript Neade had presented to King Charles was published as *The double-armed man, by the new invention: briefly shewing some famous exploits atchieved by our Brittish bowmen, with severall portraitures proper for the pike and bow* (1625).

In response to Neade's petition for authority to teach the use of the combined bow and pike, and for a proclamation to be issued for its general adoption, a commission and proclamation were drawn up by Lord Justice Heath but delayed because the lord keeper would not approve them without the agreement of other lords. In July 1633 Neade again petitioned the council, his request this time being granted and the proclamation issued. The following year Neade and his son, also William Neade, were granted a patent for the manufacture of the weapon and its quiver.

Despite the earlier royal encouragement, Neade's invention was not taken up, the bow having by this time been ousted from the battlefield by the musket. Neade, describing himself and his son as 'instructors in archery to the king' (*CSP dom.*, 1637, 171), complained to the king in 1637 that, despite several demonstrations of his weapon, he had exhausted his entire estate of £600 to no avail, and that through the bad example of the City of London, archery was now generally neglected. There was no official response to these pleas and, apart from some references to his book, nothing further is known of Neade or his son.   W. A. SHAW, *rev.* ANITA MCCONNELL

Sources W. Neade, *The double-armed man, by the new invention: briefly showing some famous exploits atchieved by our Brittish bowmen, with severall portraitures proper for the pike and bow* (1625); repr. (1971) · State papers domestic, 1633–4, PRO [Docquet of 17/8/1633], 243, no. 70; 244, no. 52 · *CSP dom.*, 1637, 127, 171 · J. Hewitt, *Ancient armour in Europe* (1859), 705

Neagle, Dame Anna [real name Florence Marjorie Robertson] **(1904–1986)**, actress and film producer, was born in Forest Gate, Essex, on 20 October 1904, the only daughter

Dame Anna Neagle (1904–1986), by Sir Cecil Beaton

and youngest of three children of Herbert William Robertson, a captain in the merchant navy, and his wife, Florence Neagle. She was educated at the high school, St Albans, and at Wordsworth's Physical Training College, South Kensington, London. After being a student dance teacher, from 1925 to 1930 she appeared in the chorus of revues produced by André Charlot and Charles Cochran.

In 1930 she changed her name to Anna Neagle. Her first significant film part was in *Goodnight Vienna* (1932), directed by Herbert Sydney *Wilcox (1890–1977), whom she married in 1943. They had no children. Wilcox directed thirty-two films with Neagle. Her first major film success was in *Nell Gwyn* (1934), and she gradually became synonymous with the historical picture, especially when Wilcox directed her in *Victoria the Great* (1937), an unexpectedly popular and critical success. It won the *Picturegoer* gold medal award and the gold cup at the Venice film festival. Neagle and Wilcox went to America to publicize its release and on their return repeated the formula successfully in Technicolor with *Sixty Glorious Years* (1938).

Anna Neagle went to America in 1939 and made four films with RKO studios: *Nurse Edith Cavell* (1939) and three musical comedies, *Irene* (1940), *No, No, Nanette* (1940), and *Sunny* (1941). She was the first actress to appear on the cover of *Life* magazine. On her return to Britain she started work on a film of the life of the aviator Amy Johnson, *They Flew Alone* (1941). Her next film was *Yellow Canary* (1943), about a Women's Royal Naval Service intelligence worker mistaken for a Nazi spy.

In 1945 Neagle's films became less heroic, and more escapist light entertainment, as she continued to straddle her film career with stage appearances and tours. She appeared in the film *I Live in Grosvenor Square* (1945), co-starring Rex Harrison, and went on an Entertainments

National Service Association (ENSA) tour in Europe in the play *French without Tears*. After the Second World War Neagle starred in a distinctive series of musical comedies with Michael Wilding. The first of the 'London series' was *Piccadilly Incident* (1946), which won the *Daily Mail* national film award, as did its successor, *The Courtneys of Curzon Street* (1947). For her performances in both films Neagle received the *Picturegoer* gold medal. The third film in the Neagle–Wilding partnership was *Spring in Park Lane* (1948).

Aware of her previous success in 'biopics', Herbert Wilcox directed Neagle as Odette Sansom, a Special Operations Executive undercover agent, who had been tortured by the Nazis, in the film *Odette* (1950). As a result Neagle was appointed an honorary ensign (1950) of the First Aid Nursing Yeomanry, an appropriate award for an actress who went on to play Florence Nightingale in *The Lady with a Lamp* (1951).

In 1957 Anna Neagle produced *These Dangerous Years*, starring Frankie Vaughan, and was directed for the first time by a person other than Herbert Wilcox (Cyril Frankel) in *No Time for Tears* (1957). After her first box-office flop, *The Lady is a Square* (1958), financial problems beset Neagle and Wilcox and her attempt to start a dance school failed. Eventually, however, theatre appearances helped to resuscitate her flagging career.

Neagle was distinctive for her ability to maintain a 'regal presence' on screen. She was an 'English' beauty with a striking bone structure, who maintained her dancer's figure throughout her life. She could look equally at home in a glamorous ball gown or a practical flying-suit. Despite her variety of parts, her portrayals of heroines firmly placed her as a British icon in a patriotic style of film-making. She was appointed CBE in 1952 and DBE in 1969. She also received the freedom of the City of London (1981) and the order of St John (1981). Her final appearance was as the Fairy Godmother in *Cinderella* at the London Palladium that year. Anna Neagle, whose home latterly was at 117B Hamilton Terrace, London, died on 3 June 1986 from breast cancer at a nursing home, Clare House, Oakcroft Road, West Byfleet, Surrey, and was buried in the City of London cemetery, Manor Park, London. A service of thanksgiving was held in Westminster Abbey on 20 October 1986. SARAH STREET, *rev.*

Sources A. Neagle, *It's been fun* (1949) · A. Neagle, *There's always tomorrow* (1974) · microfiche jackets, BFI · d. cert. · *The Times* (4 June 1986) · *The Times* (12 June 1986) · *CGPLA Eng. & Wales* (1986)
Archives FILM BFI NFTVA, prints of films
Likenesses photographs, 1907–74, Hult. Arch. · Bassano studio, photographs, 1931, NPG · M. Barclay, oils, 1940, NPG · C. Beaton, photograph, NPG [*see illus.*]
Wealth at death £151,267: probate, 15 Sept 1986, *CGPLA Eng. & Wales*

Neagle, James (1765–1822), engraver, was born on 25 July 1765. Nothing is known of his family, although he may have been of Irish descent. He was admitted to the Royal Academy Schools in 1786 and became proficient in line engraving, specializing in book illustrations, of which he executed a very large number, after designs by contemporary artists such as Thomas Stothard, Robert Smirke, Henry Fuseli, Gavin Hamilton, and Henry Singleton. These included plates for John Boydell's letterpress edition of *The Dramatic Works of Shakespeare* (1802), two of which were after Francis Wheatley and two after Smirke. For this publication he also engraved, after a drawing by Josiah Boydell, the Shakespeare monument in Stratford church. In addition Neagle produced six plates, after Fuseli, for A. Chalmers's *Shakespeare* (1805).

Neagle was often commissioned by the firm of Cadell and Davies, for whom he engraved plates for works such as J. C. Murphy's *Travels in Portugal* (1795)—for which he received £21 for one plate—and William Lisle Bowles's *Sonnets* (1798)—for which he was paid 10 guineas a plate—as well as a portrait of Laurence Sterne, which earned him 8 guineas. Extant receipts indicate that he could expect, on average, 10 guineas per plate. Neagle's work can also be found in John Sharpe's *British Classics*, Edward Forster's translation of *The Arabian Nights* (1802), B. H. Malkin's translation of *Gil Blas* (1809), Taylor Combe's *Ancient Terra-Cottas in the British Museum* (1810), and J. C. Murphy's *Arabian Antiquities of Spain* (1813–16), and he contributed to the engraving of John Flaxman's designs of *The Odyssey* (1805). One of his most important works was *The Royal Procession in St Paul's on St George's Day* (1789), from a drawing by Edward Dayes. In 1801 he was a witness for the prosecution in the lawsuit brought by the engraver Jean-Marie Delattre against the painter J. S. Copley to recover the price of a plate made from the latter's *Death of Chatham*. At this time he lived at 20 St Chad's Row, Gray's Inn Road, London, having previously lived at 7 (and 8) Acton Street, Gray's Inn Road. By 1816 he was at 39 Clarendon Square, Somers Town; he then emigrated to America, and died in Philadelphia on 24 June 1822. His son John B. Neagle practised as an engraver in Philadelphia until his death in 1866.

F. M. O'DONOGHUE, *rev.* VIVIENNE W. PAINTING

Sources Redgrave, *Artists* · T. Dodd, 'History of English engravers', BL, Add. MSS 33394–33407 · W. S. Baker, *American engravers and their works* (1875) · Free Library of Philadelphia, autographs of engravers collection · S. C. Hutchison, 'The Royal Academy Schools, 1768–1830', *Walpole Society*, 38 (1960–62), 123–91 · H. Hammelmann, *Book illustrators in eighteenth-century England*, ed. T. S. R. Boase (1975) · Bénézit, *Dict.*
Archives Free Library of Philadelphia, rare book department, autographs of engravers collection
Likenesses crayon drawing, BM

Neal, Daniel (1678–1743), Independent minister and historian, was born in London on 14 December 1678. His parents died when he was very young, and he was raised by his maternal uncle in London. In September 1686 he enrolled at the Merchant Taylors' School, and from approximately 1696 to 1699 he studied for the ministry at Thomas Rowe's dissenting academy in Newington Green, Middlesex. About 1699 he left London for the Netherlands, where he studied at the University of Utrecht for two years under Gerhard de Vries, Joannes Georgius Graevius, and Peter Barman, and at the University of Leiden for one year. He returned to London in 1703 in the company of Martin Tomkins and Nathaniel Lardner, and a year later became an assistant to Dr John Singleton, pastor of an Independent chapel in Aldersgate Street. Neal succeeded Singleton and was ordained pastor at Loriner's Hall on 4 July 1706. The congregation grew and moved to a large chapel in Jewin Street. This became Neal's parish for the rest of his career.

Neal became a prominent London minister and a friend of such eminent dissenters as Phillip Doddridge and Isaac Watts. Like Watts, Neal did not take sides during the Salters' Hall controversy in which dissenting ministers debated whether subscription to the Trinity should be compulsory. He did participate in a series of Salters' Hall lectures against Catholicism in 1734.

On 22 June 1708 at St Katharine by the Tower, London, Neal married Elizabeth (d. 1748), only daughter of Richard Lardner (1653–1740), and the sister of Nathaniel *Lardner (1684–1768), Presbyterian minister. They had two daughters and one son, Nathaniel. One of their daughters married Joseph, son of Neal's friend and fellow minister Dr David Jennings, and the other married Neal's assistant, William Lister of Ware, Hertfordshire. Neal was a dedicated, hard-working minister who also found time for scholarly research. His first work, the two-volume *History of New England*, was published in 1720. This was a well-documented history which interpolated many extracts from Neal's sources into his smoothly written narrative. In his preface Neal praised New England's religious freedom and pointedly contrasted it with what he perceived to be England's continuing intolerance. Neal's history was well received in the American colonies and won him an honorary MA degree from Harvard College in 1721. A year later he wrote the introduction to *A Narrative of the Method and Success of Inoculating the Small Pox in New England, by Mr. Benj. Colman*, which defended Lady Mary Wortley Montagu's campaign to promote inoculation for smallpox in the face of widespread resistance from the medical and clerical establishment. The pamphlet caught the attention of Princess Caroline, who met Neal, complimented him, and introduced him to the prince of Wales.

The first volume of Neal's *History of the Puritans* appeared in 1732, but the idea of writing such a work had been contemplated years earlier by prominent dissenting clergy, such as Edmund Calamy (1671–1732) and John Evans. Evans was the prime mover. He planned to write the history of the puritans to 1640 and to leave Neal to cover the period from 1640 to 1688. Having collected documents for the work, Evans died in 1730, and Neal inherited the entire project.

In a published sermon of 1730 Neal urged his congregation to pray 'that all penal laws for religion may be taken away and that no civil discouragements may be upon Christians of any denomination for the peaceable profession of their faith, but that the Gospel may have free course' (Okie, 457). The years in which the *History of the Puritans* was published coincided with a campaign to repeal the Test and Corporation Acts, which barred nonconformists from public and municipal office. Deputies representing dissenting congregations in London began petitioning parliament for repeal in 1732.

The prefaces to Neal's four volumes make it clear that the *History of the Puritans* was designed as a historical argument against the Test and Corporation Acts. The dissenters are described as 'his majesty's most dutiful and loyal subjects' who were being unfairly penalized. Neal backs the ongoing movement 'to petition for a repeal or amendment of these acts'. 'Enthusiasts or Jews' should also be granted religious freedom, according to Neal (Okie, 458). Roman Catholics, however, posed a threat to the state and should not be freed from their religious disabilities.

Although Neal opposed the penal laws, he remained a firm supporter of the whig ministry. His *Letter from a Dissenter to the Author of The Craftsman* (1733) rejected the call by the pseudonymous Caleb D'Anver for dissenters to ally with reformed tories and join the opposition country party. Lauding England's 'free constitution' and Bishop Benjamin Hoadly's latitudinarian views, Neal maintained that the ministerial 'friends of liberty' probably had postponed repeal because they feared that the tories would instigate 'Church in Danger' rioting (Okie, 458).

Neal made the historical case for repeal by presenting the dissenters' puritan ancestors as paladins of liberty and of the English constitution, and argued that liberty was the fruit of Tudor–Stuart puritanism. He foreshadowed those twentieth-century historians, such as William Haller, who have seen liberty as the outgrowth of puritan individualism. 'All the arguments against the growth of the prerogative', Neal wrote, 'are said to be founded on Puritan principles' (Okie, 458).

The History of the Puritans was an impressive performance. No history written before the twentieth century traced the history of puritanism in such lucid detail. The history was unusual also in its attention to the role of 'the people' in historical events, as, for example, protests by the City crowd on behalf of parliament during the 1640s (Okie, 461). Neal's work contained relatively few of the tedious transcriptions that characterized most contemporary English histories, and he also fashioned a well-written narrative.

Neal's *History* found a wide audience. There were two later English editions in the eighteenth century, a Dublin edition, and more than ten editions and reprints in the nineteenth century, including several American editions. Anglican clerics, however, assailed Neal's history. Isaac Maddox and Zachary Grey denounced the work in several pamphlets. They were encouraged to do so by Maddox's patron Edmund Gibson, bishop of London, and by Thomas Sherlock, bishop of Salisbury. Neal responded to Maddox's assault in *A Review of the Principal Facts Objected to in the First Volume of The History of the Puritans* (1734).

Neal was prone to 'a lowness of spirits, and to complaints of an indisposition in his head' throughout his life (Toulmin, 32). His health declined as he worked on the *History*. He suffered increasingly serious strokes of paralysis and took the waters in Bath in an unsuccessful effort to alleviate them. He died in London on 4 April 1743, only five months after retiring from the ministry, and was buried in Bunhill Fields; his funeral sermon was preached by Dr David Jennings. His widow died in 1748. LAIRD OKIE

Sources L. Okie, 'Daniel Neal and the puritan revolution', *Church History*, 55 (1986), 456–67 · *DNB* · J. Toulmin, 'Life of Daniel Neal', in D. Neal, *The history of the puritans or protestant nonconformists*, ed. J. Toulmin, new edn, 1 (1822) · W. Wilson, *The history and antiquities of the dissenting churches and meeting houses in London, Westminster and Southwark*, 4 vols. (1808–14) · *IGI*
Likenesses S. F. Ravenet, line engraving (after J. Wollaston), NPG; repro. in D. Neal, *The history of the puritans*, 2nd edn (1754) · J. Van den Berghe, stipple (after J. Wollaston), BM, NPG; repro. in D. Neal, *The history of the puritans*, ed. J. Toulmin, rev. edn, 5 vols. (1793–7)

Neal, Ernest Gordon (1911–1998), biologist and schoolmaster, was born on 20 May 1911 at 106 St Johns Road, Hemel Hempstead, Hertfordshire, the youngest child in the family of two sons and two daughters of the Revd Frederick Neal (d. 1952), a Baptist minister, and his Scottish wife, Margaret Owen, *née* Keith (d. 1959), daughter of a manufacturer of ivory goods. He was educated at Taunton School from 1926 to 1929. Although he would have liked to study medicine, his family could not afford it, and he enrolled in evening classes in botany, zoology, and chemistry at Chelsea Polytechnic, teaching at Highfield School, a preparatory school, during the day. He graduated with a second-class honours degree from London University in 1934. After teaching and working as a demonstrator in the zoology department of Chelsea Polytechnic for a year, he took a teaching job at Rendcomb College, a small boarding-school for boys near Cirencester. On 30 April 1937 he married Helen Elizabeth (Betty; b. 1913), daughter of George Sutherland Thomson, a dairying and agricultural consultant; they had three sons.

Although Neal's application to be registered as a conscientious objector during the Second World War was rejected, he was deemed unfit to serve as a medical orderly in the armed forces, and remained at Rendcomb until 1946, when he moved to Taunton School as biology master and in 1948 became head of science. Always keen to involve his pupils in ecological projects and field trips, he published a book for schools, *Woodland Ecology*, in 1953. He became second master in 1960, and from 1960 to 1966 was also housemaster of a senior house. He retired in 1971, and with his son Keith wrote *Biology for Today* (1974; rev. edn, 1983), an O level textbook.

Neal's interest in nature began as a child when he accompanied his father on butterfly-watching expeditions, and he later took up nature photography as a hobby: he published *Exploring Nature with a Camera* (1946), containing many of his black and white photographs, including pictures of the effects of the 'ice rain' of early 1940. He first saw badgers in the wild in 1936, and as he became fascinated by their ecology and behaviour, he began to photograph them. After the success of *The Badger* (1948), the first in the Collins New Naturalist series of monographs, which ran to five editions and included the first colour photograph of wild badgers at night, he was in demand as a lecturer. In 1949 he made a short film of badgers, which he was asked to show at a meeting of the Zoological Society of London. This led to his making a longer film, with Professor Humphrey Hewer, which took

three years to complete and which was shown on BBC television in 1954. Neal became a regular broadcaster, appearing as a member of the panel of *Country Questions* in the late 1950s, and started to make television programmes for schools in 1961.

A founder of the Mammal Society of the British Isles (later the Mammal Society) in 1954, Neal started the badger group, which organized a national sett survey over many years: he chaired the society from 1974 to 1980, and was elected president in 1980. At the same time he was conducting research into the reproductive cycle of the badger, which formed the basis of the dissertation he submitted for a London University PhD in 1960. In the 1970s he campaigned for legislation to protect badgers from extermination by farmers and landowners, and the first Badger Act was passed in 1973, protecting badgers but not their setts. In 1975, with growing evidence that badgers were implicated in infecting cattle with bovine tuberculosis, the government set up a consultative panel of the Ministry of Agriculture, Fisheries and Food on badgers and tuberculosis, and Neal was invited to be a member, serving for fifteen years. Gassing of badgers became illegal in 1982, and setts were given full protection in the Badgers Act of 1991. As part of his efforts to win over public opinion, in 1977 Neal organized *Badger Watch*, a series of live television programmes on five consecutive nights at a badger sett in Gloucestershire. He was advisory editor for the Blandford Mammal Series, contributing the volume *Badgers* (1977), and later became editor of the Helm Mammal Series. He published *The Natural History of Badgers* (1986), revised as *Badgers* in 1996 with the help of Chris Cheeseman.

Neal visited Africa for the first time in 1962, and in 1969 he accepted an invitation to study the banded mongoose and other small nocturnal carnivores in the Queen Elizabeth National Park in Uganda, work which he summarized in *Uganda Quest* (1971). He became interested in the ecology of Africa, and was invited to be a guest lecturer for Swan Hellenic and Ecosafaris, accompanying wildlife safaris in east Africa and the Seychelles until 1990. He contributed *On Safari in East Africa: a Background Guide* (1991) to the Collins Natural History Series.

Neal was elected a fellow of the Institute of Biology in 1963, and in 1966 he was given the Sir Stamford Raffles award by the Zoological Society of London. He was appointed MBE in 1976 for his work as chairman of the Somerset Trust for Nature Conservation, which he had helped to found. A practising Christian all his life, he was a deacon of Albemarle Baptist church in Taunton. His autobiography, *The Badger Man: Memoirs of a Biologist*, was published in 1994. He died on 5 April 1998 at Dial House, 38 Park Avenue, Bedford. He was survived by his wife, Betty.

ANNE PIMLOTT BAKER

Sources E. G. Neal, *The badger man: memoirs of a biologist* (1994) · *The Independent* (14 April 1998) · *The Times* (22 April 1998) · b. cert. · m. cert. · d. cert.
Likenesses photograph, repro. in Neal, *Badger man* · photograph, repro. in *The Independent* · photograph, repro. in *The Times*
Wealth at death under £180,000: probate, 1998, *CGPLA Eng. & Wales*

Neal, Mary Clara Sophia (1860–1944), social worker and folk-dance collector, was born on 5 June 1860 at 21 Noel Road, Edgbaston, Birmingham, the eldest of the three children of David Neal (1834–1918), button manufacturer, and his wife, Sarah Ann, *née* Smith (1833–1914). The family was prosperous, but Clara Sophia, as she was then known, felt that her life was snobbish and hypocritical. In February 1888 she was one of a number of 'ladies of leisure, culture, refinement and devotion' (Bagwell, 25–6) who joined the recently formed Methodist West London Mission, becoming 'Sisters of the People', unpaid social workers among the poor of Soho and Marylebone. At this point she took the name 'Mary' by which she was henceforth known.

One of Neal's special tasks was the running of a club for working girls, and in 1891 she was joined in this by Emmeline Pethick, her closest friend for the rest of her life. In 1895 they left the mission and established their own Espérance Girls' Club, later linked with a commercial tailoring establishment called the 'Maison Espérance', independently putting into practice the gospel of socialism. Important innovative elements in their work were the use of drama and dancing, and also the introduction of an annual country or seaside holiday for the girls.

After Emmeline's marriage to Fred Lawrence in 1901, she was succeeded by Herbert MacIlwaine as musical director. In 1905 he suggested that the girls might enjoy the folk-songs then being collected by Cecil Sharp. This was so successful that Neal asked for dances which might have a similar popularity. Sharp recalled seeing the Headington Quarry Morris Dancers in 1899 and gave her William Kimber's address. Neal promptly took a train to Oxford and a hansom cab to Headington Quarry, where she found Kimber and arranged for him to come to London to teach his dances to the girls. On 15 February 1906 the club held a belated new year party at the Passmore Edwards Settlement and the songs and dances were greeted with immense enthusiasm, Laurence Housman telling Neal that she and her girls must show the country what they had discovered.

On 3 April 1906 a public concert was held, preceded by an introductory lecture by Sharp. This was a defining moment in the history of the folk revival. Both Sharp and Neal felt that they had become instruments in a direct and transforming restoration of a lost English heritage. For Neal there was the added incentive that the girls of the Espérance Club were themselves to be the means by which this might happen, teaching the songs and dances in towns and villages throughout England. She revelled in her role as publicist and organizer of this new national movement, the Association for the Revival and Practice of Folk Music, later to become the Espérance Guild of Morris Dancers. Bernard Partridge's cartoon, 'Merrie England Once More' (*Punch*, 13 November 1907), symbolized the hopes and expectations which were being engendered.

Unfortunately there were differences of approach between Neal and Sharp. Sharp, the professional educationist, was concerned with scholarly accuracy. Neal, the philanthropic social worker, was more directly concerned

Mary Clara Sophia Neal (1860–1944), by unknown photographer

with the joy of the actual dancer: she believed in the power of the material to transmit itself, and regretted the necessity for books of instruction. From 1910 to 1914 there was a bitter struggle between Sharp's English Folk Dance Society (EFDS) and Neal's guild. At the time it was by no means clear that Sharp would be the winner. Neal had many influential supporters; she had her popular *Espérance Morris Books*; she had recruited a men's morris side before Sharp achieved this; she had friendly contacts with many traditional dancers; she had the use of the restored Crosby Hall for her guild meetings; and she had Clive Carey as a highly capable musical director and collector.

But the First World War brought the cessation of Espérance activity and Neal became involved in pensions administration on the Isle of Dogs. In west Sussex after the war she still had tentative thoughts of reviving her role in the folk world. But this was no longer possible: the future lay with Sharp and the EFDS, a more stable, middle-class affair, with a professional educational basis. She never again became directly involved in folk activity, although privately she encouraged Rolf Gardiner in his quest for independence from the EFDS. One big new commitment in 1920 was her adoption of Herbert MacIlwaine's son, Anthony, after he was orphaned. In 1925 she moved to Littlehampton, Sussex, where for twelve years she worked as a magistrate, particularly concerned with children's cases. A measure of belated public recognition came in 1937 when she was made CBE 'for services in connexion with the revival of folk songs and dances'.

In 1906 Neal had been at the inaugural meeting of the Women's Suffrage and Political Union, actually taking the minutes on that occasion, and she remained a firm supporter of the suffrage movement. Her unorthodox religious views were centred in an intense personal sense of mysticism. In person she was tall and imposing, with vivid blue eyes and an equally notable sense of humour. In 1940, when Littlehampton was affected by the war, she went to stay with the Pethick-Lawrences at Gomshall in Surrey and remained there until she died from cancer on 22 June 1944, at The Retreat, Rad Lane, Peaslake, Shere, Surrey. She was cremated in Woking two days later.

ROY JUDGE

Sources M. Neal, '"As a tale that is told": the autobiography of a Victorian woman', priv. coll. • R. Judge, 'Mary Neal and the Espérance morris', *Folk Music Journal*, 5 (1985–9), 545–91 • E. Pethick-Lawrence, *My part in a changing world* (1938) • P. Bagwell, *Outcast London, a Christian response: the West London Mission of the Methodist Church, 1887–1987* (1987) • N. W. F. [Franks], 'Factory girls: the club and the new political economy', *The Associate* (April 1900), 13–20 • E. Pethick-Lawrence, *The Times* (28 June 1944) • correspondence with Clive Carey, Vaughan Williams Memorial Library, London, Clive Carey MSS • private information (2004) • d. cert. • b. cert. • *CGPLA Eng. & Wales* (1944)

Archives priv. coll., MS unpublished autobiography | Vaughan Williams Memorial Library, London, Dean–Smith collection, annotated extracts from unpublished autobiography • Vaughan Williams Memorial Library, London, corresp. with Clive Carey

Likenesses C. Carey, photograph, 1911, repro. in Neal, '"As a tale that is told"', p. 150; priv. coll. • photograph, 1937, repro. in *Folk Music Journal*, 5 (1989), front cover; priv. coll. • photograph, English Folk Dance and Song Society [*see illus.*]

Wealth at death £1382 14s. 9d.: probate, 13 Sept 1944, *CGPLA Eng. & Wales*

Neal [Neale], **Thomas** (b. c.1519, d. in or after 1590), Hebrew scholar, was born at Yate, Gloucestershire. He was educated at Winchester College (1531–8), and New College, Oxford, of which he became a fellow in 1540. He graduated BA on 16 May 1542, MA on 11 July 1546 and was admitted BTh on 23 July 1556. His linguistic and theological abilities were recognized in the 1540s by Sir Thomas White, the founder of St John's College, Oxford, who provided him with a pension of £10 per annum for teaching undergraduates. One of his more illustrious students during this time was Bernard Gilpin.

Having spent some time in Paris, Neal returned to England during Mary's reign and became chaplain to Edmund Bonner, bishop of London. He was appointed rector of Thenford, Northamptonshire, in 1556. In 1559 he was made regius professor of Hebrew at Oxford. But it appears that he was not welcomed with open arms by the dean and chapter of Christ Church, the college to which his chair was linked, for it took two letters from the privy council to persuade the college authorities to pay his salary. This initial difficulty with Christ Church may explain Foster's comment that 'he entered himself of Hart Hall' (Foster, 3.1054) and found new lodgings at the west end of New College. Like many of his contemporaries in Elizabethan Oxford, Neal was a product of the Marian reaction, 'always continuing constant to the Roman persuasion'

(Fuller, *Worthies*, 1.384). According to the *Dictionary of National Biography*, citing Pits's *De illustribus angliae scriptoribus*, he was responsible for fabricating the Nag's Head story which was put about to discredit the validity of Matthew Parker's consecration as archbishop of Canterbury in 1559. It was alleged that because Parker could find no one to consecrate him, a group of clergy met in the Nag's Head tavern in London and performed an invalid ceremony. Pits claimed that Neal witnessed the proceedings. But the story is not substantiated by any other source.

Neal played a prominent part in Queen Elizabeth's seven-day visit to Oxford in 1566. His detailed record of the occasion formed the basis of Richard Stephens's 'A brief rehersal of all such things as were done in the University of Oxford during the Queen's Majesty's abode there'. He also presented to the queen 'a book of all the prophets translated out of the Hebrew by him and a little book of Latin verses' describing the colleges and halls of Oxford (Wood, *History and Antiquities*, 2.158). The latter was published by Hearne in his edition of Dodwell's *Parma equestri*. A speech of thirteen lines and a poem of five stanzas, both written in Hebrew, which he composed to mark the occasion, are extant in manuscript (Bodl. Oxf., MS Bodley 13).

Neal's adherence to Catholicism may have been the reason why he resigned his professorship in 1569. 'His religion being more Catholic than Protestant ... and always dreading his being called into question for his seldom frequenting the church and receiving the sacrament' (Wood, *Ath. Oxon.*, 1.250), he retired to Cassington, near Oxford, where he spent the rest of his life. The parish church contains his epitaph, dated 1590, which he wrote himself. It is presumed that he died soon afterwards, but neither the date of his death nor the place of his burial is known.

Neal is significant in the history of scholarship as one of the few regius professors in sixteenth-century Oxford who left direct evidence that he knew Hebrew. Though they contain some orthographical oddities, both the speech and the poem written to commemorate the royal visit to Oxford bear witness to Neal's proficiency not only in the classical Hebrew of the Bible but also in the later Hebrew of the rabbis. They contain several phrases and idioms peculiar to the rabbinic texts of the post-biblical period. His familiarity with rabbinic Hebrew is further illustrated by his Latin translation of the late medieval Jewish exegete Rabbi David Kimchi's commentary on Haggai, Zechariah, and Malachi, published in Paris in 1557 and dedicated to Cardinal Pole. Neal's literary remains demonstrate that he was among the growing number of English Christian Hebraists who found rabbinic commentaries relevant for dealing with perplexing questions of Hebrew philology and biblical exegesis. It was owing to Neal, and others of like mind, that the insights of medieval rabbis were utilized by those who produced the most influential English translation of the Bible ever made, the Authorized Version of 1611.

G. LLOYD JONES

Sources Wood, *Ath. Oxon.*, 1st edn, vol. 1 • J. Strype, *Annals of the Reformation and establishment of religion ... during Queen Elizabeth's* *happy reign*, new edn, 1 (1824) · *Hist. U. Oxf.* 3: *Colleg. univ.*, 357 · Foster, *Alum. Oxon.* · A. Wood, *The history and antiquities of the colleges and halls in the University of Oxford*, ed. J. Gutch (1786) · C. Plummer, ed., *Elizabethan Oxford: reprints of rare tracts*, OHS, 8 (1887), 192–205 · Fuller, *Worthies* (1811), 1.384 · epitaph, Cassington church, Oxfordshire · *DNB*

Archives Bodl. Oxf., MS

Neale. *See also* Neal, Neele, Neile, Neill.

Neale, Adam (1778?–1832), military physician and author, was born in Scotland and educated in Edinburgh, where he graduated MD on 13 September 1802, his thesis being published as *Disputatio de acido nitrico* (1802). It is possible that he was the Adam Neall who had been apprenticed to the Edinburgh surgeon James Russell in 1792. He was admitted a licentiate of the Royal College of Physicians, London, on 25 June 1806.

In July 1808 Neale was appointed physician to the forces, a position he held during the Peninsular War, when he was also one of the physicians-extraordinary to the duke of Kent. In 1809, in *Letters from Portugal and Spain*, he published an account of the operations of the armies under Sir John Moore and Sir Arthur Wellesley, from the landing of the troops in Mondego Bay to the battle of Corunna. Neale subsequently visited Germany, Poland, Moldavia, and Turkey, where he was physician to the British embassy at Constantinople, and in 1818 he published a description of his tour in *Travels through some Parts of Germany, Poland, Moldavia, and Turkey*.

In 1814 Neale settled at Exeter, but he moved to Cheltenham in 1820, 'where his stay was as stormy as it was short' (Munk, 37). He quickly attracted attention by publishing a pamphlet in which he cast doubt on the genuineness of the waters served to visitors at the principal spring, entitled *A letter to a professor of medicine in the University of Edinburgh respecting the nature and properties of the mineral waters of Cheltenham*. This created a notable controversy, and Neale's claims were variously refuted by Dr Thomas Jameson of Cheltenham, William Henry Halpin, and Thomas Newell. The dispute was ended by the publication of a satirical pamphlet entitled *Hints to a Physician on the Opening of his Medical Career at Cheltenham* (1820). As a result of the controversy Neale was obliged to return to Exeter after only a few months in Cheltenham.

In 1824 Neale was an unsuccessful candidate for the office of physician to the Devon and Exeter Hospital. He then went to London, and lived for some time at 58 Guilford Street, Russell Square. He died in Dunkirk on 22 December 1832. His sons were Erskine *Neale and William Johnstoune *Neale. A daughter, Sydney, married the topographer Samuel Rowe.

Neale was a fellow of the Linnean Society, and in 1828 he published a book on the chemical and medicinal properties of ergot of rye and, in 1831, *Researches to Establish the Truth of the Linnaean Doctrine of Animal Contagions*.

GORDON GOODWIN, *rev.* CLAIRE E. J. HERRICK

Sources A. Peterkin and W. Johnston, *Commissioned officers in the medical services of the British army, 1660–1960*, 1 (1968), 191 · Munk, *Roll* · N. Cantlie, *A history of the army medical department*, 1 (1974) · R. L. Blanco, *Wellington's surgeon general: Sir James McGrigor* (1974), 89, 92 · *GM*, 1st ser., 103/1 (1833), 191 · P. J. Wallis and R. V. Wallis, *Eighteenth century medics*, 2nd edn (1988)

Neale, Sir Alan Derrett (1918–1995), civil servant and author, was born on 24 October 1918 at 12 Spencer Place, Leeds, the only child of William Augustus Neale (1884–1941), a director of A. J. Neale, a prosperous, family-owned gentlemen's shirt makers and outfitters in the City, and his wife, Florence Emily, *née* Derrett (1886–1966). His father's family (who originated from Nympsfield, Gloucestershire) was large and musically talented, and Neale inherited both a love of music and performing skill. He was educated first at Highgate School, where he was a contemporary of Anthony Crosland. (He later shared lodgings at Oxford with Crosland and worked for him when he was president of the Board of Trade.) He excelled in English, German, and music (piano) and was active in school societies. He then won an open exhibition in modern languages to St John's College, Oxford, where he read philosophy, politics, and economics, taking a wartime shortened degree in 1940. In the Second World War he served in the intelligence corps from 1940 until 1945, achieving the rank of captain. His work on deciphering German signals, using language skills developed at school, culminated in his being appointed MBE (military), an honour that gave him special pleasure. In 1946 he entered the civil service, through the post-war reconstruction competition. He was appointed to the Board of Trade, then second in standing only to the Treasury, as an assistant principal, and rose steadily in that department over the next twenty-two years.

In 1952 Neale was awarded a Commonwealth Fund fellowship to study for a year in the United States, an experience which strongly influenced him. His topic resulted in 1960 in a book, *The Anti-Trust Laws of the United States*, intended primarily for British businessmen. Extraordinarily for a book by a non-lawyer and Englishman it became for some twenty-five years a standard text for United States law students. It was regarded by high authorities as the best general introduction, showing great understanding of US case law and of the historical and political context. Neale developed a lifelong interest in the competition laws of different countries and in the conflicts that arise when they require different standards of behaviour by international businesses. As late as 1988 he collaborated with an American lawyer, R. L. Stephens, in a further study of these conflicts, *International Business and National Jurisdictions*, based on Stephens's doctoral thesis at Oxford.

In 1956 Neale was appointed principal private secretary to Sir David Eccles. On 25 September that year he married Joan Frost (*b.* 1920), the only daughter of Harry and Hilda Frost, and a Board of Trade colleague whom he had got to know well when they were both working in Geneva on the negotiations of a round of the General Agreement on Tariffs and Trade. They had one son. In 1960 a fellowship at the Harvard Center for International Affairs resulted in

Neale's monograph, *The Flow of Resources from Rich to Poor* (1961). Back at the Board of Trade he was promoted to under-secretary (1963) and deputy secretary (1967). In 1968 he transferred to the Treasury and was promoted to second permanent secretary in 1971, responsible for overseas finance and monetary policy. He was much concerned with the currency turmoil following the breakdown of the Bretton Woods agreement, and with the efforts to reduce exchange rate instability. He was made CB in 1968 and KCB in 1972.

In 1973 Neale became permanent secretary of the Ministry of Agriculture, Fisheries and Food, where he remained until his retirement in 1978. It was not the easiest task for an incomer to head a department expert in the technicalities of agricultural policy, especially during the change from a department being largely master of a British policy to one having to negotiate European measures within the framework of the common agricultural policy. It is a tribute to Neale's human skills that he rapidly achieved the respect and confidence of his new colleagues and of the industry. Working with ministers with differing attitudes to Europe, he steered policy issues deftly without getting bogged down in the detail. Those who had previously seen him dealing mainly with policy matters found that he brought the same skills of analysis and decision-making to his management role.

After retirement Neale joined the Monopolies and Mergers Commission as a member in 1981, and was a deputy chairman from 1982 to 1986. He put to good use his wide knowledge of competition policy. He had less belief in the value of the efficiency audits of public sector bodies, which were then prominent in the commission's tasks. The subsequent major gains in productivity, achieved after privatization in bodies supposedly audited as reasonably efficient, may show that his scepticism was warranted. From 1987 to 1991 he was deputy chairman of the Association of Futures Brokers and Dealers, where he brought his experience to strengthen the organization's procedures, particularly for self-regulation.

Neale was of rather less than average height, a neat and distinguished figure, with a slightly sardonic air and a wry but piercing humour. Colleagues respected his intellect, knowledge, and grasp of issues, which made him a shrewd operator with other departments. He was notable for the clarity and precision of his English and for his ability to explain complex topics in simple terms. He may have appeared reticent to some, for he separated his work from his home life and private interests. But, without being lavish in conferring praise, he was considerate to colleagues and gave sympathetic help to anyone with a personal problem. He was an able pianist and particularly enjoyed playing Bach; a great gardener, loving old and shrub roses; and a keen tennis player in youth. At the Reform Club he regularly played bridge and snooker, a game that he enjoyed with one of his former ministers, Fred Peart. As chairman of the club, he promoted the case for the admission of women members and was disappointed that this was not achieved before his term of

office ended. He died of cancer of the prostate and emphysema at his home, 95 Swains Lane, Highgate, London, on 21 March 1995 and was cremated at Golders Green crematorium. He was survived by his wife and son.

WILLIAM KNIGHTON

Sources WWW, 1991–5 · *The Times* (29 March 1995) · *Daily Telegraph* (10 April 1995) · private information (2004) [Lady Neale] · personal knowledge (2004) · register, St John's College, Oxford
Likenesses photograph, repro. in *The Times*
Wealth at death £426,506: probate, 20 May 1995, *CGPLA Eng. & Wales*

Neale, Edward Vansittart (1810–1892), Christian socialist and co-operative movement activist, was the only son of Edward Vansittart, rector of Taplow, and his second wife, Anne, daughter of Isaac Spooner of Elmdon. His father took the surname Neale under the will of Mary, widow of Colonel John Neale of Allesley Park, his kinsman. Born at Bath on 2 April 1810, Neale was educated at home under the influence of William Wilberforce, a relative. He matriculated on 14 December 1827 at Oriel College, Oxford, where he came into contact with both the Noetics and the Tractarians, who led him to reject the evangelicalism of his upbringing. After graduating BA in 1831, gaining third-class honours in classics and a second class in mathematics, he toured Europe, proceeded MA in 1836, entered Lincoln's Inn, and was called to the bar on 4 May 1837. He married, on 14 June 1837 at St George's, Hanover Square, London, Frances Sarah, eldest daughter of James William Farrer, master in chancery, of Ingleborough, Yorkshire, and widow of the Hon. John Scott, eldest son of John, first Lord Eldon; they had five children.

Neale was greatly influenced by Frederick Denison Maurice's *The Kingdom of Christ* (1838), which convinced him that all men were brothers in Christ and that it was the duty of each to live for all. Keenly interested in social reform, as a consequence, Neale studied the socialist systems of Fourier (whom he admired), Saint-Simon, and others in the 1840s and published his analysis, *The Characteristic Features of some of the Principal Systems of Socialism*, in 1851. He also joined the utilitarian Law Amendment Society and published two books in support of radical land reform to break the aristocratic monopoly of land ownership: *The Real Property Acts of 1845* (1845) and *Thoughts on the Registration of the Title of Land* (1849). He also published *Feasts and Fasts* (1845), an account of the development of the laws relating to sabbath observance and religious festivals.

In 1850, and owing to Maurice's involvement, Neale visited the London Working Tailors' Association, begun by the Christian Socialists' Society for Promoting Working Men's Associations. He studied their work, in turn sharing his knowledge of continental socialism, and was invited to join the council of promoters. Neale was central in shifting the focus of the movement from promotion of self-governing workshops to co-operation on a larger scale. He funded and founded the first London co-operative stores in Charlotte Street, Fitzroy Square, and advanced capital for two unsuccessful builders' associations. Initially ignorant of northern co-operation on the Rochdale and redemptionist models, Neale became a swift convert to consumers' co-operation and became allied with many former Owenites, including Lloyd Jones, in the process. He established the wholesale Central Co-operative Agency without the knowledge and against the wishes of the council, and an attempt was made to exclude from the council both Neale and his collaborator Thomas Hughes. The promoters and the agency continued to work together, but Neale sought to catholicize co-operative socialism by founding the short-lived Co-operative League in 1852, as a forum for Christian, Owenite, and secularist socialists to exchange ideas and information.

Following the 1852 engineers' lock-out, Neale chaired a meeting of the metropolitan trades, held at St Martin's Hall on 4 March, in support of the Amalgamated Society of Engineers. He gave it financial assistance and published a defence of the strikers' actions, *May I not Do What I Will with my Own?*, in 1852. When the men were forced to return to work on the employers' terms, Neale purchased the Atlas ironworks, Southwark, where he established a co-operative association. The scheme ended in total failure. The agency was at the same time involved in difficulties, and the loss on both schemes fell entirely on Neale, bringing his losses in supporting co-operative ventures to an estimated £40,000.

Meanwhile Neale's activity in other directions was incessant. He had given evidence before the select committee on the savings of the middle and working classes in 1850. The resulting Industrial and Provident Societies Act (1852) led to a great development of co-operation and Neale closely associated himself with the northern movement. This, however, did not prevent him from keeping in touch with metropolitan Christian socialism, now centred on the Working Men's College, where he took a class in political economy for two terms. He frequently acted as legal adviser to co-operative societies, which sought his aid in the revision of rules for registration. He prepared, wholly or in part, all the amendments proposed in the act of 1852; the Consolidation Act (1862); and the Industrial and Provident Societies Act (1876). He was a member of the executive committee appointed by the London conference of delegates from co-operative societies (July 1852), a foreshadowing of the later co-operative board; and, in addition to lectures and pamphlets, he found time to write *The Co-operator's Handbook, Containing the Laws Relating to a Company of Limited Liability* (1860) and *The Anthology of Thought and Nature Investigated* (1863). He also spent some months in Calcutta winding up the affairs of a branch of the failed Albert Insurance Company. Neale was keenly interested in the formation of the North of England Co-operative Wholesale Society (1863), and drafted their rules for registration. He was one of the founders of the Cobden Mills in 1866 and the Agricultural and Horticultural Association in 1867, which aimed to introduce co-operation into agriculture. He helped inaugurate

the annual co-operative congresses and, on the establishment of the central board (in 1872), he was elected a member of the London section. In 1875 Neale succeeded William Nuttall as general secretary to the Co-operative Union. He received a salary of £250 a year for his official work, but acted gratuitously as legal adviser to the central board until 1878, when his remuneration was increased to £350. Devoting himself entirely to his work he took lodgings in Manchester, visiting his family only once a week, and published *A Manual for Co-operators* in 1881. His succession to the Bisham Abbey estate in November 1885 made no difference to his routine, and his tireless work for co-operation earned him the respect of all those involved in the movement.

Neale was for seventeen years a director of the Co-operative Insurance Company, and for sixteen years a member of the committee of the Co-operative Newspaper Society. Throughout his life he kept up a large correspondence with foreign co-operators, and frequently attended the continental congresses. In 1875 he visited America, with a view to opening up a direct trade between the English co-operative stores and the farmers of the western states. A diary of this visit was published in the *Co-operative News*. In August 1890 Neale took part in a conference on the relation of the Oxford University extension movement to working-class education. Between 1869 and 1875 he published five works on theological questions.

Neale resigned the general secretaryship of the Co-operative Union on 11 September 1891, at the age of eighty-one. Even then he did not entirely give up work in the cause of co-operation. On the formation of the Christian Social Union he became a member of the Oxford University branch of that organization, wrote for the *Economic Review*, and, a few months before his death, read a paper before the F.D.M., a private society named after Frederick Denison Maurice, on Robert Owen. He had been for some time suffering from a painful illness, aggravated by earlier neglect of his own health. He died at 6 Bentinck Street, Manchester Square, London, on 16 September 1892, and was buried in Bisham churchyard, Berkshire. A Vansittart Neale scholarship for the sons of co-operators was founded at Oriel College in February 1890 from the subscriptions of co-operators in various parts of the country.

Beatrice Webb's portrayal of Christian socialists as narrow-minded impractical theorists whose efforts had little to do with the success of co-operation has long distorted the truth of Neale's place in the history of the movement. Neale was instrumental in shaping the destiny of co-operation in the later part of the nineteenth century, improving its legal position, and shaping its administrative apparatus. As his biographer states, Neale was driven by an 'unrelenting compulsion to reconstruct society' and founded 'co-operation in its modern form, as an organised movement' (Backstrom, 2, 5).

MATTHEW LEE

Sources P. N. Backstrom, *Christian socialism and co-operation in Victorian England: Edward Vansittart Neale and the co-operative movement* (1974) · T. Christensen, *Origins and history of Christian socialism, 1848–1854* (1962) · E. R. Norman, *The Victorian Christian socialists* (1987) ·

C. Raven, *Christian socialism, 1848–1854* (1920) • P. R. Allen, 'F. D. Maurice and J. M. Ludlow: a reassessment of the leaders of Christian socialism', *Victorian Studies*, 11 (1967–8), 461–82 • B. Webb, *The co-operative movement in Great Britain* (1891) • *DNB*

Archives Bisham Abbey, Buckinghamshire • Co-operative Union, Holyoake House, Manchester, corresp. • Warks. CRO, deeds, family and legal papers | Col. U., Seligman collection, corresp. • W. Yorks. AS, Kirklees, letters to George Thomson • Wisconsin Historical Society, Madison, R. T. Ely MSS, letters

Wealth at death £14,533 17s. 5d.: resworn probate, May 1893, *CGPLA Eng. & Wales* (1892)

Neale, Elizabeth (1822–1901), Anglican nun, was born at Harrow Weald on 14 July 1822, the youngest of the four children of Cornelius Neale (1789–1823), an unsuccessful playwright and Anglican clergyman, and his wife, Susanna, daughter of John Mason *Good, a distinguished London physician. Following the premature death of her father, the strongest influence in Elizabeth's early life was her widowed mother, whose faith had a sternly Calvinist strain, and she and her brother and sisters were brought up to regard life as a constant battle against fallen human nature, in which only an unremitting attention to religious duty could avail. While she was never to lose this early spirit of religious devotion, like her sisters and her brother, the hymnologist John Mason *Neale, it was to find expression in the Anglo-Catholic tradition rather than the evangelicalism of her youth.

Following her husband's death Susanna Neale settled first in Shepperton and then in Brighton. Elizabeth and her sisters were educated at home while their brother John studied at Cambridge, where he came under the influence of the Oxford Movement. As a result of his example Elizabeth became involved in the work of the Tractarian parish of St Paul's, Brighton. Like many educated middle-class young women of the period she sought a role for herself beyond that of caring for her increasingly invalid mother, and became involved in parochial visiting and the running of a small orphanage for girls.

In 1857 Elizabeth Neale was invited by the Revd Charles Lowder to establish an Anglican sisterhood to assist him and his newly founded order of missionary priests in their work in the east London parish of St George-in-the-East. She was able to relinquish the care of the children in her Brighton orphanage to the Sisterhood of St Margaret, which her brother had founded at East Grinstead in Sussex, and her own Community of the Holy Cross began work with five sisters in the toughest part of east London dockland. As she later recalled, the sisters were often the object of ridicule on the streets and even of violence, as on one occasion when a drunken woman cut her hand with a knife. Gradually, however, the sisters won the respect of the poor whose homes they visited, a feeling that was reinforced by the heroic feats of nursing which they undertook during the cholera epidemic of 1866.

Elizabeth Neale's Community of the Holy Cross was not the first Anglican sisterhood to be founded; that honour fell to the Park Village Sisterhood in London in 1845. But it shared a number of features with other early orders, most notably its socially stratified organization, in which choir sisters were aided by lay sisters who did much of the menial work. The concentration on rescue work among prostitutes was also characteristic of the early sisterhoods, and Mother Elizabeth gained much help and advice from Harriet Monsell, the founder of a religious community at Clewer.

Elizabeth Neale's particular genius was, however, evident in two features of her community. In her *Community of the Holy Cross: Short Account of its Rise and History* (1887) she laid great emphasis on the missionary rationale behind her work, which meant that small numbers of sisters were sent to a wide variety of locations, including Bristol, York, and Sheffield, at the request of local clergy; it was only in 1887, with the building of the convent at Haywards Heath in Sussex, that the community became more institutionalized in its organization and outlook. Also, unlike in the case of other early sisterhoods, Elizabeth Neale succeeded in steering her community clear of the controversy which surrounded the creation and work of Anglican religious orders for women. In later years she was a formidable figure both physically and spiritually, and she could be severe—one sister later recalled her boxing the ears of those who disobeyed her—but she never lost the affection and loyalty of her community. In 1896 she relinquished the position of superior because of failing health. She died on 21 February 1901 at the convent, and was buried on 25 February at St Wilfrid's Church, Haywards Heath (reburied in the community's churchyard in 1957). She was one of the most successful of a generation of pioneering women who sought and found fulfilment and independence beyond the narrow confines of Victorian expectations of a woman's allotted role in society.

SEAN GILL

Sources E. Neale, *Community of the Holy Cross: short account of its rise and history* (1887) • A. Russell, *The Community of the Holy Cross, Haywards Heath* (1957) • Sister Miriam, *John Mason Neale: a memoir* (1895) • C. Lowder, *Ten years in St George's mission* (1867) • L. E. Ellsworth, *Charles Lowder and the ritualist movement* (1982) • E. Towle, *John Mason Neale: a memoir* (1907) • 'Necrologium', Community of the Holy Cross, Rempstone Hall, Leicester, Gleanings MSS • 'Reminiscences', Community of the Holy Cross, Rempstone Hall, Leicester, Gleanings MSS

Archives Community of the Holy Cross, Rempstone Hall, Rempstone, 'Necrologium' | Community of the Holy Cross, Rempstone Hall, Rempstone, Gleanings MSS

Likenesses photograph, *c.*1862, Community of the Holy Cross, Rempstone Hall, Rempstone, bound volume of photographs • photograph, 1887, Community of the Holy Cross, Rempstone Hall, Rempstone, bound volume of photographs; repro. in Russell, *Community of the Holy Cross*, facing p. 12 • portrait, Community of the Holy Cross, Rempstone Hall, Rempstone

Neale, Erskine (1804–1883), Church of England clergyman and author, born on 12 March 1804 at Exeter, in Devon, was the elder son of Dr Adam *Neale (1778?–1832) and his wife, Margaret Young, and the brother of William Johnstoune *Neale (1812–1893). He was educated at Westminster School from 1815 to 1816, and at Glasgow University from 1818 to 1824. He attended Emmanuel College, Cambridge, from 1825, graduating BA in 1828 and MA in 1832. He was lecturer at St Hilda's Church, Jarrow, co. Durham, in 1828, and was ordained deacon in 1829 and priest in 1830. Neale was appointed vicar of Adlingfleet, Yorkshire, in 1835, rector of Kirton, Suffolk, in 1844, and vicar of Exning with Lanwade, Suffolk, in 1854. He was also chaplain to Frederick, fourth Earl Spencer, and to the earl of Huntingdon. On 9 April 1856 he married Elizabeth Ann Scovell, eldest daughter of John Scovell, an author. A daughter, Georgiana, was born in the winter of 1859–60; she had at least one sibling, a sister named Mary Henrietta.

A dedicated Christian with liberal social views, Neale became a popular author. Among his sixteen or so books was the semi-autobiographical *The Life-Book of a Labourer* (1839) and *The Bishop's Daughter* (1842), his only novel. An active freemason, Neale's *Stray Leaves from a Freemason's Note-Book* was published anonymously in 1846. He developed an attractive style, with touches of Dickensian humour.

Experiences of a Gaol Chaplain, published in 1847, was entirely fictitious but dealt seriously with prison reform. It reflected his admiration for Elizabeth Fry, whose name he insisted 'deserves to be hallowed' (p. 399). Blaming much of crime on the 'folly and barbarism of the Game Laws', Neale believed that education, cheap food, and employment would reduce crime (ibid., 202). The theme of *The Closing Scene*, published a year later, was that however convenient in life sceptical views might be, they were poor supports when death was near. He returned to this idea in his last important book, *Sunsets and Sunshine* (1862): in this work he reflected on Lola Montes's life, arguing that 'The retrospect of an existence devoted to pleasure ... must strew with thorns a dying pillow' (*Sunsets and Sunshine*, 16). Neale also wrote a dramatic tract (the proceeds of which went to the Church of England Scripture Readers' Society) dealing with a notorious London murder in 1849, committed by Frederick and Marie Manning.

Neale was noted as a collector of papers, letters, and autographs, many relating to the duke of Kent, commonly blamed for the Gibraltar mutiny of 1802; Neale's father, a physician with the forces in the Peninsular War, had admired the duke. After the duke's death in 1820 Neale waited in vain for a military expert to clear his name, before assuming the task himself and publishing *The Life of Edward, Duke of Kent* in 1850. This biography of Queen Victoria's father succeeded beyond expectation, becoming (and indeed remaining) the chief source of information about him. All Neale's books were in demand, and several were reprinted.

The Crimean War stimulated Neale to write *My Comrade and my Colours* (1854), a shilling paperback about the Napoleonic wars. After he had moved to Exning, his last parish, in 1854, Neale wrote little more; he was busy with parish affairs, including old charities, such as the Shepherd's Charity, and the provision of poorhouses, and had too the responsibilities of a family. He was highly regarded in the village, and some of his sermons were printed. Neale died on 23 November 1883 at his vicarage. He was memorialized by an impressive monument in Exning church and was buried in the churchyard.

Another Erskine Neale, also an Anglican clergyman and an author, is sometimes confused with the subject of this article. This alternative Erskine Neale held cures in Yorkshire and Suffolk, and was the author of *The Living and the Dead* (1827), wrongly attributed (with other works) to Erskine Neale (1804–1883) in the *Dictionary of National Biography*.   BRENDA COLLOMS

Sources Venn, *Alum. Cant.* · E. Neale, *The life-book of a labourer, by a working clergyman* (1839) · *N&Q*, 6th ser., 12 (1885), 465 · *N&Q*, 7th ser., 1 (1886), 31–2, 115, 156 · Crockford (1875) · private information (1996) · *Ars Quatuor Coronatorum*, 18 (1905), 50
Archives BL, letters to Royal Literary Fund, loan 96 · NL Scot., letters to Blackwoods
Wealth at death £9649 17s. 9d.: probate, 21 Dec 1883, *CGPLA Eng. & Wales*

Neale, Sir Harry Burrard, second baronet (1765–1840), naval officer and politician, born on 16 September 1765, was the eldest son of Lieutenant-Colonel William Burrard (1712–1780), governor of Yarmouth Castle on the Isle of Wight, and his second wife, Mary, the daughter of Dr Joseph Pearce, of Lymington. William Burrard's elder brother, Harry Burrard (d. 1791), was created a baronet in 1769. The younger Harry Burrard was the first cousin of General Sir Harry Burrard. After attending Christchurch grammar school he entered the navy in 1778 on board the *Roebuck* with Sir Andrew Snape Hamond, and was at the capture of Charlestown in April 1780. He was afterwards in the *Chatham*, with Hamond's nephew Captain Douglas, and took part in the capture of the French frigate *Magicienne* off Boston on 2 September 1781. In 1783 he returned to England as acting lieutenant of the *Perseverance*. He was afterwards with Sir John Hamilton in the *Hector*, and in 1785 was in the *Europe* in the West Indies, and was officially thanked for saving five men from a wreck during a hurricane. On 29 September 1787 he was promoted lieutenant of the *Expedition*. In 1790 he was in the *Southampton* with Keats, and afterwards in the *Victory*, Lord Hood's flagship. On 3 November 1790 he was promoted commander of the *Orestes*, employed in the preventive service. During the same year he was returned to parliament for the family seat of Lymington, which he represented until 1802, again in 1806–7, from 1812 to 1823, and from 1832 to 1834.

On the death of his uncle Sir Harry Burrard on 12 April 1791, Burrard succeeded to the baronetcy, and on 1 February 1793 he was promoted captain and appointed to the frigate *Aimable*, in which he accompanied Lord Hood to the Mediterranean; there he was actively employed with the fleet and in charge of convoys for the Levant. He returned to England towards the end of 1794, and by royal licence, dated 8 April 1795, assumed the name and arms of Neale, on his marriage on 15 April to Grace Elizabeth (d. 1855), the daughter and coheir of Robert Neale of Shaw House, Wiltshire; they had no children.

Neale was shortly afterwards appointed to the command of the *San Fiorenzo* (42 guns), stationed for some time at Weymouth, in attendance on the king. On 9 March 1797 the *San Fiorenzo*, in company with the *Nymphe*, captured the French frigates *Resistance* and *Constance* off Brest. She was at the Nore when the mutiny broke out, but her crew refused to join it. She was ordered to anchor under the stern of the *Sandwich*; however, a few days later she escaped, under fire. This was a major blow to the mutiny, and on 7 June a meeting of London merchants and ship-owners, at the Royal Exchange, passed a vote of thanks to Neale and the officers and seamen of the *San Fiorenzo*. Neale continued in the *San Fiorenzo*, and on 9 April 1799 was in company with the *Amelia* (38 guns) off Lorient, where three large frigates were lying in the outer road, ready for sea. In a sudden squall the *Amelia* was partly dis-masted, and the French frigates slipped their cables and sailed towards the *San Fiorenzo*. The *Amelia*, however, quickly cleared away the wreck, and the two ships, keep-ing together, repelled the attack; the French, having lost severely, returned to Lorient.

In 1801 Neale was appointed to the *Centaur* (74 guns), from which he was moved to the royal yacht. In May and June 1804 he was one of the lords of the Admiralty under Earl St Vincent, but in July returned to the yacht. The fol-lowing year he was appointed to the *London* (98 guns), one of the small squadron under Sir John Borlase Warren which captured the French ships *Marengo* and *Belle Poule* on 13 March 1806. The two ships were actually brought to action by the *London*, but after an hour the frigate *Amazon*, having come up, engaged and captured the *Belle Poule*, while the *Marengo* (74 guns), under the personal command of Admiral Linois, seeing the *Foudroyant*, Warren's flag-ship, drawing near, surrendered to the *London* after a run-ning fight of more than four hours. Neale was again at the Board of Admiralty between February 1806 and April 1807, during the 'Ministry of the Talents'.

In 1808 Neale was captain of the fleet under Lord Gam-bier, with whom, in 1809, he was present at the abortive attack on the French ships in Basque Roads. On 31 July 1810 he was promoted rear-admiral, and from 1811 to 1814 com-manded a squadron on the coast of France, with his flag first in the *Boyne* and afterwards in the *Ville de Paris*; he often acted for Lord Keith, the commander-in-chief, who was frequently ashore. On 4 June 1814 he was advanced to vice-admiral, on 2 January 1815 was nominated a KCB, and on 14 September 1822 was made GCB. He was commander-in-chief in the Mediterranean from 1823 to 1826, a post which then carried with it a GCMG. In 1824 his prompt action enforced the observance of the 1816 treaty on the dey of Algiers, though not until bomb vessels had been sent from England and the squadron was in position for opening fire. Neale became admiral on 22 July 1830, and in August 1832 was offered the command at Portsmouth. When Sir Thomas Foley died in January 1833 the offer was repeated, on the condition that he resign his recently obtained seat in the House of Commons. Neale refused the command on these terms, pointing out that the condi-tion was unprecedented and therefore insulting. The case was brought up in the house, but Sir James Graham, then whig first lord, publicly maintained that, as the Admiralty was responsible for its appointments, it had authority to make what stipulations it judged necessary. In private Graham admitted that he wanted to remove Neale from the House of Commons because he was not a supporter of the government.

Neale died at the Royal York Hotel, Brighton, on 7 Febru-ary 1840, and was buried at Walhampton, near Lymington. He had been a local benefactor, and his coffin was carried to his grave by twenty-four poor labouring men. He was succeeded in the baronetcy by his brother the Revd George Burrard, rector of Yarmouth on the Isle of Wight. A memorial obelisk was erected on Mount Pleasant, opposite the town of Lymington, of which he was lord of the manor, and which he had then represented in parlia-ment for forty years. Neale was a minor landowner, a polit-ical admiral, and a favourite of George III and William IV, and his career spanned three major wars; he served with distinction in all of them, and was known throughout the service for his straightforward and open conduct.

J. K. LAUGHTON, *rev.* ANDREW LAMBERT

Sources Letters of … the earl of St Vincent, whilst the first lord of the admiralty, 1801–1804, ed. D. B. Smith, 2, Navy RS, 61 (1927) · Selections from the correspondence of Admiral John Markham, ed. C. Markham, Navy RS, 28 (1904) · L. B. Namier, The structure of politics at the acces-sion of George III, 2 vols. (1929) · Cumbria AS, Carlisle, Graham MSS · HoP, Commons · The Keith papers, 3, ed. C. Lloyd, Navy RS, 96 (1955) · Letters and papers of Admiral of the Fleet Sir Thos. Byam Martin, GCB, ed. R. V. Hamilton, 3, Navy RS, 19 (1901) · GM, 2nd ser., 13 (1840), 540 · d. cert.

Archives Hants. RO, political and election papers · Hants. RO, papers · New York Historical Society, notes relating to Algiers | BL, corresp. with Sir T. B. Martin, Add. MSS 41364–41369 · Cumbria AS, Carlisle, Graham MSS · NMM, letters to Lord Keith

Likenesses C. Turner, mezzotint, pubd 1812 (after M. Brown), BM · J. B. Lane, stipple, 1822 (after W. Beechey), BM · M. Brown, portrait · G. Childs, lithograph (after C. S. Le Bailly), BM

Neale, James (*bap.* 1722, *d.* 1792), biblical scholar and Church of England clergyman, was baptized on 12 Novem-ber 1722, at St Paul's, Covent Garden, Westminster, the son of Robert Neale, apothecary of that parish, and his wife, Mary. He was elected exhibitioner at Christ's Hos-pital, London, on 14 May 1731 and admitted sizar at Pem-broke College, Cambridge, on 4 July 1739; he graduated BA in 1743 and proceeded MA in 1746. From 1747 until 1762 he was master of Henley-on-Thames grammar school, Oxfordshire, which flourished greatly under his leader-ship; he also served as curate of Bix, Oxfordshire, under its rector the orientalist Thomas Hunt (1696–1774), whom Neale describes as having been 'a father to me in a thou-sand instances' (Neale, *Funeral Sermon*, vi). He was subse-quently curate of Aldbourne, Wiltshire.

Neale was an able classical and oriental scholar and an inventive preacher. At Henley he held private meetings for prayer that attracted many from outside his family circle but also generated official hostility. Having been forced to vacate his post he published *Select Hymns for Public and Private Worship of Real Christians* (1763), in which he attacked tithes but upheld subscription to the Thirty-Nine Articles. Neale moved to London, where he preached in the open air near Mayfair Chapel. In 1771 his literal trans-lation of Hosea appeared; it was based on the Hebrew text and defended the idea of the presence of the doctrine of the Trinity in the Old Testament.

Neale died in 1792. He had three sons who attended university—James (1748–1828), Robert (*b.* 1751/2), and John (1755/6–1841)—two of whom, James and John, entered the Church of England clergy. James, who graduated BA from St John's College, Cambridge, in 1771, became perpetual curate of Allerton Mauleverer, Yorkshire, and died at Botley, Hampshire, on 10 November 1828. His third son was **William Henry Neale** (*bap.* 1785, *d.* 1855), theological writer, baptized at Littlehampton, Sussex, on 12 May 1785. He was elected to Christ's Hospital in April 1793, where he gained an exhibition, and admitted sizar of Pembroke College, Cambridge, on 11 February 1803; he graduated BA in 1808 and proceeded MA in 1810. On 8 February 1808 he was appointed to the mastership of Beverley grammar school, Yorkshire, which he resigned in December 1815. In November 1823 he became chaplain of the county bridewell in Gosport, Hampshire, for whose inmates he composed a manual of spiritual instruction and where he remained until 1850. On 5 March 1840 he was elected FSA, but had withdrawn from the society by 1847.

Neale's publications included *The Mohammedan System of Theology* (1828), which denied that Islam was divinely inspired and contrasted its teachings unfavourably with Christianity; a sermon originally preached in the parish church at Portsmouth, *The Christian's Duty in Perilous Times* (1829); *The Different Dispensations of the True Religion* (1843); and a new edition of his grandfather's translation of Hosea (1850). In 1853 he accepted nomination as a poor brother of the Charterhouse, London, and died there on 20 January 1855.

GORDON GOODWIN, *rev.* SCOTT MANDELBROTE

Sources G. A. T. Allan, *Christ's Hospital exhibitioners to the universities of Oxford and Cambridge, 1566–1923* (1924), 38, 50 · J. Neale, *The funeral sermon of John Sarney* [1760] · J. Neale, *A sermon (in substance) preached abroad* (1771) · J. Neale, *The prophecies of Hosea* (1771) · W. H. Neale, 'Preliminary observations', in J. Neale, *The prophecies of Hosea*, 2nd edn (1850), 5–6 · *GM*, 1st ser., 93/2 (1823), 463; 98/2 (1828), 571; 2nd ser., 13/1 (1840), 416 · Venn, *Alum. Cant.* · Foster, *Alum. Oxon.*, 1715–1886, 3.1009 · W. H. Neale, *The Mohammedan system of theology* (1828) · G. Oliver, *The history and antiquities of the town and minister of Beverley* (1829), 279 · private information (1894, 2004) [master, Pembroke Cam.] · J. S. Burn, *A history of Henley-on-Thames* (1861) · d. cert. [William Henry Neale]

Neale, Sir John Ernest (1890–1975), historian, was born at Liverpool on 7 December 1890, the son of a master builder, Arthur Neale, whose wife, Mary Emily Latham, supported herself and her three sons by turning seamstress when her husband died in 1895. His early life cultivated in Neale a dedication to what is vulgarly called the protestant work ethic, coming as he did from dissenting rather than establishment stock. He attended the Blue Coat School in Liverpool, leaving at fourteen and preparing for university entrance at night school. He entered Liverpool University and graduated with second-class honours in history in 1914, to commence graduate work on William Cobbett. There seems to be little or no record of his life in the war years, although there are reports of time spent in Malta. He had already transferred from Liverpool to London to undertake research in Tudor history under A. F. Pollard,

Sir John Ernest Neale (1890–1975), by Howard Coster, 1940s

and in 1919 he returned to a junior post at University College, London. Apart from two years as professor of modern history at Manchester (1925–7), Neale remained at University College for the remainder of his career. In 1927 he became *de jure* F. C. Montague's successor as Astor professor of English history, but *de facto* he was Elisha to Pollard's Elijah. As head of department *ex officio*, like Pollard before him, he was absolute monarch until the day of his retirement in 1956. He built up a formidable and very professorial history department. His career was also bound up with the Institute of Historical Research, which Pollard had founded in 1921, and where every Monday evening for many decades Neale presided over the postgraduate seminar which he had inherited from Pollard. He was never absent from the institute's annual Anglo-American Conference of Historians, and rejoiced in the collegiality which joined American with British historians of the sixteenth century, and which attracted many Americans to his seminar. However, he visited the United States on only one occasion, in 1958. Following in the Pollard tradition, Neale was one of the last of the old-style academic power brokers. But, unlike Pollard, he was a rotund, genial, and often amusing man, universally known as Jimmy Neale, after a concert performance in his early days which linked him with Sunny Jim, a character used to promote a brand of breakfast cereal.

That Neale became the historian of Elizabethan England (for his generation) was doubtless a consequence of Pollard's reluctance to share the reign of Henry VIII with anybody else. By the same token, when Sir Geoffrey Elton became Neale's pupil in 1946, he was directed back to the reign of Henry VIII. Neale's researches, which were to come to full fruition in the books which he published in later years, took him into some of the technical intricacies of Elizabethan parliamentary history, the subject of all his early scholarly articles. But Neale would never be content to communicate only with fellow professionals. In 1934 he published the book which made his name, *Queen Elizabeth*. Lytton Strachey's *Elizabeth and Essex* may have been a provocation. The Elizabeth biography also arose from a fruitful engagement with the publisher Jonathan Cape, who shared with Neale an enthusiasm for making history popular. *Queen Elizabeth*, in common with many titles in the Jonathan Cape Bedford Historical Series, appeared, so as not to put off 'the general reader', without any scholarly apparatus, so that it is impossible to know what some of the sources were.

Neale had written a biography, not a general history of Elizabeth's reign (he had no taste for writing textbooks), so it was inevitable that he should have been charged with making the queen larger than her context, even larger than life. Rumours were rife that he was in love with Queen Elizabeth, which did not disturb Elfreda Skelton, a pupil, and historian of the court of Star Chamber, whom Neale had married in 1932. (The Neales were survived by their daughter, Stella.) But Neale was hard at work on the deep pile (as it were) of Elizabethan political, and especially parliamentary, culture which would lead to the trilogy of books published between 1949 and 1957. The first of these, *The Elizabethan House of Commons*, uncovered, with painstaking research in archives all over the country, the political clout of the gentry, who, through systems of clientage, occupied most of the seats in the Commons which were supposedly the property of townsmen. At about the same time, Neale delivered his British Academy Raleigh lecture, 'The Elizabethan political scene', a landmark in our understanding of Elizabethan politics.

Then came Neale's *Elizabeth I and her Parliaments*, two volumes published (inevitably by Jonathan Cape) in 1953 and 1957. It is important to notice the title. These never claimed to be all-encompassing histories of the Elizabethan parliaments. Their subject was the ongoing clash between an autocratic queen, who placed unusual restrictions on the freedom of parliament to offer counsel, and the aspirations of the Commons, heightened by the religious zeal of puritanism. Neale knew that he was writing what he regarded as the headline stories, not the grinding business of bills and acts, which filled the inside of the newspaper, and which Sir Geoffrey Elton insisted made up the real business of an English parliament. But Neale's 'whiggishness', the instinct, shared with and perhaps derived from Pollard, to look for the first shoots of the modern parliamentary constitution, coupled with his urge to write an accessible, readable history, led to what Elton denounced as an over-dramatic, and even, in that respect, superficial, account of what these parliaments were about. Neale's claims for the historical originality and momentousness of the Elizabethan parliaments were also scouted by medievalists, and especially by Professor J. S. Roskell. Yet the encounters between monarch and Commons, which make his arresting narrative, certainly happened, and, as Neale recounted them, make an unforgettable chapter in English history.

The tragedy of Neale's career was in the way that he chose to spend the nearly twenty years of his retirement. He had the ambition to write the biography of Elizabeth's last favourite, the earl of Essex, which we still to this day lack. It would have made an appropriate, enveloping, diptych with his *Queen Elizabeth*. But he was hijacked by what he called the 'biographical' approach to history. This was not so much a biographical as a prosopographical approach, famously applied by Sir Lewis Namier to the history of eighteenth-century politics. To analyse the political processes of an age through the very small print of many political careers had paid dividends in *The Elizabethan House of Commons*. But in the three Elizabethan volumes of the History of Parliament, which contained much rich biographical information, the last thing to emerge was a history of parliament. Not only was Neale personally preoccupied with the distracting labours which this large enterprise entailed, they dominated his seminar at University College, to the exasperation of those present who had little interest in these biographical minutiae. Neale expected to write the introduction to these volumes, but found that he had little to add to what he had already published on the subject. When they appeared in 1981, six years after his death at his home, 57 Penn Road, Beaconsfield, Buckinghamshire, on 2 September 1975, they were no longer attributed to Neale, who, to add insult to injury, the chairman of the editorial board suggested had never been a hands-on editor.

Neale received all the honours due to a leading historian of his generation, including honorary degrees from seven universities. He was elected to the British Academy in 1949 and knighted in 1955, letting his colleagues in University College, London, know that he still wished to be addressed as plain Professor Neale. There was, of course, no question of Christian names.

PATRICK COLLINSON

Sources J. Hurstfield, 'John Ernest Neale, 1890–1975', *PBA*, 63 (1977), 403–21 · *DNB* · personal knowledge (2004) · CGPLA Eng. & Wales (1975)

Archives SOUND BL NSA, 'Master of arts: Sir John Neale in conversation with Joel Hurstfield', NP888W

Likenesses H. Coster, photograph, 1940–49, NPG [see illus.] · W. Stoneman, photograph, 1949, NPG · M. Gerson, photograph, repro. in S. T. Bindoff, J. Hurstfield, and C. H. Williams, eds., *Elizabethan government and society: essays presented to Sir John Neale* (1961), frontispiece

Wealth at death £81,269: probate, 17 Nov 1975, CGPLA Eng. & Wales

Neale, John Mason (1818–1866), Church of England clergyman and author, was born at 40 Lamb's Conduit Street, London, on 24 January 1818, the first child and only son of the Revd Cornelius Neale (d. 1823) and his wife, Susanna Good (d. 1860). His youngest sister was Elizabeth *Neale (1822–1901). His father had been senior wrangler at Cambridge in 1812, and was elected fellow of St John's College in 1813, but had decided against ordination, preferring his literary and theatrical pursuits. He wrote verse fluently, and took an interest in education. In 1816 he married Susanna, whose father, John Mason *Good, was a London doctor with linguistic and literary talents. Both families were strongly evangelical, and in 1820 Cornelius experienced a conversion, which led him to study theology and be ordained. His premature death left his son and three younger daughters to the care of their mother.

John Mason Neale (1818–1866), by William Walker & Sons

Susanna Neale moved her family to Shepperton, where her son was taught by the rector, William Russell, with whom he maintained a lifelong correspondence. As his mother sought a better climate for her health, Neale moved from school to school: Blackheath in 1829, Sherborne in Dorset in 1833 (where he distinguished himself by writing prize-winning essays in Latin and English), and Farnham, Surrey, in 1835. He won a scholarship to Trinity College, Cambridge, in 1836, where he was acknowledged to be the best classicist of his year; his weakness in mathematics, however, meant that he failed the mathematical tripos, and under the rules then obtaining at Cambridge he was unable to proceed to classical honours and had to accept a pass degree in 1840.

The foundation of ecclesiology Neale's real work at Cambridge, however, was his theological transition from evangelicalism to Anglo-Catholicism. It was not so much the Oxford Movement and Tractarianism that influenced Neale's development as his passion for antiquarianism. This was first acquired as he studied under James Challis (1803–1882) for his university entrance examination, developed thereafter in his church tours as an undergraduate with his friend Edward Boyce, and reinforced by his reading of Hurrell Froude's *Remains* (1838–9). He began to see architecture as illustrating theological and liturgical as well as aesthetic principles, much as he had learned to read scripture symbolically and typologically. With his friends Edward Boyce and Benjamin Webb (1819–1885) he founded the Cambridge Camden (later Ecclesiological) Society in 1839 to define correct principles of church architecture and decoration, ritual and music. The ecclesiologists held the Gothic—and particularly the fourteenth-century decorated style—as the ideal church architecture, not just aesthetically but also liturgically and theologically. In 1843 Neale and Webb published *The Symbolism of Churches and Church Ornaments*, their translation and edition of the *Rationale divinorum officiorum* by William Durandus. This thirteenth-century text set out the significance of every detail of church architecture and furnishing. By emphasizing chancel and altar, and by removing triple-decker pulpits and comfortable box pews, the ecclesiologists shifted the emphasis from meeting-house to sanctuary, from preaching to sacrament. The use of music, of incense, and of colour in stained glass, tile, and vestments was intended to involve all the worshipper's senses and offer a foretaste of the heavenly Jerusalem. William Butterfield's All Saints, Margaret Street, was the London exemplar of ecclesiological principles, as expounded by Neale and his fellows in a number of pamphlets and tracts, and from 1841 to 1868 they produced a monthly publication entitled *The Ecclesiologist*. Their influence is visible in the concept and fabric of Victorian churches throughout Britain and the colonies.

Ordained deacon in 1841, Neale accepted the post of chaplain at Downing College, but he resigned after only weeks. He went temporarily to St Nicholas's, Guildford, to be curate to William Henley Pearson, later Pearson-Jervis. Charles Richard Sumner, the strongly evangelical bishop of Winchester, refused him a licence in the diocese, however, and Neale had to give up the parochial ministry he had begun with great enthusiasm. Ordained priest in May 1842, he was offered the living of Crawley in Sussex, where once again he entertained visions of establishing a model parish, making plans for its ecclesiological and social reform, as well as for his marriage to Sarah Norman Webster (1814?–1873), the daughter of Thomas Webster (d. 1840), rector of St Botolph's, Cambridge, and vicar of Oakington. His strength was unequal to his plans, however, and a diagnosis of consumption prevented his institution to the living. After their wedding on 27 July 1842 Neale and his wife divided their time between England and Madeira. Neale's health improved, and he was able productively to pursue his linguistic studies and his literary work. During the anxious time which surrounded John Henry Newman's decision to leave the Church of England in 1845 for Roman Catholicism he wrote frequent and encouraging letters to his friend Benjamin Webb, reassuring his fellow Anglo-Catholics, much as he did several years later in his pamphlet *A Few Words of Hope in the Present Crisis of the English Church* (1850). That crisis was the Gorham judgment, in which the privy council overturned a church court ruling in a decision deplorably (for Tractarians) significant for church and state relations, and for the theology of baptism. He needed also to sustain his ecclesiological colleagues during the attack upon the Cambridge Camden Society by Francis Close (1797–1882), the evangelical rector of Cheltenham. The society was briefly dissolved as a result of the furore which followed the publication of Close's *The Restoration of Churches is a Restoration of Popery* (1845), though it was soon reconstituted in London as the Ecclesiological Society.

Warden of Sackville College In 1846 Neale was appointed by the patrons (Lady De La Warr and her husband, the fifth earl) to the wardenship of Sackville College, East Grinstead. The college was a charity founded in 1608 by the second earl of Dorset; it consisted of a warden's house, a chapel, a refectory, and housing for a small number of pensioners. Neale entered with enthusiasm upon the work, renovating the buildings, beginning with the chapel, and re-establishing the chapel services provided for in the college statutes. Not surprisingly, Neale's renovations and practices were models of good ecclesiology, and equally unsurprising was the reaction among some of those who observed the changes. The bishop of Chichester, Ashurst Gilbert Turner, deplored what he considered extreme practices in his diocese; when in 1847 the new chapel appointments were brought to his attention he inhibited Neale from celebration and other clerical functions in the diocese. Neale and his patrons understood that the college itself was outside the jurisdiction of the bishop, but they lost the argument in a case brought before the court of the arches in 1848. Although the inhibition was not formally lifted until 1863 Neale obeyed it to the letter, celebrating only privately. That was not the only controversy associated with his wardenship of Sackville College. When Neale changed the customary coffin and pall provided for a pensioner's burial, complaints and even a riot in 1851 ensued. Moreover, his own assistant warden (and later successor), John Henry Rogers, spent much of the six years following his appointment in 1853 in various legal and journalistic efforts to condemn Neale for so-called papist practices and remove him from the wardenship.

In 1854 Neale established a sisterhood, the Society of Saint Margaret, to provide nursing—initially for the college pensioners but soon, under the leadership of Ann Gream, the daughter of the rector of Rotherfield, for the poor of the neighbourhood. Following training at Westminster Hospital, and despite the dangers of their new profession, the sisterhood flourished. Neale was their chaplain. Assuming that the bishop's inhibition applied to churches in the diocese, he celebrated privately for them in the house they occupied close to the college. In 1857 one of the newest sisters, Emily Scobell, died of scarlet fever and left her estate of £400 to the sisterhood. She had entered upon her new life as Sister Amy against the wishes of her father, John Scobell, the rural dean of Lewes. After her death he accused Neale of inveigling his daughter into the sisterhood for the sake of her estate. A riot took place at her funeral in Lewes, and as a result of the

controversy the sisters temporarily lost episcopal support. Nevertheless, they continued and expanded their work; by 1865 they needed a new convent, and Neale was able before his death to preside over the laying of the cornerstone of a new building designed by George Edmund Street.

Sackville College was Neale's home for twenty years; there he and his wife raised their five children: Agnes, Cornelius, Mary, Katherine (usually known by her second name, Ermenild), and Margaret. In 1850 he declined the post of provost of St Ninian's in Perth, Scotland, preferring to remain in England to serve the Church of England. Many another would have kept Sackville College a sinecure or a place of retirement; even with his innovations, it provided Neale with only a limited round of responsibilities. Ministering to the pensioners and later to the sisters constituted important duties, but they were predictable ones, and allowed time for his remarkably productive writing.

Writings and assessment Standing at his desk in his book-crammed study just under the nursery, Neale wrote tirelessly in his various projects to improve readers' understanding of Christian history, Anglican theology, and liturgical practice. He wrote for clergy and laity, for adults and children; he wrote history, fiction, biography, sermons, travelogue, and poetry, both original and in translation. One early and continuing task was his share of publications of the Ecclesiological Society. In addition to numerous contributions on hymnody, liturgy, and Christian symbolism to its journal Neale wrote some of the most influential of the society's early pamphlets, including *A Few Words to Church Builders* (1841), *A Few Words to Church Wardens on … Church Ornament*, nos. 1 and 2 (1841), *Twenty-Three Reasons for Getting Rid of Church Pues* (1841), and *Church Enlargement and Church Arrangement* (1843).

Neale's lifelong work, begun in Madeira, was a *History of the Holy Eastern Church* in three volumes: *The Patriarchate of Alexandria* (1847), a *General Introduction* (1850), and *The Patriarchate of Antioch*, edited by George Williams after Neale's death (1873). A number of Anglo-Catholics were interested in the Eastern church, among them Edward Pusey and William Palmer of Magdalen College. Palmer, whom he visited in 1846, referred Neale to many sources and to like-minded contacts in the Orthodox church, such as Andrey Nikolayevich Muravyov, under-procurator of the Holy Governing Synod, and Yevgeny Ivanovich Popov, chaplain to the Russian embassy in London. Neale saw the Eastern church as maintaining the strongest traditional links with the teachings of the fathers, unaffected by either the Reformation or the claims of papal superiority; moreover, he saw doctrinal similarities between Anglican and Eastern churches, and considered Eastern practices, such as the veneration of icons, congruent with his own ecclesiological understanding of the importance of material symbols even in matters spiritual. Altogether his sympathy for Eastern orthodoxy was remarkably intelligent and respectful, though his researches were limited chiefly to printed materials (albeit in a score of languages), and he had a tendency from time to time to see clearer parallels than someone with a different purpose might perceive.

In addition to the history, Neale wrote other works designed to improve Anglican familiarity with Eastern Christianity. They included his most popular novel, *Theodora Phranza* (1853–4), and several other works of fiction with Eastern settings; *The Liturgies of SS Mark, James, Clement, Chrysostom and Basil*, with R. F. Littledale (1859); and *Voices from the East: Documents on the Present State and Working of the Oriental Church* (1859). The most influential was his *Hymns of the Eastern Church* (1862), which gave Victorian hymnologists and eventually Victorian congregations some taste of Orthodox hymnody. The book's contents are less translations than selections, adaptations, and even hymns largely of Neale's own composition, though Eastern in style; among the best-known are 'The day of resurrection', 'Come, ye faithful, raise the strain', and 'O happy band of pilgrims'.

Neale's contribution to hymnody went far beyond his Eastern hymns: his translations from the Latin restored medieval hymns to Anglican use. Many were still sung a century and a half later: his translations from Venantius Fortunatus, 'Sing, my tongue, the glorious battle' and 'The royal banners forward go'; the centos from *Hora novissima, tempora pessima*—'Brief life is here our portion', 'To thee, O dear, dear country', and 'Jerusalem the golden'; and such others as 'Blessed city, heavenly Salem (Christ is made the sure foundation)', 'Jesu! the very thought is sweet', 'Before the ending of the day', 'Draw nigh, draw nigh [O come, O come], Emmanuel', 'Of the Father once begotten', and 'All glory, laud and honour to thee Redeemer King'. True to the theory he laid out in his article 'English hymnology: its history and prospects' in the *Christian Remembrancer* (October 1849), his *Mediaeval Hymns and Sequences* (1851) included translations in the metre of the originals, allowing them to be sung to their old tunes. Under the auspices of the Ecclesiological Society Neale collaborated with Thomas Helmore to produce *The Hymnal Noted* (1851 and 1854); intended for choral use rather than reading pleasure, it was the most important volume in the revival of plainsong in Anglican churches and the restoration of an English Catholic hymnody. His authority was consulted by others, such as the compilers of *Hymns Ancient and Modern* (1860), the best-selling and most inclusive hymnbook of the period. Like other Tractarians, Neale approved the principle of reserve; his dislike of Methodist and much contemporary hymnody was founded on his distrust of its subjectivity and sentimentalism. It was another of Neale's principles that hymns should inculcate sound doctrine: since much of English hymnody was written in the Calvinist tradition, it is not surprising that he found much to criticize, particularly in the works of Isaac Watts, whose hymns he knew from his own evangelical upbringing to be sometimes frightening. One of his earlier collections, *Hymns for Children* (1842), was the result of his childhood experience; *Hymns for the Sick* (1843) was the product of his later experience of ill health. Other hymnological contributions included two volumes of carols, *Carols for*

Christmastide (1853) and *Carols for Eastertide* (1854). His most famous carol, 'Good King Wenceslas', appeared not in a hymn collection but in one of his children's books, *Deeds of Faith* (1849).

Books for children might be expected to sell more copies than abstruse volumes of church history, and Neale's income depended in part upon such titles as *English History for Children* (1845), *Triumphs of the Cross: Tales and Sketches of Christian Heroism* (1845), *Stories from Heathen Mythology and Greek History for the Use of Christian Children* (1847), *Stories for Children from Church History* (1850, 1851), and *Evenings at Sackville College: Legends for Children* (1852).

The history of the Church of England in the nineteenth century is one of revival and renewal: by the end of the century Anglican worship bore Neale's stamp in its buildings, its furnishings and decorations, its hymns, and its revitalized sisterhoods. He was by no means a single force, although he worked in social obscurity—under disapproval or suspicion from his neighbours and superiors. His tireless correspondence and extensive publication connected him with a much wider world. Shy in unfamiliar or public surroundings, Neale was enthusiastic and even zealous in private or in print. He did not know half-measures, and compromise he rejected. The controversy that sometimes encroached upon his routine or threatened his concentration seems only to have strengthened his resolve. Less tangible was the result of his sustained work for *sobornost*, the harmony and unity of Christians in their various communions, and in particular the greater understanding between the English and the Orthodox churches.

Though his intellectual strength and versatility were great, Neale's physical health was never strong. He was tall and angular, and seemed often distracted, perhaps because he was short-sighted as well as wrapped up in a dozen simultaneous projects. His smile was warm and winning, however, and he was tender toward his children, although he expected much of them. Two operations in 1866 failed to restore him to health, and he died at the age of forty-eight on the feast of the transfiguration, 6 August 1866, at Sackville College; he was buried in the churchyard in East Grinstead on 10 August. In his lifetime he had received little official recognition (apart from an honorary degree from Trinity College, Hartford, Connecticut) and no church dignitary attended the funeral of the warden of Sackville College. The centenary of his death, however, was marked by ceremonies attended by the archbishop of Canterbury.   SUSAN DRAIN

Sources A. G. Lough, *John Mason Neale: priest extraordinary* (1975) • A. G. Lough, *The influence of John Mason Neale* (1962) • L. Litvack, *John Mason Neale and the quest for sobornost* (1994) • *Letters of John Mason Neale*, ed. M. S. Lawson (1910) • W. Jowett, *A memoir of the Rev. Cornelius Neale* (1834) • E. A. Towle, *John Mason Neale: a memoir* (1906) • Sister Miriam, *John Mason Neale: a memoir* (1895) • J. Julian, ed., *A dictionary of hymnology*, rev. edn (1907) • B. Rainbow, *The choral revival in the Anglican church, 1839–1872* (1970) • G. Rowell, *The vision glorious: themes and personalities of the Catholic revival in Anglicanism* (1983)

Archives LPL, corresp., literary MSS, and papers • W. Sussex RO, letters and papers as warden of Sackville College | BL, letters to

W. E. Gladstone, Add. MSS 44384–44406 · LPL, corresp. with Benjamin Webb · LPL, letters to Cecil Wray
Likenesses W. Walker & Sons, photograph, NPG [*see illus.*] · photograph, repro. in Lough, *John Mason Neale*, frontispiece
Wealth at death under £3000: probate, 31 Oct 1866, *CGPLA Eng. & Wales*

Neale, John Preston (1780–1847), architectural draughtsman, is best remembered for his views of the nation's country houses, churches, and public buildings. Neale's parentage, background, and training are obscure. He is known to have had a brother and two sisters, and to have found early employment as a clerk in the General Post Office in Lombard Street, London. Neale's first exhibited works at the Royal Academy were two drawings of insects in 1797, and the earliest anecdote of Neale records his meeting in spring 1796 with John Varley, the watercolour painter, while Neale was in search of specimens in Hornsey Wood. The two began a lifelong friendship and collaborated on a work entitled *The Picturesque Cabinet of Nature* (published in 1796), for which Varley made the landscape drawings and Neale etched and coloured the plates.

Neale exhibited further drawings of insects at the Royal Academy in 1799, 1801, and 1803, but from 1804 to 1844 he exhibited topographical drawings and landscapes there and at the Society of Painters in Oil and Water Colours (1817–18), the British Institution (1808–43), and the Society of British Artists. Some of his works were in oil but his reputation rests on his architectural drawings, which are executed carefully with the pen and tinted with watercolours. In 1816 he began publishing the *History and Antiquities of the Abbey Church of St. Peter, Westminster* (2 vols., 1818–23), with a descriptive text by Edward Brayley. Neale's intense, dark scenes, peopled with enigmatic characters and 'executed in the highest style of the English burin' (Neale and Brayley, unpaginated), helped to fulfil the text's antiquarian purpose of producing a complete record of this 'national structure', and the illustrations serve now as an important historical record of the abbey's sculpture (the original drawings are in the Norfolk Record Office).

Neale's engraved drawings of Westminster Abbey were individually dedicated, and the practice of finding income through flattering drawings of the property of the church and aristocracy guided Neale's career. He next began, in 1818, his *Views of the Seats of Noblemen and Gentlemen in England, Wales, Scotland, and Ireland* (first series, 6 vols., 1824; second series, 5 vols., 1824–9); the entire work comprised no fewer than 732 plates. In 1824–5 he published, with John Le Keux, *Views of the most Interesting Collegiate and Parochial Churches in Great Britain*, but the work was discontinued after the issue of the second volume. Besides these works he published *Six Views of Blenheim, Oxfordshire* (1823); *Graphical Illustrations of Fonthill Abbey* (1824); and *An Account of the Deep-Dene in Surrey, the Seat of Thomas Hope Esq.* (1826). Many other works contain illustrations from his pen and pencil, and collections of his drawings and engravings after his works are held at the Guildhall, the Victoria and Albert Museum, London, Nottingham Castle Museum, and the West Yorkshire Archive Service.

Neale died at Tattingstone, near Ipswich, on 14 November 1847, leaving a £500 life assurance policy to his son, the Revd Edward Pote Neale (*b.* 1800), himself an amateur topographical draughtsman who exhibited at the Royal Academy on a number of occasions after 1817. Neale also left to his son and second wife, Sarah Matilda, his publications, original sketches, paintings, and frames and his correspondence relating to the *Seats of Noblemen and Gentlemen* (which he asked to remain in the family as evidence 'of what may be accomplished by labour'). Neale requested that he be buried in the same grave as his first wife, Ann, under the inscription: 'John Preston Neale, architectural and landscape painter … he was the laborious author and illustrator of … Westminster Abbey and of several elegant publications.'　　　　　R. E. GRAVES, *rev.* M. G. SULLIVAN

Sources Redgrave, *Artists* · Bryan, *Painters* · J. L. Roget, *A history of the 'Old Water-Colour' Society*, 1 (1891), 168–70 · *Ipswich Express* (23 Nov 1847) · J. Macauley, 'J. P. Neale and the views of Scotland', *Scottish country houses 1600–1914*, ed. I. Gow and A. Rowan (1995), 217–27 · will, PRO, PROB 11/2065, sig. 865 · S. Houfe, *The dictionary of 19th century British book illustrators and caricaturists*, rev. edn (1996) · Graves, *Brit. Inst.* · Graves, *RA exhibitors* · *The Royal Watercolour Society: the first fifty years, 1805–1855* (1992) · J. P. Neale and E. W. Brayley, *The history and antiquities of the abbey church of St Peter, Westminster*, 2 vols. (1818–23) · W. W. Rouse Ball and J. A. Venn, eds., *Admissions to Trinity College, Cambridge*, 4 (1911), 185 · d. cert.
Archives NA Scot., corresp. relating to 'Views of [Scottish] seats', GD 38/2/71–2 · Norfolk RO, drawings of Westminster Abbey, letters received, publishers' accounts, COL/8/12–14 · V&A NAL, corresp., MSL/1980/57/1–17 | Bodl. Oxf., letters and bills to Sir T. Phillipps
Wealth at death left £500 to son Edward from life assurance policy with Licensed Victuallers Co; also had unstated amount from 'Artists [Annuity?] Fund' with provision for wife to receive £50 p.a.; left £10 and all household property to second wife; some possessions to son Edward; 'cabinet of insects' to grandson (also Edward); left publications to son; original sketches for 'Westminster Abbey', eleven volumes of 'Views of seats'; also bound letters, other paintings, frames, drawings; £5 each to brother Jacob, sisters Ann and Elizabeth 'for mourning': will, PRO, PROB 11/2065, sig. 865

Neale, Samuel (1729–1792), Quaker minister, was born in Dublin on 9 November 1729, the eldest son of the four children of Thomas Neale (*d.* 1746) and his wife, Martha (*d.* 1735), both of whom were Quakers. His mother died when he was six, whereupon his father emigrated to America, leaving the children to be brought up by relatives in Ireland. Aged seventeen Samuel succeeded to Christianstown, the family estate near Rathangan, co. Kildare, which remained his home until 1760. From about 1747 to 1750, he was apprenticed to a Dublin merchant, possibly a tanner. He spent his youth in hunting, coursing, and 'frequenting the playhouse'. In his twenty-second year he heard the Quaker ministers Catherine Payton and Mary Peisley preach in Cork. Neale underwent a conversion experience and became a Quaker minister himself. From 1752, initially with William Brown, an American Friend, he travelled in the ministry through Ireland, England, Holland, and Germany. In 1756 he visited Scotland, and subsequently many times visited England.

From August 1770 to September 1772 Neale was in America on a ministerial visit, accompanied by Joseph Oxley. He travelled on horseback to most of the meetings, from

New England to the Carolinas. While in America he influenced John Woolman to make his fateful journey to England in 1772; on his return he brought back to Ireland the anti-slavery message of Anthony Benezet. On 17 March 1757 he married his mentor Mary *Peisley (1718–1757) but she died suddenly three days later. In 1760 he married Sarah Beale (1724–1793) of Cork and settled near that city at Springmount, Glanmire, becoming the partner of a paper manufacturer employing fifty people. For many years his melodious voice was the only one heard in the otherwise silent quietist Cork meeting.

Neale, who was physically large with a pleasing countenance, was interested in the anti-slavery cause, education, and gardening. He died, childless, of gangrene, at Cork on 27 February 1792, and was interred at the Quaker burial-ground there on 2 March. He had been a minister for forty years. He prepared the journals and letters of Mary Peisley for publication (1795); his own journals were first published in Dublin in 1805. PETER LAMB

Sources S. Neale and M. Neale, *Some account of the lives and religious labours of Samuel and Mary Neale* (1845) · R. S. Harrison, *A biographical dictionary of Irish Quakers* (1997) · *The records and recollections of James Jenkins*, ed. J. W. Frost (1984), 60–61 · eighteenth-century diary (possibly that of Joshua Beale, 1720–1789), priv. coll. · J. Whitney, *John Woolman, Quaker* (1943), 345 · R. Vaux, *Anthony Benezet: from the original memoir*, ed. W. Armistead, rev. edn (1859)

Likenesses silhouette, Religious Society of Friends, Dublin, MS Box 56, Series 4, Package 1

Wealth at death part owner of paper works; house

Neale, Thomas (*d.* in or before 1643). *See under* Neale, Thomas (1641–1699).

Neale, Thomas (*fl.* 1657). *See under* Neale, Thomas (1641–1699).

Neale, Thomas (1641–1699), projector and politician, was the only son of Thomas Neale of Warnford, Hampshire, and Lucy Uvedale. The senior **Thomas Neale** (*d.* in or before 1643) was in turn the eldest son of Sir Thomas Neale (*d.* 1621), of Warnford, Hampshire, one of the auditors of Queen Elizabeth and James I. Walter Neale, the soldier, may have been his uncle. Thomas was admitted to the Middle Temple in 1630, and was the author of *A treatise of direction how to travell safely and profitably into forraigne countries*, published in London in 1643. This work, which was originally written in Latin, is dedicated to the author's brother, William Neale. It is a pedantic little treatise, full of quotations from the classics, but devoid of a solitary hint from the writer's own experience. A second edition appeared in 1664. Complete copies have a portrait of the author by W. Marshall. Neale married on 15 September 1632 Lucy, third daughter of Sir William Uvedale of Wickham, Hampshire. His son, the projector, was born in Warnford, and was educated at Clare College, Cambridge. In 1664, the year in which he became a fellow of the Royal Society, he married Elizabeth (*d.* 1683), daughter of Sir John Garrard of Lamer Park, Wheathampstead, Hertfordshire, and widow of Sir Nicholas Gould of London. At the time, her fortune was said to be £80,000.

In the following years Neale was appointed to a number of local offices, and formed other ties to various localities

Thomas Neale (1641–1699), by unknown artist, 1694

in southern England. He was a commissioner for the assessment in Hampshire, 1663–79, and sheriff, 1665–6. He received the freedom of Winchester in 1666, Lymington in 1667, and Portsmouth in 1668; and served as JP in Hampshire, 1668–80, Middlesex, 1680–86, Westminster, 1680–89, and Kent, 1680–89, 1692–9. He was also deputy lieutenant of Hampshire, 1669–80, and commissioner for recusants, 1675.

Neale enjoyed a lengthy parliamentary career, his first success being at Petersfield where he was returned at the by-election of 1668. Described as 'a moderately active Member' (Watson, 129), he was teller in seven divisions and served on sixty committees in the Cavalier Parliament. In 1666 Neale became free of the East India Company and in 1670–71 was assistant in the Royal Adventurers into Africa. Towards the end of the Cavalier Parliament he fell into desperate financial straits, the result of his unfortunate decision to engage in the brewing industry, but before the beginning of the last session, 1677, he 'reached an understanding with Danby, to whom he supplied detailed accounts of the debates' (Watson, 130), and his fortunes revived. In 1678 he was made groom-porter at £600 per annum, a post he was to keep until his death, and between 1679 and 1685 served as groom of the bedchamber. As groom-porter he took responsibility not only for ensuring that the king's apartments were supplied with dice, cards, and gaming tables, but also for adjudicating in disputes which might arise there or on the bowling greens. In 1684 his role was widened to include the licensing or suppression of gaming houses, with powers to prosecute those who kept unlicensed premises. Subsequently, in a bid to check cheating, he was to claim that he had invented 'mathematicks' (*CSP dom.*, 1690–91, 128), a kind of dice on the manufacture of which he sought a fourteen-year monopoly in 1690. At the same time as he was developing his court connection he continued to serve in parliament, being returned in 1679 in both the March and the

October elections for Ludgershall, where he was again successful in 1685. In 1689 he won Stockbridge and then returned to Ludgershall, which he represented in 1690, 1695, and 1698.

Neale also enjoyed a long association with the Royal Mint. In 1677 he was one of the commissioners appointed to inquire into irregularities there and in the following year he was granted the reversion of the office of master worker, held by Henry Slingsby. At the time financial irregularities had put Slingsby's position seriously at risk and were to continue to do so with the result that in 1680 he was formally suspended and control of the mint was placed in the hands of three commissioners, Sir John Buckworth, Charles Duncombe, and James Hoare sen. Neale replaced Buckworth in 1684, the year in which he also became a commissioner, again with Duncombe and Hoare, for the manufacture of a new issue of tin coins. Following Slingsby's ultimate disgrace and surrender of his patent, Neale finally took over sole control of the mint in 1686, at £500 per annum. Although the surety normally asked of a master worker at this time was £2000, Neale's reputation for being irresponsible with money had so far preceded him that he was bound in no less a sum than £15,000.

As his tracts, such as *A Proposal for Amending the Silver Coins of England* (1696), and numerous reports from the mint to the Treasury show, Neale certainly interested himself to some extent in the coinage problems of the time and had some involvement in the day-to-day running of the mint. Nevertheless, he employed a deputy, John Fauquier, a future director of the Bank of England, and then, in 1696, sought to bring in Samuel Sheppard, a London merchant to whom he was heavily indebted. The Treasury objected to this arrangement, preferring instead to support Thomas Hall, chief clerk of the mint, who was appointed assistant to Neale during the great recoinage of silver, 1696-8. In 1697 Neale successfully withstood a critical report of a parliamentary committee of inquiry into malpractices at the mint. His initials, N. C. A. P. (Neale, *custos artifex primus*, master and worker), occur on a number of medals signed F. D. W., by F. D. Winter, a minor English engraver who is remembered not as an employee of the mint but as an indifferent copier of other artists' designs.

Neale enjoyed a considerable reputation as a projector. In 1691 he petitioned for a grant for the right to search for mines royal in Maryland and Virginia and became one of the assistants with Henry Harris, chief engraver at the mint, in the new Company of Tapestry Makers. In 1693 he not only obtained a patent on wire screens used for separating flour and meal but also became deputy governor of the Mines Company. In the same year he floated a lottery of 50,000 lots at 10s. each, out of which were to come 250 prizes of between £2 and £3000 and a management fee for himself of 10 per cent. In 1694 he went further still, organizing the great lottery loan, secured by 5 Wm & Mary c. 7 upon a tax on salt, beer, and other liquors to raise £1 million towards the war effort. Subsequently, he was a subscriber to the National Land Bank proposed in 1695. The

project for which he is perhaps best remembered today was his property development in Westminster, the celebrated Seven Dials.

Neale, 'the Lord of Lotteries' (*An Elegaick Essay*, 1700), whose mission in life according to one contemporary was 'to on teach the Great Ones and the Small, How to get Money, and Spend it all' (ibid.), died at Whitehall on 17 December 1699. His likeness, much resembling that of James II, is preserved on a contemporary medalet which bears on the reverse a globe surmounted by Fortune, with the inscription 'Non eadem semper' ('not always the same'). The office of groom-porter was claimed by Neale's son, even though he was considered to be 'unqualified for the place … not knowing how to manage play' (*Buccleuch MSS*, 2.634). Some months later, on 1 June 1700, Sir J. Stanley reported that on his coming up to town he had found Neale dead of a fever. The last of his line, he was possibly the Thomas Neale, esquire, of Whitehall whose will was proved on 3 June.

Thomas Neale (*fl.* 1657), engraver, worked in the style of Wenceslaus Hollar. He engraved, copying Hollar, twenty-four plates of Holbein's 'Dance of Death'. The first plate is dated 'Paris, 1657', and the plates are signed 'T. N.', or with his name in full. Nagler supposes him to have engraved the plates for the eighth edition of John Ogilby's *Fables of Æsop*, and states that he engraved some of the plates for Barlow's *Diversae avium species* (Paris, 1659).

C. E. CHALLIS

Sources P. Watson, 'Neale, Thomas', HoP, *Commons, 1660-90* · C. E. Challis, 'Mint officials and moneyers of the Stuart period', *British Numismatic Journal*, 59 (1989), 157-97 · C. E. Challis, ed., *A new history of the royal mint* (1992) · J. Redington, ed., *Calendar of Treasury papers*, 1, PRO (1868) · CSP dom. · PRO, TI/48 no. 52 · PRO, E351/2095-2106 · PRO, PROB 11/456 · N. Luttrell, *A brief historical relation of state affairs from September 1678 to April 1714*, 3 (1857), 160-61; 4 (1857), 595, 650 · DNB · *An elegaick essay upon the decease of the groom-porter, and the lotteries* (1700) · Evelyn, *Diary*, 5.158, 177, 193 · *Report on the manuscripts of his grace the duke of Buccleuch and Queensberry … preserved at Montagu House*, 3 vols. in 4, HMC, 45 (1899-1926), vol. 2, pp. 631, 633-4, 639-40, 652-3 · E. Hawkins, *Medallic illustrations of the history of Great Britain and Ireland to the death of George II*, ed. A. W. Franks and H. A. Grueber, 2 vols. (1885), vol. 1, p. 637; vol. 2, pp. 104-5, 744 · VCH *Hampshire and the Isle of Wight* · J. A. Neale, *Supplement to charters and records of Neales of Berkeley Yate and Corsham* (1927)
Likenesses W. Marshall, portrait, *c.*1664 (T. Neale, *fl.* 1657), repro. in T. Neale, *A treatise of direction*, 2nd edn (1664) · silver and copper medal, 1694, BM [*see illus.*] · silver, reverse plain, and copper medal (after medalet, *c.*1694), BM

Neale, Walter (*fl.* 1617-1639), army officer and explorer, used a coat of arms of the Neale family of Leicestershire and Northamptonshire, although nothing is known of his parentage or background. He has often been confused with Walter Neale (*d.* 1612/13), the son of William Neale, auditor to Elizabeth I. Neale the explorer was evidently a military man, various petitions indicating that he began his career about 1617. He served as a captain under Count Ernest of Mansfield on the side of the elector palatine in both Bohemia and the Rhine country. In February 1625 he petitioned the king for a grant of 2000 decayed trees in the New Forest in lieu of the month's pay of £460 due to his company. In February 1629 he again petitioned for relief, 'his debts being clamorous and his wants insupportable' (*CSP dom.*, 1628–9, 480).

One of Neale's petitions to the government may have brought him to the attention of the army treasurer, John Mason, and hence into speculative colonial ventures backed by Mason and Sir Ferdinando Gorges, which were Anglican in character. In particular, they planned to exploit the North American fur trade by tapping the source of fur further inland, and thereby gaining an advantage over French and Dutch competition. From a base at the mouth of the Piscataqua River (the first river northwards outside the area granted to the Massachusetts Company) Neale was to use the local river system to travel west in search of the great inland lake that would facilitate the fur trade. The lake provided the name of the company, Laconia. Neale set sail from England in April 1630 in the 80 ton ship *Warwick*, arriving at the beginning of June. With the Atlantic base of Laconia secured and two trading stations established at South Berwick and Strawberry Bank (near Portsmouth), Neale ventured into the interior, and later claimed to have made 'greater discovery of the interior than was ever made before' (Preston, 139), but he failed to find the great lake, hindered as he was by the lack of navigable rivers and the absence of horses. He was ordered to return to England, leaving the Piscataqua settlements on 15 July 1633, and sailing from Boston on 15 August.

In October 1633 Neale was referred to as 'Lady Sydenham's full cousin german' and recommended as someone who had brought 'very good grain from New England' (*CSP dom.*, 1633–4, 230). In January 1634 he was recommended by the king to the lord mayor of London as captain of the artillery garden. After four years in command of the city's artillery Neale petitioned for the place of governor of New England. By 1639 he was lieutenant-governor of Portsmouth, Hampshire, and was last heard of in July of that year.   Gordon Goodwin, *rev.* Stuart Handley

Sources R. A. Preston, 'The Laconia Company of 1629: an English attempt to intercept the fur trade', *Canadian Historical Review*, 31 (1950), 125–44 · N. Adams, *Annals of Portsmouth* (1825), 19–26 · C. W. Tuttle, *Capt. John Mason, the founder of New Hampshire*, ed. J. W. Dean (1887) · D. E. Van Deventer, *The emergence of provincial New Hampshire* (1976) · *Documents and records relating to the province of New Hampshire … 1623–1686*, ed. N. Bouton (1867) · J. Savage, *A genealogical dictionary of the first settlers of New England*, 14 vols. (1971), vol. 3, p. 265 · *CSP dom.*, 1623–5, 487; 1628–9, 480; 1633–4, 230, 443; 1639, 32, 391 · *CSP col.*, 1.134–5, 140, 285 · J. B. Felt, *The ecclesiastical history of New England* (1855), vol. 1, pp. 155, 165, 190–91

Neale, Sir William (1609/10–1691), royalist army officer, was the third son of John Neale of Wollaston, Northamptonshire, and his wife, Elizabeth, daughter of Sir Richard Conquest of Houghton Conquest, Bedfordshire. The Neales of Wollaston and Hanging Houghton had come to Northamptonshire from Staffordshire and were the younger branch of the Buckinghamshire, Bedfordshire, and Warwickshire family; in 1618 William Neale's father was recorded as son and heir of John Neale sen. William's eldest brother, Sir Edmund Neale, knight (*b.* 1600/1),

appeared in arms briefly as a royalist and compounded for his estates at one tenth of their value, £746, a fine reduced to £582 as his estates were encumbered.

William Neale, perhaps as a younger brother less concerned for the risk to his property in a largely parliamentarian area, joined the king's forces and served throughout the war. He attached himself to Prince Rupert, the royalist cavalry commander, and quickly rose to favour, becoming his scoutmaster general. He was chosen by Rupert to take the news of the capture of Cirencester to Oxford and was knighted there by the king on 3 February 1643. At the successful relief of Newark in March 1644 he was said to have been instrumental in saving the prince's life by a timely blow, and he was one of the commissioners appointed to agree the terms of withdrawal with the defeated commander, Sir John Meldrum.

While Rupert was at Chester before the Newark march he had appointed Neale governor of Hawarden Castle, Flintshire, with the consent of the owner, the earl of Derby. It was one of the protective screen of strong places with which the cavaliers hoped to defend Chester from Sir William Brereton's encircling forces. A problem of another claimant to the command appears to have been resolved, for Neale's wife, Helen, sister of Major-General Randle Egerton, was in occupation from 1645 until the end of the war. Neale supplied intelligence from north Wales as well as military materials for the garrison of Chester; sent 120 men to the king's army on the Naseby campaign; and entertained the king himself for a night in September 1645. He surrendered the castle, on instructions from the king, on 16 March 1646.

Although Neale was a highly regarded officer—a warrant for a baronetcy had been drafted in February 1646, with the usual fee waived, but was apparently not acted on—nothing is known of his career in the years following royalist defeat. Unlike his eldest brother he did not compound, but this may be an indication of his poverty rather than absence abroad. That he remained an irreconcilable royalist is suggested by his arrest in Lancashire in 1656 and his taking part in the Booth rising in 1659, when he was captured in arms in August. He was rewarded after the Restoration with another attempt to promote him baronet, but like the last this failed: possibly on this occasion for lack of funds. He remained in obscurity, living in London from the late 1670s onwards upon the charity of a kinsman, and eventually achieving note (in John Aubrey's work) only as one of the last of the old cavaliers. His last years were afflicted with 'gowtes' which 'emaciated him extremely' (*Brief Lives*, 2.93). He died in Gray's Inn Lane, aged eighty-one, on 24 March 1691 and was buried three days later near the west door of St Paul's, Covent Garden. He had two daughters and a son, William, an officer in the guards who died three years before him.

William Neale was, according to Anthony Wood, 'a stout proper man [i.e. big and brave] and a good soldier' (Wood, *Ath. Oxon.*, 3.902). Aubrey remembered him 'as not lesse than 6 foot high: very beautiful in youth—I remember him: and of great courage, but a great plunderer and cruell' (*Brief Lives*, 2.93). He was well respected by his superiors and commonly described as 'the worthy bearer' of the messages he carried from one commander to another during the civil war.   IAN ROY

Sources The letter books of Sir William Brereton, ed. R. N. Dore, 2 vols., Lancashire and Cheshire RS, 123, 128 (1984–90) • *Brief lives, chiefly of contemporaries, set down by John Aubrey, between the years 1669 and 1696*, ed. A. Clark, 2 (1898), 93 • *Memoirs of Prince Rupert and the cavaliers including their private correspondence*, ed. E. Warburton, 3 vols. (1849) • *Diary of the marches of the royal army during the great civil war, kept by Richard Symonds*, ed. C. E. Long, CS, old ser., 74 (1859); repr. with new introduction by I. Roy as *Richard Symonds' diary of the marches of the royal army* (1997) • W. Neale, letter to Gilbert Byron, NL Wales, Clenennau papers, 598 • Wood, *Ath. Oxon.*, new edn, vol. 3 • *CSP dom.*, 1656–7, 173; 1659–60, 148; 1667, 368 • W. C. Metcalfe, ed., *The visitations of Northamptonshire made in 1564 and 1618–19* (1887), 118 • J. P. Earwaker, ed., 'A baronet's warrant', *The Genealogist*, 6 (1882), 211–12 • W. A. Shaw, *The knights of England*, 2 (1906), 215 • J. Rushworth, *Historical collections*, new edn, 3 (1721), 11–12, 308 • P. Young, *Naseby: the campaign and the battle, 1645* (1985) • M. Noble, *Memoirs of the protectorate-house of Cromwell*, 2 vols. (1784) • M. A. E. Green, ed., *Calendar of the proceedings of the committee for advance of money, 1642–1656*, 2, PRO (1888), 1064
Archives NL Wales, Clenennau letters
Wealth at death see *Calendar of the proceedings*, vol. 2, p. 1064

Neale, William Henry (*bap.* 1785, *d.* 1855). *See under* Neale, James (*bap.* 1722, *d.* 1792).

Neale, William Johnstoune Nelson (1812–1893), lawyer and novelist, was baptized at Withycombe Raleigh, Devon, on 24 December 1812, the second son of Adam Carruce *Neale (1778?–1832), military physician and author, and his wife, Margaret Johnston Young. His brother was Erskine *Neale (1804–1883), Church of England clergyman and author. In 1824 Neale entered the navy, and was awarded a medal for his services on board the *Talbot* at the battle of Navarino in 1827. On 17 January 1833 he became a student of Lincoln's Inn, but subsequently migrated to the Middle Temple, where he was called to the bar on 25 November 1836. He went to the Oxford circuit, and also practised at the Shropshire and Staffordshire sessions. Between 1839 and 1840 with Basil Montagu he published a two-part handbook entitled *The Law of Parliamentary Elections*. On 12 December 1846 he married Frances Herbert, daughter of Captain Josiah Nisbit RN and eldest grandchild and coheir of Viscountess Nelson.

In addition to his legal work, Neale wrote several novels which capitalized on his experiences in the navy, many of which achieved considerable popularity. His mentor and model was Frederick Marryat. Neale's first and probably most popular novel was *Cavendish, or, The Patrician at Sea* (1831), published when he was only eighteen years of age. *Will-Watch: from the Autobiography of a British Officer* (1834) contains an account of Neale's public quarrel in 1834 with Marryat over Neale's novel *The Port Admiral* (1833). Neale challenged Marryat to a duel, Marryat declined the challenge on the grounds of Neale's 'social inferiority', and the two men went on to have an embarrassing scuffle in Trafalgar Square on Guy Fawkes night (Sutherland, 457; Watson, 706). This conflict did not seem to damage Neale's popularity, however, as he went on to have further novelistic successes, among them *Paul Periwinkle, or, The Press-Gang* (1841), which was illustrated by Phiz (Hablot K. Browne), and *The Naval Surgeon* (1841), which was reprinted in 1858, and again in 1861 in volume six of the *Naval and Military Library*.

In 1859 Neale was appointed recorder of Walsall, a post he held until his death at 11 Promenade Terrace, Cheltenham, on 27 March 1893.

GORDON GOODWIN, rev. MEGAN A. STEPHAN

Sources J. Foster, *Men-at-the-bar: a biographical hand-list of the members of the various inns of court*, 2nd edn (1885), 336 • J. Sutherland, *The Longman companion to Victorian fiction* (1988), 457 • F. W. Bateson, ed., *The Cambridge bibliography of English literature*, 3 (1940), 499 • Allibone, *Dict.* • *The new Cambridge bibliography of English literature*, [2nd edn], 3, ed. G. Watson (1969), 953, 706 • *BL cat.*

Nearne, Jacqueline (1916–1982). *See under* Women agents on active service in France (*act.* 1942–1945).

Neate, Charles (1784–1877), pianist and composer, was born on 28 March 1784 in London, the son of a brewer. He was taught the piano by James Windsor of Bath and the cello by William Sharp. He later studied the piano with John Field and composition with Joseph Woelfl. He made his first public appearance in 1800 in the Lenten oratorio performances at Covent Garden. On 2 March 1806 Neate was admitted a member of the Royal Society of Musicians, and in 1808 he published his first work, the piano sonata in C minor, op. 1. He was one of the founder members of the Philharmonic Society in 1813.

In 1815 Neate spent three months in Munich studying counterpoint with Peter von Winter before moving on to Vienna, where he delivered an order to Beethoven from the Philharmonic Society for three new concert overtures. He spent eight months in Vienna and Baden, and formed a close friendship with Beethoven, meeting him almost daily; although Beethoven refused to teach him composition, he agreed to comment on his works, and recommended he take lessons from Emanuel Forster. Neate's string quartet was performed in Vienna in December 1815. He returned to London at the beginning of 1816 with a number of manuscript copies of works for which Beethoven hoped he would find an English publisher, including the violin concerto and the string quartet op. 95. However, he failed to arouse any interest in them, and the three overtures commissioned by the Philharmonic Society were not well received, only one, *Namensfeier*, even being performed.

In 1816 Neate married Catherine Mary Cazenove, a descendant of Huguenot immigrants; the couple had one son. In London, he built up a reputation as one of the best pianists and teachers, and his pupils included Charles Salaman. In 1820 he gave the first performance in England of Beethoven's piano concertos no. 3 in C minor, op. 37, and no. 5 in E♭, op. 73 at concerts of the Philharmonic Society, and also, in 1825, of Weber's *Konzertstück*.

Neate continued to correspond with Beethoven, and in 1824 he was asked by the Philharmonic Society to invite him to England to conduct his works, and also to compose one symphony and one concerto to be given their first performances in London. In the end Beethoven did not come, but he sent his ninth symphony, which received its first performance in England on 21 March 1825. Neate's connection with Beethoven lasted long after the latter's death, as in 1845 the director of the British Museum sent him to Aix-la-Chapelle to meet Anton Schindler with a view to acquiring his large collection of Beethoven manuscripts, but he was outbid, and the collection went to Berlin. Neate retired about 1856. He died in Brighton on 30 March 1877.

Neate's compositions were mainly for the piano, and include two sonatas, two trios, three select movements for two pianos (1823), a fantasia for piano with cello obbligato (1825), forty-seven preludes (1827), a hundred impromptus (1830), variations on 'Rule, Britannia' dedicated to Queen Victoria, and a song, 'Victoria's Sceptre o'er the Waves' (1845). In Neate's *An Essay on Fingering … together with some General Observations on Pianoforte Playing* (1855), most of the examples were taken from Beethoven's piano works.   ANNE PIMLOTT BAKER

Sources E. Anderson, 'Charles Neate: a Beethoven friendship', *Festschrift Otto Erich Deutsch* (1963), 196–202 · D. W. MacArdle, 'Beethoven and the Philharmonic Society of London', *Music Review*, 21 (1960), 1–7 · D. W. Hadley, 'Beethoven and the Philharmonic Society of London: a reappraisal', *Musical Quarterly*, 59 (1973), 449–61 · 'Sketch of the state of music in London', *Quarterly Musical Magazine and Review*, 2 (1820), 373–91, esp. 383–4 · 'Beethoven: his portrait and—its blot!', *MT*, 42 (1901), 15–16 · *New Grove* · A. W. Thayer, *Life of Beethoven*, ed. E. Forbes (1964), 614ff, 929ff · Boase, *Mod. Eng. biog.* · C. Salaman, 'Recollections: Charles Neate', *Concordia* (16 Oct 1875), 395–6 · C. Salaman, 'Recollections: Charles Neate', *Concordia* (30 Oct 1875), 428

Wealth at death under £800: probate, 5 May 1877, *CGPLA Eng. & Wales*

Neate, Charles (1806–1879), scholar and politician, was born on 13 June 1806 at Adstock, Buckinghamshire, the fifth of the eleven children of Thomas Neate, rector and minor landed gentleman of Alvescot, Oxfordshire, and his wife, Catherine, daughter of the Revd William Church. In rural England Neate acquired a lasting love of field sports (he was to be a well-known rider and steeplechaser); more unusually, in Restoration France he acquired an exceptional mastery of French at the Collège Bourbon, Paris. There the poet and critic Charles Augustin Sainte-Beuve was one of his schoolfellows, and he obtained a prize for French composition, open to all the schools of France. Neate matriculated as a commoner of Lincoln College, Oxford, on 2 June 1824; he was scholar 1826–8, and graduated first-class in 1828. The same year he was elected fellow of Oriel College, where Newman, G. A. Denison, and James Fraser were among his associates; he also wrote for Blanco White's *London Review*, then almost an Oriel house magazine. Neate was called to the bar at Lincoln's Inn in 1832. An unfortunate fracas with Sir Richard Bethell, afterwards Lord Westbury, ended his career there in 1839, but it was characteristic of Neate that later, as an MP, he opposed the vote of censure on the 'old scoundrel', as he was in the habit of styling Westbury (*The Times*, 4 and 5 July 1865).

With his legal ambitions over, Neate acted as private secretary to the chancellor of the exchequer, Sir Francis Baring, between 1839 and 1841, and published in 1842 a tract in favour of the whig policy of a fixed duty on corn. But he soon returned to Oxford and lived off his Oriel fellowship for the remainder of his life, neither marrying nor (unlike most of his contemporaries) becoming a clergyman. Neate was a devoted Anglican but, remaining at arm's length from the theological divisions which racked Oriel in the 1840s, he turned to the management of the college estates. As senior treasurer of the college (1846–9), he evinced a strong sympathy with the tenants, whose difficulties in the wake of the repeal of the corn laws in 1846 drew him briefly towards Disraeli and protectionism. But Neate was also a respectable scholar, and acted as examiner in the school of law and history in 1853–5, and as lecturer in these subjects at Oriel in 1856. In 1857 he was appointed Drummond professor of political economy. Loosely associated with the liberal political economy of his predecessors such as George Rickards, and having a strong interest in legal history, Neate proved a strident critic of the landed interest, a proponent of increased, even graduated, direct taxation, an orthodox monetary theorist, and, more unusually, a supporter of trade unions.

Neate was no mere don, and by the 1850s he was also deeply involved in the civic life of Oxford. He served as a university nominee on the board of health at the time of the cholera epidemic in 1854, as a poor-law guardian, and as a street commissioner. Yet he was increasingly at odds with the university on several issues, which led him to criticize its part in local bodies, and to support the claims of the townspeople and the poor. This growing identification with the town led to his election as its Liberal MP in 1857 but he was soon unseated, for bribery by his agents. As his period as Drummond professor ended in 1862, Neate looked once more to politics and was elected as MP for Oxford in 1863, when he stood as a conservative Liberal but, with his usual love of paradox, on the popular and democratic side of the party.

In the house Neate proved a diligent MP, chairing a committee on the regulation of mines and speaking effectively on a number of issues. He took a notable interest in legal reform, and acted as one of a small group of campaigners for the abolition of capital punishment. He was ready to defend the claims of the university against governmental interference, favouring university reform until it was taken up by the government, and then resenting its imposition. But he was also ready to support the claims of the town against university intrusion and opposed, for example, votes for resident dons in the second Reform Bill. He also took up important issues such as the Thames navigation and played a prominent part in supporting the siting of the Great Western Railway workshops at Oxford in 1865, the abandonment of which he felt 'will be a calamity to both City and University' (Neate to Richard Potter; 16 June 1865, PRO, Great Western railway records, Rail 129). He retired from parliament in 1868 but continued to live in Oxford, serving on its local board and as clerk to the market. He died at his home, 14 Bradmore Road, Oxford, on 7 February 1879 and was buried at Alvescot on 13 February.

Eccentric in manner, gaunt and uncouth in appearance, occasionally fiery in temper, Neate was generous, dependable, and chivalrous, widely esteemed for his fearless honesty and outspokenness. Lacking scholarly perseverance, his keen mind expressed itself better in witty epigrams, humorous verse, or elegant composition in French and Latin; he frowned upon the modern expert, who was slowly beginning to displace the older, rounded scholars of unreformed Oxford. A 'cosmopolitan' among Oxford dons (W. Tuckwell, *Reminiscences of Oxford*, 1900, 18–19) and a worthy citizen, Neate failed to achieve the high distinction expected of him.   A. C. HOWE

Sources T. Mozley, *Reminiscences, chiefly of Oriel College and the Oxford Movement*, 2 vols. (1882) · A. Howe, 'Intellect and civic responsibility: dons and citizens in nineteenth-century Oxford', *Oxford: studies in the history of a university town since 1800*, ed. R. C. Whiting (1993), 12–52 · *Oxford Chronicle and Berks and Bucks Gazette* (15 Feb 1879) · J. W. Burgon, *Lives of twelve good men*, [new edn], 2 vols. (1888–9) · Bodl. Oxf., Dep. Hughenden · *Hansard 3* (1857); (1863–8) · *Clarke's New Law List* (1832–9) · *DNB*
Archives Oriel College, Oxford, essay · Oriel College, Oxford, bound volume of printed notes ['Opuscula'] | Bodl. Oxf., Disraeli MSS, letters · PRO, Great Western railway records, RAIL 129, 130
Likenesses steel-engraved portrait, Oriel College, Oxford
Wealth at death £2114 16s. 8d.: administration, 25 June 1883, *CGPLA Eng. & Wales*

Neave, Airey Middleton Sheffield (1916–1979), intelligence officer and politician, was born at 24 De Vere Gardens, Knightsbridge, London, on 23 January 1916. He was the elder son, in a family of two sons and three daughters, of Sheffield Airey Neave (1879–1961), a distinguished entomologist, of Mill Green Park, Ingatestone, Essex, and his wife, Dorothy (d. 1943), daughter of Lieutenant-Colonel Arthur Thomson Middleton JP of Ayshe Court, Horsham.

Education and wartime service The family moved to Beaconsfield, where Airey Neave attended the Montessori School, and then, from 1925, St Ronan's preparatory school, Worthing, whence in 1929 he went to Eton. While there, he visited Germany in 1933 to learn German, a skill that proved of great value in wartime; he witnessed Nazi methods in seizing power, and on his return wrote a prizewinning essay predicting that Hitler's advent meant war. In a parliamentary speech of 1975 he referred to this experience when stressing the need in Northern Ireland to ban unofficial uniforms employed to intimidate the population (*Hansard 5C*, 894, 27 June 1975, 914). He later recalled that as an undergraduate at Merton College, Oxford, he had done all too little academic work, and he obtained third-class honours in jurisprudence in 1938. But he also recalled diverging from undergraduate socialist and pacifist fashions; convinced that war would come, he became a second lieutenant in the Territorial Army and bought and read the works of Clausewitz in the belief that they must be understood. Thereafter his personality, outlook, and career were understandably moulded by the first climacteric in his career: the extraordinary events he

Airey Middleton Sheffield Neave (1916–1979), by Neil Libbert

witnessed as a young man during and immediately after the Second World War.

The war interrupted his legal training in London, and shortly before war began he volunteered for service. After six months in Essex and Hereford in a searchlight training regiment, Neave joined the Royal Artillery and in February 1940 was posted to Boulogne; as a subaltern in the retreat of May 1940 he participated in the battle of Calais, winning the Military Cross, and later described the episode in his *The Flames of Calais* (1972). Wounded there, he was captured, and was imprisoned in Poland at Torun, whence he escaped only to be recaptured. His admiration for the Poles prompted his later campaign to commemorate the Katyn massacre, just as his interrogation by the Gestapo reinforced his lifelong defence of the individual against the state. Imprisoned in the maximum security prison at Colditz, and after one failed attempt, Neave made a particularly bold and well-planned escape in January 1942, the first British prisoner to do so, and returned to London through Switzerland, Vichy France, and Gibraltar. Depressed, and experiencing a strong sense of persecution, he met his father on the platform at Ingatestone and felt unable to speak: 'it was not a time for words. No sentence which I could have selected would have seemed appropriate' (Neave, 153). It was Diana Josceline Barbara Giffard [*see below*] who lifted the gloom: at a cocktail party 'I was standing in a corner talking to a red-haired girl, and laughed with her at simple things. I found in her the confidence I needed … for the first time since I was a prisoner I was gay again.' (ibid., 155). They were engaged within weeks, married on 29 December 1942, and had two sons and one daughter.

Neave brought back valuable intelligence information, and was soon at MI9, helping European resistance movements and planning escape routes for allied airmen, as described in his book *Saturday at MI9* (1969). He was called to the bar at the Middle Temple in 1943, and in 1945 joined the British War Crimes Executive to collect evidence against prominent Nazi war criminals. As a lieutenant-colonel and assistant secretary to the international military tribunal, he had the strange experience of serving the charges on the leaders of his wartime captors. In view of his wartime sufferings, wrote Lord Birkett, Neave's conduct was all the more commendable for performing his role 'with ability, tact and unwearied patience' (preface to Neave, 8). By the end of the war Neave's many honours included in 1945 the DSO and TD with clasp, the US bronze star, and the order of Orange Nassau. Later, in 1947, he was appointed OBE.

MP for Abingdon Neave established a practice at the bar, and from 1949 to 1951 was officer commanding intelligence school no. 9 (TA), which later became 23 SAS regiment. With his *They Have their Exits* (1953), movingly describing his wartime escapes in terse novelistic prose, he helped to pioneer the insider description of wartime espionage at a time when all could not be revealed—though *The Colditz Story* by Patrick Reid (like Neave a Conservative candidate) had come out the year before. Neave later took a pride in his five semi-autobiographical books, the last of which was *Nuremberg* (1978), based on notes made at the time by a 29-year-old who had observed the imprisoned Nazi leaders closely.

Neave's heart did not lie in the law but in politics, and after contesting Thurrock (1950, where he was soundly defeated) and Ealing North (1951, where he was only 120 votes behind the successful candidate), he was elected Conservative MP for the Abingdon division of Berkshire in a by-election of July 1953, a seat which he retained with comfortable margins for the rest of his career. With some difficulty Neave nerved himself to make his maiden speech on 29 July 1953, having chosen a topic which became a speciality: national defence policy. Together with his other favourite topics—science and aviation—this reflected powerful interests within his own constituency. Reticent, dressed in black lawyer-like suits, by no means a star speaker, and talking even to friends in almost conspiratorial tones, he was easily underestimated. None the less, his career soon took off. In 1954 he became parliamentary private secretary first to the minister of transport and civil aviation John Boyd-Carpenter, and then in 1954–6 to the colonial secretary Alan Lennox-Boyd. He diverged neither to right nor left from the government line during the Suez crisis, and in January 1957 became joint parliamentary secretary to the minister of transport, H. A. Watkinson. In January 1959 he moved up to parliamentary under-secretary at the Air Ministry, but then suffered the heart attack which forced him to resign.

As long as Edward Heath's authority prevailed within the party, Neave's ministerial career was stalled, despite Neave's support for entering the E. E. C. Neave therefore assumed the role of conscientious back-bencher and constituency MP instead. A close observer, a keen listener, unflamboyant, and ready to learn, he was cautious, methodical, patient, even slow; yet he was also decisive, self-sufficient, and independent-minded. His parliamentary speeches, always well briefed but previously limited in range, broadened out during the 1960s into advocating (with ultimate success) compensation for concentration camp victims at Sachsenhausen, state pensions for old

people who had been excluded from the national insurance scheme of 1948 (also successfully), and (unsuccessfully) the release of Rudolf Hess from prison. Keen for parliament to retain its role in shaping opinion and concerned that the public knew so little about it, Neave in 1966 wanted the television cameras let in. His defence of parliament's rights against the executive was all of a piece with his wartime memories of Nazism and with the wary eye he kept on Soviet ambitions: democracy requires assiduous defence. He chaired the British standing conference on refugees (1972–4) and was United Kingdom delegate to the United Nations high commissioner for refugees (1970–75). A governor of Imperial College from 1963 to 1971, he held directorships in concerns involving engineering, energy, and science. He joined the House of Commons select committee on science and technology in 1965 and was its chairman from 1970 to 1975.

Bringing Thatcher to power A career which had precociously required courage of the highest order made new demands at its second climacteric when Neave was fifty-nine, for in 1975 he perceived and seized the chance of supplanting Heath as party leader by Margaret Thatcher. Why? He was no devotee of what were later known as 'Thatcherite' monetarist and privatizing policies, if only because his specialist parliamentary concerns had never included the economy. Nor had his parliamentary speeches in 1970–74 publicly revealed disillusion with the Heath government. Heath's supporters once defeated made much of personal revenge as a motive. It was widely alleged, though denied by Heath in his memoirs, that in 1959 Heath as chief whip had told Neave on returning to parliament after recovering from his heart attack that his career was finished; 'anyone who doubts the effect of personal feeling in politics has only to examine this episode', wrote Norman Fowler in his memoirs (N. Fowler, *Ministers Decide*, 1991, 14). However this may be, Neave from October 1974 pressed one candidate after another to stand against Heath: Joseph, Whitelaw, Du Cann, and from early January 1975 after all else had failed, Thatcher, six weeks after she had decided to stand.

As he brought with him between fifteen and twenty votes previously committed to Du Cann, and wide contacts accumulated from his earlier efforts, Neave could now marshal his conspiratorial and tactical skills and steely determination behind a candidate unlikely to succeed. Yet his brilliant campaign played off the tendency of Heath's supporters to exaggerate his chances, thereby tempting into the Thatcher camp supporters of other candidates who feared an outright Heath victory. After defeating Heath on the first ballot by 130 votes to 119, Thatcher triumphed over Whitelaw on the second ballot by 146 votes to 79. Neave now became head of Thatcher's private office and shadow secretary of state for Northern Ireland. He then set out to consolidate Thatcher's position by deploying a back-bencher's grasp of parliamentary opinion and by working closely with Whitelaw to hold the party together and prevent it from moving too far to the right. Not that his public image was always moderate: in June 1978 his anti-socialism and his fierce loyalty to

Thatcher led him into a speech (incredulously received by Labour) which likened the Labour government's interventionism to the structures that had prepared the way for Nazi totalitarianism. None the less, Neave's war record, his quiet but determined patriotism, and his concern for the rule of law and for national security located him in the Conservative mainstream.

Northern Ireland secretary His preoccupation with terrorism in Northern Ireland focused attention on these characteristics and advertised his commitment to a further strand of Conservatism: the union. Before Thatcher became party leader Neave had privately told her that Northern Ireland was the only portfolio he wanted. His physical courage and intelligence contacts equipped him admirably for some aspects of his new role. He immediately launched out on courageously forthright parliamentary speeches attacking terrorism in all its dimensions: its undemocratic attempt to coerce the majority, its contempt for law, its inhumane methods. His sympathies lay with the ordinary citizen of Northern Ireland: bombed, bullied, and beset by conflicting hatreds. He often visited Northern Ireland and, referring in parliament on 27 June 1975 to their sufferings, said he found it 'moving to meet these people' (*Hansard 5C*, 894, 27 June 1975, 915). A propaganda war was under way, and on 17 December 1976 he told parliament that psychological operations against the terrorists must be organized through the media: 'instead of the dead-pan news items every day about death, injury, destruction and sorrow … there ought to be a concerted attack on these mindless barbarians' (ibid., 922, 17 Dec 1976, 1944). He told parliament on 8 December 1977 of his shock at the hatred so evident on the faces of wanted men in police photographs. These are, he said, 'not glorious republicans but bloody murderers' (ibid., 940, 18 Dec 1977, 1691). Terrorists were criminals who should be treated as such, and he personally inclined towards capital punishment. Provisional Sinn Féin and Provisional IRA were for him inseparable, and he believed that terrorist morale would wilt before a governmental policy of no compromise. No wonder the terrorists detested him.

All this aligned Neave with the Ulster Unionists and also with Thatcher's unionist instincts, but in this area of Conservative policy—as in others before 1979—a publicly announced rightward shift risked alienating 'middle opinion' and widening out divisions within the party. Furthermore, as events in the 1990s were to show, 'counterterrorism' could not unaided defeat terrorism, and Neave showed small sign of seeing this. He felt that if British troops were withdrawn the Catholic minority would suffer most, but he did not think power-sharing politically feasible. All that he would concede was a return of power to local authorities within a Northern Ireland that remained under direct rule.

Neave knew well enough, though, that his public stance on Northern Ireland endangered his life, and for that reason frequently changed his place of residence. His memory of Nazi interrogation made him keen at the very end of his life to root out any brutality detected in British order-keeping forces if he became secretary of state for Northern Ireland. 'I myself was interrogated by the Gestapo', he told Gerry Fitt, 'and, Gerry, it leaves its mark on you' (*The Guardian*, 31 March 1979). Neave's last contribution to a parliamentary debate, on 16 March 1979, concerned the Bennett report on police interrogating procedures, during which he praised 'the dedication and courage' of the Royal Ulster Constabulary (*Hansard 5C*, 964, 16 March 1979, 966). On 30 March a bomb planted by the Irish National Liberation Army under his car exploded as he drove up the ramp of the House of Commons car park, and with both legs blown off he died in hospital an hour later. Nobody has ever been charged with his murder. This, the third and final climacteric of Neave's remarkable career, advertised the fragility of democracy and the ruthlessness of its enemies, yet also had the effect of confirming his leader in her unionist instincts. 'We do not expect these things to happen in this country', said Thatcher in her parliamentary tribute on 2 April 1979, 'but somehow they have happened here' (ibid., 965, 2 April 1979, 907). At the end of her famous statement on 4 May when first entering 10 Downing Street, she said: 'and finally, one last thing: in the words of Airey Neave, whom we had hoped to bring here with us, "There is now work to be done"' (M. Thatcher, *The Collected Speeches of Margaret Thatcher*, 1997, 94). A memorial lecture was founded in Neave's memory, and the first in the series, on 3 March 1980, was delivered by the prime minister whose career Neave had done so much to advance.

Diana Neave Airey Neave's wife and fellow Conservative Party worker, **Diana Josceline Barbara Neave Airey** [née Diana Josceline Barbara Giffard], Baroness Airey of Abingdon (1919–1992), was born at 16 Alexander Square, Kensington, London, on 7 July 1919, the daughter of Thomas Arthur Walter Giffard MBE, JP (1882–1971), landowner and county councillor, of Chillington Hall, Wolverhampton, and his wife, Angela Erskine Giffard (née Trollope). Educated privately in England and abroad, she was quartermaster of an RAF hospital in 1939, and worked later with the Foreign Office (political warfare executive) and Polish ministry of information in London. After her marriage to Airey Neave her charm, beauty, and loyalty brought her skills as a hostess and party worker to the aid of her husband's career, and she helped him with the research for his books. In writing the last of them, *Nuremberg* (1978), he said that he 'was inspired … by my wife … without whose encouragement and devotion I could not have completed it'. Given the happiness of their marriage, her courageous response to his assassination was remarkable, and was widely praised at the time. 'I want only to be worthy of Airey', she told Thatcher (*Hansard 5C*, 965, 2 April 1979, 907). Strong-willed and dedicated to her husband's causes, she was within two days of his death at her desk as a volunteer sorting mail in Conservative central office, convinced that he would have wanted her there to help Thatcher to victory. On accepting a life peerage, she assumed by deed poll the name Airey as her surname and title, saying that it made her 'feel closer to him' (*The Independent*, 1 Dec 1992). In 1980 she received the freedom of the City of London. She was happy to talk about her husband in private but discouraged any biography. She was a member of the North Atlantic assembly from 1983 to 1984, and of the select committee on European Communities (subcommittee F) from 1986 to 1987. She was president of the Anglo-Polish Conservative Society, a trustee of the National Heritage Memorial Fund from 1980 to 1988, of the Imperial War Museum from 1984 to 1990, of the Dorney Wood Trust from 1980, and of the Stansted Park Foundation from 1983. She died at Charlbury, Oxfordshire, after a long illness on 27 November 1992.

BRIAN HARRISON

Sources private information (1986) · personal knowledge (1986) [DNB] · The Times (16 Nov 1979) · W. Churchill, The Observer (1 April 1979) · Daily Telegraph (31 March 1979) · Hansard 5C · CGPLA Eng. & Wales (1979) · CGPLA Eng. & Wales (1993) [Baroness Airey] · 'Baroness Airey of Abingdon', The Times (2 Dec 1992) · A. Morrow, 'Diana Neave: a woman of courage', Daily Telegraph (25 June 1979) · 'Baroness Airey of Abingdon', The Independent (1 Dec 1992), 13 · W. D. Rubinstein, ed., The biographical dictionary of life peers (New York, 1991) · L. Cheshire, 'Airey Neave', Postmaster (1980), 15–17 · A. Neave, They have their exits (1953) · b. cert. [Diana Joscelyn Barbara Giffard] · m. cert.

Archives HLRO, papers | GL, corresp. with publishers · U. Leeds, Brotherton L., corresp. with Sir Harry Legge-Bourke | FILM BFI NFTVA, news footage | SOUND IWM SA, oral history interviews

Likenesses photograph, 1974, Hult. Arch. · photograph, 1976, Hult. Arch. · N. Libbert, photograph, Hult. Arch. [see illus.]

Wealth at death £58,912: probate, 17 July 1979, CGPLA Eng. & Wales · £498,822—Diana Josceline Barbara Neave: probate, 4 June 1993, CGPLA Eng. & Wales

Neave, Caroline Hannah (1781–1863), philanthropist, was born on 23 March 1781, one of the seven children of Richard Neave (1731–1814), later first baronet, and his wife, Frances (d. 1830), the fourth daughter of John Bristow of Quidenham Hall, Norfolk. Nothing is known of her early life. In 1822 she founded and ran an asylum to shelter a small number of the more 'orderly' discharged prisoners in Westminster. In December of that year the Tothill Fields Asylum came to the attention of the British Ladies Society (itself founded by Elizabeth Fry in 1821 to promote the reformation of female prisoners) as presenting some encouraging instances of reformation in the nine months that it had been established. A few members of the society were asked to investigate and report on whether they should interfere or promote the enlargement of the concern. Encouraged by the orderly appearance of the women and the obvious benefit resulting from the care and instruction bestowed on them, the visitors recommended a financial donation to the refuge. Caroline Neave was invited to become a member of the society, an invitation which she accepted in April 1823.

In 1824 the British Ladies Society considered opening an asylum for 'vicious female children'. They publicized the idea, and when several subscriptions had been received and deposited in a bank a prospectus was drawn up for the asylum and school of reformation. In January 1825 several other philanthropic societies also agreed that such an institution was needed. Trusting that funds would continue to accumulate, the British Ladies Society authorized

a subcommittee, with Caroline Neave as its head, to provide suitable accommodation for a few children. The new foundation, in Chelsea, was called Manor Hall Asylum; it was later taken over by the Female Philanthropic Society.

The children received at the asylum were shoplifters or thieves' apprentices; one little girl had given a man a key to enter her parents' home, allowing him to steal all their money. As a measure of the asylum's success, only two children were recommitted to prison and only four had returned to crime. No corporal punishment was used; if they were disobedient the girls aged between seven and thirteen years were placed in solitary confinement. The girls were kept busy from morning to night with housework and needlework, learning skills which would be useful to them whether they married or they entered domestic service.

Caroline Neave lived in Thurlow Lodge, Clapham, for most of her life, but later moved to 49 Gloucester Street, Warwick Square, London. In 1833 she helped to establish a visiting committee in Coldbath Fields prison with Elizabeth Fry, who had become a personal friend. She died unmarried on 7 December 1863 at 49 Gloucester Street. She had been a member of the British Ladies Society for forty years and had worked in prisons, refuges, and as a convict-ship visitor, but the Manor Hall Asylum had been the special object of her care. She continued her labours to within a week of her death.

AMANDA PHILLIPS

Sources Burke, Peerage · British Ladies Society meeting minutes, 1823–5, Hackney RO, London · British Ladies Society meeting minutes, 1833, Hackney RO, London · Memoir of the life of Elizabeth Fry, with extracts from her letters and journal, ed. [K. Fry and R. E. Cresswell], 2 vols. (1847) · d. cert.

Neaves, Charles, Lord Neaves (1800–1876), judge, was born in Edinburgh on 14 October 1800, the son of Charles Neaves, a solicitor, of Forfar, who was afterwards clerk of the justiciary court, Edinburgh, and belonged to an old Forfarshire family long settled in the town of Forfar. His mother was possibly Margarate Montgomery Atkin, who married a Charles Neaves at Canongate, Edinburgh, on 24 December 1794. The original name of Neave was altered to Neaves by the father. Charles Neaves was educated at the high school and university in Edinburgh, and after a brilliant academic career was called to the Scottish bar in 1822. He soon gained an extensive practice, and even in his early years was engaged in many difficult and important cases. On 19 December 1835 he married Eliza, daughter of Coll Macdonald of Dalness, writer to the signet. They had at least one daughter.

In 1841 Neaves was appointed advocate-depute when Sir William Rae was lord advocate, and he retained this position for four years. From 1845 to 1852 he was sheriff of Orkney and Shetland. On the resignation of Lord President David Boyle in May 1852 Neaves was appointed solicitor-general for Scotland in Lord Derby's administration. He held office until Derby's resignation in January 1853, and in April 1854 was made a judge in the court of session, taking the title of Lord Neaves, to fill the vacancy caused by the death of Lord Cockburn. Five years afterwards he was appointed a lord of justiciary, and he filled this office until his death on 23 December 1876, at 7 Charlotte Square, Edinburgh. His wife survived him.

In his profession Neaves was regarded as one of the greatest 'case lawyers' of his day. His tenacious memory enabled him to quote apposite decisions with unfailing accuracy, and he was one of the foremost authorities on criminal law in Scotland. His reputation as a literary man was almost equally great: he was 'one of the greatest humorists on the bench' according to one memoirist (Knight). For more than forty years he was a regular contributor of prose and verse to *Blackwood's Magazine*. His satires were published as *Songs and Verses, Social and Scientific* (Edinburgh, 1868; 2nd edn., 1872). He also wrote on philology, and was an accomplished classical scholar. He received the degree of LLD from Edinburgh University in 1860 and was elected lord rector of St Andrews University in 1872 and 1873. Although in most respects a conservative he was reputedly well disposed towards the movement for the teaching of women at universities.

A. H. MILLAR, *rev.* ROBERT SHIELS

Sources F. J. Grant, ed., *The Faculty of Advocates in Scotland, 1532–1943*, Scottish RS, 145 (1944) · J. C. Smith, *Writings by the way* (1885), 468–81 · private information (1894) · *Men of the time* (1875) · Boase, *Mod. Eng. biog.* · W. A. Knight, *Some 19th century Scotsmen* (1903) · IGI
Archives NL Scot., legal opinions | NL Scot., corresp. with Blackwood's and verses · U. Edin. L., letters to David Laing
Likenesses wood-engraving (after photograph by J. Horsburgh), NPG; repro. in *ILN* (6 Jan 1877)
Wealth at death £78,740 2s. 5d.: confirmation, 14 Feb 1877, *CCI*

Nechtan mac Derile (d. 732), king of Picts, was overking of the Picts between 706 and 724 and again in 729. Nechtan, the Irish form of this Celtic name, is the one almost invariably used in the Irish annals and in regnal lists. Bede, writing c.731, used a Pictish form, Naiton; Derile is perhaps not Celtic. Nechtan succeeded his brother Brude in 706. A third brother, Ciniod, was killed in 713. In that year, perhaps consequentially, Talarg son of Drostan 'was imprisoned by his brother [surely his half-brother] the king Nechtan' (A. O. Anderson, 1.214).

Early in his reign Nechtan was making 'an assiduous study of ecclesiastical writings' (Bede, *Hist. eccl.*, 533), though Bede does not suggest that Nechtan himself was literate; this determined him to bring his kingdom into line with Rome in certain matters of Christian observance. To counter native opposition he sought instruction from Ceolfrith (d. 716), abbot of Bede's own monastery, whose written reply, or a version of it, addressed to 'the most excellent and glorious lord the king Naiton', was later copied by Bede into his history (ibid., 553). It dealt chiefly with rules for fixing the date of Easter within the first lunar month of the year. The identification of that month in a particular year required the use of lunar tables; and Ceolfrith had been assured that correct nineteen-year-cycle tables were already in Nechtan's hands. The letter was read aloud and translated in the presence of Nechtan and 'many learned men'; an assembly of nobles was also present. The king then caused correct tables to be disseminated 'throughout all the provinces of the Picts', and tables of the old eighty-four-year cycles to be 'obliterated'.

Nechtan had sought advice also on the form of the clerical tonsure, and he now ordered the adoption of the 'tonsure of St Peter' (a complete crown). In response to a further request Ceolfrith sent him *architecti* to build a stone church in the Roman fashion in honour of St Peter; it is not known where in Pictland this church was built. Nechtan's reforms are usually supposed to have been made about 710, though Bede does not give a precise date.

Besides a native Pictish clergy Nechtan's kingdom contained, says Bede, many daughter houses of Iona. In 717 he expelled their people, 'the *familia* of Iona' (A. O. Anderson, 1.217), across Drumalban into the country of the Scots. It is not known why he did this, for in 716 Iona itself had adopted the Roman Easter; it may be that those evicted represented a faction which had refused to conform.

In 724 annals record the *clericatus* of Nechtan: he was no longer a layman. He was succeeded by Drust, possibly a nephew. This seems not to have been a voluntary abdication, since in 726 Nechtan 'was made prisoner by the king Drust' (A. O. Anderson, 1.222). In the same year Drust was ousted by Alpin (perhaps his brother). In 728 Alpin *rex* was in turn crushed by Oengus son of Forgus (d. 761) and disappears from the Pictish record. Nechtan appears to have become king again. But in 729 some of his people were beaten by people of Oengus in a battle fought at *stagnum Loochdae* ('lake of the black goddess'), perhaps at the Scottish–Pictish frontier near Tyndrum. Several of the dead, who are named, are described as *exactatores* of Nechtan (literally tax gatherers, administrators of some kind). As usual, the annalist leaves the affair unexplained. This is the only mention in the annals of Ulster of Nechtan after his imprisonment in 726. He was succeeded by Oengus and died in 732.

MARJORIE O. ANDERSON

Sources *Ann. Ulster* · A. O. Anderson, ed. and trans., *Early sources of Scottish history, AD 500 to 1286*, 2 vols. (1922); repr. with corrections (1990) · Bede, *Hist. eccl.* · M. O. Anderson, *Kings and kingship in early Scotland*, rev. edn (1980), 248, 263, 266, 273, 280, 287 · K. H. Jackson, 'The Pictish language', *The problem of the Picts*, ed. F. T. Wainwright (1955), 129–66 · E. Fernie, 'Early church architecture in Scotland', *Proceedings of the Society of Antiquaries of Scotland*, 116 (1986), 393–411 · W. Reeves, *The life of St Columba* (1857), 67 · M. Miller, 'Eanfrith's Pictish son', *Northern History*, 14 (1978), 47–66, esp. 66 · W. J. Watson, *The history of the Celtic place-names of Scotland* (1926), 50 · A. A. M. Duncan, 'Bede, Iona and the Picts', *The writing of history in the middle ages: essays presented to Richard William Southern*, ed. R. H. C. Davis and J. M. Wallace-Hadrill (1981), 1–42

Nechtan Morbet [Nechtan Morbreac] (d. 481?). *See under* Picts, kings of the (*act. c.*300–*c.*900).

Neck, Sir Joshua van, first baronet (1702–1777), merchant and financier, was born in The Hague on 5 January 1702, one of the six sons of Cornelis van Neck, paymaster-general of the land forces of the United Provinces, and his wife, Anna de Greeff. Four of his five brothers followed their father into public service, most conspicuously Lambert, pensionary of Rotterdam, and Abraham, attorney-general of the province of Holland. In 1718 another older brother, Gerard, settled as a merchant in London, where

Joshua joined him in 1722, first as assistant and later as partner. In 1732 van Neck married Marianne, daughter of Stephen Daubuz, a Huguenot merchant of London. They had two sons and four daughters, of whom Elizabeth married Thomas Walpole, MP and merchant of London, son of Horatio *Walpole, first Baron Walpole of Wolterton; and her sister Margaret married his brother Richard Walpole, London banker and MP.

The firm of Gerard and Joshua van Neck was a general merchant, but unusually active in placing the capital of fellow Dutchmen (and other continentals) in the British public funds and company shares. The sums so entrusted made it a power among London houses subscribing to public loans, particularly during the wars of 1744–63. Already one of the four leading underwriters in 1744, it was to be one of the two houses that arranged the closed subscription loans to the government in the difficult winters of 1745–6 and 1757—loans subsequently attacked by Sir John Barnard as too favourable to the promoters. In all known surviving lists of such subscriptions in the 1750s and 1760s (1757, 1759, 1767), the Van Neck firm took the largest share. It was also an important military remittance contractor during the Seven Years' War.

The van Necks had developed valuable trading and political connections in France, particularly with the Parisian Protestant firm of Thellusson, Necker & Co., which was able to get them recognized as agents of the French court. Their greatest coup was the highly remunerative commission to buy tobacco in London in 1730–65 for the French tobacco monopoly (which then imported most of its leaf from Britain). So important was this and so adept were the participants that the farmers-general and the van Necks were able to persuade both the French and British governments to permit the continued shipment of British tobacco to France during the wars of 1744–8 and 1756–63. This traffic also permitted the firm to act as a channel of communications between the two governments in wartime. For his financial and other services Joshua van Neck was created a baronet on 14 December 1751.

The childless Gerard van Neck died on 17 August 1750, leaving an estate estimated at £240,000, almost three-fifths of which went to his brother Joshua. In 1750 the firm was reorganized as a partnership between van Neck, his son-in-law Thomas Walpole, and D. J. Olivier. In 1765 Walpole broke with his father-in-law and set up his own firm, carrying off the French tobacco contract in the process. Even so, van Neck could be described at his death as 'one of the richest merchants in Europe' (*GM*). If, in the lifetime of Gerard, their family world appeared to be very much that of the Dutch Reformed and Huguenot expatriate communities in London, their social horizons expanded considerably after the Walpole marriages. Van Neck died on 5 March 1777 and was succeeded in the baronetcy by his elder son, Gerard.   JACOB M. PRICE, *rev.*

Sources J. M. Price, *France and the Chesapeake: a history of the French tobacco monopoly, 1674–1791*, 2 vols. (1973) • C. Wilson, *Anglo-Dutch commerce and finance in the eighteenth century* (1941) • *GM*, 1st ser., 47 (1777), 147 • will, PRO, PROB 11/1029, sig. 138

Likenesses A. Devis (*Conversation piece*), repro. in Price, *France and the Chesapeake* • van Loo, portrait, repro. in Wilson, *Anglo-Dutch commerce*

Wealth at death one of the richest merchants in Europe: *GM*

Neckam [Neckham, Nequam], **Alexander** (1157–1217), scholar and abbot of Cirencester, was born at St Albans, Hertfordshire, in September 1157, on the same night as Richard I. Alexander's mother, Hodierna, was chosen as Richard's foster mother; she suckled both children together. Alexander received his early education in the town of St Albans, whose grammar school was one of the most prestigious in twelfth-century England. As a young scholar he travelled to Paris, where he spent the years *c.*1175–1182 teaching the arts, and hearing lectures on theology, canon law, medicine, and, finally, civil law. In his *Laus sapientiae divinae*, he describes himself as 'a little pier of the Petit Pont', that is, as a member of the school on Paris's Petit Pont made famous by the Englishman Adam of Balsham (Adam de Parvo Ponte) in the 1130s. He returned to England, probably in 1183, and taught for a year or two at the school of Dunstable, dependent on St Albans Abbey. When Alexander had been master at Dunstable for about a year, he was invited to head the school at St Albans. The abbot of St Albans is said to have written punningly to him: 'Si bonus es venias; si nequam, nequaquam' ('If you are good, come; if good for nothing, don't bother'). It is not known how long he taught at St Albans, but by the 1190s he was teaching theology in the schools at Oxford. A sermon of his survives in which he appeals for funds for the restoration of the church of St Frideswide, Oxford, which burnt in 1190. He also tells, in his commentary on the Song of Songs, how when he was lecturing publicly in theology at Oxford he was a strong partisan of the view that the feast of the Conception of the Virgin should not be solemnly celebrated. He decided to lecture as if it were an ordinary day, but every year, whether by chance or by providence, he became ill and unable to meet his classes. His students noted the fact and privately rebuked him, and he changed his view on the contentious subject.

Alexander left Oxford to join the Augustinian canons of Cirencester some time between 1197 and 1202, and there he continued to teach and to write. During the early years of the thirteenth century he acted as an ecclesiastical judge-delegate and carried out several assignments on behalf of the king. In 1213 he was chosen abbot of Cirencester, and he was one of the churchmen who travelled to Rome in 1215 to attend the Fourth Lateran Council. He died at Kempsey, a manor of the bishop of Worcester, on 31 March 1217, and was buried in Worcester Cathedral. His tombstone, much worn, survives in the cathedral.

The proper spelling of Alexander's surname has been much debated. R. W. Hunt argued for Nequam, and his judgement has been followed by many scholars. G. F. Wedge reviewed the evidence, and argued persuasively for the view that Nequam is best understood as a punning variation on an original toponymic surname, Neckam or Necham. Neckam is the most likely original form of the name: although Alexander and his contemporaries spelt his name in a variety of ways, they almost certainly pronounced it 'Neckam'.

Like many famous writers, Neckam was credited with more than he actually wrote, but his authentic works are more than enough to justify his reputation as 'one of the most remarkable scholars of the second half of the twelfth century' (Raby, 2.118). He was a grammarian, an encyclopaedist, theologian, homilist, commentator, and poet. His earliest works are pedagogical, probably dating from his years in Paris and as schoolmaster at Dunstable and St Albans. They include the *De nominibus utensilium*, a discussion of objects of everyday life organized by topic (if you are setting up a household, going out for a ride, about to besiege a city, and so on), a commentary on Martianus Capella (*De nuptiis Philologiae et Mercurii fabula*), and two collections of fables, a *Novus Avianus* (six fables) and a *Novus Aesopus* (forty-two fables).

From Alexander's years as a theology master at Oxford date his gloss on the Psalms, his commentary on the Athanasian creed, records of scholastic disputed questions, and a large number of sermons.

Probably dating from his years as a canon of Cirencester is his largest work, the *De naturis rerum*, a five-book commentary on Ecclesiastes. Books 1 and 2 treat of the natural world, while books 3 to 5 concern theology. Also belonging to these years are the (lost) *Laus beatissime virginis*, the *Solatium fidelis animae* (on the hexaemeron or six days of creation), and his very popular *Corrogationes Promethei*, a grammatical treatise, and a commentary on difficult words in the Old and New testaments, which Alexander subsequently translated into a versified form. Finally, to these years should be assigned Alexander's commentaries on Proverbs and the Song of Songs, his programme for clerical study (*Sacerdos ad altare*), and a scholastic theological *summa*, the *Speculum speculationum*.

During the final years of his life Alexander completed his *Laus sapientiae divinae*, a masterful, versified 'pageant of the wonders of the world' (Rigg, 121). He added a *Suppletio defectuum* (supplement) to the *Laus* before his death. Also to his years of service as abbot of Cirencester belong the *Corrogationes novi Promethei*, a lively poem describing the sins to which an abbot is susceptible; the *Super mulierem fortem*, a commentary on the 'strong woman' of Proverbs 31: 10–31; and three books *De commendatione vini*, which begin with praise of Bacchus and Noah for having invented wine and end with reflections on the beneficial effects of wine in the eucharist. Neckam has also been credited with nine hymns to the Virgin and four to Mary Magdalen, as well as many short poems and epigrams.

JOSEPH GOERING

Sources R. W. Hunt, *The schools and the cloister: the life and writings of Alexander Nequam*, rev. M. Gibson (1984) · A. G. Rigg, *A history of Anglo-Latin literature, 1066–1422* (1992) · *Alexander Nequam: 'Speculum speculationum'*, ed. R. M. Thomson (1988) · G. F. Wedge, 'Alexander Neckam's *De naturis rerum*: a study, together with representative passages in translation', PhD diss., University of Minnesota, 1967 · F. J. E. Raby, *A history of secular Latin poetry in the middle ages*, 2nd edn, 2 vols. (1957)

Archives Bodl. Oxf., fragment of 'De nobis utensilium' · Bodl. Oxf., sermons

Necker, Louis Albert (1786–1861), geologist, was born on 10 April 1786 in Geneva, eldest son of Jacques Necker (d. 1825), professor of botany and magistrate in Geneva, and Albertine (1764–1841), daughter of Horace Benedict de Saussure (1740–1799). As well as the famous alpine geologist and naturalist as grandfather on his mother's side, Necker's family included several other distinguished members, notably the famous novelist and authoress Madame de Staël. Geneva provided a fertile, highly cultured background for his early education, his schooldays finishing in 1800. He then pursued a course of higher studies for four years, probably at the academy in Geneva. In July 1803, with his father, he made his first journey into the Alps.

Already conversant with mineralogy and geology, Necker arrived in Scotland, aged twenty, in 1806 in order to continue his studies at the University of Edinburgh. He thus became one of several visiting students, including Richard Griffith (1784–1878), from Dublin, to attend the classes of Robert Jameson (1774–1854), professor of natural history from 1804. Jameson had studied briefly under A. G. Werner in Freiburg and established the Wernerian Natural History Society in Edinburgh in 1808, to promulgate Werner's teaching on the classification and origin of rocks.

The young, sociable Louis Necker was soon introduced to many of the leading figures in Edinburgh society at that time—such as John Playfair, Sir James Hall, Lord Webb Seymour, and others who had been associated with James Hutton (1726–1797) in the Royal Society of Edinburgh, founded in 1783. Hutton had first communicated his theory of the earth to that society in 1785 and thus Necker was ideally placed to take full advantage of the opposing Huttonian (Plutonist) and Wernerian (Neptunist) schools of thought in Edinburgh. The energetic Necker embarked on a series of tours throughout Scotland while based in Edinburgh. Beginning in the winter of 1806–7, he explored the coast of Fife, the islands of the Forth, and the coast of Berwickshire as far as St Abb's Head. In May 1807 he spent some time in Arran, being persuaded by the field evidence of Hutton's ideas on the origin of granite, namely that granite had crystallized out of a fluid state by means of fusion. In August that year he travelled as far as Staffa and first visited the Isle of Skye, to which he was later to return permanently.

On 9 April 1808 Jameson read a paper to his newly formed society in Edinburgh, 'On colouring geognostical maps'. No evidence exists that Jameson himself ever made such maps; Hutton, in his extensive travels, amassed a collection of specimens but made no geological map, although his friend John Clerk of Eldin illustrated the localities they visited together. Necker's unique achievement, based largely on his own tours, was to construct the earliest known geological map of the whole of Scotland. This he presented to the newly formed Geological Society of London on 4 November 1808. Hand-coloured and based on Thomas Kitchin's 1778 map of Scotland at about 12½ miles to the inch, the 'Explanation' of the rock divisions used employs both Huttonian and Wernerian principles. Unfortunately, the accompanying memoir has not survived and the map itself lay in almost complete obscurity until 1939 when it was printed in colour and published for the Edinburgh Geological Society. Although riddled with errors and omissions, it is nevertheless a remarkable document.

Necker returned to Geneva to occupy the chair of mineralogy and geology from 1810. The journal of his Scottish tours was eventually published there in three volumes in 1821, as *Voyage en Écosse et aux Îles Hébrides*. He continued making extensive tours and published several other works. In 1832, Necker accompanied J. D. Forbes (1809–1868), the pioneer Scottish glaciologist, on his first alpine tour, the two becoming close friends. Necker had never married, and the death of his mother on 13 April 1841 affected him deeply. He settled in Portree on the Isle of Skye for the last twenty years of his life, maintaining his wide range of scientific interests, especially in making barometrical observations. He died on 20 November 1861, aged seventy-five, at Portree, and was buried in the old churchyard there. NORMAN E. BUTCHER

Sources V. A. Eyles, 'Louis Albert Necker, of Geneva, and his geological map of Scotland', *Transactions of the Edinburgh Geological Society*, 14/2 (1948), 93–127 · J. D. Forbes, *Proceedings of the Royal Society of Edinburgh*, 5 (1862–6), 53–76 · NA Scot., SC 29/44/11/258-60
Likenesses portrait (aged twenty; after miniature, 1806), repro. in Eyles, 'Louis Albert Necker', pl. 6
Wealth at death £2112 6s. 2d.: confirmation, 16 Dec 1862, NA Scot.,SC 29/44/11/258-60

Necton, Humphrey (*d.* 1303), Carmelite friar and theologian, was born of a wealthy family in Norfolk and joined the order at Norwich. He studied at Cambridge University, where he was the first member of his order to become a doctor of theology. The contemporary chronicler of Barnwell Priory noted that Necton had gained his licence to incept as a result of the intercession of the bishop of Ely, William of Louth, and that this occurred soon after the Carmelites had moved to their new site in the centre of town in 1292. On 23 March 1299 Necton was acting as vicar-general, when he wrote a letter to the king appealing for the return of an errant friar. He lectured in the Carmelite studium in Cambridge until his return to Norwich, where he died in 1303 and was buried in the Carmelite house there. None of his works survives, but Bale saw a book of fourteen Sunday sermons which he attributed to Necton and recorded a *Questiones theologie* without incipit. In his later printed *Catalogus*, Bale adds *Lecturae scholasticae* and *Super articulis theologicis* without incipits. RICHARD COPSEY

Sources Bale, *Cat.*, 1.312–13 · Emden, *Cam.*, 420, 680 · J. W. Clark, ed., *Liber memorandum ecclesie de Bernewelle* (1907), 212 · J. Bale, Bodl. Oxf., MS Bodley 73 (SC 27635), fols. 51v, 79, 118v, 217v · J. Bale, BL, Harley MS 3838, fols. 21, 55v–56, 161v · J. Bale, Bodl. Oxf., MS Selden supra 41, fol. 155 · J. Bale, *Illustrium Maioris Britannie scriptorum … summarium* (1548), fol. 107 · *Commentarii de scriptoribus Britannicis, auctore Joanne Lelando*, ed. A. Hall, 2 (1709), 313 · J. Pits, *Relationum*

historicarum de rebus Anglicis, ed. [W. Bishop] (Paris, 1619), 388 · Tanner, *Bibl. Brit.-Hib.*, 542

Ned Môn. *See* Jones, Edward (*fl.* 1771–1840).

Nedeham, James (*d.* 1544), architect, was the son of Christopher Nedeham, citizen and carpenter of London, and the grandson of John Needham of High Needham, Derbyshire. He was made free of the London Carpenters' Company in 1514, served as warden between 1515 and 1533, and was master in 1534, 1535, and 1542. He designed a louvre for the Mercers' Hall in 1521 and was employed abroad as a military carpenter during the war between England and France from 1522 to 1525. On his return he was granted a sinecure as a gunner in the Tower of London; in 1526 he was advanced to the post of senior gunner.

Shortly afterwards Nedeham entered the employment of Cardinal Thomas Wolsey, with a senior post in the administration of the building works at York Place; he continued to be employed on the site after Wolsey's fall. In February 1530 he contracted to build wooden galleries round three sides of the garden of the London house of the marquess of Exeter. He was then described as 'one of the Kynge's Master Carpenters' (Salzman, 576), but it was only in March 1531 that he was appointed to the post of master carpenter of the king's works, following the death of Humphrey Coke. Eighteen months later, in October 1532, he was promoted to take overall control of the works as surveyor. He was the first craftsman to direct the organization, succeeding a long line of clerical administrators, and his appointment suggests the need for greater technical knowledge in a period of increased royal building activity.

The rapidity of Nedeham's promotion was undoubtedly a tribute to his architectural skills, but also owed something to the strength of his connections. His family was of armigerous status and as a former servant of Wolsey he was well known to both the king and Thomas Cromwell, for whom he was working in a private capacity at the time of his appointment to the surveyorship. His successful resistance to greater financial scrutiny of his accounts by the comptroller is, perhaps, a further mark of the trust that he enjoyed from Cromwell and the king.

During Nedeham's period as surveyor there was little change in the organization of the works, but his surviving particular books give a vivid picture of the extent of his responsibilities and the constant travel between the large number of sites where work was in progress. He drew plans, made designs, dispensed advice, and, as Ransome comments, 'there is every reason to suppose that when a new house was built under [his] direction, or an old one repaired, he helped to make the necessary designs' (*History of the King's Works*, 3.13). He probably designed the roof over the great hall at Hampton Court Palace (1532–3) and, among other projects, was responsible for the building of the Jewel House in the Tower of London (1535–6), the fitting up of St Augustine's, Canterbury, to receive Anne of Cleves (1539), and the domestic conversion of monastic buildings at Dartford and Rochester (1539–42).

In 1544 Nedeham accompanied the king to Boulogne

and he died there on 22 September, having made his will the same day. Although he was buried in the church of Our Lady in Boulogne, he was commemorated by a monument (now destroyed) erected in 1605 by his grandson in the parish church of Little Wymondley, Hertfordshire, where he had acquired the dissolved priory in April 1538, which remained the family seat until 1733. At the time of his death he also owned property in Gracechurch Street, London, and elsewhere in Hertfordshire, Berkshire, Essex, and Kent. He left a substantial amount of plate and cash and was survived by his wife, Alice (formerly Merrey and/or Goodyer), five sons, and two daughters.

MALCOLM AIRS

Sources H. M. Colvin and others, eds., *The history of the king's works*, 3–4 (1975–82) · J. Harvey and A. Oswald, *English mediaeval architects: a biographical dictionary down to 1550*, 2nd edn (1984), 210–13 · L. F. Salzman, *Building in England down to 1540*, rev. edn (1967), 575–7 · H. Chauncy, *The historical antiquities of Hertfordshire* (1700), 109–11 · R. Clutterbuck, ed., *The history and antiquities of the county of Hertford*, 2 (1821), 549–50 · L. Lyell and F. D. Watney, eds., *Acts of court of the Mercers' Company, 1453–1527* (1936), 531 · B. Marsh, J. Ainsworth, and A. M. Millard, eds., *Records of the Worshipful Company of Carpenters*, 7 vols. (1913–68), vol. 3, p. 211

Archives BL, particular book, Add. MS 10109 · Bodl. Oxf., particular books · Nott. Arch., accounts · Nott. Arch., particular book · PRO, particular book, E101/504/2 · U. Nott. L., particular books | Bodl. Oxf., Rawlinson MSS · Longleat House, Wiltshire, Longleat MSS · U. Nott., Newcastle MSS

Wealth at death over £500; plus extensive property in London, Hertfordshire, Berkshire, Kent, and Essex: will, PRO, PROB 11/30, sig. 21

Neden, Sir Wilfred John (1893–1978), civil servant, was born on 24 August 1893 at 27 Kimberley Road, Kennington, London, the son of John Thomas Neden, a commercial traveller selling seeds, and his wife, Margaret, *née* Hulme. After attending St Olave's Grammar School, Southwark, Neden took a regular commission in the army in 1914. During the First World War he was promoted to lieutenant, but his hopes of a regular army career were dashed when he lost a foot in the Gallipoli landing. He was mentioned in dispatches for his bravery. He subsequently left the army in 1922 and embarked on a career in the Ministry of Labour. On 10 September 1925 he married Jean Kate (1893/4–1965), the daughter of David James Lundie, a printer's reader. They had a son and a daughter.

Neden's early years at the Ministry of Labour were spent in its employment exchanges, which then faced the problems of mass unemployment. His experience of the exchanges gave him confidence in their ability during the Second World War to handle conscription, which he directed. In 1946 he was appointed an under-secretary in the ministry and in 1948 became its director of organization and establishments, overseeing the ministry's staff and premises and its extensive regional and local organization.

In 1954 Neden was unexpectedly switched to the ministry's top industrial relations post when he was appointed chief industrial commissioner. He served in this post until 1958 and was knighted in 1955. The appointment was surprising, for Neden had no experience in industrial relations. The job required him to run the ministry's industrial relations department and, on behalf of the minister, to provide conciliation in negotiations that could be exacting, frequently frustrating, and at all times difficult. However, his rigorous sense of fairness won him respect from both employers and unions and served him well in his new job. His robust personality led him to be more assertive than any of his immediate predecessors, and he rapidly became a figure to be reckoned with. He was not afraid to lose his temper, nor averse to lecturing and even bullying negotiators if he thought that his aims would be achieved thereby.

Neden's period as chief industrial commissioner was difficult, for it coincided with deteriorating British industrial relations. The difficulties were increased by the Conservative government's shift in strategy; alarmed at the pace of inflation, it began to move away from conciliating the unions and to resist, and urge employers to resist, wage claims. This brought into question the Ministry of Labour's traditional function of impartial conciliation. The problem was faced by Neden in its most acute form in the London bus workers' dispute during the winter of 1957–8. Having been asked by the two sides for his help, Neden was telephoned by Harold Watkinson, then minister of transport, and was bluntly told to desist from any action that could result in a wage increase. Neden always strongly resented the intervention of others in his conciliation work and made no attempt to disguise this resentment, whether it came from officials of the TUC, from employers, or from cabinet ministers; he thought taking sides in this manner would be wrong. Instead, he proposed to Iain Macleod, then minister of labour, that an outside committee be created to help the parties reach an agreement. Macleod was initially hesitant, but did not prevent Neden from making his offer. However, when Macleod reported to the cabinet on 24 January 1958 he was overruled by his colleagues, who feared that conciliation would be seen as a surrender to the unions and so weaken the government's anti-inflationary credentials. Consequently Macleod repudiated Neden's plan—an action without precedent and 'the breaking-point in the dialogue of trust that had hitherto existed between the ministry and the TUC' (Goodman, 169). A seven-week strike ensued in which 1,600,000 working days were lost and which ended in the defeat of the union. Macleod's reputation was thereby salvaged, indeed enhanced. Neden, however, felt badly let down and humiliated. He had considered resigning but decided not to do so. However, he was bitterly angry and never forgave Macleod for the incident.

Neden retired from the Ministry of Labour in August 1958. Like several of his predecessors, he was a disappointed man, disillusioned with politicians and with their ways. He was the last chief industrial commissioner to devote his time entirely to industrial relations and conciliation. His successors were not allowed, as Neden had done, to press employers for concessions. Nor were they allowed the same public prominence that Neden had attracted during the struggles of 1957 and 1958 and which had irritated Macleod, antagonized other civil servants, and led to complaints to Neden's permanent secretary by the head of the civil service.

With a rubicund face and an artificial leg whose thump was a familiar sound in the corridors of the Ministry of Labour, Neden was a robust and colourful figure. After more than thirty years as a civil servant, he retained something detectably military in his bearing: not least his directness, and at times bluntness of speech. After his retirement from government service he served as deputy chairman of the British Overseas Aircraft Corporation from 1960 to 1963. His wife died in 1965, and on 11 February 1967 he married (Louie) Violet Ryan (*b.* 1900/01), the daughter of Lewis Robert Ball, a taxation officer. Neden died at his home, 36 Forest Drive, Keston Park, Keston, Kent, on 11 April 1978. His second wife survived him.

HUGH PEMBERTON

Sources E. Wigham, *Strikes and the government, 1893–1974* (1976) · *The Times* (15 April 1978) · G. Goodman, *The awkward warrior* (1979) · N. Fisher, *Iain Macleod* (1973) · R. Shepherd, *Iain Macleod* (1994); repr. (1995) · N. Fishman, '"Spearhead of the movement"? the 1958 London busworkers' strike, the TUC and Frank Cousins', *British trade unions and industrial politics*, ed. A. Campbell, N. Fishman, and J. McIlroy, 1 (1999) · G. Ince, *The ministry of labour and national service* (1960) · b. cert. · m. cert. [Jean Kate Lundie] · m. cert. [Louie Violet Ryan] · d. cert. · *WWW* · Burke, *Peerage* (1959)
Wealth at death £58,595: probate, 27 Sept 1978, *CGPLA Eng. & Wales*

Nedham [Needham], **Marchamont** (*bap.* **1620**, *d.* **1678**), journalist and pamphleteer, was baptized on 21 August 1620 at Burford, Oxfordshire, the only known child of Marchamont Nedham of Derbyshire (*c.*1594–1621) and Margery, daughter of John Collier, host of The George inn, Burford. The name was frequently spelt Needham, and rhymed, according to one contemporary ballad, with 'freedom'. Marchamont senior matriculated at St John's College, Oxford, and gained his BA from Gloucester Hall on 19 February 1612; thereafter he was an attendant on Lady Elizabeth Walter, *née* Lucas, sister to John, Lord Lucas, and wife to Sir William Walter of Sarsden, near Burford. The year after Marchamont senior's death Margery married Christopher Glynn, vicar of Burford and master of its free school; accordingly young Marchamont was educated by his stepfather. From 1634 Nedham attended All Souls College, Oxford, subscribing on 22 January 1636 as a chorister, probably indicating a scholarship. He obtained his BA on 24 October 1637, and moved to St Mary Hall, Oxford. Soon after he obtained the place of an usher or undermaster at Merchant Taylors' School in London. For unknown reasons he abandoned this sinecure, perhaps during the turbulent events of 1641, to become an under-clerk at Gray's Inn, where he developed the legal knowledge that informed his later political thought. At some point during these years he also found time to study medicine.

Mercurius Britanicus and parliamentarianism Nedham moved prodigiously onto the public stage in the summer of 1643, when he became the author or editor of the parliamentarian weekly newsbook *Mercurius Britanicus*. He thus joined the first generation of news editors who were editors before they were pamphleteers. *Britanicus*, which appeared between August 1643 and May 1646, was apparently commissioned in response to the royalist *Mercurius Aulicus*, the Oxford newsbook which had created an enthusiastic readership in the south of England and Wales, not only among those loyal to the king. Nedham joined with Thomas Audley to produce a periodical combining counter-propaganda with news and witty political analysis. It is not clear who took the senior role in the day-to-day composition of the text, as was common in the collaboratively produced newspaper press of the seventeenth century, but the early issues show signs of Nedham's deft touch, and from October 1644 he was in sole control.

Nedham's powerful writing, his unwavering hostility to presbyterianism, and lack of sympathy with the king were soon to attract much hostile press. This became acute following an intervention which was long to survive in the memories of seventeenth-century readers and which caused his first friction with the authorities. When the correspondence of Charles I was seized at the battle of Naseby in July 1645 parliament recognized the propaganda value it represented, and permitted the king's private letters to be put on display and published in print. Nedham reprinted the letters in *Britanicus* with antipathetic annotations, and crossed the boundaries of permissible criticism when he presented a mocking 'Hue and Cry' after the king that referred to Charles's speech impediment (*Mercurius Britanicus*, 92, 4 Aug 1645). Nedham was reprimanded by the House of Lords, but his position on the civil war and the king's responsibility became more uncompromising. In May 1646, at a time of fragile negotiations between the Scots and English, he published an editorial in *Britanicus* that described Charles as a tyrant and suggested that he was endeavouring to set the two crowns of England and Scotland against each other. Nedham was imprisoned for two weeks in the Fleet, and the House of Lords extracted from him a £200 surety for future good behaviour and a promise that he would write no more pamphlets. The promise did not keep him quiet for long, and he soon returned to journalism. He may also have published pamphlets during this period, though without acknowledgement. Internal evidence suggests that he may have authored, or had a hand in, a considerable number of anonymous pamphlets during the 1640s and 1650s. His style was imitable, however, and his mode of arguing influential, and most attributions must remain uncertain.

Mercurius Pragmaticus and royalism By 1647 Nedham had been practising as a physician for at least a year, and supported himself with this occupation for a while—the title-page of one 1646 pamphlet, *Independencie No Schisme*, describes him as a 'Med[ical] Pr[actitioner]'—but the call of the press brought him before the king at Hampton Court in 1647. Having obtained royal forgiveness he undertook a new weekly newsbook, *Mercurius Pragmaticus* (September 1647 – May 1649). Written in a more vitriolic vein than *Britanicus*, 'Prag' was for a while the darling of the royalist cause. Nedham was probably assisted by other hack writers in its production, and it seems likely that he abandoned his editorship in January 1649, but his name was exclusively associated with the title. In rebarbative editorials Nedham denounced the English parliament and the Scots for betraying their king and suggested that they conspired to murder him; he condoned the royalist war effort as a second civil war broke out, following a revitalized propaganda campaign, in spring 1648; and he satirized the army grandees and mocked the inability of the London authorities and the 'beagles' of the press to hunt him down. In the first editorial he advised 'in the midst of *jest* I am much in *earnest*' (*Mercurius Pragmaticus*, 1, 21 Sept 1647). This was fundamental to his rhetoric when writing for parliament, king, or republic: he would couch serious political analysis and argument in a jocular style, 'to tickle and charme the more *vulgar phant'sies*' (*Mercurius Britanicus*, 1, Aug 1643). Each issue began with a short facetious ballad (an innovation which started a fashion); Nedham, later seeking to curry favour with Charles II, gathered these into a single narrative and published them as *A Short History of the English Rebellion* (1661). *Pragmaticus* also contained surprisingly detailed reports on parliamentary proceedings, particularly in the lower house; it is unlikely that Nedham was able to attend the Commons in disguise, and it seems possible that he had a mole in the house, perhaps Speaker William Lenthall, a fellow Burford man. During the same period Nedham may have edited another royalist newsbook, *Westminster Projects, or, The Mysterie of Darby House, Discovered* (March–June 1648), a scathing putative exposure of the conspiratorial Derby House committee, in which English and Scottish representatives discussed reform of church and state.

The reasons for Nedham's change of political allegiance are unclear. In the light of his later alterations hostile pamphleteers would accuse him of being an unprincipled turncoat, a man who would serve any munificent master; and historians have for the most part assented to this view. Certain consistencies and rapidly changing circumstances suggest that a more generous interpretation is possible. In July 1646 Nedham wrote a pro-toleration pamphlet, *Independencie No Schisme*, which revealed a considerable degree of anti-Scottish sentiment in its anti-presbyterian stance. In May 1647 he wrote, to be published a month later, *The case of the kingdom stated, according to the proper interests of the severall parties ingaged*, a pamphlet that suggests continuing commitment to the cause of religious toleration and a suspicion that its best hopes lie with the king's cause. A commercial success, it foregrounded a mode of political analysis which was implicit in *Britanicus*; it analysed the 'interests' of various parties and identified the most satisfactory resolution, given the circumstances, for all of them. Drawing on the interest-theory formulated by the duc de Rohan, itself derived from Machiavelli and Guicciardini, this was not an original contribution to political thought, but Nedham may have been the first to use the method to analyse an existing situation and predict future behaviour and outcomes, and to publish his counsel as propaganda. It was a method he was to use again and again, and which he would popularize; but its underlying moral ambivalence did little to soften his reputation for Machiavellian self-interest.

Nedham's critique of Pride's Purge and the ensuing move to try the king was impassioned. As the inevitable indictment and execution approached he became dispirited and relinquished his editorship, though he returned briefly with *Mercurius Pragmaticus (For King Charles II)* (April–May 1649). His circumstances, in hiding in London, were less than commodious, and the pursuit of the authorities was discomforting. One incident caused him to flee the metropolis and hide at the house of Peter Heylyn, at Minster Lovell near Burford. Eventually the council of state succeeded in tracking him down; on 15 June 1649 it ordered the serjeant-at-arms to apprehend him, which was accomplished several days later.

Classical political theory and service to the republic Nedham spent three months imprisoned in Newgate, though he escaped and was re-arrested in August. On the first of that same month he published a short pamphlet, *Certain Considerations Tendered in All Humility* (1649), apologizing for his transgressions but recommending that the new 'free state' treat him and other offenders with prudent lenience (p. 9). The pamphlet is significant for its extensive use of Roman precedent; Nedham had encountered a similar classicism in the literature of the engagement controversy, and would soon develop the language of classical republicanism for present purposes. Anthony Wood suggests that at Newgate he was 'brought into danger of his life' (Wood, *Ath. Oxon.*, 3.1181), but was pardoned at the intercession of Lenthall and John Bradshaw (who would later remember Nedham in his will). The solicitation of these friends may have been responsible for provoking another change of heart: on 14 November he took the engagement and was released. The archives are silent for the next few critical months. Then on 8 May 1650 his conversion to republican principles was announced with the publication of *The case of the Common-Wealth of England stated, or, The equity, utility, and necessity, of a submission to the present government; cleared out of monuments both sacred and civill, against all the scruples and pretences of the opposite parties*. This used interest-theory to counsel royalists, Scots, presbyterians, and Levellers to submit to the new regime; but its argument developed beyond mere de factoism into an eloquent statement of classical republicanism, drawing on Sallust, Suetonius, Aristotle, Tacitus, Livy, Machiavelli, Guicciardini, Bodin, and others. A second edition the same year added extensive quotations from two royalist theorists, Salmasius and Hobbes, that supported Nedham's position on the necessity of submission to governments. Nedham disarmingly began his preface:

> Perhaps thou art of an Opinion contrary to what is here written: I confesse, that for a Time I my self was so too, till some Causes made me reflect with an impartial eie upon the Affairs of this new Government.   (sig. A2r)

The tract made it clear that Nedham had once again shifted his allegiances.

The council of state quickly rewarded Nedham, with a payment on 24 May of £50 for his writings, to which was added an annual salary of £100 'whereby he may subsist while endeavouring to serve the commonwealth' (*CSP dom.*, *1650*, 174), paid for a year in the first instance (subsequent payments were usually quarterly, though the records are incomplete). In return Nedham presented them on 8 June with a prospectus for a new state newsbook, *Mercurius Politicus* (June 1650 – April 1660), a name chosen to reflect the government's opposition to 'the despotick forme of rule'. He proposed 'to sayle in a middle way, between the Scylla and Charybdis of Scurrility and prophanes', as he had in his earlier periodicals, but set about this with a new seriousness of purpose, beginning with the serialization as editorials of excerpts from *Case of the Common-Wealth* (French, 2.310–11). By this means he publicized and promoted in a highly accessible form the political theory of late humanism. In editing *Politicus* Nedham had at hand the resources of the office of John Thurloe, secretary to the council and head of the republic's secret service. This provided an excellent basis for foreign reporting, reflecting the government's interests and foreign policy. Nedham supplemented this very substantial intelligence network with other correspondents distributed across Britain and continental Europe. Accordingly the news content of *Politicus* was exceptionally distinguished, and it compared favourably to publications in France, Germany, and the Low Countries, as contemporary readers observed. Other collaborators in the project included Milton, who served as licenser to *Politicus* through 1651, and who became a close and enduring friend of Nedham's; and John Hall, another pensioner of the republic who worked as a literary odd-job man—though no specific nature, nor any estimate of extent, can be offered for their contributions. In its early months *Politicus* was the doyen of the Commonwealth's radicals, making remarkable proposals for political reform, including, in January 1651, political union with the Netherlands. From October 1651 until August 1652 Nedham included a new series of editorials which were later published, in subtly revised form, as *The Excellencie of a Free State* (1656), a key text in British republicanism, and one which may have endangered his rapprochement with the increasingly anti-republican protectorate government. None the less, through the ten years of *Politicus* (a period which made it the most enduring news periodical before the *London Gazette*) this radicalism declined, particularly when Nedham was called upon to support an entrenched protectorate.

Protectorate writings and career What seems like a further abandonment of political ideas had a deeper congruity. Nedham soon turned against the Rump of the Long Parliament, owing to its prevarication and failure to introduce fresh elections (for which *Politicus* called, while speculating on alternative modes of government). When Cromwell dissolved the Rump in April 1653 Nedham was relatively quiet. During the nominated assembly that followed Nedham began working as a spy, motivated by his own political convictions, to detect the underground activities of Fifth Monarchists; he disliked the strong religious influence on government and was concerned that the assembly would impose a religious settlement contrary to liberty of conscience. In a report on 16 November

he called for the introduction of 'some solid Fundamentals, in reference to the State both of Religion & Politie' (Bodl. Oxf., MS Rawl. A. 8, fols. 129–31). The 'Instrument of government', the constitution of the protectorate introduced in December 1653, realized this suggestion. Nedham penned a cogent defence of the constitution, *A True State of the Case of the Commonwealth* (1654), which presented the instrument sympathetically and emphasized its republican elements. One 1652 editorial from *Politicus* appeared in *True State*; here, as elsewhere, Nedham can be seen reiterating certain principles in shifting political contexts, but also calculating, in a pragmatic if not Machiavellian manner, how certain political ends might best be achieved or advocated in imperfect circumstances. Behind these shifting positions can be seen a commitment to the non-intervention of the state in religious matters and to liberty of conscience, to the separation between legislative and executive powers, but otherwise the rejection of the utopian ideal of a perfect system of government (whether monarchical or republican) which would fit any circumstances.

The single greatest influence on Nedham's political thought was Machiavelli's *Discourses on Livy*, though he was also inspired by Aristotle and Sallust; from Rohan he learned some of the practical applications of theory, and he found Hobbes's materialism and de factoism provocative. The primary end of government was stability, and a republican mixed constitution (in which the part of monarchy might be represented by something other than a king) was the best means of achieving it. His repeated affirmations of popular sovereignty as the one true foundation of government suggest a genuine belief, though one compromised in practice by his ongoing suspicion of the English people: the people had to be forced to be free until educated into good citizenship. His qualified support of the Rump (particularly the radical circle around Henry Marten and Thomas Chaloner) and subsequently of Cromwell was based upon a faith that they were the best temporary means to create a fixed government able to teach the people liberty. Nedham did not sketch any constitutional blueprints, though a series of mainly Machiavellian axioms emerge from his writings. Fundamental to stability was a separation between church and state, and he was prepared to endorse a national church and tithes provided liberty of conscience was simultaneously protected; he rarely wrote about religion, perhaps because it was a divisive topic. A republic should be prepared and able to expand its territories, and he envisaged that a free Britain would become a threat to neighbouring princes; in order to do so it would have to be an armed state, ready for defence. In recognition of the foundation of all government in the people's consent, parliaments should be free, frequent, and of limited duration. Security, political consent, and freedom of conscience are the natural rights and liberties of the people, and therefore it was their duty to protect them. All of Nedham's 'thought' was, however, shaped by the forms in which he expressed it, and even these abstract principles were extraordinarily malleable to the particular polemical circumstances and contexts in which he articulated them.

The formal innovations for which Nedham was responsible as a news editor included the introduction of regular advertising of diverse products and services. Nedham would later edit the first periodical devoted solely to advertising, the *Public Adviser* (May–September 1657). This made *Politicus* highly profitable; far from being a subsidized instrument of state propaganda, its revenues were such that on one occasion the protector's council awarded a share in the profits to a state servant by way of reward. *Politicus* was read widely, not only across Britain but also throughout Europe, and not only among expatriates and those sympathetic to the Commonwealth and Nedham's politics. A 1660 attack on Nedham and *Politicus* averred: ''tis incredible what influence they had upon numbers of inconsidering persons ... This was the *Goliah* of the *Philistines*, the great Champion of the late Usurper, whose Pen was in comparison of others like a Weavers beam' (*A Rope for Pol*, 1660, 'Advertisement').

The only evidence of Nedham's first marriage is the baptism of his only known child, a son named Marchamont, on 6 May 1652 at St Margaret's, Westminster. The mother's name was given as Lucy Nedham. Nothing further is known about either wife or son. On 7 July 1652 Nedham was admitted to Gray's Inn, the register recording that he then resided in 'the City of Westminster' (Foster, *Register*, 261). Among other activities during the years of the Commonwealth Nedham translated John Selden's *Mare clausum* as *Of the Dominion, or, The Ownership of the Sea* (1652), a work of renewed relevance during the First Anglo-Dutch War, for which he was rewarded with a princely £200 on 10 February 1653. Translating commissions appeared at this time, and it was during these years that he developed his close friendship with John Milton, secretary for foreign tongues to the council of state. Milton's nephew Edward Phillips later described Nedham as a 'particular friend' of Milton; Wood as his 'great crony' (Darbishire, 44–5, 74). The council relied on Nedham, like Milton, to liaise with members of the book trade. On 7 August 1654 Nedham reported to the court of the Stationers' Company, then in turmoil, on 'the proceedings in the Companies affaire depending before the Councell' (Stationers' Hall, court book C, fol. 292r); for this they gave him a gratuity of £20. On 17 April 1655 the council took his salary away, along with John Hall's, while Milton's was lowered. This may have prompted Nedham to submit a paper recommending reform of the press, to discuss which the council of state appointed a committee on 24 April 1655. By 4 May his salary was restored, and between August and October the council introduced new orders regulating printing. One of the consequences of these was that Nedham enjoyed, from October 1655, a monopoly of periodical news, though it is doubtful that he was the architect of the new regulations. That same month Nedham produced a partner journal to Thursday's *Politicus*, *The Publick Intelligencer*, appearing on Mondays and reproducing much of the same material, but none the less a commercial success.

The publication of revised *Politicus* editorials as *The Excellencie of a Free State* in 1656 may have involved a political miscalculation, as it aligned Nedham with the republican opposition in the spring of that year. *Excellencie* championed popular sovereignty and the rotation of political offices in government as a necessary preventative of corruption. Like Milton, Nedham felt disenchanted with Cromwell and the conservative tendencies of the protectorate, but the following year he conducted himself more prudently, not objecting to 'The humble petition and advice', and defending its religious arrangements. When John Goodwin attacked the triers and ejectors system of clerical appointment Nedham responded with *The Great Accuser Cast Down* (1657), a work which contradicted his previous critiques of the established church and the interference of the secular magistrate in propagating the gospel. A pamphlet response described Nedham as 'that mercenary soul that for an handful of earth shall be hired to assassinate the greatest fame and reputation' (D. F., *A Letter*, 2). Goodwin denounced him as 'a man that curseth whatsoever he blesseth, and blesseth whatsoever he curseth' (Goodwin, sig. A3v).

The Restoration: victim and apologist Even before Cromwell's death Nedham began writing anti-restoration propaganda, aware of the shaky foundations of the government. On 23 November he walked in Cromwell's funeral procession, perhaps close to the secretaries for tongues, who included Milton and Andrew Marvell. On 13 May 1659, however, he fell victim to conflict within the government, when parliament suspended him from his editorship of *Politicus*. Nedham was by no means silenced, and his *Interest will not Lie* (1659), a pamphlet arguing that a Stuart restoration would be contrary to the interests of all parties, was published three days before the restoration of his own editorship on 15 August. His tenure was not to last for long. After Charles Stuart's declaration of Breda on 4 April 1660 Nedham's case was hopeless, and on 9 April the council of state once again dismissed him from his editorship. His final parting shot, both seeking to prevent the Restoration and disavowing the consequences that would follow if his ministrations were ignored, was a fictional, satirical letter, *Newes from Brussels* (*c.*23 March 1660), purporting to be written by a cavalier anticipating the revenge that he and his king would exact if and when they returned to England.

Nedham went into hiding; printed pamphlets suggested he had fled to the Netherlands. The vociferousness of the numerous attacks on Nedham at the Restoration—many of which associated him with Milton—testified to his effectiveness as an editor and pamphleteer. Their ferocity was exceptional even by contemporary standards, perhaps because he once espoused the king's cause as its most able propagandist and then abandoned it. Anthony Wood's brief biography, which borrowed heavily (and without acknowledgement) from Restoration attacks, presented the most ameliorated seventeenth-century view:

> He was a person endowed with quick natural parts, was a good humanitarian, poet and boon droll: and had he been constant to his cavaleering principles he would have been

beloved by, and admired of, all; but being mercenary and valuing money and sordid interest, rather than conscience, friendship, or love to his prince, was much hated by the royal part to his last, and many cannot endure to hear him spoken of. (Wood, *Ath. Oxon.*, 3. 1183)

Two contemporary descriptions of Nedham's appearance survive, both hostile: a ballad describes Nedham at Amsterdam as 'hawk-nos'd', long-haired, and wearing two earrings—'His Visage smeager is and long, / His Body slender; but his Tongue / … has a Grace, / Becomming no such Traitor's face' (*O. Cromwell's Thankes*, 14); while an earlier pamphlet sketches him as 'a man of low stature full set, blacke haire, hollow-hearted, empty scull'd' (*Aulicus his Hue and Cry*, 1). No known portrait survives.

It was a surprise to many, certainly to the authors of hostile pamphlets, that Nedham was not exempted from the Act of Oblivion or Bill of Indemnity in August 1660. In September, according to Wood, he obtained a pardon under the great seal and returned to London; this enabled him to save his neck when set upon, as in Oxford in 1661 when he was assailed at St Mary's Church (Wood, *Ath. Oxon.*, 3.1182). No one was surprised when he published royalist propaganda, including an anti-Cromwellian ballad, *The Cities Feast* (April 1661), and *A Short History of the English Rebellion* (1661). His *A Discourse Concerning Schools and School-Masters* (May 1663) suggested reform of schools to prevent heterodoxy. In April 1663, aged forty-two, Nedham, then living in St Andrew Undershaft, remarried. His bride was Elizabeth Thompson (*b*. 1630/31, *d*. after 1678) of the parish of Holy Trinity, London, a widow aged thirty-two.

Physician and anti-whig pamphleteer Nedham had resumed his career as a physician. The diary of Bulstrode Whitelocke, the interregnum parliamentarian and ambassador, records that Nedham attended on him in this capacity on 29 March 1665. It was perhaps with some irony that he suggested, in *A Discourse Concerning Schools*, that old nonconformist schoolteachers would be less dangerous if licensed to 'practise Physick' (p. 8). His major contribution to medical theory was the controversial *Medela medicinæ* (1665), which acknowledged 'M. N. *Med. Londinens*' as its author. In this he argued that Galenic principles of medicine were corrupt and useless, that modern diseases were different from ancient, and that liberty should be permitted in the practice of physic in order rationally to develop new chemical remedies. He also added a commentary to Edward Bolnest's *Medicina instaurata* (1665) espousing a similar stance, and a preface to Franciscus de le Boë's *New Idea of the Practice of Physic* (1675), which responded dismissively to some attacks on his works allegedly commissioned by the College of Physicians.

Nedham thereafter practised quietly for most of his remaining years. Nothing is heard of him after 1665 until 1676, when, in probably the strangest of his shifts in allegiance, he wrote three pamphlet attacks on the earl of Shaftesbury in answer to Shaftesbury's *Letter from a Person of Quality*. These were *A Pacquet of Advices and Animadversions Sent from London to the Men of Shaftesbury* (1676), *A Second Pacquet of Advices and Animadversions* (1676), and *Honesty's Best Policy, or, Penitence the Sum of Prudence* (early 1678), all

published anonymously. Their primary aim was to play upon fears and memories of the civil wars by linking Shaftesbury's allies with the '*Old Faction*' of 1641, the 'good old cause' of which Nedham had himself once been an ally (Nedham, *Answer*, 2). Nedham spoke against his former political commitments by justifying the long prorogation of parliament, defending bishops, and showing himself prepared to speak in favour of divine right monarchy; yet he continued to blame presbyterian conspiracy as the root of the troubles. His former acquaintance, and perhaps friend, Marvell wrote bitterly that Nedham had been

> hired by the Conspirators at so much a sheet, or for day wages; and when that is spent, he shall for lesse mony Blaspheme his God, Revile his Prince, and Belye his Country, if his former Books have Omitted any thing of those Arguments; and shall Curse his own Father into the Bargain. (Marvell, 121)

Wood and Robert Ferguson the Plotter identified Edmund Warcup and Thomas, earl of Danby as the paymasters. Nedham's final work, probably more revealing of his own beliefs, was *Christianissimus Christianandus* (1678), the second of two anti-French pamphlets, calling for an immediate war.

Nedham died intestate, 'suddenly' according to Wood,

> in the house of one Kidder in D[ev]ereux Court near Temple-bar in London, in sixteen hundred seventy and eight, and was buried on the 29th of Novemb. (being the vigil of St. Andrew) at the upper end of the body of the church of St. Clement's Danes, near the entrance into the chancel. (Wood, *Ath. Oxon.*, 3.1181)

He did not die in poverty: the administrator of his estate posted a bond in December that year. The inscription on Nedham's grave was removed two years later, conceivably defaced, in rebuilding work. He was survived by his wife, Elizabeth. Nedham's capacity to switch sides, often injudiciously, has marred his name ever since. His reputation as 'the politick Shuttle-cock' (*Character of Mercurius Politicus*) and the practical orientation of his writings have discouraged the recognition that his journalism or political writings merit. In eighteenth-century America, however, he was named as a champion of liberty, alongside Milton, Marvell, and Algernon Sidney, and *The Excellencie of a Free State* was read by and, as far as time can permit us to say, influenced the fathers of the constitution.

JOAD RAYMOND

Sources Bodl. Oxf., MS Rawl. A. 8 · court book B, Stationers' Hall · parish register, Burford, Oxon. RO · *CSP dom.*, 1641–60 · *JHL*, 5–13 (1642–81) · *JHC*, 3–9 (1642–87) · J. Foster, *The register of admissions to Gray's Inn, 1521–1889, together with the register of marriages in Gray's Inn chapel, 1695–1754* (privately printed, London, 1889), 261 · J. L. Chester and J. Foster, eds., *London marriage licences, 1521–1869* (1887) · Foster, *Alum. Oxon.* · *Fourth report*, HMC, 3 (1874) · *Fifth report*, HMC, 4 (1876) · J. M. French, *The life records of John Milton*, 5 vols. (1949–58) · *The diary of Bulstrode Whitelocke, 1605–1675*, ed. R. Spalding, British Academy, Records of Social and Economic History, new ser., 13 (1990) · T. Wright, ed., *Political ballads published in England during the Commonwealth* (1841) · D. F., *A letter of addresse to the protector occasioned by Mr. Needhams reply to Mr. Goodwins book* (1657) · J. Goodwin, *Triumviri* (1658) · *O. Cromwell's thankes* (1660) · [F. Cheynell?], *Aulicus his hue and cry* (1645) · A. Marvell, *An account of the growth of popery*

(1677) • R. Ferguson, *The third part of no protestant plot* (1682) • *Character of Mercurius Politicus* (1650) • J. Frank, *Cromwell's press agent: a critical biography of Marchamont Nedham, 1620–1678* (1980) • *DNB* • Wood, *Ath. Oxon.*, new edn, 3.1180–90 • D. Masson, *The life of John Milton*, 7 vols. (1859–94) • B. Worden, '"Wit in a roundhead": the dilemma of Marchamont Nedham', *Political culture and cultural politics in early modern England: essays presented to David Underdown*, ed. S. D. Amussen and M. A. Kishlansky (1995), 301–37 • B. Worden, 'Marchamont Nedham and the beginnings of English republicanism, 1649–1656', *Republicanism, liberty, and commercial society, 1649–1776*, ed. D. Wootton (Stanford, CA, 1994), 45–81 • B. Worden, 'Milton and Marchamont Nedham', *Milton and republicanism*, ed. D. Armitage, Q. Skinner, and A. Himy (1995), 156–80 • A. N. B. Cotton, 'London newsbooks in the civil war: their political attitudes and sources of information', DPhil diss., U. Oxf., 1972 • J. Raymond, 'The cracking of the republican spokes', *Prose Studies*, 19 (1996), 255–74 • Wing, *STC* • C. Nelson and M. Seccombe, eds., *British newspapers and periodicals, 1641–1700: a short-title catalogue of serials printed in England, Scotland, Ireland, and British America* (1987) • administration, PRO, PROB, 6/53, fol. 158v • H. Darbishire, ed., *The early lives of Milton* (1965) • *IGI*

Archives BL, Northumberland MS 552 • BL, Oxenden MSS, Add. MSS 28001–28004 • Bodl. Oxf., Clarendon MS 34 • Bodl. Oxf., Thurloe State MSS, MSS Rawl. A 55–59 • Longleat House, Wiltshire, Whitelocke MS XIII • PRO, state papers, SP 16, SP 18, SP 29

Wealth at death see administration, PRO, PROB 6/53, fol. 158v

---

Needham, Charles, fourth Viscount Kilmorey (c.1637–1660), nobleman and royalist insurgent, was the elder son of Robert Needham, second Viscount Kilmorey (d. 1653), and his second wife, Eleanor (1596/7–1666), widow of Gilbert Gerard, Lord Gerard of Gerard's Bromley, and daughter of Thomas Dutton of Dutton, Cheshire; his parents' marriage settlement was dated 31 October 1636. Nothing is known of his early life. Following the death of his father, in 1654 his mother persuaded his stepbrother, Robert Needham, third Viscount Kilmorey (1608/9–1657/8), whose marriage to her daughter Frances Gerard (d. 1636) had been childless, to surrender his interest in the family estates in favour of Charles. The first stages of the transfer were completed in August that year, and financial provision was made for Robert. On 27 February 1655 Charles, described as resident in Covent Garden, married at St Paul's Church there Bridget (d. 1696), eldest daughter and coheir of Sir William Drury of Drury House (site of the Drury Lane Theatre) and Beesthorpe, Norfolk, and his wife, Mary Cockayne. The land transfer was completed on 10 September, and Charles began to exercise full rights of ownership. Finally, in January 1657 Robert signed over his personal property to Charles and to his younger stepbrother, Thomas. On Robert's death either the same month or in early January 1658, Charles succeeded as fourth Viscount Kilmorey.

In 1659 Kilmorey joined in the rebellion of Sir George Booth and the earl of Derby, which was defeated by John Lambert. It was reported on 21 August that 'Sir Thomas Middleton, the Lord Kilmorrey, with other Gentlemen, with 5 colours of horse, made no small haste from Chirk castle to Chester' (Atkinson, *Tracts*, 176). The following day came news that Kilmorey had been taken prisoner with Major Peter Brooke MP. Kilmorey was held for some days at Chester before being transported to London. On 29 October 1659 the county committee at Shrewsbury wrote to the committee for compounding asking permission to seize the estates of large landowners active during the rising, including those of Kilmorey. On 27 February 1660 he was released from prison by order of the Commons, and the sequestration of his estates was suspended, but he died later in the year. He was succeeded as fifth and as sixth viscount by his sons Robert Needham (1655–1668) and Thomas Needham (c.1659–1687). On 24 June 1663 his widow married Sir John *Shaw (d. 1680), and on 15 February 1681 Sir John *Baber (1625–1704) became her third husband. She died in 1696 and was buried on 11 July at Eltham, Kent.   STEPHEN WRIGHT

Sources GEC, *Peerage* • H. Harrod, *The history of Shavington in the county of Salop* (1891) • G. Davies, *The restoration of Charles II, 1658–1660* (1955) • J. A. Atkinson, ed., *Tracts relating to the civil war in Cheshire, 1641–1659: including Sir George Booth's rising in that county*, Chetham Soc., new ser., 65 (1909) • *Mercurius Politicus* (18–25 Aug 1659) • *Mercurius Politicus* (7 Sept 1659), 715 • *JHC*, 7 (1651–9) • Foster, *Alum. Oxon.* • W. H. Hunt, ed., *The registers of St Paul's Church, Covent Garden, London*, 3, Harleian Society, register section, 35 (1906), 6, 34

Needham [née Moyle], **Dorothy Mary** (1896–1987), biochemist, was born in London on 22 September 1896, one of the three daughters (there was also a son) of John Thomas Moyle, a civil servant at the Patent Office, and his wife, Ellen Daves. Dorothy was educated in Cheshire at Claremont College, Stockport, a private school run by her aunt, and at St Hilary's, Alderley Edge. She entered Girton College, Cambridge, in 1915. After graduation in 1919, she began research, supported by a grant from the Department of Scientific and Industrial Research, under Sir Frederick Gowland Hopkins at the Sir William Dunn Institute of Biochemistry, Cambridge. Hopkins, having worked with Sir Walter Fletcher on lactic acid in muscle, interested Dorothy in the biochemistry of muscle contraction. She won the Gamble prize at Girton College in 1924 for an essay on the structure, function, and chemical constitution of different types of striated muscle. In 1925–8 she was a Beit memorial medical research fellow, gaining her PhD in 1926.

On 13 September 1924 Dorothy Moyle married (Noël) Joseph Terence Montgomery *Needham (1900–1995) with whom she had a close affinity in ideas and attitudes. There were no children of the marriage, a fact which served to deepen their relationship and their many shared interests, especially an unshakeable commitment to Christianity and socialism. They rarely collaborated in research, except during summer vacations spent in marine biology laboratories where they micro-injected amoebae and sea-urchin eggs with pH and rH indicators to determine the reaction of the cytoplasm.

Between 1928 and 1940 Dorothy Needham taught widely both at Cambridge, where she gave advanced lectures on muscle biochemistry, and in America, France, Belgium, and other countries. Her most important research work dates from this period when O. Meyerhof, O. Warburg, and she, independently, elucidated the chemical changes by which glucose is broken down in the cell

Dorothy Mary Needham (1896–1987), by Walter Stoneman, 1947

to yield the energy-rich compound adenosine triphosphate (ATP). She also studied the roles of pyruvic, succinic, and lactic acids, and transamination. Her influence in the Cambridge laboratory was profound, largely owing to her sympathetic gentleness combined with penetrating intelligence and a quiet sense of humour. She was affectionately known as Dophi to those who worked closely with her and who often remained her lifelong friends. Among her numerous post-graduate research students, some later attained high academic positions.

During the Second World War Dorothy Needham was a member of the chemical defence group led by Professor Malcolm Dixon for the Ministry of Supply. In 1940–43 she worked on the effects of chemical weapons such as mustard gas on the metabolism of skin and bone marrow. She was also a member of the Biochemical Society committee (1941–3). In 1944 she accompanied her husband to Chungking (Chongqing), China, where he was appointed scientific counsellor at the British embassy and she was associate director of the Sino-British co-operation office which he established. During this period she contracted tuberculosis from which she only slowly recovered after her return to the Sir William Dunn Institute in 1945. She was awarded the ScD degree at Cambridge in that year and in 1948 was elected FRS, one of the earliest women fellows. Joseph Needham had been elected in 1941 and Dorothy's election made the Needhams the Royal Society's first married couple.

Despite her academic distinction Dorothy Needham

never held a pensionable post in the biochemical laboratory, but throughout her working life she received numerous research grants from various national bodies. During 1946–52 she worked on enzyme biochemistry on a grant from the Medical Research Council; afterwards, until 1955, she received a grant from the Broodbank Fund of Cambridge University. This was followed by work on smooth muscle for the Agricultural Research Council in 1955–62. She also received a Foulerton gift donation from the Royal Society in 1961–2 and a Leverhulme award in 1963, the year in which she retired after forty years spent in active research.

From 1967 Dorothy Needham devoted herself to writing her *magnum opus*; entitled *Machina carnis*, it was a historical account of studies in the biochemistry of muscular contraction. Published in 1971, this book represented the culmination of her life's work on the link between the uptake of oxygen and the binding of phosphates in energy-rich bonds in muscle tissue and it remains a unique and authoritative contribution to the history of muscle biochemistry. In 1972 she collaborated with Dr E. Bülbring in organizing for the Royal Society the first British symposium on the chemistry and physiology of smooth muscle. At the time of her death she was working with Mikuláš Teich on a documentary history of biochemistry which was published in 1991.

Dorothy Needham was an honorary fellow of three Cambridge colleges: at Lucy Cavendish College, which she was instrumental in establishing, she became a foundation fellow in 1965; at Girton, her own college, she became an honorary fellow in 1976; and at Gonville and Caius College, where Joseph Needham was master for eleven years (1965–76), she became an honorary fellow in 1979. As the wife of the master and hostess at the events and festivities held in the master's lodge, she was deeply appreciated by many members of Caius, both senior and junior. Her fellowship there pleased her greatly; she was the first woman to be admitted and was, for a long time, the only woman fellow.

Dorothy Needham's chief hobby and relaxation was painting in watercolours and her travels all over the world provided opportunities for recording scenes and events which she experienced. Paying tribute to her in November 1988, Joseph Needham said, 'she retained a certain innocence, and a complete freedom from worldliness'. This was echoed by many of her students, who loved her for her qualities of kindness, warmth, and patience, while admiring her keen intelligence and strength of mind. In retirement, after leaving Caius in 1976, she began to show the early signs of Alzheimer's disease and very gradually she declined. She died peacefully at her home, 42 Grange Road, Cambridge, on 22 December 1987, at the age of ninety-one. The funeral service was held on 31 December at Caius College chapel, followed by cremation.

N. G. COLEY

Sources *The Times* (26 Dec 1987) · *The Independent* (11 Jan 1988) · *WWW, 1981–90* · *Catalogue of the papers and correspondence of Dorothy Mary Moyle Needham*, ed. T. Powell and P. Harper (1990) · D. M. Needham, 'Women in Cambridge biochemistry', *Women scientists: the*

road to liberation, ed. D. Richter (1982), 153–63 · J. Needham, *The Caian* (1987–8), 128–31 · b. cert.
Archives CUL, corresp. and papers · Girton Cam. | CAC Cam., corresp. with A. V. Hill · CUL, corresp. with Joseph Needham · U. Sussex, letters to J. G. Crowther
Likenesses W. Stoneman, photograph, 1947, NPG [*see illus.*] · Ramsey & Muspratt, photograph, 1976 · photograph, 1976 · W. Stoneman, double portrait, photograph (with Joseph Needham) · W. Stoneman, photograph, RS
Wealth at death under £70,000: probate, 28 March 1988, *CGPLA Eng. & Wales*

Needham, Elizabeth [*known as* Mother Needham] (*d.* 1731), procurer, kept a 'notorious disorderly House' in Park Place, near St James's Street, London. She is said to have been employed by the infamous Colonel Charteris, and in *Don Francisco's Descent into the Infernal Regions*—a satire published upon Charteris's death in February 1732—she is represented as proposing in hell to marry the colonel, much to the latter's horror and disgust. She is represented in the first plate of Hogarth's *A Harlot's Progress* (1731) in the courtyard of The Bell inn, Wood Street, cajoling with flattering promises the then innocent Moll Hackabout on her arrival in London. She is depicted as a middle-aged woman, simpering beneath her patches, and well dressed in silk. The male figure leaning on his stick, and leering at the maid from the inn door, is supposed to represent Charteris himself, while behind him stands his factotum, Jack Gourley.

After enquiries by the magistrate Sir John Gonson, Mother Needham was committed by Justice Railton to the Gate House on 24 March 1731, convicted of keeping a disorderly house on 29 April, and ordered to stand in the pillory over against Park Place on 30 April 1731. Contemporary journals describe her lying upon the pillory on her face, as well as paying a number of beadles and other persons to protect her from injury. Despite these precautions she was so severely pelted by the mob that her life was put in danger. She actually died on 3 May 1731, killed apparently by the fear of having to return to the pillory.

Aside from her appearance in Hogarth's series Needham was also referred to in Mary Davyr's play *The Accomplish'd Rake* (1727), and as 'pious Needham' in Pope's *Dunciad*. Pope states in a note that she 'was a matron of great fame, and very religious in her way', her constant prayer being that she might get enough by her profession to leave it off in time and make her peace with God. *Mother Needham's Lamentation*, first printed in the *Daily Journal* on 8 May 1731, was published as a six penny pamphlet later in the year.   THOMAS SECCOMBE, *rev.* PHILIP CARTER

Sources *Daily Advertiser* [London] (1 May 1731) · *Grub Street Journal* (25 March 1731) · *Grub Street Journal* (29 April 1731) · *Grub Street Journal* (6 May 1731) · *Daily Journal* (8 May 1731) · R. Paulson, *Hogarth*, 1 (1991) · A. Pope, *The Dunciad*, ed. J. Sutherland (1943), vol. 5 of *The Twickenham edition of the poems of Alexander Pope*, ed. J. Butt (1939–69); 3rd edn [in 1 vol.] (1963); repr. (1965)
Likenesses W. Hogarth, engraving (after portrait by W. Hogarth [destroyed by fire]), repro. in W. Hogarth, *The harlot's progress, or, The humours of Drury-Lane* (1732), pl. 1

Needham, Francis Jack, first earl of Kilmorey (1748–1832), army officer and politician, was born on 5 April 1748, the third son of John Needham, tenth Viscount Kilmorey (1711–1791), and his wife, Anne (1707/8–1786), the daughter of John Hurleston of Newton, Cheshire, and the widow of Geoffrey Shakerley of Somerford, Cheshire. His long army career began on 17 December 1762 as a cornet in the 18th dragoons. He exchanged into the 1st dragoons in 1765 and advanced to lieutenant in 1771. In May 1774 he became captain of the 17th dragoons and the following year he went to America with the regiment. He saw action in New York, Pennsylvania, and Virginia and was made a major in the 76th Highland regiment, with which unit he served until the surrender at Yorktown. In 1783 he was promoted to the lieutenant-colonelcy of the 104th regiment, but exchanged the same year to the 1st foot guards. On 20 February 1787 he married Anne (*d.* 1816), the second daughter of Thomas Fisher of Acton and his wife, Margaret Pigot; they had two boys and eight girls. In 1793 Needham became an aide-de-camp to the king, and during the opening years of the French war he served in Flanders and France.

Needham is best remembered for his actions in Ireland during the 1798 uprising, where he served as a major-general, having been promoted in 1795. On 9 June 1798 he defended Arklow against about 20,000 insurgents with a hastily gathered garrison of about 1500 men, mostly militia, fencibles, and yeomanry. The rebels attacked in two columns, but Needham's intelligent defensive preparations and superiority in firepower, particularly the use of grapeshot, proved decisive, and the attack was repulsed after several hours of severe fighting. Some contemporaries criticized Needham, claiming that he considered retreat and that Arklow was saved only by the resolution of his second in command, Colonel Skerritt of the Durham fencibles. Needham's capability was further questioned after the battle of Vinegar Hill on 21 June 1798, when his late arrival thwarted General Lake's plan to encircle the insurgent army and close off their retreat. Many insurgents escaped through what became known as Needham's Gap. In a later action at Wicklow Gap, when he again failed to rendezvous on time, Lord Shannon complained that 'this Needham is always late' (Shannon to Boyle, 6 July 1798, Shannon MS D2607/A3/3/102). His critics mischievously dubbed him 'the late General Needham' (Wheeler and Broadley, 156) and there were even rumours that he had deliberately allowed the escape at Vinegar Hill. Needham undoubtedly felt the pressure, complaining to Lake that muddled and ambiguous orders left 'the troops themselves and my own character … at stake' (Dublin army letters, MIC 67/1, fols. 53–4, 30 June 1798). Nevertheless, the Arklow allegations were refuted by the officers of the Durham fencibles, whereas Needham himself noted that before the engagement at Vinegar Hill sudden countermanding orders following a long march left his men utterly exhausted. Later writers suggest that his behaviour was due to a cautious awareness of the danger of ambush in an enclosed country. Indeed, at Wicklow Gap, although he was unable to bring his infantry up in time, Needham sent cavalry forward to engage the rebels.

Needham remained on the Irish staff until 1802, when he was promoted lieutenant-general. He became involved in politics at about this time. The political potential of the Needhams' Irish property lay dormant through neglect of their interest in the borough of Newry, near their seat at Mourne Park. In 1806, after incurring heavy electioneering expenses, Needham was returned for Newry. While he was not an active member, and made only one speech, he generally voted with the government. He vacated his seat on elevation to the peerage as twelfth Viscount Kilmorey in 1818 and was succeeded as MP by his eldest son, also called Francis Jack. Following his elevation in the peerage as Viscount Newry and Morne and earl of Kilmorey in 1822, he tried unsuccessfully to become a representative peer. He had received the colonelcy of the 5th veteran battalion in 1804 and that of the 86th regiment in 1810, and was made a full general in 1812. He was popular with the soldiers who served under him and with his tenantry. He died on 21 November 1832 at Shavington Hall, Shropshire, the family's English seat, and was buried at Adderley church. A. F. BLACKSTOCK

Sources PRO NIre., Needham MSS, D 2638/D/2 · Needham to Lake, 10 June 1798, PRO, HO 100/73, fols. 219–20 · Dublin army letters, PRO NIre., MIC 67/1, fols. 49, 53–4 · G. A. H. McCoy, *Irish battles* (1969), 273–315 · D. Gahan, *The people's rising: Wexford, 1798* (1995) · H. F. M. Wheeler and A. M. Broadley, *The war in Wexford* (1910) · GEC, *Peerage* · Burke, *Peerage* (1921) · *The manuscripts of J. B. Fortescue*, 10 vols., HMC, 30 (1892–1927), vol. 8 · P. J. Jupp, 'Needham, Hon. Francis', HoP, *Commons, 1790–1820* · Shannon to Boyle, 6 July 1798, PRO NIre., Shannon MSS, D 2607/A3/3/102 · R. Musgrave, *Memoirs of the different rebellions in Ireland* (1801), 437–43, 478–9 · E. Lodge, *The peerage of the British empire*, [new edn] (1854) · *DNB*
Archives PRO NIre., family MSS | BL, corresp. with Sir Robert Peel, Add. MSS 40222–40238, *passim* · PRO NIre., Foster-Masserlene MSS · U. Southampton L., Wellington MSS
Wealth at death extensive property in Ireland; family prospered from trade of port of Newry: PRO, NIre., Needham MSS; PRO, NIre., D 2638/G/81

Needham, James. See Nedeham, James (d. 1544).

Needham, Sir John (d. 1480), justice, was the third son of Robert Needham of Cranage, a hamlet of Holmes Chapel, Cheshire, and Dorothy, daughter of Sir John Savage of Clifton. He studied at Gray's Inn, becoming a reader in (conjecturally) the autumn of 1440. He farmed the manor of King's Bromley, sat for Newcastle under Lyme in the parliaments of 1442, 1447, and January 1449, was retained by St Thomas's Priory, Stafford, and was associated with the Tuchets of Markeaton, Derbyshire (the lords Audley). However, his principal early connections were in Shropshire, where in 1438 he took a lease of the manor of Shavington (which he later bought) and became a JP for the county in 1440. Needham probably read at Gray's Inn for a second time in Lent 1447, and in 1449 he became common serjeant of London, in which capacity he was elected to represent the city in the parliament of 1449–50. It was unusual for an outsider to be appointed to a legal post in the city, but Needham had clients there, and was perhaps also indebted to the influence of a putative relative, Richard Needham, mercer and sheriff, who himself sat for London in the parliament of 1460.

At the same time as he was advancing in the law in London, Needham was in process of moving the focus of his local interests back to Cheshire. He had been king's serjeant-at-law in the county palatine since 29 September 1439, and in 1450 was a key figure in the appeal of the Cheshire gentry against the palatinate's being included in national taxation. He may well have drafted the text of the petition, and was certainly one of those given powers of attorney to present it. The petition was a success, and may also have drawn Needham to royal notice, for on 28 November 1450 he was appointed deputy justice at Chester. Promotion at Westminster came next. In February 1453 Needham was called to the coif, probably giving a third law reading at Gray's Inn in the Lent vacation before the actual creation in July. A year later he was retained temporarily as a king's serjeant. Appointed to the northern assize circuit in 1454, he became second justice at Lancaster on 13 July 1456. On 9 May 1457 he joined the bench of the common pleas, and on 9 November 1458 was promoted chief justice at Lancaster. Throughout the 1450s he had been active on government commissions, and in 1456 sat with the other judges to scrutinize plans to liquidate the royal debt. In 1459 he began to attend parliament again, as one of the royal lawyers in the Lords.

Needham seems to have been very much a professional. Although he had served on Lancastrian commissions of oyer and terminer, Edward IV made good use of him in his efforts to pacify the country at large. The crisis of 1460–61 had also seen the death of the chief justice of Chester, the earl of Shrewsbury, and had brought much of the palatinate to a halt. Needham was placed in temporary charge, first in commission and then as chief justice, until Lord Stanley took over when he reverted to deputy justice on 2 January 1462. Needham's efforts clearly pleased. He was knighted at Elizabeth Woodville's coronation in 1465, and when Edward IV remodelled the judiciary in 1471, Needham was one of six judges retained, being moved to become secondary justice (senior puisne) in king's bench. In 1473 he was one of ten new councillors added to an enlarged council for the young prince of Wales.

Needham had substantial property in Cheshire and Shropshire, including one moiety of Cranage inherited from his father, and the second half which he had purchased, and he built the bridge over the River Dane at Cranage. He is said to have married Margaret, youngest daughter of Randle Mainwaring of Peover, and widow of William Bromley of Baddington. The judge died without heir on 25 April 1480 and his property passed to his brother's family, later earls of Kilmorey. His tomb with a memorial brass in Holmes Chapel has been destroyed but an Elizabethan transcription of the epitaph is extant. E. W. IVES

Sources D. J. Clayton, *The administration of the county palatine of Chester, 1442–85*, Chetham Society, 3rd ser., 35 (1990) · G. Ormerod, *The history of the county palatine and city of Chester*, 2nd edn, ed. T. Helsby, 3 vols. (1882) · Sainty, *Judges* · Sainty, *King's counsel* · Baker, *Serjeants* · S. E. Thorne and J. H. Baker, eds., *Readings and moots at the inns of court in the fifteenth century*, 1, SeldS, 71 (1954) · E. W. Ives, *The common lawyers of pre-Reformation England* (1983) · inquisition post mortem, Ches. & Chester ALSS, CHES 3/51/1 Hen.

VII/4 · H. D. Harrod, *The muniments of Shavington* (1891) · *The manuscripts of the earl of Westmorland*, HMC, 13 (1885); repr. (1906), 358–74 [earl of Kilmorrey] · *Chancery records*

Needham, John Turberville (1713–1781), Roman Catholic priest and natural scientist, was born in Middlesex on 10 September 1713, the eldest son of John Needham (*d.* 1730?) of Hilston, near St Maughan's in Monmouthshire, who practised as a barrister in London, and his wife, Martha Lucas. The father died young, leaving four children: John Turberville; Robert (1717–1791), who became a Franciscan and took the name Joseph; Francis, who married and became a bookseller in London; and Susannah, about whom nothing further is known. John studied under the secular clergy at the English College at Douai from 1722 to 1736, with an absence of thirteen months in 1729–30, due to illness. He was ordained priest at Cambrai on 31 May 1738. From 1736 to 1740 he taught first rhetoric then logic in the college. In 1740 he was sent to England as assistant master at the Catholic school at Twyford, near Winchester. On 12 January 1744 he left England for Lisbon to teach philosophy in the English College there, but on 3 July 1745 he cut short his lectures and returned to England for health reasons.

While at Twyford, Needham made microscopic observations of blighted wheat, and in Lisbon he investigated the organs of the squid, producing the first description of its milt sac, now called Needham's sac. These and other observations were published by his brother Francis as *An Account of some New Microscopical Discoveries* (1745), translated into French as *Découvertes faites avec le microscope* (1747). This was soon followed by *A Letter from Paris, Concerning some New Electrical Experiments* (1746).

On 22 January 1747 Needham became the first English Catholic priest to be elected to the Royal Society of London. A report on his further microscopical studies was published in *Philosophical Transactions* (1748), and at greater length as *Observations upon the generation, composition and decomposition of animal and vegetable substances* (1749) and *Nouvelles observations microscopiques* (1750). The comte de Buffon, with whom Needham collaborated in Paris in the summer of 1748, made prominent use of Needham's findings in the second volume of his *Histoire naturelle* (1767). Among other things, Needham established that microorganisms do not grow from eggs, and proposed a theory according to which all living organisms develop from non-living matter at a microscopic level; this conflicted with the prevailing view that organisms were individually 'preformed' either in the egg or in the seed and simply grew in size once the process of maturation was triggered. His theory was widely misrepresented by preformists as an attempt to revive the long-disproved notion of spontaneous generation.

From 1751 to 1767 Needham acted as a tutor to young Catholic gentlemen on the grand tour, travelling extensively in France and Italy and to a lesser extent in the Low Countries and the British Isles, and also visiting Geneva. His first appointment was to accompany the seventh earl of Fingall and Mr Philip Howard of Corby in Cumberland, a future agricultural improver. Later he travelled with the eleventh Viscount Gormanston and Mr Charles Townley, a nephew of the John Townley whose French translation of *Hudibras* Needham edited for publication (3 vols., 1757).

Needham failed to obtain a chair in experimental physics at the University of Louvain in 1759, and in 1761 he unsuccessfully applied for a royal pension in Paris. In March 1762 Lord Tavistock, Edmund Rolfe, and Haughton James jointly donated 'a purse of £300 for Needham to prosecute his discoveries' (Ingamells, 699). From 1762 to 1767 he was tutor to Charles Dillon (1745–1813), eldest son of Henry, eleventh Viscount Dillon. In Turin in January 1765 he met James Boswell and John Wilkes. Boswell, who took great pleasure in his 'learned and solid conversation' (Brady and Pottle), visited him several times and accompanied him to the opera, while Wilkes described him as 'the most agreeable object I have seen here', and 'that agreeable gentleman' (Almon, 2.122).

During his years as a tutor Needham published an essay on Milton (1754) and, as *Observations des hauteurs* (1760), a number of height readings taken in the Alps. In *De inscriptione* (1761) he suggested that the Chinese alphabet might be derived from Egyptian hieroglyphs. This hypothesis, based on a superficial similarity between some Chinese characters and the inscriptions on an Egyptian bust in Turin, excited great but short-lived controversy in scholarly circles. Needham himself translated into French a letter from the Jesuit missionary Father Cibot, which finally demolished the idea (*Lettre de Pekin*, 1773).

In Geneva, in the summer of 1765, Needham joined an ongoing pamphlet controversy on the subject of miracles, propounding the view that an omnipotent creator could create local exceptions to the general laws of nature. As a result he found himself subject to a personal attack by the deist Voltaire, who accused him of encouraging atheism by his 'materialist' theories on the generation of life, a provocation which led to further pamphleteering in the following months. The Voltaire–Needham exchanges were later published as *Questions sur les miracles* (1769). In his *Idée sommaire, ou, Vüe générale du système physique & métaphysique de Monsieur Needham sur la génération des corps organisés* (1776), Needham was later to write against attempts by atheists such as the Baron d'Holbach to use his findings to support extreme materialist views.

At the end of 1767 Needham retired to St Gregory's College, Paris, and on 26 March 1768 he became a corresponding member of the Académie Royale des Sciences, Paris. In 1768 Count Cobenzl, minister-plenipotentiary of the Austrian Netherlands, founded a *société littéraire* in Brussels. In a memorandum on possible candidates for director of the society, the comte de Nény wrote: 'as concerns M. Needham, he enjoys throughout Europe the just consideration which his talents, his morals, and his profound knowledge merit' (Mailly, 12). He was offered the position and was installed the following year. His vigorous lobbying contributed to the survival of the society after Cobenzl's death in 1770, and to its more secure endowment, in 1772, as the Académie Impériale et Royale des Sciences et Belles-Lettres, of which he remained director until May 1780.

On his appointment Needham was nominated to a canonry in the collegiate church of Dendermonde, which in 1773 he exchanged for another at Soignies in Hainault. Throughout his time as director of the Brussels academy he engaged in research of a practical nature on cattle fever, corn blight, honey production, soil fertility, mining, minerals, iron smelting, and electromagnetism, none of which had any lasting scientific significance. He also accompanied Nathaniel Pigott on a four-month expedition to determine the exact longitude and latitude of the main towns of the Austrian Netherlands. In his last months he was sharing a house in Brussels with a small group of English Catholics, including Theodore Augustus Mann and Francis Needham's widow, Winifred Sherwood. He died in Brussels on 30 December 1781 and was buried there in the vaults of the abbey of Coudenberg. An obituary by the Abbé Mann was published in *Mémoires de l'Académie de Bruxelles* (1783) and later in the *Monthly Review* (1784).

An active member of the intellectual community of his time, Needham corresponded widely, and edited or translated, besides those already mentioned, works by Lazzaro Spallanzani, Thomas Pownall, and Charles, third Earl Stanhope. He was elected to many learned societies, including the Society of Antiquaries of London (1761), the Royal Basque Society (1771), the Société d'Émulation of Liège (1779), and the Society of Antiquaries of Scotland (1781). Remarks by Boswell and Wilkes suggest that by the mid-1760s Needham was himself becoming one of the sights of the grand tour. All personal testimony agrees that he was both a pleasant companion and a man of unusual openness and probity. Boswell expressed surprise that someone with such extensive knowledge of the world could still be so 'worthy' (Brady and Pottle). As a scientist he was over-confident in generalizing from a narrow experimental base or a superficial similarity of data, failings generally viewed indulgently by most contemporaries, although Gibbon, who described him elsewhere as 'my friend Needham', claimed to be 'revolted' by his superficiality and dogmatism (Ingamells, 699). The *Needhamiella*, an Australian flowering shrub of the order Epacridaceae, was named in his honour. After his death his wide-ranging library of scientific, literary, and religious works was sold at auction, and copies of the *Catalogue des livres de feu M. l'Abbé Needham* (1782) are still to be found in some libraries. PAUL ARBLASTER

Sources Gillow, *Lit. biog. hist.*, 5.157–60 · R. G. Mazzolini and S. A. Roe, *Science against unbelievers: the correspondence of Bonnet and Needham, 1760–1780* (1986) · J. Ingamells, ed., *A dictionary of British and Irish travellers in Italy, 1701–1800* (1997), 699 · *Boswell on the grand tour: Italy, Corsica, and France, 1765–1766*, ed. F. Brady and F. A. Pottle (1955), vol. 5 of *The Yale editions of the private papers of James Boswell*, trade edn (1950–89), 32–44, 74–5, 80 n. · G. Anstruther, *The seminary priests*, 4 (1977), 195–6 · P. J. Van Beneden, 'Needham (l'Abbé John Turberville)', *Biographie nationale*, 15 (1899) · *DNB* · P. R. Harris, ed., *Douai College documents, 1639–1794*, Catholic RS, 63 (1972), 115, 118 · M. Sharratt, ed., *Lisbon College register, 1628–1813*, Catholic RS, 72 (1991), 152 · E. Mailly, *Histoire de l'Académie Impériale et Royale des Sciences et Belles-Lettres de Bruxelles*, 1 (Brussels, 1883) · *The correspondence of the late John Wilkes*, ed. J. Almon, 5 vols. (1805), 2.122 · G. Scott, *Gothic rage undone: English monks in the age of Enlightenment* (1992) · *Catalogue des livres de feu M. l'Abbé Needham* (Brussels, 1782) · J. Lavalleye, *L'Académie Royale des Sciences, des Lettres, et des Beaux-Arts de Belgique, 1772–1972* (1973)
Archives U. Leeds, Brotherton L., letters | Bibliothèque Publique et Universitaire de Genève, Geneva, corresp. with Charles Bonnet
Likenesses J. B. Garand, miniature, 1755, NPG · H. Edridge, miniature (after J. Reynolds), Holburne of Menstrie Museum, Bath

Needham, (Noël) Joseph Terence Montgomery (1900–1995), biochemist and historian, was born on 9 December 1900 at 2 Westbury Gardens, Loats Road, Clapham, London, the only child of Joseph Needham (1853–1920), physician and anaesthesiologist, and his second wife, Alicia Adelaide, *née* Montgomery (1872–1945). Born in the last months of the Victorian era, he became one of twentieth-century Britain's most original and wide-ranging intellects.

Background and education Needham grew up in a cosmopolitan, middle-class home that was regularly troubled by clashes between parents who differed markedly in age, temperament, and outlook. His volatile, musically gifted mother, a native of Ireland with a passion for that country, was an accomplished composer of popular songs. His scientifically minded father was a rationalistic physician of Francophile tastes, who rose from modest Derbyshire origins to become one of Harley Street's first anaesthesiologists. The perpetual disagreements between them were exemplified in their calling their son Terence and Noel respectively, leaving it to him to settle eventually on Joseph, as a compromise of sorts.

During boyhood Needham attended Dulwich School and read widely in the large library built up by his father. The latter, who had been active in the Oxford Movement in his youth but who later adopted a philosophical theology, made a point of cultivating an intellectual openness in his son towards diverse religious and philosophical points of view. For his secondary education the younger Needham was sent to Oundle School, where a broad, forward-looking curriculum had been put in place by the headmaster, F. W. Sanderson. Needham's years there nurtured strong interests in the experimental sciences, history, and philosophy, but also awakened a taste for socialist politics that was foreign to his family milieu. After spending summer holidays during the First World War assisting his father at surgery, he was inducted into the Royal Navy for a brief stint as a surgeon sub-lieutenant after finishing school.

In the autumn of 1918 Needham proceeded to Cambridge with the intention of reading medicine, and the medical reputation of Gonville and Caius led him to choose that college. The decision had enduring consequences, for he remained a member of Caius in one capacity or another for the rest of his life. Following the advice of his undergraduate tutor, W. D. Hardy, he chose to read chemistry as well as biological fields of study. In due course he found himself inspired by the lectures of Frederick Gowland Hopkins and Rudolph Peters, pioneers in developing British biochemistry. The unexpected death of his father in 1920 threw his family into emotional and

(Noël) Joseph Terence Montgomery Needham (1900–1995), by Ramsey & Muspratt, 1937

financial disarray. Joseph's mother showed increasing signs of mental instability, and Hopkins came to play the joint role of surrogate parent and academic mentor. After taking a double second in the natural science tripos, Needham went to Berlin to work in a research laboratory and polish his German. On his return to Cambridge he was awarded the Ben Levi studentship in biochemistry, which enabled him to pursue doctoral research from 1922 to 1924 on the metabolism of inositol in the developing egg.

While much of his time as a student was naturally devoted to scientific work, this was never Needham's only area of activity. Attracted to the idea of a close religious community, he entered the oratory of the Good Shepherd, an Anglican order, whose vows included a commitment to celibacy. He also served as secretary of the Cambridge student branch of the Guild of St Luke, a society aimed at promoting spirituality among doctors and medical students. In this capacity he organized an annual series of lectures on comparative religion, history, and philosophy, an activity that brought him into contact with leading scholars in those fields. That undertaking resulted in the publication of his first book, the edited volume *Science, Religion and Reality* (1925), which featured contributions by such diverse figures as Lord Balfour, Arthur Eddington, Bronislaw Malinowski, W. R. Inge, and Charles Singer.

Early career in biochemistry By the time that volume appeared Needham's student days were behind him, and his life had changed substantially. He was awarded his doctorate in 1924, and on 13 September in the same year, after deciding against taking religious vows, he married Dorothy Mary Moyle (1896–1987) [see Needham, Dorothy

Mary], another promising biochemist, four years his senior and of Quaker background. Soon thereafter, he was elected to the Caius fellowship that he held for the rest of his life. The security afforded by this position enabled him to put aside thoughts of qualifying as a physician and to focus instead on building a research career in Hopkins's newly established Dunn Institute for Biochemistry.

At the Dunn Institute, Needham proceeded to develop innovative biochemical approaches and techniques which threw new experimental light on questions pertaining to embryology, his special research interest. His investigations in this field, pursued both in Cambridge and at leading marine research stations during the summers, resulted in a steady series of path-breaking papers before being crowned in 1931 with the publication of the three volumes of *Chemical Embryology*. Having been appointed university demonstrator in Cambridge University's department of biochemistry in 1928, he was promoted in 1934 to the Sir William Dunn readership, which he held until his retirement from the department in 1966. Throughout the late 1920s and 1930s he and Dorothy played central roles in forging the spirited mix of intellectual creativity and vibrant social engagement that characterized life at the Dunn Institute in those days. The Hopkins presentation volume *Perspectives in Biochemistry* (1937), which he edited with D. E. Green, and the commemorative volume *Hopkins and Biochemistry* (1949), which he edited with Ernest Baldwin, testify to its vigorous research atmosphere.

One of the intellectual constants throughout Needham's career was a deep concern with understanding what he saw as the major forms of human experience. In the late 1920s and early 1930s he focused on the relations between science and religion and laid out his personal philosophy in the two volumes entitled *The Sceptical Biologist* (1929) and *The Great Amphibium* (1932), the latter comprising lectures delivered to the 1931 general conference of the Student Christian Movement. These years also saw him seriously immersing himself in historical studies, especially on topics bearing on the history of science, a subject to which he and Dorothy were first introduced by Charles and Dorothea Singer. The ideas of the Soviet delegates to the 1931 Second International Congress of the History of Science impressed Needham, J. D. Bernal, and other progressive British scientists with the strengths of the Marxist approach, which they then proceeded to elaborate in original ways in their own historical works.

At about the same time Needham was turning his attention to new scientific horizons as well. In 1932 he joined together with J. H. Woodger to form the Theoretical Biology Club, a small but distinguished group devoted to effecting a revolution in the biological sciences through intensive collaboration of specialists in diverse disciplines and sub-disciplines. Their goal converged with the similar agenda pursued by the Rockefeller Foundation at this time, and Needham teamed up with C. H. Waddington in a Rockefeller-funded collaborative project that they hoped would crack one of the great scientific puzzles of the time, the identity of the 'organizer' responsible for inducing embryological differentiation. His 1935 Terry lectures at Yale sketched a vision for an integration of bio-chemistry and experimental morphology that would allow for systematic investigation of the entire range of organizing relations from the molecular to the anatom-ical level. Results of his 1930s work on morphogenetic hormones, which fleshed out his innovative notion of the cyto-skeleton, were presented in the massive *Biochemistry and Morphogenesis*, which appeared in print in 1942, the year after he became a fellow of the Royal Society.

By this time Needham's intellectual reputation was already well established abroad as well as in Britain. After a first trip to the United States in 1929, when he was visit-ing professor at Stanford University, he returned in 1935 to give named lectures at Cornell University and Oberlin College as well as at Yale. On returning to the UK he served as the Royal College of Physicians' Sharpley lecturer for 1935–6. The next academic year saw him give the Herbert Spencer lecture at Oxford, before proceeding on an invited lecture tour of Poland, which awakened an abid-ing love for that country. After the outbreak of the Second World War in September 1939 he toured universities across the United States and Canada. In 1940 he delivered the Comte memorial lecture in London and the Schiff lec-ture at Cornell. The latter, entitled 'The Nazi attack on international science', served effectively to mobilize American scientific opinion in favour of the anti-fascist cause.

Engagement with politics Politically, Needham remained an active member of the Labour Party throughout his adult life, but the late 1920s and the depression years wit-nessed a steady radicalization of his views and a rapid expansion in his political involvement. Soon after their marriage he and Dorothy had become devoted members of the revolutionary Christian socialist community headed by Conrad Noel at Thaxted, Essex. (The connection with Thaxted may have stimulated his interest in morris dancing; he became an active member of the Cambridge Morris Men, and played an important role in the forma-tion of the Morris Ring in 1934.) Shortly thereafter they were introduced to the Marxist classics during their sum-mertime research excursions by the remarkable Paris-based, French-Canadian biologist Louis Rapkine, who quickly became a close friend. At a practical level the Needhams joined J. D. Bernal and other young left-wing scientists during the early 1930s in revivifying the Associ-ation of Scientific Workers as an activist trade union. Needham served as its representative on the Cambridge Trades Council into the 1940s. During the mid- and late 1930s he joined with other left-wing colleagues in pushing the Royal Society's Social Responsibility for Science Move-ment towards concern for issues of pressing popular con-cern, such as health care, nutrition, and civil defence. In a similar vein he was active both in Solly Zuckerman's Tots and Quots group, which agitated for better government funding of science, and in the Cambridge Scientists' Anti-War Group. He also served both as treasurer of the Cornford-McLaurin Fund, which raised funds for British

volunteers fighting in the Spanish Civil War, and as chair-man of the Cambridge branch of the Socialist League, Stafford Cripps's short-lived ginger group which agitated in the Labour Party for opposition to colonialism and in favour of an anti-fascist united front. Needham's vision of the integral place of scientists within progressive move-ments informed his contributions to the edited volume *Christianity and the Social Revolution* (1935), and in the Comenius memorial volume *The Teacher of Nations* (1942), undertaken in collaboration with the exiled Czech presi-dent Eduard Beneš, as well as in his essays of the 1930s and early 1940s, which were collected in *Time the Refreshing River* (1943) and *History is on our Side* (1946).

First contacts with China A new dimension was added to Needham's life around the time of Japan's invasion of China in 1937, with the arrival in Cambridge of Wang Yinglai, Shen Shih-chang (Shen Shizhang), and Lu Gwei-Djen (Lu Guizhen) (1904–1991), promising graduate stu-dents who impressed him with their scientific talents and introduced him to their culture. Fascinated by the history and civilization of a society that struck him as intensely different from his own, he soon began learning the lan-guage with the help of Lu. The attachment they formed then lasted the rest of their lives, and the discussions he had with her about his work on the history of Western sci-ence and technology led them to the idea of writing a modest comparative study of China's record in that regard. With this objective in mind Needham started read-ing classical Chinese texts with Gustav Haloun, then pro-fessor of Chinese at Cambridge.

By the time Britain entered the war in Asia, Needham had gained sufficient acquaintance with China for him to be invited in 1942 to visit the country as the representative of the Royal Society. Seeing the crying needs of Chinese scientists for equipment and communication with the outside world, he proposed the establishment of a wartime liaison bureau. He was authorized to found the Sino-British scientific co-operation office, an inter-governmental body backed jointly by the Ministry of Pro-duction and the British Council. While serving as its director from 1943 to 1946, he was scientific counsellor at the British embassy in Chongqing. On Lu's advice he dis-tanced himself from the colonial mentality characteristic of many Foreign Office officials and instead immediately organized a team that included both British and Chinese nationals in positions of responsibility. This step contrib-uted to the credibility and effectiveness of his enterprise and led to his being appointed adviser to the Chinese Resources Commission as well as to the Chinese armed forces. In Chongqing he developed good working rela-tions not only with Chiang Kai-shek and members of the Guomindang administration, but also Zhou Enlai and Guo Moruo, with whom the Needhams were on friendly terms. Over his years in China Joseph toured many parts of the country unoccupied by the Japanese, lecturing widely on scientific topics and publishing regular reports in *Nature*. His travels enabled him to form personal relationships with many members of China's scientific élite, as well as with leading historians, social scientists, and religious figures. Many of his travel diaries and reports from this period (though naturally not those subject to Foreign Office embargo) were later included in *Science Outpost* (1948), co-edited with Dorothy Needham.

UNESCO The success of his wartime liaison work in China led Needham to envision the establishment of a similar international body geared to building up the scientific capacity of the non-industrialized countries after the war. After obtaining support for this suggestion from the then Chinese foreign minister, T. V. Soong, Needham proceeded to make his case to key political and scientific figures in the major allied countries. Though initially meeting a certain amount of resistance, including among senior officials of the Royal Society, the idea was eventually incorporated into the constitution of UNESCO when that organization was formally established in November 1945.

When Julian Huxley, another Tots and Quots member, was named UNESCO's first director-general, he quickly invited Needham to return to Europe to head the science division. Though concerned about staying away any longer from research, Needham readily agreed. During his two years in that position from March 1946 he successfully put in place what he saw as the two essential pillars of the new organization, namely, the network of field science co-operation offices modelled on his earlier office in China, and a system of grant-in-aid to the international scientific associations. However, he was deeply disappointed by Washington's blocking such funding to left-wing associations as well as by what he saw as its bureaucratic heel-dragging in making UNESCO's international scientific work effective. It was therefore with a sense of relief that he returned to academic life in Cambridge.

Science and Civilisation in China Once resettled in Cambridge, Needham conscientiously resumed his lecturing in biochemistry, but it was the history of Chinese science, technology, and medicine that had his heart. Even before he had left home in 1942 he had conceived the notion of a major project on this subject. Throughout his travels in China he had systematically collected relevant materials, while discussing the nature of China's historical development with all and sundry. The ideas of Chi Chao-ting (Ji Zhaoding), Wang Yanan, and Wu Dakun especially influenced his thinking on this subject, as did those of Karl Wittfogel, whom he met in New York. On returning to Europe after the war he was accompanied by Wang Ling, a young Academia Sinica researcher with special interests in the history of mathematics and chemistry, who assisted him on the new project. In 1950 they outlined a plan for a seven-volume work that would be entitled *Science and Civilisation in China*. But, as they proceeded to work on it, another crisis was about to break.

While passionately immersing himself again in his academic research, Needham continued to speak out strongly on issues of international importance; he remained a vocal critic of Western imperialism and cultural arrogance, and he advocated a dialogue of civilizations, in which each stood to gain from respectfully engaging with the others. Disturbed by the prospect of China again becoming cut off from the West by cold war pressures after the civil war, he became a leading Western voice calling for understanding rather than condemnation of the revolution. Following the outbreak of the Korean War he lent his voice to calls for an international investigation of communist charges that American forces were using biological weapons. The difficulties of finding first-rate scientists to serve on the international scientific commission set up in China for this purpose led him to agree to participate as a leading member himself. On returning to the UK he addressed a series of public meetings where he publicized the commission's report condemning the Americans. Widely denounced in parliament and the press as a traitor and a stooge, he had to weather a furious storm of calls for him to be removed from his academic posts, and he became *persona non grata* in the United States.

The first, introductory volume of *Science and Civilisation in China* was published by Cambridge University Press in 1954, the year that the Geneva conference formally ended the war in Korea. The second volume, on the attitudes of the various schools of philosophy to the investigation of nature, appeared in 1956. While these volumes laid out the series' essential historiographical framework and examined the broad philosophical context, they nevertheless constituted initial forays into the subject. Reactions to them were a striking mixture of high praise offset by scepticism towards Needham's claims for China's scientific distinction and by hostility towards his Marxist historiographical framework. Volumes three to six were to be devoted to what could justifiably be considered the core subject matter of the series, namely, the distinct branches of science, pure and applied. Needham organized his treatment of these fields according to what he considered to be an ascending order of complexity, starting with mathematics and astronomy, and then proceeding in turn through the various divisions of physics, chemistry, and biology.

With the publication in 1959 of volume three, on mathematics and astronomy, published in collaboration with Wang Ling, the series reached the scientific heart of the matter, and a broad consensus soon emerged that the undertaking was a monument of scholarship. Over the next two decades the *Science and Civilisation in China* series ballooned as an unanticipated wealth of materials came to light. Volume four on physics and engineering was divided into three books published between 1962 and 1971. The rich Chinese alchemical tradition was allotted a total of four books, which appeared as distinct parts of the fifth volume on chemistry and chemical technologies between 1974 and 1983. As Needham worked on each subject, he constantly collected materials and made drafts for later parts of the series, sometimes publishing these exploratory or advance versions on their own. A cluster of essays analysing the socio-economic structure of Chinese society, which he considered responsible for inhibiting the emergence of modern science in China, circulated widely in the collection entitled *The Grand Titration* (1969), while *Clerks and Craftsmen in China and the West* (1970) brought together papers on aspects of the history of physics, engineering, and medicine. Volumes five, six, and seven were all in progress at his death.

The demands of carrying out a scholarly venture of this magnitude did not prevent Needham from involving himself in political and religious activities. In 1955 he co-founded the Great Britain–China Friendship Association, and addressed its inaugural conference in a lecture ('The past in China's present') that interpreted Mao's revolutionary policies in terms of perennial concerns within Chinese civilization. After serving as the president of that association for the next decade, he joined Joan Robinson, Roland Berger, and Derek and Hong-ying Bryan in 1965 to form the Society for Anglo-Chinese Understanding. He served as its president for the next thirty-five years. His Marxism and his frank support for socialism in China and elsewhere opened him to periodic criticism from academic quarters and the press from the early 1950s onward. Once the monumental character of *Science and Civilisation in China* was established, the criticism often took the form of acknowledging his scholarship, but condemning him for political naïvety. If there was some truth to this charge, his attitudes towards Chinese politics were more discriminating than some critics suggested. He considered it his duty, however, to try to promote dialogue between East and West, and to keep channels of communication open, rather than joining the chorus of denunciation that predominated in Western establishment circles before the 1970s.

Master of Gonville and Caius College In 1966 Needham became master of Gonville and Caius College for the first of two five-year terms, after having served since 1959 as president of the fellows. His election as a dark-horse candidate underlined the college's character as a research institution, and his conciliatory, inclusive approach to governance helped foster constructive relationships in what had previously been a distinctly fractious fellowship. Besides constituting a form of recognition of the importance of his scholarship, the new position helped him carry his *magnum opus* forward towards completion in various ways, including allowing him to expand his growing collection of materials into the spacious master's residence. He was appointed a lay reader at Thaxted parish church in the same year he took up the mastership, and he regularly preached there and in his own college's chapel over the next twenty years. His years as master also witnessed his receiving a growing number of honorary degrees from universities around the world. He served as president of the International Union of History and Philosophy of Science from 1970 to 1973. In 1971 he was made a fellow of the British Academy in recognition of his historical work, thus becoming the only person to have been elected to that body and to the Royal Society for separate bodies of work.

Like Joan Robinson, Needham welcomed Mao's cultural revolution for the egalitarian, anti-bureaucratic principles proclaimed in its name, but difficulties in meeting scientific colleagues and friends during his 1972 visit brought home the movement's negative effects on intellectuals. In 1978 he published a long article in *Nature* indicating its disastrous effects on China's scientific development. Thereafter he paid less attention to developments in Chinese domestic politics, but generally approved of Deng Xiaoping's new course on account of the reaffirmation it involved of intellectual work and the expanded opportunities it offered for communications between China and the West. Suppression of the democracy movement in June 1989 shocked him and elicited a rare public expression of disappointment and dissent. The next year saw him resign as president of the Society for Anglo-Chinese Understanding, in the process of scaling back his activities and entrusting his scholarly project to others.

During his second term as master of Caius it had dawned on Needham that he was unlikely to be able to complete the grand project he had begun. He consequently undertook to expand the roster of collaborators working on the *Science and Civilisation in China* project. Among the new contingent of senior scholars who joined him on the project were the University of Chicago librarian Tsien Tsuen-Hsuin, a leading specialist in the history of printing, and Ray Huang, who specialized in the evolution of the Chinese fiscal and monetary systems. At the same time Needham began enlisting a modest cohort of promising younger scholars to help in preparing the still outstanding parts of the series. The appearance in 1984 of Francesca Bray's treatise on Chinese agriculture began the trend to publish volumes by individual authors other than Needham in the series.

The Needham Research Institute A major turning point in Needham's life came in 1976, when he stepped down as master of Caius and was faced with the prospect of moving most of his vast collection of books and papers elsewhere. He and Lu Gwei-Djen decided then to take the opportunity to incorporate their personal libraries into a specialized research institute, henceforth to be owned and administered by the East Asian History of Science Trust (UK), the educational charity they established at this time. In the medium term the trust had two pressing aims: completion of the *Science and Civilisation in China* project, and arranging for a permanent home for the institute. Peter Burbidge, the Cambridge University Press production manager who had overseen editorial processes on the series since its inception, became the first chairman of the trustees; but he stepped aside when the Labour peer Lord Roll, former head of the Bank of England, agreed to serve in that capacity. Soon thereafter two sister trusts were founded in Hong Kong and the United States for purposes of fund-raising, at which they proved highly effective during the late 1970s and the 1980s.

The establishment of the institute, temporarily housed first on Cambridge University Press grounds, then nearby on Brooklands Avenue, marked a new stage in the *Science and Civilisation in China* project. The hiring of a full-time librarian and the systematic cataloguing of the collection transformed an invaluable set of scholarly materials into an accessible academic resource. The collaborative spirit that had always informed the project now took new forms as members of the core team assembled by Needham and Lu interacted fruitfully with one another and with a steady stream of academic visitors, including a growing number of project collaborators. Within a few years the strategy of recruiting a new generation of scholars bore fruit in a variety of ways, most obviously in major contributions to the series on such subjects as agriculture, botany, printing, textiles, military technology, sugar production, forestry, and mining. In the long term the encouragement given to younger researchers, whether contributors to Needham's series or not, also secured for the East Asian History of Science library—later renamed the Needham Research Institute—a significant international role in laying the foundation for future scholarship on the history of East Asian science, technology, and medicine.

As the institute's director and associate director respectively, Needham and Lu devoted much energy to planning and arranging for the construction of a permanent new home for the institute. A meeting in 1977 with the millionaire David Robinson secured the latter's agreement that a suitable building could be located in the grounds of the Cambridge college he was in the process of endowing. Academic engagements in East Asia and the United States (once Needham was again granted a visa to visit there in 1978) helped the overseas trusts and other friends to publicize the institute's work. Major grants from the National Science Foundation in the United States and the National Institute for Research Advancement in Japan assisted significantly in the new burst of research on the *Science and Civilisation in China* project that occurred at this time. Generous donations by Tan Sri Tan Chin Tuan in Singapore as well as by foundations and individuals in Hong Kong, Taiwan, the People's Republic of China, and the United States allowed the construction of the permanent institute to proceed. Despite some disputes among the trustees over the institute's administration and priorities, the first two segments of the new building, including the central library block, were completed in 1987. The move to the permanent building took place in the autumn of that year.

Final years Dorothy Needham, afflicted for years by Alzheimer's disease, lived just long enough to see the library installed in its new premises. Though her death, on 22 December 1987, shook Needham, he recovered gradually over the following months. An inaugural conference marking the formal opening of the new institute was held in 1989. Needham and Lu were married on 15 September that year, after he succeeded in persuading her it was not too late to do so. In 1990 he passed the directorship of the institute to Ho Peng Yoke, a stalwart collaborator on the Science and Civilisation in China project since the 1950s. Scholars gathered from around the world to pay Needham their respects later that year when the institute hosted the sixth international conference on the history of Chinese science. The third and final wing of the institute was opened in 1991.

Needham's immense grief at the death of Gwei-Djen on 28 November 1991 was aggravated by a lonely sense that he had lost nearly all his contemporaries, and over the following years he also suffered increasingly from a variety of physical ailments, including Parkinson's disease. At the same time he had the good fortune to remain lucid mentally and to be shored up by people who cared for him. While labouring away until the end on various projects, he enjoyed the pleasure of receiving major new honours in his last years. In 1990 he was awarded the Fukuoka Asian cultural prize in Japan; and the Chinese government presented him with the order of the Bright Star in 1991. In 1992 he was named a Companion of Honour, and the year before his death UNESCO awarded him its Einstein medal.

Needham died peacefully at his home, 2A Sylvester Road, Cambridge, on 24 March 1995, in the company of his carers and his close friend Elinor Shaffer. The respect and affection felt for him in Cambridge and wider afield were attested by the size of the congregation that packed Great St Mary's Church on 10 June 1995 to participate in the suitably multicultural service organized in his memory by the fellows of his college.   GREGORY BLUE

Sources M. Goldsmith, *Joseph Needham: 20th-century Renaissance man* (1995) · S. K. Mukherjee and A. Ghosh, *The life and works of Joseph Needham* (1997) · J. B. Gurdon and B. Rodbard, *Memoirs FRS*, 46 (2000), 367–76 · G. Blue, 'Joesph Needham: a publication history', *Chinese Science*, 14 (1997), 90–132 · G. Blue, 'Joesph Needham, heterodox Marxism and the social background to Chinese science', *Science and Society*, 62 (1998), 195–217 · S. I. Habib and D. Raina, *Studying the history of science: dialogues with Joseph Needham* (1999) · M. Teich and R. Young, *Changing perspectives in the history of science: essays in honour of Joseph Needham* (1973) · Lu Gwei-Djen, 'The first half-life of Joseph Needham', *Explorations in the history of science and technology in China*, ed. Li Guohao, Zhang Mengwen, and Cao Tiangin (1982), 1–38 · Huang Hsing-Tsung, 'Peregrinations with Joseph Needham', *Explorations in the history of science and technology in China*, ed. Li Guohao, Zhang Mengwen, and Cao Tiangin (1982), 39–76 · *The Times* (27 March 1995) · *Daily Telegraph* (27 March 1995) · *The Guardian* (27 March 1995) · *The Independent* (27 March 1995) · *The Independent* (29 March 1995) · *The Independent* (30 March 1995) · *The Independent* (24 April 1995) · *New York Times* (27 March 1995) · *WWW* · private information (2004) · personal knowledge (2004) · b. cert. · m. certs. · d. cert.

Archives CUL, scientific, personal, and family papers · Gon. & Caius Cam., papers relating to Gonville and Caius College · IWM, papers relating to chemical and biological warfare · Needham Research Institute, Cambridge, East Asian History of Science Library, papers | Bodl. Oxf., corresp. relating to Society for Protection of Science and Learning, MSS SPSL · PRO, corresp. with Sir Henry Dale, CAB 127/222 · Rice University, Houston, Texas, Woodson Research Center, Huxley papers, corresp. with Sir Julian Huxley · Wellcome L., Singer papers, corresp. with Charles Singer

Likenesses Ramsey & Muspratt, photograph, 1937, NPG [*see illus.*] · J. Wood, portrait, oils, 1963, Gon. & Caius Cam. · photograph, repro. in *The Times* · photograph, repro. in *The Independent* (27 March 1995) · photographs, repro. in www.nri.org.uk/Joseph.htm, 24 Oct 2002 · two photographs, repro. in Gordon and Rodbard, *Memoirs FRS*, 366 and 373

Wealth at death £899,478: probate, 28 Nov 1995, *CGPLA Eng. & Wales*

Needham, Marchamont. *See* Nedham, Marchamont (*bap.* 1620, *d.* 1678).

Needham, Peter (*bap.* 1682, *d.* 1731), classical scholar, was born at Stockport and baptized there on 15 February 1682. He was son of the Revd Samuel Needham (1649/50–1718) who, after keeping a private school at Bradenham, Norfolk, was appointed master of Stockport grammar school. Peter attended his father's school at Bradenham until he entered St John's College, Cambridge, in 1693; he matriculated, in 1696. Prior to this he had been elected Billingsley scholar in 1693. He graduated BA (1696), MA (1700), BD (1707), and DD (1717). From 12 April 1698 to March 1716 he was a fellow of St John's College. In 1706 he left Cambridge to become rector of Ovington, Norfolk. Five years later he was appointed vicar of Madingley, and became rector of both Whatton, Leicestershire, and Conington, Cambridgeshire, in 1713. In the following year a prebend in the church of St Florence, Pembrokeshire, was conferred on him, and in 1717 the rectory of Stanwick, Northamptonshire, where he rebuilt the rector's house at a cost of £1000.

Needham was an accomplished scholar in both Latin and Greek. He published editions of the *Geoponica*, dedicated to John Moore, bishop of Ely; the *Characters* of Theophrastus; and Hierocles' *Commentary on the Golden Verses of Pythagoras*, dedicated to his patron the lord chancellor, William, Earl Cowper. Needham also devoted much labour to the text of Aeschylus, and his manuscript collections were freely used by Anthony Askew, Samuel Butler, and Bishop Charles James Blomfield in their editions of that dramatist. Bernard de Montfaucon, the editor of the Benedictine edition of *St Chrysostom* (1718), also acknowledged his debt to Needham, whom he described as 'vir doctissimus amicissimusque' ('a most learned and amiable man').

Needham was a frequent correspondent of Thomas Hearne, who complained in 1705 of Needham's failure to acknowledge the help that he derived from Oxford libraries when compiling his edition of *Geoponica*. Later, however, Hearne described him as 'an ingenious, learned gentleman', if 'a most rash whig'; Hearne examined many Greek manuscripts for him in the Bodleian Library (*Remarks*, 1.78, 3.123). Needham was also praised by the Cambridge antiquary William Cole. He died at Stanwick on 6 December 1731. SIDNEY LEE, *rev.* PHILIP CARTER

Sources Venn, *Alum. Cant.* · *Remarks and collections of Thomas Hearne*, ed. C. E. Doble and others, 11 vols., OHS, 2, 7, 13, 34, 42–3, 48, 50, 65, 67, 72 (1885–1921) · P. Needham, *Geoponica*, BL, Harleian MS 6876 [MS epitaph] · PRO, PROB 11/650, fols. 38r–40r

Needham, (Amy) Violet (1876–1967), children's writer, was born on 5 June 1876 at 9 John Street, Berkeley Square, London, the younger daughter of Colonel Charles Needham (1844–1934) and his wife, Hendrika Amelie Charlotte Vincentia (Amy) de Tuyll de Serooskerken (1854–1936), a Dutch heiress. Charles Needham was the illegitimate but acknowledged son of Francis Jack, second earl of Kilmorey (1787–1880), and Priscilla Anne, daughter of Captain Sir William Hoste RN (1780–1828). Needham entered the 1st Life Guards, served in the Egyptian campaign (1882), and commanded the regiment (1888–92), but his addiction to gambling brought financial difficulties; the family moved house frequently during Violet's youth as his fortunes changed.

Violet and her sister, Evelyn Norah (1874–1967), were educated at home and became fluent in French, Italian, and German. They accompanied their parents when their father was military attaché in Rome (1895–1901); later the family lived in London and at their country house, Tylehurst, Forest Row, Sussex, where Violet became friendly with the alpinist Douglas Freshfield (1845–1934). Visits were paid to her mother's relatives in France, Austria, and the Netherlands. After her parents' deaths she moved to 1 Spanish Place, Marylebone, London, and in the early 1950s joined her widowed sister at Horton Hall, Gloucestershire.

Violet Needham was physically plain, but dressed elegantly and had great personal charm. She remained a Victorian lady, but took to motoring (rather dangerously) and was a heavy smoker of Turkish cigarettes, using a special oval shagreen holder. She once gave her hobbies as gardening and wood chopping, but she also painted and did needlework. Although she published nothing until the age of sixty-three, she had always told stories to young relatives, particularly her four nephews. In 1918 they urged her to write down the latest bedtime story; it was sent to various publishers but was rejected as too adult for children. Twenty years later a niece-in-law showed it to William Collins; on his own children's recommendation he published it in 1939 as *The Black Riders*. Eighteen children's books followed, as well as short stories and articles. Only at the age of eighty, following a car accident, did she cease writing.

Violet Needham's most popular stories belong to a sequence of eight set in a group of Ruritanian countries clearly modelled on pre-1914 Austria–Hungary. *The Black Riders* (1939), *The Emerald Crown* (1940), *The Stormy Petrel* (1942), *The House of the Paladin* (1945), and their sequels are a heady mixture of romantic backgrounds, swift action, and spine-chilling suspense, with characters remarkable among the children's books of the period for having real moral dilemmas, and faults as well as virtues. She was particularly good at portraying children in relation to adults and at drawing convincing villains. Again unusually, she did not hesitate to kill off major characters. Her books are marked by the importance of loyalty and a firm sense of *noblesse oblige*—all her heroes and heroines are decidedly upper-class—with an underpinning of strong but unbigoted faith (she was an Anglican), sincere but not sanctimonious. The books were well illustrated by Joyce Bruce, a Gloucestershire neighbour, who worked closely with her to match the drawings to the author's imagination.

Violet Needham's works also include three contemporary English stories with supernatural elements, *The Horn of Merlyns* (1943), *The Bell of the Four Evangelists* (1947), and *Pandora of Parrham Royal* (1951); two Ruritanian historical stories, *The Woods of Windri* (1944) and *The Changeling of Monte*

Lucio (1946); and a historical tale, *The Boy in Red* (1948), dealing with William the Silent and using as a setting Clingendaal near The Hague, a house belonging to Dutch relatives.

Violet Needham's heyday was the 1940s, when her books reached a wide audience through being broadcast on *Children's Hour*, and her young readers included Auberon Waugh, Antonia Fraser, A. S. Byatt, and Alice Thomas Ellis. She died of heart failure at Horton Hall, Gloucestershire, on 8 June 1967. She was cremated, and her ashes scattered at Little Sodbury Manor, Gloucestershire. After a period of neglect her works began to arouse interest in the 1980s; the Violet Needham Society was formed in 1985.   HILARY CLARE

Sources private information (2004) · *Souvenir* [journal of the Violet Needham Society], 32 (1996) · V. Needham, *The stormy petrel*, 2nd edn (1971) · A. Fraser, *The pleasure of reading* (1992) · A. Thomas Ellis, *Daily Telegraph* (1 Oct 1993) · A. Waugh, 'Review of *The Oxford companion to children's literature*', *Sunday Telegraph* (29 April 1984) · b. cert. · d. cert.
Archives priv. coll.
Likenesses photographs, priv. coll.
Wealth at death £80,830

Needham, Walter (*bap.* 1632, *d.* 1691), physician and anatomist, was the son of Gervase Needham (*d.* 1649), vicar of Bishops Castle, Shropshire, and his wife, Ann. He was baptized on 28 December 1632 at Bishop's Castle. Educated as a queen's scholar at Westminster School, he matriculated at Trinity College, Cambridge, at Easter 1650. In 1654 he graduated BA and on 25 July 1655 he was admitted a fellow of Queens' College.

Needham remained in Cambridge until the summer of 1660, when, having obtained a licence to practise, he left the university to study medicine for a short time in Shropshire under the guidance of a Dr Smith. In 1662 he went to Oxford. There he attended anatomy lectures and became closely involved with the researches of Thomas Willis, Robert Boyle, Thomas Millington, and Richard Lower. His reputation as an anatomist was already known in the scientific circles of the day; in 1668 William Croone had described him to Samuel Hartlib as 'like to prove one of the rarest anatomists that hath beene in the world' (Frank, 181).

Needham subsequently returned to Cambridge, and took the degree of doctor of physic from Queens' College on 5 July 1664. In December 1664 he was admitted an honorary fellow of the College of Physicians.

On 4 August 1667 Needham's *Disquisitio anatomica de formato foetu* was licensed to be printed. This work owed much to his time in Oxford. In it Needham was mainly concerned with quite technical aspects of the anatomy and physiology of the human foetus, on which his work was not surpassed for over half a century. The book was dedicated to Robert Boyle, with whose work on respiration and air Needham had been involved while at Oxford (Frank, 60). In *Disquisitio* Needham states that he was living a long way from London.

Needham was elected a fellow of the Royal Society on 20 June 1667 and was an active participant until 1678, at one time being closely involved with (unfulfilled) plans for an anatomy lectureship for the society (Hunter, *Royal Society*, 41). On 7 November 1672 Needham was appointed physician to the Charterhouse in succession to George Castle. In 1673 he read a paper before the Royal Society giving the results of some experiments he had made in conjunction with Richard Wiseman on the value of Denis's newly discovered liquor for stopping arterial bleeding. From about 1673 to 1675 he served as anatomical lecturer to the Company of Surgeons. The syllabus of his lectures survives in the British Library (Frank, 283).

By 1681 Needham was living in Great Queen Street, Broad Sanctuary, London. He was created an actual fellow of the Royal College of Physicians under the charter of James II, alongside a number of physicians active in the Royal Society, including Hans Sloane; he was admitted on 12 April 1687. He died on 5 or 16 April 1691, and was buried obscurely in the church of St Giles-in-the-Fields, London (*Life and Times of Anthony Wood*, 3.358). Injunctions were out against him at the time of his death to seize both body and goods.

Needham was held in high esteem by some of his contemporaries, and, according to Wood, had a large practice. Sydenham, in the dedicatory epistle of his *Observationes medicae* (1676), recalls 'the sagacious Master Walter Needham, Doctor of Medicine, an ornament both to his profession and to literature' (Dewhurst, 30). However, certain of his contemporaries had a less high opinion of him; in 1687 a Doctor Pitt complained to the College of Physicians that Needham always pressed his medicines on patients and refused almost all consultations (Clark, 339).

D'A. POWER, *rev.* PATRICK WALLIS

Sources Venn, *Alum. Cant.* · Munk, *Roll* · *Old Westminsters*, vols. 1–2 · M. Hunter, *The Royal Society and its fellows, 1660–1700: the morphology of an early scientific institution* (1982) · M. Hunter, *Science and society in Restoration England* (1981) · H. J. Cook, *The decline of the old medical regime in Stuart London* (1986) · R. G. Frank, *Harvey and the Oxford physiologists* (1980) · G. Clark and A. M. Cooke, *A history of the Royal College of Physicians of London*, 1 (1964) · Wood, *Ath. Oxon.: Fasti*, new edn · K. Dewhurst, ed., *Dr Thomas Sydenham (1624–1689)* (1966) · *The life and times of Anthony Wood*, ed. A. Clark, 5 vols., OHS, 19, 21, 26, 30, 40 (1891–1900) · A. G. Matthews, *Walker revisited* (1948) · *The record of the Royal Society of London*, 4th edn (1940)
Archives BL, Sloane MSS 631, 1761

Needler, Benjamin (1620–1682), clergyman and ejected minister, was born on 29 November 1620 at Laleham in Middlesex, the son of Thomas Needler. He was admitted to Merchant Taylors' School in London on 11 September 1634 and was made head scholar in 1640. He went up to St John's College, Oxford, in June 1642, matriculating on 1 July. Although he was elected to the fellowship of St John's in 1645 his support for parliament meant that he did not reside in the college during Oxford's period as the royalist capital. He returned to Oxford in 1648 as the assistant to the parliamentary visitors of the university, who conferred upon him the degree of BCL on 14 April. Needler, however, resigned his fellowship in 1651 when he married Mary Culverwell (*d.* 1665), the daughter of the Cambridge Platonist Nathaniel *Culverwell.

Needler was chosen as the rector of the London parish of

St Margaret Moyses on 8 August 1648 and soon instituted the presbyterian discipline. He attended meetings of the first London classis and was elected by that body as a delegate to the London Provincial Assembly. Needler was among the presbyterians who met at Sion College to oppose the army's interference with the parliament and the trial of Charles I. He was a signatory of the London presbyterian ministry's *Serious and Faithful Representation* to Lord General Fairfax in January 1649 protesting against the army's *coup d'état*, and later signed the ministers' *Vindication* of that protest. His association with the London presbyterian ministers is further shown by the poem he contributed to the collection commemorating the death of Jeremiah Whitaker in 1654.

Needler was ejected from St Margaret Moyses in August 1662 but remained with the nonconforming London presbyterian brethren as a preacher. The nonconformist leader Richard Baxter noted that Needler was 'a very humble, grave, and peaceable divine' (*Reliquiae Baxterianae*, 3.94). In 1655, before his ejection, he published a work of practical divinity on the first five chapters of Genesis. He was also a regular orator at the presbyterian morning exercises from 1660, notably preaching on the mortification of lusts, and was reported preaching at Finsbury Fields in 1669.

Like many of the inhabitants of London Needler suffered during the plague of 1665–6, losing his wife and two of his daughters. After 1669 he retired to North Warnborough in Hampshire, where he kept private conventicles until he died in October 1682. In his will he requested that he should be buried without a sermon and he was laid to rest in the village of Odiham in Hampshire on 20 October 1682. He was survived by his second wife, Naomi (*d.* 1692/3), and by four children—two sons, Culverwell and Benjamin, and two daughters, Mary and Anne. **Culverwell Needler** (*bap.* 1656, *d.* in or after 1710), clerk, who was baptized at St Margaret Moyses on 5 March 1656, was appointed as an additional writing clerk to the House of Lords on 25 March 1679 and later was selected as the clerk-assistant to the House of Commons. He held this post until December 1710 when he was disabled by palsy.

E. C. VERNON

Sources Calamy rev., vol. 3 · *Reliquiae Baxterianae, or, Mr Richard Baxter's narrative of the most memorable passages of his life and times*, ed. M. Sylvester, 1 vol. in 3 pts (1696), pt 3 · S. Ashe, *Living loves betwixt Christ and dying Christians* (1654) · *A serious and faithful vindication of the ministers* (1649) · *The nonconformist's memorial ... originally written by ... Edmund Calamy*, ed. S. Palmer, 2 vols. (1775) · T. Case, *The morning exercises methodized* (1660) · JHC · C. J. Robinson, ed., *A register of the scholars admitted into Merchant Taylors' School, from AD 1562 to 1874*, 1 (1882), 136 · Foster, *Alum. Oxon.* · JHL · *The manuscripts of the House of Lords*, 4 vols., HMC, 17 (1887–94), vol. 1, p. 172 · will, PRO, PROB 11/371, fols. 207–8 · *The manuscripts of the Marquess Townshend*, HMC, 19 (1887), 143
Wealth at death £200 from bonds given to tradesmen; plus household chattels: will, PRO, PROB 11/371, fols. 207–8

Needler, Culverwell (*bap.* 1656, *d.* in or after 1710). *See under* Needler, Benjamin (1620–1682).

Needler, Henry (*bap.* 1685, *d.* 1760), musician, son of John Needler, was baptized at Horley, Surrey, on 23 September 1685. He entered the Excise Office as a young man, becoming accountant for the candle duty in 1710 and accountant-general in 1724. His lifelong passion, however, was for music. His father gave him his first lessons on the violin, and he studied with Daniel Purcell and the younger John Banister. He was prominent in musical circles, playing in Thomas Britton's concerts and in concerts at private houses. He knew Handel, and was an active member of the Academy of Vocal Music. He was a great admirer of Corelli, and is said to have been the first to play his concertos in England. He made extensive transcriptions from music in libraries in Oxford; twenty-seven volumes are in the British Library. Having married late in life, Needler left no children at his death on 8 August 1760. He left a life interest in the Needler family property at Horley to his widow, Hester, and her sister Elizabeth. He was buried at Frindsbury, near Rochester, Kent. Hester Needler composed a volume of anthems, which is in the British Library.

L. M. MIDDLETON, *rev.* K. D. REYNOLDS

Sources New Grove · Grove, *Dict. mus.* (1927) · J. Hawkins, *A general history of the science and practice of music*, 5 vols. (1776) · *IGI*
Likenesses C. Grignion, engraving (after Mathias), repro. in Hawkins, *History*

Needler, Henry (*bap.* 1690, *d.* 1718), poet and essayist, was baptized on 3 October 1690 at Horley, Surrey, the son of Henry Needler and Rose Watson. Needler was educated at a 'private school' in Reigate. In 1708 he entered the Navy Office, where he became a friend of William Duncombe; in his leisure hours he applied himself to reading the classics and the intensive study of logic, metaphysics, and mathematics. As early as 1711 Needler complained of severe pain in his head, and this gradually became more violent; eventually he became insane. He died of a 'fever' on 21 December 1718, and was buried in All Saints' Church, Frindsbury, near Rochester, Kent.

Needler's miscellaneous writings were published by Duncombe in 1724, second and third editions appearing in 1728 and 1735 (*Works ... Consisting of Original Poems, Translations, Essays, and Letters*). The poems are unremarkable, including a number of competent translations from the Latin and several pieces of biblical paraphrase. 'To Sir Richard Blackmore, on his poem, entitled "Creation"' is of some interest as a response to Sir Richard Blackmore's laboriously 'physicotheological' didactic poem. More notable are the essays, which are partly modelled on those of *The Spectator* and other contemporary periodicals: obvious examples are 'On the excellency of divine contemplation' and 'On the beauty of the universe', the second on a characteristic theme. The essay-like 'familiar letters', mostly dating from 1709–11, touch on a variety of moral and philosophical themes, and are of particular interest on account of the intellectual influences they reflect. In a letter (November 1711) to his friend John Hughes Needler warmly praises John Norris's Neoplatonic *Theory of the Ideal World*; and in a letter (3 December 1711) to Duncombe he expresses admiration for the '*Philosophical Meditation*' in *The Moralists* by Anthony Ashley Cooper, third earl of Shaftesbury, going on to attempt an imitation of Shaftesbury's rhapsodic prose in a passage on the manifestations of the deity in the physical universe. An important additional letter to Duncombe was later published by John Duncombe. Needler emerges as highly sensitive, introspective, and intellectually curious. In his preface to the *Works* Duncombe pays tribute to Needler's personal qualities. ROBERT INGLESFIELD

Sources *The works of Mr. Henry Needler*, ed. W. Duncombe, 2nd edn (1728) · *The works of Mr. Henry Needler*, ed. W. Duncombe, 2nd edn (1728); facs. edn with introduction by M. Allentuck (1961) · *IGI* · J. Duncombe, ed., *Letters by several eminent persons deceased*, 2nd edn, 3 vols. (1773)

Neel, (Louis) Boyd (1905–1981), conductor and medical practitioner, was born on 19 July 1905 at 30 Ulundi Road, Blackheath, London, the only child of Louis Anthoine Neel, a paint manufacturer, and his wife Ruby Le Couteur; both families came from Jersey. He was educated at the Royal Naval College at Osborne and Dartmouth, which he left to study medicine at Gonville and Caius College, Cambridge (BA, 1926). He then went to St George's Hospital, London, and became MRCS Eng. and LRCP Lond. (1930). Meanwhile he grasped every chance to conduct amateurs, took lessons at the Guildhall School of Music, and listened to Sir Thomas Beecham, Wilhelm Furtwängler, Bruno Walter, and Toscanini, at home and abroad. While still in medical practice he founded the Boyd Neel Orchestra, which made its début at the Aeolian Hall, London, on 22 June 1933; Neel delivered a baby later that night.

For reasons of economy and repertory the group was small and at first consisted mostly of students. At the time little romantic, let alone baroque, string music was played, and then only by symphony orchestras; Neel saw a gap waiting to be filled. He brought forward works by Dvořák, Elgar, Grieg, Gustav Holst, and Tchaikovsky. The *Fantasia on a Theme by Thomas Tallis* of Vaughan Williams, Ernest Bloch's *Concerto grosso* no. 1, and Stravinsky's *Apollon Musagète* were in the orchestra's twentieth-century repertory; and *Variations on a Theme of Frank Bridge*, composed by Benjamin Britten for them to play at the 1937 Salzburg Festival, launched both the composer's reputation internationally and their own. Based on eighteen strings with harpsichord who worked together regularly, the orchestra developed a true and distinctive chamber style, finely suited to the concertos of Mozart (often with Kathleen Long or Frederick Grinke) and to revivals of composers such as Torelli, Vivaldi, and Geminiani. A debonair and restrained figure on the podium, Neel had an instinctive gift for just tempos and lucid textures in Bach and Handel. Among the orchestra's notable releases, those of Handel's concerti grossi op. 6, ground-breaking when they were recorded (1936–8), stood the test of time when they were reissued in the critically informed 1970s.

Though Neel returned to practising medicine throughout the Second World War, he also performed at the National Gallery concerts in London. He then branched out into opera, conducting briefly for Sadler's Wells (1945–7) and D'Oyly Carte (1948–9), and also took the Sir Robert Mayer children's concerts. Even during the war the Boyd Neel Orchestra managed to celebrate its tenth anniversary, for which Britten composed his *Prelude and Fugue*. Then came their widespread tours: in Britain and elsewhere in Europe, in Australia and New Zealand in 1947, in Scandinavia in 1950, in Canada and the USA in 1952. In 1950 Neel published *The Story of an Orchestra*, and in 1985 *My Orchestras and other Adventures*; he also contributed the chapter on string music to *Britten: a Commentary* (ed. Donald Mitchell and Hans Keller, 1952).

The success of the Canadian tour of 1952 led to Neel's move to Toronto in 1953 as dean of the Royal Conservatory of Music and head of the university faculty of music (he became a naturalized Canadian in 1961). Without academic musical training Neel might have seemed a figurehead, but, finding the premises inadequate, he immediately turned his energy to planning the Edward Johnson Building, named after the great Canadian tenor. Opened in 1961 this provided the reorganized faculty with an opera theatre, a concert hall, rehearsal, lecture, and practice rooms, a library, and many other facilities, all air-conditioned and soundproofed. Neel's good humour and skill in communication stood him well in his relationship with both the university and the community (where he was highly regarded), and found another outlet in his work as a popular lecturer and broadcaster.

In 1954 Neel founded the Hart House Orchestra, a chamber group similar to his London one (which, directed by R. Thurston Dart, who had played continuo for Neel, became the Philomusica). Neel had quickly realized that Canada trained more performers than it could then employ, and that a professional orchestra based on the university would stimulate the community, and he himself needed active music-making. The Hart House Orchestra toured widely over North America, and visited the Brussels World Fair in 1958 and Aldeburgh, at Britten's invitation, in 1966. Neel was also in demand as a guest conductor, particularly after he retired in 1971 from his academic post, where his work had substantially raised the prestige of music in the university. A relaxed, buoyant figure, and a convivial homosexual, he became one of the best-known, most influential musicians in his adopted country. He was appointed CBE (1953) and a member of the order of Canada (1973). He was an honorary member of the Royal Academy of Music. He died in Toronto on 30 September 1981. DIANA McVEAGH

Sources B. Neel, *My orchestras and other adventures: the memoirs of Boyd Neel* (1985) · B. J. Edwards, 'Neel, (Louis) Boyd', *Encyclopedia of music in Canada*, ed. H. Kallmann, G. Potvin, and K. Winters (1981), 671; 2nd edn (1992), 937 · personal knowledge (2004) · D. McVeagh and E. Schabas, 'Neel, (Louis) Boyd', *New Grove*, 2nd edn

Archives SOUND BL NSA, oral history interview · BL NSA, performance recording · BL NSA, *Talking about music*, 237, 1LP0203298 S1 BD2 BBC TRANSC

Likenesses E. Auerbach, photograph, c.1975, Hult. Arch.

Neele, Henry (1798–1828), poet and writer, was born on 29 January 1798 in the Strand, London, where his father carried on business as a map and heraldic engraver. He was educated at a private school at Kentish Town and was afterwards articled to a solicitor and admitted to practice after the expiration of the usual period. He never relinquished his profession, but his attention was mainly devoted to literature.

In January 1817, while still serving his articles, Neele published at his father's expense *Odes, and other Poems*, betraying the influence of William Collins. This book attracted the attention of Dr Nathan Drake, who highly commended it. A second edition was printed in July 1820, and in March 1823 *Poems, Dramatic and Miscellaneous* appeared, inscribed to Joanna Baillie. This volume obtained considerable success, making Neele a popular contributor to magazines and annuals; he continued to produce tales and poems for these during the remainder of his short life. He prepared in 1826, and delivered in 1827, a course of lectures on English poetry that was published after his death, and which, if unoriginal, exhibits a sensitive perception of poetical beauty and a correct taste. An edition of Shakespeare by Neele, issued in parts, was soon discontinued for want of support.

In 1827 Neele published a collected edition of his poems in two volumes and in the same year he produced his *Romance of English History* in three volumes. The latter is a collection of tales illustrative of romantic passages in English history, one of a series of five works on the histories of the chief nations of the world composed by various authors as commissions from the publishing firm of Edward Bull. It was written in six months and the overstrain of composition and research was believed to have been the cause of the untimely fate of the author, who was found dead in bed at his home, Castle Street, Oxford Street, Marylebone, Middlesex, on 7 February 1828, having cut his throat under the delusion that his private affairs had become hopelessly embarrassed. The coroner's inquest returned a verdict of insanity. Neele left a widow, Jemima Mary Ann.

No symptom of a disordered mind appears in Neele's writings, which, although tinged with poetical melancholy, are always lucid and coherent; his conversation was said to have been cheerful and vivacious and he was irreproachable in every relation of life. Neele's *Literary Remains* (1829) included his 'Lectures on English poetry' and a number of tales and poems, some never before published, others collected from periodicals.

As a poet, Neele can hardly claim higher rank than that of an elegant and natural versifier, as he had neither sufficient originality of thought nor force of expression to produce any considerable effect. His lyrics are characterized by sincerity and spontaneity, but his dramatic attempts are grievously defective in truth of representation. His short stories frequently exhibit considerable power of imagination and description; especially notable is one in which the legends of the Wandering Jew and Agrippa's magic mirror are very happily combined. His romantic illustrations of English history were popular in their day, but the curious dialect that was then considered to represent medieval English is now entirely out of date.

RICHARD GARNETT, rev. M. CLARE LOUGHLIN-CHOW

Sources 'Memoir', H. Neele, *The literary remains of ... Henry Neele* (1829) • *The Times* (11 Feb 1828) • *GM*, 1st ser., 98/1 (1828), 276–7 • N. Drake, *Winter nights*, 2 vols. (1820) • [Clarke], *The Georgian era: memoirs of the most eminent persons*, 3 (1834) • Allibone, *Dict.* • administration, PRO, PROB 6/205, fol. 221r

Likenesses H. Meyer, stipple, BM, NPG; repro. in J. Britton, *The autobiography of John Britton*, 2 vols. (1849–50)

Neele [Neale], **Sir Richard** (*d.* 1486), justice, was probably the son of Gervase Neele of Shepshed, Leicestershire, rather than, as has been supposed, of another Richard Neele who was MP for Leicestershire in 1442. The younger Richard Neele trained as a lawyer at Gray's Inn, where he gave readings in autumn term 1442 and Lent term 1449. He appears to have been in London by 8 June 1439, when he witnessed a charter for Walter Moyle (*d.* 1479/80), also a future justice, though some years Neele's senior, and a fellow member of Gray's Inn. In 1448 Neele became a JP for Leicestershire, and in the same year was appointed a gaol delivery justice at Leicester. Also in 1448 he was employed as counsel, though apparently in a junior capacity, by the city of Exeter. In 1450 he was a commissioner to levy a subsidy in Leicestershire, and was also appointed to investigate riots in Nottinghamshire; during the following decade he was regularly employed by the crown as a commissioner, usually in Leicestershire and the midlands. In 1456, for instance, he was to inquire whether a supposed Leicestershire man was in fact a Scot, in 1457 to investigate the capacity of his native county to provide archers.

It would appear that Neele had Yorkist affiliations, for on 26 July 1461 he was granted an annuity of £40 by Edward IV in return for his good services; the grant was specifically exempted from the Act of Resumption passed in November of that year. He was created a serjeant in November 1463, and on 12 August 1464 was promoted to king's sergeant. In 1467–8 he was the earl of Kent's steward for the earl's lands in Leicestershire. Having served on a number of important commissions of oyer and terminer, including two in 1468 headed by the king's brothers, Neele was appointed a justice of king's bench on 18 April 1469, with a salary of 110 marks (£73 6s. 8d.). At the same time he began to be appointed to the commissions of the peace in the ridings of Yorkshire. Reappointed a king's bench justice on 9 October 1470, he remained in office during the readeption of Henry VI. But he remained in favour with Edward IV, who on 17 June 1471, as part of a reorganization of the judiciary, moved Neele to the court of common pleas, with the same salary as before. That Edward regarded Neele as trustworthy is shown by his being appointed a JP in politically sensitive areas, in Northumberland and Westmorland in the 1470s, and in Cumberland in the early 1480s. He also continued to serve in Yorkshire, while in 1475 he was a feoffee for the king's friend Lord Hastings. He appears to have been knighted in either 1477 or 1478.

Service in the north would have brought Neele into close contact with the king's brother, Richard, duke of Gloucester. Reappointed to the common bench on 21 April 1483, he retained his place when the duke usurped the throne as Richard III. He was a trier of petitions in Richard's only parliament, in January 1484, and was one of the commissioners appointed to investigate the treason of

William Colyngbourne at the end of that year. But following the battle of Bosworth he was reappointed to the common bench by Henry VII, on 13 October 1485. He had already been reappointed to the Leicestershire bench on 27 September, but according to a year-book report died, apparently suddenly, on 15 June 1486. He had married twice. His first wife, Isabel, daughter and coheir of William Ryddynges of Prestwold, brought him the manor of Prestwold and was the mother of his son and heir, Christopher, who was appointed to sit alongside his father on the Leicestershire bench between 1483 and 1485. Isobel died on 23 May 1476, and Neele married Agnes, daughter and heir of John Seyton of Martinsthorpe, Rutland, and widow of William Fielding of Lutterworth. But Neele was buried beside Isobel in Prestwold church, where his effigy, in judicial robes, survives on an incised tombstone slab.

R. J. SCHOECK

Sources Chancery records · E. W. Ives, *The common lawyers of pre-Reformation England* (1983) · Baker, *Serjeants*, 163, 528 · Sainty, *Judges*, 27, 70 · N. Doe, *Fundamental authority in late medieval English law* (1990) · *The reports of Sir John Spelman*, ed. J. H. Baker, 2, SeldS, 94 (1978), 369 n. 2 · *Letters and papers of John Shillingford, Mayor of Exeter, 1447–50*, ed. S. A. Moore, CS, new ser., 2 (1872), 148–52 · *RotP*, vols. 5–6 · *Year-books of the reigns of Edward V, Richard III and Henry VII* [1555–9] · R. I. Jack, ed., *The Grey of Ruthin valor: the valor of the English lands of Edmund Grey, earl of Kent, … from the ministers' accounts of 1467–1468*, Bedfordshire Historical RS, 46 (1965), 64 · S. E. Thorne and J. H. Baker, eds., *Readings and moots at the inns of court in the fifteenth century*, 1, SeldS, 71 (1954), xxxii · *CPR, 1477–1485*

Likenesses grave slab, incised portrait, Prestwold church, Lincolnshire

Negretti, Henry Angelo Ludovico (1818–1879), maker of scientific instruments, was born Enrico Angelo Ludovico Negretti on 13 November 1818 at piazza Volta 664, Como, in Italy, the second son of seven children of Paolo Negretti (1785–1851) and his first wife, Costanza, daughter of Gaetano Corti. His three sisters died in infancy. He and his brothers sought employment abroad, rather than follow their father in operating a horse-drawn coach service over the St Gotthard Pass.

Negretti moved to England in 1830, aged twelve, and appears to have learned his instrument skills under two established makers: Caesar Tagliabue, a barometer and thermometer maker from Como, long resident at 23 Hatton Garden, London, and Francis Augustus Pizzala, at 4 Dorrington Street. During 1840 Negretti traded under his own name as a glass-blower at 2 Dorrington Street and 20 Greville Street, and the following year moved into Angelo Tagliabue's former workshop at 19 Leather Lane, recently acquired by Jane Pizzi, whose late husband Valentine had been a barometer maker in Cross Street. The partnership of Pizzi and Negretti continued until 1844, after which Negretti continued trading from the same address, moving briefly to 9 Hatton Garden before forming his partnership with Joseph Warren Zambra (1822–1897) at 11 Hatton Garden in 1850. Zambra had worked for his father as a glass-blower and had been in partnership with John Tagliabue at 11 Brooke Street for four years before joining Negretti. Negretti and Zambra were part of the burgeoning Anglo-Italian community around Leather Lane and Hatton Garden known as Little Italy, consisting mainly of street musicians, but including picture frame and looking-glass makers, and a small group of instrument makers from the Como area.

On 1 July 1845, Negretti married Mary, daughter of Samuel Peet, a tavern keeper of 20 Yardley Street, at the Roman Catholic church of St John the Evangelist in Islington. For the next nine years they mainly lived above the shop, moving in 1854 to 2 Grosvenor Villas, Junction Road, Holloway, where they were host to Garibaldi during his visit to London that year. Of three daughters born at Leather Lane, only Maria Louisa survived infancy. Henry Paul Joseph was born at Hatton Garden on 16 April 1851, and Carolina Cherubima after the move to Holloway.

The skill of the Negretti and Zambra partnership was immediately apparent when, exhibiting at the 1851 Great Exhibition at Hyde Park, they were the only English instrument makers to receive a prize medal for meteorological instruments, and were appointed instrument makers to the queen, Greenwich observatory, and the British Meteorological Society, of which Negretti was elected a fellow in 1855. Their self-registering maximum thermometer, patented in 1856, was praised by the astronomer royal. Over the following years their patents were in joint names making it impossible to associate specific skills with either partner. They initiated the process of enamelling the back of thermometer tubes, a feature which at the time they did not consider important, but which quickly became standard practice. In 1857 they made a pressure-resistant deep-sea thermometer for Admiral Fitzroy, and in 1863 carried out improvements at his suggestion to make mercurial barometers withstand the concussion of naval guns. Negretti was present at the trials of these on HMS *Excellent*. James Glaisher used their instruments in his 1862 balloon ascents, Negretti often installing the instruments himself. The firm's 1859 catalogue described 2134 items and instruments and this range doubled a few years later. Increasing sales required larger workshop facilities; they moved to 1 Hatton Garden in 1859, to 103 in 1867, and to 38 Holborn Viaduct in 1869. Premises were also taken in succession at 68, 59, and 45 Cornhill, and a retail outlet at 122 Regent Street was acquired from the instrument makers John Newman & Sons in 1862. They also became well established as photographic equipment makers and suppliers at 120 Crystal Palace.

Among the Italians in London, Negretti enjoyed a patriarchal popularity; his purse was open to the poor and his time never wanting in their service. He was naturalized as a British subject on 11 April 1862. When Garibaldi visited London again in 1864, Negretti led the Italian reception committee and on 7 September 1865 was created cavaliere of the order of St Maurice and Lazarus by the king of Italy. The same year he also headed another Italian committee, which secured the free pardon of Serafino Pelizzoni. This man had been found guilty of murdering Michael Harrington on 26 December 1864 at the Golden Anchor, Saffron Hill, after the dying victim had mistakenly identified him for his cousin, Gregorio Mogni. Justice was done only when Negretti took out a private prosecution against Mogni, who confessed to killing Harrington in self-defence and received a five-year prison sentence. The case achieved notoriety by obliging the judiciary to reconsider the first verdict.

In 1874 the family moved to Cricklewood. Negretti spent more time in Italy in his later years and had a residence at Como, but in 1878 travelled to Argentina. His health was not good when he sailed and was further impaired by the travelling. Over the following year it continued to deteriorate, and he died of pleuropneumonia at his home, Cricklewood House, on 24 September 1879 and was buried at Highgate cemetery. He was survived by his wife, both daughters, and his son, who succeeded him as Zambra's partner. The company of Negretti and Zambra prospered, moving to successively larger premises over the next century, diversifying into aircraft and industrial instruments in 1920, but succumbing to take-over in 1981 by Western Scientific.
JOHN K. BRADLEY

Sources *The Times* (29 Sept 1879), 11d · *Kilburn Times and Western Post* (3 Oct 1879), 3a · *Quarterly Journal of the Meteorological Society*, 6 (1879–80), 72–4 · *ILN* (4 Oct 1879), 323 · P. A. Negretti, 'The story of Negretti and Zambra', *Recorder* [N and Z House Magazine] (Jan 1948) · P. A. Negretti, 'Henry Negretti: gentleman and photographic pioneer', *Photographic Collector*, 5 (1984), 96–105 · P. A. Negretti, personal notes · *The Post Office London directory* (1835–75) · W. J. Read, 'History of the firm Negretti and Zambra', *Bulletin of the Scientific Instrument Society*, 5 (1985), 8–10 · W. J. Read, 'The development of scientific instruments of Negretti and Zambra', in J. T. Stock and M. V. Orna, *The history and preservation of chemical instruments* (1986), 211–16 · *A treatise on meteorological instruments: explanatory of their scientific principles, method of construction, and practical utility*, Negretti and Zambra (1864) · *Negretti and Zambra centenary, 1850–1950*, Negretti and Zambra [1950] · 'Negretti and Zambra, 1850–1950', *Instrument Practice*, 4 (1949–50), 367–73 · J. Juxon, *Lewis and Lewis* (1983) · D. R. Green, 'Little Italy in Victorian London', *Camden History Review*, 15 (1988), 2–6 · L. G. Rule and D. Rider, 'The flame of the lamp', *Glass*, 44/8 (1967), 348–54 · L. G. Rule and D. Rider, 'The flame of the lamp: part II', *Glass*, 44/9 (1967), 402–5 · L. G. Rule and D. Rider, 'The flame of the lamp: part III', *Glass*, 44/10 (1967), 456–9 · L. G. Rule and D. Rider, 'The flame of the lamp: part IV', *Glass*, 44/11 (1967), 508–9 · L. Sponza, *Italian immigrants in nineteenth-century Britain* (1988) · Highgate cemetery register, Grave no. 23466

Archives Sci. Mus., Negretti and Zambra

Likenesses photographs, repro. in *ILN* · photographs, repro. in *Quarterly Journal of the Meteorological Society*

Wealth at death under £60,000: probate, 17 Oct 1879, *CGPLA Eng. & Wales*

Arthur George Negus (1903–1985), by unknown photographer

Negus, Arthur George (1903–1985), antiques expert and broadcaster, was born on 29 March 1903 in Reading, Berkshire, the only child of Arthur George Negus (d. 1920), cabinet-maker, from Huntingdonshire, and his wife, Amy Julia Worsley (d. 1925). He left Reading School in 1920 to join his father in his business making and restoring furniture. His father also owned a small shop, attached to his workshop, where he sold pieces of antique furniture, and when he died, ten months later, Negus took over the shop and began to go to auction sales, building up a business as an antique dealer. In 1926 he married Irene (Queenie) Amy Hollett (b. 1908); they had two daughters.

Negus later worked for Reading Fine Art Galleries, travelling round England buying antique furniture, but after the beginning of the Second World War the showrooms were requisitioned, and he joined the police war reserve in 1941, spending the war as a clerk in the Criminal Investigation Department. In 1946 he joined Bruton Knowles & Co., a firm of fine art auctioneers and estate agents in Gloucester, taking charge of the antique furniture side of the business. There he worked as an appraiser, and prepared the catalogues for auction sales in private houses. He became a partner in 1972.

When John Irving, a producer with the west region of the BBC in Bristol, had the idea for an antiques quiz on television, Negus, well known in the west of England for his skill in valuation, was asked in 1965 to take part as one of the resident experts in the first series of *Going for a Song*, in which two 'customers' competed in identifying and valuing objects which had been secretly valued by the two experts. An instant success, the series was transferred to national television later that year. Although Negus thought it was so popular because the participants often discussed quite inexpensive objects, which the viewers might have at home, it was Negus himself who was the real reason for its success. His enthusiasm and affable manner endeared him to viewers, and he was able to talk in an interesting and authoritative way about a wide variety of objects, even though he only claimed to have any expertise in English period furniture. Audience surveys showed that the only criticism of the show concerned the 'customers', who often did not know very much, and so did not contribute to the interest of the programme. *Going for a Song* ran until 1977. It was soon joined in 1966 by *Talking about Antiques* on the Home Service (later Radio 4) of the BBC, in which Arthur Negus and Bernard Price described and discussed photographs of antiques sent in by listeners. The *Antiques Roadshow*, in which he took part until 1983, travelled around the country discussing antiques, and became even more popular than *Going for a Song*. Other television shows included *Pride of Place* in 1966, in which he visited houses such as Hardwick Hall, Corsham Court, and Saltram House, describing the contents, while John Betjeman talked about the architecture, and *On the Road*, where he travelled in a yellow Rolls-Royce along old mail-coach routes such as that from London to York. He made many programmes in the *Collector's World* series on such topics as furniture restoration, longcase clocks, and the history of the chair. Although at first he turned down invitations such as one in 1966 to join *Call my Bluff* on the grounds that he had a business to run, he soon became a well-known television personality, making guest appearances in *The Two Ronnies* and *The Generation Game*. He was equally popular with radio audiences, and gave frequent talks on *Woman's Hour*. A guest on *Desert Island Discs* in 1967, he chose Ralph Edwards's *Dictionary of English Furniture* as his one luxury. Although he had never spoken in public before 1965, he was soon much in demand, and gave talks all over the British Isles.

Negus published *Going for a Song: English Furniture* (1969; 5th edn 1977), and his autobiography, *A Life Among Antiques* (1982). It was largely through him that the world of antiques was opened up to ordinary people, who were inspired to search in their own attics for treasures. He became a freeman of the City of London in 1976, and in 1982 he was appointed OBE. Arthur Negus died on 5 April 1985 at his home, 31 Queens Court, Queens Road, Cheltenham.   ANNE PIMLOTT BAKER

Sources A. Negus, *A life among antiques* (1982) · A. Negus, *Going for a song: English furniture* (1969) · *The Times* (8 April 1985) · files, BBC WAC, M 31/2, 208/1; M 26/140/1; WE 8/44313; SU 3/10/1; R 73/369/1 · *WWW*
Archives BBC WAC | Glos. RO, corresp. with Burton, Knowles & Co., auctioneers and estate agents, relating to antiques | FILM BBC WAC
Likenesses photograph, Hult. Arch. [*see illus.*] · photographs, repro. in A. Negus, *Life among antiques*, pp. 45, 54–5, 109
Wealth at death £95,027: probate, 24 July 1985, CGPLA Eng. & Wales

Negus, Francis (*bap.* **1670**, *d.* **1732**), soldier and courtier, was born in the parish of St Paul's, Covent Garden, and baptized on 3 May 1670, the eldest son of Francis Negus and his wife, Elianore Boone. His father was surveyor of the mews and, in 1685–8, secretary to the duke of Norfolk. In 1687 Negus was appointed ensign in the Holland regiment (subsequently the Buffs), and by 1694 had risen to the rank of major. He served under William III in Flanders, where he was taken prisoner, and in the expedition of 1702 to Vigo and Cadiz. The following year he was appointed brevet lieutenant-colonel by Marlborough.

In 1704 Negus married Elizabeth, daughter of William Churchill. In 1717 he succeeded his father-in-law as MP for Ipswich and served until his death in 1732. He also held several prestigious court positions. In 1715 he was appointed joint commissioner and, two years later, sole commissioner, for executing the office of master of the horse, a position which he held until the death of George I. He was appointed avener and clerk-martial to George II in June 1727 and master of his majesty's buckhounds a month later. He was ranger of Swinley Chace, lieutenant and deputy warden of Windsor Forest, one of the commissioners of the lieutenancy of Middlesex, and a freeman of Westminster.

Negus is reputed to have popularized, and given his name to, a concoction of wine (originally port wine), hot water, and sugar. On one occasion he is said to have prevented a discussion between a number of prominent whigs and tories from becoming an ugly dispute by diluting the wine in this manner. Thereafter the mixture was nicknamed 'negus'. The name probably arose from Negus's custom of inviting the junior officers to take wine with him. His concoction became fashionable in the regiment and, as a compliment to their colonel, was named after him. A near contemporary, Thomas Vernon (1704–1753) of Ashton, recommended negus highly: 'After a morning's walk, half a pint of white wine, made hot and sweetened a little, is recond very good. Col. Negus, a gent of tast, advises it, I have heard say' (*N&Q*, 1st ser., 10). Negus died at his seat at Dallinghoo, Suffolk, on 9 September 1732. On his death, verses appeared in the *Ipswich Gazette*, commencing 'Is Negus gone? Ah! Ipswich, weep and mourn'.

Samuel Negus (*fl.* **1724**), printer, who was probably a poor relative of Francis Negus, in 1724 published a list of printing houses in the City of London and Westminster. On the strength of this, and possibly through the patronage of Francis, he was given a letter-carrier's position in the Post Office.

THOMAS SECCOMBE, *rev.* CHRISTINE CLARK

Sources J. Haydn, *The book of dignities: containing lists of the official personages of the British empire*, ed. H. Ockerby, [new edn] (1890) · *GM*, 1st ser., 2 (1732) · *GM*, 1st ser., 69 (1799) · *N&Q*, 10 (1854), 10 · *N&Q*, 6th ser., 11 (1885), 189 · Dr Doran, *London in the Jacobite times*, 2 vols. (1877) · HoP, *Commons*

Negus, Samuel (*fl.* **1724**). *See under* Negus, Francis (*bap.* 1670, *d.* 1732).

Negus, Sir Victor Ewings (**1887–1974**), laryngologist, was born on 6 February 1887 in Tooting, London, the third son of a solicitor, William Negus (*d.* 1924/5), lieutenant for the county of Surrey, and his wife, Emily, *née* Ewings (*d.* 1939). Educated at King's College School and King's College, he entered King's College Hospital in 1909 with a Sambrooke exhibition and qualified MRCS, LRCP in 1912. Earlier in 1912 he had been usher in Westminster Abbey at the funeral of Lord Lister. Influenced as a student by St Clair Thomson, the renowned otorhinolaryngologist, he completed his house appointments at the old King's College Hospital in the Strand and, no doubt on St Clair Thomson's recommendation, became a clinical assistant to Charles Hope and Lionel Colledge at the Hospital for Diseases of the Throat, Golden Square. At the outbreak of the First World War he joined the Royal Army Medical Corps and saw action as a regimental medical officer to a machine-gun battalion in the first battle of Ypres. This left

Sir Victor Ewings Negus (1887–1974), by Elliott & Fry, 1956

him with tinnitus throughout his life. He was posted with the 3rd Lahore division to Mesopotamia in 1916, and was awarded the Mons star, and mentioned in dispatches.

Negus graduated MB BS (London) in 1921 and a year later gained the FRCS and became house surgeon at the Hospital for Diseases of the Throat. His developing interest in laryngology was enhanced by study with Emil-Jean Moure in Bordeaux, and Chevalier Jackson in Philadelphia, before he joined St Clair Thomson's department at King's College Hospital as clinical assistant. Here, with the collaboration of a Mr Schranz, of the Genito-Urinary Company in London, he redesigned Chevalier Jackson's endoscopes and tracheostomy tubes. Negus's instruments have since been in use throughout the world.

Negus's work on the evolution, development, and comparative anatomy of the larynx won him in 1924 the gold medal in the MS examination of the University of London, and the John Hunter medal for 1925-7. It was published in 1929 as *Mechanisms of the Larynx*. He was appointed junior surgeon at King's in 1924, surgeon in 1931, senior surgeon in 1940, and consulting surgeon in 1946. At the Royal College of Surgeons (RCS) he was Arris and Gale lecturer in 1924 and Hunterian professor in 1925, was co-opted as a member of council to represent otorhinolaryngology in 1947, and was a member of the court of examiners and one of the first examiners in the special fellowship in otorhinolaryngology. A president of the Listerian Society from 1939 to 1941, he was awarded the Lister medal in 1954. Negus was granted the fellowship of King's College in 1945 at the conclusion of the Second World War, during

which he served in the Emergency Medical Service at Horton Hospital, Epsom. A member of numerous otolaryngological societies at home and overseas, Negus was elected president of the Thoracic Society (1949–50), of the section of laryngology of the Royal Society of Medicine (1942), and of the British Association of Otorhinolaryngologists (1951). He presided over the International Congress of Otolaryngology in 1949 and the 1954 annual meeting of the Collegium Oto-rhino-laryngologicum Amicitiae Sacrum, both held in London. He served as honorary treasurer of the collegium for 20 years. He was an honorary FRCS of Edinburgh and of Ireland. Negus was knighted in 1956.

His early interest in the larynx was later developed by Negus into an interest in the function of the nose in olfaction and respiration. This work was stimulated by the retrieval of elements of the Onodi collection, held in the Hunterian Museum of the RCS, which had been largely destroyed by bombing in 1941. Adolf Onodi of Budapest demonstrated his anatomical preparations of the accessory sinuses to a meeting of the Society of Hungarian Ear and Throat Specialists in 1900. These were later acquired by the RCS and were classified by Thomas (Tubby) Layton of Guy's Hospital in 1934. Negus not only sought to replace the human collection but also added a comparative animal collection. The results of this work, which was largely undertaken while he was at the Ferens Institute of the Middlesex Hospital (1952–62), were published in 1958 in his book *Comparative Anatomy and Physiology of the Nose and Paranasal Sinuses*. The *Biology of Respiration* appeared in 1965. In addition to his research books Negus joined his mentor Sir St Clair Thomson in producing the fourth edition of his *Diseases of the Nose and Throat*, published in 1937. Thomson died before the publication of the fifth edition in 1948, but his contribution was fully acknowledged by Negus, who published the sixth edition alone in 1955. This book, which is still used for reference, was Negus's major literary contribution to clinical medicine.

On leaving the council of the RCS in 1954 Negus became involved as a trustee of the Hunterian collection; later catalogues of the surviving Hunterian specimens were published under his chairmanship. He also wrote *The History of the Hunterian Trustees* (1965) and *The Artistic Possessions at the Royal College of Surgeons of England* (1967). For this work and for his distinction in laryngology Negus was awarded the honorary gold medal of the RCS in 1969.

Negus was no less energetic when not at work. He played tennis to the age of seventy and in winter he regularly played golf against the staff and students at King's and later at the Middlesex Hospital. He loved to contribute scripts in doggerel verse for the medical students' Christmas shows. He was hardly ever beaten at billiards and had a passion for salmon fishing. In 1939 he moved to Haslemere, Surrey, where he enjoyed gardening and in particular felling trees. In the early 1950s he, as was fashionable among surgeons at the time, acquired a farm. It progressively became too much for him and he gradually reduced his commitments, spending his last years in a flat in Hindhead.

Negus was a friend and adviser to his young assistants. His advice was carefully considered and reliable in the long term, although not everybody realized it at the time, and some thought it unprogressive. He was keen that his trainees should earn their apprenticeship, as he believed that the harder path would in the end achieve a fuller life and greater satisfaction. He was naturally rather gloomy and did not suffer fools gladly. He was very much a teaching hospital man. This exterior, however, concealed kindness and a droll sense of humour.

On 14 January 1929 Negus married Winifred Adelaide Gladys (Eve; 1901–1979), daughter of Robert Rennie, an engineer. She accompanied him throughout the world and illustrated his many books. They had two sons, one of whom, David, became a consultant surgeon. Negus died at his home, 4 Nutcombe Height, Hindhead, Surrey, on 15 July 1974. His body was cremated at Guildford crematorium on 18 July.   NEIL WEIR

Sources E. H. Cornelius and S. F. Taylor, *Lives of the fellows of the Royal College of Surgeons of England, 1974–1982* (1988) • *The Times* (17 July 1974) • *BMJ* (27 July 1974) • *The Lancet* (27 July 1974), 234–5 • private information (2004) • m. cert. • d. cert. • *WWW* • *Medical Directory* (1962)
Archives RCS Eng., memoirs, mainly of First World War
Likenesses Elliott & Fry, photograph, 1956, NPG [*see illus.*] • C. G. Fletcher, photograph, 1965 • A. John, pastel sketch, priv. coll.
Wealth at death £5756: probate, 4 Sept 1974, *CGPLA Eng. & Wales*

Negus, William (*c.*1559–1616), Church of England clergyman, was possibly related to the unidentified Marian exile Richard Nagors, who subscribed to the new discipline in Frankfurt in April 1557. Negus matriculated as a sizar from Trinity College, Cambridge, at Easter 1573, graduated BA in 1578, and is next found in Ipswich early in 1584, having accepted the position of assistant town preacher. By June that year he had joined the conference of ministers in the Stour valley known to posterity as the Dedham classis.

Differences had already arisen between Negus and Robert Norton, common preacher of Ipswich, probably because Negus objected to Norton's holding the rectory of Aldeburgh, Suffolk, along with his preachership. The town was soon riven by factional strife, and by October Negus had been suspended by the bishop of Norwich, Edmund Freake. While in London in February 1585 to petition (successfully) for restoration to his ministry, Negus was offered the rectory of Leigh, Essex, by Robert, third Lord Rich. Although his Dedham colleagues urged him to remain in Ipswich if reasonable terms could be negotiated, Negus accepted Rich's offer and was instituted to Leigh by John Aylmer, bishop of London, on 31 March 1585.

While never cited in the Essex archdeaconry court for nonconformity Negus spent the rest of his life parrying the triennial visitations of five successive bishops of London. In July 1586 John Aylmer suspended him for refusing to state categorically that he would wear the surplice if one were provided. Negus's own account of the interview survives, along with a petition from his parishioners that he would not desert them for 'such a trifle', particularly since they understood that the surplice was enjoined only

'at some times' and that he would 'not be urged any further' (Peel, 1.274–5).

Yet Negus never abandoned the path of ritual nonconformity. In 1589 he was again admonished to wear the surplice by Aylmer's visitors. In 1604, with James I demanding subscription to Whitgift's articles as the badge of inclusion within the Church of England, he was probably suspended by Richard Bancroft, for he stated in court on 22 March 1605 that he remained unsatisfied about 'the lawfulness and expediency' of the ceremonies (LMA, DL/C/618, 250). Restored in January 1606 by the more sympathetic Richard Vaughan, Negus then clashed with Vaughan's successor, Thomas Ravis, in late 1607. Summoned before Ravis in December, he wrote a letter pleading illness which was handed in by Ezekiel Culverwell. His case was nevertheless transferred to high commission, and with three other Essex clergy, including Culverwell, Negus was finally deprived of his benefice at Lambeth on 20 March 1609.

Negus lived on in Leigh and died there in January 1616; he was buried in Leigh church on the 8th. His original will, dated 16 August 1615 and proved on 4 March 1616, survives (Essex RO). After a bequest of £3 6s. 8d. to the poor of Leigh, his remaining assets went to his sons, Samuel, Joseph, and Jonathan, and his daughter, Mary. The bulk of his evidently extensive library—including 'written notes appurtaining to my studies and scholarly exercises'—was bequeathed to Jonathan, then a Cambridge undergraduate. Joseph was appointed executor in the absence of Samuel, 'now at sea'. John Simmes, Negus's successor as rector of Leigh, was appointed overseer, receiving his copy of Foxe's book of martyrs 'as a pledge of my love and brotherly affection towards him'.

In 1619 Jonathan Negus, later vicar of Prittlewell, Essex, published his father's only known work, *Man's Active Obedience, or, The Power of Godliness*, with a dedication to Sir Thomas Smythe (or Smith), the governor of the East India Company, and prefaces by Simmes and Stephen Egerton. Since the dedication alludes to Smythe's 'good affection and respect' for William Negus and the 'liberal allowance' granted for some years to Jonathan, it has been surmised that Smythe, cousin by marriage of Ezekiel Culverwell, subsidized Jonathan's studies at King's.

                                                                          BRETT USHER

Sources Venn, *Alum. Cant.*, 1/3.240 • C. H. Garrett, *The Marian exiles: a study in the origins of Elizabethan puritanism* (1938) • P. Collinson, *The Elizabethan puritan movement* (1967) • K. Fincham, *Prelate as pastor: the episcopate of James I* (1990) • R. G. Usher, ed., *The presbyterian movement in the reign of Queen Elizabeth, as illustrated by the minute book of the Dedham classis, 1582–1589*, CS, 3rd ser., 8 (1905) • N. Bacon, *The annalls of Ipswche*, ed. W. H. Richardson (1884) • A. Peel, ed., *The seconde parte of a register*, 2 vols. (1915) • N. Tyacke, *The fortunes of English puritanism, 1603–1640* (1990) • London diocesan call books of visitation, 1586–1607, GL, MS 9537/6–10 • London diocesan act books of office, 1605–9, LMA, DL/C/304–7, 618 • Essex RO, D/ABW 27/225 [orig. will] • parish records, Leigh, Essex
Wealth at death under £500: will, Essex RO

Nehru, Jawaharlal (1889–1964), prime minister of India, was born in Allahabad on 14 November 1889, the eldest child of the lawyer and politician Motilal *Nehru (1861–

Jawaharlal Nehru (1889–1964), by Yousuf Karsh, 1956

1931), and of his second wife, Swarup Rani. He had two younger sisters, the elder of whom was Vijayalakshmi *Pandit (1900–1990). Nehru was doted on by his parents and brought up in luxury.

Education, marriage, and early career From his mother Nehru learned Hindu legend and folklore, while a Muslim retainer told him stories of the uprising of 1857. But his father wanted for him the best that British education could offer and in 1905 took him to England and had him admitted to Harrow School. Joe Nehru, as he was known, was a good pupil but not specially distinguished in any way. After two years he moved to Trinity College, Cambridge, where again he made no mark. In 1910 he obtained a second class in part one of the natural sciences tripos and joined the Inner Temple. On being called to the bar in 1912 he returned to India and for the next four years led an aimless life in Allahabad. He accompanied his father to the high court but had no interest in a legal career. In politics, too, he had no deep involvement.

Nehru married in Delhi on 8 February 1916 a bride selected by his father. Kamala (c.1899–1936), daughter of Jawaharmal Kaul, the owner of a flour mill in Delhi, was a Kashmiri Brahman, as was Nehru—hence the caste honorific pandit (Brahman), which was often used but which he disliked. Ten years younger than her husband, Kamala lacked a Western education and in the Nehru household felt bitterly conscious of her inadequacies. In November 1917 a daughter, Indira [see Gandhi, Indira], was born. Kamala's health was poor, and by 1920 she showed incipient signs of tuberculosis.

In June 1914 Nehru was drawn into active politics by Annie Besant. His first public speech was to protest against the demand that Mrs Besant give pecuniary security for good behaviour under the Press Act. He withdrew his application to join the Indian Defence Force, constituted on the lines of the Territorial Army, and became one of the secretaries of the Home Rule League in Allahabad. He also helped to run *The Independent*, the newspaper started by his father in 1918 to express the viewpoint of the Indian National Congress.

Nationalist leader In 1919, when Mahatma Gandhi launched his campaign of civil disobedience, Nehru at last found a cause meriting his full dedication. Gandhi seemed to offer effective leadership in contrast to other Indian politicians. The response of British public opinion to the shooting of an unarmed crowd in Amritsar in April 1919 cast doubt on British goals for India, and the worth of the proposed constitutional reforms. Nehru accepted without reserve Gandhi's moral preoccupations and, though he later moved away from many of them, the deep personal bond between him and Gandhi remained unbroken until Gandhi's death in 1948.

In 1920 Nehru by chance found himself involved in peasant unrest in the United Provinces, his home province. He encouraged the peasants to organize themselves and formulate their demands. He was impressed by their stoicism, though he was not as yet fully aware of their economic wretchedness. In December 1921 he was arrested for unlawful activity and, though sentenced to prison for six months, was released after three months on technical grounds. Baffled by Gandhi's having called off civil disobedience in February 1922, after a mob had caused the deaths of several constables by setting fire to a police station, he yet remained a loyal campaigner and organized spinning, boycott, and picketing in his province. In May 1922 he was back in prison, this time for eight months. Released in January 1923 through a general amnesty in the province, he found the Congress divided, with his father the leader of a group wishing to return to electoral politics and Gandhi opposed to this strategy. His inclinations were with Gandhi and, torn by the conflict of loyalties, he supported the compromise which permitted members to contest the elections to the legislative council without leaving the party. Drawn against his will into municipal politics, he won widespread respect during his two years as chairman of the Allahabad municipal board from April 1923. In December 1923 he was appointed a general secretary of the Congress.

Kamala lost an infant son in 1924 and her health was deteriorating. So in March 1926 Nehru accompanied her to Europe with their daughter to seek medical treatment, and settled in Geneva. Kamala's health showed little improvement, but Nehru took advantage of his stay to read widely and to make contact with left-wing movements in Europe. In February 1927 he attended, as the representative of the Indian National Congress, the International Congress against Colonial Oppression and Imperialism in Brussels. He now gave emphasis to the economic side of imperialism, developed contacts with nationalists in China and Latin America, and gained an international perspective. Joined by his father, in November 1927 he visited the Soviet Union, where he was impressed especially by what he saw of rural reconstruction and the fight against illiteracy.

In November 1927 Nehru returned to India with pronounced radical views and, at the December session of the Congress, forced through a resolution proclaiming independence rather than dominion status as India's objective. He also formed the Independence for India League as a pressure group within the Congress to work for political freedom and economic change. But both the resolution and the League amounted to little. Nehru was more effective in organizing a boycott of the statutory (Simon) commission appointed (without any Indian members) by the British government to consider the working of the 1919 constitutional reforms. At Lucknow in November 1928 Nehru, participating in a procession protesting against the arrival of the commission, was beaten up by the police. He also found time during this year, while wandering around the country, to try to educate his daughter by writing to her about the early history of humanity. These letters were published in 1929 as *Letters from a Father to his Daughter*.

In November 1929 Nehru presided over the annual session of the All-India Trade Union Congress at Nagpur and the next month at Lahore over the annual session of the Congress, which was now, after a year's notice, committed to independence and civil disobedience. In his presidential address he asserted that he was a republican and a socialist, and would like the Congress to commit itself to ending the domination of any class; but he recognized that the immediate task was to acquire political power.

Civil disobedience, gaol, and Indian independence Early in 1930 Congress again launched a non-violent campaign of resistance under Gandhi's leadership. Its initial thrust was against the official salt monopoly. Nehru took charge of the civil disobedience campaign to manufacture salt in Allahabad district and sold packets of contraband salt. In April 1930 he was arrested and sentenced to simple imprisonment for six months. Lodged in Naini gaol, he was released in October but was arrested again after a week and sentenced to rigorous imprisonment for two years plus five months in default of fines. In prison again, he took up the writing of letters to his daughter, tracing the history of humanity.

In January 1931 Nehru was released, along with other leading Congressmen, to facilitate the effort at a settlement between Gandhi and the viceroy, Lord Irwin. Bereft of the support of his father, who died on 6 February 1931, he was disillusioned with the terms of the truce reached in March 1931. But he loyally accepted Gandhi's decision and devoted his attention to the agrarian crisis caused by the current economic depression in the United Provinces. The harassment or eviction of tenants by Indian landlords for their inability to pay rents led him to consider a no-rent campaign. He was arrested in December 1931 and sentenced to imprisonment for two years.

In gaol, mostly at Dehra Dun, Nehru recommenced writing to his daughter; the letters were published in 1933 as *Glimpses of World History*. He was released in August 1933, but arrested in February 1934 for sedition and sentenced to simple imprisonment for two years. Lodged first in a prison in Calcutta and then shifted to Dehra Dun gaol, he was released for eleven days in August 1934 as Kamala's health had worsened. He was then taken to Almora gaol, which was near the sanatorium to which she had been admitted. He wrote in these months his autobiography, which was published in 1936 and became a best-seller in Britain.

In May 1935 Kamala proceeded to Europe for treatment and, her condition becoming critical, Nehru's sentence was suspended to enable him to join her. She died at Lausanne on 28 February 1936. Elected in his absence as president of the Congress, Nehru returned to India to lead the party in the elections to the newly powerful provincial legislatures created by the Government of India Act of 1935. He campaigned throughout the country, travelling over 50,000 miles in five months, presided over the sessions of the Congress at Lucknow in April and at Faizpur in December 1936, and did more than any other individual to ensure an overall Congress victory. But he did not favour the acceptance of office which followed in eight provinces.

In the summer of 1938 Nehru visited the republican side of the battle-front in the Spanish Civil War, met politicians of all parties in Britain, and declined to meet Nazi officials in Germany, but went to Prague to demonstrate solidarity with the Czech government in their resistance to Hitler. The next year he visited China. The only activity within India at this time which gave him satisfaction was the chairmanship of the national planning committee set up by the Congress. He regarded this work as paving the way for the creation of a socialist economy within a democratic structure in free India. His priorities created tensions with other Congressmen, and with Gandhi himself; but Nehru was not prepared to divide the Congress on 'socialist' issues.

On the outbreak of war in September 1939 Nehru's sympathy was with the allies, and he was eager that Britain should make it possible for the Indian people to join the war against fascism. But the expected response was not forthcoming. Instead, he was arrested in October 1940 for anti-imperialist speeches and sentenced to imprisonment for four years. In Dehra Dun gaol he started to write a second volume of his autobiography, but this was later incorporated into an analysis of India's past. In December 1941 he was released following an official decision to release all political prisoners. In March 1942 he was the principal spokesman of the Congress in discussions with Sir Stafford Cripps, who went to Delhi as the emissary of the British cabinet to seek to end the political deadlock and to gain Indian political co-operation in the war. Nehru was keen on a settlement which would enable the Congress to co-operate in the war effort, but the Cripps mission was a failure. Thereafter Nehru was unable to prevent a collision between the Congress and the government. Gandhi planned a Quit India movement of renewed civil disobedience, and on 9 August 1942 Nehru, along with other senior Congress leaders, was arrested. The Congress working committee was detained at Ahmednagar Fort without communication with the outside world. Here Nehru completed *The Discovery of India* (1946), a survey of India's history emphasizing the composite culture which in his view had held the country together over the years. He was released on 15 June 1945. He had spent altogether almost nine years in prison.

In the subsequent negotiations for the transfer of power from British to Indian hands, with M. A. Jinnah and the Muslim League now claiming a separate homeland for India's Muslims, Nehru hoped that, if the right to secede were granted, the Muslims would shed their fears and not in fact exercise that right. But the situation increasingly seemed to be one of insoluble conflict and escalating violence. In September 1946 Nehru became vice-president of the executive council in the provisional government. He held the external affairs portfolio and in that capacity he convened in March 1947 at New Delhi an Asian relations conference to enable the leaders of Asia to come together. (Here he asserted that a free India would develop an active concern in world affairs and would pursue an independent policy compatible with her own national interests. Self-respect demanded consideration of every issue on its merits and commitments only to the principles of anti-colonialism and racial equality and to the promotion of peace.) The provisional government meanwhile was unable to function normally once the representatives of the Muslim League joined it, and Nehru and the Congress recognized that partition of the country had become inevitable. (The degree of inevitability, the nature of Muslim demands, and Congress's response remain one of the most disputed aspects of India's recent history, however.) He worked closely with the last viceroy, Earl Mountbatten of Burma, and in May 1947 he persuaded Mountbatten to revise his current plan and avoid the danger of India being fragmented. The two dominions of India and Pakistan came into being on 15 August 1947. Mountbatten stayed on in India as governor-general. Lady Mountbatten became Nehru's close friend and, until her death in January 1960, helped to mitigate his loneliness.

Prime minister of India Nehru was sworn in as prime minister in 1947 and held the office until his death. His first task was to subdue the turbulence in India caused by the large-scale massacres and migrations which followed partition. The climax of communal violence was the assassination of Mahatma Gandhi by a Hindu fanatic in January 1948. Nehru denounced Hindu chauvinist feeling and insisted that in a free India Muslims should be treated as equal citizens.

Relations with Pakistan were also tense. The ruler of Kashmir, a former princely state, delayed acceding to either India or Pakistan. To force the issue, tribesmen from Pakistan entered the state and advanced on Srinagar, the capital. The ruler now acceded to India and Indian troops were flown out to push back the tribesmen. Nehru secured the appointment of Sheikh Abdullah, a popular leader with secular views, as chief minister. He also offered to hold a plebiscite, after law and order had been restored, to ascertain the views of the people on the future of Kashmir, and referred the issue of Pakistan's perceived aggression to the United Nations. Although disappointed by the failure of the Security Council to reach a quick decision, Nehru agreed on 31 December 1948 to the ceasefire suggested by a commission sent out by the United Nations. This left a third of Kashmir in Pakistan's hands.

In August 1953, on Sheikh Abdullah's own position vacillating in favour of an independent Kashmir, Nehru permitted him to be dismissed and subsequently imprisoned. Nehru reconciled himself to the holding of a plebiscite and the possible loss of Kashmir to Pakistan, but reversed his position in 1954, when Pakistan concluded a military alliance with the United States. Nehru's contention was that this brought the cold war to south Asia and that Pakistan was seeking to settle the issue with superior American arms. Nehru was of Kashmiri descent himself, but many Indians recognized that the issue of Kashmir, and its presence with a Muslim majority in the Indian Union, was a vital and visible proof that India was a secular and not a Hindu state.

Nehru saw the political advantages of India remaining in the Commonwealth, and in April 1949 persuaded the Commonwealth prime ministers to agree to continued Indian membership even after she became a republic on 26 January 1950. Nehru found the Commonwealth a useful multiracial association for the exchange of views, and he resisted demands in India from time to time, and especially during the Suez crisis in 1956, that India withdraw from the Commonwealth. In 1961 he was among those responsible for securing South Africa's withdrawal by warning of the dangers of the Commonwealth disintegrating if apartheid were tolerated.

Foreign policy and non-alignment Nehru established diplomatic relations with the Soviet Union and appointed his sister Vijayalakshmi Pandit as India's first envoy to the USSR. He did not align India with either the United States or the Soviet Union, but at the start his sympathy was with the Western powers. In September 1948 he conveyed to the United States that there was not the least chance of India lining up with the Soviet Union in war or in peace. In October 1949 he visited the United States and emphasized repeatedly that detachment in the cold war did not imply indifference on basic issues such as freedom, justice, and aggression. He was well liked by the American public, but his discussions with President Truman and senior officials at Washington, where Vijayalakshmi Pandit was now ambassador, were not fruitful. Relations were soured by what Nehru regarded as the American tilt towards Pakistan and by American dislike of Nehru's support for the recognition of the People's Republic of China.

Nehru's sponsorship of mainland China was not born of any sentimental pan-Asian considerations. He thought that China's admission to the United Nations would make it easier for her to function normally in world affairs rather than as an outlaw state. Containment through friendship was also for India a preferable alternative to heavy expenditure incurred in building defences in the Himalayas. When, in 1950, China occupied Tibet, Nehru protested because he felt that India, while recognizing China's suzerainty over Tibet, had a right to express an interest in the maintenance of Tibet's autonomy. On China objecting to such intervention, Nehru avoided an open breach and discouraged the Dalai Lama from fleeing to India. In 1954 he concluded a treaty with China providing for the abandonment by India of all extra-territorial privileges in Tibet. But he missed the opportunity this provided for securing Chinese recognition of what was now a long common boundary defined for the most part, in India's view, by custom, usage, and tradition. To the Soviet Union Nehru was driven closer by circumstances. He tried to keep the problem of Kashmir out of the cold war; but from January 1952 the Soviet Union exercised its veto in the Security Council on all resolutions on Kashmir which were slanted against India. Nehru visited China in September 1954 and the Soviet Union in June 1955. He found his hosts eager to please, but Nehru retained his critical sense.

This non-aligned approach provided Nehru in the 1950s with a pivotal role in the world. His leadership enabled India to arrange in 1953 for the repatriation of prisoners taken in the Korean War and to implement the peace settlements in Indo-China in 1954. He was forthright in opposing racial discrimination in Africa and resisted, in all ways short of war, attempts to hold on to empire or to promote domination by settlers. He gave the lead at the Asian–African Conference at Bandung in Indonesia in April 1955 and facilitated the acceptance of the People's Republic of China by most of the participating countries. Relations with the United States also improved at the time of the Suez crisis in October 1956, when both India and the United States condemned the Anglo-French invasion of Egypt. In December 1956 he visited Washington, and, despite the feeling that he had been tardy in condemning Soviet action in Hungary, he was given a warm welcome by President Eisenhower.

Parliamentary democracy Within India, Nehru's main achievement was the establishment on firm grounds of parliamentary democracy. He made sure that the constitution which came into effect when India became a republic provided for adult suffrage, and toured the country incessantly to explain issues to a largely illiterate people and to teach them the value of the vote. In his time three general elections were held: in 1952, 1957, and 1962. He created the machinery of cabinet government and built up healthy traditions in the two houses of parliament. He strengthened a free press and enabled the judiciary to function with independence and full authority to protect the fundamental rights laid down in the constitution. Under Nehru's guidance India transformed herself from a traditional and passive into an open and participant society.

To buttress the parliamentary system at the local level Nehru elaborated schemes of community development and planned the setting up in all groups of villages of a council, a co-operative, and a school. In October 1952 fifty-five community projects covering about 17,000 villages were inaugurated; and in 1953 national extension services

to provide trained workers were set up. By 1956 community development covered over a quarter of rural India. This policy did not succeed in improving the economic condition or strengthening the self-reliance of the peasant, but it helped in promoting political awareness.

In building a democratic system, Nehru utilized the Indian National Congress, which had a network of committees and cadres reaching down to every town and village. His relations with the deputy prime minister, Vallabhbhai Patel, were not without friction, but after Patel's death in December 1950 Nehru repulsed a challenge from within the party in 1951 to his secular approach. He was president of the party from 1951 to 1954, and even thereafter his control of the Congress was unquestioned. Throughout his years as prime minister the party was in office at the centre and, except for the two years 1957 to 1959 in the southern state of Kerala, in all the provinces. So relations between the central and the state governments caused Nehru no problems. He allowed the Congress parties in the states to choose their leaders and permitted these chief ministers to exercise autonomy. He utilized the Congress as a cementing force and to secure wide support for his policies. He himself functioned as a national rather than as a party leader. His bona fides were accepted by left-wing parties, and after 1951, when the Indian Communist Party renounced violent methods and agreed to work the parliamentary system, Nehru, approving of many of the party's objectives, permitted it to function and in 1957 to form a ministry in Kerala after it had secured a majority in the elections. He dismissed it two years later with reluctance as he believed that it had lost popular support, but he did not regard the Communist Party with its new tactics as posing a threat to the democratic process. On the right he regarded the Conservative Party which was formed in 1959 with contempt. The only political party which he regarded as threatening the unity of India was the Hindu Communal Party, and he gave it no quarter.

In internal administration Nehru had to act against his will in 1956, when he was obliged by public opinion to agree to the redrawing of provincial boundaries on the basis of languages. He regarded this as a marginal problem which merited low priority, but saw that the passions roused in all parts of the country by the love of local languages would, if not appeased, weaken the sense of community in India. He also gave way on the question of the continuation of English as an all-India language. While himself fluent in English and a sensitive writer of English prose, he believed that Hindi, spoken over a large part of northern India, and not English, known only to a small minority, should be the language linking the whole country. He therefore favoured the gradual abandonment of the use of English as an official language and its study only as a second language. In line with this, the constitution of 1950 stated that English would be used as an official language, in addition to Hindi, only until 1965. But, faced with agitation in southern India against the imposition of Hindi, Nehru realized that it endangered Indian unity and recognized the fear of the non-Hindi-speaking people that a ban on English would handicap them in the search for employment. So in 1959 he pledged that there would be no imposition of any language by decree and English would remain an associate, additional language for an indefinite period; the final decision on the replacement of English by Hindi would rest with those sections of the Indian people who did not know Hindi as a local language. In 1963 he translated this assurance into permissive legislation, providing that English 'may' continue to be used after 1965, in addition to Hindi, for the official purposes of the Union and in parliament. He was unwilling to provide an explicit commitment that English would continue as an official language for ever, as this seemed to him unnecessary and even constitutionally improper; but he ensured that the protagonists of English need have no cause for concern. The use of English as an official and a linking language continues to this day.

Economic and social policy One of the greatest problems facing independent India was economic development. Nehru recognized that it was an essential condition of genuine national freedom, and the only way eventually to meet the legitimate aspirations of India's peoples. In the late 1930s he had begun to concern himself with planning for India's economic future, and in March 1950 he constituted a planning commission, and from 1951 initiated a series of five-year plans, considerably influenced by the Soviet example. The objective was to create a self-reliant, self-generating modern economy, with a strong public sector in heavy and strategic industries, and a regulated private sector. The plan was to produce capital goods and growth through industrialization and import substitution: the state was to play the dominant role, controlling strategic and basic production, but leaving some space in other areas for a tightly controlled private sector. Following his personal commitment to furthering 'the scientific temperament', Nehru also encouraged India's atomic industry and the harnessing of her great rivers for energy production through several large dam projects. This broad range of planning undoubtedly helped to transform the economy in a way the imperial government neither wished nor would have been able to do. It provided the technological base for industrial development, created the facilities required for modern manufacture, and in the first decades of independence greatly increased industrial production, consumption of energy, and access to a broader range of consumer goods. Simultaneously India developed its capacity for conventional defence and raised a large corps of scientists, engineers, and technicians, despite the heavily arts-oriented educational system inherited from the British raj. It soon became clear, however, that Nehru's economic strategy was failing to address problems of large-scale poverty and poor agricultural production, problems which in turn hampered industrial growth, limiting domestic savings and the home market, and making India even more dependent on foreign aid and food imports. Consequently, by the end of the 1950s a new emphasis was given to family planning, in response to a now rapidly increasing population, and to bolstering agricultural production by various means. In the longer term it also became evident that tight state control of the economy was hampering growth and producing what came to be known as a 'licence-permit raj'. In the late 1980s Nehru's grandson Rajiv Gandhi began dismantling the Nehruvian system, a process furthered by his successors in the 1990s after India's near international bankruptcy. However, it should be remembered that Nehru was dealing with the burdensome economic inheritance of an imperial regime at a time when the main examples of radical economic change and growth were the industrialization patterns of the Western world and of the Soviet Union, long before the dramatic successes of the export-led economies of south-east Asia in the later twentieth century provided alternative models.

Nehru's economic strategy emphasized growth rather than issues of distribution of goods and resources. However, in 1955 he committed the Congress to the creation of a 'socialistic pattern of society'. His socialism was always more an ethical pledge than a doctrinal belief, reflecting the need to raise standards of living and provide more equality of opportunity rather than to further any dogma. He had realized by the mid-1950s that industrial growth had to be accompanied by an increase in agricultural productivity. Part of this new concern for agriculture was his decision to promote service co-operatives in every village as a prelude to co-operative farming over the next three years. The latter part of his strategy petered out; and none of Nehru's rural plans really tackled the fundamental investment and technological constraints on agricultural production. One of India's essential rural problems was still that of radically unequal access to land. Nehru had expedited the abolition of the largest landed estates soon after 1947, but had not ensured that this was followed up by redistribution of land to the peasantry, with security of tenure. Here the democratic process itself proved a hindrance, as the powerful and landed sector contrived to block truly radical land reform.

On social reforms, too, Nehru did not act quickly and fully: again he was hampered by widespread social conservatism and vested interests. He secured the statutory abolition of untouchability in 1955, and made its public practice a criminal offence. But the law by itself was not enough to ensure equality and opportunities for the most deprived and degraded in Hindu society. He assiduously proclaimed the need for a 'scientific temper' in modern society, for the prevalence of reason and logic to ensure civilized behaviour. But, while he gave emphasis to the promotion of higher education and set up five institutes of technology and several national laboratories in various branches of pure and applied sciences, he failed to give priority to the directive in the constitution that free education should be provided by 1961 for every child up to the age of fourteen.

Entrenched obscurantism also stood in the way of the creation of the fully secular society to which Nehru attached prime importance. He wished religion to play no part in public life, and embedded this principle in the constitution. But his implementation of secular principles was incomplete. He failed to act, because of legal difficulties, on the resolution of 1948 of the constituent assembly banning political parties which exploited religion. He was opposed to the banning of cow slaughter, but allowed it to be included among the directive principles of state policy in the constitution. Above all, while in favour of a uniform civil law for all Indians as recommended in the constitution, he did not sponsor legislation imposing it. He had recognized from before independence the need to elevate the status of Indian women. But he did not wish to hurt the prejudices of Muslims immediately after partition by revising their personal laws. In 1951 he sponsored changes in the civil law only as regards Hindus. Monogamy was enforced on Hindu men, and rights of divorce, inheritance, and property were granted to Hindu women. But the lack of a uniform civil law in India has been a major hindrance to the development of an equal and secular society.

International relations From 1956, when Nehru's reputation in India and the world was at its peak, problems and relations with other countries became more pressing. Believing that China had accepted India's stand that her northern boundary was established and not negotiable, he was surprised at Chinese incursions at three points across the border between Tibet and the Indian province of Uttar Pradesh and by the building of a road traversing Aksai Chin in Kashmir which linked Sinkiang (Xinjiang) with western Tibet. Nehru regarded these not as unfriendly acts but as matters for discussion. But the problem broadened in March 1959 with his humanitarian act of granting asylum to the Dalai Lama, who fled to India from Tibet. China's vituperative criticisms were not toned down by Nehru's directive to the Dalai Lama to refrain from political activity. In September 1959 China asserted that the whole boundary was unsettled and claimed about 40,000 square miles of what India regarded as her territory in Kashmir and in the north-east. Nehru decided that this could no longer be a matter for confidential correspondence between governments and informed parliament. The public reaction was intense and limited Nehru's scope for manoeuvre. It also drew India closer to the United States, and President Eisenhower was received cordially when he visited Delhi in December 1959.

Nehru was convinced that India's boundary was a firm one, sanctified by history, but he was anxious to avoid hostilities with China and willing to negotiate any minor rectifications that she might desire. He invited the Chinese prime minister, Zhou Enlai, to Delhi, but their talks in April 1960 were inconclusive. Thereafter China stepped up her incursions. Nehru persisted in his policy of avoiding confrontation, sending out patrols and establishing posts in Indian forward areas not taken over by China, and awaiting negotiations for a final settlement. He acted on the assumptions that China would not mount a large-scale offensive and that, if she did, Indian armed forces would be able to resist effectively and that such a war between India and China would not be confined to the border areas and would involve other countries.

Nehru had prevailed on Zhou to agree to officials on both sides examining the evidence pertaining to the boundary; and in the time thus gained he was able to turn his attention to other problems. In September 1960 he visited Pakistan to sign the agreement which had been reached on the distribution of the Indus Canal waters. The public goodwill created by this visit could not be translated into progress on the Kashmir question. Nehru's proposal that the ceasefire line, with a few adjustments, be converted into an international frontier was not acceptable to Pakistan. Later that year he went to New York to attend the session of the general assembly of the United Nations and sought to promote talks between the United States and the Soviet Union on disarmament. He also supported the intervention of the United Nations in the Congo and, at a time when India needed her troops at home, dispatched, at the request of the secretary-general of the United Nations, a brigade to the Congo. This was testimony of both his belief that the United Nations was an indispensable international organization and his commitment to freedom in Africa.

In September 1961, at the Conference of the Non-Aligned Countries in Belgrade, Nehru's influence was the decisive factor in giving priority to the urgent issue of disarmament over the receding issue of colonization. He criticized the Soviet resumption of nuclear testing, and this dampened the enthusiasm of his hosts when he proceeded from Belgrade to Moscow. But he did prevail on the Soviet authorities to be more responsive to suggestions for nuclear disarmament. In November 1961 he went to the United States to meet President Kennedy. Their personal meeting was not a success. Nehru was uncertain of Kennedy's resolution and popular backing, while Kennedy felt that Nehru was aloof, indifferent, and tired. But the relations between the two countries continued to be cordial. At Kennedy's request Nehru used his influence in Hanoi and Moscow to secure a ceasefire in Laos.

On his return to India, Nehru was confronted with a crisis developing over the Portuguese settlement of Goa, in western India. After the British withdrawal from India in 1947 and the transfer of the French settlements in 1954, the only foreign possessions in India were the pockets of Portuguese territory. No solution short of merger with India was acceptable to Nehru, but he sought to secure a peaceful transfer and to avoid the use of force as long as possible. Now, with reports of increased Portuguese repression and fading hopes of internal revolt or international intervention, especially by the United States, Nehru sanctioned the occupation of Goa by Indian troops in December 1961. It weakened Nehru's standing abroad as a champion of peaceful methods.

In 1962 China, attaching no importance to the reports of the officials who assessed the evidence regarding the border, continued to spread into Kashmir, and in September made an incursion south of the boundary east of Bhutan, which had been formalized by a treaty in 1914. The next month her troops moved across both the western and the eastern sectors of the boundary in large numbers. Though the Soviet Union, involved in the Cuban crisis, expressed for the first time sympathy for the Chinese position, and

India appeared to be isolated, Nehru's morale was unshaken. He took direct charge of the defence portfolio and secured military supplies from western Europe and the United States. But to make it easier for the Soviet Union to revert to its earlier position friendly to India, he did not declare war on China or even break off diplomatic relations, refer the issue of Chinese aggression to the United Nations, or seek to form any military alliance. But his hopes of the Indian army drawing the Chinese onto the plains and holding them there were dashed. Indian resistance was instead offered on the mountain tops and was easily dispelled. In this critical situation, on 17 November he appealed to Kennedy for the dispatch of fighters to protect Indian cities from attack from the air, for assistance to the Indian Air Force in air battles, and for the loan of bombers to enable India to strike at Chinese bases and airfields. Kennedy promised to be as responsive as possible. But on 21 November the Chinese declared a unilateral ceasefire and withdrew from Indian territory in the eastern sector.

To Nehru the Chinese aggression was a personal as well as a national betrayal. He had extended his friendship and sponsored China's cause in the world; and for China to have given the impression to him and the Indian people that she recognized India's northern boundary and expected only some rectifications, to have crept gradually and by stealth into inaccessible and sparsely populated Indian territory, and then to have challenged the validity of the whole boundary and mounted large-scale offensives was to him a breach of faith. But he utilized the military setbacks to draw the people closer together. He accepted the proposals of Ceylon and five other non-aligned countries that a demilitarized zone be created in the western sector by the Chinese withdrawing 20 kilometres from their advanced position; and talks on the boundary recommenced thereafter. The Chinese rejection of these proposals strengthened Nehru's diplomatic position.

Final years and death Nehru's health, sustained for years by regular yoga exercises, began to decline from April 1962, when a viral infection of the urinary tract brought on low intermittent fever, which he took nearly a month to shake off. But he never fully got rid of the infection and from this time a slight puffiness round the eyes was always noticeable. Recognizing that the end could not be far off, he took the first step in preparing for the succession by persuading the Congress Party in 1963 to direct all its leading members except himself to withdraw from office in order to devote themselves to organizational work. On 6 January 1964, at the Congress session in Bhubaneswar in Orissa, he suffered a mild stroke on the left side, and he inducted back into office Lal Bahadur Shastri, his henchman in Uttar Pradesh, ostensibly to assist him in his work, but in fact making clear whom he wished to replace him.

Nehru also took steps to settle, if possible, the Kashmir problem. In 1963 he had agreed, on the initiative of Britain and the United States, to resume talks with Pakistan. His objective was still a final settlement of Kashmir along the ceasefire line, and Pakistan's insistence on the transfer of almost the whole state led to the collapse of the talks. In 1964 he had Sheikh Abdullah released, and approved of his going to Pakistan to assess ways of reaching a settlement. Nehru himself was thinking in terms of a confederation of India, Kashmir, and Pakistan. But no tangible progress had been made when in Delhi, in the early hours of 27 May 1964, Nehru suffered a rupture of the abdominal aorta and died that afternoon. He was cremated the next morning on the bank of the Jumna River. The site has been planted with trees to form Shanti Vana (Wood of Peace) as a memorial to him.

Assessment To have resisted imperialism, denounced fascism, transformed the nature of the Commonwealth and saved it from possible disintegration over South Africa, stood up for the rights of the African people, and shown the way for countries to steer clear of the cold war while being concerned with the problems of the world, places Nehru among the leading statesmen of the twentieth century. The shadows are created by his failure to stabilize India's relations with Pakistan and the deterioration of her relations with China. Seeking to eliminate in India the influence of religion in public life, he could not concede that Kashmir should be a part of Pakistan merely because the majority of its inhabitants were Muslims. The impact of the cold war in south Asia precluded in his opinion the possibility of a plebiscite; and his imaginative idea of a confederation was foreclosed, even if at all acceptable to Pakistan, by his death. The uneasy peace with China he sought to maintain with friendly, patient, and pragmatic diplomacy; but China was not to be deflected by such an attitude.

Within India Nehru consolidated a nation, established a democratic system and trained the people to work it, constructed a model for economic development, and set the country on the path to growth. But his belief in a phased approach led him to neglect agriculture until the late 1950s, and he gave social justice a low priority. He did not enforce land reforms, introduce universal primary education, or improve the status of all Indian women. He did not recognize that the growth of the population, unless controlled, would nullify every aspect of economic development. He insisted that India, as a whole, was not very heavily populated and family planning was only a part of the larger movement for raising the people's standard of living; and this would be attained by education and economic planning. But offsetting all the shortcomings of Nehru's policies was his provision of objectives—unity, democracy, secularism, the self-respect of developing nations—which have become, thanks to his hold on the public mind, which is second only to that of Mahatma Gandhi, part of the general consciousness of the Indian people.

Nehru was a handsome man, 5 foot 7 inches in height, and of a light, olive complexion. His premature baldness was usually concealed under a Gandhi cap. He discarded Western clothes in 1950 and dressed in a buttoned-up tunic with a red rose in the buttonhole and tight-fitting breeches. During summers in India he wore what is now known as a Nehru jacket. Entirely different from his mentor and confidant Mahatma Gandhi, Nehru none the less had great charisma, felt by the millions of his own compatriots and those many from abroad who found in him a profoundly attractive personality, and a sensitive interpreter of different cultures to each other.   S. GOPAL

Sources S. Gopal, *Jawaharlal Nehru*, 3 vols. (1975–84) · M. Brecher, *Nehru: a political biography* (1959) · J. Nehru, *Jawharlal Nehru: an autobiography, with musings on recent events in India* (1936) · M. J. Akbar, *Nehru: the making of India* (1988) · *Selected works of Jawaharlal Nehru*, ed. S. Gopal and others, 15 vols. (1972–82) · *Selected works of Jawaharlal Nehru*, ed. S. Gopal and others, [2nd ser.], 28 vols. (1984–) · private information (2004)

Archives Nehru Museum, New Delhi, corresp. and papers | BL OIOC, corresp. with S. K. Datta, MS Eur. F 178 · Bodl. Oxf., corresp. with Lord Monckton · Bodl. Oxf., letters to E. J. Thompson · HLRO, corresp. with Lord Samuel · NA Scot., corresp. with Lord Lothian · Nehru Memorial Library, papers of the All-India congress committee · Nehru Memorial Library, V. Pandit papers [sister] · Nehru Museum, New Delhi, Motilal Nehru MSS · PRO, corresp. with Sir Stafford Cripps, CAB 127/57 143 · U. Leeds, Brotherton L., corresp. with Henry Drummond-Wolff | FILM BFI NFTVA, *The dynasty*: 'The Nehru-Gandhi story', BBC2, 2 Aug 1997 · BFI NFTVA, current affairs footage · BFI NFTVA, documentary footage · BFI NFTVA, news footage · IWM FVA, actuality footage · IWM FVA, documentary footage · IWM FVA, home footage · IWM FVA, news footage | SOUND BL NSA, 'From raj to Rajiv: revolution by consent', 12 Aug 1987, B2622/3 · BL NSA, documentary recordings · BL NSA, oral history interview · IWM SA, documentary recordings · IWM SA, oral history interview

Likenesses photographs, *c.*1899–1971, Hult. Arch. · Y. Karsh, photograph, 1956, NPG [*see illus.*] · J. Epstein, bust, Nehru Memorial Museum and Library, New Delhi · E. I. Halliday, portrait, India House, London · S. Roerich, portrait, Parliament House, New Delhi

Motilal Nehru (1861–1931), by unknown photographer, after 1920

Nehru, Motilal (1861–1931), lawyer and Indian nationalist, was born at Agra on 6 May 1861, the posthumous son of Ganga Dhar Nehru, a minor police official in Delhi under the Mughal ruler until the latter was deposed by the British in 1858. Taught Arabic, Persian, and Urdu at home, Nehru studied at the government schools at Allahabad and Cawnpore, and the Muir Central College at Allahabad. He left before graduation and, passing the *vakil*'s (lawyer's) examination, set up legal practice at Cawnpore in 1883. Three years later he moved to Allahabad, where there was a high court. He had married in 1882, after his first wife died, Swarup Rani Thussu, and had a son, Jawaharlal *Nehru, and two daughters, the elder of whom was Vijayalakshmi *Pandit.

Specializing in various branches of the civil law, Nehru soon became one of the leaders of the Allahabad bar, and lived in lavish style, entertaining a wide circle of friends, British and Indian. He visited England in 1899 and was excommunicated from his Brahman caste for refusing to do penance for travelling overseas. Throughout his life he firmly repudiated caste restrictions. He took a vague interest in politics and from 1888 to 1892 attended the annual sessions of the Indian National Congress. In 1907 he presided over the United Provinces provincial conference and three years later was elected to represent Allahabad in the legislative council of the province.

Nehru at this time believed in constitutional agitation for political reforms. In 1910 he became chairman of the board of directors of *The Leader*, a newspaper started in Allahabad to give voice to moderate opinion, and the next year he attended the imperial durbar at Delhi. But in 1917 he was persuaded by Annie Besant to become president of the Home Rule League in Allahabad. He also was drawn to Mahatma Gandhi, who had already won over Jawaharlal Nehru. The son had a strong influence on the father. Nehru was critical of the reforms proposed by the British government in 1918. Disappointed with the attitude of *The Leader*, he started his own newspaper, *The Independent*, which lasted three years.

In 1919 Nehru served as a member of the committee set up by the Congress to assess the consequences of the action of General Dyer in firing on an unarmed crowd at Amritsar and the imposition of martial law in the Punjab. Later that year he presided over the annual session of the Congress at Amritsar. In 1920 he participated in the campaign of civil disobedience led by Gandhi, and changed his way of life. He handed over his palatial residence to the Congress and built a smaller home for himself, took to wearing *khaddar* (homespun cotton), abandoned his legal practice, and resigned from the legislative council. In December 1921 he was arrested and sentenced to prison for six months.

Critical of Gandhi for calling off the civil disobedience

campaign in February 1922 because of a mob setting fire to a police station, Nehru, on his release from Naini gaol, helped to form the Swaraj (Freedom) Party within the Congress to work for entry into the legislative councils enlarged and reformed in 1919, wherein opposition would embarrass the government. The Congress permitted this deviation from non-co-operation. In 1923 Nehru was elected to the central legislative assembly and became the leader of the opposition. A skilled parliamentarian, he organized the defeat or delay of the finance and other official bills. But Nehru agreed to serve on the committee for considering ways and means of recruiting Indian officers for the army, and this opened the door for others to go further and join the government. So in March 1926 Nehru put forward a 'national demand' for the immediate drafting by a representative conference and enactment by parliament of a constitution conferring full dominion status on India. When this was rejected by the assembly Nehru and his colleagues walked out.

This was virtually the end of the Swaraj Party and Nehru returned to the mainstream of the Congress under Gandhi's leadership. He had resumed legal practice in 1926 but supported the boycott of the statutory (Simon) commission into the working of the 1919 reforms. As the constructive side of the boycott, an all-party group was formed with Nehru as chairman to determine the principles of a constitution for India. The Nehru report, published in August 1928, stated that dominion status was the immediate objective, with 'full responsible government' transferred to the people of India. Instead of Muslims having separate electorates as enacted in the reforms of 1909 and 1919, whereby they voted for Muslim candidates, there should be reservation of seats for ten years for minorities in provinces, or a common electorate voting for candidates of a certain religion.

In December 1928 Nehru presided over the annual session of the Congress at Calcutta, and it was resolved that if the British government did not accept the Nehru report by the end of 1929 the Congress would revert to the demand for independence and resort once more to a campaign of non-violent non-co-operation. Efforts in 1929 at a compromise proved futile, and in March 1930 Gandhi initiated civil disobedience. Nehru was sentenced in June to imprisonment for six months and joined his son in Naini gaol. Together they were taken in August to see Gandhi in Yeravda gaol in Poona for talks which might lead to a settlement; but these came to nothing. Back in Naini gaol, Nehru was released in September on grounds of ill health. He died of pulmonary emphysema in Lucknow on 6 February 1931.   S. GOPAL

Sources J. Nehru, *Jawharlal Nehru: an autobiography, with musings on recent events in India* (1936) · L. R. Nair, ed., *Motilal Nehru birth centenary souvenir* (1961) · S. P. Chablani and P. Chablani, eds., *Motilal Nehru* (1961) · B. R. Nanda, *The Nehrus* (1962) · *Selected works of Motilal Nehru*, ed. R. Kumar and D. N. Panigrahi, 6 vols. (1982–95)
Archives Nehru Museum, New Delhi | Nehru Memorial Museum and Library, New Delhi, Jawaharlal Nehru MSS | FILM IWM FVA, news footage · IWM FVA, documentary footage | SOUND BL NSA, documentary recordings

Likenesses photograph, after 1920, Nehru Memorial Museum and Library, New Delhi [*see illus.*] · D. P. R. Chowdhury, statue, outside Parliament House, New Delhi · K. S. Kulkarni, Parliament House, New Delhi

Neil, Eric (1918–1990), physiologist, was born in Maryport, Cumberland, on 15 February 1918, to Major George Neil (1880–1978) and his wife, Florence, *née* Waite (1880–1982). His father, from whom he inherited a passion for history and a love of the Cumbrian hills, was an inspector of schools. He was educated at Queen Elizabeth School, Darlington (1925–33), and Heath grammar school, Halifax. From 1937 he studied medicine at the University of Leeds, graduating MB, ChB in 1942. An honours BSc in physiology (1939), gained in the department of Professor Albert Hemingway, was to influence his subsequent career, so that after a year as house surgeon and casualty officer, the years 1942 to 1950 were spent in the department of physiology at Leeds, first as demonstrator, then as lecturer.

On 16 April 1946 Neil married Anne Baron Parker, daughter of T. J. M. B. Parker and Evelyn Maud Parker, whom he had taught during her medical studies, and who subsequently worked as a community physician in London. They had two daughters, Jane, a solicitor, and Georgina, a teacher of handicapped and infant children.

The preclinical school of the Middlesex Hospital medical school had been evacuated from London to Leeds during the Second World War, and a deep friendship and mutual respect developed between Neil and Samson Wright, professor of physiology of the Middlesex Hospital medical school. This led to Neil's move in 1950 to London, to Samson Wright's department at the Middlesex, first as senior lecturer and then as reader. After Samson Wright's death in 1956 he succeeded him as John Astor professor of physiology, a position which he held until his retirement and appointment as emeritus professor in 1984.

While in Leeds, Neil became interested in the effects of temperature on acid–base balance and blood gas transport, work which formed the basis of his MD thesis, awarded with distinction in 1944. This interest proved opportune, for it coincided with the introduction of induced hypothermia as an adjunct to the developing field of open-heart surgery, and led to an important series of papers in collaboration with E. Brewin, a member of the pioneering cardiothoracic surgical team at Guy's Hospital, and F. Nashat, then visiting from Baghdad. These revealed that a progressive metabolic acidosis developed during hypothermia, due to depressed liver metabolism; they paved the way for major advances in patient management. Neil reviewed the findings in the keynote lecture to the European Congress of Cardiology at Stockholm in 1956. The DSc awarded by Leeds University (1953) recognized these and other research achievements.

About 1950, often in collaboration with Swedish colleagues, including S. Landgren and Y. Zotterman, Neil began investigating the reflex control of the circulatory and respiratory systems and the mechanisms of excitation of the receptors involved, topics which dominated his research for the next 30 years. Using electrophysiological techniques to study impulse discharges in their afferent nerves, he made notable advances in the understanding of the factors determining arterial baroreceptor activity. A similar approach was subsequently used to investigate cardiac receptors and the chemoreceptors of the carotid body. For the latter studies he devised together with N. Joels a perfused carotid body preparation which enabled him to apply his considerable biochemical knowledge to unravelling the metabolic processes within the organ. Later work with R. O'Regan demonstrated the role of efferent nerves in modulating the activity of carotid body chemoreceptors. Many of the studies of cardiovascular reflexes were described in *Reflexogenic Areas of the Cardiovascular System* (1958), written in collaboration with C. Heymans, and the equally classic *Circulation* (1971), written jointly with B. Folkow, reflected Neil's interest in the circulation in general. Neil was also a dedicated and stimulating teacher of both undergraduate and postgraduate students, and with C. Keele was responsible for the editions of Samson Wright's *Applied Physiology* published during the three decades following Wright's death.

Neil was elected to membership of the Physiological Society in 1945 and to honorary membership in 1984. He served on the committee (1956–60) and was particularly proud of the improvement in the society's finances during his period as treasurer (1961–7). A fluent and highly entertaining speaker, he enlivened many Physiological Society dinners. He also served as treasurer on the committee of the International Union of Physiological Sciences (1968–71, 1971–4), and was elected for two terms as president of the council of IUPS (1974–7, 1977–80). His many honours included FRCP (1978), honorary foreign membership of the Royal Academy of Medicine of Belgium (1978), and honorary MD Ghent (1977).

The Neils' house in Highgate, London, was a second home to a constant procession of students, colleagues and physiologists from abroad. An accomplished pianist, Neil often delighted guests with his playing. Retirement enabled him increasingly to indulge his other major passion, Venice and Venetian painting, of which he had a formidable knowledge. He died of a heart attack on 8 May 1990 at his home, 53 Talbot Road, and was buried in Highgate cemetery on 22 May. He was survived by his wife and daughters.   NORMAN JOELS

Sources personal knowledge (2004) · private information · R. G. O'Regan, 'Eric Neil (1918–1990): an appreciation', *Advances in Experimental Medicine*, 360 (1994), 1–3 · WWW

Likenesses H. E. Lewis, photograph, 1957, Wellcome L., Physiological Society archives · M. E. Rosenberg, photograph, 1981, Wellcome L., Physiological Society archives · photographs, Wellcome L., Physiological Society archives

Wealth at death £121,730: probate, 1990, *CGPLA Eng. & Wales*

Neil, Robert Alexander (1852–1901), classical scholar and orientalist, was born on 26 December 1852 at Glengairn manse, Glengairn, near Ballater, Aberdeenshire, the second son of Robert Neil, minister of the *quoad sacra* parish of Glengairn, and his wife, Mary, *née* Reid. Both parents were from Aberdeenshire families which had produced many clergymen and medical men. Robert was educated at the local school, but was taught classics by his father. In

1866, while only thirteen, he entered Aberdeen University, having obtained a small scholarship at the annual bursary competition. At the end of the session he was first prizeman in William Geddes's class. In 1870 he graduated at Aberdeen with first-class honours in classics, and shared the Simpson Greek prize.

The following winter Neil acted as an assistant in the university library and next year studied anatomy and chemistry with the intention of graduating in the medical faculty. He soon changed his mind and in 1873 he was elected a classical scholar of Peterhouse, Cambridge. Under the tuition of J. S. Reid, A. W. Verrall, and Richard Shilleto, he made such rapid progress that in 1875 he won the Craven scholarship, as well as obtaining a college prize; and in 1876 graduated as second classic. He was also highly distinguished in the year's examination for chancellor's medals. Soon afterwards he was elected a fellow of Pembroke College, where until his death he was a classical lecturer, although his public lectures were given for many years at Peterhouse. The following year he published 'Notes on Liddell and Scott' in the *Journal of Philology* (7, 1877, 200–05); but his teaching work left him little time for writing, which his cautious and fastidious nature made a laborious task.

Soon after completing his degree Neil began to read with the university's first professor of Sanskrit, Edward Byles Cowell. For the rest of his life Neil spent one or two afternoons a week in term time working with Cowell. In the earlier years they read parts of the Rig-Veda, Indian drama, grammar, and philosophy, but gradually they turned their attention to Buddhist literature. Under their joint names there eventually appeared *The Divyāavadāna: a collection of early Buddhist legends now first edited from the Nepalese Sanskrit MSS in Cambridge and Paris* (1886), founded on the collation of a number of Sanskrit manuscripts which were supplied to the editors from the libraries of Cambridge, Paris, and St Petersburg. After the publication of this work Neil took up the study of Pali, and formed one of the band of scholars who under Cowell's superintendence translated into English *The Jātaka, or, Stories of the Buddha's Former Births* (6 vols., 1895–1907). Neil's own contribution forms part of volume 3 (1897; 151–286).

During these years Neil was also busy with classical work. His *Knights of Aristophanes* was published posthumously in 1901, the only substantial evidence of his classical scholarship. It concentrates much scholarship and delicate observation of Aristophanic Greek, evident less in the editor's text-critical acumen and solution of unusually difficult passages than in the nicety of his lexical definitions (see, for example, Appendix 1, 'The particle ge'), the wide-ranging provenance of his literary comparisons (see, for instances, the introduction, x, xiii, xiv), and his careful treatment of ordinary questions and small matters: the net result being, as one early reviewer noted (Richards, 354), good commentary on little touches characteristic of Aristophanes and on issues of contemporary Attic life. Neil frequently lectured on the history of Greek comedy, Pindar, and Plato; and on these subjects he accumulated much knowledge. He was also familiar with all work done in the comparative philology of the classical languages, Sanskrit, and Celtic. His emendation of a corrupt word, *asageuonta*, in Bacchylides into *aōteuonta* was at once accepted by the Greek scholar Richard Jebb.

Besides his professional work as a classical lecturer, as university lecturer on Sanskrit (a post to which he was appointed in 1883), and as the university instructor in that language for the Indian Civil Service (1886–89; 1892–1901), Neil took much interest in architecture and knew intimately the cathedrals of western Europe. He was interested in women's education, and before his college work became very heavy he lectured at both Girton and Newnham. Especially in work with individual students, his kindliness, care, and quiet humour attracted even the less scholarly. The sensitivity and breadth of his literary interest, which extended to much contemporary language and literature, ensured that he expounded prescribed texts in an engagingly humane manner, thereby complementing the strict linguistic demands of the classical tripos. He was popular in Cambridge society, and amid his duties regularly spared time to solve difficulties for his friends. As a long-standing syndic of Cambridge University Press, he helped many young scholars with advice as their work passed through the press. He also served for four years on the council of the senate.

Neil evidently retained a lifelong affection for Aberdeen University, encouraging its abler classical students in their quest for admission to Cambridge, notably James Adam. In 1891 Aberdeen University conferred upon him the honorary degree of LLD. Neil took a keen interest in Scottish history and literature, and was for long a member of the Franco-Scottish Society. In 1900, on the death of C. H. Prior, he became senior tutor of Pembroke. He died after a brief illness on 19 June 1901, and was buried in the churchyard at Bridge of Gairn, not far from his birthplace. He was unmarried. In appearance Neil was a little over average height and strongly built, with brown hair and large expressive eyes.   PETER GILES, *rev.* JOHN HARDY

Sources H. Richards, 'Recent editions of the plays of Aristophanes', *Classical Review*, 16 (1902), 354–7 • 'Prefatory note', *The knights of Aristophanes*, ed. R. A. Neil (1901) • *Cambridge University Calendar* (1873) • *Cambridge University Calendar* (1875) • *Cambridge University Calendar* (1876) • J. R. Tanner, ed., *Historical register of the University of Cambridge … to the year 1910* (1917) • A. M. Adam, 'Memoir', in J. Adam, *The religious teachers of Greece: being Gifford lectures on natural religion delivered at the University of Aberdeen*, ed. A. M. Adam (1908), i–lv • J. Adams, *Cambridge Review* (24 Oct 1901) • *British Weekly* (27 June 1901) • *Alma Mater* [Aberdeen University] (20 Nov 1901) • personal knowledge (1912) • private information (1912) [family] • *WWW*, 1897–1915 • bap. reg. Scot.
Wealth at death £7946 16s. 10d.: resworn administration, Feb 1902, *CGPLA Eng. & Wales* (1901)

Neil, Samuel (1825–1901), schoolmaster and writer, born in Edinburgh on 4 August 1825, was the second of the three sons of James Neil, an Edinburgh bookseller, and his wife, Sarah Lindsay, a connection of the Lindsays, earls of Crawford. On the death of James Neil from cholera in 1832, the family went to live in Glasgow. After education at the old grammar school there, Neil entered the University

of Glasgow; while an undergraduate, he assisted the English master in the high school and worked for the *Glasgow Argus* (of which the poet Charles Mackay was editor), and other newspapers. On 7 April 1848 he married Christina Gibson, the youngest daughter of Archibald Gibson, who had served in the navy and had been with Nelson at the battle of Trafalgar. For a time Neil was a private tutor, and then master successively of Falkirk charity school in 1850, of Southern Collegiate School, Glasgow, in 1852, and of St Andrew's School, Glasgow, in 1853. Finally he was rector of Moffat Academy from 1855 to 1873.

Neil combined much literary activity with his work in education. He promoted in 1857, and edited during its existence, the *Moffat Register and Annandale Observer*, the first newspaper published in Moffat, and he wrote regularly for other Scottish periodicals and educational journals. In 1850 he planned, and from that date until 1873 edited, the *British Controversialist* (40 vols. in all), a monthly magazine published in London for the discussion of literary, social, and philosophic questions. He himself contributed numerous philosophical articles, many of which he subsequently collected in separate volumes. Of these his *Art of Reasoning* (1853) was praised for its clarity and conciseness by John Stuart Mill, George Henry Lewes, Archbishop Whately, and Alexander Bain. Other contributions to the *British Controversialist* were published independently, under the titles of *Elements of Rhetoric* (1856), *Composition and Elocution* (1857), and *Public Meetings and how to Conduct them* (1867).

On resigning his rectorship of Moffat Academy in 1873 Neil settled in Edinburgh, devoting himself to English literature, and especially to Shakespeare. He founded and was president of the Edinburgh Shakespeare Society, and gave the annual lecture from 1874 until his death. To the *British Controversialist* in 1860 he contributed a series of papers which he reissued in 1861 as *Shakespeare: a Critical Biography*. The work enjoyed a vogue as a useful epitome of the facts, although Neil accepted without demur the forgeries of John Payne Collier. It was translated into French and German. Neil, who was a frequent visitor to Warwickshire, issued a guide to Shakespeare's birthplace at Stratford upon Avon as *The House of Shakespeare Described* (1871), and he edited the *Library Shakespeare* (3 vols.) in 1875, besides several separate plays for school use. His other publications included *British History* (1856), *Student's Handbook of Modern History* (1857), *Martin Luther* (1863), and *The Art of Public Speaking* (1867). Neil edited and compiled a large part of *The Home Teacher: a Cyclopaedia of Self-Instruction* (6 vols., 1886).

Neil took a leading part in educational and philanthropic affairs in Edinburgh, where he was on intimate terms with professors John Stuart Blackie, Henry Calderwood, John Veitch, and David Masson. He helped to found the Educational Institute of Scotland for granting fellowships to teachers. He compiled a book of poems by and about blind people, entitled *Dark Days Brightened*, for the Craigmillar School for the Blind in Edinburgh, which he managed for some years.

In 1900 Neil's health failed. He died on 28 August 1901,

while on a visit at Sullom manse, Shetland, the residence of his son-in-law, the Revd Charles Davidson, and was buried on 1 September in Sullom churchyard. His wife predeceased him on 26 January 1901. They had three sons and five daughters, of whom one son and three daughters, all married, survived him.

W. B. Owen, *rev.* Nilanjana Banerji

Sources J. Love, *The schools and schoolmasters of Falkirk* (1898) · C. Davidson, *Ardrossan and Saltcoats Herald* (20 Sept 1901) · *Educational News* (7 Sept 1901) · *Moffat Express* (5 Sept 1901)
Likenesses white alabaster sculpture, 1853 · G. Barclay, portrait; formerly in possession of his daughter, 1912
Wealth at death £176 14s. 10d.: confirmation, 11 Aug 1902, *CCI*

Neild, James (1744–1814), penal reformer and philanthropist, was born on 24 May 1744 at Knutsford, Cheshire. His father's death left his mother to support Neild and his four siblings by continuing her business as a linen draper. After a very brief education Neild lived for two years with an uncle, a farmer, but at the end of 1760 he obtained a position with a London jeweller and was later employed by Mr Hemming, the king's goldsmith. Here he learned to engrave, model, and draw, as well as to fence. In 1770 a legacy from his uncle enabled him to set up in business as a jeweller in St James's Street, London. The venture proved successful and in 1792 he retired with a fortune. Neild became actively involved in penal reform after visiting a fellow apprentice imprisoned for debt at the king's bench. Subsequently he inspected Newgate and Wood Street prisons in London, Derby prison, Liverpool bridewell, the Chester dungeons, and, before 1770, prisons at Calais, St Omer, Dunkirk, Lille, and Paris. He was particularly exercised by the number of people confined for petty levels of indebtedness and, after hearing a sermon preached by the Revd Weeden Butler in February 1772, formed a fund-raising committee which by payment of £81 secured the release of thirty-four prisoners. The success of this venture led to the establishment in May 1773 of the Society for the Relief and Discharge of Persons Imprisoned for Small Debts (also known as the Thatched House Society). In his capacity as treasurer, a position he held until his death, Neild made weekly visits and reports on prisons in London and the surrounding area. In his *Account of the Society* (1799), Neild explained its policy of prioritizing the release of 'worthy' cases, notably men with families, who were less than £10 in debt. By the end of the century the society had secured the freedom of 16,405 prisoners at a cost of £41,748.

In 1778 Neild married Elizabeth Camden (d. 1791), eldest daughter of John Camden of Battersea, Surrey; they had three children, Elizabeth, who died in childhood, and two sons, William (1779–1810) and John Camden *Neild (1780–1852). In 1779 Neild extended his survey of prison conditions to Flanders and the German states. Two years later he contracted gaol fever at Warwick and ill health, combined with business interests, interrupted his philanthropic work for a time. In addition to publishing on the aims of his society Neild wrote an *Account of Persons Confined for Debt in the Various Parts of England and Wales* (1800), of which the third edition (1808) incorporated the results

James Neild (1744–1814), by Samuel De Wilde, 1804

of his visits to Scottish prisons. These tours were also discussed in a journal and in letters to his friend the physician John Coakley Lettsom. On Lettsom's advice Neild published vivid and alarming extracts from this correspondence as 'Prison remarks', serialized in the *Gentleman's Magazine* between 1803 and 1813. Neild's series proved popular, and in 1809, during a second tour of England and Scotland, he was presented with the freedom of the cities of Glasgow, Perth, Paisley, Inverness, and Ayr. In 1812, with the help of Weeden Butler, he published the *State of the Prisons in England, Scotland and Wales*, in which he reiterated his long-running campaign against imprisonment for debt. Neild lived the final part of his life at 4 Cheyne Walk, Chelsea, London, but also owned property outside the capital estimated at a value of £250,000. He was appointed high sheriff for Buckinghamshire in 1804 and also served as JP for Kent, Middlesex, and Westminster.

Neild died at his Chelsea home on 16 February 1814. He was survived by his younger son alone, his wife and elder son, William, having died on 30 June 1791 and 19 October 1810 respectively. After his death opinion turned against Neild, who was known to have severely treated this son, forcing him to leave England for the West Indies, where he practised as a barrister before ill health required him to return in 1810. Such was the criticism of Neild's actions that Lettsom found it impossible to raise sufficient support to erect a statue in honour of his late friend.

G. Le G. Norgate, *rev.* Stephen M. Lee

Sources *Memoirs of the life and writings of the late John Coakley Lettsom*, ed. T. J. Pettigrew, 3 vols. (1817), vol. 2, pp. 191–218 · D. E. Owen, *English philanthropy, 1660–1960* (1964) · M. De Lacy, *Prison reform in*

Lancashire, 1700–1850 (1986) · H. Tattam, *A short memoir of the late J. C. Neild* (1852)

Archives BL, corresp. with Charles Weeden and Charles Butler, Add. MS 19025
Likenesses S. De Wilde, oils, 1804, NPG [*see illus.*] · F. Pulham, miniature, Royal Collection · silhouette, line engraving, NPG; repro. in *GM* (1817)
Wealth at death approx. £250,000

Neild, John Camden (1780–1852), miser, the son of James *Neild (1744–1814), prison reformer, and his wife, Elizabeth, *née* Camden (d. 1791), was born on 3 May 1780, probably in St James's Street, London. He was educated at Eton College from 1793 to 1797, and then at Trinity College, Cambridge, graduating BA 1801 and MA 1804. On 9 February 1808 he was called to the bar at Lincoln's Inn. Succeeding in 1814 to the whole of his father's property, estimated at £250,000, he developed into a confirmed miser, and the last thirty years of his life were wholly and successfully devoted to accumulating wealth. He lived in a large house, 5 Cheyne Walk, Chelsea, but it was so meanly furnished that for some time he did not have a bed to sleep on. His dress consisted of a blue swallow-tailed coat with gilt buttons, brown trousers, short gaiters, and shoes that were patched and generally down at the heels. He never allowed his clothes to be brushed because, he said, it destroyed the nap. He continually visited his numerous estates, walking whenever it was possible; he never went to the expense of a greatcoat, and always stayed with his tenants. While at North Marston, Buckinghamshire, about 1828 he attempted to cut his throat, and his life was saved only by the prompt attention of his tenant's wife, a Mrs Neale. Unlike other celebrated misers—such as Daniel Dancer or John Elwes—he occasionally indulged in acts of benevolence. He had a considerable knowledge of legal and general literature, and to the last retained a love for the classics.

Neild died at 5 Cheyne Walk, Chelsea, on 30 August 1852, aged seventy-two, and was buried in the chancel of North Marston church, Buckinghamshire, on 9 September. By his will, after bequeathing a few trifling legacies, he left the whole of his property, estimated at £500,000, to 'Her Most Gracious Majesty Queen Victoria, begging Her Majesty's most gracious acceptance of the same for her sole use and benefit'. Two caveats were entered against the will, but were subsequently withdrawn. The queen increased Neild's bequests to the three executors from £100 to £1000 each; she also provided for his servants, for whom he made no provision, and secured an annuity of £100 to Mrs Neale, who had frustrated Neild's attempt at suicide. In 1855 Queen Victoria restored the chancel of North Marston church and inserted a window to Neild's memory.   G. C. BOASE, rev. H. C. G. MATTHEW

Sources *The Times* (8 Sept 1852) · *The Times* (26 Oct 1852) · *ILN* (18 Sept 1852), 222 · *ILN* (30 Oct 1852), 350 · *ILN* (29 Sept 1855), 379–80 · Venn, *Alum. Cant.* · *GM*, 1st ser., 87/1 (1817), 305–9 · *GM*, 2nd ser., 38 (1852), 429–31 · *GM*, 2nd ser., 39 (1853), 570 · J. Timber, *English eccentrics and eccentricities* (1866) · R. Chambers, ed., *The book of days: a miscellany of popular antiquities in connection with the calendar*, 2 vols. (1863–4) · H. Tattam, *A short memoir of the late J. C. Neild of Chelsea* (1852) · J. Wright, *The poor relations of the late miser Neild* (1855)
Archives Bucks. RLSS, estate papers

John Camden Neild (1780–1852), by unknown artist

Likenesses portrait, Royal Collection [*see illus.*]
Wealth at death approx. £500,000: *DNB*; Boase, *Mod. Eng. biog.*

Neile, Sir Paul (*bap.* 1613, *d.* 1682×6), courtier and patron of science, was born in Westminster, London, where he was baptized at St Margaret's on 11 May 1613. His father was Richard *Neile (1562–1640), bishop of Lichfield and Coventry, and later archbishop of York. He was admitted a fellow-commoner at Pembroke College, Cambridge, in 1627; he matriculated in 1628 and graduated BA in 1631. He was knighted by Charles I at Bishopthorpe, his father's palace near York, on 27 May 1633; he was described as of Hutton Bonville, an estate near Northallerton that he held until at least 1667. As a measure of the regard in which the family was held by the king, Archbishop Neile was able to secure a royal pardon for his son when Sir Paul was indicted for the manslaughter of a carman and other felonies in January 1636.

Neile married Elizabeth, sister of Gabriel Clarke, archdeacon of Durham. Their first son, William *Neile (1637–1670), born at Bishopthorpe, became a mathematician of distinction. A second son, Richard, disinherited by Sir Paul because of his involvement in escapades considered discreditable to the family, subsequently became sheriff of Northumberland and was knighted in 1686. There were two daughters.

Neile was returned for Ripon in the Short Parliament of April–May 1640, and he was one of the Yorkshire gentry who signed the Yorkshire engagement in support of the royalist cause. During the protectorate he was associated with the circle of natural philosophers and mathematicians at Oxford that centred around Seth Ward, Savilian professor of astronomy, and John Wilkins, warden of Wadham College. The young Christopher Wren was a part of this group, as was Neile's son William, who entered Wadham as a gentleman commoner in 1652.

Neile's particular contribution was the provision of the longest and most powerful telescopes that had been produced in England for Ward's observatory at Wadham, and these were used by Wren in developing his theory of Saturn's rings. They were constructed by the prominent London optical craftsman Richard Reeve (*d.* 1666), at Hill

House, White Waltham, Berkshire, a property leased by Neile from 1653; Neile is credited by Wren with the detailed direction of Reeve's work. The most impressive telescope, of 36 feet focus, he donated for Wren to use on the latter's appointment as professor of astronomy at Gresham College, London, in 1657. To the diarist John Evelyn, writing in 1656, Neile was 'Sir P. Neale famous for his optic-glasses' (Evelyn, 3.172). The Gresham telescope was demonstrated to Charles II in October 1660, and then at the king's request was moved to the garden at Whitehall Palace. Further telescopes were made for use as diplomatic and royal gifts.

In November 1660 Neile was one of the twelve members at the foundation meeting of the Royal Society. He played a prominent part in its business in the 1660s and early 1670s, though he remained associated with practical optics, his only communication was a 'Discourse on cider', which was printed by John Evelyn in his *Sylva* of 1664. Neile became a gentleman usher to the privy chamber in 1662, and his influence with the king was of continuing value to the society.

Neile inherited, but then dissipated, his father's fortune. His financial interests appear to have been in land and minerals. In 1670 he was one of the original adventurers listed in the royal charter of the Hudson's Bay Company. He is noted in Treasury records from 1671 as a member of a number of official commissions, notably as a commissioner for appeals in excise. From 1673 to 1677 he was MP for Newark, but he did not sit. In his will of 1682 Neile was recorded as resident at Codnover Castle, Derbyshire. He died in London before February 1686; Margaret, dowager countess of Marlborough (widow of William Ley, fourth and last earl), was sole executor.

A. D. C. SIMPSON, *rev.*

Sources C. A. Ronan and H. Hartley, 'Sir Paul Neile, FRS (1613–1686)', *Notes and Records of the Royal Society*, 15 (1960), 159–65 · T. Birch, *The history of the Royal Society of London*, 4 vols. (1756–7); repr. with introduction by A. R. Hall (1968), vol. 1 · M. Hunter and S. Schaffer, eds., *Robert Hooke: new studies* [London 1988] (1989), 33–61 · M. Hunter, *The Royal Society and its fellows, 1660–1700: the morphology of an early scientific institution* (1982) · H. Hartley, ed., *The Royal Society* (1960), 159–65 · *VCH Berkshire*, 3.174, 176 · *VCH Yorkshire North Riding*, 1.401–2 · D. Lysons and S. Lysons, *Magna Britannia: being a concise topographical account of the several counties of Great Britain*, new edn, 1 (1813), 405–6 · C. Wren, letter to P. Neile, 1 Oct 1661, RS, Early Letters, W.3.2 · *CSP dom.*, 1635–73 · W. A. Shaw, ed., *Calendar of treasury books*, 1–9, PRO (1904–31) · M. A. E. Green, ed., *Calendar of the proceedings of the committee for compounding … 1643–1660*, 5 vols., PRO (1889–92); repr. (1967) · Evelyn, *Diary*, 3.172–3, 285–6

Neile, Richard (1562–1640), archbishop of York, was born in King Street, Westminster, and baptized at St Margaret's, Westminster, on 11 March 1562, the second of nine children of Paul Neile (*d.* 1574), a tallow-chandler, and his wife, Sybil (*née* Hasinge?) (*d.* 1611). His father died when Richard was twelve, and in 1575 his mother married Robert Newell (*d.* 1602); the Newells had two sons, the elder of whom, Robert *Newell (1576–1642), became very close to his half-brother. Neile was educated at Westminster School as a townboy, and in 1580 won a scholarship to St John's College, Cambridge, on the recommendation of

Richard Neile (1562–1640), by unknown artist, *c.*1620

the dean, Gabriel Goodman, who described him as 'a poor and a fatherless child, of good hope to be learned' (Le Neve, vol. 1, pt 1, 137–8). According to critics like Alexander Leighton, Neile was a veritable 'dunce' and the 'schoolmaster was never off his breach' (Leighton, 66), something that Neile himself engagingly acknowledged in 1627 when he confessed with self-deprecating humour that he had been 'counted an heavy-headed lubber' at school (Smart, 3). Even later in life he is reported to have stopped a schoolmaster from flogging a child on the grounds that it had not done him much good. Nevertheless, Neile graduated BA in 1584, proceeded MA in 1587, was ordained deacon and priest by Bishop Richard Howland of Peterborough on 6 July 1589, and proceeded BD in 1595 and DD in 1600.

Early career Neile never acquired a college fellowship, nor a mastership, although his name was suggested for at least three Cambridge colleges, Magdalene, Clare, and Corpus Christi, between 1595 and 1603. Yet he had acquired powerful patrons, most notably Lord Burghley, who presented him in November 1590 to Cheshunt vicarage, Hertfordshire, in the parish of which lay Burghley's country residence of Theobalds. About this time Neile also became a household chaplain to Burghley, and on his death in 1598 filled the same role for his son and political heir, Sir Robert Cecil. Further preferment came, with the rectory of Toddington, Bedfordshire (1598) and, from Bishop Anthony Watson of Chichester, the treasurership of the cathedral (1598) and then a canonry (1604). These

Chichester livings were treated as sinecures. Through Robert Cecil's influence Neile was admitted as master of the Savoy in London in 1602. In July 1603, at the age of forty-one, he became a royal chaplain and, more crucially, clerk of the closet, a post he was to occupy for the next twenty-nine years. Worldly success may have come to Neile relatively late in life, but access to James I—with whom he seems to have struck up an instant rapport—transformed the rest of his career.

On 5 November 1605 this local man was installed as dean of Westminster, probably owing to the combined influence of Sir Robert Cecil and Richard Bancroft. Neile proved to be a model dean: 'his five years' decanate was in fact crowded with every kind of activity, from building and repair work, and the increasing of revenues, to the refurnishing of the church, the overhaul of the charters and registers, and innumerable acts of charity' (Tindal Hart). His activities at Westminster suggest that Neile had now clearly joined that group of theologians identified as 'proto-Arminians' who took their intellectual inspiration from Lancelot Andrewes and who sought to return to the 'beauty of holiness'; Neile favoured high ceremonial, fine church music, all conducted with 'order and decency' in buildings fit for the purpose, upon which he was quite prepared to lavish money.

Neile was not only the first dean of Westminster to have been born locally; he was also the first married dean. It is evident from Westminster records and adjustments that had to be made to the dean's lodgings that Neile was already married by 1605, but the precise date is unknown. His wife was Dorothy (d. 1647), daughter of Christopher Dacre (d. 1593) [see under Dacre family] and Alice Knyvett, and thus a cousin of Katherine Howard (née Knyvett), countess of Suffolk, a relationship noted in the proceedings of the Essex annulment case in 1613. She also seems to have won the affection of Neile's friends and to have played her own part later in making Durham House home to so many allies in the 1620s [see Durham House group]; she was left gifts in the wills of Richard Butler, John Buckeridge, and Augustine Lindsell. The couple's only surviving son, later Sir Paul *Neile, was not born until 1613.

First three bishoprics, 1608–1617 On 2 July 1608 Neile was elected bishop of Rochester, the first of a record six sees to be held in sequence by one bishop in the Church of England; the appointment was confirmed on 8 October and he was consecrated at Lambeth the next day. It was a doubly good promotion, for he was allowed to keep the deanery of Westminster *in commendam*. That year this bishop of humble origins began to use a quartered coat of arms, although an official grant does not seem to have been given until November 1612; he continued to use the original, elaborate version in preference to the simpler, specified in the grant. Apparently on the advice of John Buckeridge, Neile appointed William Laud as his personal chaplain in August 1608, and so began a partnership which was to see them both in high office as archbishops of York and Canterbury respectively in the 1630s. Thanks to Neile, Laud gave his first sermon at court in September 1609 and gained several minor preferments including a

reversion to a Westminster canonry, and vital support with the king when his election as president of St John's College, Oxford, was disputed in 1611. Little evidence survives of Neile's Rochester episcopate, but it did bring him his first appearance in the House of Lords in 1610 when he stoutly defended the role of bishops in that chamber.

On the translation of George Abbot from Lichfield to London in 1610, Neile was elected bishop of Lichfield and Coventry on 12 October, and swiftly confirmed as such on 6 December. This see hardly represented promotion for Neile, and it was a move which he had strongly opposed one year before, but owing to the death of Archbishop Richard Bancroft in 1610 and the rapid advance of his rival Abbot, it became a good tactical move. Neile was granted the right to hold Clifton Campville *in commendam*, together with several of his Chichester livings; he was also able to pass Westminster to George Mountain and Rochester to John Buckeridge, which in turn freed the presidency of St John's College, Oxford, for his chaplain Laud. There is little evidence of Neile's impact on his sprawling diocese, but he took with him a growing band of followers, including his chancellor from Rochester, Robert Masters, and his personal secretary William Easdall, just starting an illustrious career as a church lawyer. He continued to patronize William Laud in the difficult years ahead. More notoriously, he was involved in the sad case of the trial for heresy of Edward Wightman, who was condemned for blasphemy on the doctrine of the Trinity and in 1612 became the last person to be burnt at the stake for heresy in England.

Despite scant diocesan records at Lichfield and Coventry, it is noteworthy that it was in this diocese that Neile confirmed his reputation for being fierce with nonconformists. His arrival was greeted with gloom by puritans like William Bradshaw who prayed 'Lord keep us from Rochester' for 'Neile was the man, whom all the pious, as well private men as ministers, in these parts mis-doubted would do the most mischief' (S. Clarke, *A Generall Martyrologie*, 1660, 'Lives', 61). Neile used the Wightman case as an excuse to suspend the prominent puritan Arthur Hildersham and to suppress lectures at Burton upon Trent and at Repton. It is also notable that he was helped in handling these cases by his growing entourage consisting of William Laud, Richard Butler, Benjamin Carrier, and Richard Clayton, all members of the Arminian wing of the Church of England. It is moreover in this diocese that evidence emerges of Neile's interest in the observance of due ceremony in churches, particularly with relevance to the taking of the sacraments. Early in 1611 the authorities at St Michael's, Coventry, were instructed by the king himself to receive the sacraments kneeling, rather than standing or sitting; this came after the intervention of Neile who had apparently desired 'to effect this by good means and gentle perswasions rather than by legal proceedings' (W. Dugdale, *Antiquities of Warwickshire*, 1656, 151). In the parliamentary proceedings of 1614 Neile was accused of discouraging ministers 'from preaching twice in one day; for that contrary he would hinder their preferment, and hath put down divers lectures' (Jansson,

371). No wonder then that when Neile left the diocese Edward Vaughan welcomed his successor with the hope that 'we in these parts and in your jurisdiction may have a more peaceable proceeding in our preaching' (E. Vaughan, *A Plaine and Perfect Method for the Easie Understanding of the Whole Bible*, 1617, sig. A4r).

In an episode of equal notoriety to the Wightman case, Neile sat on a commission appointed to try the Essex marriage annulment case in 1613, together with 'Nullity' Bilson (Thomas Bilson, bishop of Winchester), and later Lancelot Andrewes. It was claimed that for his subservience in voting for the annulment, clearly complying with the king's wishes, Neile was advanced to the see of Lincoln in 1614, a post which might otherwise have gone to Robert Abbot, the archbishop's brother, who with Bishop John King had opposed the annulment. Neile did not stay long at Lincoln, although for time enough to leave traces of more of his strong views about clerical nonconformity in surviving accounts of visitations held in this diocese. He was informed by his officials in 1614 that 'lecturing hath brought many of God's holy and good ordinances into contempt, as public prayer, reading of the scriptures and receiving of the blessed sacraments' (Venables, 46). Neile identified ten major centres of nonconformity and bore down heavily on over sixty ministers, including the young but already celebrated John Cotton of Boston.

Neile's time at Lincoln offers further evidence of his close relationship with the king, for records relating to a clerical benevolence of 1614 show him coaxing, wheedling, threatening, and exhorting his clergy to raise money in a particularly zealous fashion. Neile may have felt that he owed King James such strong support because he had played a small part in the collapse of the so-called Addled Parliament of 1614. His inflammatory words in the Lords suggesting that a conference with the Commons would surely lead to 'undutiful and seditious speeches unfit for us to hear' (*Hastings MSS*, 4.253) were almost certainly deliberately leaked to the Commons, and Neile was forced to make an abject apology. Yet this was only one incident among many in what gained this parliament its sobriquet, and was not one seen in the end by contemporaries as terribly significant. It should not cast a stain on any full assessment of Neile's career as a bishop in the House of Lords, for from the outset of that career in 1610 until his final parliamentary session in 1629 he proved exemplary in his conscientious attendance and his commitment to committee work, even if his views were often contested in the Commons.

Durham and London, 1617–1628 The great breakthrough in Neile's career came in 1617, when he attended King James on a tour to Scotland. Bishop James of Durham died in May 1617 and the king instantly granted the see to Neile. He was confirmed bishop of this prestigious and wealthy diocese in October 1617, and in the decade that followed the cathedral witnessed an unprecedented series of deaths of canons which fortuitously enabled Neile to provide posts for his protégés. This soon earned Neile the reputation as the great patron of the Arminian faction and master of what became known as *Durham House, a reference to those intellectuals such as Augustine Lindsell, John Cosin, and John Buckeridge whom he gathered around him, and also to his house in the Strand where so many of them found London quarters. This was a matter of great concern to opponents who picked up that the success of new legislation such as the 1626 proclamation for peace and quiet in the church depended on 'how those of Durham House will render the meaning thereof' (J. Ussher, *Works*, ed. C. Elrington, 1847, 15.356). And on the occasion of Francis White's consecration as bishop of Carlisle in December 1626, it was asked: 'is a consecration now translated from Lambeth to Durham House?' (T. Birch, *The Court and Times of Charles I*, 1848, 1.179–80).

Durham House may have proved to be Neile's most famous residence, and its members such as Cosin, Lindsell, Buckeridge, and Laud all had illustrious careers in the church, but this should not distract attention from those who had worked with Neile earlier in his career, or those who came later. Cambridge contacts like Richard Clayton and Richard Butler were recruited to his entourage during the early 1600s; fellow royal chaplains like Richard Meredith and Benjamin Carrier both fell by the wayside for different reasons. Neile's loyal lawyers Edward Lively and William Easdall were both recruited before Durham and stayed with him until the end at York. Neile had the capacity to attract loyal, like-minded colleagues throughout his life, and later recruits such as Benjamin Laney, Edward Burby, and John Neile all had good careers in the church.

According to Peter Heylyn, Laud's biographer, at Durham Neile:

> presently set himself on work to repair the palaces and houses belonging to it which he had found in great decay; but so adorned and beautified them in a very short space, that they that saw them could not think they were the same. (Heylyn, 74)

It was at Durham that Neile revealed more fully than ever his liturgical preferences, as the communion table was moved to the east end where later a stone altar was erected, church music was valued with the construction of a new Dallam organ, and services transformed in a manner which was ridiculed in the parliamentary session of 1629, but which also aroused the fears of many like John Pym and William Prynne that their church was being undermined from within. At the end of the parliamentary session of 1629 the speaker was held in the chair before parliament could be prorogued, and those who were Arminians were branded as traitors to the state. A parliamentary remonstrance of June 1628 had already named Neile and Laud as leaders of that group. Yet they had also risen too high to fear failure, for they had been made privy councillors in April 1627, backed the forced loan which Abbot opposed, and in consequence already ran the Church of England as Abbot was temporarily sequestered.

Neile had already more than proved his worth as a civil servant in a rather unusual role while at Durham; unlike his predecessor Bishop William James, he was appointed lord lieutenant of the county palatine more or less automatically in November 1617. As such he presided over the local troops and summer musters during the war years of the 1620s, a very unusual role for a bishop. Voluminous correspondence survives for this period and points to Neile's administrative efficiency, unflappability, cost-awareness, and shrewd use of local gentry—Catholic and protestant alike.

Bishop of Winchester and archbishop of York, 1628–1640

In November 1628 Neile was nominated for Winchester, another prestigious see, and one which he must have thought would have been his final resting place; he was duly elected in December and received the temporalities in February 1629. He gave Laud, now bishop of London, valuable support in high commission cases held at that time, most notably including some concerning London churches in which the parishioners had constructed seats around the communion table, to which Neile retorted angrily that they thought themselves 'worthy to sit above the Lord's board in his own house' (Gardiner, 302). He argued equally fiercely in favour of the divine right of episcopacy when Leighton's case came before Star Chamber in 1630. He served on commissions dealing with the poor and for the repair of St Paul's in 1631, both matters on which he had shown interest for much of his life.

In February 1632 came the call to help his friend Laud in another capacity, namely that of archbishop of York, following the deaths in rapid succession of George Mountain and then Samuel Harsnett. The appointment was given royal assent on 3 March and confirmed on 19 March, enthronement taking place in Neile's absence on 16 April 1632. Much else took place without him in the early years of his incumbency, for he was still a valued member of the privy council, attending its meetings in the winter and spring months until 1636. Reunited with his lawyer protégé William Easdall, Neile became famous for the speed and efficiency with which he set about bringing changes to the northern province as a result of his metropolitical visitation held in 1633–4. In his annual report to the king in January 1634 Neile complained that his commissioners had found much amiss in the dioceses of Carlisle and Chester, where 'it was scarce clear that the communion table was any whit respected and where ministers preached much as they wished regardless of the Book of Common Prayer' (PRO, SP 16/259/78, fol. 2v). By 1636 he was able to report that things were much improved on all fronts as he had goaded Bishop John Bridgeman into action, instituted a major campaign to repair and beautify churches, clamped down hard on nonconformist ministers, and restricted the activities of lecturers.

In his campaign to repair churches Neile seems to have led the way in the country, acting on the authority of a proclamation of 1629 rather than waiting for the king's pronouncement after the celebrated case of St Gregory's in 1633. Prior to that he was the first bishop to order that the communion table be railed in churches. It is also clear that, thanks to his partnership with able church lawyers like Easdall and Mottershed, Neile was more effective than many bishops in getting compliance with such orders. The act books of his chancery court pay ample tribute to the success of roving commissioners who followed

up the work of his visitation commissioners with regard to church fabric cases. Over three-quarters of the churches and chapels in the northern province are known to have been repaired and 'beautified' during the 1630s.

Character and reputation

Neile published little himself and preferred to surround himself with able chaplains who did his preaching for him, hence Heylyn's endorsement that he had more able men about him than any other of his time. His edition of *M. Ant. de Dominis Archbishop of Spalato, his Shiftings in Religion*, published in 1624, is a relatively practical account of the debates held with the archbishop pending his return to Rome. It could be argued, however, that the portrayal of Spalato's views on puritans, even citing some bishops as fellow travellers, was helpful to the general Arminian cause. Copies of Neile's episcopal visitation articles survive for Lichfield and Coventry (1611), Lincoln (1614), Durham (1624 and 1627), Winchester (1628 and 1631), and York (1632–3, 1636, and 1640). They reveal a pragmatic administrator who asked questions carefully without giving too much offence, and constitute a fairly traditional set of articles based on a cross between those of his mentor Richard Bancroft and those of William Chaderton, inherited from Lincoln. The Durham articles of 1624 possibly reveal a more confident and radical approach as Neile asked questions about the practice of confession which he favoured and showed clear hostility to nonconformists.

Neile was a devoted Londoner who, despite his sojourn in six dioceses, always spent the bulk of the year in London, until at last in 1636 ill health robbed him of the ability to travel easily. His key residences were in Westminster and then Durham House in the Strand, while both Winchester and York afforded comfortable London residences. Neile seems to have used his membership of Gray's Inn (gained in 1609) and Doctors' Commons (May 1612) to good effect to recruit able young clergymen and civil lawyers right up until his time at York. He was also very loyal to Cambridge where again voluminous correspondence survives from well into the 1620s, particularly when Neile and his chaplains were involved in recruiting support for the successful campaign of the duke of Buckingham to become chancellor in 1626.

Neile was the 'political fixer' of the Arminian party who used his court connections and the favour of James I to good advantage to support and promote his colleagues when their views were far from popular. His influence was critical when Laud became president of St John's, Oxford, in 1611, when the Abbot brothers accused Laud and Howson of favouring popery in 1615, and when Laud offended his bishop and others by moving the communion table at Gloucester in 1616. His influence was vital as a strong bishop of Durham and his chaplains played a key role behind the scenes in the publication of the controversial works of Richard Mountague in 1624 and 1625. But he was more than an astute political operator at court. Neile was also an extremely able administrator, a bishop who seems to have been able to motivate his colleagues and command great loyalty and respect from his civil lawyers, diocesan officials, and servants. In spite of his fierce reputation with puritan ministers, he was also able to say in later life that he 'never deprived any man; but have endeavoured their reformation with meekness and patience' (PRO, SP 16/345/85, fol. 6). Neile's pragmatic approach in each of his dioceses seems to have made him an effective leader and communicator with clergy and gentry alike.

A devoted family man, Neile ensured his own success as a diocesan administrator in part by his shrewd use of nepotism. His elder brother William kept house for him for over twenty years; his brother-in-law William Holmes took over that role in 1625; and his half-brother Robert Newell worked with him in three dioceses. Those who married into his family, like Gabriel Clarke and Edward Burby, benefited with promotion. His nephews, notably Richard and John Neile, gained livings under his patronage, the former at Winchester, the latter at York. Pluralist though he was in the early years of his career, the case of the nephew with the same name has confused many historians into thinking that Richard Neile was still a pluralist in the 1630s; this was not the case. His devoted civil lawyers Edward Liveley and William Easdall were made to feel part of the family, both acting as godparents to Neile's grandchildren, while Liveley was the family lawyer to whom Neile entrusted his family affairs on his death.

Death and legacy Neile died in York on 31 October 1640. According to his arch-enemy William Prynne 'this prelate being scarce Parliament proof, to prevent all questioning; at the approach of this present Parliamentary Assembly fell sick and died, being now gone to answer all his episcopal extravagancies before a greater tribunal' (Prynne, 1.224): this is surely a harsh judgement on a man of seventy-eight. Neile was buried in York Minster and neither his son, Sir Paul, nor his widow, Dorothy, seems to have seen fit in the turbulent years that followed to create any grand memorial. They returned to London and were buried in St Benet Fink, London, in 1686 and on 3 May 1647 respectively.

In his will dated 23 June 1640 Neile revealed his commitment to the Church of England as established under Elizabeth I by rejoicing in the fact that he was born in the same year as the Thirty-Nine Articles were ratified. He bequeathed a ring given to him by Christian IV of Denmark to his son, Sir Paul, left money for members of the Newell and Holmes families, and touchingly provided all servants of his household at the time of his death with a year's salary each. Such concern for those who worked for him was a constant feature in his life, for he used to provide money for his household and for the poor when on progresses to visit property when dean of Westminster, corresponded in familiar terms with servants in Durham, and when archbishop of York once stopped his carriage to give money to the poor. All this was probably in memory of his own humble origins.

Neile had clearly become quite wealthy by the time he died, for he notes in his will that it might be difficult to provide an annuity of £200 per annum for his wife because he had just lent King Charles £2000. Much of this wealth may have been founded on the acquisition of rights to various coal mines when at Durham in the 1620s, and Neile's administrative skills on behalf of his dioceses were scarcely likely to be at his own expense. Yet his reputation was that of a bountiful patron, generous benefactor, and exemplary bishop in the restoration of church property, notably his episcopal palaces at Rochester, Lincoln, Durham, and York. In a funeral sermon given at the death of his eminent chaplain John Cosin in 1672, Neile was remembered as 'Vir Architectonicus' ('Man of Architecture'; I. Basire, *A Funeral Sermon on the Death of John Cosin*, 1673, 77). Early in his career as dean of Westminster, Neile was also providing money to aid scholars go to Cambridge, just as he later supported the initiatives of others like John Williams who were able to be more generous.

At least twenty books from Neile's collection were presented to York Minster Library by Ferdinando, Lord Fairfax, commander of the parliamentary forces that took York in 1644. The books may have been seized from Neile's palace at Cawood. Many of them carry the inscription 'R. Neale et amicorum' and some have a motto, 'Vivit redemptor quid desperam' ('The redeemer lives; of what should I despair?'). Other books carrying this motto have been located in the British Library. The books at York are a mixture of classical and theological texts (Homer, Cicero, Ovid, Sallust, Euripides, St John Chrysostom, Titelmann), but the sample is too small to allow firm conclusions to be drawn from this reading matter. Quite a few writers dedicated books to Neile, despite his practical rather than academic proclivities. These included the noted early naturalist Edward Topsell, whom Neile seems to have helped when dean of Westminster, the theologians John and Francis White, and the even more distinguished Thomas Jackson; the latter two served as Neile's chaplains. Of course, some dedications came from enemies such as William Prynne. On a more positive note, Thomas Procter re-dedicated his manuscript treatise 'The parishioners clayme for their vicars mayntenance' to Neile in 1638 in recognition of all that Neile had achieved in the restoration of Yorkshire churches. ANDREW FOSTER

Sources A. W. Foster, 'A biography of Archbishop Richard Neile (1562–1640)', DPhil diss., U. Oxf., 1978 · A. Foster, 'The function of a bishop: the career of Richard Neile, 1562–1640', *Continuity and change: personnel and administration of the Church of England, 1500–1642*, ed. R. O'Day and F. Heal (1976), 33–54 · A. Foster, 'Church policies of the 1630s', *Conflict in early Stuart England: studies in religion and politics, 1600–1642*, ed. R. Cust and A. Hughes (1989), 193–223 · A. Foster, 'The struggle for parliamentary representation for Durham, 1600–41', *The last principality*, ed. D. Marcombe (1987), 176–201 · A. Foster, 'Archbishop Richard Neile revisited', *Conformity and orthodoxy in the English church, c.1560–1660*, ed. P. Lake and M. Questier (2000), 159–78 · N. Tyacke, *Anti-Calvinists: the rise of English Arminianism, c.1590–1640* (1987) · W. Prynne, *Antipathie of the English lordly prelacie*, 1 (1641), 224 · K. Fincham, *Prelate as pastor: the episcopate of James I* (1990) · K. Fincham, ed., *Visitation articles and injunctions of the early Stuart church*, 2 vols. (1994–8) · J. Davies, *The Caroline captivity of the church: Charles I and the remoulding of Anglicanism, 1625–1641* (1992) · D. Pearson, 'The libraries of English bishops, 1600–40', *The Library*, 6th ser., 14 (1992), 221–57, esp. 250 · J. Le Neve, *Lives and characters of the bishops since the Reformation* (1720), vol. 1, pt 1, pp. 137–8 · A. Leighton, *Epitome* (1646), 66 · P. Smart, *A short treatise of* *altars* (1629), preface, 3 · A. Tindal Hart, *A house of kings*, ed. E. F. Carpenter (1966), 144 · M. Jansson, ed., *Proceedings in parliament, 1614 (House of Commons)* (1988), 370 · Rev. Precentor Venables, ed., 'The primary visitation of the diocese of Lincoln by Bishop Neile, A.D. 1614', *Associated Architectural Societies' Reports and Papers*, 16 (1881–2), 46 · *Report on the manuscripts of the late Reginald Rawdon Hastings*, 4 vols., HMC, 78 (1928–47), vol. 4, p. 253 · P. Heylyn, *Cyprianus Anglicus* (1668), 74 · S. R. Gardiner, *Reports of cases in the courts of star chamber and high commission*, CS, 39 (1886), 302 · PRO, SP 16/259/78, fol. 2*v* · PRO, SP 16/345/85 fol. 6 · parish register, St Margaret's, Westminster, 11 March 1562 [baptism] · S. H. Cassan, *The lives of the bishops of Winchester*, 2 vols. (1827)

Archives Coll. Arms · U. Durham L., corresp. and papers | BL, Add. MSS · BL, Burney MSS · BL, Harley MSS · BL, Lansdowne MSS · Bodl. Oxf., Eng. Hist. MSS · Bodl. Oxf., MSS Rawl. · Bodl. Oxf., Tanner MSS · Borth. Inst., archbishop's registers (31, 32); Neile's subscription book (bk 2); visitation court books; precedent book 2 · CUL, Add. MSS · CUL, Baker MSS · Durham Cathedral, Mickleton and Spearmans MSS · Durham Cathedral, Bishop Neile's register; enrolment books · GL, parish registers · Leeds Central Library, Thomas Procter 'Parishioners clayme for their vicars maytenance' · Leicester Cathedral, clerical subsidies · Lichfield Cathedral, joint RO, dean and chapter account book · Lincoln Cathedral, Red book; visitation book 1614; dean and chapter act book; lease books · PRO, CAL State Papers Domestic, Elizabeth I, James, Charles I; privy council registers; signet office docquet books · Rochester Cathedral, dean and chapter lease book · Rochester Cathedral, Neile's register · U. Durham L., dean and chapter act book · U. Durham L., lease registers · Westminster Abbey, dean's book · Westminster Abbey, dean and chapter act books · Westminster Abbey, treasurer's accounts · Winchester Cathedral, Neile's register; patent book; lease registers; dean and chapter act book · York Minster Library, dean and chapter act books, lease books, files, book collection

Likenesses oils, *c.*1620, St John Cam. [*see illus.*] · portrait, *c.*1670 (for Bishop Cosin) · oils, copy, 19th cent., Bishopthorpe Palace, York · engraving, 1822 (after oil painting at St John Cam.) · double portrait, stained-glass window (with Cosin), St John the Evangelist, Leeds

Wealth at death over £3000 excl. loan of £2000 to King Charles I: will, Cassan, *Lives of the bishops*

Neile, William (1637–1670), mathematician, was the eldest son of Sir Paul *Neile (*bap.* 1613, *d.* 1682×6) and his wife, Elizabeth, *née* Clarke, and the grandson of Richard *Neile, archbishop of York, in whose palace at Bishopthorpe he was born on 7 December 1637. He entered Wadham College, Oxford, as a gentleman commoner in 1652, but did not matriculate until 1655; meanwhile his talent for mathematics was nurtured by John Wilkins and Seth Ward. In 1657 he became a student at the Middle Temple. In the same year, at the age of nineteen, he gave an exact rectification of the cubical parabola (the calculation of a straight line equal to a curve), and communicated his discovery—the first of its kind—to Brouncker, Wren, and others of the Gresham College Society. His demonstration was published in John Wallis's *De cycloide* (1659, p. 91).

Neile belonged to the privy council of Charles II; he was elected a fellow of the Royal Society on 7 January 1663 and a member of the council on 11 April 1666. He took part in the extended debate about the laws of motion, and his own theory of motion was communicated to the society on 29 April 1669. He undertook astronomical observations with instruments erected on the roof of his father's residence, Hill House, White Waltham, Berkshire.

Neile died at Hill House in his thirty-third year, on 24 August 1670, 'to the great grief of his father, and resentment of all virtuosi and good men that were acquainted with his admirable parts' (Wood, 902). He was buried in the parish church of White Waltham, where a monument commemorated him. Hearne said of him:

> He was a virtuous, sober, pious man, and had such a powerful genius to mathematical learning that had he not been cut off in the prime of his years, in all probability he would have equalled, if not excelled, the celebrated men of that profession. Deep melancholy hastened his end, through his love for a maid of honour, to marry whom he could not obtain his father's consent. (*Itinerary of John Leland*, 144)

An earlier attack of jaundice may, however, have contributed. A. M. CLERKE, *rev.* ANITA MCCONNELL

Sources *The correspondence of Henry Oldenburg*, ed. and trans. A. R. Hall and M. B. Hall, 4–5 (1967–8) · T. Birch, *The history of the Royal Society of London*, 4 vols. (1756–7); repr. with introduction by A. R. Hall (1968), vol. 2. pp. 361, 460 · *VCH Berkshire*, 3.174, 176 · *VCH Yorkshire North Riding*, 1.401–2 · C. Hutton, *A philosophical and mathematical dictionary*, new edn, 2 vols. (1815) · *The itinerary of John Leland the antiquary*, ed. T. Hearne, 2nd edn, 9 vols. (1744) · Wood, *Ath. Oxon.* · M. Hunter, *The Royal Society and its fellows, 1660–1700: the morphology of an early scientific institution* (1982), 36, 68

Archives RS, letters to Henry Oldenburg

Neill, Alexander Sutherland (1883–1973), founder of Summerhill School, was born in Forfar in Scotland on 17 October 1883, the fourth son and fourth of the thirteen children (one of them stillborn) of George Neill (*d.* 1937), schoolmaster, and his wife, Mary (1854–1934), daughter of Neil Sutherland, who worked in the docks at Leith. Both his parents were teachers and he attended his father's school at Kingsmuir. His upbringing was within a Calvinist culture and a rigid pattern of order, against which many of his own beliefs were a strong reaction.

Neill left school at fourteen to become first a clerk and then a draper's apprentice, but soon returned to his father's school as a pupil teacher, although he failed to win a place at teacher training college. He worked harder to pass the matriculation requirements of Edinburgh University in 1908, rapidly deserting the study of agriculture for that of English. More significantly, he was a lively editor of the student magazine and went to London to find work on the fringes of publishing and journalism. A leg injury kept him (temporarily) out of the army in 1914, and he accepted an appointment as temporary headmaster in Gretna Green School. His work as teacher and as publicist now merged, and in 1916 appeared the first of many books, *A Dominie's Log*. Significantly, too, the *Weekly Dispatch* discovered him and he was never thereafter to be short of publicity. His distrust of the conventional curriculum and of public examinations, his belief in freedom rather than orthodox discipline, and his capacity to provoke criticism were already evident. 'I send my Tommie to school to learn, not to dig in the garden', objected one parent.

In 1917 Neill joined the army and was commissioned as an artillery officer. He became a friend of the unconventional reformer Homer Lane, whom he was to acknowledge as the strongest influence upon his whole life and through whom, albeit unsystematically, he encountered

Alexander Sutherland Neill (1883–1973), by Ishbel McWhirter, 1964

the ideas and practices of Sigmund Freud. His first book had already brought him some fame, and he taught for a short while at the King Alfred School in Hampstead. His advanced views on self-government by pupils offended the restrained liberal customs of that well-known progressive school, and he was obliged to resign.

Neill became in 1920 the joint editor with Beatrice Ensor of *Education for the New Era* and so joined that loosely articulated, and often disputatious, group of educational reformers that had emerged in the last decade. Beatrice Ensor was a founder member of the Ideals in Education group which had grown up around Edmond G. A. Holmes after his retirement from his majesty's inspectorate of schools and the publication in 1911 of his deeply influential *What is and What Might Be*. Bertrand Russell and his wife, Dora, opened Beacon Hill School in 1927, and Dartington Hall began its life in 1925. Rousseau, Pestalozzi, Froebel, Dewey, and Freud were the ill-assorted intellectual patrons of these educational novelties.

The New Education Fellowship—'new' was the keynote of these hopeful years after the war—was part of these loosely related developments although Neill himself was contemptuous of attempts to induct the young into a 'higher life' or the cultivation of 'good taste'. For him, the important task was to free children from fear, to replace an emphasis on intellect with one on emotion, rather than to teach or instruct. 'No man is good enough to tell another how to live. No man is wise enough to guide another's footsteps.'

Neill went in 1921 to the international section of a new school at Hellerau, near Dresden, where he developed more confidently his theories or intuitions on the ways in which the young should be reared. The new school, trapped within a bureaucratic system and threatened by the economic crisis of the time, collapsed in 1924, and Neill moved (after a brief but unsuccessful attempt to continue his school in Austria) with five pupils and his partner's wife (whom he was later to marry) to start a tiny school at Lyme Regis in Dorset, in a rented house called Summerhill. Three years later, with some thirty pupils, they moved to Leiston in Suffolk. By 1934 there were seventy pupils: Neill and Summerhill had become, and for the rest of his life remained, synonymous. The school attracted a steady stream of comment, criticism, and visitors. During the Second World War it was removed to Ffestiniog in north Wales, which Neill hated. It was formally inspected after the return to Suffolk and Neill himself commented on the liberalism of an educational system which allowed his own creation to flourish. Nevertheless, it remained in difficulties after the war, and by 1960 numbers had declined to twenty-five.

Neill, in spite of his considerable gifts as author and publicist, chose always to concentrate on his work for the relatively small number of (often disturbed) children whose lives he could directly influence within his own boarding establishment. He preferred to be described as 'author and child psychologist'. 'I do not want to be remembered as a great educator, for I am not, but because I tried to abolish fear in schools.' Nor was his thinking systematic: for him, Summerhill was a demonstration and not an experiment. The influence of Freud was largely mediated through his intense relationship with Homer Lane. After 1937 the influence of Wilhelm Reich was similarly potent. His underlying principles and prejudices remained clear: 'Let us think of a bad school. I mean a school where children sit at desks and speak when they are spoken to.'

Neill's life and polemics contributed at many points to the swings in mood and policy which marked education in Britain and other countries during the twentieth century. The early reform movements with which he was associated in the 1920s articulated a reaction against the horrors of the First World War and the blind obedience to authority which many of his contemporaries so profoundly distrusted. He was deeply sympathetic to liberal and progressive causes in the 1930s, abandoning only slowly and reluctantly his early enthusiasm for the Soviet experiments: he was unsurprisingly refused entry to the United States in 1950, at the height of the reaction in that country to the perceived threat of communism. In 1960 his book on Summerhill (composed of a series of extracts from earlier works) was published in the United States in the same month as the election as president of John F. Kennedy, and it appealed directly both to a national mood of optimism and to a prevailing sense of disenchantment with the achievements of public education in that country. Two million copies were sold within the decade.

Neill nevertheless viewed with some alarm the founding of an American Summerhill Society, rejecting the notion that anything so particular as his creation could be organized or generalized. In his native country he took little interest, and had little confidence, in mainstream education and tended to underemphasize the substantial changes which took place during his own lifetime. Some, but never all, of his ideas became part of the so-called progressive movement in educational thought and policy which distinguished the 1960s, reaching a peak of public recognition with the publication in 1968 of the report of the Plowden committee on primary education. His work received less attention in the last three decades of the century as very different attitudes towards the purposes and nature of education came to predominate.

Neill was twice married: on 9 September 1926 to Ada Lillian Lindesay Neustätter (*b*. 1871), an Australian, a matron at his school. She was the former wife of Dr Otto Neustätter and the daughter of Walter Lindesay Richardson MD. She died in 1944, and on 14 April 1945 he married Ena May Wood [*see below*], with whom he had a daughter. He could not afford to retire, even if he had wished to, and died at the age of eighty-nine at the Cottage Hospital, Aldeburgh, on 23 September 1973. He was cremated at Ipswich. Unimpressed by honours, he had nevertheless accepted the honorary degrees of MEd from Newcastle in 1967, LLD from Exeter in 1968, and DUniv from Essex in 1971.

Neill was survived by his second wife, **Ena May Neill** [*née* Wooff] (1910–1997). She was born at Offham Road, West Malling, Kent, on 29 May 1910, the daughter of Ernest George Wooff, grocer's assistant, and his wife, Ethel Sophie May. She trained as a nurse in London but gave up nursing to marry, on 5 March 1932, William Albert (Bill) Wood (*b*. 1909/10), a commercial artist. The couple separated and their son, Peter, was sent to Summerhill, while Ena worked in London in a photographic studio. When the school moved to Wales she accepted Neill's offer of employment as a cook but gradually took over the running of the school after managing a measles epidemic and nursing Neill's first wife through her final illness. After their marriage, and the school's return to Suffolk, she took over the practical organization of the school, and after Neill's death in 1973 she formally became head, and continued to run it according to his principles. She remained head until her retirement in 1985, when she was succeeded by their daughter, Zoe Readhead. Ena Neill died at Aldeburgh and District Community Hospital, Suffolk, on 26 October 1997.   H. G. JUDGE

Sources J. Croall, *Neill of Summerhill: the permanent rebel* (1983) · J. Croall, ed., *All the best, Neill: letters from Summerhill* (1983) · A. S. Neill, *Summerhill: a radical approach to education* (1960) · A. S. Neill, *Neill! Neill! Orange peel* (1973) · J-F. Saffange, *Libres regards sur Summerhill: l'œuvre pédagogique de A. S. Neill* (1985) · *The Times* (25 Sept 1973) · *The Guardian* (6 Nov 1997) [E. M. Neill] · *The Times* (11 Nov 1997) [E. M. Neill] · R. E. Hemmings, *Fifty years of freedom: a study of the development of the ideas of A. S. Neill* (1972) · R. J. W. Selleck, *English primary education and the progressives, 1914–1939* (1972) · R. Skidelsky, *English progressive schools* (1969) · W. A. C. Stewart, *The educational innovators, 2: Progressive schools, 1881–1967* (1968) · m. certs. [A. S. Neill] · b. cert. [E. M. Neill] · m. cert. (1933) [E. M. Neill] · d. cert. [E. M. Neill]
Archives BL, corresp. with Society of Authors, Add. MS 63311 · Internationaal Instituut voor Sociale Geschiedenis, Amsterdam, corresp. with Dora Russell · McMaster University, Hamilton, Ontario, corresp. with Bertrand Russell · U. Lond., Institute of Education, corresp. with World Education Fellowship | FILM BFI NFTVA, current affairs footage
Likenesses I. McWhirter, oils, 1964, Summerhill School, Leiston, Suffolk · I. McWhirter, oils, 1964, Scot. NPG [*see illus.*] · I. McWhirter, ink drawing, 1965, NPG · photograph, 1969, Hult. Arch. · A. Thornhill, bronze head, Scot. NPG

Neill, Ena May (1910–1997). *See under* Neill, Alexander Sutherland (1883–1973).

Neill, James George Smith (1810–1857), army officer in the East India Company, was born on 27 May 1810 at Craigie, near Ayr, the eldest son of Colonel William Neill of Burnweill and Swendridge, Muir, Ayrshire, and his wife, Caroline, whose maiden name was Spiller. He was educated at Ayr and at Glasgow University. On 31 October 1835 Neill married Isabella (1816–1875), daughter of Colonel Warde of the 5th Bengal cavalry and assistant to the resident at Nagpur, with whom he had three daughters and seven sons.

India, Afghanistan, and Burma, 1826–1854 Neill obtained a cadetship in the Madras army of the East India Company's service in 1826. He landed at Madras on 1 June 1827 and with the assistance of the governor of the Madras presidency, Sir Thomas Monro, who was married to one of Neill's relatives, was posted on 5 June to the 1st regiment of European infantry (later renamed the 1st Madras fusiliers) quartered in Masulipatam Fort. Neill was commissioned an ensign on 5 December 1826, promoted lieutenant on 7 November 1828, and was made adjutant of the fort on 15 September 1829, retaining this post until his regiment marched to Kamptee. While stationed at this new garrison he was made quartermaster and interpreter to the right wing of the regiment on 1 May 1831. On 7 March 1834 Neill was nominated adjutant and shortly afterwards was selected to command the resident of Nagpur's escort.

Neill left Calicut on 1 January 1837 on sick furlough and travelled to Europe, but returned to Madras on 25 July 1839, before his leave expired, in the vain hope of being employed during the First Anglo-Afghan War. Sir Robert Dick obtained an appointment for Neill on the staff on 23 March 1841 as deputy assistant adjutant-general in the Ceded Districts. While holding this appointment he wrote a short history of his regiment. On 5 January 1842 he was promoted brevet captain, and on 25 June he was made aide-de-camp to Major-General Woulfe. Neill was promoted captain on 2 January 1843, and major on 25 March 1850.

When the Second Anglo-Burmese War broke out in 1852 Neill resigned his staff appointment, rejoining his regiment, which had been ordered on active service. *En route* he was appointed to the staff of Sir Scudamore Steele, commanding the Madras troops in Burma as deputy assistant adjutant-general. Neill served with distinction throughout the campaign and at the end of the war remained at Rangoon in command of the Madras contingent. He was actively employed under Sir John Cheape in suppressing insurrections near Thurygyeen, Bassein, and

James George Smith Neill (1810–1857), by unknown photographer

elsewhere. On 9 November he was promoted lieutenant-colonel. A combination of constant hard work and the harsh climate meant Neill contracted a near fatal fever in 1854 and he returned to England to recuperate.

Crimean War, 1855–1856 After the outbreak of the Crimean War, General Robert Vivian, formerly adjutant-general of the Madras army, appointed Neill as second-in-command of an Anglo-Turkish force he had been selected to lead. Neill was given the rank of colonel on the staff and in April 1855 travelled to Constantinople. He was appointed to command a Turkish division in camp at Büyükdere, on the Bosphorus, where he was busily occupied until July bringing it into a state of efficiency and discipline. Neill was then appointed president of a commission, composed of British officers and Turkish officials, set up to inquire into outrages committed by General Beatson's Bashhi-Bazoukhs. On 27 July it began work at the British embassy with full powers to try to discipline any offenders. Severe punishment was meted out to any men convicted of theft, which helped improve morale and discipline among the troops. Neill reported that the excesses committed were due primarily to lax discipline, and suggested various steps required to improve this state of affairs. For his work Neill received the thanks of Lord Stratford de Redcliffe, the ambassador, who directed General Beatson to either adopt the commission's recommendations or to resign his command.

Neill displayed considerable ability in organizing and reforming the Turkish contingent; he sacked twelve officers, including a brigadier-general, three lieutenant-colonels, and three majors incapable of performing their duties. When the war ended Neill returned home and spent the remainder of his leave with his family. On 20 February 1857 he sailed for India and landed at Madras on 29 March, intending to rejoin his regiment. The 1st Madras fusiliers, however, had just been sent on active service in the Persian Gulf, forming part of the expedition under Sir James Outram. Neill was preparing to depart for Bushehr when news arrived, on 6 April, that the war was over. Two weeks later the regiment reached Madras. On 29 April

Neill assumed command of the regiment as Colonel Stevenson was compelled by poor health to return to England.

Indian mutiny, 1857 The news that several Indian regiments of the Bengal army had mutinied at Meerut and Delhi reached Madras on 16 May 1857. Neill embarked the 1st Madras fusiliers aboard ship two days later fully equipped for active service, in accordance with instructions, and on 24 May they landed at Calcutta. The regiment was immediately sent by river, road, or train to Benares. Neill captured the imagination of the shaken European population when he promptly arrested the stationmaster and both the engineer and the stoker of the train, who had threatened to depart without all his men according to the timetable. When Neill arrived at Benares on 3 June and heard that another Indian regiment had mutinied at Azamgarh, he immediately insisted on the disarmament of the garrison. During a badly mismanaged attempt to disarm the 37th native infantry the following day its sepoys mutinied. On Neill's orders an artillery battery, supported by the 10th foot and Madras fusiliers, immediately opened fire upon the sepoys who, during the confusion, were aided by men from the Ludhiana Sikh regiment, who had also been attacked in error. Neill promptly relieved Brigadier George Ponsonby, the garrison commander, who seemed incapable of dealing with the situation. This decision was later confirmed and Neill was appointed a brigadier-general in nominal command of the Hyderabad contingent. Neill zealously meted out retribution to captured mutineers or those suspected of complicity in the revolt, who were executed without due process. Hanging parties went out into the surrounding area and took vengeance on anyone even vaguely implicated in the rebellion in an attempt to pacify the disaffected local population.

Neill took energetic steps to restore British authority in Allahabad and the surrounding area. On 12 June 1857 the bridge of boats was captured from the rebels allowing the safe passage of a further 100 reinforcements to the fort. The fort's artillery bombarded nearby villages and suburbs harbouring rebel troops on 13 June; they were then cleared by the infantry, and the following day the last remaining potential source of danger to the fort was removed when the Sikh troops were quartered outside the fort's walls. Over the following week the surrounding villages were cleared of mutineers and suspected rebels by the Sikh and Madras fusiliers. Neill vigorously enforced martial law in Allahabad and reprisals were meted out without mercy to captured sepoys or suspected rebels, who were immediately executed. A steamer, carrying twenty marksmen and a howitzer, was also sent up the Jumna River; the force killed large numbers of rebels gathered along its banks. Neill also began amassing sufficient stores and transport, collected from the surrounding area, for the large force which now assembled at Allahabad to relieve the beleaguered garrisons at Cawnpore and Lucknow. For his services since the beginning of the rebellion he was rewarded by being promoted colonel in the army and appointed an aide-de-camp to Queen Victoria.

Major-General Sir Henry Havelock arrived at Allahabad on 30 June and assumed command of the moveable column detailed to relieve Lucknow. When Sir Henry Havelock marched out towards Cawnpore on 7 July at the head of just under 2000 men, a bitterly disappointed and resentful Neill was left behind with 200 men to hold Allahabad and ensure the prompt dispatch of both reinforcements and stores to the front. Neill made it no secret that he felt he should be in command of the moveable column, although he was mollified when an order reached him on 15 July from the acting commander-in-chief, Sir Patrick Grant, directing him to hand over responsibility for the town when the next senior officer arrived and to act as Havelock's second-in-command. Five days later Neill reached Cawnpore, which had been captured on 17 July 1857, now believing that the authorities had serious misgivings about Havelock's ability as a commander and had complete confidence in his own. The meeting between these two officers was less than cordial. When Neill arrived Havelock brusquely instructed him that he had no powers of command, and when Havelock marched out towards Lucknow five days later Neill was left in Cawnpore.

On assuming command at Cawnpore Neill immediately launched an enquiry into the massacre of Sir Hugh Wheeler's garrison at the Sati Chaura *ghat* and the death of the surviving women and children in the *bibigarh*. Upon learning of the atrocities committed by Nana Sahib, Neill, a deeply committed Old Testament Christian, decided to mete out an eye for an eye and a tooth for a tooth and make an example that he fervently believed would serve as a warning to all the rebels in India. On 25 July 1857 the following order was issued:

> The well, in which are the remains of the poor women and children so brutally murdered by this miscreant, the Nana, will be filled up, and neatly and decently covered over to form their grave; a party of European soldiers will do so this evening, under the superintendence of an officer. The house in which they were butchered and which is stained with their blood, will not be washed nor cleaned by their countrymen; but Brigadier-general Neill has determined that every stain of that innocent blood shall be cleared up and wiped out, previous to their execution, by such of the miscreants as may be hereafter apprehended, who took an active part in the mutiny, to be selected according to their rank, caste, and degree of guilt. Every miscreant, after sentence of death is pronounced upon him, will be taken down to the house in question, under a guard, and will be forced into cleaning up a small portion of the bloodstains; the task will be made as revolting to his feelings as possible, and the provost marshal will use the lash in forcing any one objecting to complete his task. After properly cleaning up his portion the culprit is to be immediately hanged, and for this purpose a gallows will be erected close at hand. (Kaye, *History of the Sepoy War*, 2.399)

This draconian order, deliberately intended to offend Hindu and Muslim religious sensibilities, was enthusiastically carried out by the men under his command and won wide support throughout India.

Neill was left with only 300 infantry, half a battery of European artillery, and twelve gunners to hold Cawnpore when Havelock advanced into Oudh, despite the presence of large numbers of rebels in the surrounding area. He was instructed to defend the trunk road in the neighbourhood of the city, maintain communications with Allahabad and Cawnpore, strengthen the defences on both sides of the River Ganges, and finally to set up a secure ferry service across the river using two steamers.

Havelock's moveable column crossed the Ganges and successfully defeated a large rebel force occupying two fortified villages at Unao on 29 July, but after suffering heavy casualties from cholera, dysentery, and enemy action at Basiratganj he decided to halt at Mangalwar, as without further reinforcements it was impossible to reach Lucknow. This decision caused consternation and bitter disappointment in Cawnpore, prompting Neill to write an insubordinate letter to Havelock criticizing his actions, which earned a sharp rebuke from his furious superior. A further advance from Mangalwar was repulsed by the rebels, and Cawnpore itself was threatened by large bodies of rebel sepoys. A sally by two armed steamers upriver checked the rebel advance, but on 10 August 4000 men and five guns massed at Bithur. As a large part of Neill's force was now incapacitated by sickness he sent word to Havelock that he was unable to keep open his communications and had barely sufficient forces to hold Cawnpore if attacked. Havelock returned to Cawnpore and on 16 August attacked and dispersed the enemy concentration at Bithur before retiring on the town. Relations between Neill and Havelock were now badly strained. Neill maintained his intemperate attitude towards his superior in a series of letters sent to his close friend Sir Patrick Grant. Although Grant tried to impress upon Neill the necessity of loyally supporting his immediate superiors, his letters had little effect, and shortly afterwards Sir Colin Campbell took over command in India. Neill began a similar correspondence with Major-General Sir James Outram, *en route* to take command of the force moving on Lucknow, in which he also harshly criticized Havelock. Despite the bitter acrimony now evident between the two men, Havelock took Neill with him when he advanced towards Lucknow after receiving further large reinforcements, placing him in command of the right wing of his force, consisting of the 5th and 48th foot, the Madras fusiliers, and Maude's battery of artillery.

Neill marched out with the 1st brigade on the morning of 25 September towards the embattled residency, but almost immediately his men were met by a murderous crossfire from rebel guns and muskets. He pressed his attack, instructing Maude's battery to silence the enemy guns while his infantry cleared several walled enclosures packed with enemy troops on either side of the road. Neill led on horseback from the front, charging two guns firing straight down the road in one village at the head of the Madras fusiliers; the guns were captured despite heavy losses. Only slight resistance was met as the advance continued along the banks of the Gumti River around the outskirts of Lucknow until the British column reached the road leading towards the residency. When the British force approached the mess house and the *kaisarbagh*, rebel troops redoubled their efforts and for 200 yards the column was exposed to an incessant hail of bullets and grape-shot from the surrounding buildings. Further confusion was caused when the column entered a large square in the city where rebels firing from the tops of houses on all sides inflicted heavy casualties. While trying to regulate the movement of troops rushing through an archway at the end of the square that led towards the residency, Neill was shot dead by a rebel marksman. His body was rescued by Captain J. B. Spurgin, his brigade-major, and carried to safety on a gun carriage. On the evening of 26 September 1857 Neill was buried under cover of darkness in a church-yard within the Lucknow Residency.

The death of Brigadier-General Neill caused widespread shock and grief in India and England, where it was felt that the Indian army had lost a resolute, brave, and ener-getic officer who had been one of the first to stem the tide of the revolt. As Lord Canning later wrote in his dispatch on the relief of Lucknow:

> Brigadier-general Neill, during his short but active career in Bengal, had won the respect and confidence of the Government of India; he had made himself conspicuous as an intelligent, prompt, and self-reliant soldier, ready of resource, and stout of heart.   (Kaye, *Lives of Indian Officers*, 2.577)

Despite repeated insubordination and his savage treat-ment of captured sepoys and rebels at Allahabad and Cawnpore, which ironically hardened resistance among the local populace, statues of Neill were erected in his memory in India and England. The official *Gazette* also later announced that, had Neill lived, he would have been made a KCB, and his wife was later invested with the insig-nia and allowed to enjoy the title and precedence to which she would have been entitled had her husband survived. His widow also received a large pension from the East India Company.   T. R. MOREMAN

Sources J. W. Kaye, *Lives of Indian officers*, new edn, 2 vols. (1904) • H. C. Wylly, *Neill's blue caps*, 2 (1923) • S. N. Sen, *Eighteen fifty-seven* (Delhi, 1958) • C. Hibbert, *The great mutiny, India, 1857* (1978) • cadet papers of James George Neill, BL OIOC, L/MIL/9/165, fols. 124–8 • *DNB* • By a staff officer [J. G. S. Neill], *Historical record of the Honour-able East India Company's first Madras European regiment* (1843) • J. W. Kaye, *A history of the Sepoy War in India, 1857–1858*, 3 vols. (1864–76) • J. C. Marshman, *Memoirs of Major-General Sir Henry Havelock*, new edn (1876) • T. A. Heathcote, *The military in British India: the development of British land forces in south Asia, 1600–1947* (1995)
Archives NL Scot., journal | N. Yorks. CRO, letters to Sir H. Have-lock
Likenesses C. Baugniet, lithograph, pubd 1858, BL OIOC, P623 (F186) • Noble, statue, Wellington Square, Ayr • G. Stodart, stipple (after photograph by Kilburn), BM, NPG • photograph, NAM [*see illus.*] • portrait, repro. in Wylly, *Neill's blue caps*, frontispiece

Neill, Patrick (*bap.* 1665, *d.* in or after 1704), the first printer in Belfast, was baptized at Glasgow High Church on 12 November 1665, the son of David Neill, a Glasgow bookbinder (*b.* 1630), and Mary Hamilton. On 6 December 1688 he married Agnes Blaw (*b.* 1670), sister to his assistant James *Blow at Culross, Perthshire. Patrick and Agnes baptized three children in Glasgow: Elizabeth (*b.* 1691), John (*b.* 1692), and Patrick (*b.* 1694). In 1691 Patrick Neill,

described as a bookbinder, was admitted burgess and guild brother in Glasgow.

In 1694 Patrick Neill and James Blow set up the first press in Belfast at the request of the current sovereign (mayor) of Belfast, William Craford, although whether this was in an official capacity as printers to the town is unclear. Both Craford and the prominent Presbyterian bookseller and merchant Brice Blair are presumed to have been partners in Neill & Co. A letter written in 1719 by Wil-liam King, archbishop of Dublin, to the archbishop of Canterbury claimed an unnamed book dated 1694 had been printed illegally in Belfast. The book has been recently identified as *The Confession of Faith*, and the copy in question resides in Christ Church Library, Oxford (Drennan, 193). The next surviving book printed by Neill is Robert Craghead's *An Answer to the Bishop of Derry's Second Admonition* (1697).

Of thirty-six items attributed to the Neill press, some twenty-eight have survived into modern times. Most do not identify the printer or place of printing, but nine works dated 1699–1700 state 'P Neill & Company', and from the years 1700–03 there are three works stating 'P Neill'. Whether this change implies the dissolution of the partnership is unclear. The last identifiable work by Neill is *Dreadful Warnings with Seasonable Advice* (1703). The Neill press published works by authors of the Presbyterian per-suasion, the *Confession of Faith* volume (1694, 1700) and *Psalms of David in Meeter* (1699, 1700), stating that they were approved by the general assembly of the Church of Scot-land. A copy of the Psalms was presented to the Belfast First Presbyterian Church by David Smith, who was sover-eign when it was printed in 1700. It is unique among early Belfast printed books in having a fine binding of tortoise-shell and silver. The first item advertised in a list of books printed and sold by Neill at the end of Edward Pearse's *The Great Concern* (1700) is the New Testament. This is sup-ported by fragments of St Mark's gospel found in end-papers of Neill's edition of Robert Craghead's *Advice for Assurance of Salvation* (1702). Of literary interest are *The Bible the Best New-Years-Gift*—an edition of John Taylor's *Verbum sempiternum* printed in 1699—and a 1700 edition of Alexan-der Montgomerie's *The Cherrie and the Slae*.

Benn states that Patrick Neill died 'about 1705' (Benn, 427). Patrick's will, dated 1704, names the surviving child-ren as 'John, James and Sarah, and I recommend my son John to the care of my brother Blow to teach him the trade I taught him' (ibid., 428). There is no evidence of any of them surviving into adulthood or subsequently being involved in the printing trade; the Neill press was taken over by James Blow about 1705. Given the close family rela-tionship between Neill and James Blow, whose family had lived at Castlehill, Culross, for over 180 years, the death recorded on 9 July 1724 of 'Patrick Neill, sometime sta-tioner at Culross, late bookbinder of Glasgow' raises the possibility that Patrick Neill did not die *c.*1705, or suggests a close relative with the same name and occupation (McCann, 128).   ANTHONY S. DRENNAN

Sources W. McCann, 'Patrick Neill and the origins of Belfast printing', *Six centuries of the provincial book trade in Britain*, ed. P. Isaac

(1990), 125–38 · G. Benn, *A history of the town of Belfast* (1877), 425–36 · A. S. Drennan, 'On the identification of the first Belfast printed book', *The Library*, 7th ser., 1 (2000), 193–6 · E. R. M. Dix, 'List of books and tracts printed in Belfast in the seventeenth century', *Proceedings of the Royal Irish Academy*, 33C (1916–17), 73–80 · Glasgow old parish register

Archives Linen Hall Library, Belfast

Neill, Patrick (1725–1789), printer, was born in Haddington, Haddingtonshire, and baptized on 9 August 1725, one of eight children of Robert Neill and Jean Paxtoun. In 1739 he was apprenticed to James Cochran of Edinburgh, a printer of the *Scots Magazine*. Ten years later the booksellers Gavin Hamilton and John Balfour, seeing the opportunities for a new Scottish trade in reprinting, and wanting to give the Scottish book a name in the world, selected the 24-year-old Neill as their printing partner. The contract for Hamilton, Balfour, and Neill (the young printer used the second comma in imprints to set off his name) was signed on 7 December 1749, and the firm began at Whitsunday 1750. While the salary of £25, rising to £30 in the second year, was only about the wage of an Edinburgh journeyman, the arrangement allowed Neill to prosper. He contributed two-fifths of the starting capital of £320 and shared the profits proportionally. From 1750 to 1762 Neill managed for the firm its reprints of English and French titles, its production of university theses and textbooks, and its original work in science, medicine, history, law, philosophy, and literature, and for a brief period (1759–61) he also ran its newspaper, the *Edinburgh Chronicle*. In his fine printing of the classics, Neill quickly produced the look Hamilton and Balfour had achieved in their celebrated *Virgil* of 1743: on the title-page of his edition of Volusene's *De animi tranquillitate dialogus* (1751), the few words of type appear to float off the surrounding white space.

The printing house was originally located in the Royal Infirmary, where Hamilton was treasurer, in a ward on the third floor of the west wing and in a room at the top of a stair. When Hamilton and Balfour became printers to Edinburgh University in 1754, Neill moved the operation into the college, where the partners rented the Low Library and the printing house below. All the printing materials and equipment used there, including three presses and quantities of Wilson, Baine, and Caslon type, are described in an inventory Neill drew up in 1764. Of the six apprentices he took on in the early years, the most notable was William Smellie, who was given the privilege of attending university classes, and in 1758 composed and corrected the edition of Terence that won a silver medal from the Edinburgh Society. James Macpherson, creator of Ossian, was Neill's corrector of the press for a few months in 1759, and his *Fragments of Ancient Poetry* was printed there the next year.

Neill appears to have had a peaceable temperament. His calm handling of authors is seen in the marked proof sheets for William Maitland's *History of Edinburgh* (1753), where he is imperturbable in the face of the author's bullying complaints, and in his written comments on the proofs for *A Dissertation on the Numbers of Mankind* (1753).

There he politely reproves the author, Robert Wallace, for lateness: 'Mr. Wallace may please know, that the first page & a few more Sentences marked thus X are not marked by the Copy, because he did not return it' (Edinburgh University Library, La.II.96/2, sig. 1). These proof sheets, Wallace's containing some corrections by David Hume, also illustrate the changes in spelling and punctuation made to authors' copy at Neill's press.

The *Edinburgh Chronicle* was an ambitious undertaking, with an interest in literature and drama (James Boswell contributed theatrical reviews in 1759) and in readers' observations. Walter Ruddiman, publisher of the *Caledonian Mercury*, attacked Hamilton and Balfour when the paper went from twice-weekly to tri-weekly in September 1759, saying they had broken an agreement with the scholar Thomas Ruddiman, and they prudently dropped their names from the colophon as publishers. The printer John Reid, brought in as a partner to Neill, did not have the money he promised and was let go. In the number for 17 December 1760 Neill inserted a paragraph accusing a Glasgow shoemaker of the rape and death of a young girl, a false story that had been passed on to him. He was subsequently fined £10 for defamation, at a trial in which he described his editorial practices. The *Edinburgh Chronicle*, reduced to a weekly publication, stopped in March 1761, and Neill returned 5450 stamped sheets to his London agent, William Strahan.

Although Hamilton and Balfour broke up in 1762, the name Hamilton, Balfour, and Neill was used for another year, and Neill continued to print in the college until 1769, when his firm moved to Old Fishmarket Close. Neill was in partnership with Robert Fleming senior and junior from September 1764 to March 1767. He brought his brother Adam Neill into the firm (the relationship is shown in Patrick's ledger), and Adam ran the partnership with the Flemings from 1764 to 1774. The Neill ledgers give insight into the business of printing in Edinburgh at the time, showing costs of printing and paper, and identifying the type employed in titles. Much of the business was legal work, but the Neills also printed for authors and for members of the Edinburgh trade, including John Balfour, Kincaid and Bell, and the Flemings, and for C. and E. Dilly of London. It was a lucrative operation. In 1771 Patrick was able to retire, at forty-six, to become a country squire. In 1772 he bought a farm and house at Redpath, in the Berwickshire parish of Earlston, and in 1778 he married Katherine Brown there. He died at Redpath on 28 January 1789, aged sixty-three. The firm he founded, Neill & Co., continued in Edinburgh until 1973.

WARREN McDOUGALL

Sources M. McLaren, ed., *The house of Neill, 1749–1949* (1949) · W. McDougall, 'Gavin Hamilton, John Balfour and Patrick Neill: a study of publishing in Edinburgh in the 18th century', PhD diss., U. Edin., 1974, 183–6 [P. Neill, 1 Sept 1764, 'Printing materials belonging to Mr. Patrick Neill', printing ledger, fol. 13] · W. McDougall, 'The publication of William Maitland's *History of Edinburgh*', *Scottish Book Collector*, 2/10 (1991), 11–13 · P. Neill, marked proof sheets of W. Maitland's *A history of Edinburgh*, U. Edin. L., MS Dh.6.73 · P. Neill, marked proof sheets of R. Wallace's *A dissertation on the numbers of mankind*, U. Edin. L., MS La.II.96/2 · W. McDougall,

'Hamilton, Balfour, and Neill and *The Edinburgh Chronicle*', *Scottish Book Collector*, 2/11 (1991), 24–8 • P. Neill, 'The petition of Patrick Neill, printer in Edinburgh,' 9 Feb 1793, with 'Information for John Finlay merchant-shoemaker in Glasgow', 29 Nov 1762, *Session Papers* [Signet Library], 70/35 • P. Neill to James Sinclair, 18 June 1763, NL Scot., MS Dep. 196 • P. Neill, printing ledger, 1764–7; A. Neill, printing ledger, 1767–73, NL Scot., MS Dep. 196 • W. McDougall, 'A catalogue of Hamilton, Balfour and Neill publications, 1750–1762', *Spreading the word: the distribution networks of print, 1550–1850*, ed. R. Myers and M. Harris (1998), 187–232 • bap. reg. Scot. • *Scots Magazine* (1789), 52

Neill, Patrick

Neill, Patrick (1776–1851), naturalist and printer, was born in Edinburgh on 25 October 1776. He became head of the large printing firm of Neill & Co., but devoted his considerable leisure time to scientific pursuits, particularly botany. He became first secretary of the Wernerian Natural History Society in 1808, and, the following year, of the Caledonian Horticultural Society. He held the latter post for forty years.

In 1806 Neill published *A Tour through Orkney and Shetland*, a work which exposed the miserable conditions then endured by the islanders. He was the author of the article 'Gardening' in the seventh edition of the *Encyclopaedia Britannica*, which was subsequently published under the title of *The Flower, Fruit, and Kitchen Garden* (1840). In 1817 he made a tour through the Netherlands and the north of France, his account of which was published in 1823.

Neill was an active gardener and garden designer. It was under his direction, in 1820, that the West Princes Street Gardens in Edinburgh were laid out and planted with 77,000 trees and shrubs. His own garden, at Canonmills Cottage, near Edinburgh, was renowned for its exotics, and was always open to fellow naturalists. Of equal note was his collection of live animals, 'cats, parrots, cockatoos, and animals of rare stamp, which were allowed full liberty in his establishment' (Waller). His interest in zoology led to several publications including *Proofs that the Beaver was a Native of Scotland* (1819).

Neill was fellow of the Linnean and Edinburgh Royal societies, and honorary LLD of Edinburgh University. He died unmarried at Canonmills on 3 September 1851, several months after having suffered a stroke. He was buried at Warriston cemetery, Edinburgh. Among his various charitable bequests was one of £500 to the Caledonian Horticultural Society to found a medal for distinguished Scottish botanists or cultivators, and a similar sum to the Royal Society of Edinburgh for a medal for distinguished Scottish naturalists. He is botanically commemorated by the rosaceous genus *Neillia*.

B. D. JACKSON, rev. PETER OSBORNE

Sources private information (1894) • *Proceedings of the Linnean Society of London*, 2 (1848–55), 191 • *Gardeners' Chronicle* (18 Oct 1851), 663–4 • R. K. Greville, *Algae Britannicae* (1830), introduction, 4, 25 • *GM*, 2nd ser., 36 (1851), 548 • *The lithology of Edinburgh, by the late John Fleming*, ed. J. Duns (1859), 15–16 • B. W. Crombie and W. S. Douglas, *Modern Athenians: a series of original portraits of memorable citizens of Edinburgh* (1882), 115 • *Journal of Botany, British and Foreign*, 28 (1890), 55 • J. F. Waller, ed., *The imperial dictionary of universal biography*, 3 vols. (1857–63) • Desmond, *Botanists*, rev. edn
Archives NL Scot., corresp. with George Combe • NL Scot., corresp. with Archibald Constable • Royal Museum, Edinburgh, letters to Sir William Jardine • U. Edin. L., corresp. with Robert Jameson • U. Newcastle, Robinson L., letters to Sir Walter Trevelyan
Likenesses R. M. Hodgetts, mezzotint, pubd 1837? (after J. Symt), BM • B. W. Crombie, etching, 1847, NPG
Wealth at death bequests of at least £1000: *DNB*

Neill, Stephen Charles

Neill, Stephen Charles (1900–1984), church historian and ecumenical worker, was born on 31 December 1900 at Edinburgh, the third child in the family of four sons and two daughters of northern Irish evangelical parents, Charles Neill and his wife, Margaret Penelope, daughter of James Monro CB. His father was ordained as a minister in the Church of Ireland, and was a low-churchman and fundamentalist. Both parents had a strong interest in the conversion of India, and Neill's sister spent all her life as a missionary in India. Neill was sent to be educated at Dean Close School at Cheltenham. He went on to Trinity College, Cambridge, and was placed in the first class of part one of the classical tripos (1920) and part two of both the classical tripos (1922) and the theological tripos (1923). Cambridge classical dons later regarded him as one of the ablest classical students they met between the two world wars. He then wrote a thesis on the Cappadocian fathers of the fourth century AD and their relationship with Neoplatonic philosophy. On this thesis he won a fellowship at Trinity College.

Neill held the fellowship only a short time, for in 1924 he decided to go as a missionary to south India. There his astonishing ability at languages soon gave him a mastery of Tamil, in which he could preach and write fluently. He also learned Sanskrit and made himself an authority on the early Hindu religious texts. He wrote (in English) some modest but charming little books about his parish life in India. In 1930 he became warden of a theological college at Tirumaraiyur, and in 1939 was elected bishop of Tinnevelly. He was full of energy, often on a bicycle. He preached brilliantly in English or Tamil and had high standards for his clergy. Here he began his ecumenical interest. The various Christian denominations in south India were wondering how it would be possible to have a united south India church. Neill understood the theological as well as the practical problems and took a prominent part in the delicate negotiations which led up to the formation of the Church of South India in 1947.

But before the achievement of unity a disaster of health struck Neill. He began to suffer the incidence of mental aberration and a continuous weariness through insomnia and pain through headaches. The other Indian bishops believed that it was impossible for him to go on as a bishop and in 1944 asked him to resign his see.

Neill returned to Cambridge and became chaplain to his college and a lecturer in the faculty of divinity. He also became well known as a preacher, lecturer, and conductor of missions throughout England. He could talk at length without notes, his voice was attractive, his experience rare, and his capacity to illustrate his points wide-ranging. He fascinated the young, and not only the young, with his tale of Christianity spreading across the globe at a time when in Europe it seemed to be in recession.

In 1947 G. F. Fisher, the archbishop of Canterbury, made

Stephen Charles Neill (1900–1984), by Shelburne Studios

Sources K. Cragg and O. Chadwick, 'Stephen Charles Neill, 1900–1984', *PBA*, 71 (1985), 603–14 · *The Times* (24 July 1984) · *The Times* (3 Aug 1984) · private information (1990) · *WWW* · *CGPLA Eng. & Wales* (1984)
Likenesses Shelburne Studios, photograph, British Academy [*see illus.*] · photograph, repro. in Cragg and Chadwick, 'Stephen Charles Neill, 1900–1984', facing p. 603
Wealth at death £166,298: probate, 13 Nov 1984, *CGPLA Eng. & Wales*

him his assistant bishop for ecumenical work. He moved to Geneva to be near the World Council of Churches. But the problems of health recurred. Part of 1950 he spent in hospital, and in February 1951 the archbishop asked him to resign.

Neill now became a writer and a traveller for the World Council of Churches. He lived in Geneva, helped to edit the *Ecumenical Review*, edited (with Ruth Rouse) *The History of the Ecumenical Movement* (1954), an important and original achievement, and started a series called World Christian Books which published between 1952 and 1970 seventy books under his editing or direction. The intention was to help the education of the developing ministries in the churches of the developing world. He wrote several of the books himself. This post at Geneva, the publications, and the travel on behalf of the World Council or for the International Missionary Council made him a well-known figure in the world church. The best known of his books to the English public was a Pelican entitled *Anglicanism* (1958).

From 1962 to 1967 Neill was a lecturer in Christian missions and ecumenical theology, with the title of professor, at the University of Hamburg. His interest was the question how far the expansion of Christianity into Asia and Africa depended on the European imperial mission, and how it would free itself from that inheritance once the imperial mission ended. This phase was marked by *A History of Christian Missions* (1964), *Colonialism and Christian Missions* (1966), and *The Church and Christian Union* (1968). For these and other works he was elected a fellow of the British Academy in 1969.

From 1969 to 1973 Neill was the first professor of philosophy and religious studies at the University of Nairobi. Then he retired to Wycliffe Hall at Oxford to write the history of Christianity in India. The first volume was published in 1984, the second a year after his death which occurred on 20 July 1984 at Wycliffe Hall. He never married. He held eight honorary degrees, and took the Cambridge DD when he was seventy-nine.

OWEN CHADWICK, rev.

Neilson, Adelaide [*real name* Elizabeth Ann Brown; *known as* Lizzie Ann Bland; *married name* Elizabeth Ann Lee] (**1848–1880**), actress, was born on 3 March 1848 at 35 St Peter's Square, Leeds, the daughter of an unmarried strolling player, Ann Brown, later known as Mrs Bland. The name of her father is unknown (though it appears on her marriage certificate as Pera Lizon); she later claimed that letters to her mother which she had discovered in a locked drawer revealed that he was a Spanish nobleman. As a child she lived at Skipton and worked at Green Bottom Mill, Guiseley, where she attended the Wesleyan Methodist Sunday school. She was a quick pupil and at an early age recited passages from her mother's playbooks. She then became a nursemaid in a local family, until in 1861, having apparently learned the secrets of her parentage, she ran away to London, calling herself Lizzie Ann Bland.

Her early experiences in London were harsh; she worked as a seamstress and behind the bar in a public house near the Haymarket, where she acquired a reputation as a Shakespearian declaimer. She was not seen on the stage, however, until 1865, when she appeared at Margate as Julia in Sheridan Knowles's *The Hunchback*, under the name of Lilian Adelaide Lessont; she soon changed her name yet again, and it was as Adelaide Neilson that she achieved fame. In the meantime, on 30 November 1864 (using yet another name, Lilian Adelaide Lizon), she had married Philip Henry Lee, a graduate of Brasenose College, Oxford, and the son of the rector of Stoke Bruerne, near Towcester; Lee had apparently taken a great interest in her before their marriage, and had sent her to a ladies' academy. They were divorced in 1877.

Neilson made her London début in July 1865 at the Royalty Theatre. Her performance as Juliet made a profound impression on the critics in her sparse audience. Such theatrical knowledge as she possessed at that time had been obtained from John Ryder, whose pupil she was. She was a remarkable beauty of a 'Spanish type', with large dark eyes and a musical voice. This performance led to her engagement at the Princess's Theatre, where on 2 July 1866 she was the original Gabrielle de Savigny in Watts Phillips's *The Huguenot Captain*; in the same year she played the eponymous Victorine in a revival of that drama at the Adelphi, a role for which her peculiarities of accent and manner were considered to render her particularly suitable. In 1867 at the same theatre she was the original Nelly Armroyd in Phillips's *Lost in London*. She returned fairly frequently to Guiseley, and was financially generous towards her mother.

On 25 September 1868 Neilson was seen as Rosalind at the Theatre Royal, Edinburgh, after which she appeared as Pauline in Bulwer-Lytton's *The Lady of Lyons* and Julia in

Adelaide Neilson (1848–1880), by Mora

£25,000 with which she endowed a theatrical charity, the Adelaide Neilson Fund.

Adelaide Neilson won great praise from Joseph Knight, her *Dictionary of National Biography* biographer. He wrote from personal knowledge that,

> As a tragedian she has had no English rival during the last half of the [nineteenth] century. Her Juliet was perfect, and her Isabella had marvellous earnestness and beauty … In comedy she was self-conscious, and spoiled her effects by over-acting … The best of her original parts were Amy Robsart and Rebecca. It is not easy to see how these could have been improved.

J. GILLILAND

Sources C. Scott, *The drama of yesterday and today*, 2 vols. (1899) · *The life and reminiscences of E. L. Blanchard, with notes from the diary of Wm. Blanchard*, ed. C. W. Scott and C. Howard, 2 vols. (1891) · H. B. Baker, *The London stage: its history and traditions from 1576 to 1888*, 2 vols. (1889) · Ward, *Men of the reign* · E. Stirling, *Old Drury Lane*, 2 vols. (1881) · D. Cook, *Nights at the play* (1883) · C. E. Pascoe, ed., *The dramatic list*, 2nd edn (1880) · *The Times* (Aug 1880) · S. D'Amico, ed., *Enciclopedia dello spettacolo*, 11 vols. (Rome, 1954–68) · Hall, *Dramatic ports*.

Likenesses T. E. Gaunt, chalk drawing, 1880 (after N. Sarony), NPG · Lock & Whitfield, woodburytype photograph, NPG · Mora, photograph, NPG [*see illus.*] · ivory miniature, priv. coll. · photograph, repro. in J. Hollingshead, *Gaiety chronicles* (1898) · photographs, NPG · portraits, Harvard TC

Wealth at death under £25,000: probate, 30 Aug 1880, CGPLA Eng. & Wales

The Hunchback. She then spent some time performing in Birmingham before creating the part of Lilian in Westland Marston's *Life for Life*, at the Lyceum in London in March 1869. At the Gaiety in October 1869 she played the first Mme Vidal in *A Life Chase* by John Oxenford and Horace Wigan, and the first Mary Belton in H. J. Byron's *Uncle Dick's Darling*; during a performance of the latter, she was hit on the head by a piece of falling scenery and had to retire in favour of an understudy. The following April she was back at the Gaiety, as Julia in a revival of *The Hunchback*. In May 1870 at St James's Hall she began a series of dramatic readings from a variety of plays, interspersed with commentary. In 1871 she appeared at Drury Lane in a number of adaptations of Scott's novels, notably as Amy Robsart in *Kenilworth* and Rebecca in *Ivanhoe*, and in Shakespeare, drawing much admiration and a salary of £400 a week.

A series of farewell performances at the Queen's Theatre (in *Romeo and Juliet* and *The Lady of Lyons*) preceded Neilson's departure for New York. In America she was extremely popular, reputedly earning £700 a week for her performances as Beatrice, Isabella, and Lady Teazle. She returned to America in 1874, 1876, and 1879, adding Viola in *Twelfth Night* and Imogen to her repertory. In 1876 she appeared at the Haymarket as Isabella and as the heroine of Tom Taylor's *Anne Boleyn*. Her last original part was Queen Isabella in *The Crimson Cross*, which was seen for the first time at the Adelphi on 27 February 1879.

Neilson's last visit to America ended in July 1880, and soon after returning to England she left for Paris, complaining of ill health. On 15 August 1880 she drank a glass of iced milk in the Bois de Boulogne, was seized with what was apparently a gastric attack, and died the same day. After a post-mortem her body was taken to London and buried at Brompton cemetery. She left an estate of some

Neilson, George (1858–1923), historian and antiquary, was born at Horseclose Farm, Ruthwell, Dumfriesshire, on 7 December 1858, the only child of Edward Neilson (1830–1861), captain in the mercantile marine, and his wife, Janet Paterson (1831–1903). His father died in Buenos Aires, and Neilson was brought up at Horseclose Farm, which belonged to his mother's family. He was educated at Cummertrees parish school and, from January 1872 to Christmas 1873, at King William's College, Isle of Man. After serving an apprenticeship at a writer's office in Dumfries, he attended the Scottish law class of Professor Robert Berry at Glasgow University in 1879–80, gaining first place in the class. In 1880–81 he again distinguished himself in the conveyancing class. He qualified as a solicitor in 1881 and in 1884 became a principal in Messrs Stodart and Neilson, writers, at 58 West Regent Street, Glasgow. He was appointed procurator fiscal of police in Glasgow on 6 November 1891. He also became fiscal of the Glasgow dean of guild court on 2 November 1899, and on 29 December 1909 he was appointed the first stipendiary police magistrate of Glasgow. He held this office until May 1923, when he resigned on grounds of ill health. He also made an unsuccessful application for the chair of Scottish history at Edinburgh University in 1901.

Neilson married on 24 June 1892 Jane Ann Richardson (1859–1945), daughter of Thomas Richardson, cattle dealer, of Hexham, and his wife, Ann Short. They had one son, who died aged three on 14 March 1894, and one daughter.

Neilson possessed an alert mind and a keen enthusiasm for research. He was eager to direct the attention of others to subjects that interested him and often placed at their disposal the fruits of his own studies. Beginning with studies of his native south-west Scotland, by his thirtieth year he had gained a firsthand knowledge of the sources of early Scottish history and of the antiquities of Scottish law and became a charter scholar and expert paleographer. His combination of charter scholarship with the study of records, chronicles, place names, and topography blazed a trail for Scottish medieval studies. The reading of *Bracton's Notebook*, edited by Frederic William Maitland in 1887, led him to send to Maitland in 1889 the manuscript of a study that he had made of the origin and early history of the duel. Maitland was enthusiastic, and Neilson's *Trial by Combat*, dedicated to his teacher Robert Berry, was published at Glasgow in 1890. It was favourably received and remains valuable. Terse, pointed, and illuminating, it was a pioneering examination of an obscure field, in particular making clear the distinction between the judicial duel and the duel of chivalry.

Up to the date of his death in 1906, Maitland was in close correspondence with Neilson, although they met only twice. Maitland constantly applied to him for guidance and information on questions of Scottish law and history. Neilson formed similar, though less intimate, relations with other scholars, especially Mary Bateson, J. H. Round, Andrew Lang, F. J. Haverfield, H. C. Lea, and F. Liebermann. In the field of medieval studies he came to represent Scotland in the eyes of students south of the border. Scholarly and enthusiastic, he devoted much time to solving the problems of others. In 1894 he published *Peel: its Meaning and Derivation* and in 1899 *Annals of the Solway*, both admirable examples of the work of a learned antiquary. An active interest in Romano-British archaeology led to *Per lineam valli* (1891), which opened up new lines of inquiry about Hadrian's Wall, while he also edited *The Antonine Wall Report* of the Glasgow Archaeological Society (1899).

Neilson devoted many years to the study of middle Scots verse. He sought to claim for John Barbour the authorship of a series of alliterative poems and, in his *Huchown of the Awle Ryale, the Alliterative Poet* (1902), to identify Huchown with Sir Hugh of Eglinton and to assign certain poems to him. He carried on a controversy about these matters in the pages of *The Athenaeum* and elsewhere for years, and in the course of it became friendly with Henry Bradley, F. J. Furnivall, W. P. Ker, W. W. Skeat, and others. These relationships were always extremely amicable, as Neilson inspired liking even in his opponents. His arguments for the thesis that he maintained were ingenious but no longer command support. It may be claimed, however, that his writings and the replies that they called forth revived an interest in an area of literature that had fallen into neglect.

In 1902, on the invitation of the University of Glasgow, Neilson delivered a course of lectures on early Scottish literature, and in 1903 the university conferred on him the honorary degree of LLD. Latterly he returned to legal and feudal history. In 1912, at the invitation of the Society of Antiquaries of Scotland (of which he was then a vice-president), he delivered the Rhind lectures in archaeology on 'Scottish feudal traits'. In 1918, after delay owing to the First World War, the record commissioners issued the *Acta dominorum concilii, 1496–1501*, edited by Neilson and Henry Paton. The substantial introduction was Neilson's work. It contains many interesting suggestions and speculations, and was the stimulus for much subsequent work on the origins of the Court of Session.

From 1903 to his death, much of Neilson's time was devoted to the *Scottish Historical Review*, founded in that year; every issue of the journal included some form of contribution, signed or anonymous, from his pen, and he had a large share in its direction.

After suffering for more than a year from a malignant disease of the stomach and bowel, Neilson died at his home, Wellfield, 76 Partickhill Road, Partick, Glasgow, on 15 November 1923.

D. BAIRD-SMITH, *rev.* HECTOR L. MACQUEEN

Sources *Proceedings of the Society of Antiquaries of Scotland*, 29–59 (1891–1924) · U. Glas., Neilson MSS · NL Scot., Neilson MSS and charters · b. cert. · d. cert. · old parish records, Annan, Dumfriesshire · old parish records, Ruthwell, Dumfriesshire · King William's College, Isle of Man, Alumni Register, 133 · matriculation albums, U. Glas., Archives and Business Records Centre, R8/1/6 · calendars, 1880–82, U. Glas. · Mitchell L., Glas., Strathclyde regional archives · pamphlets, NA Scot., 10/13 · *The Post Office directory of Glasgow* (1880–1923) · *F. W. Maitland: letters to George Neilson*, ed. E. L. G. Stones (1976) · *Scots Law Times* (11 June 1898), 29 [portrait] · *Scottish Law Review*, 39 (1923), 353 · D. B. Smith, 'George Neilson', *Transactions of the Glasgow Archaeological Society*, new ser., 7 (1924), 351–5 · G. Macdonald, *Proceedings of the Society of Antiquaries of Scotland*, 58 (1923–4), 1–2 · *Proceedings of the Society of Antiquaries of Newcastle upon Tyne*, 4th ser., 1 (1923–4), 161–2 · J. T. T. Brown, *SHR*, 21 (1923–4), 144–5 · *Glasgow Herald* (16 Nov 1923) · A. L. Davidson, 'George Neilson, LLD, FSA', *The Gallovidian*, 15 (1913), 1–7 · E. L. G. Stones, 'Memoir', in E. L. G. Stones, A. L. Murray, and D. Stevenson, *Miscellany one*, Stair Society, 26 (1971), 1–10 · d. cert. [Jane Ann Neilson]

Archives NL Scot., collections and papers · U. Glas. L., papers | CUL, letters to F. W. Maitland

Likenesses W. Strang, etching, 1910; formerly in possession of Mrs. Neilson · photograph, U. Glas., MSS Gen 1114 (JJ) · photograph, U. Glas., Department of history · photograph, repro. in *Scots Law Times*, 6 (1898), 28 · photograph (in old age), repro. in Smith, 'George Nielson', facing p. 352 · photograph, repro. in *Glasgow Herald* (17 Nov 1923), 5

Wealth at death £4645 4s. 8d.: confirmation, 24 Jan 1924, *CCI* · £205 8s. 5d.: additional estate, 12 Sept 1924, *CCI* · £14 14s. 2d.: additional estate, 12 Dec 1924, *CCI*

Neilson, James Beaumont (1792–1865), engineer and inventor of the hot blast in iron manufacture, was born on 22 June 1792 at Shettleston, then a village near Glasgow, the son of Walter Neilson, a millwright, and Barbara *née* Smith. His father subsequently became an engine-wright at Govan colliery. Neilson received an elementary education until the age of fourteen, and while still at school he helped to supervise a condensing engine built by his father. He then became a 'gig-boy' on a winding engine at Govan.

Two years later, showing an enthusiasm for mechanics, Neilson was apprenticed to his elder brother John, an engineman at Oakbank, near Glasgow, and worked as his brother's fireman. During his spare time he also managed to acquire some knowledge of physics and chemistry from Anderson's Institution in Glasgow. His brother became a prominent engineer and designed and constructed the *Fairy Queen*, one of the first iron steam boats to sail on the Clyde.

In 1814 Neilson was appointed, with a salary of £70–£80, to the post of engine-wright of a colliery at Irvine, where he made various improvements. A year later he married Barbara Montgomerie of Irvine, who brought him a dowry of £250; and this enabled them to live when Neilson's employer's business failed, and he lost his job. The couple migrated to Glasgow, where Neilson was appointed foreman of the Glasgow gasworks although aged only twenty-five. Five years later he became manager and engineer of the works, and he maintained his connection there for thirty years. He introduced several important improvements in both the manufacture and the utilization of gas, notably the employment of clay retorts, the use of sulphate of iron as a purifier, and the swallow-tail jet, which subsequently came into general use. He encouraged his employees, many of whom were illiterate, to educate themselves, and established a workers' institute, complete with library, lecture-room, laboratory, and workshop.

In the 1820s Neilson began the research which led to his discovery of the value of hot blast in iron manufacture. This contradicted current practice, for finding that iron was produced by blast furnaces in greater quantity and of better quality in winter than in summer, the ironmasters had concluded that this was due to the lower temperature of the blast in winter. So strongly were they convinced of the truth of this that they had even adopted artificial refrigeration of the blast. Neilson discovered that this theory had no basis in fact, and he was convinced that the superior yield of the blast furnaces in winter could be explained, in part at least, by increased moisture of the air in summer. It was, however, the comparative inefficiency of the blast in one particular case, in which the blowing engine, instead of being near the furnace, was half a mile away, that alerted him to research which led ultimately to his breakthrough. Neilson concluded that the effects of distance between the furnace and blowing engine would be overcome if the blast was heated by passing it through a red-hot vessel, by which its volume, and therefore the work done by it, would be increased. Experimenting on gas and on an ordinary smith's fire, he found on the one hand that heated air in a tube surrounding the gas-burner increased the illuminating power of the gas, and on the other that by blowing heated air instead of air at its ordinary temperature into the fire its heat was much more intense. The overall heat loss was greatly reduced. Neilson therefore concluded that the blast would be made more efficient by heating it, not by refrigerating it.

Because the ironmasters stuck to their view about the benefit of cold air in the smelting process, they were reluctant to allow Neilson to try the hot blast in their furnaces. Even those who were willing to participate objected to alterations in their furnaces which Neilson wanted for a full-scale trial of his invention. Despite the delay, the hot blast was eventually tested to 200 °F at the Clyde ironworks, so successfully that Charles Macintosh

(1766–1843), the inventor of the waterproof, Colin Dunlop, and John Wilson of Dundyvan entered into a partnership with Neilson to patent and exploit the invention. Ultimately, on Dunlop's retiral, the partnership consisted of Neilson, Macintosh, and Wilson, Neilson being entitled to six-tenths of the profits, Macintosh to three-tenths, and Wilson to one-tenth. Separate patents were filed in 1828 for England, Scotland, and Ireland, that for England being dated 11 September, those for Scotland and Ireland 1 October. The complete specification was dated 28 February 1829. In 1832 Neilson became a member of the Institution of Civil Engineers in London.

Neilson and others soon improved the equipment. After five years' trial at the Clyde ironworks it was found that with the hot blast—ultimately raising the temperature to 600 °F—the same amount of fuel produced three times as much iron, and that the same amount of blast did twice as much work as the cold blast. A subsidiary benefit was that, whereas with the cold blast coke—at least in Scotland—had to be used, with the hot blast raw coal could be substituted, with considerable savings. In Scotland the invention was linked to the use of hard splint coal, which proved a major benefit. It allowed the exploitation of low grade black band ironstone, which, following its discovery by David Mushet (1772–1847), had been relatively uneconomic in iron manufacture because of high fuel costs. In 1839 the proprietor of one estate in Scotland derived a royalty of £16,500 from black band, although before the hot blast it had yielded him nothing. Later English anthracite coal, which could not be used in smelting iron with the cold blast, could be deployed using hot blast.

From the outset, controversy surrounded both the originality and patent rights of the hot blast. In 1832 the ironmasters the Bairds of Gartsherrie, new entrants to the industry and hence less bound by tradition, were the first openly to challenge Neilson's patent. Their protracted negotiations for a licence failed and they refused to pay the licence duty, claiming they were not using Neilson's process and were not bound to pay any licence duty. This challenge was quickly followed by others, and by 1833 Neilson and his partners were conducting legal cases against two other iron companies, which, like that against the Bairds, were pursued vigorously until payment was forthcoming. Neilson was also successful in the English courts, which explains the continued adherence of the Scottish ironmasters to the licence. They could hardly complain, because the Scottish pig-iron industry grew rapidly in the 1830s, partly in response to enhanced demand and partly as a result of the technological advance occasioned by Neilson's process.

In the later 1830s Neilson saw the early struggles and difficulties give way to widespread adoption of his invention, even if it did not go entirely unchallenged. By 1840 all the furnaces in Scotland were blown with hot blast, except one at Carron, while in England and Wales fifty-eight ironmasters had taken out licences. Income from the rights, which had been meagre at the outset, rose steadily to reach £30,000 per annum by 1840. Licences were issued at the rate of 1s. per ton, sufficient, Neilson and his partners thought, to make the patent remunerative, but not so high as to encourage widespread evasion or attack on the patent's validity.

However, in August 1839 the Bairds again refused to pay the licence duty, and so began a four-year legal battle, which at one stage saw the patentees pursuing twenty separate court actions against different companies in England and Scotland, culminating in the final and greatest challenge to Neilson's patent. Although the Scottish ironmasters formed an association to resist the validity of Neilson's patent in 1840, the first test case was brought against the English opposition. The case began in January 1841 with Neilson's declaration of his claim against the Harford Company and closed finally in November of the same year with a decision in favour of the patentees.

Meantime the Scottish ironmasters had chosen the Household Coal Company (which despite its name was a small iron producing concern) as a vehicle for their revived fight north of the border. When the case ultimately came to trial in April 1842, the patentees were awarded the verdict on all counts. However, on appeal to the House of Lords, a retrial was granted, though the law lords made it clear that they agreed with the verdict and only allowed the appeal on a technicality. Further litigation in this case was thus delayed until the following year and, more critically, the Bairds themselves avoided a trial until after the expiry of Neilson's patent on 1 October 1842.

When it reached the court of session in May 1843 the scale of the action of *Neilson v. Baird* made it a *cause célèbre*. The trial in Edinburgh lasted ten days, a record at the time, 102 witnesses were called, and the costs of the action were over £40,000. The principal attacks on Neilson focused on his originality and whether or not similar processes had been developed by others, but Lord Justice General Boyle was not convinced and summed up in the patentees' favour. The pursuers were awarded £4867 16s. in lieu of profits, and £7000 for damages. But what was by then known as the 'great hot-blast affair' was far from over, with Neilson preparing a further case against the Bairds, covering the period from May 1840 to the expiry of his patent and claiming £160,000 in lieu of profits, £20,000 in damages, and £500 towards costs. He also sought a retrial of the Household case and continued an action against William Dixon, another prominent ironmaster. When these were settled out of court the Bairds followed suit. By an agreement of 26 January 1844, not only were they forced to admit that the patent was valid and had been infringed, but they also had to pay the patentees £160,000 in damages and costs. James Baird, in the moment of this devastating defeat, made a typically defiant gesture of signing a cheque on the spot for the total sum.

Despite patent evasions and lawsuits, Neilson prospered financially and in 1847 resigned as manager of the Glasgow gasworks, buying a property in the Isle of Bute, belonging to the marquess of Bute, with whom he was friendly. In 1851 he moved to Queenshill near Tongland in the Stewartry of Kirkcudbright, where he actively promoted local improvements, founding an institution similar to that which he had established for the workmen of the Glasgow gasworks. He was elected a fellow of the Royal Society in 1846. In 1859, in the course of a discussion on H. Martin's paper on 'Hot ovens for iron furnaces', read at Birmingham to the Institution of Mechanical Engineers, Neilson gave an interesting account of his research and invention.

Neilson was apparently an upstanding and puritanical individual. At the Disruption he left the established Church of Scotland, and joined the Free Church. Following the death of his first wife he married Jane Gemmell, who predeceased him, dying at Bridge of Allan on 29 July 1863. Neilson died on 18 January 1865 at Queenshill and was buried at the Glasgow necropolis on 27 January. He was survived by four sons and three daughters.

Whether or not Neilson's invention was entirely original, he certainly demonstrated considerable ingenuity and formidable business skills in pursuing the application of the hot blast and asserting his patent rights. He and his partners therefore contributed substantially to the rapid expansion of the British iron industry during the second quarter of the nineteenth century, when pig-iron production quadrupled, its estimated gross value tripled, and the percentage of exports more than doubled.

FRANCIS ESPINASSE, *rev.* IAN DONNACHIE

Sources T. B. Mackenzie, *The life of J. B. Neilson, F.R.S.: the inventor of the hot blast* (1928) · R. D. Corrins, 'The great hot-blast affair', *Industrial Archaeology*, 7 (1970), 233–63 · A. Birch, *The economic history of the British iron and steel industry, 1784–1879* (1967) · C. K. Hyde, 'The adoption of the hot blast by the British iron industry: a reinterpretation', *Explorations in economic history*, 10 (1972–3), 281–93 · C. K. Hyde, *Technological change and the British iron industry, 1700–1870* (1977) · J. Butt, 'The Scottish iron and steel industry before the hotblast', *Journal of the West of Scotland Iron and Steel Institute*, 73 (1965–6), 193–220 · *DSBB* · W. K. V. Gale, *The British iron and steel industry: a technical history* (1967) · P. L. Payne, *Colvilles and the Scottish steel industry* (1979) · d. cert.

Archives Mitchell L., Glas. | NA Scot., court of sessions records · Royal Society of Procurators Fiscal of Glasgow, Hill collection · U. Glas., Murray MSS · University of Strathclyde, Glasgow, Baird MSS

Likenesses Brodie, bust, Kelvingrove Art Gallery and Museum, Glasgow · bust, repro. in *Memoirs and portraits of one hundred Glasgow men*, 2 (1886) · portrait, priv. coll. · portrait (*The hot blast partners*), University of Strathclyde, Collins Art Gallery

Neilson, John (1776–1848), publisher and politician in Canada, was born on 17 July 1776 at Dornald, Balmaghie, Kirkcudbrightshire, the son of William Neilson and Isabel Brown. In 1791 he joined his elder brother Samuel at Quebec to help him run the publishing firm of Brown and Gilmore; when Samuel died in 1793 he took over the business. He was a Presbyterian, but on 6 January 1797, at Trois-Rivières, he married the Roman Catholic Marie-Ursule Hubert, the niece of the Catholic bishop of Quebec. They had at least ten children, some of whom died in infancy. The boys were brought up Presbyterian, the girls Roman Catholic. This arrangement showed a willingness to compromise and a respect for French traditions which characterized Neilson's political as well as his private life.

Neilson soon became a successful printer, publisher, and bookseller, running his business with a keen eye for detail, a tenacity in following up unpaid accounts, and a determination to get the best staff and equipment even if these were not available close at hand. He was king's printer, and official commissions accounted for much of his business. He also published several newspapers, most importantly the *Quebec Gazette*, the largest weekly in the Canadas, and books including religious works and school textbooks. In addition he was a successful bookseller and a retail and wholesale stationer.

In 1818 Neilson was elected to the assembly of Lower Canada for the county of Quebec as a member of the Canadian party (he handed control of his business to his eldest son, Samuel, in 1822). The party, headed by Louis-Joseph Papineau, sought to wrest power from the largely British official clique which dominated the executive and legislative councils and strongly promoted union with Upper Canada. In 1823 Neilson and Papineau went as delegates to London with petitions from Lower Canada against the bill proposing union between Upper and Lower Canada, and the measure was abandoned. In 1828 Neilson again went to London to present the assembly's complaints against the administration of Lord Dalhousie, who was subsequently censured by the select committee of that year, which was much influenced by Neilson's testimony. In the assembly Neilson generally supported Papineau, but as the latter became increasingly revolutionary, anti-clerical, and anti-British, personal relations between the two broke down. In 1833 he distanced himself from the radicals and in 1834 he was defeated at the polls. Increasingly he was associated with the moderates among the British minority, and he assisted in the formation of constitutional associations and represented them in London in 1835; however, his efforts to find a political solution to the crisis in Lower Canada that would prevent a rebellion were in vain.

From 1838 to 1840, after the rebellion had been suppressed and the constitution suspended, Neilson served on the special council for the government of the two provinces. However, he continued to oppose the union of the Canadas, and thereby regained some of his popularity with the French-Canadian nationalists. He was elected to represent some of his old constituency in the assembly of the united provinces of Canada in 1841 and was allied with the French-Canadian minority in the assembly, which opposed demands for responsible government. In 1843–4 he supported the policies of the governor-general, Sir Charles Metcalfe, and in 1844 he became speaker of the assembly. He campaigned for the Conservatives in the election of 1844 and shortly afterwards was appointed to the legislative council, on which he served until his death.

Throughout his life Neilson was active in an extraordinarily wide range of Quebec affairs, from the Presbyterian church, to the theatre, education for adults and children, the Literary and Historical Society, agriculture, immigration, the fire service, and the treatment of prisoners and the insane, as well as in the upbringing of his many children. From the autumn of 1847 he suffered from respiratory illness, and he died on 1 February 1848 in Cap-Rouge, Lower Canada, and was buried in the cemetery of the Presbyterian church in Valcartier, near Quebec. He left a considerable estate. In politics he had consistently sought gradual reform and greater self-government. He was one of the few members of the Montreal business community to show real sympathy for the needs of the French-Canadian majority in Lower Canada, yet in both the crisis of the mid-1830s and that of the mid-1840s he found himself without significant allies in French Canada.

G. P. MORIARTY, *rev.* ELIZABETH BAIGENT

Sources S. Chassé, R. Girard-Wallot, and J.-P. Wallot, 'Neilson, John', *DCB*, vol. 7 · J. E. Hare and J.-P. Wallot, *Les imprimés dans le Bas-Canada, 1801–1840* (1967)
Archives Archives Nationales du Québec | Archives Nationales du Québec, Bourassa MSS · Archives Nationales du Québec, Duvernay MSS · Archives Nationales du Québec, Papineau MSS

Neilson, John (1778–1839), grocer and benefactor, was born on 14 December 1778 in Paisley, Renfrewshire, the second son in a family of five children of John Neilson, merchant and grocer of Paisley Cross, and his wife, Elizabeth *née* Sclater of Paisley. He was probably educated at Paisley grammar school until he was about fourteen years, when he entered his father's business as an apprentice. In 1810 he was admitted to the Paisley Merchants' Society and two years later joined his brother James and his father as a partner in the firm. Following the death of their father, the brothers continued in the business until James died in 1831. The firm was well established and prosperous, but a fire at Paisley Cross in 1833 which destroyed it and the family home above had a profound effect on John. Shortly afterwards he purchased an estate on the outskirts of Paisley, retired from business, and lived quietly at Nethercommon until his death there on 6 November 1839. He never married, and was buried in Paisley Abbey.

A reserved bachelor with no interests beyond commercial affairs, it is not known what motivated Neilson to leave £17,181 to found a school and provide clothing for boys from poor backgrounds or those whose parents had died 'without leaving funds … or who from misfortune … or from want of means … are unable to give a suitable education to their children'. His trustees, one of whom was his nephew, were invested with the 'most ample and unlimited powers' provided they purchased land for building within five years of his death, named the school the John Neilson Institution, and based the syllabus on the scriptures. By 1844 they had purchased a feu at Oakshawhead (the tradition that this was the site of a Roman camp was disputed in the twentieth century). The site was one of the most commanding in the town. So too was the John Neilson Institution; its architect, Charles Wilson of Glasgow, created an elegant, human-scaled building in the Palladian style.

The decision to restrict the number of foundationers and to admit fee-paying pupils, boys and girls, proved controversial. The trustees were accused of misinterpreting

Neilson's original wishes and it was not until legal opinion was sought by both sides that the matter was resolved, and pupils paying fees, kept deliberately low, were admitted.

From its opening in April 1852 about one-third of the school roll benefited from Neilson's settlement, and in 1874 provision was made to include girls, especially those who wished to train as teachers. Educationally and academically the school flourished, and as the curriculum was extended beyond the elementary to include classics, mathematics, and modern languages the school soon gained a reputation throughout the west of Scotland as a first-rate seminary. Nevertheless the trustees had to grapple with increased financial problems and by the twentieth century fee-paying pupils greatly outnumbered foundationers. The problem was solved in part by the school's abandonment of its independent status, becoming absorbed in the Scottish public school system. By the 1920s it was being administered by the Renfrewshire education authority, which continued to provide free places and subsidize the low-fee policy.

In 1968 the school was integrated into the new comprehensive system and a new building was erected about a mile away. In the early 1980s the original school was closed, but was saved from demolition by being designated a building of outstanding architectural and historical interest. In 1992 it was converted into private residential flats, with the name John Neilson Institution being retained. However, no school of that name now exists in Neilson's native town.

GEORGE STRONACH, rev. MAUREEN DONOVAN LOCHRIE

Sources W. M. Metcalf, *The John Neilson Institution* (1902) · Centenary Commitee, *The John Neilson Institution, 1852–1952* (1952) · trade directory, Paisley, 1810 · trade directory, Paisley, 1812 · trade directory, Paisley, 1820 · *Paisley Advertiser* (9 Nov 1839) · *Paisley Advertiser* (16 Nov 1839) · *Paisley Herald* (10 Oct 1846) · *Paisley Daily Express* (21 Nov 1980) · *Paisley Daily Express* (April 1992)
Likenesses portrait, *c.*1820; formerly at John Neilson Institution, Paisley
Wealth at death over £17,181: will

Neilson, Julia Emilie (1868–1957), actress and theatre manager, was born in Tottenham Court Road, London, on 12 June 1868, the only child of Alexander Ritchie Neilson, a silversmith and jeweller, and his wife, Emily Davis, who was one of an unusually gifted Jewish family of five sisters, no fewer than seven of whose offspring became professional actresses. Her widowed mother later married William Morris, a solicitor; his deceased first wife had been the actress Florence Terry, member of an even more illustrious theatrical dynasty and elder sister to the actor Fred Terry, who was by then Julia's husband.

Educated initially at two local private schools but showing little scholastic aptitude, Julia was sent to Germany at the age of twelve to be 'finished' at a cosmopolitan boarding establishment in Wiesbaden, where she learned French and German and discovered a pronounced talent for music. After returning to London three years later she was enrolled at the Royal Academy of Music, at first to study the piano; before long, however, she was found to

Julia Emilie Neilson (1868–1957), by Barraud, pubd 1889

possess a fine mezzo-soprano voice and was advised to concentrate on singing with a view to a career in opera or on the concert platform. Having already won several prizes she made her first public appearance, while still a student, at the St James's Hall on 1 April 1887, but after gaining some experience of amateur dramatics she was given an introduction to W. S. Gilbert, who auditioned her and encouraged her to abandon music for the theatre. It was he, too, who arranged for her to make her acting début as Cynisca, the jealous wife, with Mary Anderson as Galatea in a charity matinée of his *Pygmalion and Galatea* at the Lyceum Theatre on 21 March 1888, and then to play Galatea opposite Lewis Waller in a similar matinée at the Savoy on 16 May.

Thanks to Gilbert's coaching, to which Neilson always acknowledged a profound debt, these performances helped to secure a formal engagement with Rutland Barrington at the St James's Theatre for the 1888–9 season, following which she was invited by Beerbohm Tree to become a member of his company, initially on tour and subsequently at the Haymarket Theatre—a meteoric rise to prominence for a young woman of twenty-one after little more than twelve months in the profession. She remained at the Haymarket for five years, creating such leading roles as Drusilla Ives in Henry Arthur Jones's *The Dancing Girl* (1891), Lady Isobel in his *The Tempter*, and Hester Worsley in Oscar Wilde's *A Woman of No Importance* (both 1893). She married Fred *Terry (1863–1933), a fellow artiste in the company, in 1891. After a brief engagement at the Adelphi Theatre she returned to the Haymarket, now under the management of Lewis Waller, in January

1895 to become the first Lady Chiltern in *An Ideal Husband*; in December she accompanied John Hare on a five-month tour of the United States, opening at Abbey's Theater in New York as Agnes in the American première of Arthur Wing Pinero's *The Notorious Mrs Ebbsmith*. On her return she joined George Alexander at the St James's to portray Princess Flavia in Anthony Hope's *The Prisoner of Zenda* (1896), staying with him for two years and playing, among others, her first Shakespearian roles, Rosalind in *As You Like It* (1896) and Beatrice in *Much Ado about Nothing* (1898). After rejoining Beerbohm Tree, now at Her Majesty's Theatre, she appeared as Constance in *King John* (1899) and Oberon in *A Midsummer Night's Dream* (1900).

The same year saw Neilson take a fateful step which did much to determine the remainder of her career, when, following a tour of *As You Like It*, she embarked upon London management with her husband. They mounted their first joint production, Paul Kester's *Sweet Nell of Old Drury*, at the Haymarket on 30 August. Not only did this inaugurate an acting and managerial partnership which lasted for thirty years, but it established a model for their subsequent offerings, mostly historical romances or comedy melodramas that made few intellectual demands on the spectator but ravished the eye with exquisite costumes and stylish period settings. Among the most successful were *The Scarlet Pimpernel* by Baroness Orczy and J. M. Barstow (New Theatre, 1905) and *Henry of Navarre* by William Devereux (New, 1909), which, with *Sweet Nell*, became their mainstay for many provincial tours and one to the United States in 1910; others, like *For Sword or Song* by Robert Legge and Louis Calvert (1903), *Dorothy o' the Hall* by Paul Kester and Charles Major (1906), *The Popinjay* by Boyle Lawrence and Frederick Mouillot (1911), *Mistress Wilful* by Ernest Hendrie (1915), *The Borderer* (1921), *The Marlboroughs* (1924), and William Devereux's *The Wooing of Katherine Parr* (1926), were equally capable of drawing large and extraordinarily loyal audiences. Each provided both actor–managers with a prime role in which they could shine, but which scarcely challenged their creative resources, a fact which makes it difficult to assess the true calibre of Julia Neilson's acting. She possessed a compelling stage presence, admirable diction, a vibrant personality, and striking physical beauty which aged gracefully. If not a great actress, she was certainly highly accomplished and dearly loved by the thousands to whom she gave so much pleasure.

After her husband's death in 1933 Neilson appeared twice more on the stage, in the farce *Vintage Wine* by Seymour Hicks and Ashley Dukes at Daly's in 1934 and Heron Carvic's *The Widow of Forty* at the Q in 1944, and was guest of honour at a testimonial luncheon held in London in 1938 to mark her fiftieth anniversary as a performer. She died in hospital in Hampstead, after a fall at her home, on 27 May 1957, and was cremated at Golders Green two days later. Her son, Dennis (1895–1932), and daughter, Phyllis Neilson-Terry (1892–1977), also enjoyed distinguished theatrical careers.   DONALD ROY

Sources J. Neilson, *This for remembrance* (1940) • *The Times* (28 May 1957) • *The Times* (30 May 1957) • S. D'Amico, ed., *Enciclopedia dello*

spettacolo, 7 (Rome, 1960) • *Who was who in the theatre, 1912–1976*, 3 (1978) • *Men and Women of the Day*, 2 (1889) • *Men of the time* (1887) • *WWW, 1951–60* • E. Reid and H. Compton, eds., *The dramatic peerage* [1891] • *The Times* (10 June 1957) • *The Times* (5 June 1957) • J. Parker, ed., *The green room book, or, Who's who on the stage* (1909) • D. Hines and H. P. Hanaford, *Who's who in music and drama* (1914) • F. Terry, 'My wife and I', *Strand Magazine*, 49 (1915), 635–42 • R. Mander and J. Mitchenson, 'A tribute on her eightieth birthday', *Theatre World* (June 1948), 10, 12

Likenesses photograph, 1887, repro. in *Men of the time* (1887) • Barraud, photograph, pubd 1889, NPG [*see illus.*] • five photographs, 1896–1920, repro. in Neilson, *This for remembrance* • M. Beerbohm, pen-and-pencil caricature, V&A • Buchel & Hassall, lithograph, NPG • group portrait, photograph (with family), repro. in Neilson, *This for remembrance* • photograph (in old age), repro. in *The Times* (28 May 1957) • photographs, repro. in Neilson, *This for remembrance* • photographs, NPG

Neilson, Laurence Cornelius (*c*.1760–1830), organist, was born in London. His father had been born in Copenhagen. At the age of seven he went with his parents to the West Indies. After the failure of their turtle fishery, and his father's death, he returned with his mother to London. He studied music under Valentine Nicolai, and began teaching at Nottingham and Derby. He was organist for two years at Dudley, Worcestershire, and in 1808 took over the pupils of Samuel Bower at Chesterfield. His compositions, none of which is important, include a *Book of Psalms and Hymns*, twelve flute duets (1800), marches for the piano (1810), and songs.

Neilson died in Chesterfield in 1830. His son, E. J. Neilson, was one of the ten foundation students of the Royal Academy of Music.

J. C. HADDEN, *rev.* ANNE PIMLOTT BAKER

Sources Brown & Stratton, *Brit. mus.* • [J. S. Sainsbury], ed., *A dictionary of musicians*, 2 vols. (1824)

Neilson, Peter (1795–1861), poet and mechanical inventor, was born at Glasgow on 24 September 1795, the seventh child and youngest son among the nine children of George Neilson, calenderer, and his wife, Janet Galbraith. George Neilson was descended from the Neilsons of Camoquill, near Balfron, Stirlingshire, and he settled at an early age in Glasgow. Peter was educated at Glasgow high school and at the University of Glasgow before being sent to learn business in various city offices. He then joined his father in exporting cambric and cotton goods to America. On returning from a visit to the United States he married his cousin Elizabeth Robertson (*d*. 1831) on 11 September 1820. In 1822 he returned to America with his wife and infant daughter. The store of information he amassed while carrying out his business activities was eventually published on his return in *Six Years Residence in America* (1828). Written in 'a clear and accurate manner', the book is 'replete with lively incident and anecdote' (Neilson, x). The death of his wife on 27 October 1831 caused him to seek solace in religion, and he wrote numerous poems on scriptural themes. Two of these, 'The Millennium' and 'Scripture Gems', were published in 1834.

In 1841 Neilson settled in Kirkintilloch, Dunbartonshire, where his maiden sister, 'an accomplished lady' who also ran 'a seminary for the education of young ladies' (Neilson, xi), looked after him and his family of three daughters and one son. In 1846 he proposed improvements to the lifebuoy, which the lords of the Admiralty deemed worthy of being patented, but he shrank from the expense. Continuing his literary efforts, he wrote a remarkable little work on slavery entitled *The Life and Adventures of Zamba, an African Negro King; and his Experiences of Slavery in South Carolina* (1846). Ostensibly only edited by Neilson, this work in some respects foreshadowed *Uncle Tom's Cabin*. He also contributed a series of practical articles on cotton supply for Britain to the *Glasgow Herald*.

On 8 January 1848 Neilson wrote a patriotic letter to Lord John Russell, suggesting iron-plate ships, and enclosing a plan of invention. He wrote:

> Britain's best policy … consists in her being able totally to prevent an enemy from ever planting foot on her hallowed shores … with six, or even four, steam vessels, constructed and armed in the peculiar manner which I am now able to describe, an invading fleet of 100 sail, might not only be greatly annoyed, but almost totally destroyed in the space of two hours.   (Neilson, xiii–xiv)

In 1855 he further corresponded on the subject with Lord Panmure and Admiral Earl Hardwicke, and apparently his proposals were adopted, though not formally acknowledged. After the building of the *Warrior* and the *Black Prince*, according to his plan, Neilson suggested inside as well as outside plates and summed up his views in *Remarks on Iron-built Ships of War and Iron-plated Ships of War* (1861). Shortly afterwards he published another pamphlet on the defence of unfortified cities such as London.

In his latter years Neilson suffered from heart disease and bronchitis, and he died at Eastside, Kirkintilloch on 3 May 1861. He was buried beside his wife, in the burial-ground near the north-west corner of Glasgow Cathedral.

Neilson's *Poems* appeared in 1870, edited with a memoir by Dr Whitelaw, who took the opportunity to castigate the government for slighting Neilson and his inventions, arguing that it was 'one more example of those sons of intellect and mechanical genius, who, sacrificing thought and labour for their country, go down to the grave unhonoured and unrequited' (Neilson, xxiii). The poems in the collection feature Neilson's representations of biblical and historical figures from David to George Washington.

T. W. BAYNE, *rev.* JANE POTTER

Sources P. Neilson, *Poems* (1870) [incl. memoir by W. Whitelaw] · b. cert. · m. cert. · d. cert.
Likenesses portrait, repro. in Neilson, *Poems*

Neilson, Samuel (1761–1803), United Irishman, the son of Alexander Neilson, a Presbyterian minister, was born at Ballyroney, co. Down, in September 1761. Educated at home by his father and then at a neighbouring school, he displayed a remarkable aptitude for mathematics. At the age of sixteen he joined his elder brother John, a woollen draper in Belfast, as an apprentice. He married a Miss Bryson, the daughter of a highly respectable and wealthy Belfast merchant, William Bryson, in September 1785. Striking out on his own, Neilson soon established one of the largest woollen warehouses in Belfast, and he traded widely in Irish-made silks and linen as well. But his business began to decline as his interest in politics rose. In 1790 he served as an electoral agent for the young Robert Stewart (afterwards Viscount Castlereagh) in his successful contest for the parliamentary seat for County Down against the pro-government candidate Lord Hillsborough (afterwards the marquess of Downshire). At the same time Neilson was also a member of the gentry-dominated Northern Whig Club and of a secret committee of democratic radicals within the 1st (Green) Belfast volunteer company. Frustrated, however, with the moderate whiggism of the Irish opposition in advancing the cause of parliamentary reform in Ireland, Neilson and his fellow middle-class radicals pursued a new strategy, uniting Catholic and protestant to mobilize public opinion to pressure the parliament to reform itself. 'Our efforts for reform hitherto have been ineffectual', he proclaimed in the summer of 1791, 'and they deserve to be so, for they have been selfish and unjust, as not including the rights of Catholics in the claims we put forward for ourselves' (Madden, 1.79). In October 1791 Neilson and the secret volunteer committee launched the Society of United Irishmen, and invited Theobald Wolfe Tone to Belfast to draft its resolutions, calling for radical parliamentary reform, Catholic emancipation, and a union of Catholic and protestant to achieve them both. As its chief organizer, Neilson may properly be considered the founder of the society. He was also instrumental in establishing a bi-weekly newspaper, the *Northern Star*, launched in January 1792 to propagate the principles of the United Irishmen. Editor, and originally one of twelve shareholders, Neilson assumed sole proprietorship of the paper in 1794, a paper meant to make propaganda and not profit. Circulation figures peaked at 5000 and until its suppression in 1797 the *Northern Star* surpassed the *Belfast News-Letter* as the most popular newspaper in Ulster, twice inviting government prosecution for seditious libel, and twice acquitted. The prohibitive legal costs were met partly by Neilson himself, who committed much of his substantial fortune of £5000 to the service of the United Irishmen.

If his contribution to the radical movement had only been as the editor of the influential *Northern Star*, Neilson would still deserve pride of place among United Irish leaders. But as an active organizer and shrewd strategist, he made an even greater contribution. His secret committee of volunteers seems to have directed and co-ordinated the affiliated system of United Irish clubs in Belfast and its environs, and when the organization opted for an insurrectionary strategy and mass recruitment after 1794, Neilson remained one of the central directors. He was also in close and frequent contact with United Irish and Catholic Committee leaders in Dublin and was described by William Drennan as too sympathetic to the Catholics. With Catholic Committee member John Keogh and Theobald Wolfe Tone, Neilson intervened in calming sectarian conflicts between protestant Peep o' Day Boys and Catholic defenders in Rathfriland, co. Down, in 1792. When the revolutionary United Irishmen began to court defender support after 1795, he headed a committee to forge links with John Magennis, leader of the co. Down defenders.

Referred to as the 'Tandy of Belfast' (after James Napper Tandy, the Dublin civic activist), Neilson was well known to the authorities as the principal leader of the northern United Irishmen. In September 1796 government troops ransacked the offices of the *Northern Star* and arrested Neilson along with many other known United Irish leaders. After a brief stint in solitary confinement at Newgate, Dublin, he was removed to the newly built Kilmainham gaol. The surviving letters of the United Irishmen imprisoned there from 1796 to 1798 make light of what must have been oppressive and unhealthy conditions. Subscriptions were raised among the rank and file to provide some comforts for the imprisoned leaders, but the physical and psychological effects of incarceration took their toll. Neilson fell out temporarily with his close friend and comrade Henry Joy McCracken. It took McCracken's sister and Neilson's wife to get the two men to talk to one another again. Victims of cold, damp, and vermin, the prisoners were constantly afflicted by illness. One antidote to the physical and psychological torments of imprisonment was alcohol, and Neilson emerged after seventeen months' confinement in Kilmainham with an irreparably broken constitution and a drinking problem.

Neilson also emerged as a poor man, and it was the charity of a friend, Dublin Catholic merchant John Sweetman, that supported Neilson and his family. Neilson was released from Kilmainham on condition that he refrain from seditious activity, a pledge he soon disregarded. New arrests were decimating the United Irish leadership, and after the arrest of the Leinster directory at Oliver Bond's house in March 1798, Neilson joined Lord Edward Fitzgerald as one of the five central directors of the national United Irish organization. With a warrant out for his arrest, Lord Edward went into hiding and planned a United Irish rising for May 1798, while Neilson travelled extensively about the country attending to its preparation. He recklessly took no precautions when he returned to Dublin to consult with Lord Edward in his hiding place, alerting the Dublin authorities to the republican aristocrat's whereabouts and leading to his arrest. This led to a later unfounded rumour that Neilson had betrayed Fitzgerald. On 22 May a reward of £300 was offered for Neilson's arrest and on the next day he was taken, after a ferocious resistance, outside Newgate, where he was plotting Lord Edward's rescue. He was reputed to have been drunk.

After the failed risings in Leinster and Ulster in May and June of 1798, the government was left with eighty-odd prisoners, who constituted much of the leadership of the United Irishmen. With witnesses refusing to come forward in public, the government entered a pact on 29 July 1798 with the leaders, requiring that the prisoners give full details of the movement but without implicating any individuals by name. In return they asked permission to emigrate. Neilson was examined before the committees of the lords and commons on 9 August 1798. After ten months' imprisonment in Dublin he was, despite being confined to bed with a high fever, transported with the other prisoners to Fort George in Scotland on 19 March 1799. The United States would not accept the would-be emigrants, and Europe was closed to them by war. He was released in July 1802, the American authorities having relented on his entry, but Neilson eluded the authorities and returned to Ireland. He was sheltered by Bernard Coyle in Dublin and then proceeded with the assistance of James Hope to Belfast, where he remained for three or four days to visit friends and relatives. He secured passage to America in December 1802 and was contemplating starting an evening newspaper when he died suddenly of apoplexy on 29 August 1803 at Poughkeepsie, New York. He was buried there. His widow remained in Belfast, where she embarked on her own business, and her five children attained respectable positions in life. She died in November 1811. Neilson's only son, William Bryson, died in Jamaica of yellow fever in 1817.

An engraved portrait of Neilson based on a miniature is included in Madden's *United Irishmen*. He was a tall, handsome man, of great strength but even greater boldness and determination. From the early 1790s he aimed for an independent Irish republic, but would have accepted radical parliamentary reform. Government tyranny, however, he insisted, justified the United Irish recourse to armed insurrection.

A short sketch of Neilson's life by Bernard Dornin was published in New York in 1804 and reprinted in Walter Cox's *Irish Magazine* in September 1811. Another sketch appeared in the *Dublin Morning Register* of 29 November 1831. Both accounts were superseded by R. R. Madden in his *United Irishmen* (2nd ser., 1, 1842–6). As one of the chief leaders of the United Irishmen, Neilson is a recurring character in the documentary and secondary sources on the United Irishmen, including the Rebellion manuscripts of the National Archives of Ireland, the Pelham manuscripts in the British Library, the published correspondence of major political figures such as Beresford, Castlereagh, Cornwallis, and Grattan, and the memoirs of United Irishmen such as Theobald Wolfe Tone and Charles Hamilton Teeling.   NANCY J. CURTIN

Sources N. J. Curtin, *The United Irishmen: popular politics in Ulster and Dublin, 1791–1798* (1994) · R. R. Madden, *The United Irishmen: their lives and times*, 2nd ser., 1 (1842) · M. Elliott, *Partners in revolution: the United Irishmen and France* (1982) · M. Elliott, *Wolfe Tone: prophet of Irish independence* (1989) · M. H. Thuemte, *The harp new strung* (1994) · R. Jacob, *The rise of the United Irishmen* (1937) · W. T. W. Tone, *Life of Theobald Wolfe Tone*, 2 vols. (1826) · J. Smyth, *The men of no property* (1992)

Archives University of Rhode Island Library, corresp. and papers | BL, Pelham MSS · CKS, Pratt MSS · NL Ire., Rebellion MSS · PRO, home office papers relating to Ireland · PRO NIre., Drennan MSS

Likenesses engraving (after miniature), repro. in R. R. Madden, *The United Irishmen: their lives and times* · group portrait, coloured lithograph (*The United Irish patriots of 1798*), NPG · oils, Ulster Museum, Belfast

Neilson, William [Uilliam Mac Néill] (**1774–1821**), minister of the Presbyterian General Synod of Ulster and grammarian, was born at Rademon, Crossgar, co. Down, on 12 September 1774, the fourth child of the seven sons and one daughter of Moses Neilson (1739–1823), minister of Kilmore, and his wife, Catherine (1740–1827), eldest daughter of Andrew Welsh, minister of Ardstraw, co. Tyrone, and a descendant of John Knox. Neilson attended Rademon Academy, his father's school, and matriculated in 1789 at Glasgow University. There he studied under George Jardine, who filled the chair of logic, and John Young, professor of Greek. Excelling in Greek, Neilson 'displayed such superior intellectual acquirements as gained the highest prizes' (D'Alton and O'Flanagan, 346). After two years at Glasgow he returned to Rademon to teach in his father's school and to study for the ministry. It seems likely that it was during this time too that he studied the literary Gaelic of ancient manuscripts, under Patrick Lynch, schoolmaster and copyist, of nearby Loughinisland. Spoken Gaelic, in which his father was proficient, he is believed to have had from infancy.

Licensed to preach in 1796, Neilson was ordained minister of Dundalk by Armagh presbytery on 23 December of the same year. He soon after married Jane Warnock (c.1775–1834), who, states a reliable informant, was 'almost certainly one of the Warnock family who had a small property outside Portaferry' (private information). They had five children: one son and four daughters. Neilson's 'classical and mercantile school' in Clanbrassil Street, Dundalk, which was to have many distinguished alumni, was founded in 1797. During Dr Moses Neilson's moderatorship of the General Synod of Ulster in the turbulent year of 1798, the minister of Dundalk entered his father's pulpit at Rademon to preach in Gaelic. At the end of the service a yeomanry officer arrested him, seized his manuscript, and, on a charge of preaching treason and sedition, marched him to Downpatrick gaol. In court the next day, on giving as requested a translation of his harmless discourse, he was released.

Neilson spent much of 1798 abridging the English–Irish dictionary by O'Begley and MacCurtin (published at Paris in 1732); this fairly substantial manuscript was later acquired by the National Library of Ireland. It is said to have been his *Greek Exercises* with its *Key*, first published in 1804, that earned for him the degree of DD from Glasgow University in 1805. The work went into several editions, including a few in the United States. A total of ten works by William Neilson are recorded: of some of his published writings no copies have survived, nor is there any extant evidence of a Hebrew grammar ascribed to him, though he was known to have been 'a distinguished Hebraist, when Hebrew scholars were few' (*Irish Book Lover*).

The work for which Neilson is remembered, however, is his *Introduction to the Irish Language* (1808). The primary authority for the long-defunct Gaelic dialect of south-east Ulster, it was used as a textbook by such scholars as Douglas Hyde and Eoin Mac Néill, co-founders of the Gaelic League. In June 1806, soon after he had completed the manuscript of his Gaelic grammar, Neilson's church conferred upon him the highest honour in her gift, when, like his father before him, he was chosen moderator of the General Synod of Ulster. No sooner had his major work appeared than the country's premier learned society, the Royal Irish Academy, elected him a member, on 30 November 1808.

In 1818 Neilson accepted the double appointment of headmaster of the classical school and professor of Latin, Greek, Hebrew, Irish, and oriental languages at the Belfast Academical Institution. But his tenure of office was short, for he died there of rheumatic fever about midnight on 26–7 April 1821. On his deathbed he learned that he had been appointed professor of Greek at Glasgow, in succession to his old mentor, John Young. He was buried in Rademon on 29 April. SÉAMAS Ó SAOTHRAÍ

Sources S. Ó Saothraí, *An ministir Gaelach Uilliam Mac Néill* (1992) [annotated biography; incl. bibliography] · S. Ó Saothraí, 'William Neilson', *County Louth Archaeological and Historical Journal*, 22 (1989), 20–28 · S. Ó Saothraí, 'Dr Neilson's Irish grammar', *Bulletin of the Presbyterian Historical Society of Ireland*, 20 (1991), 5–11 · W. I. Addison, *A roll of graduates of the University of Glasgow from 31st December 1727 to 31st December 1897* (1898) · W. I. Addison, ed., *The matriculation albums of the University of Glasgow from 1728 to 1858* (1913) · Blackwood MS, Neilson/Nelson pedigree, Linen Hall Library, Belfast · W. D. H. McEwen, *Funeral address … at the grave of Rev. W. Neilson* (1821) · *DNB* · J. Magee, 'Neilsons of Rademon and Down', *Familia: Ulster Genealogical Review*, 2/4 (1988), 63–77 · *Records of the General Synod of Ulster, from 1691 to 1820*, 3 (1898) · J. McConnell and others, eds., *Fasti of the Irish Presbyterian church, 1613–1840*, rev. S. G. McConnell, 2 vols. in 12 pts (1935–51) · minute book, 1808, Royal Irish Acad. · J. R. Fisher and J. H. Robb, *Royal Belfast Academical Institution: centenary volume, 1810–1910* (1913) · B. Ó Buachalla, *I mBéal Feirste cois cuain* (1968) · S. Ó Casaide, *Irish language in Belfast and county Down* (1930) · J. Nelson, 'William Neilson', *Belfast literary society, 1801–1901*, ed. [G. Smith] (1902) · J. A. Pilson, *History … of Belfast and annals of county Antrim* (1846) · J. D'Alton and J. R. O'Flanagan, *History of Dundalk* (1864) · J. Jamieson, *The history of the Royal Belfast Academical Institution, 1810–1960* (1959, [1960]) · private information (2004) [J. McRobert] · *Irish Book Lover*, 13 (1921–2), 13

Likenesses T. C. Thompson?, miniature, repro. in Nelson, 'William Neilson'; formerly in possession of the Royal Belfast Academical Institution

Wealth at death widow and children had to vacate official Institution residence at his death

Neligan, Dorinda (1833–1914), headmistress and suffragette, was born on 9 June 1833 in Cork, the fifth daughter of Thomas Neligan, a lieutenant in the army. She was educated at home by her mother, a woman of great culture, and later in Germany and Paris before becoming a 'finishing governess'. From August 1870 to March 1871 she served with the Red Cross in France during the Franco-Prussian War, being in sole charge of the wounded at Metz during the siege. In direct contravention of orders, she personally sawed up a supply of wooden desks, found in the basement of the makeshift hospital, for fuel to keep the frozen men warm.

Just three years later, without ever having had either any formal higher education or experience of teaching in schools, Dorinda Neligan was appointed by the Girls' Public Day School Company (GPDSC), under the patronage of Mrs Maria Grey, to be one of the first headmistresses of a girls' high school in Britain. Croydon High School for Girls, undenominational and 'classless' like all GPDSC schools, began with eighty pupils in 1874. By 1876 the roll had already risen to 175. In the early days Miss Neligan had to run the gauntlet of criticism from ill-wishers. There had originally been objections to the very founding of the

Dorinda Neligan (1833–1914), by Sir James Jebusa Shannon, c.1901

school: a local newspaper suggested that it would bankrupt existing private girls' schools in the area; neighbours feared intolerable noise disturbance from the girls in the playground; others simply did not want 'strong-minded' women encouraging girls to be dissatisfied with life at home. Once the school was in existence some parents objected to the teaching of physiology. In 1875 two local shareholders of the Croydon school alleged that Miss Neligan evaded the GPDSC's printed regulations and was not enough of a disciplinarian. She was fully vindicated, however, by the GPDSC's education committee and then by the council of the GPDSC, and continued with her school policy of no rewards and no punishments (Kamm, 61). She fully believed that girls would be sufficiently motivated by the joy of learning in itself and that their sense of honour would lead them voluntarily to admit to any shortcomings. Whereas Miss Buss looked upon girls as potential devils, Miss Neligan tended to treat them as potential angels (GPDST Newsletter, 1958, 33).

An enthusiastic teacher, Miss Neligan could inspire interest in subjects as diverse as German poetry, Italian art, foreign travel, Gladstone's politics, and the Bible. 'There was nothing narrow, nothing conventional about Miss Neligan' (Croydon High School Record, 1924, 9). She was gifted with a fine presence, a most beautiful speaking voice, and a lively sense of humour, all of which combined with her intelligence and practical ability to make her a commanding personality for her staff and pupils at Croydon for twenty-seven years. The close connection between her school and university education for women was made clear in 1890 when she invited Miss A. J. Clough, principal

of Newnham College, Cambridge, to present the Croydon girls with their Cambridge local examination certificates. Most important of all, she transmitted to her women teachers and pupils her own values of compassion, moral courage, and independent-mindedness.

After retiring in 1902 Dorinda Neligan devoted her time and energy to the struggle for women's suffrage. On one occasion, on refusing, as a voteless woman, to pay her rates, she had her silver teapot 'distrained'. On 18 November 1910 Miss Neligan, by then seventy-seven years old, volunteered, together with the scientist Hertha Ayrton, Dr Elizabeth Garrett Anderson, Dr Louisa Garrett Anderson, Mrs Cobden-Sanderson, and Princess Sophia Duleep Singh, to form the first group of a Women's Social and Political Union deputation headed by Mrs Pankhurst to petition Asquith, the prime minister, in the Commons. They met in Parliament Square with some very rough treatment, being 'thrown from side to side by police and hooligans alike' (Sharp, 220–21). Some of the 'hooligans' were very possibly plain-clothes police. Winston Churchill, when home secretary in 1911, refused to grant an inquiry into the allegations of police brutality on that 'black Friday'—though urged to do so by Lord Robert Cecil, who had seen the medical evidence relating to the women's injuries. Miss Neligan was arrested for allegedly 'assaulting a police constable' that day, but no charges were brought. Her student, colleague, and friend of many years, Eleanor Roper, testified that Dorinda Neligan absolutely 'hated war' (GPDST Newsletter, 1958, 31). She died, of heart disease and acute bronchitis, at her home, Oakwood House, 5 Sydenham Road, Croydon, on 17 July 1914, just a fortnight before the outbreak of the First World War. There is a brass tablet to her memory in Croydon parish church and a portrait of her by Shannon in Croydon high school.

SYBIL OLDFIELD

Sources E. Roper, 'Dorinda Neligan, 1833–1914', 1958, GPDST Archives, 26 St Anne's Gate, London, GPDST Newsletter • J. Kamm, Indicative past: one hundred years of the Girls' Public Day School Trust (1971) • L. Magnus, The jubilee book of the Girls' Public Day School Trust, 1873–1923 (1923) • E. Sharp, Hertha Ayrton, 1854–1923: a memoir (1926) • 'Croydon High School for girls: the laying of the memorial stone', Croydon Advertiser and Surrey County Reporter (19 July 1879) • M. C. T. M. [M. Tipple], 'Miss Neligan: an appreciation', Croydon High School Record (1924) • T. Loyd-Lindsay, Report of the executive committee of the British National Society for Aid to Sick and Wounded in War, July 1871 (1871)
Archives Girls' Public Day School Trust, London, archives
Likenesses J. J. Shannon, oils, c.1901, Croydon High School for Girls [see illus.]
Wealth at death £2166 8s. 6d.: probate, 19 Sept 1914, CGPLA Eng. & Wales

Neligan, John Moore (1815–1863), physician and dermatologist, was born in Clonmel, co. Tipperary. His father was a medical practitioner who died when he was young; his mother was Macella, daughter of William Hayes, of co. Limerick. Neligan graduated MD at Edinburgh in 1836, and practised in Clonmel for a few months. He then moved to Cork, where he lectured on materia medica and medical botany at the private school of anatomy, medicine, and surgery in Warren's Place. In 1840 he moved to Dublin, and lived at 17 Merrion Square East for many years. In 1841 he was appointed physician to the Jervis Street Hospital. He was also on the staff of the Dublin school in Peter Street, where he lectured on materia medica (1841–6), and went on to lecture in medicine (1846–57), following the resignation of Sir Dominic Corrigan.

In 1844 Neligan published *Medicines, their Uses and Mode of Administration*, a compilation of all the drugs mentioned in the London, Scottish, and Irish pharmacopoeias and some others. Though valuable to medical practitioners, it was not an original work. The seventh edition, edited by Rawdon Macnamara, appeared posthumously in 1867. Neligan's knowledge of materia medica led to his appointment to the committee of the board editing the *British Pharmacopoeia*. Neligan was friendly with Robert James Graves the identifier of Graves' disease (thyrotoxicosis), who entrusted Neligan with editing the second edition of his *Clinical Lectures on the Practice of Medicine* (1848).

Neligan was one of the early British dermatologists. He first published *Diagnosis and Treatment of Eruptive Diseases of the Scalp* (1848), followed by *A Practical Treatise on Diseases of the Skin* (1852); the second edition, edited by T. W. Belcher, appeared posthumously in 1866. Although mainly a compilation from standard authors, it was much read and increased his practice. Like most doctors who acquire fame as a dermatologist he also produced a coloured *Atlas of Skin Diseases* (1855), which was mainly a compilation from standard authors. Neligan followed Sir William Wilde as editor of the *Dublin Quarterly Journal of Medicine* (1849–61).

Neligan married Kate, daughter of the Revd and Hon. Mrs Gumbleton of Curraglass House, Waterford; they had no children. He died somewhat unexpectedly after a week's exacerbation of uraemia, on 24 July 1863, at Clonmel House, Blackrock, co. Dublin; he had been ill for some time. NORMAN MOORE, *rev.* GEOFFREY L. ASHERSON

Sources *BMJ* (1 Aug 1863), 130 · *The Lancet* (1 Aug 1863), 140 · C. A. Cameron, *History of the Royal College of Surgeons in Ireland* (1886) · J. T. Crissey and L. C. Parish, *The dermatology and syphilology of the nineteenth century* (1981)
Wealth at death under £7000: probate, 10 Sept 1863, *CGPLA Ire.*

Nelson family (*per.* 1780–1958), publishers and printers, entered the book trade in the early nineteenth century with the bookselling activities of Thomas Neilson or Nelson, son of a Stirlingshire farmer. He founded the bookselling, printing, and publishing firm in Edinburgh, which became Thomas Nelson & Sons in 1858 and remained in family hands until 1962.

Thomas Nelson senior and the launch of a dynasty Thomas Nelson (1780–1861) was born Thomas Neilson in the village of Throsk near Stirling in Scotland, the son of William Neilson, a farmer, and his wife, Lilias Gibson. He was baptized on 1 October 1780 at St Ninian's, Stirling, and was brought up with the strict religious outlook of the Reformed Presbyterian church (covenanters). He became briefly a teacher at sixteen, and also worked in a local distillery, but eventually left the family farm for London to undertake an apprenticeship with a bookseller at 35 Paternoster Row, abandoning an opportunity to go to the West Indies. After two years in London he returned to Edinburgh in 1798, to set up a business as a secondhand bookseller trading from a small half-timbered shop with its booth opening onto the street at the head of the West Bow, near St Giles's Cathedral.

At some point Nelson realized the existence of a market for cheap editions of standard, non-copyright works which he initially attempted to satisfy by publishing in monthly parts well-known religious texts such as *Pilgrim's Progress* and *Scots Worthies*, then by issuing what became the Nelson hallmark, reprints of classics such as *Robinson Crusoe*, *The Vicar of Wakefield*, and Goldsmith's *Essays*. From these beginnings the emphasis was on price—he produced inexpensive books accessible to a new reading public of the skilled working classes. Nelson employed the still uncommon process of stereotyping to reduce production costs over a large print run. To circumvent hostility towards reduced profit margins from the book trade, he found alternative outlets, such as direct sales at fairs and markets, and vacant shops rented temporarily in the smaller towns and burghs of Scotland. Thus Nelson established the publishing 'holy trinity' of wide distribution, mass production, and low costs. The first authenticated year of Nelson's operation as a publisher was 1818 when, after restricted growth due to lack of capital, the firm opened a bank account and the company name, with that of its founder, changed from Neilson to Nelson, to accommodate frequent misspelling. Thomas made a joke of it: 'Like the naval hero of the same name, I have had to sacrifice an "i" in a good cause' (Ramsay, 4).

On 15 March 1814 Thomas Nelson married Margaret Sibbald Black of Kinghorn, Fife. They had a large family. Three of the five sons later entered the business: William (1816–1887) [*see below*], Thomas (1822–1892) [*see below*], and Peter (*d.* 1871). Their eldest daughter, Anne, married George *Brown (1818–1880), who was the leader of the Liberal Party in Upper Canada until killed by an assassin. A son of this couple later joined the family firm.

The business continued to expand until in 1829 Nelson took the unprecedented step of employing a 'bagman', James Macdonald, the first publisher's representative, to hawk the firm's wares around Scotland and the north of England. It was not initially a successful experiment, orders coming from only one Aberdeen bookseller. The religious nature of many of Nelson's early publications reflected the strict religious outlook of his family. John A. H. Dempster suggests that the early history of Thomas Nelson & Sons conforms to a common early nineteenth-century model. The founder of the publishing house, actuated by zeal to spread the word of God, commences general, secular publishing as an adjunct to this. Succeeding generations inherit the prosperous business but none, or only a diluted form, of the religious motivation. The religious output decreases in proportion to the whole but often remains a steady income generator on the back list. This categorization perhaps ignores the evangelism of the educator: the urge to spread knowledge through good, cheap books across a wide section of the population, a mission which lay, however implicitly, behind the story of Thomas Nelson & Sons until its last years.

William and Thomas junior: the second generation William Nelson (1816–1887) and **Thomas Nelson junior** (1822–1892) controlled the firm of Thomas Nelson & Sons throughout the second half of the nineteenth century. William Nelson was born in Edinburgh on 13 December 1816 and was educated at the high school, where he won the classical gold medal. In 1835 he abandoned his studies at Edinburgh University to help his ailing father run the business. Thomas Nelson was also born in Edinburgh, on 25 December 1822, and followed his eldest brother through Edinburgh high school, leaving at seventeen to assist William. They gave fresh energy to the expansion of the firm, which still dealt only in reprints. William concentrated on marketing, Thomas on editing and production.

In 1844, at Thomas senior's request, Thomas junior opened a London office at 35 Paternoster Row, the place of his father's apprenticeship. Peter Nelson ran this branch for a time but was never made a partner. A new printing house at Hope Park in Edinburgh was built in 1845, where the complete book manufacturing process was carried out under one roof, with a payroll of over 400 employees. In 1850 Thomas perfected a rotary press, demonstrated at the Great Exhibition in the following year, but because he refused to patent his invention, little fame and no fortune resulted from the many clones which competitors built. A continuous web of paper-fed cylinders holding curved stereotype plates passed the printed paper under a serrated knife for cutting into sheets: a principle on which all newspaper presses were based until well into the twentieth century. Thomas also undertook experiments with coated paper for use with half-tone blocks.

On 24 July 1851 William married at St Cuthbert's Church, Edinburgh, Catherine Inglis (d. 1904), daughter of Robert Inglis of Kirkmay, Fife. They had two sons (neither of whom entered the family business) and four daughters.

In 1854 Thomas—normally the stay-at-home brother—established at William's suggestion a branch of Thomas Nelson & Sons in New York at 42 Bleecker Street, the first branch of a British publishing house in the USA. It later proved a sound investment for reasons not altogether to do with publishing, providing opportunities for investment and for profitable imports during the American Civil War.

In his early days with the firm William reduced stock holdings by rebinding reprints in a more attractive cloth finish, taking to the road himself to sell them, travelling as far as Liverpool, via Carlisle, on his first expedition. The repackaging, coupled with an increased discount, was successful: booksellers who may have earlier despised Nelsons' list now subscribed eagerly. Perhaps also publishing a cheap reprint of a work too popular to ignore, MacKnight on the epistles, blackmailed them into recognizing the upstart firm.

Thomas Nelson & Sons continued to expand and now began publishing stories of adventure and travel for young people, 'moral books', and educational titles generally. The former were especially suitable as Sunday school and church, or indeed weekday school, prizes, featuring elevating and wholesome contents, attractive presentation, and reasonable price. The work of R. M. Ballantyne fitted well into this category. *The Young Fur Traders* (1856) was written at the suggestion of William Nelson out of Ballantyne's own experiences with the Hudson's Bay Company, the first of seven major titles including *Coral Island* (1858) published by Nelsons. Harriet Beecher Stowe was another moral, humane Nelson author, while illustrators included artists like Landseer and David Scott. Lesser-known figures important in their time were Charlotte Maria Tucker, who used the pseudonym A. L. O. E. (A Lady of England), and Evelyn Everett-Green. The former was, like Ballantyne, possessed of a Christian mission in her writing. She was, also like Ballantyne, extremely prolific: Nelsons advertised forty-seven of her titles, new and reprints, in 1875: by 1894 there were sixty. Copyright was bought outright on acceptance of the manuscript, the author receiving no other payment or royalty from Nelsons.

Ballantyne protested against such exploitation, reputedly calling William 'a mean old codger' (Quayle, 95). This is in contrast with William's personal benevolence towards the indigent, especially towards the dependants of former employees. Ballantyne certainly felt that he was the victim of sharp practice when he set the popularity of works issued by Nelsons against the sums paid for their copyright: £50 for *The Young Fur Traders*, £60 for his second novel *Ungava* (1857) and for *Coral Island*, rising to £75 for *Martin Rattler* (1858). When in 1860 Nelsons refused, apparently with a sad lack of commercial foresight, to allow him to retain the copyright in a new work, he took the only sanction open to him and removed future titles to another publisher. Nelsons further refused, in 1865, to allow him to buy back the copyright to his early titles, which continued to be best-sellers, and Ballantyne saw not a penny more for them.

Thomas Nelson senior died on 23 March 1861, after a period of failing health. His sons had taken on all responsibility for the firm over the previous ten years, and the secondhand bookshop had by this time grown into a business giving work to hundreds.

On 30 April 1868 Thomas Nelson junior married Jessie (1846–1919), daughter of James Kemp of Manchester and South America. They had five children: a son, Thomas Graeme, who died aged eighteen months; two other sons, Thomas Arthur (1877–1917) [*see below*] and Ian Theodore (1878–1958) [*see below*], who later carried on the family business; and two daughters. Thomas Nelson was politically liberal, and a member of the Free Church of Scotland, but had few or no interests outside his work: his obituary in *The Scotsman* comments that he had no desire for holidays, and found it impossible to delegate.

William continued to travel widely for both business and leisure, visiting the American offshoot on several occasions, and on one transcontinental tour in 1870 narrowly escaped capture by raiding Sioux. Although not a 'public man', he, like his brother, espoused liberal politics, and was particularly known for his support of the restoration of historic buildings in Edinburgh, including parts of Edinburgh Castle and St Bernard's Well on the Water of Leith.

A fire devastated Hope Park in 1878, causing damage estimated between £100,000 and £200,000, only partly covered by insurance. William Nelson witnessed the destruction: the fire had broken out in the back of the building at about three in the morning, and the whole building was soon in flames. By the time that William arrived at the scene just over an hour later, the roof had already fallen in and the flames, fanned by a strong east wind, carried the fire rapidly throughout the works. 'Not a book or sheet of paper was saved' (Wilson, 173–4).

Within two months Thomas Nelson & Sons were back in operation, albeit on a limited scale, and within two years the production works moved to a new site at Parkside near Arthur's Seat in Edinburgh. The calamity brought the fortuitous benefit of investment in new plant from which a flood of inexpensive reprints, schoolbooks, prize books, and religious books poured—with the corollary of low profit margins. From 1878 to 1881 fiction represented, again, according to John Dempster's calculations, 40 per cent of the books printed but only 10 per cent of the firm's total profit. Furthermore, 17 per cent of the fiction titles produced 53 per cent of the profit. The inescapable conclusion is that most of the fiction published by Nelsons, non-copyright reprints notwithstanding, made very little money.

The Education Acts after 1870 stimulated tremendous demand for good, inexpensive learning materials, and Nelsons responded with the Royal Readers series, which sold in vast quantities throughout the British empire and was followed by the Royal School series. The educational market was monitored through correspondence with educationists, contacts with school boards at home and abroad, and inspecting the products of rivals such as Blackie and Arnold. Between 1878 and 1881 educational books represented 25 per cent of total output but, according to calculations by John Dempster, yielded 88 per cent of the firm's total profit. Nelsons introduced the first school atlases and Thomas is credited with the introduction into these of lines of latitude and longitude, and of the scale in English miles. (Not long before his death he bought a controlling interest in John Bartholomew & Co., the cartographical and geographical specialists.) *The Highroads of History* (1907), *The Highroads of Literature*, and *The Highroads of Geography* (both 1911) remained on the company's back list for over forty years. Nelsons also published periodicals, the most successful being the *Children's Paper*, issued from 1855 until 1925. From 1895 the *Practical Teacher* appeared under its imprint, carrying, like many other Nelsons periodicals, a high proportion of advertising for Nelsons' publications: possibly they were regarded partly as a promotional medium for the firm.

William died on 10 September 1887 and Thomas on 20 October 1892. Both were millionaires. The obituary of Thomas published in *The Bookseller* stresses the high production values of the Nelsons' books: 'they were better printed, better illustrated and more tastefully bound than any other books of their class' (*The Bookseller*, 7 Nov 1892).

Thomas Arthur Nelson and Ian Theodore Nelson: forward to the twentieth century Until Thomas Nelson junior's two sons, Tommy and Ian, could take over the business, the firm was directed under trusteeship by their Canadian cousin George Brown, who later continued as partner with them. John Buchan noted that he revolutionized the financial side of the business, introducing an up-to-date American accounting system.

Thomas Arthur [Tommy] **Nelson** (1877–1917) was born in Edinburgh in 1877 and was educated at Edinburgh Academy and University College, Oxford, where he gained a rugby blue. He also played rugby for Scotland. While at Oxford his friends included John Buchan and E. R. Balfour, whose sister Margaret he later married. (They apparently had no children.) Tommy's younger brother **Ian Theodore Nelson** (1878–1958) was born in Edinburgh.

Tommy Nelson continued the family tradition of innovation in mass publishing, becoming managing director in practice if not in title, and initiating a number of popular series. The New Century Library included titles by Dickens, Thackeray, and Scott, 'handy for the pocket or knapsack, and especially suitable for railway reading'. The Sixpenny Classics, later Nelsons Classics (from 1903), eventually consisted of over 400 volumes and included works by James, Conrad, and Wells. From 1907 the Nelson Library, selling at 7*d*., offered reprints of copyright works in still familiar, at least to denizens of secondhand bookshops, red and gold cloth bindings. The Shilling Library provided copyright titles of general literature, while several foreign series catered for languages other than English. Credit must be paid to Nelsons as one of the forerunners of Allen Lane's sixpenny Penguins or the British equivalent of Tauchnitz. Among a limited number of new books was the Nelson biography of Edward VII, on sale in an edition of 120,000 copies within three days of his death.

Late in 1906 Tommy Nelson also brought John Buchan, author, politician, and later as Lord Tweedsmuir governor-general of Canada, his friend from Oxford days, into the firm, where for some years he was largely responsible for editorial policy. Buchan was inspired by the principles that were Nelsons' from its earliest days: to place good books within the means of as many people as possible. He took charge of a weekly published by Nelsons, the *Scottish Review*, attempting to slough off its dour, worthy image as a house journal of the United Free Church of Scotland. Brown and the Nelsons envisaged it as the centre of a new Edinburgh-based Enlightenment when they bought the rights. There was a consensus that a periodical covering all matters Scottish—political, literary, and social—was needed. However, despite contributing lengthy items each week, Buchan could not sustain the necessary sales at 1*d*. a copy to keep it afloat, and it closed at the end of 1908.

In these years the American branch continued to flourish. In 1901 it published the American Standard Version of the Bible from a dedicated factory in Brooklyn, and in 1903 the American Thomas Nelson & Sons became a New York corporation wholly owned by the parent British company. It was also innovatory in popular publishing, issuing the *Nelson Encyclopaedia* on a loose-leaf principle to subscribers.

In 1907 a new factory was constructed which could produce 200,000 books a week. Reprint series of foreign language works increased, and the name Thomas Nelson & Sons appeared over branches in France and Germany. Business in Canada expanded with a Toronto branch opening in 1914. In *Memory Hold-the-Door* (1940) John Buchan wrote of that period: 'We were a progressive concern, and in our standardised Edinburgh factories we began the publication of cheap books in many tongues' (p. 146). The languages included French, German, Magyar, and Spanish, and printing in Russian was under consideration. John Buchan became a director of Nelsons in 1915 when it became a limited company, signing a contract which expired in 1929. The book which brought Buchan lasting popular success, *The Thirty-Nine Steps* (1915), is dedicated to Tommy Nelson in memory of a long friendship, and a joint affection for 'that elementary type of tale which the Americans call the "dime novel" and which we know as the "shocker"—the romance where the incidents defy the probabilities, and march just inside the borders of the possible'. The need to be doing something (that he was writing *The Thirty-Nine Steps* at the time did not count) preoccupied Buchan in the early months of the First World War. He was also anxious that the denial of foreign markets, the loss of manpower, and general exigencies of wartime should not lead to the temporary rundown and long-term decline of Nelsons. He proposed an ongoing history of the war, published in monthly parts (it was initially issued fortnightly) and when Hilaire Belloc declined the invitation to write it, Buchan undertook the challenge himself. Each issue, of about 50,000 words, published from 1915 to 1919, was seized upon by a public eager for clear, authoritative accounts of the war and represents a staggering feat of stamina and consistency. Over the same period another Nelson author, Edward Parrott, produced *The Children's Story of War*, also in instalments and also giving a regularity to the business. Both Tommy and Ian served on the western front, while retaining their interest in the family firm.

The take-over of the publishing house of T. C. and E. C. Jack in 1915, strong in children's titles, consolidated the company's future direction. After Tommy's death in action at the battle of Arras on 9 April 1917 (he served in the Lothian and Borders horse, and later in the tank corps), Ian became head of the firm. In 1919 Thomas Nelson junior's original rotary press, which was interred in Germany since its exhibition at a Leipzig trade fair in 1914, was returned intact.

Between the wars Nelsons expanded its educational list. Buchan brought in Sir Henry Newbolt as editorial adviser in this field, establishing new series: The Teaching of English and The Teaching of History, and a new range of school readers, Reading for Action, and Read and Remember. Buchan's collaboration continued long after his departure in 1929: at that point he did not renew his contract, given increased commitments in his political career. In any case, much of the excitement disappeared from the business on the death of Tommy. When 35 Paternoster Row was destroyed in the blitz, Nelsons shared the fate of many other publishers, but in 1948 the firm celebrated its 150th anniversary as well as release from the restrictions of wartime and after.

Ian Nelson remained head of the firm until his death on 14 April 1958 and was succeeded by his son Ronnie. Nelsons nurtured its overseas textbook markets in the newly established Commonwealth in the same way as it had forged links in the old empire. During the 1960s branches were opened in Australia, Nigeria, and Kenya, but in order to sustain its publications in a global market, Nelsons was absorbed into the Thomson Organization in 1962. Soon afterwards the production plant in Edinburgh was separated from the publishing division, which became permanently based in London. In 1968 the printing division was sold to the Edinburgh company Morrison and Gibb and the Parkside works were eventually demolished to make way for new insurance company buildings. In 1969 the American company was sold to Royal Publishers Incorporated of Nashville, Tennessee, which retained the name Thomas Nelson & Sons. The London firm continued to trade until January 2000, when it merged with Stanley Thornes to become Nelson Thornes, a combined subsidiary of the Dutch company Wolters Kluwer.

HELEN WILLIAMS and ALISTAIR MCCLEERY

Sources J. Buchan, *Memory hold-the-door* (1940) · J. A. H. Dempster, 'Thomas Nelson & Sons in the late nineteenth century: a study in motivation, part 1', *Publishing History*, 13 (1983), 41–87 · J. A. H. Dempster, 'Thomas Nelson & Sons in the late nineteenth century: a study in motivation, part 2', *Publishing History*, 14 (1983), 5–63 · *The Bookseller* (8 Oct 1887) · *The Bookseller* (7 Nov 1892) · A. Ramsay, *Nelson the publisher* (c.1981) · E. Quayle, *Ballantyne the brave* (1967) · *Thomas Nelson & Sons: two centuries of success* (1987) · J. T. Winterich, 'The American Thomas Nelson & Sons celebrates its first 100 years', *Publishers' Weekly* (30 Oct 1954) · 'A great conflagration', *Edinburgh Evening News* (5 Nov 1932) · J. Adam Smith, *John Buchan and his world* (1979) · D. Wilson, *William Nelson: a memoir* (1889) · *The Scotsman* (12 Sept 1887) · *The Scotsman* (21 Oct 1892) · 'Thomas Nelson', *Proceedings of the Royal Society of Edinburgh*, 19 (1891–2), lviii–lxii · *The Times* (17 April 1917) · *DNB* · www.thomasnelson.com · D. Finkelstein and H. Holmes, eds., *Thomas Nelson & Sons: memories of an Edinburgh publishing house* (2001)

Archives NL Scot., corresp. relating to Edinburgh Castle [William Nelson] · U. Edin., archives |SOUND Napier University, Edward Clark Collection, Scottish Archive of Printing and Publishing Records, Nelson Reminiscence Project

Likenesses W. Brodie, marble bust, 1880 (William Nelson), Scot. NPG · wood-engraving (Thomas Nelson), NPG; repro. in *ILN* (29 Oct 1892)

Wealth at death Thomas Nelson, senior · William Nelson · Thomas Nelson, junior: sealed 16/3/1893 London · Thomas Arthur Nelson: £470,782, of which £219,300 represents holding in Nelson & Sons: *The Times* 27 June 1917 · Ian Nelson: £166,283 personal estate in England and Scotland: *The Times* 12 June 1958

Nelson, Sir Alexander Abercromby (1814–1893), army officer, was born at Walmer, Kent, on 30 June 1814. He was educated at the Royal Military College, Sandhurst, and on

6 March 1835 was appointed ensign 40th foot, in which regiment his two brothers, and later his son, also served. He became lieutenant on 15 March 1839, and was in sole charge of the commissariat of the Bombay column during the operations under Sir William Nott at Kandahar and in Afghanistan in 1841–2. He accompanied the Bombay column, under Colonel Stack, which went from Ferozepore to join Sir Charles James Napier in Sind, was present at the battle of Hyderabad on 24 March 1843, and was thanked by the governor-general of India and the Bombay government. He was aide-de-camp to Sir Thomas Valiant at the battle of Maharajpur on 29 December 1843, and had a horse shot under him. On 31 July 1846 he was promoted captain. He was appointed adjutant of the Walmer depot battalion on 7 April 1854, but immediately afterwards was made deputy assistant adjutant-general, and subsequently brigade major, at Portsmouth, which post he held during the period of the Crimean War and Indian mutiny. He became major unattached on 6 June 1856, lieutenant-colonel on 9 December 1864, and colonel on 9 December 1869.

Deputy adjutant-general in Jamaica from December 1864 to October 1866, in 1865 Nelson was appointed brigadier-general to command the troops at St Thomas-in-the-East at the time of the Morant Bay insurrection (October). He was active in its suppression and punishment, with extensive reprisals—including shooting, hanging, flogging, and hut burning—for the murders committed by the rebels. Following the removal by Governor Eyre of George William Gordon, a local politician believed guilty of fomenting the rebellion, from Kingston to Morant Bay, where martial law was operative, Nelson ordered Gordon's trial by court martial. Gordon was tried for high treason by a court martial presided over by Lieutenant Herbert Charles Alexander Brand RN (d. 1901), found guilty, and sentenced to death. Nelson confirmed the sentence, as did Eyre, and Gordon was executed (23 October). For his role in the suppression Nelson was thanked by the government and voted a 200 guinea testimonial by the planter-dominated Jamaica house of assembly.

In Britain the suppression of the Jamaica rebellion was bitterly controversial, condemned by radical politicians and Exeter Hall negrophiles who formed the Jamaica committee—denounced by Carlyle as 'rabid Nigger-Philanthropists, barking furiously in the gutter' (Carlyle, 3.210)—but defended by the Eyre defence committee. The Jamaica committee initiated the 'Jamaica prosecutions' of key participants in the suppression. John Stuart Mill and Peter Alfred Taylor, both radical MPs and members of the Jamaica committee, in 1867 brought a private prosecution against Nelson and Lieutenant Brand on the charge of murdering Gordon. After initial proceedings at Bow Street magistrates' court in February, in April the case was brought before a Middlesex grand jury at the central criminal court, the Old Bailey, to decide whether the accused should be indicted and tried. Indicative of the case's importance, the charge was delivered by Lord Chief Justice Cockburn. For nearly six hours he expounded on martial law and the case, criticizing the evidence on which

Gordon had been convicted as 'evidence so morally and intrinsically worthless … so utterly inconclusive' (Annual Register, 1867, pt 2, 238). He apparently, in effect, asked for an indictment, but the grand jury, possibly bemused by so many hours of legal oratory, decided there was 'no true bill', acquitting Nelson and Brand.

Nelson was assistant adjutant-general, Cork district (1867) and Gibraltar (1873–6); lieutenant-governor of Guernsey from May 1879 to 1883; and a JP for Middlesex. He became major-general in 1880, and retired lieutenant-general in 1883. He was made CB in May 1875 and KCB in May 1891. He married in 1846 Emma Georgiana (d. 1892), daughter of Robert Hibbert of Hale Barns, Altrincham, Cheshire. Nelson died at his residence, Walmer, Bath Road, near Reading, on 28 September 1893.

ROGER T. STEARN

Sources Army List · LondG (1846) · The Times (30 Sept 1893) · P. Macrory, Signal catastrophe: the story of a disastrous retreat from Kabul, 1842 (1966) · J. A. Norris, The First Afghan War, 1838–1842 (1967) · Annual Register (1867) · B. Semmel, The Governor Eyre controversy (1962) · R. Hyam, Britain's imperial century, 1815–1914: a study of empire and expansion (1976) · T. Carlyle, Critical and miscellaneous essays, collected and republished, another edn, 3 (1905) · W. L. Clowes, The Royal Navy: a history from the earliest times to the present, 7 vols. (1897–1903), vol. 7 · Boase, Mod. Eng. biog. · Burke, Peerage (1892) · DNB

Wealth at death £1370 4s. 8d.: resworn probate, Jan 1894, CGPLA Eng. & Wales (1893)

Nelson, Sir Amos (1860–1947), cotton manufacturer, was born on 31 January 1860 at Winewall, near Colne, Lancashire, the eldest son of James Nelson (1831–1912), an overlooker, and his wife, Mary Ann, née Hartley. Although he came from a hand-loom weaving family, James Nelson began work in a power-loom weaving factory in 1842 and by 1867 had risen from the position of weaver to overlooker to mill manager at the Cotton Tree mill of Critchley and Armstrong at Colne. It was in this mill that Amos was first employed at the age of eight as a half-timer; he had begun full-time work by the age of thirteen and was employed in a range of occupations before being apprenticed as an overlooker when he was sixteen. By the 1880s the family, six children in all, was an example of a highly successful Lancashire working-class family, but in 1881 the closure of the mill threatened its prosperity.

James Nelson invested his savings of £1200, considerable for a working man, in buying 100 looms and renting room and power in nearby Nelson. He was joined in this venture by his son Amos, who, at the age of twenty-one, had already saved £200. Nelson and Burnley were the centres of the 'room and power' system in weaving, a system by which a successful working man could transform himself into an entrepreneur through renting both room and power in a weaving shed, thus needing to buy only the looms. The effect of the system was to reduce the start-up costs for new business, easing entry for those families who had been able to save a modest sum.

The firm, James Nelson & Son, was a remarkable success story. By 1895 it had erected mills at Valley Road, Walverden, in Nelson, and was operating some 1200 looms. The firm continued to grow, and in 1912, on the death of James Nelson, owned some 3000 looms. Its success lay in seeking

Sir Amos Nelson (1860–1947), by Lafayette, 1930

out specialist markets in which it could obtain a premium for its cloth. Having first concentrated on the market in China, the firm moved into the more prosperous home and European markets. It was also the first to introduce the sateen trade into Nelson. During the period of James Nelson's life there appears to have been a division of responsibility between the two men in the firm, the father managing production and the son responsible for finance and policy, including marketing.

In 1914, after his father's death, Amos Nelson set up a private limited company in which he chaired the board. The firm continued its pre-war success and by the end of the First World War had further expanded its capacity by buying spinning and doubling firms and creating an integrated enterprise. By 1922 Nelson controlled 3700 looms as well as more than 300,000 spindles and 60,000 doubling spindles.

Business success also brought with it considerable personal wealth. Nelson had married Mary Driver (1861–1931) of Winewall, Colne, in 1879, and they had three sons and two daughters. They lived initially in Nelson before moving to the Manor House at Thornton in Craven, near Skipton, Yorkshire, and in 1919 Nelson acquired Gledstone Hall and estate, also near Skipton, with the intention of modernizing it. He invited Edward Lutyens, the distinguished architect, to draw up plans. Lutyens, who had a reputation for over-spending, produced plans that were too expensive, and Nelson, who had been knighted in 1922, instead asked him to build a new hall to a budget of £40,000. The hall, which was built between 1923 and 1927,

cost £120,000, and although some of the estate's 6000 acres provided an income the cost, coinciding with a depression in the cotton industry, severely taxed Sir Amos's finances. The hall was one of Lutyens's finest buildings.

Gledstone Hall was not Nelson's only project at the end of the war. The firm built a sports and social club in Nelson as a memorial to those employees who had given their lives during the conflict. As the largest employer in the town, and with a record for paying the highest wages, Nelson's was regarded as a good place to work, and the new sports and social club further enhanced this reputation.

The inter-war crisis in the Lancashire cotton industry presented the firm and Sir Amos with their most formidable challenge. The initial post-war depression forced the company to suspend production for three months in 1921, and, while there was some recovery after an intensive marketing operation in the United States of America, the firm responded far more quickly than most of its rivals to the need to adapt. Nelson followed three strategies. The first was to diversify by moving into artificial silk (rayon). He set up two subsidiary companies, Lustrafil Ltd, which by 1924 was producing viscose yarn at Valley Mills, and Nelson Silk Ltd, at Lancaster, making acetate yarn from 1929.

The second aspect of Nelson's strategy was to move away from selling 'grey' (unfinished) cloth through merchant distributors. Instead the company began to develop its own commercial outlets, giving direct access to buyers. Nelson acquired five subsidiary companies in Bradford and Manchester which specialized in selling the firm's branded products at home and abroad. Many contemporary manufacturers were critical of the merchant sector, but Sir Amos was one of the few to act positively by supplanting it.

The third strategy was to reduce costs in cotton weaving by a system of 'more loom' weaving in the Valley Mills. This was a system by which weavers minded six or eight looms, rather than the traditional four, but were paid at new rates which enabled employers to cut overall costs. The more looms system was a common response by employers in cotton weaving in the 1930s and was the cause of major industrial unrest in Lancashire weaving between 1929 and 1932. Nelson's policy differed from that of most employers in that he introduced a more looms system on semi-automatic looms, rather than the traditional Lancashire looms, enabling him to pay higher wages than his competitors. His proposed more looms system attracted opposition not from the trade unions, but rather from his fellow employers, who felt his proposals undermined their own position. They therefore attempted to prevent him from implementing an agreement with the local trade union, the Nelson Weavers' Association. It was a measure of the growing desperation of the cotton industry that in 1931 Nelson chose to ignore the policy of the Cotton Spinners' and Manufacturers' Association and introduced a local agreement.

Sir Amos established a reputation as an industrial conciliator during the 1928 weavers' lock-out in Nelson. The dispute had been sparked by the fining of John Husband, vice-president of the Nelson Weavers' Association, and for seven weeks some 7000 weavers were locked out by their employers over a 1s. fine. Encouraged by the town's Labour mayor, Andrew Smith, to intervene, Sir Amos proposed to employ the Nelson Weavers' vice-president in his own mills, but he infuriated his fellow employers by suggesting an experimental scheme whereby there was no fining in the town. The county employers' organization, the Cotton Spinners' and Manufacturers' Association, threatened to take action against him if he did not withdraw, though when the dispute was finally settled John Husband was employed at Valley Mills.

The inter-war years also brought personal sadness for Nelson when his first wife died. In 1931 he married his second wife, Harriet, *née* Hargraves (1896–1966), the daughter of his agent at Gledstone; they had one son.

Sir Amos was active in local politics, sitting as a Liberal on the Nelson town council between 1900 and 1910 and holding the office of mayor between 1903 and 1906. He left the council in 1910, when he broke with the Liberal Party over the issue of free trade, having become convinced that tariff reform was the solution to Britain's economic problems. It was this issue which persuaded him to stand as Conservative parliamentary candidate in 1923 for Nelson and Colne. Despite his local popularity, he was defeated by the Labour candidate, Arthur Greenwood.

The outbreak of war in 1939 changed the economic position of the cotton industry, but recovery did not come until after the war, when from 1945 to 1951 there was a sellers' market in cotton cloth. During this period Sir Amos chose to convert the firm from a private to a public company. Profits had risen substantially in the period 1936–46, and the public company, employing 2600 workers, was capitalized at £1.2 million. Nelson remained chairman of the new company but his tenure was short-lived, as he died on 13 August 1947 at Gledstone Hall. He was buried at St Peter's Church, Marton in Craven.   ALAN FOWLER

Sources W. G. Rimmer and A. Fowler, 'Nelson, Sir Amos', *DBB* · *Nelsons of Nelson: the story of James Nelson Ltd, 1881–1951* (1951) · *Nelson Leader* (15 Aug 1947) · *Textile Mercury* (22 Aug 1947) · *Nelson Leader* (4 Oct 1912) · A. Fowler and L. Fowler, *The history of the Nelson Weavers' Association* (1984) · 'Nelson's new knight', *Nelson Leader* (6 Jan 1922) · W. R. Mitchell, 'Sir Amos in the country', *The Dalesman* [n.d.] [photocopy in Pendle District Central Library] · J. Alcorn, 'To the stables born', *Lancashire Evening Telegraph* (5 Nov 1984) · D. Nelson, 'Biography of Sir Amos Nelson', priv. coll.
Archives Pendle District Library, Nelson, newspaper cuttings, Nelson file [largely photocopies]
Likenesses Lafayette, photograph, 1930, NPG [*see illus.*] · R. Brundrit, oils, priv. coll. · photographs, priv. coll.
Wealth at death £444,246 3s. 2d.: probate, 31 Dec 1947, CGPLA Eng. & Wales

Nelson [*née* Abbat], **Ann** (1769/70–1852), coach proprietor and innkeeper, was probably the Ann Abbat, daughter of Robert and Ann Abbat, baptized at St Mary's, Whitechapel, on 11 March 1772. On 18 January 1790 she married Edward Nelson at St Leonard, Shoreditch. In December of the same year Nelson was admitted to the Innholders' Company, his inn being the Blue Boar, Whitechapel. By the time of his death, in June 1800, he had moved to The Bull inn, Aldgate. He expected his wife to continue the business, since his will provided for the payment of an annuity out of it 'in case my said wife shall find the business answer her expectations' (PRO, PROB 11/1345, 186). Ann Nelson was subsequently the most substantial of the very small number of female coach proprietors, rivalled only by Sarah Ann Mountain.

Ann Nelson's coaches served mainly the roads into East Anglia, but her most prestigious coach was the Exeter Telegraph, which set off from The Bull at 4.30 a.m. and completed the 176 mile journey within the day. In 1836 she had eighteen departures a day from London. Harris, writing in the mid-1880s, described her as follows:

> Up between five and six, and sometimes earlier, in the morning, dressed in a cap of a peculiar fashion, which I cannot pretend to describe, Mrs. Nelson was quite a character, active and bustling about. She made up considerably over a hundred beds in her house … and she lodged and boarded about three dozen of her coachmen and guards, whose comfort and convenience she studied with great care, their tariff being considerably lower than that of her customers … A most active and energetic woman. (pp. 157–67)

By the late 1830s she appears to have left the coaching side of the business to her son John and concentrated on the innkeeping side, and was described in the 1841 census as an innkeeper. The inn then catered chiefly for corn merchants and others in the corn trade.

Ann Nelson had three sons and one daughter (Rebecca). The eldest son, Robert (*b.* 1791), was admitted to the Innholders' Company in 1825, his inn then being the Three Nuns, Aldgate, and in the 1830s he had an innkeeping and coaching business at the Belle Savage, Ludgate Hill, employing about 400 horses. In 1836 he was London's fourth largest coach proprietor. He is recorded as having been 'at times rather peculiar and brusque to persons he came in contact with'. John (1794–1868) was admitted to the Innholders' Company in 1820, when he was described as a coachmaster at The Bull inn, Aldgate. He successfully made the transition to the railway age, and became an omnibus proprietor, particularly of a line of omnibuses called the Wellington between Stratford, the Bank, and Westbourne Grove, and was said to have died very wealthy. George, born in 1796, at one time drove the Nelsons' Exeter night coach. Ann Nelson died at 22 Aldgate High Street on 11 October 1852, aged eighty-two.   DORIAN GERHOLD

Sources d. cert. · Innholders' Company, freedom admissions, GL, MS 6651 · parish register, Aldgate, St Botolph, GL, MS 9232/30 · *IGI* · S. Harris, *The coaching age* (1885), 157–67 · *Robson's London Directory* (1836) · census returns, 1841 · PRO, PROB 11/2162, 56 · PRO, PROB 11/1345, 186 · PRO, IR 26/1944, 998
Wealth at death under £1500: PRO, death duty registers, IR 26/1944, 998

Nelson, David (*d.* 1789), gardener and plant collector, of unknown background, was brought to the attention of Sir Joseph Banks by James Lee of the Vineyard Nursery, Hammersmith, in April 1776. Banks had him appointed plant collector on the *Discovery*, captained by Charles Clerke, for

James Cook's third voyage to the Pacific; his annual salary was £35 and he had only three months' training before the expedition.

The *Discovery* touched at Cape Town, Kerguelen Island, Van Diemen's Land, New Zealand, Tonga, Tahiti, and other islands in the Pacific including Hawaii (until then undiscovered by Europeans), then Kamchatka and Macao, returning to England on 6 October 1780. Nelson collected herbarium material and seeds at every opportunity: his collection of *Eucalyptus obliqua*, made in Van Diemen's Land in January 1777, was the material on which the genus was based; he collected at least 136 species on the island of Hawaii during a four-day attempted ascent of Mauna Loa. He also introduced *Rosa rugosa*, from Kamchatka. Banks later sent 200 packets of Nelson's seed collections to J. A. Murray at Göttingen, where Chinese sumac (*Rhus chinensis*), collected in Macao, was raised. Nelson had also collected insects, to be described by J. C. Fabricius in 1787, and acquired a grasp of Pacific languages.

Nelson seems then to have been employed at what was to become the Royal Botanic Gardens, Kew, but, in November 1783, Banks arranged that he go on HMS *Swift* to west Africa. However, the ship was recalled when it reached Plymouth in March 1784. Three years later, in March 1787, Nelson was appointed botanist (with William Brown from Kew as assistant) on William Bligh's voyage to bring the breadfruit from the Pacific to the British West Indies. In May, Banks and Nelson, together with the assistant surveyor of the Navy Board at Wapping, selected and modified the *Bethia*, which became HMS *Bounty*: Nelson's salary was £50 with a £25 kit allowance and free messing. The expedition left Spithead on 23 December 1787, with 800 clay pots for the trees and room for the water they would need, and reached Tahiti on 26 October 1788. Nelson botanized on the way and supervised the planting of fruit trees in Van Diemen's Land, where he collected some seventy new or interesting plant species. The *Bounty* left Tahiti on 4 April 1789 with 1005 breadfruit plants as well as ornamental plants and supplies but, on 30 April, the crew, including Brown (who was later murdered on Pitcairn Island), mutinied and soon threw the breadfruit plants into the sea: Bligh and his followers, including Nelson, who was his confidant, were cast off in an open cutter. Nelson was taken ill at sea, but when they touched the Australian coast his knowledge allowed them to gather edible plants, including fern-roots. Bligh navigated to Kupang, Timor, which was reached on 15 June. Bligh successfully sought permission from the Dutch authorities for Nelson to botanize on Timor but Nelson then contracted an 'inflammatory fever' and died at Kupang on 20 July 1789. He was buried next day behind the chapel in a grave later occupied by the French gardener, Anselme Riedlé (*d.* 1801), and the German gardener, Alexander Zip-[p]elius (*d.* 1828).

Nelson's fortitude during the mutiny and its aftermath was praised by Bligh; Clerke wrote of him as 'one of the quietest fellows in Nature' (St John). Bligh named 'Nelson's Hill' (possibly the hill subsequently named Mount Mangano, South Bruny, Tasmania) after him as he had

been the first European to climb it. His herbarium collections are preserved at the Natural History Museum, London and a number of plants, especially from Hawaii, were named after him; Robert Brown proposed at first to give the generic name *Nelsonia* to a group of Australian tree-ferns but eventually settled on an enigmatic Acanthacea.

D. J. MABBERLEY

Sources H. St John, 'Biography of David Nelson, and an account of his botanizing in Hawaii', *Pacific Science*, 30 (1976), 1–5 · G. Mackaness, *The life of Vice-Admiral William Bligh RN, FRS*, new edn (1951) · H. B. Carter, *Sir Joseph Banks, 1743–1820* (1988) · D. J. Mabberley, *Jupiter botanicus: Robert Brown of the British Museum* (1985) · M. van Steenis-Kruseman, 'David Nelson', *Flora Malesiana*, 1 (1950), 382–3 · J. Britten, 'William Anderson (†1778) and the plants of Cook's third voyage', *Journal of Botany, British and Foreign*, 54 (1916), 345–52 · R. Desmond, *Kew: the history of the Royal Botanic Gardens* (1995) · E. J. Willson, *James Lee and the Vineyard Nursery, Hammersmith* (1961) · Desmond, *Botanists*, rev. edn · *The voyage of the Bounty's launch as related in William Bligh's despatch to the Admiralty and the journal of John Fryer, with an Introduction by O. Rutter* (1934) · *Sir Joseph Banks: a global perspective* [London 1993], ed. R. E. R. Banks and others (1994)

Archives NHM

Nelson, Edward Theophilus (1874–1940), barrister and local politician, was born on 22 October 1874 in Georgetown, Demerara, British Guiana, the first son of Philip Nelson, a builder. Details of his mother are not known. Edward Nelson was of African descent, whose antecedents in the British colony had been freed from slavery in 1838, but not from the struggle for economic and social improvement. Progress was difficult, but the development of elementary schools and compulsory education from 1876 was beneficial to some. The cost of fees for secondary schooling was prohibitive for most Guianese, but by the 1880s a few scholarships for the most gifted pupils were available. In 1894 the first Guianese of African descent won a scholarship to attend a British university, despite the objections of the local sugar planters who dominated the colony. Nelson was one of the few who benefited from these very limited educational opportunities. He attended St Philip's School, Demerara, and in January 1898 he arrived at Oxford University to study law at St John's College. He was recorded as a commoner, meaning that he received no financial support from the college, so his higher education must have been paid for by a Guianese scholarship. This may have been supplemented by his own family, although the economic circumstances of his parents are not known.

Nelson seems to have been generally well regarded in his university career. He was elected president of the college debating society, was elected to membership of the essay society, and played cricket for the college eleven in 1900. He also won election as secretary, and later treasurer, of the Oxford Union. He was nominated as secretary by the president, Raymond Asquith, the son of the future prime minister Herbert Asquith. In a letter to his father the younger Asquith described Nelson as a:

West African [*sic*] Nigger, called Nelson for some reason, black as pitch and a staunch patriot; I think his voice and teeth pulled him through; the former is a most magnificent

Edward Theophilus Nelson (1874–1940), by unknown photographer, 1912 [detail]

organ, like the sound of heavy guns at sea.   (J. Jolliffe, *Raymond Asquith: his Life and Letters*, 1980, 64)

The casual racism of parts of this description, no doubt unexceptional for its time, combined with the admiration for Nelson's vocal abilities and his 'patriotism', convey something of the mixed feelings that Nelson must have evoked among some fellow students. He took third-class honours in jurisprudence and graduated with a BA in 1901.

Nelson was called to the bar at Lincoln's Inn in November 1904. He then established a legal practice at 78 King Street, Manchester, and by 1906 was living in an affluent middle-class suburb just south of the city, in Stamford Road, Bowdon, Cheshire. By 1909 he had moved a short distance to the equally salubrious surroundings of 49 Cecil Road, Hale, Cheshire, where he was to reside until he died in 1940. At some stage later he married, although nothing is known of his wife and she appears to have predeceased him. The couple had one daughter, May, who was still living in the family home at the time of her father's death, along with a niece named Vera Austin. The members of the family regularly attended St Peter's Church, and were described as 'generally very popular in the district' by a contemporary (Green, 'Edward T. Nelson', 152). The same source opined that 'coloured people were a bit thin on the ground' in Hale at the time, although an African-Caribbean doctor had also settled there by the 1930s. In these overwhelmingly white and bourgeois surroundings, the black barrister Edward Nelson and his family seemed to have assimilated into the local community well. Nelson himself remained a keen cricketer and played for Bowdon cricket club. A photograph also survives of him as a member of the first eleven

of Hale cricket club in 1912. A young, handsome, clean-shaven, black man, quite short, dressed in college cap, blazer, and white flannels, he looks fully at ease among his white team-mates.

Nelson shot to wider fame, however, when he was involved in a sensational murder case played out in the courts in 1909–10. In November 1909 a 49-year-old businessman of Stalybridge, George Harry Storrs, was stabbed to death at his home. A cousin of Storrs, Cornelius Howard, was accused of the murder, and in the committal proceedings held in Dukinfield he was defended by Edward Nelson. Howard was eventually committed to trial at Chester in March 1910, where he was acquitted, although Nelson was not involved in the proceedings at this point. Subsequently a second man, Mark Wilde, was charged with the murder, and Nelson did represent him at his trial at the Chester assizes in October 1910. Nelson conducted a spirited and able defence, and he engineered a dramatic twist in the case when he made Howard and Wilde stand side by side in front of the jurors, casting doubt on the evidence of identification. After a long and impressive summing-up for the defence by his barrister, Wilde was acquitted. Nelson's name had been made, particularly because he was a comparatively young member of the bar, but also because he had won a highly unusual case in which two men had been separately charged with, and acquitted of, the same murder.

In 1919 Edward Nelson was involved in another much publicized court case, which had some connection with his African-Caribbean origins. In the summer of that year racial tensions in Liverpool began to rise. Many black workers were sacked because white employees refused to work with them, and there were numerous black men, mostly demobilized soldiers and sailors, who were unemployed and stranded in the city. An ugly racist mood developed on the streets, and by mid-June black men were being attacked frequently. On 5 June, after a white mob had stabbed a West Indian, eight of his black acquaintances attacked the group of Scandinavians whom they believed responsible. Police subsequently raided lodging houses inhabited by black seamen, and wholesale rioting broke out. One African-Caribbean seaman, Charles Wootton, fled from his lodgings and was pursued down to the Queen's Dock by a crowd of two to three hundred white people. He was thrown into the water, pelted with rocks, and drowned. For the next week anti-black rioting was widespread, with white gangs 'savagely attacking, beating and stabbing every negro they could find', according to a police report, and, as a local magistrate put it, these events made the name of Liverpool 'an abomination and disgrace to the rest of the country' (Fryer, 301, 303).

The following November fifteen black men were tried in connection with the events of 5 June, on charges of riotous assembly and assault. Their defence counsel was Edward Nelson, whose fees were paid by the African Progress Union. This was a London-based black civil rights group led by the prominent black activist and Labour councillor in Battersea, the Liverpool-born John Richard Archer. The case against the men was based mainly on identification by police and bystanders, much of which was unreliable and at times contradictory, and five of the fifteen accused were acquitted. The other ten, however, received prison sentences of between eight and twenty-two months. Nelson, described variously in press reports as 'a coloured gentlemen' and 'a native barrister', was able to cast doubt on much of the evidence presented by the prosecution, and was reported as conducting the defence 'with great clearness and ability' (*Liverpool Daily Post and Mercury*, 8, 10 Nov 1919).

Edward Nelson's subsequent work was confined to more mundane legal matters and to public service in local government. His good standing in his local community had been demonstrated in 1913 when he was elected to the Hale urban district council. He remained on the council until his death, twice serving as chairman of the council, and also chairing the library committee from 1920 and the rating and valuation committee from its inception in 1925. He had a great interest in literature, and one of his ambitions was to have a public library established in Hale. He also became an acknowledged expert on the legal and technical aspects of rating and evaluation, receiving recognition for this not only in Hale but also at a regional and national level. He became the first chairman of the Cheshire Urban District Councils Association in 1929, and in 1936 he was elected to the executive committee of the Urban District Councils Association of England and Wales.

Nelson suffered from ill health in later life, and he died of myocarditis at his home, 49 Cecil Road, Hale, Cheshire, on 3 August 1940. His financial affairs must also have deteriorated, for he left no will and his effects were the subject of administration, amounting to less than £50. Yet the heartfelt tributes in the local press from his colleagues on Hale council attested to the high esteem in which he was held (*Sale Guardian*, 9 Aug 1940). Next to a picture of Edward Nelson showing a white-haired and distinguished-looking black man, they averred that he was one of Hale's 'best and most loved adopted sons', a 'clever, wise and trusted colleague', and a 'genuine and kind-hearted friend'. He had possessed a 'quiet and modest demeanour' and a 'keen legal mind', and he had been admired for 'his sincerity of purpose, his marked ability, and his untiring zeal in the service of the community'. His funeral service at St Peter's Church, Hale, and interment at Altrincham cemetery on 7 August 1940, were attended by a large gathering with representatives from local government, the legal profession, Hale Conservative Club, Altrincham police force, and many other public and commercial interests in the area. Only the mention of 'relatives of British Guiana and Trinidad' on one wreath, and another from 'members of the Manchester International Group', sounded an echo of his African-Caribbean roots.

SAM DAVIES

Sources *Sale Guardian* (9 Aug 1940) · J. P. Green, *Black Edwardians: black people in Britain, 1901–1914* (1998), 183–219 · J. P. Green, 'Edward T. Nelson (1874–1940)', *New Community*, 12 (1984–5), 149–54 · P. Fryer, *Staying power: the history of black people in Britain* (1984), 298–316 · V. T. Daly, *A short history of the Guyanese people* (1975) · R. T. Smith, *British Guiana* (1962) · A. Murphy, *From the empire to the Rialto: racism and reaction in Liverpool, 1918–1948* (1995), 1–42 · *Liverpool Daily Post and Mercury* (June–Nov 1919) · J. Goodman, *The stabbing of George Henry Storrs* (Columbus, Ohio, 1983) · V. Sillery, *St John's College biographical register, 1875–1919* (1981) · matriculation records, Oxf. UA · d. cert.

Likenesses photograph, 1912, Sale Library, Trafford [*see illus.*] · photograph, repro. in *Sale Guardian*

Wealth at death £49 17s. 6d.: administration, 26 June 1941, CGPLA Eng. & Wales

Nelson, Eliza (1827–1908). *See under* Craven, Henry Thornton (1818–1905).

Nelson [*née* Woolward], **Frances Herbert** [Fanny], **Viscountess Nelson** (1761–1831), wife of Horatio Nelson, the daughter of William Woolward (*d.* 18 Feb 1779), the senior judge of the island of Nevis in the West Indies, and his wife, Mary, the sister of John Richardson Herbert, president of the council of the island, was born on Nevis, and was baptized in May 1761. On 28 June 1779 she married Josiah Nisbet MD, who, while visiting England, died at Salisbury on 5 October 1781, leaving her with an infant son, also named Josiah. She was then dependent on her widowed uncle, for whom she acted as hostess at his plantation house, Montpelier.

A good-looking woman with the genteel manners of her social standing, in May 1785 Fanny Nisbet met Horatio *Nelson, captain of the frigate *Boreas*, who visited Nevis while he was unpopular for enforcing the Navigation Act against illegal American trading in the West Indies. She was regarded as sophisticated by her friends, who recommended that she might 'make something of' him, as she had 'been in the habit of attending to these odd sort of people' (Clarke and M'Arthur, 1.78).

Twice disappointed in love, Nelson was then ripe for marriage, so, seen in the setting of an elegant house on an exotic island, Fanny Nisbet must have seemed the ideal match for a naval officer—as indeed she would have been to most, other than Nelson. Much of their courtship was conducted by letter, he often using the term 'esteem' rather than 'love'.

The couple were married at Montpelier on 11 March 1787, with Prince William Henry (later William IV) as best man. After returning to England, where Nelson remained unemployed for five years, they lived in the chilly Parsonage House at Burnham Thorpe in Norfolk, where she, accustomed to black slaves, had the services of village servant-girls. She loathed the cold and damp, and it was noted by her father-in-law that 'Mrs N. takes large doses of the bed' (Matcham, 65). It seems that Nelson often took responsibility for household tasks, such as ordering provisions and loose covers for the furniture.

Fanny Nelson bore her husband no children, but Nelson was fond of his stepson and, when he returned to sea in 1793, took the boy with him for training as a naval officer. Fanny packed his bags inefficiently and fussed about her husband and son in her letters, and thereafter a note of irritation sometimes showed in Nelson's replies. After he won fame by boarding two Spanish ships at the battle of Cape St Vincent she pleaded, 'I sincerely hope, my dear

Frances Herbert Nelson, Viscountess Nelson (1761–1831), by Henry Edridge

husband, that all these wonderful and desperate actions—such as boarding ships you will leave to others' (*Dispatches and Letters*, 2.359); he was not inspired by such cosseting.

Yet when Nelson returned from the disastrous attack on Tenerife having lost his right arm, Fanny came into her own as his nurse. When the couple dined with Lord Spencer, first lord of the Admiralty, Lady Spencer noted that 'his attentions to her were those of a lover' (*Diary of Frances, Lady Shelley*, 39). When, in 1798, he destroyed the French fleet at the battle of the Nile she was touchingly proud of him. But by the time her letters reached him he was at Naples and in love with Emma, Lady *Hamilton, who provided the encouragement and sexual excitement that his wife did not. Thereafter his letters to Fanny became increasingly terse and he fell out with his stepson. She continued to write him long letters, full of family and social news, and once asked if she could join him in the Mediterranean, a suggestion he instantly rejected. So she busied herself setting up a new household for him at Roundwood, a new house on the outskirts of Ipswich, Suffolk.

Rumours about Nelson and Lady Hamilton eventually reached Fanny, and in 1800 their reunion in London was tense. There were embarrassing scenes when they dined with the Spencers, and at the theatre, and finally he left her and joined the Hamiltons in a *ménage à trois*, making an annual allowance to his wife of about £1800 (Oman,

446). Fanny repeatedly attempted reconciliation. When she wrote, 'Do my dear husband, let us live together. I assure you again I have but one wish in the world, to live with you. Let everything be buried in oblivion, it will pass away like a dream', the letter was returned to her and on the envelope was written, 'Opened by mistake by Lord Nelson but not read' (Nelson MSS, vol. 3, Monmouth Museum).

Encouraged by Lady Hamilton, most of Nelson's family, with the notable exception of his father, rejected Fanny, nicknaming her 'Tom Tit' (because of her bird-like gait) and Josiah 'the Cub'; Nelson himself joined in the denigration. Throughout she bore herself with dignity and, after her husband's death at Trafalgar, was treated with the respect due to his widow and granted an annual pension of £2000 for life.

While Emma Hamilton was increasingly disregarded by the Nelson family, the latter now began making up to Fanny. She took a house in Upper Harley Street, London, and moved easily in the quieter reaches of London society; her acquaintances included William IV, the duke of Wellington, and Lord Byron. Her son and his family were her principal interest; four of her seven grandchildren—all the grandsons—died in her lifetime. The eldest survivor, also named Frances, remembered her kissing a miniature of Nelson and saying to her, 'When you are older, little Fan, you may know what it is to have a broken heart' (Keate, 265). In 1807 she moved to Exmouth in Devon, where she and Nelson had spent a happy holiday, and where Josiah, now a successful businessman, lived. She first occupied 6 The Beacon, overlooking the sea, and from 1829 a smaller house nearby in Louisa Place. After Josiah's sudden death on 9 July 1830, her health deteriorated, and she died on 6 May 1831, probably at her London home, 28 Upper Harley Street, or possibly when staying with her cousin Mrs Fanny Franklyn, who was with her when she died, at her house, 26 Baker Street. Baker Street was then a modern street that Nelson had once told Fanny he detested. She was buried on 18 May beside her son in the churchyard of St Margaret and St Andrew at Littleham, near Exmouth.

Fanny Nelson had given her husband the secure domestic base from which he began his twelve years of mounting fame, but she was unable to keep up with the demanding complexities of his character. After the separation she conducted herself with magnanimity—unlike many of those who were close to him when he was ashore and out of his element.   J. K. LAUGHTON, *rev.* TOM POCOCK

Sources E. M. Keate, *Nelson's wife: the first biography of Frances Herbert, Viscountess Nelson* (1939) · *Nelson's letters to his wife and other documents, 1785–1831*, ed. G. P. B. Naish, Navy RS, 100 (1958) · *The dispatches and letters of Vice-Admiral Lord Viscount Nelson*, ed. N. H. Nicolas, 7 vols. (1844–6) · J. S. Clarke and J. M'Arthur, *The life of Admiral Lord Nelson*, 2 vols. (1809) · T. J. Pettigrew, *Memoirs of the life of Vice-Admiral Lord Viscount Nelson*, 2 vols. (1849) · M. E. Matcham, *The Nelsons of Burnham Thorpe* (1911) · *Diary of Frances, Lady Shelley*, ed. R. Edgcumbe, 2 vols. (1912–13) · M. W. Warner, *A portrait of Lord Nelson* (1963) · T. Pocock, *Horatio Nelson* (1987) · C. Oman, *Nelson* (1947) · C. Hibbert, *Nelson: a personal history* (1994) · E. H. Moorhouse, *Nelson in England: a domestic chronicle* (1913) · parish register (baptism), Nevis, West Indies, May 1761 · parish register, Stratford-sub-Castle church, Wiltshire, Oct 1781 [burial, Josiah Nisbet]

Archives NMM, financial corresp. and papers · NMM, letters and legal papers | BL, Spencer MSS · Monmouth Museum, Nelson MSS · NMM, letters to Lord Nelson · Royal Naval Museum, Portsmouth, Nelson MSS

Likenesses D. Orme, watercolour, 1798, NMM · oils, *c.*1800, NMM · H. Edridge, watercolour, Royal Naval Museum, Portsmouth [*see illus.*]

Nelson, Sir Frank (1883–1966), intelligence officer, was born at Bentham, Gloucestershire, on 5 August 1883, the son of Henry Ellis Hay Nelson, general manager of the Army and Navy Auxiliary Co-operative Supply, and his wife, Catherine Haviland. After education at Bedford grammar school and Heidelberg, he went to India to work in a mercantile firm in Bombay in which he rose to become senior partner. In the First World War he served in the Bombay light horse. Subsequently he was chairman of the Bombay chamber of commerce and its representative on the Bombay legislative council (1922–4) and president of the associated Indian chamber of commerce (1923). In 1924 he was knighted and returned to England. He was Conservative member of parliament for Stroud from 1924 to 1931 when the depression forced him to resign to concentrate on his business interests.

On the outbreak of war in 1939 Nelson was employed on intelligence work in Basel, but this came to an end with the fall of France when he returned to England. Even before 1939 it had been recognized that the government would have to weaken any potential enemy by political subversion, sabotage, and other clandestine operations. When war broke out the work suffered from lack of co-ordination, for it was split up among several bodies, responsible to different authorities. By 1940, when the British were left to fight the axis powers alone, co-ordination was more than ever essential. The war cabinet consequently decided on 16 July 1940 that all these functions were to be put in the charge of a new body, the Special Operations Executive (SOE), with Hugh Dalton, who continued to be minister of economic warfare, at its head. Dalton records that the prime minister then said to him, 'And now set Europe ablaze'. He at once divided SOE into three bodies—SO1 for underground propaganda, SO2 for unacknowledgeable action, sabotage, and the support of resistance in enemy-occupied territory, and SO3 for planning. In August 1940 Dalton appointed Nelson to be head of SO2. The functions of SO3 were assumed by SO2 in January 1941, and in the following August those of SO1 by a separate body called the political warfare executive. From that point Nelson was responsible for all the remaining activities of SOE.

Nelson had a formidable task. Not only was there not a single agent in enemy-occupied France, but SOE was a new body for which no precedent existed. As such it incurred the suspicion and jealousy of the established secret organizations of the Foreign Office and the service ministries, all of which were professional bodies which had existed for many years and which were concerned by the inevitable amateurishness at first displayed by SOE. Another difficulty was recruitment, for by the

autumn of 1940 most men of ability were employed elsewhere. Above all Nelson found he had to obtain for SOE facilities, such as secret wireless sets, aircraft for parachute training and getting agents into Europe, and special devices for sabotage. But it was no easy task to get these scarce resources unless SOE could show results, and without the resources there could be no results. Finally, he had somehow to gain the confidence of Whitehall and the services.

Nelson set to work at once with tireless energy, and surrounded himself with a group of able people, notably Colin Gubbins, who at first took charge of the important job of training and operations and was to finish the war as head of SOE. Gradually Nelson overcame the difficulties by his unshakeable integrity of purpose. It was a disappointment to him when in early 1941 the chiefs of staff ruled against supplying secret armies in Europe by air in favour of the bombing offensive. But he persisted, and by the winter of 1941 SOE was in touch with agents and supporters in most of the countries of occupied Europe. Above all, Nelson made people believe that, given facilities, results could be achieved. In less than two years SOE had become an established force with the confidence of the chiefs of staff, and was recognized in every theatre of war. It is no disparagement of his successors to say that he created the groundwork without which SOE's later successes in Europe and the Far East would have been impossible.

But Nelson was never physically strong, and in 1942 his health began to fail. He resigned in May, was appointed KCMG, and subsequently held appointments as an air commodore in Washington and Germany. He had married in 1911 Jean, daughter of Colonel Patrick Montgomerie; they had one son. She died in 1952 and he then married Dorothy Moira Carling. He died in Oxford on 11 August 1966. His second wife survived him.

B. Sweet-Escott, *rev.*

Sources H. Dalton, *The fateful years: memoirs, 1931–1945* (1957) · M. R. D. Foot, *SOE in France: an account of the work of the British Special Operations Executive in France, 1940–1944*, 2nd edn (1968) · M. R. D. Foot, *Resistance* (1976) · B. Sweet-Escott, *Baker Street irregular* (1965) · personal knowledge (1981) · *The Times* (13 Aug 1966)
Likenesses Elliott & Fry, photograph, NPG

Nelson, (Henry) George, second Baron Nelson of Stafford (1917–1995), engineer and businessman, was born on 2 January 1917 in Stretford, Manchester, the only son and younger child of George Horatio *Nelson, first Baron Nelson of Stafford (1887–1962), engineer and industrialist, and his wife, Florence Mabel (known as Jane; 1888–1962), only daughter of Henry Howe JP for Leicestershire. His father was chairman of the English Electric Company Ltd from 1933 until his death. Nelson was educated at Oundle School, winning an exhibition to King's College, Cambridge. After graduating with a second in mechanical sciences in 1937, he gained practical experience working for Renault and the Societé de Construction de Batignolles in Paris and Sulzers Bros and the Brown Boveri Company in Switzerland for two years before joining English Electric. On 8 June 1940 he married Pamela Roy, younger daughter of Ernest Roy Bird, solicitor, and Conservative MP for Skipton from 1924 to 1933. They had two sons and two daughters.

In 1939 Nelson was appointed superintendent of the Preston works, where he was in charge of the change from locomotive to aircraft production in preparation for the war. As assistant works manager in 1940–41 and deputy works manager in 1941–2, he was one of those involved in the manufacture of Hampden and Halifax bombers for the Air Ministry. When English Electric took over the aero-engine manufacturer D. Napier & Son Ltd in 1942 at the request of the Ministry of Aircraft Production, Nelson was appointed managing director and was responsible for the development and production of the Sabre engine, used in the Typhoon fighter bomber and the Tempest fighter aircraft. Altogether 4500 Sabre engines had been delivered by the end of the war, after which Nelson and the chief engineer Herbert Sammons concentrated on the development of a turboprop engine.

A director of English Electric from 1943, and an executive director of Marconi Wireless Telegraph Company, taken over by English Electric in 1946, Nelson moved from Napiers in 1949 to become deputy managing director of English Electric; he became managing director in 1956, when his father gave up that position to his son. Although very much in the shadow of his father, who wanted his son to succeed him and who made sure that he was appointed a director or deputy chairman of most of the subsidiary companies of the group, Nelson continued to concentrate on military aviation as chairman of English Electric Aviation Ltd at the Preston works, where he oversaw the successful production of the Canberra bomber, Britain's first jet bomber, and the supersonic Lightning fighter. Later, English Electric merged its aviation and guided weapons interests with those of Vickers-Armstrongs and Bristol Aircraft to form the British Aircraft Corporation (BAC) in order to develop the TSR2, the successor to the Canberra bomber, in accordance with the government's requirements for the aircraft industry. Nelson then became one of the two deputies to the first chairman, Lord Portal, and he remained deputy chairman of BAC until 1977.

When his father died in 1962 Nelson was appointed chairman and chief executive of English Electric. He had wanted to be chairman and managing director, but the board opposed this, appointing instead two deputy managing directors. During the next six years Nelson was responsible for modernizing the management structure of the company, devolving responsibility to the heads of different product groups, but he did not promote younger men, preferring to retain his father's key advisers, men mainly in their sixties, as heads of these new groups. Under Nelson the company moved into the civil nuclear power field as part of the consortium forming the Atomic Power Construction Company Ltd, which built the Sizewell and Hinckley Point nuclear power stations. The company also expanded into the growth areas of computers and electronics, especially after the acquisition of Elliott Automation in 1967.

English Electric had tried to merge with the General Electric Company (GEC) in 1960 in order to increase the light electrical side of its business, but the talks had broken down. In 1968 Arnold Weinstock, managing director of GEC since 1963, who in 1967 had taken over its other main rival, AEI, approached English Electric with a proposal for a merger. Nelson, who had just fought off a bid from Plessey Company, agreed, under pressure from the government's industrial reorganization committee, interested in rationalizing the heavy electrical industry, and from the company's merchant bankers, Lazards, who did not think English Electric could survive a takeover battle. Nelson was appointed chairman of the newly merged company, and to start with it was known as the General Electric and English Electric Companies, but Weinstock closed English Electric House in the Strand in London and moved the staff to GEC's head office. It was clear from the start that Weinstock was in charge: of the eleven senior managers appointed, ten were from GEC or AEI. But Nelson admired Weinstock, and the two worked well together. While Weinstock closed factories and reduced the workforce, Nelson travelled overseas in pursuit of orders, and when he retired as chairman in 1983 GEC was the largest electrical engineering company in Britain, and the third largest in Europe, after Philips and Siemens.

Nelson served on many public bodies. He was a member of the civil service selection board from 1956 to 1961; vice-chairman of the government's Advisory Council on Middle East Trade from 1959 to 1963, leading official trade missions to the United Arab Republic in 1960 and to Iraq in 1961; a director of the Bank of England from 1961 to 1987; a member of the Advisory Council on Technology from 1964 to 1970; chairman of the National Defence Industries Council from 1971 to 1977; and president of the Sino-British Trade Council from 1973 to 1982. He was interested in education, lecturing on industrial management for the mechanical sciences department at Cambridge University from 1947 to 1949, and he headed the appeal for funds to establish the London and Manchester business schools in the 1960s. From 1966 to 1979 he was chancellor of Aston University, which created him honorary DSc in 1966. He was awarded the Benjamin Franklin medal by the Royal Society of Arts in 1959, for his work in scientific industrial development.

A modest and generous man, Nelson was respected by his colleagues, but he was considered less dynamic than his father at English Electric, where he was nicknamed Half-Nelson. He died on 19 January 1995 in the Stafford Clinic. His funeral was at the Holy Trinity Church, Eccleshall, Staffordshire, on 24 January. He was survived by his wife and four children. The elder son, Henry Roy George Nelson, succeeded him as third Baron Nelson. A memorial service was held at St James's, Piccadilly, London, on 21 March 1995.   ANNE PIMLOTT BAKER

Sources R. Jones and O. Marriot, *Anatomy of a merger: a history of GEC, AEI, and English Electric* (1970), 289–324 · S. Aris, *Arnold Weinstock and the making of GEC* (1998) · C. H. Wilson and W. Reader, *Men and machines: a history of D. Napier and Son, Engineers, Ltd, 1808–1958*

(1958), 153–71 · C. Gardner, *British Aircraft Corporation: a history* (1981) · G. Tweedale, 'Nelson, Henry George 2nd Lord Nelson of Stafford', *DBB* · *English Electric and its People* (Sept 1962) · A. Whyte, *The war diary of the English Electric Company Ltd* (1945) · Burke, *Peerage* · *WWW, 1991–5* · *Cambridge historical register* · *The Times* (21 Jan 1995) · *The Times* (23 Jan 1995) · *The Times* (22 March 1995)
Likenesses J. Gunn, portrait, 1958, priv. coll. · photograph, repro. in Jones and Marriott, *Anatomy of a merger* · photograph, repro. in *English Electric and its People* (Sept 1962) · photograph, repro. in *English Electric and its People* (Feb 1959) · photograph, repro. in *The Times* (23 Jan 1995)
Wealth at death £1,268,147: probate, 20 March 1995, *CGPLA Eng. & Wales*

Nelson, George Horatio, first Baron Nelson of Stafford

(1887–1962), electrical engineer and company manager, was born at 102 Church Road, Islington, London, on 26 October 1887, the eldest child in the family of two sons and one daughter of George Nelson, textile merchant, of Muswell Hill, Middlesex, and his wife, Emily Walsh Lewis. He was educated at City and Guilds Technical College, where he worked under Silvanus Thompson. After gaining a diploma and the Mitchell exhibition, he moved on, with a Brush studentship, to the Brush Engineering Company at Loughborough. He then joined the British Westinghouse Company in Manchester, becoming chief outside engineer at Trafford Park in 1911, and chief electrical superintendent in 1914. In 1913 he married Florence Mabel (Jane; 1888–1962), only daughter of Henry Howe JP, for Leicestershire. They had one son and one daughter.

At Westinghouse, Nelson was responsible for the manufacture and installation of steam and hydro-electric power equipment and electric traction equipment in various parts of the world. He remained with the same company when it joined the Metropolitan Vickers Group, becoming manager of the Sheffield works of Metropolitan Vickers Electrical Company in 1920, and stayed at the works, which specialized in electric traction, for ten years. Sir Holberry Mensforth, who had been works manager at Trafford Park, and who had subsequently joined the English Electric Company, then persuaded Nelson to become English Electric's managing director. When Mensforth retired in 1933 Nelson was appointed chairman and managing director.

Nelson set the English Electric Company on its feet, expanding the work force, handling men and contracts with great skill, and fully understanding the engineering aspect of his company. In 'clearing the decks' he made some bold, far-ranging, and usually correct decisions which were to alter and broaden the whole concept of the business. When the rearmament programme began he spent many months trying to persuade service chiefs of the contribution his organization could make, and finally won a contract for seventy-five Hampden bombers. These were followed by 2470 Halifax bombers and 2730 tanks. By the end of the war, English Electric was undertaking the production of the Canberra bomber to its own design, which was one of the most successful of its time.

In 1942 Nelson went to the United States and Canada as chairman of the United Kingdom tank mission to discuss

George Horatio Nelson, first Baron Nelson of Stafford (1887–1962), by Harold Knight, exh. RA 1942

a joint policy for tank production. He served on the heavy bomber group committee of the Air Ministry from 1939 to 1945, on the reconstruction joint advisory council in 1943–4, on the higher technological education committee in 1944–5, and was chairman of the census of production committee in 1945. He was president of the Federation of British Industries in 1943–4, a most difficult period.

After the war, English Electric acquired Marconi's Wireless Telegraph Company, which increased Nelson's responsibilities. He also found time to develop his interest in technical education. His own companies provided much technical training, and he served on the governing body of the Imperial College of Science and Technology, on the court of governors of Manchester College of Science and Technology, and on the governing body of Queen Mary College, London. He was president of the Institution of Electrical Engineers in 1955, and of the Institution of Mechanical Engineers in 1957–8. He served as prime warden of the Goldsmiths' Company in 1960. In 1955 Imperial College made him an honorary fellow and granted him an honorary diploma. In 1957 he received an honorary LLD from Manchester. The previous year he received the freedom of Stafford.

Nelson received a knighthood in 1943, a baronetcy in 1955, and was raised to the peerage as first Baron Nelson of Stafford in 1960. Nelson died at the premises of the English Electric Company, in Stafford, on 16 July 1962 and was succeeded by his son, Henry George *Nelson (1917–1995), who became chairman of the General Electric Company Ltd from 1968, chancellor of Aston University, and a member of the court of the Bank of England.

C. S. NICHOLLS, *rev.*

Sources *The Times* (17 July 1962) · private information (1981) · b. cert. · d. cert. · *CGPLA Eng. & Wales* (1962)
Likenesses H. Knight, oils, exh. RA 1942, NPG [*see illus.*] · W. Stoneman, two photographs, 1947–58, NPG · H. Knight, oils, *c.*1948 · M. Codner, double portrait, 1955 (with his daughter), London office, English Electric Co. · M. Codner, portrait, 1955, London office, English Electric Co. · black and white sketch, 1955, Inst. EE · J. Gunn, double portrait, 1958 (with his son), London office, English Electric Co. · C. D. Capinpop, portrait, 1960, Stafford office, English Electric Co.
Wealth at death £78,350 17*s.* 11*d.*: probate, 4 Sept 1962, *CGPLA Eng. & Wales*

Nelson, Horatio, Viscount Nelson (1758–1805), naval officer, third surviving son (out of a family of eleven) of the Revd Edmund Nelson (1722–1802), rector of Burnham, and his wife, Catherine (1725–1767), daughter of Maurice Suckling, prebendary of Westminster, was born at Burnham Thorpe, Norfolk, on 29 September 1758. His father's family were Norfolk clergymen; his mother was a great-niece of Sir Robert Walpole and a cousin of Horatio, second Lord Walpole, who was the boy's godfather. She died when he was nine, leaving his father to bring up eight children on a small income. Horace, as he was called at home, went to the Royal Grammar School at Norwich, then Sir John Paston's School at North Walsham.

Early service, 1770–1792 In the autumn of 1770 the Falkland Islands crisis led to naval mobilization, and Nelson's uncle, Captain Maurice *Suckling, was appointed to command the 64-gun *Raisonnable* at Chatham. The boy was keen to go to sea, and on 1 January 1771 he joined the ship at Chatham. Presently the crisis was resolved and most of the navy paid off, but Captain Suckling was appointed to the guardship *Triumph*, lying in the Thames. This was no place to learn seamanship, so Suckling sent his nephew on a voyage to the West Indies in a merchantman commanded by one of his former petty officers. He returned fourteen months later, on the way to being an experienced seaman, and with a prejudice against the navy which took him some time to overcome. In 1773 he managed to get himself taken by Captain Skeffington Lutwidge of the *Carcass*, one of two ships sent to test the possibility of an ice-free passage across the north pole. They barely escaped from the ice north of Spitsbergen, and the young Nelson barely escaped from a polar bear on an unauthorized expedition from his ship. Soon after their return to England in October 1773 Nelson joined the frigate *Seahorse* going out to the East Indies. In her he served two years, visiting Madras, Calcutta, Ceylon, Bombay, and Basrah. In the autumn of 1775 he fell gravely ill and almost died. He returned to England in September 1776 aboard the frigate *Dolphin*, emaciated and depressed, to learn that his professional prospects had strikingly improved: his uncle had become controller of the navy. Immediately he was appointed acting lieutenant of the *Worcester*. In April 1777 he passed his examination for lieutenant at the Navy

Horatio Nelson, Viscount Nelson (1758–1805), by Sir William Beechey, 1800

Office—the controller, as usual, presiding at the examining board. Next day he received his commission as second lieutenant of the frigate *Lowestoffe* (Captain William Locker), bound for Jamaica. Locker was a pupil of Sir Edward Hawke and an admirer of his bold and aggressive tactics. He and Nelson became warm friends, and in later life Nelson acknowledged Locker as his formative professional influence.

The *Lowestoffe*'s initial task in the West Indies was to enforce the blockade of the rebellious American colonies, but in February 1778 war broke out with France. A new commander-in-chief, Sir Peter Parker, made the controller's nephew an officer of his flagship with a view to further advancement. His relief in the *Lowestoffe* was Lieutenant Cuthbert Collingwood. In October Nelson learned that his uncle had died, but by then Parker had seen enough of Nelson to judge his merit for himself. In December he became commander of the brig *Badger*, patrolling the Mosquito Shore. In June 1779 he was promoted captain of the frigate *Hinchinbrook*. By the age of twenty-one he had risen as far, and as fast, as talent or influence could carry a sea officer, for promotion to flag rank was strictly by seniority, from the top of the captains' list.

In the absence of his new ship, Nelson took command of part of the harbour defences of Port Royal against an expected French attack. On 1 September he took over the *Hinchinbrook* and sailed for the Mosquito Shore again. Britain was now at war with Spain, and Major-General John Dalling, the governor of Jamaica, prepared a scheme to attack Central America by a force to ascend the Rio San

Juan in boats from the Mosquito Shore to Lake Nicaragua. Being now familiar with that coast, Nelson was appointed to escort the troops to their landing. The convoy reached the bar of the San Juan on 24 March 1780. Experience soon demonstrated the soldiers' inability to handle their boats, so Nelson with fifty sailors and marines volunteered to accompany them. The river was low in the dry season and the passage difficult, but on 10 April they reached the fort of San Juan, the only substantial defence of the river. Nelson was for an immediate assault, but the soldiers insisted on a regular siege, which took eighteen days. By the time the Spaniards surrendered the rains had begun and most of the British were dead or dying of tropical fevers. Nelson was among the sick, and was dispatched downriver by canoe. He arrived at Jamaica near death, and in September, still very ill, he was sent to England under the care of his friend Captain William Cornwallis of the *Lion*.

After convalescing at Bath, Nelson visited his family at Burnham, and in the autumn took command of the frigate *Albemarle*, escorting convoys in the North Sea. In April he took a convoy across the Atlantic to the St Lawrence, then cruised off Boston, where he had a narrow escape from a squadron of four French ships of the line. In September 1782 he was at Quebec, where he fell in love with the daughter of an army officer and with difficulty tore himself away. At New York in November he met the king's son, Midshipman Prince William Henry, with whom he was to remain friendly all his life. From there the *Albemarle* went to the West Indies, where in March Nelson with three other small ships made an unsuccessful attack on the French garrison of Turk's Island. Soon after came news of peace negotiations, and in June 1783 the *Albemarle* returned to England to pay off.

There was little employment for a sea officer in peacetime, so Nelson decided to use his time to learn French. In October he and a brother officer left for St Omer, where, however, he spent his time mainly with a Miss Elizabeth Andrews, daughter of a visiting English clergyman. He hoped to marry her, but she was unwilling and he had no money. In January 1784 he returned to England, still single and monoglot. Two months later he was appointed to command the frigate *Boreas*, going out to the Leeward Islands. The terms of the recent peace treaty with the United States did not modify the Navigation Acts, which thus forbade American ships from trading to the remaining British colonies. The sugar islands, however, grew very little but cash crops, and depended on imported food and raw materials, almost all of which came from American ports in American ships. The intention of the British government was that British, Irish, or Canadian producers and shippers should benefit at the expense of the Americans—and of the West India planters, who faced a tripling of their costs, if not actual famine. In practice it was impossible to divert the flow of trade overnight, and since no transitional arrangements had been provided for, means had to be found to circumvent the acts and allow American ships to bring in their indispensable cargoes. Nelson arrived to find that two young frigate captains, the

brothers Cuthbert and Wilfred Collingwood, had already begun to disrupt these arrangements by applying their standing orders to the letter, and he enthusiastically joined them. This led to immediate clashes with the naval commander-in-chief, Sir Richard Hughes, and the governor of Antigua, General Sir Thomas Shirley, in which Nelson told them their duty in confident, not to say arrogant, language. 'Old respectable officers of high rank, long service and of a certain life', Shirley replied, with some restraint, 'are very jealous of being dictated to in their duty by young Gentlemen whose service and experience do not entitle them to it' (*Nelson's Letters from the Leeward Islands*, 37–8). Nelson's intemperate zeal made him very unpopular in the islands and generated lawsuits which made it impossible for him to go ashore for some time.

Nelson was nevertheless able to land at Nevis, where in the spring of 1785 he met the young widow Frances Herbert (Fanny) Nisbet *née* (Woolward; 1761–1831), [*see* Nelson, Frances Herbert], daughter of a local judge and niece of the leading planter of the island, for whom she kept house. Indeed he first met her small son Josiah, with whom he was discovered playing under a table. She was charming and gentle, he was lonely and susceptible. Soon they were engaged. In November 1786 the arrival of Prince William Henry, now a frigate captain too, ended Nelson's social isolation, as the prince insisted on taking Nelson (temporarily the senior officer on the station) on his tour of the islands. He gave away the bride when Nelson married Frances Nisbet at Nevis on 11 March 1787. In June the *Boreas* sailed for home, soon followed by Mrs Nelson in a merchant ship. Nelson and his wife spent the next five years in England on half-pay, much of the time with his father in Norfolk. Frances, who had lived all her life in the West Indies, was severely tried by Norfolk winters in a draughty parsonage, while Nelson fretted at inactivity and was still troubled by lawsuits arising from his West Indian command. Moreover, after five years the couple were still childless.

The Mediterranean, 1793–1797 Nelson was released from inactivity by the approach of war with revolutionary France. In January 1793 he was appointed to command the 64-gun *Agamemnon* fitting out at Chatham. In May she sailed to join the Mediterranean Fleet under Lord Hood, then blockading the French fleet in Toulon. In August the local authorities surrendered Toulon to Hood to protect themselves from the terror meted out by the republicans. Hood urgently needed troops if he was to defend the town, and Nelson was sent on a diplomatic mission to Naples to seek help from King Ferdinand IV. On his return to Toulon in October, Nelson was detached to join a squadron under Commodore Robert Linzee. On the 22nd, off Sardinia, he encountered a squadron of French frigates and engaged the *Melpomene* (40 guns), but she was rescued by her consorts. With Linzee he endured a frustrating diplomatic visit to Tunis, where the bey was sheltering a French convoy. In December Hood was forced to evacuate Toulon, and Nelson, at Leghorn in Christmas week, had to deal with shiploads of distraught refugees. In January

1794 Hood entrusted Nelson with the blockade of Corsica and co-operation with the Corsican patriots under Pasquale Paoli, who were trying to throw off French rule. Co-operation with the British army was more difficult, but in spite of General David Dundas's refusal to support it, Hood undertook the siege of Bastia with the squadron's marines alone. Nelson landed to take command on 4 April, and on 23 May Bastia surrendered. In June, this time in conjunction with the army, Nelson was once again ashore besieging Calvi. On 12 July he was wounded in the face by stones thrown up by an enemy shot, and never recovered the sight of his right eye. Calvi surrendered on 10 August. The *Agamemnon* spent the winter cruising between Leghorn, Genoa, and Corsica or blockading the coast of Provence, refitting as necessary at Leghorn, where Nelson took comfort with a local mistress and occasionally brought her to sea with him.

In March 1795 the French fleet (seventeen ships of the line) made a sortie from Toulon in the hope of retaking Corsica. The Mediterranean Fleet (fifteen ships of the line, including one Neapolitan), under its acting commander-in-chief, Vice-Admiral William Hotham, intercepted them, and in the course of a straggling engagement on 13–14 March took two ships from the fleeing enemy. The *Agamemnon* was faster than the rest of the fleet, and Nelson had the leading share in the success, but he was thoroughly dissatisfied with Hotham's caution and believed a decisive victory could have been achieved. 'My disposition can't bear tame and slow measures. Sure I am, had I commanded our fleet on the 14th, that either the whole French Fleet would have graced my triumph, or I should have been in a confounded scrape' (*Nelson's Letters to his Wife*, 204). On 14 July a similar affair took place, in which another French ship was taken, but to Nelson's disgust Hotham again recalled his headmost ships as the French closed their own coast. Nelson was now put in command of a small detached squadron supporting the Austrian army and blockading Genoa, nominally neutral but increasingly French-controlled. Nelson imposed the blockade on his own initiative, well understanding the risk of being disowned by government and ruined by private lawsuits: 'Political courage in an officer abroad is as highly necessary as military courage', he wrote (Oman, 171). During the summer of 1795 the *Agamemnon* and her squadron were active against French shipping and coastal positions along the Ligurian coast, while Nelson grew more and more dissatisfied with the inactivity of the Austrian army. At the end of November they were heavily defeated and retreated inland.

In January 1796 the new commander-in-chief, Sir John Jervis, arrived on the station. He and Nelson took to one another at once: in April Jervis appointed him a commodore, in June he hoisted his broad pendant in the *Captain* (74 guns), and in August Jervis (stretching his authority) made him an established commodore with a flag captain—in all but name an acting rear-admiral. Meanwhile the strategic situation was deteriorating rapidly, as the French armies under General Bonaparte continued their advance across northern Italy, and Spain was forced into

the war on the side of France. The position of the Mediterranean Fleet was now precarious. In the autumn the government took the decision to abandon Corsica and withdraw the fleet from the Mediterranean. In practice slow communications obliged Jervis and Sir Gilbert Elliot, the viceroy of Corsica, to take many critical decisions themselves, guessing ministers' intentions. The evacuation of Corsica in the face of advancing French troops was perilous, and it was largely thanks to Nelson's determination that Elliot, the entire garrison, and nearly all their stores were safely retrieved from Bastia in October and landed on Elba, now the last British refuge in the Mediterranean, while the fleet withdrew to Gibraltar. On 15 December Nelson with two frigates alone was sent back on a perilous rescue mission. On the way they met two Spanish frigates, and Nelson in the *Minerve* captured the *Santa Sabina* after a very severe fight. Her captain was Don Jacobo Stuart, great-grandson of James II. Next day the appearance of a Spanish fleet forced Nelson to abandon his prize, but the two frigates escaped to reach Porto Ferrajo on Christmas day. Thence they removed Elliot and the naval stores, but the general, having received no orders, insisted on remaining. Sailing on 29 January 1797 Nelson learned at Gibraltar that both the Spanish and British fleets had passed through the straits and hastened to follow them. Having actually passed through what may have been the Spanish fleet in the night without being detected, Nelson rejoined Jervis on 13 February and returned to the *Captain*.

Action was now imminent, and thanks to efficient scouting by his frigates Jervis was informed of the size and movements of the Spanish fleet. Next morning, about 25 miles west of Cape St Vincent, they were sighted ahead in hazy weather. The Spaniards were in two groups, totalling (as it seemed) twenty-seven ships of the line, though in fact the smaller group was a convoy (laden with quicksilver) and its close escort, and there were only twenty-two Spanish battleships present, of which the seventeen in the main body did most of the fighting. Jervis had expected to engage twenty-nine Spanish ships with his fifteen, but the British were well aware of the poor efficiency of their late allies, and Jervis rightly judged that 'the circumstances of the war in these seas, required a considerable degree of enterprise' (*Dispatches and Letters*, 2.333). Jervis deftly cut between the two Spanish forces, then tacked in succession to attack the main body from the rear. This tactic of 'rolling up' an ill-formed enemy from the rear was something of a British speciality, which had brought victory to Anson, Hawke, and Rodney. Initially it went well, but a bold attack by Vice-Admiral Don Juan Joaquín Moreno, commanding the Spanish convoy, held up Jervis and the centre of his fleet, leaving the leading ships unsupported. At this moment Don José de Córdoba y Ramos, the Spanish commander-in-chief, signalled to his leading ships to bear up and attack the British rear, a manoeuvre which might well have retrieved his situation if it had been smartly carried out. Seeing the risk, Jervis ordered Rear-Admiral Charles Thompson with his rear division to tack in order to frustrate the Spanish move.

Thompson did nothing, but Nelson (fourth from the rear) wore out of line and cut across to join the head of the British line, to leeward of the Spaniards, thus blocking their move. With part of the British to leeward of the Spanish main body and others coming up to windward a fierce battle developed, in the course of which the *Captain* was considerably damaged. She was in action with the *San Nicolas* and *San Josef* when Captain Cuthbert Collingwood in the *Excellent* came up on the other side of them and fired with such effect that the Spanish ships collided in confusion. Seeing the opportunity, and with his own ship now almost unmanageable, Nelson ran aboard the *San Nicolas* and himself led one of the two boarding parties which leapt aboard. There was bloody fighting, but it was soon over. The much bigger *San Josef*, however, was still alongside, though heavily pounded by another British ship from the other side. Before the Spaniards could rally, Nelson led the boarders onward and took her too:

> and on the quarterdeck of a Spanish first-rate, extravagant as the story may seem, did I receive the swords of the vanquished Spaniards; which as I received I gave to William Fearney, one of my bargemen, who put them with the greatest sang-froid under his arm.　(ibid., 2.343)

At the end of the day the Spanish fleet was decisively defeated, losing four prizes, though the great four-decker *Santissima Trinidad*, the ambition of every British captain, narrowly escaped.

The victory was the fruit of teamwork by a fleet which Jervis had trained to a peak of efficiency. Nelson greatly contributed by wearing out of line, but it is going much too far to call this 'disobedience', or to make him solely responsible for the success of the day. Jervis had previously ordered him to use his initiative in such a case, and he acted in accordance with the admiral's tactical intentions. Nelson's boarding party was the most spectacular moment of the day. To board an undefeated enemy was a bloody and desperate move; for a flag officer to lead in person, and take not one but two ships bigger than his own, had no precedent, even though the two ships in question had first been battered for two hours by a total of five British ships. Nelson would in any event have emerged from the battle a public hero, but he took steps to make sure. Sir Gilbert Elliot had witnessed the action from a frigate. One of his staff, Colonel John Drinkwater, was a successful author, and to him Nelson gave an interview intended for the press. He also sent another narrative for publication to his old friend Captain Locker. 'Nelson's patent bridge for boarding first-rates', as the press called it, instantly captured the public imagination. This glamorous heroism, easily understood by laymen, eclipsed in the public mind the efficient teamwork and gallantry of his brother officers, among whom Nelson's skill in managing his public image caused some resentment. Rewards for the action were distributed according to rank. Jervis, who had already been offered a barony, received an earldom instead. Nelson, having let his preference be known, became a knight of the Bath rather than a baronet like the other junior flag officers: he had no heir to inherit a baronetcy, and it carried no star and ribbon to wear in public. At the same time he was promoted rear-admiral in the course of seniority.

Tenerife and the Nile, 1797–1798 After the battle of St Vincent the Spanish fleet stayed in Cadiz, while Jervis (now earl of St Vincent) established a blockade and considered means of forcing the Spanish fleet to sea. To this end he made his blockade as tight and aggressive as possible. An inshore squadron under Nelson's command was anchored at the mouth of the harbour, so close in that they could easily distinguish the ladies of Cadiz walking on the ramparts. Then in May and June 1797 the mutinies at Spithead and the Nore paralysed the navy in home waters and threatened disaster. In St Vincent's ships discipline was tight and morale was high, so in the aftermath of the mutinies many of the most disaffected ships were sent to join the Mediterranean Fleet. When the *Theseus* arrived 'in great disorder' her captain was removed and Nelson, his flag captain Ralph Willett Miller, and several of his favourite officers turned over to her. Within a fortnight a note was left on the quarter-deck from the ship's company:

> Success attend Admiral Nelson God bless Captain Miller we thank them for the officers they have placed over us. We are happy and comfortable and will shed every drop of blood in our veins to support them, and the name of the *Theseus* shall be immortalised as high as *Captain*'s ship's company.
> (*Nelson's Letters to his Wife*, 326)

There was only one Nelson, however, and many troubled ship's companies. St Vincent showed no mercy and no spirit of compromise towards mutinous men or idle officers, but he well understood that inactivity had been one of the springs of discontent in the Channel Fleet, and he made sure that his fleet was not inactive. On the night of 3–4 July an attempt was made to bombard Cadiz from a bomb-vessel, protected by ship's boats. A few days before, some British boats had shown marked reluctance to come to close quarters with the Spanish gunboats. When they counter-attacked this time, Nelson in person led the British boats in his barge. There was desperate hand-to-hand fighting, in which Nelson's life was saved by his coxswain John Sykes, who put out his own arm to receive a cutlass blow aimed at Nelson's head. Nelson mentioned Sykes in his dispatch (an almost unheard-of honour for a rating) and got him promoted. Once again Nelson had shown extraordinary personal courage and risked his life in circumstances where no flag officer would normally be found—but he had good reason to do so, for the shaky morale and discipline of the navy called for outstanding leadership.

Two further bombardments were attempted with limited success before St Vincent and Nelson turned to a more promising operation. A rich treasure ship was reported to be sheltering in Santa Cruz, Tenerife, in the Canary Islands. A well-planned raid promised to gain a good prize, occupy the men, and dishearten the Spaniards, so Nelson was dispatched to undertake it. Two landing attempts on 22 July, however, only succeeded in alerting the defences. Then a deserter's information persuaded the captains to make another attempt, and Nelson consented. This time the plan was for a direct frontal assault of the town in darkness, relying on speed to overwhelm the strong defences. Everyone knew it was very risky, and their assessment of the defences was optimistic. Though the governor, General Antonio Gutiérrez, had fewer than 800 regular troops (including some French seamen) and about as many local militiamen (mostly without firearms), the defenders were well led, well trained, and in good heart. Even so, if the whole British force of 1000 had rushed the mole, as planned, they might well have succeeded, for it was defended by fewer than 100 men. Unfortunately the defences were alert, strong currents swept the boats along the shore, and only a few, including Nelson's, reached the mole. As he stepped from the boat he was wounded in the right arm. His stepson Lieutenant Josiah Nisbet got him aboard a boat and back to the *Theseus*, where his arm was amputated. In the town Captain Thomas Troubridge and the survivors of the landing parties were able to negotiate a surrender by which they were returned to their ships. After a chivalrous exchange of letters between Nelson and Gutiérrez, the defeated British force sailed away on 27 July.

Dejected and in great pain, Nelson returned to England. There, however, he was still the hero of Cape St Vincent, his recent check was blamed on others, and he was soon cheered up by the adulation of the crowds and the congratulations of his brother officers, though his wound continued to give him severe pain until the ligatures finally came away in November. Over the winter he was lionized everywhere in London, and the hero's public devotion to his wife was widely noted. At the same time he longed to return to duty. Finally he sailed on 10 April 1798 to rejoin St Vincent off Cadiz.

The strategic situation was critical. A very large expedition was known to be preparing at Toulon for an unknown destination. Austria, driven out of the war at the peace of Campo Formio in October 1797, would not re-enter without a British fleet in the Mediterranean to guard her southern flank and protect her protégé, the kingdom of the Two Sicilies. In these circumstances St Vincent was ordered to detach a small force on reconnaissance into the Mediterranean. Nelson joined his flag at the end of the month, and was at once sent towards Toulon with three ships of the line and four frigates. Meanwhile the government had at last made up its mind to risk stationing a proper fleet in the Mediterranean again, leaving home waters with no margin whatever in the face of threatened invasion. On 24 May St Vincent received a reinforcement of eight sail of the line, and the same day he detached ten to join Nelson.

Meanwhile Nelson had met disaster. His new flag captain, Captain Edward Berry, had won Nelson's heart by his gallantry in battle, but he had never commanded a big ship before, and experience was to prove him an indifferent seaman and a poor manager of men. In the early hours of 21 May the *Vanguard* was completely dismasted in a gale; only fine seamanship by Captain Alexander Ball of the *Alexander* got the flagship in tow and saved her from

driving on the coast of Sardinia. Since the other ships in company did not suffer severely, the *Vanguard*'s accident must be attributed to bad seamanship, and it came at the worst possible moment. The day before the storm, the French expedition had sailed from Toulon: thirteen ships of the line and 400 transports laden with troops, all under the command of General Bonaparte. While the *Vanguard* repaired her damage in a Sardinian bay, the French passed unseen. As soon as she was fit for sea, Nelson hastened to the rendezvous where his frigates had been ordered to wait ten days for him. He arrived on the eleventh day, 9 June; they had left to seek him elsewhere and they never found him. Two days earlier Thomas Troubridge had joined him with the reinforcements. Nelson now had a fleet to command, for the first time, and an enemy to seek, but he had no information on where the French had gone and no frigates to help him find them.

First looking on the Italian coast, Nelson headed south on information that the French had been seen off Sicily. On 17 June he sent Troubridge into Naples, where he obtained vague promises of support and definite information that the French had gone towards Malta. South of Sicily on 22 June a neutral merchantman informed Nelson that the French had taken Malta from the knights of St John and sailed again on the 16th for an unknown destination. They had not appeared in Sicily, the obvious target, and the wind ruled out anywhere to the westward; so in the teeth of probability Nelson decided they were bound for Egypt. Calling back the ships then chasing some French frigates in the distance, lest the fleet become separated, he pushed for Alexandria with all speed. What he did not know was that the neutral's information was in one critical respect wrong: the French had sailed from Malta on the 19th, not the 16th. The distant frigates were actually the outliers of their fleet, and the two flagships were then only 60 miles apart. On 28 June the British squadron sighted Alexandria, only to find the port empty and no news of the French. On the 30th he sailed again, sick at heart at having wrongly guessed the enemy's intentions. Next day the French fleet, which had proceeded more slowly and on a more northerly course, anchored off Alexandria and prepared to land its troops. On 20 July Nelson was back at Syracuse, where the fleet watered and victualled, but found no information. On the 24th he sailed, still convinced the French must be somewhere in the eastern Mediterranean, and meaning to search in the Aegean. Then at last, on the 28th, he received definite intelligence that the French were in Egypt. At noon on 1 August the British were close enough to Alexandria to see the harbour crammed with French transports, but no sign of the men-of-war. The only other anchorage on the coast was Abu Qir Bay, 10 miles to the northward. By midafternoon the French fleet was in sight, anchored in the bay in a single line.

The wind was blowing into the bay, so—accepting the risks of fighting in shoal water and gathering darkness— Nelson ordered an immediate attack, the ships forming a rough line as they stood in. Rounding the island of Abu Qir which marked the southern entrance of the bay, they hauled up to reach the head of the line. Captain Thomas Foley of the *Goliath*, the leading ship, observing the French ships lying at single anchor, correctly deduced that they must have enough deep water ahead and inshore to swing, and so crossed the head of the enemy line and came down the inshore side, where the French had not even cleared for action. The next three ships did the same, while Nelson and the rest of the fleet took the outside berth. Vice-Admiral François Paul de Brueys d'Aigalliers had stationed his weakest ships at the head of his line on the assumption that it could not easily be attacked: instead they received an overwhelming onslaught without the rest of the fleet to leeward being able to help them. The British worked methodically down the line until they came to the flagship, the 120-gun *l'Orient*, usually reckoned the largest warship in the world. She seriously damaged the *Bellerophon*, which was driven out of action, but then caught fire herself. Late that evening she blew up with an explosion which stunned both French and British and brought all fighting to a halt for some time. Later the action resumed, but all through the night the French rear division, under Rear-Admiral Pierre Charles de Villeneuve, made no attempt to come to their comrades' assistance. Next morning, when most of the British ships were too much damaged to follow, Villeneuve made his escape with two ships of the line and two frigates. He left behind eleven battleships and two frigates taken or sunk by a squadron of thirteen ships of the line (one of which ran aground and did not get into action) and one 50-gun fourth rate. 'Victory is certainly not a name strong enough for such a scene', Nelson wrote to his wife (*Nelson's Letters to his Wife*, 399).

Naples and Palermo, 1798–1800 Nelson had been wounded in the head during the night and seems to have been heavily concussed, but he had sufficiently recovered the next morning to organize divine service to give thanks for victory—to the surprise of a generation of officers to whom public religion afloat was very unusual. His next task was to supervise repairs to his fleet and send news of the battle. An officer was dispatched overland to India to warn the East India Company that Bonaparte was in the Orient. He arrived safely, but Nelson's dispatches home were lost when the *Leander* (50 guns) met and was taken by another survivor of the battle, the 74-gun *Généreux*, with the result that rumours of the battle circulated throughout Europe for some time before definite news. In Britain Nelson (and those who had entrusted so vital an operation to so young an officer) had come in for some criticism for missing the French. The contrast when a victory of such stunning completeness was announced was overwhelming. The public was overjoyed and ministers were intensely relieved: Lord Spencer, the first lord of the Admiralty, fainted on hearing the news. All over Europe Britain's potential allies heard of the battle with an enthusiasm which in due course was translated into a new coalition against France.

The Two Sicilies was the most exposed of all countries to French aggression and the most intensely relieved at the victory. When Nelson finally reached Naples aboard the crippled *Vanguard* on 22 September, he was received by the court and people amid scenes of enthusiasm barely short of hysteria. The British minister, Sir William Hamilton, was naturally prominent in the rejoicing, and his theatrical wife, Emma *Hamilton, Lady Hamilton (*bap.* 1765, *d.* 1815), still more so. Under their care Nelson began to recover from his wound and from the intense strain of the previous months. But this 'country of fiddlers and poets, whores and scoundrels' (*Dispatches and Letters*, 3.138) irritated him, and on 15 October he sailed with some relief to take care of the blockade of the French garrison of Malta, where the islanders had risen against their new masters and confined them to the fortifications. On 5 November he was back in Naples.

Nelson's reward for his unprecedented victory was to be made a peer, Baron Nelson of the Nile. Ministers felt they could not be more generous to a subordinate commander, technically under St Vincent's orders, but Nelson and many others remembered that St Vincent himself had been made an earl for much less. Other sovereigns were more forthcoming. The Ottoman sultan created a new order of chivalry to invest him with, and added the *chelengk*, a diamond plume taken from his own turban. There was more to turn his head, for in Naples he found himself dealing with high policy and diplomacy in conjunction with Sir William Hamilton and Queen Maria Carolina, the real head of her husband's government, which was dominated by a small group of her favourites, mostly brought in from Austrian service. The queen advocated an aggressive foreign policy, intended to provoke French attack and force Austria into war. Daughter of the Empress Maria Theresa, sister of two emperors, and mother-in-law of the reigning emperor, the queen was happy to treat her husband's kingdom as a pawn in a private foreign policy designed to overthrow the French republicans and avenge her murdered sister Queen Marie Antoinette. Hamilton had long since become an uncritical adherent of the queen, and Nelson had no idea how unpopular she and her policy were among informed Neapolitans. His orders were to support the kingdom against the French, and he readily fell in with, and encouraged, the queen's policy. Overbearing the king's well-founded misgivings about the quality of his army, Nelson lent his support to the offensive. On 28 November Leghorn surrendered to his ships, and next day King Ferdinand entered Rome in triumph. One week later the French counterattacked, and the Neapolitan army instantly disintegrated.

Nelson now had to organize the secret evacuation of the royal family, their treasure, and servants in the face of advancing French troops and a loyal populace determined to prevent their king and queen deserting. They sailed on 23 December for Palermo, enduring on passage a severe storm during which the youngest prince died in Lady Hamilton's arms. Her resolution during a horrifying voyage which reduced the other passengers to prostration and despair aroused Nelson's admiration. The court disembarked at Palermo on 26 December, and Nelson moved ashore to live with the Hamiltons. Still exhausted, overworked, and unwell, uncomfortable at the disastrous results of his meddling in foreign affairs, resentful at the Admiralty for what seemed to be its slighting treatment and at his wife for the fewness of her letters, Nelson badly needed emotional support, and from Lady Hamilton alone he received it. Vivacious and uninhibited even by the relaxed standards of the Bourbon court, she threw herself, and drew him, into an extravagant social round of spectacles, drinking, and gambling. Emma Hamilton's earlier career as a courtesan had taught her skills which might have overcome a more sophisticated and less vulnerable man than Nelson. By February their relationship had passed beyond dalliance. Her friendship with the queen and her intimacy with the hero of the hour placed her at the centre of affairs, and she relished the position.

In Naples, meanwhile, a French satellite republic had been established, led by many of the aristocracy and educated classes. The lower classes of town and country remained loyal to the Bourbons, and in February a Calabrian nobleman, Cardinal Fabrizio Ruffo (a former papal minister, but only technically a clergyman), landed to raise the country against the 'Jacobins'. This he did with such success that by April the French and their friends were confined to Naples and a few fortresses. At the same time Nelson sent ships which blockaded Naples and retook the islands in the bay. All this while the king and queen insisted that Nelson must remain at Palermo in person to protect them. Then in early May a naval crisis developed: the French fleet escaped from Brest and entered the Mediterranean. St Vincent was ill ashore and his second, Lord Keith, with fifteen sail of the line off Cadiz, was unable to block Vice-Admiral Eustache Bruix with twenty-four. The allied forces in the Mediterranean were scattered and vulnerable: Rear-Admiral John Thomas Duckworth had four ships of the line at Minorca; Nelson four at Naples, three off Malta, one at Palermo, and two in the Levant; while the Russian Admiral Fyodor Fyodorovich Ushakov had fifteen at Corfu. There was little to stop Bruix, had he acted boldly, from defeating them all in detail and relieving Bonaparte's army in Egypt. The British had to concentrate urgently. On 12 May Nelson heard of Bruix's approach, drew in his ships, and cruised for a week off the eastern end of Sicily. On the 29th he was back at Palermo and on 13th June he sailed for Naples with Neapolitan troops aboard. Next day, however, he received news of the French fleet from Lord Keith, now commander-in-chief of the station, which caused him again to cruise to the east of Sicily. He then returned to Palermo to resume his expedition to Naples, where he arrived on 25 June. He was there on 13 July, when he received the first of three orders from Keith to come himself to Minorca, threatened by Franco-Spanish attack, or at least send all the ships he could spare. He refused to obey, on the grounds that Naples was more important than Minorca. For this he was subsequently reproved by the Admiralty. No other officer would have got off so lightly, for he was in no position to judge of the strategic situation, and his refusal to concentrate as ordered left the fleet open to defeat in detail.

On his arrival at Naples Nelson found that Cardinal Ruffo had concluded an armistice with the besieged rebels which guaranteed them safe passage to France. The senior British officer present, Captain Edward Foote of the frigate *Seahorse*, had signed this with reservations, but Nelson at once cancelled it. It appears that he was legally justified in doing so, but his wisdom is more doubtful. Nelson's political opinions were conservative and uncomplicated: he hated Frenchmen and Jacobins. Ruffo, in a time of civil war when most views ran to extremes, urged reconciliation as the only means to rebuild a divided kingdom. He was well placed to do so, for his devotion to the throne was unquestionable, but he was not of the queen's party. Nelson, who understood nothing of Neapolitan politics, doubted his loyalty and despised his moderation. He overruled the cardinal and insisted on unconditional surrender. The rebels duly marched out and embarked on ships which they believed would carry them to safety, but instead they were handed over to the restored Neapolitan government and many of them executed. Nelson has been accused of treachery, but it appears he honestly believed that the rebels had surrendered in full knowledge that the armistice had been cancelled. Nelson spoke no foreign tongue, and there is room to suspect Sir William and Lady Hamilton, his interpreters, of deceit; they both had personal reasons to hate the rebels, and long residence in Naples had accustomed them to chicanery which was quite foreign to his nature. At the same time Commodore Francesco Caracciolo, former senior officer of the Neapolitan navy and latterly commander of the republic's naval forces, was discovered in hiding, handed over to a Neapolitan court martial, and condemned to death. Caracciolo was respected by British officers, who lamented his fate; but having unquestionably taken up arms against his sovereign he was guilty of treason, and neither Nelson nor anyone else could have saved his life. What was unnecessary and ungenerous was to hurry him to a demeaning death, refusing him even a priest.

On 8 August Nelson returned to Palermo, where he spent most of the next ten months ashore. From August to December 1799 he was acting commander-in-chief of the Mediterranean. Nelson's actions at Naples were approved by his own government and very highly approved by King Ferdinand, who created him duke of Bronte. Only much later did doubts begin to circulate. What few of his naval colleagues had any doubt about at the time was his conduct at Palermo. Officers who admired and loved him were appalled to see him enslaved to Emma Hamilton, heedless of his reputation and duty. Since the French fleet did not return to the Mediterranean and the French armies were driven out of Italy, the activities of the squadron could be left to subordinates. When Bonaparte escaped from Egypt in August 1799, Nelson was not at sea to intercept him. In London ministers were as alarmed as Nelson's friends by what they heard from Palermo, but they had to handle the public hero with care. When Keith returned to command in January 1800 he ordered Nelson to join him at sea to inspect the blockade of Malta. On 18 February, south of Sicily, his flagship captured the *Généreux* (74 guns), one of the survivors of the Nile. Almost at once, however, Nelson returned to Palermo. In April he was briefly off Malta again, this time with the Hamiltons on board. By this time Lady Hamilton was pregnant, though her ample figure long concealed the fact. At home Lord Spencer had lost patience and all but ordered him to haul down his flag.

Since Keith refused to allow Nelson to take a battleship home, he took the ships from the blockade of Malta without orders and landed at Leghorn on 14 July, accompanied by the Hamiltons (for Sir William too had been replaced) and by Queen Maria Carolina on her way to visit her relatives in Vienna. Narrowly escaping the French armies, once more advancing across Italy, the party proceeded to Ancona, crossed the Adriatic in a Russian frigate to Trieste, and thence travelled to Vienna, Prague, Dresden, Magdeburg, and so down the Elbe to Hamburg. Everywhere Nelson was received with the greatest honour; everywhere close observation of the *tria juncta in uno* (as Emma Hamilton called their *ménage à trois*) aroused mingled amusement, regret, and disgust. 'It is really melancholy', noted Sir John Moore when he met them at Leghorn, 'to see a brave and good man, who has deserved well of his country, cutting so pitiful a figure' (*Diary of Sir John Moore*, ed. J. F. Maurice, 1.367).

The Baltic, 1800–1802 The party landed at Great Yarmouth on 6 November 1800. Along the road to London they were received with public celebration. In London there were further dinners and honours, but there was also the inevitable meeting with Lady Nelson and the inevitable parting. Much of the reputation Nelson had won at the Nile had now faded in the recollections of those who had heard of Palermo or had encountered him with the Hamiltons. He appeared at court covered with foreign decorations which he did not yet have permission to wear, and was pained to be received coldly by that most faithful of husbands, George III. In the upper reaches of society many followed the king's example. It was in some ways a relief to be promoted vice-admiral in January 1801 and appointed second in command of the Channel Fleet under his old chief St Vincent, flying his flag in his own prize the *San Josef*. On the other hand Emma Hamilton was heavily pregnant, and he himself was tormented with jealous fears which she skilfully played upon. On 29 January, in great secrecy, she was delivered of a girl, duly named Horatia. There is some evidence that there was a twin: Nelson was not told, and never knew of Emma's earlier child, then aged twenty.

The same day he received this news, Nelson learned that he was to be second in command of a fleet for the Baltic, under Vice-Admiral Sir Hyde Parker. St Vincent, about to become first lord of the Admiralty in the new administration, had a high opinion of Parker, and there could be no question of giving Nelson an independent command after the events of the past fifteen months. The task of the new fleet was to frustrate the armed neutrality, a dangerous combination of Denmark, Sweden, and Russia acting under the tsar's direction, and effectively in French interests, which threatened to shut off the supply of timber and naval stores on which the Royal Navy depended. After a brief reunion with Lady Hamilton, Nelson joined the fleet assembling at Yarmouth. There he found his commander-in-chief newly married at the age of sixty-one to a girl of eighteen, and showing no enthusiasm for an early departure. 'Consider how nice it must be laying abed with a young wife, compared with a damned cold raw wind', he wrote to Troubridge, now St Vincent's second at the Admiralty (Laughton, 1.418). Suppressing whatever comparisons may have risen to his mind, St Vincent wrote a private note hastening Parker to sea, and they sailed on 12 March. Parker did not go out of his way to discuss his plans with Nelson, nor did he consult the several Baltic experts who had been attached to his fleet, although the situation was delicate and he needed all the intelligence he could get. War had not been declared and diplomatic negotiations continued; if fighting was necessary, Parker had to decide whom to attack and how. Nelson wanted to ignore the Danish fleet, which was in no condition to put to sea, and strike straight at that part of the Russian fleet which was laid up in Reval, while the remainder was still frozen in Kronstadt. This would have been the boldest and safest course, tackling the real core of the alliance rather than the reluctant Danes and Swedes, but it was too bold for Parker. After much hesitation he agreed to risk the passage of the Sound, where the much feared Danish batteries did them no damage and the Swedes did not fire at all. On 30 March they anchored in sight of Copenhagen.

The month lost by Parker's idling had allowed the Danes to put the defences of Copenhagen into a formidable condition, but fortunately for the British they had moored their ships along rather than across the channels leading towards the city, so that they could be attacked one after the other as at the Nile. Moreover the line along the King's Deep in front of the city was strongest at the key point off the dockyard where the Tre Kroner Fort marked the angle of the two channels, and weakest at its further, southern end. Nelson saw that that end could be attacked by a fleet which came up the Holland's Deep, rounded the end of the Middle Ground shoal, and came back down the King's Deep. It would not even be necessary to subdue the strongest part of the defences in order to get bomb vessels within range of the city and force a negotiation with the Danes. On 1 April Nelson was detached to attack with twelve smaller ships of the line, while Parker with the bigger ships waited offshore. That evening he anchored at the southern end of the Middle Ground. At dawn the next morning, with a favourable southerly wind, the British ships weighed anchor to attack. Almost at once things miscarried. Without reliable charts or pilots, the British thought the deepest part of the channel was further from the Danish ships than it was, and kept too far to seaward. One ship grounded before the action began, and two more grounded on the farther side of the channel, at very long range. The remaining nine fought at the relatively long range of a cable (240 yards), reducing the effectiveness of their gunnery, though subsequent sounding showed that they could have run right alongside the Danish line, and even doubled it, as at the Nile. The Danish defences were stronger than anticipated, partly because the low, raft-like floating batteries moored between their ships had not been counted from a distance, and their guns were served with great gallantry. The result was a slow and hard-fought victory, with several ships suffering severely before the superiority of British gunnery began to tell. Fortunately the strongest part of the Danish defences around the Tre Kroner Fort to the north was largely or entirely out of range, and though the ships here were fully rigged and manned, they made no attempt to intervene in the battle. Parker, whose eight ships were supposed to have worked up towards the town from the north to check such a move, advanced so slowly that he could have done nothing to assist. Nevertheless time was on Nelson's side. By 1.30 p.m. British gunnery had clearly mastered the southern defences. Commodore Olfert Fischer had abandoned his burning flagship, twelve more ships were largely or completely out of action, and the way was open for the British bomb vessels to get within range of the city. At this point Parker, still 4 miles away, hoisted the signal of recall, made 'general' (directed to each ship individually). Had the signal been obeyed it would have transformed victory into catastrophe, for Nelson's ships could have withdrawn only across the face of the undefeated northern defences, in front of which several of them subsequently ran aground when attempting this move after the cease-fire. Angry and agitated at his superior's folly, Nelson turned to his flag captain and said 'You know, Foley, I have only one eye—and I have a right to be blind sometimes' and, putting the telescope to his blind eye, 'I really do not see the signal'. Fortunately Nelson's captains, seeing that he had not repeated Parker's signal, copied him in disobeying the commander-in-chief, while his second, Rear-Admiral Thomas Graves, reluctantly repeated the signal, but hoisted it in such a position that it was invisible to most of the squadron, while keeping Nelson's signal for 'close action' at the masthead.

Meanwhile most of the Danish ships in the southern line were out of action, several on fire, but still being hit both by British ships in front and by Danish batteries trying to fire over or between them from the city behind. To save further slaughter, Nelson now sent a message with a Danish-speaking officer proposing a truce. At the time some British officers thought this a skilful *ruse de guerre*, and later Danish historians have suggested that had the proposal not been accepted Nelson would have been defeated. It is true that British lives as well as Danish were saved by the cease-fire, but by then Nelson had clearly won the battle and Copenhagen was exposed to bombardment. Virtually ignoring Parker, Nelson now negotiated in person with Fischer (whom he had known in the West Indies) and later with the crown prince, effective head of the Danish government. In these discussions Nelson's uncomplicated approach to diplomacy showed to best effect. Language was not a problem, since both the crown prince and his naval aide-de-camp spoke English. Domestic politics

were not involved and the international situation was essentially simple: fear of Russia had forced Denmark into the armed neutrality, and fear of Britain had to force her out of it. Nelson wanted a truce of sixteen weeks, sufficient to sail up the Baltic and deal with the Russian fleet. The Danes eventually agreed to fourteen, having heard (some time before the British did) of the murder of Tsar Paul and correctly guessing that Russian policy might change.

After the battle Sir Hyde Parker occupied himself (to the disgust even of his friends) in filling the places of dead officers with his own followers who had not been engaged in the battle. Nelson, physically and emotionally exhausted, and convinced that further fighting was unlikely, was preparing to return to England on sick leave when on 5 May Parker received orders to hand over his command to Nelson and himself return to England. The arrival of unofficial accounts of the battle soon after Parker's dispatches had convinced ministers that he had to be replaced at once, and revived their confidence in Nelson. The prospect of command and activity revived Nelson himself, as it always did. On the 6th he took command, and next day he sailed for Reval. There he found the new Russian government conciliatory, and with no further need of fighting in the Baltic he returned to England, landing at Yarmouth on 1 July. With great generosity he counselled the indignant Parker not to demand an inquiry into his conduct, which could only have damaged his reputation and gilded Nelson's.

Nelson was now a viscount, and the disastrous effects of Lady Hamilton had been largely wiped from his reputation. His friends, especially St Vincent and Troubridge at the Admiralty, intended to prevent him falling into the same situation again by keeping him busy. On 27 July he was appointed to command the local anti-invasion forces in the channel. The appointment of a vice-admiral to what was essentially a captain's command was justified by the necessity of quieting public alarm, but it is difficult to believe that this was the sole motive. Emma Hamilton certainly did not believe it. Correctly identifying her real rivals, she worked Nelson up to a jealous irritation which damaged his relationship with St Vincent and ruined his long friendship with Troubridge. However he undertook his new command with his customary energy. On the night of 15 August he organized a boat attack on French invasion craft moored at the mouth of Boulogne harbour, but the enemy were forewarned and the attack was driven off with loss. By this time peace negotiations were under way, and on 1 October an armistice with France was signed.

Mediterranean and West Indies, 1802–1805 The peace of Amiens, finally ratified in 1802, provided Nelson with nineteen months of rest. In September Lady Hamilton had bought for him Merton Place, Surrey, and there he now settled with the Hamiltons. His relatives were frequent visitors, having swiftly deserted Lady Nelson and echoed Emma Hamilton's spiteful remarks about her; only his old father declined to break off relations with her.

He died in 1802, and that summer Nelson and the Hamiltons went on a triumphal progress across England and south Wales to visit Sir William's Pembrokeshire estates. Refreshed and rewarded by public acclaim, Nelson returned to a house which Lady Hamilton had turned into a sort of shrine to himself. His old friend Sir Gilbert Elliot, now Lord Minto, recorded his impressions on a visit in March 1802:

> The whole establishment and way of life is such as to make me angry, as well as melancholy; but I cannot alter it, and I do not think myself obliged or at liberty to quarrel with him for his weakness, though nothing shall ever induce me to give the smallest countenance to Lady Hamilton … She is high in looks, but more immense than ever. She goes on cramming Nelson with trowelfuls of flattery, which he goes on taking as quietly as a child does pap. The love she makes to him is not only ridiculous, but disgusting.   (*Life and Letters*, 3.242)

The public was almost as fully informed about their relationship as Minto was, for the print shops were full of suggestive allusions to the famous household. All this while the bare appearance of propriety was assured by the presence of Sir William. When he died on 6 April 1803 all three were in London, and diplomatic relations with France were worsening rapidly. On 14 May Nelson was appointed commander-in-chief of the Mediterranean Fleet, and two days later war against France was declared. On the 18th he hoisted his flag in the *Victory* at Portsmouth, next day he sailed, and in July he joined the fleet already off Toulon.

His function there was to protect Malta and Gibraltar, to keep in check the French Mediterranean squadron, and above all to prevent it escaping through the straits to participate in Napoleon's invasion schemes. With the *grande armée* encamped around Boulogne, it was essential that the French squadrons be prevented from uniting and coming up the channel. It was very difficult to mount a close blockade of Toulon in the face of frequent offshore gales in winter and the mountains behind the port, from which the blockaders could be seen far out to sea. Nelson was insistent that he never meant to blockade the place, but to watch it from a distance, far enough to tempt the French out, near enough to catch them when they came. To this end he often used an anchorage in the Maddalena Islands, off the northern end of Sardinia, where water and fresh provisions were plentiful. Throughout eighteen weary months of observation, usually at sea, far from a base, for long periods acutely short of naval stores, Nelson devoted great care to keeping his ships in repair and his men supplied with fresh food. Always careful of morale, he deliberately varied his cruising grounds to provide new sights and experiences. Visiting from ship to ship was allowed whenever the weather permitted boatwork, while the men were encouraged to take part in music, dancing, and theatricals.

This routine went on all through 1804. In May of that year Nelson learnt that at Christmastide Lady Hamilton had borne him another daughter, who died soon afterwards. By the end of the year Nelson was unwell and hoping for leave, but then Napoleon crowned himself as emperor, Spain entered the war as a French ally, sharply worsening the situation of the Mediterranean squadron, and on 19 January 1805 at Maddalena Nelson heard that the French fleet had sailed from Toulon, eluding his frigates. Once again he had to endure a frustrating search with little information. As Villeneuve's squadron had last been seen steering south-east, Nelson searched to the eastward as far as Alexandria once more, and was back at Malta on 19 February when he discovered that the French had been driven back to port by gales. On 4 April, off Majorca, he learned that the Toulon fleet was at sea again. This time Villeneuve, warned by a neutral merchantman of Nelson's whereabouts, succeeded in getting out of the Mediterranean without being intercepted, and in the face of persistent headwinds, it was not until the beginning of May that Nelson was able to get through the straits in pursuit. The problem now was to guess where in the world Villeneuve, and the Spanish ships he had collected from Cadiz, might be bound. An obvious possibility was northward to join the other French squadrons, enter the channel in overwhelming force, and cover Napoleon's invasion. This was the greatest risk, to counter which the standing practice of British admirals in such a situation was to fall back on the western approaches and join the Channel Fleet. Sir John Orde, commanding the squadron off Cadiz, had done so already, and Nelson was preparing to follow suit when, off Cape St Vincent, he learned from a Portuguese warship that Villeneuve's ships had steered westward, across the Atlantic.

Nelson had now to take a difficult strategic decision. He had to assume that no other British admiral yet knew the movements of the Toulon fleet. If he did not pursue and mark it, untold damage might be done to British interests in the West or even East Indies. On the other hand, the French plan might be (and in fact was) a feint, designed to lure as many British ships as possible away from European waters before the invasion. Information might have reached the Admiralty and caused them to detach other squadrons, fatally weakening the Channel Fleet at the critical moment. Weighing these factors, Nelson decided to follow Villeneuve across the Atlantic. After only a brief pause to water and revictual, his squadron (which had been at sea more or less continuously for twenty-two months) set out westward, eleven ships of the line pursuing eighteen. Although he did not know it, at almost the same moment his old friend Collingwood had been detached with a squadron from the Channel Fleet under orders to do the same thing, unless he heard that Nelson had gone before him, but learning of Nelson's movements he took Orde's place off Cadiz instead.

Nelson left the Portuguese coast on 11 May, only three days before Villeneuve reached Martinique. Villeneuve's orders were to wait there for the Brest squadron, which was to escape and join him before they returned in overwhelming force to sweep away whatever British squadrons had not been decoyed away from the channel. Nelson reached Barbados on 8 July to receive what seemed to be precise intelligence that the French were attacking Trinidad. This mistaken information led him south and wasted much time, but even so he was close behind Villeneuve.

On 10 June he was off Montserrat, the same day that Ville-neuve, off Anguilla only 150 miles to the northward, sailed for home. Though he was still supposed to be waiting for the Brest squadron, he was unnerved by the news of Nel-son's arrival and determined to escape while he could. Three days later Nelson set off in pursuit. Not knowing Villeneuve's destination, he steered to Cadiz to return to his station, but he also sent the brig *Curieux* to warn the Admiralty of the enemy's movements. She not only made a fast passage but sighted Villeneuve's squadron and was able to report that they were steering for Ferrol. With this information the Admiralty was in time to order a reinforcement to Sir Robert Calder, who was cruising off that port. On 22 July, in fog, Calder's fourteen ships of the line intercepted Villeneuve's Franco-Spanish fleet, now of twenty. There followed a confused action in which the Spaniards did most of the fighting and lost two ships. The following two days were clearer and Calder could have renewed the action, but chose to regard the preservation of his squadron as a priority. For this he was subsequently disgraced, since in the strategic situation the crippling or even loss of his ships would have been a price well worth paying to knock out the combined fleet. Nelson saw this, as the other admirals did, and an officer of Calder's experi-ence should have done the same.

Nevertheless Calder's action did have a major strategic effect: it further demoralized Villeneuve and led him to abandon his orders to push for Brest. Instead he took ref-uge in Vigo, then on 2 August moved to Corunna. On the 13th he sailed with the ships from Ferrol, but turned south instead of north. On the 20th he entered Cadiz, while Col-lingwood's little squadron skilfully drew off to a safe dis-tance. Nelson meanwhile had landed at Gibraltar on 20 July, the first time in almost two years that he had been ashore. There he concerned himself with redisposing the ships in the Mediterranean, until on the 25th he had news that the *Curieux* had seen Villeneuve steering for the Bay of Biscay. At once Nelson headed north to rejoin the Channel Fleet, but a headwind forced him to stretch out into the Atlantic. Instead of meeting Villeneuve coming south, as he might otherwise have done, Nelson joined Lord Corn-wallis off Brest, where he left the bulk of his squadron and himself proceeded to Portsmouth.

Disappointed at his failure to catch the enemy, and ill as he so often was when frustrated, Nelson returned to his residence, Merton Place, on leave. He was astonished to find that his unsuccessful pursuit across the Atlantic and back had fired the public imagination almost as much as a victory. He was now beyond common popularity. He could not appear in public without being instantly mobbed and cheered. In August Minto

> met Nelson to-day in a mob in Piccadilly and got hold of his
> arm, so I was mobbed too. It is really quite affecting to see
> the wonder and admiration, love and respect, of the whole
> world; and the genuine expression of all those sentiments at
> once, from gentle and simple, the moment he is seen. It is
> beyond anything represented in a play or a poem of fame.
> (*Life and Letters*, 3.363)

Adored in the streets of London, adored at home at Merton, Nelson soon recovered his health and began to discuss with his naval friends how he might fight the great fleet the enemy had gathered. He was also in discussions with the ministers of William Pitt's new administration, for his reputation as a strategist now stood nearly as high as his fame as a tactician and fighter. He knew that he was likely to return to high command soon.

Trafalgar, 1805 Nelson landed at Portsmouth on 19 August, the day before Villeneuve reached Cadiz, but the enemy's whereabouts were not at once known in England. Very early on the morning of 2 September Captain Henry Blackwood of the frigate *Euryalus* called at Merton on his way from Portsmouth to the Admiralty carrying Colling-wood's dispatches announcing that Villeneuve had entered Cadiz. 'I am sure you bring me news of the French and Spanish fleets,' Nelson exclaimed, 'and that I shall have to beat them yet.' Following Blackwood to town, Nelson was reappointed that day to the Mediterranean command, including Collingwood's squadron off Cadiz. He already believed that Villeneuve was bound into the Mediterranean again, and he was right. Napoleon had now abandoned his invasion scheme and issued orders for Villeneuve to take the combined fleet into the Mediterra-nean to support the intended French invasion of the Two Sicilies. Late on the evening of 13 September Nelson left Merton and next day he re-embarked in the *Victory*, having to push through a cheering crowd to reach the water's edge and step into his boat. On the 28th the *Victory* joined Collingwood off Cadiz, and Nelson took command. Imme-diately he moved the fleet further out to sea, to encourage the enemy to sail, while keeping a careful watch on their movements with his frigates. Almost as soon as he arrived signs of imminent movement were reported from Cadiz, and early on 19 October the enemy began to get under way. Nelson made no attempt to close until they were well at sea, but his frigates continued to give him very full information of Villeneuve's movements. During the night of the 20th the two fleets closed, and at dawn on the 21st they were in sight.

The morning was fine, with a very light westerly wind. The combined fleet was heading south with a view to opening the straits, in what was meant to be a single line, with a flying squadron under the Spanish admiral Don Federico Gravina ahead and to windward. Nelson's fleet was in its cruising formation of two columns, running before the wind towards the enemy. His tactics have given rise to a great deal of controversy since it is not clear exactly how he intended to fight, nor how closely he fol-lowed his own intentions. For thirty years naval tactics and signalling had been developing rapidly, and Nelson, like his opponents, was familiar with many methods of concentrating on some part of an enemy's fleet. His own ideas were always flexible and eclectic, and their object was not so much to follow any theoretical scheme as to throw the enemy into confusion by swift and unexpected movements. 'On occasions', he had written earlier, 'we must sometimes have a regular confusion, and that appar-ent confusion must be the most regular method which could be pursued on the occasion' (Laughton, 1.424). Before the battle he circulated a plan of attack in three divisions, the third to be kept to windward under a trusted officer with discretion to throw it into action at a decisive point: 'I think it will surprise and confuse the enemy. They won't know what I am about. It will bring forward a pell-mell battle, and that is what I want' (*Dispatches and Letters*, 7.241). In the event five ships were away watering on the Moroccan coast, and with only twenty-seven against the enemies' thirty-three Nelson went into action in two columns. Contrary to all precedent, both he and Collingwood in their powerful flagships were at the head of their respective columns instead of in the middle, and the British went into action under full sail including studding sails, so that they closed much faster than the enemy could have expected. Even so their progress was slow in the light airs, and there was ample time to prepare for battle, for last-minute letters to be written, and for Nelson to 'amuse' the fleet with the newly introduced 'telegraph' system, which for the first time allowed an officer to compose signals in his own words: 'England expects every man will do his duty.'

Seeing the enemy bearing down towards his rear, Villeneuve ordered his fleet to wear together, thus reversing its formation and direction. This further disorganized an already loose formation and introduced a pronounced curve in the combined fleet's line. Possibly against Villeneuve's wishes, Gravina's squadron of observation bore up and prolonged the rear (as it now was) of the line, instead of keeping its station to the windward. The combined fleet was now steering northwards, back towards Cadiz, and Nelson probably interpreted the move as a last-minute scramble for safety. Perhaps this caused him to modify his tactics, for instead of turning parallel to the enemy at the last minute, and then bearing up together to cut through the enemy line at many points (the plan he had circulated beforehand), Nelson's column held on, initially towards the enemy van, then altering course to starboard to cut nearly vertically through the middle of the combined fleet. Collingwood's column had already cut into the rear. This unconventional head-on approach was dangerous, but besides gaining time it concealed Nelson's intentions from the enemy until the last moment. Initially fighting at a great advantage against the isolated leaders of the British columns, the centre and rear of the allied line were now subjected to a growing onslaught as ship after ship came into action. Gravina's squadron of observation, now absorbed into the rear and engaged by Collingwood's ships, was not in a position to take any initiative, and the unengaged van under Rear-Admiral Pierre Étienne Dumanoir le Pelley, which was, did nothing until the battle was already lost. Firing began about noon, and the battle was virtually over by about 5 p.m., with seventeen prizes in British hands and another burnt.

About 1.15 p.m., as he walked the quarterdeck with his flag captain, Thomas Masterman Hardy, Nelson was hit by a musket-ball fired from the mizzen-top of the French *Redoubtable* alongside. The ball entered his left shoulder,

passed through a lung, and lodged in his spine. It seems unlikely that it was aimed specifically at him; the quarter-deck was crowded and he cannot have been clearly visible through the dense smoke of battle even at 20 yards, nor was a musket accurate at such a range, especially fired from aloft in a rolling ship. Contrary to myth, he was wearing an old uniform coat with inconspicuous cloth replicas of his decorations. There is no evidence that he deliberately sought or recklessly courted death, though he was certainly well enough aware of the risks of action. He was carried below to the cockpit, where he lay in great pain but conscious until just before he died at 4.30 p.m.

After the battle and the gale which followed, the dismasted *Victory* was towed to Gibraltar, where she arrived on the 28th. Her men made good their claim to bring Nelson's body home: 'they have behaved well to us', one of them wrote, 'for they wanted to take Ld. Nelson from us, but we told Captn., as we brought him out we would bring him home, so it was so and he was put into a cask of spirits' (Pocock, *Horatio Nelson*, 333). The body lay in state for three days in the Painted Hall of Greenwich Hospital, where the arrangements all but disintegrated under the pressure of crowds far greater than the authorities had expected. On 8 January 1806 it was carried up the Thames to Whitehall Stairs, and next morning the funeral procession wound through the streets from the Admiralty to St Paul's Cathedral. Huge, silent crowds watched the cortège, and many felt that the most moving part was not the elaborate catafalque or the numerous soldiers, but the seamen of the *Victory* carrying her battle ensigns. At the final moment of the ceremony, as the coffin was lowered through the floor of the nave to its resting place directly beneath the dome, the seamen were supposed to fold the colours and lay them on the coffin—instead of which, they tore them up and each saved a piece as a memorial of their lost commander.

Apotheosis At every level of society, among those who knew him personally and those who knew only his name, the news of Nelson's death was received as a personal grief. Collingwood, most reserved and private of men, wept, and so did many other officers and men. 'My heart, however, is sad, and penetrated with the deepest anguish', wrote Blackwood.

> A victory, such a one as has never been achieved, yesterday took place … but at such an expense, in the loss of the most gallant of men, and best of friends, as renders it to me a victory I never wished to have witnessed. (*Dispatches and Letters*, 7.224)

A boatswain's mate of the *Victory* was unable to pipe the men to quarters for tears. Joy in 'our victory, in which we gained and lost so much' (*Public and Private Correspondence*, 164) was almost submerged by the universal sense of loss. The immortal hero was hailed as an undying inspiration to his countrymen. Very soon he was being painted at the moment he was struck down in compositions closely modelled on the deposition of Christ from the cross. Relics associated with him were as eagerly sought (and as frequently forged) as those of any saint. Yet Nelson, as virtually all his contemporaries knew, was not in all respects a saint. His private life had been distressingly public and less than edifying. His contemporaries canonized him as the supreme example of courage, leadership, and self-sacrifice—but also of fallible humanity, warmth, and generosity. The great wars against France yielded many other heroes, men of undoubted gallantry and signal achievements, but they were for the most part classical heroes in marble: austere and distant. Nelson was flesh and blood, and he felt uniquely close even to those who had never met him. 'When I think,' wrote his chaplain, 'setting aside his heroism, what an affectionate, fascinating little fellow he was, how dignified and pure his mind, how kind and condescending his manners, I become stupid with grief for what I have lost' (Morrison, 2.274).

Nelson's reputation suffered some eclipse in the years after the war. The publication of his correspondence with Emma Hamilton and the high-water mark of the evangelical revival reminded people of his less admirable characteristics. The national memorial to him in Trafalgar Square (largely paid for by subscriptions from the navy) was not finished until 1843, by which time hundreds of other Nelson monuments already existed throughout the English-speaking world. The 'immortal memory' began to revive in the middle years of the nineteenth century, and reached its apogee in the years before the First World War, when the Navy League promoted the cult of Trafalgar day as a central part of its campaigns, and the navy itself adopted the celebration as part of its traditions. Nelson was now a symbol of imperial Britain and its overarching seapower, and a talisman against anxiety. Whatever strengths other imperial and naval powers might gain, they could not have Nelson—though they tried, for the Nelson cult was strongly promoted in both the Japanese and German navies. By this time Nelson the man (and, as a natural result, Nelson the leader of men) had largely been forgotten in Nelson the hero, and his heroism was looked for not in his humanity but in formulas. Admirals (the majority) who knew nothing of naval history justified their views with half-remembered quotations from the great man. The Admiralty demonstrated how well prepared the navy was for future war by publishing, in 1913, the report of a weighty official committee on Nelson's tactics at Trafalgar.

In spite of this preparation the First World War failed to yield the second Trafalgar which the Royal Navy and the public expected, but the disappointment did not cause a revulsion from Nelson, as it so easily might have done. Instead the late-Victorian Nelson was dismantled, and behind the façade new biographers began to discover the human figure as well as the hero. Dramatists and filmmakers presented his life (usually his life with Emma Hamilton) in vivid, not to say garish, colours. In the 1920s the Society for Nautical Research led a successful campaign to preserve and reconstruct the *Victory*, which has ever since presented a powerful physical and visual image of Nelson and the navy of his day. During the Second World War Nelson was a real, and in many ways a realistic,

inspiration to his countrymen: Churchill reckoned Alexander Korda's 1942 film *Lady Hamilton* was worth four divisions in morale. Since then Nelson has never ceased to fascinate, and he remains a lively subject of historical research, a perennial favourite of biographers, an inspiration for the Royal Navy, and an icon of popular culture.

No one-dimensional explanation can account for Nelson's extraordinary popular status in his own lifetime and ever since. As a sea officer he excelled in most, though not all, areas of his profession. He was not an outstanding seaman by the very high standards of the navy of his day, and his handling of diplomacy and strategy, though improving with experience, suffered from his ignorance of languages and his uncertain feel for politics. As a tactician, however, he deployed a unique combination of very thorough training, delegation to trusted subordinates, and an uncompromising determination to achieve total victory. 'He possessed the zeal of an enthusiast,' Collingwood wrote, 'directed by talents which Nature had very bountifully bestowed upon him, and everything seemed, as if by enchantment, to prosper under his direction. But it was the effect of system, and nice combination, not of chance' (*Private Correspondence*, 167). He achieved at sea the same practical and psychological revolution as the French revolutionary generals had achieved on land, ushering in an age when victory meant not a modest advantage, but the total destruction of the vanquished. In Minto's words, 'there was a sort of heroic cast about Nelson that I never saw in any other man, and which seems wanting to the achievement of *impossible things* which became easy to him' (*Life and Letters*, 3.374). Instead of the centralized control which was the ambition of most admirals, because it seemed the essential prerequisite for success, Nelson practised initiative and flexibility.

> Without much previous preparation or plan he has the faculty of discovering advantages as they arise, and the good judgement to turn them to his use. An enemy that commits a false step in his view is ruined, and it comes on him with an impetuosity that allows him no time to recover. (*Private Correspondence*, 130)

In this he built upon the methods of several of his predecessors, including Anson, Hawke, and St Vincent, but he applied them with a unique openness and generosity of spirit. Warm and friendly among his brother officers, Nelson was equally direct and approachable to his men. It was typical of him to mention ratings by name as his companions in arms, to go around the gun decks after an action shaking hands with the men. Though other officers might be more advanced in their social views, or more relaxed as disciplinarians, Nelson alone gained his people's hearts.

> He added to genius, valour, and energy, the singular power of electrifying all within his atmosphere, and making them only minor constellations to this most luminous planet … it was his art to make all under him love him, and own his superiority without a ray of jealousy. (Harris, 4.311)

Just the same was true ashore among the millions who never knew Nelson personally. In part they were inspired by his extraordinary gallantry. Though he never wantonly risked his life, no flag officer ever exposed himself with such heroism or bore so many wounds to show it. No other British officer had such a record of victory, in the long years of endurance against France when victories were so scarce. But Nelson the public hero was also Nelson the public scandal, the figure of contradictions who could be admired, deplored, and even ridiculed all at once. James Gillray's reaction to his death was an engraving of the dying Nelson transported aloft to immortality, surrounded by Captain Hardy, a seaman holding aloft a captured French flag marked 'Vive l'Empereur françois', and the weeping Britannia. Death and glory are depicted with unfeigned emotion—but the figure of Hardy is a caricature of George III, the seaman is Prince William Henry, and the corpulent, theatrical Britannia is unmistakably Emma Hamilton.

The key to Nelson's extraordinary appeal lay in the combination of ardour and naïvety. He threw himself into all his undertakings with 'ardent, animated patriotism panting for glory' (Clark and M'Arthur, 2.267, quoting the surgeon of Nelson's flagship at Copenhagen). He was a stranger to half-measures, to reservations, to fears. Uninterested in appearances, he burnt with direct, uncompromising, and entirely unfeigned zeal. Nervous, irritable, sometimes anguished and often ill with the strain of unsupported responsibility, he never tried to conceal his feelings. His vanity was as artless as the rest of his personality, and went with an extraordinary generosity which rejoiced at the successes of his friends and lamented the misfortunes even of rivals like Hyde Parker and Calder who had treated him badly. His naked thirst for glory was part of his vulnerability and insecurity. He needed emotional support: from the many close friends he found among the officers he worked with, from the world at large, and from women. It was his misfortune that when he needed it the most, in 1798, his wife was far away and his best friend's wife was close at hand. His naïve ardour, the inexperience of a man brought up from boyhood in a masculine society, did not help him to resist temptation—and there is no doubt that he deeply longed to have an heir. Yet Nelson was devoutly and unashamedly religious, in a generation where public displays of religion were unusual if not shocking. In taking Lady Hamilton as his mistress he violated his most fundamental beliefs. Though he quieted his conscience with easy phrases, it is too obvious that his behaviour was at its worst whenever he was with her and its best when he was at sea, among his naval colleagues, with nothing to distract him from his duty. It is not necessary to present Lady Hamilton as the scheming harpy who seduced the innocent hero, though she was quite capable of calculation and deception. He was responsible for his own fall, and at bottom he knew it. Vulnerable and weak as a man, Nelson was also a leader of unequalled ardour, courage, generosity, and professional genius: 'in many points a really great man,' as Minto put it, 'in others a baby' (Life and Letters, 3.370). In that extraordinary combination lies something of his appeal to successive generations. N. A. M. RODGER

Sources DNB · The dispatches and letters of Vice-Admiral Lord Viscount Nelson, ed. N. H. Nicolas, 7 vols. (1844–6) · A. Morrison, Collection of autograph letters: the Hamilton and Nelson papers, 2 vols. (privately printed, 1893) · Nelson's letters to his wife and other documents, 1785–1831, ed. G. P. B. Naish, Navy RS, 100 (1958) · Nelson's letters from the Leeward Islands, ed. G. Rawson (1953) · A selection from the public and private correspondence of Vice-Admiral Lord Collingwood, interspersed with memoirs of his life, ed. G. L. Newnham-Collingwood, 4th edn (1829) · The private correspondence of Admiral Lord Collingwood, ed. E. Hughes, Navy RS, 98 (1957) · Memoirs of Admiral the Right Hon. the earl of St. Vincent GCB &c, ed. J. S. Tucker, 2 vols. (1844) · Private papers of George, second Earl Spencer, ed. J. S. Corbett and H. W. Richmond, 4 vols., Navy RS, 46, 48, 58–9 (1913–24) · The Keith papers, ed. W. G. Perrin and C. Lloyd, 3 vols. (1927–55) · The letters of Lord St. Vincent, 1801–1804, ed. D. B. Smith, 2 vols. (1921–7) · O. Warner, The life and letters of Vice-Admiral Lord Collingwood (1968) · J. K. Laughton, ed., 'Miscellaneous letters', The naval miscellany, 1, Navy RS, 20 (1902), 387–444 · Life and letters of Sir Gilbert Elliot, first earl of Minto, from 1751 to 1806, ed. countess of Minto [E. E. E. Elliot-Murray-Kynynmound], 3 vols. (1874) · A. Fremantle, ed., The Wynne diaries, 3 vols. (1935–40) · H. C. Gutteridge, Nelson and the Neapolitan Jacobins: documents relating to the suppression of the Jacobin revolution at Naples, June 1799 (1903) · T. S. Jackson, ed., Logs of the great sea fights, 1794–1805, 2 vols. (1899–1900) · 'Letters of Lord Nelson, 1804–5', The naval miscellany, ed. W. G. Perrin, 3, Navy RS, 63 (1928), 171–90 · E. P. Brenton, Life and correspondence of John, earl of St Vincent, 2 vols. (1838) · G. S. Parsons, Nelsonian reminiscences: leaves from memory's log (1843) · Diaries and correspondence of James Harris, first earl of Malmesbury, ed. third earl of Malmesbury [J. H. Harris], 4 vols. (1844) · J. S. Clarke and J. M'Arthur, The life and services of Horatio Viscount Nelson, duke of Bronte, vice-admiral of the white, 2 vols. (1840) · C. Oman, Nelson (1947) · O. Warner, A portrait of Lord Nelson (1958) · T. Pocock, Horatio Nelson (1987) · J. S. Corbett, The campaign of Trafalgar, 2nd edn, 2 vols. (1919) · E. Desbrière, The naval campaign of 1805: Trafalgar, ed. and trans. C. Eastwick, 2 vols. (1933) · O. Feldbæk, Slaget på Reden (1984) · J. Drinkwater Bethune, A narrative of the battle of St. Vincent, with anecdotes of Nelson before and after that battle, 2nd edn (1840) · B. Lavery, Nelson and the Nile (1998) · M. Battesti, La Bataille d'Aboukir 1798 (1998) · D. Pope, The great gamble (1972) · C. White, 1797 Nelson's year of destiny: Cape St. Vincent and Santa Cruz de Tenerife (1998) · F. Fraser, Beloved Emma (1985) · E. C. Freeman and E. Gill, Nelson and the Hamiltons in Wales and Monmouthshire, 1802 (1962) · T. Pocock, The young Nelson in the Americas (1980)

Archives Admiralty Library, London, order book, MS 200 · BL, corresp. and MSS, Add. MSS 30260, 34274, 34902–34992, 35191, 36604–36613, 40094–40095, 43504, 46356; Egerton MSS 1614, 2240 · BL, letters and papers, RP 345, 356, 366, 376 [copies] · Harvard U., Houghton L., log books and corresp. with Lady Hamilton · Hunt. L., corresp. and MSS · Hydrographic Office, Taunton, Admiralty Library, order book · Karpeles Manuscript Library, corresp. and papers · Nelson Museum and Local History Centre, Monmouth, corresp., letter-books, logs, papers · NMM, corresp. and MSS · Royal Naval Museum, Portsmouth, personal letters and official orders · U. Mich., Clements L., corresp. · United States Naval Museum, corresp. · Wellcome L., accounts and MSS | BL, Bridport MSS, Add. MS 35191 · BL, MSS and corresp. with Alexander Davidson, Add. MS 28333, Egerton 2240 · BL, letters to Lady Hamilton, Egerton MS 1614 · BL, letters to second Earl Spencer · Bucks. RLSS, corresp. with Lord Hobart · Centre for Polar Archives, Washington, DC, records of the case arising between Nelson and Benjamin Tucker · Cornwall RO, letters to Spiridion Foresti [copies] · Devon RO, corresp. with first Viscount Sidmouth · L. Cong., corresp. with Sir George Cockburn · NA Scot., letters to Lord Melville · Nelson Museum and Local History Centre, Monmouth, Llangattock MSS · NL Scot., corresp. with Sir Thomas Graham · NMM, letters to Sir Edward Berry · NMM, letters to duke of Clarence · NMM, corresp. with William Cornwallis · NMM, letters to Ross Donelly · NMM, letters to Sir John Duckworth · NMM, corresp. with Hugh Elliott · NMM, corresp. with Lord Hood · NMM, letters to Lord Keith · NMM, corresp. with Sir Charles Middleton · NMM, letters to Lord Minto · NMM, corresp. with Frances Nelson · NMM,

Phillips and other MSS • NMM, letters to Lord St Vincent • Royal Naval Museum, Portsmouth, McCarthy MSS and other collections • Royal Naval Museum, Portsmouth, letters to Hercules Ross • Shrops. RRC, corresp. with Joseph Brame • Trafalgar House, Bridport, Nelson-Ward MSS • United States Naval Academy Museum, Annapolis, Maryland, corresp.

Likenesses J. F. Rigaud, oils, 1781, NMM • C. Collingwood, drawing, c.1785, NMM • H. P. Bone, miniature, c.1797 (after L. F. Abbott), NPG • R. Shipster, stipple, pubd 1797 (after Rigaud), BM, NPG • L. F. Abbott, portraits, 1797–8, NMM • L. F. Abbott, oils, 1798, NMM • W. Evans, stipple, pubd 1798 (after H. Edridge), BM, NPG • J. Gillray, caricature, etching, pubd 1798 (*Extirpation of the plagues of Egypt*), NPG • D. Orme, stipple, pubd 1798, NPG • H. Singleton, pencil drawing, 1798, NMM • J. de Vaere, Wedgwood medallion, 1798, Wedgwood Museum, Stoke-on-Trent • mezzotint, pubd 1798, NPG • G. Head, oils, 1798–1800, NPG • C. Grignion, drawing, 1799, Royal United Services Institution, London • L. Guzzardi, oils, 1799, Museo di San Martino, Naples; version, Gov. Art Coll., NMM • W. Beechey, oils, 1800, NPG [*see illus.*] • H. Füger, oils, 1800, NPG • Granger, stipple, pubd 1800 (after L. F. Abbott), NPG • J. Hoppner, oils, 1800, NMM • P. Roberts, stipple, pubd 1800 (after L. F. Abbott), NPG • J. Schmidt, pastel drawing, 1800, NMM • J. Young, mezzotint, pubd 1800 (after L. Guzzardi), BM, NPG • oils, c.1800, NMM • W. Beechey, oils, 1801, St Andrew's Hall, Norwich • M. H. Keymer, oils, 1801, NMM • J. Rising, oils, 1801, NMM • Thallor and Ransom, marble bust, 1801, NMM • S. de Koster, oils, 1801–3, NMM • J. Hoppner, oils, c.1801–1805, Royal Collection • H. Edridge, watercolour drawing, 1802, NPG • W. Goldsmith, double portrait, watercolour drawing, c.1802 (with Lady Hamilton), Gov. Art Coll. • L. Gahagan, bust, 1804, Victoria Art Gallery, Bath • H. H. Meyer, stipple, pubd 1805 (after J. Hoppner), BM, NPG • B. Pearce, silhouette, 1805, NPG • E. Scriven, stipple and line engraving, pubd 1805 (after R. Bowyer), NPG • medallion, 1805 (plaster replica; after W. Tassie), Scot. NPG • A. W. Devis, oils, 1805–7, NMM • C. Andras, wax effigy, 1806, Westminster Abbey • E. Scriven, stipple, pubd 1806 (after after A. W. Devis), BM, NPG • C. Turner, mezzotint, pubd 1806 (after J. Hoppner), NG Ire. • J. Golding, line engraving, pubd 1808 (after L. F. Abbott), BM, NPG • W. H. Worthington, line engraving, pubd 1808 (after R. Bowyer), BM, NPG • J. Flaxman, statue on monument, 1809, St Paul's Cathedral, London • C. Turner, mezzotint, pubd 1823 (after R. Bowyer), BM, NPG • A. S. Damer, bust, 1827, Royal Collection • F. Chantrey, marble bust, 1835, Royal Collection • F. Chantrey, marble bust, 1835, NPG • W. Read, stipple and line engraving, pubd 1836 (after L. F. Abbott), BM, NPG • E. H. Baily, statue on Nelson's Column, 1839–43, Trafalgar Square, London • S. Freeman, stipple and line engraving, pubd 1844 (after L. F. Abbott), NPG • L. F. Abbott, oils, NPG • L. F. Abbott, oils, Scot. NPG • G. Cruikshank, etching, NPG • A. W. Devis, group portrait, oils (*The death of Nelson*), NMM • D. Maclise, group portrait, fresco (*The death of Nelson*), Palace of Westminster, London; study, Walker Art Gallery, Liverpool • S. W. Reynolds, coloured engraving (after J. P. Knight), Wellington Museum, London • R. Shipster, stipple (after L. F. Abbott), NPG • R. S. Syer, mezzotint (after L. F. Abbott), BM, NPG • R. Westmacott, bronze statue, Bull Ring, Birmingham • J. Young, mezzotint (after J. Rising), NPG • metal relief, NPG • pastel drawing, Scot. NPG • sketch (of head; after W. Beechey, 1801), NPG

Nelson, Sir Hugh Muir (1833–1906), politician and pastoralist in Australia, was born at Kilmarnock, Ayrshire, Scotland, on 31 December 1833, the son of William Lambie Nelson LLD (*d.* 1887), a Presbyterian minister and sheep farmer, and his wife, Agnes, *née* Muir. He was educated at Edinburgh high school and Edinburgh University, where he did not graduate, but came under the influence of Professor John Wilson, a contributor to the tory *Blackwood's Magazine* under the pseudonym Christopher North. Nelson emigrated to Queensland with his family in 1853, and became a storekeeper's clerk in Ipswich. Later he took

farming work and managed sheep stations for his father and others, including Eton Vale from 1862 to 1872. In August 1870 he married Janet, the daughter of Duncan McIntyre, at Toowoomba, and they eventually settled on the 40,000 acre Loudon estate near Dalby, which Nelson acquired with his brother-in-law Watts. They prospered, and sold out for £60,000 just before the financial crash of 1893.

Nelson entered Queensland politics as chairman of the Wambo divisional board in 1880, and was elected to the state legislative assembly for Northern Downs in 1883, having unsuccessfully contested the same electoral district in 1879. Following the boundary reorganization of 1888 he represented the subdivision of Murilla for the remainder of his active political career. He became secretary for railways in June 1888 in the ministry led by his political mentor Sir Thomas McIlwraith, and continued as secretary for railways and public works under the premiership of Boyd Dunlop Morehead until August 1890. He was leader of the opposition throughout 1891. Under the 'Griffilwraith' coalition he was briefly vice-president of the executive council and acting colonial treasurer, and he served McIlwraith as treasurer from March 1893 before succeeding him as premier in October 1893. He combined this office with those of vice-president of the executive council and colonial president (until August 1896), chief secretary (from March 1895), and treasurer (August 1896 to March 1898).

Nelson's premiership came at a time of economic and social upheaval, to which he reacted with political caution and budgetary austerity. Twice, in May 1893 and in February 1896, he intervened to save the Queensland National Bank, by which means he rendered 'his greatest and shrewdest service to colonial capital and bourgeois society' (*AusDB*). The Peace Preservation Act, which he originated during the failed shearers' strike of 1894, became a cornerstone of the future conduct of industrial relations. Nelson won contemporary repute as a constitutional authority, and opposed the federation of the Australian states.

Nelson was created KCMG in 1896, and represented Queensland at the diamond jubilee of Queen Victoria in 1897; while in England he was sworn of the privy council and received honorary degrees from Oxford and Edinburgh. He resigned the premiership on 13 April 1896 and his seat in the assembly soon afterwards. From 29 July 1898 he served as president of the legislative council, and from 1904 to 1905 was lieutenant-governor of Queensland. He founded the Royal Agricultural Society of Toowoomba and the Austral Association and was president of the Royal Geographical Society of Australasia (Queensland), the Colonial Political Association, and the Queensland Club. He took an interest in New Guinea, to which he made several visits.

Nelson died at his residence, at Gabbinbar, Middle Ridge, Toowoomba, on 1 January 1906, and was buried in Toowoomba cemetery after a state funeral under Presbyterian rites. He was survived by his wife, two sons, and three daughters. A physically imposing man, Nelson was a ruthless and effective politician, who could none the less be both humorous and reflective in private.

C. A. HARRIS, *rev.* H. J. SPENCER

Sources D. B. Waterson, 'Nelson, Sir Hugh Muir', *AusDB*, vol. 10 · *Brisbane Courier* (2 Jan 1906) · *WW* · **Archives** Queensland State Archives, Brisbane, Australia, premier's corresp. | State Library of Queensland, South Brisbane, John Oxley Library, Palmer–McIlwraith MSS · **Wealth at death** £26,292: Waterson, 'Nelson, Sir Hugh Muir'

Nelson, Ian Theodore (1878–1958). *See under* Nelson family (*per.* 1780–1958).

Nelson, Isaac (1809–1888), minister of the Presbyterian Church in Ireland, was born in Belfast, the son of Francis Nelson, a grocer of Barrack Street, Belfast. After attending local schools in Belfast, Nelson served as assistant classical master at Belfast Academical Institution for nine years. He was licensed to preach in Belfast in 1837 and on 27 August 1838 he was ordained minister of First Comber, succeeding Revd J. McCance. On 31 March 1842 he returned to the parish of Belfast, where he was installed in Donegall Street (Cliftonville) Presbyterian Church. A considerable linguist, whose daily scripture readings with his sister could be conducted in French, German, Greek, or Hebrew, Nelson was described by one historian of Irish Presbyterianism as 'a man of great mental powers and an eloquent, although a hesitating speaker. In almost every case he cast his lot with the "minority"' (Latimer, 494). Many of his contemporaries, however, explained his frequent hostility to the general assembly as a matter of personal bitterness resulting from his having been passed over for a chair in Greek.

Opposing the more popular trends in the evangelical protestantism of his day, Nelson was author of several pamphlets whose titles indicate his doctrinal position: *An answer to the Rev. Professor Killen's Defence of revivalism, assurance and the witness of the spirit* was published in Belfast in 1867, with a similar *Answer* addressed to the Revd John MacNaughton in 1888. Nelson particularly objected to the 'enthusiasm' which surrounded the Ulster revival of 1859. He regarded lay preaching as dangerous and dismissed the supposed 'physical manifestations' and dramatic conversion experiences which characterized this religious movement as displays of excess and emotion without spiritual foundation. His most controversial and best-remembered attack, written in response to the Revd William Gibson's *The Year of Grace*, was *The Year of Delusion* (Belfast, 1860). Although his own tone was vitriolic and his language extreme, there is little doubt that Nelson's criticisms of the extravagances of the revival had some validity. Gibson, evidently seeing the weight of some of Nelson's criticisms, considerably modified his second edition of *The Year of Grace* to omit much of the original material on 'manifestations'.

Nelson resigned his ministry in 1880 to become home rule member of parliament for county Mayo, a position he held for five years. He died in Belfast on 8 March 1888, and was buried in Shankhill graveyard. According to the Revd George Magill, who gave the funeral sermon, he came to regret his parliamentary career; the same oration also referred, however, more generally to his 'mistakes' and 'misdirected judgment', declaring that his love of controversy sometimes led him to express feelings unworthy of a superior mind. Nelson's strong-minded individualism provides a good example of the continuing debates within nineteenth-century Ulster Presbyterianism.

MYRTLE HILL

Sources J. McConnell and others, eds., *Fasti of the Irish Presbyterian church, 1613–1840*, rev. S. G. McConnell, 2 vols. in 12 pts (1935–51), pt 12 · *A history of congregations in the Presbyterian Church in Ireland, 1610–1982*, Presbyterian Church in Ireland (1982) · A. R. Scott, 'The Ulster revival of 1859', PhD diss., TCD, 1962 · W. T. Latimer, *A history of the Irish Presbyterians*, 2nd edn (1902) · M. Hill, 'Assessing the awakening: the 1859 revival in Ulster', *Church and people in Britain and Scandinavia* [York 1995], ed. I. Brohed (1996) · G. Magill, 'Wisdom justified of her children', 1888 [funeral sermon] · I. Nelson, *The year of delusion* (1860) · I. Nelson, *An answer to the Rev. Professor Killen's Defence of revivalism, assurance and the witness of the spirit* (1867) · I. Nelson, *An answer to the Rev. John McNaughton's Defence of revivalism, assurance and the witness of the spirit* (1888)

Nelson, James (1710–1794), author and apothecary, was born on 22 April 1710, the son of Thomas Nelson, an apothecary. He may have been the James Nelson apprenticed to Thomas Manning on 6 August 1717 and to Ferdinando Watkins on 8 July 1724. Nelson was admitted to the Society of Apothecaries by patrimony on 5 March 1744 and joined the livery in 1758 when he was living in Red Lion Street, Holborn, London. Nelson was well known in contemporary literary circles, and wrote two highly praised works: *An essay on the government of children under three general heads: health, manners, and education* (1753), and *The affectionate father, a sentimental comedy; together with essays on various subjects* (1786). In this various moral lessons were taught in the form of a play. Nelson died in London on 19 April 1794, three days before his eighty-fourth birthday, according to the *Gentleman's Magazine*. C. R. B. Barrett, in his *A History of the Society of Apothecaries* (1905), claims that Nelson had a daughter who married a Mr Gabb.

G. P. MORIARTY, *rev.* MICHAEL BEVAN

Sources private information (2004) [D. Cook, Society of Apothecaries] · *GM*, 1st ser., 63 (1793), 389 · *GM*, 1st ser., 23 (1753), 508 · P. J. Wallis and R. V. Wallis, *Eighteenth century medics*, 2nd edn (1988) · Nichols, *Lit. anecdotes*, 9.14

Nelson, John (1653?–1734), merchant, was the son of Robert Nelson, a lawyer resident at Gray's Inn, London, and Mary (*b.* 1623), daughter of Edmund Temple and Eleanor Harvey. Mary's uncle was Sir Thomas *Temple, governor of Nova Scotia from the Restoration of 1660. It was as his great-uncle's protégé that John Nelson travelled to Boston and was appointed deputy governor in 1670. Following the death of Sir Thomas in 1674 Nelson established himself as a merchant, trading with French army officers of what was new French Acadia. In the early 1680s he negotiated with the French authorities to allow English ships to fish in Acadian waters.

About 1682 Nelson married Elizabeth Tailer (*d.* 1734), daughter of William Tailer of Dorchester, near Boston, and niece of William Stoughton, the Massachusetts magistrate and later lieutenant-governor of the royal dominion of New England (created in 1686). The marriage brought Nelson into contact with leading figures in the government of the newly established colony. However, his continued association with French Acadian traders distanced him from New England's governor, Sir Edmund Andros. Nelson took part in the rising by the Boston militia that replaced Andros's government, and for a short period he sat on the council of safety established thereafter.

In September 1691 Nelson was captured by French forces during an attempt to set up a trading port at Port Royal, Acadia, after its plunder by Sir William Phipps. Nelson's capture led to his imprisonment in Quebec. In the year following his arrest he learned of a proposed French attack on Boston and engaged two French deserters to carry a warning to Phipps, now governor of Massachusetts. The message was discounted and, after his role was discovered, Nelson was sent to France and finally detained at the inland prison of Angoulême. In 1695 he was moved to the Bastille, and a year later he was released on parole. He reached London in early 1696 and over the next year provided the English Board of Trade with information and proposals for future policy concerning Acadia.

Nelson returned to America in 1698 and settled on Long Island in Boston harbour, where he resumed trading with French Acadian merchants. In later life he attempted, without success, to establish the family's claim to what was now English Nova Scotia, through his second son, Paschal. Another of his and Elizabeth's six children, Mehitable, married Robert Temple; with him Nelson initiated what became the family's long-standing involvement in land speculation in New England. He died at Robert Temple's residence on Noddle's Island in Boston Harbour, on 16 November 1734, three weeks after the death of his wife.   PHILIP CARTER

Sources *DNB* · R. R. Johnson, 'Nelson, John', *ANB* · R. R. Johnson, *John Nelson, merchant adventurer: a life between empires* (1991) · Burke, *Peerage*

Nelson, John (*bap.* 1707, *d.* 1774), Methodist preacher, was born in or before August 1707 at Birstall in the West Riding of Yorkshire, the eldest of the four children of William Nelson (1685–1723), stonemason, and his wife, Dorothy Smith (*d.* 1741). The record of his baptism at St Peter's Church, Birstall, on 17 August 1707 confirms the inaccuracy of the ascription of Nelson's birth to October 1707 in printed editions of his journal. Lacking a formal education, Nelson followed his father's trade as a stonemason, working in his native West Riding and later as far afield as London. On 26 June 1727 he married Martha Webster (*d.* 1774); the marriage produced four children, Elizabeth, David, William, and Charles. His autobiographical journal, published in 1767, which has been compared with John Bunyan's *Grace Abounding to the Chief of Sinners* for its vivid imagery, reveals that Nelson's spiritual pilgrimage before 1750 was rooted in a childhood experience as he listened to his father read from the twentieth chapter of the book of Revelation. Nelson remained, however, 'like a wandering bird, cast out of the nest' until he heard John Wesley preach at Moorfields in London, when his 'heart

beat like the pendulum of a clock' and his soul was 'filled with consolation, through hope that God for Christ's sake' would save him (Nelson, 11–12). He subsequently wrestled with his inner convictions until 'his heart was set at liberty from guilt and tormenting fear and filled with a calm and serene peace' in October 1739 (Nelson, 16). On his return to Birstall at Christmas 1740 he recounted his conversion experience to his relatives and friends, and engaged in evangelism from his cottage. In May 1742 John Wesley, his 'father in the gospel', travelled to Birstall to encourage him in the work, observing that 'the whole town wore a new face' as a result of 'the artless testimony of one plain man' whose 'word sounded forth to … all the West Riding of Yorkshire' (Hargreaves, 10). Episcopal visitation returns for 1743 confirm the profusion of Methodist activity around Birstall, unparalleled elsewhere in the vast diocese of York.

Nelson preached initially from the doorway of his cottage, usually with his mason's hammer and trowel 'stuck within the string of his leather apron' (Telford, 3.59). As his reputation as a preacher grew he often encountered opposition, particularly from unsympathetic clergymen, alehouse keepers, and hostile mobs. He was pelted with eggs and potatoes at Leeds and at Manchester a stone hurled from the edge of the crowd lacerated his head. His opponents had him impressed for military service against the Jacobites at Halifax in 1744, but, following his discharge from the army, secured by the intervention of Selina, countess of Huntingdon, he returned to Birstall, where he helped to build the first Methodist preaching-house in Yorkshire. 'We are now building our preaching house', he wrote to John Wesley in August 1750, 'so that I am employed all the day in hewing stone and at night in calling upon sinners to repent and believe the gospel' (Laycock, 119). John Wesley observed in 1751 that he found the societies in Yorkshire, chiefly under the care of John Nelson, 'all alive, strong and vigorous of soul … and increased in number from 1800 to upwards of 3000' (ibid., 125). By 1767 statistical returns to the Wesleyan conference reveal that membership in the Birstall circuit had reached 1491, and membership of the other Yorkshire circuits evangelized by Nelson constituted almost a quarter of the total Methodist membership.

Nelson often accompanied John Wesley on his preaching missions, travelling as far afield with him as Cornwall and the Isles of Scilly. In 1747 Nelson was one of four lay and four ordained preachers who met with John and Charles Wesley to consider and determine the doctrines, discipline, and practice of 'the people called Methodists'. Like the Wesleys, Nelson opposed secession from the Church of England. He remained committed throughout his life to a forthright, fervent, evangelical style of preaching, advising Charles Wesley that: 'no other preaching will do in Yorkshire but the old sort, that comes like thunderclaps upon the conscience'. Between 1765 and 1774 Nelson was stationed at Leeds, Bristol, Derbyshire, Newcastle, Yarm, and York. By 1769, however, the health of this stout, broad-shouldered evangelist, who has been described as 'one of John Wesley's sturdiest itinerants' was failing (Rack, 218). He suffered from 'a considerable degree of lameness' and 'was compelled to lean upon a man's shoulder for support whilst preaching' (Laycock, 308). He died suddenly at Leeds on 18 July 1774, following an apoplectic stroke compounded by gout. The news of his death brought 'a weeping multitude' onto the streets of Leeds and a procession nearly half a mile long followed his corpse to Birstall, where he was buried in the churchyard of St Peter's. His death proved such a shock to his wife, who had never fully recovered from the miscarriage she had suffered when she had been attacked by a mob at Wakefield in 1755, that she followed her husband to the grave within two months. The epitaph added to Nelson's tomb in 1910, describing him as 'coadjutor of John Wesley and pioneer of Methodism in Yorkshire' (Cradock, 311), recognizes that without Nelson's support John Wesley's distinctive Methodist doctrines and discipline would not have gained such a rapid ascendancy amid the plethora of religious societies which emerged from the evangelistic initiatives of Moravians, Inghamites, and others in Yorkshire in the 1730s and 1740s.   JOHN A. HARGREAVES

Sources J. Nelson, *Journal* (1767) · J. Telford, ed., *Wesley's veterans*, 3 (1912) · A. E. Keeling, *John Nelson: mason and missionary* (1892) · J. A. Hargreaves, ed., *The Wesleys and west Yorkshire* (1988) · J. C. Hartley, *John Nelson and the evangelical revival in west Yorkshire* (1988) · J. W. Laycock, *Methodist heroes in the great Haworth round, 1734–84* (1909) · J. Cleeve, 'John Nelson's native place', *Methodist Recorder*, 29 (1898), 77–81 · N. V. Rhodes, 'John Nelson's house', *Proceedings of the Wesley Historical Society*, 34 (1963–4), 125 · H. C. Cradock, *A history of the ancient parish of Birstall, Yorkshire* (1933) · will, Borth. Inst. · parish registers, Birstall, W. Yorks. AS, Wakefield · correspondence of John Nelson, JRL, Methodist Archives and Research Centre, MAM PLP 78 · H. D. Rack, *Reasonable enthusiast: John Wesley and the rise of Methodism* (1989)
Archives JRL, Methodist Archives and Research Centre, corresp. with Charles Wesley, MAM PLP 78
Likenesses engraving, 1773 (aged sixty-six), BM · marble bust, 1846; formerly at Wesley Chapel, Birstall [stolen] · J. Sowden, coloured etching (in the Bradford Dungeon), Birstall Methodist Church; repro. in Keeling, *John Nelson*, 73 · engraving, repro. in Nelson, *Journal*, frontispiece
Wealth at death approx. £50: will, 1774, Borth. Inst.

Nelson, John (*bap.* 1726, *d.* 1812), statuary and mason, was baptized on 9 April 1726 at St Andrew's Church, Penrith, Westmorland, the son of Richard and Ann Nelson, of whom nothing is otherwise known. He received a 'liberal education', possibly at Penrith grammar school, but from his birth until 1759, when he appears in the registers of St Anne's, Soho, Westminster, with his wife, Hannah (*d.* 1802), whom he married about 1751, details of his life are unrecorded. By 1759 he had become a skilled carver in wood and marble, and in view of his later expertise was perhaps employed by Sir Henry Cheere. About 1762 he was recruited by Thomas Ffarnolls Pritchard as a journeyman for Pritchard's Shrewsbury workshop. Nelson remained in his employment until 1770 and along with John Vanderhagen and others he was responsible for carving a remarkable collection of Gothic and rococo chimneypieces, overdoors, mirror frames, and girandoles, as well as fine masonry details and marble mural monuments in the style of Cheere. Nelson was probably the principal carver,

because when Pritchard moved out of Shrewsbury in 1770 Nelson took a joint tenancy of his house and yard, and he became the sole tenant there after the death of his former master in 1777. Shortly before Pritchard's death Nelson was made free of the Shrewsbury Carpenters' and Bricklayers' Company, and about this time his trade card laconically advertised his skills as 'Statuary, Carver (in wood and stone) and Marble Mason ... Monuments, Chimney Pieces etc. neatly executed'. To this he might have added picture and mirror frames.

From the 1770s Nelson executed numerous mural monuments in Shropshire and adjacent counties and in north Wales. Initially these were in a restrained rococo style characteristic of Pritchard and Cheere, using multi-coloured marbles and similar decoration; in later years, though they remained colourful, his works were more austerely classical. Nelson was widely employed in town and county. He contrived a marble seat for a water closet for the first Lord Clive at Oakly Park and worked there and at Walcot Park (both in Shropshire) on masonry work and marble chimneypieces through the 1770s and 1780s. He carved the lions at the front and rear of The Lion inn in Shrewsbury in 1777, and when his patron there—John Ashby, a leading attorney—died in 1779 he made his monument at nearby Westbury. There he also carved a fine royal arms for the parish church and provided a sundial. When the new St Chad's, Shrewsbury, was built in 1791, he was responsible for the freestone Corinthian and Ionic capitals on the tower and interior architectural details. At Hawkstone in 1795 he executed the statue of Sir Rowland Hill for the column in the park as well as a pair of sphinxes at one of the entrances, and in 1796 he provided a statue of Roger of Montgomery for Sir William Pulteney at Shrewsbury Castle.

As a masonry contractor Nelson built two curious round, domed toll-houses on Worcester Bridge in the late 1770s, to the design of John Gwynn. Both on his tombstone and on his drawing and contract for rebuilding a bridge over the Rea at Meole Brace near Shrewsbury in 1789, he is described as an architect. His contemporaries preferred to remember him as a sculptor, and his daybook of 1799–1805 records funerary inscriptions on ledger slabs, freestone headstones and tombs, marble mural monuments, and simple tablets, for gentry, clergy, and more humble people in churches and graveyards in Shropshire, Denbighshire, and Montgomeryshire. He died on 17 April 1812 at House of Correction Shut, Shrewsbury, and was buried locally at St Mary's Church five days later. The *Gentleman's Magazine* stated that his

> abilities as a statuary will be long remembered in this and the neighbouring counties where specimens of his ingenuity may be seen in many of the churches and in the mansions of the nobility and gentry.

> By noble men is Nelson prais'd,
> Such selfish praise is spar'd,
> In busts to others merits rais'd,
> He has his own declar'd.
> (*GM*, 492)

JAMES LAWSON

Sources R. Gunnis, *Dictionary of British sculptors, 1660–1851* (1953); new edn (1968) · J. Ionides, *Thomas Ffarnolls Pritchard of Shrewsbury etc. Ludlow* (1999) · *GM*, 1st ser., 82/1 (1812), 492 · *VCH Shropshire*, vol. 8 · trade card, [n.d.], Shrops. RRC, Watton's cuttings, 6001, vol. 1 · H. Owen and J. B. Blakeway, *A history of Shrewsbury*, 2 (1825), 404 · D. Whitehead, 'John Gwynn, R.A. and the building of Worcester Bridge, 1769–86', *Transactions of the Worcestershire Archaeological Society*, 3rd ser., 8 (1982), 31–45, esp. 37, 41 · *IGI* · parish register, St Mary, Shrewsbury, 22 April 1812 [burial] · parish register, St Andrew, Penrith, 9 April 1726 [baptism]
Archives Shrewsbury School, daybook of funerary inscription

Nelson, Richard John (1803–1877), army officer and author, was born on 3 May 1803 at Crabtree, near Plymouth, Devon, the son of Richard Thomas Nelson (*d.* 1842), army officer, and his wife, Catharine. His baptism on 4 May 1803 was recorded at Eggbuckland, and early education given at a private school in Tamerton Foliot, both villages nearby. He was a gentleman cadet at the Royal Military Academy, Woolwich, from 25 March 1818 until about 1822, but his commission as second lieutenant in the Royal Engineers was delayed until 7 January 1826 by reduction in the established strength of the corps. Following field instruction at Chatham from March 1826 to March 1827, he was posted for service in Bermuda. Illness resulted in his returning to Woolwich and Plymouth, for the period April to October 1828, but he otherwise remained in Bermuda until July 1833, being promoted lieutenant on 22 May 1829. A member of the Plymouth Institution, he published an article on the geology of Jersey, Channel Islands, in 1830. In Bermuda he supervised defensive construction works but in his leisure time initiated studies on geology and coral reefs—communicating his findings to the Geological Society of London via its president, G. B. Greenough, in 1834 (published 1837) and, much later, to the Linnean Society of London through its president in 1876. He also made elegant pencil sketches, now preserved in the Bermuda archives.

After a period of unemployment and leave, Nelson was stationed at Woolwich from June to October 1835, but from December 1835 until December 1838 served in southern Africa, at the Cape of Good Hope. When again militarily unemployed, on 6 August 1839 he married Lucy (1807/8–1896), daughter of Thomas Howard, silversmith, at the parish church of St Margaret, Ipswich, Suffolk. From September 1839 to March 1841 he served at Plymouth, but from April 1841 he was again posted overseas, to Canada, where he was promoted second captain on 1 September of that year. He was granted sick leave from July 1842 until January 1843, but then sent to Ireland until June 1846; while there he was one of the six editors of, and a major contributor to, the first edition of a massive three-volume *Aide-mémoire to the Military Sciences* by G. G. Lewis, H. D. Jones, R. J. Nelson, and others (1846–52). Promoted captain on 1 April 1846, he served in England at Devonport, Plymouth, from June 1846 to August 1848, and then in south Wales at Pembroke Dock until May the next year. From July 1849 until invalided home in October 1851 he served in the Bahamas, where again he devoted his leisure time to the study of island geology and coral formation, and later (1852, published 1853) communicated these observations to the Geological Society of London (via Sir Charles Lyell, as his eyesight was then failing). Nelson's remaining years of military service were mostly spent in his native Devon. He was promoted brevet major on 14 June 1854, regimental lieutenant-colonel six days later, and on 20 June 1857 became a colonel in the army. From September 1858 he returned to Canada, on appointment as commanding royal engineer at Halifax, Nova Scotia. He returned to England in August 1861, and retired on full pay with promotion to major-general on 5 February 1864.

During his military career Nelson contributed seventeen articles to *Professional Papers of the Corps of Royal Engineers*. He wrote on a variety of topics, including coastal defences, suspension bridges, convict labour, and a lunar tide on Lake Michigan. He also contributed several papers on wood, including 'Remarks and experiments on various woods, foreign and domestic', which has been credited as a notable contribution to the development of nineteenth-century building technology. He also wrote the second part of a memorandum on the Bahama tornado of 1850, and a work on the learning of the German language. After retirement he lived at Stoke Damerel, Plymouth, until his death at 12 Penlee Villas on 18 July 1877 from a three-month 'disease of the stomach'. His wife died later, on 9 January 1896, and was buried with him and his ancestral family of a century earlier in Stoke Damerel churchyard. They had no children.   E. P. F. ROSE

Sources *Army List* (1827–77) · R. F. Edwards, ed., *Roll of officers of the corps of royal engineers from 1660 to 1898* (1898) · T. W. J. Connolly, 'Notitia historica of the corps of royal engineers', Royal Engineers Library, Chatham · *Professional Papers of the Corps of Royal Engineers*, 4th ser., 3–5 (1839–42); 4th ser., 7 (1845); new ser., 1 (1851); new ser., 6–7 (1857–8); new ser., 10–12 (1861–3) · *Royal Engineers Journal* (Sept 1877) · J. M. Weiler, 'Army architects: the royal engineers and the development of building technology in the nineteenth century', PhD diss., University of York, 1987 · parish register (baptism), Devon, Eggbuckland · m. cert. · d. cert. · *DNB* · private information (2004) [West Devon RO]
Archives NHM
Likenesses photographs, Royal Engineers Library, Chatham
Wealth at death under £1500: probate, 8 Aug 1877, *CGPLA Eng. & Wales*

Nelson, Robert (1656–1715), philanthropist and religious writer, was born in London on 22 June 1656. He was the only survivor of the three children of John Nelson (*d.* 1657) and his wife, Delicia (or Delitia) Roberts (*d.* 1703). John Nelson, of a Suffolk family, was a wealthy Levant Company merchant, and Delicia was the sister of Sir Gabriel Roberts, also of the Levant Company and prominent in City affairs.

Early life and travels Robert was one when his father died, and his mother and Gabriel Roberts as guardian brought him up. He became a pupil at St Paul's School but left after only two or three years, probably when the school was destroyed in the great fire of London in 1666. He and his mother then lived at Driffield, Gloucestershire, where he was educated by the rector of nearby Suddington, George Bull, afterwards bishop of St David's. He did not return to St Paul's when the school was rebuilt after the fire. He and his mother each subscribed 1 guinea to the rebuilding of

St Paul's Cathedral. He was entered as a fellow commoner at Trinity College, Cambridge, in 1678, but never resided and took no degree. Gabriel Roberts was a friend of John Tillotson, dean of Canterbury and subsequently archbishop of Canterbury; Nelson likewise became a close friend of Tillotson. Nelson had been a schoolboy friend of Edmond Halley, apparently when they were at St Paul's before the fire, and they remained good friends as young men and throughout Nelson's life. In late 1680, when Tillotson and Halley were already fellows of the Royal Society, Nelson also was elected FRS, although he was not admitted until 1695 because he was abroad for many years until then. The grounds for Nelson's election were, as was frequent at the time, not recorded, but were probably a general interest in the society and likely support of it. In 1680 Halley proposed to visit astronomers in France and Italy, and Nelson joined him. They set out for Paris at the end of 1680 and on their way from Boulogne to Paris they saw the brilliant tail of the spectacular comet of 1680. They arrived in Paris on Christmas eve to stay in the fashionable and cultured quarter of St Germain-des-Près, and Halley observed the great comet with Jean-Dominique (Giandomenico) Cassini at the Observatoire. They were received in exalted circles and entertained Cardinal D'Estrées to a feast for St Bartholomew. Tillotson had recommended them to the English ambassador, Henry Savile, and while in Paris, Nelson received an offer of a place at court through the interest of Savile's brother, the marquess of Halifax. Nelson's family, on Tillotson's advice, declined it for fear of the moral corruption of the court; Nelson and Halley none the less retained the regard of Savile. In May they moved to Saumur, where they stayed with Miss Griggs, a friend of Tillotson. Letters between Nelson and Tillotson contain much information about the friends' stay in Paris and Saumur. They left Saumur for Rome in July. They travelled by way of Bordeaux, by the incomplete Canal du Midi, and by Avignon, Leghorn, Florence, and Siena, and arrived in Rome at the end of October. Almost nothing is known of their stay there. Halley met at least one of the members of the Accademia Fisica-Matematica of Mgr Ciampini associated with Queen Kristina of Sweden, and may have followed up earlier contacts between the accademia and the Royal Society. Nelson stayed on after Halley left in December, and met his future wife, Lady Theophila Lucy (1654–1706), the second daughter of the earl of Berkeley and the widow of Sir Kingsmill Lucy. Two years older than Nelson, she had a son and daughter from her first marriage. Nelson and she returned to England in 1682 and were married on 23 November 1682, after a delay because of Lord Grey of Warke's abduction of her younger sister when he was already married to their elder sister. In Rome, Theophila had known Cardinal Philip Howard and had corresponded with Bossuet, the bishop of Meaux, and she became a Roman Catholic, probably after her marriage. Tillotson tried unavailingly to regain her for the Church of England. She and Nelson both wrote controversial religious pamphlets, hers in 1686 from the Roman Catholic side and his against transubstantiation. Theophila's health was weak and she and Nelson lived for a while in Aix-la-Chapelle; Nelson paid a brief visit to England in 1688.

Nonjuror Nelson believed in the hereditary right of James II and on the accession of William and Mary he moved with his family to Rome and Florence. He corresponded with Lord Melfort, the envoy of James II to the pope, passing on to him such news, mostly inaccurate, as he had had of the campaigns in Ireland. He and his family returned to England in 1691 to Blackheath. Tillotson was now William's archbishop of Canterbury and Nelson asked him if he could properly attend church when prayers were said for monarchs he did not recognize. Tillotson said he could not, and Nelson joined the nonjuring community of those who could not take the oaths of allegiance to William on account of the fealty they had already sworn to James II. No further letters between Nelson and Tillotson are known, but evidently their close relation was not broken for Nelson attended Tillotson in the last two nights of his final illness and Tillotson died in his arms on 22 November 1694. Nelson was instrumental in obtaining an increase of pension for Mrs Tillotson, who had been left in difficult circumstances. When in 1695 Nelson was formally admitted to the Royal Society, some of his nonjuror friends were also fellows, such as Samuel Pepys (a past president) and Sir Anthony Deane, the naval constructor: the society did not impose oaths of allegiance or abjuration. Nelson's closest friend at this time was the nonjuring priest John Kettlewell, whose life he proposed to write but did not complete. Kettlewell persuaded Nelson to begin devotional writings. George Hickes, later a nonjuring bishop and a neighbour in Ormond Street, Nathaniel Spinckes, also later a nonjuring bishop, and Pepys's clerk Bowdler were other prominent nonjurors whom Nelson knew in London; in Francis Cherry's house at Shottisbrooke he also met Henry Dodwell who had been expelled from his Oxford chair, and Francis Brokesby. When Bishop Lloyd died in 1710, Bishop Ken was the only remaining bishop deprived in 1689. He desired that the nonjuring schism should end and Nelson rejoined the established church, taking communion from his friend Sharp, the archbishop of York. He none the less remained committed to the Stuart family and hereditary right.

The religious societies Throughout his years as a nonjuror Nelson was on good terms with many of the established church, and he supported its philanthropical activities. Many churchmen and others became concerned at the growing licentious behaviour, anti-clericalism, and ignorance of mainstream Christian doctrine that followed the revolution of 1688–9. In the last decades of the seventeenth century 'religious societies' of young men were formed to counteract the licentious manners of the time by encouraging prayer and religious study and attendance at holy communion every Sunday. There were related societies for the reformation of manners, which sought to shame and prosecute notorious evil-livers. The societies started by Dr Thomas Bray following his attempts to set up the established church in Maryland were of far greater effect. He formed the Society for Promoting Christian Knowledge (SPCK) in 1698 to distribute tracts and especially to encourage the practice of confirmation and preparation for it. Nelson was an early member and among the most effective on the committee. He was also an active member of the Society for Propagation of the Gospel (1701), which derived from the SPCK and carried its work to North America; and of the Associates of Dr Bray who provided libraries for country clergy. The effects of Nelson's part in founding those societies continue to this day in the vigorous activity of the SPCK and the missionary work of the Church of England. Nelson also had some indirect connection with the later rise of Methodism. Samuel Wesley, the father of John and Charles, had a religious society in his parish of Epworth and was an early out-of-town corresponding member of the SPCK. Nelson canvassed support for Samuel and his wife when the Epworth rectory was burnt down and they were in distress. One of the books from which John Wesley at Oxford derived his pietistic attitudes was Nelson's *The Practice of True Devotion*. John Wesley was also a corresponding member of the SPCK, which helped to support him and Charles Wesley in Georgia. The Wesleys, like Nelson, were devout high-churchmen, and like him, Bray, and their associates, deeply concerned at the ignorance and deprivation of the mass of people in England. Methodism is in some sense a child of Dr Bray's projects, but unlike those it eventually separated from the established church.

Religious writings Nelson was best known in his own day for his religious writings and in particular for *A Companion for the Festivals and Fasts of the Church of England* (1704). He provided, in the form of a catechism, an account of the saint or other occasion for each of the days for which there were special services in the Book of Common Prayer of 1662. That was followed by a homily on aspects of the Christian life associated with the festival or fast, by the collect for the day, and other appropriate prayers. It was very popular, there were more than forty editions, and it was translated into German and Welsh. The SPCK distributed it widely and the Episcopal church of the United States of America adopted it. Its popularity must have been in part because it provided convenient material for sermons on the major holy days. It is firmly of its time. Biblical criticism and historical study of the lives of saints have made some of the material out of date, while the ethical and moral precepts reflect the social and political presuppositions of Nelson's day. Much of his other writing is concerned with contemporary controversies. He wrote against transubstantiation and other Roman Catholic doctrines, but held that the holy communion was a material sacrifice and not simply a memorial. He advocated frequent communion in the Church of England. He corresponded with Bossuet about the theological writing of George Bull on the Nicene creed and the divinity of Christ, which they both admired.

Nelson promoted the building of a number of churches. He and his mother each subscribed a guinea for the church of King Charles the Martyr in Tunbridge Wells, and he was a member of the parliamentary commission set up to build fifty new churches in London—only a few were in fact built. He solicited contributions for the erection of a church in Rotterdam for the entourage of the duke of Marlborough from 1703 onwards: that church was torn down at the beginning of the twentieth century but the pulpit survives in Lincoln Cathedral and some of the panelling is in the hall of Selwyn College, Cambridge. Pepys was one whom he asked for a contribution, in a letter in which he advised Pepys that the nonjuror Spinckes of Winchester Street, where Halley had property, might serve him as a pastor.

Last years and assessment Nelson lived in Ormond Street from 1703. His mother died that same year and his wife on 26 January 1706. He was elected to the council of the Royal Society for 1711 to 1712, at the time of the rancorous dispute of Flamsteed with Newton and Halley about the publication of Flamsteed's Greenwich results, and attended meetings of the society rather sporadically until 1714. At the end of his life, ill with asthma and dropsy, he moved to the house of his cousin Mrs Wolf, a daughter of Sir Gabriel Roberts, in Kensington, and there he died on 16 January 1715. He was buried in a new cemetery in Lamb's Conduit Fields, the first interment there.

The political and religious history of the late seventeenth and early eighteenth century is often presented in terms of deep hostility between parties such as whig and tory, high church and latitudinarian, nonjuror and conformist, and so on. Nelson, in his own life and in the SPCK, shows how glib a view that is. A nonjuror who maintained a respectful correspondence with Bossuet, Nelson supported the work of the established church in many ways, and with others kept up unbroken connections, personal, social, and institutional, between established and nonjuring confessions. The membership of the SPCK was still broader, embracing many nonconformists (only excepting Quakers and Roman Catholics) and members of the Presbyterian Church of Scotland, while early Methodism owes much to the ideals and practices of Nelson and others like him in the SPCK and the Society for the Propagation of the Gospel. Nelson is one of many contemporaries of varied churchmanship and political allegiance who could join together in common aims and who cannot be confined by any one political or ecclesiastical label.

ALAN COOK

Sources C. F. Secretan, *Memoirs of the life and times of the pious Robert Nelson* (1860) · A. Cook, *Edmond Halley, charting the heavens and the sea* (1998) · T. Birch, *The life of the Most Reverend Dr John Tillotson, lord archbishop of Canterbury* (1752) · T. Lathbury, *A history of the nonjurors* (1845) · R. Nelson, *A companion for the festivals and fasts of the Church of England* (1704) · journal book, 1680–95, RS · council minutes, 1711–12, RS · C. Rose, 'The origins and ideals of the SPCK, 1699–1716', *The Church of England, c.1689–c.1833*, ed. J. Walsh and others (1993), 172–90

Archives BL, biographical papers, Add. MSS 45511–45512 · NL Ire., letters and papers | BL, corresp. relating to George Bull, Add. MS 41667 · Bodl. Oxf., Rawlinson MSS

Likenesses G. Kneller, oils, Stationers' Company; copies, priv. coll., Society for Promoting Christian Knowledge · G. Kneller, oils, U. Oxf., Examination Schools · G. Vertue, line engraving (after G. Kneller), BM, NPG; repro. in R. Nelson, *An address to persons of quality and estate* (1715)

Wealth at death substantial legacies: will, Secretan, *Life and times*

Nelson, Sydney (1800–1862), composer, was born in London on 1 January 1800, the son of Solomon Nelson. Showing musical ability when quite young, he was adopted by a gentleman who gave him a good musical and general education. He was for some time a pupil of George Smart, and eventually became a teacher in London. From *c*.1840 until 1843, when he was elected an associate of the Philharmonic Society, he was in partnership with Charles Jeffreys (1807–1865) as a publisher and music seller. Nelson composed much of their output, and claimed to have written about eight hundred ballads, some of which were published under an assumed name. He also wrote several comic operas, which were staged at such London theatres as the Lyceum between 1829 and 1851. Among his other works were a burletta, *The Grenadier*, produced by Madame Vestris at the Olympic; *The Cadi's Daughter*, performed after *Macbeth* for William Macready's farewell benefit; and *The Village Nightingale*, with words by H. T. Craven, his son-in-law. He had a grand opera, *Ulrica*, in rehearsal at the Princess's Theatre, but, owing to some dispute, it was not produced. In addition, he was the author of *Instructions in the Art of Singing* and composed many duets, trios, pianoforte pieces, and songs; some of the latter, such as 'The Pilot' and 'The Rose of Allandale', attaining considerable popularity. One project that he undertook was to arrange a musical and dramatic entertainment with members of his family, with which he went on tour to the USA, Canada, and Australia.

Nelson died at Russell Square, London, on 7 April 1862 and was buried at West Ham. He left a widow, Sarah Nelson, and a son, Alfred Nelson.

J. C. HADDEN, *rev.* DAVID J. GOLBY

Sources F. Kidson, 'Nelson, Sydney', *New Grove* · private information (1894) · Boase, *Mod. Eng. biog.* · *CGPLA Eng. & Wales* (1862)
Wealth at death under £450: probate, 5 May 1862, *CGPLA Eng. & Wales*

Nelson, Thomas (*fl.* 1580–1592), bookseller and ballad maker, is of obscure origins. In October 1580 he was made free of the Stationers' Company by the bookseller Garret Dewes, and it is therefore unlikely that he was the Thomas Nelson of Clare College, Cambridge, who graduated BA twelve years previously. He may instead have been the Thomas Nelson baptized on 4 June 1555 at St Lawrence Jewry or at St Mary Magdalen, Milk Street, London. On 24 June 1583 Nelson took an apprentice.

Between 1584 and 1585 Nelson's shop was at the west door of St Paul's Cathedral; it moved to London Bridge in 1586, the year in which he was arrested by officers of the Stationers' Company for an unnamed offence. In 1591 his shop was at the great south door of St Paul's, and in 1592 he was said to be dwelling in Silver Street near the sign of the Red Cross. The last entry for a work on his account in the Stationers' register is for 14 August 1592, and in December that year he was named in the will of Jarrett Anderson, who bequeathed him his walking-stick.

The Stationers' register from 1583 to 1592 records a number of ballads and topical works licensed to Nelson, few of which have survived, but among these four were by Nelson himself. His *A short discourse: expressing the substaunce of all the late pretended treasons against the queens maiestie* (1586), in verse, proved popular, and was also printed for two other booksellers, William Wright and Edward White (three times). In 1590 Nelson wrote a verse epitaph on Sir Francis Walsingham and an account of the Fishmongers' pageant of that year; and in the following year, *The blessed state of England. Declaring the sundrie dangers which by God's assistance, the queen's maiestie hath escaped.*

It is not known when Nelson died. ELERI LARKUM

Sources *STC, 1475–1640* · H. G. Aldis and others, *A dictionary of printers and booksellers in England, Scotland and Ireland, and of foreign printers of English books, 1557–1640*, ed. R. B. McKerrow (1910) · *IGI* · Venn, *Alum. Cant.* · *DNB*

Nelson, Thomas (1780–1861). *See under* Nelson family (*per.* 1780–1958).

Nelson, Thomas, junior (1822–1892). *See under* Nelson family (*per.* 1780–1958).

Nelson, Thomas Arthur (1877–1917). *See under* Nelson family (*per.* 1780–1958).

Nelson, William (*b.* 1652/3), legal writer, was the second son of William Nelson of Chaddleworth, Berkshire. He matriculated at Trinity College, Oxford, on 16 July 1669 aged sixteen, and recovered his caution money in 1672 without having taken a degree. He was admitted to the Middle Temple on 16 June 1673, and called to the bar on 9 May 1684. He was called to the bench of the inn on 25 October 1706, but failed to act upon the call.

A successful practitioner in the court of chancery, Nelson's numerous literary works displayed considerable legal learning, but despite his low opinion of the writings of others, Nelson's own works were not invariably accurate or useful. In 1704 he published *Office and Authority of a Justice of the Peace*, a successful work including information on the duties of many other local government officials, which reached a twelfth edition in 1745 and no doubt drew upon Nelson's experience as chairman of the Sussex sessions. This was followed in 1709 by *Rights of the Clergy of Great Britain*, abridging the relevant law under alphabetical heads but seldom making clear statements of principle. In 1714 came the *Lex testamentaria* on the laws concerning last wills, which was followed in 1717 by the anonymous *Law of Evidence* and the *Reports of Special Cases in the Court of Chancery*. The former, one of the first works to be published on the English law of evidence, digested the cases without attempting to extract underlying principles. The latter claimed to be largely transcribed from the manuscript of a late attorney-general, and to contain reports most of which had never previously been printed or of points which had not previously been noticed, though several of the reports had already appeared in print elsewhere.

In 1725–6 Nelson published his three-volume *Abridgment of the Common Law*. This work, not entirely accurate, was taken by Charles Viner to have been copied largely from William Hughes's abridgment (1660–63). It consisted of a digest of cases subsequent to the abridgements of Anthony Fitzherbert (1514–16) and Robert Brooke (1573), Nelson regarding the medieval year-book reports as merely a 'rhapsody of antiquated law, written in a barbarous and unpolished language' (W. Nelson, *Abridgment of the Common Law*, vol. 1, preface). Nelson's *Abridgment* contained no statutes, possibly because he had some part in a consolidation of previous abridgements of the statutes which appeared at about the same time. Nelson may also have been the compiler of an anonymous digest, *Readings upon the Statute Laws*, published in 1723–5. In 1727 appeared *Laws of England Concerning Game*, which reached a sixth edition in 1762. Of lesser works, there appeared in 1717 editions of John Manwood's treatise on the forest laws, first published in 1598, which Nelson altered considerably in contents and arrangement in the fourth edition, and of Thomas Blount's law dictionary, first published in 1667, to which Nelson claimed to have added nearly 3000 words. In 1718 Nelson issued a translation and abridgement of Edward Lutwyche's reports of cases in the court of common pleas, 1682–1704. This was of very little value, and was stigmatized by Charles Viner as 'a reproach and dishonour to the profession' (Viner, *Abridgment*, vol. 17, preface). In 1719 came a preface to John Lilly's posthumous *Cases in Assize*, and in 1725 appeared an edition of reports in chancery during the time of Lord Nottingham (1673–81), remarkable for its marginal comparisons of English and Roman law but not of high authority. Nelson may have edited the final version of John Cowell's controversial law dictionary, *The Interpreter*, which appeared in 1728. It is also possible that Nelson was the reporter of the fifth volume of *Modern Reports*, for which he wrote a preface, and he may have had an editorial supervision over all the volumes in that series. The date and place of his death are not known.   N. G. Jones

Sources H. A. C. Sturgess, ed., *Register of admissions to the Honourable Society of the Middle Temple, from the fifteenth century to the year 1944*, 1 (1949), 187 · Foster, *Alum. Oxon.* · Trinity College, Oxford, admission book · W. H. Maxwell and L. F. Maxwell, eds., *English law to 1800*, 2nd edn (1955), vol. 1 of *A legal bibliography of the British Commonwealth of Nations* (1938–58) · Holdsworth, *Eng. law*, 6.556, 562, 617 · Holdsworth, *Eng. law*, 11.307 · Holdsworth, *Eng. law*, 12.162, 164, 175, 334, 365, 381, 623–4 · J. W. Wallace, *The reporters*, 4th edn (1882), 380, 395–6, 423, 480 · J. D. Cowley, *A bibliography of abridgments, digests, dictionaries and indexes of English law to the year 1800* (1932), x, xxxvi–xliv, lvi–lvii, 103–4, 110 · minutes of parliament, 1706–10, Middle Temple archives, London · J. G. Marvin, *Legal bibliography, or, A thesaurus of American, English, Irish and Scotch law books* (1847), 184, 354, 481–2 · IGI · C. Viner, *A general abridgment of law and equity*, 17 (1743)

Nelson, William (1711–1772), merchant and politician in America, was born in Yorktown, Virginia, the son of Thomas Nelson (1677–1745), a merchant, and Margaret Reade (d. 1719x23). He was sent to England for his education; it is not known which school he attended, but he spent some time in Penrith, Cumberland, and did not return to Virginia until 1732. He was appointed JP at the York county court, and entered the family mercantile firm, a flourishing business with intermittent links to the slave trade, by which time he was described as 'a young Gentleman of merit and fortune' (BL, Sloane MS 4054, fols. 304–7). On 9 February 1738 he married Elizabeth Carter Burwell (b. 1718), who was from an old and distinguished Virginia family. The union produced six sons, five of whom lived to maturity. Thomas (1738–1789), the eldest, entered Christ's College, Cambridge, and was a signatory to the Declaration of Independence.

Under the terms of his father's will Nelson came into a substantial inheritance which included the family business and 3270 acres of land. The overall value of Thomas Nelson's land must have been considerable as besides the major portion conveyed to William Nelson it included cash bequests amounting to £10,000. Nelson managed his plantations and the business with careful efficiency. In the course of time his landholdings rose to nearly 30,000 acres, on which he produced large quantities of tobacco. His trading company developed into one of the most prosperous Virginia-owned firms. Goods for his wholesale and retail trade were imported from eight or ten British companies in London and the Atlantic ports; Nelson himself was part-owner of one or two merchant vessels. In a land without banks, Nelson lent considerable sums of money and he was able, unlike many of Virginia's citizens, to remain free of debt.

This accumulated wealth underpinned Nelson's immensely successful public career. After ten years on the county court he was elected to the house of burgesses from York county, and he quickly emerged as an important member of that body. In 1745 Nelson was appointed to the council, which served as an advisory body to the governor, the court of highest appeal in the colony, and the upper house of the legislature, and he remained a member until his death. He was joined on the council by his brother Thomas in 1749, and over the middle decades of the eighteenth century they represented perhaps the strongest single family influence in Virginia government. Governors did little without consulting him. When Governor Lord Botetourt died in 1770, Nelson as the senior member of the council was acting governor until Lord Dunmore arrived in 1771.

As a member of the council, Nelson remained silent on the emerging contest with the mother country, although in private he was a strong defender of Virginia's 'rights' within the empire. Despite the repeal of the Stamp Act he remained restive under the Navigation Acts, which, he said, placed 'cruel Impositions and clogs on our trade'. In his stated opinion, English politics were corrupt, and it was a farce for the English people to consider themselves as being 'the Freest people on Earth'. In contrast America was the land of hope where 'brave men' came during 'the usurpation of the last century' and 'laid the Foundation of what may in future ages become a mighty Empire' (Nelson and Nelson, letter-book).

Nelson died on 19 November 1772. 'The Chief ornament of the Country is gone', wrote one commentator, while another stated that 'no man amongst us … was more strenuous in promoting the true Interest of his Country, whether view'd in a political or commercial light' (Mason, 281, 285–6). He was buried at Yorkhampton parish church in Yorktown.   EMORY G. EVANS

Sources E. G. Evans, 'Nelson, William', *ANB* • E. G. Evans, 'The Nelsons: a biographical study of a Virginia family in the eighteenth century', PhD diss., University of Virginia, 1957 • E. G. Evans, *Thomas Nelson of Yorktown: revolutionary Virginian* (1975) • W. Nelson and T. Nelson, letter-book, 1766–75, Library of Virginia, Richmond, Virginia • *The correspondence of William Nelson as acting governor of Virginia, 1770–1771*, ed. J. C. Van Horne (1975) • J. P. Greene, 'A mirror of virtue for a declining land: John Camm's funeral sermon for William Nelson', *Essays in early Virginia literature honoring Richard Beale Davis*, ed. J. L. Lemay (1977) • H. R. McIlwaine and others, eds., *Executive journals of the council of colonial Virginia*, 6 vols. (1925–66) • H. R. McIlwaine, ed., *Legislative journals of the council of state*, 2nd edn (1979) • H. R. McIlwaine and J. P. Kennedy, eds., *Journals of the house of burgesses of Virginia, 1619–1776*, 13 vols. (1905–15) • F. N. Mason, *John Norton and Sons, merchants of London and Virginia ... 1750–1795* (1937) • *The papers of George Washington*, ed. W. W. Abbot and others, [10 vols.] (1983–) • *The official letters of Francis Fauquier: lieutenant governor of Virginia, 1758–1768*, ed. G. Reese, 3 vols. (1980) • 'Berkeley manuscripts', *William and Mary College Quarterly*, 6 (1897–8), 135–52, esp. 143–5 • *Parks's Virginia Gazette* (10 Feb 1738) • *Parks's Virginia Gazette* (10 Oct 1745)
Archives College of William and Mary, Williamsburg, Virginia, corresp. • Colonial Williamsburg Foundation, corresp. • L. Cong., corresp. • Library of Virginia, Richmond, letter-book • Library of Virginia, Richmond, corresp. • University of Virginia, Charlottesville, corresp. • Virginia Historical Society, Richmond, corresp.
Likenesses R. Feke?, oils, repro. in Evans, *Thomas Nelson of Yorktown*; priv. coll.
Wealth at death substantial: Evans, *Thomas Nelson*; *Virginia Magazine of History and Biography*, 43, 190–92

Nelson, William, first Earl Nelson (1757–1835), Church of England clergyman, was born on 20 April 1757 at Parsonage House, Burnham Thorpe, Norfolk, the eldest son of Edmund Nelson (1722–1802), rector of Burnham Thorpe, and his wife, Catherine, *née* Suckling (1725–1767), and brother of Horatio *Nelson, Viscount Nelson. He was educated with his brother at the Royal Grammar School, Norwich, until 1769, and then at the William Paston School, North Walsham. In 1778 he graduated from Christ's College, Cambridge, and in 1781 proceeded MA. Nelson was ordained in the same year, and in 1784 was appointed curate at Brandon-Parva in Norfolk. Hankering after the adventurous life at sea led by his brother, he persuaded Horatio to engage him as chaplain to his command, the frigate *Boreas*, later that year. However, the discomforts of shipboard life and of the tropics affected him greatly; he left the ship at Antigua and was formally discharged from the service in October 1786.

On his return to Norfolk in November Nelson married Sarah (d. 1828), daughter of the Revd Henry Yonge; the couple had two children, Horatio (or Horace) and Charlotte, and Nelson settled down to his curacy, transferring in 1797 to Hilborough, in Norfolk, where his father had been rector. The brothers corresponded continually in this period and when Viscount Nelson, his mistress Emma, Lady Hamilton, and her husband settled at Merton Place in Surrey in 1802, William Nelson and his family were frequent guests. Close relationships subsequently developed between Lady Hamilton and Charlotte, whom Hamilton instructed in the ways of society, and between

her and Sarah Nelson in whom Hamilton found an ally in her campaign of denigration against Viscountess Nelson.

Nelson continually asked for help from his brother in ecclesiastical promotion, prompting a verse which included the lines:

> But, to return to this same worthy Vicar,
> Who loves, you say, good eating and good liquor,
> Know, Lady, that it is our earnest wish
> That we, ere long may greet him—Lord Archbish.
> (Pettigrew, 2.121)

In January 1802 Nelson was awarded a doctorate of divinity from the University of Cambridge; in the following year the DD degree was conferred on him by Oxford when his brother and Sir William Hamilton were also granted honorary degrees. In May 1803 he was appointed a prebendary of Canterbury. After his brother was killed at the battle of Trafalgar on 21 October 1805 Nelson presided over the lavish funeral arrangements. As a proxy for his dead brother he succeeded as Baron Nelson of the Nile and the following month was created Viscount Merton and Earl Nelson of Trafalgar and Merton, also succeeding to the dukedom of Bronte in Sicily in 1806. He and his heirs were granted an annual pension of £5000 in perpetuity and £100,000 to purchase an estate; in 1814 he bought Stanlynch Park, near Downton in Wiltshire, and named the mansion Trafalgar House. His life was blighted when his son Horatio died of typhoid in 1808 and the titles passed to his nephew, Thomas Bolton, son of his sister Susannah, who changed his surname to Nelson. Nelson was described as a large, heavily built man with a somewhat coarse-featured, fleshy face; 'his own voice very loud and he exceedingly and impatiently deaf'.

After his brother's death Nelson was accused by Lady Hamilton of concealing the last codicil of his will, which benefited her, but this was unjustified because law officers had already decided that it was invalid. However, he and his wife distanced themselves from Lady Hamilton and resumed friendly relations with his brother's widow.

A year after the death of Sarah Nelson in 1828 Nelson married Hilaire (d. 1857), daughter of Rear-Admiral Sir Robert Barlow and widow of George Ulric Barlow. Nelson died in London on 28 February 1835. His daughter, who had married Baron Bridport in 1810, now succeeded to the Sicilian title of duchess of Bronte. Nelson's widow later married George Thomas Knight; she died in 1857. The earldom continued through descendants of his nephew but the annuity was ended in 1947 and Trafalgar House was sold in the following year.   TOM POCOCK

Sources *The dispatches and letters of Vice-Admiral Lord Viscount Nelson*, ed. N. H. Nicolas, 7 vols. (1844–6) • M. E. Matcham, *The Nelsons of Burnham Thorpe* (1911) • W. Gérin, *Horatia Nelson* (1970) • O. Warner, *A portrait of Lord Nelson* (1965) • C. Oman, *Nelson* (1947) • E. Hallam Moorhouse, *Nelson in England* (1913) • C. Hibbert, *Nelson: a personal history* (1994) • T. Pocock, *Horatio Nelson* (1987) • *The Hamilton and Nelson papers*, ed. A. Morrison, 2 vols. (privately printed, London, 1893–4) • T. J. Pettigrew, *Memoirs of the life of Vice-Admiral Lord Viscount Nelson*, 2 vols. (1849)
Archives BL, corresp., Add. MS 34992 • Canterbury Cathedral archives, account book and diary • NMM, corresp. and papers

Likenesses G. Hayter, group portrait, oils (*The trial of Queen Caroline, 1820*), NPG · J. Hoppner, oils

Nelson, William (1816–1887). *See under* Nelson family (*per.* 1780–1958).

Nelson, Wolfred (1791–1863), doctor and rebel in Canada, was born in Montreal on 10 July 1791, the third son of William Nelson, a schoolmaster, and Jane Dies, the daughter of a wealthy American loyalist who had moved to Canada after the revolution. He was educated at his father's school at William-Henry, known as Sorel, before being apprenticed in December 1805 to Dr C. Carter, an army surgeon of Sorel. He received his surgeon's licence in February 1811, and after practising in Sorel served as a surgeon during the Anglo-American War of 1812–14 to a militia battalion based at St Denis-sur-Richelieu. Both town and battalion were overwhelmingly French Canadian, and his army service, subsequent practice in St Denis, and marriage in 1819 to Charlotte-Josephte Noyelle de Fleurimont, with whom he had seven children, changed him from an anti-French-Canadian tory to a pro-French-Canadian reformer. In 1827 he contested the borough of Sorel against James Stuart, attorney-general for Lower Canada, and won by two votes, but for unknown reasons he did not seek re-election in 1830. Instead he consolidated his medical practice, opened a distillery, and became a justice of the peace.

An outspoken supporter of the *patriote* party, Nelson became increasingly radical. By the mid-1830s the British government had made a number of concessions to critics in Canada, and it is at least arguable that the nationalists were driven not by opposition to old abuses, but by a desire for power. Nelson was clearly one of the most radical of the *patriotes* and one of the earliest advocates of armed rebellion. In May 1837 he organized the first of many 'anti-coercion' meetings, losing his commission as magistrate as a result. In October 1837 he was made chairman of the Assemblé des Six Comtés, and his angry, rousing speeches led the government to issue a warrant against him for high treason. The *patriote* leadership decided to resist arrest, arm themselves, and declare the independence of Lower Canada, and Nelson became effectively the military leader of the rebels. As a brigade under Colonel Charles Gore advanced on St Denis, Louis-Joseph Papineau fled, but Nelson mobilized the *patriotes* for battle. He defeated Gore's first attack on 23 November, and his victory galvanized the *patriotes*, but after defeats elsewhere he abandoned St Denis on 1 December, leaving Gore to advance and burn his property. Arrested before he could reach the United States, Nelson was imprisoned in Montreal, until in 1838 Lord Durham, the governor-general, acting on his own responsibility and anxious to avoid an inflammatory trial, banished him and seven other *patriotes* to Bermuda. The sentence was declared invalid by the imperial government and the *patriotes* were released in Bermuda.

Nelson and his family settled in Plattsburgh, New York, where he established a medical practice before returning to work in Montreal in 1842, after his close friend the attorney-general Louis-Hippolyte LaFontaine had removed any legal obstacles. From 1844 to 1851 he represented Richelieu in the assembly, becoming again the Anglophone exponent of French-Canadian nationalism and an advocate of responsible government. In 1848, when Papineau returned from exile and attempted to regain his leadership of French Canadians, Nelson exposed the former's desertion of the *patriotes* of St Denis in 1837, thereby destroying Papineau's reputation. In 1848–9, despite bitter opposition, he helped prepare the contentious Rebellion Losses Bill, which compensated people for losses incurred in 1837–8. He retired from politics in 1850, but in 1851 was made inspector of prisons and 1859 chairman of the board of prison inspectors, offices for which as an ex-inmate he was uniquely well qualified. In 1854–6, as the first elected mayor of Montreal, he sought to improve the regulation of public services and the provision of welfare. He never ceased to practise medicine, and he and his son Henry are credited with having performed the first operation in Canada using anaesthetics. In 1854 he published a pamphlet in English and French on the prevention of cholera. He died in Montreal on 17 June 1863. He is remembered for the sincerity and passion of his political beliefs and his integrity and compassion in both public and professional life.

Wolfred's younger brother Robert (1794–1873) followed him into the medical profession (qualifying in 1814), into the army (during the Anglo-American War of 1812–14), into politics (in 1827 as a reformer), and finally into armed rebellion (in 1837). At the end of 1837 he fled to the United States and in February the following year led an invasion of Canada. After its failure he established the secret society of Frères-Chasseurs with lodges throughout Lower Canada, but his attempt to foment rebellion in November 1838 was a complete fiasco. He went to California where, after winning and losing a fortune in the gold rush, he practised as a doctor, like Wolfred publishing a work on cholera. He died in New York in 1873.

ELIZABETH BAIGENT

Sources *DCB*, vol. 9 · F. Ouellet, *Lower Canada, 1791–1840: social changes and nationalism*, ed. and trans. P. Claxon (Toronto, 1980) · E. K. Senior, *Red coats and patriotes: the rebellions in Lower Canada, 1837–8* (1985) · *Dictionnaire des parlementaires du Québec, 1792–1992* (1993) · J. Schull, *Rebellion: the rising in French Canada, 1837* (1970) · *DNB*
Archives NA Canada
Likenesses J. J. Girouard, soft pencil or charcoal, NA Canada · oils, McGill University, Montreal, McCord Museum

Nelthorpe, Richard (*d.* 1685), conspirator and rebel, was the son of James Nelthorpe of the Charterhouse, London. Nelthorpe was admitted to Gray's Inn on 7 December 1669, and later became a member of the Green Ribbon Club. He supported Algernon Sidney's efforts to win a seat in the House of Commons, travelling with him, Sir Henry Ingoldsby, Sir William Waller, and William Lord Howard of Escrick to Amersham for the by-election in December 1680. The following April an informer reported that Nelthorpe had been at the Dolphin tavern, in Lombard Street, London, when Howard accused the king of fabricating the

Popish Plot and asserting that the queen deserved the worst of deaths; Nelthorpe, Colonel Roderick Mansell, and others reputedly concurred. On the eve of Shaftesbury's trial in November 1682, Nelthorpe, the whig attorney Richard Goodenough, and the linen draper Francis Jenks allegedly discussed the assassination of Charles; Nelthorpe was supposedly prepared to donate a horse, saddle, and weapons to the assassins, and Jenks and Goodenough each offered £100. Although these charges are probably baseless, they likely arose because of Nelthorpe's dislike of the king. Described by Sir Christopher Musgrave as 'a black man, high nosed, [with] pox holes in his face' (*Le Fleming MSS*, 192), Nelthorpe was living in Soho Square, London, where such political dissidents as Captain Thomas Walcott, Colonel John Rumsey, and Nathaniel Wade also resided.

By the autumn of 1682 Nelthorpe had become involved in the Rye House cabal (as it later became known) that typically met in the chamber of the attorney Robert West in the Middle Temple. The conspirators, who included Goodenough, Rumsey, John Row of Bristol, and the minister Robert Ferguson, discussed both a general uprising and assassination, but Nelthorpe opposed the latter as dishonourable. According to West's later confession, Nelthorpe thought a general rebellion was 'agreeable to the general bent of the people' (BL, Add. MS 38847, fol. 94v). Members of the cabal were republicans, whose proposed polity included a role for a prince with very weak powers (ibid., fol. 96v). In March 1683 Nelthorpe, West, and another man were observed studying the defensive works of the Tower of London, a likely target in an uprising. During this period Nelthorpe assisted Algernon Sidney, who was part of the cabal around the duke of Monmouth planning a general insurrection. In particular, Nelthorpe was helping Sidney deal with Scottish allies, and for this purpose recommended that Sidney also use Aaron Smith, another radical lawyer. Nelthorpe in turn helped keep West apprised of the Monmouth cabal's discussions. This was the origin of the much twisted allegation later made by Josiah Keeling, the plotter who turned informer, that Nelthorpe had been present at Lord William Russell's house when the arrest of the lord mayor was contemplated. When the plotters learned that Keeling had informed the government of their activities, Nelthorpe and others discussed their options at Walcott's house on 18 June 1683. With Edward Norton, Nelthorpe reported Keeling's betrayal to Russell and expressed their desire to take up arms. When Russell demurred, Nelthorpe and Goodenough fled. The following day, the government issued a warrant to search Nelthorpe's chambers, and on the 23rd it offered a reward of £100 for his apprehension. Nelthorpe and Goodenough made their way to Scarborough, where they found a ship to take them to the Netherlands on the 24th. The government indicted Nelthorpe for high treason on 12 July, having three witnesses against him.

By August 1683 Nelthorpe had reached Vevey, Switzerland, where he unsuccessfully urged Edmund Ludlow to lead an uprising. With security a constant concern, Nelthorpe, Ferguson, and Wade paid Row to stay in Switzerland, fearing he might turn informer. Like various other exiles, Nelthorpe used an alias (Gardner). Periodically, he was in contact with Monmouth, Waller, and John Locke. He seems to have spent considerable time in Amsterdam, though he also resided in Cleves until a complaint from the English government prompted the elector of Brandenburg to insist that he leave. With Wade, Ferguson, and other radicals, he participated in Monmouth's rebellion. After the disaster at Sedgemoor, he and the minister John Hickes escaped to Moyles Court, home of the widow Alice Lisle, whose husband John had been a regicide. Captured there, Nelthorpe was taken to London, imprisoned in Newgate, and interrogated on 9 August 1685. He denied having conspired to kill Charles, though he admitted he knew about plans for an insurrection. Following sentencing on 27 October, he was hanged, drawn, and quartered at Gray's Inn gate on the 30th. In his last speech he professed that he had thought it his duty to hazard his 'life for the preservation of the Protestant religion and English liberties, which [he] thought invaded, and both in great danger of being lost' (Tutchin, 185).

Nelthorpe owned estates in Nottinghamshire and co. Durham as well as a house at Seacroft, Yorkshire. His wife, Susannah, who would serve as a messenger for the radicals during their exile, petitioned in July 1683 for reinstatement of her husband's real and personal property on the grounds that most of it (which included an estate at Clayworth, Nottinghamshire, worth £120 p.a.) had been inherited from her ancestors, and that her grandfather, a royalist, had been killed in the civil war and his estate sequestered. The privy council advised her to apply to the attorney-general if anything irregular had been done. Nelthorpe's grandfather had imprisoned the royalist Sir John South in the civil war and obtained his estate in co. Durham, which at that time had been worth £1500 p.a. South's grandson sought its return in the summer of 1684, but was instead given the estate in Nottinghamshire, pending an inquest. Nelthorpe was the father of five children. William III reversed his attainder in June 1689.

RICHARD L. GREAVES

Sources PRO, SP 29/415, 425–429, 436 · BL, Lansdowne MS 1152 · BL, Add. MS 38847 · BL, Harley MS 6845 · *CSP dom.*, 1683, 1–2; 1683–5 · R. L. Greaves, *Secrets of the kingdom: British radicals from the Popish Plot to the revolution of 1688–89* (1992) · J. Tutchin, *A new martyrology*, 3rd edn (1689) · Ford, Lord Grey, *The secret history of the Rye-House plot: and of Monmouth's rebellion* (1754) · W. A. Shaw, ed., *Calendar of treasury books*, 7, PRO (1916) · J. Scott, *Algernon Sidney and the Restoration crisis, 1677–1683* (1991) · J. Foster, *The register of admissions to Gray's Inn, 1521–1889, together with the register of marriages in Gray's Inn chapel, 1695–1754* (privately printed, London, 1889) · *A true account of the proceedings against John Ayloff, and Richard Nelthorp esquires* (1685) · Wilmington to Halifax, 29 Aug 1683, BL, Althorp MSS, C2 · N. Luttrell, *A brief historical relation of state affairs from September 1678 to April 1714*, 1 (1857), 362 · *The manuscripts of S. H. Le Fleming*, HMC, 25 (1890)

Archives BL, Add. MS 38847 · BL, Althorp MSS, C2 · BL, Harley MS 6845 · BL, Lansdowne MS 1152 · PRO, state papers, SP 29/415, 425–429, 436

Nemon, Oscar (1906–1985), sculptor, was born in Osijek, Slavonia, eastern Croatia, on 13 March 1906, the elder son and second of the three children of Mavro Nemon, pharmaceutical manufacturer and a member of the Jewish community in Osijek, and his wife, Eugenia Adler. As a youth he practised modelling in clay at a local brickworks and he participated in local exhibitions in 1923 and 1924. After his unsuccessful application for admission to the Akademie der Bildenden Künste in Vienna (where one of his uncles owned a bronze foundry) he spent many months there, long enough to meet Sigmund Freud of whose dog Topsy he made a portrait, on the completion of which he was allowed to make his great brooding over-life-size seated figure of Freud himself (bronze, 1930–31, corner of Fitzjohn's Avenue and Belsize Lane, London). He also modelled a portrait of Princess Bonaparte in Vienna.

In 1925 Nemon obtained a bursary from his native city to study at the Académie Royale des Beaux-Arts in Brussels, where he won the gold medal for sculpture. A one-man exhibition of his portrait heads was mounted there in the Palais des Beaux-Arts, and his sculptures were also shown by the Galerie Monteau in December 1934 and January 1939. For some years during this period he shared a house with the surrealist painter René Magritte. While in Brussels he did not lose touch with Osijek, for in 1928 he made the monument *June Victims* for the city.

To avoid the antisemitic threats of the Nazis, Nemon decided, on the advice of his lifelong friend and confidante Madame Simone Spaak, to take refuge in England just before war broke out in 1939. (With the exception of his sister, his entire family perished during the Holocaust.) That year he married Patricia, daughter of Lieutenant-Colonel Patrick Villiers-Stuart; the couple had a son and two daughters. In 1948, Nemon was naturalized. He was fortunate to be given English lessons by Sir H. Max Beerbohm, whose bust (Merton College, Oxford) he had sculpted about 1941. Having had to abandon most of a dozen years of studio work, including a 20 foot clay model, *Le pont*, of which only photographs have been preserved, he had to start again in a new country, with but a few introductions, some sympathy, and little money. He settled in Oxford and set to work, and in 1942 a small exhibition of portraits was arranged there at Regent's Park College. Through Albert Rutherston, Ruskin master of drawing in the university, he came to the notice of John Rothenstein, director of the Tate Gallery (bust, Tate collection), and of Sir Karl Parker, keeper of the department of fine art in the Ashmolean Museum (reduced half-length terracotta, Ashmolean Museum, Oxford). He was befriended by the classical scholar G. Gilbert A. Murray, not far from whose house he built Pleasant Land, his studio–residence on the north slope of Boars Hill overlooking Oxford.

For the convenience of his royal sitters Nemon was allotted a lofty studio in St James's Palace where he modelled the busts of Elizabeth II (in the hall, Christ Church, Oxford), Queen Elizabeth, the queen mother (Grocers' Hall, London), Earl Mountbatten of Burma, and Prince Philip, duke of Edinburgh. There he also created what must be considered his most successful series, the monumental effigies of Sir Winston Churchill, of which more than a dozen larger-than-life busts and compositions are in public places. Other wartime heroes who sat to him were Dwight D. Eisenhower, Earl Alexander of Tunis (Imperial War Museum, London), Viscount Montgomery of Alamein (1955; Whitehall, London, and Brussels), Lord Freyberg, Lord Portal of Hungerford, and Lord Beaverbrook (Beaverbrook Art Gallery, Fredericton, New Brunswick, Canada). Notable personalities of the post-war period whom he portrayed include Harold Macmillan (*c*.1959; Oxford Union Society) and Margaret Thatcher (1978; Conservative Central Office, London). Besides many other portraits in clay (terracotta), plaster, bronze (his chosen material for finished works), and stone, he designed many monuments and a series of brilliantly handled small reliefs in Plasticine, a medium which allowed him to show bold outlines in fine modulated wiry relief to accentuate the low relief of the figures; these were cast in plaster to give them permanence. His last major work was a monumental memorial to the Royal Canadian Air Force, which was unveiled by Queen Elizabeth in Toronto in 1984.

Throughout his career, Nemon modelled in clay directly from life, rapidly making many small studies in the tradition of the great baroque master Gianlorenzo Bernini, though unlike him he never made preliminary drawings. He animated his sitters with a sequence of droll stories and observations told with turns of phrase that betrayed his earlier fluency in Serbo-Croat, German, and French. He was thus able to evoke in them a variety of moods from which he essentialized both likeness and typical poses. Although deft in modelling, he never hurried his work. If he talked on with an accentuated drawl, amusingly, and with originality of thought and phrase, he pondered long and with penetration towards the final form of the portrait on a larger scale. He seemed to feel that the form, capable of modification by his sitter's changes in mood and age and physique, was ever elusive. He was a perfectionist, always aware of the eternal dilemma of the portraitist: how to catch in a single finite form the unceasing mobility of feature and mood. His preferred foundries were those of Morris Singer and occasionally, for smaller pieces, the Burleigh Field art foundry in High Wycombe, Buckinghamshire.

An exhibition of Nemon's work was held at the Ashmolean Museum in 1982. Shortly afterwards he was honoured by the tenth Biennale Slavonaca, which in the event became a memorial exhibition in the Galerija Likovnih Umjetnosti in the city of his birth. Oscar Nemon died on 13 April 1985 in the John Radcliffe Hospital, Oxford, having been working on models for a portrait of the princess of Wales up to the last. His studio effects and models and several cases of assorted photographs, letters, and other papers, including a manuscript autobiography, have been preserved. GERALD TAYLOR, *rev.*

Sources *Sculptures of our time* (1982) [exhibition catalogue, AM Oxf.] · V. Kusic, *Okcar Nemon, 1906–1985* (Osijek, Croatia, 1985) [exhibition catalogue, Galerija Likovnih Umjetnosti, Osijek, Nov–Dec 1985] · *Oxford Times* (19 April 1985) · *The Times* (16 April 1985) ·

personal knowledge (1990) · private information (1990) · *CGPLA Eng. & Wales* (1985)

Archives Beaverbrook Art Gallery, Fredericton, New Brunswick, Canada · Christ Church Oxf. · Conservative Central Office, London · Grocers' Hall, London · IWM · Oxford Union

Likenesses photograph, 1955, Hult. Arch. · B. Warhurst, photograph, repro. in *The Times*

Wealth at death under £40,000: administration, 7 Oct 1985, *CGPLA Eng. & Wales*

Nennius [Ninnius, Nemniuus] (*fl. c.*770–*c.*810), scholar, is commonly, but most certainly incorrectly, regarded as the author of the early ninth-century Cambro-Latin historical compilation *Historia Brittonum*. The ascription to Nennius occurs in just one of the numerous recensions of the text, the so-called 'Nennian recension', which survives in five medieval manuscripts. The earliest and primary recension (the Harleian) offers no identity for the author, while most others attribute the text, equally erroneously, to Gildas. No original copy of the Nennian recension survives, but between 1164 and 1166, at the Cistercian abbey of Sawley, Yorkshire, three different scribes collated the same (now lost) copy of the recension with the Gildasian recension which is now in Corpus Christi College, Cambridge, manuscript 139. The Nennian material was accordingly added to this manuscript as a series of interlinear and marginal annotations plus the prologue and this composite text is the archetype of all other copies of this recension. The Nennian recension seems to have been created in north Wales (possibly Anglesey) in the first half of the eleventh century, probably by a scribe called Euben (Owain) under the direction of his clerical *magister*, Beulan; and it was probably at this stage that the prologue attributing the *Historia* to Nennius was composed. This prologue describes him as *Ninnius Eluodugi discipulus* ('Ninnius disciple of Elfoddw'). If Elfoddw is the bishop of Bangor of that name who in 768 was responsible for bringing the Welsh church into conformity in the Paschal question and who died in 809, and assuming the connection with Ninnius is reliable, then Nennius would have lived at some time between about 770 and 810. Furthermore, Nennius may be identified with the Nemniuus said to have composed an alphabet based on Old English runic 'futhorc', but adapted to Old Welsh orthography, which is preserved in a manscript written in 817. This would suggest that the historical Nennius was a Welsh scholar with linguistic interests and specifically with a familiarity with things English, perhaps explaining in part why the creators of the Nennian recension believed him to have been the author of the *Historia*.

The true author of the *Historia Brittonum* remains anonymous. From internal chronological calculations it can be determined that the work was composed in 829–30, perhaps in Gwynedd or more specifically at the court of Merfyn Frych (*fl.* 825–844). However, the author himself was possibly a cleric originally from the border region of south-east Wales, possibly around the minor kingdoms of Buellt and Gwrtheyrnion. The contents of the text suggest that, as well as Old Welsh and Latin, the author knew Old English (like Nemniuus) and perhaps even some Old Irish. The statement in the erroneous 'Nennian prologue'

that Nennius had simply 'made a heap' of all that he had found has long inclined scholars to take a dim view of the work and its author; but modern analysis demonstrates that it warrants closer attention. In fact, the *Historia Brittonum* represents the earliest extant example of continuous historical writing in Wales and is an instance of early medieval synchronizing history especially common in Ireland. It seeks to trace the history of the Britons (that is, the Welsh) as descendants of the legendary eponymous Trojan immigrant 'Britto' (or the Roman consul 'Brutus') down to the late seventh century. It lacks any absolute dates, but creates a relative chronological structure from Roman imperial lists and Anglo-Saxon regnal lists and genealogies, as well as standard Christian computistical calculations. Within this structure are synchronized a variety of legendary, hagiographic, aetiological, etymological, and literary materials in an effort to create something approaching a coherent narrative. Much of the information thus incorporated certainly cannot be taken at face value and there are instances of error and miscalculation by the author; but the final product is a commendable, if problematic, attempt at historical writing based on very limited sources.

Analysis of the sources used in the *Historia Brittonum* provides a brief glimpse into the cultural and scholarly milieu of the royal court of Merfyn Frych, for which there is other evidence. Native Welsh matter includes: a battle-catalogue poem of Arthur; a life of St Garmon of Powys (identified with Germanus of Auxerre); the legend of Ambrosius Aurelianus, or Emrys Wledig; plus local place-name legends. Much of this material is unique to the *Historia* and, despite its historical unreliability, is therefore a witness to Welsh literature and pseudo-historical writing in the early ninth century. The list of Arthur's battles, for example, demonstrates an early stage in the growth of the Arthurian legend. Similarly, the otherwise unknown life of Garmon, in describing the saint's dealings with Cadell Ddyrnllug and Vortigern, preserves important aetiological traditions about the kingdoms of Powys and Gwrtheyrnion. Materials of English significance include traditions about the Kentish settlers Hengist and Horsa and their dealings with Vortigern and various Anglo-Saxon regnal lists and genealogies, as well as Bede's *Historia ecclesiastica*. The author also appears to have had access to sources of originally Irish provenance, including some lives of St Patrick (or parts thereof) plus what was probably an earlier version of the synchronizing pseudo-history *Lebor Gabála Érenn* ('Book of the conquest of Ireland'); and these should perhaps be taken alongside other indications of cultural contacts between the court of Merfyn Frych and Ireland.

Thus, despite its obvious difficulties as a primary source and the erroneous attribution to Nennius, the *Historia Brittonum* is an important work, providing unique if problematic information about the sixth and seventh centuries as well as giving an insight into early ninth-century Wales. Indeed, its significance is reflected in the number of times it was copied and reworked throughout the middle ages (including, as the *Lebor Bretnach*, or 'Book of the

Britons', a translation into Middle Irish made in the eleventh century). The main copy of the Harleian recension has inserted into its text the *Annales Cambriae* and the Harleian genealogies, both important Welsh historical sources composed in Dyfed under Owain ap Hywel Dda. Finally it should be stressed that the *Historia Brittonum* constituted an important source and model for the *Historia regum Britanniae* of Geoffrey of Monmouth (*d.* 1155).

DAVID E. THORNTON

Sources T. Mommsen, ed., *Chronica minora saec. IV. V. VI. VII.*, 3, MGH Auctores Antiquissimi, 13 (Berlin, 1898) • Nennius, *'British history' and 'The Welsh annals'*, ed. and trans. J. Morris (1980) • R. Derolez, *Runica manuscripta: the English tradition* (1954), 157–9 • D. N. Dumville, *Histories and pseudo-histories of the insular middle ages* (1990)

Neot [St Neot] (*d.* in or before **878**), monk and hermit, lived in Cornwall at some time probably in the mid-ninth century and was subsequently venerated as a saint. His name is preserved in modern St Neot, Cornwall, and St Neots, Huntingdonshire. No source contemporary with his lifetime records any detail concerning his life, and therefore every detail, including even the spelling of his name, is a matter of uncertainty. He is first mentioned in the life of King Alfred by Asser, who reports that on one occasion Alfred had gone to Cornwall to do some hunting and made a detour to the church where St 'Gueriir' lies in peace; Asser adds that 'St Niot now lies there as well' (*Life of Alfred*, chap. 74). Asser was writing in 893, and the events to which he refers took place before the battle of Edington in 878, which must accordingly be the *terminus ante quem* for the death of the saint. Unfortunately the identity of the church cannot be determined with absolute certainty: St 'Gueriir' is unknown, and is possibly an error for Guenyr or Gwinear, an Irish saint who was culted in the far west of Cornwall. It is probable, nevertheless, that the church in which the saint's remains were preserved is modern St Neot on Bodmin Moor, some 8 miles from Bodmin. This inference is confirmed by the next surviving source in which Neot is mentioned, namely the *Vita prima sancti Neoti*, composed some time in the mid-eleventh century by a British-speaking native of Cornwall. In this text (c. 5) it is related that Neot went to Cornwall to seek retreat as a hermit, and chose a place called 'Neotestoc', 'some ten mile-stones [*lapidibus*] from St Petroc's monastery', that is to say, from Bodmin. The implication is that Neot was buried in a church near or on the site of his hermitage.

The *Vita prima sancti Neoti* supplies further information concerning Neot's life, but it is difficult to know how much (if any) is historical fact, and how much is hagiographical fiction. Thus it is said (c. 1) that Neot was born 'in the territory of the eastern Britons which is now called England' (the name Niot or Neot cannot be explained in terms of Germanic philology, however, and is arguably Cornish). He became a monk of Glastonbury (c. 2), and learned monastic discipline there under Prior Æthelwold. (If this prior is taken to be identical with Bishop Æthelwold, who spent the 940s and early 950s at Glastonbury, was *decanus* or 'dean' there, and who died in 984, then the *Vita* is patently anachronistic on this point.) According to

the life, Neot next sought out his hermitage on Bodmin Moor, where he spent seven years (cc. 5, 6). He subsequently went to Rome (c. 6), on his return from where he went back to the site of his hermitage, where he built a monastery and where he was visited by King Alfred, whom he castigated for his evil behaviour before giving him his blessing (cc. 8, 9). Neot subsequently died—the day of his death, 31 July, is given, but not the year—and after seven years the church in which he was buried was rebuilt and his remains translated and rehoused in its northern side (c. 10). The hagiographer next describes the advent of Guthrum and the viking armies in England and the problems they posed for King Alfred (c. 11); and then relates the famous story of how Alfred, having taken refuge at a swineherd's cottage near Athelney, was so absorbed in his problems that he failed to notice that the bread being baked by the swineherd's wife was burning (c. 12). Neot later appeared to Alfred in a dream and helped secure the king's victory over the vikings at the battle of Edington (cc. 13–16).

The remainder of the *Vita prima sancti Neoti* pertains to the translation of St Neot's relics to Neotesberia (modern St Neots in Huntingdonshire). According to the hagiographer, Neot appeared in a dream to the sacristan of Neot's church in Cornwall and instructed him to steal the relics; having done this, the sacristan was pursued by the inhabitants of 'Neotestoc', but found refuge with a powerful English landowner named Æthelric and his wife, Æthelflæd (c. 18). Æthelric endowed a church on the River Ouse at St Neots, where the saint continues to perform miracles, and where his translation is celebrated on 7 December (cc. 21–3).

Although the hagiographer's narrative lacks any chronological frame of reference, it squares roughly with the evidence of other (post-conquest) sources. From book 2 of the later twelfth-century *Liber Eliensis* (which is based on an earlier twelfth-century treatise entitled *Libellus quorundam insignium operum beati Æthelwoldi episcopi*, itself a Latin translation of a lost tract in Old English dating from the period of Æthelwold's bishopric), it is learned that a layman named Leofric and his wife, Leofflæd, in combination with Bishop Æthelwold and Abbot Byrhtnoth of Ely, established *c.*980 a monastery at Eynesbury, Huntingdonshire, now known as St Neots (*Liber Eliensis*, bk 2. 29); and this monastery is known to have possessed the relics of St Neot no later than *c.*1014. It would seem, though the *Liber Eliensis* makes no mention of the fact, that the stolen relics of St Neot were received at Eynesbury during the approximate period between 980 and 1014, whence the foundation came in due course to be known as St Neots. The Leofric mentioned in the *Liber Eliensis* is possibly identical with a landowner who had frequent dealings with Æthelwold and who owned estates at Brandon; since no layman named Æthelric is found in contemporary records, it is likely that the author of the *Vita prima sancti Neoti* simply confused the names of the monastery's founder and his wife. In any event, the cult of St Neot soon spread to other centres: according to Orderic Vitalis, Crowland claimed to have acquired the saint's relics in the early eleventh century; and by c.1080 a relic of the saint was owned at Bec in Normandy. The *Vita prima sancti Neoti* served as a quarry for later hagiographers: for a late eleventh-century homily on the saint in Old English and for a Latin life, known as *Vita II* or the 'Bec' life, which probably dates from the twelfth century. St Neot is recorded (but sporadically) in litanies and liturgical calendars from the mid-eleventh century onwards. The universal feast of St Neot is 31 July; but he was also commemorated in south-west England and Cornwall on 20 October, and at St Neots, Huntingdonshire, on 7 December.   MICHAEL LAPIDGE

Sources D. Dumville and M. Lapidge, eds., *The annals of St Neots, with Vita prima sancti Neoti* (1985), vol. 17 of *The Anglo-Saxon Chronicle*, ed. D. Dumville and S. Keynes (1983–) · *Asser's Life of King Alfred: together with the 'Annals of Saint Neots' erroneously ascribed to Asser*, ed. W. H. Stevenson (1904) · *Alfred the Great: Asser's Life of King Alfred and other contemporary sources*, ed. and trans. S. Keynes and M. Lapidge (1983) · E. O. Blake, ed., *Liber Eliensis*, CS, 3rd ser., 92 (1962) · G. C. Gorham, *The history and antiquities of Eynesbury and St Neot's*, 2nd edn (1824) · G. H. Doble, *S. Neot, patron of St Neot, Cornwall, and St Neot's, Huntingdonshire* (1929)

Nepean, Sir Evan, **first baronet** (1752–1822), politician and colonial governor, was born on 19 July 1752 at the Green Dragon, St Stephens by Saltash, Cornwall, and baptized on 25 August, the second son of the five children of Nicholas Nepean (c.1700–1772), the innkeeper of the Green Dragon, and his second wife, Margaret Jones, the daughter of Evan Jones from Glamorgan. His father came from a landowning family, originally from Gurlyn, St Just in Penwith. The young Nepean and his two brothers were painted, dressed in yellow coats, against the background landscape of the Hamoaze, by Arthur Devis. On 28 December 1773 he joined HMS *Boyne* at Devonport, as a civilian clerk. Having been appointed purser by admiral's warrant on 31 October 1775 in the *Falcon* at Boston, he joined Admiral Molyneux Shuldham on 30 April 1776, and returned with him in the *Bristol* to Spithead in February 1777. He was discharged on 21 April 1777, and on 24 April was appointed purser and secretary to Lord Shuldham in the *Ocean* at Plymouth, where he joined on the same day. He did not continue with Shuldham on the latter's appointment as port admiral in Plymouth, but by special resolution of the Board of Admiralty was appointed purser in the *Achilles* at Deptford, on 3 February 1778. He moved to the *Hero* on 1 September 1778, and from there he exchanged in April 1780 into the *Foudroyant* under Captain John Jervis, and remained on her books until 25 June 1782. Nepean, however, had been appointed by Lord Shelburne under-secretary of state at the newly formed Home Office on 3 March 1782. This astonishing promotion suggests that his naval service had included some intelligence work as well as normal purser's duties. His qualities were acknowledged by Jervis, who noted his 'superior talent for business, unremitting diligence and integrity' (HoP, *Commons*).

On 6 June 1782 Nepean married Margaret (or Harriett) Skinner, the daughter of Captain William Skinner and the granddaughter of General William Skinner, chief engineer of Great Britain, at Greenwich church. They appear to have had six sons and two daughters, according to Nepean's memorial in the parish church at Loders.

At the Home Office, Nepean was involved in the negotiations for the peace of 1783, regulations for the government of Ireland, the conviction or pardoning of convicts, and arrangements for botanical expeditions. These last included Bligh's search for breadfruit in the *Bounty* and Archibald Menzies's voyage with Captain George Vancouver in the *Discovery* to the Pacific coast of America in 1790. He also planned, with Arthur Phillip, the first convict settlement in New South Wales, in 1788.

Nepean had responsibility for 'Money paid for Foreign Secret Service' by the home department, though the actual payments were delegated to William Pollock, the chief clerk. The agents paid in Rotterdam up to 1815 were from the Wolters and Hake families, who were first paid for naval intelligence in the Seven Years' War. Nepean appointed William Clarke and twelve assistants to watch suspect foreigners and dissident nationals in London in the 1780s and paid members of the embryo Channel Island correspondence.

This multiplicity of responsibilities and his unremitting labour affected Nepean's health, and from 1789 he was forced to spend time each year recuperating at Bath or in the country. From March 1783 he held the sinecure appointment of naval officer in Grenada, Dominica, and Barbados, and from December 1791 to May 1792 he was in the West Indies, qualifying himself for the better-paid sinecure of clerk of the peace and chief clerk of supreme court, in Jamaica, procured for him by Lord Grenville in appreciation of his achievements and to prevent him 'killing himself by his labours' (HoP, *Commons*). Grenville appointed John King as law clerk in 1791, then co-under-secretary in 1792, providing essential assistance for the extra work resulting from the Police Justices Act of June 1792. William Huskisson joined the Home Office team in January 1793 on the passing of the Alien Act. With adequate division of labour Nepean's health improved. Huskisson noted that he was admired and respected for his kindness, his 'upright and honourable conduct', and an 'indefatigable attention to business' (HoP, *Commons*). He counted William Pitt and Henry Dundas among his personal friends, while George III relied on his discretion to the extent that he dealt with him direct on day-to-day government business and for problems of the household.

In 1794 Nepean left the Home Office with Henry Dundas for the new department of war and colonies. Privately, Dundas was described as the 'mere funnel of Nepean' (HoP, *Commons*), who continued his intelligence work in conjunction with William Huskisson (who moved with them). In 1795 he became secretary of the Admiralty under Lord Spencer but remained a key figure in foreign and home secret service. In 1797 the king decreed that 'Mr Nepean alone must be employed' in the 'executive part of the nautical arrangements' for a secret plan to invade Spanish settlements in South America from the Cape of Good Hope, and 'no one be permitted to copy his letters' (*Later Correspondence of George III*, 2.537–8).

In 1796 Nepean entered parliament for Queenborough.

In 1799 he bought Loders Court, near Bridport, Dorset, and in January 1802 successfully contested that borough, but was noted for not speaking in the house. He was created a baronet on 16 July 1802 and sworn of the privy council by 1804, but his direct access to George III led to his political downfall. His arrangements with naval commanders in the 1803–4 Anglo-French conspiracy to overthrow Napoleon, although authorized by the prime minister, Addington, were concealed from Lord St Vincent and Admiral Markham and provoked naval disapproval. He succeeded William Wickham as chief secretary to the lord lieutenant of Ireland in February 1804, against his better judgement. George III's hope was that Nepean's 'habits of business and good temper will … remove some of the inconveniences which have of late too often occurred' (Later Correspondence of George III, 4.183), but Pitt later thought his lack of parliamentary skills made him unsuitable for the position. He proved to be out of his element in Dublin, working with men to whom he was unknown and accused of indecision by Lord Hardwicke, who went from initial praise to outright dislike, accusing him of undermining his lord lieutenant's position through his access to the king and his influence with Lord Sidmouth. He left Ireland in mid-May, and since Dundas, now Lord Melville, had succeeded St Vincent, he returned to the Admiralty as a junior lord in September 1804. In February 1806, disregarded by Lord Grenville, his official career ended, but his reputation was untarnished. He remained a privy councillor, continued to represent Bridport until 1812, and kept the sinecure in Jamaica until 1819.

In 1812, aged sixty, Nepean accepted the East India Company's appointment as governor of Bombay, where he remained until 1819. This posting gave him scope for his long-term botanical interests. He corresponded with Sir Joseph Banks on the subject of plants and seeds that he sent back to England, notably the best varieties of vines, teak, and peach trees from Persia, and 'every species of flowering plants' from the west coast of India. Most were consigned to Milne, a nurseryman of Fulham, and a few to Banks. On his return he was made a fellow of the Royal Society on 4 May 1820 and high sheriff of Dorset in 1822.

Nepean died at Loders on 2 October 1822 and was buried in the family vault in Loders church on 16 October. Lasting memorials to him are found in the place name Nepean in Ontario, Canada, the Nepean River, in New South Wales, and Nepean Island off Norfolk Island in the Pacific Ocean.   ELIZABETH SPARROW

Sources R. Nelson, *The home office, 1782–1801* (1969) · PRO, ADM 6, ADM 1/484 · PRO, FO 38/1 · PRO, Nepean MSS, NEP MS 89/006, pts 1–2, NEP 3 · A. Cobban, 'British secret service in France, 1784–1792', *Aspects of the French Revolution* (1968), 192–224 · A. Cobban, 'Beginnning of the Channel Islands correspondence', *Aspects of the French Revolution* (1968) · *The later correspondence of George III*, ed. A. Aspinall, 5 vols. (1962–70) · *The correspondence of King George the Third from 1760 to December 1783*, ed. J. Fortescue, 6 vols. (1927–8) · BL, Add. MS 69077, accts 3 Feb 1790 – 7 June 1791; Add. MS 38769, fols. 89–91 · R. G. Thorne, 'Nepean, Evan', HoP, *Commons, 1790–1820* · W. Dawson, 'The Banks letters: a calendar of the manuscript correspondence', 1958, NHM · M. Sydenham and J. A. Sydenham, *Nepean: a noble name for our noble city* (Nepean, Ontario, The Nepean Museum, 1990) · *Selections from the correspondence of Admiral John Markham*, ed. C. Markham, Navy RS, 28 (1904) · parish register, 25 Aug 1752, Saltash, Cornwall [baptism] · will, proved, 30 Oct 1772, Cornwall RO [Nicholas Nepean] · will, proved, 27 March 1823, PRO · *Sherborne Mercury* (1747) · *Sherborne Mercury* (1763) · *Sherborne Mercury* (1769) · *Sherborne Mercury* (1772) · GM, 1st ser., 92/2 (1822), 373 · *Annual Register* (1822) · J. Ehrman, *The younger Pitt, 3: The consuming struggle* (1996), 632, n.4 · DNB · Burke, *Peerage* (1840)

Archives BL, corresp., Add. MSS 21142, 69077 · BL, secret service notebook, Add. MS 69078 · BL OIOC, corresp., MSS, letter-book, MS Eur. D 666, MS Eur. D 1095 · BL OIOC, corresp. relating to India · Mitchell L., NSW, corresp., MSS · New York Historical Society, corresp. · NMM, corresp. and papers · PRO, corresp., C104/182 | BL, corresp. with Joseph Banks, Add. MSS 33978–33982 · BL, corresp. with J. Bentham, Add. MSS 33541, 33543 · BL, corresp. with Lord Bridport, Add. MSS 35195–35201 · BL, corresp. with third earl of Hardwicke, Add. MSS 35643–35755 · BL, letters to Lord Nelson, Add. MSS 34905–34936 · BL, Spencer MSS, letters to second Earl Spencer · BL, letters to Sir Thomas Thompson, Add. MS 46119 · BL OIOC, corresp. with Lord Buckinghamshire, MS Eur. B 325 · BL OIOC, corresp. with lords Elphinstone and Hastings, MS Eur. F 87–89 · Bucks. RLSS, corresp. with Scrope Barnard · Morgan L., letters to Sir James Murray-Pulteney · NA Scot., corresp. with Henry Dundas · NL Ire., letters to Lord Bolton · NL Scot., corresp. with Lord Minto · NMM, corresp. with Richard King · NMM, corresp. with Sir C. Middleton · PRO, letters to William Pitt, PRO 30/8 · PRO NIre., corresp. with Lord Castlereagh · U. Mich., Clements L., Sydney MSS

Likenesses attrib. Gainsborough, oils, 1788, priv. coll. · oils, c.1800 (after Gainsborough?), Admiralty, London

Wealth at death wealthy; considerable property in Dorset left in trust: will, PRO

Nepean, Nicholas (*bap.* 1757, *d.* 1823). *See under* New South Wales Corps (*act.* 1789–1810).

Nerford [Narford], **Robert** (*d.* 1225), soldier, was the son of Richard Nerford, from whom he inherited the manor of Nerford in Norfolk. His marriage to Alice, daughter of John Pouchard, brought 40 acres of land called Lingerescroft, situated in the water-meadows between Creake and Burnham, which she inherited from her grandfather Sir William Pouchard. In 1206 they founded there a small chapel for their private use, dedicating it to St Mary of the Meadows. His wife's sister married Reyner de Burgh, whose two sons, Hubert de Burgh (*d.* 1243) and Geoffrey de Burgh, became justiciar and bishop of Ely respectively.

In 1215 Nerford was granted lands in Kent and was one of the keepers of ships and sail in 1216 when he also received lands belonging to a knight in the service of the Bigod family. Hubert de Burgh's defeat of the French in a naval battle off Sandwich on 24 August 1217 (St Bartholomew's day) prompted Nerford, with his wife's agreement, to commemorate the victory (in which Nerford had also taken part) in the form of a hospital dedicated to St Bartholomew. The foundation, which centred on the original chapel in Norfolk, was endowed with a further 40 acres, a windmill, and the advowson of two churches under Nerford's patronage. The master, William Geysle, four chaplains, and an unspecified number of lay brothers were to feed and clothe thirteen poor men. Grants of alms, rents, and land were made by leading local families, and in January 1226, after Robert's death, the hospital's popularity was sufficient for the archbishop of York to issue an indulgence of twenty days for those who contributed to its support.

Royal recognition included permission in 1223 for an annual fair on the vigil and feast of St Bartholomew (later extended to the Annunciation, the translation of St Thomas, and St Nicholas) and a grant of twenty oaks from the 'Kingeswod'. With Alice's consent, the master adopted the Augustinian habit in 1227, and hospital and chapel merged to become a priory of regular canons. A papal bull (undated) confirmed the priory's possessions and ordained observance of the rule of St Augustine. Nearing death, Alice resigned patronage of the priory to the crown, whereupon Henry III elevated its status to that of an abbey. Papal permission was received in October 1231.

A dispute with William L'Enveise over lands in North Creake was eventually settled in 1220 in Nerford's favour, by which time he was receiving 20 marks a year as constable of Dover Castle. In 1224 he was given land in Ketton, Rutland, and paid for work abroad as an ambassador. He died in 1225. An additional dedication to the chapel of the hospital may have been to commemorate Nerford's eldest son, Nicholas, who was survived by his brothers, Richard and John.   A. J. MUSSON

Sources Chancery records · Curia regis rolls preserved in the Public Record Office (1922–) · A. L. Bedingfeld, ed., A cartulary of Creake Abbey, Norfolk RS, 35 (1966)

Nerudová, Vilemína Maria Franziška. See Hallé, Wilma, Lady Hallé (1838?–1911).

Nervo, Jimmy [real name James Henry Holloway] (1897–1975), acrobat and comedian, was born on 2 January 1897 at 3 Ashwin Street, Dalston, Hackney, London, the son of Captain George Holloway, circus owner, and his wife, Belvina Gee. Nervo was born into one of the great Victorian circus families and from earliest childhood was trained in the skills of wire-walking, juggling, acrobatics, and comedy. He made a solo appearance at the age of twelve at the Bedford Theatre in Camden Town, and in adolescence toured as an acrobat and wire-walker with his brothers in a variety act, The Four Holloways. On leaving that act he took the name Nervo from a livewire, trouble-prone character in a cartoon strip. From 1917 he worked for two years as an acrobatic comedian in one of Fred Karno's touring troupes.

In 1919 he met the juggler Teddy *Knox and formed a double act which made its first appearance at the Bradford Alhambra at the end of that year. Nervo and Knox devised a robust physical act, and made a reputation for themselves as exquisite slapstick comedians and burlesque dancers. They enjoyed early success in 1919 with a burlesque of Léonide Massine's Russian Ballet, currently enjoying a vogue at Oswald Stoll's London Coliseum, and followed this up with other celebrated burlesques, such as their drag Greek dance, 'The Fall of the Nymph'. One of their most celebrated routines, reputedly devised as they lurched on a transatlantic liner, consisted of their engaging in a hotly contested slow-motion wrestling bout; another, which would be much imitated, had them as ballet dancers manhandling a large balloon.

They appeared frequently in pantomime in the early twenties and also worked in revue on both sides of the Atlantic. In 1923 they travelled to New York with The Whirl of the World. This was followed by appearances with the Ziegfeld Follies and a tour of the United States on the Orpheum circuit. In 1925 they devised a show, Young Bloods of Variety, in which their penchant for anarchic practical joking was given free rein. In ways that broke the conventional divisions between acts in variety they intruded into other acts on the bill, including that of juggler Eddie Gray, to create an effect of comedic pandemonium. Gray might find his clubs greased or his neck being tickled through the curtain as he juggled, or he might be interrupted at a delicate moment in his act by a shower of cabbages from the flies. Similarly, Nervo and Knox showed little respect for the boundaries between audience and stage by taking their performances out into the auditorium: occupying boxes and throwing rice over the stalls or dressing as usherettes and directing audience members to wrong seats.

The style found its fullest expression in the *Crazy Gang, the group with whom Nervo and Knox would be associated from its first appearance in November 1931 until its final performance in May 1962. While Bud Flanagan came to embody the defining sentiment of the gang, Nervo was seen as its guiding comic intelligence. With Knox and Gray he had established the tone of the gang's comedy, ranging between drag burlesque and extravagant audience-threatening slapstick, and he remained a source of its comic innovations. He was not distinctive in physical appearance, lacking Flanagan's air of cherubic roguishness, Charlie Naughton's baby-face, or Eddie Gray's mustachioed seediness, but was marked more by a physical agility and expressive energy befitting his stage name.

With the Crazy Gang, Nervo was, as one commentator has put it, 'virtually in residence' at the London Palladium between 1932 and May 1940, when the war ended their regular activities. He married Minna Scott (b. 1904/5), a dancer and daughter of Wilhelm Schimmler, restaurant owner, on 2 October 1939, following the outbreak of war. Nervo and Knox toured extensively during the war, playing morning and afternoon shows at the Liverpool Empire and entertaining troops at home and in Italy, France, and Belgium. In 1945 they appeared in the revue For Crying out Loud at the Coliseum and in variety at the Victoria Palace.

After the war Nervo and Knox were reputedly the highest-paid entertainers on the British stage (in 1937 they were said to have taken out an insurance policy for £20,000 against having a tiff) and continued to enjoy top billing (as well as the principal dressing rooms) on Crazy Gang shows. With the Crazy Gang, re-formed in 1947, they appeared in a succession of long-running revues at the Victoria Palace and in numerous royal variety performances at the Palladium. With the demise of the gang Nervo went into a prosperous and contented retirement and was often seen sailing his boat Lady Campbell on the upper Thames. He died on 5 December 1975 at Westminster Hospital in London, survived by his wife.   DAVID GOLDIE

Sources M. Owen, The Crazy Gang: a personal reminiscence (1986) · J. Fisher, Funny way to be a hero (1973) · R. Wilmot, Kindly leave the stage! (1985) · The Times (6 Dec 1975) · R. Busby, British music hall: an *illustrated who's who from 1850 to the present day* (1976) • R. Hudd, *Roy Hudd's cavalcade of variety acts* (1997) • I. Bevan, *Top of the bill: the story of the London Palladium* (1952) • B. Green, ed., *The last empires: a music hall companion* (1986) • CGPLA Eng. & Wales (1976) • b. cert. • m. cert. • d. cert.

Likenesses photographs, 1936–59, Hult. Arch. • C. Beaton, group portrait, photograph, NPG; *see illus. in* Crazy Gang (*act.* 1931–1962)

Wealth at death £99,978: probate, 24 Feb 1976, CGPLA Eng. & Wales

Nesbit, Alfred Antony (1854–1894). *See under* Nesbit, John Collis (1818–1862).

Nesbit, Anthony (*bap.* **1778**, *d.* **1859**), schoolmaster and land surveyor, was the son of Jacob Nesbit, farmer, of Long Benton, near Newcastle upon Tyne, where he was baptized on 3 May 1778. In the preface to his *Treatise on Practical Arithmetic* (1826) Nesbit states that he was educated 'under the direction of some of the first commercial and mathematical preceptors in the kingdom', and that, having a decided predilection for teaching, he became a schoolmaster at an early age. He lived successively at Whitby, Malton, Scarborough, Bridlington, and Hull. In 1808–9 he was an under-master at Preston grammar school, as appears from a communication to the *Lady's Diary* for 1809. On the title-page of his *Treatise on Practical Land Surveying* (1810) he describes himself as 'land surveyor and teacher of the mathematics at Farnley, near Leeds'. About 1814 he set up a school at Bradford, moving in 1821 or thereabouts to Manchester, where his school in Oxford Road became well known. About 1841 he moved to London, and started a school at 38 Lower Kennington Lane, Lambeth.

Nesbit's books had a considerable reputation in their day, especially in the north of England. As well as the works mentioned above he published *A Treatise on Practical Mensuration* (1816), *A Treatise on English Parsing* (1817), *A Treatise on Practical Gauging* (1822), and *An Essay on Education* (1841). His sons, John Collis *Nesbit and Edward Planta Nesbit, took part in the compilation of the last-named work. Some of his books went through several editions, and his *Land Surveying*, revised by successive editors, retained its popularity throughout the nineteenth century, the twelfth edition appearing in 1870.

Nesbit was an excellent teacher, though somewhat severe; in the preface to his *Arithmetic* he laments that an over-fond parent too often 'prohibits the teacher from using the only means that are calculated to make a scholar of his son'. He contributed to the mathematical portions of the *Lady's Diary*, *Enquirer*, and *Leeds Correspondent*. Nesbit died at 38 Lower Kennington Lane, Lambeth, in London, on 15 March 1859, and was buried in Norwood cemetery.

R. B. PROSSER, *rev.* C. A. CREFFIELD

Sources Boase, *Mod. Eng. biog.* • *GM*, 3rd ser., 6 (1859), 547

Nesbit, Charlton (1775–1838), wood-engraver, was born on 22 August 1775 at Swalwell, co. Durham, on the south bank of the Tyne, the son of a keelman. Nothing is known of his early life before he was apprenticed to Thomas Bewick of Newcastle upon Tyne on his fourteenth birthday, 22 August 1789 [*see* Bewick, Thomas, apprentices]. A note between Bewick and his partner Ralph Beilby refers to

their prospective employee being given an evening meal followed by a demonstration of printing on the rolling press. A charge of 13*s*. 6*d*. was recorded for Nesbit's indentures on 5 June 1790 and, although terms of 7*s*. to 9*s*. a week were discussed, half-yearly payments of £5 4*s*. on 22 February and 22 August were settled on, beginning in February 1793. This delay of wages was probably accounted for by the want of a premium paid by either his parents or a sponsor. The final record of Nesbit's apprentice wage was made on 22 August 1796; he then continued in the workshop at £1 1*s*. a week until he left for London at the end of 1797. Throughout his time he would have witnessed the preparation of all the engravings for the first volume of *History of British Birds*, published in 1797. The vignette of a bird's nest and eggs which appears at the head of the preface is known to be his work, as are the majority of the head- and tailpieces in the *Poems of Goldsmith and Parnell*, printed and published by William Bulmer in 1795.

In 1796 Nesbit engraved a view of St Nicholas's churchyard, Newcastle, after a drawing by his fellow apprentice Robert Johnson (who died in tragic circumstances in October that year) which was intended to raise funds to support Johnson's parents. At 12 by 15 inches, made up from twelve pieces mounted on an iron base, this was thought to be the largest work executed on end-grain boxwood up to that time, and it won the silver palette award from the Society of Arts.

Bewick wrote of Nesbit in his *Memoir*:

> The first of my pupils who made a figure in London, after my Brother, as a Wood Engraver, was Charlton Nesbit—he went at a nick of time, when wood cuts seemed to claim something like universal attention & fortunately for that Art it was under the guidance of the ingenious John Thurston who pencilled his designs stroke by stroke on the Wood, with the utmost accuracy & it would appear that Nesbit was the first, by his mechanical excellence to do justice to these designs. (*Memoir*, 199)

The first part of Nesbit's career in London continued to 1815, during which time his work, particularly when in collaboration with Thurston, established him as one of the leading wood-engravers of the day; judged on technical skill alone, he was probably the best of Bewick's pupils. The principal books in which he was involved during this time, often in company with others, were the edition of Wallis and Scholey of Hume's *History of England* (1804–); the second volume of Way's translation of *Le Grand's fabliaux* (1800); a frontispiece, after Thurston, to Bloomfield's *Farmer's Boy* (2nd edn, 1800); an edition of Butler's *Hudibras* (1801); Cowper's *Poems* (1808); Ackermann's *Religious Emblems* (1809); Baxter's *Sacred Writings Illustrated* (1811); and Somervile's *Hobbinol, Field Sports and Bowling Green* (1813). It seems that an inheritance and the onset of ill health took him back to Swalwell, where he remained until 1830. During this semi-retirement he engraved little, but a letter from the printer William Savage of 18 March 1817, then preparing his *Practical Hints on Decorative Printing* (1822), tells Nesbit to expect a block carrying a drawing of 'Rinaldo and Armida' by Thurston 'allowed by those who have seen it to be the finest … that ever was made on Wood'. Savage reminded him that, through this, he ought to 'produce some specimen' to prove his 'continued superiority over all your competitors. … What are you doing at Swalwell? All the Engravers on Wood here have more than they can do … Do not bury yourself any longer'. Robert Branston's and John Thompson's work of the same size was to be included, and Luke Clennell, 'who had given up engraving on wood', had now been 'roused … to engrave a subject, which he believes will be superior to any other'. Although Branston turned out to be his only rival, W. J. Linton judged the engraving to have been Nesbit's finest (p. 170). The exercise was enough to 'rouse' him to return to his graver: he produced a number of excellent cuts for the Lee Priory Press of Sir Egerton Brydges which eventually appeared collected in Edward Quillinan's *Woodcuts and Verses* (1820). Some of Nesbit's best work is also to be found in the first and second series of Northcote's *Fables* (1828, 1833). This latter may well have prompted his return to London in 1830. Nesbit engraved a portrait of Bewick after Nicholson for Charnley's edition of the *Select Fables* (1820); it has often attracted notice, but was damned by Bewick as 'not worth a Pin' (letter to J. F. M. Dovaston, 18 Nov 1823), and by his daughter Jane as a 'vile caricature' (Pease Collection). Contributions to an edition of White's *Selborne* (1836) and Latrobe's *Scripture Illustrations* (1838) were completed before Nesbit's death, which took place at Queen's Elm, Brompton, London, on 11 November 1838.

Much of Nesbit's work before Thurston's death in 1822 was dominated by the draughtsman's manner; idiosyncrasies which identify his hand are hard to discern beyond a liking for bare forked tree branches on the edges of his smaller landscape vignettes and flowers and grasses showing as sparkling points of light in dark foregrounds. Thurston himself enjoined Bewick to direct the attention of his apprentices to Nesbit's figures. Compared with that of his fellow engravers in some collaborative ventures, Nesbit's work often displays a greater richness of effect. His signature, 'CNesbit' or 'CN' in a flourished script, is sometimes seen.   IAIN BAIN

Sources *A memoir of Thomas Bewick written by himself*, ed. I. Bain (1975); rev. edn (1979) • W. J. Linton, *The masters of wood-engraving* (1889) • Beilby–Bewick workshop account books, Tyne and Wear Archives Service, Newcastle upon Tyne, 1269 • R. Robinson, *Thomas Bewick: his life and times* (1887) • J. Boyd, *Bewick gleanings* (1886) • W. Chatto and J. Jackson, *A treatise on wood engraving* (1839) • *Select fables* (1820), Pease Collection, Newcastle upon Tyne [annotated by J. Bewick] • W. Savage, letter to Nesbit, 18 March 1817, priv. coll.
Archives Laing Art Gallery, Newcastle upon Tyne, collection • priv. coll., Thomas Bewick, family and business corresp. • Tyne and Wear Archives Service, Newcastle upon Tyne, collection, incl. Beilby–Bewick workshop account books, 1269

Nesbit [*married name* Bland], **Edith** (1858–1924), writer, was born on 15 August 1858 at 38 Lower Kennington Lane, London, the youngest of five children of John Collis *Nesbit (1818–1862), who owned the agricultural college where she was born, and his wife, Sarah Green, *née* Alderton (1818–1902). Her grandfather was the schoolmaster and land surveyor Anthony *Nesbit (*bap.* 1778, *d.* 1859). As well as her sister Mary (1852–1871) and brothers Alfred Antony

Edith Nesbit (1858–1924), by James Russell & Sons, pubd 1905 [right, with her daughter]

*Nesbit (1854–1894) [*see under* Nesbit, John Collis] and Harry (1855–1928), Edith (or Daisy, as she was called) had a half-sister Sarah (Saretta) from her mother's first marriage. Another brother, John, had died aged six before she was born. All their lives changed when her father, John Nesbit, died quite suddenly in March 1862. For a year or two Sarah Nesbit continued to run the college, but Mary was ill with tuberculosis, and needed a warmer climate. The family moved, first to the seaside at Brighton, and then to France, and the younger children were sent to boarding-schools. Edith alternated between hated schools or equally hated relatives, and idyllic holidays reunited with her brothers. These extreme contrasts made her childhood peculiarly memorable: 'When I was a little child I used to pray fervently, tearfully, that when I should be grown up I might never forget what I thought and felt and suffered then', she wrote, in 'My school-days', and she never did.

In 1871 Mary, who had been briefly engaged to the poet Philip Bourke Marston, died, and Sarah settled her family at Halstead on the North Downs, Edith's favourite home. Here she wrote her first poems, and sent them off for publication. Four years later the family moved back to London, and in 1877 Edith met Hubert *Bland (1855–1914), who was working as a bank clerk with her fiancé, a young man called Stuart Smith. She fell in love with Bland at once, and by the end of 1879 she had left home, called herself Mrs Bland, and was expecting his child. The couple were married on 22 April 1880 in a register office, and their son Paul was born two months later. Bland continued to spend half of each week with his widowed mother and her paid companion, Maggie Doran, who also had a son by him, though Edith did not realize this until later that summer when Bland fell ill with smallpox. With characteristic optimism, she forgave him, befriended Maggie, and set about supporting the household by writing sentimental poems and short stories, and by hand-painting greetings cards. A daughter, Mary Iris, was born to the Blands in 1881.

Bland was a disciple of Thomas Davidson, founder of the Fellowship of the New Life, and Henry Hyndman of the Social Democratic Federation, and in 1884 Edith followed Bland into the Fabian Society. Here she became an 'advanced woman', abandoning Victorian corsets in favour of flowing Liberty gowns, cutting her hair short, and smoking cigarettes; she told her friend Ada, 'I really surprise myself sometimes' (Briggs, 68). Among her new friends she now counted Eleanor Marx, Olive Schreiner, Clementina Black, Charlotte Wilson, and Annie Besant.

With Hubert (often out of work) Edith wrote two novels, *The Prophet's Mantle* (1885) and *Something Wrong* (1886), about the early days of the socialist movement, under the pen-name Fabian Bland, and their son, born in 1885, was named Fabian. In February of the following year Edith gave birth to a stillborn child, and her friend Alice Hoatson came to look after her. But Alice was also pregnant by Bland. She joined the Blands as their housekeeper in a *ménage à trois*, and a daughter, Rosamund, was born in November 1886. Edith passed the baby off as her own (as again with Alice's son by Hubert, John). Life in such circumstances was not without its tensions, but Hubert's infidelities licensed Edith to pursue her own interests, and she fell in love, first with Bernard Shaw, and later with a series of young admirers. The poet Richard Le Gallienne was charmed by her 'tall lithe boyish-girl figure, admirably set off by her plain "Socialist" gown, with her short hair, and her large vivid eyes' (Briggs, 154); she could indeed be charming, flirtatious, and even imperious.

In 1896 Edith began to write up her memories of her schooldays for the *Girls' Own Paper* (October 1896 – September 1897); doing so stimulated her to write the earliest adventures of the Bastables, and their quest to restore their fallen family fortunes, as told in *The Story of the Treasure-Seekers* (1899). With the creation of Oswald Bastable, she knew that she had discovered a highly original way of writing about and for children, and from this point in her career she never looked back. She now invented the children's adventure story, more or less single-handed, adding to it fantasy, magic, time-travel, and a delightful vein of subversive comedy. The next ten years or so saw the publication of all her major work, and in the mean time she was also composing poems, plays, romantic novels, ghost stories, and tales of country life.

In 1899 the Bland family moved to Well Hall, a handsome eighteenth-century house at Eltham, where Edith wrote the rest of her children's books, though her progress was interrupted by the unexpected death of Fabian in the autumn of 1900, from what ought to have been a simple operation; she never entirely recovered from his loss. She was working on the further adventures of the Bastables, *The Wouldbegoods* (1901), and at the same time she had also begun writing a serial for the prestigious *Strand Magazine* about some children who find a sand-fairy (or 'psammead') at the bottom of a sand-pit in Kent (*Five Children and It*, 1902). The same children then hatch a phoenix egg on their nursery fire in *The Phoenix and the Carpet* (1904) and, after travelling the world on a magic carpet, they discover time-travel in *The Story of the Amulet* (1906). All these were first serialized in the *Strand Magazine* (where they were delightfully illustrated by H. R. Millar) and were then published in book form. In 1906 Nesbit finished her most popular (and sentimental) book, *The Railway Children*, the story of how Bobby, Peter, and Phyllis recover their lost father, who has been mistakenly arrested for spying (with an echo of the Dreyfus affair).

Nesbit also wrote many amusing fairy-stories, collected in *The Book of Dragons* (1899), *Nine Unlikely Tales* (1901), *The Magic World* (1912), and elsewhere. *The Enchanted Castle* came out in 1907, and was followed by two interlinked books about going back into English history—*The House of Arden* (1908), and *Harding's Luck* (1909), the story of a slum child. Her last major achievement was *The Magic City* (1910), a utopian fantasy in which Philip enters the miniature city he has made and becomes its saviour, with Lucy's help. The book begins with a miniature city built on a table top from a variety of everyday objects (upturned bowls, nursery bricks, chess pieces, cigarette papers, among other things), and in 1912 Nesbit was invited to build such a city for the Children's Welfare exhibition at Olympia, London. Out of that came *Wings and the Child* (1913), her reflections on the role of imagination in children's play—a book that admits that, at some level, she felt that she was 'only pretending to be grown-up' (*Wings and the Child*, 6). At heart she was still a child.

Despite their emotional ups and downs, Edith's political views were strongly coloured by Hubert's, and her books reflect both his socialism (her sense of what it might mean to be poor or a servant), and also his impatience with the suffragettes (mocked in the bossy Pretenderette in *The Magic City*): 'Votes for Women! Votes for children! Votes for dogs!', he would sneer. Hubert suffered from heart trouble and died unexpectedly on 14 April 1914. Despite their bohemian marriage, Edith was desolated, and lost much of her former energy. She struggled on at Well Hall during the early years of the First World War, taking in paying guests and undergoing a serious illness of her own (caused by a duodenal ulcer). In the summer of 1916 she met Thomas Terry Tucker, known as 'the Skipper' (1856/7–1935), a widowed marine engineer who asked her to marry him. Her older children disapproved—Tucker spoke with a broad cockney accent and never wore a collar—but she had been 'shivering in a sort of Arctic night', as she explained to her brother Harry (Briggs, 373), and accepted with delight. They were married on 20 February 1917 at St Peter's Roman Catholic Church, Woolwich, London (Edith had always been attracted to Catholicism, though she never adopted it completely). She particularly appreciated Tucker's single-minded devotion to her.

By now it was clear that Well Hall could no longer be kept up, so she and Tucker bought two former army huts at Jesson St Mary's on Romney Marsh, close to Dymchurch. They were immediately christened the Long Boat and the Jolly Boat, and are still there, though the handsome Well Hall has gone. Edith, a heavy smoker all her life, now fell ill. The 'Duchess of Dymchurch' (as she had sometimes been called) lay in her four-poster bed, looking across the marsh towards the 'little low hills of Kent' which she had always loved. She died on 4 May 1924 and was buried beneath a spreading elm in the quiet churchyard of St Mary's in the Marsh.

Nesbit's stories for the *Strand Magazine* were enormously and deservedly popular. They were much admired by other writers, including Rudyard Kipling and H. G. Wells, both of whom in turn influenced her. She was the first modern writer for children, and her reputation as a key contributor to the 'golden age' of children's literature (with James Barrie, Frances Hodgson Burnett, Kenneth Grahame, and Beatrix Potter) remains high. A very successful film of *The Railway Children* was released in 1970, and that book, *Five Children and It*, and *The Phoenix and the Carpet* have all been effectively adapted for television. Although Nesbit's humour is sometimes too sophisticated and literary for children of the early twenty-first century, her books have continued to delight new readers and to inspire imitations.   JULIA BRIGGS

Sources E. Nesbit, 'My school-days', *Girls' Own Paper*, 18/875–924 (Oct 1896–Sept 1897); repr. as E. Nesbit, *Long ago when I was young* (1966), repr. (1974) • E. Nesbit, *Wings and the child* (1913) • J. Briggs, *A woman of passion: the life of E. Nesbit, 1858–1924* (1987) • D. L. Moore, *E. Nesbit: a biography* (1933); rev. (1967) • N. Streatfeild, *Magic and the magician: E. Nesbit and her children's books* (1958) • A. Bell, *E. Nesbit* (1960) • N. MacKenzie and J. MacKenzie, *The first Fabians* (1977) • B. Ruck, *A story-teller tells the truth* (1935) • E. Jepson, *Memories of an Edwardian and Neo-Georgian* (1937) • d. cert.

Archives Greenwich Local History Library, corresp. and literary papers | BL, corresp. with Macmillans, Add. MS 54964 • BL, corresp. with George Bernard Shaw, Add. MS 50511 • BL, corresp. with Society of Authors, Add. MS 56762 • BLPES, letters to Fabian Society • Greenwich Local History Library, letters to C. H. Grinling • LUL, letters to Sir Francis Galton • NYPL, Berg collection, corresp. with Morris Colles and J. W. Pinker • Ransom HRC, corresp. with John Lane • University of Illinois, Urbana-Champaign, letters to H. G. Wells

Likenesses J. Russell & Sons, photograph, pubd 1905, NPG [see illus.] • R. Bryden, woodcut, repro. in Briggs, *Woman of passion*

Wealth at death £660: probate, 1924, *CGPLA Eng. & Wales*

Nesbit, John Collis (1818–1862), chemist and educationist, was born on 12 July 1818 at Bradford, Yorkshire, the son of Anthony *Nesbit (*bap.* 1778, *d.* 1859), teacher of mathematics and land surveyor. He was educated at home and assisted his father in the school which the latter had established in Bradford about 1814, moving to Manchester about 1821. Though at first he followed his father's choice of subject, he soon became attracted to chemistry, and once it became clear that this interest was paramount he was placed under the guidance of John Dalton. He also attended lectures on electricity given by William Sturgeon. His practical skill enabled him to construct scientific instruments for sale, using the proceeds to buy books

on chemistry. He sold an electric battery he had made to the Manchester Mechanics' Institute for 30 guineas.

In Manchester, Nesbit began his career as a public lecturer, acquiring great facility as a speaker upon scientific subjects. He took a leading part in the management of his father's school upon its removal to London in or about 1841. In the same year there appeared his father's *An Essay on Education*, which he and his brother Edward Planta Nesbit had helped to prepare. The *Essay* clearly shows that the Nesbits were inspired by Pestalozzian methods of instruction. Their school in London was one of the first to introduce the teaching of natural science into an ordinary school course, the instruction being given partly by Nesbit himself and partly by the botanist Charles Johnson (1791–1880) and the geologists John Morris (1810–1886) and George Fleming Richardson (1796–1848). Particular attention was paid to chemistry, especially as applied to agriculture, and each pupil received practical instruction in the laboratory. Eventually the school became the Chemical and Agricultural College, at 38 Lower Kennington Lane, with Nesbit as its principal.

As the use of superphosphates and other artificial manures became general, Nesbit began to undertake commercial analyses for farmers and manufacturers. New laboratories were built, and he developed a large practice as a consulting and analytical chemist. His other main interest was geology, and he was elected a fellow of the Geological Society and of the Chemical Society in 1845. Reasoning from certain geological indications, he was led to suspect the existence of phosphatic deposits in the Ardennes, and in the summer of 1855 he discovered several important beds of coprolites in that region.

On 22 January 1851 Nesbit married a widow, Sarah Green, *née* Alderton (1818–1902). Their daughter Edith *Nesbit (1858–1924) wrote many popular children's stories, some of which have become classics. A son, Alfred Antony Nesbit [see below], became, like his father, an analytical chemist.

Nesbit lectured widely to farmers' clubs, and in 1856 published four lectures chosen with the aim of familiarizing the general public with his subject. One dealt with a topic to which he devoted much time and energy in his last years. 'I know', he wrote, 'that there are parties in London who are making several thousands a year by adulterating manures' (*On Agricultural Chemistry and the Nature and Properties of Peruvian Guano*, 1856, 50). His lecture described methods of detecting this practice.

The book also included a previously published pamphlet on Peruvian guano, which, because of its rich content of phosphorus and nitrogen, became the most highly valued of natural fertilizers. Deposits, mainly the droppings of vast flocks of a Peruvian cormorant, accumulated on islands just off Peru to a depth of over 50 metres, and their export accounted for over a half of that country's income. In a later work, Nesbit classified and gave detailed chemical analyses of all the imported guanos with which he was acquainted (*The History and Properties of the Different Varieties of Guano*, 1859). In addition to other pamphlets on manures he also wrote articles for scientific and agricultural periodicals. He was a prominent member of the Central Farmers' Club.

Nesbit, died at the house of a friend, Elm Bank House, Barnes, on 30 March 1862. His son **Alfred Antony Nesbit** (1854–1894) was born in London, on 25 August 1854. An analytical chemist, he for some years had a laboratory at 38 Gracechurch Street, London. In 1883 he patented an improved ink for postmarking postage stamps, having earlier pointed out the ease with which the postmark could be removed. His few published experiments are of no significance. He died on 19 March 1894.

R. B. PROSSER, *rev.* E. L. SCOTT

Sources *ILN* (19 April 1862), 394 · A. C. Ramsay, *Quarterly Journal of the Geological Society*, 19 (1863), xxxi · *Quarterly Journal of the Chemical Society*, 15 (1862), 495–6 · personal knowledge (1894) · m. cert. · d. cert. · b. cert. [Alfred Nesbit]
Likenesses wood-engraving, NPG; repro. in *ILN* (18 April 1862)
Wealth at death under £9000: probate, 25 April 1862, *CGPLA Eng. & Wales*

Nesbitt family (*per. c.*1717–*c.*1900), merchants and bankers, came to prominence with **Albert Nesbitt** (*d.* 1753), a son of Andrew Nesbitt (*d.* 1692) and his wife, Anne Lindsay. Presumably born in Ireland, he was introduced about 1717, most likely by a kinsman, to the firm of Gould, Baltic merchants in London. In 1729 he married Elizabeth (*d.* 1781), sister of his business partners, Nathaniel Gould (*d.* 1738) and his brother John (*d.* 1740); they had a daughter, Rachel.

Albert Nesbitt and the Gould brothers became the sole partners in the firm after the deaths of the latters' uncle, Sir Nathaniel *Gould, in 1728 and their father, John Gould, in 1736. The firm was based in Coleman Street until about 1752 when it moved to 8 Bishopsgate Within. It was the chief house in the city dealing with Irish business: its partners acted principally as bill agents between London and Ireland, and had many distinguished Irish clients, including members of the Conolly family. Albert, a man of sound judgement, directed the firm's business away from the Baltic to include the import of wines from Bordeaux and elsewhere to London and Ireland. He took as apprentices three of his brother Thomas's younger sons, Arnold [*see below*], Albert (*d.* 1776), and Alexander (*bap.* 1730, *d.* 1772).

Albert Nesbitt's commercial success enabled him to move from the city to a suburban villa at Putney about 1738 and to buy estates in Sussex, at Ringmer in 1741, at Whyly in East Hoathly in 1750, and at Winchelsea in 1751. The wealth engendered by the firm, and his family and business connections, through the Goulds, with the Pelhams allowed him to enter parliament, sitting on the Treasury interest for Huntingdon in 1741 and for Mitchell in Cornwall in 1747. He died on 12 January 1753 in his coach near London on the Bath Road and was buried on 19 January at Putney.

The business was carried on by Albert's nephew **Arnold Nesbitt** (*bap.* 1721, *d.* 1779), a younger son of his brother Thomas and Thomas's second wife, Jane Cosby (*d.* 1771), an Irish heiress. Arnold was baptized in Kilmore Cathedral near Cavan in Ireland on 27 March 1721, was apprenticed to his uncle by 1744, and was his partner by 1753. The wealth of the firm and the continued patronage of the Pelhams allowed him, like his uncle, to represent the Treasury interest in parliament and to buy more properties in Sussex, Icklesham Manor in 1760 and at Winchelsea between 1753 and 1767. He briefly succeeded his uncle at Mitchell in 1753, and sat for Winchelsea from 1754 to 1761 when the duke of Newcastle requested that he stand down. An ambitious and enterprising man, he rejected Newcastle's control, successfully challenged the Treasury interest there in law suits called the Winchelsea causes, and after 1769 controlled one of the borough's two seats. He sat again in 1770 but, having established his influence there beyond doubt, chose instead to sit from 1774 for Cricklade in Wiltshire, the borough and hundred of which he had bought during his exclusion from Winchelsea.

Arnold Nesbitt's domestic base in London was the counting house in Bishopsgate, the lease of which had been devised to him by his uncle, until about 1772 when he moved to a newly built house in Grafton Street. In the same year the firm moved to 18 Aldermanbury where it remained until 1802. In 1750 Arnold Nesbitt was prosperous enough to lease a suburban villa at Keston, Kent, where he lived until about 1760, when he moved to another at West Wickham, also in Kent. He is known to have had liaisons with four women: Nancy Parsons; Martha Yeates, by whom he had two sons, Colebrooke Nesbitt and Arnold Nesbitt (1756–1813); Ann Dryland, later Stevenson (1735–1783), by whom he had a son John (*bap.* 1761); and another by whom he had a daughter, Elizabeth or Frances Moore. In 1758 Nesbitt married Susanna, daughter of Ralph Thrale and sister of his close friend Henry Thrale, the Southwark brewer. He consequently became part of the social circle formed around Samuel Johnson from 1765 at Thrale's houses in Streatham and Southwark which included Sir Joshua Reynolds, David Garrick, and Oliver Goldsmith.

Under Arnold Nesbitt's leadership, banking and remitting to Ireland, where clients included Thomas Conolly (1738–1803), remained the chief business of the firm. To it he added the import of sugar and rum from estates in Grenada and the West Indies, and, from 1756, the supply under government contract of provisions and money for troops in the American colonies. Sir George Colebrooke, bt (1729–1809), was his chief associate in those enterprises, and in the founding of a cambric manufactory in Winchelsea in 1761 and of a bank in Dublin in 1764.

Both Colebrooke and Nesbitt suffered a severe reverse in the financial crisis of June 1772. Heavy borrowing after 1772 and the burden of his government contracts may have hastened Nesbitt's death. He was unwell in March 1779 and, according to Samuel Johnson, did not fight his illness (*Letters of Samuel Johnson*, ed. B. Redford, 1992–1994 3.371). He died in Grafton Street on 7 or 12 April 1779 and was buried in Icklesham church on 18 April. Examination of his affairs showed that he was insolvent.

Unresolved chancery proceedings and debts to the Treasury allowed the business to continue uninterrupted under the direction of Arnold Nesbitt's nephew **John** [i] **Nesbitt** (1745/6–1817), whom he had taken as a partner after the death of his brother Albert in 1776. A younger son of Arnold's eldest brother Cosby Nesbitt and Cosby's wife, Anne Enery, John Nesbitt was presumably born in Ireland and was apprenticed to his uncle as a youth. When in the city he lived in the Aldermanbury counting house and, possibly from 1776, outside London in the villa at Keston either inherited or bought from the younger Albert Nesbitt.

John Nesbitt's cousin and apprentice, the younger Arnold Nesbitt, also lived in the counting house. In 1784 they were joined by Edward Stewart and until 1802 the firm was usually called Nesbitt and Stewart. The younger Arnold later left, and was replaced by John Nesbitt's nephew, John [ii] Nesbitt (d. 1853). The type of business remained similar, although in 1797 the firm ceased to act for Thomas Conolly after his repeated failure to take up bills presented to him.

The elder John Nesbitt moved to a house in Grafton Street about 1787. He, too, was a member of parliament and sat for Winchelsea (1780–90), Gatton (1790–96), and Bodmin (1796–1802). He was a friend and political ally of Charles James Fox who proposed him for Brooks's in 1783. A connoisseur of wines and paintings, he was from 1796 to 1802 the owner of the version of Gainsborough's *Blue Boy* later in the Huntington Library. His career was overshadowed by his uncle's insolvency, and, because of it, he was forced into bankruptcy in 1802 and his connection with the firm ended. The Keston house was sold and the lease of that in Grafton Street given up.

At the request of the prince regent, with whom he had enjoyed a friendship, John [i] Nesbitt was appointed a commissioner of hackney carriages in 1814. In 1815 he secured the discharge by statute of Arnold Nesbitt's estate from his debt to the Treasury and afterwards reduced the remaining debt to £26,114 by negotiation. He died in Bolton Street, where he had lived from about 1807, on 15 March 1817 and was buried in the parish of St George, Hanover Square, on 22 March. From 1803 his nephew John [ii] Nesbitt was based at 16 Tokenhouse Yard and the firm, staffed by younger members of the Nesbitt family, continued as general provision merchants in the city and Southwark until the early twentieth century.

JANET H. STEVENSON

Sources J. H. Stevenson, 'Arnold Nesbitt and the borough of Winchelsea', *Sussex Archaeological Collections*, 129 (1991), 183–93 · E. Cruickshanks, 'Nesbitt, Albert', HoP, *Commons, 1715–54* · E. Cruickshanks, 'Nesbitt, Arnold', HoP, *Commons, 1715–54* · L. B. Namier, 'Nesbitt, Arnold', HoP, *Commons, 1754–90* · R. G. Thorne, 'Nesbitt, John', HoP, *Commons, 1790–1820* · registered copies of wills, PRO, PROB 11/799, fols. 185–8; PROB 11/1052, fols. 187–192v; PROB 11/1593, fol. 349r–v · chancery proceedings, PRO, C11/215/21; C12/579/8; C12/585/6; C12/1989/33 · NA Ire., Lucas-Clements muniments, BR/CAV/18 · transcript of registers of Kilmore Cathedral, NL Ire., MS 4487 · TCD, Conolly MSS 3974–3984 · E. Sussex RO, Sayer MSS · parish register, St George's, Hanover Square, 22 March

1817 [burial] · register of marriages, 1641–1754, Mercers' Hall, London · W. Musgrave, *Obituary prior to 1800*, ed. G. J. Armytage, 4, Harleian Society, 47 (1900), 277 · A. C. Hare, *Parish register of Putney in the county of Surrey*, 2 (1915), 315 · *GM*, 1st ser., 87/1 (1817), 375 · *London Chronicle* (13–15 April 1779) · monument, Icklesham church · *GM*, 1st ser., 28 (1758), 611 · rate books, London borough of Wandsworth local history collections, Battersea, London · rate books, City Westm. AC · land tax assessments, GL, MS 11316 · land tax assessments, CKS, Q/RPL 200 · *The Jenkinson papers, 1760–1766*, ed. N. S. Jucker (1949), 331, n. 1

Archives BL, letters to duke of Newcastle, etc., Add. MSS 32863–32988, *passim* [Arnold Nesbitt]

Likenesses J. Reynolds, portrait, 1759–61 (Arnold Nesbitt) · T. Gainsborough, oils, 1766–79 (Arnold Nesbitt), repro. in Stevenson, 'Arnold Nesbitt and the borough of Winchelsea', p. 194; priv. coll.

Wealth at death £20,500; extensive estates and legacies; plus silver and gold plate; Albert Nesbitt: will, PRO, PROB 11/799, fols. 185–8 · insolvent; Arnold Nesbitt: will, PRO, PROB 11/1052, fols. 187–192v · bankrupt from 1802; bequeathed chattels only; John [i] Nesbitt: will proved, 21 June 1817, bankruptcy records, PRO, B3/3690 and B4/26; will, PRO, PROB 11/1593, fol. 349r–v

Nesbitt, Albert (d. 1753). *See under* Nesbitt family (*per. c.1717–c.1900*).

Nesbitt, Arnold (*bap.* 1721, *d.* 1779). *See under* Nesbitt family (*per. c.1717–c.1900*).

Nesbitt, Cathleen (1888–1982), actress, was born on 24 November 1888 at 1 Liscard Grove, Liscard, Cheshire, the eldest of the five children of Thomas Nesbitt and his wife, Mary Catherine Parry. Thomas Nesbitt was a young naval lieutenant who subsequently became the captain of a tramp steamer, the *County Antrim*, owned by the County Shipping Line, of Belfast. At that point, when Cathleen was seven or eight years old, the Nesbitts moved to Belfast.

Cathleen was educated at Victoria College, Belfast. The family's financial circumstances were very narrow and her schooldays were scarred by privation. Later this situation eased somewhat and the family moved once again, this time to London. About this time Cathleen spent a year at a school in Lisieux, France. The move to London had been prompted partly by her mother's desire to live there and partly by Cathleen's growing interest in the theatre. She had been bewitched by it ever since she had been taken, at the age of eight, to see Sarah Bernhardt in *La dame aux camélias* at the Belfast theatre. Settled in London in 1907 she became a pupil of the actress Rosina Filippi, who in addition to playing regularly in the London theatres also gave lessons in acting to young aspiring professional performers. Cathleen Nesbitt proved an apt recruit; almost immediately after completing her training she made her first professional London appearance at the Royalty Theatre in 1910 in a play now long forgotten, *The Master of Mrs. Chilvers*. When this closed she at once secured a place in W. B. Yeats's Irish Players, in Dublin, and with them went to New York, causing something of a sensation there for her playing of Molly Byrne (the part originally played five years before by Sara Allgood) in J. M. Synge's *The Well of the Saints*.

Back in London in 1912 Cathleen Nesbitt was cast as Perdita in Granville Barker's famous and innovative production of *The Winter's Tale* at the Savoy Theatre; she had originally been cast as Mopsa—one of the two comic servants—but was promoted during the course of rehearsals to the much more important part. Several contemporary critics refer not only to the sense of freshness and innocence that she conveyed in this role but also to her extreme physical beauty, though she herself, in her autobiography, complains constantly of having been 'too fat' and describes her shape at that time as being roughly equivalent to that of a pillar box. Be that as it may it was her playing of Perdita that first attracted the attention of the poet Rupert *Brooke, who was so smitten by her that he went back to see the play twice more, in spite of the fact that he had an irrational and rooted prejudice against women on the stage. 'I'd better state before going further', he said to her in a letter of 1913, 'that as a matter of fact I loathe women acting in public' (Jones, 372); and in a later letter he added 'I hope you'll be giving up this beastly stage business soon' (ibid., 394). But in spite of the wild infatuation that she (along with others, both men and women) felt for Brooke she was not about to give it up 'soon'—or indeed ever: she played her last part in 1980, at the age of ninety-two.

There can be little doubt that Cathleen Nesbitt was deeply and genuinely in love with Brooke, as—in his way—he was with her. During 1912 and 1913 they saw a great deal of each other. But her early years of hazard and penury had given her a gritty personality and a staunchly realistic outlook on life: she was not easily fooled. In spite of the perfervid tone of the sonnets and poems that Brooke addressed to her ('Cathleen! Loveliest creature! Nymph divine! / Unhoped for, unapproachable, yet mine!') she measured him shrewdly. Long after his death she recalled:

> Like all artists who have a neurotic strain he would always have needed another woman … I felt if I were married to him I would probably suffer a great deal, because I thought there was no chance of his ever being a one woman man. (Jones, 367)

So she continued with her career, play after play. And, from 1922 onward, film after film—thirty-seven of them between 1922 and 1975—and dozens of television plays.

In 1920 Cathleen Nesbitt was invited by Charles Morgan, at that time president of the Oxford University Dramatic Society, to play Cleopatra in the Shakespeare *Antony and Cleopatra*. Cecil Ramage, president of the Oxford Union, was Antony. 'On the last night there was a farewell party and we danced together continually' (Nesbitt, 146). Sentiments from the play seem to have slopped over into off-stage life ('Let's have one other gaudy night'); at the end of the dance he proposed marriage to her and was accepted. They married—unhappily as it turned out—in 1921. They had two children: Mark, born in 1922, and Jennifer, born in 1925.

Cathleen Nesbitt was equally at home in plays of fluff and frivolity and in sterner plays of greater consequence. Among the latter may be noted her roles in G. K. Chesterton's *The Man who was Thursday* (New York, 1916), *The Merchant of Venice* (London, 1919), John Webster's *The Duchess of Malfi* (London, 1920), and Thomas Otway's *Venice Preserv'd* (London, 1921). She also appeared in more modern plays—as Jennifer Dubedat in Bernard Shaw's *The Doctor's Dilemma* (London, 1923), in Flecker's *Hassan* (London, 1923), and as Jessica in Granville Barker's *The Madras House* (London, 1926). In later life she continued to appear on stage, with roles in two of T. S. Eliot's plays: *The Cocktail Party* (Edinburgh, 1949) and *The Family Reunion* (Guildford, 1964), in which she took the part of Amy. She also played in Enid Bagnold's *The Chalk Garden* (on tour in the USA in 1957) and in a version of Henry James's *The Aspern Papers* (Chichester, 1978). Among those confections of the lighter sort perhaps the most notable is her playing—aged over ninety but looking about sixty—of Mrs Higgins in *My Fair Lady*, on tour in America in 1980. Equally sought after in England and in the United States she crossed the Atlantic many times as offers of parts reached her sometimes in one country, sometimes in the other.

It would be false to describe Cathleen Nesbitt as a great actress: she was never that. However, she was a steady, sturdy professional: meticulous, reliable, and infinitely capable. Her professional career was astonishingly continuous: in a profession notorious for its hazards and sudden vicissitudes she was never out of work for more than a month or so in a career spanning seventy years. In 1975 she published her autobiography, *A Little Love and Good Company* (the title is from George Farquhar's *The Beaux' Stratagem*)—a pleasant, chatty, sentimental, quite undistinguished piece of work containing a plethora of conventional commendatory adjectives of a very clichéd kind and the names of many well-known actors and actresses of the twentieth century in both England and America. She was appointed CBE in 1977, and died in London on 2 August 1982.

ERIC SALMON

Sources C. Nesbitt, *A little love and good company* (1975) · N. Jones, *Rupert Brooke* (1999) · I. Herbert, ed., *Who's who in the theatre*, 17th edn, 2 vols. (1981) · *The Times* (4 Aug 1982) · E. Salmon, *Granville Barker: a secret life* (1983) · personal knowledge (2004) · *CGPLA Eng. & Wales* (1982) · b. cert.

Archives Col. U., corresp. with Anita Loos | FILM BFI NFTVA, performance footage | SOUND BL NSA, documentary recordings · BL NSA, performance recordings

Likenesses Sasha, group portrait, photograph, 1930, Hult. Arch. · C. Beaton, pencil drawing, NPG · photographs, repro. in Nesbitt, *A little love* · portraits, Trinity College of Music, London, Mander and Mitchenson theatre collection

Wealth at death £110,678: probate, 25 Nov 1982, *CGPLA Eng. & Wales*

Nesbitt, Colebrooke (1755/6–1798), army officer, was one of two natural sons of Arnold *Nesbitt (*bap.* 1721, *d.* 1779) [*see under* Nesbitt family], a prominent merchant and banker in the City of London and MP for Winchelsea in Sussex and Cricklade in Wiltshire, and Martha Yeates (*fl.* 1756–1798). From 7 June 1773, when he became an ensign in the 32nd regiment of foot, in which he was gazetted lieutenant on 25 October 1775, his career followed the usual advancement by purchase. He became a captain in the 82nd on 5 January 1778 and a major in the 19th on 3

May 1782. He transferred to the 52nd on 9 May 1789 and was gazetted lieutenant-colonel on 21 June 1789, brevet colonel on 26 February 1795, local major-general on 3 May 1796, an aide-de-camp to George III, also in 1796, and major-general on 8 January 1798.

Nesbitt is presumed to have served in Ireland with the 32nd, in North America with the 82nd, and in the West Indies with the 19th. With the 52nd he took part in the Third Anglo-Mysore War of 1790 against Tipu Sultan. On 21 December 1791 he led the successful assault on the hill fort of Savanadrug without loss to the British. That victory helped prepare the way for Lord Cornwallis's final and successful attack on Tipu's stronghold at Seringapatam, which began on 6 February 1792. During the preliminary stages Nesbitt's insistence on adhering to clearly erroneous orders for an assault on the mosque redoubt, although achieving the establishment of the right-hand division before Tipu's camp outside Seringapatam, resulted in heavy British casualties.

On 1 January 1795 Nesbitt was appointed inspector-general of all the foreign corps raised for the crown after the outbreak of war with France in 1793. His brief was to muster all the corps already serving or about to be engaged to serve as part of the British army on the continent, and his correspondence and reports show that he carried out his tasks energetically and efficiently. He was based in Hanover, chiefly at Stade on the River Elbe, throughout 1795 and in the autumn of 1796. Early in 1796 he established a London office in John Street, near Berkeley Square, though he was sometimes at Southampton to oversee the embarkation and disembarkation of troops.

On 26 or 27 May 1797 the duke of York sent Nesbitt, as 'an officer whose discretion and prudence could be thoroughly depended upon' (*Later Correspondence of George III*, 2.582), to take command at Gravesend during the naval mutiny at the Nore. The same qualities may have occasioned his appointment in January 1798 as commander of an expeditionary force to Haiti.

The moiety of an estate in Grenada which Arnold Nesbitt devised to him in tail male in 1779 may have been his chief source of income. He had married Elizabeth Sneyd (1766/7–1835), the daughter of his father's friend Jeremy Sneyd, at St George's, Hanover Square, on 7 November 1789. They had one son, Douglas, and two daughters, Mary Elizabeth Emma and Caroline. From 1798 the Nesbitts had a leasehold house in St James's Place, Piccadilly. They also had a house at Crookham, and often stayed with Jeremy Sneyd at Testwood House.

Nesbitt's only known liaison was with Christiana Skellhorn, who, as Christiana Nesbitt, was living with their daughter Carolina at Brunswick in Germany in 1798. His closest friends were Major-General Sir James Craig, Colonel John Moore (both of whom received bequests in his will), Major-General George Don, and Robert Ballard Long, for whom he negotiated the succession to the lieutenant-colonelcy of Ferdinand Hompesch's mounted riflemen in February 1798. Accompanied by Long, Nesbitt embarked at Portsmouth on 6 February 1798 as commander of an expeditionary force to Haiti, but while becalmed at Cowes

fell ill with 'a violent bowel complaint' (PRO, PRO 30/8/150, fol. 153), possibly caused by an intestinal obstruction. After putting in at Funchal, Madeira, for treatment, he eventually returned to London, where he died, at his home in St James's Place, on 21 July 1798. He was buried in the south vault of St James's, Piccadilly, on 25 July.

JANET H. STEVENSON

Sources PRO, WO 1/173, 247–54, 373–5, 409–10, 413–14, 433–4; WO 1/898, 31–2, 35–8, 71–6, 91–4, 99–102, 111–12; WO 1/899, 107–10, 115–18, 143–6, 191–6, 207–10, 223–8, 235, 239, 243–51, 255, 259–60, 263, 333, 349, 373, 397, 409, 421, 425, 433, 437, 445, 463, 471, 479, 483; WO 1/900, 5, 9–12, 21–5, 99–104, 119, 131–2, 185, 193–5; WO 4/292, 114–15, 242–3, 271; WO 4/367, 40–41, 87–8, 91–2, 101, 108, 193, 227–30, 247–8, 371, 443, 490, 493; WO 6/25, 136–9 · BL, Don MSS, Add MSS 46703, fol. 144r–v, 46704, fols. 116–280, 46705, fols. 1–230v, 49710, fols. 200–46 · BL, Windham MSS, Add MSS 37862, fols. 289–293v, 37874, fol. 195, 37875, fol. 64, 37876, fol. 84 · PRO, Chatham MSS, PRO 30/8/150, fols. 147–54 · M. L. Ferrar, *Officers of the Green Howards: Alexandra, princess of Wales's own Yorkshire regiment, formerly the 19th foot, 1688 to 1920* (1920), 67 · W. S. Moorsom, ed., *Historical record of the fifty-second regiment (Oxfordshire light infantry), from the year 1755 to the year 1858* (1860), 42–51 · *The later correspondence of George III*, ed. A. Aspinall, 5 vols. (1962–70), vol. 2, pp. 582–3 · Fortescue, *Brit. army*, vol. 3 · *Army List* (1774–98) · *The register book of marriages belonging to the parish of St George, Hanover Square*, 2, Harleian Society, register section, 11 (1886), 32; 3, Harleian Society, register section, 22 (1896), 128 · *GM*, 1st ser., 68 (1798), 811 · parish registers, St James's, Piccadilly, vols. 22–3, City Westm. AC · rate books, Pall Mall ward, City Westm. AC · register of wills, PRO, PROB 11/1316, fols. 235v–242 · register of wills, PROB 11/1052 [Arnold Nesbitt's will], fols. 187–192v

Likenesses silhouette, Green Howards regimental museum, Richmond, North Yorkshire

Wealth at death half an estate in Grenada; several bequests amounting to over £500, together with the remainder of his unspecified estate: will, PRO, PROB 11/1316, fols. 235v–242

Nesbitt, Cosby Lewis (1806–1853), army officer, was born in London on 1 April 1806, the eldest child (of four) and only son of Major (later Lieutenant-General) Alexander Nesbitt (1778–1849), 3rd dragoon guards, and his wife, Jane Gregory (d. 1858). On 27 March 1824 Nesbitt was commissioned second lieutenant in the 1st battalion, 60th regiment (King's Royal Rifle Corps), and became lieutenant (by purchase) on 2 June 1825. He served in Portugal in 1826 and 1827 as part of a force under General Sir Edward Blakeney, sent to assist the Portuguese against a threatened Spanish invasion. On 18 December 1828 he was promoted captain. From 1830 to 1841 Nesbitt served at Malta, Gibraltar, and the Ionian Islands and then in Jamaica, where he assumed temporary command of the 2nd battalion upon the death from yellow fever of the commanding officer. On 10 August 1841 he was promoted major in the 1st battalion, then he returned to England to join it.

Nesbitt was afterwards stationed in Ireland (1843–5), Canada (1845–7), England (1847–8), and then again in Ireland (1848–51), where he remained until his departure with his battalion for the eastern Cape Colony to fight in the Cape Frontier War. On 26 July 1844 he had been promoted second lieutenant-colonel of the 1st battalion and shortly after was appointed to command the 2nd battalion, after a dispute over the succession had been resolved in Nesbitt's favour by the commander-in-chief, the duke of Wellington. Nesbitt and his battalion embarked, on 5

July 1851, at Queenstown, Ireland, bound for the Cape, arriving at Simonstown on 20 September and disembarking at East London in the eastern Cape on 3 October. Almost immediately the 60th rifles were drawn into operations against the Ngqika (Gaika) Chief Maqomo in the Kroomie Mountains; these operations lasted the remainder of the month. Until the end of February 1852 Nesbitt's battalion was engaged in skirmishes, cattle raids, and crop destruction. Between March and September the same year further operations against the Ngqika chieftains were carried out by Nesbitt's battalion in the Waterkloof and Amatola Mountains. Nesbitt was mentioned in the dispatch of the governor and commander-in-chief, Sir Harry Smith, at the conclusion of the operations.

With the restoration of peace on the frontier in March 1853, the 2nd battalion worked on road construction in the province of British Kaffraria (annexed in December 1847). Nesbitt himself took an active part in the planning of roads in conjunction with the Royal Engineers. In September he was appointed commandant of British Kaffraria, superseding Major-General Yorke. During a tour of inspection of forts and outposts, on 1 October 1853, while attempting to ford the flooded Keiskamma River, Nesbitt was swept from his horse and drowned. He was buried in the military cemetery at King William's Town on 10 October. He was unmarried. Nesbitt was an able and popular officer, esteemed by both officers and men. In 1857 his brother officers placed a memorial tablet in Holy Trinity Anglican Church in Geneva, Switzerland, where his parents had retired. Nesbitt's gravestone in the military cemetery in King William's Town (closed in 1865) was defaced by vandals and was finally removed by the South African war graves board, c.1968, when the cemetery was landscaped. His name, however, appears on a granite obelisk commemorating those persons interred there. A watercolour portrait (now at the Royal Green Jackets Museum, Winchester), probably painted when he was a subaltern, depicts a young man with an oval face, dark curly hair, and prominent eyes.

F. G. RICHINGS

Sources F. G. Richings, 'A tragedy at Hobb's Drift, British Kaffraria, October 1853', *Journal of the Society for Army Historical Research*, 76 (1998), 21–33 · L. Butler, *The annals of the king's royal rifle corps*, 2–3 (1923–6) · *Hart's Army List* (1853) · *Records of 2nd battalion, king's royal rifle corps* (1895) · W. R. King, *Campaigning in Kaffirland* (1853) · 1829 officers' records, PRO, WO 25/769 no. 62 · register of marriages, baptisms, and burials, English Episcopal Church, Geneva

Likenesses watercolour, c.1825, Royal Green Jackets Museum, Winchester, Hampshire

Wealth at death £2844 6s.: PRO, death duty registers, IR 26/279, p. 76

Nesbitt, John (1661–1727), Independent minister, was born in Northumberland on 6 October 1661. He possibly entered Richard Frankland's academy, Natland, either in June 1674 or January 1675, but was certainly sent to Edinburgh University to be educated for the ministry; a John Nisbett graduated at Edinburgh University on 24 March 1680. He had to leave Edinburgh some time in 1680 or 1681 for being the 'chief contributor of burning the pope in effigie' in the presence of the duke of York (Ridpath, 43, 44). He was subsequently usher at a school in Bishop's

Hall, Bethnall Green, Middlesex, kept by the ejected vicar of West Ham, Essex, Thomas Walton. He then worked as tutor to the family of Matthew Richardson in Mile End, but soon after had to leave the country for political reasons. It is not clear whether he was fleeing to the Netherlands or was *en route* to study at Utrecht, but in 1683 he was arrested in Essex 'on suspicion of complicity with the Rye House Plot' (Gordon, *Freedom after Ejection*, 316). He was imprisoned in the Marshalsea for four months, and on his release, adopting the name of White, he went to the Netherlands. There he became an accomplished classicist, well read in the church fathers and in history, and was an occasional preacher to the English congregation at Utrecht in 1688.

After the revolution of 1688 Nesbitt returned to London and became a member, on 16 December 1690, of Stepney Independent Church. In the Common Fund survey, compiled between 1690 and 1692, he is recorded as a minister 'not fixed to particular Congregations … Mr Nesbet … Att Neere Rope-makers Alley, in Little moor fileds, an evening Lords day lecture at Mr Williams, now wth Dr Chauncey' (Gordon, *Freedom after Ejection*, 3). On 10 December 1689 at St James's, Duke Place, London, he married Elizabeth, the only daughter of Isaac *Chauncy (1632–1712), Independent minister at the meeting in Bury Street, London, and his wife, Jane; they had a son, Robert *Nesbitt (d. 1761), who became a physician. In 1691 he succeeded George Cokayne as pastor of the Independent church in Hare Court, Aldersgate Street, London, where he remained for over thirty years. He was an exceedingly popular preacher, famous for his use of similes; he retained his evangelical Calvinism, yet resisted the prevalent tendency to a merely didactic style. In Addison's *Spectator* (317, 4 March 1712) he is caricatured as Mr. Nisby in extracts from an imaginary diary of one of his hearers.

Nesbitt was appointed a manager of the Common Fund on 9 May 1692 and took part in the survey of dissenting congregations and ministers undertaken between 1690 and 1692. After the failure of the Happy Union between the Presbyterians and Congregationalists, Nesbitt appears in the Congregational Fund minutes in 1696 as correspondent for a large number of counties, especially the northern counties, and took a large part in managing the fund's affairs. He helped to prepare during 1717–18 the dissenting statistics known as the Evans list, supplying the lists for Northumberland, Cumberland, and Westmorland and obtaining the Staffordshire list. His figures for Cumberland and Westmorland vary so much from those returned by Thomas Dixon of Whitehaven that the Evans list manuscript (in DWL) explicitly distinguishes between the two sets of returned figures. In 1697 Nesbitt was elected to a merchants' lectureship at Pinners' Hall, in succession to Nathaniel Mather, and soon afterwards was joined by Matthew Clarke (1664–1726). Lecturing on the same day they drew crowded audiences for nearly thirty years. Together with Matthew Mead, George Griffith, Stephen Lobb, and Richard Taylor, Nesbitt published a *Declaration Against Antinomian Errors* in 1699. However he could be persuaded to publish only six of his sermons, three of which were funeral sermons for fellow ministers: Thomas Gouge, John Russell, and Richard Taylor; the other three were sermons addressed to young people.

Nesbitt was a subscriber in the Salters' Hall conference of 1719, and though not prominent in public affairs did much to secure the cohesion and unity of his own denomination. Matthew Clarke resigned as his assistant in 1705, and was succeeded by James Naylor (d. 1708), John Conder, and John Hurrion. In 1723 Nesbitt was seized with paralysis, which disabled him from work. He died on 22 October 1727 aged sixty-six and was buried at Bunhill Fields. Hurrion, who succeeded him as minister, preached his funeral sermon, which was subsequently published as *The Christian's Hidden Life*. Nesbitt was survived by his wife.

JONATHAN H. WESTAWAY

Sources A. Gordon, ed., *Freedom after ejection: a review (1690–1692) of presbyterian and congregational nonconformity in England and Wales* (1917), 3, 23, 36, 80, 121, 161, 168, 186, 316 · DNB · W. Wilson, *The history and antiquities of the dissenting churches and meeting houses in London, Westminster and Southwark*, 4 vols. (1808–14), vol. 1, pp. 283–6; vol. 3, pp. 282–6 · A. Gordon's annotated *DNB*, vol. 40, 1894, JRL · E. Calamy, *An historical account of my own life, with some reflections on the times I have lived in, 1671–1731*, ed. J. T. Rutt, 2nd edn, 1 (1830), 144–5 · F. Nicholson and E. Axon, *The older nonconformity in Kendal* (1915), 541 · J. Dunton, *The life and errors of John Dunton*, new edn, 2 vols. (New York, 1969), 681 · J. Evans, 'List of dissenting congregations and ministers in England and Wales, 1715–1729', DWL, MS 38.4 · *Calamy rev.*, 509 · G. Ridpath, *An answer to the Scotch Presbyterian eloquence* (1789), 43, 44 · *The Rev. Oliver Heywood … his autobiography, diaries, anecdote and event books*, ed. J. H. Turner, 2 (1883), 9 · J. Hurrion, *The Christian's hidden life* (1728) · *Calendar of the correspondence of Philip Doddridge*, ed. G. F. Nuttall, HMC, JP 26 (1979), 15 · will, PRO, PROB 11/617, sig. 239 · IGI

Likenesses J. Faber senior, mezzotint, 1709, BM · G. White, mezzotint (after J. Wollaston), BM, NPG

Nesbitt, John (1745/6–1817). *See under* Nesbitt family (*per. c.*1717–*c.*1900).

Nesbitt [*née* Davis], **Mary** (1742/3–1825), courtesan and adventuress, was born Mary Davis, of unknown parentage, but was alleged to have been born 'in a wheelbarrow' in Covent Garden ('History of the Tête-à-tête'); she was also called Polly Davis. She was a strikingly beautiful artist's model, first sitting to Sir Joshua Reynolds in 1764. Her career as a courtesan may have been directed by the King of Hell, Simon Luttrell, later first earl of Carhampton, who was possibly her seducer (*Autobiography, Letters and Literary Remains of Mrs Piozzi*, ed. A. Hayward, 2, 1861, 23). This connection, allied to Mary's fiery character, may perhaps have earned her the sobriquet Hellfire Davis. Luttrell introduced her to Alexander Nesbitt (*bap.* 1730, *d.* 1772), youngest of the three sons of Thomas Nesbitt (*d.* 1750), who were in partnership as merchants and bankers in the City of London. Luttrell encouraged Mary's marriage to Nesbitt, on 25 February 1768, at St Martin-in-the-Fields, and was both a witness to it and a trustee of Mary's marriage settlement, by which Nesbitt settled on her for life his new house and its estate at Upper Norwood in Surrey. The couple also lived in London at 10 Buckingham Street.

According to a 'Tête-à-tête' pen portrait of 1775, by 1769 Mary's contemptuous treatment of Nesbitt and her continued connections with the *demi-monde* had caused his

Mary Nesbitt (1742/3–1825), by Sir Joshua Reynolds, 1781

insanity. He certainly suffered a mental collapse and was confined in private lodgings near Blackfriars; he died in 1772. The story of Mary and Nesbitt was told, and Mary's behaviour vilified, by Junius in his letter of 27 November 1771. By 1771 Mary had become the mistress of the Hon. Augustus John *Hervey (1724–1779), naval officer, second son of John *Hervey, Lord Hervey of Ickworth (1696–1743), and Mary Lepell [*see* Hervey, Mary]; Hervey became third earl of Bristol in 1775, when his alliance with Mary was pilloried in the aforementioned 'Tête-à-tête' portrait, and Mary was again castigated for abusing her husband. Mary and Hervey lived together, apparently faithfully, at Norwood House, at 6 St James's Square, and at Ickworth House, Suffolk, but were prevented from marrying when the earl's divorce petition was dismissed, in 1779, because of his collusion in his wife Elizabeth's 1769 action to have their marriage declared void. Referred to by the earl, in his will, as his 'dear valuable and best friend', Mary was both an executor and legatee of the will, the trusts of which were performed only after a dispute with the earl's brother the Hon. William Hervey, Mary's fellow executor, was resolved in her favour in chancery in 1783. She received the manor and advowson of Evedon, other land in Lincolnshire, and £5000 from the sale of about 186 acres in Suffolk. She also received a share of the stock and furniture at 6 St James's Square and at Ickworth, valued at £7378 12s. 11d.

Mary Nesbitt's financial and professional acumen was thereafter devoted to enlarging the Norwood estate and to establishing herself on the fringes of political life. She exercised influence and patronage in her salon at Norwood, which was frequented by men such as George Rose, secretary to the Treasury, and young aspirants to political office. Her travels and activities in diplomatic circles on the continent during the French Revolution suggest that she may have been employed as a government agent in Pitt's covert attempts to restore the French monarchy. Celebrating her achievements on 25 September 1797, the *Morning Chronicle* acknowledged that 'this celebrated woman', despite 'the miscellany of her life', had 'acquired an elevation … which she has preserved with dignity', using 'her influence with the great in favour of the unfortunate' (*Early Married Life of … Lady Stanley*, 432–3). In the early nineteenth century straitened financial circumstances occasioned the letting of Norwood House and Mary's frequent residence abroad, in 1821 at Montreuil-sur-Mer, Pas-de-Calais, and in 1822 in Switzerland. She is presumed to have died, aged eighty-two, in Paris, where she was buried on 4 November 1825, and not, as the earl of Bristol had requested in his will, with him at Ickworth.

JANET H. STEVENSON

Sources J. H. Stevenson, 'The Nesbitts of Norwood House: a footnote to Junius', *Surrey Archaeological Collections*, 82 (1994), 169–79 · muniments of the Convent of Our Lady of Fidelity, Central Hill, London · 'History of the tête-à-tête annexed, or, Memoirs of the Hon. Capt. H—y and Mrs. N—t', *Town and Country Magazine*, 7 (1775), 9–12 · chancery proceedings, PRO, C 12/433/30, C 12/937/21 · chancery entry books of decrees and orders, PRO, C 33/460, fols. 155–156v · will of Augustus Hervey, earl of Bristol, PRO, PROB 11/1059, fols. 98–100 · will, PRO, PROB 11/1709, fol. 24 · *The letters of Junius*, ed. J. Cannon (1978), 315–19 · *The miscellaneous works of Hugh Boyd, the author of the 'Letters of Junius'*, ed. L. D. Campbell, 2 vols. (1800), vol. 1, pp. 17–18, 143–9 · *Journals of the Hon. William Hervey, in North America and Europe, from 1755–1814*, ed. S. H. A. Hervey, Suffolk Green Books, no. 14 (1906) · *The early married life of Maria Josepha, Lady Stanley*, ed. J. H. Adeane (1899) · J. Wardroper, *Kings, lords and wicked libellers: satire and protest, 1760–1837* (1973), 73 · *Croydon inclosure award*, ed. J. C. Anderson (1889) · court books of Croydon and Waddon manors, LPL, no. 1960 (1774–95), ED/1920 (1809–18) · Lambeth inclosure award, LPL, TO57 · plan of the Norwood estate, 1830, LPL, TR30 · Evedon land tax assessments, Lincs. Arch., KQS 9 · PRO, RG 33/60
Likenesses J. Reynolds, oils, 1764 (as Circe), Smith College Museum of Art, Northampton, Massachusetts; repro. in A. R. Warwick, *The phoenix suburb: a South London social history* (1972), pl. 7 · O. Humphrey, miniature, 1770, repro. in G. C. Williamson, *The life and works of Ozias Humphrey* (1918), 176 · J. Reynolds, oils, 1781, Wallace Collection [*see illus.*]

Nesbitt, Robert (*d.* 1761), physician, was the son of John *Nesbitt (1661–1727), Independent minister, and his wife, Elizabeth. He was born in London, and on 1 September 1718 entered as a medical student at Leiden, where he attended the lectures of Boerhaave and the elder Albinus, and graduated MD on 25 April 1721. After his return to England he practised in London as a physician. He became licentiate of the Royal College of Physicians on 25 June 1726, was created MD at Cambridge on 15 June 1728, and was admitted a fellow on 30 September 1729, having been a candidate at the same date in the preceding year. He filled the office of censor in 1733, 1738, 1742, 1745, and 1748, became elect on 22 August 1748, and was conciliarius in 1750, 1754, and 1758. He was appointed Lumleian lecturer for five years on 23 March 1741. Nesbitt had been elected FRS as early as 15 April 1725, and two years later contributed to the *Transactions* a paper 'On a

subterraneous fire observed in the county of Kent' (*PTRS*, 7, 1727, 195). He married Deborah Wilkes, whose sister Martha was married to James Douglas, the anatomist.

Nesbitt published, besides his Leiden thesis, *Human osteogeny explained in two lectures read in the anatomical theatre of the surgeons of London, anno 1731, illustrated with figures drawn from life* (1736). A German translation by Johann Ernst Greding appeared at Altenburg in 1753. In these lectures he first mentions the formation of the bone in membrane, as well as cartilage, and gives an accurate description of the stages of the development of the human skeleton. Nesbitt died in London on 27 May 1761.

G. LE G. NORGATE, *rev.* CLAIRE L. NUTT

Sources Munk, *Roll* · R. W. Innes Smith, *English-speaking students of medicine at the University of Leyden* (1932) · J. Dobson, 'Pioneers of osteogeny', *Journal of Bone and Joint Surgery*, 30B (1948), 551–5 · *GM*, 1st ser., 31 (1761), 284 · *The record of the Royal Society of London*, 4th edn (1940) · Venn, *Alum. Cant.*
Likenesses J. Nesbitt, oils, RCS Eng.

Nesfield, William Andrews (*bap.* 1794, *d.* 1881), watercolour painter and landscape gardener, was born in Chester-le-Street, co. Durham, and baptized there on 16 June 1794, the elder son of the Revd William Nesfield, later rector of Brancepeth, and his first wife, Elizabeth, eldest daughter of John and Elizabeth Andrews of Shotley Hall, Northumberland. This estate passed into chancery rather than going to Mrs Nesfield on her father's death in 1792. After her death in 1808, the Revd William Nesfield married Marianne, aunt of Anthony Salvin, the future architect, business partner, and brother-in-law of her stepson. William Andrews Nesfield spent two unhappy years at a preparatory school in Winchester, followed by a still less happy year at Winchester College. Two years at the grammar school in Bury St Edmunds were more congenial, and hero worship of a cousin, in whose home he lodged, turned his ambitions towards the army rather than the church, for which he had been intended. He spent two terms at Trinity College, Cambridge, however, before becoming a cadet at the Royal Military Academy, Woolwich, in 1809. There he was taught drawing by Thomas Paul Sandby, son of the watercolourist Paul Sandby. In 1812, through the good offices of his mother's sister, the marchioness of Winchester, he obtained a commission in the 95th regiment. In the autumn of 1813 he sailed for service in the Peninsular War, where he was at St Jean de Luz and the attack on Bayonne. Family connections then won him the appointment as extra aide-de-camp to Sir Gordon Drummond, commanding in Upper Canada during the 1812 war with the United States. In 1814 he was present during the American attack on Fort Erie, which cost 500 British casualties. After two years travelling with Drummond in Canada, and a further year at Sandhurst and on half pay, he resigned in 1818 to become a watercolourist.

Nesfield took lessons from (Anthony Vandyke) Copley Fielding, was elected associate and member of the Society of Painters in Water Colours (now the Royal Watercolour Society) in February and June 1823, and was a regular exhibitor until his resignation in 1852. He was famous for his cascades, seeking subjects in Piedmont and the Swiss Alps, but more often in Wales, Killarney, Staffa, Scotland, and the north of England. Among the colleagues with whom he toured were David Cox, William Evans of Eton, John Varley, Clarkson Stanfield, Edwin Landseer, William Havell, and J. D. Harding. After visiting Switzerland in 1820 he settled in London, at first in lodgings with Salvin, and later, after their respective marriages to sisters and a brief period in Bath, in one of a pair of villas built by Salvin for the two couples at Fortis Green, Muswell Hill, Middlesex. From 1842 until his death, the Nesfields lived in London at 3 York Terrace, Regent's Park. His wife, whom he married on 13 July 1833, was Emma Mills (d. 1874), a connection of his stepmother and a granddaughter of William Markham, archbishop of York. There were two sons, William Eden *Nesfield and Markham (1841–1874), both of whom assisted their father in his business. From about the time of his marriage a new career as a landscape gardener, often in collaboration with Salvin, was occupying more of his time, and eventually it took over entirely. However, as he told Sir William Hooker at Kew, he regarded landscape gardening as 'the Art of painting with Nature's materials' (Nesfield to Hooker, 2 Feb 1846, Letterbook 24, no. 433, RBG Kew). Cascades played their part, although he was best-known for his parterres, but according to Shirley Evans, his biographer, 'his accomplishments were many and various' (S. Evans, 'William Andrews Nesfield: an introduction to his life and work', in Ridgway, Nesfield, 7). For two decades he was the most sought-after designer in the country, working at Arundel Castle, Sussex; Trentham Park, Staffordshire; Alnwick Castle, Northumberland; Clumber Park, Nottinghamshire; Crewe Hall, Cheshire; Woolverstone Hall, Suffolk; and many other seats, as well as advising on improvements to London parks, particularly St James's, and Kew Gardens. In all he was consulted at over 200 sites. He was a forceful character with strong ideas as to the formality of parterres, and how the eye should be led to a view of the horizon unrestricted by clumps or belts of trees. Avenues should have a point, and to this end he approved 'the judicial use of the axe' (ibid., 8). Something of this no-nonsense assurance, perhaps a product of his military training, can be seen also in his painting style. Despite Ruskin's praise in Modern Painters (1.344) for his 'extraordinary feeling both for the colour and the spirituality of a great waterfall', his watercolours are merely thoroughly well done, rather than essays in poetic imagination. Examples of Nesfield's works are in the British Museum and the Victoria and Albert Museum, London, and several of his drawings were engraved for J. P. Lawson's Scotland Delineated (2 vols., 1854). He died at his home, 3 York Terrace, Regent's Park, London, on 2 March 1881, leaving under £5000. A portrait of him by John Moore, and a drawing dated 1840 by James Duffield Harding, are owned by his descendants.

THOMAS SECCOMBE, rev. HUON MALLALIEU

Sources J. L. Roget, A history of the 'Old Water-Colour' Society, 1 (1891), 432, 522–3; 2 (1891), 82–4 · C. Ridgway, ed., William Andrews Nesfield, Victorian landscape architect [York 1994] (1996) · S. Evans, Country Life (8 April 1993) · S. Evans, Country Life (12 May 1994) · C. L. Ridgway, Country Life (27 July 1989) · CGPLA Eng. & Wales (1881) · IGI
Archives Castle Howard archives, North Yorkshire, MSS
Likenesses J. D. Harding, drawing, 1840, priv. coll. · J. Moore, portrait, priv. coll.
Wealth at death under £5000: probate, 14 March 1881, CGPLA Eng. & Wales

Nesfield, William Eden (1835–1888), architect, was born on 2 April 1835 in Bath, the eldest child of William Andrews *Nesfield (bap. 1794, d. 1881), watercolour painter and landscape architect, and his wife, Emma Mills (d. 1874), daughter of the Revd Henry Foster Mills and granddaughter of William Markham, archbishop of York. He attended Eton College (1844–9), where his father was drawing master, and showed an early interest in architecture. He took drawing lessons from J. K. Colling and J. D. Harding and was articled first to William Burn from 1851 to 1853, and then to his uncle by marriage Anthony Salvin from 1853 to 1856. Periodic trips to the continent, particularly between 1857 and 1861, resulted in his acclaimed Specimens of Mediaeval Architecture (1862). His only other publication, 'The late Mr. Anthony Salvin', appeared in The Builder in 1881. The Royal Institute of British Architects holds several of Nesfield's early sketchbooks which reveal the influence of A. W. N. Pugin and Viollet-le-Duc, whose work he traced and sketched. During his apprenticeships and the first decade of practice Nesfield shared a close friendship and three-year partnership (1866–9) with R. Norman Shaw.

Nesfield played a key role in the development of the Old English and Queen Anne revivals; indeed his designs were integral to the course of British architecture in the 1860s and 1870s, and reflect a wide range of influences: Gothic and classical, vernacular and medieval, Dutch and Japanese. Certain projects anticipated major stylistic shifts: the wing at Combe Abbey, Warwickshire (1861–5), and Cloverley Hall, Shropshire (1865–70), foreshadowed the Old English style. Others initiated new styles: the lodge at Regent's Park (1864) introduced the Old English style to London, and two years later the lodge at the Royal Botanic Gardens, Kew, helped conceive the Queen Anne revival. Kinmel Hall, Abergele, north Wales (1868, 1871–4) was a landmark project within the Queen Anne revival and found renewed fame thirty years later with the neo-Georgians. In particular, Nesfield's lodges illustrate his genius for amalgamating disparate elements into a harmonious design, the most elegant of which is the lodge at Kinmel Park (1868).

Nesfield worked throughout England and Wales and occasionally in Scotland. Country house commissions include Sproughton Manor, Suffolk (1863–4), Lea Wood, West Derby, Liverpool (1870–76), Plas Dinam, Montgomeryshire (1872–4), and Loughton Hall, Essex (1876–8). Country house additions and alterations include Farnham Park, Buckinghamshire (1865), Bodrhyddan, Flintshire (1872–3), and Gloddaith Hall, Denbighshire (1875–6). He designed numerous estate buildings at Shipley Hall, Derbyshire (1860–62), Crewe Hall, Cheshire (1860–66),

William Eden Nesfield (1835–1888), by Sir William Blake Richmond, c.1859

Croxteth Park, West Derby, Liverpool (1861–70), Broadlands, Hampshire (1870–78), and Kiplin Hall, North Riding of Yorkshire (1875–81). Other significant commissions include Romsey Elementary Boys' School (later a library), Hampshire (1870–72), Gibson, Tuke and Gibson Bank (later Barclays), Saffron Walden, Essex (1873–4), and additions to Newport grammar school, Essex (1875–8). Although he altered or rebuilt a dozen or more churches, he never designed a church from start to finish.

While his father's landscapes echoed the architecture of the site, Nesfield's architecture was informed by the landscape. Furthermore, Nesfield patterned his unorthodox business practices after his father: he developed a parity between himself and his patrons, was inordinately selective in his commissions and clients, favoured freedom of design over prestigious commissions, and eschewed self-promotion. He repeatedly collaborated with artists, particularly the painter Albert Moore and the sculptor James Forsyth. He renounced his associate membership of the Royal Institute of British Architects, yet actively participated in the Foreign Architectural Books Society.

A heavy drinker, something of a womanizer, and the occasional sparring partner of J. M. Whistler, Nesfield retired—still a bachelor—in his mid-forties. At fifty, on 3 September 1885, he married Mary Annetta Backwell (1845–1922), a divorcée and the daughter of the architect John Sebastian *Gwilt [see under Gwilt, Joseph]. One week short of his fifty-third birthday, on 25 March 1888, he died at his home, 45 Buckingham Road, Brighton, of scirrhoma of the liver.   NINA JAMES-FOWLER

Sources N. James-Fowler, 'Landscape into architecture: William Andrews Nesfield and William Eden Nesfield', PhD diss., U. Lond., 1997 · R. P. Spiers, 'William Eden Nesfield's drawings', *RIBA Journal*, 2 (1894–5), 605–11 · J. Forsyth, *Architectural Association Notes*, 16 (1901), 109–11 · J. Turner, 'William Eden Nesfield (1835–1888): some houses', *Canterbury School Review*, 1 (1990), 16–26 · A. Saint, *Richard Norman Shaw* (1976), 44–53 · CGPLA Eng. & Wales (1888) · b. cert. · m. cert. · d. cert.

Archives LPL, Incorporated Church Building Society records · RIBA BAL, sketchbook · V&A, department of prints and drawings | Canadian Centre for Architecture, Montreal, drawings, with Richard Norman Shaw, for remodelling of Kinmel Park

Likenesses J. E. E. Brandon, pencil drawing, 1858, NPG · W. B. Richmond, pencil and chalk drawing, c.1859, NPG [see illus.]

Wealth at death £13,065 18s. 11d.: probate, 4 Aug 1888, CGPLA Eng. & Wales

Nesham, Christopher John Williams (1771–1853), naval officer, was the son of Christopher Nesham, a captain in the 63rd regiment, and his wife, Mary Williams, the sister of William Peere Williams-Freeman, admiral of the fleet, and a relative of Lord North. He entered the navy in January 1782 on board the *Juno*, with Captain James Montagu, and was present at the action off Cuddalore on 20 June 1783. On his return to England in 1785 he was for some time in the guardship *Edgar* at Portsmouth, commanded by Captain Adam Duncan, and in the frigate *Druid*. In March 1788 he was sent to a college in France, and was still there at the outbreak of the revolution. He was at Vernon, in Normandy, in October 1789, when a crowd fell on a corn merchant named Planter who was accused of wishing to starve the town. Nesham, with two others, rescued Planter. One of the first acts of the municipality on the restoration of order was to confer citizenship on Nesham (17 November). In January 1790 he was summoned to Paris, where he was presented by the assembly with a uniform sword of the national guard and a civic crown was placed on his head.

The following June Nesham was appointed to the *Salisbury*, bearing the flag of Vice-Admiral Milbanke, who had as his flag captain Edward Pellew. On 17 November 1790 he was promoted lieutenant, and during the next two years he served in the channel under the immediate command of Keats and Robert Moorsom. In 1793 he was appointed to the *Adamant* (50 guns), in which he served on the West Indian, Newfoundland, and home stations. In 1797 he was her first lieutenant in the North Sea, when, during the mutiny and through the summer, she carried the flag of Vice-Admiral Richard Onslow. She afterwards took part in the battle of Camperdown, and on 2 January 1798 Nesham was promoted commander of the sloop *Suffisante*. In 1802 he married his cousin Margaret Anne (d. 1808), the youngest daughter of Thomas, first Lord Graves; they had one daughter.

On 29 April 1802 Nesham was advanced to post rank, and from October 1804 to February 1805 was captain of the *Foudroyant*, in the Bay of Biscay, with the flag of his kinsman and connection Rear-Admiral Sir Thomas Graves. In

March 1807 he was appointed to the *Ulysses* (44 guns), which he took out to the West Indies and commanded at the capture of Marie Galante in March 1808. In July 1808 he was moved into the *Intrepid* (64 guns), and in her, the following February, took part in the capture of Martinique, where he served on shore under the immediate command of Commodore Sir George Cockburn and superintended the transport of the heavy guns and mortars. On 15 April 1809 the *Intrepid* suffered severely in an unsuccessful attack on two French frigates under the guns of Fort Mathilde of Guadeloupe, and in December she returned to England and was paid off. In 1830–31 Nesham commanded the *Melville* (74 guns) in the Mediterranean. In July 1833 he married Elizabeth, the youngest daughter of Colonel Nicholas Bayly, the brother of the first earl of Uxbridge, of the third creation. He retired as rear-admiral on 10 January 1837, but was replaced on the active list on 17 August 1840. He became vice-admiral on 9 November 1846 and admiral on 30 July 1852. He died at Exmouth, Devon, on 4 November 1853, aged eighty-two.

J. K. LAUGHTON, *rev.* ANDREW LAMBERT

Sources D. Syrett and R. L. DiNardo, *The commissioned sea officers of the Royal Navy, 1660–1815*, rev. edn, Occasional Publications of the Navy RS, 1 (1994) • O'Byrne, *Naval biog. dict.* • *GM*, 2nd ser., 41 (1854), 316 • J. Marshall, *Royal naval biography*, 2/2 (1825), 587 • Boase, *Mod. Eng. biog.*

Ness, Christopher (1621–1705), Independent minister, was born at North Cave, Yorkshire, on 26 December 1621, the son of Thomas Ness, husbandman. He attended a school run by the local vicar, John Seaman, before being admitted to St John's College, Cambridge, on 17 May 1638. He graduated BA early in 1642 and became curate to his uncle William Brearcliffe at South Cliff and subsequently preached at Holderness and Beverley (also in the East Riding), where he was appointed master of the grammar school by the corporation in 1649. In 1651 Ness succeeded Dr Samuel Winter as rector of nearby Cottingham, and in 1656 he became a preacher at Leeds. At the Restoration the zealously Calvinist Ness was at odds with the equally Arminian vicar, John Lake, later bishop of Chichester. Ejected following the Act of Uniformity in 1662, Ness supported himself as a private preacher and schoolmaster in the West Riding parishes of Clayton, Morley, and Hunslet, where he bought a house in 1667. He also published a tract on the plague in London, *Peace Offerings and Lamentations* (1666). Licensed as an Independent in Leeds on 1 May 1672, he opened a church there in 1674. He got into trouble almost immediately, being excommunicated four times and convicted for schismatical assemblies. When a writ was issued against him in 1675, Ness fled to London; by March 1676 his Leeds congregation were claiming that he had deserted them, having denied them the Lord's supper even before his departure.

In London, Ness ministered to a meeting at Salisbury Court, Fleet Street. From here he published works of practical divinity, including *The Crown and Glory of a Christian* (1676) and *A Christian's Walk and Work on Earth until he Attain*

to Heaven (1678). During the exclusion crisis he issued *A Distinct Discourse and Discovery of the Person and Period of Antichrist* (1679), dedicated to the whig leader Lord Shaftesbury, *A Protestant Antidote Against the Poison of Popery* (1679), dedicated to parliament, which Ness hoped would be 'a new sharp threshing instrument (having teeth) in the hands of the Lord' (sigs. A2v–A3), and *The Signes of the Times* (1681). Ness used recent comets and an impending 'great conjunction' of Saturn and Jupiter to argue for imminent apocalypse in tracts like *A Philosophical and Divine Discourse Blazoning upon this Blazing Star* (1681). *A Compleat and Compendious Church-History*, dedicated to Patience Ward, the whig lord mayor, went through two editions in 1680 and 1681. Organized in a framework of trumpets, vials, and seals derived from the book of Revelation, it presented church history as a series of Satan's failed 'Plots' against God. Ness attempted to defend Shaftesbury from John Dryden's satire in *A key (with the whip) to open the mystery of iniquity of the poem called, Absalom and Achitophel* (1682). Dryden replied in the preface to *The Medall* (1682). In addition to anti-Catholicism, Ness employed secular whig arguments, asserting that royal prerogative became monstrous by devouring 'Privilege of Parliament', 'Liberty', and 'Property' (*Signes of the Times*, 29). His biography of Pope Innocent XI, *The Devil's Patriarck* (1683), boasted an introductory epistle from no less a foe of Antichrist than Titus Oates. (John Dunton, the publisher, claimed to have sold the whole edition in a fortnight.) Ness was persecuted after the whig defeat, and was sought for arrest on the charge of publishing in 1684 an elegy for Nathaniel Partridge, another dissenting minister. He left London some time later.

Ness was back in London by 1690, certifying Woodmonger's Hall, Duke's Place, as a meeting-place on 3 October 1693. He published a massive four-volume biblical commentary, *A Compleat History and Mystery of the Old and New Testaments* (1690–96). One of his last publications, *An Antidote Against Arminianism* (1700), was a classic defence of Calvinist predestinarianism and was reprinted into the nineteenth century. The frontispiece portrait depicts a burly man with heavy jowls. Ness died in London on 26 December 1705, and was buried at Bunhill Fields cemetery on 29 December. In his will, dated from Deptford, Kent, on 21 April 1701, he left property in Hunslet and over £300, naming his daughters Mary Newby and Elizabeth Beaumont and granddaughter Hannah Britland; nothing is known of his wife.

WILLIAM E. BURNS

Sources Venn, *Alum. Cant.* • *Calamy rev.* • *VCH Yorkshire East Riding* • Greaves & Zaller, *BDBR*, vol. 2 • will, PRO, PROB 11/485, sig. 249 • W. E. Burns, *An age of wonders: prodigies, politics, and providence in England, 1657–1727* (2002)

Likenesses line engraving (aged fifty-six), BM, NPG; repro. in C. Ness, *An antidote against Arminianism* (1700)

Wealth at death £370: will, PRO, PROB 11/485, sig. 249

Nessán (*d.* 556). *See under* Munster, saints of (*act. c.*450–*c.*700).

Nest (*b.* before 1092, *d. c.*1130), royal mistress, the daughter of *Rhys ap Tewdwr, king of Deheubarth (*d.* 1093), and

Gwladus, daughter of Rhiwallon ap Cynfyn of Powys, features prominently in the history of west Wales in the reign of Henry I. Her father was killed on campaign in Brycheiniog in 1093 and his kingdom was largely overrun by Anglo-Norman settlers. Nest first appears in 1108 as the wife of Gerald of *Windsor (d. 1116x36), castellan of Pembroke, placed for safety in his castle of Cenarth Bychan. It seems likely that this was her first marriage, which was doubtless made soon after 1097, when Gerald came to power as Count Arnulf's (and later King Henry's) steward in Pembrokeshire. By 1109 she already had two sons and a daughter with Gerald, and he and they were with her at Cenarth Bychan when Owain ap Cadwgan of Powys, her cousin, broke into the castle. She acted promptly to save husband and children, but was abducted by Owain. This attack on Gerald and Nest was the excuse for a co-ordinated assault by the Anglo-Normans and their Welsh allies on Powys, driving Owain into temporary exile in Ireland.

By virtue of the marriage, Nest's brother Gruffudd was able to take refuge with Gerald at Pembroke from time to time between 1115 and 1117, during his guerrilla campaign to recover the kingship of Deheubarth, which indicates that Nest maintained an ascendancy over her husband. Certainly she was a woman of some character and independence. It was probably during *Henry I's campaign against Powys in 1114 that she was seduced by him, or seduced him, and conceived an illegitimate son, called Henry after his father but brought up in Gerald's household. A relationship with Stephen, constable of Cardigan, produced another son, Robert, but this may have been after Gerald's death, which took place at some time later in Henry I's reign, certainly before 1130 when the Fleming sheriff Hait accounted for Pembroke at the exchequer. Nest also had a son with this Hait—it almost seems as though sleeping with Nest was a routine requirement among the barons of Pembrokeshire in the early twelfth century.

The great number of grandchildren of Nest in later twelfth-century Wales and Ireland are recorded by one of them, *Gerald of Wales. He notes coolly that because of her the lords of Haverford were the only significant family in west Wales not linked to him by blood. Nest's date of death is unknown. Gerald records that she had eight sons and two daughters. The eldest were William Fitzgerald of Carew, and Maurice *Fitzgerald of Llansteffan, who were born before 1108; she had also by that date had a daughter Angharad, who married William of Barry, the father of Gerald of Wales. With Gerald of Windsor she had a later son, *David, bishop of St David's (d. 1176). Henry, her royal bastard, became lord of Narberth and died in the service of Henry II in Anglesey in 1157. William, her son with Hait the Sheriff, became lord of St Clears. *Robert fitz Stephen, her son with Stephen the Constable, held Cardigan and part of Cemais. There were besides two sons with fathers whose identities Gerald does not note, Hywel and Walter. However, Hywel might have been another son of Stephen the Constable, as he had a claim on Lampeter, one of Stephen's acquisitions in Ceredigion before 1136. A further

daughter, Gwladus, has no father attributed to her, but she is said to have made a marriage to a baron of west Wales.

DAVID CROUCH

Sources T. Jones, ed. and trans., *Brut y tywysogyon, or, The chronicle of the princes: Red Book of Hergest* (1955) · *Gir. Camb. opera* · J. Williams ab Ithel, ed., *Annales Cambriae*, Rolls Series, 20 (1860) · I. W. Rowlands, 'The making of the march: aspects of the Norman settlement in Dyfed', *Anglo-Norman Studies*, 3 (1980), 142–57

Nethersole, Sir Francis (*bap.* 1587, *d.* 1659), diplomat and politician, was baptized at Kingston, Kent, on 26 February 1587, the second son of John Nethersole of Wymondeswold, Kent, and his wife, Perigrinia, daughter of Francis Wilsford. He matriculated as a pensioner from Trinity College, Cambridge, at Easter 1603 and was elected to a scholarship on 12 April 1605; he graduated BA in 1606, and obtained a minor fellowship at Trinity in 1608 and a major fellowship on 23 March 1610, the year he graduated MA. He became a popular tutor and on 11 December 1611 was elected public orator of the university. In the following year he published an address in Latin prose which he had delivered before the vice-chancellor on the death of Prince Henry, and added a short epitaph in verse by himself, and elegies in Latin and Greek by Andrew Downes. He displeased James I during a visit to Cambridge with Prince Charles, whom he addressed as 'Jacobissime Carole' and 'Jacobule', but his literary taste was sufficiently respected to lead Edmund Bolton to nominate him in 1617 as one of the class of 'essentials' in his projected academy of literature.

In 1619 Nethersole left academia for the world of politics, diplomacy, extensive travel, and many frustrations. He accepted the post of secretary to James Hay, Viscount Doncaster, whom James dispatched on a lavish embassy to the Holy Roman empire to negotiate a settlement in the rapidly intensifying struggle over Bohemia between the king's son-in-law, Elector Palatine Frederick V, and Ferdinand Habsburg, the reigning king of Bohemia (the conflict which was to become the Thirty Years' War). While the embassy was under way Ferdinand was elected Holy Roman emperor, and Frederick seized the former's Bohemian crown, which seemed to some to demand an alteration in English policy. Upon returning to England, Nethersole was knighted at Theobalds on 19 September 1619 and concurrently appointed the English agent to the princes of the protestant union and secretary to the king's only daughter, Elizabeth, wife of the elector palatine. James granted him annuities worth £356 for these positions. Nethersole left for Prague in the following year.

When Nethersole arrived in August 1620 he quickly assessed the dire military situation facing the new regime and tried repeatedly to persuade Elizabeth to leave for a safer location. She refused out of loyalty to her husband and their cause. After the defeat of their forces at the battle of White Mountain in November 1620 Nethersole accompanied the princess in her flight from Prague, though she allowed him to return briefly to secure the papers that he had left behind. He accompanied her dutifully for much of the ensuing journey across the empire to The Hague. Frederick and Elizabeth then dispatched him to England to obtain an army for the recovery of the Palatinate, which had been invaded by Spanish troops, but James sent him back, now as an envoy to the palatine court-in-exile in The Hague, with orders to pacify Frederick instead. The effort failed.

In 1622 Frederick defied his father-in-law, resolved to retake his patrimonial lands by force, and went to the Palatinate incognito by way of Paris, accompanied by Nethersole, whose copious correspondence vigorously defended this course of action. Soon afterwards, however, James ordered Nethersole to assist Lord Chichester in a mission to persuade Frederick to break off his military campaign in favour of peace negotiations in Brussels. Nethersole obeyed but with great misgivings. Frederick eventually relented, though the negotiations failed to prevent the Spanish from taking Heidelberg. In the autumn Nethersole was sent to England to complain to James and Charles about the failure of a pacific policy in the face of Spanish and Habsburg treachery.

Nethersole's travelling did not abate. In 1623, while Prince Charles and the duke of Buckingham were in Madrid trying to finalize the Spanish match, Frederick recalled Nethersole to The Hague and then sent him to Spain. His ostensible assignment was to deliver a congratulatory, conciliatory letter to King Philip IV and a pair of diamond pendants from Elizabeth to the Infanta María, but he was also to deliver a special plea to Charles that he not go through with the marriage until he had obtained adequate promises for Frederick's full restoration. Nethersole reached the prince in Segovia, just after he had left the Escorial, and the infanta, for good. The secretary's mission coincided with the desired effect. From Segovia Charles issued his secret instructions to delay indefinitely the marriage by proxy that he had just agreed to.

From 1624 Nethersole balanced his work for the exiled elector and his wife with a growing participation in English politics. In or prior to that year he married Lucy (1593/4–1652), the daughter and heir of Sir Henry Goodere of Warwickshire. On 31 January 1624 Nethersole was elected MP for Corfe Castle, Dorset. He was re-elected for the same constituency to Charles I's first and third parliaments in 1625 and 1628. In 1624–5 he was more an observant correspondent than an active participant, sending numerous reports to Sir Dudley Carleton, the English ambassador in the Netherlands. He tried to succeed Carleton in that office but failed to procure it. In the parliament of 1628 he was more active. He endorsed a petition from both houses for the execution of the laws against Jesuits, Catholic priests, and seminarians, and he presented the Commons with a bill requiring all MPs to take an oath to forswear private interest and only vote for what was just and beneficial to the glory of God and the welfare of the king and kingdom. Nethersole risked censure by suggesting that the two preceding parliaments had been dissolved because of a group of wilful, passionate MPs, who in forgetting their duty to king and country were 'no less dangerous' to the Commons than the perpetrators of the notorious Gunpowder Plot (*A Bill Drawn Up*, 1659). He warned of ruin in the state if the parliament of 1628 were dissolved summarily. Nethersole sent detailed reports of the proceedings to the Princess Elizabeth throughout. In 1629 he returned to The Hague with his wife. In November he applied for the office of master of requests but did not receive it. In December 1631 he was back again in London.

Thomas Fuller wrote of Nethersole's service to the Princess Elizabeth, 'it is hard to say whether he was more remarkable for his doings or his sufferings in her behalf' (Fuller, *Worthies*, 85). For years Nethersole petitioned the English government to relieve palatine debts. He sold his plate on their behalf and lent them money. His wife even bought clothes for the 'Queen of Bohemia'.

It was a bitter charge for Nethersole to convey to Elizabeth Charles I's condolences after the death of her husband in 1632. Thereafter he intensified his efforts to help her, which actually led to his undoing. In May 1633 Nethersole finally managed to obtain permission from Charles to raise a voluntary contribution or benevolence to recover the Palatinate for Frederick's son and heir. French forces were poised to take palatine fortresses after the Swedes evacuated. He procured an advance of £31,000 from two London merchants, citing Lord Craven as a guarantor, but before the legal documents authorizing the collection were prepared the scheme was leaked to the public. When Lord Craven's support proved uncertain Nethersole saw his chances for success vanish. He then charged Lord Goring, a member of Queen Henrietta Maria's household, with frustrating the plan by revealing it prematurely. The queen defended Goring and Charles became convinced that Nethersole had misled him. He was ordered to keep to his house and to apologize formally to Goring. The benevolence was cancelled. Nethersole tried to regain royal favour by offering strategic advice about military affairs in the Palatinate.

Importunate, desperate letters from Elizabeth then led Nethersole to make an even greater blunder. In December 1633 he forwarded an extract to the king's secretary, having appended a message in his own hand, to the effect that James I had already lost the Palatinate once through negligence, and that Charles appeared determined to let it happen a second time. The king was grossly offended and ordered Nethersole's arrest. When informed of his fate Nethersole wrote Elizabeth a furious note warning her not to rely on her brother for charity. In order to place his papers in safe custody he evaded capture for a few days, but he was soon apprehended and taken to the Tower. He was released at the end of April 1634, but not until the king had obtained a formal promise from Elizabeth, who had defended Nethersole, never to employ him in her service again. Nethersole then withdrew to Polesworth, Warwickshire, to property which his wife had inherited. By March 1636 the king had relented and allowed him to be received once again at court.

In his religion Nethersole is known to have been protestant, but not much is certain beyond that. Many ardent supporters of the palatine couple were dedicated Calvinists, and Nethersole obtained the vicarage of Polesworth for a minister who was ejected after the Restoration for non-conformity. In his letters, however, communion is mentioned reverently as 'the blessed sacrament', and his taking it was repeatedly the occasion for a conciliatory letter to a former rival or enemy, but that may have been merely for form's sake. He appears to have been on amicable terms with William Laud and once delivered a prayer book for him to Secretary Conway. Nethersole despised Catholics but did not sympathize with radical puritans either. He certainly supported a national church established by law, and his later writings show support for, or at least acceptance of, episcopacy.

During the civil war Nethersole's sympathies were at first for parliament, but he quickly chose neutrality. Thereafter his attitude was conciliatory, though increasing sympathy for the royalist cause is discernible. In 1643 he prepared a proposal for peace between the king and parliament with the goal of preventing the Scots from taking charge of affairs in England, but he did not publish it for fear of being accused of partiality by either side. The unfolding of the revolution forced him to break his silence. From August 1648 to January 1649 he published several pamphlets, at first anonymously, suggesting that both sides had committed injustices and needed to make peace. Nethersole denied that the original struggle could be legitimately called a 'war of religion'. He proposed a general pardon and the free election of annual parliaments until the nation had been fully pacified. Greatly opposed to the regicide, he published an open attack on John Goodwin for his defence of the army's violent design on the king.

Lucy Nethersole died on 9 July 1652, at the age of fifty-eight, and was buried in Polesworth church. In 1653, after protracted litigation, Nethersole finally compounded his estates. About the same time, in accordance with his wife's desire, he built and endowed a free school at Polesworth.

The political chaos of 1659 incited Nethersole, aged about seventy-three, to publish again. He reprinted a pamphlet by William Ashhurst which defended king and parliament against the Levellers' *Agreement of the People* in 1648. In the context of 1659 the work was easy to construe as an argument in favour of the restoration of the monarchy, a bicameral parliament, and the established church. He also supplied the members of the Long Parliament with copies of *A Bill Drawn Up*, a pamphlet containing the bill and speech that he presented to the House of Commons in 1628. It was another gesture for the sake of restoration, which he did not live to see. He died in August 1659 at Polesworth, where he had requested to be lain next to his wife. An inscribed stone to his memory was placed in the church in 1859. Being childless he left his estates to his nephew John Marsh, son of his sister Ann and Thomas Marsh of Brandred. In addition he left over £1145 in bequests to poor parishioners, his alma mater, and various relatives.

B. C. PURSELL

Sources *CSP dom.*, *1603–49* · Venn, *Alum. Cant.* · PRO, state papers, German states, 81/20–35 · *DNB* · B. C. Pursell, 'The constitutional causes of the Thirty Years' War: Friedrich V, the Palatine crisis, and European politics, 1618–1632', PhD diss., Harvard U., 2000 · J. Rushworth, *Historical collections*, new edn, 8 vols. (1721–2) · R. Lockyer, *Buckingham: the life and political career of George Villiers, first duke of Buckingham, 1592–1628* (1981) · M. A. E. Green, *Elizabeth electress palatine and queen of Bohemia*, ed. S. C. Lomas, rev. edn (1909) [based on M. A. E. Green, 'Elizabeth, eldest daughter of James I', *Lives of the princesses of England*, 5 (1854), 145–573] · C. Oman, *Elizabeth of Bohemia* (1938) · R. E. Ruigh, *The parliament of 1624: politics and foreign policy* (1971) · C. Russell, *Parliaments and English politics, 1621–1629* (1979) · will, PRO, PROB 11/307, sig. 22 · P. R. Sellin, 'John Donne: the poet as diplomat and divine', *Huntington Library Quarterly*, 39 (1975–6), 267–75 · E. McCabe, 'England's foreign policy in 1619: Lord Doncaster's embassy to the princes of Germany', *Mitteilungen des Instituts für Österreichische Geschichtsforschung*, 58 (1950), 457–77 · Fuller, *Worthies* (1662), 2.85

Archives PRO, state papers, German states, 81/20–35 | BL, corresp. with Sir Walter Aston, Add. MSS 36444–36445, *passim* · BL, letters to Lord Carlisle, Egerton MSS 2593–2597, *passim* · BL, letters to Sir Robert Naunton and Sir George Calvert, Add. MS 5950

Likenesses P. Oliver, miniature, 1619, V&A

Wealth at death bequests totalled £1145 plus 100 marks; outstanding mortgage to nephew Michael Biddulph for £2350: will, PRO, PROB 11/307, sig. 22

Netter [**Walden**], **Thomas** (*c.*1370–1430), theologian and Carmelite friar, came from Walden, Essex, and was often described for this reason as Thomas Walden. His parents, whose names were John and Matilda, seem to have been of humble origin, their surname perhaps indicating his father's trade.

Early life and public career Netter was probably born about 1370. He was ordained acolyte on 19 September 1394, subdeacon on 5 June 1395, and priest on 23 September 1396, all as a member of the London Carmelite convent. At some point, probably in the years after this final ordination, he studied in Oxford; by 1409 he was a bachelor of theology, and later became doctor of theology. He was elected prior provincial of the Carmelite order in England in 1414, and remained in office at least until 1426, and probably until his death; he was evidently an active and influential leader of the order, consulted on many issues by those within it and by others. At some stage he was appointed as confessor to Henry V, and, judging by Bale's extracts from his correspondence, was highly regarded by the king; he preached at the king's funeral in 1422. He continued as confessor to Henry VI. As such he crossed with the king to France in April 1430; he died in Rouen on 2 November 1430 and was buried in the Carmelite church there.

Netter attended the Council of Pisa in 1409, though his part in it seems to have been small. He was not one of the English delegation to the Council of Constance, but may have attended briefly in 1414; he certainly followed the proceedings of the council closely, especially where these concerned John Wyclif (d. 1384) and Jan Hus. He was invited by Giovanni Grossi, prior-general of the Carmelites, to attend the Council of Siena (1423–4), an invitation he refused on grounds of the damage done to his own health and to his order by his previous absence.

Netter was used by Henry V as an envoy to King Władysław of Poland in May 1419, and to Michael Küchmeister, grand master of the Teutonic knights. The purpose of the mission was to secure peace between these two rulers, and between Küchmeister and the duke of

Lithuania. the emperor Sigismund had offered to adjudicate between the rulers, and had asked Henry V for his assistance in this; by July all three had agreed to suspend hostilities for a year, and to accept the emperor's judgment. Netter was a witness to these agreements, but apparently did not stay until Sigismund's decision was given on 6 January 1420; by mid-November he was back in England. Extracts from some of the letters concerning Netter's participation in this embassy were transcribed by Bale. On the journey to Poland, Netter visited Vienna, where he consulted the Jewish community about their habits of confession and penance.

Opponent of Lollardy Netter's chief fame rests on his activities in opposition to Wyclif and the Lollards. As he himself points out, he was too young to have known Wyclif or the first generation of Oxford followers, but he mentions William Woodford as one of his masters, though not claiming personal acquaintance. His knowledge of debate in Oxford on questions raised by Wyclif early in the reign of Henry IV was doubtless gained while he was studying there. At some point he and a *confrater*, William, at the instigation of an unnamed nobleman, arranged to debate with the Lollard Peter Payne in Oxford on the subjects of pilgrimages, the eucharist, images, the religious orders, and mendicancy; Payne failed to appear for the meeting. This must have been before 1414, by when Payne had left England, but an earlier date is more likely, probably about 1406–9. Netter's first presence at a trial for heresy was at that of John Badby in 1410 (the accused, described as a tailor—*sartor*—must have been Badby, not William Taylor, in view of the reference to Thomas, duke of Exeter, as chancellor); he is not mentioned in the official record, and may have been an observer only. In the trial of Sir John Oldcastle in 1413 he was named as one of the official assessors; the contemporary records do not mention Netter's part in the questioning, though the later account by John Bale ingeniously elaborates on this from details taken from Netter's *Doctrinale fidei ecclesiae*. Although Netter mentions John Purvey, and a book taken from Purvey in prison, he does not seem to have been involved in any inquiry into Purvey's heresy. Netter also participated in the trial of William Taylor before Archbishop Henry Chichele in February 1423, and in that of William White before Bishop William Alnwick at Norwich in September 1428.

The *Doctrinale fidei ecclesiae* Netter's most important contribution was, however, his vast *Doctrinale fidei ecclesiae*, a detailed refutation of the views of John Wyclif, whose teaching Netter saw as the pernicious origin of the religious and, in his view, civil disobedience of the Lollards, and more distantly the source of the errors of Jan Hus and the Hussites. Apart from the abortive debate with Payne, there is some evidence that Netter's experiences in Oxford may have sown the seeds of this vast project. In 1409 a committee of twelve Oxford men, not including Netter, was set to list the erroneous conclusions of Wyclif as these could be found in a number of the master's writings; the committee reported in 1411. In one copy of this

list, that in the *Fasciculi zizaniorum* (though details reveal that this cannot have been recorded until 1436), an extra four conclusions not found elsewhere are said to have been added by Thomas Netter; Netter also seems to have been in correspondence with five of the members of the committee, though since only two of the letters survive, and those only in later extracts, it is not clear that the letters were prompted by the inquiry.

The *Doctrinale* survives in a large number of manuscripts, both in England and on the continent, in a form that may be deceptively uniform. It consists of six books, almost always grouped into three parts: books 1–4 as the first, book 5, *De sacramentis*, as the second, and book 6, *De sacramentalibus*, as the third, the last two constituting each a volume as long as the first. Books 1–4 were sent together to Pope Martin V (r. 1417–1431) with a letter of dedication, implying that the composition may have been a response to a request from Henry V. The latest datable event mentioned in this first part is the condemnation of Wyclif's forty-five articles by the Council of Constance on 4 May 1415. The form of this first part, however, may suggest that its four books have different origins. Books 1 and 2, respectively *De capite ecclesiae Jesu Christo* ('Concerning Jesus Christ the head of the church'—though actually much concerned with the philosophical background to Wyclif's errors) and *De corpore Christi quod est ecclesia* ('Concerning the body of Christ which is the church'), conform to the pattern of the later books 5 and 6: they quote extracts from Wyclif's writings, each of which is precisely located; set against these are quotations from the fathers, again precisely located, and used to refute Wyclif.

But the third and fourth books, *De religiosis perfectis in lege Christi* ('Concerning men of religion made perfect in the law of Christ') and *Quomodo religiosi in ecclesia Dei possunt licite exigere victum suum* ('How men of religion in the church of God can lawfully demand their maintenance'), though they concern issues that Wyclif discussed at length, rarely quote Wyclif or indeed refer to him; they seem to be more generalized defences of the religious orders and their means of support, rather than directed at a specific opponent. As such these two books may originally have been written separately, though book 4 is linked back to book 3 (bk 4, ch. 15 to bk 3, ch. 12), and perhaps before books 1 and 2, and only secondarily incorporated into the *Doctrinale*; book 3 at least must have originated as an Oxford determination, since its opening submits the work to the authority of the chancellor (Netter, *Doctrinale*, bk 3, *Protestatio authoris*). Book 5, the largest part of which concerns the eucharist, was probably begun before Henry V's death on 1 September 1422 (ibid., bk 5, prologue), but was finished after it (ibid., bk 5, *peroratio, et operis dedicatio*, 'final dedication'); the latest event mentioned is the burning of William Taylor for heresy on 1 March 1423 (ibid., bk 5, *doctrina* 11). The acknowledgements of parts 1 and 2 from Martin V are dated respectively 1 April 1426 and 8 August 1427. References in book 6 to the trial of William White *hoc anno* make it clear that its composition was under way in late 1428, and was still proceeding six months later (ibid., bk 6, ch. 66, 140; ch. 99); as it stands the book cannot have been finished much before Netter left for France in April 1430. Netter intended further material, since there are subjects promised at the start of book 6 which are not covered within it.

Netter's learning and outlook The *Doctrinale* is an immense work of scholarship, which shows that its author had access to an enormous library, most of it presumably at the London Whitefriars. Netter declares his intention of following Wyclif's own preference for writers of antiquity, as the best means of establishing the heresiarch's biased interpretation; the most frequently quoted patristic authors (as in Wyclif) are Augustine, Jerome, and Gregory, while the only commonly used medieval sources are Hugh of St Victor and Robert Grosseteste (both used by Wyclif). Canon law is rarely cited. Little use is made of earlier refutations of Wyclif: Woodford is never quoted, while Dymoke's answer to the twelve conclusions of the Lollards is mentioned only a few times. Netter used extensively the 267 conclusions condemned in 1415 by the Council of Constance. His first-hand knowledge of Wyclif's Latin writings was considerable, but not exhaustive. He quotes most extensively from the late *Trialogus*, a conveniently ordered summary of Wyclif's final positions, and the even later *Opus evangelicum*; there are many quotations from the *De papa*, *De eucharistia*, *De apostasia*, *De symonia*, *De blasphemia*, and from a considerable number of the shorter polemical writings. Of Wyclif's sermons, however, Netter only seems to have known the set on the Sunday epistles (which he cites extensively), while those on the Sunday gospels he mentions once only and then declaredly second-hand; since the *Sanctorale* sermons, for the festivals of saints, contain material equally unacceptable to Netter, it must be concluded that he did not know them. Equally, though he discusses Wyclif's views on dominion extensively, he cites *De dominio divino* once only, and *De civili dominio* only a handful of times, and then only in a section not concerned with dominion. A fair number of the texts cited by Netter no longer survive in manuscripts of English origin (*Trialogus*, *De potestate pape*, *De eucharistia* most notably). Where Netter obtained them is unfortunately unclear. Netter's knowledge of the Lollard movement was in some respects similarly patchy, and was necessarily limited for the early stages by his arrival in Oxford at the earliest some ten years after Wyclif's death.

Though Netter was present at many of the celebrated trials between 1410 and 1428, and uses details from his experience especially in book 6, he shows no sign of apprehending the appeal of aspects of the Lollard movement's beliefs to ordinary lay people. Equally his anxiety to refute the doctrinal errors of Wyclif in every minute particular means that he never confronts the defects in the contemporary church to which, at least in some regards, those errors relate. The demands of polemic, and the rigidity of his method of argument, prove a straitjacket; Netter's own positive ideas emerge only rarely.

Continental connections The writing of this enormous, academic anti-Wycliffite treatise in the 1420s may seem an anachronism in view of the decline of support for Wyclif in Oxford University following the enactment of Archbishop Thomas Arundel's *Constitutions* in 1409, and the increasing persecution of the Lollard sect especially after Oldcastle's rising in 1414. But, though Netter evidently expected a native readership for his work (and an abbreviation was made in 1491 by Bishop John Russell of Lincoln as an aid to those investigating heretics), it is clear that his aim was as much directed at the continent: the *Doctrinale* was intended to re-establish the orthodox credentials of the English church after the notoriety that an English heretic had gained at the Council of Constance, both in his own right and as the alleged theological begetter of Jan Hus (see, for instance, bk 1, *epistola nuncupatoria*, 'dedicatory epistle', bk 5, *doctrina* 10). Netter had learned much about the ideas of Hus and his followers through reports of the proceedings at Constance, and perhaps also during his journey to Poland in 1419—travelling as he did via Vienna, he must have passed through areas with a substantial Hussite population.

A number of manuscripts of the *Doctrinale* survive on the continent, some probably deriving from the dedicatory set sent to Martin V, but some originating from interest in it during the Council of Basel. Ironically, Cardinal Giuliano Cesarini at Basel lent a copy to the Hussite Procop for Peter Payne, by then a spokesman of the Hussite church; it was also used there by both sides of the debate, by the utraquist Rokycana, and by his orthodox opponents Giovanni da Ragusio and Heinrich Kaltenstein, and a two-volume set now in Cracow was copied at the council. Netter's purpose could backfire: Andreas Gałka, a Hussite sympathizer in Poland, commented that much could be learned of Wyclif's ideas by reading Netter. Netter's work continued to be used both as a source-book of heresy, and as a model for its refutation, right through until the seventeenth century. Its dissemination was aided by three printed editions in the sixteenth century, two from Paris and the third from Salamanca, and a final edition of 1757 from Venice (citations here give references by book and chapter number, common to all manuscripts and editions).

Netter's other writings and attributions John Bale, whose interest in Netter as a fellow Carmelite antedated his conversion to reform and his departure from the order, lists fifty-three works by Netter, thirty-five with incipits, in his *Catalogus*; unfortunately, in his *Index*, which indicates the manuscripts in which Bale had seen the works, he gives only a short descriptive paragraph and no manuscripts. Doubtless this was because his knowledge had derived from the holdings of the East Anglian Carmelite houses. Four of the works Bale lists are sections or the whole of the *Doctrinale*. Several could be the incipits of Netter's letters from which Bale transcribed extracts surviving in his notebook (now Bodl. Oxf., MS Bodley 73, fols. 94v–103v). In one of the extracts, from a letter to Thomas Rodeburne (d. 1442), Netter mentions his own recently written *De divinatione*; since Rodeburne is described as archdeacon of Sudbury, this lost work must have been written later than 1414. One text, a brief rebuttal of the forty-five articles of Wyclif and Hus circulating at the Council of Constance, though not mentioned by Bale, does survive (Bodl. Oxf., MS Bodley 825, fols. 1–18v; Magd. Oxf., MS Lat. 4, fols. 271–82; printed in Netter, *Doctrinale*, ed. Blanciotti, 1757, pt 3, cols. 1029–48); its authenticity seems reasonable. Less certainly, the *Questiones terminorum naturalium* in Vienna, Österreichische Nationalbibliothek, MS 4878, fols. 53–60, beginning 'Queritur utrum difficile non sit', is attributed by the scribe to Netter; its incipit varies only slightly from a work in Bale's list. Another text, in the Bodleian Library, Oxford, MS Bodley 676, fols. 149–156v, though unattributed in the manuscript, has the same incipit as that given by Bale for Netter's *Introductiones naturalium*. Thomas Tanner adds some details to the material in Bale: he lists with incipit an address given by Netter in Ludlow in the jubilee of the Carmelite Robert Mascall, bishop of Hereford, in 1416, and, again with incipits, *Orationes* and letters beyond those mentioned by Bale; unfortunately, he does not detail his source.

Among the works attributed to Netter by Bale is what he describes as *Fasciculus zizaniorum Vuicleui* ('Bundle of Wyclif's weeds'), which Bale undoubtedly knew in the manuscript now in the Bodleian Library, MS e Museo 86 (as his manifold notes there witness). This is a collection of materials, most of which relate to the struggles of the orthodox against Wyclif and his followers (though some items list academic heresies of an earlier date). The material of earliest origin consists of three, partially incomplete, determinations which the Carmelite John Kenningham (*d.* 1399) delivered in the Oxford schools against Wyclif; the latest is an account of the trial of William White in Norwich in 1428, at which Netter was present. The manuscript as it stands has been convincingly shown to date from after Netter's death: the names of the twelve Oxford men who produced in 1411 the list of heresies from Wyclif's books are supplemented by their later positions, one of which (that of Robert Gilbert, said to be later bishop of London) was not held until 1436; there is also a note added on the first leaf giving the date 1439. Equally some of the contents derive from a date some thirty years before Netter can have been involved in the fight against heresy (and the Kenningham debate may antedate his birth). The volume is certainly of Carmelite origin, since by far the largest amount of material in it is by men of that order. It seems likely that the compilation reflects Carmelite concern with heresy over a long period, and was supplemented from time to time with new material. Netter's contribution to the whole is possible, but its extent unclear: of the trials at which he was present, those of Oldcastle and White are included, that of William Taylor is only very briefly covered, and that of John Badby is absent. It is absolutely clear, however, that this work should be removed from the writings of Netter.

John Leland, in his description of the London Carmelite house library, states that Netter gave many books to it, though without providing any precise indication of which of the sixty-one volumes came from his gift; among the holdings Leland noted are a three-volume set of the *Doctrinale*, and some of the works used or mentioned in it. Three surviving manuscripts (now Bodl. Oxf., MS Bodley 730, Cassian's *Collationes*; Oxford, Trinity College, MS 58, a glossed psalter; Cambridge, St John's College, MS I.15, computistical material) contain a note that they were part of Netter's gift to the London Carmelites.

ANNE HUDSON

Sources *Thomæ Waldensis … doctrinale antiquitatum fidei Catholicæ ecclesiæ*, ed. B. Blanciotti, 3 vols. (Venice, 1757–9) · B. Zimmerman, ed., *Monumenta historica Carmelitana* (1907), 442–82 · J. Bale, notebooks, Bodl. Oxf., MSS Bodley 73, Selden supra. 41 · J. Bale, notebooks, BL, Harley MSS 1819, 3838 · G. Wessels, ed., *Acta capitulorum generalium ordinis fratrum B. V. Mariae de Monte Carmelo*, 1 (Rome, 1912), 150, 159 · E. Weise, ed., *Die Staatsverträge des deutschen Ordens in Preussen im 15. Jahrhundert*, 1 (Königsberg, 1939), documents nos. 133–40 · E. Joachim, *Regesta historico-diplomatica ordinis S. Mariae Theutonicorum, 1198–1525*, ed. W. Hubatsch, 2 (Göttingen, 1948), 225–31 · M. Dogiel, ed., *Codex diplomaticus regni Poloniae et magni ducatus Lituaniae*, 4 (Vilnius, 1764), document no. 87 · Bale, *Cat.*, 1.569–71 · Reg. Braybrooke, GL, fols. 36v, 40, 42v · E. F. Jacob, ed., *The register of Henry Chichele, archbishop of Canterbury, 1414–1443*, 3, CYS, 46 (1945), 167–8 · J. D. Mansi, *Sacrorum conciliorum nova, et amplissima collectio*, 27 (Florence, 1784), 401 · [T. Netter], *Fasciculi zizaniorum magistri Johannis Wyclif cum tritico*, ed. W. W. Shirley, Rolls Series, 5 (1858) · J. Crompton, 'Fasciculi zizaniorum [pts 1–2]', *Journal of Ecclesiastical History*, 12 (1961), 35–45, 155–66 · M. Harvey, 'The diffusion of the *Doctrinale* of Thomas Netter in the fifteenth and sixteenth centuries', *Intellectual life in the middle ages: essays presented to Margaret Gibson*, ed. L. Smith and B. Ward (1992), 281–94 · Tanner, *Bibl. Brit.-Hib.*, 746–8 · J. Bale, *A brefe chronycle concernynge the examinacyon and death of the martyr syr J. Oldecastell* (1544) · *Commentarii de scriptoribus Britannicis, auctore Joanne Lelando*, ed. A. Hall, 2 (1709), 438–41 · D. J. Dubois, 'Thomas Netter of Walden, O.C. (*c.*1372–1430)', BLitt diss., U. Oxf., 1978 · K. S. Smith, 'The ecclesiology of controversy: scripture, tradition and church in the theology of Thomas Netter of Walden, 1372–1430', PhD diss., Cornell University, 1983 · M. Hurley, 'A pre-tridentine theology of tradition: Thomas Netter of Walden (d. 1430)', *Heythrop Journal*, 4 (1963), 348–66

Archives Bodl. Oxf., MS Bodley 676, fols. 149–59v · Bodl. Oxf., MS Bodley 825, fols. 1–18v · Magd. Oxf., MS lat. 4, fols. 271–82 | Österreichische Nationalbibliothek, Vienna, MS 4878, fols. 53–60 · Bodl. Oxf., MS e Museo 86

Netterville, John, second Viscount Netterville of Dowth

(*d.* 1659), landowner and army officer, was the eldest son of Nicholas *Netterville, first Viscount Netterville of Dowth (1581–1654), and his first wife, Eleanor Bathe (*d.* 1634) of Drumcondra, co. Dublin. Nicholas Netterville was created viscount during an intermission of relaxation in the official pressure on Irish recusancy; his was one of a number of honours designed to conciliate, and secure Catholic goodwill and financial support. In 1623 John Netterville married Elizabeth Weston (*d.* 1654), daughter of Sir Richard *Weston, the chancellor of the exchequer (later first earl of Portland and lord treasurer), a reputed Roman Catholic and certainly a man with strong recusant connections and sympathies. Netterville was knighted on 22 November 1625.

Netterville was one of those who, in November 1632, petitioned the newly appointed lord deputy, Thomas Wentworth, Lord Wentworth, not to enforce the recusancy laws against Irish Catholics. Despite, or perhaps because of, his activism, Netterville was awarded the command of an infantry company on the regular establishment some time between 1629 and 1633. He displaced Sir John Clotworthy, who later emerged as an inveterate enemy of Wentworth and acted as the principal Irish protestant liaison with the English parliamentary opposition. For a Roman Catholic to secure a peacetime captaincy in the Irish standing army was singularly unusual; the Weston connection may explain this.

At the outbreak of the 1641 rising Netterville commanded a company comprising part of the garrison defending Drogheda from Irish Catholic insurgents. The siege lasted from November 1641 to March 1642, with the insurgents blockading the town and launching periodic assaults. During one almost successful attempt a party of insurgents infiltrated the town with the connivance of sympathetic townspeople, but the alarm was raised before they could open the gates. Netterville was suspected of being the leader of the fifth-columnists and accused of 'giving groundless alarms, raising false rumours and infusing evil dispositions into the minds of the townsmen' (Archdall, 4.212). The *Commentarius Rinuccinianus*, on the other hand, asserts that the matter arose out of a guardroom quarrel between Netterville and Charles Moore, Viscount Drogheda. Moore spoke disparagingly of the Irish indiscriminately as rebels and Netterville took strong exception to this and forced him to withdraw the remarks. However, the exchange was overheard by the protestant dean of Armagh, Nicholas Bernard, who alleged to the governor, Sir Henry Tichburne, that Netterville was looking for a way to let the besiegers into Drogheda. At any event Netterville had left Drogheda by mid-January 1642 and subsequently returned to his own home at Dowth, co. Meath, some 4½ miles to the west.

In March 1642 Ormond, commander of the government forces in Leinster, marched to relieve Drogheda, though the insurgents had, by then, retreated. In an attempt to regularize his standing Netterville went to Ormond at his camp at Garristown, co. Meath. Ormond sent him to Dublin on 12 March 1642. The lords justices were sympathetic to the emergent parliamentarian faction and inclined to attribute collective guilt to Irish Catholics for the rising and subsequent atrocities against protestant settlers. Consequently they imprisoned Netterville and actively collected evidence of treasonable involvement with the insurgents.

The main charge against Netterville was that after leaving Drogheda for Dowth he had consorted with, and entertained, the besiegers at his home. The 8000 or so besiegers occupied a ring of strong points surrounding Drogheda; with the Mac Mahon encampment of Tullyallen just 2 miles from Dowth, it was inevitable that soldiers would be quartered on Netterville. His case, then, had wider implications for the imputed collective guilt of Catholic landowners in general. As the reconquest of Ireland from the insurgents went ahead, as was expected in the summer of 1642, nearly all would be found to be implicated at least as deeply as Netterville. This would then serve as justification for the wholesale land confiscations envisioned by the Adventurer's Acts of 1642.

Netterville pleaded that a one-hundred-strong party of rebels forced their way into his house 'against his will' (extracts of Sir John Netterville's petition) and that he and his half dozen man servants were powerless to resist. He further pleaded that as 'everyman's intention is best proved by his action' (ibid.) so his loyalty could be inferred from the fact that he surrendered himself to Ormond 'with the first opportunity' (Archdall, 4.213). His plea of non-belligerency was doubtless complicated by the fact that his younger brother, Luke Netterville, MP for Swords in the 1640 parliament, was the acknowledged leader of the insurgents in the north of co. Dublin while his father, Nicholas Netterville, along with his neighbour Nicholas Preston, Viscount Gormanstown, were the main insurgent leaders in co. Meath. Evidence from his servants implicated Netterville, though they later retracted these accusations and claimed they were extorted by 'menace and threatening with the rack' (deposition of Streete, Aylmer, and Aylmer).

As it happened Netterville's case did not transpire to be the central precedent invoked against other Catholic landowners. He was kept imprisoned in Dublin Castle, and by the time of his release in April 1643 the political and military situation had been transformed. The outbreak of civil war in England, among other factors, caused the reconquest to falter and the insurgents to consolidate their position as confederate Catholics. Ormond had replaced the lords justices and Charles I was already working towards a rapprochement with his Irish Catholic subjects with a view to securing their assistance. Netterville's petition for release, and his claim that evidence against him of complicity in the rising was 'extorted by menaces with the rack' then, were received more sympathetically (extracts of Sir John Netterville's petition). On his release he at once joined the Leinster confederate army led by Thomas Preston, uncle of Viscount Gormanstown. He was present during the latter part of the siege and capture of the fortified protestant settlement at Ballinakill, Queen's county.

Netterville's subsequent role in the confederate Catholic regime and the wars of the 1640s is obscure. Viscount Netterville was 'treasurer general' for the province of Leinster and two other family members (probably his brothers), Patrick and Richard, were insinuated into posts as receivers and commissioners for revenue.

Netterville served as captain of an under-strength troop in the cavalry regiment of Thomas Dillon, Viscount Dillon of Costello-Gallen, during the early phase (1649–50) of the Cromwellian reconquest. The regiment's combat record was undistinguished; during the debacle of Baggot Rath (August 1649) the soldiers under Dillon's command refused to advance in support of their beaten comrades and, again, in March 1650 they refused to march to relieve Kilkenny from Cromwell's siege. Netterville's position in Dillon's regiment suggests that, like his commander, he was aligned with the 'Ormondist' faction of Irish Catholics who subordinated their religious aspirations to their loyalty to the Stuarts.

The Cromwellian Act of Settlement of 1652 exempted from pardon for life or estate both Sir John Netterville and his father, Viscount Netterville. They were not arrested, however, and Viscount Netterville died in 1654. By virtue of being a well-connected Englishwoman Sir John Netterville's wife, Elizabeth, was treated with some sympathy by the Cromwellian regime and, in April 1653, she secured an order allowing her one fifth of the profits of her husband's estates. Later she was allowed to retain temporary possession of the manors of Dowth and Proudfootstown, yielding an annual rental of £200, 'scarce the eight part of her husband's estate' (*CSP Ire.*, 1647–60, 630). Lady Elizabeth then went to England 'laying her case before kindred and friends … with much sorrow of heart for the space of many months and with the grief and the toil … in half a year's time she brought herself to an untimely end' (ibid.). She was buried in St Giles-in-the-Fields, Middlesex, on 16 September 1654. In February 1657 Lord Protector Cromwell ordered that the Netterville family retain Dowth and Proudfootstown until a definite arrangement was made. This order was ignored and the family (three daughters and five sons) evicted. It is most likely that Netterville had earlier accompanied his wife to England. He died in London and was buried in St Giles-in-the-Fields on 3 September 1659, the day after he made his will.   Pádraig Lenihan

Sources J. Netterville, extracts of petition, TCD, MS 816, fol. 202 · deposition of Richard Streete, Andrew Aylmer, and Robert Aylmer, TCD, MS 816, fol. 204 · B. McGrath, 'Parliament men and the confederate association', *Kingdoms in crisis: Ireland in the 1640s, essays in honour of Dónal Cregan*, ed. M. Ó Siochrú (2001), 103–4 · *CSP Ire.*, 1633–47, 109, 534; 1647–60, 180, 629–31 · B. O'Ferrall and D. O'Connell, *Commentarius Rinuccinianus de sedis apostolicae legatione ad foederatos Hiberniae Catholicos per annos 1645–1649*, ed. J. Kavanagh, IMC, 1 (1932), 265 · J. Lodge, *The peerage of Ireland*, rev. M. Archdall, rev. edn, 4 (1789), 212–13 · V. Treadwell, *Buckingham and Ireland, 1616–28* (Dublin, 1998), 110 · GEC, *Peerage* · *The manuscripts of the marquis of Ormonde*, [old ser.], 3 vols., HMC, 36 (1895–1909), vol. 1, pp. 228, 234–5

Netterville, Luke de (*d.* 1227), archbishop of Armagh, was a member of an Anglo-Norman family in Ireland, associated in Louth and Meath with the Verdons and Lacys. He was in Ireland before 1189 and by 1202 was archdeacon of Emly. In or before 1206 he was made archdeacon of Armagh, probably on the understanding that he would succeed the Irish archbishop of Armagh, Echdonn Mac Gilla Uidhir, who had been made archbishop against the wishes of King John in 1202. The diocesan chapter of Armagh in 1216 chose Netterville as archbishop of the primatial see, by then vacant; but their act was annulled on the ground that the assent of the crown of England had not previously been obtained. After a money composition a new election was held, under royal authority, and Netterville was appointed to the archbishopric. On 6 July 1218 the king wrote to the pope saying he had given his assent to Netterville's election, and asking for papal confirmation. The pallium was sent to him from Rome, and he received consecration from Stephen Langton.

In Ireland Netterville was overshadowed by the archbishop of Dublin, Henry of London. He maintained Armagh's claims to control over the county of Louth against the bishopric of Clogher. He introduced the Dominicans into Drogheda in 1224 and resided in the same town among the Augustinian canons of St Peter's. At one point—possibly during the invasion of Hugh de Lacy, the temporarily dispossessed earl of Ulster, in 1223–4—he and the community of St Peter's were forced to flee and seek shelter in the house of Llanthony Secunda near Gloucester. Netterville died on 17 April 1227, and was buried at the Cistercian monastery of Mellifont.

J. T. Gilbert, rev. B. Smith

Sources J. Ware, *De praesulibus Hiberniae* (1665) · H. S. Sweetman and G. F. Handcock, eds., *Calendar of documents relating to Ireland*, 5 vols., PRO (1875–86), vol. 1 · J. T. Gilbert, ed., *Chartularies of St Mary's Abbey, Dublin: with the register of its house at Dunbrody and annals of Ireland*, 2 vols., Rolls Series, 80 (1884) · J. T. Gilbert, ed., *Register of the abbey of St Thomas, Dublin*, Rolls Series, 94 (1889) · E. St J. Brooks, ed., *The Irish cartularies of Llanthony prima and secunda*, IMC (1953) · A. Gwynn, 'Armagh and Louth in the 12th century', *Seanchas Ardmhacha*, 1 (1954–5), 1–11

Netterville, Nicholas, first Viscount Netterville of Dowth (1581–1654), politician, was the only son of John Netterville (*d.* 1601), politician, of Dowth, co. Meath, and Eleanor, daughter of Sir James Gernon of Kilmacoole, co. Louth. Little is known about his boyhood or youth but it is possible that he followed the tradition of attendance by family members (including his father) at the inns of court in London. At the age of twenty he succeeded to the family estates on his father's death. He also inherited the Dowth estate of his uncle Richard *Netterville, who died in 1607.

Richard Netterville had incurred the wrath of the Elizabethan authorities for his intractable constitutional opposition to the cess and other policy measures, but Nicholas's tenure as the principal member of his generation of the Netterville family was relatively untroubled by controversy for almost four decades. A notable recusant like his uncle, Nicholas was one of the most extensive landowners in the Old Englishry of Ireland. He had estates in counties Wexford and Westmeath, as well as in his native co. Meath where, besides the family properties, he held a very large number of impropriated rectories. The cordiality of his relations with the crown was marked by his advancement to the peerage as Viscount Netterville of Dowth on 3 April 1622. He eventually took his place in the Irish House of Lords at the subsequent meeting of parliament in July 1634. As one of the leading Old English lords he took part in the negotiation of the graces in the mid-1620s, and in 1627 he was proposed for appointment as a colonel in a new Irish army on the recommendation of his father-in-law, Sir John Bathe.

Nicholas had married Eleanor (*d.* 1634), daughter of Sir John Bathe of Drumcondra, co. Dublin, and Athcarne, co. Meath, probably shortly after 1600 and certainly before 1620; the couple had five daughters and eight sons, two of whom entered the Society of Jesus. After Eleanor's death in 1634, Netterville married Mary (*d.* in or after 1642), daughter of John Brice, alderman of Drogheda, and widow successively of John Hoey, serjeant-at-arms, and Sir Thomas Hibbots, chancellor of the exchequer. There were no children born of this second marriage.

Although he was in conflict, along with many of his fellow Old English, with the lord deputy, Thomas Wentworth, in the mid- to late 1630s, Netterville retained his allegiance to the royal government. When rebellion broke out on 23 October 1641 he immediately offered his services along with other lords of the pale to the lords justices in Dublin but these were rejected. He then retired to his country estates and eventually joined his heir, John *Netterville, second Viscount Netterville, and four other sons, and the other lords of the pale in the insurrection. He was declared an outlaw on 17 November 1642 and his estates were declared forfeit, but throughout the insurgency Netterville repeatedly declared his loyalty to Charles I. He engaged in the negotiations through the agency of the earl of Clanricarde for a truce to be concluded with the king in the early stages of the rebellion.

When the Catholic confederacy at Kilkenny met Netterville was a representative for co. Dublin and he took the oath of association on 26 July 1644. He was appointed treasurer-general of the supreme council of the confederation. When Archbishop Rinuccini arrived in Ireland, Netterville was one of three commissioners sent by the confederates to escort the papal envoy through Cork, Limerick, and Tipperary to Kilkenny. Even though he subscribed the oath for the full restoration of Catholicism in Ireland he later became active against Rinuccini's mission.

After the Cromwellian campaign in Ireland, Netterville and his heir, John, were listed among those excepted from pardon for life and estate in 1652, but neither man was personally molested. Netterville died in 1654 and was buried in Monkstown, co. Dublin; his eldest son, John, succeeded to the title.   COLM LENNON

Sources J. Lodge, *The peerage of Ireland*, rev. M. Archdall, rev. edn, 4 (1789) • GEC, *Peerage* • *CSP Ire.*, 1611–14 • M. Ó Siochrú, *Confederate Ireland, 1642–1649* (1999) • A. Clarke, *The Old English in Ireland, 1625–1642* (1966) • D. Cregan, 'Irish Catholic admissions to the English inns of court, 1558–1625', *Irish Jurist*, new ser., 5 (1970), 95–114 • DNB

Netterville, Richard (*c.*1545–1607), lawyer, was the second son of Lucas or Luke Netterville (*d.* 1560), of Dowth, co. Meath, second justice of the court of queen's bench, and Margaret, daughter of Sir Thomas Luttrell, of Luttrellston, co. Dublin. Netterville had an elder brother, John, who inherited the bulk of their father's property and was MP for County Meath in 1585–6. While a law student Richard Netterville signed the twenty-four articles of 1562 protesting at the cess, which was a range of government impositions. This was drawn up and signed by twenty-six Old English law students at the inns of court.

Netterville succeeded in building a successful and extremely lucrative career as a lawyer but continued to be concerned about erosion of Old English wealth, property rights, and power. In 1577 he was sent with Barnaby Scurlocke and Henry Burnell by members of the Old English élite on a mission to Elizabeth I to seek redress from a cess imposed by Sir Henry Sidney, the lord deputy, who had undertaken the government of Ireland under a form of contract with the crown. Sidney learned of the mission and wrote a letter to the queen which attempted to discredit it and paint Netterville as ungrateful, dangerous, and not far short of revolutionary: 'he was the younger

sonne of a meane Family and second Justice of one of the Benches borne to nothinge and yet onelye by your Majestyes Bountye lyveth in better countenaunce than ever his father did or his elder brother dothe'. Despite having gained great favour at Elizabeth's hand, he was 'as sedicious a Varlett and as great an Impugner of English Governement as any this Land bearethe and calls for severe dealing with' (*DNB*). Netterville and his companions were arrested and imprisoned for impugning the queen's right to levy cess independently of the parliament or grand council, but, on giving security, were released in August 1577, because of the plague in the Fleet. They were pardoned before the end of the year and the cess was reduced in amount. The mission, though only partially successful, can be seen as one of many attempts to control the common law prerogatives of the crown and their abuse in Ireland under Sidney. Netterville's behaviour suggests he was a moderate man who nevertheless acted on the strength of his convictions.

Netterville was very successful at building a landed estate. By 1607, in addition to his house and land at Corbally, co. Dublin, he possessed substantial amounts of land in several parts of Ireland, including Meath, counties Dublin, Louth, Carlow, Tipperary, Kilkenny, and Galway. In 1585 he was returned to the Irish parliament as MP for co. Dublin. He died at his house at Corbally on 5 September 1607, and was buried in Donabate, co. Dublin. His wife, who survived him, was Alison, daughter of Sir John Plunket of Dunsoghly, chief justice of the king's bench in Ireland. They had no children. His heir, Nicholas *Netterville, was the son of his elder brother John, and became first Viscount Netterville of Dowth in 1622. Thus he provided for a great aristocratic estate. Netterville left a life interest in his estates to his wife and lands at Corbally and elsewhere to Luke Netterville, a younger son of his heir.

ANDREW LYALL

Sources DNB • J. G. Crawford, *Anglicizing the government of Ireland: the Irish privy council and the expansion of Tudor rule, 1556–1578* (Dublin, 1993) • C. Brady, *The chief governors: the rise and fall of reform government in Tudor Ireland, 1536–1588* (1994) • F. E. Ball, *The judges in Ireland, 1221–1921*, 2 vols. (1926); repr. (1993) • *Calendar of exchequer inquisitions, county Dublin* (Dublin and Carlow), vol. 1, pp. 353–4

Archives PRO, SP 63

Nettlefold, Joseph Henry (1827–1881), screw manufacturer, was born in London on 19 September 1827, the son of John Sutton Nettlefold (1792–1866) and his wife, Martha Chamberlain (1794–1866), both Unitarians. What was to become the future firm of Guest, Keen, and Nettlefold (GKN) began when John Nettlefold opened an ironmonger's shop at 54 High Holborn, London, in 1823, and in 1826 a watermill at Sunbury-on-Thames to make iron woodscrews; this was followed in 1834 by a steam-powered factory in Baskerville Place, off Broad Street in Birmingham, the centre of the screw trade.

The crucial breakthrough came in 1854, with the purchase of the United Kingdom rights of an American patent for the manufacture, by steam machinery, of a revolutionary woodscrew with a pointed end, which acted as its own gimlet. John Nettlefold needed £30,000 to buy

Joseph Henry Nettlefold (1827–1881), by unknown photographer

the patent and to begin manufacture; his wife's brother, Joseph Chamberlain, invested £10,000, becoming an equal partner in Nettlefold and Chamberlain, and sending his own son, also named Joseph *Chamberlain, to look after the investment. The older generation of both families remained in London; the new partnership was managed by Joseph Nettlefold, his elder brother Edward, and the younger Joseph Chamberlain. A factory was built in Heath Street, Smethwick, on the canal and railway on the outskirts of Birmingham; it comprised 20,000 square feet in two single-storey sheds. By 1864 it had 600 employees.

When the Chamberlains left the firm in 1874, Joseph Nettlefold moved into the void thus created. In 1878, on his brother's death, he became chairman and prime mover in the creation of a limited liability company in 1880. By then the Smethwick factory had trebled in size, and new offices had been built in Broad Street. It was Nettlefold too who organized the building up of the firm's virtual monopoly of the woodscrew trade in Britain. These two operations went together, for additional capital was needed to buy up competitors, and iron and wire suppliers. The neighbouring firm, Birmingham Screw, was acquired; this permitted further extension at Smethwick.

Not much is known of Nettlefold's personality. He was educated in a nonconformist academy; his abilities lay in mathematics, engineering, and business administration. An obituary said that his tastes were simple, and that he was wholly free from a sense of personal importance. He became a member of the Institution of Mechanical Engineers in 1860. He was a benefactor to the city, leaving twenty-five pictures by David Cox to the Birmingham Art Gallery (on condition that it opened on Sundays). He also left £1000 to the King's Heath and Moseley Institute.

Nettlefold was a man of great business capacity, and his leadership established the prosperity of the company for a decade after his death; thereafter it declined, until it was acquired by Arthur Keen, of Guest, Keen & Co., in 1902.

In 1867 Nettlefold married a Catholic, Mary Maria (b. 1835), daughter of John Seaborne of Birmingham. They had three daughters, none of whom was connected with the family business. Nettlefold died of an apoplectic seizure on 22 November 1881, at his Scottish home, Allean House, near Pitlochry, Perthshire.

BARBARA M. D. SMITH, rev.

Sources Institution of Mechanical Engineers: Proceedings (1882), 9–10 · E. Jones, Innovation and enterprise, 1759–1918 (1987), vol. 1 of A history of GKN · DBB · private information (1993) · CGPLA Eng. & Wales (1882)
Likenesses photograph, repro. in Jones, Innovation and enterprise, pl. 55 [see illus.]
Wealth at death £287,887 5s. 1d.: probate, 30 Jan 1882, CGPLA Eng. & Wales

Nettles, Stephen (fl. 1595–1647), Church of England clergyman, was born in Shropshire; further details of his background are unknown. He was admitted a pensioner at Queens' College, Cambridge, on 25 June 1595, graduated BA in 1599, and proceeded MA in 1602 (a degree incorporated at Oxford on 13 July 1624). He was a fellow of Queens' for several years, and commenced BD as a member of Corpus Christi College, Cambridge, in 1611. He was briefly rector of Alderton, Suffolk, in 1608–9.

From 1610 to 1644 Nettles was rector at Lexden. He was also vicar of two other Essex parishes: he held Great Tey from 1617 until 1623, when he exchanged it with Timothy Rogers for Steeple. Nettles lived at Lexden, whose parish register records the baptisms of four children: Mark (1615), Rebecca (1620), Stephen (1623), and, after the death of his namesake, another Mark (1626). The register is silent as to the name of the mother of the first child; the other three entries name Stephen's wife as Rebecca. It is likely that there was an eldest son who does not appear in Lexden parish register: though the identification must remain uncertain, he could plausibly be John Nettles, who was rector of Lexden from 1657 to 1669.

In 1625 Nettles published An Answer to the Jewish Part of Mr Selden's History of Tithes (1625). This was a closely argued, but rather narrow, tract designed to reiterate from a close reading of the scriptures in Hebrew the obligation to pay tithes to the clergy; Nettles published it after his earlier criticism of Selden in a sermon had encountered opposition. If this was at Lexden, it provides further evidence of objections to Nettles's ministry, in a parish where he had been successful after a dispute in pursuing his own, more immediate claims for the payment of tithes. His predecessor at Lexden had been a godly preaching minister, but Nettles was of a different mettle. He was a pluralist and conformist, who was reported as saying that 'the booke of comon Prayer is an absolute Rule to walke by' (BL, Add. MS 5829, fol. 50). In 1629 he signed the petition of the conformable ministers of Essex against Thomas Hooker, the puritan lecturer, and on occasion he presided over the Colchester archdeaconry church court at Lexden.

In 1644 a range of accusations were entered against Nettles before the Essex committee for scandalous ministers. These included various moral failings. It is not possible to ascertain whether these, sometimes stereotypical, accusations were true, but the real burden of the complaint was his failure to perform his clerical duties to the satisfaction of his godly parishioners. Although appointed before Sir Thomas Lucas, elder brother to Sir John Lucas, acquired the manor and living, Nettles's politics mirrored that of this strongly loyalist family. He was accused of failing to give notice of the fast days prescribed by parliament and of ostentatiously flouting them by inviting others to dine with him; he had failed to take or administer the vow and covenant (the oath of loyalty imposed by parliament following Waller's plot in May 1643) and he later refused to pay the parliamentary assessment. In 1649 Stephen Nettles junior, presumably his son, had his estate seized for his part in the royalist defence of Colchester during the second civil war. Nettles was evicted from his living in 1644, but internal divisions within the parish allowed him to reintrude himself briefly in 1647. The last secure record for Nettles is, appropriately, an order by the Essex county committee for him to reimburse his successor for tithes wrongly collected during his reintrusion. There is a record of a 'Steven Nettils, a strainger' buried on 7 August 1657 in Aldenham, Hertfordshire, where the John Nettles who became rector of Lexden also lived.   JOHN WALTER

Sources Walker rev. · S. Nettles, An answer to the Jewish part of Mr Selden's history of tithes (1625) · Venn, Alum. Cant. · Foster, Alum. Oxon. · W. Cliftlands, 'The "well-affected" and "the country": politics and religion in English provincial society, c.1640–c.1654', PhD diss., Essex University, 1987 · BL, Add. MS 5829, fols. 49–52 · PRO, SP 16/152/4 · H. Smith, The ecclesiastical history of Essex under the Long Parliament and Commonwealth [1933] · Essex RO, D/ABW 51/186 · VCH Essex, 9.391–401 · R. Newcourt, Repertorium ecclesiasticum parochiale Londinense, 2 (1710) · H. Smith, 'Some omissions in Newcourt's Repertorium', Transactions of the Essex Archaeological Society, new ser., 17 (1923–5), 23–7, esp. 25 · J. H. Round, ed., Register of the scholars admitted to Colchester School, 1637–1740 (1897) [also pubd as appx to Transactions of the Essex Archaeological Society, new ser., 4 (1893)] · IGI · R. Freeman Bullen, 'Catalogue of beneficed clergy in Suffolk, 1551–1631', Proceedings of the Suffolk Institute of Archaeology and Natural History, 22 (1934–6), 294–333

Nettleship, Edward (1845–1913), ophthalmic surgeon, was born on 3 March 1845 at the family home in Gold Street, Kettering, Northamptonshire, the fourth of the seven children of Henry John Nettleship (1807–1870), solicitor, and his wife, Isabella Ann (1818–1898), daughter of the Revd James Hogg, vicar of Geddington, Northamptonshire. As he did not possess the remarkable aptitude for the classics of his brothers, Henry *Nettleship, John Trivett *Nettleship, and Richard Lewis *Nettleship, his early education was confined to Kettering grammar school (until 1860). His enthusiasm for natural history suggested a vocation for farming and he was sent to the Royal Agricultural College at Cirencester. Study there (1861–3), and his subsequent courses in London, simultaneously at the Royal Veterinary College and King's College Hospital, proved his academic ability. He graduated MRCVS and as a licentiate of the Society of Apothecaries in 1867.

For some months Nettleship returned to the Royal Agricultural College as a lecturer, before deciding to concentrate on human medicine, influenced against his own preference by his family. In 1868 he obtained the membership of the Royal College of Surgeons and, two years later,

its fellowship. He had the good fortune to attract the patronage of the polymath Jonathan Hutchinson, initially as his assistant at the London Hospital and the Blackfriars Hospital for Skin Diseases. In 1869 Nettleship published the first description of the skin disorder urticaria pigmentosa.

On 22 January 1869 Nettleship married Elizabeth Endacott Whiteway (b. 1843/4) from Compton in Devon, daughter of Richard Whiteway, a farmer, and the sister of a college friend; there were no children. To secure his professional future, they considered emigration to New Zealand, but experience as Hutchinson's assistant at Moorfields Eye Hospital encouraged Nettleship to specialize. By so doing he deviated from his mentor's teaching; nevertheless, their association matured into lifelong friendship. Nettleship's choice of ophthalmology was facilitated by his appointment as librarian and curator of the museum at Moorfields (1871–3). He seized this opportunity for research, and subsequent publications established his credentials as a meticulous scientific investigator, initially on eye pathology and later on a wide range of clinical topics.

Nettleship left Moorfields for the post of medical superintendent at the Ophthalmic School at Bow (1873–4). This difficult work, with pauper children in isolation because of ocular infections, resulted in a Local Government Board commission for him to report on conditions in the metropolitan poor-law schools. Thereafter his career prospered, with staff appointments at the South London Ophthalmic Hospital (1873–8), St Thomas's Hospital (1878–95), Great Ormond Street Hospital (1880–81), and Moorfields (1882–98).

Contemporaries regarded Nettleship as a sound diagnostician and a methodical, if not brilliant, surgeon. The popularity of his textbook The Student's Guide to Diseases of the Eye (1879) reflected his teaching ability, and from 1888 to 1891 his workload was increased by appointment as dean of the St Thomas's medical school.

Nettleship's stature in the speciality was recognized by both colleagues and patients. A founder member of the Ophthalmological Society of the United Kingdom, he was chosen as its president (1895–7). His private practice, begun in 1875 and conducted from 5 Wimpole Street, London, flourished. In May 1894, under the scrutiny of considerable press interest, he operated on the former prime minister William Ewart Gladstone, to extract a cataract. Two years later Nettleship examined Queen Victoria for the same condition, but advised against surgery.

Nettleship retired from clinical practice in 1902 and concentrated on the application to his speciality of the developing science of genetics. His former colleagues and students marked his retirement by founding the Nettleship medal 'for the encouragement of scientific ophthalmic work'. Nettleship's pioneering series of papers on inherited eye disease inspired a school of successors and was acknowledged in 1912 by fellowship of the Royal Society.

The early influence of his authoritarian mother and the absence of children of his own may have contributed to the austere, reserved façade that Nettleship presented to outsiders. This was particularly apparent in 1907, when he was embroiled in the dispute over the care of the children of his late niece, Ida, and Augustus John, their unconventional father. His pupils, patients, and friends were aware, though, of the underlying warmth and generosity of his character, which complemented the energy and determination he applied to his researches. Born into a staunch Church of England family, Nettleship joined the positivists in 1873. In later life he actively supported the eugenics movement, while engaged on a study of albinism with Karl Pearson.

Prostatic surgery in 1911 led to distressing complications, and Nettleship's recovery was interrupted by the development of cancer of the lower bowel. Despite treatment with radiotherapy, he died at his home, Longdown Hollow, Hindhead, Surrey, on 30 October 1913; after cremation at Woking on 3 November, his remains were interred at St Stephen's Church, Shottermill, on 4 November. His wife survived him.   WILLIAM A. BRANFORD

Sources J. B. Lawford, 'Edward Nettleship', in J. Bell, *The treasury of human inheritance*, 2: *Anomalies and diseases of the eye* (1922), ix–xv [Nettleship memorial vol.] · private information (2004) · M. Jay, 'Remembrances of things past: Nettleship's two pedigrees of retinitis pigmentosa, a historical postscript', *Survey of Ophthalmology*, 27 (1983), 264–8 · *BMJ* (8 Nov 1913), 1261–2 · *The Lancet* (8 Nov 1913), 1354–5 · S. Stephenson, 'The late Mr Edward Nettleship', *The Ophthalmoscope*, 2 (1913), 767–9 · *The Times* (1 Nov 1913), 11 · W. C. Marshall, 'Mr Edward Nettleship F.R.S.', *Eugenics Review*, 5 (1913–14), 353–4 · D'A. Power and W. R. Le Fanu, *Lives of the fellows of the Royal College of Surgeons of England, 1930–1951* (1953) · M. Holroyd, *Augustus John: a biography*, 2 vols. (1974–5) · M. Reid, *Ask Sir James* (1987) · W. B. Shelley and J. T. Crissey, *Classics in clinical dermatology* (1953) · m. cert. · d. cert. · *CGPLA Eng. & Wales* (1913)

Archives CUL · RS · UCL, Institute of Ophthalmology · UCL, corresp. and papers | BL, Congreve MSS · BL, letters to W. E. Gladstone, Add. MSS 44518–44526 · CUL, corresp. with Charles C. Hurst · UCL, Pearson MSS

Likenesses photograph, *c.*1912, UCL · Gainsborough Studio, photograph, repro. in Lawford, 'Edward Nettleship' · photograph, repro. in *Veterinary Journal* (1913), 543–4 · photograph, repro. in E. T. Collins, *History of Moorfields Eye Hospital* (1929), pl. xvii

Wealth at death £26,768 10s. 4d.: probate, 1 Dec 1913, *CGPLA Eng. & Wales*

Nettleship, Henry (1839–1893), Latin scholar, was born on 5 May 1839 at Kettering, Northamptonshire, the eldest of the six sons of Henry John Nettleship (1807–1870), solicitor, of Kettering, and his wife, Isabella Ann (1818–1898), daughter of the Revd James Hogg. Nettleship attended Mr Darnell's Preparatory School, Market Harborough, before going in 1849 to the new Lancing College, and then in 1852 to Durham School, whose headmaster was Edward Elder, for whose character and attainments Nettleship always retained the utmost admiration. In 1854 Nettleship followed Elder to Charterhouse, and became a 'gown-boy' by winning an open foundation scholarship in 1855. Among his Charterhouse friends and contemporaries was Richard Claverhouse Jebb. In April 1857 he gained an open scholarship at Corpus Christi College, Oxford, of which John Conington, as Latin professor, was a fellow. He gained a first in moderations, and won the Hertford scholarship and the Gaisford prize for Greek prose in 1859; and,

Henry Nettleship (1839–1893), by unknown engraver, pubd *c.*1893 (after Elliott & Fry)

though he only achieved a second in *literae humaniores* in 1861, in the same year he won one of the two Craven scholarships, and in 1862 a fellowship at Lincoln College which he retained until 1871 (MA 1863). In 1863 he won the chancellor's prize for a Latin essay, on the civil war in America. He was tutor and librarian of Lincoln College (1862–8), and an assistant master at Harrow (1868–73), under Dr H. M. Butler. In 1870 he married Matilda, daughter of the Revd Thomas Henry Steel, another Harrow master. With his intellectual aims and interests Nettleship could hardly feel quite at home in a public school, though he was valued by his Harrow pupils and colleagues; it was a welcome relief when in Michaelmas 1873 he returned to Oxford as fellow of Corpus and joint classical lecturer at Corpus and Christ Church. In 1878 he was elected to the Corpus professorship of Latin and held it with success and distinction until his death. Though he never played a very prominent part in university politics, Nettleship was one of the academic reformers who believed a university should be organized for learning and research as well as undergraduate education. In this, Nettleship was to some extent influenced by Mark Pattison, to whom he owed much, and of whom he always spoke highly. It was probably from Pattison's advice that Nettleship decided to see a German university. With an introduction from Pattison to Professor E. Hübner, Nettleship went in 1865 to Berlin, matriculating there and attending lectures as a student during a summer semester. In the 1870s he was one of the Oxford 'Germanizers', and he became a keen proponent of new honours schools. His impression of German learning and modes of study he recorded in his sketch (reprinted in his *Lectures and Essays*) of Professor Moritz Haupt. Nettleship already possessed scholarship, in the English sense of the term; but Haupt made him aware that this was only a beginning, and that a larger and more critical view of ancient literature was requisite to make a philologist. Nettleship's Oxford teacher Conington, who had done much towards reviving the study of Latin in the university, was a peculiar scholar, studying almost exclusively a few 'best authors'; in his later years he lapsed into translation, and chose to address the general public rather than academe. Nettleship, however, eschewed translation, and saw that, to understand an ancient author, one must know much more than what is contained in the pages of his book. This larger conception was shown in his first published work, his completion of Conington's Virgil (1871), to which he prefixed an important introduction on the ancient critics and commentators on Virgil, and again in his *Suggestions Introductory to the Study of the Aeneid* (1875), and *Ancient Lives of Virgil* (1879). In 1877 he was diverted from these studies by an invitation to prepare for the Clarendon Press a new Latin dictionary; and he decided not to revise an existing dictionary, as his predecessors did, but to produce a new work by a fresh reading of the ancient texts and authorities. Failing to obtain the hoped-for collaboration, Nettleship worked single-handed for several years before he finally relinquished the task as too great for any one man. The main results of these years of labour were printed as *Contributions to Latin Lexicography* (1889), which Professor J. E. B. Mayor characterized as a 'genuine piece of original work, necessary to all serious students of the Latin language'; its importance was also recognized abroad. During these severe and technical studies Nettleship never lost his hold on literature, and he had long intended a history of Roman literature. From a sense of duty, however, he felt bound to agree to a request from Oxford University Press to complete the Nonius his friend and pupil J. H. Onions of Christ Church had undertaken and, by his death in 1889, left unfinished. Though difficult, it was a job for which Nettleship possessed unique qualifications; and he was devoting himself to it with his usual thoroughness when his fatal illness overtook him.

Nettleship combined with his devotion to scholarship a fine sense for language and literary form. As F. Haverfield wrote:

> He was willing to plunge deep into laborious and abstruse detail, but he kept throughout a clear sense of the ultimate meaning of it all. The deification of detail, the favourite fault of Kleinphilologie, was his abhorrence. His researches into Latin glossaries, into Verrius Flaccus, Nonius, and the rest, were carried through with the distinct consciousness that the results would illustrate the whole vocabulary of Latin, as well as the efforts made by the Latins themselves to study their own language. (*Classical Review*, 370)

And he never forgot that the final end of all lexicography is to throw light on literature and history. Opinions varied on his lectures, but with a few pupils in his room 'the inspiration was unmistakable and unforgettable' (ibid., 370). His contemporaries considered him a great scholar.

Nettleship read much modern literature and was interested in recent philosophical speculation, but his passion was for music. Even as a schoolboy he wanted to study it seriously. His desire to understand the theory and methods of the great German composers increased as he grew older, and in his later years he systematically studied the works of J. S. Bach. He was an accomplished pianist. Opposed to tests and other impediments to freedom of thought and enquiry in matters of religion, he had a serious religious vein, and had no sympathy with the coarser forms of theological liberalism. Interested in politics, he was a keen Liberal until the 1885 Home Rule Bill, when he became a Liberal Unionist. In his later years he was also interested in issues of popular education, women's higher education, and women's trade unionism.

Nettleship contributed many articles and reviews to *The Academy*, *Journal of Philology*, and *Classical Review*, and some to American and German classical journals. He superintended edition after edition of Conington's Virgil and Persius, bringing them up to date and incorporating valuable additions of his own. He edited for the Clarendon Press the *Essays of Mark Pattison* (1889), and the second edition of Pattison's *Casaubon* (1892). With J. E. Sandys, he revised and edited the English translation of Seyffert's *Dictionary of Classical Antiquities* (1891). He contributed to the third edition of Smith's *Dictionary of Greek and Roman Antiquities*, and contributed a critically edited text of Virgil to the Cambridge Corpus Poetarum. His essay entitled 'The present relations between classical research and classical education in England' appeared in *Essays on the Endowment of Research* (1876), edited by Dr Appleton. His other publications included *The Roman Satura* (1878), *Ancient Lives of Vergil, with an Essay on the Poems of Vergil in Connection with his Life and Times* (1879), and *Lectures and Essays on Subjects Connected with Latin Literature and Scholarship* (1885).

Nettleship was shy, diffident, hesitant, and sometimes abrupt in manner, inclined to hero-worship, and with a strong sense of injustice. Following influenza in January 1892 and prolonged illness, he died at his home, 17 Bradmore Road, Oxford, on 10 July 1893. He was survived by his wife.

INGRAM BYWATER, rev. ROGER T. STEARN

Sources *The Times* (11 July 1893) · Foster, *Alum. Oxon.* · *Classical Review*, 7 (1893), 369–72 · *Oxford Magazine* (18 Oct 1893), 7 · private information (1894) · personal knowledge (1894) · Boase, *Mod. Eng. biog.* · *Hist. U. Oxf.* 6: *19th-cent. Oxf.*

Archives Bodl. Oxf., notes and corrections to *Ancient lives*, 1879, MS Eng. misc. d. 113

Likenesses wood-engraving, pubd *c.*1893 (after photograph by Elliott & Fry), NPG [*see illus.*]

Wealth at death £1301 9*s.*: probate, 19 Aug 1893, *CGPLA Eng. & Wales*

Nettleship, John Trivett (1841–1902), animal painter, was born at Kettering, Northamptonshire, on 11 February 1841, the second son of Henry John Nettleship, solicitor, and brother of Henry *Nettleship, Richard Lewis *Nettleship, and Edward *Nettleship. His mother was Isabella Ann, daughter of James Hogg, vicar of Geddington and master of Kettering grammar school. Music was hereditary in the family, and Nettleship was for some time a chorister at New College, Oxford. Afterwards he was sent to the cathedral school at Durham, where his brother Henry had preceded him. Having won the English verse prize on 'Venice' in 1856, he was taken away comparatively young in order to enter his father's office. There he remained for two or three years, finishing his articles in London. Though admitted a solicitor, and in practice for a brief period, he decided to devote himself to art, for which he had shown an aptitude from childhood. Accordingly he entered himself as a student at Heatherley's and at the Slade School in London, but to the last he was largely independent and self-taught. His first work was in black and white, not for publication, but to satisfy his natural temperament, which always led him to the imaginative and the grandiose. However, none of the designs conceived during this early period was ever properly finished. They include biblical scenes, such as *Jacob Wrestling with the Angel* and *A Sower Went Forth to Sow*, which show the influence of William Blake. Nothing was published under his own name except a poor reproduction of a *Head of Minos* in the *Yellow Book* (April 1904). But the illustrations to *An Epic of Women* (1870), by his friend Arthur William Edgar O'Shaughnessy, are his; and his hand may likewise be traced in a little volume, *Emblems*, by A. Cholmondeley (1875), where his name erroneously appears on the title-page as 'J. J. Nettleship'. On 15 April 1876 he married Adaline Cort, daughter of the otologist James Hinton; she survived him with three daughters. The eldest, Ida, studied at the Slade School and was married to Augustus John; she died in Paris in 1909.

Nettleship delighted in physical activity: he rode to hounds as a boy, took boxing lessons from a famous prize-fighter when he went to London, is reputed to have walked to Brighton in a day, and accompanied a friend, Henry Cotton, on a mountaineering expedition to the Alps, for which they trained barefoot. It was this delight in physical prowess and in wild life that now induced him to become a painter of animals. He made studies, almost daily, in London's zoological gardens; and for twenty-seven years (1874–1901) exhibited large-scale paintings of lions, tigers, and so on at the Royal Academy and for most of the period at the Grosvenor Gallery. *Puma Devouring a Peacock*, in many respects 'his strongest and most characteristic' work (Bryan, *Painters*, 4.14), was exhibited at Burlington House. Though always noble in conception and often effective in grouping and in colour, these pictures failed somewhat in technique. At one time more than a dozen of them were exhibited together in the Corn Exchange at Gloucester; but a scheme for purchasing the collection fell through, and they were dispersed. In 1880 Nettleship was invited to India by the Maharaja Gaikwar of Baroda, for whom he painted a cheetah hunt as well as an equestrian portrait; he was thus able to observe animals in their natural habitat. In his later years he worked in pastel, and, painting his old subjects on a smaller scale, acquired a wider measure of popularity.

Nettleship's interests were not confined to painting. In 1868 he published a volume of essays on Robert Browning's poetry (enlarged third edition published as *Robert Browning: Essays and Thoughts*, 1895). The book prompted an intimate friendship between the poet and his critic. Another book that shows both his power of literary expression and his opinions about his own art is *George Morland and the Evolution from him of some Later Painters* (1898). He illustrated a number of books, including *Natural History Sketches among the Carnivora* by A. Nicols (1885) and *Icebound on Kolguev* by A. B. R. Trevor Battye (1895).

After a long and painful illness Nettleship died at 33 Beaumont Street, London, on 31 August 1902, and was buried at Kensal Green cemetery. A memorial tablet in bronze, designed by Sir George Frampton, with the aid of two fellow artists who were born in the same town as Nettleship, Sir Alfred East and Thomas Cooper Gotch, has been placed in the parish church at Kettering.

J. S. COTTON, *rev.* MARK POTTLE

Sources personal knowledge (1912) · H. Cotton, *India and home memories* (1911) · Graves, *RA exhibitors* · Mallalieu, *Watercolour artists* · Wood, *Vic. painters*, 2nd edn · J. Johnson and A. Greutzner, *The dictionary of British artists, 1880–1940* (1976), vol. 5 of *Dictionary of British art* · *The Times* (2 Sept 1902) · *The Times* (10 Sept 1902) · S. H. Pavière, *A dictionary of British sporting painters* (1965) · Bryan, *Painters* (1903–5) · *CGPLA Eng. & Wales* (1902) · m. cert.
Wealth at death £1330 18s. 5d.: probate, 24 Oct 1902, *CGPLA Eng. & Wales*

Nettleship, (Richard) Lewis (1846–1892), philosopher, was born on 17 December 1846 in Kettering, Northamptonshire. He was the son of Henry John Nettleship, a Kettering solicitor, and Isabella Ann Nettleship, the daughter of the Revd James Hogg. His five brothers included Henry *Nettleship, Latin scholar, John Trivett *Nettleship, painter and critic, and Edward *Nettleship, ophthalmic surgeon. He was educated first at a preparatory school at Wing, Buckinghamshire, and afterwards at Uppingham School under Edward Thring. Nettleship was elected to a scholarship at Balliol in 1864, and went to reside at Oxford in October 1865. He won a long series of university distinctions—the Hertford scholarship in 1866, the Ireland in 1867, the Gaisford Greek verse prize in 1868, a Craven scholarship in 1870, and the Arnold prize in 1873. Like his brother Henry, he disappointed expectations by taking only a second in *literae humaniores* (1869). His failure to gain a first was the result of his enthusiasm for philosophical idealism which at that time was regarded with hostility at Oxford.

Nettleship was elected to a fellowship at Balliol in 1869, and in the following year Jowett appointed him to a tutorship. As a tutor he eventually came to take the place of his friend, Thomas Hill Green, in the philosophical teaching of the college. Although remaining a layman, and abandoning conventional Christianity, he exercised a considerable pastoral influence. The strong and lasting impression he made on his pupils and friends, who included Arnold Toynbee and Henry Scott Holland, was largely due to his extremely interesting personality—a strange combination of intellectual acuteness with singular modesty and diffidence in matters of opinion. He never married, but nurtured a passionate, unreciprocated attachment from about 1880 until his death. Besides possessing the family love of music, Nettleship was fond of all outdoor exercise, especially walking and mountaineering, in which he sought relief from an unhappy and self-questioning temperament. As an undergraduate he rowed in his college boat. He died on 25 August 1892 from exposure in the course of an attempt to ascend Mont Blanc, and was buried at Chamonix.

During his lifetime Nettleship published little. A major historical project based on his Arnold prize essay, 'The Normans in Italy and Sicily', occupied him for several years but he ultimately handed over to A. L. Smith the collection of materials he had made for a book on the subject. He was invited by the Society for the Promotion of Christian Knowledge to write a book on Platonism but this too was abandoned. Of the original works that Nettleship did publish during his life the most significant are an essay, 'The theory of education in Plato's *Republic*', contributed to *Hellenica*, edited by Evelyn Abbott, an article on T. H. Green's philosophy in *Contemporary Review* (May 1892), and a valuable memoir of T. H. Green. This memoir is as much philosophical as biographical and Nettleship regarded it as among his best work. It was appended to the third volume of the *Works of T. H. Green*, which he edited after Green's death in 1882. Some of Green's posthumously published works required a great deal of intervention to bring the manuscripts to a finished state, and Nettleship's editing of Green's *Lectures on the Principles of Political Obligation* has been criticized. It has been suggested that these lectures display an account of the common good which differs from that found elsewhere in Green's writing and that the most likely explanation of this inconsistency is that Nettleship corrupted the text. However, close examination of the manuscript does not support this accusation.

Nettleship's *Philosophical Lectures and Remains* were published posthumously. These include his best-known work, afterwards published separately, the *Lectures on Plato's Republic*, which is still consulted. Here as elsewhere his work is characteristic of a generation of idealist philosophers whose thought was strongly marked by a reformist social conscience for which neither Christianity nor utilitarianism was any longer an adequate expression. His interpretation of Plato offers a conception of community which is both a denial of utilitarian individualism and a secular reinterpretation of Christian values.

INGRAM BYWATER, *rev.* C. A. CREFFIELD

Sources *Philosophical lectures and remains of Richard Lewis Nettleship*, ed. A. C. Bradley and G. R. Benson, 2 vols. (1897) • *The Times* (27 Aug 1892) • *Uppingham School Magazine* (Nov 1892) • M. Richter, *The politics of conscience: T. H. Green and his age* (1964) • F. M. Turner, *The Greek heritage in Victorian Britain* (1981) • P. Hinchliff, *Benjamin Jowett and the Christian religion* (1987) • Craig A. Smith, 'The individual and society in T. H. Green's Theory of Virtue', *History of Political Thought*, 2 (1981), 187–201 • P. Harris and J. Morrow, 'Did Nettleship corrupt Green's lectures?', *History of Political Thought*, 6 (1985), 643–6
Likenesses G. Girardot, oils, 1893, Balliol Oxf. • photograph, repro. in Bradley and Benson, eds., *Philosophical lectures and remains of Richard Lewis Nettleship*
Wealth at death £1444 0s. 3d.: probate, 30 Nov 1892, CGPLA Eng. & Wales

Neubauer, Adolf (1832–1907), Hebrew scholar, was born at Bitsche, Kottesó, Trentsen, in northern Hungary, on 7 March 1832, the son of Jacob Neubauer, a Jewish merchant and Talmudic scholar, and his wife, Amalie, *née* Langfelder. Intended by his father to become a rabbi, Neubauer was taught Hebrew by his cousin, Moses Neubauer, also a Talmudic scholar. About 1850 he taught at the Jewish school at Kottesó; soon afterwards he left for Prague, where he attended the lectures of the critical rabbinical scholar S. J. L. Rapoport, learned French, Italian, and Arabic, studied mathematics, and finally, on 15 December 1853, matriculated at Prague University. Between 1854 and 1856 he studied oriental languages at the University of Munich.

In 1857 Neubauer moved to Paris, where he resided until 1868, except for visits to various libraries to examine manuscripts, and a period in Jerusalem, where he held a post at the Austrian consulate. In Paris he discovered the manuscript room at the Imperial Library and met orientalists and Judaeo-Arabic scholars, such as Salomon Munk, Joseph Derenbourg, and Ernest Renan. It was at Paris that Neubauer found as his life's vocation the study, description, and publication of medieval Jewish manuscripts. In 1861–2 he began his scholarly career by publishing in the *Journal Asiatique* (vols. 18–20) extracts and translations from a tenth-century lexical work of David ben Abraham, of Fez, whose manuscripts he had found in a Karaite synagogue in Jerusalem. In 1866, after a visit to St Petersburg, he published *Aus der Petersburger Bibliothek*, which consisted of excerpts from related manuscripts held in the library there.

Neubauer pursued his interests in Palestine, and in 1863 he won the prize offered by the Académie des Inscriptions et Belles-Lettres for a critical exposition of the geography of Palestine, as set forth in the two Talmuds and other post-biblical Jewish writings. His first important work, *La géographie du Talmud: mémoire couronné par l'académie*, appeared in 1868, and placed its author in the first rank of rabbinical scholars, despite its occasional errors.

Neubauer had visited Oxford in 1866 in order to examine the collection of Hebrew manuscripts held in the Bodleian Library. Although the printed Hebrew books held in the library had been catalogued shortly beforehand (between 1852 and 1860) by Moritz Steinschneider, the manuscript collection was still untouched. In 1868 the curators invited Neubauer to catalogue the Hebrew manuscripts, and Oxford became his home until 1901. The catalogue which eventually appeared in 1886 contained descriptions of 2602 manuscripts (many consisting of between twenty and fifty distinct works). It was accompanied by an atlas of forty facsimile plates, illustrating the Hebrew palaeography of different countries and periods.

Despite his involvement with Hebrew manuscripts, Neubauer still found time for other literary work. He was appointed sub-librarian of the Bodleian Library in 1873, and he greatly expanded foreign collections and added especially to the oriental department of the library's holdings. Neubauer was in 1890 the first to recognize the value for Jewish literature of the genizah or depository attached to a synagogue, in which manuscripts no longer in use were put away. He eventually obtained for the Bodleian as many as 2675 items from the genizah at Old Cairo. These consisted frequently of several leaves, and many were of considerable interest and historical value. Neubauer began to catalogue these fragments, with very detailed descriptions, publishing a preliminary volume in 1886, but the work was completed and published by his successor, A. E. Cowley, in 1906.

During 1875 Neubauer also edited from a Bodleian and a Rouen manuscript the Arabic text of the eleventh-century Hebrew dictionary (the 'Book of Hebrew roots') of Abu-'l-Walid; this was a work of extreme importance in the history of Hebrew lexicography (which had been known before only through excerpts and quotations). Edward Pusey encouraged Neubauer to publish in 1876 a catena of more than fifty Jewish expositions of Isaiah 53, which was followed in 1877 by a volume of translations. In the same year there appeared, in the twenty-seventh volume of *L'histoire littéraire de la France*, a long section entitled 'Les rabbins français du commencement du XIVe siècle', which (though its literary form was due to Renan) was based throughout upon materials collected by Neubauer. A continuation of this work, 'Les écrivains Juifs français du XIVe siècle' (in volume 31 of *L'histoire littéraire*, 351–802), based similarly on materials supplied by Neubauer, appeared in 1893. These two volumes on the French rabbis remained the most important result of Neubauer's industry and learning. They include information drawn not only from Hebrew and German journals, but also from unpublished manuscripts in the libraries of Oxford, Paris, the south of France, Spain, Italy, and other countries.

In 1884 Neubauer was appointed reader in rabbinic Hebrew at the University of Oxford. In 1887 he published a Hebrew volume of medieval Jewish chronicles and chronological notes (a second volume appeared in 1895). He also issued, in 1878, a previously unknown Aramaic text of the book of Tobit, from a manuscript acquired in Constantinople for the Bodleian Library; and in 1897 he edited the original Hebrew of ten chapters of Ecclesiasticus from some manuscript leaves which had been discovered in a box of fragments from the Cairo genizah. A frequent contributor to learned periodicals, Neubauer wrote four articles entitled 'Where are the ten tribes?' for the *Jewish Quarterly Review* (1888–9), and contributed essays to the Oxford *Studia Biblica* in 1885, 1890, and 1891.

In 1890 Neubauer's eyesight began to fail him. He resigned from the library in 1899 and from the university in 1900. He continued to live in Oxford until 1901, when he moved to live with his nephew, Dr Adolf Büchler in Vienna. Büchler, who was also a rabbinical scholar, returned to England in 1906, when he was appointed vice-president of Jews' College, London. Neubauer died (unmarried) in the following year, on 16 April 1907, while living in London with Büchler at 18 Tavistock Square.

Neubauer's careful scholarship and integration into Oxford University life, helped perhaps by his failure to observe Jewish practices, ensured that he was accepted in English society. He was created MA of Oxford by diploma in 1873, and he was elected an honorary fellow of Exeter College in 1890. He received an honorary PhD from the University of Heidelberg, was made an honorary member of the Real Academia de la Historia at Madrid, and became a corresponding member of the Académie des Inscriptions et Belles-Lettres in Paris.

S. R. DRIVER, rev. SINÉAD AGNEW

Sources *The Times* (8 April 1907), 8 · *Jewish Chronicle* (8 April 1907), 8 · *Jewish World* (19 April 1907), 13 · *Jewish Chronicle* (8 March 1901), 12–13 · Allibone, *Dict.* · *Allgemeine Zeitung des Judentums* (3–10 Jan 1908)
Archives Bodl. Oxf., lecture notes
Likenesses L. C. Taylor, oils, 1900, Bodl. Oxf. · photograph, repro. in *Jewish Chronicle* (8 March 1901)
Wealth at death £10,912 13s. 5d.: probate, 1907, CGPLA Eng. & Wales

Neuberger, Albert (1908–1996), biochemist, was born on 15 April 1908 at Hassfurt, Germany, the first of the three children of Max Neuberger (1877–1931), cloth merchant and businessman, and Bertha, *née* Hiller (1888–1974), both religious Jews. He was educated first at home, mainly by private teachers or clergymen, with much emphasis on classics, including Latin and Greek, then at a *Gymnasium* in Würzburg, where he also studied mathematics and physics, but not biology or chemistry. In addition he was given a remarkably good Jewish education, which had a permanent impact on his life. During his medical studies at the University of Würzburg, Neuberger took courses in chemistry, and his interest in the subject continued throughout his career. He also spent some time in a research laboratory in Berlin where he established a lasting friendship with Ernst Chain, one of the many future Nobel prizewinners with whom he became closely associated. After receiving in 1931 a summa cum laude medical degree from the University of Würzburg, Neuberger worked for a short time as a clinician. As soon as Hitler came to power in January 1933 he left Germany and went to London.

Neuberger adapted rapidly to the British way of life and mastered the English language. In 1936 he obtained a PhD degree from the University of London for studies on the electrochemistry of amino acids and proteins, carried out under the guidance of Sir Charles Harington, and remained to continue his postdoctoral research there. Just before the outbreak of the Second World War he moved to the department of biochemistry at Cambridge University, headed by Frederick Gowland Hopkins, and at the time one of the world centres of biochemical research. Unlike many refugees from Nazi Germany, Neuberger had a comfortable life at Cambridge, since he was awarded the prestigious Beit memorial fellowship (1936–40). For some time during the war he served as consultant in nutrition to the medical directorate, general headquarters, India command. On 14 September 1943 he married Lilian Ida (*b.* 1912), daughter of Edmond Dreyfus and Marguerite (*née* Herz) from Basel.

From 1950 to 1955 Neuberger was head of the department of biochemistry at the National Institute for Medical Research, Mill Hill. He then moved to St Mary's Hospital medical school, where he was appointed professor of chemical pathology. During 1958–62 he also served as principal of the Wright–Fleming Institute of the hospital, a position held earlier by Sir Alexander Fleming. At sixty-five Neuberger retired from St Mary's and moved to Charing Cross Hospital medical school, where he continued to do research and to publish scientific articles until he was in his eighties.

Among Neuberger's many contributions to biochemistry the most important are in the area of glycoproteins, proteins that contain sugars in their molecules. This class of compound includes all antibodies and blood clotting factors, as well as many hormones, enzymes, and other body constituents. Their importance is also highlighted by the fact that a major product of the biotechnological industry is the glycoprotein erythropoietin, used for treatment of dialysis patients, with annual worldwide sales of over $5 billion. A seminal paper he published in the *Biochemical Journal* in 1938, showing that in ovalbumin, a protein from egg white, the sugar is an integral part of the molecule, marks the starting point of modern glycoprotein research. Subsequent work in his laboratory, mainly with Robin Marshall, led in 1963 to the discovery of the nature of the chemical bond that holds the protein and sugar together. It was the first of its kind to be understood, and was subsequently identified in many other glycoproteins isolated from animals, plants, and micro-organisms. Neuberger also carried out outstanding work on the porphyrins, vital constituents of haemoglobin of blood and of chlorophyll of green plants. Research done by him in the late 1940s to the middle 1950s, and in parallel by David Shemin at Columbia University, New York, contributed to the elucidation of the biosynthesis of the porphyrins. It also helped to explain the biochemical defect in acute porphyria, a disease believed to be the cause of George III's illness.

Neuberger was an inspiring teacher and had numerous students and co-workers, many of whom made illustrious careers for themselves. The most prominent was Fred Sanger, twice Nobel laureate, in 1958 for elucidating the amino acid sequence of insulin, and then in 1980, together with Walter Gilbert, for a method for DNA sequencing. Sanger obtained his doctorate under Neuberger's guidance in 1943 for work on protein metabolism and also studied with him the nutritive value of potatoes, within the framework of the war effort. He regarded Neuberger as his main teacher 'both by instruction and by example'.

Neuberger was elected to the Royal Society in 1951, and derived enormous pride from the election to the society in 1993 of his youngest son, Michael, a noted biochemist at the Medical Research Council Molecular Biology Laboratory, Cambridge. It was one of the rare cases of father and son both being FRS. In 1959 he received the Heberden medal of the Royal Society of Medicine, in 1960 the Frederick Gowland Hopkins medal of the Biochemical Society, and in 1973 he was elected an honorary member of that society. In the previous year he had become foreign honorary member of the American Academy of Arts and Sciences. In 1964 he became CBE. He received honorary doctorates from the University of Aberdeen (1967), the Hebrew University of Jerusalem (1968), and the University of Hull (1981).

Neuberger also rendered many services to the scientific community and to society in his country, in Israel, and elsewhere. In England he was a member of, among others, the Medical Research Council, the Agricultural Research Council, and the Council of Scientific Policy. He also served as chief editor of several leading scientific journals, including the *Biochemical Journal* (1947–55; chairman of the editorial board, 1967–9), and as associate managing editor of *Biochimica et Biophysica Acta* (1968–81). He was chairman of the governing body of the Lister Institute of Preventive Medicine from 1971 to 1988; when the building housing the research laboratories was closed, he established, from the proceeds of the sale, the Lister fellowships in medical research that have had an enormous impact on young scientists in Britain. In 1976 he was elected warden of Golders Green synagogue. Although an irregular attender, he accepted, having concluded that the long-term survival of Jewry was possible only along the lines of traditional Judaism.

Since the 1960s Neuberger and his wife had become closely attached to Israel, visiting the country frequently: he even went back to his Hebrew, which he had studied in childhood. During this period Neuberger devoted much time and energy to the Hebrew University, Jerusalem, serving for almost two decades as chairman of the academic committee of its board of governors.

Neuberger was a warm and kind person, a family man, modest and unassuming, with a clear penetrating mind and balanced views, who was liked and admired by many and whose advice was often sought. He was a polymath, deeply interested in the humanities, law, history, and Judaism. His hobbies were sailing (when young) and travel (until old age). He had an interesting and varied life and was blessed with an exceptionally happy marriage. The Neubergers had four sons, each of whom made a successful career in a different field: the Hon. Sir David (*b.* 1948) in law, James Max MD FRCP (*b.* 1949) in medicine, Anthony John MA MBA PhD (*b.* 1951) in economics, and Michael Samuel BSc PhD FRS (*b.* 1953) in molecular biology. A daughter, Janet, born in 1957, died in 1985. Neuberger died on 14 August 1996 of pneumonia, heart problems, and complications of diabetes, at his home, 37 Eton Court, Eton Avenue, Hampstead, London. He was buried at Bushey cemetery, Bushey, Hertfordshire. He was survived by his wife.

NATHAN SHARON

Sources A. Neuberger, 'Early work on the glycoprotein of egg albumin', *Trends in Biochemical Sciences*, 13, 398–9 · A. Neuberger, 'An octogenarian looks back', *Selected topics in the history of biochemistry: personal recollections III*, ed. G. Semenza and R. Jaenicke (Amsterdam, New York, 1990), 21–65 · A. Neuberger, 'Recollections: my interest in protein and glycoprotein chemistry', *Protein Science*, 6 (1990), 1119–21 · N. Sharon, 'Albert Neuberger (1908–1996): founder of modern glycoprotein research', *Glycobiology*, 7/3 (1997), x–xiii · personal knowledge (2004) · private information (2004) [family] · *The Times* (22 Aug 1996) · *CGPLA Eng. & Wales* (1996)

Archives RS · University of Bath, National Cataloguing Unit for the Archives of Contemporary Scientists | Bodl. Oxf., corresp. with Peter Mitchell · Bodl. Oxf., Society for Protection of Science and Learning File · Trinity Cam., corresp. with R. L. M. Synge | FILM Biochemical Society, 39 Portland Place, London, a two-hour video of Professor Neuberger in conversation with Professor Robin Marshall and Dr Gerge Tait

Likenesses photograph, repro. in *The Times* · photograph, repro. in Sharon, 'Albert Neuberger'

Wealth at death £1,019,354: probate, 20 Nov 1996, *CGPLA Eng. & Wales*

Neufmarché, Bernard de (*d.* 1121×5?), landowner, was the son of Geoffroi de Neufmarché, custodian of the castle of Le Neufmarché-en-Lion, Normandy, where Bernard was probably born, and of his wife, Ada, daughter of Richard de Heugleville. Bernard was a distant kinsman of William I through his mother. He had one brother, Drogo, who became a monk at St Évroul. Bernard probably did not participate in the Norman conquest of England. However, he had entered the service of William I by *c.*1085, when he witnessed a settlement made in Normandy before William between Gulbert de Alfait and the abbey of Fécamp. He was in England by 1086–7, witnessing William's 'foundation charter' to Battle Abbey. He does not appear in Domesday Book. Between 1086 and 1088 he was granted lands in Herefordshire (including Burghill, Brinsop, and Much Cowarne) by either William I or William II. At about the same time, Bernard married Nest (also known as Agnes), daughter and heir of the Herefordshire lord *Osbern fitz Richard [*see under* Richard Scrob], and granddaughter of the north Welsh king *Gruffudd ap Llywelyn. Through Nest, Bernard acquired further lands in Herefordshire, including Bodenham and Berrington. His English properties also included Pattingham in Shropshire, Hardington in Somerset, and the church of Speen, Berkshire.

In 1088, Bernard de Neufmarché participated in the rebellion against William II, joining the force which attacked Worcester. He may have been drawn into the rebellion by his father-in-law, and was apparently not punished for his actions. Also in 1088, he seems to have embarked upon his conquest of the minor Welsh kingdom of Brycheiniog, for late in 1088 he made a grant of Glasbury in Brycheiniog, together with Much Cowarne church, to St Peter's, Gloucester. This may have been a 'first fruits' offering. By 1093, Bernard was probably in possession of the Welsh capital of Brycheiniog, Talgarth, and in that year, the south Welsh king Rhys ap Tewdwr was killed near Aberhonddu by the Norman invaders of Brycheiniog. His death cleared the way for Bernard to annex the whole region, establishing himself and his feudal vassals in new castles and fiefs there. His main castle (which he may have commenced building before 1093) was at Aberhonddu, at the confluence of the rivers Honddu and Usk, where he also established the borough of Brecon. The motte is still standing, although none of Bernard's building survives. In the period 1094–6 he endured a number of setbacks in Brycheiniog as a result of the Welsh revolt of those years. However, his castles held out and he rapidly regained control. About 1100 he established the church of St John the Evangelist at Brecon; and he and his wife endowed it with lands in Brycheiniog and England, granting the whole as a dependency to Battle Abbey. With Bernard's consent, the monks of Battle established Brecon

Priory at this church. It may be that Bernard's foundation of the priory near the site of his victory over Rhys was done in emulation of William I's foundation of Battle itself. Bernard was also a benefactor of Auffray, a Norman church with strong links to his family. His activities in Brycheiniog threatened the rights of the diocese of Llandaff: he was among the magnates addressed on behalf of that church by Pope Calixtus II in 1119.

Bernard de Neufmarché had at least two children from his marriage to Nest: a son, Philip, who predeceased him, and a daughter, Sybil. In 1121 Sybil married Miles of *Gloucester who inherited Bernard's rights and lands as a result (some of them came to Miles at the time of the marriage). Gerald of Wales recorded a tradition of another son of Bernard and Nest, Mahel, who was deprived of the inheritance by his mother's perjury. The veracity of this is doubtful, however: Mahel, if he existed, may have been an illegitimate son of Bernard. The date of Bernard's death is not known: it seems to have occurred between 1121 and 1125.   K. L. MAUND

Sources Ordericus Vitalis, *Eccl. hist.* · E. Searle, ed., *The chronicle of Battle Abbey*, OMT (1980), 86–8 · John of Worcester, *Chron.*, s.a. 1088 · R. W. Banks, ed., 'Cartularium prioratus s. Johannis evang. de Brecon', *Archaeologia Cambrensis*, 4th ser., 14 (1883), 18–49, 137–68, 221–36, 274–311 · J. Williams ab Ithel, ed., *Annales Cambriae*, Rolls Series, 20 (1860), s.a. 1093, 1096 · T. Jones, ed. and trans., *Brut y tywysogyon, or, The chronicle of the princes: Peniarth MS 20* (1952), s.a. 1091 [1093], 1094 [1096] · T. Jones, ed. and trans., *Brut y tywysogyon, or, The chronicle of the princes: Red Book of Hergest* (1955), s.a. 1090 [1093], 1092 [1096] · T. Jones, ed. and trans., *Brenhinedd y Saesson, or, The kings of the Saxons* (1971), s.a. 1091 [1093], 1094 [1096] [another version of *Brut y tywysogyon*] · *Reg. RAN*, 1.62, 113, 207, 220, 300, 325; appx xxxii · W. H. Hart, ed., *Historia et cartularium monasterii Sancti Petri Gloucestriae*, 1, Rolls Series, 33 (1863), 64–5, 80, 88, 314–15 · *Gir. Camb. opera*, 4.28–9 · J. G. Evans and J. Rhys, eds., *The text of the Book of Llan Dâv reproduced from the Gwysaney manuscript* (1893), 93 · *ASC*, s.a. 1088 [text E]

Neuhoff, Theodor Stefan von, Baron von Neuhoff (1694–1756), king of Corsica, was born in Cologne on 24 August 1694, second child and only son of Anton, Baron von Neuhoff (*d.* 1695), of a Westphalian family, and Amelia, the daughter of a draper of Viseu near Liège. The origin of the family's baronial title has not been found. Finding himself *déclassé* by this match, Anton had given up an appointment in the service of the bishop of Münster and moved away from his ancestral area of the county of Mark. Shortly after his son's birth he died, leaving a modest estate of 11,000 florins; his widow then married a customs official at Metz called Marneau and had another daughter, who was later the wife of a parliamentary counsel at Metz called Gomé-Delagrange.

Theodor von Neuhoff seems to have been brought up at first by a relation on his father's side before being sent at the age of ten to the Jesuit school in Münster. After some years there, in 1709 or before, he became a page to Elisabeth Charlotte of the Palatinate, duchess of Orléans (known generally as Madame), at Versailles. On her recommendation he was later commissioned in the army of the elector of Bavaria; contracting heavy gambling debts, however, he evaded his creditors and went to Paris to lodge with his sister, now countess de Trévoux. According to a report relayed by Madame, his stay there was abruptly terminated by an argument in which he tried to kill his brother-in-law, and he again fled, this time to London. The other sources on Neuhoff's early life are silent on this affair, ascribing his departure to the pressure of further debts.

By 1716 Neuhoff had entered the service of the Swedish minister in the Netherlands, Baron Goertz. When Goertz was executed in March 1719, Neuhoff was on a mission for him to Cardinal Alberoni in Spain, and chose to remain there, obtaining a commission in a Spanish regiment through the influence of the powerful minister Ripperda.

It was at about this time that Neuhoff is stated to have married 'Lady Sarsfield', the daughter of an Irish peer at the Spanish court, 'Lord Kilmallock'. This would most naturally mean a daughter of David Sarsfield (killed 1710), titular Viscount Sarsfield of Kilmallock (the title had in fact been forfeit since 1691), a colonel of dragoons in the Spanish service and governor of Badajoz. However, Ruvigny, in his *Jacobite Peerage*, suggested that she was a daughter of Patrick *Sarsfield, who was created earl of Lucan by the exiled James II in 1691; his son James Sarsfield, Jacobite second earl of Lucan (1693–1719), was also in Spanish service. The marriage did not last long, as in 1720 Neuhoff abandoned his pregnant wife in the Escorial (in some accounts, taking her jewels with him) and went to Paris. His wife may have followed him there; a manifesto issued (apparently by Neuhoff himself) in Cologne in 1740 states that she died in Paris in 1724, in childbed of a daughter who also died. Whether there is any truth in this, and if so whether the daughter was Neuhoff's, is unclear, as the sources imply that he stayed only a brief while in Paris. According to the letters of the duchess of Orléans, he once again absconded from his sister's house, this time with 200,000 livres of her husband's money.

Between 1720 and 1732 Neuhoff is said to have travelled a great deal, being at least twice in London and several times in Italy, occasionally using the pseudonym Etienne Romberg. In 1732 he was in Genoa, at a time of great tension between that republic and its recalcitrant possession Corsica. According to one account he achieved a semi-official status as intermediary between the Corsican agents at Leghorn and the Genoese authorities. This undoubtedly exaggerates his role, although he was certainly known to the leaders of the Corsican party from this date. Corsican sources state that Neuhoff presented himself at this stage as an English nobleman, and encouraged inferences that he was acting on behalf of the British authorities. His only connections with Britain at this time were his occasional letters to George II recounting Jacobite activity and his own strenuous efforts to prevent it.

It is unclear at what point Neuhoff saw an opening for himself in Corsica. In early 1736, however, he was in Tunis, where his associates included two alchemically inclined monks who claimed to have developed a 'universal medicine' and a Sicilian doctor called Buongiorno. With their assistance he obtained arms, munitions, and other supplies on credit, and loaded them aboard a British vessel commanded by a Captain Dick, who may have been under the impression that the enterprise had official British support. They sailed for Corsica, with two redeemed slaves and some hangers-on, and on 12 March 1736 arrived at Aleria. In a letter to the rebel leaders Neuhoff offered himself as their king, requiring only that they guarantee religious freedom to non-Roman Catholics.

The offer was accepted. Corsica had long been regarded as a kingdom within the dominions of the kings of Aragon and then the doges of Genoa, and the rebels had already granted the title 'royal highness' to their three leaders, the 'primates' of the kingdom, Giacinto Paoli, Andrea Ceccaldi, and Luigi Giafferi. According to contemporary observers, these three found it a useful publicity-winning device to complete the picture with a king, however unsuitable the individual chosen. Neuhoff was installed in the episcopal palace in Aleria and crowned on 14 April, under a constitution which decreed his title hereditary by male primogeniture.

King Theodor's rule in Corsica manifested itself largely in the making of appointments (not all agreeable to the three primates) and the liberal distribution of titles, some of which were nobiliary while others were grades within the order of Deliverance (or Redemption). A silver and copper coinage was issued, struck from very poorly cut dies, the silver showing on one side the Virgin and, on the other, a shield with the arms of the Neuhoffs (three links of a chain) impaling those of the island (a Moor's head). Apart from a brief campaign in June, Neuhoff left military activities against the Genoese to the rebel commanders who had led them before. His own main assault on the Genoese was a robust reply to a long denunciation they had published of him and his dubious antecedents. But his rhetoric could not hide the disappointing lack of the supplies, munitions, and money that he had promised since the outset. As far as the rebel leaders were concerned he had served his purpose, and by the autumn his position in the island was perilously weak. On 4 November he published an edict creating a system of regency and, with Costa, his secretary of state, left for the coast. Disguised as a priest, he landed at Leghorn on 14 November.

In the five years that followed, Neuhoff travelled as ceaselessly as before, and was as frequently in debt, but managed with backing from a small group of Dutch merchants to mount two more abortive missions to Corsica. Among his followers were two nephews, both called Frédéric de Neuhoff, who both spent considerably more time and suffered much greater hardship in active support of the rebels in the island than he. Neuhoff now viewed Corsica as a family matter; in a letter of 1740 to his brother-in-law, Gomé-Delagrange, he claimed that his rights there derived not only from popular election as king, but also by inheritance from a Neuhoff ancestor who had been viceroy of the island and feudal lord of its southern part in the early tenth century.

In 1742 Neuhoff seems, briefly, to have gained rather more powerful support. Having been for an unknown period in London, he sailed in November for Leghorn, and thence, at the end of January 1743, for Corsica, with two

British men-of-war and 400 Austrian deserters and Corsican exiles. His arrival had been announced in an edict drafted for him by General Braitwitz (commander of the Austrian army in Tuscany), Count de Richecourt (French minister to Florence), and Burrington Goldsworthy (British consul at Leghorn). On reaching Corsica he received the compliments of the rebel leaders and sailed around the coast distributing small amounts of arms, powder, and ammunition. But there was now a Genoese-sponsored, 5000-strong, French expeditionary force in the island; on a second journey towards the end of February, aware of the weakness of his position, he did not even disembark. In fact the British had not agreed to support him: Horace Mann, minister to Tuscany (and Goldsworthy's superior), had from the outset renounced any involvement or responsibility in the enterprise, and in April orders were addressed to the commander of the Mediterranean Fleet expressly forbidding it. Having achieved little, Neuhoff travelled incognito to Florence where he had a long interview with Mann, in the course of which he apparently claimed to be the uncle of Amalie Sophie van Wallmoden, countess of Yarmouth, George II's mistress. (Lady Yarmouth's family, the Wendts, were certainly related to the Neuhoffs.) Mann continued to advise that Britain do nothing to assist Neuhoff. His requests for support from other quarters were rebuffed, although Corsica remained the centre of much international interest, and another plan to sail for Corsica in 1745 was scotched by Mann. In September 1747 Neuhoff was expelled from Tuscany.

After a period in Germany and the Netherlands, Neuhoff moved to London in January 1749. Using the name Baron Stein, he stayed at first with the Dutch envoy, Hendrik Hop, who with the Hanoverian minister Baron Münchhausen presented him to London society. In March 1749, at the house of the diplomat Sir Luke Schaub, he met Horace Walpole. But by the following December he was again seriously in debt, and shortly before Christmas he was arrested and imprisoned in the king's bench prison for a specific sum of £400.

Much visited in gaol over the ensuing three years by sightseers and well-wishers, Neuhoff appointed many of them to the order of Deliverance. Among those so honoured was Colonel Frederick [see Frederick, Felice], who later claimed to be his son. According to the *Gentleman's Magazine*, while a prisoner Neuhoff married on 25 July 1751 Miss Edmonston of Panton Square, 'a lady of beauty and fortune' (*GM*, 1st ser., 21, 1751, 332), but the marriage is not mentioned by any other source. His financial plight did not visibly alter, and the public interest in him waned somewhat. A subscription inaugurated by Walpole in *The World* in February 1753 raised only £50. Walpole attributed this to the notoriously bad character of the beneficiary, and complained that so far from being grateful, Neuhoff had threatened to sue the publisher of *The World* for misnaming him; but the satirical style of the announcement and its title 'Date obolum Belisario' were unlikely to have earned his approval, or encouraged donations.

Neuhoff's release was eventually secured, with Walpole's help, under the Insolvency Act of 1755. Registering his claim to the kingdom of Corsica as his only asset, and assigning it to his creditors (in a document later acquired by Walpole and exhibited at Strawberry Hill), he left gaol on 5 or 6 December 1756 and took up residence with a tailor in Little Chapel Street, Soho. But exhausted by his long imprisonment he fell ill immediately, and died there a few days later, on 11 December 1756. He was buried in an unmarked grave in the churchyard of St Anne's, Soho; a monumental inscription composed and paid for by Walpole was placed on the exterior of the church, and survives to this day. A neighbouring public house is still called the King of Corsica. A different form of immortality was bestowed by Voltaire, who included Theodore among the deposed monarchs depicted in chapter 26 of *Candide*. This scene was the basis for the opera *Il re Teodoro in Venezia* by Giovanni Paisiello and Giambattista Casti, which Walpole saw in London in December 1787. He thought it of poor quality, but reported that the emperor Joseph II was delighted with it, believing it to be a satire on the king of Sweden.

Theodore was frequently caricatured, but two engravings are known that may derive from reliable portraits. One, signed J. V. Schley and dated 1737, shows him fully wigged, moustachioed, and dressed in vaguely oriental garb, standing on the coast as if just arrived in Corsica. Another, more idealized, is signed I. I. Haid, and shows him clean-shaven in a short wig and rich, courtly dress. A third engraving sometimes reproduced as a portrait of Neuhoff is in fact from a painting by Van Dyck of the seventeenth-century Parisian collector Everard Jabach. Walpole's plan of sending William Hogarth to the king's bench prison to portray Neuhoff there, as related to Horace Mann in a letter of 25 July 1750, does not seem to have borne fruit.

C. E. A. CHEESMAN

Sources A. Le Glay, *Théodore de Neuhoff, roi de Corse* (1907) • *Histoire des révolutions de l'isle de Corse … et l'élévation de Théodore I sur le trône de cet état* (1738) • *The history of Theodore I, king of Corsica* (1743) • *Correspondance de Madame duchesse d'Orléans*, ed. and trans. E. Jaeglé, 2nd edn, 3 vols. (1890) • *Mercure Historique et Politique* (April 1740) [The Hague] • PRO, SP 85/13 [various dates] • PRO, SP 89/39/323–4 [1737] • *Mémoires de Rostini*, ed. P. Lucciana and L. Lucciana, trans. M. Letteron, 2 vols. (1882) • Walpole, *Corr.* • fondo Corsicae (eighteenth century), Archivio di Stato, Genoa
Archives Archivio di Stato, Genoa | PRO, State Papers, SP 85/13
Likenesses J. V. Schley, engraving, 1737, BM • I. I. Haid, engraving, BM
Wealth at death none: Walpole, *Corr.*, 1756

Neurath [*née* Itzig], **Eva Urvasi** (1908–1999), publisher, was born in Berlin on 22 August 1908, the youngest of five daughters of Rudolf Itzig, a Jewish clothier, who, after suffering from a breakdown, died when she was eight. Her mother, an art gallery proprietor who greatly influenced her, then married a solicitor called Kahn who worked for the Universal Film AG (UFA), Germany's largest motion picture company. She spent her youth working as a film extra (notably in F. W. Murnau's *Faust* in 1926) and was rewarded with a German shepherd puppy. She grew up in a prosperous, well-educated, and politically engaged family—her mother was an ardent socialist committed to women's rights—and spent her childhood in a villa in Berlin Tempelhof. She was mainly an autodidact, having left school at fourteen, in protest when some of her Jewish friends were expelled.

Eva Itzig then worked for a prominent auctioneer, publisher, and antiquarian bookseller, Paul Graupe, where she met her first husband, an editor, Ernst Jutrosinski. She married him aged eighteen shortly after she had been fired by Graupe. After the end of her marriage, which lasted a year, she started working for an antiquarian book-selling couple, the Rosenbergs, who committed suicide when Hitler came to power. In 1934, after converting to Judaism (her mother was non-Jewish), she married Wilhelm Feuchtwang, an industrial adviser and patent broker, and son of the chief rabbi of Vienna, whom she had met through her first husband. They had one son, the distinguished Chinese anthropologist Professor Stephan Feuchtwang. Wilhelm was arrested in 1937 suspected of assisting Jews to transfer funds abroad (he was released because of his Austrian nationality), but on the day of the *Anschluss* the family fled to Rotterdam. They had left just in time: the Gestapo visited the Feuchtwangs' flat in Berlin just a few hours after their departure.

The family arrived in England after a year in the Netherlands. At the outbreak of the Second World War Wilhelm was interned on the Isle of Man as an enemy alien. Facing starvation, and considering employment as a domestic, Eva lived with her son in Highgate, London, in a house owned by Martin Freud's mistress. Here she received news of her husband from a fellow internee, Walter *Neurath (1903–1967), production director of Adprint, a London 'book-packaging' company, also from Vienna. Neurath, who had been asked by Wilhelm to help his wife and son, introduced Eva to the refugee publisher Wolfgang Foges of Adprint, who was a 'packager' of interesting, good-quality illustrated books; these he later sold to other publishers, who finally produced and distributed them. Adprint's most distinguished work during and just after the Second World War was the series Britain in Pictures under the Collins imprint, which Walter Neurath had overseen, and which proved his loyalty to England in the eyes of the authorities, leading to his early release from internment. Eva Feuchtwang became involved with this series, which included such titles as George Orwell's *The English People* (1947), Rose Macaulay's *Life among the English* (1942), and John Piper's *British Romantic Artists* (1942), and by the end of the war she was head of the art department. These volumes showed great expertise in quality colour reproductions of works of art, and the first use of the 'integrated spread': unusually superb illustrations were incorporated into the text, rather than appearing in a separate plate section at the back or middle of the book.

On 21 September 1949, having left Adprint, Walter and Eva established Thames and Hudson with their life savings, backed by the printer John Jarrold and the engraver Wilfred Gilchrist. Amicably divorced from Wilhelm, Eva

married Walter on 6 August 1953, after the death of Walter's first wife (with whom he had two children, Thomas and Constance). From the beginning Thames and Hudson, situated near the British Museum, specialized in books on art, and was particularly successful in originating a paperback series, the World of Art, which consists now of some 150 titles on different artists and movements in art written by experts, but for popular consumption. Walter was the expert publisher, and Eva the aesthetic visionary behind such works as *The Book of Kells* (1974) and *The Bayeux Tapestry* (1985). Eva was also involved with H. C. Robbins Landon's five-volume biography of Haydn and the photographic works of Roloff Beny. On the death of Walter Neurath in 1967, Eva Neurath became chairman of Thames and Hudson (she insisted on using this term for herself), with Walter's son Thomas as managing director. She was closely involved with the business for the rest of her life. One of her last great efforts was, over three sleepless nights, to approve every sheet of the catalogue of the Francis Bacon retrospective at the Tate Gallery, London, in 1985.

Eva Neurath's large house in Highgate, London, filled with splendid Biedermeier furniture, was a centre of intellectual warmth. When invited for tea, one would almost always find her reading a book—Heine for instance—despite her poor eyesight in later life. She delighted in music (when interviewing a prospective editor, she might talk about Beethoven rather than publishing), in her villa in Tuscany, in her beautiful and stylish appearance, but above all in producing at Thames and Hudson books that reflect her great respect for the arts. She spoke of the difficult times she had lived through, both with seriousness and sometimes with a delicate snort of laughter. She would never, she said, have become the person she became in England had it not been for 'that chap' in Germany, as she called Hitler. She had heart trouble in her final years, and on her deathbed said, 'I know that I am dying, but my mind won't let me'. She died on 27 December 1999 at the London Clinic, 20 Devonshire Place, Westminster.　　　　DAVID PLANTE

Sources *The Guardian* (6 Jan 2000) · *The Times* (4 Jan 2000) · *Daily Telegraph* (4 Jan 2000) · *The Independent* (3 Jan 2000) · m. cert. [Walter Neurath] · d. cert. · *CGPLA Eng. & Wales* (2000)
Likenesses photograph, 1958, repro. in *Daily Telegraph* · photograph, repro. in *The Guardian* · photograph, repro. in *The Times*
Wealth at death £1,027,064—gross; £1,005,619—net: probate, 21 Aug 2000, *CGPLA Eng. & Wales*

Neurath, Walter (1903–1967), publisher, was born in Josef-städterstrasse, Vienna, on 1 October 1903, the only child of Alois Neurath (1872–1934) and his wife, Gisela Fröhlich (d. 1944). The Neurath family came from Bratislava and Alois Neurath arrived in Vienna aged twenty-one; he worked in a bank until he was twenty-eight, when he founded his own business as a wholesale importer of tea, coffee, and luxury foods. Walter Neurath spent his entire childhood in Vienna, where he was educated at the Volks Schule and the Real Gymnasium from which he matriculated with distinction. He then attended the University of Vienna where he studied art history, archaeology, and history, becoming, in 1922, a member of the Institute for Art History. At the same time he worked for the art book publisher Würthle & Sohn and organized various art exhibitions—including one in Paris—of nineteenth-century French paintings from Viennese collections. He also lectured on art history to the Austrian equivalent of the Workers' Educational Association.

Neurath was a founder member of Neustift ('new foundations'), a small left-wing commune of intellectuals with a radical approach to both life and culture which included the psychoanalyst Bruno Bettelheim, whose seminal work on the German concentration camps, *The Informed Heart*, Neurath was to publish with great success nearly forty years later. In 1925 Neurath married Lilly Kruk (a marriage which was dissolved in 1933) and, because of his father's ill health, joined and ran the family firm, thus acquiring considerable routine business skills. On his father's recovery in 1929 Neurath turned to full-time publishing, with a strong interest in printing and typography. He joined the Verlag für Kulturforschung ('publishing house for cultural research'), and Zinner Verlag, which published fiction and where, after six months, he was made production director. There he published a number of illustrated books, and the German language translations of English and American books. The rise to power in Germany of the Nazi party effectively closed the main German language market for this Jewish firm which therefore decided to close down.

From 1935 to 1937 Neurath worked as an educational publisher, developing new illustration techniques and creating, as general editor, a series of illustrated textbooks for children designed as an educational counter-influence to Nazi ideology. The books had a strong democratic and anti-totalitarian bias and were translated into seven foreign languages by like-minded publishers abroad. In 1937 Neurath was appointed manager of the Wilhelm Frick publishing house, where he continued to commission and publish both illustrated books on the arts and anti-Nazi propaganda. However, on the occupation of Austria by the Nazis he was ordered to cease publishing immediately and a Nazi-approved 'Commissar' was appointed to run the house.

Because of his anti-Nazi publishing activities, Neurath was soon on the Gestapo lists and, after several near misses and a period in hiding, managed to escape to England on 1 June 1938, taking with him his second wife, Marianne Müller (1909–1950), a schoolteacher. His sponsor for entry into England as an alien was Frances Margesson, wife of Captain (later Viscount) Margesson; the Neuraths stayed with the Margessons at Boddington, near Rugby, for some five years and their son Thomas was born there. Neurath was offered work by a company called Adprint, run by a fellow refugee, Wolfgang Foges. He soon became the production manager and both designed and produced the celebrated King Penguin series. It was originally intended to print this series in Czechoslovakia, but Germany's invasion of that country also meant that the books, published by Allen Lane of Penguin Books, were printed in England. Belonging as he did to a European

tradition of publishing where the series was the norm if not the rule, Neurath frequently thought in series terms rather than single volumes. Thus, after the success of what were in effect Penguin's first hardcover books, the beautifully made, jewel-like King Penguins, he developed a larger and more ambitious series called Britain in Pictures, edited by W. J. Turner.

A formidably scholarly and erudite man, Neurath had a genius for making illustrations an integral part of a book, placing them prominently on the page together with the words to which they were related, rather than banishing them to the plates section in the centre or (worse still) at the back of the book. Britain in Pictures married skilful picture research and fine design and printing with significant texts from George Orwell (*The English People*), Rose Macaulay (*Life among the English*), John Piper (*British Romantic Artists*), Michael Ayrton (*British Drawings*), and Jacquetta Hawkes (*Early Britain*); the series eventually comprised more than 100 volumes.

Just as the series was about to be launched the Second World War broke out, leading to paper rationing which was based on publishers' output in preceding years. A new firm, Adprint had no proper track record with which to secure a paper ration. The 'book packager' emerged, becoming a significant part of book publishing in the second half of the twentieth century. The packager put together author and subject and looked after the design of a book all the way through to complete production by a publisher with an adequate paper ration; it was that publisher whose name appeared on the jacket, spine, and title-page of the book. Neurath's brilliant series was actually successfully published by Collins, who also took on his next project, the even more numerous and more permanently successful New Naturalist series, edited by Julian Huxley. At a stroke, Adprint and Neurath had become a significant force in quality illustrated book publishing in Britain. The path was, however, not wholly smooth or unbroken: Neurath was not yet a naturalized British subject and was dispatched to an internment camp in the Isle of Man, alongside the Amadeus Quartet and other distinguished and blameless European artists and intellectuals viewed as 'enemy aliens'. Happily, aware that the Britain in Pictures series had considerable propaganda value, a friendly civil servant, Richard Cowell, managed to get Neurath released rapidly and he was soon back at work, with eventual naturalization as a British subject to follow.

Neurath stayed with Adprint, which was, however, less successful once the war ended. The firm had been financed by Tennants and its head, Lord Glenconner, lost faith in Foges and offered the managing directorship to Neurath, who declined it. He had more ambitious ideas and, on an exceedingly modest capital of £7000, departed to found Thames and Hudson in September 1949. His own contribution was his life savings of £3000; his co-directors included his Adprint colleague Eva Feuchtwang (who contributed her own savings of £150) and—shrewdly on Neurath's part—the printer John Jarrold and the process engraver Wilfrid Gilchrist. The firm's first book was a translation of a photographic work, *English Cathedrals*, by the Swiss photographer and publisher Martin Hürlimann. Happily this was successful and Neurath built on his American connections. The publishing house was named after the rivers of London and New York, to signify its ambition to publish on both sides of the Atlantic. However, the point was frequently missed in the business world and letters addressed to Mr Thames and Mr Hudson were often received.

Because of Neurath's high reputation in America and because editing, design, printing, and binding were then much cheaper in England and Europe than in the United States, American art book publishers such as Abrams and the great museums such as the Metropolitan and the Museum of Modern Art in New York not only appointed Thames and Hudson as their representative, but also relied on the firm to package some of their more complex art historical books, as well as publishing under the firm's imprint in the UK. Thames and Hudson thus simultaneously established its Anglo-American business and acquired an immediate turnover base and a niche in the English publishing market. Neurath's second wife, Marianne, had died in 1950, and on 6 August 1953 he married his longtime colleague Eva Feuchtwang (*b*. 1908) who, as Eva Neurath, was his full business partner as well as his wife and made an essential contribution to the success of the firm.

At that time the leading art book publishing house in England was the Phaidon Press, established by Neurath's fellow Viennese refugee Bela Horovitz, who had transferred his existing business to London in 1938. Their books were of the conventional kind, separating text and plates and rarely using colour. The Neuraths, having already established the integration of text and illustrations, also pioneered the use of a much higher proportion of colour illustration which, because of its much greater engraving and printing costs, was a brave departure in the 1950s. Neurath invariably not only planned his books on an Anglo-American axis but also aimed at the European market, producing books which were simultaneously translated into the principal western European languages and printed for publishers both in the major publishing countries such as France, Germany, Italy, and Spain and also, provided that the subject was sufficiently accessible, in Dutch, Finnish, and the three Scandinavian languages. Eventually even the problem of publishing key books such as Herbert Read's *A Concise History of Modern Painting* (1959) in Japanese was mastered.

Read's volume was part of a series, the World of Art, which was to be (and still is) one of the mainstays of the Thames and Hudson list. Neurath was not only the first publisher to produce art books at readily affordable prices—a World of Art title with approximately 100 pictures in colour would, typically, cost no more than a decent biography—but also the first to foresee the rise of the quality original paperback. By putting the World of Art into paperback form he could issue the books at prices which fitted student budgets, and the best titles in the series, such as Read's work or Michael Levey's *From Giotto to*

Cézanne (1962), which had over 500 colour illustrations, went on student reading lists all over the world, in as many as twenty languages, and sold by the hundred thousand. This had as powerful an impact on international art education as Allen Lane's Penguins had in making the possession of works of literature, biography, and other genres open to all, regardless of income, a point once made appreciatively to Neurath by Lane himself.

On the same principles of international co-production, Neurath also published in the fields of architecture, photography, archaeology, and history. Distinguished scholars responded to his enthusiasm, to the prospect of escaping the confines of a university press, to the idea of seeing their words sensitively illustrated by staff picture researchers who had studied their own disciplines, and, above all, to having their work reach an international market not previously available to them. Neurath had a considerable persuasive gift in attracting the leading figures in their subjects and historians such as H. R. Trevor-Roper, Asa Briggs, and A. J. P. Taylor were happy to join their art-historical colleagues in these ventures. When he got Glyn Daniel, then the editor of *Antiquity*, to edit for Thames and Hudson a new series of archaeological books called Ancient Peoples and Places, neither could have foreseen the publication of more than 100 separate titles. And when Richard Cowell retired from the civil service, Neurath—never a man to forget a favour—engaged him as a consultant editor and he created a successful series of books on the classics entitled Aspects of Greek and Roman Life.

A connoisseur of art, Neurath was often the first publisher to recognize the talents of new artists, and he published the first books on painters such as Sidney Nolan, Arthur Boyd, Jackson Pollock, and many more. He also had an enviable collection of drawings by Egon Schiele and works by Oskar Kokoschka, who was a lifelong friend as well as author. He built a beautiful house, Dolphin Villa, in Tuscany—the emblem of the firm is a dolphin—and in London lived in a fine eighteenth-century house in Highgate village. On 26 September 1967 Neurath succumbed to cancer which he had fought heroically for many months, working to the last to ensure that the substantial business he had created would continue without him, but on the principles he had established. His widow, Eva, became chairman, his son Thomas managing director, and his daughter Constance a director. He was buried on 2 October in Highgate cemetery, not far from the grave of Karl Marx, to whom he had always granted a certain sceptical admiration.

Neurath was a tall, strongly built man who, with his heavy beetle brows and glasses which partially concealed intense, deep-set blue eyes, could be saturnine in repose but, when energized, became formidable, immensely charming, and indeed lovable. More or less until his death, the working day at Thames and Hudson began with all the departmental heads assembled in his office, to be confronted by their own pile of the day's post opened by the office manager, and already read by Neurath, who would comment and question all present volubly and in an English—which was after all his second language—that was sharply elegant and larded with telling neologisms. 'This book', he would proclaim of the occasional failed title, 'has not been published. It has been *privished*.' Of another: 'It's been published to the *exclusion* of the public.' A generous and supportive employer, Neurath could be quick to anger, but the explosions were soon over. He did, however, have an almost phobic inability to say 'Well done' to a subordinate or colleague. On one occasion, when one of his staff had just pulled off a considerable commercial coup, he asked what currency had been used for the transaction. On being told that it was in sterling on the day that the Germans had just massively revalued their currency, his only comment was: 'What a pity you didn't do the deal in Deutschmarks.' However, an hour later the employee was summoned and given an immediate rise, and a significant sum to be used to buy paintings.

After Neurath's death, Thames and Hudson endowed an annual Walter Neurath memorial lecture, first at Birkbeck College in the University of London and then at the National Gallery in London. The lecture is always published as an illustrated book and, for the first thirty years at least, was delivered by scholars who had been published personally by him. It was a fitting memorial to one of the many German-speaking Jewish refugees who had such a deep influence on British cultural life. Neurath was, a little shamefully perhaps, awarded no decoration in Britain, but his native Austria gave him the Goldene Ehrenzeichen (the approximate equivalent of CBE).

T. G. ROSENTHAL

Sources family and company archives, Thames and Hudson, London • personal knowledge (2004) • private information (2004) • b. cert. • *The Times* (27 Sept 1967) • *CGPLA Eng. & Wales* (1968)
Archives Thames and Hudson, London, family and company archives
Likenesses O. Kokoschka, drawing, priv. coll. • photographs, priv. coll.
Wealth at death £18,139: probate, 29 Jan 1968, *CGPLA Eng. & Wales*

Neustadt, Ilya [Ilie] (1915–1993), sociologist, was born on 21 November 1915 near Odessa, Russia, the youngest of five children of Nicolai Neustadt, a prosperous grain and sunflower seed merchant, and his wife, Maria. In the turmoil following the Russian revolution his family decided to cross the Dniester into Bessarabia, which in 1918 became part of Romania. Neustadt was educated chiefly in Bucharest, and his early interests were in biology. He considered training as a doctor or as a professional musician, being a highly talented violinist. However, as a Jew he found the political climate in Romania increasingly threatening, so he decided to continue his university education in a new country and in a new field, the social sciences. He travelled to Belgium and entered the Liège School of Economics, where he specialized in international politics and law. In 1939 he completed and published his doctoral thesis, *Le problème de l'organisation internationale en Europe centrale, 1919–39*. But events in Europe now forced him into the third migration of his life and in

1940 he found a place on one of the last ferries to leave Belgium for Britain.

As a refugee in London, Neustadt managed to obtain a bursary from the London School of Economics, where he intended to continue his studies in politics under the supervision of Harold Laski. However, he was instead referred to Morris Ginsberg, professor of sociology, and in this somewhat haphazard way came to the subject that was thereafter to occupy—in effect to be—his life. Working with Ginsberg, he obtained his second doctorate with a thesis entitled 'Some aspects of the social structure of Belgium' (1944), which focused on the changing middle classes.

In the immediate post-war years academic posts in sociology were hard to come by, and Neustadt (who was naturalized in 1948) stayed on for some time at the London School of Economics as a library assistant. Eventually his opportunity came, with his appointment in 1949 as lecturer in sociology in the department of economics at the University College of Leicester. It was an opportunity that he took with striking results. At first he taught single-handed all the sociology courses on offer at Leicester. In 1954, however, a department of sociology was established, Neustadt was promoted to senior lecturer, and he acquired a highly influential colleague in Norbert Elias. The department then slowly grew and in 1959, after Leicester received its university charter, Neustadt was able, with Elias's help, to devise a new sociology degree with a strong comparative emphasis. In 1962 a chair in sociology was created and Neustadt was appointed to it. Subsequently, he was able to promote a far more rapid expansion of the department. By the time of his retirement in 1981 it comprised over thirty permanent staff, making it one of the largest in Britain.

The department that Neustadt created was distinguished yet more by its quality than by its size. In his selection of junior lecturers, as well as students, he showed a remarkable capacity for talent-spotting. As in the 1960s and 1970s the demand for sociologists increased in other universities, including Oxford and Cambridge, Leicester products were greatly sought after, and the department regularly lost its promising youngsters to highly attractive offers from elsewhere. Neustadt never resented this, but rather took pride in the role played by his protégés in developing sociology in Britain and in what T. H. Marshall aptly called 'the legacy of Leicester'. He was at least in part repaid by the many distinguished contributions to his Festschrift, edited by Anthony Giddens and Gavin Mackenzie, *Social Class and the Division of Labour* (1982). Nevertheless, Neustadt could still be reckoned the victim of his own success. His time and energy were almost totally absorbed by his constant struggle to sustain his department and by his unwavering commitment to teaching, at which he excelled—his inaugural lecture was entitled 'Teaching sociology' (1965). He was thus left with little opportunity to pursue his own academic interests. His one involvement in a major research project was begun in 1957–8 while he was visiting professor of sociology at

Accra, and led eventually to his editing (with Walter Birmingham and E. N. Omaboe) the two-volume *A Study of Contemporary Ghana* (1966–7).

In retirement Neustadt hoped at last to be able to write his long-planned study of Auguste Comte. He received an invitation to spend a year as an academic visitor at Nuffield College, Oxford. Unfortunately, though, the Parkinsonism that had afflicted him for some years grew more severe and he became reluctant to move far from his house in Leicester. He died at Leicester General Hospital on 16 February 1993, and was buried in the Jewish cemetery, Leicester. He never married but to the end of his life kept a circle of devoted friends and for long maintained his reputation as a splendid host.

JOHN H. GOLDTHORPE

Sources T. H. Marshall, foreword, *Social class and the division of labour: essays in honour of Ilya Neustadt*, ed. A. Giddens and G. Mackenzie (1982) · BLPES, T. H. Marshall MSS · *The Independent* (19 Feb 1993) · *The Times* (2 March 1993) · naturalization cert. · personal knowledge (2004) · *CGPLA Eng. & Wales* (1993)
Archives priv. coll.
Likenesses photograph, repro. in Giddens and Mackenzie, eds., *Social class and the division of labour* · photograph, repro. in *The Independent* · photograph, repro. in *The Times*
Wealth at death £278,757: probate, 4 May 1993, *CGPLA Eng. & Wales*

Neuton, John (*c*.1350–1414), canon lawyer, was born in the diocese of Norwich, but was brought up in the diocese of York, according to his ordination record in the register of Bishop Thomas Arundel. By the end of November 1375 he had qualified as BCL, presumably at Cambridge, while another entry in the act book on 1 December of that year further describes him as an advocate of the consistory court. It seems unlikely, therefore, that he could have been born much later than 1350, both because the BCL degree entailed at least five years of legal studies after preparation in the arts, and also because appointment as an advocate was customarily restricted to relatively senior practitioners at the bar of the consistory court. Although Neuton was practising as an advocate at least as early as 1375, and appears occasionally as a commissary judge of the consistory, his formal admission as an advocate took place only on 23 January 1377. An act book entry for 1378 shows that, in addition to his legal practice, he was also lecturing that year as an inceptor in civil law at Cambridge.

Neuton had received the degree of DCL by 20 September 1379, the date on which Bishop Thomas Arundel of Ely (*d*. 1414) appointed him as the official-principal, or presiding judge, of the episcopal consistory. Although the court's jurisdiction derived from the bishop of Ely and covered the entire diocese, it habitually held its sittings and transacted its other business in Cambridge, in part no doubt because Cambridge was easier of access than Ely, and in part because the lawyers who clustered around the university furnished the nucleus of a well-trained and competent bar. The consistory customarily transacted its formal business in the parish church of the official-principal, and

during Neuton's period in office it met in St Mary-without-Trumpington-Gate (Little St Mary's). Neuton presided over the consistory there until Bishop Arundel was translated to York in 1388, and he continued to do so during the first two years of the pontificate of Arundel's successor, John Fordham (*d*. 1425).

Although Neuton was named as rector of Rattlesden in his home diocese of Norwich some time before 1379, he remained a layman until after his appointment as official-principal, and was ordained a priest only on 10 March 1380. His patron, Archbishop Arundel (as he was by then), did not forget his former official-principal and legal adviser. By the end of 1390 he had brought John Neuton to join his administration at York as vicar-general of the diocese, canon, and treasurer of the minster. Neuton thus became in effect Arundel's second in command. He was also at least once employed on royal business, when in the autumn of 1393 he took part in negotiations for peace with France. When Arundel was translated to the archbishopric of Canterbury in 1396, however, Neuton remained at York and retained his position there under archbishops Waldby (*d*. 1398), Scrope (*d*. 1405), and Bowet (*d*. 1423), the last two of whom were, like Neuton, former officials-principal of the Ely consistory.

Neuton was appointed master of Peterhouse in 1382, while he was still living in Cambridge and Arundel was still bishop of Ely, and he retained the mastership until 1397, long after he had taken up residence at York. This situation created difficulties for the college, which had to keep a stream of messengers almost constantly riding the roads between Cambridge and York, a problem that became particularly acute when the college was involved in complicated affairs, such as appropriating the living of Cherry Hinton. Presumably the inconvenience of having a non-resident master was more than offset by the benefits that flowed from Neuton's powerful ecclesiastical connections. The library at Peterhouse also profited considerably from Neuton's mastership, for Neuton, like Arundel, was a shrewd and aggressive collector of books and gave the college numerous valuable items from his collection. York Minster, too, benefited from Neuton's bibliophilia. When Neuton died in the summer of 1414 he bequeathed the nucleus of his collection of law books to the minster library, to hold in trust for his nephews against the time when they would in their turn enrol as students of law.

JAMES A. BRUNDAGE

Sources Ely diocesan records, CUL, E.D.R. D/2/1; G/1/2; G/1/3 · register 14, Borth. Inst. · *Documents relating to the university and colleges of Cambridge*, Cambridge University Commission, 3 vols. (1852) · M. Bateson, ed., *Cambridge gild records*, Cambridge Antiquarian RS, 39 (1903) · C. I. Feltoe and E. H. Mins, eds., *Vetus liber archidiaconi Eliensis*, Cambridge Antiquarian Society, 48 (1917) · M. Aston, *Thomas Arundel* (1967) · D. M. Owen, *The medieval canon law: teaching, literature and transmission* (1990) · D. M. Owen, 'The records of the bishop's official at Ely', *The study of medieval records: essays in honour of Kathleen Major*, ed. D. A. Bullough and K. L. Storey (1971), 189–205 · Emden, *Cam.* · [J. Raine], ed., *Testamenta Eboracensia*, 1, SurtS, 4 (1836), 364–71
Archives CUL, Ely diocesan records

Nevay, John (*c*.1606–1671/2), Church of Scotland minister, was a nephew of Andrew Cant, a leading covenanter. He married Ann Sharp, widow of Richard Halyburton, merchant of Edinburgh. The couple had one son, who married Sarah Van Brakel, a Dutch national. Nevay was educated at King's College, Aberdeen, and graduated MA in 1626. He became tutor to the master of Ramsay, and later chaplain to John Campbell, earl of Loudoun, also an adherent of the covenanting party. He was admitted minister of New-milns, Ayrshire, in 1637. A presbyterian and covenanter, he was strongly opposed to all forms of set prayer in public worship. He was a member of the general assemblies of 1646, 1647, and 1649, and attended regularly as a member of the church commission of 1648. Appointed chaplain to David Leslie, commander of the covenanting forces, he was present at the slaughter of the garrison of Dunaverty Castle, Argyll, in 1647. Nevay was accused of having led the Mauchline rising against the 'engager' regime in the following year, but denied emphatically that he had been 'a raiser of that tumult' (*Letters and Journals of Robert Baillie*, 3.53). Exonerated under an act of parliament of 1649, he was named one of the commissioners for visiting the University of Aberdeen. He took an active part in raising the western army, which was defeated by Cromwell at Dunbar in September 1650. On the division of the kirk in 1651 Nevay sided with the 'protesting' minority, which formed a separate church under the protection of the English administration. In 1654 he was appointed commissioner for authorizing admissions to the ministry within the bounds of Glasgow and Ayr.

A man 'of very considerable parts and bright piety' (Wodrow, 1.317), Nevay wrote the fifty-two sermons which were published at Glasgow in 1748 under the title *The Nature, Properties, Blessings, and Saving Graces of the Covenant of Faith*. He was an 'acute and distinct' preacher (*Letters of Samuel Rutherford*, clxxxix), who is also said to have written a version of the Song of Solomon in Latin verse, and thirty-nine sermons on Christ's temptation. Two Latin stanzas, apparently of his authorship, are prefixed to the sermons of James Borstius (published at Utrecht in 1696). In 1647, he was appointed by the assembly to revise Rous's version of the last thirty psalms. Contemporary assessments of Nevay's character reflect the deep divides caused by the religious and political troubles of the day. For Henry Guthrie, bishop of Dunkeld, he was the 'bloody preacher' who instigated the massacre at Dunaverty (Mathieson, 2.71); but to the presbyterian diarist Alexander Brodie of Brodie he was 'a good man' whose death saved him 'from the evil to com' (*Diary*, ed. Laing, 325).

At the Restoration, Nevay was banished from the king's dominions, and went to the Netherlands. In 1662 the English government demanded his expulsion from the latter country, along with that of his close friends Robert Mcuard and Robert Traill. Placards to this effect were issued by the Dutch authorities, but not pursued. For some years he corresponded regularly with his former congregation of Newmilns. Nevay died, probably at Rotterdam, about January 1672. VAUGHAN T. WELLS

Sources *Diary of Sir Archibald Johnston of Wariston*, 2, ed. D. H. Fleming, Scottish History Society, 2nd ser., 18 (1919) · *The letters and journals of Robert Baillie*, ed. D. Laing, 3 vols. (1841–2), vols. 2–3 · W. Steven, *The history of the Scottish church, Rotterdam* (1832, 1833) · R. Burns, memoir, in R. Wodrow, *The history of the sufferings of the Church of Scotland from the Restoration to the revolution*, ed. R. Burns, 1 (1828) · *Letters of Samuel Rutherford*, ed. A. Bonar (1984) · *The diary of Alexander Brodie of Brodie* (1863) · *Fasti Scot.*, new edn · [J. Howie], *Biographia Scoticana, or, a brief historical account … of the most eminent Scots worthies* (1775) · W. Makey, *The church of the covenant, 1637–1651* (1979) · J. K. Hewison, *The covenanters*, 2 vols. (1908) · W. Mathieson, *Politics and religion … in Scotland*, 2 vols. (1902) · J. Nicoll, *A diary of public transactions and other occurrences, chiefly in Scotland, from January 1650 to June 1667*, ed. D. Laing, Bannatyne Club, 52 (1836); repr. (1886) · *DNB*

Nevay, John (1792–1870), poet, was born in Forfar on 28 January 1792, the son of Alexander Neave, a weaver, and his wife, Elizabeth Halket. He was educated in Forfar schools, one of his teachers being James Clarke, a friend of Burns, and developed an appreciation of his natural surroundings, and of poetry. By trade he was a handloom weaver. He published *A Pamphlet of Rhymes* in 1818, and a second *Pamphlet* three years later. *Emmanuel*, a sacred poem, appeared in 1831. He was a close friend of Alexander Laing (1787–1857), the Brechin poet, and he contributed 'Mary of Avonbourne' to his *Angus Album* in 1833. He published *The Peasant* in 1834, and *The Child of Nature* the following year. Widely recognized by literary men, Nevay corresponded with Ebenezer Elliot, and found an appreciative critic in John Wilson, who inserted 'The Yeldron' in one of the 'Noctes ambrosianae' (in *Blackwood's Edinburgh Magazine*, 1835). Other publications during his lifetime were *Rosaline's Dream* (1853) and *The Fountain of the Rock* (1855). He is said to have written prose tales in various periodicals, and to have contributed to the *Edinburgh Literary Journal*. The Chevalier de Chatelain apparently translated several of Nevay's lyrics into French, and German translations were also made (Wilson, 122). Nevay had been married, to Jean Edward, but was a widower at the time of his death in Manor Street, Forfar, on 4 May 1870.

T. W. BAYNE, *rev.* SARAH COUPER

Sources C. Rogers, *The modern Scottish minstrel, or, The songs of Scotland of the past half-century*, 4 (1857), 257–60 · J. G. Wilson, ed., *The poets and poetry of Scotland*, 2 (1870), 122 · private information (1894) [W. D. Latto, Miss Ewen, A. Lowson] · bap. reg. Scot. · d. cert.

Neve, Cornelius de [Cornelius Le Neve] (*b.* before **1594**, *d.* **1678**), portrait painter, is first recorded in a list of members of the Dutch church in London on 31 October 1594. He must still have been a child as he was living with his father, Cornelius de Neve van Ghistele, a Netherlandish painter, who had married Elisabeth Goddens van Maseick, the widow of Jan Davidts, at the Dutch church, Austin Friars, on 21 August 1593. Some time before 1609 Elisabeth must have died, and his father remarried, his new wife being Sara Pookes (*d.* 1618). With his father's death his stepmother married John de Critz the younger. His relationship with the de Critz family led de Neve towards a style relatively uninfluenced by Van Dyck. The artist's early work is similar to that of Michiel Miereveldt, as may be seen by his portrait of Richard and Edward Sackville as boys, signed and dated 1637 (Knole, Kent). De Neve also

Cornelius de Neve (*b*. before 1594, *d*. 1678), self-portrait

seems likely to have painted Richard Steward, dean designate of St Paul's Cathedral and Westminster, as is suggested by a watercolour copy by George Perfect Harding (NPG). In 1627 the Painter–Stainers' Company unsuccessfully attempted to prosecute de Neve along with other foreign artists (including Orazio Gentileschi, Daniel Mytens, George Geldorp, J. van Belcamp, Hendrick Corneliszoon Vroom, Hendrick van Steenwyck, and Abraham van der Doort) for failing to obey the company's ordinances. What is apparently a self-portrait painted about 1650 is inscribed by an eighteenth-century hand as 'Mr. Le Neve, a famous painter' (Ashmolean Museum, Oxford). This work is related to a larger group of pictures in the Ashmolean of individuals related to the de Critz family. Another work, painted in 1651 and of Nicholas Fiske, may also be by de Neve, as it is signed 'C. D. N.' (Ashmolean Museum). The artist is mentioned among Sir Edward Dering's accounts for 1648 and 1649. According to Vertue, in the last year of his life de Neve drew Elias Ashmole's portrait, and a painted version still exists (Merevale Hall, Warwickshire), demonstrating a shift in his style towards that of Thomas de Critz. De Neve died in 1678, supposedly 'aged about seventy' (MacGregor, 299). **P. G. MATTHEWS**

Sources M. Whinney and O. Millar, *English art, 1625–1714* (1957), 81 · E. K. Waterhouse, *The dictionary of British 16th and 17th century painters* (1988), 202 · E. Waterhouse, *Painting in Britain, 1530–1790*, 4th edn (1978), 79 · A. MacGregor, ed., *Tradescant's rarities* (1983) · Mrs R. Lane Poole, ed., *Catalogue of portraits in the possession of the university, colleges, city and county of Oxford*, 3 vols. (1912–25) · Vertue, *Note books*

Likenesses C. de Neve, self-portrait (family group), Petworth House, West Sussex · C. de Neve, self-portrait, oils, AM Oxf. [*see illus.*]

Neve, Jeffery. *See* Le Neve, Jeffrey (1579–1653).

Neve, Timothy (1694–1757), Church of England clergyman and antiquary, was born at Wotton, in the parish of Stanton-Lacy, near Ludlow, Shropshire, the son of Paul Neve, bailiff of the same place. He was educated at Ludlow School and admitted sizar of St John's College, Cambridge, on 10 November 1711, graduating BA in 1714. In 1716 he became master of the free grammar school at Spalding, Lincolnshire.

Ordained priest at Lincoln on 22 June 1718, he ministered at Spalding parish church, and was in 1718 admitted a member of the Gentlemen's Society at Spalding, where he acted as librarian. To this society he communicated several papers including, in 1727, essays on the invention of printing and Britain's first printers, and on Bishop Kennett's donation of books to Peterborough Cathedral. He left Spalding about 1729, when a successor at the school was appointed, and moved to Peterborough, where he was minor canon from 24 March 1729 until 1745. While there he was secretary and joint founder, along with Joseph Sparke, the registrar of Peterborough, of the Gentlemen's Society, founded on the lines of the Spalding society.

In addition to his antiquarian pursuits Neve had an interest in natural phenomena; and he contributed at least two items to the *Philosophical Transactions* of the Royal Society. These were accounts of '2 Parhelia, or Mock Suns', seen on 30 December 1735, and of aurora borealis seen on 11 December 1735, as well as another in 1741.

On 4 November 1722, at the church of St John the Baptist, Peterborough, Neve married Compton Rowell (*d.* 1733); they had four children, of whom two were surviving in 1741—a son, Timothy *Neve (1724–1798), also a Church of England clergyman, and a daughter, who subsequently married a Mr Davies. His second wife, whom he married on 26 February 1750, was Christina, daughter of the Revd Mr Greene of Drinkstone, Bury St Edmunds, and sister to Lady Danvers of Rushbrooke, Suffolk.

Neve was chaplain to Dr Thomas, bishop of Lincoln, and by him nominated prebendary of Lincoln, first of the North Kelsey stall (1744–8), then of Nassington stall (1747–57). On 28 March 1747 he was also collated archdeacon of Huntingdon. For twenty-eight years (1729–57) he was rector of Alwalton, Huntingdonshire, a living attached to his Lincoln prebend. He died there on 3 February 1757, and was buried in Alwalton church, in the north transept of which an epitaph to his memory was erected.

W. A. SHAW, *rev.* ROBERT BROWN

Sources *An account of the Gentlemen's Society at Spalding, being an introduction to the Reliquiae Galeanae* (1784), no. 20 [3/1] of *Bibliotheca topographica Britannica*, ed. J. Nichols (1780–1800) · Nichols, *Illustrations* · Nichols, *Lit. anecdotes* · A. Chalmers, ed., *The general biographical dictionary*, new edn, 32 vols. (1812–17) · private information (1894) · W. Hustler, ed., *Graduati Cantabrigienses* (1823) · *IGI* · *Fasti Angl., 1541–1857*, [Bristol] · *GM*, 1st ser., 68 (1798), 85–6

Neve, Timothy (1724–1798), Church of England clergyman and religious writer, born at Spalding, Lincolnshire, on 12 October 1724, was the only surviving son of Timothy *Neve (1694–1757), Church of England clergyman, and his first wife, Compton Rowell (*d.* 1733). He was admitted at Corpus Christi College, Oxford, on 27 October 1737, at the age of thirteen, and was elected scholar in 1737 and fellow in 1747. He graduated BA (1741), MA (1744), BD (1753), and DD (1758). In 1759 Neve was one of the preachers at the Chapel Royal, Whitehall, and on 23 April of that year he was appointed rector of Middleton Stoney, Oxfordshire, on the nomination of Bishop Green of Lincoln. He resigned this living in 1792 in favour of his son, the Revd Egerton Robert Neve (1766–1818). In 1762 he was appointed by his college to the rectory of Letcombe Bassett, Berkshire, but he left in 1763 on his preferment to the more valuable rectory of Geddington, Northamptonshire, which he kept for the rest of his life. From 1783 to his death Neve held the Lady Margaret professorship of divinity at Oxford and the sixth prebendal stall in Worcester Cathedral. He was also chaplain of Merton College, Oxford, and a Bampton lecturer.

Neve was a fellow of the Literary Society at Spalding from 1746 and became its correspondent in Oxford. In 1766 he published *Animadversions upon Mr. Phillips's History of the Life of Cardinal Pole*, a vindication of the doctrine and character of the reformers from the attacks made on them by the Roman Catholic priest Thomas Phillips (1708–1784). Neve's copy, with numerous notes made by him and with several letters inserted from John Jortin, Charles Townshend, and others, is in the British Library. Phillips responded in an appendix to his history, which was reprinted in 1767 and 1773. In addition to individual sermons Neve published his Bampton lectures in *Eight Sermons* (1781). His *Seventeen Sermons* appeared posthumously in 1798, and six letters addressed to him by Maurice Johnson on antiquarian topics are printed in the *Bibliotheca Topographica Britannica* (3.417–35).

Neve was partially paralysed for several years before his death, which occurred in Oxford on 1 January 1798. He was survived by his wife, Ann, and their three sons and two daughters. His widow was described by G. V. Cox as 'a gay old lady' (Cox, 155), who lived for many years opposite Merton College.　　W. P. COURTNEY, *rev.* EMMA MAJOR

Sources Foster, *Alum. Oxon.* · *GM*, 1st ser., 68 (1798), 85–6 · will, PRO, PROB 11/1301, sig. 51 · *ESTC* · *IGI* · T. Fowler, *The history of Corpus Christi College*, OHS, 25 (1893), 282, 405 · G. V. Cox, *Recollections of Oxford*, 2nd edn (1870), 155 · *Fasti Angl.* (Hardy), 3.85, 519 · Nichols, *Lit. anecdotes*, 6.70, 99–100, 134 · J. C. Blomfield, *History of the present deanery of Bicester, Oxon*, 8 pts (1882–94), 4.80–81

Wealth at death everything to wife: will, PRO, PROB 11/1301, sig. 51

Nevell, John (*d.* 1697), naval officer, was descended from a junior branch of the Nevilles of Abergavenny. He served as a volunteer in the fleet during the early part of the Third Anglo-Dutch War and in 1673 was promoted lieutenant of the *French Ruby*. On 29 June 1675 he was appointed to the *Sapphire*. The captain, Thomas Harman, died on 9 September 1677 while fighting an Algerine corsair; his replacement, Cloudesley Shovell, became a lifelong friend. In November 1679 Nevell commanded eighteen seamen in a battle with Moors attacking Tangier. Arthur Herbert, commander-in-chief of the Mediterranean squadron,

appointed him second lieutenant of his flagship, the *Bristol*, on 23 December 1680 and sought to appoint him to the command of the Ann yacht, which served the Tangier garrison, on 23 February 1681 'in justice to Mr Nevills merit whose behaviour on many occasions has struck envy itself dumb'. An argument over the right to make the appointment resulted in Nevell's discharge on 10 June and appointment as first lieutenant to the *Bristol*. He played an important role in the peace negotiations with Algiers in April 1682 and once the treaty was signed was left as consul at Algiers by Herbert, who thought him 'much fitter to serve the king as a sea captain than in the post he now is, for I am afraid his head is not very well turned that way'. His appointment was meant to be temporary and Herbert also signed a blank commission for him to be captain of the *Bristol*. His wife, Mary Nevell, petitioned Charles II in 1683 to send him home since suits had been entered against him which could lead to the ruin of his family, and that same year he took over the *Bristol* and returned to England.

On the duke of Monmouth's rebellion in 1685 Nevell was appointed captain of the *Rupert* with a warrant to fit the ship out as a flagship for Herbert, for use should the political crisis deepen. The rebellion was crushed before the ship was ready whereupon he was appointed captain of the *Garland*, a guardship at Portsmouth. On 1 August 1686 he was appointed to the *Crown*, and accompanied Sir Roger Strickland to the Mediterranean. In the summer of 1687 he carried Sir William Trumbull to Turkey and early in 1688 carried soldiers to Scotland. Through a friend of Herbert, who was in the Netherlands with the prince of Orange, he was appointed on 25 September 1688 to the *Elizabeth*, and served as Sir John Berry's flag captain in February 1689. In March he was appointed captain of the *Henrietta*, which vessel was ripped from her anchorage in Plymouth Sound on 25 December, driven aground, and broken up. In February 1690 he was appointed to the *Royal Sovereign*, Torrington's flagship at the battle of Beachy Head, and in September to the *Kent*. He was present at Marlborough's reduction of Cork in October and at the trial of the earl of Torrington on the *Kent* in December 1690. The *Kent* was one of the ships of the Red squadron which broke the French line at Barfleur on 19 May 1692. Edward Russell considered Nevell 'a good man' and in July 1692 detailed him to intercept and report any attempt by ships from St Malo to join the Brest fleet. In the following January he was appointed first captain of the *Britannia*, the flagship of the three admirals, on 7 July was promoted to rear-admiral of the blue, and in August was appointed commander-in-chief of ships intended for the Baltic. In December, with his flag in the *Royal Oak*, he went out to the Mediterranean as second in command under Sir Francis Wheler. On 19 February 1694 when Wheler and a large part of the squadron were lost in a storm, Nevell escaped, collected the shattered remains of the fleet, and went to Cadiz to refit. He continued in the Mediterranean until April 1696.

In October Nevell was appointed commander-in-chief

in the Mediterranean, and drew up his will on 2 November, leaving his property to be equally divided between his wife, Mary, and his two daughters, Mary and Elizabeth, with £50 each to his two sisters, Elizabeth Nevell and Martha Carpenter. He sailed in the *Cambridge* the next day, was promoted to vice-admiral on arrival at Cadiz, and was ordered to proceed at once to Madeira and the West Indies in response to intelligence that a strong French fleet under De Pointis had been sent there. He met Captain George Mees at Madeira and they proceeded to Barbados (17 April), then to Antigua (3 May 1697). On receiving a 'flying report' that the French were at Cartagena, Nevell sailed to intercept them. He sighted De Pointis's fleet on the night of 27–8 May and a three-day running fight took place as Nevell gave chase. On 30 May Nevell and De Pointis engaged each other briefly and the *Cambridge*, Nevell's flagship, lost its mainsail, with other English ships also sustaining damage. These misfortunes allowed De Pointis to elude Nevell and return to France. Nevell arrived at Cartagena, the rendezvous point for his scattered fleet, on 1 June to find that De Pointis's buccaneer allies had sacked and plundered the town and the inhabitants had taken shelter in the woods. He sailed on to Havana where he hoped to find the treasure galleons he was to escort back to England carrying, it was said, 10 or 12 million sterling. On arrival on 23 July he found that the governor not only declined the escort, having no orders for it, but would not allow the English ships to enter the harbour to get water. Great numbers of his men had already died from yellow fever including, on 19 July, Rear-Admiral Mees. Nevell sailed on 25 July for Florida, then Virginia, anchoring in the James River in August. There he, too, died of yellow fever, on 17 August 1697, and the same day was carried onshore and buried at Elizabeth City county church. The *Cambridge* fired forty guns in salute while the rest of the squadron fired 'by the half minute 372 guns'. Nevell's wife survived him. J. K. LAUGHTON, rev. PETER LE FEVRE

Sources A. Herbert, letterbook, 1678–83, Yale U., Beinecke L., Osborn Collection, fb 96, 98, 152, 251, 257, 269–70 · PRO, SP Foreign, Algiers, SP 71/2, pt 3 · ship's disposition book, PRO, ADM 8/1, fols. 193v, 207v · captain's journal, *Garland*, PRO, ADM 51/384/2 · paybook, *Rupert*, PRO, ADM 33/119 · journal 6, captain's journal, *Crown*, 1686–8, PRO, ADM 51/3817 · D. Hepper, *British warship losses in the age of sail, 1650–1859* (1994), 13 · paybook, *Kent*, PRO, ADM 33/137 · E. Russell, 'Characters of captains, Nov. 1691', Folger, Rich MS xd 451 (98) · P. Aubrey, *The defeat of James Stuart's armada, 1692* (1979), 141 · PRO, ADM 2/12, 123, 352, 420 · journal 5, captain's log, *Cambridge*, esp. 17 Aug 1697, PRO, ADM 51/151 · journal 2, captain's log, *Breda*, PRO, ADM 51/130 · *The Sergison papers*, ed. R. D. Merriman, Navy RS, 89 (1950), 299–311 · will, PRO, PROB 11/441, fol. 227r **Archives** PRO, admiralty MSS · U. Nott., department of manuscripts and special collections, naval journal | BL, corresp. with Sir William Trumbull · CKS, corresp. with Alexander Stanhope, U1590/031 · Yale U., Herbert letterbook **Wealth at death** see will, PRO, PROB 11/441, fol. 227r

Nevile, Sir Sydney Oswald (1873–1969), brewer, was born on 12 July 1873, at 2 Gordon Houses, Scarborough, the thirteenth of the fifteen children of the Revd Christopher Nevile (1806–1877), landowner, and rector of Wickenby, in Lincolnshire, and his wife, Mary Anne, daughter of Robert Tooth, brewer and hop grower of Swift's Park, Cranbrook,

Kent. The Neviles were a well-connected family with large estates, but Christopher Nevile's death in 1877, when Sydney was four, produced financial problems which restricted his education to the somewhat sporadic tuition of Mr Travers's Preparatory School in Bognor. His mother decided on a brewing pupillage for him, since her brothers had done well in Australia, establishing a major brewery, Tooth's of Sydney. In January 1888 Sydney became an articled pupil at Ebenezer Robins & Son's Hove brewery, paying £100 a year. After two years he joined a larger concern, Brandon's Putney brewery, in London, for a further six months' pupillage. In July 1890, when only seventeen, he was appointed assistant brewer there to T. K. Amos, with a salary of £100 a year.

Nevile's precocity in a conservative industry was further demonstrated when, on Amos's premature death in 1896, he became Brandon's head brewer at the age of twenty-two. He was probably the youngest in such a post in the country. Brandon's quickly expanded, mainly through the free trade, and Nevile took the eye as a promising London brewer with a wider vision than most. It was no surprise when he left the company in 1919 to become a managing director of Whitbread & Co., a much larger and more prestigious company. By that time he had become a nationally known figure in the trade, advocating moderation in drinking and the introduction of improved public houses as the best way to ward off the temperance lobby.

It was during the two world wars that Nevile was at his most influential. In the First World War he often acted as one of the industry's representatives in negotiations with the government. He became a member of the central control board (liquor traffic) from 1917 to 1921. This was Lloyd George's substitute for brewing nationalization, where, despite overt opposition from several quarters in the industry, Nevile adopted a positive response, advising on brewing at Carlisle (where the brewery was state-owned), and ensuring that his enthusiasm for improved pubs was turned into reality. His role in nationalized brewing was a long-term one, since he served on the council of state management districts until 1955. He was also a member of the Hop Control Committee, 1917–23, and an influence on the Licensing Act of 1921. President of the Brewers' Society in 1938–40, he used his earlier experience to good effect in the Second World War, producing a more harmonious relationship with government, while protecting brewing interests large and small. He was chairman of the brewing advisory committee appointed by the Ministry of Food, 1940–46, where he gave clear and authoritative advice on fuel and transport economies. He also played a full part in post-war reconstruction, serving on the Morris committee on war-damaged licensed premises, 1942–4. He was knighted in 1942, and in 1946 married Madeleine de Lacy, daughter of Dr C. A. Wickham, of Willesborough, Kent.

At Whitbread, Nevile was for three decades the only director to be recruited from outside the families of the old partnership. He was also one of the company's longest-serving directors, acting as a managing director until 1946 and as an ordinary director until 1968. By orchestrating important mergers in the inter-war years, he was a key figure in Whitbread's emergence as a national brewer. The development of the company's beer brands, marketing, and retailing were particular interests. He helped to establish the Improved Public House Company, a subsidiary which managed Whitbread's large improved pubs in the London area. He also encouraged the company to spend more on advertising. Indeed, his ideas were taken to a national stage when he promoted the Brewers' Society's collective advertising campaign of 1933, based on the themes 'Beer is best' and 'Beer—the best long drink in the world'. He spent his later years pressing for better training for licensees. Nevile's many positions in the brewing industry included the posts of president of the Institute of Brewing (1919–21), master of the Brewers' Company (1929–30), and chairman of the National Trade Defence (subsequently Development) Association (1946–8). He also gave evidence to the royal commission on licensing of 1929–31. Outside the industry, he was a council member of the Federation of British Industries, 1922–58, and vice-president in 1958.

Sir Sydney Nevile combined a disarming conviviality and wit with tremendous energy and a shrewd business brain. He was also a keen oarsman, and later an enthusiastic yachtsman. The initiator of a new era of 'responsible drinking', he was one of the most influential brewers of the twentieth century. He died at his home, 9 Mill Road, Worthing, on 3 September 1969, survived by his wife.

TERRY GOURVISH

Sources T. R. Gourvish and R. G. Wilson, *The British brewing industry, 1830–1980* (1994) • S. O. Nevile, *Seventy rolling years* (1958) • B. Ritchie, *An uncommon brewer: the story of Whitbread, 1742–1992* (1992) • D. M. Fahey, 'Nevile, Sir Sydney Oswald', *DBB* • *WWW* • *Brewing Trade Review* (March 1919) • *Brewing Trade Review* (Feb 1942) • *Brewing Trade Review* (Sept 1969) • *Journal of Institute of Brewing* (1919) • *The Times* (4 Sept 1969) • *The Times* (12 Sept 1969) • Nevile MSS, Whitbread Archives, London, W/40 • b. cert. • d. cert.
Archives Whitbread Archives, London
Likenesses photograph, 1962, repro. in Gourvish and Wilson, *The British brewing industry* • P. Phillips, portrait, repro. in Ritchie, *An uncommon brewer*, 94 • photographs, repro. in Nevile, *Seventy rolling years*
Wealth at death £49,409: Fahey, 'Nevile, Sir Sydney Oswald'

Nevill family (*per. c.*1793–1973), copper smelters and colliery proprietors, was founded by **Charles Nevill** (1753–1813), born in May 1753, probably on the 2nd, either at Birmingham or Stafford, the youngest of the seven children of Thomas Nevill (*c.*1723–*c.*1783) of Lichfield and his first wife, Elizabeth Parrock, who died soon after his birth. He entered the Birmingham copper trade at a young age, and became recognized as an important Birmingham button maker in the 1780s. He married, first, Sarah Willets (*d.* 1782) of Rowley Regis, Staffordshire, in 1777, and second, in 1784, Martha (*c.*1746–1821), daughter of Richard Janion of Colchester and widow of William Acton. There were three children from the first marriage, and one son, Richard Janion Nevill [*see below*], from the second. Charles became a shareholder in the Birmingham Mining and Copper Company in the early 1790s, moving to south Wales about 1793 to manage the company's new copper smelting works at Swansea, Glamorgan.

The short sailing distance between copper ore-rich Cornwall and the coastal coalfield of south-west Wales led to most of Britain's copper smelting capacity being concentrated into a small area around Swansea at the beginning of the nineteenth century, the resulting heavy demand on the local collieries causing serious coal supply and cost problems. Llanelli, Carmarthenshire, a small seaport town 12 miles west of Swansea, possessing a proven but undeveloped coalfield, attracted Charles Nevill's attention as a suitable location for a profitable copper smelting enterprise. He entered into partnership with other industrialists to raise the required capital, the company of 'Daniell, Savill, Guest, and Nevill, coppersmelters' being formed in March 1805. Nevill quickly took up permanent residence in the town to supervise the construction and commissioning of the Llanelli copperworks and its associated dock. A committed Wesleyan from his early years, he also found time to establish a large Sunday school shortly after his arrival. The company became both a copper smelting and coalmining concern with the purchase of local collieries in 1807. Charles Nevill died at his Llanelli home, Vauxhall House, on 20 November 1813, aged sixty, and was buried in Llanelli churchyard. It was later written of him 'it was he made the Copperworks, and the Copperworks made Llanelly' (Mee, xxxiii) and there is little doubt that his advent had laid the foundations of Llanelli's long-term industrialization.

Richard Janion Nevill (1785–1856), youngest son of Charles, born at Summer Hill, Birmingham, on 22 November 1785, assumed local control of the company on his father's death. In 1812 he married Anne (*c.*1782–1863), eldest daughter of William Yalden (*d.* 1810), originally of Lavington, Hampshire, and his wife, Anne, who were resident at Llanelli from about 1784. The Nevills lived at Glanmor House, a newly built house near the copperworks, and there were eight children from the marriage. Richard Janion expanded the copperworks and collieries throughout his years of control, diversifying the company into brass, yellow metal, lead and silver smelting, and shipping; additional industrial interests were acquired outside Llanelli. Changes in partnership led to alterations in the company name—Daniell, Savill, Sons, and Nevill in 1817, Daniell, Son, and Nevill in 1819, Daniell, Nevill & Co. in 1824, and Sims, Willyams, Nevill, Druce & Co. in 1837. The company was responsible for some 13 per cent of Britain's copper production by 1833, making it the nation's joint third largest copper smelting concern, a position it maintained over the following two decades. Separate from the company's affairs, Richard Janion also had personal involvement in banking, industrial shareholding, the timber trade, shipping, land purchase, and mineral leasing, to the extent that it was often difficult to distinguish between his interests and those of the company, clarification of ownership being sought on more than one occasion by his partners. He moved to Llangennech Park, a mansion 5 miles from Llanelli, in 1834, and was appointed a magistrate in 1835 and high sheriff of Carmarthenshire a year later; he was also locally active in support of the Conservative Party at that time.

Richard Janion Nevill suffered a stroke and died at Llangennech Park on 14 January 1856, aged seventy. He was buried on 18 January in Llangennech parish churchyard. At the time of his death the company was still one of Britain's premier copper smelters employing some 550 in its copperworks, and a major coalmining concern employing more than 1000 and responsible for almost 3 per cent of the total production of the south Wales coalfield. Surviving evidence yields a contradictory picture of the person who controlled Llanelli's industrial development for more than forty years. Reported as hot-tempered, and certainly a ruthless man of business employing child labour in his collieries up to 1842, he nevertheless provided aid at personal loss during times of grain shortages, built a large British school, the Copperworks School, for his workmen's children in 1848, and was involved in Anglican church provision and endowment to the time of his death. The attendance at his funeral was unprecedented for Llanelli, some 3000, including most of the company's workforce, forming the procession to the churchyard.

Charles William Nevill (1815–1888), eldest son of Richard Janion, born at Glanmor House on 7 May 1815, assumed local control on his father's death, having been a partner since 1841. He was educated at Swansea grammar school and Rugby School. He married in 1841 Jane (1820–1894), daughter of David Davies of Swansea, and they lived initially at Glanmor House and, from about 1850, at a newly built residence, Westfa House, in the village of Felin-foel, near Llanelli. Six out of ten children of the marriage survived to adulthood, Hugh [*see below*] being the only son. The company's smelting works and collieries flourished during the first two decades of his control, but then steadily contracted under the combined effects of the general decline in Britain's copper and lead smelting industries, caused by previous ore exporting countries starting their own smelting, and the working to exhaustion of the profitable seams at the company's collieries; and he became the first member of his family to preside over a decline in the company's fortunes. Unconnected with changes in partnership, the company name changed to Nevill, Druce & Co. in 1873.

Charles William was particularly active in public life. A magistrate since 1838, he was also deeply involved in the poor-law guardians, the board of health, the harbour commissioners, and the school board. He was a deputy lieutenant of Carmarthenshire, the high sheriff in 1868, and the MP (Conservative) for the Carmarthenshire United Boroughs from 1874 to 1876. Strongly ecumenical in outlook, he supported the provision of nonconformist chapels at Llanelli and helped fund the building of the Anglican church at Felin-foel. At the age of sixty-six ill health confined him to his home, causing his withdrawal from participation in most affairs. He died at Westfa on 7 June 1888 aged seventy-three, and was buried in the graveyard of Felin-foel church.

Richard Nevill (1817–1892), the second son of Richard Janion, became an industrialist in his own right, involved in Llanelli's iron, tinplate, and manufacturing industries for most of his working life. He was born at Glanmor House on 6 June 1817 and educated at Thornbury, near Bristol. He married about 1849 Mary Sophia (*b.* 1821), daughter of Joseph Willis of Crewkerne, Somerset, and lived at Felin-foel House near his brother's residence of Westfa. There were three children from the marriage. Initially, he joined his father at the Llanelli copperworks but in 1839 left to become a partner in the Wern ironworks, a small foundry originally established at Llanelli by his uncle William Yalden junior. He expanded this into a large concern, known locally as Nevill's foundry, specializing in the manufacture of heavy machinery, works and marine engines, boilers, and other products. He was also involved in the establishment and management of iron and tinplate works in and around Llanelli. He did not particularly involve himself in public affairs, although he acted as a magistrate and was deputy lieutenant of Carmarthenshire and occasional chairman of the poor-law guardians. He was a staunch Conservative and a pillar of the Anglican church, involved with his brother in the establishment of the church at Felin-foel. In later years he suffered from heart problems, and he died suddenly on 5 June 1892, aged seventy-four, while visiting his wife's birthplace at Crewkerne.

William Henry Nevill (1822–1894), the fifth son of Richard Janion, worked for his father's company for many years before becoming a builder of iron sailing and steam ships. He was born at Glanmor House on 15 September 1822 and educated at Bridgnorth, Shropshire, before joining the company as an assistant to his father. About 1857 he married Rachel Louisa Fry of Woodford, Essex, a granddaughter of Elizabeth Fry the reformer and philanthropist. They lived initially at Llangennech Park, then moved to Ferryside, some 12 miles from Llanelli, in 1870. There were six children from the marriage.

His family's long experience of shipping and metalliferous industry undoubtedly led William Henry into shipbuilding at a time when iron was replacing wood in ship construction, and in 1852 he took over an existing shipyard and invested in his brother Richard's ironworks, the Old Lodge, which supplied plates and other iron products to the yard. Considerable investment was made, but little appears to have been produced in the way of ships in the 1850s and substantial losses must have resulted. Shipbuilding ceased and he became a junior partner in his father's company, acting as manager of the Cambrian lead and silver works which had commenced smelting in 1848. Shipbuilding was restarted on a much larger scale in 1863 at a time of expansion and prosperity in national and local trade, with the ships initially supplied to a new company, the Llanelly Iron Shipping Co. Ltd, in which he and his brothers Charles William and Richard were substantial investors. At least twenty-three sailing ships and two steamships were built to Lloyd's highest classification over the following decade, ten of the sailing ships being purchased by the new company. Unfortunately, the boom shipping market of the 1860s soon slumped and there was little demand for well-built, but expensive, sailing vessels from the smaller shipyards. William Henry withdrew from shipbuilding, selling the yard in 1874 and closing the Old Lodge ironworks two years later.

A talented person with a number of diverse patents to his name, William Henry had been unsuccessful in his business life, facing bankruptcy on two separate occasions and being kept from insolvency by his brothers at considerable cost to the family's finances. He died of heart failure at his home, Robert's Rest, Ferryside, on 8 September 1894, aged seventy-one.

Hugh Nevill (1855–1924), the only son of Charles William, born at Westfa House on 9 March 1855, was educated at Winchester College and at Oxford. In 1886 he married Maud (b. 1858/9), daughter of Frederick Elkington of Wolverley, Worcestershire, but previously a copper smelter at Burry Port, near Llanelli. There were no children from the marriage. Involved in the company since his father's health failed in the early 1880s, Hugh was admitted as managing partner in 1889 but found himself presiding over a declining concern. Copper smelting ceased in 1894, subsequent activity concentrating on small-scale refining and the manufacture of copper sheets, plates, and wire; the lead and silver works closed in 1896, and the last remaining colliery was abandoned in 1907. The company's dock and local railway system were separated from the parent concern in 1911 with the formation of Nevill's Dock and Railway Ltd, the company itself becoming Nevill, Druce & Co. Ltd in 1920. Unlike his father, Hugh hardly involved himself in public life, acting only as a magistrate. He left his home at Burry Port to live in Cobham, Surrey, shortly before his death from heart disease in a London clinic on 14 January 1924, aged sixty-eight.

Richard Austin Nevill (1867–1946), son of William Henry, born at Llangennech Park on 24 September 1867, married about 1896 Gertrude Emily (1869–1958), daughter of William Roderick of Llanelli and his wife, Maria. There were three daughters and one son, Charles William [see below], from the marriage. He qualified as a mining engineer and was appointed manager of the Llanelli copperworks in 1894. The natural family successor to his childless cousin Hugh, he was admitted to the partnership in 1913, but then spent the duration of the First World War on active service, reaching the rank of lieutenant-colonel and being awarded the DSO for gallantry in the Dardanelles. He became managing director of the two limited companies after his cousin's death in 1924 and set about rationalizing operations, closing the refineries and hot rolling mills, and concentrating on the cold rolling of copper plates and the drawing of electrical wire. Active in public life, he was awarded the territorial decoration for his involvement in the Territorial Army, and was chairman of the Llanelli magistrates, a member of the governing body of the Church in Wales, and also a committed Rechabite who often lectured members of his workforce on the evils of drink. He was made a freeman of the borough of Llanelli in 1923 and acted as a deputy lieutenant of Carmarthenshire. He died of heart failure at his home, Brondeg, Ferryside, on 11 January 1946, aged seventy-eight.

Charles William Nevill (1907–1973), son of Richard Austin, born at Ferryside on 16 August 1907, was the last member of his family involved in the town's industrial and public life. Educated at Clifton College, Bristol, he married in 1947 Philippa (b. 1916), daughter of Captain H. P. Farrell of Karachi, India. He joined the company in 1925 and was appointed a director just before the start of the Second World War. During war service he attained the rank of lieutenant-colonel, was mentioned in dispatches, and was appointed OBE. He became chairman and managing director of the two limited companies on his father's death in 1946. The dock closed in 1951, and the copperworks became a copper wire and cable manufacturing subsidiary of a national company in 1961, although both Nevill's Dock and Railway Ltd and Nevill, Druce & Co. Ltd continued in existence, with Charles William remaining as their lifelong principal. Active in public life, he was a magistrate, became lord lieutenant of Carmarthenshire in 1967, and was made honorary colonel of the 4th (volunteer) battalion of the Royal regiment of Wales in 1972. He suffered a stroke shortly before Christmas 1972 and died at Llanelli General Hospital on 2 January 1973, aged sixty-five; his death marked the end of his family's 168 years of continuous involvement in Llanelli's industrial life.

The Nevill family was instrumental in ensuring that Llanelli developed into a major centre of heavy industry. The first Charles Nevill and his son Richard Janion were the leading participants, building an industrial empire of national importance which attracted other investors and businesses to the town. The family's long-term commitment to the area provided stability of employment through many difficult periods, the company's reputation as considerate employers by the standards of the day being reflected in particularly good labour relations. The working to exhaustion of the company's coalfield and the adherence to obviously declining copper and lead interests in the late nineteenth century, when steel and tin-plate manufacturing were becoming the staple industries of south Wales, hastened the family's economic decline and ensured its eventual disappearance from the industrial life of the region.

R. PROTHEROE JONES and M. V. SYMONS

Sources NL Wales, Nevill papers · Llanelli Public Library, local collection archives · *Cambrian* (18 Jan 1856) · *Cambrian* (25 Jan 1856) · *Llanelly and County Guardian* (14 June 1888) · *Llanelly and County Guardian* (14 Feb 1889) · *Llanelly and County Guardian* (9 June 1892) · *Llanelly and County Guardian* (17 Jan 1918) · *Llanelly Mercury* (13 Sept 1894) · *Llanelly Mercury* (27 Sept 1894) · *Llanelly Mercury* (17 Jan 1946) · *South Wales Press* (9 April 1924) · *Llanelli Star* (6 Jan 1973) · J. Innes, *Old Llanelly* (1902) · A. Mee, *Llanelly parish church: its history and records* (1888) · Carmarthen RO, Francis Jones collection, D/FJ/5 · N. Harvey, 'The Nevilles of England', 1966, priv. coll. · R. Craig, 'W. H. Nevill and the Llanelly Iron Shipping Company', *National Library of Wales Journal*, 10 (1957–8), 265–80 · West Glamorgan Archive Service, Swansea, D/D Xav (1838–72) · D. ab Owen [D. Bowen], 'Hanes Llanelli', 1856, Llanelli Public Library · M. V. Symons, *Coal mining in the Llanelli area*, 1 (1979) · census returns for the Llanelli districts, 1841, 1851, 1861, 1871, 1881, 1891 · d. cert. [Richard Janion Nevill]

Archives Carmarthenshire RO · NL Wales | Llanelli Public Library, local collection archives · West Glamorgan Archive Service, Swansea, D/D Xav
Likenesses oils, c.1845 (Richard Janion Nevill), priv. coll.

Nevill, Charles (1753–1813). *See under* Nevill family (*per.* c.1793–1973).

Nevill, Charles William (1815–1888). *See under* Nevill family (*per. c.*1793–1973).

Nevill, Charles William (1907–1973). *See under* Nevill family (*per. c.*1793–1973).

Nevill [*née* Walpole], **Lady Dorothy Fanny** (1826–1913), hostess and horticulturist, was born on 1 April 1826 at 11 Berkeley Square, London. She was the youngest in the family of three sons and two daughters of Horatio Walpole, third earl of Orford, and his wife, Mary, daughter of William Augustus Fawkener, envoy-extraordinary at St Petersburg. She spent her childhood at the family seats at Wolterton in Norfolk and Ilsington in Dorset, and at the house in Berkeley Square. She received no formal education, but was taught Italian, French, Greek, and Latin by an excellent governess, Eliza Redgrave, sister of the painter Richard Redgrave.

Despite their rank, the Walpoles were on the fringes of society: Lord Orford gambled, and his son Horatio eloped with the notorious Lady Lincoln. Lady Dorothy was introduced to London society in 1846, during the course of which season her name was linked with those of several young men. Her reputation was damaged by rumours, which suggested a liaison with Disraeli's friend and associate George Smythe, and she was hastily married to her cousin Reginald Henry Nevill (1807–1878) on 2 December 1847. He was twenty years her senior, and had inherited considerable wealth from a Walpole uncle. He was the son of the Revd George Henry Nevill (the son of George Nevill, first earl of Abergavenny) and his wife, Caroline Walpole. Lady Dorothy and her husband had six children, four of whom (one daughter and three sons) survived to adulthood.

In 1851 the Nevills acquired, in addition to their London house at 45 Charles Street, an estate in west Sussex known as Dangstein, near Petersfield, with a large neo-Grecian mansion, built in the 1830s. Reginald looked after the large estate, while Lady Dorothy took charge of the house and the 23 acre garden. The latter soon became celebrated in horticultural circles, particularly for the collection of exotics, housed in its seventeen hothouses, which were the subject of no fewer than twelve articles in the gardening press. Lady Dorothy soon struck up a friendship with William Hooker at Kew, with whom she exchanged plants and letters; and the relationship continued with his son and successor, Joseph Hooker. She was on friendly terms with most of the leading horticulturists of the time, and was able to provide Charles Darwin with a number of rare plants.

As well as these exotics, the garden at Dangstein, tended

Lady Dorothy Fanny Nevill (1826–1913), by Henry Richard Graves, 1855

by thirty-four gardeners, had one of the earliest herbaceous borders, a pinetum, exotic birds and animals, a flock of pigeons with Chinese whistles attached to their tails (Lady Dorothy's 'aerial orchestra'), a silkworm farm, and a museum with some of her numerous collections— snuffboxes, corset buttons, silhouettes, wax medallions, lockets, and many similar objects. As well as collecting these trivia, Lady Dorothy was a serious collector of eighteenth-century porcelain and pictures, particularly anything relating to her ancestor Horace Walpole, fourth earl of Orford (1717–1797).

Lady Dorothy's habit of collecting extended to people. Her salon at 45 Charles Street, modelled on that of Lady Molesworth, was eagerly attended by politicians, writers, artists, scientists, and soldiers. Disraeli was a close friend (family tradition held that he was the father of her youngest son, Ralph), and her salon was at its most influential in 1866–8. She was a strong Conservative and founder member of the Primrose League, but her dinner-table was by no means sectarian: Richard Cobden was as likely to dine with her as the second duke of Wellington or the prince of Wales. After her husband died in 1878 she moved to Stillyans, in east Sussex, where she also had a garden, but thereafter most of her entertaining was done in London. In her 'quaintly episcopal' robes, she sought out celebrities, entertaining Joseph Chamberlain (with whom she shared a passion for orchids) before his acceptance at other aristocratic tables, and the radicals Joseph Arch and H. M. Hyndman. Eclectic in her collection of guests, she had a deep horror of change, which became more pronounced as she grew older, an aversion which is reflected in her comments on the declining standards of high society.

As well as a book on silkworms, and another on her Walpole ancestors, Lady Dorothy wrote (with assistance from her son Ralph) three selective autobiographical volumes: *The Reminiscences of Lady Dorothy Nevill* (1906), *Leaves from the Notebooks of Lady Dorothy Nevill* (1907), and *Under Five Reigns* (1910). She died on 24 March 1913 at her home at 45 Charles Street, London.   W. R. TROTTER, *rev.* K. D. REYNOLDS

Sources R. Nevill, *The life & letters of Lady Dorothy Nevill* (1919) · G. Nevill, *Exotic groves: a portrait of Lady Dorothy Nevill* (1984) · W. R. Trotter, 'The glasshouses at Dangstein and their contents', *Garden History*, 16/1 (1988), 71–89 · V. Surtees, *Charlotte Canning* (1975) · S. Weintraub, *Disraeli: a biography* (1993)
Archives Yale U., Farmington, Lewis Walpole Library, journal | BL, letters to T. H. S. Escott, Add. MS 58788 · Bodl. Oxf., letters to Disraeli · Bodl. Oxf., letters to Mrs Disraeli · Bodl. Oxf., letters to Lord Lovelace · NL Scot., letters to Lord Haldane, MSS 6020–6040 · U. Birm. L., corresp. with Joseph Chamberlain and Mary Chamberlain · U. Leeds, Brotherton L., letters to Sir E. W. Gosse
Likenesses G. F. Watts, engraving, 1843, NPG · H. R. Graves, portrait, 1855, NPG [*see illus.*] · H. J. Brooks, group portrait, oils (*Private view of the old masters exhibition, Royal Academy, 1888*), NPG · K., chromolithograph caricature, NPG; repro. in *VF* (6 Nov 1912)
Wealth at death £36,317 6s. 8d.: probate, 29 May 1913, *CGPLA Eng. & Wales*

Nevill, Sir Edward (*d.* 1705), judge, was the second of the three sons (there were at least three daughters) of Henry Nevill of Bathwick in Somerset. Admitted to Gray's Inn in 1650, he was called to the bar in 1658, and became an ancient of that inn in 1676. By the mid-1670s he had embarked upon a career of loyal service and advancement under the Stuarts. The king appointed him deputy lieutenant of Nottinghamshire on 28 July 1675, on the recommendation of the earl of Ogle. He was knighted in June 1681 on the occasion of an address he delivered to the king in his capacity as the recorder of Bath. Nevill was created serjeant-at-law on 21 January 1685, and James II appointed him king's serjeant upon his accession later that year. On 11 October 1685 James further promoted him to the position of baron of the exchequer.

Nevill was dismissed from this position on 21 April 1686 for refusing to uphold James's broad interpretation of the dispensing power. When the Convention Parliament of 1689 asked him to describe the circumstances of his dismissal, he stated that the king had sought his opinion on four separate occasions on his claim to have the authority to repeal all penal laws against religious dissenters. In his first three interviews he gave his opinion that the king had no such powers of dispensing, and he maintained this position during his fourth interview despite the chancellor's open threat of dismissal. Nevill received his dismissal eight days later, a casualty of James's purge of the courts.

Nevill returned to public life during the deliberations of the Convention Parliament in the role of expert legal counsel. On 30 January 1689 he was invited to appear before the House of Lords to give his opinion on the constitutional question of whether there existed an original contract between king and people upon which royal government is based. Like the other judges consulted, Nevill affirmed the existence of an original contract, although

there was no mention of it in the law books. In his opinion contracts *per se* originated in man's first submission to government, a fact not mitigated even by conquest: 'In conquests the government puts the laws upon them [the governed], yet in a little time that becomes an original contract. It must of necessity be implied by the nature of government' (*House of Lords MSS*, 2.1689–90). In this way he contributed to the growing consensus that kings held their titles not from God immediately but from God mediately with the community's sanction.

On 18 March 1689 Nevill was again sworn in as baron of the exchequer under King William's settlement of the courts. His patent was renewed on 20 April 1689, changing the condition of his tenure from the king's pleasure to good behaviour. Thereafter all barons of the exchequer held their office on condition of good behaviour. On 30 October 1691 he was translated from the exchequer to the court of common pleas, where he took his place above justices Rokeby and Powell due to his seniority in the bench. Nevill continued in this position under Queen Anne, who reappointed him on 23 June 1702. During these years he assisted in several of the state trials, where he 'seems to have acted an honest and independent part on the bench' (Foss, *Judges*, 399). Nevill died on 8 August 1705 and was buried in Hammersmith Chapel, Fulham, Middlesex, on 11 August. His wife, Frances, is named in his will, dated 1 July 1703, but nothing else is known of her; they had no heir.   MARY S. REDD MAGNOTTA

Sources Baker, *Serjeants* · J. H. Baker, *An introduction to English legal history*, 3rd edn (1990) · Foss, *Judges*, vol. 7 · E. Foss, *Biographia juridica: a biographical dictionary of the judges of England … 1066–1870* (1870) · Sainty, *Judges* · C. Weston and J. Greenberg, *Subjects and sovereigns: the grand controversy over legal sovereignty in Stuart England* (1981) · *The manuscripts of the House of Lords*, 4 vols., HMC, 17 (1887–94), vol. 2 · will, 1 July 1703, PRO, PROB 11/482, sig. 104 · IGI
Wealth at death house and 'outhouses' at Bedford Walke; plate; employed servants; left annuities of £20 each for sister Dorothy and brother Ralph; 40s. p.a. to William Spawkings; £100 in apprenticeships to educate boys; £500 to sister Katherine to pay mortgage; small grants to aunt, nieces, and nephews; grants of 20s. each to sixty-six poor people: will, 1 July 1703, PRO, PROB 11/482, sig. 104

Nevill, Henry. *See* Payne, Henry (*d.* 1705?).

Nevill, Hugh (1855–1924). *See under* Nevill family (*per. c.*1793–1973).

Nevill, Meresia Dorothy Augusta (1849–1918), political activist, was born on 14 December 1849 at 29 Upper Grosvenor Street, London, the eldest of the four surviving children of Reginald Henry Nevill (1807–1878) and Lady Dorothy Fanny (1826–1913), daughter of Horatio Walpole, third earl of Orford, and Mary Walpole, *née* Fawkener.

The outstanding influence in Meresia Nevill's life was undoubtedly her mother, Lady Dorothy, a notable society hostess and a woman with extensive connections in the world of politics and literature. Her early years were spent at Dangstein, Sussex, where Lady Dorothy guided the education of her three sons and only daughter, and where Meresia studied with a governess. In keeping with upper-class custom she was presented at court in 1871, but by all accounts her coming out as a débutante was an unhappy experience, made the more awkward perhaps by signs of the St Vitus's Dance from which she suffered all her life. A 'manly' young woman, with cropped hair and a deep gruff voice, hers might have been the lot of the dutiful, unmarried daughter: becoming social secretary and companion to her busy and sometimes difficult mother. However, from an early age she demonstrated a marked interest in public affairs, and embarked on a productive life in politics. Her powerful talents for organization and public speaking were nurtured within the embryonic Primrose League and Ladies' Grand Council. A generous inheritance from her father precluded any financial need to marry, and consequently there was no impediment to a political career that consumed much energy and took her on speaking tours around the country.

Although mainly a tory stronghold, Lady Dorothy's London home in Charles Street, Berkeley Square, attracted men and women from across the political spectrum. Disraeli had been a neighbour and close friend, and it was at her famed luncheon table in the 1880s that members of the so-called Fourth Party discussed the idea of the Primrose League. Eschewing her mother's less partisan views, but acquiring her taste for politics, Meresia Nevill became an 'uncompromising Tory', which she steadfastly remained all her life. Having joined the Primrose League on 6 February 1884, once women were admitted to membership, Meresia and Lady Dorothy were among those attending the inaugural meeting of the Ladies' Grand Council the following year. Appointed honorary treasurer at her mother's prompting, Meresia remained on the executive committee of the Ladies' Grand Council in that capacity until 1904, when she became honorary secretary, and then a vice-president until her death in 1918.

The Corrupt Practices Act of 1883, which forbade the payment of canvassers at elections, indirectly paved the way for the Dames of the Primrose League to provide an 'army of unpaid substitutes'. Meresia Nevill was perhaps the person most instrumental in directing this new force in politics. From her organizational base at the league headquarters in Victoria Street, Westminster, she transformed the Dames into an efficient organization of backroom constituency workers, which quickly became the envy of other political parties. Guy Nevill was later to observe that 'Like Boadicea she led an army', and could be seen at election time wheeling around the streets of London in her blue and white dog cart (*Exotic Groves*, 166). Any apprehensions about the public nature of this new political activity for women were quickly dispelled by the success of their efforts at the general elections of 1885, 1892, and 1895. She publicized the work of the league in effective speeches at habitation meetings around the country and in articles in society magazines. While thus developing the political skills of a great many women—she likened canvassing to political district visiting—she was none the less lukewarm on the feminist implications of their work, and always maintained the official league line

on women's suffrage: that it was a matter of personal opinion which should not be made an object of league policy. Her own views on the subject are not recorded.

Meresia Nevill remained her mother's indispensable companion—'my sheet anchor and rudder'—both at social functions on behalf of Erridge habitation at the family home of Lord Abergavenny and at their London residence in Charles Street until Lady Dorothy's death in 1913 (*Life and Letters*, 287). When the First World War broke out the Ladies' Grand Council, with Meresia Nevill at the centre of activities, turned its attention to fundraising for the war effort. After an illness of a few months she died of cancer on 26 October 1918 at 29 Sloane Gardens, London.

LINDA WALKER

Sources G. Nevill, *Exotic groves: a portrait of Lady Dorothy Nevill* (1984) · L. Walker, 'Party political women: a comparative study of liberal women and the Primrose League, 1890–1914', *Equal or different: women's politics, 1800–1914*, ed. J. Rendall (1987), 165–91 · *Reminiscences of Lady Dorothy Nevill*, ed. R. Nevill (1906) · *Primrose League Gazette* (1887–1918) · *Primrose League Gazette*, 26 (Nov 1918), 3 · R. H. Nevill, *The life and letters of Lady Dorothy Nevill* (1919) · J. H. Robb, *The Primrose League, 1883–1906* (1942) · M. Pugh, *The tories and the people, 1880–1935* (1985) · b. cert. · d. cert. · CGPLA Eng. & Wales (1919)
Likenesses photograph, repro. in *Primrose League Gazette*, 26 (Nov 1918)
Wealth at death £34,241 2s. 3d.: probate, 17 Feb 1919, CGPLA Eng. & Wales

Nevill, Richard (1817–1892). *See under* Nevill family (*per.* c.1793–1973).

Nevill, Richard Austin (1867–1946). *See under* Nevill family (*per.* c.1793–1973).

Nevill, Richard Janion (1785–1856). *See under* Nevill family (*per.* c.1793–1973).

Nevill, Samuel (*bap.* 1697, *d.* 1764), politician in America and journal editor, was baptized on 4 November 1697 at Colwich, Staffordshire, England, the son of John Nevill (*bap.* 1669) and his wife, Mary. He did not attend university but acquired extensive learning and literary refinement. He became well versed in law after moving to London about 1717. He also demonstrated an instinctive bent for journalism as the London *Morning Post*'s editor. A member of the Church of England, he married Ann Doleman (1692–1755) on 27 October 1718; they had no surviving children.

Family connections drew Nevill to America in 1736. His sister Sarah (1699–1735) and brother John (1702–1774) had emigrated to Perth Amboy, New Jersey, a modest port near New York. In 1736 Samuel Nevill was bequeathed his sister's estate; she had inherited it from her husband, Peter Sonmans (1667–1734). Nevill's inheritance linked his fortunes with the East Jersey proprietors—heirs of the partnership given title by Charles II to all territory in East Jersey, who retained ownership of any acreage not privately held when that colony merged into New Jersey in 1702. Through Sonmans, Nevill could claim 22 per cent of all unpatented lands, as well as 22 per cent of any tracts that reverted to the proprietors as a result of defective title claims.

Enormous incentive thus existed for East Jersey proprietors to sue landowners for their property. Before the proprietors' charter from Charles II could be proclaimed, the earliest settlers occupied several townships where titles still remained uncertain. Land registration, moreover, had long been error-prone in New Jersey, where overlapping surveys and lost deeds made ownership precarious. By 1736 the eastern proprietors and their heirs were challenging possession to as much as 330,000 acres, from which Nevill might have expected to receive £60,000 to £120,000.

Nevill emerged as one of New Jersey's leading politicians less than a decade after emigrating; he won election to the assembly in 1743 and became speaker in 1744. Controversy soon ensued from his efforts to dispossess farmers occupying 17,540 acres that he claimed as Sonmans's property. Although he appears to have had no formal legal training, Nevill orchestrated a campaign of legal harassment by filing numerous and costly eviction suits designed to sap his opponents' financial ability to resist. After Nevill lost a crucial case in court, strong evidence surfaced that his brother John had suborned two jurors into swearing perjured affidavits, which enabled the chief justice, another eastern proprietor, to vacate the judgment against him. These allegations contributed to Nevill's loss of the speakership in 1746.

The proprietors' legal offensive meanwhile encountered violent and broadly based resistance, as crowds blocked evictions and rescued offenders from gaol. Having failed to win passage of draconian measures to quell the unrest, even after regaining the speakership in 1748, Nevill left the assembly in 1751. From 1749, however, he had struggled to restore order as the second-ranking justice in the colony's supreme court. He showed striking coolness and courage at circuit court sessions to indict or try protesters, even as their sympathizers packed his hearings and scowled menacingly. Unperturbed by threats against his property and life, Nevill relentlessly hounded his antagonists. In consequence he became one of New Jersey's most hated men, but hastened the end of the disturbances. Nevertheless, Nevill returned to the assembly in 1754 and resumed the speaker's chair in 1759.

On 22 August 1755 Nevill's first wife died, and on 23 October 1757 he married Mary Walker. There were no surviving children of this marriage either. Nevill meanwhile ranked as an unusually learned jurist and erudite man of letters. He published the first compilation of his colony's laws in 1752. From 1758 to 1760 he edited monthly issues of New Jersey's first periodical, the *New American Magazine*, which continued for twenty-seven volumes, longer than any previous colonial magazine except one.

Nevill's career entered its twilight in May 1763 when failing health forced him to resign the speakership. But for this sudden decline he would have been appointed the colony's chief justice in 1764. Simultaneously respected and reviled within New Jersey, Samuel Nevill died at Perth Amboy on 27 October 1764 and was buried there at St Peter's Church. His second wife survived him.

Thomas L. Purvis

Sources W. A. Whitehead, *Contributions to the early history of Perth Amboy and adjoining country* (1856), 120–24 • T. L. Purvis, 'Disaffection along the millstone: the petition of Dollens Hegeman and anti-proprietary sentiment in eighteenth-century New Jersey', *New Jersey History*, 101 (1983), 61–82 • J. Ashton, 'Parker, James', *ANB* **Archives** New Jersey Archives, Trenton, journal of the New Jersey assembly • New Jersey Historical Society, Newark, Robert Hunter Morris papers

Nevill, Wilfred Percy (1894–1916), army officer, was born on 14 July 1894 at 15 Canonbury Park, North Islington, London, a younger son—among nine children of whom seven survived childhood—of Thomas George Nevill (1852–1903), coal merchant (of George Nevill & Son, Hoxton) and managing director of Kelly's Directories, and his wife, Elizabeth Ann, *née* Smith (1856–*c*.1948). The family was affluent, and staunchly Anglican. Following T. G. Nevill's death they moved to Tennyson's House, Montpelier Road, Twickenham, Middlesex. Nevill, called Billie or Bill by his family, from 1902 to 1908 attended Penrhyn Lodge, Westgate-on-Sea, Kent, a small 'dame preparatory school', where he became captain of the school, gained cricket, football, and hockey colours, topped the bowling averages, and won the shooting prize. From 1908 to 1913 at Dover College, a small Victorian public school, he was notably successful at games: he played in the first fifteen, the first eleven—as captain in 1913, and scoring 107 not out against 6th flotilla, RN—and the first hockey eleven, and was a member of the school running team. In 1913 he was head prefect and head of School House. He was a sergeant in the Officers' Training Corps, active in the debating society, and on the committee of the school branch of the Navy League. In October 1913 he was admitted a pensioner at Jesus College, Cambridge, where he read for the classics tripos, intending to become a schoolmaster. Jesus was then known as a sporting college, and he played hockey for it. He also enjoyed winter sports and London musicals and reviews.

In November 1914 Nevill was commissioned second lieutenant—one of 'K's pups' (*Billie*, 72)—in the 8th battalion of the East Surrey regiment, whose depot was at Kingston, a few miles from his home. The 8th was a service battalion, a Kitchener's New Army unit, and was in the 18th (eastern) division commanded by Major-General F. I. Maxse. After a month's course at the Royal Military College, Sandhurst, in December 1914, Nevill trained with his battalion in England, was promoted lieutenant (dated from 11 April 1915), and went to France with the battalion in July 1915. From August he served in the trenches, and in September he was promoted captain (backdated to 11 April 1915). He liked army life and applied for a regular commission. In November 1915 he was appointed a regular second lieutenant in the East Yorkshire regiment—he wrote, 'Never heard of 'em before. I'm trying to get transferred to 1st E.S.R.' (*Billie*, 73)—though he continued to serve in the 8th East Surreys with the temporary rank of captain. He hoped after the war to serve in India. He wrote letters home to his family: in them he appears cheerful, jaunty, and confident of ultimate British victory. Concerned about inadequate religious provision—he wrote home in April 1916, 'it's disgraceful how few services we get out here' (*Billie*, 174)—he held services for his unit. He may have been informally engaged to his sweetheart, Alice (Muffie or Muff) Schooling (*b*. 7 June 1898), who had been his next-door neighbour in Twickenham until her family moved to Hastings: her family assumed that the couple would have married had Nevill survived.

The 18th division was part of the Fourth Army, commanded by General Sir Henry Rawlinson, which in 1916 was to attack the German lines at the Somme. On leave in England in May Nevill bought footballs for his company to dribble across no man's land in the offensive: he hoped that it would help their advance. There had been similar uses of footballs previously, but it is not known whether he had heard of them. At 7.27 a.m. on Saturday 1 July 1916, the first day of the battle of the Somme, Nevill went over the parapet, kicking off his football, and led his company across no man's land towards the German lines and Montauban. He was shot in the head and killed, just outside the German wire. He was buried in Carnoy military cemetery, Somme.

Nevill was one of over 19,000 British killed that day: available statistics indicate that the most vulnerable rank was captain. Nearly 1000 officers were killed, and of these very few gained individual recognition from the wider public. However, Captain Nevill and his footballs were featured in the local and national press: the *Illustrated London News* published a dramatic drawing by Richard Caton Woodville, 'The Surreys Play the Game!', and the *Daily Mail* published a verse, 'The Game'. Nevill's deed was commemorated by his regiment, and the story was subsequently retold in successive accounts of the Somme. His letters home were preserved by his family, and were later edited as *Billie: the Nevill Letters, 1914–1916* (1991) by Ruth Elwin Harris. Nevill is commemorated, with other men from east Twickenham, on the war memorial in St Stephen's Church, near his family home.

ROGER T. STEARN

Sources *Billie: the Nevill letters, 1914–1916*, ed. R. E. Harris (1991) · *The Dovorian*, 26–8 (1912–14) · *The Dovorian*, 30 (1916) · *Dover College Register, 1871–1924* (1924) · *ILN* (29 July 1916) · private information (2004) [F. H. Willmoth, Jesus College archives, Cambridge; P. E. Thomson, Margate library; D. Crouch, Westgate-on-Sea] · H. W. Pearse and H. S. Sloman, *History of the east Surrey regiment*, 2 (1923) · M. Langley, *The east Surrey regiment (the 31st and 70th regiments of foot)* (1972) · A. Gray and F. Brittain, *A history of Jesus College, Cambridge*, rev. edn (1979) · M. Middlebrook, *The first day on the Somme, 1 July 1916* (1971); repr. (1984) · H. Cecil and P. Liddle, eds., *Facing Armageddon: the First World War experienced* (1996) · T. Wilson, *The myriad faces of war: Britain and the Great War, 1914–1918* (1986) · P. Simkins, *Kitchener's army: the raising of the new armies, 1914–16* (1988) · J. M. Winter, *The Great War and the British people* (1985) · P. Parker, *The old lie: the Great War and the public-school ethos* (1987) · J. R. de S. Honey, *Tom Brown's universe: the development of the Victorian public school* (1977) · B. Bond, *A victory worse than defeat? British interpretations of the First World War* (1997)

Archives IWM, MSS

Likenesses photograph, 1915, repro. in Harris, ed., *Billie: the Nevill letters*

Nevill, William, first marquess of Abergavenny (1826–1915), party manager, was born on 16 September 1826 at Longford Hall, Shropshire, the eldest son and heir of William Nevill, the fourth earl of Abergavenny (*d*. 1868), of Eridge Castle, Frant, near Tunbridge Wells, and of Nevill Hall, Abergavenny, and Caroline, daughter of Ralph Leeke, of Longford Hall, Shropshire; he had one brother and three sisters. From his father's succession to the peerage in 1845 until his own succession in 1868, he was styled Viscount Nevill. He was educated at Eton College. In 1848 he married Caroline (*d*. 1892), daughter of Sir John Vanden-Bempde-Johnstone, second baronet, of Hackness Hall, Scarborough, with whom he had five sons and five daughters. In 1849 he was commissioned in the 2nd Life Guards.

After early years of conventional country and sporting pursuits Nevill developed a consuming interest in working to restore the fortunes of the Conservative Party as it struggled, during the leadership of Lord Derby and Benjamin Disraeli, to regain the confidence of the country after the split under Peel in 1846. Nevill never sought a Commons seat nor much figured in a public role in the Lords; he had no ambition to influence or participate in decisions of high policy. He remained consistently through his long life content to work in the background of politics as organizer, fund-raiser, adviser, and manager-activist for the Conservative cause in the constituencies. He took to heart Disraeli's point that the Conservative Party depended much more than the Liberal on a comprehensive and efficient system of organization. In this 'backroom' sphere Nevill came to have an unrivalled reputation as the 'tory bloodhound' for his assiduous application to electioneering and raising the money to fund it. He was instrumental in founding the Junior Carlton Club in 1864; he was one of the group which started the *Yorkshire Post* in 1866; he took over superintendence of the National Conservative Registration Association. He came to have a bond of friendship with and admiration for Disraeli, which was warmly reciprocated.

Nevill was primarily responsible for moving Markham Spofforth out of the party's firm of legal advisers, Messrs Baxter, Rose, Norton & Co., to take over the party agency on the retirement of Philip Rose in 1859, and worked steadily with him until Spofforth was replaced by J. E. Gorst in 1870. With Gorst (party agent 1870–77, 1880–82), a rather prickly 'tory democrat', Abergavenny (as he had become) was never on easy terms; nor was he much at ease during G. C. T. Bartley's brief and troubled term (1883–5). W. B. Skene (1877–80) suited Abergavenny better, but it was not until the arrival at Central Office from Kent in 1885 of R. W. E. Middleton that the Conservative leaders found a principal agent who suited their requirements, and who collaborated smoothly with the concurrent chief whip, who had also 'come under Lord Abergavenny's eye', Aretas Akers-Douglas.

Abergavenny's most important political insight was to

see that the party 'out of doors' would become of immensely greater consequence with the semi-democratic 'occupier' borough franchise of the second Reform Act of 1867. Despite a stubborn reluctance on Disraeli's part, Abergavenny pushed through the arrangements leading to the inauguration in November 1867 of the Conservative National Union, by which the multifarious Conservative local associations and societies were gathered together in permanent institutional form. It is altogether characteristic of Abergavenny's political covertness that Disraeli—who ruthlessly snubbed that inauguration—should none the less be credited with it as the genius of 'popular toryism'. Abergavenny followed through the logic of assimilating the provincial Conservative elites by founding in 1883 the Constitutional Club, which effectively in 1887 incorporated the Beaconsfield Club of 1879. He was by this time virtual manager of both the Carlton and Junior Carlton clubs.

Abergavenny settled into a station of singular prestige in the innermost Conservative councils: the 'Grand Panjandrum'; the 'electioneering Warwick', *grand seigneur* of the 'Kent gang' of party managers. He was principal trustee of the party fund; he was supreme promoter and vetter of patronage; he greatly assisted Lord Salisbury and Lord Randolph Churchill to come to terms in 1884. He was rewarded by Disraeli with a marquessate (of Abergavenny) in 1876 and by Salisbury with a Garter in 1886. He was lord lieutenant of Sussex from 1892 to 1905, and honorary colonel of the Kent and Sussex yeomanry regiments.

An imposing yet genial aristocratic figure, Abergavenny made Eridge Castle a centre famed for party hospitality. He features in the various memoirs of his cousin by marriage, Lady Dorothy Nevill. After 1905 ill health obliged him to retire from active party service and he died at Eridge on 12 December 1915, in his ninetieth year, and was buried in the family vault in the church at Eridge Green. *The Times* marked his death as worthy of a news item in its own right, not a mere obituary.   R. T. SHANNON

Sources *The Times* (13 Dec 1915) · R. Shannon, *The age of Disraeli, 1868–1881: the rise of tory democracy* (1992) · R. Shannon, *The age of Salisbury, 1881–1902: unionism and empire* (1996) · *Reminiscences of Lady Dorothy Nevill*, ed. R. Nevill (1906) · P. Cohen, 'Disraeli's child, a history of the conservative and unionist party organisation', 1964, Conservative Central Office · T. W. H. Escott, *Randolph Spencer Churchill* (1895) · H. J. Hanham, *Elections and party management: politics in the time of Disraeli and Gladstone* (1959) · A. M. Brookfield, *Annals of a chequered life* (1930) · GEC, *Peerage*
Archives E. Sussex RO | Bodl. Oxf., letters to Benjamin Disraeli · Bodl. Oxf., Hughenden MSS · CKS, Chilston MSS · CKS, letters to Aretas Akers-Douglas · Hatfield House, Hertfordshire, Salisbury MSS
Likenesses Ape [C. Pellegrini], lithograph, repro. in *VF*, 7 (1875), pl. 207 · group portrait, photograph, repro. in E. A. Akers-Douglas, *Chief whip: the political life and times of Aretas Akers-Douglas, 1st Viscount Chilston* (1961) · portrait (in life guards uniform), Eridge Castle, Kent · portrait (in Garter robes); on loan to East Sussex county council · wood-engraving (after photograph), repro. in *ILN*, 68 (1876), 61
Wealth at death £173,680 14s. 9d.: probate, 5 April 1916, CGPLA Eng. & Wales

Nevill, William Henry (1822–1894). *See under* Nevill family (*per. c.*1793–1973).

Neville [de Neville] **family** (*per. c.*1267–1426), gentry, was prominent in Lancashire and Yorkshire. The family was founded by Geoffrey de *Neville (d. 1285), younger brother of Sir Robert de *Neville (d. 1282) of Raby, and probably a knight. Both supported the crown in the civil wars of Henry III's reign, and it was probably at the end of the conflict (by February 1267) that Geoffrey acquired Hornby, near Lancaster, with other property in Lancashire, the West Riding of Yorkshire, and Lincolnshire by his marriage to the daughter and heir of John de Longvillers. After Geoffrey's death his widow, **Margaret de Neville** (d. 1319), recovered custody of these estates to hold of the crown on condition that she did not remarry without licence. As licence was granted to her in 1293, and as she was summoned to perform military service in Gascony in 1294 and against the Scots in 1300, it seems that she may have remarried. She was vigorous in pursuing a number of lawsuits to protect her rights in her estates. Her son John de Neville (b. 1269, d. in or before 1309) married a certain Pernel or Petronilla (d. 1346×9) but appears to be otherwise unknown. Their son **John Neville** (1299/1300–1335), however, began the family's long personal association with the house of Lancaster. His grandmother had held Hornby Castle of Thomas, earl of Lancaster, by knight service, and John became a member of the latter's household, suffering forfeiture and the imposition of a fine of £500 after the earl's defeat by the forces of Edward II at Boroughbridge in 1322. The fact that payment of the fine was to be spread over five years suggests that he was not regarded as an incorrigible rebel, and in 1324 he was summoned to attend a great council and to serve the crown on the continent. After Edward's deposition in 1327 John was rehabilitated in an amnesty for former adherents of the earl, having only paid £50 of his fine. He then helped to usher in the personal rule of Edward III by his part in the arrest of Roger Mortimer, earl of March, at Nottingham Castle in October 1330. This was a violent and dangerous enterprise in which men were killed, and John was pardoned for his involvement in two deaths before being rewarded with royal grants of land in Berkshire, Dorset, and Shropshire. He was summoned to fight against the Scots in 1335, but died before the end of that year.

John was apparently unmarried, and the inheritance passed to his cousin **Sir Robert** [ii] **Neville** (*fl.* 1344–1373), the son of Robert [i], a younger son of Geoffrey de Neville: this Robert was possibly the man of that name who had distinguished himself against the Scots in Edward I's reign. Robert [ii] embarked on a promising career of administrative and military service, acting as a commissioner of the peace in Lancashire in 1344 and 1346 and a keeper of the peace in the West Riding in 1350, and seeing active service at Crécy (1346) and elsewhere in France. By 1344 his son with his first wife, Joan, daughter and heir of Henry Atherton of Lancashire, **Sir Robert** [iii] **Neville** (d. 1413), had married Margaret, daughter of the merchant and royal financier Sir William de la *Pole and sister of

Michael de la *Pole, the future earl of Suffolk. However, the Nevilles' association with this eminent but controversial family appears to have been a factor in plunging Robert [ii] into serious financial difficulties. By 1355 he was imprisoned as a debtor in Newgate, and was released in 1362 after clearing some of his debts only to be committed to the Fleet prison. His troubles do not seem to have been resolved until at least 1367, when property in Kent which he had forfeited was restored to him. This had presumably come to him by his second marriage, to Elizabeth, daughter of Thomas St Laurence and widow of Sir Roger Kirkeby of Horton Kirby, Kent. Both she and her husband, who seems to have taken no further part in public life, were still living in 1373.

Robert [iii] Neville entered the service of Edward, the Black Prince, and received an annuity of 100 marks from him in 1357 after distinguishing himself in the previous year at Poitiers. He was subsequently associated with the prince's brother John of Gaunt, duke of Lancaster, with whom Robert's brother-in-law Michael de la Pole had close political links in the later years of Edward III's reign. Robert served overseas with Gaunt in 1369 and 1370 before becoming a prominent figure in the administration of Yorkshire for at least thirty-five years. He was a knight of the shire for that county in 1377 and 1380, and figured regularly on commissions of the peace and of oyer and terminer. These were mainly in the West Riding; those in the East Riding, especially (as in 1377, 1390, and 1397) in the vicinity of Beverley, may be explained by his employment as steward of two archbishops of York, Alexander *Neville and Thomas Arundel. More specific commissions ranged from the restoration of order in 1382 after the peasants' revolt and the protection of England in 1385 from French invasion to more parochial issues, such as the investigation of murder, the suppression of cattle theft, and the maintenance of the highways. Leading northern magnates with whom he was associated on commissions included Gaunt, Henry Percy, earl of Northumberland, and his own kinsman Ralph *Neville of Raby, the future earl of Westmorland. Robert was in receipt of an annuity of £20 from Gaunt and was named in the duke's will in 1399 as his 'trescher Batcheler'. He appears to have remained an active supporter of the house of Lancaster after Henry IV's usurpation in 1399. He may have been keeper of the king's castle of Pontefract at the time of Northumberland's revolt in 1405. He was still serving as a commissioner of the peace in Yorkshire in the year before his death. His son Sir Thomas Neville had died by 1387, and Robert [iii] was survived in 1413 by two daughters, Margaret and Joan, and Thomas's daughter Margaret. She had put the seal on the Lancastrian connection by her marriage by 1404 to Gaunt's legitimized son Thomas *Beaufort, earl of Dorset (1412) and duke of Exeter (1416). Margaret acquired the Neville estates but did not produce an heir and predeceased her husband. On his death in 1426 the Neville inheritance was divided between the elder Margaret and Joan's son, Sir John Langton.

PETER MCNIVEN

Sources GEC, *Peerage*, new edn, 9.487–91 · *Chancery records* · *VCH Lancashire*, 8.192–4 · M. C. B. Dawes, ed., *Register of Edward, the Black Prince*, 4 vols., PRO (1930–33), vol. 3, p. 306; vol. 4, p. 219 · [J. Raine], ed., *Testamenta Eboracensia*, 1, SurtS, 4 (1836); [J. Raine], ed., 3, SurtS, 45 (1865), 238 · *Thomae Walsingham, quondam monachi S. Albani, historia Anglicana*, ed. H. T. Riley, 2 vols., pt 1 of *Chronica monasterii S. Albani*, Rolls Series, 28 (1863–4), vol. 1, p. 100 · *The register of William Greenfield, lord archbishop of York, 1306–1315*, ed. W. Brown and A. H. Thompson, 2, SurtS, 149 (1934), 159–62

Neville, Alan de (*d. c.*1176), administrator, probably took his name from Neuville in Normandy. He is first recorded in 1138, in the retinue of Count Waleran of Meulan, whose butler he became with an annual fee of 100s. About this time he married a daughter of a baron of the honour of Pont Audemar. Having served Count Waleran during most of Stephen's reign, about 1153 Neville transferred his allegiance to the Angevins, and by 1156 he held land in Lincolnshire, on which he several times received remittance from the geld. Pardons he received between 1168 and 1171 from paying his share of amercements laid on seven wapentakes there, all except one of them in Lindsey, indicate that it was in Lindsey that his holdings mainly lay. It is not certain whether he was related in any way to several other Nevilles active in Lincolnshire in the reign of Henry II, or to the Neville family established probably on the abbot of Peterborough's fee at Walcot in 1086. Alan de Neville may have been involved in forest administration by 1159, when he received a royal gift out of the income from Savernake Forest in Wiltshire; in 1158 he received royal land worth £32 a year at Marlborough in the same county, which he held until his death; by 1170 he also held land in Bedwyn, Homington, and Grafton there. The first mention of pleas, probably forest pleas, held by him occurs in Wiltshire in 1163. Neville supported the king in his quarrel with Archbishop Thomas Becket, and was twice excommunicated by the latter—in 1166 and 1168. About 1166 he was appointed Henry II's chief forester, and he held forest pleas in many counties in 1166 and 1167. According to Roger of Howden, Neville remained chief forester until his death, when he was succeeded by Thomas son of Bernard. Neville's death took place about 1176.

Alan de Neville was widely hated for the vigour with which he enforced the forest laws. The chronicler of Battle Abbey said that he used the power the king had given him to enrich his master by harrying various counties of England with numerous and unaccustomed inquiries; since he feared neither God nor man, he spared no man of rank, whether churchman or layman. Confirmation that great men feared him comes from an official source; the treasurer, Richard fitz Nigel, reported that the justiciar Robert, earl of Leicester, obtained a special writ from the king in order more easily to avoid the pressing demands of Neville's men (*Alaniorum*). When Neville was dying, a monastic community asked the king for Neville's body for burial; the king replied 'I will have his wealth, you shall have his corpse, and the demons of Hell shall have his soul' (*Chronicle of Battle Abbey*, 223). The memory, or at least the reputation, of his activities was still strong during the minority of Henry III, when juries in several counties blamed him personally for the wide extension of the forest boundaries in Henry II's reign. His heirs probably included the Thomas and Ivo de Neville who received a pardon of a fine on his land at Grafton in 1178. Hugh de Neville (d. 1234), sometimes said to have been his grandson, later served Richard I, John, and Henry III as chief forest justice, and Hugh's son John also served Henry III. In 1168 another Alan de Neville, the 'other Alan', also held land in Lindsey. He was probably the 'Alan de Neville junior' who held forest pleas in 1169–70 and was active in Lincolnshire, and is likely to have been a close relative. The Alan whose widow held royal land at Amesbury in Wiltshire in 1190 was presumably the younger Alan, who was dead by Michaelmas that year.   DAVID CROOK

Sources Pipe rolls · W. Stubbs, ed., *Gesta regis Henrici secundi Benedicti abbatis: the chronicle of the reigns of Henry II and Richard I, AD 1169–1192*, 2 vols., Rolls Series, 49 (1867) · E. Searle, ed., *The chronicle of Battle Abbey*, OMT (1980), 220–23 · L. C. Loyd, *The origins of some Anglo-Norman families*, ed. C. T. Clay and D. C. Douglas, Harleian Society, 103 (1951), 72–3 · *Materials for the history of Thomas Becket, archbishop of Canterbury*, 5, ed. J. C. Robertson, Rolls Series, 67 (1881), 73 · Chancery Miscellanea, PRO, C 47 · R. Fitz Nigel [R. Fitzneale], *Dialogus de scaccario / The course of the exchequer*, ed. and trans. C. Johnson (1950), 58–9 · D. Crouch, *The Beaumont twins: the roots and branches of power in the twelfth century*, Cambridge Studies in Medieval Life and Thought, 4th ser., 1 (1986)

Neville, Alexander (c.1332–1392), archbishop of York, was a younger son of Ralph *Neville, fourth Lord Neville of Raby (c.1291–1367), and his wife, Alice (c.1300–1374), daughter of Hugh, Lord Audley. John *Neville, fifth Baron Neville, who became a leading figure among the northern baronage, was his eldest brother. Born in or about 1332, sixteen years later Alexander Neville was already a student at Oxford, where he lodged in a hostel with his brother Thomas. The latter became a prominent university clerk and canon of York Minster who was elected bishop of Ely shortly before his early death on a visit to Avignon in 1361. Alexander's own academic credentials are difficult to assess. He was a master of arts by 1357, when he received licence to study at a university for five more years. In 1361 he described himself as a scholar in civil law; but he never went on to acquire a higher degree in any university faculty. For a young clerk of such elevated aristocratic origins, academic qualifications were not in any case of prime importance, especially as Alexander Neville never entered royal governmental service. His noble birth however brought him ecclesiastical preferment from an early age. When he was only fourteen, and at the petition of no less a person than David II of Scots (a prisoner in England since his defeat at the battle of Neville's Cross in 1346), he received a papal dispensation to hold a benefice with cure of souls. Five years later, in February 1351, he acquired his first known living, the rectory of Kirkby Misperton in the North Riding of Yorkshire. Later in the same year Alexander Neville was also rector of Aysgarth in Wensleydale; and during the following decade (despite the fact that he was only ordained priest as late as June 1365) he was promoted to canonries at York Minster and prebends in each of the two collegiate churches of Darlington and Howden.

In the case of a clerk of such exclusively northern connections and benefices, it is not a little surprising that on 16 August 1361 Alexander Neville was made archdeacon of Cornwall by papal provision. Whatever the reasons for this unusual appointment, Neville's strenuous attempts to make good his claim to the archdeaconry not only dominated his career for the next ten years, but also revealed the reckless disregard for higher authority that was later to characterize his rule as archbishop of York. Although Neville is recorded as a king's clerk by 1365, Edward III became increasingly reluctant to accept him as archdeacon of Cornwall. Nevertheless the future archbishop was prepared not only to suffer imprisonment (in 1367) but also to pursue his cause at the curia in person. Although he eventually dropped his case there, he continued to reside at Avignon, apparently in an attempt to win a greater prize still. Quite unpredictably, and against the background of untypically confused attitudes within the English government and church, he was more fortunate than he could ever have expected. By January 1371 he had been promoted to the archdeaconry of Durham. Much more surprisingly, a month after the death of Archbishop Ralph Thoresby in early November 1373, the York Cathedral chapter (quite probably under pressure from the northern nobility) elected Alexander Neville as his successor. Four months later still (on 16 April 1374), and with no opposition from the English crown, Pope Gregory XI (r. 1370–78) duly provided him to the archbishopric. Neville immediately ended his residence at the curia, the temporalities were restored on 4 June, and he was formally enthroned in York Minster on 18 December of the same year.

Within a few months of Alexander Neville's return to Yorkshire the church of York was to experience the dangers of having as its archbishop—quite untypically—a clerk of local aristocratic origins who had no previous training in either royal or diocesan administration. Almost immediately Neville's pontificate was disfigured by an ugly series of disputes and altercations, most startlingly perhaps when the mayor of Hull allegedly snatched the archiepiscopal crozier from his hands. Much more dangerous was the archbishop's determination to exercise his metropolitan and diocesan authority to the utmost. In 1376 he was rebuked by Edward III for his 'unheard-of and unusual actions' in securing a papal bull authorizing him to visit York's suffragan diocese of Durham (*Historiae Dunelmensis*, cxliii); and five years later another storm of protest greeted Neville's attempt to use this bull during the vacancy at Durham created by the death in 1381 of Bishop Thomas Hatfield. Equally abortive, and much more disastrous for Neville's reputation, were his jurisdictional assaults on the great collegiate chapters of Ripon, Beverley, and York Minster itself. In every one of these disputes, probably all best interpreted as attempts by the archbishop to wrest lucrative patronage from the hands of the established Yorkshire clerical affinity created by Archbishop Thoresby, Neville gravely underestimated the power of his opponents.

At Beverley Minster, Neville's determination to visit the

chapter and lesser clergy there in early 1381 led to the most notorious 'clerical strike' in late medieval English history. His long and scandalous dispute with the canons of Beverley not only undermined his spiritual authority as archbishop, but also led to his dangerously close personal involvement in the savage urban conflicts between the so-called *potentiores* and *mediocres* who dominated town life in Beverley during the 1380s. Although Alexander Neville played an important role in defending the northern border against the more than usually dangerous threats of a Scottish invasion in 1383–4, his preoccupation with local disputes within Yorkshire itself seems to have delayed his direct involvement in the bitter national political factions of the period. However, in 1385 the archbishop took the unexpected and fateful step of joining Richard II's intimate court circle, partly no doubt because of the local political alliance he had recently forged with the king's leading counsellor, Sir Michael de la Pole of Hull (d. 1389), partly because of Richard's desire to enlist the active support of at least one powerful prelate, and partly no doubt because of Neville's own urgent need for protection in the highest quarters.

After a decade in which he had resided more or less continuously at his castle of Cawood, a few miles south of York, and rarely left his diocese at all, Neville was therefore now plunged into the perils of national politics at their most volatile. Although a member of the continual council appointed by parliament in late 1386 to further the good governance of the realm, he was clearly mistrusted by Richard II's opponents from the start [see Lords appellant]. Yet despite Thomas Walsingham's claim that he was the most militant of the royal advisers, it is difficult to know whether Neville ever exercised much real influence on public events. After accompanying Richard during the latter's perambulations through the country in 1387, he seems to have appreciated that he was likely to fall victim to those magnates most vehemently hostile to the king. Shortly after the earls of Arundel, Gloucester, and Warwick threatened to raise arms against Richard on 11 November 1387, Neville fled northward from London, but in mid-June 1388 was captured off Tynemouth while trying to cross the North Sea in a small boat, and was returned to civic custody in Newcastle. Meanwhile, at the Merciless Parliament of February 1388, after he had been charged with a wide variety of alleged acts of misgovernance, evil counsel, and corruption, the archbishop was declared guilty of treason. Unlike his fellow traitors he was not sentenced to death; but his claims to any continued authority in the English church and state were cleverly and effectively terminated, when on 3 April 1388 Pope Urban VI (r. 1378–89) was persuaded to translate him to what was in effect the purely titular see of St Andrews. As Neville had no hope of occupying that bishopric in the face of an established Clementist rival supported by the Scottish crown, he was forced into exile. After visiting Paris and Rome to argue his cause in 1389–90 he moved on to Brabant, and is said to have served as a parish priest in Louvain before dying and being buried there in the Carmelite church on 16 May 1392. Although he died intestate,

he was not to be entirely forgotten, either by his many enemies or his fewer friends. In the September parliament of 1397, at Richard II's request, Alexander Neville was posthumously declared a loyal servant of the English realm.   R. B. DOBSON

Sources register of Alexander Neville, 1374–88, Borth. Inst., Reg. 12 • J. Raine, ed., *The historians of the church of York and its archbishops*, 2, Rolls Series, 71 (1886), 422–5; 3 (1894), 284–6, 380 • *Historiae Dunelmensis scriptores tres: Gaufridus de Coldingham, Robertus de Graystanes, et Willielmus de Chambre*, ed. J. Raine, SurtS, 9 (1839), cxliii–cxliv • R. G. Davies, 'Alexander Neville, archbishop of York, 1374–1388', *Yorkshire Archaeological Journal*, 47 (1975), 87–101 • S. W. Calkin, 'Alexander Neville, Archbishop of York, 1373–1388: a study of his career with emphasis on the crisis at Beverley in 1381', PhD diss., U. Cal., Berkeley, 1976 • R. B. Dobson, 'Beverley in conflict: Archbishop Alexander Neville and the minster clergy, 1381–8', *Medieval art and architecture in the East Riding of Yorkshire*, ed. C. Wilson, British Archaeological Association Conference Transactions, 9 (1989), 149–64 • R. B. Dobson, 'The authority of the bishop in late medieval England: the case of Archbishop Alexander Neville of York, 1374–88', *Miscellanea historiae ecclesiasticae*, 8, ed. B. Vogler (Brussels, 1987), 181–91 • A. F. Leach, 'A clerical strike at Beverley Minster in the fourteenth century', *Archaeologia*, 55 (1896–7), 1–20 • R. B. Dobson, 'The later middle ages, 1215–1500', *A history of York Minster*, ed. G. E. Aylmer and R. Cant (1977), 44–110 • J. R. L. Highfield, 'The English hierarchy in the reign of Edward III', *TRHS*, 5th ser., 6 (1956), 115–38 • Emden, *Oxf.*

Archives Borth. Inst. • Borth. Inst., register, Reg. 12

Neville, Alexander (1544–1614), author, was the sixth of the eleven children of Richard Neville (c.1510–1599) of South Leverton, Nottinghamshire, and his wife, Anne (b. c.1512), daughter of Sir Walter Mantell of Heyford, Northamptonshire, and aunt of the poet Barnabe *Googe. Thomas *Neville (c.1548–1615), who became dean of Canterbury, was a younger brother. Early in Alexander's life his parents moved to Canterbury, where his father died on 3 August 1599. Neville was admitted to St John's College, Cambridge, and matriculated on 10 November 1559, but there is no evidence that he resided at the university. He was almost certainly not there in 1564 when the university presented a collection of verses, mostly Latin, to Queen Elizabeth on her visit, as so accomplished a Latinist would surely have been among the contributors. Whether or not he spent time in Cambridge, Neville seems to have continued his studies at one of the inns of court. Although his name does not appear in any of the printed registers, he was one of the five friends associated with Gray's Inn who challenged George Gascoigne, wishing entry to that inn, to win his place by writing verses to them. In 1581, perhaps because in that year his brother Thomas was senior proctor, Neville proceeded MA, at Cambridge.

After his first dalliance with Cambridge, and with the inns of court, Neville became secretary to Matthew Parker, archbishop of Canterbury, and to his successors, Edmund Grindal and John Whitgift. There is some evidence that he shared Parker's interest in early ecclesiastical manuscripts. Tanner records that a cartulary of St Gregory's (now CUL, MS Ll.2.15) originally bore on its cover a Latin couplet 'Injuriosa quid non delebis vetustas! Et tamen O nobis quae monumenta reservas' ('Consuming time, what will you not devour? Yet what memorials spare you to this hour!') and Neville's signature dated 1565. It was certainly at Parker's prompting that Neville undertook his best-known work: *De furoribus Norfolciensium Ketto duce* (1575; *STC* 18478). An account of the 1549 Norfolk rising, it has a verse history of Norwich, an account of its antiquities and office-holders, and a chart of the descent of the British and Irish kings appended. The book is dedicated to Parker and has prefixed verses by Thomas Drant. An injudicious reference on page 132 to the sheep-like demeanour of the Welsh levies summoned to suppress the rebellion gave offence to the government, and later in 1575 the book was reissued twice, now dedicated to Archbishop Grindal of York, with varying cancellantia for the offending sheet (*STC* 18478a and b). Neville also published an apology in May 1576: *Ad Walliae proceres apologia* (*STC* 18477). In 1615 the original text was published in an English translation by R. Woods: *Norfolkes furies, or, A view of Ketts campe: necessary for the malecontents, with a table of maiors and sheriffes of this worshipfull city of Norwich* (*STC* 18480).

The style of the Latin narrative of *De furoribus* is lively and elegant. Neville's skill in Latin had already been demonstrated in 1560 by his translation into fourteeners of Seneca's *Oedipus*, subsequently printed in 1563 and then found worthy of inclusion, in a version which was extensively but tacitly revised and stressed the author's youth at the time of its first composition, in Thomas Newton's anthology of Seneca translations, 'Seneca his Tenne Tragedies', published in London in 1581. The Stationers' Register records on 3 May 1577 that Neville was 'appointed to translate' Livy and imposed a ban on rival attempts, but no manuscript of this translation has yet been identified. In 1587, however, he edited *Academiae Cantabrigiensis lachrymae tumulo nobilissimi Equitis, D. Philippi Sidneii sacratae* (*STC* 4489), a collection of verses by members of Cambridge University on the death of Sir Philip Sidney, the first of the many such collections of occasional verses from the universities to be printed. To this Neville himself contributed preliminary and final verses and a lengthy prose preface. The volume is dedicated to the earl of Leicester, who had tried in 1585 to employ Neville and his brother to bring pressure to bear on Whitgift to further the interests of the protestants in the Low Countries; a letter from Neville to Whitgift on this topic survives in the Lansdowne manuscripts. Neville became MP for Christchurch, Hampshire, in 1585, and also sat for Peterborough in 1597 and for Saltash, Cornwall, in 1601. He is not, however, known to have made any contribution to the proceedings of any of these three parliaments.

Neville married Jane (1537–1606), daughter of Richard Duncomb of Morton, Buckinghamshire, and his wife, Margaret, *née* Cheyney, and widow of the herald Sir Gilbert Dethick, who died in 1584, and, previously, of William Naylor, a chancery clerk, who died in 1571. She died on 9 November 1606, and was buried at Stepney.

Neville himself died on 4 October 1614 in the extramural London ward of Bishopgate and was buried on 9 October in Canterbury Cathedral, where the dean erected a monument to commemorate both his brother and himself. Badly damaged in the eighteenth century, it represented Alexander kneeling in armour. His will shows him to have been a generous and a wealthy man. He made ample provision for his domestic servants and left £120 per annum to his brother the dean, now also master of Trinity College, Cambridge; £200 to his nephew George; and £200 to Barnaby Goche, son of the poet and master of Magdalene College, Cambridge. In a codicil made on 9 September 1614 he bequeathed £100 to the 'new intended library at Cambridge when and wheresoever erected, provided it be within six years' (PRO, PROB 11/124, sig. 102).

ELISABETH LEEDHAM-GREEN

Sources will, PRO, PROB 11/124, sig. 102 · biographical notes, St John Cam. · Venn, *Alum. Cant.* · J. Strype, *The life and acts of Matthew Parker*, new edn, 3 vols. (1821) · Arber, *Regs. Stationers* · A. Neville, *De furoribus Norfolciensium Ketto duce* (1575) · A. Neville, *Ad Walliae proceres apologia* (1576) · A. Neville, *Academiae Cantabrigiensis lachrymae tumulo nobilissimi equitis, D. Philippi Sidnei sacratae* (1587) · IGI · *STC, 1475–1640* · HoP, *Commons, 1558–1603*, 3.121 · Tanner, *Bibl. Brit.-Hib.* · *DNB* · J. Strype, *The life and acts of ... John Whitgift* (1718) · E. M. Spearing, 'Alexander Nevile's translation of Seneca's *Oedipus*', *Modern Language Review*, 15 (1920), 359–63 · J. Venn, ed., *Grace book Δ* (1910) · BL, Lansdowne MSS 16, 45 · A. M. Woodcock, ed., *Cartulary of the Priory of St Gregory, Canterbury*, CS, 3rd ser., 88 (1956) · W. Somner, *The antiquities of Canterbury*, ed. N. Battely, rev. edn (1703) · G. Gascoigne, *A hundreth sundrie flowres bounde up in one small poesie* (1572), 360–63 · verses for Queen Elizabeth, CUL, Add. MS 8915 · cartulary of St Gregory's, Canterbury, CUL, MS Ll.2.15 [once owned by Neville]

Archives BL, Lansdowne MSS 16, 45

Likenesses effigy, Canterbury Cathedral

Wealth at death over £700 in money, £120 p.a. for life to brother; also lease of a 'great messuage or tenement', the King's Head, in West Cheap, held of Canterbury dean and chapter; further lease, of Winwold parsonage, Leicestershire, held from Trinity College, Cambridge: will, PRO, PROB 11/124, sig. 102

Neville, Anne. *See* Anne (1456–1485).

Neville, Anne (1605–1689), abbess of Pontoise, whose baptismal name was Mary, was the third daughter of Sir Henry Neville (*b.* before 1580, *d.* 1641), later Lord Abergavenny, and his first wife, Lady Mary Sackville (*d.* before 1616). Mary Vavasour, the abbess of the Benedictine convent in Brussels, said that Anne Neville had her education from her mother, described as a fervent Catholic who instructed her daughter in her own religion. Little is known of Anne Neville's life before she joined the Benedictines. She professed at the Ghent house in 1634 and subsequently was given a number of important offices including novice mistress, dean, and councillor.

Anne Neville's personal qualities and her family connections led the abbess, Mary Knatchbull, to take her to England to try to secure the repayment of royal debts to the convent incurred when Charles II was in exile. Anne Neville was in England with two other nuns in June 1663 and was able to use family connections at court to secure the payment of the annuity of £500 that Mary Knatchbull had negotiated earlier. During her stay she spent time when she could with her family including her sister-in-law, the dowager Lady Abergavenny, and Frances Neville, described as her sister. She remained in England for four years during which time she was able to resolve some problems related to dowry payments and develop personal contacts with Catholic families.

On her return to the order in 1667 Anne Neville's exact future was still undecided. The abbess of the English convent in Dunkirk, where she had stopped on her way to Ghent, invited her to remain, but there was another invitation from Abbess Eugenia Poulton at the new foundation at Pontoise. With the consent of Mary Knatchbull, the superior of the order, Anne Neville went to Pontoise and after Abbess Poulton's death in December 1667 she was elected abbess by a unanimous vote. Such was her modesty that she commented on the favourable reaction to her election: 'Though I blush and hold this and severall things of this nature improper for me to wright' (Rumsey, 60). She explained her limited response by writing that she could find no one willing to take on the task of annalist and was herself unwilling to comment on the praise she had received.

Like several others at the time Pontoise was a convent with financial difficulties. The nuns had moved from Boulogne but had kept their property in the town. This had increased the borrowings needed to buy suitable premises in Pontoise. Anne Neville's 'Annals' and her other manuscripts reveal real understanding of the problems facing superiors and a sensible pragmatic approach to finding solutions. Pontoise was a convent with friends in high places in both the English and French courts. However, this did not prevent the non-payment of dowries, the main source of income. Some significant gifts of precious items were received but while these indicated the favour with which the convent was regarded by Catholic exiles, they did not meet bills. It took some negotiating before the abbess was able, in 1669, to recover money that was still tied up in property in Boulogne, the site of the initial foundation. However, with her careful management the existence of the Pontoise house continued, although finances remained precarious.

As abbess Anne Neville took her responsibilities very seriously. She wrote a lengthy 'Instructions for superiors' completed in 1676, outlining the duties and obligations of all officials in the convent for the purpose of sound management. In it she offered practical advice particularly on how the young girls entering the convent should be treated, and the importance of keeping accounts. The register of members giving details of both choir nuns and lay sisters was kept largely in her hand, with each nun having her obituary carefully recorded.

Abbess Anne Neville's 'Annals', which end abruptly in 1685, are an essential source for the history of the Benedictine communities in Flanders. She wrote for an audience, and her writing shows awareness of her role as a reporter, selecting material, drawing together information from a number of sources, and interpreting motives and actions of key figures, male and female. This can be seen strongly in her analysis of the reasons for the difficulties following the convent's foundation at Ypres in 1665. She argued that it should be treated as a time of trial; she failed to find weaknesses in the sisters who opened the new house, but

concluded that in such circumstances good intentions were not enough for success. As annalist she acknowledged her sources carefully, quoting extensively from Abbess Mary Vavasour in Brussels and including a letter from Charles II in her account.

Pontoise remained a small house, but through her writing, her travelling, and her connections, Abbess Anne Neville extended her influence outside its walls. Her extensive writings reveal the love she had for her community, her understanding of management issues, and her qualities of leadership. In her own obituary her nuns recorded the qualities they particularly admired in her, focusing on her care for the individual, her ability to comfort and advise, giving each of them her undivided attention, as well as her religious zeal. Anne Neville died on 15 December 1689 having governed her convent for twenty-two years.

CAROLINE M. K. BOWDEN

Sources A. Neville, 'English Benedictine nuns in Flanders, 1598–1687', ed. M. J. Rumsey, *Miscellanea, V*, Catholic RS, 6 (1909), 1–72 · 'Registers of the English Benedictine nuns at Pontoise, now at Teignmouth, 1680', *Miscellanea, X*, Catholic RS, 17 (1915), 248–326 · D. Rowland, *An historical and genealogical account of the noble family of Nevill, particularly of the house of Abergavenny* (1830) · GEC, *Peerage*
Archives Buckfast Abbey, Devon, diary and religious writings | St Mary's Convent, Buckfastleigh, Devon, duties and customs · St Mary's Convent, Buckfastleigh, Devon, book for superiors · St Mary's Convent, Buckfastleigh, Devon, register of the Pontoise nuns · St Mary's Convent, Buckfastleigh, Devon, annals of the five communities

Neville, Cecily. See Cecily, duchess of York (1415–1495).

Neville, Charles, sixth earl of Westmorland (1542/3–1601), magnate and rebel, was born between 18 August 1542 and 28 August 1543, the second, but only surviving, son of Henry *Neville, fifth earl of Westmorland (1524/5–1564) [see under Neville, Ralph, fourth earl of Westmorland (1498–1549)], magnate, and his first wife, Anne (d. in or after 1549). She was the daughter of Thomas *Manners, first earl of Rutland (c.1497–1543), courtier and soldier, and his second wife, Eleanor. He was raised a Catholic at the family seat of Raby Castle, co. Durham. His father was a notable supporter of Mary I, and this influence significantly coloured Neville's later political allegiance. He was styled Baron Neville between 1549 and 1564. Although only a child, he signed a letter proclaiming Mary queen on 19 July 1553.

Neville married Jane (1537–1593), daughter of Henry *Howard, earl of Surrey, and his wife, Frances, probably in 1563 or 1564. The couple had at least five children before 1570, including a son styled Lord Neville (1569–1571). His brother-in-law was Thomas *Howard, fourth duke of Norfolk (1538–1572), nobleman and courtier. The fifth earl of Westmorland died on 10 February 1564 and his heir sat in the House of Lords from 30 September 1566. Although the family held the earldom of Westmorland, the principal Neville estates were in the north-east, mainly in co. Durham. Unlike the Percy family, the Nevilles were noted as good landlords, whose tenants held by lease for term of years (usually twenty-one year leases). A royal surveyor after 1569 commented that in the lordship of Brancepeth, co. Durham, 'the lands ... are very good ... and not improved of long tyme past. The tenants hold all by Indenture for term of years, the fermes very good and the tenants wealthy and substantial ... and have moche land for their rent' (PRO, E 164/37). This was essential if the Nevilles were to maintain a strong military retinue. Westmorland's affinity was built on his social status as one of the leading northern magnates, with a right to rule within his lordship. He had a great household and dispensed patronage through appointment of his officers and servants, who, in turn, were bound to him. Although rare within the Neville household, several members of the leading local gentry families did hold office under Westmorland. These gentry, including the Salvins, Lilburnes, and Claxtons, however, were more prominent among Westmorland's wider following. The bulk of Westmorland's affinity was made up of substantial yeomen, including the Newbies of Raby and the Jacksons of Brancepeth.

Westmorland brought a degree of infamy to the family name through his undoubtedly significant contribution to the northern uprising in 1569. He was, however, more of a bungling malcontent than a cold, calculating rebel leader. The detail of his involvement in the unrest in the north represents an anatomy of treachery. Family members such as his father's younger brother Christopher *Neville (*fl.* 1549–1575) and his northern friends, encouraged an attitude of rebellion. The countess of Westmorland supported this attitude and promoted her brother's interests. Marriage to her may well have dangerously politicized Westmorland, who found himself in the midst of a complex web of discontented individuals. Francis Russell, second earl of Bedford, thought him to be loyal to the crown in 1565, when he met him at Morpeth, Northumberland. Although Westmorland was capable of concealing, albeit briefly, his true political aspirations as shown by his appointment as a commissioner for musters for co. Durham in spring 1569, he was keen to attack the government but initially recoiled from rebellion as a stain on his honour. At first he seems to have been practising 'oppositional politics', acting provocatively regarding religious change but not coming out into open rebellion (James, *Society, Politics, and Culture*, 306). Westmorland's 'wicked counsellors' persuaded him that the regime was implacably opposed to him and would destroy him (*CSP dom.*, addenda, 1566–79, 107–8). His sense of fear and isolation was exacerbated fatally when Norfolk, whom he had been supporting in his intrigues to marry Mary, queen of Scots, abandoned him when summoned to court to explain himself. Elizabeth I demanded that Thomas Radcliffe, third earl of Sussex, lord president of the council of the north, bring Westmorland and Thomas Percy, seventh earl of Northumberland, to London to declare their allegiance. Both earls refused to do so, rode to Durham on 14 November, and raised the standard of revolt. On seizing Durham the rebels entered the cathedral, pulling down the communion table and unlawfully restoring the mass.

The nature of Westmorland's and Northumberland's designs to release Mary from imprisonment at Tutbury in Staffordshire quickly became clear to Henry Carey, first Baron Hunsdon, who recommended her removal south. It is equally clear that the uprising, which began on 9 November, sought to turn back the clock with the restoration of Catholicism as the national religion. In early December, after surrounding Barnard Castle, co. Durham, the rebels seized Hartlepool, an important strategic point. Hartlepool provided the potentially vital communication line with the continent, the expected source of much needed assistance. A further advance was made on Darlington, co. Durham, and subsequently on York. Sussex advanced from Hull against the rebels and this went some way to forcing a rebel retreat on 24 November, although the main reason was the approach of a ten-thousand-strong royal army from the south. Furthermore, the government had outwitted its enemies, since while the rebel advance was centred upon Clifford Moor, Yorkshire, Mary had been quietly and discreetly moved to Coventry. The government response to the crisis was highly successful; as the rebels retreated in disarray, no doubt hoping to hold the north and give battle against the royal forces, the leaders were proclaimed traitors at Windsor on 26 November. Within a few days the rebel army disbanded in a quite hopeless situation. Westmorland had conspired against the crown at home, and was known to be in touch with the Spanish ambassador, Guerau de Spes, who contacted Fernando Alvarez de Toledo, third duke of Alva. Alva was not interested and the conspirators contacted Pius V because Philip II would not sanction rebellion. In 1571 Westmorland was formally attainted, and his estates in Durham became the property of the crown. In exile, he received a pension from Philip of 100 crowns a month.

As a result of the northern uprising Elizabeth's government was exposed to a serious risk. The level of vengeance, when it came, was heavy even by Tudor standards. Executions, serving as a warning to others, took place in every village that had offered practical assistance to the campaign of insurgency. More than 800 rebels were executed, though the major leaders escaped into exile. One remarkable feature of the rising was that it was almost entirely bloodless. Indeed, the greatest number of fatalities occurred during the seizure of Barnard Castle, when five soldiers died accidentally while leaping over the walls in a desperate effort to desert. In fact, the principal targets of the rebels were economic, involving the firing of barns, the destroying of crops, and the killing of the livestock of the loyal gentry.

Westmorland and Northumberland fled to Scotland, where the former benefited from the protection of Sir Thomas Ker, laird of Ferniehirst in Roxburghshire. Northumberland was not quite so fortunate. Seeking refuge at Liddesdale, Roxburghshire, he was promptly handed over to the Scottish regent, James Stewart, earl of Moray. In 1570 Westmorland sailed from Aberdeen to the Spanish Netherlands, never to return to his native country. Fellow rebels Leonard Dacre, Richard Norton and his sons, and

Thomas Markenfield also reached the safety of the Spanish Netherlands.

Westmorland apparently made a number of unsuccessful attempts to return to England. Sir Robert Constable, the celebrated English spy, tried to persuade him to return and seek a formal pardon; despite a tie of kinship existing between the two men, the effort failed to persuade the earl. In fact, the government attempted to kidnap Westmorland on two occasions, in 1575 and 1586. While in exile, he continued to display a political appetite, forming a friendship with Don John of Austria and serving in the Spanish army in 1580 as a colonel in an English refugee regiment. He still meddled in English affairs, though. In 1572 he involved himself in the Ridolfi plot, campaigning vigorously for support from Philip at Brussels. Westmorland continued to demonstrate considerable commitment to Catholicism, making a pilgrimage to Rome in 1581. In 1583 he was appointed captain of all the English forces under Alessandro Farnese, duke of Parma, and was almost captured at Terneuzen in July 1584. He again joined Parma in 1588 during the Armada campaign, confirming a lifelong tendency to consort with the enemies of the crown, plotting with others on several occasions to foment an invasion of England.

The countess of Westmorland, a single-minded and determined supporter of her husband, died in 1593 and was buried at Kenninghall, Norfolk, on 30 June. She had remained in receipt of a pension since her husband's exile: initially £200 per annum, later increased to £300 per annum after Westmorland's attainder. Westmorland's life as a political exile bore heavily upon his character. He spent his twilight years in loose living, running up heavy debts. Lack of a sufficiently high pension had a considerable bearing upon his protracted negotiations for marriage in Flanders. While contemplating the prospect of a second marriage, to a daughter of Jean Grusset Richardot, president of the council of Artois, he died at Nieuwpoort in Flanders on 16 November 1601. Westmorland's life was sadly wasted as a result of political intrigue and exile from his homeland. At his death his cousin Edmund *Neville (b. before 1555, d. in or after 1620), only son and heir of Richard Neville, became the claimant to the earldom, while the baronies of Neville fell into permanent abeyance. Among several known portraits of the sixth earl of Westmorland, a three-quarter length one is illustrated in Daniel Rowland's *An Historical and Genealogical Account of the Noble Family of Nevill* (1830). It shows a man of strong physical character.

ROGER N. McDERMOTT

Sources GEC, *Peerage* · DNB · *CSP dom., 1547–80; 1598–1601* · D. Rowland, *An historical and genealogical account of the noble family of Nevill, particularly of the house of Abergavenny* (1830) · D. M. Loades, *Politics, censorship, and the English Reformation* (1991) · A. Fletcher and D. MacCulloch, *Tudor rebellions*, 4th edn (1997) · *CSP for., 1569–71; 1583–4; 1586–8* · C. Sharp, ed., *Memorials of the rebellion of 1569* (1840) · M. James, *Family, lineage, and civil society: a study of society, politics, and mentality in the Durham region, 1500–1640* (1974) · M. James, *Society, politics, and culture: studies in early modern England* (1986)
Likenesses portrait, repro. in Rowland, *Historical and genealogical account*, 44 · portrait, repro. in Sharp, *Memorials*, vol. 1, p. 364

Neville, Christopher (*fl.* 1549–1575), rebel, was the fourth son of Ralph *Neville, fourth earl of Westmorland (1498–1549), administrator and soldier, and his wife, Katherine (d. 1555), daughter of Edward Stafford, third duke of Buckingham, and his wife, Eleanor. Little is known about his education and upbringing. Before he entered the household of one of his father's friends or colleagues, tutors probably educated his brothers and him. On the death of his father in 1549, his elder brother Henry Neville, fifth earl of Westmorland, leased to him the manor of Kirkbymoorside in the North Riding of Yorkshire, where he appears to have resided.

Neville married Anne (d. after 1570), daughter and heir of John Fulthorpe, of Hipswell in the North Riding, and widow of Francis Wandesford, but they had no children. She had a son, Christopher, from her first marriage, who married Elizabeth, daughter of Sir George Bowes, and who fought for Elizabeth I against his stepfather at the siege of Barnard Castle. Anne Neville's dower lands made up the bulk of her husband's estate but it was an unhappy marriage because of his behaviour. He reputedly kept a mistress, Katherine, whose husband, William Barkley, or Smith, was provided with the rectory of Kirkbymoorside. She twice sent him a ring while he was in hiding in Scotland and he was genuinely fond of her. Neville acquired a reputation for a hot temper. In May 1554 he was involved in a violent incident at the Gatherley races, near Richmond, Yorkshire, when he brought a group of Neville supporters to see one of his own horses run and a quarrel broke out with members of the rival Rokeby, Bowes, and Wycliffe families. This resulted in Neville being badly injured himself, and the death of one of his opponents. He seems to have escaped any judicial inquiry, probably owing to the influence of his family. The feud continued through the 1550s and 1560s and these families opposed the Nevilles in 1569, when they were involved in the defence of Barnard Castle, co. Durham. Neville was a recognized Catholic and his wife came from a family with Catholic sympathies. In 1561 he probably had a Catholic priest, Anthony Salvin, a deprived prebendary of Durham, living with him at Kirkbymoorside.

Neville was among those disgruntled with the 1559 religious settlement and the encroachment of southerners, like Thomas Radcliffe, third earl of Sussex, lord president of the council of the north, into northern offices, especially in the marches. His nephew, Charles *Neville, sixth earl of Westmorland, and he were among the principals implicated in the northern uprising in 1569. Neville was one of the principal members of Westmorland's clientele. Bowes reported to Sussex that Neville was one of those most responsible for encouraging his nephew to rebel. Thomas Percy, seventh earl of Northumberland, confessed that Neville was one of those first privy to the conspiracy (Sharp, 34, 202). He was with his brother Cuthbert Neville [see below] at the fateful gathering at Westmorland's castle at Brancepeth, co. Durham, on 10 November 1569 and was in the party at Durham Cathedral on the 13th which overthrew the communion table and celebrated mass.

On 16 November Neville led a party of horsemen through Cleveland, Yorkshire, to raise the Neville tenantry about Kirkbymoorside, and set up altars in the parish churches and ordered the clergy to celebrate mass. By the 29th he is reported to have taken Hartlepool, co. Durham, with 300 men and to have held it for Westmorland and Northumberland as a possible place of disembarkation for reinforcements from abroad. He seems to have been constantly on the move, for on 1 December he was at the siege of Barnard Castle, where he issued an order to muster men there, but a few days later he was encountered with a well-armed body of 500 horsemen at Piercebridge, co. Durham. He was active, well-organized, and energetic in prosecuting complete rebellion.

When Westmorland and Northumberland broke up their forces, Neville accompanied them to Hexham and then crossed with them and a number of the other rebel leaders into Scotland, where they sought refuge with the Kerrs and Scotts and other adherents of Mary, queen of Scots. Neville was sheltered for a time by Sir Walter Scott at Branxholme, from where Sussex demanded his apprehension by the regent, James Stewart, earl of Moray, but early in February 1570 Bowes reported to Sir Thomas Gargrave that Neville was once more around Brancepeth. Soon afterwards he escaped, probably by way of Aberdeen, to Flanders. He had already been formerly exempted by the queen's proclamation from any pardon and was in May 1571 attainted for treason and his estates were confiscated by the crown. In fact, these lands were not great: Kirkbymoorside had been left as a life-interest to the dowager countess of the fifth earl and she seems to have leased them to Ralph Bowes of Barnes, co. Durham; and property near Barnard Castle, which he had obtained through his wife, passed to his stepson. Neville first settled in Louvain in 1571, but by 1575 he was at Brussels where he was receiving a small pension of 30 crowns a month from Philip II. He died in exile.

Cuthbert Neville (*fl.* 1549–1569) was also a rebel who took part in the northern uprising in 1569. It is unknown whether or not he married. He lived at Brancepeth and played a leading role in the occupation of Durham Cathedral in November 1569. He was reported for restoring the altars and for commanding a number of the clergy to assist at the rebels' services. He also was attainted and went into exile, in the Spanish Netherlands, where he died. G. BRADLEY

Sources C. Sharp, ed., *Memorials of the rebellion of 1569* (1840); repr. with foreword by R. Wood as *The rising in the north: the 1569 rebellion* (1975) · *CSP dom.*, addenda, 1566–79 · *The state papers and letters of Sir Ralph Sadler*, ed. A. Clifford, 2 vols. (1809) · *VCH Yorkshire North Riding*, 1.105, 112, 136, 513–14; 2.48, 56 · H. Aveling, *Northern Catholics: the Catholic recusants of the North Riding of Yorkshire, 1558–1790* (1966), 40, 64, 84 · T. F. Knox and others, eds., *The first and second diaries of the English College, Douay* (1878), 299 · *Dodd's Church history of England*, ed. M. A. Tierney, 5 vols. (1839–43), vol. 3, p. 86 · H. J. Swallow, *De nova villa, or, The house of Nevill* (1885), 133 · A. Forster, 'Bishop Tunstall's priests', *Recusant History*, 9 (1968), 190, 195 · A. Fletcher and D. MacCulloch, *Tudor rebellions*, 4th edn (1997) · M. James, 'The concept of honour and the northern rising, 1569', *Society, politics and*

culture: studies in early modern England (1986), 270–307 · GEC, *Peerage* · DNB

Neville, Cuthbert (*fl.* 1549–1569). *See under* Neville, Christopher (*fl.* 1549–1575).

Neville, Edmund (*b.* before 1555, *d.* in or after 1620), peerage claimant, was the son and heir of Richard Neville (*d.* 1590), who held the manors of Penwyn and Wyke Sapie in Worcestershire, and Barbara Arden of Park Hill in the same county. As a young man, according to his letter of 1620 to Philip III, he fled 'the persecution of Queen Elizabeth' to serve in the Spanish army of Flanders, where he fought at the sieges of Maastricht (June 1579), Tournai (1581), and Oudenarde (June 1582), in 1583 at sieges at Dunkirk, Bergues, Nieuport, and Dixsmunde, and in 1584 at Ypres (GEC, *Peerage*, 12 (2).561). His letters of 1580 to 1583 indicate he had routine duties near Brussels in 1580, at Mons in Hainault in 1581, and later in east Flanders at Nivelles. In 1580 he informed the secretary of state, Sir Francis Walsingham, that he wished 'to be relieved from following foreign princes and to enter the service of my natural prince' (*CSP dom.*, 1580–1625, 25). In 1583 he lamented his poverty through the loss of his pension and of the income due to his wife, Jane Martignis, who held lands in Hainault, as a result of the French invasion. He claimed to be looked on with suspicion in the Spanish Netherlands. In summer 1584 he returned to London, where he encountered Dr William Parry. Another of Walsingham's informants, Parry had a plan to assassinate the queen, which he confided to Neville, possibly acting as an agent provocateur. In the event, Neville's deposition to Walsingham against Parry helped to convict him of treason, though Neville too came under suspicion of conspiracy and was sent to the Tower. Although Burghley arranged his 'pardon for treasons' (Murdin, 2.782) in April 1585, his pleas for release were refused. In 1585 he reported 'the poor gentlewoman his wife … was dead in his absence' and in January 1588 he married Jane Smyth (*d. c.*1646) privately (Surtees, 4.162). He was released in late 1598.

For years Neville, like his father, had assumed a mistaken claim to the barony of Latimer as heirs male to John, fourth Lord Latimer, when the barony was in fact descendible to Latimer's daughters as heirs general. In 1601, following the death in exile of his cousin Charles *Neville, the attainted sixth earl of Westmorland, he was determined to succeed him as seventh earl. He was at first successful in securing the support of James VI of Scotland for, after James's accession to the English throne, Neville reminded him that he had been assured by the courtiers Patrick Murray and the earl of Roxburghe 'of all the entailed lands of Nevill' (Surtees, 4.164–5). He also drew attention to assurances he had received from James's ambassadors to London, Mar and Kinloss, and suggested that he had supported James's succession during Elizabeth's reign. During his progress south in April 1603 the king was heard to say 'he would give title' to Neville of Westmorland (*Salisbury MSS*, 15.26, 16.450). However, in October 1603 James, declining to rule on the title, granted Neville an annuity of £600 'during pleasure' but named him merely 'Edmond Nevell of Latymer claiming of right to be Earl of Westmorland' (Devon, 62). Though Neville's claim had merit, the courts, in 1604, refused to approve it.

Ten years later Neville tarnished his reputation by his liaison with Francelliana Townsend, which led him to retire to Flanders in 1614. Archbishop Abbot warned the English agent Trumbull, 'he is a beggar and a bankrout to a high degree … being sued in the Ecclesiasticall court by his former wife, hee hath used strange delaies' (*Downshire MSS*, 5.78–9) and James was 'well rid of him'. Poverty-stricken, Neville begged Philip III's aid, citing his war record. Fresh humiliation occurred in 1624 when Francis Fane was created earl of Westmorland, following a large gift to Buckingham. Neville's wife, Jane, as 'countess of Westmorland and widow', petitioned Charles I in February 1636 for the arrears of the annuity settled on her by James, perhaps at the time of her husband's flight. Neville appears to have died in Brussels some years before, in or after 1620.

A. J. LOOMIE

Sources GEC, *Peerage*, new edn, vols. 7, 12/2 · J. Strype, *Annals of the Reformation and establishment of religion … during Queen Elizabeth's happy reign*, new edn, 3–4 (1824) · M. A. Philips, 'Parry (ap Harry), William', HoP, *Commons, 1558–1603* · CSP dom., 1580–1636 · CSP for., 1580–93 · R. Surtees, *The history and antiquities of the county palatine of Durham*, 4 (1840) · *Report on the manuscripts of the marquis of Downshire*, 6 vols. in 7, HMC, 75 (1924–95), vol. 5 · *Calendar of the manuscripts of the most hon. the marquis of Salisbury*, 3, HMC, 9 (1889); 15–16 (1930–33); 23 (1973) · F. Devon, ed. and trans., *Issues of the exchequer: being payments made out of his majesty's revenue during the reign of King James I*, RC (1836) · *A collection of state papers … left by William Cecill, Lord Burghley*, ed. W. Murdin, 2 (1759)
Archives PRO, State Papers, domestic and foreign
Wealth at death possible small pension from Spain

Neville, Edmund. *See* Sale, Edmund (1604/5–1647/8).

Neville, Edward, first Baron Bergavenny (d. 1476), nobleman, was probably the youngest surviving son of Ralph *Neville, first earl of Westmorland (c.1364–1425), and his second wife, Joan *Beaufort (1379?–1440), legitimated daughter of *John of Gaunt, duke of Lancaster (1340–1399). He founded the baronial house of Abergavenny (the form, adapted from Bergavenny, which was in use in the mid-sixteenth century and was used by successive holders of this title after 1730), which is the only noble branch of the Neville family to survive in the male line to the present day.

In 1426 'dominus de Bourgevenny' was one of the young lords summoned to Leicester to be knighted by the infant Henry VI on Whitsunday (19 May). Edward Neville owed his place among the English peerage to his marriage with a great heiress, Elizabeth (1415–1448), daughter of Richard Beauchamp, earl of Worcester (c.1397–1422), and his wife, the Despenser heiress, Isabel (1400–1439). This advantageous match, which took place in 1424, cost Earl Ralph the sum of 2000 marks, about two years' income from Elizabeth Beauchamp's lands, which did not come into her husband's possession until March 1436. This situation arose because Richard, earl of Worcester, who died on 18 March 1422 of injuries sustained at the siege of Meaux,

never had seisin of the Welsh marcher lordship of Abergavenny, or his patrimony in England. His father, William *Beauchamp, first Baron Bergavenny (c.1343–1411), had given his wife, the redoubtable Lady Joan (1375–1435), a life interest in all his lands. Royal favour and the extinction of a great magnate family, that of the Hastings earls of Pembroke, had enabled Sir William to found and endow a cadet branch of the Beauchamp family. By an entail made on 20 February 1396 he settled the lordship of Abergavenny on the male line of his elder brother, Thomas *Beauchamp, earl of Warwick (1337×9–1401), in default of male issue among his own descendants; this settlement excluded Elizabeth Beauchamp and enabled Sir William's nephew, Richard *Beauchamp, earl of Warwick (1382–1439), to inherit the lordship of Abergavenny on the death of Lady Joan in 1435. He was Elizabeth's stepfather, as he had married the Despenser heiress, Isabel, as his second wife in 1423. The English manors inherited by Edward Neville's wife, Elizabeth, had been formerly owned by the Hastings and Arundel families and were declared to have a taxable value of 1000 marks a year in 1436. After 1450 the Neville barons of Abergavenny ranked with the English higher nobility in landed wealth, but promotion to an earldom did not take place until 1784.

The male line of the Beauchamp earls of Warwick was extinguished by the death on 11 June 1446 of Earl Richard's only son, Henry, first (and last) duke of Warwick (1425–1446). His heir was his only child, the Lady Anne of Warwick, who was three years old when her father died. Edward Neville and his wife, Elizabeth, saw this girl's minority as an opportunity to lay claim to the lordship of Abergavenny, but they did not resort to litigation. Probably in the autumn of 1446 Neville took possession of Abergavenny Castle by force and in October Henry VI ordered Richard, duke of York (the greatest of the Welsh marcher lords and Neville's brother-in-law), to expel him. Elizabeth Beauchamp died on 18 June 1448, but, despite his wife's death, Neville continued to pursue his claim to the disputed lordship. Following the death of the child heiress, Anne, on 3 January 1449, Neville obtained royal licence on 14 July to enter on the lordship of Abergavenny, but he could not defeat the well-founded title of his powerful nephew, the earl of Salisbury's eldest son and heir, the newly created earl of Warwick, Richard *Neville (1428–1471), who had married Anne Beauchamp (1426–1493), Duke Henry's sister, in 1436. Despite his failure to make good his claims, Edward Neville was summoned to parliament as Baron Bergavenny in September 1450, and his heirs inherited that dignity. Between 1450 and 1512, by a remarkable anomaly, the barons of Abergavenny were not in possession of the Welsh marcher lordship from which they took their peerage title.

Edward Neville did not have the abilities of his capable elder brothers, Richard *Neville, earl of Salisbury (1400–1460), and William *Neville, Lord Fauconberg, afterwards earl of Kent (1401?–1463), and he took little part in war or politics. He supported the government headed by Richard, duke of York, as lord protector in 1454, when Salisbury was made (on 1 April) lord chancellor. As a landowner in Kent, where he had his principal residence at Birling, near Maidstone, he could not escape involvement in the civil war when his nephews, the earls of Warwick and March (the future Edward IV), invaded England from Calais in June 1460. He was with them at the battle of Northampton, fought on 10 July, which ended the rule of the house of Lancaster. After the change of dynasty in 1461 Neville helped to put down Lancastrian resistance in northern England late in 1462, but he held aloof from the political and dynastic upheavals of 1469–71. After Edward IV's final victory Bergavenny was one of the peers who, on 3 July 1471, in the parliament chamber at Westminster, swore an oath of loyalty to the infant Edward, prince of Wales (afterwards Edward V), as his father's heir. His public activities in his later years appear to have been confined to serving on commissions in Kent, and he died on 18 October 1476.

Shortly after the death of his first wife, Elizabeth, Neville married his kinswoman (and mistress) Katherine (d. c.1478), daughter of Sir Robert Howard, and sister of John, Lord Howard (d. 1485), created duke of Norfolk by Richard III in 1483. The papal dispensation needed for this union was granted by Pope Nicholas V on 15 October 1448. From his second marriage Neville had two sons who died childless, and three daughters.

Neville's heir, **George Neville** (1436–1492), his second but only surviving son with Elizabeth Beauchamp, succeeded him as the second Baron Bergavenny. As a child, he had been in the household of Edmund Beaufort, duke of Somerset (d. 1455), who became lieutenant-general in France, and George was one of the hostages given to the victorious French when Rouen was surrendered in October 1449. After the death early in 1449 of the infant Beauchamp heir, Anne, he was found to be coheir, with the late Duke Henry's sister, Anne Beauchamp (1426–1493), of the Despenser lands formerly held by his grandmother, Isabel, countess of Warwick (d. 1439). Except perhaps for a brief interlude during the summer of 1470, when Warwick had been forced into exile in France, George Neville was never able to obtain seisin of that part of his family inheritance, which included the valuable lordships of Glamorgan and Morgannwg. His cousin Richard Neville, earl of Warwick, succeeded in keeping control of the whole of the Despenser estates, in the right of his wife, Anne. Shortly before Henry VI became insane in July 1453, Somerset's attempt to gain custody of George Neville's share of the Despenser lands led to conflict with Warwick, who supported Richard, duke of York, at the first battle of St Albans, fought on 22 May 1455. George Neville came of age in 1457; he fought on the Yorkist side at the battle of Tewkesbury on 4 May 1471, and was knighted by Edward IV. The second Lord Bergavenny was a supporter of Richard III, whose territorial possessions included the lordships of Abergavenny and Glamorgan and Morgannwg. Like most of the English peerage he was absent from the battle of Bosworth and he proved loyal to Henry VII. His heir, George *Neville, third Baron Bergavenny (c.1469–1535), was granted the castle and lordship of Abergavenny by Henry VIII on 18 December 1512. Other sons with his

first wife, Margaret Fenne (d. 1485), were Sir Edward *Neville (b. in or before 1482, d. 1538) and Sir Thomas *Neville (b. in or before 1484, d. 1542).   T. B. PUGH

Sources contract between the earls of Warwick and Westmorland, 1424, Longleat House, Wiltshire, Wilton MS 342 • Rymer, *Foedera*, 1st edn, vol. 10 • N. H. Nicolas, ed., *Proceedings and ordinances of the privy council of England*, 7 vols., RC, 26 (1834–7), vol. 5 • J. Stevenson, ed., *Letters and papers illustrative of the wars of the English in France during the reign of Henry VI, king of England*, 2 vols. in 3 pts, Rolls Series, 22 (1861–4) • W. Dugdale, *The baronage of England*, 2 vols. (1675–6) • 'Select committee … on the dignity of a peer', *Parl. papers* (1821), 9.165, no. 709; (1826), vols. 6–9, nos. 391–4 • S. Bentley, ed., *Excerpta historica* (1830) • G. Williams, ed., *Glamorgan county history*, 3: *The middle ages*, ed. T. B. Pugh (1971) • R. I. Jack, 'Entail and descent: the Hastings inheritance, 1370–1436', *BIHR*, 38 (1965), 1–19 • GEC, *Peerage*
Likenesses group portrait, miniature, Bibliothèque Nationale, Paris

Neville, Sir Edward (b. in or before **1482**, d. **1538**), courtier, of Addington Park, Kent, was a younger son of George *Neville, second Baron Bergavenny (1436–1492) [see under Neville, Edward (d. 1476)], and his first wife, Margaret Fenne (d. 1485), and as such a brother of George *Neville, third baron, with whom his fortunes were inextricably linked. He owed his early advancement to George's personal standing with the Tudor dynasty, and perhaps to a lesser degree to another of his brothers, Sir Thomas *Neville, who was a councillor successively to Henry VII and Henry VIII, as well as speaker of the House of Commons in the parliament of 1515.

Neville was to make his name as a courtier and in the military campaigns in the opening years of Henry VIII's reign. He first entered the royal service as a squire of the body, in which capacity in 1509 he attended Henry VII's funeral, and subsequently rose to be a gentleman of the privy chamber, where he was in frequent attendance upon the king. Physically he resembled Henry VIII before the king became corpulent. George Cavendish tells of a banquet given by Cardinal Wolsey which was interrupted by the arrival of masquers. The cardinal was deceived, or pretended to be, in identifying Neville in his vizard as the king: 'A comely knyght of goodly personage that mych resembled the Kynges person in that Maske than any other' (Cavendish, 27–8). This coincidence gave rise to speculation that Neville was a royal bastard, but there is no evidence that Henry VII had any illegitimate offspring. Neville was not only a notable masquer. He was also an accomplished singer with a liking for 'merry songs'. He possessed a talent for extempore verses, often of current topicality. One example from the mid-1530s has survived—he 'trusted knaves should be put down, and lords should reign one day' (*LP Henry VIII*, 3/2, no. 765).

Neville shared Henry VIII's twin passions for jousting and hunting: he was one of the principal challengers at court for over a decade from the opening of the reign, and had become master of the buckhounds by 1516. His enthusiasm for the mock warfare of the court almost involved him in dynastic tragedy. In January 1510 Henry VIII and William Compton, both disguised, challenged courtiers in impromptu jousts at Richmond: 'The Kynge ranne never openly before'. Neville ran against Compton, and 'hurte hym sore, and [he] was likely to dye'. For a moment there was alarm that the wounded man was the king until Henry 'discovered' himself (*Hall's Chronicle*, 513). This episode only served to endear Neville to the king, who showed his favour by selecting Neville as one of the English representatives at the spectacular tournaments held outside Paris on the eve of Princess Mary's coronation as queen of France in 1514. He was the recipient of new year's gifts from Henry VIII, who also stood as godfather to his second son (but eventual heir), Henry. In 1513 Neville served in the vanguard of the army royal which successfully besieged Tournai, and for his valour in its capture he was knighted. He fought again in France in 1523 under the duke of Suffolk, and once more three years later. As a courtier he took part in an embassy to François I in 1518, and he was present at the Field of Cloth of Gold two years later.

Following the downfall of the third duke of Buckingham in spring 1521, in which his elder brother Bergavenny was involved as the duke's son-in-law, Sir Edward was banned from the king's presence on the grounds of having himself favoured the duke. Over ten months later the prohibition was lifted, and he resumed his old intimacy with his royal master, if not, perhaps, on quite the same terms of unfettered familiarity. In 1532 he accompanied Henry VIII to Calais for his meeting there with the French king, and later that year he succeeded Sir Henry Guildford as the king's standard-bearer. He acted as a sewer to Queen Anne Boleyn at her coronation feast in the summer of 1533. Neville combined official duties at court with a place on the local bench in Kent from 1526. In late 1533 his local eminence received official recognition when he was nominated one of the knights for Kent for a vacancy in the parliament of 1529, but with what outcome is not known. In June 1534 he obtained the important constableship of Leeds Castle, and with it a role in the administration of extensive estates. Some time before 1524 he had married Eleanor, daughter of Andrew Windsor, later first Baron Windsor, keeper of the great wardrobe, and widow of Ralph, ninth Baron Scrope of Masham, who had died in 1515. They had seven children.

Although Neville emerged unscathed from the twists and turns of fortune that beset his elder brother's career, he fared less well after Bergavenny's death in 1535. His close kinship with the Poles and Courtenays, through marriages largely contrived by Bergavenny, proved his eventual undoing. His own innate conservatism provoked the irritation of Thomas Cromwell, and changes in the personnel of the privy chamber left him increasingly isolated. He ruefully observed: 'The king keepeth a sort of knaves here that we dare not speak; and if I were able to live, I would rather live any life in the world than tarry in the privy chamber' (*LP Henry VIII*, 13/2, no. 804). Even so, enough of the king's earlier affection remained for Henry VIII to warn him against keeping company with the marquess of Exeter. But, following Exeter's arrest, and in particular after the examination of Sir Geoffrey Pole in the autumn of 1538, Neville was accused of implication in the Pole conspiracy, and in particular of abetting Cardinal Reginald Pole. He was alleged to have called Henry VIII 'a beast and worse than a beast' (ibid.). The imperial ambassador called him 'good Edward Neville', observing how he had reproached Sir Nicholas Carew for looking to the French king for remedy rather than Emperor Charles V (Dodds and Dodds, 2.320). Under questioning the marchioness of Exeter suggested that Neville had dabbled in prophecy. Although he staunchly maintained his innocence and at his trial on 4 November declared himself not guilty, he was attainted of high treason. He was beheaded at the Tower on 9 December 1538 and buried the same day in the chapel of St Peter ad Vincula there. He was survived by his wife. In the summer of 1539 his attainder was confirmed by act of parliament (31 Hen. VIII c. 15), but within four years his son Edward obtained restoration in the blood (34 and 35 Hen. VIII c. 36). On the death of Sir Edward's nephew, the fourth Baron Bergavenny, without heirs male, in 1587 the Neville estates passed to his grandson Edward, and by a decision of 1604 which assigned a place in the House of Lords to his great-grandson Edward the family title passed to his descendants.

ALASDAIR HAWKYARD

Sources *LP Henry VIII*, vols. 1–14 · *Report of the Deputy Keeper of the Public Records*, 3 (1842), appx 2 · A. Luders and others, eds., *Statutes of the realm*, 11 vols. in 12, RC (1810–28) · GEC, *Peerage*, vol. 1 · T. Benolt and R. Cooke, *The visitations of Kent taken in the years 1530–1 … and 1574*, ed. W. B. Bannerman, 1, Harleian Society, 74 (1923) · G. Cavendish, *The life and death of Cardinal Wolsey*, ed. R. S. Sylvester, EETS, original ser., 243 (1959) · HoP, *Commons, 1509–58* · *Hall's chronicle*, ed. H. Ellis (1809) · H. M. Dodds and R. Dodds, *The Pilgrimage of Grace, 1536–7, and the Exeter conspiracy*, 2 vols. (1915) · D. R. Starkey, *The reign of Henry VIII: personality and politics* (1985) · CIPM, *Henry VII*, vol. 1 · W. A. Shaw, *The knights of England*, 2 vols. (1906)
Archives PRO, SP 1

Neville, Edward. *See* Scarisbrick, Edward (1639–1709).

Neville, Elizabeth, Lady Neville. *See* Willoughby, Elizabeth, Lady Willoughby and *suo jure* Lady Latimer (d. 1395), *under* Willoughby family (*per.* c.1300–1523).

Neville [*née* Manners], **Frances**, Lady Bergavenny (d. 1576), writer, was the third daughter of the ten children of Thomas *Manners, first earl of Rutland (d. 1543), and his second wife, Eleanor Paston (d. 1550). By 1554 she had married Henry Neville, fourth Lord Bergavenny or Abergavenny (d. 1587), and they had one daughter, Mary (1554–1626), who married Sir Thomas Fane and unsuccessfully claimed the barony on the death of her father. Collinson cites a letter by the puritan preacher Edward Dering attacking Lord Abergavenny for 'ungodly talke', 'unclennes', and 'riot' (Collinson, 301). Lady Abergavenny wrote pious works. Her *Praiers* in prose and verse were later published in the second lamp of *The Monument of Matrones* (1582), Thomas Bentley's anthology of protestant women writers' prayers. In a deathbed dedication of her work to her daughter, she calls her work 'a jewell of health for the soule, and a perfect path to paradise, verie profitable to be used of everie faithfull Christian man and woman' (Aburgavennie, 139). Her collection includes sixty-seven pages of prose prayers for private use and public worship linked to varied occasions and times of day; a metrical prayer against vices; a five-page acrostic prayer based on Mary Fane's name; and a concluding acrostic prayer based on her own name. She died in 1576.

ELAINE V. BEILIN

Sources F. Aburgavennie [F. Neville, Lady Bergavenny], 'The praiers made by the right honourable Ladie Frances Aburgavennie', *The monument of matrones*, ed. T. Bentley (1582), 139–213 [the second lampe] · Burke, *Peerage* (1978) · E. V. Beilin, *Redeeming Eve: women writers of the English Renaissance* (1987) · P. Collinson, 'A mirror of Elizabethan puritanism: the life and letters of "Godly Master Dering"', *Godly people: essays on English protestantism and puritanism* (1983), 288–324 · DNB · J. Strype, *Annals of the Reformation and establishment of religion … during Queen Elizabeth's happy reign*, new edn, 4 vols. (1824) · J. Strype, *Ecclesiastical memorials*, 3 vols. (1822) · J. Cave-Browne, 'Knights of the shire for Kent', *Archaeologia Cantiana*, 21 (1895), 198–243 · J. F. Wadmore, 'The knight hospitallers in Kent', *Archaeologia Cantiana*, 22 (1897), 232–74

Neville, Geoffrey de (d. 1225), baron, was the younger son of Alan de Neville (d. 1190), and nephew of Gilbert de Neville, an ancestor of the Nevilles of Raby. He was probably connected with Hugh de Neville (d. 1234). Geoffrey de Neville first appears as the recipient of grants from King John in 1204. In 1207 he was briefly a household steward, and was then appointed king's chamberlain, a post that he held until the end of his life; in the same year he was briefly sheriff of Wiltshire. In 1210, Neville was sent with reinforcements to Poitou; and in 1213 he was sent on an embassy to Raymond, count of Toulouse, and Petro II, king of Aragon. In the next year he was again in Poitou, to secure for John the support of the Poitevin barons, and his fidelity was rewarded by further grants of lands belonging to the barons in opposition. During July and August 1214 Neville was seneschal of Gascony; and during July and August 1215 he was seneschal of Poitou. Both posts were lost to Reginald de Pontibus. On 1 October 1215, he was with John at Lincoln, where he received the grant of Scarborough Castle; he later received grants of money to enable him to fortify it. During the winter he was employed in defending the castle, and the city of York, against the rebel barons. Early in 1216 he was appointed to the shrievalty of Yorkshire, a post that he held until 1223. Neville remained faithful to John to the end.

In 1217 Neville attested the reissue of Magna Carta. In March 1218 he had his tenure of Yorkshire confirmed at the old farm; the surplus was to be used to sustain the royal castles of Scarborough and Pickering. The same year, he was present when Llywelyn ab Iorwerth (d. 1240) submitted to Henry III, and he was commissioned to take possession of certain castles in Wales. He was again appointed seneschal of Poitou and Gascony in May 1218, and in 1219 he was in Gascony opposing Hugh de Lusignan, who was besieging Niort. Neville wrote to Henry in late May of that year, threatening to start for the Holy Land unless he were better supported from home; at some point before September he wrote again, saying that unless steps were taken to defend Poitou and Gascony it was no

good his remaining there. In October he returned to England. He landed at Dover on 1 November 1219, leaving William Gauler in charge of Gascony. He left behind him debts incurred in the king's service, and in 1220 the citizens of Dax petitioned for repayment. In the same year he was dispatched to Scotland on business connected with the marriage of the king's sister to Alexander II. On 23 January 1221 he was summoned to meet Henry at Northampton to concert measures against the earl of Albemarle, who had seized Fotheringhay Castle. In 1222 he undertook to pay £100 for the guardianship of Alexander de Neville, probably a second cousin, who held lands in Lincolnshire, Yorkshire, and Cumberland. On 4 December in that year Neville was commissioned to see that the compromise arranged between Hugh de Lusignan and certain towns in Gascony was carried out; in the following year Lusignan wrote to Henry complaining of the conduct of Neville's successor, Savari de Mauléon, and recommending Neville's reappointment. Although this suggestion was not adopted, Neville was in Poitou in 1223 and 1224, and again with Richard, earl of Cornwall, in 1225. By 26 December 1225 he had died, presumably on this final trip to Gascony.

Geoffrey de Neville married Mabel, daughter and coheir of Adam fitz Swane, who founded the abbey of Monk Bretton, Yorkshire. They had two sons, John and Alan. John was granted custody of Pickering and Scarborough castles on his father's death, and was in the battle of Chesterfield with Robert Ferrers, earl of Derby, in 1264, and subsequently fought on the barons' side at Evesham. Geoffrey de Neville should not be confused with a namesake who died in 1194, and was the great-grandfather of Robert de Neville (d. 1282); the two Geoffreys may have been cousins.

A. F. POLLARD, rev. S. D. CHURCH

Sources *Chancery records* (RC) · *CPR, 1216–25* · P. Chaplais, ed., *Diplomatic documents preserved in the Public Record Office*, 1 (1964) · H. C. M. Lyte and others, eds., *Liber feodorum: the book of fees*, 3 vols. (1920–31) · H. Hall, ed., *The Red Book of the Exchequer*, 3 vols., Rolls Series, 99 (1896) · Rymer, *Foedera*, new edn, vol. 1/1 · Rymer, *Foedera*, 3rd edn, vol. 1/1 · *Pipe rolls* · W. W. Shirley, ed., *Royal and other historical letters illustrative of the reign of Henry III*, 2 vols., Rolls Series, 27 (1862–6) · Paris, *Chron.*

Neville, Geoffrey de (d. 1285), baron, the son of Geoffrey de Neville, lord of Raby, co. Durham, and younger brother of Robert de *Neville of Raby (d. 1282), came to prominence as a member of Prince Edward's military household, which he had joined by 1259. He took an active part in the barons' wars, siding, like most of his family, with the king. In 1264 he was with Prince Edward, and was captured at the battle of Lewes, but was soon exchanged for Robert of Newington, who had been made prisoner by the king at Northampton. On Edward's escape in 1265 Neville again joined him; he was present when Edward recaptured Dover, and was left in charge as constable of the castle. In February 1266 he was granted the right of free market in his wife's town of Appleby, Lincolnshire.

In October 1270 Neville was appointed chief justice of the forests beyond Trent, an office he held until his death. In 1270 he also served as one of four justices on eyre to hear pleas of the forest beyond Trent. In 1275 he was appointed chief assessor in Cumberland and Lancashire of the fifteenth granted by the prelates, earls, and barons. In 1277, 1282, and 1283 he was summoned to serve in the military campaigns against Llywelyn. He acted as one of the executors of his brother Robert in 1282, and in 1283 he was present at the Shrewsbury parliament. He also served frequently as a justice on commissions of oyer and terminer, especially in the north.

Neville's wife was Margaret de *Neville (d. 1319) [see under Neville family], daughter and heir of John de Longvillers, whom he married before February 1267. She brought him almost all the estates he eventually possessed, including Hornby, Lancashire, and Hutton Longvillers, Yorkshire. Title to some of these manors was challenged in Edward I's quo warranto inquiries, and possession of Hutton Longvillers passed subsequently to John de Lovetot. Margaret and Geoffrey had five sons: John Neville, born on 10 August 1269, from whom were descended the Nevilles of Hornby; Geoffrey, Robert, Edmund, and William. Margaret, the only known daughter, married Robert of North Milford; their son John died childless. Neville died, apparently suddenly, shortly before 26 March 1285, the king's final order to him as chief justice of the northern forests having been issued on 28 January 1285.　　　　A. F. POLLARD, rev. ROBERT C. STACEY

Sources Chancery records · CIPM, 2, no. 575 · The historical works of Gervase of Canterbury, ed. W. Stubbs, 2 vols., Rolls Series, 73 (1879–80) · [W. Illingworth], ed., Placita de quo warranto temporibus Edw. I, II, et III, RC (1818) · GEC, Peerage

Neville, George (1432–1476), administrator and archbishop of York, was the fourth and youngest surviving son of Richard *Neville, fifth earl of Salisbury (1400–1460), and Alice (c.1406–1462), the daughter and heir of Thomas Montagu, fourth earl of Salisbury (d. 1428); his elder brothers were Richard *Neville, earl of Warwick and Salisbury (the Kingmaker), Sir Thomas Neville, and John *Neville, Marquess Montagu. He was of royal blood through three lines: in particular his paternal grandmother Joan Beaufort, countess of Westmorland (d. 1440), half-sister of Henry IV. He was related through marriage to almost every noble dynasty in England. It was primarily this lineage—'his blood, virtue and cunning' (Proceedings … of the Privy Council, 6.168)—that prompted the protectorate council in 1454 to nominate him to the next vacant bishopric in England. His own rank and qualities notwithstanding, he seems throughout to have accepted the political lead of Salisbury and Warwick and was apparently disorientated by the latter's death.

Early advancement Richard was always destined to succeed to his father's earldom and Thomas and John pursued secular careers, but from an early age George Neville was scheduled for an ecclesiastical career. There was good family precedent for it. His great-grandfather's brother Alexander Neville (d. 1392) had been archbishop of York, and Salisbury's brother Robert *Neville (d. 1457) was successively bishop of Salisbury and Durham. Not surprisingly, George Neville secured rapid and early promotion. His way was smoothed by papal dispensations in 1447 and

1452 and by the patronage of a succession of well-born relatives. He was only nine or ten in 1442 when he was collated to a canonry in Salisbury Cathedral, he was only thirteen or fourteen when he added the exceptionally valuable 'golden prebend' of Masham in York Minster in 1446, and he was only twenty-four on his elevation to the episcopate in 1456 when, however, his consecration was delayed two years until he reached his twenty-seventh year. By then he held the two archdeaconries of Durham and Northampton, five prebends, one rectory, and the mastership of the hospital of St Leonard's, York: a substantial haul that does not compare with some earlier pluralists. Naturally Neville did not serve them himself: he was too young; he was not ordained subdeacon until 1453 or priest until 1454 and was allowed to exercise his episcopal functions by suffragans for two years until he was consecrated; he had a papal licence in 1452 to visit the archdeaconry of Durham by deputy; and he was in any case studying at Oxford. There is no evidence that he had any experience in pastoral affairs or ecclesiastical administration before he was promoted bishop.

Education and learning The separation of the duties and rewards of a bishop during George Neville's two years as bishop-elect were denounced as scandalous by the religious controversialist Thomas Gascoigne (d. 1458), but it would not be fair to regard Neville merely as an aristocrat masquerading in clerical clothing and exploiting ecclesiastical preferment for secular ends. Admittedly Neville's career illustrates many aristocratic qualities: conspicuous consumption, notably in buildings, books, and the splendid feasts that accompanied each stage of his career; pride of lineage; love of display and ceremony; and the patronage of kinsfolk, neighbours, and other dependants. But rank alone no longer normally sufficed for promotion to the episcopate, which was open only to graduates. Like other aristocratic bishops Neville was educated for his new intended role and indeed became a man of learning and culture not unworthy of his ecclesiastical office, even if he did not possess the legal expertise more common among the contemporary episcopate. Perhaps as early as 1448 he was studying at Balliol College, Oxford: a 'northern' college—in that its masters and students came from England north of the River Nene—with natural associations with the former Balliol lordship of Barnard Castle, co. Durham, now a possession of Neville's family. There he graduated BA in 1450 and MA in 1452; he supplicated for his doctorate of theology in 1457 at the unusually early age of twenty-five, but may not actually have received the degree.

On each occasion Neville's progress was speeded by special graces: he did not complete the whole undergraduate course, was excused from the administrative and teaching requirements of a regent master, and had only two disputations to his credit as a doctor. However, he had lectured on the Bible and the Sentences, delivered the necessary public sermons, and distinguished himself at Bishop Reginald Pecock's trial in 1457 by denouncing Pecock for criticizing the early Christian fathers, to whom Neville himself was passionately committed. Neville possessed conventional works on Aristotelean philosophy, canon law, and theology, and several books were dedicated to him. He is also credited with fostering the revival of Greek studies. While he is unlikely to have learnt Greek himself, he certainly learnt to write in Greek script; he patronized the Greek scholars Emanuel of Constantinople and George Hieronymos, who presented him with books, and he was said to be a friend of Bessarion, the so-called 'Greek cardinal'. Most obviously, he developed his rhetorical gifts for use in diplomacy, and his sophistication impressed even the Italians. Only at the end of his life, it is reported, did his interest in scholarship desert him.

As befitted a scholar of his rank and income, George Neville lived in some luxury in chambers at Balliol, and celebrated his master's degree with a particularly splendid feast that required the relaxation of university regulations. His patronage was valued by his college, by the university, and by individuals: twelve contemporaries shared his graces in 1450 and 1452; the distinguished scholar John Shirwood (d. 1493) was his protégé; he acted as feoffee for Balliol College; he presumably contributed to those buildings that bear his arms at Balliol, Lincoln, and Queen's colleges and at the Divinity School; he gave five silver staves for the university bedels in 1457; and he was elected and twice re-elected chancellor of the university in 1453–7, perhaps only relinquishing office in response to pressure from a king suspicious of the university's loyalty. Far from being an inactive absentee as chancellor, he has left considerable evidence both of his activity and concern. He is credited with saving Lincoln College from dissolution in 1462. His further term (1461–72), as the first chancellor appointed for life, was different: he was no longer expected to be resident but was intended to be an absentee chancellor well placed to advance the university's interests. In 1461 he secured a charter from Edward IV confirming and slightly extending the university's privileges. It was only at Edward IV's command that he was removed in 1472.

Bishop of Exeter George Neville owed his nomination to the next vacant bishopric in 1454, and his provision to Exeter on 4 February 1456, to the king's madness and the domination of his government by Neville's uncle, Richard, duke of York (d. 1460), as protector, and his allies, among whom George's father Salisbury and brother Warwick were prominent. This actually involved overriding the king's own personal preference for John Hales and involved some confusion at the papal curia, where contradictory recommendations were received by Pope Calixtus III (r. 1455–8). Others whom the protectorate council promoted were York's brother-in-law Thomas Bourchier (d. 1486) as archbishop of Canterbury, and the duke's cousin William Gray (d. 1478) as bishop of Ely. George Neville's political career effectively commenced late in 1459, when his father, brothers, and York rebelled and were exiled and attainted, although he himself initially avoided implication, his loyalty being commended by King Henry. Following the landing of the Yorkist earls in June 1460 Neville was among the bishops who met them at Southwark and

took their oaths of allegiance to Henry VI, and he accompanied the earls to Northampton and mediated on their behalf with the king. After the battle, the capture of the king, and their return to London, he became chancellor of England on 25 July—a post that was confirmed by Edward IV on 10 March 1461 and one he held continuously until June 1467. Following the earl of March's election as Edward IV by the Yorkist peers, who included the bishop himself, on 3 March 1461, it was Neville who preached next day in support of Edward's case at St John's Fields; it was also he who won over Francesco Coppini, bishop of Terni and papal legate. As chancellor he preached the sermons that opened Edward IV's first and second parliaments.

One justification for George Neville's promotion to Exeter was supposedly the need to bring order to a remote see. However, he can only be said with confidence to have visited it once during his nine-year episcopate, in 1459 (it is possible that he was there in 1462 and 1464, but the evidence is inconclusive). He may have undertaken a formal visitation in 1459, since he was in the diocese from at least 10 March to 4 November. But the west country was unfamiliar to him and to his family, whose cause he did not seek to advance there. He made John Shirwood chancellor of the diocese, but he cannot otherwise be shown to have tried to install his own men in the cathedral chapter, or to build up the position of the Nevilles in Devon and Cornwall. At first he resided in Oxford, then from 1458 at his episcopal residence at Temple Bar in London, administering his diocese from afar and through deputies: his register survives. It is an indication of his connections and, perhaps, avarice that he was allowed even as the bishop of a wealthy see to retain the mastership of St Leonard's, York, and the prebend of Masham for a while, until he resigned them in 1458 and 1459 respectively. In 1462 he was reappointed master of St Leonard's and occasionally resided there.

Archbishop of York On 15 March 1465 Neville was translated by Pope Paul II (r. 1464–71) to the archbishopric of York, a diocese that was both more prestigious and more congenial to himself. He himself came from the northern province, and it was there that his family was most powerful. In 1461, even before he became archbishop, he and his brother Warwick had established a College of St William of York, whose splendid half-timbered premises survive, to incorporate the chantry chaplains of York Minster; unfortunately it was inadequately endowed. Proceeding northwards in August he was enthroned on 28 September in the presence of six other bishops, six abbots, four earls, and five barons. The splendour of his enthronement feast at Cawood has become legendary: there survives a full description of the menu and details of the 6000 guests. The two royal dukes of Suffolk and Gloucester, two earls, and three bishops sat at high table, and thirty-one heads of religious houses at the second table. His brother Warwick was steward, his other surviving brother, John, was treasurer, Lord Willoughby was carver, and the duke of Buckingham's son was cup-bearer. Thereafter, although often absent, Neville visited his diocese each year. He held a provincial council in April 1466 that promulgated constitutions. The archbishopric was a new power base and source of patronage for Neville's family. He relied on his brothers, appointing Warwick as steward of Ripon in 1466, and on northern graduates. At least three of his principal officials—Edmund Chaderton, Thomas Barowe (d. 1499), and John Shirwood—moved on his death into the service of Warwick's residual heir as husband of his daughter Anne, Richard, duke of Gloucester.

The two archbishops, Bourchier and Neville, were cousins, members of the high nobility, and churchmen. Apart from politics, they concerned themselves with the liberties of the church, for which they sought more effective protection. Even before his translation to York Neville worked for this objective, both as a member of the Canterbury convocation and as chancellor. However, a charter protecting clergy against writs of prohibition issued by the royal courts proved insufficient, and all their efforts to secure parliamentary compensation, for which a charitable subsidy—that is, a voluntary tax—was voted in 1463, proved unsuccessful.

Chancellor of England As chancellor of England from 1461 to 1467 George Neville was apparently diligent and competent. In the early years the beleaguered and inexperienced Edward IV relied heavily on Neville's brothers Warwick and John—the latter from 1464 earl of Northumberland—for overcoming Lancastrian resistance and conducting foreign relations. While Neville undertook some negotiations, with France at St Omer in September 1463 and Scotland in May 1464 and late 1465, he resided almost continually in London, presiding not only over chancery but also over the royal council and hence the central administration as a whole. He therefore lived mainly in and around London, after 1465 principally at his archiepiscopal house York Place in Westminster, and acquired a country house on the forfeited estate of Moor Park in Rickmansworth, Hertfordshire, which he rebuilt and allegedly furnished luxuriously.

Neville's career and political stance followed that of his brother Warwick closely, although it is clear that on some issues he was independent. Edward IV's advancement of new favourites after 1464 and his adoption of a pro-Burgundian foreign policy weakened the influence not only of Warwick, but of George Neville too. Warwick was absent in France in the summer of 1467, when the Woodvilles were at the height of their prestige. Parliament met at the same time as the celebrated tournament between Anthony Woodville and Antoine, count of La Roche, the Bastard of Burgundy, which was staged both to flaunt the standing of the Woodvilles and to demonstrate Edward's leanings towards Burgundy. Chancellor Neville was not allowed to open parliament on 3 June, and on 8 June the king came to his house where he lay sick and deprived him of the great seal. He was also refused exemption from the 1467 Act of Resumption and thus lost those lands he had been granted, including Moor Park. Finally, late in 1467, the king forwarded to him a papal letter nominating Thomas Bourchier as cardinal of St Cyriac—not, as Neville

had hoped, himself. Edward was taking malicious advantage of his Neville mentors, who had guided his early rule so effectively, and was making the parting much more acrimonious than it need have been. The earl of Warwick did not take his loss of power quietly: tensions built up between the Nevilles and the royal favourites. At this stage the archbishop's services as a mediator were of value: an outward reconciliation was achieved early in 1468 at Nottingham, George Neville was again in favour, and there was talk of his restoration as chancellor. This did not happen; however, early in 1469 he recovered his resumed lands once again as reward for his services. But the breach was not healed.

Involvement in civil war The Crowland continuator attributes the breach between Warwick and the king principally to differences of foreign policy, but Warwick was also concerned about the succession to his various lands and titles, and not least the need to find husbands of high standing and influence for his two daughters. For the elder, Isobel, he had selected the king's own brother George, duke of Clarence, but Edward IV refused his permission and worked to prevent the necessary papal dispensation, which Warwick was openly seeking. It was Archbishop Neville who secured it, even using the king's representative and drawing on his own connections at the curia, notably the legate Stefano Trenta. The archbishop then performed the service of marriage on 11 July 1469 at Calais, where Warwick was captain, outside the jurisdiction of the archbishop of Canterbury. This was a splendid occasion, attended by five knights of the Garter.

George Neville then accompanied Warwick and Clarence back to England, where both declared their approval for an ostensibly popular manifesto denouncing Edward IV's favourites (especially the Woodvilles) supposedly composed by the Yorkshire rebels led by Robin of Redesdale, but actually inspired, like the rebellion itself, by the archbishop, duke, and earl. The king underestimated the opposition: his army was defeated at Edgcote in 1469; his favourites Rivers, Pembroke, and Devon were executed; and the king himself was arrested by the archbishop at Warwick's manor of Olney, Buckinghamshire, and imprisoned first at Warwick and then at Middleham. With the king in custody, the Nevilles governed in his name; Archbishop Neville presided over affairs in London, while the earl sent directions from his residences in Warwickshire and Yorkshire. The new regime proved unviable. Archbishop Neville proceeded northwards before 10 September and met the king, who had had to be released, accompanying him south from York to Moor Park.

Edward IV spent the rest of 1469 reconstructing his power base in consultation with his great council. Relations with the Nevilles were extremely tense. George Neville was not directly implicated in the Lincolnshire rebellion in the spring of 1470 or in Warwick's invasion in the late summer but as soon as Warwick had landed it was he and Lord Sudeley who removed Henry VI from the Tower of London. He was again appointed chancellor and opened parliament on 26 November, preaching the customary sermon on an appropriate text, 'Turn, O backsliding children, saith the Lord, for I am married into you' (Jeremiah 3:12). He was rewarded with the grant of Woodstock, Oxfordshire, and three adjoining manors. When Edward IV invaded to recover his throne, George Neville remained in London and was instructed by Warwick to keep Edward out of London, which he found that he could not do. He therefore treated with the king, seeking his forgiveness, and did not oppose his entry on 11 April, whereupon he was arrested.

Last years Following the disaster of Barnet on 14 April, where both his brothers were killed, George Neville's future was far from obvious. His political career appeared to be over, but, not yet forty, he had potentially several more decades as archbishop of York. Edward IV pardoned him formally as early as 16 April, but did not give him his liberty until 4 June. He swore allegiance to the king's eldest son and heir, and was living once again at Moor Park at Christmas 1471, when he entertained John Paston: probably he was not permitted to go north to his archdiocese. He was the king's guest at Windsor, and Edward planned to return the visit to the Moor. Neville may, however, have been dabbling in treason again: in the week before Palm Sunday (22 March) 1472 at Moor Park and afterwards at Windsor, he allegedly received one John Bank, yeoman of Otley, Yorkshire, read letters he brought from other obscure Yorkshiremen, and discussed with him an uprising designed to dethrone the king. Neville was unable to provide them with money, but expressed his support, apparently in the presence of Chaderton, his personal treasurer. So the subsequent indictment runs. It does not sound very substantial; if true, it suggests that he had lost his grasp on reality. Admittedly there were many reports of plots in 1472, and the earl of Oxford, Neville's brother-in-law, raided both St Osyth, Essex, and St Michael's Mount, Cornwall, with French support: however, the indictment against Neville does not mention Oxford. Nevertheless, Edward IV arrested the archbishop, brought him to the Tower during the night of 25–6 April 1472, and dispatched him to prison at Calais. The king seized his temporalities, Moor Park with goods allegedly worth £20,000, and converted a jewelled mitre into a crown. The moral for the chronicler Warkworth was that 'such goods as were gathered with sin were lost with sorrow' (Warkworth, 26). Perhaps this was the intention. Had the archbishop been set up?

So secretly was Neville borne away that at first he was thought to be dead. He was indicted of treason and Edward IV wished at least to deprive him of his see, but found, like earlier and later monarchs, that it was not easy to remove an archbishop. Neville is reported to have been thoroughly dispirited by his imprisonment, abandoned learning, and dabbled in alchemy: Master John Shirwood, who visited him, taught him the game of arithomachia as a distraction. Probably he was already suffering from kidney stones. However, he had friends at the papal court and in England who campaigned on his behalf. Among them in November 1472 was even Richard, duke of Gloucester,

the husband of George's niece Anne Neville, but it was not until 11 November 1474 that the archbishop was again pardoned and released on the intervention of Pope Sixtus IV (r. 1471–84). On 19 December he landed at Dover and spent Christmas at Cardinal Bourchier's house at Knole, Kent. He is recorded at Westminster and mainly at Bisham Priory, Berkshire, the Salisbury family mausoleum, where his brothers lay, and was apparently at Gloucester, perhaps visiting his archiepiscopal peculiar, at Easter 1475. Presumably he was still not yet allowed to visit his northern province, and he played almost no part in its administration, save in theory. When Edward IV invaded France, Archbishop Neville accompanied him to Calais, perhaps because, like the duke of Exeter, he was still considered too dangerous to leave behind. Thereafter, though ill, he finally proceeded northwards to his archbishopric, but died at Blyth in Nottinghamshire on 8 June 1476, and was buried in York Minster. He left no will and founded no chantry, and no tomb is recorded.   MICHAEL HICKS

Sources G. I. Keir, 'The ecclesiastical career of George Neville, 1432–76', BLitt diss., U. Oxf., 1970 · Emden, *Oxf.* · M. A. Hicks, *'False, fleeting, perjur'd Clarence': George, duke of Clarence, 1449–78*, rev. edn (1992) · King's Bench Indictments, ancient indictments, PRO, KB 9/41 · C. L. Scofield, *The life and reign of Edward the Fourth*, 2 vols. (1923) · R. L. Storey, 'Episcopal king-maker in the fifteenth century', *Church, politics and patronage in the fifteenth century*, ed. B. Dobson (1984), 82–98 · N. H. Nicolas, ed., *Proceedings and ordinances of the privy council of England*, 7 vols., RC, 26 (1834–7), vol. 6 · *Fasti Angl., 1300–1541*, [Exeter] · J. Warkworth, *A chronicle of the first thirteen years of the reign of King Edward the Fourth*, ed. J. O. Halliwell, CS, old ser., 10 (1839) · N. Pronay and J. Cox, eds., *The Crowland chronicle continuations, 1459–1486* (1986)

Archives Borth. Inst., register · Devon County RO, Exeter, register

Neville, George, second Baron Bergavenny (1436–1492). *See under* Neville, Edward, first Baron Bergavenny (d. 1476).

Neville, George, third Baron Bergavenny (c.1469–1535), nobleman and courtier, of Birling, Kent, was the eldest son of George *Neville, second Baron Bergavenny (1436–1492) [see under Neville, Edward (d. 1476)], and his first wife, Margaret Fenne (d. 1485). Although he was a descendant of the second marriage of Ralph Neville, first earl of Westmorland, his territorial connections were not with the north but with East Anglia, Surrey, Sussex, and Kent. His peerage title had originated in his paternal grandfather's marriage to Elizabeth Beauchamp, the heir to the lordship of Abergavenny, which, however, passed by marriage to other members of the Neville family and eventually escheated to the crown, so that the younger George Neville's father and grandfather never held it. The lordship was granted to Bergavenny by Henry VIII on 18 December 1512.

When his mother died in 1485 George Neville was said to be about sixteen. Two years earlier, despite his youth, he had attended the coronation of Richard III, when he was knighted, presumably on account of his kinship with Anne Neville, the queen consort. Through Elizabeth of York, who became Henry VII's queen, he was equally closely linked with the Tudor dynasty. Having succeeded

George Neville, third Baron Bergavenny (*c*.1469–1535), by Hans Holbein the younger

to his father's peerage in 1492 and obtained livery of his inheritance not long after, Bergavenny came to public attention in 1497 when he helped Henry VII defeat the Cornish insurgents at Blackheath. He did not waver in his allegiance, though later allegations that immediately before the battle he had tried to persuade his kinsman Edmund de la Pole, earl of Suffolk, to desert with him to the rebels may hint at a measure of personal cowardice in a crisis. Whatever lay behind Bergavenny's apparent hesitation in rising to his task, it was not held against him at the time. Likewise the departure of Suffolk (who was also the principal Yorkist claimant) for the continent without licence in 1501 did Bergavenny no harm initially. Indeed, both then and later he was often involved in court and government business.

From January 1497 onwards Bergavenny took his place in the House of Lords, and was regularly named as a trier of petitions, in other words advising the crown on subsidiary legislation. He was equally at home in the local affairs of the south-east. Alone of the contemporary peerage under Henry VII, he became a member of the king's council, with what was evidently a reasonable record of attendance. Like other nobles he honoured both Henry VII and Henry VIII by his frequent attendance at court, and was conspicuous as a jouster there until middle age. From 1501, when he witnessed the reception of Katherine of Aragon at Richmond, he was also a frequent attender at important state occasions, including Henry VIII's meetings with the French king at the Field of Cloth of Gold and with the emperor at Gravelines, both in 1520. As a close friend of Henry VIII and a royal councillor he enjoyed the unusual privilege in 1519 of receiving his diet (a food allowance) at court.

Bergavenny first got into serious trouble in 1506 when, contrary to the Statute of Liveries, he persisted in retaining a body of 470 dependants. It may be significant that this was also the year in which the earl of Suffolk was brought back to England and imprisoned in the Tower—thereafter the government was apt to be suspicious of the earl's associates. Indicted in 1507 for illegal retaining, Bergavenny was fined £100,000 and forbidden to visit Kent, Surrey, Sussex, or Hampshire without royal consent. Edmund Dudley later named him as one who had suffered at Henry VII's hands. When Henry VIII became king, however, he cancelled the fine, granted him a pardon, and within three years restored him to the royal council. In 1513, two years after his first nomination, he was elected to the Order of the Garter. During that year's expedition to capture Tournai and in the subsequent expedition to relieve Guînes, his retinue included an impressive Welsh contingent. But although he shared the young king's passion for jousting this did not save Bergavenny from further accusations of illegal retaining under a regulation of 1464. Following his part in the jousts at Greenwich to honour the Scottish queen in May 1516 an information was laid against him in king's bench, but he escaped virtually unscathed, only being 'put out of the Council chamber' (*LP Henry VIII*, 2/1, no. 1959). In the period before this unfortunate episode the king had helped promote the career of his younger brother Richard in the order of St John of Jerusalem and nominated another brother, Thomas *Neville, as speaker of the Commons in the parliament of 1515.

Bergavenny's first two marriages—to Joan Fitzalan, a daughter of the eleventh earl of Arundel, and then to Margaret Brent, daughter of a Kentish gentleman—were childless but strengthened his territorial links in the south-east, and guaranteed his political ascendancy there. This was further enhanced by his marriage about June 1519 to Lady Mary Stafford, a daughter of the third duke of Buckingham, with whom he had six surviving children, including Henry Neville (*d.* 1587), who succeeded him as fourth baron and whose wife was Frances *Neville (*d.* 1576). Buckingham's downfall in 1521 seriously harmed Bergavenny's career. Having been kept a prisoner in the Tower for almost a year, he admitted to concealing the duke's treason. He surrendered all his offices, including the reversion of the lord wardenship of the Cinque Ports granted to him twelve years previously, agreed to sell his house at Birling to the king, and submitted to a fine of 10,000 marks, before receiving a royal pardon. Thereafter, the crown continued to demand his services at court, in parliament, in the country, and at war, but treated him more warily. He was not reinstated on the royal council, and he was excluded from the reception of Charles V in May 1522. Even so, he remained on the local bench for Kent. His treatment at the hands of Cardinal Wolsey and Thomas Cromwell rankled with him. He felt aggrieved by his reduced political stature and by the lingering doubts as to his loyalty. In September 1533 he confided in the imperial ambassador about his disillusionment, while at the same time expressing support for the proposed marriage of Princess Mary to Reginald Pole. Less reliable evidence of his continuing dissatisfaction comes from after his death. The marquess of Exeter is alleged to have observed that if Bergavenny had lived to witness the Pilgrimage of Grace in 1536, he would have supported the insurgents with 10,000 men. His younger brother Sir Edward *Neville was executed for treason in 1538.

Even if Bergavenny had grounds for dissatisfaction, his public actions in his closing years did much to mend relations between him and the Henrician regime. In July 1530 he was one of the signatories to the petition urging Pope Clement VII to dissolve Henry VIII's marriage to Katherine of Aragon, and as a mark of renewed favour, perhaps owing to an effort to woo his continuing support for the king's divorce, he was permitted in the same year to buy back Birling, now surplus to royal needs. In 1532 he witnessed the submission of the clergy. In the following summer he was considered a possible regent during the king's absence abroad to meet François I of France. About this time his presence at court took visual form, for Hans Holbein drew a portrait of him wearing a hat, and also made a miniature based on it. A further sign of renewed confidence in him came in 1535, when the rising Thomas Cromwell discussed the possibility of a marriage between his own son and Bergavenny's niece.

Some time shortly before 24 January 1530, when he settled estates on her, Bergavenny married his fourth wife, Mary Brooke, or Cobham, a sister of the ninth Lord Cobham; she had previously been his mistress. Their union reinforced the pattern of his earlier matrimonial ties by strengthening his regional dominance in Kent. By the time of his death he had consolidated this by a series of projected marriages for his daughters, to his ward the ninth Lord Dacre of the South and to the sons of Sir Thomas Cheyne of Shirland. In the spring of 1535 his concern over the implications of the recently enacted Statute of Uses led Bergavenny to seek clarification on certain points involving his wife (then pregnant), children, and executors before making a new will. On 4 June he made this at his house at Eridge in Sussex, and died on 13 or 14 June. He was buried at Birling. The entailment of his estates made in his will was confirmed by an act of parliament (2 and 3 Philip and Mary c. 22) twenty years later.

ALASDAIR HAWKYARD

Sources GEC, *Peerage*, vols. 1, 3 · M. Mercer, 'Kent and national politics, 1437–1534', PhD diss., U. Lond., 1995 · *LP Henry VIII*, vols. 1–9 · J. Gairdner, ed., *Letters and papers illustrative of the reigns of Richard III and Henry VII*, 2 vols., Rolls Series, 24 (1861–3) · W. C. Richardson, *Tudor chamber administration* (Baton Rouge, 1952) · H. Miller, *Henry VIII and the English nobility* (1986) · C. G. Bayne and W. H. Dunham, eds., *Select cases in the council of Henry VII*, SeldS, 75 (1958) · C. Rawcliffe, *The Staffords, earls of Stafford and dukes of Buckingham* (1978) · G. W. Bernard, ed., *The Tudor nobility* (1992) · *CPR, 1485–1509* · will, PRO, PROB 11/25, fols. 259–63 · W. A. Shaw, *The knights of England*, 2 vols. (1906) · P. G. Begent and H. Chesshyre, *The most noble Order of the Garter: 650 years* (1999) · J. A. Guy, *The cardinal's court: the impact of Thomas Wolsey in star chamber* (1977) · G. G. Cruickshank, *Army royal: an account of Henry VIII's invasion of France* (1969) · HoP, *Commons, 1509–58*, 3, 7–11 · *CIPM, Henry VII*, vol. 1 · T. Benolt and R. Cooke, *The visitations of Kent taken in the years 1530–1 … and 1574*, ed. W. B. Bannerman, 1, Harleian Society, 74 (1923)

Likenesses H. Holbein, drawing, repro. in J. Rowlands, *Holbein: the paintings of Hans Holbein the younger* (1985) · H. Holbein, miniature, repro. in R. C. Strong, *Artists of the Tudor court: the portrait miniature rediscovered, 1520–1620* (1983) [exhibition catalogue, V&A, 9 July – 16 Nov] · H. Holbein the younger, drawing, Wilton House, Wiltshire [*see illus.*]

Neville, George (1509–1567). *See under* Neville, Richard, second Baron Latimer (c.1467–1530).

Neville, Grey (1681–1723), politician, was born in the parish of St Giles-in-the-Fields, London, on 23 September 1681, the elder son of Richard Neville (1655–1717) of Billingbear, Berkshire, and his wife, Catharine, the daughter of Ralph Grey, Baron Grey of Werke. His father, who represented Berkshire in seven parliaments, was the third son of Richard Neville (1615–1676) of Billingbear, a gentleman of the privy chamber. Grey himself was elected as a whig MP for Abingdon on 10 May 1705; his tory opponent, Sir Simon Harcourt, unsuccessfully petitioned against his return. On 14 February 1708 he married Elizabeth, the daughter of Sir John Boteler of Woodhall, who had a substantial dowry of £8000. The couple had one daughter, who died in infancy. Also in 1708 Grey was elected MP for Wallingford, and in February 1715 and March 1722, through the influence of his brother Henry in the local Grey of Warke estates, for Berwick. An undistinguished and unambitious backbencher, he supported the act for naturalizing foreign protestants in 1708 and voted for the impeachment of Dr Sacheverell, both actions indicating low-church sympathies. He supported Walpole in the schism of 1717 and voted with the majority which threw out the ministry's Peerage Bill in 1719.

Neville's most prominent action in parliament was his defence in 1721 of ministers implicated in the South Sea scandal. He defended Charles Spencer, earl of Sunderland, saying that he hated the South Sea Company's promoters but 'on such trivial evidence he himself would be for even one that was accused of murdering his father', and opposed the bill to include John Aislabie, former chancellor of the exchequer, in the confiscation of directors' estates.

Neville died on 24 April 1723 at Billingbear, only six years after succeeding his father. He was very popular with the dissenters, and left a sum of money to Jeremiah Hunt, pastor of the congregational church at Pinner's Hall, to preach a sermon after his death, insisting that his name should not be mentioned. He was survived by his wife, who died on 16 November 1740. His brother Henry, born on 17 August 1683, succeeded to the Billingbear estates, and assumed the additional name of Grey.

G. LE G. NORGATE, rev. TIMOTHY VENNING

Sources R. R. Sedgwick, 'Neville, Grey', HoP, *Commons* · *JHC* · D. Rowland, *An historical and genealogical account of the noble family of Nevill, particularly of the house of Abergavenny* (1830) · *The historical register*, 8 (1723)

Likenesses G. White, mezzotint, 1720 (after M. Dahl), BM, NPG

Neville, Sir Henry (c.1520–1593). *See under* Henry VIII, privy chamber of (*act.* 1509–1547).

Neville, Henry, fifth earl of Westmorland (1524/5–1564). *See under* Neville, Ralph, fourth earl of Westmorland (1498–1549).

Neville, Sir Henry (1561/2–1615), diplomat and courtier, was the son of Sir Henry Neville (*d.* 1593) of Billingbear, Berkshire, and his second wife, Elizabeth (*d.* 1573), daughter of Sir John Gresham. His father was, as the funerary monument erected in his honour by his son in the parish church at Waltham St Lawrence declared, 'descended of the Nevilles at Abergavenny, who were a branch of the House of Westmorland' (*VCH Berkshire*, 3.183). Like his associates Sir Henry Sidney, Sir Nicholas Throckmorton, Sir Henry Killigrew, and, above all, Sir William Cecil, Sir Henry the elder's blend of forward protestantism, commitment to public service, and willingness to reward himself for it ensured that his son inherited a substantial estate. It was concentrated in Berkshire around the parish of Billingbear, at the highest point of which he began to construct a substantial brick Elizabethan manor house around the time his son was born. As a keeper of Windsor Forest, high steward for Reading, deputy lieutenant for Berkshire, and, from 1588, lord lieutenant, Sir Henry the elder retained his links with the court while maintaining a reputation for diligence in his locality.

Henry Neville the younger matriculated from Merton College, Oxford, on 20 December 1577, aged fifteen (being created MA on 30 August 1605). His tutor was Henry Saville, later warden of the college, whose advice he continued to seek throughout his career. They both went on a continental tour in 1578, spending at least part of the journey with Philip Sidney and visiting Padua, Venice, and Prague. Neville sat as MP for New Windsor in the parliament of 1584–5 alongside his father (who was MP for the county of Berkshire) and was also returned from the same borough for the parliaments of 1586–7 and 1588. In the last, however, he chose to sit for the county of Sussex since, following his marriage in December 1584 to Anne (*d.* 1632), daughter of Sir Henry *Killigrew (*d.* 1603), Cornish politician and diplomat, he and his wife had set up residence at Mayfield, Sussex. The latter was a country house that had come to the Neville family in 1579 on the death of Sir John Gresham, uncle of Henry's mother, Elizabeth. Through this property Neville became a Sussex ironmaster and, possibly with Burghley's help, secured a large share of the market in the sale of small ordnance in Sussex in the 1590s. After his father's death there were lawsuits in chancery with his stepmother, Sir Henry the elder's third wife, also Elizabeth, daughter of Sir Nicholas Bacon. So it was not until 1595 that he was able to establish himself locally as the successor to his family estates in Berkshire and return to Billingbear, selling Mayfield in 1597. He was deputy lieutenant for the county in 1596 and sat in the parliament of 1597 for the Cornish borough of Liskeard. His wife's sister Elizabeth had married Jonathan Trelawny, high steward for Liskeard, and the two families were apparently close. Trelawny named Neville as his executor in his will, and guardian of his two sons.

In February 1599, manoeuvred by Robert Cecil, and despite his own protestations that he had neither title nor means to sustain such an appointment, Neville was nominated resident ambassador to France. He secured a knighthood before he left and Cecil agreed to the appointment of the capable Ralph Winwood as his secretary; Jonathan Trelawny accompanied them. His letters of instruction concentrated on the vexed question of the debts owed by Henri IV to Elizabeth I as a result of her assistance during the wars of the Catholic league. With the peace of Vervins (May 1598) Henri IV was less beholden to Elizabeth and correspondingly less concerned to resolve the issue. Before he left Neville collected as much detail as he could about the numerous bonds on which the debt was based, constructing an inventory of it, totalling £401,734 16s. 5½d. 'If I come not thoroughly furnished of my proofs in every point, I shall but minister them some colourable pretext of delay, which they will lie in wait for' (*Salisbury MSS*, 9.72).

Neville's embassy was a frustrating and inconclusive interlude. He arrived in France on 3 May 1599 and met English merchants in Rouen to hear their complaints against French customs duties. He had his first audiences with the king on 13 and 22 May, raising both the issues that would dominate the subsequent year of embassy: French depredations of English merchant shipping and the debt. Both proved intractable and, as the year wore on, Neville became more concerned at the declining influence of protestants at the French court in the wake of the edict of Nantes. His greatest fears, however, were reserved for the activities of the Scottish ambassador at the French court whom he saw as seeking to draw James VI into a Catholic orbit. By December 1599 Neville wanted nothing more than to be 'a hermit in Ashridge or the forest, and do penance for the faults committed here' (*CSP dom.*, 1598–1601, 379). In March he was chosen as a commissioner for the peace negotiations with the plenipotentiaries from the Spanish Netherlands at Boulogne. He openly distrusted the intentions of the delegates from the archdukes and was frustrated in his attempts to renew the Anglo-French alliance concluded at the treaty of Blois in 1572. When the conference broke down in July 1600 he was given leave to return to England for a month and he arrived back in London on 6 August.

Immediately Neville became embroiled in intrigue surrounding the earl of Essex's conspiracy; this almost ruined his career and risked his life. While pointedly refusing the queen's explicit instructions to return to France he had secret meetings with the earl of Essex in late September and October, their country houses being no more than 10 miles away from one another in Berkshire and Oxfordshire. Although he played no direct part in the emerging conspiracy of Essex and his associates he was no doubt sympathetic to the more aggressively protestant dimension that Essex would have given to foreign affairs. He met the earl of Southampton and Sir Charles Danvers, prominent among Essex's companions, on Candlemas day in London, where he was given outline details of the intended plot. When Essex's armed rebellion failed on 8 February, Neville's reluctance to leave for France evaporated. Essex revealed the surprising news of Neville's involvement on 21 February and a warrant was issued for his arrest, which took place as he was taking ship at Dover. He was imprisoned in the Tower, brought before the council on 8 July, dismissed from his ambassadorship, and fined £5000. It was a heavy price to pay, given that his embassy had also cost him, according to his own estimate, £4000 in sales of his estates. During prolonged negotiations to secure his freedom he agreed to pay his fine in yearly instalments of £1000 and, on James I's accession, he was eventually released on 10 April 1603 by royal warrant.

Neville lived the life of a frustrated courtier for the remainder of his public life, at times malcontent, capable of more influence than appeared on the surface, but never able to secure the preferment he yearned for. In the first Jacobean parliament of 1604 he was elected MP for the borough of Lewes and his name was 'muttered' as speaker. When Salisbury considered resigning the secretaryship Sir Dudley Carleton thought he would have been a good replacement, but the occasion never arose. He was regarded as the popular choice to succeed Salisbury when the latter eventually died in 1612, but the king had no love for popular choices. His role in the Jacobean parliaments was a testimony to his zeal for courting protestant causes and exerting influence. In 1605 he served on thirty-eight committees, especially those dealing with the problems of the Catholic minority and the vexed question of supplying the king's needs. He had his fair share of ambitious projects that offered to satisfy the latter and, at the same time, alleviate his own necessities. These must have been pressing, since he had a son who was of an age to be knighted and three daughters who needed husbands and dowries, as well as two nephews to support at Oxford.

Neville increasingly looked to commercial ventures to relieve his debts and in 1613 he lent his weight to a project to open up the overland route from India. In 1610 his efforts to secure the great contract led him to mediate between king and Commons in November. The effort proved fruitless. In July 1612 he used his influence with the king's favourite, Robert Carr, Viscount Rochester, to secure a meeting with the king in Windsor Great Park. As part of his efforts to secure the secretaryship he presented a plan of action in a memorial that advised the recall of parliament and the granting of concessions that did not infringe the prerogative but which would, so he assured the king, win substantial supply from the Commons. In the end, however, Ralph Winwood, his erstwhile clerk in Paris, was made secretary and Neville refused Rochester's offer of the office of treasurer of the chamber by way of compensation. In the privy council in February 1613, and then again in the Addled Parliament of 1614, the memorial was discussed, but the outcome demonstrated its flaws. In the winter of 1614–15 he suffered the ignominy of having the potentially profitable patent to prosecute those despoiling royal forest, on which he had set his store,

denied him by the council. By then Neville was incapacitated by gout in both legs and afflicted by jaundice, scurvy, and dropsy. He died in London on 10 July 1615.

Of the Nevilles' sons, Sir Henry, the eldest, succeeded his father and died in 1629. William, the second son, became a fellow of Merton College, Oxford. Charles died in 1626. Richard became sub-warden of Merton and became the ancestor in the female line of the Nevilles, barons of Braybrooke. Edward, a fellow of King's College, Cambridge, died in 1632. Of their six daughters, only one, Anne, remained unmarried. The others, in order of age, married as follows: Elizabeth to William Glover, then Sir Henry Berkeley, and lastly to Thomas Duke; Catherine to Sir Richard Brooke; Frances to Richard Worseley, and then Jerome Brett; Mary to Sir Edward Lewknor; and Dorothy to Richard Catlyn.   M. GREENGRASS

Sources Berks. RO, Neville MSS, D/En · PRO, C 3/24616 [suit with Elizabeth Neville]; SP 78/43, fols. 25–60 [letters of instruction for embassy] · R. Winwood, *Memorials of the affairs of state in the reigns of Queen Elizabeth and King James I*, ed. E. Sawyer (1725) · *The letters of John Chamberlain*, ed. N. E. McClure, 2 vols. (1939) · *CSP dom.*, vols. 3–6 and addenda · *The works of Francis Bacon*, ed. J. Spedding, R. L. Ellis, and D. D. Heath, 14 vols. (1857–74) · *Calendar of the manuscripts of the most hon. the marquis of Salisbury*, 24 vols., HMC, 9 (1883–1976) · *JHC*, 1 (1547–1628) · O. L. Duncan, 'The political career of Sir Henry Neville: an Elizabethan gentleman at the court of James I', PhD diss., Ohio State University, 1974 · S. Gardiner, *History of England from the accession of James I to the disgrace of Chief Justice Coke, 1603–1616*, 2 vols. (1863) · R. Lacey, *Robert, earl of Essex* (New York, 1971) · T. E. Hartley, ed., *Proceedings in the parliaments of Elizabeth I*, 3 vols. (1995) · T. Moir, *The Addled Parliament of 1614* (1958) · A. Harding, 'Neville, Henry (1562–1615)', HoP, *Commons, 1558–1603* · N. M. Fuidge, 'Neville, Sir Henry I (d. 1593)', HoP, *Commons, 1558–1603* · Foster, *Alum. Oxon.* · *Surrey Archaeological Collections*, 2 (1864), 187, 210, 245 · G. M. Bell, *A handlist of British diplomatic representatives, 1509–1688*, Royal Historical Society Guides and Handbooks, 16 (1990), 101–2 · V. M. Howse, *Shellingford: a parish history* (1978)

Archives Berks. RO, corresp. and papers · PRO, SP 78/43–4 · PRO, diplomatic corresp., PRO 30/50 | BL, Cotton MSS Calig. E.ix–x, Vespasian F.x., Titus F.iv · BL, Lansdowne MS 161

Likenesses oils, *c*.1600, Audley End, Essex · W. N. Gardiner, stipple (after unknown artist, *c*.1600), BM, NPG; repro. in F. G. Waldron, *The Biographical Mirror*, 3 vols. (1795–1810) · attrib. B. Rebecca, portrait, oils, Audley End, Essex · portrait, priv. coll.

Neville, Henry (1620–1694), politician and political writer, was the second son of Sir Henry Neville (d. 1629) of Billingbear, near Windsor, Berkshire, and Elizabeth (1595–1669), daughter of Sir John Smythe of Westenhanger, Kent; his grandfather was Sir Henry *Neville (1561/2–1615). By 1633 he was already married to Elizabeth Staverton, heir of Richard Staverton (d. 1636) of Heathley Hall in Warfield, Berkshire. She died childless and probably young, and Neville came to possess most of the Staverton properties; years later, 'his barbarous usage of the woman that brought him the estate' was recalled by a hostile observer (*Clarendon State Papers*, 4.249). On 29 January 1636 he matriculated at Oxford, entering Merton College, and then moved to University College; he left the university without a degree. He is certified as having taken the protestation oath to defend the protestant faith on 11 May 1641, when he was styled as of Heathley, Berkshire. Soon after, he made an extended tour on the continent, especially of Italy, which his older brother, Richard (1615–1676), seems already to have visited in 1636 in the company of James Harrington. He stayed chiefly in Florence and Rome during 1643–4, and made a further visit to Venice. Among his friends dating from this trip were the Florentine lawyer Ferrante Capponi and Bernardo Guasconi (Bernard Gascoigne); Guasconi later fought in Neville's brother's royalist regiment of horse in 1644. In 1645 Neville returned to England.

In the spring of 1647 Neville anonymously published *The Parliament of Ladies*, lampooning prominent women associated with the parliamentary side. This libertine parody of the parliamentary publications common at the time was soon reprinted with various additions later that year; its popularity is also reflected in the published answers to it and imitations, as well as a continuation that may well be Neville's work, *The Ladies, a Second Time, Assembled in Parliament* (1647). A few years later appeared the comparable *Newes from the New Exchange, or, The Common-Wealth of Ladies* (1650), published in two editions, which also elicited some responses.

In April 1649 Neville was chosen a recruiter MP (that is, as a replacement for an MP who had sided with the king) at Abingdon, Berkshire, which election was then successfully supported against the opposition of the godly Henry Vane by Neville's second cousin Algernon Sidney and probably by Henry Marten, a fellow Berkshire landowner who had previously been elected from that county. Neville could thus play his part in 'the emergence for the first time in the Rump of an effectively coordinated radical party', especially in consort with the republican Marten and Thomas Chaloner, reputed a 'gangue' of wits (Worden, *Rump Parliament*, 218; *Writings and Speeches of Oliver Cromwell*, 2.376). He was soon active in committees. In November 1651 he was elected to the council of state, where he played a part in foreign policy, especially in relation to the Netherlands and to Scotland. He failed to be re-elected to the council a year later. After the battle of Worcester, the increasing tension in the Rump between the army and the civilians found Neville conspicuously on the latter side. The expulsion of the Rump in April 1653 he seems to have greeted as an opportunity for a better constitution, which he sought to promote in a tract that went unpublished.

After the dissolution of the Rump, Neville was 'so obnoxious to Cromwell as to be banished from London in 1654' (*DNB*). In August 1655 and again the next year he returned to the city under special licence. The visit in 1656 followed from his failure to win a seat in parliament from Reading, where his election had been peremptorily blocked by the Cromwellian interest. Rather than concede the authority of the instrument of government, he successfully went to court to sue the sheriff of Berkshire for damages, and his wrongs were published in the broadside *Nevill versus Strood: the State of the Case* (1656) and in *A true and perfect relation of the manner and proceeding, held by the sheriffe for the county of Berk: at Redding, upon the 20th. of Aug. last 1656* (1656). Such resistance to Cromwell long delighted republicans (*Memoirs of Edmund Ludlow*, 2.35).

Neville's relationship to the political philosopher James Harrington was so close that Thomas Hobbes suspected Neville's hand in *Oceana*, and his 'constant friendship' to Harrington from the 1650s until long after the Restoration finds a warm tribute from John Aubrey (*Brief Lives*, 1.293). Neville's 'bitterness towards His Highness and the Government' was also seen in *A Copy of a Letter from an Officer in the Army* of 1656 (*Fifth Report*, HMC, 148). Much of Neville's subsequent political writing also shows Harrington's influence, as do Neville's positions in debate on constitutional matters, where he was consistently indifferent to the claims of the one, and instead attentive to the balance between the few and the many.

After Oliver Cromwell's death, Neville was finally returned to parliament for Reading on 30 December 1658 in another disputed return. Having been confirmed by order of the house, he then encountered charges of atheism and blasphemy on 16 February 1659, which were debated at length but inconclusively. He was charged with having 'said ten years ago that nothing could be said for the Scripture which could not be said for the Alcoran' and seemed to prefer reading Cicero to the Bible (*Clarendon State Papers*, 4.152). He was a very active speaker. In foreign policy, he regretted Cromwell's war with Spain and wished to avoid embroilment in the war between Sweden and Denmark. In constitutional discussions, he shaded his reluctance to recognize the 'other house' with suspicions of corruption and placemen. After the army's usurpation in April 1659, he was among the republicans who tried to prescribe a new constitutional settlement as *The Armies Dutie* (2 May 1659); when the army instead restored the Rump, Neville presented in parliament the republican proposals voiced in *The Humble Petition of Divers Well-Affected Persons* (6 July 1659). On 19 May 1659 he was placed on the new council of state. His zeal against the house of Cromwell appears from his satire *Shufling, cutting, and dealing, in a game at pickquet: being acted from the year, 1653. to 1658. By O.P. and others* (1659). He remained cold to the claims of the army and later that year sharply opposed the committee of safety. He was a prominent figure in the republican Rota Club which met in London between November 1659 and February 1660, but his Harringtonian prescriptions for present political occasions tended to be camouflaged in more conciliatory terms of the ancient constitution. This emerged in his speeches in parliament in 1659 as well as in tracts from his hand just before the Restoration. He may well have been behind a broadside recommending a committee to consider Harrington's 'Propositions for setling the Government of this Commonwealth' (*A Proposition in Order to the Proposing of a Commonwealth or Democracie*, 14 June 1659). That he continued to seek a strongly republican compromise is revealed in his *Letter Sent to General Monk* (dated 29 January 1660), where Neville nominated another smaller committee for settlement that might forestall any oligarchic or monarchical outcome.

After the Restoration Neville returned to a more private

life in Berkshire. The government viewed him with persistent misgivings, and in October 1663 he was arrested on suspicion of being implicated in the so-called Yorkshire rising, and lodged in the Tower. There being no evidence against him, he successfully petitioned for liberty the following year, and obtained a pass to travel abroad in May. Having maintained his Italian connections in the two decades since his first visit, he now returned there for three years, during which time his correspondence shows him to have been chiefly in Florence, at the court of Ferdinand II of Tuscany, and Rome, where his brother was still writing to him in June 1667. Neville had returned to England by the time he published *Isle of Pines* (1668), which was licensed on 27 June 1668. In this libertine fantasy, a shipwreck leaves George Pine with four women survivors on a mild and fertile island, soon copiously populated by their offspring, whose rapid increase in numbers is charted. The success of this publication may be measured in the successive editions in which it appears, including an attempted piracy in North America; in its immediate continuation in *A New and Further Discovery of the Islle of Pines* (licensed 27 July 1668); and in its popularity on the continent, where it found translation into Dutch, French, Italian, German, and Danish—these translations were in turn republished into the eighteenth century, not least in compilations of narratives of travel and discovery. Although back in England, Neville retained his Italian acquaintance. He attended the young Cosimo on his ducal visit to England, which included a stop with Neville at the family seat at Billingbear on 14 May 1669. In the decade to come, the grand duke corresponded with Neville and had his English agent consult with him about books to buy. Neville has also long been associated with the English translation of Machiavelli's *Works* published by John Starkey in 1675, and republished in 1680, 1694 (reissued 1695), and 1720. The *Works* includes a letter attributed to Machiavelli, but dated a decade after his death, which defends him from the worst imputations against him; from an early date Neville was thought to be the author of this letter, although it may have been an earlier forgery brought back, as the preface claims, from his visit to Italy in the 1640s.

In the Restoration Neville preserved his reputation as a republican, but apparently without any too close ties to the opposition to the Stuart court or crown. In November 1669 much was made of his presence in London; a decade later he and John Wildman were reported to be with George Villiers, second duke of Buckingham, on a political errand to France. In May–June 1679 he was in London in the company of George Savile, marquess of Halifax. At this date Neville wrote his most enduring political treatise, *Plato redivivus*, a dialogue in great part between an English gentleman, who resembles Neville, and a noble Venetian. Here Neville's Harringtonian arguments of earlier years are much expanded. They are now trained on the Restoration monarchy at the time of the exclusion crisis, with much freedom of reflection on the causes and cure for the present troubles of state. Ostensibly reconciled to monarchy, Neville now sees it as consistent with the

Harringtonian principle that 'Dominion is founded in property' (Robbins, 89). England had historically been governed by a limited or mixed monarchy, featuring an appropriate balance of crown and aristocracy, which had since Bosworth field 'been decaying for near two hundred years' (ibid., 81). Modern more absolute monarchy had destroyed that balance, even though the ever widening distribution of property meant that the gentry should have acquired more rather than less 'empire' by the present day. Neville's remedies for this growth of court power went beyond the whig proposals of recent years, which in his view addressed only the effects rather than 'the causes of our misfortunes' (ibid., 133–4). This allows him to disavow whig radicalism, especially the exclusion of James, duke of York, from the throne, while pressing further with his ultimately republican recommendations. Adducing many classical, some biblical, and also modern examples, with guidance from 'the divine ... the incomparable Machiavel' (ibid., 81, 155), he advocates that the present distribution of property find some better reflection in constitutional arrangements. But he also urges that the ancient constitution should issue in a much more popular form of government, in which monarchy plays a much smaller part. Thus he finally demands more revolutionary changes after all, even as he protests 'the less change the better' (ibid., 192), aiming to devolve the executive powers of the crown to councils elected from and under the control of parliament, in a system of rotation, and with a reduction in the independence of the Lords.

Plato redivivus seems to have been brought to the press in October 1680, at the time of the second Exclusion Parliament, and was published by John Starkey in time for the Oxford parliament (it finds notice by 7 February 1681); a second edition with some extra anti-clerical material and comment on exclusion soon followed. John Locke gave a copy to James Tyrrell. In the 1680s it met with a number of hostile responses. It was republished in 1698, 1737, and 1763, sometimes in association with Harrington's works; a modern edition with a fine biographical introduction is available in *Two English Republican Tracts* (1969), edited by Caroline Robbins.

From the early 1670s, at least, Neville seems to have stayed in London at an address in Silver Street, near Covent Garden, until his death in September 1694. He was buried in the parish church of Warfield, Berkshire. The burial he wished 'to be without "Jewish ceremonies," eating and drinking, and that "unprofitable form of words" in the prayer-book' (Robbins, 19). His will made provision for his nieces, personal servants, and the poor of the village; his property went in great part to his nephew Richard Neville. NICHOLAS VON MALTZAHN

Sources Foster, *Alum. Oxon.* · C. Robbins, ed., *Two English republican tracts* (1969) · A. M. Crinò, 'Lettere inedite italiane e inglesi di Sir Henry Neville', *Fatti e figure del Seicento anglo-toscano: documenti inediti sui rapporti letterari, diplomatici e culturali fra Toscana e Inghilterra* (Florence, 1957), 173–211 · Berks. RO, Neville family papers, D/EN · B. Worden, 'Harrington's *Oceana*: origins and aftermath, 1651–1660', *Republicanism, liberty, and commercial society, 1649–1776*, ed. D. Wootton (1994), 111–38 · B. Worden, 'Marchamont

Nedham and English republicanism', *Republicanism, liberty, and commercial society, 1649–1776*, ed. D. Wootton (1994), 45–81 · B. Worden, 'Republicanism and the Restoration, 1660–1683', *Republicanism, liberty, and commercial society, 1649–1776*, ed. D. Wootton (1994), 139–93 · W. C. Ford, 'The Isle of Pines', 1668: an essay in bibliography (1920) · N. von Maltzahn, 'Henry Neville and the art of the possible: a republican *Letter sent to General Monk* (1660)', *Seventeenth Century*, 7 (1992), 41–52 · Wood, *Ath. Oxon.*, new edn · *Diary of Thomas Burton*, ed. J. T. Rutt, 4 vols. (1828) · *CSP dom.*, 1633–41 · E. Chaney, *The grand tour and the great rebellion* (1985) · *Fifth report*, HMC, 4 (1876) · R. Ashcraft, *Revolutionary politics* (1986) · Sheffield University, Hartlib papers 29/5/98A · Oxon. RO, University College papers, P2/M51/9:3 · *JHC*, 6 (1648–51) · *The poems and letters of Andrew Marvell*, ed. H. Margoliouth, rev. P. Legouis, 3rd edn, 2 vols. (1971) · J. Scott, *Algernon Sidney and the English republic* (1988) · B. Worden, *The Rump Parliament, 1648–1653* (1974) · *The writings and speeches of Oliver Cromwell*, ed. W. C. Abbott and C. D. Crane, 4 vols. (1937–47) · *DNB* · *The memoirs of Edmund Ludlow*, ed. C. H. Firth, 2 vols. (1894) · *Brief lives, chiefly of contemporaries, set down by John Aubrey, between the years 1669 and 1696*, ed. A. Clark, 2 vols. (1898) · L. Naylor and G. Jagger, 'Neville, Richard', *HoP, Commons, 1660–90* · *Calendar of the Clarendon state papers preserved in the Bodleian Library*, 4: 1657–1660, ed. F. J. Routledge (1932)

Archives Berks. RO, corresp. and papers, incl. family material

Neville, (Thomas) Henry Gartside (1837–1910), actor, was born at Manchester on 20 June 1837. He was the son of John Neville (1787–1874), the manager of the Queen's Theatre, Spring Gardens, and his second wife, Marianne, the daughter of Captain Gartside of Woodbrow, Saddleworth, Yorkshire. He was the twentieth child of a twentieth child, both being the issue of a second marriage. A brother, George, was also an actor.

At the age of three Neville was brought on the stage in his father's arms as the child in *Pizarro*. He forfeited all help from his father by refusing to join the army like other members of the family, and in 1857, at Preston, under Edmund Falconer, he took to the stage as a profession. When John Vandenhoff made his farewell performance on 29 October 1858, at the Theatre Royal, Liverpool, Neville played Cromwell to the tragedian's Cardinal Wolsey in *King Henry VIII*. Following a stern noviciate in the north of England and in Scotland, he made his début in London at the Lyceum Theatre, under Madame Celeste, on 8 October 1860, as Percy Ardent in a revival of Boucicault's *The Irish Heiress*. After further provincial engagements he spent four years at the Olympic under Robson and Emden (1862–6). The experience proved the turning point in his career. In May 1863 he was the original Bob Brierley in Tom Taylor's *The Ticket-of-Leave Man*, a character in which he made the success of his life. He played it in all some 2000 times. In May 1864, while Taylor's play was still running, Neville also appeared as Petruchio in the afterpiece *Catherine and Petruchio*, and was highly praised for his speaking of blank verse. In October 1866 he was the first professional to take the part of Richard Wardour in Wilkie Collins's *The Frozen Deep*, a character originally performed by Charles Dickens.

Neville's impassioned and romantic style of acting, which gave a character to the Olympic productions, contrasted with the over-charged, highly coloured style then current at the Adelphi. But early in 1867 he migrated to the Adelphi, where he was the original Job Armroyd in Watts Phillips's *Lost in London* and the original Farmer Allen in Charles Reade's version of Tennyson's *Dora*. In August 1867, on Kate Terry's farewell, he played Romeo to her Juliet, and the following December he was the original George Vendale in Dickens and Collins's *No Thoroughfare*. In November 1868 *The Yellow Passport*, Neville's own version of Victor Hugo's *Les misérables*, was produced at the Olympic with himself as Jean Valjean. At the Gaiety in 1869 he played an important role in W. S. Gilbert's first comedy, *An Old Score*.

From 1873 to 1879 Neville was lessee and manager of the Olympic Theatre. After experiencing failure in 1873 with H. J. Byron's comedy *Sour Grapes* and James Mortimer's *The School for Intrigue*, he scored numerous successes through his acting of Lord Clancarty in Taylor's *Lady Clancarty* and with John Oxenford's *The Two Orphans* in 1874, and also in the part of Franklin Blake in Wilkie Collins's *The Moonstone* in 1877. From 1879 he played for two years at the Adelphi, opening there as Perrinet Leclerc in Clement Scott and E. Mavriel's *The Crimson Cross*. He proved a popular Charles Surface in a successful revival of *The School for Scandal* at the Vaudeville in February 1882. A little later he was supporting Madame Modjeska in the provinces as the Earl of Leicester in Lewis Wingfield's *Mary Stuart* and as Jaques in *As You Like It*.

Thereafter Neville confined himself chiefly to playing romantic heroes in melodrama. In September 1885 he was the original Captain Temple in Pettitt and Harris's *Human Nature* at Drury Lane, and after playing in many similar pieces he went to America in 1890 with Sir Augustus Harris's company to appear as Captain Temple. He opened at the Boston Theatre and performed in the role for 200 nights (the play had been renamed *The Soudan*). He was in London again at the Princess's in 1892. During the succeeding fourteen years he continued, with occasional interruptions, to originate prominent characters in the autumn melodramas at Drury Lane. His last appearance on the stage was at His Majesty's at a matinée on 29 April 1910, when he played Sir Oliver in Sir Herbert Beerbohm Tree's revival of *The School for Scandal*, which was also the last great engagement of Lionel Brough and Hermann Vezin.

Neville's art reflected his buoyant, breezy nature and his generous mind. He believed that the principles of acting could be taught, and in 1878 established a dramatic studio in Oxford Street, in whose fortunes he continued to take an interest for many years. In 1875 he published a pamphlet giving the substance of a lecture on *The Stage, its Past and Present in Relation to Fine Art*, which was later published as a book. He also wrote half a dozen plays, including *The Violin-Maker*, *The Duke's Device*, and *The Great Metropolis*, the last in collaboration with William Terriss.

Although he lived for the theatre, Neville was a man of varied accomplishments. He was a prominent freemason. He painted, carved, and modelled, took a keen interest in sport, and was a volunteer and crack rifle shot. He was also a man of sound business capacity, and long managed the George Hotel at Reading. He was a freeholder in Berkshire, Lancashire, Kent, and Middlesex.

Neville died at 4 Esplanade, Seaford, Sussex, on 19 June 1910, from heart failure as the result of an accident, and was buried at Denshaw, Saddleworth, Yorkshire. He was survived by the four sons from his marriage to Henrietta Waddell.   W. J. LAWRENCE, *rev.* NILANJANA BANERJI

Sources *Daily Telegraph* (20 June 1910) · B. Hunt, ed., *The green room book, or, Who's who on the stage* (1906) · J. Parker, ed., *The green room book, or, Who's who on the stage* (1907–9) · E. Reid and H. Compton, eds., *The dramatic peerage* [1891]; rev. edn [1892] · C. E. Pascoe, ed., *The dramatic list*, 2nd edn (1880) · *WWW* · P. Hartnoll, ed., *The Oxford companion to the theatre*, 3rd edn (1967) · E. D. Cook, *Nights at the play* (1883) · J. Knight, *Theatrical notes* (1893) · R. J. Broadbent, *Annals of the Liverpool stage* (1908) · Hall, *Dramatic ports.* · H. Morley, *The journal of a London playgoer from 1851 to 1866* (1866) · *Era Almanack and Annual* (1887) · *CGPLA Eng. & Wales* (1910)

Likenesses T. W. Walton, oils, 1874, Garr. Club · C. R. Fitt, cartes-de-visite, NPG · Lock & Whitfield, woodburytype, NPG; repro. in *The Theatre* · London Stereoscopic Co., cartes-de-visite, NPG · E. Matthews & Sons, lithograph, NPG · Rotary Photo Co., photograph, NPG · caricature, repro. in *The Hornet* (31 May 1876) · caricature, repro. in *Entr'acte Annual* (6 Jan 1877) [plate] · woodburytype, carte-de-visite, NPG · woodcuts and lithographs, Harvard TC

Wealth at death £18,671 11s. 5d.: probate, 21 Nov 1910, *CGPLA Eng. & Wales*

Neville, Hugh de (*d.* 1234), royal forester, was apparently the son of a Ralph de Neville, and a grandson of the notoriously unpopular chief forester of Henry II, Alan de *Neville. Hugh performed many governmental tasks, but the most important of them was the execution of his office as chief justice of the forest, or chief forester, under Richard I and John, continuously from 1198 to 1216, and again under Henry III from 1224 to 1229. According to Matthew Paris, he was brought up at the court of Henry II as an intimate of Richard. His service to the crown, however, began at the end of Henry's reign, when he was the keeper of two baronies in Northumberland. Richard, near the beginning of his reign, in December 1189, granted Neville the manor of Hallingbury in Essex. Neville accompanied the king on crusade, and was present at the siege of Jaffa in 1192, giving an account of it to the Essex chronicler Ralph, abbot of Coggeshall. Matthew Paris tells a story of his encounter with a lion in the Holy Land, which may however have derived only from Neville's use of the device of a man slaying a lion on his seal, since it is not mentioned by earlier writers.

In 1198 Neville received the office of forester from Richard, following which he held a forest eyre, criticized by the chronicler Roger of Howden, himself a forest justice in the 1180s, as a torment to the men of the kingdom. From Richard I he also received Joan, elder daughter of Henry of Cornhill, as his wife, between 1195 and 1200. He had paid 100 marks for her custody in 1194, and the marriage eventually brought him a half share of the barony of Courcy through his wife's mother, Alice de Courcy. As well as retaining his forest office under John, Neville also remained in office as sheriff of Essex and Hertfordshire, from 1197 to 1200, and served again in 1203–4; he was later sheriff of Hampshire, from 1210 to 1212. He also held the Wiltshire castles of Marlborough and Ludgershall for much of the reign, as well as other castles for shorter periods. Other royal favours came in the form of the custody of estates, while in 1204 he was granted the manor of Arnold in Sherwood Forest. As chief forester he was largely free of supervision by the king's exchequer at Westminster; he held his own exchequer of the forest, which is known to have sat at Marlborough and Nottingham, and was directly accountable to the king, who, however, sometimes intervened personally. Neville's position during John's reign was very powerful, since he was one of the king's closest advisers and agents, but his relationship with his royal master was a turbulent one. Several times he had to pay large fines to the king when his actions did not find favour. His wife may have been one of the women who suffered from the amorous attentions of the king, since in 1204 she made a fine of 200 shillings 'to lie one night with her husband' (*Rotuli de oblatis et finibus ... tempore Regis Johannis*, ed. T. D. Hardy, RC, 1835, 275). In 1212 Neville was forced to pay a fine of 6000 marks, ostensibly for allowing the escape of two knights captured at Carrickfergus in 1210, but it seems also to have covered his misdeeds in administering the northern forests and his tenure of the lands of the bishopric of Salisbury during the interdict. Soon afterwards he was dismissed as sheriff of Hampshire, and as keeper of the county and forest of Cumberland, which he had held since 1209; some of the debt was, however, pardoned later. He witnessed Magna Carta in 1215, but before John's death joined the baronial party, to whom he brought the possession of Marlborough Castle.

His defection cost Neville his forest office and some of his lands. Although by the end of 1217 he had made peace with the new king, Henry III, he was out of favour for some years, despite his ability to beg favours from his kinsman Ralph de Neville, then keeper of the king's seal. He was eventually re-appointed chief justice of the forests in England on 17 January 1224, in succession to Brian de Lisle, his position being confirmed in April that year. His period of office coincided with the final attempts to implement the terms of the charter of the forest (1217) concerning the forest boundaries, which it had been conceded would exclude from the forests woods afforested by Henry II, Richard I, and John, except their demesne woods. Earlier efforts to resolve the disputes which then arose between the government and the counties, under the chief justiceships of John Marshal and Brian de Lisle, had been unsuccessful, and in October 1224 Hugh was ordered to keep the forest within the same boundaries that it had attained before the outbreak of civil war in 1215. The return of John's forest justice thus brought a temporary return to John's forest policy. In 1225, however, the reissue of the charter in return for a grant of taxation immediately led to another attempt to settle the boundaries, with Hugh himself leading those making the perambulations in most counties. Some were successful, but early in 1227 the young Henry III intervened personally, disputing the boundaries which had been specified by the jurors in some counties. Some of the jurors were dealt with by Neville, who also held forest eyres following the settlement of the disputes. He was removed from office on 8 October

1229 and replaced by John of Monmouth and Brian de Lisle jointly.

Neville's first wife Joan apparently died some time after December 1224. By April 1230 he had married, as his second wife, Beatrice, widow of Ralph de Fay (d. c.1223) and one of the five daughters and coheirs of Stephen of Turnham. Matthew Paris mistakenly recorded Neville's death under 1222, but in fact he died shortly before 21 July 1234. Following Paris, later historians (including the author of the Neville article in the *Dictionary of National Biography*) erroneously distinguished a Hugh de Neville (d. 1222) from his 'son' (d. 1234). Neville was buried at Waltham Abbey in Essex, which he had patronized. His son John, who followed him as chief justice of the forests between 1235 and 1244, was also buried there after his death in 1246. Neville had another son, Henry, who predeceased him in 1218, and at least one daughter, Joan. DAVID CROOK

Sources *Radulphi de Coggeshall chronicon Anglicanum*, ed. J. Stevenson, Rolls Series, 66 (1875) • *Chronica magistri Rogeri de Hovedene*, ed. W. Stubbs, 4, Rolls Series, 51 (1871) • Paris, *Chron.*, vol. 3 • W. W. Shirley, ed., *Royal and other historical letters illustrative of the reign of Henry III*, 1, Rolls Series, 27 (1862) • N. Vincent, 'Hugh de Neville and his prisoners', *Archives*, 20 (1992), 190–97 • GEC, *Peerage* • D. Crook, 'The struggle over forest boundaries in Nottinghamshire', *Transactions of the Thoroton Society*, 83 (1979), 35–45 • S. Painter, *The reign of King John* (1949) • Lord Treasurer's remembrancers, pipe rolls, PRO, E372 • *Chancery records* • R. Ransford, ed., *The early charters of the Augustinian canons of Waltham Abbey, Essex, 1062–1230* (1989) • duchy of Lancaster miscellanea, PRO, DL41 • D. A. Carpenter, *The minority of Henry III* (1990)

Neville, Sir Humphrey (c.1439–1469), rebel, of Brancepeth, co. Durham, was the son of Sir Thomas Neville of Slingsby, Yorkshire, the third son of Sir John Neville (d. 1420), who was the eldest son of Ralph *Neville, first earl of Westmorland. He was thus the nephew of the second earl, Ralph *Neville. His mother was Elizabeth, daughter of Henry, fifth Baron Beaumont. He came to prominence in the late 1450s as a Lancastrian against the Yorkist junior branch of the family. In March 1457 he was granted the stewardship of Richmond during the minority of Henry Tudor, an empty grant since the lordship was occupied by the earl of Salisbury. A more tangible reward came his way from the forfeited estates of the earl in 1459 in the parkership of Caplebank in the lordship of Middleham.

By 6 May 1461 Humphrey Neville had succeeded his uncle John, Lord Neville, killed on the field of Towton, as bailiff of Hexham. A month later he joined Lord Ros and others in a Lancastrian raid into co. Durham. He was captured near Brancepeth, imprisoned in the Tower of London, and attainted in November. In February 1462, by which time he appears to have succeeded his father, he was pardoned and granted his life provided he remained in prison and did not seek to regain his forfeited lands. But a year later he escaped and fled to Northumberland where he 'made commotion of people' (*RotP*, 5.511). In June 1463 Lord Montagu was commissioned to receive him back into the king's grace. He was pardoned again and received 'great and large bounties from the king' (ibid.): his estates, with one exception, were restored and he was knighted.

Nevertheless in August he was harassing the prior of Durham and by the spring of 1464, 'as an unkind and unnatural man' (ibid.), had turned again, joining the duke of Somerset and other rebels in Northumberland. In March 1464, north of Newcastle, he attempted to ambush Lord Montagu who was escorting Scottish ambassadors north to the border; a day later Montagu fought off a larger force at Hedgeley Moor. Neville does not appear to have been in the Lancastrian army defeated two months later at Hexham; but he was, with Sir Ralph Grey, defending Bamburgh when it was besieged by Montagu in June. The castle was subjected to a heavy bombardment. After his fellow commander was seriously wounded, Neville negotiated a surrender in exchange for his own and the garrison's liberty.

Neville probably had no intention of giving his allegiance to Edward IV in 1464. Within a short while he withdrew to the remote dales of Hexhamshire and for five years maintained the Lancastrian cause as a brigand. By August 1466 his 'assemblies, gatherings and commotions' (PRO, Durh 3/49/2) were causing serious disturbances of the peace in the bishopric. Three years later he seized the opportunity of Warwick's rebellion against Edward IV and the king's captivity in Middleham Castle to escalate the conflict. His rising, which Warwick had not the authority on his own to repress, forced the earl to release the king. The two then rapidly moved against Neville, scattered the insurgents, and captured him and his brother Charles. Humphrey and Charles were taken to York and executed on 29 September 1469. Humphrey pursued his family feud against the Nevilles of Middleham as obdurately as he maintained the Lancastrian cause. Edward IV's repeated willingness to pardon him and spare his life was ill-judged but sprang from calculation rather than misplaced leniency, for Sir Humphrey Neville was after 1461 the acting head of the earl of Westmorland's family, which the new king was anxious to win over.

A. J. POLLARD

Sources *RotP*, vol. 5 • *Chancery records* • PRO, Durham chancery records, Durh 3 • J. Raine, ed., *The priory of Hexham*, 2 vols., SurtS, 44, 46 (1864–5) • J. R. Lander, 'Attainder and forfeiture, 1453–1509', *HJ*, 4 (1961), 119–51, esp. 127 n. • C. Ross, *Edward IV* (1974) • A. J. Pollard, *North-eastern England during the Wars of the Roses: lay society, war and politics, 1450–1500* (1990) • J. Warkworth, *A chronicle of the first thirteen years of the reign of King Edward the Fourth*, ed. J. O. Halliwell, CS, old ser., 10 (1839)

Neville, Jill Adelaide (1932–1997), writer and broadcaster, was born on 29 May 1932 in Sydney, Australia, the eldest of the three children of Clive Henry Neville, scion of a family of distinguished Australian soldiers, who became a colonel, and his wife, Elizabeth (Betty), a newspaper columnist, daughter of the Sydney diva Laura McKnight. Gifted, imaginative, sensual, passionate, and possessing a great sense of drama, Jill Neville was determined from an early age to be an actress, dancer, or writer. Worried at her dreamy impracticability, her father sent her to the regimented, patriotic Osborne Ladies College in the Blue Mountains, which the headmistress, who called herself 'Admiral', referred to as her 'Boat'. Though Neville enjoyed eccentricity, she hated school and emerged tougher and even more resolved to have an audacious life.

Jill Neville was sent by her mother to a business college, where she learned to type. She became an audio typist at the *Daily Mirror* in Sydney, and began to publish poems and stories in small magazines. With her beauty, intelligence, vivacity, humour, and gargantuan appetite for life, at seventeen she was already a star among the more bohemian elements of the Sydney literary world. Drawn to interesting and experienced men, she included among her beaux the cricketer-turned-sportswriter Keith Miller; the painter and roué Norman Lindsay; Max Harris, who wrote on arts and literature in his syndicated column; and the journalist and gossip columnist Murray Sayle. But Neville longed for the romance of London and worked hard as a secretary in a travel agency to earn the money to buy an 'under 21' ticket to England. The journey took more than seven weeks; on board ship she began an affair with the young poet Peter Porter.

After getting a job at the BBC as a typist she soon became a journalist and set up home in a houseboat on the Thames, plunging into Soho artistic life and creating her own salon. Though Neville was Porter's muse, her life was too exciting to allow her affair with him to flourish and he suffered greatly as it hit the rocks. Self-pitying poems such as 'To Jill Neville, cold as night' did not help the relationship, and in 1954 Porter went back to Australia for almost a year to recover. She portrayed him as the neurotic Seth in her first novel, *Fall Girl* (1966), but, like most of her lovers, he remained a lifelong friend. On Neville's houseboat, friends from Australia such as Murray Sayle, along with newcomers including Barry Humphries, met an eclectic bunch of Londoners, acquired at pubs and clubs like the French House and Muriel's, or during parties in garrets and basements. An account of Neville's party to greet her mother when she came to check on her daughter involved a West Indian saxophonist, overwhelmed by drink and marijuana, falling into the Thames. That might have been apocryphal, but there is ample testimony to the occasion when two of her suitors came to blows and she had to rescue them both from the river.

A disastrous marriage in 1960 to the South African poet and broadcaster Peter Duval-Smith (*d.* 1967) produced a daughter. They divorced in 1962. By now Neville was earning well as a copywriter for J. Walter Thompson and other advertising agencies, where she worked with creative people such as Fay Weldon and Assia Wevil. Her deep friendship with Elizabeth Smart, author of *By Grand Central Station I Sat Down and Wept*, proved seminal, for Smart fulfilled the roles of mother and guru, encouraging the talent Neville showed in her stories in *Harpers & Queen* and the *London Magazine*. The crisp and witty Soho-based *Fall Girl*, which dealt with, among other things, her affair with Robert Lowell, attracted comparisons with Anaïs Nin and Jean Rhys and was so successful that she turned freelance writer/journalist and copywriter.

The notoriety of Neville's newly arrived brother Richard with his iconoclastic magazine *Oz* exposed her to a drug-filled hippie world that she found intellectually, morally, and aesthetically repellent; in 1967, the year *The Girl who Played Gooseberry* was published, she moved to Paris. Like many of her circle there, she became caught up in the *évenements* that, along with a stormy affair with Italian anarchist Angelo Quattrocchi, inspired *The Love Germ* (1968), a hilarious chronicle of the progress of a sexual disease through a chain of Parisian revolutionaries.

On 5 November 1970 Neville married the journalist David Paul Leitch, with whom she moved back to London. After she published *The Living Daylights* (1974) they separated and she took their son to Australia, where her struggles as a returned émigré provided the background to *Last Ferry to Manly*. When this was published in 1983, she was back in London, flourishing as a newspaper, radio, and television reviewer, still writing poems and stories, and revelling in her innumerable friends. During the 1980s she presented *Cover to Cover*, a BBC2 book programme. She found great contentment in her partnership with, and later marriage (in 1993) to, her old friend, the biologist Lewis Wolpert (*b.* 1929).

Swimming the Channel (1993), a chronicle of infatuation set in London and Paris, was well received, but Neville's finest novel was her last. Sensual as ever, the fiercely personal *The Day We Cut the Lavender* (1995) drew painfully on the horrors she had experienced as she rescued her daughter from drug addiction. Yet probably her outstanding literary achievement was the contemporaneous brilliant, savage, hilarious play about Robert Graves and Laura Riding, *The Poet and the Goddess, or, Astonished Always*, which simultaneously conveyed her profound understanding of creativity, language, and love and her contempt for the silliness of ungrounded intellectuals; it was never staged commercially.

Jill Neville was strikingly beautiful, tall, with hazel eyes, long auburn hair, and a rangy yet sensual elegance. She died of cancer at her home, 63A Belsize Park Gardens, London, on 11 June 1997 and was cremated at Golders Green crematorium on 17 June.   RUTH DUDLEY EDWARDS

Sources *The Guardian* (13 June 1997) · *The Times* (14 June 1997) · *The Independent* (12 June 1997) · personal knowledge (2004) · private information (2004)
Likenesses C. Ware, two photographs, 1966, Hult. Arch.
Wealth at death £30,696: probate, 21 Oct 1997, *CGPLA Eng. & Wales*

Neville, John (1299/1300–1335). *See under* Neville family (*per. c.*1267–1426).

Neville, John, fifth Baron Neville (*c.*1330–1388), soldier and landowner, was the eldest son of Ralph *Neville, fourth Lord Neville (*c.*1291–1367), and Alice (*c.*1300–1374), daughter of Hugh, Lord Audley, of Stratton Audley in Oxfordshire.

Childhood and military career The date of his birth is uncertain: he was described as between twenty-eight and thirty years of age at his father's death in 1367, but he served in Gascony in 1345 and at Nevilles Cross, under his father, in 1346. It is therefore likely that he was well over thirty when his father died, and he was probably born about

1330. His first marriage was made within the circle of northern noble families into which he had been born: some time before 1364 he married Maud, daughter of Henry *Percy, second Lord Percy of Alnwick. His early career was spent in the service of Edward III and his companions-in-arms, mainly in France. He twice campaigned in Gascony with Henry of Grosmont, earl of Lancaster, in 1345 and 1349. In 1359–60 he served with Edward III on the Rheims campaign, and according to Froissart was knighted after a successful foray up to the walls of Paris. In the mid-1360s, however, he formed the connection with John of Gaunt which was to be of great significance for his future career. He had taken Gaunt's fee since 1366 at the latest, and in 1370 was retained by him for life at a fee of 50 marks a year in time of peace and 500 marks a year in time of war. He contracted to bring a retinue of twenty men at arms and twenty mounted archers to serve his lord in war, increasing to fifty men-at-arms and fifty archers for war in Scotland. He was one of Gaunt's most important retainers, and the retinue which he undertook to contribute to Gaunt's wars was one of the largest of all those for which evidence survives. He accompanied Gaunt and Edward, the Black Prince, on the Spanish expedition of 1367 which culminated in the battle of Nájera. At some point during the campaign, however, he was captured by the Castilians, and Gaunt made a payment towards his ransom. He was made a knight of the Garter in 1369, and had attained the rank of banneret by 1370. He held office as admiral of the north from 30 May 1370 until 6 October 1371.

Failure in Brittany and its aftermath In June 1372 Neville was appointed one of the ambassadors to negotiate an alliance between Edward III and the duke of Brittany, and in the following month he engaged to take a force of 299 men-at-arms and 300 archers to Brittany in fulfilment of the terms of the alliance. The expedition's departure was delayed until October, apparently because of difficulty in assembling ships for transport. Neville was appointed captain of Brest, and he remained there until 1374. The arrival of his expedition provoked the French to invade the duchy and lay siege to Brest. The duke failed to come to its rescue, and on 6 July 1373 Neville agreed to surrender the fortress if it were not relieved within one month. He handed over twelve hostages as guarantors of the agreement. The earl of Salisbury led an expedition to relieve the fortress, but the French declined to give battle and Neville demanded the return of the hostages.

Neville was owed substantial sums by the duke of Brittany at the end of his service there; some of the money was repaid by an annuity assigned on the duke's lands around Richmond in Yorkshire. The duke's indebtedness compelled him to mortgage his Richmond lands to Neville for a sum in excess of 2000 marks, some of which was eventually repaid to Neville by the government of Richard II in 1377 'in consideration of the great impoverishment of the duke' (CPR, 1377–81, 74).

In November 1371, some months before his departure for Brittany, Neville was appointed steward of the royal household. He may have owed his appointment to Gaunt, though the duke of Brittany, as Edward III's son-in-law, also had influence at court. His ties with the court and his involvement in Breton affairs perhaps explain his friendship with William *Latimer, Lord Latimer, who was chamberlain of the household and had served in Brittany in the 1360s. Latimer, like Neville, had estates in north-east England, and although the two were much of an age Neville was to marry his daughter and heir Elizabeth. The marriage took place some time before Latimer's death on 28 May 1381, by which time Elizabeth was twenty-one or perhaps a little older. Under the terms of Latimer's will his feoffees were instructed to enfeoff Neville with the lands they held on Latimer's behalf; Neville was to pay Latimer's feoffees 3000 marks, and he and his heirs were to bear the Latimer arms.

Impeachment of Neville, 1376 Neville's position in the household, his links with Gaunt and Latimer, and his association with military failure in Brittany made him one of the chief objects of the hostility of the Commons in the Good Parliament of April 1376. According to the Anonimalle chronicle, the Commons demanded the dismissal of the king's councillors, and on 26 May Edward III agreed to remove Neville, Latimer, and Alice Perrers, the king's mistress, from his council. On 2 June Neville was deprived of his office as steward. After Latimer was removed from the council, the Commons proceeded to impeach him. According to Walsingham, Neville spoke up in Latimer's defence, saying it was unworthy for so substantial a peer of the realm to be impeached by such people. The speaker of the Commons, Sir Peter de la Mare, ordered Neville to be silent and told him to look to his own fate, for the Commons had yet to deal with him.

Whether Neville's intervention hardened the attitude of the Commons towards him is difficult to judge, but when he in his turn was impeached the charges against him were less serious than those against Latimer. The Commons alleged that he had bought up royal debts and defrauded the creditors, notably Reginald Love, a London merchant, and the executors of 'la dame de Ravensholm' (probably Margaret, widow of Sir John Ravensholm: she had died on 10 September 1375). They also accused Neville of taking to Brittany in 1372 a retinue that was both inexperienced and smaller than he had contracted, and been paid, for. As a result, several fortresses in Brittany had been lost. Neville defended himself vigorously against both charges. Love, who had perhaps been pressurized by Neville's friends at court, withdrew his accusation, but Neville was eventually ordered to make restitution to the Ravensholm executors. As far as the Breton expedition was concerned, Neville told the Commons that he had engaged to take only 100 men. His terms of engagement in 1372 suggested otherwise, and it is possible that Neville had attempted to make a profit for himself out of the contract. However, it is hard to see why he should have deliberately sailed with a seriously under-strength retinue, and the discrepancy may have another, if undiscoverable, explanation. The Commons requested that he should be punished according to his deserts, and Walsingham says that he was ordered to pay a fine of 8000 marks.

Neville's fortunes revive All the penalties imposed by the Good Parliament were set aside in the subsequent parliament which met in January 1377 and in which Gaunt's influence was preponderant. Neville's impeachment had little long-term effect on his career, but he never again held office in the household of either Edward III or Richard II. His years at court, and his connection with Gaunt and Latimer, probably brought him substantial benefits. His marriage to Elizabeth Latimer was followed by his acquisition of most of the Latimer inheritance at his father-in-law's death in 1381. His connection with Gaunt probably lay behind his acquisition in 1379 of the reversion of the barony of Bolbec in Northumberland, which belonged to the wife of another of Gaunt's retainers, Sir Ralph Hastings. Neville already held the neighbouring barony of Bywell, and this transaction enabled him to establish a substantial interest in a county where hitherto the Percy family had been dominant. During his time as steward of the household he acquired the custody of two important Yorkshire inheritances, those of William Everingham and John Mowbray, and he began to acquire lands in Cumberland. His dealings with the duke of Brittany brought him influence in Richmond: in October 1374 the duke had appointed him governor of 'the county of Richmond', and after the confiscation of Richmond from the duke in 1381 Neville was confirmed as governor for life. By this time he was evidently a man of considerable wealth. Not only was he able to provide a mortgage for the duke of Brittany, but in 1372 and 1373 he lent Gaunt money to finance his military expeditions, and in 1386 he lent Richard II 2000 marks. In January 1383 Richard II acknowledged that he owed Neville £7000, some of which may have been payment for his service on the Scottish border. £300 of the debt was assigned on the farm of the earldom of Richmond.

Neville also expressed his wealth and ambition in other ways. On 10 May 1378 Bishop Hatfield granted him licence to crenellate his manor of Raby, and between 1381 and 1388 he undertook the construction of the Neville gateway, on which are displayed the shields of Neville himself, his wife Elizabeth Latimer, and St George and the Garter. He was also responsible for the construction of Clifford's Tower and the extension of Joan's Tower, thus in effect remodelling the west front of the castle. On 26 April 1382 he was licensed to crenellate his castle at Sheriff Hutton, and he probably inaugurated the substantial building programme there, although it was completed only after his death. At Durham Cathedral he contributed '500 pounds or marks' towards the cost of the so-called 'Neville screen', the choir reredos made of Caen stone, which was completed in 1379. It is possibly the work of the royal mason Henry Yevele, whom Neville may have known during his time as steward of the royal household. At about the same time he also paid for a new base 'of marble and alabaster' for the shrine of St Cuthbert, which cost over £200, and he commissioned the tomb in which he is buried and which stands in the south aisle of Durham Cathedral.

All this conspicuous expenditure suggests a determined attempt on Neville's part to elevate his family to the front rank of English nobles. It is entirely in keeping with the rising importance and wealth of the family that, if the Westminster chronicler is to be believed, Richard conferred on him the title earl of Cumberland during the Scottish campaign of 1385. However it has been argued that as a protest against the king's largesse the parliament of October 1385 refused to ratify the grant. Certainly it never took effect, and the family's acquisition of a title did not occur until John Neville's heir, Ralph, was created earl of Westmorland in 1397.

Further military service Although Neville moved away from the court after 1376, he continued to serve the crown in a military capacity. In June 1378, following the capture by the French of Sir Thomas Felton, the seneschal of Gascony, Neville was appointed to succeed him. He engaged to serve with his own retinue of 6 knights, 193 esquires, and 200 archers. Once again Neville's departure was delayed by difficulties in obtaining ships, and he did not sail until September 1378. He remained in Aquitaine until late 1380 or early 1381, and achieved some success in recapturing fortresses from the French, particularly in the Médoc.

After his return to England the rest of his military career was played out on the Scottish border. He had held office as warden of the eastern march between 1368 and 1371, and again after his return from Brittany. In June 1377, shortly after the accession of Richard II, he was appointed keeper of Bamburgh Castle for life. Throughout these years he served as one of the wardens of the marches, generally in the eastern march though sometimes in the western, or in both. He also served on various commissions undertaking negotiations with the Scots. As head of a family with substantial territorial interests in Durham, Northumberland, and Yorkshire such duties were expected of him, and of course his retinues as warden were paid for by the exchequer, but here too his connection with Gaunt was significant. The tension between Gaunt and Henry Percy, earl of Northumberland, following Percy's refusal to allow Gaunt entry into Alnwick Castle during the peasants' revolt probably explains the division of the eastern march into a Neville and a Percy sphere of influence in December 1381 with a 'middle march' consisting mainly of Percy lands being created for the earl of Northumberland. The conflict between Gaunt and Percy was not resolved until the parliament of 1384, and the expedient of creating a middle march for Percy was followed again in August 1383, when Neville was reappointed warden of the eastern march. Neville's increasing importance in the affairs of Northumberland in these years is also evident in his appointment as a justice of the peace there in 1380, 1381, 1382, and 1385. He also served regularly in the same capacity in the North Riding of Yorkshire in these years.

Final years, death, and family Neville brought a retinue of 200 men-at-arms and 300 archers to Richard II's Scottish expedition in 1385: this was a larger retinue than that of any lord except Gaunt, the duke of Gloucester, the earl marshal, and the earl of Northumberland. This, however, was to prove his last major campaign, though he was appointed commander of all forces against the Scots in March 1386. By now he was probably in his mid-fifties, and he did not accompany Gaunt on his expedition to Castile in 1386. Although his brother Alexander *Neville, archbishop of York, moved close to the court in these years and rose high in Richard II's favour, only to be forced into exile and accused of treason by the king's opponents in 1388, Neville himself evidently did not seek to regain the status at court which he had enjoyed a decade earlier. He was appointed to supervise and defend the marches following the English defeat at Otterburn in August 1388, but he took no part in the Anglo-Scottish warfare of that summer. He died at Newcastle on 17 October 1388. He was buried beside his first wife in the tomb that he had commissioned in the 1370s; the tomb remains, somewhat mutilated, in the south aisle of Durham Cathedral, close to the tombs of other members of his family.

With Maud, his first wife, Neville had two sons and at least four daughters. His elder son, Ralph *Neville (c.1364–1425), was created earl of Westmorland in 1397. His younger son, Thomas (b. c.1366), married Joan, daughter and sole heir of William, Lord Furnivall. Joan had died by 1401, and he married as his second wife Ankaret, widow of Sir Richard Talbot of Goodrich, Herefordshire; she died on 14 March 1407. Of his daughters, Elizabeth became a nun; Alice (d. 1433) married William, Lord Deincourt (d. 1381); Matilda married a William Scrope, who was probably not the younger son of Sir Geoffrey Scrope of Masham. Eleanor married Ralph, Lord Lumley (b. c.1361), whose wardship Neville had acquired in 1384: he was executed for his part in the rising against Henry IV in January 1400, but she never remarried and survived into the 1440s. A fifth daughter named Iolande is mentioned by the nineteenth-century historian of the family, though without any supporting evidence. Neville had two children with his second wife, Elizabeth Latimer, later Elizabeth *Willoughby [see under Willoughby family (per. c.1300–1523)]: John (1382–1430) and Elizabeth. After Neville's death she married Robert Willoughby of Eresby (c.1349–1396) and died on 5 November 1395.   ANTHONY TUCK

Sources Accounts Various, PRO, E 101 · inquisition post mortem, PRO, C 136/56 · PRO, Durham 3/2 IPM · BL, Add. MS 32097 · CCC Oxf., MS 495 · Chancery records · RotP, vols. 2–3 · V. H. Galbraith, ed., The Anonimalle chronicle, 1333 to 1381 (1927) · Œuvres de Froissart: chroniques, ed. K. de Lettenhove, 25 vols. (Brussels, 1867–97) · A. Goodman, John of Gaunt: the exercise of princely power in fourteenth-century Europe (1992) · S. Walker, The Lancastrian affinity, 1361–1399 (1990) · J. Sherborne, War, politics and culture in fourteenth-century England, ed. A. Tuck (1994) · G. Holmes, The Good Parliament (1975) · C. R. Young, The making of the Neville family, 1166–1400 (1996) · John of Gaunt's register, ed. S. Armitage-Smith, 2 vols., CS, 3rd ser., 20–21 (1911) · John of Gaunt's register, 1379–1383, ed. E. C. Lodge and R. Somerville, 2 vols., CS, 3rd ser., 56–7 (1937) · N. B. Lewis, ed., 'Indentures of retinue with John of Gaunt, duke of Lancaster, enrolled in chancery, 1367–1399', Camden miscellany, XXII, CS, 4th ser., 1 (1964), 77–112 · Historiae Dunelmensis scriptores tres: Gaufridus de Coldingham, Robertus de Graystanes, et Willielmus de Chambre, ed. J. Raine, SurtS, 9 (1839) · [J. Raine], ed., Testamenta Eboracensia, 6, SurtS, 106 (1902) · RotS · Chronicon Galfridi le Baker de Swynebroke, ed. E. M. Thompson (1889) · M. Jones, Ducal Brittany, 1364–1399 (1970) · M. Hislop, 'The castle of Ralph fourth Baron Neville at Raby', Archaeologia Aeliana, 5th ser., 20 (1992), 91–7 · C. Wilson, 'The Neville screen', Medieval art and architecture of Durham Cathedral, ed. P. Draper and N. Coldstream, British Archaeological Association Conference Transactions [1977], 3 (1980), 90–104 · A. Tuck, 'The Percies and the community of Northumberland in the later fourteenth century', War and border societies in the middle ages, ed. A. Tuck and A. Goodman (1992), 178–95 · H. J. Swallow, De nova villa (1885) · [J. Raine], ed., Wills and inventories, 1, SurtS, 2 (1835), 38–42
Likenesses tomb effigy, Durham Cathedral
Wealth at death see Raine, ed., Wills and inventories; PRO, C 136/56; PRO, Durham 3/2 IPM, fols. 112–13

Neville, John, Marquess Montagu (c.1431–1471), magnate, was the third son of Richard *Neville, fifth earl of Salisbury (1400–1460), and Alice (1406–1462), daughter and heir of Thomas *Montagu, fourth earl of Salisbury.

Early career and Yorkist allegiance Neville was knighted, with his younger brother Thomas and the king's half-brothers, Edmund and Jasper Tudor, by Henry VI at the Tower of London on 5 January 1453, but this association with the royal circle did not last. By the following summer he was a protagonist in the quarrel between the Percys and the Nevilles that was ultimately to ally the Nevilles with Richard, duke of York (d. 1460), in opposition to the crown. The dispute had its origins in the growing power of Thomas Percy, Lord Egremont, the second son of the earl of Northumberland, in the west march. In the summer of 1453 John Neville had gone in search of Percy at Topcliffe, near Thirsk, but had failed to find him. Serious violence seems also to have been avoided in August, when the Percys intercepted the Nevilles at Heworth Moor, on the outskirts of York. It erupted finally on 31 October in the following year when John and Thomas Neville joined battle with Egremont at Stamford Bridge and took him prisoner.

The 'battle' of Stamford Bridge took place during Henry VI's mental collapse and the first protectorate of the duke of York. The protectorate ended with the king's recovery in December 1454, leaving York and those who had been associated with him vulnerable to attack from within the court circle. As events began to slide towards civil war the Nevilles emerged as the duke's leading allies. John Neville fought at the first battle of St Albans (22 May 1455), and it was partly on his advice that Sir William Skipwith lost his offices on the duke's estates for failing to accompany York to battle. John was rewarded with a half share of the forfeited offices. On 25 April 1457 Neville married Isabel, the daughter and coheir of Sir Edmund Ingaldesthorpe (who had died the previous year) and Joan, the sister and eventual heir of John Tiptoft, earl of Worcester. In 1459 he was with his father Salisbury when their forces were intercepted at Blore Heath by supporters of Henry VI. The skirmish was a victory for Salisbury, but Neville ventured too far in pursuit of the losers and was captured, with his brother Thomas and Sir Thomas Harrington. They thus avoided involvement in the rout of the Yorkists at Ludlow, but were attainted at the Coventry parliament along with the rest of York's supporters. They were not released from custody until the summer of 1460, when the exiled Yorkists successfully invaded England and defeated the Lancastrians at the battle of Northampton on 10 July. On 22

August Neville and his wife were restored to their land and his attainder was reversed by parliament in October.

John Neville was not present at the battle of Wakefield on 30 December, at which Salisbury and Thomas Neville, along with York and his son Edmund, earl of Rutland, were killed. He had remained in London with his elder brother Richard *Neville, earl of Warwick. It was probably in the aftermath of the battle, when the Yorkists were seeking to strengthen their representation among the lords, that John became Baron Montagu. He witnessed a council minute as 'J. Montagu' on 28 January 1461. He was with Warwick at the second battle of St Albans on 17 February 1461, and was captured there. Unlike some of his fellow captives he was not executed, but was sent prisoner to York, where he remained until Edward IV's victory at Towton on 28 March clinched the Yorkist possession of England. When Edward IV returned south for his coronation, Neville remained in the north. In June 1461 he raised the Lancastrian–Scottish siege of Carlisle, and in September, with his brother Warwick, gained control of Alnwick.

Yorkist commander in the north Over the next three years John Neville was a central figure in the military operations against the Lancastrian strongholds in the north. He was responsible for the capture of Naworth in July 1462 and of Bamburgh at the end of that year. In July 1463 he and Warwick lifted the siege of Norham. In 1464 what had hitherto been a war of attrition culminated in Yorkist victory in the field under John Neville's leadership. By that time Scotland was considering the advisability of a *rapprochement* with the Yorkist regime and the Neville brothers were given responsibility for the negotiations. On his way to meet the Scottish envoys, John Neville was intercepted on 25 April at Hedgeley Moor, north of Alnwick, by the Lancastrian forces under Henry Beaufort, duke of Somerset. Neville was able to beat off the attack and continued on his way to meet the envoys and conduct them to Newcastle. That done, he went in search of the Lancastrian army and attacked it near Hexham on 15 May. The battle was a complete Yorkist victory. Henry VI's leading northern supporters were either killed in battle or captured and executed soon afterwards.

Neville's service was well rewarded by Edward IV. On 23 May 1461 he received a personal summons to parliament as Lord Montagu, confirming his earlier elevation. On 21 July he was made steward of the duchy of Lancaster lands in Norfolk, Suffolk, and Cambridgeshire. In March 1462 he took his father's stall as a knight of the Garter and in the following May was granted nine manors in Norfolk, Leicestershire, Nottinghamshire, and Lincolnshire. On 26 May 1463 he was made warden of the east march, his brother Warwick holding the west march. A year later, on 27 May 1464, his victory at Hexham was recognized, and his identification with the north confirmed, by his creation as earl of Northumberland. In the following August he was granted all the Percy estates in Northumberland forfeited after Towton, including Alnwick, Warkworth, and Prudhoe. In March 1466 he was granted the duchy of Lancaster honours and castles of Tickhill, Knaresborough, and Pontefract, along with other duchy lands, which were intended to contribute £1000 p.a. towards the money due to him as warden of the east march, for which he had so far received no payment. In July 1466 he was made sheriff of Northumberland for life.

As Warwick grew increasingly disaffected in the late 1460s, John Neville's loyalties remained with the crown, and when Warwick rebelled, with the king's brother George, duke of Clarence, in 1469, Neville took no part in their proceedings. The rising allowed Warwick and Clarence to remove some of Edward's closest associates, and Edward IV himself was captured, but the two men were unable to govern convincingly in the king's name and Edward was back in control by the beginning of October. Warwick's treason, although nominally forgiven by the king, evidently prompted Edward IV to consider installing a counterweight to the Nevilles in the north. On 27 October he released Henry Percy, son and heir of the third earl of Northumberland, from captivity in the Tower. Richard and John Neville and the duke of Clarence had been the main beneficiaries of the Percy forfeiture, and although for a time Percy's release had no sequel, it was obvious that the restoration of his land and title was imminent.

Shift of lands and switch of allegiance Edward's grievance was, however, only against Clarence and Warwick. His continuing regard for John Neville was emphasized by the betrothal of his daughter Elizabeth to Neville's son George, who was made duke of Bedford on 5 January 1470. Edward was also anxious to compensate Neville for the impending loss of his Percy lands. On 22 February 1470 Neville surrendered his share of the Percy estates. Five days later, on 27 February, he was formally granted, for his good service against the Scots and rebels, lands of the earldom of Devon in the south-west, including Tiverton, Plympton, and Okehampton. The final stage of the transfer came on 25 March when Henry Percy was restored to the earldom of Northumberland and its estates, and John Neville was made Marquess Montagu.

The move was to prove a major misjudgement on Edward IV's part, but it should not be interpreted as a thoughtless snub to Montagu. It was, rather, intended to reward his loyalty (and recognize his skill in dealing with opposition) by giving him a major new power base in another disaffected region. The lands given to Montagu had previously been held by Humphrey Stafford, one of the victims of Warwick's rising in 1469, and his death had left a power vacuum in an area where the Yorkists still had relatively little local support. Montagu's new lands and responsibilities amounted to much more than the 'pyes neste' of which he later complained (Warkworth, 10). But his connection with the north had been seriously weakened, as was emphasized on 24 June when he surrendered the wardenship of the east march to Henry Percy.

In the short term Montagu seemed to accept the change. He did not support the rebellion of his brother and Clarence in the spring of 1470 which led to their exile, or, apparently, the flurry of unrest in the north in July and August. But when Warwick and Clarence landed in the south of England with French and Lancastrian backing in September, Montagu declared in their favour. Edward IV, caught unawares by his defection, fled with his supporters to the Low Countries, and Henry VI was restored as king of England.

Montagu was rewarded by the new regime, receiving the wardship of his wife's cousin the young earl of Worcester and of the heir of the last Lord Clifford. But on balance he lost by his action. His own priority was clearly to recover some of his northern influence, but without reversing the restoration of Henry Percy, which was hardly possible given the family's tradition of loyalty to Lancaster, there was a limit to what could be done for him. Montagu regained the wardship of the east march on 22 October and was also confirmed in his possession of Wressle—a former Percy property which the family had not recovered after its forfeiture in the reign of Henry IV, and which had been granted to Montagu in 1465. But the other Percy lands were beyond his reach, and the rehabilitation of the Lancastrian Courtenays threatened his possession of much of the land which he had received in compensation.

Death in battle and children Edward IV returned to England with Burgundian backing in the following spring. He landed in Holderness on 14 March, which brought him close to the Percy sphere of influence, but Northumberland made no move to block his advance. Montagu, who had been given power of array in the north, also took no action, and when Edward passed close to Pontefract, where he was based, 'in no wyse trowbled hym, ne none of his fellowshipe, but sufferyd hym to passe in peaceable wyse' (*Historie of the Arrivall of Edward IV*, 6). The author of the *Arrivall* emphasizes that Montagu was unable to muster local support sufficient to oppose Edward, but he also suggests that Montagu let him pass with good will. However, Montagu subsequently joined his brother at Coventry and fought against Edward at Barnet on 14 April 1471, when both the brothers were killed. After their bodies had been displayed in St Paul's, they were taken for burial at Bisham Priory, Berkshire.

With his wife Montagu had one surviving son, George, and five daughters: Anne, who married Sir William *Stonor [see under Stonor family (per. c.1315–c.1500)]; Elizabeth, the wife of Thomas, Lord Scrope of Masham, and Sir Henry Wentworth; Margaret, the wife of Thomas Horne, Sir John Mortimer, and Charles Brandon, duke of Suffolk; Lucy, the wife of Sir Thomas Fitzwilliam and Sir Anthony Brown; and Isabel, who married William Huddleston. George Neville, who had been created duke of Bedford, was not only his father's heir, but the heir male of Richard Neville, earl of Warwick. Although neither had been attainted, George did not inherit the Neville lands and in 1478 lost his dukedom on the grounds that he could not support the estate. His betrothal to Elizabeth of York was already a dead letter. He died on 4 May 1483.

Isabel Ingaldesthorpe outlived Montagu and married Sir William Norreys, with whom she had a son, William, and two daughters, Alice and Joan. She died on 20 May 1476 and was buried with Montagu at Bisham, where their daughter Elizabeth directed a tomb to be built over them.

ROSEMARY HORROX

Sources *Chancery records* · GEC, *Peerage*, new edn · R. L. Storey, *The end of the house of Lancaster* (1966) · B. P. Wolffe, *Henry VI* (1981) · R. A. Griffiths, *The reign of King Henry VI: the exercise of royal authority, 1422–1461* (1981) · C. L. Scofield, *The life and reign of Edward the Fourth*, 2 vols. (1923) · C. Ross, *Edward IV* (1974) · R. Somerville, *History of the duchy of Lancaster, 1265–1603* (1953) · M. A. Hicks, 'False, fleeting, perjur'd Clarence': George, duke of Clarence, 1449–78 (1980) · J. Warkworth, *A chronicle of the first thirteen years of the reign of King Edward the Fourth*, ed. J. O. Halliwell, CS, old ser., 10 (1839) · J. Bruce, ed., *Historie of the arrivall of Edward IV in England, and the finall recoverye of his kingdoms from Henry VI*, CS, 1 (1838) · CIPM, Henry VII, 1, no. 210 onwards

Neville, John, third Baron Latimer (1493–1543), nobleman, was born on 17 November 1493, the eldest son and heir of Richard *Neville (c.1467–1530), second baron, and Anne, daughter and heir of Sir Humphrey Stafford of Grafton, Worcestershire, and Blatherwyk, Northamptonshire. The poet William *Neville was one of his many younger brothers; William's dealings with a magician in 1532 hint at tensions between John and himself. By 1520 John Neville had married Dorothy, daughter of Sir George de Vere and sister of John de Vere, fourteenth earl of Oxford. Dorothy died on 7 February 1527 and on 20 June 1528 her husband obtained a licence to marry Elizabeth, daughter of Sir Edward Musgrave of Hartley, Westmorland, and Edenhall, Cumberland. Finally, in the summer of 1534 he took as his third wife *Katherine (1512–1548), daughter of Sir Thomas Parr of Kendal, Westmorland, and widow of Sir Edward Borough.

When Henry VIII mounted an invasion of northern France in 1513, Neville joined the expeditionary force, and after the capture of Tournai he was knighted at Lille on 14 October. By 1522 he was acting as his father's spokesman in consultations with the ruling élite of northern England; he served as a JP in the North Riding in 1528–39, the liberty of Ripon in 1538, the West Riding in 1538–41, and the East Riding in 1538–41; in June 1530 he became a member of the king's council of the north. In autumn 1529 he was elected to the Reformation Parliament as one of two knights of the shire for Yorkshire; however, following his father's death in December 1530 and his own succession to the Latimer barony, he became a member of the Lords, first taking his seat on 16 January 1531. Soon afterwards, on 17 March 1531, he obtained livery of his father's lands, although, as late as April 1534, he had still not paid all that was due to the king or various bequests contained in his father's will.

Although he had signed the letter sent to Pope Clement VII in 1530 in favour of Henry VIII's divorce, and may even under the influence of his third wife Katherine have acquired evangelical sympathies, Latimer came under considerable suspicion during the Pilgrimage of Grace. Early in October 1536, as the leading magnate in Mashamshire (where he had his principal residence of Snape Castle), an area prominent in the uprising, and as the archbishop of York's steward at Ripon, he was urged to prevent the spread of unrest but singularly failed to do so. No doubt it was under pressure that he was sworn to the pilgrims, probably on 14 October, but he subsequently acted as a captain of the contingent from the bishopric of Durham and Richmond, and was one of the representatives of the insurgents who put the latter's case to the duke of Norfolk at Doncaster on 27 October. He was similarly among the leaders of the rising when they gathered at York on 21 November and at Pontefract early in December. However, when on the latter occasion he asked Archbishop Lee to preach on 'whether subjects might lawfully move war in any case against their prince' (Dodds and Dodds, 1.377), it was probably in the hope of a sermon that would urge loyalty and so help bring the pilgrimage to a peaceful conclusion. Latimer took no part in Sir Francis Bigod's further insurrection in January 1537, and Norfolk (unsuccessfully) recommended his retention on the council of the north. But Thomas Cromwell not unreasonably harboured doubts about his loyalty, and when Latimer finally went to London in June he was thought to be risking death. Norfolk remained sympathetic, telling Cromwell that Latimer had been 'enforced, and no man was in more danger of his life' (*LP Henry VIII*, vol. 12/2, no. 101), and the latter took the precaution of granting the minister an annuity of £20 and also, perhaps, surrendering his London house to him. By 1538, when he purchased former monastic property at Nun Monkton and elsewhere in Yorkshire, he seems to have convinced the government of his trustworthiness; he attended parliament in 1539, 1540, and 1542; he was appointed steward of Galtres Forest in May 1542; and, later in the year, campaigned against the Scots.

Latimer died in London on 2 March 1543 and was buried in St Paul's Cathedral. In his will, dated 12 September 1542 and proved 15 March 1543, he provided for his wife, family, and servants. His son John inherited the Latimer barony; and, on 12 July 1543, his widow, Katherine, became Henry VIII's sixth wife.

KEITH DOCKRAY

Sources LP Henry VIII · JHL (1846) · [J. Raine], ed., *Testamenta Eboracensia*, 6, SurtS, 106 (1902) · HoP, *Commons, 1509–58*, 3.8–9 · GEC, *Peerage*, 7.482–4 · DNB · R. R. Reid, *The king's council in the north* (1921) · R. B. Smith, *Land and politics in the England of Henry VIII: the West Riding of Yorkshire, 1530–1546* (1970) · M. H. Dodds and R. Dodds, *The Pilgrimage of Grace*, 2 vols. (1915) · A. G. Dickens, *Lollards and protestants in the diocese of York* (1959) · R. W. Hoyle, *The Pilgrimage of Grace and the politics of the 1530s* (2001) · G. R. Elton, *Policy and police: the enforcement of the Reformation in the age of Thomas Cromwell* (1972)

Neville, Jollan de (d. 1246), justice, was the second son of Jollan de Neville of Shorne, Kent, and his wife, Amphelisia of Rolleston (Nottinghamshire). The elder Jollan died in 1207 or 1208; it was probably he, rather than his son, who served as a justice itinerant in Lincolnshire, Derbyshire, Nottinghamshire, and Yorkshire between October 1198 and February 1199. Indeed, there is no certain reference to the younger Jollan before December 1219, when he succeeded his elder brother, John, in their father's estates. These included lands in Lincolnshire and Nottinghamshire which presumably formed part of Amphelisia's inheritance. Jollan de Neville's first involvement in public

affairs took a military form, when in 1230 he went on Henry III's expedition to Brittany. In 1234–5 he served as a justice itinerant in Yorkshire and Northumberland, on the circuit led by William of York. Later in 1235 he was an assessor of that year's aid from knights' fees in Lincolnshire. Engagement in royal business did not prevent Neville's attending to his own affairs. Between 1233 and 1236 he engaged in litigation in defence of the franchises of his manor of Shorne, while in 1238/9 he was sued by both the king and Richard, earl of Cornwall, over the marriage of a ward.

In January 1241 Neville was appointed to inspect the king's castles in Lincolnshire. But he was soon once more employed on judicial business, serving as a justice itinerant under Robert of Lexinton in the west and north of England between April and November 1241. In July it was ordered that he be paid 20 marks for his expenses. In Michaelmas term 1242 he became a justice of the common bench at Westminster, a position he appears to have retained until his death. But he also acted as a justice of assize and gaol delivery in Nottinghamshire and Lincolnshire in 1243, and as a justice itinerant in Middlesex in 1244, and in Norfolk and Suffolk in 1245. A fine records his presence in the bench on 20 January 1246, but he was dead by 5 October following.

In November 1244 Neville paid 20 marks for licence to marry Sarah, widow of John Heriz. He had clearly married before, since his son and heir, another Jollan, was said to have been aged twenty-two and a half at his father's death. The fact that the younger Jollan was said to have been the nephew and heir of John de Beauchamp suggests that his mother was a member of the latter family. He had a younger brother, John, who inherited their father's lands on the death of Jollan junior between 12 November 1249 (when he came to an agreement with his stepmother over her dower) and 12 March 1250. The suggestion that the elder Jollan de Neville gave his name to the collection of exchequer records known by 1298 as the *Testa de Nevill* appears to have been first made in Dugdale's *Baronage of England* (1675). No evidence survives to support it, and in any case Jollan's expertise was judicial rather than financial.

HENRY SUMMERSON

Sources Chancery records [PRO and RC] · Pipe rolls, 2, 10 John · Pipe rolls, 3, 4 Henry III · CIPM, 1, no. 78 · H. C. M. Lyte and others, eds., *Liber feodorum: the book of fees*, 3 vols. (1920–31), 287, 570 · J. Caley and W. Illingworth, eds., *Testa de Nevill, sive, Liber feodorum in curia scaccarii*, RC (1807) [Rec. Comm.] · Curia regis rolls preserved in the Public Record Office (1922–), vol. 10, pp. 15–17 · *Bracton's note book*, ed. F. W. Maitland, 3 vols. (1887), no. 1280 · E. Mason, ed., *The Beauchamp cartulary: charters, 1100–1268*, PRSoc., new ser., 43 (1980), no. 332 · C. W. Foster, ed., *Final concords of the county of Lincoln ... 1244–1272*, Lincoln RS, 17 (1920), 281–2 · W. Dugdale, *The baronage of England*, 2 vols. (1675–6) · D. Crook, *Records of the general eyre*, Public Record Office Handbooks, 20 (1982) · S. K. Mitchell, *Taxation in medieval England* (1951), 79 · I. J. Churchill, R. Griffin, F. W. Hardman, and F. W. Jessup, eds., *Calendar of Kent feet of fines to the end of Henry III's reign*, 5 vols., Kent Archaeological Society Records Branch, 15 (1939–56), 143–4 · C. Roberts, ed., *Excerpta è rotulis finium in Turri Londinensi asservatis, Henrico Tertio rege, AD 1216–1272*, 1, RC, 32 (1835), 426, 464

Wealth at death £20 p.a. from manor of Shorne, Kent: *CIPM*

Neville [*married names* Mowbray, Strangways, Beaumont, Woodville]**, Katherine, duchess of Norfolk** (*c.*1400–1483), noblewoman, was the eldest daughter of Ralph *Neville, of Raby, first earl of Westmorland (*c.*1364–1425), and Joan *Beaufort (1379?–1440), illegitimate daughter of *John of Gaunt, duke of Lancaster (1340–1399), and Katherine Swynford (1350?–1403) [*see* Katherine, duchess of Lancaster].

Katherine Neville is first recorded on 12 January 1412, when she was married in Raby Castle to John (V) *Mowbray (1392–1432), the younger son and heir of the disgraced Thomas (I) *Mowbray, first duke of Norfolk (*d.* 1399), for whose wardship and marriage her father had in 1411 paid the enormous sum of 3000 marks. On 12 September 1415 she gave birth to their only known child, John (VI) *Mowbray, at Epworth on the Isle of Axholme, Lincolnshire. In these early years of marriage Katherine was often alone while Earl John served abroad. In March 1420 she travelled to France to join the household of Henry V's new queen, Catherine de Valois, and returned with the king and queen, but without her husband, in February 1421. Since the earl remained abroad Katherine rejoined him later that year. In May 1423 she was with Mowbray at Sandwich when he embarked on the first expedition of Henry VI's minority, and then returned to Epworth where she had probably spent most of her married life. There are only occasional glimpses of her active in administering Mowbray property during these years, but as the three surviving Mowbray receiver-general's accounts all cover years when the earl was absent for all or most of the year, and as his receiver-general travelled regularly to Epworth, it must be presumed that she was largely responsible for overseeing the estates between 1415 and 1423.

In July 1425, with Mowbray's restoration to the dukedom of Norfolk, Katherine became able to enjoy the dignity of duchess. Almost nothing is recorded of her during the last seven years of the marriage. In his first will, of 12 May 1429, the duke left Katherine all his property in Axholme, but in his nuncupative will made on the day of his death, 19 October 1432, he left her, in addition to valuables, a life interest in Mowbray lands in the Isle of Axholme, Yorkshire, Sussex, and the Gower peninsula in south Wales, and appointed her as chief executor. She is not known to have received a jointure at the time of her marriage, but what the duke had left, together with her common-law dower, she carried to Sir Thomas Strangways, a knight who had been in Mowbray's service at least since 1414. Katherine appears, from her accounts, to have been single at Michaelmas 1440. Her second marriage is first mentioned on 27 January 1442, when the couple were fined for not securing the necessary royal licence for their union. Either the marriage had remained secret for some time, or at least one of their two daughters, Katherine and Joan, was born out of wedlock for, by 25 August 1443, Thomas was dead and Katherine was married to John *Beaumont, first Viscount Beaumont (1409?–1460). No children were born to the couple and there is insufficient

evidence to determine whether or not they were particularly close. Beaumont certainly benefited from Katherine's huge Mowbray landholding and resided at times at Epworth, where he made his last will. He was killed at the battle of Northampton, on 10 July 1460.

By far the most remarkable marriage of the middle ages in terms of the relative ages of the couple was that which occurred, some time after 1465, between the aged Katherine and Sir John Woodville, a youth of less than twenty, the brother of *Edward IV's new queen, *Elizabeth Woodville. Dubbed 'a diabolical marriage' (*maritagium diabolicum*) by William Worcester (Stevenson, 2.783)—not surprisingly, as he mistakenly believed the bride to be eighty—this is a match that demands yet defies explanation. Historians have variously speculated that the duchess was forced, or that she had taken a fancy to the boy, but both theories are equally wanting in proof. It is true that the impoverished Sir John would enjoy her Mowbray and Beaumont dower lands for her lifetime, but he could hardly have hoped to do so for long. If he did, he was sadly mistaken, for he was executed on 12 August 1469, following the battle of Edgcote.

Born at a time when the Nevilles were Lancastrians, but subsequently married to the Lancastrian Beaumont as her closest Neville relatives turned Yorkist, Katherine Neville's loyalties may have been regarded with suspicion. In February 1470 a commission was set up to hear her complaint that, following the attainder of her stepson, William, Viscount Beaumont, she had been expelled from three Beaumont manors which she held for life. These she seems to have recovered. Neither her whereabouts nor her activities during the readeption of Henry VI are recorded, but in 1473 she received a general pardon from Edward IV for any offences committed before 30 September 1471. Of her later years nothing is known, and Katherine was last recorded alive in the summer of 1483 at the coronation of Richard III. By then her longevity had deprived both her Mowbray son and grandson of the bulk of their lands, and following the death of her great-granddaughter, Anne Mowbray, in 1481, she survived to deprive the Howards and the Berkeleys of their shares of these lands as coheirs. For all her longevity and her royal connections Katherine remains a shadowy figure. It seems that neither politically nor socially was she particularly active. Much of her time was taken up by administration of land, especially during her successive widowhoods, but, although she became very wealthy, with an annual income by 1470 which can seldom have been less than £1300, there is no evidence that she became a great patron or lived particularly lavishly. She had probably spent most of her life in Epworth and it was probably there that she died and was buried in the late summer of 1483.

ROWENA E. ARCHER

Sources *Chancery records* · PRO · BL, Add. MSS · BL, MS Harley 433 · Arundel Castle archives, West Sussex · Berkeley Castle, Gloucestershire, Berkeley Castle MSS · J. R. Lander, *Crown and nobility, 1450–1509* (1976) · C. Ross, *Edward IV* (1974) · E. F. Jacob, ed., *The register of Henry Chichele, archbishop of Canterbury, 1414–1443*, 4 vols., CYS, 42, 45–7 (1937–47) · J. Stevenson, ed., *Letters and papers illustrative of* *the wars of the English in France during the reign of Henry VI, king of England*, 2 vols. in 3 pts, Rolls Series, 22 (1861–4) • T. B. Pugh and C. D. Ross, 'The English baronage and the income tax of 1436', *BIHR*, 26 (1953), 1–28

Wealth at death approx. £1300 p.a., comprising her dower lands: *Chancery records*; Berkeley Castle MSS; Arundel Castle MSS

Neville, Margaret de (*d.* 1319). *See under* Neville family (*per. c.*1267–1426).

Neville, Ralph de (*d.* 1244), administrator and bishop of Chichester, was of unknown parentage and illegitimate in the eyes of the church; however, both Geoffrey de Neville (*d.* 1225), John's chamberlain, and Hugh de Neville (*d.* 1234), chief forester under Henry III, claimed kinship with him. Nothing is known of his education, though he was occasionally called 'master' by people wanting his favour, and Neville certainly favoured education, maintaining a lecturer in theology in his cathedral and supporting at least three students in the schools of Lincoln, Oxford, and Douai. It was not learning, however, but royal service upon which he based his career. He was employed by King John as a clerk of the household as early as March or April 1207, and on 29 December of that year he deposited royal treasure in Marlborough Castle. The royal records of the next four years are very scanty and Neville does not again appear until 4 January 1213. Then on 22 December 1213 at Windsor he received custody of the king's great seal to use under the supervision of the bishop of Winchester. Thus began a lifelong career in the royal chancery.

After sealing documents in England during the winter of 1213–14, in March 1214 Neville accompanied the king to France and there acted as vice-chancellor, though without the title. When the king returned to England in October, Neville's special assignment ended, but he continued to be employed by John at least until 19 May 1216. His whereabouts during the civil war are unknown, but he was at court in May 1218, and as soon as a new great seal was struck for the young Henry III and put into operation on 6 November, it was handed over to his keeping. Neville was not chancellor, that title being retained by Richard Marsh, bishop of Durham (*d.* 1226). But Marsh rarely came south, and the care of the chancery was clearly in Neville's hands. He preserved many of the letters he received, and they show how he retained the respect of all the magnates who were competing for power in the minority, as well as of the foreign powers who petitioned for his favour. Under him the chancery functioned well: the rolls of letters patent, letters close, and fines continued to record the writs authorized by king or councillors. In 1226 the liberate rolls were split from the letters close for administrative convenience, and in 1227 the charter rolls were revived. Writs originating judicial business were issued by the chancellor's own authority and were not enrolled. These writs *de cursu* tested the chancellor's sense of equity, but according to the St Albans chronicler Neville was fair and even-handed in their issuance. A register of the writs used in his time still survives. He had a clerk at the exchequer as well as one at the bench, so that he was intimately informed of the work of these powerful institutions. He himself sometimes sat with the justices or the

barons of the exchequer, and played an important part in the appointment of justices on eyre, general and special. He also continued to perform a wide variety of other tasks for the king, culminating in the regency of England in 1230, when both king and justiciar went to France.

For his services Ralph was well rewarded with ecclesiastical preferment. On 11 April 1214, while he was with King John in France, he was made dean of Lichfield. Over the next two years he was further presented by the king to the churches of Ludgershall (Wiltshire), Stretton (Shropshire), Ingham and Morningthorpe (Norfolk), Hambleden (Buckinghamshire), and Penrith (Cumberland). He was also made a canon of London and of Lincoln. Then on 28 October 1222 he was presented to the chancellorship of Chichester Cathedral, but on that same day he was elected bishop there. The royal assent was given on 1 November, and Neville received the temporalities on 3 November, but it was not until 21 April 1224 that Archbishop Stephen Langton (*d.* 1228) consecrated him, along with the newly elected bishops of Exeter and Carlisle, all in St Katherine's Chapel at Westminster. He was given hopes of even higher promotion when he was postulated by the monks of Canterbury to be their archbishop on 22 September 1231. The king gave his assent, but early in 1232 the election was quashed by the pope, acting on the advice of Simon Langton (*d.* 1248), who is reported to have described Neville as a courtier and hall clerk, unlearned and unworthy of such high office, swift of speech and bold of action, having his spirit in his nostrils, and, most damning of all, desirous of freeing England from its subjection to the Roman church.

Neville was disappointed again in 1238, when the monks of Winchester postulated him to be their bishop on or about 28 August 1238, but the king refused his assent and secured papal disapproval in 1239. In church affairs Neville showed himself cognizant of the prevailing reform movement. He had obtained papal dispensations to hold plural benefices, and to be promoted to episcopal rank despite his illegitimacy. As dean of Lichfield he had felt obliged to reform the morals of his chapter. In 1231, Matthew Paris reports, Neville refused to pay the expenses of the monks who carried his name to Rome lest he be charged with simony. In 1238 he sought the support of Robert Grosseteste (*d.* 1253), the highly respected bishop of Lincoln, in his efforts to obtain the see of Winchester, but Grosseteste refused, on the grounds that such a pursuit of office would cause Neville to appear ambitious. While his duties at court may have kept him away from his diocese, Neville employed an excellent seneschal to attend to the temporalities of the see and he appointed an official (three are known) to see to the spiritualities. He and his chapter appear to have co-existed harmoniously, and he reclaimed the treasurership from the Romans in order to give it to his brother. Outside his diocese he attempted in 1238 to settle the great quarrel between the archbishop and the monks of Canterbury, but he never went to Rome, and had papal commissions on only three occasions.

Neville's career at the chancery was not without its vicissitudes. After the death of the bishop of Durham on 1 May 1226, but before 17 May, he was promoted to be chancellor and thus to receive the considerable emoluments of the office. Soon after Henry III declared his majority in January, Neville received a grant by charter, dated 12 February 1227, of the chancellorship for life. This grant was renewed on 16 November 1228. On 14 June 1232 it was once again renewed and he was further granted the right of custody of the king's seal for life by himself or by deputy appointed by him. On 4 May 1233 his charters were again renewed, and a grant was added of the chancellorship of Ireland, also for life. Thus he strengthened his hold on the chancery at the very time that the justiciar, Hubert de Burgh (d. 1243), and the treasurer, Walter Manclerk (d. 1248), were dismissed in disgrace. Presumably he had the grace of the bishop of Winchester whom he had served in 1213 and who was the king's principal counsellor from 1232 to 1234. Neville showed himself adept at negotiating the political shoals of the mid-1230s. In 1236, however, Matthew Paris records that the king tried to remove the seal from Ralph's authority during a remodelling of royal government and that Ralph refused to surrender it, claiming to have received it by assent of the community of the realm. Some doubt has been cast on Paris's account, and he is the only chronicler to report this episode. But it is certain that two years later, when Neville was postulated to the bishopric of Winchester against the king's will, Henry did indeed force him to give up the seal at Winchester, on 28 August 1238, though he was allowed to keep the title of chancellor and to retain the revenues of office. In 1239 he is said to have been offered the custody of the seal again but declined to take up the burden. Only in May 1242, when Henry was going to France, did Neville accept some responsibility for the seal used by the regent. After Henry returned to England in September 1243, Neville gave some few charters with the great seal, but it was for a very short time, since he died between 1 and 4 February 1244.

Ralph de Neville died in the splendid London palace he had built on the New Street known ever since as Chancery Lane because of its location there. Clearly he had become a very wealthy man. He had other 'inns' at Eton and Winchester to house himself and his clerks when the court travelled there. He had obtained important gifts from the king and other men for himself and his church. His correspondence and the rolls of the bench show how carefully he attended to his estate. Often an executor of wills himself, he obtained from the king a grant of free administration of his own will, including the grain of the current year. Some few provisions of his will are known: he left two rings to the king, the gems from which the king used to decorate his great new shrine for St Edward at Westminster; he left a custody to the canons of Tortington near Arundel; he bequeathed the lands he had bought, including his London palace, to his successors as bishops of Chichester; while to the dean and chapter of Chichester he left a London house, his chapel furniture, and many ornaments as well as a large sum of money for the fabric. For the poor of the city of Chichester he endowed an annual distribution of bread which continued until the twentieth century. His body was buried behind the high altar of his cathedral, where he had established a chantry for his soul. He had previously founded a chantry for his first lord and benefactor, King John. No wonder that Neville was memorialized by Matthew Paris as a pillar of stability, fidelity, and truth. FRED A. CAZEL, JR.

Sources C. R. Young, 'Ralph de Neville, chancellor', *The making of the Neville family in England, 1166–1400* (1996), 64–81 · J. Boussard, 'Ralph Neville, évêque de Chichester et chancelier d'Angleterre', *Revue Historique*, 176 (1935), 217–33 · D. A. Carpenter, 'Chancellor Ralph de Neville and plans of political reform, 1215–1258', *Thirteenth century England: proceedings of the Newcastle upon Tyne conference* [Newcastle upon Tyne 1987], ed. P. R. Coss and S. D. Lloyd, 2 (1988), 69–80 · W. D. Peckham, ed., *The chartulary of the high church of Chichester*, Sussex RS, 46 (1946) · *Paris, Chron.* · *Ann. mon.* · H. R. Luard, ed., *Flores historiarum*, 3 vols., Rolls Series, 95 (1890) · *Chancery records* · *Curia regis rolls preserved in the Public Record Office* (1922–) · ancient correspondence, PRO, SC 1 · PRO, ancient deeds · PRO, fine rolls, C 60 · PRO, household accounts, E 101 · Bodl. Oxf. · CUL · *The historical works of Gervase of Canterbury*, ed. W. Stubbs, 2 vols., Rolls Series, 73 (1879–80) · *Roberti Grosseteste episcopi quondam Lincolniensis epistolae*, ed. H. R. Luard, Rolls Series, 25 (1861) · R. C. Stacey, *Politics, policy and finance under Henry III, 1216–1245* (1987) · *Fasti Angl.* (Hardy)

Archives PRO, SC 1

Wealth at death £140 value of residue of estate: PRO, chancery records; Peckham, ed., *Chartulary*

Neville, Ralph, fourth Lord Neville (*c.*1291–1367), soldier and administrator, was the second son of Ranulph, third Lord Neville, and Euphemia, daughter of Robert fitz Roger of Clavering, Essex, and Warkworth, Northumberland. At his father's death in 1331 he was stated to be aged forty years and more, so he was probably born *c.*1291. Little is known of his early life. His father served both Edward I and Edward II in Scotland, but Ralph Neville first comes to notice in 1318 when he was on military service in Scotland. In the following year he took part in the unsuccessful campaign to regain Berwick, which had been taken by the Scots in 1318. In an incident near the town on 6 June, according to the Bridlington annalist, the Scots killed his elder brother, Robert, known as 'the Peacock of the North', and captured him and his younger brothers Alexander and John. The annalist's date may be wrong, for the main body of English troops did not arrive at Berwick until September. On the other hand the incident may have been a skirmish unrelated to the main campaign. The Scots demanded a ransom of 2000 marks for Ralph, and he petitioned the king for help towards its payment, saying that his father had been impoverished by the ransoms for his sons. There is no evidence that Edward II made any contribution towards the ransoms. As a result of his brother's death Ralph Neville became his father's heir, and he was evidently free by 1321 when he was a retainer of Thomas, earl of Lancaster, and a signatory to the Sherburn indenture. However, he survived the destruction of the Lancastrian interest after the battle of Boroughbridge in 1322 and Edward II made use of his services on the northern border. He was keeper of Warkworth Castle by 1322, and in 1325 he was appointed one of the commissioners to maintain the truce with the Scots.

Neville's commitment to the regime of Edward II, however, was less than wholehearted. Froissart records that Henry, Lord Percy of Alnwick, and 'Li sires de Noefville' joined Isabella and Mortimer when they invaded England in September 1326. The reference is probably to Ralph and his brothers: their father was perhaps too old at sixty-four for involvement in political adventures. After the deposition of Edward II the new regime continued to make use of Neville's services on the northern border, and he became one of Percy's retainers in 1328. His ability to judge which way the political wind was blowing was again demonstrated when he supported Edward III's coup against Mortimer and Isabella in October 1330. John Neville of Hornby, who was probably a relation of the Nevilles of Raby, took part in the seizure of Mortimer and Isabella at Nottingham Castle on 19 October and slew the steward of the royal household, Hugh Turplington. Six days later, on 25 October, Ralph Neville was appointed steward of the household in Turplington's place. Neville formed part of the group of nobles who were influential at Edward III's court in the 1330s, but he maintained his links with the Percys and in January 1332 his indenture with Percy was renewed: he agreed to serve him in peace and war for life with twenty men-at-arms, and was granted tenure for life of the Percy manor of Newburn, Northumberland.

In the following year Neville became involved in the English intervention in Scotland to support the regime of Edward Balliol, who had had himself crowned king at Scone in September 1332, but had been driven out three months later. In February 1333 Neville received a gift from the king of 800 marks out of the lay subsidy; other nobles were similarly rewarded, and the probable intention was to cover the costs they expected to incur in the forthcoming campaign in Scotland. In March 1333 Neville, together with Montagu, Arundel, and Lancaster, joined Edward Balliol's march through Roxburghshire to besiege Berwick. The Anonimalle chronicle suggests that they abandoned the siege, but it is more probable that they remained there until Edward III's forces arrived before the town in early May. It is not clear whether Neville took part in the battle of Halidon Hill on 19 July 1333, after which Berwick surrendered to Edward III. Edward subsequently sent him as an envoy to Balliol's parliaments at Scone (October 1333) and Edinburgh (February 1334) with instructions to persuade Balliol to implement the Roxburgh agreement of November 1332 under which Balliol had agreed to do homage to Edward III for the kingdom of Scotland and hand over to him 2000 librates of land in southern Scotland.

Edward III now undertook a series of campaigns to restore Balliol and defend the lands ceded to England. Neville and Henry Percy were appointed wardens of the marches and of the king's lands in Scotland in August 1334, and on 29 August 1335 he was granted the custody of Bamburgh Castle for life. He was promoted to the rank of banneret by the autumn of 1334, and he brought a retinue of sixty men-at-arms and forty mounted archers to the campaign of November 1334–February 1335 in Scotland. He served again on the campaign of June–September 1335 with a retinue of eighty-five men-at-arms.

According to Robert de Graystanes, Neville was 'great with the king' in these years (Raine, *Scriptores tres*, 110), and he received appropriate rewards for his service. In 1333 Edward appointed him keeper of the temporalities of the bishopric of Durham during the vacancy following the death of Bishop Louis Beaumont, and he may have been influential in obtaining a grant of the archdeaconry of Durham for his younger brother Thomas in March 1334. In 1336 he was granted the reversion of the barony of Bywell in Northumberland, thus beginning the development of a substantial Neville territorial interest in south Northumberland [see Neville, John, fifth Baron Neville]. He may have hoped to obtain the reversion of the barony and castle of Warkworth after the death of his maternal uncle John fitz Robert of Clavering, but in 1328 Edward III had granted it to Henry Percy of Alnwick. Although Neville and Percy evidently enjoyed good relations and worked together on the king's business in Scotland and the marches, the grants made in Northumberland by Edward III in the opening years of his reign perhaps sowed the seeds of later rivalry between the two families.

Neville's service to the king was not, however, limited to the north and Scotland. Although he ceased to hold office as steward of the household on 24 March 1336, he retained his links with the court, and served on the councils of regency set up in July 1338 and again in June 1340 to govern during Edward III's absences in the Low Countries. Neville and Henry Percy of Alnwick had particular responsibility for the defence of the northern border in these years as 'Chieftains of the king', and Neville took part in the campaigns of 1338 and 1339 in Scotland. He was granted various lands in Berwickshire and Roxburghshire, although he can have held them only with difficulty.

The climax of Neville's military career came in 1346, when he was one of the commanders of the English army which defeated and captured David II at the battle of Nevilles Cross on 17 October. According to the Lanercost chronicler, Neville, whom the chronicler describes as a powerful man, brave, cunning, and much to be feared, fought so fiercely that his enemies bore the imprint of his blows after the battle. The chronicler goes on to describe how Neville and Gilbert Umfraville, earl of Angus, invaded Scotland after the battle and reimposed English authority over the lands between the border and the Firth of Forth. The tradition that he erected Nevilles Cross on the Brancepeth Road west of Durham city to commemorate the battle is probably baseless. The Anonimalle chronicle implies that the place of the battle was already called 'la Nevyle Croice' (*Anonimalle Chronicle*), though a contemporary letter giving an account of the battle merely states that it took place between Durham city 'and a certain hill called Fyndonne' (Raine, *Scriptores tres*, 435).

With David II a prisoner in England the threat from Scotland diminished, but Neville continued to serve Edward III as warden of the marches and, in 1355, as governor of Berwick. Froissart suggests that he took part in the sea battle off Winchelsea against the Castilians in August 1350, but otherwise the last years of his life seem to have been uneventful. At the time of the battle of Nevilles Cross he had probably been fifty-five years old, and in the 1350s his mind turned to spiritual matters. In 1355 he gave the church of Durham a vestment of red velvet embroidered with images of the saints, which he had received from the executors of Bishop Richard Bury as security for a debt of £100. At the same time, according to William de Chambre, he asked the prior and convent of Durham to allow him and his wife, Alice (c.1300–1374), daughter of Hugh, Lord Audley, whom he had married in January 1327, to be buried in the nave of the cathedral. His benefactions to the church and his fame as one of the victors of Nevilles Cross, a battle won under the auspices of the relics of St Cuthbert, no doubt helped persuade the prior and convent to grant permission, the first time a layman had been accorded such an honour. He died on 5 August 1367, and was duly buried at the east end of the nave of the cathedral, where a chantry was founded for his soul in the following year. Alice died on 12 January 1374. Neville had served with distinction in Edward III's wars and by his service he had brought his family to the forefront of the northern nobility.

Neville's plans for his children provide further evidence of his ambition. His wife, Alice, had previously been married to Ralph, Lord Greystoke, who had died at the age of twenty-three in 1323. Her son from this marriage, William, Lord Greystoke (1321–1359), who had been Neville's ward, remained childless for many years, and Ralph Neville as his stepfather sought to have the Greystoke lands entailed on his younger sons, on condition that they took the surname and arms of Greystoke. But in 1353 William's second wife gave birth to a son, and thus the scheme to transfer the Greystoke inheritance to the Neville cadets proved fruitless. Alice and Neville had five sons: John *Neville, the eldest; Alexander *Neville, archbishop of York from 1374 to 1388; Ralph, Robert, and William *Neville, on whom the Greystoke lands were to have been entailed. They also had four daughters, whose marriages demonstrate Neville's concern to establish links with other leading families in northern England: Euphemia (d. 1393) married first Robert, Lord Clifford, second Reginald, Lord Lucy, and third Sir Walter Heselarton; Margaret (d. 1372) married first William, Lord Ros of Helmsley (d. 1352), and second, in 1358, Henry Percy, first earl of Northumberland (d. 1408); Catherine (d. 1361) married William, Lord Dacre of Gilsland; Eleanor, however, became a minoress in the convent of the Poor Clares at Aldgate in London. ANTHONY TUCK

Sources Chancery records • 'Durham records: calendar of the cursitor's records', Report of the Deputy Keeper of the Public Records, 31 (1870), appx 2, pp. 42–168; 32 (1871), appx 3, pp. 264–330 • RotS, vol. 1 • CDS, vols. 2–3, 5 • RotP, vol. 2 • J. Stevenson, ed., Chronicon de Lanercost, 1201–1346, Bannatyne Club, 65 (1839) • Scalacronica, by Sir Thomas Gray of Heton, knight: a chronical of England and Scotland from AD MLXVI to AD MCCCLXII, ed. J. Stevenson, Maitland Club, 40 (1836) • W. R. Childs and J. Taylor, eds., The Anonimalle Chronicle, 1307 to 1334: from Brotherton collection MS 29, Yorkshire Archaeological Society, 147 (1991) • V. H. Galbraith, ed., The Anonimalle chronicle, 1333 to 1381 (1927); repr. with corrections (1970) • Historiae Dunelmensis scriptores tres: Gaufridus de Coldingham, Robertus de Graystanes, et Willielmus de Chambre, ed. J. Raine, SurtS, 9 (1839) • [J. Raine], ed., Wills and inventories, 1, SurtS, 2 (1835) • Œuvres de Froissart: chroniques, ed. K. de Lettenhove, 25 vols. (Brussels, 1867–77) • Chronicon Galfridi le Baker de Swynebroke, ed. E. M. Thompson (1889) • M. Jones and S. Walker, eds., 'Private indentures for life service in peace and war, 1278–1476', Camden miscellany, XXXII, CS, 5th ser., 3 (1994), 1–190 • J. C. Hodgson, A history of Northumberland, 6 (1902) • G. L. Harriss, King, parliament and public finance in medieval England to 1369 (1975) • J. R. Maddicott, Thomas of Lancaster, 1307–1322: a study in the reign of Edward II (1970) • R. Nicholson, Edward III and the Scots: the formative years of a military career, 1327–1335 (1965) • Tout, Admin. hist. • W. Stubbs, ed., Chronicles of the reigns of Edward I and Edward II, 2 vols., Rolls Series, 76 (1882–3) [incl. Bridlington annals] • CPR, 1324–7 • C. R. Young, The making of the Neville family, 1166–1400 (1996)
Archives PRO • PRO, records of palatinate of Durham
Likenesses alabaster effigy (Ralph Neville?), Durham Cathedral

Neville, Ralph, first earl of Westmorland (c.1364–1425), magnate, was the eldest son of John *Neville, fifth Baron Neville (c.1330–1388), and Maud (d. 1378/9), daughter of Henry, second Lord Percy of Alnwick.

Early career At his father's death in 1388 Ralph Neville was described as aged twenty-four years and more, so he was probably born about 1364. He was only sixteen when he took part in his first military expedition, accompanying Thomas of Woodstock, earl of Buckingham (d. 1397), to Brittany in 1380: according to Froissart he was knighted along with seven others at St Omer. Like his father and grandfather, however, he played out his military career chiefly on the northern border. In October 1385 he was appointed governor of Carlisle Castle jointly with Thomas, son of Lord Clifford; in March 1386 he became warden of the west march at the same time as his father was appointed warden of the east march, and in 1389, following his father's death in the previous year, his appointment as warden of the west march was renewed. In 1393–4 he took part in the negotiations for peace with the Scots that followed the negotiations held at Leulinghem in the early 1390s for a final settlement with France. He also held office as justice of the peace in the North and West ridings of Yorkshire in these years. He may have contemplated joining Richard II on his Irish expedition in 1394–5, for he appointed attorneys in November to administer his affairs while he was with the king in Ireland, but there is no other evidence that he went there.

By the 1390s the Neville family had become as powerful and important in the north as the Percys, but although Richard II had created Henry, Lord Percy of Alnwick, earl of Northumberland in 1377, the Nevilles had remained without a title, though of course they had been summoned to parliament as barons of Raby since 1295. Ralph Neville's father and grandfather had had close links with the court and both had served for a time as steward of the household of Edward III. His uncle Alexander Neville, archbishop of York, had been one of Richard's favourites and had fled into exile at the end of 1387, only to be tried for treason in his absence in the Merciless Parliament of February 1388. Ralph Neville in his turn became prominent at court in the 1390s: he was retained as a king's knight by Richard II in May 1395 at a fee of £130 p.a., and over the following two years his standing greatly increased. Perhaps Richard II saw in the Nevilles a potential counterweight to the Percys in the north; perhaps, too, the family's traditional links with the house of Lancaster stood Ralph in good stead. His father had been a retainer of John of Gaunt, duke of Lancaster, from at least 1366 until his death, and although Gaunt did not retain Ralph during his father's lifetime he was in receipt of Gaunt's fee by 1397, and was one of the executors of his will. His first wife, Margaret, daughter of Hugh *Stafford, second earl of Stafford, and Philippa, daughter of Thomas Beauchamp, earl of Warwick, died on 9 June 1396, and within a few months (certainly by 29 November 1396) he had married Joan *Beaufort (1379?–1440), widow of Sir Robert Ferrers and legitimized daughter of *John of Gaunt and his mistress, Katherine Swynford [see Katherine, duchess of Lancaster]. This marriage was a measure of the standing Neville now enjoyed at court and his close relationship with John of Gaunt: it was to have major consequences both for the Neville family and for the English nobility more generally in the mid-fifteenth century.

Neville's influence at court enabled him to pursue the family's interest in the honour of Richmond and other English lands of the dukes of Brittany, which his father had developed in the 1370s and early 1380s. In 1390 Henry Fitzhugh (d. 1425) had been granted a twelve-year lease on Richmond by the queen's feoffees; in 1395 the reversion of the lease was granted to Neville, and within a few months Fitzhugh had surrendered his interest in the honour to Neville. In November 1396 Richard granted him and his wife jointly for life another part of the Brittany lands, the manor of Penrith and Sowerby; eleven months later the grant was converted into one in tail male. There seems little doubt that Neville's marriage to Joan opened up extensive resources of patronage for him, and in view of later disputes about the descent of his inheritance it is significant that many of the grants he received at this time were made jointly to him and his wife. On the other hand, Neville had little influence on the Scottish border at this time. Between 1390 and 1396 the Percys monopolized the wardenships of the marches, and only with his temporary acquisition of the lordship of Wark-on-Tweed in February 1397 did he acquire a foothold in the eastern march.

The earl's political role, 1397–1399 In the political upheaval of September 1397 Neville remained loyal to Richard II. His importance to the king and Gaunt was demonstrated at the trial for treason of the earl of Arundel in the parliament of September 1397. According to both Walsingham and Adam Usk, Gaunt, who presided over the trial as high steward of England, ordered Neville to remove Arundel's belt and scarlet hood; Walsingham also suggests that Neville had custody of the earl of Warwick while he awaited trial on charges of treason in the same parliament.

Neville was rewarded for his loyalty by being created earl of Westmorland on 29 September 1397, and on the following day he joined other nobles in taking the oath to uphold the work of the parliament. Westmorland's attachment to Richard did not, however, survive Henry Bolingbroke's invasion of England in July 1399: his links with the house of Lancaster proved more durable than those with Richard II. When Gaunt died in February 1399 his son Henry was in exile, and Richard assumed control of the Lancastrian inheritance. He confirmed an annuity of 500 marks granted by Gaunt to Westmorland and his wife, but did so on the understanding that Westmorland was 'retained to stay with the king only' (CPR, 1396–9, 548), a restriction which Richard insisted on when confirming other Lancastrian annuities at this time. This annuity, which was assigned mainly on duchy of Lancaster lands in Yorkshire, replaced one of 400 marks granted to Joan Beaufort and her first husband. Perhaps of more importance in determining Westmorland's allegiance in 1399 was Richard's restoration of the Richmond lands to the duke of Brittany's sister in December 1398, though the

Ralph Neville, first earl of Westmorland (c.1364–1425), tomb effigy [with one of his wives]

duke himself seems to have assumed that they had been returned to him.

This action, together with the injustice of the sequestration of the Lancastrian inheritance and the king's appointment of courtiers with little interest in the region to positions of authority on the northern border, probably inclined Westmorland to throw in his lot with Bolingbroke, his brother-in-law, in 1399. According to Adam Usk, Westmorland, together with the earl of Northumberland, joined Henry at Doncaster within a few days of Henry's landing at Ravenspur, probably at the beginning of July. The two earls marched south with Henry, but Westmorland evidently did not join Northumberland in the journey to meet Richard at Conwy and persuade him to leave the castle and come, virtually as a prisoner, to meet Henry at Flint. Westmorland appears to have remained at Chester during this time, but on 20 August he and Northumberland set out with Henry and Richard for London, where Richard was lodged in the Tower. On 28 and 29 September Westmorland and Northumberland represented the earls in the delegations sent to Richard in the Tower to persuade him to resign the crown; the two earls were among the witnesses to the document which embodied Richard's supposed renunciation, and were among the proctors appointed by the estates to convey their renunciation of homage to Richard after his formal deposition. The accounts of Jean Creton and Walsingham, together with the anonymous tract entitled 'The manner of King Richard's renunciation', all suggest that Westmorland readily supported the deposition of Richard II and Henry's assumption of the crown. John Hardyng, who admittedly wrote much later and had close links with the Percys, maintained that Henry swore an oath at Doncaster that he had come only to claim his inheritance and that subsequently, when Richard was in the Tower, both Westmorland and, which is harder to believe, Northumberland, advised Henry not to 'do anything contrary to his oath' (*Chronicle*, ed. Ellis, 351). Although it has been argued that Henry was indeed guilty of perjury in taking the crown, and although there is some legitimate doubt about whether Northumberland's son Henry Percy (Hotspur) genuinely supported Henry's seizure of the throne, nothing in Westmorland's conduct in 1399 or in his subsequent attitude to Henry as king suggests that he had any serious reservations about Henry's right to be king. His family's traditional links with the house of Lancaster, and long history of service to the crown, together perhaps with a realistic appreciation of the benefits he was likely to derive from loyalty to the new regime, explain the support which Westmorland gave Henry IV throughout his reign and his service too under his son Henry V.

The conflict with the Percys Westmorland's rewards were not long in coming after Henry's accession. On the very day that Henry became king he was created marshal of England for life (though he resigned the office by 1412), and on 20 October he was granted the honour of Richmond for life: Henry IV evidently ignored its restoration to the Breton ducal family by Richard II the previous year. He also received several wardships, including that of the

Dacre estates, and he was a regular member of Henry IV's council between 1399 and 1404. He became a knight of the Garter in 1403, filling the vacancy created by the death of the duke of York in the previous year. His influence on the border was not, however, as great as he might have hoped: the wardenships of both marches were in the hands of the Percy family, and only in March 1402, with the transfer of the keeping of Roxburgh Castle to him from Hotspur, did he begin to acquire some presence in the marches. The sweeping grant of much of southern Scotland to the earl of Northumberland a year later, as a reward for his victory at Homildon Hill, did not include Roxburgh, but Westmorland's outpost there would have been surrounded by Percy territory had the Percys been able to gain possession of the territory so liberally granted to them. The exclusion of Westmorland from office in the marches in the opening years of Henry's reign may well explain the growing rivalry between the two families, and he probably saw the Percy rebellion of 1403 as an opportunity to break Percy power in the north. After the battle of Shrewsbury on 21 July 1403 Henry instructed Westmorland to raise troops and intercept the earl of Northumberland to prevent his marching south in support of the rebels. Westmorland drove Northumberland back to Warkworth Castle; then, through Lord Say, he advised Henry that the Percy castles in the north should be taken by force if necessary, and urged the king to appear in person in the north to counteract rumours put about by Percy retainers that he was dead.

Westmorland now profited substantially from his loyalty: he was granted the wardenship of the west march, which he was to hold until 1414, when his son John succeeded him. The new warden of the east march was the king's son John, later duke of Bedford, aged fourteen, but Westmorland's influence was strong there too. However, Henry may not have welcomed the prospect of Neville predominance in the north any more than that of the Percys. In the parliament of January 1404 the king pardoned Northumberland, restored his castles to him, and at the request of the Commons brought about a reconciliation between him and Westmorland. The reconciliation proved short-lived, however: in May of the following year Northumberland led a raid on Sir Ralph Eure's castle at Witton-le-Wear with the intention of capturing Westmorland, who had been staying there. Westmorland was forewarned of the attack and left the castle before Northumberland's force arrived. It may be that this was the 'opening act' of a new rebellion by Northumberland in concert with the archbishop of York, Richard Scrope, who had his own grievances against Henry IV. Northumberland perhaps hoped to neutralize his most dangerous opponent before committing himself to open revolt: his failure to do so may explain why he did not overtly support the rebellion which Scrope and the young Thomas (II) Mowbray, the earl marshal, raised in Yorkshire in late May, but instead fled to Scotland. His estates were subsequently forfeited to the crown.

Westmorland moved rapidly to quell the rebellion and prevent Percy retainers from joining forces with Scrope's men. At Topcliffe near Thirsk he defeated a group of Percy and Mowbray retainers from Cleveland, and then marched towards York. He intercepted Scrope's forces at Shipton Moor, 5 miles north of the city, on 27 May. Westmorland's forces were outnumbered by those of the rebels, and Westmorland decided to resort to parleying rather than battle. He sent envoys to Scrope asking why he was in warlike array: the archbishop replied that he would rather have peace than war, but showed the envoys the schedule of grievances against Henry IV that he had drawn up. Westmorland gave every appearance of sympathy for Scrope's demands, and invited Scrope and Mowbray to meet him and discuss them. When they met, on neutral ground between the two camps, Westmorland again expressed his sympathy with the rebels' grievances and according to Walsingham declared his willingness to persuade the king to remedy them. Westmorland concluded the meeting with a glass of wine and prevailed upon Scrope to send his forces home. No sooner had they gone, however, than he arrested Scrope and Mowbray on charges of treason and imprisoned them in Pontefract Castle to await the arrival of the king on 3 June. Five days later they were both executed. Walsingham gives the fullest and most circumstantial account of the episode, and he is borne out in essentials by both Giles's chronicle and the continuation of the *Eulogium historiarum sive temporis chronicon*. There seems little doubt that Westmorland's skilful, if duplicitous, handling of the negotiations with Scrope and Mowbray brought their rebellion to an end without great bloodshed or wider danger to the crown. Scrope proved a gullible opponent, but Westmorland demonstrated both his astuteness and his loyalty to the crown. He profited handsomely from Northumberland's fall. He and his wife were granted the Percy lordships of Cockermouth and Egremont in Cumberland and the barony of Langley in Northumberland (the former Lucy inheritance) for life, and all other Percy lands in the west march were committed to him for the time being.

Later career The Scrope rebellion, however, proved the climax of Westmorland's career. Although he was only forty-one in 1405, the rest of his life was devoted mainly to service on the northern border. He continued to hold office as warden of the west march: he indented to serve with 50 men-at-arms and 100 mounted archers in time of peace, and double that number in time of war. He was to receive £1250 p.a. in time of peace and £2500 in time of war to cover his expenses, mainly the wages of his troops, but by 1409 the crown was substantially in debt to him, as it had been to the Percys earlier in Henry IV's reign and indeed in the reign of Richard II. However, financial difficulties with the crown never threatened to undermine Westmorland's loyalty to the Lancastrian monarchy. He regularly held office as justice of the peace in Cumberland, Westmorland, and the three ridings of Yorkshire; he was appointed to commissions to negotiate with the Scots throughout the reigns of both Henry IV and Henry V, and he successfully resisted the Scottish invasion of 1417 known as the 'Foul Raid'. He was nominated a member of the council appointed under the leadership of the prince of Wales on

2 May 1410, but he was excused service on the ground that he was needed on the northern border. He does not seem to have formed close links with the prince and the group of younger nobles around the prince who were influential in politics and diplomacy as the deepening illness of Henry IV rendered him incapable of action for lengthy periods in the last three years of his reign.

When the prince succeeded to the throne as Henry V in 1413, Westmorland's relationship with him seems to have been more distant than it had been with his father. Indeed, he received what he may have regarded as something of a snub in November 1414 when the reversion of the honour of Richmond, which Westmorland held for life, was granted to the king's younger brother John, duke of Bedford. The involvement of Westmorland's son-in-law Sir Thomas Grey of Heaton in the Southampton plot against Henry V in 1415 perhaps cast a temporary cloud over Westmorland's relationship with the king. The Grey family had close links with the Nevilles; Thomas Grey had been one of Westmorland's retainers since at least 1404, and his advancement in Henry IV's reign may have owed something to Westmorland's patronage. Westmorland played an important part in the negotiations that led in 1417 to the return from Scotland and restoration to the family's honours and lands of Henry Percy, grandson of the first earl of Northumberland. There was some potential danger to the Nevilles in a Percy restoration, but the marriage of Henry Percy to Westmorland's daughter Eleanor, which Joan Beaufort may have engineered, served to bind the two families together and prevent any immediate revival of their rivalry, despite the restored earl's appointment as warden of the east march in April 1417.

Although the first folio text of Shakespeare's *Henry V* gives Westmorland, on the eve of Agincourt, the famous words:

> O that we now had here
> But one ten thousand of those men in England
> That do no work today
> (*Henry V*, IV.iii)

he did not in fact accompany the king on the campaign of 1415 and was not present at Agincourt (the first quarto text attributes these lines to the earl of Warwick). Perhaps his age—he was fifty-one in 1415—made it difficult for him readily to identify with the martial enthusiasm of the younger nobles around the king. Yet his distance from the king should not be exaggerated. Henry perhaps saw him as a loyal elder statesman; he appointed him one of his executors for the will he made before leaving for France in 1415 and again for his last will in 1422. In this will Henry bequeathed a gold goblet to both Westmorland and Joan. After Henry V's death in 1422 Westmorland's status and experience ensured his appointment to the council of regency established for the infant Henry VI.

Westmorland's family and will Like his father Westmorland devoted some of his resources to buildings which expressed his wealth and status. He continued his father's work at Sheriff Hutton Castle, where there survives a shield impaling his arms with those of Joan Beaufort, and in 1410 he obtained a licence from Bishop Langley of Durham to establish a college of priests at Staindrop church, close to Raby Castle.

Westmorland died on 21 October 1425, and was buried in the choir of his collegiate church at Staindrop. In his will he stated his wish to be buried either in Durham Cathedral or at Staindrop: the magnificent alabaster tomb at Staindrop with effigies of himself and his two wives was perhaps commissioned in London and would have been capable of being placed in either church: presumably his executors decided upon Staindrop. His second wife, Joan Beaufort, is not buried with him, even though her effigy appears on his tomb: she died in 1440 and is buried in Lincoln Cathedral.

Westmorland fathered a total of twenty-two or twenty-three children. With his first wife, Margaret, he had two sons: John (b. c.1387), who married Elizabeth Holland and died in May 1420, and Ralph (d. 1458), who married Mary (c.1394–1458), daughter and coheir of Sir Robert Ferrers of Oversley and his wife, Joan Beaufort, who later became Ralph's stepmother. He also had with Margaret six or seven daughters, whose marriages indicate Westmorland's wish to strengthen his family's links with other northern noble families: Matilda married Peter, Lord Maulay; Philippa married Thomas, Lord Dacre; Alice married first Sir Thomas Grey of Heaton, and after his execution for treason in 1415 Sir Gilbert Lancaster; Elizabeth followed family tradition and became a nun in the Minories; Anne married Sir Gilbert Umfraville of Kyme (d. 1421); and Margaret married first Richard, Lord Scrope of Bolton (d. 1420), and second William Cressener. He may have had another daughter, Anastasia, who died in infancy or childhood.

With his second wife, Joan Beaufort, Westmorland had nine sons and five daughters. The eldest son, Richard *Neville, earl of Salisbury (1400–1460), married Alice, daughter and heir of Thomas Montagu, earl of Salisbury (d. 1428); the second son, William *Neville (1401?–1463), married Joan, daughter and heir of Sir Thomas Fauconberg of Skelton, Yorkshire (d. 1407); the third son, George (d. 1469), inherited the estates of his uncle of the half-blood John Neville, Lord Latimer, but he became insane c.1450 and the custody of his lands passed to his brother Richard. George married Jane Welby. The fourth son, Robert *Neville (1404–1457), entered the church and became successively bishop of Salisbury (1427–38) and of Durham (1438–57). The fifth son, Edward *Neville (d. 1476), married Elizabeth, daughter and heir of Richard Beauchamp, earl of Worcester. He also had four sons—Henry, Thomas, John, and Cuthbert—who died in infancy or childhood. His eldest daughter with Joan Beaufort, Katherine *Neville (c.1400–1483), was married four times: to John (V) Mowbray, duke of Norfolk (d. 1432); Sir Thomas Strangways; John Beaumont, Viscount Beaumont (d. 1460); and Sir John Woodville (d. 1469). The second daughter, Eleanor, married first Richard, Lord Despenser (d. 1414), and then Henry Percy, second earl of Northumberland, who was killed at the first battle of St Albans in 1455. The third

daughter, Anne (d. 1480), married first Humphrey Stafford, duke of Buckingham, who was killed at Northampton in 1460, and second Walter Blount, Lord Mountjoy (d. 1474). The fourth daughter, *Cecily (d. 1495), married Richard, duke of York, who was killed at Wakefield in 1460: she was the mother of Edward IV and Richard III. The fifth daughter, Joan, became a nun.

Shortly after his marriage to Joan Beaufort, Westmorland embarked on a series of enfeoffments, the effect of which was to settle the greater part of his inheritance on his children with her, largely disinheriting his sons from his first marriage. The honour of Penrith, granted jointly to him and Joan in 1396, was entailed on the heirs of their bodies, and in 1398 Sheriff Hutton was settled on him and Joan jointly. When Westmorland made a will on 8 August 1400, however, it was probably not yet his intention to deprive his children from his first marriage of a substantial part of their inheritance. This will does not survive, and was in any case superseded by his final will made in 1424, but his grandson Ralph *Neville, second earl of Westmorland (d. 1484), evidently believed that it favoured the children of his first marriage, for during his dispute with Joan and her children in the 1430s over the inheritance he sought unsuccessfully to have its contents made public.

In the years after Westmorland made his first will, the disinheritance of the children with his first wife gathered pace. In 1404 Sheriff Hutton was entailed on his heirs male by Joan, and other Yorkshire lands, including Middleham, were similarly settled during Henry IV's reign. Finally, in 1417, Raby itself was settled on his children with Joan. The earldom of Westmorland had been granted in tail male and thus passed to the senior line, but the only estates left to the two sons of the senior line as a result of these enfeoffments were Brancepeth in co. Durham, the barony of Bywell and Styford in Northumberland, the manor of Cambois and other lands in Bedlingtonshire, Northumberland, some manors in Lincolnshire, the Neville Inns in London and Newcastle, and some property in Ripon. John Neville, Westmorland's eldest son from his first marriage, seems to have made no effort to prevent his virtual disinheritance, and indeed some later evidence suggests that he consented to some of the transactions, including the conveyance of Sheriff Hutton to his father's heirs with Joan. He died in May 1420, predeceasing his father.

Westmorland's final will, made at Raby on 18 October 1424, was niggardly in its legacies to his children with his first wife. Their daughters Matilda, Philippa, Alice, and Margaret received bequests of gold and silver plate, but their grandson Ralph, heir to the title, is not mentioned, and their second son, Ralph, was left the barony of Bywell and Styford, Northumberland, in tail male together with 'a flock of sheep, twenty-four cows, one bull' and some gold and silver plate (register of wills of John Kempe, fol. 495).

Westmorland's grandson Ralph, who became second earl of Westmorland at his grandfather's death in 1425, was to prove more willing than his father to attempt to reverse the first earl's dispositions, but in the event his attempts to regain much of his lost inheritance proved unsuccessful. His grandfather's scheme, described by Charles Ross as 'an ambitious family fraud' (Ross, 45), survived largely intact and the concentration of so much territorial power in the hands of Westmorland's son Richard, earl of Salisbury, and grandson Richard, earl of Warwick, was to have a major impact on English politics during the conflict between York and Lancaster in the years after 1450.   ANTHONY TUCK

Sources indentures of war, PRO, E 101 · inquisitions post mortem, PRO, C 139, C 141 · inquisitions post mortem for Durham, PRO, DUR 3/2 · BL, additional charter 20582 · chancery close rolls, PRO · *CIPM* · *CPR* · 'Annales Ricardi secundi', *Johannis de Trokelowe et Henrici de Blaneforde … chronica et annales*, ed. H. T. Riley, pt 3 of *Chronica monasterii S. Albani*, Rolls Series, 28 (1866), 155–280 · 'Annales … Henrici quarti', *Johannis de Trokelowe et Henrici de Blaneforde … chronica et annales*, ed. H. T. Riley, pt 3 of *Chronica monasterii S. Albani*, Rolls Series, 28 (1866), 280–420 · 'The manner of King Richard's renunciation', *Chronicles of the revolution, 1397–1400: the reign of Richard II*, ed. and trans. C. Given-Wilson (1993), 162–7 · *Chronicon Adae de Usk*, ed. and trans. E. M. Thompson, 2nd edn (1904) · F. S. Haydon, ed., *Eulogium historiarum sive temporis*, 3 vols., Rolls Series, 9 (1858–63) · J. A. Giles, ed., *Incerti scriptoris chronicon Angliae de regnis trium regum Lancastrensium* (1848) · *The chronicle of John Hardyng*, ed. H. Ellis (1812) · *Chroniques de J. Froissart*, ed. S. Luce and others, 9 (Paris, 1894) · register of wills of John Kempe, archbishop of York, Borth. Inst., fols. 495–6 · *RotP*, vols. 3–4 · *RotS*, vol. 2 · Dugdale, *Monasticon*, new edn · [J. Raine], ed., *Wills and inventories*, 1, SurtS, 2 (1835) · C. Given-Wilson, *The royal household and the king's affinity: service, politics and finance in England, 1360–1413* (1986) · G. L. Harriss, *Cardinal Beaufort: a study of Lancastrian ascendancy and decline* (1988) · M. Jones, *Ducal Brittany, 1364–1399* (1970) · J. L. Kirby, *Henry IV of England* (1970) · P. McNiven, 'The betrayal of Archbishop Scrope', *Bulletin of the John Rylands University Library*, 54 (1971–2), 173–213 · J. A. Petre, 'The Nevilles of Brancepeth and Raby, 1425–1499 [pt 1]', *The Ricardian*, 5 (1979–81), 418–35 · T. B. Pugh, *Henry V and the Southampton plot of 1415*, Southampton RS, 30 (1988) · C. D. Ross, 'The Yorkshire baronage, 1399–1435', DPhil diss., U. Oxf., 1950 · R. L. Storey, *The end of the house of Lancaster* (1966) · S. Walker, *The Lancastrian affinity, 1361–1399* (1990) · [J. Creton], 'Translation of a French metrical history of the deposition of King Richard the Second … with a copy of the original', ed. and trans. J. Webb, *Archaeologia*, 20 (1824), 1–423, esp. 13–239 · *Thomae Walsingham, quondam monachi S. Albani, historia Anglicana*, ed. H. T. Riley, 2 vols., pt 1 of *Chronica monasterii S. Albani*, Rolls Series, 28 (1863–4) · GEC, *Peerage*
Archives PRO, government records
Likenesses B. Howlett, etching (after C. A. Stothard; after effigy), NPG · alabaster tomb effigy, Staindrop church, co. Durham [*see illus.*] · manuscript illumination, Bibliothèque Nationale, Paris, Latin MS 1158, fol. 27*v*

Neville, Ralph, second earl of Westmorland (*b.* in or before **1407**, *d.* **1484**), magnate, was the grandson and heir of Ralph *Neville, the first earl (*c.*1364–1425). His father was Sir John Neville, who died campaigning in France in 1420, and his mother, Elizabeth Holland, daughter of Thomas *Holland, fifth earl of Kent, who died in 1422. He had licence to enter his estates, was knighted, and married Elizabeth Percy (*d.* 1437), the daughter of Sir Henry *Percy (Hotspur) and widow of Lord Clifford, in 1426. In the same year he was commissioned to maintain the truce with the Scots, which commission was renewed from time to time until 1438.

Neville's life was dominated by his struggle to recover the greater part of his inheritance (Middleham, Sheriff Hutton, Penrith, and Raby) which had been settled by his grandfather on his step-grandmother, Joan *Beaufort, the first countess (*d.* 1440), and their family, leaving him only Brancepeth in co. Durham, Bywell, Styford, and Cambois in Northumberland, Kirby Moorside in Yorkshire, manors in Lincolnshire, and properties in Newcastle, Ripon, and London. He claimed that his livelihood had thereby been reduced from an expected £2600 to £400 p.a. At first he could make little headway against the combined forces of the Beauforts (his step-grandmother, step-uncle Richard *Neville, earl of Salisbury, and Cardinal Henry *Beaufort) and Thomas Langley, bishop of Durham. In 1430 he and Joan entered recognizances not to pursue their quarrel by force. When in 1431 and again in 1436 the earl of Salisbury undertook to serve in France, Ralph Neville was bound again not to harass the earl in his absence. Moreover, Neville failed to secure a copy of an early will of his father which was deposited in the priory at Durham and was handed over to his enemies in 1435.

After Langley's death, however, and the further injury of the translation of his step-uncle Robert *Neville (1404–1457) to Durham in 1437, Westmorland at length resorted to violence, the bishopric being disrupted in 1438 by 'great rowtes and compaignies upon the field' (*Proceedings … of the Privy Council*, 4.289–90). Westmorland may have been encouraged in this course of action by *Humphrey, duke of Gloucester, for some time after October 1437 he married Margaret Cobham (*d.* 1466×71), the duke's sister-in-law. Conciliar attempts at pacification in 1438 and 1439 failed; it was only after Joan Beaufort's death in 1440, and possibly because of the ruin of *Eleanor, duchess of Gloucester, in 1441, that a way was opened for a settlement which was finally reached in August 1443. 'Settlement' is barely the right word, since it represented a crushing defeat for him. He recovered the lordship of Raby, but at the cost of conceding Salisbury's right in all the other properties in dispute and granting, as security, to Salisbury and two of his brothers, bonds to pay annuities worth over £400 should he default. His only consolation was that his countess had already been recognized as the sole heir of her father, who died in 1446. Thus did Westmorland bow to the superior might of his step-uncle.

Not surprisingly Ralph Neville carried little weight in the affairs of the kingdom or the bishopric. He did not totally neglect his political interests, for in 1448 he retained Richard Clervaux of Croft, a rising courtier, for life with a fee of 10 marks and later retained Sir Roger Conyers of Wynyard. He was called upon to mediate, with Bishop Neville among others, between the forces of the Nevilles and the Percys in October 1454, and was twice a commissioner of array: in 1459, for rival parties, to resist York, and in 1461 to resist Margaret of Anjou. But by this time his involvement was fitful if not entirely nominal, for he had succumbed to a mental disorder. William Worcester noted in his *Itineraries* that he was 'simple-minded' (*innocens homo*) and that Sir Thomas Neville, his younger brother (*d. c.*1461), once had his guardianship.

Indeed it is noticeable that it was not Westmorland but

his kinsmen who took up the family cause after 1457 when the provision of Laurence Booth to Durham brought a turn for the better in their fortunes. One of Booth's early acts, on 16 December 1457, was to appoint Sir Thomas Neville as lay steward of the palatinate in place of Thomas's namesake, Salisbury's son. Ralph Neville's brother and heir, Sir John, was nominated a justice of assize. More sweeping gains were made in 1459 when all remaining traces of Salisbury's influence in the palatinate were removed. John, now Lord Neville, was added to the commission of the peace, was made Booth's constable of Barnard Castle and, furthermore, became constable of Sheriff Hutton, forfeited to the crown, as well as being granted an annuity of £100 out of Middleham. The earl's resources were mobilized in the defence of the Lancastrian dynasty in 1460–61, the earl himself, it would seem, being brought out to lead troops raised in his name when they marched through Durham in November 1460. But hopes of a full restoration of the inheritance were dashed by defeat at Towton, Lord Neville's death on the field, and his subsequent attainder. The struggle against the junior branch, now led by the all-powerful earl of Warwick, was kept alive during the 1460s by his nephew Humphrey *Neville (c.1439–1469), but Humphrey and his brother were finally taken and executed in 1469.

Westmorland's prospects revived again with the overthrow and death of the earl of Warwick in 1471. Bishop Booth of Durham, who had his own reasons to resent Warwick and his family, was quick to promote the earl's nephew and heir Ralph, the son of John, Lord Neville (d. 1461). Ralph was restored to his title and estates by Edward IV in October 1472 at the age of eighteen. But he had already been placed on the Durham commission of the peace a year earlier (as was nominally the earl) and presided over sessions on several occasions between 1471 and 1473. He married Booth's niece, Isabel, before 20 February 1473. Shortly before Booth's translation to York in 1476 he was made lay steward of the palatinate for life. If the younger Ralph Neville was hoping thereby to have his future influence in the palatinate ensured, he was to be rapidly disappointed. The new bishop, William Dudley, immediately removed him, providing the compensation of an annuity of £20. It was perhaps in support of Ralph, as well as to promote the claims of the priory's own steward William Claxton of Old Park, a prominent servant of Westmorland, that Prior Bell wrote to the new bishop in March 1477 advising him to cherish the Nevilles since 'your lordship and they stand as one ye may rule and guide all other that do inhabit the country' (Raine, 359). But such lobbying was to no avail; Dudley and the bishopric were already in the pocket of Richard, duke of Gloucester.

The same fate befell Westmorland and his interests. It is not clear who, if anyone, took over his guardianship after the death of Sir Thomas Neville. It may be that George Neville, archbishop of York, acquired an interest, for in 1466 he and several servants of the earl of Warwick were pardoned their trespasses in acquiring the south-east Durham, Yorkshire, and Lincolnshire properties from the earl and his countess without licence. Two of these properties,

Kirby Moorside and Besely, were subsequently conveyed to Ralph, Lord Neville, and his wife, perhaps in jointure on the occasion of their marriage. It is apparent, however, that Richard of Gloucester acquired control of some of the same property. Between July 1477 and January 1479 Westmorland vested his lordship of Raby and his south-east Durham estates in the hands of his infant great-nephew (Lord Neville's son) and a panel of feoffees, the majority of whom, apart from three Booths (kinsmen of Lady Neville) and William Claxton, were the duke of Gloucester's councillors. No fewer than six of these councillors had received on behalf of their lord at Easter 1477 a formal surrender from Lord Neville of all his claims to the family estates in Yorkshire. Gloucester thereafter used Raby from time to time as his own residence. Moreover, in 1484, as Richard III he diverted £66 14s. 8d. from its revenues to support the newly established council of the north and early in 1485 appointed Geoffrey Frank his receiver there.

By 1485 Westmorland was dead. He died, aged seventy-seven or more, on 4 November 1484. He was buried in the parish church of St Brandon at Brancepeth, next to the castle in which he had probably lived for the last decades of his life. There his effigy in wood was to be found until the church was destroyed by fire in 1998. He had but two children, who predeceased him: John Neville, who died in March 1450, and a daughter, Margaret, with his second countess, who died in childhood. His was a long and tragic life, blighted for its last thirty years by ill health and ruined by his grandfather's legacy.   A. J. POLLARD

Sources PRO, Durham Chancery Records, Durh 3 · U. Durham L., archives and special collections, Durham Church Commission records, estate accounts · *Chancery records* · N. H. Nicolas, ed., *Proceedings and ordinances of the privy council of England*, 7 vols., RC, 26 (1834–7) · R. Horrox and P. W. Hammond, eds., *British Library Harleian manuscript 433*, 4 vols. (1979–83) · C. D. Ross, 'The Yorkshire baronage, 1399–1435', DPhil diss., U. Oxf., 1950 · R. B. Dobson, *Durham Priory, 1400–1450*, Cambridge Studies in Medieval Life and Thought, 3rd ser., 6 (1973) · J. A. Petre, 'The Nevilles of Brancepeth and Raby, 1425–1499 [pt 1]', *The Ricardian*, 5 (1979–81), 418–35 · J. A. Petrie, 'The Nevills of Brancepeth and Raby, 1425–1499 [pt 2]', *The Ricardian*, 6 (1982–4), 2–13 · A. J. Pollard, '"St Cuthbert and the Hog": Richard III and the county palatine of Durham, 1471–85', *Kings and nobles in the later middle ages*, ed. R. A. Griffiths and J. Sherborne (1986), 109–29 · A. J. Pollard, *North-eastern England during the Wars of the Roses: lay society, war and politics, 1450–1500* (1990) · *Historiae Dunelmensis scriptores tres: Gaufridus de Coldingham, Robertus de Graystanes, et Willielmus de Chambre*, ed. J. Raine, SurtS, 9 (1839) · *Itineraries [of] William Worcestre*, ed. J. H. Harvey, OMT (1969) · effigy, St Brandon's Church, Brancepeth, co. Durham · G. L. Harriss, *Cardinal Beaufort: a study of Lancastrian ascendancy and decline* (1988)
Likenesses drawing (after effigy), repro. in R. Surtees, *The history and antiquities of the county palatine of Durham*, 4 vols. (1816–40) · wooden effigy on tomb, Brancepeth parish church, co. Durham; destroyed by fire, 1998
Wealth at death approx. £600 p.a.: Harriss, *Cardinal Beaufort*

Neville, Ralph, fourth earl of Westmorland (1498–1549), magnate, was the second son of Ralph, Baron Neville (who died soon after his birth), and Edith (d. 1529), daughter of Sir William Sandys of the Vyne. Born on 21 February 1498, he succeeded to the earldom of Westmorland, as his father's only surviving son, on the death of his grand-father Ralph Neville, third earl, in 1499. A ward of Edward *Stafford, third duke of Buckingham, during the later part of his minority, he was betrothed to Buckingham's daughter Elizabeth [see Howard, Elizabeth]. When she instead married Thomas Howard, later third duke of Nor-folk, Neville married Stafford's second daughter, Kather-ine (d. 1555), and they had eighteen children, including the rebel Christopher *Neville (fl. 1549–1575). Present at Henry VIII's extravagant encounter with François I of France at the Field of Cloth of Gold in June 1520, and his meeting with the emperor Charles V at Gravelines a few weeks later, he also participated in the reception of the emperor when he visited England in 1522. Knighted in Scotland by the earl of Surrey in 1523, he became a knight of the Garter in June 1525 and a privy councillor by Febru-ary 1526. In July 1530 he signed the letter to Pope Clement VII urging him to accede to Henry VIII's desire for an annulment of his marriage to Katherine of Aragon, and in May 1536 he was one of the peers who tried Anne Boleyn; in November 1537 he attended the funeral of Jane Sey-mour.

Westmorland principally served the crown in the north of England and on the Anglo-Scottish border. In 1522 and 1523 he actively campaigned against the Scots; from Octo-ber 1525 to September 1526 he held office as deputy cap-tain of Berwick and vice-warden of the east and middle marches; and he headed the team of envoys responsible for concluding a truce with Scotland in January 1526. In May 1534 he served on the commission inquiring into alle-gations of treason against Lord Dacre. In the same month, when Cuthbert Tunstall, bishop of Durham, was sus-pected of disloyalty, he and the earl of Cumberland made a search of the bishop's palace at Auckland but found no incriminating evidence. In June and July 1535, he was among those charged to suppress disorders in Northum-berland, Cumberland, and Westmorland.

Westmorland's conduct during the Pilgrimage of Grace was not without ambiguities. There were some who believed he was sympathetic to the rising, but although he sent his young son to the rebel musters, together with the banner of St Cuthbert, it would appear that he acted under duress, having been captured by the Richmond-shire commons after being deserted by his own retinue. He managed to inform the duke of Norfolk of his difficul-ties, and the king continued to trust him, in a letter of 7 November 1536 commenting on 'the danger he has been in from the rebels', and on his having preserved himself from 'thinfection of their traitorous poison' (LP Henry VIII, vol. 11, no. 1003). Henry VIII promised a reward, but in a letter of 17 March 1537 Norfolk described the earl as 'a man of such heat and hastiness of nature' as to be unsuit-able for appointment as warden of the east and middle marches (LP Henry VIII, vol. 12/2, no. 667). In fact the office was one that Westmorland was very anxious to avoid, unlike Norfolk, who may well have been disparaging him as a potential rival. But it may be significant that in 1538 an anonymous writer described Westmorland as 'of a great power, without wit or knowledge' (LP Henry VIII, vol. 13/2,

no. 732), a judgement perhaps echoed by an earlier per-ception of his wife as one that 'rather playeth the part of a knight than of a lady' (LP Henry VIII, vol. 12/1, no. 345). Whatever his deficiencies, Westmorland became a mem-ber of the reconstituted council of the north on 14 January 1537, and it was he who was charged to protect the east and middle marches when Edward Seymour, earl of Hert-ford, invaded Scotland in May 1544. Westmorland died on 24 April 1549 and was buried at Staindrop, co. Durham, near Raby Castle; his widow lived until 14 May 1555 and was buried on the 17th at St Leonard, Shoreditch, in London.

Henry Neville, fifth earl of Westmorland (1524/5–1564), succeeded to the title on his father's death. Probably not yet in his teens when he was effectively taken hostage dur-ing the Pilgrimage of Grace, as early as June 1541 he was charged to deputize for his father 'if the Scots should make a sudden ruffle' (LP Henry VIII, vol. 16. no. 879); in January 1543 he was ordered to be ready, at forty-eight hours warning, to enter Scotland; he participated, in Sep-tember 1545, in a major raid over the Scottish border; and he acted as an ambassador to Scotland in 1552 and 1557. A member of the council of the north by May 1549, he became lord lieutenant of the bishopric of Durham in May 1552. In April 1557, after the protestant exile Thomas Stafford had seized Scarborough Castle and proclaimed himself protector of the realm, Westmorland crushed this small-scale rising and, at the end of May, became general of the horse in northern England; for most of 1558, moreover, he served as lieutenant-general of the north.

However, the fifth earl's interests clearly extended beyond northern and Anglo-Scottish affairs. As an adoles-cent he had accompanied Henry VIII to Blackheath to receive Anne of Cleves in January 1540. He was knighted by Henry at Boulogne on 30 September 1544 and served as king's carver in 1545. On 26 February 1551 he became a privy councillor, probably because the duke of Northum-berland saw him as an appropriate substitute for Cuthbert Tunstall, bishop of Durham, who had been under arrest since the previous August. In 1552 he was made a knight of the Garter. When Edward VI died on 6 July 1553, Westmor-land, who had signed the letters patent of 16 June settling the crown on Lady Jane Grey, seems at first to have con-tinued to associate with Northumberland, and may even have accompanied him to Cambridge. But he soon dec-lared for Princess Mary, and at her coronation on 1 Octo-ber bore the second sword and cap of maintenance. In Feb-ruary 1558, for his services to Henry VIII, Edward VI, and Mary, he received generous grants of land in Lincolnshire and Yorkshire, and, soon after Elizabeth's accession on 17 November 1558, he was even spoken of as a possible hus-band for the new queen.

The fifth earl's career was certainly not without blem-ish, however. At an early age, on 3 July 1536, he had mar-ried Lady Anne (d. in or after 1549), second daughter of Thomas *Manners, first earl of Rutland. The marriage clearly ran into difficulties, for by October 1546 Henry Neville had been committed to the Fleet prison not only for heavy gambling debts (to remedy which he was inveigled into buying a magical ring which would enable him to invoke angelic assistance) but also his 'unnatural enterprise' in plotting the deaths of both his wife and his father (*LP Henry VIII*, vol. 20/2, no. 212). He admitted that, despite Anne's 'good and gentle nature', his own 'naughty living and neglect of her' had helped bring him to this plight (ibid., no. 421), and in March 1547 his father was ordered to take him back and pay his debts. In October 1552 he was once more in trouble, this time on charges of secretly conspiring to seize treasure at Middleham and rob his mother, but again he soon regained his liberty. By then, perhaps, he had already married his second wife, Jane, daughter of the Yorkshire knight Sir Roger Cholmeley, and, following her demise, he went on (controversially) to marry her sister Margaret, widow of Sir Henry Gascoigne, some time before 21 June 1560. Westmorland died at Kelvedon in Essex on 10 February 1564 and his will, dated 18 August 1563, was proved at York on 22 September 1564. He bequeathed his soul to God alone, and his body to be buried at Staindrop, where he and his first two wives are still commemorated by wooden effigies; his third wife, to whom he left an annuity of £100 and other bequests, long survived him, being eventually buried at St Dunstan-in-the-West, London, on 2 April 1570. The earldom of Westmorland passed to his only surviving son, Charles *Neville. He also left seven daughters, one of them illegitimate. KEITH DOCKRAY

Sources GEC, *Peerage*, new edn, 12/2.553–8 · DNB · *LP Henry VIII* · APC, 1542–70 · CPR, 1547–58 · *The chronicle and political papers of King Edward VI*, ed. W. K. Jordan (1966) · C. Wriothesley, *A chronicle of England during the reigns of the Tudors from AD 1485 to 1559*, ed. W. D. Hamilton, 2 vols., CS, new ser., 11, 20 (1875–7) · D. E. Hoak, *The king's council in the reign of Edward VI* (1976) · M. H. Dodds and R. Dodds, *The Pilgrimage of Grace, 1536–1537, and the Exeter conspiracy, 1538*, 2 vols. (1915); repr. (1971) · M. Bush, *The Pilgrimage of Grace: a study of the rebel armies of October 1536* (1996) · R. W. Hoyle, 'Thomas Master's narrative of the Pilgrimage of Grace', *Northern History*, 21 (1985), 53–7 · R. W. Hoyle, *The Pilgrimage of Grace and the politics of the 1530s* (2001) · [W. Greenwell], ed., *Wills and inventories from the registry at Durham*, 2, SurtS, 38 (1860), 1–6

Likenesses wooden effigy, Staindrop church, co. Durham

Neville, Richard, fifth earl of Salisbury (1400–1460), magnate, was the eldest son of Ralph *Neville, first earl of Westmorland (c.1364–1425), and his second wife, Joan *Beaufort (d. 1440), daughter of *John of Gaunt, duke of Lancaster. He was thus the nephew of *Henry IV and close kinsman of all three Lancastrian kings. The reversion of the greater part of the Neville inheritance, including Penrith, Sheriff Hutton, Middleham, and Raby had been conveyed to him before he came of age. His moulding as a Lancastrian magnate was completed with his marriage by 1422 to Alice (c.1406–1462), sole daughter and heir of Thomas *Montagu, earl of Salisbury (1388–1428).

Political career, 1420–1452 By 1425 Sir Richard Neville was already launched in his public career. He succeeded his elder half-brother, John, Lord Neville, in the wardenship of the west march in 1420. In this capacity he participated in the negotiations at Durham that completed the release of James I and the signing of a seven-year truce with the Scots in 1424, renewed in 1430. His closeness to the royal family was marked by his serving as a carver at the coronation of Queen Catherine in 1421, the grant of the stewardship of the Lancastrian lordship of Pontefract in 1425, and his acting as constable of England at the coronation of Henry VI on 6 November 1429. By this time, following the death of his father-in-law on 3 November 1428, he had become earl of Salisbury.

In the early summer of 1431 Salisbury crossed to Calais to join his king in Rouen, providing the escort, it would seem, for his uncle, Cardinal Henry *Beaufort (1375?–1447). He was there at the time of the trial of Jeanne d'Arc, and attended the coronation of Henry VI as king of France in Paris on 16 December. By now clearly identified as a member of Beaufort's faction, in 1432 and 1433 he received further grants of office in the duchy of Lancaster, including the stewardship of Tickhill in southern Yorkshire. Nevertheless his interests still lay primarily in the Scottish marches. In July 1434 Salisbury took over from the earl of Northumberland the wardenship of the east march. He laid down strict conditions; prompt payment of his wages, the repair of Berwick within four months, and settlement of his arrears for the west march. These conditions were not met and in 1435 he resigned both wardenships. His replacements in both, the earls of Northumberland and Huntingdon, in their turn resigned in 1436. These upheavals are unlikely to have been caused solely by financial difficulties; it is conceivable that the parties were caught up, in ways no longer discernible, in the political manoeuvrings of the duke of Gloucester and Cardinal Beaufort.

As far as Salisbury was concerned a way out was found by his agreeing to serve once more in France, this time in the company of his young brother-in-law, *Richard, duke of York (d. 1460), who was nominated the king's lieutenant in France in February 1436. His retinue was mustered on landing at Honfleur on 7 June. After campaigning in the Pays de Caux, and recovering Fécamp and neighbouring places, he saw little further action. By early 1437 he was serving as York's lieutenant-general, primarily engaged, it would seem, as a councillor. York's appointment lapsed in March 1437, though it was not until November that he was relieved. Salisbury probably returned to England earlier, for he began to receive a series of generous grants from the crown on 20 September.

Salisbury's return home coincided with the first emergence of Henry VI from his minority, and with the successful assertion of Cardinal Beaufort's primacy in the transitional government established at a great council on 12 November. Salisbury himself, no doubt as Beaufort's nominee, was sworn in as a councillor on the same day. He rapidly established himself as one of the central figures at court and in council of the group who, first under Beaufort and then around the duke of Suffolk, became dominant in the government of the realm. From November 1437 until the autumn of 1442 he was one of the more assiduous lay councillors, and thereafter, while his attendance was less frequent, he remained very much at the heart of affairs. He played a prominent role in the negotiations at

Westminster in the summer of 1445, was one of those who arrested the duke of Gloucester at Bury St Edmunds in 1447, and rallied several times to the defence of the crown: to suppress Cade's revolt in 1450, to assert royal authority in the west country in September 1451, and to face down the duke of York at Dartford in February 1452. He survived the fall of the duke of Suffolk largely unscathed.

Securing an inheritance, 1428–1443 Salisbury exploited his position at court to reinforce and extend his power in the north of England. His first priority was to secure his inheritance and title. Since the title of earl of Salisbury had been created in tail male in 1337, and Earl Thomas had a male heir (his childless uncle Sir Richard Montagu), Richard Neville's succession to the title had to be determined in May 1429 by the royal council in the name of the king; a decision that the king himself subsequently confirmed in 1443. Burdened with dower, and clouded by the claim of Sir Richard Montagu to the endowment of the earldom, the acquisition of his countess's inheritance was complex and, as Neville complained, costly. While Richard and Alice immediately entered her deceased mother's estates, they lost the endowment of the earldom. Ultimately the inheritance was worth some £850 p.a. to them.

Salisbury also needed to ensure his succession to the greater part of the Neville inheritance. From 1425 Penrith, Middleham, Sheriff Hutton, and Raby were in the hands of his mother. She leased Penrith, Middleham, and Sheriff Hutton to her son for a rent that was the equivalent of a dower. Salisbury saw off a vigorous challenge from his half-brother, the earl of Westmorland, after his mother's death in 1440, making doubly sure of possession by enfeoffing the northern estates in the hands of Cardinal Beaufort and others. And when the outmatched Westmorland finally came to terms in 1443 it was on Salisbury's conditions; Penrith, Middleham, and Sheriff Hutton were conceded, Westmorland's only consolation being the lordship of Raby. Furthermore Salisbury received a grant for life of two-thirds of the lordship of Richmond, a grant converted in 1449 to tail male. Thus the prospect was created of consolidating the neighbouring lordships of Middleham and Richmond into one hereditary fiefdom in north Yorkshire. The Neville lordships and Richmond secured an annual income at the time of approximately £2000; the total combined yield of the lands held by Salisbury and his countess was by 1450 not far short of £3000.

Dominance in the north Inherited land was reinforced by royal grants. In common with other Lancastrian nobles, from 1437 Salisbury continued to accumulate royal offices, in his case in the north. A further clutch of duchy of Lancaster grants came his way: the stewardship of Richmond, the stewardship of Blackburn, the forestership of Bowland, and to cap everything, in 1445, the conversion of the stewardship of Pontefract in survivorship to himself and his sons Sir Richard *Neville, afterwards earl of Warwick (the Kingmaker), and Sir Thomas Neville together with the reversion of the remaining duchy stewardships in Yorkshire in Knaresborough and Pickering. He had

already acquired the office of chief justice of the royal forests north of the Trent and was granted the stewardship of Kendal in Westmorland as well as the custody of two parts of the Richmond fee of the lordship.

After 1437 Salisbury was also anxious to recover the wardenship of the west march, which Bishop Lumley of Carlisle had taken at the end of 1436 for seven years. In that year Salisbury had himself been granted the fee farm of the city of Carlisle, worth £80 p.a. In 1439 the earl petitioned the crown, successfully, for the reversion of the office, even at a significantly reduced salary in peacetime of just under £1000. He duly entered office again at the end of 1443 for a term of ten years. Three years later he renegotiated the term to twenty years from 1453 in survivorship with his son Sir Richard. Despite the doubts expressed by some historians, the wardenship almost certainly was a source of profit (in peacetime) as well as a source of political and military power. Salisbury himself, it is clear, exercised it by lieutenant: in 1435 his brother George, Lord Latimer; in 1450 Lord Dacre; and lastly, in 1457, his son Sir Thomas, to whom he paid a salary of £333 6s. 8d. to cover all the costs. It is likely that the warden maintained only a caretaker garrison in Carlisle in time of peace, relying on his indentured retainers and local levies to raise troops to defend the march in time of war. And the costs of retaining, as some remnants of Salisbury's estate accounts reveal in the late 1450s, were lower than his net salary, even after paying his lieutenant. In peacetime, it would seem, the warden could indeed carry the cost of some degree of underpayment. In the late 1440s, however, Salisbury did not even have to do this, as he consistently received preference at the exchequer.

To office, Salisbury added the promotion of his family. His brother Robert *Neville was provided to the see of Durham early in 1438, and put the resources of the palatinate at Salisbury's disposal. In 1434 he invested in a lucrative double deal with Richard Beauchamp, earl of Warwick, whereby his daughter Cicely married Beauchamp's heir, Henry, and his son Richard married Beauchamp's daughter Anne. He met part of the cost of the first instalment of the marriage portion from his salary as warden of the west march. Henry, while under age, inherited in 1439. Bearing in mind Salisbury's prospects and his own role as feoffee for his son-in-law's estates, it is not at all surprising that in 1439 he acted promptly to prevent his own brother, the bishop of Durham, from taking possession of the lordship of Barnard Castle on the Tees. Duke (as he had become) Henry died in 1446 just as he had reached his majority, to be followed three years later by his infant daughter Anne. In July 1449 Sir Richard Neville succeeded to the earldom in right of his wife, and was granted a significant share of the Beauchamp inheritance, including Barnard Castle abutting Richmondshire. Salisbury's own direct landed interest in the north was extended further in 1451, when he took custody of the estates of his brother Lord Latimer, who had gone insane.

By the early 1450s Salisbury and his close kinsmen controlled through land and office a swathe of northern England from coast to coast. With land and office went the power to retain. Most of the lesser peers, such as Dacre, Fitzhugh, Greystoke, and Scrope of Bolton, were in his service. Many of the leading gentry of northern Yorkshire, Cumberland, and Westmorland followed suit. Ties of service were frequently buttressed by marriage and kinship. In parts of the north, especially Richmondshire, Salisbury stood at the head of an entire network of the local élite. Basking in royal favour, commanding the resources of the duchy of Lancaster as well as the lion's share of his father's inheritance, he had assembled an all-embracing hegemony in the north. It was something of an understatement to remark of Henry VI's generosity to his kinsman, as did the act of attainder of the earl in 1459, that 'you showed your grace and bounteous grants in right ample wise' (*RotP*, 5.346).

The challenge of the Percys, 1449–1453 The rise and rise of Richard Neville did not pass unchallenged. The Cliffords, based in the north of Westmorland, and at Skipton in the West Riding of Yorkshire, felt themselves threatened, and still more importantly, the house of Percy watched on with growing dismay. Salisbury's relationship with Henry *Percy, second earl of Northumberland (1394–1455), if not close, was civil. They were brothers-in-law, Percy being married to Neville's sister Eleanor. In the 1420s, 1430s, and 1440s, through to the war of 1448–9, they worked frequently together defending the border and negotiating with the Scots. The upheaval in the wardenships in 1434–6 does not seem to have produced personal animosities. A dispute over precedence as earls which came to a head either in 1429 or 1442 was resolved in Salisbury's favour. Northumberland seems to have accepted his secondary status. Until 1450 the shrievalty of Cumberland alternated between the nominees of the two earls. And until January 1453 they seem to have co-operated in the return of MPs for Yorkshire. It was Northumberland's sons who seem to have chafed, especially the younger sons led by Sir Thomas Percy.

Perhaps the Anglo-Scottish war of 1448–9 left a bitter legacy. Henry Percy, Lord Poynings, the earl of Northumberland's heir and warden of the east march, led a raid into Scotland in October 1448 which was repulsed on the River Sark with heavy loss of life and Poynings's own capture. It is possible that Salisbury himself was held to blame for the defeat. Sir Thomas Percy fought in the war of 1448–9, and was promoted to the title of Lord Egremont in 1449. Precisely when he began disturbing the peace in Cumberland is unclear, but by November 1452 the Neville-retained sheriff was complaining of disorder prompted by 'riotous people longing to Lord Egremont' (Summerson, 441). But by then Yorkshire was in uproar too.

The sudden outbreak of disorder in Yorkshire in 1453 immediately followed the issuing of a royal licence for the marriage between Sir Thomas Neville, Salisbury's second son, and Maud Stanhope, niece and joint heir of Ralph *Cromwell, third Lord Cromwell (d. 1456), on 1 May. Maud had been widowed only in July 1452. Part of the terms of her new marriage was the settlement on the couple of the lordship of Wressle, which Cromwell had held in fee simple for life from the Percy inheritance. It is plausible that

the Percys had envisaged recovering this property on Cromwell's death, and even that it was 'pencilled in' for Egremont. The Percy response was instantaneous, with attacks on the properties of the Nevilles and their retainers. Salisbury's younger sons, Sir Thomas and Sir John *Neville, retaliated in kind. A summer of uproar reached a climax at Heworth on the outskirts of York at the end of August when the Percys ambushed the Neville wedding party as it rode from Lincolnshire to Sheriff Hutton.

***Rapprochement* with York, 1453–1454** The outbreak of violence in Yorkshire and Cumberland was sudden and largely unforeseen. Royal response to it was prevented by the king's mental collapse early in August 1453. At this stage Salisbury and Northumberland were still able to limit the scale of conflict. In October 1453, facing each other in force near Topcliffe, they held back. Mediation might yet have been found, had not the dispute become entangled in the wider conflict over the government of the kingdom during Henry VI's incapacity, in which Salisbury allied himself with the duke of York. In October 1453 he supported York's claim to take precedence in the council; he went along with the imprisonment of the duke of Somerset and later was part of the majority of councillors to reject the queen's claim to exercise the powers of a regency. By February 1454 it was apparent that he was one of York's principal supporters, and when, after Chancellor Kemp's death in March, York was appointed protector of the realm, Salisbury was himself immediately made chancellor.

Salisbury's realignment, not just his becoming chancellor, was remarkable. His whole career, from which he had benefited hugely, had been founded on close kinship to the royal family and favour at court. Consequently Salisbury might have been expected to stand by his cousin Edmund Beaufort, duke of Somerset, and Northumberland, with a family history of questionable loyalty to the house of Lancaster, to throw in his lot with York. It is not possible fully to explain why the opposite happened. There is no doubt that Salisbury had remained closer to York than many at court. Not only was he his brother-in-law; he had also, at eleven years his senior, been something of a mentor to the young duke in England and France. In 1450 it was to Salisbury that York wrote when he wanted a hearing at court for his case for financial support in Ireland. Salisbury and Warwick were also both acceptable as mediators on the field at Dartford. At the same time there are signs that Salisbury, after the fall of Suffolk, no longer enjoyed such high favour. He lost the fee farm of Carlisle in the Act of Resumption of 1450, and it could not have pleased him when in July 1452 it was regranted to Lord Poynings, while a month later William Percy was provided to the bishopric of Carlisle. More ominous perhaps was the attempted settlement on the king's half-brother, Edmund Tudor, of the lordship of Richmond in November 1452, especially as Salisbury already held it as a hereditary grant.

But these straws in the wind do not alone explain such a volte-face. Of greater significance is the wider political context, in particular the repercussions of two other baronial disputes in 1453: the quarrel between Lord Cromwell and the duke of Exeter over possession of Ampthill and the earl of Warwick's dispute with the duke of Somerset over custody of part of the lordship of Glamorgan. Late in 1453 York, Salisbury, Warwick, and Cromwell united to ensure that power during Henry VI's illness did not fall into their rivals' hands. In the circumstances there was much to recommend Salisbury's decision to back York and thereby remain close to the centre of power. In the event the realignment proved to be the decisive moment in both Salisbury's career and the fate of the house of Lancaster.

The advantages were immediate. York himself initially took on the task of pacifying Yorkshire, in the summer of 1454 coming down with a powerful commission of oyer and terminer, which resulted in the condemnation of the Percys and the imposition of heavy fines. The violence continued, but in October a clash at Stamford Bridge, near York, led to the capture of Egremont and his brother Sir Richard by the younger Nevilles. The Percys were committed to prison as debtors.

Civil war, 1455–1459 Neville triumph, however, was short-lived. After Christmas 1454 the king recovered. The protectorate came to an end, Somerset was restored, Northumberland became high in favour, and at the end of March 1455 Salisbury was removed from office. York and his allies withdrew from court. On hearing that Somerset intended to proceed against them at a special council meeting at Leicester, they raised troops and marched rapidly to intercept the king and his entourage at St Albans. In the fight that followed on 22 May Somerset and Northumberland were both killed; and the king fell once more under the control of the Yorkists. The government that now emerged, formalized as a second protectorate in the autumn, was again founded on the principle of collective conciliar rule. Although Salisbury was not restored to the chancellorship, he was a regular attender at council, and early in 1456 he succeeded Lord Cromwell as chief steward of the duchy of Lancaster in the north, and secured for his son George *Neville (1432–1476) promotion to the diocese of Exeter. By the beginning of 1456, however, it became apparent that this revival of enforced conciliar government could not work. York surrendered the protectorate in February, and power subsequently shifted back into the hands of his enemies, now given a lead by the queen.

It would appear too that after St Albans Salisbury began to play second fiddle to his eldest son. Warwick, by his title, held precedence over his father; his wealth was greater; and he seems to have been less troubled about opposing the king and killing his enemies than his father. By early 1456 he had become the dominant Neville and York's principal lieutenant. Salisbury himself withdrew to his northern estates, strengthening and extending his local influence. It was only with great reluctance that he agreed finally to return to court and the council chamber, to participate in the planned reconciliation of the warring factions early in 1458, and did so only in some strength. On 24 March York and the Nevilles agreed to pay compensation to the sons of those that fell at St Albans, and to forgo the fines imposed in 1454 on Egremont. Egremont was even granted the disputed manor of Wressle by the king. For a while Salisbury and his family were accepted back in the fold. Notably a marriage was agreed between Salisbury's son Sir John Neville and the queen's ward Isabel Ingaldesthorpe, who was also the earl of Worcester's heir. And in May Salisbury joined Warwick and others as ambassadors to negotiate with the duke of Burgundy.

But it was a hollow reconciliation. In November 1458 Queen Margaret asserted her unchallenged control of government, and Warwick narrowly escaped with his life. Salisbury withdrew once more to the north, and there resolved to take full part with the duke of York. What precisely this meant is hard to tell, for in most respects he had been full party to the duke since 1454. Perhaps plans for a new rebellion were discussed and agreed. Certainly that is what happened a year later. In early September 1459 the Yorkist lords planned to present their case in strength to the king. Salisbury called his retainers together and set out from Middleham on 2 September. A detachment occupied Knaresborough Castle, but the main body marched south. They were intercepted at Bloreheath near Newcastle under Lyme on 23 September. The royal force was defeated, and despite suffering heavy casualties, including the capture of his sons Sir Thomas and Sir John, Salisbury and the remnant pressed on to join York and Warwick at Worcester. There in the cathedral they issued a solemn declaration of their own loyalty, and an appeal to the king to rid himself of his evil ministers. But a royal army, outnumbering them, was rapidly moving up. They retreated to Ludlow and drew up for battle at Ludford Bridge on 12 October. That night, however, the lords broke camp and fled: York with his younger son, the earl of Rutland, making his way to Ireland; Salisbury and Warwick with York's heir, the earl of March, to Calais.

Rebellion and death, 1460 In a parliament called to Coventry in November Salisbury and several of his retainers were condemned for treason and their estates confiscated. Throughout the winter a sustained effort was made by the Lancastrians to dislodge the Yorkist lords from Calais, but to no avail. In late June 1460 the latter themselves landed at Sandwich and marched on London. Salisbury was left to hold the city and blockade the Tower, while the main force marched on to confront and defeat the Lancastrians at Northampton, returning in triumph to the city with the person of the king on 16 July. The Lancastrian garrison in the Tower surrendered three days later. Power over the king's person as well as his government was now asserted. The royal household was purged, with Salisbury taking the post of king's chamberlain. At the same time he and Warwick jointly took command of the duchy of Lancaster as its stewards. A parliament was called for October to reverse the attainders of 1459. When it met, the duke of York formally claimed the throne on 10 October.

But York's claim was not met with the anticipated universal acclaim. There was even reported opposition from high in the Yorkist camp. For three weeks the matter was debated, until eventually a compromise was hammered out which recognized York as Henry VI's heir. However, while the Yorkists had concentrated on the consolidation of power at Westminster, they had lost control of the north, where Queen Margaret regathered her forces. At the end of November, York and Salisbury set out to face the Lancastrian challenge. They marched as far as York's castle of Sandal near Wakefield, where Christmas was spent. It is highly likely that they had underestimated the strength of the Lancastrian forces and advanced too far; they certainly found themselves cut off. On 30 December, out foraging in strength or even attempting a break-out, York and Salisbury were caught in the open field and overwhelmed. Sir Thomas Neville as well as York was slain; Salisbury was taken alive, brought to Pontefract and there on the following day lynched by the mob, who, it was said, 'loved him not' (Davies, 107). His severed head was set on one of the gates of York.

The man and his career It is hard to suppose that many of the commons had ever loved Richard Neville. He was, however, remembered by at least two of his servants: Robert Constable, who died in 1454 and made bequests both to him and to his countess, and John Cartmell, who in 1470 founded a chantry in Middleham parish church for the souls of the earl and countess. Salisbury was a hardheaded, ambitious man, who had built for himself an unprecedented hegemony in the north. To many he no doubt received his just deserts on 31 December 1460. Nevertheless his career is an enigma. His power had been founded on his close blood relationship with the king and a family commitment to the dynasty. He was an experienced servant of the crown as soldier, diplomat, and councillor, perhaps rightly 'named prudence' by Yorkist propaganda in 1460. Yet all this apparently came to nought after 1454. The explanation may lie in the emergence of Warwick in 1455. Salisbury was of the generation that had participated in collective conciliar rule for two or more decades. His time had passed. Warwick's generation was less committed to the dynasty, less willing to tolerate Henry VI's failings and more ruthless in its actions. It is just possible that it was Salisbury who opposed York's bid for the throne in 1460; and that he had been deliberately kept in the dark until the last possible moment by Warwick and York, who knew that he would not countenance the deposition of his cousin. This is perhaps the kindest that can be said of a man who betrayed the dynasty to which he owed everything.

Salisbury was initially buried in the Dominican friary at Pontefract. He was subsequently reinterred with chivalric ceremony on 15 February 1463 in the Montagu family mausoleum at Bisham Priory, Berkshire, according to the terms of his will. The Salisbury roll of arms, now in the possession of the duke of Buccleuch, was probably drawn up to mark the occasion and contains a stylized representation of Salisbury and his countess. His will had been made on 10 May 1459, not long before he set out for Bloreheath. He made conventional bequests to his children: his sons, the earl of Warwick, Sir Thomas (who died at Wakefield), Sir John Neville, later Marquess Montagu, and

George Neville, bishop of Exeter, later archbishop of York, and his daughters, Joan, countess of Arundel, Alice, Lady Fitzhugh, and Eleanor, Lady Stanley; and provided for the marriage portions of Katherine, who was then betrothed to William Bonville, Lord Harrington, and Margaret, who was to marry John de *Vere, thirteenth earl of Oxford. His second daughter, Cicely, dowager duchess of Warwick, had already died. His widow outlived him only by two years. The provision for masses for his soul was meagre.

A. J. POLLARD

Sources PRO · Chancery records · RotP, vol. 5 · N. H. Nicolas, ed., Proceedings and ordinances of the privy council of England, 7 vols., RC, 26 (1834–7), vol. 6 · [J. Raine], ed., Testamenta Eboracensia, 2, SurtS, 30 (1855), 239–46 · [J. Raine], ed., Wills and inventories, 1, SurtS, 2 (1835), 69–71 · R. Somerville, History of the duchy of Lancaster, 1265–1603 (1953) · J. S. Davies, ed., An English chronicle of the reigns of Richard II, Henry IV, Henry V, and Henry VI, CS, 64 (1856) · J. de Wavrin [J. de Waurin], Anchiennes cronicques d'Engleterre, ed. E. Dupont, 3 (1863) · R. L. Storey, The end of the house of Lancaster (1966) · A. J. Pollard, North-eastern England during the Wars of the Roses: lay society, war and politics, 1450–1500 (1990) · G. L. Harriss, Cardinal Beaufort: a study of Lancastrian ascendancy and decline (1988) · H. Summerson, Medieval Carlisle: the city and the borders from the late eleventh to the mid-sixteenth century, 2, Cumberland and Westmorland Antiquarian and Archaeological Society, extra ser., 25 (1993) · R. A. Griffiths, The reign of King Henry VI: the exercise of royal authority, 1422–1461 (1981) · J. L. Watts, Henry VI and the politics of kingship (1996) · M. A. Hicks, 'The Neville earldom of Salisbury, 1429–71', Wiltshire Archaeological Magazine, 72 (1977–81), 141–7 · A. Payne, 'The Salisbury Roll of Arms', England in the fifteenth century [Harlaxton 1986], ed. D. Williams (1987), 187–98 · M. W. Warner and K. Lacey, 'Neville vs. Percy: a precedence dispute, circa 1442', Historical Research, 69 (1996), 211–17 · GEC, Peerage, new edn, 11.395–8 · M. A. Hicks, Richard III and his rivals: magnates and their motives in the Wars of the Roses (1991), 356–8 · J. Stevenson, ed., Letters and papers illustrative of the wars of the English in France during the reign of Henry VI, king of England, 2/2, Rolls Series, 22 (1864), 775 [Worcester's Annals]

Likenesses manuscript illumination, Bibliothèque Nationale, Paris, Latin MS 1158, fol. 27

Wealth at death £3000: Hicks, Richard III, 356–8; Pollard, North-eastern England, 91

Neville, Richard, sixteenth earl of Warwick and sixth earl of Salisbury [called the Kingmaker] (1428–1471), magnate, was born on 22 November 1428, the eldest son of Richard *Neville, fifth earl of Salisbury (1400–1460), and Alice (c.1406–1462), daughter of Thomas *Montagu, fourth earl of Salisbury.

Early life and the Warwick inheritance As a child aged six Neville was betrothed to Anne Beauchamp (1426–1492), daughter of Richard *Beauchamp, thirteenth earl of Warwick, and his second countess, Isabel Despenser, as part of a double contract in which his sister Cicely married Anne's brother, Henry, the heir to the earldom. Through this marriage, which cost his father over £3000, he was to succeed to the title and much of the inheritance of the Beauchamps and Despensers. Little is known of Neville's youth. He was knighted by Henry VI in or before 1445. As the son of a courtier high in favour he appears to have joined, with his brother-in-law Henry *Beauchamp (d. 1446), the group of young noblemen in personal attendance on the king, for in the letters patent first conferring the title of earl of Warwick on him in 1449, specific reference is made to his service about the king's person. The

Richard Neville, sixteenth earl of Warwick and sixth earl of Salisbury (1428–1471), manuscript drawing [above, with his wife, Anne, and their descendants, including (right) their daughter Isabel and her husband, George, duke of Clarence]

same letters refer to his service in Scotland. It is possible that from 1446, when his father renegotiated an extended contract as warden of the west march in order to include Sir Richard as joint warden for twenty years from 1453, he was already acting as his father's lieutenant. He may have seen military service in the war of 1448–9.

Neville's life was transformed by his succession to the earldom of Warwick, when he had not yet reached his twenty-first birthday, in the summer of 1449. Two lives had stood between him and this dignity: those of his brother-in-law Henry, who died in 1446, and the latter's infant daughter and sole heir Anne, who herself died in 1449. Henry's next heir was his full sister Anne, Neville's wife. In her right he became earl. He stood to enter a vast inheritance, with three constituent elements: the Beauchamp estates which Anne inherited from her father; the Despenser estates, in which she was the joint heir of her mother; and the lordship of Abergavenny in which she was also joint heir. With so much at stake, it is not surprising that his succession was challenged by Anne Beauchamp's elder half-sisters and their husbands, two of whom exercised significant influence at court. Richard Beauchamp had three daughters with his first countess, Elizabeth Berkeley—Margaret, married to John *Talbot, first earl of Shrewsbury; Eleanor, married to Edmund *Beaufort, first duke of Somerset; and Elizabeth, married to George Neville, Lord Latimer. The earl of Shrewsbury, as husband of the eldest daughter, claimed the title himself; all three claimed a share of the inheritance.

The doctrine of the exclusion of the half blood should have given Richard Neville an untroubled succession to the Beauchamp inheritance. This it largely did, in spite of claims by the half-sisters based on settlements made in 1423 and 1425. The Despenser inheritance was nominally divided between Anne and her young nephew George Neville, the heir to Edward, Lord Bergavenny, though in the event Richard and Anne were able at first to secure George's share, the lordship of Glamorgan in south Wales, as well. They also contrived to take possession of the lordship of Abergavenny itself. Moreover, in spite of plausible claims by the half-sisters, Warwick in 1450 forcibly occupied the chamberlainship of the exchequer which had been hereditary to the Beauchamps, but was deprived of it in 1451. The case was referred to the exchequer court, but not determined before the king fell ill in 1453.

In the early 1450s the young Warwick was probably too preoccupied with other commitments, and above all with taking possession (not always peaceably) of his complete inheritance, to have played much part in politics. He became a councillor on his promotion to the earldom, but is not recorded as having attended at all between the end of July 1450 and March 1453. He rallied to the king's side at Dartford in February 1452. But it would appear that while Edmund, duke of Somerset, was dominant at court, he kept his distance. And when Somerset took the custody of the young George Neville's lordships of Glamorgan and Morgannwg from Warwick in June 1453, even though their committal to him had been renewed three months earlier, he responded immediately with violence, occupying Cardiff and Cowbridge castles, which in July he refused to surrender to the king's commissioners. It is not surprising that in the prolonged crisis following the king's collapse in August 1453 Warwick was anxious to see Somerset removed from power. He thus became an early ally of Richard, duke of York, although there is no evidence to identify their sharing a common cause before.

During the first protectorate Warwick was happy to play second fiddle to his father, now the chancellor. While he attended council regularly, and accompanied York on his progress into Yorkshire in May 1454, he received little reward other than the reinforcements of his rights in the earldom of Warwick, a judgment in his favour over the chamberlainship of the exchequer, and a similarly favourable settlement of disputes over the remaining Beauchamp estates. For Warwick, support of York and the first protectorate was largely a means of finally securing his inheritance.

The lord of Calais, 1455–1458 It is not surprising that Warwick followed York and his father into outright opposition to the restored duke of Somerset in 1455. He had retired from council by 5 February. With York and his father he withdrew in March to the north, where they immediately began to raise troops. With an army behind them they marched up to London, intercepting the king and a hastily strengthened entourage at St Albans on 22 May. Warwick played a decisive role in the victory that followed: it was he who made the first breach of the town's defences; and judging by the amends he later undertook to make, he was responsible for the death of Lord Clifford, if not of Somerset himself, whose heir, Henry, earl of Dorset, he took into his own custody.

In the aftermath of St Albans, Warwick displaced his father as York's right-hand man. His prominence was noted in the first session of the parliament that met on 9 July. And something of a stir was caused by his accusation that the ageing Lord Cromwell, his father's close ally, had caused the recent battle. Towards the end of the second protectorate, on 9 February 1456, it was he who came into parliament backed by armed men to shield York. At this stage York and Warwick were particularly anxious to secure the latter's appointment to the captaincy of Calais.

The captain of Calais controlled the only significant standing army in the kingdom. Warwick was nominated to its command in August 1455. But the garrison's wages were deeply in arrears and the government heavily in debt to the Company of the Staple which organized the trade and dominated the government of the town. Neither the garrison nor the company would accept a new captain until their debts had been settled. But a deal was struck in January 1456 which guaranteed wages and repayments of debts. The settlement survived York's dismissal as protector, and Warwick's appointment was confirmed by the king in April. It was not, however, until Somerset's principal lieutenants, lords Rivers and Welles, had been persuaded to step down that Warwick was able to take up the post in July and put in his own commander, his uncle William *Neville, Lord Fauconberg.

For the next four years Calais became Warwick's base. During the summer of 1456 he was still a frequent attender at council, but it is clear that he was already marked out by Queen Margaret as one of the chief threats to the dynasty. At the Coventry council in the autumn, after the queen had made a bid to take over the government, he alone besides York was apparently made to swear an oath of loyalty. Thereafter he was excluded from the council and withdrew to Calais. Starved of funds with which to pay the garrison, he took matters into his own hands: in the spring of 1457 he was reported to have thanked the inhabitants of Canterbury and Sandwich for supplying Calais and begged them to continue. Already there were rumours that the French would lay siege to the town. The attack, when it came, was a raid on Sandwich in August 1457, in effect an attack on Warwick's supply lines. It was soon put about, perhaps by Warwick's agents, that Queen Margaret herself had encouraged the raid. In the event the government had little choice but to commission him to keep the sea and ensure that he was paid to do so.

The threat to Calais and the fear of invasion in 1457 may have helped inspire the attempt at general appeasement that was made early in 1458. While not apparently summoned to the great council held at Westminster in February and March, Warwick nevertheless arrived in strength from Calais and accepted the award of 24 March which involved his paying reparations to the young Lord Clifford and making a contribution to the foundation of a chantry for the victims of St Albans in the abbey there. As befitted the new spirit of reconciliation, he was rewarded with further payment for his fleet and an additional commission to tackle piracy. In fact appeasement only encouraged Warwick to display his contempt for royal authority more openly. In May he attacked a Castilian fleet, and his men, though not unscathed, came away with valuable booty. A few weeks later he seized the Bay fleet of the Hanseatic league as it passed through the straits of Dover, in flagrant violation of a truce concluded two years earlier.

Warwick also used his position in Calais to open up independent lines of communication with both Charles VII of France and Philip the Good of Burgundy. He was commissioned by the crown to negotiate on its behalf in 1458, and it is apparent from Burgundian sources that he also negotiated secretly on behalf of the duke of York. By the autumn of 1458 Warwick's enemies had enough evidence of his insubordination to persuade the king's council that action should be taken against him. He was summoned to a council meeting at Westminster in November to account for his behaviour. He later claimed that a brawl between his servants and others of the king had been an attempt on his life. Thereafter both sides began to prepare for war.

The beginnings of civil war, 1459–1460 By his illegal but spectacular exploits in the channel Warwick managed to keep the Calais garrison paid and loyal, and also to win popular approval in Kent and the home counties, a consideration that enabled him to move with a degree of impunity between London and Calais, flaunting his insubordination. He carried out another spectacular act of piracy against a combined Spanish and Genoese fleet in the summer of 1459. But by this time he, Salisbury, and York had finalized their plan to strike at their enemies at court. They had kept away from a council meeting summoned at Coventry in June, and had been indicted for their failure to attend. They now planned to move in strength on the king's reinforced entourage in the midlands.

Salisbury raised his northern retainers, York called up men from the Welsh marches, and Warwick brought some 600 men of the Calais garrison. They finally made their rendezvous at Worcester at the end of June, and solemnly swore their loyalty to the crown in the cathedral before sending demands to the king for the removal of his evil ministers. Pressed by the Lancastrian army, however, they retreated to Ludford Bridge, before Ludlow, where they endeavoured to make a stand. But the desertion of some of the Calais garrison under Andrew Trollope decided the issue. On the night of 12 October the duke, his sons, Salisbury, and Warwick, broke camp and fled, York and his younger son, the duke of Rutland, going to Dublin, Warwick, Salisbury, and the duke's heir, Edward, earl of March, making their way to Calais.

The rebellion had been a fiasco. The greater part of the nobility had rallied to the crown and rejected the Yorkist claim to speak for the realm. Even before the rout of Ludford a parliament had been summoned to Coventry to meet on 20 November. There the Yorkists were condemned, attainted for treason, and stripped of their property. At the same time immediate action was taken to dislodge Warwick from Calais. On 9 October he had been replaced as captain by the young Henry, duke of Somerset. By the end of the month Somerset had raised troops and crossed the channel, but though he seized Guînes Castle, the Yorkist earls entered Calais itself on 2 November, and maintained themselves there throughout the winter, in spite of constant attack. A government embargo on trading through Calais probably proved counter-productive, because it drove the staplers into Warwick's arms. The attempt to take Calais was further hindered by support Warwick received from the people of Kent, and the garrison's own vigorous counter-attacks, including a raid on Sandwich in January 1460, which destroyed a fleet being gathered to reinforce Somerset, and captured Lord Rivers and other Lancastrian captains.

Warwick himself sailed to Dublin in March 1460 to confer with York. What they there decided has ever since remained controversial. Later Edward IV remembered that voyage as being of great significance to his future, for Warwick brought back with him 'the gretest joye and consolacion erthly' (PRO, DL 37/32/79). There is reason to suppose that Warwick and York not only agreed an invasion plan, but also determined that York would usurp the throne, though Warwick would maintain the dissemblance that the collective aim still remained the removal of evil ministers. Having flooded Kent with reformist propaganda, the Calais lords landed at Sandwich at the end of June, and entered London on 2 July. And, having sworn with his fellow earls a solemn oath in St Paul's that he was the true subject of the king, and leaving Salisbury to blockade the Tower, Warwick marched on with the earl of March to face Henry VI at Northampton on 10 July. The battle, fought in pouring rain, was brief, its outcome aided by desertion in the king's camp. Warwick gave orders to spare the commons. His men made straight for the king's tent, where the duke of Buckingham, the earl of Shrewsbury, Viscount Beaumont, and Lord Egremont were killed defending him. The king, once more, became a guest of the Yorkists.

The making of King Edward, 1460–1461 The victors returned to London, from where Warwick made a brief visit to Calais, to consolidate his position there, before riding to Shrewsbury. There he met York, who was now bearing the arms of England as if he were king, in mid-September. Parliament had been summoned for October, and Warwick returned to London. York, after a circuitous and stately progress to rally support, arrived at Westminster when parliament was already in session. He strode into the Lords' house and walked straight to the chair of state. But, instead of acclamation, he faced a stony silence. It is not at all clear what happened. But although the dominant account, carried most fully by Waurin, reports that the earls and their supporters were to a man taken by surprise and reluctant to acknowledge York as king, it beggars belief that Warwick and March, at least, had not been privy to York's plans, probably since the spring. Perhaps

they hoped to orchestrate a 'popular' election, overriding the likely opposition of men like Warwick's own uncles, the earl of Salisbury and Lord Fauconberg. It seems probable that Warwick had for some months been party to an elaborate charade, concealing his and the duke's true intentions even from their kinsmen, until York finally made his public claim to the throne.

The Act of Accord of 31 October 1460, which left Henry VI on the throne, but recognized York as his heir and protector of the realm, was an expedient that could only be imposed by the sword. On 30 December York was overwhelmed and killed at Wakefield. Salisbury and Warwick's brother, Sir Thomas Neville, also lost their lives. The victorious Lancastrian army marched south. Warwick, who had remained in London with the king and to conduct the second session of parliament which convened in January 1461, frantically raised troops in the south-east, painting an alarming picture of the rapacious intent of the northerners who were then descending on the southern counties. With these levies, and with the dukes of Norfolk and Suffolk at his side, on 12 February he marched out of London to face his enemies. But he was outmanoeuvred and routed at the second battle of St Albans on 17 February. Fleeing westward, he and the remnants of his army were rallied by Edward, the new duke of York, fresh from victory at Mortimer's Cross earlier in the month. They marched immediately on London, arriving in time to prevent the city falling to the hesitant Queen Margaret, who, on hearing of their approach, withdrew. Warwick and Edward, already styling himself true heir to the throne, entered the city on 27 February. Five days later, having been 'elected' by a hastily gathered assembly, Edward took possession of the throne.

Edward IV immediately set about the task of pursuing the retreating Lancastrians northwards, Warwick raising reinforcements in the midlands, before rejoining the king's host at Leicester on 16 March. The armies met on the field of Towton, south-west of York, on 29 March, the victory being carried after a titanic struggle by the divisions under the command of the new king and Lord Fauconberg—Warwick himself may have been less to the fore in the battle as a result of his having been wounded in the leg while forcing the River Aire on the previous day. There was no immediate rest. When the victorious king went back to Westminster and his coronation, Warwick was left in overall command of the north, commissioned to suppress continuing disorder in Yorkshire, to co-ordinate resistance to Lancastrian counter-attacks in Durham and the west march in June, and to oversee the submission of the castles of Dunstanburgh and Alnwick, thereby leaving only Bamburgh untaken in Northumberland. The north seemed to be sufficiently secure by the autumn for Warwick to return to Westminster to attend the parliament summoned to meet on 4 November.

'The governor of the realm', 1461–1464 Edward IV owed his throne to Warwick and his kinsmen. It was a debt fully acknowledged in the rewards heaped upon the earl. He was made great chamberlain of England, master of the king's mews, warden of the Cinque Ports, and constable of

Dover Castle, all for life. His captaincy of Calais was renewed, and he became admiral of England by the end of 1461. In the north his wardenship of the west march was confirmed, to which was added the wardenship of the east march until 1463, when his brother, John *Neville, later Marquess Montagu, succeeded him. He was made steward of the duchy of Lancaster in both the north and south parts, and granted all the stewardships of the duchy in Yorkshire. He received liberal grants of the confiscated estates of his defeated enemies including parts of the Percy estates in Yorkshire, and later, the honour of Cockermouth in Cumberland, as well as the Clifford lordship of Skipton. Commines later repeated the greatly exaggerated rumour that these rewards were worth 80,000 crowns (£16,000) a year; they were certainly worth several thousand pounds.

Warwick had also inherited his father's estates, and after the death of his mother in 1462, her inheritance and dower too. The earldom of Warwick produced an income for him of over £5000 p.a., the Neville and Montagu estates a further £2000. With an annual income from all sources of over £10,000 in the early 1460s, he was spectacularly wealthy, far outstripping any other subject of the king. It is not at all surprising that contemporaries viewed him in the opening years of Edward's reign as the real ruler of England. 'My lord of Warwick … has made a new king of the son of the duke of York'. So wrote the papal legate, Francesco Coppini, to the duke of Milan in April 1461 (CSP Milan, 1385–1618, 69). Bishop Kennedy of St Andrews, who had negotiated with him, wrote a year or two later that he was the 'governor of the realm of England under King Edward' (Waurin, 3.173–4). 'They have but two rulers', joked the governor of Abbeville in a letter to Louis XI, 'M de warwick and another whose name I have forgotten' (ibid., 3.184). He was, Commines considered, like a father to Edward IV. But it was largely to foreign observers that Warwick appeared all powerful. In reality the relationship between the two was more of a partnership between mighty subject and insecure king, and it would be entirely wrong to suppose that Warwick was the sole author of royal policy during these early years.

He was certainly indispensable. In the first two years of the reign Warwick's main preoccupation was defending northern England against the combined assaults of Lancastrians and Scots. The far north had apparently been pacified by the end of 1461, and in the summer of 1462 Warwick concluded a truce with the regent of Scotland, Mary of Gueldres. In October of that year Margaret of Anjou, backed by the French, landed in Northumberland and took the castles of Alnwick and Bamburgh, whereupon the Scots renounced the truce. Warwick immediately raised the north to recover the castles, while the king also called out his household. Edward was struck down with measles at Durham, and it was left to Warwick to co-ordinate the recovery of the castles by early January 1463. The earl was presumably party to the king's insistence that clemency should be shown to rebels, including Sir Ralph Percy and Sir Humphrey Neville of Brancepeth (the respective heads of their families), who were even

entrusted with the custody of the recovered castles. He certainly felt sufficient confidence in the settlement to travel south in February to undertake the solemn interment of the remains of his father and brother at Bisham Priory, and then on to the opening of the second parliament of the reign at Westminster in April.

The confidence was misplaced, however, for in the spring Percy and others went over once more to Queen Margaret. Once more, too, the Scots took advantage by laying siege to Norham. While the king in parliament sought and received a grant of taxation to raise an army against the Scots, Warwick raised the north again, relieved Norham in June, and raided into Scotland. The royal expedition never materialized, however, and the Lancastrians were left, for the time being, undisturbed in their possession of the Northumbrian castles and their control of the county of Northumberland. It had been determined to isolate the rebels and Scots diplomatically before taking to the field again.

Warwick had maintained his diplomatic contacts with Burgundy and France while engaged in the defence of the north. Although the opening of negotiations for a tripartite settlement with Burgundy and France was left in the hands of his brother, the chancellor George *Neville, and his lieutenant of Calais, John, Lord Wenlock, at a conference at St Omer, in October 1463 Warwick himself was commissioned to treat with Scottish ambassadors at York for a renewal of the truce in December. But by late March he was back in London to open negotiations with French ambassadors, led by Jean de Lannoy. The truce was confirmed, a proposal for Edward IV to marry Louis XI's sister-in-law, Bona, daughter of the duke of Savoy, was discussed, and agreement was reached for further talks at St Omer in the summer. Warwick himself wrote to Louis XI encouraging the king to believe that Edward IV was sympathetic. But the talks never materialized. Lord Wenlock was sent to sue for a postponement to October, while Warwick himself returned north, first to complete the truce with the Scots, and then to join his brother John in the final reduction of the Northumbrian castles in July. Now revenge was exacted on the enemies of Neville, as some two and a half dozen of the Lancastrian leaders were summarily executed in relay at Newcastle, Middleham, and York. Montagu for his services was raised to the earldom of Northumberland.

The king's marriage and foreign affairs, 1464–1467 Negotiations for a French marriage were postponed in the summer for a good reason: on 1 May Edward IV had secretly married Elizabeth Woodville. The secrecy of Edward's marriage, and the fact that it was not revealed until Warwick pressed at a council meeting in late September for instructions for his forthcoming embassy concerning the king's projected French alliance, make it clear that Edward feared the reaction of Warwick and others. He knew that his choice of bride would not meet with approval, because of both her background and the political implications of the match. By choosing to marry in secret he risked adding insult to injury, for he clearly continued to allow Warwick to believe that he was eligible.

The manner, as much as the fact, of the marriage, while it reveals the extent to which the king was in awe of Warwick, was also a declaration of independence, marking a turning point in the relationship between the two.

Warwick himself put on a brave face. He gallantly escorted the new queen on her first ceremonial public appearance at Michaelmas; and he swallowed his pride over the deceit. He was no doubt to some extent mollified in the following spring by the grants of Cockermouth, Egremont, and the shrievalty of Westmorland, as well as by the promotion of his brother George to be archbishop of York. There was no visible rift. In July 1465 he was at hand to escort the recently captured Henry VI through London to his imprisonment in the Tower. But it is notable that he had not been present at the queen's coronation on 26 May 1465 and distanced himself, or was distanced from, the new courtly society with which the king surrounded himself. Indeed, the sumptuous installation of George Neville at York on 22 September, while it celebrated the Neville triumph in the north, might also be seen as a riposte to the other coronation in the south.

Yet Warwick was still prominent in foreign affairs. In May 1465 he headed a powerful embassy empowered to treat at will with Burgundy and France. But the outbreak of civil war in France prevented any progress being made. It was not until the spring of 1466 that the commission was reissued. This time the ambassadors were to discuss with Burgundy possible ways of ending the trade war then raging, and also a proposed marriage between Charles, count of Charolais, the heir to Burgundy, and Edward's sister Margaret. It is likely that it was at this meeting in April that a personal antipathy between Warwick and Charolais was born. A similar marriage alliance and truce with France were discussed. Throughout 1466 and into 1467 a stream of envoys passed between England, France, and Burgundy. It soon became apparent that Warwick was advocating a French alliance, while the king, encouraged by the queen's father, Richard Woodville, Earl Rivers, who was created treasurer in March, moved towards a Burgundian alliance.

In October 1466 the king concluded a secret non-aggression pact with Charolais, and followed up with negotiations for a marriage and the end to the commercial war. All this was opposed by Warwick. Nevertheless, Edward, to increase the pressure on Burgundy, was keen to encourage rival French negotiations. Warwick was sent on a further embassy to France in May 1467, being lavishly, almost regally, entertained by Louis XI in Rouen. On offer were a marriage, a pension, generous commercial concessions to offset lost markets in Flanders, and, in exchange for an alliance against Burgundy, a promise to discuss English claims in France. With these terms carried by French envoys, Warwick returned to England in June, only to discover that his brother George had been dismissed as chancellor. In his absence, too, further negotiations between England and Burgundy had been conducted behind the scenes of the great sporting event of a tournament. These had been cut short by the death of Philip the Good. The French envoys were largely ignored by the king, and the

day they left the king announced the renewal of his pact with Charolais, now Duke Charles of Burgundy.

Estrangement, 1467–1469 By midsummer 1467 Warwick knew that he had lost the argument over the direction of foreign policy. He cannot have been deceived by the king. He knew that the French and Burgundians were being played against each other. But he had become personally committed to a French alliance, perhaps flattered by the attention given him by Louis XI, perhaps himself boasting that he could deliver. It now dawned on him how little influence he still had with the king. In pique he withdrew to his estates in the north of England.

The disagreement over foreign policy was the occasion of the breach between Edward and Warwick. But it was not the cause. The cause lay at home. For three years the earl had been progressively marginalized. As the star of Earl Rivers waxed, so his waned. He had been powerless to stop the string of favourable marriages arranged for the benefit of Rivers's family since 1466, which included that of Anne Holland, the heir of Exeter, promised to Montagu's son, George, but now given to Rivers's grandson, the queen's son Thomas Grey. He found too that the king would not contemplate the marriage of his elder daughter, Isabel, to *George, duke of Clarence.

Warwick and Edward became estranged because in the last resort the king could not rule indefinitely under the shadow of his mighty subject while the earl could not accept any diminution of his special status and power. It is not simply that Warwick was arrogant, haughty, acquisitive, and ambitious (all of which he was). The king also handled him unwisely and insensitively. It was injudicious of Edward IV to reward him so lavishly at the beginning of the reign, and to have delegated so much power and authority to him then; it was weak of him later to allow so much scope to Earl Rivers to exploit his position as the queen's father for factional ends; and it was foolish, not in itself to be deceitful in his relationship with Warwick, but to let it become so apparent that he was duplicitous. Warwick had good cause to be aggrieved in 1467.

John Warkworth later wrote that after the announcement of the king's marriage 'there rose great dissension ever more' between the king and Warwick; and that after the dismissal of George Neville:

> the earl of warwick took to him in fee many knights, squires and gentlemen as he might, to be strong; and King Edward did that he might to feeble the Earl's power. And yet they were accorded many diverse times: but they never loved together afterward.   (Warkworth, 3)

The earl could indeed command formidable strength. The twin pillars of his power lay in the north and in Calais. While many families traditionally allied to the Percys remained unreconciled, he and his brothers made Yorkshire a virtual family fiefdom. His dominance extended into Cumberland and Westmorland, and into co. Durham, and he established an iron grip on Calais and its English approaches. In 1467 he withdrew to Yorkshire, and it is possible that he retained more men there, although he already had a powerful affinity in the county at his command. Calais was held loyal to him by his deputy Lord Wenlock.

In other parts of England, where Warwick might have been expected to wield a similar power, he was more vulnerable. In Cumberland, although he was warden of the west march, captain of Carlisle, and the lord of Cockermouth, his control, as events were to demonstrate, was less complete. In Warwickshire and Worcestershire, where Richard Beauchamp, earl of Warwick, had once ruled all, he had never been able to establish his own hegemony. He had been hindered by being an outsider by birth, held back by the early dispute over the inheritance, and, in the late 1450s cut out by the rival power of the court while he had based himself in Calais. Consequently, although he had men and retainers there at his disposal, the west midlands were never a major source of strength. He exercised even less authority in south Wales, where after 1461 Edward IV had already promoted William, Lord Herbert, later earl of Pembroke, as his principal agent. The military might at Warwick's disposal thus lay largely in the north and Calais, but above all in north-eastern England. First and foremost he was a Neville.

But Warwick could also draw on his popular appeal. The fame won by the earl as a naval hero before 1460 lingered on, a fame that he deliberately tapped after 1468 by promoting a popular, though unwinnable, war at sea against the Hanse. His hospitality was legendary. Everywhere he travelled he kept open house; it was said that anyone who came in could take away as much meat as he could load onto a dagger. In the last years of his life, as in 1459–61, he never hesitated to stir up risings, whether in Yorkshire or Kent, to advance his own political cause. There was enough latent popular discontent, whether begotten of residual Lancastrian sympathies or of disappointment with the perceived inadequacies of Yorkist rule, to give Warwick ample opportunity for mischief-making. The earl's skill as a rabble-rouser was a further reason for Edward IV to fear him as an opponent.

It took time for Warwick and Edward to fall out irrevocably. As Warkworth said, they were accorded divers times. Over the winter of 1467–8 Warwick stayed away from court. Incriminating evidence about his doubtful loyalty came to light. He was embarrassed by the revelation that he had secretly sought a papal dispensation for the marriage of Isabel to the duke of Clarence. A captured messenger from Margaret of Anjou reported that it was widely said in France that his sympathies now lay with the house of Lancaster. He was summoned to court to answer the charge, but refused to come. Edward conceded that he would·accept his denial from Yorkshire. Yet it was true that there was talk of that kind in France, whether well founded or not. Moreover Warwick kept constantly in touch with Louis XI through their intermediary William Moneypenny; and Moneypenny's reports to the king encouraged him to think that Warwick was already plotting rebellion.

Rebellion, however, was at this time unlikely. Edward IV kept the truculent Warwick sweet by granting him the profitable wardship of Francis, Lord Lovell. Besides, the earl had in his charge Edward's youngest brother, Richard, duke of Gloucester. In January 1468, through the mediation of his more flexible brother George, Warwick relented and attended a council meeting, called in his own country at Coventry, where he was reconciled with lords Herbert and Stafford, but not with Rivers and the latter's son Lord Scales. Back at court and council in July he participated in the ceremonial departure of Margaret of York for her wedding to the duke of Burgundy, escorting her from London to Dover. His influence probably helped determine the declaration of war against the Hanse in the same month.

Plans by now were well under way for a renewal of war with France. But Louis XI was assiduous in stirring up trouble in England, and in July 1468 a Lancastrian agent named Cornelius revealed under torture that Lord Wenlock was involved in a Lancastrian plot; and the involvement of Wenlock implicated Warwick. On this occasion they both escaped. Any hopes that Edward had that war with France might unite his fragmenting kingdom were dashed. The reconciliation at court was paper thin; popular disturbances recurred in Kent, Yorkshire, and elsewhere. By the beginning of 1469, after the revelation of yet another Lancastrian conspiracy—involving this time John de Vere, earl of Oxford—there was widespread dissatisfaction with Edward's regime, especially the rule of the faction under Earl Rivers. The time was ripe for Warwick to put himself at the head of this discontent.

Rebellion, 1469–1470 Warwick's plans were well laid. They involved the suborning of Clarence and the organizing of a further 'popular' rising in the north while he was away from the region. His path was cleared early in 1469 by the recall of Richard of Gloucester, now sixteen, to court. Dissembling until the eleventh hour, Warwick maintained the pretence of his reconciliation. For the safe keeping of the sea he was given command of a fleet which he ostentatiously sent to harass the west coast of France. In April he represented his king at a meeting at St Omer with Charles of Burgundy and the emperor Friedrich III. In May he attended the installation of Charles as a knight of the Garter at Windsor. Edward was so totally taken in that he set off on pilgrimage to Walsingham in June, convinced that all differences were a thing of the past.

It was then that Warwick struck. There had already been two risings in Yorkshire in the spring of 1469, both stirred by Percy supporters and suppressed with ease by John Neville, now Marquess Montagu. Now a third, at first stirred by Percy supporters and now under the leadership of a Robin of Redesdale, revealed itself in June to be a rebellion of Warwick's northern affinity led by a member of the Conyers family, whose head, Sir John, was Warwick's steward and constable of Middleham. Warwick himself, taking his daughter Isabel, Clarence, and Archbishop Neville with him, sailed over to Calais, and there on 11 July Isabel and Clarence were married. On 12 July he and his new son-in-law published a manifesto condemning the covetous rule of the king's evil ministers, headed by Earl Rivers, and calling upon the commons of Kent to join him for the reform of the commonwealth at Canterbury. This the Kentishmen did, and in a repetition of the campaign of 1459 the lords set off for Coventry to join the northern rebels. But before they did so the king's forces, under William Herbert and Humphrey Stafford (now earls of Pembroke and Devon), had been overthrown at the bloody battle of Edgcote on 26 July. Herbert and his brother Richard were captured and executed in cold blood a few days later; Stafford fled, but was seized by a mob in Bridgwater in Somerset and lynched; Earl Rivers and his son John were caught in the Forest of Dean and murdered; all no doubt on Neville orders. The king, until the last moment unaware of the defeat of his army, was taken by Archbishop Neville at Olney.

Warwick's victory was complete. Edward IV was first imprisoned at Warwick, and then later in August, presumably for safer keeping, was moved north to Middleham. Already a parliament had been summoned in his name to York on 22 September. The rumour spread in France that Warwick was planning to depose him and place Clarence on the throne. Perhaps he was, but before parliament met the escalating general disorder—and especially a rising by Sir Humphrey Neville in upper Tynedale which Warwick could not suppress without royal authority—forced his hand. An agreement was reached with the king, who was released. The rebellion was suppressed, but Edward returned to Westminster in state, and a free man.

It would seem that over the winter of 1469–70, in a series of great councils, an attempt was made to structure a new regime agreeable both to the king and to Warwick. It was reported by Sir John Paston that the king 'hathe good langage' of the earl, but, ominously, that 'hys howsholde men have other langage' (*Paston Letters and Papers*, 1.410). It was a precarious entente. The promotion of the young duke of Gloucester to office in south Wales may have been acceptable to Warwick. The restoration of Henry Percy as earl of Northumberland, by successive stages between 27 October and 1 March as a means of belatedly clipping Neville wings in Cumberland, Northumberland, and Yorkshire, was not. By then Warwick and Clarence were plotting further rebellion, this time, it soon became apparent, without doubt to depose Edward. Disturbances in Lincolnshire provided the opportunity. Richard, Lord Welles, and his son Sir Robert attacked Sir Thomas Burgh, the master of the king's horse. The king could not allow such an assault on one of his senior servants to pass unpunished (perhaps as intended). But the recklessness of Sir Robert Welles, who it was later revealed had been instructed to lure the king north where he would be confronted by Warwick's men in strength, lost the day. Welles was routed near Erpingham on what became known as Losecote Field and, before his execution, implicated Warwick and Clarence. Knowing what was afoot, Edward IV marched north to York to confront the Richmondshire rebels, as Warwick and Clarence shadowed him and Montagu raised the marches. In this game of cat and mouse, Warwick's nerve broke first. Finding that Lord Stanley would not come out for him, he turned and fled. And although Edward gave chase, the earl managed to take boat at Dartmouth early in April. Denied support in Southampton, and access to Calais, despite the sympathy of Lord Wenlock, the earl's party, which included his countess and daughters, finally put ashore at Honfleur on 1 May, and became the guests of Louis XI.

The remaking of King Henry, 1470–1471 In England Edward IV began the process of dismantling Warwick's power. He dismissed the earl's lieutenant of the west march, Lord Fitzhugh, and put in his own man, Sir William Parr. In August the duke of Gloucester was made full warden. Lord Howard was sent to take command of Calais. Henry Percy was made warden of the east march. Warwick's estates were untouched, perhaps pending formal attainder, with the exception of Barnard Castle, which was granted to Bishop Booth of Durham. Beyond this the king did not go, perhaps expecting to decide the issue once and for all on the field of battle.

Louis XI lost no time in taking advantage of the situation. He immediately sought to effect a reconciliation between Warwick and Margaret of Anjou. This might have been a long-term objective—rumours to that effect, some possibly started by Louis himself, had circulated since 1466. On the other hand, Louis might have been only a recent convert to a plan to which some in Margaret of Anjou's circle had been working for some time. Warwick appears to have readily agreed, but only after much persuading did Margaret put her name to a deal which involved the marriage of her son, *Edward, prince of Wales, to Warwick's daughter *Anne, on condition that Warwick and Clarence secured control of England before she and her son came over. On 22 July Warwick was formally reconciled to the house of Lancaster, and agreed to restore Henry VI.

The earl wasted no time. Warwick's plan, yet again, was to mount a decoy to draw Edward IV north, while he himself slipped the blockade on his ships in the Seine to land on the south coast. As planned, Lord Fitzhugh led a rising of men in Richmondshire and Cumberland. They melted away before Edward's advance and soon sued for pardon, which was granted to them on 10 September. But the plan nearly came unstuck because Warwick's flotilla could not get out of port until a storm scattered his enemies' ships. Fortunately Edward had lingered in the north. When Warwick and Clarence landed on 13 September with the earls of Oxford and Pembroke, they raised the country in the name of Henry VI. Whereas Warwick's rebellions in 1469 and earlier in 1470 had received only lukewarm support, now thousands flocked to the Lancastrian colours. Edward IV, returning to confront his enemies, learnt that Montagu to his rear was planning not to join him, but rather to attack him. Now caught in the very trap he had avoided six months earlier, he and a small party of faithful followers hurriedly abandoned their troops, took to the sea at Bishop's Lynn on 2 October, and fled to the Netherlands. England lay at Warwick's feet.

Warwick entered London in triumph on 6 October. Henry VI had already been released from the Tower and was in the care of Bishop Waynflete of Winchester. He was a pitiful figure, incapable of ruling. Warwick assumed the position of the lieutenant of the realm, leading an interim government pending the return of Margaret of Anjou and the prince of Wales. A parliament was summoned to Westminster on 26 November, the principal purpose of which was to attaint the rebel duke of York, calling himself Edward IV, and grant the duchy to Clarence. Ambassadors from France were received to finalize a treaty of alliance. On their return to France in December they were able to assure Margaret of Anjou that Warwick was in full command; she then set out on her journey for England.

But events moved faster than Queen Margaret. Louis XI now declared war on Burgundy. Duke Charles, who had initially kept his distance from his uninvited guest, fitted out an expedition as speedily as he could to help Edward IV recover his kingdom. By the end of February both Edward IV and Margaret of Anjou were held up in port by contrary winds waiting to sail to England. Edward put to sea first and with his small band landed at Ravenspur on the Humber on 14 March. Warwick's preparations had been thorough, but Edward was able to establish himself in Yorkshire because of the tacit support of the earl of Northumberland. Reinforced by his household men as he moved south, and unchallenged by his enemies, he marched on to confront Warwick at Coventry. Warwick was confident that, when joined by Clarence from the west country and the troops under Montagu and the earl of Oxford who had been shadowing Edward, he would have the overwhelming strength to crush him. But his strategy was undermined by the betrayal of Clarence, who on 3 April went over to his brother. Nevertheless Warwick met up with his more reliable Lancastrian allies, and then pursued Edward towards London. On 14 April, Easter Sunday, the two armies finally faced each other in thick morning fog just north of Barnet. In the bad visibility the battle lines became confused. The earl of Oxford routed Hastings's men opposite him, but on regrouping and returning to the field attacked not the rear of Edward IV as he believed, but Montagu's flank, which fought back. Montagu fell and the Lancastrian line broke. Warwick took to his horse and fled, but was caught and killed. After all was over the bodies of the Neville brothers, stripped of their armour, were brought back to London and there displayed for three days in St Paul's, so that all could see that the mighty earl of Warwick was dead. The bodies were then handed over to Archbishop Neville for burial in the family vault at Bisham.

Warwick's last will and testament has not survived. Of his religion nothing is known. His widow lived until 1492. Having landed at Weymouth on the day of his death, she hastened into sanctuary at Beaulieu Abbey. There she was kept for two years under guard, until in 1473 she was taken into the care of Richard of Gloucester, who had married her daughter Anne, and was taken to Middleham Castle. She was disinherited by Edward IV so that his brothers could share the spoils of the Warwick inheritance. Only after the succession of Henry VII did she receive any kind of justice, and that on the condition that she 'voluntarily' made over her inheritance to the crown.

Assessment and reputation Warwick died at the age of forty-two. During his meteoric career he had dazzled the courts of northern Europe with his power and flamboyance. He was already reputed to be the 'proud setter-up and puller-down of kings', as Shakespeare later called him (W. Shakespeare, 3 *Henry VI*, III.iii). But he overreached himself. It could be said that he lacked that quality for which his father was noted: prudence. He was a consummate intriguer, dissembler, and manipulator, but his political career led nowhere. He had but two daughters: Isabel, born in 1451, who married Clarence, and Anne, born in 1456, who married Edward, prince of Wales. It is perhaps because after 1465 he despaired of producing a male heir that he became obsessed with making first one and then the other of his daughters queen of England, an ambition he was to achieve posthumously when the younger became queen as the consort of the third Yorkist, *Richard III.

It is likely that in his preoccupation with his national and international ambitions Warwick neglected the roots of his power in England. One reason why he fell to Edward IV in 1471 was his inability to raise enough men to fight for him. His great north-eastern affinity had done all it could: it rose four times in four years at his command; but on the fourth occasion in April 1471 it was isolated by the course of events. So little had he attended to his interests in Cumberland, on the other hand, that the men of Carlisle and the west march went over to Edward IV under Sir William Parr, and he never established himself in the midlands. It is ironic that it was at Coventry in 1471 that he endeavoured to rally military support that was not forthcoming in sufficient strength. An air of desperation is revealed in his personal postscript to a summons (written at Warwick) to Sir Henry Vernon of Haddon: 'never fail me now' (*Rutland MSS*, 1.4). And it is symptomatic that fail him is just what Vernon did. For all his wooing of the commons, when it came to the final trial of strength, Warwick's neglect of the political nation in the localities away from his own roots left him vulnerable.

Warwick's military reputation was founded on his feats at sea. His control of the channel in 1459–61 was a significant factor in the Yorkist victory. On land he was an incompetent general, notwithstanding his enthusiasm for artillery in the field as well as in siege warfare; and this, strategically and tactically, was his undoing. It was said that he preferred not to fight on foot in the press, as did his contemporaries, most notably Edward IV, but to command from the rear on horseback: an approach hardly calculated to inspire confidence in his men. At Barnet, for once, he was persuaded to fight on foot; and from that final defeat there was no escape. Wary on the field of battle, he had no qualms about killing prisoners afterwards. It is arguable that it was he who, from the first battle of St Albans onwards, was responsible for making the summary execution and murder of defeated opponents common practice in the Wars of the Roses.

Warwick the Kingmaker was unique. Holding what had earlier been four separate earldoms, he enjoyed wealth and exercised influence on a scale arguably never matched before or since by a nobleman who was not directly of the royal blood, and that at a time when the crown itself was weak. It was this fortuitous conjunction of circumstances that made him in effect the arbiter of English politics for fifteen years. On the whole he has not enjoyed a good historical reputation. Building on Burgundian hostility and Edward IV's embittered propaganda in 1471, a view was quickly established that he was motivated only by insatiable ambition and overweening self-regard. Shakespeare portrayed a man driven by injured pride to revenge himself on Edward IV. J. R. Lander has placed a similar emphasis on 'a career which resentment progressively and finally completely dominated' (Lander, 120). But the leitmotif for most modern historians has been his 'contumacious ambition' (Ross, 137): he 'devoted himself with single aim to the acquisition of power for himself and his family' (*DNB*).

Yet there is an alternative tradition. Beginning with Yorkist propaganda in 1460 which described him as the 'flower of manhood', he has been admired as the exemplar of true nobility and promoter of the common weal. So he appeared in the mid-sixteenth-century *A Myrroure for Magistrates*. To Lord Lytton in his romantic novel of 1843, *The Last of the Barons*, Warwick was a hero, 'a man who stood colossal amidst the iron images of the Age—the greatest and the last of the old Norman chivalry—kinglier in pride, in state, in possessions, and in renown, than the king himself' (Bulwer-Lytton, 3), who was driven to rebellion by outrage at Edward IV's attempted seduction of his daughter Anne (a fiction based on a comment in Hall's *Union of the Houses of Lancaster and York* that Edward had attempted the virtue of one of the earl's female relations). Oman at the end of the nineteenth century praised his exceptional powers of leadership and his ability to use his position to articulate popular sentiment. P. M. Kendall in his over-imaginative biography of 1957 followed Lytton's lead. Hicks, too, in his 1998 biography restated the case for Warwick as the very model of medieval nobility who died representing public opinion.

The truth probably lies between the two extremes. He was undoubtedly ambitious and unwilling to accept any role other than first subject in the realm. But perhaps it should also be recognized that his birth, wealth, and status placed him unavoidably at the centre of affairs, and that his erratic course was determined as much by self-preservation as by self-aggrandizement. His vast inheritance stood on shaky foundations, each element open to counter-claim. It was thus essential for him to retain influence at court so as to ensure untroubled possession. Furthermore, his grievances against an immature and inexperienced Edward IV were real. In the later 1460s he and his brother George were pushed aside by a faction led by the queen's father, Earl Rivers. He may genuinely have believed that England's future lay in close diplomatic and commercial ties with France. This was an eccentric and unrealistic policy, but it might not have been adopted solely as a mask to cover an insatiable ambition. His

exploitation of popular grievances for political ends, however, even if deriving from a genuine concern for the common good, threatened the very fabric of the social order. When all is said and done, Warwick became too colossal and too wayward for the long-term stability of the late fifteenth-century kingdom of England; it is entirely appropriate that his career inspired the cult board game Kingmaker, which has been aptly described as a feudal version of Monopoly.   A. J. POLLARD

Sources duchy of Lancaster chancery rolls, PRO, DL 37/32/79 · *Chancery records* · *RotP*, vol. 5 · N. Davis, ed., *Paston letters and papers of the fifteenth century*, 2 vols. (1971–6) · J. S. Davies, ed., *An English chronicle of the reigns of Richard II, Henry IV, Henry V, and Henry VI*, CS, 64 (1856) · A. H. Thomas and I. D. Thornley, eds., *The great chronicle of London* (1938) · 'John Benet's chronicle for the years 1400 to 1462', ed. G. L. Harriss, *Camden miscellany, XXIV*, CS, 4th ser., 9 (1972) · J. de Wavrin [J. de Waurin], *Anchiennes cronicques d'Engleterre*, ed. E. Dupont, 3 (1863) · J. Warkworth, *A chronicle of the first thirteen years of the reign of King Edward the Fourth*, ed. J. O. Halliwell, CS, old ser., 10 (1839) · J. G. Nicholls, ed., 'Chronicle of the rebellion in Lincolnshire, 1470', *Camden miscellany, I*, CS, 39 (1847) · 'The manner and guiding of the earl of Warwick at Angers', *Original letters illustrative of English history*, ed. H. Ellis, 2nd ser., 1 (1827), 132–5 · P. de Commines, *Memoirs, 1461–83*, ed. M. Jones (1972) · J. Bruce, ed., *Historie of the arrivall of Edward IV in England, and the finall recoverye of his kingdomes from Henry VI*, CS, 1 (1838) · C. L. Scofield, *The life and reign of Edward the Fourth*, 1 (1923) · C. Ross, *Edward IV* (1974) · R. A. Griffiths, *The reign of King Henry VI: the exercise of royal authority, 1422–1461* (1981) · R. L. Storey, *The end of the house of Lancaster* (1966) · P. A. Johnson, *Richard, duke of York, 1411–1460* (1988) · J. L. Watts, *Henry VI and the politics of kingship* (1996) · G. L. Harriss, 'The struggle for Calais: an aspect of the rivalry between Lancaster and York', *EngHR*, 75 (1960), 30–53 · C. Carpenter, *Locality and polity: a study of Warwickshire landed society, 1401–1499* (1992) · A. J. Pollard, *North-eastern England during the Wars of the Roses: lay society, war and politics, 1450–1500* (1990) · J. R. Lander, *Crown and nobility, 1450–1509* (1976) · M. A. Hicks, *Richard III and his rivals: magnates and their motives in the Wars of the Roses* (1991) · M. A. Hicks, *'False, fleeting, perjur'd Clarence': George, duke of Clarence, 1449–78* (1980) · M. Hicks, *Warwick the Kingmaker* (1998) · C. W. Oman, *Warwick the Kingmaker* (1891) · H. Summerson, *Medieval Carlisle: the city and the borders from the late eleventh to the mid-sixteenth century*, 2, Cumberland and Westmorland Antiquarian and Archaeological Society, extra ser., 25 (1993) · A. Gross, *The dissolution of the Lancastrian kingship: Sir John Fortescue and the crisis of monarchy in fifteenth-century England* (1996) · E. G. E. L. Bulwer-Lytton, *The last of the barons* (1843) · *Hall's chronicle*, ed. H. Ellis (1809) · P. M. Kendall, *Warwick the Kingmaker* (1957) · *Thys rol was laburd and finished by Master John Rows of Warrewyk*, ed. W. Courthope (1859); repr. as *The Rous roll* (1980) · GEC, *Peerage*, new edn · A. Goodman, *The Wars of the Roses* (1981) · *CSP Milan* · *First report*, HMC, 1/1 (1870); repr. (1874) · *DNB*

Archives Warks. CRO, letter to Lord Ferrers of Chartley

Likenesses T. Rous, drawing, c.1484, BL, Add. MS 48976, Rous roll, no. 57 · B. Rebecca, oils, 1775–1800, Audley End House, Essex · manuscript, University of Ghent, Belgium, Ghent MS 234 · manuscript drawing, BL, Cotton MS Julius E.iv, art. 6, fol. 28 [*see illus.*]

Wealth at death approx. £7000: Hicks, *Richard III*, 339, 356–8; Pollard, *North-eastern England*, 91

Neville, Richard, second Baron Latimer (*c.*1467–1530), soldier, was the son of Sir Henry Neville, who died at Edgcote, on 25 or 26 July 1469, and his wife Joan (*d.* 1470), daughter of John Bourchier, Baron Berners. He inherited his title and lands in twenty-four counties, together with the principal seat of Snape Castle in Richmondshire, on the death of his grandfather George Neville in December 1469. His great-uncle Thomas Bourchier, cardinal-archbishop of Canterbury, gained his wardship and marriage in May 1470 for £1000; royal receivers minded his lands. In 1478 he was knighted. Richard Neville's strengths were loyalty to the crown and military service. He was with the army that went north after the earl of Northumberland's assassination in 1489, served with Henry VII's captains in Brittany in 1492, and joined the earl of Surrey at Flodden in 1513, where he fought in the vanguard and signed the challenge to James IV. The earl of Shrewsbury summoned him for 'secret council' in September 1522 regarding war against the duke of Albany. He appeared at Henry VII's court festivals in 1488 and 1489, joined the escort for Princess Margaret (*en route* for Scotland) between Tadcaster and York in 1503, and witnessed Wolsey's receipt of his cardinal's hat in November 1515.

About 1490 Latimer married first Anne, daughter of Sir Humphrey Stafford of Grafton, Worcestershire, who predeceased him. They had at least thirteen children, including John *Neville, third Baron Latimer (who married Katherine Parr), William *Neville (*b.* 1497, *d.* in or before 1545), and George [*see below*]. In July 1522 he was granted a licence to marry Margaret, the widow of Sir James Strangwishe. He attended the trial of the earl of Warwick and Perkin Warbeck in November 1499, having had livery of his lands in May 1491; and he served as a JP in all three Yorkshire ridings from 1493, in Westmorland from 1503, and in Beverley and Ripon while the York archbishopric was vacant under Henry VII. He was also high steward of Ripon while Wolsey was archbishop. In July 1530 he signed the petition praying Pope Clement to hasten his decision as to Henry VIII's divorce. He died at Snape Castle in December the same year, and was buried with his wife, Anne, in Well church, Yorkshire.

Latimer's son **George Neville** (1509–1567) was born on 29 July 1509. He was admitted BTh at Oxford in August 1541, and supplicated for the degree of DTh in July 1541, a title that he subsequently used. He was witness in two treason cases, in 1532 against his brother William *Neville, and in 1538 against a member of King Henry VIII College, Oxford. He prospered from family livings and pluralism, becoming rector of Bolton, Cumberland, from 1538, and rector of North Lew, Devon, from 1540. He benefited from dispensations to hold additional benefices, serving as master of St Michael's Hospital in Well from at least 1546, rector of Burton Latimer, Northamptonshire, from 1552 until at least 1561, and rector of Rothbury, Northumberland, from 1566, a grant perhaps influenced by the earl of Northumberland, a relative by marriage. Additionally he was archdeacon of Carlisle and rector of Salkeld, Cumberland, from at least 1548, rector of Spofforth, Yorkshire, from 1560 until his death, and of Morland, Westmorland, from 1562 until his death. He was buried on 6 September 1567, in Well church, Yorkshire.　　　　　L. L. FORD

Sources *LP Henry VIII*, vols. 1–3, 5, 13 · *CPR*, 1461–7, 71; 1467–77, 94, 205, 207, 209; 1485–1509 · T. C. Horsfall, *Notes on the manor of Well and Snape in the North Riding of the county of York* (1912) · GEC, *Peerage*, new edn, 7.479–84 · *Reg. Oxf.*, 1.196 · *Calendar of the fine rolls*, PRO, 20 (1949), 247, 260, 264, 267 · Rymer, *Foedera*, 1st edn, 12.490–94; 14.405–7 · H. Ellis, ed., *Original letters illustrative of English history*, 1st ser., 1 (1824), 85–7, 228–32 · A. H. Thomas and I. D. Thornley, eds., *The great chronicle of London* (1938); repr. (1983), 291 · Hunt. L., Ellesmere MS 2654, fol. 16v · BL, Cotton MS Julius B.xii, fols. 32r, 48v, 50r, 51v, 53r, 54v, 64v · Francis, Lord Latimer and F. Redmayne, *Well* (1922) · J. Raine, ed., *Wills and inventories from the registry of the archdeaconry of Richmond*, SurtS, 26 (1853) · W. Dugdale, *The antiquities of Warwickshire illustrated* (1656) · *VCH Northamptonshire*, 3.181 · *VCH Northumberland*, 15.309 · *VCH Yorkshire North Riding*, 1.349–54 · C. J. Ferguson, 'Bolton church, Cumberland', *Transactions of the Cumberland and Westmorland Antiquarian and Archaeological Society*, 3 (1877–8), 1–8 · W. Whellan, ed., *The history and topography of the counties of Cumberland and Westmoreland* (1860), 115, 621, 802 · LPL, MS 318, fols. 365v–359r · BL, Lansdowne MS 860a–b, vol. 1, fol. 371 · BL, Egerton MS 3385B, fol. 2 · D. S. Chambers, ed., *Faculty office registers, 1534–1549* (1966) · Emden, *Oxf.*

Wealth at death £809 in gifts and annuities; £562 in goods and chattels; farmhold at Leake; George Neville: will, 4 Sept 1567

Neville, Richard. *See* Griffin, Richard, third Baron Braybrooke (1783–1858).

Neville, Richard Aldworth. *See* Griffin, Richard, second Baron Braybrooke (1750–1825).

Neville, Richard Cornwallis, fourth Baron Braybrooke (1820–1861), archaeologist, the third son of Richard *Griffin (formerly Richard Aldworth Neville), third Baron Braybrooke (1783–1858), and his wife, Jane (1798–1856), daughter of Charles *Cornwallis, second Marquess Cornwallis [*see under* Cornwallis, Charles, first Marquess Cornwallis], was born in Charles Street in the parish of St George, Hanover Square, London, on 17 March 1820. He was educated at Eton from 1832 to 1837 when he was gazetted an ensign and lieutenant in the Grenadier Guards on 2 June. He served with that regiment in Canada during the rebellion in the winter of 1838, narrowly escaping drowning in the St Lawrence on 5 November the same year. He was promoted to lieutenant and captain on 31 December 1841 before retiring from the service on 2 September 1842.

For some years, aided by his sister, Neville devoted himself to the study of natural history, and to the investigation of the Bronze Age, Roman, and Saxon remains in the neighbourhood of Audley End, Essex, and ultimately attained a distinguished position among the practical archaeologists of his day. At one period geology was his favourite pursuit, and he formed a collection of fossils, which he presented to the museum at Saffron Walden. He also brought together a beautiful series of stuffed birds. At Audley End he created, entirely through his own exertions, a museum of antiquities of every period, which consisted chiefly of objects brought to light at the Roman station at Great Chesterford, or at other sites of Roman occupation in the vicinity of Audley End, and at the Saxon cemeteries excavated under his directions near Little Wilbraham and Linton in Cambridgeshire during 1851 and 1852. He published the results of these excavations, together with a catalogue of his collection of finger rings. He was elected a fellow of the Society of Antiquaries on 25 March 1847, and from time to time made communications to that body regarding his explorations (see *Archaeologia*, 32, 350–4, 357–6). He also contributed memoirs to the *Journal of the British Archaeological Association* (3, 208–13). He was a frequent contributor to the *Journal of the Archaeological Institute* (6, 14–26, 8, 27–35, 10, 224–34, 11, 207–15, 13 1–13), and was vice-president of the institute in 1850. To the *Transactions of the Essex Archaeological Society* he supplied a list of potters' names on Samian ware (1, 141–8), and notes on Roman Essex (1, 191–200), and on the death of John Disney in 1857 he was elected president of the society. Neville's detailed and careful descriptions of his excavations, together with the artefacts he collected, remain fundamental to the study of Bronze Age barrows, Roman sites, and Anglo-Saxon cemeteries in the Cambridge region.

On 27 January 1852 Neville married Lady Charlotte Sarah Graham Toler (1826–1867), sixth daughter of the second earl of Norbury. In March 1858 he succeeded as fourth Baron Braybrooke. He was hereditary visitor of Magdalene College, Cambridge, high steward of Wokingham, Berkshire, and vice-lieutenant of the county of Essex. He died at Audley End on 22 February 1861.

G. C. BOASE, rev. RICHARD SMAIL

Sources GEC, *Peerage* · *GM*, 3rd ser., 11 (1861), 201 · *The Times* (23 Feb 1861) · C. Fox, *The archaeology of the Cambridge region* (1923)
Archives Berks. RO · CUL, diary of military life in Canada, incl. report of a rebellion at Beauharnois · Essex RO, archaeological papers · PRO · U. Cam., Museum of Archaeology and Anthropology, corresp., drawings, excavation notes, finds registers, etc. | S. Antiquaries, Lond., letters to Charles Roach Smith relating to Roman finds at Great Chesterford
Likenesses M. Bras, carte-de-visite, NPG
Wealth at death under £90,000: resworn probate, June 1862, *CGPLA Eng. & Wales* (1861)

Neville, Richard Neville Aldworth (1717–1793), diplomatist and politician, only son of Richard Aldworth of Stanlake, Berkshire, and Catherine, daughter of Richard Neville MP, of Billingbear, Berkshire, was born Richard Neville Aldworth on 3 September 1717. He was educated at Eton College (1728–32), where he was a close friend of Lord Sandwich, Lord Rochford, Lord Orford, Owen Cambridge, and Jacob Bryant. On 12 July 1736 he matriculated at Merton College, Oxford, but instead of finishing his course he travelled abroad. In 1739 he visited Geneva, and passed every winter there until 1744, joining other English visitors—John Hervey, earl of Bristol, William Windham, Benjamin Stillingfleet—in 'a Common Room' for 'an hour or two after dinner' (Coxe, 74); he also took part in private theatricals in which he played, among other parts, Macbeth, and Pierrot in pantomime. He was a good linguist in French and Italian as well as an accomplished classicist. In 1744 he went to Milan and Florence and returned to England before the end of 1745. It is probable that he met his wife, Magdalen Calendrini (d. 1750), while abroad. She was the daughter of Francis Calendrini, the first syndic of Geneva; they were married in 1748.

At the general election of 1747 Neville became MP for Reading. Through the influence of his political patron, Lord Fane, he came to the attention of the duke of Bedford, who appointed him as his under-secretary of state for the southern department on 13 February 1748; he held office until his leader's resignation, on 12 July 1751. He also served as joint secretary to the council of regency in 1748

and 1750. Aldworth was returned for Wallingford in Berkshire in 1754 and for Tavistock in Devon in 1761, which he represented until 1774.

In August 1762 Aldworth assumed the name and arms of Neville and succeeded to the estates of Billingbear, following the death of his aunt Elizabeth, countess of Portsmouth. In politics he joined the duke of Bedford in supporting Lord Bute's government and from September 1762 he acted as the duke's secretary at the peace negotiations in Paris. Walpole credits Neville with causing a delay in the signature of the preliminaries until the capture of the *Havannah* had become known. Bedford acknowledged in generous terms Neville's aid when writing to Egremont, secretary of state, on 10 February 1763, and by way of reward Neville was made paymaster of the band of pensioners. On 15 February he arrived in England with the definitive treaty, which had been signed on 10 February at Paris and which was received by the king and Lord Bute. Neville soon returned to Paris to act as plenipotentiary until the arrival of the earl of Hertford, Bedford's successor as ambassador, on 17 October 1763. While at Compiègne in August John Wilkes visited him. On taking leave of Neville, Louis XVI gave him his picture, set with diamonds, and the duc de Choiseul treated Neville with unusual consideration.

After Neville's settlement again in England he took no prominent part in public affairs. He lost office when Rockingham came to power in June 1765 and he failed to regain it in Grafton's government. He suffered from gout and died at Billingbear after a lingering illness, on 17 July 1793.

He was survived by his two children: Frances, who married Francis Jalabert, and Richard Aldworth, who became second Baron Braybrooke [see Griffin, Richard].

G. LE G. NORGATE, rev. R. D. E. EAGLES

Sources R. S. Lea, 'Aldworth, Richard Neville', HoP, *Commons* · M. M. Drummond, 'Aldworth, Richard Neville', HoP, *Commons* · D. B. Horn, ed., *British diplomatic representatives, 1689–1789*, CS, 3rd ser., 46 (1932) · D. Rowland, *An historical and genealogical account of the noble family of Nevill, particularly of the house of Abergavenny* (1830) [table v] · Burke, *Peerage* · Foster, *Alum. Oxon.* · W. Playfair, *British family antiquity*, 9 vols. (1809–11) · W. Coxe, *Literary life and select works of Benjamin Stillingfleet*, 2 vols. (1811), 1.73–80, 98–107, 160–74; 2.165 · *Correspondence of John, fourth duke of Bedford*, ed. J. Russell, 2 (1842), 93; 3 (1846), 93, 195, 199, 203, 212, 246, 252–4 · *The Grenville papers: being the correspondence of Richard Grenville ... and ... George Grenville*, ed. W. J. Smith, 2 (1852), 29, 52, 57–8, 99 · H. Walpole, *Memoirs of the reign of King George the Third*, ed. G. F. R. Barker, 4 vols. (1894) · J. Ingamells, ed., *A dictionary of British and Irish travellers in Italy, 1701–1800* (1997), 12 · *GM*, 1st ser., 18 (1748), 188, 235 · *GM*, 1st ser., 20 (1750), 187, 233 · *GM*, 1st ser., 32 (1762), 448 · *GM*, 1st ser., 33 (1763), 314, 561 · *IGI*
Archives Berks. RO, notebooks on debates in House of Commons · Essex RO, Chelmsford, diary, accounts, commonplace books, and memoirs · PRO, MSS as under-secretary of state and secretary to Paris embassy, PRO 30/50
Likenesses J. Vanderbanck, oils, 1739, Gov. Art Coll., Audley End House, Essex · J. Zoffany, oils, 1761, Gov. Art Coll., Audley End House, Essex · Basire, engraving, repro. in Coxe, *Literary life* · Tomkins, engraving (after portrait by J. Zoffany)

Neville, Sir Robert de (d. 1282), baron, was the son of Geoffrey fitz Robert (later Geoffrey de Neville; d. in or before

1242), and the paternal grandson of Robert fitz Meldred, lord of Raby, and of Robert's wife, Isabel de Neville, whose surname was borne by her descendants. The identity of Robert's mother has been confused. He has been identified in the past as the son of a Geoffrey de Neville who died in 1249 and Margaret de Longvillers, but the latter's husband died in 1285 (and a Geoffrey de *Neville of Hornby was probably Robert's younger brother), while the Geoffrey whose inquisition post mortem was taken in July 1249 had a wife called Mabel. The point is settled by a Lincolnshire final concord of 1247, which refers to Robert de Neville and his mother, Joan.

Neville held land in Burreth, Lincolnshire, by 1242, and inherited Raby in co. Durham from Robert fitz Meldred in 1254. In 1251 he and his brother took venison in Galtres Forest for the king's Christmas, and in 1252 Robert de Neville had a grant to enclose land into tillage in his manor of Sutton in Galtres, Yorkshire. In 1255 he was given deer to stock his park at Raby, and in 1256 was licensed to hunt hare, fox, and cat with his dogs throughout the forest in Yorkshire. Neville became prominent in northern politics in the late 1250s. As sheriff of Northumberland from January to November 1258, during the unsettled minority of Alexander III, king of Scots, he was one of those entrusted with prosecuting the English royal family's interests in Scotland. He visited the young queen, Henry III's daughter Margaret, 'for solace and succour', and received and escorted political refugees and embassies. Neville was appointed captain for the defence of York and counties beyond Trent on 12 June 1263, and sheriff of Yorkshire on the following day, holding office until June 1264. Within this period he was one of the royalist barons who sought Louis IX's arbitration in December 1263. Local administration was disturbed, and it was recognized in 1269 that Neville had been so impeded by John d'Eyville and others that he could scarcely exercise office between Michaelmas 1263 and the battle of Lewes (14 May 1264), when Simon de Montfort appointed William Boszeall sheriff; in 1274 it was agreed Neville could not account for 1263–4, nor Boszeall for 1264–5, because of the impediments they suffered. Neville was also justice of the forests north of the Trent in 1258 and 1261–5, and at various times custodian of the castles of Bamburgh, Newcastle, Scarborough, and York.

Throughout and beyond these excessively demanding times Neville performed more usual military and administrative services. He was listed under protection for service in Wales in 1257, summoned with service to London in April 1260, to Chester in August following, to London in October 1261, to Welsh campaigns in 1263 and 1264, and to the Hilary parliament of 1265. Summoned to join the attack on Kenilworth in 1266, he was apparently admitted to the king's peace there, which jars given his conspicuously loyal career. In 1267 he was assigned to hear pleas arising from the disinheritance of the rebels, and received other judicial commissions, while in the field of taxation he supervised the fifteenth in Northumberland and Westmorland in 1275. He was present at the Westminster council that found against Llywelyn in 1276, and at the hearing of the earl of Gloucester's claims to Bristol. Summoned to perform military service against Llywelyn in 1277, he offered service by his son John; he was given protection going beyond seas in 1278, but when summoned to military service in 1282 was reported to be infirm. He had died by 20 August 1282. His place of burial is uncertain; the Greyfriars and Blackfriars at York, and Staindrop church, have all been suggested. His heir was his grandson Ranulf, then aged twenty or twenty-one. His sons were obviously born of an earlier marriage than that to his surviving wife Ida, earlier widow of Roger Bertram, and afterwards wife of John fitz Marmaduke. Neville's elder son, confusingly another Robert, who predeceased him, married Mary, coheir of Ralph fitz Ranulf, who brought Middleham to the Neville family.

HELEN M. JEWELL

Sources Chancery records · CIPM, 2, nos. 435, 483 · F. Palgrave, ed., *The parliamentary writs and writs of military summons*, 1 (1827), 758 · W. Brown, ed., *Yorkshire inquisitions of the reigns of Henry III and Edward I*, 1, Yorkshire Archaeological Society, 12 (1892), 254, 259 · H. C. M. Lyte, ed., *Liber feodorum: the book of fees*, 2 (1923), vol. 2, p. 1061 · C. T. Clay and D. E. Greenway, eds., *Early Yorkshire families* (1973), 67 · R. F. Treharne and I. J. Sanders, eds., *Documents of the baronial movement of reform and rebellion, 1258–1267* (1973), 283 · W. W. Shirley, ed., *Royal and other historical letters illustrative of the reign of Henry III*, 2, Rolls Series, 27 (1866), 252 · W. Farrer and others, eds., *Early Yorkshire charters*, 12 vols. (1914–65), vol. 2, pp. 127–9 · Foss, *Judges*, 2.429–30 · C. W. Foster, ed., *Final concords of the county of Lincoln … 1244–1272*, Lincoln RS, 17 (1920), 45 · CDS, vol. 1 · '*Registrum palatinum Dunelmense': the register of Richard de Kellawe, lord palatine and bishop of Durham*, ed. T. D. Hardy, 4 vols., Rolls Series, 62 (1873–8) · *Calendar of the fine rolls*, PRO, 1 (1911), 168 · *Calendar of the charter rolls*, 6 vols., PRO (1903–27), vol. 2, p. 140; vol. 3, pp. 135–6 · CClR, 1272–9, 44; 1279–83, 318

Wealth at death CIPM · £148 16s. 8½d., value of Raskelf, Sutton, and Sheriff Hutton, Yorkshire: Brown, ed., *Yorkshire inquisitions* · in debt to king: *Calendar of the fine rolls*

Neville, Sir Robert (fl. 1344–1373). See under Neville family (per. c.1267–1426).

Neville, Sir Robert (d. 1413). See under Neville family (per. c.1267–1426).

Neville, Robert (1404–1457), bishop of Durham, was the fourth surviving son of Ralph *Neville, first earl of Westmorland (c.1364–1425), and Joan *Beaufort (d. 1440), daughter of *John of Gaunt, duke of Lancaster. He was destined for the church from childhood, being granted in 1411 (when he was seven or eight) licence to hold any benefice with cure of souls on entering his eighteenth year. Preferment came earlier, however, for his father's ally, Bishop Thomas Langley of Durham, collated him in 1413 to his first prebend, that of Eldon, in Auckland collegiate church. By the time he was fifteen he was well provided for, with the rectory of Spofforth and a string of prebends, all in the diocese of York. He must have owed these to the patronage of Archbishop Henry Bowet, another great Lancastrian churchman.

Neville owed his further promotion to his uncle, Henry *Beaufort, bishop of Winchester, who took him into his household. He travelled to the Council of Constance in Beaufort's entourage, leaving England in August 1417. Still only a boy of thirteen, he stayed in Constance rather than continuing on pilgrimage with Beaufort to the Holy Land in 1418, probably returning to England early in 1419. He then seems to have gone up to Oxford, for on 1 July 1420 he was granted licence of non-residence from his prebend in Beverley Minster for three years, and was later described as master of arts in papal letters. On 23 December 1422 he became provost of Beverley.

Neville was provided to Salisbury in a disputed election in 1426–7. He was nominated by the royal council in July 1426, even though under canonical age. The chapter elected their dean. The deadlock was not broken until a year later when Beaufort appealed directly to Martin V on his nephew's behalf, with the result that Neville was provided on 9 July 1427 despite his youth, the pope having been 'moved solely by the cardinal's prayer, desiring to please him alone' (Harriss, 173). He received the temporalities on 10 October, and was consecrated on the 26th. Although there is some evidence of Neville's personal involvement in diocesan affairs, and he does appear to have been a resident bishop, he was also usually an inactive one, and during his episcopacy the diocese became in effect an extension of Beaufort's ecclesiastical network.

Robert Neville's provision to Durham was similarly manipulated in the Beaufort interest. Fortuitously Bishop Langley died on 20 November 1437, just after Cardinal Beaufort had reasserted his authority on the royal council. Only a week later Neville was nominated, while the temporalities were placed in the hands of his brother, Richard *Neville, earl of Salisbury. Although the letter to Eugenius IV in the king's name extolled Robert Neville's supposed virtues and suitability, the real reason was to protect the interests in the palatinate of his mother, the dowager countess of Westmorland, and his family against her stepson, the second earl. Neville was elected by the prior and convent on 27 January, but actually translated by the pope from Salisbury even on that same day.

The new bishop's mother and brother and their servants duly took command of the palatinate. Robert Neville himself was somewhat out of his depth, unable to cope with the violent reaction of the earl of Westmorland. His enthronement was postponed and the king's council stepped in to attempt to restore order. In 1439, following the death of Richard Beauchamp, earl of Warwick, and perhaps influenced by Prior John Wessington of Durham, on whom he came to rely for spiritual guidance, he added to the confusion by his attempt to recover the Beauchamp lordship of Barnard Castle for the liberty of St Cuthbert by force. Yet, since his own brother, the earl of Salisbury, was the father-in-law of the new earl and a feoffee of the lordship, as he must surely have known, he was quickly and humiliatingly forced to withdraw. The death of Neville's overbearing mother on 13 November 1440 finally cleared the way for a general settlement and pacification of the palatinate: the earl of Westmorland received the Durham lordships, and Bishop Robert himself was at length enthroned on 11 April 1441. His episcopacy was thereafter uneventful. He entertained the king in 1448 and received from him an extension of his palatine rights into Northallerton, which proved, however, to be unenforceable.

With all four of Bishop Neville's brothers taking substantial fees, and the administration in the hands of Richard Neville's servants, the palatinate of Durham became unequivocally part of the hegemony of the earl of Salisbury in northern England and its resources were placed at his disposal. The wider political significance of the subordination of Durham to Neville interests became apparent in the 1450s. While at first Robert kept his distance from the quarrel in Yorkshire between his family and the Percys (he acted as a mediator on one occasion), he sent the constable of Norham, Sir Robert Ogle, with a contingent to the first battle of St Albans (22 May 1455) which played a decisive role in the Yorkist victory.

Robert Neville was a man not blessed with an outstanding intelligence; his education seems to have been rudimentary, and, with one disastrous exception, he seems always to have done what the dominant members of his family wanted. While he was routinely appointed to border commissions, it is highly likely that he delegated his responsibilities to others, and especially to his brother, William *Neville, Lord Fauconberg, and the latter's deputies. He was usually resident on his estates in co. Durham and Yorkshire, on which he left his mark mainly as a builder—of the Bedern at Beverley as the provost's residence, of the exchequer on Palace Green in Durham to house the palatine administration, and of the castle at Crayke in the North Riding of Yorkshire. He was a patron of the hospital of St John the Baptist and St John the Evangelist at Sherborne, Dorset, founded in his last year as bishop of Salisbury. He may well have fathered three acknowledged children, the Thomas, Ralph, and Alice for whom he made provision in his will, their mother perhaps also being remembered as betrothed to Thomas Marley. Not the greatest ornament of the late medieval English church, he died at Auckland Palace on 9 July 1457. Even in death he was ineffectual, for his executors failed to prove his hurried eleventh-hour will, and with apt irony his sequestered goods were granted on 31 July to the enemy of his family, Sir John Neville, brother of the earl of Westmorland, and others. He was buried in the south aisle of Durham Cathedral, and not in the galilee chapel, next to Bede, as he had wished. His tomb was defaced by the Scots in the mid-seventeenth century.

A. J. POLLARD

Sources PRO, Durham Chancery records, DURH 3 · U. Durham L., archives and special collections, Durham Church Commission records, estate accounts · W. Hutchinson, *The history and antiquities of the county palatine of Durham*, [2nd edn], 1 (1823), 411–17 · Emden, *Oxf.*, 2.1350 · R. B. Dobson, *Durham Priory, 1400–1450*, Cambridge Studies in Medieval Life and Thought, 3rd ser., 6 (1973) · VCH Wiltshire, vol. 3 · A. J. Pollard, *North-eastern England during the Wars of the Roses: lay society, war and politics, 1450–1500* (1990) · A. J. Pollard, 'The crown and the county palatine of Durham, 1437–1494', *The north of England in the age of Richard III*, ed. A. J. Pollard (1996), 67–87 · G. L. Harriss, *Cardinal Beaufort: a study of Lancastrian ascendancy and decline* (1988) · *Historiae Dunelmensis scriptores tres: Gaufridus de Coldingham, Robertus de Graystanes, et Willielmus de Chambre*, ed. J. Raine, SurtS, 9 (1839) · CEPR letters, 6.247

Likenesses MS illustration, Bibliothèque Nationale, Paris, MS Lat. 1118, fol. 27; repro. in C. Ross, *The Wars of the Roses* (1976), 30

Wealth at death approx. £2500–£3000: Pollard, *North-eastern England*, 49

Neville, Robert (*b.* 1640/41, *d.* in or before 1694), Church of England clergyman and playwright, was born in London, the son of Robert Neville of Sunninghill Park, Berkshire, and his wife, Mary Umfreville, daughter of Andrew Umfreville of Farnham Royal, Buckinghamshire. He was educated at Eton College, from where he was elected to King's College, Cambridge, where he was admitted scholar, aged sixteen, on 17 April 1657. He graduated BA in 1661, proceeded MA in 1664, and was created BD by royal mandate on the occasion of Charles II's visit to Cambridge in 1671. He was ordained deacon at Ely on 20 September 1662 and priest at St Asaph on 25 July 1663. Neville was a fellow of King's between 1660 and 1664, under the provostship of James *Fleetwood, and went on to marry Fleetwood's daughter, probably before 22 May 1671, when he was instituted, on the presentation of Sir Rowland Lytton, to the rectory of Anstey, Hertfordshire, which had become vacant by Fleetwood's resignation. Neville and his wife had two sons: Fleetwood, who became rector of Rampton, Cambridgeshire, and Robert (*b.* 1670/71), who followed his father as rector of Anstey.

Neville was the author of *The Poor Scholar* (1673), a comedy in five acts, partly in prose and partly in verse. Of this the critic and biographer Gerard Langbaine the younger wrote, 'I know not whether ever it was acted, but I may presume to say 'tis no contemptible play for plot and language' (Langbaine, 385). Neville also published many sermons, including *The Great Excellency, Usefulness, and Necessity of Humane Learning* (1681), which was preached before the university at Great St Mary's, Cambridge, and which was concerned with the nature of human and divine knowledge. 'Were not our Church furnished with learned and able men,' Neville declared, 'the church of Rome would soon come in upon us, on our ignorant blind side and make her advantage' (*Great Excellency*, 30). Neville died some time before 7 June 1694, when he was succeeded in the rectory by Thomas Fairmeadow.

CAROLINE L. LEACHMAN

Sources Venn, *Alum. Cant.* · G. Langbaine, *An account of the English dramatick poets* (1691), 385 · R. Clutterbuck, ed., *The history and antiquities of the county of Hertford*, 3 (1827), 344 · T. Harwood, *Alumni Etonenses, or, A catalogue of the provosts and fellows of Eton College and King's College, Cambridge, from the foundation in 1443 to the year 1797* (1797), 251

Neville [Fauconberg], **Thomas** [called the Bastard of Fauconberg] (*d.* 1471), naval commander and rebel, was one of at least two illegitimate sons of the Yorkist commander William *Neville, Lord Fauconberg (*d.* 1463) in right of his mad wife and, from 1461, earl of Kent. Lord Fauconberg was next brother to Richard Neville, earl of Salisbury, uncle to Salisbury's son Richard Neville, earl of Warwick, and was one of their closest allies on the northern borders, at Calais, and at sea. On his death in 1463 his bastards may have transferred to Warwick's service and served him at sea, for Warwick, like Salisbury and Kent before him, was keeper of the seas, had his own ships, and was besides captain of Calais and warden of the Cinque Ports. Such

possibilities are speculation, for Thomas Neville's life is almost wholly undocumented: the identity of his mother, his date of birth, whether he married, and his residence are all unknown.

Neville was already adult on 4 March 1470, when he was paid £50 for maritime service against the Hanse, but he deserted, joining the fleeing Warwick off Calais in late April, and preyed on Burgundian ships, some of which were restored at Louis XI's insistence. In October 1470 he invaded England and entered London with Warwick and then deputized for him as admiral with the grandiose title of 'captain of the navy of England and men of war both by sea and land'. He engaged in piracy against the Portuguese, perhaps as far west as Brittany, and failed to thwart Edward IV's invasion from Burgundy. In late April 1471, following Warwick's defeat at Barnet, he landed in Kent, raising an army from the Calais veterans and the leaders and commons of the chief Kentish towns, and asked leave to pass through London. The city refused permission and informed him of Edward IV's victory at Tewkesbury, which did not deter him. His objective is obscure, but may have been to liberate Henry VI with a view to further resistance. With several thousand men, a core of hardened veterans, a train of ordnance, and a fleet that enabled him to cross the Thames at will, he launched a series of attacks on London from the south and east from 10 to 14 May, destroying the gate on London Bridge and briefly taking Aldgate, but was repulsed with heavy loss of life by Londoners stiffened with the noblemen whom Edward had left behind. His ships withdrew on 14 May, Neville himself and the Calais contingent on 18 May, and the rest of his men were abandoned. As he was still potentially troublesome, Neville negotiated a pardon (10 June) in return for surrendering forty-seven ships at Sandwich to the duke of Gloucester as lord admiral on 27 May. On 16 June he had a protection to accompany Gloucester northwards, where the duke had succeeded to Warwick's lands and offices and needed to win over his retainers. By 11 September he had been arrested at Southampton. He was dispatched to Gloucester in the north and executed; his head was placed on London Bridge facing Kent, and his brother, who was wounded, took sanctuary at Beverley. It is uncertain why Neville died, allegedly for a new offence, perhaps for collaboration with die-hard opponents of Edward IV. The details are not recorded, for he was not tried by common law, but presumably by the law of arms by Gloucester in his capacity as constable of England.

MICHAEL HICKS

Sources J. Warkworth, *A chronicle of the first thirteen years of the reign of King Edward the Fourth*, ed. J. O. Halliwell, CS, old ser., 10 (1839) · C. F. Richmond, 'Fauconberg's Kentish rising of May 1471', *EngHR*, 85 (1970), 673–92 · N. Pronay and J. Cox, eds., *The Crowland chronicle continuations, 1459–1486* (1986) · P. W. Hammond, *The battles of Barnet and Tewkesbury* (1990) · R. Britnell, 'Richard, duke of Gloucester and the death of Thomas Fauconberg', *The Ricardian*, 10 (1994–6), 174–84 · A. H. Thomas and I. D. Thornley, eds., *The great chronicle of London* (1938) · C. Ross, *Edward IV* (1974) · N. Davis, ed., *Paston letters and papers of the fifteenth century*, 2 (1976)

Neville, Sir Thomas (*b.* in or before 1484, *d.* 1542), lawyer and speaker of the House of Commons, was the fifth son of George *Neville, second Baron Bergavenny (1436–1492) [see under Neville, Edward (d. 1476)], and his first wife, Margaret, daughter of Hugh Fenne, and given his position in the family he must have been born in or before 1484. He married first Katherine, daughter of Humphrey, first Baron Dacre of Gilsland, and widow of George, eighth Baron Fitzhugh, with whom he had his only child, Margaret; and second, on 28 August 1532, Elizabeth, widow of Robert Amadas (d. 1532), a London goldsmith who supplied plate and jewels to the royal court.

Neville's service to the crown seems to have originated in his legal expertise, though little evidence survives concerning his early career as a lawyer. A member of Gray's Inn, by 1515 he headed the list of those practising at the bar by virtue of his knighthood, and in 1518 he was listed as a 'pleader' in the king's court. He also received a fee of £3 6s. 8d. as Katherine of Aragon's counsel. Between 1516 and 1527 he frequently attended council meetings, and played an active role in both Star Chamber (where he was appointed by Thomas Wolsey to hear poor men's causes) and the court of requests. His annual fee of £86 as councillor had risen to £100 in 1514 'for good counsel and attendance about the king to be made' (Roskell, 317–20). By 1522 only Neville and Sir Thomas More of the secretaries and masters of requests had access to the king. Between 1517 and 1518 and from 1522 Neville featured in the ad hoc conciliar committees which dealt with justice, and in the 1526 division of subjects between councillors he was assigned to matters of law. In 1527 he heard cases alone. His legal connections extended into personal ones—he was the grandson of Thomas Palmer, a London lawyer, his son-in-law Sir Robert Southwell was master of the rolls, while of his executors, his cousin Sir Thomas Willoughby was chief justice of common pleas and Sir John Baker was chancellor of the exchequer.

Neville's most significant legal work lay in the field of liveries, in which he was active from about 1514, supervising the processes whereby the heirs of tenants-in-chief obtained possession of their estates. In 1518 he became keeper of the king's wards. Under his management liveries began to be dealt with separately from wardships, and in 1529 he was formally appointed to oversee all liveries of possessions in England, Wales, and Calais with Robert Norwich, chief justice of common pleas. His later colleagues were Richard Rich (1535) and John Hynde (serjeant-at-law; 1537), but Neville effectively remained in charge until his death in 1542, when the office became part of the new court of wards and liveries.

Neville's parliamentary experience before 1515 is unknown; he may have been a member for Kent, and while under-sheriff of London (1509–14) he was asked to speak to his father about bills in which the city was interested. Neville was presented by the House of Commons as their choice of speaker on 8 February 1515, and after the customary disclaiming speech he was accepted into office and knighted by the king in the presence of both houses, which the compiler of the Journals of the House of Lords thought an unprecedented distinction. While there is no direct evidence for his performance, the provision of a

second subsidy plus a tenth and fifteenth to meet the deficit of £64,000, and the handling of contentious matters of ecclesiastical jurisdiction including the Hunne and Standish cases, made this a far from easy session to handle, and Neville was well recompensed for his efforts.

Neville does not appear to have continued a parliamentary career, but remained connected to the court. He had daily livery in the king's household in 1519. He was a signatory of the treaty of universal peace and the marriage treaty with France in 1518, and in 1520 was present at the Field of Cloth of Gold, and the meeting with the emperor Charles V in Canterbury. He was a leading mourner at the funeral of Sir Thomas Lovell in 1524, and received a new year's gift from the king in 1533. He does not appear to have been present at Anne Boleyn's coronation, nor at the baptisms of Prince Edward and Princess Elizabeth, but he was at Dover at the end of 1539 as one of the group of courtiers who welcomed Anne of Cleves. The disgrace of his brother George *Neville, third Baron Bergavenny, and the purge of Kent justices in the wake of the fall of Buckingham in 1521 made no difference to his own career, though he acquiesced to the surrender of his brother's main manor of Birling to the crown; the execution for treason of another brother, Sir Edward *Neville, in 1538 had no repercussions for Sir Thomas, who received indictments from Surrey for the trial of Sir Edward's alleged co-conspirator, the marquess of Exeter.

Throughout his career Neville served the king as a county commissioner in Kent, Surrey, Sussex, and Middlesex, whether for taxation or for justice and local administration. He was a knight of St John, and worked with the prior of the order, Sir Thomas Docwra, in Star Chamber. He had a house at Bridewell from Docwra, but they had to surrender it to the king at Wolsey's request in 1523. His success in office made him wealthy enough to lend money to leading courtiers: Charles Brandon, duke of Suffolk, pawned jewels to Neville for £700, and Henry Percy, fifth earl of Northumberland, owed him over £570 in money and plate. In 1532 he was steward of the abbey of Westminster, and hoped to be high steward of the abbey of Malling in Kent, competing with Sir Thomas Wyatt for the grant of the abbey and offering Cromwell 500 marks for it after its dissolution. Eventually it was granted to Cranmer, and for £400 Neville was granted the manor of Shelwood in Surrey and other lands belonging to the dissolved priory of Marton.

Neville's early successes seem to have been made possible by good relations with Wolsey, but he knew that Cromwell was the coming man when Wolsey was under praemunire in November 1529. After the cardinal's fall, Neville was on the commission inquiring about his lands in Kent. Neville corresponded with Cromwell both about personal and political matters. In 1535 he tried to persuade him of the advantages of a marriage between his daughter and Cromwell's son Gregory, but her lack of land seems to have prevented the match. However he was 'comforted in [his] disappointment' by Cromwell's choice instead of Robert Southwell, 'who has many virtues' (LP

Henry VIII, 8, no. 365). Later that year he informed Cromwell of the death of his brother Bergavenny, hoping for his favour in executing the will and enclosing a gold token, and requesting him to be good to Bergavenny's son, a royal ward. He offered Cromwell 'his house of the Yoke' for the king on progress in 1538. As a JP he reported traitorous conversations and bills about the supremacy to Cromwell, and thanked him for his support against the 'complaints of persons … who hate him because he serves the king by ministering his laws with true justice' (LP Henry VIII, 13/1, no. 318).

It is possible that Neville and Cromwell had a similar evangelical outlook: Neville was the patron of Thomas Becon, who dedicated his Christmas Bankette (1542) and Potacion for Lent (1543) to him, describing how rigorously Neville had tested his work against the 'touchstone of the scriptures' and generously entertained him at table, and hoping that God would help him to execute justice. After the fall of Cromwell, however, Neville continued to serve the crown, and payments to his servants suggest some kind of attendance at court in 1541. He corresponded with the privy council in that year about an affray on his land and the investigation of a seditious priest in Maidstone, suggesting that business continued as usual. Neville died on 29 May 1542 and was buried in Mereworth church in Kent, commemorated in a memorial brass.

CATHARINE DAVIES

Sources HoP, Commons, 1509–58, 3.10–11 • LP Henry VIII, vols. 1–17 • J. S. Roskell, The Commons and their speakers in English parliaments, 1376–1523 (1965) • J. A. Guy, Politics, law and counsel (2000) • J. A. Guy, The cardinal's court: the impact of Thomas Wolsey in star chamber (1977) • M. St C. Byrne, ed., The Lisle letters, 6 vols. (1981) • T. Becon, The early works of Thomas Becon, ed. J. Ayre, 2 vols., Parker Society, 11–12 (1844) • M. Zell, 'Early Tudor JPs at work', Archaeologia Cantiana, 93 (1978), 125–143 [1978 for 1977] • E. W. Ives, The common lawyers of pre-Reformation England (1983) • W. H. Dunham, 'The members of Henry VIII's whole council', EngHR, 59 (1944), 187–210 • will, PRO, PROB 11/29 • JHL, 1 (1509–77) • J. L. Chester and G. J. Armytage, eds., Allegations for marriage licences issued by the bishop of London, 1, Harleian Society, 25 (1887)
Archives LMA, journal 11 | PRO, Foreign and Domestic, Henry VIII, SP 1
Likenesses memorial brass, St Laurence Church, Mereworth, Kent
Wealth at death see will, PRO, PROB 11/29

Neville [Nevile], **Thomas** (c.1548–1615), college head and dean of Canterbury, was a younger son of Richard Neville (c.1510–1599) of South Leverton, Nottinghamshire, and Anne, daughter of Sir Walter Mantell of Heyford, in Northamptonshire. Alexander *Neville (1544–1614), who became Archbishop Parker's secretary, was his brother. Thomas was born in Canterbury, where his father retired in his latter years. He entered Pembroke College, Cambridge, proceeded BA in 1569, and in November 1570 was elected a fellow of the college. Among the fellows was Gabriel Harvey, and the two became bitter enemies, Neville even going as far as to non placet the grace for the admission of Harvey to his master of arts degree. In 1580 he was appointed senior proctor of the university. In 1582

Thomas Neville (c.1548–1615), by unknown artist

he was made master of Magdalene College, on the presentation of Lord Thomas Howard, later first earl of Suffolk, and grandson of Thomas Lord Audley of Walden, the founder. Shortly afterwards he was appointed chaplain to the queen, who in 1587 conferred on him the second prebend in Ely Cathedral; and about this time he was presented to the rectory of Doddington-cum-March, in the Isle of Ely.

In 1588 Neville was elected vice-chancellor of the university, but held office for only one year, a year disturbed by the disciplinary measures he was obliged to take against Francis Johnson, the future separatist, and Cuthbert Bainbrigg, fellows of Christ's College, for preaching objectionable sermons. He received the DD in 1589 and in 1590 was appointed dean of Peterborough. In 1592, in conjunction with other deans and prebendaries, he took a prominent part in soliciting an act of parliament confirming them in their rights and revenues, which were at that time in danger of being confiscated under the pretext that they were derived from concealed lands and belonged rightly to the crown. In February 1593, perhaps at the instance of Archbishop John Whitgift, he was appointed by the queen to the mastership of Trinity College, and on his entering office his arms were emblazoned in the Memoriale of the college, an honour never vouchsafed, according to the compiler of that volume, to any preceding master. In March 1594 he resigned the rectory of Doddington for that of Teversham, near Cambridge. He continued to rise in the royal favour, and on 28 June 1597 was installed as dean of Canterbury, resigning his deanery at Peterborough. As he had done at Trinity, Neville worked to improve the quality of the music at Canterbury, bringing George Marston from Cambridge to be organist and master of the choristers. During his regime wind instruments were brought into use at major festivals, and both the music library and repertory were greatly expanded.

Neville, in conjunction with and acting under the directions of Whitgift, took a leading part in repelling the attacks on Calvinistic doctrine made in the university by Peter Baro and William Barrett in 1595. He was greatly esteemed and trusted by the archbishop, and on the death of Elizabeth was chosen by him to convey to King James in Scotland the united greetings of the clergy of England on his accession. Whitgift also appointed him one of his executors.

When James I visited Cambridge in March 1615, Neville kept open house for the royal train at Trinity lodge, with sumptuous hospitality. He was prevented by palsy from waiting personally on the king, but before his departure James visited Neville in his apartments, and with his own hands helped him to rise from his knees, observing that 'he was proud of such a subject'. Neville died at Trinity lodge on 2 May of that year, and was interred on 7 May in Canterbury Cathedral, in the ancient chantry in the south aisle, which he had designed to be the burial place of his family.

Neville never married, died wealthy, and was thus enabled to leave to his college what Fuller terms 'a batchelor's bounty'. His claims to be remembered by posterity rest chiefly on his great services to the foundation, where, to quote the expression of Hacket, 'he never had his like for a splendid, courteous, and bountiful gentleman' (Willis and Clark, 2.474 n.4). In order to carry out his plans for the adornment and extension of the college, he obtained permission from Elizabeth to lease the lands and livings for a period of twenty years (instead of ten years, as before). His first improvement was to remove the various structures belonging to the King's Hall, Michaelhouse, and Physick Hostel, which encumbered the area of what is now the great court; and, assisted by the architect Ralph Symons, to erect, or alter in their present form, most of the buildings (except the chapel) now surrounding it. The *Memoriale* notes:

> When he had completed the great quadrangle and brought it to a tasteful and decorous aspect, for fear that the deformity of the hall, which through extreme old age had become almost ruinous, should cast as it were a shadow over its splendour, he advanced 3,000l. for seven years out of his own purse, in order that a great hall might be erected answerable to the beauty of the new buildings. Lastly, as in the erection of these buildings he had been promoter rather than author, and had brought these results to pass more by labour and assiduity than by expenditure of his own money; he erected at a vast cost, the whole of which was defrayed by himself, a building in the second court adorned with beautiful columns, and elaborated with the most exquisite workmanship, so that he might connect his own name for ever with the extension of the college. (Willis and Clark, 2.475)

During his administration Trinity assumed the leading position among Cambridge colleges that it has enjoyed ever since; the number of scholars and fellows had risen to more than 300 by the time of his death. He also contributed to the college library, bequeathing to it thirty volumes of patristic writings from Canterbury Cathedral Library, and was a benefactor to Eastbridge Hospital in his native city.

In his will, dated 12 October 1614, Neville similarly distributed favours at both Canterbury and Cambridge, leaving 20 marks to be shared out among the poor of Canterbury on the day of his funeral, and £40 to Trinity to buy a piece of plate. There were bequests to several colleagues in both places, but Neville seems to have been principally anxious to provide for his numerous servants, to whom he bequeathed money, clothes, and furniture. One servant, Elizabeth, 'comonlie called black Bes', received an annuity of £5, which after her death was to be applied to the upkeep of Neville's monument in Canterbury Cathedral. Another, Edward Whitgreve, was appointed residuary legatee and sole executor, as the man 'unto whome my poore estate is best knowne and of whose trust and faithefulnes I have had for manie yeares sufficient testimonie' (PRO, PROB 11/126, fols. 410–411v). The will was challenged after Neville's death by a group of his kinsmen, apparently alleging that he was *non compos mentis* when he made it, but its validity was upheld in the prerogative court of Canterbury. Neville had arranged for his memorial at Canterbury long before his death. Begun in 1599, it was a large monument, with effigies of the dean in clerical garb and his brother Alexander (who predeceased him by less than a year) in armour, both kneeling in prayer. Originally in a chantry chapel on the south side of the nave, its remains now stand in the cathedral's south choir aisle. Thomas Neville was remembered as a princely figure, 'non eius academiae tantum sed totius Europae celeberrimus' ('celebrated not only in his own university but throughout Europe'; Cowper, 92–3). It is to be noted that he himself wrote his name Nevile, hence, probably, his motto, *Ne vile velis*. Contemporaries usually pronounced his name 'Nevis'.

J. B. MULLINGER, *rev.* STANFORD LEHMBERG

Sources P. Collinson, P. N. Ramsay, and M. Sparks, eds., *A history of Canterbury Cathedral* (1995) · J. B. Mullinger, *The University of Cambridge*, 2 (1884) · chapter act books, Canterbury Cathedral Library · PRO, PROB 11/126, fols. 410–411v · H. C. Porter, *Reformation and reaction in Tudor Cambridge* (1958) · R. Willis, *The architectural history of the University of Cambridge, and of the colleges of Cambridge and Eton*, ed. J. W. Clark, 2 (1886), repr. (1988) · J. M. Cowper, ed., *The memorial inscriptions of the cathedral church of Canterbury* (1897), 92–3 · Cooper, *Ath. Cantab.*, vol. 2

Likenesses oils, deanery, Canterbury [*see illus.*] · tomb effigy, Canterbury Cathedral · two oil paintings, Trinity Cam.

Wealth at death wealthy; £300 p.a.: will, PRO, PROB 11/126, fols. 410–411v

Neville, Sir William (*c.*1341–1391), Lollard, was the fifth son of Ralph *Neville, fourth Lord Neville (*c.*1291–1367), of Raby, and his wife, Alice (*c.*1300–1374), daughter of Hugh, Lord Audley; he was the younger brother of John *Neville, fifth Baron Neville, and Alexander *Neville, archbishop of York. His career is sometimes uncertain, because another William Neville held lands in Nottinghamshire and Yorkshire, both counties with which he had connections.

Nothing is known of Neville's career before about Michaelmas 1366 when he married Elizabeth, daughter and coheir of Sir Stephen Waleys (d. 1347), who brought him lands in Yorkshire. They do not appear to have had any children. Neville served in France in 1370 and 1372, but his early promotion to office was possibly due to his brother John, steward of the household from November 1371, whom he succeeded as admiral of the north in 1372. He held the office until 1378. Both during and after this period he was named, along with others, to inquire into foreign merchants' complaints about the pillaging of goods at sea. In Edward III's later years he was associated with the court party, and in 1376 was one of the mainpernors (sureties) responsible for ensuring Lord Latimer's appearance in the Good Parliament. Neville's brother also was impeached then, but he himself remained unscathed.

In December 1376 Neville entered the future Richard II's service, and other favours followed the new king's accession: an annuity was confirmed to him in 1378, and in 1381 he was named a knight of the chamber, a post he held for life. In May 1381 he was appointed justice of the forest north of the Trent (a post sufficiently lucrative to be exchanged in 1387 for lands worth 200 marks p.a.) and in November 1381 constable of Nottingham Castle for life. Neither office was a sinecure, for he received various instructions to act in both, bailing individuals accused of forest offences or defining the terms of custody of prisoners in the castle, but it is uncertain whether it was he or his namesake who undertook duties as a local justice in Nottinghamshire. Although he spent much of his time there, he served on an embassy to France in 1383 and in the same year was associated with Michael de la Pole and other court knights in paying certain sums of money to John of Gaunt. In 1386 he was named to survey the port of Orwell as a precaution against a feared French invasion.

Although Archbishop Alexander Neville granted him a pension of £40 p.a. from the archiepiscopal lands, he was not affected by his brother's fall during the appellants' crisis; indeed he was apparently trusted by them. His pension was continued from the forfeited lands and he was given custody of some of the appellants' victims, including his fellow household knight, Sir Simon Burley. After Richard II regained power, between August and December 1389, Neville and other alleged *Lollard knights were regular attenders at council meetings. In 1390, however, he and Sir John Clanvow, another Lollard suspect, went to fight the Muslims in Tunisia. Later they travelled east on pilgrimage, but both died near Constantinople, Clanvow on 17 October 1391 and Neville two days later, on 19 October. Their tombstone survives in the Archaeological Museum of Constantinople.

Neville and Clanvow had known each other since at least 1376 as mainpernors for Lord Latimer. The charge of Lollardy was made against them in 1387 by the chronicler Thomas Walsingham, and of the knights named they were the two against whom the allegations can be most easily upheld. Clanvow actually identified himself with the Lollards in his tract The Two Ways, while the evidence against Neville dates from 1387, when Wyclif's follower

Nicholas Hereford was arrested in Nottingham. Neville petitioned that he should be transferred from the town gaol to his custody in the castle, 'because of the honesty of his person', even though Hereford had long been excommunicated. It is not clear when they first showed a sympathy for radical religious ideas nor are their precise beliefs certain. There is no evidence that they supported eucharistic heresy, nor did they share some Lollards' pacifist views. Most probably they favoured the puritanical piety displayed in Clanvow's work.

JOHN A. F. THOMSON

Sources Chancery records · Thomae Walsingham, quondam monachi S. Albani, historia Anglicana, ed. H. T. Riley, 2 vols., pt 1 of Chronica monasterii S. Albani, Rolls Series, 28 (1863–4) · L. C. Hector and B. F. Harvey, eds. and trans., The Westminster chronicle, 1381–1394, OMT (1982) · K. B. McFarlane, Lancastrian kings and Lollard knights (1972)

Neville, William, earl of Kent (1401?–1463), soldier and baron, was the second son of Ralph *Neville, first earl of Westmorland (c.1364–1425), and his second wife, Joan *Beaufort (d. 1440), daughter of *John of Gaunt, duke of Lancaster. He married, before 28 April 1422, Joan (1406–1490), the heir to the barony of Fauconberg of Skelton in Cleveland, in whose right he was first summoned to parliament in 1429. She was mentally handicapped, being described in 1463 as an imbecile (fatua) and idiot from birth. Her father, Sir John Fauconberg, who was probably also insane, had died in 1407 when she was a year old, and it is likely that her wardship had been granted to Westmorland, who used her inheritance to provide for his second son.

William Neville was knighted in 1426 by Henry VI alongside his half-brother Ralph *Neville, second earl of Westmorland. Little is known of his career, until at the age of thirty-five he joined the expedition led by his young brother-in-law *Richard, duke of York (d. 1460), which sailed to Normandy at the beginning of June 1436. He was soon promoted to a significant command, becoming before the end of the year lieutenant-general for the conduct of the war in the central zone of the Norman marches, with his headquarters at Évreux and Verneuil, of which towns he was made captain. For the next six and a half years, with his fellow lieutenants-general, lords Talbot and Scales, he was one of a trio of field commanders who carried the defence of the duchy.

Following the death of Richard Beauchamp, earl of Warwick, in the spring of 1439, Fauconberg became a member of the interim ruling council of the duchy. In 1440, alongside Talbot and Scales, he participated in the recovery of Harfleur under the command of his kinsman Edmund *Beaufort, later duke of Somerset (c.1406–1455). But during the siege a relieving French force, which had been unable to break the blockade, had seized Louviers and Conches south of the Seine, and thereby established in Fauconberg's sector a salient which reached to the banks of the Seine. Most of the following two years were taken up with attempts to dislodge the enemy. But though Conches was recovered in 1442, Évreux was lost, and the salient could not be removed.

Fauconberg had been on active service for six years when in June 1443 he was sent by York in a deputation to Westminster to plead for more support. He had served with distinction in difficult circumstances. With resources stretched to the limit, and competing demands on his services, it was hardly a result of his negligence that the French had been able to make significant inroads on his front in 1440–42. Yet, while he had lost ground, with his fellow commanders he helped achieve the overall military objective of retaining possession of most of the duchy of Normandy after 1435, thus paving the way for the truce of Tours in 1444. The value of Fauconberg's service was recognized in 1440 by his elevation to the Order of the Garter, appropriately to the stall vacated by the earl of Warwick.

William Neville did not return to France for five years. His services were needed elsewhere. Already, in March 1443, he had been appointed captain of Roxburgh. Since 1441, too, he had not only been the steward of Durham, but had also held the military command of the bishopric on behalf of his brother, Robert *Neville. In the autumn of 1443 he took up these posts in person, even presiding over the Durham halmote courts in October. For the most part, however, he was absent from Durham; how much time he devoted to Roxburgh is unknown. In 1448, however, as the truce came under strain, he returned to France, but was seriously wounded and captured in May 1449 when Charles VII seized Pont de l'Arche. He was a prisoner for over three years. Not until October 1452 were his agents licensed to travel to Normandy to negotiate his release. It was probably to help him meet the cost of his ransom that in 1449, and again in 1451, steps were taken to guarantee the payment of his mounting arrears as captain of Roxburgh.

Fauconberg was probably released in the spring of 1453. He immediately joined the royal council, which he continued to attend during the protectorate of Richard of York. He remained at court in the spring of 1455 after the withdrawal of York and Fauconberg's brother Richard *Neville, earl of Salisbury, acting as a go-between in the weeks leading up to St Albans. And he was in the royal army at the battle, probably protecting the king's own person. Shortly afterwards he was appointed joint constable of Windsor. However, following the appointment of his nephew, Richard *Neville, earl of Warwick, as captain of Calais, his main interests focused on England's last remaining possession in France. In June he was sent to reassure the garrison that its wages would be paid; in the following year, after the end of York's second protectorate, he became its *de facto* lieutenant. Yet throughout these years Fauconberg retained his personal connections at court. It was not until after Queen Margaret seized power in November 1458, and he was removed from the constableship of Windsor, that he became fully identified with the Yorkist cause which his kinsmen had for several years espoused.

When Warwick set out from Calais in September 1459 to join his father and York in rebellion, Fauconberg remained behind. He thus avoided attainder and forfeiture. After the rout of Ludford, however, he was drawn fully into the conflict, organizing the successful defence of Calais against a determined attack by the duke of Somerset. When in June 1460 the Yorkists launched their counter-attack, it was Fauconberg who established a bridgehead at Sandwich. And it was he who led the attack at Northampton on 10 July. His movements in the following months are uncertain, but it is possible that, as the most experienced Yorkist soldier, he accompanied the untried Edward, earl of March, on his campaign in the marches of Wales which culminated in the victory at Mortimer's Cross on 2 February 1461. Certainly when Fauconberg marched out of London at the head of the Yorkist advance guard in pursuit of Margaret of Anjou, on 11 March 1461, he was leading contingents from Wales as well as Kent. It was he who forced the crossing of the Aire on 28 March; and he played a prominent role in the defeat of the main Lancastrian army at Towton on the following day. Shortly after the battle he became captain of Newcastle upon Tyne.

The veteran commander was well rewarded for his services in establishing Edward IV on the throne. On the eve of the parliament that met in November 1461 Fauconberg was created earl of Kent and appointed steward of the king's household. In August 1462 he was granted a substantial patrimony in the west country, carved out of the forfeited estates of the Courtenays. But there was no rest from active service. In July he was appointed admiral of England, but failed to intercept the French fleet carrying Margaret of Anjou and reinforcements to Northumberland. Nevertheless he joined the king on land in his march north in the autumn, and assisted Warwick in the recovery of the Northumbrian castles. He died, of what cause it is not known, on 9 January 1463, possibly before Alnwick. He was buried at Guisborough Priory, of which house he was patron by virtue of his title as Lord Fauconberg. He left three daughters: Joan, aged thirty, who died without heirs; Elizabeth, aged twenty-eight, who married Richard Strangways, son and heir of Sir James *Strangways, speaker of the House of Commons in 1461; and Alice, aged twenty-six, wife of John Conyers, heir of Sir John Conyers. His estates, valued for income-tax purposes at £325 in 1436, were divided between the Strangways and Conyers families. He fathered at least two illegitimate sons, one of whom, Thomas *Neville (the Bastard of Fauconberg), was executed for treason in 1471. The barony of Fauconberg fell into abeyance, but his widow, still officially certified as insane, married a household servant (perhaps to provide for her care) and lived until 1490 when she died at the age of eighty-four.

William Neville, one of the sons of Ralph, earl of Westmorland, represented in the family portrait in Paris, Bibliothèque Nationale, MS Lat. 1158, fol. 27, was described in 1460 as 'little Fauconberg', and also as 'a knight of great reverence' (*English Chronicle*, 91). He was a distinguished soldier, admired by his contemporaries, who rendered selfless and costly service to the house of Lancaster in

France and Scotland. A reluctant rebel, he remained personally closer to Henry VI, and served him loyally for longer, than any other of his kinsmen. Yet it was largely his military expertise and experience that carried the Yorkists to victory in 1460–61.   A. J. POLLARD

Sources king's remembrancer, exchequer accounts various, PRO, E. 101 · estate accounts, Durham, Church Commission records · PRO, Durham chancery records, Durh 3 · BL, Add. MS · Bibliothèque Nationale, Paris, manuscrits français · *Chancery records* · *La chronique d'Enguerran de Monstrelet*, ed. L. Douët-d'Arcq, 6 vols. (Paris, 1857–62) · *Chronique de Mathieu d'Escouchy*, ed. G. Du Fresne de Beaucourt, new edn, 3 vols. (Paris, 1863–4) · J. S. Davies, ed., *An English chronicle of the reigns of Richard II, Henry IV, Henry V, and Henry VI*, CS, 64 (1856) · J. Stevenson, ed., *Letters and papers illustrative of the wars of the English in France during the reign of Henry VI, king of England*, 2 vols. in 3 pts, Rolls Series, 22 (1861–4) · GEC, *Peerage*, new edn, 5.281–6 · A. J. Pollard, *John Talbot and the war in France, 1427–1453*, Royal Historical Society Studies in History, 35 (1983) · A. J. Pollard, *North-eastern England during the Wars of the Roses: lay society, war and politics, 1450–1500* (1990) · R. A. Griffiths, *The reign of King Henry VI: the exercise of royal authority, 1422–1461* (1981) · C. L. Scofield, *The life and reign of Edward the Fourth*, 1 (1923) · H. L. Gray, 'Incomes from land in England in 1436', *EngHR*, 49 (1934), 607–39
Likenesses miniature (possibly William Neville), Bibliothèque Nationale, Paris, Latin MS 1158, fol. 27
Wealth at death approx. £1100: Gray, 'Incomes from land'; Pollard, *North-eastern England*, 347

Neville, William (*b.* 1497, *d.* in or before 1545), poet, was born on 15 July 1497, the second son of Richard *Neville, second Baron Latimer (*c.*1467–1530), and his wife, Anne, daughter of Sir Humphrey Stafford; his brother was John *Neville, third Baron Latimer (1493–1543). He married before 1 April 1529, Elizabeth, daughter of Sir Giles Greville, with whom he had a son, Richard, and two daughters, Mary and Susan.

In his youth Neville may have been in the household of Cardinal Wolsey. On a number of occasions from 1524 he is recorded as commissioner of the peace for Worcestershire. He held or occupied by his marriage various estates in Worcestershire and Gloucestershire. The lands bequeathed to the couple by Elizabeth's father appear to have been the subject of protracted litigation during the late 1520s and 1530s. In a petition of 1534 to Thomas Cromwell Neville laments that 'owing to my great losses I am so empoverished, I am not able to sue by course of law for redress of wrongs' (*LP Henry VIII*, 7, no. 1649).

In 1532 Neville was accused of treason by one Thomas Wood, who alleged that he had prophesied the death of Henry VIII and claimed that he would become earl of Warwick. Similar charges were levelled in March 1533 by his former chaplain Sir Edward Legh. There is no record of the consequences of such allegations. He appears to have died in or before 1545, when his estate is known to have been in the possession of his son, Richard.

Neville is the author of an allegorical dream vision, 'The Castell of Pleasure', in which a dreamer, Desire, is led by Morpheus to the eponymous castle. There he encounters, among others, Beauty, with whom there are exchanges by various allegorical personages. On waking he laments the mutability of human affairs. Verses by Robert Copland preface and follow the poem, which is much influenced by the poetry of Stephen Hawes. Copies survive in editions by Henry Pepwell of 1518 and Wynkyn de Worde, probably of 1530.   A. S. G. EDWARDS

Sources *LP Henry VIII*, 7, no. 1649 · Bodl. Oxf., MS Ashmole 837, fol. 177 · *STC, 1475–1640* · Burke, *Peerage* (1924)

Nevin, Thomas (1686–1745), non-subscribing Presbyterian minister, was born at Kilwinning, Ayrshire, the son of Robert Nevin of Kilwinning. His grandfather Hugh Nevin was vicar of Donaghadee, co. Down, from 1634 to 1652. He was educated at Glasgow University, whence he matriculated on 25 February 1703, describing himself 'Scoto-Hibernus'. It is not known when he graduated but he styled himself MA in a publication of 1725. He trained for the ministry, was licensed by Down presbytery on 26 July 1709, and spent a year as a probationer in Dublin in 1709. On 20 November 1711 he was ordained minister of Downpatrick by Down presbytery, and a new meeting-house in Stream Street was built for him. When the subscription controversy broke out in 1720 Nevin refused to subscribe to the Westminster confession at the general synod of 1721, yet made strong profession of his faith in Christ's deity. In April 1722 he travelled to London to confer with Edmund Calamy and others on the prospects of the non-subscribers, especially in reference to the income provided by the *regium donum*.

Early in 1724 Charles Echlin, a layman of the Church of Ireland church at Bangor, co. Down, charged Nevin with Arianism. Nevin responded by suing for defamation against Echlin. To support Echlin's case an affidavit was sworn on 27 May 1724 by Captain William Hannyngton of Moneyreagh, co. Down, and two others to the effect that in the previous December Nevin had asserted in conversation that 'it is no blasphemy to say Christ is not God' (Reid and Killen, 3.178). This confirmed the suspicions of the subscribing party, who believed that their opponents were hiding their Arian views beneath the issue of subscription. Nevin published a letter on 11 June 1724 in which he explained that the conversation had been on the duties of the civil magistrate; he had argued that to deny Christ's divinity, though a sin, was not a blasphemy deserving of civil punishment. The matter was brought before the general synod, which met at Dungannon on 16 June 1724, by Samuel Henry, minister of Sligo, and a ten-day trial ensued. The synod required Nevin to make an immediate declaration of belief in the deity of Christ, which he refused to do on the grounds that 'to clear himself, by any such method, was directly sinful' (ibid., 3.182). The synod voted on 26 June to cut him off from ministerial communion, but unusually he was neither deposed nor excommunicated, nor removed from his congregation.

In July 1724 Nevin's action against Echlin came on at the Downpatrick assizes. The judge called for a definition of Arianism, which was supplied by John Mears. On hearing the evidence the judge pronounced Echlin's charge 'unmeaning, senseless, and undefined', although it is not known whether he awarded Nevin damages. When the Down presbytery met in August, Mears, who was clerk, flouted the synod's ruling and called Nevin's name as usual. Nevin's supporters called for his case to be reheard, whereupon the subscribers withdrew. At the September meeting Mears was removed from the clerkship and Nevin's name struck off the roll. Nevin was admitted to the non-subscribing presbytery of Antrim when it was excluded from the synod in 1726. He published two accounts of his trial, in 1725 and 1728; the second was in response to a pamphlet by the orthodox subscriber Robert McBride, *Overtures Transmitted by the General Synod, 1725, in a Fair Light* (1726).

Nevin married either one of the daughters of James Fleming, minister of Lurgan, or the daughter of Thomas Boyd of Glastry. He had at least two sons, Thomas and William, both of whom matriculated from Glasgow University in 1737 and became ministers. Nevin died in March 1745, and his funeral sermon was preached at Downpatrick by Alexander Colvill on 24 March. He was succeeded as minister by his son William (*d.* 1780), whose second son, William, also served as minister of Downpatrick.   ALEXANDER GORDON, *rev.* S. J. SKEDD

Sources T. Nevin, *The tryal of Thomas Nevin* (1725) · 'Progress of non-subscription to creeds', *Christian Moderator*, 2 (July 1827), 110–14 · J. S. Reid and W. D. Killen, *History of the Presbyterian church in Ireland*, new edn, 3 (1867), 165–82 · T. Witherow, *Historical and literary memorials of presbyterianism in Ireland, 1623–1731* (1879), 286–94 · T. Witherow, *Historical and literary memorials of presbyterianism in Ireland, 1731–1800* (1880), 332 · *Records of the General Synod of Ulster, from 1691 to 1820*, 3 vols. (1890–98) · J. S. Reid, *History of congregations of the Presbyterian church in Ireland*, ed. W. D. Killen (1886), 119 ff. · [E. Calamy], *An historical account of my own life*, 2nd edn, 2 vols. (1830), 2.479 ff. · W. I. Addison, ed., *The matriculation albums of the University of Glasgow from 1728 to 1858* (1913), 18 · J. McConnell and others, eds., *Fasti of the Irish Presbyterian church, 1613–1840*, rev. S. G. McConnell, 2 vols. in 12 pts (1935–51), 119, 169

Nevinson [Nevynson], **Christopher** (*d.* 1551), civil lawyer and Benedictine monk, was the eldest son of Rowland Nevinson of Briggend in the parish of Wetheral in Cumberland. His cousin Stephen *Nevinson was also a civil lawyer and came from a minor Westmorland gentry family. Christopher Nevinson started his career as a Benedictine monk, and in 1536 was sub-prior of the abbey of Holme Cultram in Wetheral, asking with others for a commission to appoint a new abbot. The seven years before the dissolution were full of intrigue and dissension, and four different abbots were in charge in the period. Nevinson may then have come to the notice of a royal official as a man of promise. He was sent by the abbey to study at Cambridge, where he became a bachelor of civil law in 1533–4, doctor of civil law in 1538, and advocate and member of Doctors' Commons in 1539.

In 1538 Nevinson was allowed with the other monks of Holme Cultram Abbey to hold a benefice and to change habit. On 28 May 1538 he became commissary-general to Archbishop Cranmer, who at first had difficulty in finding him a benefice. As commissary he exercised the archbishop's spiritual and ecclesiastical jurisdiction in the province of Canterbury. From 1541 onwards he was granted several leasehold estates—Adisham parsonage, the manors of Eastry, Wingham, and Teynham, and a *maison dieu* in Romney Marsh among others—and found offices and lands for several of his family. He contributed to a loan to the king in 1542 as commissary of Canterbury. In 1543 he was granted for life the office of registrar of the archbishop's high court and court of arches.

Nevinson married Anne, the daughter of Henry Bingham and Jane Cranmer, sister of Archbishop Thomas. The conspirators in the prebendaries' plot later said that Jane committed bigamy when she married her second husband, John Monnings. They went on to hint that Nevinson had committed buggery with a kitchen boy in the archbishop's palace. There were several other complaints against Nevinson, and he became known as the hated commissary. He had in his library books by Bullinger, Calvin, Bucer, and Pietro Martire Vermigli (known as Peter Martyr), but he was more than a closet radical, for he was heavily involved in defending Cranmer against his conservative attackers in the plot of 1543. He gave up his position at Adisham church to John Bland, who railed against popery and became a protestant martyr under Mary.

Under Edward VI, Nevinson served on several church commissions. In 1547, now confirmed by Cranmer in the office of commissary for his lifetime and as official of the archdeacon of Canterbury, he issued a new set of visitation articles for cathedrals generally and for London, Norwich, Ely, and Westminster, with an insistence on a preaching ministry and use of the vernacular in services. He was a commissioner for the trial in 1549 of Anne, countess of Sussex, for 'errors of scripture', and for the process against George von Parre, an Anabaptist follower of Joan Bocher. Finally he was present as one of the king's visitors at Peter Martyr's disputation at Oxford in May and June 1549.

Nevinson died between 17 March 1551, when he made his will, describing himself as a civil lawyer of Adisham, Kent, and 12 September, when it was proved. He remembered many of his family, but particularly his wife, his son Thomas, and his daughter Jane. He left silver, money, and leases, some to his wife for life with remainder to his son. He appointed his cousin Stephen Nevinson as executor with Archbishop Cranmer one of the supervisors. He was buried at Adisham. His widow had married Thomas Wyseman by 1564, when they brought a case in chancery concerning the lease of Nonington against Stephen Nevinson and evidently won, because they later sold it. Christopher Nevinson's son Thomas died in 1590.

DUNCAN HARRINGTON

Sources CKS, PRC 32/24, fols. 62*v*–66*v* · PRO, PROB 11/35, fols. 24–5*v* · dean and chapter register U, Canterbury Cathedral Archives, fols. 13, 75, 76, 171, 184, 189, 190, 204 · *VCH Cumberland*, 2.162, 170–3 · D. S. Chambers, ed., *Faculty office registers, 1534–1549* (1966), 123 · D. MacCulloch, *Thomas Cranmer: a life* (1996), 204, 304–5, 312, 323, 369, 608–9, 633–5 · *LP Henry VIII*, 18/2.329–30, 359 · PRO, E179/124/254 · B. M. Hogben, 'Preaching and reformation in Henrician Kent', *Archaeologia Cantiana*, 101 (1985), 169–85 · W. F. Shaw, *Liber Estriae* (1870), 95, 234 · W. Berry, *County genealogies: pedigrees of the families in the county of Kent* (1830), 390–91 · PRO, C 3/188/84, 8 Feb 1564/5 · J. Nicolson and R. Burn, *The history and antiquities of the counties of Westmorland and Cumberland*, 1 (1777), 451–2 · Venn, *Alum. Cant.*

Nevinson, Christopher Richard Wynne (1889–1946),
painter and journalist, was born on 13 August 1889 in John
Street, Hampstead, London, the only son of Henry Woodd
*Nevinson (1856–1941), writer, journalist, and foreign cor-
respondent, and Margaret *Nevinson, née Wynne Jones
(1858–1932), a leading suffragette and a writer. He was educated at University College School, Hampstead, and then
at Uppingham School, Rutland (1904–7), where excessive
bullying caused his early departure. He returned to London and began to study art, first at the St John's Wood
School of Art (1907–8), and then at the Slade School of Fine
Art (1908–12), where Mark Gertler, Dora Carrington, Stanley Spencer, William Roberts, and David Bomberg were
among his contemporaries. He began to exhibit regularly,
painting in an impressionist style, and gained the interest
of older artists, including Charles Ginner, Harold Gilman,
and Spencer Gore, but not that of the assistant professor,
Henry Tonks, who advised him to quit art. Nevinson left
the Slade School in the summer of 1912 and travelled to
Paris. There he befriended the Italian futurist painter
Gino Severini and soon afterwards introduced the fragmented imagery of futurism into his own paintings, with
mixed results. In due course Severini introduced him to
Filippo Marinetti, the futurist leader and polemicist,
already well known in England for his bombastic performances. When Marinetti visited London in 1913, he was
enthusiastically welcomed by Nevinson, and also by
Wyndham Lewis, the self-appointed spokesman for
nearly every young independent abstract artist then comprising the English avant-garde. Lewis was eager for radical artistic change, and futurism was a noisy, freely available, anti-establishment aesthetic; but by the spring of
1914 Lewis had changed his mind: he feared an Italian
takeover of abstract art in England. When—on 7 June
1914—Nevinson and Marinetti published *Vital English Art*, a
brash futurist manifesto wrongly claiming the support
and signatures of nearly all the British independents,
Lewis pounced, incensed. Vilifying Marinetti and Nevinson in print, he announced vorticism, an art movement of
1914–15 which attacked British aesthetic values in semi-
futurist terms through the pages of his own magazine
Blast—whose name Nevinson had coined. The ensuing furore denied Marinetti a voice in Britain and, temporarily
but seriously, discredited Nevinson among the English
avant-garde.

It is arguable that Nevinson made his greatest contribution to futurism—and to his own reputation—in his very
vocal role as Marinetti's proselytizing acolyte, and not
through his paintings. His work was often uneven and
owed too much of its style to Severini. However, his
retreat from pure abstraction worked in Nevinson's
favour, for, in the wake of *Blast*, he gave the press an
accessible form of contemporary art to debate. Critics and
readers alike tended to accept his paintings, whereas they
were unable or unwilling to come to terms with the icy
abstraction of vorticism. Nevinson called himself a futurist until late in 1915, even using the name in the vorticist
exhibition catalogue of the same year. Thereafter, until

Christopher
Richard Wynne
Nevinson (1889–
1946), self-portrait,
1911

his death in 1946, he was outspoken in his rejection of all
group affiliations.

In 1915 Nevinson married Kathleen Mary Knowlman;
they had one son, who died in infancy. He experienced the
First World War at first hand as a Red Cross orderly (1914–
15), and with the Royal Army Medical Corps in France and
Flanders (1915–16) before illness led to his military discharge in 1916. From 1915 he executed and exhibited several harshly emotive images of the war in a futurist idiom,
including *La mitrailleuse* (exh. London Group, 1915; Tate
collection), whose merits were argued by well-placed
admirers and detractors alike (Cork, *A Bitter Truth*). By the
end of 1915 Nevinson had completely disavowed futurism
(to Lewis's delight) but did not mention this when he
requested employment as an official war artist from the
Ministry of Information in April 1917: official correspondence shows that Britain's head of propaganda, C. F. G. Masterman, was disappointed with the non-futuristic outcome of Nevinson's official commission. Instead, his work
at, and derived from, the western front after the end of
June 1917 (such as *Paths of Glory*, 1918) was a form of painterly journalism, respected by many artists and by a wide
public following an exhibition at the Leicester Galleries,
London, in 1918. This, and the publication of two illustrated books (*British Artists at the Front: C. R. W. Nevinson*,
1918; *The Great War: Fourth Year: Paintings by C. R. W. Nevinson*,
1918), meant that, by the armistice of 1918, Nevinson's
reputation in Britain, France, and the United States was
assured. However, his peacetime painting lacked the bite
of his wartime images, and it was soon criticized: he may
have entered journalism in self-defence, but in doing so
he found an alternative métier. Nevinson's popularity as
an outspoken artist gained him easy access to the features
columns of many newspapers, and he was a frequent contributor to the *Daily Express* and the *Daily Mail*. From 1920
until 1940 they carried his strident, maverick diatribes,
aimed at society at large, and at the establishment in all its
forms—for example, 'Women growing more and more
beautiful' (*Daily Mail*, October 1929) and 'Once more, this

ridiculous Royal Academy' (*Daily Express*, May 1930). He also wrote regularly for other journals such as the *New Statesman*, the *Strand Magazine*, and *Harper's Bazaar*, and the variety, salacity, and often uncompromising savagery of his egocentric articles remains enormously entertaining. However, his autobiography, *Paint and Prejudice* (1937), is marked and marred by a strong undercurrent of confrontational right-wing xenophobia, and some of his private correspondence in the Imperial War Museum in London is explicitly racist: true signs of the times to which he was such a conspicuous contributor.

A series of strokes in 1942 and 1943 ended Nevinson's career as a painter, and his unjustly neglected prints form his last continuous body of work. Many views of London, New York (1919–21), and southern England, including several executed for London Transport, are outstanding, but his last major commission—as an official war artist in 1940—completely lacked his former vigour. Variously viewed by his contemporaries as charming, aggressive, and neurotic, he was the only artist among the young, pre-1914 British avant-garde who had adopted wholeheartedly the bellicose ideals of Italian futurism. Nevinson died of heart disease on 7 October 1946 at his home, 1 Steeles Studios, Haverstock Hill, Hampstead, London.

JULIAN FREEMAN

Sources correspondence files, First World War and Second World War, IWM, 2 vols. · R. Cork, *Vorticism & abstract art in the first machine age*, 2 vols. (1976–7) · R. Cork, *Vorticism and its allies* (1974) [exhibition catalogue, Hayward Gallery, London, 27 March – 2 June 1974] · R. Cork, *A bitter truth: avant-garde art and the Great War* (1994) · I. Jeffrey, 'C. R. W. Nevinson: artist celebrity', *C. R. W. Nevinson, 1889–1946*, ed. H. Gresty (1988) [incl. bibliography; exhibition catalogue, Kettle's Yard, Cambridge] · C. R. W. Nevinson, *Paint and prejudice* (1937) · *Nash and Nevinson in war and peace: the graphic work, 1914–20* (1977) [exhibition catalogue, Leicester Galleries at the Alpine Club Gallery, London] · J. Rothenstein, *Modern English painters*, 1–2 (1952–6) · picture collection, IWM · J. E. C. Flitch, in C. R. W. Nevinson, *The Great War: fourth year: paintings by C. R. W. Nevinson* (1918) [essay] · CGPLA Eng. & Wales (1947) · M. Walsh, *C. R. W. Nevinson: this cult of violence* (2002)

Archives IWM, corresp. · Tate collection

Likenesses C. R. W. Nevinson, self-portrait, oils, 1911, Tate collection [see illus.] · photograph, 1912 (as student), Slade School of Fine Art, London · B. Seale, bronze bust, 1930, NPG · H. Coster, photographs, 1935, NPG · photographs, c.1935–1946, Hult. Arch. · H. Leslie, silhouette, 1936, NPG · R. O. Dunlop, portrait · H. L. Oakley, silhouette drawing, NPG · portraits, priv. coll.

Wealth at death £8154 6s. 9d.: probate, 1 March 1947, *CGPLA Eng. & Wales*

Nevinson, Evelyn Jane. *See* Sharp, Evelyn Jane (1869–1955).

Nevinson, Henry Woodd (1856–1941), social activist and journalist, was born at 5 South Fields Place, Leicester, on 11 October 1856, the second son of George Nevinson, a solicitor, and his wife, Maria Jane, *née* Woodd, who raised him in a strictly evangelical atmosphere. He won a scholarship at Shrewsbury School and later a junior studentship at Christ Church, Oxford, where he matriculated on 10 May 1875. He was placed in the second class in both classical moderations (1877) and *literae humaniores*, graduating BA

Henry Woodd Nevinson (1856–1941), by Sir William Rothenstein, 1924

in 1879. He retained an interest in the classics, especially Greek drama.

After taking his degree, and spending a short time at Westminster School teaching Greek, Nevinson studied German literature during two sojourns in Germany (mainly at Jena). His first book, *Herder and his Times* (1884), was followed by a volume on Schiller (1889) and, many years afterwards, by another on Goethe (1931). As a child Nevinson had developed a keen interest in military affairs, which led him, as a young man, to study the German army, to advocate conscription, and, after training, to command a company of cadets in the East End of London. Although he grew to hate war, he never lost his academic interest in military history.

At Oxford, Nevinson had been deeply influenced by the principles of Christian socialists and the impressive personality of John Ruskin, and after returning to England from Germany he worked at Toynbee Hall, settling in Whitechapel in London. He also lectured on history at Bedford College, and acted as secretary to the London Playing Fields Committee. He gradually became more radical through his exposure to the miseries of poverty, and by 1889 had joined the Social Democratic Federation of H. M. Hyndman; Marxism, however, was never congenial to him. As an agnostic who disliked all dogmatic systems, his ethical and political outlook was similar to that of his friends Peter Kropotkin and Edward Carpenter. On 18 April 1884 Nevinson married Margaret Wynne Jones (1858–1932) [see Nevinson, Margaret Wynne], with whom he had one daughter and one son, the painter Christopher

Richard Wynne *Nevinson. After her death he married in 1933 Evelyn Jane *Sharp (d. 1955), suffragette and novelist. He spent time living among the working classes and depicted the life of the labouring people in *Neighbours of ours* (1895), which was written in cockney dialect. In later years he joined the Labour Party.

In 1897 Nevinson was made the *Daily Chronicle*'s correspondent in the Graeco-Turkish War. For the next thirty years he chronicled, mainly through eyewitness reports, most of the wars and civil disturbances of the day. He was sent by the *Daily Chronicle* to report on the Second South African War, visited Russia during the abortive revolutionary movement of 1905–6, went to India for the *Manchester Guardian* in 1907–8, and was with the Bulgarians during the First Balkan War. During the First World War he was a correspondent on the western front and at the Dardanelles, where he was wounded. He published *The Dardanelles Campaign* in 1918. In 1926, at the age of seventy, he went to Palestine, Syria, and Iraq to report for the *Manchester Guardian*.

As a war correspondent Nevinson was always scrupulously careful in gathering his facts, and his writing often inspired those struggling towards freedom. However, writing was not his only form of service. He helped to organize relief for the Macedonians (1903) and the Albanians (1911), and to found the Friends' Ambulance Unit in Flanders (1914). When incensed at the outrages of the Black and Tans in Ireland he used the platform as well as the printed page in order to rouse public protest. The most difficult, however, of all his crusades was that which he conducted against what he saw as the virtual slavery of bonded labourers in Portuguese Angola. After a journey into the interior in 1904–5 he returned to the malaria-infested plantations of São Tomé and Principe, encountering skeletons of perished slaves along the way. His writings aimed to make clear to the consciences of his fellow Englishmen the human price of their taste for cocoa. Eventually the leading cocoa firms boycotted the produce of those islands; some of the slaves were repatriated, and, after prolonged controversy, the accusations which he had made in *A Modern Slavery* (1906) were confirmed by the government's white paper published in 1914. Nevinson suffered from a painful tropical disease for many years after the journey.

A strong supporter of female suffrage, Nevinson was friends with the suffragette Evelyn Sharp for many years before they married. In 1909 he rejected a job offer from the *Daily News* as a protest against its stance on women and the vote.

Nevinson wrote good and clear prose. His *Plea of Pan* (1901) was perhaps his most accomplished piece of writing. From 1907 to 1923, while Massingham was editing *The Nation*, Nevinson, whenever he was in England, contributed 'middle' articles (essays written to order and to a prescribed space). He wrote well on an astonishing variety of topics, ranging from humour to grave commentary on history and life. His travel articles were collected in several volumes, of which the best-known were *Essays in Freedom* (1909), *Essays in Rebellion* (1913), *Between the Wars* (1936), and

Running Accompaniments (1936). He also published a few poems. A selection of his work was published posthumously as *Essays, Poems and Tales of Henry W. Nevinson* (1948). His personal experiences were recorded in three autobiographical volumes: *Changes and Chances* (1923), *More Changes, More Chances* (1925), and *Last Changes, Last Chances* (1928); the latter two volumes were abridged by Ellis Roberts in *Fire of Life* (1935).

Nevinson was a handsome man, who carried himself with a noble air which earned him the nickname of the Grand Duke. His blend of humanity, compassion, and daring made him a popular figure in his own lifetime. Twice in his old age friends arranged a banquet in his honour and made him a presentation. In 1938 he was president of the London PEN Club; he received the honorary degree of LLD from the University of Liverpool in 1935, and that of LittD from the University of Dublin in 1936. In 1939 he was elected an honorary student of Christ Church, Oxford. Nevinson died at the vicarage, Chipping Campden, Gloucestershire, on 9 November 1941.

H. N. BRAILSFORD, rev. SINÉAD AGNEW

Sources *The Times* (10 Nov 1941), 6 · Foster, *Alum. Oxon.* · H. W. Nevinson, *Changes and chances* (1923) · H. W. Nevinson, *More changes, more chances* (1925) · H. W. Nevinson, *Last changes, last chances* (1928) · Allibone, *Dict.*, suppl. · M. Farbman, ed., *Political Britain* [1929] · b. cert. · m. cert. · d. cert. · *CGPLA Eng. & Wales* (1942)
Archives Bodl. Oxf., corresp. and papers, incl. diaries; letters | BL, corresp., Add. MS 57040 · Bodl. Oxf., corresp. with John Masefield · HLRO, letters to David Soskice · JRL, letters to *Manchester Guardian* · King's Lond., Liddell Hart C., corresp. with Sir B. H. Liddell Hart · Sheff. Arch., letters to Edward Carpenter · U. Leeds, Brotherton L., letters to Edward Clodd · W. Sussex RO, letters to Wilfrid Scawen Blunt, MS 1988
Likenesses W. Rothenstein, chalk drawing, 1919, NPG · W. Rothenstein, sanguine drawing, 1924, NPG [see illus.] · W. Stoneman, photograph, 1939, NPG · T. R. Annan, photograph, NPG · J. Southall, oils, Christ Church Oxf.
Wealth at death £12,902 15s. 11d.: resworn probate, 8 Jan 1942, *CGPLA Eng. & Wales*

Nevinson, John. *See* Nevison, John (d. 1684).

Nevinson [née Jones], **Margaret Wynne** (1858–1932), women's rights activist, was born at Vicarage House, Lower Church Gate, Leicester, on 11 January 1858, the daughter of the Revd Timothy Jones (c.1813–1873/4) and his wife, Mary Louisa (c.1830–1888). Her father, vicar of St Margaret's Church, Leicester, was a classical scholar who taught her Latin and Greek alongside her five brothers. Her mother had more traditional notions of appropriate pursuits for her only daughter. A brief, unhappy spell in an Oxford Anglican convent school was followed by finishing school in Paris. The unexpected death of her father increased Margaret's wish to live independently. She tried governessing, then went to Cologne as a pupil teacher in a professor's family. In the early 1880s she became a classics mistress at South Hampstead high school, London. She also studied for examinations in Education, German, and Latin, becoming one of sixty-three women who gained the title and diploma of lady literate in arts in 1882 from St Andrews University.

On 18 April 1884 in London Margaret Jones married a

Margaret Wynne Nevinson (1858–1932), by Lena Connell, *c.*1910

childhood friend, the journalist Henry Woodd *Nevinson (1856–1941). They spent a year in Germany, Henry studying at Jena University while Margaret resumed teaching English. Their daughter (Mary) Philippa, who became a talented musician, was born in Germany. After returning to London (encouraged by Samuel and Henrietta Barnett) they moved to workmen's flats in Whitechapel. Margaret Nevinson taught French evening classes at Toynbee Hall and helped with St Jude's Girls' Club. She then became a rent collector in artisans' dwellings. In 1887 the Nevinsons moved to Hampstead. Their son, born in August 1889, was the artist Christopher Richard Wynne *Nevinson. His autobiography describes growing up as part of the Hampstead intelligentsia. His mother was 'always a pioneer', from her shingled hair and hatred of lace curtains to her espousal of modern art, European outlook, and commitment to social justice (C. R. W. Nevinson, 6). In 1901 the Nevinsons bought a house in Downside Crescent, Haverstock Hill, where Margaret lived for the rest of her life. By now Margaret and Henry's lives were running along separate grooves, not least because of the latter's night newspaper work. Henry also became a war correspondent so was frequently away for months. The marriage suffered though they never formally separated.

Margaret Nevinson was a school manager for twenty-five years, initially for the London school board in the East End, then for the London county council (north St Pancras). In 1904 she became a Hampstead poor-law guardian,

determined to root out inefficiency and expose anomalies, particularly where they had an impact on poor women. Her greatest contribution was probably not so much through the weekly meetings she attended so regularly as in publicizing the problems of the poor law. She did this through talks to women's suffrage groups, articles, and stories. In 1918 she published twenty-six tales known as *Workhouse Characters*. These included one story which had earlier been turned into a one-act play called *In the Workhouse*. Performed in 1911 in the Kingsway Theatre by Edy Craig's Pioneer Players, it dramatized the fact that a married woman could be compelled to remain in a workhouse simply because of her husband's marital authority. The stir this provoked helped change the law in 1913. Gender-specific legislation discriminating against married women was increasingly the focus of Margaret Nevinson's writings whether through pamphlets such as *The Legal Wrongs of Women* (Women's Freedom League, 1923) or via her thinly disguised autobiographical stories, *Fragments of Life* (1922).

Margaret Nevinson joined a number of women's suffrage groups. A committed Christian, she was a member of the Church League for Women's Suffrage, spoke for the Cymric Suffrage Union (her father, originally from Lampeter, was a Welsh speaker) and was treasurer of the Women Writers' Suffrage League. Her main commitment was, however, to the Women's Freedom League (WFL). She was a founder member in 1907, became treasurer of the Hampstead branch and was widely known as a witty speaker with a good stock of stories. She frequently invoked classical and biblical themes to illustrate points. She participated in passive resistance such as the suffrage picket outside parliament.

An early trainee in massage, during the war Margaret Nevinson treated wounded Belgian soldiers. Although she had refused to speak on behalf of parties or causes other than suffrage prior to gaining the vote, once enfranchised she supported the Liberal Party. She also lectured on the League of Nations and became a vice-president of the Women's Peace Crusade. In 1927 she was elected to the committee of the Society of Women Journalists. Her most significant post-war public service was, however, as a pioneer female justice of the peace. Nominated by the WFL, in June 1920 she became the first woman in London to adjudicate at criminal petty sessions. With her experience and self-confessed 'passion for justice' and 'devotion to logic' (M. W. Nevinson, 254), she again played a crucial role in Hampstead's affairs. She also visited the United States to study the American probationary system. In 1921 she was one of three women appointed to the lord chancellor's London county justices advisory committee. Margaret Nevinson's autobiography was published in 1926. Her final years were lonely ones, plagued by depression. She died of kidney failure at her Hampstead home, 4 Downside Crescent, on 8 June 1932. She was buried on 11 June at St Stephen's, Rosslyn Hill, London.

ANGELA V. JOHN

Sources M. W. Nevinson, *Life's fitful fever* (1926) · C. R. W. Nevinson, *Paint and prejudice* (1937) · H. W. Nevinson, *Changes and chances*

(1923) • *The Vote* (9 Dec 1909) • *The Vote* (30 July 1920) • *The Vote* (17 June 1932) • *Hampstead Gazette* (10 June 1932) • *The Times* (9 June 1932) • minute book, LMA, Hampstead board of guardians archives, Hp BG cols. 30–44 • *Toynbee Record*, LMA, A/TOY/26/11/11 • appointment of magistracy, LMA, LTCY/86 • *Manchester Guardian* (9 June 1932) • *Daily Telegraph* (9 June 1932) • H. W. Nevinson, diaries, Bodl. Oxf. • A. J. R., ed., *The suffrage annual and women's who's who* (1913) • m. cert. • d. cert. • *Leicestershire Mercury* (23 Jan 1858) • parish registers, Leics. RO [baptism] • W. Harris, 'H. W. Nevinson, Margaret Nevinson, Evelyn Sharp: little-known crusaders', *English Literature in Transition, 1880–1920*, 45 (2002), 280–305

Archives LMA, Hampstead board of guardians minute book, Hp BG cols. 30–44

Likenesses L. Connell, photograph, *c*.1910, The Women's Library [*see illus.*] • T. Fall, photograph, repro. in *The Vote* (9 Dec 1909) • photograph, repro. in *The Vote* (30 July 1920) • photograph, repro. in *The Vote* (17 June 1932)

Wealth at death £2830 10s. 7d.: probate, 28 Aug 1932, *CGPLA Eng. & Wales*

Nevinson [Nevynson], **Stephen** (*c*.1520–1580), biographer and ecclesiastical lawyer, was born about 1520, the second son of Richard Nevinson of Newby, Westmorland. His first cousin Christopher Nevinson was diocesan commissary to Thomas *Cranmer, archbishop of Canterbury, and married Cranmer's niece. This family connection with the central figure of the English Reformation was crucial for Nevinson's career as an academic and ecclesiastical administrator: fervently protestant, he was also fiercely ready to defend his own interests against his like-minded superiors. Already, when noted in 1544 as pensioner of Christ's College, Cambridge, he had moved south to Kent, as he was described as a scholar from the newly refounded King's School, Canterbury. He proceeded BA at Trinity College in 1544–5, commenced MA in 1547–8 and LLD in 1552–3. Soon after 1544 he became fellow and tutor of Trinity College, Cambridge. Among his pupils, the poet George Gascoigne, who had Westmorland connections, commemorated his teaching in the 199th stanza of his *Dulce bellum inexpertis*. In 1551/2 he accounted for rents at Cranmer's manor of Wingham, Kent, on behalf of Christopher Nevinson's young son Thomas, and, in accordance with a provision in Christopher's will of 1551, was described as Thomas's guardian in a Kentish chancery suit of 1556–8.

Under Mary I, Nevinson seems to have left Cambridge, but remained in the circle of former Cranmer servants and associates determined to preserve the archbishop's writings and reputation. He may already have married Elizabeth, daughter of Reyner Wolfe, one of Cranmer's principal publishers. He gained custody of Cranmer's theological notebooks, preserving them jealously until 1563, when Matthew Parker, archbishop of Canterbury, had to bring privy council pressure to bear on him to surrender them. Nevinson is the likeliest candidate for authorship of the anonymous eyewitness life of Cranmer which was published by the Camden Society in 1859 in *Narratives of the Reformation*. This author was undoubtedly also the anonymous editor E. P. of a section of Cranmer's theological notebooks, published in 1556 (probably at Wesel) as *A Confutation of Unwritten Verities*, which overlaps in some editorial textual material with the anonymous life. A pseudonymous Eusebius Pamphilus also produced

an English translation of an anti-Spanish tract by Luther, published at Strasbourg and London in 1554: *A Faithful Admonition of a Certain True Pastor and Prophet*, whose translator's preface has similarities to these two works. The three texts share a fervent evangelical fury directed at the Marian regime and reproof of England's rulers for allowing it to happen, and Cranmer emerges as a heroic figure from the anonymous life, which provides intimate and affectionate personal detail about his career. The attribution of the life to Nevinson is dependent on a number of clues: the author talks of his memory stretching back 'above thirty years', which for a man writing *c*.1557 would be compatible with arriving in Cambridge early in the 1540s; he has a particular interest in printing, suggestive of the man whose father-in-law was a prominent evangelical printer; above all, Nevinson was the custodian in 1563 of the very notebooks that had provided the material for *A Confutation of Unwritten Verities*.

On Elizabeth's accession Nevinson soon emerged from retirement to a new and different career. On 25 January 1559 he had a lease from the dean and chapter of Carlisle of tithe corn at Morland, Westmorland, previously leased by his recently deceased father. On 22 July 1559 he was appointed one of the commissioners for the royal visitation of the dioceses of Oxford, Lincoln, Peterborough, and Coventry and Lichfield, and in September 1560 was among commissioners beginning a metropolitical visitation of Canterbury Cathedral; by 16 October 1560 he had been appointed commissary for Canterbury diocese, the office formerly held by Christopher Nevinson. John Bale, writing to Parker on 30 July 1560, spoke admiringly of Nevinson's unrivalled knowledge of the canons of early church councils. On 2 January 1561 Edmund Grindal, bishop of London, ordained him both deacon and priest, and the same day Parker presented him to the wealthy rectory of Saltwood, Kent, in succession to Alexander Nowell. On 23 November 1562 he was presented to the eighth prebend in Canterbury Cathedral, in succession to Cranmer's former secretary, Pierre Alexandre. In the convocation of 1563 Nevinson as *procurator cleri Cant.* headed the list of subscribers to the Thirty-Nine Articles, and in February 1563 he was prominent in speaking and signing in favour of proposed reforms to the Book of Common Prayer, possibly with Parker's encouragement.

In 1566 John Parkhurst, bishop of Norwich, an old friend of Reyner Wolfe, appointed Nevinson vicar-general in his diocese. Nevinson was zealous for the rights of his new office, disrupting the work of Parker's metropolitical visitation in the diocese in 1567. He nevertheless kept a keen eye on his Canterbury income, earning Parker's annoyance by seeking in March 1568 to retain his whole profits from his prebend despite his non-residence. His relationship with Parkhurst also deteriorated: on 9 February 1569 Parkhurst collated him rector of Stiffkey, Norfolk, but the title was doubtful and Nevinson refused to risk paying first-fruits to the crown. By 19 April 1569 Parkhurst wrote to him reproachfully, regretting his resignation as vicar-general after two years of threatening to do so. On 12 June 1570 Nevinson, by now in attendance on Parker once more, resigned Stiffkey to Lord Keeper Sir Nicholas Bacon, having used his father-in-law, Wolfe, as an intermediary. The transaction took place at Wolfe's London house. Soon there came the compensation that Nevinson had requested the lord keeper to grant him, Westbere rectory, Kent, on 21 June 1571, on Wolfe's petition. However, Nevinson was still a presence in Norwich in August 1571, when the city's mayor, embroiled in a dispute with the Norwich Strangers' Church, vainly sought to persuade Parkhurst to allow him and two other leading city preachers to confront one of the Stranger ministers in debate.

In July–October 1570, when Parker held an ordinary visitation of Canterbury Cathedral, Nevinson was ordered to examine suspected traditionalists among the petty canons and vicars-choral. He demonstrated his continuing protestant militancy when he wrote from London to Lord Burghley on 25 May 1572, urging (with a wealth of biblical and classical allusion) that no mercy should be shown to those disaffected to the queen, no doubt meaning Mary, queen of Scots, and Thomas Howard, duke of Norfolk. On 1 November 1570 Nevinson had obtained a licence to hold three benefices simultaneously, but this does not seem to have been required until 19 August 1577, when the crown presented him to the wealthy rectory of Romaldkirk, Yorkshire. He no doubt remained in Kent or London, since his mother-in-law had bequeathed him use of a chamber in her London house in 1574. At that time Archbishop Cranmer's widow, Margarete, was probably yet another member of this crowded household, as she had moved in with the Wolfes after the breakdown of her third marriage, to Bartholomew Scott. Nevinson made his will on 31 December 1579, and died before 15 June 1580, when a successor was appointed to his Canterbury prebend. His widow was left a bed formerly belonging to Reyner Wolfe; his executor was George Boleyn, dean of Lichfield and a former colleague at Canterbury, who proved his will on 12 October 1581. No children are recorded.   DIARMAID MACCULLOCH

Sources D. MacCulloch, *Thomas Cranmer: a life* (1996), esp. appx 1 · P. M. Black, 'Matthew Parker's search for Cranmer's "Great notable written books"', *The Library*, 5th ser., 29 (1974), 312–22 · BL, Lansdowne MS 443, fol. 195*r* · *Correspondence of Matthew Parker*, ed. J. Bruce and T. T. Perowne, Parker Society, 42 (1853) · *CPR, 1575–8*, no. 2634 · Cumbria AS, Carlisle, D/LONS/L5/2/17 · *Miscellaneous writings and letters of Thomas Cranmer*, ed. J. E. Cox, Parker Society, [18] (1846), 1–19 [repr. in *A confutation of unwritten verities*] · *The complete works of George Gascoigne*, ed. J. W. Cunliffe, 1 (1907), 180 · M. Luther, *A faithful admonition of a certayne true pastor and prophete, sent unto the Germanes at such time as certain great princes went about to bryng alienes into Germany … with a preface of M. Philip Melancthon*, trans. Eusebius Pamphilus [1554] [Ger. orig., *Warnung an seine lieben Deudschen*] · *Registrum Matthei Parker, diocesis Cantuariensis, AD 1559–1575*, ed. W. H. Frere and E. M. Thompson, 3 vols., CYS, 35–6, 39 (1928–33), 353 · H. Gee, *The Elizabethan clergy and the settlement of religion, 1558–1564* (1898), 97, 160 · *The recovery of the past in early Elizabethan England: documents by John Bale and John Joscelyn from the circle of Matthew Parker*, ed. T. Graham and A. G. Watson (1998), 27 · W. P. Haugaard, *Elizabeth and the English Reformation: the struggle for a stable settlement of religion* (1968) · *The letter book of John Parkhurst, bishop of Norwich*, ed. R. A. Houlbrooke, Norfolk RS, 43 (1974–5) · R. Hovenden, ed., *The visitation of Kent, taken in the years 1619–1621*, Harleian Society, 42 (1898) · will, consistory court of Canterbury probate register, vol. 34, CKS, PRC 32/34, fol. 166 · *Fasti Angl., 1541–1857*, [Canterbury] · GL, MS 9535/1, fols. 98v, 99r · J. G. Nichols, ed., *Narratives of the days of the Reformation*, CS, old ser., 77 (1859), 218–33 [for anonymous 'Life and death of Thomas Cranmer, late Archbishop of Canterbury', from BL, Harley MS 417, fols. 90–93] · prerogative court of Canterbury, wills, 1574, PRO, PROB 11/56, sig. 32 [will of Joan Wolfe] · chancery, early chancery proceedings, PRO, C 1/1457/13 · exchequer, king's remembrances, ecclesiastical documents, PRO, E135/25/31, fol. 18 · special collections, ministers' and receivers' accounts, PRO, SC 6/Edw VI/240 · state papers domestic, Elizabeth I, PRO, SP 12/86/50 · *The papers of Nathaniel Bacon of Stiffkey*, ed. A. H. Smith and others, [4 vols.], Norfolk RS (1979–) · J. Strype, *Annals of the Reformation and establishment of religion … during Queen Elizabeth's happy reign*, new edn, 4 vols. (1824) · Venn, *Alum. Cant.*, 1/3.245 · 'Kentish wills: genealogical extracts from sixteenth-century wills in the consistory court at Canterbury', *Miscellanea Genealogica et Heraldica*, 5th ser., 5 (1923–5), 215

Nevison [Nevinson], **John** [William] (*d.* 1684), highwayman, was born at Wortley in the West Riding of Yorkshire. Details of his birth are uncertain. There is absolutely no reason to believe that he was born in 1639, the date that became enshrined in pamphlet accounts of his life. It is possible that he is the John Nevinson, son of John Nevinson, who was baptized at Tankersley (the parish in which Wortley lay) on 10 September 1648. His mother's name was Elizabeth. Nevison's parents, the nonconformist minister Oliver Heywood was told, had been brought up profanely, while Nevison himself had married his wife (also Elizabeth?) in an alehouse. During his life Nevison was always known by the name John.

Nothing is known of John Nevinson before the mid-1670s, by which time his activities as a highwayman were being investigated by local magistrates as they interrogated a variety of unreliable witnesses among his associates. George Skipwith of Howden, in the West Riding, examined in March 1676, described the men he knew by the names of Tankered and John Brace (or Bracy) as 'men who live by robbing' and mentioned as their companion Edmund Bracy (Raine, 221). He believed that John Brace was really John Nevinson, who had lived for a time at Burton Agnes in the East Riding and now lived beyond Pontefract. Skipwith pinpointed a couple of safe houses that the men had, at Tuxford in Nottinghamshire and Wentbridge in Yorkshire. He was rather vaguer as to the details of actual crimes: when he went to see them at Wentbridge in the hope of borrowing money from them, their landlady told Skipwith how, after there had been a robbery of excisemen, the two highwaymen had been able to pay off their bills with her and each buy a horse. Picked up in January 1677 for a burglary in Mansfield, Nottinghamshire, Elizabeth Burton was more informative. She had fallen in with John Nevison and his associates Edmund Bracy, Thomas Wilbore, Thomas Tankerd, John Bromett, and William (or Robert) Everson—'all highwaymen'—who had kept her for two years in a house in Newark (Raine, 260). They kept a room at the Talbot at Newark where they used to divide up their spoils. She listed a number of their robberies, committed in groups of two to six in south Yorkshire, Lincolnshire, and Nottinghamshire, which she remembered from the shares of the proceeds that she was given. When Nevison, Everson, and Bromett robbed a shopkeeper of about £300 on the road between Grantham and Stamford, for instance, her share paid for her lodgings for three months; when all six committed a robbery near Royston, in Yorkshire, their takings were £250, from which she received two gold pieces, enough silver to pay for six months' lodging, and 6s. 8d. to buy some shifts. In February 1677 Robert Holgate of Grimethorpe told how he had tried to buy from Nevison what he must have known was a stolen horse, a 'daple gray Gelding, and … bloudy faced' (PRO, ASSI 45/12/1/56A). Holgate gave it a trial ride through Barnsley, where he was evidently spotted on such a distinctive horse so that the original owner, Jeremiah Peele of Pontefract, was able to track him down.

In March 1677 Nevison was tried at the York assizes for the theft of Peele's horse and for a highway robbery committed near Wombwell: a wallet stolen during the latter theft had been found hidden behind a chest in his widowed mother's house. The indictments gave his place of residence as Wortley. Convicted, he was pardoned on condition of transportation upon his offer to inform against his accomplices, although it is uncertain how far he kept his side of the bargain. He was still a prisoner in York Castle awaiting transportation in July 1681. Later that year he was taken out of gaol to be enlisted in a company of soldiers bound for the fever-ridden outpost of Tangier. He immediately ran away and in October the Yorkshire magistrate Sir John Reresby met the king to urge a reward of £20 for his recapture, warning that Nevison 'had threatned the death of severall justices of the peace' (*Memoirs of Sir John Reresby*, 235). A notice duly appeared in the *London Gazette*. To renewed highway robbery in Yorkshire, Nottinghamshire, and Derbyshire, a further charge was added: that Nevison had murdered Fletcher, constable of Howley in the parish of Morley in the West Riding. Despite the reward Nevison remained free for over two years. 'I have seene him passe ordinarily in the road', Heywood recorded, 'he led his horse lately down the street in Wakefield, was generally known, yet none were so hardy as to lay hands on him' (Heywood, 4.58). He was also running an effective protection racket, as carriers and drovers paid him off or lent him money not to be troubled by him. He was finally captured on 6 March 1684 while he sat drinking at an alehouse in Sandal by William Hardcastle, aided by the local constable and another man. He was taken to York, where the assizes were sitting. As he was in breach of the terms of his pardon by still being in England no further trial was needed, and he was condemned by the judge, who 'told him he must dye, for he was a terrour to the country' (Heywood, 4.57). He was hanged at the Knavesmire, York's place of execution, on 15 March. He went to the gallows 'somewhat stupid'—presumably either stupefied with drink or in a state of psychological collapse—and before he was turned off confessed to having killed Fletcher in self-defence (Heywood, 4.57). He was buried at St Mary Castlegate, York, the following day.

'He is gone at last, and hath left much debt at severall ale-houses in the country where he haunted', was Oliver Heywood's epitaph on Nevison:

this poor man at last found and confest that his sabbath-breaking, drinking, lewd company and course had brought him to that shameful end, its said he was a papist and had his pardon in his bosom, Oh that all his thievish and drinking companions might learn by his example to leave their wicked ways and fear god! (Heywood, 4.58)

However, Nevison received rather different memorials in both chapbook literature and in local popular memory. *The Yorkshire rogue, or, Capt. Hind improv'd; in the notorious life and infamous death of that famous highwayman*, published in London in the year of his execution, provided the template for a narrative which was endlessly recycled and elaborated on in chapbooks well into the nineteenth century, and which helped place Nevison as one of the three archetypal highwaymen in the popular imagination— alongside James Hind and Claude Duval—in the years before the development of the legend of Dick Turpin. This literature drew on some genuine incidents in his life but otherwise mixed plausible circumstantial detail with a generic set of picaresque adventures. It was the chapbooks who rechristened Nevison William—the name by which he became universally known—and had him born in Pontefract (a bigger and better known place than his actual place of birth). It was also the chapbooks that credited him with the royalism appropriate to any respectable Restoration highwayman, claiming that he had served under James, duke of York, in Flanders in the 1650s (a claim given some plausibility by the early date of birth they gave him). Nevison was also celebrated in ballad. *The High-Way Mans Advice to his Brethren, or, Nevison's Last Legacy to the Knights* was a London broadside probably produced to capitalize on the news of his death: Nevison's name was just a peg to hang the song on. 'Bold Nevison', extant in Yorkshire in the mid-nineteenth century, which included verses describing the killing of Fletcher and the capture at Sandal, portrayed him as a Robin Hood figure.

Chapbook and ballad generally showed little sense of place, but Nevison also lived on in local memory. Elizabeth Nevison, reputedly either his wife or even his mother and reported as aged 109 at the time of her death, did not die until 1732. In March 1745 the Yorkshire apothecary Arthur Jessop recorded the death of a Mr Hardcastle of Wakefield: 'It was his grandfather that took Nevison' (*Two Yorkshire Diaries: the Diary of Arthur Jessop and Ralph Ward's Journal*, Yorkshire Archaeological Society, vol. 117, 1952, 97). The local historian Norrisson Scatcherd, born in 1780, who dismissed most tales about Nevison as 'Grub Street fabrications', claimed as authority for his own retelling of the murder of Fletcher that, 'Such was the account, which in my boyish days I received from people seventy or eighty years old' (Scatcherd, 253, 252). In the version he first knew Nevison had shot Fletcher while struggling to break free; from Thomas Robertshaw, a descendant of local gamekeepers, he heard that the murder weapon was a short dagger which, so Robertshaw's grandfather had told him, had been found all bloody thrust into the thatch of a nearby cottage. West Riding tradition, no doubt involving more than an element of invention over the years, and as much created as recorded by antiquarians, had by the early nineteenth century attached Nevison's name to various artefacts and places. 'Nevison's chair', for instance (which Hardcastle allegedly took from the inn where he had captured Nevison), was bought by a vicar of Sandal and placed in the parish church where it remains today. 'Nevison's leap', a ravine between Pontefract and Ferrybridge, was where he was supposed to have escaped from his pursuers by a daring piece of horsemanship. A stone marked the spot where he had killed Fletcher.

The most famous story attaching to Nevison's name— that it was he, rather than Dick Turpin, who made the famous ride from the south to York to establish an alibi— does not appear in the chapbook accounts. It shows, rather, how apparently local memory was shaped by antiquarian enthusiasm and creativity. Certainly, the story of the ride attached itself to Turpin's name only at the turn of the eighteenth and nineteenth centuries, some sixty years after his death, while a version of it, dated to Charles II's reign, was current by the early eighteenth century. In Alexander Smith's account the ride was from Barnet in Hertfordshire to York. In the version told by Daniel Defoe, which was taken up by those who claimed that Nevison made the ride, the incident took place in 1676 and the journey was even longer, from Gadshill on the London–Rochester road. The highwayman committed the robbery about 4 a.m. and arrived in York the same afternoon, making sure that he got noticed by speaking to the lord mayor of York on the bowling green at about 8 p.m. With his alibi secured the highwayman was duly acquitted when the case came to trial. However, if anybody actually made the ride, it was not Nevison, and in truth his name does not appear attached to the story until well into the nineteenth century. Both Defoe and Smith named the highwayman as Swift Nicks, and despite antiquarian assertions to the contrary, this was not a nickname of Nevison's. Swift Nicks (or Nix) was remarkably successful at concealing his true name and even on royal pardons only appeared as 'Swift Nix, gent', although proclamations against highwaymen in 1668 and 1669 gave Clarke as an alternative name. Pardoned twice, in 1667 and 1670, he was granted a captain's commission in Ireland in 1674, where he died a violent death in 1687.

The nineteenth century saw completed the transformation of John Nevison, thief, murderer, and protection racketeer, into the more romantically acceptable gentleman of the road William Nevison. Macaulay mentioned him briefly but sympathetically in his *History of England*, largely providing a sanitized version of the chapbook accounts, while Dickens (who with his house on Gadshill had his own reasons of local patriotism to be interested in the story) recounted the story of Nevison's ride to York.

TIM WALES

Sources J. Raine, ed., *Depositions from the castle of York relating to offences committed in the northern counties in the seventeenth century*, SurtS, 40 (1861), 219–21, 259–62 · *The Rev. Oliver Heywood … his autobiography, diaries, anecdote and event books*, ed. J. H. Turner, 4 (1885), 57–9 · R. Blakeborough, *The hand of glory and further grandfather's tales and legends of highwaymen and others*, ed. J. Fairfax-Blakeborough (1924), 212–28 · S. Holmes, *Nevison the highwayman* (1990) · *Memoirs of Sir John Reresby*, ed. A. Browning, 2nd edn, ed.

M. K. Geiter and W. A. Speck (1991), 235 · northern circuit assize rolls: Yorkshire 28 Charles II [1677], PRO, ASSI 44/24 · information of Josias Windle, 22 Dec 1676, PRO, ASSI 45/11/3/127 · informations of Richard Burrowes and Valerius Hales, 22 March 1677, and of Robert Holgate, 9 Feb 1677, PRO, ASSI 45/12/1/55A, 56A · examinations of Elizabeth Burton, 3 Jan 1677 and others, PRO, ASSI 45/12/1/7–9 · gaol calendars, Yorkshire, 13 March and 24 July, 32 Charles II, 3 July 33 Charles II, PRO, ASSI 47/20/6 · northern circuit pardon, July 1679, PRO, C 82/2851 · *LondG* (27–31 Oct 1681) · N. Scatcherd, *The history of Morley in the parish of Batley and West Riding of Yorkshire* (1830), 251–4 · T. Gent, *The ancient and modern history of the … city of York* (1730), 227–8 · T. B. Macaulay, *The history of England from the accession of James II*, new edn, 1, ed. C. H. Firth (1913), 174 · J. W., *A full and complete history of the lives, robberies and murders, of all the most notorious highwaymen* [n.d., 1726?] · *The lives and adventures of Jack Shepherd, Dick Morris, William Nevison and Sawney Beane* (1839) · G. Spraggs, 'Outlaws and highwaymen: the history of the highwaymen and their predecessors, the medieval outlaws', www. outlawsandhighwaymen.com · D. Defoe, *A tour thro' the whole island of Great Britain*, 2 vols. (1927), vol. 1, pp. 104–5 [incl. introduction by G. D. H. Cole] · A. Smith, *A compleat history of the lives and robberies of the most notorious highwaymen*, 3 vols. (1719–20), vol. 2 · *CSP dom.*, 1667; 1670 · private information (2004) [C. B. Herrup] · parish register, Tankersley, transcript, Society of Genealogists

Nevoy, Sir David, Lord Nevoy (d. 1683), judge, was the son of John Nevoy of Nevoy, Forfarshire. He was a regent of St Leonard's College, St Andrews, but was deposed in 1649, his place being filled by a William Jamieson. He was admitted advocate on 27 November 1649, and acted for a time as sheriff-depute of Forfarshire under the Cromwellian union. He married, on 21 April 1653, Margaret, fourth daughter of Sir Patrick Hay, laird of Pitfours. He was knighted and appointed an ordinary lord of session on 25 June 1661, assuming the title Lord Reidie, but afterwards that of Lord Nevoy. His appointment in place of Viscount Oxford, who was named to the commission but never installed, appears significant in that he was admitted without trial. The lords of session took the occasion to declare:

> whensoever the King's Ma[jes]tie shall nominate any persoun to the place of ane Ordinar Lord of Session, that before his admission the persone shall be tryet and examined by the remanent Lordes, and give proof of his literature and knowledge of the laws and practicks of the Kingdome. (Brunton and Haig, 379–80)

Nevoy also held office as a commissioner of excise for the shire of Forfar in March 1681. He died in the autumn of 1683.

J. A. HAMILTON, *rev.* DEREK JOHN PATRICK

Sources G. Brunton and D. Haig, *An historical account of the senators of the college of justice, from its institution in MDXXXII* (1832) · *The diary of Mr John Lamont of Newton, 1649–1671*, ed. G. R. Kinloch, Maitland Club, 7 (1830) · *Reg. PCS*, 3rd ser., vol. 7 · J. Nicoll, *A diary of public transactions and other occurrences, chiefly in Scotland, from January 1650 to June 1667*, ed. D. Laing, Bannatyne Club, 52 (1836) · F. J. Grant, ed., *The Faculty of Advocates in Scotland, 1532–1943*, Scottish RS, 145 (1944)
Archives BL, letters to Charles II and Lauderdale, Add. MSS

New South Wales Corps (act. 1789–1810), army regiment, was established in May 1789 to serve only in garrison in Britain's first antipodean colony. Three companies were raised by December 1789 and arrived with the Second Fleet in June 1790. Two more were added in 1791 and a further company was made up of men from the marines detachment already in the colony. At its peak, in 1802, the corps numbered 680 men (when the total population of the colony was about 5000) and at least 1640 served over the twenty years of its time in New South Wales. A large number were skilled men and, given that military duties were rarely full-time, played an important part in town life. This was made all the easier by the fact that large numbers either brought wives with them or lived with local women (mainly convicts) who could help in the management of their civilian affairs. Numbers of non-commissioned officers ran public houses, for instance, and were influential men within Sydney. Like the officers, the men and women of the corps therefore played an important part in the economic fortunes of the colony.

The corps's initial commander, and its colonel for most of its history, was **Francis Grose** (1758?–1814), the eldest son of the antiquary Francis *Grose (bap. 1731, d. 1791) and his wife, Catherine, née Jordan (1733?–1774). Grose's military career had begun in 1775 when he was commissioned ensign in the 52nd regiment. He was promoted lieutenant that year. He served as a captain in the 85th and 51st regiments in the American War of Independence. A fellow officer in the 51st was Henry Phipps, afterwards third baron and first earl of Mulgrave, who became an important patron. Grose returned to Britain in 1779, after having received wounds in America, and spent two years as a recruiting officer. In 1783 he was placed on half pay as a major in the 96th regiment, where he remained until he was appointed lieutenant-governor of New South Wales and commandant of the New South Wales Corps in 1789. His first duty was the raising of soldiers, and he did not arrive at Port Jackson until February 1792.

Early years of the corps Grose appointed the first three captains of the corps in June 1789: **Nicholas Nepean** (bap. 1757, d. 1823), William *Paterson (1755–1810), and William Hill. Nepean was baptized at Saltash, Cornwall, on 9 November 1757, one of the five children of Nicholas Nepean (c.1700–1772), an innkeeper, and his second wife, Margaret Jones. He was the younger brother of the highly influential Sir Evan *Nepean, first baronet, under-secretary of state in the Home department and a client of Sir Joseph Banks. Nicholas Nepean had joined the marines as a second lieutenant in December 1776, and after active service in the American War of Independence, like Grose, became a recruiting officer in the later phase of the war. On 21 April 1784, at Stoke Damerel in Devon, Nepean married Johanna Francina Carolina (1767?–1845), the daughter of Major Wedikind of the 11th Hanoverian regiment; they had four daughters. His wife and children did not accompany him to Australia. He arrived in Sydney in June 1790 and was acting commanding officer of the corps until Grose's arrival.

The army lists show that more than seventy officers were commissioned into the New South Wales Corps between its formation in 1789 and its return to Britain in 1811. Of these, sixty-two men served in the critical years between their arrival in 1790 and the military insurrection against Governor William Bligh in 1808. They were not young; indeed, their average age on arrival in New South Wales was 29.4 years. The older officers included

Thomas Brabyn (aged thirty-seven), the surgeon John Harris (thirty-six), and the irascible, ill-tempered Nicholas Bayly (thirty-five). The youngest officers were John Piper (aged nineteen), John *Macarthur (twenty-three), and the Montreal-born Edward Abbott (twenty-six). These were primarily career officers who had developed networks of interest and commercial and social contact. Most officers had patrons. Bayly was the son of another Nicholas Bayly, MP for Andover, Hampshire, and was a nephew of Henry Paget (formerly Bayly), first earl of Uxbridge. George *Johnston was under the protection of Hugh Percy, second duke of Northumberland, and Joseph Foveaux [see below] was the client of General Richard Fitzpatrick, second son of the earl of Upper Ossory. Patronage was a juggling act. A patron could never be taken for granted, and officers oiled the relationship with gifts of Australian birds, marsupials (especially wombats), and botanical specimens. Nothing in New South Wales which crawled, flew, swam, or burrowed was safe from being killed, preserved, and shipped to Great Britain.

The majority of officers were born in England, but there were three prominent Irishmen—Lieutenant William Cummings, surgeon John Harris, and William Minchin, the adjutant at the time of the military mutiny in 1808. Paterson and Hugh and John Piper were Scots, Abbott was from Canada, and Francis Barralier was French. Among the English-born officers there was no geographical concentration.

The officers of the corps lived from the start in an uneasy relationship of conflict and co-operation. Macarthur attempted to have Nepean court-martialled on their arrival in New South Wales as the result of an argument during their journey, and John Harris attacked Nepean for using the men under his command for his own profit while stationed at Parramatta from May 1791. Aside from specific charges relating to conduct, officers were concerned with points of honour and duels were frequent. Macarthur nearly killed Paterson in 1801, and Nepean, Foveaux, and Hill were all involved in conflict.

The departure of Governor Arthur Phillip in December 1792 left Francis Grose in charge of New South Wales, and Grose's initiatives during this time provided incentives for the officers to involve themselves with the development of the colony. Grose made land grants of 25 acres available to serving members of the corps who requested them; he believed that encouraging the officers to farm would lead to New South Wales becoming self-sufficient. This had not been achieved by the time Grose left Australia in December 1794, but many officers had farming or surveying experience which played a prominent role in identifying fertile land. Several were committed farmers, and one officer, Archibald Bell, had wanted to bring his Alderney cow to New South Wales, alongside his pregnant wife and nine living children. The transport commissioners had found the whole project 'totally impractical'. John Macarthur became a leading landowner and was the most prominent of the officers who laid the foundations of large-scale wool-farming in New South Wales; George Johnston, with the support from Britain of the duke of

Northumberland, established Australian horse-breeding. Several officers had scientific interests which underpinned their economic enterprises. Grose's botanical concerns were recognized by his fellowship of the Linnean Society. Paterson had explored in southern Africa in 1777–9 and became a fellow of the Royal Society. Macarthur showed a keen interest in the Aboriginal people and, like William Cox and Thomas Hobby in the Hawkesbury Valley (which began to be opened up during Grose's administration of the colony), was on good terms with them. This interest in the Aborigines did not prevent the corps from efficiently destroying resistance to British settlement in the Hawkesbury Valley, although Cox and Hobby seem to have been less bloodthirsty than their soldiers, who also held land in the area.

Changes in personnel Francis Grose never returned to New South Wales; he was eventually promoted major-general in January 1805, when posted to Gibraltar. Twice, in 1808 and 1809, he applied to become governor of New South Wales, but was rejected. His first wife died on 12 January 1813, and he married Elizabeth Paterson, née Driver (1760x75–1825), William Paterson's widow, in April 1814. By this time he was a lieutenant-general. Grose died at his home in Croydon, Surrey, on 8 May 1814.

Nicholas Nepean had been dispatched to Britain in September 1793, eventually rising to the rank of lieutenant-general in 1814. He died at Newton Abbot, Devon, on 18 December 1823. William Paterson thus became commanding officer of the New South Wales Corps on Grose's departure. When Paterson returned to Britain on sick leave in August 1796, **Joseph Foveaux** (*bap.* 1767, *d.* 1846) took charge of the corps. Foveaux was baptized in Millbrook church, Bedfordshire, on 6 April 1767, the son of Joseph Foveaux, steward to the earl of Upper Ossory at Ampthill Park, Bedfordshire, and his wife Elizabeth, née Wheeler. He entered the 60th regiment as an ensign on 10 May 1789, but on 5 June purchased a lieutenancy in the New South Wales Corps, advancing to captain on 6 April 1791. He arrived in Sydney in 1792, and in May that year was appointed commandant at Parramatta. By late 1793 he had begun a relationship with a convict, Ann Sherwin (*d.* 1840); they had a daughter, Ann Noble Foveaux (*b.* 1801), and eventually married at All Saints, Derby, England, in 1814. Foveaux was acting commanding officer of the New South Wales Corps from August 1796 to November 1799, when Paterson returned to Sydney. During his time in New South Wales he established a flock of 1027 sheep, which he sold in 1800 to John Macarthur on becoming acting lieutenant-governor of Norfolk Island. Foveaux established his reputation as an administrator by harnessing the scarce resources of Norfolk Island to reinforce the small settlement there, but in 1803 he had to apply the British government's order that part of the population of the overworked island be transferred to Van Diemen's Land. On sick leave in Britain from early 1805, Foveaux persuaded the British government to accept his plan by which the entire population of Norfolk Island should be transferred, with all property owners receiving compensation from the government but those of high moral character receiving a second year of convict labour, food, and clothing. Foveaux's plan was adopted by the government and implemented by Governor William Bligh, with resistance from the islanders. Foveaux was sent back to New South Wales in 1807, with orders to assume responsibility for the population that remained on Norfolk Island, but in the event he found the corps in mutiny against Bligh and assumed the government of the colony.

Social relations Foveaux was not alone in taking a female partner from among the convicts, and for the corps marriage was the exception rather than the rule. Grose had arrived in the colony with his wife and sister-in-law, and Paterson, Archibald Bell, William Cox, and William Patullo all brought their wives to Australia, but Nicholas Nepean had left his wife at home, and found a number of consolations in Sydney. Of other officers, Neil MacKellar had a long, loving relationship with Sarah Cooley, with whom he had two sons and three daughters; Adjutant Thomas Rowley had four children with the convict Elizabeth Selwyn; and George Johnston lived for many years with Esther Abrahams, a Jewish convict he met on the voyage to Australia, whom he finally married in 1814.

The regiment seems to have accepted relationships with convict or former convict women. However, Quartermaster Thomas Laycock suffered badly when his wife left him in 1805 because of a heated dispute over their housekeeper. Laycock threatened to fight his brother officers for calling his mistress 'an infamous strumpet' and urged his son, Lieutenant Tom Laycock, to join him in 'calling them out'. After thirty-three years in the army, Laycock was cashiered. More successful were Anthony Fenn Kemp, who after a number of liaisons married Elizabeth Riley, the sister of the merchant Alexander Riley, with whom he had seven sons and two daughters; and John Piper, who married the daughter of a convict, Mary Jane Shears, in 1816, by which time their family consisted of four boys and Sarah, the result of an earlier liaison. By 1826 the couple was able to commission Augustus Earle to produce two huge portraits, latterly in the Art Gallery of New South Wales. In these the former officer wears a uniform of his own design, while his wife is resplendent in a red dress set off by a crown.

The officers were nominally Christian but most had little time for religion. William Hill's evangelicalism did not stop him fighting duels. Grose was an Anglican, highly suspicious of Methodists, and William Lawson, one of the conquerors of the Blue Mountains in 1813, was a devout Presbyterian. William Cox, who professed radical views, was sceptical of religion, but most officers saw it as a necessary and useful part of society, something akin to Voltaire's 'social cement'.

Freemasonry attracted many officers. In 1802, during the visit of the French expedition led by Nicholas Baudin, Captain Anthony Fenn Kemp was received into the Rose Croix lodge, much to the chagrin of Governor Philip Gidley King. The informer against Fenn Kemp was Lieutenant John Brabyn, himself a mason, and a member of the secret lodge within the New South Wales Corps. Brabyn's lodge was loyalist and formally Christian, and opposed the advance of the secular, radical, republican French model of freemasonry introduced by Baudin. There is evidence in 1803 that both Paterson and Sergeant-Major Thomas Whittle were freemasons, and on Norfolk Island in the early nineteenth century Captain John Piper allowed a lodge to operate freely without government interference.

Politics was of great concern. Most officers mirrored the opinions of their patrons, but a number had well-developed political philosophies. Johnston, Foveaux, and Macarthur were whigs; Macarthur's plans for the economic self-sufficiency of New South Wales were influenced by the ideas of Jeremy Bentham. These opinions balanced the tory beliefs held by Grose and Paterson. Whigs and tories did not hold a duopoly. William Cummings, born in Ireland, was suspected of radical sentiments, and Ensign George Bond, probably a 'friend of liberty', was accused of being involved in a military mutiny on the convict transport *Barwell* in 1798.

The overthrow of Bligh Sergeant-Major Whittle's egalitarian leanings contributed towards the mutiny that overthrew Bligh from the government of New South Wales in 1808. Bligh had ordered the demolition of Whittle's house as part of his replanning of Sydney. Whittle formed an alliance with Macarthur (who had resigned his commission in the corps in 1804), whose mercantile interests were threatened by Bligh's vision of an agrarian New South Wales. The two fanned opposition to Bligh among the soldiers. Macarthur's trial, for resisting Bligh's attempt to build on his land, asked the six officers who sat on the bench alongside Judge-Advocate Richard Atkins to condemn their former colleague for defending his property rights; the officers refused to condemn Macarthur. Bligh intended to charge them with treason, even though there was no court in New South Wales that could try the officers. The episode confirmed to Macarthur and his allies, who included Lieutenant William Minchin, one of the officers on the bench at Macarthur's trial, that Bligh intended arbitrary government, and legitimized any move to overthrow Bligh. As Macarthur directed the march on Government House on 26 January 1808, he told the troops that 'the Memorable day shall be the most Glorious day the New South Wales Corps ever experienced' (Atkinson, 289). Once Bligh was under arrest, Johnston assumed authority as lieutenant-governor, but real power was in the hands of Macarthur.

Joseph Foveaux returned to New South Wales on 28 July 1808, and instead of reinstating Bligh assumed the government himself, superseding both Johnston (whom he outranked) and Macarthur. Foveaux's rule enhanced his reputation for efficiency, seeking to reduce expenditure and restricting the liquor trade, but, while the British government's response to the mutiny accepted the end of Bligh's administration, it also envisaged the recall of the New South Wales Corps and its replacement by the 73rd regiment led by the new governor, Lachlan Macquarie. Macquarie was sworn in on 1 January 1810, assuming authority

from William Paterson, who had superseded Foveaux as lieutenant-governor in January 1809. Some officers of the corps had feared that Macquarie would put them under arrest, but although Macquarie brought a proclamation communicating the government's displeasure towards the rebels, in the first months of his rule the new governor relied very much on Foveaux. Among Macquarie's early initiatives was one to promote marriage; of the 174 marriages in the first six months of 1810—about equal to the number of marriages in the period 1807–9—two-thirds were of soldiers of the New South Wales Corps, who had to marry before returning to Britain or transferring to the 73rd regiment or the veteran company. The corps, renamed the 102nd regiment, departed for Britain during 1810.

Foveaux escaped a court martial and continued to rise through the army, being promoted major-general on 4 June 1814 and lieutenant-general on 22 July 1830. He died on 20 March 1846 at his home, 21 York Buildings, New Road, London, and was buried in Kensal Green cemetery, London, alongside his wife. Many other officers and soldiers of the corps chose to remain in New South Wales; it is impossible to write the history of early Australia without acknowledging them.

The officers of the New South Wales Corps have been the subject of myth and legend. Most of the writing about them is antiquarian and anachronistic. Many did use their position to charge high prices for imported goods and employed the legal system in the colony to appropriate large estates, against the interest of the small settlers, but most would not have thought this unreasonable behaviour at the time, given that the soldiers went out to New South Wales to make their fortunes. They did not destroy morality and submerge the convict colonies in rum; it was true that several officers traded in alcohol, but others, such as Foveaux, used their positions of authority to restrict the business. Most were not men of the first rank, but it was they who laid much of the foundation of early Australia.   GEORGE PARSONS

Sources A. Atkinson, *The Europeans in Australia: a history*, 1: *The beginning* (1997) • B. H. Fletcher, 'Grose, Francis', *AusDB* • V. Parsons, 'Nepean, Evan … and Nicholas', *AusDB* • A.-M. Whitaker, *Joseph Foveaux: power and patronage in early New South Wales* (2000) • 'Joseph Foveaux', www.geocities.com/joseph_foveaux/joseph_foveaux. htm, 12 Aug 2002 • [F. Watson], ed., *Historical records of Australia*, 1st ser., 1–8 (1914–16) • F. M. Bladen, ed., *Historical records of New South Wales*, 7 vols. (1892–1901) • B. H. Fletcher, 'Foveaux, Joseph', *AusDB* • B. H. Fletcher, *Landed enterprise and penal society: a history of farming and grazing in New South Wales before 1821* (1976) • P. Statham, ed., *A colonial regiment: new sources relating to the New South Wales corps, 1789–1820* (Canberra, 1992)
Archives Mitchell L., NSW, corresp. and papers [Francis Grose]

Newall [*née* Phillpotts], **Dame Bertha Surtees** (1877–1932), educationist and Scandinavian scholar, was born in Bedford on 25 October 1877, the second of three daughters of James Surtees Phillpotts (1839–1930), headmaster of Bedford grammar school, and his wife, Marian Hadfield Cordery (1843–1925). She was the fifth of six children to survive childhood. She apparently had little formal education, but with the extramural aid of the masters of her

Dame Bertha Surtees Newall (1877–1932), by J. Palmer-Clarke

father's school she managed to win the gold medal of the Société Nationale des Professeurs de Français en Angleterre in February 1897. Gaining a scholarship to Girton College, Cambridge, where she studied between 1898 and 1901, she won a first in French and German in the medieval and modern languages tripos. Cambridge degrees were at that time closed to women so she took an MA degree from Trinity College, Dublin, in 1905 (subsequently becoming DLitt there). In the years before the First World War she worked intensively on developing her knowledge of Scandinavian history and archaeology and increasing her firm grasp of the Scandinavian languages. She showed a particular flair for Icelandic, for which she had the personal tutorage of the eminent Icelandic scholar Eiríkur Magnússon (1833–1913), then underlibrarian at the University Library, Cambridge. Phillpotts proceeded to win the Pfeiffer scholarships to Girton in 1903–4 and 1905–6, before becoming librarian of Girton (1906–9) and secretary to Baron Anatole von Hügel at the museum of archaeology and ethnology at Cambridge (1909–13). In 1913 she was elected the first Lady Carlisle fellow of Somerville College, Oxford. There she made the influential acquaintance of Gilbert Murray.

In 1903 Phillpotts made her first trip to Iceland, spending the summer learning Icelandic in the household of high court judge Jón Jensson. During a further year of study in Copenhagen she encountered other important Icelandic scholars, including Finnur Magnússon and Sigfús Blöndal. Attracted since childhood to outdoor pursuits such as walking and sailing, she also made visits to

Iceland mainly for walking holidays in 1905, 1909, 1910, 1912, and 1914. On these largely unguided trips across the harsh Icelandic landscape she was usually accompanied by female friends from college. Her expeditions, and especially that undertaken in 1909 when she walked a total of about 500 miles around the country, wearing out several pairs of shoes on the way, astounded even the Icelanders (the Icelandic newspaper, *Ísafold*, 28 Aug 1909).

Of all the Europeans involved in Scandinavian studies during this time, Phillpotts probably had the most firsthand knowledge of the countries involved: she was certainly the first woman to enter the male realms of Scandinavian studies on an academic basis, and in 1911 became only the second woman to be elected as fellow to the Society of Northern Antiquities in Copenhagen. She also worked continuously to improve the opportunities and status of other women students. She visited other Nordic countries, spending the war years working as a clerical assistant at the British legation in Stockholm, where she later served as private secretary to the minister, Sir Esme Howard. For this she was appointed OBE in 1918.

On her return to England in 1919 Phillpotts became the principal of Westfield College, London, and was a member of the consultative committee of the Board of Education. In 1922 she succeeded her aunt, Katharine Jex-Blake, as mistress of Girton, a position she held until 1925 (during which time Girton at last received its charter). She then stepped aside to give more time to her ailing father. In 1926, however, she accepted a lecturing position in Scandinavian studies at the University of Cambridge, and subsequently became director of Scandinavian studies and head of other foreign languages. She was the sole female member of the statutory commission for the University of Cambridge (1923–7), and was also a member of the statutory commission for the University of London (1926–8).

Bertha Phillpotts was not a prolific author, but her main works have exerted continuing influence. Her first book, *Kindred and Clan in the Middle Ages and after* (1913), concerning the clan society of the medieval Germanic peoples, is still regularly quoted by historical anthropologists, and her final work, *Edda and Saga* (1931), has only recently been replaced as one of the best general introductions to early Icelandic literature. Phillpotts's most daring and original work, *The Elder Edda and Ancient Scandinavian Drama* (1920), which proposed a dramatic origin for some of the Eddic poems, has been under-rated. By the end of the twentieth century, the inspired and far-sighted arguments expressed in this book at last appeared to be gaining some vindication (see, for example, Terry Gunnell, *The Origins of Drama in Scandinavia*, 1995, and Ursula Dronke, *The Poetic Edda*, 2, 1997).

Phillpotts was made a DBE in 1929 and two years later married her friend Hugh Frank *Newall (1857–1944), emeritus professor of astrophysics at Cambridge. She died of cancer at their home, Madingley Rise, Madingley Road, Cambridge, on 20 January 1932, and was buried in the Tunbridge Wells cemetery.   TERRY GUNNELL

Sources G. Harlowe, 'Bertha Phillpotts and Iceland', unpublished lecture presented to the Viking Society for Northern Research, 31 May 1986 · *The Times* (21 Jan 1932) · *The Times* (25 Jan 1932) · *The Times* (29 Jan 1932) · *Manchester Guardian* (21 Jan 1932) · *Manchester Guardian* (5 Feb 1932) · *Manchester Guardian* (7 May 1932) · *Manchester Guardian* (13 June 1932) · *Cambridge Review* (29 Jan 1932) · *Danbrit* (1932) · K. T. Butler and H. I. McMorran, eds., *Girton College register, 1869–1946* (1948) · letters written by Phillpotts to her family and Eiríkur Magnússon [provided by Geoffrey Harlowe, James Surtees Phillpotts, and Landsbókasafn Íslands] · *Ísafóld* (28 Aug 1909), 223 · T. Gunnell, 'Dame Bertha Phillpotts and the search for ancient Scandinavian drama', *Anglo-Scandinavian cross-currents, 1850–1914*, ed. I.-S. Ewbank (1999), 84–113 · T. Gunnell, *The origins of drama in Scandinavia* (1995) · *The poetic Edda, 2: the mythological poems*, ed. and trans. U. Dronke (1997), 353–5, 386–403 · d. cert.

Archives Girton Cam., G. C. P. P. Phillpotts notes, papers, letters, drafts, lectures, etc. | Bodl. Oxf., letters to Gilbert Murray · National Library of Iceland, letters to Eiríkur Magnússon, Lbs 2189, a, 4to, 11 bindi, a

Likenesses P. A. de Laszlo, oils, 1921, Westfield College, London · H. Somerville, oils, 1927, Girton Cam. · photograph, *c.*1932, NPG · J. Palmer-Clarke, photograph, NPG [*see illus.*]

Wealth at death £14,496 14*s.* 0*d.*: probate, 3 May 1932, *CGPLA Eng. & Wales*

Newall, Cyril Louis Norton, first Baron Newall (1886–1963), air force officer, was born on 15 February 1886 at Mussooree in north-west India, the only son and the second child of Captain (later Lieutenant-Colonel) William Potter Newall, of the Indian army, and his wife, Edith Gwendoline Caroline Norton. He was educated at Bedford School and the Royal Military College, Sandhurst, and was commissioned in the Royal Warwickshire regiment on 16 August 1905. He went with his regiment to India, transferred to the Indian army, and served from September 1909 on the north-west frontier with King Edward's Own Gurkha rifles. During an exercise, he and his Gurkhas were 'annihilated' while still at breakfast by a force led by Hugh Dowding, who later achieved greater fame as head of Fighter Command (1936–40).

While on leave in England in 1911 Newall learned to fly at Larkhill, Salisbury Plain, and instructed in India before returning permanently to England in 1914. He joined the Royal Flying Corps as a captain and instructed at the Central Flying School, Upavon, Wiltshire. In March 1915 he was promoted major and from September prepared 12 squadron for service in France, under his command. Although he was not yet thirty, he gave up flying and concentrated on efficient management—a skill much needed by so new a service. His pilots and observers regarded him with limited respect until 3 January 1916, when he faced up to a challenge on the ground with as much courage as any man could show in the air. Noticing smoke emerging from a wooden shed where some 2000 bombs were stored on his airfield at St Omer, Newall ordered hoses to be brought up, walked calmly into the shed (followed by three corporals), dragged several bombs to safe places, and helped put out the fire. An eyewitness recalled 'a dirty and blackened figure, very unlike his usual immaculately turned-out self', busily rolling 'red-hot bombs out of harm's way' (Pollard, 25). He was awarded the Albert medal (first class, gold) on the personal recommendation of General Trenchard, head of the Royal Flying Corps in

Cyril Louis Norton Newall, first Baron Newall (1886–1963), by Reginald Grenville Eves, 1940

France; those who helped him received the second-class (bronze) version of that medal.

Newall returned to England in February 1916 on promotion to lieutenant-colonel to command a training wing. In December he went back to France as head of 9 wing (seven squadrons), and during 1917 he organized numerous long-distance reconnaissances and raids. 41 wing (later renamed 8 brigade, with five squadrons) was formed under his command at Ochey, near Nancy, in October 1917 to specialize in raids on Germany. That brigade, led by Newall as a brigadier-general from December, joined Trenchard's independent bombing force after May 1918. Its actual achievements were small, but both Trenchard and Newall became convinced that the morale impact of bombing on Germans had been devastating.

Granted a permanent commission as a group captain in August 1919, Newall served as deputy director of personnel (1919–22), commander of the school of technical training (for apprentices) at Halton, Buckinghamshire (1923–5), and head of operations and intelligence in the Air Ministry (1926–31). He was promoted air commodore in January 1925 and air vice-marshal in January 1930. From 1931 to 1934 he fulfilled his one and only overseas posting—to Cairo, as head of RAF Middle East. In January 1935 he became air member for supply and organization, a newly created position in which he was responsible for aircraft supply, bases, and stores at a time of rapid expansion. It has often been alleged that he had reached the limit of his capabilities when he was promoted air marshal in June 1935 and knighted (KCB) in July.

In September 1937, however, and much to the surprise and disappointment of Dowding, Sir Edgar Ludlow-Hewitt, and Sir Wilfrid Freeman—all of whom have been supposed to be his superiors in every respect—Newall was appointed chief of the air staff on the recommendation of Lord Swinton, secretary of state for air, as successor to Sir Edward Ellington. Dowding and Freeman were probably too abrasive and too severe on senior colleagues of ordinary ability to thrive in that appointment, but it may be that Ludlow-Hewitt possessed all Newall's qualities, in addition to a stronger grasp of bombing capabilities in particular and air force organization in general. Trenchard and Salmond, though retired, remained influential and soon regretted their failure to oppose Newall's elevation—which brought with it promotion to air chief marshal and a GCB in 1938.

Sir John Slessor, who worked closely with Newall in the late 1930s, described him as 'the prime architect of the wartime air force' (Slessor, 241); this high praise is not echoed by other contemporaries or subsequent historians, but Slessor was certainly one of the RAF's shrewdest high commanders. Newall was an orthodox disciple of Trenchard, who believed that a powerful bomber force would probably deter an aggressor; if not, it would certainly wreck his economy very quickly; and no effective fighter defence was possible. In fact, just such a defence—based on radar and heavily armed monoplane fighters—was then being developed in Fighter Command (under Dowding), while in Bomber Command Ludlow-Hewitt was bluntly informing the Air Ministry that a Trenchardist 'knock-out blow' lay far in the future.

Newall, though ignorant of modern bomber or fighter issues, and lacking the staff college experience—as pupil or teacher—that might have broadened his mind, failed to remedy his ignorance. On the other hand, he played a key part in the decisions to order Hurricane and Spitfire fighters and to construct 'shadow' factories, where aircraft were produced in quantity at a time of urgent need, and when the administrative machinery for aircraft development and production was reorganized in 1938. He rejected accepted wisdom that there would be no special demand for an aircraft repair organization if war came, and just such an organization did in fact play a vital part in boosting aircraft supply to the RAF, not only during the battle of Britain but throughout the war.

Instead of spending time with Dowding and Ludlow-Hewitt, his principal commanders, Newall remained in his office, vainly resisting the government's growing emphasis on fighters rather than bombers. He learned nothing from the Luftwaffe's conduct of operations during the Spanish Civil War and even asserted that its adroit support of ground forces was a gross misuse of air power. He therefore resisted demands for similar support of British and French soldiers in the event of (and then in the face of) a German invasion of France. He failed to realize that his bombers could cause significant damage to German targets only if they operated from French bases. When German forces occupied the channel coast, and the Luftwaffe prepared to attack targets in south-east England, he still thought it best to employ bombers against 'strategic' targets far behind the front line. As Sholto Douglas (a senior assistant) observed, Newall was 'an absolute bag of nerves' by 1940. 'He worked at his desk in the Air Ministry during the day, and he had a cell underground where he used to work and sleep at nights. He never left the place' (Douglas to Wright, 2 July 1963).

Newall certainly did more in May and June 1940 than some admirers of Dowding have admitted to resist Churchill's readiness to send British fighters to assist the French in an obviously lost cause. Newall had sacked Ludlow-Hewitt in April and wished to get rid of Dowding also, but Churchill's objection—and a succession of desperate crises—thwarted him. From May onwards he was himself under growing pressure. A memorandum composed by Wing Commander Edgar Kingston-McCloughry (a member of the Air Ministry's directorate of war organization), and circulated anonymously, castigated Newall as 'A Weak Link in the Nation's Defences': his mental capacity was inadequate, his practical experience was limited, his character and personality were weak, and he lacked judgement and foresight (Ritchie). Whatever his merits as a diligent manager, it was clear by mid-1940 that Newall was unable to galvanize the Air Ministry, regarded by Churchill as 'a most cumbersome and ill-working administrative machine', into the alertness required in wartime.

Lord Beaverbrook (appointed minister of aircraft production by Churchill in May) eagerly backed the campaign against Newall, partly because he agreed with Kingston-McCloughry and partly because Newall opposed many of the actions of the new ministry. By September Beaverbrook was receiving powerful support from Trenchard and Salmond, director of armament production in that ministry. They recognized Newall's general weakness, but they also had two particular fears: that he would prove unable to resist growing pressure for the creation of an Army Air Corps to give direct support to ground forces, and that he no longer believed absolutely in the bomber doctrine. Unlike Trenchard and Salmond, Newall had come to recognize that his bomber force was quite incapable, at least in the near future, of causing serious injury to Germany and was more usefully employed helping Fighter Command to prevent an invasion of Britain. Trenchard went over Newall's head on 25 September, writing directly to Churchill to urge that Bomber Command be used solely against 'strategic' targets in Germany. Churchill agreed on 2 October that Newall should go, and Portal replaced him on 25 October 1940.

After three hard years, made harder by Britain's unreadiness for war, by France's shockingly sudden collapse, and by increasingly bitter criticism from powerful, unscrupulous men, Newall was more than ready to go. Promotion to marshal of the RAF and appointment to the Order of Merit at the end of 1940, plus a nice long rest as governor-general of New Zealand from February 1941 to April 1946 (rewarded by a barony in June 1946), consoled him. He took no further part in public affairs, wrote no memoirs, and made no speeches. At the close of the twentieth century no historian had yet closely examined his work in the critical years 1935–40.

In 1922 Newall married May Dulcie Weddell, who died on 29 September 1924. He then married, on 16 April 1925 in Cannes, Olive Tennyson Foster, the only daughter of Mrs Francis Storer Eaton of Boston, Massachusetts. They had a son and two daughters. A slim man, always neatly dressed, Newall was even-tempered and had a ready smile and a pleasant voice: he was at his best in small gatherings, where he listened more than he spoke. He died at his London home, 37 Welbeck Street, on 30 November 1963, and was survived by his wife; his son, Francis (*b.* 1930), succeeded to the title.   VINCENT ORANGE

Sources S. Ritchie, 'A political intrigue against the CAS: the downfall of ACM Sir Cyril Newall', *War & Society*, 16/1 (May 1998), 83–104 · H. Probert, *High commanders of the RAF* (1991) · A. O. Pollard, *Leaders of the RAF* [1940] · J. C. Slessor, *The central blue: recollections and reflections* (1956) · S. Douglas and R. Wright, *Years of combat* (1963) · S. Douglas and R. Wright, *Years of command* (1966) · *The Times* (2 Dec 1963) · J. P. Ray, *The Battle of Britain: new perspectives* (1994) · *DNB* · *CGPLA Eng. & Wales* (1964) · P. P. O'Shea, *An unknown few* (1981), 50–53

Archives PRO, papers, AIR 8/235–299 · Royal Air Force Museum, Hendon, corresp. and papers | Bodl. RH, corresp. with C. Walker **Likenesses** W. G. de Glehn, oils, 1931, priv. coll. · photograph, 1939, Hult. Arch. · R. G. Eves, oils, 1940, IWM · R. G. Eves, oils, 1940, NPG [*see illus.*] · O. Birley, oils, 1941, priv. coll. · C. Beaton, photograph, 1942, NPG

Wealth at death £6830: probate, 19 Feb 1964, *CGPLA Eng. & Wales*

Hugh Frank Newall (1857–1944), by Olive Edis, *c.*1926

Newall, Hugh Frank (1857–1944), astrophysicist and educational benefactor, was born at Ferndene, near Gateshead, on 21 June 1857, the youngest of six children of Robert Stirling *Newall (1812–1889), engineer, and his wife, Mary, daughter of Hugh Lee Pattinson FRS (1796–1858), metallurgical chemist and astronomer. At the London Exhibition of 1862 R. S. Newall acquired two discs of crown and flint glass, which Thomas Cooke (1807–1868) the following year contracted to figure and mount as a 25 inch refractor. The task took longer than anticipated, but the telescope was finally completed and mounted at Ferndene in 1871; this instrument shaped Hugh Newall's life and work.

After attending J. M. Furness's private school, Newall was educated at Rugby School (1872–1876), then entered Trinity College, Cambridge, in 1876 as a pensioner. In 1880 he obtained a junior optime in the mathematical tripos, and a second class in the natural sciences tripos. At Rugby Newall fell in love with (Susannah) Margaret (1850–1930), seven years his senior, daughter of his house master, the Revd Charles Arnold (*d.* 1878). Despite his parents' reservations, they married on 21 June 1881. An appointment in 1881 as assistant master at Wellington College was terminated in 1884 by Newall's poor health. He spent the next three years partly abroad and his first three papers, written in those years, indicate interests in natural phenomena; the last, written jointly with J. J. Thomson (1856–1940), induced an invitation in 1886 to become his personal assistant and demonstrator in experimental physics at the Cavendish Laboratory, and in 1887 Newall became senior demonstrator, with special interest in laboratory spectroscopy.

In March 1889 Newall senior offered his refractor to Cambridge. For the impecunious university and observatory, the offer presented real problems, especially the recurring expense of staff. R. S. Newall died in April before the offer was accepted, and to implement his father's wish, Newall offered to work the 'Newall telescope' from 1890 for five years without stipend, an offer renewed several times; he also contributed to its removal to a separate building on the observatory site. The Newalls built Madingley Rise, a fine house, next to the observatory; it became famed for gracious hospitality and as a cultural centre drawing astronomers, scientists, and music lovers of many nationalities.

Astrophysics was changing from small-scale sampling to quantitative collection of high-quality photographic observations. Great ingenuity was needed to adapt the telescope for photography and faint star spectroscopy. Newall designed a one-prism slit spectrograph, in 1895 began to study stellar spectra, and from 1896 pioneered in this country work on radial velocities. He then designed a four-prism spectrograph (1899). Those years of work and delicate observations yielded the independent discovery that Capella was a binary star (1899). Despite having only one assistant, paid by himself, Newall competed with H. C. Vogel at Potsdam and W. W. Campbell at Lick Observatory and proved 'that high-precision stellar spectroscopy was possible … in Britain' (Milne, *Nature*, 456). In 1895 Newall deduced descending currents at the sun's surface near spots. He took part in six eclipse expeditions after 1898, and specialized in studying the solar corona. From 1906 he undertook a long study of sun-spot cycles to derive how the rotation of the sun differed from rigid body models. In 1916 he shared the identification of hydrocarbons in the solar spectrum, and in 1918 obtained the spectrum of Nova Aquilae.

Newall's researches introduced new fields of enquiry to the observatory and thereby established astrophysics at Cambridge. In 1892 he refused to direct the Cambridge observatory, thus maintaining his freedom to research. The new director and Lowndean professor was Robert S. Ball (1840–1913), who did very little observing but divided his time between official duties, lecturing, mathematical researches, and popular lecturing and writing. Newall became assistant director in 1904; at that time he was unencumbered by university duties and, through his continued presence and successful astrophysical research, attracted several excellent students who won the Isaac Newton studentships, established in 1890 by Frank McClean (1837–1904), and then sought research opportunities. Newall's scientific responsibilities soon increased. In 1904 a bequest from McClean 'to the Newall Observatory' (Stratton, 14) brought £5000 for equipment, which Newall invested in solar apparatus. Crucially, however, he maintained his broader contribution to astrophysics by instigating and partly funding a new graduate post, an assistantship in astrophysics. These initiatives made Newall's observatory a natural beneficiary in 1908 of the Royal Society's donation of William Huggins's twin telescopes and spectroscopes. They were accommodated in the Astrophysical Building provided by Newall where they were re-mounted. Other gifts followed including E. H. Grove-Hills's valuable solar apparatus in 1909.

In 1882 J. Norman Lockyer (1836–1920) became the controversial beneficiary of government funding for a new lectureship in physical astronomy at the Board of Education's new Normal School of Science at South Kensington. In 1887 he became professor, and director with a budget and staff for the separate Solar Physics Observatory (SPO) there. The government's annual grant to the observatory was its principal regular subsidy for solar research. In 1906 the board needed the site, and decided to relocate the SPO. Newall's work had established the potential of Cambridge as an alternative location and in mid-1909 the board stunned Lockyer by announcing negotiations with Cambridge, where Newall had already in January been elected a fellow of Trinity College, then to a new chair of astrophysics established for him (which he occupied without stipend until his retirement in 1928). The coincidence of Newall's academic rise and the board's announcement suggests intrigue. Joseph Larmor (1857–1942), Lucasian professor of mathematics and a member of the board's committee, had manoeuvred the Cambridge interest: their friend Thomson at the Cavendish Laboratory was building a great school of experimental physics, and spectroscopy was crucial; John Strutt, third Baron Rayleigh (1842–1919), who had been Cavendish professor of experimental physics in 1879–84, latterly with a special interest

in physical optics, in 1908 became chancellor of the university; the ground was fertile. Newall was enabled to negotiate that the board make a sufficient capital grant for buildings, and transfer instruments and an enhanced SPO annual grant of £3000 to Cambridge. When this was effected in 1913, merged with Newall's installations it became the separate and independently constituted Solar Physics Observatory, Cambridge; Newall directed it and had a staff of six. On his retirement in 1928 Newall endowed his chair, thereby consolidating astrophysics as an academic subject, especially since PhD degrees had meanwhile become available at Cambridge, in 1920.

Cambridge had not felt the need for a formal school of astronomy. The subjects were examined within the faculties of mathematics or physics, and especially since the early 1900s graduate students had a range of research opportunities under two directors at the observatory. In 1909 Newall founded the Observatory Club to promote interaction and access between all staff and students, and regular meetings became a tradition; in 1910 he published an elementary book on spectroscopy. Newall's initial generosity had made it possible to accept the 'Newall telescope'. His successful research, and development of facilities often at his own expense, precipitated a major shift first of private and then of government resources which established astrophysics as an academic discipline at Cambridge, which university then dominated observational astrophysics in Britain until 1935.

Newall was elected FRS in 1902, and a fellow of the Royal Astronomical Society in 1891; he served on its council continuously for forty-three years from 1893, as secretary from 1897 to 1901, and as president from 1907 to 1909. He was president of the Cambridge Philosophical Society in 1914–16. Between 1883 and 1927 he published sixty-three papers, principally in the journals of those three societies and the *Astrophysical Journal*, of which he was on the editorial board. He was awarded an honorary degree of LLD by Durham. Newall was very active in the International Union for Cooperation in Solar Research, and in 1919 served on committees of the new International Astronomical Union of which in 1925 he was vice-president.

Newall was a natural philosopher of the old school, with no frontiers between his broad interests in science and art. He could afford not to press his many scientific projects to a conclusion; he loved the mysteries in science and nature, but disliked modern theories that explained them away. His colleague E. Arthur Milne emphasized that 'the coming of astrophysics to Cambridge … was almost entirely due to [Newall's] personal work and striking character' (*Obits. FRS*, 727). Mechanically skilful, an expert in optical design, he hated mechanical music, typewriters, or transport, and persisted with his brougham and pair. The Newalls gardened, farmed 50 acres, and travelled as widely as they read and entertained. Newall was profoundly influenced by his lifelong friendship with the American astrophysicist George Ellery Hale, who shared his wide interests.

Margaret Newall was a distinguished pianist who gave concerts in Cambridge, and accompanied and assisted her husband in his eclipse expeditions. After her death, childless, in 1930, Newall in June 1931 married their close friend Dame Bertha Surtees Phillpotts (1877–1932), Scandinavian scholar and sometime mistress of Girton College, who was already seriously ill and died seven months later. Newall's career was much more significant than his published work. By his marked contributions to stellar and solar spectroscopy and then the institutional development of his observatory, and nurturing of graduate students, he earned his rank as 'one of the fathers of astrophysics in Great Britain' (Milne, *Nature*, 457). He died peacefully at Madingley Rise on 22 February 1944.

E. A. MILNE, *rev.* ROGER HUTCHINS

Sources E. A. Milne, *Obits. FRS*, 4 (1942–4), 717–32 · F. J. M. Stratton, *Monthly Notices of the Royal Astronomical Society*, 105 (1945), 95–102 · E. A. Milne, *Nature*, 153 (1944), 455–7 · J. B. Hearnshaw, *The analysis of starlight: one hundred and fifty years of astronomical spectroscopy*, new edn (1990) · A. J. Meadows, *Science and controversy: a biography of Sir Norman Lockyer* (1972), 292–4, 296–9 · H. D. Babcock, *Publications of the Astronomical Society of the Pacific*, 56 (1944), 146–8 · *Journal of the British Astronomical Association*, 54 (1943–4), 75 · A. M. Clerke, *Problems in astrophysics* (1903) · H. C. King, *The history of the telescope* (1955); repr. (1979) · A. McConnell, *Instrument makers to the world: a history of Cooke, Troughton & Simms* (1992) · H. Wright, *Explorer of the universe: a biography of George Ellery Hale*, 2nd edn (1994) · W. W. Bryant, *A history of astronomy* (1907) · H. H. Stephenson, *Who's who in science* (1913) · *WWW, 1941–50* · E. A. Milne, *Cambridge Review* (22 April 1944), 269–72 · m. cert. (1881) · d. cert.
Archives Cambridge Observatory, archives, MS diary | CUL, Hale MSS (George Ellery), corresp. with G. E. Hale, Caltech microfilms, films 10504–10600, rolls 27, 35 · CUL, letters to Sir George Stokes, Add. 7342, 7656 · RAS, letters, RAS papers 55 · RAS, RAS letters, letters to the Royal Astronomical Society · RGS, letters to Sir David Gill [p. 163]
Likenesses photograph, 1910, Hunt. L., Hale Observatory Archive · W. Stoneman, photograph, 1917, NPG · O. Edis, photograph, *c.*1926, NPG [*see illus.*] · G. Clausen, pencil drawing, 1928, Trinity Cam. · G. F. Watt, oils, 1929, Cambridge Observatory
Wealth at death £117,311 0s. 6d.: probate, 9 June 1944, *CGPLA Eng. & Wales*

Newall, Robert Stirling (1812–1889), engineer and astronomer, was born at Dundee on 27 May 1812, the son of Walter Newall, merchant, and his wife, Janet Hair. He started work in a mercantile office at Dundee, but soon joined the London office of Robert McCalmont, where he was employed to carry out tests on the rapid generation of steam, before spending two years promoting McCalmont's business interests in America. On his return, hearing about the wire ropes used in mines in Saxony, he entered into partnership with Liddell and Gordon to manufacture wire rope and colliery equipment in a factory at Gateshead on the Tyne.

The patent for wire rope filed by Newall in 1840 enabled him to move into the new field of submarine cable manufacture in 1850. Telegraph cables consisted of a copper core insulated with gutta-percha, and to protect them on the sea-bed they were encased within wire rope, a process covered by Newall's specification. His firm thus secured the contract to armour the first Dover–Calais cable in 1851, after which he received so many orders that by 1854 he had a complete monopoly and was obliged to employ

subcontractors, usually based in London, to handle the work. Newall's experience with colliery winding gear stood him in good stead when he designed and built paying-out machinery for the cable-laying vessels. He accompanied some of the cable-laying expeditions, notably those in the Mediterranean. In July 1859 he was on board HMS *Cyclops*, laying the Red Sea cable, when he and other crew members went to the rescue of the P. & O. steamer *Alma*, wrecked on a nearby reef. When several of Newall's cables failed because they were too lightly armoured, the firm withdrew from the submarine cable business for several years, returned briefly in 1869–70, then abandoned it. There was in any case a thriving market in wire ropes for haulage, for ships' rigging, and for factory use generally.

On 14 February 1849 Newall married Mary, youngest daughter of Hugh Lee *Pattinson FRS, a retired metallurgical chemist of Newcastle and, like Newall, a keen amateur astronomer. Between 1848 and 1852 Newall made a series of drawings of the sun, and in 1860 he sought to purchase a large telescope from Thomas Cooke of York, a precision engineer and scientific instrument maker, who had previously supplied Newall with telegraph apparatus. On a visit to the 1862 exhibition in London, Newall saw, on the stand of Messrs Chance, glassmakers, two great discs of top-quality flint and crown glass, sufficient to work into a 25 inch achromatic lens—larger than any then in existence. He was able to buy them for £500 each, and sought quotations from Cooke and Thomas Grubb, the only two craftsmen capable of handling the order. In his eagerness for the contract Cooke seriously underestimated the time needed to prepare the glasses and to construct the massive telescope and its clockwork drive, promising a delivery date of about one year. The lens was exhibited at the Newcastle meeting of the British Association in 1863. Years passed; Newall grew ever more impatient at what he saw as Cooke's laziness, although he must have known from his contacts within the Royal Astronomical Society that Cooke had other major contracts to fulfil. From time to time Newall put in a supervisor and made token progress payments, but when the supervisor left Cooke's men turned to more immediately profitable work. Their former friendship evaporated, as Newall threatened and Cooke became plaintive. As the telescope was too large to assemble within the factory—the tube was 32 feet long and it weighed 9 tons—it was assembled in the open space beside York's city wall. Newall's bullying tactics hastened Cooke into an early grave in 1868, and he pressed his claims to the point where, in 1879, he tried to force Mrs Cooke and her sons into liquidation. The telescope was handed over in 1871. Newall had intended to observe with it in Madeira, but, being kept in England by pressure of business, he had it erected in the garden of his house, Ferndene, near Gateshead. Its towering bulk impressed visitors, but cloudy skies largely prevented its use. His offers to lend it, in 1875 to a proposed physical observatory and in 1879 to the Cape observatory, were declined. In March 1889, shortly before his death, he presented the telescope and its dome and auxiliary equipment to the University of Cambridge, where his son Hugh Frank *Newall became observer. Many years later, it was transferred to Greece.

Newall served as mayor of Gateshead in 1867 and 1868, and was alderman of the borough and a JP. He was active on the River Tyne commission in 1876 and was always willing to advise on matters connected with engineering. He was elected to the Royal Astronomical Society in 1864, and to the Royal Society in 1875, and in 1879 he became a member of the Institution of Mechanical Engineers. He was decorated with the order of the Rose of Brazil in 1872, and awarded a DCL by the University of Durham in 1887. He died at Ferndene on 21 April 1889; his wife survived him.

A. M. CLERKE, rev. ANITA MCCONNELL

Sources *Monthly Notices of the Royal Astronomical Society*, 50 (1889–90), 165–7 · *PRS*, 46 (1889), xxxiii–xxxv · *Nature*, 40 (1889), 59–60 · *The Times* (25 April 1889), 7a · *The Times* (7 July 1859), 5a–b · *The Athenaeum* (27 April 1889), 541 · *Annual Register* (1889), 141 · N. Lockyer, *Stargazing, past and present* (1878), 119, 302 · C. L. F. André, *L'astronomie pratique et les observatoires en Europe et en Amérique*, 1: *Angleterre* (Paris, 1874), 142 · *The Observatory*, 12 (1889), 197, 229 · *Newcastle Daily Leader* (23 April 1889) · A. McConnell, *Instrument makers to the world: a history of Cooke, Troughton & Simms* (1992), 53–4 · D. W. Dewhirst, 'The Newall telescope', *Journal of the British Astronomical Association*, 80 (1969–70), 493–5 · b. cert.
Likenesses bronzed plaster plaque, 1868 (after G. Simonds), U. Cam., Observatories Syndicate
Wealth at death £167,881 3s. 5d.: resworn probate, Dec 1889, *CGPLA Eng. & Wales*

Newall, Sybil Fenton [Queenie] (1854–1929), archer, was born at Hare Hill, Littleborough, near Rochdale, on 17 October 1854, the eldest daughter of the ten children of Henry Newall (1815–1886), merchant, and his wife, Maria Fenton (1832–1901). The Newall family traced an unbroken succession from the reign of Henry IV. Her father owned a large estate at Hare Hill, where all ten children were born. Her maternal grandfather, John Fenton (1792–1863), was elected Liberal member of parliament for Rochdale in 1832 and represented the constituency as a 'radical reformer' and friend of Bright and Cobden for two periods until his retirement in 1841.

Queenie Newall, who had independent financial means, never married, and lived in Cheltenham with her younger sister Margaret Fenton Newall. In 1905 they joined the fashionable Cheltenham archers club. Queenie won four of the five regional archery meetings held in 1907, and soon began to make a name for herself in the sport. Lady archers shot the national round, which was 48 arrows from 60 yards, and 24 arrows from 50 yards on each day of the two-day event.

The 1908 Olympic games took place in London, and the archery contest was held in the White City stadium on 20 and 21 July. Alice Legh, the finest woman archer of the era, had chosen not to compete, and Queenie's main rival was expected to be Lottie Dod, still considered by many to be the greatest all-rounder in the history of British women's sport. Conditions were dreadful on the first day as wind and driving rain swept across the stadium, affecting the flight of the arrows to such an extent that officials had to stop the contest at one stage. Miss Newall trailed Miss Dod by ten points, but on the second day the weather improved and Queenie soon took the lead and won the gold medal by a clear 43 points, with a total of 688. At the age of 53 years 275 days Queenie Newall was still, by the end of the twentieth century, the oldest woman to have won an Olympic medal.

At the national championships held soon after the Olympics, Alice Legh beat her by 151 points, but Queenie Newall won the championship in 1911, and retained the title in 1912, when it was held in her home town. She continued competing after the First World War, her last recorded score being with the Cheltenham archers in September 1928. She died at her home, Ellingham House, Pittville Lawn, Cheltenham, on 24 June 1929.

JAMES W. BANCROFT

Sybil Fenton [Queenie] **Newall** (1854–1929), by unknown photographer, 1908 [at the Olympic games in London]

Sources J. W. Bancroft, *Olympic champions in Manchester* (1993) · T. A. Cook, *The fourth Olympiad: the official report of the Olympic games of 1908* (1909) · H. Fishwick, *The history of the parish of Rochdale in the county of Lancaster* (1889) · *Gloucestershire Echo* (24 June 1929) · I. Buchanan, *British Olympians: a hundred years of gold medallists* (1991) · census returns for Littleborough, 1851 · P. Cant, *History of Cheltenham archers, 1857–1975* (1976) · Burke, *Gen. GB* · b. cert. · d. cert.

Likenesses photograph, 1908, Hult. Arch. [*see illus.*] · photograph, repro. in Cook, *Fourth Olympiad* · photograph, repro. in Buchanan, *British Olympians*, 13 · photograph, repro. in Bancroft, *Olympic champions*, 11

Wealth at death £3081 18s. 4d.: probate, 19 Oct 1929, *CGPLA Eng. & Wales*

Newark. For this title name *see* Leslie, David, first Lord Newark (1601–1682).

Newark, Henry of (*d.* 1299), archbishop of York, probably took his name from Newark-on-Trent in Nottinghamshire, at that time part of the diocese of York. He is recorded as holding property in the town, and he caused to be built a chantry chapel in the churchyard of the parish church of St Mary Magdalen, for his own soul and for the souls of his ancestors, but nothing is known of his parentage. His relationship to Master William of Newark (*d.* 1286), archdeacon of Huntingdon and at one time official of Richard of Gravesend, bishop of Lincoln, and to another William of Newark, who succeeded the archbishop in his Southwell prebend of North Muskham, is also unclear, and it remains uncertain whether the ties were of kinship or geography. In a letter written in 1298 about the vacancy of the mastership of the Gilbertine order of Sempringham, the archbishop refers, in recommending the appointment of the prior of St Catherine's outside Lincoln to be master, to having been brought up in the order himself. Where precisely he received his education, and from which university he ultimately obtained his master's degree, is unknown, but the earlier Gilbertine link seems to have been with the priory of St Catherine's outside Lincoln, the patrons and appropriators of the parish church of Newark.

Newark came to prominence as a royal clerk in the service of Edward I and is found on several missions as a trusted royal emissary: to the papal curia in 1276–7; on an embassy to Scotland in 1290; in the arranging of a truce with France and of treaties with Gueldres and Flanders in 1296. In 1279 he was one of the royal custodians appointed to administer the vacant see of York after the death of Archbishop Giffard. He saw service as a clerk of Giffard's successor, Archbishop Wickwane (*d.* 1285), being commissioned in 1279, along with another future archbishop, Thomas of Corbridge (*d.* 1304), to deal with the business of the election of Robert of Scarborough as dean of York Minster. He was also used by Wickwane in his dispute with the bishop of Durham. Newark's close connection with the administration of the northern archbishopric continued when he was appointed vicar-general of the diocese in 1288 by Archbishop Romeyn, who was about to accompany Edward I to Gascony, Béarn, and Aragon. After an unsuccessful attempt to obtain admission to the rectory of Barnby near Newark in 1270, ecclesiastical preferment

came steadily in the form of canonries and prebends at cathedral or collegiate churches. He was granted the prebend of Colwall at Hereford, the prebend of Buckland Dinham at Wells, the prebend of North Muskham at Southwell, the prebend of Brownswood at St Paul's, London, and a succession of prebends at York: Holme Archiepiscopi, Strensall, and Weighton. Newark also held the rectory of Bassingham, in the Lincoln diocese but only some 8 miles from Newark, until his consecration. Higher preferment came in the form of a royal grant, during an archiepiscopal vacancy at York, of the archdeaconry of Richmond in 1279, and with his election as dean of York Minster in 1290.

The death of Archbishop Romeyn led to Newark's being unanimously elected to the archbishopric by his fellow canons on 7 May 1296. The king assented to the election on 5 June following, and the temporalities were granted on 22 June 1297. Later in that year Newark summoned a council of the clergy of York province which granted the king the subsidy he had demanded. After some considerable delay the pope gave permission for the bishops of Durham and Carlisle to consecrate him and in the event he was consecrated by Antony (I) Bek, bishop of Durham (*d.* 1311), assisted by the bishops of Coventry and Lichfield, St Asaph, and Cork, in York Minster on 15 June 1298. But within a year his household clerks were recording in his register that the archbishop was very ill at his manor house of Cawood near York; he died on 15 August 1299 and was buried in York Minster. The record of Newark's brief pontificate survives in twenty-nine folios, a fragment of the original register of his acts, which nevertheless shows him to have been an active administrator even when obviously dogged by ill health. At his death he made testamentary provision for four chaplains to celebrate daily in York Minster for the souls of the king and queen, and of the archbishops of York. His chantry chapel in Newark churchyard did not long survive, and in 1313 permission was given for it to be pulled down, on condition that Archbishop Newark should be commemorated in a chantry within Newark parish church. DAVID M. SMITH

Sources *The register of John le Romeyn … 1286–1296*, ed. W. Brown, 2 vols., SurtS, 123, 128 (1913–17) · *The register of William Giffard, lord archbishop of York, 1266–1279*, ed. W. Brown, SurtS, 109 (1904) · *The register of William Wickwane, lord archbishop of York, 1279–1285*, ed. W. Brown, SurtS, 114 (1907) · C. T. Clay, ed., *York Minster fasti*, 2 vols., Yorkshire Archaeological Society, 123–4 (1958–9) · W. H. Dixon, *Fasti Eboracenses: lives of the archbishops of York*, ed. J. Raine (1863) · J. Raine, ed., *The historians of the church of York and its archbishops*, 3 vols., Rolls Series, 71 (1879–94) · *Fasti Angl., 1066–1300* · Emden, *Oxf.*, 3, appx · R. Brentano, *York metropolitan jurisdiction and papal judges delegate, 1279–1296* (1959) · Chancery records · *DNB* · P. Chaplais, ed., *Treaty rolls preserved in the Public Record Office*, 1 (1955) · R. G. Griffiths and W. W. Capes, eds., *Registrum Thome de Cantilupo, episcopi Herefordensis*, CYS, 2 (1907) · R. M. T. Hill, ed., *The rolls and register of Bishop Oliver Sutton*, 8 vols., Lincoln RS, 39, 43, 48, 52, 60, 64, 69, 76 (1948–86) · *Calendar of the manuscripts of the dean and chapter of Wells*, 2 vols., HMC, 12 (1907–14) · *Calendar of papal registers*

Archives Borth. Inst., register 5

Newark, William (*d.* 1509), composer, is of unknown parentage, although he was possibly related to Henry Newerk of Greenwich (whose will was made in 1482). Admitted to the Confraternity of St Nicholas (a fraternity of the parish clerks and professional church musicians of London and its environs) in 1476, he was appointed gentleman of the royal household chapel by 1477. As such he received corrodies from Edward IV and Henry VII: at St Mary's Priory, Thetford (1479, confirmed 23 November 1480), the abbey of St Benet of Hulme, Norfolk (1487), and Gloucester Abbey (1492). An annual grant of £20, from the royal manor of Bletchingly, Surrey, was given by Richard III on 6 April 1485. Newark became master of the choristers of the Chapel Royal in September 1493, with an annual grant of 40 marks for the choristers' teaching and maintenance, and retained this position until September 1509, shortly before his death.

After 1493 Newark's duties included the devising of Christmas entertainments at court; although his surviving compositions are exclusively secular songs, he also wrote liturgical music (on 31 December 1500 he was paid for his polyphony for the feast of St Nicholas). About 1500 he received from the abbot of Battle Abbey payment of 5s. 8d. for various pieces supplied by him. Seven of his songs, three of which are for three voices and four for two voices, survive in the Fayrfax manuscript (BL, Add. MS 5465), an early sixteenth-century songbook associated with the household of Henry VII or that of his son Arthur, prince of Wales. An eighth song, 'A my herte, I knowe you well' (in the same source), has also been attributed to Newark. The two-voice 'The farther I go, the more behynde' sets an early fifteenth-century stanza in rhyme-royal by John Halsham. Another two-voice song, 'So fer I trow from remedy', exemplifies Newark's style in the appearance of extended melismas at phrase-endings, and in his use of repeated rhythmic cells and imitation. Newark made his will on 5 November 1509, and it was proved by his wife and executor, Agnes (d. 1511), on 13 November. He died and was buried at Greenwich.   MAGNUS WILLIAMSON

Sources A. Ashbee and D. Lasocki, eds., *A biographical dictionary of English court musicians, 1485–1714*, 2 vols. (1998) · F. L. Kisby, 'The royal household chapel in early Tudor London, 1485–1547', PhD diss., U. Lond., 1996 · J. Stevens, ed., *Early Tudor songs and carols*, Musica Britannica, 36 (1975) · J. Stevens, *Music and poetry at the early Tudor court* (1961); repr. with corrections (1979) · R. Bowers, 'Early Tudor courtly song: an evaluation of the Fayrfax Book (BL, Additional MS 5465)', *The reign of Henry VII* [Harlaxton 1993], ed. B. Thompson (1995), 188–212

Newbald, Geoffrey (*d.* 1283), justice and administrator, was of unknown origins. He is first recorded in 1266, employing an attorney for litigation against Walter of Blythburgh. In 1268 he was himself an attorney for Richard Daniel, steward of William de Valence (*d.* 1296), and also an executor for Nicholas Meuling. The following year he witnessed a charter between William de Valence and Roger Bertram. In 1270 he was involved in a dispute with the priory of Monks Horton, concerning the latter's incumbency of the church of Bradbourne in Kent.

In 1274 Newbald was keeper of the bishopric of Durham, and was ordered to provide from its revenues the necessary expenses for Alexander III, king of Scots, to attend Edward I's coronation. In the same year Newbald heard pleas and assizes in Durham and was commissioned to inquire into those lending money on usury in the realm. In 1275 he was an assessor of the fifteenth in the counties of Norfolk and Suffolk. He seems to have specialized in mercantile law and over the next seven years was frequently commissioned to inquire concerning the export to Flanders of wool and other merchandise contrary to the king's prohibition. In 1276 he received a writ to hold pleas and assizes in the liberty of Dunstable and in the following year replaced John of Mettingham (*d.* 1301), who had a serious illness, in hearing assizes in Norfolk and Suffolk. During this period he was also for two years (1276–8) the attorney of the king's kinsman Maurice de Craon. In 1277 Newbald became chancellor of the exchequer, a post he held for the next six years.

In 1276 Geoffrey Newbald or his namesake was parson of the church of Rathmore in Ireland. A year later Newbald was presented to the church of Rothbury in the diocese of Durham, although his admission was refused by the bishop. He was granted the deanery of St Martin's-le-Grand in London in 1280 and two years later a prebend in Hereford Cathedral. In 1281 an order was given for him to receive five bucks of the king's gift from Waybridge Forest, Huntingdonshire. He died towards the end of January 1283.   A. J. MUSSON

Sources Chancery records · J. C. Sainty, ed., *Officers of the exchequer: a list* (1983) · *Select cases concerning the law merchant*, 2, ed. H. Hall, SeldS, 46 (1930) · J. R. Scott, ed., 'Charters of Monks Horton Priory', *Archaeologia Cantiana*, 10 (1876), 269–81, esp. 278
Archives BM, seal

Newberry, Percy Edward (1869–1949), Egyptologist, was born in Islington, London, on 23 April 1869, the younger son of Henry James Newberry, a woollen warehouseman, of Lewisham, and his wife, Caroline Wyatt. He was educated at King's College School and King's College, London. As a child he had a particular interest in botany, which he studied in London and at Kew. He was a gifted artist and illustrator who came to archaeology through these skills. Unlike his contemporary Howard Carter, of Tutankhamun fame, Newberry lacked natural ability, but he became an expert copyist. While still a young student he was introduced to the Egyptologist Reginald Stuart Poole of the British Museum, who served as a mentor. From 1884 to 1886 Poole enlisted Newberry to help with the administration of the newly founded Egypt Exploration Fund (later to become Society). The work brought the young Newberry into contact with such Egyptological luminaries as Amelia Edwards, Flinders Petrie, and F. Ll. Griffith. As a result he made Egyptology the focus of his life and studied it intensively. Petrie made use of Newberry's botanical expertise to identify the botanical remains found during his excavations in the Fayyum Depression. Newberry presented a paper to the British Association on the plant species in the excavations in 1888, as well as contributing chapters to Petrie's monographs on Hawara (1889) and Kahun (1890).

In 1889 Newberry's mentor, Griffith, advocated an archaeological survey of Egypt to be conducted under the aegis of the Egypt Exploration Fund. The fund adopted the scheme in 1890. As part of this ambitious project, Newberry was sent out to the Nile valley to head an expedition to investigate the tombs of Middle Kingdom nomarchs at Beni Hasan and El Bersha from 1890 to 1894. Much of the work involved copying tomb paintings, in which he was joined by Howard Carter. Newberry was uncompromising in his requirements. 'Mechanical exactitude of facsimile-copying is required rather than freehand or purely artistic work', read the survey's instructions. Newberry followed them to the letter, unlike the more gifted Carter, who believed in observing 'the fundamental Laws of Egyptian Art'. Newberry was conservative in his copying, but produced an impressive body of work. In 1893–4 he published his two-volume monograph *Beni Hasan*, which remains a definitive account of the tombs there. His competence established after five years with the fund, Newberry operated as a freelance excavator in the Theban necropolis from 1895 to 1901. His patrons included Lord Amherst, the marquess of Northampton, and the American excavator Theodore Davis.

On the strength of this fieldwork and his broad experience, Newberry was appointed the first Brunner professor of Egyptology at the University of Liverpool in 1906, where he took an MA in 1909. On 12 February 1907 he married Essie Winifred (1878–1953), daughter of William Munn Johnston, a Liverpool shipowner, of Bromborough, Cheshire. There were no children of the marriage. He held the Brunner chair until 1919, when he was nominated university reader in Egyptian art. During those years he was an influential member of the faculty. He was active in many learned societies and elected a fellow of King's College, London, in 1908. He was appointed OBE in 1919. In 1923 he served as president of the anthropology section of the British Association. His association with the Egypt Exploration Society lasted for sixty-five years. He was elected vice-president shortly before his death. He was vice-president of the Royal Anthropological Institute in 1926. In 1929 he accepted the chair of ancient Egyptian history and archaeology at the University of Egypt in Cairo, a post he held for four years.

Newberry's publications included a noteworthy series of monographs, among them the Archaeological Survey volumes on Beni Hasan, *El Bersheh* (2 parts, 1895), *The Amherst Papyri* (1899), *The Life of Rekhmara*, a vizier of the pharaohs Tuthmosis III and Amenhotep II (1900), and *Scarabs* (1906). His *Short History of Ancient Egypt* (1904), written with John Garstang, was widely read. Newberry also compiled three volumes of the great *Catalogue général* of the Cairo Museum. Throughout his career Newberry wrestled with a backlog of unpublished work, which he never completed. His unfinished manuscripts, notebooks, and papers were presented by his widow to the Griffith Institute at Oxford University.

A gentlemanly, urbane man, who never achieved the fame of Flinders Petrie or Howard Carter, Percy Newberry was an important figure in Egyptology who influenced several generations of young Egyptologists. He devoted much of his career to fostering others' researches through the Egypt Exploration Society and played an important part in organizing the society's work at the pharaoh Akhenaten's capital at Tel el Amarna in the 1930s. He was responsible for recording many heavily damaged tombs, of which his copies are often the only record. He died at his home, Winkworth Hill, Hascombe, near Godalming, Surrey, on 7 August 1949.   BRIAN FAGAN

Sources DNB · *Journal of Egyptian Archaeology*, 36 (1950) · W. R. Dawson and E. P. Uphill, *Who was who in Egyptology*, 3rd edn, rev. M. L. Bierbrier (1995) · H. F. V. Winstone, *Howard Carter* (1991) **Archives** U. Oxf., Griffith Institute, biographical notes relating to nineteenth-century Egyptologists and other papers · U. Oxf., Griffith Institute, corresp. and papers, incl. copies, notes, photographs | Bodl. Oxf., corresp. with J. L. Myres · Egypt Exploration Society, London, corresp. with Egypt Exploration Society · U. Oxf., Griffith Institute, corresp. with Jaroslav Cerny **Likenesses** A. Lipczinski, group portrait, oils, 1915, U. Lpool **Wealth at death** £2897 16s. 4d.: probate, 21 April 1950, *CGPLA Eng. & Wales*

Newbery, Thomas (*fl.* 1653–1658). *See under* Newbery, Thomas (*fl.* 1563).

Newbery, Elizabeth (1745/6–1821), bookseller and publisher, is of obscure origins. Family correspondence describes her father as 'Bryant the trunk merchant'— probably the James Bryant at the corner of St Paul's 'facing Cheapside'—but nothing else is known of her background or early life. She was later married to Francis *Newbery (*d.* 1780) [*see under* Newbery, Francis], the nephew of John Newbery. Francis had worked for his uncle and inherited the publishing business with John's son Francis and his stepson Thomas Carnan, but they quarrelled, and Francis set up his own premises at 20 Ludgate Street. On her husband's death, Elizabeth inherited his business in January 1780; his will appointed her sole executor. In 1786 fire destroyed a large part of the stock, and for part of 1787 Elizabeth lived at 37 Ludgate Street.

Beginning with Charles Welsh, the first biographer of John Newbery, scholars have tended to assume Elizabeth had a merely caretaking role in the history of the prestigious Newbery firm. Evidence to support this position is tenuous, derived largely from the surviving account books of Richard Johnson, a hack writer and compiler who provided the Newberys with a substantial number of manuscripts between 1770 and 1792. These records show payments and records of orders from Elizabeth in 1780 and 1785; after that date they refer only to Abraham Badcock, her manager. Contemporary accounts of Badcock make clear his talents, but this is as much an argument for Elizabeth's business acumen as for her secondary role. During her twenty-two-year tenure Elizabeth published over 300 juvenile titles, three out of four under her sole imprint. The moral and didactic writing which dominated her list in comparison with that of John Newbery reflected the contemporary market rather than any inherent lack of his light-hearted touch. As John Newbery and then her husband had done, Elizabeth used internal publisher's 'puffs' to sell her wares, and she expanded the bookselling business, maintaining stock from other publishers for sale in her catalogues and shop. Her control spanned the decades in which children's books became an established branch of the publishing industry, and her list included abridgements of Richardson and Fielding, English writers such as Sarah Trimmer and Priscilla Wakefield, and versions of traditional tales including the 'Cries of London' and the 'Arabian Nights'. She employed the engraver Thomas Bewick, most notably to illustrate Arnaud Berquin's *Looking-Glass for the Mind* (1792) and J. H. Wynne's *Tales for Youth* (1794). She published the geographical games of the Abbé Gaultier and commissioned a historical game which she published jointly with John Wallis. She collaborated with other publishers including Vernor and Hood, and Francis's cousin Thomas Carnan, and after Carnan's death she reprinted titles from the Carnan–Newbery list as well as her own. She also published over 200 adult titles, but these were often joint ventures and her participation may have been merely financial. The only appearance of Elizabeth's imprint before 1780 was the *Middlesex Journal* for 1772–3 but her name appeared on the January issue of the *Gentleman's Magazine* immediately following Francis's death. A few books with her imprint appeared after the sale to Harris, suggesting she retained an interest in publishing, and her obituary in the *Gentleman's Magazine* describes her as adding 'many an useful and engaging work to the stock of juvenile literature' built up by John and Francis Newbery.

In 1802 Elizabeth sold the business to John Harris (who had succeeded Abraham Badcock as her manager after Badcock's death in 1797). She died in Clapham on 21 October 1821, aged seventy-five, 'after an illness of 16 years, endured with uncommon fortitude and resignation' (*GM*, 377). According to an 1830 letter by a Newbery descendant, Elizabeth had remarried, but throughout her career had 'continued the business and retained on the shop and title pages, the name that had been to her so prosperous'. However, her will, drawn up in 1820, was also in the name of Newbery, and her obituary makes no reference to a second marriage. Elizabeth also continued to receive dividends from an inherited share in the Stationers' Company English stock which she would have lost had she remarried. Given the value of her estate—some £20,000 in specific bequests—dividends of approximately £5 a year would not seem worth the hiding of a second marriage. Her will is interesting for the careful provision of money for female relatives and dependants. The money designated for her surviving sister, Susanna, who received the bulk of the estate, and that for Susanna's daughter, was to be held in trust in such a fashion that it could not be used by their husbands. Among the smaller bequests are those to young Newbery and Bryant relations, to the daughters of John Harris the younger, and to her servants. The executors, John Harris the elder, George Royde, William Bryant, and John Harris the younger were given £50 each for their trouble but Royde also received a separate legacy of £3000. John Harris or, failing him, his son, was granted the right to purchase the one-twelfth share in the *Gentleman's Magazine* that Elizabeth had inherited from Francis.

JILL SHEFRIN

Sources F. J. Harvey Darton, *Children's books in England: five centuries of social life*, rev. B. Alderson, 3rd edn (1982) · *GM*, 1st ser., 91/1 (1821), 377 · *London booktrades database* · A. Le B. Newbery, *Records of the House of Newbery, 1274–1910* (1911) · [*E.*] *Newbery's catalogue of instructive and amusing publications* (1800) · S. Roscoe, *John Newbery and his successors, 1740–1814: a bibliography* (1973) · J. R. Townsend, *Trade and plumb-cake for ever, huzza! The life and work of John Newbery, 1713–67* (1994) · M. J. P. Weedon, 'Richard Johnson and the successors to John Newbery', *The Library*, 5th ser., 4 (1949–50), 25–63 · C. Welsh, *A bookseller of the last century, being some account of the life of John Newbery* (1885)

Wealth at death £20,000 in specific bequests; incl. £6000 to sister, £3000 to two nephews, £2000 to another nephew, £500 to brother-in-law, £300 to great-nephews, £3000 to George Royde, £200 to executors, £300 to cousin's daughters, £160 and mourning clothes to two servants, £600 plus £10; £400 to Newbery children, 57 guineas to John Harris the younger's daughters; plate, glass, and china; wearing apparel: will, 25 Oct 1821

Newbery, Francis (d. 1780). *See under* Newbery, Francis (1743–1818).

Newbery, Francis (1743–1818), publisher, born in Reading on 6 July 1743, was the son of John *Newbery (bap. 1713, d. 1767), publisher, and his wife, Mary Carnan. He was educated at Ramsgate, Kent, and Hoddesdon, Hertfordshire, then entered Merchant Taylors' School in 1758 and matriculated at Trinity College, Oxford, on 1 April 1762. In 1766 he moved to Sidney Sussex College, Cambridge, but took no degree in either university. Newbery had studied chemistry and medicine but on the death of his father in 1767 he was urged by Samuel Johnson and Robert James to continue the business of publishing and selling patent medicines which he had inherited as the only surviving son. He took Thomas Carnan as partner in the bookselling business at 65 St Paul's Churchyard, although Carnan also continued to publish independently, specializing in almanacs and successfully challenging the monopoly of the Stationers' Company in 1775. On 29 May 1770 Newbery married Mary, the sister of Robert *Raikes, the Gloucester printer and founder of the Sunday school movement, who brought him a dowry of £3000. After the death of Oliver Goldsmith following an overdose of Dr James's fever powder in 1774, Newbery, who had inherited the patent from his father, wrote a lengthy statement in defence of the medicine. He became a freeman of the Goldsmiths' Company in 1777. After a quarrel Carnan and Newbery dissolved their partnership in 1779, Newbery moving to no. 45 at the east end of St Paul's Churchyard, where he concentrated on the selling of patent medicines. Carnan continued at no. 65 until his death in 1788 when he was briefly succeeded by Francis Power, the son of Michael Power and Mary, the daughter of John Newbery. Francis Newbery was a scholar, poet, and lover of music. His passion for the violin and amateur theatricals had detracted from his studies and Dr Johnson offended him by telling him that he had better give his fiddle to the first beggar-man he met, on the grounds that the time required for practice interfered with professional pursuits. Many of Newbery's poems were set to music by Dr William Crotch (1775–1841) and others. Callcott set his poem 'Hail all the dear delights of home' to music as a glee. His translations from the classical authors, particularly Horace, were published in *Donum amicis: Verses on Various Occasions* (1815). He was appointed a commissioner of taxes and published several works on that subject in the period 1799–1801. Newbery's profits from the patent medicine business enabled him to indulge his love of field sports on his Sussex estate, Heathfield Park, which he purchased in 1791. He died there on 17 July 1818.

Newbery's cousin, also named **Francis Newbery** (d. 1780), was the son of Francis Newbery, a baker of Easthampstead, Berkshire. Bound to William Faden, a printer of Wine Office Court, Fleet Street, on 3 August 1756, he was made free of the Stationers' Company on 4 September 1764. He was established in business by his uncle John Newbery at 15 Paternoster Row, London, in 1765. It was he who first published Goldsmith's *The Vicar of Wakefield* in 1766 together with Benjamin Collins, although probably acting for John Newbery. He moved to 20 Ludgate Street, at the corner of St Paul's Churchyard, in 1768 and relations with the firm of Carnan and Newbery became increasingly hostile. He owned a share of the *Gentleman's Magazine* from 1767 until his death. He was succeeded by his widow, Elizabeth, *née* Bryant (1745/6–1821), who retained the name Newbery after her remarriage and published over 500 books, most of them for children, as well as puzzles and games. She retired in 1802 when John Harris (1756–1846) acquired the business on condition of paying her an annuity of £500 a year. Harris continued the Newbery tradition of publishing children's books, selling the business to Grant and Griffith in 1843.

IAN MAXTED

Sources S. Roscoe, *John Newbery and his successors, 1740–1814: a bibliography* (1973) · J. R. Townsend, *John Newbery and his books: trade and plumcake for ever, huzza!* (1995) · C. Welsh, *A bookseller of the last century, being some account of the life of John Newbery* (1885) · J. Rose, 'John Newbery, Thomas Carnan, Francis Newbery', *The British literary book trade, 1700–1820*, ed. J. K. Bracken and J. Silver, DLitB, 154 (1995), 224–6 · Venn, *Alum. Cant.* · A. le B. Newbery, *Records of the house of Newbery from 1274 to 1910* (1911)
Likenesses portrait, repro. in Newbery, *Records of the house of Newbery*

Newbery, Francis Henry [Fra] (1855–1946), art educationist and painter, was born on 15 May 1855 in Membury, Devon, the second son and third of the six children of William Newbery (c.1824–1897), a shoemaker born in Stockland, Devon, and his wife, Mary Elliot (c.1820–1888), of Bridport, Dorset. The family moved about 1858 to Bridport. Newbery attended Bridport general school from 1860 to 1874, where he qualified as a teacher. From 1871/2 to 1875 he studied at the Bridport School of Art, where he became a certificated art master. The same year he obtained a post as art master at the City Corporation Middle Class School, Cowper Street, London, then from 1877 to 1881 he taught at the Grocers' Company's School in Hackney Downs. Newbery enrolled as a general student at the National Art Training School at South Kensington in 1877, and in 1881 he won a scholarship as a full-time 'Art Master in Training'.

In 1885 Newbery was appointed as headmaster of the Glasgow School of Art, where he established himself as a first-class pedagogue and organizer. His educational philosophy emphasized the importance of a thorough

Francis Henry Newbery (1855–1946), by Maurice Greiffenhagen, 1913

technical training, an immersion in artistic tradition, and the need for students to discover their own artistic individuality. He sought to employ artists as teachers, rather than the certificated art masters approved by the Department of Science and Art. Through the Glasgow School of Art Club, which he initiated in 1885, he encouraged a broader approach to art than that prescribed by the department's national course of instruction, and by 1897 Newbery's school was consistently gaining more awards in the department's annual national competitions than other schools of art.

In 1893 Newbery had taken advantage of additional funding made available through the Technical Instruction Acts (1887–1892) and opened a series of craft workshops. His encouragement of collaboration between four students, Charles Rennie *Mackintosh (1868–1928), Herbert McNair (1868–1953), Frances *Macdonald (1873–1921) [see under Mackintosh, Margaret Macdonald], and Margaret Macdonald *Mackintosh (1864–1933), and his promotion of their and other students' work in British and continental exhibitions, won the school an international reputation. This was further aided by exposure of students' work in British and continental art periodicals such as *The Studio*, for which Newbery also wrote. His organization of the Scottish section at the international Exhibition of Modern Decorative Art at Turin (1902) gained Newbery the title of *cavalliere ufficiale dell'ordine della corona d'Italia*.

Newbery played a part in the selection of Charles Rennie Mackintosh as the architect of the Glasgow School of

Art's new premises and between 1897 and 1909 collaborated closely with him over the details of its design and building.

In 1901 the Glasgow School of Art became the first central institution for art under the Scottish education department, with control over its own curriculum and increased funding, enabling Newbery to make prestigious international appointments to his staff. The teaching, especially that in architecture, was reorganized largely on the continental *beaux arts* model. Of the crafts which were taught in the school, probably the most distinctive was embroidery, carrying the Glasgow decorative art style well into the twentieth century. Newbery's school was unusual in employing large numbers of women, many of whom, like Newbery's wife, Jessie Wylie Rowat (1864–1948) [*see* Newbery, Jessie Wylie, *under* Glasgow Girls], whom he married on 28 September 1889, had previously been students.

As a painter Newbery was closely allied with the Glasgow Boys, with whom he exhibited internationally. Like several of them he often chose field workers and fishermen as subjects, as well as children—primarily his two daughters, Margaret Elliot (*b.* 1890) and Mary Arbuckle (*b.* 1892). Many of his paintings were produced at Walberswick in Suffolk, which he visited from 1883 to 1915, including *Sole a levante e luna a ponente* (*c.*1901; Galleria Civica d'Arte Moderna e Contemporanea, Turin) and *The Warden of the Marshes* (*c.*1899; Museo Nacional de Bellas Artes, Santiago, Chile). After his retirement in 1917 Newbery settled in Corfe Castle, Dorset, where he continued to paint until 1932. His most important late works were decorative schemes for Bridport town hall (1923–7) and at the church of the Holy Ghost and St Edward, Swanage (1924–30). Newbery died at his home, Eastgate, East Street, Corfe Castle, on 18 December 1946 and was buried there in the West Street cemetery. Examples of his paintings are held in the National Gallery of Scotland, Edinburgh, and the Hunterian Museum and Art Gallery, University of Glasgow.

GEORGE RAWSON

Sources G. Rawson, 'Francis Henry Newbery and the Glasgow School of Art', PhD diss., U. Glas., 1997 · G. Rawson, *Fra H. Newbery: artist and art educationist, 1855–1946* (1996) · Glasgow School of Art Archives, Newbery, testimonials, 1885 · F. Newbery, letter, *Dorset Year Book* (1926), 120–21 · G. E. Todd, *Who's who in Glasgow in 1909* (1909), 158 · census returns for Bridport, 1861, 1871 · Bridport general schools, Dorset RO, S117 · Bridport council minutes, 1923–7, Dorset RO, DC/BTB · Bridport News (Aug 1871–1875) · Grocers' Company's School, GL, MSS 11633/1, 11634/1 · annual reports, 1886–1901, Glasgow School of Art, Glasgow School of Art Archives · minutes, 20 May 1885, Glasgow School of Art, Glasgow School of Art Archives · Department of Science and Art, *1st–46th Reports* (1854–99) · Department of Science and Art, *Directories* (1887–1900) · T. Howarth, *Charles Rennie Mackintosh and the modern movement* (1997) · J. Burkhauser, *Glasgow Girls* (1990) · d. cert. · b. cert.
Archives Glasgow School of Art, testimonials · NA Scot. · NL Scot., letters | Dorset RO, schools records, council minutes · GL, Grocers' Company's School archive · Glasgow School of Art, general administration · Glasgow School of Art, minutes, reports
Likenesses A. McFarlane Shannan, bronze bust, 1895, Glasgow School of Art · M. Greiffenhagen, oils, 1913, Glasgow Art Gallery and Museum [*see illus.*] · F. H. Newbery, group portrait, oils, 1913 (including self-portrait; *The building committee of the Glasgow School of Art*), Glasgow School of Art · H. Muspratt, photograph, *c.*1930, Glasgow School of Art · photographs, Glasgow School of Art
Wealth at death £5459 8s. 6d.: probate, 19 June 1947, *CGPLA Eng. & Wales*

Newbery, Jessie Wylie (1864–1948). *See under* Glasgow Girls (*act.* 1880–1920).

Newbery, John (*d.* in or after **1585**), traveller, began his working life as a London merchant. In 1579, backed by the merchants Edward Osborne and Richard Staper, who two years later led moves to found the Levant Company, Newbery travelled overland to Marseilles, and from there by ship to Syrian Tripoli, a journey that appears to have been more a reconnaissance than an active trading mission. In 1580 he sailed once more to Tripoli, and from there passed to Aleppo. With him was William Barret, later the Aleppan consul of the Levant Company. At Aleppo they separated; Newbery moved eastwards, disguised as a Muslim trader to avoid adverse attention, and travelled via the cities of Baghdad and Basrah to Hormoz. He remained there for six weeks, by the end of which time he had become a relatively competent speaker of Arabic. However, some members of a colony of Venetian merchants resident in the city, fearing English competition, showed hostility to him and expressed their suspicions of his motives to the Portuguese captain of the city; he interviewed the Englishman but, persuaded of his good intentions, remained cautiously friendly.

Newbery's return journey was even more notable. Leaving Hormoz on 1 August 1581, he paused at Lar to hire a Jewish servant, and went on from there to Shiraz. After resting in the city for two weeks he decided to move northwards, passing in turn through the cities of Esfahan, Kashan, Qom, and Tabriz. In the latter city he made contact with some Armenian merchants who had done business with Thomas Banister during his visit some twelve years earlier. From Tabriz he moved westwards through Asia Minor, visiting Ararat, Erivan, Erzurum, Tokat, and Bursa, near the shores of the Aegean. He and his servant entered Constantinople on 9 March 1582. Rather than take ship for England, Newbery boarded a Greek Black Sea trader, and passed through the Dardanelles to the Danube estuary. Via Iaşi, Khotin, and Kamenets, he travelled overland to Poland, and finally to the Baltic port of Danzig. There he found a Hull ship and obtained passage to England. He set foot in his own country once more on 31 August 1582.

The rigours of a journey beyond the dreams of most Englishmen appear only to have whetted Newbery's appetite. Almost immediately he planned a further, even more protracted expedition to exploit the commercial opportunities he had discerned during his travels. Between November 1582 and February 1583 he visited John Dee and Richard Hakluyt, with whom he appears to have been closely acquainted, to obtain all available English intelligence upon Arabia and India. He sailed from England on 11 March 1583, carrying letters of introduction from Elizabeth I to the kings of Cambay (Gujarat) and China. He had the company of three fellow travellers: the merchant

Ralph Fitch, the jeweller William Leach (or Leades), and an artist, James Storie. They arrived at Aleppo on 20 May. For ten days they remained in the city, purchasing local wares to add to trade goods provided by their backers (principally English cloths and haberdasheries) worth about £1300, of which £200 was reserved for their own profit. From Aleppo they passed overland by camel to Baghdad, arriving on 20 June. From there the small party travelled via Basrah to Hormoz, which they reached on 4 September. They hired a shop in the city from which to sell their English goods. Almost immediately the same Venetian merchants who had resented Newbery's presence two years earlier began assiduously to broadcast stories of the interlopers' heretical practices and their collusion with the Portuguese pretender, Dom Antonio. This time the captain of the town responded aggressively. On 10 September the four Englishmen were committed to prison, pending their transfer to Goa for interrogation.

By 20 November 1583 they had been carried by sea to the Indian subcontinent, and were committed to Goa prison, where they remained for twenty-two days (except James Storie, who obtained his freedom by the drastic expedient of agreeing to enter a monastery). Their liberation was due to the intercession of the archbishop of Goa and two Jesuits, one of whom was an Englishman, Thomas Stephens. Remarkably, much of the English party's money and property had been transferred to Goa also, and this was now restored. The Englishmen rented a house in the city and commenced trading, but the strict supervision under which they had been placed soon inclined them to attempt to flee Portuguese-held territory. On Whit Sunday 1584, taking all but a small proportion of their property (which they left in their house to deflect suspicion), the three merchants went to a river nearby—ostensibly to picnic there. They did not return. Passing slowly northwards by stages, they reached Agra by the end of the year, and remained there until 28 September 1585. Thereafter they separated. Leach remained to ply his jeweller's trade at Fatehpur, where the local king gave him a house and six slaves; Newbery determined to return to Aleppo, and thereafter to England; while Fitch continued his epic journey eastwards. Somewhere between Agra and Aleppo Newbery died from unknown causes. His body was not recovered.

Newbery was an assiduous correspondent, writing letters from Aleppo, Baghdad, Basrah, Hormoz, and Goa. Their tone suggests a man of pronounced piety and, unremarkable in one who had penetrated an unknown continent more comprehensively than any Englishman before him, considerable stoicism in adversity. The Flemish traveller Linschoten, who called him the 'principall' of his small party, reported unequivocally good opinions of his demeanour and integrity at Goa.

JAMES McDERMOTT

Sources R. Hakluyt, *The principal navigations, voyages, traffiques and discoveries of the English nation*, 5–6, Hakluyt Society, extra ser., 5–6 (1904) · S. Purchas, *Hakluytus posthumus, or, Purchas his pilgrimes*, bk 8 (1625); repr. Hakluyt Society, extra ser., 21 (1905) · D. B. Quinn, ed., *The Hakluyt handbook*, 2 vols., Hakluyt Society (1974) · The writings and correspondence of the two Richard Hakluyts, ed. E. G. R. Taylor, 2 vols., Hakluyt Society (1935) · A. C. Wood, *A history of the Levant Company* (1935); repr. (1964) · *The private diary of Dr John Dee*, ed. J. O. Halliwell, CS, 19 (1842)

Newbery, John (*bap.* 1713, *d.* 1767), publisher, was born in Waltham St Lawrence, Berkshire, where he was baptized on 9 July 1713, the son of Robert Newbery, farmer. He was taught in his village school but read widely and in 1730 he was employed by William Carnan, printer of the *Reading Mercury and Oxford Gazette*. On the death of Carnan in 1737 Newbery inherited a share of his estate, and in the summer of 1739 he married Mary, his late employer's widow, who was six years his senior. In 1740 he toured England in search of business opportunities and later that year he published in Reading *The Whole Duty of Man* by Richard Allestree, the first book to appear under his imprint. In the next two or three years, at the Bible and Crown, Market Place, Reading, he established a local circulating library, became a wholesaler of draper's goods, and set up a body of forty-three agents to widen the circulation of the *Reading Mercury*.

Late in 1743 Newbery established a shop in London at the Bible and Crown, near Devereux Court, outside Temple Bar. In 1745 he moved to the Bible and Sun (later numbered 65) in St Paul's Churchyard. Newbery's first London publication was *A Little Pretty Pocket-Book* (1744) 'intended for the instruction and amusement of little Master Tommy and pretty Miss Polly'. It was the first of many books designed specifically for children, and the motto on the frontispiece, '*Delectando monemus*—instruction with delight', reveals the influence of Locke's ideas on education. While Newbery was not the first to publish books for children—Thomas Boreman's series of ten *Gigantick Histories* (1740–43) must have been an influence on him—he was the first to create a separate list of works for children and regularly to employ or commission illustrators and authors, although he himself was almost certainly the author of some of the titles. Newbery was an imaginative publicist, advertising widely in newspapers in Britain and North America, offering discounts for teachers buying in bulk, and making use of promotional offers. In 1746 he acquired the patent for Dr Robert James's fever powder and lost no opportunity to market it. Thus the father of Margery Meanwell, the heroine of Newbery's most popular children's book, *The History of Little Goody Two-Shoes*, was 'seized with a violent fever in a place where Dr. James's Fever Powder was not to be had, and where he died miserably'. After the orphaned Margery, through her diligence, had overcome many difficulties to become a headmistress her pupils read no fewer than forty-two of Newbery's publications, all thoughtfully listed at the back of the third edition of the work. Newbery produced what could be considered the first children's encyclopaedia, *The Circle of the Sciences*, in seven volumes (1745–8) and the first children's periodical, the short-lived *Lilliputian Magazine* (1751). Another innovative publication was *Mercurius Latinus* (1746), which for thirty-one issues reported the news in Latin. Many of the works in his juvenile library were attractively issued in flowered paper covers and he also devised a number of educational games to teach spelling, reading, writing, and arithmetic. Newbery's adult list also demonstrated an awareness of his market; *The Ladies Complete Pocket-Book* appeared annually from 1750 to 1789 and he published several best-sellers, such as Isaac Bickerstaff's *Love in a Village* (1763), with at least eight editions within a year.

In 1750 Charles Burney introduced Newbery to Christopher *Smart, five times winner of Cambridge University's Seatonian prize for poetry. Newbery published all the winning poems between 1751 and 1756. In 1752 Smart married Newbery's stepdaughter Anna Maria Carnan; after bouts of insanity Smart was committed to St Luke's Hospital in 1757, and later to a private asylum for the insane, but Newbery continued to support him and his family, financially and by publishing his work. Another unfortunate associated with Newbery was Dr William Dodd, executed for forgery in 1777, who worked for the *British Magazine*, established in 1760, which was edited by Smollett and in which Newbery had an interest. Dodd also, from 1760 to 1767, acted as editor of the *Christian's Magazine*, which was established by Newbery.

Newbery engaged several prominent authors, at times supporting them with great generosity, although he prudently maintained an account of any cash advances he made. When Oliver Goldsmith was arrested for debt in 1762 he purchased a third share in the uncompleted *Vicar of Wakefield* and paid for Goldsmith's accommodation at Canonbury Tower, Islington (owned by a relative of Newbery), to allow him to write without interruptions. He also paid him £42 for a two-volume *History of England* for children (1764) and £21 for *The Traveller* (1764), on which he had paid an advance of £11 in 1763, but on Newbery's death Goldsmith still owed him about £200. Newbery also published works by Samuel Johnson, including *The Rambler* (1761) and *The Idler* (1761); this last work originally appeared in Newbery's *Universal Chronicle, or, A Weekly Gazette*, which Newbery established on 15 April 1758 and which continued until 1760. Newbery had interests in several other newspapers and periodicals, and on 12 January 1760 he established the long-running daily *Public Ledger*, which first published Goldsmith's *Citizen of the World* and which only later assumed its present character of a commercial news-sheet.

Goldsmith and Johnson have immortalized two aspects of Newbery's character: his generosity and his constant industry. In Goldsmith's *The Vicar of Wakefield* the sick and penniless Dr Primrose, stranded in a tavern, is lent money to pay his bills by:

> none other than the philanthropic publisher in St Paul's Churchyard, who has written so many little books for children. He called himself their friend, but he was the friend of all mankind. He was no sooner alighted than he was in haste to be gone, for he was ever on business of the utmost importance.

Johnson underlines Newbery's incessant activity in an affectionately satirical portrayal in *The Idler*:

> that great philosopher Jack Whirler, whose business keeps him in perpetual motion, and whose motion always eludes his business; who is always to do what he never does, who

cannot stand still because he is wanted in another place, and who is wanted in many places because he stays in none ... overwhelmed as he is with business, his chief desire is to have still more. (*The Idler*, 19 Aug 1758)

This continuous industry meant that when Newbery died, on 22 December 1767 at his house in St Paul's Churchyard, he was a wealthy man, although most of his money came not from publishing but from the sale of Dr James's fever powder and some thirty other patent cures. He was succeeded in business by his son Francis *Newbery. His contribution to children's literature is recognized by the Newbery medal, which has been awarded in the United States each year since 1922 to an outstanding book for children.

IAN MAXTED

Sources S. Roscoe, *John Newbery and his successors, 1740–1814: a bibliography* (1973) · J. R. Townsend, *John Newbery and his books: trade and plumcake for ever, huzza!* (1995) · C. Welsh, *A bookseller of the last century, being some account of the life of John Newbery* (1885) · J. Rose, 'John Newbery', *The British literary book trade, 1700–1820*, ed. J. K. Bracken and J. Silver, DLitB, 154 (1995), 216–28 · A. le B. Newbery, *Records of the house of Newbery from 1274 to 1910* (1911)
Archives Free Library of Philadelphia, MSS

Newbery, Ralph (*b.* in or before **1536**, *d.* **1603/4**), bookseller, was freed by the London Stationers' Company on 21 January 1560, at which date he was at least twenty-four. Although details of his parentage and background are unknown Newbery may have been from Berkshire, as three of the many apprentices he bound during his career came from that county; these included a relative, John Newbery from Waltham St Lawrence, and Newbery also held property in the county. Succeeding to the printer Thomas Berthelet's sales outlet Newbery was based in Fleet Street from 1560 until his death. Newbery entered his first publications in the Stationers' register in spring 1560 and took his first apprentice in 1561. He published infrequently between 1560 and the late 1570s, but early publications included Heinrich Bullinger's *Fiftie Godlie and Learned Sermons*, Bishop Thomas Cooper's *A Briefe Exposition*, Sir Geoffrey Fenton's *Golden Epistles*, two works by the Spanish bishop Antonio de Guevara, and the *Zodyake of Lyfe* by Marcellus Palingenius. In July 1577 he entered into the Stationers' register *An Abstract of All the Penall Statutes* by Ferdinand Pulton with the printer and bookseller Richard Tottell and the bookseller Robert Walley, upon condition that the copyright would be held by Tottell until his death, whereupon it would be passed successively to Newbery and Walley for life. Newbery's edition of Caspar Huberinus's *A Riche Storehouse, or Treasurie, for the Sicke* (1578) carried a dedication from the bookseller to Lady Catherine Howard, probably the great-granddaughter of the third duke of Norfolk, whose arms were printed facing the dedication.

Newbery's printer of choice at this time seems to have been Henry Middleton, but from 1578 he often published with the bookseller and printer Henry Bynneman (who had first collaborated with Newbery in 1573), and from 1581 to 1582 they were jointly the assigns of Richard Tottell and the queen's printer, Christopher Barker. In April 1582 Bynneman and Newbery appeared before the governing body of the Stationers' Company to agree to share the publication of an edition of Thomas Cooper's *Thesaurus linguae Romanae et Britannicae*. Following the death of Bynneman in 1583 Newbery and the printer Henry Denham (who had first printed for Newbery in 1565) took over many of his copyrights, including his printing privilege for dictionaries and chronicles. In January 1584, in their capacity as Bynneman's assigns, they yielded the rights to ten titles to the Stationers' Company for the benefit of poor members; Newbery himself also gave up eight titles, including Bullinger's *Sermons* and William Lambard's *Perambulation of Kent*. In December he and Denham underlined their rights to Bynneman's printing privilege 'whiche doe belonge unto them by vertue of the queenes pryviledge and grante' by making a series of blanket entrances in the Stationers' register covering all manner of chronicles and dictionaries (Arber, *Regs. Stationers*, 2.438). From 1586 he was publishing with the bookseller George Bishop and the following year they became deputies of Christopher Barker, effectively taking over the mantle of queen's printer until Barker's death in 1599. Newbery appeared before the Stationers' Company's court (of which he was now a member) in March 1587 to seek permission to publish a new edition of Bullinger, which was granted on the basis of various financial and commercial conditions. Two years later an unspecified dispute between Newbery and Richard Tottell was referred to arbitration by the company. In 1592–3 Newbery appears to have bought the manor of Beenhams in the parish of Waltham St Lawrence. He was elected in March 1594 as one of the stock-keepers for the group of stationers who had succeeded to the privileges formerly held by John and Richard Day; the following year he was named as one of ten partners for the publication of one of the books covered by these privileges, Foxe's *Book of Martyrs*. He was also involved in the group of stationers who controlled the printing privileges of William Seres.

During these years Newbery had risen steadily through the ranks of the Stationers' Company. Made a liveryman on 29 June 1570 he served terms as renter warden (1578–9 and 1579–80), under warden (1583–4 and 1584–5), upper warden (1589–90 and 1591–2), and master (1598–9 and 1601–2). His gift of a standing cup to the company was probably made about the time of his service in the higher corporate offices. In January 1602 he transferred his rights to John Stow's *Chronicle* to Thomas Adams and his cousin John Newbery, in March he drew up his will, and from that year his shop was managed by two former apprentices, John North and Roger Jackson. In the same year he bought an interest in the manor of Woolley in the parish of White Waltham, Berkshire. Newbery's last attendance at the company's governing body was on 6 June 1603 and on 14 August he added a codicil to his will. The exact date of his death is unknown, but while he was definitely dead by 19 June 1604, when a receipt for his bequest of £15 to Bridewell Hospital was issued to the Stationers' Company, he was probably dead by 23 April 1604 when the company ordered that an account be drawn up of his stock. Newbery's wife, Elizabeth (*d.* in or after 1607), and his son, Francis, were principal beneficiaries of the will, but the will also stipulated that his stock of books at Stationers' Hall, including copies of the *Book of Martyrs*, and his parts in the Seres and Day privileges 'shalbe sould by the discretion and assistance' of the Stationers' Company 'to the moste advantage and benefitt' with one quarter of the money going to the poor of the company and a quarter each to Bridewell Hospital, Christ's Hospital, and his local parish of St Bride's respectively (PRO, PROB 11/109, fol. 234*v*). Newbery's shop passed to Roger Jackson in 1604. Newbery's widow was evidently still alive when probate of the will was finally granted on 24 April 1607; Elizabeth may have been the Mrs Newbury whose share in the Stationers' Company's joint stock venture was sold in July 1615. Francis married Mary, the daughter of Sir Henry Rowe, lord mayor of London for 1607–8, and died at Woolley manor about 1651; he was buried in White Waltham parish.

I. GADD

Sources STC, 1475–1640 · DNB · private information (2004) [M. Treadwell, M. Turner] · will, PRO, PROB 11/109, sig. 30 · W. W. Greg and E. Boswell, eds., *Records of the court of the Stationers' Company, 1576 to 1602, from register B* (1930) · W. A. Jackson, ed., *Records of the court of the Stationers' Company, 1602 to 1640* (1957) · H. R. Plomer, *Abstracts from the wills of English printers and stationers from 1492 to 1630* (1903) · H. G. Aldis and others, *A dictionary of printers and booksellers in England, Scotland and Ireland, and of foreign printers of English books, 1557–1640*, ed. R. B. McKerrow (1910) · Arber, *Regs. Stationers* · VCH *Berkshire*, 3.173, 181 · W. H. Rylands, ed., *The four visitations of Berkshire*, 2, Harleian Society, 57 (1908), 182–3

Newbery, Thomas (*fl.* 1563), author, is known only for his work *Dives pragmaticus*, printed by Alexander Lacy in April 1563. The book, a quarto of eight pages, offers itself as particularly suited to teaching children and servants how to 'rede and wryte' the names of various 'wares and implements' (sig. A1*r*). The work comprises a prose preface from the author, who professes himself to be a merchant, and a long list in verse of various goods on sale. According to E. M. Field, such lists of everyday objects were an established way of instructing young children. Newbery's exuberant celebration of commercial activity is tempered at the end of the poem by a number of moral strictures, including exhortations to avoid gambling, fornication, excess in apparel, and blasphemy, and, perhaps surprisingly, to watch expenditure. The one remaining copy of *Dives pragmaticus* is in the Althorp Library, now at Manchester. Henry Huth reprinted the text in *Fugitive Tracts* (1875). The *Dictionary of National Biography* erroneously suggests that the author may have been a London publisher of the same name, who printed (among other things) *A briefe homily wherein the most comfortable and right use of the Lords supper is very plainly and openly delivered* in 1580. This publisher was in fact one Ralph Newberie.

Another **Thomas Newberry** (*fl.* 1653–1658) was a printer and bookseller, whose shop was at the Three Golden Lions, near the Royal Exchange in London, and who regularly published works by J. Brinsley and E. Reyner, author of *Rules for the Government of the Tongue*.

CATHY SHRANK

Sources H. Huth, *Fugitive tracts written in verse* (1875) · E. M. Field, *The child and his book*, 2nd edn (1891) · J. Ritson, *Bibliographia poetica* (1802) · *A briefe homily wherein the most comfortable and right use of the*

Lords supper is very plainly and openly delivered (1580) • W. T. Lowndes, *The bibliographer's manual of English literature*, ed. H. G. Bohn, [new edn], 6 vols. (1864) • *STC, 1475–1640* • Wing, *STC*

Newbigin, (James Edward) Lesslie (1909–1998), missionary and theologian, was born on 8 December 1909 at 4 Tanquerville Terrace, Jesmond, Newcastle upon Tyne, the second child of Edward Richmond Newbigin (1863–1940), shipping merchant, and his wife, Annie Ellen Affleck (*d.* 1962). His father was of Northumbrian, and his mother of Scottish descent. Both parents were convinced Presbyterians. His father was the owner and manager of a shipping company based in Newcastle upon Tyne, but was interested in a radical approach to national issues. After primary schooling in Newcastle and secondary as a boarder at the Quakers' Leighton Park School, near Reading, Newbigin gained entrance in 1928 to Queens' College, Cambridge, where he read geography and economics with a view to joining his father's firm. His energies were soon occupied with debating and with the Student Christian Movement (SCM). At a camp for unemployed men in south Wales in the summer of 1929, he saw, in a sleepless night of worry at his own failure to handle such a situation, a vision of Christ on the cross reaching 'down to the most hopeless and sordid of human misery, and yet promis[ing] life and victory' (Newbigin, 12)—a conviction that was to shape the rest of his life.

A year later, at an SCM conference, in a moment of quiet prayer Newbigin believed he received an unambiguous 'order' to offer for ordination, and was startled by a suggestion later that day that he join the SCM staff when he graduated in 1931. So he went to Glasgow as one of two Scottish secretaries, the other being Helen Stewart Henderson (1907–1999), daughter of the Revd Robert Henderson. Newbigin quickly knew he was to share his life with her. In fact, because of the strict rules of the Church of Scotland for its missionaries, they could not marry until 20 August 1936, just before they set out for India. Meanwhile Newbigin made good use of his two years of working with students and the three of theological studies at Westminster College, Cambridge, to develop an unusually penetrating and clear intelligence. A short book, *Christian Freedom in the Modern World* (1937), in response to Macmurray's *Freedom in the Modern World* of 1932, was finished on the boat.

During an initial intensive period of study of Tamil, in which he became outstandingly fluent, indeed eloquent, Newbigin suffered a severe leg injury in a bus accident and had to return to Scotland. On returning to India in September 1939 the Newbigins were stationed in Kanchipuram, Madras, where as 'district missionary' until 1946 Newbigin gained a profound respect for the people of humble villages and for the potential of the Christian leaders among them. He was increasingly drawn into discussions towards the unity of three denominations (Presbyterian and Congregational, Methodist, Anglican)—to such good effect that in the epoch-making service on 27 September 1947 inaugurating the united Church of South India he was one of the fourteen new bishops consecrated. His diocese was Madurai and Ramnad, in south-east Tamil

Nadu, where he was soon immersed both in the innerchurch work of preaching and caring for the congregations and in the wider care for the health, economic possibilities, and political prospects of the total community, which involved him in searching discussions with leading Hindus.

On leave in 1946–7 Newbigin faced the bitter arguments in Britain over this pioneering inter-church union, and he provided a deeply theological approach to their resolution in his first major book, *The Reunion of the Church: a Defence of the South India Scheme* (1948, revised edn, 1960). The reputation this earned him was heightened by his *A South India Diary* (1951, revised edn, 1960), a winning portrait of a church growing from its local roots and of a caring, imaginative bishop. In August 1948 he shared, as a delegate of the Church of South India, in the inaugural Amsterdam assembly of the World Council of Churches (WCC), with many of whose leaders and staff he was acquainted from SCM days. He served on the group drafting the assembly's *Message* and presented to the plenary session its eventual text, largely his own work. So began an oft-repeated story within that council: Newbigin, like William Temple between the wars, almost always proved able to produce from complex debates a text of shining clarity and good sense, offering a reconciling, forwardlooking view that earned general agreement.

The Madura years saw Newbigin active alike on the Indian church scene and on the international level, where the advent of air travel made it possible for him to share in key meetings of both the WCC and the International Missionary Council (IMC); the IMC's founding conference in Edinburgh in 1910 had provided the essential impetus for the WCC, and it was now actively debating integration with it. In 1952 he delivered the Kerr lectures at Glasgow, published as his second major book, *The Household of God* (1953), on the nature of the church. In 1957—to his surprise, indeed dismay—he was approached about becoming general secretary of the IMC, an appointment confirmed by its 1958 assembly in Ghana. So he left India in mid-1959, by which time he had delivered lectures at Harvard, published in 1961 as *A Faith for this One World?*, and written for the IMC an influential quasi-manifesto, *One Body, One Gospel, One World: the Christian Mission Today* (1958).

Based at first in London, from 1962 in Geneva, Newbigin was widely acclaimed as the leader of the 'world mission' constituency later gathered in the division of world mission and evangelism of the WCC—travelling, preaching, writing, and consulting and being consulted by church leaders in every continent. One of his major contributions was the section report on unity from the WCC's third assembly (1961). This for the first time offered a vision of what God's will and gift of unity could look like, starting from the local level with 'all in each place who are baptized into Jesus Christ and confess him as Lord and Saviour' and climaxing with a vision of Christians who have

a corporate life reaching out in witness and service to all and who at the same time are united with the whole Christian fellowship in all places and all ages in such wise that ministry and members are accepted by all, and that all can act and speak together as occasion requires for the tasks to which God calls his people.   (*The New Delhi Report*, 1962, 116)

Newbigin also took a leading role in the world mission conference at Mexico in 1963 under the theme 'Mission on six continents', at which the old, hurtful distinction between 'sending' and 'receiving' churches could be overcome in the agreement that Christ's mission was now entrusted to each local church to pursue in its own place and way, with the support—and on occasion correction—of all other local churches: a vision of catholicity in mission that remains a keystone of the ecumenical movement. *The Relevance of Trinitarian Doctrine for Today's Mission* (1963) brought his distinctive theological approach to a wider audience.

Yet Newbigin did not altogether enjoy the Geneva years, and was happy to be elected bishop in Madras and to return to India with his wife Helen—their four children (three daughters and a son) by now grown up—in mid-1965. His years there brought constant demands on him from the local, national, and international levels. He remained active in the WCC, especially in its 'faith and order' commission. Addresses continued to appear in book form: *Honest Religion for Secular Man* (1966), his riposte to the debate around John Robinson; *The Finality of Christ* (1969), originally given in Yale University; and *The Good Shepherd: Meditations on Christian Ministry in Today's World* (1974, revised edn, 1977).

In 1974 Newbigin and his wife travelled back to retirement in the UK by local transport, carrying only two suitcases and a rucksack from Madras to Munich. Forbidden to cross Iraq or Syria, they hitch-hiked with a friendly Turkish workman from Tabriz to the Armenian border, and thence to Erzurum and Cappadocia. They had decided to live in Birmingham, in order that Newbigin could serve the Selly Oak Colleges as a part-time lecturer in mission studies. His work there resulted in *The Open Secret: Sketches for a Missionary Theology* (1978, second edn, 1995). He was also soon caught up in many other activities, not least in the United Reformed church (URC), in which the English Presbyterians had united with the Congregationalists, and which was pursuing the possibility of further unity with the Methodists and the Church of England. Newbigin served as the URC's national moderator in 1978–9, also as one of its representatives on the churches' unity commission, whose plan for 'covenanting for unity' of 1980 fell victim, like the Anglican–Methodist unity scheme ten years earlier, to an insufficient majority among the clergy in the general synod of the Church of England, though not without a hard-fought battle also in the URC.

In *The Light has Come: an Exposition of the Fourth Gospel* (1982), Newbigin published a magisterial commentary on St John, while *Unfinished Agenda: an Autobiography* (1985, second edn, 1993) provided an engaging, fast-paced, and attractively humble record. Addresses and articles continued to pour from his portable typewriter. Notable among them were 'The welfare state' for Westminster

Abbey's Gore lecture; 'What is "a local church truly united"?' for the *Ecumenical Review*; 'A Christian perspective on the city' for *Faith in the City of Birmingham*, a twenty-page summary of the theology many had missed in the national report *Faith in the City*; *Your Kingdom Come* (1979), biblical reflections on the theme of the WCC's world mission conference at Melbourne in 1980; *Mission in Christ's Way* (1987), in preparation for the next at San Antonio, Texas, in 1989; and *Come Holy Spirit—Renew the Face of the Earth*, a lecture towards the 1991 WCC assembly in Canberra. As a former director of the world mission commission he was a guest at the Texas conference, giving an outstanding impromptu after-hours address. In November 1996 he flew, his last major journey, to spend a few days at the corresponding conference in Salvador de Bahia, Brazil, where his brief but far-sighted contribution was welcomed with great warmth.

Meanwhile Newbigin had given fifteen years to what he called 'the most intensely missionary period of my life', engaging at depth with the underlying assumptions and unspoken convictions of the 'Western, post-Enlightenment' culture that was spreading all over the world and sapping the foundations of religious traditions, including Christian faith. This began when a planning group of the British Council of Churches, considering a major 'church and society conference' for 1984, ran into uncertainty. Newbigin offered to draft a sketch of what its discussions could be indicating, and within ten days had sent a fifty-page manuscript which many who read it, including both the Anglican and Roman Catholic archbishops, found deeply exciting. It became *The other Side of 1984: Questions for the Churches* (1983), sold worldwide in many different languages and editions. It was followed during the next ten years by *Foolishness to the Greeks: the Gospel and Western Culture* (1986), *The Gospel in a Pluralist Society* (1989), *Truth to Tell: the Gospel as Public Truth* (1991), and three chapters in *Faith and Power: Christianity and Islam in 'Secular' Britain* (1998)—all pursuing his passionate concern for the nature of truth and obedience to God's will in a society and culture that had grown indifferent to this entire genre of question. In these years he lectured frequently in Europe and North America, with a memorable visit to India for the fiftieth anniversary of the IMC's Tambaram world mission conference.

After a move to live in sheltered housing in London in 1992, Newbigin was often invited to speak at Holy Trinity, Brompton, sanctuary for evangelicals and charismatics—hardly his lifelong supporters but among whom he found an attentive audience for his central theological concerns. A heart-warming service in September 1997 celebrated his fifty years as a bishop, all spent in leadership of united and uniting churches. Despite a number of health scares in earlier years, it was only at Christmas 1997, on a visit to his eldest daughter in Manchester, that his heart started to give out; he died, not without thought-provoking reflections shared with those visiting his bedside, in south London on 30 January 1998. His funeral service was at the Dulwich Grove URC on 7 February, led jointly by a Nigerian

Anglican and a British URC minister; his body was cremated at nearby Norwood the same day. A memorial service was held in Southwark Cathedral on 28 March. He was survived by his wife, Helen, and their four children.

Newbigin was one of relatively few British Christians to have reshaped the thinking and witness of the worldwide church in the twentieth century. He was noted for his combination of five characteristics. In his speaking and writing, he stood out for the fluency of his rigorous, yet unfailingly attractive, fair, and persuasive argument with major strands in current debate. This was invariably grounded in an unshakeable belief in the centrality of God, and in God's initiatives in Jesus and in the Spirit, as the deepest fact and truth underlying everything else. He discerned the universal horizon of whatever he dealt with, whether the dilemmas of a Western welfare state or a dialogue with Hindu friends in India or Handsworth. He always held together in a profound wholeness and integrity both faith and life, both religious teachings and social practice, both the concerns of an individual and the needs of society, God's purposes for both the church and the world. All of these were bathed in the courtesy and infectious laughter of a man who had long since forgotten how to think of himself more highly than he ought to.

MARTIN CONWAY

Sources L. Newbigin, *Unfinished agenda: an autobiography* (1985) [rev. edn, 1993] · M. Conway, 'God-open, world-wide, and Jesus-true: Lesslie Newbigin's faith pilgrimage', *Mid-Stream* [Indianapolis, USA], 34/1 (Jan 1995), 21–33 [in shortened form, *Epworth Review*, 21/3 (1994), 27–36] · G. Wainwright, *Lesslie Newbigin: a theological life* (2000) · *The Times* (31 Jan 1998) · *The Scotsman* (31 Jan 1998) · *Daily Telegraph* (3 Feb 1998) · *The Independent* (4 Feb 1998) · *The Guardian* (6 Feb 1998) · *The Guardian* (14 Feb 1998) · WWW · personal knowledge (2004) · private information (2004) · E. Jackson, *Walking in the light* [forthcoming] · G. Hunsberger, *Bearing the witness of the spirit* (Grand Rapids, Michigan, 1998)
Archives Bishop Newbigin Institute for Church and Mission Studies, Royapeltah, Madras 600014 · U. Birm., Orchard Learning Resources Centre, corresp. and papers | World Council of Churches, Geneva, Switzerland, archives | Leighton Park School, Reading, records and some old boy activities · NL Scot., archives of Church of Scotland Foreign Missions Council · U. Birm., archives of Student Christian Movement
Likenesses D. McPhee, photograph, repro. in *The Guardian* (6 Feb 1998) · photograph, repro. in *Epworth Review*, 21 (1994) · photograph, repro. in *The Times* · photograph, repro. in *Daily Telegraph* · photograph, repro. in *The Independent* · photographs, repro. in Newbigin, *Unfinished agenda*
Wealth at death very little

Newbigin, Marion Isabel (1869–1934), geographer and biologist, was born in Alnwick, Northumberland, one of five daughters and three sons in the family of James Lesslie Newbigin, pharmacist. Her sister Maude was lecturer in history and deputy principal of the Day Training College, Portsmouth. A third sister, Alice, held a post at the Edinburgh College of Agriculture. All five of the daughters of James Newbigin were strong supporters of the feminist cause.

Marion Newbigin was educated at the Edinburgh Association for the University Education of Women, University College, Aberystwyth, and the extramural School of Medicine for Women, Edinburgh. In 1893 she took a University of London BSc; she was awarded a DSc (London) in 1898.

While a student at Edinburgh, Marion Newbigin had come under the influence of J. Arthur Thompson, whom she later succeeded as lecturer in biology and zoology at the School of Medicine for Women. She was a distinguished teacher and an outstanding lecturer. Her original research at this period, carried out in the laboratories of the Royal College of Physicians, concerned studies on coloration in plants, crustaceans, and fish. Several papers resulted from this work, some being joint publications with N. D. Paton and other collaborators. Also worthy of note were her contributions to the analysis of collections brought back by the *Challenger* expedition of 1872–6. Her monograph *Colour in Nature* appeared in 1898. Her second book, *Life by the Sea Shore* (1901), which resulted from work at the Marine Biological Station, Millport, remained a classic for many years.

In 1902 Marion Newbigin became editor of the *Scottish Geographical Magazine*, the position she held until her death. Her career in geography began at a time when, in Britain, this field had yet to be fully established as an academic discipline. One of the founders of modern British geography, she stressed the value of biological principles applied to human geography. She was one of the first British geographers whose interests covered the whole range of the field, and this breadth is reflected in her many writings. Her *Animal Geography* (1913) and *Ordnance Survey Maps* (1913) were pioneering works. *Aftermath* (1920), dealing with the territorial questions raised by the Versailles settlement, was a remarkable essay in political geography. Her most valuable contributions, however, were probably those relating to the Mediterranean region; they included *Geographical Aspects of Balkan Problems* (1915) and *Southern Europe* (1932), her last major publication. She travelled widely, and in *Frequented Ways* (1922) expressed the hope that 'something of the intense joy of travel shines through the pages'.

Much of Marion Newbigin's work was directly educational, and her *Introduction to Physical Geography* (1912) remained a student stand-by for many years. She long acted as examiner in geography for various institutions, and her influence on the training of the next generation of geographers was substantial. She was president of the geographical section of the British Association in 1922; the following year she received the Royal Scottish Geographical Society's Livingstone gold medal. Under her able and accomplished editorship, which lasted over three decades, the *Scottish Geographical Magazine* became one of the most respected periodicals in the field.

Marion Newbigin's home in Edinburgh was shared with her sisters Hilda and Alice, and later, on her retirement, Maude. Marion Newbigin died at her home, 2 Chamberlain Road, Edinburgh, on 20 July 1934.

MARY R. S. CREESE, rev.

Sources *Scottish Geographical Magazine*, 50 (1934), 331–3 · *Geographical Review*, 24 (1934), 676 · W. N. Boog Watson, 'The first eight ladies', *University of Edinburgh Journal*, 23 (1967–8), 227–34 · CGPLA

Eng. & Wales (1934) • M. R. S. Creese, *Ladies in the laboratory? American and British women in science, 1800–1900* (1998) • A. M. C. Maddrell, 'Scientific discourse and the geographical work of Marion Newbigin', *Scottish Geographical Magazine*, 113 (1997), 33–41 • A. S. Mather, 'Geddes, geography and ecology: the golden age of vegetation mapping in Scotland', *Scottish Geographical Magazine*, 115 (1999), 35–52

Archives U. Edin. L., university archives | NL Scot., corresp. mainly with Sir Patrick Geddes

Wealth at death £6020 13s. 6d.: confirmation, 10 Sept 1934, *CCI*

Newbold, Sir Douglas (1894–1945), colonial governor, was born on 13 August 1894 at Tunbridge Wells, the seventh and youngest son of William Newbold (*d.* 1900) of Warwickshire and his wife, Eleanor Isabel Ferguson (*d.* 1942). His father's business interests took him frequently to the USA and Mexico. His mother was the daughter of Colonel David Ferguson of the American army, and she presided over their large family after her husband's death in 1900. In Tunbridge Wells, Newbold was the prankster and the favourite in the family of six brothers and four sisters, and his mother became the dominant influence in his life until her death. He never married. Within his close family in rural Kent, Newbold absorbed a romantic fascination with ancient archaeology that remained with him throughout his life in the more remote regions of the Middle East and the Sudan. In 1907 he followed his brothers to Uppingham School as a scholar. There his insatiable curiosity was strengthened by a deep appreciation of the human condition, symbolized by a fierce individualism that never left him. His success at Uppingham sent him to Oriel College, Oxford, in 1913 as a classical scholar, but his career was interrupted in 1914 by the outbreak of the First World War and a commission in the Dorset yeomanry and the cavalry machine-gun corps. He served in Mudros in Greece, in Egypt against the Senussi in 1915, and also in Palestine, where he was wounded at Zeitun after the fall of Gaza in November 1917. His time in the Middle East, supported by a thorough knowledge of the Bible, also proved to be of scholarly interest that led to his study of the classical and Arab medieval geographers.

After the war Newbold returned to Oxford and Oriel for another year before joining the Sudan political service whose administration in the remote regions of the Nile basin appealed to his romantic temperament. He arrived in the Sudan in 1920 and was sent to the Kordofan province as an assistant district commissioner where, aided by his Arabic studies, he began to fulfil his ambition to explore the remote regions of the country. He undertook exploration by camel and car into the Libyan desert in 1924, 1927, and 1930 in search of the legendary oasis of Zerzura. His experience and success among the nomads of the west resulted in his transfer to the Beja of the Red Sea hills in eastern Sudan, after a brief sojourn in Khartoum as deputy assistant civil secretary in 1924–5. His fascination and fondness for the nomadic Beja (Rudyard Kipling's 'Fuzzy-Wuzzy') thereafter became the paramount interest of his life. His most happy years were those spent as district commissioner, nomad administrator, and deputy governor, Beja, from 1926 to 1932. His return to Kordofan

Sir Douglas Newbold (1894–1945), by Elliott & Fry

as governor in 1933 made him the chief administrator of the nomadic peoples he had known as a young district commissioner. He was made an OBE in 1933. Promoted deputy civil secretary in 1938, he was also made a CBE. He was appointed civil secretary the following year, and remained in this post—the chief administrative officer of Sudan—until his death.

Newbold's years as civil secretary were devoted to war and political transition in the Sudan, during which he never lost his composure or his concern for the Sudanese. As a district commissioner and governor he had protected the Sudanese from commercial and political exploitation. In war he now defended them from foreign invasion and attempted to create institutions to satisfy their growing political aspirations without sacrificing the social benefits and individual liberties bestowed by paternal but autocratic imperial rule. During his early years he had established a close bond of affection and trust with the great tribal sheikhs which as civil secretary he had greater difficulty in retaining when challenged by younger, educated Sudanese aspiring for greater political control of Sudanese affairs. The Second World War and Newbold's death prevented progress towards self-government. As the chief executive officer of Sudan, he had to organize its defence and the campaigns against the Italians in Ethiopia and Libya, while continuing civil administration in the Sudan with limited human and material resources, all of which intruded upon his ideas for imperial reform and political innovation in which Western representative institutions were perhaps not the solution. Despite being made a KBE in 1944 in recognition for his service to the empire this conundrum troubled him deeply and was only partially resolved in 1945 by the convening of the advisory council for northern Sudan.

Newbold was an intellectual, but also an imperial and pragmatic administrator. An insatiable and prolific writer of letters, he was the author of many articles on exploration and archaeology which were published in *Antiquity*, the *Geographical Journal*, and *Sudan Notes and Records*. A selection of his letters, papers, and lectures were published in 1953 under the title *The Making of the Modern Sudan*. In these Newbold expressed his enthusiasm for education, not only to instil greater professionalism in British colonial administration, but also to lay the foundation for a new Sudan. He perceived 'a golden chance to use all our powers, moral, intellectual and physical, for the benefit of some of the finest people in the world' (*DNB*). He never lost sight of the need for educational advance as a condition of popular government and a responsible civil service. He was one of the most influential founders of the Khartoum University College.

Newbold did not recover after being thrown from his horse during an outing in Khartoum. Exhausted by the demands of war, the politics of the coming peace, and an abscess in his hip brought on by years of growing osteoarthritis, he died in the Khartoum Hospital on 23 March 1945 and was buried at Khartoum the following day. He left his library to Gordon Memorial College, now the University of Khartoum, where his portrait hangs.

ROBERT O. COLLINS

Sources K. D. D. Henderson, ed., *The making of the modern Sudan: the life and letters of Sir Douglas Newbold* (1953) · U. Durham L., department of palaeography and diplomatic, Sudan archive, Douglas Newbold MSS · *DNB* · *CGPLA Eng. & Wales* (1945) · *The Times* (26 March 1945)
Archives U. Durham L., Sudan Archive, war diary, photographs, etc. · U. Oxf., Griffith Institute, notes on the history and archaeology of the Beja tribes of the eastern Sudan | Bodl. RH, corresp. with M. Perham · U. Durham L., letters, mainly to Sir Christopher Cox · U. Durham L., corresp. with J. Longe
Likenesses Elliott & Fry, photograph, NPG [*see illus.*] · oils (posthumous), University College, Khartoum, Newbold Memorial Library
Wealth at death £18,069 9s. 1d.: administration, 18 Sept 1945, *CGPLA Eng. & Wales* · £2911 2s. 11d.—in England: administration, 3 April 1947, *CGPLA Eng. & Wales*

Newbold [*née* Neilson], **Marjory** (1883–1926), socialist and communist, was born on 29 May 1883 at Winton Terrace, Beith, Ayrshire, the second of four children of Alexander Neilson, cabinet-maker, and his wife, Mary Steven Fettes. Marjory Neilson was brought up in a comfortable upper working-class household. Her father had sufficient income to support her into higher education after an excellent career at Beith Academy. She studied arts subjects at Glasgow University from 1902 to 1905 but failed to gain enough passes to graduate.

While at university, Marjory Neilson broke from her Presbyterian background and became an atheist, feminist, and socialist, joining the Independent Labour Party and the growing socialist Sunday school movement in Glasgow. By 1908 she had entered the teaching profession and until 1916 taught in Wishaw public school, a large elementary school in industrial Lanarkshire. Here,

encountering deprived children in overcrowded classrooms with few resources, she committed herself to the political struggle for fundamental reform of education, health, welfare, and housing provision for working-class families.

For several years, Marjory Neilson was a leading member of the thriving Wishaw branch of the Independent Labour Party (ILP) and—unusually for a woman—a prominent socialist on the west of Scotland scene. She pioneered and supervised the Wishaw socialist Sunday school which, from 1909, promoted fellowship and working-class solidarity among a large membership of children and adults. She undertook a wide range of other political responsibilities and was variously ILP branch chairperson, lecture and literature secretary, political education officer, delegate to the Scottish divisional council of the ILP between 1912 and 1916, agent in local and parliamentary elections, and secretary to Wishaw Housing Council, as well as an active member of the Scottish Socialist Teachers' Society.

The impact of the First World War tested Marjory Neilson's existing anti-militarist and pacifist beliefs. After her marriage on 16 June 1915 to (John Turner) Walton *Newbold (1888–1943), then a research student, who was also involved in socialist politics, she had to resign from school teaching. This allowed her to devote her energies to antiwar politics, initially as organizing secretary in Scotland for the No Conscription Fellowship. By 1916 Marjory Newbold had moved leftwards, rejecting individual pacifism and, like her husband, openly identifying with Marxism. In late 1917 and early 1918 she worked for the Hands Off Russia Committee. Already in London, Marjory also worked closely with the young socialist movement, taking political education classes and, while in Manchester in 1919–20, led the small pro-communist National League of Working Youth. Concurrently, she was secretary of the local group of the left-wing movement inside the ILP in the campaign to win the rank and file to revolutionary politics.

As fraternal delegate from those revolutionary groups, Marjory Newbold journeyed incognito to Russia in the summer of 1920 to participate in the Second Congress of the Third (Communist) International. In Petrograd, she briefed Communist International officials on the left ILP campaign to affiliate with the emerging Communist Party, and researched Soviet policies and provision for women and children. After her return from Moscow in September, her health, already poor, rapidly deteriorated and by the spring of 1921 a fatal strain of tuberculosis was diagnosed. Dora Russell, a travelling companion to Russia, recalled Marjory as

> small, very thin and pale and not unlike the ILP leader James Maxton. Like so many communists I was to meet then and later she was totally convinced and dogmatic and willing to make any sacrifice for the cause. I liked Marjory and her spirit, her courage and her endurance, but her physical strength was not enough.   (Russell, 85)

Although one of several hundred ILP members who joined the Communist Party in April 1921, Marjory was too ill for further active political life. She helped with Walton Newbold's electoral campaigns in 1922 and 1923, but after a long period of illness she died on 15 November 1926 at the family home, Bellscauseway, Beith, from acute pulmonary tuberculosis and was buried in Beith cemetery. Although politically active for a comparatively short time, Marjory Newbold made a distinctive contribution to the labour and socialist movement.   ROBERT DUNCAN

Sources R. Duncan, 'Marjory Neilson Newbold: tribute to a socialist pioneer', *Scottish Labour History Review*, 6 (winter 1992), 4–7 • memoir, JRL, Newbold MSS • J. Muir, *An anatomy of a socialist: the life and times of Marjory Newbold* (1984) • *Wishaw Press* (1908–16) • *Young Socialist* (1917–18) • *Forward* (1909–10) • matriculation album and academic record for Marjory Neilson, U. Glas. • *The International* (14 Aug 1920) • *Motherwell Times* (19 Nov 1926) • D. Russell, *The tamarisk tree*, 3 vols. (1975–85), vol. 1, p. 85 • Beith monumental inscriptions book (tombstones), Cunninghame District Council Archive, Irvine, Scotland • b. cert. • m. cert. • d. cert.
Archives JRL, MSS
Likenesses photograph, 1920, Scottish Trade Union Congress Offices, Glasgow, Gallacher Memorial Library • photograph, c.1920, repro. in *The International*, 7 • photograph (as a young woman), priv. coll. • portraits, repro. in Duncan, 'Marjory Neilson Newbold'

Newbold, Thomas John (1807–1850), army officer in the East India Company and oriental scholar, son of Francis Newbold, surgeon, of Macclesfield, Cheshire, was born in Macclesfield on 8 February 1807. He was commissioned ensign in the 23rd regiment Madras light infantry in 1828, and arrived in India in the same year. He passed very creditably examinations in Hindustani (1830) and Persian (1831), and from 1830 to 1835 was quartermaster and interpreter to his regiment. He went to Malacca in 1832, and became lieutenant in 1834. While in command of the port at Lingy, he detained a boat which had carried supplies to one of the indigenous belligerents between whom the government of Malacca wanted to maintain neutrality. When he was prosecuted by the owner the legality of the seizure could not be maintained, but Newbold's conduct was approved by the court, and he was reimbursed his expenses. He arrived at the Madras presidency with a detachment of his regiment in August 1835, and was approved aide-de-camp to Brigadier-General E. W. Wilson, commanding the Ceded Districts, an appointment which he held until 1840. He was made deputy assistant quartermaster-general for the division in 1838, and deputy assistant adjutant-general and postmaster to the field force in the Ceded Districts in 1839.

During his three years' residence in the Strait of Malacca, where he had constant contact with the chiefs on the Malayan peninsula, Newbold had accumulated materials for several papers contributed to the journals of the Asiatic societies of Bengal and Madras. These papers formed the basis of his *Political and statistical account of the British settlements in the Straits of Malacca … with a history of the Malayan states on the peninsula of Malacca* (2 vols., 1839), forty copies of which were taken for the court of directors of the East India Company. Newbold also devoted much time to the investigation of the mineral resources of India. He visited the Kupput Gode range of hills in the southern Maratha country, where he obtained specimens

of gold-dust, the iron mines of the Salem district, the lead mines of the Eastern Ghats, the diamond tracts, and many other localities. He was one of the leading authorities on the geology of southern India, which he investigated with great thoroughness. The results of his observations were published from time to time in the *Journal of the Asiatic Society* and other scientific periodicals.

Newbold left India on leave early in 1840, and visited Jebel Nakas in the Sinai peninsula in June that year. He was elected a member of the Asiatic Society on 5 June 1841, and during a residence of some months in England read several papers before the society. He also persuaded it to address a letter to the pasha of Egypt, protesting against the demolition of the ancient remains by his officers. Newbold was an accomplished oriental scholar. As early as 1831 he formed the project of compiling an account of some Persian, Hindustani, Arabic, Turkish, and Malayan poets, with extracts from their compositions; and he published a notice of some Persian poets in the Madras *Journal of Literature and Science*. He presented to the Asiatic Society manuscripts, artefacts, and geological specimens. Among the manuscripts was Shah Muhammad Kamal's *Majma ulintikhab*, which formed the subject of a correspondence between Newbold and Garcin de Tassy, upon the latter's publication in the *Journal Asiatique* of his 'Sâadi, auteur des premières poésies hindoustanies'.

Newbold was promoted captain on 12 April 1842, and was recalled to India in the following May. Arriving at Madras, he was appointed assistant to the commission at Kurnool, at a salary of 200 rupees, in addition to his military allowances, and also to command the horse. He was assistant to the agent to the governor of Fort St George at Kurnool and Bunganahilly from 1843 to 1848, when he was appointed assistant to the resident at Hyderabad. He was permitted to go to Egypt for two years in June 1845.

Among other subjects of Newbold's investigations were the geology of Egypt, the Chenchwars, a wild people inhabiting the Eastern Ghats, the Gypsies of Egypt, Syria, and Persia, the ancient sepulchres of Panduvaram, North Arcot, the sites of Ashteroth, of Hai or Ai, the royal city of the Canaanites, and of the 'seven churches of Asia'. Forty-six scientific papers by Newbold were listed in the Royal Society's catalogue. He died at Mahabaleshwar, India, 'too early for his fame' (Burton), on 29 May 1850.

W. A. S. HEWINS, *rev.* ROGER T. STEARN

Sources *Annual Register* (1850) • *GM*, 2nd ser., 35 (1851) • W. F. B. Laurie, *Some distinguished Anglo-Indians* (1875) • T. A. Heathcote, *The military in British India: the development of British land forces in south Asia, 1600–1947* (1995) • A. Harfield, *British and Indian armies in the East Indies, 1685–1935* (1984) • private information (1894) [India Office] • I. Burton, *The life of Captain Sir Richard F. Burton*, 2 (1893)
Likenesses lithograph, BM

Newbold, (John Turner) Walton (1888–1943), journalist and politician, was born on 8 May 1888 at Culcheth, Leigh, Lancashire, the only child of Thomas Robinson Newbold (c.1846–1926), corn merchant, and his wife, Elizabeth Turner. His Irish Quaker and Liberal father was the principal formative influence, and the socially conscious boy developed a passion for history and radical politics. He was educated at Barrow in Furness grammar school (1900–02) and Buxton College, Derbyshire, before, a gangly six-footer with a chronic nasal catarrh condition, he entered Manchester University in 1905. He gained an ordinary BA in 1910 and an MA in history in 1912, before beginning historical research into early mercantile capitalism in England.

At university Walton, as he was known, became politically active, joining the Fabian Society in 1908 and the Independent Labour Party (ILP) in 1910, and in 1912 he was a leading figure in the University Socialist Federation. From 1912 he campaigned against militarism, briefing the Labour and ILP leaders. During 1913–14, as an investigative journalist with the ILP weekly *Labour Leader*, he produced articles and big-selling pamphlets exposing interests behind the defence industries. As platform speaker he warned of the danger of impending war and argued for conversion of arms expenditure into social reconstruction. *How Europe Prepared for War, 1871–1914* (1916) was his first substantial publication on the international arms race.

On 16 June 1915 Newbold married Marjory Neilson (1883–1926) [*see* Newbold, Marjory], schoolteacher, peace activist, and socialist. Radicalized by the First World War, he abandoned individual pacifism, campaigning for the No Conscription Fellowship and collective war resistance. In 1916 he contested military service, to be rejected on health grounds.

By early 1917 Newbold became a Marxist, joined the left wing of the British Socialist Party, and contributed extensively to the left-wing press. From October 1917 he championed the Bolshevik Revolution, although even in his brief communist phase (1921–4) he never advocated the primacy of the single vanguard revolutionary party, preferring to work with a range of socialist groups for the defeat of capitalism and imperialism. For Newbold, building socialist cadres and promoting Marxist worker education were vital concerns. To this end, he was a driving force in the Plebs League and Labour College movement. Action research for the trade union and labour movement was also a major commitment through high-level participation in the Labour Research Department until 1926.

At the general election of 1918 Newbold contested Motherwell and Wishaw as ILP and Bolshevik candidate. Between 1918 and 1921 he was a leading activist in the Hands Off Russia and Hands Off Ireland campaigns and in the left-wing movement within the ILP to win affiliation to the Communist International. Failure to achieve this objective led, reluctantly, to membership of the new Communist Party of Great Britain in April 1921.

Newbold was a high-profile activist in the Communist Party. During 1921–3 he was arguably the most prolific journalist in the party press. At the general election of November 1922 he won Motherwell constituency as a Communist and Labour candidate, making history as the first avowed elected Communist MP.

In a short, hectic career as MP Newbold proved an effective revolutionary tribune. In parliament he consistently pursued the united front policy of the Communist Party;

upheld principled, vigorous stands on Ireland, defence and international issues; and promoted alternative socialist strategies. While defending the Soviet Union, he was suspended from the House of Commons briefly in May 1923. During 1923 he was often abroad on Communist International concerns, in Germany during the Ruhr crisis, and on four occasions attended conferences in Moscow and Leningrad.

However, Newbold's disagreement with the ultra-leftism of the Communist International, his defeat in the general election of 1923, together with physical exhaustion and political burn-out led to disillusionment with revolutionary politics and his eventual resignation from the Communist Party in August 1924. Renewing allegiance to Labour and the ILP, he resumed lecturing for the Plebs League and research work, preparing *The Railways, 1825–1925* (1925); a study of the steel industry (1925); and, for the Miners' federation, supporting evidence to the Samuel commission.

Newbold's wife and father both died in 1926. Now financially independent, he travelled widely in North America and Europe during the late 1920s. As unofficial envoy for MacDonald, Snowden, and Thomas, he interviewed and lobbied leading politicians and businessmen and researched new developments in the world of capital. He also visited Germany several times to spy on industrial and chemical plant and report on potential for rearmament.

In January 1928 Newbold joined the Social Democratic Federation (by then a reformist rump affiliated to the Labour Party), whose policies were close to his revised views on defence of an island, socialist Britain; between 1929 and 1931 he edited the *Social Democrat*. Appointed by Snowden, he also served on the Macmillan committee on finance and industry, where he adopted a maverick stance opposing proposals to bail out ailing capitalists. In the 1931 crisis he supported the National Government and finally abandoned socialist commitments. Thereafter, he made no impact on the political scene. *Democracy, Debts and Disarmament* (1933), his largest and last book, was an idiosyncratic review of the rise and fall of finance capital. In 1935 he gave evidence to the royal commission on the private manufacture of and trading in arms, urging the location of defence industries in depressed areas.

In his final years Newbold became increasingly eccentric, and his politics are difficult to unravel. In failing health, he contracted tuberculosis by 1937. In 1936 he joined the Catholic church, not as a communicant but ostensibly to study Catholic statecraft. He lived in Éire from 1937 to 1941 and continued to write press articles on strategic issues. He moved to Glasgow in 1941 and died of tuberculosis in Ruchill Hospital on 20 February 1943. He was buried in Eastwood cemetery. ROBERT DUNCAN

Sources R. Duncan, 'Newbold, John Turner Walton', *DLB*, vol. 10 · JRL, Newbold MSS · R. Duncan, 'The papers of John Turner Walton Newbold, 1888–1943: an introductory guide', *Bulletin of the John Rylands University Library*, 76 (1994), 195–203 · R. Duncan, 'Motherwell for Moscow: Walton Newbold, revolutionary politics and the labour movement in a Lanarkshire constituency, 1918–22', *Scottish*

Labour History Journal, 28 (1993) • K. Morgan and R. Duncan, 'Loitering on the party line: the unpublished memoirs of J. T. Walton Newbold', *Labour History Review*, 60/1 (1995) • *WWBMP*, vol. 3 • J. Klugmann, *History of the communist party of Great Britain*, 1 (1968) • S. Macintyre, *A proletarian science* (1980) • *Forward* (1915) • *Motherwell Times* (1918) • *Labour Leader* (1915–16) • *Workers Weekly* (1922–4) • b. cert. • d. cert.
Archives JRL, corresp. and papers | Glos. RO, letters to Morgan Philips Price • People's History Museum, Manchester, Communist Party of Great Britain archive • U. Oxf., Ruskin College, letters to James Middleton and Lucy Middleton
Likenesses photograph, 1922, repro. in Klugmann, *History*, 168–9 • photograph, 1923

Newbolt, Sir Henry John (1862–1938), poet and writer, was born at St Mary's vicarage, Bilston, Staffordshire, on 6 June 1862, the elder son and eldest of the three children of Henry Francis Newbolt (1823/4–1866), vicar of St Mary's Church, Bilston, and his second wife, Emily (*d.* 1921), second daughter of George Bradnock Stubbs, of Walsall and Blymhill, Staffordshire. Newbolt was educated at Clifton College and in 1881 was awarded a scholarship at Corpus Christi College, Oxford, where he took a first in classical moderations (1882) and a second in *literae humaniores* (1885). In 1887 he was called to the bar by Lincoln's Inn, London. He practised law for twelve years, contributing largely to the *Law Digest*; but during this time he was steadily tending towards literature. On 15 August 1889 Newbolt married Margaret Edina (*b.* 1867/8), fourth daughter of the Revd William Arthur Duckworth of Orchardleigh, Frome, Somerset (an estate which later formed the scene of Newbolt's romance *The Old Country*, 1906). Both courtship and marriage were unconventional, as Margaret originally refused him on the basis of her close relationship with her cousin Ella Coltman; her consent was obtained only by Newbolt's assurances that Ella would not be deserted. Ella became in effect a third member of the household, and about two years after the wedding Newbolt and she became lovers, with Margaret aware of the arrangement, and Ella moving into the house. 'Neither woman appeared jealous of the other, perhaps because their lover was careful to divide his favours equally' (Chitty, 91), to the extent of keeping a careful 'account sheet' (ibid.) of the number of nights in a month that he slept with each. Newbolt and Margaret had two children: Celia (*b.* 1890), and Francis (*b.* 1893). The details of this unconventional domestic life seem at variance with Newbolt's standard reputation as a latter-day Victorian, and suggest that he was a more complex figure than is usually supposed.

Newbolt's first book, *Taken from the Enemy*, appeared in 1892 and was followed by *Mordred*, a tragedy in blank verse, published in 1895; in the following year Andrew Lang printed six of Newbolt's poems in *Longman's Magazine*, and 'Drake's Drum', immediately famous, appeared in the *St James's Gazette*. Newbolt himself relates how after reading this poem his friend Robert Bridges declared, 'It isn't given to a man to write anything better than that'. It was included in *Admirals All* (1897), four editions of which raced into circulation within a fortnight. Many books followed from 1898 to 1932, various in theme, but consistent in the fastidious care expended on their making. Newbolt

Sir Henry John Newbolt (1862–1938), by Meredith Frampton, 1931

also edited the *Monthly Review* during its brief lifetime (1900–04).

During the First World War Newbolt served at the Admiralty and the Foreign Office, and was finally controller of wireless and cables. In 1923 he undertook the completion in two volumes (4 and 5) of the official *History of the Great War: Naval Operations*, the first three volumes of which had been written by Sir J. S. Corbett. He was conscientious in honorary service: he served on many commissions and committees, and on bodies such as the Royal Literary Fund and the Royal Society of Literature. He was a trustee of the National Portrait Gallery from 1928 to 1937. In 1915 he was knighted and appointed CH in 1922. He received honorary degrees from the universities of Bristol, Glasgow, St Andrews, Sheffield, Toronto, Oxford, and Cambridge, and in 1920 he was elected an honorary fellow of his college.

Newbolt's name will always be associated with the Edwardian heyday of empire. His poetry is now little read, although it still figures in anthologies, and the late twentieth century saw something of a revival of critical interest in his work, with a selected edition (1981), a critical study (1994), and a biography (1997). Poems like 'Drake's Drum' and 'Vitaï lampada' (with its famous refrain of 'Play up, play up, and play the game') have always remained popular. These stirring expressions of a certain sort of Englishness remain in the national memory, alongside similar things by Kipling and Elgar. Many of Newbolt's best-known poems, like 'Clifton Chapel', are rooted in the ethos of the public school, though his later verse is less robust and can even be dreamy. The poets who influenced him most were Shelley, Keats, D. G. Rossetti, and William Morris. Modern poetry, even after the war, for him meant the Georgians.

Newbolt lived and worked in a literary world that naturally overlapped with the world of public affairs. He divided his time between his Wiltshire country house and his London base at the Athenaeum, devoting as much energy to public duties as to writing. He was known as a patriot but he was not a jingoist. In one poem he praises the *Dictionary of National Biography* as a record of Englishmen who 'keep the Nelson touch' but in a letter of 1916 he complains that the word *patriot* 'ought to be forbidden'. He came to regard his call to 'play the game' as a 'Frankenstein's Monster that I created'. W. B. Yeats told him in April 1902 that his patriotism was of the finer sort 'that lays burdens upon a man, & not the patriotism that takes burdens off' (*Collected Letters*, 63). His chairing of the government committee which produced the Newbolt report (1921) on the teaching of English in England was innovative at the time and remains a landmark in discussions of the question.

Walter de la Mare recalled of Newbolt:

> His faith in Christianity and the influence of tradition, social, historical, and literary, was paramount in his mind and work. He was haunted too by the seductive problem of time, not that of the clock but of the self within, and by a 'sense of the past' allied to the idea of the supreme consciousness, contained in a poem included in *A Perpetual Memory* (a collection of his later poems published posthumously in 1939). 'Pre-incarnation', so to speak, is indeed the theme of his *Aladore* (1914)—love-allegory, fantasy, reverie, fairy-tale; so simple and limpid in its imposed archaic style that it may conceal its depth and its full meaning. In part for this reason it was his Benjamin among his own books.

Newbolt was a lucid speaker and a lively conversationalist. He was not a born story-teller, but his romances have a grace of their own. In his criticism he held true to tradition, but was too urbane to be dogmatic. He was a zealous admirer of Thomas Hardy, though being himself an enthusiast by nature, who could hardly avoid a tendency to optimism. Spare in figure, aquiline in face, with a finely moulded head and a dominant nose, alert in speech and laughter, he surveyed the world from grey-blue eyes at once intent and contemplative. In spite of so many pursuits that called him away from it, poetry was his inmost and lifelong devotion. Henry Newbolt died at his London home, 29 Campden Hill Road, Kensington, on 19 April 1938.   DAVID GERVAIS

Sources *DNB* · H. Newbolt, *My world as in my time* (1932) · M. Newbolt, ed., *The later life and letters of Sir Henry Newbolt* (1942) · S. Chitty, *Playing the game: a biography of Sir Henry Newbolt* (1997) · D. Winterbottom, *Henry Newbolt and the spirit of Clifton* (1986) · V. F. Jackson, *The poetry of Henry Newbolt: patriotism is not enough* (1994) · *Selected poems of Henry Newbolt*, ed. P. Dickinson (1981) · *The collected letters of W. B. Yeats*, 3, ed. J. Kelly and R. Schuchard (1994) · m. cert. · d. cert.

Archives BL, letters to William Archer, Add. MS 45293 · BL OIOC, corresp. with E. F. Younghusband, MS Eur. F 197 · Bodl. Oxf., corresp. with Robert Bridges · CAC Cam., letters to Sir F. C. D. Sturdee and related papers · CUL, corresp. with the marquess of Crewe · NA Scot., corresp. with A. J. Balfour · NL Scot., corresp. with Blackwoods · NMM, corresp. with Sir Julian Corbett · U. Leeds, Brotherton L., letters to Sir Edmund Gosse

Likenesses W. Strang, pencil drawing, 1897, Tate collection · W. Strang, etching, *c.*1898, NPG · W. Stoneman, photograph, 1917, NPG · T. Spicer-Simson, plasticine medallion, *c.*1922, NPG · M. Frampton, oils, 1931, NPG [*see illus.*] · E. Kapp, drawing, Barber Institute of Fine Arts, Birmingham · photograph, NPG

Wealth at death £7190 15*s.* 4*d.*: probate, 24 June 1938, *CGPLA Eng. & Wales*

Newbolt, William Charles Edmund (1844–1930), Church of England clergyman and theologian, was born on 14 August 1844 at Somerton, Somerset, the fourth and youngest son of the Revd William Robert Newbolt (1801/2–1857), rector of Somerton, and his wife, Ann Frances Dorrien, daughter of Magens Dorrien Magens, of Hammerwood, East Grinstead. As a small boy Newbolt enjoyed 'playing at church' (Newbolt, 14) in the nursery. He attended Somerton grammar school, then a small preparatory school at Weston-super-Mare. In 1857 he went to Uppingham School, Rutland, where the headmaster, Edward Thring (1821–1887), exerted the first significant spiritual influence on his life. In 1863 he went to Pembroke College, Oxford. There he came under the influence of Edward Pusey, Henry Liddon, and Edward King of Cuddesdon, and adopted their Tractarian principles. Never a distinguished scholar, he graduated with a second class in classical moderations (1865) and a third in *literae humaniores* (1867): BA (1867), MA (1869). He had a further year reading at Oxford but no professional clergy training.

In 1868 Newbolt was ordained deacon and in 1869 priest and for two years (1868–70) worked as a curate in one of the then foremost Tractarian parishes at Wantage, Berkshire, under its vicar, William John Butler (1818–1894). In 1870 he married Fanny Charlotte (d. 1923), fourth daughter of William Weld Wren of 27 Gower Street, London; they had one son and two daughters. On his marriage he was nominated as vicar of Dymock, Gloucestershire, by Frederick Lygon, sixth Earl Beauchamp (1830–1891), high-church layman and Conservative politician, and in 1877 Beauchamp nominated him for the parish of Malvern Link, Worcestershire. In both parishes he applied the principles of parochial management he had learned at Wantage.

At Malvern Link Newbolt was in close touch with Worcester. In 1886 the dean of Worcester, Lord Alwyne Compton (1825–1906), became bishop of Ely, and in 1887 invited Newbolt to succeed Dr Herbert Mortimer Luckock (1833–1909) as principal of Ely Theological College. This was for Newbolt the beginning of the most important work of his life. The theological college had been founded in 1876 by Bishop James Russell Woodford (1820–1885) on the pattern of Samuel Wilberforce's college at Cuddesdon, Oxfordshire, and opened in 1881 with the aim of providing for ordinands a spiritual and professional training in accordance with Tractarian ideals of the priestly life. In 1856 and 1857 Dr Henry Parry Liddon (1829–1890) had published in the periodical *Ecclesiastic and Theologian* an essay, 'The priest in his inner life', which suggested the lines along which the devotional life of the clergy should be developed, and it was on these lines that Newbolt worked at Ely. He brought to his task the knowledge of and sympathy with human nature gained by his pastoral work, besides the example of his own strong and disciplined character.

On the death in 1890 of Liddon, Lord Salisbury asked Liddon's brother whom he thought Liddon would have wished to succeed him as canon of St Paul's. The answer was 'the Principal of Ely'. In that year Newbolt was installed canon of St Paul's, and he held the canonry until his death. St Paul's then held a great place in the religious life of London and England generally—Newbolt wrote, 'there was a glamour about St Paul's at this time' (Newbolt, p. 171)—with Richard William Church (1815–1890), Henry Scott Holland (1847–1918), and Robert Gregory (1819–1911) notable among the clergy, and Sir John Stainer (1840–1901) the organist. Newbolt entered enthusiastically into the spirit and plans of the chapter; he wished to make the cathedral the central church of London, the spiritual home of the metropolis and the empire, where the Anglican liturgy was perfectly rendered throughout the year.

Newbolt was a fluent and facile, but painstaking, preacher. His sermons were carefully prepared; excellently phrased, and delivered with ease and grace; interesting and fresh, and showed wide reading and generous culture. For many years they reached a wide public through the *Church Times*. He made no attempt to grapple with the intellectual and social problems of the time; he was content to commend goodness and faithfulness and the Tractarian piety which he had known all his life. He was an unswerving champion of Tractarian orthodoxy, and of views about the inspiration of the Bible and Sunday observance which were considered obsolete.

In 1893 Newbolt founded the St Paul's Lecture Society to provide lectures and retreats for the young men employed and living in the surrounding businesses. Later he also founded the Amen Court Guild which had about 400 members and associates: sixty of its members were killed in the First World War, and are commemorated in the crypt of St Paul's.

Arguably Newbolt's greatest achievement was his work for the spiritual life of the clergy. At St Paul's he continued and developed the ministry he had begun at Ely. Every year he conducted retreats for priests and heard their confessions; he published many books of counsel and admonition containing the meditations which he had given in retreat. *Speculum sacerdotum* (1893) was the most characteristic and successful of these. He also edited, with Dr Darwell Stone, the *Oxford Library of Practical Theology*. Newbolt's theological standpoint changed very little during his long life, remaining true to the ideals of Butler and Liddon. He was so convinced of the excellence of the religious life implied in the prayer book of 1662 that he felt some hesitation in following recent developments which went beyond what the prayer book enjoined. In his prime he was a leading speaker in convocation, and for some years he was returned at the head of the poll as representative of the London diocese clergy in convocation and the church assembly. In 1921 he published his memoirs, *Years that are Past*.

His final years were overshadowed by his wife's mental illness during her last thirty years. He died on 12 September 1930 in London.

J. F. BRISCOE, rev. GEORGE HERRING

Sources W. C. E. Newbolt, *Years that are past: being some recollections of a long life* (1921) · DNB · Foster, *Alum. Oxon.* · WWW, 1929–40 · Crockford (1902) · *CGPLA Eng. & Wales* (1930)
Likenesses photograph, repro. in Newbolt, *Years that are past*, frontispiece
Wealth at death £8238 11s. 8d.: probate, 17 Oct 1930, *CGPLA Eng. & Wales*

Newbould, William Williamson (1819–1886), botanist, born at Sheffield on 20 January 1819, was the son of Henry Newbould, a merchant trading with Russia, and Mary, daughter of William Williamson of Buntingford, Hertfordshire. An interest in botany dating from his time at a preparatory school near Doncaster deepened when he went up to Trinity College, Cambridge, in 1838. There he attended the lectures of Professor J. S. Henslow, and became friendly with C. C. Babington and Frederick Townsend, who were to be among the leading field botanists of his generation. After graduating in 1842 he embarked on a series of plant-hunting trips to various parts of the British Isles, five of them with Babington. During these he consolidated his expertise as a taxonomist.

Meanwhile, Newbould had also taken holy orders. Ordained deacon in 1844 and priest in 1845 (the year in which he also graduated MA), he held curacies first at Bluntisham, Huntingdonshire, and then, in 1848, at Comberton, Cambridgeshire. On 18 October 1855 he married Mary Louisa Kendall, daughter of William Kendall, an officer in the 4th dragoons. Despite a growing family (eventually five sons and a daughter), he nevertheless refused at least one living on conscientious grounds and about 1860 resolved to take advantage of his private means to leave the service of the church (except for a later spell of temporary duty at Honington, Warwickshire) and devote his days to his scholarly interests. He moved to London and thereafter spent almost all of each winter in the botanical department or reading room of the British Museum—his lithe, spare figure was long a familiar sight in the latter. In 1863 he was elected a fellow of the Linnean Society.

Marrying his wide knowledge of British botany to antiquarian leanings, Newbould now made a unique role for himself as a disseminator of early plant records to the increasingly numerous botanists who were compiling local or county floras. Every one of those issued in the years 1860–91 owed far more to his editorial and scholarly assistance than he allowed their authors to acknowledge; in the words of one of his obituarists, he was 'the very incarnation of self-abnegation ... nothing was to him a source of greater happiness than to place his time, his brains, his critical experience freely at the disposal of some younger man who seemed in need of them' (Hillhouse). Deeply averse to having anything published in his name, he insisted on disclaiming all responsibility for the fifth volume of the *Supplement to English Botany* (1863), which was credited to him on the title-page. That he was persuaded in his last years to allow his name to appear as co-signatory to the introduction to the second edition (1883) of H. C. Watson's great compendium, *Topographical Botany*—on which he had indeed bestowed much labour—must be accounted a triumph. The silent presence of a kind of all-pervading ghost was always more to his taste. Eighteen volumes of manuscript lists in the botany library of the Natural History Museum testify to his unwearying diligence, as did his herbarium, later incorporated in that museum's general collection. As further memorials, his name is borne by two species of blackberry and by a beautiful genus of Bignoniaceae, *Newbouldia*.

In addition to botany, Newbould was also interested in phrenology (as a child he had been nursed on the knee of the great phrenologist Spurzheim). A total abstainer and almost a vegetarian, he exhibited practical sympathy with others, especially the poor. After he moved to London he lived first in Turnham Green and later for a period more centrally in Regent's Park, and eventually moved to Kew Green in 1879. At one time he had contemplated taking up residence at Oxford, but was deterred by the inaccessibility of that university's early herbaria, which were then housed in a loft reached only by a shaky ladder. After he was knocked down by a cab he suffered a bout of pneumonia followed by heart failure, and died at Kew on 16 April 1886; he was buried in Fulham cemetery on 20 April. The number of obituaries that appeared, several of them of exceptional length, reflected a general wish that the scale of his anonymous services should at last be publicly acknowledged, and how widely he had been revered for his unfailing helpfulness. D. E. ALLEN

Sources [G. S. Boulger], *Journal of Botany, British and Foreign*, 24 (1886), 159–60 · W. Hillhouse, 'The late Rev. W. W. Newbould … a few personal reminiscences', *Midland Naturalist*, 9 (1886), 160–63 · *Proceedings of the Linnean Society of London* (1883–6), 145–6 · *Gardeners' Chronicle*, new ser., 25 (1886), 569 · *Transactions of the Botanical Society* [Edinburgh], 17 (1887–91), 15–17 · J. Ardagh, 'W. W. Newbould and his manuscripts', *North Western Naturalist*, 22 (1947), 223–5 · m. cert.

Archives Hitchin Museum and Art Gallery, notes · NHM, notebooks · RBG Kew, botanical catalogue and papers · U. Cam., department of plant sciences, notes on Babington's *Manual of botany* and transcription of Pulteney's *Catalogue of English plants* · U. Oxf., department of plant sciences, notes

Likenesses photograph, NHM, department of botany

Wealth at death £14,804 10s. 1d.: probate, 7 Aug 1886, *CGPLA Eng. & Wales*

Newburgh. For this title name *see* Stuart, Katherine [Katherine Livingston, Viscountess Newburgh] (d. 1650); Livingston, James, of Kinnaird, first earl of Newburgh (1621/2–1670); Radcliffe, Charlotte Maria, *suo jure* countess of Newburgh (1694–1755) [*see under* Radcliffe, James, styled third earl of Derwentwater (1689–1716)]; Eyre, Margaret Radclyffe-Livingstone-, styled countess of Newburgh (1800–1889).

Newburgh, Henry de. See Beaumont, Henry de, first earl of Warwick (d. 1119).

Newburgh, William of (b. 1135/6, d. in or after 1198), Augustinian canon and historian, belonged to a family that may have originated in Bridlington or an area nearby, according to statements in his *Historia rerum Anglicarum*. He was educated from boyhood in the Augustinian priory of Newburgh, and spent most if not all of his life as a member of that community. The evidence of his chronicle suggests that he died in or soon after 1198. Apart from the *Historia rerum Anglicarum*, which was his major work, William wrote a number of sermons which are found together with his history, and a commentary on the Song of Songs begun before 1196, which he interpreted as a hymn in praise of the Virgin Mary. An attempt has been made to identify him with a certain William, canon of Newburgh, whose name appears in a charter of the period. Between 1160 and 1165 this William married Emma de Peri, an heiress of considerable lands, and subsequently retired to Newburgh as a canon between 1182 and 1183. The identification seems unlikely, for there is nothing in the *Historia rerum Anglicarum* to suggest experience of the world outside the cloister. Despite his own accomplishments William came from a house with no tradition of historical writing. He was encouraged in his historical work by Ernald, abbot of Rievaulx (d. 1199), while his commentary on the Song of Songs was written at the request of another Cistercian, Roger, abbot of Byland (d. c.1199). William's Cistercian contacts were important and were to prove a significant influence upon his writing.

The *Historia rerum Anglicarum* itself seems to have been composed in a comparatively short period between 1196 and 1198. The work has the appearance of being an early draft which was never revised. The history is divided into five books, and each book into a number of chapters, an indication of William's attempt to structure his narrative, and give it some kind of literary form. After a brief prologue in which he looks back with approval to the work of Gildas and Bede, his first book covers the period from 1066 to 1154. The second book deals with the reign of Henry II from Henry's accession in 1154 to 1174. The third book takes the history from 1175 to Henry's death in 1189, while the final two books cover more limited periods, concluding in 1194 and 1198 respectively. The history is of particular value for its account of the reign of Henry II, and especially for the early years of that reign, which are not well covered by other sources. As the narrative breaks off suddenly in May 1198, it seems likely that William died while still working on this section of his history.

William of Newburgh is a writer whose reputation has remained consistently high among modern readers. Like Ailred (d. 1167), with whose writings he was almost certainly acquainted, William wrote in a good, clear Latin style. He knew something of Latin literature, quoting from Virgil and Horace, and was acquainted with the work of the early church fathers such as Augustine and Gregory. It is, however, the broad range of his narrative, and the critical qualities that he exhibits, that distinguish his work. Although William appears to have spent the whole of his life at Newburgh, he put together a narrative which extended over much of Christendom, and which, as regards England, included an account of the major political events of the century in which he lived. William's interest in northern events is also evident. His chronicle is an important source of information on the Cistercian settlement in the north, the northern archbishops, and the attack on the Jews in York in 1190. In writing his history William used only a few identifiable sources. Among those accounts that can be identified are the chronicles of Symeon of Durham and Henry of Huntingdon (or perhaps their likely source, the Durham compilation known as the *Historia Anglorum post obitum Bedae*), which he used for the opening part of his work, the Anglo-Norman poem of Jordan Fantosme, which was used for the events of the 1170s, and the *Itinerarium regis Ricardi* of Richard of Devizes, which was a source for the third crusade. A lost biography of Richard I, by the king's chaplain, Anselm, may have been a source for William's account of the king's captivity. Apart from these writings much of his information came from contemporaries. Although he rarely names them, he is careful to indicate whether or not his informants were eyewitnesses of a particular event. Thus he says that his account of the Council of Rheims in 1148, and of Raymond of Antioch on the second crusade, came from people who were there. An eyewitness provided him with information on events in London in 1196. Elsewhere he says that an abbot, an archdeacon, or a monk, related some particular piece of information to him. It seems likely that several of these informants came from William's contacts within the Augustinian order, as well as from neighbouring Cistercian houses which through their founders had close links with the Anglo-Norman aristocracy.

As his work indicates, William possessed historical ability of a high order. Apart from the range of his narrative, and the care with which he indicated his sources, the quality of his writing is also evident in his treatment of some of the major controversies of the twelfth century. His independence of judgement is clearly seen in his account of the quarrel between Henry II and Thomas Becket, in which he considered neither party to be free from blame, criticizing Henry for the manner in which he dealt with the matter of criminous clerks, and Becket for his obstinacy in resisting the king's decree. He wrote from a similar viewpoint when describing the 'pointless conflict' (William of Newburgh, *Historia rerum Anglicarum*, ed. R. Howlett, Rolls Series, 1884, *Historia*, 444) between Canterbury and York. His well-informed, well-balanced, and realistic account of the massacre of the Jews at York in 1190 made no attempt to conceal the atrocities that were committed nor his own condemnation of these acts. Nowhere is William's critical judgement seen to better advantage than in his treatment of Geoffrey of Monmouth's history. William was not misled by Geoffrey's story. In the opening to his work he denounced what he termed its 'impudent fabrications' (*impudentia mentitur*; Newburgh, *Historia*, 18), and argued that Bede would have mentioned Arthur if that ruler had existed. He pointed out errors in Geoffrey's account, including the presence of kingdoms and archbishops unknown to history. If William displayed a certain partiality in denouncing Geoffrey's work while accepting other fictions, he revealed, at least with regard to Geoffrey's history, a soundness of judgement that was

not always found among his successors in the field of historical writing. None the less, despite William's criticism, Geoffrey's history 'swept away opposition with the ruthless force of a great epic' (Kendrick, 7). As William himself divined, the appeal of Geoffrey's history lay not in its truth, but in the fact that it provided the British with a noble and romantic past.

Remarkable as the *Historia rerum Anglicarum* was as a piece of historical writing, William's work inevitably reflected the intellectual milieu in which it was written. Twelfth-century chroniclers lacked the techniques available to a modern historian: William made some errors of fact, and his chronology was not always accurate. Thus he was six years in arrears in his date for the Council of Oxford of 1166, on which he provides the fullest surviving account. He did, however, attempt to construct as reliable a narrative as possible, and his use of documents, including the texts of papal letters, illustrates his appreciation of the value of such sources. Like Bede he had an interest in the miraculous. In particular he wrote at length about the miracles and marvels that he claimed had been seen in twelfth-century England. Some of his best stories concern the raising of the dead, and have their parallels in Icelandic literature. Among such ghost stories was one given on the authority of Stephen, archdeacon of Buckingham, concerning a dead man who forced his unwelcome attentions upon the living until finally a letter from the saintly Bishop Hugh of Lincoln (*d.* 1200), placed upon the dead man's body, ensured a satisfactory end to these activities.

As his association with Abbot Ernald indicates, William's history was from the start intended for an audience wider than that of his own community. The *Historia rerum Anglicarum* survives in nine copies. One copy (BL, Stowe MS 62) belonged to Newburgh Priory, and may have been written in William's own's lifetime. Not surprisingly his work was especially popular among the Cistercians. Although no surviving manuscript can be assigned to Rievaulx, it is certain that a copy of his work would have been found there, and also at Byland. Copies of his history were in the possession of the Cistercian houses of Rufford and Buildwas, while the Cistercian annals of Stanley in Wiltshire follow an incomplete text of William's work. The *Historia rerum Anglicarum* was also known within the Augustinian order. The Augustinian abbey of Osney in Oxfordshire owned a thirteenth-century copy, and at the end of that century Walter of Guisborough, an Augustinian canon, used William's account as a main source for his own chronicle. Members of other orders were familiar with the work. In the fourteenth century both the Anonimalle chronicle in its opening section, and Nicholas Trevet in his annals utilized William's account. Judged by the standards of its day the *Historia rerum Anglicarum* was a remarkable achievement and the forerunner of what was to become an important tradition of chronicle writing by Augustinian canons in the north of England.

JOHN TAYLOR

Sources R. Howlett, ed., *Chronicles of the reigns of Stephen, Henry II, and Richard I*, 4 vols., Rolls Series, 82 (1884–9), 1.11–408; 2.415–500 · *William of Newburgh's 'Explanatio sacri Epithalamii in matrem sponsi'*, ed. J. C. Gorman, *Spicilegium Friburgense*, 6 (1960) • R. Jahncke, *Guilelmus Neubrigensis: ein pragmatischer Geschichtsschreiber des zwölften Jahrhunderts* (1912) • A. Gransden, *Historical writing in England*, 1 (1974), 263–8 • N. F. Partner, *Serious entertainments, the writing of history in twelfth century England* (1977), 51–113 • K. Norgate, 'The date of composition of William of Newburgh's *History*', *EngHR*, 19 (1904), 288–97 • H. E. Salter, 'William of Newburgh', *EngHR*, 22 (1907), 510–14 • B. Dickins, 'A Yorkshire chronicler', *Transactions of the Yorkshire Dialect Society*, 5/35 (1934) • T. D. Kendrick, *British antiquity* (1950)

Archives BL, Stowe MS 62 • Bodl. Oxf., MS Rawl. B.192 • LPL, Lambeth MS 73

Newby, (Percy) Howard (1918–1997), writer and broadcasting administrator, was born on 25 June 1918 at a nursing home in Crowborough, Sussex, the son of Percy Newby, a baker, and his wife, Isabel Clutsom Bryant. The family lived at Lime Street, Nether Stowey, Somerset. Newby was educated at Hanley Castle Grammar School, Worcestershire, and, being unable to afford university, St Paul's Teacher Training College, Cheltenham.

After a short period as a schoolteacher Newby was called up into the Royal Army Medical Corps on the outbreak of the Second World War, and served first with the British expeditionary force in France (1939–40) and then in Egypt as a corporal stretcher-bearer with the Eighth Army. In 1942 he was seconded by the army to be a lecturer in English literature at Fuad 1st University (Cairo University), where he remained until 1946. His experiences there provided the inspiration for his first two novels, *Journey to the Interior* (1945) and *Agents and Witnesses* (1947), which quickly established Newby's reputation as a promising new writer. He won an Atlantic award in 1946 and the Somerset Maugham award in 1948.

On 12 July 1945 Newby married Joan (*b.* 1921/2), an agricultural worker, daughter of Henry Charles Thompson, and in 1946 he returned to Britain as a freelance writer. An initial approach to the BBC failed, but on the intervention of Geoffrey Grigson he was invited to broadcast occasional short stories, book reviews, and talks, and he became a fiction reviewer for the BBC house journal *The Listener*. In 1949 he finally joined the BBC as a talks producer. He was originally designated the 'short story expert' on the grounds of his own writing experience, and went on to specialize in literary talks series, including *First Reading* (a 'literary magazine of the air') and *Literary Opinion*, a monthly series of arts talks.

In 1958 Newby became controller of the Third Programme, BBC radio's flagship arts network, at a time when its morale was low and it was reeling from financial cutbacks. Reserved and self-effacing, he was described by Ved Mehta in the *New Yorker* as 'a quiet, unworldly, rather sphinx-like man, whose large head and tightly drawn mouth gave him a cerebral look' (*New Yorker*, 18 May 1963), though the *Manchester Guardian* likened him to the jockey Sir Gordon Richards, 'even down to the bright, darting eyes, the aggressive chin and the head of smartly cropped hair' (*Manchester Guardian*, 4 Nov 1958). The appointment of such an uncompromisingly literary figure was taken as an encouraging sign, as was the collegiate atmosphere that Newby fostered in production meetings. Under his control the Third Programme supported many young writers, including Tom Stoppard, while one of the trainees he recruited was the young Dennis Potter. Newby did not, as many had hoped, defend the Third Programme against the controversial proposals outlined in the document *Broadcasting in the Seventies*. Change was, however, all but inevitable, and in 1969 Newby became the first controller of the Third Programme's replacement, Radio 3.

In 1971 Newby became director of programmes, radio, where he was responsible among other things for consolidating news and current affairs coverage and introducing consumer programmes and phone-ins. Some considered his introverted and consultative style less successful at this level of management, and he was accused of failing to fight his corner. Nevertheless he succeeded Ian Trethowan as managing director of BBC radio (1975–8), where he sought to broaden audience appeal in the face of financial constraints (promoting, for instance, the simultaneous broadcast of music on television and radio), and sparked controversy when he suggested that the BBC might cut back on its orchestras (in particular, the BBC's training orchestra, the Academy of the BBC, which he disbanded). Created a CBE in 1972, Newby left the BBC in 1978 after almost thirty years' service. He served as chairman of the English Stage Company from 1978 to 1984.

While at the BBC Newby continued to publish as a novelist. Writing at evenings and weekends, he maintained a steady output of books, publishing thirteen between 1950 and 1977. Many of these drew on his wartime life in Egypt, most successfully his ninth novel, *The Picnic at Sakkara* (1955). This story of the relationship between an academic and an Egyptian student planning to assassinate him was generally regarded as his best work and was praised for its 'almost Chaplinesque humour' (*Daily Telegraph*, 15 Sept 1997). Witty, atmospheric, and often complex of plot, Newby's fiction received plaudits during his career from, among others, Evelyn Waugh and Graham Greene (who considered him much underrated). In the 1950s the American critic Anthony West described him as 'the only English writer with anything approaching genius to be produced by his generation so far' (*The Times*, 9 Sept 1997). But Newby failed to fulfil his early promise, as the wry detachment of his earlier novels gave way to a laboured Jungian symbolism. In 1969 he won the first Booker prize for his fourteenth novel, *Something to Answer for* (from a shortlist that included Iris Murdoch and Muriel Spark), but it was not considered to be among his best work.

As well as writing twenty novels, Newby published a book of short stories, two short works for children, critical works (including a British Council pamphlet, *The Novel, 1945–50*), and three books on Middle and Near Eastern history. He maintained a rigid separation between his literary and administrative careers, and characteristically vetoed an adaptation of one of his novels while controller of Radio 3. His only novel to draw on his experiences at the BBC was *Feelings have Changed*, published after his retirement in 1981, in which fictionalized versions of Louis MacNeice and Laurence Gilliam appear. His last published novel was *Something about Women* (1995), by which time his fame as a writer had faded.

Newby died from a heart attack at his home Garsington House, Oxford Road, Garsington, Oxfordshire, on 6 September 1997. He was survived by his wife and two daughters. His ashes were interred in the churchyard at St Mary's, Garsington, on 20 October. SIÂN NICHOLAS

Sources A. Thwaite, 'P. H. Newby', *The Independent* (9 Sept 1997) · *Daily Telegraph* (15 Sept 1997) · H. Carpenter, 'Broadcasting House sphinx', *The Guardian* (8 Sept 1997) · *The Times* (9 Sept 1997) · H. Carpenter, *The envy of the world: fifty years of the BBC Third Programme and Radio 3, 1946–1996* (1996) · A. Briggs, *The history of broadcasting in the United Kingdom*, 4 (1979) · private information (2004) [R. Cowles] · b. cert. · m. cert. · d. cert.

Likenesses photograph, repro. in Thwaite, 'P. H. Newby' · photograph, repro. in *Daily Telegraph*

Wealth at death £232,588: probate, 26 Nov 1997, *CGPLA Eng. & Wales*

Newby, Peter (1745–1827), Roman Catholic schoolmaster and author, was born at Horncop Hall, near Kendal in Westmorland, the son of William Newby (1702–1772), a waller and land agent, and his wife, Elizabeth Carter (*c*.1707–1772), of Thistleton, Lancashire. After attending the Catholic preparatory school operated by Dame Alice Harrison at Fernyhalgh, near Preston, Lancashire, Newby was an ecclesiastical student at the English College, Douai, from 1757 to 1764. On returning to England in January 1764, having decided not to proceed to holy orders as his parents had hoped, Newby was rejected by his family and forced to seek his own way in the world.

Two major influences shaped Newby's subsequent career. Employment as a steward on a Guineaman from November 1764 to January 1766 awakened his humanitarianism. On a return voyage from Liverpool to Jamaica via west Africa, where he stayed for five months, Newby witnessed at first hand the horror of the transatlantic slave trade. Next, the inspiring mentorship of the Revd Bartholomew Booth (1732–1785), an enlightened and unorthodox Anglican schoolmaster, completed his education and perfected his teaching skills. As a teacher of French and Latin at Booth's two highly successful private academies, at Woolton Hall near Liverpool (1766–72) and at High Beach near Waltham Abbey in Essex (1772–3), Newby discovered the many advantages of offering an unusually wide curriculum.

In 1773 Newby opened his own academy for boys at Burton in Kendal, Westmorland, even though Catholic schools were still officially proscribed. There his pioneering approach to education attracted significant patronage from the rising Catholic middle class of the north of England. The growth of the academy caused it to move, first in 1775 to Great Eccleston, in the Fylde area of Lancashire, and in 1780 to Gerard Hall, Haighton, near Fernyhalgh, where it remained until 1797.

Though Newby was the first schoolmaster in Lancashire to register his academy officially after the passing of the 1791 Catholic Relief Act, his success was short-lived. The migration of English Catholic schools from continental Europe to England during the French Revolution created new competition, forcing Newby to abandon teaching in

1797. He set up as a printer and bookseller in Preston, specializing in Catholic devotional literature. When this venture failed around 1805, he was once again forced to offer private tuition, but soon fell into the penury which characterized the last twenty years of his life.

Newby's marriage at Childwall, Lancashire, on 15 May 1768 to Elizabeth Gant (*c*.1743–1782) of Prescot, and the couple's happy family life following the birth of their five children between 1769 and 1782, first inspired the schoolmaster to write poetry. Composed between 1771 and 1790, Newby's verse never received wide public acclaim owing to the poet's natural diffidence. His *Six Pastorals* (1773), of which the copy in the Beinecke Library at Yale is the only known surviving example, was published anonymously; and his longest single work, *The Wrongs of Almoona, or, The African's Revenge* (1788), an anti-slavery poem dedicated to William Cowper, appeared under the pseudonym A Friend to All Mankind. Newby's *Poems* (1790), published in two volumes with the support of some 340 subscribers, were written essentially for private purposes, 'to alleviate disappointments, or to encounter domestic misfortunes' (*Poems*, Preface). The combination of their late classicism and limited readership resulted in their being soon forgotten.

Newby's most enduring achievement was in founding the Broughton Catholic Charitable Society, created in 1787 to alleviate distress following a smallpox epidemic in the Fylde. Acting as its secretary for twenty years until 1807, he established an organization which was still carrying out its charitable work at the close of the twentieth century. Taken together, Newby's career exemplifies the vitality of Catholic life in pre-emancipation England. Peter Newby died on 16 December 1827 at his home in Hill Street, Friargate, Preston, and was buried in the cemetery attached to the Catholic churches of St Wilfrid and St Mary, Preston, on 19 December. MAURICE WHITEHEAD

Sources J. Malone, *Peter Newby: friend to all mankind* (1964) · M. Whitehead, *Peter Newby: 18th century Lancashire recusant poet* (1980) · M. Whitehead, *The academies of the Reverend Bartholomew Booth in Georgian England and revolutionary America* (1996) · Gillow, *Lit. biog. hist.* · P. Whittle, *The history of the borough of Preston*, 2 (1837) · Kirk MSS · Oscott College, Birmingham, Collectanea Anglo-Catholica, 3 [fols. 1123–1126] · P. R. Harris, ed., *Douai College documents, 1639–1794*, Catholic RS, 63 (1972)

Likenesses J. Barney, stipple (after portrait by T. Barrow, *c*.1785), NPG; repro. in P. Newby, *Poems* (1790)

Newby, Thomas Cautley (1797/8–1882), publisher and printer, was possibly born in Staffordshire. His parents' names are unknown. Having started in business about 1840, Newby by 1843 had offices in London at 65 Mortimer Street, Cavendish Square, a year later at 72 Mortimer Street, and from 1849 to March 1874 at 30 Welbeck Street, Cavendish Square. About two-thirds of the titles he published were fiction, the rest were non-fiction works such as history, biography, memoirs, travel accounts, translations, and a few works of poetry, drama, and music.

Newby has won literary notoriety as the publisher of first novels by Emily and Anne Brontë (Ellis Bell and Acton Bell), *Wuthering Heights* and *Agnes Grey*, in a single three-volume edition of December 1847. Newby first asked for a deposit of £50 to cover costs of publication, but kept the corrected proofs until the successful appearance of Charlotte Brontë's (Currer Bell's) *Jane Eyre*, published by Smith Elder in October 1847. Newby then printed fewer than the agreed number of Emily's and Anne's novels and left most errors uncorrected. When Anne sent him her second novel, *The Tenant of Wildfell Hall* (1848), Newby offered it to Harper Brothers of New York for publication in America, implying it was by Currer Bell. Charlotte Brontë's biographer Elizabeth Gaskell had to be restrained from exposing Newby as a warning to other writers, initially naming him as one of the 'three people I want to libel'. She referred to him as 'the mean publisher to be gibbetted' (*Letters of Mrs Gaskell*, 418).

In 1847 Newby also published Anthony Trollope's first novel, *The Macdermots of Ballycloran*, after holding the manuscript for over a year. Newby had agreed to divide the profits after costs but evidently printed only enough copies to reimburse himself and barely advertised, so Trollope got nothing.

Two other well-known writers lost money from Newby's publishing of their first novels: Eliza Lynn Linton with *Azeth, the Egyptian* (1847) and Charlotte Riddell with *Zuriel's Grandchild* (1855). On occasion Newby verged on plagiarism. In 1844 he published William North's *Anti-Coningsby, or, The New Generation Grown Old. By an Embryo M. P.*, a satire on Benjamin Disraeli's *Coningsby, or, The New Generation* (1844) and in 1845 North's *The Impostor, or, Born without a Conscience: by the Author of 'Anti-Coningsby'*. After publication of George Eliot's highly lauded *Adam Bede* (1859), Newby advertised *Adam Bede, Junior: a Sequel*, to be published in 1859, causing an angry exchange of letters in *The Times*: G. H. Lewes declared that Eliot was not the first to suffer from Newby's method of trading, but Newby blithely asserted his innocence with respect to the two Brontës.

In spite of shifty practices, Newby satisfied a legion of minor writers who repeatedly offered him manuscripts; for example, he published about twenty-two novels by [Mrs?] Robert Mackenzie Daniel, about fourteen novels by George Payne Rainsford James (*Leonora d'Orco*, 1857, became a best-seller), a number of sea romances by Francis Claudius Armstrong, and historical romances by Louis Alexis Chamerovzow. In non-fiction he responded astutely to contemporary interest in great men, foreign countries, the occult, self-help, scientific enquiry, the military, religion, sport, and the arts.

Thomas Cautley Newby died on 14 June 1882 at his daughter's home, 12 Westbourne Gardens, Folkestone, Kent, aged eighty-four; he was survived by a daughter, the next of kin, Marion Garling.

ELISABETH SANDERS ARBUCKLE

Sources Boase, *Mod. Eng. biog.* · *English catalogue of books* (1831–) · M. Allott, ed., *Emily Brontë, 'Wuthering Heights': a casebook* (1970) · J. Barker, *The Brontës: a life in letters* (1998) · J. A. Sutherland, *Victorian novelists and publishers* (1976) · N. Cross, *The common writer: life in nineteenth-century Grub Street* (1985) · G. Haight, *George Eliot: a biography* (1968) · *The letters of Mrs Gaskell*, ed. J. A. V. Chapple and A. Pollard (1966) · V. Glendenning, *Anthony Trollope* (1992) · J. Barker, *The Brontës* (1994) · P. A. H. Brown, *London publishers and printers, c.1800–* 1870 (1982) · W. Gérin, *Emily Brontë* (1971) · *CGPLA Eng. & Wales* (1882) · d. cert.
Wealth at death £38: administration, 1882, *CGPLA Eng. & Wales*

Newbyth. For this title name *see* Baird, Sir John, Lord Newbyth (*bap.* 1620, *d.* 1698).

Newcastle. For this title name *see* Butler, Pierce, styled third Viscount Galmoye, and Jacobite earl of Newcastle (1652–1740).

Newcastle under Lyme. For this title name *see* Holles, Thomas Pelham-, duke of Newcastle upon Tyne and first duke of Newcastle under Lyme (1693–1768); Clinton, Henry Fiennes Pelham-, ninth earl of Lincoln and second duke of Newcastle under Lyme (1720–1794); Clinton, Henry Pelham Fiennes Pelham-, fourth duke of Newcastle under Lyme (1785–1851); Clinton, Henry Pelham Fiennes Pelham-, fifth duke of Newcastle under Lyme (1811–1864).

Newcastle upon Tyne. For this title name *see* Cavendish, William, first duke of Newcastle upon Tyne (*bap.* 1593, *d.* 1676); Cavendish, Margaret, duchess of Newcastle upon Tyne (1623?–1673); Cavendish, Henry, second duke of Newcastle upon Tyne (1630–1691); Holles, John, duke of Newcastle upon Tyne (1662–1711); Holles, Thomas Pelham-, duke of Newcastle upon Tyne and first duke of Newcastle under Lyme (1693–1768).

Newcastle, Hugh (*fl.* 1320), Franciscan friar and theologian, probably entered the order at Newcastle, Northumberland. He was sent to Paris, where he attended the lectures of Duns Scotus (*d.* 1308), and incepted as doctor of theology, and perhaps also as doctor of canon law. He attended the general chapter of the Franciscan order that met at Perugia in 1322, and was one of those who issued a famous letter to Pope John XXII (*r.* 1316–34), begging him not to reverse decrees issued by former popes upholding as orthodoxy the doctrine that Christ and the apostles had owned nothing of their own, but had lived in an absolute poverty (which the Franciscans sought to emulate). It is not known when he died, but he was buried in the convent at Paris.

Newcastle wrote a treatise, *De victoria Christi contra Anti-Christum*, which Bartolomeo da Pisa admired. Manuscripts of this work are at Paris and Vienna, and it was printed at Nuremberg in 1471. More than twenty manuscripts of his 'Commentaries on the *Sentences*' survive. Their content is entirely conventional.

A. G. LITTLE, *rev.* JENNY SWANSON

Sources L. Wadding, *Annales minorum*, ed. J. M. Fonseca and others, 2nd edn, 6 (1733) · F. Stegmüller, ed., *Repertorium commentariorum in sententias Petri Lombardi*, 1 (Würzburg, 1947) · P. V. Doucet, 'Commentaires sur *Les sentences*', *AFH* (1954), 128ff. · A. G. Little, *The Grey friars in Oxford*, OHS, 20 (1892), 167 · C. L. [C.-V. Langlois], 'Hugues de Novo Castro, frère mineur', *Histoire littéraire de la France*, 36, ed. C.-V. Langlois (Paris, 1927), 342–9 · L. Amorós, 'Hugo von Novo Castro O. F. M. und sein Kommentar zum ersten Buch der Sentenzen', *Franziskanische Studien*, 20 (1933), 177–222

Newcomb, Thomas (1681/2–1765), poet, was the son of William Newcomb, of Westbury, Shropshire, who was termed 'pleb' when Thomas matriculated at Oxford on 15 April 1698 aged sixteen. At Corpus Christi College Newcomb was a chorister in 1699, and a 'clerk' from 4 July 1700; he also met the poet Edward Young, his most significant literary associate. Newcomb took the degree of BA in 1704 and became chaplain to Charles Lennox, first duke of Richmond. He was rector of Stopham in Sussex from 1705 to at least 1723. He was also rector of nearby Barlavington from 1707 until his death.

Newcomb began his literary career in 1709 with *An Epistle from the Duke of Burgundy to the French King*, a panegyric on Marlborough, returning to the theme with *Pacata Britannia* (1713), on the treaty of Utrecht. His satiric voice was established with *Bibliotheca: a Poem. Occasion'd by the Sight of a Modern Library* (1712), along lines suggested by Jonathan Swift's *Battle of the Books*; it contains virulent attacks on many modern writers, especially Daniel Defoe and Richard Bentley, a panegyric on Richard Steele, and a vision of the goddess Oblivion, whose resemblance to Alexander Pope's Dulness was noted by John Nichols and Joseph Warton. Newcomb read to Young his *Ode … to the Memory of … the Countess of Berkeley* (in memory of the duke of Richmond's daughter) in May 1717, and Young sent it to Edmund Curll, with the suggestion that he should publish it. Curll published not only the poem, but Young's letter, which Young, who was associated with Joseph Addison's opposition to the earl of Berkeley, then denied having written. Newcomb testified on his behalf in the subsequent public quarrel. Curll also published Newcomb's translations of Latin poems by Addison and John Philips. In 1721, in an effort to advance his reputation, Newcomb published a translation of *The Roman History of C. Velleius Paterculus*; some errors were pointed out in an alternative translation by J. Paterson the following year. In 1723 Newcomb published by subscription a Miltonic epic in twelve books, *The Last Judgment of Men and Angels*, with his own portrait as frontispiece. It was dedicated to the earl of March, who succeeded that year to the title of duke of Richmond. Also in 1723, Giles Jacob's *Poetical Register* praised Newcomb as 'a Man of Wit and Learning, and an Excellent Poet' (2.118–19), and claimed that he was the great-grandson (by descent on his mother's side) of Edmund Spenser. It was also said that his father was a 'worthy Clergyman, now Living, in *Herefordshire*'.

Under the second duke's patronage Newcomb continued his series of patriotic encomia: *An Ode to the Queen* (1727), on the coronation; further odes to the duke of Newcastle (1732), Walpole (1742), the duke of Cumberland (1746), Sir Edward Hawke (1747); and *Verses Left in a Grotto in Richmond Garden* (1744) on the battle of Dettingen, at which the second duke of Richmond had been present. His *Miscellaneous Collection of Original Poems* (1740) was expressly assembled to defend Walpole's administration. He attacked Thomas Woolston and other freethinkers in *Blasphemy as Old as the Creation* (1730), and produced some Young-like moral satires in *The Manners of the Age* (1733). *The Woman of Taste* (1733), a riposte to Bramston's *Man of Taste*,

is also ascribed to him, as are *A Supplement to One Thousand Seven Hundred Thirty-Eight* (1738), a reply to Pope, and *A Supplement to … 'Are these things so?'* (1740) in answer to James Miller's poem.

In 1743 Young told Philip Yorke of Newcomb's regret that Yorke would not allow Newcomb's *Collection of odes and epigrams, occasioned by the success of the British and confederate arms in Germany* (1743) to appear under his patronage. Young visited Newcomb at Richmond in March 1744. In 1757 Newcomb issued two poetical versions of 'Contemplations' by James Hervey, 'after the manner of Dr. Young' (a collected edition of such versions, dedicated to Arthur Onslow, appeared in 1764); in 1760 he published *The Retired Penitent*, a poem based on a text by Young, whose collaboration in the publication was advertised on the title-page. Newcomb was still producing patriotic panegyric: *Vindicta Britannica* (1758) on the Royal Navy (censured by the *Gentleman's Magazine* for its inflammatory jingoism), and odes to the king of Prussia (1758) and the queen (1761). His *Novus epigrammatum delectus, or, Original State Epigrams* (1760) was dedicated to Pitt. In 1762 Newcomb sent Young some verses, perhaps *On the Success of the British Arms* (1763); Young sent a warm reply to 'My Dear Old Friend', praising the verses and Newcomb's translation of Gessner's *Death of Abel*, attempted in the style of Milton (also 1763). Newcomb was apparently claiming to be eighty-seven, though he was only eighty. In a letter of 1763 to the duke of Newcastle, one of his patrons, Newcomb similarly overestimates his age, and complains of gout, rheumatism, and the stone. The third duke of Richmond had settled £10 a year on him; but he was still in need of funds. On 8 May 1764 Newcomb, who had been living in Hackney in 'rather distressed circumstances' (Nichols, *Select Collection*, 7.161), wrote to Newcastle to complain that his £80 salary for officiating at the local chapel had been stopped; he sent a Latin character of Wilkes and other papers in the hope that Newcastle would contribute to a collection on his behalf. Other begging letters of this time, to Lord Hardwicke and Charles Yorke, also survive. Newcomb died at Hackney in 1765 and was buried there on 11 June. Newcomb's later works all received reviews, but Nichols, collecting some of them in 1781, evidently had great difficulty in establishing authorship and collecting biographical material.

Newcomb made his will (PRO, PROB 11/910/267) on 20 May 1752 during an illness (his recovery from a fever in 1732, with the aid of Dr Gardiner, is recorded in BL, Add. MS 4456, 12). At the time of his son's marriage Newcomb had settled £150 of 'Old South Sea Annuities' on him; he now further bequeathed him all his sermons, manuscripts, and books, apart from such religious items as his widow should choose for her own use (the library was in fact sold in 1766). The son and daughter were each to receive a ring of 20*s*. in value. His 'Sister James' was to receive £5. Everything else went to his 'beloved Wife', Susanna, whom he made sole executor and to whom administration was granted on 1 July 1765.

PAUL BAINES

Sources *The correspondence of Edward Young, 1683–1765*, ed. H. Pettit (1971) · Foster, *Alum. Oxon.* · T. Fowler, *The history of Corpus Christi College*, OHS, 25 (1893) · [G. Jacob], *The poetical register, or, The lives and characters of all the English poets*, 2 vols. (1723) · H. Leek, 'The Edward Young–Edmund Curll quarrel: a review', *Papers of the Bibliographical Society of America*, 62 (1968), 321–35 · J. Nichols, ed., *A select collection of poems*, 8 vols. (1780–82), vols. 3–4, 7 · Bodl. Oxf., MSS Rawl. 1.451, 18.144 · A. Forster, *Index to book reviews in England, 1749–1774* (1990) · GM, 1st ser., 28 (1758), 601 · Nichols, *Lit. anecdotes*, 3.637 · R. D. Lund, 'From Oblivion to Dulness: Pope and the poetics of appropriation', *British Journal for Eighteenth-Century Studies*, 14/2 (1991), 171–89

Archives BL, letters to the duke of Newcastle, Add. MS 32948, fol. 381; Add. MS 32958, fol. 343; Add. MS 32992, fol. 294 · BL, letters to C. Yorke, Add. MS 35637, fol. 102

Likenesses J. Faber junior, mezzotint (after H. Hawkins), BM; repro. in T. Newcomb, *The last judgment of men and angels* (1723)

Wealth at death not insolvent, but little monetary estate; bequests to value of £7; plus books and papers: will, 1765, PRO, PROB 11/910, sig. 267

Newcombe, Thomas, the elder (1625×7–1681), printer, was the son of Thomas Newcomb, a yeoman of Dunchurch, Warwickshire. He was bound as an apprentice to the London printer Gregory Dexter on 8 November 1641, and was freed into the Stationers' Company by Dexter and Richard Cotes on 6 November 1648. Ten days later he married Ruth (*d.* 1653), widow of the London printer John Raworth, at Holy Trinity-the-Less, succeeding to Raworth's business based on Thames Street. Their first child, Hannah, was baptized in the parish of St Benet Paul's Wharf in September 1649; the couple had six children in all, including a pair of non-identical twins who were baptized on 18 October 1653 six days before their mother was buried in the same parish. Newcombe apparently remained a resident at Thames Street in the parish until his death.

Newcombe printed Descartes's *A Discourse of a Method* in 1649, the first work of Descartes to appear in English. He was imprisoned briefly in September 1649 for printing John Lilburne's *Outcry of the Young Men and Apprentices of London*; he was freed only on condition he entered into a recognizance of £300 binding him not to print any seditious or unlicensed books. The following year he took the first of sixteen apprentices. He was elected to the Stationers' Company livery in April 1653. He was a notable publisher of interregnum newsbooks and periodicals, including *Mercurius Politicus* (1651–60) and the *Public Intelligencer* (1655–60).

Following the Restoration Newcombe became the manager of the re-established king's printing house. He served as a common councilman for the ward of Castle Baynard between 1663 and 1667. The printer of the *Philosophical Transactions* of the Royal Society between 1665 and 1670, Newcombe was also involved in printing Henry Muddiman's *London Gazette*, reprinting it in London during its initial phase when it was being published in Oxford (to where the court had moved because of the plague) in late 1665, and then becoming its sole printer once it relocated to the capital in February 1666 following the return of the court. The fire of 1666 destroyed Newcombe's business premises and he, along with the king's printing house, relocated to the Savoy, where his business

remained until his death. His position after the fire was such that he became one of those figures who dominated the London book trade. In July 1668 his business was recorded as having three presses, one proof press, seven compositors, five pressmen, and an apprentice, making this one of the largest printing houses in the city. Over his career, he printed a significant number of literary works including works by Abraham Cowley (principally *Poems*, 1656), John Dryden (*Of Dramatick Poesie*, 1668), John Fletcher, Fulke Greville, Philip Massinger, Thomas Middleton, Thomas Shadwell, and John Suckling.

In December 1675 Newcombe was elected to the Stationers' Company's governing body and in the same month he and the printer Henry Hills received a thirty-year patent to follow the expiration of the reversion of the patent for the king's printing house in 1710. Two years later both men were formally recognized as the king's printers. Newcombe served as under-warden for 1679–80, and was elected as upper-warden in July 1681, but did not serve his term out, dying on 26 December 1681 in the '55 year of his age' (Dugdale, 285). His body was laid in state in Stationers' Hall ahead of a large funeral procession on 2 January 1682, which was attended by senior members of the company and about 200 'Gentlemen, Members of the said Company and others' (*Impartial Protestant Mercury*, 1). His body was carried to his home town of Dunchurch for burial; a memorial is recorded by Dugdale. His will, drawn up on 22 December 1681 and proved on 11 January 1682, left his interest in the king's printing house to his executors in trust to pay annuities to two siblings and to ten poor or aged printers; he also left legacies to the poor of the parishes of St Benet Paul's Wharf and Dunchurch.

Newcombe's son, **Thomas Newcombe the younger** (*bap.* 1651, *d.* 1691), succeeded to his father's business. He had been baptized on 31 August 1651 at St Benet Paul's Wharf, London, and, bound to his father on 18 December 1666, was freed by patrimony into the Stationers' Company in October 1672. He bound his first of five apprentices in October 1676 and was elected to the livery in the same month. The following February he married Dorothy Young (1660/61–1718), a sixteen-year-old from London Bridge. He was sworn as king's printer on 1 February 1682, and in 1686 his printing house was recorded as operating five presses. He remained active at the Savoy until July 1688, when Edward Jones took over the printing of the *London Gazette*. Whether this date marks the end of Newcombe's association with the book trade is unclear. He died on 27 March 1691. His will, dated 2 March and proved on 12 April 1691, described him as a gentleman of Wandsworth, Surrey. The bulk of his estate, including property at Westminster and London, and his business was left to his wife, Dorothy. He left £600 to establish almshouses at Dunchurch and was buried there, as he requested, alongside his father. His interest in the king's printing house was passed to Dorothy but in February 1694 she was declared of unsound mind and her person and property were assigned to John Williams, who had succeeded her husband as manager of the king's printing house. Within four months, however, she had recovered and remarried; her annual income from property and printing interests was estimated at this date to be £439. Her new husband, Richard Hutchinson, died in August 1695. In July 1708 she was once again declared a 'lunatique' and did not recover before her death in February 1718; Williams was again made responsible for her person and property during these last ten years of her life (Haig, 163). I. GADD

Sources DNB · private information (2004) [M. Treadwell, Trent University, Canada, and M. Turner, Bodl. Oxf.] · D. F. McKenzie, ed., *Stationers' Company apprentices*, [2]: *1641–1700* (1974) · Wing, *STC* · H. R. Plomer and others, *A dictionary of the booksellers and printers who were at work in England, Scotland, and Ireland from 1641 to 1667* (1907) · A. F. Johnson, 'The king's printers, 1660–1742', *The Library*, 5th ser., 3 (1949), 33–8 · R. L. Haig, 'New light on the king's printing office, 1680–1730', *Studies in Bibliography*, 8 (1956), 157–67 · court books, Stationers' Hall, London · P. Morgan, *Warwickshire apprentices in the Stationers' Company of London, 1563–1700*, Dugdale Society, 25 (1978) · C. W. Miller, 'Thomas Newcomb: a Restoration printer's ornament stock', *Studies in Bibliography*, 3 (1950–51), 155–70 · C. W. Miller, 'In the Savoy: a study in post-Restoration imprints', *Studies in Bibliography*, 1 (1948–9), 41–6 · W. Dugdale, *The antiquities of Warwickshire illustrated*, rev. W. Thomas, 2nd edn, 2 vols. (1730) · will, PRO, PROB 11/369, sig. 7 [T. Newcombe sen.] · will, PRO, PROB 11/404, sig. 70 [T. Newcombe jun.] · *Impartial Protestant Mercury*, 73 (30 Dec 1681–3 Jan 1682) · C. Nelson and M. Seccombe, eds., *British newspapers and periodicals, 1641–1700* (1987) · C. Nelson and M. Seccombe, *Periodical publications, 1641–1700: a survey with illustrations* (1986)

Newcombe, Thomas, the younger (bap. **1651**, d. **1691**). See under Newcombe, Thomas, the elder (1625×7–1681).

Newcome, Henry (bap. **1627**, d. **1695**), clergyman and ejected minister, was born in Caldecot in Huntingdonshire and baptized there on 27 November 1627, the fourth of the seven sons and one daughter of Stephen Newcome, the vicar of Caldecot, and his wife, Rose Williamson, a daughter of Henry Williamson, vicar of the nearby parish of Connington, a native of Salford, Lancashire. Newcome was educated at home by his father until 1641; he then attended the free school at Congleton in Cheshire, where his eldest brother, Robert, was schoolmaster. Newcome's parents died in the last days of January 1642 and were buried together in the same grave on 2 February. The brothers returned to Huntingdonshire, where the two eldest Newcome brothers, Robert and Richard, undertook the care and upbringing of the younger children. Henry Newcome entered St John's College, Cambridge, 'at the heat of the wars' in 1644 (*Autobiography*, 7). Although his education was interrupted by civil war, he graduated BA in 1647 and subsequently MA in 1651. In 1647 Newcome returned to Congleton, where he took up the post of schoolmaster formerly occupied by his brother.

Although only twenty years old, Newcome started preaching in the Congleton and Astbury area of southeast Cheshire, where he attracted the attention of, and became reader to, John Ley, vicar of Astbury and member of the Westminster assembly. With Ley's encouragement he was ordained as presbyterian minister in Sandbach, Cheshire, on 22 August 1648. On 6 July 1648 he married Elizabeth Mainwaring (bap. 1617, d. 1701), the third daughter of Peter and Jane Mainwaring of Smallwood, Cheshire, against the advice of friends, although no reason for such opposition is recorded. Henry and Elizabeth Newcome

Henry Newcome (bap. 1627, d. 1695), by Robert White

had five children: Rose, born 24 April 1649; Henry, born 28 May 1650; Daniel, born 29 October 1652; Elizabeth, born 11 November 1655; and Peter, born 5 November 1656. The eldest and youngest sons, Henry and Peter, are mentioned separately below.

From 1646 until his death Newcome kept a diary, of which only one volume for 1661–3 survives, and which was published by the Chetham Society as volume 18 of the old series in 1846. Newcome also wrote an autobiography for the guidance of his children, as a record of his life and a justification of his actions. It reveals Newcome to be an anxious man, with a tendency to worry and an active conscience. A heavily abridged version of this autobiography was also published by the Chetham Society in 1852 as volumes 26 and 27 of the old series as a popular edition of the text, but which omits much of interest to the student of puritanism and early nonconformity in the north-west. The complete manuscript as well as the surviving diary are both now in the care of Chetham's Library in Manchester.

Ministry in the 1650s Through his marriage to Elizabeth Mainwaring Newcome became connected to Cheshire gentry families, notably the Mainwarings of Kermincham and the Davenports of Marton. Henry and Elizabeth Newcome's first home was some rooms provided for them by

Henry Mainwaring at Kermincham, and it was through the influence of this connection that Newcome was appointed, first, curate at Goosetry in Cheshire and, subsequently, in 1650, minister at Gawsworth. Although Newcome deplored the execution of the king, and was impressed neither by Oliver Cromwell nor the Rump Parliament, he was constrained to take the engagement. This necessity troubled his conscience, and in time he repented his action and noted 'I looked always upon myself as a Non-engager' (*Autobiography*, 25). On 20 October 1653 Newcome attended a meeting of ministers at Knutsford exercise where the Cheshire voluntary agreement for mutual support and advice was discussed. Although intended to function along presbyterian lines, the parties to the agreement had none of the powers usually found in a formally convened classis.

Between 1650 and 1657 Newcome not only ministered to the congregation at Gawsworth; he actively sought out other like-minded men who shared with him the ideal of a fully reformed national church. He became part of a circle of friends which met in the home of his close friend and mentor John Machin at Seabridge in Staffordshire (now a suburb of Newcastle under Lyme). Throughout the early years of the 1650s, together with Machin, Thomas Leadbeater of Holmes Chapel, and others, Newcome took part in private days of devotion and participated in preaching tours in the towns of south-east Cheshire, north-west Staffordshire, and northern Shropshire. Newcome was so impressed by Machin's example that following his death in 1664 Newcome and Leadbeater collaborated in preparing *A faithfull narrative of the life and death of that holy and laborious preacher, Mr. John Machin* (London, 1671). Published anonymously, it was attributed to Newcome by Matthew Henry.

Newcome remained happily at Gawsworth until 1657, when, with a growing family, he felt the need to find a more remunerative post. He considered an invitation to become minister to the parish of St Julian in Shrewsbury. However, following the death of Richard Hollinworth he was offered the post as assistant minister at the former collegiate church of St Mary, St George, and St Denys (now Manchester Cathedral), and the family moved to Manchester. On 13 July 1659 Newcome signed the 'Proposition for Accommodation between Congregational and Presbyterian ministers' in the wake of rising radical sectarian activity in the region. On 1 August 1659 Sir George Booth's Cheshire rising broke out and, although he claimed not to have taken any active part in it, Newcome was said to have been involved. Although he was undoubtedly sympathetic to Booth's plans, it is clear that Newcome was deeply worried by his connection with the uprising and feared that it might do material harm to his position.

The Restoration and ejection Henry Newcome welcomed the restoration of the monarchy in 1660, and on 24 May 1660, at a day of thanksgiving held in the church at Manchester, preached his sermon *Usurpation Defeated and David Restored* (London, 1660). He prudently acknowledged the king's free pardon and declared his loyalty to the monarchy before the mayor of Newcastle under Lyme on 14 June 1660. Nevertheless, he deplored the frivolity of the celebrations surrounding the Restoration:

> We found May-poles in abundance as we came, and at Oakham I saw a morris-dance, which I had not seen of twenty years before. It is a sad sign the hearts of the people are poorly employed when they can make a business of playing the fool as they do. (*Autobiography*, 121)

He nevertheless continued to believe in the ideal of a fully reformed, national church, based on sound government and organized religious practice. In 1660, when presbyterians still hoped for some accommodation within the restored episcopal church, he wrote in support of a structured system to Richard Baxter, who was then engaged in the Savoy conference and the debates regarding church settlement:

> I never was yet so satisfied with my own performances in the administration of the ordinance, but I could prefer a prescribed form before any contrived way of my own, and I believe many modest men are of the same minde. (*Calendar*, 2.7)

Between 1660 and the Act of Uniformity in 1662, Newcome continued to preach in Manchester and in the surrounding towns and to conduct the twice monthly lecture at Stockport. When collegiate status was restored to the parish church in Manchester he hoped to be appointed fellow. A petition to the king on his behalf was raised and supported by Sir George Booth, other local gentry, and town officers. An order from the king directed the warden and fellows to consider Newcome's appointment; however, the appointments had already been made and he had missed his chance. Following the implementation of the Act of Uniformity on 24 August 1662, Newcome hoped for some days that a last-minute reprieve might be granted. He preached his last sanctioned sermon at Dunham, the home of Sir George Booth, on 31 August, and thereafter considered himself ejected. His conscience would not let him conform just to obtain a living. Worldly interest, he believed, would 'hinder my preferment in another world' (MS A3 123, p. clxx).

After ejection Following the Act of Uniformity Newcome continued to attend private days of devotion, to preach at funerals, and voluntarily to perform tasks akin to those of a parish priest, visiting the sick and giving comfort and advice. On at least two occasions, one in 1665 and another in 1668, he baptized the children of friends, despite being unauthorized so to do. Following the Five Mile Act he left Manchester and moved to Ellenbrook in the parish of Worsley, to the house of Thomas Topping, 6 miles northwest of Manchester. There, he and his wife apparently stayed for twenty years, although he seems to have stayed regularly in Manchester.

Under the declaration of indulgence in 1672, and supported by a petition to the king from the inhabitants of Manchester, Newcome was licensed to preach at 'a house near the college' (Turner, 2.678). He was a visitor to Hogton Tower in Lancashire, a meeting-place for many Lancashire nonconformists. He also preached at Cocky Chapel in the parish of Middleton. The rector of Middleton preached there once a month, but the association with non-conformity persisted. A meeting-house was built so close to the chapel 'that the congregations may hear one another sing psalms' (Gastrell, vol. 2, pt 1, 105). In 1677 Newcome visited London and preached at Richard Baxter's lecture in Fetter Lane. In June 1685, following Monmouth's rebellion, he was suspected of being involved and his house searched for arms. Although he expected imprisonment, no charges were brought against him.

Despite this nonconformist activity Newcome still attended services in the episcopal church. His son Henry recorded that in October 1685, 'my fa[ther] mo[ther] and sister were with me at the sacrament and complyed in the gesture of kneeling' (MS 922.3, N21, diary, 1696–1713, p. 70). In July 1684 he attended the metropolitan visitation at Nantwich with his son Henry and daughter Rose. At this period he appears to have been a partial or occasional conformist, which drew criticism from separatists and conformists alike. He deplored the disruptive effect of strife surrounding religion, and blamed hardline episcopacy for driving presbyterianism towards separatism. Although ejected, he remained on good terms with friends who conformed.

In the absence of a living, how Newcome supported himself, his wife, and family is unclear. He was not a wealthy man, and at certain periods of his life he had been chronically short of money. He was very worried about establishing his sons creditably. The eldest and youngest had to be maintained at Oxford, and the second son, Daniel, appears to have been a black sheep whose activities came home to roost upon the father. Newcome frequently expressed his gratitude to sympathetic and generous friends who made donations. Bequests left to him and other ejected ministers in local wills suggest the support of sympathetic laity.

Following James II's second declaration of indulgence in 1687, Newcome was preaching at a barn owned by his friend Thomas Stockton. After the Act of Toleration in 1689, he seems to have become reconciled to being excluded from the church and in April 1693 he became a moderator of the general meeting of ministers of the United Brethren in Lancashire. In June 1693 land was bought in Plungens meadow (later Cross Street) and the first nonconformist meeting-house in Manchester was built by the congregation which met at Stockton's barn. Newcome's account of the scheme seems to lack enthusiasm. Nevertheless, he preached the sermon at the first service in the chapel on 24 June 1694.

In addition to the publications mentioned above, between 1660 and his death Newcome published the following sermons: *The Sinners Hope* (London, 1660); *An Help to the Duty in and Right Improvement of Sickness* (London, 1685); and *A Plain Discourse about Rash and Sinful Anger* (London, 1693). A further sermon, *The Covenant of Grace Effectually Remembered* (London, 1682), has been attributed to Newcome, but why such attribution has been made is unclear from the text of the sermon.

Death Henry Newcome died in Manchester on 17 September 1695 aged sixty-eight and was buried in Cross Street Chapel three days later; John Chorlton, his assistant, preached the funeral sermon. Encomiums came from John How, a nonconformist friend from London, and another eminent nonconformist, William Bagshaw of Ford Hall in Derbyshire, summed up his career thus: 'That he had the voice of the learned, and that the Lord spake by him, Lancashire, Cheshire, Staffordshire, Shropshire, etc. have many witnesses' (*Autobiography*, 294).

Cross Street Chapel, later to become a Unitarian meeting-house, was wrecked by the Jacobite mob in 1715. The replacement chapel, enlarged over the years, stood on the same spot until December 1940, when it was badly damaged by bombing during the blitz in Manchester. The chapel, rebuilt in 1959, was demolished and rebuilt yet again, on the same site, in 1997. The remains of Henry Newcome and others were removed and reinterred in Manchester's southern cemetery. A memorial stone was laid, inscribed as follows:

> Sacred to the memory of Rev. Henry Newcome MA., founder of non-conformity in Manchester, and of those other Ministers, members and adherents of Cross Street Chapel who were buried in its graveyard 1695–1846. Their remains now rest either beneath Cross Street and Chapel Walks or were reinterred in this place in the year of our Lord, 1996.

Newcome's will and inventory were proved at Chester in April 1696. In it he described his outward estate as 'very small and inconsiderable'. His inventory valued his goods and chattels at £174 15s. 8d. He left the estate to his wife, Elizabeth, and their daughter Rose, 'who I know will not leave hir [Elizabeth] in hir old age and infirmity'. After Elizabeth's death the estate was to be divided between the daughters. His wife and the eldest son, Henry, were appointed executors, and Henry was charged to 'doe all he can to make his aged mother's life as comfortable as he can' (will and inventory of Henry Newcome, Lancs. RO, WCW 1696). Elizabeth Newcome died in February 1701, aged eighty-four, and was buried beside her husband in Cross Street Chapel.

Henry Newcome's sons Henry Newcome junior (1650–1713), Church of England clergyman, was the eldest son of Henry and Elizabeth Newcome. He was born in Gawsworth parsonage on 28 May 1650 and baptized in the parish church on 2 June. On 24 April 1677 he married Elizabeth Taylor (d. 1725) of Middleton, Lancashire, in Middleton church. They had four daughters and three sons. Newcome followed his father's example and recorded his life story in a manuscript deposited at Manchester Central Library (Archives and Local Studies) as a diary for 1696–1713, but which also contains autobiographical material from his youth.

Newcome's early education was sparse, which he attributed to constant bouts of ill health and the inadequacy of the schoolmaster. When the family moved to Manchester, however, he attended Manchester grammar school and subsequently in March 1666 he entered St Edmund Hall, Oxford. Newcome senior's reasons for sending his son to Oxford, rather than Cambridge, where he himself had been educated, were thus:

Two motives my father had for the choice of this house, One for the name of the Doctors good government, the other that there was no Preferment to tempt me to early conformity before I was capable of judging concerning the controversies about ceremonies and Discipline.   (MS 922.3, N21, diary, 1696–1713, pp. 6–7)

However, by the time Newcome took his degree in 1670, he had decided to conform and was ordained deacon in May 1673 and priest in June 1674. He was appointed curate of Shelsey in Worcestershire prior to his ordination. Probably through family influence he was inducted as rector of Tattenhall in Cheshire on 30 July 1675, and took up the appointment in February 1676.

Newcome continued as vicar of Tattenhall until 1701, when he was presented the living as rector of Middleton in Lancashire. He published his sermon *Divine Goodness, a Pattern for All* (London, 1689), which he preached before the Chester assize in September 1689, and *The Complete Mother* (London, 1695), a treatise intended to persuade all mothers to nurse their own children. Henry Newcome died on 19 May 1713 and was buried at Middleton on 22 May, survived by his wife and four of their children. In his will, proved at Chester on 24 October 1713, he divided his estate between his wife and children and made his wife, Elizabeth, sole executrix. No inventory appears to have survived. Elizabeth Newcome was buried at Middleton on 27 January 1725.

The youngest son of Henry Newcome senior, **Peter Newcome** (1656–1738), who like his eldest brother became a Church of England clergyman, was born in Gawsworth parsonage on 5 November 1656 and baptized in the parish church on 11 November. In August 1681 he married Ann Hook (*c*.1661–1726) of Hook in Hampshire; they had twelve children. Little is known of his early education. He followed his brother Henry to Oxford in March 1675, and graduated BA in 1678 and MA in 1681. He also conformed, and was ordained in 1679 or 1680. Shortly afterwards he became curate of Hook in Hampshire. In 1683 he was inducted vicar of Aldenham in Hertfordshire; he stayed there until 1704, when he was presented the living as vicar of Hackney, Middlesex. In 1714 he bought the advowson of Shenley rectory in Hertfordshire. The Newcome family remained patrons of the living until it was sold in 1902, and, except for two short periods in the eighteenth century, his son Peter Newcome (1684–1744), grandson Peter *Newcome (1727–1797), and other descendants were incumbents. Peter Newcome published *Peccata in deliciis* (London, 1686), *A Sermon Preached … April 16 1696* (London, 1696), and *A Catechetical Course of Sermons* (London, 1700).

Ann Newcome died on 17 August 1726, aged sixty-five. Peter Newcome died on 5 October 1738, aged eighty-two, and was buried beside his wife in Hackney churchyard. No will for Peter Newcome appears to have survived.

CATHERINE NUNN

Sources autobiography of Henry Newcome, Chetham's Library, Manchester, MS A3123 · *The autobiography of Henry Newcome*, ed. R. Parkinson, 2 vols., Chetham Society, 26–7 (1852) · *The diary of the Rev. Henry Newcome, from September 30, 1661, to September 29, 1663*, ed. T. Heywood, Chetham Society, 18 (1849) [Chetham's Library, Manchester, MS A140] · H. Newcome jun., diary, Man. CL, Manchester Archives and Local Studies, MS 922.3.N21 · [H. Newcome], *A faithful narrative of the life and death of … Mr. John Machin* (1671) · *Calendar of the correspondence of Richard Baxter*, ed. N. H. Keeble and G. F. Nuttall, 2 vols. (1991) · B. Nightingale, *Lancashire nonconformity*, 6 vols. [1890–93] · G. L. Turner, ed., *Original records of early nonconformity under persecution and indulgence*, 3 vols. (1911–14) · F. Gastrell, *Notitia Cestriensis, or, Historical notices of the diocese of Chester*, ed. F. R. Raines, 2/1, Chetham Society, 19 (1849) · calendar for July and August 1998, Cross Street Chapel, Manchester · wills and inventories, Lancs. RO, WCW 1696, 1713 · J. E. Cussans, *History of Hertfordshire*, 3 vols. (1870–81) · D. Lysons, *The environs of London*, 4 vols. (1792–6) · D. Lysons, *Supplement to the first edition of 'The environs of London'* (1811) · parish register, Middleton, Lancashire · parish register, Astbury, Cheshire · parish register, Gawsworth, Cheshire
Archives Chetham's Library, Manchester, MS autobiography, diary and commonplace book · Chetham's Library, Manchester, funeral sermons [Henry Newcome] · Man. CL, diary and MSS [Henry Newcome]
Likenesses Mr Cunney, portrait, 1658; known to be at the Lancashire Independent College, Whalley Range in 1894 · J. Bull, line engraving, NPG; repro. in [J. Birt], ed., *The Manchester socinian controversy* (1825), frontispiece · G. Vertue, line engraving (Newcome, Peter), BM · R. White, line engraving, BM, NPG [*see illus.*] · woodcut, repro. in T. Baker, *Memorials of a dissenting chapel* (1884), frontispiece
Wealth at death £174 15s. 8d.: will and inventory, WCW 1696, Lancs. RO

Newcome, Henry, junior (1650–1713). *See under* Newcome, Henry (*bap.* 1627, *d.* 1695).

Newcome, Peter (1656–1738). *See under* Newcome, Henry (*bap.* 1627, *d.* 1695).

Newcome, Peter (1727–1797), antiquary, was born at Wellow, Hampshire, where he was baptized on 6 October 1727, the eldest of the three children of Peter Newcome (1684–1744), rector of Shenley, Hertfordshire, from 1742 to 1744, and his wife, Ann Haskar. His grandfather was Peter Newcome (1656–1738), youngest son of the ejected minister Henry *Newcome (*bap.* 1627, *d.* 1695). Having been educated at Hackney School, Newcome entered Queens' College, Cambridge, in November 1743, from where he graduated as a bachelor of laws in 1750. He was ordained priest on 22 December 1751 and the following December was instituted rector of Shenley, the advowson of which had been purchased by his mother in 1742, which he held until his death. He was also a prebend of Llandaff from March 1757 and of St Asaph from May 1764, a position that he passed to his brother, Henry, on being presented to the sinecure rectory of Darowen, Montgomeryshire, in 1766. By the appointment of his friend J. Heathcote, Newcome preached two Lady Moyer lectures in St Paul's Cathedral, both of which were well received, and was the last preacher on that endowment. In 1786 he was made rector of Pitsea, Essex, on the gift of Sir Gilbert Heathcote.

The author of a Latin poem, *Maccabeis* (1787), Newcome is best known for *The History of the … Abbey of St. Alban* (1793–5), the first part of which considers the history of the abbey from its Anglo-Saxon origins to the reign of Edward III, and the second part the period from *c*.1340 until the Reformation. In this history, which draws heavily on the medieval chronicles of Matthew Paris and

Thomas Walsingham, Newcome gave the first comprehensive account of the lives of the abbots of St Albans and the history of its dependent cells—work that helped to underpin the first detailed architectural descriptions of the church, such as that by E. W. Brayley (*Beauties of England & Wales*, 7, 1808), which began to appear from the early nineteenth century onwards. Newcome never married and died on 2 April 1797 at the house of his sister, Ann, at Hadley, near Barnet, Middlesex, from an inflammation of the lungs caused by a neglected cold.

GORDON GOODWIN, *rev.* NICHOLAS DOGGETT

Sources R. Clutterbuck, ed., *The history and antiquities of the county of Hertford*, 1 (1815), 485–7 · J. E. Cussans, *History of Hertfordshire*, 3/1 (1881), 320, 323 · *GM*, 1st ser., 67 (1797), 437 · Nichols, *Lit. anecdotes*, 9.134–5 n. · Venn, *Alum. Cant.*, 1/3.247 · *Fasti Angl.* (Hardy), 1.90; 2.268 · E. Roberts, *The hill of the martyr: an architectural history of St Albans Abbey* (1993), 188–9 · *IGI* · will, PRO, PROB 6/173, fol. 348v
Wealth at death under £600: will, PRO, PROB 6/173, fol. 348v

Newcome, William (1729–1800), Church of Ireland archbishop of Armagh and theologian, was born at Abingdon, Berkshire, on 10 April 1729. He was the second son of Joseph Newcome, vicar of St Helen's, Abingdon, and rector of Barton in the Clay, Bedfordshire. He was educated at Abingdon grammar school, and in 1745 won a scholarship at Pembroke College, Oxford. He subsequently moved to Hertford College, Oxford, and graduated MA (1753) and DD (1765). He was elected a fellow of Hertford in 1753, and afterwards its vice-principal, and was an eminent tutor; among his pupils in 1764–5 was Charles James Fox.

In 1765, when Francis Seymour Conway, then earl of Hertford, was appointed lord lieutenant of Ireland, he took Newcome with him as his chaplain. Newcome was consecrated bishop of Dromore on 27 April 1766. He was translated to Ossory on 13 April 1775 and to Waterford and Lismore on 5 November 1779. Finally he was made archbishop of Armagh and primate of all Ireland on 27 January 1795, during the short-lived viceroyalty of Earl Fitzwilliam.

Newcome's elevation to the primacy was said to be on the insistence of George III; he had no English patron but Fox, who was not then in power. His appointment was described by James Caulfeild, Lord Charlemont, as the reward of character, principles, and erudition. His private fortune was large; he was able to pay without difficulty a sum of around £16,000, in lieu of improvements, to the heirs of his predecessor, Richard Robinson, Baron Rokeby. In his primary visitation of the province (1795) he strongly urged the neglected duty of clerical residence. He spent large sums on the improvement of the cathedral and palace at Armagh, and though quiet and domestic in his own tastes he provided hospitality appropriate to his position as primate. During his whole episcopal career he was an exemplary prelate.

Newcome devoted most of his time to biblical studies, chiefly exegetical, and especially with a view to an amended English version of the scriptures. His first important publication was *An Harmony of the Gospels* (1778), which was based on the work of Jean Leclerc, the Greek text being given with various readings from Johann Jacob Wettstein. In this work Newcome criticized Joseph Priestley's adoption (1777) of Nicholas Mann's 1773 hypothesis limiting Christ's ministry to a single year. Priestley defended himself in his English *Harmony* (1780), and Newcome replied in a small volume, *The Duration of Our Lord's Ministry* (1780). The controversy was continued in two pamphlets by Priestley and one by Newcome (1781), and was concluded by a private letter from Newcome to Priestley (19 April 1782). While he held his ground against Priestley, on another point Newcome subsequently revised his *Harmony* in *A Review of the Chief Difficulties … Relating to Our Lord's Resurrection* (1791). In this work he returned to the hypothesis of the Socinian writer George Benson. An English *Harmony*, on the basis of Newcome's study in Greek, was published in 1802 and reprinted in 1827.

As an interpreter of the prophets Newcome followed Robert Lowth, the discoverer of the parallelisms of Hebrew poetry. Newcome's *Attempt towards an improved version, a metrical arrangement, and an explanation of the twelve minor prophets* (1785) remains his best work, in which he claims to give 'the critical sense … and not the opinions of any denomination'. In his notes Newcome made frequent use of the manuscripts of Thomas Secker. Newcome followed this publication with *An Attempt towards an Improved Version … [of] Ezekiel* (1788). These were parts of a larger plan presented in *An Historical View of the English Biblical Translations* (1792), with suggestions for a revision. Newcome himself worked at a revision of the whole English Bible. The New Testament part was printed as *An Attempt towards Revising our English Translation of the Greek Scriptures* (1796); the text adopted was the first edition (1775–7) of Johann Griesbach, and there were numerous notes. The work was withheld from publication until after Newcome's death; as the impression was damaged in crossing from Dublin, the number of copies for sale was small. In 1808 the Unitarians issued, anonymously, an *Improved Version upon the Basis of Archbishop Newcome's New Translation*. The adaptations, for a sectarian purpose, were mainly the work of the Unitarian minister Thomas Belsham, whose arguments were angrily refuted on 7 August 1809 by Newcome's friend Joseph Stock, bishop of Killala and Achonry. In addition Newcome published three sermons (1767–72) and *Occasional and Private Instruction, an Important Part of the Pastoral Duty* (1795). He also published *Observations on Our Lord's Conduct as a Divine Instructor* (1782), with subsequent English reprints.

Newcome married twice. Details of his first wife, with whom he had a daughter, Susanna, are unknown. His second marriage, to Anna Maria Smyth, produced a large family. Newcome died at his residence at St Stephen's Green, Dublin, on 11 January 1800 and was buried in the chapel of Trinity College, Dublin.

ALEXANDER GORDON, *rev.* J. FALVEY

Sources B. Bradshaw and others, 'Bishops of the Church of Ireland from 1534', *A new history of Ireland*, ed. T. W. Moody and others, 9: *Maps, genealogies, lists* (1984), 392–438 · H. Cotton, *Fasti ecclesiae Hibernicae*, 6 vols. (1845–78) · R. Mant, *History of the Church of Ireland*, 2 vols. (1840) · Burtchaell & Sadleir, *Alum. Dubl.* · J. J. Falvey, 'The Church of Ireland episcopate in the eighteenth century', MA diss., University College, Cork, 1995 · will, PRO, PROB 11/1343, sig. 430 ·

R. J. Hayes, ed., *Manuscript sources for the history of Irish civilisation*, 11 vols. (1965)
Archives Glos. RO, letters to Robert Hughes · Sheff. Arch., Wentworth Woodhouse MSS, corresp. with Earl Fitzwilliam
Likenesses H. Hamilton, oils, 1798, Pembroke College, Oxford · C. Knight, stipple and line engraving, pubd 1803 (after portrait by Hamilton), NG Ire. · portrait, Hertford College, Oxford · portrait; in possession of Archbishop of Armagh, 1867
Wealth at death over £9500—plus possessions (horses, carriages, furniture, etc.): will, PRO, PROB 11/1343, sig. 430

Newcomen, Elias (1547/8–1614), author and schoolmaster, was born at Barking, Essex, the son of Charles Newcomen of London, an officer in the exchequer, and Joan, daughter and coheir of Richard Nightingale of Bourne or Brentwood in Essex. Charles was the second son of Bryan Newcomen, owner of the family estates at Saltfleetby, Lincolnshire. Elias matriculated as a pensioner from Clare College, Cambridge, at Michaelmas 1565, and graduated BA from Magdalene College in 1569, MA in 1572. He was elected a fellow of Magdalene, also in 1572, but the master Roger Kelke immediately ejected him on the grounds that Newcomen had, through court influence, obtained royal nomination to his fellowship directly, without having first obtained Kelke's own recommendation, in accordance with the college statutes. It is clear that Kelke identified Newcomen with a group of puritan malcontents, whom he sought to exclude by asserting his own powers of nomination. The case generated great controversy between the fellows, most of whom supported Newcomen, and Kelke, whose appointment as master was 'most disastrous to the college' according to its historian (Purnell, 56). Newcomen was unable to secure the reversal of his ejection.

Newcomen probably did sympathize with men such as Thomas Cartwright, and he was certainly a zealous protestant. His *Defence and True Declaration of Thinges Lately done in the Lowe Countrey* (c.1571) was a translation of a work presented to the emperor, the electors, and other German princes assembled at Speyer, and published in Latin in 1570 following the duke of Alba's military campaign against the rebels in the Netherlands. The book 'containeth a great deal of matter of good historical knowledge' to be used against the 'poisonous kind of parasites and rumour spreaders', whom Newcomen identified with the papists. After his ejection from Magdalene Newcomen earned a living as a schoolmaster. He opened a school near London which, according to Cooper, was successful in attracting an average of twenty or thirty pupils, the 'children of worshipful parents', but its whereabouts have not been established.

On 26 August 1579 a licence was granted for the marriage of Elias Newcomen and Prothesa (or Prophetia) Shobridge, of St Leonard, Shoreditch; they had two children, Thomas and Thomasine. In 1586 Newcomen applied for the headship of the Merchant Taylors' School, vacant through the resignation of Richard Mulcaster, but his candidature was unsuccessful. On 10 May 1588 he was ordained deacon, aged forty. In 1594 he was instituted to the vicarage of Stoke Fleming, near Dartmouth, the first of his family to settle in the area. His son Thomas became a prosperous merchant in Dartmouth, was prominent in its resistance to royalist siege in 1643, and was grandfather to another Thomas Newcomen (d. 1729), the inventor of the steam engine. The will of Elias Newcomen, proved on 2 August 1614, was signed 'lieing at the point of death, 12 July 1614': the brass to his memory in Stoke Fleming church is dated the following day. It records:

> Elias old lies here intomb'd in grave,
> But Newcomin to heavens habitation.
> In knowledge old in zeale, in life most grave,
> Too good for all who line in lamentation.
> Whose sheep and seed with heavy plaint and moan
> Will say too late Elias old is gone.
> The xiii July 1614.
> (Allen, 21)

STEPHEN WRIGHT

Sources Venn, *Alum. Cant.* · Cooper, *Ath. Cantab.* · J. Strype, *The life and acts of John Whitgift*, new edn, 3 vols. (1822) · W. Fletcher, *The family of Newcomen of Saltfleetby* (1898) · J. S. Allen, 'Thomas Newcomen (1663/4–1729) and his family', *Transactions* [Newcomen Society], 51 (1979–80), 11–24 · M. Hine, 'Pedigree of Thomas Newcomen', *Transactions* [Newcomen Society], 9 (1928–9), 105–8 · E. K. Purnell, *Magdalene College* (1904) · A. R. Maddison, ed., *Lincolnshire pedigrees*, 2, Harleian Society, 51 (1903), 715 · F. W. M. Draper, *Four centuries of Merchant Taylors' School, 1561–1961* (1962)
Likenesses brass sculpture, Stoke Fleming church, Devon
Wealth at death £103 2s. 6d.: Allen, 'Thomas Newcomen', p. 21

Newcomen, Matthew (d. 1669), clergyman and ejected minister and religious controversialist, was the second son of Stephen Newcomen (1557/8–1629), vicar of St Peter's, Colchester, Essex.

Early career After education under William Kempe at the Royal Grammar School, Colchester, on 8 November 1626 he matriculated from St John's College, Cambridge, having been elected the second scholar on the foundation of Robert and Mary Lewis. He graduated BA early in 1630 and proceeded MA in 1633. He spent some time studying with John Rogers, lecturer of Dedham, Essex, and seems to have acted as assistant to Nehemiah Rogers (no relation) at Messing, Essex, in 1632 before being licensed as curate to Thomas Mott at Stoke by Nayland, Suffolk. At the episcopal visitation in 1636 he failed to show the documents he claimed to have received from the bishop of Ely but he was simply admonished and told to conform to episcopal injunctions.

When John Rogers died on 18 October 1636, Newcomen was recommended as his successor in the lectureship at Dedham by John Knowles, a friend from university and now lecturer at Colchester. In this post Newcomen won his reputation as a godly minister, perhaps establishing his popularity with his congregation with a laudatory poem, *A Mournefull Epitaph upon the Death of John Rogers*, circulated in manuscript and published in 1642. More importantly he proved to be an acclaimed preacher. Dr Collins, who had known him for thirty years, stated in the preface to Newcomen's funeral sermon:

> that he never knew any that excelled him, considering him as a *minister in the pulpit, a disputant in the schools*, and a *desirable companion*. In the first capacity, his gift in prayer was incomparable. He was a solid, painful, pathetick, and

perswasive preacher.   (J. Fairfax, *The Dead Saint Speaking*, 1679, preface)

In his published works Newcomen placed a strong emphasis on pastoral responsibilities, particularly on the role of the minister as a reconciliatory agent in dispute, and he seems to have met with some success in this field at Dedham. His preaching drew godly visitors from Colchester and won him invitations to preach along the Stour valley, receiving accolades from lay and clerical listeners alike. One piece of practical evidence for his popularity survives from an appearance at the lecture at Stowmarket, Suffolk, where his friend Thomas *Young was vicar. When he preached there in November 1641 more food was required at the lecture dinner, 'being abundance of ministers when Mr Newcomen, and a quart of wine they sent for' (A. G. H. Hollingsworth, *The History of Stowmarket*, 1844, 145–6). He seems to have been untroubled by the episcopal authorities in these years, which may be because of a combination of Bishop William Juxon's underachieving regime and Dedham's advantage of being in the far northeast corner of the diocese. Certainly, there were no later allegations that he had conformed during the 1630s, allegations that were often cast about during the sharp debates among the godly in the 1640s.

That is not to say that Newcomen hid his light under a bushel. He preached in support of the godly candidates during the electioneering of the spring of 1640. When the Short Parliament was dissolved and puritan insecurity and uncertainty were at their height he gave a particularly bold sermon at Dedham. He bemoaned the numbers of godly ministers, 'so many burning and shining lights' whose flames had been 'quenched' and predicted his own imminent silencing. He warned his congregation against the temptation of apostasy and advised them to steel themselves for persecution by reading John Foxe's *Acts and Monuments*. It should be noted that, in good Foxeian style, he was promoting resolve and a determination to undertake passive resistance; he was not suggesting or legitimizing resistance to the magistracy.

London circle of ministers and Smectymnuus Once the Long Parliament had been called, Newcomen spent more and more of his time in London. To a degree, his marriage encouraged this. Earlier in 1640 he became the third husband of Hannah Raven (*d.* 1675), widow of Gilbert, who had been rector of St Mary's Stoke, Ipswich, Suffolk, daughter of Robert Snelling, a former MP for the town, and sister of the first wife of Edmund *Calamy (1600–1666). Indeed, Calamy proved to be a critical clerical contact in London and his pulpit at Aldermanbury was one that welcomed Newcomen. From November 1640 the latter took part in weekly meetings at Calamy's house, meetings at which the clerical contribution to the godly cause was discussed and, as far as possible, controlled. In addition to Calamy, he was joined by Young, Stephen *Marshall, Cornelius Burges, John White, and William *Spurstowe. This group played an important part in several ways. It provided, in effect, the management committee for the ministers' 'petition' and 'remonstrance', signed by more than 700 clergymen and delivered to the House of Commons on 23 January 1641; several petitions were collected and collated by this group.

Newcomen played a more visible role in some of the most famous pamphlets in the early part of the ecclesiological debate. His initials provided two letters for the acronym Smectymnuus, the others belonging to Marshall, Calamy, Young, and Spurstowe. The first tract, *An Answer*, appeared in February 1641, providing a rebuttal of the work of Joseph Hall, then bishop of Exeter, which had defended divine-right episcopacy. The alternative form proposed by the Smectymnuans is fairly inexact, growing out of the stock of limited or 'primitive' episcopacy but remaining vague at this stage. On the other hand, *An Answer* delivered a harsh and lengthy critique of Laudian-style episcopacy, verging on the vitriolic. At the end of June the second Smectymnuan tract, *A Vindication*, responded to Bishop Hall's reply to *An Answer*. It shares a great deal with the initial treatise, expanding issues raised there, but there are also passages which seem to advocate something akin to presbyterianism. Part of the reasoning behind this reticence is revealed in a meeting in November 1641. The puritans were anxious to present a united front against the episcopal *status quo*, minimizing the internal ecclesiological differences of the godly supporters of reform. Thus Newcomen was among many of the leading clerics who adopted an agreement to avoid ecclesiological in-fighting in the short term.

Parliament and the Westminster assembly Newcomen was called to preach to the houses of parliament at their fasts on several occasions through the 1640s, and was plainly popular as his sermons were usually printed by the order of the houses. He was most popular in the first half of the decade. His concern, here as elsewhere, was to maintain unity against the common enemy. For instance, in *The Craft and Cruelty of the Churches Adversaries* (1643), delivered on 5 November 1642, he provided a skilfully set and politically sensitive analysis on the anniversary of the Gunpowder Plot, at a moment when the call to unity was critical. Having selected as his text Nehemiah 4: 11, he followed the idea of hidden enemies to give a (heavily weighted) history lesson, tracing the occurrence of Catholic plots against Elizabeth and James VI and I, moving on to the 1630s, portraying the Laudians as a popish fifth column.

A desire for reconciliation of godly people who shared the heart of the matter was also a recurring element in Newcomen's work in the Westminster assembly. Among the first to be summoned, he delivered the opening sermon before the assembly and both houses of parliament, setting out the scale of their task and calling upon them to prove equal to the responsibility; it was published as *Jerusalems Watchmen* (1643). He was taken onto the third committee formed on Monday 10 July 1643 whose job was to deal the eighth, ninth, and tenth of the established articles of the Church of England. On a related issue, with John Arrowsmith and Anthony Tuckney, Newcomen drew up the catechism to be issued by the assembly. In its debates on the reform of church government, Newcomen emerged as a convinced presbyterian but always with an eye to the peaceful accommodation of the Independents. In November 1643, when the Independents were being denounced as quasi-separatists, he tried to defuse the situation with a very open definition of a true church, based solely on faith and practice of worship, leaving government as a less loaded issue. It was, therefore, natural that in November 1644 he should be appointed to a committee created to discuss the objections to presbyterianism put forward by Thomas Goodwin and Philip Nye. The growing feeling, heightened by external pressures over the following months, was that the Independents should make their scheme explicit rather than exist in counterpoint to the proposals of the majority. Thus Newcomen proposed in April 1645 that as 'dissenting brethren' they should be recognized as an official committee of the assembly, giving them an opportunity to set out their stall, to present a model of church government with supporting scriptures and reasons. The Independents accepted the proposal but it foundered on their insistence that they should deliver their model piece by piece, as the presbyterian scheme had emerged.

Newcomen's peaceful tone and his advocacy of unity should not be overstated. He was only prepared to go so far to find a peaceful settlement. On 3 November 1643 he joined a committee with the considerable task of assessing all the Antinomian literature pouring from the unregulated presses of the metropolis. In a more subtle way, a similar understated conviction emerged in October 1644. The divines were debating the question of excommunication through the church at Ephesus. Newcomen took it as given, and refused to shift, that the starting point was the classis rather than the particular congregation. Such resolution, founded upon a concern to avoid provoking God's disfavour, was at its most explicit when in July 1643 he warned the House of Commons against a peace with the enemy which would 'tolerate anything in the Church of England that might make him to be at war with us' (*Jerusalems Watchmen*, 1643, 33).

At this point Newcomen was close to the centre of parliamentary politics but as the spectrum shifted through the 1640s he and ministers of his ilk became less so. With many of his colleagues in the assembly he was outraged when parliament issued an ordinance effectively uniting church and state and so he worked on 19 March 1646 with English ministers and the Scottish commissioners on a form asserting ecclesiastical power by divine right, and on 20 March with a subcommittee with Stephen Marshall, Richard Vines, and Lazarus Seaman to draft a petition as a response. The petition delivered to parliament on 23 March was suitably caustic, clearly setting out the assembly's affronted conscience. Newcomen outlined what he considered to be the boundaries of parliamentary power in religion in his last published sermon to the Commons, delivered on 30 December. *The All-Seeing Eye of God* pointed out that 'the Magistrate cannot give men a heart to know and love the truth' (p. 47), but he could provide the legal framework within which men were obliged to confront it, 'laws to restrain and punish errours and blasphemies that are against the truth'. 'The vows of God' were upon MPs

'for the extirpation of heresie, superstition, schisme, profanenesse, and of whatsoever is contrary to sound Doctrine and the power of godlinesse, as well as of Popery and Prelacy' (p. 48).

Newcomen played a critical role in drawing up the 'Essex testimony' and the 'Essex watchmen's watchword' of 1648 and early 1649 respectively, supporting similar statements by the London ministers. The 'Essex testimony' praised the solemn league and covenant and the confession of faith, *Directory for the Publique Worship of God*, and the 'Humble advise for church government', the last three products of the assembly, and went on to express regret over the toleration of what were seen as heresies and blasphemies. It was signed by 129 ministers from all over the county. Newcomen concurred with the criticism but he did not feel in a position to voice the approval of the assembly. The 'Watchword' is a more lengthy document with fewer signatures, perhaps as a consequence of its hurried distribution. It voices similar concerns but also presents serious misgivings about the *Agreement of the People*, expressing surprise at the conclusion of the conflict. The opening aims of the war win approval but regret is made plain in that a war broached to protect religion and the king has produced the opposite results. Newcomen not only signed the 'Watchword' but can be traced explaining and promoting the two across Essex. Despite these serious misgivings about the ways religious politics were developing, he still had an eye to the art of the possible, recognizing the *status quo* by helping to organize presbyterianism in the county, assisting with the practicalities and taking his place on the classis for Dedham.

Later career Newcomen seems effectively to have withdrawn from politics at the centre from the late 1640s, although further works appeared from Smectymnuus in 1654. He became an assistant to the commission of triers of scandalous ministers for Essex in 1654 and town lecturer of Ipswich, Suffolk, as successor to his friend Stephen Marshall upon the latter's death in 1655. His place among the fraternity of East Anglian godly ministers is hinted at by his funeral sermon for Samuel Collins, minister of Braintree, Essex, delivered in 1657 and published in 1658. Perhaps his experience here gave rise to *Irenicum, or, An essay towards a brotherly peace and union between those of the congregational and presbyterian way* (1659), which has been credited to him.

Newcomen made a brief return to centre stage shortly after the Restoration. In March 1661 he was summoned to join the Savoy House conference by Edmund Calamy. The intention was to bring twelve bishops and twelve presbyterian clergymen together to provide a review of the Book of Common Prayer as part of the pursuit of a more comprehensive Church of England. The conference failed due to the lack of common ground and partly due to Richard Baxter's intransigence, and any success would have been likely to have received short shrift from parliament. Newcomen was, according to Baxter, a dogged assistant. However, he left London rather quickly, having to apologize to Baxter for leaving without saying goodbye. He showed little willingness to compromise with the settlement. He was created DD on 10 October 1661 but quickly declined the offer of a royal chaplaincy and implored Baxter to dissuade Calamy from accepting a bishopric. It would certainly have been reasonable if he was feeling frustrated or under threat; a weaver from Boxted, Essex, was reported to have said that 'he would be one of the first to pull [him] from the pulpit and roast him alive' (Walter, 336).

Newcomen was faced with a more personally costly test of his convictions when he was required to declare his adherence to the settlement in order to keep his ministry in 1662, as set down in the Act of Uniformity. He resolved to refuse and delivered his last sermon as lecturer of Dedham on 22 December 1662, calling upon his congregation to find good preaching where they could but, as in 1640, advocating passive resistance. His initial plan was to remain as a deprived minister and he eventually consulted John Collins as to whether he should accept a call to preach in the Netherlands. Evidently Collins responded in a positive fashion, as shortly afterwards Newcomen preached his final sermon on English soil (published as *Ultimum vale*, 1663) before his departure to become pastor of the English church in Leiden in December 1662. He seems have become well settled in Leiden. He was disturbed by a call for his return by a royal proclamation issued on 26 March 1666 as a response to the outbreak of the Anglo-Dutch war but friends at home worked to have him excepted on the grounds of ill health and in any case he became a Dutch citizen. He died in Leiden about 1 September 1669 during an outbreak of plague and had a well-received funeral sermon delivered in Dedham by John Fairfax, the ejected minister of Barking, Suffolk. Newcomen was survived by his wife, Hannah, and son Stephen. Baptized at Dedham on 17 September 1645, Stephen had been admitted as a student of philosophy to Leiden University on 28 May 1663.

Matthew's older brother, **Thomas Newcomen** (*c*.1603–1665), Church of England clergyman, was born in Colchester about 1603 and educated at the Royal Grammar School there. On 6 November 1622 he was elected as the first Lewis scholar at St John's College, Cambridge; he graduated BA early in 1625. He was ordained deacon and priest in London on 24 September 1626. In 1628 he proceeded MA and became rector of St Runwald's and Holy Trinity, both in Colchester. He was a devotee of Laudianism, a religious style which sat uneasily in the puritan traditions of the town. His religious campaign was conducted with remarkable insensitivity. He introduced altar rails despite considerable opposition within his parishes and refused to serve the eucharist to communicants who were unwilling to kneel at the rails. It was particularly unfortunate that he employed the external forces of ecclesiastical courts and the high commission to enforce Laudianism, touching a sensitive nerve with a corporation concerned about civic autonomy. There was a long and bitter legal struggle over the question of excommunication. His behaviour was brought to the attention of a wider public when he was central to the conviction bemoaned in John Bastwick's *Letany* (1637), and he also appeared in William Prynne's *A Quench-Coale* (1637).

The conflict came to a head at midnight on 22 August 1642. Newcomen was chaplain to Sir John Lucas, whose plans to take arms and supporters to the king were exposed. Newcomen was known to be a royalist, having made it clear in a sermon that he thought that the '*Scots were damnable* Rebells for invading the kingdom' (Walter, 199). Both men were taken into the hands of outraged Colchester people and Newcomen was severely beaten and threatened with death. A considerable quantity of arms was found in Lucas's house, on which Newcomen had made the servants swear an oath of secrecy. The two men were placed in the town gaol before the House of Lords had them placed in separate prisons in London. Newcomen was held until 24 September.

However, in November 1643 Newcomen was presented by the earl of Salisbury, whose chaplain he had become, to a living at Headbourne Worthy, near Winchester. Since he held on to his Essex livings he was charged by the county committee there in April 1644 on five counts referring back to alleged conduct in the 1630s. It is not clear whether he was sequestrated. On 3 August 1646 at St Bartholomew-the-Less, London, he married Blanch Brewer, widow. In 1653 the triers admitted him to the rectory of Clothall, Hertfordshire, another of Salisbury's livings. Following the Restoration Newcomen proceeded DD in October 1660 and was also given a prebend at Lincoln. He died in 1665, the admonition for his will being granted on 20 February. At least two sons, Thomas and Stephen, survived him.

TOM WEBSTER

Sources Venn, *Alum. Cant.* · *Calamy rev.*, 363 · T. W. Davids, *Annals of ecclesiastical nonconformity in Essex* (1863) · H. Smith, *The ecclesiastical history of Essex* (1932) · W. Hunt, *The puritan moment* (1983) · T. Webster, *Godly clergy in early Stuart England: the Caroline puritan movement, c.1620–1643* (1997) · J. Reid, *Memorials of the Westminster divines* (1811) · R. S. Paul, *The assembly of the Lord: politics and religion in the Westminster assembly and the 'Grand debate'* (1985) · K. Sprunger, *Dutch puritanism* (1982) · F. Bremer, *Congregational communion* (1994) · J. Walter, *Understanding popular violence in the English revolution* (1999) · *Walker rev.*, 159 [Thomas Newcomen]
Archives Harvard U., Houghton L., sermons | DWL, 'Minutes of the sessions of the assembly of divines from August 1643 to March 25 1652'

Newcomen, Thomas (*c*.1603–1665). *See under* Newcomen, Matthew (*d.* 1669).

Newcomen, Thomas (*bap.* 1664, *d.* 1729), ironmonger and inventor of the atmospheric steam engine, was born at Dartmouth, Devon, and baptized at St Saviour's Church on 28 February 1664, one of two sons of Elias Newcomen (*d.* 1702), a freeholder, shipowner, and merchant, and his wife, Sarah (*d.* 1667). His grandfather was Thomas Newcomen (*d.* 1652), a merchant venturer and shipowner, who may have led the Dartmouth Newcomens away from the established church to join the Baptists. His great-grandfather was Elias Newcomen (1547/8–1614), rector of Stoke Fleming, near Dartmouth, who married Prothesa Shobridge of Shoreditch in 1579. Shortly after the death of Thomas's mother, Elias married, on 6 January 1668, Alice Trenhale of Kingswear and it was she who brought up Thomas.

Early career in Dartmouth Newcomen is said to have served an engineering apprenticeship in Exeter. No indentures have been found, nor does his name appear as a freeman of Dartmouth; however, it appears that nonconformist apprentices were excluded from the lists of freemen of Dartmouth owing to the prevailing political situation. He commenced trading as an ironmonger in Dartmouth about 1685. Besides local dealings, he traded with the Foleys in the midlands at least between 1694 and 1700, purchasing iron in quantities of up to 10 tons from mills at Cookley, Wolverley, Wilden, and Stourton. On 13 July 1705, at the age of forty-one, Newcomen married Hannah (d. 1756), daughter of Peter Waymouth of Malborough, Devon. Their three children were Thomas (d. 1767), who became a sergemaker at Taunton, Elias (d. 1765), an ironmonger, who married Hannah Waymouth of Exeter, and Hannah, who married William Wolcot, a surgeon.

In 1707 Newcomen either renewed or took out new leases for a number of properties in Dartmouth. The chief of these was where he lived in North Town, abutting Higher Street in the west and Lower Street in the east. There were also some 'cellars or ground rooms' that may have been the site of his workshops, where he was to experiment. Newcomen's partner was John Calley (1663–1717), a glazier and member of an ancient Dartmouth family.

Newcomen and Savery Thomas *Savery (1650?–1715) was a member of a family of prosperous merchants in Totnes. On 25 July 1698 he was granted a fourteen-year patent for 'Raising water and imparting motion to all sorts of mill-work by the impellant force of fire, useful for draining mines, serving towns with water and working all kinds of mills in cases where there is neither water nor constant wind' (patent no. 356, 1698). It was in 1699 extended by twenty-one years to 1733. Savery's pump relied on a vacuum to raise water to a vessel and the use of high-pressure steam to force this water to an appropriate height. The device was limited by atmospheric pressure in order to force water to the vessel and by the available technology to build vessels and pipework to withstand the high pressures necessary to force water to any great height. Nevertheless, Savery developed the principle using two receivers and demonstrated this to the Royal Society in June 1699. In 1702 he published *The Miner's Friend*, in which he described and illustrated his pump in its final form. He appears to have abandoned his efforts at mine drainage about 1705 although pumps for other purposes were installed after this date.

The date at which Newcomen commenced his experiments is not certain. Marten Triewald, who came to England from Sweden in 1716 and met both Newcomen and Calley, was impressed with their engine and assisted in the erection of an engine at Byker colliery, near Newcastle upon Tyne, in 1717. He later wrote:

> Now it happened that a man from Dartmouth named Thomas Newcomen, without any knowledge whatsoever of the speculations of Captain Savery, had at the same time also made up his mind in conjunction with his assistant, a plumber by the name of Calley, to invent a fire machine for

drawing water from the mines. He was induced to undertake this by considering the heavy cost of lifting water by means of horses, which he found existing in the English tin mines. These mines Mr Newcomen often visited in the capacity of a dealer in iron tools with which he used to furnish many of the tin mines … For ten consecutive years Mr Newcomen worked at this fire-machine. (*Marten Triewald's Short Description*)

Another contemporary, Stephen Switzer, stated:

> I am well informed that Mr. Newcomen was as early in his invention as Mr. Savery was in his, only the latter being nearer the court had obtained his patent before the other knew it; on which account Mr. Newcomen was glad to come in as a partner to it. (S. Switzer, *An Introduction to a General System of Hydrostaticks and Hydraulicks*, 2, 1729, 325–6)

Writing in 1730, Dr John Allen stated:

> It is now more than thirty years since the engine for raising water by fire was at first invented by the famous Captain Savery, and upwards of twenty years that it received its great improvement by my good friend the ever memorable Mr. Newcomen, whose death I very much regret. (J. Allen, *Specimena ichnographica*, 1730, art. 12)

Newcomen's engine was essentially different from that of Savery and comprised a large rocking beam with arch heads, to which chains were connected. At one end these chains were connected to a piston able to move in an open-topped cylinder fixed above a domed-top boiler. From the other end the pump rods descended into the mine, where they were fixed to the pumps. The boiler produced steam at just above atmospheric pressure, which entered the cylinder when the piston was raised. Cold water was then injected directly into the cylinder from an overhead tank, condensing the steam and creating at least a partial vacuum beneath the piston. Atmospheric pressure then pushed down the piston, raising the pump rods. Depending on the type of pump, this either raised the water, or, when the vacuum was broken by the admission of more steam, allowed the pump rods to act upon a force pump as they descended. The injection water was supplied from an overhead tank, itself fed by an in-house pump operated by a plug rod suspended from a small arch head on the beam. This plug rod also served, by a series of plugs and catches, to operate the levers which moved the valves and caused the engine to operate in irregular but continuous motion. The engine was thus capable of construction by available technology and was enlarged in capacity by the increasing ability to cast and machine larger cylinders and to build larger boilers. The cylinders and valves were at first of brass but from the early 1720s many were of iron.

Savery demonstrated his pump with two receivers to the Royal Society in June 1699. It would seem that a demonstration of Newcomen's engine took place in London in October or November 1712, for in correspondence between John Spedding of Whitehaven and Sir James Lowther in London there is reference to 'Capt. Savery's invention' and 'the engines for raising water'. Spedding wrote, 'I am glad you have found so great a satisfaction in the experiments you have seen for raising water' (Spedding to Lowther, 26 Nov 1712, Cumbria AS, Carlisle, D/LONS/W). At this date mine engineers were well aware of Savery's pump and the reference must be to the New-comen engine.

J. T. Desaguliers referred to what is recognized as New-comen's first successful engine, built in 1712:

About the year 1710 Thomas Newcomen, Ironmonger and John Calley, glazier, of Dartmouth, ... anabaptists, made then several experiments in private, and having brought [their engine] to work with a piston, &c, in the latter end of the year 1711 made proposals to draw the water at Griff, in Warwickshire; but their invention meeting not with reception, in March following, throu' the acquaintance of Mr. Potter of Bromsgrove, in Worcestershire, they bargain'd to draw water for Mr. Back of Wolverhampton where, after a great many laborious attempts, they did make the engine work; but not being either philosophers to understand the reason, or mathematicians enough to calculate the powers and to proportion the parts, very luckily by accident found what they sought for. (J. T. Desaguliers, *Experimental Philosophy*, 2, 1744, 532)

Desaguliers stated that the condensation by injection of water inside the cylinder (rather than outside, according to Savery's practice) was discovered accidentally, and that the engine was rendered self-acting by the ingenuity of Humphrey Potter, a boy employed to mind the engine, who contrived a series of catches and strings worked from the beam, by which the several valves were opened and closed in due order.

The accuracy of some aspects of Desaguliers's accounts has been questioned and extensive research has failed to establish the identity of 'Mr. Back'. The engine was certainly fully self-acting by 1717 as depicted in a print by Henry Beighton that year.

It is known that the 1712 engine was built on a site in or near Lady Meadow, Coneygree coalworks, Tipton, Staffordshire, within sight of Dudley Castle, therefore becoming known as the 'Dudley Castle Engine'.

The engine is shown on a print of 1719 by Thomas Barney of Wolverhampton which has explanatory text detailing all the parts and quoting many sizes. The cylinder is 21 inches in diameter and 7 feet 10 inches high, and the engine made twelve strokes per minute, each stroke lifting 10 gallons through 51 yards perpendicularly.

Newcomen's engine gains acceptance Following the undoubted success of this engine a number of others were built in which Newcomen himself was involved. They included those at Griff colliery, Warwickshire, April 1714; Bilston, 1714; Woods mine, Hawarden, Flintshire, 1714–15; Moore Hall, Austhorpe, Leeds (where John Calley became ill and died), 1714–15; and Stone Pitts, Whitehaven, Cumberland, November 1715.

After Savery's death a joint-stock company was launched, known as the 'Proprietors of the invention for raising water by fire'. The nature of Newcomen's association with Savery within his broad patent becomes clear from an opinion dated 1 July 1720 by Sir Thomas Pengelley, a leading lawyer who stated:

Thomas Savery ... divided the profit to arise by his invention into 60 shares and sold divers of them ... and after his death ... his executors sold all the rest. One Mr. Newcomen having made considerable improvements to the said invention, the Proprietors in 1716 came to an agreement amongst

themselves and with the said Newcomen and by indenture in persuance of articles made between Savery and Newcomen they agreed to add 20 shares to the 60 which were to be had by Newcomen in full of his improvement and of the said agreement. (BL, Add. MS 22675, fols. 27–28)

Shortly afterwards the *London Gazette* (11–14 August 1716) announced:

Whereas the invention for raising water by the impellant force of fire, authorized by Parliament, is lately brought to the greatest perfection, and all sorts of mines, &c., may be thereby drained and water raised to any height with more ease and less charge than by the other methods hitherto used, as is sufficiently demonstrated by diverse engines of this invention now at work in the several counties of Stafford, Warwick, Cornwall, and Flint. These are therefore, to give notice that if any person shall be desirous to treat with the proprietors for such engines, attendance will be given for that purpose every Wednesday at the Sword Blade Coffee House in Birchin Lane, London.

All the counties mentioned are known to have had Newcomen engines, though the site of that in Cornwall remains uncertain.

The proprietors also licensed others for royalties to build engines including in the United Kingdom, Stonier Parrott, George Sparrow, Henry Beighton, members of the Potter and Hornblower families, and Henry Lambton, together with others abroad. The spread of the use of the engine was both remarkably rapid and widespread, some 104 being known before the expiry of the patent in 1733.

Newcomen was in Bristol in 1722 where he went 'designing to turn his engines or part of them into cash' (PRO, C11/1247/38, 39). In 1725 he wrote from Dartmouth to Lord Chief Justice King concerning 'a new invented wind engine' ('A holograph letter'). He spent much time in London during 1727–8 and is also recorded as being at the foundry of Harrison and Waylett, London, on 29 January 1728. Perhaps his last official document was on 5 July 1729, when William Baddiford was bound to Arthur Holdsworth and Thomas Newcomen for £61.

Final years and death Newcomen was involved with the engine and other inventions for the remainder of his life. He was strong in his Baptist faith throughout, as indicated by a letter to his wife in December 1727, and by his acting as pastor at Dartmouth. That he was well respected can be seen by references in correspondence between James Lowther and John Spedding at Whitehaven where 'nothing was wanting to be explained or can admit of disputes afterwards' (Spedding to Lowther, 7 Oct 1715, Cumbria AS, Carlisle, D/LONS/W/MISC), and 'There is nothing that will do our business so well and be less liable to accidents than the engine, and ... 'tis the cheapest, safest and best way of keeping the colliery dry' (ibid., 7 Jan 1719).

Lowther further commented, in February 1727, 'Mr. Newcomen is a perfect honest man and had helpt to make this matter easy, he owns none of the rest that had Fire Engines have bin so fair with them as we have' (Lowther to Spedding, 18 Feb 1727, Cumbria AS, Carlisle, D/LONS/W/MISC) and in February 1728, 'I have a letter this day from honest Mr. Newcomen' (ibid., 6 Feb 1728). 'We have bin very successful from first to last in the timeing of things about the Fire Engine, which I should hardly have ventured upon if I had not mett with such a very honest good man as Mr. Newcomen who I believe would not wrong any body to gain ever so much' (Devon RO, DD 68495, no. 4320). Newcomen died on 5 August 1729 in London, at the house of Edward Wallin. He had the advice of two 'Skilful Physitians' every day and a nurse continually with him and he departed 'without a sigh or groan'. The *Monthly Chronicle* noted 'About the same time [7 August] died Mr. Thomas Newcomen, sole inventor of that surprising machine for raising water by fire' (*Monthly Chronicle*, 2 Aug 1729, 169). He was buried on 8 August in the nonconformist burial-ground at Bunhill Fields, Finsbury, London.

Although improvements were made to the details and workmanship, Newcomen's engine remained little changed for almost three-quarters of a century until it was gradually superseded by that of Watt, with a separate condenser, patented in 1769. Even then many Newcomen type engines continued to be built.   JOHN S. ALLEN

Sources L. T. C. Rolt and J. S. Allen, *The steam engine of Thomas Newcomen*, [rev. edn] (1977); repr. (1997) · J. S. Allen, 'The 1712 and other Newcomen engines of the earls of Dudley', *Transactions* [Newcomen Society], 37 (1964–5), 57–84, pls. I, II · J. S. Allen, 'Some early Newcomen engines and the legal disputes surrounding them', *Transactions* [Newcomen Society], 41 (1968–9), 181–201 · J. S. Allen, 'The introduction of the Newcomen engine from 1710–1733', *Transactions* [Newcomen Society], 42 (1969–70), 169–90 · J. S. Allen, 'The introduction of the Newcomen engine from 1710–1733', *Transactions* [Newcomen Society], 43 (1970–71), 199–202 [first addenda] · J. S. Allen, 'The introduction of the Newcomen engine from 1710–1733', *Transactions* [Newcomen Society], 45 (1972–3), 223–6 [second addenda] · J. S. Allen, 'Bromsgrove and the Newcomen engine', *Transactions* [Newcomen Society], 43 (1970–71), 183–98, pl. XLI · J. S. Allen, 'The 1715 and other Newcomen engines at Whitehaven, Cumberland', *Transactions* [Newcomen Society], 45 (1972–3), 237–68, pls. XXXVI, XXXVII · J. S. Allen, 'Thomas Newcomen (1663/4–1729) and his family', *Transactions* [Newcomen Society], 51 (1979–80), 11–24 · J. M. H. Elton and J. S. Allen, 'Edward Short and the Newcomen engine at Bilston, Staffs.', *Transactions* [Newcomen Society] [forthcoming] · A. Smith, 'Steam and the city: the committee of proprietors of the invention for raising water by fire, 1715–1735', *Transactions* [Newcomen Society], 49 (1977–8), 5–20 · A. Smith, 'Engines moved by fire and water', *Transactions* [Newcomen Society], 66 (1994–5), 1–25 · G. J. Hollister-Short, 'The introduction of the Newcomen engine into Europe', *Transactions* [Newcomen Society], 48 (1976–7), 11–24 · J. R. Harris, 'The employment of steam power in the eighteenth century', *History*, new ser., 52 (1967), 165 · S. Lindqvist, *Technology on trial: the introduction of steam power technology into Sweden, 1715–1736* (1984) · I. H. Smart, 'The Dartmouth residences of Thomas Newcomen and his family', *Transactions* [Newcomen Society], 60 (1988–9), 145–60 · 'A holograph letter of Newcomen communicated by Conrad Matschoss, Dr. Ing. PhD', *Transactions* [Newcomen Society], 2 (1921–2), 115–17 · Devon RO, Newcomen family papers, DD 68945 · Cumbria AS, Stray colliery papers, D/LONS/W · E. Hughes, *North country life in the eighteenth century*, 1 (1952) · PRO, C11/1247/38, 39 · *Marten Triewald's Short description of the atmospheric engine, published at Stockholm, 1734*, ed. and trans. R. Jenkins (1928) · parish register (baptism), Dartmouth, St Saviour's
Archives Devon RO, family MSS

Newcourt, Richard, the elder (*bap. c.*1610, *d.* 1679), topographical draughtsman and cartographer, was baptized at Washfield, Devon, the second son of Philip Newcourt and Mary Tucker, of Tiverton, Devon. Philip Newcourt was the third son of John Newcourt and his wife, Mary, widow of George Hext, of Pickwell, Devon. On 23 September 1633 Richard Newcourt was granted admonition of the will of Sir Edward Hext, his father's half-brother, and on 16 May 1657 he received permission to act in the same capacity for Elizabeth, the widow of Sir John Stawell of Cothelstone, Somerset, and daughter of Sir Edward Hext. He came to possess an estate at Somerton, Somerset, some time after 1641, where he resided. Newcourt married Anne Gibbs and had two sons, Richard (the younger) and Jerrard, and two daughters, Elisabeth, who predeceased him, and Mary, who married Thomas Spicer of Somerton.

Newcourt drew a number of views of religious houses for his friend Sir William Dugdale. Those views were engraved by Wenceslaus Hollar and published in Dugdale's *Monasticon Anglicanum* between 1655 and 1673. Newcourt's most important cartographic work was a map view of London, engraved by William Faithorne the elder, and published in 1658. Entitled *An Exact Delineation of the Cities of London and Westminster and the Suburbs Thereof*, the map provides a particularly important record of London as it was before the great fire of 1666. Though lacking some of the fine detail of earlier maps, it delineated significantly the extent of the recently enlarged suburbs (Glanville, 22–4). Newcourt went on to produce a map of Sedgemoor for Dugdale's *History of Imbanking*, published in 1662 (Fisher, 2). It is likely that Newcourt's knowledge of the metropolis moved him to formulate first a design to rebuild the palace of Whitehall that was never presented (Colvin, *Archs.*, 588), and later a plan for rebuilding the city following the fire (Guildhall Library, MS 3441). His grid-based plan appears to have been influenced by the ideal city form found in continental Europe. The design comprised fifty-five identical rectangular blocks, each with a central parish church, that were arranged around a large central square, with four smaller squares, central upon each quarter of the city. The lesser squares were assigned to house St Paul's Cathedral, markets, and the Guildhall. Having drafted three 'mapps' and an explanatory pamphlet, Newcourt sent them to his son Richard *Newcourt in London. In a letter probably written in early 1667, Newcourt questioned his son regarding his maps, Richard having failed apparently to submit them to the king for consideration. In practical terms Newcourt's plan was not executed partly because it ignored the existing topography and also because it required the destruction and rebuilding of as much again of the surviving city and suburbs (Brett-James, 299), yet, a postscript in the explanatory pamphlet makes it clear Newcourt would have accepted staged redevelopment. It is, however, likely that Newcourt's grid and block plan was an inspiration for the formative layout of two North American cities—Philadelphia, Pennsylvania, and Savannah, Georgia, established in 1683 and 1733 respectively (Porter, 165–6). Newcourt died at Somerton in 1679 and was buried there, as was his wife, who had predeceased him. In his will, dated 25 March 1675 and proved on 4 July 1679, he left his estate at Somerton, later known as Ivythorn, to his second son Jerrard.   CRAIG SPENCE

Sources J. Fisher, *A collection of early maps of London, 1553–1667* (1981) • R. Newcourt, 'Mapp[s] of the designe for ye Cytie of London', *c.*1666, GL, manuscripts section, MS 3441 • Colvin, *Archs.* • Redgrave, *Artists* • P. Glanville, *London in maps* (1972) • N. G. Brett-James, *The growth of Stuart London* (1935) • T. L. Stoate, ed., *The Somerset protestation returns; and lay subsidy rolls, 1641–2* (1975) • will, 4 July 1679, PRO, PROB 11/360, sig. 89 • *VCH Somerset*, vol. 3 • S. Porter, *The great fire of London* (1996) • Dugdale, *Monasticon* • L. Fagan, *A descriptive catalogue of the engraved works of William Faithorne* (1888)
Archives GL, post-great fire plans, MS 3441
Wealth at death over £203 and property of Somerton, Somerset: will, PRO, PROB 11/360, sig. 89

Newcourt, Richard (*d.* 1716), notary public and author, was the eldest son of Richard *Newcourt (*bap. c.*1610, *d.* 1679), topographical draughtsman, of the Newcourt family of Somerton, Somerset, and Anne, daughter of John Gibbs esquire of South Parrott, Dorset. His place and date of birth are unknown. He matriculated at Oxford University as a servitor of Wadham College on 9 December 1653, but did not graduate. He then became a notary public. From about 1662 he was clerk to Alexander Dyer, a proctor of the court of arches, and was admitted as a proctor of the court on 5 June 1668. In August 1669 he was appointed principal registrar of the diocese of London, holding the post until he resigned in May 1696.

On 25 July 1670 Newcourt married, at St James's, Paddington, Elizabeth, daughter of Peter Lane, rector of St Benet Paul's Wharf from 1662, and vicar or perpetual curate of St James's from 1669. Both of their daughters died in infancy and Elizabeth was buried on 24 October 1672. By 1674 Newcourt had married his second wife, Mary, and they may have lived in the parish of St Benet's, where their children were baptized, although apparently not at Doctors' Commons. Richard, who was baptized in 1675, was the only one of their children to survive infancy.

Using the records in his custody, and drawing on other collections and printed histories, by 1700 Newcourt had compiled a history of the diocese of London, which was published in two volumes in 1708 and 1710 as *Repertorium ecclesiasticum parochiale Londinense: an ecclesiastical parochial history of the diocese of London*. The first volume contains accounts of the cathedral and clergy of St Paul's, the bishops and deans, and the parishes in London, Middlesex, and those parts of Buckinghamshire and Hertfordshire within the diocese. The second volume consists of an account of the parishes in Essex. Newcourt acknowledged the assistance of Dr Matthew Hutton in compiling the lists of the clergy of St Paul's before 1306 and for the parishes drew on a manuscript compiled by Richard Smith. Some time between 1688 and 1700 he also prepared an abstract, perhaps afraid that the full work would not be published: neither the abstract nor his manuscript additions were published, nor was his history of the bishops of England to 1710.

Newcourt and his wife were not resident in the City in 1695 and by 1710, when he made his will, lived in Greenwich. He added a codicil on 6 January 1716, shortly after Mary's death. He died soon afterwards, and was buried at Greenwich on 26 February that year. He bequeathed to St Bartholomew's Hospital two houses in St Helen's parish, London, land at Rotherhithe, Surrey, and Odiham, Hampshire, and £300 in East India bonds. He also left £10 to his sister, Mary Spicer of Somerton. His executor and residuary legatee was Edward Alexander, the bishop of London's secretary, who had helped prepare the *Repertorium*. Thomas Hearne, who mistakenly calls him Thomas Newcourt, describes him as a nonjuror and a 'man of true integrity' (*Remarks*, 2.265). STEPHEN PORTER

Sources LMA, P87/JS/1 • W. A. Littledale, ed., *The registers of St Bene't and St Peter, Paul's Wharf, London*, 4 vols., Harleian Society, register section, 38–41 (1909–12) • 'Act books of the Archbishop of Canterbury, 2, 1666–70', LPL, 136 • R. Newcourt, *Repertorium ecclesiasticum parochiale Londinense*, 1 (1708), preface • *DNB* • PRO, PROB 11/551/54 • *Remarks and collections of Thomas Hearne*, ed. C. E. Doble and others, 2, OHS, 7 (1886), 265 • G. D. Squibb, ed., *The visitation of Somerset and the city of Bristol, 1672*, Harleian Society, new ser., 11 (1992) • R. B. Gardiner, ed., *The registers of Wadham College, Oxford*, 1 (1889), 201 • Foster, *Alum. Oxon.*
Archives BL, additions to *Repertorium*, Add. MS 5833 • Canterbury Cathedral, archives, index and supplement to *Repertorium*, Add. MSS 53, 54 • Essex RO, Chelmsford, draft of the Essex portion of *Repertorium* | Bodl. Oxf., MSS Gough London 15, 16
Likenesses B. Lens, ink miniature, V&A • J. Sturt, engraving (after portrait, formerly in possession of Lord Coleraine), repro. in Newcourt, *Repertorium ecclesiasticum parochiale Londinense*, frontispiece • J. Sturt, line engraving, NPG

Newdegate. *See also* Newdigate.

Newdegate, Charles Newdigate (1816–1887), politician, was born at Harefield Park, Uxbridge, Middlesex, on 14 July 1816, the only child of Charles Parker Newdigate Newdegate, and his wife, Maria, daughter of Ayscoughe Boucherett, of Willingham, Lincolnshire. He was educated at Eton College from 1829, at King's College, London, and at Christ Church, Oxford, from 1834 to 1837. He took his BA in 1849, his MA in 1859 and his DCL in 1863. His father died in 1833, leaving him the estate at Harefield, and on the death of his great-uncle Francis Parker Newdigate in 1835, he also inherited Arbury Hall, near Nuneaton, in Warwickshire. Charles was thus the eventual heir of his great-grandmother's redoubtable cousin, Sir Roger *Newdigate, and the extensive family estates were reunited under his ownership. His mother lived until 1868 and took an intense interest in her son's career.

His father's early death meant that Newdegate entered on adult life already a substantial country gentleman, for whom parliamentary ambitions beckoned. He was first elected for North Warwickshire at a by-election in March 1843, and was to hold the seat continuously for forty-two years. He described himself as 'attached to the principles of the Constitution as established in 1688'. Protestantism and protectionism were to be the two dominant themes of Newdegate's career in a pattern which was early marked out by his opposition to the Maynooth Act in 1845, and his prominent role in 1846 in the resistance to the repeal of the corn laws. After the split in the Conservative Party Newdegate was, until March 1850, a protectionist whip, a post which had particular importance in view of the party's initial vacuum of effective Commons leadership.

Newdegate was, with both tongue and pen, a lifelong opponent of free trade. His speeches in the Commons

Charles Newdigate Newdegate (1816–1887), by Camille Silvy, 1866

were supported between 1849 and 1852 by a series of published letters to Henry Labouchere and J. W. Henley, and in 1855 by his *Collection of the Customs' Tariffs of All Nations*. His essential argument was that free trade caused capital to flow out of the country, and hence benefited foreigners and impoverished the nation. He was to republish some of his earlier statements in 1870, and perceived the depression of the later 1870s as a vindication of his standpoint.

Underlying Newdegate's protectionism was a fervent patriotism, linked to a romantic tory vision of social cohesion, which found its distinctive expression in his passionate defence of the protestant constitution in church and state, particularly against the perceived dangers of Roman Catholicism. Although he collaborated in this cause with evangelicals, his own religion and motivation were of a more traditionally Anglican kind. He was from an early stage an active member of the National Club, founded in 1845 to provide a focus for parliamentary protestantism. In the later 1840s he opposed attempts to repeal the remaining penal statutes against Catholics, and in 1851 he unsuccessfully sought decisive legislative measures against the new Roman Catholic episcopal hierarchy. By 1852 he had had ample cause to recognize that both Lord Derby and Disraeli lacked his own die-hard commitments on protectionism and protestantism, and when Derby offered him the vice-presidency of the India Board of Control, he turned the post down. The inevitable compromises that office would have required were entirely foreign to his nature.

During the next fifteen years Newdegate became established as a leading advocate of the defence of the established church and of unbending constitutional protestantism. During the 1850s he supported Richard Spooner's campaign for the repeal of the Maynooth endowment, and led the eventually unsuccessful resistance to Jewish emancipation. In 1858 he again demonstrated his independence by turning down Derby's offer of the presidency of the Board of Health. Having also declined the offer of a peerage from Palmerston, Newdegate was in the later 1860s a prominent opponent in the Commons both of the abolition of compulsory church rates and of the disestablishment of the Church of Ireland.

Meanwhile Newdegate maintained the wider fabric of anti-Catholic agitation through his active support of the Protestant Alliance and his financial subsidies to newspapers which assisted in the propagation of his views. Increasingly his zeal against Rome became focused in a campaign for the regulation of convents, an obsession driven by his sincere belief that nuns were victims of sinister authoritarian manipulation which deprived them of the constitutional liberties of British subjects. He developed his arguments in published speeches and pamphlets. In April 1864 Newdegate asked the House of Commons to set up a select committee to investigate monasteries and convents. The motion was defeated but attracted sufficient support for Newdegate to feel justified in making similar attempts in 1865 and 1869. In 1870, to his own astonishment, Newdegate's motion was successful. However, the triumph was short-lived because the select committee when it reported in 1871 completely failed to vindicate his suspicions and hence strengthened rather than weakened the position of conventual institutions. Thereafter Newdegate's campaign gradually lost credibility.

The aftermath of the general election of 1880 brought Newdegate once again to a position of prominence, as he mounted a challenge in the courts to the admission to the Commons of the atheist Charles Bradlaugh on the grounds that affirmation was illegal. Newdegate was initially successful, thus excluding Bradlaugh from parliament until 1886, but subsequent appeals on technicalities left him with heavy legal costs.

By 1885 Newdegate's health was deteriorating, while the third Reform Act divided his old constituency. Accordingly he retired from parliament at the general election. His long political career as an archetypal independent back-bencher had been distinguished by consistency and integrity rather than by any significant or lasting achievement. As a speaker he had a stately, solemn, and old-fashioned style, and despite his passionate commitment to lost causes, he held the respect of his contemporaries in virtue of his unimpeachable honesty and his scrupulous personal courtesy. Such qualities led to the suggestion that he might have been a suitable candidate for the speakership; he was sworn of the privy council in February 1886.

Newdegate took an active part in county life, as a justice of the peace for both Middlesex and Warwickshire, as a deputy lieutenant for Warwickshire, and an officer in the Middlesex militia. As a landlord he was conscientious and well regarded, and supported religious and educational charities. In private life he was thoroughly genial and sociable. He was a fine horseman, whose favourite recreations were hunting and shooting.

Newdegate died at Arbury Hall on 9 April 1887, and was buried on 16 April in Harefield church, which had earlier been extensively restored at his expense. He was unmarried and, on his death, his estates passed to his second cousin Lieutenant-General Sir Edward Newdigate Newdegate under the terms of a will which by excluding any Roman Catholic from inheriting sustained the struggles of his life from beyond the grave.   JOHN WOLFFE

Sources W. L. Arnstein, *Protestant versus Catholic in mid-Victorian England: Mr Newdegate and the nuns* (1982) · *The Times* (11 April 1887) · T. W. Reid, *Cabinet portraits* (1874) · J. Wolffe, *The protestant crusade in Great Britain, 1829–1860* (1991) · G. I. T. Machin, *Politics and the churches in Great Britain, 1832 to 1868* (1977) · R. Stewart, *The foundation of the conservative party, 1830–1867* (1978) · Warks. CRO, Newdegate papers · P. Smith, *Disraelian Conservatism and social reform* (1967)
Archives Warks. CRO, corresp. and papers | Bodl. Oxf., corresp. with Sir Thomas Phillipps · LPL, letters to A. C. Tait · Lpool RO, letters to fourteenth earl of Derby · W. Sussex RO, letters to duke of Richmond
Likenesses T. Say, oils, 1855–6, Arbury Hall, Nuneaton, Warwickshire · C. Silvy, photograph, 1866, NPG [*see illus.*] · Ape [C. Pellegrini], chromolithograph caricature, NPG; repro. in *VF* (13 Aug 1870), 66 · portrait, repro. in *ILN*, 90 (1887), 458 · wood-engraving, NPG; repro. in *ILN* (23 April 1887)
Wealth at death £11,616 8s. 11d. in personal estate: probate, 9 June 1887, *CGPLA Eng. & Wales* · £8318 p.a. for Arbury, £2524 p.a. for Harefield, rental income in 1873: will, 1887, Arnstein, *Protestant versus Catholic*

Newdigate [née Fitton], **Anne**, **Lady Newdigate** (1574–1618), gentlewoman and letter writer, was born in October 1574 and baptized at Gawsworth, Cheshire, on 6 October, the elder daughter of Sir Edward *Fitton (1548/9–1606) and his wife, Alice (d. 1627), daughter of Sir John Holcroft of Holcroft. Details of her education are unknown, but she learned to write effectively and to move confidently in the circles of nobility and gentry to which her birth gave her access. Perhaps in an attempt to widen these circles, Sir Edward had his daughter married on 30 April 1587 at St Dunstan and All Saints, Stepney, to John Newdigate [**Sir John Newdigate** (1571–1610)], eldest son of John *Newdigate (1542?–1592) and his first wife, Martha Cave (d. 1575). The bridegroom, himself only sixteen that March, may have been the 'Master Newdigate' who accompanied the earl of Derby on his 1585 embassy to Paris, and he had active kinship ties with leading south midlands families, including the Knollys. However, as a result of Newdigate senior's indebtedness and tangled settlements, his eldest son's substantial maternal inheritance was swallowed up, and the income assured the young couple was very much less than anticipated. Consequently, Anne later claimed, they both lived at her father's expense for seven years. While Anne remained with her parents, sometimes in London, her husband was sent in January 1588 to Brasenose College, Oxford. Here he was joined by William Whitehall (d. 1636/7), younger son of a

Staffordshire gentleman, who was to become his chief steward; neither stayed to graduate.

About 1595 the young couple took up residence at their main estate at Arbury, near Nuneaton, Warwickshire, acquired ten years earlier by Newdigate senior. Although they were newcomers to the county, and at that time enjoyed a notional income of only about £300 to £400 a year (with a further £240 from the rump of the family's Middlesex estate near Harefield), by 1600 John had been placed on the commission of the peace; he was knighted in 1603. He energetically, if not always profitably, exploited all the agricultural possibilities of his estates, and took a close interest in his coalmines at Griffe, but still found time for a strenuous programme of improving reading. His compositions included many pious confessions and resolutions, an address to James I on his accession, an obituary for Warwickshire grandee Sir Fulke Greville (d. 1606), and exhortatory jury charges, replete with classical allusion and biblical phraseology. The calling of godly magistrate to which he aspired proved somewhat compromised by his role as a landlord: in the aftermath of the 1607 enclosure rebellion he was prosecuted, along with other local landowners, in Star Chamber, and encountered accusations of greed and hypocrisy from humbler neighbours.

John and Anne Newdigate had five surviving children—Mary (1598–1643), John *Newdigate (1600–1642), Richard *Newdigate (1602–1678), Lettice (1604–1625), and Anne (1607–1637). Their identifiable godparents—Sir William Knollys (chamberlain of the royal household); Sir Richard Leveson (vice-admiral); Sir John Tonstal (gentleman of the bedchamber); Lettice, Lady Paget; and Elizabeth, Lady Grey—stand testimony to the continuing importance to the family of elevated social connections, and provide some explanation for their survival on the fringes of the upper gentry despite repeated financial difficulties. These connections were largely maintained by Anne Newdigate. Revealed in her account books as a capable manager, she was also valued as a friend and confidante. While still under her father's roof she had received correspondence from Lady Arabella Stuart and Elizabeth Vere (née Cecil), countess of Oxford. Her departure from London to the provinces drew a lament from Sir Henry Cary, but did not result in the isolation he envisaged. Through her great-uncle Francis Fitton (d. 1608), husband of the dowager duchess of Northumberland and a prime mover in the Newdigates' affairs, Anne kept abreast of their business and friends in London. Lady Lucy Percy; Margaret, Lady Hoby; Lady Grey; and Elizabeth, Lady Ashburnham, were among female correspondents; among male, Sir Fulke Greville's avuncular letters betokened deep respect, while those of Francis Beaumont of Bedworth showed appreciation of Anne's epistolary skills and grasp of literate culture. Sir William Knollys unfolded the disastrous career at court of Anne's sister, Mary *Fitton, and confided his unrequited love for the maid of honour, while Sir Richard Leveson, then Mary's favoured lover, wrote in the winter of 1604–5 of attempts to secure for Anne the place of royal wet-nurse. The Fittons recorded their anger at their younger daughter's conduct, and sought Anne's conciliatory skills when great families such as the Egertons took an unwelcome interest in Mary's affairs.

All Lady Newdigate's skills were tested when, in late March or early April 1610, after some weeks' illness, Sir John died, probably at Arbury Hall, leaving an estate overburdened by provision for his children and vulnerable to the depredations of wardship. He was buried in April at Harefield, Middlesex. Leaning delicately on the old connection between her family and his, and emphasizing her own fitness as a devoted breast-feeding mother for the role, Lady Newdigate successfully appealed to the master of the wards, Sir Robert Cecil, for the guardianship of her son. Although she faced powerful competition from the likes of the Harringtons of nearby Coombe Abbey, 'your letter to my Lord', reported Philip Mainwaring from court, 'was so passionate and moveinge as you did not need any better means for obtayninge your desyer' (Warks. CRO, CR 136, B277).

Thereafter, Lady Newdigate rejected offers of marriage (including one from Beaumont) and, aided by William Whitehall, threw herself into maximizing estate revenues and placing her children in society. The same resources of written persuasion and useful friends were deployed to prosecute litigation, market agricultural produce, and seek marriage partners for Mary and John. As its new master, Knollys was the key to influencing wards business, kin such as the Crewe and Croke families were retained to give legal support, Sir Anthony Chester of Chicheley and Sir Henry Slingsby were enlisted in the search for advantageous marriages, and Sir John Tonstal provided an entrée to the royal court, where Lady Newdigate and Mary attended a masque in 1617. Lady Newdigate oversaw her children's academic and musical education with care, took them to associate with the Egerton circle at the Newdigates' former home at Harefield Place, and hired a house in Hackney in October 1615 to ease access to the metropolis. She returned permanently to Warwickshire in the autumn of 1617, her health deteriorating from an unspecified illness which manifested itself in a swelled leg, but continued vigorous direction of family business. She died early in July 1618. She was buried that month at Harefield, where she had erected a monument to her husband extolling his 'faithful love'. Such was her success in managing her family and property that the overseeing of both passed smoothly to William Whitehall, her chief executor, for the remaining three years of young John Newdigate's minority.   VIVIENNE LARMINIE

Sources The registers of the parish church of Gawsworth, 1557–1837, Ancient Monuments Society (1955) · Warks. CRO, Newdegate papers, CR 136 · V. M. Larminie, *Wealth, kinship and culture: the seventeenth-century Newdigates of Arbury and their world*, Royal Historical Society Studies in History, 72 (1995) · V. Larminie, 'Fighting for family in a patronage society: the epistolary armoury of Anne Newdigate, 1574–1618', *Early modern women's letter writing, 1450–1700*, ed. J. Daybell (2000) · W. Yorks. AS, Leeds, Yorkshire Archaeological Society, Slingsby MSS, DD211, DD56/M2 · A. E. Newdigate-Newdegate, *Gossip from a muniment room* (1897)

Archives Warks. CRO, account books, corresp., settlements, papers | W. Yorks. AS, Leeds, Yorkshire Archaeological Society, letters to Sir Henry Slingsby

Newdigate, Sir Henry Richard Legge (1832–1908), army officer, was born at Astley Castle, Nuneaton, Warwickshire, on 24 December 1832, the seventh son of Francis Newdigate and Barbara Legge, daughter of the third earl of Dartmouth. He was born into a large family and was educated at Eton College before purchasing a commission as second lieutenant in the 2nd battalion, the rifle brigade, in September 1851. His elder brother Edward was already serving in the same regiment, and Edward's career in many ways mirrored Henry's own. In June 1854 Henry purchased his lieutenancy, and sailed with the regiment to the Crimea. He was present at the battle of the Alma, in which the rifle brigade was heavily engaged, and in March 1855 was promoted captain in the field and given a company command. He was, however, appointed to depot duties thereafter, and to his disappointment had no further chance to distinguish himself. In 1857 Newdigate was sent to India with the troops to suppress the mutiny. He took part in the action at Cawnpore and the relief of Lucknow. His energy and adaptability apparently brought him to the notice of his superiors, and he was selected to join an experimental camel corps, with which he served throughout the central Indian campaign. Although his service was appreciated by his commanding officer and recognized by the award of a brevet majority, he saw no further active service for the next twenty years.

Newdigate was promoted substantive major in May 1868. In June 1875 he was appointed to the command of the 4th battalion of the rifle brigade, which was then stationed in India. In 1878 in the Second Anglo-Afghan War Newdigate was attached to the Peshawar valley field force. He served throughout the war, but much of the fighting—and therefore laurels—fell to Major-General Roberts, who emerged from it with a reputation which overshadowed the officers under his command. Newdigate commanded the Kurram valley field force from April 1880 until it was disbanded the following autumn, but was disappointed that he had found no opportunity to shine. The campaign earned him a brevet colonelcy and the CB, but was his last opportunity to command troops in the field. His appointment as commander of the 4th battalion having expired, he returned to the United Kingdom, and the rest of his career was spent in several significant but unglamorous peace-time appointments. Between 1883 and 1886 he commanded the rifle depot at Winchester, and in 1886 he married Phillis, the daughter of the Revd Arthur Shirley. They had one son and three daughters. In December 1886 he was promoted major-general, and in 1888 he was appointed to the command of the infantry brigade in Gibraltar. He left in 1897, when he was created KCB. He was made colonel commanding the rifle brigade in June 1897, and retired in April 1898. His wife died in 1906. He died at Northgate House, Warwick, on 17 January 1908 from the effects of a seizure he had suffered a week before. He was buried on 21 January near his home at Allesley, near Coventry. Newdigate's career in many ways typified the late

Victorian officer class; he was a competent soldier who lacked the flair and luck to achieve popular renown and royal favour, but instead progressed steadily through service in a number of campaigns and peace-time posts to achieve high rank.   IAN KNIGHT

Sources *The Times* (18 Jan 1908) · *WWW*
Archives Warks. CRO, letters incl. those to his brother Francis William
Wealth at death £4509 13s. 3d.: resworn probate, 15 Feb 1908, *CGPLA Eng. & Wales*

Newdigate [Newdegate], **John** (1542?–1592), landowner, was born at Beaconsfield, Buckinghamshire, probably on 2 February 1542, the eldest and only surviving son of John Newdigate (1513–1565), lawyer, of Lincoln's Inn and of Harefield, Middlesex, and of his first wife, Mary, daughter of Robert Cheney of Chesham Bois, Buckinghamshire. From Eton College he was admitted on 25 August 1559 as a king's scholar to King's College, Cambridge. His admission to Lincoln's Inn on 23 January 1557 had probably been honorary, during his father's readership: unlike his ancestors, who had for several generations augmented their income from estates in Surrey and Middlesex by pursuing successful careers as lawyers, Newdigate began an academic life. He contributed verses celebrating Martin Bucer, Paul Fagius, and the restoration of religion in Britain to a Cambridge University collection of 1560, later published in Basel as *Martini Buceri scripta Anglicana fere omnia* (1577). He became a fellow of King's in 1562, graduated BA early in 1564, and then went to the University of Prague, where he may have proceeded MA. However, following the death of his father on 16 August 1565, his studies were cut short and he returned to England to take possession of his inheritance.

On 7 December 1568 at Harefield, Newdigate married Martha (d. 1575), daughter and coheir of Anthony Cave of Chicheley, Buckinghamshire, and of Elizabeth (*née* Lovett), who as a widow had become his father's second wife in 1559 or 1560. Visitations credit the couple with eleven children, but given the brevity of their marriage this is implausible; only two sons and a daughter are known to have survived infancy—John *Newdigate (1571–1610) [*see under* Newdigate, Anne], William (1571–1587×92), and Crisolde or Grisell. Newdigate had first been mooted as a possible MP (for Clitheroe) while still at Cambridge. In 1571, his wealth and status enhanced by his marriage, he entered the Commons as junior knight of the shire for Middlesex, the senior knight being his uncle, Francis Newdigate, first steward and then husband of Anne, dowager duchess of Somerset. Neither was active in the house, but from about 1573 John was a JP of the quorum for his county.

Newdigate's career had reached its apex. Following Martha's death on 22 November 1575, he embarked on a series of injudicious marriages, financially crippling lawsuits, and effectively fraudulent property transactions. Some time before 1580 he married Mary Smith, reputedly Martha's gentlewoman. She 'brought nothing' to the family, her stepson John later claimed, '& what ruines followed her entry ther are to[o] many witnesses' (Warks.

CRO, CR 136, B1273). Before December 1584 the couple had two sons, Henry (d. 1629) and Robert (d. 1592×1604). By 1586 Mary had died and Newdigate had married Winifred Wells, who came from Staffordshire; a daughter, Winifred, was baptized at St Andrew's, Holborn, on 8 July that year. At an unknown date Newdigate also fathered a son, Rawley (d. 1642), absent from extant family settlements and attendant legal wrangles but amicably recognized by his eldest stepbrother.

Newdigate's evident expectations of providing for his various children partly by his uncle Francis's generosity were challenged when, on Francis's death in January 1582, his lands in Westminster, Surrey, Staffordshire, and Lincolnshire proved to have been bequeathed to the Seymour family. Disputing the circumstances of the will, Newdigate took on the earl of Hertford and became embroiled in long-drawn-out legal arbitration. Outlawed for debt in 1584, the following year he exchanged the core of his valuable Harefield estate for the more modest estate at Arbury, near Nuneaton, Warwickshire, belonging to Sir Edmund Anderson, chief justice of common pleas. This failed to arrest his financial decline. In April 1587 he made a good match for his eldest son, John, with Anne, daughter of Sir Edward Fitton, but secured it by making settlements on the young couple which were incompatible both with arrangements for his other dependants and with the desperate money-raising expedients of high entry fines and wood-felling implemented at Arbury. Settlements were further compromised in April 1591 when Newdigate mortgaged all his manors in Buckinghamshire, Warwickshire, and Middlesex to Sir George Cary for £2000. In December the privy council ordered an investigation of Fitton's allegations of conspiracy by Newdigate and his kinsman John Croke of Studley to circumvent his other obligations in order to provide for Crisolde's marriage to Croke's neighbour Edmund Shillingford or Izard.

His affairs tortuously entangled, Newdigate died, perhaps in the Fleet prison, London, on 26 February 1592, and was buried the same day at St Mildred Poultry. Within weeks his widow remarried: described as of Chignall Mary and James, Essex, on 22 March she obtained a licence to marry Walter Stanley of Brackenborough, Middlesex. After some difficulty, the Stanleys obtained Winifred's jointure, and continued to enjoy it for many years. Newdigate's surviving children were left to fight each other in the courts over their depleted and encumbered inheritances.   VIVIENNE LARMINIE

Sources settlements and papers relating to Newdigate's lands, Warks. CRO, CR 136, B847, B1103–4, B1254–5, B12611–12, B1273–5, B1314, C338, C344, C381, C1717, C1785, C1828, C1909, C2205–9, C2711, and CR 136/Middlesex · W. Sterry, ed., *The Eton College register, 1441–1698* (1943) · W. P. Baildon, ed., *The records of the Honorable Society of Lincoln's Inn: admissions*, 1 (1896) · *Middlesex parish registers: marriages* 5 (1914), 38 · T. Milbourn, *The history of the church of St Mildred, Poultry* (1872), 34 · J. G. Nichols, 'The origin and early history of the family of Newdegate', *Surrey Archaeological Collections*, 6 (1874), 227–67 · N. M. Fuidge, 'Newdigate, John', *HoP, Commons, 1558–1603* · M. Blatcher, 'Newdigate, Francis', *HoP, Commons, 1558–1603* · G. J. Armytage, ed., *Middlesex pedigrees*, Harleian Society, 65 (1914), 67 · J. L. Chester and G. J. Armytage, eds., *Allegations for marriage licences issued by the bishop of London*, 1, Harleian

Society, 25 (1887), 197 • V. M. Larminie, *Wealth, kinship and culture: the seventeenth-century Newdigates of Arbury and their world*, Royal Historical Society Studies in History, 72 (1995) • W. P. Baildon, ed., *The records of the Honorable Society of Lincoln's Inn: the black books*, 1 (1897) • H. W. Pointer, 'Coats of arms in Surrey churches, pt 1', *Surrey Archaeological Collections*, 48 (1943), 61–112, esp. 105

Archives Warks. CRO, MSS, incl. deeds and settlements, CR 136

Newdigate, Sir John (1571–1610). *See under* Newdigate, Anne, Lady Newdigate (1574–1618).

Newdigate, John (1600–1642), gentleman and diarist, was born on 28 May 1600, the elder son and second child of John (later Sir John) *Newdigate (1571–1610) [*see under* Newdigate, Anne], of Arbury, Warwickshire, and his wife, Anne *Newdigate (1574–1618), daughter of Sir Edward *Fitton (*d.* 1606) and Alice Holcroft. From 1607 he was with his younger brother Richard *Newdigate (1602–1678) educated at home by Henry Simpson, an Oxford graduate. Following the death of his father in 1610 his mother obtained his wardship and actively, if unsuccessfully, sought for him both a bride and a knighthood before she too died, in July 1618. Newdigate then passed into the guardianship of her executor, the family steward and friend, William Whitehall (*d.* 1637).

On 17 October 1618 Newdigate and his brother were admitted to Trinity College, Oxford, from where they matriculated on 6 November. Under the tutelage of Robert Skinner, future bishop of Worcester, they studied a broad curriculum and began lasting friendships with several midlands gentlemen, most notably Gilbert Sheldon, the future archbishop; Newdigate did not participate in any of the formal degree exercises. He was entered in the pension book of Gray's Inn in July 1620 but it was the Inner Temple to which he went in November and to which, on 28 January 1621, he gained a special admittance at the request of his kinsman Paul Ambrose Croke. By prior arrangement he shared with Edward Holte, the son of Sir Thomas Holte of Aston near Birmingham, chambers that had been Sir Thomas Coventry's. Although as a consequence of wardship and other business Newdigate gave constant attention to litigation and to his retained lawyers, who included members of the Croke and Crewe families, there is no evidence that he studied for the bar. Instead, he cultivated his social contacts, continued his lute lessons, and patronized London theatres.

Shortly after attaining his majority, on 27 June 1621 Newdigate married at St Dunstan and All Saints, Stepney, Susanna (*bap.* 2 Jan 1597, *d.* 1654), only surviving child of Arnold *Lulls (*fl.* 1584–1642), goldsmith and jeweller, and his first wife, Susanna de Beste (*d.* 1597). Lulls offered a handsome £5350 portion with his daughter, while Newdigate and his trustees, William Whitehall and Sir John Tonstal of Croydon, urgently sought cash to discharge debts and to supply John's siblings' portions. However, it became increasingly evident through the 1620s that the full sum promised by Lulls would not materialize, despite Richard Newdigate's efforts to extract it from various guarantors among the London Dutch community, and the insecurity that had characterized Newdigate finances in previous generations continued. None the less Newdigate remained on good terms with his father-in-law, who through the decade served as one of his sources of news from London and abroad.

Following their marriage John and Susanna Newdigate took up residence at Arbury: a stillborn son was buried there in 1622, and probably another in 1623. In the year from November 1625 Newdigate served as sheriff of Warwickshire, and by 1630 he was on the commission of the peace. Probably through the influence of his kin in the north-west he was elected to the 1628 parliament as member for Liverpool. After taking his seat in the company of many friends and cousins he annotated the stirring sermons given to the Commons by Richard Sibbes and others, and kept a diary of the proceedings. However, while he captured the apocalyptic mood of the moment, was well informed about the national and international political scene, and successfully resisted payment of the unpopular distraint of knighthood, Newdigate does not seem to have desired a public life: he was an inactive magistrate, increasingly absent from Warwickshire.

For a time Newdigate energetically pursued mixed farming at Arbury, and between 1623 and 1627 on a leased estate at Dallington, Northamptonshire. Horse breeding and racing became a particular passion. Coalmining at Griffe brought fluctuating returns and in 1632 a reprimand from the privy council for undermining the public highway. By this date, however, Newdigate had begun selling and mortgaging his property and was living mainly at Ashtead, Surrey. In March 1633 he moved to a farm in Croydon, finally leasing out the Arbury estate in 1637. At Croydon he planted fruit trees obtained from the Tradescants at Lambeth, acquired pictures, bought contemporary books and (especially) plays, and collected and wrote verse. There is some inconclusive evidence that he was involved in playwriting in the 1620s, and Gilbert Sheldon as early as 1623 noted his friend's fondness for 'strong lines'. The influence of John Donne and in particular of his *Paradoxes* is evident in Newdigate's commonplace book, notably in a poem of his own composition 'Upon a painted gentlewoman', dated August 1637. The death that year of Jane, Lady Burdett, who had been at the centre of a literary circle to which Newdigate evidently belonged, prompted his only printed work. Appended to Thomas Calvert's funeral sermon, *The Wearie Souls Wish*, finally published in 1650, were celebratory verses by, among others, Newdigate and his friend Sir George Gresley of Drakelowe; the former's contribution was a robust depiction of a scholarly woman.

Gresley and the Burdetts were known as puritans, but in the late 1630s Newdigate's circle also included Laudians. He heard Sheldon preach at the Chapel Royal during Lent 1639 and exchanged presents with his Croydon neighbour, Archbishop William Laud. On 5 August 1641 he conveyed land in his Warwickshire parish of Chilvers Coton to trustees who included Sir John Tonstal and Samuel Bernard, vicar of Croydon; his nephew later endorsed the deed 'for the use of the Archbishop of Cant. Laud, tho not mentioned in the grant' (Warks. CRO, CR 136, C879). In the following year he answered neither the king's nor parliament's summons to arms in Warwickshire.

On 5 November 1642 Newdigate moved most of his goods to London, and, after a lifetime punctuated by ill health, he died on 16 November at his brother's house at Leaden Porch, Holborn. While the truncated Newdigate estates went to his brother Richard, the bulk of his surviving personal effects were left to his wife, and all his books to Gilbert Sheldon. On 18 May 1646 Susanna Newdigate married Simon Edmonds, haberdasher and sheriff-elect of London, at St Antholin, Budge Row. She died in May 1654, leaving to her new husband's family and to her stepsisters an extensive and valuable collection of jewellery, including Newdigate's wedding ring 'of gold set with sixteen diamonds' (PRO, PROB 11/233, fol. 41).

VIVIENNE LARMINIE

Sources Warks. CRO, Newdigate papers · V. M. Larminie, *Wealth, kinship and culture: the seventeenth-century Newdigates of Arbury and their world*, Royal Historical Society Studies in History, 72 (1995) · V. Larminie, ed., 'The undergraduate account book of John and Richard Newdigate, 1618–1621', *Camden miscellany, XXX*, CS, 4th ser., 39 (1990), 149–269 · Bodl. Oxf., MS Eng. poet. e. 112 · R. C. Johnson and others, eds., *Proceedings in parliament, 1628*, 6 vols. (1977–83) · will, PRO, PROB 11/191, sig. 4 · will, PRO, PROB 11/233, fol. 41 [Susanna Edmonds, wife] · W. B. Bannerman, ed., *The registers of St Mary the Virgin, Aldermanbury, London*, 1, Harleian Society, register section, 61 (1931)

Archives Bodl. Oxf., commonplace book, MS Eng. poet. e. 112 · Warks. CRO, MSS

Newdigate, Sir Richard, first baronet (1602–1678), lawyer and landowner, was born on 17 September 1602 at Arbury Hall, Warwickshire, the younger son of Sir John *Newdigate (1571–1610) [see under Newdigate, Anne] and his wife, Anne *Newdigate (1574–1618), and younger brother of John *Newdigate (1600–1642). Having attended school in Coventry from September 1617, he matriculated from Trinity College, Oxford, on 6 November 1618. Under his tutor Robert Skinner, vice-president of the college, he worked diligently and participated in disputations, but he did not graduate. Admitted to Gray's Inn on 3 July 1620, he took up residence that November. An industrious student who frequented sermons, he acted as his brother's London agent and cultivated the family's connections in the City and at the inn, especially the Egertons and Lord Chief Justice Sir Randolph Crewe.

Called to the bar on 24 June 1628, Newdigate rapidly established a profitable practice in chancery. On 2 February 1632 he married at St Bartholomew-the-Great, West Smithfield, Juliana or Julian (*bap.* 1610, *d.* 1685), daughter of Sir Francis Leigh (*d.* 1610) of Newnham Regis, Warwickshire, and Mary, daughter of the late lord chancellor, Thomas *Egerton, first Viscount Brackley (1540–1617). Within a few months the young couple won a long-running lawsuit brought by Juliana and her trustees (including Crewe) against her brother Francis *Leigh, Baron Dunsmore (*d.* 1653), to secure her inheritance. Newdigate raised £6400 on top of the £2600 portion for the purchase of an estate at Theddingworth, Leicestershire, although the couple resided in Fetter Lane, and from 1634 at Leaden Porch, Holborn. Between 1633 and 1650 they

had eleven children, of whom two daughters and three sons survived to adulthood. The Newdigates' personal and professional circle is indicated by their godparents, who included John Egerton, first earl of Bridgewater, and other aristocratic Egertons and Leighs; the courtiers Mary Curson, countess of Dorset, and George Goring, Lord Goring; and the office-holder Sir William Slingsby.

In 1642 Newdigate took a lieutenancy of horse in the parliamentarian forces, but his direct military activity seems to have been limited and short-lived. Following his brother's death that December, he inherited the encumbered family estates in Warwickshire and at Brackenborough, Middlesex, and used his own money to discharge mortgages and other obligations. He was involved in the impeachment of Archbishop William Laud, and in 1644 acted as one of the prosecution counsel in the trial for conspiracy of Connor Macguire, Lord Enniskillen. A bencher at Gray's Inn from 1645, he became a commissioner for gaol delivery in Warwickshire that year and of militia in Middlesex in 1648, served as a JP in both counties and in Leicestershire, and was nominated as a commissioner for the great seal in 1646.

Apparently a genuine religious and political moderate, Newdigate enjoyed the confidence of a spectrum of contemporaries. While temperamentally careful and cautious, he was prepared to take on delicate briefs and to tread an independent line. By the later 1640s he was acting for a number of recusants and royalist delinquents, including his once estranged brother-in-law Francis Leigh, now earl of Chichester. In 1647 he defended Denzil Holles and the other MPs impeached for opposition to the self-denying ordinance and (perhaps at the instigation of his old Trinity friend Gilbert Sheldon) the University of Oxford in its unsuccessful attempts to resist parliamentary visitation. He maintained close contact with Sheldon after the latter's release from prison in October 1648, having stood bail for him, and associated with moderate former parliamentary commanders Basil Feilding, earl of Denbigh, and Ferdinando Hastings, earl of Huntingdon. In 1650 he chose as godfathers for his youngest child both Sir Edward Leche of the Derbyshire county committee and sequestered royalist Thomas Leigh, Baron Leigh of Stoneleigh. His younger daughter Mary (*b.* 1635) was by the summer of 1652 married to George Parker, from the puritan and moderate parliamentary family of Willingdon, Sussex.

Created serjeant-at-law in February 1654, Newdigate was admitted on 23 June, with Parker and German Pole of Radbourne, Derbyshire, husband of his daughter Anne (*b.* 1633), as his patrons. He had already been appointed by Oliver Cromwell on 30 May as a justice of upper bench. It was later claimed that he intended to refuse the office, but was persuaded to accept by politically moderate and royalist friends. If so, they were rewarded when, in the aftermath of Penruddock's rising, Newdigate dismissed the case against the insurgents who came before him at York assizes on the ground that levying war against the protector was no treason in law. On 1 May 1655 he and fellow justice Francis Thorp were discharged, but he was restored on 13 June 1657, only to bail at the western assizes that summer sisters who had helped their brother escape punishment for involvement in the same rising. Reappointed by Richard Cromwell on 29 September 1658 and by parliament in May and June 1659, he continued to extend mercy to similar accused, and is credited with having intervened to save the life of Sir Henry Slingsby.

On 19 January 1660 Newdigate reached the apex of his career when he was appointed by parliament as lord chief justice. In the spring he was confirmed as a JP and a commissioner of the great seal. Irregularly, he was still chief justice when returned as MP for Tamworth to the Convention Parliament, but he may never have taken his seat. At the Restoration he was not reappointed as a justice of the renamed king's bench, but he was recreated serjeant on 23 June 1660. Soon after, according to his son Richard *Newdigate (1644–1710), he became so seriously ill that 'for three months his life was despaired of, insomuch as Dr Sheldon, elect Bishop of London … came from Whitehall every day to pray by him' (Warks. CRO, CR 136, C1946–7). Sheldon appealed to Edward Hyde for Newdigate's restoration to the judiciary, but reported to his friend on 6 November that the crown had chosen to impose a delay as a penance for interregnum office-holding.

Newdigate never regained his place, but his legal practice prospered. On the marriage of his eldest son in December 1665 he settled on Richard all his Warwickshire lands, but still had £10,000 to spend between 1665 and 1676 on property in Warwickshire, Leicestershire, Northamptonshire, and Kent, and thousands more for moneylending and for leases and mortgages in Sussex and Derbyshire. In 1677, after protracted negotiations, he purchased Harefield Place, Middlesex, the estate alienated by his grandfather. That July, in belated recognition of his services to royalists during the 1640s and 1650s, he was given a baronetcy, conferred without payment of the usual fee: concerned that he would be supposed to have bought it, he accepted with reluctance. Prudent, sober, and pious, and absorbed to the end with the efficient running of estate and family business, he died on 14 October 1678 and was buried at Harefield parish church. His widow died on 9 December 1685. Of their sons, Richard succeeded as second baronet, Robert (1648–1694) practised as a lawyer from Hillingdon, Middlesex, and established a landed family in Derbyshire, and Thomas (1650–c.1717) became a serjeant-at-law based in Sussex and Nottinghamshire.

VIVIENNE LARMINIE

Sources Warks. CRO, CR 136, esp. B828, B832, C1946–7 · V. M. Larminie, *Wealth, kinship and culture: the seventeenth-century Newdigates of Arbury and their world*, Royal Historical Society Studies in History, 72 (1995) · V. Larminie, ed., 'The undergraduate account book of John and Richard Newdigate, 1618–1621', *Camden miscellany, XXX*, CS, 4th ser., 39 (1990), 149–269 · Baker, *Serjeants* · Sainty, *Judges* · M. W. Helms, A. M. Mimardière, and B. D. Henning, 'Newdigate, Richard', HoP, *Commons, 1660–90* · R. J. Fletcher, ed., *The pension book of Gray's Inn*, 1 (1901) · [B. Whitelocke], *Memorials of the English affairs* (1682), 101, 679 · C. H. Firth and R. S. Rait, eds., *Acts and ordinances of the interregnum, 1642–1660*, 3 vols. (1911), vol. 1, p. 1239; vol. 2, p. 1435 · W. A. Shaw, ed., *Calendar of treasury books*, 5, PRO (1911), 693, 1429, 1431 · *The Clarke papers*, ed. C. H. Firth, 3, CS, new ser., 61 (1899), 32, 38; 4, new ser., 62 (1901), 284 · *CSP dom., 1677–8*, pp. 206, 300–01 · A. M. Burke, ed., *Memorials of St Margaret's Church, Westminster* (1914), 79 · E. Gooder, *The squire of Arbury: Sir Richard Newdigate, second baronet, 1644–1710, and his family* (1990) · J. Harington, *The diary of Sir John Harington, MP, 1646–53*, ed. M. F. Stieg, Somerset RS, 74 (1977), 42 · J. S. Cockburn, ed., *Somerset circuit assize orders, 1640–1659*, Somerset RS, 71 (1971) · GEC, *Baronetage*

Archives Warks. CRO, letters, notes, and accounts | Bodl. Oxf., letter to G. Sheldon, Tanner MS 41, fol. 94

Likenesses G. Soest, oils, Arbury Hall, Warwickshire · miniature, Arbury Hall, Warwickshire

Newdigate, Sir Richard, second baronet (1644–1710), landowner and mining entrepreneur, was born on 5 May 1644, the eighth child and third (but first surviving) son of Richard *Newdigate (1602–1678) and his wife, Juliana (c.1610–1685), sister of Sir Francis Leigh, Baron Dunsmore, later earl of Chichester. He claimed William Fuller (1608–1675) as his old schoolmaster, and was admitted to Gray's Inn in 1654 when his father was created sergeant. Matriculating at Christ Church, Oxford, on 21 March 1661, he was still in residence in 1662, but left without a degree. However, he retained lasting links with Oxford, especially through correspondence with the dean of Christ Church, John Fell (1625–1686).

After his first marriage, on 21 December 1665 to Mary (1646–1692), daughter of Sir Edward Bagot of Blithefield, Staffordshire, Newdigate settled at Arbury Hall, the family seat near Nuneaton in Warwickshire. Here, in addition to acting as broker for certain Birmingham gunsmiths and drawing up proposals for a canal between the Severn and the Avon, he embarked on increasingly ambitious and costly schemes for the improvement of his estates. To his house were added an elaborate private chapel, grandiose stables, and gardens which impressed his contemporaries. A comprehensive five-volume study of his parish, Chilvers Coton, undertaken for him between 1681 and 1684, provides a uniquely detailed and accurate picture of landownership, land use, and community structure at this time.

Newdigate's particular enthusiasm was reserved for his coal mines, and he considered himself such an expert on them that 'it was morally impossible that he should fail' (Newdigate, *The Case*). His inventiveness extended to the construction of a waterway to carry coal from Arbury to Nuneaton (1687), the pioneering use of gunpowder blasting, and the installation of a 'great water wheel' to drain the pits (1707). The wheel cost about £2360, but soon after Newdigate's death it was superseded by a Newcomen engine. Investment was heavy; returns habitually fell short of Newdigate's over-optimistic expectations.

Newdigate's private writings reveal a pious, orthodox Anglican, and he had friends in the Caroline clerical establishment. However, he had an acrimonious dispute with the incumbent at one of his family's residences at Harefield, in Middlesex, and his uncompromising anti-popery and chosen political stance brought accusations of overfamiliarity with 'fanatics'. Appointed in 1675 to the Warwickshire commission of the peace, on which he was fairly active, he soon displayed wider ambitions. An abortive attempt in early 1678 to enter the war against France brought charges of levying troops without a warrant. His unsuccessful candidacy for a county seat in both elections of 1679 alienated a majority of the Warwickshire gentry, who were critical of his 'country' stance and personal demeanour. In November 1679 the lords Denbigh and Brooke gained his dismissal both from the magistrates' bench and from his position, briefly, as gentleman of the privy chamber. Yet two months later he was offered a peerage and, 'despite abominable foul play' (Newdigate to Conway, *CSP dom.*, *1680–81*, 43–4), reported to Edward, earl of Conway, the vindication of his behaviour at the summer assizes. Elected to the Oxford parliament of 1681, he made contact with Monmouth, but had his considerable armoury confiscated after the Rye House plot and had to work hard after James's accession to prove his loyalty. Restored to the bench and returned to the Convention Parliament in 1689, he continued an active and loyal magistrate to William III.

In the last decade of Newdigate's life, his once affectionate relations with most of his seven daughters and four surviving sons deteriorated. Their petition in 1701 to have him declared insane was withdrawn after arbitration, but rifts reopened after his second marriage, to Henrietta (*d.* 1739), daughter of Thomas Wigginton, contracted on 6 August 1703 but acknowledged only after a court of arches case in 1704. Newdigate's outrage at his 'persecution' was manifested in a colourful, but largely unconvincing, pamphlet in 1707. There were no surviving children from this marriage.

Newdigate died in London on 4 January 1710 and was buried with his ancestors at Harefield. His heir, Richard, whose so-called 'hellish contrivances' (WCRO, CR136, C1977) led to his exclusion from Newdigate's will, inherited by prior settlement an estate overburdened by debt.   VIVIENNE LARMINIE

Sources Warks. CRO, Newdegate papers, CR136 · [R. Newdigate], *The case of an old gentleman persecuted by his son* (1707) · Marriott Letters, BL, Add. MS 34730, fols. 41–71 · *CSP dom.*, *1678*, 84; *1679–80*; *1680–81*, 43–4; *July–Sept 1683*, 190, 201; *1685*, 32, 33, 62; *1696*, 72, 94, 103, 254; *1697*, 240–41, 248 · *JHL*, 17 (1701–4), 47a, 57a, 58b, 70a, 72b, 73b · *JHC*, 10 (1688–93) · *Warwick County Records (Quarter Sessions, 1674–1682)*, 7 (1946) · *Warwick County Records (Quarter Sessions, 1682–1690)*, 8 (1953) · *Warwick County Records (Quarter Sessions, 1690–1696)*, 9 (1964) · Foster, *Alum. Oxon.*, *1500–1714*, 3.1060 · J. Foster, *The register of admissions to Gray's Inn, 1521–1889, together with the register of marriages in Gray's Inn chapel, 1695–1754* (privately printed, London, 1889), 266 · A. W. A. White, *Men and mining in Warwickshire* (1970) · E. Gooder, *The squire of Arbury: Sir Richard Newdigate, second baronet, 1644–1710, and his family* (1990) · J. Houston, ed., *Index of cases in the records of the court of arches*, British RS, 85 (1972), 278 · *CSPD*, *1680–1*, 43–4 · Will of Sir Richard Newdigate, WCRO, CR136, C1977 [probate copy] · *WCRO*, CR136 B262–4 · *CPSD* (1679–80), 280 · Lady Newdigate-Newdegate [A. E. Garnier], *Cavalier and puritan in the days of the Stuarts* (1901)
Archives Warks. CRO, corresp., diaries, personal accounts, and papers · Warks. CRO, Arbury Library, commonplace book, M. I. 351/7: item 35 | Folger, Newsletters from Sir Joseph Williamson and others to Newdigate, his father and ?, 1674–1715, MSS L. c. 1–3950 · Folger, letters, incl. to Sir Walter Bagot, MS X.d.435
Likenesses P. Lely, oils, Arbury Hall, Nuneaton, Warwickshire
Wealth at death estate rental *c.*£5500 p.a., but debts of £56,256 10s: Gooder, *Squire of Arbury*, 179–90; Warks. CRO, CR136, C1978

Newdigate, Sir Roger, fifth baronet (1719–1806), politician and architect, was born on 20 May 1719 at his family's seat, Arbury Hall, Warwickshire, the seventh son and the youngest of the eleven children of Sir Richard Newdigate, third baronet (1668–1727), landowner, and his second wife, Elizabeth (1681–1765), the daughter of Sir Roger Twisden, second baronet, of Bradbourne, Kent. He was educated at Westminster School (1727–35), and while there inherited the baronetcy, upon the death, in 1734 at the age of nineteen, of his last surviving brother, Sir Edward Newdigate, fourth baronet. He matriculated at University College, Oxford, on 9 April 1736, having earlier been rejected by the whig-inclined Christ Church, possibly on account of his friendship with the tory MP for Oxford University, William Bromley. Shortly after being awarded an MA on 16 May 1738, he embarked upon his first grand tour (1738–40), beginning with an element of formal instruction at Angers, western France. Throughout his life he was an earnest scholar, and during his grand tour filled notebooks with sketches and detailed descriptions of the architectural sights of Italy, taking a particular interest in the Roman period. He married on 31 May 1743 Sophia (1718–1774), the daughter of the politician Edward Conyers and his wife, Mathilda Fermor, and the sister of John Conyers, tory MP for Reading. Following her death on 9 July 1774, he returned to Italy for a second grand tour (1774–6), and amassed a large collection of paintings, statues, and other artefacts, including two candelabra from Hadrian's villa, which he donated to Oxford University. He also made the acquaintance of the antiquary and artist Giovanni Piranesi; Newdigate purchased the Italian's works and they studied together over several months. After returning home he married his second wife, Hester Mundy (1737–1800), on 3 June 1776; she was the daughter of Edward Mundy and Hester Miller of Shipley, Derbyshire.

Newdigate was an early exponent of the Gothic revival in architecture and, beginning in 1748, was, over the course of fifty years, to remodel Arbury Hall, hitherto a conventional Elizabethan mansion, into 'the most impressive 18th-century Gothic house in England, Horace Walpole's Strawberry Hill not excepted' (Tyack, 9). He employed several architects to assist him in effecting this transformation, notably Sanderson Miller, Henry Keene, and Henry Couchman, but virtually every detail was approved by and inspired by Newdigate himself. Dramatic fan vaulting and the juxtaposition of classical statues in Gothic niches decorate the house's interior.

Newdigate's passion for Gothic architecture was also evident in the substantial contribution he made to the design and funding of alterations to the interior of the dining hall at University College, Oxford, in 1766, and also in his advice to his relation Lady Pomfret during the construction of her Gothic revival 'castle' in London during the late 1750s. Newdigate's friendship with Lady Pomfret was instrumental in her decision to donate a substantial, if miscellaneous, collection of classical statuary, known as the Arundel or Pomfret marbles, to Oxford University

Sir Roger Newdigate, fifth baronet (1719–1806), by Arthur Devis, c.1756–8 [in his library at Arbury Hall, Warwickshire]

in 1755. In addition to his generosity towards University College, Newdigate made substantial bequests to the university itself, including, upon his death, funds sufficient to establish an annual prize, known as the Newdigate, of 20 guineas for the finest undergraduate composition on a classical theme.

Newdigate was MP for Middlesex from 1742, but lost his seat at the general election of 1747. This was due in no small measure to a tide of anti-Jacobite feeling; although Newdigate was not a supporter of the Stuarts, his opposition to the nobleman's regiments raised against the Young Pretender in late 1745 appeared to count against him. As he had issued a warning in the Commons against leaving the country undefended as early as January 1745, and had called for the militia to be re-established, he had reason to feel aggrieved by his defeat and had little involvement with Middlesex affairs thereafter. There was some vindication for Newdigate and a clear demonstration of his sincerity when the militia was re-established for the Seven Years' War, during which he served as major of the Warwickshire regiment. He was a diligent 'soldier'; his leadership and, somewhat more surprisingly, his tact and patience at this time, particularly concerning the animosity between Colonel Lord Denbigh and Lieutenant-Colonel George Shirley, ensured that his regiment was one of the least ineffective of the county militias.

Newdigate re-entered public life in 1751, when he was elected MP for Oxford University (where he had been awarded an honorary DCL in April 1749), a seat he held until his surprise resignation in 1780. William Blackstone promoted Newdigate's interest assiduously in the only

two elections for the Oxford University seats to be contested during this time (1751 and 1768), and the close nature of their friendship can be seen in the influence of Blackstone's writings upon the clearest extant enunciation of Newdigate's constitutional views, his 'Essay on party', with its picturesque description of the constitution as a structure of 'Gothic majesty' altered and 'polished even to Corinthian elegance' by the revolution of 1688. Blackstone also provided Newdigate and his friend and kinsman Sir Charles Mordaunt with important legal advice during their failed efforts to persuade the Commons to declare the tories Sir James Dashwood and Viscount Wenman as the MPs elected for Oxfordshire in the famous election of 1754.

Newdigate was a high-church tory. He was opposed to unnecessary continental entanglements, and in 1757 voted against William Pitt's proposals to pay subsidies to foreign powers. His vote for a reduction in the land tax in 1767 reflected his distaste for high taxes, and his steadfast belief in the independence of MPs led him to vote for Dunning's motion in 1780. Notwithstanding his professed desire 'not to lose the country gentleman in the courtier' (Namier, 72), he had the highest regard for the institution of the monarchy and for George III personally. Indeed, since by the 1760s being a tory had become more a state of mind than denoting membership of an organized party, he turned into something of a government supporter, particularly during the premierships of George Grenville and Lord North.

Newdigate was determined in his opposition to further relaxation of religious disabilities. He pressed for the repeal of the Jewish Naturalization Bill of 1753, and in the early 1770s opposed the proposed abolition of the requirement that students at Oxford and Cambridge subscribe to the Thirty-Nine Articles of the Church of England at matriculation. However, his efforts to compel Lord North to oppose relief for protestant dissenting clergy and teachers from such a subscription had failed by 1779. Newdigate also endured the ridicule of the House of Commons for demanding, almost as a lone voice, that the official remembrance day for Charles I's 'martyrdom' (30 January) be retained—in which, nevertheless, he was successful.

In local and private life, as in national and public life, Newdigate was diligent and devout. He cast a patrician eye over his Warwickshire domain, personally tending to sick tenants, and funded a workhouse and a school in the estate village of Chilvers Coton. He had little interest in fox or stag hunting but was a keen fisherman and member of local bowling and book clubs. His voice carried much weight among the county élite; he was a JP and a deputy lieutenant and in the 1750s played a leading part in selecting Warwickshire's tory MPs.

During the second half of his life Newdigate reopened the coal seams on his estate at Arbury. It was an ambitious industrial scheme, utilizing steam technology and taking advantage of the recent construction of turnpike roads, notably that from Coventry to Leicester, and the Coventry and Oxford canals, all of which he helped to administer and fund. Following his retirement from parliament in

1780 he was to devote most of his energy to these profitable local pursuits, and in his old age he rarely left Arbury Hall.

Newdigate enjoyed the company of women; he was close to his mother, who had brought him up single-handed since he was eight years old, and he encouraged the favourite sisters of both his wives to live with them at Arbury. Although both marriages proved childless, he and his wives shared a love for children, and many of his relatives' offspring were to visit Arbury remarkably frequently. Lady Hester Newdigate went so far as to adopt Sally Shilton, the daughter of a local buckle maker, with a view to training her as an opera singer. This formed the basis of George Eliot's short story 'Mr Gilfil's Love-Story' in her first fictional book *Scenes of Clerical Life* (1858). Although Eliot grew up on the Arbury estate an entire generation after Newdigate's death, her portrayal of him as Sir Christopher Cheverel is a discerning one.

Newdigate had a humourless, self-righteous, and occasionally ill-tempered disposition, and yet was affectionate, loyal, creative, and benevolent. His considerable estate passed to the descendants of his uncle Francis Newdigate (d. 1723) when he died at Arbury, aged eighty-seven, on 23 November 1806. He was buried at Harefield church, Middlesex. His obsessive note-taking, retention of correspondence, and diary-keeping have produced a huge archive whose great scholarly value is marred only by its lack of structure and his minute handwriting.

ANDREW I. LEWER

Sources *The correspondence of Sir Roger Newdigate of Arbury, Warwickshire*, ed. A. W. A. White, Dugdale Society, 37 (1995) · L. B. Namier, *Personalities and powers* (1955) · P. D. G. Thomas, 'Sir Roger Newdigate's essays on party, c.1760', *EngHR*, 102 (1987), 394–400 · A. W. A. White, 'Economic growth in eighteenth century Warwickshire: a study of the rise of the Warwickshire coal industry with special reference to Sir Roger Newdigate (bart.) of Arbury, estate owner and coalmaster', PhD diss., U. Birm., 1972 · G. Tyack, *Warwickshire country houses* (1994) · M. McCarthy, *The origins of the Gothic revival* (1987) · A. Newdigate-Newdegate, *The Cheverels of Cheverel Manor* (1898) · G. Eliot, *Scenes of clerical life* (1858) · G. M. Ditchfield, 'The subscription issue in British parliamentary politics, 1772–1779', *Parliamentary History*, 7 (1988), 45–80 · A. C. Wood, 'The diaries of Sir Roger Newdigate, 1751–1806', *Proceedings of the Birmingham Archaeological Society*, 78 (1962), 40–55 · *Hist. U. Oxf. 5: 18th-cent. Oxf.* · W. R. Ward, *Georgian Oxford: university politics in the eighteenth century* (1958) · J. Brooke, 'Newdigate, Sir Roger', HoP, *Commons, 1754–90* · I. Doolittle, *William Blackstone: a biography* (2001) · *Old Westminsters*, 2.688 · Warks. CRO, CR 136/B 831, CR 136/ A637 · W. Goatman, *Harefield and her church* (1947) · E. Gooder, *The squire of Arbury: Sir Richard Newdigate, second baronet, 1644–1710, and his family* (1990)

Archives BL, corresp. relating to his election for Oxford, Add. MS 38457 · LMA, election diary · Warks. CRO, corresp., diaries, journals, and papers

Likenesses W. Hoare, oils, 1748, Arbury Hall, Warwickshire; repro. in White, ed., *Correspondence of Sir Roger Newdigate*, 138–9 · A. Devis, oils, c.1756–1758, Arbury Hall, Warwickshire [*see illus.*] · G. Romney, oils, 1793, Arbury Hall, Warwickshire; repro. in Newdigate-Newdegate, *Cheverels of Cheverel Manor*, frontispiece · T. Kirkby, oils, 1806 (after G. Romney?), University College, Oxford

Wealth at death sixth largest landowner in Warwickshire in late eighteenth century; coal mines, canal and turnpike stock, and large landholdings in Middlesex; bequeathed estates to great- grandson of his uncle; also life interest in Arbury Hall to another grandson of his uncle: White, 'Economic growth', 45

Newdigate, Sebastian [St Sebastian Newdigate] (1500–1535), Carthusian monk and Roman Catholic martyr, was born on 7 September 1500 at Harefield, Middlesex, the seventh of seventeen children of John Newdigate (d. 1528), serjeant-at-law, and his wife, Amphyllis (d. 1544), daughter and heir of John Neville of Rolleston, Nottinghamshire, a kinsman of the earls of Westmorland. The family was influential politically, and Newdigate was brought up at court. He may have spent time at Cambridge University, and later became a favoured member of Henry VIII's privy chamber. Newdigate married Katherine, daughter of Sir John Hampden of Great Hampden and widow of Henry Ferrers. They had two daughters, Amphyllis and Elizabeth.

Following Katherine's death, Newdigate entered the London Charterhouse. His elder sister Jane Dormer (1496–1571), wife of Sir Robert Dormer of Wing, Buckinghamshire, visited the prior to question Sebastian's suitability for so strict an order, after life at court. Nevertheless Newdigate was admitted, was ordained deacon on 3 June 1531, and had become a priest before he died. His family was exceptionally devout: two brothers were knights of St John, two sisters became nuns, at Syon and at Holywell, and Jane Dormer was renowned for her piety. In the later 1520s Newdigate was himself involved in the confiscation of protestant books in London, where he brought to light the activities of the radical heretics known as the Christian Brethren. The London Charterhouse was at the forefront of the propaganda war against protestantism in England. In May 1535, after the community refused to accept Henry VIII's supremacy over the English church, Prior Houghton and two other Carthusian priors were martyred. A few days later Newdigate and two fellow monks were arrested. They were imprisoned for a fortnight, chained to pillars by their necks and legs, standing in their own excrement to encourage them to capitulate. The king allegedly visited Newdigate, trying to persuade him to recant with alternate entreaties and threats. All three monks stood firm and were condemned for treason. On 19 June they were dragged on hurdles to Tyburn, where they were hanged and quartered, and their remains displayed around the city.

Newdigate is said to have been quite tall, well-proportioned, and attractive. He was lively and pleasant, and behaved with directness and honesty. His courageous death, as one of eighteen Carthusians martyred under Henry VIII, inspired others to adhere to Roman Catholicism, notably members of his own family. He was beatified in 1886 and canonized as one of the forty martyrs of England and Wales in 1970. VIRGINIA R. BAINBRIDGE

Sources M. Chauncy, *Historia aliquot martyrum Anglorum* (1888) · M. Clifford, *The life of Jane Dormer, duchess of Feria* (1887) · J. Strype, *Ecclesiastical memorials*, 3 vols. (1721), vol.1 · L. E. Whatmore, 'The Carthusians under Henry VIII', *Analecta Cartusiana*, 109/1 (1983) · *LP Henry VIII*, vol. 8, *addenda* · N. Sanders, *De origine ac progressu schismatis Anglicani* (1585) · D. Knowles [M. C. Knowles], *The religious* *orders in England*, 3 (1959) • S. Brigden, *London and the Reformation* (1989)

Newell, Edward John (1771–1798), informer, was born on 29 June 1771 at Downpatrick, co. Down, Ireland, one of two children of Robert Newell and his wife, who were both of Scottish extraction. His rebellious youth in Dublin led to an estrangement from his parents, and he left briefly in 1789 to become a sailor. After returning to Dublin he found employment in a painting and glazing business and later in a glass-staining workshop. Becoming restless, he travelled to Limerick, where he failed in business. His parents refused to help him because of his membership of the Defenders, a secret society. At the beginning of 1796 Newell went to Belfast, where he joined the Society of United Irishmen. Lodging at 61 Mill Street, he worked as a miniature painter and met through business one George Murdoch and his son, Robert, staunch government supporters, with whom he became friendly, so much so that he informed George Murdoch of a United Irish plot to assassinate him. Murdoch reported this to the authorities and the prospect of imprisonment pushed Newell into becoming an informer in early 1797. His deep knowledge of United Irish activity in Belfast made him a highly valuable acquisition. Newell's information was sent straight to Edward Cooke, the under-secretary for Ireland at Dublin Castle.

In April 1797 Cooke sent Newell to Newry, co. Down, in order to uncover United Irish sympathizers there. General Gerard Lake, the northern commander, whose orders were to follow Newell's instructions and accede to his financial demands, accompanied him. Later that month Newell informed the authorities of plans by members of the Monaghan militia to murder their protestant officers. Back in Belfast, the macabre ritual of Newell walking around at night with a military escort, in army dress with his face blackened, pointing out United Irish suspects, led to much consternation in the town. In May his brother, Robert Newell, criticized Newell in the radical newspaper the *Northern Star* for violating every principle of confidence, honour, and manhood. In the same month Newell was lodged, entertained, and financially rewarded in Dublin Castle by Cooke. He provided the secret committee of the Irish House of Lords, whom he later referred to as 'old whores' (Newell, 42–3), with damaging testimony, much of it fabricated. He later claimed that he received £2000 for the information that led to the confinement of 227 men and the forced flight of many others. He was to waste much of his money on a wild and lascivious lifestyle; he contracted a venereal illness in Dublin in 1797.

In early 1798 Newell resolved to discontinue his career as an informer, citing an altercation with George Murdoch as the main reason. He arranged to go to England and resume his miniature painting under the name of Johnson. Newell eloped with Murdoch's wife and lived with her for twelve days before abandoning her and notifying Murdoch of her whereabouts. He wrote an account of his time as an informer, saying that he wanted to make restitution for the perjuries and crimes he had committed. In his *Apostacy of Newell*, printed in 1798 in Belfast and not

London as stated, he confessed to having been bribed into giving information, much of it false, to the authorities. He acknowledged, for example, that the Revd Sinclair Kelburn, one of his victims, was barely known to him, save for a brief conversation they once had in the street.

Newell found lodgings at Donegore, co. Antrim, in the house of one McQuiston, and he began to make overtures towards his one-time United Irish colleagues. He had hoped to escape to the United States, but in June 1798 he was murdered, undoubtedly by United Irishmen. One account states that he was thrown into the sea while being conveyed to a ship bound for America. Another version is that Newell was shot dead near Roughfort, co. Antrim, and was buried in the nearby district of Templepatrick.

KENNETH L. DAWSON

Sources E. J. Newell, *The apostacy of Newell* (1798) • C. Dickson, *Revolt in the north: Antrim and Down in 1798* (1960) • R. R. Madden, *The United Irishmen: their lives and times*, 2nd edn, 1st ser. (1857) • N. J. Curtin, *The United Irishmen: popular politics in Ulster and Dublin, 1791–1798* (1994) • O. Knox, *Rebels and informers: stirrings of Irish independence* (1997) • J. T. Gilbert, ed., *Documents relating to Ireland, 1795–1804* (1893); repr. (1970) • NA Ire., Rebellion MSS, 620 collection • *DNB*
Archives NA Ire., corresp. with Edward Cooke, Rebellion Papers (620 collection)
Likenesses mezzotint, 1798 (after self-portrait by Newell), NPG; repro. in Madden, *United Irishmen*; copy, Down County Museum, The Mall, Downpatrick, County Down

Newell, Robert (1576–1642), Church of England clergyman, was born in Westminster, the son of Robert Newell (d. 1602) and Sybil Neile (d. 1611), who had been married at St Margaret's, Westminster, in April 1575. His mother had three surviving sons from her first marriage to Paul Neile, William, Walter, and Richard *Neile (1562–1640), who had a distinguished career in the church which benefited Newell greatly. Educated first at Westminster School, Newell matriculated from Richard's college, St John's, Cambridge, about 1595 and graduated BA in 1597. Possibly through the influence of the Cecil family, Neile's patrons, in 1599 he became rector of Wormley, Hertfordshire. The following year he proceeded MA, was incorporated with Neile at Oxford, and on 26 October was ordained priest in London by John Sterne, suffragan bishop of Colchester, with letters testimonial provided by Neile and William Baylie, archdeacon of Peterborough.

In 1605 Newell became vicar of Cheshunt, Hertfordshire, a Cecil living which he took over from Neile on the latter's promotion to the deanery of Westminster. It was through Dean Neile (from 1608 also bishop of Rochester) that he gained his first significant clerical appointments—in 1607 the reversion to a canonry in Westminster and, on his resignation of Wormley in 1610, the rectory of Islip, Oxfordshire, a living in the gift of the dean and chapter of Westminster. Following Neile's translation to Lichfield also in 1610, the same year Newell took a Chichester prebend and succeeded his stepbrother as treasurer of Chichester Cathedral (although he seems to have regarded both as sinecures), and also gained from him the Lichfield prebend of Pipa Parva; he exchanged the last for the wealthier prebend of Colwich in 1613. On 17 September 1612 at St Giles Cripplegate, London, he married Elizabeth Clarke, sister of Gabriel Clarke, one of Neile's chaplains; they had five children—Sybil, Richard, Dorothy, Elizabeth, and John.

When it was rumoured in 1614 that he might gain the living of Clifton Campville, which eventually went to John Overall, Newell was described as a royal chaplain. On Neile's translation to Lincoln the same year Newell duly gained a Lincoln prebend and became subdean of the cathedral. That April—on Neile's collation—he attained his most important clerical position, that of archdeacon of Buckingham, a post he held until his death. Again in 1614, Cecil family patronage accounted for his appointment as rector of Clothall, Hertfordshire. In October 1620 Neile, now bishop of Durham, gave Newell a Durham prebend, but there is little evidence that he ever resided either in Durham or Buckinghamshire, where, presumably through local gentry patronage, he also acquired the rectory of North Crawley in 1631. Instead he concentrated on his duties at Westminster, where he finally took possession of his prebend in April 1620; he resigned his Chichester prebend in 1622. He always took his work at the abbey seriously and was part of a group of canons led by Peter Heylin who took over its running after the sequestration of Dean John Williams in 1637.

While Newell undoubtedly benefited from the patronage of his illustrious stepbrother, he appears to have been an able and efficient clergyman in his own right. He served Neile conscientiously when the latter was dean of Westminster and appears to have moved out of his stepbrother's shadow most effectively when in the diocese of Lincoln. It was the latter diocese which seems to have claimed his affections, for his will notes bequests to Lincoln of communion pots and £1000 for the cathedral fabric fund. He also made generous provision for the poor of various places, particularly Clothall, in memory of his wife's family. John Clarke, a fellow Lincolnshire minister, dedicated his *Holy Oil for the Lamps of the Sanctuary* to Newell in 1628. Records of the archdeaconry of Buckinghamshire, including his surviving visitation returns for 1626, 1627, 1630, 1635, 1637, and 1639, suggest that he shared Neile's interest in observing all church ceremonies with due order and dignity, and in aptly fitted surroundings. They reveal a man concerned for order and ceremony, one who insisted that people should receive communion kneeling.

Newell was still treasurer of Chichester Cathedral, when he died on 21 June 1642 at Winchester; he was buried in Winchester Cathedral. His will, not proved until 1646, suggests that he died relatively well off, for he left several hundred pounds each to various members of the extended Neile/Newell family, including Gabriel Clarke, John Neile, and Edward Burby, with whom he was probably staying when he died. His wife had predeceased him. Their elder son, Richard, successively a member of three Cambridge colleges, Emmanuel, St John's, and Peterhouse, at the last of which he was a fellow from 1639 to 1642, followed his father into the church. He succeeded his father as subdean of Lincoln Cathedral in 1641, but was sequestered shortly before his death in 1645.

ANDREW FOSTER

Sources Venn, *Alum. Cant.* · A. W. Foster, 'A biography of Archbishop Richard Neile (1562–1640)', DPhil diss., U. Oxf., 1978 · E. R. C. Brinkworth, 'The Laudian church in Buckinghamshire', *University of Birmingham Historical Journal*, 5/1 (1955), 31–59 · William Neile's diary, Prior's Kitchen, Durham, Hunter MS 44, item 17 · signet office docquet book, PRO, SO.3.5 · J. L. Chester, ed., *The marriage, baptismal, and burial registers of the collegiate church or abbey of St Peter, Westminster*, Harleian Society, 10 (1876) · *Fasti Angl., 1541–1857,* [Chichester] · *Fasti Angl., 1541–1857,* [Lincoln] · PRO, PROB 11/93, sig. 72 · K. Fincham, ed., *Visitation articles and injunctions of the early Stuart church*, 2 (1998) · PRO, SP 16/375/54 · A. Foster, 'The dean and chapter, 1570–1660', *Chichester Cathedral: an historical survey*, ed. M. Hobbs (1994), 85–100

Newell, Robert Hasell (1788–1852), artist and author, was born in Colchester, Essex, the younger son of Robert Richardson Newell, surgeon. Newell's brother, Charles Hazell Newell, was baptized on 1 November 1780 at St Mary the Virgin (at The Walls), Colchester, when his mother's name was recorded as Sarah. After attending Colchester School he was admitted pensioner of St John's College, Cambridge, on 22 April 1795, and was elected scholar on 2 November 1796. He graduated BA in 1799 as fourth wrangler, and proceeded MA in 1802, and BD in 1810. On 1 April 1800 he was admitted fellow, was lecturer from 1800 to 1804, and acted as dean of the college from 1809 to 1 June 1813, when he was presented to the college rectory of Little Hormead, Hertfordshire. On 27 September that year he married, at Little Hormead, Mary Alexander. Their son, Charles Alexander Newell, was baptized there on 8 June 1818. He was for twenty-six years also curate of Great Hormead. He died on 31 January 1852, aged sixty-four. A memorial inscription to Newell was placed in Little Hormead church, where he was presumably buried.

Newell was a good amateur artist, having studied under the watercolourist William Payne (*fl.* 1800). His edition of *The Poetical Works of Oliver Goldsmith* (1811 and 1820), in which he attempted to ascertain, chiefly from local observation, the actual scene of 'The Deserted Village', is embellished with drawings by him, engraved in aquatint by Samuel Alken. He likewise illustrated his *Letters on the Scenery of Wales* (1821), the drawings being engraved in aquatint by T. Sutherland. In 1845 he published *The Zoology of the English Poets Corrected by the Writings of Modern Naturalists.*

GORDON GOODWIN, rev. ANNETTE PEACH

Sources G. Meissner, ed., *Allgemeines Künstlerlexikon: die bildenden Künstler aller Zeiten und Völker*, [new edn, 34 vols.] (Leipzig and Munich, 1983–) · J. E. Cussans, *History of Hertfordshire*, 3 vols. (1870–81) · *IGI* · Venn, *Alum. Cant.*

Newenham, Sir Edward (1734–1814), politician, younger son of William Newenham (1696?–1738), landowner, of Coolmore, co. Cork, Ireland, and Dorothy Worth (*c.*1693–1734), whose father, Edward, was baron of the exchequer in Ireland, was born on 5 November 1734. After attending Dr Thompson's school at Leixlip, co. Kildare, he was admitted to Trinity College, Dublin, in March 1751 but he did not graduate. In February 1754 he married Grace-Anne

Burton (*b. c.*1735), the eldest daughter of Sir Charles Burton, MP for Dublin City. They had eighteen children. It was his wife's marriage portion which enabled him to purchase the lucrative collectorship of the excise for co. Dublin in 1764. He was knighted in the same year for his efforts as high sheriff of co. Dublin. He was equally forceful in combating smuggling in north co. Dublin as collector of the excise, and in countering the Whiteboys in co. Tipperary as a magistrate in 1767.

Newenham's perception, articulated at the time of the Whiteboys, that 'most of the resident Papists of this kingdom would be peaceable subjects' but for the activities of returned 'Jesuits and friars' (*Freeman's Journal*, 9 Sept 1766), caused him to oppose Catholic relief following his election to the House of Commons for the borough of Enniscorthy in 1769. However, it was his opposition to Lord Townshend's scheme to divide the revenue board that caused his dismissal from the excise in 1772. This posed him severe financial problems, reinforced his conviction that the British government in Ireland and America was embarked on a despotic policy, and precipitated him onto a more overtly radical course. Following in the footsteps of Charles Lucas, he oversaw the elaboration in 1773–5 of a 'test' committing electoral candidates not to 'entertain' voters and to be guided in their actions by their constituents. Few were willing to change their practices, but it proved personally advantageous to Newenham as he secured the Dublin County seat that had twice eluded him in 1768 at the 1776 general election. Energized by this and by the example of the American colonists, whose cause he championed, he ensured that radical patriotism had a voice in the Irish Commons in the late 1770s. His influence was limited. He was, he conceded, 'not eloquent enough to captivate the ears of the House' (Black, 3.364), and his policies and egregious manner obliged him to cede to more moderate and to more respectable voices.

The low esteem in which Newenham was held is vividly illustrated by John Beresford's observation, following their duel in 1778, that it pained him 'to risk my life on an equal footing with such a man' (*Beresford*, 1.23). Despite this, Newenham was not without political guile. His attachment of a clause providing for the repeal of the test oath demanded from Presbyterians to a bill seeking to repeal disabilities against Catholics in 1778 ensured its repeal in 1780. In 1779 he played a leading part in the famous volunteer protest of 4 November, which hastened the concession of free trade, and he was a consistent advocate of the reform of the Anglo-Irish constitutional connection in the early 1780s.

Following 'the glorious and full emancipation from the usurped dominion of any foreign legislature' (*The Parliamentary Register*, 1.367), which was how he described legislative independence, Newenham re-animated parliamentary reform by offering a proposal to disfranchise revenue officers in May 1782. This was lost, but in 1783–4 he participated in the Grand National Convention of volunteer delegates and obtained leave from the House of Commons to bring on 'the business of a parliamentary reform'

(ibid., 2.225) before yielding to Henry Flood, who presented the purely 'Protestant reform' Newenham favoured. It was rejected then and again in March 1784, as were Newenham's other legislative initiatives in the busy 1783–4 session, namely proposals for a commercial treaty with America and for protecting duties to relieve manufacturers in Dublin. He also resisted the administration's attempt to 'subvert the inestimable liberty' of the people (ibid., 3.185) by curbing the press, and from 1785 he actively opposed the commercial propositions, the Dublin Police Bill, and other government measures he deemed incompatible with political 'virtue'. Indeed, such was his reputation that the Irish administration intercepted his correspondence in 1784. His contacts with Benjamin Franklin, George Washington, and other international patriots were more a testament to his vanity than to his consequence for, though he continued to articulate the radical proposition that his purpose as an MP was 'to take care' of his constituents, his instinctive conservatism took over in the early 1790s when he opposed Catholic enfranchisement on the ground that it 'would entirely destroy the protestant establishment in church and state' (ibid., 12.190).

As befitted someone who in 1795 described himself as 'a friend to the Protestant ascendancy' (*The Parliamentary Register*, 15.245), Newenham devoted his remaining years to its defence. Having expended the inheritance that eased his finances in the 1780s, he did not stand for election in 1797. He made his last political speech in support of the arch-conservative John Claudius Beresford in 1802. He died at his home, Retiero, Blackrock, co. Dublin, on 2 October 1814.   JAMES KELLY

Sources J. Porter, P. Byrne, and W. Porter, eds., *The parliamentary register, or, History of the proceedings and debates of the House of Commons of Ireland, 1781–1797*, 17 vols. (1784–1801) · *An edition of the Cavendish Irish parliamentary diary, 1776–1778*, ed. A. R. Black, 3 vols. (Delavan, WI, 1984–5) · J. Brady, *Catholics and Catholicism in the eighteenth-century press* (1965) · *The manuscripts of his grace the duke of Rutland*, 4 vols., HMC, 24 (1888–1905), vol. 3 · J. Kelly, 'Parliamentary reform in Irish politics, 1760–90', *The United Irishmen: republicanism, radicalism and rebellion*, ed. D. Dickson and others (1993), 74–87 · Falkland [J. R. Scott], *A review of the principal characters of the Irish House of Commons* (1789) · D. Wecter, 'Benjamin Franklin and an Irish "enthusiast"', *Huntington Library Quarterly*, 4 (1940–41), 205–34 · E. A. Coyle, 'Sir Edward Newenham: the 18th century Dublin radical', *Dublin Historical Record*, 46 (1993), 15–30 · J. Hill, *From patriots to unionists: Dublin civic politics and Irish protestant patriotism, 1660–1840* (1997) · *The correspondence of the Right Hon. John Beresford, illustrative of the last thirty years of the Irish parliament*, ed. W. Beresford, 2 vols. (1854) · *DNB* · GEC, *Peerage* · Burke, *Gen. Ire.* (1976) · E. Lodge, *Peerage, baronetage, knightage and companionage of the British empire*, 81st edn, 3 vols. (1912) · Burtchaell & Sadleir, *Alum. Dubl.*
Archives NA Canada, diary · NA Canada, diary of visit to France | Belvoir Castle, Leicestershire, Rutland MSS · BL, corresp. with Robert Peel, Add. MSS 40221–40238 · Hist. Soc. Penn., Franklin MSS · NA Canada, diary · PRO, letters to William Pitt, PRO 30/8
Likenesses engraving, 1778, repro. in *Hibernian Magazine* (March 1778); copy, NL Ire. · F. Wheatley, group portrait, oils, 1779 (*The volunteers in College Green*), NG Ire.; similar watercolour group portrait, V&A

Newenham, Frederick (1807–1859), painter of portraits and historical subjects, is known to have been related to

Robert O'Callaghan Newenham (1770–1849), but his parentage is unknown. He was born in co. Cork but subsequently moved to London.

Newenham exhibited at the Royal Academy for the first time in 1838, giving his address as 30 Soho Square, London. He was commissioned to paint companion portraits of Queen Victoria and Prince Albert for the Junior Service Club in 1842. They were exhibited at the Royal Academy in 1844 and helped establish him as a fashionable society portrait painter, particularly of women. His portrait of Queen Victoria was presented to HMS *Vincent* in 1959. He continued to exhibit at the Royal Academy until 1855, sending a total of nineteen pictures, most of which were portraits. He also contributed seventeen subject pictures, many of which were large, to the British Institution from 1841 to 1852. Titles included *Arming for Battle* (1841), *Jenny's Lament* (1849), *Cromwell Dictating to Milton* (1850), *Queen Mary Beatrice Taking Shelter under the Walls of Old Lambeth Church* (1851), and *Princess Elizabeth Examined by the Council* (1852).

Newenham's historical picture *Princess Elizabeth Examined by the Council* was in the collection of Salford Museum, but in 1948 its condition was considered beyond repair (presumably war damage) and it was destroyed. Some of his portraits were engraved, including that of George, third Lord Mountsandford, which was engraved in stipple by Frederick Christian Lewis and published by Newenham himself at 3 Thayer Street, Manchester Square, London, in 1831. Frederick Newenham died at Bethlem Hospital, London, on 21 March 1859.   JILL SPRINGALL

Sources W. G. Strickland, *A dictionary of Irish artists*, 2 vols. (1913) · *GM*, 3rd ser., 6 (1859), 548 · B. Stewart and M. Cutten, *The dictionary of portrait painters in Britain up to 1920* (1997) · Graves, *Artists* · Graves, *RA exhibitors* · Wood, *Vic. painters*, 3rd edn · R. Ormond, *Early Victorian portraits*, 2 vols. (1973) · d. cert.
Likenesses engraving (mezzotint), NPG

Newenham, John (*d.* 1390), administrator, was on the evidence of the location and patronage of his early benefices a Cheshire man in the service of Edward, the Black Prince, who presented him to the rectory of Cheadle and the vicarage of Over in 1349, and to the chantry of St Nicholas, Nantwich, in 1353, and who in 1349 petitioned the pope on his behalf. Newenham had business or personal links with three men who were also associated with the Black Prince: Ralph Basset of Drayton, for whom he acted as attorney during Drayton's pilgrimage to the Holy Land (1360–61) and overseas journeys in the king's service (1368); Edward Despenser (*d.* 1375), with whose widow he acted in property transactions; and Sir Thomas Ferrers, a long-serving member of the prince's staff, of whose will he was an executor. Edward III presented him to Farndish, Bedfordshire, in December 1349, to Thundersley, Essex, in November 1360, and to a prebend in the royal free chapel of Wolverhampton before March 1361; the royal grant of Bishophull prebend (Lichfield) proved ineffective.

Newenham perhaps entered crown service *c.*1360, and in April 1361 he and Thomas Minot, a former privy seal clerk, were apparently serving in Ireland. Newenham was appointed a chamberlain of the exchequer on 21 February 1365, and served until 30 September 1369. His duties included the payment of wages to archers guarding the coast at Portsmouth and Southampton in 1369. During these years he served on a number of *ad hoc* commissions—for example, of oyer and terminer in Suffolk in 1366, and to visit four royal free chapels in the west midlands in 1368—and in this decade his ecclesiastical career also prospered greatly; he acquired prebends in the cathedrals of Wells (1363 and 1367), Lincoln (1364), and Lichfield (1365), and the deanery of the royal free chapel of Wolverhampton (1368). A continuing thread in his church career was the acquisition of benefices in Wales and Cheshire: the treasurership of Llandaff Cathedral by exchange in 1360, two prebends in St John's College, Chester (1361 and 1365), the churches of Gumfreston, Dyfed, in 1374 and Wolvesnewton, Gwent, in 1379. Newenham is not known to have held any crown office after 1369, and from 1374 virtually disappears from the public records. He had apparently relinquished all his cathedral prebends by *c.*1380. In 1389 he exchanged Poynings rectory in Sussex for Little Burstead, Essex, his last benefice. His short will left modest bequests to Burstead church and to the rector of St Andrew's, Holborn, Middlesex, and named Master John Dorne, clerk, and Isabella atte Crofte as his executors. It was dated 16 September 1390 and proved on the 25th of the same month. **Thomas Newenham** (*d.* 1393/4), administrator, may have been John Newenham's brother. He is first recorded in 1340, as a chancery clerk, and as a king's clerk was presented to St Mary's, Drogheda, Louth, in 1342, though he was only ordained (as both deacon and priest) in 1370. His most important benefice was the rectory of Newbury, Berkshire, which he held from 1369 until his death, and he also obtained an unidentified prebend at Llandaff. His career was centred upon the chancery, where he became a clerk of the first grade in 1369. In 1371 he received petitions in parliament, while in 1377, and again in 1386, he was one of the commissioners given custody of the great seal when the chancellor was abroad. He had interests in Surrey and Kent, and probably London, and in 1369 acquired property in Warwickshire; he also appears to have been active as a moneylender. Thomas Newenham was still employed in the king's service on 27 March 1393, but was dead by 25 May 1394.

A. K. MCHARDY

Sources D. Jones, *The church in Chester, 1300–1540*, Chetham Society, 3rd ser., 7 (1957) · *Chancery records* · *Fasti Angl., 1300–1541*, [Bath and Wells] · *Fasti Angl., 1300–1541*, [Lincoln] · *Fasti Angl., 1300–1541*, [Coventry] · *Fasti Angl., 1300–1541*, [Welsh dioceses] · M. C. B. Dawes, ed., *Register of Edward, the Black Prince*, 4 vols., PRO (1930–33) · J. C. Sainty, ed., *Officers of the exchequer: a list* (1983) · F. Devon, ed., *Calendar of papal letters*, 3–4 (1835) · F. Devon, ed. and trans., *Issue roll of Thomas de Brantingham*, RC (1835) · Tout, *Admin. hist.* · GEC, *Peerage*, new edn · 'Register of wills of Consistory Court of London I', GL · B. Wilkinson, *The chancery under Edward III* (1929) · *Registrum Simonis de Sudbiria, diocesis Londoniensis, AD 1362–1375*, ed. R. C. Fowler, 2, CYS, 38 (1938) · *CCIR, 1392–6*, 138 · *CPR, 1391–6*, 416
Wealth at death approx. £1 5s. 8d.—bequests: will, GL

Newenham, Thomas (*d.* 1393/4). *See under* Newenham, John (*d.* 1390).

Newenham, Thomas (1762–1831), writer on Irish affairs, second son of Thomas Newenham (1729–1766) of Coolmore, co. Cork, and his second wife, Elizabeth (*d*. 1763), eldest daughter of William Dawson, was born on 2 March 1762. Sir Edward Newenham was his uncle. He entered Trinity College, Dublin, on 3 July 1776, but does not appear to have taken a degree.

Elected member for Clonmel, co. Tipperary, in the Irish parliament of 1798, Newenham was one of the steadiest opponents of the Act of Union. After 1800 he appears to have lived principally in England, at Ellesmere, Cheshire, and at Gloucester and Cheltenham. After the union, he believed that the ignorance of Irish affairs by English politicians would lead to injustice, and he investigated the resources and capabilities of Ireland, in the hope that his published evidence would influence public opinion in England. He became one of the principal authorities on the Irish economy. Newenham also tried to promote the reunion of the Catholic and protestant churches. In his correspondence with James Warren Doyle, Roman Catholic bishop of Kildare and Leighlin, he suggested a conference between ten divines on each side, who should formulate articles of primary importance and obligation as the groundwork of a new catechism, but his suggestion was refused. In March 1825 Newenham was requested to give evidence before the parliamentary committee on the state of Ireland. Unable through illness to do so, he laid before the committee the manuscript of *A Series of Suggestions and Observations Relative to the State of Ireland* (1825), in which he expressed the opinion that the political claims of the Irish Catholics were well founded, but that conceding these claims would no longer have 'a prominent and effectual tendency to insure tranquillity in Ireland'.

Newenham was a major of militia. He married Mary, daughter of Edward Hoare of Factory Hill, co. Cork. They had two sons and a daughter. He died at Cheltenham on 30 October 1831.

Newenham wrote a number of pamphlets on Catholic emancipation and Irish affairs. His book *The Natural, Political and Commercial Circumstances of Ireland* (1808) was reviewed in the *Edinburgh Review* by T. R. Malthus, who criticized Newenham for what he considered a failure to provide hard facts on Ireland's economy.

W. A. S. HEWINS, *rev.* MARIE-LOUISE LEGG

Sources GM, 1st ser., 101/2 (1831), 474 · W. J. Fitzpatrick, *The life, times and correspondence of the Right Rev. Dr Doyle, bishop of Kildare and Leighlin*, new edn, 2 vols. (1880) · [T. Malthus], review of T. Newenham, *The natural, political and commercial circumstances of Ireland*, *EdinR*, 14 (1809), 151–70 · Burtchaell & Sadleir, *Alum. Dubl.* · Burke, *Gen. GB*
Archives NL Ire. | Derbys. RO, letters to Sir R. J. Wilmot-Horton · TCD, corresp. with William Shaw Mason

Newhall. For this title name *see* Pringle, Sir Walter, Lord Newhall (1664?–1736).

Newhaven. For this title name *see* Cheyne, Charles, first Viscount Newhaven (1625–1698); Cheyne, William, second Viscount Newhaven (1657–1728).

Newitt, Dudley Maurice (1894–1980), chemical engineer, was born on 28 April 1894 in London, the second son in the family of four sons and three daughters of Edward James Dunn Newitt, a ballistics engineer, and his wife, Alice Gertrude Lewis, daughter of a craftsman in Windsor. After secondary school at Wandsworth, in 1910 he was appointed assistant chemist at the Nobel's explosives factory, Ardeer, Scotland, which enabled him to attend evening classes at the Glasgow and West of Scotland Technical College, to study for the London University external BSc in chemistry. He passed his intermediate BSc in 1912, and planned to continue studies for higher degrees while being paid as an elementary schoolteacher. The advent of the First World War changed this programme drastically.

Newitt joined up with the East Surrey regiment, and he was drafted to the Indian Army Officer Reserve in November 1914. After some service on the north-west frontier with the 54th Sikhs, he was transferred to the 53rd Sikhs in Mesopotamia, where he shared in the capture of Kut and of Baghdad, battles with heavy losses. For a time he was second in command of his battalion, and he was mentioned in dispatches. He was appointed adjutant in 1917, and shared in the memorable entries into Damascus and Jerusalem. In 1918 he received the Military Cross for his participation in the capture of Samaria, and was promoted major. He continued as a regional administrator in Syria up to his demobilization in 1919.

In 1919 Newitt married Alix, daughter of Angele Schaeffer, hotel owner, of Rouen; she had been a friend of the family for a long time. She died in 1923 at Nice, giving birth to their first child, who was stillborn. After his five stirring war years, and his marriage, Newitt returned to pursue his career in chemical research with tenacity, but under less strenuous conditions. He enrolled as an undergraduate in chemistry in the Royal College of Science in South Kensington, and passed his BSc with first-class honours and a governor's medal for skills in chemistry in 1921. He went on to postgraduate studies in chemical engineering with Professor J. W. Hinchley and research in fuel technology with Professor W. A. Bone at Imperial College. Newitt became one of Bone's leading research colleagues. Together with Bone and with another colleague, D. T. A. Townend, he published numerous researches and a monograph, *Gaseous Combustion at High Pressures* (1929). Newitt obtained higher external degrees at London University (PhD 1924, DSc 1930).

In 1933 Newitt married his second wife, Dorothy Wallis Arthur Garrod (*d*. 1953), daughter of George William Arthur Garrod (Wallis Arthur), a concert party agent. They had a son and a daughter. In the early 1930s established university posts were few. Newitt's first senior teaching appointment at Imperial College was in 1936. Its title, reader in high pressure technology, marked an abiding feature of his interest in researches at high pressures. In 1940 he published a weighty monograph, *The Design of High Pressure Plant and the Properties of Fluids at High Pressures*.

The Second World War stopped any further sheltered academic growth for Newitt, who was appointed scientific director of Special Operations Executive in 1941. In this post he had to supervise the invention, manufacture, and supply of every kind of gadget to secret agents in enemy-occupied country, to further their operations of sabotage. He did not return to university affairs until 31 May 1945, as the first Courtaulds professor of chemical engineering at Imperial College. This highlighted his many commitments in the development of chemical engineering science as a distinctive academic discipline in Britain, including his office as president of the British Institution of Chemical Engineers (1949–51). Eight of his former students later became university professors.

In 1952 Newitt became head of department, and had much to do with the planning and building (from 1954 to 1967) of a large modern home for chemical engineering and chemical technology at Imperial College. He was skilful at delegating and the leader of what he liked to term 'a mettlesome team'. In 1956 he was appointed pro-rector of Imperial College, a post he held until his retirement in 1961. He gave untiring services to the student community.

Newitt's many human qualities made him much sought after for numerous public professional duties, such as council member of the Royal Society (1957–9), chairman of the Water Pollution Board (1950 onwards), member of the scientific advisory committee of the TUC, and member of the Federation of British Industry committee to set up a college of technology at Delhi. For several years Newitt gave powerful support to international collaboration on thermodynamic reference standards, and, in particular, steam tables.

Newitt was elected FRS in 1942. His many honours included the Rumford medal of the Royal Society (1962) and the Osborne Reynolds, Moulton, and Hawksley medals of the engineering institutions. He was appointed a fellow of Imperial College, and honorary DSc of the universities of Toulouse (1961) and Bradford (1969).

Newitt was a clubbable man who astonished his friends with his zest for travelling rough by sea and by land over enormous distances, but whose hospitality in his own home at Runfold made up for this. Newitt died on 14 March 1980 at his home, 21 Crooksbury Road, Runfold, Farnham, Surrey. A. R. UBBELOHDE, rev.

Sources A. R. Ubbelohde, *Memoirs FRS*, 27 (1981), 365–78 · personal knowledge (1986)

Wealth at death £20,273: probate, 30 July 1980, *CGPLA Eng. & Wales*

Newland, Abraham (1730–1807), banking official, was born at either King Street or Castle Street, in Southwark, Surrey, on 23 April 1730, one of twenty-five children of William Newland, miller and baker of Southwark and of Grove, Buckinghamshire, and Ann Arnold, William Newland's second wife. It is not known where he was educated, but his neat hand and his competence in arithmetic secured him a post as clerk at the Bank of England in 1748. Over the years Newland's tireless activity and attention to business carried him through various promotions and he became chief cashier in 1782. His signature on Bank of England notes became so familiar that they were known

as Abraham Newlands. His fame in this respect was commemorated in several popular jingles, one such being:

> I have heard people say,
> That sham Abram you may,
> But you must not sham Abraham Newland.
> (*N&Q*, 442)

When the House of Lords appointed a committee of secrecy in 1797 to evaluate the outstanding demands of the Bank of England, Newland was summoned as a witness. In his evidence, given on 28 March 1797, he gave an account of the Treasury bills due to the bank and of the sums repaid each month over the previous two years. He also described how business was conducted between the bank and the exchequer. After 1799 his growing infirmities obliged him to entrust the management of exchequer bills to a cashier, Robert Astlett, to whom Newland was probably distantly related and whom he had brought into the bank some twenty years earlier. Astlett embezzled some of these bills, and Newland had to give evidence against him at the Old Bailey in 1803, an event which caused him much grief and further hastened his decline.

During his twenty-five years as chief cashier Newland slept in his apartments in the bank. He acquired a small house at 38 Highbury Place, north of London, which he rented to a young widow named Mary Ann Cornthwaite, and to this semi-rural retreat his carriage brought him after business hours. Newland was a cheerful and agreeable companion who enjoyed a glass with friends and the retailing of jokes and stories. He was of middle height, and portraits show him with a somewhat corpulent figure. He was an avid reader across a wide range of subjects. In politics he supported the monarchy. He loved music, and played the violin until prevented by the increasing deafness which had afflicted him over thirty years. Deafness also caused him to give up regular attendance at church, leading some to suspect the sincerity of his religious opinions. Newland held that 'man lived, died, and there ended all respecting him'.

Newland amassed a fortune, said to be worth £200,000 in stock and £1000 in revenue from estates, by living modestly and speculating in Pitt's loans, a certain amount of which was always reserved for the cashier's office. When he resigned from the bank on 18 September 1807 he needed no pension and the directors decided to present him with plate worth 1000 guineas, appropriately inscribed, but he did not live to receive it. He retired to his house at Highbury, where Mrs Cornthwaite cared for him until his death on 21 November 1807. Eighteen coaches followed his body to St Saviour's, Southwark, where he was buried on 28 November. A small memorial tablet was set up in the south choir aisle by Mrs Cornthwaite.

In his later years Newland had made regular annual payments to the most needy of his numerous relatives, and in his will he made further disbursements of his government stocks to provide annuities to twenty-six of them or their children, and to Mrs Cornthwaite.

ANITA MCCONNELL

Sources W. M. Acres, *The Bank of England from within, 1694–1900*, 2 vols. (1931) · J. D. Collier, *The life of Abraham Newland* (1808) · W. Granger and others, *The new wonderful museum, and extraordinary magazine*, 1 (1803), 326–9 · *GM*, 1st ser., 77 (1807), 1086 · Bank of England wills register, 1807, 270/1, no. 40 · J. Clapham, *The Bank of England: a history*, 2 vols. (1944) · *N&Q*, 5 (1852), 442 · *N&Q*, 7th ser., 12 (1891), 78, 172
Likenesses S. Drummond, oils, Bank of England, London · G. Romney, oils, Bank of England, London

Newland, Henry Garrett (1804–1860), Church of England clergyman and author, was born in London, the son of Colonel Bingham Newland. From 1809 to 1816 he lived with his father in Sicily, and from there he was sent to school at Lausanne, Switzerland, to learn French for a year. Newland then returned to England, and in 1823 he matriculated from Christ's College, Cambridge, afterwards migrating to Corpus Christi College and graduating BA in 1827 and MA in 1830. After being ordained priest in 1829, he was, in September that year, presented to the rich sinecure rectory of Westbourne, Sussex; he also held two or three important curacies in the diocese of Chichester until January 1834, when he became vicar of Westbourne.

Always a high-churchman, Newland was greatly influenced by the Tractarians. At Westbourne he introduced a daily choral service and detailed instruction of candidates for confirmation; he built new schools, encouraged membership of friendly societies, and restored the church building. His efforts earned him the nickname the Pope of Westbourne, and during the so-called 'papal aggression' crisis of 1850 local opposition to his innovations forced him to defend them in a number of pamphlets. In 1855 Henry Phillpotts, bishop of Exeter, persuaded him to take up the living of St Marychurch, near Torquay, Devon, with the task of restoring order to a parish disrupted by several years of opposition to Tractarian practices. His diplomatic efforts to calm the situation largely failed, and from 1857 his health began to deteriorate as a result. He died (unmarried) at St Marychurch on 25 June 1860.

Newland's published works all reflected his experiences of parish life. *Confirmation and First Communion* (1854) was a substantial contribution to pastoral theology, while his *Three Lectures on Tractarianism* delivered in Brighton in 1852 were designed to explain and defend the movement to a popular audience; after their delivery he received numerous letters of support. *Village Clubs* (1855) advocated friendly societies, and *Increase of Romanism in England* (1851) was his response to the popular outcry against Tractarians as the originators of the 'papal aggression'. More than a dozen other sermons, pamphlets, and tracts all expand on these themes. GEORGE HERRING

Sources R. N. Shutte, *A memoir of the late Henry Newland* (1861) · Venn, *Alum. Cant.*

Newland [Nailheart], **John** (d. 1515), abbot of St Augustine's, Bristol, was also known as Nailheart, a name that was given visual form in the rebus of a bleeding heart, pierced with three nails between the initials J. N., which he adopted and which appears on several of the buildings for which he was responsible. Nothing is known of his early life; it has been assumed that he came from Newland in the Forest of Dean, but he may have been a member of the Newland family of Long Ashton, near Bristol. He was a bachelor of theology, and in 1502 is said to have supplicated for the degree of doctor from Oxford, although the result is not known.

Newland was elected abbot of St Augustine's on 6 April 1481 and devoted himself to the efficient management of the abbey's finances and to extensive building work. He kept the office of treasurer and cellarer in his own hands, and the surviving accounts show the financial affairs of the abbey in good order with a large surplus of income over expenditure, in spite of all the expense of building. Building work during his abbacy included numerous churches, houses, and barns on the abbey estates, including five new barns in the parish of Berkeley and the fine barn that survives at Ashleworth, Gloucestershire. He was responsible for the reconstruction of the abbey cloisters, prior's lodging, and gatehouse, for work on the chancel, transepts, and bells of the abbey church, and he began the task of replacing the twelfth-century nave, a project that was not completed until the nineteenth century. His concern to protect his abbey's rights over its precinct led to a bitter quarrel with the mayor and officials of Bristol which lasted from 1491 to 1496, when a compromise was reached through the mediation of Cardinal John Morton, archbishop of Canterbury (d. 1500).

Newland compiled a chronicle (published as *Abbot Newland's Roll*) of the history of the Berkeley family, together with notes on the foundation of the abbey and details of the abbots. The chronicle was continued after his death and records his death on 2 June 1515. He was buried on the south side of the lady chapel where his effigy shows him attired for mass, with a staff and jewelled mitre. At his feet two angels hold a shield with his rebus. J. H. BETTEY

Sources I. H. Jeayes, 'Abbot Newland's roll', *Transactions of the Bristol and Gloucestershire Archaeological Society*, 14 (1889–90), 117–30 · G. Beachcroft and A. Sabin, eds., *Two compotus rolls of St Augustine's Abbey, Bristol*, Bristol RS, 9 (1938) · A. Sabin, 'Compotus rolls of St Augustine's Abbey, Bristol for 1503–4 & 1506–7', *Transactions of the Bristol and Gloucestershire Archaeological Society*, 73 (1954), 192–207 · A. Sabin, ed., *Some manorial accounts of St Augustine's Abbey, Bristol*, Bristol RS, 22 (1960) · Emden, *Oxf.* · J. Smyth, *Lives of the Berkeleys* (1883), vol. 1 of *The Berkeley manuscripts*, ed. J. Maclean (1883–5), 2 · J. Smyth, *A description of the hundred of Berkeley* (1885), vol. 3 of *The Berkeley manuscripts*, ed. J. Maclean (1883–5), 54 · Wood, *Ath. Oxon.*, 1st edn, 1.639–40 · B. Willis, *A history of the mitred parliamentary abbies and conventual cathedral churches*, 1 (1718), 128 · B. Willis, *A survey of the cathedrals of York, Durham, Carlisle … Bristol*, 2 vols. (1727), vol. 2, p. 767 · *The registers of Robert Stillington, bishop of Bath and Wells, 1466–1491, and Richard Fox, bishop of Bath and Wells, 1492–1494*, ed. H. C. Maxwell-Lyte, Somerset RS, 52 (1937), 796, 832, 838 · J. Britton, *The history and antiquities of the abbey and cathedral church of Bristol* (1830), 16–18 · E. Ralph, ed., *The Great White Book of Bristol*, Bristol RS, 32 (1979), 2–3, 17–67
Archives Berkeley Castle, Gloucestershire, Berkeley MSS

Newlands, Benjamin Edward Reina (1842–1912). *See under* Newlands, John Alexander Reina (1837–1898).

Newlands, James (1813–1871), architect and civil engineer, was born in Edinburgh on 28 July 1813, the son of Thomas Newlands, a rope maker, and his wife, Janet, *née* MacKay.

He was educated at the Edinburgh high school and at Edinburgh University where he was a student of John Leslie and excelled in mathematics and natural philosophy. In 1827 he began working in the office of Thomas Brown, architect to Edinburgh corporation, and became a skilled draughtsman. From 1833 to 1836 he assisted David Low, professor of agriculture at Edinburgh, on a large work on agriculture concerned with the laying out of farms and the design of farm buildings (probably his work *On Landed Estates*, 1844). About 1838 Newlands also began to study chemistry, another of Low's interests. For most of the next decade Newlands was in private practice as an architect and surveyor. He is said to have designed the manses for several Scottish churches, and to have been valuing agricultural land in connection with railway bills. He had also by this time become an accomplished painter, exhibiting at the Royal Scottish Academy, and was a skilled flautist. On 11 August 1845 he married Joanna Handerson at St Cuthbert's Church, Edinburgh; she died in 1848.

On 26 January 1847 Newlands was appointed, from among five candidates, engineer to Liverpool corporation at a salary of £700 (ultimately raised to £1300). This was a new post established by the 1846 Liverpool Sanitary Act, which also established the first medical officership of health, held by Dr William Henry Duncan. While some large towns, including Liverpool, employed surveyors to look after town buildings, and while some metropolitan sewers commissions employed sanitary engineers, the Liverpool post was the first for a municipal engineer who would be concerned with comprehensively improving the health, amenity, and efficiency of the city.

During his first year in office Newlands carried out a detailed survey of the city on a scale of 1 inch to 20 feet. His first report of April 1848 included plans for a complete system of sewers, but addressed much else as well. It has been rightly said that it 'elucidates with clearness and precision almost every matter connected with the sanitary arrangements of a great population' (*PICE*, 229). Indeed, in many ways it presaged the structural changes that characterize Haussmann's Paris. Much concerned with access of light and air, Newlands proposed regulations on building height, street width, and room size. He proposed a series of boulevards along the parliamentary boundary, and to rebuild courtyard housing to allow communal cooking, baking, and washing. Newlands's sewer scheme was adopted, and while most of his other suggestions were deemed too radical to be adopted in full, he was successful in leading Liverpool to undertake responsibility for municipal services in many areas. Newlands's report pioneered both the regulation of housing and the provision of new public housing, as well as the provision of baths, washhouses, and swimming baths. Supplementary reports appeared every few years reviewing the sanitary progress of the city and identifying new needs.

While in many ways Newlands's efforts paralleled those of Edwin Chadwick, who was attempting to establish state responsibility for sanitary reform, the two were not close. Newlands's survey, carried out by private practice surveyors, undermined Chadwick's claim that a corps of military engineers should do such work; Newlands's successful working relationship with Liverpool council seemed to indicate that successful sanitation was not necessarily predicated on the existence of a general board of health.

In 1855 Newlands took leave from his post to advise on the sanitation of army camps in the Crimea. In 1860 he published *The Carpenter and Joiner's Assistant*, a treatise that went through five editions during his life and was republished in 1890. He was elected associate member of the Institution of Civil Engineers in 1848, and to full membership in 1857.

The first municipal engineer, Newlands was also for more than twenty years an exemplar of the profession which was only beginning to take formal shape at the end of his life. He quietly managed to begin the transformation of many aspects of the urban landscape by introducing a concept of urban planning, all the while maintaining popularity with all segments of the community in a city where there were deep political divisions. By the late 1860s he was being treated for the effects of chronic bronchitis and exhaustion through overwork. Rest cures did not help. In early June 1871 he moved to a role as consulting engineer, and died six weeks later, on 15 July. Crowds lined the route of his funeral procession. He was buried in the Liverpool necropolis. CHRISTOPHER HAMLIN

Sources *PICE*, 33 (1871–2), 227–31 • C. Hamlin, 'James Newlands and the bounds of public health', *Transactions of the Historic Society of Lancashire and Cheshire*, 143 (1993), 117–40 • B. D. White, *A history of the corporation of Liverpool, 1835–1914* (1951) • J. K. Walton and A. Wilcox, eds., *Low life and moral improvement in mid-Victorian England: Liverpool through the journalism of Hugh Shimmin* (1991) • *Liverpool Mercury* (17 July 1871) • *Liverpool Mercury* (21 July 1871) • J. Newlands, *Report to the health committee of the borough of Liverpool, on the sewerage and other works, under the Sanitary Act* (1848) • P. J. Waller, *Democracy and sectarianism: a political and social history of Liverpool, 1868–1939* (1981)
Archives Liverpool Central Library, reports
Likenesses G. E. Ewing, bust, 1872, National Museums and Galleries on Merseyside
Wealth at death under £8000: resworn probate, 1871/3

Newlands, John Alexander Reina (1837–1898), chemist, was born on 26 November 1837 in Southwark, London, the second son of the Revd William Newlands, a Presbyterian minister, and his wife, Mary Sarah Reina. His early education came chiefly from his father. In 1856 he enrolled at the Royal College of Chemistry and studied for a year under A. W. von Hofmann, before becoming assistant chemist to J. T. Way at the Royal Agricultural Society. He energetically supported various social reforms in England, and in 1860 he spent several months with British volunteers fighting for Garibaldi in the Risorgimento (his mother was of Italian descent).

On 1 June 1862 Newlands married Jane Rickings, daughter of James Rickings, a farmer. From 1864 he was a consulting analytical chemist in London; he also taught at St Saviour's Grammar School, the School of Medicine for Women, and the City of London College. In 1868 he became chief chemist in a sugar refinery at the Victoria docks, owned by James Duncan, with whom he devised

John Alexander Reina Newlands (1837–1898), by unknown photographer

ideas in its *Journal*. Newlands's tables did contain errors and anomalies, but after 1869, when more accurate and comprehensive studies by Mendeleyev and J. Lothar Meyer began to appear, he argued for recognition of his priority. When the Royal Society awarded Mendeleyev and Lother Meyer its Davy medal for the discovery of the periodic law, Newlands renewed his campaign; he eventually received the Davy medal in 1887, but was never elected a fellow of the Royal Society. Newlands died on 29 July 1898 at his home, 1 Mildenhall Road, Lower Clapton, London, survived by his wife, daughter, and a son.

Benjamin Edward Reina Newlands (1842–1912), chemist, was born on 23 January 1842 in Southwark, the son of William Newlands and Mary Sarah Reina. He was the younger brother and business partner of John Alexander Reina Newlands. Like his elder brother he studied at the Royal College of Chemistry, and also worked under J. T. Way at the Royal Agricultural Society. From 1863 he was chemist to J. Gibbs & Co., leaving to join his brother at Duncans in 1873. He was a council member of the Society of Chemical Industry, and he published a paper on the manufacture of aluminium sulphate from bauxite in its *Journal* in 1882. He was married, and had a daughter, Mary. After his brother's death he continued with their chemical consultancy business for a number of years. He died of Bright's disease at Summerville, Eastoke, Hayling Island, Hampshire, on 7 August 1912.   MICHAEL A. SUTTON

Sources *Nature*, 58 (1898), 395–6 · *Journal of the Society of Chemical Industry*, 17 (1898), 743 · *DSB*, vol. 10 · W. A. Smeaton, 'Centenary of the law of octaves', *Journal of the Royal Institute of Chemistry*, 88 (1964), 271 · J. V. Van Spronsen, *The periodic system of the elements* (1969) · A. R. Ling, *JCS*, 103 (1913), 764–5 [obit. of Benjamin Newlands] · m. cert. · *CGPLA Eng. & Wales* (1898) · d. cert. [Benjamin Newlands]
Likenesses photograph, University of Pennsylvania Library, Philadelphia [*see illus.*] · portrait, repro. in D. McDonald and L. B. Hunt, *A history of platinum and its allied metals* (1982), 336
Wealth at death £4541 4*s*. 6*d*.: probate, 11 Nov 1898, *CGPLA Eng. & Wales*

and patented several technical improvements. The business eventually declined, and in 1886 he returned to private practice, in partnership with his brother Benjamin [*see below*]. The connection with sugar continued, as the brothers, with C. G. W. Lock, published *Sugar: a Handbook for Planters and Refiners* (1888), based on an earlier work by Lock and others.

Despite his marginal position in the academic world, Newlands earned a place in chemical history by his partial anticipation of D. I. Mendeleyev's periodic law, developed in several papers in the *Chemical News* between 1863 and 1866, and republished in his *On the Discovery of the Periodic Law* (1884). Though unaware of A. E. Béguyer de Chancourtois's general classification of the elements, Newlands knew that J. B. Dumas had identified 'families' of similar elements and noted numerical relationships among their atomic weights. On listing all the known elements in order of ascending atomic weight, Newlands noticed that elements with similar properties occurred at regular intervals. In 1864 he asserted that 'the eighth element starting from a given one is a kind of repetition of the first, like the eighth note of an octave in music' (*Chemical News*, 20 Aug 1864, 94), and in 1865 he formalized this relationship as the 'law of octaves'. His proposal met with opposition and even ridicule—G. C. Foster suggested ironically that he should arrange the elements in alphabetical order—and the Chemical Society refused to publish his

Newley, (George) Anthony (1931–1999), entertainer and songwriter, was born on 24 September 1931 at 230 High Street, Hackney, London, the son of (Frances) Grace Newley, of Clapton Park, London. His father (whom he did not know as a child) was a local builder. At a later stage Newley acquired another name, George, but he was always known as Anthony. He attended Mandeville School for Boys in Clapton but was evacuated, during the blitz, to Morecambe, Lancashire, where George Pesckett, a former music-hall performer, engendered his interest in the theatre. Back in London after the war, he worked briefly in an insurance office before answering an advertisement for the Italia Conti stage school. This led almost immediately to the launch of his career when he was picked, aged sixteen, for the title role in a film, *The Adventures of Dusty Bates* (1947). His cheeky cockney personality made him a natural for the Artful Dodger in David Lean's *Oliver Twist* (1948). With a contract from the Rank Organisation, he became an established character actor of plucky vitality in films like *Here Come the Huggetts* (1948, during the filming of which he later claimed to have lost his virginity to

(George) Anthony Newley (1931–1999), by David Redfern

Diana Dors) and *The Cockleshell Heroes* (1955), a tale of dashing wartime exploits, also starring Jose Ferrer and Trevor Howard.

An important development in Newley's stage career was an appearance in the surreal West End revue *Cranks* (1955), devised by the choreographer John Cranko. On 30 August 1956 he married the dancer and actress (Elizabeth) Ann (*b.* 1933/4), daughter of Basil Lynn. There were no children of the marriage. Newley spent the late 1950s touring England with his own variety show and finally secured pop-star status in the film *Idle on Parade* (1959), a send-up of an Elvis Presley movie. He became a national heart-throb. His ambitions fired, he cut records, made a bizarre comedy television series called *The Strange World of Gurney Slade* (1960), and finally moulded these various strands into one of the defining stage musicals of the era, *Stop the World—I Want to Get Off* (1961), a zany morality tale of the Newley character, Littlechap, seeking fame and fortune ('Gonna build a mountain') and lamenting his wasted life in a song that became an instant and enduring popular classic, 'What kind of fool am I?'

The co-author with Newley was the composer and lyricist Leslie Bricusse, and the two men tried to repeat their huge success with another Chaplinesque, allegorical sequence of 'little man' routines in *The Roar of the Greasepaint—the Smell of the Crowd* (1964). The show never opened in London, but did well in America, where its ebullient, audience-pleasing score, including songs like 'A wonderful day like today', 'The Joker', and 'Who can I turn to?', added to Newley's reputation among such fellow artistes as Sammy Davis jun., Andy Williams, and Tony Bennett,

all of whom recorded many items, and enjoyed many hits, from the Bricusse–Newley catalogue.

Newley was a high-profile success story of the 1960s. His marriage to Ann Lynn ended in divorce in 1963, the year in which he met and married, at the height of his West End fame, the actress and film star Joan Henrietta Collins (*b.* 1933), with whom he had two children, Tara and Sacha. The couple divorced in 1970, by which time Newley was more at home in America, living in Hollywood (he made his American film début in the leading role of *Doctor Dolittle* in 1967), belting out his songs in Las Vegas, and greeting his audience with a signature gesture, his raised right arm, at the end of a noisy bid for their sympathy. This show of a public bleeding heart was more appealing in America than in Britain. He bore the scars of a disrupted childhood—his father made himself known to him only late in life—like a badge, one felt, in his stage persona. But this facet of his personality undoubtedly fuelled his extraordinary talent for producing songs of searing emotional power and melodic vigour. And he sang them with a rasping intensity and a curdling vibrato that sometimes made him an object of parody.

Newley's third marriage, to the airline hostess Dareth Dunn, also produced two children, Shelby and Christopher, but it too ended in divorce (in 1989). From the mid-1980s Newley suffered from cancer. He had one kidney removed and returned to England in 1992 to live with his mother in Esher, Surrey. A West End comeback in a long-cherished project, *Scrooge* (1996), written by Leslie Bricusse, was a disappointing failure. He shared the last seven years of his life with the fashion designer Gina Fratini, succumbing finally to his disease at Jensen Beach, Florida, on 14 April 1999. Gina Fratini survived him.

Newley's two big stage shows did not survive well. London revivals of both in the late 1980s were unkindly received by the critics. But the songs survived. One of Newley's later collaborators, the lyricist Herbert Kretzmer—with whom Newley worked on what the magazine *Playboy* called 'a zany erotobiography', the movie *Can Hieronymous Merkin Ever Forget Mercy Humpe and Find True Happiness?* (1969)—rated him a true original, 'driven by the need to innovate and contemptuous of repetition or the following of fashion' (*The Independent*).

MICHAEL COVENEY

Sources *The Independent* (16 April 1999) · *The Times* (16 April 1999) · *Daily Telegraph* (16 April 1999) · *The Guardian* (16 April 1999) · K. Gänzl, *The British musical theatre*, 2 (1986) · b. cert. · m. cert. [Elizabeth Ann Lynn]

Archives Boston University, Mugar Memorial Library, corresp., diaries, and MSS

Likenesses photographs, 1948–*c.*1962, repro. in *The Guardian* · photographs, 1948–72, repro. in *Daily Telegraph* · double portrait, photograph, 1960–64 (with Joan Collins), repro. in *The Independent* · D. Redfern, photograph, Redferns Music Picture Library, London [*see illus.*] · photograph, repro. in *The Times* · photographs, Hult. Arch.

Newlin, Thomas (*bap.* 1688, *d.* 1744), Church of England clergyman, the son of William Newlin, rector of St Swithin's, Winchester, was baptized there on 29 October 1688. He was a scholar of Winchester College from 1702

until 1706, the year in which he was elected demy of Magdalen College, Oxford. He graduated BA on 26 June 1710, and proceeded MA on 7 May 1713 and BD on 8 July 1727. He was a fellow of Magdalen from 1717 to 1721. He married Susanna (1690–1732), daughter of Martin and Sarah Powell of Oxford, probably in 1721, when his fellowship was concluded, but they had no children. Together they repaired the ancient priory of Sele, held with the living of Beeding, Sussex, in 1724 at a cost of £200.

Newlin was a strenuous advocate of education in original languages, and frequently preached in Latin and English before the University of Oxford. He seems to have been a popular preacher, and it is easy to understand how, for example, his *One and Twenty Sermons on Several Occasions* (1726) went through three editions: though grounded in scholarship and reason, his printed sermons reveal a range of emotion from sadness to joy and sympathy to righteous indignation, and they touch upon a wide variety of topics relevant to his audience. He could preach with detailed arguments and intricate logic, and he could move the ordinary person in his parish with words of encouragement or admonition. Like most divines of his day he railed against deism and heterodoxy, but he could also tenderly counsel his flock and speak of the grace and goodness of God. Newlin was clearly in the high-church tradition—this is very strongly demonstrated in his 30 January sermon, in which he displayed a deep loathing for 'republicanism'—but he was also a peacemaker who pleaded for understanding in order to heal the political and religious divisions in the church. He could, in addition, be surprisingly gentle with dissenters, despite the fact that he considered them to be schismatics.

An air of sadness seems to have permeated his personal life; this can be detected in Newlin's sermons and is, perhaps, what gives them some of their power and pathos. Susanna died in 1732, at the age of forty-two. Newlin did not remarry and was evidently ill for much of the time, since a large portion of his will is devoted to rewarding the woman who took care of him. The only relatives he mentioned were a spinster sister (Constantia) and two cousins. He died at Beeding on 24 February 1744, and was buried in a vault in the parish church on 2 March. An epitaph in the church, noting that his works were 'a lasting monument', nevertheless praised his 'worth and shining abilities' (*GM*). J. S. CHAMBERLAIN

Sources PRO, PROB 11/732 · BL, Duncan MSS, Add. MS 32326, vol. 68, fol. 314 · E. Turner, 'The Marchant diary', *Sussex Archaeological Collections*, 25 (1873), 163–203, esp. 191 · *GM*, 1st ser., 55 (1785), 424 · *DNB* · Foster, *Alum. Oxon.* · T. F. Kirby, *Winchester scholars: a list of the wardens, fellows, and scholars of … Winchester College* (1888)
Wealth at death £45; plus clothing, furniture, and books: will, PRO, PROB 11/732

Newlyn school (*act.* 1882–*c.*1900), painters, were based in the fishing village of Newlyn, in west Cornwall. Here they found companionship, a mild climate, and the opportunity to paint *en plein air*, using local people as models. Their paintings were tonal and silvery, combining accuracy of detail with story-painting always so dear to British hearts. Each year throughout the 1880s and 1890s an important group of paintings exhibited at the Royal Academy came from Newlyn.

Walter Langley (1852–1922) described himself as 'the first figure painter to depict incidents in the life of the fisherfolk' (Fox and Greenacre). He was born into a working-class family in Irving Street, Birmingham, on 8 June 1852, the eighth of the eleven children of William Langley, a tailor, and his wife, Mary Ann, *née* Robinson. He was educated at Hurst Street Unitarian Mission School, Birmingham, and at the age of thirteen was apprenticed to a lithographic printer. He trained in drawing and industrial design at the Birmingham School of Design and gained a scholarship to study decorative design at the South Kensington Schools, London, but he was increasingly drawn towards painting. On 26 August 1876 he married Clara Perkins (*d.* 1895).

With financial assistance from a Birmingham businessman Langley moved to Newlyn in 1882. Soon after his arrival he produced some of his finest work, effectively capturing moments of personal crisis experienced by the fishermen's families. At this time he painted almost entirely in watercolour and became a leading exhibitor with the Institute of Painters in Water Colours. In the 1890s he returned to the use of oil colour and produced such major works as *Never Morning Wore to Evening but some Heart did Break* (1894; Birmingham Museums and Art Gallery); its title was taken from Tennyson's *In Memoriam*, which proved to be one of the most popular of all late Victorian scenes of tragedy. Following the death of Clara in August 1895 Langley married secondly, in 1897, Ethel Pengelly. Langley lived in Newlyn for ten years before moving to nearby Penzance, where he died on 22 March 1922 at 18 Clarence Street.

Edwin Harris (1855–1906), another Birmingham painter, trained with Langley at Birmingham School of Art, where he taught for two years before continuing his studies at the Royal Academy in Antwerp. He spent some months in Newlyn in 1881, and by 1883 was resident there. In contrast to the sombreness of Langley his painting depicts the quiet hours of happiness in the cottagers' lives. He left Newlyn in 1895 and spent the remainder of his life in Birmingham. Fred Hall (1860–1948) went to Newlyn in late 1883 and left in 1898. He was born at Stillington, Yorkshire, where his father was a doctor. He attended Lincoln School of Art and, like Harris, the Royal Academy in Antwerp. His landscape studies are more impressionist than those of his contemporaries in Newlyn, and he also had a gift for caricature.

Frank Bramley (1857–1915) was arguably the most talented and dedicated of the Newlyn painters. He was born at Sibsey, Lincolnshire, on 6 May 1857, the son of Charles Bramley and his wife, Harriet. Like Hall he trained at Lincoln School of Art and the Royal Academy in Antwerp. He went to Newlyn in the winter of 1884. His principal subject was the figure, with a concern for mood and character. Trained in the discipline of northern painting his work tended more towards tonality, less towards colour. One of the finest emotional statements of late nineteenth-century art was his *A Hopeless Dawn* (1888;

Chantrey Bequest, Tate collection), a scene of tragic loss set in the intimate theatre of Bramley's small room in Newlyn. In 1891 he married Katherine, daughter of John Graham of Huntingstile, Grasmere, Westmorland. In 1893 he was elected associate of the Royal Academy, of which he became academician in 1911. In 1894 he left Newlyn; his final years were spent in Grasmere. He died on 10 August 1915.

The arrival of Stanhope Alexander *Forbes (1857–1947) in Newlyn in January 1884 marked a turning point for the artists' colony. Forbes was to become the leading figure in the group; he possessed a capacity for action and a practical genius that propelled their work upon a national stage. During his first months in the village he painted *Fish Sale on a Newlyn Beach* (1885; Plymouth Museum and Art Gallery), which depicts the glistening beach at low tide, a heavy sky over a slate-blue sea. The fishing fleet is anchored offshore and fish are being unloaded and offered for sale on the beach. When the painting was exhibited at the Royal Academy in 1885 it was much admired for its freshness and accuracy of observation. Forbes was the first of the Newlyn painters to be elected to the Royal Academy, as associate in 1892 and as academician in 1910.

Not all who came to Newlyn had the abilities or the ambitions of Langley, Bramley, or Forbes. Ralph Todd (1856–1932) had little success at the Royal Academy but exhibited regularly in Birmingham. A number of other painters were not resident in Newlyn for long periods but came on visits or used it as a sketching-ground. They include William John Wainwright (1855–1931) and Henry Detmold (1854–1924), both from Birmingham; Leghe Suthers (1856–1924) and William Banks Fortescue (c.1855–1914), both from Southport, in Lancashire. William Teulon Blandford Fletcher (1859–1936) was one of the few Londoners in the group.

The Slade School of Fine Art, founded as part of University College, London, attracted some of the most talented of the younger generation, including a number who went to Newlyn. Henry Scott Tuke (1858–1929) made his first extended visit in 1883 but he was mainly associated with his home town of Falmouth. Thomas Cooper Gotch (1854–1931) settled in Newlyn in 1887 and remained there until his death. Percy Robert Craft (1856–1934) arrived in the village in February 1885 and stayed there for about two years, before joining the artists' community in St Ives. Albert Chevallier Tayler (1862–1925) went to Newlyn in the late summer of 1884 and was an irregular resident over a period of eleven years. Frank Wright Bourdillon (1851–1924) had a painting career of about twelve years, most of it spent in Newlyn. In June 1892 he gave up painting to become a missionary.

Norman *Garstin (1847–1926) was born at Cahirconlish, co. Limerick. He was already thirty-one before he began to train in art at the Royal Academy in Antwerp, and in Paris, and went to Newlyn in 1886. His smaller sketches—studies of sea and landscape—captured the transient effects of light, but his most robust painting is undoubtedly *The Rain*

it Raineth every Day (1889; Penlee Gallery and Museum, Penzance), which depicts the wide, rain-soaked expanse of the promenade between Newlyn and Penzance. Garstin also had talent as a writer; from 1895 he was a regular contributor to the *Studio Magazine* with a feature, 'Studio talk', in which the work of the Newlyn and St Ives artists was chronicled.

Elizabeth Adela Armstrong (1859–1912) [*see* Forbes, Elizabeth Adela] was born in Ottawa and educated in England. She studied at the South Kensington Schools, London, and at the Art Students League, New York. Later, chaperoned by her mother, she travelled to Europe and painted in Germany, France, and the Netherlands. In November 1885 she made her first visit to Newlyn, although she was not a resident there until her marriage, to Stanhope Alexander Forbes. She painted with a delicacy and clarity that few of the Newlyn painters could match and discovered a theme that she made her own—the village children. Her painting *School is out* (1888), exhibited at the Royal Academy in 1889, is a sympathetic description of the children as individuals. In that year Forbes had his own success at the same exhibition, with *The Health of the Bride*, an equally warm portrayal of a village wedding; the work was purchased by Sir Henry Tate and later formed part of his gift to the nation of sixty-eight pictures that led to the formation of the Tate Gallery.

By the turn of the century Newlyn had changed; the harbour had been enlarged and the fishing trade greatly expanded. This commercial development made it much less interesting to the artists, and many left. Stanhope and Elizabeth Forbes made a decision to stay, and in 1899 opened a school of painting in Newlyn; this marked the beginning of a new era in the artistic life of the village. The school continued until the Second World War, surviving Elizabeth Forbes's death in 1912 and Stanhope Forbes's subsequent marriage, in 1915, to Maudie Palmer.

TOM CROSS

Sources R. Langley, *Walter Langley: pioneer of the Newlyn art colony* (1997) · T. Cross, *Shining sands: artists of Newlyn and St Ives, 1880–1930* (1994) · C. Fox and F. Greenacre, *Artists of the Newlyn School, 1880–1900* (1979) · M. L. Birch, *Stanhope A. Forbes and Elizabeth Forbes* (1906) · G. M. Waters, *Dictionary of British artists working 1900–1950* (1978) · IGI · WWW, 1897–1915
Archives Tate collection, corresp., record book on sales of works [Stanhope Forbes] · Tate collection, MSS | Penlee Gallery and Museum, Penzance
Likenesses S. Forbes, portrait, 1891 (Elizabeth Armstrong), Penlee Gallery and Museum, Penzance · S. Forbes, self-portrait, oils, 1891, Aberdeen Art Gallery · bronze medallion (Stanhope Forbes), Passmore Edwards Art Gallery, Newlyn, Cornwall · photograph (Stanhope Forbes), NPG

Newman, Arthur (*fl.* 1607–1619), poet and essayist, was the son and heir apparent of William Newman of Ludgvan, Cornwall. He entered Trinity College, Oxford, before 1607, though his name does not appear in the matriculation books of the university; he subscribed to the Thirty-Nine Articles on 3 June 1614. It seems, however, from an entry in the bursar's book, that his caution money was returned to him in 1618, when he probably left Oxford. On

19 October 1616 he was admitted a student of the Middle Temple, London.

Newman's works indicate a lively personality and an incisive mind, which sought the reality beneath appearances. *The Bible-Bearer* (1607) was dedicated to Hugh Browker, protonotary of the common pleas. Also found under the title *Two Faces under a Hood, or, The Cloake of Hypocrisie, Worn Thred Bare, now Newly Turned*, it is in prose and describes itself as a 'shrewd satire upon all hypocritical, puritanical, and sanctified sinners, all trimmers, timeservers, and holy cameleons, or conformists to any preachers, parties, or fashionable principles, who are only politically pious for profit or preferment'. Newman's second work was published some years later and concerns opposing views on women, *Pleasures vision: with deserts complaint, and a short dialogue of a womans properties, betweene an old man and a young* (1619); it is dedicated to his kinsman Sir George Newman (1562–1627) of Canterbury. A facsimile edition appeared in 1840 under the editorial supervision of E. V. Utterson. Thomas Park says Newman 'is a writer who, from the brevity rather than the inferiority of his productions, may be deemed a minor poet; his verses are moral, harmonious, and pleasing' (Brydges, 2.155).

THOMPSON COOPER, rev. JOANNA MOODY

Sources Watt, *Bibl. Brit.*, 2.701 • W. T. Lowndes, *The bibliographer's manual of English literature*, ed. H. G. Bohn, [new edn], 2 (1864), 1667 • E. Brydges, *Censura literaria: containing titles, abstracts, and opinions of old English books*, 2 (1806) • Foster, *Alum. Oxon.* • Wood, *Ath. Oxon.*, new edn, vol. 3 • W. C. Hazlitt, 'Arthur Newman', *N&Q*, 3rd ser., 6 (1864), 27

Newman, Arthur Shean (1828–1873). *See under* Newman, John (*bap.* 1786, *d.* 1859).

Newman, Edward [*pseud.* Rusticus] (**1801–1876**), naturalist, was born on 13 May 1801 at Hampstead, Middlesex, the eldest of four sons of Quaker parents, George Newman (1774–1845), a leather manufacturer, and his wife, Ann Prichard, of Godalming, Surrey. Both parents nurtured his love for natural history, and he developed a 'very, very early predilection for butterflies' (Newman, *Memoir*, iii). From 1812 to 1817, he attended a Quaker boarding-school at Painswick, Gloucestershire, where the master, Oade Roberts (brother of the botanical writer Mary Roberts), further developed Newman's fondness for natural history.

In 1817 Newman became engaged in his father's new business as a wool-stapler, at Godalming. However, he did not take an active interest in the business, and was often absent from work, pursuing his interests in natural history. In 1826, when his father's business was abandoned, they moved to London and entered into a rope-making business at Deptford, where Newman remained until about 1837. About this time, Newman entered into a partnership as a printer with George Luxford (Luxford & Co.), at Ratcliff Highway.

On 11 August 1840, at Cheltenham parish church, Newman married Maria Preston, daughter of Charles Henry Hale, and his wife, Elizabeth (*née* Butler). Maria was not a Quaker, and as a result Newman had been disowned by the Society of Friends by the end of 1840. Newman and his wife had at least five children including: Charles Bevington (*b.* 31 July 1841) who died at Gwalior, India, on 4 September 1867; Maria Bradley (*b.* 5 Sept 1842) who married, in 1868, Henry Tuke Mennell (1835–1923); Ellen Elizabeth (*b.* 23 April 1844) who married, in 1873, Samuel Tuke Mennell (1845–1923); Thomas Prichard (*b.* 3 June 1846) who married, in 1879, Jane Elizabeth Hutchinson (1857–1928); and Marion Whitehead (*b.* 12 May 1849) who died on 14 March 1854.

Following his marriage in 1840, Newman moved to Wellclose Square, where he resided for the next two years, while maintaining a 'nominal residence' in Deptford. In 1849 he moved to York Grove, Peckham, Surrey. In 1865 he was reinstated as a member of the Society of Friends. He bought out George Luxford's business, and moved the firm to Devonshire Street, Bishopsgate, where he ran the firm until he retired, in 1870 (his son, Thomas, then became manager of the works).

Throughout his life, Newman devoted his leisure to scientific study, and became intimate with some of the leading London naturalists. In 1826 he was one of the four founders of the Entomological Club, and became editor of the *Entomological Magazine* which ran from 1832 to 1838, to which he contributed fifteen out of the sixty-three articles in the first volume. When the rules of the Entomological Club were codified in 1836 he was re-elected as curator. At this time, the cabinet and library were situated at Newman's residence, 21 Union Street, Deptford, and the collections were open to naturalists from 1836 to 1841. In 1833 he was elected a fellow of the Linnean Society, and in the same year he played an important role in the founding of the Entomological Society of London. He was elected a member of the first council, and in 1853–4 he was president of the society. He was also a fellow of the Zoological Society, the Royal Microscopical Society, and the Zoologico-Botanical Society of Vienna, as well as an honorary member of the Entomological Society of France, that of Pennsylvania, and of the Botanical Society of Edinburgh.

Newman's publications up to 1838 focused on entomological subjects. His first paper, in 1831, 'Polyommatus argiolus, melitaea euphrosyne and selene', was published in the *Magazine of Natural History*, and a year later his more important work, *Sphinx vespiformis: an Essay*, appeared; it was regarded as an attempt at a new system of classification. In 1832 he began an anonymous series of notes in the *Magazine of Natural History*, which were reprinted in 1849 as *The Letters of Rusticus*, chiefly discussing the bird and insect life of Surrey. His pseudonym, Rusticus, was a secret known not even by his closest friend, the naturalist Edward Doubleday (1810–1849). In 1835 he published the *Grammar of Entomology*, of which a more extended second edition was issued in 1841, under the title *A Familiar Introduction to the History of Insects*; this was later issued as *The Insect Hunters, or, Entomology in Verse* (1858). In 1840 he published not only his *Notes on Irish Natural History* but also *A History of British Ferns*, which was printed by Luxford. Newman drew his own cuts for the latter work, which was issued as a second and third edition in 1844 and 1854, respectively, and a fourth edition (1864).

In 1840 Newman established, and edited, *The Entomologist*, which was merged into its successor, *The Zoologist*, from 1843 until 1863. He was the sole editor of the latter from 1843 until 1876, and issued thirty-four volumes. A non-believer in Charles Darwin's theories, Newman used his journals as anti-evolutionary vehicles. From June 1841 to June 1854 he contributed to another venture of his own, *The Phytologist*, a monthly magazine edited by Luxford. From 1858 until his death Newman was also natural history editor of *The Field* newspaper, to which he contributed a valuable series of notes on economic entomology—he was a great advocate of the use of insect predators in controlling harmful pests.

In March 1861 Newman received a testimonial from about seventy colleagues in 'high appreciation of services rendered in the promotion and diffusion of scientific knowledge'. In the same year his popular work on British oology, *Birdnesting*, was issued, followed, in 1864, by a popular fourth issue (without cuts) of *British Ferns*. He also revived *The Entomologist* and released the *Dictionary of British Birds* (1866), which reflected his later interest in ornithology, *Natural History of British Moths* (1869), and a companion work, *British Butterflies* (1869–71). In 1870 J. Greene (1824–1906) published *The Insect Hunter's Companion*, to which Newman contributed a chapter on Coleoptera (a further edition appeared in 1880). He died at his home in York Grove, Peckham, on 12 June 1876, and was buried at Nunhead cemetery. YOLANDA FOOTE

Sources T. P. Newman, *Memoir of the life and works of Edward Newman* (1876); repr. (1980) · 'Preface', *The Zoologist* (1876) · *Journal of Botany, British and Foreign*, 14 (1876), 223–4 · Smith's Friends' books, 2, 236–7 · *Entomologist's Monthly Magazine*, 13 (1876–7), 45–6 · J. F. M. Clark, 'Science, secularization, and social change: the metamorphosis of entomology in nineteenth-century England', DPhil diss., U. Oxf., 1994 · 'Dictionary of Quaker biography', RS Friends, Lond. [card index] · CGPLA Eng. & Wales (1876) · DNB

Archives NHM, notebook · Oxf. U. Mus. NH, corresp. · RS Friends, Lond., family corresp.

Likenesses portrait, 1866, repro. in Newman, *Memoir*

Wealth at death under £25,000: probate, 2 Aug 1876, CGPLA Eng. & Wales

Newman, Edward Arthur (1918–1993), computer engineer, was born on 27 April 1918 at 9 Coleridge Road, Walthamstow, London, the elder of the two sons of Edward Charles Newman, a manual worker and later a postal sorter, and his wife, Amy Cecilia, *née* Harvie. He was educated at Kingsbury county school (1929–36), and at University College, London, from where he graduated BSc in physics in 1939. He then started research aimed ultimately at the degree of PhD, but this work was suspended because of the war and never completed, and after a brief period working for Masteradio Ltd he joined the research laboratories of Electric and Musical Industries Ltd (later EMI) at Hayes, Middlesex, in 1941. This was to prove a crucial move because he was assigned to work with a genius in electronic circuit design, Alan D. Blumlein, who was

Edward Arthur Newman (1918–1993), by unknown photographer, 1966

developing an airborne radar system known as H_2S. Newman gained a thorough knowledge of Blumlein's distinctive rigorous approach to circuit design, and of the ingenious circuits he had developed to handle the streams of pulses of current which were used to generate the outgoing pulsed radio signal and to represent the reflected incoming signal. When Blumlein was killed in an air crash in June 1942 while testing H_2S, Newman took over responsibility for part of the subsequent production of operational radar sets, and for the training of those testing them; after the war he worked on the development of advanced circuits for television cameras. Meanwhile, on 9 September 1944 he married a schoolfriend, Helen Maud Green (1920/21–c.1988), daughter of Alfred Green, a clerk. There were three sons and one daughter of the marriage.

In September 1947 Newman left EMI to move to the National Physical Laboratory (NPL) in Teddington. There Alan Turing, later well known for his wartime work on code-breaking, had produced a brilliant outline design for a stored-program electronic digital computer in late 1945, which was ahead of all other such work in the world at that time. Newman was recruited to provide the specialist knowledge needed to implement these plans, in which streams of pulses of current, and sound waves in a mercury tank, were used to represent the data and instructions in the computer. Turing soon left the NPL for a period of sabbatical leave from which he did not return, but the two had a month to get to know each other, discovering a common interest in cross-country running which they practised together. This friendship was maintained, and Newman later visited Turing several times in

Manchester; both enjoyed debate, unconventional ideas, and a comfortably disorganized lifestyle. After Turing's departure the NPL assembled a balanced team to design and build a prototype computer based on his plans. F. M. Colebrook led the group, which combined the logical design skills of J. H. Wilkinson, D. W. Davies, and others with the practical engineering experience of Newman and D. O. Clayden. Blumlein's techniques made an important contribution. The result was the Pilot ACE, one of the first stored-program electronic digital computers in the world, which ran its first program at the NPL on 10 May 1950; it went on to provide the world's first commercial computing service. Newman's key contribution to this achievement ensured him a permanent place among the founders of the computer revolution which was to sweep the world in the following fifty years.

Newman's next task was to lead a group investigating the use of computers in office work. In 1957 the NPL held a course attended by twenty-four representatives of government departments, who then went out into the civil service to spread the new gospel of office automation. One of those who attended, Douglas Wass, later joint head of the home civil service, remembered forty years on how influential the course had proved to be in his career, and particularly commended 'the enthusiasm and dynamism of an electronics engineer called Ted Newman' (Yates, 54–5).

Newman was an irrepressible, perceptive, cheerful man of wide interests and sometimes maverick originality. This combination of innovative ability (he held twenty-six patents) with a strong and friendly personality gained him rapid promotion, and he reached the grade of senior principal scientific officer in 1955 at the age of thirty-seven. This meant that he was responsible for several research projects simultaneously. At different times these included teaching machines, computer reliability, visual pattern recognition, and speech recognition. From 1963 he also helped to manage the advanced computer techniques project, which provided government support for the British computer industry. In all these projects there were others who did much of the detailed work; Newman loved discussion and argument and contributed in his own way, making comments and suggestions which provoked those more directly involved into new lines of thought. He published twenty-five scientific papers on computer engineering, pattern recognition, and related topics. He retired from the NPL in December 1977 and took up a visiting professorship in computer science at Westfield College, London.

Outside work Newman's interests were active and practical. At various times they included running, cycling, building his family home (at Oxshott, Surrey), country dancing, and gardening. His marriage having ended in divorce, in 1982 he went to live with (Kathleen) Margaret Page, *née* Johnson (b. 1922), a teacher, and the widow of an NPL colleague. He died at their home, 113 New Haw Road, Addlestone, Surrey, from cancer of the stomach, on 7 August 1993, and was cremated at Woking crematorium.

DAVID M. YATES

Sources D. W. Davies, 'Edward Arthur Newman', *IEEE Annals of the History of Computing*, 17 (1995), 64–6 • *The Times* (17 Aug 1993) • D. M. Yates, *Turing's legacy: a history of computing at the National Physical Laboratory 1945–1995* (1997) • private information (2004) • personal knowledge (2004) • student records, UCL • A. Hodges, *Alan Turing: the enigma* (1983); repr. (1992) • E. W. Burns, 'A. D. Blumlein: engineer extraordinary', *Engineering Science and Education Journal* (Feb 1992), 19–33 • b. cert. • m. cert. • d. cert.

Likenesses photograph, 1966, National Physical Laboratory, Teddington, Middlesex [*see illus.*]

Wealth at death £311,659: probate, 1993, *CGPLA Eng. & Wales*

Newman, Ernest [*formerly* William Roberts] (1868–1959), music critic, was born William Roberts in Everton, Lancashire, on 30 November 1868, the only child of Seth Roberts, a tailor, and his second wife, Harriet Spark, whose first married name was Jones. Both parents also had families by their first spouses. William Roberts was brought up in the Anglican faith which he later violently rejected. From an early age he studied the piano and as a boy became interested in vocal music, especially opera. He attempted some composition and studied harmony and counterpoint without formal instruction. He quickly became acquainted with a large quantity of music, including all the Wagner operas, through reading scores, a practice he later advocated with enthusiasm. From St Saviour's School in Everton he won a scholarship to the middle school of Liverpool College and graduated as a student at University College, Liverpool, in 1886, having studied English literature, philosophy, and art. He intended to pursue a diplomatic career, but due to ill health he was unable to take the examinations for the Indian Civil Service before reaching the age limit of nineteen. Instead he became a clerk in the Bank of Liverpool (1889–1903), meanwhile contributing to a number of progressive journals, not only on music but on literature, religion, and philosophical subjects.

Newman became president of the Liverpool branch of the National Secular Society in 1894 and began contributing to Charles Bradlaugh's journal, the *Nationalist Reformer*. It was at the National Secular Society that he met J. M. Robertson and initiated a friendship that continued until Robertson's death in 1933. Robertson's writings, especially his *New Essays towards a Critical Method* (1897), exercised a decisive influence, reflected in his lifelong study of the philosophy of criticism and in the preface to his first book, *Gluck and the Opera* (1895), which he wrote as Ernest Newman. The pseudonym was intended to signify his outlook as a 'new man in earnest', but it corresponded to some psychological need, since he thereafter adopted it in private as well as public life, although he never legally ratified the change. In 1897 he published *Pseudo-Philosophy at the End of the Nineteenth Century*, a criticism from the point of view of 'aggressive Rationalism' of writings by Benjamin Kidd, Henry Drummond, and A. J. Balfour, under the name Hugh Mortimer Cecil, but he did not use this name again. This volume was a penetrating and cogent refutation of mock scientific writing and subjective theological speculation. It displayed the three most prominent characteristics of his critical thought: scepticism, dialectic skill, and passion for accuracy.

Although Newman had often referred to music in his writings on other subjects, it was not until 1894 that he began to write regularly on the subject. His first articles were written for Granville Bantock in his *New Quarterly Musical Review*. He also owed to Bantock commissions to write programme notes for his concerts and later (in 1903), when Bantock was principal of the Birmingham and Midland Institute school of music, an invitation to join the staff. In 1905 Newman published his *Musical Studies* and left Birmingham to become music critic of the *Manchester Guardian*. His trenchant pen and independence of view sometimes upset the Hallé committee and Hans Richter, but established his critical reputation as a champion of Bruckner, Sibelius, Strauss, and Elgar.

From the very start of his career as a music critic Newman tackled head-on the most perplexing aesthetic issues of the day. He convincingly challenged accepted notions and the opinions of renowned philosophical thinkers—as when, for example, during the course of his second book, *A Study of Wagner* (1899), he denounced Herbert Spencer's theories of the origin and function of music. In 1906 the *Birmingham Post* recalled him to Birmingham, where he remained until 1919. During these years he wrote studies of Wagner (1899 and 1904), Strauss (1908), Elgar (1906), and Hugo Wolf (1907). This last book remained for thirty years the best monograph on its subject and was translated into German. In 1914 came *Wagner as Man and Artist*, which showed Newman's analytical powers, his independence—it was critical of *Mein Leben* and consequently not well received at Bayreuth—his appreciation of the Wagnerian music drama, and his extreme care over documentation. In the second chapter Newman makes his position regarding the composer's philosophical intentions unequivocal, writing of 'one of the most curious of Wagner's hallucinations—the idea that the musical stage can be the dispenser of profound philosophy' (*Wagner as Man and Artist*, 19). Here for the first time is the expression of Newman's inability to accept the ideological framework of Wagnerian music drama; he may have abandoned rationalist propaganda, but not the tenets of his philosophical position. This book led him on to his great work: *The Life of Richard Wagner*, in four volumes published between 1933 and 1947. This in turn gave rise as a by-product to a study, *The Man Liszt* (1934). In counteracting the false portrait of Liszt built up by earlier biographers Newman went to the other extreme. His rationalist perspective prejudiced him against accepting Liszt's religious conviction, which in turn blinded him to other qualities. Making a case through carefully selecting information was a feature of Newman's criticism which could be as misleading as it was persuasive; *The Man Liszt* tarnished his critical integrity.

In 1919 Newman moved from Birmingham to London, where he had been appointed music critic of the Sunday newspaper, *The Observer*. He joined the *Sunday Times* in 1920 and remained with that newspaper until his retirement in 1958 (but had a five-month stint in 1923 as guest critic of the *New York Evening Post*). During these years he not only wrote regular reviews and a more substantial weekly article, but also a large number of programme notes, weekly articles for the *Manchester Guardian* (1919–24) and the *Glasgow Herald* (1924–8), and a huge number of articles for music periodicals. From 1930 he made weekly broadcasts on music for the BBC, as well as writing a sporting column for the *Evening Standard*.

Newman's lack of sympathy for the main trends in contemporary music, and his disillusionment with the apparent chaos of criticism in responding to it, led him to attempt a philosophy of criticism in his *A Musical Critic's Holiday* (1925). In an age in which the past and future of music seemed irreconcilable it was natural for a rationalist to try to discern standards that maintained continuity in order to give criticism an objective basis. While his attempt to provide a physiology of criticism in *The Unconscious Beethoven* (1927) had no lasting impact, his efforts to bring a psychological perspective to the biography of composers were more significant.

A collection of his articles was published in 1919 entitled *A Musical Motley*, and from the *Sunday Times* two other selections were made by Felix Aprahamian in 1956 and 1958. These serve to show Newman's great range, which was sometimes overlooked because of his undoubted predilection for the nineteenth century and for opera. On the latter he published his most enduring and widely read works: *Opera Nights* (1943), *Wagner Nights* (1949), and *More Opera Nights* (1954). He had translated most of Wagner's opera texts by 1912 and he translated Felix Weingartner's *On Conducting* (1906) and Schweitzer's *J. S. Bach* (1911).

Newman was married twice: first, on 3 February 1894, to Kate Eleanor Woollett (d. 1918), daughter of Henry Woollett, an artist descended from the engraver William Woollett; second, in 1919, to Vera Agnes Hands, daughter of Arthur Hands, a Birmingham jeweller. There were no children of either marriage.

Newman rigidly refused all honours until in extreme old age he no longer had the energy to decline them. Finland conferred on him the order of the White Rose in 1956; Germany the Grosse Dienstkreuz in 1958; and the University of Exeter the DLitt in 1959. In 1955 he was presented with a Festschrift, a collection of essays by colleagues and admirers: *Fanfare for Ernest Newman*, edited by Herbert van Thal, who later edited a further selection of Newman's writings in *Testament of Music* (1962). A large collection of Newman's notebooks, correspondence, and other papers was donated to the Lila Acheson Wallace Library at the Juilliard School, New York, in 1976 by Walter Legge.

Ernest Newman died at Tadworth, Surrey, on 7 July 1959 and was cremated two days later. He was survived by his second wife.   NIGEL SCAIFE

Sources V. Newman, *Ernest Newman* (1963) · H. G. Farmer, 'Ernest Newman as I saw him', memoir, 1962, U. Glas. · W. Blissett, 'Ernest Newman and English Wagnerism', *Music and Letters*, 40 (1959), 311–23 · *CGPLA Eng. & Wales* (1959) · *DNB* · *New Grove*
Archives Juilliard School, New York, collection | BL, corresp. with Society of Authors, Add. MS 56763 · Bodl. Oxf., letters to Bertram Dobell · JRL, letters to *Manchester Guardian* · NL Scot., letters

to D. C. Parker |SOUND BL NSA, documentary recording · BL NSA, performance recording

Wealth at death £17,043 6s. 9d.: probate, 2 Sept 1959, *CGPLA Eng. & Wales*

Newman, Francis (d. 1660), colonial governor, of whose parents and background nothing is known, emigrated to New Hampshire in 1638, and then moved to New Haven, Connecticut. In his barn in New Haven in June 1639 the constitution of the colony was formulated. His first appointment to civic office occurred in August 1642 when he was made an ensign in the New Haven trained band. He was subsequently promoted to lieutenant in the artillery in March 1645, and then lieutenant in the trained band in May 1652, but he resigned the following month. He was made a surveyor of roads and bridges in October 1644, and in March 1645 he became a judge of New Haven, serving until May 1653. In 1646 he took over as temporary secretary of the general court of New Haven, becoming secretary in October 1647, and again serving until May 1653. He was married by 1649, when his wife, whose name is not mentioned, was accused of making disparaging comments about the wife of Lancelot Fuller.

In May 1653 Newman was chosen as an assistant governor of New Haven, a post he combined with that of secretary of the council. That year he was one of a deputation sent to Peter Stuyvesant, governor of the New Netherland, to obtain satisfaction for Dutch encroachments in the colony. In 1654 he was elected a commissioner of the united colonies (serving as the alternative commissioner in 1656–7). Having served as an assistant governor and secretary since 1653, he was elected governor in May 1658. In September 1659 he was arrested at Connecticut by one Henry Tomlinson of Stratford as a protest against the imposition of a new tax on wine and liquors, but the general court at New Haven forced Tomlinson to apologize and give security for good behaviour. Newman attended a meeting as governor in June 1660, but was reported absent and ill from a meeting on 17 October. He died at New Haven on 18 November 1660, leaving his widow, Mary, his estate being valued at £430 in an inventory after his death. His funeral was paid for by the public purse. His widow went on to marry the Revd Nicholas Street, and died on 13 December 1683.   GORDON GOODWIN, rev. STUART HANDLEY

Sources J. Savage, *A genealogical dictionary of the first settlers of New England*, 3 (1861), 274 · *Appleton's cyclopaedia of American biography*, ed. J. G. Wilson and J. Fiske, 6 vols. (1894), 4.504 · C. J. Hoadly, *Records of the colony and plantation of New Haven, 1638–49* (1857) · C. J. Hoadly, *Records of the colony or jurisdiction of New Haven, 1653–65* (1858) · D. L. Jacobus, *List of officials civil, military and ecclesiastical of Connecticut colony, 1636–77* (1935), 40 · *New Haven town records, 1649–62*, ed. F. B. Dexter, New Haven Colony Historical Society (1917) · IGI

Wealth at death £430 2s. 7d.: inventory, Hoadly, *Records of the colony or jurisdiction*, 400

Newman, Francis William (1805–1897), classical scholar and moral philosopher, was born at 17 Southampton Street, Bloomsbury Square, London, on 27 June 1805. His father, John Newman (1767–1824), a banker, was of Dutch descent and his mother, Jemima (1772–1836), of Huguenot extraction, was a sister of the paper manufacturer Henry

Francis William Newman (1805–1897), by Herbert Watkins, 1858

Fourdrinier. Like his two older brothers, Frank (as he was known) attended the large school of the Revd George Nicholas at Great Ealing, where the senior classical master, the Revd Walter Mayers, was an important influence in his evangelical conversion in 1819. A few years after the failure of the bank of Ramsbottom, Newman, and Ramsbottom in 1816, Newman's father was on the verge of bankruptcy. On leaving school, therefore, he lodged at Oxford with his brother John Henry *Newman for a year prior to matriculating from Worcester College in November 1822.

Oxford and Dublin   While his brother would soon adopt more 'sacramentalist' opinions, the evangelical faith of the undergraduate Frank Newman was more enduring. In 1823 Walter Mayers became curate of Over Worton, near Deddington, and Newman spent some vacations helping his former teacher with his pupils. This was when he first met Mayers's sister-in-law Maria Rosina Giberne, for whom he later developed an unrequited love. In June 1826 his elder brother (who had paid for his studies) wrote that Frank's double first 'has astonished all Oxford' (*Letters and Diaries*, 1.292), and the mathematical examiners were so impressed by his 'extensive attainments and superior ability' that they presented him with two suitably inscribed works by Lagrange and Laplace (Daniel and Barker, 199). In a rare gesture of acclaim, the assembly rose to welcome the 21-year-old when he took his degree. On 29 November he was elected to a fellowship at Balliol, where he was soon noted for his dislike of the corn laws and his support for Catholic emancipation; in 1827 he was also a teacher in Thomas Byrth's Sunday school in the parish of St Clement's.

In September 1827 Newman moved to Delgany, co. Wicklow, where for a year he tutored the sons of Edward Pennefather (later chief justice of queen's bench), whose brother-in-law, the Revd John Nelson Darby, soon became a powerful influence in Newman's development. Although Darby had not yet seceded from the church, Newman was impressed by his self-sacrificial mode of living and his scorn for the 'worldly' Erastianism of the establishment. It was in Ireland that he first attended a nonconformist chapel, became acquainted with other dissatisfied evangelicals at Trinity College, Dublin, and learned of Anthony Norris Groves, who was soon to leave for Baghdad in 1829 as a freelance missionary. On his return to Oxford Newman was identified with other radical evangelicals such as B. W. Newton, who, with Darby, would soon be involved in the early Brethren movement, but he also assisted his brother in parish visiting at Littlemore. Maria Giberne's rejection of his proposal of marriage and Darby's arrival in Oxford in May 1830 seem to have precipitated Frank's decision to resign his fellowship at Balliol and, with John Vesey Parnell (later second Baron Congleton) and Edward Cronin, to join Groves's missionary venture in Baghdad. Before he left, however, he reimbursed his brother for the expenses of his education at Oxford.

Traveller and 'doubter' Newman's *Personal Narrative in Letters, Principally from Turkey in the Years 1830–3* (published, with revisions, in 1856) displays his avid interest in the society and economic viability of the countries through which he was travelling, though his party avoided sightseeing as such. Having left Dublin for Bordeaux in late September, they travelled overland to Marseilles, from where they sailed to Cyprus and then to Syria. They arrived at Latakia in late December, but a combination of circumstances including sickness, death, and civil disturbances (following the Russo-Turkish War of 1828–9) detained them at Aleppo for well over a year. Newman, discovering that Christianity was easily confused with Englishness, began to study Arabic, took up smoking, and adopted Syrian dress. Late in 1831 he nearly died of fever, but in April 1832 the party finally left Aleppo. Surviving a variety of dangers, including that of being stoned by an angry crowd after some injudicious Bible distribution at Aintab, they eventually reached Mosul in June, from where they took a raft down the Tigris to Baghdad.

Although Newman later recalled a conversation in Aleppo with a carpenter whose Muslim faith made a 'lasting impression' on him (Newman, *Phases of Faith*, 32), he was far from abandoning his evangelical beliefs. He still had the highest regard for Groves's missionary ideal, but his own emphatic concern with moral and social issues was out of tune with the resigned 'other-worldliness' of his missionary colleagues, and after three months he set out for home with the biblical scholar John Kitto. Passing the cliff of Behistan, about three years before Sir Henry Rawlinson began to transcribe its trilingual inscription which made possible the decipherment of cuneiform, they travelled by way of Tehran and Tabriz to Constantinople. From there they set sail, and after a two-month voyage arrived in England in June 1833.

Almost at once Newman unsuccessfully renewed his proposal of marriage to Maria Giberne, but by late August his brother John learned from Hurrell Froude that Frank was expected to marry Maria (*c*.1806/7–1876), the daughter of Sir John *Kennaway (1758–1836) of Escott, Devon, though the wedding did not take place until 22 December 1835. In late 1834 Newman was appointed as classical tutor at Bristol College to lecture in the place of the principal who was in weak health. At this time his profession of Christianity was still strictly Trinitarian, as can be seen from his letter to Charles Golightly of 12 November 1834, but his independence of thought had led Darby and others to question his orthodoxy. In consequence, although Maria Kennaway was associated with the Brethren (and continued to be until her death), Newman became a Baptist, and in 1836 was baptized in Broadmead Chapel, Bristol. It was shortly after this that he became friendly with the poet John Sterling, the eldest of whose orphan sons he adopted in 1844.

Newman's crucial break with traditional Christianity occurred when he was classical professor at Manchester New College for six years prior to his appointment in July 1846 as Latin professor at University College, London. At Manchester his holiness was 'reverenced' by Mrs Gaskell (*Letters of Mrs Gaskell*, 87), and his *Catholic Union* (1844) was a plea for a non-dogmatic 'church of the future', but he was moving to a more radical position. Although his *History of the Hebrew Monarchy* and *The Soul: its Sorrows and Aspirations* were not published until 1847 and 1849, they are the fruit of the crisis in his thinking during the early 1840s, when his 'free critical inquiry' caused him to abandon the idea of biblical authority. This, in turn, led to his realization that arbitrary, external moral authorities must be relinquished, and that 'each worshiper sees by a light within him and is directly dependent on God' (Robbins, 107). The publication in 1850 of *Phases of Faith* provoked considerable indignation—not least in Henry Rogers's *The Eclipse of Faith* (1852)—but Newman's autobiographical account of how his earlier religious attitudes had been 'pruned and chastened by the sceptical understanding' (*Phases of Faith*, 175) found many sympathetic readers. Although later in the century his pioneer rationalism would be forgotten, at the time it answered to the needs of a generation of 'honest doubters' including the young Marian Evans (George Eliot), who hailed him in 1849 as 'our blessed St Francis' (Willey, 31).

Newman's first years at the University of London were not without administrative controversy. In February 1848 he had accepted the principalship of University Hall, a newly established centre for liberal dissenting students, but his criticisms of the hall's structural arrangement led him to resign in November. Similarly, as an outspoken champion of women's rights Newman had supported the establishment of Bedford College, where he delivered his lectures on political economy, but in 1851 he resigned his professorship at the college and his place on its council in protest at the dismissal of a colleague, the Revd Thomas Wilson, for his heterodox theology.

Translations and other writings As a classics teacher Newman strove to treat Greek and Latin as spoken languages and to put them in a modern context by using his translations of *Hiawatha* (1862) and *Robinson Crusoe* (*Rebilius Cruso*, 1884). He introduced the Italian pronunciation of Latin and his lectures were always delivered without notes, but he was irritated by the many students who were content to 'scrape through their degree' (Sieveking, 115) and he had difficulty in establishing much rapport with his pupils. Significantly his commentaries on Aeschylus and Euripides appeared only in the 1880s, after his retirement. His English translation of *The Iliad* (1856) was intended to be read by 'working men', and he therefore presented it in ballad form using prosaic (and sometimes archaic) language. When Matthew Arnold, in his essay *On Translating Homer* (1861), pilloried the work as pedantic and ignoble, his hostility to Newman was probably partly related to his earlier complaint that, in *Phases of Faith*, Newman 'bepaws the religious sentiment so much that he quite effaces it to me' (Arnold, 115). Newman's ruthless demolition of the Christian establishment was part of the 'anarchy' from which Arnold was trying to salvage a Christian 'culture'. Newman was deeply hurt by Arnold's attack, but his reply in *Homeric Translation in Theory and Practice* (1861) was more concerned with the need for an accurate contextual understanding of Homer than with poetry.

Francis Newman's linguistic talents found expression in his enquiries into a remarkable range of ancient languages. He had a working knowledge of cuneiform, published a *Libyan Vocabulary* (1882) from which he proposed to recover the ancient Numidian language, and was keenly interested in the pre-classical Italic languages. Building on the pioneering work of Lepsius and other German scholars, he produced for English readers an edition of the Umbrian *Iguvine Inscriptions with Interlinear Latin Translation and Notes* (1864) and *First Steps in Etruscan* (1892). His insatiable appetite for these researches was reflected in some forty years of correspondence with the biblical orientalist John Nicholson of Penrith. He also published a *Handbook* (1866) and *Dictionary of Modern Arabic* (2 vols., 1871) and a *Kabail Vocabulary* (1882, 1887).

On the Defective Morality of the New Testament (1867) is one of numerous works by Newman in which it is clear that his difficulties with traditional Christianity were as much moral as historical. Haunted and appalled by any form of injustice and suffering, Newman's capacity for moral indignation was almost proverbial. *The Crimes of the House of Hapsburg Against its Own Liege Subjects* was his protest in 1853 against the exile of Mazzini and other nationalists whom Newman had befriended, and in the same year he edited an English selection of Kossuth's speeches. Later he published his *Reminiscences of Kossuth and Pulszky* (1888). A similar abhorrence of imperial exploitation informed his criticism of British rule in Ireland and India.

Naturally he supported American abolitionists, but many of his political objectives were less fashionable. As early as 1860 he argued in the *Westminster Review* for a system of international arbitration to reduce the danger of war. In *English Institutions* (1865) he opposed hereditary aristocracy, called for the involvement of the Indian people in the government of India, and proposed the establishment of fourteen provincial councils in Great Britain and Ireland elected by universal suffrage. He fervently believed in the right of women to vote, and his 'Marriage laws' in *Fraser's Magazine* (August 1867) argued that married women should be allowed to be independent property owners. He was a relentless critic of the Contagious Diseases Act of 1864, which he sarcastically referred to as the 'Safe-Harlot-Providing Law' (Sieveking, 380). His delight at the establishment of the National Agricultural Labourers' Union in 1872 was a natural corollary to his support for the Land Nationalisation Society, of which he was later vice-president. He was aware of his isolation in many of these causes and in 1881 wrote with some despondency that he was 'ashamed to be an Englishman … I look on ministers in the House as nearly our worst nuisance' (ibid., 356).

Character and later life Observers often felt that Newman was inclined to become a crusader rather too readily—all the more so after 1862, when he relinquished the chair of Latin in London, and, as emeritus professor after 1865, moved back to Clifton, Bristol, in 1866. His humane attitude to animals and his opposition to vivisection might be regarded as an extension of his wider concern for the oppressed, but his obsessive preoccupation with what he saw as the evils of vaccination, alcohol, smoking, and the eating of meat meant that he was perceived as being only on the fringes of serious reform. The grave dignity of his dark complexion and aquiline nose was diminished by fastidious eccentricities (epitomized by the rug, with a hole in the middle for his head, worn over three overcoats) and by his total lack of humour.

At heart, Francis Newman's priorities were still religious, and from 1865 their development can be traced in some twenty contributions to the series of publications issued by his fellow freethinker Thomas Scott. Although he was critical of Unitarian dogma, his friendship with James Martineau, dating back to 1840, contributed to a softening of his position, and in 1876 he joined the British and Foreign Unitarian Association, of which he was later vice-president. On 16 July 1876 his wife died in Weston-super-Mare, where they had been living for a few years. On 3 December 1878 he married his wife's devoted friend, Eleanor Williams (b. 1823/4), who was then aged fifty-four, the daughter of John Williams, a builder. It was Newman's practice, after breakfast, to conduct family prayers, a selection of which he published in 1878. He eventually considered himself a Christian in the sense that he believed the Lord's prayer to be 'the highest and purest in any known national religion' (Sieveking, 343), though he regarded immortality as no more than a possibility. In his later years he regularly visited his brother John, with whom his relationship was courteous but detached. Although many readers felt that his *Contributions Chiefly to* the Early History of the Late Cardinal Newman (1891) was needlessly caustic, the book demonstrates how much Francis had retained of the earlier evangelical tradition which John had abandoned. Writing to Edwin A. Abbott in 1892 he observed: 'while I cannot be a Christian if weighed in any historical balance yet my moral and spiritual sentiment is unchanged since I joyfully surrendered myself to God in 1819'. In his last years he continued writing, but was hampered by increasingly weak eyesight and partial paralysis. He died on 4 October 1897 at 15 Arundel Crescent, Weston-super-Mare, where he was buried in the cemetery on 9 October. He was survived by his second wife. An appropriate tribute was paid at his funeral to his 'enthusiasm for righteousness' and 'his sympathy with downtrodden and oppressed people' (ibid., 345).

Newman's last work, *Mature Thought on Christianity* (1897), was posthumously edited by his old friend, the secularist G. J. Holyoake, who had also been reared as an evangelical and had similarly rejected Christianity in the 1840s. Holyoake later recalled his admiration for Newman's moral integrity and intellectual powers, insisting that theism had rarely seemed so 'enchanting' as it had appeared in the life of Francis Newman (Holyoake, 1.201).

TIMOTHY C. F. STUNT

Sources F. W. Newman, *Phases of faith, or, Passages from the history of my creed*, 6th edn (1860); repr. (1970) · F. W. Newman, *Contributions chiefly to the early history of the late Cardinal Newman*, 2nd edn (1891) · I. G. Sieveking, *Memoir and letters of Francis W. Newman* (1909) · *The letters and diaries of John Henry Newman*, ed. C. S. Dessain and others, [31 vols.] (1961–) · B. Willey, *More nineteenth century studies: a group of honest doubters* (1956); another edn (1980), 11–52 · W. Robbins, *The Newman brothers: an essay in comparative intellectual biography* (1966) · T. C. F. Stunt, 'John Henry Newman and the evangelicals', *Journal of Ecclesiastical History*, 21 (1970), 65–74 · T. C. F. Stunt, *From awakening to secession: radical evangelicals in Switzerland and Britain, 1815–35* (2000) · LPL, Golightly MS 1808 [F. W. Newman letter to C. P. Golightly, 12 November 1834], pp. 180–81 · F. W. Newman, letter to E. A. Abbot, 28 March 1892, [formerly in Pusey Oxf.] · M. Arnold, *Letters to A. H. Clough*, ed. H. F. Lowry (1932) · G. J. Holyoake, *Bygones worth remembering*, 2 vols. (1905) · C. H. Daniel and W. R. Barker, *Worcester College* (1900), 199 · S. O'Faolain, *Newman's way* (1952) · M. J. Tuke, *A history of Bedford College for Women, 1849–1937* (1939), 69–76 · H. H. Bellot, *University College, London, 1826–1926* (1929), 256–8 · *Remains of Thomas Byrth … with a memoir of his life by the Rev. G. R. Moncreiff* (1851), 101–2 · *The letters of Mrs Gaskell*, ed. J. A. V. Chapple and A. Pollard (1966), 86–91 · T. Kabdebo, *Diplomat in exile: Francis Pulszky's political activities in England, 1849–1860*, East European Monographs, no. 56 (*East European Quarterly*, Boulder, 1979) · m. cert. · d. cert. · *DNB* · A. M. Schellenberg, 'Prize the doubt: the life and work of Francis William Newman', PhD diss., U. Durham

Archives Birmingham Oratory, files · Bodl. Oxf., letters [copies] · Boston PL, corresp. · Hunt. L., corresp. · LUL, corresp. · UCL, corresp. and MSS · Worcester College, Oxford, corresp. | Birmingham Oratory, letters to J. H. Newman and others · BL, letters to W. E. Gladstone, Add. MSS 44397–44786, *passim* · BL, letters to Toulmin Smith, RP 831 · Bodl. Oxf., letters to A. H. Clough and others, MS Eng. lett. · Co-operative Union, Holyoake House, Manchester, letters to G. J. Holyoake · CUL, letters to Lord Kelvin · DWL, corresp. with Henry Crabb Robinson · Harris Man. Oxf., J. Martineau MSS, letters to J. Martineau and others, 4, 1–152 · Harvard U., Houghton L., letters to J. H. Allen · JRL, letters to W. E. A. Axon · LPL, letters to C. P. Golightly and W. Trower, Golightly MS 1808, pp. 176–81 · LUL, letters to J. R. Mozley and others · Orszàgos Széchényi Könyvtàr, Budapest, corresp. with F. A. Pulszky [photocopies in UCL] · Pusey Oxf., letters to Edwin A. Abbott [photocopies] · U. Lpool, letters to John Thom and Hannah Thom · W. Yorks. AS, Leeds, letters to William Shaen and Mrs Shaen · Worcester College, Oxford, letters to C. H. O. Daniel

Likenesses H. Watkins, photograph, 1858, NPG [*see illus.*] · J. Davies, photograph, *c.*1876, repro. in Sieveking, *Memoir* · G. Bainsmith, bronze bust, *c.*1885; LUL, 1909 · J. Banks, photograph, NPG · J. Davies, photograph (after daguerreotype, 1851), repro. in Sieveking, *Memoir*

Wealth at death £791 8s. 2d.: resworn probate, Feb 1898, *CGPLA Eng. & Wales* (1897)

Newman, Sir George (1870–1948), medical officer of health, was born on 23 October 1870 at 14 Broad Street, Leominster, Herefordshire, the fourth child and second son of Henry Stanley Newman, a Quaker and for many years editor of *The Friend*, and his wife, Mary Anna, *née* Pumphrey. He began his education at a local dame-school before becoming a boarder at Sidcot School in Gloucestershire in 1881, then at Bootham School in York, 1885–8. At the age of twelve he resolved to become a missionary, though his father, himself the founding secretary of the Friends' Foreign Missionary Society, favoured a career in the Indian Civil Service. Some time in 1886, however, Newman read John Lowe's *Medical Missions* and decided that medicine was his calling. He sat and failed the matriculation examination of Edinburgh University in October 1887, but passed on his second attempt six months later, and began his studies at the university in May 1888.

Early years in medicine Newman's early years as a medical student were undistinguished. He devoted much of his energy to religious activities, reviewing books for *The Friend* and joining the University Christian movement. Here he fell under the spell of the liberal evangelical Henry Drummond, who subsequently became a close friend and a model for Newman's own increasingly rationalistic faith. During his second year in Edinburgh Newman began holding weekly services in a lodging house in the Cowgate, experiencing for the first time the circumstances of slum life. He was equally shocked by the moral laxity of his fellow medical students, among whom he preached temperance. In 1890 he became one of the secretaries of the Medical Students' Christian Association. By 1892 he was applying himself more conscientiously to his medical studies, winning distinctions in medicine, surgery, obstetrics, and public health in the spring of that year, and graduated MB.

Shortly thereafter Newman moved to London. He became assistant physician to the London Medical Mission in the parish of St Giles-in-the-Fields in December 1892, but found the institution deficient in Christian spirit and resigned four months later. He continued to be involved in running a girls' club in the neighbourhood, however, and late in 1893 he became the warden of Chalfont House, a Quaker settlement in Bloomsbury. By this time his evangelical energies were increasingly being channelled into public health work, which he had studied in Edinburgh under Sir Douglas Maclagan. While at the medical mission he had addressed public meetings on temperance, and in February 1893 he began lecturing on

Sir George Newman (1870–1948), by Margaret Lindsay Williams, exh. RA 1935

hygiene and ambulance work for Essex county council. He also spent two years working part time for the medical officer of health to the Strand board of works, Francis Allan, collecting evidence for Allan's inquiry into the living conditions of the local population. In autumn 1894 Newman began studying at King's College, London, for the Cambridge diploma in public health, which he obtained in October 1895. Also in 1895 he took the Edinburgh MD and gold medal with a historical dissertation on the decline of leprosy in England and India, which he studied in the library of the prominent Quaker surgeon Jonathan Hutchinson. The dissertation won the university's Alison prize for medical jurisprudence and public health, and was published by Hutchinson's New Sydenham Society.

In January 1896 Newman was appointed part-time demonstrator at King's College, London, at a salary of £100 per annum, teaching practical classes under the professor of bacteriology, Edgar Crookshank. The post also provided him with the opportunity to conduct bacteriological research, which resulted in the publication of a book, *Bacteria*, in 1899 and, with Harold Swithinbank, *The Bacteriology of Milk* in 1903. In March 1896 Newman applied unsuccessfully for the post of medical officer of health to Clerkenwell. Later that year he was offered a position as a medical inspector to the Local Government Board to oversee the practice of vaccination, but Newman wished to pursue a wider perspective on public health and turned it down. In January 1897 he was appointed part-time medical officer to the Holborn board of guardians. In April that year he became engaged to Adelaide Constance, the daughter of Samuel Thorp of Alderley Edge. An accomplished artist, she was herself a member of the Society of Friends, and the couple met through their common involvement in the Frideswide Girls' Club. They married in August 1898 and moved into a home in Woburn Square, Bloomsbury, though Newman retained the wardenship of

Chalfont House. Meanwhile he was becoming increasingly involved in the liberal wing of the Society of Friends, though he did not always find favour among more conservative Quakers; in February 1900 a group of Friends publicly criticized him as a vivisectionist. He began editing *The Friends' Quarterly Examiner* at the end of 1899, and continued to do so anonymously for the next forty years; he took particular pleasure in the lively leaders that he wrote from 'The House of the Four Winds'.

Public health work Newman's career in public health was by this time beginning to gain momentum. In October 1897 he was offered the post of government bacteriologist to the India Office to study and advise on the control of plague, but he was increasingly of the view that Britain's public health needs must come before those of the dominions, and he declined the appointment. On 1 April 1900 he was appointed part-time consulting medical officer for Bedfordshire at a salary of 50 guineas. Also in April 1900 he was made temporary medical officer of health to Clerkenwell, whereupon he resigned from the wardenship of Chalfont House and from his demonstratorship at King's College. In June 1900 he secured his first permanent full-time position as medical officer of health to the new metropolitan borough of Finsbury, a poor and overcrowded area of London with a growing immigrant population and very high death rates, especially among children.

Newman's first real test as a public health doctor came with an outbreak of smallpox in the summer of 1901. He initiated a policy of intensive surveillance, isolation, and investigation of contacts, to which he attributed the comparatively small number of deaths in the area under his jurisdiction. He was also concerned at the very high death rate from tuberculosis in the borough, to combat which he instituted strict inspections of food outlets including dairies, ice-cream parlours, and the meat trade, and established a scheme of voluntary notification and inspection of cases coupled with instruction in healthy living habits. These initiatives secured him a position on the council of the National Association for the Prevention of Tuberculosis, but had little impact on the incidence of the disease in Finsbury. Increasingly Newman was coming to the view that tuberculosis and other infectious diseases were as much an index of moral as of physical ill health, and must be countered by moral education as much as medical intervention. This view informed his campaigns against infant mortality in particular. In 1904, with charitable funds, he opened a milk depot under the control of the Finsbury Social Workers Association. Here nursing mothers received not only clean milk, but also education in infant management and the maintenance of a hygienic home environment. The milk depot was officially taken over by the borough council in 1906. In the same year Newman published *Infant Mortality: a Social Problem*, which described his work in Finsbury and the philosophy behind it. During this period he also served as a smallpox consultant, lecturer, and examiner to the Royal Sanitary Institute; as a member of the council of the Society of Medical Officers of Health; and from 1905 as lecturer in public health to St Bartholomew's Hospital medical school. He collaborated with Sir Arthur Whitelegge on a thoroughly revised edition of the latter's *Hygiene and the Public Health*, which appeared in 1905, and in 1907 his own book on *The Health of the State* was published.

Into central government In 1906 Newman was contacted by Beatrice Webb, who had recently been appointed a member of the royal commission on the poor laws. Webb was keen to use the commission as a forum in which to argue for the creation of a universally available state medical service under the control of the public health authorities. Newman sympathized with her ideas and presented evidence to the commission that became a key source for many of the arguments she incorporated into her minority report of 1909. Most importantly, he put forward the view that under an appropriately organized system of state medicine the provision of personal health care by general practitioners might be oriented to the work of preventive as much as curative medicine. Through his association with Webb, Newman also met her friend and ally Sir Robert Morant, permanent secretary to the Board of Education. It came as a surprise to Newman when, presumably through Morant's advocacy, in August 1907 he was offered the new post of chief medical officer to the Board of Education, with responsibility for setting up a new school medical service. He took up the post in December, at a salary of £1200. Newman's appointment met with outspoken hostility from many in the medical profession, who feared that the school medical service represented an encroachment of state medicine on private practice, and from the London county council, who initially refused to implement the scheme of medical inspection that Newman drew up. In recognition of his work for the service Newman received a knighthood in the new year's honours list for 1911.

In 1911 the government passed the National Insurance Act, which provided, among other things, for the establishment of a system of national health insurance to provide free medical care to a significant proportion of the working population. This scheme, which eventually came into being in 1913, fell far short of the vision of a state medical service that Webb had sketched for the royal commission on the poor laws. Nevertheless, the act of 1911 created opportunities for further expansion in specific aspects of public health medicine. Most notably, it made special provision for the treatment of tuberculosis cases, and in 1912 a departmental committee chaired by Lord Astor was appointed to recommend an appropriate scheme of services. Newman served on this committee, where he helped to ensure that tuberculosis treatment was brought under the aegis of the public health authorities and was expanded to cover not just the insured but the entire population. The committee also considered how best to make use of the penny per insured person that the National Insurance Act set aside for medical research, and in June 1913 its recommendations resulted in the establishment of the Medical Research Committee (later Council). Five months later Newman was offered the post of secretary to the new committee. He was tempted

to accept, in the hope that the committee would provide a base from which to further his aim of creating a state medical service, but in the end he decided that he would be able to do more for public health if he remained with the Board of Education and the school medical service.

The outbreak of war led to serious delays in the development of the school medical service as government funds were reallocated, local education authorities cut back their inspection programmes, and doctors enlisted in the forces. Newman's energies, too, were diverted into war-related work. In May 1915 he was appointed medical officer to the central control board for liquor traffic, established under the defence of the realm regulations to minimize manpower wastage due to alcohol. In this capacity he was able to give practical expression to his temperance sentiments, particularly by promoting the establishment of factory canteens as an alternative to the attractions of the public house. Four months later he was also appointed chairman of the Health of Munition Workers Committee of the Ministry of Munitions, which oversaw research into a variety of problems including industrial fatigue, TNT poisoning, and other conditions. He also undertook war work in a voluntary capacity. In autumn 1914 he became involved in the establishment of the Friends' Ambulance Unit, which provided medical care for soldiers and civilians in the war zone, and following the introduction of conscription in 1916 he helped to negotiate exemptions for Quakers serving with the ambulance unit. With all this on his plate he felt unable to continue his lectureship at St Bartholomew's Hospital and resigned in January 1916. His contribution to the national effort was officially acknowledged when he was appointed KCB in 1918.

Ministry of Health By 1916 the government was beginning to give serious thought to the problems of post-war reconstruction. Among the schemes under consideration was the creation of a new Ministry of Health which would unify responsibility for the various medical services scattered around different departments of government. For the next three years Newman worked closely with Morant, who from 1911 had overall charge of the national insurance administration, and Christopher Addison, the minister for reconstruction, to draw up a scheme for combining the medical functions of national insurance and the Local Government Board in a single administrative department. Fulfilment of this scheme was delayed by political resistance from poor law and insurance interests, but on 1 April 1919 Newman was appointed chief medical officer to the Local Government Board, and two months later the new ministry was constituted with Newman as chief medical officer, Morant as permanent secretary, and Addison as minister. They envisaged a new kind of ministry in which the medical staff would be given parity of status and remuneration with the lay officials, in contrast to the distinctly subordinate position of technical experts in the old Local Government Board. They were only partially successful in securing this aim, however. Newman was given a salary of £2100, subsequently raised to £2300 in June 1921, but not the official rank of permanent secretary that he hoped for; although he was given the right of direct access to the minister this was an *ad hominem* concession and did not attach to the post of chief medical officer.

Newman's influence within the ministry was subsequently undermined when Morant died suddenly from influenza in March 1920, to be replaced by the far more conservative figure of Arthur Robinson, and again when Addison was forced to resign as minister in the following year. Though Newman remained in post until retirement in 1935, when he was appointed GBE, he was unable to effect any further major reforms in medical administration. Much of his energy was devoted to summarizing the state of the nation's health in a series of monumental annual reports to the ministers of health, and to reiterating his personal vision of preventive medicine in a wide range of official memoranda and public lectures, including the annual oration to the Hunterian Society in 1926; the Dodge lectures, 'Citizenship and the survival of civilization', at Yale University in 1926–7 (published in 1928); the Charles Hastings lecture of the British Medical Association in 1928; the Linacre lecture at Oxford University in the same year; the Halley Stewart lectures, 'Health and social evolution', in 1930; the University of London's Heath Clark lectures, 'The rise of preventive medicine', in 1931; and the Harveian oration to the Royal College of Physicians in 1932. He also served as crown nominee on the General Medical Council, 1919–39, and was latterly its senior treasurer. He enjoyed good relations with leading medical men—the patrician culture in which they moved evidently appealed to him—and he did much to persuade them that the concerns of private practice could be reconciled with the demands of state medicine. He was made an honorary fellow of the Royal College of Surgeons in 1928, and subsequently of the New York Academy of Medicine; he received the Bisset-Hawkins gold medal from the Royal College of Physicians in 1935, and the Fothergill gold medal from the Medical Society of London in the same year.

Later years with the Board of Education As well as serving as chief medical officer to the Ministry of Health Newman retained the post of chief medical officer to the Board of Education until his retirement, with the aim of ensuring co-ordination between the school medical service and other health services. He oversaw renewed expansion of the school medical service after provision of treatment by local education authorities was made compulsory under the Education Act of 1918, but in the context of inter-war economic depression his privileging of health education over more material forms of provision provoked frustration among many public health doctors. He also used his position at the Board of Education to pursue reforms in medical education, which he saw as another means of reorienting doctors towards the practice of preventive as well as curative medicine. In particular he was firmly of the view that control of clinical training should be taken away from the élite private practitioners who dominated

the work of the teaching hospitals at the start of the twentieth century and handed over to university based academic teachers.

In 1908, when the Board of Education had begun to award grants to medical schools, Newman had acquired the leverage to start nudging clinical teaching into more academic channels. Then in 1913 the royal commission on the University of London urged that clinical teaching in several of the metropolitan medical schools should be brought entirely under university control. Working first through the Board of Education then subsequently, from 1919, as medical assessor to the new University Grants Committee, Newman was largely responsible for the negotiations which led to the establishment of full-time university chairs of medicine, surgery, and gynaecology in a number of schools. He also played a major part in drafting the 1921 report of the Athlone committee on postgraduate medical education, which paved the way for the establishment of the London School of Hygiene and Tropical Medicine in 1924.

Thereafter, however, the initiative in the reform of medical education passed increasingly to the Medical Research Council, and Newman's distinctive view that medical training should serve the needs primarily of general practice and preventive medicine tended to be forgotten. The universities appreciated his efforts, however, and his honorary degrees included a DCL from the University of Durham (1919), a DSc from Oxford (1936), and the LLD from London, Edinburgh, McGill, Toronto, Glasgow, and Leeds.

Newman was rather short in stature, but made up for this by his vivacious and dramatic manner in conversation and his eloquence in lectures. As a politician and administrator, he inclined towards an evangelical faith in the power of the written word, as his enormous literary output attests; as a result he was most effective when working with others more pushy than himself, and by far his most fruitful period was marked by his partnership with Morant. He largely withdrew from public life after his retirement, though he found the time to publish *The Building of a Nation's Health* in 1939, and to speak at the centenary of the Quaker journal, *The Friend*, in 1943. His wife died in April 1946; they had no children. Newman himself died at The Retreat, York, on 26 May 1948, and was buried in the historic Quaker burial-ground at Jordans.

STEVE STURDY

Sources M. A. E. Hammer, 'The building of a nation's health: the life and work of George Newman to 1921', PhD diss., U. Cam., 1995 • W. F. Bynum, 'Sir George Newman and the American way', *The history of medical education in Britain*, ed. V. Nutton and R. Porter (1995), 37–50 • *The Friend* (4 June 1948) • S. Sturdy, 'Hippocrates and state medicine: George Newman outlines the founding policy of the ministry of health', *Greater than the parts: holism in biomedicine: 1920–1950*, ed. C. Lawrence and G. Weisz (1998), 112–34 • *The Lancet* (5 June 1948), 888–9 • *BMJ* (5 June 1948), 1112–17 • *The Times* (27 May 1948) • R. Acheson and P. Poole, 'The London School of Hygiene and Tropical Medicine: a child of many parents', *Medical History*, 35 (1991), 385–408 • d. cert.

Archives Herefs. RO, corresp. and papers • PRO, diary • Wellcome L., corresp. • Wellcome L., papers | Birm. CA, letters to Elizabeth Cadbury • Bodl. Oxf., Christopher Addison MSS • Bodl.

Oxf., corresp. with Viscount Addison and other papers · PRO, Ministry of Health and Board of Education files

Likenesses W. Stoneman, photograph, 1918, NPG · M. L. Williams, oils, exh. RA 1935, London School of Hygiene and Tropical Medicine [see illus.]

Wealth at death £58,618 4s. 9d.: probate, 30 July 1948, CGPLA Eng. & Wales

Newman, Henry (1670–1743), missionary society administrator, was born on 10 November 1670 at Rehoboth, Massachusetts, the eldest of the three sons of Noah Newman (c.1646–1678), a Congregational minister, and his wife, Joanna (d. 1679), the daughter of Henry Flint, a nonconformist minister of Roxbury, Massachusetts. His grandfather was a puritan divine who emigrated from England to Massachusetts about 1636. After attending free schools in Massachusetts, Newman went to Harvard College in 1683 to prepare for the Congregational ministry, but the college was becoming more liberal in outlook, and the influence of its tutors, who introduced their students to recent Anglican writings, eventually led him into the Church of England. He acquired there also an interest in mathematics and astronomy, which led him to produce two almanacs—*Harvard's Ephemeris* (1690) and *News from the Stars* (1691).

Newman graduated BA in 1687 and MA in 1690, and remained at Harvard as librarian until 1693. He then had a commercial career, trading with Europe principally in Newfoundland fish until 1703, when he settled in England. He was employed by Charles Seymour, sixth duke of Somerset, until about 1708.

In 1703 Newman became a corresponding member for Newfoundland of the Society for Promoting Christian Knowledge (SPCK), founded by Dr Thomas Bray, and in 1708 was appointed its secretary. He was suited for the post. He knew Latin and French, his American connection was valuable when the society was extending its work across the Atlantic, and his support of the house of Hanover strengthened the position of Bray and his friends, who did not want to see the society involved in the struggle for the succession to the throne in Queen Anne's reign.

Newman was a modest, retiring man and avoided prominence for himself. He was unmarried and content with his canaries and his cats. He clearly joined in the discussion at the society's meetings, but he never referred in the minutes to any view expressed by himself; and he did not leave London to visit any of the society's members in their homes. His main task was to engage in the correspondence concerned with the society's interests. In his first five years he wrote more than 6000 letters, besides making abstracts of all the letters the society had received. The drafts of his letters have been preserved in the SPCK's archives. They provide nearly all the information about him and a full account of the work of the society during those years.

Through his correspondence Newman succeeded in putting into effect the society's decisions. He dealt with many subjects as the society's activities steadily widened. While its original purpose, as he explained, was 'to encourage the erection of charity schools and to disperse good books' (Cowie, 22), it was led into other enterprises, which often caused Newman serious problems. Notable was his failure to induce Anglican missionaries to go to India, which caused the society to support German Lutherans there despite high-church criticism.

In addition, Newman's philanthropic concern led him to support such causes as Thomas Coram's Foundling Hospital and James Oglethorpe's settlement of Georgia. He served also as colonial agent for New Hampshire from 1709 to 1720, representing the colony's interests to the British government, especially in its lengthy boundary dispute with Massachusetts.

Newman worked for the SPCK until he died of asthma at his home in Bartlett's Buildings, Holborn, on 15 June 1743. He was buried in the churchyard of St Andrew's, Holborn, on 17 June. He was notable for his sincere but modest personal religion, which found expression in a broad-minded attitude towards others and a wish to devote himself to their welfare.   LEONARD W. COWIE

Sources L. W. Cowie, *Henry Newman: an American in London, 1708–43* (1956) · W. K. Lowther Clarke, *Eighteenth-century piety* (1944) · H. P. Thompson, *Thomas Bray* (1954) · W. K. Lowther Clarke, *A history of the SPCK* (1959) · M. G. Jones, *The charity school movement: a study in eighteenth century puritanism in action* (1938) · S. E. Morison, *Three centuries of Harvard* (1936) · H. Newman, correspondence, CUL, SPCK MSS · minute books, CUL, SPCK MSS · parish register, St Andrew's, Holborn [burial]

Archives Bucks. RLSS, letters relating to translation of New Testament into Arabic · CUL, SPCK MSS, abstract of correspondence, letters, minute-books · CUL, letter-books | Christ Church Oxf., Wake MSS · Commonwealth Relations Office, East India Company MSS · CUL, letters to John Stype · Harvard U., Hollis MSS · LPL, corresp. with Society for Propagating the Gospel in Foreign Parts · PRO, Colonial Office MSS

Newman, Jeremiah Whitaker (1759–1839), surgeon and physician, son of Arthur Newman, surgeon, of Ringwood, Hampshire, and his wife, Joanna, was born on 7 April 1759. He was apprenticed to a London surgeon, Alexander Reid, in 1773. Newman became a member of the Company of Surgeons and was in practice at Ringwood in 1783. Ill health led to his moving to Dover, where he made the acquaintance of the antiquary Sir Thomas Mantell and his wife, and he lived with them for many years. He was a delightful companion at all times, 'full of anecdote and energy, intelligence and originality' (GM, 594). Newman married Mary Shoulder at St Mary the Virgin, Dover, on 17 November 1790. On 9 December 1790 Newman was admitted an extra-licentiate of the Royal College of Physicians, London. He was a favourite with the eccentric Messenger Monsey, the resident physician at Chelsea Hospital, of whom he wrote (but did not publish) an amusing memoir.

Newman's principal work, published anonymously, was *The lounger's commonplace book, or, Miscellaneous anecdotes: a biographic, political, literary, and satirical compilation*, 4 vols. (1796–99). He also wrote *A short inquiry into the merits of solvents, so far as it may be necessary to compare them with the operation of lithotomy* (1781) and *An essay on the principles and manners of the medical profession; with some occasional remarks* on the use and abuse of medicines (1783). These two tracts were republished in 1789 under the title of *Medical Essays, with Additions*. He settled on his own estate at Ringwood, Hampshire, where he died on 27 July 1839.

THOMPSON COOPER, rev. MICHAEL BEVAN

Sources P. J. Wallis and R. V. Wallis, *Eighteenth century medics*, 2nd edn (1988) · Munk, *Roll* · [J. Watkins and F. Shoberl], *A biographical dictionary of the living authors of Great Britain and Ireland* (1816) · *GM*, 2nd ser., 12 (1839), 323 · *GM*, 2nd ser., 25 (1846), 594 · *GM*, 2nd ser., 26 (1846), 153 · *GM*, 2nd ser., 39 (1853), 226 · *N&Q*, 9 (1854), 258 · *N&Q*, 3rd ser., 5 (1864), 500n. · Watt, *Bibl. Brit.* · d. cert. · IGI

Newman, John (*c.*1677–1741), Presbyterian minister, was born in or near Banbury in Oxfordshire. Details of his parents are unknown but he was schooled by the Revd Samuel Chapman, probably at Yoxford in Suffolk; later he was prepared for the ministry at the academy run by John Woodhouse at Sheriff Hales, Shropshire. In 1695 he was appointed assistant to Joseph Read at Dyott Street Chapel in Bloomsbury, London, and the following year he was made assistant to Nathaniel Taylor at Salters' Hall. He was early recognized as a rising star within dissent, and he was ordained in October 1697, before he came of age. He continued as assistant to Taylor's successor, William Tong, until 1716, when he was made co-pastor. In 1727 he was appointed senior pastor, an office which he held until his death. In 1724 he added the position of the Tuesday Merchants' lecturer at Salters' Hall to his tasks.

Newman was a highly popular preacher and attracted large numbers in his early years at Salters' Hall. He preached to crowded congregations without notes and 'had an admirable method of reaching the conscience, and exposing the secret devices of the human heart' (Jones, 183). A long ministry of this duration could only mean a falling off of popularity at some stage but 'when his popularity declined, so did not he; he lost that but nothing else; but preached better Sermons when he had fewer hearers' (Barker, 25).

Newman married about 1706, although details of his wife's identity have not been found; his eldest son, Samuel (1707–1735), was his assistant at Salters' Hall from 1728. Newman was a subscriber in 1719 in the Salters' Hall debate and his theology was traditional; he was not affected by the doctrinal disputes of the day but he was noted for his pastoral work and for the attention that he gave to his family. His published work was limited to sermons.

Newman died at Sion College, London, on 25 July 1741, after a few days' illness, and was buried on 31 July at Bunhill Fields with his wife, who had predeceased him. The address at the graveside was given by Philip Doddridge, an old friend, who said of Newman that 'He was one Lord's day in the Pulpit … the next in Paradise … And now he has gone the way of all the Earth, buried in Silence, and covered with the Clods of the Valley' (Barker, 30–31).

ALEXANDER GORDON, rev. ALAN RUSTON

Sources J. Barker and P. Doddridge, *Resignation to the will of God, consider'd, in a funeral sermon for … John Newman* (1741), 22–41 · W. Wilson, *The history and antiquities of the dissenting churches and meeting houses in London, Westminster and Southwark*, 4 vols. (1808–14), vol. 2, pp. 33–6 · C. Surman, index, DWL · will, PRO, PROB 11/711, sig. 209 · W. D. Jeremy, *The Presbyterian Fund and Dr Daniel Williams's Trust* (1885), 128 · J. A. Jones, ed., *Bunhill memorials* (1849), 182–3 · IGI

Likenesses J. Hopwood, stipple (after portrait by unknown artist), BM, NPG; repro. in Wilson, *History and antiquities of dissenting churches*, vol. 2, facing p. 33 · oils, DWL

Wealth at death see will, PRO, PROB 11/711, sig. 209

Newman, John (*bap.* 1783, *d.* 1860), maker of scientific instruments, was baptized at St Giles, Camberwell, on 27 June 1783, one of two sons and two daughters—Mary (*bap.* 1779) and Jane (*bap.* 1781)—of Robert and Mary Newman of Windmill Row, Camberwell. He and his brother, George (*bap.* 1785), were together apprenticed on 1 October 1799 to Philip Brock, a lesser-known mathematical instrument maker of Fetter Lane, in the City of London. In 1807 John took his freedom in his master's livery, the Company of Makers of Playing Cards. From this time he traded independently, initially from 11 Windmill Row, Camberwell, on the southern margins of London. By 1809 he had moved to Lisle Street, off Leicester Square, Westminster, where he remained until 1827, trading as a chemical and philosophical instrument maker.

Newman's lifelong association with the Royal Institution, based in Albemarle Street, on the north side of Piccadilly, began about 1809. Accounts show that he not only supplied standard laboratory apparatus and chemicals, but also acted as laboratory assistant, cleaning and repairing the instruments. He helped to prepare the theatre for the demonstrations of Humphry Davy, William Thomas Brande, and other lecturers, and it was in connection with one such lecture that an incident of some significance occurred. On 22 February 1813, as the Royal Institution Managers' Minutes (5.353) recorded:

> Mr Harris the superintendent of the House reported that on Friday evening last, hearing a great noise in the lecture room, he went to see the cause of it. When he found Mr Payne and Mr Newman at high words and Newman complained of having been struck by Payne for representing to him his neglect of duty in being absent when he should have attended on Mr Brande.

Payne was promptly dismissed. A week later, the minutes recorded (5.355):

> Sir Humphry Davy has the honour to inform the Managers that he has found a person who is desirous to occupy the situation in the Institution lately filled by Mr Payne. His name is Michael Faraday. He is a youth of 22 years of age and as far as Sir Humphry Davy has been able to observe or ascertain, he appears well fitted for the situation.

Faraday was duly engaged.

There is no evidence that Newman had applied to fill the vacancy. Clearly he had already developed a clientele that numbered some of the leading scientists of his day, as well as supplying the trade. In 1818 he made a copper waterbottle to Davy's designs for John Ross's polar expedition; it was a failure, though a sturdy iron sampler which he constructed for the chemist Alexander Marcet was sent on Edward Parry's first Arctic expedition of 1819 and appeared to function effectively down to 300 fathoms. Newman was also employed by the Revd Edward Daniel Clarke, professor of mineralogy at Cambridge, to make an oxy-hydrogen blowpipe, which was described in Clarke's

The Gas Blow-Pipe (1819). In 1822 he made a standard barometer for the Royal Society, and later supplied similar standards to several major observatories.

In April 1828 the Royal Institution awarded the Fuller silver medal to Newman and allowed him to style himself 'philosophical instrument maker to the Royal Institution'. Newman promptly moved into more prestigious premises at 122 Regent Street. At about this time he married Elizabeth, who came from Southwark. They set up house at 82 Albany Street, Camden Town, and raised two sons and two daughters.

Robert Hare, writing to the American scientist Joseph Henry in 1837, stated: 'In London you will find a great number of shops in which philosophical instruments are sold. The persons so engaged are generally scientific men ... I do not like Newman, 122 Regent Street ... he is however much employed' (*Papers of Joseph Henry*, 3.151). In April 1837 Henry bought a number of instruments from Newman, and described him as 'a ... much older man than I imagined' (*Papers of Joseph Henry*, 3.237).

Many scientists and explorers commissioned special apparatus from Newman; Sir Charles Wheatstone and Isambard Kingdom Brunel were among his customers, as were the major colleges and institutions. From the large number of surviving instruments, many of ingenious and imaginative design, and of first-rate quality, his high reputation was certainly justified. The citation for his award of the council medal at the Great Exhibition of 1851 praises for its originality, excellence, and perfection, his air-pump, the best in the exhibition.

Newman's son John Frederick joined him in business until December 1859 when their partnership was dissolved by mutual consent and Newman retired from business. A Richard Newman who signed a shop receipt in 1839 may have been his other son, but his role in the firm is unknown. Newman died at his home, 26 High Street, Camden Town, on 5 July 1860. His son's business did not last long and the premises were almost immediately taken over by the rival firm of Negretti and Zambra, about whose barometers Newman had made some disparaging remarks in earlier years. Newman's will showed that he owned or leased much property in Camden Town, Woolwich, and Camberwell, in addition to the lease of 122 Regent Street. HOWARD DAWES

Sources minutes of the proceedings of the managers of the Royal Institution, Royal Institution of Great Britain, London, vols. 4–9 (1809–60) · *A catalogue, of philosophical instruments* (1822) [sale catalogue, J. Newman, 8 Lisle St, Leicester Square, London] · J. Newman, *A catalogue of philosophical instruments* (1827) · H. Davy, 'A description of the apparatus...for bringing up water from certain depths in the sea', *Journal of the Society of Arts*, 5 (1818), 231–3 · A. Marcet, 'On the specific gravity and temperature of sea waters', *PTRS*, 109 (1819), 161–208 · CUL, Royal Greenwich Observatory papers, Airy correspondence · *The papers of Joseph Henry*, ed. N. Reingold and others, [8 vols.] (Washington, DC, 1972–), vol. 3, pp. 151, 237 · will of J. Newman, 12 Sept 1860 · R. T. Gunter, *Early science in Cambridge* (1937) · d. cert. · parish register, St Giles Church, Camberwell, 1783, Surrey [baptism] · census returns, 1851

Archives Meteorological Office Museum, artefacts · MHS Oxf., artefacts · Royal Institution of Great Britain, London, artefacts ·

Royal Scottish Museum, Edinburgh, artefacts · Sci. Mus., artefacts · Whipple Museum, Cambridge, artefacts

Wealth at death under £3000: probate, 12 Sept 1860, *CGPLA Eng. & Wales*

Newman, John (*bap.* **1786**, *d.* **1859**), architect, was baptized at St Sepulchre's Church, Holborn, London, on 8 July 1786, the son of John Newman (*d.* 1808), wholesale dealer in leather, of Skinner Street, Snow Hill, and a common councillor of the ward of Farringdon Without. His grandfather William Newman was sheriff of London in 1789–90. In 1819 Newman married Eliza Frances, daughter of the Revd Bartholomew Middleton, subdean of Chichester.

Nothing is known of Newman's education or architectural training, although he is presumed to have visited Italy, having, in 1807, exhibited at the Royal Academy a drawing of the remains of the temple of Jupiter Tonans in Rome. By 1809 he was working for Sir Robert Smirke on the building of Covent Garden Theatre. His most important building was the Roman Catholic church of St Mary, Blomfield Street, Moorfields (1817–20), for which he exhibited drawings at the Royal Academy in 1819 and 1821. Howard Colvin noted that, 'for the first time in nineteenth-century London, the Mass was given a dramatic setting comparable to that in continental churches' in this 'ambitious and cleverly designed ... outstanding building' (Colvin, *Archs.*, 700). Newman was also responsible for a terrace of houses in Duke Street, Southwark, with wharves and warehouses behind them, built when the line for the new London Bridge was decided in 1824; the Islington proprietary school, Barnsbury Street (1830); the School for the Indigent Blind in St George's Fields, Southwark (1834–8), in the Gothic style; and St Olave's Girls' School, Maze Pond, Southwark (1839–40). He exhibited several of his designs at the Royal Academy between 1807 and 1838.

From about 1815 Newman was one of the three surveyors in the commission of sewers for Kent and Surrey, and helped to prepare a report in 1843. He was also clerk of the Bridge House estates for over thirty years. He held several surveying appointments, including that to the commissioners of pavements and improvements for the west division of Southwark, and to Earl Somers's estate in Somers Town, St Pancras, London. He was honorary architect to the Royal Literary Fund from 1846, and to the Society of Patrons of the Charity Children's anniversary meeting in St Paul's Cathedral.

Newman also built up a collection of antiquities which he found in the London area, including a colossal bronze head of Hadrian from the bed of the Thames, now in the British Museum. The collection formed the subject of two papers delivered by Charles Roach Smith to the Society of Antiquaries in 1837 and in 1842. His collection was sold by auction at Sothebys in 1848. He was a fellow of the Society of Antiquaries from 1830 until 1849, and was elected a fellow of the Institute of British Architects in 1834.

Newman retired in 1850. He died on 3 January 1859 at the house of his son-in-law Dr Alexander Spiers, the lexicographer, at Passy, near Paris.

Arthur Shean Newman (1828–1873), architect, the son

of John Newman, was born at the Old Bridge House, Southwark, on 3 May 1828 and baptized at St Olave's Church, Southwark, on 18 March 1829. In 1858 he entered into partnership with Arthur Billing, and designed many churches, including St James's, Kidbrooke (1867), Christ Church, Somers Town (1868), and Holy Trinity, Penge (1872). He also restored Stepney church. He was surveyor to Guy's Hospital and to the St Olave's district board of works for many years, and succeeded to some of his father's appointments. Newman died on 3 March 1873, leaving a widow, Phoebe, and a son, Arthur Harrison Newman (d. 1922), who succeeded to his practice.

BERTHA PORTER, rev. ANNE PIMLOTT BAKER

Sources Colvin, *Archs.* · *Dir. Brit. archs.* · Boase, *Mod. Eng. biog.* · Graves, *RA exhibitors* · IGI · *CGPLA Eng. & Wales* (1873) [Arthur Shean Newman]
Archives RIBA, nomination papers · RIBA BAL, drawings collection · RIBA BAL, biography file
Wealth at death under £3000—Arthur Shean Newman: probate, 25 May 1873, *CGPLA Eng. & Wales*

Newman, John Henry (1801–1890), theologian and cardinal, was born on 21 February 1801 at 80 Old Broad Street in the City of London. His father, John Newman (d. 1824), was a banker, the son of a London grocer, who originally came from Cambridgeshire. His mother, Jemima (d. 1836), was the daughter of Henry Fourdrinier, a paper maker, whose family were originally French Huguenot refugees, and the sister of Henry Fourdrinier (1766–1854). They had married in 1799 and John Henry was their first child of six. Francis William *Newman (1805–1897) was one of his brothers.

Formative years In 1803 the family moved to 17 Southampton Street (later Southampton Place), Bloomsbury. They were sufficiently well off to own another Georgian house, in the country—Grey Court House near Ham Common, Surrey. In 1808 Newman was sent to Ealing School, a well-known private boarding-school. Saved from the ordeals of a public school—he managed later to avoid being sent to Winchester—he enjoyed school life. Apart from his academic studies (in which he excelled) and games (in which he had no interest), he acted in Latin plays, played the violin, won prizes for speeches, and edited periodicals, in which he wrote articles in the style of Addison. This happy childhood came to an abrupt end in March 1816 when the financial collapse after the Napoleonic wars forced his father's bank to close. While his father tried unsuccessfully to manage a brewery at Alton, Hampshire, Newman stayed on at school through the summer holidays because of the family crisis.

The period from the beginning of August to 21 December 1816, when the next term ended, Newman always regarded as the turning point of his life. Alone at school and shocked by the family disaster, he fell ill in August. Later he came to see it as one of the three great providential illnesses of his life, for it was in the autumn of 1816 that he underwent a religious conversion under the influence of one of the schoolmasters, the Revd Walter Mayers,

John Henry Newman (1801–1890), by Heath & Beau, 1861

who had himself shortly before been converted to a Calvinistic form of evangelicalism. Newman had had a conventional upbringing in an ordinary Church of England home, where the emphasis was on the Bible rather than dogmas or sacraments, and where any sort of evangelical 'enthusiasm' would have been frowned upon. In fact, his conversion lacked the kind of emotional upheaval associated with evangelicalism, although the theology he learned from Mayers and the books Mayers lent him were certainly Calvinistic: he believed he was 'elected to eternal glory' (Newman, *Apologia*, 17). However, it was not the Calvinism (which he was to abandon) that was important, but the fact that the dogmas of Christianity, particularly the Trinity, now became real to him in a way that they had not been before. Of the evangelical authors recommended by Mayers, the most important was the biblical commentator Thomas Scott, whose autobiography, *The Force of Truth* (1779), recounted his conversion from Unitarianism to Trinitarian Christianity. The other critical influence was Joseph Milner's *History of the Church of Christ* (1794–1809), which contained long extracts from the church fathers; Newman was thrilled by the picture they presented of the early church. At the same time, however, he read Thomas Newton's *Dissertation on the Prophecies* (1754–8), a book that convinced him that the pope must be the Antichrist predicted in scripture. On the personal level, the effect of his conversion was that he felt that God was calling him to the kind of sacrificial service, such as missionary work, that would involve celibacy: 'it would be the will of God that I should lead a single life' (Newman, *Apologia*, 20).

In 1817 Newman entered Trinity College, Oxford, when he was still only sixteen. In May 1818 he won a college scholarship. His first published writing was an anti-Catholic verse romance, *St Bartholomew's Eve* (1818), which he wrote with his close college friend John William Bowden. His final examinations in 1820 were an unexpected disaster, failing as he did altogether in mathematics and achieving only a fourth (the lowest class) in classics. He had been expected to get a double first but he was exhausted through overwork. Since his scholarship was for nine years, he was able to return to Oxford, and on 12 April 1822 he was elected to a fellowship by examination at Oriel, a college which prided itself on its ability to discern academic potential.

Fellow of Oriel Newman's evangelical views soon began to be undermined by the liberal atmosphere of the Oriel common room, which was famous for its Noetics such as Thomas Arnold who believed in the primacy of reason in theology. Among them was Richard Whately, whose famous *Elements of Logic* (1826) Newman helped to compose, and whose importance in teaching him to think for himself Newman later recognized. However, he was still sufficiently under the influence of Mayers to decide to take holy orders while still teaching, and in 1824 he was ordained deacon (and a year later priest) and appointed curate at St Clement's, a working-class parish in east Oxford. Throwing himself energetically into pastoral work, he came to believe that the standard evangelical distinction between 'nominal' and 'real' Christians did not work in practice. This realization seemed to be supported by the fact that St Paul had not divided Christians into the converted and the unconverted, an observation Newman owed to another of the Noetics, Edward Hawkins, who stressed that tradition was needed as well as scripture. He also began to abandon the doctrine of imputed righteousness in favour of that of baptismal regeneration, the rejection of which was seen as marking out the true evangelical.

Whately was responsible for Newman's first serious publication, an article in 1824 for the *Encyclopaedia metropolitana* on Cicero, who clearly influenced Newman's rhetorical style as a controversialist. A further two articles in the *Encyclopaedia*, on Apollonius of Tyana and miracles in the Bible, followed in 1826. In spite of the shyness that affected him all his life, Newman had begun to come out of his shell at Oriel. In 1825 Whately became principal of the tiny, run-down Alban Hall and invited Newman to become vice-principal. One important result of this close collaboration was Whately's impressing on Newman's mind the idea of the church as a divine body separate from the state. But in 1826 he resigned both this post and his curacy on being appointed a tutor at Oriel.

Newman later wrote that the influences leading him in a religiously liberal direction were abruptly checked by his suffering first, at the end of 1827, a kind of nervous collapse brought on by overwork and family financial troubles, and then, at the beginning of 1828, the bereavement of his beloved youngest sister, Mary, who died suddenly. There was also a crucial theological factor: his fascination since 1816 with the fathers of the church, whose works he began to read systematically in the long vacation of 1828.

Ironically, but not altogether surprisingly, Newman had supported his mentor, Edward Hawkins, in his successful candidature for the vacant Oriel provostship at the beginning of 1828 against the high-church John Keble, whom he hardly knew. One consequence was that Newman now succeeded Hawkins as vicar of the university church of St Mary's. At first Hawkins supported Newman in his role as a reforming tutor, determined to raise both the religious tone of the college and also its academic standards. But the volte-face by the Tory government in granting Catholic emancipation in 1829 led to a sharp division between Hawkins, who supported this liberal measure and therefore the re-election of Sir Robert Peel as MP for the Anglican university, and Newman, who was part of the successful opposition to what was seen as treachery on the part of the political party of the established church. The Peel affair coincided with a new tutorial system drawn up by Newman with the collaboration of his colleagues Richard Hurrell *Froude and Robert Isaac Wilberforce. Its purpose was to strengthen the academic and pastoral relationship between the undergraduate and his individual tutor. But Hawkins strongly disapproved of the attempt to change the role of the tutor from that of a lecturer with responsibility for discipline to that of a personal moral tutor, and in 1830 informed Newman that no further students would be sent to him.

Freedom from teaching duties meant that Newman had no difficulty in accepting a commission in 1831 to write a history of church councils. Instead, he ended up by writing *The Arians of the Fourth Century* (1833). As a work of historical theology, it reflects Newman's own reaction against the religious liberalism of the day. But while insisting on the necessity of dogmatic formulations, Newman was also careful to acknowledge the inadequacy of human language to express the mysteries of faith—an awareness which stemmed from his discovery of the early church's principle of 'economy', which also had a practical application in the way in which Christianity was taught. This economical method of imparting truths was connected with the primitive practice of 'reserve', which, Newman pointed out, was the reverse of the current evangelical preaching of the atonement to arouse feelings that would lead to conversion. This reticence in the face of transcendent mystery was to become a hallmark of Tractarianism.

On 8 December 1832 Newman set sail from Falmouth for the Mediterranean with Richard Hurrell Froude, who was going abroad for his health, and his father. Because of an outbreak of cholera, the first place they were able to visit properly was Corfu, where Newman tried to find out what he could about the Orthodox church. He was disconcerted to find how like the Roman Catholic church it was in its veneration of Mary and the saints and its liturgical ceremonies. Even more disconcerting was Rome, where they arrived in March 1833: here was the 'eternal' city of the apostles, martyrs, and saints, from where the gospel had come to England; but this same city which so impressed and moved Newman, and where there seemed so much to admire in the devotions and piety of the people, was also, so he still believed, the city of a corrupt and superstitious religion. All this time his thoughts were never far from home, where the Reform Bill, which threatened the position of the established church, had been passed in 1832, and where the Irish Church Reform Bill, which threatened to suppress ten sees of the church in Ireland, was before parliament. In March he sent off the first poems he and Froude were writing for a regular verse section, to be called (and in 1836 published as) 'Lyra apostolica', in the *British Magazine*, a review recently started by Hugh James Rose, a Cambridge high-churchman, in defence of the church.

Instead of accompanying the Froudes home in April, Newman decided to revisit Sicily, where he fell seriously ill of gastric or typhoid fever. Many were dying from the epidemic, but Newman was confident that he would live: 'God has still work for me to do' (Newman, *Autobiographical Writings*, 127). When he came later to write a graphic account of his fever, he looked back on it as the third of the three pivotal illnesses in these formative years. On his way home, while at sea, he wrote 'Lead, kindly light', which, with its mood of thanksgiving and trust, has become a famous hymn. He arrived back in Oxford on 9 July 1833. Five days later Keble preached the assize sermon from the pulpit of the university church, published as *National Apostasy*, protesting against state interference in the Church of England. Newman always regarded that day as the beginning of the Oxford or Tractarian Movement.

The Tracts If the 'Lyra apostolica', which began appearing in June 1833, were the first literary productions of the Oxford Movement, the next were a series of papers by Newman, later published as *The Church of the Fathers* (1840), which he began sending in August 1833 to the *British Magazine*. The first, which appeared in October 1833, pointed out that the early Christian church had depended not on the state but on the people. It was preceded by the publication on 9 September 1833 of Tract 1 (*Ad clerum*) of the Tracts for the Times, which was on the doctrine of the apostolic succession and was anonymously written by Newman. The Tracts were his idea, and he insisted on publishing them himself rather than allowing a board to authorize and supervise their publication, since 'living movements do not come of committees' (Newman, *Apologia*, 39). Indeed, Newman was against any kind of formal association to organize the movement, because it would involve compromises and inhibit individual action, preferring to build up a network of personal contacts among sympathizers throughout the country, particularly through the circulation of the Tracts. These soon aroused furious controversy, were increasingly in demand, and began to attract new writers, including the regius professor of Hebrew, Edward Bouverie Pusey. Accusations of exaggeration and extremism did not surprise Newman: an element of excess, he thought, was an inevitable part of fighting for a true cause, in this case the protection of the church against state encroachment and the preservation of the apostolic faith against such liberal plans of reform as Thomas Arnold's proposal to make the Church of England more doctrinally comprehensive in order to avert the threat of disestablishment.

In March 1834 the first volume of Newman's *Parochial Sermons* was published (the whole series appeared from 1834 to 1842, reprinted in 1868 as the first six volumes of *Parochial and Plain Sermons*). As well as being one of the great classics of Christian spirituality, the pastoral sermons he preached in St Mary's were almost as central to the Oxford Movement as the Tracts. Unlike the latter, they deliberately avoided controversial issues, although the theology that underlay Newman's preaching was clearly influenced by his reading of the Greek fathers, as can be seen in the emphasis on the incarnation and the resurrection, the indwelling of the Holy Spirit and the sacraments, and the sense of the mystery of the Christian revelation. However, the profound influence they exerted at the time lay in their call to holiness, a call which could not be dissociated from the charisma of the preacher himself, who avoided all the usual oratorical devices of the pulpit but whose rapt intensity and low, soft, but strangely thrilling voice left unforgettable memories with many of his listeners. J. C. Shairp recalled: 'He laid his finger—how gently, yet how powerfully!—on some inner place in the hearer's heart, and told him things about himself he had never known till then' (J. C. Shairp, *Studies in Poetry and Philosophy*, 1868, 248).

The *via media* The most obvious criticism of the Tracts was that they were undermining the protestant character of the Church of England. In answer, Newman wrote two Tracts in 1834 to the effect that the English church was 'reformed' but also Catholic, occupying a *via media* or middle position between protestantism and Roman Catholicism. He welcomed, therefore, the chance to develop this view of the Anglican *via media* in October, when he was asked by one of the contributors to the Tracts to take over a theological debate he was having with a French priest called Jean-Nicolas Jager in the pages of *L'Univers* newspaper. Newman sent one lengthy letter translated into French before Christmas and the first part of a second letter in July 1835, but the controversy came to an end and the second part was never published. However, Newman was able to make use of the correspondence when he came to formulate his statement of the Anglican *via media* in the *Lectures on the prophetical office of the church, viewed relatively to Romanism and popular protestantism* (1837), which were delivered in 1836 in St Mary's. While admitting that Anglo-Catholicism was as yet more of an unrealized theory than a reality, he argued that it approximated far more closely to primitive Christianity than either protestantism, which neglected the church referred to in the creed, or Roman Catholicism, which substituted the authority of the church for that of the testimony of antiquity.

Concerned as he was with the urgent need to show that Tractarianism was not the same as Roman Catholicism, Newman also continued to battle against theological liberalism. In 1835 he published Tract 73, later republished as *On the Introduction of Rationalistic Principles into Revealed Religion*. He blamed evangelicalism for the subjectivity of modern religion, and explained Schleiermacher's theology as an attempt to justify intellectually a religion of feelings. He dated the beginning of open hostility between the Tractarians and the liberals to a sharp exchange he had with R. D. Hampden at the end of 1834 over an (unsuccessful) bill to remove the obligation to subscribe to the Thirty-Nine Articles at Oxford and Cambridge. It was, however, embarrassing for a Tractarian to have to insist on the articles, which were seen as the protestant title deeds of the established church, as the means of protecting the Anglican, and indeed religious, character of the university. Hampden had been appointed in 1832 to one of the vacant Oriel tutorships after the enforced resignation of Newman and his colleagues; then in March 1834 he had been elected to the chair of moral philosophy, for which Newman had also applied, not with any enthusiasm but because he thought the position might help the Tractarian cause. Much more serious was the appointment of Hampden in February 1836 as regius professor of divinity. A few days later Newman brought out a pamphlet, *Elucidations of Dr Hampden's Theological Statements*, attacking Hampden's liberal theology.

As vicar of St Mary's, Newman was in a position to put Tractarian principles into practice: he had begun daily morning prayer in church in 1834, as well as an evening service once a week, and after Easter 1837 he began an early communion service on Sundays. He had privately been using the Roman breviary for more than a year, having chosen Hurrell Froude's own copy from his books as a memento of his beloved friend, who had died after a long illness in 1836. Froude's papers were entrusted to Newman and Keble, and it was decided to begin by publishing his 'Private thoughts', which, Newman thought, revealed the kind of heroic saintly figure that the movement needed for a model, although he was afraid that the details of Froude's fasting and the very un-evangelical nature of his religious journal would increase the fear that the Tractarians were really crypto-papists.

Newman's second major attempt to establish an Anglican *via media* came with his *Lectures on Justification*, delivered in 1837 and published in 1838. He wanted to show that both the protestant theory of justification by faith alone and the Roman Catholic doctrine of justification by works were incomplete truths. The way through this apparently impassable Reformation controversy lay, for Newman, in the Johannine and Pauline doctrine of the indwelling of the Holy Spirit, who both justifies and sanctifies. Newman has been criticized for misrepresenting Luther, who was ostensibly his chief target, but the lectures remained a formidable indictment of popular evangelicalism, with its preoccupation with conversion and

faith. Polemical as it was, the book—considered by some to be Newman's most brilliant theological work—was certainly a pioneering model of ecumenical theology in its resolution of a historic controversy by changing the terms of reference and setting the problem in a wholly new perspective.

In the summer term of 1838 Newman gave another series of lectures in the Adam de Brome Chapel at St Mary's entitled 'Lectures on the scripture proof of the doctrines of the church', most of which were published as Tract 85. The Anglican or *via media* position was that the creed is to be found not on the face of, or literally in, scripture, as protestant evangelicals claimed, but implicitly in it. This contrasted with the Roman Catholic view that tradition provides another source of revelation. The only other possibility was the liberal protestant denial that Christianity has an objectively ascertainable creed or doctrine. The lectures contain some of Newman's most brilliant biblical criticism, particularly in regard to the literary form of scripture.

As Newman had feared, the publication of the first two volumes of Froude's *Remains* in February 1838 had caused a stir, and even some alarm, among the less adventurous of the Tractarian supporters. As a result, a project to translate the Roman breviary, in which he was involved, was dropped. Meanwhile, opponents of the Tractarians decided to launch an appeal for the erection of a monument in Oxford to the protestant martyrs Cranmer, Ridley, and Latimer, as a kind of test of the loyalty of Newman and others to the Church of England. Newman, who refused to acknowledge them as representative of Anglicanism, had no intention of subscribing. In spite of, or because of, all the controversy and criticism, Newman had never felt more confident about the Tractarian cause. The Tracts had become best-sellers. He himself had taken on the editorship of the *British Critic* in January 1838, with the idea of its becoming the organ of the Tractarians. There, in the spring of 1839, at what he was to recall as the high point of the movement, he published an article, 'The state of religious parties'. After asserting that the Oxford Movement should be seen as part of the Romantic movement (in which Newman's favourite novelist Walter Scott was especially singled out) or a larger spiritual awakening after the rationalism of the eighteenth century, he argued that while liberalism was too cold to appeal and evangelicalism too inconsistent and unreal to convince, there existed an alternative to unbelief on the one hand and Roman Catholicism on the other, namely the *via media* of Anglo-Catholicism.

Doubts about the Church of England and Tract 90 It was only three or four months later, in the summer vacation of 1839, that the first real doubt about the Anglican position assailed Newman. He had returned to his study of the early church and was rereading the history of the Monophysite heresy, when quite suddenly he was struck by the way in which at the Council of Chalcedon the pope had upheld the Catholic orthodox faith while the heretics had divided into an extreme and a more moderate party. What impressed him was the similarity to the current situation, with Rome on one side, protestantism on the other, and Anglicanism in the middle. Then in September his attention was drawn by a friend to an article in the *Dublin Review* by Nicholas Wiseman, the rector of the English College in Rome, on the Donatist schism in the African church, but with special reference to the Anglican claim. He was struck forcefully by the maxim of St Augustine quoted in the article: 'Securus judicat orbis terrarum' ('the verdict of the whole world is conclusive'). The principle that 'the deliberate judgment, in which the whole Church at length rests and acquiesces, is an infallible prescription and a final sentence against such portions of it as protest and secede' (Newman, *Apologia*, 117) not only seemed to offer the key to understanding the whole course of ecclesiastical history but also to destroy the theory of the *via media*. The excitement of the moment passed away, but Newman's confidence in the notion of an Anglican *via media* was gone for ever. However, his objection to the doctrinal accretions of Rome remained, as well as his deepseated antipathy to popery dating back to his evangelical conversion, which still had a strong emotional, although no longer intellectual, hold on him.

In February 1841 Newman wrote his first sustained work of satire, a series of letters to *The Times* entitled 'The Tamworth reading room', a riposte to a speech by Sir Robert Peel on the replacement of religion by education and knowledge as the moral basis of a new pluralist society. In his bitingly sarcastic defence of faith as the foundation of individual and social morality, Newman anticipated some of the central themes of his later educational and philosophical writings.

Since 1839 Newman had been worried not only about his own belief in Anglicanism but also about the difficulty of preventing younger Tractarians from leaving a church in which the devotions and externals of a more developed Anglo-Catholicism had not yet come into being for the Church of Rome, which offered what they saw as the fullness of both Catholic doctrine and devotion. The crucial problem posed by the apparently protestant Thirty-Nine Articles led to Newman's publishing his highly contentious Tract 90 on 27 February 1841 which demonstrated, sometimes with what were considered by some to be intellectual sleights of hand, how the articles of the Anglican church were 'patient of a Catholic interpretation'. He argued, some protestants believed disingenuously, that the articles were not intended to exclude those Anglicans of Catholic sympathies but to protest against the errors of so-called popery. On 16 March the vice-chancellor, heads of colleges, and proctors issued a public censure—only a few hours before Newman's *A Letter Addressed to the Rev R. W. Jelf* appeared in his defence. In it he condemned the popular religion of popery, while at the same time comparing it to the kind of popular protestantism that existed in what he argued was the essentially Catholic Church of England. However, he agreed to a demand by his bishop, Richard Bagot, bishop of Oxford, that no further Tracts should be published.

In the summer vacation of 1841, as in 1839, Newman put aside controversy to return to his patristic studies, and

again was assailed by doubts about the Anglican position. This time it was the Arian heresy—he was busy translating St Athanasius for the Library of the Fathers, a project he and Pusey had begun planning in 1836—which presented a disturbing parallel to the contemporary situation. Again, there were the same divisions: the extreme Arians, the semi-Arians, and Rome; again the truth lay not with the *via media* but with Rome. This was the first of the three blows that, Newman was later to say, finally broke him. The second was the series of condemnations of Tract 90 that the bishops began issuing. The third was the agreement, which became law in 1841, between the Prussian and English governments to set up a bishopric in Jerusalem that would alternate between an Anglican and a Lutheran or Calvinist; politically it would give protestantism a position in the Holy Land, but ecclesiologically it was anathema to the Tractarians. Newman's only defence of the Church of England now was that it still had the apostolic succession and the creed, as well as the ecclesiological note of holiness.

The development of doctrine Newman's parish of St Mary's included the village of Littlemore, 2 miles outside Oxford, where Newman had had a church—also St Mary's—built in 1836. In February 1842 he moved out to a row of cottages nearby which he had leased. Not only did he want to get away from controversy in Oxford but since 1840 he had been seriously thinking of trying to found some kind of monastic or religious community, if only because he felt that the lack of religious life in the Church of England would drive the younger, more advanced Tractarians into the arms of Rome. His own objections to Rome were somewhat shaken at the end of 1842, when Charles Russell, a professor at the seminary in Maynooth, sent him an English translation of some unexceptionable sermons by the Neapolitan St Alphonsus Liguori, where, if anywhere, one might have expected to find the kind of extreme Mariolatry that was assumed to be part of the popular Catholicism or popery that Newman had denounced. He did find that some passages on the Virgin Mary had been omitted as unsuitable for English-speaking readers, but this seemed to show that there was a devotional pluralism in the Roman church. In December 1842 he sent a retraction of his more extreme anti-Roman statements to an Oxford newspaper.

On 2 February 1843 Newman preached the last of his Oxford University sermons (published under that title in the same month), 'The theory of developments in religious doctrine'. His argument that the apostolic church had an implicit if not an explicit knowledge of later doctrinal formulations relied upon key ideas he had worked out in the six sermons on the relation between faith and reason which he had preached between 1839 and 1841. Newman defined faith as the kind of implicit rather than explicit reasoning which depends not on evidences but on 'antecedent probabilities' or presumptions, which in the case of religion would be determined by one's moral dispositions. The originality of these sermons lay in their refusal to assume the Enlightenment's opposition of faith and reason and to abandon (like Schleiermacher) religion's claim to truth by conceding to science all factual knowledge and claiming for religious statements emotional, imaginative, and existential significance. Instead, Newman defined faith in terms of a wider concept of reasoning than had been current since the seventeenth century. The epistemology of these sermons, the most seminal of his writings, contained the seeds of his later educational and philosophical thought.

Early in September 1843 Newman resigned as vicar of St Mary's, believing that he no longer had the confidence of the bishops and feeling less and less confident himself about his own position in the Church of England. On the 25th he preached at Littlemore his last sermon as an Anglican, 'The parting of friends', taking as his text the same verse of the Psalms which he had taken for the first sermon he ever wrote: 'Man goes forth to his work and to his labour until the evening.'

Not only was Newman's own position becoming more and more untenable, but the movement itself seemed to have a momentum which led irresistibly towards Rome. In December 1843 Newman decided to discontinue the series of lives of the English saints which he had begun editing, as it was impossible to write sympathetically about pre-Reformation saints without betraying a sympathy for things Roman Catholic. His conviction that the Church of England was in schism was now greater than his belief that certain Roman Catholic dogmas were not true developments of the original revelation. In the course of 1844 he revealed to friends that he was on the verge of joining the Roman Catholic church; holding the convictions that he did, he now needed only to be certain that he was not under some delusion. At the end of 1844 he resolved to write a book on the question of doctrinal development, and to seek admission to the Roman Catholic church if the writing of the book did not alter his opinions. In February 1845 the heads of the Oxford colleges voted to permit convocation to vote on a censure of Tract 90. When convocation met on 13 February, W. G. Ward's *Ideal of a Christian Church* was censured and Ward was stripped of his degrees. Only the intervention of R. W. Church, the senior proctor, prevented, by a procedural device, a vote on Newman.

The *Essay on Development* and reception into the Catholic church Newman began to send instalments of the *Essay on the Development of Christian Doctrine* to the printers in late September 1845. It was never properly completed (though it was published that year), as the author had decided to become a Roman Catholic on the strength of the argument already advanced and felt there was no more to be said. His thesis was that since a living idea is necessarily a developing idea, and development brings out rather than obscures the original idea, doctrinal development is to be expected and indeed welcomed in Christianity. But if so, then an infallible authority is needed to distinguish true from false developments in the unfolding of a revelation that claims to be objectively true. Catholicism is the only form of Christianity that shows a continual development that purports to be guaranteed by authority, and modern Catholicism seemed ostensibly to be the historical continuation of early Christianity. Nevertheless Newman proposed, albeit tentatively, seven notes to distinguish authentic developments from corruptions: an idea has not been corrupted

> if it retains one and the same type, the same principles, the same organization; if its beginnings anticipate its subsequent phases, and its later phenomena protect and subserve its earlier; if it has a power of assimilation and revival, and a vigorous action from first to last. (*Essay on the Development of Christian Doctrine*, 171)

The *Essay on Development* is Newman's best-known theological work and remains the starting point for modern Catholic theology of doctrinal development.

On 3 October 1845 Newman resigned his fellowship at Oriel College. On 9 October he was received into the Roman Catholic church by Blessed Dominic Barberi, the Italian Passionist missionary. At the end of the month he went to Oscott College, near Birmingham, to be confirmed by Nicholas Wiseman, then president of the college and also coadjutor to the vicar apostolic of the midland district. Wiseman offered Newman and the other converts from the Littlemore community the use of the old Oscott College (renamed Maryvale by Newman). Newman stayed there from February to September 1846, when he left for the College of Propaganda in Rome to study for the priesthood.

The Oratory Dismayed by the state of theology at Rome which preceded the Thomist revival, Newman was also worried by the critical reaction to his *Essay on Development*, which leading theologians felt had gone too far in applying the principle of development. However, Rome gave him the opportunity of visiting the Oratory of St Philip Neri. The idea of founding an Oratory in England had been originally suggested by Wiseman: as a community of secular priests living together under a rule but not vows, the Oratory offered a form of religious life without having to join a religious order, as well as the opportunity to combine a pastoral apostolate with educational and intellectual work. Ordained a priest on 30 May 1847, a month later Newman began an Oratorian novitiate in Rome with other members of the Maryvale community. Five months later he was confirmed as superior of the new English Oratory, and on 1 February 1848 the Birmingham Oratory was formally set up at Maryvale. Two weeks later Newman somewhat reluctantly admitted to the community F. W. Faber and his Brothers of the Will of God. Faber, a poet and former fellow of University College, Oxford, had come over to Rome a few weeks after Newman, bringing with him a group of young men from his Anglican parish, who were living in community with him at St Wilfrid's, Staffordshire.

Newman himself was in the process of publishing (anonymously) his first novel, *Loss and Gain: the Story of a Convert*. The book is partly autobiographical, not least in its preoccupation with finding a real as opposed to unreal religion. The hero's discovery of the objective reality of Catholic worship was meant to reflect Newman's own experience after his conversion, particularly his fascination with the reservation of the sacrament making Christ 'really' present in every Catholic church. The inconsistencies of the comprehensiveness of the Church of England and of Anglo-Catholicism are amusingly satirized in what are probably the most memorable parts of a novel of which the chief claim to originality lies in the introduction of a new kind of introspective self-questioning into English fiction (see K. Tillotson, *Novels of the Eighteen-Forties*, 1954).

Maryvale and later St Wilfrid's were intended only as temporary sites for the new community, and in February 1849 the Oratory was formally set up in a disused gin distillery in Alcester Street, Birmingham. At the opening Newman preached a sermon, later published as the first of *Discourses Addressed to Mixed Congregations* (1849), which are more rhetorical than his Anglican sermons, sometimes in a rather Italianate manner. The working-class parishioners were not the educated congregation that was supposed to be the object of the new English Oratory's apostolate, and London would obviously have been a more suitable place, but Newman personally welcomed the opportunity to combine ordinary pastoral with academic and intellectual work. In May the two original communities, which increasingly took different approaches and were too large for a single Oratory, split, and another Oratory was founded under Faber in London. Faber's exuberant style had already caused Newman problems with a series of translations of continental lives of the saints, the extravagant and even sensational character of which had offended 'old Catholics', including W. B. Ullathorne, the new vicar apostolic, who had succeeded Wiseman after the latter's appointment to London.

At the invitation of the London Oratorians, Newman in the summer of 1850 delivered *Lectures on Certain Difficulties Felt by Anglicans in Submitting to the Catholic Church*. They were a response to the privy council's decision in the Gorham case that baptismal regeneration was not an essential doctrine of the Church of England, which caused a crisis for Anglo-Catholics and brought many over to Rome, including Henry Edward Manning. Urging, often to great satirical effect, that common sense shows that Anglo-Catholicism is inconsistent and unreal, Newman recounted how his own study of the early church led him to recognize that the church of the fathers was identical with the Roman Catholic church.

After the restoration of a Roman Catholic hierarchy to England in September 1850, Wiseman, who had been made a cardinal, issued a triumphalist pastoral letter 'from out the Flaminian gate', which was read out in churches on 20 October. Against this so-called papal aggression a 'no-popery' agitation flared up, and in response Newman delivered another series of lectures in Birmingham in the summer of 1851, published as *Lectures on the Present Position of Catholics in England*. Regarded by Newman as his best-written book (it contains his best satire), it aimed to reveal the inconsistencies and the unreality of the powerful British anti-Catholic tradition. The fifth of the lectures contained a denunciation of Giacinto Achilli, a former Dominican priest who had become a protestant after being found guilty of sexual assault. Brought to England in 1850 by the Evangelical Alliance, he had toured the country speaking to packed audiences. Relying on the information in Wiseman's published (but anonymous) indictment of Achilli, Newman had been advised that libel proceedings were highly unlikely as no action had been taken against Wiseman, who would easily be able to prove his allegations. In November 1851 Achilli denied on oath all the charges against him, an affidavit which enabled him to institute criminal rather than civil proceedings against Newman. Unfortunately, not only had Wiseman mislaid the crucial documentary evidence which would have stopped the case, but he failed to enable the two Birmingham Oratorians who had gone to Italy to obtain the evidence they needed. The necessary documents and evidence were found too late to prevent Newman from being committed to trial on a criminal charge for which he was liable to a year's imprisonment.

The Catholic University of Ireland Newman was not only busy with the preparations for the new Oratory house that was being built in Edgbaston but was also preoccupied with the establishment of a new Catholic university in Ireland. In April 1851 Paul Cullen, then archbishop of Armagh and afterwards of Dublin, had asked him for his advice and also to give some lectures. After the majority of Irish bishops had refused to support the new non-denominational Queen's Colleges, Rome had urged them to set up a Catholic university on the lines of the University of Louvain in Belgium. In November the organizing committee, headed by Cullen, appointed Newman the first president. In May and June 1852 Newman delivered five of the *Discourses on the Scope and Nature of University Education* (1852), which became the first half of *The Idea of a University* (1873).

In these classic lectures Newman defended the idea of a liberal education within a confessional religious context against both utilitarian attacks and anti-intellectual clericalism. The skilful rhetoric contrived to do justice to the complexities of the Irish situation, as well as to argue for the central place of theology among the branches of knowledge, but without detriment to the ideal of a liberal education, which for Newman meant essentially an intellectual training of the whole mind. The *Lectures and Essays on University Subjects* (1859), a collection of addresses and papers delivered and written while Newman was rector of the university, and which later became the second half of *The Idea of a University*, offered specific application of the more theoretical ideas of the first part, particularly in arguing that there need be no conflict between theology and science, which should respect each other as different ways of understanding the world.

The Achilli trial took place at the end of June 1852, when the jury decided that Newman had been unable to prove all his charges, which was practically impossible. Still, he had won a moral victory, and *The Times* in a leading article commented that Catholics could not expect justice in a British court. In January 1853 the prejudice of the jury was implicitly acknowledged by the judge, who let Newman off with a fine of £100. In July 1852 he had celebrated the revival of Catholicism in his famous sermon 'The second spring', which was delivered at the first provincial synod of the new ecclesiastical hierarchy held at Oscott—when, however, he warned that it might turn out to be like an uncertain English spring.

It was not until October 1853 that Newman received from the university committee a mandate to start the university. But during October and November he was already engaged to give a course of lectures in Liverpool, published as *Lectures on the History of the Turks in its Relation to Christianity* (1854), which were delivered against the background of hostilities between Orthodox Russia and Muslim Turkey. In January 1854, much to Newman's disapproval, Britain and France became involved on the side of Turkey in what soon became the Crimean War. In March Newman began sending a series of letters, 'Who's to blame?', to the *Catholic Standard*, which contained his first real foray into political theory.

Newman had as yet received no official recognition from the Irish bishops, who were divided about the feasibility of the university and suspected Cullen of wanting sole control over it. Wiseman's idea of Newman's being made a titular bishop to give him more authority was scotched by last-minute reservations on the part of Cullen. In February 1854 Newman arrived in Ireland to consult and take soundings, as well as to advertise the university. He found a distinct lack of enthusiasm, not only among some of the bishops but particularly among the educated Catholic laity, who saw no need for a Catholic, let alone a clerical, university in the denominationally mixed community of Ireland. Irish nationalists like Archbishop MacHale of Tuam were also hostile to any English involvement. It was not until May 1854 that the bishops formally approved the university's statutes and the appointment of Newman as rector. Newman immediately began a weekly *Catholic University Gazette*, in which during 1854 he published a series of articles, later collected as *Office and Work of Universities* (1856). These developed his educational thought, not least his emphasis on the importance of the student–teacher relationship, as well as his ideal of a university which would combine the college tutorial principle of Oxford with the university professorial system of a continental university like Louvain, where the rector and professors rather than heads of colleges governed the university. On 3 November 1854 the university opened with about twenty students in residence and another forty expected.

At the end of July 1855 Newman resumed work on a second novel, begun in 1848. *Callista* (1856) remains interesting as an imaginative attempt to recreate the world of the primitive church—in this case third-century Africa—where an analogy between the situation of the early Christians facing persecution in the Roman empire and that of Catholics in nineteenth-century Britain is clearly intended to strike the reader. But it is also a much more profound exploration of the process of conversion (here from unbelief to Christian faith) than that of his earlier *Loss and Gain*, as well as containing a strikingly existential theology of hell.

In October 1855 a long and bitter dispute between the Birmingham and London oratories began. Ostensibly, it was over the latter's successful application to Rome for a dispensation from the clause in the Oratorian rule, adapted by Newman for England, which forbade the spiritual direction of nuns. Newman felt he had not been properly consulted, and the Birmingham Oratory resented the fact that when the dispensation came in November it seemed to be intended for both oratories. There were two connected reasons why an apparently trivial difference turned into such a deep alienation: almost from the beginning not only had there been inevitable tensions between two communities under two such different superiors but a disagreement about the nature of the Oratory itself had emerged, with Newman insisting on the intellectual apostolate and Faber on the exclusively spiritual and devotional mission of the Oratory. Faber and his companions had moved to London, which meant that their Oratory was now in a much more prominent situation than the mother house and potentially in a position to dictate to the Birmingham house. Although oratories were meant to be autonomous and independent, there was nevertheless a common rule governing the two oratories, for which Newman as the founder of the English Oratory was responsible, so that any dispensation or ruling from Rome inevitably affected both houses. Anxious to ensure that no ruling from Rome to one of the English oratories should be binding on the other, and that no interpretation of the rule should be made by one Oratory without the other's knowing, Newman set off at the end of December 1855 for Rome, where he had a satisfactory audience with Pope Pius IX. The final, formal separation of the oratories took place with the London Oratory's successful application in the summer of 1856 for a separate foundation brief.

In May 1856 a university church was opened on ground next to the University House in St Stephen's Green in Dublin. Newman had from the beginning hoped to found an Oratory which would provide chaplains for the university. The university sermons he preached there were published in *Sermons Preached on Various Occasions* (1857), in which a principal theme is the importance of Christian humanism combining the religious and the intellectual which, he thought, had characterized St Philip Neri and the Oratory from the beginning.

In spite of the difficulty of finding students because of the low level of secondary education in Ireland and the failure of those Irish and English Catholics who could afford to do so to support the university, the project was not a complete failure: the medical school was a success as was the launch of an academic journal entitled *The Atlantis*. Newman's official leave of absence from the Birmingham Oratory expired in 1857, when he sent his resignation to the Irish bishops. He felt it was impossible to be both provost of the Birmingham Oratory and rector of the university, and indeed his absences during vacations were a constant source of tension between him and Cullen. But there were other serious disagreements: Cullen wanted the kind of discipline that would have been appropriate for a seminary; Newman thought that he should be allowed to appoint the vice-rector; and most significant of all, Cullen refused to countenance a lay finance committee and strongly disapproved of Newman's appointment of laymen, including leading Irish nationalists, to chairs. Newman agreed to stay on temporarily as part-time rector, but finally resigned in 1858. In retrospect he thought he had been wrong not to have insisted on certain conditions before accepting the rectorship. He also considered the pope ill-advised to have tried to found a Catholic university in Ireland.

The laity Newman realized that the tensions between laity and clergy, which had hampered his efforts in Dublin, were not peculiar to Ireland, but were a feature of the increasingly ultramontane nineteenth-century church. In March 1859 he reluctantly agreed to take on temporarily the editorship of the popular liberal Catholic magazine *The Rambler*, which was threatened by ecclesiastical censure, as the only person acceptable to the bishops on the one hand and the editor, Richard Simpson, and the chief proprietor, Sir John Acton, on the other. Newman fully supported a lay Catholic magazine concerned to encourage the intellectual life of Catholics, but disapproved of its critical attitude towards authority and of theological articles by untrained laymen. In May he received a letter of complaint from John Gillow, a professor of theology at Ushaw seminary, about a passage which Newman had written in the May issue upholding the right of lay Catholics to express their views on matters which concerned them, such as educational standards in Catholic schools. Gillow had particularly complained about Newman's pointing out that the laity had even been consulted before the definition of the immaculate conception in 1854. Newman's point, however, was not that their opinion had been sought but that the fact of their faith had been ascertained. On the advice of his bishop, he decided to resign after the July number, in which he set out a scholarly and theological defence of the role of the laity in the famous article 'On consulting the faithful in matters of doctrine'. His first point was that 'consulting' was used in the sense in which a doctor consults the pulse of his patient and not that in which the patient consults the doctor. The laity's faith was important because the *consensus fidelium* witnessed to the tradition of the church, as during the Arian heresy in the fourth century when the laity was more faithful than the episcopate in witnessing to the doctrine of the divinity of Christ.

Gillow again wrote to complain that Newman appeared to be denying the church's infallibility. Newman replied that he had admitted only a temporary suspension of function on the part of the teaching authority at the time. An official complaint was made to Rome by Bishop Brown of Newport. At the request of Bishop Ullathorne, Newman wrote to Wiseman to say that he was ready to comply with any demands the Holy See might make. The list of objectionable passages drawn up by the Congregatio de Propaganda Fide (under which England, as a quasi-missionary country, came) was never forwarded by Wiseman (then a sick man) to Newman, who assumed the matter was closed. The Roman authorities, on the other hand, assumed that Newman's failure to offer an explanation proved his disobedience.

Newman's *Apologia* The disappointments and setbacks of the past decade had taken their toll on Newman, and in the summer of 1861 he was advised by his doctor to rest for several months. Not only was he exhausted but he was deeply depressed. After all his trials as an Anglican, his Catholic life seemed to be almost uniformly unsuccessful. Apart from the Irish university and *The Rambler*, there had been the abortive affair of the translation of the Bible, with which he had been entrusted by the English bishops in 1855—although Wiseman did not see fit to inform him officially until 1857. He had agreed to undertake a work that was hardly congenial to him, and made preliminary preparations; but after a request from the American bishops to co-operate in a joint translation, he never heard any more about the project from the English hierarchy. Ever anxious to encourage Catholic education, he had responded to the need for a new type of Catholic school, which would provide the kind of education that the public schools offered and that the middle-class converts particularly wanted for their children, by opening the Oratory School in 1859. Faber's disapproval of the undertaking as un-Oratorian influenced Wiseman, who had taken the London Oratory's side in the quarrel with Birmingham, and the school was also resented by the existing Catholic schools which were run on very different lines.

On 30 December 1863 Newman was sent anonymously a copy of the January number of *Macmillan's Magazine*, containing a review by the Revd Charles Kingsley (1819–1875), a successful novelist and regius professor of modern history at Cambridge, in which he accused Newman in particular, and the Roman Catholic church in general, of preferring cunning to truth. The ensuing correspondence with the publisher and Kingsley was published by Newman as a satirical pamphlet in February 1864 and elicited a highly favourable review by the literary critic R. H. Hutton, who scornfully dismissed Kingsley's pamphlet of rejoinder. Long used to aspersions on his integrity, Newman now decided to take advantage of an attack by such a well-known public figure to write an apologia for his conversion, which would finally convince the protestant public that he had not been an agent for popery as a Tractarian and that his submission to Rome was entirely sincere. The resulting classic autobiography—more theological than spiritual—appeared in weekly pamphlets to take advantage of the publicity aroused by the controversy. The pressure was enormous, but Newman shared the strain of remembering the Oxford Movement with old Anglican friends, who lent him letters and offered advice and criticism. The pamphlets were published as a volume in 1864 entitled *Apologia pro vita sua*. In the last chapter Newman undertook a general defence of Catholicism, particularly the infallibility of the church, which he directed not only at protestants and sceptics, but also more covertly at Catholic ultramontanes, against whom he urged a balanced theology of authority and freedom, in which the interaction, even conflict, of the magisterium and the theologians was depicted as creative and necessary for the life of the church. It was his second significant contribution to a theology of the church.

Against the ultramontanes Not only was the *Apologia* a bestseller, making Newman financially secure for the first time since he became a Catholic, but the reviews were almost universally favourable, especially the nonconformist ones, and there was no doubt about the support of the vast majority of the Catholic clergy. It was a turning point, and Newman's depression lifted. Nor did it return when his next project, the possibility of founding an Oratory in Oxford, was foiled. When in August 1864 he was offered the chance of buying a 5 acre plot of ground, he was asked by Bishop Ullathorne to establish a church and mission in Oxford. Ullathorne made it clear that he would not countenance a Catholic college being built, as had been mooted by the original buyer. The idea of an apostolate to the Catholic undergraduates who were already at Oxford appealed to Newman. News of the possibility alerted the English ultramontanes, and H. E. Manning, who was now Wiseman's closest aide, obtained an instruction from Rome to the English bishops to hold an extraordinary meeting, as a result of which Catholics were formally warned against attending protestant universities— an inevitable pronouncement given the official Catholic opposition to 'mixed' education. Newman was convinced that the ultramontanes' real fear was not that the faith of Catholic undergraduates would be undermined, but that he, Newman, would be able to exert an important influence in forming an educated laity. Newman sold the land, but bought a smaller plot in case the situation should change.

In the summer of 1865 Newman published in the Catholic periodical *The Month* his poem *The Dream of Gerontius*. In the depths of his depression he had seriously thought he might be about to die, and it seems to have been this prospect of death which led to his writing the poem later made famous in Edward Elgar's oratorio. The verses 'Praise to the Holiest in the height' became one of the most famous hymns in the English language. The poem contained, like the treatment of hell in *Callista*, a deeply spiritual depiction of purgatory, very different from the conventional one of a place of physical punishment. Another controversial work followed in January 1866: the publication of E. B. Pusey's *Eirenicon* in 1865, in answer to Manning's pamphlet of 1864 (ostensibly attacking Pusey but also implicitly criticizing the *Apologia*), led to Newman's writing his *Letter to Pusey*. While complaining about the contradiction between Pusey's professed desire for Christian unity and his provocative citation of extreme Marian devotions in the Roman Catholic church as though they were obligatory or typical, Newman took the opportunity to dissociate himself from the devotionalism of Faber as well as the ultramontanism of converts such as Manning (who had succeeded Wiseman as archbishop of Westminster) and W. G. Ward, the lay editor of the *Dublin Review*. Apart from pointing out that Catholic Mariology

was essentially the same as that of the fathers and that the Virgin Mary's intercessory role was quite distinct from actual invocation of her, Newman also observed that a popular religion like Catholicism was inevitably open to abuse and corruption, a point which represented a further stage in his developing ecclesiology.

After yet another request from Bishop Ullathorne to undertake the Oxford mission, the Birmingham Oratory in April 1866 conditionally agreed to build a church on the smaller plot of land for which it would provide a priest. Ullathorne assured a somewhat reluctant Newman, who was adamant that his only motive in becoming involved was to look after Catholic undergraduates, that the policy of discouraging rather than forbidding Catholics from going to Oxford would continue unless there were a substantial increase in numbers. At the end of the year Ullathorne told Newman that permission had been given by Rome for an Oxford Oratory, but concealed the directive that Newman himself was not to reside there lest his presence should encourage Catholics to send their sons to Oxford.

Donations had already begun coming in when, in March 1867, the Congregatio de Propaganda Fide complained that it had received a report that the Oratory School was actively preparing boys to go to Oxford. In fact it was doing no more than other Catholic schools, but the complaint meant that the school would have to discontinue the special tuition needed. The letter from Rome was the result of English ultramontane dismay that permission for an Oxford Oratory had been given. Then in April a report appeared in an English Catholic newspaper to the effect that the pope had decided that Newman was too theologically unsound to be allowed to go to Oxford. The bishop now revealed the instruction which he had suppressed on the ground that it concerned an eventuality which had not been contemplated. However, the newspaper report provoked a published protest signed by many prominent lay Catholics in favour of Newman. His closest confidant at the Oratory, Ambrose St John, went to Rome to defend both the school, of which he was in charge, and Newman himself. There he found that the authorities still held *The Rambler* article against Newman, who had apparently never answered the charges against it, but were otherwise interested only in maintaining the official policy against 'mixed' education; personal hostility to Newman and what he stood for seems to have been confined to the English ultramontanes. After Propaganda Fide, at the instigation of Manning, had ordered the English bishops to issue a much stronger prohibition against Catholics attending non-Catholic universities, Newman formally resigned the Oxford mission.

For years now Newman had been trying to work out a philosophy of faith in the face of the growing deChristianization of modern society. In his *Oxford University Sermons* he had argued that religious belief involved the same kind of informal reasoning that was unhesitatingly employed in other areas without accusations of irrationality. The problem still remained as to whether one could talk of attaining certitude, when the kind of certainty involved was clearly so different from the object-ive certainty of logically necessary propositions and empirically verifiable factual statements. At last in August 1866, while on holiday in Switzerland, he decided that he had been wrong to start from the problem of certitude, since certitude was a kind of assent, which in turn must be distinguished from inference. The discovery was the beginning of nearly four years of strenuous work on *An Essay in Aid of a Grammar of Assent* (1870).

Newman began by distinguishing between the assent one makes to a proposition and the conclusion one draws from an inference, arguing that assenting and inferring were two distinct kinds of activity. Assent might be 'notional' or 'real', depending on whether one's appre-hension of a proposition was notional or real. Newman's usage can be confusing because, although 'notional' seems to mean what is abstract or general, and 'real' what is concrete and individual, nevertheless the distinction is not in fact between sense perceptions and mental abstrac-tions but between experiential and non-experiential knowledge. Thus a mental act may bring before the mind a more vivid image than a sensible object. Newman argued that conscience can suggest the existence of God if intimations of conscience are seen as the echoes of a magisterial voice suggestive of a God of whom we gain a real image from, and in, these dictates of conscience. Arguing that, where formal logical inference is impos-sible, it is the cumulation of probabilities which leads to certainty, Newman pointed out that assent to the truth of non-logical propositions involves personal judgement. This judgement, similar to Aristotle's *phronesis*, Newman called the 'illative sense', which operates more or less implicitly and instinctively, without formal verbal analysis.

Written by a disciple of Bishop Joseph Butler from within a pragmatic philosophical tradition, the *Grammar of Assent* inevitably found little favour with Catholic scho-lastic philosophers. Well aware that the alleged weakness of the work was its failure to provide a criterion of cer-tainty, Newman's originality lay in recognizing that the truths in question were not empirically or logically dem-onstrable.

Papal infallibility In June 1867 the pope announced that a general council was to be held. Newman was immediately alarmed that the ultramontanes would press for a defin-ition of papal infallibility. But he refused three invita-tions, including one from Pope Pius IX himself, to attend as a theological consultor on the grounds that he had no aptitude for committee work nor the kind of professional expertise that would be needed. In January 1870 he received a letter from Bishop Ullathorne deploring the way in which the ultramontanes were lobbying for a def-inition. Newman thought a definition was uncalled for, as there was no heresy threatening papal authority, and also dangerous, because there had not been sufficient prepar-ation and study to justify such a sudden and unnecessary development. Newman's extremely strong response to the bishop was leaked to the newspapers. In fact, the actual definition that was passed by the majority of the

bishops in July 1870 struck Newman as so moderate as to constitute a defeat for the ultramontanes.

The loss of Rome by the pope in September 1870 meant the end of the Papal States and of his temporal power, about which Newman, to the annoyance of the English ultramontanes, had been less than enthusiastic. Perhaps his new spiritual powers—which Newman thought popes had acted on in practice for at least 300 years—were after all providential: at least they would give the church an enhanced central authority against attempts by the state to control local churches. Still, Newman knew only too well that the definition would cause a lot of problems for Catholics, particularly in protestant countries. History, however, seemed to show that declarations of councils were modified in the sense of being qualified and comple-mented by later councils.

In November 1874 W. E. Gladstone—influenced by the excommunicated Catholic J. J. I. von Döllinger—pub-lished a best-selling pamphlet alleging that the infallibil-ity definition had not only deprived Catholics of their intellectual freedom but also put their civic loyalty into serious question. Newman saw his opportunity to disown the extreme ultramontanism of Manning, which had partly inspired Gladstone's outburst. The resulting *Letter to the Duke of Norfolk* (the leading Catholic layman), which was actually, like the *Letter to Pusey*, a short book, was pub-lished in January 1875. In it Newman pointed out that all doctrinal pronouncements of councils and popes required the interpretation of theologians, just as the meaning of the laws of the legislature had to be deter-mined by lawyers. Moreover, magisterial definitions of an abstract nature had to be applied to concrete situations and to admit of exceptions. Theology, too, had its own principles and rules, not least that of minimizing the force and scope of a teaching, which were an important part of the church's tradition. The most famous part of the *Letter* was Newman's raising of a toast to 'the pope if you please—still to conscience first, and to the pope after-wards' (*Letter to Pusey*, 114). Newman admitted the possibil-ity of conscientious disobedience to a papal edict, but not to a papal teaching, which, since it had to be of a general nature, could not represent a practical dictate to the indi-vidual.

Last years Although the *Letter to the Duke of Norfolk* was Newman's last book, it was not his last word on ecclesio-logy. In 1877, as part of the process of republishing his Anglican and Catholic writings in a uniform series, he added a lengthy preface to the *Lectures on the Prophetical Office*. In his *Essay on Development*, which he was to reissue in a greatly revised edition in 1878, he had argued that the dogmas of Catholicism were not corruptions but develop-ments of the original revelation. In the 1877 preface he maintained that the superstitions and abuses of power to be found in the history of the Catholic church were not corruptions of its theology (which would be rationalism), but of the church's other two 'offices', namely its worship and government. The anomalies to be found in Catholi-cism resulted from the church's difficulty in combining all three offices at the same time, and while Newman saw theology as predominant, since without its subject matter, revelation, the church would not be a political power or a religious rite, nevertheless he allowed that at times theology had to take into account and respect the devotions of popular religion and also even 'political' considerations, as the church is the church militant as well.

In May 1877 Newman was sent one of the three drawings made of him by a friend, Lady Coleridge. As well as the famous voice, people who met him for the first time were particularly struck by his strangely mysterious expression, which was evidently evoked better in her portraits than in others (including that painted by J. E. Millais *c*.1881). Unlike W. T. Roden's portrait (1874?), which emphasized Newman's keen sensitivity, Lady Coleridge succeeded in integrating it with the resoluteness and strength that also marked his character.

In December 1877 Newman received a surprise invitation from Trinity College, Oxford, to become its first honorary fellow, an honour which he deeply appreciated, particularly as his memories of Trinity were happier than those of Oriel—as he had indicated in the famous account in the *Apologia* of his taking leave of Oxford in 1846. This was followed by an even greater honour in 1879, when he was made a cardinal by the new, more liberal Pope Leo XIII. Although such a dignity seemed quite alien to him, he felt that he had no alternative but to accept the red hat: not only would it end all suspicions of his orthodoxy and his commitment to the Catholic church but it would also signify that ultramontanism was not the only acceptable kind of Catholicism and would mark the beginning of a new openness in Rome, as the pope intended. In his *biglietto* speech, Newman adverted to the significance of his elevation, while at the same time affirming his lifelong opposition to that liberalism which rejects dogma and the objectivity of religious truth.

In 1881 *Select Treatises of St Athanasius* was published in two volumes, a greatly revised and altered version of the edition Newman had contributed to the Tractarian Library of the Fathers, which completed the uniform edition of the works. But it was not the last of his publications. In 1882 he published, with a preface, *Notes of a Visit to the Russian Church in the Years 1840, 1841*, which had been compiled by William Palmer while he was a Tractarian fellow of Magdalen; Palmer had recently died after becoming a Catholic. Then in 1884 Newman published an article in *Nineteenth Century* on the problem of the inspiration of scripture, which was more sophisticated than the prevailing Catholic theory of the time in arguing that it was the biblical writers, not the writings themselves, who were directly inspired. And finally, in October 1885, in an article in the *Contemporary Review*, he defended himself against the frequent charge of scepticism which was made against him, later to be put forward with force by Leslie Stephen in 'Cardinal Newman's scepticism' (*Nineteenth Century*, Feb 1891), in emphasizing conscience and imagination in religious belief rather than so-called reason.

From the latter half of 1886 Newman's health began to fail, and he celebrated mass for the last time on Christmas day 1889. On 11 August 1890 he died of pneumonia at the Birmingham Oratory. He was buried on the 19th in the grave of Ambrose St John at the Oratory country house at Rednal, outside Birmingham. The pall over the coffin bore his cardinal's motto *Cor ad cor loquitur* ('Heart speaks to heart'). On his memorial tablet were inscribed the words he had chosen: *Ex umbris et imaginibus in veritatem* ('Out of shadows and phantasms into the truth').

Posthumous reputation The many eulogies which followed Newman's death included the first important literary biographical study (1891), by R. H. Hutton, whose highly favourable review in *The Spectator* of Newman's original pamphlet against Kingsley had been a turning point in Newman's eventually successful battle to prove his integrity as a Tractarian and as a convert to Rome. But even though Kingsley's crude attack had been discredited, Hutton's short critical life did not have the field to itself. In the same year Newman's younger brother Francis published *Contributions, Chiefly to the Early History of the Late Cardinal Newman*, a portrait which depicted him as authoritarian and imperious as well as having been for long a covert Romanist if not papist, just as Kingsley had claimed. As a young man, Francis Newman had been influenced by the founder of the Plymouth Brethren and his extreme protestant views had not only necessitated his resigning his fellowship at Balliol but had also led to his elder brother, in his most ardently Tractarian phase, breaking off ordinary relations on the ground that Francis was a schismatic sectarian, whose theological views would eventually end in unbelief, a prophecy that was fulfilled.

The centenary of the Oxford Movement in 1933 stimulated two more critical psychobiographies: Frank Leslie Cross's *John Henry Newman*, which echoed Bishop Samuel Wilberforce's review in the *Quarterly Review* of the *Apologia* in portraying a resentful Newman, whose failures stemmed from his own diffidence and excessive dependence on authority, whether Anglican or Roman, and *Oxford Apostles* by Geoffrey Faber, the great-nephew of Father Faber, which attempted to debunk the spiritual ideals of the Tractarians by means of a Freudian analysis according to which Newman's friendship with Hurrell Froude was at least subconsciously homosexual. So far from the world of Freud were Newman and his contemporaries that his wish to be buried in the same grave as his faithful friend Ambrose St John caused not the slightest comment at the time, let alone scandal or even embarrassment on the part of the ecclesiastical authorities. In assessing such speculations as those of Faber, the anachronistic assumptions of a later age should be avoided: not only was the Oxford of the Tractarians an exclusively male environment, and moreover a culture in which the concept of affectionate friendship without any sexual implications was taken for granted, but also it needs to be borne in mind that the early Victorians were uninhibitedly emotional in expressing their feelings, sometimes in language open to misunderstanding in an age preoccupied by sex; in this they were quite unlike a later generation of Victorians who were moulded by the ethos of the public school as shaped by Thomas Arnold of Rugby and intended for the training of stiff-upper-lip imperial administrators. Again, while Newman's strongly held conviction about the value of clerical celibacy for the Church of England led him to feel less than sympathetic to the marriages of fellow Tractarian clergy, it has to be recalled that not only did Newman himself confess that he was tempted at times by marriage right into his late twenties—notwithstanding the call to celibacy which he had felt so powerfully at the time of his 1816 conversion—but also in 1840 he completed his remarkable account of his illness in Sicily with some poignant reflections on the sacrificial nature of celibacy that entailed the loss of the sympathetic intimacy which only a wife could provide.

It is perhaps significant that the strongest defence of Newman's character has come from a woman, Meriol Trevor, in her two-volume biography *Newman: the Pillar of the Cloud* and *Newman: Light in Winter* (1962), a study so overtly defensive as to seem partisan to many. Yet it was a deeply 'feminine' empathy that enabled Newman to have close and enduring friendships with a number of women, especially during the Catholic years. In his *John Henry Newman: a Biography* (1988) Ian Ker argued that the key to understanding Newman's temperament and to making a balanced judgement on the notorious question of Newman's sensitivity is to recognize this 'feminine' side of Newman but to emphasize also the no less pronounced 'masculine' aspects of his personality. It was, Ker maintained, the unusual combination of these vibrantly sensitive and unflinchingly tough elements in his character that accounts for the very different reactions that Newman continues to arouse. It is crucial for understanding his rift with the London Oratorians, and particularly with Faber, who had not simply offended Newman personally by what Newman perceived as their disloyalty and ingratitude but had done so over an issue which involved important matters of principle that drew out of Newman a characteristic refusal to compromise or to use the kind of diplomatic language that would have helped smooth things over. While there need not be much argument over whether Newman's sensitivity did not sometimes, unsurprisingly, verge on the hypersensitive and touchy, the fact is that what seems to his admirers to be an impressive integration of sensitiveness with firmness and directness into a wholeness of personality will always, no doubt, seem to others with a different outlook more like touchiness aggravated by dogmatic inflexibility and tactless obstinacy.

It was not only Newman's character that came under critical scrutiny immediately after his death. Edwin A. Abbot's *The Anglican Career of Cardinal Newman* (1892) was the first of a series of posthumous attacks on his theology and thought, often again only repeating contemporary reactions. Here, as opposed to the criticisms of his personality, a much greater measure of agreement has become possible through the publication of Newman's letters and papers and through recent developments in philosophy as well as theology. Abbot's criticism of Newman for credulously sacrificing reason to faith, in relying on antecedent probability as opposed to demonstrable evidence, and in allowing his imagination to dominate his intellect

was answered by Henri Bremond in his sympathetic *Newman: essai de biographie psychologique* (1906; Eng. trans. *The Mystery of Newman*, 1907), which, however, had the effect of highlighting the old charge of scepticism by presenting Newman as an anti-intellectual proponent of a Schleiermachian religion of the heart. The fear that Newman would be condemned along with the modernists who claimed his support lay behind Wilfrid Ward's *The Life of John Henry Cardinal Newman* (1912), which sought successfully to expound the careful balance of Newman's theological stance as a Catholic, caught as he was between the ultramontanes on the one side and the liberals on the other, while at the same time so stressing his sufferings during his Catholic period as to leave an excessive impression of depression and hurt.

It is an irony that the very charge of irrationality which was brought against Newman by secular and liberal Anglican critics, whose idea of rationality was derived from the Enlightenment, was also the criticism made by Roman Catholic philosophers and theologians whose scholasticism was quite alien to Newman's thought on faith and reason, which itself bears obvious resemblances to the writings of Coleridge and Kierkegaard in the nineteenth century and of the phenomenologists and the later Wittgenstein in the twentieth century. Furthermore, 'What more than anything else has altered the situation and restored Newman to decisive relevance are developments in the philosophy of science, which have, for the first time in the modern era, cast doubt upon the credentials of science itself as an avenue to truth' (B. Mitchell, 'Newman as a philosopher' in Ker and Hill, 237). Basil Mitchell has drawn the analogy explicitly:

> the paradigm instance of factual knowledge, by comparison with which the claims of religion were thought to be problematic, can no longer be made to serve this purpose. Yet, of course, scientists do unhesitatingly rely upon the validity of scientific method. ... Their situation is, thus, curiously analogous to that in which Newman found himself as he struggled to analyse the nature of reason and its relation to Christian Faith. (ibid., 238)

If the originality of Newman's philosophy is only just beginning to be appreciated and understood, the same is not true of his theology, which received its full vindication at the Second Vatican Council (1962–5), when the Roman Catholic church turned away from scholasticism and back to scriptural and patristic sources. Not only did the council, of which Newman has often been called the 'Father', adopt the kind of ecclesiology which had led Newman into so much trouble with the authorities, but his views on revelation, on the rights of conscience, on ecumenism, and on the need for the Catholic church's renewal and adaptation to the modern world all anticipated the teachings of the council.

In 1991 Pope John Paul II declared Newman to be 'Venerable', the first formal step to canonization. Certainly the most significant Roman Catholic theologian of the nineteenth century, he has also come to be seen as the most seminal of modern Catholic thinkers. Within the English context, he was the most important Anglican theologian since Hooker, as well as being one of the great Victorian prose writers.

IAN KER

Sources *The letters and diaries of John Henry Newman*, ed. C. S. Dessain and others, [31 vols.] (1961–) · J. H. Newman, uniform edition of works, 36 vols. (Longmans, Green and Co., London, 1868–81) · J. H. Newman, *Autobiographical writings*, ed. H. Tristram (1956) · I. Ker, *John Henry Newman: a biography* (1988) · V. F. Blehl, *John Henry Newman: a bibliographical catalogue of his writings* (1978) · J. R. Griffin, *Newman: a bibliography of secondary studies* (1980) · J. H. Newman, *Apologia pro vita sua*, ed. M. J. Svaglic (1967) · G. Faber, *Oxford apostles* (1933) · *Letters and correspondence of John Henry Newman during his life in the English church*, ed. A. Mozley, 2 vols. (1891) · R. W. Church, *The Oxford Movement: twelve years, 1833–45* (1891) · R. H. Hutton, *Cardinal Newman* (1891) · W. Ward, *The life of John Henry Cardinal Newman*, 2 vols. (1912) · L. Bouyer, *Newman: his life and spirituality*, Eng. trans. (1958) · M. Trevor, *Newman: the pillar of the cloud* (1962) · M. Trevor, *Newman: light in winter* (1962) · C. S. Dessain, *John Henry Newman* (1966) · J. H. Newman, *Newman the Oratorian: his unpublished Oratory papers*, ed. P. Murray (1969) · J. H. Newman, *The philosophical notebook of John Henry Newman*, ed. E. Sillem, 2 vols. (1969–70) · M. J. Svaglic and C. S. Dessain, 'John Henry Newman', *Victorian prose: a guide to research*, ed. D. J. DeLaura (1973) · J. H. Newman, *The idea of a university*, ed. I. T. Ker (1976) · J. H. Newman, *An essay in aid of a grammar of assent*, ed. I. T. Ker (1985) · I. Ker and A. G. Hill, eds., *Newman after a hundred years* (1990) · S. Gilley, *Newman and his age* (1990) · T. Vargish, *Newman: the contemplation of mind* (1970) · D. J. DeLaura, *Hebrew and Hellene in Victorian England* (1969) · J. Coulson, *Newman and the common tradition* (1970) · A. D. Culler, *The imperial intellect: a study of Newman's educational ideal* (1955) · C. F. Harrold, *John Henry Newman: an expository and critical study of his mind, thought and art* (1945) · W. E. Houghton, *The art of Newman's 'Apologia'* (1945) · J. Holloway, *The Victorian sage: studies in argument* (1953) · M. J. Ferreira, *Doubt and religious commitment: the role of the will in Newman's thought* (1980) · H. Graef, *God and myself: the spirituality of John Henry Newman* (1967) · O. Chadwick, *From Bossuet to Newman: the idea of doctrinal development* (1957) · N. Lash, *Newman on development: the search for an explanation in history* (1975) · R. C. Selby, *The principle of reserve in the writings of John Henry Cardinal Newman* (1975) · J. H. Walgrave, *Newman the theologian: the nature of belief and doctrine as exemplified in his life and works*, Eng. trans. (1960) · E. J. Miller, *John Henry Newman on the idea of church* (1987) · T. Merrigan, *Clear heads and holy hearts: the religious and theological ideal of John Henry Newman* (1991)

Archives Archives of the British Province of the Society of Jesus, London, letters · Archives of the Irish Province of the Society of Jesus, Dublin, letters · Birmingham Oratory, corresp., literary MSS, and papers · BL, letters, RP 2708, 2752 [photocopies] · Bodl. Oxf., letters [copies] · Boston College, Massachusetts, papers · Brompton Oratory, London, letters · Claremont Colleges, California, Honnold/Mudd Library, papers · Clifton Roman Catholic diocese, Bristol, letters · College of the Holy Cross Library, Worcester, Massachusetts, letters · Coshel and Emly Diocesan Archives, letters · CUL · Douai Abbey, Woolhampton, Berkshire, letters · Duke U., Perkins L., papers · FM Cam., observations on the Preteus-Menelaus letters · L. Cong., papers · Newman College Library and Information Services, collection of his life and works · NL Wales, family letters [transcripts] · Pusey Oxf., corresp. · St John's Seminary, letters · Trinity College, Oxford, letters · University of Notre Dame, Indiana, letters · Ushaw College, Durham, letters, mainly personal · Venerable English College, Rome, letters | Archbishop's House, Drumcondra, Dublin, P. Cullen MSS · Arundel Castle, West Sussex, corresp. with the duke of Norfolk, S. L. Pope, J. R. Hope-Scott, and others · Balliol Oxf., letters to Tom Arnold · Balliol Oxf., corresp. with J. E. C. Bodley · BL, corresp. with W. E. Gladstone, Add. MSS 44360–44506 · BL, letters to F. S. Hayden, RP827 · BL, letters, mostly to Thomas Hayden, RP2708 [copies] · BL, corresp. with William Maskell, Add. MSS 37824–37825 · BL, letters to Royal Literary Fund, loan 96 · Bodl. Oxf., letters to Acland family · Bodl. Oxf., letters to William Bright · Bodl. Oxf., letters to J. W. Burgon · Bodl. Oxf., letters to H. T. Ellacombe · Bodl. Oxf., corresp. with H. E. Manning · Bodl. Oxf., corresp. with Mozley family · Bodl. Oxf., letters to Edwin Palmer · Bodl. Oxf., letters to Mark Pattison · Bodl. Oxf., corresp. with Joseph Blones White · Bodl. Oxf., letters to Robert Wilberforce · Bodl. Oxf., letters to Samuel Wilberforce · Brompton Oratory, letters to F. W. Faber · Campion Hall, Oxford, letters to Gerard Manley Hopkins · CKS, letters to W. B. Woodgate · College of the Holy Cross Library, Worcester, Massachusetts, letters to Edwin Palmer · CUL, letters to Lord Acton · CUL, letters to Sir Rowland Blemmerhassett and A. S. Griffin · Dublin Roman Catholic Diocesan Archives, letters, mostly to Paul Cullen · English Congregation of Dominican Sisters, Stone, corresp. with Catherine Balhurst and Margaret Hallahan · Georgetown University, letters to Thomas Hayden · Keble College, Oxford, corresp. with H. P. Liddon, John Keble, and others · LPL, corresp. with Ampele Burslett-Coutts · LPL, corresp. with Charles Golightly · LPL, letters to Isaac Williams · Magd. Oxf., letters to J. R. Bloxam · Magd. Oxf., letters to M. J. Routh · NRA, priv. coll., letters to the Revd W. Hook · NRA, priv. coll., letters to family and others · Oriel College, Oxford, letters to David Brown · Oriel College, Oxford, corresp. with Edward Hawkins · Pembroke College, Oxford, letters to Peter Renouf · Pusey Oxf., MSS · Pusey Oxf., corresp. with J. R. Bloxam · Pusey Oxf., R. W. Church MSS · Pusey Oxf., letters to E. S. Ffoulks · Pusey Oxf., letters to Henrietta Woodgate · U. Edin., New Coll. L., letters to Jane Whyte and Alexander Whyte · U. Reading L., agreements with F. H. Rivington · Ushaw College, Durham, letters to Charles Newsham · Ushaw College, Durham, letters to John Walker · Ushaw College, Durham, letters to Henry William Wilberforce · Westm. DA, corresp. with J. B. Morris and others · Westm. DA, corresp. with E. H Thompson

Likenesses R. Westmacott, bust, marble, c.1841, Birmingham Oratory · G. Richmond, likeness, coloured chalk, 1844, NPG · W. C. Ross, miniature, ivory, c.1845, Birmingham Oratory · Heath & Beau, photograph, 1861, Birmingham Oratory [*see illus.*] · T. Woolner, bust, marble, 1866, Keble College, Oxford · W. T. Roden, portrait, oils, 1874? Keble College, Oxford · J. F. Coleridge, likeness, black and white chalk, 1874–5, Park Place Pastoral Centre, Wickham, Hampshire · W. W. Oulen, portrait, oils, 1880, Birmingham Oratory · J. E. Millais, portrait, oils, c.1881, NPG · H. R. Barraud, print, carbon, c.1888, NPG

Wealth at death £4206 10s. 11d.: probate, 27 Feb 1891, *CGPLA Eng. & Wales*

Newman [*formerly* Neumann], **Maxwell Herman Alexander** (1897–1984), mathematician, was born in Chelsea, London, on 7 February 1897. He was the only child of Herman Alexander Neumann, a German working as secretary in a small company, and his wife, Sarah Ann Pike, who was of farming stock and an elementary schoolteacher. In 1908 he went to the City of London School, and in 1915 he gained a scholarship to St John's College, Cambridge. He gained a first class in part one of the mathematical tripos in 1916, the year in which he changed his name to Newman by deed poll. Much of the next three years he spent in the army, returning to Cambridge in 1919. In 1921 he was a wrangler in part two of the mathematical tripos, with a distinction in Schedule B. He was elected to a fellowship at St John's in 1923 and appointed a university lecturer in 1927. He studied in Vienna in 1922–3, and spent the year 1928–9 on a Rockefeller research fellowship at Princeton University in fruitful collaboration with J. W. Alexander.

Newman was among the pioneers of combinatory (or geometric) topology and wrote important papers on it in the late 1920s. Earlier definitions of combinatory equivalence, based on subdivision, had hit snags. Newman had the bold idea of using only three elementary 'moves' for

Maxwell Herman Alexander Newman (1897–1984), by Walter Stoneman, 1939

defining equivalence, none resembling subdivision. He developed all the desirable definitions and theorems for combinatorial manifolds, and also showed that his definition of equivalence encompassed earlier definitions and resolved their difficulties. In the 1930s, apart from continued work on combinatory topology, he wrote a seminal paper on periodic transformations in Abelian topological groups and an admirable book, *Elements of the Topology of Plane Sets of Points* (1939). In the early 1940s he wrote on logic and Boolean algebras.

During the Second World War, in 1942, he joined the government code and cypher school at Bletchley Park. There he became familiar with an important, German army cipher system, the *Lorenz Schlüsselzusatz 40* (the SZ40, dubbed 'Tunny' by the Bletchley codebreakers); it was a non-Morse teleprinter system of higher grade than the Enigma. Following an error by a German cipher clerk, the SZ40 had been 'broken', sight unseen, mainly by Colonel John Tiltman and W. T. Tutte. Under Major Tester, a section called the Testery was started for routinely applying, by hand, methods similar to those used by Tiltman and Tutte. This was possible because the kind of error mentioned above often occurred. Newman joined the Testery but felt he was not good at the work and disliked it. He realized that it should be possible to perform the statistical aspects with the help of rapid, special-purpose electronic machinery employing paper tape and photoelectric cells, and with A. M. Turing proposed the logical requirements for

such machinery. These requirements formed the basis of actual machines, culminating with the Colossus, for which the head engineer was Tom Flowers of the Post Office Research Station, which devoted about half of its total effort to the project. The section at Bletchley that used the machinery was headed by Newman and was called the Newmanry. The flexibility of the Colossi was such that they could be used for purposes additional to those for which they were originally intended, especially when no longer relying on mistakes made by German cipher clerks. (The German air force was covered well enough by reading the Enigma.) The Colossus Mark II had about 2500 tubes (valves). Apart from important new engineering concepts, it incorporated some ideas of Donald Michie and Jack Good, Max's first two cryptanalytic assistants.

Colossus was the world's first large-scale electronic, as distinct from electromagnetic, computer, but was not intended to be for general purposes. At first each Colossus was operated by a cryptanalyst working with a 'Wren' (a member of the Women's Royal Naval Service). The staff of the Newmanry consisted of about twenty cryptanalysts (including some distinguished mathematicians), about six engineers, and 273 Wrens. Newman ran this large section with the natural authority of a father figure, but in a democratic spirit. He took pleasure in the achievements of his staff, and originality flourished.

From 1945 to 1964 Newman was the Fielden professor of mathematics at Manchester University. He went there convinced that general-purpose computers were on the horizon, and he was active in persuading the authorities to build one at Manchester. The main engineer was Tom Kilburn. Newman ran the mathematics department effortlessly, attracting a formidable succession of fine mathematicians and getting the best out of them. After he retired from Manchester in 1964 he spent the next three years abroad, at the Australian National University (ANU), Rice University, Texas, and again at ANU. This period saw a second burst of mathematical research in geometric topology, culminating in an engulfing theorem for topological manifolds, published in 1966. This extended to topological manifolds what was already known of combinatorial manifolds, namely that the Poincaré conjecture is true for manifolds of dimension greater than four. His essentially Hilbertian interpretation of the nature of mathematics and science was described in his presidential address to the Mathematical Association (1959), where he said, among other things, that 'the pleasure and enlightenment to be obtained [from modern mathematics] is all the greater if we are thoroughly at home on one floor before starting to move to the next' (*Mathematical Gazette*, 43, 1959, 171).

Newman was a very gifted pianist and a good chess player. His technique for solving chess problems was to consider the function of a seemingly irrelevant piece. He enjoyed reading, claiming once to have read everything—among Russian novelists he preferred Pushkin to Dostoyevsky. At first contact perhaps austere, he was in fact a splendid companion. Typical of his quiet wit, in the face of wartime delays, was his topological comment 'It's wonderful how many different shapes the neck of a bottle can take'. He was elected FRS in 1939. In 1959 he was awarded the Sylvester medal of the Royal Society and in 1962 the De Morgan medal of the London Mathematical Society. He was given an honorary DSc by the University of Hull in 1968, and in 1973 St John's made him an honorary fellow.

In 1934 Newman married Lyn Lloyd, daughter of John Archibald Irvine, a Presbyterian minister; she was a writer. They had two sons. After her death in 1973 he married in the same year Dr Margaret Penrose (d. 1989), daughter of the physiologist John Beresford Leathes, and widow of Professor Lionel Sharples Penrose. Newman died in Cambridge on 22 February 1984.

SHAUN WYLIE, rev. I. J. GOOD

Sources J. F. Adams, *Memoirs FRS*, 31 (1985), 437–52 · personal knowledge (1995, 2004) · private information (1990) · P. J. Hilton, *Bulletin of the London Mathematical Society*, 18 (1986), 67–72 · F. H. Hinsley and A. Stripp, eds., *Codebreakers: the inside story of Bletchley Park*, pbk edn (1994) · N. Metropolis, J. Howlett, and G.-C. Rota, eds., *A history of computing in the twentieth century* (1980)
Archives King's AC Cam., corresp. and papers, mostly relating to A. M. Turing
Likenesses W. Stoneman, photograph, 1939, NPG [*see illus.*] · photograph, repro. in Hilton, *Bulletin of the London Mathematical Society* · photograph, repro. in Adams, *Memoirs FRS*, opposite p. 437
Wealth at death £127,126: probate, 27 June 1984, *CGPLA Eng. & Wales*

Newman, Robert (1858–1926), concert manager, was born on 26 July 1858 at 121 Regent Street, London, the son of Charles Newman, a job master who had contracts to supply horses to the royal mail, and his wife, Emiline Maria, *née* Love. His first employment, as a stock jobber, ended in bankruptcy after two years in 1887, when he was twenty-nine. He then studied singing in Italy, ran a concert agency in London, and, from 1888 until December 1889, studied singing at the Royal Academy of Music. He sang professionally as a bass for six years, and was chosen by Sir Hubert Parry to sing the title part in the first performance of his oratorio *Job*, at the Gloucester festival in 1893. Lacking exceptional abilities as a singer, however, Newman went into partnership with an Oxford Street concert agent named Farley Sinkins. They leased Covent Garden Theatre for a series of Promenade Concerts in autumn 1893, employing a good quality orchestra of 100 players conducted by Frederick H. Cowen. The opening of the Queen's Hall complex in Regent Street that same year brought Newman the great opportunity of his life: he became its first lessee and manager. The first official concert in the large hall took place on 2 December 1893 and included a performance of Mendelssohn's *Hymn of Praise* conducted by Cowen, with a choir hand-picked by Newman. He was confident of a large public for good-quality orchestral music at the Queen's Hall and planned a continuous series of Promenade Concerts during the summer, aiming through lower prices to attract a larger and less affluent audience while fashionable society was away and no good music was available. He approached Henry Wood, as yet hardly known on the concert platform, early

in 1895 to conduct them. Financial support was provided by Dr George Cathcart, a well-known throat specialist. The first concert took place on 10 August 1895. The excellence of the programmes (which always included a new work and favoured little-known Russian and French music) and the high orchestral standards were immediately noted in the press. Thus began a partnership that lasted for thirty-two years and created an entirely new audience, repertory, and status for orchestral music in London.

Until 1902 Newman managed the Queen's Hall entirely alone. He added Saturday Afternoon Symphony Concerts in January 1897 and Sunday Afternoon Concerts, begun in the face of much sabbatarian opposition, later that year. He invited the leading continental conductors and orchestras, and the Queen's Hall soon became the focus for London's concert music. Notable early events included two London music festivals, in 1899 and 1902, in which the celebrated Lamoureux Orchestra under its founder and the Queen's Hall Orchestra under Wood shared the programmes. In 1902 Newman became bankrupt as a result of the failure of a venture in theatrical management. A syndicate chaired by the financier and philanthropist Edgar Speyer was created to underwrite the orchestra, and the music publisher Chappell took the lease of the Queen's Hall, retaining Newman as manager until 1906. Soon after the outbreak of the First World War Chappell also assumed proprietorship of the orchestra, which it renamed the New Queen's Hall Orchestra; Newman continued as its manager. The later support of the orchestra and Promenade Concerts by the BBC was first negotiated, unsuccessfully, by Newman shortly before his death; he was the constant factor in changing commercial conditions.

Newman was a man of few words and a formal manner but unfailing courtesy, single-minded and straightforward in all his dealings. He was a bulky, commanding figure with a heavy, well-groomed black moustache, very blue eyes, and a stern expression. He worked his musicians hard but sympathetically, regularly observed his concerts, and sought to make them physically attractive. In 1904 he fiercely resisted the still prevalent deputy system that undermined standards; he opposed the strong anti-German feeling in 1914 by reinstating German works—especially Wagner—in the programmes, for which they were famous. He died on 4 November 1926 at a nursing home at 40 Belsize Grove, Hampstead, of acute entero-colitis (from which he had suffered for three months), at the age of sixty-eight, and was interred in Hampstead cemetery, Fortune Green Road, on 8 November. He was survived by his wife, Florence Maud Newman; two children are recorded, a son and a daughter (married as Mrs E. F. Andrews). His family residence at time of death was 246 Finchley Road, London.

MICHAEL MUSGRAVE

Sources d. cert. · *MT*, 67 (1926), 1134 · *The Times* (6 Nov 1926) · R. Elkin, *Queen's Hall, 1893–1941* [1944] · H. J. Wood, *My life of music* (1938) · P. A. Scholes, *The mirror of music, 1844–1944: a century of*

musical life in Britain as reflected in the pages of the Musical Times, 2 vols. (1947) · R. Pound, *Sir Henry Wood* (1969) · R. Newmarch, *Henry Wood* (1904) · b. cert. · 'The Queen's Hall', *MT*, 34 (1893), 739 · *MT*, 35 (1894), 27, 340 · *MT*, 36 (1895), 480 [promenade concerts] · *MT*, 43 (1902), 600 [promenade concerts] · *CGPLA Eng. & Wales* (1927)
Likenesses photograph, repro. in Pound, *Sir Henry Wood*, 38
Wealth at death £1439 4s. 10d.: probate, 4 Jan 1927, *CGPLA Eng. & Wales*

Newman, Samuel (1602–1663), biblical scholar, was baptized on 24 May 1602 at Banbury, Oxfordshire, the son of Richard Newman, of a family 'more *Eminent* and more *Ancient* for the Profession of the True *Protestant Religion*, than most in the Realm of *England*' (Mather, 113–14). Biographical information on Newman is extremely scarce; even his acquaintance Cotton Mather, writing a brief life of Newman in 1702, complained that 'our *History* of him is necessarily Creepled with much Imperfection' (ibid., 114). He matriculated at Magdalen College, Oxford, on 3 March 1620, aged seventeen, and graduated BA from St Edmund Hall on 17 October in the same year. After Oxford, Newman entered the clergy, but his clerical career was interrupted by repeated official prosecution on account of his puritanism. He was compelled to move no fewer than seven times over the following eighteen years, leading Mather to remark that 'although we might otherwise have termed him a *Presbyter* of *One* Town by *Ordination*, we must now call him an *Evangelist* of *many*, through *Persecution*' (ibid., 114). In 1638 he moved to New England, initially settling in Dorchester, Massachusetts, for about a year and a half, before moving on to Weymouth, where he remained for five years. In 1644 he moved for the last time and established a congregation in Rehoboth, Massachusetts, which he named after the biblical city of Genesis 26: 22, where 'the Lord hath made room for us, and we shall be fruitful in the land' (ibid., 114). Newman's major work, his *Large and Complete Concordance to the Bible in English*, was published in London in 1643, expanding upon the earlier concordances compiled by Clement Cotton (New Testament, 1622; Old Testament, 1627); it went through nine editions up to 1720. He died in Rehoboth on 5 July 1663; whether he married or had children does not appear to have been recorded. DAVID WILSON

Sources C. Mather, *Magnalia Christi Americana*, 7 bks in 1 vol. (1702), 113–16 · Wood, *Ath. Oxon.*, new edn, 3.648 · Foster, *Alum. Oxon., 1500–1714* · *Reg. Oxf.*, vol. 2/4 · *DNB* · parish register, Banbury, 24 May 1602, Oxon. RO [baptism]

Newman, Sydney Cecil (1917–1997), television producer, was born in Toronto, Ontario, Canada, on 1 April 1917, the son of an Orthodox Jewish shoe salesman who had moved to Canada from Russia. He was educated at Ogden public school, Toronto, and then at the Central Technical School, Toronto, where he qualified as a commercial artist. Between 1935 and 1941 he worked as a stage painter and as an industrial designer, moving to New York in 1938. He joined the national film board of Canada as a splicer in 1941. Under the guidance of the board's founder and chairman, John Grierson, he became a documentary director, a

producer in 1944, and head of production in 1947, winning several awards. In 1944 he married Margaret Elizabeth (Betty) McRae (d. 1981); they had three daughters, Deirdre, Jennifer, and Gillian.

Newman's involvement with television began in 1949–50 when he spent a year on secondment to NBC in New York. He moved to the Canadian Broadcasting Corporation (CBC) in 1953 as director of outside broadcasts, features, and documentaries. However, he saw the potential for applying the techniques he had learned in documentaries to the emerging form of television drama, and in 1954 became the CBC's drama supervisor, producing *General Motors Theatre*.

Several of Newman's CBC plays were also broadcast in Britain by the BBC, leading to a visit to Britain in 1956. There he saw John Osborne's *Look Back in Anger*, which changed the direction of his career. Struck by Osborne's insight into post-war British society, in 1958 he accepted the position of head of drama at ABC, the ITV contractor for the north of England and the midlands at weekends. ABC produced ITV's Sunday evening play strand, *Armchair Theatre*, where Newman developed what he called 'agitational contemporaneity' (Sendall, 338). Anxious to hold on to a wide audience with diverse educations, experiences, and expectations, who 'would not have time to wait for Godot' (*The Armchair Theatre*, 17), he declared that it was necessary to 'exclude from my programme all Shakespeare, all the classics, all costume drama' and concentrate on situations which the greater part of the audience would find familiar (Wiseman). He encouraged his authors to develop plays from points of controversy, such as social mobility, labour problems, and sexual identity. Critics of this policy castigated him as the 'abominable showman', alleging that cultural breadth was being sacrificed to the pursuit of ratings. None the less, at ABC he secured the services of respected authors who had previously avoided television, such as Harold Pinter and Angus Wilson. He also devised ITV's most commercially successful drama series of the 1960s, *The Avengers*.

During 1962 Newman was approached by Hugh Greene, director-general of the BBC, to take up the position of head of drama at BBC television. Greene believed that the application of Newman's house style to BBC television drama would help to lure viewers from ITV and help with the demand for new drama for the BBC's second television channel, which would start broadcasting in 1964. Newman took up his new position in January 1963, and embarked on a restructuring of his department, dividing the renamed drama group into divisions responsible for plays, series, and serials. Central authority was strengthened by separating the roles of the producer and director, directors working to producers rather than commissioning work themselves, as had been BBC practice. The department's responsibilities were broadened by the transfer of populist drama series and those aimed at a young audience from light entertainment and children's programmes respectively. His controversialist agenda and manner—he was described by Peter Luke as 'a cross between Ghenghis Khan and a pussy-cat' (Shubik, 9)—had already won him press attention at ABC, but this increased at the BBC, where he was almost as much the target of the self-appointed guardians of public morality as Hugh Greene. He alienated some of the staff he inherited, who considered that he promoted two-dimensional characterization and unsubtle exposition.

Newman's strategy was epitomized in *The Wednesday Play*, which began in 1965. Its producers included James MacTaggart and Tony Garnett, and the strand included perhaps the most memorable plays of the Newman era, such as early work by Dennis Potter. The two most controversial plays were two directed by Ken Loach, confronting urban deprivation and the failure of the welfare state to deal with social breakdown: *Up the Junction* (1965), written by Nell Dunn, and *Cathy Come Home* (1966), written by Jeremy Sandford. Newman's other major legacy to BBC television was *Doctor Who*, a science-fiction adventure series made up of episodic serials set in historic and futuristic settings, first broadcast on 23 November 1963. Newman devised the lead character, the Doctor, a nameless elderly man from a non-earthly civilization whose intellectual brilliance would be obscured by his eccentric manner and inability to control his highly advanced time–space machine, which Newman's colleagues decided should be called a 'tardis' and have the exterior appearance of a police telephone box while being of near-infinite space within. Newman intended that the programme would avoid science-fiction clichés and concentrate on encouraging children's interest in history and science. The introduction of Terry Nation's malevolent metal-clad aliens, the Daleks, into the series helped the programme become a success with audiences but, in moving the series towards a 'monster of the week' format, compromised Newman's original intentions. None the less he continued to defend the series for most of the rest of its twenty-six year run.

The structure of the BBC drama group, and the escalation of its output under Newman's leadership—he once calculated that the department produced 250 different programmes in 1963, and 720 in 1968—removed him from the immediate creative process, and he chose not to renew his contract in December 1967. Instead, he became an executive producer at Associated British Picture Corporation, the parent company of ABC, but financial uncertainty and then the takeover of the company by EMI prevented him from making any films, and he left in July 1969. In January 1970 he returned to Canada to become adviser to the chairman of the Canadian radio and television commission, and in August that year he became film commissioner at the national film board of Canada. There his struggle to persuade his film-makers to produce work with a mass audience in mind made him enemies, as did his attempts to reduce the influence of those he perceived as Quebec separatists in the Francophone production division. His contract was not renewed in 1975.

Newman's wife, Betty, died in 1981, the same year that he was made an officer of the order of Canada. A few years later he returned to London as a freelance producer and consultant. His periods at ABC and the BBC had come to be regarded as a 'golden age' of television drama, as political and financial pressure in the 1980s was marking the end of his cherished single play. Many interviewers were chiefly interested in his connection with *Doctor Who* and *The Avengers*; he acknowledged the success of these series but would also use the opportunity to warn against television drama becoming purely an escapist form. He returned to Canada in the early 1990s, and died of heart failure at Wellesley Central Hospital, Toronto, on 30 October 1997. He was survived by his partner, Marion McDougall, and his three daughters. His funeral was held at St James-the-Less Church, Toronto, on 3 November 1997.

Matthew Kilburn

Sources M. Hearn, 'A cross between Genghis Khan and a pussy-cat', *Doctor Who Magazine*, 260 (14 Jan 1998), 26–31 • B. Sendall, *Origin and foundation, 1946–62* (1982), vol. 1 of *Independent television in Britain* (1982–90) • BBC WAC • A. Briggs, *The history of broadcasting in the United Kingdom*, rev. edn, 5 (1995) • I. Shubik, *Play for today: the evolution of television drama* (1975) • D. B. Jones, *Movies and memoranda: an interpretative history of the National Film Board of Canada* (1981) • T. Wiseman, 'Keeper of the public's drama', *Time and Tide* (7 June 1962) • *The Listener* (14 Dec 1967) • M. Wiggin, 'Sydney of the kitchen sink', *Sunday Times* (4 Jan 1970) • *The armchair theatre: how to write, design, direct and enjoy television plays* (1959) • J. J. Jacobs, 'Newman, Sydney', *Museum of Broadcast Communications encyclopedia of television*, ed. H. Newcomb, 3 vols. (1997) • 'Stranger than fiction', *Starlog* [UK edn], 1 (2000) • D. Taylor, *Days of vision: working with David Mercer* (1990) • *Toronto Star* (31 Oct 1997) • *The Gazette* [Montreal] (1 Nov 1997) • G. Evans, *In the national interest: a chronicle of the National Film Board of Canada from 1949 to 1989* (1991) • H. Thomas, *With an independent air* (1977) • biographical files, BFI [microfiche]

Archives BBC WAC • BFI, biographical files [microfiche] | FILM BFI NFTVA

Likenesses photograph, *c*.1962, BFI • photograph, *c*.1962–1967, repro. in Hearn, 'A cross between Genghis Khan and a pussy-cat', pp. 26, 31 • Emmwood, caricature, 1964, repro. in *Daily Mail* (29 June 1964) • S. Payne, photograph, 1985, repro. in *Cult Times Special*, 15 (2000), 61; priv. coll.

Newman, Thomas (*c*.1564–1594), bookseller and publisher, was born at Newbury, Berkshire, the son of John Newman, clothworker, of Newbury. He was apprenticed, probably aged fourteen, to Ralph Newbery for eight years from Michaelmas 1578, was made free of the Stationers' Company on 25 August 1586, and set up in business the following year. He published with Thomas Gubbin, his own first entry at Stationers' Hall being on 18 September 1587.

In 1591 Newman published a poor text of *Astrophel and Stella* and some other poems, without the consent of Sir Philip Sidney's family or of Samuel David, author of twenty-eight of the poems, and without entering the book at Stationers' Hall. The book was seized on 18 September, apparently at the order of Lord Burghley. Newman, however, seems to have persuaded those in authority that he had acted in good faith, and later in the year he published a second edition of *Astrophel* alone. This was corrected, albeit very unsatisfactorily, from what appears to have been a superior manuscript, perhaps supplied by the Sidneys themselves.

Also in 1591 Newman bought Henry Middleton's shop in St Dunstan's Churchyard, with his books, for £150. The last entry under Newman's name in the Stationers' registers is in June 1593. He was buried at St Dunstan-in-the-West, Fleet Street, on 2 April 1594. His widow published one book, in 1594, as E. Newman.

H. R. TEDDER, rev. ANITA MCCONNELL

Sources Arber, *Regs. Stationers*, vols. 1–2 · R. L. Steele, 'Printers and books in chancery', *The Library*, new ser., 10 (1909), 101–6 · parish register, St Dunstan-in-the-West, 2 April 1594, GL, MS 10342 · C. R. Wilson, '*Astrophil and Stella*: a tangled editorial web', *The Library*, 6th ser., 1 (1979), 336–46 · J. Ames, *Typographical antiquities, or, An historical account of the origin and progress of printing in Great Britain and Ireland*, ed. W. Herbert, 3 vols. (1785–90), vol. 3, pp. 1355–6 · *STC, 1475–1640*

Newman, Thomas (1691/2–1758), Presbyterian minister, was born in London, the son of Thomas Newman (1665–1742), a tradesman. His father, who had been born in Cloth Fair near London's Smithfield during the worst period of the great plague, was a dissenter and, fearing that James II would deprive protestants of their liberty, had transcribed the whole Bible into shorthand over the course of six months (now in DWL, MS 28.1). Newman was probably educated at Dr John Ker's academy at Highgate. On 9 March 1710 he matriculated from Glasgow University but took no degree. After returning to London he received his first 'impressions of genuine religion' (Wilson, 2.148) from the preaching of the Presbyterian minister Dr John Evans, whose congregation, to which his family belonged, met first at Hand Alley, Bishopsgate Street, then from 1729 at New Broad Street, Petty France.

In 1718 Newman became assistant to Dr Samuel Wright at Blackfriars. He was ordained at the Old Jewry on 11 January 1721 by Wright and Edmund Calamy. His confession of faith, which was printed at the time, upheld orthodox views of the Trinity yet was also indicative of his later theological position. The Blackfriars congregation was one of the most respectable Presbyterian congregations in London, having been gathered by Matthew Sylvester and served by Richard Baxter and Calamy. It met at Meeting House Court, Knightrider Street, until 1734, when it moved to Little Carter Lane, Doctors' Common, a place 'scarcely equalled by any place of worship among the Dissenters in London' (Wilson, 2.107). Newman remained with the congregation as assistant minister from 1718 to 1746, and as pastor in succession to Wright from 1746 until his death. He was a member of the Presbyterian board and a trustee of Dr Williams's Trust. His memorialist Edward Pickard thought he had 'few equals' as a preacher, and described his subjects as 'practical and important. His language strong and nervous. His manner serious and striking. And his appeals to the heart forcible and pungent' (Pickard, 33–4).

On the outbreak of the Salters' Hall controversy over the question of whether dissenting ministers should subscribe to the Westminster confession, Newman sided with the non-subscribing ministers. This was consistent with his belief in the individual's freedom of conscience and his rejection of any human formulation of doctrine. He forcefully expressed these theological principles in a short paper which was written on 1 June 1752, when he

was aware of his approaching death, and was published posthumously. He maintained that he always declared 'what I believed to be the truths of the gospel' as he found them, no matter that they may have differed from 'a public faith, synodical determinations, or (O monstrous absurdity!) from religious sentiments established by law' (Pickard, 43). Newman's hatred of bigotry, not least among fellow Presbyterians, led him to advocate tolerance towards the Church of England but not towards the Roman Catholic church. His principal publications, *Piety Recommended as the Best Principle of Virtue* (1735) and *The Progress of Vice* (1738), were concerned with matters of moral and practical religion; likewise moral issues predominate in the two volumes of his sermons that were published posthumously in 1760.

Newman, who was married and had a family, suffered from poor health for many years and died in London on 6 December 1758, aged sixty-six. He was buried privately in Bunhill Fields on 17 December. His funeral sermon was preached by his successor at Little Carter Lane, Edward Pickard. His widow, Elizabeth, died on 25 December 1776 in her seventy-third year.

W. A. SHAW, rev. MARILYN L. BROOKS

Sources W. Wilson, *The history and antiquities of the dissenting churches and meeting houses in London, Westminster and Southwark*, 4 vols. (1808–14), vol. 2, pp.107, 147–53 · E. Pickard, *The Christian's confidence and joy in the views of death and judgment* (1759) · *DNB* · J. A. Jones, ed., *Bunhill memorials* (1849), 183 · W. D. Jeremy, *The Presbyterian Fund and Dr Daniel Williams's Trust* (1885), 138–9 · DWL, MS Wilson, H. 3, nos. 95–6
Likenesses J. Macardell, mezzotint (after S. Webster), BM, NPG

Newman, William (1577–1640), Roman Catholic priest, was from Staffordshire. He was at Douai in 1594 and was arrested in England in 1601 and condemned to death for his religion, being charged with aiding the escape of a priest from the home of Anne Line. At the intercession of a noble lady at court the death sentence was commuted to banishment and exile. He went to Seville, where he studied and was ordained priest in 1606. In May 1609 he was sent to Lisbon to take charge of the English residence near St Catherine's Church. This was a house for priests which was supported by donations from the duke of Braganza and the archbishop of Lisbon. Among the duties of the rector was that of visiting ships coming from the British Isles, acting as interpreter and seeing that they conformed to the requirements of the Inquisition. This might entail a search for subversive literature and taking note of any protestants who might be thought to be a threat to the security of the state. There was also chaplaincy work on behalf of English sailors.

Newman's predecessor, Nicholas Ashton, had bequeathed property to the residence and Newman wished to use the Ashton legacy to found a seminary for the training of priests for the English mission. He visited Madrid and entered negotiations with Thomas More, the agent for Douai College, in order to further this scheme. It was on one of these visits that he made contact with Pedro Coutinho, a retired Portuguese soldier who was anxious to leave some of his fortune for the founding of a religious house and who had recently been told of the plight of Catholics in England. On learning of this the Jesuits considered that Newman had betrayed his trust since they regarded the opening of seminaries in the Peninsula to be their sole responsibility and he was consequently deprived of his chaplaincy. However, the negotiations went ahead and the papal brief founding the college was issued on 22 September 1622. Although it was Newman who brought together the patronage of Pedro Coutinho and the interests of the English secular clergy he was never president of the college, but he was always concerned with its affairs. His idea that the college should be restricted to students of philosophy and theology did not, however, prevail and from the early days younger boys were also accepted to study the humanities.

Newman became a curate of the Royal Hospital in Lisbon and chaplain at St George's Fort, where he lived much honoured and respected. While ministering at the hospital during an outbreak of sickness he caught a fever and died, on 4 July 1640. He was buried in the college chapel and he left 2000 crowns to the college in his will.

MICHAEL E. WILLIAMS

Sources M. Sharratt, ed., *Lisbon College register, 1628–1813*, Catholic RS, 72 (1991), 130–31 · G. Anstruther, *The seminary priests*, 2 (1975), 230–31 · *Dodd's Church history of England*, ed. M. A. Tierney, 5 vols. (1839–43), vol. 4, pp. 128–33, ccliii–cclxii · M. E. Williams, 'The origins of the English College, Lisbon', *Recusant History*, 20 (1990–91), 478–92 · Ushaw College, Durham, Lisbon collection, William Newman MSS · W. Croft and [J. Kirk], *Historical account of Lisbon College* (1902) · private information (2004)
Archives Ushaw College, Durham, Lisbon collection
Wealth at death bequest to Lisbon College

Newman, William Lambert (1834–1923), ancient historian and philosopher, the second son of Edmund Lambert Newman, solicitor, of Cheltenham, was born at Cheltenham on 21 August 1834. He was educated at Cheltenham College (1846–51) and at Balliol College, Oxford, which he entered as a scholar in 1851 and where his tutors were Benjamin Jowett, James Riddell, Edwin Palmer, and Henry Smith. He won the Hertford scholarship (1853) and the Ireland scholarship (1854), obtained first classes in classical moderations (1853) and in *literae humaniores* (1855), and while still an undergraduate was elected a fellow of his college (1854).

As lecturer in history for the schools of *literae humaniores* and of law and modern history from 1858 to 1870, Newman exercised a unique influence on the teaching of history and political philosophy at Oxford; those who attended his lectures described them with great unanimity as the best they ever heard. There was then no regular system of inter-collegiate lectures, but Balliol was constantly asked by other colleges to permit their students to attend Newman. Among those who heard him were the philosophers T. H. Green (afterwards his close friend and colleague), Thomas Case, Edward Caird, and R. L. Nettleship; the historians J. L. Strachan-Davidson and Evelyn Abbott; the lawyers R. T. Reid and W. R. Anson; and, among others, Andrew Lang, John Addington Symonds, F. Y. Edgeworth, and the earl of Kerry. In spite of frequent absences owing to ill health, and of a weak voice and rapid delivery, Newman's importance as a teacher was quite equal to that of Jowett and Green: he was effectively the founder of a new school of ancient history. His treatment of the subject in his lectures was novel in its independence and imagination, in the wide range of modern history and law from which he drew his illustrations, and in the connection between history and philosophy which he always maintained and which became characteristic of *literae humaniores*. He was a reformer in university politics, outlining his ideas for strengthening the professoriate on German lines in his evidence to the select committee on Oxford and Cambridge university extension (July 1867). His mentor, Jowett, acknowledged his learning and genius, though doubted his judgement, and considered him 'to be absolutely without the religious sense' (*Dear Miss Nightingale*, 99).

In 1868 Newman was appointed university reader in ancient history, but in 1870 ill health obliged him finally to leave Oxford. From that time he lived in retirement at Cheltenham, preparing the edition of Aristotle's *Politics* which was his principal monument, reading everything that bore upon the subjects of his interest, making endless notes on odd scraps of paper in his tiny handwriting, and corresponding with other scholars. Although partially lame, he took his country walk almost daily, and was a keen observer of birds.

While at Oxford Newman published only an essay on the land laws in the manifesto of the university liberals, *Questions for a Reformed Parliament* (1867), having been called to the bar by Lincoln's Inn in the same year. Newman's essay, which expounded the view of many mid-Victorian radicals that the social evils of the time could be attributed to the concentration of land ownership into a few hands, was a masterpiece of noble English. While he had always in view the ethical principles which should govern the tenure of land, he never overlooked historical and practical considerations; in thus holding the balance between philosophy and practice this early work exhibited a notable quality of his edition of the *Politics*, of which the first two volumes were published in 1887. The first was occupied by an introductory essay which was virtually a treatise on political philosophy. The third and fourth volumes appeared in 1902. The whole work belonged to the grand, leisurely type of scholarship, in which even notes have a literary quality, and the views of others (sometimes even when they did not deserve it) were discussed with courteous fullness. The hurried or perfunctory student found little in Newman's work to encourage him; the minute pedant who had no sense of proportion might have spoken slightingly of it. But for soundness of interpretation, copiousness of illustration, and mature wisdom its value was permanent. The degree of honorary LittD was conferred on him by Cambridge University in 1900.

Newman died at the Imperial Nursing Home, Cheltenham, on 3 May 1923. He was unmarried. He retained his fellowship of Balliol until his death, but for many years refused to accept the stipend, and left a considerable benefaction to the college in his will.

A. W. PICKARD-CAMBRIDGE, *rev.* M. C. CURTHOYS

Sources private information (1937) · personal knowledge (1937) · E. S. Skirving, ed., *Cheltenham College register, 1841–1927* (1928) · I. Elliott, ed., *The Balliol College register, 1833–1933*, 2nd edn (privately printed, Oxford, 1934) · O. Murray, 'The beginnings of Greats, 1800–1872: ancient history', *Hist. U. Oxf. 6: 19th-cent. Oxf.*, 520–42 · C. Harvie, *The lights of liberalism* (1976) · *Dear Miss Nightingale: a selection of Benjamin Jowett's letters to Florence Nightingale, 1860–1893*, ed. V. Quinn and J. Prest (1987)
Wealth at death £34,638 11s. 10d.: probate, 22 June 1923, *CGPLA Eng. & Wales*

Newmarch, Charles Henry (1824–1903), Church of England clergyman and author, born at Burford, Oxfordshire, on 30 March 1824, was the second son of George Newmarch, solicitor, of Cirencester, and his wife, Mary. After studying at Rugby under Dr Arnold from August 1837, following in the footsteps of his elder brother, George Frederick, who had joined that school in 1830, Newmarch spent some time in the merchant navy, travelling in the East. In 1847 he published *Five Years in the East* under the pseudonym of R. N. Hutton. It attracted favourable reviews, and was followed in 1848 by *Recollections of Rugby, by an Old Rugbeian* and a novel, *Jealousy*. Settling in Cirencester, Newmarch showed keen interest in local antiquities, and in 1850 wrote with James Buckman (1814–1884) *Illustrations of the Remains of Roman Art in Cirencester*. In 1851 he was instrumental in the foundation of the *Cirencester and Swindon Express*, which was soon amalgamated with the *Wilts and Gloucester Standard*. He was joint editor of the paper and, until the end of his life, a regular contributor under the name of Rambler. In 1868 he published with his brother an account of the Newmarch pedigree.

Newmarch matriculated at Corpus Christi College, Cambridge, in 1851, graduating BA in 1855. On 6 February 1855 he married, at Leckhampton, Anne Straford of Cheltenham and Charlton Kings; the couple had two sons and three daughters. After taking holy orders in 1855, he was from 1856 to 1893 rector of Wardley-cum-Belton, Rutland, and rural dean of the district from 1857 to 1867. He was greatly interested in agricultural matters, contributing much to *Bell's Life* on the subject; he championed the cause of village labourers, who in turn defended him against the attacks of Joseph Arch, when Arch visited Belton in his tour of the village districts in 1872. Newmarch took an active part in the building of churches in Rutland, and restored the chancel of his parish church. Increasing deafness led to his retirement in 1893 to 37 Upper Grosvenor Road, Tunbridge Wells, where he died on 14 June 1903. One daughter survived him. A tablet to his memory was erected in Belton church in 1912.

W. B. OWEN, rev. NILANJANA BANERJI

Sources *The Times* (20 June 1903) · *The Guardian* (1 July 1903) · Venn, *Alum. Cant.* · Crockford (1902) · A. T. Mitchell, ed., *Rugby School register, 1: From April 1675 to April 1842* (1901) · *CGPLA Eng. & Wales* (1903)
Wealth at death £8903 9s. 10d.: probate, 7 July 1903, *CGPLA Eng. & Wales*

Newmarch [*née* Jeaffreson], **Rosa Harriet** (1857–1940), writer on music, was born at 29 Lansdowne Place, Leamington Spa, on 18 December 1857, the daughter of Samuel John Jeaffreson, a doctor, and his wife, Sophy Kenney, and

Rosa Harriet Newmarch (1857–1940), by Howard Coster, 1931 [with the Russian singer Fyodor Chalyapin]

the granddaughter of the playwright James *Kenney. On 19 June 1883 she married Henry Charles Newmarch, a surveyor; they had a daughter, Elsie, and a son, John. All her work appeared under her married name. In 1897 she made the first of many visits to Russia, the country of whose music, together with that of Czechoslovakia, she was to pioneer English appreciation. Working in the Imperial Public Library in St Petersburg under the supervision of Vladimir Stasov, she made herself familiar with Russian music, and in England put her energy and enthusiasm into awakening a wider interest in Russian composers with a long series of lectures, books, articles, and programme notes. She also translated a number of Russian operas for English performance. A close friend of Sir Henry Wood, she encouraged performance of Russian music at the Proms, and became an eloquent advocate of it in her capacity as official programme-note writer to the Queen's Hall Orchestra between 1908 and 1919 (her work continued to appear until 1928).

Mrs Newmarch's last visit to Russia was made in the summer of 1915. When political events made further travel difficult, she turned her attention to the music of the Czech lands. Her writings had already aroused much appreciation among Czech musicians, and she was invited to the country, with her daughter, as a gesture of thanks by the conductor and composer Karel Kovařovic in 1919. Their travels included a visit to Moravia, where she met Janáček. Her advocacy of his music, then barely known in England, included a sympathetic review of *The*

Cunning Little Vixen when she went to Prague in 1925 as correspondent of *The Times*, and in the following year she was the prime mover in Janáček's visit to England. In gratitude, he dedicated his *Sinfonietta* to her.

Sir Henry Wood wrote that Mrs Newmarch's programme notes (which were republished in book form) were 'not merely a synopsis of the works she treats, but … beautiful specimens of English literature' (Wood, 232). As with much of her work, their somewhat subjective descriptive manner has dated, but they served to help appreciation of a great deal of the new music that Wood was introducing to Proms audiences, sometimes at her prompting. Similarly, her study of Tchaikovsky (1900), while interesting enough to have warranted a reissue in 1969, has long been superseded, though her translation of Modest Tchaikovsky's *Life and Letters of P. I. Tchaikovsky* remains valuable. Her importance rests not on her scholarship, though she was thorough and meticulous (and contributed useful essays on Russian composers to the second, third, and fourth editions of *Grove's Dictionary*), but on her eloquent, and successful, appeal to English audiences on behalf of Russian and Czech music at a time when taste was still largely ruled by German symphonic music and Italian opera. She also introduced Sir Henry Wood to Sibelius's music, and wrote a monograph on it (1944). Other useful books included *The Russian Opera* (1914, reissued 1972) and *The Music of Czechoslovakia* (1942, reissued 1969). Her energy and enthusiasm of mind were retained into old age. She died at Percival's Hotel, Heene Terrace, Worthing, Sussex, on 9 April 1940.

JOHN WARRACK

Sources *New Grove* · H. Wood, *My life of music* (1938) · J. Vogel, *Leoš Janáček: his life and work* (1962) · R. Newmarch, *The concert-goer's library of descriptive notes* (1928–48) · A. Jacobs, *Sir Henry Wood* (1994) · b. cert. · m. cert. · d. cert.

Likenesses H. Coster, three photographs, 1931, NPG [*see illus.*]

Wealth at death £5386 19s. 11d.: probate, 6 July 1940, *CGPLA Eng. & Wales*

Newmarch, William (1820–1882), economic statistician, was born at Thirsk, Yorkshire, on 28 January 1820 and left school at an early age to take a clerical post with a distributor of stamps. At a time when an able, industrious clerk could aspire to managerial status in the financial world, young Newmarch seized every opportunity to raise his position. After a further stint as a clerk—this time with the Yorkshire Fire and Life Office—he moved on to the Wakefield branch of the banking firm of Leatham, Tew & Co. and assumed the post of second cashier at the age of twenty-three. No doubt it was there that he acquired his interest in assembling and analysing monetary statistics, for his first substantial research project, which explored fluctuations in the issue of bills of exchange, was explicitly inspired by work that Leatham (his employer) had published in the early 1840s. After three years at Wakefield, Newmarch—now married—was again ready to expand his horizons. He moved to London in 1846, joined the staff of the *Morning Chronicle* (where he wrote articles on economic questions), and became second in command of the London branch of the Agra Bank.

In 1847 Newmarch joined the Statistical Society of London. This represented a turning point in his self-propelled educational progress. It put a young man, keen to learn, into regular informal contact with the capital's leading statisticians and economic commentators. He could not have found a better research school in which to develop and demonstrate his talent for collecting and organizing the statistical data relevant to significant questions about national economic trends, events, and policies. In his first paper, read to the Statistical Society in early 1850, he showed that Lord Overstone, a distinguished authority on banking and currency issues, had offered an opinion to a parliamentary bank charter committee that was at variance with the facts ('An attempt to ascertain the magnitude and fluctuations of the amount of bills of exchange', *Journal of the Statistical Society*, 14, 1851, 156). Newmarch's view that it is essential to ascertain the relevant facts before offering an opinion must have commended him to many members of the Statistical Society who were unreceptive to abstract economic theorizing. It was particularly congenial to Thomas Tooke and other critics of the 1844 Bank Charter Act. Shortly afterwards, in the early 1850s, the ageing Tooke accepted Newmarch's offer to collaborate with him in updating his four-volume *History of Prices* (1848), so that it could cover the momentous economic events of recent years. Tooke's preface to volumes 5 and 6 made it clear that the bulk of this massive final instalment was attributable to his 'zealous and industrious collaborator' ('Preface' to T. Tooke and W. Newmarch, *History of Prices*, 1857, 5.ix). It created widespread interest because it offered a statistically based interpretation of, and reasoned commentary on, a remarkable sequence of profound economic changes—including the introduction of free trade, the 1844 Bank Charter Act, the French revolution of 1848–51, the Irish famine and migration, the gold discoveries in Russia, California, and Australia, and the Crimean War. The two volumes were soon translated into German, and Newmarch became a corresponding member of the Institut de France. Afterwards he was invited to give evidence to a succession of parliamentary bodies inquiring into monetary or fiscal questions, beginning with the 1857 select committee of the House of Commons on the Bank Acts. Even the Royal Society, which was not noted for its appreciation of either economists or businessmen, elected him a Fellow.

Meanwhile, Newmarch energetically pursued his business and journalistic activities, steadily extended the range of his personal contacts among economists, bankers, and other influential businessmen, and moved up the managerial hierarchy. In 1852 he became secretary to the Globe Insurance Company and engineered its amalgamation with the Liverpool and London Insurance Company. In December of that year he was elected a member of the Political Economy Club, and in 1855 he became the club's treasurer. He published a pamphlet (based on a series of articles he had written for the *Morning Chronicle*), *The New Supplies of Gold* (1853), to which he had induced a governor of the Bank of England to contribute an authoritative appendix on the gold coinage. In 1855 he became an honorary secretary of the Statistical Society and for the next twenty-five years he was one of its most conscientious and valued members: he served as a member of the society's council, editor of its *Journal*, and, to the end of his life, as a trustee. When the society abandoned its practice of nominating 'ornamental' presidents its choice naturally fell upon Newmarch and he was elected for the 1869–71 term in succession to Gladstone. Before then, in 1862, he became manager of Glyn, Mills, and Currie, a prominent banking firm, which he served with dedicated efficiency until forced by ill health to retire in 1881.

In spite of the fact that Newmarch was primarily an active businessman, he participated in a variety of learned societies. In addition to the Statistical Society and the Political Economy Club he regularly attended the meetings of similar groups, such as the Adam Smith Club (which he founded), the Cobden Club, the Society of Bankers, and the Institute of Actuaries (of which he was a fellow). He was also a member of the Reform Club. His literary output was prolific, much of it published anonymously in leading journals and newspapers. He began (and carried on) the *Economist* 'Commercial history of the year' and invented its first price index. The research papers he read to the Statistical Society ranged over a variety of subjects, from an assessment of Pitt's war loans raised during the years 1793–1801 to an analysis of electoral statistics for the counties and boroughs of England and Wales over the twenty-five years since the 1832 Reform Act; his last research study, on the growth of international trade, appeared in the 1878 *Journal of the Statistical Society*. He also published a selection of pamphlets, some of which expanded articles written for journals or newspapers, including *Political Perils* (1859), a spirited defence of political reforms proposed by Lord Derby's administration. All of these pamphlets were openly controversial. Indeed, most of Newmarch's publications were designed to contribute to a topical debate.

The controversy with which Newmarch was most persistently and consistently involved was the argument between the currency and banking schools that revolved around the monetary policies embodied in the Bank Charter Act of 1844. He shared Tooke's view that the currency school's emphasis on currency (as opposed to credit) control was totally misguided and that the level of currency in circulation was determined by the level of prices and incomes, rather than the reverse. Newmarch himself broke new ground in tracing the way that the mid-century influx of new gold stimulated demand first in the countries mining it, then in their trading partners, and so on, with diminishing repercussions through the world trade network. He was also in advance of his time in stressing the effects of an increase in demand on the level of investment. By refusing to swallow the crude quantity theory of money that underpinned current monetary orthodoxy, and demonstrating that the connections between prices and metallic currency in circulation were more complex in practice than an algebraical formula could usefully identify, he injected a distinctive element of realism into the controversy. He insisted, for example, in the last volume of the *History of Prices*, that a comparison of data on price changes as between 1851 and early 1857 did not justify the inference that the influx of gold had raised commodity prices; he argued that a full explanation of price movements invariably required analysis of the factors affecting supply and demand (Tooke and Newmarch, 6.232–3). Newmarch's faith in his inductive methodology was elaborated in his presidential address to the economics and statistics section of the British Association for the Advancement of Science in 1861 ('The progress of economic science during the last thirty years', *Journal of the Statistical Society*, 24, 1861, 451–71). There he asserted that the most important advance in economic science over the preceding three to four decades had been the substitution of systematic observation for deductions arrived at by geometrical reasoning.

Given his ferocity as a controversialist, it would not be surprising if Newmarch had had enemies. The evidence is, however, that he had innumerable friends and that even those who disagreed with his passionately held opinions admired his indefatigable search for basic data, his mastery of his business as a bank manager, and his realistic approach to economic analysis. Robert Giffen, who knew Newmarch well, paid warm tribute (in his own inaugural address as president of the Statistical Society) to the older man's generosity of spirit, to his unstinted service to the society and its members, and to his substantial research contribution.

In 1881 Newmarch's only son, William T. Newmarch, also a member of the Statistical Society, died after a painful illness, and Newmarch himself retired from his post as bank manager after suffering a stroke. He had another stroke, however, in the following year and he died on 23 March at 3 Sulyarde Terrace, Torquay, Devon, leaving his widow, Elizabeth Newmarch, his only daughter, and his son's widow.

PHYLLIS DEANE

Sources T. Tooke and W. Newmarch, *A history of prices and the state of circulation during the nine years 1848–56*, 6 vols. (1857) · T. E. Gregory, *An introduction to Tooke and Newmarch's 'History of Prices'* (1928) · *Journal of the Statistical Society*, 45 (1882), 117–20 [obits. repr. from *The Statist*, *The Times*, and *The Economist*] · W. A. G., *PRS*, 34 (1882–3), xvii–xix · R. Giffen, 'President's inaugural address', *Journal of the Statistical Society*, 45 (1882), 519–23 · J. L. Mallett, ed., *Political Economy Club … minutes of proceedings 1899–1920*, 6 (1921), 327–51 · CGPLA Eng. & Wales (1882)

Archives Royal Statistical Society, London, corresp. and papers | Mitchell L., Glas., Glasgow City Archives, letters to John Strang

Wealth at death £56,203 9s. 10d.: probate, 9 June 1882, CGPLA Eng. & Wales

Newmarket, Adam of [Adam de Novo Mercato, Adam de Novo Foro] (*d.* in or before **1247**), justice, was a member of the family of Neufmarché, which was established in south Yorkshire soon after the Norman conquest. His mother was Denise de Pusat. This Adam de Novo Foro, or (more usually) de Novo Mercato, held four knights' fees from King John in the honour of Tickhill. He served with the king in Ireland in 1210, and in 1211 offered him 60 marks and three palfreys to obtain his mother's dower. But he was one of those northern barons who were drawn by their indebtedness to the king into alliance with Robert Fitzwalter and other dissidents, so that in 1213 he was imprisoned in Corfe Castle and had to surrender his sons John and Adam as hostages. Perhaps because Adam the son was kept in custody until March 1219, Adam the father is not known to have involved himself in the baronial revolt which was effectively ended by the battle of Lincoln in 1217, although he was associated with one of its leaders, Gilbert de Gant, claimant to the earldom of Lincoln, from whom he was later recorded as holding three knights' fees at Whatton and Hawksworth, Lincolnshire.

Adam of Newmarket was appointed to hear an assize of mort d'ancestor in Yorkshire in 1215, and to be one of the justices for Lincolnshire, Nottinghamshire, and Derbyshire when the eyres resumed in 1218 at the end of the civil war. In 1226 he was employed in the collection of the fifteenth in Yorkshire; in 1232 he was named as a justice for the eyre in Nottinghamshire, Derbyshire, Cambridgeshire, and Huntingdonshire, though there is no evidence that he sat outside the first two counties; and in 1234 he again sat as a justice on eyre at York and Beverley. The special assizes he heard, the last of them in 1231, were all in Yorkshire, Derbyshire, or Nottinghamshire. He was not appointed a justice for any eyres after 1234, though he was still living in 1241, when he was named last among thirteen leading northern barons summoned to Chester for a Welsh campaign. He was dead by September 1247, when his grandson and heir, Sir Adam of *Newmarket, did homage for his lands in Tickhill. ALAN HARDING

Sources Chancery records · H. C. M. Lyte and others, eds., Liber feodorum: the book of fees, 3 vols. (1920–31) · Pipe rolls, 3 Henry III, 191 · D. Crook, Records of the general eyre, Public Record Office Handbooks, 20 (1982) · I. J. Sanders, English baronies: a study of their origin and descent, 1086–1327 (1960)

Newmarket, Sir Adam of

Newmarket, Sir Adam of [Sir Adam de Novo Mercato] (b. in or before **1226**, d. in or before **1291**), baronial leader, was the son of John of Newmarket, one of the sons of Adam of *Newmarket, justice. In 1253 Henry III granted him a Tuesday market at his manor of Carlton, Lincolnshire, and a fair there at Whitsun. That same year he was granted respite of knighthood until the knighting of his overlord, Edmund de Lacy, earl of Lincoln, which took place in 1255. He was summoned for service in Scotland in 1256 and for Welsh campaigns in 1257, 1277, and 1282. Between September 1263 and May 1264 he was reported among rebels 'going through the county of York with standards unfurled' (Jacob, 270). In December 1263 he was the first of the two named representatives of the barons at King Louis's arbitration at Amiens, and he appears among the half-dozen rebel lords captured by the king at Northampton on 5 April. After Simon de Montfort's victory at Lewes a month later he was appointed to keep Lincoln Castle, and in March 1265 he was warden of the vacant archbishopric of York. In July 1264 he rose to be steward of the royal household, and for nine months authorized safe conducts for envoys and important visitors to the royal court, dealt with foreign cloth merchants, and witnessed such royal acts as the appointment of a new chancellor. Meanwhile his men supplanted the sheriffs of Yorkshire

and Lincolnshire, so that after the battle of Evesham some northern knights lost their lands because they were 'of the company of Sir Adam de Novo Mercato' (Calendar of Inquisitions Miscellaneous, 1, no. 851). He made peace with the victorious king under the terms of the dictum of Kenilworth, but this period may have left him in financial difficulties. In 1265 and 1278 he was involved in dealings with Mosseye and Hagin, king's Jews of London, and in 1276 he received the king's licence to sell his houses in the cities of York and Lincoln. He died on or before 30 August 1291, the month in which his widow, Cecily, a daughter of Alexander de Neville, was given back the lands which Adam of Newmarket had held in Lincolnshire as of her inheritance. ALAN HARDING

Sources Chancery records · H. C. M. Lyte and others, eds., Liber feodorum: the book of fees, 3 vols. (1920–31) · I. J. Sanders, English baronies: a study of their origin and descent, 1086–1327 (1960) · Ann. mon., vol. 4 · E. F. Jacob, Studies in the period of baronial reform and rebellion, 1258–1267 (1925) · Calendar of inquisitions miscellaneous (chancery), PRO, 1 (1916), 851

Newmarket, Thomas

Newmarket, Thomas (fl. 1371–1384), mathematician, was quite probably born and brought up in Newmarket and by 1371 was an MA and regent master at Cambridge. In 1376 he was granted leave to study for a further year at Cambridge, although it is not known in what subject. A tract De passione arth[r]etica or De passionibus juncturarum is ascribed (in Bodl. Oxf., MS Ashmole 1481) to Thomas Newmarket; this could suggest some medical training, but other evidence is lacking. After various ecclesiastical preferments, Newmarket was in 1384 appointed by the archdeacon of Ely to be 'master of glomery', or superintendent of the Cambridge grammar schools, a post which may give plausibility to occasional reports of grammatical or rhetorical texts by him. After 1384 he disappears from the records.

Two mathematical or quasi-mathematical works may with fair confidence be assigned to Thomas Newmarket. The first, found in Oxford, Bodleian, MS Digby 81, is a commentary on the Carmen de algorismo of the thirteenth-century French Franciscan, Alexander de Villa Dei, a didactic poem on reckoning with Hindu-Arabic numerals. The introduction to Newmarket's lengthy prose commentary ascribes the art to an Indian philosopher named Algus and includes a philosophical discussion of the ontological status of numbers. J. O. Halliwell, in his 1839 edition of Alexander's work, quoted from a different commentary, found in British Library, Royal MS 12 E.i, and ascribed it to Thomas Newmarket; he was followed in this by R. R. Steele. But the attribution appears to be groundless. It may be noted that the commentaries in both the Royal and the Digby manuscripts accompany a more complete version of Alexander's text than that found in the standard editions.

The second work is a commentary on a compotus (or computus, a work on calendrical reckoning), which Newmarket, followed by his cataloguers, regarded as being by the abbot Dionysius Exiguus (fl. c.500), but is in fact another didactic poem by Alexander de Villa Dei, known as Massa compoti (found in Cambridge, Peterhouse, MS 184, and Bodl. Oxf., MS Digby 81, and edited by Steele in *Compotus Fratris Rogeri*). As Newmarket points out, it avoids discussion of underlying causes and aims itself at the ecclesiastic or common man, here placed together in antithesis to the mathematician or astronomer. Newmarket's introduction speaks also of the virtues of writing in verse form, and of the early history of the calendar; he includes a citation of 'Pompeyus romanus' (probably Numa Pompilius is intended) as beginning the year at the winter solstice, which Newmarket says was then on the first day of January.

Other mathematical works are sometimes ascribed to Thomas Newmarket, but, it would seem, for little better reason than proximity in the manuscript codices.

GEORGE MOLLAND

Sources Emden, *Cam.*, 432 · Bodl. Oxf., MS Digby 81 · J. O. Halliwell, ed., *Rara mathematica, or, A collection of treatises on the mathematics and subjects connected with them* (1839) · R. Steele, *The earliest arithmetics in English*, EETS, extra ser., 118 (1922) · R. Bacon, *Compotus Fratris Rogeri: accedunt 'compotus' Roberti Grossecapitis Lincolniensis Episcopi, 'Massa compoti' Alexandri de Villa Dei*, ed. R. Steele, Opera Hactenus Inedita Rogeri Baconi, 6 (1926) · Peterhouse, Cambridge, MS 184 · H. Rashdall, *The universities of Europe in the middle ages*, ed. F. M. Powicke and A. B. Emden, new edn, 3 vols. (1936) · W. H. Black, *A descriptive, analytical and critical catalogue of the manuscripts bequeathed unto the University of Oxford by Elias Ashmole*, 2 vols. (1845–66) · G. F. Warner and J. P. Gilson, *Catalogue of Western manuscripts in the old Royal and King's collections*, 4 vols. (1921)
Archives Bodl. Oxf., MS Ashmole 1481 | BL, Royal MS 12 E.i · Bodl. Oxf., MS Digby 81

Newnes, Sir George, first baronet (1851–1910), newspaper proprietor and politician, born on 13 March 1851 at Glenorchy House, Matlock, was the youngest of the six children of the Revd Thomas Mold Newnes (*d.* 1883), Congregational minister, and his wife, Sarah (*d.* 1855), daughter of David Urquhart of Dundee. He was educated at Silcoates School, Yorkshire, Shireland Hall, Birmingham, and for two terms at the City of London School. At sixteen he was apprenticed to a wholesale haberdasher in the City, subsequently travelling in haberdashery and managing a shop in Manchester. In 1875 Newnes married Priscilla, daughter of the Revd James Hillyard.

On 24 August 1881, reading the *Manchester Evening News*, Newnes's attention was arrested by an item, 'A runaway train'. In that moment he conceived the idea of a journal made up entirely of entertaining and interesting anecdotes—'tit-bits' as he called them. He failed to obtain outside financial backing for his idea, but scraped together sufficient to produce the first number of his weekly journal, which appeared on 22 October 1881. Within two hours he had sold 5000 copies. *Tit-Bits* was to be the matrix of twentieth-century popular journalism. A man of business, all bustle and energy, by bold innovation—prize competitions, free insurance schemes, and treasure hunts—and an unerring sense of the prejudices and preferences of his lower middle-class readers, Newnes ensured his journal's commercial success. But he sought also to improve the literary diet of the masses. It was his earnest hope that readers of *Tit-Bits*, saved at least from reading the worst, might develop an interest in better

Sir George Newnes, first baronet (1851–1910), by Sir Benjamin Stone, 1901

forms of literature. A token of his earnestness was the way he scrutinized every line printed, and he would remove anything he thought unduly lurid, sensational, or smutty. As the contents improved so did the sales. Within a decade *Tit-Bits* provided Newnes with an annual income of £30,000.

W. T. Stead, the most celebrated journalist of the day, who had been Newnes's contemporary at Silcoates, agreed to edit a new digest of journals, to be called the 'Sixpenny Monthly'. Before its first appearance, in January 1890, it had metamorphosed into the weekly *Review of Reviews*. Two such very different men were never likely to work comfortably together. Newnes distrusted Stead's judgement, fearing writs for libel and even imprisonment. After six months the partnership was dissolved by mutual agreement, Stead buying out Newnes for £3000, 'a fair and reasonable price'. Newnes, always concerned about the welfare of his employees, retained the extra editorial staff he had engaged for the *Review of Reviews*. He was contemplating a new kind of magazine to employ them. On style and typography he was undoubtedly influenced by American journals, but it was H. Greenhough Smith who gave Newnes the idea that was to become the *Strand Magazine*—a monthly, each issue complete in itself, like a book, all stories and articles lavishly illustrated. The first number appeared in January 1891, and the print of 300,000 sold out completely. Monthly sales were soon to exceed half a million, and the *Strand* became a perennial best-seller. The magazine exercised an important and beneficial influence upon English short-story writing. It also created and enhanced the reputations of many graphic artists, like Sidney Paget (1860–1908), the first illustrator of Conan Doyle's immortal detective, Sherlock Holmes.

In 1885 Newnes entered parliament as Liberal member for Newmarket; he held the seat for ten years. When defeated in the 1895 election he took it with very good humour. Almost immediately he was offered the safe Liberal seat of Swansea, which he held from 1900 until his retirement in January 1910. His single distinction as an MP was to be nominated one of the best-dressed men in the house. If he said little, he was particularly valued by Lord Rosebery as a press magnate prepared to buy and maintain newspapers favourable to the Liberal cause. Newnes was duly rewarded in 1895 with a baronetcy 'for political services', a euphemism for subsidizing Liberal newspapers. The citation, however, also acknowledged Newnes's 'good work … in the cause of healthy popular literature'.

In 1892, when W. W. Astor bought, in the tory interest, the previously Liberal *Pall Mall Gazette*, Newnes seized the opportunity to found a new Liberal paper. 'The scheme will find favour with the leading men of the party,' he correctly told E. T. Cook, who became the first editor of the *Westminster Gazette*. From 1896, under J. A. Spender's editorship, the 'pea-green incorruptible', as *Punch* dubbed the *Westminster Gazette*, was unchallenged as the honourable, influential, Liberal, heavyweight newspaper. But its circulation was never better than 25,000, and with an advertising revenue of a mere £40,000, the *Westminster* was a commercial flop. Newnes would not have it cheapened or vulgarized to increase sales, for nothing should imperil its influence among serious readers. In time the ever mounting debt of the *Westminster* wearied even Newnes. In 1908 it was at last sold to a Liberal syndicate headed by Sir Alfred Mond (1868–1930), but continued to lose money.

Newnes's publishing company was one of the first to receive a stock exchange quotation. When the company was restructured in 1897, Newnes was appointed permanent governing director. He was joined on the board by his son, Frank, straight down from Cambridge and more interested in and knowledgeable about golf than publishing, who replaced Lewis Tomalin. The other key board member was Edward Hudson. The Newnes publishing empire expanded to include *Country Life* (1897), *Woman's Life* (1898), the first women's weekly magazine, and the *World-Wide Magazine* (1898), the offspring of an excess of travel and adventure stories submitted by *Strand* readers. But not all was success; some new journals were short-lived, artistic and commercial failures. There was the imaginative and original four-coloured twopenny weekly, *The Million*. A morning penny newspaper, the *Daily Courier*, edited by Newnes himself and designed to compete with Harmsworth's new, halfpenny *Daily Mail*, crashed within four months. There was also a disastrous venture in Sunday newspapers when Newnes acquired the venerable *Weekly Dispatch*. Newnes's religious scruples would not allow him to employ the same means as the *Dispatch*'s main rivals, the *News of the World* and *Lloyd's Sunday News*, to win and boost circulation. Eventually he was forced to sell out to Harmsworth for £25,000.

Newnes's capacities as an editor had always been limited. *Tit-Bits* exercised a strong sentimental grip and he never altogether rid himself of his delight in scraps of information. His business sense, however, was always acute until, from the mid-1890s, it was undermined and finally overthrown by the ravages of diabetes and alcohol. Public displays of hopeless drunkenness probably cost him elevation to the peerage. As his condition worsened, he would disappear from home, sometimes for weeks at a time. He lost a fortune speculating wildly on oil and rubber. In the City remaining confidence in his business acumen was destroyed, and his company's share quotation and dividends plummeted. In the end his estate was entirely swallowed by debt.

As a son of the manse, Newnes had appeased his conscience about his sudden and enormous wealth by demonstrations of practical concern for the welfare of the less fortunate, public benefactions, and service in parliament. His gifts included a fine library for the citizens of Putney, where he had his London residence; a cable railway for his birthplace, Matlock; and a cliff railway at Lynton where he had his country house. Newnes and his wife had two sons; the death of the elder boy, aged eight, devastated him. The second son, Frank Hillyard (1876–1955), served as a Liberal MP from 1906 until 1910 and was involved in publishing and a range of commercial concerns. Newnes died at Lynton on 9 June 1910, where he was buried. His last years had been tragic for him, his family, and the managers of his various business interests. He deserves, however, to be remembered as the masterful head of a great publishing company, genial, generous, and inspiring. He was the supreme innovator in an industry that succeeded by imitating success. That others imitated him so successfully and made fortunes from his ideas, pleased rather than annoyed Newnes. It had been his enterprise that forged the means to assail illiteracy and gratify the first mass reading public. He believed it was enough 'to give wholesome and harmless entertainment to hard-working people craving a little fun and amusement'. If this was, in his own words, 'no great ambition', none could deny that he succeeded in it completely.   A. J. A. MORRIS

Sources S. Friederichs, *The life of Sir George Newnes* (1911) · *The Times* (10 June 1910) · *Tit-Bits* (25 June 1910) · R. Pound, *The Strand Magazine, 1891–1950* (1966) · S. E. Koss, *The rise and fall of the political press in Britain*, 2 vols. (1981–4) · *DNB* · *WW*
Archives CAC Cam., corresp. with W. T. Stead
Likenesses B. Stone, photograph, 1901, NPG [*see illus.*] · O. Wheatley, bronze bust, 1911, Putney Library · Spy [L. Ward], caricature, chromolithograph, NPG; repro. in *VF* (31 May 1894) · B. Stone, photographs, NPG
Wealth at death £174,153 1s. 1d.: administration with will, 9 Aug 1910, CGPLA Eng. & Wales

Newnham, William (1790–1865), general medical practitioner, was born on 1 November 1790 at Farnham, Surrey, the son of John Newnham, a surgeon apothecary, and his wife, Mary Dowden (1756–1830). He is thought to have attended the grammar school in Farnham. Having decided to pursue a medical career, he studied at Guy's Hospital, London, where he was a favourite pupil of Sir Astley Cooper. He also studied in Paris. About 1810 he returned to the town of his birth where he practised medicine for the next forty-five years. In 1826, some years after commencing practice, he obtained the licence of the Society of Apothecaries. Newnham was twice married: first in 1813—his wife died within the year, on 31 December—and second in 1821, to Caroline (c.1792–1863), youngest daughter of Christopher Atkinson, vicar of Wethersfield, Essex. They had eight children, six of whom, three sons and three daughters, survived beyond childhood. Two of the sons became clergymen while a third, Christopher Atkinson Newnham, became a medical practitioner in Wolverhampton.

Newnham joined the Provincial Medical and Surgical Association (PMSA; British Medical Association from 1855) in 1836, and regularly attended its anniversary meetings, even when they were held far from his Surrey home. He became a member of the association's council about 1843. His main interest in the PMSA was its Benevolent Fund for the relief of 'distressed medical men and their families' (*Transactions of the Provincial Medical and Surgical Association*, 4, 1837, xv). He was not, as has sometimes been suggested, the founder of the fund, for this was established before Newnham joined the association, but by 1840 he was taking a close interest in the fund committee's activities. Several times in the early 1840s he either seconded or moved the adoption of its annual reports, often using the occasion to urge PMSA members to contribute generously to its coffers. In 1844 he told the association that he had personally written to 504 medical practitioners in pursuit of donations. In 1847 he succeeded William Conolly as the fund's treasurer; before long he also became its honorary secretary. Under his influence the size of the fund, and hence its utility, grew substantially. So strong was the link between Newnham and the fund that in 1856, the year after he ceased to be an office holder, *The Lancet* called him the 'founder of the Benevolent Fund of the Association' (9 Aug 1856, 173)—an estimation with which the *British Medical Journal* later concurred.

In early and middle life Newnham acquired a reputation as a 'very skilful and eminent medical practitioner' (*GM*, 798). His particular medical interest lay within the fields of gynaecology and obstetrics, on which subjects he was the author of a number of articles. In 1850 he read a paper entitled 'Case of malformed and imperforate vagina' at the PMSA's Hull meeting. Newnham was a prolific author, writing on several other aspects of medicine and health, including phrenology and human magnetism. His book *Some Observations on the Medicinal and Dietetic Properties of Green Tea* (1827) was dedicated to Astley Cooper. He also published a *Memoir of the Late Mrs Newnham* (1830), which was a biography of his mother, and several works on spiritual, religious, and educational subjects. Among the latter were *A Tribute of Sympathy to Mourners* (1817), which went into a 7th edition in 1834, *The Principles of Physical, Intellectual, Moral and Religious Education* (2 vols., 1827), and *Man in his Physical, Intellectual, Social, and Moral Relations* (1847).

Newnham was a member of the Royal Society of Literature and a prominent local figure in Farnham. Among the positions he held in the town were a directorship of Farnham Gas Company and a trusteeship of Farnham Water Company. He also ran the Farnham Female School of Industry, which his mother had founded in 1813.

In 1856 failing health obliged Newnham to relinquish his medical practice. He moved to 9 Belvedere Terrace, Tunbridge Wells, Kent. His wife died in 1863. In the autumn of 1865 he suffered an attack of paralysis; some two weeks later, on 24 October, he died at home of the 'chronic cerebral disease' which had afflicted him for six or seven years (*Medical Times and Gazette*, 28 Oct 1865, 484).

P. W. J. BARTRIP

Sources DNB · Boase, *Mod. Eng. biog.* · *London and Provincial Medical Directory* (1866) · *Medical Times and Gazette* (28 Oct 1865), 484 · *GM*, 3rd ser., 19 (1865), 798 · W. Newnham, *Memoir of the late Mrs Newnham* (1830) · *Provincial Medical Directory* (1847) · *BMJ* (28 Oct 1865) · private information (2004) · E. Smith, *Victorian Farnham* (1971) · N. Temple, *Farnham buildings and people* (1973) · P. J. Wallis and R. V. Wallis, *Eighteenth century medics*, 2nd edn (1988)

Likenesses J. Andrews, portrait, 1857

Wealth at death under £16,000: probate, 1 Dec 1865, *CGPLA Eng. & Wales*

Newport. For this title name *see* individual entries under Newport; *see also* Blount, Mountjoy, first earl of Newport (c.1597–1666).

Newport, Alexander of [*called* Alexander the Mason] (*fl.* c.1235–1257), master mason, was the son of Odo of Newport in Lincoln. First recorded in the mid-1230s, by 1240 he had become master mason of the fabric of Lincoln Cathedral, and it was probably in that capacity that between 1245 and 1248 the dean and chapter granted him a messuage in Pottersgate on a repairing lease. Although large claims have sometimes been made for the influence and importance of Alexander's work, these cannot be substantiated; indeed, it is probable that the most innovative work on the cathedral was done before he took up office. But the lower stages of the existing crossing tower, rebuilt after a collapse in either 1237 or 1239, would have been his work, and this had an effect on subsequent towers at Newark and Stamford. Alexander may also have been responsible for the remodelling of Lincoln's west front, for the galilee, and for the beginnings of work on the Angel Choir; the latter was undertaken c.1256, the year before he is last documented as master mason. He had died by 1270. With his wife, Thecia, he had two daughters: Maud, who became a nun at Stamford; and Thecia, who married Lawrence of Ingilby.

HENRY SUMMERSON

Sources J. Harvey and A. Oswald, *English mediaeval architects: a biographical dictionary down to 1550*, 2nd edn (1984), 6 · P. Kidson, 'St Hugh's choir', *Medieval art and architecture at Lincoln Cathedral*, ed. [T. A. Heslop and V. A. Sekules], British Archaeological Association Conference Transactions, 8 (1986), 29–42 · P. Kidson, 'Architectural history', *A history of Lincoln Minster*, ed. D. M. Owen (1994), 14–46 · C. Wilson, *The Gothic cathedral* (1990)

Newport, Andrew (*bap.* 1622, *d.* 1699), royalist conspirator and politician, was baptized on 30 November 1622 at High

Ercall, Shropshire, the second son of Richard *Newport, first Baron Newport (1587–1651), and his wife, Rachel (d. 1661), daughter of Sir John Leveson of Kent. Andrew was the younger brother of Francis *Newport, first earl of Bradford (1619–1708). He matriculated from Christ Church, Oxford, on 3 July 1640. His father and elder brother were both active royalists, and High Ercall was one of the garrisons held longest for the king in Shropshire, but it is doubtful whether Andrew took part in the civil war. His name does not appear in any list of persons fined for delinquency.

Newport's real services to the royalist cause began under the protectorate, and from 1657 he acted as treasurer for money collected among the English cavaliers for the king's service. He belonged to the energetic and sanguine section of younger royalists, headed by John Mordaunt, who opposed the cautious policy recommended by the Sealed Knot. Charles II, in his instructions to Mordaunt on 11 March 1659, writes:

> I desire that Andrew Newport, upon whose affection and ability to serve me I do very much depend, and know he will act in any commission he shall be desired, may be put in mind to do all he can for the possessing Shrewsbury at the time which shall be appointed. (DNB)

Newport accordingly played a very active part in preparing the rising of July 1659, warning very late in the day that there were insufficient arms in readiness. When the rising failed Newport was arrested. He spent four months in the Tower, and was released on a bail of £1500.

After the Restoration Newport became an esquire of the body, had an estate worth £800 p.a. settled on him, was proposed for the order of the Royal Oak, and in 1662 was captain of a foot company at Portsmouth. He was comptroller of the great wardrobe from 1667 to 1681, and a commissioner of customs, 1681–4. He sat for Montgomeryshire in the parliament of 1661–78, for Preston in that of 1685, and for Shrewsbury from 1689 to 1698. From the fall of Clarendon, which he supported, and by which he also profited, Newport was fairly consistent in his loyalty to court interests in parliament, appearing in the category of 'thrice vile' in Shaftesbury's celebrated taxonomy. The regime of James II helped persuade Newport to accept the Williamite coup, but he remained a firm tory, refusing to sign the Association in 1696. He died unmarried on 11 September 1699 and was buried in the chancel of Wroxeter church, Shropshire.

In the preface to the second edition of Defoe's *Memoirs of a Cavalier* (printed at Leeds, c.1750) the publisher identifies Newport as the author. Another edition, published in 1792, is boldly entitled *Memoirs of the Honourable Colonel Andrew Newport*. There is no warrant for this identification in the statements of the preface to the 1720 edition, and the account given of his own services in Germany and in the civil war by the hero of the memoirs is incompatible with the facts of Newport's life. An examination of the contents of the memoirs shows conclusively that it is a work of fiction. C. H. FIRTH, rev. SEAN KELSEY

Sources *The letter-book of John, Viscount Mordaunt, 1658–1660*, ed. M. Coate, CS, 3rd ser., 69 (1945) · D. Underdown, *Royalist conspiracy in England, 1649–1660* (1960) · E. Cruikshank, 'Newport, Hon. Andrew', HoP, *Commons, 1660–90*, 3.136–7 · GEC, *Peerage* · will, PRO, PROB 11/453, fols. 75r–77r · A. Davies, *Dictionary of British portraiture*, 1 (1979)
Archives BL, Add. MSS
Likenesses school of P. Lely, oils, Weston Park, Staffordshire
Wealth at death disposed of real estate in Shropshire and Montgomeryshire and made gifts and bequests to a value in excess of £800: PRO, PROB 11/453, fols. 75r–77r

Newport, Christopher (*bap.* 1561, *d.* 1617), privateer and colonist, was baptized at Harwich, Essex, on 29 December 1561, the son of Christopher Newport, himself a Harwich shipmaster, and his wife, Jane. Young Christopher was serving on the *Minion* of London in 1580 when he jumped ship at Bahia, Brazil, but by 1584 he was back in England, an inhabitant of Limehouse, a hamlet of Stepney, Middlesex, where on 19 October he married Katherine Procter, and where in 1594 and 1599, representing Limehouse, he was chosen a vestryman. War with Spain gave Newport his opportunity. The Spanish seizure of English ships in 1585 led to privateering reprisals and Newport was soon active: in 1587, at the attack on Cadiz, as master's mate of John Watts's *Drake*, and in 1589 as master of Robert Cobb's *Margaret* of London. Newport captained Watts's *Little John* in 1590, making his first independent Caribbean privateering voyage and losing his right arm while attacking two Spanish treasure ships off Cuba. On 29 January 1591 he married his second wife, Ellen Ade, and as captain of Cobb's *Margaret* that year he combined Barbary trade with Caribbean privateering. From 1592 to 1595, however, when captaining the *Golden Dragon*, which belonged to Cobb's partner John More, Newport kept to the West Indies. In 1592—evidence of his increasing reputation—he was given command of a flotilla of privateers and he pioneered attacks on the towns of the Spanish Caribbean. On his return he helped to capture the *Madre de Dios* off the Azores and he was chosen to sail her to England.

Between 1587 and 1595 Newport had been, however successful, merely an employee of leading London merchants. In 1595 his status changed when, on 1 October, he married Elizabeth Glanfield, a London goldsmith's daughter. Thereafter, with two Glanfields and three others, he owned the heavily armed *Neptune*, in which he raided the Spanish Caribbean almost annually until 1603. After peace was signed in 1604 he returned to the region to trade, in 1605 bringing back live from Hispaniola two young crocodiles and a wild boar, which he presented to the king. From these voyages Newport gained an unrivalled knowledge of Caribbean waters, and thus, in 1606, command of the Virginia Company's first fleet. He sailed from the Thames on 20 December in the *Susan Constant*, was delayed in the Downs all January, yet, sailing by the Canaries and the West Indies, he entered Chesapeake Bay in Virginia, America, on 26 April 1607. Here Newport's sole command ended. Sealed instructions brought from London appointed a council of seven, Newport being one, and ordered him to spend two months exploring the region before returning to England by May. Delays had made this timetable impossible; he could afford merely a week (21–7 May), reaching only the falls of the James. He returned to Jamestown the day after a major attack by Native Americans on it and, since swift fortification was essential, he lent sailors for the task. Within the fort he played the peacemaker, according to Gabriel Archer, but Edward Maria Wingfield, the short-lived first president of the colony, implicitly blamed Newport for inadvertently setting Archer and Bartholomew Gosnold against him. On 22 June Newport sailed for England, promising to return in November. From Plymouth on 29 July he wrote enthusiastically to the earl of Salisbury about the gold he was carrying, and by 12 August he had reached London. To the disappointment of investors, the ore was worthless, but Newport optimistically promised to bring better next time. In the *John and Francis* on 2 January 1608 he reached Jamestown, resuming his place on the council, seemingly as president. Half the colonists were dead, and the colony's survival depended on the Algonquian chief Powhatan. Newport secured supplies of corn from Powhatan, and he then spent a month refining ore and settling matters before sailing for England on 10 April. Another fast crossing of the Atlantic brought him to the Thames on 21 May. Again he wasted no time. In the autumn he was back in Virginia bringing seventy colonists, ceremonial gifts for Powhatan, and instructions to find Ralegh's lost colony, or the Pacific Ocean, or gold. Captain John Smith, now the colony's president, disliked both Newport's courting of Powhatan and his fruitless expedition up the James to Monacan. Again Newport did not tarry long, reaching England by mid-January 1609.

In 1609 the Virginia Company was reformed. A second royal charter, which named Newport among its many adventurers, altered the form of government and in May Newport led a fleet of nine vessels to the colony. Sir Thomas Gates, a veteran of the Dutch wars, went as deputy governor, Sir George Somers was admiral, and William Strachey secretary. Though these three were ordered to cross in separate ships Newport carried them all in the *Sea Adventure*. The fleet was to pass west of the Canaries and 'steere away directly for Virginia without touching at the West Indies' (Purchas, 19.1). This new shorter route produced disaster. On 24 July a storm scattered the fleet and drove the *Sea Adventure* on to the Bermudas, but without loss of life. The islands' resources carried the survivors through the winter of 1609–10 and, after an earlier attempt failed, they reached Jamestown on 23 May. Finding it 'so full of misery and misgovernment' (ibid., 44), Gates decided to abandon it, but the arrival of the governor, Lord De La Warr, reversed this decision. When appointing his council De La Warr named Newport vice-admiral of Virginia, yet in early September Newport was back in England.

In 1611 Newport made his last voyage to Virginia (17 March–12 May), carrying Sir Thomas Dale to the colony. There Newport spent some three months, building at Jamestown a 'bridge' or quay. Departing about 20 August he reached home in late October. In appreciation the Virginia Company granted Newport thirty-two shares worth £400, which were converted after his death into 1600 acres. Another 300 were added for six men that Mrs Newport sent out in 1619, the whole perhaps being assigned at Newport News, which commemorated the captain. In 1612 Newport became a principal master of the Royal Navy, a post to which he had been granted the reversion in 1606. Thereafter Newport served the East India Company, this change perhaps being caused by an altercation with Sir Thomas Dale in 1611: Dale had pulled Newport's beard, threatening to hang him for a remark Newport had made about Sir Thomas Smith. Newport made three voyages to Bantam for the East India Company. On his first (7 January 1613–10 July 1614), in the *Expedition*, he carried Sir Robert Shirley, the shah's envoy, dropping him at the mouth of the Indus in late September, and reaching Bantam on 17 December, when Thomas Best reported him 'not very well' (Foster, *The Voyage of Thomas Best*, 74). Filling his holds swiftly Newport left on 2 January 1614 and was in the Downs on 10 July. Delighted with his efficiency, the company made no difficulty over his private trading and they 'gratified' him with 50 jacobuses, coins worth 22s., 'for landing the ambassador, discovering the Persian gulf, and a trade in the river Syndus, and bringing his men home in health with so little loss' (*CSP col.*, 2.318).

In September 1614 Newport began dickering with the company over his next voyage, in the end accepting the status of vice-admiral, a wage of £15 a month, and command of the *Lyon*, which would carry out Sir Thomas Roe as ambassador to the Mughal emperor. This second voyage (24 January 1615–August 1616) was as swift as his first. Though Roe was a former commander at sea, Newport allowed him no part in the conduct of the voyage. Not surprisingly, Roe wrote:

> It goes against my stomach (that am very moderate) to be denied a candle, or a draught of beer of a steward, without asking the captain's leave: whom yet, I must say, used me well: but loved that I should know his authority, and then denied me nothing. (Strachan, 60)

From Surat, where Roe was dropped on 25 September 1615, Newport went on to Calicut (3 March 1616) and Bantam (1–16 May) before returning to England.

Before his third voyage Newport on 16 November 1616 made his will, 'being to go with the next wind and weather, captain of the Hope' (PRO, PROB 11/132, sig. 92). With him as master's mate went his son Christopher. By 16 May 1617 they were in Saldanha Bay and on 15 August at Bantam. Shortly after his arrival Newport died and was buried there. In her return the *Hope* called again at Saldanha Bay, where on 27 April 1618 young Christopher made his will. Proved even before his father's, it made his brother John and sister Elizabeth his chief beneficiaries. His father's will left most of his property, including a house and garden on Tower Hill, London, to his widow for life (she was still alive in 1624) and then to John and Elizabeth. The latter was also to have £400 on marriage or at age twenty-one. An erring daughter, Jane, was all but cut from the will.

DAVID R. RANSOME

Sources K. R. Andrews, 'Christopher Newport of Limehouse, mariner', *William and Mary Quarterly*, 11 (1954), 28–41 · K. R. Andrews, *Elizabethan privateering: English privateering during the Spanish war, 1585–1603* (1964) · K. R. Andrews, *Trade, plunder and settlement:*

maritime enterprise and the genesis of the British empire, 1480–1630 (1984) • P. L. Barbour, ed., *The Jamestown voyages under the first charter, 1606–1609*, 2 vols., Hakluyt Society, 2nd ser., 136–7 (1969) • *CSP col.*, vols. 1–3 • *The embassy of Sir Thomas Roe to the court of the great mogul, 1615–1619*, ed. W. Foster, Hakluyt Society, 2nd ser., 1–2 (1899) • W. Foster, ed., *The voyage of Thomas Best to the East Indies, 1612–14*, Hakluyt Society, 2nd ser., 75 (1934) • W. Foster, ed., *The voyage of Nicholas Downton to the East Indies, 1614–15*, Hakluyt Society, 2nd ser., 82 (1939) • S. M. Kingsbury, ed., *The records of the Virginia Company of London*, 4 vols. (1906–35) • D. B. Quinn, A. M. Quinn, and S. Hillier, eds., *New American world: a documentary history of North America to 1612*, 5 vols. (1979) • M. Strachan, *Sir Thomas Roe, 1581–1644: a life* (1989) • S. Purchas, *Hakluytus posthumus, or, Purchas his pilgrimes*, 20 bks in 4 vols. (1625); repr. 20 vols., Hakluyt Society, extra ser., 14–33 (1905–7) • parish register, Essex, Harwich, Essex RO • parish register, Stepney, St Dunstan's, London, LMA [marriage] • G. W. Hill and W. H. Frere, eds., *Memorials of Stepney parish* (privately printed, Guildford, 1890–91) • will, PRO, PROB 11/132, sig. 92 • will, PRO, PROB 11/132, sig. 85 [Christopher Newport, son]
Wealth at death £400 and property: will, PRO, PROB 11/132, sigs. 85, 92

Newport, Francis, first earl of Bradford (1619–1708), politician, was born in Shropshire on 23 February 1619, the son and heir of Richard *Newport, first Baron Newport (1587–1651), and his wife, Rachel Leveson (d. 1661), of Halling, Kent. He was baptized on 12 March 1619 at Wroxeter, Shropshire, and was educated at Gray's Inn (admitted 12 August 1633), the Inner Temple (admitted November 1634), and Christ Church, Oxford, where he matriculated on 18 November 1635.

Clarendon claimed that in the early 1640s Newport's father 'had the best estate of any gentleman' in Shropshire (Clarendon, *Hist. rebellion*, 2.339), and Francis Newport was selected member of parliament for Shrewsbury for the Short Parliament in April 1640 and again in November 1640 for the Long Parliament. As an MP he voted against Strafford's attainder in April 1641, though in the crisis preceding the outbreak of civil war he took a moderate line, hoping that Charles I 'would come nearer his parliament' (*Fifth Report*, HMC, 147). On 28 April 1642 he married Diana Russell (1624–1695), youngest daughter of the reformist Francis *Russell, fourth earl of Bedford, but by the summer of 1642 he was drifting towards the king's camp. In June 1642 he obtained a leave of absence from the Commons, and in August Simonds D'Ewes noted that he supported the commission of array in Shropshire. It seems likely that much of his wife's £7000 dowry went to support the royalist cause. It is certain that he organized his father's purchase of a peerage in October 1642 and, using his friend Sir Edward Hyde as a go-between, paid £6000 for his father's barony. He was a captain of horse in the royalist army after January 1644, but his military career was brief. Captured near Oswestry in late June 1644 he remained a prisoner until March 1648, when he and his father were jointly fined £10,000 for their royalism. He succeeded his father as second Baron Newport in February 1651.

Newport remained an active royalist conspirator after his release, and was arrested in June 1655 and again in 1657. At liberty in the summer of 1659 he participated in an abortive plot to seize Shrewsbury for Charles II. The king rewarded Newport's service by appointing him lord

lieutenant of Shropshire on 26 July 1660. In 1666 he received a grant of Shrewsbury Castle. He grew more important at court after the king named him comptroller of the household and a privy councillor in 1668, and, in 1672, treasurer of the household. On 11 March 1675 Charles II promoted him Viscount Newport of Bradford in Shropshire. But as an ally of Arlington's he lost political ground following Danby's rise. In November 1675 he voted with the opposition to address the king for a dissolution of the Cavalier Parliament, elected in 1661. As a result he was forbidden the king's presence, though he retained his court office.

In succeeding years Newport continued to side with the king's opponents in the Lords, supporting their causes on several occasions. This probably accounts for his dismissal from the council in 1679. He was not, however, a rigid whig. He compromised his principles on at least one important issue, and voted with the court on exclusion. This flexibility earned him the characterization 'vile' from Shaftesbury, and ensured that he kept his offices under the crown. Although rumours suggested that he would lose all his offices in 1681, Newport clung to his lieutenancy and court posts even after James II's accession. He was finally dismissed from all office in 1687, having failed to pledge his support for repeal of penal legislation. At the revolution he strongly supported the prince of Orange, playing an active role in the Convention, where he described James II in early February 1689 as merely 'a private man' and 'no more King' (*Correspondence of Henry Hyde*, 2.259).

William III reinstated Newport to his offices and in 1691 appointed him cofferer of the household, a post he lost at Anne's accession in 1702. In March 1694 William raised him another step in the peerage, as earl of Bradford, a reward for his support of the ministry in the House of Lords. In 1704 he resigned his lieutenancy in favour of his son Richard, and played a limited political role thereafter. He died on 19 September 1708 at Richmond House, Twickenham, Middlesex, and was buried at Wroxeter on 4 October. According to John Macky, Bradford 'had a great deal of wit, is a just critic, a judge and lover of poetry, painting, and nice living: hath been a handsome man', but was 'always a great libertine' (*Memoirs of the Secret Services*, 58). He was particularly well known for his art collection, which included works by Van Dyck, Dobson, and Poussin.

VICTOR STATER

Sources DNB • GEC, *Peerage* • Clarendon, *Hist. rebellion*, 2.339; 6.112 • *Fifth report*, HMC, 4 (1876), 147–60 • N. Luttrell, *A brief historical relation of state affairs from September 1678 to April 1714*, 1–3, 5 (1857) • A. Browning, *Thomas Osborne, earl of Danby and duke of Leeds, 1632–1712*, 1 (1951), 93–4, 167; 3 (1951), 126, 129 • *Memoirs of the secret services of John Macky*, ed. A. R. (1733), 58 • W. H. Coates, A. Steele Young, and V. F. Snow, eds., *The private journals of the Long Parliament*, 3 vols. (1982–92), vol. 1, p. 144; vol. 3, pp. 284, 454 • *Calendar of the manuscripts of the marquess of Ormonde*, new ser., 8 vols., HMC, 36 (1902–20), vol. 5, p. 488; vol. 6, p. 78 • Evelyn, *Diary*, 4.169–70, 402–3, 416, 444–5, 468 • H. Horwitz, *Parliament, policy and politics in the reign of William III* (1977), 105, 132 • L. G. Schwoerer, *The declaration of rights, 1689* (1981), 128, 203, 238 • K. H. D. Haley, 'Shaftesbury's lists of the lay peers and members of the Commons, 1677–8', *BIHR*, 43 (1970), 86–105 • *The correspondence of Henry Hyde, earl of Clarendon,* and of his brother Lawrence Hyde, earl of Rochester, ed. S. W. Singer, 2 (1828), 259 · P. R. Newman, *Royalist officers in England and Wales, 1642–1660: a biographical dictionary* (1981), 273 · J. C. Sainty, ed., *List of lieutenants of counties of England and Wales, 1660–1974* (1979), 113 · G. S. Thomson, *Life in a noble household, 1641–1700* (1937), 39, 50

Archives Bolton Central Library, estate papers · NL Scot., corresp.

Likenesses G. Kneller, oils, *c.*1682–1690, Weston Park, Shifnal, Shropshire · M. Dahl, oils, Weston Park, Shifnal, Shropshire

Newport, George (1803–1854), entomologist, was born on 4 February 1803 in Canterbury, the first of four children of William Newport (1777–1843), a local wheelwright, and Sarah Gillham (1778–1859) of Hackington. He attended day school in Canterbury and on 15 June 1818, he was for seven years unwillingly apprenticed to his father's trade, partly as a result of the latter's sudden bankruptcy, and took his freedom in June 1826. An autodidact and amateur entomologist, Newport became a member of the Canterbury Philosophical and Literary Institution, which in 1826 employed him as its general exhibitor. In 1828 William Henry Weekes of Sandwich accepted Newport as an unpaid surgical apprentice, during which time Newport depended on loans from friends. On 16 January 1832 he began medical studies at the University of London. His tuition fees were waived by the faculty (whose staff included Robert Edmond Grant, the comparative anatomist). After receiving dual diplomas from the Society of Apothecaries and the College of Surgeons in 1835, he was appointed house surgeon at the Chichester Infirmary. He resigned in January 1837 and moved back to London, where his practice at 30 Southwick Street declined as he devoted increasing time to his entomological studies.

From 1824 Newport conducted experiments and field research (often in Richborough, Kent) focusing on the link between insect structure and function. His first paper was published in 1832 in the *Philosophical Transactions of the Royal Society*; it was followed, over the next twenty-five years, by a total of forty-six papers in prominent scientific journals of the day. The papers often concerned the embryology and development of millipedes, centipedes, and parasitic Hymenoptera, and exemplified his passion to find universal principles encompassing invertebrates and vertebrates. Other works include his collaboration in Peter Mark Roget's controversial Bridgewater treatise, *Animal and Vegetable Physiology Considered with Reference to Natural Theology* (1834), the entry for Insecta in Robert Todd's *Cyclopaedia of Anatomy and Physiology* (1836–9), and *Catalogue of the Myriapoda in the British Museum* (1856). The Agricultural Society of Saffron Walden awarded him a medal in 1838 for his essay on the turnip sawfly, *Athalia centifoliae* (later *Athalia rosae*), then causing significant crop damage.

In the 1840s Newport received increasing professional recognition, including election as a fellow to the Royal College of Surgeons of England in 1843 and the presidency of the Entomological Society of London (in 1843 and 1844). He was also elected a fellow of the Royal Society in 1846 and of the Linnean Society in 1847. In the latter year, on 1 July, he was awarded a civil-list pension. However, it was Newport's meticulous experiments in his three famous frog papers, 'On the impregnation of the ovum in the Amphibia' (1851, 1853, 1854), that brought him most renown. In them, he concluded that sperm penetrate, and do not merely contact, the egg, and that the point of sperm entry determines the median plane of the developing embryo. For the first of these, he was awarded his second royal medal from the Royal Society in 1851.

Newport was 'tenacious of his opinions and over-anxious for his own fame' (Bell, 298), and engaged in protracted battles in print. The most prominent took place between 1836 and 1838 in the pages of *The Lancet* with his former mentors, Grant and Marshall Hall. Calling Newport an 'ungrateful parasite' (*The Lancet*, 1, 1836–7, 747), they accused him of plagiarism and challenged the award to him of the royal medal for animal physiology in 1836 for his paper on the nervous system of the privet hawk moth, *Sphinx ligustri* (1834) and for another on the respiration of insects (1836). The basis of their attack was as political as scientific. Other disputes concerned the Linnean Society's censorship of his conversion of force theory in his 1845 paper on the oil beetle, *Meloë cicatricosus* (Newport believed that inorganic forces, such as light or electricity, were mutually interconvertible with 'vital' forces). His conversion of force theory also figures in the frog papers with his censored concept of 'sperm-force'. In addition, there were also conflicts caused by Newport's printed criticisms of other naturalists' research. Despite these 'painful collision[s] with his fellow naturalists' (Bell, 298), Newport was well regarded abroad, holding corresponding memberships in European and American scientific societies. He was also one of the British authors 'who had a significant impact' on Charles Darwin (M. Di Gregorio, xxxiii). His love of his subject matter informs his prose, making even the intimate behaviour of parasites enjoyable reading.

Newport was adept at minute dissection using only a single lens. He was ingenious in his experimental designs, and supplied his own detailed illustrations. His avocations included designing heraldic arms, genealogy, Canterburian archaeology, and sketching. He remained a bachelor. After contracting a fever on one of his scientific excursions in the marshlands of Shepherd's Bush, Middlesex, he died on 7 April 1854 at his home, 55 Cambridge Street, Hyde Park, London. He was buried at Kensal Green cemetery where a monument was raised for him by the Linnean and Royal societies. Newman called him 'the most profound physiological entomologist that this country has produced' (Newman, 51).

Despite recognition in its day, Newport's work fell into oblivion, and was rediscovered over thirty years later by Wilhelm Roux, father of modern embryology. Roux concluded that such obscurity was 'the usual fate of singular achievements that surpass the imaginative faculties of their contemporaries' (Roux, 211).

JENNIFER D. COGGON

Sources DSB · *Literary Gazette* (15 April 1854), 350 · *PRS*, 7 (1854–5), 278–85 · *Proceedings of the Linnean Society of London*, 2 (1848–55), 309–12 · T. Bell, 'Anniversary meeting', *Proceedings of the Linnean Society of*

London, 2 (1848–55), 297–9 • E. Newman, *Transactions of the Entomological Society of London*, new ser., 3 (1854–6), 51–3 • A. Desmond, *The politics of evolution: morphology, medicine and reform in radical London* (1989) • V. G. Plarr, *Plarr's Lives of the fellows of the Royal College of Surgeons of England*, rev. D'A. Power, 2 vols. (1930) • *GM*, 2nd ser., 41 (1854), 660–61 • *DNB* • J. Farley, *Gametes and spores: ideas about sexual reproduction, 1750–1914* (1982) • *The Lancet* (25 Feb 1837–21 April 1838) [correspondence to the editor from George Newport, Robert Grant, and Marshall Hall] • private information (2004) • G. Newport, family tree, Linn. Soc., MS 236 • *Charles Darwin's marginalia*, ed. M. A. Di Gregorio and N. W. Gill (1990) • W. Roux, 'Beiträge zur Entwickelungs mechanik des Embryo', *Archiv für mikroskopische Anatomie*, 29 (1887), 157–212

Archives Linn. Soc., corresp.

Likenesses Field, silhouette, Linn. Soc. • G. Newport, self-portrait, pen-and-ink drawing, Linn. Soc. • photograph (after portrait), Linn. Soc.

Wealth at death subscription limited to 1 guinea jointly set up by Royal Society, London, and Linnean Society, London, to raise money to buy tombstone for grave, implying that he was not well off when he died: *GM*, 661

Newport, Sir (Simon) John, first baronet (1756–1843), politician, was born on 24 October 1756, the eldest son of Simon Newport (1727–1817), merchant and banker at Waterford, and Elizabeth Riall (*b. c.*1735) of the Clonmel banking family of the same name. Educated at Eton College, where he established a lifelong friendship with William Grenville, later Lord Grenville, at Queen's College, Oxford, and at Lincoln's Inn, he was called to the Irish bar in 1780 but he did not practise. Returning to Waterford and to a partnership in his father's bank, he signalled that he was possessed of political ambitions when he accepted the nomination of the volunteers of co. Waterford to represent them in the Grand National Convention that assembled in Dublin in November 1783. Elected to the convention's general committee, which was charged with preparing a plan of reform, he was a vocal but not inflexible advocate of the need to 'invigorate' the constitution by eradicating the 'bashaws—the aristocratical evils who stalked over the land, to the destruction of the rest of the community' (*History of … the Volunteer Delegates*, 59, 92–3). He was convinced, arising out of his own observations, that the exercise of 'undue influence' in the county of Waterford had 'produce[d] the most mischievous effects to the freedom of election' and he illustrated that this was also the case elsewhere in the kingdom with his impressive *State of the Borough Representation in Ireland* (1832), which achieved a wide readership (ibid., 96).

Newport emphasized his liberal credentials by marrying, on 1 October 1784, Ellen Carew (*c.*1750–1819), daughter of Shapland Carew, whose brother Robert Shapland was the 'popular' MP for Waterford between 1776 and 1800. Obliged, as a result, to put his own parliamentary ambitions on hold, Newport occupied himself during the 1780s and 1790s with local matters. He was, for example, a member of the committee that oversaw the construction between 1786 and 1794 of a bridge over the River Suir, linking Waterford with its hinterland. More controversially his advocacy of Catholic relief in January 1792, when a majority of local freemen and freeholders favoured continuing 'protestant ascendancy', won him the applause of local Catholics, while his elevation to the baronetcy on 25

August 1789, arising out of his friendship with William Grenville, also enhanced his profile. Regarded by some as the most powerful figure in Waterford politics by the mid-1790s, he demonstrated his independence of mind by signing a petition in favour of a union in 1799. Arising out of the Act of Union and profiting from 'the good wishes' of Lord Grenville, Newport secured the representation for the Waterford constituency after a tense and acrimonious contest with the sitting conservative MP, William Alcock, in December 1803 (*Fortescue MSS*, 7.69–70). It was the first of nine consecutive election successes.

At Westminster, Newport quickly found a prominent niche in the ranks of the Grenvillite opposition and because of his banking background he earned a reputation as one of the leading spokesmen on Irish finance and banking matters. Though 'his plain, practical and sober style' did not much impress, he more than made up for his limitations in this sphere by his energy and commitment, and during his first two years in the Commons he contributed to or initiated debates on subjects as varied as defence, security, the abolition of the slave trade, the need for pauper lunatic asylums in Ireland, and Catholic relief (Jupp, HoP, *Commons, 1790–1820*, 4.664). As a result, when others declined the position Newport was appointed chancellor of the Irish exchequer on 25 May 1806 in the short-lived Grenville ministry. He proved an effective minister. Attentive to detail and mindful of his own constituency and the interests of his whig colleagues, his administrative priority was to put in place a reformed and efficient system for the collection and administration of the revenue. Though the combination of illness, deriving from the onerous burden of work he undertook, and the premature collapse of the ministry some thirteen months after his appointment ensured that Newport's legacy as chancellor was modest, his reputation as a liberal and reforming politician was enhanced. Back in opposition, where he was to spend pretty much the rest of his political career, Newport lived up to his nickname—'the Political Ferret'—by pursuing successive ministers across a broad front. The misuse of public money was one matter he pursued tirelessly, but he advocated a more reforming and less coercive style of government in Ireland with equal enthusiasm. In this context the cause of Catholic relief and of its corollary, the 'unqualified censure of the odious principle on which the Orange societies of Ireland are founded', assumed an appropriately prominent place on his political agenda (*Fortescue MSS*, 10.465). A supporter, when it was first raised in 1808, of the suggestion that the state should be allowed to exercise a veto on the appointment of Catholic ecclesiastics in return for the removal of obstacles in the way of Catholics sitting in parliament, Newport overcame his dislike of 'the unhappy and infatuated line' (ibid., 9.231) pursued by the Catholic hierarchy and his apprehension that emancipation would unleash 'malignant and destructive passions' (HoP, *Commons, 1790–1820*, 4.665–6). In association with Daniel O'Connell he pressed for Catholic relief in the 1820s, and in the early 1830s advocated a variety of reforms. Newport's decision not to stand for election in 1832 after thirty years in parliament brought the curtain down on the active political career of 'one of the most consistent, indefatigable, useful and best informed members in the house' (Hamilton, 59). He was comptroller-general of the exchequer from 1834 to 1839, when he retired with a pension of £1000. He died at his residence, Newpark, near Waterford, on 9 February 1843, more than twenty-three years after his beloved wife. He was buried on 15 February in Waterford Cathedral and was succeeded by his nephew, the Revd John Newport (d. 1859).   JAMES KELLY

Sources W. P. Burke, 'Newport's Waterford Bank', *Journal of the Cork Historical and Archaeological Society*, 2nd ser., 4 (1898), 278–86 · T. P. Power, 'Electoral politics in Waterford city, 1692–1832', *Waterford history and society*, ed. T. P. Power and W. Nolan (1992), 227–64 · *The history of the proceedings and debates of the volunteer delegates of Ireland, on the subject of parliamentary reform* (1784) · GEC, *Baronetage*, vol. 5 · P. J. Jupp, 'Newport, Sir Simon John', HoP, *Commons, 1790–1820* · P. J. Jupp, *William Grenville, 1759–1834* (1985) · *The manuscripts of J. B. Fortescue*, 10 vols., HMC, 30 (1892–1927) · F. G. Hall, *The Bank of Ireland, 1783–1946*, ed. G. O'Brien (1949) · B. Inglis, *The freedom of the press in Ireland, 1784–1841* (1954) · *The correspondence of Daniel O'Connell*, ed. M. R. O'Connell, 8 vols., IMC (1972–80) · F. B. Hamilton, *Picture of parliament containing a biographical dictionary of the Irish members* (1831) · B. Jenkins, *Era of emancipation: British government of Ireland, 1812–1830* (1988) · A. D. Macintyre, *The Liberator: Daniel O'Connell and the Irish party, 1830–1847* (1965) · *DNB* · *Annual Register* (1843) · Foster, *Alum. Oxon.* · Burke, *Peerage* · Burke, *Gen. Ire.* (1912)
Archives Bodl. Oxf., Newport–Grenville corresp., MS Eng. lett. d. 80 · NA Ire., MS 482 · NL Ire., MS 796 · Queen's University, Belfast, corresp. and MSS, MS 7 | BL, corresp. with Lord Grenville, Add. MSS 58970–58971 · BL, corresp. with Robert Peel, Add. MSS 40225–40365 · BL, corresp. with Lord Wellesley, Add. MSS 37306–37313, 37416 · Lpool RO, letters to E. G. Stanley · NL Ire., Monteagle MSS 13370–13372, 13353, 13362 · NL Scot., corresp. with William Elliot · NL Scot., Elliott of Wells MS 12917 · TCD, corresp. with Lord Donoughmore · TCD, letters to William Shaw Mason · U. Durham L., corresp. with second Earl Grey
Likenesses J. Ramsey, oils, c.1810; formerly in possession of Charles Newport JP, Waterford, 1858 · H. Brocas, engraving, 1811, NG Ire.; repro. in *Hibernian Magazine* (June 1811) · R. Cooper, stipple, pubd 1826 (after drawing by S. C. Smith), NPG, NG Ire. · T. Lupton, mezzotint, pubd 1828 (after J. Ramsey), BM, NPG, NG Ire.

Newport, Maurice. *See* Ewens, Maurice (c.1611–1687).

Newport, Richard (d. 1318), bishop of London, first occurs in Bishop Richard of Gravesend's will, dated 12 September 1302, where he is described as archdeacon of Colchester and the bishop's official. At some point he held the prebend of Islington in St Paul's and was a residentiary canon there. At the time of Gravesend's death (9 December 1303) Newport had become archdeacon of Middlesex. He was one of Gravesend's executors, and had custody of the spiritualities during the vacancy of the see. Gravesend bequeathed him a volume of decretals worth 10 marks. He served as Bishop Ralph Baldock's vicar-general in 1305–6 and on 5 June 1306 was one of those who excommunicated at St Paul's Robert I, king of Scots, and the murderers of John Comyn. In 1313 he was commissary for Bishop Walter Reynolds of Worcester (d. 1327) in settling a dispute between the Dominicans and the University of Oxford. He is later described by the *Flores historiarum* as *doctor in decretis*. In the latter part of 1316 he was elected dean of St Paul's, but did not take up office, possibly because soon

afterwards, on 27 January 1317, he was elected bishop of London. The royal assent was given on 11 February, the election was confirmed on 26 March, and on 15 May Newport was consecrated by Walter Reynolds at Canterbury. Newport died suddenly at Ilford on 24 August 1318, and was buried in St Paul's four days later. His tomb was defaced at the Reformation. By an ordinance of 1309 he made provision for two priests to pray for his soul, and left 40s. annually for the keeping of his obit. In 1315 he gave a house to the almoner of St Paul's for the maintenance of two choristers for two years after their voices had broken.   C. L. KINGSFORD, *rev.* M. C. BUCK

Sources R. C. Fowler, ed., *Registrum Radulphi Baldock, Gilberti Segrave, Ricardi Newport, et Stephani Gravesend*, CYS, 7 (1911) · W. H. Hale and H. T. Ellacombe, eds., *Account of the executors of Richard, bishop of London, 1303, and of the executors of Thomas, bishop of Exeter, 1310*, CS, new ser., 10 (1874) · *Fasti Angl., 1300–1541*, [St Paul's, London] · R. R. Sharpe, ed., *Calendar of wills proved and enrolled in the court of husting, London, AD 1258 – AD 1688*, 2 vols. (1889–90) · W. S. Simpson, ed., *Documents illustrating the history of St Paul's Cathedral*, CS, new ser., 26 (1880) · W. Dugdale, *The history of St Paul's Cathedral in London*, new edn, ed. H. Ellis (1818) · H. R. Luard, ed., *Flores historiarum*, 3 vols., Rolls Series, 95 (1890) · W. Stubbs, ed., *Chronicles of the reigns of Edward I and Edward II*, 2 vols., Rolls Series, 76 (1882–3) · Emden, *Oxf.* · H. Wharton, *Historia de episcopis et decanis Londoniensibus* (1695) · W. S. Simpson, ed., *Registrum statutorum et consuetudinum ecclesiae cathedralis Sancti Pauli Londinensis* (1873) · G. Hennessy, *Novum repertorium ecclesiasticum parochiale Londinense, or, London diocesan clergy succession from the earliest time to the year 1898* (1898) · *Chancery records*
Archives GL, register, MS 9531/1
Wealth at death see will, BL, Harley MS 4080, fol. 38, cited in Hennessy, *Novum repertorium*; Sharpe, ed., *Calendar*, vol. 1, p. 281

Newport, Richard, first Baron Newport (1587–1651), royalist army officer, was born on 7 May 1587, the son of Sir Francis Newport (c.1555–1623) of High Ercall and Eyton-on-Severn, Shropshire, MP for Shropshire in the parliament of 1593, and his wife, Beatrice, daughter of Rowland Lacon of Willey, Shropshire. He matriculated from Brasenose College, Oxford, on 19 October 1604 and graduated BA on 12 June 1607. On 2 June 1615 Newport was knighted at Theobalds by James I. By 1615 he had married Rachel (d. 1661), daughter of Sir John *Leveson of Hales Whornes Place, Kent, and sister and coheir of Sir Richard Leveson of Trentham, Staffordshire, and Lilleshall, Shropshire. Their eldest surviving son was Francis *Newport, first earl of Bradford.

Following his father's death on 5 March 1623, the estates that Newport inherited made him probably the richest man in Shropshire and were the basis of his considerable influence in the county. He was sheriff of Shropshire in 1627 and was appointed to the council in the marches of Wales. He was a knight of the shire in the parliaments of 1614, 1624–5, 1625, and 1628, usually alongside Sir Andrew Corbet. This sequence was broken in 1621–2, when he sat for the borough of Shrewsbury, and again in 1626 when, probably with Newport's agreement, his brother-in-law Sir Richard Leveson was returned for the county. In both religion and in politics Newport seems to have been a man of moderation. His patronage of the young Richard Baxter, his son's schoolfellow, suggests that he did not share the violent hostility towards puritans of many in that region, while he seems not to have been involved, even in informal discussions, in the elections of 1640.

In the summer of 1642 Newport was certainly involved in strenuous efforts to compose the differences between the partisans of king and parliament. He urged his brother-in-law Leveson to persuade James Stanley, Lord Strange (then en route for Shropshire for the king), not to press him to declare for the king, in order that he might continue his efforts at accommodation. Neither Newport nor his sons signed the declaration and protestation agreed upon by the Shropshire grand jury on 8 August as an oath of loyalty to the royalist cause. Both sides were acutely aware that in Shropshire Sir Richard Newport 'had a very powerful influence upon that people' (Clarendon, *Hist. rebellion*, 2.339). His conciliatory stance encouraged parliamentarians to make efforts to enlist him on their side.

But the parliamentarian county committee was disappointed. When Colonel Hunt made preparations for the defence of Shrewsbury as the king approached, Newport 'craved and laboured' with Sir Francis Ottley to try and dissuade Hunt from raising volunteers, and did not appear with them. These men now:

> grew discouraged, though they had appeared before the militia ... and fell off, looking upon Sir Richard as a man of vast estate ... And after this, the said Sir Richard was one of the forwardest of the [king's] commission of array, being one himself, to remove the [county] magazine ... to Bridgnorth and Ludlow. (Phillips, 4–5)

Newport—'a man of undoubted affections and loyalty to the King and to the government both in Church and State'—doubtless acted on principle both in resisting the choice of sides as long as possible and then, when a choice was unavoidable, in aligning with his king. But he also exacted a price for his allegiance. Francis Newport let Edward Hyde know that, 'if his father might be made a baron, he did believe he might be prevailed with to present his majesty with a good sum of money'. The king was initially hostile to the idea, but when he returned to Shrewsbury from Chester at the end of September, needing cash urgently for the forthcoming campaign, 'in a few days it was perfected'. Sir Richard Newport 'presented the sum of £6000 to his majesty; whereupon all preparations for the army were prosecuted with effect', and by a patent of 14 October, Newport was created Baron Newport of High Ercall (Clarendon, *Hist. rebellion*, 2.339–40), the title deriving from Newport's principal residence in Shropshire.

Newport was a prisoner of war by 14 March 1643, when the parliamentarian committee at Coventry was instructed to hold him until further notice. However, he was released or exchanged; on 2 February 1644 he was at Shrewsbury, writing to warn Prince Rupert, who was proposing to make the town his headquarters, of its lack of provisions. On 3 March he wrote to the prince again, this time from Oxford. The letter was chiefly concerned with military news, but Newport was also anxious to scotch a

rumour that he had tried to flee the country upon receiving a summons from the prince, a report which conflicted both with his presence at Oxford and by 'my waiting upon you at Newport' (presumably Newport Pagnell in Bedfordshire, which Rupert had occupied in October 1643) (BL, Add. MS 18981, fol. 78). Newport was reported to have been present at Bristol when it was besieged in September 1645 by the New Model Army, and the following month he found himself a prisoner again, this time at Stafford. Newport managed to gain his release, but at this point seems to have accepted the hopelessness of the king's military position. Taking refuge at Moulins in France, 'Sir Richard, alias Lord Newport', as the committee for compounding pointedly styled him, faced sequestration and massive losses (Green, 2.925). The joint fine for Newport and his son Francis was initially set at £16,687, but following strenuous protests this was reduced in January 1646 to £9436.

High Ercall was one of the last royalist bastions to fall, in March 1646; its works were slighted and its moat drained. On 13 April the committee for compounding received a letter from Newport, who was still in France, applying for a pass to London 'to perfect his composition' (Green, 2.925). Granted this on 21 May, he did not appear, and in his absence it was agreed that Lady Newport should be permitted to compound on his behalf. In his will, signed on 12 November 1648, Newport bitterly resented his misfortunes: 'By the malignity of the recent times, my family is dissolved, my chief house, High Ercall, is ruined, my household stuff and stock sold from me for having assisted the king' (PRO, PROB 11/217).

On 22 March 1649 the House of Commons issued an order fixing at £10,000 the fine to be paid jointly by the Newports, father and son. Of this, £8260 13s. 4d. was received by the Shropshire committee. Lady Newport seems to have experienced continuing difficulties with the estate, arising from the hostility of the sequestration commissioners and the refusal by recalcitrant ministers to pay rents on their holdings. Her husband remained in France, partly for fear of parliamentarian vengeance. His absence did not go unnoticed at Westminster, but on 25 March 1650 the Commons was assured that his residence abroad had been 'certified by Sir Theo Mayerne, and Dr Lempriere to be for the cure of the numb palsy' (Green, 2.926). He died on 8 February 1651 at Moulins; his widow died in London on 31 January 1661.

STEPHEN WRIGHT

Sources W. Phillips, 'Sequestration papers of Sir Richard first Baron Newport and Sir Francis, his son', *Transactions of the Shropshire Archaeological and Natural History Society*, 2nd ser., 12 (1900), 1–38 • M. A. E. Green, ed., *Calendar of the proceedings of the committee for compounding ... 1643–1660*, 2, PRO (1890) • Foster, *Alum. Oxon.* • *VCH Shropshire*, vols. 2–3, 10–11 • Clarendon, *Hist. rebellion* • letters of Lord Newport to Prince Rupert, BL, Add. MS 18981, fols. 24, 78 • J. E. Auden, 'Ecclesiastical history of Shropshire during the civil war, Commonwealth and Restoration', *Transactions of the Shropshire Archaeological and Natural History Society*, 3rd ser., 7 (1907), 241–307 • JHC • J. J. Clarke, 'Newport, Francis II', HoP, *Commons, 1558–1603* • will, PRO, PROB 11/217, sig. 126, fols. 176v–177r

Newport, Sir Thomas (late 1450s?–1523), knight of the hospital of St John of Jerusalem, was probably born in the late 1450s. He had entered the order of St John by 1478, when he was in Rhodes (he must have been at least eighteen when he became a hospitaller). He was almost certainly among the defenders of the island against the Turks in the siege of 1480. He was licensed to return to England in March 1489, in which year he became preceptor (the officer in charge) of Newland in the West Riding of Yorkshire, to which he added the lease of Dalby and Rothley, both in Leicestershire, in 1493, and a grant of Temple Bruer, Lincolnshire, in 1495, both by the grace of the order's master, Pierre d'Aubusson. In 1501, while still at home, he was elected turcopolier, or head of the English knights (with responsibility for the coastguard) in Rhodes. On 10 March 1503, on condition that he resign this dignity, he was made bailiff of Eagle in Lincolnshire, the fourth ranking dignity of the *langue* or 'tongue' of England (the association of British born hospitallers). On 2 September 1503, being summoned to Rhodes, he had authority given him to anticipate the revenues of his commanderies (preceptories) for three years; he was thus enabled to raise £306 13s. 4d. in 1505 to fund his journey. He set out the same year, wintered in Venice, and had reached the Aegean by May 1506. He remained there until September 1508, serving on a number of commissions and holding the important office of procurator of the common treasury.

Newport was evidently a good man of business. He recovered the Leicestershire manor of Heather, of which it had lost control, for his order and, in reward, on 28 June 1505 a lease of it was granted to his brother Richard, also a professed hospitaller. Between 1489 and 1503 Sir Thomas filled the important office of receiver-general for the order's common treasury in England. In this capacity he was responsible for the collection of the payments from subsidiary estates known as *responsiones*, which he then sent via Venice to Rhodes. During this time he probably lived just outside London, at St John's Gate, Clerkenwell, and became known at court. He probably spent more time at Eagle and his other commanderies after 1503, but was still often in London on the order's business. Under Henry VIII he was often put in the commission of the peace for Lincolnshire and Leicestershire, and his name appears as one of those ready in 1513 to serve the king abroad.

Newport was also urgently needed at Rhodes, and after his royal service he raised £1000 by leasing his commanderies. He set out in the summer of 1513, travelling through Germany to Venice. With him went his fellow hospitaller Thomas Sheffield. At Venice they stayed some time. They had brought letters from Henry VIII, and were received as his ambassadors. A formal audience was granted them by the senate on 3 September, and Troian Bollani made a formal report to the senate on 10 September of the slender political information he had derived from them. Newport reached Rhodes before 15 November, and stayed there, owing to the directions of Fabrizio del Carretto, the grand master of the order, longer than anticipated. In 1516 he captured some Turkish transports and brought them into Rhodes. Occasionally he wrote home, either to the king or to Wolsey; the last letter preserved was written in 1517, and in it he reports that the Turkish fleet was only 40 miles off, while the Rhodians were ready under four captains, of whom he was one.

Newport subsequently returned home, and attended the Field of Cloth of Gold in 1520. But having received news that Rhodes was again under siege he set out once more for the eastern Mediterranean in 1522, but was drowned 'in the sea of Spain' on 24 January 1523 (National Library of Malta, archives of the knights, cod. 54, fol. 93*v*). After the prior of England, Thomas Docwra, Newport was the richest and most prominent English hospitaller of his generation, with an income between 1503 and 1523 of perhaps £800, on which he paid *responsiones* of £270 10s. 6d. in the early 1520s.

W. A. J. ARCHBOLD, *rev.* G. J. O'MALLEY

Sources National Library of Malta, archives of the knights, codices 16, 54, 283, 284, 79, 81, 82, 389–95, 397–404, 406–10 • BL, Cotton MS Claudius E.vi • BL, Lansdowne MS 200 • *LP Henry VIII*, vols. 1–3 • *CSP Venice, 1202–1519* • A. J. Gabarretta and J. Mizzi, eds., *Catalogue of the records of the order of St. John of Jerusalem in the Royal Malta Library*, 1, 2 (1964–78) • R. C. Mueller, *The Venetian money markets: banks, panics and the public debt, 1200–1500* (1997) • J. Nichols, *The history and antiquities of the county of Leicester*, 4 vols. (1795–1815) • Dugdale, *Monasticon*, new edn, vol. 6 • J. Caley and J. Hunter, eds., *Valor ecclesiasticus temp. Henrici VIII*, 6 vols., RC (1810–34), vols. 4–5
Wealth at death approx. £800 p.a.—total annual value of preceptories in 1535: *Valor ecclesiasticus*; Dugdale, *Monasticon*

Newsam [Nusam, Newsham], **Bartholomew** (c.1530–1587), clockmaker, was probably born in or near York, although the details of his birth and parentage remain obscure. Bartholomew had an elder brother, William, who appears to have been about twenty years older and may have acted *in loco parentis*. William was a locksmith in Coney Street, York, and made the keys for the chest which housed the great seal of the City of York in 1541. By the early part of the reign of Elizabeth I, Bartholomew was established in London in the parish of St Mary-le-Strand, and on 10 September 1565 he married Parnell Younge in that church; they had at least fourteen children, the majority of whom appear to have died in infancy, since only four are mentioned in Newsam's will. When William Newsam died in February 1569, Bartholomew inherited a moderate estate including premises in Coney Street, York.

Newsam was a skilled craftsman and on familiar terms with many figures at court. On 8 April 1573, he leased from the crown 'a tenement in Stronde Way [the Strand] (abutting … on the garden of Somerset Place towards the Thames on the south and on the highway leading to Westminster on the north) … for 30 years from Lady Day 1573 for a yearly rent of 26s. 8d.' On 4 June 1583, Newsam received under the privy seal '32s. 8d. for mending of clockes' during the previous year, suggesting that he was an employee of the queen. On 5 August 1583 Newsam wrote to 'his very speciall good friend' Sir Francis Walsingham 'to be mindfull unto her Majstie of my booke concerninge my long and chargable suite, wherein I have procured Sir Philip Sydney to move you' (*CSP dom.*). On 6 September 1583, Newsam registered on the patent rolls investments in several parcels of land in Wymondham (Norfolk), Fleet (Lincolnshire), St Clement Danes (Middlesex), and Llanlluney (Pembrokeshire). Newsam died on 17 January 1587 and was buried on 9 February in the parish church of St Mary-le-Strand. It is unclear whether he ever officially occupied the post of clockmaker to Elizabeth I, although he was clearly an employee of the crown. An undated note among the state papers domestic (which has been attributed to 1590) grants the office of clockmaker to the queen to him in place of Nicholas Urseau, who was dead. However, this date would be three years after Newsam's own death, so it is conceivable that this grant was never issued.

Newsam's will is dated 7 January 1587, ten days before he died. In it he mentions four surviving children, William, Edward, Margaret, and Rose, all in their minority. Newsam bequeathed his tools to his son Edward, 'should he follow the trade of clockmaker', otherwise they were to be passed to John Newsam, undoubtedly a relative. Less than three months after Newsam's death, his widow married his cousin George Tuke, a haberdasher, on 2 May 1587 at St Mary-le-Strand. Probate of Newsam's will was delayed for six years until 18 December 1593, possibly for the period of the minority of Newsam's children. Disagreement between them and Tuke led to chancery litigation on 18 April 1594. Newsam's eldest son, William, brought an action on behalf of his brother and sisters against his mother and her new husband for control of property in his father's estate.

Newsam is considered to have been one of the most important and influential figures in the clock making world of his time. Prior to Newsam, the trade in London had been dominated by foreign makers brought to England; he was among the first English clockmakers whose skills were recognized by the crown and whose clocks are judged equal to those of his foreign contemporaries. He also made sundials. Some pieces by him survive, including notable examples in the British Museum. The period following Newsam's death saw major expansion in English clock making to the degree that London became an important centre for clock and watch manufacture with English makers being considered among the best in the world. ADRIAN FINCH

Sources A. A. Finch, V. J. Finch, and A. W. Finch, *Antiquarian Horology and the Proceedings of the Antiquarian Horological Society* · *CSP dom.*, 1581–90, 117 · parish registers, St Mary-le-Strand Church, Westminster · patent rolls, PRO, C 274 Reg. 25, pt 12, fol. 26v · York Civic Records: Henry VIII, 33 · *Chancery Proceeding* (18 April 1594)
Archives BM, clock · BM, mathematical instruments

Newsam, Sir Frank Aubrey (1893–1964), civil servant, the third son of William Elias Newsam and his wife, Alice Mary Chambers, was born on 13 November 1893 in Barbados, where his father held a modest civil service post. From Harrison College, Barbados, he went to St John's College, Oxford, in 1911, with an open scholarship in classics.

After taking his degree in 1915, with second classes in classical moderations and *literae humaniores*, he was commissioned in the Royal Irish regiment and later served with the 1st battalion 30th Punjabis. He saw active service in Ireland (where he was wounded in the Easter rising), Belgium, France, the Punjab, and Afghanistan. He was awarded the MC and was mentioned in dispatches. On demobilization he taught classics at Harrow for a short time; and then in July 1920, having passed the civil service examination, he joined the Home Office.

Newsam began in the children's division. Although this was perhaps the one division in the Home Office least suited to his taste, his energy and strong personality soon made an impression. His career followed an unusual pattern. In 1924 the permanent under-secretary of state—the formidable Sir John Anderson—chose him as his private secretary, came to trust him, kept him in that post for three years after his promotion to principal in 1925, and then appointed him as principal private secretary to the home secretary. Newsam held this key post for five years, serving Sir William Joynson-Hicks, J. R. Clynes, Sir Herbert Samuel, and Sir John Gilmour. As Anderson, who was clearly destined for greater things, devoted more and more of his time to non-Home Office matters, and as he was succeeded in 1932 by a Treasury nominee who knew little of the Home Office, Newsam became a powerful and authoritative figure at the centre of the office. He also learned a good deal about the ways of politicians and parliament.

Newsam at last returned to ordinary divisional duties in 1933 as assistant secretary in charge of a new division. For a start, he handled the controversial bill which became the Betting and Lotteries Act 1934, but his main task was to address the problems caused by the disorders resulting from the activities of the British Fascists. He had a large responsibility for the Public Order Act 1936, which proved to be effective. In 1938 he moved to head the criminal division and set about preparing a major criminal justice bill, which in the event had to be put off until 1948.

At the beginning of the war Newsam, now an assistant under-secretary of state, went for a few months to Tunbridge Wells as the principal officer to the regional commissioner located there, but was brought back to take overall charge of the criminal and aliens divisions. Then in April 1941 he was promoted to be the deputy under-secretary of state with special responsibility for security. The permanent under-secretary of state, Sir Alexander Maxwell, was totally unlike Newsam in character, but they worked well together, especially over the detention of suspect British subjects and aliens under defence regulation 18B and the wartime aliens order. When the Americans came into the war Newsam took the lead in negotiations about handling criminal offences by members of the US forces, resulting in the United States of America (Visiting Forces) Act 1942. Finally, as the war came to an end, he worked hard and effectively on the restoration of the Channel Islands after the German occupation.

The police service, however, was becoming Newsam's

prime interest. There were too many small police forces unable to provide the specialist services which were increasingly needed. Following some rolling up under wartime powers, the Police Act 1946 abolished, at a stroke, nearly all non-county borough forces, and made provision for further amalgamations. Separate from this, Newsam headed a committee of police and local authority representatives studying the whole future shape of the service. In particular he secured agreement on new schemes of training for all recruits and on setting up a new national staff college, this last project becoming something of a personal crusade. It gave him great satisfaction to secure for the college's permanent home a magnificent house at Bramshill, near Hartley Wintney, with enough land for new buildings. In 1947 he was the first chairman of the board of governors, and kept this post for the rest of his career.

In 1948 Newsam succeeded Maxwell as head of the office. The home secretary at the time was Chuter Ede. He had already seen a good deal of Newsam, and concurred in his promotion. But the two men were utterly unlike, and Ede did not altogether trust Newsam's judgement. Although there was no open falling out Ede saw to it that he remained firmly in charge, and the relationship, for three years, was a somewhat uneasy one. Newsam got on well with three other home secretaries under whom he served—Sir David Maxwell-Fyfe, Gwilym Lloyd-George, and R. A. Butler. Newsam was a man of action, and ready when necessary to give tough advice and to take tough decisions. But on the fundamental issue which underlies so much of the work of the Home Office—the balance between public order and individual liberty, between the powers of the state and the interests of the citizen—in the end, like his predecessor, he would always tend towards seeking a liberal solution.

A principal concern throughout was advising the home secretary on capital cases. Newsam was gravely concerned when Maxwell-Fyfe, contrary to his recommendation, decided to let the law take its course in the case of Derek Bentley. He was also shaken by the discovery in 1953 that a convicted murderer, Christie, might have committed the crime for which Timothy Evans had been hanged in 1950. He worked out a distinction between capital and non-capital murder, and saw his concept embodied in the Homicide Act 1957. But it did not last—unlike the provision in that act which introduced into English law the defence of diminished responsibility.

Newsam was not greatly interested in organization, but he was a born leader. He chose people he could trust, without much regard for rank, and gave them considerable authority. He tended to concentrate his own energies on the aspects of the Home Office which particularly appealed to him—notably crime and criminal law, prison administration, emergencies, and especially the police, with occasional bursts of activity in the aliens department. One spectacular intervention was when it came to be known that an individual who was claiming political asylum was being forcibly detained on a ship in the Thames. Newsam sent his lawyers to obtain a writ of habeas corpus from the lord chief justice, and the commissioner of police then led a boarding party of 120 policemen to rescue the individual.

Newsam chaired (with some enthusiasm) the state management districts council, and also the fire brigades advisory council. But he really came into his own as chairman of the official committee on emergencies. Most of the problems arose from strikes, when it was a question of doing everything possible to maintain essential supplies and services. There was, though, one grave emergency of a different kind. The east coast floods in 1953 killed 300 people and affected 25,000 houses. Newsam sat at the centre directing the activities of large numbers of troops and civilians on repairs and defences, R. A. Butler later writing that 'Newsam had almost literally taken charge of the country … and secured achievements that would have surprised Canute' (Butler, 199).

Newsam contributed to one embarrassing heritage. On his advice the home secretary, Lloyd-George, authorized an intercept on the telephone of a known criminal in order to help the bar council in an inquiry into the professional conduct of a barrister. The row which erupted when it became known that an intercept had been used for this purpose led Butler, who had succeeded Lloyd-George, to set up the Birkett committee inquiry into the scope of telephone tapping.

Newsam retired in 1957, well beyond the normal age. He had never served outside the Home Office, apart from his few months in Tunbridge Wells which were, technically, under the Ministry of Home Security, and had never had much to do with other permanent secretaries and the central departments. Within his own field, though, he had been an extremely effective operator. Quick to go to the heart of a problem, a superb chairman of a meeting, an eloquent (if not very witty) speaker, he had a strong personality and tremendous drive. If at times he showed impatience with those who differed from him, he would in the end always listen. Quite good-looking, with a touch of the Caribbean, he had about him an aura of power and authority. In conversation, he would sometimes come out with an unexpected bit of knowledge, or quote by heart some passage from Aeschylus. But he also drank quite a lot, was an inveterate gambler on horse-racing, and enjoyed dancing and social occasions. Butler summed him up as 'an original'.

On 28 December 1927 Newsam married Natalie Janet Elsie (Jean; b. 1898/9), daughter of James McAuslin, monumental mason of Pietermaritzburg, South Africa. When the war came she went to live in Wylye, Wiltshire, developed a taste for country living, and rarely went to London. Newsam went to Wylye most weekends, but not all, and continued to live in London after he retired. She survived him. Although they did not see much of each other they remained on good terms. There were no children.

Newsam was appointed CBE in 1933, KBE in 1943, KCB in 1950, and GCB in 1957. He was a commander in the Norwegian order of St Olaf. He published *The Home Office* in 1954. His health had begun to deteriorate during his last year or two in office, and his only major commitment in retirement was to serve as a highly regarded member of the newly formed police committee of the British Transport Commission. He died of cancer at his London home, 25 Blomfield Road, Paddington, on 25 April 1964.

ALLEN OF ABBEYDALE

Sources Baron Butler of Saffron Walden [R. A. Butler], *The art of the possible: the memoirs of Lord Butler* (1971) · *The Times* (27 April 1964) · personal knowledge (2004) · private information (2004) [keeper of the archives, St John's College, Oxford] · Home Office staff records · British Transport Police · m. cert. · d. cert. · earl of Kilmuir [D. P. Maxwell-Fyfe], *Political adventure* (1964) · WWW
Archives PRO, papers relating to royal commission on capital punishment, HO 317/4 | JRL, letters to the *Manchester Guardian*
Likenesses W. Stoneman, photograph, 1943, NPG · W. Stoneman, photograph, 1954, NPG
Wealth at death £2301: probate, 4 June 1964, CGPLA Eng. & Wales

Newsham, Richard (*d.* 1743), maker of fire engines, was born in London; his date of birth and parentage are unknown. He described himself as a maker of pearl buttons in his patents of 1721 (no. 439) and 1725 (no. 479) relating to 'a water engine for extinguishing fires'. Whereas most hand-operated pumps ejected the water in spurts, Newsham's engine incorporated a vessel to maintain a constant pressure on the water, expelling it in a steady stream. A similar design had been proposed by Nicholas Mandell, whose engine was patented in 1712, but Newsham improved on the existing arrangement by moving the pump handles from the end to the sides, where several men could operate them, and he designed an effective mechanism to transmit their up-and-down movement to the pistons, which were accurately made and balanced. In form his engines were long and narrow so as to pass through doorways, and they were manufactured in a range of sizes, depending on the number of firemen available to replenish the water and to work the handles.

In 1725 Newsham, who by then was established in Cloth Fair, by Smithfield, in the City of London, issued a broadsheet describing how his engines 'played before the King [George II] and the Nobility at St James, with so general an approbation that the largest was instantly ordered to be left for the use of the Royal palace aforesaid' (Guildhall Library, broadside 11.130). He was, however, obliged to compete with an engine maker named Fowke, of Wapping. Both men issued pamphlets and Newsham claimed in the *Daily Journal* of 7 April 1726 that his engine could throw water to the height of the gilded grasshopper on the Royal Exchange, some 160 feet above the ground. Doubts have been cast on the veracity of this claim (Blackstone, 57–60), but Newsham's engines were certainly soundly constructed and a number of examples survive in museums, in working order. They were supplied to fire insurance companies, to the Admiralty for ships of the Royal Navy, to various provincial towns, and in 1730 two machines were ordered by the city of New York.

Newsham's first marriage produced at least one son, Lawrence, and two daughters, but the name of his wife is not known. He was described as widower when he married widow Mary Matthew on 4 December 1728 at St Katharine by the Tower. Her son John became his apprentice

and was still under age when Newsham, who was ailing when he made his will in 1741, died at the beginning of April 1743 and was buried on 4 April in the churchyard of St Bartholomew-the-Great, Smithfield. His second wife also predeceased him. After small bequests to his sister Esther, his married daughters Mrs Shaw and Ann Dollison, and nephew George Ragg, and provision for John Matthew's apprenticeship to continue, Newsham left his thriving engine business to Lawrence.

Lawrence, whose date of birth and marriage to his wife, Christian, are unknown, died childless in April 1744, leaving the business to be run equally by his cousin George Ragg and Christian, who was to live in the house adjoining the engine workshop. Christian married George Ragg in June 1744; he died in 1758, leaving the business to his brother Richard. Christian died in 1761. The business continued trading as Newsham and Ragg of Cloth Fair until 1765.

ANITA McCONNELL

Sources J. T. Desaguliers, *A course of experimental philosophy*, 2 (1744), 505–19 · 'Richard Newsham of Cloth Fair, London, engineer', 1725, GL, broadside 11.130 · H. E. Gillingham, 'The first fire engines used in America', *Quarterly Bulletin of the New York Historical Society* (July 1936), 63–74 · G. V. Blackstone, *History of the British fire service* (1957), 57–60 · *Daily Journal* (7 April 1726) · will of Richard Newsham, 1743, PRO, PROB 11/725, sig. 126 · will of Lawrence Newsham, 1744, PRO, PROB 11/733, sig. 101 · will of George Ragg, 1758, PRO, PROB 11/840, sig. 275 · will of Christian Ragg, 1761, PRO, PROB 11/862, sig. 32 · parish register, St Bartholomew-the-Great, Smithfield, London, 4 April 1743 [burial]
Wealth at death left house at Spitalfields; small cash bequests; thriving business: will, 1743, PRO, PROB 11/725, sig. 126

Newsholme, Sir Arthur (1857–1943), public health official and epidemiologist, was born on 10 February 1857 in Haworth, Yorkshire, the fourth son of Robert Newsholme (*d. c.*1861), wool stapler or merchant, and his second wife, Phoebe, daughter of John Binns, wool comber, of Haworth. Robert Newsholme had been Patrick Brontë's churchwarden, but after Newsholme's death, when his son Arthur was four years old, Phoebe raised the children in a stricter Wesleyan environment. Newsholme attended a Wesleyan Sunday school and a free grammar school in Haworth before spending a year at Keighley grammar school. He aspired to a position in the Indian Civil Service, but in 1873 he was forced to withdraw from University College, London, because of family problems, probably financial. He returned to Bradford where his mother was then living. Only then did he consider medicine as a career, and he began a medical apprenticeship in Bradford. In the autumn of 1875 he returned to London and entered St Thomas's Hospital medical school, with the aid of a small inheritance he was permitted to take before his majority. He had a brilliant career as a medical student, winning prize money every year. He became a licentiate of the Society of Apothecaries in 1876, took his MB in 1880, and earned his MD and a gold medal in 1881. He held resident posts at St Thomas's, Tottenham Hospital, and at the Evelina Hospital for Children, London.

In 1881 Newsholme married Sara (*d.* 1933), daughter of William Mansford, farmer, of Marlborough, Lincolnshire; there were no children. Newsholme established a general practice on High Street, Clapham, in 1883, and supplemented his income by tutoring medical students and editing a series of science textbooks for schoolchildren. He first took an interest in public health in 1882, when he began lecturing on basic physiology and hygiene to teachers at elementary schools whose pupils would face questions on these subjects in the Department of Science and Art's examinations. Newsholme wrote his first books to exploit this market; *Hygiene: a Manual of Personal and Public Health* (1884), *School Hygiene: the Laws of Health in Relation to School Life* (1887), and *Lessons on Health: Containing the Elements of Physiology and their Application to Hygiene* (1890) all sold very well and went through several editions. In 1884 he became part-time medical officer of health (MOH) for Clapham and earned his diploma in public health from London University the following year. He was not formally trained in vital statistics or epidemiology. He learned these subjects in his years at Clapham by studying the annual reports of William Farr and John Simon. Newsholme soon prepared a practical textbook on vital statistics. *The Elements of Vital Statistics* (1889) became a standard textbook for medical officers of health and was issued in a revised edition as late as 1923.

Newsholme made public health his sole occupation in May 1888, when he was appointed full-time MOH for Brighton. During his twenty years in the town he built a model local authority public health programme—first by more rigorously pursuing established preventive strategies in environmental sanitation and in inspection of meat and food; and then by expanding the work of the sanitary department into newer areas: the prevention of infant diarrhoea, housing reform, the notification of infectious diseases and case tracing, and a much expanded use of hospital isolation of infectious diseases. His best-known work in Brighton was probably the tuberculosis programme he helped to develop, which relied on voluntary notification of cases and municipally financed institutional treatment. Between 1905 and 1908 Newsholme published a series of studies on the epidemiology of tuberculosis, which culminated in his monograph, *The Prevention of Tuberculosis* (1908). In this work he attempted to show that institutional segregation of those suffering from pulmonary tuberculosis, most often in poor-law institutions, was the prime reason for the decline in tuberculosis mortality. While in Brighton, Newsholme also undertook important epidemiological studies of scarlet fever, diphtheria, epidemic diarrhoea, and rheumatic fever. His studies of the latter three diseases in the middle and late 1890s attempted to identify environmental factors which could account for the epidemic pattern of these diseases which, he was convinced, contagion alone could not explain. His investigation of scarlet fever not only helped to clarify the etiology of this puzzling disease, it also led to a highly effective municipal system of surveillance and response to milk-borne outbreaks of the illness.

In February 1908 Newsholme became the medical officer of the Local Government Board, a position he held until 1919. He was thus the central health authority's medical adviser during a period that saw important changes in the nation's health programmes: national health insurance was initiated and national programmes were established to combat tuberculosis, venereal disease, and infant mortality. Newsholme opposed important portions of Lloyd George's National Insurance Bill, fearing that they would compromise public health work in local authorities, particularly on tuberculosis. Between 1909 and 1913 he was the major force behind the orders from the Local Government Board that required the notification of tuberculosis cases and that encouraged local authorities to take steps to prevent the disease. Newsholme also played an important role in designing and implementing the venereal disease service that was hastily put in place following the final report of the royal commission on venereal disease in February 1916. His most important epidemiological studies at the Local Government Board were his five reports of infant, childhood, and maternal mortality, which appeared between 1910 and 1916 as supplements to his annual reports. These were the most comprehensive empirical studies of these subjects in English to date. By the time the final report appeared, the Local Government Board was locked in bitter competition with the Board of Education for the control of the nation's emerging programme to promote infant and child health. Newsholme resigned in March 1919 to avoid serving in the new Ministry of Health under his rival in this conflict, George Newman, chief medical officer of the Board of Education.

Newsholme had a very active retirement: he lectured on public health administration at the newly created School of Hygiene and Public Health at Johns Hopkins University between 1919 and 1921; he wrote and delivered public addresses on a variety of public health topics on both sides of the Atlantic; and he undertook for the Milbank Fund a major study of European health-care systems. His three-volume series, *International Studies on the Relation between the Private and Official Practice of Medicine* (1931), presented a detailed description of conditions in individual nations, whereas his *Medicine and the State: the Relation between the Private and Official Practice of Medicine* (1932) offered a synthesized discussion accessible to a more general reader. In August and September 1932, Newsholme visited the Soviet Union with John Kingsbury, secretary of the Milbank Fund. The result was their book, *Red Medicine: Socialized Health in Soviet Russia* (1933). In his remaining ten years of life Newsholme wrote a two-volume autobiographical history of public health, *Fifty Years in Public Health* (1935) and *The Last Thirty Years in Public Health* (1936). He was widowed in 1933 and then suffered a lengthy decline in his own health. He died on 17 May 1943 at his home, the White House, Durrington, Worthing, Sussex, at the age of eighty-six.

Newsholme was a prolific writer. His bibliography contains twenty-five book titles, several of which appeared in subsequent editions, over 160 articles and book chapters, some three dozen annual reports and supplemental reports, and numerous pamphlets. He was a leading figure in the public health world, serving as a council member of the Society of Medical Officers of Health, as president of the society (1900–01), and twice as editor of its journal, *Public Health* (1892–6 and 1906–8). He was a regular examiner for the diploma of public health at London, Oxford, and Cambridge universities. He became a member of the Royal College of Physicians in 1893, served as the college's Milroy lecturer in 1895, and became a fellow in 1898. In 1907 he was president of both the Royal Society of Medicine's section on epidemiology and the British Medical Association's section on state medicine. In 1912 he was made CB, and in 1919 advanced to KCB.

JOHN M. EYLER

Sources J. M. Eyler, *Sir Arthur Newsholme and state medicine, 1885–1935* (1997) · *DNB* · A. Newsholme, *Fifty years in public health: a personal narrative with comments* (1935) · A. Newsholme, *The last thirty years in public health: recollections and reflections on my official and post-official life* (1936) · J. M. Eyler, 'The sick poor and the state: Arthur Newsholme on poverty, disease, and responsibility', *Framing disease: studies in cultural history*, ed. C. Rosenberg and J. Golden (1992), 275–96 · J. M. Eyler, 'Policing the food trades: epidemiology, hygiene, and public administration in Edwardian Brighton', *History of hygiene: proceedings of the twelfth International Symposium on the Comparative History of Medicine—East and West*, ed. Y. Kawakita, S. Sakai, and Y. Otsuka (1991), 193–225 · J. M. Eyler, 'The epidemiology of milk-borne scarlet-fever: the case of Edwardian Brighton', *American Journal of Public Health*, 76 (1986), 573–84 · *BMJ* (29 May 1943), 680–81 · *The Lancet* (29 May 1943), 696 · *CGPLA Eng. & Wales* (1943)
Likenesses W. Stoneman, photograph, 1919, NPG · H. J. Whitlock and Son, photograph, 1931 (with Mrs Newsholme), Wellcome L.
Wealth at death £10,790 14s. 5d.: probate, 14 Aug 1943, *CGPLA Eng. & Wales*

Newsom, Sir John Hubert (1910–1971), educationist, was born in Glasgow on 8 June 1910, the elder son (there were no daughters) of Hubert Nash Newsom and his wife, Dorothy Elliott. His brother died young. His father, having served as an army officer in South Africa, held various administrative jobs in India, Britain, and Ireland. John Newsom, after attending schools in England, Scotland, and Ireland, went to the Imperial Service College from 1924 to 1928 from where he won a scholarship to the Queen's College, Oxford. He went down in 1931 with a second in philosophy, politics, and economics. The same year he married Barbara Joan, daughter of Louis Day, who worked in the building industry; they had one son and one daughter.

Between 1931 and 1938 Newsom was engaged in social work in the London area, the midlands, and the northeast. His interest in social service began while at Oxford; he had no income but his scholarship and he supported himself by unskilled work in the East End of London during vacations, living in lodging-houses and rented rooms. This pre-Orwellian experience gave rise to a remarkable book, written when he was only nineteen and published in 1930 by his friend Basil Blackwell under the title *On the Other Side*.

Newsom's main work in education began in 1939 when he was appointed deputy county education officer for

Sir John Hubert Newsom (1910–1971), by Walter Bird, 1964

Hertfordshire, having arrived in the county in 1938 in connection with Home Office plans for civil defence and evacuation. In 1940, still only twenty-nine, he became county education officer, a post he held until 1957.

During this time Hertfordshire became a leading education authority with, in particular, a national and international reputation for school building. Newsom had little administrative and no schoolteaching experience but he had flair and enthusiasm and an individual style which permeated his administration. He was a skilled manipulator inside county hall: his close relationship with R. S. McDougall, county treasurer, helped forward the rapid and costly expansion of the education service. Between them they devised a way of decentralizing control of much day-to-day spending—each head had a budget, cheque book, and bank account. Critics disputed how much real difference this made: heads welcomed it and the vote of confidence it signified.

With a large influx of population to London county council housing estates and three new towns, Hertfordshire's school building needs were great. The secret of Hertfordshire's success in this field was the close co-operation between C. H. Aslin, the county architect, and Stirrat Johnson-Marshall, his deputy, and Newsom and his deputy, Sidney Broad. The moving spirit was Johnson-Marshall, who overcame the shortage of building materials and labour by prefabricated methods, and (more important) insisted on a new and creative relationship between the architects and the educators. Newsom instinctively responded and encouraged his staff to do so too. Newsom had early come to the belief that good education deserved the best physical environment. He wanted children to encounter original works of art and persuaded Hertfordshire to build up a collection, which included work by Barbara Hepworth, Henry Moore, and Ben Nicholson, among many others. For many years the contract for each new school included provision for a mural or a piece of sculpture. But before Newsom departed the philistines had whittled away at the budget and the policy was abandoned. In 1954 he was appointed CBE.

In 1957 Newsom resigned on health grounds and joined the board of Longmans, Green & Co. Ltd, the educational publishers. It was intended to reduce his workload but in the event the respite was brief. On the death of a colleague he found himself in the managing director's chair. Newsom never became an expert publisher, but he knew a lot about running a big organization and he cheerfully applied to Longmans the arts he had learned in local government.

In 1961 Newsom joined the Central Advisory Council for Education (England) as deputy chairman to Viscount Amory—who was promptly sent to Canada as governor-general—and it fell to Newsom to conduct the inquiry into the education of children of average and below average ability which resulted in *Half our Future* (the Newsom report) in 1963.

The report was compassionate and practical. It showed Newsom's concern for social disadvantage, and it located education's opportunities and limitations within the complex of social and economic forces at work in English cities. The concerted policies it advocated were taken up again by the Central Advisory Council in Lady Plowden's report on primary education (1967), when Newsom served as deputy chairman, and in the community development policies subsequently adopted by the Department of the Environment, but the large resources needed to make a reality of educational priority areas were never forthcoming. In 1964 Newsom's services were recognized by the award of a knighthood.

From 1966 to 1968 Newsom was chairman of the Public Schools Commission set up by the first administration of Harold Wilson. The commission's task was unsatisfactory from the start: it was to serve as a substitute for action; to keep an election promise, not to formulate policy. Its suggested ways of integrating the public schools with the maintained sector were never seriously considered and its useful study of 'boarding need' was largely ignored. Newsom took it philosophically but he was aware that he had been used and did not enjoy the experience.

Among Newsom's many other interests were various committees and institutions connected with the arts. He was a member of the Arts Council from 1953 to 1957. He was a vice-chairman of the National Youth Orchestra, a governor of the Royal College of Art, the British Film Institute, Haileybury and the Imperial Service College, and St Edmund's College, Ware, an honorary fellow of Queen's College, Oxford (1969), and an honorary FRIBA. He

received an honorary LLD from the University of Pennsylvania. In 1964 he became the first chairman of the Independent Television Authority's education advisory council. He served on government committees on colonial education, public libraries, and charitable trusts. From 1966 to the time of his death he was chairman of the Harlow Development Corporation. He was made an officer of the Légion d'honneur in recognition of a brief period of secret service in Europe on secondment from Hertfordshire at the end of the war.

A fluent and combative writer and broadcaster, Newsom's best known book was *The Education of Girls* (1948) in which he argued the unfashionable case for more emphasis on home making and the domestic arts.

Newsom's inner seriousness was combined with a cheerful and amusing manner. Brought up an Anglican, he became an agnostic for a time, before joining the Roman Catholic church in 1946. His deep humanitarian ideals never dimmed the mischievous sense of humour which made him excellent company. He was a good cook; given to hospitality, interested in all around him, especially young people with their way to make. Even his little weaknesses had charm. He clearly loved being an establishment figure, knowing the top people, and being in the know, while retaining somewhere at the back of it all a radical commitment to those social and religious values which had once made him throw in his lot with those *On the Other Side*. He died at Sawbridgeworth, Hertfordshire, on 23 May 1971.   STUART MACLURE, *rev.*

Sources *The Times* (24 May 1971) · private information (1986) [M. Ollis] · personal knowledge (1986) · *CGPLA Eng. & Wales* (1971)
Likenesses W. Bird, photograph, 1964, NPG [*see illus.*]
Wealth at death £17,536: probate, 8 Sept 1971, *CGPLA Eng. & Wales*

Newsome, James (1824–1912), equestrian performer and circus proprietor, the son of Christopher and Mary Newsome, was baptized in Newcastle upon Tyne on 1 June 1824. His elder brother, Timothy (1813–1890), was a celebrated lion tamer. James was indentured to William Batty, the lessee of Astley's Amphitheatre, London, in 1836, and became famous as a horse tamer, trainer, and trick rider. He was a great favourite with circus audiences both in London and the provinces.

On 17 May 1846 Newsome married Pauline Hinné [**Pauline Newsome** (*c.*1825–1904)], an equestrian performer with whom he sometimes rode in double acts. Hinné was a member of a famous French circus family, the fourth daughter of Johann Hinné and his wife, Franzisca, *née* Zinsberger, and was born in Berlin. She travelled to Britain with her family about 1845 and became principal dancer on horseback at Astley's. Following their marriage, the couple sought their fortunes abroad and spent six years with Franconi's Cirque Olympique at Paris, where Newsome was engaged as principal horseman. Afterwards the Newsomes visited Belgium and Germany, and returned to England late in 1852 with their three daughters, Adelaide, Emma, and Marie. Three more daughters, Ella, Pauline, and Virginie, were born in Britain. The Newsomes initially joined Hernandez and Stone's circus, with whom James

Newsome went into partnership in 1854–5. He became a partner with Pablo Fanque for the 1855–6 season.

In 1853 Pauline Newsome toured for the season as 'Madame Pauline Newsome's French Troupe', and repeated the experience in 1856. By 1859 Newsome's circus was established. The company travelled the country, staying several weeks or months at each venue, and using specially erected buildings rather than tents. The family prospered; Madame Newsome directed the business arrangements of the circus, while her husband was horse trainer and equestrian director. All six of the Newsome daughters were equestrian performers, and were noted in the hunting field as well as in the ring.

A fire at their circus in Edinburgh in 1887 causing damage estimated at £7000 brought about a change in the family's fortunes, and they were forced to sell up in 1889 after a poor season in Sunderland. The family dispersed to other circuses, and eventually Pauline and James Newsome retired to Cleethorpes, where they lived near their daughter Virginie, who was now married. Pauline Newsome died there on 25 September 1904; James Newsome survived her until 1 January 1912. They were both buried in the Beacon Avenue cemetery, Cleethorpes.

JOHN M. TURNER

Sources T. Frost, *Circus life and circus celebrities* (1875) • *The Bailie* (1 Jan 1879) • *World's Fair* (10 June 1911) • *World's Fair* (6 Jan 1912) • *World's Fair* (20 Jan 1918) • *World's Fair* (10 Dec 1927) • *Newcastle Daily Chronicle* (2 Jan 1812) • *Grimsby Daily Telegraph* (3 Jan 1912) • *Grimsby News* (9 Jan 1912) • *Edinburgh Courant* (16 Sept 1879) • J. W. MacLaren, *Edinburgh memories and some worthies* (1926) • *Era Annual* (1913) • G. Speaight, *A history of the circus* (1980) • A. Enevig, *Cirkus Hinné* (Odense, 1992) [P. Hinné] • *Grimsby News* (28 Sept 1904) [Pauline Hinné] • *Newcastle Daily Chronicle* (5 June 1866) • *Era Almanack and Annual* (1905) [Pauline Hinné] • *Bradford Observer* (11 Oct 1866) [Pauline Hinné]
Likenesses W. Cooper, photograph (Pauline Hinné), repro. in Enevig, *Cirkus Hinné* • engraving, repro. in *The Bailie*, 324 • photograph, repro. in *The Eastern Daily Telegraph*

Newsome, Noël Francis (1906–1976), broadcasting executive, was born on 25 December 1906 in Pill St George, Somerset, the younger child and only son of Herbert Newsome, a country doctor, and his wife, Christine Marguerite, daughter of William Gibbs, owner of a hardware shop, of Redditch, Worcestershire. He was educated at Oundle School and won an exhibition to Magdalen College, Oxford, where he was awarded a first in modern history in 1928. He then joined the *Bristol Times and Mirror* before moving to the *Bristol Evening Times* in 1930, as a sub-editor. When the paper ceased publication early in 1932 he helped to launch the *Bristol Evening Post*, and acted as foreign editor until December 1932, when he joined the *Daily Telegraph* as a sub-editor and leader writer. On 22 October 1932 he married Pauline Astbury (b. c.1905), of Barnt Green, near Birmingham, daughter of an engineer; they had one son. Early in 1934 Newsome went to Kuala Lumpur to be assistant editor of the *Malay Mail*, and started a daily column under the title 'The man in the street', in which he gave his opinions on the news of the day, but his views were deemed too radical for the readership. He was

also made Malayan correspondent of the London *Daily Mail*. In November 1935 he sailed for England to rejoin the *Daily Telegraph*, as a foreign news sub-editor, and by the end of 1936 he was in charge of the foreign news pages, in which he made clear his opposition to appeasement.

On 1 September 1939 Newsome was appointed to the BBC as assistant, overseas news, and in December was made European news editor, in charge of the central news desk. From the start he saw the role of the BBC in Europe as part of the propaganda effort to win the war, acting as a reliable news service: 'all news and views … must … serve the one real and fundamental propagandist aim of helping us to win this war as rapidly as possible' (N. F. Newsome, notes for European sub-editors, 12 Feb 1940, BBC WAC). Convinced that the presentation of news must be accurate, he protested in June 1940 when the European news service was given information about the Norwegian campaign that was deliberately intended to be misleading, as he was afraid that this might have damaged the BBC's reputation abroad for reliability. He thought that all foreign-language news broadcasts should give the same version of the news, and to this end he issued daily directives to the foreign-language news editors, who then compiled their own bulletins. In addition from spring 1941 he became known to millions of listeners as 'the man in the street', broadcasting several times a week for over three years as part of the news service in English to Europe: talks that were translated into other languages and heard all over Europe. These broadcasts were made on his own initiative. Inspired by hatred of the Nazis and a passionate belief in England as the liberator of Europe, he tried to convey the views of British citizens on the news of the day. Though never a communist he felt great admiration for the Soviet Union. His second wife edited a volume of his talks: *'The Man in the Street' Talks to Europe* (1945).

The BBC European service moved to Bush House, in the Strand, in March 1941, and after the overseas service was reorganized and a separate European division created Newsome was appointed to the new post of director of European broadcasts in December 1941. The controller of the European division, Ivone Kirkpatrick, reorganized the service into separate foreign-language sections, each with its own editor responsible for all output in that language. Newsome continued his daily directives and weekly notes, and his daily news conferences, managing to retain a considerable degree of independence from the government's political warfare executive (PWE), based at Woburn Abbey, which was supposed to guide the policy of the BBC European service. But some heads of the regional sections, which numbered twenty-two by the end of 1942, ignored his directives. Hugh Carleton Greene, head of the German section, and Darsie Gillie, head of the French section, in particular disliked Newsome's approach, and disliked being told what to do. They thought that the selection of news should be relevant to the country to which it was being addressed, and they thought Newsome ignorant and misguided: it was 'one of our contributions to the war effort to see that no traces of Newsome's directives were ever seen' (Tracey, 78). There was a continuous struggle between Newsome and the regional editors as Newsome tried to ensure that the European service acted as an entity: he complained that some editors followed their own line, acting as 'a series of guerrilla bands or groups of partisans' (directive of 18 June 1942, BBC WAC). He worried that although the central news desk was supplying them with excellent material much of its output was not being used. But Newsome's optimism and enthusiasm were important in the early years of the war, when most of the news was bad news, and his confidence in Britain's ultimate victory helped to keep hope alive in the occupied countries.

In 1942 Newsome and his first wife divorced, and in July he married Shiela Grant Duff (b. 1913), granddaughter of Sir Mountstuart Elphinstone Grant Duff (1829–1906) and daughter of Lieutenant-Colonel Adrian Grant Duff (1869–1914) and his wife, Ursula, daughter of John Lubbock, first Baron Avebury. A foreign correspondent in the 1930s, she set up the Czech section of the BBC European service in 1942, and in that year published *A German Protectorate: the Czechs under Nazi Rule*. They had one daughter but were divorced, in the mid-1950s. On 23 April 1955 Newsome married, as his third wife, Barbara (b. 1927/8), daughter of Ralph Harry Rowberry, cabinet-maker, with whom he had two sons and one daughter.

Newsome was awarded the OBE in 1943, but after the D-day landings there was less need for his crusading spirit at the BBC, and in October 1944 he was seconded as chief of the radio section of the psychological warfare division (PWD) of the Supreme Headquarters Allied Expeditionary Force (SHAEF), where he worked from Radio Luxemburg. He resigned from the BBC in May 1945 and unsuccessfully contested the seat of Penrith and Cockermouth in the general election, as the Liberal candidate; he was chairman of the committee that advised on the reconstruction of the Liberal Party in 1945. He edited *Europe* (1944) and *Europe Liberated* (1945), two issues in magazine form of what was intended to become a series, with the aim of furthering the cause of a united Europe.

In December 1945, after a few months working as a political correspondent for the *News of the World*, Newsome was appointed the first director of recruitment at the Ministry of Fuel and Power, with the task of attracting young men into the coalmines. He moved to the National Coal Board in September 1947 to set up and direct the public relations department, and when he resigned in May 1948 he went to Harry Ferguson Ltd, tractor manufacturer, as public relations officer. He later became a director of Harry Ferguson Research Ltd, in Coventry. On behalf of Harry Ferguson he preached the need for the adoption of Ferguson's price-reducing scheme and the mechanization of world agriculture, as part of the fight against world hunger. Another crusade, again inspired by Ferguson, concerned road safety, and he urged the adoption of the Ferguson formula for all-wheel-control (four-wheel drive) for motor vehicles. Newsome also campaigned on environmental issues. He became the first chairman of the Warwickshire branch of the Conservation Society, in

1971, and was chosen 'Midland man of the year' by the media in 1972, after he had exposed the indiscriminate dumping of cyanide waste in the midlands. He campaigned against the building of the M40 motorway in 1973, and helped to organize the national War on Waste conference and exhibition in 1975.

Newsome died on 1 May 1976 in Warwick Hospital; his body was cremated. He was survived by his wife, Barbara.

ANNE PIMLOTT BAKER

Sources M. Stenton, *Radio London and resistance in occupied Europe* (2000) · A. Briggs, *The history of broadcasting in the United Kingdom*, rev. edn, 3 (1995) · G. Mansell, *Let truth be told: fifty years of BBC external broadcasting* (1982) · BBC WAC · M. Tracey, *A variety of lives: a biography of Sir Hugh Greene* (1983), 71–88 · H. Grisewood, *One thing at a time* (1968), 131–51 · N. Newsome, 'Galley proof to microphone', *British Evening Post* (30 Dec 1942) · *A noble combat: the letters of Shiela Grant Duff and Adam von Trott zu Solz*, ed. K. von Klemperer (1988) · Burke, *Gen. GB* (1952) · *The Times* (10 May 1976) · *The Times* (18 May 1976) · *Daily Telegraph* (3 May 1976) · CAC Cam., Newsome papers [incl. unpubd transcript of first vol. of his autobiography, 'Haunting spectre', 1968] · C. Fraser, *Harry Ferguson* (1972) · b. cert. · m. cert. [B. Rowberry] · d. cert.
Archives BBC WAC, texts of daily directives · CAC Cam., corresp. and papers
Likenesses photograph, 1943, Hult. Arch. · photograph, repro. in Newsome, 'Galley proof to microphone' · photograph, repro. in *Evening News* (28 Dec 1945)
Wealth at death £10,460: probate, 1976, CGPLA Eng. & Wales

Newsome, Pauline (c.1825–1904). *See under* Newsome, James (1824–1912).

Newsome, Stella Winifred (1889–1969), women's activist, was born on 28 July 1889 at 3 Museum Terrace, Leicester, the daughter of George Newsome (1841–1909), wholesale grocer, and his wife, Caroline Louisa Rice (b. 1859). Little is known of her childhood and education, though by profession she was a schoolteacher. Newsome's life was shaped by her twin commitment to campaigning for women's equality and creating a historic record of feminist activity. She became involved in the Leicester branch of the Women's Social and Political Union (WSPU) about 1911. Under the direction of its local organizer, Margaret West, she took part in militant activities, setting light to pillar boxes and raiding golf courses. Like other members of the WSPU she was angered by the halt to suffrage activity during the First World War and disapproved of Christabel Pankhurst's jingoism. As a result she left the union.

About 1916 Newsome moved to London and may have worked with the Borough branch of the United Suffragists. She went on to join the Women's Freedom League, and became secretary to its mid-London branch. In the 1930s she served on its executive committee, and between 1954 and 1958 was honorary secretary to the organization. After the extension of the franchise in 1918 Newsome campaigned to secure a new position for women based on economic and social equality. In November 1920 the National Federation of Women Teachers called a demonstration on the issue of equal pay for equal work: Newsome was a member and, in the run-up to the march, spoke on the issue to London women's organizations. She was not a high-profile activist, but worked hard behind the scenes. For many years she was an executive member of the Six Point Group, and focused particularly on broadening the educational opportunities of girls.

From the mid-1940s to her death, Newsome was secretary to the Suffragette Fellowship and effectively its archivist. She placed high value on documenting the movement and commemorating its participants. In 1954, with Edith How-Martyn and Elsa Gye, she compiled the commemorative roll of honour to suffragette prisoners. She was secretary to the Pethick-Lawrence Portrait Fund, and contributed many suffragette obituaries to *Calling All Women*—the fellowship's journal. As part of the celebrations marking the fiftieth anniversary of the Women's Freedom League she wrote an account of its history: *Women's Freedom League, 1907–1957* (1957).

Newsome was active right up until her premature death. Shortly after the fellowship celebrated her eightieth birthday she was involved in a road accident from which she never regained consciousness. She died unmarried on 11 November 1969 at her home, 26 West End Lane, West Hampstead, London, and was cremated at Golders Green on 24 November.   GAIL CAMERON

Sources *Calling All Women* (Feb 1970) · *Hampstead and Highgate Express and News* (21 Nov 1969) · M. Pugh, *Women and the women's movement in Britain, 1914–1959* (1992) · *Votes For Women*, 4th ser., 9/432 (Dec 1916), 232 · *Votes For Women*, 4th ser., 9/436 (Feb 1918), 336 · *The Vote*, 21/574 (22 Oct 1920), 239 · 'Trafalgar Square meeting', *The Vote*, 21/577 (12 Nov 1920), 259 · *CGPLA Eng. & Wales* (1971) · b. cert.
Archives Museum of London, London, Suffragette Fellowship collection · Museum of London, London, David Mitchell collection [78.83/51]
Wealth at death £228: probate, 14 May 1971, *CGPLA Eng. & Wales*

Newstead, Christopher (1597–1660x63), Church of England clergyman, was baptized on 13 November 1597, one of four sons of Robert Newstead (*d.* 1611/12) of South Somercotes, Lincolnshire, and his wife, Jane (*d.* in or after 1611), daughter of George Lacon of Coates. He matriculated from St Alban Hall, Oxford, on 22 November 1616, when he was described as 'aged eighteen', but there is no record of his graduation, although he has been linked with the 'son of Thomas' Newstead who proceeded BD on 21 April 1631. In 1620, in answer to Joseph Swetnam's *The Arraignment of Lewd, Idle, Froward and Unconstant Women*, he published *An Apology for Women, or, Womens Defense*, with a preface addressed to Mary Villiers, countess of Buckingham. It observes that 'men were more perfect by nature, but women by industry … Eve then tempted Adam, but now Adame tempts Eve' (p. 3), and argues that women are often more pious and chaste than men, and outdo them in fortitude and loyalty in love.

Between 1621 and 1628 Newstead acted as chaplain to Sir Thomas Roe, during the latter's embassy to Constantinople. Shortly after his return to England, and on the deprivation of Edmund Rood, he was presented by the crown to the vicarage of St Helen, Abingdon, Berkshire. Inducted on 20 June 1629, he became at the same time *ex officio* vicar of the town's other parish of St Nicholas, until in May 1635 John Stone became vicar there. On 3 September 1631 Newstead was licensed to marry Mary (*d.* 1645x50), daughter of Anthony Fulhurst of Great Oxenden, Northamptonshire. By February 1640, when Edmund

Rood was reinstated, Newstead had resigned from St Helen's; it was later alleged (1644) that this was in order to escape defending a suit brought against him by parishioners who claimed, among other complaints, that he had ejected Rood's children from their home while their parents were absent.

In 1642 Newstead, who through Sir Thomas Roe's influence was Archbishop William Laud's preferred candidate for the vacant living of Stisted, Essex, became embroiled in disputes over the exercise of patronage in the county. Rival candidates temporarily prevailed, but on 23 May 1643 Newstead was appointed to Stisted by the House of Lords. Newstead's eventual arrival in the parish provoked violent resistance. On 16 June 1643 he complained to the Lords 'that women threw stones at him and reviled him and his friends' and that he had been prevented from entering the church (*JHL*, 6.97b). On 20 March 1644 Newstead was charged by the Essex committee against scandalous ministers (supervised by the earl of Manchester) with fourteen articles; there were reports about his ministry at Abingdon, and it was alleged that while at Stisted he had promoted ceremonies distasted by the parishioners and buried many bodies with crosses on their breasts. He had refused to take the covenant himself, but administered it to others.

Newstead was sequestered from Stisted, but on 24 July 1645 the committee for plundered ministers granted a fifth of the rectorial income to his wife, Mary. Within a few years she had died, and Newstead married on 8 January 1651 at St Peter-le-Poer, London, Mary Etherege, *née* Powney (*bap.* 1612, *d.* 1699), of Maidenhead, widow of Captain George Etherege (*d.* 1650) and mother of the playwright George Etherege. Newstead had been appointed by the committee for plundered ministers as a preacher in Maidenhead before 29 August 1650, for on that date he petitioned the committee for compounding to be allowed time for the payment of his own composition. This depended upon his claim for £800 upon the sequestered estates of his nephew Robert Newstead, the son and heir of his eldest brother, Herbert (*d.* 1641/2), who may have been a captain in the royalist army, imprisoned at the fall of Newark, and who had compounded for his delinquency in 1646. On 7 February 1655 Newstead petitioned again, complaining that he had been awarded an augmentation of £50 p.a. for the chapel of St Mary the Virgin in the parish of Bray with Maidenhead, but had lost the place because the Triers refused to approve him in view of his earlier sequestration at Stisted. Three ministers, Philip Nye, Nicholas Lockier, and Peter Sterry, were appointed to enquire into his loyalty to the state and his fitness to preach. On 15 July 1656, despite his having acquired certificates from Major-General Goffe and the commissioners for Berkshire, three more ministers were deputed to make enquiries. And on 18 August 1657 Nye and yet another three ministers were instructed 'to speak with Mr Newstead and certify concerning his fitness to be restored to his ministrations there' (*CSP dom.*, 1657–8, 69). Whether Newstead was ever reinstated at Maidenhead is uncertain, but he was restored at Stisted in 1660. On 25 August 1660

Newstead was collated to the prebend of Caddington minor, in the cathedral of St Paul's; he was dead before the collation of his successor, Robert Breton, on 7 March 1663.   STEPHEN WRIGHT

Sources *Walker rev.* · Foster, *Alum. Oxon.* · *JHL*, 5–6 (1642–4) · *JHC*, 3 (1642–4) · M. A. E. Green, ed., *Calendar of the proceedings of the committee for compounding … 1643–1660*, 5 vols., PRO (1889–92) · M. A. E. Green, ed., *Calendar of the proceedings of the committee for advance of money, 1642–1656*, 3 vols., PRO (1888) · *CSP dom.*, 1655–8 · A. R. Maddison, ed., *Lincolnshire pedigrees*, 2, Harleian Society, 51 (1903) · A. E. Preston, *The church and parish of St Nicholas, Abingdon: the early grammar school, to end of sixteenth century*, OHS, 99 (1935) · BL, Add. MS 5829, fols. 18–21 · Wood, *Ath. Oxon.*, new edn · *Fasti Angl., 1541–1857*, [St Paul's, London] · *Letters of Sir George Etherege*, ed. F. Bracher (1974) · IGI

Newte, John (1656–1716), Church of England clergyman, was born on 15 January 1656 and baptized at home six days later at Ottery St Mary, Devon, the son of Richard *Newte (*bap.* 1613, *d.* 1678) and his wife, Thomasine (*d.* c.1679/80), daughter of Humphrey Trowbridge (or Trobridge) of Crediton. His father had been sent by the triers to Ottery St Mary as lecturer after he had been deprived of the rectory of the Clare and Tidcombe portions of the parish of St Peter's, Tiverton. In December 1656 Richard Newte was admitted as rector of Heanton Punchardon, near Barnstaple, until the Restoration enabled him to return to Tiverton. The memory of the travails of the father (recounted in John Walker's *Sufferings of the Clergy* from the information provided by John) doubtless shaped the highchurch and tory attitudes of the son.

John Newte was educated at Blundell's School, Tiverton, Exeter College, Oxford (where he matriculated on 12 July 1672), and Balliol College, Oxford, having been appointed to the fellowship reserved for former members of Blundell's in 1676. He graduated BA in 1676 and MA in 1679. He was incorporated into Cambridge in 1681, possibly with a view to pursuing his studies there, but the duties of church and parish claimed him for the rest of his life.

Newte was ordained deacon at Michaelmas 1678. His mother presented him to the rectory of Tidcombe portion, Tiverton, on 5 February 1679 on an archiepiscopal dispensation for his institution at so young an age. He was ordained priest on 8 October 1679. Shortly afterwards he was appointed a chaplain to the king and on 5 March 1680 his elder brother, Richard, presented him to be rector of Pitt portion, Tiverton, with a second archiepiscopal dispensation to hold in plurality with Tidcombe. With the stipends of two portions and income from land acquired either by inheritance or through marriage John was financially secure. He married Edith, daughter of William Bone of Faringdon. Their only child, Mary, predeceased them, and Edith died 13 February 1705.

The best indicator of Newte's devotion to his parish duties lies in the gifts he made, the duties he undertook in life, and the bequests he made in his will. Examples are the personal care he gave to the country chapel of Cove; the £100 he donated towards building the chapel of St George, Tiverton, the foundation stone of which he laid on 5 December 1714; and his involvement first as deputy governor and then as governor of Tiverton Hospital. His most remarkable bequest was to the poor of St Sidwell's, Exeter, to pay for bibles, prayer books, and two specified books of devotion (Richard Allestree's *The Whole Duty of Man* and Robert Nelson's *The Practice of True Devotion*). After the life interest of two named relatives expired, he left land to Balliol College to found an exhibition for a scholar at Blundell's School.

In Newte the Society for the Propagation of Christian Knowledge (1699) had an enthusiastic supporter. He founded a small charity school in 1701 at his own expense and by 1713 more than 100 poor children were being clothed and educated in schools he had founded. He left land with which to found charity schools in Cove and Cullompton. He is best remembered for raising the money, despite dissenting opposition, to install an organ in St Peter's, Tiverton, in 1696—thought to be the first in a parish church in the west of England. He preached and published a sermon justifying the use of music in worship, which was attacked in print in 1698. This drew forth a learned response from the nonjuror Henry Dodwell the elder vindicating Newte. The only other piece Newte published was a sermon on the religious duty of paying tithes and the impiety of withholding them (1711), occasioned perhaps by the legal victory of the owners of a new horse malt mill in resisting payment.

Newte died at Tidcombe on 7 March 1716, and was buried in St Peter's, Tiverton, five days later. He bequeathed to St Peter's his father's and his own books, in all 250, to found a parochial library, and prints (of 'King Charles the first in his devotionall posture', and of Laud, Strafford, and Montrose) which reflect his tory high-church principles, together with his own portrait, which depicts 'a fresh coloured alert man mouth pursed for an enigmatic smile; a double chin; face sleek and oval' (Chalk, 169); they are still held at the church.   MICHAEL G. SMITH

Sources A. Welsford, 'Mr. Newte's library in St. Peter's Church, Tiverton [2 pts]', *Report and Transactions of the Devonshire Association*, 106 (1974), 17–31; 107 (1975), 11–20 · M. Dunsford, *Historical memoirs of the town and parish of Tiverton in the county of Devon* (1790), 150–53, 207, 287, 288, 293, 331–2, 457 · will, PRO, PROB 11/551, fols. 294v–296v · E. S. Chalk, *A history of the church of St. Peter, Tiverton in the diocese of Exeter* (1905), 45, 66, 142, 169 · A. Warne, *Church and society in eighteenth century Devon* (1969), 55, 132–3 · register of Ottery St Mary, Devon RO, 46/30 PR 6 · Bishop Lamplugh's register, Devon RO, Chanter 25 · Bishop Lamplugh's ordination register, Devon RO, Chanter 51 · register, St Peter's Church, Tiverton, 1711–33, Devon RO [baptism, marriage, burial] · E. H. W. Dunkin and C. Jenkins, eds., *Index to the act books of the archbishops of Canterbury, 1663–1859*, pt 2, British RS, 63 (1938), 121 · Foster, *Alum. Oxon.* · *Walker rev.*

Archives St Peter's Church, Tiverton, Devon, Newte parochial library, MSS

Likenesses M. Vandergucht, line engraving (after T. Foster), NPG · portrait, St Peter's Church, Tiverton, Devon

Wealth at death approx. £5000—valuation of estate left to Balliol College: will, PRO, PROB 11/551, fols. 294v–296v; Dunsford, *Historical memoirs*, 153

Newte, Richard (*bap.* 1613, *d.* 1678), Church of England clergyman, the third son of Henry Newte, the first town clerk of Tiverton after its incorporation in 1615, was baptized on 24 February 1613 at St Peter's, Tiverton. He was educated at Blundell's School and Exeter College, Oxford, where he matriculated in February 1632 and graduated BA in June 1633, MA in May 1636, and was a fellow of the college from 1635 to 1642. He became a domestic chaplain to George Digby, son of the earl of Bristol, in 1641.

Most of Newte's ministry was in the parish of Tiverton which was divided into four portions, three held by rectors and the fourth by King's College, Cambridge. Newte was instituted into the Tidcombe portion on 24 September 1641 and a month later admitted to the Clare portion, the advowson of which was held by his father. According to John Walker (who will have had the story from Richard's son John *Newte) he continued 'a constant Preacher' there for about two years before deciding to travel on the continent with other scholars including Dr Pocock and Dr Lockey (although Pocock's travels, at least, do not match this chronology) (Walker, 2.316). He left Thomas Long, an Oxford pupil of his, in charge of his benefice until he returned in 1646 to find that the war had reduced his parsonage of Clare to ruins as well as four adjoining houses of which he held the leases. Plague was raging in Tiverton and he cared assiduously for his parishioners, even holding services in a field when he found that the people were too fearful of infection to come to church.

Once the danger of plague had passed Newte was subjected to a succession of attacks on his position as rector. The first was the requirement to employ Lewis Stukeley, an Independent, to act with him, and to pay him £100 per annum. Then he was brought before the commission of triers in 1650 and sequestered. In September 1651 he let his portions of Tiverton parish to three clerics for five years for £240 p.a., but he refused to leave his rectory. Attempts were made to drive him out by billeting rough soldiers on him and encouraging a mob to disturb his house at night. Even so he was still termed rector of Tidcombe and Clare when the parish register recorded the baptism of his eldest son on 31 May 1654. (Newte had married Thomasine, daughter of Humphrey Trobridge of Trobridge, near Crediton; they had in all seven sons and three daughters.) Newte had moved to Ottery St Mary before his second son, John, was born there in January 1656. He held a lectureship there worth £20 per annum, a contrast to his Tiverton benefice valued between £300 and £400 per annum. At Ottery he gathered a following from as far afield as Exeter but also opponents who harassed and abused him and caused his dismissal. Then he was presented to the parish of Heanton Punchardon in December 1656 by the royalist Colonel Basset, and enjoyed four peaceful years.

Newte regained Clare and Tidcombe at the Restoration and became chaplain to Lord De La Warr; in 1666 he was appointed chaplain to Charles II though excused attendance at court because of the long distance to travel and also because he suffered from gout. He was offered the deaneries of Salisbury and Exeter but refused them. He died at Tiverton on 10 August 1678 and was buried seven days later in the chancel of St Peter's, Tiverton. His wife outlived him, and he was succeeded as rector of Tidcombe by his son John.   MARY WOLFFE

Sources J. Walker, *An attempt towards recovering an account of the numbers and sufferings of the clergy of the Church of England*, pt 2 (1714), 316–18 · J. Prince, *Danmonii orientales illustres, or, The worthies of Devon* (1701); 2nd edn (1810) · parish register, Tiverton, St Peter's, 24 Feb 1613 [baptism] · parish register, Tiverton, 31 May 1654 [son's baptism] · parish register, Ottery St Mary, Jan 1656 [son's baptism] · parish register, Heanton Punchardon, 1656–60 · parish register, Tiverton, St Peter's, 17 Aug 1678 [burial] · M. Sampson, *A history of Tiverton* [forthcoming] · M. Dunsford, *Historical memoirs of the town and parish of Tiverton* (1790) · W. Harding, *The history of Tiverton*, 2 vols. (1845–7) · E. S. Chalk, *History of St Peter's Church Tiverton* (1905) · Foster, *Alum. Oxon.* · *Fourth report*, HMC, 3 (1874), 2–114, esp. 36 [House of Lords] · *Seventh report*, HMC, 6 (1879), 1–182, esp. 104, 107 [House of Lords] · *DNB* · 'Newte, John', *DNB* · will, PRO, PROB 11/357, sig. 101 · PRO, PROB 11/398, sig. 25 [will of Henry Newte] · *Walker rev.*, 119
Wealth at death everything left to wife; had endowed a fellowship of Balliol College, Oxford, for a Blundell boy in 1676 with £1000: will, PRO, PROB 11/357, sig. 101

Newth, Samuel (1821–1898), college head, was born on 15 February 1821 in the parish of Christchurch, south London, the youngest son of Elisha Newth (c.1775–1858) and his wife, the eldest daughter of J. Killick. His father was an early convert of Rowland Hill (1744–1833), and later served as his assistant minister for nearly thirty years at the Surrey Congregational chapel. Newth's childhood was spent under the sway of distinct religious influences, and he came into contact with all the leading Congregationalists of the time. His father instructed him in Greek, Latin, Hebrew, French, and Italian, after which, in 1837, he entered Coward College. He graduated BA and then MA in the University of London with high mathematical honours, and after ordination settled, in 1842, at Broseley, Shropshire, where for three years he was minister of the Congregational chapel. While there, Newth married the daughter of John Aldridge of Christchurch, Hampshire, on 18 May 1843; they had a large family. In 1845 he was appointed professor of classics and mathematics at Western College, Plymouth, one of the Congregational colleges for training candidates for the ministry. While holding this appointment he published two elementary textbooks on natural philosophy, *The Elements of Statics, Dynamics, and Hydrostatics* (1851) and *A First Book of Natural Philosophy* (1854); their clearness and simplicity of treatment made them standard textbooks.

In 1855 Newth was appointed professor of mathematics and ecclesiastical history at New College, St John's Wood, in north London, another of the Congregational colleges, where he remained until 1889. In 1867 he added the teaching of classics to his other duties, and in 1872 succeeded Robert Halley as principal of the college, holding the post together with the professorships of New Testament exegesis and ecclesiastical history until his resignation in 1889.

Newth's great work lay in the influence which he exerted as principal of New College on the minds of the divinity students who came under his care. Although his rule was strict, he gained their affection and esteem. A careful and accurate scholar, he was appointed in 1870 as a member of the company of New Testament revisers, and he took an active part in the revision which was completed in 1880. He described the work of the revisers, together with a historical sketch of the whole question of biblical translation, in *Lectures on Bible Revision* (1881). He was also the author of numerous articles in the *Cyclopaedia of Biblical Literature*, and edited *Chambers of Imagery* (1876), a series of sermons by his brother, the Revd Alfred Newth, to which he contributed a memoir of the author. In 1875 the degree of DD was conferred upon him by the University of Glasgow, and in 1880 he was elected chairman of the Congregational Union of England and Wales, while he also officiated as chairman of the London Congregational board and organized the Congregational library at the Farringdon Street Memorial Hall. Newth died at his home, 3 Perrhyn Road, Acton, Middlesex, on 29 January 1898.

ARTHUR HARDEN, rev. DAVID HUDDLESTON

Sources *Congregational Year Book* (1899), 62, 195–7 · J. Waddington, *Congregational history*, 5 (1880), 552–6 · *The Times* (31 Jan 1898), 10 · Boase, *Mod. Eng. biog.* · *Nature*, 57 (1897–8), 322 · *ILN* (5 Feb 1898), 177 · A. Peel, *The Congregational two hundred, 1530–1948* (1948)
Archives BL, New Testament revision notes, MSS 36279–36290 · DWL, notebooks, lecture and sermon notes
Likenesses J. Cochran, stipple and line engraving (after photograph by Mayall), NPG · Elliott & Fry, photograph, NPG · oils, DWL · print (after photograph by A. D. Cain), repro. in *Congregational Year Book* · print (after photograph by Russell & Sons), repro. in *ILN*
Wealth at death £6642 1s. 2d.: probate, 5 March 1898, CGPLA Eng. & Wales

Newton. For this title name *see* Oliphant, Sir William, Lord Newton (1550–1628); Legh, Thomas Wodehouse, second Baron Newton (1857–1942).

Newton, Sir Adam, first baronet (d. 1630), royal official, whose parentage is unknown, was a native of Scotland. He graduated MA from the University of Glasgow in 1582. He spent some part of his early life in France, passing himself off as a priest and teaching at the college of St Maixent in Poitou. There, for some time in the 1580s he instructed the theologian André Rivet in Greek. After his return to Scotland Newton was 'professor of laws' in the new University of Edinburgh from 1590 to 1594, when he was ejected. He was appointed tutor in 1599 to Prince Henry, eldest son of James VI. Thomas Birch thought him 'thoroughly qualified … both by his genius, and his skill in the learned and other languages, and was distinguished by the neatness and perspicuity of his Latin style' (Birch, 14). On 26 June 1605 he received a present of gilt plate, weighing 266 oz, on his marriage to Katharine (d. 1618), daughter of Sir John *Puckering, lord keeper of the seal to Elizabeth I in 1592–6, whose son was also a pupil of Newton. In October 1604 Newton had apparently been promised by the king the deanery of Durham, but when it became vacant there was competition for the post and Newton was able to call upon Prince Henry to support his claims. Newton was duly installed as dean on 27 September 1606; he then served as an absentee. In 1607 he purchased the manor of Charlton in Kent for £4500, where between 1607 and 1612 he built a 'goodly brave house' (Philipott, 96). In August 1609 he

received £2000 in lieu of his grant of the privilege of letting certain tenements in the Tower. In 1610 Prince Henry was given a separate household, in which Newton served as his secretary.

Following the death of Prince Henry in November 1612 Newton became receiver-general in the household of Prince Charles, relinquishing to Thomas Murray (1564–1623) his claim to the secretaryship. In June 1613 Newton was one of three men granted a special licence for eleven years to use a new method of 'steeping all kind of corn and grain in a certain liquor' (*Court and Times*, 1.246–51), which was said to improve yields. In 1620 he sold the deanery of Durham, and on 2 April 1620 he was created a baronet. In the same year he translated into Latin the first six books of Pietro Sarpi's history of the Council of Trent, which followed his translation of James I's *Discourse Against Conrade Vorstius*. The accession of Charles I saw Newton appointed secretary to the council, and the death of Fulke Greville, Lord Brooke, in September 1628 saw the reversion of the office of secretary to the marches of Wales (worth £2000 p.a.), which he had gained in 1611, fall to him. Newton died on 13 January 1630 and was buried at Charlton on the following day. He left four daughters, one of whom, Elizabeth (d. after 1658), married Sir Edward *Peyto [see under Peyto family], and one son, Henry, who changed his name to Puckering upon succeeding his uncle Sir Thomas Puckering [see Puckering, Sir Henry].

STUART HANDLEY

Sources GEC, *Baronetage* · will, PRO, PROB 11/158, sig. 112 · *Fasti Angl.* (Hardy), 3.299 · *Hasted's history of Kent: corrected, enlarged, and continued to the present time*, ed. H. H. Drake (1886), 120, 143 · T. Philipott, *Villare Cantianum, or, Kent surveyed and illustrated* (1659), 96 · *The court and times of James the First*, 2 vols. (1848), vol. 1, pp. 246–51 · T. Birch, ed., *The life of Henry, prince of Wales* (1760), 14–15, 66–7, 218, 372 · Mr Des Maizeaux [P. Des Maizeaux], *The dictionary historical and critical of Mr Peter Bayle*, 2nd edn, 3 (1736), 360 · J. Nichols, *The progresses, processions, and magnificent festivities of King James I, his royal consort, family and court*, 1 (1828), 600 · CSP dom., 1603–10, 536; 1611–18, 60, 186 · Calendar of the manuscripts of the most hon. the marquess of Salisbury, 18, HMC, 9 (1940), 29, 141, 279 · private information (2004) [C. J. Fordyce]

Newton, Alfred (1829–1907), zoologist, was born on 11 June 1829 at Les Délices, Geneva, the fifth son in the family of six boys and four girls born to William Newton (1782–1862) of Elveden, Suffolk, plantation owner and MP, and Elizabeth (1789–1843), daughter of Richard Slater Milnes of Fryston, MP for York. The family, of Lincolnshire origin, moved to Elveden in 1813 from their sugar plantations in St Croix in the West Indies, which they retained. William Newton was MP for Ipswich; he was also a JP in Norfolk. Alfred was born as they returned from a holiday in Italy. His closest family relationship was with his younger brother, Edward, who shared his lifelong interest in birds and to whom he wrote almost daily in his adult years. A childhood fall from a table in Elveden Library caused a permanent lameness in Alfred's right leg, necessitating his use of a stick. In 1882 he ruptured the tendon in his left leg and thereafter remained, in his words, 'a four-legged man' (Wollaston, 279–80).

Newton entered Magdalene College, Cambridge, in 1848, won two successive annual English essay prizes, and graduated BA in 1853. Election to the Drury travelling fellowship allowed him ten years of ornithological study. With John Wolley, he visited northern Scandinavia (1855) and went to Iceland (1858) in search of the last nesting place of the great auk. He visited the West Indies and North America in 1857 and Madeira in 1862. In the latter year he abandoned his long-held intention to take holy orders, a decision he never regretted. He was already at the forefront of ornithology, having played a leading role in founding the British Ornithologists' Union (1858) and its journal *Ibis*. He drew attention to Wolley's studies after the latter died in 1859 and began to catalogue the collection of eggs which Wolley bequeathed to him. The first volume of the massive *Ootheca Wolleyana* was published in 1864 but so cautious and painstaking were Newton's working methods that further volumes did not appear until 1902, 1905, and 1907.

In 1864 Newton visited Spitsbergen. Thereafter his travels were confined to summer voyages around the coasts of the British Isles in search of seabirds with Henry Evans. This was largely due to his appointment as professor in the new chair of zoology and comparative anatomy at Cambridge in March 1866; he held this office until his death. At Cambridge he took seriously the task of developing this embryonic discipline into a rigorous science. It is unlikely that a better candidate could have been found. Always resident during term-time, he was prominent in university affairs and greatly expanded the university's zoological museum by his personal patronage. He presented both his own and Wolley's extensive collections of birds' eggs, partly perhaps because the cotton wool in which they were stored aggravated his hay fever. He knew himself to be one of the worst lecturers, reading from notes in a desperately dry fashion (and later appointing William Bateson to lecture for him). However, he encouraged every undergraduate with any interest in natural history and the informal Sunday evening talks in his rooms became a fond memory for many renowned zoologists. Among his plain furniture, threadbare carpets, and drab wallpaper, surrounded by piles of books and papers in which he could readily find any item he sought, he was always ready with a humorous story or with considered advice and opinion given with the admirable clarity of expression which also marked his writings.

Newton contributed to many journals and books, including the article on ornithology in the ninth edition of *Encyclopaedia Britannica*. He edited *Ibis* from 1865 to 1870, after which other work curtailed his active involvement in the British Ornithologists' Union; the *Zoological Record* (1871–3), for which he declined payment, so concerned was he to see it succeed; and volumes 1 and 2 of Yarrell's *British Birds* (1871 and 1882). His methodical insistence on accuracy frustrated the publishers and, refusing to be rushed, he relinquished responsibility for the final two volumes. Preparation of his greatest work was also ponderous but the four-volume *Dictionary of Birds* (1893–6) was a precise, thorough, and succinct exposition of contemporary ornithology.

Newton took particular interest in extinct species such as the dodo and the great auk, and the great bustard which had recently disappeared from Britain, so it was as natural that he should have championed protective legislation as it was that his leadership should have been so level-headed, treading a line between his sympathy for egg collectors and his wariness of misguided sentimentalists. His paper to the British Association at Norwich in 1868 led directly to the first of many protective acts, the 1869 Sea Birds Preservation Act. He served on the council of the British Association and chaired its committee for studying bird migration (1880–1903). He was vice-president of the Zoological Society and the Royal Society, being elected FRS in 1870 and receiving its medal, and that of the Linnean Society, in 1900. He provided the fledgeling Society for the Protection of Birds with its first guinea in 1889.

Despite his two sticks, Newton was noted for his strong, lofty build, alert countenance, and bushy side whiskers. His outward lack of emotion and sometimes grim exterior hid a warm heart and a kind, courteous, and faithful personality with a deep affection for and understanding of others. He disliked untruthfulness and prevarication, and could not abide inaccuracy. He was critical in the best sense of the word. Fiercely independent both in contending with his physical disability and in his thoughts, he was utterly opposed to change in many things, expressing his opinions forcefully, for example, on alterations to dining practices at Magdalene and the introduction into the college chapel of both women and music. Yet he took defeat with grace and good humour and never indulged in subsequent criticism or recrimination. He was perhaps more liberal, though never incautious, in scientific matters. He quickly embraced Darwin's theory of evolution and Michael Foster's experimental methods in physiology. His wisdom and inspiration had a lasting impact on the science of ornithology. He never married. On 7 June 1907, in his rooms in the Old Lodge at Magdalene, his heart failed following a bout of dropsy. He was buried in St Giles's cemetery, Huntingdon Road, Cambridge.

DAVID E. EVANS

Sources A. F. R. Wollaston, *Life of Alfred Newton* (1921) · *DNB* · *The Ibis*, 9th ser., 1 (1907), 623–33 · A. G., *PRS*, 80B (1908), xlv–xlix · private information (2004)

Archives CUL, lecture notes · Magd. Cam., corresp. · U. Cam., department of zoology, corresp. and papers · U. Cam., Museum of Zoology, corresp. and papers | BL, letters to Thomas Rupert Jones, Add. MS 45927 · BL, letters to Henry Scherren, Add. MS 38794 · BL, letters to Alfred Russel Wallace, Add. MSS 46435–46436 · Elgin Museum, letters to George Gordon · Gilbert White Museum, Selborne, Hampshire, Oates Memorial Library, letters to Rashleigh White · NHM, corresp. with Andrew Bloxham · NHM, letters to Albert Gunther · NHM, corresp with Sir Richard Owen and William Clift · NRA, priv. coll., letters to Sir Norman Moore · RBG Kew, letters to William Hooker · Royal Literary and Scientific Institute, Bath, letters to Leonard Blomefield · U. Hull, Brynmor Jones L., letters to John Cordeaux · U. Oxf., Edward Grey Institute of Field Ornithology, letters to Sir Philip Manson Bahr · Wellcome L., letters to Henry Lee

Likenesses C. W. Furse, oils, 1890, U. Cam., department of zoology • L. Dickinson, oils, 1891, Magd. Cam. • R. Faulkner, photograph, repro. in Wollaston, *Life* • C. M. Newton, sketch (*The Professor*), repro. in Wollaston, *Life*

Wealth at death £14,934 15s. 9d.: probate, 2 Aug 1907, CGPLA Eng. & Wales

Newton, Alfred Pizzey (1830–1883), watercolour painter, was born at Rayleigh in Essex. His mother was of Italian descent. Newton became interested in art when he moved to London at the age of fifteen and was apprenticed to Messrs Dickenson, a firm of printsellers and publishers in Bond Street. He subsequently studied watercolour and opened a studio in Maddox Street for pupils during the London season. Newton first exhibited at the Royal Academy in 1855, showing views of the western highlands. Queen Victoria commissioned a drawing for the princess royal's wedding in January 1858, and Newton also made sketches for the queen in the area around Inverlochy Castle in Inverness-shire. In 1858 he was elected an associate of the Old Watercolour Society (OWS); in all, he exhibited 249 drawings with the OWS and five with the Royal Academy. Most of Newton's works were atmospheric highland scenes showing effects of light and weather. It was said that in the severe winter of 1860 he continued with his drawing *Mountain Gloom* despite a frost so intense that he was forced to mix his colours with pure whisky instead of water. This picture was subsequently sent to the Philadelphia exhibition, where Newton was awarded a diploma of merit.

In the 1860s Newton also exhibited drawings of Italian scenes and some English studies, mostly done in Essex—such as *South Benfleet* (V&A)—or in Cheshire and Merseyside. His wife, Jessie, whom he married on 28 April 1864, was the second daughter of Edward Wylie of Rock Ferry, Birkenhead; they had five children and lived in London at 44A Maddox Street, Regent Street. In portraits Newton appears with short dark hair, a full black beard, and a 'southern type of feature' (Roget, 2.417). According to his obituarist in the *Liverpool Mercury* of 17 September 1883 Newton 'was much liked for his genial disposition—was of a frank lively nature, and well known for his lively stories he would tell of his adventures in Scotland and elsewhere'.

Newton was elected a full member of the OWS in 1879 and in the following year his picture *Mountain Pass* had place of honour at the society's exhibition. It was, the critic of *The Spectator* commented, 'a very beautiful picture … a rough, grand effect of light and shadow, such as throws most water-colour landscape painting into the shade'. In autumn 1882 Newton travelled to Athens where he painted his final pictures, but by now his health was failing and he died on 9 September 1883 at his father-in-law's house at 14 Rock Park, Rock Ferry, Birkenhead. Remaining works were sold by Christie, Manson, and Woods on 29 April 1884, for up to £162. The Victoria and Albert Museum in London holds seven drawings by Newton. His most usual signature was 'Alfred P. Newton'.

SIMON FENWICK

Sources J. L. Roget, *A history of the 'Old Water-Colour' Society*, 2 vols. (1891) • Bankside Gallery, London, Royal Watercolour Society MSS • *ILN* (27 Oct 1883) • *The Spectator* (1 May 1880) • *Liverpool Mercury* (17 Sept 1883) • Mallalieu, *Watercolour artists* • m. cert.

Archives V&A NAL, corresp. and MSS | Bankside Gallery, London, Royal Watercolour Society MSS

Likenesses photograph, c.1863, Bankside Gallery, London, Royal Watercolour Society MSS • wood-engraving (after photograph by Elliott & Fry), NPG; repro. in *ILN* (27 Oct 1883)

Wealth at death £460 12s. 11d.: administration, 17 Nov 1883, CGPLA Eng. & Wales

Newton, Ann. *See* Dawson, Nancy (*bap.* 1728, *d.* 1767).

Newton, Arthur Francis Hamilton (1883–1959), athlete, was born at 7 Glentworth Terrace, Weston-super-Mare, Somerset, on 20 May 1883, the son of Henry Newton, clergyman, and his wife, Selina Elizabeth Saunders. He was educated at Bedford and at Banham in Norfolk. In 1901 he travelled to South Africa to join his brother, and was employed in clerical work in Durban before becoming a teacher. Following a visit to England in 1909, when he joined the cross-country running club Thames Hare and Hounds, he decided to settle in South Africa permanently, and in 1911 acquired a 1350 acre farm in Natal from the union government. He had no experience in farming, but by 1914 his finances appeared secure. The war intervened; Newton served as a trooper in the Natal light horse, and as a dispatch rider, providing his own motorcycle.

On his return Newton found his farm in a state of neglect; African workers had burnt much of his pasture land and destroyed his farm implements. Investment in cotton production was a failure, for which he blamed the native affairs department of the union government. He was left with no labour for his farm, and was denied compensation by the government for the considerable improvements in roads and buildings which he had made to the surrounding area. He saw publicity as the only way of bringing attention to his case. He later recalled: 'genuine amateur athletics were about as wholesome as anything on this earth; any man who made a really notable name at such would always be given a hearing by the public' (Newton, *Running in Three Continents*, 11). He decided to enter the Comrades Marathon, a 54½ mile race between Durban and Pietermaritzburg, which had attracted considerable interest when it had first been held the previous year. Newton began training on 1 January 1922, but although he considered himself naturally fit, he found that he could not cover 2 miles without stopping. Even this effort left him stiff for four days. After a few weeks of experimentation he decided to disregard conventional schemes of training and apply his own common-sense principles to his preparation, which he later developed into a coherent approach to training that emphasized consistency and volume. The results were successful: he won the Comrades Marathon in 1922 and 1923, set a world record for 50 miles on the road, and in 1924 travelled to England where he broke the London-to-Brighton record with a time of 5 hr 53 min. 43 sec.; his time for the marathon distance in this run was 9 minutes faster than the time of the best British runner in the 1924 Olympics. Newton was described by Walter George, who acted as a timekeeper for this and many of Newton's other record attempts in England, as 'the most phenomenal distance runner the world has ever known' (Newton, *Running*, foreword).

Newton returned to South Africa and won the Comrades Marathon in 1924 and 1925. His athletic reputation gained a considerable amount of publicity for his case against the union government, and he had meetings with General Smuts and General Hertzog, but was offered no compensation; in 1925 he decided to emigrate to Rhodesia to be in a 'British country'. The loss of his farm had left him impoverished and he was forced to begin the 770 mile journey on foot. Embarrassed by his financial circumstances, Newton walked at night to avoid recognition. The newspapers gave much publicity to his disappearance, and in Natal a 'shilling fund' was opened to offer him support; it raised over £1200. After eight days' walking he was lent a bicycle on which he reached the border with Rhodesia, but was initially refused entry as he had neither money nor an offer of employment. After working for mining companies in Messina and Northern Rhodesia, he was offered employment in Bulawayo, Southern Rhodesia, on condition that he would organize an athletics club. Newton lectured on training and racing and helped to found the Bulawayo Harriers, and broke the amateur records for 60 and 100 miles on roads. In 1927 he travelled to England to race and in January 1928 broke the 100-mile record between Bath and London, where he finished at Hyde Park Corner in front of an estimated 50,000 spectators in a time of 14 hr 22 min. 10 sec.

Later in 1928 Newton began competing as a professional. He entered the first professional Trans-Continental Race between New York and Los Angeles, but injury forced him to withdraw when well ahead of the field. In the 1929 race he suffered a similar misfortune, when he was run over by a car and left with a broken shoulder. On both occasions he was employed by the race organizers as technical director and did much to encourage the remaining competitors, as well as observing them and developing his theories on distance running. He formed a friendship with the Southampton-based Peter Gavuzzi and the two were involved in a series of races in Canada, America, and Britain. As a professional Newton broke the 24-hour record at Hamilton, Ontario, in 1931, achieving 152 miles 540 yards, and the Bath-to-London 100-mile record again on 20 July 1934, when aged fifty-one, with a time of 14 hr 6 min.

This was Newton's last race, although he continued to run and cycle, and was very much involved with development of road running; he was an honorary coach to the Road Runners Club. He lived alone in Ruislip, Middlesex, where he wrote a series of influential books and articles on training, and was visited by some of the world's leading athletes and coaches, who could expect to receive conversation, tea, and slices of yellow Madeira cake. Percy Cerutty, the Australian coach to John Landy and Herb Elliot, stayed with Newton in the 1950s. From 1951 an annual race was held between London and Brighton, and the trophy was awarded in Newton's name; in old age, as his eyesight failed him, he used to stand and listen to the runners in the annual Polytechnic Marathon. On his death at Hillingdon Hospital, Hillingdon, Middlesex, on 7 September 1959, he was acknowledged as the father of modern long-distance running. Those who knew him remembered his generous hospitality, honesty of purpose, charm of manner, and the stream of encouraging letters he wrote to his friends. On Newton's passing, one added, 'there has departed also the greatest gentleman of them all' (*The Times*).

M. A. BRYANT

Sources D. F. Macgregor, 'Arthur Newton', unpublished account of Newton's life · A. F. H. Newton, *Running in three continents* (1940) · A. F. H. Newton, *Running* (1935) · *The Times* (13 Sept 1959) · b. cert. · d. cert.
Likenesses photograph, 1924–34, repro. in Newton, *Running* · Swaine, photograph, repro. in Newton, *Running*, frontispiece · photograph, repro. in A. F. H. Newton, *Commonsense athletics* [1947], frontispiece · photographs, repro. in A. F. H. Newton, *Racing and training* (1949)
Wealth at death £2634 11s. 7d.: probate, 5 Feb 1960, CGPLA Eng. & Wales

Newton, Benjamin (1677–1735), Church of England clergyman, was born at Leicester on 8 December 1677. He was the son of the Revd John Newton (c.1638–1711), fellow of Clare College, Cambridge, vicar of St Martin's, Leicester, and master of Sir William Wigston's Hospital, Leicester (1680), and his wife, Mary. Later John Newton was rector of Taynton (1696–1710), and prebendary of Gloucester (1690–1711).

Benjamin Newton was educated first at the grammar school in Leicester. Admitted sub-sizar at Clare College, Cambridge, on 29 January 1694, he received his BA in 1698 and an MA on 7 July 1702. Sir Nathan Wright presented him with the crown living of Allington, Lincolnshire, in 1704. He married, first, in 1707, Jane, daughter of John Foxcroft, vicar of Nuneaton; they had one son, John (fl. 1712–1790). On 12 January 1719 he married Mary (d. c.1725), daughter of Benjamin King DD, prebendary of Gloucester, and they had three children, including Benjamin [see below]. Benjamin and Jane Newton settled in Gloucester in 1708 after his election by the corporation of the city as curate of St Nicholas's, Gloucester, and his installation as a minor canon of the cathedral.

In December 1709 Newton succeeded to the living of Taynton, Gloucestershire, by the gift of the dean and chapter. On 3 August 1712 he was appointed headmaster of the Gloucester Cathedral school, and resigned his stall at the cathedral. However, he gave up this position in September 1718, finding it allowed him little time for personal study. After being reinstalled as minor canon on 30 November 1723 Newton became librarian of the cathedral library on 29 September 1731, a position that was 'one of the most pleasing stations of my life' (Newton, 1.12). He was presented to the vicarage of Llantwit Major, Glamorgan, on 29 January 1733, and resigned his living at Taynton, retaining, however, the rectory of St Nicholas's, Gloucester, where he continued to reside.

Newton died at Gloucester of pleurisy on Good Friday, 4 April 1735, and was buried on Easter Sunday, 6 April 1735, in St Nicholas's Church, Gloucester. Thirty-one of his sermons were published posthumously as *Sermons Preached* on *Several Occasions*, 2 vols. (1736), with a memoir by New-ton's eldest son, John, who was educated at Corpus Christi College, Cambridge (BA and MA, 1738), and became rector of Taynton, Gloucester (1737–1754), and vicar of Brook-thorpe (1754–90).

Another son, **Benjamin Newton** (*bap.* 1722, *d.* 1787), Church of England clergyman, was baptized at St Peter's, Gloucester, on 28 August 1722, the child of Benjamin and his second wife, Mary King. Having been admitted to Cor-pus Christi College, Cambridge, in 1739, Benjamin junior transferred to Jesus College on 4 November 1740. He received a BA (1743) and an MA (1747), and was a fellow of Jesus College from 1746 to 1761. After being ordained dea-con at Ely in December 1744, and priest at Norwich in June 1747, Newton served as curate of Whittlesford, Cam-bridgeshire (1748–52), vicar of St Clement's, Cambridge (1749), and vicar of Guilden Morden, Cambridgeshire (1755–63). He became vicar of Sandhurst, Gloucestershire, in 1763, and lived there for the rest of his life. In addition Newton served as rector of St John's, Gloucestershire, and vicar of St Aldate, Gloucestershire, from 1768 to 1787. He died in Gloucester, apparently unmarried, on 29 June 1787.

At his death Newton was described as a divine of excel-lent moral character, 'genius and learning', 'luminous understanding', and 'brilliance of imagination'. These qualities enabled him to become 'one of the most valuable members of society' (*GM*, 57.640). His published works included two sermons: *The Church of England's Apology for the Use of Music in her Service* (1760); and *The Influence of the Improvements of Life on Principle, Considered* (1758), preached before Cambridge University on 30 January 1758. Also attributed to him was *Another Dissertation on the Mutual Sup-port of Trade and Civil Liberty* (1756).

CHARLOTTE FELL-SMITH, *rev.* ROBERT D. CORNWALL

Sources B. Newton, *Sermons preached on several occasions*, 2 vols. (1736), 1.4–16 · Venn, *Alum. Cant.* · *GM*, 1st ser., 5 (1735), 218 · *GM*, 1st ser., 57 (1787), 640
Likenesses G. Vandergucht, line engraving (after Robbins), BM, NPG; repro. in Newton, *Sermons preached on several occasions*

Newton, Benjamin (*bap.* 1722, *d.* 1787). *See under* Newton, Benjamin (1677–1735).

Newton, Benjamin Wills (1807–1899), leader of the Ply-mouth Brethren and religious writer, was born at Ply-mouth Dock on 12 December 1807, the only child of Quaker parents, Benjamin Newton, a draper of Plymouth Dock, who died eleven days before the birth of his son, and his widow, Anna (1782–1877), a daughter of Roger Tref-fry of Lostwithiel, in whose Anglican family Newton lived until the age of twelve. He was educated at the grammar schools of Lostwithiel and Plymouth, and tutored by the Revd Thomas Byrth of Diptford, before matriculating at Exeter College, Oxford, in 1824. He became a fellow of Exe-ter College at the age of only eighteen in 1826, two years before obtaining first-class honours in classics. He took his degree in 1829.

At Oxford, influenced by Henry Bellenden Bulteel, he experienced an evangelical conversion which brought him into a circle of somewhat radical Calvinist piety. In 1830 he was involved in the removal of J. H. Newman from the local secretaryship of the Church Missionary Society, and in the following year abandoned the idea of taking holy orders. His marriage on 12 March 1832 to Hannah Abbott, a daughter of John Abbott, a flour merchant of Ply-mouth, was only the ostensible reason for the vacation of his fellowship in the same year, as he had already in effect seceded from the Church of England.

Back in Plymouth he worked with John Nelson Darby and became a leader of the newly formed community at Providence Chapel who were soon nicknamed Plymouth Brethren. He was an elder of the assembly in Raleigh Street, Plymouth, until 1840, and when the church moved to Ebrington Street he was an elder there until 1847. His energies were mainly given to evangelism and the study of prophecy; his *Thoughts on the Apocalypse* (1844) was widely circulated and his *Aids to Prophetic Enquiry* (1848) ran to several editions. He also tirelessly opposed the teaching of Catholics, Irvingites, and the Quakers, whose commu-nion he had earlier abandoned. Of his Quaker relatives who followed him in this course Samuel Prideaux Tre-gelles and the banker Samuel Lloyd were the most prom-inent. His writings were extensive; the British Library lists more than seventy separate items.

In 1847 Darby and other Brethren who had previously been critical, both of his eschatology and of his authori-tarian style of leadership, accused Newton of Christo-logical heresy. The death of his wife in 1846 and the acri-mony of controversy led Newton to leave Plymouth in December 1847. He moved to London, where for many years he regularly preached in a chapel in Bayswater. His published writings were valued by a wide circle of biblical students but his later life was spent in a secluded retire-ment.

Newton's second wife, Maria (1815–1906), whom he mar-ried on 24 April 1849, was the daughter of William Haw-kins of the Madras civil service. Their only child, Maria Anne Constantia, died aged five in 1855. Newton died at his home, 2 Clanricarde Gardens, Tunbridge Wells, on 26 June 1899.   TIMOTHY C. F. STUNT, *rev.*

Sources H. H. Rowdon, *The origins of the Brethren, 1825–50* (1967) · T. C. F. Stunt, 'John Henry Newman and the evangelicals', *Journal of Ecclesiastical History*, 21 (1970), 65–74 · JRL, Christian Brethren Arch-ive · *CGPLA Eng. & Wales* (1899) · T. Stunt, *From awakening to secession: radical evangelicals in Switzerland and Britain 1815–35* (2000)
Archives JRL, corresp. and papers
Wealth at death £22,010 13s. 2d.: resworn probate, Oct 1899, *CGPLA Eng. & Wales*

Newton, Sir Charles Thomas (*bap.* 1816, *d.* 1894), archae-ologist, was born at Clungunford, Shropshire, where he was baptized on 15 September 1816, the second son of Newton Dickinson Hand Newton (formerly Hand; 1778–1853), vicar of Clungunford and later vicar of Bredwardine and rector of Brobury, Herefordshire, and his wife, Maria Julia, *née* Wyatt (1780–1866). Educated at Shrewsbury

Sir Charles Thomas Newton (*bap.* 1816, *d.* 1894), by John Jabez Edwin Mayall

School during Samuel Butler's headmastership, he matriculated at Christ Church, Oxford, on 17 October 1833. There he was a friend of John Ruskin, who mentioned him in *Praeterita*, and held a studentship from 1835 to 1861, graduating BA in 1837 with a second class in *literae humaniores* and MA in 1840.

Despite family opposition, Newton entered the British Museum in 1840 as assistant in the department of antiquities under Edward Hawkins. Here he took advantage of the opportunity to study at first hand a wide range of antiquities, including coins, and acquired a thorough training in curatorship. He was active in the Archaeological Institute, writing papers for their annual meetings and serving as one of the secretaries at the 1846 meeting. In 1847 he published an important article in the *Classical Museum* on the mausoleum at Halicarnassus. Other papers at this period show him already making an English contribution to the study of classical archaeology, which had been initiated on the continent by Winckelmann.

In 1852 Newton resigned from the British Museum on appointment as vice-consul at Mytilene. From April 1853 to January 1854 he served as acting consul at Rhodes. His time in the East was described in *Travels and Discoveries in the Levant* (1865). In addition to consular duties he was authorized to serve the interests of the museum by acquiring antiquities through excavation and purchase. His excavations on Kalymnos in 1854 and 1855, financed by Lord Stratford de Redcliffe, the British ambassador at Constantinople, yielded many inscriptions for the British Museum. Also in 1855 he unearthed the bronze serpent

from Delphi in the hippodrome at Constantinople and visited Bodrum (ancient Halicarnassus) for the first time. After a second visit in the following spring he obtained a government grant of £2000 together with naval and military support for an expedition to retrieve some lions from the mausoleum immured in the castle of St Peter and to excavate the site of the mausoleum itself. This was eventually found in an unexpected location first pointed out by Robert Murdoch Smith RE. Newton never acknowledged Smith's observation, and most later writers accepted his implicit claim to have identified the spot himself. The expedition also explored neighbouring sites, and Newton's report, *A History of Discoveries at Halicarnassus, Cnidus, and Branchidae* (1862), was his major archaeological publication. Its illustrations included lithographs after photographs taken by Corporal B. Spackman RE, Newton having been one of the first archaeologists to include a photographer on his staff.

While on leave in London in 1858 Newton met the artist Ann Mary Severn [*see* Newton, (Ann) Mary], daughter of the commercially unsuccessful painter Joseph *Severn. Newton proposed marriage, but this was impractical since her income was needed to keep her family solvent. On 10 June 1859 Newton became consul at Rome, but when Hawkins eventually resigned from the museum, the department of antiquities was divided into three and Newton, as the favoured candidate of Panizzi, was appointed to the new post of keeper of Greek and Roman antiquities in January 1861. With the support of Newton and others, Joseph Severn succeeded him as consul at Rome. Now free from her financial commitments, Mary Severn married Newton on 27 April 1861. They had no children, and in 1866 she died of measles at 74 Gower Street, London. Newton later moved to 2 Montagu Place.

Newton's excavations had greatly enriched the collections of the British Museum, and as keeper he added many important acquisitions from new excavations conducted by others, from old collections, and from the market. Between 1864 and 1874 alone he obtained special grants of over £100,000 to purchase the Farnese, the Pourtalès, and the Blacas collections, and two important groups assembled by the dealer Castellani. Newton was indefatigable in his efforts to obtain these grants, urging the importance of the acquisitions on the museum's trustees, writing to the press, and even making a direct approach to the government through his personal acquaintance with Gladstone, himself a classical scholar. Excavators who worked with Newton's active support on behalf of the museum included A. Biliotti at Bodrum and in Rhodes; George Dennis in Sicily, in Cyrenaica, and around Smyrna; Sir Robert Hamilton Lang in Cyprus; R. P. Pullan at Priene; Robert Murdoch Smith and E. A. Porcher at Cyrene; and J. T. Wood at Ephesus.

Newton's administrative burdens did not restrict his scholarly work. Seeing himself primarily as a historian, he stressed the value of epigraphy and initiated the series of volumes on *The Collection of Ancient Greek Inscriptions in the British Museum*, serving as chief editor of the first three

(1874–90) and himself editing the inscriptions he had excavated on Kalymnos in the second (1883). His pioneering articles on Greek inscriptions were republished in French and German. He wrote a series of detailed guidebooks to the museum's collections and papers in *The Academy*, *Edinburgh Review*, and elsewhere on current archaeological topics, including perceptive notices of Schliemann's work at Troy and Mycenae. Several papers were reprinted as *Essays on Art and Archaeology* (1880). Newton was himself a pioneer in the study of Bronze Age material from the excavations of Biliotti and Schliemann.

When consul in Rome Newton confided to his friend A. H. Layard that he enjoyed lecturing and wondered whether he could pursue such a career in England. In 1855, at the suggestion of H. G. Liddell, Lord Palmerston had offered him the regius professorship of Greek at Oxford, with a view to fostering the study of classical archaeology there, but he had been unable to accept since the salary was inadequate. When the Yates chair of classical archaeology was created at University College, London, in 1880, Newton was allowed to accept the appointment without relinquishing his keepership at the museum. He also lectured as antiquary to the Royal Academy and read papers to the Royal Society of Literature and the Society of Antiquaries.

As classical archaeology developed into a separate discipline and the existing archaeological societies tended to become more insular in outlook, new organizations arose. Newton was closely involved in the foundation of three: the Society for the Promotion of Hellenic Studies, to which he gave an inaugural address in June 1879; the Egypt Exploration Fund, founded in 1882; and the British School at Athens, opened in November 1886. His friends and pupils, led by the earl of Carnarvon, subscribed to a testimonial fund and in 1889 presented him with a marble portrait bust of himself by Sir Joseph Boehm, later housed in the British Museum; at his own request the balance of the fund was given to the British School at Athens, where part was spent on studentships and part on books.

Newton was by this time old and frail. In 1885 he had resigned his posts at the British Museum and the Royal Academy, and in 1888 he gave up the Yates chair. He died at Adelaide House, Westgate-on-Sea, Kent, on 28 November 1894 and was buried at Kensal Green, London, on 4 December.

Tall and distinguished in appearance (and bearded from his time in the East), Newton was fond of society and skilled in conversation. His wife's early death was a bitter blow, hardly softened by his Anglican faith, and in later years his manner was habitually austere, although he allowed himself to relax when travelling in Greece. His assistants were expected to meet his own exacting standards, and his approval, when given, was highly valued.

Honorary fellow of Worcester College, Oxford, from 1874, Newton became DCL of Oxford in 1875, LLD of Cambridge and PhD of Strasbourg in 1879, CB on 16 November 1875, and KCB on 21 June 1887. He was a member of the Society of Dilettanti, fellow of the Society of Antiquaries of London, corresponding member of the Institut de France, honorary member of the Zentraldirektion des Deutschen Archäologischen Instituts (Berlin), and honorary member of the Accademia dei Lincei (Rome).

B. F. COOK

Sources B. F. Cook, 'Sir Charles Newton, KCB (1816–1894)', *Sculptors and sculpture of Caria and the Dodecanese* [British Museum classical colloquium, 1994], ed. I. Jenkins and G. B. Waywell (1997), 10–23 · R. C. Jebb, 'Sir C. T. Newton', *Journal of Hellenic Studies*, 14 (1894), xlix–liv · R. C. Jebb, *Classical Review*, 8 (1895), 81–5 · S. Lane-Poole, 'Sir Charles Newton, KCB, DCL, LLD', *National Review*, 24 (1894–5), 616–27 · E. Gardner, 'Sir Charles Newton, KCB', *Annual of the British School at Athens*, 1 (1894–5), 67–77 · E. Sellars, 'Sir Charles Newton', *Revue archéologique*, 25 (1894), 273–81 · S. Smith, *Illustrious friends. The story of Joseph Severn and his son Arthur* (1965) · *The Times* (30 Sept 1894) · B. F. Cook, *Relief sculpture of the Mausoleum at Halicarnassus* [forthcoming] · I. Jenkins, *Archaeologists and aesthetes in the sculpture galleries of the British Museum, 1800–1939* (1992) · P. Gardner, *Autobiographica* (1933) · Foster, *Alum. Oxon.* · H. Waterhouse, *The British School at Athens: the first hundred years* (1986) · census returns, 1871 · parish register, baptism, Clungunford, Shropshire, 15 Sept 1816 · *CGPLA Eng. & Wales* (1894)
Archives BL, corresp. and papers, Add. MSS 31980, 46889–46890, 50850 · BM · PRO, accounts and vouchers, T64/374 | BL, corresp. with W. E. Gladstone, Add. MSS 44407–44785, *passim* · BL, letters to Sir Austen Layard, Add. MSS 38981–39115, *passim* · BL, Panizzi MSS · BL, letters to Philip Bliss, Add. MSS 34576, 34582 · Bodl. Oxf., letters to H. W. Acland · NL Wales, letters to Johnes family · PRO, letters to Lord Odo Russell, FO918
Likenesses H. W. Phillips, oils, *c*.1850, BM · B. Spackman, photographs, 1856–7, BM · A. M. Newton, cartoon, 1861–6, priv. coll. · Lock & Whitfield, woodburytype photograph, 1883, NPG · W. Story, marble head, 1888, U. Lond., Institute of Classical Studies · J. E. Boehm, marble bust, 1889, BM · J. J. E. Mayall, photograph, NPG [*see illus.*] · P. Naumann, wood-engraving, BM, NPG; repro. in *ILN* (8 Dec 1894) · M. Severn, red chalk drawing, BM · drawing, photographic copy, BM; repro. in D. M. Wilson, *The British Museum* (2002) · etching (after drawing, attrib. M. Newton), BL · photograph, repro. in A. Michaelis, *Ein Jahrhundert kunstarchäologischer Entdeckungen*, 2nd edn (1908)
Wealth at death £16,602 14s. 8d.: probate, 27 Dec 1894, *CGPLA Eng. & Wales*

Newton, Ernest (1856–1922), architect, was born in London on 12 September 1856, the fourth son of Henry Newton, then resident agent for the Sturt property in Hoxton, and his wife, Mary Lockyer. Educated at Uppingham School, Rutland, under Edward Thring, he entered the office of Richard Norman Shaw in June 1873, and after three years as an assistant began to work independently in 1879. In Shaw's office he came into contact with E. S. Prior, Mervyn Macartney, G. C. Horsley, and, later, W. R. Lethaby. The early meetings of this group for discussion of architectural matters ultimately developed into the Art Workers' Guild, the most important and enduring of the groups and guilds of the arts and crafts movement. To Shaw himself, and particularly to Philip Webb, Newton owed a conception of architecture as art, as a mode of personal expression rather than an exercise in archaeology or a professional occupation. That his mature work was marked by a serenity and a simplicity is due to his own interpretation of the work of Webb and Lethaby rather

Ernest Newton (1856–1922), by Arthur Hacker, 1916

than to the somewhat dramatic vigour of his master's work.

Like other pupils of Shaw, Newton passed into private practice with the help of a major piece of work in the House of Retreat, Lloyd Square, Clerkenwell (1880–83), and possibly also a small development at Grove Park in south-east London for the earl of Northbrook (1879), now mostly demolished. Both were in the Shaw manner. For the first ten years of his career he was working mainly on small suburban houses, particularly in the Chislehurst and Bickley areas of Kent, showing how orderliness of plan and unity of materials could give an effect of breadth to minor works—a lesson not lost upon the next generation of architects. Like many architects starting out on their careers he published his work in two books, *A Book of Houses* (1890) and *A Book of Country Houses* (1903), thereby illustrating a number of his earlier houses for a wider public. He married in 1881 Antoinette Johanna, the eldest daughter of William Hoyack, merchant of Rotterdam; they had three sons.

Bullers Wood, Chislehurst, Kent (1888–9), was Newton's first large work (later altered). Here an earlier stuccoed house was encased and enlarged to form what was in effect a new house, carefully combining liveliness of elevation with a quiet dignity which was to be his hallmark. It is thought of in terms of wall and window, roof and chimney, while other architects were still thinking in terms of style and period. This is important, because it throws light on all Newton's subsequent work. Lethaby,

the former colleague who was one of his oldest friends and who took over charge of works at the church of St Swithun, Hither Green (*c*.1890–1895), during an illness, wrote that Newton was 'aiming rather at sound and expressive building than at style imitations' (*The Builder*, 122, 3 Feb 1922, 19). He was using traditional elements and materials but not designing in a way which copied any specific style. It could be said that, although he fully agreed with Webb's and Lethaby's more philosophical approach to design in architecture, his contribution was to make of it a domestic architecture for every day.

The houses of the two decades either side of 1900 were Newton's main achievement. He was extraordinarily stable in his method of designing, and usually produced variations on single themes, such as the very similar pair, one in a free neo-Georgian—Luckley, Wokingham, Berkshire (1906)—the other much more vernacular—Ludwick Corner, Welwyn Garden City, Hertfordshire (1907). Such houses could be built at the scale of a country house, as at Flint House, Goring, Oxfordshire (1913). He also favoured a more compact type of house, often, however, quite large and usually in a free neo-Georgian style, from Redcourt, Haslemere, Surrey (1894), and Steep Hill, Jersey (1899), to Dawn House, Winchester, Hampshire (1907), Feathercombe, Hambledon, Surrey (1910), Lukyns, Ewhurst, Surrey, (1911), and Norsbury House, Sutton Scotney, Hampshire (1919). Like many arts and crafts architects he also carried out works to older buildings, restoring and extending houses such as Upton Grey Manor House, Hampshire (1907; with a Gertrude Jekyll garden), The Greenway, Shurdington, Gloucestershire (1910), and, one of his major works, Oldcastle, Dallington, Sussex (1912), where he extended a medieval house of the Sussex Weald.

Newton's work outside the domestic field was limited, but he designed the church of St Swithun at Hither Green, Kent (*c*.1890–1895), and added the tower to the church of St George, Bickley, Kent (1904–5), as well as the little Roman Catholic chapel of Sts Gregory and Augustine, Oxford (1911), and, executed by his son W. G. Newton, also an architect, the memorial shrine and hall at Uppingham School, Rutland (1921), the elevation of the latter of which is based on the hall of the Elizabethan Kirby Hall in Northamptonshire.

Ernest Newton was elected president of the Royal Institute of British Architects in 1914. In 1916 he voluntarily undertook onerous public work in connection with the issue of building licences, to the detriment of his health. In 1918 he was awarded the royal gold medal of the RIBA on the recommendation of its council. He was elected an associate of the Royal Academy in 1911 and Royal Academician in 1919, and created CBE in 1920. He died at his home, 17 Blomfield Road, Maida Hill, London, on 25 January 1922.

As a man Newton had a facility for making friends in every walk of life and at various time keenly pursued the study of the Dutch language, the violin, acting, French conversation and literature, and the technique of watercolour. He had a notably candid mind and an unusually frank admiration for attainments which he lacked himself. He had a very great facility for taking pains, and a candid dislike of pedantry and fanaticism, all of which were reflected in his architecture.

W. G. NEWTON, rev. RICHARD MORRICE

Sources W. G. Newton, *The work of Ernest Newton, RA, containing a list of his works* (1925) · R. Morrice, 'Ernest Newton', *The architectural outsiders*, ed. R. Brown (1985), 172–88 · E. Newton, *A book of houses* (1890) · E. Newton, *A book of country houses* (1903) · *CGPLA Eng. & Wales* (1922) · d. cert.
Archives RIBA BAL, corresp. relating to Pierrepont House, Frensham · V&A
Likenesses A. Hacker, oils, 1916, RIBA [*see illus.*] · Elliott & Fry, photograph, NPG
Wealth at death £11,313 4s. 9d.: probate, 4 March 1922, *CGPLA Eng. & Wales*

Newton, Frances Emily (1871–1955), Arab apologist and missionary, was born on 4 November 1871 at Mickleover Manor, near Derby, the daughter of Charles Edmund Newton, banker, and his second wife, Mary Henrietta Moore (d. 1893). She and her numerous sisters were educated by a governess and brought up on strict evangelical principles. From an early age she took an active part in her mother's charitable works in the village, and later organized a youth club for local boys.

In 1888 Newton went to Palestine to visit her stepsisters Constance, a Mildmay deaconess, and Edith, a Church Missionary Society (CMS) missionary, who were both working in Jaffa, and in the following year she was recognized by the CMS as a voluntary helper. During this time she began to learn Arabic and travelled extensively throughout Palestine and Jordan. In 1893 her mother's death, and her own considerable private means, allowed her to offer herself full-time to the CMS on a non-stipendiary basis, like her sister Edith. Her training consisted of district nursing and social work in Birmingham and, from 1894, missionary training at The Olives, the CMS training centre in Hampstead. She was formally accepted as a missionary on 17 December 1894 and sailed for the Palestine mission in Jaffa on 3 October 1895.

Here Newton's work consisted initially of teaching and evangelism, with the help of an Arab bible-woman, though she later took charge of the medical mission in Jaffa. Between 1903 and 1905 she was in Britain, where she undertook some theological study at Westfield College, London. On returning to Palestine in 1905 she was sent to Nazareth, where she administered four girls' schools in the town and a further six in the surrounding villages. Much of her time was occupied in visiting these schools and supervising the Arab teachers. Her entrepreneurial efforts to raise money for the schools by selling local craftwork to tourists led to her first serious clash with the CMS.

More serious was Newton's lengthy debate with the home committee, which began in 1912, over the status of women missionaries and their spheres of influence. After much correspondence and several meetings while on leave in Britain it became clear that nearly twenty-five years of experience of Arab society and fluency in Arabic were not enough to give her the authority of a male clergyman. The CMS found itself unable to 'contemplate that women missionaries should be placed in that position of responsibility over the male workers which they naturally and rightly exercise over their own sex' (G. T. Manley, 29 Sept 1914, CMS archives, G3 P/L14). On 15 June 1915 she withdrew from the list of CMS missionaries, though she remained a committed supporter.

Frances Newton was on leave in Britain when war broke out in August 1914. Initially she volunteered for the women's police force, with a beat in Leicester Square. However, she was soon back serving the Arab cause, as travelling secretary of the Syria and Palestine Relief Fund, set up by Rennie MacInnes, Anglican bishop in Jerusalem. Her efforts helped to raise £150,000 to alleviate distress throughout the area. From 1917 she was the fund's representative on a joint committee with the Red Cross and the order of St John of Jerusalem, and a year later was made a lady of grace of the venerable order of St John of Jerusalem in recognition of this work; she later became a dame of justice of the order. By then she had also been drawn to a greater understanding of Arab nationalism, and had met both T. E. Lawrence and the emir Feisal in London. Feisal was later to be her guest on Mount Carmel after the French took control of Syria.

In 1919 Newton was finally able to return to Palestine and took up residence on Mount Carmel. Here she busied herself with social work among the Arabs of Haifa and the surrounding district, acting as prison visitor and probation officer. She was largely responsible for the appointment of the first women's welfare inspector, Margaret Nixon, and was herself a member of the National Council of Women. However, her attempts to work with Henrietta Szold of the Hadassah women's movement came to nothing. She was the only woman called to give evidence to the land commission in 1930. In 1927 the journalist Owen Tweedy described her as 'comely but podgy—tall & masterful & with the hell of a temper and always having rows. She has been years in Palestine … pro-Arab and seeing the Jews through Red—blood-red—spectacles' (Tweedy diary, 4 May 1927, St Ant. Oxf., Middle East Centre). This was confirmed by Norman Bentwich, attorney-general of Palestine, himself a Jew, who recalled 'Effie' Newton (as he mistakenly called her) as 'incurably anti-Jewish, intensely critical of the Administration, a principal supporter of the Arab cause, both with her brains—for she was clever—and with her money, because she was also rich' (Bentwich, 65).

As Arab–Jewish relations worsened throughout the 1930s, and civil unrest increased, the British police and later the army were called upon to deal with an escalation of violence and intimidation, from both Arab fighters and the Zionist Haganah. Newton was one of the founders of the Arab Centre in London, which published material defending the Arab cause and holding up for scrutiny the methods of the British administration in dealing with unrest. The pamphlet *Punitive Methods in Palestine*, published in March 1938, was attacked in the House of Commons by the colonial secretary, W. G. A. Ormsby-Gore, as 'all lies' (*Hansard 5C*, 333, 24 March 1938, 80). This and a later pamphlet, *Searchlight on Palestine*, were the cause of a banning order issued on 4 October 1938 by the high commissioner, Sir Harold MacMichael. Newton was then in London following a trip to Geneva to lobby the League of Nations on the situation in Palestine. The banning order was not rescinded until September 1943, but by then the political situation was irredeemable.

Newton's autobiography, *Fifty Years in Palestine*, a personal and closely argued political memoir, was published in 1948, the year the British mandate was terminated. The creation of the state of Israel and the collapse of the Arab cause in Palestine caused her great distress, but she kept open house for Arab nationalists in London and continued to use her personal wealth in supporting relief services for Palestinian refugees. Proceeds from the sale in 1951 of her house in Haifa were devoted to maintaining a girls' school in Nazareth run by the Jerusalem and the East Mission.

Frances Newton suffered a heart attack in her sleep and died at her home, Flat 8, 9 Wilbraham Place, Chelsea, on 11 June 1955. Fittingly for a political activist, her funeral was held at the church of St Simon Zelotes, Milner Street, Chelsea, on 18 June and was followed by cremation at Putney Vale the same day. She left a substantial sum of money to the bishop in Jerusalem to provide medical services for Palestinian refugees in Jordan. In 1927 Owen Tweedy quoted a British official as saying that Newton had 'the exterior of an English woman and the mind of a Palestinian' (Tweedy diary, 4 May 1927, St Ant. Oxf., Middle East Centre). She herself believed that her work for the Arabs of Palestine was in the spirit of the motto of the order of St John of Jerusalem: 'Pro Fide Pro Utilitate Hominum' (Newton, *Fifty Years*, 109).   CLARE BROWN

Sources F. E. Newton, *Fifty years in Palestine* (1948) · U. Birm. L., special collections department, Church Missionary Society archive · St Ant. Oxf., Middle East Centre, Jerusalem and the East Mission · St Ant. Oxf., Middle East Centre, Owen Tweedy MSS · N. Shepherd, *Ploughing sand: British rule in Palestine, 1917–1948* (1999) · T. Segev, *One Palestine complete: Jews and Arabs under the British mandate* (2000) · N. Bentwich and H. Bentwich, *Mandate memories, 1918–1948* (1965) · I. M. Okkenhaug, '"The quality of heroic living, of high endeavour and adventure": Anglican mission, women, and education in Palestine, 1888–1948', diss., University of Bergen, 1999 · b. cert. · d. cert.

Archives St Ant. Oxf., Middle East Centre, Jerusalem and East Mission archives · U. Birm., Church Missionary Society archives

Wealth at death £44,675 2s.: probate, 31 Aug 1955, CGPLA Eng. & Wales

Newton, Francis (*d.* 1572), dean of Winchester, was the son of Sir John Newton, or Cradock, of Gloucester (*d.* 1568), and his wife, Margaret, the daughter of Sir Anthony Poyntz. Sir John and Margaret had eight sons and twelve daughters, one of whom, Frances, married William Brook, Lord Cobham. Francis Newton was educated at Michaelhouse, Cambridge, graduating BA in 1549. Twenty Latin verses by him appeared in the collection of memorial poems for Martin Bucer put out by John Cheke in 1551, and he proceeded MA in 1553. He was not one of those who chose exile on the accession of Mary in the latter year. In

1555 he was among the regents who subscribed to the fifteen Catholic articles imposed on the university by Stephen Gardiner, now restored as chancellor, to replace the protestant forty-two. During the following months he was nevertheless removed from his fellowship at Jesus, and probably lived quietly in retirement for the rest of the reign.

On 23 December 1559 Newton received letters patent for the prebend of North Newbald, in York Minster, and was installed in April 1560. On his return to Cambridge that year, he became a fellow of Trinity College, and proceeded BD in 1561 and DD in 1563. Meanwhile the master of Trinity, Robert Beaumont, suggesting some discreet changes in September 1561 among the Cambridge heads, proposed Newton as a suitable master of Jesus, but he was not appointed. However, he served as vice-chancellor in 1563, and accordingly took a prominent part in the entertainment of Elizabeth on her visit to Cambridge the following year.

On 14 April 1565 Newton received letters patent as dean of Winchester, and was installed a month later. Following the death of his brother Theodore [*see below*], the queen wrote to Archbishop Parker on 17 January 1569, at the suit of their sister-in-law Lady Cobham, requesting him to bestow Theodore's prebendal stall at Canterbury on Francis. Possibly to Parker's embarrassment (Leicester had also urged the suit as a way of pleasing Elizabeth), he had to reply that he had installed a successor to Theodore four days earlier. At Winchester, Newton lived in harmony with his bishop, Robert Horne, although a visitation of 1571 suggests that between them they had let the cathedral fabric fall into disrepair. Somewhat mysteriously, Newton died overseas at some time before 15 November 1572, when his brother Henry was granted letters of administration.

Francis Newton's brother **Theodore Newton** (1531/2–1568/9), also a Church of England clergyman, graduated BA from Christ Church, Oxford, early in 1549, and proceeded MA early in 1552. In that year he contributed to the memorial volume of verses for Henry and Charles Brandon, the two boy-dukes of Suffolk who had died together of the sweating sickness. Presented by a kinsman to the rectory of Badgeworth, Somerset, he was the only Marian exile among the sixty-nine incumbents deprived during Mary's reign in the diocese of Bath and Wells. The cause of his deprivation seems to have been insufficiency of orders rather than marriage. On 5 November 1555 he was received into John Knox's congregation at Geneva, and apparently remained there until his return to England.

On 20 October 1559 Newton received letters patent as canon of the first prebend at Canterbury, and was installed three days later, despite continuing doubts about his orders. Perhaps in order to dispel them he was ordained, or reordained, deacon by Bishop Grindal of London on 25 January 1560, as MA, of Bath and Wells diocese, aged twenty-eight. On 16 June following he was appointed rector of Ringwould, Kent, and in September 1567 was instituted rector of St Dionis Backchurch, London, on the presentation of the dean and chapter of Canterbury. He had died before 13 January 1569, when his successor was installed in his Canterbury prebend. He was buried in the cathedral chapter house. His will survives among the Canterbury diocesan probate archives (Reg. 31, fol. 174).

STANFORD LEHMBERG

Sources F. Bussby, *Winchester Cathedral, 1079–1979* (1979) · treasurers' books, Winchester Cathedral Library · PRO, PROB 6/2, fol. 17v · Venn, *Alum. Cant.*, 1/3.252 · J. B. Mullinger, *The University of Cambridge*, 2 (1884) · H. C. Porter, *Reformation and reaction in Tudor Cambridge* (1958) · C. H. Garrett, *The Marian exiles: a study in the origins of Elizabethan puritanism* (1938) · *Fasti Angl.*, 1541–1857, [Canterbury] · G. Hennessy, *Novum repertorium ecclesiasticum parochiale Londinense, or, London diocesan clergy succession from the earliest time to the year 1898* (1898) · Cooper, *Ath. Cantab.*, 2.308

Newton, Francis Milner (1720–1794), portrait painter, was born in London in 1720 and baptized at St Andrew's, Holborn, London, on 31 January 1728, the son of Edward Newton and his wife, Mary Ann, daughter of Smart Goodenough of Barton Grange, Corfe, near Taunton, Somerset. Newton was a pupil of the German artist Marcus Tuscher (1705–1751). He also studied at the St Martin's Lane Academy, London. Although Newton worked as a professional portrait painter, his historical significance lies in the role he played in the formation and organization of art institutions. In 1753 Newton was involved in formulating the initial plans for a national academy of art. Two years later, in 1755, he was appointed secretary to a committee of artists formed for a similar purpose. On 12 November 1759 a further meeting of artists was held at the Turk's Head tavern, Newton acting once more as secretary. This meeting resulted in the first exhibition held by the artists of Great Britain in the gallery of the Society for the Encouragement of Arts, Manufactures, and Commerce, to which Newton contributed a portrait. In 1761 a schism took place among the exhibiting artists. Newton joined the seceding body, who exhibited thereafter at Spring Gardens. In 1765 this group obtained a charter as the Incorporated Society of Artists. Once more Newton was appointed secretary. In 1768 a further schism took place, which resulted in the ejection of a number of the directors and of the secretary, Newton, from the Incorporated Society. These artists formed a new society, the Royal Academy of Arts, under the patronage of the king, George III. Newton was elected as its first secretary. In Zoffany's painting *The Academicians of the Royal Academy* (Royal Collection) Newton is depicted conversing with the academy's treasurer, Sir William Chambers, and the president, Sir Joshua Reynolds, an indication presumably of his own influential role within the institution. Ellis Waterhouse, who described Newton's paintings as 'completely undistinguished', concluded disparagingly that he was 'the sort of person who becomes a committee secretary' (Waterhouse, *18c painters*, 256). According to his fellow academicians Joseph Nollekens and John Inigo Richards, Newton possessed an 'avaritious & narrow mind', while Joseph Farington described him as 'frivolous, & pettish, with troublesome Office Pomp' (Farington, *Diary*, 2.407; 10.3609). Thomas Gainsborough, who clearly found him a stickler for rules, referred to him as 'that puppy Newton' (*Letters*, 76). The academicians were more appreciative of Newton's wife, Frances, whose famous veal and ham pie was served to the academy's committee in a large dish. Newton exhibited a total of eight portraits at the Royal Academy from 1769 to 1774. Only one has been identified, a portrait of the bishop of Winchester, exhibited in 1772. After 1774 Newton appears not to have exhibited. In 1769 he is recorded as living at Mortimer Street, and in 1771 at nearby Portland Street. He also had a house in Hammersmith for some years. When the Royal Academy moved to William Chambers's new Somerset House in 1780 Newton was given a suite of rooms there. In 1783 he suffered from an unspecified illness, although he continued as secretary until his retirement from the post in 1788. A silver cup was presented to Newton on his retirement, and his portrait is among those drawn by George Dance (engraved by William Daniell), and preserved in the library of the Royal Academy. In addition to his academic position, Newton held the office of muster master for England, and often wore the Windsor uniform, an outfit designed by the king for use by his family and friends. At some point Newton's cousin Goodenough Earle, who had inherited the Barton Grange property, appointed him as guardian to his only daughter. On her death Newton inherited the property and retired to Barton Grange, where he lived for the rest of his life. He died there on 14 August 1794, having caught a chill following an evening out with friends. He was buried at Corfe. He left one child, Josepha Sophia, who married twice; on her death without issue in 1848 the property passed to a cousin, Francis Wheat Newton.

MARTIN POSTLE

Sources Redgrave, *Artists*, 2nd edn · S. C. Hutchison, *The history of the Royal Academy, 1768–1986*, 2nd edn (1986) · Waterhouse, *18c painters* · *The letters of Thomas Gainsborough*, ed. J. Hayes (2001) · Farington, *Diary* · will, PRO, PROB 11/1249, sig. 426 · IGI
Archives RA, corresp.; papers
Likenesses G. Dance, drawing, 1793, RA · Daniell, engraving (after G. Dance) · J. Zoffany, group portrait, oils (*The academicians of the Royal Academy*), Royal Collection
Wealth at death properties in Bloomsbury and Southwark and funds in securities to wife; estate in Somerset to daughter: will, PRO, PROB 11/1249, sig. 426

Newton, George (1601/2–1681), clergyman and ejected minister, was a native of Devon and the son of a clergyman. He matriculated from Exeter College, Oxford, on 17 December 1619, aged seventeen, graduated BA on 14 June 1621, and proceeded MA on 23 June 1624. Ordained priest at Exeter on 21 September 1628, he began his ministry at Bishop's Hull, Somerset, but on 7 April 1631 was instituted to the vicarage of St Mary Magdalene in the nearby town of Taunton, on the presentation of Sir William Portman and Robert Hill. When in 1633 clergy were ordered to read Charles I's Book of Sports in their churches Newton complied—obedient, as he said, to the commandment of man—but he went on to recite Exodus 20, the ten commandments, telling his congregation that they might resolve the contradiction themselves by opting to follow the one or the other. He married twice: nothing is known of his first wife; he seems to have married his second wife, Mary (d. 1645), in or before 1642.

During the greater part of the civil war, when Taunton was contested for by royalists and parliamentarians—to whom many of its citizens were inclined to adhere—Newton resided at St Albans, his wife's former home. There he preached in the abbey church, and in 1644 was serving as interim vicar of St Albans. In 1645 when Robert Blake, the parliamentarian governor of Taunton, began in earnest to break the royalist siege, Newton returned there. On 11 May 1645 his sermon 'I am the Lord; I change not' was delivered amid exultant cries of 'Deliverance! deliverance!' as the besiegers withdrew. He published it as *Mans Wrath and Gods Praise* (1646), and thereafter annually on 11 May he preached in gratitude for 'the gratious deliverance from the strait siege'; his sermon for 1652 was also published.

In 1646 Newton was a signatory with William Prynne and others of a letter favouring the setting up of presbyterian classes in Somerset. From 1654 under the protectoral ordinance he served in company with Independents as a trier of ministers for Somerset. In 1655 the zealous Joseph Alleine (1634–1668) joined him as assistant at St Mary's. Alleine's tireless emphasis on 'domestic religion'—involving frequent home visiting—chimed well with Newton's own ideals and practices. He was named in Robert Blake's will (dated 1655) as a trustee for the distribution of a legacy of £100 for the poor of Taunton.

In 1660 Newton published *An Exposition with Notes*, of John, chapter 17, based on weekly sermons to his congregation. Under the terms of the Act of Uniformity, on 27 August 1662 he was ejected from his living, although he was still living in Taunton in 1664–5, when he paid hearth tax for a house in North Street. In his last sermon at St Mary's he prayed that if he could not serve God in one way he might do so more earnestly in another. Certainly whenever and wherever it seemed safe to do so he contrived to preach, and his sermons were well regarded for their unembellished style and 'profitable' content, but at length, according to Anthony Wood, he was apprehended and for some years imprisoned. None the less, he preached at the funeral of his former assistant, Alleine, in 1668; the sermon was published in 1672 as an annexe to *The Life and Death of Mr Joseph Alleine*. Newton was licensed as a presbyterian minister at Taunton on 2 May 1672 but by 1677 was ministering to a congregationalist meeting in Paul Street. In March 1680 he was presented for nonconformity at the assizes. Newton died in Taunton on 12 June 1681 and was aptly enough buried in the chancel of his old church, with a monument to his memory. In his will dated 7 October 1679 he bequeathed land in Ireland and the leasehold of Thornfalcon Manor, where he had recently been living. He named two sons, Francis and Thomas, a daughter, Susanna, married to local presbyterian minister John Musgrave, and two grandchildren.

IVAN ROOTS

Sources *Calamy rev.*, 364–5 · *Reg. Oxf.* · *The nonconformist's memorial … originally written by … Edmund Calamy*, ed. S. Palmer, [3rd edn], 3 vols. (1802–3) · D. Underdown, *Somerset in the civil war and interregnum* (1973) · J. Stoughton, *Ecclesiastical history of England: the church of the Restoration*, 2 vols. (1870) · C. Stanford, *Joseph Alleine: his companions and times* [1861] · J. R. Powell, *Robert Blake: general-at-sea* (1972) · C. H. Firth and R. S. Rait, eds., *Acts and ordinances of the interregnum, 1642–1660*, 3 vols. (1911) · Foster, *Alum. Oxon.* · *ESTC* · *Walker rev.*, 198

Likenesses engraving (after painting by Bocquet), repro. in Palmer, ed., *The nonconformist's memorial*

Newton, Gilbert Stuart (1794–1835), artist, was born at Halifax, Nova Scotia, Canada, on 20 September 1794, the twelfth and youngest son of the Hon. Henry Newton (*d.* 1803), collector of his majesty's customs, and his wife, Ann, daughter of Gilbert Stuart, a Boston snuff grinder, and sister of Gilbert *Stuart (1755–1828), the portrait painter. Newton's parents left Boston in 1776 but when his father died in 1803 the family returned to Charlestown near Boston. Newton was destined for a commercial career but, showing an interest in painting, had lessons from his uncle and 'almost lived in' his house (Mason, 48). Newton is recorded as 'invariably' contradicting his teacher (ibid., 49). Having shown some promise as an artist, he travelled with an elder brother in 1817 to Italy, where he studied for about a year; this included time in Florence. On his way to London he stayed in Paris sometime between late September and late November 1817, and there met the artist Charles Robert Leslie, with whom he travelled back to England via Brussels and Antwerp.

Newton's first exhibit at the Royal Academy in 1818 was a self-portrait. His first exhibit at the British Institution was in 1819. This was *Falstaff Escaping in the Buck Basket* from Shakespeare's *Merry Wives of Windsor*, a type of literary and humorous subject which was to characterize most of his output and on which his reputation was built. In this he was influenced both by C. R. Leslie's growing success as a painter of literary subjects and domestic and everyday scenes and, as was the case with Leslie, also by his close and frequent contact with that gentle observer of English life and manners, the American author Washington Irving. He first met Irving in London in 1818 and exhibited a portrait of him at the Royal Academy in 1820 (priv. coll.). As a member of a small circle of American artists established in London which included Benjamin West and Washington Allston, he must have learned much from having access to their studios though there is no evidence of his having been a pupil of any of them. He was admitted as a student to the Royal Academy Schools on 15 January 1820.

The picture that established Newton's reputation was *The Importunate Author* from Molière's *Les fâcheux*, exhibited at the British Institution in 1821 and bought by the discerning collector Thomas Hope for 50 guineas. T. G. Wainewright, writing in the *London Magazine*, thought the expressions of the characters 'true and humourous; the costume correct and well arranged; the back ground appropriate and walk-inviting' (Wainewright, 439). For Newton colour was an important element of painting. In Paris with Wilkie in September 1821 he copied Veronese's *Marriage Feast of Cana* for this reason. Colouring in his exhibited pictures was frequently referred to by critics: a British Institution exhibit of 1826, *Deep Study*, was

Gilbert Stuart Newton (1794–1835), by Stephen James Ferris, 1883 (after self-portrait, 1821)

described as 'the climax of beautiful and harmonious colouring' (*Literary Gazette and Journal of Belles Lettres*, 92). C. R. Leslie, too, commented that Newton was 'blessed with an exquisite eye for colouring' (Dunlap, 301). With this, his dashing style of paint handling, and his ordinary draughtsmanship Newton's work conformed well with what in his time was deemed to be very much the British style of art, and in this context it is worth pointing out that when Newton was elected Royal Academician in 1832 it was to the place formerly held by John Jackson, a painter similarly renowned for his skills in handling and colour.

Socially highly agreeable, Newton was as popular as his art, and this undoubtedly helped his early career as a portraitist: his most famous sitter was Sir Walter Scott, whose portrait he exhibited at the Royal Academy in 1825. In London he exhibited twenty-seven pictures at the Royal Academy between 1818 and 1833 and twenty-two at the British Institution between 1819 and 1831. He attracted important patrons, among them George IV, the earl of Essex, the earl of Carlisle, the marquess of Lansdowne, the duke of Bedford, Robert Vernon, and John Sheepshanks. Much of Newton's work was engraved, and this secured him some reputation in Europe as well as reinforcing that which he also had in America. His fondness for producing fancy portraits of pretty women meant that his paintings were also engraved for keepsake volumes. In English public collections he is represented in the Tate and the Victoria and Albert Museum, London.

With what Washington Irving described as 'a naturally delicate' constitution, Newton appears to have been prone to illness (Irving to Leslie, 15 March 1823, Leslie,

2.140). This might have been connected with the undoubted neurotic streak in him: for example, after the success of his 1821 British Institution picture he confessed '[I] am terribly nervous lest I should not get as good a subject for my next' (Irving, 1.372). When with Wilkie in France in 1825, he was unwell. In October 1831 illness led to him take a voyage to America. There, in 1832, he heard that he had been elected a Royal Academician and in February he married Sarah (Sally) Williams Sullivan (1810–1892), with whom he had a child. They returned to England in November 1832, but during his time abroad Newton perhaps showed the first signs of madness. Samuel Morse heard that he 'made himself quite conspicious and rather obnoxious' in Boston (Morse to Cooper, 28 Feb 1833). By January 1834, 'in a sad serious excited state, but … recovering', as Constable described him, he was in an asylum (*Constable's Correspondence*, 107). Newton died in a Chelsea asylum on 5 August 1835. C. R. Leslie had often visited him there and described Newton's circumstances in some detail in his *Autobiographical Recollections*. He was buried on 13 August 1835 at St Mary's Church, Wimbledon, where a monument, designed by Francis Chantrey, was raised to him by a few fellow academicians. As an artist Newton's influence was in the end slight, though Richard Redgrave singled out *The Vicar of Wakefield Reconciling his Wife*, the picture that secured Newton's election as an associate of the Royal Academy in 1828, as the work 'that originally inspired me' (*Richard Redgrave … a Memoir*, 265). It was one of the most eminent of his artist friends, John Constable, who on hearing of his death most accurately summed up his place in history: 'He is a real & great loss to the art—and (after all) he will be more missed as a man (if possible) than as an artist' (*Constable's Correspondence*, 128).

ROBIN HAMLYN

Sources *GM*, 2nd ser., 4 (1835), 439 · *DNB* · G. C. Mason, *The life and works of Gilbert Stuart* (New York, 1879) · W. C. Dunlap, *A history of the rise and progress of the arts of design in the United States*, 2 vols. (New York, 1834), repr. with an introduction by J. T. Flexner and R. Weiss (1969), vol. 2, pp. 300–06 · *Appleton's cyclopaedia of American biography*, ed. J. E. Wilson and J. Fiske, 4 (New York, 1888) · C. R. Leslie, *Autobiographical recollections*, ed. T. Taylor, 2 vols. (1860) · Graves, *RA exhibitors* · S. C. Hutchison, 'The Royal Academy Schools, 1768–1830', *Walpole Society*, 38 (1960–62), 123–91, esp. 173 · *Literary Gazette*, 216 (10 March 1821), 153 · T. G. Wainewright, review, *London Magazine*, 3/16 (April 1821), 439 · A. Cunningham, *The life of Sir David Wilkie*, ed. P. Cunningham, 3 vols. (1843) · [W. Irving], *Life and letters of Washington Irving*, 3 vols. (New York, 1869) · *Literary Gazette and Journal of Belles Lettres*, 473 (11 Feb 1826), 92 · L. Park, ed., *Gilbert Stuart: an illustrated descriptive list of his works*, 4 vols. (New York, 1927), vol. 2, p. 278 · Redgrave, *Artists* · [S. Newton], 'Some old letters', *Scribner's Monthly*, 13/9 (Jan 1875), 354 · S. F. B. Morse, letter to J. F. Cooper, New York, 28 Feb 1833, Smithsonian Institution, Washington, DC, Morse papers [microfilm], vol. 2, fol. 9821 · *John Constable's correspondence*, ed. R. B. Beckett (1962–78), vol. 3, pp. 107, 128 · *Richard Redgrave … a memoir compiled from his diary*, ed. F. M. Redgrave (1891)
Likenesses G. S. Newton, self-portrait, exh. RA 1818 · S. J. Ferris, etching, 1883 (after self-portrait by G. S. Newton, 1821), BM, NPG [see illus.]

Newton, Sir (Leslie) Gordon (1907–1998), journalist, was born at 17 Grand Avenue, Muswell Hill, Middlesex, on 16 September 1907, the second son of John Newton, a prosperous plate glass merchant, and his wife, Edith Sara, *née*

Sir (Leslie) Gordon Newton (1907–1998), by unknown photographer, 1966

Goode. Educated at Blundell's School in Devon (his parents had by then moved to Minehead in Somerset, about 30 miles away), he was good enough as a violinist to be leader of the school orchestra. At Sidney Sussex College, Cambridge, he read economics and became a running blue. He graduated with an upper second-class degree in 1929 and joined the family glass business (it had been founded by his grandfather), but it collapsed the following year, leaving the family destitute. With the onset of the great depression, job opportunities were few and far between; so, at his father's suggestion, he set up in business on his own account, acquiring (for £120) a struggling mirror-making firm in the East End of London. He sold the company in 1933 and invested the modest proceeds in a motor car accessory business, which promptly went bust after his partner absconded with the cash.

After a dispiriting and hungry period unsuccessfully looking for work, in 1935 Newton was offered by Maurice Green, the editor of the *Financial News*, a job as a cuttings clerk at £4 a week. On 26 October the same year he married Peggy Ellen Warren (1909/10–1995), daughter of Walter William Warren, commercial manager. They had one son, Henry. By the time of his marriage Newton had already transformed himself from cuttings clerk into an all-purpose journalist; a glutton for work, he was promoted rapidly, and became the paper's news editor in 1939. A few months later, with war imminent, he joined the Honourable Artillery Company (HAC) as a gunner, and later became something of a gunnery expert. The following year he was commissioned, and remained with the HAC for the duration of the war, having turned down the offer of a job in intelligence.

On demobilization as a major in 1945 Newton returned to the *Financial News*, which had just acquired from the *Daily Telegraph*'s owner, Lord Camrose, the property and title of its fierce rival the *Financial Times* (*FT*), and was made features editor and leader writer of the post-merger *FT*. Four years later Hargreaves Parkinson, who had succeeded Green at the *Financial News* in 1938 and gone on to become the first editor of the merged paper, became ill and retired. Much to Newton's surprise and to that of most others, the chairman, Brendan Bracken, who had masterminded the merger, chose him ahead of the hot favourite, Harold Wincott, to fill the vacancy. It was an inspired appointment.

During his long editorship of the *FT*, which lasted until his self-imposed retirement at sixty-five in 1972, Newton successfully transformed the paper from little more than a City news-sheet to a substantial international newspaper with a worldwide reputation. He greatly improved the paper's quality, strengthening, deepening, and internationalizing its core coverage of finance, business, economics, and politics, and at the same time cautiously broadening out into other fields—most notably, egged on by his even longer-tenured managing director, Garrett Moore (subsequently eleventh earl of Drogheda), the arts. At the time Newton assumed the editorship the paper's circulation was below 60,000; by the time he relinquished it twenty-three years later it was well over three times as large and rising fast. It is a flattering tribute to his achievement that several newspapers around the world chose to print their financial sections on pink paper. He was a great editor: among the most successful, and most idiosyncratic, of British newspaper editors of the twentieth century.

In at least two respects Newton was a lucky editor. For one thing, he was in the right place at the right time. The merger in 1945 had left the new *FT* with an unchallenged UK dominance in what was to prove the great growth sector of post-war journalism. He was fortunate, too, in his proprietors: first, the Eyre family in the shape of the Eyre Trust, dominated by the forceful and enigmatic Bracken, who had been Churchill's Man Friday during the war; and subsequently, from 1957, the bafflingly diversified Pearson group, then still very much a family business. As a matter of policy they both left Newton to edit the paper in his own way without interference, and gave him their total backing whenever the powerful or influential sought to complain about anything that had appeared in the paper. This enabled Newton, in turn, to give his unqualified support to the journalist who had caused the offence. There was no more striking example of this than the take-over battle for British Aluminium during the winter of 1958–9, a watershed event in the evolution of the modern City of London, in which the go-getting, parvenu merchant bank S. G. Warburg took on and eventually defeated the serried (and appalled) ranks of the old City establishment, led by Lazards. The *FT*'s influential 'Lex' column, at that time written by Arthur Winspear, came down in favour of Warburgs, and Newton stood by Winspear—despite the fact that Lazards was also owned by the Pearson group.

Newton would not have enjoyed for long the unquestioned support of his proprietors had he not been so manifestly on top of his job. The great mystery was quite what it was that made him a great editor. So far from being larger than life, he appeared the most ordinary and unprepossessing of men. The Clement Attlee of newspaper editors, he frequently resembled no one so much as Mr Pooter. Wholly unpretentious, he was also—unlike Attlee—devoid of guile. To some extent it was his extraordinary ordinariness that enabled him to understand with unerring instinct what it was that the ordinary *FT* reader wanted to read. He had no need to seek guidance from what subsequently came to be known as focus groups, and had no time for this negation of leadership, either. Quite early on in his editorship the management commissioned a survey to discover how the readers would like to see the paper improved. The answer came back loud and clear: more share tips. Newton had no hesitation in locking the report in his bottom drawer and resolutely ignoring it.

Incapable of any great insight, Newton was also completely without affectation, and success never went to his head. If he never saw things in any great depth, he always saw them clearly, and was not to be sidetracked or fooled. A man of few words, he usually knew what he wanted, and even more clearly what he didn't want, even though he was frequently unable to articulate either what it was that he wanted or why he didn't want what he didn't want. And far more often than not he was right. In appearance Newton was lean and trim, of slightly above average height, with spectacles perched on a prominent aquiline nose, and a mouth that turned down at the corners, which frequently gave the impression of disapproval even when none was intended.

During the 1950s, his first decade of editorship, when the essentials of the paper's transformation were established, Newton's recruitment policy was unique. He picked graduates straight (national service apart) from Oxford and Cambridge, preferably with a first-class honours degree, although good seconds were tolerated, with no journalistic experience or training of any kind, and set them to write for the paper straight away. This had three advantages. First, perhaps helped by the fact that there were no individual by-lines in those days, he could mould them into the sort of journalists he wanted: he never wrote himself, but was very much a 'hands-on' editor. Second, since they were not members of the National Union of Journalists (NUJ), he could pay them significantly less than the NUJ minimum wage: seared by his own early experiences, he was always very careful with money, his own and the paper's alike. And third, since at that time all other national newspapers foolishly insisted on two years' apprenticeship in the provinces first, Newton was able to take the pick of those Oxbridge graduates who were attracted to the journalist's trade.

Among those Newton recruited to the *FT* in this way during the 1950s, many of whom went on to make a name for themselves, were Samuel Brittan, Jock Bruce-Gardyne, George Bull, John Higgins, Patrick Hutber, Nigel Lawson, Geoffrey Owen, William Rees-Mogg, Michael Shanks, and Christopher Tugendhat. As this list suggests, he insisted, at that time, that journalists had to be men. He was prepared to recruit Shirley Williams from Oxford, but she was confined to the syndication department and was never allowed to write. Later on he abandoned this last policy, with the recruitment of Sheila Black, the wife of the then editor of the *Daily Mirror*: she became not merely a valued colleague but a close friend (one of very few) and confidante of Newton's, a relationship which for many years was of great importance to him.

For the graduate direct intake of Newton's early years the *FT* was in some ways like a postgraduate education, both in journalism at the feet of a chain-smoking, gin-drinking (though always sober) principal, and in practical economics and finance on the job and from each other. This innovative and highly successful recruitment policy came to an end during the 1960s, when the NUJ succeeded in imposing a closed-shop agreement on Fleet Street (as the national newspapers were then known), and laid down the criterion of two years' active journalistic experience as the necessary prerequisite for an NUJ card. But by then Newton had already established the nature and quality of the paper he wanted; what lay ahead was organic growth (he tried but failed to persuade his proprietors to acquire *The Times* when the Astors put it up for sale in 1966) and the conquest of overseas (notably European) markets.

Wider recognition of Newton's achievement was surprisingly long in coming. It was not until 1966, after he had been editor for seventeen years (longer than the total tenure of most national newspaper editors), that he won a journalist of the year award, the same year that he accepted Harold Wilson's offer of a knighthood. He received a Granada Television special award in 1970.

After his retirement in 1972 Newton took on a number of board appointments, but his post-*FT* business career, notably his chairmanship of the Vavasseur group, a financial conglomerate which came to grief in the 1973–4 secondary banking collapse, was little happier than his earlier business experiences before he had become a journalist. As he put it in his memoirs, with his characteristic directness and understatement, 'When I retired I was offered four or five directorships and accepted the chairmanship of two companies, both of which were to cause me more worry than anything I had experienced in the previous 25 years' (Newton). A much more agreeable aspect of his long retirement by the banks of the Thames was that it enabled him to indulge to the full his passion for fly-fishing, which despite progressively failing eyesight he continued to enjoy up to the age of eighty-seven. He was always pleased (if sometimes surprised) at the subsequent success of so many of his protégés, who for many years came together to honour him at the annual dinner of the Gordon Newton Society, which George Bull and John Higgins had initiated in 1975.

Newton also began writing his autobiography, but after 20,000 words he was dissatisfied and gave it up. Instead, a slim volume of engaging but rather scrappy and poorly edited reminiscences was privately printed in a limited edition on the occasion of his ninetieth birthday in 1997. Its title, *A Peer without Equal*, was a Newtonism: a unique species of malapropism which he from time to time spontaneously came out with, much to the delight of those who worked for him. This particular one he had coined in the course of his obituary of Harold Wincott in 1969, the only article he wrote in all his twenty-three years as editor of the *FT*. He died of old age and cerebrovascular disease at his home, Thamesfield, Wargrave Road, Henley-on-Thames, Oxfordshire, on 31 August 1998, two weeks short of his ninety-first birthday. His wife, Peggy, had predeceased him in 1995, and their son, Henry, had predeceased them both. Newton devoted the best years of his life single-mindedly to the *Financial Times*, and that paper is his memorial.

NIGEL LAWSON

Sources G. Newton, *A peer without equal: memoirs of an editor*, ed. M. Rutherford (1997) · D. Kynaston, *The Financial Times: a centenary history* (1988) · G. Bull, 'A peculiar kind of genius', *British Journalism Review*, 9/1 (1998), 20–31 · *Financial Times* (2 Sept 1998) · *The Times* (3 Sept 1998) · *Daily Telegraph* (3 Sept 1998) · *The Independent* (3 Sept 1998) · *The Guardian* (3 Sept 1998) · *WWW* · private information (2004) · personal knowledge (2004) · b. cert. · m. cert. · d. cert.
Likenesses photograph, 1966, Press Association Photo Library, London [*see illus.*] · photograph, 1966, repro. in *The Guardian* · photograph, 1967, repro. in *Daily Telegraph* · photograph, repro. in *The Times* · photograph, repro. in *The Scotsman* (10 Sept 1998)
Wealth at death £345,638—gross; £334,668—net: probate, 18 Nov 1998, *CGPLA Eng. & Wales*

Newton, Harry Robert (*bap.* 1828, *d.* 1889). *See under* Newton, Sir William John (1785–1869).

Newton, Henry. *See* Puckering, Sir Henry, third baronet (*bap.* 1618, *d.* 1701).

Newton, Sir Henry (1650–1715), diplomat and judge, was baptized at Romford on 20 August 1650, the eldest son of Henry Newton of Highley, Essex, and his wife, Mary, daughter of Richard Hunt of Essex. He matriculated at St Mary Hall, Oxford, on 17 March 1665, aged fourteen, graduated BA in 1668, and proceeded MA in 1671 and BCL in 1674. He was still at St Mary Hall in August 1676 when his sister was licensed to be married. He transferred to Merton College and received his degree of DCL on 27 June 1678. He was admitted an advocate of Doctors' Commons on 23 October 1678. While in practice at Doctors' Commons, Newton lived in the parish of St Benet Paul's Wharf. By 1683 he had married Sarah; a daughter, Sarah, was baptized at St Benet on 15 November that year, but was buried a few days later. Within the next few years his wife also died and Newton married Mary, daughter of Thomas Manning of St Dunstan-in-the-West, London. Their daughter, Mary, was baptized on 4 February 1690. Subsequently two further children, Catherine and Henry, were baptized in the parish, Henry only living a few weeks.

Newton acted as one of the counsel for Henry Compton, bishop of London, when he was called before the ecclesiastical commission in 1686 over the issue of allowing John Sharp to preach against Roman Catholicism. Newton succeeded Sir Thomas Exton as chancellor of the diocese of London early in 1689; Rupert Browne believed that 'he will make a good figure in that place' (*Downshire MSS*, 1.305). He also served as principal official to the archdeacon of Essex. From a letter Newton wrote to Sir William Trumbull in

October 1694 it would appear that he had acted as an Admiralty advocate, stepping into a vacancy caused by the dismissal of William Oldys 'when there was no person to supply the place' (ibid., 1.451). On 26 January 1694 he had been sworn 'the King's Counsel' (Admiralty advocate), and this had caused him to forfeit his private practice and had damaged him financially. In his quest for compensation he mentioned that some people had regarded him as the deputy of Fisher Littleton, but that he had received the 'whole fees for the time, as advocate of the Admiralty'. In the event Newton officially succeeded Littleton on 16 March 1697. On 23 February 1699 his old friend Lord Chancellor John Somers appointed Newton a master in chancery, a post he retained until 20 August 1701.

In November 1704 Newton received his credentials as envoy-extraordinary to Genoa and Tuscany. In January 1705 he was at The Hague, finally reaching Florence in May. He spent most of his time in Florence, following the Florentine court when it went to Leghorn (with its important English merchant factory) and Pisa. From September 1706 to June 1707 he lived in Genoa, where one of his servants was murdered. As envoy he provided a constant stream of reports back to England; he also had to deal with trading disputes and, having obtained the right of the merchants at Leghorn to practise their religion, he had to make the Anglican chaplain at Leghorn, Basil Kennet (brother of White Kennet), his personal chaplain to reduce the harassment he had to endure. While abroad Newton also executed various artistic and agricultural commissions for his Oxford contemporary and friend Lord Somers, the duke of Marlborough (statues for Blenheim), and Bishop Compton of London (seeds). In 1708 Newton revealed that he had 'been advocate general for the Admiralty' for many years, with Nathaniel Lloyd acting as his deputy while he was abroad; the death in October of Prince George, who had been head of the Admiralty, led him to hope that the arrangement would be continued. In July 1709 he received the news that he had been named as master of St Katherine's Hospital in London, and an intimation that before too long this would require his presence in England. Newton seems to have argued successfully for an extension of his embassy, but in May 1710 he was informed that his recall was imminent. This news may account for Newton's visit to Rome, where he was at the end of May. While in Italy he had several works published in Latin, and was admitted a member of the Academia della Crusa. This was matched on 4 May 1709 by his election to the Royal Society. In April–May 1711 Newton was in Genoa to take his leave of the republic, and then he returned home.

Newton was still chancellor of the diocese of London, master of St Katherine's, and Admiralty advocate. He continued in the latter post until 28 October 1714. On 1 December 1714 he was made a judge of the Admiralty court and he was knighted on 4 March 1715. Newton died suddenly on 29 July 1715, and was buried in the Mercers' Company chapel in London. His family even received a letter of commiseration from Pope Clement XI, who had been a regular correspondent of Newton. He was survived by his wife and two daughters: Mary (*d.* 1737), who married Henry Rodney, of Rodneystoke, Somerset, and was the mother of Admiral George Bridges *Rodney; and Catherine (*d.* 1755), who married Colonel Francis Alexander (*d.* 1722), and then Lord Aubrey *Beauclerk. STUART HANDLEY

Sources G. C. Gebaueri [G. C. Gebauer], *Georgii Christiani Gebaueri … Narratio de Henrico Brenkmanno* (Göttingen, 1764) • Foster, *Alum. Oxon.* • G. D. Squibb, *Doctors' Commons: a history of the College of Advocates and Doctors of Law* (1977), 183 • J. C. Sainty, ed., *Admiralty officials, 1660–1870* (1975), 98, 141 • D. B. Horn, ed., *British diplomatic representatives, 1689–1789*, CS, 3rd ser., 46 (1932), 73–4, 78 • W. A. Littledale, ed., *The registers of St Bene't and St Peter, Paul's Wharf, London*, 1, Harleian Society, register section, 38 (1909), 45, 53, 55, 57 • BL, Add. MSS 61153, fols. 172–202; 61518–61520; 61651 • E. Carpenter, *The protestant bishop, being the life of Henry Compton* (1956), 220, 366 • *The letters and dispatches of John Churchill, first duke of Marlborough, from 1702 to 1712*, ed. G. Murray, 5 vols. (1845), vol. 4, pp. 377, 680; vol. 5, p. 257 • *Report on the manuscripts of the marquis of Downshire*, 6 vols. in 7, HMC, 75 (1924–95), vol. 1, pp. 305, 451–2 • T. D. Hardy, *A catalogue of lords chancellors, keepers of the great seal, masters of the rolls and principal officers of the high court of chancery* (1843), 97 • will, PRO, PROB 11/547, sig. 163

Archives BL, Blenheim papers, Add. MSS 61518–61520, 61651 • CKS, letters to Alexander Stanhope

Likenesses B. Fariat, line engraving (after copper medal by M. Soldani-Benzi), NPG • M. Soldani-Benzi, copper medal, BM

Newton, Sir Isaac (1642–1727), natural philosopher and mathematician, was born on 25 December 1642 in the manor house of Woolsthorpe, near Colsterworth, about 7 miles south of Grantham, Lincolnshire, the only and posthumous son of Isaac Newton (1606–1642), yeoman farmer, and his wife, Hannah (*c.*1610–1679), daughter of James Ayscough, gentleman, of Market Overton, Rutland. His family could trace its roots to John Newton of Westby, a village near Grantham; John Newton's grandfather Simon Newton was a husbandman whose name appeared among taxpayers listed in Westby in 1524. The family clearly had industry and ability, each generation inching up the local hierarchy. Thus the son of John Newton of Westby styled himself yeoman in his will of 1562, a step above husbandman, and successive wills indicate that the family flourished until its members could be counted among the most prosperous farmers in the district. They were also prolific, so that the area south of Grantham came to be sprinkled with numerous thriving Newton families, descended from Simon Newton of Westby.

Early years and education Isaac Newton's own endowment was secure. One of his ancestors had purchased a farm in Woolsthorpe for a son, Richard; the manor of Woolsthorpe was added in 1623, and the combined estate was inherited by Newton's father in 1641. His mother, Hannah, brought a property worth £50 per annum to the marriage—her brother William occupied the rectory of Burton Coggles, 2 miles east of Woolsthorpe. As soon as the estate was settled Newton's parents married, in April 1642, but six months later, early in October, his father died, leaving a pregnant widow. For a yeoman, he also left a considerable estate, which would bear upon the prospects of his unborn son. In addition to extensive lands, there were goods and chattels valued at £459, including a flock of 235 sheep and 46 head of cattle, possessions in

Sir Isaac Newton (1642–1727), by Sir Godfrey Kneller, 1702

excess of the average at that time. Although it is impossible to assess accurately, an annual value of £150 appears to be a reasonable estimate of the estate.

Isaac Newton was born on Christmas day, a tiny baby. He was not expected to survive and his mother delayed his baptism until 1 January 1643. The next recorded event in his life was more than three years later, when his mother married the Revd Barnabas Smith, left her first-born son with her parents in Woolsthorpe, and went off to the rectory of North Witham, 1½ miles south of Woolsthorpe, to rear a second family. Smith was wealthy, with an estate worth £500 per annum in addition to the rectory. There is some evidence that Newton, who never mentioned his stepfather, hated him, and he probably did not care for his grandparents either. He recorded no affectionate recollection of his grandmother, and made no mention whatever of his grandfather. The animosity was shared; grandfather Ayscough pointedly omitted him from his will. The unpleasant aspects of Newton's mature personality may have had their roots in this traumatic period.

The family were reunited in 1653, when Smith died and Newton's mother returned to Woolsthorpe with his half-brother and two half-sisters. By this time Newton's education had begun in day schools in neighbouring villages, undoubtedly thanks to his Ayscough upbringing. At least in the Revd William Ayscough, who held an MA from Cambridge, and probably in other family members, the Ayscoughs had a history of education, whereas neither Newton's father nor his uncles on the paternal side were able to sign their names. His education continued when, less than two years after the return of his mother to Woolsthorpe, he was sent off to the free grammar school of King Edward VI in Grantham.

In Grantham, Newton lodged with an apothecary, a Mr Clark. About his studies very little is known but it may be assumed that the master, a Mr Stokes, did what nearly every schoolmaster of the age did—that is, he concentrated on building a mastery of Latin. At any rate, about the middle of his undergraduate career, Newton began to compose as readily in Latin as in English. Although mathematics does not figure in the Newton papers from this time, a recent discovery has indicated that Stokes had more than ordinary mathematical competence, and he may have played some role in directing Newton down this path. However, the stories that survived in Grantham had to do with other things, with building models, including a working model of a windmill, constructing sundials, and frightening the townspeople with a lantern attached to a kite. There was apparently a schoolboy romance with the stepdaughter of his landlord (though hers is the only account of it): years later, the young woman, then Mrs Vincent, was one of two people from Grantham that Newton recalled with pleasure.

Late in 1659, as he neared the age of seventeen, Newton's mother called him home from school to take charge of her considerable estate. The experiment was a disaster. Newton wanted none of it. He had discovered the world of learning, and there his heart lay. Set to watch the sheep, he would, it was said, build models of water-wheels while the sheep wandered into the neighbours' fields, leaving his mother to pay for the damage. Stokes had assessed his student's potential and offered to remit the fee if Newton were to return, and the Revd William Ayscough likewise urged his sister to let the young man prepare for the university. In the autumn of 1660 she relented. Newton returned to Grantham, and nine months later he departed for Cambridge.

Undergraduate years Newton arrived in Cambridge on 4 June 1661 and the following day presented himself at Trinity College, where he was entered in the books as a sub-sizar. Sizars and sub-sizars—the college does not appear to have made a distinction between them—were poor students who earned their keep by performing menial tasks. Although less segregated in Trinity than in other colleges, they were nevertheless a lower order who, for example, were not allowed to dine with the other students.

Newton's status as sizar raises questions. Heir to the lordship of a manor, son of a widow who can only be described as wealthy, he was used to being served, not to serving. Two explanations that are not mutually exclusive present themselves. His mother had begrudged him a full grammar school education, and she may have been unwilling to send him to the university on any other terms (his patchy undergraduate accounts that survive seem to suggest a stingy allowance). Alternatively he may have gone to Trinity as the sizar of Humphrey Babington, a fellow of the college who had Lincolnshire connections, whose sister was the wife of the apothecary in Grantham with whom Newton had stayed. Babington held the rectory of Boothby Pagnell, not far from Woolsthorpe; Newton stayed at Boothby Pagnell for part of the time he was home during the plague, and a number of other details

connect the two men. Babington was resident in Trinity only four or five weeks of the year and may have needed someone to watch over his affairs.

In any event it is safe to assume that Newton's lowly status as a sub-sizar served to magnify his isolation from other students. He formed a friendship with one, John Wickins, who became his chamber fellow and, like Newton, stayed on as a fellow of the college. Although a number of others who were students with Newton also became fellows and lived in the college with him for thirty-five years, there is no evidence from either side of any relationships between them. His isolation as a student, extending a pattern already manifest in grammar school, formed the initial chapter of an isolation within the university that continued until he left. After his departure he never corresponded with anyone he had known there.

Evidence of Newton's studies comes from the reading notes that he kept, especially those in one notebook. They show that his tutor, Benjamin Pulleyn, set him a curriculum the roots of which stretched back four centuries to the establishment of the medieval universities. Its focus was Aristotle: Newton read Aristotelian logic, Aristotelian ethics, and Aristotelian rhetoric, all preparations for the study of Aristotelian philosophy. Johannes Magirus's *Physiologiae peripateticae* furnished his first serious introduction to natural philosophy—Aristotelian natural philosophy, of course, as the name of the book implies.

In what became his characteristic style, Newton made notes from both ends of the notebook. It is significant that he did not finish reading any one of the texts he was set, and suddenly, apparently early in 1664, although nothing fixes the date with certainty, he broke off his reading in the established curriculum to pursue a different line of study. There is no hint of tutorial guidance. By every indication, Newton launched his new course alone. In the notebook some 200 pages in the middle remained empty. On one of them he entered a title, 'Questiones quaedam philosophcae' [*sic*], and he set down forty-five headings under which to gather information from his new reading (CUL, Add. MS 3996, fols. 88–135). Later he copied a slogan under the title: 'Amicus Plato amicus Aristoteles magis amica veritas'. Neither Plato nor Aristotle appeared again in the 'Quaestiones'. What did appear, significantly, were notes from Descartes, then reported in Cambridge, as in Paris, as the leading exponent of a revolutionary new philosophy. Descartes's writings he digested in a way he had never digested the readings prescribed by the curriculum. He also took notes from Walter Charleton's English digest of Pierre Gassendi, from Galileo's *Dialogue*, and from the writings of Robert Boyle, Thomas Hobbes, Kenelm Digby, Joseph Glanville, and Henry More, all in their way exponents of unauthorized philosophical positions, and interested in the new science.

The 'Quaestiones quaedam' launched Newton's career in science. They set out his initial interest in a number of key phenomena, such as the cohesion of bodies, capillary action, the expansion of gases, and surface tension, that

continued to occupy central places in his ongoing speculations on the nature of things. Also noted was his first concern with the question of colours, the problem of motion,
and the cause of gravity in terrestrial bodies. More than
anything else, the 'Quaestiones' considered the relative
merits of the Cartesian and the Gassendist (that is, atomist) versions of the mechanical philosophy, and began to
lean towards the latter.

Anni mirabiles, 1665–1666 One of the central stories in the
Newton legend concerns the *annus mirabilis*, the marvellous year of discovery to which all of his later achievements in science could be traced. Newton himself helped
to inaugurate the story in an often quoted passage that
dates from much later:

> In the beginning of the year 1665 I found the Method of
> approximating series …. The same year in May I found the
> method of Tangents of Gregory & Slusius, & in November
> had the direct method of fluxions & the next year in January
> had the Theory of Colours & in May following I had entrance
> into ye inverse method of fluxions.

Nor were his discoveries confined to mathematics. Newton went on to claim that:

> the same year I began to think of gravity extending to ye orb
> of the Moon & (having found out how to estimate the force
> with w^{ch} [a] globe revolving within a sphere presses the
> surface of the sphere) from Keplers rule of the periodical
> times of the Planets being in sesquialterate proportion of
> their distances from the center of their Orbs, I deduced that
> the forces wch keep the Planets in their Orbs must [be]
> reciprocally as the squares of their distances from the
> centers about wch they revolve: & thereby compared the
> force requisite to keep the Moon in her Orb with the force of
> gravity at the surface of the earth, & found them answer
> pretty nearly. All this was in the two plague years of 1665–
> 1666. For in those days I was in the prime of my age for
> invention & minded Mathematicks & Philosophy more than
> at any time since.   (CUL, Add. MS 3968.41, fol. 85)

As Newton's words make clear, the legend should at least
speak of *anni mirabiles*, in the plural, yet the historical evidence shows that much of the work mentioned was less
complete than his words imply—it is now generally
agreed that only with hindsight can the bulk of Newtonian science be traced to this early date. Never mind: the
achievement of these years, measured by any standard
other than that of the Newton legend, remains marvellous in the full sense of the word.

In 1664 mathematics seized Newton's attention, and in
mathematics the marvellous years were most fully realized. When the surviving record of mathematical study
during the following two years is considered it is hard to
believe that he had time for anything else. By his own
account, which his niece's husband, John Conduitt, wrote
down, he was self-taught in mathematics:

> He bought Descartes's Geometry & read it by himself …
> when he was got over 2 or 3 pages he could understand no
> farther than he began again & got 3 or 4 pages farther till he
> came to another difficult place, than he began again &
> advanced farther & continued so doing till he made himself
> Master of the whole without having the least light or
> instruction from any body.   (King's Cam., Keynes MS 130.10,
> fol. 2v)

With Descartes's *Geometry*, Newton studied the wealth of

commentaries included in the second Latin edition. He
also absorbed the Dutchman Franz van Schooten's *Miscellanies*, William Oughtred's *Clavis*, the works of François
Viète on algebra, and the writings of John Wallis on infinitesimals. Within a year, working on his own, Newton had
made himself the master of the new analysis created by
earlier mathematicians of the seventeenth century. Gradually his reading notes transformed themselves into original investigations, and he launched forth on the sea of
mathematics as an independent explorer.

The central mathematical discoveries Newton's first major
discovery came in quadratures, or what is now called integration. Following a method he found in Wallis, he set out
to determine the area, in the first quadrant, of a segment
under a circle. From earlier analysts he knew how to
evaluate areas under curves of the simple power series
such as $y = x$, x^2, x^3 …, and Wallis had also taught him that
the pattern observed in the results applies equally to frac-
tional and negative exponents, and that with polynomials
the area is the sum of areas under the separate terms, each
computed according to the same rule. But what was one to
do with curves such as $y = (1 - x^2)^{1/2}$, the circle, or $y = 1/x$, the
equilateral hyperbola? Expanding and improving on Wal-
lis's method, Newton arrived at the binomial theorem
which expresses such areas as infinite series. In his enthusiasm for his new discovery he utilized the area under the
equilateral hyperbola to calculate the logs of 1.1, 1.01, and
a few more numbers to 55 places (*Mathematical Papers*,
1.101–41). Added to the procedures he inherited, the binomial expansion gave Newton a general method of quadratures by which he could find the area under virtually every
algebraic curve then known to mathematics.

One of the central problems that the new analysis dealt
with was drawing tangents to curves, essentially differentiation. In this case, Newton initially followed the
approach of Descartes, which determined the normal to a
curve, which is perpendicular to the tangent, at a given
point. Always seeking to generalize, he worked out an
algorithm valid for any equation to determine the subnor-
mal, the distance along the x axis between the x
co-ordinate of a point on a curve and the place where the
normal to that point cuts the axis.

Patterns, which Newton did not fail to note, began to
emerge. The formulae for the subnormals seemed related
to those for squaring the same curves. The idea occurred:
would it be possible to use the patterns to define curves
that could be squared? As Newton pursued the idea he
called upon the concept that areas under curves are generated by lines in motion. He was soon rewarded with what
is recognized today as the fundamental theorem of the
calculus—the inverse relation of differentiation and integration (*Mathematical Papers*, 1.221–33).

In the autumn of 1665 Newton extended the kinematic
approach he had used for areas to tangents. He began to
think of curves being generated by the motion of a point.
If the equation of a curve expresses how x and y vary in
relation to each other, the point that traces the curve will
move at a rate compounded from the velocities of x and y,
and the slope of the tangent at any point will be the ratio

of their velocities. Let p be the velocity of x, and q the velocity of y. Newton derived an algorithm for determining the ratio of q/p (the derivative of y with respect to x) from the equation of the curve. His name for the method now beginning to emerge, the fluxional method (from the past participle of the Latin verb *fluere*, to flow) expressed the intuitive concept of motion with which he sought to escape from the complexities of infinitesimals, which he considered dubious concepts in mathematics.

The autumn of 1665 passed in feverish activity until, in a paper dated 13 November, Newton summarized his results, which solved the various problems in mathematics on which he had been focusing his attention. With their solution he seemed to lose interest and the manuscripts indicate that he did not touch mathematics again for six months. In May 1666 he returned to draft two successive versions of a general paper, and then, after another pause, a third version in October. He gave it the title 'To Resolve Problems by Motion these Following Propositions are Sufficient' (*Mathematical Papers*, 1.400–48). In the paper Newton spelt out the inverse algorithms for tangents and quadratures and applied them to a number of problems such as determining centres of curvature, and rectifying certain curves. Even though no one at the time knew of the existence of the tract of October 1666, Newton had become Europe's leading mathematician.

From the manuscripts it appears that Newton dropped mathematics once more and did not concern himself with it during the following two years. In the future he returned to mathematics at intervals: he worked on his fluxional method a number of times, mostly seeking to place it on a more secure foundation; he composed a pathbreaking investigation of cubics; and he explored interpolation theory and projective geometry. As the years passed his returns to mathematics became less and less frequent, and increasingly it was external impulses that set him to work. As he said, he never again minded mathematics so closely.

Optics and mechanics There was other fare on which to feast. Whereas Cartesian and atomist philosophers considered light to be homogeneous, in the 'Quaestiones quaedam', as Newton considered colours, he had set down his first suggestion of the heterogeneity of light. He thought of an experiment to test whether the rays that provoke the sensation of blue may be refracted more than the rays that provoke red: colour one end of a thread red and the other blue; when the thread is viewed through a prism the two ends should appear disjoined. He tried it, and they did. There, for the time being, he left the topic. By Newton's own testimony, somewhat later he was trying to grind lenses of elliptical and hyperbolic cross-section. Descartes had demonstrated that such lenses would refract parallel rays, those from a star for example, to a perfect focus, as spherical lenses do not. Newton realized that, while Descartes had assumed the homogeneity of light, the experiment with the thread seemed to demonstrate the opposite. Even if he succeeded in grinding the non-spherical lenses, they would not produce a perfect focus. At this point, Newton abandoned the lenses and

took up an experimental investigation of the heterogeneity of light.

Newton's primary tool was an established instrument in optics, the prism. Into his darkened room he admitted a narrow beam of light through a hole in the shutter and refracted the beam through a prism onto a wall 22 feet away. This arrangement, especially the long trajectory giving enough distance for the refracted beam of finite cross-section to spread, altered the conditions of earlier experiments of which he had read and adapted the experiment to his own question. If light were homogeneous, the refracted beam ought to have cast a round image on the wall: instead it painted a spectrum five times as long as it was wide.

Newton recorded his investigation in an essay he entitled 'Of colours', entered into another of his student notebooks, probably early in 1666 (CUL, Add. MS 3975, 1–20). The new theory he began to elaborate inverted a tradition of more than 2000 years in Western science and philosophy, according to which light as it comes from the sun, pure and homogeneous, either is or appears white and colours arise from its modification. For Newton, light as it comes from the sun is a heterogeneous mixture of rays that differ in the sensations of colour they cause. Sensations of white and shades of grey are caused by the mixture; phenomena of colour arise from the separation of the mixture into its components, which for Newton are primary and immutable. Because the rays differ also in their degree of refrangibility, the prism disperses the incident beam into a diverging spectrum.

At that time Newton did not carry his work in optics to the same level of completeness that his mathematics had reached. The heterogeneity of light he subjected to a rigorous investigation, devising other experiments to separate white light into its components. He carefully eliminated the possibility that the spreading spectrum could be an accidental result of imperfections in the glass. Colours analogous to the prismatic spectrum, however, are a tiny fraction of all the phenomena of colours, most of which are associated with solid bodies. Newton was convinced that the other phenomena also arise from processes of separation, caused by the differing tendencies of rays to be reflected more readily from some surfaces than from others. A couple of experiments in the essay 'Of colours' spoke to this issue, one of them the first, relatively crude, production of Newton's rings, which would be, in a more refined state, the foundation of his approach to the colours of solid bodies. Another experiment, also relatively crude in comparison to later ones, illustrated the reassembly of the separated rays to produce the sensation of white—a demonstration essential to the theory. Not wholly free from the long tradition, Newton still spoke at this time largely in terms of two colours, red and blue. He had seized what remained the central idea of all his work in optics, the heterogeneity of light, but it is not wholly true that, in the language of his later statement, he 'had the Theory of Colours' in 1666.

During roughly the same period Newton also took his first steps in mechanics. Two of the 'Quaestiones quaedam' dealt with motion, and he had seemed at that point to embrace the atomistic doctrine that a principle of motion inheres in bodies. Not long thereafter, in another notebook, which he called the 'Waste book', he addressed the problem of impact (CUL, Add. MS 4004, fols. 10–15, 38*v*). Impact was a Cartesian problem. Newton considered it within a Cartesian context that started with the enunciation, in language almost identical to that in Descartes's *Principles of Philosophy*, of the principle that particles at rest or in motion retain their status unless disturbed by another body. Beyond this point, however, he diverged from Descartes, who had treated impact in terms of the force that a body in motion possesses by virtue of its motion. In contrast Newton began to define an abstract concept of force which, whatever its cause in a given case might be, set the change of motion proportional to the force exerted. He reasoned that when two bodies meet in impact each presses equally on the other, and both must undergo equal and opposite changes of motion. From this he concluded that the common centre of gravity of two isolated bodies in impact remains in an inertial state of rest or of uniform motion in a straight line. The conclusion is identical to the principle of the conservation of momentum. It appears as corollaries three and four to the laws of motion in the *Principia*.

On another problem in mechanics, circular motion, Newton remained closer to Descartes. The French philosopher, whose concept of today's 'rectilinear inertia' made circular motion a problem, set the pattern for its subsequent treatment with the idea that bodies constrained in circular motion endeavour constantly to recede from the centre. Centrifugal force, as Christiaan Huygens named it, was another force that a body possesses by virtue of its motion, but with circular motion Newton retained the concept that he replaced when he dealt with impact. Proceeding beyond Descartes he derived a quantitative measure of it, equivalent to today's formula for the radial force, mv^2/r.

Two other early manuscripts concerned with circular motion survive. In one of them Newton took up the problem he found in Galileo's *Dialogue*, an answer (imperfect in Galileo) to the argument that the earth cannot be turning daily on its axis because loose objects would be hurled into space. Newton saw that the objection could be assessed definitively with his quantitative measure of centrifugal force. From the accepted size of the earth he computed the centrifugal acceleration at the equator due to the diurnal rotation and compared it to the figure Galileo gave for the acceleration of gravity. Gravity, he found, is about 150 times greater than the centrifugal force. Then he saw that the same measure of centrifugal force gave him a means to check Galileo's figure for *g*, via the measured period of a conical pendulum. Galileo's value, it turned out, was only about half the correct one, and the objection against Copernican astronomy was doubly invalid.

In the other paper Newton substituted the values of Kepler's third law into his formula for centrifugal force and found that among the planets the force varies inversely as the square of their distance from the sun. He also compared the centrifugal force exerted by the moon in its orbit with the measured acceleration (or force for a given body) of gravity at the surface of the earth. The ratio came out as 1 to something more than 4000. In accordance with astronomical measurements, Newton was setting the distance of the moon at sixty terrestrial radii. An inverse square relation would have been $\frac{1}{3600}$, and if a correct measurement of the earth had been available, he would have reached something close to this number. Most scholars believe that this paper was what Newton had in mind when he later stated that in the comparison he 'found them answer pretty nearly'. However, that does not mean that Newton had the concept of universal gravitation in 1666—nothing in the paper spoke of an attraction. He compared gravity at the surface of the earth with the moon's endeavour to recede, and if he silently assumed that something must be checking that endeavour since the moon remains in its orbit, nevertheless nothing like a universal attraction was mentioned and the correlation proved far from exact. Of his three early investigations, that in mechanics remained the least developed. Nevertheless, he remembered the calculation and later thought that it marked a step forward in his thought.

For all its brilliance the work in mathematics, optics, and mechanics which began during the final year or eighteen months of Newton's undergraduate career nearly blighted his future prospects. To pursue his new interests he had abandoned the established curriculum. In April 1664 Trinity had an election to scholarships, the only election during Newton's undergraduate years; only those who held scholarships would later be eligible for fellowships. Whatever obstacle his private course of study presented at this point, it appears that Newton had a patron in the college, probably Humphrey Babington, and he was elected. A little over a year later he proceeded BA.

Soon thereafter plague afflicted Cambridge and before the summer was over the university had dispersed. Newton returned to Woolsthorpe. The following March, after no deaths had been reported in Cambridge for six weeks, the university convened again, but by June it was evident that 1666 would also be a plague year. Only in the spring of 1667 did the university fully resume.

Much has been made of the plague years in the Newton legend. The *anni mirabiles* have been connected with his respite at home, but the manuscript evidence does not entirely support this notion. It is true that some of his important steps were taken in Woolsthorpe. The story of the apple—that, sitting in his orchard, he observed an apple fall from its tree and from this inferred the law of gravity—was set in Woolsthorpe and was connected with his idea that gravity extends to the sphere of the moon. Newton repeated the story to William Stukeley in his old age and it was later retailed by his niece and her husband, John Conduitt, and by Martin Folkes. Moreover, the tract of October 1666, his early definitive statement of the fluxional method, had to stem from Lincolnshire. Nevertheless, all of his investigations had begun in Cambridge, where the books that put him in contact with earlier figures of the scientific revolution were available, and his manuscripts do not reveal any marked break in continuity associated with the move. The marvellous years had as much to do with a young man's expanding intellectual world as with his physical location.

Lucasian professor Only a few months after his return to Cambridge in 1667 Newton faced another decisive election, this one for a fellowship and the possibility of an indefinite stay in Trinity. By 1667 Humphrey Babington was one of the eight senior fellows of the college. Newton prevailed in the election once again, and it seems likely that Babington's support was decisive. At that time Newton became a minor fellow of Trinity and a year later, upon incepting MA, one of the college's sixty major fellows. He received an income of about £60, part of which came in the form of room and board, and virtually no prescribed duties. He could tutor if he chose, and the college records show that over the years he was tutor to a total of three fellow-commoners. The sole trace of them in his life is one letter to one father. For twenty-eight years, until he left Trinity, he was free to follow his interests wherever they might lead him.

The first step led to his appointment as Lucasian professor of mathematics, a new and not very prestigious establishment but one of only eight chairs in the university at that time. Isaac Barrow, the first Lucasian professor to hold the chair, from 1664, had not been Newton's tutor, but it is likely that Newton attended his lectures. At some point, before or in 1669, the two became sufficiently acquainted that when Barrow received a copy of Nicholas Mercator's *Logarithmotechnia* from John Collins, a mathematical intelligencer in London, he realized how closely it paralleled a single case of Newton's binomial expansion. Mercator's book led Newton to compose a tract, 'De analysi per aequationes numero terminorum infinitas' ('On analysis by infinite series'), which Barrow forwarded to Collins (*Mathematical Papers*, 2.206–47). 'De analysi', which was not published until the eighteenth century, circulated among a confined circle in 1669 and constituted the first knowledge that others beyond Trinity (or perhaps beyond Barrow) had of Newton's abilities. Together with whatever else Barrow knew about his accomplishments, it led him to secure Newton's appointment to succeed him as Lucasian professor that same year, 1669. The income from the chair, about £100 per annum, added to his income from the Trinity fellowship and from his estate, ensured Newton's material well-being while he remained in Cambridge, and saved him, because he did not need the income which ordination would have provided, from having to subscribe to the articles of the Church of England, a requirement for fellows, but one which Newton would have been unable honestly to fulfil.

The statutes of the Lucasian chair required one lecture per week during three terms each year. Barrow had silently reduced the duty to one term per year, in which Newton acquiesced. Although the evidence is ambiguous, apparently he did deliver an annual series, often to an empty hall, until either 1684 or 1687. After that he converted the position into a sinecure, as other professors were doing, until he resigned it, together with his fellowship, five years after he left the university.

In 1669 Newton chose optics for his first lectures, and at that time he polished the theory of colours into its final form. The 'Lectiones opticae' ('Optical lectures'), deposited in the Cambridge University Library as the text of his first four sets of lectures, contains all the content of book one of the ultimate *Opticks*. About then he also returned to the experiment with Newton's rings, as they are still called, which would fill book two. He pressed a lens with a 50 foot radius of curvature down on a flat sheet of glass and with dividers carefully measured the diameters of the rings he observed in the film of air between the two pieces of glass. The computed thickness of the film marked the first secure entry of science into dimensions in the order of $\frac{1}{100,000}$ of an inch. The measurements also first established the periodicity of an optical phenomenon, although Newton did not hold that light itself is periodic. The periods belonged to waves of compression in the ether, generated in his view when a corpuscle of light strikes the first surface of a film, which determine whether the corpuscle can proceed through the second surface. Newton was convinced that the films, which reveal spectra, correspond to the thickness of the particles that compose bodies, and his experiments with the rings supplied his explanation of the colours of solid bodies.

The renewed work on optics also brought Newton further onto the public stage. From the differing refrangibility of rays he concluded that chromatic aberration could not readily be eliminated from refracting telescopes. A reflecting telescope, however, would not have this defect, and Newton constructed the first known reflecting telescope early in 1669, and later a second. The telescope was about 6 inches long; it magnified about forty diameters. He was proud of his creation and showed it off, and by late 1671 news of it had reached the Royal Society in London, which asked to see the instrument. When it arrived at the end of the year it caused a sensation. The society sent notices about it to the scientific community on the continent and elected Newton a fellow on 11 January 1672.

Pleased by the response, Newton offered to send the society the discovery that had led him to the telescope—'in my Judgment the oddest if not the most considerable detection wch hath hitherto beene made in the operations of Nature'. The letter he sent on 6 February 1672 was a condensed statement of his theory of colours and some of the experiments on which it rested (*Correspondence*, 1.92–102), and the society published the paper in its *Philosophical Transactions*. His exposition effectively concealed the complicated steps by which he had arrived at his new and revolutionary theory, an approach which led to many favourable but some unfavourable responses.

Newton's equanimity quickly dissolved. Most important in this process was a condescending critique by Robert Hooke, considered the Royal Society's resident expert in optics. After nearly four months of mounting anger with

Hooke, Newton sent a long reply couched in deliberately insulting terms. Through the society's secretary, Henry Oldenburg, he also received four successive letters in which Huygens, the recognized doyen of European science, expressed his increasing reservations about Newton's theory. With Huygens, Newton did not allow himself to take the high tone he used with Hooke; nevertheless Huygens recognized Newton's irritation and refused to discuss the question further. There were also other letters (through Oldenburg) of query and criticism to which he had to reply. The number was not huge, but Newton was quickly complaining that he had sacrificed his peace, 'a matter of real substance' (*Correspondence*, 2.133). Only thirteen months after he sent this first paper to the Royal Society he requested that he be dropped from its rolls, and he informed Oldenburg that he intended 'to be no further sollicitous about matters of Philosophy' (ibid., 1.294–5). He did not pursue the resignation further, and Oldenburg simply allowed the matter to drop. Nevertheless, Newton did sever his correspondence with Oldenburg and Collins, who had been the channels for his communication with everyone else, and did attempt to regain his isolation. It was too late: the telescope and the letter on colours had introduced him to the larger world of scientific learning, which did not forget that a man of superlative quality lived and worked in Cambridge.

At the end of August 1674, when Newton was in London for a week, he made no effort to contact anyone connected with the Royal Society. When he was again in the city early the following year, however, he chose to attend the society. He found himself an object, not of criticism, but of respect. While he was there a letter arrived from Father Linus, an English Jesuit in Liège, denying that the experiment with the prism worked as Newton described it. Hooke informed the society that the experiment was beyond question, and the whole society made its support of Newton clear. He also met and conversed with Robert Boyle, whose works he had studied carefully. When Linus wrote again to the same effect in the autumn of 1675, Newton was sufficiently confident to offer another paper on optics. In fact, he sent two: a 'Discourse of observations', on the colours of thin films, which was virtually identical to the first three parts of book two of the eventual *Opticks*, and 'An hypothesis explaining the properties of light'. Based on the concept of a universal ether, the 'Hypothesis' did not confine itself to optical phenomena. It presented a general system of nature, beholden to mechanical philosophies but also pervaded with themes that derived from his recent study of alchemy, which presaged future developments in Newton's natural philosophy.

The 'Hypothesis' quickly involved Newton in new controversy. It contained two provocative references to Hooke, and at the conclusion of its reading before the Royal Society in December 1675 Hooke rose to assert that most of its content was contained in his own *Micrographia*. When the charge was relayed to Cambridge, Newton exploded in rage reminiscent of that in 1672. A letter from Hooke, who claimed that Oldenburg had misrepresented him and went on to express his esteem for Newton, led to a mollified response in which Newton likewise expressed his esteem. Their basic antagonism remained, however; it would later find occasion for further expression.

Meanwhile the controversy with English Jesuits in Liège, arising from his paper of 1672, continued to disturb Newton's peace. When Linus died his student Anthony Lucas took up the cause and soon drove Newton to distraction. 'I see I have made my self a slave to Philosophy', he stormed to Oldenburg, after he had written only a fifth letter, 'but if I get free of Mr Linus's business I will resolutely bid adew to it eternally, excepting what I do for my privat satisfaction or leave to come out after me' (*Correspondence*, 2.182–3). Eventually, after a brutal letter in which he poured his paranoia over Lucas, he refused to receive any further communication from Liège and once more attempted to isolate himself from the learned world.

It was during this period of stress that Newton learned of another man who would later figure prominently in his life, Gottfried Wilhelm Leibniz, and briefly corresponded with him, as usual not directly but through an intermediary. In May 1676 in a letter to Oldenburg, Leibniz, who had developed his system of calculus the previous autumn, asked for a derivation of two infinite series by Newton that he had received from Collins. Urged by Oldenburg and Collins, Newton composed a long letter on infinite series. Later that year, in October, he composed a second letter in response to Leibniz's enthusiastic reception of the first (*Correspondence*, 2.20–32, 110–61). Nearly forty years later, when the priority dispute raged, Newton called upon the two letters, which he referred to at that time as 'Epistola prior' and 'Epistola posterior', as evidence against Leibniz. In the 'Epistola posterior', Newton indeed approached the fluxional method, brief statements of which he concealed in indecipherable anagrams. By the time of the controversy, Newton had learned further that, on a visit to London, Leibniz also saw papers by him in Collins's possession. Not only did Newton not meet the German mathematician at the time, he rebuffed Leibniz's eager desire to communicate. Prone in any case to isolation and thoroughly agitated then both by Hooke and by Lucas, he never replied to Leibniz's response to his second epistle. Instead of an intellectual exchange at the time, he earned a bitter dispute forty years later, when he used the 'Epistolae' as ammunition against his opponent.

Theology and alchemy When Newton told Oldenburg that he intended to bid philosophy adieu, he was not issuing an idle threat; well before 1676 new interests had seized his attention. One of them was alchemy. Shortly after he composed the 'Quaestiones quaedam', Newton began to read earnestly in chemistry, and about 1669 the interest turned decidedly toward alchemy. On a trip to London he purchased the massive six-volume *Theatrum chemicum* of 1602, and in the months ahead pored over its collection of alchemical treatises, taking extensive notes. Both here and elsewhere he studied all the recognized authorities, including contemporaries such as the pseudonymous Eireneaus Philalethes (George Starkey), one of Newton's favourite authors. One student of alchemy asserts that the vast literature of the art has never been read so thoroughly. Newton assembled one of the great collections of alchemical books, which formed a significant proportion of his personal library; he made contact with clandestine circles of alchemists from whom he received manuscripts that he copied; and in the garden outside his chamber in Trinity he set up a laboratory in which he experimented.

Some time about 1670 Newton compiled a manuscript known as 'The vegetation of metals' from a phrase in its first line—'that metalls vegetate after the same laws [of Nature]'. In the paper, which is more a collection of thoughts than a connected discourse, he insisted on the distinction between mere mechanical alterations in the textures of bodies and the more subtle and noble changes wrought by vegetation. The principles of vegetable actions are 'the seeds or seminall virtues of things those are her only agents, her fire, her soule, her life' (Smithsonian Institution, Dibner Collection, Burndy MS 16). Some of the passages in 'Vegetation' are similar to parts of the 'Hypothesis … of light', composed not long after it and pervaded with themes from alchemy: in the latter Newton met a natural philosophy that spoke in terms of life and spirit rather than inert particles in motion, and in the two manuscripts its influence began to transform his mechanical philosophy of nature.

Alchemy was not Newton's only new study—there was also theology. The statutes of Trinity may have started his serious reading in theology. They required that all fellows, with the exception of the holders of two specified fellowships, be ordained to the Church of England ministry within seven years of incepting MA. Newton was never one to take an obligation lightly, and it may have been the approaching ordination that set him on serious study of theology, about 1670. In his usual style he purchased a notebook and entered a set of headings under which to collect the fruits of his reading in an orderly way (King's Cam., Keynes MS 2). He devoured the Bible, making himself a master of it to an extent that few could match, and tackled the early fathers of the church in a prodigious programme of reading that took him through all the major fathers and many lesser ones as well. Almost immediately his study found a focus. In his notebook headings such as 'Christi passio, descensus, et resurrectio' and 'Christi satisfactio, & redemptio', apparently expected to be major topics from the space allotted to them in anticipation, received very few entries. 'Deus filius' ('God the Son'), on the other hand, spilled over the smaller space originally intended for it, and the entries he did set down suggest that very early he began to see a distinction between God the Father and God the Son and to question the status of Christ and the doctrine of the Trinity.

It did not take Newton long to read himself right out of orthodoxy. He became fascinated with the theological struggle of the fourth century as a result of which trinitarianism was established as Christian orthodoxy. For Athanasius, the principal architect of trinitarianism, he developed more than a mere antipathy—passionate hatred is a better description. One of his manuscripts, 'Paradoxical questions concerning the morals & actions of Athanasius & his followers' (King's Cam., Keynes MS 10), virtually stood Athanasius in the dock and prosecuted him for an extended litany of sins. Newton enlisted himself among the disciples of Athanasius's opponent, Arius, for whom Christ was not an eternal part of the Godhead but a created intermediary between God and man, a doctrine similar but not identical to modern unitarianism.

Interpretation of the prophecies formed a major strand of Newton's theological quest—primarily the book of Revelation at first, but later Daniel as well. Newton's interest in the prophecies is well known from a volume published after his death, but that publication was a product of his old age, sanitized by him to obscure its point. The unpublished interpretation that he composed in the 1670s fitted harmoniously with his new theological stance. The prophecies foretold the great apostasy, the rise of trinitarianism. The vials of wrath of the apocalypse represent the barbarian invasions of the Roman empire—'like Furies sent in by the wrath of God to scourge ye Romans'—God's punishments of a stiff-necked people who had gone whoring after false gods (Jerusalem, Jewish National and University Library, Yahuda MS 1.4, fol. 127).

Newton's Arianism nearly terminated his academic career. Religious heterodoxy of that extent was not something Cambridge would tolerate. Not that he advertised his heretical views—far from it. Newton understood perfectly that his theological views were anathema to the established order, and the need to keep what he regarded as his most important truth to himself was a central ingredient in his notorious secretiveness. The problem was ordination, required by 1675 at the latest: Newton had moved himself beyond the possibility of ordination and in the questions that would have arisen Newton could not have concealed his heretical views. A potential avenue of escape presented itself when one of the two exempted fellowships fell vacant, but unfortunately a fellow more senior than Newton claimed it. In a letter to Oldenburg early in 1675 Newton indicated that he was laying down his fellowship. At the last minute, probably through the intervention of Isaac Barrow, by then master of Trinity, a royal mandate that exempted the Lucasian professor in perpetuity from any college requirement of ordination rescued Newton and enabled him to continue in his sanctuary, at the time devoting himself largely to writing Arian tracts and to pursuing alchemy, two activities that he indulged in private.

In the early 1680s Newton went beyond mere Arianism in his most important theological composition, 'Theologiae gentilis origines philosophicae' ('The philosophical origins of gentile theology'), as he called it in the least chaotic of its incomplete manuscripts (Jerusalem, Jewish National and University Library, Yahuda MS 16.2). The 'Origines' removed the coming of Christ from the focus of world history and treated him as merely the latest in a series of prophets sent by God to reclaim mankind from false gods. But mankind has an innate tendency to idolatry; trinitarianism, the worship of a creature as God, was only another turn in the cycle that throughout history had repeatedly perverted worship. 'What was the true religion of the sons of Noah before it began to be corrupted by the worship of false Gods', Newton wrote as the title to one chapter that he did not compose; 'And that the Christian religion was not more true and did not become less corrupt' (Jewish National and University Library, Yahuda MS 16.2, fol. 45v). In the years ahead Newton kept inserting perplexing passages drawn from the 'Origines' into his scientific work—the final paragraph of 'Query 31' in the *Opticks*, for example, and the two footnotes to the 'General scholium' added to the *Principia*. Thoroughly purged, it became his *Chronology of Ancient Kingdoms Amended* (1728). The original treatise he kept to himself.

Alchemical work continued in tandem with theology. In the early 1680s Newton began what he called the 'Index chemicus', a typical Newtonian exercise in organizing and systematizing his knowledge. Newton kept expanding the 'Index' for more than a decade. In its ultimate form—there is nothing to suggest that he thought it complete—it contained 879 separate entries that cited more than 150 separate alchemical works, extending from mythical alchemists of antiquity to Newton's contemporaries, and gave about 5000 separate page references to them (King's Cam., Keynes MS 30). He continued also to experiment. His dated experimental notes began in 1678 and continued, with a break for composition of the *Principia*, almost until his departure from Cambridge (CUL, Add. MSS 3973; 3975, 101–58, 267–83). Couched in Newton's personal set of symbols, the experimental notes have so far resisted interpretation. Now and then, however, when success seemed to crown his endeavours, he interjected notes of exultation that echo the imagery of alchemy: 'Friday May 23 [1684] I made Jupiter fly on his eagle' (CUL, Add. MS 3975, 149).

Alchemy led to an important correspondence with Robert Boyle, his first significant direct correspondence with no intermediary. In a long letter to Boyle that Newton composed in 1679 he argued, among other things, for 'a certain secret principle in nature by wch liquors are sociable to some things & unsociable to others' (*Correspondence*, 2.288–95). A paper, 'De aere et aethere', related to the letter to Boyle, asserted that particles of air repel each other 'with a certain large force' (*Unpublished Scientific Papers*, 214–20). Mechanical philosophers employed an invisible ether to explain such phenomena. The letter to Boyle introduced an ether, though it also denied that the secret principle of sociability had anything to do with the sizes of particles and pores. The second chapter of 'De aere et aethere' also started to describe such an ether. After a few lines, however, it stopped in the middle of a sentence, as though he found the exercise futile. During the following thirty-five years the concept of an ether disappeared from Newton's natural philosophy, which dealt now with forces between particles.

About this time Newton underwent a general revulsion from Descartes, the philosopher who, more than anyone else, had introduced him to the new world of scientific thought, including the mechanical philosophy. The revulsion included mathematics: Cartesian geometry, he now

declared, was 'the Analysis of the Bunglers in Mathematicks' (Hiscock, 42). Natural philosophy and religion were central to the revulsion. An essay, 'De gravitatione et equipondio fluidorum' ('On the gravity and equilibrium of fluids'), not only repudiated basic themes of Cartesian philosophy, with a passion reminiscent of his attacks on Athanasius, but accused Descartes of atheism as well (*Unpublished Scientific Papers*, 89–121).

Newton's *Principia mathematica*, 1687 Newton's mother died during the spring of 1679 and he was absent from Cambridge for six months, tending her during her final days and then settling the estate in Woolsthorpe. Immediately upon his return late in November a letter from Robert Hooke arrived, the first of a number of intrusions prompted by his earlier renown in mathematics and natural philosophy. Hooke, now secretary of the Royal Society in place of the recently deceased Henry Oldenburg, invited Newton to resume correspondence with the society. Towards that end he invited Newton's opinion on his theory that planetary motions are compounded of a tangential motion that is continually deflected by an attraction towards a central body, the remarkable idea that Hooke had expounded in his Cutlerian lecture of 1674. It proposed the idea of a general attraction, not quite universal gravitation, and it inverted the conceptualization of circular motion by focusing attention, not on centrifugal force, but on an attraction towards the centre. Every indication is that Hooke, at this point, taught Newton to conceive of circular motion in these new terms. Not long thereafter Newton coined the phrase 'centripetal force', in imitation of Huygens's word 'centrifugal'; the central theme of the *Principia* would be the quantitative exploration of the new concept, something Hooke had not achieved.

At the time Newton rejected the correspondence; he was engaged in other studies, he told Hooke, and grudged time spent on philosophy. Nevertheless, he went on to propose an experiment to demonstrate the rotation of the earth. Opponents of Copernicanism argued that bodies dropped on a turning earth would appear to fall to the west; Newton proposed that a body dropped from a high place would fall rather a tiny distance to the east because the top of a tower has a higher tangential velocity than its foot, and treating the earth as a non-resisting vacuum, he drew the path as part of a spiral that ended at the centre. That is, he converted the problem of fall on a rotating earth into the problem of orbital motion conceived according to Hooke's idea, and in the process he made a monumental blunder. Hooke corrected him; under conditions of no resistance, the body dropped would not tend to the centre but would rather return to its original height, and the path would be a sort of ellipse. In turn, Newton corrected Hooke; given a constant attraction, the body would return to its original height, not at 360°, but at about 240°. Hooke replied once more that he did not assume a constant gravity, but a force that varies inversely as the square of the distance. Here the correspondence ended. Seven years later it formed the basis of Hooke's charge of plagiarism, not of the dynamics of circular motion, but of the inverse square relation. At the time it led Newton to demonstrate for his own satisfaction that an elliptical orbit with the centre of attraction at one focus entails an inverse square force.

A year later it was nature which intruded, by way of two comets, the first one visible before dawn, then, after an interval, another in the evening sky. No one had seen a comet greater than the evening one; it stretched some 70 degrees across the sky. Within days of its first sighting Newton began to observe it closely, and systematically collected data both on this comet and on others. Through an intermediary he also corresponded about it with John Flamsteed, the astronomer royal, who was convinced that the two appearances were not two comets but a single one which reversed its direction in the vicinity of the sun. He expounded the theory in terms of a fantastic magnetic dynamics, rejected by Newton, who also resisted the notion of a single comet. Although he had recently worked out the dynamics of orbital motion, he did not apply it to the comet at this time. Comets had always been regarded as foreign bodies, altogether different from planets. Whatever ideas of attractions Newton was entertaining in 1681, they did not add up to universal gravitation.

In August 1684 Newton received a visit from Edmond Halley, and this intrusion proved to be decisive. In London, Halley had been in a discussion with Christopher Wren and Hooke about the shape of an orbit in an inverse square force field. Clearly Hooke was misled in thinking that he alone had come upon the inverse square relation. Newton had derived it twenty years earlier, and apparently Halley and Wren had done the same more recently. Both Halley and Wren admitted that they could not work out the orbital dynamics, and although Hooke claimed that he could, he did not produce a demonstration. Halley, in Cambridge, put the question to Newton, who replied at once that he had demonstrated that an orbit in an inverse square attraction must be an ellipse. When he failed to find the paper, he promised to work out the demonstration anew and send it to Halley.

As a consequence, in November, Halley received a nine-page tract known as 'De motu' ('Concerning motion'), which sketched in an orbital dynamics virtually identical to that which appears in the *Principia*. Already Newton was entertaining ideas that stretched beyond orbital dynamics. He asked Flamsteed for information about the satellites of Jupiter and Saturn and about the motion of Saturn as Jupiter approaches conjunction with it. In fact the issue of celestial motion had seized Newton's attention and expelled alchemy and theology entirely. For the following two and a half years Newton virtually cut himself off from society to pursue a problem which kept expanding in every direction and revealing new facets. Swept along by the grandeur of the theme, he finally saw a work to completion. It transformed his life, and it transformed science.

The first issue was dynamics. 'De motu' sketched an orbital dynamics but not a system of dynamics. During the early months of 1685 Newton gradually worked out what became his three laws of motion. For twenty years he had hesitated before the principle of inertia he had found in Descartes, now seeming to embrace it, now retreating, especially as he recoiled from Cartesian relativism, to the notion that a force internal to bodies sustains their motion. As he pondered over dynamics early in 1685 he realized once and for all that he could not elaborate a consistent dynamics without the principle of inertia. His first law of motion remains today the classic statement of the principle. For the second law he returned to the concept he had begun to explore in 1665 as he treated impact: the change of motion is proportional to the force impressed. The law implied a concept of quantity of matter, which Newton defined at this time and named 'mass'. The third law generalized the equal and opposite changes of motion in impact. Before the middle of 1685 Newton had defined a system of dynamics from which both Galileo's kinematics of terrestrial motion and Kepler's kinematics of celestial motion emerged as necessary consequences.

And he arrived at the concept of universal gravitation. Obviously Newton's thoughts were moving in that direction when he asked Flamsteed about the motions of Jupiter and Saturn in conjunction and when he began, as he did in 'De motu', to treat comets as planet-like bodies governed by the same attraction. Details made it more than a general idea. He realized that with pendulums he could, with great precision, test Galileo's assertion that all bodies fall with the same acceleration. 'When experiments were carefully made with gold, silver, lead, glass, sand, common salt, water, wood, and wheat', his revisions of 'De motu' record, pendulums of identical length had identical periods (Herivel, 311, 319). This is only possible if the earth attracts all the particles in those various substances in exact proportion to their quantities of matter. Kepler's third law implies that the sun attracts the planets and Jupiter attracts its satellites in exact proportion to their masses, and if the satellites remain concentric with Jupiter, the sun must attract both them and Jupiter in exact proportion to their masses. Because the moon stays in orbit around the earth, the earth must attract it, and in 1685, with a correct measure of the earth, the correlation of the moon's orbit with the measured acceleration of gravity on the earth was not pretty near but exact within an inch in the measure of g. By the third law of motion, all these orbiting bodies must also attract the bodies they orbit. Some time early in 1685 Newton concluded that every particle of matter in the universe attracts every other with a force proportional to the product of their masses and inversely proportional to the square of the distance between them.

Clearly an idea of this magnitude demanded more than a nine-page tract, and during the following two years Newton expanded 'De motu', first into an intermediate treatise in two books, and then into the three-book treatise we know. He confronted the problem inherent in his correlation of the moon's orbit with g, that he was treating the apple (in the well-known story) as though it were attracted not to the surface but to the centre of the earth. In one of

the key propositions of the *Principia* Newton demonstrated that the composite attraction exerted on external
bodies by a homogeneous sphere, made up of particles
that attract with a force inversely proportional to the
square of the distance, is directed toward its centre and
varies according to the same law. He developed an analysis
of the three-body problem that allowed him to argue with
justice that most of the perturbations of Kepler's laws
arising from the mutual attractions of bodies in the solar
system fell below the threshold of observation as it then
stood. By April of 1686 he was sufficiently satisfied with
book one to send the manuscript to the Royal Society.

In response Halley assured him that his 'Incomparable
treatise' had arrived and that the society greatly appreciated the honour of being its dedicatee. Unfortunately, he
had also to report that Hooke had raised the cry of plagiarism. Initially Newton reacted calmly enough. After he had
fed on the accusation for three weeks, however, he was in
a flaming rage:

> Now is this not very fine? Mathematicians that find out,
> settle & do all the business must content themselves with
> being nothing but dry calculators & drudges & another that
> does nothing but pretend & grasp at all things must carry
> away all the invention. (*Correspondence*, 2.435–40)

He then informed Halley that 'Philosophy is such an
impertinently litigious Lady that a man had as good be
engaged in Law suits as have to do with her' (ibid.). One of
his latest revisions of book three had been a handsome
acknowledgement of Hooke's concept of attraction. He
now slashed it out and removed every other reference to
Hooke in the manuscript except for a few indispensable
observations.

Newton also threatened to suppress book three, a matter of consequence for Halley, who was in fact the publisher after the nearly bankrupt Royal Society had handed
the manuscript to him. What Newton now threatened to
suppress would have mutilated the work to which Halley
was devoting not only his energy but his meagre
resources. By diplomatic suasion Halley calmed the
storm, but Newton did not withdraw his threat. It was
only in the spring of 1687, after he had received the copy
for book two, that Halley learned what the full content of
the book he was publishing would be.

'De motu' had contained two propositions about
motion through resisting media. Newton greatly
expanded his treatment of this problem, to which he
finally devoted book two, and altered its thrust into an
attack on Cartesian natural philosophy. On the one hand
new propositions on the resistance of physical media
showed how quickly a dense medium, like that which
filled the Cartesian universe, would bring planets to rest.
On the other hand an analysis of vortical motion demonstrated that vortices are incompatible with Kepler's laws
and that they cannot be self-sustaining. The hypothesis of
vortices, he concluded, 'is utterly irreconcilable with
astronomical phenomena and rather serves to perplex
than explain the heavenly motions' (*Mathematical Principles*, 396).

Book three proceeded then to explain the heavenly

motions in terms of attractions propagated through
empty space. The early part of the book derived the law of
universal gravitation in much the way presented above.
Newton then proceeded to employ the concept to explain,
in quantitative terms, a number of phenomena not
employed in its derivation. He redirected the analysis of
the three-body problem, developed originally to argue
that most perturbations are below the threshold of observation, to submit some perturbations to exact calculation.
Astronomers had long known of a number of irregularities in the moon's motion. By demonstrating how the
external attraction of the sun would affect the moon's
orbit around the earth, Newton shifted lunar theory from
empirical description to dynamic analysis. A similar
analysis, in which the moon and sun together were the
external sources of perturbation and the water of the
oceans was the body around the earth, offered the first satisfactory explanation of tides. Applied to the bulge of matter around the equator, the analysis derived a conical
motion of the earth's axis that gives rise to an appearance
known as precession of the equinoxes. In a final *tour de
force*, in what Newton called the most difficult demonstration in the work, he succeeded in reducing the observed
positions of the great comet of 1680–81 to a conical orbit, a
parabola in the first edition, later an ellipse.

At a number of places in the *Principia* Newton inserted
disclaimers that his book intended to assert the reality of
attractions; it merely pursued the mathematical description of observed motions. These assertions were a vain
attempt to forestall objections by mechanical philosophers to the very concept of attraction at a distance. In
fact, Newton was reshaping natural philosophy into a new
mould that allowed mathematical treatment in a way that
etherial mechanisms never could. As he drew his book to a
conclusion, he considered adding a general discussion of
forces. The *Principia* dealt with the great motions readily
observed in the heavens:

> There are however innumerable other local motions which
> on account of the minuteness of the moving particles cannot
> be detected, such as the motions of the particles in hot
> bodies, in fermenting bodies, in putrescent bodies, in
> growing bodies, in the organs of sensation and so forth. If
> any one shall have the good fortune to discover all these, I
> might almost say that he will have laid bare the whole
> nature of bodies so far as the mechanical causes of things are
> concerned. (*Unpublished Scientific Papers*, 333)

In the end he sought, also in vain, to avoid controversy by
suppressing the discussion. In an expanded version it
appeared twenty years later as 'Query 31' of the *Opticks*.

Halley received the manuscript for book two early in
March 1687, and that for book three early in April. He
engaged a second press and for four months did little
except supervise the edition. On 5 July he was able to
inform Newton that his *Philosophiae naturalis principia mathematica* ('Mathematical principles of natural philosophy')
had appeared. Never in the history of civilization has a
major theory been so fully, so clearly, or so influentially
proved.

Revolution In February 1685, not long after Newton seriously immersed himself in the *Principia*, the death of

Charles II passed the crown to his brother James II, a dedicated Roman Catholic committed to the reconversion of England to Roman Catholicism. The time it took for the crisis implicit in James's succession to reach Cambridge was precisely the time Newton needed to complete his work. On 9 February 1687, as he was polishing its final pages, a letter mandate arrived from James ordering the university to admit Alban Francis, a Benedictine monk, to the degree of master of arts and thus to the senate of the university. The letter presaged a campaign to install a Roman Catholic majority in the university. Free from the burden his master-work imposed, Newton, that reclusive fellow of Trinity College, who had sought primarily to isolate himself from the university community but who also hated popery with passion, suddenly emerged as one of its champions in resistance to James.

In April, Newton was one of eight representatives of Cambridge called to answer in London before the notorious Judge Jeffreys, and two years later, after the uprising of 1688 had ratified his courage, he was elected as one of the two Cambridge representatives in the convention parliament. Without taking a leading role, Newton stood four square with the majority who declared that the Roman Catholic James had forfeited the throne, and in general he supported the principles the uprising installed in the English constitution. After the parliament was dissolved in 1690 Newton did not stand for re-election, though later, from December 1701 to May 1702, when he was a public servant, he represented Cambridge in parliament, and once more he was inconspicuous. He stood a last time in 1705, only to be rejected in a tumult about conformity to the established church. Nothing could induce him thereafter to repeat that experience. Whatever his role in parliament, Newton's leadership in the resistance to James in Cambridge, capping the triumph of the *Principia*, which had made him one of the recognized intellectual leaders of England, promoted the recluse of Trinity into one of the university's most prominent figures.

In London, moreover, the horizons of the recluse expanded. He made new friends. As a refugee in the Netherlands, John Locke had grasped the significance of the *Principia* and when the 1688 action made it possible for him to return home he immediately sought out Newton's acquaintance. The two men had much in common, intellectual distinction of course, and a shared outlook on politics and on religion. Locke was probably the first man with whom Newton openly discussed his theological views, and for Locke had composed an essay, 'Two notable corruptions of scripture', in which he demonstrated that the two primary scriptural supports of trinitarianism had not appeared in the Bible before the fourth century. As he had done with Boyle, Newton corresponded with Locke directly rather than through an intermediary, and they remained in contact until Locke's death.

In London, Newton also met a brilliant young Swiss mathematician, Nicolas Fatio de Duillier (1664–1753), who had recently arrived from the continent. Instantly the two became very close. Fatio arrived a Cartesian. Soon he was singing in a Newtonian key. For a time he entertained

plans to edit a second edition of the *Principia*. He was one of the first men freely to explore Newton's mathematical papers, an exploration that led him to begin suggesting that Newton both preceded and excelled Leibniz in the calculus. Newton introduced Fatio to heterodox theology, the prophecies, and alchemy. The relationship, incandescent in its emotional intensity, dominated Newton's life for about five years. Fatio, who lived in London, broached the idea that Newton should find a governmental appointment there. In turn, when Fatio became ill late in 1692, Newton urged him to live with him in Cambridge, where he would provide an allowance.

There were other new friends. In the aftermath of the *Principia* young men who recognized its power sought to enlist themselves as Newton's epigoni. David Gregory of Scotland gained Newton's support, which may have been critical, for appointment as Savilian professor of astronomy at Oxford. An aspiring young divine, Richard Bentley, who had been selected to deliver the first series of Boyle lectures in defence of religion, sought Newton's comments as he prepared for publication texts that drew heavily on Newtonian philosophy. In the four letters to Bentley that Newton eventually composed, he explored the deity's relation to the creation (*Correspondence*, 3.233–54). Somewhat later Newton came to know William Whiston, who would succeed him as Lucasian professor. Between 1707 and 1710, Whiston's public avowal of theological positions he probably learned from Newton led to his expulsion from Cambridge and threatened Newton with the exposure of matters he strove always to keep secret.

The early 1690s were a period of manic intellectual activity as Newton, realizing the *Principia*'s success, sought to produce a synthesis of the new natural philosophy in the Newtonian style. He began a second edition of the *Principia*. He drew his work in optics and in the calculus together. In the end, he abandoned all of these projects, at least for the time being. Theology was not prominent in his endeavour at that time; although he did compose 'Two notable corruptions' during those years, the *Principia* marked the beginning of a hiatus of about two decades in serious theological study. For alchemy, in contrast, the *Principia* was a momentary interruption, and Newton took up the art anew even before the *Principia* was completed. Roughly half of the large volume of alchemical manuscripts that he left behind dated from the years immediately after the *Principia*. He devoted time to expanding his 'Index chemicus'; he experimented; and he composed his most important alchemical paper, 'Praxis', which went through four successive versions and seemed to claim success in the alchemical work:

> Thus you may multiply each stone 4 times & no more [he wrote in the essay's climax] for they will then become oyles shining in yᵉ dark & fit for magicall uses .... This is yᵉ multiplication in quality. You may multiply it in quantity by the mercuries of wᶜʰ you made it at first ... Every multiplication will encreas it's vertue ten times &, if you use yᵉ mercury of yᵉ 2ᵈ or 3ᵈ reaction wᵗʰout yᵉ spirit, perhaps a thousand times. Thus you may multiply to infinity. (Dibner Institute, Babson MS 420, 18a)

When Newton composed the final version of 'Praxis' in

the summer of 1693, he was in a state of acute tension. Beyond 'Praxis', some dated alchemical experiments, and a letter he began but did not finish, nothing is known of his activity that summer. In the middle of September he broke silence with two wild letters. He informed Samuel Pepys that he must withdraw from his acquaintance and see none of his other friends any more. To Locke he wrote that he was so much affected by the conviction that Locke had tried to embroil him with women 'that when one told me you were sickly & would not live I answered twere better if you were dead' (*Correspondence*, 3.279–80). Before long stories were circulating on the continent that Newton had suffered a mental derangement that lasted a number of months. Undoubtedly the stories were exaggerated, but just as undoubtedly there was a breakdown difficult to define during 1693. It brought an end to the euphoria of the early 1690s and to the plans for publication, and it effectively terminated Newton's intellectual creativity. It may have terminated his involvement with alchemy; although he did date some experiments after 1693, he abandoned the work about the time he moved to London. It also marked the end of his close relationship with Fatio, an event shattering for Newton but even more so for Fatio, who soon abandoned science and mathematics and drifted into religious fanaticism.

In the aftermath of the breakdown Newton resolved to have, as he put it, another go at the moon. The detailed lunar theory had been one of the last additions to the *Principia*, where it was clearly imperfect. Newton intended to carry the investigation to completion, and now was the time to do so. To this end he applied to Flamsteed for observations of the moon, and in the summer of 1694 he set about the task in his usual intense way. It was excruciating work, dealing with a set of corrections that could hardly be distinguished from each other. He later told one associate that 'his head never ached but with his studies on the moon' (King's Cam., Keynes MS, 130.6, Book 3). Measured by his aspiration to devise a theory accurate to 2 minutes, his efforts were a failure. Increasingly frustrated, he projected his failure onto Flamsteed, who had not, Newton claimed, supplied the observations he needed. Finally, a furious letter in July 1695 effectively ended amicable relations between the two, and not long thereafter Newton abandoned his effort.

The failure over the moon confirmed the breakdown of 1693. Realizing that his creativity was exhausted, Newton began to find the leisure Cambridge supplied more of a burden than a benefit, and when the opportunity of an appointment in London opened he seized it without hesitation. Within a month of receiving the proffered appointment, he had moved out, lock, stock, and barrel.

London and the mint Newton had been consulted on matters connected with the Royal Mint in 1695. Through the combined efforts of clippers (who clipped silver from the edges of hammered coins that had no definite outline) and coiners (or counterfeiters), English money—the silver money of daily commerce—had deteriorated alarmingly in the early 1690s. The crisis in the coinage was made worse by the simultaneous financial crisis caused by the unprecedented expenses of a war with France. In an age when professional economists did not exist the government, in 1695, sought advice from eight men known for their intellectual prowess or their experience in matters financial. The fact that Newton was one of the eight testifies to the impact of the *Principia*. Together with another six he favoured recoinage. By December the government had made its decision, and the recoinage was already under way when, late in March 1696, Newton received a letter from Charles Montagu, chancellor of the exchequer and a prominent figure in the whig junta then in control of the government, offering him the wardenship of the mint. He did not hesitate in accepting and by 2 May had installed himself in London and assumed his duties.

Montagu's letter was unambiguous in offering a sinecure. Newton had never learned how to do things halfway, however, and his personal need to escape from intellectual activity become fruitless made common cause with the need of an institution in chaos under the demands that the recoinage imposed. He gave of himself without stint. Arranging and ordering were among Newton's most basic instincts. Every time he had approached a new discipline, his first step had been an ordered collection of information. The same impulse served him well at the mint. He was by nature an administrator, and as far as can be untangled from the confused record, it appears that his presence was a significant factor in bringing about an orderly functioning of the mint and radically increasing the rate of coinage until it reached £100,000 per week at a time when, with the old coins called in, the shortage of legal tender was threatening to bring economic life to a standstill. He appears certainly to have been instrumental in setting up the five country mints called for by parliament. When the recoinage ended in the summer of 1698 the mint had coined a total of £6.8 million in two and a half years, nearly twice the total coinage of the previous thirty. Some significant portion of that record was Newton's work.

Newton soon learned that there was another dimension to his duties as warden that he had not counted on. The warden was responsible for apprehending and prosecuting clippers (who soon ceased to exist with the new coinage) and coiners (as yesterday's clippers soon became). Newton disliked the job and initially petitioned to be relieved of it. When the Treasury would not even hear of that, he plunged in with his normal intensity: he had himself commissioned as a justice of the peace in all the home counties; he took innumerable depositions in taverns and in gaols from assorted riff-raff; and he successfully prosecuted twenty-eight coiners. In all more than a hundred were pursued under his authority.

As Newton accustomed himself to a new life, aspects of the old one continued to make their appearance. In 1697 he received two challenge problems from Johann Bernoulli, who intended to show that Newton's pretended, but unpublished, method was not as powerful as the differential calculus of Leibniz and Bernoulli. John Conduitt, the husband of Newton's niece, later heard the following story, which surviving documents support: Newton came home from the mint one evening, tired, to find the problems and solved them before he went to bed. When Bernoulli shortly thereafter received from England an anonymous paper with the solutions, he understood at once whence it came—'as the lion is recognized from his claw', in his classic phrase. Newton also chose to have another try at the moon. It got no further than the previous one, and led just as quickly to another angry confrontation with Flamsteed. In 1698 there was an episode of a different sort; the French Académie des Sciences elected Newton as one of eight foreign associates.

Initially Newton moved into the warden's house in the mint, which was located between the walls of the Tower of London. He did not stay there long. By August he had installed himself in a house on Jermyn Street in Westminster, where he lived for more than a decade. In 1709 he moved to Chelsea, quickly found it unsatisfactory, and the following year transferred to St Martin's Street, south of Leicester Fields (now Leicester Square). Here he stayed until, with his health decaying in his final years, he moved to Kensington. If he did not live sumptuously, he certainly lived well, keeping a coach until his last years and a fleet of servants.

Soon after he settled in London, although the exact date is not known, Newton's niece Catherine Barton went to live with him. She was thereafter a constant part of his life, from 1717 with John Conduitt, her husband, and their daughter. Catherine Barton was a young woman approaching twenty when she arrived in London, beautiful, lively, witty, and possessed of unlimited charm. Among those who felt the charm was Charles Montagu, the earl of Halifax as he became, Newton's old friend who had secured his appointment at the mint. The relationship of Catherine Barton and Halifax was known to the gossips of London, who passed it on to Voltaire, who broadcast it to the world. It was not merely gossip. In 1706 Halifax drew up a codicil to his will leaving Catherine £3000 and all his jewels 'as a small Token of the great Love and Affection I have long had for her' (Earl of Halifax [C. Montagu], *Works … Earl of Halifax*, 1715, 1716, iv–vi). Seven years later a second codicil replaced the first, now bequeathing £5000 plus a grant during her life of the rangership and lodge of Bushey Park (adjacent to Hampton Court) and the manor of Apscourt in Surrey. Flamsteed, who drew malicious pleasure from the news, valued the house and lands at £20,000, a small fortune with the additional £5000. Ambiguities cloud the picture, but it is impossible not to accept that Catherine Barton was Halifax's mistress and that Newton must have been aware of the relationship. In the nineteenth century this information was unacceptable and was therefore denied (but in any case it has no bearing on Newton's scientific achievement).

Newton's career at the mint brought him back to reality. It did not take him long to understand the true state of affairs. Historically the warden had been the institution's highest officer but in fact, after a reorganization in 1666, the master (that is, the master coiner) had assumed that role. He controlled the accounts—even the warden

received his salary through the hands of the master. Not only was his salary higher than the warden's, but he received a set payment, or 'profit', from each pound of precious metal coined. When Newton arrived Thomas Neale was the master. He treated the position as a sinecure so that Newton, who had been offered a sinecure, ended up shouldering many of his duties. Not only did Neale receive a salary of £500 to Newton's £400, but his profits from the recoinage, to which he contributed almost nothing, mounted above £22,000. Almost at once after he assumed office in the mint, Newton, who knew that Neale was in poor health, began to familiarize himself in detail with all its operations. No warden had ever before become master but when Neale obliged by dying at the end of 1699 the appointment immediately went to Newton, and this despite the fact that his patron Montagu had fallen from power. He took office on 25 December, his birthday. The don from Cambridge had learned how to swim in the dangerous waters of London.

During more than twenty-seven years as master Newton's average income was about £1650, though it varied widely from year to year. In 1701, a year of heavy coinage, his income reached nearly £3500 and he decided to resign his fellowship and chair in Cambridge. The War of the Spanish Succession quickly brought coinage to a standstill; his total profit from coining in 1703 was £13. With peace, the pace picked up again. In 1715 his total income came to £4250, and in years of peace he averaged about £2250. Very few governmental positions carried a salary higher than that, and Newton died a wealthy man.

For all the trauma the recoinage imposed on English society, silver was allowed to remain undervalued so that it quickly disappeared to be sold abroad as bullion. The shortage of silver coins became a serious inconvenience, and over the years the Treasury called upon the master of the mint to offer advice. Papers with titles such as 'Observations upon the valuation of gold and silver in proportion to one another' urged that the value of the guinea, a gold coin, be set significantly lower than its current rate of 21s. 6d. Eventually a government which ignored his advice longer than it should have, and then acted only half way, lowered the value to 21s.; what proved to be the permanent value and later the definition of the guinea is a small fraction of Newton's legacy.

President of the Royal Society The Royal Society hardly figured in Newton's activities during the first seven years of his residence in London. The society stood at a low ebb, with leadership lacking, interest declining, and finances in chaos. The death of Robert Hooke in March 1703 removed an obstacle to Newton's active participation, and at the annual meeting on 30 November of that same year the Royal Society looked to a real natural philosopher for leadership and elected Newton as president. He continued as president, dominating the society's affairs, until his death.

Master of the mint and president of the Royal Society: Newton had moved a long way from the reclusive don who had isolated himself in his chamber in Trinity, and Queen Anne added a further plum to his pudding in 1705. Halifax, who needed a block of supporters in the House of Commons, persuaded Newton to stand once more for Cambridge in the election that year. This was the election that provoked the noisy demonstrations by students against nonconformity and determined Newton, who was not elected, never to run again. However, the election also had another effect. On the occasion of a visit by Queen Anne to the university Halifax organized what was really a campaign rally in which he received an honorary doctorate, and his brother was knighted along with Halifax's candidate for parliament. Thus Newton became Sir Isaac Newton, the first scientist in Europe so honoured (whatever the political calculations that lay behind it).

To the Royal Society, Newton brought the same organizational talent that he had brought to the mint, and the same inability to ignore an obligation. Whereas the previous two presidents, prominent political figures, had attended a total of three meetings during the space of eight years, Newton presided at more than three out of four, and during the twenty years that followed 1703, until age imposed constraints, failed to preside at only three sessions of the council. His first concern was the content of meetings. To the first one over which he presided he brought along Francis Hauksbee to perform experiments with his air pump. Hauksbee became a fixture. His experiments, first with the air pump and then on electricity and capillary action, published as *Physico-Mechanical Experiments* in 1709, elevated him to the status of a well-known scientist in his own right, and some of his discoveries, especially those related to electricity, influenced Newton. When Hauksbee died in 1713, Newton found an equally capable replacement in J. T. Desaguliers, a Huguenot refugee.

Likewise the finances of the society revived under Newton's administration. A society on the verge of bankruptcy in 1703 was able to purchase a home of its own in 1710. Since its establishment, the society had met in Gresham College. In the summer of 1710 a house in Crane Court off Fleet Street, owned by Dr Edward Browne, the son of Sir Thomas Browne, came up for sale. Newton moved quickly so that the society could buy it for £1450. There were additional expenses of £710 for repairs and renovation, but the society had only £550 in ready cash; gifts poured in, however, and in less than six years the society had retired all the debt and was able to invest an additional bequest in bank annuities.

The Royal Society provided a setting for Newton's second major publication, *Opticks*. On 16 February 1704, two and a half months after he assumed the chair, Newton presented the book to the society. The overwhelming majority of its content dated from the late 1660s and early 1670s: in the 1690s he had rewritten his optical lectures of 1669–72 into book one; with the exception of the section on coloured phenomena in thick transparent plates, work done during 1689, even the prose of book two repeated a paper written in 1672. What was new were the 'queries' that formed the bulk of book three. There were sixteen in the first edition, to which he added seven more (those numbered 25 to 31 in current editions of *Opticks*) in the Latin

edition of 1706. In the twenty-three queries of 1704–6 Newton offered a general statement, couched in rhetorical questions that demanded affirmative answers, of his programme in science:

> Have not the small Particles of Bodies certain Powers, Virtues, or Forces, by which they act at a distance, not only upon the Rays of Light for reflecting, refracting, and inflecting them, but also upon one another for producing a great Part of the Phaemonema of Nature [the final query began]? For it's well known, that Bodies act one upon another by the Attractions of Gravity, Magnetism, and Electricity; and these Instances shew the Tenor and Course of Nature, and make it not improbable but that there may be more attractive Powers than these. For Nature is very constant and conformable to her self.

When he wrote these words, and others to the same effect, the eight queries (numbered 17 to 24 in current editions) asserting the existence of a universal ether that offered quasi-mechanistic accounts of these forces did not exist. Newton added them to the second English edition as age brought on timidity. The *Opticks* of 1704–6, generalizing the message of the *Principia*, issued a manifesto of his new programme. The mechanical philosophy with its imagined mechanisms of imagined particles was out. Forces mathematically defined, explaining observed motions in a quantitatively precise manner, formed the centrepiece of Newtonian science. Modern science has shaped itself accordingly.

The same *Opticks* also contained at the end the first full papers in mathematics that Newton made public. He had been aware of Leibniz's publication of his differential calculus and of the renown it had brought him. Although word circulated about the Newtonian method of fluxions, the manuscripts of which only a small number studied, the only text expounding it in print was a brief précis of 'De quadratura' in Wallis's *Opera*. 'Tractatus de quadratura curvarum' ('A treatise on the quadrature of curves') changed that situation, and 'Enumeratio linearum tertii ordinis' ('Enumeration of lines of the third order'), though not on fluxions, further displayed his mathematical prowess. They may be looked upon as a preliminary salvo in the battle that would be joined with Leibniz over priority in the discovery of the calculus.

A new confrontation with Flamsteed also arose from Newton's office of president. The failure with lunar theory still rankled. Newton was convinced that Flamsteed had a trove of observations that would enable him to achieve success. Therefore, only a few months after he assumed the chair, he went down to Greenwich, full of pretended benevolence, asking if he might recommend the publication of Flamsteed's observations to Prince George, the consort of Queen Anne. There were few things that Flamsteed wanted more, and the prince's agreement to finance the publication was immediately gained. In the process Newton also succeeded in getting the project into his own hands. The group of referees in charge of publication, which he headed, paid no attention to Flamsteed's desires or advice and proceeded towards the publication of the data that Newton most wanted. It did not take long for the seemingly friendly relations at the beginning of the project to degenerate into outright hostility, and there they remained until Prince George died near the end of 1708, bringing publication to a temporary halt before it had progressed very far.

Newton was unwilling to let the matter stand. In 1710, as he embarked on a second edition of the *Principia* in which he would perforce deal again with lunar theory, he arranged for the queen to appoint the Royal Society as visitor, that is, supervisor, of the observatory, and from this position of power he again set out to publish Flamsteed's catalogue of the fixed stars and selected other observations, with expenses to be borne by the Treasury. This time there was no pretence of co-operation—tense antagonism reigned from the beginning. Newton had an imperfect copy of the catalogue from the earlier episode and, as visitor, forced Flamsteed to hand over observations from which Halley was able to fill in the lacunae. Thus, in 1712, *Historia coelestis*, with a shameful preface that denigrated Flamsteed, issued from the press. As he completed edition two of the *Principia*, Newton struck out fifteen references to Flamsteed, but his reliance on Flamsteed's observations of the great comet prevented him from reducing the astronomer royal to non-existence.

This was not yet the end of the affair. In 1714 the death of Anne led to the fall of the tory government and the return of the whigs. When Halifax died the following year Newton's patron disappeared, whereas Flamsteed had one in the lord chamberlain, the duke of Bolton. Through Bolton, Flamsteed obtained an order that all unsold copies of the *Historia coelestis*, about 300, be delivered to him. Separating out some pages, he consigned the rest, including the catalogue of fixed stars, to the flames. Already he had begun, at his own expense, to print the catalogue and his observations in the form he had always wanted. The pages he saved from Newton's edition, his early observations before the construction of his great mural arc in 1689, became volume one in his edition. When he died in 1719, he had nearly completed volume two, the observations with the mural arc. His widow and two former assistants oversaw the printing of volume three, mostly the catalogue of the fixed stars. In 1725 *Historica coelestis Britannica* appeared, a landmark in the history of observational astronomy, and a monument to Newton's failure to reduce Flamsteed to subservience.

The priority dispute The climax of the struggle with Flamsteed coincided with a number of other crises in Newton's life. On 5 May 1711 an angry confrontation with Craven Peyton, warden of the mint, signalled the deterioration of their relationship. Tension continued at a high level until the death of Anne in 1714 and the fall of the tory government with which Peyton was allied led to the appointment of a new warden. During the same period, beginning in this case in 1709, Newton engaged himself in a second edition of the *Principia*, which taxed his time and energy until its completion in 1713. And with the Royal Society's receipt, on 22 March 1711, of a letter from Leibniz, the long smouldering dispute between him and Newton over priority in the invention of the calculus finally

burst into open flame. The seven years from 1709 to 1716, when Leibniz died, were among the most stressful in Newton's life.

Newton had been thinking about a second edition of his masterpiece almost from the day it first appeared, but the specific timing of the edition owed less to Newton than to Richard Bentley, now master of Trinity, who was determined to woo Newton's support for his efforts to reform and rejuvenate the college. Bentley arranged the edition and functioned as its publisher. He appointed one of his young protégés, Roger Cotes, only twenty-seven years old but already Plumian professor of astronomy at Cambridge, as editor, and in 1709 Newton and Cotes got down to work. Bentley's choice could hardly have been more fortunate. Despite Newton's early, repeated suggestions that he not give himself too much trouble, Cotes insisted on going over the copy with a fine-tooth comb, and in the end succeeded in luring Newton into a serious discussion of his work. As a result the second edition of the *Principia* contained a number of major emendations that greatly enhanced its value. Today only historians of science refer to the first edition; the *Principia* that has shaped Western scientific tradition is substantially the second edition, very modestly modified in a third edition shortly before Newton's death.

Initially the two men found little more than details to discuss, and by the middle of 1710 the edition had moved swiftly through book one and well into book two, not far short of two-thirds of the entire work, before they struck the issue of a fluid's resistance to motion through it. This was an important topic, the heart of Newton's argument against Cartesian philosophy. In the first edition it had rested on a dubious experimental basis, and difficulties continued to appear as Newton performed new experiments in London and fundamentally revised the theory. At the time when the confrontation with Flamsteed was boiling over and when Newton's relationship with Peyton at the mint was in a state of acute tension while heavy coinage imposed additional strain, the press simply came to a halt until the problem was resolved. For all the effort, the section on the resistance of fluids remained the *Principia's* weakest part. Meanwhile, printing hardly advanced through the rest of 1710 and through 1711. By the end of 1711 the dispute with Leibniz was beginning to expand to include their philosophical differences, and the new edition, important as it was in its own right, acquired additional urgency. Devoting himself to it seriously once more Newton, ably assisted by Cotes, drove it to completion without another major interruption.

At the beginning of book 3, a new 'rule of reasoning in philosophy' ('rule 3') flung down the experimental gauntlet in challenge to Leibniz's more speculative philosophy. Other changes late in book two and in book three emphasized a concomitant advantage of Newtonian philosophy: its ability to calculate natural phenomena, such as the speed of light and the rate of precession of the equinoxes, with quantitative precision. The two major additions to the work, a long preface by Cotes and a concluding

'General scholium' by Newton, both stressed the differences that separated Newtonian philosophy from its continental rival. The 'General scholium', one of Newton's last testimonies about his vision of the scientific enterprise, began with a repudiation of mechanical philosophies in general: 'The hypothesis of vortices is pressed with many difficulties', he asserted, difficulties that he proceeded to detail. Moreover, the order of the cosmos seemed incompatible with mechanical necessity and demanded not merely a creator at the beginning but his abiding presence. In one of his most quoted passages, which argued that mechanical causes could not explain gravity, Newton proclaimed anew the difference that separated his philosophy from speculative, mechanical ones:

> But hitherto I have not been able to discover the cause of those properties of gravity from phenomena, and I feign no hypotheses … And to us it is enough that gravity does really exist, and act according to the laws which we have explained, and abundantly serves to account for all the motions of the celestial bodies, and of our sea.
> (*Mathematical Principles*, 547)

As the edition neared completion there arose a final crisis. Nikolaus Bernoulli, the nephew of Johann Bernoulli, visited London, where he told Newton's friend Abraham De Moivre that his uncle had found an error in proposition 10 of book three. The error seemed to indicate that Newton did not understand second differentials, and Newton had no intention of allowing any such thing to appear in print, especially with the priority dispute in full blaze. In a *tour de force* for a man of nearly seventy, he located the source of the error and corrected it. Proposition 10 had long since been printed. A whole sheet had to be set anew, together with the last two pages on the previous sheet, which were glued onto the stub of the original, mute testimony to the late correction. Johann Bernoulli, Leibniz's supporter, who had intended to use the mistake as evidence that Newton's fluxional method was inferior to the differential calculus, was furious to find that Newton had not attributed the correction to him.

At the end of June 1713 the long labour reached its fulfilment and the second edition emerged from the press. Unfortunately the controversy with Leibniz had no similar termination. The conflict had long been simmering, since 1684 to be exact, when Leibniz first began to publish his calculus without mentioning the correspondence of 1676 by which he knew that Newton had a similar method. Newton grumbled about it but took no action. In 1699 he did co-operate in the publication, in volume three of Wallis's *Opera*, of his two letters to Leibniz in 1676 plus other letters that testified to his progress by the year 1673. That same year, 1699, in a mathematical tract, Fatio de Duillier, who had seen Newton's papers and heard his complaints, bluntly asserted his priority and only a little less bluntly accused Leibniz of plagiarism. For his part, Leibniz made similar charges against Newton in reviews that he published anonymously. To one of those charges a young Oxford don, John Keill, a protégé of James Gregory, replied directly in a paper published in the *Philosophical*

Transactions in 1708, again asserting Newton's priority and accusing Leibniz of plagiarism. When he eventually saw the paragraph in question, Leibniz wrote to the Royal Society, of which he was a member. His letter, received on 22 March 1711, demanded that Keill publicly recant.

Newton's papers contain an enormous record of his personal response to Leibniz's letter, as he went back over his own papers and reconstructed the order of events. At meetings of the society during April he recounted the history of his method. Newton had trained himself in empirical historical research in his theological investigations, and that capacity, with its command of factual details, he brought to the priority dispute. He appears to have participated in composing Keill's reply to Leibniz, and he certainly composed the covering letter from Hans Sloane, secretary of the Royal Society, that accompanied it.

Leibniz, in no way satisfied to see his demanded apology refused, replied in a letter received early in 1712. Distinguishing between Keill and Newton, expressing his regard for the latter (in contradiction to his anonymous reviews) but asserting his equal right as an independent discoverer, he threw himself on the society's sense of justice. Newton made an unexpected riposte by having the society appoint a committee to sit in judgement. The society, that is, Newton, liked to refer to it as a committee made up of gentlemen of several nations; in fact it was composed of Newton's followers plus Frederick Bonet, the minister in London of the king of Prussia, who allowed himself to be co-opted. Newton himself wrote the committee's report, drawing upon what was by then a year's research in his records. In a ringing condemnation of Leibniz and a full endorsement of Newton, the report insisted that there were not two independent methods but a single one, and cited the correspondence of 1676 together with Leibniz's access to Newton's papers on his visit to London in that year to convict him of plagiarism. The society went on to publish the report, together with the factual basis in the early correspondence that gave it weight, in a volume, *Commercium epistolicum D. Johannis Collins, et aliorum de analysi promota* ('The correspondence of the learned John Collins and others relating to the progress of analysis'), copies of which it sent about through the learned society of Europe. Newton put the volume together, of course, and he later reviewed it at great length, anonymously, in the *Philosophical Transactions*.

It was out of the question that so blatantly partial a publication as the *Commercium epistolicum* should settle the issue. Leibniz replied in his own way, avoiding the ground of historical details that Newton commanded and emphasizing instead the differences of the two methods and the superiority of his own. Proposition 10 of book two saw heavy duty. Like Newton, Leibniz tried to conceal his own role in the dispute, in his case by relying on anonymous publications and the testimony of others. The dispute refused to die, and it refused to confine itself to the principal figures. Nor was it confined to mathematics, as differences in natural philosophy and eventually theology crept in. In a letter to the princess of Wales, who had been his protector in Germany, Leibniz criticized Newton's published understanding of the relation of God to the creation. Out of the letter came a correspondence on related issues between Leibniz and Samuel Clarke, the leading theologian in England at the time and a dedicated Newtonian, who defended Newton's position and possibly had Newton's assistance in composing his part of the correspondence. The exchange went through five rounds, ten letters in all, each longer than its predecessor, and would no doubt have continued indefinitely, like the priority dispute, had Leibniz not died on 4 November 1716.

If the Clarke–Leibniz correspondence perforce came to an end, the priority dispute had generated too much heat and involved too many additional men, especially Johann Bernoulli on the one hand and John Keill and Brook Taylor on the other, to extinguish itself. For another six years letters passed back and forth and literary journals published attacks and replies. Eventually these too ran down, and at last silence, if not peace, reigned.

Final years During the final decade of his life Newton spent some of his time attending to his scientific legacy. A second English edition of the *Opticks* in 1717 scarcely touched the text but added eight new queries, which partially compromised with orthodox mechanical philosophy by reasserting the existence of a cosmic ether, a concept he had consciously excluded from his philosophy since about 1680. The compromise was more apparent than real. If the new ether explained gravity and optical phenomena in a seemingly familiar manner, its structure of particles that repelled each other at a distance incorporated the very notion that mechanical philosophers found inadmissible. In 1721 a third English edition, which scarcely differed from the second, appeared. Meanwhile, a second Latin edition (1719), in the language of international scholarship, was more important. Together with two French editions (1720 and 1722) it carried Newton's conclusions in optics, which heretofore had not spread much beyond Britain, to the continent. Newton also participated in a 1726 third edition of the *Principia*, which did not begin to rival the second in the importance of its emendations.

Newton also functioned as a scientific expert for the government. In 1714, after hearings in which Newton testified along with others, parliament offered a large monetary prize for a method of determining longitude at sea. A board of longitude, on which, inevitably, Newton sat, was established to judge submitted proposals. Until death delivered him, one of his duties was to read these proposals, most of them verging on the absurd.

It was theology rather than science, however, that dominated the consciousness of the ageing man. Some time between 1705 and 1710 he returned to the subject he had largely ignored for two decades, and theology formed the principal staple of Newton's intellectual life from that time until his death. Like his late efforts in science, those in theology confined themselves mostly to reshuffling earlier ideas. This he did at enormous length, so that an immense volume of manuscripts testifies to his activity (Jewish National and University Library, Yahuda MSS 6, 7,

15, 25, 26, 27; King's College, Cambridge, Keynes MSS 3–9; Bodl. Oxf., MSS New College 361.1–3). One theme unites much of it. Newton had become a prominent man of the world who did not intend to compromise his position by publicly espousing opinions that had passionately stirred an isolated young don in Cambridge. Much of his effort was devoted to laundering those opinions to obscure their radical thrust.

The most radical of Newton's theological endeavours had been his 'Theologiae gentilis origines philosophicae', which he transformed into the *Chronology of Ancient Kingdoms Amended*, as the manuscript published soon after his death was entitled. In 1716 an Italian visitor to England, Abbé Antonio Schinella Conti, both Newton's confidant and a familiar figure in the court, mentioned Newton's new principles of chronology to the princess of Wales, who immediately wanted to see the treatise. Newton had no intention of surrendering a manuscript he considered potentially damaging. Because he could not refuse a royal command, he hastily composed an 'Abstract', later called the 'Short chronology', which put the work in a shape, little more than a list of dates, which Newton deemed suitable for the princess's eyes.

The 'Abstract' had its own history. When Conti left England he carried with him a copy, which he showed about Paris. French scholars in chronology rejected its apparently arbitrary truncation of ancient history, and one of them arranged to publish a translation of it together with a refutation. Thus Newton was drawn into another controversy, which was not as bitter and not as prolonged as the priority dispute but was sufficiently sharp nevertheless. When he died his heirs found the completed manuscript of the *Chronology*, which they immediately sold to a publisher for £350.

Newton also returned to his study of the prophecies. Here too he obscured the radical, Arian thrust of his early interpretation, partly by placing Daniel rather than Revelation at the centre so that the rise of trinitarianism, the object of his odium, was less prominent, and in general by converting the work into a set of rambling commentaries that had no obvious point. At his death he left a completed treatise and a newer, still incomplete one. Advisers to his heirs melded the two into one and added three additional chapters that Newton had not considered part of either; eventually *Observations upon the Prophecies of Daniel, and the Apocalypse of St. John* (1733) appeared.

Other theological manuscripts, which did not find publication in the eighteenth century and remained largely unknown until the mid-twentieth, were more reminiscent of the earlier stance, though here too Newton couched them in a milder idiom. One of these, which survives in multiple versions, bore the name 'Irenicum'. On the surface it presented a programme of common beliefs on which all Christians could agree, but this programme dispensed with all the distinctive doctrines of Christianity and reduced religion to two principles, love of God and love of neighbour. 'This was the religion of the sons of Noah established by Moses & Christ still in force' (King's Cam., Keynes MS 3, 5–7). 'Thus you see there is but one law for all nations', he stated in another paper, 'the law of righteousness & charity dictated to the Christians by Christ to the Jews by Moses & to all mankind by the light of reason & by this law all men are to be judged at the last day' (Keynes MS 7, 2–3). Only within a very confined circle did Newton discuss such opinions. Publicly he performed as a trustee of the chapel on Golden Square, and as a member of the commission established by parliament to oversee the construction of fifty new churches in the expanding suburbs of London, and of the commission to supervise the completion of St Paul's Cathedral.

In June 1717 a young man who figured prominently in the rest of Newton's life read a paper to the Royal Society on the site of the Roman city Carteia, in Spain, and two months later he gave Catherine Barton married respectability. Not only was John Conduitt the husband of Newton's favourite niece, he was also an unabashed hero worshipper of Newton himself. To his determination to assemble a record of the great man is owed many of the details known about Newton, and to him also is owed the preservation of Newton's papers. Through negotiation with the other heirs the Conduitts obtained possession of the papers, and when their only child, Catherine, married John Wallop, Viscount Lymington, the papers passed to the Portsmouth family, which later donated the bulk of them to Cambridge University Library. Conduitt himself, who acted unofficially as Newton's deputy at the mint during the final two years, succeeded him as master.

Conduitt and William Stukeley set down much of the accepted picture of Newton the man. Conduitt reported that he was of medium stature, though Thomas Hearne called him short. Both agreed that he was plump, but this must have come with age for his early portraits show no such thing. Count Luigi Ferdinando Marsigli, who met him in 1723, was struck by his small wizened figure, and reported that, like many English scholars, he was unable to converse fluently in Latin. In general he was silent, a man who spoke little in company. Humphrey Newton (no relation), his amanuensis for five years in Cambridge, saw him laugh only once; Stukeley, trying unsuccessfully to mitigate the image of constant gravity, said that he could easily be brought to smile if not to laugh.

The first portrait of Newton (1689), by Kneller, shows him at the height of his powers, immediately after the *Principia*. Kneller painted at least three more portraits, the last when Newton was about eighty. During his London years portraiture became something of an obsession with Newton. Beyond those by Kneller, there were two by Thornhill, three by Vanderbank, and at least seven others, one or two of which may be copies, plus a sketch by Stukeley, a medal by the engraver at the mint, and two ivory busts (nearly identical with each other) and three ivory plaques by Le Marchand.

During his last five years Newton's health steadily deteriorated. There was a serious illness during the spring of 1722, and a more serious one in January of 1725. On 2 March 1727 he presided over a meeting of the Royal Society, was exhilarated by the experience, but overtaxed himself and collapsed the following day. He never recovered. In his most significant act as he lay dying, he refused to take the sacrament of the Church of England. On 15 March he seemed somewhat better but immediately declined again and died on 20 March 1727.

Newton's death did not go unnoticed. He lay in state in the Jerusalem Chamber in Westminster Abbey, and, with the pall borne by the lord chancellor and five high-ranking aristocrats, was interred on 28 March in a prominent position in the nave, where in 1731 his heirs erected an extravagant monument. Few, however, have found the final lines of the inscription extravagant: 'Let Mortals rejoice That there has existed such and so great an Ornament to the Human Race'. There has never since been a time when Newton was not considered either the greatest scientist who ever lived or one of a tiny handful of the greatest. His *Principia* marked the culmination of the scientific revolution, which ushered in modern science, and through its legacy the work may have done more to shape the modern world than any other ever published.

RICHARD S. WESTFALL

Sources *The correspondence of Isaac Newton*, ed. H. W. Turnbull and others, 7 vols. (1959–77) · *The mathematical papers of Isaac Newton*, ed. D. T. Whiteside, 8 vols. (1967–80) · *The optical papers of Isaac Newton*, ed. A. E. Shapiro (1984–) · *Sir Isaac Newton's mathematical principles of natural philosophy and his system of the world*, trans. A. Motte, rev. F. Cajori, 2 vols. (1934) · *Isaac Newton's Philosophiae naturalis principia mathematica*, ed. A. Koyré, I. B. Cohen, and A. Whitman, 2 vols. (1972) · I. Newton, *Opticks*, 4th edn (1952) · *Unpublished scientific papers of Isaac Newton*, ed. A. R. Hall and M. B. Hall (1962) · *Isaac Newton's papers and letters on natural philosophy and related documents*, ed. I. B. Cohen (1958) · PRO, Mint MSS, 19.1–5 · King's Cam., Keynes MSS · Jewish National and University Library, Jerusalem, Yahuda MSS · CUL, Portsmouth MSS, Add. MSS 3958–4006 · Massachusetts Institute of Technology, Dibner Institute, Babson MSS · Smithsonian Institution, Washington, DC, Burndy MSS, Dibner collection · Bodl. Oxf., MSS New College, 361.1–4 · I. B. Cohen, *The Newtonian revolution* (1980) · I. B. Cohen, *Introduction to Newton's 'Principia'* (1971) · A. Koyré, *Newtonian studies* (1965) · J. W. Herivel, *The background to Newton's 'Principia'* (1965) · B. J. T. Dobbs, *The Janus faces of genius: the role of alchemy in Newton's thought* (1991) · A. E. Shapiro, *Fits, passions, paroxysms: physics, method and chemistry and Newton's theories of colored bodies and fits of easy reflection* (1993) · F. E. Manuel, *A portrait of Isaac Newton* (1968) · R. S. Westfall, *Never at rest: a biography of Isaac Newton* (1980) · K. A. Baird, 'Some influences upon the young Isaac Newton', *Notes and Records of the Royal Society*, 41 (1986–7), 169–79 · D. B. Meli, *Equivalence and priority: Newton versus Leibniz* (1993) · J. B. Brackenridge, *The key to Newton's dynamics* (1995) · S. Chandrasekhar, *Newton's 'Principia' for the common reader* (1995) · F. De Gandt, *Force and geometry in Newton's Principia*, trans. C. Wilson (1995) · B. J. T. Dobbs, *The foundations of Newton's alchemy, or, The hunting of the greene lyon* (1975) · K. Figala, *Newton as alchemist* (1979) · C. W. Foster, 'Sir Isaac Newton's family', *Reports and Papers of the Architectural Societies of the County of Lincoln, County of York, Archdeaconries of Northampton and Oakham, and County of Leicester*, 39, Part 1 (1928), 1–62 · A. R. Hall, *Philosophers at war: the quarrel between Newton and Leibniz* (1980) · W. G. Hiscock, *David Gregory, Isaac Newton and their circle* (1937) · A. Koyré, 'A documentary history of the problem of fall from Kepler to Newton', *Transactions of the American Philosophical Society*, new ser., 45 (1955), 329–95 · D. McKie and G. R. De Beer, 'Newton's apple', *Notes and Records of the Royal Society*, 9 (1951–2), 46–54, 333–5

Archives Andrews University Library, Berrien Springs, Michigan, papers relating to Christ's second coming · Babson College Library, Wellesley, Massachusetts, corresp. and papers · BL, corresp. and papers, Add. MSS 4294, 5751, 6489, 25424, 44888 · Bodl. Oxf., papers relating to alchemy · CUL, corresp. and papers ·

FM Cam., notebook with shorthand notes, lists of expenses · Hants. RO, papers · Jewish National and University Library, Jerusalem, corresp. and papers relating to theology, chemistry, and alchemy · King's AC Cam., corresp. and papers · Leics. RO, inventory of goods and list of MSS · LPL, 'Trigonometriae fundamenta' · Massachusetts Institute of Technology, Cambridge, Dibner Institute for the History of Science and Technology · Morgan L., notebook and papers relating to coinage and astronomy · NRA, priv. coll., corresp. and papers · NRA, priv. coll., Mint account · RS, corresp. and papers relating to Commercium epistolicum · Smithsonian Institution, Washington, DC, corresp. and papers · Stanford University, California, papers relating to alchemy and astronomy · Trinity Cam., corresp. and papers · U. Edin. L., mathematical papers | Bodl. Oxf., papers relating to chronology, Bible, and church history · Bodl. Oxf., corresp. with John Flamsteed · Bodl. Oxf., corresp. with John Locke · CUL, corresp. with Cotes · CUL, corresp. with John Flamsteed · PRO, papers relating to the Mint, MINT 19 · RS, letters to Henry Oldenburg

Likenesses G. Kneller, oils, 1689, Portsmouth estates · D. Le Marchand, ivory medallion, after 1696, RS · J. Croker, medal, after 1700, Royal Mint, London · G. Kneller, oils, 1702, NPG [*see illus.*] · C. Jervas, oils, 1703, RS · W. Gandy, oils, 1706, Col. U., Rare Book and Manuscript Library, David Eugene Smith Collection · J. Thornhill, oils, 1710, Trinity Cam. · J. Thornhill, oils, 1710, Portsmouth estates · D. Le Marchand, ivory bust, 1714, Sotheby Parke Bernet & Co. · D. Le Marchand, ivory bust, c.1718, BM · D. Le Marchand, ivory plaque in high relief, 1718, Sotheby Parke Bernet & Co. · T. Murray, oils, 1718, Trinity Cam. · G. Kneller, oils, 1720, Petworth House, Sussex · W. Stukeley, sketch, c.1720, RS · G. Kneller, oils, c.1723, Portsmouth estates · M. Dahl?, oils, 1725 (after Vanderbank?) · E. Seeman, oils, 1725 (after Vanderbank?) · J. Vanderbank, oils, 1725, Trinity Cam.; version, RS · J. Vanderbank, oils, 1726, RS · oils, c.1726 (after Seeman? or Vanderbank?) · oils, c.1726, NPG · J. M. Rysbrack?, plaster death mask, 1727, Trinity Cam.; iron cast, NPG · J. M. Rysbrack, marble bust, 1733, Royal Collection · L. F. Roubiliac, marble statue, 1755, Trinity Cam. · sculpture on halfpenny, 1793, NPG · G. B. Black, lithograph (aged sixty-four; after W. Gandy junior), BM, NPG · J. Faber junior, mezzotint (after J. M. Rysbrack), BM · J. Faber junior, mezzotint (after J. Vanderbank), BM, NPG · J. Goldar, line engraving (after G. Kneller), NPG · J. Macardell, mezzotint (after E. Seeman), BM, NPG · C. Richter, engraving (after miniature), Col. U., Rare Book and Manuscript Library, David Eugene Smith Collection · J. M. Rysbrack, reclining statue on monument, Westminster Abbey · J. Simon, mezzotint (after G. Kneller), BM

Wealth at death £32,000—liquid assets

Newton, James (c.1664–1750), physician and botanist, was the son of James Newton (1639–1718), physician and botanist. According to the Leeds antiquary Ralph Thoresby, he was born at Leeds and apprenticed there to a tinsmith (Noble, 280), but this is probably misidentification. Newton senior was a tireless botanical collector who had worked throughout the British Isles and in the Netherlands; he was acquainted with Professor Paul Hermann at Leiden, James Sutherland at the Edinburgh Physic Garden, Sloane, and Ray. According to its preface, he began his *Complete Herbal* about 1668, the first part consisting only of a table of authors cited and 175 etched plates, on which several thousand plants were depicted, with their English names, many copied from earlier herbals, plus an index. In later life he compiled the second part, a universal and complete history of plants with their icons, commencing with the apples, some of which was set up in type. A third part was interrupted by his death. A further incomplete manuscript, with no title, is in the library of

the Natural History Museum. By 1698 he was in London, where he established a madhouse in the former Clerkenwell Manor House in Wood's Close, by the Islington turnpike. An advertisement for this institution, dated c.1674, suggests he and his son took in both paying and non-paying guests. He died there in 1718, and was buried at St James's, Clerkenwell. His herbarium and his copper plates, also his property, were bequeathed to his sons Caleb (d. 1722) and James.

It is not known where James Newton junior studied medicine—perhaps at Leiden. He married twice: his first wife, Alice, died in 1703; a son, James (1714–1786), and daughters Zenobia, Mary, and Hester were born of his second marriage, in 1713, to Hester Chaddock (1673–1759). Newton continued as keeper and physician of the madhouse inherited from his father. He was also a keen botanist; among the specimens growing in the garden surrounding the madhouse, the *Daily Post* noted in August 1730 'a white lily, having a cluster of roots from the uppermost end of the stalk, a rarity never before seen in this country'. Newton died at his asylum on 5 November 1750 and was buried in the old ground at St James's, Clerkenwell, a week later.

His son, James Newton, matriculated at Christ Church, Oxford, migrated to Corpus Christi, and graduated BA in 1736. In the same year he was instituted to the living of Nuneham Courtenay, near Oxford. In 1752 he arranged for the publication of his grandfather's *Complete Herbal*, with a portrait, and a dedication to Lord Harcourt. It went through six or seven editions, up to 1805. The destruction of medieval Nuneham and its church in 1759 to make way for Lord Harcourt's new park clearance of Nuneham is believed to have been the inspiration for Oliver Goldsmith's poem *The Deserted Village*. Newton lived unhappily in his new house, ministering to a declining congregation, until his death in 1786.   ANITA McCONNELL

Sources O. Goldsmith, *The deserted village* (1993) · R. Hunter and I. Macalpine, *Three hundred years of psychiatry, 1535–1860* (1963), 200–01 · GM, 1st ser., 20 (1750), 525 · J. Britten and J. E. Dandy, eds., *The Sloane herbarium* (1958), 170–72 · B. Henrey, *British botanical and horticultural literature before 1800*, 2 (1975), 10–14 · parish registers, St James, Clerkenwell · will, James Newton sen., PRO, PROB 11/565, sig. 164 · will, Revd James Newton, PRO, PROB 11/1139, sig. 109 · *A biographical history of England, from the revolution to the end of George I's reign: being a continuation of the Rev. J. Granger's work*, ed. M. Noble, 3 (1806), 280 · W. Roberts, 'Some little known botanists', *Gardeners' Chronicle*, 3rd ser., 65 (1919), 147 · administration, PRO, PROB 6/127, fol. 212

Likenesses oils, Bodl. Oxf. · portrait, Carnegie Mellon University, Pittsburgh, Hunt Botanical Library · print, NPG

Newton, John (1621–1678), mathematician, was probably born at Lavendon, Buckinghamshire, the son of Humphrey Newton, gentleman, and his second wife, Sibyl, née Tyringham. He entered Oundle School in 1627, became a commoner at St Edmund Hall, Oxford, in 1637, and graduated BA in 1641 and MA in 1642. Wood describes him as a 'learned, but capricious and humorous person' (Wood, *Ath. Oxon.*, 3.1190). He was married and had children, though further details of his family are not known.

VERA EFFIGIES IOHĀNIS
NEWTON   ÆTAT·39
    1 6   6 0

John Newton (1621–1678), by unknown engraver, 1660

argued strongly for the teaching of mathematics in English. Claiming support from Francis Bacon he wrote that:

> all the Arts should be taught our Children in the English Tongue, before they learn the Greek or Latin Grammar, by which means many thousands of Children would be fitted for all Trades, enabled to earn their own Livings, and made useful in the Commonwealth. (*Cosmographia*, 1679, published posthumously)

In his illustrated *School Pastime for Young Children* (1669), one of a number of books designed to supply the means of teaching a wider and more practical curriculum, he ordered:

> Let this Book be given to Children, to delight themselves withall as they please, with the sight of the Pictures, and making them as familiar to themselves as may be, and that even at Home, before they be put to School.

Newton died on 26 December 1678 at Ross, and was buried two days later in the chancel of the parish church of St Mary the Virgin.   GRAHAM JAGGER

Sources W. G. Walker, *A history of the Oundle schools* (1956) · parish registers, Ross, 1671–1727, Herefs. RO · parish registers, Lavendon, Buckinghamshire, 1620–21, Bucks. RLSS · Chapter act book, 1672–3, Hereford Cathedral · E. G. R. Taylor, *The mathematical practitioners of Tudor and Stuart England* (1954) · *DNB* · Foster, *Alum. Oxon.* · Wood, *Ath. Oxon.*

Likenesses line engraving, 1660, NPG; repro. in J. Newton, *Mathematical elements* (1660) [*see illus.*]

Newton, John (1725–1807), slave trader and Church of England clergyman, was born on 24 July 1725 in Wapping, London, the only child of John Newton (*d.* 1750), master mariner in the Mediterranean trade, and his first wife, Elizabeth (1705?–1732), whose maiden name was probably Seatliffe. Two days later he was baptized at the Independent chapel in Old Gravel Lane, Wapping, where his mother attended and where David Jennings was the minister. He remembered his mother as 'a pious and experienced Christian', and at her knee he learned the hymns and catechisms of Isaac Watts and was nurtured in the piety of old dissent. She died of tuberculosis when John was only six. His father remarried after his mother's death, but John's relationship with both his father and his stepmother was distant, and his religious training ceased. His stepmother, Thomasina, was the daughter of a substantial tenant-grazier in the parish of Aveley in Essex, and he lived with her family while his father was away at sea. Newton eventually had two half-brothers, William and Harry, and a half-sister, Thomasina. For two years (1733–5) he was sent to a boarding-school at Stratford in Essex, where he began to learn Latin. From the age of eleven (1736) he went to sea with his father and made several voyages with him before 1742. The elder Newton was drowned on 29 June 1750, when he was governor of Fort York under the Hudson's Bay Company.

Slaver Newton recounts the story of his early life in his autobiography, *An Authentic Narrative of some Remarkable and Interesting Particulars in the Life of —* (1764), in which he weaves together the themes of religious conversion and romantic love with his seafaring career. Newton's adolescence was a time of fluctuating passions. On a journey to Kent he visited George and Elizabeth Catlett, friends of his

Following the Restoration, Newton was made chaplain to the king and was created DD in 1661. He became vicar of Ross, Herefordshire, in 1660, and rector of Stretton Sugwas, Herefordshire, in 1661. In 1662 Newton resigned the living of Stretton Sugwas, and in the same year was made rector of Upminster, Essex, which position he held until his death. He was installed as prebendary of Cublington, Herefordshire, on 24 March 1673 but resigned the following year.

Being a royalist, Newton received no preferment during the interregnum and supported himself by teaching mathematics and astronomy. He wrote a connected series of books on these subjects, all in English, advocating the use of decimal arithmetic. It was his 'chief and principal aime to shew how much of trouble may be avoyded in computing the motions of the heavenly bodies, if only the form of our Tables were changed from Sexagenary into Decimall' (*Astronomia Britannica*, 1657).

As vicar of Ross, Newton had other concerns: to the local landowners he wrote that Ross lacked only two things, 'a comfortable subsistence for Gods Minister, and a competent endowment for a good school' (*The Scale of Interest*, 1668). He worked tirelessly for the reform of the local tithing system, and succeeded in obtaining a private act of parliament in 1671. Under the terms of this act Newton became rector of Ross in 1674 following the death of the previous rector, John Cooke. In the field of education he

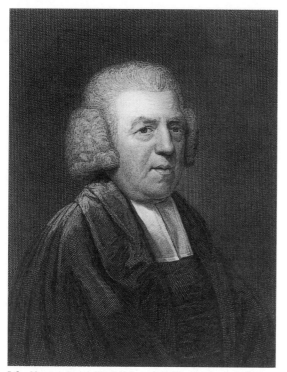

John Newton (1725–1807), by Joseph Collyer the younger, 1807
(after John Russell, 1788)

late mother, and fell immediately in love with their eldest daughter, Mary Catlett, known as Polly (1729–1790), whom he would later marry. He prolonged his visit and thereby evaded his father's plans to send him to a sugar estate in Jamaica to be set up in business. Returning at the close of 1743 from a voyage to Venice, during which he began his decline into 'apostasy', he again evaded his father's plans by a protracted visit to the Catlett family. Before another business opportunity could be found he was press-ganged on board HMS *Harwich* in the tense days just before France formally declared war on England (during the War of the Austrian Succession, 1739–48). Newton soon attempted to desert but he was caught, put in irons, whipped, and degraded from the office of midshipman to common seaman. As he watched the English coastline recede, at the end of 1744, knowing his ship was bound for a five-year voyage to the East Indies, he claimed it was only his love for Mary that kept him from attempting to murder the captain or commit suicide.

The day before his ship was due to leave Madeira he contrived to be transferred to a merchant vessel in the African slave trade. His behaviour during this whole period involved ribald and blasphemous language; he also alludes vaguely to sexual misconduct. After six months trading he determined to stay on the Guinea coast of Africa to work in the onshore trade, hoping to make his fortune as a slave factor on one of the Plantanes islands off the coast of Sierra Leone. Instead during the next two years he suffered illness, starvation, exposure, and ridicule as his master, a man named Clow, used him brutally.

Newton always marked this point as the nadir of his spiritual journey.

Newton's father had arranged for a fellow captain to look for him on his next voyage to the Guinea coast, but meanwhile Newton had found a new master under whom his prospects had so improved that when the captain located him he could barely be persuaded to leave Africa. The ship, the *Greyhound*, returned to England along the triangular Atlantic trade route, via Brazil and Newfoundland, but encountered a severe north Atlantic storm in the winter of 1748. On 21 March, Newton was awakened in the middle of the night to find that the ship was breaking apart and filling fast with water, and a man was already swept overboard. Newton muttered his first prayer for mercy in many years. When the ordeal was over he and most of the crew had survived the storm but were left with very little food or water and a ship out of repair. Newton began to read the Bible and other religious books. By the time the ship at length reached Ireland he considered himself no longer an 'infidel'. In his diary he would always thereafter remember 21 March as the anniversary of his conversion. Indeed the very last entry he made in his diary, as an eighty-year-old man, was a commemoration of this event.

In terms of his later evangelical theology, however, this was Newton's awakening of conscience more than his true repentance. He was not yet a 'true believer': that came six months later. On his return to England he was helped by Joseph Manesty of Liverpool, a friend of his father's, to obtain a position as first mate on board the *Brownlow*, a slave-trading ship bound for the Guinea coast and the West Indies (1748–9). He hoped to return to England having proved himself worthy to make a proposal of marriage to Mary Catlett. It was on this voyage, in Africa, that Newton found himself unable to live up to his new spiritual and moral obligations. Only a violent fever returned him to seriousness about his soul. Delirious, he crept to an isolated spot on the island where the ship had stopped and he cast himself before God in an act of surrender, trusting himself wholly to the atonement of Christ. From this moment, he claimed, he experienced a new sort of peace and power over sin. He returned to England and married Mary on 12 February 1750.

After his marriage Newton made three voyages as master of slave-trading ships, the *Duke of Argyle* (1750–51) and the *African* (1752–3 and 1753–4). On his last voyage he met a fellow captain, Alexander Clunie, who acquainted him with the progress of evangelical revival in England. Consequently when a convulsive fit caused Newton to leave the maritime trade, later in 1754, he frequented religious meetings in London and was soon drawn into the revival associated with George Whitefield and with John and Charles Wesley. Through his contact with dissenters and Calvinistic Methodism, and through his personal study, he became a convinced Calvinist himself.

Newton has sometimes been accused of hypocrisy for holding strong religious convictions at the same time as being active in the slave trade, praying above deck while his human cargo was in abject misery below deck. He was not, however, within the orbit of evangelicals such as John Wesley, who had advanced views against slavery, until he had already left the sea. He was a typical European of his time. Later in life he had deep regrets and repented of his involvement in the traffic, supported William Wilberforce in his abolition crusade, gave evidence to the privy council, and wrote a tract supporting abolition, *Thoughts upon the African Slave Trade* (1787).

Curate in charge In August 1755 Newton took up a civil service post as tide surveyor at Liverpool, where his duties included inspecting import cargoes and checking for smuggled goods. The Seven Years' War meant that traffic dropped off at the port so Newton used all his spare time to pursue private studies in divinity. Having become proficient in Latin while at sea he now taught himself Greek, and began to learn Hebrew and Syriac. Soon he was one of the leading evangelical laymen in the region, widely acquainted with 'awakened clergy' up and down the country. His acquaintance included Whitefield and Wesley, as well as Yorkshire ministers of all denominations, such as Henry Venn of Huddersfield, William Grimshaw of Haworth, Henry Crooke of Hunslet, and John Edwards of Leeds. He was nicknamed locally Young Whitefield and soon hosted large religious meetings in his own home. It was natural that he began to have thoughts of entering the ministry himself, in 1757. Branded a Methodist he was unsuccessful, during the winter of 1758–9, in several applications for orders in the Church of England. The secretary to the archbishop of York wrote to Newton: 'His Grace thinks it best for you to continue in that station which Providence has placed you in' (*Dartmouth MSS*, 3.173). It was in fact seven frustrating years before he achieved ordination. Newton's churchmanship was far from settled during these years. He contemplated at least three opportunities among the Independents (serving a locum in Warwick for three months in 1760), one among the Methodists, and one among the Presbyterians; he also took his application for orders (in most cases at least twice) to the bishops of Chester and Lincoln, to two archbishops of York, and to the archbishop of Canterbury. When he finished writing his autobiography, in 1764, he was still hoping a bishop would ordain him despite his many disappointments.

In the end that draft of his autobiography acted like a curriculum vitae, which Thomas Haweis used to introduce Newton's case to the young evangelical nobleman Lord Dartmouth. In April 1764 the earl provided a letter of introduction that pacified the bishop of Chester, Edmund Keene, when Newton needed the bishop to authenticate his letters testimonial. Lord Dartmouth also used his influence to overcome the remaining obstacles with the archbishop of York, Hay Drummond, and the bishop of Lincoln, John Green, in whose diocese the living of Olney lay—the living which Lord Dartmouth intended for Newton. At long last Newton received deacon's orders, on 29 April 1764, from the bishop of Lincoln; he was priested several weeks later on 17 June. He could fairly be said to have ended his own seven years' war. A little later that same year Newton's *Authentic Narrative* appeared in print and it immediately established his place as one of the leading evangelicals in the revival. It went through ten British and eight American editions before the end of the century and was quickly translated into several other languages.

In the event Newton became curate-in-charge rather than vicar of Olney in Buckinghamshire, for Moses Browne (the vicar since 1754) chose not to resign the living when he moved to take up the chaplaincy of Morden College, Blackheath. Olney was a market town located in low, open country on the north-west bank of the River Ouse. The parish included approximately 2000 inhabitants, chiefly artisans and tradesmen. It was well known for its production of bone lace, a cottage industry which had been important locally since religious refugees from France and the Low Countries had brought the trade with them generations earlier. William Cowper described the inhabitants of Olney in Newton's time as 'the half-starved and ragged of the Earth' (*Letters and Prose*, 2.91). Newton's stipend was only £60 a year but the wealthy evangelical merchant John Thornton allowed him an additional £200 a year for hospitality and to help the poor.

Indeed Newton was so successful in helping the poor that he raised the pique of the local nonconformists. The Independent John Drake found his methods 'Jesuitical'. There was an important puritan–nonconformist history in the region but that constituency had been weakened by the earlier preaching of Whitefield and by the ministry of Moses Browne. Drake claimed that Newton's preaching and pastoral care gave the dissenting interest a 'mortal wound'. During his sixteen years at Olney, Newton established a variety of services and society meetings, which became very popular; the church became so crowded that a gallery was added. With Olney as his base Newton made forays into adjacent parishes to speak at cottage prayer meetings. He also exchanged pulpits with ministers further away, such as John Berridge of Everton, or went on preaching tours, visiting evangelical clergy in Yorkshire or in London. He maintained warm friendships with dissenters locally, such as the Independent minister William Bull of Newport Pagnell. Though he would not exchange pulpits with dissenters they would frequently visit each other's homes, society meetings, and churches. While known for being tolerant of those with whom he differed he rejected both the Arminianism and the perfectionism of Wesley as well as the high Calvinism prevalent among some Baptists. He liked to call himself 'a sort of middleman'.

By the end of Newton's ministry in Olney his encouragement of lay religiosity and his ecumenical spirit caused him problems since several of the laymen in his parish, such as the carpenter Thomas Raban (*d.* 1784), who had got a taste for public speaking, challenged his authority and eventually seceded from the church. After a serious fire in the town in 1777, Newton tried to restrain the parish from behaving recklessly on the forthcoming Guy Fawkes night. He claimed that the Baptists 'in a body' set themselves against him, and his own house was later threatened by mob violence. From that point forward he had thoughts of leaving Olney.

Collaboration with Cowper In 1767 the poet William Cowper, having recently come to evangelical convictions, settled at Olney to be near Newton. Cowper shared in the religious life of the parish and in 1771 he and Newton began to collaborate formally on a project to publish a volume of their collected hymns. It was to be a sort of mutual Festschrift, celebrating their friendship and spiritual ideals. With the onset of Cowper's third bout of serious depression in 1773, however, the whole project was cast into doubt, for from that point Cowper wrote very few more hymns. In the end Newton decided, nevertheless, to publish what they had. Many of the *Olney Hymns* (1779) addressed specific situations in the parish but the hymnbook became popular more widely. Newton's most famous contributions are 'Glorious things of thee are spoken', 'How sweet the name of Jesus sounds!', 'Approach, my soul, the mercy-seat', and 'Amazing grace'. The style and tone of these hymns fit somewhere between the sobriety of old dissent in Isaac Watts's *Hymns and Spiritual Songs* (1707) and the exuberance of Wesleyan Methodism in the standard *Collection of Hymns, for the Use of the People called Methodists* (1780).

Soon after Cowper's death in 1800, a long and often bitter debate commenced over the causes of his dementia and religious melancholy. Some blamed the emotionalism of evangelicalism for aggravating his mental illness while others laid the blame specifically on Calvinism. The belief that Newton's influence had served to undermine Cowper's sanity was long perpetuated by Robert Southey's *Life of Cowper* (1835). The debate continued throughout the nineteenth and early twentieth centuries with very little fresh work in source criticism and a great deal of *parti pris*. Newton's life has all too often functioned as merely an episode in the poet's melancholy. Although there were temporary breaches in their friendship Newton continued to treat Cowper with tenderness, acting the part of a spiritual counsellor. He wrote to Cowper in 1780:

> I know not that I ever saw you for a single day since your calamity came upon you, in which I could not perceive as clear and satisfactory evidence, that the grace of God was with you, as I could in your brighter and happier times. (*Works*, 6.162)

Indeed it was at Olney that Newton emerged as a well-known spiritual writer, 'the St. Francis de Sales of the Evangelical movement, the great spiritual director of souls through the post' (Balleine, 84). Although Newton published sermons and even a *Review of Ecclesiastical History* (1770)—which may have suggested to Joseph Milner the idea of his *History of the Church of Christ*—his favourite medium was the familiar letter; he came virtually to think in quarto sheets folded once. In 1774 he collected and published twenty-six of his letters on religious subjects, which had earlier been published in the *Gospel Magazine* under the pen name Omicron. His three letters on growth in grace (originally written to John Thornton in 1772) have

frequently been printed from the Omicron series as a classical statement of evangelical spirituality. Newton's later collection of more personal letters, *Cardiphonia, or, The Utterance of the Heart* (1780), established his place as the gentle casuist of the evangelical revival. Included in *Cardiphonia* is Newton's correspondence with Thomas Scott, the biblical commentator whom Newton helped to convert, after much debate, from Socinianism. Over 500 of Newton's letters of spiritual advice were published during his lifetime or shortly afterwards.

Evangelical in the city In January 1780 Newton accepted the offer from John Thornton of the benefice of St Mary Woolnoth with St Mary Woolchurch, Lombard Street, London. The living was worth just over £260 a year and the church itself had been built by Nicholas Hawksmoor, in 1727, in a fashionable, baroque style. This was an important city living at a time when William Romaine was the only other evangelical incumbent in London. Newton took up residence at Hoxton Square, near Newington Road, in 1780, and then in 1786 at Coleman Street Buildings, just inside London Wall and close to his church. Unlike his extensive parish ministry at Olney, St Mary Woolnoth was for Newton chiefly a pulpit since the church looked out on a highly mobile, cosmopolitan population with little parochial identity. In 1786, during the Handel commemoration, he preached and published fifty sermons on the libretto of the *Messiah*. Throughout his ministry in London people came from afar to hear him, and his congregations were large. However when he was awarded the degree of DD by the University of New Jersey in 1792 he chose not to recognize the honour, feeling that his behaviour in Africa as a young man disqualified him from doing so.

Increasingly Newton gained the status of a patriarch within the emerging evangelical party, and his home was regularly crowded with younger ministers eager to glean wisdom from him. Richard Cecil and William Jay were present to record much of Newton's casual table talk. William Wilberforce called on Newton for advice during the crisis of his evangelical conversion in 1785; Claudius Buchanan, who later served as chaplain in India, was converted by a sermon at St Mary Woolnoth and later became Newton's curate; Newton visited Charles Simeon at Cambridge and Hannah More at Cowslip Green. He was also involved in the founding of the Eclectic Society, in 1783, which would become famous as the matrix of the Church Missionary Society and of the *Christian Observer* magazine. He continued to represent an affable, winsome evangelicalism within the Church of England, and his Calvinism became, if anything, more moderate as he grew older. He told William Jay that he used Calvinism in his ministry like sugar in his tea: 'I do not give it alone and whole; but mixed and diluted.' This is also a good example of his epigrammatic wit and homely anecdotal style of communication, in and out of the pulpit. Yet in the troubled 1790s he felt the need to defend his churchmanship in an *Apologia* (1784), where he made clear his reasons for staying within the Church of England; it satisfied few of his dissenting friends.

Final years Newton's wife died in 1790 of cancer, and though he was able to preach her funeral sermon his sense of loss was as deep as his love for her had been devoted. He published his *Letters to a Wife* in 1793, in which he poignantly traced the lines of his grief in meditations recorded in his own interleaved copy. Newton and his wife had no children of their own but they adopted two of their orphan nieces on the Catlett side of the family. Elizabeth (Eliza) Cunningham, daughter of James and Elizabeth Cunningham, came into their home in 1783 but died while still a child, in 1785, and Newton wrote up an account of her childhood faith. Elizabeth (Betsy or Eliza) Catlett was the daughter of George Catlett and had been adopted earlier, in 1774. After his wife's death, Newton depended upon Betsy. In 1801 she experienced a period of derangement and was confined to Bethlem Hospital, much to Newton's distress. After her recovery she married an optician named Smith; both remained at Coleman Street Buildings to take care of Newton as his sight failed and his health deteriorated. He died peacefully on 21 December 1807 and was buried by the side of his wife in St Mary Woolnoth on 31 December; both bodies were re-interred at Olney in 1893.

The most famous image of Newton is an engraving by Joseph Collyer the younger, after a portrait by John Russell. In addition to his published works Newton left behind many manuscripts, comprising largely spiritual journals, sermons, and letters. His archive is now divided among several repositories, the chief of which are the Cowper and Newton Museum, Olney; Lambeth Palace Library, London; and Firestone Library, Princeton University.

Interpretations of Newton's life have varied. Almost every generation since his death has seen sympathetic or inspirational biographies and these have largely affirmed Newton's emblematic sense that his life was a symbol of divine grace to hardened sinners. Richard Cecil's *Memoirs of the Rev. John Newton* (1808) was squarely in the tradition of Newton's own autobiography; Josiah Bull's more carefully researched *John Newton of Olney and St. Mary Woolnoth* (1868) was likewise filiopietistic. These volumes are also the chief repositories of information and anecdotes about Newton. In contrast to these interpretations Newton has often appeared as an unsympathetic foil to William Cowper in biographies of the poet. On a broader canvas historians, and particularly ecclesiastical historians, have consistently portrayed Newton as a warm, genial, Christian man and a devoted minister, one of a number of evangelical clergy who helped to raise the spiritual tone of the Church of England in the eighteenth century.

D. BRUCE HINDMARSH

Sources D. B. Hindmarsh, *John Newton and the English evangelical tradition between the conversions of Wesley and Wilberforce* (1996) [incl. bibliography] · J. Bull, *John Newton of Olney and St. Mary Woolnoth* (1868) · R. Cecil, *Memoirs of the Rev. John Newton* (1808) · *The works of the Rev John Newton*, 6 vols. (1808) · B. Martin and M. Spurrell, eds., *The journal of a slave trader (John Newton), 1750–1754* (1962) · D. B. Hindmarsh, 'The Olney autobiographers: English conversion narrative in the mid-eighteenth century', *Journal of Ecclesiastical History*,

49 (1998), 61–84 · B. Martin, *John Newton: a biography* (1950) · J. Pollock, *Amazing grace: John Newton's story* (1981) · *Autobiography of William Jay*, ed. G. Redford and J. A. James (1854) · *The manuscripts of the earl of Dartmouth*, 3 vols., HMC, 20 (1887–96), vol. 3 · *The letters and prose writings of William Cowper*, ed. J. King and C. Ryskamp, 5 vols. (1979–86) · G. R. Balleine, *A history of the evangelical party in the Church of England*, new edn (1951) · R. Cecil, *The life of John Newton*, ed. M. Rouse (2000)

Archives Cowper and Newton Museum, Olney, Buckinghamshire, corresp., MSS, and notebooks · GL, corresp. and sermon notes · LPL, corresp. and papers · NMM, log as master of a slaver · Princeton University Library, Firestone Library, collection and other MSS · Princeton University Library, corresp. relating to history of Church of England, MSS of hymns, and notebook · U. Birm. L., letters from wife and sermon notes | BL, letters to W. Cowper, Egerton MS 3662 · Bodl. Oxf., corresp. with William Wilberforce · Bristol Baptist College, letters to John Ryland jun. · CUL, corresp. with John Thornton · DWL, letters to David Jennings · Hist. Soc. Penn., letters of Newton · LPL, corresp. with William Bull · Lpool RO, letters to David Jennings · McMaster University, Hamilton, Ontario, MS memoir of William Cowper · Ridley Hall, Cambridge, letters to John Thornton · U. Birm. L., Church Missionary Society archive

Likenesses engravings, 1781–8, NPG · J. Collyer the younger, line engraving, 1807 (after J. Russell, 1788), BM, NPG [*see illus.*] · two engravings, in or before 1809, NPG · oils, Cowper and Newton Museum, Olney, Buckinghamshire

Wealth at death see will, 4 Feb 1808, PRO, PROB 11/1474

Newton [*née* Severn], **(Ann) Mary** (1832–1866), painter, was born in Rome on 29 June 1832, the daughter of Joseph *Severn (1793–1879), the painter and friend of Keats, and his wife, Elizabeth Montgomerie (*d.* 1862). One of six children in an artistic family, she was first taught to draw by her father; after the Severns returned to England in 1841, she studied with George Richmond. In 1857 she took lessons from Ary Scheffer in Paris. By the time she was twenty Mary Severn was building up a flourishing practice, becoming the family breadwinner as her father fell into debt. At first she specialized in portraits of children, working in crayon, chalk, pastel, or watercolour, and travelling from one great house to another; most of these family portraits are still in private collections. She began exhibiting at the Royal Academy in 1852, with *The Twins* (priv. coll.), a double portrait of her younger brother and sister. Commissions from the French imperial court and from aristocratic British sitters recommended her to Queen Victoria, for whom she made portraits of the queen's children and nephew (Royal Collection, Windsor Castle, Berkshire) as well as copies of old masters.

On 27 April 1861 Mary Severn married the archaeologist Sir Charles *Newton (*bap.* 1816, *d.* 1894), keeper of Greek and Roman antiquities at the British Museum, London. She worked with him at the museum, making large-scale drawings of Greek sculpture for his public lectures and illustrations for his *History of the Discoveries at Halicarnassus, Cnidus, and Branchidæ* (2 vols., 1862–3). Her wryly observed sketches and caricatures offer an informal glimpse of the strains and triumphs of their collaboration. Together they toured the eastern Mediterranean, where Mary drew archaeological finds for Charles's *Travels and Discoveries in the Levant* (1865). Their travelling companion was the young artist Gertrude Jekyll; the two women sketched local scenes and people and also recorded the adventures of their own party among the makeshift, exhilarating, and sometimes dangerous conditions of nineteenth-century travel. Some of Mary Newton's watercolour portraits and landscapes from the Levant were exhibited at the Dudley Gallery in London in 1866.

In the 1860s Mary Newton worked increasingly in oils, still concentrating on portraits and figures while developing a richer use of colour; examples include a striking self-portrait (exh. RA, 1863; National Portrait Gallery, London), a sympathetic and well-received portrait of Mrs Liddell (exh. RA, 1865), and an Arthurian subject from Tennyson, *Elaine* (exh. RA, 1863). She died at her home, 74 Gower Street, London, on 2 January 1866, of measles, at the age of thirty-three; she had no children. Her husband survived her. Little of her work is on public view and her engaging and spirited personality found much of its expression in private letters, sketches, and notebooks. She was a fully professional artist, an accomplished portraitist, and one of several Victorian women who, in the opinion of a contemporary reviewer (*The Times*, 7 May 1863), if the academy were not closed to women, 'should write R.A. after her name'.

ROWENA FOWLER

Sources S. Birkenhead, *Against oblivion: the life of Joseph Severn* (1943) · S. Birkenhead, *Illustrious friends: the story of Joseph Severn and his son Arthur* (1965) · *GM*, 4th ser., 1 (1866), 435–6 · *The Times* (23 Jan 1866) · *The Times* (7 May 1863) · *Catalogue of drawings by Max Beerbohm and Mrs Newton* (1922) [exhibition catalogue, Oxford Arts Club] · *DNB*
Archives BM, Charles Newton MSS · Keats Memorial Library, London, Severn family MSS · NRA, priv. coll., Furneaux family MSS
Likenesses M. Newton, self-portrait, oils, 1863, NPG · M. Newton, self-portrait, pencil, Keats Memorial Library, London

Newton, Sir Richard (*d.* 1448), justice, was the son of John Cradock of Newtown in Montgomeryshire and his wife, Margaret, daughter of Sir Owen Moythe of Castle Odwyn and Fountain Gate. It is not known when he was born. Trained as a lawyer at the Middle Temple, London, he was created serjeant-at-law in 1425 under the name of Richard Newton, and became a king's serjeant in 1430. But he had earlier connections with Bristol, where he had become recorder by December 1430, and with Wales, being appointed before September 1426 by Humphrey, duke of Gloucester, to be justice itinerant in the latter's courts in Pembrokeshire. In 1438 he headed a general commission of oyer and terminer in Carmarthenshire and Cardiganshire, but away from Westminster his interests were increasingly confined to south-west England, where he was often a royal commissioner and justice of assize. Newton was appointed a justice of common pleas on 8 November 1438, and less than a year later, on 17 September 1439, chief justice of that court, being granted £93 6s. 8d. and two robes yearly in addition to the usual fee. He was knighted by the following July. In 1441 he was appointed an arbitrator in one of several attempts to resolve the dispute over the inheritance of Thomas, Lord Berkeley, while between 1439 and 1447 he four times acted as a trier of petitions to parliament from Gascony and lands overseas.

Newton was clearly an important and influential justice, whose arguments and decisions are often recorded in the year-books. In 1442 his argument in Dogge's case seems to have been effective in persuading his fellow judges to decide that an action of *assumpsit* lay against a vendor of land who deceitfully failed to complete an oral contract. Until then, a promisor could only be sued for non-feasance (failing to perform an agreed act) if the contract was in writing, whereas a debt could be enforced without writing; but Newton said it would be 'amazing law' if a bargain could be made which only bound one party. This celebrated decision paved the way for a general contractual remedy through *assumpsit*. Newton made his will on 28 November 1448, and died on 13 December following. He was survived by a widow, Emma, or Emmota, variously described as the daughter of Sir Thomas Perrott or of John Hervey of London; she may have been his second wife. He also left a son, John, who by 1443 had married Isabel, daughter of Thomas Chedder of Somerset. He bequeathed his body to Yatton church in Somerset, where his legacy financed a bell, and where he is still represented by the effigy of a judge on an altar-tomb.

HENRY SUMMERSON

Sources will, LPL, Reg Stafford A 169, 169v · *Chancery records* · E. Foss, *Biographia juridica: a biographical dictionary of the judges of England … 1066–1870* (1870), 480 · Baker, *Serjeants* · N. Doe, *Fundamental authority in late medieval English law* (1990) · C. M. Gray, 'Plucknett's "Lancastrian" constitution', *On the laws and customs of England*, ed. M. S. Arnold, T. A. Green, S. A. Scully, and S. D. White (1981), 195–230 · W. S. Holdsworth, *A history of English law*, 3rd edn, 3 (1923) · J. T. Driver, 'Parliamentary burgesses for Bristol and Gloucester, 1422–1437', *Transactions of the Bristol and Gloucestershire Archaeological Society*, 74 (1955), 60–127 · Sainty, *Judges*, 47, 69 · Sainty, *King's counsel*, 9
Likenesses effigy, Yatton church, Somerset

Newton, Richard (1676–1753), educationist and college head, was born on 8 November 1676 at Yardley Park, Northamptonshire, the youngest son of Thomas Newton, landowner, of Lavendon, Buckinghamshire, and his wife, Katherine (*d.* 1680), daughter of Martin Hervey of Weston Favell, Northamptonshire. He was educated at Westminster School, where he was made king's scholar in 1690, and then proceeded to Christ Church, Oxford, in 1694. He graduated BA in 1698, MA in 1701, and BD in 1708, and became a doctor of divinity in 1710. After a brief period as a tutor at his old college he was preferred to the rectory of Sudborough in Northamptonshire, in which county his mother's family had originated. He held this living from 1704 until 1748 but invariably deputed the services to a curate; during a short spell of intermittent residence he instructed pupils at this country location. Newton was twice married; his first wife was Catherine, daughter of Andrew Adams of Wetton, Northamptonshire, with whom he had one daughter, Jane, who married the Revd Knightley Adams. Newton's second wife was Mary (1698/9–1781), the fifth daughter and ninth child of Sir Willoughby Hickman of Gainsborough and Ann Anderson; this marriage was childless.

In 1710 Newton's reputation as a tutor led to his appointment as principal of Hart Hall in Oxford. This hall of the university had only slowly shaken off its reputation for religious recusancy. Newton immediately interested himself in reforming the curriculum and in schemes to turn the endowments of the surviving halls to better use. Soon his schemes for improving Hart Hall, both physically and academically, ran into local opposition. In particular the hall's neighbour All Souls coveted some of the ground on which Newton proposed to build. An effort was made to distract Newton from this site by Dr George Clarke, a powerful fellow of All Souls. Clarke schemed to persuade Newton to exchange halls with William King, principal of St Mary's Hall, in the hope that Newton might then erect his new foundation where St Mary's stood.

Nothing came of this design. Instead Newton reverted to the possibility of expanding the institution of which he was head. In 1720 he published his *Scheme of Discipline* to reform Hart Hall. However his plans, which included elevating the hall into a college, again ran into opposition both from All Souls and from its landlord, Exeter College. Newton's combative approach and the hostility of the bishop of Exeter, Exeter's visitor, stalled the project. Concurrently Newton faced adversaries from within Hart Hall itself; there his powers as principal were absolute, and in exercising them to the full he made enemies. A few, restless under the principal's dictatorship, in 1723 seceded to other colleges; their actions, damaging alike to the precarious finances of Hart Hall and to its reputation, had to be resisted.

Newton was quick to print justifications of his conduct, whether in relation to the mutinous body of undergraduates or his battles with other colleges. However, by 1737, after protracted disputes, the obstructionism of Exeter College and its visitor had ended. The way was cleared for Newton to realize his ambition of making Hart Hall a college. Endowments for thirty-two undergraduates were to be secured. Minute attention was devoted to every aspect of the pedagogic and financial regulation of the establishment. Newton himself set an example by bestowing a rent charge from his own properties in Buckinghamshire on the foundation. However this did not suffice and he had to solicit more benefactions, work on which he was still engaged when he died. He also envisaged a complex of new buildings in the classical style. A chapel, financed by subscriptions, had already been erected shortly after his appointment as principal; he preached at its consecration in 1716. Part only of the planned quadrangle was built, in an austere neo-Palladian style reminiscent of Newton's earlier connections with the architectural innovators Dean Aldrich at Christ Church and Dr George Clarke. In 1740 Newton secured a royal charter for the new establishment, Hertford College. Its statutes were the work of Newton and embodied his ideas on education; in the light of long experience these diverged from what he had proposed in 1720. He would oversee tutors and students with equal strictness. Regular and rigorous academic exercises were to guarantee scholastic standards. Great power reposed in the principal, who doubled as bursar. The principal, in a manner more appropriate to a hall than to a college, selected fellows. Future principals, following Newton's own example, were to be chosen exclusively from

alumni of Westminster and Christ Church. Newton was keen, too, that an economical regime should attract undergraduates from less affluent backgrounds and compete for members against other colleges within the university. As principal he watched vigilantly over the domestic economy of the house. He calculated that the annual expenses of an undergraduate could be cut to about £31. He also waged an unavailing battle against the distractions that seduced the young from their studies. His frugal regimen at Hertford of 'small-beer and apple dumplings' was easily mocked.

In 1748 Newton resigned his Northamptonshire living in order to concentrate on his college duties. As part of his academic work he translated the *Characters* of Theophrastus from Greek into Latin. Among his pupils had been Henry Pelham, who in 1752, as first lord of the Treasury, had Newton preferred—belatedly—to a canonry in Christ Church Cathedral. However, Newton did not long enjoy the dignity, and died at Lavendon Grange, Buckinghamshire, on 21 April the following year. He was buried in Lavendon church, survived by his second wife, who died on 5 July 1781.

Newton exhibited a ruthlessness perhaps necessary to overcome the hostility of Oxford colleagues towards his schemes of educational regeneration. He dissented from the notion that the head of any college should act simply as an innkeeper. The objectives of education were, he insisted, 'piety, learning and good manners' (R. Newton, *University Education*, 1726). His foundation attracted entrants, thanks to its blend of scholastic seriousness and prudent economy. Nevertheless, his uncompromising approach made enemies and thus slowed the achievement of his design. In addition it may have prevented his securing the ample benefactions that alone could have put the foundation on a secure footing. By 1820 Hertford College had collapsed physically, having already ceased to exist as a legal corporation in 1805. It would require refoundation later in the nineteenth century.

TOBY BARNARD

Sources S. G. Hamilton, *Hertford College* (1903) · T. C. Barnard, introduction, in R. Newton, *Rules and statutes for the government of Hertford College* [1998] · A. Goudie, ed., *Seven hundred years of an Oxford college: Hertford College, 1284–1984*, new edn (1999), 43–5 · *DNB*
Archives BL, Newcastle MSS, Add. MSS
Likenesses oils, Hertford College, Oxford · oils, Bodl. Oxf.

Newton, Richard (1777–1798), caricaturist and miniature painter, was probably born in London, the son of Richard Newton (d. 1796), a haberdasher who later let properties near the Drury Lane Theatre. Little is known of the younger Newton's early life and artistic training. His earliest surviving print was engraved when he was eleven and his talent was certainly well developed by the age of fourteen, when he joined the radical publisher William Holland (1757–1815), either as an apprentice or as a paid draughtsman. In that year, 1791, his name appeared on a number of prints, the earliest being *A Sketch of the Highlife* (27 May), one of many published by Holland mocking the king and queen.

Newton's brief career coincided with the upsurge of political caricature in England during the era of the French Revolution. His employer, Holland, was one of several print publishers who made 'the singly issued satire, hand-coloured with transparent watercolour washes … one of the most important products of the London print trade' (Alexander, 7). In Newton he found an expert draughtsman capable of the rapid work and comic creativity needed to produce marketable satire. He published over a dozen of Newton's prints in 1792, culminating in November in perhaps the most radical, *Liberty and Equality*, in which the king is depicted walking uncomfortably alongside a plebeian who flourishes a copy of Paine's *Rights of Man*.

In February 1793 Holland was sentenced to a year's imprisonment for selling Paine's *Letter Addressed to the Addressers, on the Late Proclamation*. In his absence Newton published some prints under his own name from the Oxford Street print shop of his employer. He appears to have begun publishing on his own account as early as November 1791, when he issued *A Visit to the Royal Cole Pit*, which ridiculed the alleged miserliness of the king and queen. The clergy were another of his favourite targets and his satire was at its most cutting in *Fast-Day!*, issued on 19 April 1793 to coincide with a day of national fasting decreed by the king and depicting four grotesquely fat parsons gorging from a table laden with food and drink. In a similar vein was *Which Way shall I Turn Me?* (July 1794), which shows a parson torn between a young woman reclining seductively on a couch and a roasting pig with a bottle of wine.

While Holland was in Newgate, Newton visited him there and produced a series of portrait groups of inmates and visitors, including one featuring Holland with the veteran reformer John Frost and the radical John Horne Tooke. Holland's release in the spring of 1794 marked the beginning of an intensive phase for Newton, and by December 1796 he etched over 100 singly issued prints, in addition to the plates for an edition of Sterne's *Sentimental Journey*. He also produced two works in the 'progress' genre, *Progress of an Irishman* and *Progress of a Scotsman*, thereby becoming one of the pioneers of the narrative 'strip' on a single plate which prefigured the comic strip of the modern day. In the autumn of 1794 he painted a large watercolour of Holland's exhibition rooms thronging with society figures, in a parody of contemporary engravings of Royal Academy exhibitions. The depiction of both the viewers and the exhibits is subtly subversive; among the prints depicted in the background are Newton's social satires *Who shall Wear the Breeches?* and *Wearing the Breeches*, in which the voluptuous young wife asserts her dominance over her husband.

Holland's imprisonment made him more cautious about his political targets, and this may have increased Newton's desire to branch out on his own. The death of his father in 1796 may also have provided the necessary means, for early in 1797 he opened, at 13 Brydges Street, Covent Garden, his Original Print Warehouse. He supplemented his income here by offering 'warranted strong likenesses for half a guinea in miniature', and he evidently harboured the ambition to paint portraits (Hill, xvi). In August 1797 he produced an engaging self-portrait, which shows a realism and an elegance absent from some of his satirical work.

Released from Holland's employment, Newton's radicalism reasserted itself, and in May 1797 he published *Head—and Brains*, a pen-and-watercolour drawing that caricatured the symbiotic relationship between George III and William Pitt: from a single neck their two heads emerge, the king's much the larger but the prime minister's seemingly the more powerful. Among the best prints of this period is *Treason!!!* (19 March 1798), in which an artisan John Bull 'capers with hands on hips', playfully directing 'a blast from his posterior' at a portrait of the king, while a much-caricatured Pitt cries out: 'That is Treason, Johnny' (George, 6.434–5). This was one of Newton's last works: he fell ill in the spring of 1798 and died in London on 8 December of that year.

Newton's early death curtailed a talent that was still in the making. And although he left nearly 300 singly issued prints and over eighty plates in books, he was soon forgotten. Holland continued to sell his prints until his own death in 1815, but they were not afterwards reissued, unlike those of Newton's more famous contemporary James Gillray. Perhaps because of the vulgarity of some of his work, and also its radicalism, he was neglected by the Victorians. It was not until Francis Klingender's London exhibition of caricature in 1944 that public attention was again drawn to his 'enormous comic vitality' (Alexander, 55). He was 'an extraordinarily original and "modern" humorist' (ibid., 56), whose 'comic simplification and exaggeration of line' are closer to the cartoons of the twentieth century than to the academic art of the eighteenth (Donald, 8).   MARK POTTLE

Sources D. S. Alexander, *Richard Newton and English caricature in the 1790s* (1998) · F. D. Klingender, ed., *Hogarth and English caricature* (1944) · D. Hill, *The satirical etchings of James Gillray* (1976) · D. Donald, *The age of caricature: satirical prints in the reign of George III* (New Haven, Connecticut, 1996) · F. G. Stephens and M. D. George, eds., *Catalogue of political and personal satires preserved … in the British Museum*, 6–7 (1938–42) · M. Bryant and S. Heneage, eds., *Dictionary of British cartoonists and caricaturists, 1730–1980* (1994) · *GM* (1798), 1089 · Redgrave, *Artists*

Likenesses R. Newton, self-portrait, 1797, repro. in Alexander, *Richard Newton*

Newton, Robert (1780–1854), Wesleyan Methodist minister, the sixth child and fourth son of the six sons and two daughters of a Wesleyan farmer, Francis Newton (1732–1816), and his wife, Anne Booth (1742/3–1826), was born at Roxby, in the North Riding of Yorkshire, on 8 September 1780. Four of Francis Newton's sons became Wesleyan ministers. After attending the village school Robert assisted his father on the farm, but sought every opportunity for reading and self-improvement. He was 'awakened' by the woman preacher Mary Barritt and converted in a prayer meeting on 26 February 1798. After working in public prayer meetings he became a local preacher. In the same year (1798) he became a probationer Wesleyan minister. He married Elizabeth (1779/80–1865), the second child of Captain John Nodes of Skelton, near York, in 1802. They had at least eight children.

Received into full connection in 1803, Newton's ministry, with the exception of London in 1812–14 (which he disliked for the committee work involved), was spent in northern towns, notably Liverpool, Leeds, and Manchester. His clear, musical voice and verbal fluency, coupled with an impressive physical bearing and pleasing delivery, rapidly rendered him the leading popular preacher of the standard Wesleyan doctrines. Though often making a deep impression, it was said that he seldom made instant conversions. A critical contemporary claimed that 'No man living, perhaps, carries on such an extensive trade, with so moderate a capital' (Beaumont and Everett, 246). He usually travelled at least 6000 miles a year, increased to 8000–10,000 when railways became available. He specialized in anniversary, charitable, and special occasions, and particularly overseas missions. He is believed to have collected more money for religious objects than any of his contemporaries. Though serving his own town chapels on Sundays, he spent the weekdays preaching far away, and from 1833 had an assistant minister to attend to his circuit work. He was president of the Wesleyan conference four times, in 1824, 1832, 1840, and 1848, as well as being secretary of the conference nineteen times from 1821. In 1840 he successfully visited the United States as the official representative of the British conference to the American Methodist Episcopal church. If his friend Jabez Bunting was a master of administration and conference proceedings, Newton was an active enforcer of conservative Wesleyan ministerial control. In 1834–5 he led the expulsions of Joseph Rayner Stephens and Joseph Beaumont. He opposed the American revivalist James Caughey's campaigning in England. In 1835 he canvassed tory Wesleyans in opposition to Lord John Russell's election in Tiverton.

In appearance Newton stood about 6 feet tall; with an erect but not stiff bearing, he was well proportioned, with dark hair until old age. He published several single sermons, tracts, and short stories. His *Sermons on Special and Ordinary Occasions* (1856) was published posthumously by J. H. Rigg. Newton died at Easingwold, near York, on 30 April 1854, and was buried in the churchyard there on 4 May.   HENRY D. RACK

Sources T. Jackson, *Life of Rev. Robert Newton D. D.* (1855) · W. R. Ward, *Religion and society in England, 1790–1850* (1972), 153, 157, 162, 175, 247 · J. Kent, 'The Wesleyan Methodists to 1849', *History of Methodism in Great Britain*, ed. R. E. Davies, A. R. George, and G. Rupp, 2 (1978), 231–4 · *Life of Rev. Robert Newton* (1864) · B. Gregory, *Side lights on the conflicts of Methodism during the second quarter of the nineteenth century, 1827–1852*, popular edn (1899), 202, 268–70, 400, 421 · [J. Beaumont and J. Everett], *Wesleyan takings*, 2nd edn, 2 vols. (1840), 232–50 · letters of R. Newton, JRL, Methodist Archives and Research Centre, MAM PLP 79–12 · *DNB*

Archives John Wesley's Chapel, Bristol, letters · JRL, Methodist Archives and Research Centre, corresp.

Likenesses J. Cochran, engraving (after W. Gush), repro. in Jackson, *Life*, frontispiece · T. A. Deane, engraving (after J. Jackson), repro. in Jackson, *Life*, frontispiece · J. Ellingworth, lithograph, BM · W. Gush, oils, Methodist Publishing House, London · J. Jackson, oils, Methodist Publishing House, London

Newton, Robert Guy (1905–1956), theatre and film actor, was born in Shaftesbury, Dorset, on 1 June 1905, the only son among the three surviving children of Algernon Cecil Newton (1880–1968), a landscape painter and Royal Academician, and his first wife, Marjorie Emelia Balfour Rider, a writer. He was educated at Newbury grammar school and in Switzerland. His first stage appearance was in a walk-on part in Shakespeare's 1 *Henry IV* in November 1920 at Birmingham Repertory Theatre, where he worked variously as a scenery painter, stage hand, assistant stage manager, and actor. In 1923–4 he toured in Canada, South Africa, Australia, and the West Indies before returning to make his London début at Drury Lane in June 1924 in *London Life*. In late 1925 he appeared in *The Ring o'Bells*, but between 1926 and 1928 he toured the provinces, and worked in Canada as a lumberjack and on a cattle ranch.

Back in London, Newton played in *My Lady's Mill*, *Her Cardboard Lover*, and *Byron* (1928–9) before appearing, in July 1929, as Hugh Devon in Noël Coward's *Bitter Sweet* at His Majesty's. The play ran for over a year. In May 1931 he made his New York début at the Times Square Theatre when he succeeded Laurence Olivier as Victor Prynne in Coward's *Private Lives*. After playing in *I Lived With You* at the Prince of Wales and reprising at the Duchess an old Birmingham repertory role, Jesse Redvers in *The Secret Woman*, Newton assumed in 1932 the management of the Grand Theatre in Fulham, which he ran for two years as the Shilling. He sought to offer 'good plays at a price everyone could afford' (*The Times*, 21 April 1956), and appeared himself in most productions, but it was not a particularly successful venture. 1932 also saw his film début, a bit part in *Reunion*. He continued busily in a variety of stage roles through the 1930s, including Horatio—which, 'though a trifle lacking in solidity and too highly strung, is spoken well and with understanding' (*The Times*, 6 Jan 1937)—to Laurence Olivier's Hamlet at the Old Vic in early 1937. Thereafter the stage virtually lost him to films. Many of these were good: *Fire over England*, *Dark Journey*, *Farewell Again*, and *The Squeaker*, all released in 1937; *Vessel of Wrath* and *Yellow Sands* (both 1938), *Jamaica Inn* (directed by Hitchcock), *Poison Pen*, and *Gaslight* (all 1939), *Busman's Honeymoon* and *Bulldog Drummond Sees it through* (both 1940). But it was only when he appeared as Bill Walker, a 'slum ne'er do well', in *Major Barbara*, the 1941 film version of G. B. Shaw's play, that his film career really took off. Although now in the forces, he next played Jim Mollison to Anna Neagle's Amy Johnson in *They Flew Alone*, and the tyrannical Scottish hatter James Brodie in *Hatter's Castle*, both in 1941, before returning to the Prince of Wales as Slim Grisson in *No Orchids for Miss Blandish*, by J. H. Chase and R. Nesbitt, in July 1942.

During the Second World War, Newton was in the Royal Navy for four years, chiefly serving aboard a minesweeper, but he did appear on screen in 1944, as Frank Gibbons in *This Happy Breed*, a huge popular success directed by David Lean from Coward's play, and as Pistol in Olivier's *Henry V*. After the war he toured as Randy Jollifer in *So Brief the*

Spring, a part he played also in a short run at the Wimbledon theatre early in 1946. This was his last stage performance, apart from his appearance in *Gaslight* by Patrick Hamilton at the Vaudeville in June 1950. His first post-war films of note were *Night Boat to Dublin* (1946) and Carol Reed's *Odd Man Out* (1947) in which he played the crazy artist Lukey. In this year he was the number three attraction at the British box office. These films were followed by *Snowbound*, Lean's *Oliver Twist*, in which he memorably portrayed Bill Sikes, and his first American film, *Kiss the Blood off my Hands* (all 1948), and *Obsession* (1949). Newton's first American film might have been *Wuthering Heights* (1939) after its director, William Wyler, had wired producer Sam Goldwyn: 'Have found Heathcliff … amazing young English actor … much better than Olivier' (Berg, 322), but he was overridden.

In 1950 Newton was cast in the role for which he is best remembered: Long John Silver in Disney's *Treasure Island*. His colourful, swaggering characterization has been an inspiration to many actors seeking to portray a pirate and contributed unfairly to his being generally considered a ham actor. He did, though, reprise the role in the Australian film *Long John Silver* (1954), and in a 1955 television series of the same name, as well as appearing as *Blackbeard the Pirate* (1952). One notable reference book called him a 'star character actor with a rolling eye and a voice to match; a ham, but a succulent one' (Halliwell, 525). He gave, though, a most restrained performance as Dr Arnold in *Tom Brown's Schooldays* (1951). Films in his American period included *Soldiers Three*, for which he 'arrived practically every morning incoherent with booze' (Granger, 214), *Les misérables* (as Javert) and *Androcles and the Lion* (both 1952), *The Desert Rats* (1953), and *The High and the Mighty* (1954). In England he took over Charles Laughton's role in *Vessel of Wrath*, now called *The Beachcomber* (1954). His last film role was as the detective Inspector Fix in the all-star extravaganza *Around the World in Eighty Days* (1956).

Shortly after receiving a bankruptcy notice in March 1954, Newton left England; he did not return. Early in 1956 he was sued for breach of contract over his leaving the production of *Trilby and Svengali* during filming. Newton's drinking caused many problems, and gave him a reputation for unreliability. David Niven wrote:

> With just the right amount on board he could be fascinating, for he was a highly intelligent, erudite, kindly and knowledgeable man, but once he had taken the extra one … he changed gear and became anything from unpredictable to a downright menace.   (Niven, *Empty Horses*, 322)

Niven added that, sadly, 'his charm was so great and when he took only a couple of drinks, his entertainment value was so spectacular that there was always some idiot who would press him to take the fatal third and fourth' (ibid., 327). Newton's contract for *This Happy Breed* stipulated that his fee would be docked by £500 each time he was drunk on the set. So great a threat to health had his drinking become that he managed to keep his promise to producer Mike Todd not to drink throughout the shooting of *Around the World in Eighty Days*. But a few weeks after its completion he was called back to reshoot a scene; it was

clear that he had 'fallen off the wagon', and very shortly afterwards he was dead.

Although often rebellious and nonconformist, Newton's real persona was more often honest, gentle, sensitive, and warm-hearted, most unlike some of the dastardly characters he created on the screen. In his spare time he enjoyed reading and walking, shooting and fishing, and particularly cooking. He was married four times, first on 7 November 1929 to Margaret Petronella Millicent Walton (*b.* 1904/5), with whom he had two daughters, thirdly to Natalie Newhouse, with whom he had a son, and lastly to Vera Budnick (*d.* 2000), with whom he also had a son. The name of his second wife is not known. He died of a heart attack on 25 March 1956 in Beverly Hills, Los Angeles, California. He was buried at Westwood Memorial Park, Los Angeles.   ROBERT SHARP

Sources *Who was who in the theatre, 1912–1976*, 4 vols. (1978) · *The Times* (23 Jan 1956) · *The Times* (27 March 1956) · D. Niven, *The moon's a balloon* (1972), 281–2 · D. Niven, *Bring on the empty horses* (1976), 320–28 · E. Katz, *The international film encyclopedia* (1982), 857 · L. Halliwell, *Halliwell's filmgoer's companion* (1977) · S. Granger, *Sparks fly upwards* (1981) · A. S. Berg, *Goldwyn* (1989) · b. cert. · m. cert.

Likenesses photographs, 1936–76, Hult. Arch. · R. S. Sherriffs, ink drawing, NPG

Newton, Samuel (*bap.* 1629, *d.* 1718), local politician and diarist, was baptized on 5 April 1629 in St Mary-the-Less, Cambridge, son of John Newton, painter, and his wife, Alice, *née* Hales. Newton married Sarah Wellbore (*d.* 1716), daughter of John Wellbore, draper of Cambridge, on 20 January 1659. He became a Cambridge freeman on 8 January 1661, at which time he and Sarah acquired stalls in Sturbridge fair. Sarah Newton took further fair stalls with her sister, Susanna Ellis, mother of John Ellis, the future under-secretary of state. Newton served as treasurer of Cambridge corporation in 1664–5; he became a common councilman in 1667 and an alderman the following year. He only accepted the latter dignity when, upon opening the Bible at random, he read a passage in the book of Psalms and concluded 'it was by divine appointment that I was chose to the Bench' (*Diary*, 29). In 1671 Newton became mayor, giving both the traditional self-effacing oration and the customary entertainments upon entering office. Charles II visited Cambridge soon afterwards and as mayor Newton was among those who kissed the king's hand. After his mayoral year, Newton remained an alderman and presided in Cambridge at the proclamation of James II in 1685. But, like more than 2000 other urban officers nationwide, Newton was removed by royal mandate in 1688 as James tried to remake England's local leadership to promote his policy of religious toleration. Newton and the others were restored in October of that year. He continued as an alderman until his death, serving frequently as a justice of the peace.

As an attorney Newton witnessed oaths and signatures, offered legal advice, and prepared deeds, wills, and bonds, as attested by the formularies of legal instruments among his surviving papers. He was an occasional legal adviser to

Cambridge corporation, especially in poor law cases. Newton became auditor of Trinity College in 1669, registrar of Pembroke College in 1673, and in 1674 registrar of Trinity jointly with his cousin William Ellis. From these engagements, from fees paid by occasional boarders and apprentices, and from his market stalls and land holdings, Newton earned sufficient income to install a small organ in his home and to have his only surviving child, John, instructed in music. Samuel and Sarah Newton had two other sons, both named Samuel, who died in infancy. A Sarah Newton, born in 1672, was most likely the daughter of Samuel and Sarah Newton's nephew, named Samuel, and his wife, also named Sarah.

Newton continued to attend Cambridge corporation meetings intermittently throughout his eighties. He was among a small group of tory corporation members challenged in a 1714 lawsuit for illegally admitting freemen in order to control the outcome of parliamentary voting. Newton audited the accounts of Trinity College until 1714, though his faltering signature after 1705 reveals the creeping effects of age; the last college accounts of his lifetime were signed by his son, who had become his deputy. Newton died on 21 September 1718, and was interred four days later next to his wife, who had died two years earlier, in St Edward's Church, Cambridge. A memorial to Samuel and Sarah was placed in the church, next door to which they had lived most of their fifty-seven years of marriage. Samuel left the bulk of an estate that comprised lands in Cambridge and its vicinity, as well as numerous fair and market booths, to his son, John, who died fifteen months later, apparently without having married.

Newton is most significant for the diary he kept from the Restoration in 1660 until the year before his death, a rare example of a diary by a seventeenth-century urban leader. In it he shows his care for social and political propriety, a commitment to monarchy that made him ask God's blessing on the newborn prince of Wales in June 1688, and an equal commitment to the established church which caused him to celebrate the acquittal of the seven bishops that same month. This combined allegiance to king and church left Newton, like many provincial leaders, feeling ambivalent in the face of James II's promotion of Catholics and protestant dissenters in 1687–8 and probably relieved to have regained his former position at the time of the revolution of 1688. While careful in his observance of the sacrament, his dreams and other omens proved an object of equal interest. The diary and surviving correspondence reveal his concern for his family and his interest in its social advancement, especially his worries about his son's changing professional ambitions.

PAUL D. HALLIDAY

Sources Samuel Newton diary, Downing College Library, Cambridge · *The diary of Samuel Newton, alderman of Cambridge (1662–1717)*, ed. J. E. Foster, Cambridge Antiquarian RS, 23 (1890) · common day books, Cambridge corporation, Cambs. AS, Shelf C/8 and 9 · parish register, Cambridge, St Mary-the-Less, Cambs. AS, 5 April 1629 [baptism] · parish register, Cambridge, St Edwards, Cambs. AS [marriage, burial] · will, Cambs. AS, WR:300 · commonplace books of Samuel Newton, BL, MSS Harleian 4115–4116 · corresp. of Samuel Newton, BL, Add. MS 28931, fols. 51, 84; Add. MS 28932,

fols. 102–3v, 129 · S. Newton, letter to S. Pepys, 1695, Bodl. Oxf., MS Autograph. d.24, fols. 49–50 · declaratio computi, 1652–1698 and 1700–1778, Trinity Cam. · king's bench crown side rule books, quo warranto against Samuel Newton, et al., 1714, PRO, KB21/29/27 · C. H. Cooper and J. W. Cooper, *Annals of Cambridge*, 4–5 (1852–1908) · *VCH Cambridgeshire and the Isle of Ely*, vol. 3 · PRO, PROB 11/565, sig. 197, fols. 335–6
Archives BL, Harley MSS 4115–4116 · Downing College, Cambridge, diary
Wealth at death various fair booths and lands in Cambridge area: will, Cambs. AS, WR:300

Newton, Theodore (1531/2–1568/9). *See under* Newton, Francis (d. 1572).

Newton, Thomas (1544/5–1607), translator and Church of England clergyman, was born in Cheshire, the eldest son of Edward and Alice Newton of Butley. He studied at Macclesfield grammar school with John Brownswerd, and then reportedly attended Trinity College, Oxford, before matriculating (November 1562) at Queens' College, Cambridge, and, some time later, returning to his old college at Oxford. From 1565 to 1567 he stood in for the absent Brownswerd as headmaster at Macclesfield; the dedication to a published translation from Cicero places him in Greenwich in June of 1569, but he subsequently returned to Butley, from which several publications between 1570 and 1583 are dated. He was ordained deacon on 25 March 1578 (at which time his age was given as thirty-three) and priest on 16 April 1579; on 4 June 1583 he became rector of Little Ilford, Essex, where he appears to have spent the rest of his life (though continuing to identify himself as Thomas Newtonus Cestreshyrius and occasionally revisiting his home town; a 1586 publication is dated from Butley). At least in his early years as rector he was out of favour with the puritans, who in 1585 put his name on a list of non-preaching clergy and identified him as 'a great drunkard' (Powell, 6.171). There is record of two sons, Emanuel and Abel (*bap.* 1587), and one daughter, Grizell, who married Edward Weekes. Anthony Wood's failure to mention Emmanuel suggests that he may have died young, and he does not appear in Newton's will.

Newton's first publication, in early 1569, appears to have been a broadside elegy on the death of Lady Knowles (Catherine Carey, wife to Sir Francis Knollys). Between 1569 and 1596 he published perhaps twenty books, on a wide range of subjects. These include translations of Guglielmo Grataroli, *A Direction for the Health of Magistrates and Studentes* (1574); Agostino Curione, *A Notable Historie of the Saracens* (1575); Levinus Lemnius, *The Touchstone of Complexions* (1576) and *An Herbal for the Bible* (1587); Martin Luther's commentary on the epistles of Peter and Jude (1581); Lambert Daneau, *True and Christian Friendshippe* (1586); an anonymous *Olde Mans Dietarie* (1587); Andreas Gerhard Hyperius, *The True Tryall and Examination of a Mans Owne Selfe* (1587); and Matthew Parker's funeral sermon on Martin Bucer (1588). He is probably the translator of Pedro Mexia's *A Pleasaunt Dialogue, Concerning Phisicke and Phisitions* (1580). He introduced and may have had a hand in editing four tales by Bandello, translated from French versions by Robert Smythe (*Straunge, Lamentable, and Tragicall Hystories*, 1577). Newton compiled *Approved Medicines and*

Cordiall Receiptes (1580) from various sources, prepared Brownswerd's Latin poems for publication (1589), and reworked John Stanbridge's popular *Vocabula* (1577, with Newton's improvements surviving in numerous later editions). He could be the T. N. who edited Henry de Bracton's *De legibus et consuetudinibus Angliae* (1569). Newton's most consequential editorial work resulted in the publication of John Leland's Latin epigrams (1589); without Newton's efforts most of them would probably have been lost. A manuscript version of the collection, accompanied by a letter from Newton to John Stow, survives in the Bodleian; its readings are not always those of the published book, and give some sense of the trouble that went into establishing its text.

In the late 1570s and early 1580s Newton was particularly occupied with classical literature. Early in his career he published English versions of Cicero's *De senectute*, *Paradoxa Stoicorum*, and *Somnium Scipionis* (1569–70); in 1577 he reworked them (complaining that they had been rushed into print) and added a version of *De amicitia* for *Fowre Severall Treatises of M. Tullius Cicero*. He introduced *A View of Valyaunce* (1580) as a translation (supposedly not his own) of the (lost) Roman history of Rutilius Rufus; it is actually an abridgement of Appian's *Iberikê* (a complete version of which, by another translator, had appeared in 1578). In 1581 Newton edited *Seneca his Tenne Tragedies*, collecting translations (some already in print) by Jasper Heywood, Alexander Neville, Thomas Nuce, and John Studley, and adding his own of the *Thebais* (*Phoenissae*) to complete the set. These were the only English versions of Seneca's tragedies available during the English Renaissance, and their influence has been a recurring object of scholarly study. A twentieth-century edition featured a respectful preface by T. S. Eliot; Edward Phillips remembered Newton's *Thebais* in his *Theatrum poetarum* (1675) and, presumably on its evidence, confidently assigned to Newton authorship of the two parts of *Tamburlaine the Great*, even though Marlowe's far more plausible claim had by then already been staked.

Newton's dedications and commendatory verses, in both Latin and English, appeared in over two dozen published sites during his lifetime: the earliest in 1575 (in John Banister's *A Needefull, New, and Necessarie Treatise of Chyrurgerie*), the last in 1597 (in John Gerard's *Herball*). They testify to a significant network of contacts sustained for over two decades within Elizabethan literary and intellectual circles. An edition of John Heywood's *Workes* (actually his epigrams) published in 1587, the first since the author's death, included an elegiac verse epilogue by Newton. Stow included a poem by Newton celebrating Leicester's return from the Netherlands in his continuation of Holinshed's *Chronicle* (1587); despite its politically sensitive content, it was one of the passages to escape 'castration' by the archiepiscopal censor. There was in their time a readership for such poems independent of their original context and purpose; Newton himself gathered some fifty of his Latin poems—encomia of the powerful as well as book prefaces and fatherly advice to Emanuel and Abel—and published them as a supplement to his edition of

Leland's similar efforts. (They were reprinted in that form as recently as 1970.) The volume rated approving mention by Thomas Nash and Francis Meres. Thomas Warton, giving Newton a paragraph in his *History of English Poetry*, praised his commendatory verses for their 'classical clearness and terseness', and suggested that he was the first Englishman since Leland to achieve these qualities in Latin elegiacs (Warton, 878).

Newton appears by the end of his life to have been of modestly comfortable means. He died at Little Ilford in May 1607 and was buried in his church the same month; a will dated 27 April and proved at Canterbury on 13 June makes specific bequests of almost £300.

GORDON BRADEN

Sources DNB · Cooper, *Ath. Cantab.*, 2.452–4 · Wood, *Ath. Oxon.*, new edn, 2.5–12 · Venn, *Alum. Cant.*, 1/3.253 · T. Warton, *The history of English poetry*, 3 (1781); repr. (1870), 877–9 · B. E. Harris, *A history of the county of Chester*, 3 (1980), 237 · W. R. Powell, ed., *A history of the county of Essex*, 6 (1973), 171 · F. B. Williams, *Index of dedications and commendatory verses in English books before 1641* (1962), 136 · Foster, *Alum. Oxon.* · L. Bradner, *Musae Anglicanae: a history of Anglo-Latin poetry, 1500–1925* (1940), 29–30 · H. B. Lathrop, *Translations from the classics into English from Caxton to Chapman, 1477–1620* (1933); repr. (1967), 200–02
Archives Bodl. Oxf., John Stow MSS
Wealth at death bequests of almost £300: will, proved, 13 June 1607, PRO, PROB 11/110, sig. 53

Newton, Thomas (1704–1782), bishop of Bristol, was born at Lichfield on 1 January 1704, the son of John Newton (c.1671–1754), a brandy and cider merchant, and his first wife, Isabel (d. 1705), the daughter of a clergyman named Rhodes. Newton was educated at Lichfield grammar school, and in June 1717 passed to Westminster School, where in 1718 he was nominated to a scholarship by George Smalridge, bishop of Bristol and a native of Lichfield. Having been captain of the school in 1722, he matriculated at Cambridge University the following year and was elected into a scholarship at Trinity College in 1724. This distinction did not stave off later regrets that he had not continued to Christ Church, Oxford, with William Murray, later first earl of Mansfield, and other friends. He graduated BA in 1727 and MA in 1730, and was also made a fellow of Trinity. He was ordained deacon on 21 December 1729 and priest in February 1730 by Edmund Gibson, bishop of London. Meanwhile his father had married, as his second wife, the sister of Dr Andrew Trebeck, first rector of St George's, Hanover Square (1725–59); he made Newton his curate, and selection as reader at the Grosvenor chapel enabled him to gain speedy acceptance as a fashionable West End cleric. He was appointed tutor to the son of George, second Baron Carpenter of Killaghy (d. 1749), in whose house he lived for some years, which gave him the opportunity to begin collecting books and pictures.

In 1738 Zachary Pearce, vicar of St Martin-in-the-Fields, appointed Newton morning preacher at the proprietary Spring Gardens chapel. Newton's acquaintance Mrs Anne Deanes Devenish (her first husband was the playwright

Thomas Newton (1704–1782), by Sir Joshua Reynolds, 1773

Nicholas Rowe) meanwhile introduced him to Frederick, prince of Wales, and to William Pulteney, leader of the opposition to Walpole. Pulteney, who was created earl of Bath in 1742 and made Newton his chaplain, was thereafter his main patron and mutual confidante. Bath secured for Newton in 1744 (appointed 16 April) the rectory of St Mary-le-Bow, whereupon he gave up his Trinity fellowship and the Spring Gardens chapel; in 1745 he took his DD degree. He preached some loyal sermons during the Jacobite rising of 1745 and received some threatening letters in consequence, but no preferment. He attracted favourable notice from Prince Frederick by helping Mrs Devenish to prepare a new edition of Rowe's works for the edification of the prince's children, and in 1747 he was chosen lecturer at St George's, Hanover Square. He married the rector's eldest daughter, Jane Trebeck (c.1716–1754), on 18 August of that year; she was, Newton wrote, an 'unaffected, modest, decent young woman' (*Works*, 1.25) who saved him the trouble of housekeeping. They had no children and lived in her father's house.

Having shown his capacities in editing Rowe, Newton was encouraged by his patron Zachary Pearce (himself a clerical Miltonist) to begin work on John Milton. In 1749 he published his variorum edition of Milton's *Paradise Lost*, with a life and elaborate notes, and in 1752 the remaining poems. Eight editions of the *Paradise Lost* appeared by 1775 and Newton made £735 by it. It was dedicated to Bath but also brought Newton the acquaintance of John Jortin and William Warburton. The edition, with its rigorous use of original documents and collation of all previous editions, is highly rated by literary scholars and has been described as 'scrupulously definitive' (Moyles, 73).

Bath meanwhile lost no opportunity of pressing the secretary of state, Thomas Pelham-Holles, first duke of Newcastle, on behalf of his chaplain (whom Newcastle had promised to protect). Newton had better luck with Augusta, princess dowager of Wales, who named him her chaplain after receipt of his sermon preached in March 1751 on her husband's death, an event presented as 'the most fatal blow that this nation has felt for many, many years' (*Works*, 1.53). This reflected the genuine admiration and esteem that Newton had come to have for the prince and his family. Newton himself knew bereavement in June 1754, when both his father and his wife died within days of each other. He creatively poured his grief into his *Dissertation on the prophecies, which have been remarkably fulfilled, and are at this time fulfilling in the world*, the first volume of which appeared in the winter. It was dedicated to Archbishop Thomas Herring and had been perused in manuscript form by Pearce, Warburton, and Jortin. In 1755 Newton was appointed Boyle lecturer, and he pursued the prophetic theme in these lectures, which were finally published in their entirety in 1758. In all there were twenty-six dissertations on the subject, ranging from Noah to the modern papacy, with the main argument that, despite the range of time, place, and cultures, scriptural prophecies had 'a visible connexion and dependency, an entire agreement one with another' (*Works*, 1.775). The dissertation had gone into twenty editions by 1835. Its popularity both reflected and contributed to the persistence of the prophetic mode (and with it anti-papalism) as a key element in eighteenth-century Anglican apologetics, one that was at least as important as miracles. By choosing this subject Newton reclaimed it for orthodoxy and seized the initiative from Arians such as William Whiston and, most recently, Bishop Robert Clayton of Clogher.

For all Bath's reminders to Newcastle, higher preferment was slow in coming for Newton, though the duke had him in mind for several vacancies, including the deanery of Christ Church, Oxford, in 1752. Royal objections dished Newton on that occasion but by 1756 Newcastle at last believed himself in a position to offer Bath's protégé a prebend in Westminster Abbey, only to find that the supposed vacancy had not occurred. Newton had to wait until 18 March 1757 for that place and was meanwhile appointed a chaplain to George II. In October 1757 Archbishop John Gilbert of York obtained for him the sub-almonership, and in June 1759 made him precentor of York. In 1760 he was made president of Sion College and on 20 January he preached the sermon at Lambeth, when William Warburton was consecrated bishop of Gloucester.

The death of Dr Andrew Trebeck in 1759 deprived Newton of his London house; again he sought a partner who could housekeep and act the elegant wife, and found her in the Hon. Elizabeth Vaughan, daughter of John, second Viscount Lisburne (c.1695–1741) and widow of the Revd Mr Hand. They married in Norfolk on 5 September 1761. Thirteen days later Newton obtained the bishopric of Bristol on the translation of Philip Yonge to Norwich, part of a series of appointments to the bench made that year; he was consecrated on 28 December. Newton had the backing of John Stuart, third earl of Bute, thanks to his contacts with Princess Augusta, as well as the approval of Newcastle and Archbishop Thomas Secker. Though the see brought him only £300 p.a. he had to resign the Westminster prebend, the precentorship of York, the lectureship of St George's, and the sub-almonership. He was, however, appointed a prebendary of St Paul's (fourth canon) on 5 December 1761. When, in 1763, Pearce desired to resign the see of Rochester and the deanery of Westminster he hoped for Newton as his successor and, with the support of Lord Bath, supplicated the king's agreement, which was provisionally given. At this point the Grenville administration intervened, anxious to keep a controlling grip on church patronage; Pearce was not allowed to resign, though Grenville advised Newton that better things were intended for him. In 1764 Grenville recommended Newton for the see of London without success, and later in the same year offered him the Irish primacy on the death of Archbishop George Stone. An increasingly infirm Newton declined, and lost his main political ally on Grenville's departure from office in 1765.

As bishop of Bristol he bore out in his actions his sense that Catholicism was on the increase by preventing Romanists from erecting a public chapel in Clifton, after a private word with the priest, who was 'obliged to me for my candour' (Newton to George Grenville, 27 May 1765, BL, Add. MS 57819, fols. 51–2). Otherwise his impact on the Bristol diocese was limited; he criticized the neglect of their duties by members of the Bristol chapter, but made no attempt to rectify matters. He was not much involved in politics and rarely spoke in the House of Lords. He usually took the ministerial side, except on the repeal of the Stamp Act, a measure to which he ascribed all the subsequent American troubles. He had no time for the parliamentary opposition to North's government, accusing it of having 'fostered and cherished the rebellion in America' (Works, 1.122). He voted against the bill of 1772 for the relaxation of religious subscription and devised his own version of the oath.

On Archbishop Secker's death in 1768 Newton hoped for translation, and George III (who knew the bishop well through the Kew connection) desired arrangements by which he would become bishop of London. The Grafton ministry opposed this plan but had to make Newton dean of St Paul's (8 October 1768), although he voluntarily resigned St Mary-le-Bow at the same time. Newton professed himself well pleased: 'the manner in which it has been given me greatly enhances the favour & the pleasure' (Newton, to Z. Pearce, 15 Sept 1768, Westminster Abbey Muniments, 64610). A severe illness followed in the winter of 1768–9, making it hard for the new dean to attend services at St Paul's; he remained in residence at the deanery and spent most summers at Bristol until 1776, travelling into Dorset on confirmation tours. His poor health made him stop attending parliament in the mid-1770s and he bought a house at Kew Green for future summer use. He continued to collect books and pictures, and tried to secure a proposal whereby Joshua Reynolds and other academicians would decorate St Paul's Cathedral at their own expense. Richard Terrick, bishop of London, claimed that the scheme tended towards popery and it was abandoned. Newton, however, improved his own deanery and increased the income of the see of Bristol to £400 p.a. Ground down by ill health (he attended only one chapter meeting annually at St Paul's between 1777 and 1780) he spent the last years of his life revising, correcting, and preparing his abundant literary works. These included an autobiography, completed just before his death at the deanery on 14 February 1782. He was buried on 28 February in the vaults of St Paul's Cathedral, and a monument by Thomas Banks was erected in Bow church by his widow, showing Religion and Sculpture deploring his loss, with an inscription by Elizabeth Carter. There had been no children of the marriage.

Newton's works were published in 1782 in three volumes. They contain the autobiography, the volumes on the prophecies, and a number of dissertations and sermons. The autobiography is a rare piece of eighteenth-century self-portraiture by a bishop and shows Newton as a mildly ambitious churchman and convinced Christian, happy to abide by the conventions of contemporary society. His critical comments in the autobiography on authors such as Gibbon and Johnson invited posthumous retaliation in kind—Johnson called him 'a gross flatterer' (Boswell, Life, 4.286)—but they should not overlay the bishop's achievements. He had a keen appreciation of the fine arts and, as a literary editor and biblical scholar, possessed a competence and a productivity that few of his colleagues on the bench could match. There is much to be said for Boswell's judgement that Newton's 'labours were certainly of considerable advantage both to literature and religion' (ibid., 4.286n.), none more so than *Dissertation on the Prophecies*, a work that helped his contemporaries to make sense of their world and strengthened the national sense of protestant identity in his lifetime and down to the revolutionary wars of the 1790s.   NIGEL ASTON

Sources *The works of … Thomas Newton*, 3 vols. (1782) • *GM*, 1st ser., 24 (1754), 291 • *GM*, 1st ser., 31 (1761), 430 • *GM*, 1st ser., 52 (1782), 95 • *GM*, 1st ser., 56 (1786), 994 • A. L. Reade, *Johnsonian gleanings*, 1 (privately printed, London, 1909), 36; 3 (1922), 123 • S. Shaw, *The history and antiquities of Staffordshire*, 1 (1798), 147 • J. Jackson, *History of the city and cathedral of Lichfield* (1805), 224–6 • *VCH Staffordshire*, 14.125 • *Old Westminsters*, 2.690 • Venn, *Alum. Cant.*, 1/3.253 • *Fasti Angl., 1541–1857*, [St Paul's, London], 220 • *Fasti Angl., 1541–1857*, [Chichester], 317, 424 • *Fasti Angl., 1541–1857*, [Canterbury], 157, 366 • *Fasti Angl., 1541–1857*, [Ely], 92 • *Fasti Angl., 1541–1857*, [Bristol], 13 • G. Hennessy, *Novum repertorium ecclesiasticum parochiale Londinense, or, London diocesan clergy succession from the earliest time to the year 1898* (1898), 58, 308 • M. Walsh, *Shakespeare, Milton and eighteenth-century literary editing: the beginnings of interpretative scholarship* (1998) • R. G. Moyles, *The text of 'Paradise lost': a study in editorial procedure* (1985) • N. Hitchin, 'The evidence of things seen: Georgian churchmen and biblical prophecy', *The power of inspired language in history, 1300–2000*, ed. B. Taithe and T. Thornton (1997), 119–39 • Nichols, *Illustrations*, 6.311 • Dealtary letters, Bodl. Oxf., MS Eng. lett. d. 122 • E. Pyle, *Memoirs of a royal chaplain, 1729–1763*, ed. A. Hartshorne (1905), 286, 289–90 • G. M. Ditchfield, 'The subscription issue in British parliamentary politics, 1772–1779', *Parliamentary History*, 7 (1988), 45–80 • Walpole, *Corr.*, 2.321, 323; 10.145; 29.254, 259;

38.364–5 · J. H. Jesse, *Memoirs of the life and reign of King George the Third*, 2nd edn, 3 vols. (1867), vol. 2, p. 35 · Boswell, *Life*, 4.285–6, 532 · private information (2004) [G. M. Ditchfield]
Archives BL, letters to Thomas Birch, Add. MSS 4315, 5847 · BL, letters to George Grenville, Add. MS 57819, fols. 51–2 · St Paul's Cathedral, GL, dean's registers, MS 25630, nos. 28–9 · Westminster Abbey, London, muniments room, letters to Zachary Pearce, WAM 64598–64616
Likenesses R. Earlom, mezzotint, pubd 1767 (after oils by B. West), BM · J. Reynolds, oils, 1773, LPL [*see illus.*] · T. Banks, monument, Bow church · J. Collyer, engraving (after portrait by J. Reynolds), repro. in *Works of … Thomas Newton*, vol. 1 · B. West, oils, Trinity Cam. · engraving, repro. in *New Christian Magazine* (1783) · engraving (after monument by T. Banks), repro. in *Works of … Thomas Newton*, vol. 1

Newton, William (*bap.* 1730, *d.* 1798), architect, was baptized at St Andrew's Church, Newcastle upon Tyne, on 20 December 1730, the son of Robert Newton (*d.* 1789), a shipwright, who became an architect–builder, and his wife, Mary Robley (?). His first documented architectural work was the repair of Simonburn church, Northumberland, which he undertook with his father in 1762. He was described as an 'eminent architect' by the *Newcastle Courant* when he married Dorothy Bell (*d.* 1789) on 31 May 1763; the couple had six sons and six daughters. The Newcastle corporation commissioned him to build St Anne's Chapel in 1764–8, an elegant and beautiful building, and also an asylum for lunatics, in 1765–7. He became architect to William Ord at Benwell, near Newcastle, in 1765; in the same year he built a church, a parsonage house, and a cupola bridge for Ord at his estate at Whitfield, Northumberland. In 1769 Newton started speculative building in Charlotte Square in Newcastle; his next commission in the town was for the new assembly rooms, erected in 1774–6. The success of the assembly rooms meant that Newton was in great demand to build houses for the gentry and rich merchants in Northumberland.

In Northumberland, Newton designed a number of late Georgian country houses in a simple neo-classical style with reminiscences of Paine and Adam: Howick Hall, for Sir Henry Grey (1781–2), and Backworth Hall, for Ralph William Grey jun. (1778–80), were characteristic examples. Sometimes an addition to an older house was needed, which Newton provided by making the old house into kitchen offices, and building reception rooms in front. His houses were usually plain, with canted bays or a columned entrance to give distinction to the façade. One of his later works was the remodelling of Newcastle exchange and guildhall in 1795–6; his health was now failing, and David Stephenson collaborated in the work. Newton died on 29 April 1798 at Green Court, Newcastle, where he lived, and was buried in St Andrew's Church, Newcastle, on 2 May.   MARGARET WILLS

Sources Colvin, *Archs.* · P. Lowery, 'William Newton: an eminent architect?', *Northern Architect*, 5th ser., 1 (winter 1994–5), 15–17 · *Newcastle Courant* (4 June 1763) · J. C. Hodgson, 'Two eighteenth century Newcastle worthies: Samuel Hallowell, surgeon, and William Newton, architect', *Proceedings of the Society of Antiquaries of Newcastle upon Tyne*, 3rd ser., 6 (1913–14), 26–31 · T. Sopwith, *The strangers' pocket-guide to Newcastle upon Tyne and its environs* (1838), 66 · *A history of Northumberland*, Northumberland County History Committee, 15 vols. (1893–1940), vol. 15, pp. 178–9 · Northumbd RO,

Blacketts of Matfen, ZBL 269/69 · Fenham journal no. 1, Northumbd RO, Blackett-Ord [Whitfield], MS 324 E14 · Northumbd RO, Anderson of Little Harle papers, MS 660/1/3 · Northumbd RO, Ralph Grey of Backworth papers, MS 753 · Tyne and Wear Archive Service, D/NCP/16/1 (1–2) · *Northumberland*, Pevsner (1957) · parish register (baptism), St Andrew, Newcastle, 20 Dec 1730 · parish register (marriage), St Mary, Gateshead, 31 May 1763 · parish register (death), St Andrew, Newcastle, 29 April 1798 · parish register (burial), St Andrew, Newcastle, 2 May 1798
Archives Northumbd RO, Newcastle upon Tyne · Tyne and Wear Archives Service, Newcastle upon Tyne
Likenesses J. Newton, stipple (after A. Cozens), BM · J. Newton, stipple (after R. Smirke), BM, NPG; repro. in *Vitruvius* (1791) · W. Newton, self-portrait, Indian ink drawing, BM
Wealth at death £5740; plus two freehold and two leasehold properties: Hodgson, 'Two eighteenth century worthies'

Newton, William (1735–1790), architect, born probably at Holborn, London, on 27 October 1735, was the eldest son of James Newton, a cabinet-maker of Holborn. His father claimed to be related to Sir Isaac Newton and his mother, Susanna, was the daughter of Humphrey *Ditton (1675–1714), mathematical master at Christ's Hospital. William was admitted to Christ's Hospital in November 1743, and on leaving the school in December 1750 was apprenticed to the architect William Jones. He was afterwards in the London office of Matthew Brettingham. He began to exhibit at the Society of Artists in 1760, and also exhibited at the Free Society of Artists in 1761 and 1783, and showed two reconstructions of Roman houses at the Royal Academy in 1776.

By 1764 Newton had established his own practice. His drawings in the collection of the Royal Institute of British Architects suggest that he was trained in the Palladian tradition but developed a neo-classical style for which a visit to Rome in 1766, from which he returned early the following year, was no doubt a preparation. He had a fairly extensive practice in and around London, but gained no major commissions. In 1769 he competed unsuccessfully for the Royal Exchange at Dublin, in 1774 for the church of St Alfege, London Wall, and in 1775, with a neo-classical design, for that of St Mary's, Battersea. From time to time he assisted William Jupp the elder (1734–1788), for whom he designed the ballroom and eating-room of the London tavern, Bishopsgate Street Within (1768; dem. 1876), and probably also the entrance to Carpenters' Hall (1779; dem. 1876), for which there is a design among his drawings. His interiors were decorated in an elegant 'antique' style comparable to that of the Adam brothers.

In February 1781 Newton became assistant to James Stuart (1713–1788), surveyor of Greenwich Hospital, and in September 1782 succeeded Robert Mylne (1733–1811) as clerk of the works there. Mylne had been dismissed by the governors after a disagreement with James Stuart, who was then engaged in rebuilding the chapel after its destruction by fire in 1779. As clerk of the works Newton was closely involved in the design as well as the execution of the chapel, the rebuilding of which was not completed until 1790. When Stuart died in February 1788, Newton hoped to succeed him as surveyor, but was passed over in favour of Sir Robert Taylor. The latter died within a year, but Newton's claims were again set aside by the appointment of John Yenn. Newton thought of resigning, disinclined to work under a younger man he considered less eminent in the profession than himself. In the event he did not do so but pressed, unsuccessfully, for an admission from the governors that, as the effective architect of their chapel, he was entitled to professional remuneration in addition to his salary as clerk of the works. The governors did not accept that they had any additional financial obligation towards him.

In 1771 Newton published the earliest English translation of the first five books of Vitruvius, under the title *The architecture of M. Vitruvius Pollio: translated from the original Latin by W. Newton, architect*. He was also the author of *Commentaires sur Vitruve*, written in French but published in London in 1780, and helped to edit and complete the second volume of Stuart's *Antiquities of Athens*, which, though dated 1787, was not published until after its author's death in 1788. Newton translated the remaining five books of Vitruvius: the text was printed and most of the plates finished before his death in 1790. A complete edition of Vitruvius was published in two volumes in 1791 by his brother and executor James Newton 'from a correct manuscript prepared by himself'. William Newton's achievement in producing the earliest English translation of Vitruvius was little recognized during his lifetime or thereafter. His literal adherence to the original text did not make for easy reading or understanding, although his notes were commended for their intelligence.

In February 1790 Newton obtained three months' leave of absence from Greenwich in order to take a course of sea-bathing. His health was failing through overwork, and he died at Sidford, near Sidmouth, Devon, on 6 July 1790. His will was proved on 7 August 1790 and mentions his brother James, his wife, Frances, his late sister Elizabeth Thompson, and his sister Susanna O'Kely. A collection of more than 100 drawings by Newton was presented to the Royal Institute of British Architects in 1891, together with some of his papers.   ALAN MACKLEY

Sources Colvin, *Archs.*, 702–4 · E. Harris and N. Savage, *British architectural books and writers, 1556–1785* (1990), 464–6 · J. Lever, ed., *Catalogue of the drawings collection of the Royal Institute of British Architects: L–N* (1973), 128–44 · *DNB*
Archives RIBA, papers relating to Royal Naval Hospital, and papers
Likenesses J. Newton, stipple, 1791 (after R. Smirke), BM, NPG; repro. in J. Newton, ed., *The architecture of M. Vitruvius Pollio*, trans. Newton (1791) · J. Newton, stipple (after A. Cozens), BM · W. Newton, self-portrait, Indian ink drawing, BM

Newton, William (1750–1830), poet, was born on 25 December 1750, at Cockney Farm, near Abney, Eyam, Derbyshire, the son of George Newton, a carpenter, and Mary Bagshout. He attended a dame-school, and then worked in the carpentry trade. He soon showed skill in constructing spinning-wheels, and was articled for seven years as machinery carpenter in a mill in Monsaldale. With his spare means he purchased books, chiefly poetry, and his own efforts at poetry were soon noticed by Peter Cunningham (d. 1805), then curate to Thomas Seward at Eyam.

On 20 April 1778 Newton married Helen Cook (1753–1830) in Tideswell, Derbyshire, and they had several children. In the summer of 1783 he was introduced to Anna Seward, who corresponded with him until her death, and called him 'the Peak Minstrel' (Rhodes, 76–7). She showed his verses to William Hayley and other literary friends, who formed a high opinion of them. Beyond a sonnet to Seward, verses to Peter Cunningham, and others in a Sheffield newspaper, few have survived. In return, sonnets were addressed to Newton by Cunningham, Seward, and Lister, and Seward also wrote an 'Epistle to Mr. Newton, the Derbyshire Minstrel, on receiving his description in verse of an autumnal scene near Eyam', in September 1791 (*Poetical Works*, ed. W. Scott, 3 vols., 1810, 2.22).

After the Monsaldale mill burnt down Seward helped Newton to become partner in a cotton mill in Cressbrookdale, and he made a fortune. He died on 3 November 1830 at Tideswell, Derbyshire, and was buried there. His eldest son, William (1785–1851), is recorded as supplying Tideswell with good water at his own expense.
CHARLOTTE FELL-SMITH, *rev.* SARAH COUPER

Sources *GM*, 1st ser., 55 (1785), 169–70 · *GM*, 1st ser., 59 (1789), 212 · W. Wood, *The history and antiquities of Eyam*, 4th edn (1865), 209 · S. Glover, *The history and gazetteer of the county of Derby*, ed. T. Noble, 1 (1829), 109 · *Letters of Anna Seward: written between the years 1784 and 1807*, ed. A. Constable, 6 vols. (1811), vol. 1, pp. 221, 290, 318, 325; vol. 2, pp. 9, 171; vol. 3, p. 262; vol. 4, p. 134 · Nichols, *Illustrations*, 6.63–7 · E. Rhodes, *Peak scenery, or, Excursions in Derbyshire*, 1 (1818), 76–7 · IGI

Newton, William (1822–1876), trade unionist and journalist, was born in Congleton, Cheshire, the son of William Newton, a skilled engineer. He began an engineering apprenticeship at Kirk's foundry, Etruria, Staffordshire, at the age of fourteen, became a member of the Journeymen Steam Engine and Machine Makers' Society in 1840, and shortly afterwards moved to London. In 1842 he married Emma, daughter of Samuel Baxter, a labourer; they had one daughter.

In the course of the 1840s Newton worked his way up the trade to the position of foreman but his prominent role in union affairs resulted in his dismissal in 1848. Newton then took over the Phoenix tavern, Ratcliffe Cross, which was already the meeting place of the east London branch of the Steam Engine Makers, and used this position both further to extend the influence of the union and to launch himself into politics.

In his trade union activities Newton was a close colleague of William Allan, who became general secretary of the Steam Engine Makers in 1848, and together they led the movement towards the fusion of a number of craft organizations into the Amalgamated Society of Engineers (ASE) in 1851, with Newton's own contribution being largely that of a persuasive publicist. In 1851 and the early part of 1852 he published and edited *The Operative*, a weekly paper which pressed the case for amalgamation. On the ASE's executive council it was Newton who moved the pioneering motion 'that all engineers, machinists, millwrights, smiths and pattern-makers cease to work systematic overtime and piece-work after 31 December 1851'

(*DLB*, 2.270). This sparked off the widely publicized 'lock-out' by the employers, which began on 10 January 1852 with the employers in London and Lancashire closing their works.

During the dispute Newton gave powerful speeches at important meetings throughout the country; a gathering at the Manchester Free Trade Hall was said to be 'the greatest indoor meeting ever held by the working class of England' (*DLB*, 2.270). In accounting for the ASE's eventual defeat Newton later emphasized the contribution of hostile reports in the press. However, it is clear that the union was quite unprepared to withstand a long dispute. As a result of his experience, Newton became for several years a strong advocate of producers' co-operatives instead of unequal industrial conflicts.

Though not directly involved in the union's affairs after its dramatic launch, Newton continued as a prominent spokesman for its case. He was active on the committee which secured the first legal recognition for trade unions under a friendly societies' act of 1855, and he gave evidence as an engineer before the select committee on masters and servants in 1856. During the London builders' dispute in 1859 a major attack on trade unions was made by the Edinburgh MP Adam Black in a lecture entitled 'Wages, trade unions and strikes'. A speech refuting Black's unsubstantiated allegations about the ASE was made by Newton in Edinburgh, and was later published. In 1867 Newton chaired the meeting called to formulate the engineers' response to the royal commission on trade unions.

In his political activities Newton played a leading part in the earliest movements for labour representation, considerably aided by his talents for speaking and journalism. In the 1852 general election in the Tower Hamlets constituency he became the country's first independent labour candidate and, though he came bottom of the poll behind two sitting middle-class radicals and a Liberal, his involvement in the engineering trade's dispute and his personal appearances on the hustings gathered him over 1000 votes. He then floated the idea of a new 'national party' to press for manhood suffrage as the key to the solution of labour's problems but, though he received some support in trade union and Christian socialist circles in London, he failed to convince the national Chartist leaders of the value of collaborating with middle-class radicals in pursuit of a single issue at this time.

Undaunted, Newton continued to press for political reform through his other newspaper ventures, *The Englishman* (1853–4) and the *East London Observer* (1858–76), becoming president of the Labour Representation League and an enthusiastic Gladstonian Liberal. In the 1868 general election he stood again for Tower Hamlets, this time as a radical Liberal with strong local support, but once again came bottom of the poll, this time partly because of faction fighting within the labour movement itself. His final unsuccessful attempt to enter parliament was in a straight fight against a Conservative at a by-election in Ipswich in 1875; his candidature testified to his national standing, reflected both in his having been invited by the local branch of the Labour Representation League and in the wider interest shown in his campaign speeches.

Newton was much more successful in local politics. He was a member and subsequently chairman of the Stepney vestry, and from 1862 until his death served as the Mile End vestry's representative on the Metropolitan Board of Works, which he also eventually chaired. Both in his committee work on such public services as sanitation and water supply, and in his newspaper coverage of poor-law issues, he was a champion of coherent London-wide policies. One of his contributions to the debate on London local government in 1870, calling for 'one great central authority' (*DLB*, 2.273), was widely circulated, and he consistently advocated the equalization of local poor rates to prevent the heaviest financial burdens falling on the districts of the city least able to pay.

William Newton was an important pioneer of labour organization in both the industrial and the political spheres. He was a heavily bearded, thoughtful-looking man, remembered for his remarkable eloquence, which allowed him both to inspire masses of men with large ideas and to persuade committees about detailed schemes. However, little is recorded about his personal life. He died at his home, 41 Stepney Green, London, on 9 March 1876, having been ill for a while with a number of complaints, including Bright's disease. He was survived by his wife. ALASTAIR J. REID

Sources *DLB*, 2.270–76 · F. E. Gillespie, *Labour and politics in England, 1850–1867* (1921) · J. B. Jefferys, *The story of the engineers, 1800–1945* [1946] · *CGPLA Eng. & Wales* (1876) · m. cert. · d. cert.

Wealth at death under £6000: probate, 30 March 1876, *CGPLA Eng. & Wales*

Newton, Sir William John (1785–1869), miniature painter and photographer, born in Thornhaugh Street, Bedford Square, London, was the son of James Newton (1748–1804), engraver, and his wife, Abigail, *née* Post, of Thornhaugh Street. James Newton worked closely with his elder brother, the architect William Newton (1735–1790), and engraved many plates for his brother's translation of Vitruvius's *De architectura* (as *The Architecture of M. Vitruvius Pollio*, 2 vols., 1791). As an engraver he worked in both line and stipple and engraved some mythological subjects after Claude Lorrain, Marco Ricci, and Francesco Zuccarelli, as well as a few portraits.

William John Newton entered the Royal Academy Schools, London, on 15 January 1807 as an engraver, and his early efforts include an ink and wash drawing of Joseph Richardson MP, after Martin Archer Shee (British Museum, London). From 1808, however, he worked solely as a miniature painter, and he soon established himself as one of the most fashionable artists of his day. Many of his portraits were engraved. He exhibited at the Royal Academy between 1808 and 1863, though his candidature for appointment to associate was rejected in 1825.

Newton married Ann (*d.* 1856), daughter of Robert Faulder, on 30 August 1822. The couple had two children, Mary Margaret (*d.* before 1861) and Harry Robert Newton [*see below*]. He lived for many years at 33 Argyll Street, London, and then at no. 6. In 1831 he was appointed miniature painter-in-ordinary to William IV and Queen Adelaide, and from 1837 to 1858 held the same office under Queen Victoria. He was knighted in 1837.

Newton's most ambitious miniatures were three large historical groups: *The Coronation of Queen Victoria* (1838), *The Marriage of Queen Victoria and Prince Albert, the Prince Consort* (1840), and *The Christening of Albert Edward, Prince of Wales* (1842). Although his miniatures were highly regarded during his lifetime, his work suffered a lapse in critical esteem in the late nineteenth and early twentieth centuries, particularly at the hands of the critic Dr G. C. Williamson. More recent judgements have reinstated Newton 'among the best English miniaturists of his period' (Schidlof, 2.588).

Newton's contribution to the early development of photography has also been recognized. His passionate amateur interest in the subject was fired by his membership from 1833 of the Graphic Society, at which demonstrations were given of early photographic work. In 1847 he began to experiment with the calotype process invented by W. H. Fox Talbot and became associated with the Calotype Club. As a result of his experiments he was able to exhibit in 1852 photographs at the first exhibition of photography, sponsored by the Society of Arts, and in 1853 to publish the details of his technique for making calotypes. This entailed the innovative use of potassium cyanide in the process of iodizing the photographic paper to prepare it to receive the photographic image. In January 1853 he was elected vice-president of the Photographic Society of London and in 1861 was involved in a dispute regarding the proposed classification of photography at the 1862 International Exhibition in London. He upheld the view that photography should be classed as a science, not as one of the fine arts.

After his retirement Newton moved to 6 Cambridge Terrace, London, where he died on 22 January 1869. A collection of his miniatures were sold by order of the executors of his son, Harry Robert Newton, at Christies on 23 June 1890 (lots 106–72). A large group of his miniatures is in the Glynn Vivian Art Gallery and Museum, Swansea.

Newton's son, **Harry Robert Newton** (*bap.* 1828, *d.* 1889), architect, was baptized on 9 February 1828 at St James's, Westminster, London. His early schooling is unknown, but he studied under the architect Sydney Smirke. He was appointed ARIBA on 16 May 1853 and FRIBA on 4 June 1860. He practised from his father's address at 6 Argyll Street in 1868 and later from Weybridge in Surrey. He died in the Civil Service Co-operative Stores, Bedford Street, Covent Garden, London, on 14 November 1889. V. REMINGTON

Sources L. G. Zillman, *William Newton: miniature painter and photographer, 1785–1869*, History of Photography Monograph Series, special issue no. 2 (1986) • *The Times* (26 Jan 1869) • *Art Journal*, 31 (1869), 84 • L. R. Schidlof, *The miniature in Europe in the 16th, 17th, 18th, and 19th centuries*, 2 (1964), 588–9 • D. Foskett, *Miniatures: dictionary and guide* (1987), 353, 426, 607 • B. S. Long, *British miniaturists* (1929), 311–12 • B. Stewart and M. Cutten, *The dictionary of portrait painters in Britain up to 1920* (1997) • S. C. Hutchison, 'The Royal Academy Schools, 1768–1830', *Walpole Society*, 38 (1960–62), 123–91, esp. 163 •

Graves, *RA exhibitors* • G. C. Williamson, *The history of portrait miniatures*, 2 (1904), 27 • *CGPLA Eng. & Wales* (1869) • *DNB* • parish register (marriage), entry no. 270, 30 Aug 1822, London, St James's, Piccadilly • parish register (baptism), 9 Feb 1828, London, St James's, Westminster [H. R. Newton] • *Dir. Brit. archs.* [H. R. Newton] • *CGPLA Eng. & Wales* (1890)
Likenesses W. J. Newton, self-portrait, chalk drawing, BM • W. J. Newton, self-portrait, pencil and white chalk on blue paper (as a young man), BM
Wealth at death under £4000: probate, 1869, *CGPLA Eng. & Wales* • £524—Harry Robert Newton: probate, 1890, *CGPLA Eng. & Wales*

Ngata, Sir Apirana Turupa Nohopari (1874–1950), Maori

leader and politician in New Zealand, was born on 3 July 1874 at Te Araroa on the east coast of North Island, New Zealand, the first child of Paratene Ngata (1849–1924) and his wife, Katerina Naki. They were from Ngati Porou, a tribe that remained loyal to the crown during the New Zealand wars of the 1860s. Throughout his life Ngata was conspicuously loyal to the crown and empire. His father was a tribal leader, progressive farmer, storekeeper, and expert in tribal lore; his mother was a daughter of Maora Nekewhare and Abel Knox, a London whaler. Ngata once said this Pakeha ancestry was the source of his methodical habits, but otherwise he did not consider it important.

Ngata began his education at Waiomatatini native school (1880–83). He then, with a scholarship, attended Te Aute College (1883–90), an Anglican secondary school for Maori boys; under headmaster John Thornton he was drilled in the classics in preparation for matriculation and imbued with a mission to save his race from likely extinction. Then he attended Canterbury University College (1891–6), where he completed a BA in 1893 and an LLB in 1896. He was the first Maori to complete a university degree and to qualify as a lawyer, being admitted to the bar in 1897. An attractive young man, he was short and very strong.

In 1895 Ngata married Arihia Kane Tamati (*d.* 18 April 1929), daughter of Tuta Tamati, also of Ngati Porou. They had fifteen children, of whom five sons and six daughters survived to adulthood. After his admission to the bar Ngata and Arihia returned to the east coast. Instead of practising law Ngata assumed leadership of Ngati Porou farming enterprises; he expanded their flocks of sheep and invested in pasture improvement, buildings, and mechanization. He consolidated scattered fragments of land into contiguous holdings and established incorporations to manage tribal land. He also created tribal co-operatives to provide credit and market produce.

About 1900 Ngata became involved in national affairs under the guidance of James Carroll, the Maori minister for native affairs in the Liberal government. He helped Carroll to draft legislation giving Maori greater control over their land and a measure of local government through Maori councils. In 1905 Ngata won the Eastern Maori seat in the house of representatives, which he retained until 1943. He was an able parliamentarian. A skilled debater, he could get the measure of any opponent. He quickly made his mark in parliament and was appointed to cabinet in 1909, though he lost office with the Liberal party's defeat in 1912. He remained faithful to the Liberals and did not return to cabinet until the party, renamed the United Party, won the 1928 election. In the interval he continued to facilitate land reform and development, encouraging other tribes to follow the lead of Ngati Porou. During the First World War he recruited volunteers for a Maori battalion that served with distinction in the Middle East and France. His achievements were recognized in 1927 when he was made a knight bachelor, becoming the third Maori knight.

Further reward came with United's victory in 1928, when Ngata became native minister, a portfolio he had long coveted. Now fifty-four, he had the energy of a man of half his age. He entered into his new ministry with a ferocious energy that left his hapless staff trailing in his wake. He pressed ahead with land development, using state funds and initiating schemes wherever he could find under-developed Maori land and local communities willing to improve it. But his involvement with one such community was to have tragic effect. In 1929 Ngata, his wife, Arihia, and eldest son, Makarini, went to Waikato to initiate land development and to open a carved meeting-house. Makarini contracted dysentery and Arihia, nursing him at home, caught it too. Both died. Ngata was devastated.

Ngata was soon beset by another misfortune. The country was slipping into depression and the government was paring expenditure to the bone. But he pressed ahead with land development and increased expenditure. Impatient with red tape, he made decisions without consulting his officials. They were unable to keep up with the paperwork. By early 1932 Ngata was being roasted in parliament and the press. A commission of inquiry was appointed to investigate his departmental administration and land development schemes. Its report was critical of his administration, especially his personal style and contempt for bureaucratic regulations. Some of his subordinates had been falsifying accounts. He accepted responsibility and resigned from the cabinet.

Although he remained in parliament, Ngata had to watch Labour, victorious in the 1935 election, continue his land developments—with even greater expenditure of funds. When another world war started Ngata again recruited a Maori battalion, this time sending two of his sons to war. His parliamentary career finally ended when he was defeated in 1943.

Ngata now had more time for cultural and academic activities. He continued to promote the construction or restoration of carved meeting-houses, including a new house to commemorate the centennial of the treaty of Waitangi in 1840. He published Maori poetry, adding further volumes to his 1928 publication, *Nga moteatea*. From 1938 to 1950 he was president of the Polynesian Society, of which he had been a member since 1895. An active Anglican, he helped with a revision of the Maori Bible. His scholarship was finally recognized by the University of New Zealand with an honorary LittD in 1948. He became frail, though he kept working on various projects, including the Rangiatea church restoration, a memorial house

for his beloved Arihia, and preparations for the Te Aute College centennial. After Arihia's death Ngata married Te Riringi Tuhou in 1932. She died in 1948, and he married Hine Te Kira not long before his own death, following a brief illness, at Waiomatatini, North Island, on 14 July 1950. He was buried beside Arihia on a little hill behind his home at The Bungalow, Waiomatatini.

Ngata made a vital contribution to the revival of the Maori race in the early twentieth century. He used his knowledge of the European world and his professional skills to assist his people to develop and farm their land while also encouraging them to preserve their culture and maintain their identity. He was the pre-eminent Maori leader of the twentieth century.   M. P. K. SORRENSON

Sources R. Walker, *He tipua: the life and times of Sir Apirana Ngata* (2001) • M. P. K. Sorrenson, 'Ngata, Apirana Turupa', *DNZB*, vol. 3 • *Na to hoa aroha: from your dear friend: the correspondence between Sir Apirana Ngata and Sir Peter Buck, 1925–50*, ed. M. P. K. Sorrenson, 3 vols. (1986–8) • G. V. Butterworth, 'The politics of adaptation: the career of Sir Apirana Ngata, 1874–1928', MA diss., Victoria University of Wellington, 1969 • *WWW, 1941–50*
Archives Archives New Zealand, Maori affairs files • NL NZ, Turnbull L., papers | NL NZ, Turnbull L., Maori Purposes Fund Board papers • NL NZ, Turnbull L., Polynesian Society papers • NL NZ, Turnbull L., Ramsden papers | FILM New Zealand Film Archive, Wellington, 'In the shadow of Ngata', 1974 • New Zealand Film Archive, Wellington, documentary footage | SOUND BL NSA, recorded talk • National Sound Archives, Auckland, performance recordings • National Sound Archives, Auckland, recorded talks
Likenesses three photographs, 1910–52, NL NZ, Turnbull L. • D. Fraser, bronze statue, House of Parliament, Wellington; repro. in Sorrenson, ed., *Na to hoa aroha*, 3.256 • photograph (as BA graduate), Gisborne Museum, New Zealand • photograph, National Archives of New Zealand
Wealth at death £NZ56 10s.: Walker, *He tipua*, p. 394, a reference to J. A. Thorburn to E. B. Corbell, NAMA 1 19/1/699

Niall Frossach mac Fergaile (718–778), high-king of Ireland, was a member of the Cenél nÉogain dynasty of the Uí Néill and one of four sons of *Fergal mac Máele Dúin (d. 722), high-king of Ireland; his mother was Aithechdae ingen Chéin. His father, his brother *Áed Allán, and his son *Áed Oirdnide were all militarily active and powerful kings of Tara (high-kings), but Niall Frossach seems to have had a remarkably placid career, if the silence of the sources is to be believed.

Niall Frossach is one of only a handful of Irish kings in the early middle ages whose birth has been reported in the chronicles. Such records must have been made retrospectively, and the entry of 718 has an aura of legend: 'A shower of honey rained on Othan Becc, a shower of silver on Othan Mór, a shower of blood rained on the Dyke of the Leinstermen, and hence Niall Frossach mac Fergaile was so called, for he was born then' (*Ann. Ulster*, 718.7) (*frossach* means 'showery'). A similar but fuller explanation of his epithet is found in a seventeenth-century translation of a lost medieval chronicle. This reports a great famine in the early 760s (which is attested in other chronicles). Niall, in the presence of seven bishops, besought God either to take his soul or to send relief for his subjects. At once a shower of silver fell from heaven. The king rejoiced, but said, 'This is not the thing that can Deliuer us from this famine & eminent Danger'. He prayed again:

> then a second shower of heavenly honey fell, & then the K. said with Great thanksgiving as before, wᵗʰ that yᵉ third shower fell of pure wheat, which covered all the fields … soe that there was such plenty & aboundance of wheat, that it was thought yᵗ was able to maintaine manye kingdomes (*Annals of Clonmacnoise*)

Following the death of his brother Áed Allán in battle in 743, it is likely that Niall Frossach took the kingship of the Cenél nÉogain dynasty but little more: in 747, a member of the rival northern Uí Néill dynasty of Cenél Conaill died, styled by the chronicles 'king of the North', which implies that Niall was subject to him. However, in 754, another king of Cenél Conaill died, this time described merely as king of his own dynasty, and it is probable that by now Niall had achieved overlordship of the northern Uí Néill. Two years later comes the single reported military incident of Niall's career: Domnall Midi, king of Tara, led an army against Niall as far as the plain of Muirthemne in Louth. There is no report of any clash, and the event is without context.

Domnall Midi died in 763, and at some point between then and 770 Niall Frossach took the high-kingship. The chronicles say that he did so in 763, but their testimony is probably far from contemporary, for later annalists liked to regard kings of Tara as following hard on one another, which was not always the case. The remainder of the 760s are notable for violent events in Meath and the plain of Brega in which Niall was not involved but which worked in favour of Domnall's son, Donnchad Midi. Nothing is known of when and how he overthrew Niall. In 770, Donnchad led the army of the Uí Néill against the Leinstermen, and if Niall had not lost his power by this point, then the coup may have happened the following year, when Donnchad led a hosting northwards.

Niall Frossach died in 778; an addition to the annals of Ulster says that he was at the Columban monastery on Iona. He may well have been in exile, perhaps placed there by Donnchad, a friend of the Columban monastic confederation. He was married to Dúnfhlaith (*d.* 799), daughter of *Flaithbertach mac Loingsig, an earlier high-king of Ireland. His sons included Colmán (*d.* 815), Áed Oirdnide (*d.* 819), Ferchar, and Muirchertach.   PHILIP IRWIN

Sources Ann. Ulster · D. Murphy, ed., *The annals of Clonmacnoise*, trans. C. Mageoghagan (1896); facs. edn (1993), 121 · W. Stokes, ed., 'The annals of Tigernach [8 pts]', *Revue Celtique*, 16 (1895), 374–419; 17 (1896), 6–33, 119–263, 337–420; 18 (1897), 9–59, 150–97, 267–303, 374–91; pubd sep. (1993) · M. A. O'Brien, ed., *Corpus genealogiarum Hiberniae* (Dublin, 1962), 134 · M. C. Dobbs, ed. and trans., 'The Banshenchus [pt 2]', *Revue Celtique*, 48 (1931), 163–234, esp. 186 · K. Meyer, 'Das Ende von Baile in Scáil', *Zeitschrift für Celtische Philologie*, 12 (1918), 232–8, esp. 233

Niall mac Áeda [Niall Caille] (*d.* 846), king of Ailech and high-king of Ireland, was the son of *Áed Oirdnide mac Néill (*d.* 819) and Medb ingen Indrechtaich. A dynast of Cenél nÉogain, Niall first appears in the records in a dynastic war in 823, when he deposed his kinsman Murchad mac Máele Dúin and reigned as king of Ailech. Soon afterwards he became embroiled in a controversy at Armagh

when his confessor, Éogan Mainistrech, abbot of the monastery, was expelled by rivals in 827. Niall led an army south to restore Éogan, and the ensuing conflict was the important battle of Leth Cam (near Armagh), when Niall defeated the Uí Chrimthainn, a dynasty of the Airgialla among whom Armagh was situated, and their allies the Ulaid. Éogan was reinstated and Niall forced the submission of the Airgialla to his own dynasty of Cenél nÉogain, extending his lordship as far south as Armagh.

Niall was recognized as high-king in 833 on the death of the Clann Cholmáin lord and high-king, Conchobar mac Donnchado. The same year he defeated a viking army that had raided Derry, the church of St Columba. From his father, Áed, Niall had inherited an interest in Leinster affairs and he led his army south in 835 and 'ordained' Bróen mac Fáeláin as provincial king of Leinster. Having ordered affairs in Leinster to his satisfaction, on his return he raided the territory of his Uí Néill rivals, Clann Cholmáin, as far as Bodammair (Offaly). He then had to face a challenge to his overlordship from the south-west, from the Munster king Feidlimid mac Crimthainn. In 836 Feidlimid captured the abbot of Armagh, Forindán, who was visiting Kildare. What seems at first glance to be a challenge to Niall, may have fitted with his plans, for control of Armagh was contested between Forindán and a Diarmait ua Tigernáin, who could have been supported by Niall. In 838 a *rígdál mór* ('great royal meeting') was held by Niall with Feidlimid; the location is given variously as Clonfert or Cloncurry (Kildare). Any agreement made there has not survived, although the report of the meeting from a Munster chronicle with a bias towards the southern prince claims that Niall submitted to Feidlimid, while a contemporary northern chronicle has no report of the proceedings. Later events suggest that nothing was solved, since Feidlimid led an expedition to the ceremonial centre at Tara in 840 and encamped there. Niall led raids into what is now co. Offaly to destroy any support for the pretender and then, in the following year, forced the issue by confronting Feidlimid's army at Mag nÓchtair (near Cloncurry, in Kildare) as his rival was attempting to assert his lordship over Leinster. Niall won the battle and Feidlimid never returned to the north.

The viking menace had increased by this time and in 845 Niall defeated a viking band at Mag nÍtha (Donegal). His victory was the last recorded event of his life, for he drowned in the River Calann in 846 (hence the name Niall Caille) and was buried at Armagh. Niall's queen was Gormfhlaith (*d.* 861), the daughter of the high-king Donnchad mac Domnaill; their son *Áed Findliath (*d.* 879) ruled as high-king. Niall had six other known children: a daughter, name unknown, who was the wife of Conaing of Brega; and five sons, named Bróen, Dub-indrecht, Óengus, Muirchertach, and Flaithbertach.

BENJAMIN T. HUDSON

Sources Ann. Ulster · M. C. Dobbs, ed. and trans., 'The Banshenchus [3 pts]', *Revue Celtique*, 47 (1930), 283–339; 48 (1931), 163–234; 49 (1932), 437–89 · J. MacNeill, 'Poems by Flann Mainistrech on the dynasties of Ailech, Mide and Brega', *Archivium Hibernicum*, 2 (1913), 37–99 · J. H. Todd, ed. and trans., *Cogadh Gaedhel re Gallaibh* /

The war of the Gaedhil with the Gaill, Rolls Series, 48 (1867) · M. A. O'Brien, ed., *Corpus genealogiarum Hiberniae* (Dublin, 1962) · K. Meyer, 'Das Ende von Baile in Scáil', *Zeitschrift für Celtische Philologie*, 12 (1918), 232–8 · S. Mac Airt, ed. and trans., *The annals of Inisfallen* (1951) · W. M. Hennessy, ed. and trans., *Chronicum Scotorum: a chronicle of Irish affairs*, Rolls Series, 46 (1866) · AFM · F. J. Byrne, *Irish kings and high-kings* (1987) · D. Ó Corráin, *Ireland before the Normans* (1972) · E. Hogan, *Onomasticon Goedelicum* (1910)

Niall mac Áeda [called Niall Glúndub] (c.869–919), king of Ailech and high-king of Ireland, was the son of the high-king *Áed Findliath mac Néill (d. 879) and Máel Muire (d. 913), daughter of the Scottish king Cináed mac Alpin; his byname Glúndub means 'Black Knee'. A dynast of Cenél nÉogain, one of the families of the Uí Néill confederation, his three-year reign as high-king (916–19) came at the end of a lengthy career of military success. After his death he achieved a literary fame in the poems lamenting his death that were attributed to his wife, Gormlaith.

Niall became king of Ailech in 896 and for a number of years he shared the kingship with his paternal half-brother Domnall; yet he first appears in the chronicles in 905 when he and Domnall prepared to fight a duel, but were prevented by their family. Any quarrel between the brothers had been resolved by 908 when they led an expedition to Meath against the other powerful Uí Néill dynasty of Clann Cholmáin, in the course of which they burnt the ceremonial site at Tlachtga (Hill of Ward in Meath). In 912 he caused to be executed by drowning a subject prince, Cernachán mac Duilgen of the Airthir, for a violation of Armagh when Cernachán ordered the killing of a man who was in the sanctuary of the church.

Niall's half-brother Domnall retired into religious life in 911, and from then until his elevation in 916 Niall busied himself with preparation for assuming the overlordship. In 913 he invaded Connacht and defeated two kingdoms in Mayo, Uí Amalgada and Umall. The next year he turned east and raided the kingdoms of the coast, defeated the Dál nAraidi at Ravel Water (Antrim) and their southern neighbours, the Ulaid, at Carncary. That the motives for these predatory excursions were political rather than purely material is seen when, on 1 November, the Ulaid king, Áed mac Eóchacáin, submitted to Niall at Tullyhog (Tyrone). Niall followed this success in December by setting up camp at Girley for raids round Meath. He was back in Meath the following year, this time for an unusual reason. The Clann Cholmáin dynast, and then high-king *Flann Sinna mac Máele Sechnaill, had requested Niall's assistance to quell a rebellion led by Flann's sons Donnchad and Conchobar. Flann was Niall's stepfather, the second husband of his late mother, Máel Muire. Niall complied and the erring sons were forced to obey their father.

The old monarch was approaching the end of his life and after his death on 25 May 916, Niall became high-king. In recognition of his new eminence, he presided over the fair of Tailtiu (Teltown), a festival that had not been held for a number of years. Niall's brief tenure as high-king was occupied by a new foe, a group of vikings known as the 'descendants of Ivar' who were active both in Ireland and in Britain. They raided Munster, and in the summer of

917 Niall led a force south. Making camp at Tobar Glethrach, in Mag Femin (near Clonmel), he fought a battle against the vikings on 22 August, from morning until evening. Niall was victorious, although when his allies, the men of Leinster, attacked the vikings in a separate engagement, they were defeated at Glynn. For almost a month Niall remained in the south campaigning against the vikings. In 918 he fought Sihtric, the future king of Northumbria, but in 919 he decided to carry the fight to the vikings. Leading a force with troops from the north, he attacked the vikings outside Dublin at Kilmashogue (Islandbridge, Dublin). The vikings had allied with the men of Leinster for the conflict, and the battle, fought on 15 November, was a disaster for the northern army. Niall was slain, as well as many of his commanders: a list of the dead reads like a roll of the powerful families of northern Ireland. Niall was buried at Kells.

Niall had two wives: Land, daughter of Eochaid of Dál Riata, whose son was the famous *Muirchertach mac Néill (Muirchertach of the Leather Cloaks) (d. 943); and *Gormlaith (d. 948), daughter of the high-king Flann Sinna. His other children were Niall (d. 916), Conaing (d. 937), Máel Muire (d. 966), and Máel Ciaran. In addition to the fame Niall acquired through the successes of his children, he was fortunate that two poets commemorated his reign in verse. One was Cormacán mac Máele Brigti (d. 948); and his wife Gormlaith was the supposed author of poems which speak of her sorrow at the death of Niall and the emptiness of her life as a widow. One saga, preserved in the annals of Clonmacnoise, claims that Gormlaith's own death was due, in part, to her late husband. In this tale, the dowager queen awakes from sleep and sees the spirit of Niall standing by her bed. She rises and tries to embrace him, but falls and impales herself on the bedstead, receiving her death wound. To Gormlaith is credited the verse, 'My blessing on the soul of Niall; since he is gone my grief is lasting; until the giving of judgement at Domesday I shall never find a man like Niall.'

BENJAMIN T. HUDSON

Sources *Ann. Ulster* · M. C. Dobbs, ed. and trans., 'The Banshenchus [3 pts]', *Revue Celtique*, 47 (1930), 283–339; 48 (1931), 163–234; 49 (1932), 437–89 · J. H. Todd, ed. and trans., *Cogadh Gaedhel re Gallaibh / The war of the Gaedhil with the Gaill*, Rolls Series, 48 (1867) · K. Meyer, 'Das Ende von Baile in Scáil', *Zeitschrift für Celtische Philologie*, 12 (1918), 232–8 · M. A. O'Brien, ed., *Corpus genealogiarum Hiberniae* (Dublin, 1962) · E. Hogan, *Onomasticon Goedelicum* (1910) · S. Mac Airt, ed. and trans., *The annals of Inisfallen* (1951) · W. M. Hennessy, ed. and trans., *Chronicum Scotorum: a chronicle of Irish affairs*, Rolls Series, 46 (1866) · AFM · F. J. Byrne, *Irish kings and high-kings* (1987) · D. Ó Corráin, *Ireland before the Normans* (1972)

Niall mac Áeda meic Máel Ísu (d. 1139), claimant to the see of Armagh, was of the hereditary secularized ecclesiastical dynasty of Clann Sínaig, which asserted a monopoly of the headship of the church of Armagh from 966 and which opposed Máel Ísu Ua Morgair (St Malachy) as archbishop of Armagh. In 1129, on the death of Archbishop Cellach, Malachy failed to gain possession of the insignia and temporalities of the see because of the opposition and installation of Muirchertach Mac Domnaill of Clann Sínaig. On the death of Muirchertach on 17 September

1134, Malachy assumed archiepiscopal office, but Niall, whom Muirchertach had designated his successor, seized the insignia, including the *Bachall Ísu* ('staff of Jesus') and the Book of Armagh, Malachy being forced to purchase the staff in 1135. When Malachy resigned the see of Armagh in 1137, Niall attempted to retake possession but was driven out and died in 1139. M. T. FLANAGAN

Sources *Sancti Bernardi opera*, ed. J. Leclercq and others, 3 (Rome, 1963), 332–4 · *Ann. Ulster*, s.a. 1129 · W. Stokes, ed., 'The annals of Tigernach [8 pts]', *Revue Celtique*, 16 (1895), 374–419; 17 (1896), 6–33, 119–263, 337–420; 18 (1897), 9–59, 150–97, 267–303, 374–91; pubd sep. (1993), 2.366 · *AFM*, 2nd edn, 1134–7, 1139

Niall mac Eochada (*d.* 1063), king of Ulaid, was the son of Eochada mac Ardgair (*d.* 1004). He was a dynast of Dál Fiatach and his early military ventures were against members of his own dynasty: in 1012 he defeated his cousin in the 'battle of the Summits'; and in 1020 he defeated and blinded his kinsman Flaithbertach Ua Eochada. Having become king of Ulaid in 1016, he achieved supremacy in the north equally through his own efforts and through fortunate circumstances. In 1020 his rivals of Cenél nEógain were driven across Sliab Fuait by the high-king Máel Sechnaill mac Domnaill. Two years later, in 1022, Niall defeated the vikings of Dublin in a sea battle off his coast. He then turned to the Cenél nEógain client-kingdom of Airgialla and defeated them. In 1024 he invaded Dublin and took their hostages; he repeated his success two years later. The Cenél nEógain raided his lands in 1027, and in 1030 they attacked his client-kingdom of Dál nAraidi. The following year Niall carried the war to Cenél nEógain and raided their capital at Tullyhog, but his intended victims raided Ulaid in his absence. This discomfort may have emboldened Niall's rivals to rebel, for he raided the church of Cill Comber (Down) within his own province.

In 1032 the Airgialla repulsed another raid by the Ulaid, this time at Drumbanagher in Armagh. Despite these hostilities, the Airgialla may have preferred the lordship of Ulaid to Cenél nEógain, for in 1048 their king Gilla Coluim mac Écnich retired to Downpatrick, the stronghold of the Ulaid, where he died. The increased power of the Ulaid may explain the compliment paid to Niall mac Eochada in one poem—that he decided who was a peasant and who was a noble. Niall carried war southwards in 1034, when he raided the southern Uí Néill as far as 'Tech mic Mellen' (perhaps Stamullen, in Meath). Cenél nEógain attacked Niall again in 1041, and in 1044 Niall raided the southern Uí Néill kingdom of Brega, but was defeated with the loss of two hundred men.

These military reverses sent Niall looking for an alliance, which he found with the Leinster king, Diarmait mac Máel na mBó. The first sign of this union comes in 1047, when Ulaid suffered severely during a year of tremendous snows which lasted from 8 December to 17 March, and Niall's people were forced to seek relief in Leinster. In 1048 and 1049 Niall and Diarmait attacked the southern Uí Néill kingdoms of Meath and Brega. Seven years later the Uí Néill were leading raids against Niall's northern subjects, the Dál nAraidi; in 1056 the southern

Uí Néill took three thousand cows and sixty captives, and in 1059 Cenél nEógain raided the same area.

Niall mac Eochada was married to Máel Midach, with whom he had a daughter, Bean Ulad, and a son, Eochaid, whom he had made king by 1061; Niall had a second daughter named Dirbail. Eochaid's brief reign ended with his death in 1062, and Niall died on 13 November in the following year. BENJAMIN T. HUDSON

Sources *Ann. Ulster* · W. Stokes, ed., 'The annals of Tigernach [8 pts]', *Revue Celtique*, 16 (1895), 374–419; 17 (1896), 6–33, 119–263, 337–420; 18 (1897), 9–59, 150–97, 267–303, 374–91; pubd sep. (1993) · M. C. Dobbs, ed. and trans., 'The Ban-shenchus [3 pts]', *Revue Celtique*, 47 (1930), 283–339; 48 (1931), 163–234; 49 (1932), 437–89 · F. J. Byrne, *Irish kings and high-kings* (1987) · F. J. Byrne, 'Clann Ollaman Uaisle Emna', *Studia Hibernica*, 4 (1964), 54–94 · T. W. Moody and others, eds., *A new history of Ireland*, 9: *Maps, genealogies, lists* (1984)

Niall mac Maíl Shechnaill (*d.* 1061), king of Ailech, was the most powerful ruler of his time in the north-west of Ireland. His father was Máel Sechnaill (*d.* 997) and his mother was Barrfhind, daughter of Uadlusán from Mag Lemna (in Tyrone), a person of minor importance within the territories ruled by Cenél nEógain. In spite of his position, Niall mac Maíl Shechnaill largely avoided involvement in the wars between the great provincial kings which marked the eleventh century. After the death of Brian Bóruma and the succession of his much less able but long-lived son, Donnchad, the hegemony he had established was fought over by a succession of rivals to the power of Brian's dynasty, Dál Cais. Niall's achievements, however, were mainly confined to the north. Up to his succession upon the death of Flaithbertach Ua Néill in 1036, the kingship of Ailech and Cenél nEógain had been largely monopolized by the descendants of Niall Glúndub (*d.* 919) to the exclusion of the line of Niall Glúndub's brother, Domnall (*d.* 915). Domnall's son, Fergal (*d.* 938), had been king of Ailech, but otherwise his descendants, including Niall's father, Máel Sechnaill, had been acknowledged only as *rígdamna* ('king-worthy'), and no more of them became king of Ailech until Niall mac Maíl Shechnaill. Niall's succession, moreover, was secured only after three of his brothers had died in dynastic in-fighting.

During his reign Niall mac Maíl Shechnaill was not the only Cenél nEógain ruler to take a lead in war, and his relative passivity is highlighted not only by the ability of his successor, Ardgar Mac Lochlainn (*d.* 1064) to lead major expeditions before Niall's death, but also by Ardgar's successful attacks on the Connachta in both 1062 and 1063, before his death in the following year. Niall did, however, attack Cuailnge in 1044, Brega in 1045 and 1047, and Dál nAraidi in 1059; but these were minor powers compared with the Connachta attacked by his successor. The continuing alliance between Cenél nEógain and Armagh is illustrated by the ability of the abbot, Dub dá Leithi, to go on a great circuit round Cenél nEógain in 1050, from which he is said to have brought 300 cows, a feat worthy of a full-scale cattle raid. T. M. CHARLES-EDWARDS

Sources W. Stokes, ed., 'The annals of Tigernach [8 pts]', *Revue Celtique*, 16 (1895), 374–419; 17 (1896), 6–33, 119–263, 337–420; 18 (1897), 9–59, 150–97, 267–303, 374–91; pubd sep. (1993) · *Ann.*

Ulster · M. C. Dobbs, ed. and trans., 'The Ban-shenchus [3 pts]', *Revue Celtique*, 47 (1930), 283–339; 48 (1931), 163–234; 49 (1932), 437–89 · W. M. Hennessy, ed. and trans., *Chronicum Scotorum: a chronicle of Irish affairs*, Rolls Series, 46 (1866) · M. A. O'Brien, ed., *Corpus genealogiarum Hiberniae* (Dublin, 1962) · K. Meyer, ed., 'The Laud genealogies and tribal histories', *Zeitschrift für Celtische Philologie*, 8 (1912), 291–338 · F. J. Byrne, *Irish kings and high-kings* (1973)

Níall Noígíallach (d. *c.*452), high-king of Ireland, was the son of Eochu Muigmedón, said to have been king of Tara and therefore the high-king of Ireland (*rí Érenn*). Although many of the stories associated with Níall are obviously apocryphal, there is a consensus among scholars that he was a genuine historical figure who lived in the fifth century. These stories were mainly intended to justify his descendants' monopoly of the high-kingship at the expense of the Connachta, descended from Níall's brothers.

Níall is reputed to have been the son of a slave woman named Cairenn, the daughter of a British king. Eochu's queen Mongfhind hated Cairenn, and when she was pregnant with Níall attempted to cause her to abort by forcing her to carry all the water required by the royal household at Tara. However, Cairenn gave birth to a living baby on the green of Tara, but because of her fear of the magical powers of Mongfhind, she had to leave the baby unattended on the ground. The poet Tórnae saw the baby being attacked by birds and rescued him. He fostered Níall until he was of an age to assume the kingship.

Níall returned to Tara with Tórnae and met his mother, Cairenn, carrying water. He ordered her to desist from such menial work and dressed her in a purple robe. Mongfhind was angry and called upon Eochu to decide which of his sons was to succeed him. Eochu referred the matter to the smith Sithchenn, who had the power of prophecy. Sithchenn thereupon set fire to a forge in which five of Eochu's sons were at work. According to one version of the tale, Brian brought out the hammers, Fíachrae brought out a vat of beer and the bellows, Ailill brought out the weapons, and Fergus brought out a bundle of kindling with a stick of yew in it. Níall carried out the anvil, which Sithchenn interpreted as a sign that he would be king.

Some time later, the five sons got lost while hunting. They encountered a loathsome hag guarding a well. Four of them in turn asked the hag for leave to get some water. She demanded a kiss in return for the water, but each of the four refused. Níall, however, not only accepted the hag's offer of a kiss, but offered to have intercourse with her as well. Immediately she turned into a beautiful woman and revealed herself as the sovereignty of Ireland. She explained that sovereignty was usually horrible at first, since it had to be acquired by violence and savagery, but that subsequently it was fair and pleasant. She told Níall not to give any water to his brothers until they had granted him seniority over them. They agreed to do so; and when they returned home, Sithchenn announced that Níall and his descendants would hold dominion over Ireland.

Various traditions about Níall's reign are found in early Irish sources. In one text, it is said that he acquired his epithet Noígíallach, ('of the Nine Hostages') on account of the five hostages which he held from Ireland—one from each province—and the four hostages which he held from Britain. However, Thomas O'Rahilly suggested that the nine hostages were handed over by the nine subject tribes of the Airgíalla. The genealogies record that Níall had fourteen sons: Conall and Éogan were with Indiu, daughter of Lugaid mac Óengusso; the rest (including Coirpre mac *Néill) with unnamed other women. It has been argued that the military campaigns conducted by Níall and his sons caused the collapse of the power of the Ulaid in what is now mid-Ulster, and also of the power of the Laigin (Leinstermen) in Brega and Meath. Níall's son Éogan founded the dynasty of Cenél nÉogain which held the territory of Tír Eoghain ('the land of Éogan', Anglicized as Tyrone) and his son Conall founded the dynasty of Cenél Conaill which held the territory of Tír Conaill ('the land of Conall', Anglicized as Tirconnell). His son Lóegaire was the high-king of Ireland whose conversion by Patrick is described in Muirchú's life of the saint, written in the late seventh century.

It is possible that there is some historical basis in the tradition that Níall also conducted campaigns overseas, given the well-attested Irish raids on Britain in the fourth and fifth centuries. In one genealogy he is said to have been the king of the western world (*rí íarthair domuin*) for twenty-seven years. The sources variously describe his death as having taken place in Scotland, in the English Channel, or by the Alps and the year is reckoned to have been about 452. His killer is said to have been Eochu, son of Énnae Cennselach of the Laigin. Níall's body was brought home to Ireland by his warriors, who fought seven battles on the journey. When their enemies were prevailing, they raised up Níall's body to bring them victory. A tradition transmitted by the tenth-century poet Cináed ua hArtacáin holds that he was buried at a place called Ochan, which has been identified as Faughan, in Meath. There is also a tradition that when his foster father Tórnae heard of Níall's death, he himself died of grief. A short text entitled *Timnae Néill* ('The will of Níall'), relates how his various attributes and possessions were divided among eight of his sons.

The domination of most of Ireland by the descendants of Níall—the Uí Néill—is one of the most important facts of early Irish political history. The southern Uí Néill held sway over Connacht, Meath, and Leinster, while the northern Uí Néill dominated the north-west. Historians have stressed, however, that some ruling dynasties managed to have their lineages spuriously grafted onto that of Níall in the later genealogies.   FERGUS KELLY

Sources W. Stokes, ed. and trans., 'Echtra mac Echach Muigmedon', *Revue Celtique*, 24 (1903), 190–207 · M. Joynt, ed., 'Echtra mac Echdach Mugmedóin', *Ériu*, 4 (1908–10), 91–111 · K. Meyer, ed., 'Aided Néill Noígiallaig', *Archiv für Celtische Lexikographie*, 3 (1905–7), 323–4 · M. A. O'Brien, ed., *Corpus genealogiarum Hiberniae* (Dublin, 1962) · F. J. Byrne, *Irish kings and high-kings*, rev. edn (1999) · E. Gwynn, ed. and trans., *The metrical dindshenchas*, 2, Royal Irish Academy: Todd Lecture Series, 9 (1906), 36–41 · T. F. O'Rahilly, *Early Irish history and mythology* (1946) ·

P. Walsh, 'Irish *Ocha, Ochann*', *Ériu*, 8 (1915–16), 75–7 • M. Dillon, *The cycles of the kings* (1946) • K. Meyer, 'How King Niall of the Nine Hostages was slain', *Otia Merseiana*, 2 (1900), 84–92

Nias, Sir Joseph (1793–1879), naval officer, the third son of Joseph Nias, a ship insurance broker, was born in London on 2 April 1793. He entered the navy in 1807, on the sloop *Nautilus* under Captain Matthew Smith, with whom he continued in the frigates *Comus* and *Nymphen* on the Lisbon, Mediterranean, North Sea, and channel stations until August 1815. During the last few weeks of the *Nymphen*'s commission Nias, in command of one of her boats, was employed in rowing guard round the *Bellerophon* in Plymouth Sound, keeping off the sightseers who thronged to see Napoleon. He continued in active service after the peace, and in January 1818 was appointed to the brig *Alexander*, with Lieutenant William Edward Parry, for an expedition to the Arctic under the command of Sir John Ross. In February 1819 he was again with Parry in the converted bomb-vessel *Hecla*, but returned to the Thames in November 1820, and on 26 December was promoted lieutenant. In January 1821 he was again appointed to the *Hecla* with Parry, and sailed for the Arctic in May. After two winters in the ice the *Hecla* returned to England in November 1823.

In 1826 Nias went out to the Mediterranean as first lieutenant of the *Asia*, the flagship of Sir Edward Codrington, and after the battle of Navarino was promoted commander (11 November 1827) and appointed to the brig *Alacrity* (10 guns), in which he saw some sharp service against the Greek pirates who infested the archipelago; on 11 January 1829 he cut out one commanded by a noted criminal named Georgios, who was sent to Malta and duly hanged. The *Alacrity* was paid off in 1830.

Nias was advanced to post rank on 8 July 1835, and in May 1838 commissioned the frigate *Herald* (26 guns) for the East India station, which then included Australia, China, and the Western Pacific. In February 1840, when Captain Hobson RN was ordered to take possession of New Zealand in the name of the queen, he went from Sydney as a passenger in the *Herald*, and was assisted by Nias in the formal proceedings. During the First Opium War (1839–42) Nias served in the operations leading to the capture of Canton (Guangzhou), and on 29 June 1841 he was made a CB. The *Herald* returned to England in 1843, when Nias was placed on half pay. In June 1850 he commissioned the *Agincourt* (74 guns), from which in August he was moved to the *St George*, as flag captain to Commodore Seymour, then superintendent of the dockyard at Devonport, and as captain of the ordinary.

In 1852 Captain James Scott RN, in conversation with a friend at the United Service Club, made some reflections on Nias's conduct in China. Though duelling was then not quite extinct, the feeling of the navy was strongly opposed to it, and Nias took the then unusual practice of bringing an action against Scott, who, after the evidence of Sir Thomas Herbert (1793–1861) and others, withdrew the imputation, and under pressure from the lord chief justice expressed his regret, on which the plaintiff accepted a verdict of 40s. and costs. In 1855 Nias married Caroline Isabella, the only daughter of John Laing of Montagu Square, London; they had two sons and three daughters.

Nias commanded the ordinary at Devonport for the usual three years, and from 1854 to 1856 was superintendent of the victualling yard and hospital at Plymouth. He had no further service, but became rear-admiral on 14 February 1857, vice-admiral on 12 September 1863, KCB on 13 March 1867, and admiral on 18 October 1867. After his retirement from active service he resided for the most part at Surbiton, Surrey, but in 1877 moved to London, where he died, at his home, 56 Montague Square, on 17 December 1879. He was buried in the Marylebone cemetery at East Finchley. Nias was an able, resourceful, and determined officer. His promotions were secured on merit, and he was sensitive of his reputation.

J. K. LAUGHTON, *rev.* ANDREW LAMBERT

Sources A. Parry, *Parry of the Arctic* (1963) • G. S. Graham, *The China station: war and diplomacy, 1830–1860* (1978) • O'Byrne, *Naval biog. dict.* • private information (*c.*1894) • C. Ware, *The bomb vessel: shore bombardment ships of the age of sail* (1994) • Boase, *Mod. Eng. biog.* • *CGPLA Eng. & Wales* (1880)
Archives NMM, corresp. and papers
Likenesses ambrotype photograph, NPG • oils (after photograph by Maull & Co.), NPG
Wealth at death under £12,000: probate, 12 Jan 1880, *CGPLA Eng. & Wales*

Niccols, Richard (1583/4–1616), poet and literary editor, was, according to Anthony Wood, born in London, of genteel parents. He may have been the son of Richard Niccols (*d.* 1613), a lawyer of the Inner Temple, who wrote *A Day Starre for Darke Wandring Soules: Shewing the Light by a Christian Controversie*, published posthumously in 1613, the year of his death.

Niccols sailed with the earl of Nottingham as part of the fleet of Robert Devereux, second earl of Essex, which captured Cadiz in 1597. He alludes to the event in his poetry, referring to a dove that settled on the mainyard of the admiral's ship, symbolizing 'peace to the fleet, but to the foes, distress' ('England's Eliza' in *A Mirror for Magistrates*, 1610, 861). Niccols matriculated at Magdalen College, Oxford, on 26 November 1602, aged eighteen, but transferred to Magdalen Hall, where he obtained a BA on 20 May 1606. According to Wood he was 'numbered among the ingenious persons of the university' (Wood, *Ath. Oxon.*, 2.166). He appears to have moved to London and followed an unspecified profession while writing poetry for a variety of patrons. These included the families of the earl of Nottingham, Sir Thomas Wroth, and James Hay, earl of Carlisle, though how close Niccols was to any of them or how substantially they supported his work is a matter of conjecture. A number of Niccols's works are dedicated to Hay's wife, Honor, whose death he laments in *Monodia, or, Walthams Complaint* (1615).

Niccols is generally considered to have been a skilful and fluent poet rather than an original writer. He wrote a number of complaints and elegies, lamenting the recently deceased, and refers in one of his last works to the 'mournful muse' that inspired him (*Sir Thomas Overburies Vision*, 1616). His work shows a considerable debt to Edmund Spenser and, to a lesser extent, to Michael Drayton. In his first poem, *Expicedium: a funeral oration, upon the death of the late deceased princesse of famous memorye, Elizabeth* (1603), written while he was still an undergraduate, Niccols expresses his sorrow at the absence of Colin Clout, now that his queen is dead, a reference to Spenser's own death (1599) through the use of one of Spenser's most important poetic personae. The posthumously published *The Beggers Ape* (1627) is a beast fable that clearly imitates Spenser's *Mother Hubberds Tale*. *The Cuckow* (1607), dedicated to Sir Thomas Wroth, appears to owe much to Drayton's recently published poem *The Owl* (1604).

Niccols also had an eye for historical detail and accurate reporting. The *Expicedium* contains a detailed description of those present at Queen Elizabeth's funeral. *London artillery, briefly containing the noble practise of that wothie societie: with the moderne and ancient martiall exercises, natures of armes, vertue of magistrates, antiquitie, glorie and chronography of this honourable cittie* (1616), dedicated to John Jolles, lord mayor of London, appears to have been written after Prince Charles had reviewed the volunteers of London in the artillery ground. It consists of a versified history of London's defences, and owes much to the principal Elizabethan historians William Camden, John Stow, and Raphael Holinshed.

Niccols's most ambitious project was his re-editing of *A Mirror for Magistrates*, one of the most widely read and frequently reprinted literary works of the late sixteenth century. Niccols collated the previous editions of William Baldwin, Thomas Blenerhasset, and John Higgins, basing his 1610 edition on John Higgins's edition of 1587. Niccols rearranged all the poems in historical order, starting with those dealing with ancient British kings and finishing with one on Elizabeth—'England's Eliza'—which he wrote himself. He omitted four poems, mainly on Scottish subjects, from earlier editions: Baldwin's 'James I of Scotland', Francis Segar's 'Richard, Duke of Gloucester', 'James IV of Scotland', and the 'Battle of Flodden Field'. He altered the rhythm and style of many of the poems to fit in with his perception of contemporary poetic standards, and corrected some historical inaccuracies, as he noted in his preface.

Niccols added a number of his own poems at the end of the volume, under the general title 'A winter nights vision, being an addition of such princes especially famous, who were exempted in the former historie'. Dedicated to the earl of Nottingham this consisted of an induction, followed by the lives of King Arthur, Edmund Ironside, Prince Alfred, Godwin, earl of Kent, Robert Curthoise, duke of Normandy, Richard I, King John, Edward II, Edward V, Richard, duke of York, and Richard III. Part 4, dedicated to Elizabeth Clere, wife of Sir Francis Clere, opens with an induction paying tribute to Spenser, and the long poem listing Elizabeth's achievements, 'England's Eliza'. Niccols claimed that he wrote the induction at Greenwich in August 1603, where he had fled to escape the plague. The edition was reprinted in 1619 and in 1628.

Niccols also wrote *The Three Sisters Teares, Shed at the Late Solemne Funerals of the Royall Deceased Henry* (1613), dedicated to Lady Honor Hay, which has the three daughters of Albion—Angela, Albana, and Cambera—lamenting the untimely demise of a lost future leader; *The Furies, with Vertues Encomium* (1614), a collection of epigrams—a fashionable genre in the early 1600s—dedicated to a number of courtiers, including Sir Robert Wroth, Lady Honor Hay, and Lady Charatie Howard, daughter-in-law of the earl of Nottingham; and *Sir Thomas Overburies Vision* (1616), another complaint, in which the ghost of Sir Thomas Overbury, murdered in the Tower of London in 1613, points the finger at his murderer, Lady Essex, and regrets his own sinful life (the poem resembles many in Niccols's edition of *A Mirror for Magistrates*). A play, 'The Twynnes Tragedy', was entered in the Stationers' Register on 15 February 1611 and said to be 'by Niccolls', but it does not seem to have been published. Niccols is believed to have died in 1616.   ANDREW HADFIELD

Sources Wood, *Ath. Oxon.*, new edn, 2.166–8 · Foster, *Alum. Oxon.*, 1500–1714 [Richard Niccols] · STC, 1475–1640, 186 · BL cat., 236.134–5 · J. P. Collier, ed., *A bibliographical and critical account of the rarest books in the English language*, 1 (1865), 32–41 · T. Warton, *The history of English poetry*, rev. edn, ed. R. Price, 4 vols. (1824), vol. 4, pp. 86–94 · *Mirror for magistrates*, ed. J. Haslewood, 3 vols. (1815), 1.xliv–xlvi · R. Niccols, *Sir Thomas Overburies vision*, ed. J. Maidment (1873) · L. B. Campbell, ed., *Parts added to 'A mirror for magistrates'* (1946), 10–11 · DNB · Arber, *Regs. Stationers*, 3.478 · E. K. Chambers, *The Elizabethan stage*, 4 vols. (1923), vol. 3

NicDhòmhnaill [MacDonald], **Sìleas** [Sìleas nighean Mhic Raghnaill] (*c.*1660–*c.*1729), Scottish Gaelic poet, was daughter of Gilleasbaig (*d.* 1682), chief of the MacDonalds of Keppoch in Lochaber (Mac Mhic Raghnaill), and his wife, who has been identified as Mary MacMartin of the Letterfinlay family. Sìleas was thus a sister of Colla nam Bò, the next Mac Mhic Raghnaill (*d. c.*1723). She was married in 1685 to Alexander Gordon of Camdell (*d.* 1720), near Tomintoul in Banffshire, who was factor for the Lochaber lands of the Gordons of Huntly. She doubtless went to live in Gordon country then and in 1700 they acquired Beldorney Castle, near Dufftown. It seems clear that by her marriage Sìleas was able to maintain a social standing consistent with her aristocratic highland origin. There were at least five sons and three daughters of the marriage. Sìleas is perhaps best known as the Gaelic poet of the Jacobite rising of 1715, and from her extant corpus of twenty-three songs (they are not mere poems) six are primarily concerned with that event, but she has probably attracted some spurious ascriptions, since all of her extant works have depended, to various extents, on the oral tradition for survival. Some of the six (and of the twenty-three) may therefore not be her work at all, so that she cannot really be called a political poet. Instead it is likely that her high social standing and her eastern location, together with the passage of time, all helped her to develop as a new kind of songmaker in Gaelic, one not thematically limited to 'Clan and politics', D. S. Thomson's classic markers for the work of the seventeenth-century Gaelic poets (Thomson, 'Clan and politics', 116). Her songs, as far as is known, all date from after 1700 and her range of themes is notably wider than that of her predecessors. While she does not expand into nature poetry or love poetry (these were to flourish famously in Gaelic after her death), she does bring much that is new to the song tradition, including religious song, very much in the Roman Catholic dogmatic mould, and related comment on sexual mores. Her political songs on the 'Fifteen do reflect the simple Jacobite view one expects from MacDonald poets, and the presence of old conventions is clear to see. But a new extension of the idea of song as *brosnachadh*, incitement to battle, arises among Gaelic poets as the 1715 campaign gets under way. That is when the type of song sometimes called 'Oran nam fineachan Gaidhealach' ('the song of the highland clans') is first found, which some scholars see as a development of the age-old practice of listing a heroic subject's potential allies (Thomson, 'Political poetry', 192; MacInnes, 465). Songs of this new type are essentially lists of the main clans who might be expected to fight for the Stewarts, and as popular songs they could doubtless put heavy pressure on hesitant chiefs to lead their men out for James VIII (James Stuart). Both Sìleas and another MacDonald poet, Iain Dubh, composed rousing songs of this type for the 'Fifteen, so neither poet can really be credited with inventing the genre.

Sìleas makes a major contribution to the vast body of Gaelic encomium with her famous and popular song lamenting the death of Alasdair Dubh, the Glengarry chief, late in 1721. Even here, in this heroic lament where the hero is likened to the noblest of animals, the most valuable of stones, and the trees that were traditionally respected by Gaels, there are personal touches that show that Sìleas knew the man and loved him. Personal touches feature in other songs, as where she delights in her children or laments the deaths in 1720 of both her husband and daughter and, a little later, of a harper who had visited her house regularly, bringing music and news of her family in the west. It is probably in these more personal poems, for which she had few identifiable models in the heroic public poetry of her predecessors, that the modern reader will find her most approachable. Almost nothing is known of Sìleas's life after her husband's death, and that shortage of information may partly explain a number of traditions which have persisted about her religious life, including vaguely sinister trances and conversions. All that can really be said is that, while her death has been placed about 1729 on very little evidence, it is quite likely that she was buried at the ancient church of Mortlach, near Dufftown, where one of her songs relates that her husband was buried.   COLM Ó BAOILL

Sources *Bàrdachd Shìlis na Ceapaich: poems and songs by Sìleas Mac-Donald, c.1660–c.1729*, ed. C. Ó Baoill (1972) · K. Macdonald, ed., 'Unpublished verse by Sìlis Ni Mhic Raghnaill na Ceapaich', *Celtic studies: essays in memory of Angus Matheson, 1912–1962*, ed. J. Carney and D. Greene (1968), 76–87 · D. S. Thomson, 'Clan and politics', *An introduction to Gaelic poetry* (1974), 116–55 · J. MacInnes, 'The panegyric code in Gaelic poetry and its historical background', *Transactions of the Gaelic Society of Inverness*, 50 (1976–8), 435–98 · D. Thomson, 'Alasdair mac Mhaighstir Alasdair's political poetry', *Transactions of the Gaelic Society of Inverness*, 56 (1988–90), 185–213 · C. Fraser-Mackintosh, *Antiquarian notes: a series of papers regarding families and places in the highlands* (1865)

Ní Chearbhaill, Mairgréag [Margaret O'Carroll] (*d.* 1451), celebrated hostess, was the daughter of Tadhg Ó Cearbhaill (*d.* 1407), chief of Éile, and married An Calbhach Ó Conchobhair Failghe (*d.* 1458), chief of Uíbh Fhailghe. In 1433, a year of general shortage, she gave two great feasts which earned her the nickname Mairgréag an Einigh ('Margaret of the Hospitality'), one on 26 March at Killeigh, Offaly, and the other on 15 August at Rathangan, Kildare, at opposite ends of her husband's territory, to which were invited 2700 members of the Irish learned families of bardic poets, historians, and musicians, 'besides gamesters and poore men'. On 26 March she also presented two golden chalices to the church at Killeigh and arranged for the fosterage of two orphans. She oversaw that occasion from the battlements of the church, dressed in cloth of gold, surrounded by her retainers, her judges and clergy, with her husband below on horseback, marshalling the guests. In 1445 Mairgréag joined a party of Irish and Anglo-Irish aristocrats on a pilgrimage to Santiago de Compostela. On her return she negotiated an exchange of prisoners with the Anglo-Irish government without her husband's permission in order to secure the release of the son of one of her fellow pilgrims and others. She herself had five sons, Conn (*d.* 1440), Cathal (*d.* 1448), Feidhlim (*d.* 1451), Brian (*d.* 1452), and Tadhg (*d.* 1471); she also had two daughters, Mór (*d.* 1452), wife of MacWilliam of Clanricarde, and Fionnghuala (*d.* 1493), who married first Niall Garbh Ó Domhnaill (*d.* 1439), king of Tír Conaill, and second Aodh Buidhe Ó Néill (*d.* 1444), before retiring to become an Augustinian canoness at Killeigh. Extremely pious herself, Mairgréag commissioned the making of roads, bridges, churches, and missals 'to serve God and her soule', before dying of breast cancer in 1451.

KATHARINE SIMMS

Sources L. Fitzpatrick, 'Mairgréag an-Einigh Ó Cearthaill "the best of the women of the Gaedhil"', *Journal of the Kildare Archaeological Society*, 18 (1992–3), 20–38 · J. O'Donovan, ed., 'The annals of Ireland… by MacFirbis', *Miscellany of the Irish Archaeological Society*, 1 (1846), 198–302 · *AFM*, vol. 4 · A. M. Freeman, ed. and trans., *Annála Connacht / The annals of Connacht* (1944); repr. (1970) · O. Bergin, *Irish bardic poetry* (1970), 156–7, 285

Nichol, Elizabeth Pease [*née* Elizabeth Pease] (**1807–1897**), slavery abolitionist and radical, was born on 5 January 1807 in Darlington, the second of the two children of Joseph Pease (1772–1846), wool manufacturer, and his first wife, Elizabeth (1779–1824), daughter of John Beaumont, chemist, of Holborn, London, and his wife, Mary. The Peases were members of one of the great Quaker industrialist families of the nineteenth century, who played a leading role in philanthropic and humanitarian movements.

Elizabeth Pease was educated at a local school and then by a governess, but her studies were disrupted by nursing her sick mother. She suffered from poor health during her early adulthood, which was exacerbated by grief at the deaths of her parents. She did not marry until she was in her mid-forties, when she finally left the Pease family home at Feethams Mansion in Darlington. Her husband, whom she married on 6 July 1853, was Dr John Pringle

*Nichol (1804–1859), regius professor of astronomy at the University of Glasgow. He was a Presbyterian, and Elizabeth was disowned by the Society of Friends for 'marrying out'. She settled in Glasgow with her husband; on his death in 1859 she moved to Edinburgh, where she lived for the rest of her life.

Before and after her marriage Elizabeth Pease Nichol was involved in a wide variety of movements for radical reform, but she played particularly important roles in the anti-slavery, feminist, and anti-vivisection campaigns. From the mid-1830s to the mid-1860s her deepest involvement was with anti-slavery activities. She joined other women campaigning in 1837–8 for the complete emancipation of slaves in the British West Indies, and she became a central figure in the forging of a transatlantic abolitionist network from 1836 onwards. She fostered links between female anti-slavery societies in Britain and the United States, and she became one of the leading British promoters of the radical wing of the movement which was led by William Lloyd Garrison. She engaged in an extensive correspondence with American abolitionists, discussing the wide range of radical reforms which she actively supported: anti-slavery, the peace movement, temperance, the Anti-Corn Law League, Chartism, Italian and Hungarian nationalism and republicanism, and home rule for Ireland. She continued her anti-slavery activities into the mid-1860s, when she was president of the Edinburgh Ladies' Emancipation Society. She also campaigned against racial discrimination, opposing attempts at racial segregation among American Quakers and helping to set up the Society for the Furtherance of Human Brotherhood in the 1880s. She also played a vital 'behind-the-scenes' role in the British India Society, formed by her father in 1839 to campaign against debt bondage, and acted as her father's secretary and assistant, collecting information, writing leaflets and articles for the provincial press, advising the society's travelling lecturer, and encouraging ladies' anti-slavery societies to support the cause.

First alerted to the 'woman question' by American abolitionists in the 1830s, from the 1860s Elizabeth Pease Nichol became involved in the wide spectrum of feminist campaigns. She was a member of the executive committee of the Ladies' National Association, founded in 1870, which campaigned for the repeal of the Contagious Diseases Acts, and she was also a member of the committee of the Edinburgh Women's Suffrage Society, founded in 1867. In addition she was involved in promoting female education: she publicly supported women's struggle to gain medical training at Edinburgh University; she became a member of the Edinburgh committee of the Ladies' Educational Association, established in 1867; and she was elected as a member of the first school board, set up in Scotland in 1873 after the passage of the Education Act. Elizabeth Pease Nichol also worked against cruelty to animals, and from 1875 onwards this became the main focus of her activity. As a leader of the campaign against vivisection, she set up a Scottish branch of the anti-

vivisection society formed in London by Frances Power Cobbe (1822–1904).

Elizabeth Pease Nichol, with her intense blue eyes, simple dress, and Quaker bonnet, was an earnest, direct, independent-minded, and principled individual, who had an internationalist outlook and a wide circle of like-minded friends. She was also self-deprecating, and overcame her reluctance to speak in public only towards the end of her long career as a campaigner. She died on 3 February 1897 at her home, Huntly Lodge, Merchiston, Edinburgh, and was buried on 8 February alongside her husband in Grange cemetery, Edinburgh.

CLARE MIDGLEY

Sources A. M. Stoddart, *Elizabeth Pease Nichol* (1899) · C. Taylor, *British and American abolitionists: an episode in transatlantic understanding* (1974) · J. H. Bell, *British folks and British India fifty years ago: Joseph Pease and his contemporaries* [1891] · *The letters of William Lloyd Garrison*, ed. W. M. Merrill and L. Ruchames, 2–6 (1971–81) · G. H. Barnes and D. L. Dumond, eds., *Letters of Theodore Dwight Weld, Angelina Grimké Weld and Sarah Grimké, 1822–44*, 2 vols. (1934) · C. Midgley, *Women against slavery: the British campaigns, 1780–1870* (1992) · *Digest registers of births, marriages and burials for England and Wales, c.1650–1837* [1992] [Durham quarterly meeting, births digest; microfilm] · E. L. Rasor, 'Nichol, Elizabeth Pease', *BDMBR*, vol. 2 · C. Blake, *The charge of the parasols* (1990), 104, 130, 132, 168
Archives Boston PL, anti-slavery collection
Likenesses portraits, 1852–94, repro. in Stoddart, *Elizabeth Pease Nichol*
Wealth at death £15,383 4s. 4d.: confirmation, 18 March 1897, CCI · £25: additional estate, 11 Sept 1907, CCI

Nichol, John (1833–1894), literary scholar and writer, was born on 8 September 1833 at Montrose, Forfarshire, the only son of the rector of Montrose Academy and astronomer, John Pringle *Nichol (1804–1859), and his first wife, Jane Tullis (1809–1850). In 1836 the family moved to Glasgow, on John Pringle Nichol's appointment to the regius chair of astronomy at the university. His father's wide acquaintance, and the salon he kept at the observatory after 1841, exposed John Nichol at an early age to an impressive network of contacts, including De Quincey and John Stuart Mill. From 1842 to 1847 he attended the Western Academy, an experimental school where 'no child was ever flogged or constrained' (Knight, 53). Nichol thought little of it, and indeed seems to have disliked school, where he suffered from bullying. During 1845–6 he attended natural history classes in Glasgow University, and, after a year's boarding at Kelso grammar school, entered the university on a regular basis in 1848, his mind already strongly developed through society and travel (including a visit to Germany). At Glasgow, where he was taught by Robert Buchanan, he took a leading role in the Liberal cause and rectorial politics, and made the acquaintance of John Service, Henry Crosskey, and Edward Caird, the future master of Balliol. While at Glasgow, Nichol printed a collection of poetry, *Leaves* (1852), for private circulation, and edited the *Glasgow University Album* (1854), which was brought to the attention of Tennyson, De Quincey, and Sydney Dobell. Nichol's lifelong friendship with Dobell—to whose *Poems* (1875) and *Thoughts on Art, Philosophy and Religion* (1876) he contributed introductions, and to the latter a memoir—dated from a

John Nichol (1833–1894), by Sir William Quiller Orchardson, 1891

request to Dobell for a poem for the *Album*, which Nichol, with characteristic forthrightness, rejected on receipt.

In 1850 Nichol's mother, to whom he was devoted, died, and on 6 July 1853 his father married Elizabeth Pease (1807–1897), of Darlington, daughter of Joseph Pease. Elizabeth *Nichol was an ardent anti-slavery campaigner. In 1855 Nichol entered Balliol College, Oxford, where in the following year he was appointed to one of the Snell exhibitions awarded annually since the seventeenth century to outstanding students from Glasgow University. He graduated in 1859 with a first in Greats, but did not proceed MA until 1874, as his scepticism prevented him from taking the tests of religious orthodoxy while they were still in force. Initially impressed, Nichol conceived a lifelong ambivalence towards Oxford, veering from bitterness to admiration, which coloured and was coloured by his experience in the Scottish university system. None the less, he made lasting friendships, with among others Benjamin Jowett and Nichol's fellow Snell exhibitioner George Luke, who was tragically drowned in 1862. Together with Thomas Hill Green, Albert Venn Dicey, and Algernon Charles Swinburne (Walter Pater was among those who joined later), Nichol founded a reading society, Old Mortality, in which his fully formed characteristics as a thinker were displayed. His radicalism and personal knowledge of Giuseppe Mazzini (whom, together with Lajos Kossuth, his father knew) were influential on Swinburne, though, despite the later implications of Edmund Gosse and others, there is no indication that Nichol, who himself kept to a very strict regimen, was responsible for any of the poet's more colourful habits.

Shortly after Nichol took his degree his father died, on 19 September 1859, at the age of fifty-five. Barred from a fellowship, owing to his unwillingness to accept the Thirty-Nine Articles, and possibly in deference to a paternal wish that he go to the bar, Nichol was admitted to Gray's Inn on 12 November (though he appears never to have been called); meanwhile he remained a coach at Oxford. However, he was already in pursuit of a Scottish chair, and to this end his uncle, the publisher James Nichol, issued *Fragments of Criticism* (1859) for private circulation. It contains notable assessments of Carlyle and Browning, whose work Nichol was at the forefront of popularizing. In December he was a candidate for the chair of logic and English literature at St Andrews, but the appointment went to John Veitch, who subsequently also deprived Nichol of the logic and rhetoric chair at Glasgow.

On 10 April 1861 Nichol married Jane Stuart Bell (d. 1894), eldest daughter of Henry Glassford *Bell, advocate and later sheriff of Lanarkshire, and his first wife, Sophia Stewart. Nichol was fortunate in his wife, who provided him with great support throughout his career. They had three children. Nichol's son, Pringle (also a Snell exhibitioner), distressed his father by becoming a Roman Catholic; he developed something of a penchant for French literature, publishing a book on Victor Hugo. Henrietta and Lucy were the two daughters: Lucy married Professor A. A. Jack of Aberdeen.

In 1862 Nichol was elected and appointed by the crown to the new regius chair of English literature at Glasgow University, where he stayed until his early retirement in 1889. An intense if nervous man with a patriarchal Victorian beard, Nichol was, on the ample evidence of contemporary reports, an inspirational and magnetic lecturer, who was highly influential in developing the reputation of English literature as a subject. At Jowett's request he redelivered two of his 1868–9 courses at Oxford. He also prepared the way for the development of university extension lectures with widespread extra-mural addresses throughout Scotland and in England, in which he displayed 'a singularly magnetic power of raising sympathy' (Knight, 196). Although Nichols was a supporter of the traditions of Scottish student debating (in his early days at Glasgow, he attended the Dialectic Society, which in turn founded Glasgow University Union in 1885), his cosmopolitan experience led him to distrust the Scottish generalist tradition as set against the 'refinement, taste and skill' of Oxford (Davie, 83). His interest in contemporary educational debate is borne witness to in his *Address on National Education* (1869) and *Scotch University Reform* (1888). In 1865, he visited the United States, which made a profound impression on him, and no doubt led to his *American Literature* (1882). In 1867, probably during a lull in the activities of the Edinburgh-based Speculative Society, Nichol helped to found the New Speculative Society, meeting in both Edinburgh and Glasgow (there was later a St Andrews branch). In other respects, too, Nichol was still at the heart of a circle of eminence, playing host at Glasgow to Henry Wadsworth Longfellow, W. M. Rossetti, Ford Madox

Brown, William Morris, Jowett, and Swinburne, among others. In 1873 St Andrews conferred on him the honorary degree of LLD.

The grind of his teaching duties, which he took very conscientiously, combined with years of hard work, a tendency to ill health, and perhaps a native restlessness, began to dispose Nichol to leave Glasgow. In 1872, after some debate, he withdrew his name as a candidate for the chair of logic at Oxford. In 1885 he became a candidate for the newly established Merton chair at Oxford, appointment to which would have cut his lecturing load by three-quarters: but he was not appointed. Such repeated disappointments combined with his temperament and a misplaced belief in his abilities as a poet to make Nichol bitter. His plain speaking naturally won him enemies as well as friends, while his early radicalism and religious scepticism added fuel to that fire. He was an early supporter of the emancipation of women and (on the continent at least) republicanism; his politics drifted towards the Liberal Unionist right as he aged, but he seems never to have lost his doubts of conventional Christianity. He continued to enjoy recognition (in 1881, Swinburne addressed two sonnets to him), but without crystallizing his early promise. In 1889, weary with 'this perpetual teaching of roughs, and wrangling with senates' (Knight, 223), Nichol resigned his chair, A. C. Bradley being appointed in his stead.

After taking some time to travel, Nichol and his wife moved to London in 1890, where they renewed old acquaintances, including that of Jowett, whom Nichol met for the last time in September 1893. His portrait was presented at Glasgow University on 25 November 1891, and a window in the university's Bute Hall was dedicated to him. While in London, Nichol made very few public appearances, though he did make some new friends, among them Leslie Stephen. His ill health and infirmity tended to increase, and after the death of his wife on 9 January 1894 he appeared to have little to live for. Symptoms developing from a chill encountered small resistance, and John Nichol died at his home, 11 Stafford Terrace, Kensington, London, on 11 October 1894. In accordance with his wishes, he was cremated at Woking on 15 October, and the Anglican service was read. His ashes were placed near to his wife in Grange cemetery, Edinburgh.

Nichol's lasting reputation is chiefly as a figure who was important and influential in his day, and whose period cannot be understood without him. None of his eighteen books is widely remembered, though his reputation as a critic and reviewer did not fall far short of that he once held as a teacher and inspirer. His poetry, never universally admired, has now faded altogether. Neither *Hannibal* (1873) nor *The Death of Themistocles and other Poems* (1881) displays a talent for the long poem beyond that of a learned and educated man of his day, and his shorter poems are lightweight and show little development: his translations from the Latin poets and the Spenserian stanzas of his 'Ailsa Craig' alike seem clumsy and over-literary. Among Nichol's critical productions, his *English Composition* (1879)

is a powerful and precise textbook which still has its merits, and *A Sketch of the Early History of the Scottish Poets* (1871), *American Literature* (1882; 2nd edn, 1885), *Robert Burns* (1882), and *Carlyle* (1892) were innovative and show the breadth of Nichol's interests. His trenchant views, such as that 'Criticism … was but an indirect method of expressing one's own opinions' (Knight, 184) and that 'the History and Literature of every country are necessary comments on each other, and cannot be studied altogether apart' (Horner, 129), display the philosophic common sense of the tradition he exemplified, which should still commend itself to his successors in the discipline he did so much to promote.   MURRAY G. H. PITTOCK

Sources W. A. Knight, *Memoir of John Nichol, professor of English literature in the University of Glasgow* (1896) · R. D. Macleod, 'John Nichol: friend of Swinburne', U. Glas. L., GEN 1477 · G. E. Davie, *The democratic intellect: Scotland and her universities in the nineteenth century*, 2nd edn (1964) · W. B. Horner, *Nineteenth-century Scottish rhetoric* (1993) · DNB · CGPLA Eng. & Wales (1894)
Archives U. Glas. L. | BL, letters to T. H. S. Escott, Add. MS 58788 · BL, corresp. with Macmillans, Add. MS 55012 · BL, letters to Algernon Swinburne, Ashley MSS 5752, A295, A1941 · BL, letters to Theodore Watts-Dunton, Ashley MSS 5752, A 1990 · Mitchell L., Glas., corresp. with Algernon Swinburne, printed material and papers relating to Nichol [copies] · NL Scot., letters to Blackwoods
Likenesses group portrait, photograph, *c.*1851–1859, NPG · photographs, 1869–71, repro. in Knight, *Memoir of John Nichol* · W. Q. Orchardson, oils, 1891, Hunterian Museum and Art Gallery, Glasgow [*see illus.*]
Wealth at death £13,535 3*s.* 11*d.*: confirmation, 16 Nov 1894, CCI

Nichol, John Pringle (1804–1859), astronomer and political economist, was the eldest of seven children of John Nichol, a farmer from Northumberland, and Jane Forbes of Ellon, Aberdeenshire. Born on 13 January 1804 at Huntlyhill, Forfarshire, 4 miles north-east of Brechin, he was educated at Brechin grammar school, then, from 1818 to 1822, at King's College, Aberdeen; he did not graduate, but King's awarded him an honorary MA in 1857. During one of his vacations, at the age of seventeen, he was schoolmaster at Dun, and he later taught in Cupar, Hawick, and Montrose. At the same time he continued to study theology and is said to have been licensed as a minister.

While he was at Cupar the *Fife Herald* said that Nichol's excellent teaching in geography would be improved if he omitted discussion of political economy. This subject was, none the less, to preoccupy him for the next ten years, during which he wrote extensively for periodicals (as well as, in *Tait's Edinburgh Magazine* in 1833, advocating for the first time the nebular hypothesis which was to dominate his later writing). He entered into correspondence with John Stuart Mill, who became a lifelong friend. James Mill and Nassau Senior recommended him to succeed Jean-Baptiste Say as professor of political economy at the Collège de France. He was also a friend and supporter of George Combe, and of phrenology; in 1835 he worked with Combe to promote the public teaching of science in Edinburgh. On 1 August 1831 Nichol married Jane Tullis (1809–1850), daughter of Robert Tullis (1775–1831), printer and paper maker of Cupar and proprietor of the radical *Fife Herald*. Their elder child became Professor John

*Nichol, and the younger, Agnes, married William Jack, professor of mathematics at Glasgow.

Nichol was appointed regius professor of astronomy at the University of Glasgow in 1836, and was given an honorary LLD by the university the following year. He was elected a fellow of the Royal Society of Edinburgh in 1836. When William Meikleham, professor of natural philosophy, was ill in 1838–40, Nichol helped to give his lectures. His teaching included the discoveries of contemporary French scientists, and he was thus responsible for introducing Fourier's work on heat to the young William Thomson, who later praised Nichol's inspiring enthusiasm for the great French school of mathematical physics. When Meikleham died in 1846, Nichol encouraged curriculum reform and helped to engineer Thomson's appointment to the chair.

Nichol determined to move the university observatory from the Old College to a site 5 miles west of Glasgow. A charismatic lecturer, in addition to four lectures per week on applied astronomy to meet the need of men trained in engineering to be able to survey, he gave popular lectures which stimulated formation of an astronomical association which raised a public subscription for the new Horselethill observatory; completed in 1841, the observatory became his family home four years later. Nichol spent the summer of 1840 travelling on the continent with his family and visiting Munich, where he bought instruments for the observatory. By 1843 he had spent £700 without consulting his colleagues, and in addition relations were strained when an inspection of the university's instruments revealed that some had been lent to Lord Rosse, though part of the difficulty stemmed from Nichol's colleagues' Conservative politics. By 1844 the association was in debt for more than it had raised, and the university took it over. Founding the observatory was Nichol's great success, but it proved beyond his skills to bring the new Ertel meridian circle into operation. Lecturing anyway prevented much research, and he published only two astronomical papers, in 1844 and 1855, both about the moon. Apparently a poor administrator, he was dismissed by the astronomer royal, George Airy, and by Professor David Forbes as a mere showman who had high aspirations and spent enormous sums on prestige projects with no permanent result. Yet he did much to spread astronomical knowledge, and his successor, Robert Grant (1814–1892), put the instruments to excellent use.

In his first years in Glasgow, Nichol began to write popular accounts of contemporary astronomy. *Views of the Architecture of the Heavens* (1837), concerned with the origins of the universe, was like most of his work written in enthusiastic, even lavish, language. With Mill and the philosophical radicals he believed in a science of progress: progress could be seen both in the political or psychological world and in the physical world. The most dramatic example of the latter was the nebular hypothesis, which suggested that the solar system had been formed by the action of natural law upon a rotating and condensing gaseous nebula. As early as October 1833 in *Tait's Edinburgh Magazine* (4, 1833, 57–64) he cited the theory and thus laid heavy stress on the earl of Rosse's detection of the spiral structure of certain nebulae, which indicated that they were rotating; he also stressed the 'true nebulosity' of others such as the Orion nebula, which appeared to suggest that they consisted of condensing gas. Many thought him to be the author of the anonymous *Vestiges of Creation* (1844) which proved to have been written by Robert Chambers.

An anonymous reviewer of Nicol's *System of the World* (1846) pointed out 'his very liberal and very unconsidered use of words such as inconceivable, infinite, eternal … we find them applied to things which are not only quite measurable, but which have been measured' (*British Quarterly Review*, 6, 1847, 26). The same observation could be made of his later popularizations, *The Stellar Universe* (1847), *The Planetary System* (1848), and *The Planet Neptune* (1855), which are said to have been written in order to clear debts incurred in equipping the observatory. Though in declining health (his strength had been sapped by an enormous quantity of public lectures, including a tour in the United States in 1847–8), he prepared the enormous *Cyclopaedia of the Physical Sciences* (1857).

Nichol's first wife died in 1850 and on 6 July 1853 he married, at an Independent chapel in Darlington, Elizabeth (1807–1897) [see Nichol, Elizabeth Pease], daughter of Joseph Pease of Feethams, Darlington. Her uncle called it 'a union very much advised against and disapproved by all her friends' (*Diaries of Edward Pease*, 305–6). Their objections were that Nichol was not a Quaker, and that he was a 'designing' man—they may have thought that he had designs on the family's wealth. Nichol remained a lifelong radical. In 1847 he wrote an introduction for Joseph Willm's *Education of the People*, in which he called for universal education. The Hungarian patriot Lajos Kossuth, touring Britain, stayed at the observatory in 1854. In 1857 Nichol was asked to stand as the Liberal candidate for Glasgow, but declined. He died of congestion of the brain at Glenburn House, Rothesay, Isle of Bute, on 19 September 1859 and was buried five days later in the Grange cemetery, Edinburgh. JOHN BURNETT

Sources J. MacLehose, ed., *Memoirs and portraits of one hundred Glasgow men who have died during the last thirty years*, 2 (1886) • *Monthly Notices of the Royal Astronomical Society*, 19 (1858–9), 141 • *Monthly Notices of the Royal Astronomical Society*, 20 (1859–60), 131 • S. Schaffer, 'The nebular hypothesis and the science of progress', *History, humanity and evolution*, ed. J. R. Moore (1989), 131–54 • W. A. Knight, *Memoir of John Nichol, professor of English literature in the University of Glasgow* (1896) • J. Coutts, *A history of the University of Glasgow* (1909) • *The diaries of Edward Pease: the father of English railways*, ed. A. E. Pease (1907) • P. J. Anderson, ed., *Roll of alumni in arts of the University and King's College of Aberdeen, 1596–1860* (1900) • W. Stewart, ed., *University of Glasgow, old and new* (1891) • *The Times* (23 Sept 1859), 10b • d. cert. • A. M. Stoddart, *Elizabeth Pease Nichol* (1899) • *DNB*

Archives ICL, letters to Sir Andrew Ramsay • NL Scot., corresp. with George Combe • U. St Andr., corresp. with James David Forbes

Likenesses woodcut?, c.1840, repro. in MacLehose, ed., *Memoirs*, facing p. 249

Wealth at death £1934 15s. 6d.: confirmation, 6 Jan 1860, NA Scot., SC 36/48/45/671–2

Nichol [*née* Wallhead], **Muriel Edith** (1893–1983), politician, was born on 2 February 1893 at South Oak Lane, Fulshaw, Wilmslow, Cheshire, daughter of Richard Christopher Wallhead (later known as Richard Collingham Wallhead; 1869–1934) and his wife, Ellen Starnes. Her father, a journeyman house painter at the time of her birth, was an Independent Labour Party (ILP) activist who became a journalist and lecturer, and was MP for the Merthyr division of Merthyr Tudful from 1922 until 1934.

Muriel Wallhead, who received a secondary education, was an active ILP member and also an organizer and speaker for the National Union of Women's Suffrage Societies (1913–14). She became secretary of the Manchester and Salford ILP federation (1914–16) and was a propagandist in the anti-war crusade of the party, during which her father was imprisoned under the Defence of the Realm Act. At the time of her marriage, at Chorlton register office on 3 August 1920, she was employed as a welfare supervisor.

Her husband, James Nichol MA, of Bradford, the son of James Moody Nichol, an engineer's pattern maker, was a schoolteacher. Katharine Bruce Glasier, an original ILP member and founder of the Women's Labour League, was a witness to the marriage. In 1922 the Nichols moved to Welwyn Garden City as 'pioneers' and James Nichol became headmaster of the town's grammar school. They had one son.

In 1935 Muriel Wallhead Nichol, as she was known in her national political career, fought in the general election for the seat of Bradford North, but was defeated. She became involved in local politics as a member of the Welwyn Garden City urban district council from 1937 to 1945 and was chairman in 1943–4. She was appointed a justice of the peace in 1944 and remained on the bench for twenty-four years. She was active in the co-operative movement, serving on the education committee of the St Albans Co-operative Society. During the war she was chairman of the Women's Co-operative Guild's food control committee and a lecturer to the armed forces.

In the general election of 1945, Muriel Wallhead Nichol won Bradford North. Her primary domestic interests were the welfare of children, education, and housing. Her maiden speech in November 1945 was on education. She argued that the 1944 Education Act did not satisfy socialist aspirations. She was not in favour of direct-grant schools and criticized the loss of freedom of the grammar schools. Throughout the parliament of 1945–50, she raised questions about numbers and salaries of teachers, supplies of textbooks, and state scholarships. She continued to champion the cause of the grammar school.

Muriel Nichol was the one woman appointed among a group of MPs who toured India in February 1946 to report on constitutional reform. She came back a staunch supporter of Indian independence. She was a member of the Parliamentary Union delegation to Norway in 1949 and of the kitchen committee of the House of Commons. She was appointed to the Curtis committee on the care of children, set up by the Home Office in 1945 to make recommendations for legislation. Muriel Nichol was in favour of adoption, followed by boarding out and foster homes as the best course for children in care, and advocated more training for social services. She spoke for the Children's Bill in 1948 and the Adoption Bill in 1949. She was interested in better housing and criticized, in the House of Commons debate on housing on 21 October 1946, the 'miserable and cheap' building of the inter-war years. A socialist government, she maintained, must build the best-quality housing for its 'own comrades and workpeople and those who fought in the war' (*Hansard 5C*, vol. 427, col. 1406). Her ILP roots resurfaced in her opposition to the government's national service bills, in April 1947 and December 1948, introducing peacetime conscription. In March 1947 she spoke in favour of the Women's Royal Air Force becoming a permanent element within the RAF.

After defeat at Bradford in the general election of 1950, Muriel Nichol unsuccessfully contested Stockport North in 1955. Thereafter, she returned to local concerns in Welwyn Garden City, although she continued to work for the Labour Party. When Lord Attlee visited Welwyn Garden City in 1960 he described her as an 'indefatigable fighter for the Labour cause' (recalled in the *Welwyn and Hatfield Times*, 24 June 1983). She remained active after the death of her husband in 1976 and chaired the governors of two local schools for several years.

Muriel Nichol died in Queen Elizabeth II Hospital in Welwyn Garden City on 28 May 1983 of bronchopneumonia. A special commemorative meeting was held by Welwyn Hatfield district council on 23 November 1983 to honour her memory, attended by the former prime minister James Callaghan, with whom she had worked in the 1945–50 parliament.   JANET E. GRENIER

Sources *The Labour who's who* (1927), 225 · *WWBMP*, vol. 4 · *Labour Woman* (Sept 1945), 174 · *Labour Woman* (Nov 1946), 244–5 · *Labour's election who's who*, Labour Party (1950), 74–5 · *Welwyn and Hatfield Times* (3 June 1983) · *Welwyn and Hatfield Times* (24 June 1983) · *Welwyn and Hatfield Times* (11 Nov 1983) · *Welwyn and Hatfield Times* (2 Dec 1983) · *Welwyn Hatfield Review* (10 Nov 1983), 15 · *Welwyn Hatfield District News* (Dec 1983), 1 · *Hansard 5C* (1945–50) · b. cert. · m. cert. · d. cert. · *WW* (1967)

Likenesses photograph, repro. in *Welwyn and Hatfield Times* (3 June 1983); (24 June 1983); (11 Nov 1983); (2 Dec 1983)

Wealth at death £40,231: probate, 11 Aug 1983, *CGPLA Eng. & Wales*

Nicholas. *See also* Nicolas.

Nicholas (*d.* 1124), prior of Worcester, is recorded in the *Vita Wulfstani* of William of Malmesbury as being of a noble English lineage. More recently it has been speculated that he may have been connected with the family of Earl Leofric of Mercia (*d.* 1057). His parents enjoyed a close relationship with Bishop Wulfstan of Worcester (*d.* 1095), who baptized Nicholas and treated him as his special protégé. He presumably entered the cathedral priory at Worcester at an early age, as the bishop himself took charge of Nicholas's education, and later sent him to Christ Church, Canterbury, to be trained in the reformed monastic discipline introduced by Archbishop Lanfranc (*d.* 1089). There is some evidence to suggest that his English name was

Æthelred (Ægelredus) because, according to Eadmer, there was a contemporary monk of this name at Canterbury, who served in the offices of sub-prior and precentor there, and who later held office at Worcester under Bishop Wulfstan.

The friendship between Nicholas, or Æthelred, and Eadmer is clearly documented. On at least two occasions Nicholas provided information for Eadmer's historical writings: in one letter he gave details of the descent of Edward, king and martyr (d. 978)—Eadmer named his source as Æthelred; in another he offered advice on York's claims to primacy over the Scottish bishops at the time of Eadmer's election to the see of St Andrews in 1120–21—here Eadmer acknowledged Prior Nicholas (he had been prior since at least 1116). These two instances reveal Nicholas's interest in and grasp of historical events; they imply that he had studied the available chronicles and probably consulted his fellow monks Florence and John, who were at this time gathering material for the Worcester chronicle. The letter of 1120–21, for example, makes it clear that Nicholas was well versed in the complex historical background to the claims made by the archbishops of York.

Nicholas also supplied biographical information to William of Malmesbury for his *Vita Wulfstani*; the events, both anecdotal and miraculous, that he probably recounted during a visit by William to Worcester were for the most part based on his own observations as witness or participant. With his recognized historical talent he may have been one of the monks responsible for the forgery of the charter *Altitonantis*, ostensibly recording the monastic foundation of Worcester in 964, but probably concocted c.1092.

Following the death of Bishop Theulf in 1123 Nicholas unsuccessfully exerted his influence and authority on behalf of the monks of the cathedral who, in their anxiety to avoid the appointment of another secular clerk, were trying to gain the right of free election of their bishop. His death on 24 June 1124 is recorded in the chronicle of John of Worcester. JOAN GREATREX

Sources The Vita Wulfstani of William of Malmesbury, ed. R. R. Darlington, CS, 3rd ser., 40 (1928) · Willelmi Malmesbiriensis monachi de gestis pontificum Anglorum libri quinque, ed. N. E. S. A. Hamilton, Rolls Series, 52 (1870) · W. Stubbs, ed., Memorials of St Dunstan, archbishop of Canterbury, Rolls Series, 63 (1874) · Fasti Angl., 1066–1300, [Monastic cathedrals] · E. Mason, St Wulfstan of Worcester, c.1008–1095 (1990) · [H. Wharton], ed., Anglia sacra, 2 (1691) · M. Brett, 'John of Worcester and his contemporaries', The writing of history in the middle ages: essays presented to Richard William Southern, ed. R. H. C. Davis, J. M. Wallace-Hadrill, and others (1981), 101–26

Nicholas (d. 1217), bishop of the Isles (a diocese also referred to as Man, Sodor, Sudreys, and Skye), is said by the chronicle of Man to have been a native of Argyll. Following the death of Bishop Michael, probably in 1203, Nicholas was elected to succeed him. He was presumably identical with the Koli (a Scandinavian abbreviation of Nicholas) recorded by Icelandic annals as having been consecrated bishop in 1210. The delay was probably due to the campaign by the archbishop of Trondheim to secure papal confirmation of his metropolitan rights over the sees which he claimed as his suffragans, of which Man was one. Nicholas himself is known to have attended a general council of the church, which must have been the Fourth Lateran Council (1215–16). On his return from this council, Nicholas acknowledged that, in accordance with the will of his predecessor, he had received from Abbot Nicholas the pontifical staff, ring, and vestments which Michael had deposited at Furness. He died in 1217 and was buried in the monastery at Bangor, Down. It has been suggested that he resigned, but chronicle evidence for his death at this time is supported by a papal letter of 9 November 1219, referring to Nicholas 'of blessed memory, bishop of the Isles' (Theiner, no. 31).

The succession to the see of Man then became the subject of lively dispute. Ragnvald, a nephew both of King Ragnvald (Reginald) of Man and of the latter's half-brother and rival for the throne, Olaf, was installed on the king's authority, in opposition to another **Nicholas** (d. in or after 1226), abbot of Furness, known as Nicholas of Meaux. This Nicholas had been elected by his monks, who by tradition had the privilege of electing the bishops of the Isles. It was probably he, rather than his predecessor and namesake, who confirmed the monks in this privilege, and who also secured the consent to his election of the monks of Rushen, the daughter house of Furness on Man, and of the archdeacon of Man. Nicholas had begun his career in monastic houses in the East Riding of Yorkshire. Having first become an Augustinian canon at Warter, he must then have transferred to the Cistercian order, first as a monk at Meaux Abbey near Hull, and later as abbot of Furness, being recorded as receiving benediction from the bishop of Down at Melrose on 13 December 1211. Ragnvald had probably secured consecration at York, so following his own election, Nicholas obtained consecration from the archbishop of Dublin about 1217, but finding himself unable to take possession of his see, turned for help to Rome. In November 1219 Honorius III instructed the bishop of Carlisle and Pandulf, the papal legate, to order King Ragnvald to desist from his opposition to Nicholas.

Clearly Nicholas had become involved in the rivalry between Ragnvald and Olaf for the throne of Man. He had the support of Olaf, who wrote to the dean of York asking that Nicholas be consecrated, in terms making it clear that opposition to this was to be expected. But neither the pope nor Olaf was able to secure his see for Nicholas, who never set foot in his diocese and finally complained to Honorius in 1224 that he had for a long time past been exiled from it and sought permission to resign. The pope would appear to have consented, for Nicholas remained in England, where by August 1225 a portion of the church of Kellaw in the diocese of Durham had been allocated to him for his support. He seems to have joined the entourage of Archbishop Walter de Gray of York, two of whose deeds he witnessed in 1226 with the style 'formerly bishop of the Isles'. It is not known when he died. Meanwhile Ragnvald remained in effective control of the see of Man. He is recorded as carrying out a visitation of the churches of the Hebrides, and also as canonically dissolving the marriage of Olaf to King Ragnvald's sister-in-law, thereby breaking the link which had maintained a precarious peace between the two men. The result was an outbreak of hostilities which involved the kingdom in almost a decade of strife.   COLM MCNAMEE

Sources *Chronicle of the kings of Mann and the Isles*, ed. G. Broderick (1973), 26 • J. R. Oliver, ed., *Monumenta de Insula Manniae, or, A collection of national documents relating to the Isle of Man*, 2, Manx Society, 7 (1861), 7.38–68 • *Chronica monasterii de Melsa, a fundatione usque ad annum 1396, auctore Thoma de Burton*, ed. E. A. Bond, 1, Rolls Series, 43/1 (1866), 380 • J. Raine, ed., *The register or rolls of Walter Gray, lord archbishop of York*, SurtS, 56 (1872), 5, 153–4 • A. Theiner, *Vetera monumenta Hibernorum et Scotorum historiam illustrantia* (Rome, 1864) • Dugdale, *Monasticon*, new edn, 4.309; 5.246; 6/1.298; 6/2.1186 • J. Raine, ed., *The priory of Hexham*, 2, SurtS, 46 (1865), 2.94 • A. O. Anderson and M. O. Anderson, eds., *The chronicle of Melrose* (1936), 55 • G. Grub, *An ecclesiastical history of Scotland*, 4 vols. (1861), 1.306–22 • J. Dowden, *The bishops of Scotland … prior to the Reformation*, ed. J. M. Thomson (1912), 274–5 • D. E. R. Watt, ed., *Fasti ecclesiae Scoticanae medii aevi ad annum 1638*, [2nd edn], Scottish RS, new ser., 1 (1969), 199–200 • D. Knowles, C. N. L. Brooke, and V. C. M. London, eds., *The heads of religious houses, England and Wales*, 1: 940–1216 (1972), 134

Nicholas (*d.* in or after **1226**). *See under* Nicholas (*d.* 1217).

Nicholas ap Gwrgan (*d.* 1183), bishop of Llandaff, was from the Llandaff area and has sometimes been identified, on dubious grounds, as the son of *Urban, bishop of Llandaff. He was much favoured by Archbishop Theobald, who consecrated him at Canterbury on 14 March 1148.

Nicholas had been a monk at St Peter's, Gloucester, for thirty years, and remained in close touch with the abbey, providing valuable oral evidence in disputes about land. He retained contact with the family of the earls of Hereford, and helped to establish accord between William, earl of Gloucester, and the Welshmen of Glamorgan. Rarely recorded outside his own diocese, he had little contact with the royal court; the payment to him of £3 6s. 8d. by the king's writ in 1172 was a rare event. He was with his former abbot, Gilbert Foliot, in the diocese of Hereford early in the 1150s, and with Henry II at Gloucester in 1157, when the conflicting claims of the abbey and the archbishop of York were settled. He went to Canterbury on 2 October 1149 for the consecration of Walter Durdent as bishop of Coventry. Although he was said to have claimed the right to consecrate Thomas Becket in 1162, Henry, bishop of Winchester, presided while Nicholas assisted him. He did not keep clear of controversy. Between 1148 and 1150 he was in dispute with Archbishop Theobald, and Gilbert Foliot acted as peacemaker. In 1171 he joined in the coronation of Henry, the young king, and was suspended in consequence. In 1174 the new archbishop, Richard of Dover, suspended him again for a blatant infringement of the bishop of Salisbury's prerogative.

As bishop, Nicholas continued the development of his diocese, resolving disputes, fostering monastic houses, holding synods, consulting the canons in his chapter, and issuing *acta* enhanced by their attestation. He was served by archdeacons, clerics drawn from Llancarfan, canons of Llandaff, a personal chaplain, and even by Hugh, 'the bishop's monk'. He died on 3 or 4 June 1183.

DAVID WALKER

Sources T. Jones, ed. and trans., *Brenhinedd y Saesson, or, The kings of the Saxons* (1971) [another version of *Brut y tywysogyon*] • *The historical works of Gervase of Canterbury*, ed. W. Stubbs, 2 vols., Rolls Series, 73 (1879–80) • D. Crouch, ed., *Llandaff episcopal acta, 1140–1287*, South Wales and Monmouth RS, 5 (1988) • *Letters and charters of Gilbert Foliot*, ed. A. Morey and others (1967) • W. H. Hart, ed., *Historia et cartularium monasterii Sancti Petri Gloucestriae*, 3 vols., Rolls Series, 33 (1863–7) • Llanthony cartulary, PRO, C 115/K2/6683, sect. 14, nos. 1, 32–34a • M. Richter, ed., *Canterbury professions*, CYS, 67 (1973) • J. C. Davies, ed., *Episcopal acts and cognate documents relating to Welsh dioceses, 1066–1272*, 2, Historical Society of the Church in Wales, 3 (1948) • R. R. Davies, *Conquest, coexistence, and change: Wales, 1063–1415*, History of Wales, 2 (1987) • D. Walker, *Medieval Wales* (1990) **Archives** PRO, C 115/K2/6687, sect. 14

Nicholas de Farnham. *See* Farnham, Nicholas of (*d.* 1257).

Nicholas de Walkington. *See* Walkington, Nicholas of (*supp. fl.* before 1200).

Nicholas le Blund. *See* Blund, Nicholas le (*d.* 1305).

Nicholas of Fakenham. *See* Fakenham, Nicholas (*d.* 1407).

Nicholas of Hereford. *See* Hereford, Nicholas (*b. c.*1345, *d.* after 1417).

Nicholas of Lynne. *See* Lynn, Nicholas (*fl.* 1386–1411).

Nicholas, Abraham (1692–*c.*1744), writing-master, was born in London, the son of the writing-master Abraham Nicholas, who kept a school in Cusheon Court, near Austin Friars, Broad Street, and published several editions of a merchant primer entitled *The Young Accountant's Debitor and Creditor* (1711). He was the third generation of a line of writing-masters all named Abraham Nicholas; his grandfather, who died in 1692, had kept a writing school near St Mary Magdalen's, Southwark. It is most likely that he received his training in penmanship and accountancy from his father and he is known to have assisted at his school for several years. As the son's address was given as the Hand and Pen in Broad Street it has been generally assumed that he took over his father's school early in the second decade of the eighteenth century.

Nicholas's first publication, indicatively named *A Small Copy Book* (1715), was a modest affair comprising fifteen plates executed in various hands and engraved by George Bickham, the foremost specialist engraver of calligraphy. This was followed by a second edition in 1717 and a number of similar copy-books published over the next few years. In 1719 Henry Overton published Nicholas's *The Penman's Assistant and Youth's Instructor*, which included fifteen plates of round hand copy texts designed to teach young merchants the most convenient hands for effecting business. According to the Revd Mark Noble this work 'seemed to have raised his reputation' and about 1719 Nicholas moved to Clapham where he established his own boarding-school (Noble, 3.425). Although Nicholas provided two designs for George Bickham's *Penman's Companion* (1722), the only other copy-book to be published in his name was *The Compleat Writing Master* (1722). By this stage,

Nicholas had developed a highly refined level of penmanship. His skill can be assessed not only from his calligraphic performances but also from the opinion of his contemporary George Bickham, who commented in a letter to John Bowles, 'I never saw any pieces that were wrote with greater command of hand' (Noble, 3.426). Some time after the publication of *The Compleat Writing Master*, Nicholas transferred his school in Clapham to his brother James and then emigrated to Virginia where he died about 1744.

LUCY PELTZ

Sources A. Heal, *The English writing-masters and their copy-books, 1570–1800* (1931) · W. Massey, *The origin and progress of letters: an essay in two parts* (1763) · *A biographical history of England, from the revolution to the end of George I's reign: being a continuation of the Rev. J. Granger's work*, ed. M. Noble, 3 vols. (1806) · *Engraved Brit. ports.*, vol. 6 · *DNB*
Likenesses G. Bickham, line engraving, BM; repro. in A. Nicholas, *Compleat writing master* (1722) · line engraving, NPG

Nicholas, David. *See* Nicolas, Dafydd (*bap.* 1705?, *d.* 1774).

Nicholas, Sir Edward (1593–1669), government official, was born on 4 April 1593 at Winterbourne Earls, Wiltshire, the eldest son of John Nicholas (*d.* 1644) of Winterbourne Earls and his wife, Susannah Hunton (*d.* 1658). Nicholas's paternal grandfather had been a Marian exile in Frankfurt-am-Main with John Jewell, bishop of Salisbury, and the family leased Winterbourne Earls from the bishopric. John Nicholas was a lawyer often retained by the bishop, dean, and chapter of Salisbury Cathedral as well as estate steward to successive earls of Pembroke.

Education and early career Edward Nicholas studied with his younger brother Matthew Nicholas [*see below*] at Salisbury grammar school; in the household of Sir Lawrence Hyde, attorney-general to Anne of Denmark; at Winchester College; and under the tutelage of one Mr Badcock in the household of his uncle, Richard Hunton. On 25 October 1611 Nicholas matriculated from Queen's College, Oxford, and in the following year he entered the Middle Temple, where his father had chambers. In 1615–16 he travelled in France. Late in 1616, possibly through the Hyde connection, he entered the service of Sir John Dackombe, chancellor of the duchy of Lancaster. This was short employment, however, owing to Dackombe's death the following year, when Nicholas returned to the Middle Temple, perhaps intending to take up law as a profession.

But it was as an administrator and bureaucrat that Nicholas made his career. At the end of 1618 he was employed as secretary to Edward la Zouche, eleventh Baron Zouche, lord warden of the Cinque Ports. Theirs was a cordial relationship, and Nicholas later considered among his significant life experiences his discovering at Zouche's country estate of Bramshill the body of a gamekeeper inadvertently shot and killed by George Abbott, archbishop of Canterbury. Nicholas sat as the lord warden's nominee for Winchelsea in the parliament of 1621 but was active only on a few local Cinque Ports matters. He was a compulsive note-taker, however—no doubt his gentleman's education emphasized the importance of keeping commonplace books—and he wrote a fine italic script in addition to developing his own system of shorthand. These habits served him well in this parliament, when he kept a diary

Sir Edward Nicholas (1593–1669), by William Dobson, *c.*1645

which is more complete than the official House of Commons journal. As MP for Winchelsea again in 1624, he followed the same pattern.

On 24 September 1622 Nicholas married Jane (*d.* 1688), third daughter of Henry Jaye, draper and alderman, of London, who brought with her a portion of £600. After the death of her parents Jane lived in Wiltshire with her married sister Elizabeth, wife of William Hunton, Nicholas's cousin and college friend, with whom Nicholas negotiated a hard-won marriage agreement. Jane and Edward had at least four sons and at least three daughters.

Servant to the duke of Buckingham Nicholas's fortunes continued to improve in the 1620s, and took a significant upturn in December 1624 when George Villiers, first duke of Buckingham, the royal favourite, bought the place of lord warden from Zouche. On Zouche's recommendation Buckingham kept Nicholas on as clerk and soon recognized his talent for organization, financial administration, thoroughness, and honesty. Most who knew him noted his honesty, and the course of his career indicates that he may have been 'honest to a fault', unable to internalize moral objections for the sake of his own advancement. In a shuffle of offices among Buckingham's clients in 1625 surrounding Sir Albertus Morton's death, Nicholas replaced Sir Thomas Aylesbury as the duke's secretary for admiralty affairs. Buckingham subsequently obtained for him the post of clerk-extraordinary to the privy council, with a special portfolio in admiralty affairs that allowed him to be present at all council meetings. Nicholas helped organize Buckingham's 1627 expedition to La Rochelle and supervised the admiralty while the lord admiral sailed with the fleet. He had a genuine interest in the everyday administration of the navy and did much to improve it over the years he served in government.

As a result of this appointment to the council staff, Nicholas's voluminous notes and memoranda comprise a large portion of the state papers domestic from this period. They also provide numerous glimpses into his personal life. He rented accommodation adjacent to The Axe, a tavern on the west side of King Street, just outside the precincts of Whitehall Palace, to be near his work with the council. His notes, and even his parliamentary diaries, contain recipes for various medical remedies. Nicholas suffered from some sort of chronic gastrointestinal condition (which may have led to halitosis) as well as kidney stones and gout, although he was something of a gourmand. He liked dogs and birds, and his good friend Captain John Pennington of the navy sent him several exotic varieties over the years.

In 1628 Nicholas sat in parliament as MP for Dover, most important of the Cinque Ports, again keeping a diary. He lost his powerful patron Buckingham to assassination, which he witnessed at Portsmouth in August, but maintained his post in the government, briefly handling admiralty affairs directly for the king, then under a royal warrant issued on 5 September for a commission to administer the office of lord high admiral during the vacancy. He received a salary of £200 per year for this service. He was intimately involved in the attempts to settle Buckingham's debt-ridden estate, an endeavour which took almost a decade and from which he profited £500. Not long after Buckingham's death, Charles I apparently offered Nicholas the mastership of the court of wards, which he refused, not wishing to endure the envy and censure that came with it.

Admiralty and council clerk in the 1630s Nicholas managed a variety of maritime affairs for the council during the 1630s. He was one of two clerks for the Fishing Society from July 1633, and in 1634 took on oversight of ship money, auditing the sheriffs' accounts as they were paid in and keeping track of delinquents who should be called up for non-payment. Although not in line for the position, Nicholas was advanced by the king to become clerk-in-ordinary to the privy council in November 1635 on the death of William Trumbull. He retained oversight of naval matters and received a portion of the muster master-general's fees for his work in military aspects of admiralty administration. When Algernon Percy, tenth earl of Northumberland, was appointed lord admiral in 1638, Nicholas continued this work for the council, but did not serve as Northumberland's secretary. He seems to have remained on good terms with Northumberland personally, but had something of a turf battle with the lord admiral's private secretary.

During these years Nicholas's personal fortunes improved through business ventures such as moneylending and land speculation, often in partnership with John Ashburnham. His income from his estates was an estimated £1050 per year on top of an estimated annual income of £1500 from wages and fees of his offices with the council and in other minor crown posts. He was ever mindful of his good fortune, devoting a fixed percentage of his income to the service of the church. Moreover, he was assiduous in his duties at the council board, being almost constantly in attendance, often to the detriment of his relationship with his family. It was Nicholas who pushed for an alphabetical and marginal index to be instituted in the council registers at this time, and his staff took on much of the retrospective indexing. William Prynne in *Canterburies Doome* (1644) highlighted Nicholas's assiduousness from personal experience: when in April 1637 Nicholas searched his rooms in the Tower for books and papers, he was so thorough that he even looked in the close stool.

Never one to push for his own advancement, Nicholas remained uncomplainingly at his post through the crises of the late 1630s, inspiring a friend to tell him he 'affect[ed] to be a drone' (Nicholas, 128). In the summer of 1640 he was sent to York by the secretary of state Sir Francis Windebank with instructions for the king on how to conduct a great council of peers. But by the following summer there was little work for Nicholas, as Charles I lost his grip on the government and the privy council was wholly superseded. At the end of July 1641 Nicholas was making plans to live quietly at his country house near Thorpe, Surrey.

Secretary of state and civil war However, in August Charles I promised Nicholas the secretary of state's slot, vacant due to Windebank's flight from prosecution by the Long Parliament. The king did not formalize this arrangement before he travelled to Scotland, leaving Nicholas behind at Westminster with a signet and instructions to use it, but no patent of office. It was not until Charles returned that he knighted Nicholas, on 26 November 1641, and confirmed him in office. Their correspondence while the king was in Edinburgh shows that Charles recognized and trusted Nicholas's unwavering service and honest opinions, often circumventing the other, troublesome, secretary, Sir Henry Vane, to deal instead with Nicholas. But while Nicholas did the bulk of the work for the royal secretariat, he had little political influence with Charles, as evidenced by his inability to obtain for his friend Pennington the job of treasurer of the navy when Vane's son was dismissed from the position. It was also during the king's absence in Scotland that Nicholas and Queen Henrietta Maria embarked on a struggle of wills which endured for decades and ultimately terminated his career. The tone of his letters reveals that Nicholas believed she gave the king bad advice, and the king may have told her that Nicholas advised him to send away her Capuchin friars.

When Charles I and the queen left Whitehall for the country on 10 January 1642 Nicholas once again went to Thorpe, but he was shortly called on to retrieve jewels from Westminster for the queen to take to the continent. After her departure, he went north with the king, very much involved in the escalation to war, and after the raising of the king's standard his name appeared on the list of those excluded from indemnity and pardon by parliament. Nicholas took his family, including his wards, the sons of William Hunton, to live with him in the royalist capital at Oxford. His second son, Edward, there married the daughter of Sir Thomas Clayton, the master of Pembroke College, where the family lodged. As secretary of state, Nicholas was at the centre of a web of international communication and domestic information-gathering. Among his informants while at Oxford was Richard Powell, brother-in-law of John Milton.

The war cost Nicholas dearly in terms of income from his properties, loss of his goods in Westminster (to the value of £800) and at Thorpe, and the chronic inability of the king to pay his salary. In October 1643 he wrote to James Butler, marquess of Ormond, that in two years of service he had not had so much as a sixpence from the king. When the following spring his fellow secretary George Digby, Lord Digby, left England with the queen's entourage, Nicholas remained as the sole secretary at work. When his father died in December 1644 Nicholas could not attend the funeral for several reasons, including his involvement in the Uxbridge negotiations. He remained faithful to the king's service, and in September 1645 it was he who was sent by the king to discharge Prince Rupert of his commission in the royal army after the surrender of Bristol. Nicholas was one of the privy councillors who strongly opposed the king's decision to ally with the Scots in May 1646, and who signed the terms for the surrender of Oxford the following month. Under the terms, he was granted six months to settle his personal affairs; when it became apparent he would not be pardoned by parliament, he left England, as his friend John Ashburnham had done, to continue working for the king's cause.

Exile In exile Nicholas received news from England in letters written by his secretary Nicholas Oudart, sometimes in invisible lemon-juice ink for reasons of security. His long-time friend and family associate Sir Edward Hyde wrote from Jersey to consult about the history of the civil war he was writing. The queen, titular leader of the royalist exiles, was openly hostile to Nicholas, apparently offended that he did not go to Paris to seek instructions from her, and angry that he opposed all the plans concocted by her and her favourite Henry Jermyn to secure assistance from Catholics in Ireland, France, or Spain. Nicholas continued to correspond with Charles I from whom on 28 November 1648 he received what was probably a final letter, commending him for his service and loyalty, and urging him to do what he could for his own family; the king also wrote that he was recommending Nicholas for service to the prince of Wales. Nicholas described the king's subsequent execution as 'transcendantly abominable' (Nicholas, 232). While in spring 1649 Jane Nicholas prepared to go to England to try to get an income out of his estates, Nicholas was in limbo, disliked and excluded by the queen as well as by those who had turned Charles II against his father's old councillors. In

that summer Nicholas went to Jersey, where on 17 September he was sworn to the new king's privy council, although he was not formally reinstated as secretary of state.

In Charles II's government in exile Nicholas entertained numerous plots, plans, and conspiracies to reclaim England, although contemporaries and historians alike have concluded that he was not fully in the confidence of the king and his closest advisers. Increasingly impatient of slights, he insisted that he could not do the work he was given without being sworn secretary of state. Charles made some slight concessions: in February 1650 he increased the council as Nicholas had been suggesting for years and agreed that Nicholas should be sworn secretary in reversion after Robert Long, who had been the queen's private secretary and who had corrupted Nicholas's former clerk Oudart. Nicholas, opposed to the young king's alliance with the Scots, was reduced to increasing poverty and bitterness. In December 1650 he wrote to Hyde, with whom his relations were also growing tense, that he planned either to retire to Wessel, where the cost of living was lower, or to return to England to compound for his estates. But that same month Nicholas accepted Charles's commission to accompany and advise the duke of York in the Low Countries. He was in Antwerp in summer 1651 when his estates and those of Hyde in Wiltshire were confiscated and sold because they were traitors. Extremely depressed by Charles's defeat at Worcester in September, Nicholas did not obey a summons to meet him in Paris later that year. Despite this invitation he continued to feel marginalized: in December 1651 he wrote to Ormond that he would 'rather to starve in some private corner than live at court in contempt' (Ormonde MSS, 1.246). In January 1652 Nicholas commented that Charles shared the same fatal propensity to cling to 'faithless and perfidious servants' as the rest of his family (Nicholas, 259). Once he could no longer afford to stay at The Hague he would go to England 'and bid them do with me as they list' (ibid.). Hyde continued to encourage him to come to Paris, and in April Nicholas finally received from the king a promise of reward for his loyalty, although by this time the king himself was as impoverished as any exile.

In the spring of 1653 Nicholas uncovered the duplicitous activities of Colonel Bampfield, an alleged supporter of Charles II who had helped the duke of York escape from England, but who exploited his proximity to Jermyn and others in the queen's clique to spy for the Presbyterians. In November Charles gave Nicholas permission to sell a baronetcy for his own profit, but he was unable to find anyone in his circles sufficiently wealthy to buy it and complained constantly that his credit was almost exhausted. Poverty and mobility increased in 1654 as Nicholas and the royal court roamed from The Hague to Breda to Antwerp to Aix-la-Chapelle to Cologne, seeking money and accommodation. Nicholas again contemplated leaving the king for Frankfurt in order to provide for his family. His relations with Hyde became particularly strained as the latter neither obtained money for him from the king nor repaid personal loans. Furthermore, Hyde was acting as secretary of state while insisting he was protecting Nicholas's interest in the office and vehemently denying that he was cutting Nicholas out of business and confidence, and he continued to employ as his secretary Nicholas's eldest son, John, himself a future secretary of state.

Charles finally swore Nicholas as secretary of state at Aix-la-Chappelle in July 1654 on the proven disloyalty of Robert Long. Nicholas was immediately deluged with petitions from royalists desiring restoration to previous office or new preferment. He entered into close correspondence with Elizabeth of Bohemia, leading to a personal relationship that allowed him to send one of his daughters to serve in her court. In the autumn Nicholas worked with Hyde to prevent the conversion to Catholicism of the thirteen-year-old duke of Gloucester by the queen mother and her cronies. Much of Nicholas's political effort was rendered ineffectual by regular interception of his letters to England: elaborate codes proved fairly transparent. He was apparently excluded from the planning in 1655 for Penruddock's rising, and his mending of fences with Hyde after he turned over the secretary's seals broke down again as Nicholas was convinced Hyde had deliberately kept from him information on the rising.

Jane Nicholas returned from an enforced, extended, and fruitless stay in England in August 1655. In November Nicholas was among those exiles whom France agreed to expel under an Anglo-French treaty. When he was subsequently approached with a plot to assassinate Cromwell, he supported it but would not ask the king for approval. He was still personally and professionally dissatisfied early in 1656, at odds with Hyde over the latter's refusal to sanction repayment of a substantial loan to the king. Nicholas's situation appeared desperate indeed when at new year 1657 Digby rejoined the king's court at Bruges and was reinstated as secretary of state. On 7 March 1658 Nicholas's mother died at Winterbourne Earls, but he could afford neither a journey to England nor the trappings of mourning.

In January 1658 Hyde was officially appointed lord chancellor and lord keeper to Charles. He opposed Nicholas's plan, urged to the king, of putting a price on Cromwell's head in an effort to remove the obstacle to his regaining England. However, following the departure of Digby, now second earl of Bristol, from the court under suspension in April, his open conversion to Catholicism in September, and his subsequent dismissal as secretary, Nicholas's prospects looked better. He joined the court at Brussels the following month. On 8 September he gave the king the good news of Cromwell's death, and over the following year welcomed the news of instability and failure that came out of England. When in March 1660 the king, Hyde, and John Nicholas left Brussels for Breda, from where Charles issued his declaration of intent, Nicholas stayed behind in Brussels to discharge business, but he joined the king at Breda by the end of April, from which time his correspondence was immediately filled with attempts to maintain calm and to prevent unbridled retribution against the parliamentarians. On 23 May the king and a party which included Hyde and both the Nicholases boarded the *Royal Charles* for England.

Restoration secretary of state The Restoration that Nicholas had longed for and suffered for quickly turned sour for him. On 16 May 1660 William Morrice, cousin of the victorious General George Monck, was knighted and sworn secretary of state in place of Bristol. When the court resettled at Westminster, Nicholas was granted the Whitehall lodgings traditionally assigned to the senior secretary of state on the river front of the palace; but, as before, he was apparently not in the king's inner circle or among his advisers. Nevertheless, he now set about securing offices and favours for his family and royalist friends. Almost immediately he obtained for his brother Matthew Nicholas the deanery of St Paul's Cathedral, and he was helpful in getting Samuel Pepys's boss at the Admiralty the title of earl of Sandwich, for which the secretary received £100 worth of plate. John Nicholas, who was made a clerk of the signet and knight of the Bath, and knighted, collaborated with his father to procure the bishopric of Salisbury for Humphrey Henchman, who was helping Nicholas reconsolidate his landholdings in Wiltshire. Nicholas also concluded the purchase of Gillingham manor, forest, and park in Dorset from the earl of Elgin, who had mortgaged it to him before the wars.

Despite his apparent exclusion from the inner circles of the king's government, Nicholas resumed his old assiduous habits, and hired as his Latin secretary a graduate of his old college, Queen's, Joseph Williamson, later secretary of state himself. He began to accumulate the records of 1650s governments. In October 1660 Nicholas was involved in preparing for the trials of regicides including Thomas Scot. He signed the warrants for the execution of Scot and for the disinterment and hanging in December of the bodies of Oliver Cromwell, John Bradshaw, Henry Ireton, and Thomas Pride, considering this a 'wonderful' example of 'justice'. He tried to ensure that financial restitution went only to deserving supporters of the king, and not to those who had served both sides in the late conflict, but was often unsuccessful. He tended to some foreign affairs, and in May 1661 was granted a pension of 1500 dollars per annum by the king of Denmark for his role in the negotiation of a treaty between England and Denmark, but he did not seek election to parliament.

Pepys in October 1661 recorded in his diary that Nicholas's place as secretary had been given to Henry Bennet and that it was not known if this happened with or without Nicholas's co-operation. No one questioned Nicholas's loyalty, but he was unpopular with Charles II's mistresses (especially Barbara Palmer, countess of Castlemaine) and, according to Pepys, Henrietta Maria, who had never forgiven Nicholas for opposing her advice to Charles I and was in league with Castlemaine to persuade the king to be rid of him. Secretary Morrice, who anticipated promotion, was complicit in this as was Bennet, openly allied with the enemies of Hyde, now earl of Clarendon. Nicholas had warned Hyde of Bennet's untrustworthiness years before when he promoted Bennet among the exiles. Charles II was easily manipulated into asking Nicholas to step down, but sent Nicholas's old friend and business partner Ashburnham to present the request, promising Nicholas £10,000 in compensation. Nicholas replied via Ashburnham that he would yield to the king's will, but requested a larger sum of money, paid in advance. Charles instead offered Nicholas a title in addition. Ever the realist, Nicholas took the £10,000 although his wounded pride caused him to refuse the title in a show of contempt for Charles and his regime. On 15 October 1661 Nicholas surrendered the signet which provided his authority in office.

Retirement and legacy The retired secretary began looking for a house in the country where he could live in peace with his books and his pictures and write a history of the civil wars as Clarendon had done, with the assistance of Clarendon's secretary, his own son John. He also worked on a history of the Long Parliament and on his autobiography. In July 1664 he bought the manor of West Horsley, Surrey, from Sir Carew Ralegh. Late in 1665, allegedly because of ill health, Nicholas stopped attending privy council meetings. He still read letters of intelligence and news books and wrote regularly to Williamson, who was now Bennet's clerk, but his general correspondence shrank and he withdrew from public life. In August 1667 Clarendon was also dismissed from the king's service.

On 1 September 1669, Nicholas died at West Horsley; he was buried in the parish church there. His wife, Jane, survived him by another eighteen years; after she died in 1688 she was buried in his grave. In his will, drawn up on 19 December 1668, Nicholas left Winterbourne Earls, his interest in the Great Park at Windsor, and his house in the Spring Garden to his son Sir John Nicholas, with provision for his wife's use during her widowhood. All his Latin and French books, books of law and manuscripts, and estate papers also went to John, while most of his English books were to be distributed among his other sons. Among other beneficiaries were his sisters, while his cousin Charles Whittaker, who had been his clerk and secretary for many years, and his kinsman William Gauntlett were left £50 and £10 respectively for their care in time of distress. He also left £20 towards repair of the cathedral church of New Sarum. The art collection that Nicholas had assembled at West Horsley remained intact until the 1920s.

Nicholas's younger brother **Matthew Nicholas** (1594–1661), Church of England clergyman, was born on 26 September 1594. Having been educated with Edward, he graduated BCL from New College, Oxford, on 30 June 1620 and became rector of West Dean, Wiltshire, in 1621. Licensed on 3 February 1627 to marry Elizabeth, daughter of the late William Fookes, he proceeded DCL that June. In 1629 he became rector of Broughton, Hampshire, and in 1630 master of St Nicholas's Hospital at Hernham, near Salisbury. Further preferment came with the prebendal rectory of Whorwell, Hampshire, in 1637, the deanery of Bristol and vicarage of Olveston, Gloucestershire, in 1639, and a prebend at Westminster in 1642. Sequestered from these livings and offices between 1643 and early 1646, by 23 January 1646 he was a prisoner at Dartmouth, Devon. On his release, he settled near Salisbury, and in 1647 his

wife was granted fifths on all his preferments. In 1660 he was restored at West Dean and became dean of St Paul's, but he died on 15 August 1661, survived by Elizabeth, two daughters, and three sons, George, Edward, and John.

S. A. BARON

Sources CSP dom., 1625–61 · PRO, SP 16 · D. Nicholas, *Mr Secretary Nicholas, 1593–1669: his life and letters* (1955) · *The Nicholas papers*, ed. G. F. Warner, 4 vols., CS, new ser., 40, 50, 57, 3rd ser., 31 (1886–1920) · Clarendon, *Hist. rebellion* · *The diary and correspondence of John Evelyn, F.R.S.*, ed. W. Bray, new edn, 4 vols. (1891) · *Calendar of the manuscripts of the marquess of Ormonde*, new ser., 8 vols., HMC, 36 (1902–20), vol. 1 · G. E. Aylmer, *The king's servants: the civil service of Charles I, 1625–1642*, 2nd edn (1979) · R. Lockyer, *Buckingham: the life and political career of George Villiers, first duke of Buckingham, 1592–1628* (1981) · *VCH Wiltshire*, vol. 5 · Foster, *Alum. Oxon.* · will, PRO, PROB 11/330, fol. 106 · *Walker rev.*, 378

Archives BL, letters, Add. MSS 18980–18982 · BL, memoranda books, Add. MSS 62927, 63076 · BL, family and personal papers, Add. MSS 37816–37823, 41202, 44925–44926, Egerton MSS 2533–2562, see Eg. Ch. 417–426, 486–503 · Bodl. Oxf., privy council minutes · Hunt. L., letters · JRL, corresp. · NL Scot., papers · PRO, SP 16 · Surrey HC, corresp. and papers · Surrey HC, papers relating to Scotland | BL, Egerton MSS 2533–2562; Add. MSS 4180, 31954 · BL, letters to Sir G. Downing, Add. MS 22919 · Christ Church Oxf., Sir Richard Browne papers · Hunt. L., letters to Lord Loughborough · Leics. RO, corresp. with earl of Winchilsea

Likenesses W. Dobson, oils, c.1645, NPG [see illus.] · A. Hanneman, oils, c.1652–1653, Wilton House, Wiltshire · P. Lely, oils, c.1662, NPG · P. Lely, portrait, 1665–8, repro. in Nicholas, *Mr. Secretary Nicholas* · A. Hertochs, line engraving (after A. Hanneman, c.1652–1653), BM, NPG

Wealth at death see will, PRO, PROB 11/330, fol. 106

Nicholas, Henry. *See* Niclaes, Hendrik (1502–c.1580).

Nicholas, Matthew (1594–1661). *See under* Nicholas, Sir Edward (1593–1669).

Nicholas, Robert (*bap.* 1595, *d.* 1667), judge, was born to a gentry background, the eldest son of John Nicholas of Devizes and Roundway, Wiltshire, and his wife, Mary. He was baptized on 21 September 1595 at St James Southbroom in the parish of Bishop's Canning. He matriculated at Queen's College, Oxford, on 11 May 1610 at fifteen years of age, taking his BA on 17 May 1613 and entering the Middle Temple on 11 November that year. He was called to the bar on 23 November 1621. He served as recorder for Devizes in 1639 and in 1640 served as commissioner in Wiltshire for raising money for the defence of the realm and the payment of the parliament's debts. At this time he also held the farm of All Cannings, Wiltshire.

Nicholas was elected on 23 October 1640 to represent the borough of Devizes in the Long Parliament and over the next two years emerged as a supporter of the parliamentarian cause and a critic of the administrative and ecclesiastical policies of Charles I's government during the personal rule of 1629–40. He played prominent roles in the proceedings against the king's leading counsellors Thomas Wentworth, earl of Strafford, and Archbishop William Laud. Although he was not one of the managers of the evidence against Strafford, in April 1641 he joined with John Pym and Oliver St John in calling for the earl's attainder on a charge of high treason for his conduct in both Ireland and England during the previous decade. He argued that the earl's actions in subverting the fundamental law of the land was also a compassing of the king's death because 'the Law [was] the soule of the political body' and 'to destroy the law is to destroy the kingdome and the king in it' (BL, Harley MS 164, fol. 981r). The king declared him a rebel in 1642 and he subsequently served, along with Sir John Maynard, Samuel Brown, and John Wilde, as one of the managers of the evidence against Archbishop Laud—a task he undertook with occasionally foul-mouthed enthusiasm. While his precise views on religion at this time are unclear, it is safely assumed that he was a strong opponent of the Laudian episcopate and the ecclesiastical innovations of the 1630s. His role in Laud's impeachment also suggests an Erastian tendency that emphasized the role of the civil magistrate and in particular parliament in the ordering of ecclesiastical affairs. He served on the subcommittee of accounts for Wiltshire in November 1646 and on 30 October 1648 the House of Commons raised him to the serjeantcy, probably as a prelude to judicial appointment. He was named to the high court erected for the trying of the king but like most of the common law bar and bench did not serve.

Nicholas survived Pride's Purge and about 17 February 1649 he took the dissent from the Long Parliament's vote of 5 December 1648 in favour of continuing talks with the king. In May 1649 the council of state appointed him counsel for the Commonwealth in proceedings against the Leveller leaders John Lilburne, William Walwyn, and Richard Overton. On 1 June 1649 he became a judge of the newly renamed upper bench and on 13 June he resigned his office as recorder of Devizes. On 1 April 1650 he was named a commissioner to establish a new high court of justice and also in that year he gave the sum of £30 to the poor of the parishes of St John's and St Mary's, Wiltshire. After his appointment to the bench he returned to the Rump only occasionally to oppose proposals for law reform flowing from the Hale commission. He became a baron of the exchequer during Hilary term 1654. On 12 March 1655 cavaliers under Colonel John Penruddock seized the western circuit assize judges, Nicholas and Chief Justice Rolle, in their beds at Salisbury during the abortive royalist uprising in the west. Nicholas narrowly escaped being hanged in the market square and was freed two days later. He subsequently served on the commission of oyer and terminer for the trying of Penruddock and his confederates. Possibly sensitive to his status as an interested party, he declined to deliver the charge to the jury or otherwise play an active role in the proceedings. Cromwell appears to have removed him from office in 1657, possibly for questioning the validity of his controversial treason ordinance of 19 January 1654, but his name reappears as an assize justice in 1658. The recalled Rump Parliament reappointed him to the upper bench on 17 January 1660, and he served there until May of that year.

Nicholas was one of a group of barristers that included Peter Warburton, John Puleston, Sir Matthew Hale, and Sir John Glyn whose service on the bench during the interregnum helped assure the survival of common law values

and institutions. During his tenure on both benches he served primarily on the Oxford and western assize circuits but also occasionally on the Norfolk and midland. He was pardoned at the Restoration and his name appears as a commissioner for the raising of money in his native Wiltshire during 1660. However, Charles II declined to confirm his serjeantcy and he played no further role on the bench at Westminster. On 3 December 1664 he was accused of boasting that he had drawn up the charge against Charles I and would be prepared to do so again. The outcome of these proceedings is not known. He retired to Seend Row, Wiltshire, where he made his will, dated 6 May 1667. He was buried on 28 December 1667 at St James Southbroom where he was baptized. He appears to have been married twice and to have been survived by a son, Oliver, a daughter, Catherine, and his second wife. He was in possession of his family's estates at Roundway at his death although he died poor; the estate appears to have passed from the family's hands at that time.   D. A. ORR

Sources DNB · E. A. Andriette, 'Nicholas, Robert', Greaves & Zaller, BDBR, 2.262–3 · Foss, Judges, 6.463–5 · Baker, Serjeants, 528 · Foster, Alum. Oxon. · C. H. Hopwood, ed., Middle Temple records, 4 vols. (1904–5) · S. D'Ewes, 'Parliamentary journal of Sir Simonds D'Ewes', BL, Harley MS 164, fol. 981r · J. S. Cockburn, A history of English assizes, 1558–1714 (1972), 244–5, 273–4 · VCH Wiltshire, 7.191, 10.271, 312 · S. F. Black, 'The courts and judges of Westminster Hall during the great rebellion, 1640–1660', Journal of Legal History, 7 (1986), 23–52 · S. F. Black, 'Coram protectore: the judges of Westminster Hall under the protectorate of Oliver Cromwell', American Journal of Legal History, 20 (1976), 33–64 · D. Underdown, Pride's Purge: politics in the puritan revolution (1971), 381 · B. Worden, The Rump Parliament, 1648–1653 (1974), 320 · D. A. Orr, 'Sovereignty, state, and the law of treason in England, 1641–1649', PhD diss., U. Cam., 1997 · Keeler, Long Parliament, 285

Nicholas, Robert Carter (1728–1780), jurist and revolutionary politician in America, was born on 28 January 1728 in Williamsburg, Virginia, the third son of George Nicholas (c.1695–1734), British naval surgeon, and Elizabeth (1692–1734), eldest daughter of Robert Carter (1633–1732), of Corotoman, and widow of Nathaniel Burwell. Young Nicholas received 6200 acres in the Shenandoah valley and £5000 in trust from his grandfather. Orphaned at the age of six he was raised by his uncle John Carter of Shirley. Nicholas attended the College of William and Mary, and then was apprenticed in law. In 1750 he became common councillor of Williamsburg and began practice before the York and Warwick county courts and, by 1757, the general court. In 1752 he married Anne (1735–1786), daughter of Wilson Miles Cary and his wife, Sarah Blair, of Ceeleys, Elizabeth City county, Virginia. The couple had eight surviving children.

Nicholas was made vestryman of Bruton parish in 1754. He served as burgess for York county (1756–61) and for James City county (1765–75), a member of the inner circle from initiation. Named in 1759 to the committee instructing the colony's first permanent agent in London he continued on the committee of correspondence for over fifteen years, including five in which he was not a burgess. Though generally wary of paper currency he supported

Virginia's first venture during the Seven Years' War, countersigning most issues. He represented the York–Hampton vestry against the Revd John Camm in one of the 'parsons' causes' suits that arose because when crops failed the assembly allowed vestries to convert clerical salaries from tobacco to cash at below market prices; he won in the general court and again on appeal to the privy council. He was an active trustee of a school that a Church of England charity, Dr Bray's Associates, operated for African Americans in Williamsburg from 1760 to 1774. In late 1764 he helped to compose the legislature's constitutional objection to the Grenville ministry's proposal for a stamp tax but opposed the more aggressive resolves of Patrick Henry, revolutionary statesman, the next spring. The demise of Speaker John Robinson in 1766 revealed that, in Robinson's concurrent position as treasurer, he had not retired paper currency as required but had reissued it in loans to hard-pressed planters. Nicholas, breaking with the new speaker, Peyton Randolph, who hoped for both appointments, advocated separating the posts and became treasurer himself. Within six years he retired three-quarters of the currency outstanding. To offset deflation he instituted tax payments by bills of exchange through the London merchant John Norton and prevailed upon royal officials to mint £2500 in copper pennies for Virginia. In 1768 Nicholas helped craft the burgesses' protest against the Townshend duties. The next year, when the governor, Norborne Berkeley, fourth Baron Botetourt, dissolved the assembly for protesting the crown's intimidation of Massachusetts critics, Nicholas joined his colleagues at the Ralegh tavern to proclaim a boycott of British imports. Politics aside he admired the intellectual governor and, on his death in 1770, served on the committee to erect a statue of him in the Capitol. Commitment to public business led Nicholas to offer his legal practice to Thomas Jefferson in 1771 and, when he declined, to transfer it to Henry two years later. That same year Nicholas publicly charged the speaker's choice for rector of Bruton parish, Samuel Henley, with heresy and blocked the appointment.

In 1774, when parliament closed Boston harbour because of the city's tea party, Jefferson asked Nicholas, known for his piety, to move a day of public fasting and prayer. The new governor, John Murray, fourth earl of Dunmore, dissolved the assembly in response and the burgesses, including Nicholas, announced another boycott at the Ralegh. Provoked by an anonymous publication criticizing the fast day resolution Nicholas attributed it to the attorney-general, John Randolph, Peyton's brother, and published a bristling defence, deploring violence but blaming the British. Family clashes notwithstanding, Randolph's son Edmund married Nicholas's daughter Elizabeth in 1776. When Dunmore seized munitions in the Williamsburg magazine in April 1775 Nicholas angrily confronted him, then dissuaded citizens from rioting and kept Henry from leading militia into the city.

Nicholas attended all five Virginia conventions, serving as president during the speaker's illness in August 1775. He repeatedly sought accommodation with Britain, but,

having failed, proposed raising 10,000 troops and ordered the convention's first arms shipment from the West Indies. On the vote for American independence in May 1776 he abstained rather than cast the only negative. When George Mason proposed the declaration of rights Nicholas asked if universal freedom applied to slaves, and this led to an amendment from the pro-independence delegates that it did not. When the convention became the first House of Delegates under the new constitution Nicholas resigned as treasurer to ensure separation of powers. Early in the war he directed the Williamsburg Manufacturing Society, which produced textiles. He resisted Jefferson's effort to disestablish the Episcopal church but, when a compromise in 1776 excused dissenters from tithing without altering the church's traditional responsibility for the poor, Nicholas proposed universal exemption, which effectively achieved Jefferson's goal. The next year Jefferson's ally George Wythe defeated Nicholas for speaker. In 1779 the assembly appointed Nicholas a judge of the new high court of chancery and, *ex officio*, of the court of appeals. He died on 8 September 1780 at The Retreat, his estate in Hanover county, Virginia, where his family had moved at the outbreak of war.

JOHN E. SELBY

Sources W. J. Lescure, 'The early political career of Robert Carter Nicholas, 1728–1769', MA diss., College of William and Mary, 1961 · R. Isaac, *The transformation of Virginia, 1740–1790* (Chapel Hill, North Carolina, 1982) · J. E. Selby, *The revolution in Virginia, 1775–1783* (Williamsburg, 1988) · D. J. Mays, *Edmund Pendleton, 1721–1803: a biography*, 2 vols. (1952) · J. P. Greene, 'The attempt to separate the offices of speaker and treasurer in Virginia, 1758–1766', *Virginia Magazine of History and Biography*, 71 (1963), 11–18 · T. W. Tate, 'Nicholas, Robert Carter', ANB · *Considerations on the present state of Virginia attributed to John Randolph, attorney general, and Considerations on the present state of Virginia examined by Robert Carter Nicholas*, ed. E. G. Swem (1919) · IGI · *Virginia Magazine of History and Biography*, 9 (1901–2), 108

Wealth at death owned house and lot in Williamsburg plantation, Hanover county, Virginia: Colonial Williamsburg Foundation database; Tate, 'Nicholas, Robert Carter'

Nicholas, Thomas (1816–1879), educationist and antiquary, was born on 17 February 1816 in Trefgarn, near Solfach, Pembrokeshire. Nothing is known of his parentage and early life. During his youth he contributed to various Welsh periodicals, but the intervention of business interests and evangelical tours meant that it was not until 1841 that he first received formal education at Lancashire Independent College, Manchester, before studying at Göttingen University, Germany, where he received the degrees of MA and PhD. In 1847 he was installed as preacher at the Old Chapel, Stroud, Gloucestershire, before moving on in 1853 to Eignbrook, Herefordshire.

In 1856 Nicholas was appointed professor of biblical literature and mental and moral sciences at the Presbyterian college, Carmarthen. Although he was initially enthused by the prospect of working in such an institution, his incumbency was little short of disastrous. A torrent of complaints accused him of neglecting his pedagogical duties. His reputation as a theologian was supported by his edition of Mathias Maurice's *Social Religion Exemplify'd* (1860), but his insouciance towards the college led to his dismissal in 1862. In mitigation, his absenteeism was the result of his passion for the furtherance of higher education in Wales on non-sectarian principles. While the idea of a university for Wales was certainly not moribund, its expressions in the 1850s by Hugh Owen and others were vague and indistinct. Inspired by the ideas of Dr David Thomas, a Congregational minister at Stockwell, Nicholas wrote six seminal letters to the *Cambrian Daily Leader* in 1862–3, published in 1863 at the expense of William Williams MP, as *Middle and High Schools and University Education for Wales*. Taking either London University or the Irish Queen's colleges as his model, he envisaged in the letters the foundation of two colleges, one in the north and one in the south of Wales, which would be funded by voluntary contributions. Though liberal in his economic philosophy, Nicholas's educational philosophy was steeped in the hard-headed dictates of utilitarianism. Similarly, a university for Wales was conceived by him as part of an integrationist drive which would place Wales firmly at the heart of the British state.

In 1863, Nicholas settled in London and became the first salaried secretary of the committee of the University of Wales. Thanks to his indefatigable efforts, the committee was by 1867 able to purchase the building of the Castle Hotel in Aberystwyth, which in 1872 opened its doors as the first college of the future University of Wales. But the achievement was not without its penalties: his efforts in raising £14,000 led to increasing bouts of ill health and the Olympian presence of Hugh Owen as president of the committee grated on his sensitive disposition. On 8 November 1867, amid ever more fractious scenes, Nicholas resigned as secretary.

While Nicholas increasingly retreated after 1867 from the coteries of London-Welsh liberals, his intellectual fecundity remained undiminished. In 1868, he published *The Pedigree of the English People*, a notable work in the annals of Welsh historiography in that his ethnographical methodology fused both providential and scientific explanations. However, this work was the subject of an acrimonious lawsuit with Joseph Pike, who accused him of plagiarism. Undaunted by this controversy, he published *Annals and Antiquities of the Counties and County Families of Wales* (2 vols., 1872), in which he upheld the equal validity of Welsh and English pedigrees. Part of this larger work was printed as the *History and Antiquities of Glamorganshire and its Families* (1874). During the last three years of his life, Nicholas wrote regularly for the *London Echo* and in 1878 edited a version of Baedeker's *London*. Death intervened before he could finish his history of the Welsh. Nicholas died, unmarried, on 14 May 1879 at 156 Cromwell Road, South Kensington, London, and was buried at Hammersmith cemetery. It was only the generosity of his friends which prevented him from being buried in a pauper's grave.   W. GARETH EVANS

Sources DWB · T. R. Roberts, *Eminent Welshmen: a short biographical dictionary* (1908) · *Y Geninen*, 27 (1909), 129 · *Congregational Year Book* (1881) · *The homilist* (1877), 456 ff. · *The Athenaeum* (24 May 1879), 662–3 · E. L. Ellis, *The University College of Wales, Aberystwyth, 1872–1972* (1972), 13–16 · J. G. Williams, *The university movement in Wales* (1993), 24–30 · H. T. Edwards, *Gŵyl Gwalia* (1981), 89–95 · D. E. Davies, *Hoff Ddysgedig Nyth* (1976), 171–2 · *CGPLA Eng. & Wales* (1879) · DNB

Archives NL Wales, corresp. and papers, 3091–31061 | NL Wales, *Nicholas v. Pike* MSS, MS 3097 · U. Wales, Aberystwyth, University of Wales MSS

Wealth at death under £200: administration, 13 June 1879, *CGPLA Eng. & Wales*

Nicholas, Thomas Evan [known as Niclas y Glais] (1879–1971), poet and political activist, was born on 6 October 1879 at Y Llety, a smallholding in the parish of Llanfyrnach, Pembrokeshire, one of the five children of David (Dafydd) Nicholas (1844–1928), a farmer, and his wife, Elizabeth (Bet) Evans, *née* Thomas (1844–1937). After attending primary school at nearby Hermon, he studied for the Congregational ministry at the Gwynfryn Academy in Ammanford and was ordained at Llandeilo in 1901. On 1 October 1902 he married Mary Alice (1879–1965), the daughter of Thomas Hopkins, a watchmaker and jeweller of Ammanford. He spent a year as a minister in Dodgeville, Wisconsin, before returning to Wales to take up the pastorate of Seion in the industrial village of Glais in the Swansea valley in 1904; although he only spent ten years there, he was associated with that place for the rest of his life and was generally known in Welsh as Niclas y Glais.

Already firmly egalitarian in outlook, Nicholas was to develop his political creed, which he claimed was communist long before he had read Marx because it sprang from his Christian beliefs, in a south Wales which, over the next decade, brought harsh reminders of the clash between workers and the capitalist system: the Cambrian Combine lock-out and Tonypandy riots of 1910 and the Senghennydd pit disaster of 1913, the worst in the annals of British coalmining, were among the events which helped to shape his thinking. His early verse, published in *Salmau'r werin* (1909), *Cerddi gwerin* (1912), *Cerddi rhyddid* (1914), *Y rhyfel anghyfiawn* (1914), and *Dros eich gwlad* (1920), blazed with millenarian biblical imagery; its message was that it is not man's spiritual imperfections but the inhuman economic system under which he lives that is responsible for social injustice, oppression, and war. Having joined the Independent Labour Party (ILP) he became a prominent public speaker, a regular contributor to the Welsh column of the party's newspaper, *The Merthyr Pioneer*, and a close friend of its editor, Keir Hardie, MP for Merthyr Tudful, whose opposition to militarism he shared.

In 1914 Nicholas left Glais to become minister of Llangybi and Llanddewibrefi in Cardiganshire, where he began organizing the county's agricultural workers and lead miners and using his pulpit to denounce what he considered to be an imperialist war which was against the interests of the working class. His sermons were monitored by Home Office informers for 'treasonable' sentiments, and in 1918, after he had delivered a particularly outspoken sermon in his own chapel, there was an unsuccessful attempt to prosecute him under the Defence of the Realm Act. When he founded the No-Conscription Fellowship many chapels closed their doors to him, and at the war's end he abandoned the ministry in disgust. In the election of 1918 he stood as the ILP candidate in Aberdâr,

Thomas Evan Nicholas (1879–1971), by unknown photographer

part of Hardie's old constituency, with the backing of the local trades council, the Labour Party, and the co-operative movement. His programme was uncompromisingly anti-imperialist and socialist, supporting people's control of industry, the concept of a League of Nations, self-government for Ireland and autonomy for Scotland and Wales, and the Bolshevik Revolution of October 1917; he was defeated by the 'Britisher' candidate, Charles Butt Stanton, who polled 22,834 votes against the 6229 cast for Nicholas. It was the Russian Revolution which confirmed his Marxist ideals and inspired him to write many of the poems in which his vision of international brotherhood, peace, and proletarian solidarity was expressed.

In 1921, with his wife, Nicholas trained as a dentist, and he established practices first at Pontardawe and then at Aberystwyth, where he remained for the rest of his life. Between 1917 and 1945 he delivered more than a thousand lectures on the Soviet Union, which he had visited, and in 1920 he was a founder member of the Communist Party of Great Britain, but he did not resume his political journalism until 1937, when his column in the weekly newspaper *Y Cymro* began to appear under the title 'O fyd y werin'; one of his main concerns was to warn against appeasement of Hitler and Mussolini. He also founded at about this time, with J. Roose Williams, the short-lived paper *Llais y Werin*. On 11 November 1940 he was arrested, with his son Islwyn (one of his four children), and detained in Swansea and Brixton prisons, but the charges were shown to be spurious after a vigorous campaign was mounted by the labour movement, and they were released after two months. The fruit of this episode was *Llygad y drws* (1940), a sequence of 288 sonnets which he had scratched on a slate in his cell, copied out on toilet paper, and then arranged to be smuggled out of gaol by a sympathetic warder; an English version was translated by Daniel Hughes and others and published as *Prison Sonnets* in 1948.

Nicholas's career as a poet had two phases. Up to about 1920 he wrote, for the most part, poems of political polemic, alternately vitriolic and apocalyptic, and most effective when the bludgeon of rhetoric was supplemented by the cutting edge of irony. In his later books, notably *Terfysgoedd daear* (1939), *Canu'r carchar* (1942), *Y dyn â'r gaib* (1944), *Dryllio'r delwau* (1941), and *'Rwyn gweld o bell* (1963), the stridency of the earlier period was held in check by a greater economy of diction and control of form (particularly the sonnet), though the conflict between labour and international capitalism, and the Christian imperative to improve man's lot on earth, remained his favourite subjects. A selection of his poems (with English prose translations) appeared posthumously in the volume *Tros ryddid daear* (1981) under the aegis of Cymdeithas Niclas, the society named in his honour.

Nicholas was the most eloquent and uncompromising spokesman for the ILP and the Soviet state in the Welsh language. Acclaimed by Harry Pollitt in 1949 as 'Wales's greatest man', he combined a rigorous Marxist analysis of society with what he saw as most progressive within the Welsh radical nonconformist tradition. Among his *bêtes noires* were the capitalist system, the Roman Catholic church, and the monarchy. Communism was for him the creed which gave meaning, hope, and dignity to the lives of ordinary people, and all his writing, whether in verse or prose, was dedicated to that ideal. His poetry, while Welsh in form, is consistently socialist and internationalist in content, and awaits the wider recognition it deserves.

The poet, whose genial personality won him many friends in Wales and abroad, died at his home, Glasynys, in Elm Tree Avenue, Aberystwyth, on 19 April 1971; after a funeral service at Baker Street Independent Chapel, his ashes were scattered on a slope of the Preseli hills above Y Llety, where he had been born.   MEIC STEPHENS

Sources T. E. Nicholas, *Tros ryddid daear* (1981), introduction · T. E. Nicholas, *Proffwyd sosialaeth a bardd gwrthryfel*, ed. J. R. Williams [1972] · personal knowledge (2004) · D. T. Lloyd, 'T. E. Nicholas', *Gwŷr llên*, ed. A. T. Davies (1948) · D. Morris, *T. E. Nicholas and the Welsh communist tradition* (1998) · D. B. Rees, 'Y Parch. T. E. Nicholas (1879–1971)', *Pymtheg o Wŷr llên yr ugeinfed ganrif* (1972) · I. Pritchard, 'Thomas Evan Nicholas (1879–1971)', *Herio'r byd*, ed. D. B. Rees (1980) · m. cert. · b. cert. · d. cert.
Archives NL Wales
Likenesses photograph, NL Wales, picture collection [*see illus.*]
Wealth at death £6655: probate, 23 June 1971, *CGPLA Eng. & Wales*

Nicholas, William (1785–1812), army officer, third son of Robert Nicholas (1758–1826), of Ashton Keynes, near Cricklade, Wiltshire, MP for Cricklade (1785–90), and chairman of the board of excise (1802–22), and his first wife, Charlotte, sixth daughter of Admiral Sir Thomas Frankland, fifth baronet, was born at Ashton Keynes on 12 December 1785. Educated at a private school in Hackney, and from late 1799 at the Royal Military Academy, Woolwich, he was commissioned second lieutenant in the Royal Engineers in 1801, becoming first lieutenant on 1 July 1802. After the usual Chatham course he was employed on the Dover defences.

In spring 1806 Nicholas joined the expedition to Sicily. He was engaged at St Euphemia, and at Maida, where he was assistant quartermaster-general, and survived one incident in which a cannon ball carried away his cloak, strapped on behind him, and knocked him off his horse. He took part in the capture of Scylla, July 1806, and was then selected to accompany Sir John Moore on a tour of Sicily. He was promoted second captain on 25 August 1806. On his return he accompanied the expedition to Egypt, and was present at the capture of Alexandria and at the two actions at Rosetta; at the first of these he bravely assisted in carrying General Meade, dangerously wounded, out of the carnage in the streets of Rosetta.

Nicholas was mentioned in dispatches in February 1808 for his conduct during the defence of Scylla, where he served as assistant quartermaster-general; and he was present at the action of Bagnara. He reconnoitred the country in the western part of Sicily, and prepared a report which was highly approved, and forwarded to the secretary of state. In 1809 he was sent by Sir John Stuart on a secret mission to the Spanish army in Spain. On 20 May he joined General Blake's army at Alcanitz in Aragon, and did good service in the action. He returned to Sicily, and shortly afterwards joined the army at Ischia, on the capture of the island. He went to England at the end of 1809 to recover from a blow in the chest received in the engagement at Alexandria.

In March 1810 Nicholas went to Cadiz as second engineer officer of the defence, and on the death of Major Lefebre at Matagorda he succeeded to the command of the engineers at Cadiz. He took part in the battle of Barrosa, and with Captain Birch was publicly thanked on the field of battle by Sir Thomas Graham, who declared: 'There are no two officers in the army to whom I am more indebted than to you two; you have shown yourselves as fine fellows in the field as at your redoubts.'

On 13 February 1812 Nicholas left Cadiz for Elvas, and took part in the siege of Badajoz. On the night before that of the storming, having volunteered to reconnoitre, he stripped, and forded the inundation of Revellas, thus ascertaining the safest passage for the column. He was given the task of leading the troops of the advance to the great breach. There, after twice trying to reach the top, he fell, wounded by a musket ball in his knee, and by a bayonet in his right leg; his left arm was broken and his wrist struck by a musket ball. Despite his wounds, on seeing Colonel Macleod and Captain James fall, and hearing the soldiers ask who was to lead them, he ordered two of his men to carry him up the breach. One of them was killed at the top, and Nicholas was hit by a musket ball, which passed through his chest, breaking two ribs. This shock precipitated him from the top to the bottom of the breach. He was eventually rescued, but died on 14 April. Sir Thomas Graham wrote that no soldier ever distinguished himself more, and his heroic conduct could never be forgotten. Sir Richard Fletcher, the commanding royal engineer, placed a monumental stone over his grave. The brevet rank of major was conferred upon him on the receipt of the dispatch of Marquess Wellesley, but he did not live to know it.   R. H. VETCH, rev. ROGER T. STEARN

Sources Royal Engineers' Institution, Chatham, Royal Engineers Corps' records · J. Philippart, ed., *The royal military calendar*, 3rd edn, 5 (1820) · HoP, *Commons* · A. J. Guy, ed., *The road to Waterloo: the British army and the struggle against revolutionary and Napoleonic France, 1793–1815* (1990) · R. Muir, *Britain and the defeat of Napoleon, 1807–1815* (1996)
Likenesses E. Scriven, stipple (after B. Pym), NPG; repro. in *Royal military calendar* · engraving, Royal Engineers' Institution, Chatham, Royal Engineer Corps' records; repro. in *Royal military calendar*

Nicholl. *See also* Nichol, Nicol, Nicoll.

Nicholl, Andrew (1804–1886), landscape painter and draughtsman, was born on 4 April 1804 in Church Lane, Belfast, the second son of a boot- and shoemaker whose name is variously given as Andrew or Henry Nicholl. His elder brother, William Nicholl (1794–1840), was an amateur painter and gave him encouragement. At about the age of eighteen, Andrew Nicholl was apprenticed as a compositor with the Belfast printer Francis Dalzell Finlay, who spotted Nicholl's talent as a draughtsman. In 1824 Finlay started the newspaper the *Northern Whig*, in which Nicholl was given many puffs, although he was described as 'a delicate young man' (Adams, 29). In 1828 he made a series of 101 watercolour views of the Antrim coast, and in 1829 was commissioned by Robert Thomson of Jennymount to sketch in his grounds. Other early patrons included James Lawson Drummond and James MacDonnell.

In 1830 Nicholl went to London, probably under the aegis of his main patron, James Emerson, later Sir James Emerson Tennent. In London, Nicholl studied in the Dulwich College Gallery, then the only collection of old master paintings open to the public. Under the influence of Aelbert Cuyp, Copley Fielding, Peter DeWint, and Turner, his watercolours grew larger, more loosely painted, and more colourful. After a brief return to Belfast, Nicholl was again in London in 1832 when he exhibited at the Royal Academy for the first time, and was commissioned by Rudolph Ackermann to make drawings in the western highlands of Scotland. From then until 1834, Nicholl shuttled between London and Belfast, and made teaching excursions to Coleraine and Ballycastle. Of his many Belfast pupils, the most distinguished were James Moore (1819–1883) and Narcissus George Batt (c.1824–1898).

In October 1834 Nicholl's *Five Views of the Dublin and Kingstown Railway* appeared, and he began his association with the *Dublin Penny Journal*. He was elected an associate of the Royal Hibernian Academy in 1837, but did not become a full academician until the constitution was revised in 1860. In the mid-1830s Nicholl produced his most attractive watercolour compositions, usually featuring a bank of wild flowers in the foreground and a recognizable Irish coastal view in the background. Between about 1834 and 1840 he was one of the team of artists illustrating *Hall's Ireland*, employed by Samuel Carter Hall and his wife. Nicholl supplied the Halls with archaeological information as well as sketches. A letter from Hall to Nicholl in Belfast, dated 4 December 1840, pays compliments to 'Mrs Nicholl', indicating that the artist was by now married (Nicholl, scrapbook).

Soon afterwards, Nicholl moved to London again, and in 1842 illustrated John Fisher Murray's *The Environs of London*. In December 1844 his seven-year-old son, Robert Andrew Nicholl, died of a chest infection. Nicholl kept up the production of northern Irish scenes for sale in Belfast, and by 1845 bad copies of his work were being sold in Belfast. In July of that year, his patron Emerson Tennent was appointed colonial secretary for Ceylon; in August 1846 Nicholl followed him to the colony as 'teacher of landscape painting, scientific drawing and design' at the Colombo Academy. It seems likely that Nicholl was invited there by Tennent for the purpose of illustrating the secretary's authoritative book *Ceylon* (1859), which is still admired by Sri Lankans. Both Tennent and Nicholl were on an exploratory expedition in the central province of Kandy during the Kandyan uprising of 1848 and had to flee for their lives; Nicholl described his experiences in a long article in the *Dublin University Magazine* in 1852. Many of Nicholl's sketches still remain in the National Museum in Colombo, and among his pupils at the academy was the father of the Sri Lankan art historian Ananda K. Coomaraswamy.

Nicholl seems to have returned to London by 1849, as he exhibited views of Ceylon in the Royal Academy that year. For many years he wrote light pastoral verse, some of which was published in the *Dublin University Magazine*. From the 1850s the chronology of Nicholl's life is hard to establish, as he rarely dated his work; however, he clearly continued to shuttle between London and Belfast. In 1870 he submitted twelve watercolours of Ceylon scenes to Queen Victoria, who bought two of them, and he presented a volume of sketches of Ceylon to the British Museum print room in 1883. Nicholl died at his London house, 7 Camberwell Grove, aged eighty-two, on 16 April 1886, and a memorial exhibition was held in Belfast the following month. Nicholl's daughter Mary Anne presented fifty-six of her father's studies of the plants of Ceylon to the Royal Hibernian Academy. The Ulster Museum has a collection of over 350 works by Nicholl, mostly watercolours and antiquarian sketches; it also holds six charcoal portrait drawings of members of the Nicholl family, mostly dated 1839, by the Italian immigrant Felice Piccioni, and a portrait drawing of Andrew Nicholl, dated 1840, by the Scottish artist Charles Grey (*c*.1808–1892).

MARTYN ANGLESEA

Sources M. A. Nicholl, ed., scrapbook, Ulster Museum, Belfast · *Catalogue of watercolour drawings by the late Andrew Nicholl, RHA* (1886) [with introduction by W. Nicholl; exhibition catalogue, 55 Donegall Place, Belfast, 26 May 1886] · J. F. Johnston (?), 'Account of Nicholl's life', *c*.1890, Ulster Museum, Belfast · A. Nicholl, 'A sketching tour of five weeks in the forests of Ceylon: its ruined temples, colossal statues, tanks, dagobahs etc [pts 1–2]', *Dublin University Magazine*, 40 (1852), 527–40, 691–700 · W. G. Strickland, *A dictionary of Irish artists*, 2 vols. (1913) · [M. Anglesea], *Andrew Nicholl, 1804–1886* (1973) [exhibition catalogue, Ulster Museum, Belfast, 15 Aug – 24 Sept 1973] · *Andrew Nicholl: the plants of Ceylon* (1981) · M. Anglesea, 'Andrew Nicholl and his patrons in Ireland and Ceylon', *Studies: an Irish Quarterly Review*, 71 (1982), 130–51 · M. Anglesea, *Andrew Nicholl's views of the Antrim coast in 1828* (1982) · R. Adams, 'Andrew Nicholl', *Irish Arts Review*, 1/4 (1984), 29–34 · S. Lakdusinghe and R. K. de Silva, *Exhibition of Andrew Nicholl watercolours* (1998) [exhibition catalogue, National Museum, Colombo, 1998] · A. Deane, 'Belfast in the past', *Belfast Museum and Art Gallery Quarterly Notes*, 40 (March 1939), 1–5 · R. M. Elmes, *Catalogue of Irish topographical prints and original drawings in the National Library of Ireland* (1943) · J. Hewitt and others, *Art in Ulster: paintings, drawings, prints and sculpture for the last 400 years to 1957*, 2 vols. (1977), vol. 1 · A. M. Stewart and C. de Courcy, *Royal Hibernian Academy of Arts: index of exhibitors and their works, 1826–1979*, 3 vols. (1985–7) · [M. Anglesea], *Portraits and prospects: British and Irish drawings and watercolours from the collection of the Ulster Museum, Belfast* (1989) · M. Anglesea, 'The iconography of the Antrim coast', *The poet's place: essays in honour of John Hewitt*, ed. G. Dawe and J. W. Foster (1991), 31–44

Likenesses C. Grey, oils, 1836, priv. coll. · F. Piccioni, charcoal, *c*.1839, Ulster Museum, Belfast · C. Grey, drawing, 1840, Ulster Museum, Belfast

Nicholl, Donald (1923–1997), historian and theologian, was born in Claremount, Halifax, Yorkshire, on 23 July 1923, the son of William Nicholl (1898–1979), a brass finisher, and his wife, Mary Ann Scott (1904–1981). They had been married in the Anglican church of Claremount the previous Christmas day and it was a continuing source of joy to know that he had already been present on that occasion, two months old in his mother's womb. The family was extremely poor: Nicholl's childhood experience was one of a warm, close-knit, working-class community on the one hand, and of a burgeoning sense of personal ability on the other. In school he proved outstanding, excelling in every academic subject as well as in sport. In due course he rose, too, to be 6 feet 6 inches tall. When his teachers decided that he should specialize in history, he won a Brackenbury scholarship to Balliol College, Oxford, as well as a state scholarship. By then the war was on, but he went up to Oxford for a year before joining the army.

Nicholl's experience of personal tuition as a freshman for two terms in political philosophy by the master of Balliol, A. D. Lindsay, was breathtaking; no less formative was a term of tutorials in medieval history with Maurice Powicke, regius professor of history, a remarkable privilege. In the army Nicholl served in the ranks, first in the infantry and then in intelligence, mostly in Asia. His time in India deeply affected him, strengthening an already existing resolve to become a Catholic. In India, as later on visits to Germany and France, he discovered in Catholicism a satisfyingly international spiritual community. After returning to Oxford in 1946 he was received into the Catholic church at Blackfriars. Numerous Dominicans were ever after among his closest friends. At the same time his medieval tutor, Richard Southern, had a profound influence upon him and became another lifelong friend. On 26 July 1947 Nicholl married Dorothy Tordoff (*b*. 1923), whom he had known from schooldays. She provided the domestic stability and affectionate companionship he greatly needed to set against the life of a somewhat impractical and ascetic teacher. They had five children.

In January 1948 Nicholl began teaching at Edinburgh University as assistant to Professor Richard Pares. In 1953 he moved to Keele, where he was promoted to a professorship in 1972. Two years later, however, he became professor of both religious studies and history at the Santa Cruz campus of the University of California. For three years he was also chairman of the religious studies department. In 1980 he and his wife returned to Britain.

Nicholl's intellectual odyssey was more complex than this suggests. While he began academic life as a medieval historian, he was at the time more preoccupied with modern philosophy, to which he produced a highly stimulating guide, *Recent Thought in Focus* (1952). Only at Keele did his heart really return to medieval history. After publishing an English translation of Dante's *Monarchy* for student use, he became immersed in his one major historical study, a life of Archbishop Thurstan of York, something which grew almost naturally out of his love for Yorkshire and its greatest saint, Ailred of Rievaulx, Thurstan's contemporary. At the same time Nicholl taught himself medieval Welsh and medieval Irish, believing it essential for a historian of medieval Britain. Yet while he greatly loved Celtic literature, he wrote almost nothing in this area.

After the publication of *Thurstan* (1964), Nicholl turned overnight to modern history, having decided that he could not spend his life becoming an ever more learned medievalist. Instead he learned Russian and specialized in the field of Russian religious and intellectual history, delighting particularly in Seraphim of Sarov, Nikolai Fyodorov, and Dostoyevsky. At Santa Cruz his concerns turned increasingly to the great eastern religions, Hinduism, Buddhism, and Islam, but nothing pleased him more than his course on Dostoyevsky's *The Brothers Karamazov*, open to anyone in the 'penny university' at the Café Pergolesi. Nicholl was a magnetic lecturer, at heart more teacher than scholar. He published remarkably little but towards the end of his Californian years, urged by John Todd, he wrote his best-selling *Holiness* (1981).

Soon after returning to Europe, Nicholl was appointed rector of the Ecumenical Institute for Advanced Theological Studies at Tantur, near Jerusalem, and his four years there proved intensely demanding, a life he later described in *The Testing of Hearts* (1989 and 1998), reflecting on the round of events both inside the institute and in the relations between Jews and Palestinians. Subsequently, in nominal retirement at Betley, near Keele, he became a senior research fellow in the multi-faith centre at Selly Oak and a leader of spiritual retreats. At the same time he worked on a study entitled *Triumphs of the Spirit in Russia* (1997), a culmination of years of reflective scholarship. He died at his home, Rostherne, Common Lane, Betley, Staffordshire, on 3 May 1997, just as it was published, after struggling serenely against the advance of cancer. He was buried in Keele churchyard on 9 May 1997. *The Beatitude of Truth* (1997), a collection of papers selected by him, appeared posthumously. These two, with *Holiness* and *The Testing of Hearts*, he called his quartet, containing the spiritual legacy that he hoped would endure.

Nicholl always remained at heart a Yorkshireman, but his numerous intense friendships were worldwide. Broadly of the left but never a party man, he contributed about a hundred articles to *The Tablet*, commenting on current affairs in a way that was at once personal, sharply perceptive, and profoundly compassionate. As he matured intellectually and spiritually, his loyalty to the Catholicism he had fervently embraced in youth grew more critical but did not diminish, yet as he developed from academic historian to spiritual teacher his sense of affinity with all the world's great religions grew ever deeper.

ADRIAN HASTINGS

Sources D. Nicholl, *The testing of hearts*, 2nd edn (1998) · D. Nicholl, *The beatitude of truth*, ed. A. Hastings (1997) · D. Nicholl, 'Gratitude', unfinished autobiography, MS, priv. coll. [Dorothy Nicholl, widow] · personal knowledge (2004) · private information (2004) [Dorothy Nicholl, widow]
Archives priv. coll., MSS

Nicholl, John (*fl.* 1605–1637?), mariner and author, if a will of 1637 is his, originated from Northam, Devon. On 12 April 1605 he sailed under Captain Nicholas St John from Woolwich in the *Olive Branch*, a large fly-boat of 170 tons dispatched by Sir Oliph Leigh to reinforce the colony established by his brother, Charles Leigh, on the River Wiapoco in Guiana. On reaching the coast of Guiana, the ship was carried to leeward of the Wiapoco, which increased the 'heart-burning and malice' (Hulme and Whitehead, 66) between crew and colonists. After weeks battling against adverse winds and currents they sought fresh victuals among the islands of the Lesser Antilles and on 15 August landed on St Lucia. Archaeological evidence suggests that they were based near the present-day Vieux Fort, on the island's south coast. Initially they were well received by the native, red-painted Caribs; but the quantity of food they acquired was insufficient for both the ship's crew and the colonists to continue the voyage. While the seamen sailed off, sixty-seven colonists decided to stay and settle the island. One group, led by St John, seems to have perished in a fruitless search for gold, and most of the remainder were gradually massacred by the Caribs before, taking advantage of a truce, the surviving nineteen colonists (including Nicholl) rigged and provisioned one of the Carib piraguas (large canoes made from a single tree) and sailed from St Lucia on 26 September, only to be wrecked (5 October) on a barren island about a league from the mainland.

A small group sailed in a canoe for Venezuela; Nicholl and the remainder suffered two weeks' hunger and thirst before being rescued. They were taken to Tocuyo, then to Coro, and appeared before the local governor; but through the intervention of a friendly Fleming they escaped the galleys. After five months being well treated at Coro, Nicholl and three companions sailed on a frigate bound for Cartagena (30 April 1606), where on 10 May they were imprisoned as spies. Released after two months, Nicholl was sent in early August to Havana, from where (about 10 October) he sailed for Spain, reaching Cadiz on 15 December. Finally an accommodating English skipper landed him in the Downs on 2 February 1607. Later that year Nicholl published *An Houre Glasse of Indian Newes*, which he dedicated to Sir Thomas Smythe, governor of the East India Company. It gives a spirited account of his travails and is especially interesting on Carib agriculture and smallholding, which successfully combined traditional crops with European introductions. Nicholl was especially struck by the turtles, guavas, and hammocks made from local cotton, and by the hail of arrows and 'great Brasill swords' (Purchas, 327) employed by the horn-blowing natives. It is the most detailed and valuable account of Carib-European contacts before full-scale attempts at settlement on the islands of the Lesser Antilles in the 1620s. Little more is known of Nicholl: a John Nicoll who made his last will on 20 March 1637 was married to Anne, with two daughters, but no place of residence is given. BASIL MORGAN

Sources P. Hulme and N. L. Whitehead, eds., *Wild majesty: encounters with Caribs from Columbus to the present day* (1992), 62–79 · S. Purchas, *Purchas his pilgrimes* (1625); repr. (1906), vol. 16, pp. 324–37 · *DNB* · J. A. Williamson, *The Caribbee islands under the proprietary patents* (1926), 13–18 · K. R. Andrews, *The Spanish Caribbean* (1978) · R. Bullen, 'The first English settlement on St. Lucia', *Caribbean Quarterly*, 13/2 (1966), 29–35 · J. Nicholl, 'An houre glasse of Indian newes', BL, MS 278a4.T.P.9070619 · will, PRO, PROB 11/177, fol. 320

Nicholl, Sir John (1759–1838), judge and politician, was born on 16 March 1759, the second son of John Nicholl (c.1726–1773) of Llan-maes, Glamorgan, and his wife, Elizabeth, *née* Havard. By birth and connection one of the minor gentry of Glamorgan and heir to the small Tondu estate of his uncle Edward Powell (d. 1771), Nicholl's standing and dynastic influence in the county increased after his marriage on 8 September 1787 to Judy (*bap.* 1760, *d.* 1829)—youngest daughter and coheir of Peter Birt of Airmyn, Yorkshire, and Wenvoe Castle, near Cardiff—the success of his career in the law, and his purchase in 1804 of the Merthyr Mawr estate near Bridgend, where his friends John Luxmore (1756–1830), bishop of St Asaph, William Van Mildert, bishop of Llandaff, and Sir Christopher Cole and the Talbot family of nearby Penrice Castle were regular guests. Shelving his personal ambition to represent the county in parliament he played a decisive part in determining the outcome of contested elections in Glamorgan and Cardiff Boroughs in 1820, the election for Glamorgan in 1830 of Cole's stepson Christopher Rice Mansel Talbot (1803–1890), and for Cardiff Boroughs in 1832 of his only surviving son, John (1797–1853), who on 14 December 1821 married Talbot's sister Jane Harriot (d. 1874). Two of Nicholl's three daughters were married: Judy (b. 1791) to the Glamorgan squire and banker Charles Franks, and Katherine (1789–1830) to Luxmore's son Charles (1794–1854), dean of St Asaph.

Intended initially for the church, Nicholl received his early education at grammar schools in Cowbridge (1765/6–73) and Bristol (1773–5). On 27 June 1775 he matriculated from St John's College, Oxford, where he was elected to a founder's kin fellowship. He graduated BCL on 15 June 1780 and DCL on 6 April 1785. Admitted to Lincoln's Inn on 28 July 1775, he was not called, and on 3 November 1785 he was entered as an advocate in Doctors' Commons, where he made the acquaintance of his mentor and lifelong friend, Sir William Scott. He assisted Sir

William Grant with the inquiry into the state of law in Jersey in 1791, but was turned down for the post of Admiralty advocate that year. On 31 October 1798 he was knighted preparatory to succeeding Scott as king's advocate on 6 November 1798, and regularly briefed the privy council and secretaries of state on international law and maritime matters, including booty and prize cases and the wording of notices, correspondence, and the Amiens peace treaty of September 1801.

At the general election of 1802 Nicholl was brought into parliament for the rotten borough of Penryn by Lord de Destainville, a supporter of the Addington ministry. An effective and astute debater, he declared for Pitt in 1804 and displayed his knowledge of international law in a maiden speech in justification of his ministry's decision to wage war against Spain, 11 February 1805. Kept on by the 1806–7 Grenville ministry and returned for Hastings, Nicholl defended their order in council on neutral vessels, 4 February 1807. He declined to second the nomination of Charles Abbott for re-election as speaker in 1807, choosing to speak only on 'matters immediately connected with my profession, upon which alone I can hope to be entitled to any attention' (PRO, 30/9/15, Nicholl to Abbott, 2 June 1807). He refused the Portland ministry's offer of a seat at Rye that year, opting instead to sit for the Wiltshire borough of Great Bedwyn, which he represented on the interest of the first and second barons Ailesbury (with one brief interruption) until his retirement from parliament in 1832. Following his appointment on 6 February 1809 as dean of the court of arches and a prerogative court of Canterbury judge with a seat on the privy council, Nicholl's support for government, particularly the 1812–27 tory administration of Lord Liverpool, was more conspicuous, and his speeches proposing Abbott's re-election as speaker, on 24 November 1812, and that of his successor, Charles Manners Sutton, on 2 June 1817, were highly acclaimed. He invariably defended the interests of the established church and the Admiralty and ecclesiastical courts. He was against exempting nonconformist chapels from parish rates (16 June 1815), chaired and reported from the select committee on tithes (18 June 1816), and backed the attempts made by Joseph Phillimore in 1819 and 1820 to amend the law on marriages. He supported government over the 1820–21 Queen Caroline affair, including the omission of her name from the liturgy. From 1812, when he was first broached as a contender for the prestigious Oxford University seat, until 1825 he was one of the leading parliamentary opponents of Catholic relief. Backed by 'the Lord Chancellor [Lord Eldon], Sir William Scott, Doctors' Commons, his own college of St. John's, All Souls College, Corpus, all the leading people connected with Christ Church … (the Dean excepted), Magdalen College and the greater part of the residents' (BL, Add. MS 51659, John Wishaw to Lady Holland, 16 July 1821), and with 740 votes promised he resigned from parliament on 18 August 1821 to stand as the anti-Catholic candidate for the University of Oxford, losing by 612 votes to 519 to Richard Heber, the nominee of the chancellor of the university, Lord Grenville. Solicited to stand again in

January 1826 he declined, partly because his patron, who had been reluctant to return him for Great Bedwyn after his previous failure, forbade it. He remained a die-hard opponent of emancipation, including concessions to protestants and Jews, but chose not to declare against Peel at the Oxford University by-election in February 1829 and deemed it prudent to submit with good grace when it became law. He took the same stance when parliamentary reform, which he had resolutely opposed since it was proposed by Sir Francis Burdett on 17 May 1817, was conceded in 1832. He steered the 1827 Clerical Benefices Registration Bill and the 1829 Ecclesiastical Courts Bill successfully through the House of Commons.

Nicholl habitually devoted much time to 'regular study and fireside reading', preferring to 'leave the management of domestic concerns and family accounts' to his wife (Merthyr Mawr MSS, L/205/7). His advice to the privy council on matters affecting the Channel Islands (*White* v. *Lequense*, 1823–4) and Admiralty and ecclesiastical court cases was highly valued, and he was renowned for his sound judgments as a prerogative court judge. Among his definitive decisions he ruled in the case of *Kemp* v. *Wickes* (1809) that a Church of England priest could not refuse to bury a dissenter's child; rejected all claims against the will of George III (1822); ruled in *Dew* v. *Clarke and Clarke* (1826) that partial insanity did not necessarily invalidate a will; and in *Lillie* v. *Lillie* (1829) that the deliberate destruction of a will, without the testator's consent, did not invalidate its contents if they could be otherwise proved. In *Mytton* v. *Mytton* (1830) he ruled that a wife might divorce her husband for cruelty and adultery. He was exonerated when the cost of proceedings in his court in the case of *Evans* v. *Peddle* (1821–8) and his decisions in the Brinco (1826) and Westmeath (1826) divorce cases were questioned in the House of Commons in 1829 and 1830. Some judgments by him were rendered obsolete by the 1837 Wills Act. Despite his increasing deafness and the aspirations of Phillimore and younger men he was appointed an Admiralty court judge in 1833, and ruled in the case of the *Perth* (1838) that it befell steamships to take every possible precaution *vis-à-vis* sailing ships. He resigned from the court of arches in 1834 in favour of his nephew Herbert Jenner (afterwards Jenner-Fust; 1778–1852) whom he replaced as vicar-general to the archbishop of Canterbury.

Nicholl died at Merthyr Mawr on 26 August 1838 and was buried in the parish church in September. His will, dated 13 September 1830 with two codicils, was proved under £140,000 at the prerogative court of Canterbury on 4 October 1838. Chief of its many beneficiaries were his son, John, the heir to his estates in fee simple and residuary legatee, and his unmarried daughter, Mary Anne (1787–1844). Obituaries in *The Cambrian* and the Conservative *Glamorgan, Monmouth and Brecon Gazette and Merthyr Guardian* of 1 September 1838 noticed Nicholl's legal career, involvement in the establishment of a national school (1812) and savings bank (1817) in Bridgend and of King's College, London (1824), his support for the Society for the Propagation of the Gospel, and fellowships of the Royal Society and of the Society of Antiquaries. Sir William Holdsworth's *History of English Law* (13.691–6) testifies to Nicholl's outstanding contribution as an ecclesiastical and Admiralty court judge.   MARGARET ESCOTT

Sources corresp. and papers, priv. coll., Merthyr Mawr MSS · R. G. Thorne, 'Nicholl, Sir John', HoP, *Commons, 1790–1820* · R. G. Thorne, 'Cardiff Boroughs', HoP, *Commons, 1790–1820* · R. G. Thorne, 'Great Bedwyn', HoP, *Commons, 1790–1820* · R. G. Thorne, 'Glamorgan', HoP, *Commons, 1790–1820* · M. Escott, 'Nicholl, Sir John', HoP, *Commons, 1820–32* [draft] · PRO, Nicholl MSS, PRO 30/42 · Holdsworth, *Eng. law*, 13.691–6 · *Parliamentary Debates*, 1st ser., and new ser. [as indexed to Nicholl] · *The Times* (1795–1838) [CD-ROM] · Wilts. & Swindon RO, Ailesbury papers, 9/35/109; 1300/5753 · BL, Holland House MSS, Add. MSS 51813, 52011 · *The Cambrian* (1 Sept 1838) · *Glamorgan, Monmouth and Brecon Gazette, and Merthyr Guardian* (1 Sept 1838) · PRO, Colchester MSS, PRO 30/9/42 · *The diary and correspondence of Charles Abbot, Lord Colchester*, ed. Charles, Lord Colchester, 3 vols. (1861) · IGI · John Wishaw to Lady Holland, 16 July 1821, BL, Add. MS 51659

Archives priv. coll., Merthyr Mawr MSS, corresp. and papers · PRO, papers relating to maritime and international law, 30/42 | BL, Peel MSS, indexed items · Cardiff Central Library, Bute MSS · Glamorgan RO, Cardiff, Bute MSS · NL Wales, Bute MSS · NL Wales, Penrice and Margam MSS · NL Wales, Vivian MSS · PRO, Colchester MSS, PRO 30/9/42 · Wilts. & Swindon RO, Ailesbury papers

Likenesses P. W. Tomkins, stipple, pubd 1806 (after M. A. Shee), BM, NPG · W. Owen, oils, exh. RA 1814, St John's College, Oxford · F. Chantry, pencil drawing, NPG · T. Lawrence, portrait, priv. coll. · Meyer (after portrait by W. Owen) · W. Owen, portrait, priv. coll. · Tomkins, portrait (after M. A. Shee)

Wealth at death under £140,000: PRO, death duty registers, IR 26/1495/721

Nicholl, John (1790–1871), antiquary, born at Stratford Green, Essex, on 19 April 1790, was the only son of John Nicholl, a brewer, and Mary, daughter of Mathias Miller of Epping in the same county. Nicholl was enabled by an ample fortune to pursue uninterruptedly his researches in heraldry and genealogy. He married, on 5 October 1822, Elizabeth Sarah, the daughter and heir of John Rahn MD of Enfield, Middlesex. On 16 February 1843 he was elected FSA, and in 1859 he served as master of the Ironmongers' Company.

Nicholl collected genealogical notes made in Essex churches in six folio volumes, and filled three folio volumes with Essex pedigrees, and three others with pedigrees of the various families of Nicholl, Nicholls, or Nichols. Of the latter he made three copies, two of which he bequeathed to his own children, and a smaller third copy was left to the College of Arms. Nicholl also compiled, in three volumes, a series of genealogical miscellanea and architectural and landscape sketches and paintings made during two tours made to the continent in 1842 and 1843. In addition, he left manuscript collections for the history of Islington and notes on biblical criticism. Using the archives of the Ironmongers' Company, he compiled a history of the company in seven folio volumes, embellished with armorial bearings and illuminated initials, and illustrated with drawings of buildings and costumes. The first six of these volumes were presented to the company between 1840 and 1844. (Materials relating to his descriptions of buildings are held in the Victoria and Albert Museum.) In 1851 he printed for private circulation 'Some account of the Worshipful Company of Ironmongers', of which an improved edition was printed in 1866; the cost of both editions was defrayed by the company. Nicholl also wrote poetry, and privately printed a small edition in 1863. He was also one of the original founders of the Islington proprietary school.

Nicholl died at home at Canonbury Place, Islington, London, on 7 February 1871. He was buried in the churchyard of Theydon Garnon, Essex, on 13 February. He left three sons and two daughters.

GORDON GOODWIN, rev. MICHAEL ERBEN

Sources *Herald and Genealogist*, 7 (1873), 83–5 · Boase, *Mod. Eng. biog.* · J. G. Nichols, ed., 'Documents relating to the family of Nicholl, of Essex, with their pedigree', *The topographer and genealogist*, 3 (1858), 544–62, esp. 557–62 · E. Glover, *A history of the Ironmongers' Company* (1991) · *Proceedings of the Society of Antiquaries of London*, 2nd ser., 5 (1870–73), 143

Archives Ironmongers' Company, London · V&A NAL, collections concerning monuments, etc., of Essex chronology of the Bible

Likenesses J. G. Middleton, oils, 1851; formerly in possession of Ironmongers' Company, 1894

Wealth at death under £800: probate, 24 March 1871, *CGPLA Eng. & Wales*

Nicholls. *See also* Nichols, Nicolls, Nicols.

Nicholls, Agnes Helen (1877–1959). *See under* Harty, Sir (Herbert) Hamilton (1879–1941).

Nicholls, Arthur Frederick Crane (1911–1944), secret operations officer, was born on 6 February 1911 at 30 Compayne Gardens, Hampstead, London, the first son and middle child of Joseph Crane Nicholls (1849–1917), a stockbroker, and his wife, Josephine Orchiston Campbell (1871–1953). He was educated at Shardlow Hall, Derbyshire (1917–24), and Marlborough College (1924–9). Childhood summers were shared in Sussex and Aberdeenshire with his sister, Elisabeth. A younger brother died at birth. After the First World War, it was said, young Arthur was the only surviving male on his mother's side of the family.

After seven months at the Sorbonne and a period working at Bonn and Frankfurt in Germany, Nicholls went up to Pembroke College, Cambridge, in 1930. He graduated LLB in 1933 before becoming a member of the Inner Temple and a stockbroker with Sheppards & Co., for whom he worked until 1939.

Nicholls was mobilized shortly before the outbreak of war, having been in the Officers' Training Corps at Cambridge, commissioned in the Territorial Army (Royal Artillery) in 1933, and transferred to the supplementary reserve (Coldstream Guards) in 1937. In September 1939 he went to France with the 2nd battalion of the Coldstream Guards, but was quickly posted to the headquarters of 1st division as an intelligence officer owing to his command of French and German. In May 1940 he was evacuated from Dunkirk, where he had been aide-de-camp to General Alexander. During a brief visit back from

France on 10 January 1940 Nicholls married (Dorothy) Ann Violet Schuster (*b.* 1921), daughter of Sir (Felix) Victor Schuster, baronet and banker, and his wife, Lucy (*née* Skene), at the Royal Military Chapel, Wellington Barracks, London. Their daughter, Jennifer, was born in March 1943.

Nicholls remained on the staff of 1st division headquarters before returning to the 2nd battalion of the Coldstream Guards in June 1941. In October 1941 he went to Staff College at Camberley, from where, in March 1942, he joined the London headquarters of the Special Operations Executive (SOE). In March 1943 he volunteered for SOE service in the occupied Balkans.

That October, promoted lieutenant-colonel, Nicholls parachuted into central Albania as chief of staff of Brigadier 'Trotsky' Davies's mission to the Albanian resistance. For the next two months he performed his duties with distinction, being mentioned in dispatches. In December Davies's mission was then attacked by the Germans and forced on the run in mountains covered by 4 feet of snow. For the next three weeks the remnants of the mission remained on the move in conditions of extreme cold and fatigue, with no medical supplies and little or no food.

Tall—he was 6 feet 5 inches—and lean, Nicholls was physically less robust than others in the party, and his blood circulation was poor. By the end of the month he was already suffering from extreme frostbite in his hands and feet, but to keep going refused to remove his boots. When he finally did so, early in January 1944, both feet at once swelled up and burst. Two days later, while sheltering in a sheepfold, the party was ambushed by Albanian quislings and several men were hit. Davies was among those wounded and captured, and Nicholls assumed command of the mission; only he, another officer, Captain Alan Hare, and three partisans succeeded in making their escape. Nicholls led them on through the snow before halting in another sheepfold where he discovered he could no longer stand. He ordered Hare to abandon him and head for an SOE mission to the south.

With two partisans, Nicholls made for an SOE mission to the north. For the next fortnight he traversed enemy territory, dragged over the snow on his greatcoat, until finally found by the mission. By then he was starved and gangrenous and had dislocated a shoulder from a fall, but at once insisted on radioing a report to SOE headquarters on the fate that had befallen Davies's mission and important matters affecting allied policy. A doctor was found and Nicholls's feet were immediately operated upon, but septicaemia had taken a hold and eventually spread to the kidneys. He died in Albania on 11 February 1944.

Nicholls received a posthumous award of the George Cross. His citation concludes:

> He set an example of heroism, fortitude, courage, leadership, the will to win, and devotion to duty which has seldom been equalled and never surpassed. He carried on far longer than could normally be considered humanly possible, and this undoubtedly caused his death. (*LondG*)

One newspaper termed him 'a modern Captain Oates'

(*Daily Mail*). His widow subsequently married Archibald Dunlop Mackenzie, of Kilfinan, who too had served with SOE during the war.

First buried by the Albanians who had treated him, Nicholls was later reinterred in a formal cemetery in Tirana, but this grave was then obliterated by Enver Hoxha's communist regime after the war. In 1994 a headstone was finally erected in Tirana in the approximate area of the grave.   RODERICK BAILEY

Sources *Coldstream Gazette*, 62 (Sept 1991) · *Marlburian* (autumn 2001) · E. F. Davies, *Illyrian venture: the story of the British military mission to enemy-occupied Albania, 1943–44* (1952) · *LondG* (1 March 1946) · *Daily Mail* (2 March 1946) · *The Times* (2 March 1946) · *Daily Telegraph* (2 March 1946) · private information (2004) [special operations executive adviser; others] · b. cert. · m. cert.

Wealth at death £1588 15s. 9d.: probate, 1944, CGPLA Eng. & Wales

David Gwyn Nicholls (1936–1996), by unknown photographer

Nicholls, David Gwyn (1936–1996), Church of England clergyman and theologian, was born on 3 June 1936 at Woking, Surrey, the only son of Edward Glyndwr Nicholls (1901–1976), local government officer, and his wife, Muriel (Mimi) Gwenllian, *née* Price (1900–1970), a telephone operator. His parents were both Welsh. He was baptized at St Peter's, Old Woking, and educated at Woking grammar school (1947–54), followed by the London School of Economics (1954–7), where he gained a first-class degree in economics and received the Laski and the Gladstone prizes (1957). His advanced studies at King's College, Cambridge (1957–60), led to a PhD (1962), supervised by Alec Vidler, on the theologian and political theorist John Neville Figgis (1866–1919), whose thought continued to inspire Nicholls throughout his life. There followed a year at Yale divinity school (1960–61; STM, 1962) and one at Chichester Theological College (1961–2), where Cheslyn Jones was principal. He was ordained deacon in 1962 and priest in 1963, and held a curacy (1962–6) at St George with St John, Bloomsbury, in connection with the London University chaplaincy, under Gordon Phillips. Crucial for his later life was his move to be lecturer in government in the University of the West Indies in Trinidad (1966–73). At Oxford he received an MA when he went to Exeter College as chaplain, lecturer, and fellow (1973–8), and in 1991 a DLitt through the faculties of history and social studies. After the Exeter chaplaincy he became priest-in-charge (1978–86) and later vicar (1986–96) of Littlemore, Oxford.

For Nicholls theology and politics were one single theme. His religious tradition was distinctly Anglo-Catholic; yet he was anything but an identifiable partisan of any group, and would continually surprise his friends by saying the opposite of what they had expected to come from him. He voted Labour but deplored many Labour Party policies and its 'democratic' ossification. He opposed any sort of 'statism', and at times uttered remarks that sounded like radical Conservative opinions, or indeed like a sort of anarchism. His Anglo-Catholic views did not prevent him from being strongly critical of John Henry Newman and of some Anglican incarnationalism. On the ordination of women he was critical of the positions taken by both sides and thought that the questions as posed were often the wrong ones; he did not see the matter as one of critical urgency, and would have preferred a slower, deeper process of thought about it.

Pluralism, an emphasis inherited from Figgis, was an aspect dear to Nicholls's heart. For him the positive stress had to be on voluntary association; decentralization was better than the centralized sovereign state. But in his view voluntary associations should strive to fulfil their own needs, and should not be pressure groups seeking to persuade the state to do things for them. *The Pluralist State* (1975) was his clearest expression of this belief. His strong historical interest, especially in the Victorian period, was manifested in such books as *Church and State in Britain since 1820* (1967), *Deity and Domination: Images of God and the State in the 19th and 20th Centuries* (1989), based on his Hulsean lectures in Cambridge in 1985, and *God and Government in an 'Age of Reason'* (1995). Apart from his own major books, he did much to stimulate discussion, and was associated with research groups such as the Christendom group and the Jubilee group (a network of 'socialist Christians'); for this latter he edited a series of volumes, and he co-edited (1991) a volume of critical essays on John Henry Newman, opposing the move for his canonization. He had strong dislikes, for example for the Anglican liberalism of the Lux Mundi group, for the application of 'management' techniques in the church, and not least for Archbishop William Temple and his relation to the developing welfare state. He excelled in short pamphlets, in which he commonly touched on important issues in church–state relations, for example Thatcherism, the Terry Waite affair, and the attitudes of archbishops in general.

A second focus of Nicholls's life was the Caribbean. In his London student days he had already spent a term in Jamaica. It was in Trinidad that, on new year's day 1968, he married Gillian Sleigh (*b*. 1938), a paediatrician who became his mainstay throughout his life (he called her Gillie). Of all the islands, Haiti was to become the most distinctive for his future. In the West Indies, attendance at university committees, commonly in Jamaica, meant the use of an 'island-hopping' plane that stopped in Haiti, and he became fascinated with that country. No one at the university seemed to be doing research on the non-English-speaking islands. Haiti's history and politics quickly widened his interests to include questions of race, colour, and independence. Few English-speaking scholars, if any, knew as much about Haiti as Nicholls. Characteristically, he was doubtful whether any change of government there would do any good: change, he thought, had to come from below. His major books in this area were *Economic Dependence and Political Economy: the Haitian Experience* (1974), *From Dessalines to Duvalier: Race, Colour and National Independence in Haiti* (1979), and *Haiti in Caribbean Context: Ethnicity, Economy and Revolt* (1985). Allied with this work were his connections with the Institute of Race Relations, with Oxfam, and with the Society for Caribbean Studies in the United Kingdom, and also his contacts with St Antony's College, Oxford, and his joint seminars on race relations with Professor Kenneth Kirkwood.

Nicholls should have had a professorial position or a canonry in one of the more intellectual of the cathedrals; perhaps his interests covered too many areas for modern specialism to accept. In any case his years at Littlemore gave space for his genius to flower: a large, mainly working-class parish, many visitors from overseas, a centre for hospitality. Everyone in Littlemore knew him. The regular life of prayer and pastoral care meant much to him; but he did not confine himself to the obvious responsibilities of a parish, and made friends informally with all sorts of people whom he met, especially strangers and newcomers.

The most notable inhabitant of the vicarage was the large blue and yellow macaw from Trinidad, Archdeacon William Paley, named after the great representative of traditional natural theology, who was also in evidence at the Sunday lunch parties where sociologists from Poland rubbed shoulders with Littlemore parishioners and Indians from Cowley. On these occasions the Archdeacon flapped and screeched a little but was generally quiescent; he flew only seldom. He was more vocal, however, in his letters to the newspapers, which sometimes stimulated indignant replies. At one stage the Archdeacon actually achieved registration in the Oxford diocesan directory, and under his name Nicholls covered the Haitian elections for the *Daily Telegraph*. He died only a few days before Nicholls's own death.

Nicholls himself disliked pomp and pretentiousness. His motor cycle was as characteristic of him as his vivid dress, which often included a Latin American poncho and sandals. His taste for cigars was another symbol of the world he loved. He died suddenly on 13 June 1996, in the John Radcliffe Hospital, Oxford, as a result of an aortic aneurysm. His funeral and memorial services, attended by local people, by academics, and by eminent figures in the church, were moving and memorable. His ashes were buried in the churchyard of St Mary and St Nicholas, Littlemore, on 20 June. After his death a street close to the church was named David Nicholls Close. He and Gillian, who survived him, had no children. The David Nicholls Memorial Trust was set up to commemorate him through housing his books and papers and continuing the central interests of his life. The collection, rich in theology, politics, and above all Caribbean affairs and Haiti, is in Regent's Park College, Oxford. JAMES BARR

Sources private information (2004) [G. Nicholls] · personal knowledge (2004) · C. Matthew, *The Times* (22 June 1996) · R. Morgan, *The Independent* (18 June 1996) · P. Hirst, *The Guardian* (28 June 1996) · *Daily Telegraph* (25 June 1996) · K. Leech, *Church Times* (3 July 1996)
Archives Regent's Park College, Oxford, books and papers
Likenesses photograph, 1970, repro. in *Daily Telegraph* · photograph, priv. coll.; repro. in *The Independent* · photograph, News International Syndication, London [*see illus.*]
Wealth at death under £180,000: probate, 12 Aug 1996, *CGPLA Eng. & Wales*

Nicholls, Degory (*c*.1545–*c*.1591), college head, was the second son of John Nicholls (*d.* 1544) of Penvose in the parish of St Tudy, Cornwall, and his second wife, Isabella (*b. c*.1505), daughter of John Mohun. He matriculated as a pensioner at Peterhouse, Cambridge, in Easter term 1560, studied under John Whitgift, and took the BA degree in 1564. Elected a probationary fellow of Peterhouse on 30 March 1565, his fellowship was confirmed on 31 March 1566. The MA followed in 1567, which he incorporated at Oxford. In 1570 he became rector of Lanivet, Cornwall, under the patronage of his elder brother Humphrey, and was bursar of Peterhouse in 1570/71. As a university taxor in 1571/2 Nicholls was prominent in agitation against the university statutes of 1570, which much increased the powers of the heads of the colleges over those of the regent masters. In May 1572 he was among those nominated by 164 fellows of colleges to take steps for the 'reformation of certain matters amiss in the new statutes' (Cooper, *Annals*, 2.279). The heads of the colleges exhibited articles against the agitators, condemning Nicholls as one of those who were to be seen in Cambridge and London in clothing 'too fine for scholars' (Cooper, *Ath. Cantab.*, vol. 2). The chancellor, Lord Burghley, referred the dispute to a committee of bishops, who concluded that the 'statutes … may yet stand' and that 'these younger men have been far overseen to seek their pretended reformation by disordered means' (Heywood and Wright, 1.112).

His probably unwelcome duties as taxor fulfilled, Nicholls took the BTh degree in 1574 and preached before the university, becoming also a chaplain to Burghley. On 20 July 1577 Richard Howland, master of Magdalene College, Cambridge, was appointed master of St John's College. Lord Thomas Howard, hereditary visitor of Magdalene, held the power to appoint Howland's successor, but was a minor in ward to the crown. On 22 July 1577, Andrew Perne, master of Peterhouse, wrote to Burghley proposing Nicholls for the mastership, as 'well learned' and 'a maintainer of good order and statutes' (CUL, MS Mm.2.22, p.234), and the fellows of Magdalene expressed their 'very good liking' (ibid., 13.147) of Nicholls, to whom Burghley granted the place. Henry Copinger, a fellow of St John's, had already obtained royal letters appointing him master of Magdalene, but his success was short-lived. Howland rode up to tell Burghley of the 'unlooked for admission of

Mr. Copinger as Master upon her Majesty's letters' (ibid., 13.148), and by 16 August 1577 Nicholls was signing Magdalene accounts 'convinced that he had at last come into his kingdom' (Cunich and others, 85). At about this time Nicholls married Elizabeth (*b. c.*1552), daughter of John Bradley of Louth, Lincolnshire, and his wife, Frances Fairfax.

In 1578 Nicholls was among those appointed to confer on religion with John Feckenham, late abbot of Westminster, but in December 1578 the fellows of Magdalene complained to Burghley that Nicholls hated Welshmen, that he had his cows milked at the college hall door, and that his wife's scolding could be heard all over the college. Hatred of Welshmen brought conflict with Richard Jones, lecturer in Greek, and William Bulkeley, president of Magdalene, whom Nicholls removed, appointing his brother-in-law, John Bradley of Peterhouse, in Bulkeley's place. An uneasy compromise was subsequently reached with the fellows, and Nicholls took the DTh degree in 1581. But his mastership had failed, and in 1582 he resigned and retreated to his Cornish living at St Ervan. He held also the rectory of Cheriton Fitzpaine, Devon, and was appointed a canon of Exeter by the crown in 1579. In 1583 he obtained the rectory of Lanreath, Cornwall. He died about 1591.   N. G. JONES

Sources J. Maclean, *The parochial and family history of the deanery of Trigg Minor in the county of Cornwall*, 3 (1879) · T. A. Walker, *A biographical register of Peterhouse men*, 1 (1927) · P. Cunich and others, *A history of Magdalene College, Cambridge, 1428–1988* (1994) · *Calendar of the manuscripts of the most hon. the marquis of Salisbury*, 13, HMC, 9 (1915) · Venn, *Alum. Cant.* · J. Hurstfield, *The queen's wards: wardship and marriage under Elizabeth I* (1958) · *CSP dom., 1547–80* · *Fasti Angl.* (Hardy), vol. 1 · Rymer, *Foedera*, 2nd edn, vol. 15 · J. Heywood and T. Wright, eds., *Cambridge University transactions during the puritan controversies of the 16th and 17th centuries*, 1 (1854) · Cooper, *Ath. Cantab.*, vol. 2 · CUL, MS Mm.2.22 · C. H. Cooper, *Annals of Cambridge*, 2 (1843) · J. Venn, ed., *Grace book Δ* (1910) · A. R. Maddison, ed., *Lincolnshire pedigrees*, 1, Harleian Society, 50 (1902)

Nicholls, Edward. *See* Nichols, Edward (*bap.* 1583?, *d.* 1622?).

Nicholls, Erith Gwynne [Gwyn] (1874–1939), rugby player and businessman, was born at Flaxley, Gloucestershire, on 15 July 1874, fifth of seven children of Hartley Nicholls (1838–1924), a farmer and later a businessman, and his wife, Jane Eliza Millard (1847–1927). As a small child Gwyn Nicholls, as he was always known, joined the migration from the rural west of England to industrial south Wales which helped quadruple the size of Cardiff in the last thirty years of the nineteenth century. He was one of a number of Cardiff rugby players who were 'West countrymen by birth, but Welsh by location, adoption and inclination' (Williams, *Taff's Acre*, 41). Details of his education are unclear.

While he was a successful businessman, running a laundry company in the Cardiff area, Nicholls's fame rests firmly on rugby. He was one of the leading figures of the first great period of Welsh success, from 1900 on, in which the rugby union game became 'a prominent constituent of Welsh popular culture, a pre-eminent expression of Welsh consciousness, a signifier of Welsh nationhood'

(Williams, 1905, 86). After playing junior rugby with the Cardiff Stars and Cardiff Harlequins teams, he followed his older brother Sydney (1868–1946), who was capped four times for Wales between 1888 and 1891, to the Cardiff club. He made his first-team début in February 1893 and was awarded his first-team cap in 1894–5. In total he played 417 matches for Cardiff, the last in the 1909–10 season, was captain for four seasons, and scored 110 tries. He also played for his native Gloucestershire and briefly, in 1901–2, for Newport.

First capped for Wales against Scotland in 1896, Nicholls played twenty-four times for Wales between then and 1906, captaining the team ten times and scoring three tries and a drop goal. He married on 21 June 1905 Emmeline Helen (Nell; 1884–1928), daughter of Philip Thomas, a Cardiff coal exporter, and later that year (16 December 1905) captained the Welsh fifteen in its most famous victory of the period, 3–0 over the otherwise unbeaten New Zealand tourists. He toured Australia with the British Isles team of 1899, playing in all four test matches and scoring tries in the first two. While much of the visceral appeal of rugby in Wales has rested on flamboyantly gifted individualists, successful Welsh teams have been equally reliant on less obtrusive players who subordinate their skills to creating time and space for others. Nicholls was both exemplar and ideologue of the 'enabling' school, writing in his book *The Modern Rugby Game (and How to Play It)* (1908):

> In an ideal Welsh game, you really see fifteen great chess masters working in partnership and without consultation, each man knowing instinctively not only the best thing to be done, but that all the other fellows know it also, and are falling, or have fallen into their places accordingly.

Tall—6 feet—and powerful by the standards of the time with 'restrained but menacing power' (Smith and Williams, 129), Nicholls was often called the 'prince of three-quarters' (*Western Mail*, 25 March 1939). W. J. T. Collins reckoned him the best all-round centre he had seen in sixty years watching rugby:

> His aim was to draw and hold the defence so that the way was open for his own wing. It was in the supreme gift of judgment that he was greatest. An all-round player with all the gifts, he could make a burst for the line with a gallop or a close swerve, and he was very difficult to stop; his fielding and screw-punting to touch were remarkable for quickness, accuracy and judgment; he was a good drop kick; his tackling was of the best; and he had a masterly faculty for getting to the weak spot to strengthen defence.   (Collins, 14)

Other players deferred to Nicholls's judgement and presence, and possibly to his slight social superiority to most Welsh players. W. J. Hoare referred to the 'confidence the mere presence of Nicholls produced' (Hoare, 100). A natural choice as captain, he was at least twice persuaded out of retirement to lead Wales, and before the 1905 match against New Zealand—the origin of a rivalry that retained unusual intensity until the 1980s—innovatively prepared the team by training behind closed doors. After retiring he refereed—'wasn't I awful' (Sewell, 261), he said after his one international match, Scotland v. England in 1909—and he was a Welsh rugby union committee man and selector from 1925 to 1931. Extremely reticent, he was a reluctant committee man and results as a selector were in marked contrast to his playing success.

Nicholls's business life, in partnership with his brother-in-law Bert Winfield, also a member of the 1905 Wales team, was highly successful. Their company, Victoria Laundries, survived in the Cardiff area until the 1970s. Of his three children the second son, Geoffrey, played seven times for Cardiff in 1934–5, while his daughter, Erith Maisie, married Frank Williams (1910–59), who was capped fourteen times for Wales between 1929 and 1933. Nicholls died at his home, Fairways, Highwalls Road, Dinas Powys, Glamorgan, on 24 March 1939 after some years of ill health, ascribed to nervous trouble after diving into the sea fully clothed attempting to rescue two girls at Weston-super-Mare in August 1923. He was buried three days later in St Andrew's Church, Dinas Powys. He is commemorated by the Gwyn Nicholls gates, erected in 1949 at the Quay Street entrance, in Westgate Street, to Cardiff Arms Park. They were taken down in 1999 during the construction of the Millennium Stadium, but relocated outside the Cardiff Rugby League Football Club ground, also in Westgate Street, in 2000.   HUW RICHARDS

Sources D. Parry-Jones, *Prince Gwyn* (1999) • D. Smith and G. Williams, *Fields of praise: the official history of the Welsh Rugby Union, 1881–1981* • D. E. Davies, *Cardiff rugby club: history and statistics, 1876–1975* (1975) • private information (2004) • W. J. T. Collins, *Rugby recollections* (1948) • J. M. Jenkins, D. Pierce, and T. Auty, *Who's who of Welsh international rugby players* (1991) • G. Williams, 'Taff's acre: the pre-1900 years', *Taff's acre*, ed. D. Parry-Jones (1984) • *Western Mail* [Cardiff] (25 March 1939) • *Western Mail* [Cardiff] (28 March 1939) • G. Williams, '1905 and all that: sporting success and social function in Wales, 1880–1914', *1905 and all that: essays on rugby football, sport and Welsh society* (1991) • E. H. D. Sewell, *Rugger: the man's game* (1944) • C. Thomas, *The history of the British Lions*, pbk edn (1996) • W. J. Hoare, 'Wales 1905', *The game goes on*, ed. H. B. T. Wakelam (1936) • m. cert. • d. cert. • *CGPLA Eng. & Wales* (1939) • D. P. James, *History of Cardiff RFC*

Wealth at death £25,600 1s. 4d.: probate, 9 June 1939, *CGPLA Eng. & Wales*

Nicholls [Nicolls], **Ferdinando** (1597/8–1662), clergyman and ejected minister, came from a Buckinghamshire gentry family; his parents' names are unknown. He matriculated from Magdalen College, Oxford, on 10 November 1615, aged seventeen, graduated BA in December 1618, and proceeded MA in June 1621. He began his clerical career as curate to John White of Dorchester, Dorset, with whom he had probably been brought into contact by his brother, Matthew Nicolls, father of Matthias Nicolls (1630?–1687), who had been a lecturer at Plymouth and who later assisted White in organizing emigration to New England. In 1627 Ferdinando Nicholls moved to Sherborne, also in Dorset, but in May 1629 accompanied White to the Tower of London in an attempt to speak to Denzil Holles, MP for Dorchester, and the other members imprisoned for preventing the speaker, Sir Heneage Finch, from adjourning the Commons.

Nicholls married Mary, daughter of Oliver Littisham of Fordington, Somerset, on 12 May 1631 and the next month

became lecturer at St Mary Arches, Exeter; he was presented to the vicarage there by Bishop Joseph Hall in November 1634. He agreed with his parishioners to preach two sermons every Sunday and they undertook to pay him £80 per annum. He was an eloquent preacher although he always wrote out his sermon in full. One of his parishioners was the alderman and redoubtable puritan Ignatius Jurdain. Nicholls preached his funeral sermon in 1640 and showed his admiration for Jurdain by later publishing *The Life and Death* (1654), in which he related going to Jurdain's house after a 'frothy' sermon at the cathedral: when Jurdain picked out various passages, Nicholls thought it wonderful 'to see how a holy heart can draw comfort out of anything'.

Nicholls was presented to the living of Twickenham in 1645 by the Westminster assembly and as he did not receive the profits of the vicarage was granted an order for payment from the committee for plundered ministers. Yet his parish register suggests that he remained in Exeter: the numerous baptisms, marriages, and burials are recorded with the same regularity during the war years as before and after. In 1646 Nicholls was appointed one of three Bodley lecturers and in 1654 became the sole one for the rest of his life, receiving at first £40 per annum and later the profits of land at Hennock, purchased with the Bodley funds, but criticism suggests that he did not fulfil his commitment to lecture. In 1648 he signed *The Joint Testimonie* of Devon ministers in support of the solemn league and covenant, thus showing his Presbyterianism. After the king's execution he influenced JPs not to attend the sessions and in 1650 he revealed his opposition to the Commonwealth, being accused, with Thomas Ford, of using his pulpit for 'intemperate declarations and seditious invectives' which might endanger the safety of the state (*CSP dom.*, 1650, 74–5). However, like others, in time Nicholls became in some measure reconciled to the new regime: he became one of the commissioners for examining the conduct of the clergy in 1654, dealing with charges such as using the prayer book, encouraging Whitsun ales, wakes, and plays, and disaffection to the government. He supported the Exeter assembly of the ministers of Devon begun in 1655 and became its moderator in 1657. When thirteen of the Exeter churches were closed by the chamber of the city in 1657, St Mary Arches was retained and he was presented to the enlarged living.

At the Restoration Nicholls remained in possession of his living, but in September 1662 he was ejected. None the less, he fulfilled his desire to end his life with his congregation, dying in his church on 14 December that year during the singing of a psalm. At his burial in the chancel on 17 December there was a disturbance from over a hundred objectors protesting at the service's being according to the prayer book. Nicholls was survived by his wife and one daughter of their two sons and four daughters.

                                        MARY WOLFFE

Sources *Calamy rev.* • F. Rose-Troup, 'An Exeter worthy and his biographer', *Report and Transactions of the Devonshire Association*, 29 (1897), 350–77 • Exeter city chamber act book 10, 1651–63, Devon RO, B1/10 • F. Nicholls, *The life and death of Mr Ignatius Jurdain* (1654) •

A. Brockett, *Nonconformity in Exeter, 1650–1875* (1962) · parish registers, Exeter, St Mary Arches, Devon RO · W. J. Harte, 'Ecclesiastical and religious affairs in Exeter, 1640–1662', *Report and Transactions of the Devonshire Association*, 69 (1937), 41–72 · R. N. Worth, 'Puritanism in Devon and the Exeter assembly', *Report and Transactions of the Devonshire Association*, 9 (1877), 250–91 · Wood, *Ath. Oxon.*, new edn · Foster, *Alum. Oxon.* · *CSP dom.*, *1628–9*; *1650* · I. Gower, 'Puritanism in the county of Devon, 1570 to 1641', MA diss., University of Exeter, 1970 · W. J. Harte, 'Bodley lecture', *Devon and Cornwall Notes and Queries*, 20 (1938–9) · F. Rose-Troup, *John White* (1930) · S. K. Roberts, *Recovery and restoration in an English county: Devon local administration, 1646–1670* (1985) · *The nonconformist's memorial ... originally written by ... Edmund Calamy*, ed. S. Palmer, [3rd edn], 2 (1802) · *DNB*
Wealth at death assessed for eight hearths in 1662: Harte, 'Ecclesiastical and religious affairs in Exeter'

Nicholls, Francis [Frank] (*bap.* **1699**?, *d.* **1778**), anatomist and physician, was the second of the three sons of John Nicholls (*d.* 1714) of Trereife, Cornwall, barrister. He can probably be identified with the Francis Nicholls who was baptized on 19 January 1699 at the church of St Andrew's, Holborn. Both his parents came from Cornwall. Nicholls was educated at a private school in the country and at Westminster School before entering Exeter College, Oxford, on 4 March 1715, where his tutor was John Haviland. He graduated BA on 14 November 1718, MA on 12 June 1721, MB on 16 February 1725, and MD on 16 March 1730.

While at university Nicholls practised dissection at every opportunity. He was appointed reader in anatomy at the university and probably began lecturing in 1719. At the end of each course he went to London to study with public lecturers in anatomy there. He also travelled on the continent, attending Winslow's lectures in Paris and visiting Morgagni and Santorinus in Italy. Upon his return to England, probably in the mid-1720s, he began a medical practice in Cornwall. However, he soon abandoned this and moved to London to teach anatomy. A course in human and comparative anatomy was advertised in the *Daily Post* to begin on 6 October 1727 at the Two Black Posts in Bow Street, Covent Garden. A printed syllabus was advertised as being available.

Nicholls was elected a fellow of the Royal Society in 1728, and his next anatomy course was given in December 1729 at Mr Ranby's, Southampton Street, Bloomsbury; between 1730 and 1736 he lectured at the Druggists' Laboratory, Old Fish Street. His 1732 syllabus described

> a compleat course of human and comparative anatomy in which the Oeconomy will be explained, and the progress from Anatomy to the several branches of physick illustrated, by proper lectures on the blood, medicines, and the theory and practice of midwifery.

In that year he published in Oxford his *Compendium anatomicum*, a detailed syllabus of his lectures, amended and expanded in 1733, 1736, and 1740. By all accounts he was a very successful lecturer, attracting not only medical students but also the general public to his courses. In 1736 he lectured at a house near the Bull's Head tavern in Lincoln's Inn Fields, and charged 4 guineas for his first course, 3 for the second, and 2 for subsequent courses. By 1739 his course comprised thirty-nine lectures and he had

Francis Nicholls (*bap.* 1699?, *d.* 1778), attrib. Thomas Hudson, *c.*1745–8

moved to a corner of Lincoln's Inn Fields near Clare Market. William Hunter took this course in the winter of 1740–41, and he hoped to succeed Nicholls, who retired from teaching the following year, but Nicholls instead appointed his pupil Thomas Lawrence.

Nicholls was among the first to lecture on the minute anatomy of the tissues, and he was especially interested in the structure of the blood vessels. Before the Royal Society he demonstrated how an aneurysm could be produced in an artery when its inner coats were ruptured, while the outer remained intact. He also suggested the relationship between the nerves and blood pressure. Anatomists admired his skill in making 'corroded' anatomical preparations, in which part of an organ could be displayed by removing surrounding structures. Nicholls is often credited as the inventor of this technique, but William Cowper and Govart Bidloo had used it before him.

On 27 June 1743, at St James's, Westminster, Nicholls married Elizabeth Mead (*b.* 1705), youngest daughter of the celebrated physician Richard *Mead. Thereafter, Nicholls successfully pursued a medical practice in London, assisted by his father-in-law. Of five Nicholls children, two survived to adulthood, a son, John, and a daughter, Elizabeth.

Nicholls was elected a candidate of the Royal College of Physicians of London on 30 September 1730 and a fellow on 26 June 1732. The college named him Goulstonian lecturer in 1734, when he lectured on the structure of the heart and the circulation of the blood, and again in 1736, when he lectured on bladder stones. In November 1739 he delivered the Harveian oration, published in 1740. He was a censor in 1735 and 1746. Nicholls was named Lumleian lecturer for a five-year term on 30 August 1746; he gave the first lecture, 'De anima medica', on 16 December 1748 and it was published in 1750. Early in 1749, however, upon the death of one of the elects of the college, a physician junior to Nicholls was elected as successor. Nicholls was gravely insulted and resigned his Lumleian lectureship, withdrawing from active participation in the college. His father-in-law, Mead, resigned as an elect, probably in protest, on 9 April 1750. While no reason for this slight was given at the time, Peachey speculates that Nicholls's 'professed and militant agnosticism' was a deciding factor (Peachey, 60).

Nicholls is usually said to be the author of an anonymous 1751 pamphlet, *The Petition of the Unborn Babes to the Censors of the Royal College of Physicians of London*, which satirized several senior fellows of the college, including Dr Robert Nesbit (called Pocus in the pamphlet) and Dr William Barrowby (Barebone). The pamphlet opposed lying-in hospitals, and was answered by *A Vindication of Man-Midwifery* (1752). In 1753 Nicholls was appointed to succeed the late Hans Sloane as one of George II's physicians. His report on the autopsy of the king in 1760, in the form of a letter to the earl of Macclesfield, president of the Royal Society, was published in the *Philosophical Transactions*.

Nicholls left London for Oxford in 1762 to supervise his son John's education, and when John moved back to London to study law Nicholls retired to Epsom where he lived until his death, possibly of tuberculosis, on 7 January 1778. Nicholls's will, written in 1770, mentions property in several villages in Surrey and Sussex which had been part of his wife's jointure. Also part of Elizabeth Mead's dowry were over £6000 in South Sea stock and other securities. Nicholls also owned property in the parish of St Giles-in-the-Fields, London, which he left to his wife. He left only £20 each to his daughter, Elizabeth, and her husband, the Revd William Trinder, while the rest of his estate passed to his son. John Nicholls became a barrister at Lincoln's Inn and was MP for Bletchingley, 1783–7, and for Tregony, 1798–1802. He died in 1832. His mother, Elizabeth, was still alive at the age of ninety-two in 1798.

Frank Nicholls was an important teacher of anatomy and his style and methods greatly influenced those such as William Hunter, who made London a centre for the teaching of anatomy in the late eighteenth century.

ANITA GUERRINI

Sources G. C. Peachey, *A memoir of William and John Hunter* (1924) · Munk, *Roll* · *GM*, 1st ser., 55 (1785), 13–15 · A. Zuckerman, 'The life and works of Richard Mead', PhD diss., University of Illinois, 1965 · Foster, *Alum. Oxon.* · *IGI* · T. Lawrence, *Franci Nicholsii, M.D. … vita* (privately printed, London, 1780)
Archives Bodl. Oxf., survey of the manor of Church Stanton · Linn. Soc., drawings and papers · Royal College of Physicians of Edinburgh, lecture notes · University of British Columbia Library, Woodward Biomedical Library, lecture notes
Likenesses attrib. T. Hudson, oils, *c*.1745–1748, NPG [*see illus.*] · I. Gossets, portrait, repro. in Lawrence, *Franci Nicholsii … vita* · J. Hall, engraving (after I. Gossets), repro. in Lawrence, *Franci Nicholsii … vita*
Wealth at death £6269 trust fund; property in Ockley, Ruspor, Ifield, and London: will, PRO, PROB 11/1038, sig. 30

Nicholls, Frederick William (1889–1974), army officer, was born on 27 May 1889 at 21 Holdenhurst Road, Bournemouth, the eldest of three children and only son of Thomas Arthur Nicholls, a master photographic printer, and his wife, Sabina Mapstone. He volunteered as an infantry private in 1914, served in Mesopotamia in 1916–18, and by the end of the First World War was a lieutenant in the Royal Corps of Signals. He obtained a regular commission, and worked in the army Y service (wireless interception) in Russia in 1919, and thereafter in Afghanistan, Burma, Iraq, Persia, Palestine, India, and—in 1939–40—France.

Nicholls was *persona grata* to secret authorities; this made him useful when in November 1942 he was posted as a lieutenant-colonel to be general staff officer, grade 1 (GSO 1) (signals), to the Special Operations Executive (SOE). SOE had suffered much from rivalry with MI6, which Nicholls was able in part to appease. From 1 May 1943 he was SOE's director of signals and sat on its governing council. He was promoted brigadier in July 1944. He supervised the design and development of clandestine equipment for wireless telegraphy, and codes and ciphers, and a worldwide range of wireless communication which at peak periods handled 2 million groups a week. Without these wireless links SOE would have been helpless; with them it exercised an influence on the war out of all proportion to its size, about that of a division.

Nicholls's subordinates found him a just and generous chief, and his equals admired his judgement. So did Colin Gubbins, his chief, who had long known him. At the war's end his networks were summarily closed down, on the orders of C. R. Attlee. Nicholls devoted himself for four months to finding new work for his juniors, and retired in mid-January 1946 to settle in Wiltshire.

After the death in 1952 of his first wife, Jessie Jane Lindsay, an American, he married in March 1955 Marjorie Emilie (Marianne), daughter of Arthur West Tindall, a miller; she had served under his command in SOE's signals section, and outlived him. He had no children. He was appointed MBE (1918), OBE (1929), and CBE (1946), and received American, Danish, Dutch, and French orders. He died, at a doctor's house near his home, Staddle Barn Cottage, Coombe Bissett, near Salisbury, on 18 December 1974.

M. R. D. FOOT, *rev.*

Sources M. R. D. Foot, *SOE in France: an account of the work of the British Special Operations Executive in France, 1940–1944* (1966) · P. Lorain, *Secret warfare*, trans. D. Kahn (1984) · private information (1986) · *CGPLA Eng. & Wales* (1975) · L. Marks, *Between silk and cyanide* (1999)
Wealth at death £14,674: probate, 22 Jan 1975, *CGPLA Eng. & Wales*

Nicholls, Sir George (1781–1865), poor-law reformer and administrator, was born on 31 December 1781 in Trenithen, Cornwall, the eldest son of Solomon Nicholls (1755/6–1793) and his wife, Jane (1760/61–1849), daughter of George Millett of Helstone. Though a farmer, Solomon had served at sea as a young man, and was a man of quick temperament and adventurous spirit. George displayed these same traits, and after finishing his schooling at the parish school at St Kevern and the grammar school at Helstone eagerly accepted from an uncle an offer of maritime service with the East India Company. Upon completing the necessary tutoring in geometry, trigonometry, and navigation at Mr Weatherdon's school in Newton Abbot (1796–7), he went to sea in 1797 as a midshipman aboard a company ship bound for Bombay and China. He prospered financially and rose rapidly through the ranks, becoming a captain in 1808 at the age of twenty-seven. In 1815 a fire on board his last command, the *Bengal*, resulted in the loss of several lives and the destruction of the vessel and its uninsured cargo. Though acquitted of all blame by the company's directors, he suffered severe financial losses as a consequence of the tragedy and resigned his post.

On 6 July 1813 Nicholls had married Harriet (*d.* 14 May 1869), daughter of Brough Maltby of Southwell, Nottinghamshire, and after his resignation from the company's service the couple decided to take up residence near her family. On settling in Farndon in April 1816 Nicholls became active in parochial affairs, including managing the village school and starting a savings bank. He also began to take an active interest in poor relief, at the time considered to be in a state of crisis and the subject of parliamentary investigations. A succession of anguished books and pamphlets on the topic made the poor laws the most widely discussed social problem of the day, and most commentators had come to accept Thomas Malthus's dismal view of the law's operation. A guaranteed subsistence and the baneful operation of the allowance system were, it was claimed, producing demoralization and a disastrous growth of a pauperized population. Nicholls subscribed wholeheartedly to these views, and began to study the subject carefully.

On moving to Southwell in 1819 Nicholls resolved to take an active part in the operation of the poor laws, and became an overseer of the poor. He was appointed by the Revd J. T. Becher, who had been involved for a number of years in reforming poor relief at the local level. The two men held similar views on the need for more stringent administration of poor relief, although Becher was to prove more open to ameliorative policies towards the poor. Nicholls's deterrent policies were much closer to those embraced by a neighbouring magistrate, the Revd Robert Lowe of Bingham. The three are often referred to as the Nottinghamshire Reformers, a label that highlights the importance of the county (or indeed district within the county) as a laboratory for poor-law experimentation in the years leading up to the major national reform of 1834. Both Lowe and Nicholls came to place their faith in the eradication of outdoor relief and the offer of the workhouse as a test of destitution. As Nicholls put it in a lengthy letter to the *Nottingham Journal*, the key was to place the poor in a position in which the parish was 'the hardest Taskmaster, the closest Paymaster and the most harsh and unkind friend that they can apply to and whose aid they cannot receive without sacrificing a large portion of their independence and self respect' (Nicholls, *Eight Letters on the Management of our Poor*, 1822, 24).

When Nicholls published this letter and others on the subject in 1822 he injected himself into the national debate on the poor laws. In his pamphlet he revealed himself to be not only an ardent devotee of the workhouse test but a committed Malthusian and doctrinaire believer in classical political economy. The 'wages fund', he insisted, was in dire threat of being swallowed up by the ever advancing tide of poor relief, resulting in economic ruin if unchecked. While he mentioned the importance of basic schooling, religion, and savings banks as devices for reforming the character of the lower orders, the emphasis throughout was on managing the poor through deterrent relief policies. Nicholls denounced the destructive force of the allowance system, though in fact it had been but recently introduced into Nottinghamshire, and was responsible for relatively modest claims on the poor rates. None the less, he claimed that major reductions in poor relief had been achieved during his tenure as overseer, crediting it to the ending of outdoor relief and the establishment of a well-regulated workhouse. His work impressed the 1824 House of Commons select committee on labourers' wages, which praised his application of the principle of 'less eligibility'.

In 1823 Nicholls moved to Gloucester, there to plan, together with Thomas Telford, the construction of a canal linking the English Channel and Bristol Channel. The financial crisis of 1826 rendered this project untenable, but another scheme that he undertook shortly thereafter, the Gloucester Canal, was brought into operation in 1827. He was next engaged to attempt to rescue a financially distressed bank of considerable regional importance. While unsuccessful, Nicholls's efforts impressed the directors of the Bank of England, who offered him the post of managing their newly opened Birmingham branch. On moving with his family to Birmingham at the end of 1826 Nicholls quickly mastered the intricacies of banking, and became active in the town's civic and cultural life. It was during this period that he became well acquainted with Robert Peel, beginning a correspondence that would last until Peel's death in 1850. Declining two offers of company partnerships (one from John Gladstone), Nicholls seemed content to remain with the Bank of England, but he was about to embark on a new career as a national poor-law administrator.

With Earl Grey's reform ministry taking office in 1830, on the heels of the widespread riots of agricultural labourers (the Captain Swing riots), there was a fresh political will for major overhaul of the poor laws. The royal commission appointed in 1832 sent its investigators throughout the country to report at first hand on the prevailing system. John Cowell, the assistant commissioner for Nottinghamshire, on undertaking an inquiry at Southwell, was directed to Nicholls. Cowell's subsequent report, praising the Southwell reformers, was widely circulated, making Nicholls a likely candidate to be one of the three commissioners created by the Poor Law Amendment Act of 1834. When an offer was made to him by the prime minister, Lord Melbourne, in the summer of 1834, he accepted, even though his official salary of £2000 was considerably below the £2500 offered by the directors of the Bank of England to retain his services.

On moving with his family (now including a son and six daughters) to London, Nicholls threw himself into the arduous duties of implementing the new poor law. These included hiring staff, working out detailed office procedures, answering numerous inquiries from throughout the country, devising relief directives, negotiating with workhouse architects, and dividing the country into poor-law unions. His colleagues on the poor-law commission, Thomas Frankland Lewis and J. G. Shaw Lefevre, proving to be less informed and less doctrinaire on the poor laws than he, Nicholls forged an alliance with Edwin Chadwick, the outspoken secretary to the commission. He shared Chadwick's ardent desire to curtail outdoor relief and to move toward its complete abolition. While his colleagues, parliament, and the country generally proved unwilling to embrace such a drastic programme, Nicholls was gratified at the major savings in poor relief effected within the first two years of the new system. He was also pleased that his plan for most poor-law unions to have one large, new, well-regulated workhouse instead of a collection of existing small parish workhouses was put into practice.

Within the first year of his new position fever struck Nicholls's ill-drained Portman Square house, carrying off two of his daughters. In spite of this tragedy he was soon at work reforming the treatment of poverty in Ireland, which lacked any public system of poor relief. In 1836 a royal commission had recommended a national board to superintend public works, disseminate knowledge of improved agriculture, provide an array of social services, and facilitate emigration; poor relief was to remain in the hands of voluntary bodies. The home secretary, Lord John Russell, who wanted something more like the English poor law for Ireland, directed Nicholls to conduct his own inquiry. After a whirlwind tour of twelve counties over six weeks, Nicholls issued his report. Asserting that the Irish were a work-shy, reckless race who needed the strong medicine of a deterrent workhouse system, Nicholls called for an extension of the English new poor law to Ireland. An Irish Poor Law Bill modelled on his recommendations was passed in 1838, and he was directed to proceed to Ireland to begin implementation of the statute.

Nicholls arrived in Dublin in September 1838. In contrast to the English poor law, where powerful local interests had to be consulted and sometimes deferred to, Nicholls was given a free hand in Ireland. The country was quickly formed into 130 poor-law unions, each with its own central workhouse. He had seen to it that the Irish Poor Law Act prohibited outdoor relief, and lent his support to Lord Morpeth's bill for the suppression of mendicancy. The speed and audacity of his proceedings, however, earned him some enemies, among them the duke of Wellington, who was alarmed that Nicholls's policies regarding voting rights in poor-law electoral divisions seemed to favour the reform party over the Conservatives.

A more serious charge arose out of the land and construction transactions relating to the new workhouses; a later inquiry estimated an excess expenditure from the rates of £50,000. These and other difficulties rendered the whole Irish episode a frustrating one, and he returned to London in November 1842 under a cloud, though his integrity and honesty had not been called into question.

Nicholls found the resumption of his official duties at Somerset House an ordeal. He failed to influence his new colleagues, Sir Edmund Head and George Cornewall Lewis, who insisted on steering a cautious course in poorlaw administration. In his absence the two had succeeded in marginalizing Chadwick, Nicholls's ally in the quest to curtail outdoor relief. Furthermore the Conservatives were now in office, and the new home secretary, Sir James Graham, perhaps taking his cue from the duke of Wellington, proved icy and aloof. Even Nicholls's friendship with Peel, now prime minister, was of little help. When the poor-law commission was abolished in 1847, however, the Liberals were back in office and Nicholls was appointed permanent secretary to the poor-law board (December 1847), which took over the functions of the commission. Yet even this mark of favour represented a backward step financially, for his salary was reduced from £2000 to £1500.

A mild stroke forced Nicholls's resignation in January 1851. Made KCB (March 1851) and provided with an annual pension of £1000, he devoted the remainder of his life to writing and to various business ventures. The latter included serving as chairman of the Birmingham Canal Company and as director of the Rock Life Assurance Company. The first years of his retirement from official duties were occupied with writing poor-law histories: *A History of the English Poor Law* (1854), *A History of the Scotch Poor Law* (1856), and *A History of the Irish Poor Law* (1856). While all of these books are useful compendia of information, they are self-justifying and devoid of critical insight. He died at his home, 17 Hyde Park Street, London, on 24 March 1865, and was buried in Willesden cemetery on 30 March.

Though doctrinaire and sometimes prone to rashness, Nicholls was an able administrator who had considerable influence on the relief provisions and administrative structures of both the English and Irish poor laws. His grandson, H. G. Willink, described him as an alert, austere, and demanding figure with 'keen grey eyes under extremely bushy eyebrows', yet one who was 'absolutely devoid of affected solemnity; on the contrary, a thoroughly genial man' (Willink, lxxii). He inspired confidence in a great many leading figures, and even those most critical of his policies never questioned his personal probity and dedication to public service.

ANTHONY BRUNDAGE

Sources H. G. Willink, introduction, in G. Nicholls, *A history of the English poor law*, new edn, 1 (1904) • *DNB* • C. Knight, *The Examiner* (1 April 1865), 193 • Boase, *Mod. Eng. biog.* • A. Brundage, *The making of the new poor law* (1978) • J. D. Marshall, 'The Nottinghamshire reformers and their contribution to the new poor law', *Economic History Review*, 2nd ser., 13 (1960–61), 382–96 • S. Webb and B. Webb, *English local government*, 8/2–9/2: *English poor law history* (1929) • B. V. Heagerty, 'Ideology and social reform: the case of George Nicholls and the restructuring of poor relief in early nineteenth century England and Ireland', MA diss., University of Missouri, Kansas City, 1979 · H. Burke, *The people and the poor law in nineteenth century Ireland* (1987) · G. O'Brien, 'Workhouse management in pre-famine Ireland', *Proceedings of the Royal Irish Academy*, 86C (1986), 113–34 · G. O'Brien, 'The establishment of poor-law unions in Ireland, 1838–43', *Irish Historical Studies*, 23 (1982–3), 97–120 · d. cert.

Archives BL, corresp. with Sir Robert Peel, Add. MSS 40400–40588 · NL Wales, letters to Sir George Cornewall Lewis · PRO, corresp. with Lord John Russell, PRO 30/22 · UCL, corresp. with Sir Edwin Chadwick

Likenesses R. R. Reinagle, oils, 1834, NPG · E. U. Eddis, crayon drawing, 1839; formerly in the possession of Miss G. E. Nicholls, 1894 · photograph, 1850–1859?, repro. in G. Nicholls, *A history of the English poor law*, reissue of new edn, 1 (1904), frontispiece · J. C. Moore, watercolour; formerly in the possession of Miss E. M. G. Wingfield, 1894

Wealth at death under £80,000: probate, 5 May 1865, *CGPLA Eng. & Wales*

Nicholls, James Fawckner (1818–1883), antiquary and librarian, of Cornish ancestry, was born on 26 May 1818 at Sidmouth, Devon. His father was a builder at Sidmouth, and his mother a daughter of Captain James Fawkner of Plymouth. In 1830 he went to sea with an uncle. Two years later he was sent to school at Kentisbeare in Devon for six months. He then entered the drapery business, and after a short time bought an establishment for himself at Benwick in the Isle of Ely. He next kept a school at Ramsey, and then moved to Manchester, where he became a travelling agent for a firm of paper-stainers. In 1860 he settled at Bristol, where he ran his own paper-staining business for eight years. Finally in 1868 he was appointed city librarian of Bristol. The city library, which had been founded in 1613, had become very restrictive in terms of both the books held and access to them, and so was taken over by the city council in 1855 and reopened in 1856. Further improvements during Nicholls's time as librarian led to the opening of three free branch libraries in St Philip's (1876), St James (1877), and Bedminster (1878). All were in poor areas of the city. Nicholls was in part responsible for this reform.

Nicholls had from his earliest years devoted his leisure to antiquarian studies, and in 1876 he was elected a fellow of the Society of Antiquaries. In 1869 he published *The Remarkable Life, Adventures, and Discoveries of Sebastian Cabot*, which received mixed reviews. But he is mainly remembered for works on the history and antiquities of Bristol. After trying to establish a series of biographies of Bristolians, in 1874 he collected a series of articles originally contributed to Bristol papers, under the title *How to see Bristol: a guide for the excursionist, the naturalist, the archaeologist, and the man of business*. This was followed by other works which partly reflect his involvement in local affairs, including the visit to the city of the British Association and the establishment of the Bristol and Gloucestershire Archaeological Society in 1876. Nicholls's *magnum opus*, *Bristol Past and Present*, appeared in 1881–2. The two parts of the book dealing with the civil history of the city were by Nicholls, and a third part dealing with the ecclesiastical history was written by his colleague John Taylor. Taylor's is the better section, but the work as a whole contained

useful information. Nicholls was twice married, and left several children at his death on 19 September 1883 at Goodwick, Fishguard, Pembrokeshire.

G. LE G. NORGATE, *rev.* ELIZABETH BAIGENT

Sources *Biography and Review*, 6 (Nov 1881) · *Monthly Notes of the Library Association*, 4 (1883), 124 · review of *Bristol past and present* by J. F. Nicholls and J. Taylor, *The Athenaeum* (1 April 1882), 407–8 · *The Athenaeum* (29 Sept 1883), 405 · H. E. Meller, *Leisure and the changing city, 1870–1914* (1976) · J. Latimer, *The annals of Bristol in the nineteenth century*, [1] (1887) · I. Gray, *Antiquaries of Gloucestershire and Bristol*, Bristol and Gloucestershire Archaeological Society Records Section, 12 (1981) · C. R. J. Currie and C. P. Lewis, eds., *English county histories: a guide* (1994) · *Public libraries in Bristol, 1613–1974*, City and County of Bristol Arts and Leisure Committee (1974)

Wealth at death £208 1s. 1d.: probate, 13 Nov 1883, *CGPLA Eng. & Wales*

Nicholls [Niccols, Nicols], **John** (1555–1584?), religious controversialist and apostate, was the son of John Nicholls of Cowbridge in Glamorgan. Having studied in Wales, in 1569 he entered White Hall, Oxford, transferring to Brasenose in 1570. He left Oxford after completing his course but without taking a degree. On returning to Glamorgan he took work as a tutor to a gentleman's children, before obtaining a curacy in Withycombes in Somerset and then moving on to a cure at Whitestaunton in the same county, where he remained until 1577. In that year, however, he quit the Church of England, and from Antwerp and Rheims began a journey—literally and metaphorically—to Rome, travelling via Grenoble, Vicenza, and Milan.

On his arrival in Rome, in the spring of 1578, Nicholls voluntarily surrendered himself to the Inquisition, recanted of his protestantism, and was received both into the Roman Catholic church and also, on 28 May, into the English College; he received funding, as a Catholic source acknowledged, from 'the charity of the Sovereign Pontiff' (Foley, 3.679 n. 28). In 1580, however, Nicholls left for England, travelling via Rheims, but was arrested in Islington and imprisoned in the Tower of London. In the early 1580s members of the new wave of seminary-educated priests and Jesuits flooding into England from the continent were treated with the utmost cruelty if they proved obdurate, but with extraordinary indulgence should they apostatize—as Nicholls did, recanting his recently acquired Catholic beliefs. Aware of his impecuniosity, both Lord Chancellor Bromley and Lord Treasurer Burghley, along with others of the queen's council, urged the bishops to support him by collecting contributions, thereby providing him with the better than adequate salary of £50 p.a.

Four propaganda works, probably written in prison, and published 'by authoritye' in 1581, display Nicholls's industry on behalf of his re-adopted protestant profession: *John Niccols Pilgrimage* (1581) was an attack on the immorality of the popes, cardinals, bishops, monks, and Jesuits; *A declaration of the recantation of Iohn Nicols (for the space almost of two yeeres the popes scholar in the English Seminarie or Colledge at Rome)*, heavily influenced by the French Calvinist Philippe Duplessis-Mornay, broadcast his fulfilled desire to 'be reconciled, and received as a Member of the true Church of

Christ in England' (Wood, *Ath. Oxon.*, 1.496); a work purporting to be an address he had delivered in Rome before the most eminent churchmen, *An oration and sermon made at Rome by commandment of the four cardinals and the Dominican inquisitor*, elicited Catholic indignation and a riposte, with the help of hostile material supplied by William Allen, from the formidable Jesuit controversialist Robert Persons, *A Discoverie of J. Nicols Minister*; and to this last Nicholls replied in *An Answer to an Infamous Libel Maliciously Written and Cast Abroad Against him*.

The work which Nicholls did for the government was extended into prison sermons attempting to convert newly arrested priests held in the Tower. On Easter day 1581 he preached there to a large congregation invited by the lieutenant, Sir Owen Hopton. In June 1581 his knowledge of the personnel of the Catholic priestly mission to England was put to active use when he encountered an alumnus of the Catholic English College in Rome on a London street, identified him as a traitor, and arrested him. Around the time of the trial of the Jesuit Edmund Campion in November 1581 he was engaged in divulging the names of known Catholics.

In this busy period in which he was enjoying official favour, Nicholls was also preaching in public to congregations in London. Catholic sources, however, were reporting that Londoners 'were already tired of him' (Foley, 3.678), perhaps on account of his very ubiquity. There was also a danger that he was about to be exposed, and that a copy of the Inquisition's official text of his 1578 recantation of protestantism, which Allen and Persons were preparing for publication, would demolish his claims to sincerity as a member of the Church of England. Perhaps it was with that perilous prospect in view that Nicholls resorted to his boldest stroke yet. Late in 1582 he travelled to Rouen, where he was arrested and imprisoned, and recanted his protestantism, claiming, according to a Catholic source published in 1583, that everything he had told the English authorities as an informer against Catholics was disclosed 'either through vain-glory, envy, fear, or hopes of reward' (Wood, *Ath. Oxon.*, 1.496). Reward, however, was no longer likely to come the way of so serial an apostate. He tried to ingratiate himself with Allen in a series of letters, *Litterae ad D. G. Alenum*, which were recognized as having a certain propaganda value and were published in 1590, and in 1583 he issued a further set, *Litterae aliae ad eundem Alenum*. In June 1584 Allen reported receipt of Nicholls's letters of re-recantation. Nicholls also published, as *Literae et confessio publica* (1583), an admission that the allegations he had written during his second stay in England against the pope, cardinals, and English Catholics were lies.

His credit exhausted, Nicholls died on the continent in want and, probably, depression, most likely in 1584. He has been condemned by biographers for his want of constancy in what are assumed to be genuine, if bewildering, changes of faith and profession. Yet it may have been the case that there was a kind of cynical consistency in his animal sense of self-preservation, one actively encouraged by

the systems of religious repression and polarization under which he managed for a while to operate with some success.   MICHAEL MULLETT

Sources Wood, *Ath. Oxon.*, new edn, 1.496–7 · J. Strype, *Annals of the Reformation and establishment of religion … during Queen Elizabeth's happy reign*, new edn, 3 (1824), 61 · H. Foley, ed., *Records of the English province of the Society of Jesus*, 3 (1878), 292–3, 678–9 · *DWB*, 685 · P. McGrath, *Papists and puritans under Elizabeth I* (1967), 170 · Foster, *Alum. Oxon.* · F. Edwards, *Robert Persons: the biography of an Elizabethan Jesuit, 1546–1610* (1998), 52–3, 62 · *CSP dom.*, 1581–90, 187 · A. O. Meyer, *England and the Catholic church under Queen Elizabeth*, trans. J. R. McKee (1916); repr. with introduction by J. Bossy (1967), 504 · M. C. Questier, *Conversion, politics and religion in England, 1580–1625* (1996)

Nicholls, John Ashton (1823–1859), cotton spinner and philanthropist, was born on 25 March 1823 at Grosvenor Street, Chorlton-on-Medlock, Manchester, the only child of Benjamin Nicholls (1796–1877), cotton spinner and mayor of Manchester (1853–5), and his wife, Sarah, daughter of John Ashton and his wife, Sarah, of Manchester. His father attended the Church of England, but Nicholls was raised a Unitarian by his mother; he was taught by the Unitarian minister John Relly Beard and as a lay student (1840–44) at Manchester New College (afterwards Harris Manchester College, Oxford). Keenly interested in physical science, he joined the British Association in 1842 and the Manchester Literary and Philosophical Society in 1848. He also built an observatory and was elected a fellow of the Royal Astronomical Society in June 1849.

Having entered his father's firm during the bitter conflicts of the 1840s, Nicholls displayed a strong desire to improve the condition of the working class and to help reconcile employers and employed through personal example, voluntary endeavour, and civic action. In the vicinity of his firm, he was the linchpin of the Ancoats Lyceum, organizing numerous lectures and entertainments, 'not knowing', he wrote to Mrs R. H. Greg, 'any better way in which employers can show their sympathy with their workpeople, than by joining them in their amusements' (Nicholls to Greg, 30 Dec 1848, Quarry Bank Mill, Greg MSS).

Working-class apathy, it seems, led to the failure of the lyceum, but Nicholls did much for adult education subsequently through his popular lectures and his organizational involvement in the Manchester Athenaeum. He also set up a half-time school for factory children in Mather Street, Manchester, and acted as treasurer of the Manchester Model Secular School established by the National Public School Association. However, he was never entirely reconciled to its secular scheme and later promoted the merger between non-sectarian and denominational educational associations in Manchester in 1857.

Closely associated with the Cross Street Chapel under William Gaskell's ministry, Nicholls worked for the spiritual improvement of the working classes through the Unitarian Home Missionary Board. He also joined the Manchester and Salford Sanitary Association and spoke eloquently on the need for social improvement, temperance, working-class self-reliance, and rational recreation. In this vein, he pressed for the Sunday opening of museums and for Sunday bands in parks, a social experiment soon brought to an end by religious pressure on Manchester city council. His belief in class reconciliation was challenged by renewed industrial conflict in the mid-1850s, but in his lectures on strikes he continued to urge mutual understanding between masters and men, while critical of union 'tyranny'. This message surprised the Christian socialist Charles Kingsley, but was one which growing numbers of Lancashire employers were ready to espouse by the late 1850s.

Nicholls's experience was broadened by a long European trip in 1851, extending to the Habsburg empire, Italy, Constantinople, and Malta. In 1857–8 he travelled extensively in Canada and the United States, returning disillusioned with American notions of equality and a confirmed believer in English liberty. He declined to stand for the Liberals at Nottingham in 1859, but at his last appearance in public (24 May 1859) spoke against British intervention on behalf of Austria in Italy.

Nicholls died of 'low fever' at Eagley House, Manchester, on 18 September 1859. He never married. He was buried at Cross Street Chapel, and his funeral sermon (23 September 1859) was preached by William Gaskell, whose wife, Elizabeth, noted the passing of 'a friend of ours, a young man of some local distinction' (*Letters of Mrs Gaskell* 574). His life's work was commemorated by a tablet in Cross Street Chapel, an obelisk in Great Ancoats Street, erected by the working men to 'their invaluable friend' (Gaskell, *Christian Views*, 129) in July 1860, and by the Nicholls Hospital, an orphanage set up by his parents at a cost of some £100,000, a substantial benefaction in Victorian Manchester.

ALEXANDER GORDON, rev. A. C. HOWE

Sources W. Gaskell, *Christian views of life and death: a sermon on the occasion of the death of John Ashton Nicholls, with a sketch of his life* (1859) · *In memoriam: a selection from the letters of the late John Ashton Nicholls*, ed. [S. A. Ashton] (privately printed, Manchester, 1862) · biographical cuttings, Man. CL · *Monthly Notices of the Royal Astronomical Society*, 20 (1859–60), 131–3 · *The letters of Mrs Gaskell*, ed. J. A. V. Chapple and A. Pollard (1966) · A. Howe, *The cotton masters, 1830–1860* (1984) · Quarry Bank Mill, Wilmslow, Greg MSS

Archives Chetham's Library, Manchester, Nicholls Hospital records · Quarry Bank Mill, Cheshire, Greg MSS

Nicholls, Josias (*c*.1553–1639/40), Church of England minister and religious controversialist, was probably born in Canterbury, the son of George Nicholls, a member of the city's ruling oligarchy. At the local cathedral grammar school he was exposed to the distinctly protestant influence of the masters, Anthony Rush and John Gresshop; he proceeded to Oxford in 1570 and graduated BA on 18 March 1574. His first cure was at Yalding in the Medway valley, where he succeeded the radical printing preacher John Strowd. In 1580 he was presented to the living of Eastwell, near Ashford, by Nicholas St Leger, a staunchly protestant gentleman who had denounced Mary, queen of Scots, in parliament as that 'monstrous huge dragon and mass of the earth', and who had married the widow of Sir Thomas Finch, whose manor house dominated this tiny parish of fifteen households and seventy-two communicants.

The small scale of Nicholls's parochial obligations in Eastwell was out of proportion with his leading role among 'the ministers of Kent' who confronted John Whitgift, archbishop of Canterbury, and his drive for conformity. He was denounced in 1584 as the 'ring-leader' of those clergymen in Kent who opposed subscription to the three articles, Whitgift's standard of conformity, and who favoured further reformation of the Church of England. By his own admission, he was 'not one of the hindmost' in taking the puritan campaign into the lobbies of parliament itself, and he represented Kent at a synod of puritan ministers held at Cambridge in September 1587. In the 1590s he favoured a tactic of moderation in the expectation of a favourable political change. He placed his hopes first in Robert Devereux, second earl of Essex, to whom he dedicated *An Order of Household Instruction* (1596), and then on James VI, to whom he appealed more or less directly in *The Plea of the Innocent* (1602), an account of the variable fortunes of the godly cause under Elizabethan rule. This book included memorable and often quoted accounts of Nicholls's pastoral experiences in Kentish parishes, where congregations without experience of a preaching ministry retained a vague semi-Pelagian religion associating righteousness with the performance of conventional good works. The consequence of what Nicholls may have intended as a politic and eirenical statement was suspension, degradation, and imprisonment.

In 1604 Nicholls attended the Hampton Court conference as an observer. Two years later he was suspected of complicity in Thomas Whetenhall's *A Discourse of the Abuses now in Question in the Churches of Christ* and was fined in Star Chamber. Further troubles followed in 1614, when Nicholls was again prosecuted in Star Chamber and imprisoned in the Marshalsea for opposing the forced loan of that year. By now he lived as a schoolmaster in Loose and Maidstone. It is significant that all three of his sons, Josias, Suretonhie, and Repentance, laboured in the same profession, doubtless as frustrated preaching ministers. Nonconformity persisted in the Nicholls dynasty into at least the third generation.

The tradition that Nicholls married three times is partly borne out by the wills of the two unmarried daughters of Dudley Fenner. Morefruit made hers on 8 April 1602 making no reference to Nicholls, but in that of Faintnot, dated 16 February 1604, he is referred to as her father-in-law. Thus Joan Fenner, having in the interim been married to William Whitaker, would appear to have married Nicholls in 1602 or 1603. In old age Nicholls gravitated to London. In September 1627 he witnessed the will of Caesar Galliardello, of Holy Trinity Minories, thereafter settling in the parish. From November 1627 until May 1635 he was evidently the senior member of its ruling vestry. Unless a minister was present he always signed the minutes first, but there is no evidence that he himself acted as minister or preacher. Perhaps, as a venerable relic of the campaigns of the 1580s, he was now regarded as a quasi-presbyterian elder.

Nicholls made his will on 22 July 1639, in his eighty-sixth year, as a parishioner of St Mary-le-Bow. His younger sons received his property in Goudhurst, Loose, and in the manor of Longport, outside Canterbury. If his eldest son, Josias, should later 'be found alive' his brothers were jointly to pay him an annuity of £12 a year. There were bequests to the children of three married daughters—Mrs (Elizabeth) Ferrier, Mrs Mary Woods, and Mrs Sharpies—and provision for an annuity to Margaret, wife of Repentance, in the event of his (evidently anticipated) death. Since Suretonhie was granted probate as sole executor on 19 May 1640, Nicholls probably died in the spring of that year. PATRICK COLLINSON, *rev.* BRETT USHER

Sources P. Collinson, *The Elizabethan puritan movement* (1967) · P. Clark, 'Josias Nicholls and religious radicalism, 1553–1639', *Journal of Ecclesiastical History*, 28 (1977), 133–50 · B. Usher, 'The Cosyns and the Galliardellos: two Elizabethan musical dynasties', *The Consort*, 50 (1994), 95–110 · Foster, *Alum. Oxon., 1500–1714* · will, PRO, PROB 11/183, fols. 67r–68r · HoP, *Commons, 1558–1603*, 3.327–9 · prerogative court of Canterbury, wills, PRO, PROB 11/99; PROB 11/104
Wealth at death £500–1000 ?: will, 22 July 1639

Nicholls, Norton (1741?–1809), friend of Thomas Gray, was the only son of Norton Nicholls, a London merchant, and his wife, Jane Floyer, daughter of Lieutenant-Colonel Charles Floyer (*d.* 1731), of Richmond, Surrey, whom he had married at Somerset House chapel, London, in 1741. The elder Nicholls died young, but his widow survived him for many years. In 1756 Nicholls entered Eton College, where he was much indebted to the care of Dr Barnard and the voluntary private instruction of Dr Sumner. In 1760 he was admitted as a pensioner to Trinity Hall, Cambridge; he graduated LLB in 1766. While taking tea one day in the rooms of Lobb, a fellow of Peterhouse, mere student of the hall as he was and not yet nineteen, he was introduced to Thomas Gray. Even at that age he was well acquainted with the best Italian poets, as well as with the best classical writers; and his chance illustration of a remark 'by an apposite citation from Dante' attracted the attention of Gray, who turned and said to the youth, 'Right, sir, but have you read Dante?' The modest answer was, 'I have endeavoured to understand him.' Nicholls recalled that this incident cemented a friendship which, with the single exception of that with Richard West, was warmer than any other ever entered into by Gray, who for the future directed the youth's studies (Gray, *Correspondence*, 2.851–2). Before long, Gray considered Nicholls 'a young man worth his weight in gold' (Ketton-Cremer, 192).

In the summer of 1770 Nicholls accompanied Gray on a journey through the midland counties of Worcestershire, Shropshire, Herefordshire, Monmouthshire, and Gloucestershire. Nicholls kept the journal of their proceedings, which the poet kept in his possession, but which has not survived. The next year, at the beginning of June, on the poet's advice, he visited France, Switzerland, and Italy, and is said to have printed an account of his travels as a gift for his friends. The journey was made more interesting through his friendship with Count Firmian, the Austrian minister at Milan, by whom he was introduced to the best social circles in those countries.

On the death of his uncle, Charles Floyer, on 7 September 1766, Nicholls's income was drastically reduced, and Gray suggested he join the church. In 1767 he was ordained and then presented, through the purchase of his uncle, William Turner, to the rectory of Lound and Bradwell, near Lowestoft. He kept the living until his death. As there was no rectory, he moved, with his mother, to Blundeston House, in an adjoining parish, and spent his spare time improving its grounds. For many years, except when abroad, he spent the greater part of his time there. Even when they came into a considerable amount of money on the death of an elderly uncle, probably William Turner, who died at Richmond on 11 November 1790, Nicholls and his mother remained at Blundeston House. There in 1799 Nicholls entertained 'Admiral Duncan soon after his return to Yarmouth, crowned with the laurels won at Camperdown' (Suckling, 1.315–16, 327).

Nicholls was well informed in history, and familiar with the chief ancient and modern writers. He was fluent in French and Italian, had studied Italian art closely, and had been trained in music under the best masters. Even as late as 1790 Horace Walpole expressed the hope of hearing him sing. Some of the letters addressed to him by Gray were included in Mason's life of the poet. At the suggestion of Samuel Rogers the full correspondence, then the property of Dawson Turner, was included in the fifth volume of John Mitford's edition of Gray, together with his 'Reminiscences of Gray', his letters to Barrett, and the letters of James Brown. The volume was also issued, with a distinct title-page, as *The Correspondence of Thomas Gray and the Rev. Norton Nichols* (1843). The 'Reminiscences of Gray' were praised by John Forster as 'one of the most charming papers, at once for fulness and brevity, ever contributed to our knowledge of a celebrated man' (Forster, 2.151). The anecdotes of Gray, which were printed by Thomas James Mathias, were all derived from Nicholls. When Boswell's correspondence with Temple was discovered at Boulogne, several letters from Nicholls were contained in the collection.

Samuel Brydges called Nicholls 'a very clever man, with a great deal of erudition, but, it must be confessed, a supreme coxcomb' (Brydges, 2.88). Samuel Parr found in him 'some venial irregularities, mingled with much ingenuity, much taste, much politeness, and much good nature' (Parr, 412). Mason, less charitably, told Walpole that Nicholls 'drinks like any fish' (*Correspondence of … Walpole and … Mason*, 1.397).

Nicholls died at Blundeston from the sudden bursting of a blood vessel, on 22 November 1809, in his sixty-eighth year. He was buried in a vault on the south side of Richmond church, and an epitaph to his memory was placed on a marble slab on the south wall of the chancel. Nicholls left his books to Mathias and a large sum of money in the event, which did not take place, of his surviving one of his own near relatives. He is supposed to have been described in the *Pursuits of Literature* as Octavius, and Mathias wrote a letter on his death privately printed in 1809 and reprinted in the *Gentleman's Magazine* of 1810.

W. P. COURTNEY, *rev.* GRANT P. CERNY

Sources *Correspondence of Thomas Gray*, ed. P. Toynbee and L. Whibley, 2 (1935), 851–2; repr. with additions by H. W. Starr (1971) · R. W. Ketton-Cremer, *Thomas Gray: a biography* (1955), 191–4, 233–4, 260 · A. I. Suckling, *The history and antiquities of the county of Suffolk*, 1 (1846), 315–16, 327 · *GM*, 1st ser., 60 (1790), 1057 · *GM*, 1st ser., 79 (1809), 180 · *GM*, 1st ser., 80 (1810), 346–51 · *Extracts of the journals and correspondence of Miss Berry*, ed. M. T. Lewis, 2nd edn, 3 vols. (1865–6), vol. 1, p. 260 · J. Forster, *The life and times of Oliver Goldsmith*, 2nd edn, 2 (1854), 151 · *The works of Thomas Gray in prose and verse*, ed. E. Gosse, 3 (1884), 179; 4 (1884), 339–43 · E. Brydges, *The autobiography, times, opinions, and contemporaries of Sir Egerton Brydges*, 2 (1834), 88 · S. Parr, *Bibliotheca Parriana* (1827), 412 · *The correspondence of Horace Walpole, earl of Orford, and the Rev. William Mason*, ed. J. Mitford, 1 (1851), 392, 397 · O. Manning and W. Bray, *The history and antiquities of the county of Surrey*, 1 (1804), 428–9 · T. Phillips, ed., *Register of marriages, baptisms and burials in Somerset House chapel* (privately printed, London, [1831]), 8
Archives Yale U., Beinecke L., corresp. | Yale U., Farmington, Lewis Walpole Library, letters to Walpole

Nicholls, Sutton (*fl.* **1680–1740**), draughtsman and engraver, is remembered primarily for his bird's-eye prospects, sometimes depicting gentlemen's seats but most often representing panoramic views of the streets and squares of the City of London and Westminster. No details are known of his life, but in 1713 George Vertue included his name in a list of 'ye Engravers or Impres-gravers Burinators. Sculpture-Gravers Living in London' (Vertue, *Note books*, 2.11). As he worked almost exclusively for book publishers, the clearest picture of Nicholls's career can be derived from the various publications with which his name is associated. The first of these is Philip Ayres's *Emblems of Love in Four Languages*, which was published in 1683 by Henry Overton, who continued to employ Nicholls on an occasional basis, as an engraver of maps and views, until at least 1739. A few isolated examples, such as a greeting card designed for the parishioners of Shoreditch in 1695 and a series of grotesque emblematic plates illustrating the twelve months of the year, prove that he also took on jobbing work.

Throughout his career, however, Nicholls specialized in topographical designs and architectural elevations, many of which he either engraved or etched himself. Despite his rather 'crude and hasty draughtsmanship' (Adams, 69), the frequent inaccuracy of his views, and an apparently shaky grasp of perspective, he was repeatedly employed to produce illustrations for antiquarian accounts and topographical surveys of London. In 1724 he contributed a view of London Bridge to David Mortier's long-term publishing project entitled *Nouveau théâtre de la Grande Bretagne* (1707–26), which was a continuation of an original corpus of plates produced by Johannes Kip and Leonard Knyff in 1707. Nicholls's best works are his modest bird's-eye views of London squares and buildings, published by John Bowles as *Prospects of the Most Noted Buildings in and about London* (1724), each with a distinctive title on an engraved banderole and an assortment of foreground figures which served both as scale referents and an indication of urban life. His best-known engravings were, undoubtedly, the several unsigned ward maps he produced to illustrate John Strype's edition of John Stow's *Survey of London* (1720); the success and level of circulation

of that work can be assumed from the appearance of a sixth edition in 1754, which was further embellished with a number of plates Nicholls had originally published in *London Described* (1731). Aside from his book illustrations, Nicholls produced a few large-scale London prints, most of which were published by Henry Overton; however, one view, of the Tower of London, he published himself from the Golden Ball in St Paul's Churchyard.   LUCY PELTZ

Sources B. Adams, *London illustrated, 1604–1851* (1983) · R. Hyde, *Gilded scenes and shining prospects: panoramic views of British towns* (1985) [exhibition catalogue] · J. J. Morrison, 'Strype's Stow: the 1720 edition of *A survey of London*', *London Journal*, 3 (1977), 40–54 · Redgrave, *Artists*, 2nd edn · Vertue, *Note books*

Nicholls, Thomas (*b.* in or before **1523**, *d.* **1612**), translator, was described as the infant son of John Nycholles (*c.*1480–1523), a goldsmith of the parish of St Vedast, Foster Lane, London, in John's will of 1523. Nicholls matriculated at Easter 1544 as a sizar at Trinity Hall, Cambridge, where he was taught by Sir John Cheke for about three years. He was freed by patrimony into the Goldsmiths' Company on 20 January 1548.

Nicholls's translation of Thucydides was published in London on 25 July 1550 as *The hystory writtone by Thucidides the Athenyan of the warre which was betweene the Peloponesians and the Athenyans*; the printer has been identified as William Tylle. A royal privilege granted in February 1550 (the text of which was prefixed to the edition) protected the work from unauthorized publication for seven years so that Nicholls could continue in his intention to 'bring other profytable hystories out of frenche & latene into our sayd maternall language, to the g (Charles Edward Stuart)enerall benefyt, comodytie & profyt of all our louing Subiectes' (fol. 2*r*). With no knowledge of Greek, Nicholls based his work on the French translation by Claude de Seyssel published in Paris in 1527 which, according to Nicholls, was in turn based on the Latin translation of Laurentius Valla; Nicholls included a translation of Valla's preface in the *Hystory*. Nicholls dedicated his translation to his former tutor, acknowledging his debt to Cheke's tuition. Cheke's own position as tutor to Edward VI meant that Nicholls's *Hystory* was one of the books bought as a school book for the young king. Thucydides was not translated again until the philosopher Thomas Hobbes issued a new translation in 1676; Hobbes was critical of the earlier version in its reliance on second- or third-hand translations from the Greek, claiming that 'by multiplication of errour, he [Thucydides] became at length traduced, rather than translated into our Language' (Hobbes, sig. A3*v*).

Despite the privilege of 1550, Nicholls does not seem to have produced any further translations. In 1555 he was elected to the livery of the Goldsmiths' Company, and served as renter warden in the company in 1566. Terms as third and fourth warden of the company followed in the 1570s, but his absence from meetings of the company's governing body in 1578–9—in stark contrast to his earlier diligent attendance—suggests the onset of either financial or health problems. He married Sarah Atkinson (*d.* in or before 1612) at Mary Woolnoth, London, on 14 July 1560, and together they had at least three children: Thomas, John, and Christopher; Christopher was probably the merchant adventurer of that name who invested in the ventures of the East India Company from 1604. John *Nicholl (*fl.* 1605–1637?), the mariner, may well have been a grandson of the translator.

Nothing further is heard of Nicholls (although he may have been the Thomas Nycholls fined by the Goldsmiths' Company in 1606 for poor workmanship) until he drew up his will on 16 July 1612 in which he described himself as 'fryle of body' (GL, MS 9171/22, fol. 74v). He died at some point between that date and 27 August 1612 when the will was proved; his widow and executrix was named as Jane, indicating that he had remarried. Bequests were divided between his wife, children, and two brothers-in-law. He was buried at St Sepulchre, Holborn.

R. C. D. BALDWIN

Sources will, PRO, PROB 11/21, sig. 12 [J. Nycholles] · will, GL, MS 9171/22, fols. 74–5 · GL, MS 9168/16, fol. 153 · court letter books, Goldsmiths' Hall, London · private information (2004) [R. Kennedy] · T. A. Birrell, *English monarchs and their books from Henry VII to Charles II* (1986) · G. Birdwood and W. Foster, *The first East India Company letter book* (1893), 222, 295 · court books, BL OIOC, BI, fols. 73, 105–6; BIII; BV · Thucydides, *The history of the Grecian war*, trans. T. Hobbes (1676)
Archives Goldsmiths' Company court books, vol. I, pp. 30, 223; vol. L, pp. 73, 154–5, 415–28; vol. K, p. 61; vol. O, pp. 470, 542
Wealth at death see will, GL, MS 9171/22, fols. 74–5

Nicholls, Thomas (1532–1601), shipowner and translator, was born in or near Gloucester in 1532 and baptized that year in nearby Adlestrop, the son of John Nicholls. Apprenticed as a mercer in London on 2 October 1547, he learned his trade under, successively, Sir William Lok (1480–1550) and another mercer recorded as Daulk, and was freed in 1554. Nicholls served as secretary to the new Muscovy Company in 1555–6, exploiting links with Sir William's old associates: Anthony Hickman, a major importer of marine stores and dealer in Azorean dyestuffs, notably woad; Edward Castlin, a Baltic trader and naval victualler; and his expatriate brother, Jaime, master of the *San Jorge* regularly used out of Seville by Edward Kingsmill. In 1556 these London merchants appointed Nicholls to succeed William Edge as their resident agent in Tenerife.

The Canarian trade of Nicholls, Hickman, and Kingsmill was worth about 30,000 ducats annually, busying three ships and a pinnace by 1559, when a trading dispute over imported guns and books saw Nicholls represent Simon and Richard Grafton and Edward Kingsmill before the island's courts. During it Nicholls offended a local notary, Juan Moreno, and then frustrated the marriage ambitions of the notary's daughter, Catalina, marrying instead Annis Coleman (1539–*c*.1576) at Adlestrop in Gloucestershire on 31 January 1560. Vengefully the Moreno family cited the Calvinist observances of Nicholls and Kingsmill, their contempt for the mass, and a local colour bar as evidence of heresy before Gran Canaria's inquisitor on 12 September 1560. Nicholls sought diplomatic help, notably from Thomas Challoner, who wrote on 24 September 1560 to the Spanish ambassador in London, Conde Feria, on

Nicholls's behalf. Inquisitorial hearings began in La Laguna on 13 February 1561 for which Nicholls penned long ineffectual depositions on 23 March. Nicholls next wrote from Tenerife's prison on 14 July asking Sir William Chamberlain, England's ambassador in Spain, to intervene. On 17 August Kingsmill also asked Chamberlain to have the archbishop of Seville, as the inquisitor-general of Spain, investigate procedural irregularities in their case; Chamberlain secured their release through Hugh Tipton, an English agent in Seville. However, Nicholls was soon re-imprisoned and charged anew with heresy based on depositions made by a Jewish convert, Francesco de Coronado, in 1562. Again Nicholls wrote to Challoner, now posted to Spain as Chamberlain's successor, saying that goods worth 14,000 ducats had also been unfairly confiscated. Challoner moved to ensure Nicholls's case was decided before the inquisitors in Seville and they approved in principle on 26 April 1563. Nicholls was sent in chains to Seville on 14 March 1564 but his case was not heard until mid-January 1565. Acquittal followed in the same year but he was ordered not to leave Seville on pain of forfeiting his seized goods. On his eventual return to England these tests of his faith ensured his induction as rector of a tiny living at Widford, Gloucestershire, in 1570. He may have been the Thomas Nicholas who matriculated at Peterhouse, Cambridge, in March 1571. He would be deprived of Widford by the bishop of Oxford for his extreme Calvinist preachments in 1577.

Meanwhile Nicholls began to translate works that would inform the privy council's strategic reappraisals of the military and financial strength of the Spanish monarchy. Contacts he had made in Seville's prison brought other talented linguists to Sir Francis Walsingham's notice. On 12 October 1574 Walsingham's diary records a letter sent at the behest of Nicholls on behalf of three Bristol merchants, including John Frampton, all convicted of heresy. This intervention, which secured their release in 1575–6, injected new energy into a translation programme of key Spanish texts, and Frampton was put to work alongside Nicholls on complementary navigational and medical works. The first of Nicholls's translations was *The Pleasant Historie of the Conquest of the West India, now called New Spayne*, printed in 1578 with a dedication to Walsingham that revealed it was not based on the original Spanish version of 1552 but on an Italian translation by Agostino de Cravaliz. Nicholls also translated an intercepted dispatch sent to Philip II in March 1577 by a merchant who had just returned from China via the Philippines and New Mexico, which was published in London in 1578 as *The Strange and Marvellous Newes Lately Come out from the Great Kingdome of Chyna*.

Nicholls's first wife died about 1576 and in 1577 he married Joan Harmer (*c*.1555–1618) of Ickenham, Middlesex, but by 1580 his old trading debts forced them both into the Marshalsea debtors' prison. On 29 August 1580 Nicholls began a compensation suit for 20,000 ducats for trading losses and the sequestration of his ships in the Canaries twenty years earlier. The privy council thereupon took advice from an admiralty judge that they sanction a recovery of Nicholls's trading debts against Spanish merchandise 'concealed' within the realm. Nicholls twice wrote from the debtors' prison to Lord Burghley, first in December 1580 and then on 10 October 1581, revealing that the unsettled claim had cost him another 220 ducats to pursue in Spain. Burghley and Walsingham did not fund this claim, however, finding it more convenient to keep Nicholls confined to the Marshalsea, as he was engaged in writing an account of the sugar plantations, the natural fruits, and the main exports of the Canaries and the Azores, which was published in London in 1583 as *A Pleasant Description of the Fortunate Islands called the Islands of Canaria*. Publication was delayed because the text was first used to inform English naval operations thereabouts in support of Dom Antonio's insurrection which lasted from 1578 into 1582. Indeed, during 1581 Burghley procured a manuscript chart of the region, adding to it each island's exports in the order listed in Nicholls's text.

Legal prevarication forced Nicholls to rely on translation work and to maintain links with a Sevillian financier called 'Jacques Nicholls' before he could re-establish his shipping business about 1590. Thus as a marketing ploy Nicholls's next two translations purported to emanate from Charles V's former courtiers but were probably drawn from his own annotated books. The first claimed to reflect the ideas of Pedro Mexia, an apothecary serving the late emperor, and was entitled *A delectable dialogue wherein is maintayned a pleasant dispatch between two Spanish gentlemen concerning physick and phisitions* (1580); the other was *The strange and delectable history of the discoverie and conquest of the province of Peru, and the South Sea* (1581). Nicholls explains that he was given the original text by its author, Augustine Sarate, in Toledo in 1570 while Sarate sought funds to reassert his own claim to gold-bearing lands south of the Orinoco River. It also contains references to Nicholls's trips to the Cape Verde Islands and to fishing grounds on the vast Mauretanian shoals.

By 1596 Nicholls was correcting proofs of his *Pleasant Historie of the Conquest of the West India* for publication later that year. In 1599 Richard Hakluyt incorporated most of this booklet within his *Principal Navigations*. Nicholls's re-established trading status in London was clearer still by 1600 when he won a suit in the sheriff's court at Guildhall for payment of victualling debts against his first son, Robert (*bap.* 1561).

Nicholls died at some point between 1 April 1601, when he drew up his will, and 9 May 1601, when it was proved. He was a resident of the parish of St Leonard's, Shoreditch, Middlesex, at his death. The will shows that he owned two ships which plied from his own grain wharf complex on Maidstone's riverfront, whence his daughter, Mary, would briefly enjoy a propertied income too. His son Thomas inherited both ships while Robert would inherit a Medway lighter and forgiveness of his outstanding debts. Thomas sailed as a gunner on a Levant Company ship in 1608 but was captured by Bizertan pirates. With help from Trinity House, his mother Joan raised the ransom in 1609

by selling their Maidstone premises before taking Thomas into less risky trade along the River Nene from Whittlesea, where they both eventually died in 1618.

R. C. D. BALDWIN

Sources A. Cioranescu, *Thomas Nicholls, mercader de azucar, hispanista, y hereje, con la edicion y traduccion de su descricion de las Islas Afortunadas* (La Laguna de Tenerife, 1963), esp. 11–15, 33–57, 85–91 · A. Cioranescu, *Thomas Nichols, mercader de azucar*, Instituto Estudios Canarios Monografias, vol. 19 (La Laguna de Tenerife, 1963) · R. E. H. Hair, 'Morocco, the Saharan coast and the neighbouring Atlantic Islands', *The Hakluyt handbook*, 1, ed. D. B. Quinn; 2nd ser., 144 (1974), 190–96, esp. 191–2 · D. B. Quinn, ed., *The Hakluyt handbook*, 2, Hakluyt Society, 2nd ser., 145 (1974), 426, 573 · C. T. Martin, ed., 'Journal of Sir Francis Walsingham, from December 1570 to April 1583', *Camden miscellany, VI*, CS, 104 (1871), 22 · J. L. Chester and G. J. Armytage, eds., *Allegations for marriage licences issued by the bishop of London*, 1, Harleian Society, 25 (1887) · Venn, *Alum. Cant.* · J. W. Blake, ed., *Europeans in West Africa, 1450–1560*, 2, Hakluyt Society, 2nd ser., 87 (1942), 190–94, 273–82, 304–7, 354, 433–40, 608, · G. Connell-Smith, 'English merchant trading to the New World in the early 16th century', *BIHR*, 23 (1950), 53–67 · will, PRO, PROB 11/97, sig. 28 · *CSP dom.*, 1560–64 · register of freemen of the city of London in the reigns of Henry VIII and Edward VI, CLRO, MS 512 · *APC*, 1580–81, 182 · T. S. Willan, *Muscovy merchants of 1555* (1953), 115–16 · *IGI*

Nicholls, William (1664–1712), theologian, was the son of John Nicholls of Donington, Buckinghamshire. He was educated at St Paul's School, London, under Dr Thomas Gale, and matriculated as a commoner at Magdalen Hall, Oxford, on 26 March 1680. He later migrated to Wadham College and graduated BA on 27 November 1683. Nicholls was chosen as a probationary fellow of Merton College on 6 October 1684; he proceeded MA on 19 June 1688, BD on 2 July 1692, and DD on 29 November 1695. After taking holy orders in 1688 he became chaplain to Ralph Montagu, later first duke of Montagu. In September 1691 he became rector of Selsey in Sussex, near Chichester. He also served as rector of Bushey, Hertfordshire, from 1691 to 1693. On 12 April 1707 he was installed as canon of Chichester.

Nicholls spent much of his life in literary labours, and he suffered because of poverty in his later days. In a letter to Robert Harley, earl of Oxford (31 August 1711), he complained that he was 'forced on the drudgery of being the editor of Mr Selden's Books, for a little money to buy other books to carry on my Liturgical Work' (Nichols, 1.490). He also asked Harley to consider him for the next open prebendary stall at Westminster. He wrote several apologetics in defence of orthodox Christianity. He wrote a response to Arthur Bury's *The Naked Gospel* and published it with his *Short History of Socinianism* in 1691, and followed it with a four-part *Conference with a Deist* (1696–9). He wrote on political theology in a work entitled *The religion of a prince; shewing that the precepts of holy scripture are the best maxims of government: in opposition to the irreligious principles of Nicholas Machiavel, Hobbs, etc.* (1704). He also published the Latin treatise *Defensio ecclesiae Anglicanae* (1707 and 1708), which he translated into English in 1715. Daniel Waterland praised the book for laying out the differences between Anglicans and remonstrants and stated that while '*Episcopius, Limborch,* and *Curcullaeus* often come into the hands of our young divines who may not perhaps readily distinguish between the true and old doctrines and some novel corruptions it would be very proper for them to have such a book as Dr Nichols' at hand, for a caution to them' (Allibone, *Dict.*, 2.1426). Nicholls hoped that the book would attract the attention of foreign scholars to the excellence of the English church. Therefore, he sent Latin copies to the king of Prussia and to many eminent scholars on the continent. This led to correspondence with Daniel Jablonski, Benedict Pictet, Jean le Clerc, Johann Jacob Wettstein, and many others. After his death, a collection of these letters was presented by his widow, Catherine, to the archbishop of Canterbury on 28 October 1712. Nicholls's views were answered by James Pierce in his *Vindication of the Dissenters*, published in 1718.

Nicholls's chief work was the *Comment on the Book of Common Prayer, and Administration of the Sacraments* (1710). He published a supplement separately in 1711. The book was published by subscription and dedicated to Queen Anne. The book, which Richard Buxton suggests represented a typical perspective of the eucharist, laid out the text of the prayer book. It also provided variant readings from other prayer books, including those of 1549 and 1637, with 'copious notes' and a paraphrase, which is 'an expanded version of the text giving what Nicholls assumes is its sense' (Buxton, 158-9). In his preface, which examined the history of the development of the prayer book, he linked the changes in the 1552 edition to the influence of John Calvin and Martin Bucer. His health broke down while he was working on the *Comment*, which he wrote without the help of an anamnesis. He died on 11 April 1712 near Bath and was buried in the centre aisle of St Swithin's Church, London, on 5 May 1712. ROBERT D. CORNWALL

Sources Foster, *Alum. Oxon.* · Nichols, *Lit. anecdotes*, 1.489–93 · *Fasti Angl., 1541–1857*, [Chichester] · R. Buxton, *Eucharist and institution narrative* (1976) · Allibone, *Dict.* · J. McClintock and J. Strong, *Cyclopaedia of biblical, theological, and ecclesiastical literature*, 12 vols. (1894–5) · G. Rupp, *Religion in England, 1688–1791* (1986) · W. D. Adams, *Dictionary of English literature*, rev. edn [1879–80]; repr. (1966) · *DNB*

Archives LPL, corresp.

Likenesses Basire, line engraving (after portrait by J. Richardson), NPG; repro. in W. Nicholls, *Defensio ecclesiae Anglicanae* (1707–8) · M. Vandergucht, line engraving (after portrait by J. Richardson), BM, NPG; repro. in W. Nicholls, *Comment on the Book of Common Prayer and administration of the sacraments* (1710)

Nichols family (*per. c.*1760-1939), printers and publishers, editors of the *Gentleman's Magazine*, and known especially for their books on local history and antiquarian scholarship, came to prominence in the late eighteenth century with the gifted **John Nichols** (1745-1826), printer and writer. Nichols was born on 2 February 1745 in Islington, Middlesex, the eldest of six children of Edward Nichols (1719-1779), baker, and his wife, Anne (1719-1783), daughter of Thomas Wilmot of Beckingham, Lincolnshire. Only John and his sister Anne survived to maturity. He was educated at John Shield's Academy for Young Gentlemen in Islington (*c.*1749-1757). He was originally destined for a naval career but his uncle, Thomas Wilmot, an officer under the command of Admiral Barrington, who was to have preferred him, died in 1751, and so on leaving school

Nichols joined the Bowyer printing office, founded in 1699, and was bound apprentice at Stationers' Hall, on 6 February 1759. His master, William Bowyer the younger, who had been educated at Cambridge and had, 'for more than half a century, stood unrivalled as a learned printer' (Nichols, *Lit. anecdotes*, 3.269), set about furthering his new apprentice's education by setting him Latin exercises, accompanying him to scientific lectures, and introducing him to the authors whose works were passing through his press. Nichols had a retentive memory and was eager to learn; from his youth he was quick at everything: 'he read with rapidity ... he spoke quickly, and that whether in the reciprocity of conversation or ... in a set speech.' He also wrote 'with great rapidity; but this, he used jocularly to allow, ... did not tend to improve his hand' (Chalmers). He was soon placed in a position of trust, and in 1765 his master sent him to Cambridge to test his business acumen by trying to negotiate the purchase of a share in the management of the university press. The negotiations fell through, but Bowyer was impressed with how the young man handled the business. When he came out of his time on 4 March 1766 (he was freed at Stationers' Hall) Bowyer returned half the apprenticeship fee to his father, an accepted practice where an apprentice satisfied the conditions. Bowyer's partnership with his relative James Emonson had ended acrimoniously in 1760 and his only surviving son, Thomas, had rejected his father and the business; so on 7 April 1766 Bowyer took Nichols into partnership, and in 1767 they moved from the cramped quarters in Whitefriars to larger premises in Red Lion Passage, Fleet Street.

At St Giles-in-the-Fields, Westminster, on 22 June 1766 Nichols married Anne (1737-1776), daughter of William Cradock of Leicester, with whom he had three children. Only two, Anne (*d.* 1815), who married the antiquary and architect John *Pridden, and Sarah, lived to maturity. His wife died in childbirth on 18 February 1776, and on 11 June 1778 Nichols remarried at St Mary's, Hinckley, Leicestershire. His second wife was Martha (1756-1788), daughter of William Green of Hinckley, with whom he had seven children. Bishop Thomas Percy was godfather to a son who died young; a second son, John Bowyer Nichols [*see below*], later succeeded his father in the business; and four daughters also survived.

William Bowyer died in 1777 and Nichols, his executor, became proprietor of one the largest printing houses in London. They had printed the House of Commons *Votes* or agenda papers since 1729, and in 1767 they were appointed printers of the House of Lords *Journals*. For many years they were printers to the Society of Antiquaries and the Royal Society but both commissions were lost at the end of the century; the Antiquaries, for whom they had printed from 1736, grew dissatisfied with the Nichols press and in 1798 moved to the cheaper and more fashionable press of William Bensley. Likewise the Royal Society, for whom the firm had printed since 1761, transferred to the 'fine' printer William Bulmer in 1791. But these were rare failures. In 1773 the government commissioned the Bowyer press to print a type facsimile of the Domesday

Book. Nichols designed the type and saw the work through the press during the ten years it took to produce. 'On the correctness and beauty of this important work I am content to stake my typographical credit,' Nichols wrote (Nichols, *Lit. anecdotes*, 2.265); it is still considered remarkably accurate and complete.

In June 1778 Nichols purchased a share in the *Gentleman's Magazine* from the sister of its founder, Edward Cave. At first he had half the printing and all the folding and stitching of each issue, but in 1780 he became sole printer and took over much of the editorial responsibility from Cave's brother-in-law, David Henry, who owned the remaining shares; shortly before his death in 1792 Henry surrendered the entire editorial control to Nichols. This put him in a very strong position: the lucrative and prestigious *Gentleman's Magazine* was a key component of the Nichols press, which kept tight control of its editorial policy and production until the family sold the property to J. H. Parker of Oxford in 1856.

It might be said of Nichols, as Dr Johnson said of Cave, that 'he never looked out of the window but with a view to the Gentleman's Magazine' (Boswell, *Life*). His editorial guidance of the *Gentleman's Magazine* is manifest throughout the years of his proprietorship. His first action on taking control was to double its size; Richard Gough had been reviews editor from 1786, and Nichols now printed longer reviews, as well as giving space to literary and antiquarian contributions from readers. He gave more prominence to the obituary columns and was indefatigable in his search for data, which he encouraged his readers to check. He was fascinated by biographical facts and anecdotes and he got his readers to produce information for both the *Magazine* and his other writings. His method was to question the accuracy of his contributors in footnotes, introducing topics he was interested in under a variety of pseudonyms and then correcting his own mistakes and eliciting further information in footnotes to footnotes. By 1794 this section had become what Nichols proudly called 'a body of biography'. John Wolcot, writing under the pseudonym Peter Pindar, might satirize 'John Nichols, the death hunter', but scholars ever since have owed him an incalculable debt. The contributors to the *Dictionary of National Biography* lifted whole phrases and paragraphs from Nichols for inclusion in their biographical articles and the *Gentleman's Magazine* is given as a source some 7000 times.

Nichols's reputation as an editor, biographer, and antiquary grew with the expansion of his printing business and was inextricably linked to it. As a youth he was always scribbling poetry and with William Bowyer's encouragement he published two slim volumes, *The Buds of Parnassus* and *Islington*, in 1763. His first important editorial work was a supplementary volume to the works of Jonathan Swift in 1775 which formed volume 17 of the trade edition of Swift's works and contained an index to the whole. Further supplementary volumes followed in 1776 and 1779. This led him to a general interest in the editorial process and by a study of the work of earlier Swift editors and a close reading of the *Journal to Stella* Nichols was able to improve the accuracy and orderliness of Swift's original

texts. The list of missing works which he added to his supplement of 1779 impressed Edmund Malone and is still useful today. His interest in Hogarth derived from Bowyer's association with the artist, while Nichols's biography exemplifies his editorial and scholarly method, only affordable by an author who was his own printer. Volume 4 of Walpole's *Anecdotes of Painting in England* (1780) had stimulated public interest in Hogarth. In the following year Nichols published, with the assistance of George Steevens and Isaac Reed, *Biographical anecdotes of Mr Hogarth, and a catalogue of his works, with occasional remarks* (1781), followed by enlarged editions in 1782 and 1785. Even the critical Walpole praised the work. The fourth edition, *Biographical Anecdotes of William Hogarth* (1810), 'in two handsome quarto volumes, illustrated with 160 beautiful plates' (Nichols, *Lit. anecdotes*, 3.9n.), remains a key work.

William Bowyer's proposal in 1764 to add to Tonson's edition of *The Tatler* and *The Spectator* turned Nichols's attention to the works of Steele, and between 1789 and 1797 he printed a number of Steele's periodicals, both on his own and jointly with a consortium of other booksellers. He bought a number of Steele's letters for his edition of the *Correspondence of Sir Richard Steele* (1797) which he later donated to the British Museum.

Nichols made extensive use of the papers of George Hardinge and the elder and younger Samuel Pegge, culminating in a new, enlarged edition of the younger Pegge's *Curialia* in 1806 and of the *Miscellaneous Works in Prose and Verse of George Hardinge* in 1818. Among Nichols's other edited works are *Letters on Various Subjects to and from William Nicholson* (1809), Samuel Pegge's *Anonymania* (1809), and a new edition, with the assistance of Malone, of Fuller's *History of the Worthies of England* (1811).

Nichols was an avid collector of literary manuscripts, which he then edited and printed. His wide circle of friends, readers, and contributors had confidence in his integrity and judgement and he was thus enabled to get hold of manuscript material for the obituary pages of the *Gentleman's Magazine* which might not have been entrusted to other publishers. He also bought heavily at sales and, as literary executor of William Bowyer, George Hardinge, and Samuel Pegge, acquired further collections. His editing of one group of documents might lead to the donation of related material which he would incorporate in further, enlarged editions. *The Epistolary Correspondence of Francis Atterbury* (1783) is a case in point; it originated in the purchase of a single manuscript which he enlarged by transcribing the bishop's letters in the British Museum and then published. This produced further original material from Atterbury's relations and other 'sources of equal authenticity' which culminated in a five-volume edition of Atterbury's letters in 1799.

For Nichols, work and social life were one and the same thing, and many of those for whom he printed, often inherited from Bowyer, became his friends and helped him in his publishing projects. His method was to assess the market for a work while he pursued his own 'harmless pleasure' of editing the works of lesser known authors. Such was the case with the *Original Works of William King* which he edited in 1776; he followed this up by printing a *Select Collection of Miscellaneous Poems*, which he edited between 1780 and 1782 with the assistance of Joseph Warton and bishops Percy and Lowth. It contained biographical notices of over 150 persons and was intended to supplement the poetical collections of James Dodsley, George Pearch, and Samuel Johnson. He printed Johnson's *Lives of the English Poets*, for which he contributed biographical details, and was drawn into Johnson's circle and joined his convivial Essex Head Club, founded in 1783. Nichols gave Boswell material for the *Life of Johnson* and subsequently donated his correspondence with Johnson to the British Museum.

Nichols's love of antiquarianism, encouraged by Bowyer, cannot be dissociated from his career as a printer and editor. He was passionately concerned with disseminating historical source material which might otherwise be lost. The Bowyer–Nichols press was at the heart of the output of monumental county histories. It was through printing the first edition of John Hutchins's *History and Antiquities of Dorset*, which Nichols saw through the press between 1770 and 1774, that he first met Richard Gough, a pioneer local historian. Gough was quick to see Nichols as an ally in his plan to publicize the antiquities of Britain, and Nichols became his closest friend. During twenty years they travelled through England visiting sites of historic interest, and collaborating on many projects, of which the most ambitious was the *Bibliotheca Topographica Britannica*, which appeared in fifty-two numbers between 1780 and 1790. The highly successful *Miscellaneous Antiquities* followed (1791–1800), with Gough the chief contributor. Its opening number was a series of questions seeking information from lovers of antiquities; then came Edward Rowe Mores's *History and Antiquities of Tunstall in Kent*, which proved that a scholarly local study could have more than local appeal. Nichols drew on manuscripts in his hands or on his own historical research for other titles in the series. Gough contributed a seminal article on 'the progress of sale catalogues' to volume 3 of the *Literary Anecdotes* and Nichols one of the first attempts at a history of the Stationers' Company to the same volume. Nichols felt keenly Gough's death in 1809. As his executor he oversaw Gough's bequest of his enormous collections of local history to the Bodleian Library. Nichols worked with other antiquaries such as William Cole of Milton and A. C. Ducarel, who provided Nichols with material for his work *Royal Wills* and for the 'History and antiquities of Lambeth parish' in *Bibliotheca Topographica Britannica*, 39 (1786), which drew on Ducarel's histories of the archbishop's palaces of Croydon and Lambeth.

Nichols's reputation as an antiquary and county historian rests principally on *The History and Antiquities of the County of Leicester*. He had family connections with Leicestershire and visited there regularly. This gave him a special interest in that county, while, as a Londoner, he could remain detached. In printing county histories of Dorset, Worcestershire, and Cornwall, he had learned how to arrange the material which he collected assiduously over many years, using his contacts through the *Gentleman's Magazine* to assemble a team of over 100 writers whose work he combined with research of his own and the unpublished manuscript histories of Leicestershire by William Burton, Francis Peck, and Richard Farmer. He was at pains to include documents of county-wide interest, ranging from his own extracts from Domesday to more recent government statistics, which provided points of comparison between different parishes. His novel method of illustrating the work derived from his experience as a printer; by using a border of coats of arms round views of buildings, sculptures, and artefacts his plates provided his readers with virtually a printed county museum. Nichols had begun characteristically with a series of fifty-two short studies printed in the *Bibliotheca Topographica Britannica* (1780–90), which gradually grew into a multi-volume work in spite of the loss of much material in the fire at his printing house in 1808, which cost Nichols at least £5000. He saw the work as his most important; it has not been superseded and remains one of the best county histories.

It is as chronicler of the book trade that Nichols is pre-eminent. His interest in printing history began when he and Bowyer edited the *Origin of Printing, in Two Essays* by Conyers Middleton and Gerard Meerman (1774); a supplement by A. C. Ducarel was added in 1781. In the same year came *The biographical memoirs of William Ged, including a particular account of his progress in the art of block printing* (1781). A peak year for Nichols was 1778, when he purchased the *Gentleman's Magazine*; published Edward Rowes Mores's *Dissertation of Type Founders and Type Founderies*, having bought the manuscript and blocks at Mores's posthumous sale; and, as a private tribute to his master and partner, published a fifty-two-page pamphlet in an edition of twenty copies, *The Anecdotes, Biographical and Literary of the Late Mr William Bowyer*. This he enlarged as *Biographical and Literary Anecdotes of William Bowyer, Printer … and Many of his Learned Friends* (1782). Nichols considered it the first edition of what in the course of thirty-four years grew to be the monumental *Literary Anecdotes of the Eighteenth Century* (9 vols., 1812–15) and *Illustrations of the Literary History of the Eighteenth Century* (8 vols., 1817–58), of which four volumes came out in his lifetime and the rest were completed by his son and grandson. He used the *Gentleman's Magazine* to elicit new material, asking his readers, usually under a pseudonym, for information, and by this means assembled a wealth of anecdote and biography incorporating letters and data as they came to hand. At times the reader is overwhelmed with a mass of footnotes and footnotes to footnotes; and Walpole, while praising Nichols's meticulousness, waspishly wished that 'he would not dub so many *great*. I have known several of his heroes, who were very little men' (Walpole, *Corr.*, 8.259). Taken together, however, these two works remain Nichols's most enduring monument.

Nichols was active in the Stationers' Company throughout his career, reaching the 'summit of his ambition' when he was made master in 1804. He was well known in the trade and, as owner of one the major printing houses engaged in official printing, was deeply involved in negotiating rates of pay and conditions during the unrest in the trade after 1785. He was also involved in many charities; in 1786 he helped to get a monument erected to John Howard in St Paul's Cathedral, and in 1793 he helped to get land purchased for a sea-bathing infirmary for 'scrophulous diseases' at Margate, Kent. He was a registrar of the Royal Literary Fund and was involved in the foundation of the Royal Humane Society, on both of whose committees his son later represented him; he subscribed to local charities in St Bride's, in the City of London, and in his native village of Islington, Middlesex. He was elected an honorary member of the Society of Antiquaries of Edinburgh in 1781 and of Perth in 1785. In 1810 he was admitted a fellow of the Society of Antiquaries of London.

On 8 January 1807 Nichols fell and fractured his thigh, and in the following year, on 8 February, the printing office and warehouse in Red Lion Passage were destroyed by fire with the loss of some £30,000, of which £10,000 was uninsured. The entire book stock in the warehouse was consumed, including all the numbers of the *Gentleman's Magazine* dating back to 1783. It says much for Nichols's fortitude and his standing in the trade that at the age of sixty-three and with the help of his son, John Bowyer Nichols, he was able to recover his business and continue his numerous personal printing enterprises. Many, including Luke Hansard, offered him the use of their presses until he could find new premises. He had moved back to Islington in 1803, intending to pursue his own writing interests, but his letters to his son show that he retained control of the firm and its routine business, continuing to check proofs and liaise with other members of the book trade to the end.

Portraits of Nichols in later life depict a short, amiable man, inclined to stoutness. He possessed, however, immense energy and a powerful memory. In private life he was popular and convivial. Boswell once described him as 'joyous to a pitch of bacchanalian vivacity' (*The Yale Edition of the Private Papers of James Boswell*, vol. 4, 1986, 412). According to Hart he was the 'archetype of the successful industrious apprentice' (*Minor Lives*, xx) who became master of a flourishing printing house and was known and liked by most of the leading literary and antiquarian figures of the day. Walpole admired his modesty and intelligence and to Gibbon he was 'the last, or one of the last of the learned printers in Europe' (Edward Gibbon to John Nichols, 24 Feb 1792; Nichols, *Lit. anecdotes*, 8.557). His printing office became a focus: many correspondents who met there left manuscripts to be called for. As well as editing over 150 works by other men he contributed innumerable articles to the *Gentleman's Magazine* and wrote works containing more biographical information than all his contemporaries combined. Behind his works lay his belief that 'every book should contain within itself its necessary explanation' (Kuist, *Works*, 19), thus saving the reader the trouble of referring elsewhere. He died on 26 November 1826 at his home in Highbury Place, Islington, and was buried on 5 December in the churchyard of St Mary's, Islington.

John Bowyer Nichols (1779–1863), printer and antiquary, was born on 15 July 1779 in Red Lion Passage, Fleet Street, London, only son among the five surviving children of John Nichols and his second wife, Martha Green. His childhood was spent largely with his maternal grandfather and his great-uncle, William Iliffe, at Hinckley. From about 1784 to 1790 he was taught by the Revd William Brown at Stoke Golding, Leicestershire, and moved to St Paul's School, London, on 9 October 1790. His father bound him apprentice on 6 August 1793 while he was still at school; on leaving school in September 1796 he entered his father's printing office. On 5 August 1800 he was freed at Stationers' Hall and was made a partner in the family business. He married, at St Bride's, Fleet Street, London, on 6 June 1805, Eliza (1784–1846), daughter of John Baker, apothecary of Camberwell, Surrey, with whom he had fourteen children; three sons and five daughters survived.

J. B. Nichols started to represent his father in business in 1802. He continued to live at Red Lion Passage after his father moved to Islington, but between 1808 and 1811 he and his family found accommodation in Thavies Inn while the fire-damaged print rooms and warehouse were refurbished and the presses were moved into their living quarters above the printing office. He took an active part in managing the printing business and in producing the *Gentleman's Magazine*. William Bray, who completed Owen Manning's *History and Antiquities of Surrey*, praised Nichols's 'attention and accuracy' in revising proof sheets to the second volume in 1809 (Manning and Bray, *Surrey*, vol. 2). Between 1811 and 1815 he and his father edited volumes 3 and 4 of the second edition of William Hutchins's *History and Antiquities of Dorset*, the entire stock of volumes 1 and 2, as well as part of volume 3 which was unpublished, having perished in the warehouse fire. The firm continued the Bowyer press tradition of publishing county histories, useful experience for a budding antiquary. J. B. Nichols printed most of the major early nineteenth-century works in the field, in which he was personally interested as an antiquary and on which he lavished his typographical skill. Samuel Bentley, J. B. Nichols's cousin, joined the firm between 1812 and 1818. In 1819 the younger man oversaw a move from the premises in Red Lion Passage to 25 Parliament Street, Westminster, where the press was more conveniently situated for printing the House of Commons *Votes*, which was night work and always required with urgency.

When his father died in 1826 J. B. Nichols became sole owner of the printing house. The Nicholses had been reappointed printers to the Society of Antiquaries in 1821 and J. B. Nichols inherited lucrative printing contracts for the *Votes* and the *Journals* of the Lords. He was held in high regard for his honourable dealings and mild manner, but this did not protect him from attack during the select committees on printing for the Commons of 1828 and 1833. Luke Graves Hansard lamented his 'lack of judicious explanation' (Ford and Ford, 38) when the committee questioned him about his methods and high cost of printing.

J. B. Nichols was closely associated all his working life with editing and printing the *Gentleman's Magazine*. In 1833 he purchased the remaining shares from the descendants of Edward Cave and David Henry and in the following year transferred a portion of the property to William Pickering, publisher, of Piccadilly. A new series was begun under an editorial team which included John Mitford, Sir Frederick Madden, J. T. Mansel, John Bruce, and A. J. Kempe, but J. B. Nichols and his son John Gough Nichols [see below] retained ultimate control. In 1850 J. B. Nichols bought back Pickering's share and in 1856 sold the entire property to J. H. Parker of Oxford.

Contemporaries compared J. B. Nichols's industry to the editorial energy of his father. He took over many of his father's literary works and those of his father's friends. He shared his father's interest in the history of the book trade and in 1818 edited *The Life and Errors of John Dunton*, to which he added an index. From 1825 he helped his father edit and print Joseph Cradock's *Literary and Miscellaneous Memoirs*, and after Cradock's death in 1826 completed volumes 3 and 4. Hansard told him: 'you have added to their interest by the beauty of your typography' (letter to J. B. Nichols, 15 Jan 1828). Cradock was godfather to Nichols's second son, Robert Cradock Nichols (1824–1892), and Nichols was one of Cradock's executors. In 1828 J. B. Nichols completed the fifth volume of the *Literary Illustrations*, which had been left unfinished at John Nichols's death in 1826. Drawing on his father's and Richard Gough's large accumulation of family and business papers, J. B. Nichols edited three further volumes in 1831, 1848, and 1858. He made use of his father's *Biographical Anecdotes of Mr Hogarth* (1781) to compile his *Anecdotes of William Hogarth* (1833) and his own collection of paintings contained several works by the artist.

J. B. Nichols was an active and popular antiquary. In 1818 he was elected fellow of the Society of Antiquaries and he frequently spoke and exhibited at their meetings. From 1829 he was an original member of the Noviomagians, the Antiquaries' select and convivial dining club. He regularly hosted their feasts and held amateur dramatics at his home. In 1819, during a brief appointment as printer to the corporation of London, he published *A Brief Account of the Guildhall of the City of London*; he revised and brought up to date Ducarel's *Account of the Royal Hospital and Collegiate Church of St Katharine, near the Tower* (1824). His *Historical Notices of Fonthill Abbey, Wiltshire* (1836), compiled from the earlier works of his lifelong friend John Britton and of John Rutter, brought the history of that abbey down to the time of its destruction. Two years later he compiled *Illustrations of Her Majesty's Palace at Brighton, Formerly the Pavilion*, which included a description of the palace by E. W. Brayley. On the death in 1833 of J. T. Smith, keeper of prints at the British Museum, Nichols purchased a series of unpublished etchings which Smith had prepared for a continuation of *Vagabondiana*. He included a memoir of Smith in the collection of *The Cries of London*, which he edited with the assistance of Francis Douce in 1838. He

became a friend of Sir Richard Colt Hoare through printing his *Wiltshire* and other of his works and was a frequent visitor at Stourhead. His catalogue of the Stourhead library was privately printed in 1840 and formed the basis of a lecture on the history and contents of the library delivered on his behalf to the Wiltshire Archaeological and Natural History Society in 1854. In 1843 he edited a second edition of Richard Yates's *History and Antiquities of the Abbey of St Edmunds Bury*.

J. B. Nichols kept detailed journals of the many tours of Britain and Europe he made throughout his life, visiting places of historic or printing interest, and he encouraged other members of his family to do the same. After the death of John Nichols, Dawson Turner approached J. B. Nichols with a view to purchasing the papers and letters accumulated by his father as editor of the *Gentleman's Magazine*, *Literary Anecdotes*, and other of his works. Nichols refused the offer and over the years collected and had bound as 'Family records' thousands of letters and associated ephemera which he identified and annotated. He was, in effect, the family archivist, and the large collections of Nichols papers now scattered among public repositories and private collections would not have survived without his assiduity and care. In addition he accumulated a large library of history and topography which included thousands of illustrations, rubbings, and maps arranged by county in portfolios, which John Britton, John Adey Repton, and Maria Hackett used in their research, and he formed an important collection of artefacts ranging from Norman Romanesque sculpture to a Renaissance chimney-piece from Theobalds, Hertfordshire, which had belonged to Richard Gough.

J. B. Nichols followed in his father's footsteps in being involved in good works and learned societies. He continued to serve on the committees of the Margate Infirmary, the Royal Literary Fund, and the Royal Humane Society. He filled various public offices in Westminster and Hammersmith. He was an original member of the Camden Society, whose proceedings he printed, and he also belonged to the Archaeological Institute, the Numismatic Society, the Royal Society of Literature, the Athenaeum Club, and the Linnean, the Zoological, and the Horticultural societies. J. B. Nichols was called to the court of the Stationers' Company in 1840 and was master of the company in 1850.

In later life J. B. Nichols went blind and was cared for by his eldest daughter, Mary, who was his amanuensis and helped him in assembling the family archive. She was an exhibiting artist and amateur photographer in her own right. He died at his home at Hanger Hill, Ealing, Middlesex, on 19 October 1863 and was buried in Kensal Green cemetery on 24 October.

John Gough Nichols (1806–1873), printer and antiquary, was born on 22 May 1806 at Red Lion Passage, Fleet Street, London, the eldest son of John Bowyer Nichols and his wife, Eliza. Richard Gough was his godfather. J. G. Nichols received his earliest education at the school of Miss Roper in Islington, Middlesex, and was then educated by Dr Waite in Lewisham, Kent, from 1814 to 1816; in

January 1817 he was sent to the Merchant Taylors' School, London, which he left in 1824 to join the family printing firm in Parliament Street, Westminster. On 22 July 1843 at Chiswick, Middlesex, he married Lucy (1821–1907), eldest daughter of Commander Frederick Lewis RN of Chiswick, with whom he had three children, of whom a son and a daughter survived.

Like his father and grandfather before him, J. G. Nichols took an active part in running the printing office with its contracts with the government and learned societies. He continued the close association with the *Gentleman's Magazine*, which he helped to edit from 1826; he continued to have ultimate managerial control over it after the responsibility was shared out between 1834 and 1850. He was sole editor from 1850 until it was sold in 1856, when he continued to be a contributor. Well aware of the importance of the obituary columns, he strove to promote them all his life, and wrote numerous obituary articles. When away from home he combed the local papers for biographical details likely to have been missed by the London papers. He was founding editor of the *Collectanea Topographica et Genealogica* (1834–43), the *Topographer and Genealogist* (1846–58), the *Herald and Genealogist* (1863–74), and the *Register and Magazine of Biography* (1869). In all these he sought to print, preserve, and make accessible original sources of interest to local historians.

J. G. Nichols's enthusiasm for antiquities began in childhood. He attended meetings of the Society of Antiquaries with his father from the age of twelve and was a skilled palaeographer by the time he left school. In 1826 he assisted his grandfather with the *Progresses of James I* and he completed it (1828) after the latter's death. His first separate publication, *Autographs of Royal, Noble, Learned and Remarkable Personages* (1829), which contains extracts from more than 600 manuscript letters, did much to stimulate contemporary interest in autograph collecting and is still of scholarly interest today.

J. G. Nichols shared the family interest in county history. He assisted W. L. Bowles in the *Annals and Antiquities of Lacock Abbey* (1834) and in 1837 he contributed an account of 'The hundred of Alderbury' to Colt Hoare's *History of Modern Wiltshire*. He printed the third edition, edited by Shipp and Hodson, of Hutchins's *History of Dorset* (4 vols., 1861–74); he was at work on the second edition of T. D. Whitaker's *History of Whalley* (2 vols., 1872–6) when he died. While researching his pioneering study *Examples of Decorative Tiles, Sometimes termed Encaustic* (1841–5) J. G. Nichols corresponded with architects and china manufacturers such as Minton. His work provided an important link between archaeologists and clergymen wishing to restore their churches and was influential in reviving the art of tile making for contemporary church decoration.

J. G. Nichols was elected a fellow of the Society of Antiquaries in 1835. Among his many contributions to *Archaeologia* may be noted his comments on the work of Holbein after the discovery of his will in 1862. He was a member of the committee which considered the authenticity of the Paston letters in 1865. He was an honorary fellow of the societies of Antiquaries of Newcastle and of Scotland and

corresponding fellow of both the Massachusetts History Society and the New England Genealogical Society. He visited his friend Robert Surtees in 1830, and helped to found the Surtees Society in 1834. He also helped to found the Camden Society (1838), the Archaeological Institute (1844), and the London and Middlesex Archaeological Society (1855). He was a member of the Numismatic Society, the Surrey Archaeological Society, and the Shakespeare Society. He was a prolific contributor to all their publications. His editions of the *Chronicle of Calais in the Reigns of Henry VII and Henry VIII* (CS, 35), *The Diary of Henry Machin, 1550–63* (CS, 42), and *The Narratives of the Days of the Reformation chiefly from the Manuscripts of John Fox* (CS, 77) were among some eighteen contributions made to the society's publications. He compiled a *Descriptive Catalogue* of the society's works (1862). For the Roxburghe Club he edited *Literary Remains of Edward VI* (1857–8), *The Boke of Noblesse addressed to Edward IV, 1475* (1860), and *The Legend of Sir Nicholas Throckmorton* (1874).

The Nicholses were close friends of the Herrick family, and between 1843 and 1862 J. G. Nichols arranged their family estate and personal papers, manorial rolls, and exchequer records, 1616–23, housed at Beaumanor Park, Leicestershire. The official warrants alone comprised 2300 documents, which Nichols had bound in sixteen volumes.

J. G. Nichols represented the firm in Liverpool in 1823, when he visited Matthew Gregson. He travelled widely in Britain and on the continent; he toured the north of England and Scotland in 1830, visited Gloucester in 1832, when he stayed with T. D. Fosbroke, made numerous tours of Oxfordshire, Berkshire, Wiltshire, and Leicestershire in the course of his research, and toured Germany with John Rivington in 1841 and Ireland in 1853. He made several visits to France. He was elected to the general committee of the Royal Literary Fund in 1836 and was a trustee of the Printers' Pension Corporation from 1845. For many years he was a director of the York Buildings Waterworks Company, latterly serving as its chairman and director. He was also a governor of the Grey Coat and Blue Coat schools, Westminster. He was called to the court of the Stationers' Company in 1865 and was under-warden of the company at the time of his death.

John Gough Nichols, like his father and grandfather before him, spent a lifetime as a working printer and proprietor of one of London's major printing offices, but he is best-known as a compiler, editor, author, and printer of archaeological and heraldic works. He died of cancer at his home, Holmwood Park, Dorking, Surrey, on 14 November 1873 and was buried on 19 November at the east end of Holmwood church.

The printing business remained in the Nichols family's hands after the death of J. G. Nichols. Initially it was managed by his son, John Bruce Nichols (1848–1929), in partnership with his uncle, Robert Cradock Nichols (1824–1892), but from 1898 until his death in 1929 he was joined by his own son, John Cradock Morgan Nichols (1876–1962). In 1897 the firm moved from Parliament Street to larger premises in Orchard Street. In 1930 the business became a private limited company known as J. B. Nichols & Sons Ltd, with John Cradock Morgan Nichols at the helm. In addition to its parliamentary contracts the company also printed for the houses of the convocation of Canterbury, the national assembly of the Church of England, Harrow School, the Royal College of Music, and the Surveyor's Institution. The company ceased trading in December 1939 and much of its parliamentary work was absorbed by the Stationery Office.

JULIAN POOLEY and ROBIN MYERS

Sources Col. U., Butler Library, Nichols papers [microfilm, Bodl. Oxf., MS film 1529/1–3] · Folger Nichols manuscript collection, Folger · Nichols correspondence, Bodl. Oxf., MS Eng. lett. b. 34, fols. 145–224 · Nichols family records, vols. 14–20, c.1824–c.1854, Bodl. Oxf., MSS Eng. b. 2071–2077 · Nichols family letters, mainly to John Bowyer Nichols, 1816–1837, Bodl. Oxf., MSS Eng. c. 6165–6166 · private information (2004) · Nichols correspondence, Archibald S. Alexander Library, New Brunswick, Rutgers Special Collections and University Archives, Rutgers University, MSS 86–540 · Nichols, *Lit. anecdotes* · Nichols, *Illustrations* · J. B. Nichols, *A pedigree of the family of Nichols: registered in the College of Arms AD 1861, with additions, March 1862* · [A. Chalmers], *GM*, 1st ser., 96/2 (1826), 489–504 · A. H. Smith, 'A biography of John Nichols, 1745–1826, with a critical and descriptive account of works written and edited by him', MA diss., U. Lond., 1959 · A. H. Smith, 'John Nichols, printer and publisher', *The Library*, 5th ser., 18/3 (Sept 1963), 169–90 · *Minor lives: a collection of biographies by John Nichols*, ed. E. L. Hart (1971) · J. M. Kuist, *The works of John Nichols: an introduction* (1968) · R. C. Nichols, *Memoir of the late John Gough Nichols* (1874) · P. Peoples, 'The Folger Nichols manuscript collection: a description and analysis', PhD diss., University of Wisconsin-Milwaukee, 1980 · J. M. Kuist, *The Nichols file of the Gentleman's Magazine* (1982) · K. Maslen and J. Lancaster, eds., *The Bowyer ledgers* (1991) · C. Reed, 'A discovery in Pennsylvania: the "Tiles" guardbook of John Gough Nichols', *Journal of the Tiles and Architectural Ceramics Society*, 6 (1996), 3–13 · *GM*, 3rd ser., 15 (1863), 794–8 · *GM*, 2nd ser., 25 (1846), 217 · J. Simmons, ed., *English county historians* (1978) · C. R. J. Currie and C. P. Lewis, eds., *English county histories: a guide* (1994) · J. G. Nichols, *The hall of the chancellors* (privately printed, 1839) · A. H. Smith, 'John Nichols and Hutchins' *History and antiquities of Dorset*', *The Library*, 5th ser. 15/2 (1960), 81–95 · E. L. Hart, 'Some new sources of Johnson's *Lives*', *Publications of the Modern Language Association of America*, 65 (1950), 1088–111 · [G. E. Dunstone], *A short history of the house of Nichols* (1938) · E. L. Hart, 'An ingenious editor: John Nichols and the *Gentleman's Magazine*', *Bucknell Review*, 10 (1962), 232–42 · E. L. Hart, 'The contributions of John Nichols to Boswell's *Life of Johnson*', *Publications of the Modern Language Association of America*, 67 (1952), 391–410 · C. Phythian-Adams, 'Leicestershire and Rutland', *English county histories: a guide*, ed. C. R. J. Currie and C. P. Lewis (1994), 228–45 · J. Evans, *A history of the Society of Antiquaries* (1956) · J. Britton, *The autobiography of John Britton*, 3 vols. in 2 (privately printed, London, 1849–50) · *Luke Graves Hansard, his diary, 1814–1841*, ed. P. Ford and G. Ford (1962) · T. Faulkner, *The history and antiquities of the parish of Hammersmith* (1839) · J. Pooley, 'The diary of Mary Anne Nichols, 1823–1834: a publisher's daughter in Hammersmith', *Transactions of the London and Middlesex Archaeological Society*, 44 (1993), 171–97 · R. B. Gardiner, ed., *The admission registers of St Paul's School, from 1748 to 1876* (1884) · L. Hansard, *The auto-biography of Luke Hansard, written in 1817*, ed. R. Myers (1991) · R. Myers, 'John Nichols (1745–1826): chronicler of the book trade', *The development of the English book trade, 1700–1899*, ed. R. Myers and M. Harris (1981) · R. Rabicoff and D. F. McKitterick, 'John Nichols, William Bowyer and the Cambridge University Press in 1765', *Transactions of the Cambridge Bibliographical Society*, 6/5 (1976), 328–38 · E. L. de Montluzin, 'Attributions of authorship in the "Gentleman's Magazine", 1731–1868: a supplement to Kuist [7 pts]', etext.lib.virginia. edu/bsuva/gm [*Studies in Bibliography*, 44–50 (1991–7)] · E. L. de Montluzin, 'Attributions of authorship in the "Gentleman's Magazine", 1731–1868: a synthesis of finds appearing neither in Kuist's "Nichols file" nor in de Montluzin's "Supplement to Kuist"', etext. lib.virginia.edu/bsuva/gm, 1996 · 'J. B. Nichols and Sons to close', *British and Colonial Printer and Stationer* (7 Dec 1939), 458–9 · *English literature and history* (1988) [sale catalogue, Sothebys, London, 15 Dec 1988] · *John Bowyer Nichols: sale of books and portfolios of illustrations from Hanger Hill* (1864) [sale catalogue, Sothebys, London, 24–30 May 1864]

Archives BL, copy of *Anecdotes of Hogarth* with further notes, Add. MS 27996 [John Nichols] · BL, corresp. and papers relating to *Gentleman's Magazine*, Add. MS 63652 [John Nichols] · BL, family corresp., Add. MS 36987 [John Nichols] · Bodl. Oxf., accounts [John Nichols] · Bodl. Oxf., antiquarian and literary notes [John Nichols] · Bodl. Oxf., corresp. and papers [John Nichols] · Bodl. Oxf., family corresp. and papers [John Nichols] · Bodl. Oxf., literary notes [John Nichols] · Bodl. Oxf., notebooks [John Nichols] · Bodl. Oxf., personal corresp. and papers [John Nichols] · Col. U., Butler Library, family corresp. and papers [microfilm at Bodl. Oxf., MS film 1529/1–3] · CUL, ledger of copyrights [John Nichols] · CUL, transcript by J. B. Nichols of notes by Richard Gough [John Bowyer Nichols] · Folger, Folger Nichols manuscript collection · JRL, corresp. [John Nichols] · JRL, corresp. [John Bowyer Nichols] · LPL, antiquarian papers [John Nichols] · LUL, corresp. relating to *Gentleman's Magazine* [John Bowyer Nichols] · NL Scot., corresp. relating to the Mar peerage case and related papers [John Gough Nichols] · priv. coll. · Rutgers University, New Brunswick, Archibald S. Alexander Library, family corresp. and papers [John Nichols] · S. Antiquaries, Lond., corresp. [John Nichols] · S. Antiquaries, Lond., corresp. and papers relating to Cobham brasses [John Gough Nichols] · Trinity Cam., collections relating to *Literary illustrations* and notes relating to Hinckley [John Nichols] · Trinity Cam., notes and papers [John Bowyer Nichols] · Trinity Cam., notes from sale catalogues of Suffolk collections [John Gough Nichols] · Yale U., Beinecke L., Osborne collection, corresp. and papers | BL, letters to F. J. Baigent, Add. MS 39985 [John Gough Nichols] · BL, letters to Philip Bliss, Add. MSS 34567–34569, 34581 [John Nichols] · BL, William Cole, 'Manuscript collections', Add. MSS 5381, 5993, 6401 · BL, letters to Stacey Grimaldi, Add. MS 34188 [John Bowyer Nichols] · BL, letters to Stacey Grimaldi, Add. MSS 34188–34189 [John Gough Nichols] · BL, corresp. with Sir Frederic Madden, Add. MS 51020; MSS Egerton 2838–2848, *passim* [John Gough Nichols] · BL, corresp. with Sir Frederic Madden, MSS Egerton 2838–2845, *passim* [John Bowyer Nichols] · BL, letters to Royal Literary Fund [John Nichols] · Bodl. Oxf., corresp. with William Cuming [John Nichols] · Bodl. Oxf., letters to Francis Douce [John Nichols] · Bodl. Oxf., letters, mainly to Richard Gough [John Nichols] · Bodl. Oxf., corresp. relating to Hutchins's *History of Dorset* [John Nichols] · Bodl. Oxf., letters to Mark Noble [John Nichols] · Bodl. Oxf., letters to Sir Thomas Phillipps [John Nichols] · Bodl. Oxf., letters to John Price [John Nichols] · Bucks. RLSS, corresp. with George Lipscomb [John Bowyer Nichols] · CUL, letters to Henry Taylor [John Nichols] · Derbys. RO, Matlock, letters to Richard Gifford [John Nichols] · Herefs. RO, letters to F. R. Havergal [John Gough Nichols] · Leics. RO, corresp. with J. N. Ludford [John Nichols] · Leics. RO, letters to Rowland Rouse [John Nichols] · NL Scot., corresp. with George Paton [John Nichols] · S. Antiquaries, Lond., letters to G. S. Steinman [John Gough Nichols] · Spalding Gentlemen's Society Museum, papers relating to *Gentleman's Magazine* [John Nichols] · Stationers' Company, London, register of freemen, 4 Feb 1752 to 5 July 1796, item 38 · U. Edin. L., corresp. with James Halliwell-Phillipps [John Gough Nichols] · U. Edin. L., letters to David Laing [John Gough Nichols]

Likenesses V. D. Puyl, portrait, 1787 (John Nichols) · H. Humphrey, engraved satirical portrait, 1797 (John Nichols), Columbia Nichols collection · J. Sayers, etching, pubd 1797 (John Nichols), NPG · watercolour?, miniature, c.1800 (John Bowyer Nichols), priv. coll. · J. Wood, oils, 1804 (John Nichols), Stationers' Hall, London · J. G. Giannelli, bust, 1814 (John Nichols) · J. Jackson, watercolour, *c.*1818 (John Bowyer Nichols) • F. Hopwood, pencil, 1821 (John Bowyer Nichols), priv. coll. • Tery, engraving, pubd 1822 (John Nichols; after portrait by J. Jackson, 1811), NPG • D. Maclise, group portrait, watercolour, 1831 (John Gough Nichols), repro. in Nichols, *Memoir of the late John Gough Nichols*; priv. coll. • J. Wood, oils, 1836 (John Bowyer Nichols), priv. coll. • silhouette, 1847 (John Bowyer Nichols), repro. in 'Family records', vol. 19, Bodl. Oxf., MS Eng. b. 2076, fol. 383 • W. Behnes, bust, exh. RA 1858 (John Bowyer Nichols) • Kent and Hennah of Brighton, photograph, *c.*1860 (John Bowyer Nichols), repro. in [J. G. Nichols], *Memoir of the late John Bowyer Nichols* (1864) • photograph, 1866 (John Gough Nichols), repro. in Nichols, *Memoir of the late John Gough Nichols* • J. Basire, engraving (John Nichols; after portrait by R. C. Woolnoth, 1803) • W. Behnes, marble bust (John Nichols) • A. Cardon, stipple (John Nichols; after drawing by H. Edridge, 1814), BM, NPG; repro. in Cadell and Davies, *Contemporary portraits* • T. Cook, line engraving (John Nichols; aged thirty-seven; after portrait by F. Towne, 1782), BM; repro. in *Collections for the history of Leicestershire* (1787) • C. Heath, line engraving (John Nichols; after drawing by J. Jackson, 1811), BM, NPG; repro. in Nichols, *Lit. anecdotes*, 3 • J. H. Lynch, lithograph (John Bowyer Nichols; after portrait in chalks by S. Lawrence, 1850), BM, NPG • H. Meyer, mezzotint (John Nichols; aged sixty-six; after drawing by J. Jackson, 1811), BM, NPG; repro. in J. Nichols, *The history and antiquities of Leicestershire*, 1 (1795) • H. Meyer, stipple (John Nichols; aged eighty; after his drawing, 1825), BM, NPG; repro. in *GM*, 96 (1826), 489–504 • T. Rowlandson, engraved satirical portrait (John Nichols), repro. in 'A benevolent epistle to Sylvanus Urban, alias Master John Nichols, printer, common-councilman of Farringdon ward, and censor-general of literature …' (1790) • L. C. Wyon, medallion (John Gough Nichols with Lucy; struck to commemorate their silver wedding in 1868) • etching (John Nichols), NPG • pencil (John Nichols), repro. in R. Myers, M. Harris, and G. Mandelbroke, *Lives in print: biography and the book trade from the middle ages to the 21st century* (2002) • silhouette (John Nichols), repro. in J. C. Lettsom, *Hints designed to promote benificence, temperance and medical science* (1801) • three miniatures (John Nichols), NPG

Wealth at death £12,000—John Nichols: will, consistory court of London, 21 Dec 1826, London Metropolitan Archives, estate duty wills register 1826 N–R IR26/1101, fol. 1306, Family Records Centre, London • under £180,000—John Bowyer Nichols: will with 3 codicils proved at principal registry of the family division 1836 and re-sworn at stamp office July 1864 • under £100,000—John Gough Nichols: resworn probate, Oct 1874, *CGPLA Eng. & Wales* (1873)

Nichols, (John) Beverley (1898–1983), writer, was born on 9 September 1898 at Woodlands, Bower Ashton, Long Ashton, Bristol, the youngest of three sons of John Nichols (*d.* 1946), a wealthy solicitor, and his wife, Pauline Zoe Lilian Shalders (1866–1939). He was educated at Marlborough College following preparatory school in Torquay. Contrary to family testimony, Nichols later portrayed his early years as unhappy owing to his father's alcoholism, violence, and adultery. After an unsuccessful term at Balliol College, Oxford, in 1917, he obtained his commission in the army, as a second lieutenant in the labour corps. While he was attached to the War Office a series of open homosexual liaisons caused consternation and he was hastily transferred to Cambridge to instruct officer cadets in military strategy. Here he was made aide-de-camp to A. E. Shipley, vice-chancellor of the university, when he headed the Universities' Mission which toured America for the last three months of 1918. Nichols, strikingly handsome in uniforms of his own design, was hailed as a war hero despite not having seen any action. He acted the part with aplomb and charm, and such was his success that he

(John) Beverley Nichols (1898–1983), by Howard Coster, 1929

extended his stay in New York to cope with social engagements. He also earned his first 40 dollars for a magazine article. During the long train journeys across America he completed his critically successful novel *Prelude* (1920), partially based on his schooldays.

Nichols returned to Balliol in 1919 determined to become a celebrity. As editor he revitalized *Isis*, the student newspaper, launched *Oxford Outlook*, a leftish magazine, and cajoled the Liberal Party to finance a new club. After an initial and humiliating defeat engineered by his tory detractors, he was elected president of the union for Michaelmas term 1920 and used the position to promote himself unceasingly. When he left Oxford in 1921 with a degree in modern history (short course), having nearly been sent down for neglecting his studies, his controversial opinions, on topics such as a 'soviet of youth', were, much to his gratification, already the subject of indignant letters to the national press.

After flirting with politics and abandoning a career in law, Nichols drifted into journalism. In the *Daily News* he created a disagreeable child, Crystabel, who asked awkward questions of her parents. He later developed this satirical approach in the book *For Adults Only* (1932). His second novel, *Patchwork* (1921), set in Oxford, audaciously stated that the characters, pleasant and otherwise, were drawn from life. His next, *Self* (1922), based on Thackeray's *Vanity Fair*, was a best-seller, although Nichols later dismissed it as 'the worst novel ever written' (*The Times*). After an abortive, if adventurous, trip to Greece to write a defence of King Constantine, he travelled to Australia in 1924 to ghost the memoirs of Dame Nellie Melba. After her death he highlighted her faults in *Evensong* (1932); the dramatized version gave Edith Evans her first commercial stage success in London. His precocious autobiography *Twenty-Five* appeared in 1926 but its elegance and wit were marred by sentimentality. This tendency bedevilled his satire of the 'bright young things' in *Crazy Pavements*, autobiography posing as fiction, which startled readers in 1927 with scenes of drug-taking and sexual ambivalence, and which was thought to have influenced Evelyn Waugh's *Vile Bodies* (1930). Lawsuits were threatened but dodged.

In the 1920s Nichols also pursued a moderately successful career in the theatre. He composed the music for the revue *Picnic* in 1927, and his play *The Stag* (1929), which mixed blood sports with abortion, was produced in the West End in 1929. Directed by Raymond Massey, it proved an 'honourable failure' (Connon, 141), and indeed Nichols entitled the collected edition of his plays *Failures* (1933). He also wrote the book and lyrics for C. B. Cochran's *1930 Revue* with Ivor Novello and, when that did not gel, with Vivian Ellis.

On a lecture tour of America in 1927 Nichols was screen-tested unsuccessfully in Hollywood (he was later the romantic lead in *Glamour*, 1930, a disastrous British film). He returned in 1928 to work briefly as editor of the *American Sketch* and the trip gave him the opportunity to interview celebrities such as Charlie Chaplin for his book *The Star-Spangled Manner* (1928). In 1932 he started his popular gossip column 'Page two' for the *Sunday Chronicle*, of which he was never very proud. It lasted fourteen years.

In the 1930s the sophisticate turned garden writer. *Down the Garden Path* (1932)—a witty, fictionalized account of Nichols's experience as an amateur gardener at his weekend cottage at Glatton, near Peterborough—was enormously successful, and became his best-remembered book. Nine similar books followed. In 1932 he began to live with the actor Cyril Butcher, and their relationship lasted until Nichols's death; Nichols's pleas for sexual tolerance were unusually vocal for the period, and are found throughout his writings. At this time he also produced a play about Franz Mesmer; a popular treatment of theology, *The Fool hath Said* (1936), which applied Christian belief to the problems of sex, war, and money; and *No Place Like Home* (1936), a travel book about the Middle East.

Nichols also turned to more serious writing. His play *Avalanche* (1931) had aired his 'idealistic pacifism', as did his book *Cry Havoc!* (1933), which caused a furore; *When the Crash Comes* (1933) dramatized communist revolution in Britain. In Germany he had tackled Goebbels, and spoke of 'peace at any price' at disarmament rallies organized by the League of Nations Union in 1932, so it is a surprise to hear him in *News of England* (1938) declaring that Sir Oswald Mosley was the only politician strong enough to prevent war with Germany. He later regretted this. By contrast, he never regretted his support for Indian partition and the Muslim cause, or his vitriolic criticism of M. K. Gandhi in *Verdict on India* (1944).

With another change of tack, which could look like opportunism, Nichols turned children's story-teller with *The Tree that Sat Down* (1945), feature writer for *Woman's Own*, and detective novelist with *No Man's Street* (1954). A successful series on cats followed in the early 1960s. He further courted controversy with *A Case of Human Bondage* (1966), which condemned Somerset Maugham for the vilification of his wife Syrie, and he attacked his own father in *Father Figure* (1972). It contained three melodramatic accounts of attempted patricide which were discussed in parliament, but which were probably embellished. He further published his autobiography, *The Unforgiving Minute* (1978), collected his verse in *Twilight* (1982), and assessed himself, mystifyingly, as a failure. Having suffered from cancer for some years, he died on 15 September 1983 in Kingston Hospital following a fall at his home in Richmond. His body was cremated, and the ashes scattered at Glatton church.

BRYAN CONNON, *rev.* CLARE L. TAYLOR

Sources B. Connon, *Beverley Nichols: a life* (1991) • *The Times* (17 Sept 1983) • B. Nichols, *Twenty-five* (1926) • B. Nichols, *All I could never be* (1949) • B. Nichols, *Father figure* (1972) • B. Nichols, *The unforgiving minute* (1978) • personal knowledge (1978) • private information (1990) • b. cert. • d. cert.
Archives U. Sussex, corresp. • U. Texas, corresp. and literary papers | CAC Cam., letters to Cecil Roberts • Indiana University, Bloomington, Maugham MSS II • U. Texas, Nancy Cunard collection • University of Delaware, Newark, Sir Gerald Barry corresp.
Likenesses C. Beaton, photograph, 1920–29, NPG • H. Coster, photograph, 1929, NPG [*see illus.*] • H. Coster, photograph, 1929, NPG; *see illus.* in Cochran, *Sir Charles Blake* (1872–1951) • G. Argent, photograph, 1969, NPG • photographs, repro. in Connon, *Beverley Nichols*
Wealth at death £138,679: probate, 10 Jan 1984, *CGPLA Eng. & Wales*

Nichols [Nicholls], **Edward** (*bap.* 1583?, *d.* 1622?), sailor, was possibly the son of Simon (*d.* 1602) and Alice Nicholl (*d.* 1596) of Newhaven, Sussex, baptized on 10 May 1583 at St Michael's, Newhaven. He was probably the Edward Nicholls shown in the customs accounts of 1612 as master of the *Gilliflower*, bound for Spain. He was still master on 14 June 1615, but had been replaced by 16 June, perhaps because of his appointment to command the *Dolphin* of London, for which he was granted ship's bounty on 30 November 1615. The next year, armed with 24–8 guns, the *Dolphin* sailed for the Mediterranean, probably in the service of the Levant Company.

On 12 January 1617, homeward bound with a crew of thirty-eight, the *Dolphin* encountered off Sardinia five or six Turkish warships from the Barbary coast, each allegedly of 200 to 500 tons, with 20 to 35 guns and crews of 200 to 650 apiece, three commanded by English renegades, captains Walsingham, Kelley, and Sampson. Four attacks were made on the *Dolphin*, each by one or two ships. The *Dolphin* was hit with heavy shot, but boarding parties were repulsed with fire from the roundhouse. Nichols rejected an offer to surrender on favourable terms. When the *Dolphin* appeared to catch fire the Turks sheered off, having suffered heavy casualties. The *Dolphin* had been battered and eight to eleven members of her crew were dead or dying. Yet she had survived a fight against hopeless odds and, after repairs at Cagliari, reached England safely.

Henry Gosson of London quickly published an account of the fight by the water poet John Taylor, and then issued another version when Nichols complained that the earlier pamphlet was false and had been published without his consent. Substantially, however, the two accounts agree, sometimes word for word, although the later perhaps exaggerates the odds: for example, the *Dolphin* is said to be only 220 tons, but the ship's bounty had been geared to 280 tons.

Nichols's feat earned him admission to the Levant Company. Little else is known of him. He still commanded the *Dolphin*, outward bound, in May 1617; he may be the Captain Nicholls reported in 1621 as having seized a ship adrift in the Mediterranean; and he might be the Edward Nicholls of St Olave's parish, Southwark (a mariner of that name certainly lived there), whose will mentioning four children and containing a bequest to the poor of Newhaven was proved by his widow, Sindenie, on 18 December 1622. He was not listed in the muster of the seamen of London taken in 1629, no doubt because he was dead.

G. G. HARRIS

Sources [J. Taylor], *A fight at sea, famously fought by the Dolphin of London, against five of the Turkes men of warre and a salty the 12 of January last 1616 etc* (1617) · [E. Nichols (?)], *The Dolphins danger and deliverance* (1617) · port books, PRO, E 190/19/5; E 190/16/2; E 190/21/1; E 190/745/23; and E 190/750/17 · pell receipt books, PRO, E 401/1895 · PRO, SP [Charles I] 135 and 105/147, 148 · PRO, PROB 11/140, fol. 355 · examinations, PRO, HCA 43 · parish register, St Olave, Southwark, LMA · parish register, Newhaven, St Michael, E. Sussex RO · wills, archdeaconry of Lewes, E. Sussex RO, A11 B3, fol. 147 [Simon Nicholl]

Nichols, James (1785–1861), master printer and theological writer, was born at Washington, co. Durham, on 6 April 1785. His family moved to Bradford, Yorkshire, where James received religious instruction from John Crosse. His father encountered reverses, so James worked in a factory at Holbeck, Leeds, from 1793 to 1797, studying Latin grammar in his spare time. Eventually he attended the free grammar school, Leeds. Distinguished for his classical attainments, he became a private tutor, and after this he set up as a printer and bookseller at Briggate, Leeds. In 1813 he married Miss Bursey of Stockton-on-Tees and then had many children.

Nichols was devoted to Methodism, editing Samuel Wesley's *Poems* (1842, 1862), and in 1813 he published the proceedings of the first Methodist missionary meeting in Leeds. He contributed to the *Theological Dictionary* of the Revd Richard Watson, edited and printed the *Poetical Works* (1814) of Dr Byrom, a friend of the Wesleys, printed and published the *Wesleyan Notices Newspaper* (1854), and printed the *Arminian or Methodist Magazine* (1831–61).

Nichols also edited and printed the *Leeds Literary Observer* (vol. 1, January to September 1819, no more published), printed the *Leeds Correspondent* (vols. 1–5, January 1814 –

July 1823), and printed and published the *Christian Reporter of Political, Literary … Intelligence* (1820). In 1820 Nichols moved to London, opening a printing office at 2 Warwick Square.

Nichols loved to read Latin and Dutch biographies, the publications of famous divines of Reformation Europe, and English historians. *Calvinism and Arminianism Compared*, his best-known title, written and printed in 1824, was praised by Southey and the *Quarterly Review*. In 1831 he moved his London printing office to 45 Hoxton Square, Shoreditch. He edited and printed to acclaim Thomas Fuller's works—*Church History* (1837) and *The Holy and Profane State* (1841), for example—and many other religious tracts, such as Anthony Faringdon's *Sermons* (4 vols., 1849), as well as editing books for William Tegg. Among the thirty-nine titles he wrote, edited, or printed, the chief was Samuel Annesley's *The Morning Exercises at Cripplegate* (5th edn, 6 vols., 1844–5). His *Poetical Works of Thomson* (1849) and the *Complete Works of Young* (1855) were esteemed for their scholarship.

The Athenaeum extolled Nichols as 'one of the rare … learned printers' (7 Dec 1861, 769). Watson praised his laborious, careful research and pious spirit. By early rising and with efficiency, Nichols became a Greek, Hebrew, and Dutch scholar, accomplishing an astonishing amount of literary work, despite the cares of a large business. Endowed with a knowledge of sacred literature, he was befriended by Southey, Wordsworth, Tomline, Todd, Bunting, and Bowring. On several occasions he was invited to take holy orders in the Church of England. Dr Walter Farquhar Hook, who knew Nichols for forty years, recalled his remarkably cheerful disposition as author, editor, and family man (*Watchman Newspaper*, 27 Nov 1861, 391). He died of pemphigus at 45 Hoxton Square, Shoreditch, London, on 26 November 1861, mourned by his wife and their two surviving children, William and Councillor Nichols of Holbeck.

RALPH A. MANOGUE

Sources *The late Mr. James Nichols* [n.d., 1860x69] [incl. portraits and letter pasted on flyleaf from William Nichols to Mr Stevenson]; repr. from W. F. Hook, 'The late Mr. James Nichols', *Watchman Newspaper* (27 Nov 1861), 391 [with notes by William Nichols] · R. V. Taylor, 'Mr. James Nichols 1785–1861', *Biographia Leodiensis* (1865) · *DNB* · W. B. Todd, *Directory of Printers, 1800–1840* (1972) · *The Athenaeum* (30 Nov 1861), 705 · *The Athenaeum* (7 Dec 1861), 769 · J. Darling, *Cyclopaedia bibliographica* (1854), vol. 2 · 'The late Mr James Nichols', *GM*, 3rd ser., 12 (1862), 106 · Boase, *Mod. Eng. biog.*, vol. 2 · L. Baillie and P. Sieveking, eds., *British biographical archive* (1984), fiche 816, frames 155–6 [microfiche] · Allibone, *Dict.*, vol. 2 · *Shilling Methodist Magazine* (Jan 1862) · *Wesleyan Times* [n.d.] [with reminiscence by Mr Hare]

Archives BL, letter to Sir Robert Peel, Add. MS 40374, fol. 189 · Bodl. Oxf., letter to John Nichols and John Gough Nichols, Add. MS 40499, fol. 100

Likenesses photograph, repro. in Hook, 'The late Mr. James Nichols', *Watchman Newspaper*

Wealth at death £2000: administration, 1861, *CGPLA Eng. & Wales*

Nichols, John (1745–1826). *See under* Nichols family (*per. c.*1760–1939).

Nichols, John Bowyer (1779–1863). *See under* Nichols family (*per. c.*1760–1939).

Nichols, John Gough (1806–1873). *See under* Nichols family (*per. c.*1760–1939).

Nichols, Mary Sergeant Gove (1810–1884), campaigner for medical reform and women's rights, was born at Goffstown, New Hampshire, USA, on 10 August 1810, the second daughter and third child of William A. Neal (*d.* 1845) and Rebecca R. Neal. Her paternal grandfather was Scottish, while her mother's family were Welsh. Mary Neal was largely self-educated; her voracious reading was influenced by her father's interests as a radical democrat and her mother's universalist sympathies; she reputedly memorized classical and medical authors from an early age. On 5 March 1831 Mary Neal married Hiram Gove. His surly and domineering character, combined with four stillbirths and her need for outside intellectual interests, brought the relationship to an end in 1842.

Mrs Gove then embarked upon a lively social and intellectual life. Jacksonian democracy, antipathetic towards élites, privilege, monopoly, or restrictions on knowledge, proved a favourable climate for independent-minded women: popular education was expanding; Sylvester Graham was publicizing his theories on diet, health, and sex; Fanny Wright was endorsing 'free love'; Dr William A. Alcott was expounding communitarian ideas; and enthusiastic religion was beginning to overtake staid orthodoxy. Mrs Gove started school teaching with boarders and lecturing to women on the lyceum circuit. Already unorthodox in reading medical materials, her interest in the subject was intensified by her own persistent ill health and her unhappy marriage, several family deaths, and her brother's career as a doctor. She began giving physiology lectures to Boston ladies in 1838: her runaway success led to tours of New England, New York, Pennsylvania, New Jersey, and Ohio, and she became the first woman in America to speak in public on the subject of contraception. She also edited the Worcester *Health Journal and Advocate of Physiological Reform* from 1840. Here she reflected on the inadequacy of medical training and trained doctors for women, and also criticized overdependence on drugs, bloodletting, constricting garments, and excessive childbearing. Her advocacy of women's property rights and freedom of expression sharpened as a result of her acrimonious divorce and her lengthy battle for custody of her child and her income. She wrote numerous articles, often anonymous because of her sex, advocating healthy, wholesome diet, fresh air, and abstinence from stimulating drinks.

In 1842–3 Mrs Gove fell in love with an English teacher, Henry G. Wright, from James Pierrepoint Greaves's Ham House, near London. He introduced her to European hydrotherapy, and in her enthusiasm she launched the *Health Journal and Independent*, which lasted only one issue. In spite of this disappointment she studied techniques in a new water-cure centre in Brattleboro, Vermont, for several months in 1845 and then worked as a resident physician in a water-cure house in Lebanon, New York, before opening her own establishment in New York in May 1846. Women could neither train nor qualify as doctors, but she graduated from being a teacher to acting as a physician. She enjoyed great success as a pioneering woman treating her sisters and became an advocate of natural childbirth.

Mrs Gove campaigned both through practical example and through the press in the late 1840s. She contributed to *Godey's Lady's Book*, the *Democratic Review*, and the *Water-Cure Journal*, described her work in *Experience in Water-Cure* (1849), and wrote three novels, *Uncle John* (1846), *Agnes Morris* (1849), and *The Two Loves: Eros and Anteros* (1849). She continued her lectures on dress reform and economic independence, and her house became a centre of like-minded radicals like Albert Brisbane, the Fourierist, and Edgar Allan Poe. Amid these activities she met and eventually married, in a Swedenborgian ceremony on 29 July 1848, **Thomas Low Nichols** (1815–1901).

Nichols, born in Orford, New Hampshire, USA, had studied medicine at Dartmouth before embarking on a career as a radical democratic journalist. On one occasion a libel suit got him several months in gaol in Buffalo. He had worked in William Lloyd Garrison's abolitionist office in Boston, in Lowell, and in New York before qualifying as a doctor. By 1850 Thomas Low Nichols had become a vice-president of the American Vegetarian Society, acted as secretary of the American Hygienic and Hydropathic Association, and appointed himself permanent secretary of the Society of Public Health. In 1851 the newly wedded couple set up their American Hydropathic Institute, the first water-cure medical school: students secured diplomas following a successful three-months' training course. In 1852 they moved to West Chester, New York, where they offered summer courses in water-cure techniques. The following year, under T. L. Nichols's name, they published the sensational best-seller, *Esoteric Anthropology* (1853): to Victorian America it was sexually explicit. Finding themselves too advanced for other reformers the Nicholses began their own *Journal of Health, Water-Cure and Human Progress* in 1853. The following year Mary attacked oppressive marriage bonds in her thinly disguised autobiographical novel, *Mary Lyndon* (1854). The Nicholses vigorously campaigned for the water-cure as the basic reform, a prelude to the regeneration of mankind. These developments coincided with their movement towards communitarianism: under the influence of Fourier, the Nicholses decided to found a school with the American anarchists Josiah Warren and Stephen Pearl Andrews in the Modern Times Colony, Long Island. Delays and sensational publicity intervened and the experiment foundered.

The contemporary spiritualist craze now attracted Mary Nichols, who soon became a medium. In 1855 the Nicholses moved west to Cincinnati and established their Progressive Union in Yellow Springs, Ohio. A vegetarian water-cure community, it collapsed in 1857 when, following apparitions of St Ignatius of Loyola, the Nicholses and eight others became Roman Catholics. Self-denial, chastity, and Catholic community proved irresistible: the church provided an eternal medium of health education.

The Nicholses travelled extensively through the midwest, the south, and Texas preaching their gospel of health to priests and nuns. After returning to New York in 1861 they fled to Britain to avoid the American Civil War.

Welcomed to London by Cardinal Wiseman, the Nicholses embarked on a health campaign in Ireland. After establishing their literary credentials with the Howitts, Edmund Yates, Dickens, Robert Chambers, J. Garth Wilkinson, and others, they thrived. Mary Nichols was soon writing for periodicals—*The Athenaeum, Temple Bar, Fraser's, All the Year Round*—as well as producing two more novels, *Uncle Angus* (1864) and *Jerry* (1872). Thomas wrote a bestselling autobiography, *Forty Years of American Life* (1864), and numerous articles for *Chambers's Encyclopaedia*. A brief sojourn in Crosshill, Glasgow, during which they published the *Journal of Sanitary and Social Science* (1873), proved less successful. In the hydropathic boom they began a 'school of life' at their new water-cure centre, Aldwyn Towers, in Malvern, in 1867. There they practised medicine (Mrs Nichols claiming to have healing powers) and spiritualism, produced their *Herald of Health* (1875), and made provision for the first mass in Malvern since the Reformation. Archbishop John McCloskey of New York and Cardinal Manning were visitors. The Nicholses eventually settled in Earls Court, London, where they continued to hold seances and to busy themselves in social reforms; they campaigned against capital punishment and military conscription, and ran anti-vaccination and anti-vivisection campaigns.

In 1875 Thomas Low Nichols began his Co-operative Sanitary Company, which marketed health products including Turkish baths, soap powders, 'foods of health', cereals, egg preservers, Count Rumford soup, tonic drinks, and water filters. His pioneering firm preceded those of J. H. Kellogg, T. R. Allinson, and other health-food enthusiasts in Britain. He also inaugurated vegetarian restaurants in London, providing simple recipes for cheap, wholesome food, hygienically prepared and well cooked. In their writings and lectures to all sorts and conditions, he and his wife ceaselessly promoted vegetarianism, dress reform, the creation of garden suburbs, and temperance, co-operating with and visiting like-minded Europeans.

In later life Mary Nichols was blind for five years until Dr Charles Bell of Nottingham operated on her two cataracts. Unfortunately breast cancer and a fractured femur then curbed her activity and eventually led to her death on 30 May 1884 in Brompton, London. She was buried at Kensal Green cemetery. Age, financial pressures, the death of his wife, and the unfortunate publicity in the 'Pimlico case' made Nichols surrender the editorship of the *Herald of Health*. He moved to Sutton, Surrey, from where he continued his pamphlet publishing, and died quietly and forgotten at Chaumont-en-Vezin, in France, in 1901. Their one daughter died young.

The Nicholses were important transatlantic links in radical feminist, medical, and religious movements of the nineteenth century. They were propagandists of the platform, printed word, and varied, if ultimately unsuccessful, practical enterprises. Promoting health education,

natural birth control, and social improvement, they were at once backward-looking and progressive: they sought a reinvigorated version of the older, simpler, puritanical, and close-knit New England communal lifestyle. Self-denial and self-restraint for the common good formed a providential code which was guaranteed, for the Nicholses, through spiritualism and, ultimately, the Catholic church. Wholesome education, food, and social and sexual relations were essential: only then could man be liberated from the 'artificial' oppression of law or economic interests, and physical or spiritual contaminants. They believed that simplicity would allow the masses to look after themselves: complexity was invariably a creation of self-interested groups for their own ends. A healthy environment, pure foodstuffs, and basic necessities for all within a readily accountable democratic social order of mutual interests was their ideal.

BERNARD ASPINWALL

Sources M. S. G. Nichols, *A woman's work in the water cure and sanitary education*, 2nd edn (1869) · T. L. Nichols, *Forty years of American life* (1864) · T. S. Nichols, *Nichols' health manual: being also a memorial of the life and work of Mrs Mary S. Gove Nichols* (1887) · *Herald of Health* (1875–86) · J. B. Blake, 'Mary Gove Nichols, prophetess of health', *Proceedings of the American Philosophical Society*, 106 (1962), 219–33 · B. Aspinwall, 'Social Catholicism and health: Dr and Mrs Thomas Low Nichols in Britain', *The church and healing*, ed. W. J. Sheils, SCH, 19 (1982), 249–70 · P. Gleason, 'From free love to Catholicism: Dr and Mrs Thomas Low Nichols at Yellow Springs', *Ohio Historical Quarterly*, 70 (1961), 283–307 · S. Nissenbaum, *Sex, diet and debility in Jacksonian America: Sylvester Graham and health reform* (1980) · L. G. Stevenson, 'Religious elements in the background of the British anti-vivisection movement', *Yale Journal of Biology and Medicine*, 39 (1956), 128–57 · R. J. Lambert, 'A Victorian national health service: state vaccination, 1855–71', *HJ*, 5 (1962), 1–18 · B.-M. Stearns, 'Two forgotten New England reformers', *New England Quarterly*, 6 (1933), 59–84 · B.-M. Stearns, 'Memnonia, the launching of a utopia', *New England Quarterly*, 14 (1942), 280–95 · I. T. Richards, 'Mary Gove Nichols and John Neal', *New England Quarterly*, 7 (1934), 344–52 · d. cert.

Likenesses double portrait (with T. L. Nichols), repro. in *Nichols health manual*

Nichols, Peter (1928–1989), journalist and author, was born on 15 February 1928 in Portsmouth, the only son of Walter Ernest Nichols and his wife, Beatrice Alice Jutsum; they also had one daughter. He was educated at Portsmouth grammar school, winning an open history scholarship to St Edmund Hall, Oxford, taking up residence in October 1948 after two years' national service which included a spell with field security in Singapore. In 1949 Nichols married Marie Pamela Ffoulkes; they had two sons and two daughters. They were later divorced.

After working for a short time with the British Society for International Understanding, Nichols joined the editorial staff of *The Times* in October 1953, first in the special supplements department, and then in the foreign newsroom. He was sent to Bonn as assistant correspondent in 1954, and remained there until 1957, when he was made Rome correspondent. He used to attribute this fortunate posting to a misunderstanding; a crackle on the line between London and Bonn, when asked if he spoke Italian, his reply being taken as yes instead of the more accurate no.

Nichols remained Rome representative of *The Times* for thirty years, including a few special assignments to the Middle East, an unusually long but not wholly unprecedented stretch for a foreign correspondent. By the end of that time he could without exaggeration be described as 'the most famous Englishman in Italy' (Boyes), as well as quite simply 'an institution', the first port of call for fellow journalists, diplomats, politicians, and anyone lucky enough to come armed with an introduction. He travelled extensively, coming to know the country thoroughly from Sicily to the Alps, was familiar with its arts, literature, and archaeology, and though many of its leading politicians became his personal friends he never allowed friendship to cloud his objectivity.

Nichols made the church a subject for his special study. In 1968 he published *The Politics of the Vatican*, a survey of the papacy from the days of Constantine to those of Paul VI, a pontiff for whom he had a particular respect—a man by nature cautious, but called upon to complete the work of his more dramatic predecessor, John XXIII. 'Truly', wrote Nichols, 'he has looked every inch a great pope in his public *persona*' (p. 128).

This expertise stood Nichols and his newspaper in good stead when John XXIII called the Second Vatican Council in 1962. The council's sessions lasted for more than three years, from October 1962 to December 1965, and Nichols's covering of it was comprehensive and authoritative. After his death Cardinal Achille Silvestrini, under-secretary of state for public affairs, to whose 'warmth and approachability' Nichols paid tribute, said of him:

> He had a rare intelligence of things and men, and of ideas. He wanted to know so as to understand, and by understanding to be able to inform reliably and in depth. He was demanding and critical, sometimes severe in his judgements, but always tolerant with people, because he was a benevolent man and loved his fellow human beings. (Silvestrini)

Nichols was not a Roman Catholic, though a believing Christian. ('I was baptised an Anglican at the age of fourteen, rather to the bewilderment of my school friends.') 'I have lived in Rome throughout the whole period of what may be called the modern papacy', he wrote in *The Pope's Divisions* (1981), his much admired study of 'The Roman Catholic church today', from 'the final hermit years of Pius XII, through the brief cyclone of the reign of John XXIII, the painful complexities of Paul VI, to the pair of clumsily named John Pauls' (p. 17).

In 1977 Nichols had published a historical novel, *Ruffo in Calabria*, about a cardinal who in 1799 had led, on a white horse, a Christian army against the French republican troops who had erupted into south Italy. This was after his death made into a radio programme in which his second wife played a leading part. But his other main publication was *Italia, Italia* (1973), a social and political anatomy of the country which he loved but which he could look at with as dispassionate an eye as he had already cast on one part of it, the Vatican. 'He came to know Italy better than many Italians', said Giorgio La Malfa, leader of the Republican Party, 'and with his penetrating critical judgement helped

us all make it a better country' (Boyes). This won him Italy's book of the year prize and was translated into many languages. Other prizes which came his way included the City of Rome prize for journalism which expressed with greatest insight the contemporary problems and historic values of Rome, and the Golden Rose of Venice for his work as chairman of the Foreign Press Club of Italy in 1974 and 1976.

Nichols was a tireless worker. In addition to his contributions to *The Times* he wrote a regular column in *Il Messaggero*, was a frequent broadcaster in a rapid Italian which retained a sturdy English accent (though with his dark good looks he was often taken for an Italian), and appeared on a television interview programme with the actress Paola Rosi, who became his second wife on 7 September 1974. The couple had a son. In their sixteenth-century house on the shore of Lake Bracciano, north of Rome, they cultivated choice flowers and vegetables, entertained with taste and generosity, and led a semi-rural existence. 'We used to have a pair of peacocks, and sometimes my wife would make *fettuccine* with their eggs, incredibly delicious' (Boyes). He died there of cancer on 11 January 1989. A plaque on a wall commemorated his residence and his saying: 'in questa casa lascio il mio cuore' ('in this house I leave my heart'). He was appointed OBE in 1982, and in 1988 commendatore of the Italian Republic.

E. C. HODGKIN

Sources personal knowledge (2004) · *The Times* (12 Jan 1989) · R. Boyes, 'Tributes for *Times* man who plumbed Italy's mysteries', *The Times* (12 Jan 1989) · A. Silvestrini, 'Cardinal laments loss of great journalist', *The Times* (12 Jan 1989)
Archives SOUND BL NSA, 'Talking about his autobiography *Feeling you are behind*', 30 Oct 1965, C 208/32 · BL NSA, *With great pleasure*, BBC Radio 4, 1983, T5803 BW BD1 · BL NSA, T5889W · BL NSA, current affairs recording · BL NSA, performance recording
Likenesses photographs, News Int. RO

Nichols, Philip. See Nicolls, Philip (*fl.* 1547–1564).

Nichols, Robert Malise Bowyer (1893–1944), poet and playwright, was born at Shanklin, Isle of Wight, on 6 September 1893, the elder son of John Bowyer Buchanan Nichols (1859–1939) of Lawford Hall, Essex, artist and author and a descendant of John Nichols, the eighteenth-century antiquary. His mother was Catherine Louisa, daughter of Captain Edward Bouverie Pusey RN of Manningtree, Essex, a nephew of Dr E. B. Pusey. Nichols's brother, Sir P. B. B. Nichols, was ambassador to the Netherlands (1948–51); his sisters married George Gater and H. G. Strauss (later Lord Conesford). Educated at Winchester College and at Trinity College, Oxford (1913–14), Nichols asserted that he owed most to his own unmethodical private reading. The outbreak of the First World War cut short his university career; in October 1914 he became a second lieutenant in the Royal Field Artillery and served in France from 1915 until August 1916, after which time he spent several months in hospital. In 1917 he was attached to the Foreign Office and in the following year went with the British mission (Ministry of Information) to New York.

Having begun to write verse at school, Nichols became

one of the soldier–poets of the First World War; his *Invocation* (1915) and *Ardours and Endurances* (1917) were widely read and quoted and established him as one of the more highly acclaimed younger poets of the day. He was regarded as a sort of new Rupert Brooke, and in E. B. Osborn's noted collection *The Muse in Arms* (1917) he was represented more copiously than any other writer. Like his friends Siegfried Sassoon and Robert Graves, Nichols wrote graphic records of the battlefield, but his poetry was inherently more idealistic.

In 1921, after haunting Oxford for a time as a poetical personality, Nichols accepted the chair of English at Tokyo Imperial University. The opportunity of a closer view of Japanese art and culture suited his aesthetic habits. As a professor he sought to train new men of letters rather than competent academics. Illness disturbed his programme, but his lectures were amusing and invigorating. He became a busy and zealous essayist in the *Japan Advertiser*, writing on an abundance of subjects; among his papers there a series of articles on contemporary English novelists was the most considerable. He also translated the poems of the seventeenth-century Japanese poet Chikamatsu Monzaemon into English. In 1922 he married Norah, daughter of Frederick Anthony Denny, of Horwood House, Winslow, Buckinghamshire, and niece of the composer Roger Quilter. They had no children. In 1924 Nichols resigned his professorship and went to Hollywood, where he acted as adviser to Douglas Fairbanks senior in his film-making.

Nichols regarded himself as a writer of plays; he wrote in other genres—prose fiction in *Fantastica* (1923) and *Under the Yew* (1928), and metrical satire in *Fisbo* (1934)—but the drama *Guilty Souls* (1922), stirring but unconvincing, announced his principal object, never successfully realized. *Twenty Below* (with Jim Tully, 1927) and *Wings over Europe* (with Maurice Browne, 1932), though striking, had little success in the theatre; and his vast project *Don Juan*, about which he constantly talked, was never completed. Drama took precedence over lyrical poetry, where his promise had been first recognized; the volume *Aurelia* (1920), containing among other things a Shakespearian sonnet series, was the last of its kind from him. After 1926 he lived in England, at first at Winchelsea in Sussex, finding his pleasures in music, the fine arts, conversation, and letter-writing. In response to the Second World War he published an *Anthology of War Poetry, 1914–1918* (1943) containing a characteristic discourse in which he generously recalled the soldier–poets of his earlier years.

Nichols was tall, thin, and impulsive in movement, with a face in which the wit and the poet found expression by turns. His talk was rapid and humorous, but tending towards the defence of the lofty Romantic attitude of which he saw himself as a protagonist. His long list of heroes, often recommended to his listeners and correspondents, included Goethe and Berlioz. He wished to be a bohemian character in modern life. Confident of his powers, he was nevertheless an example of unselfish activity on behalf of the work of other authors, new or old. The

discovery of the work of the American poet Vachel Lindsay was one of his great successes. As a poet he was probably hindered rather than helped by his preoccupation with world literature; at all events he did not fulfil his ambitious or visionary schemes. In 1942 he published a selection of his poems entitled *Such was my Singing*. Nichols died at Cambridge on 17 December 1944 and was buried in Lawford, near Manningtree, Essex.

EDMUND BLUNDEN, rev. SAYONI BASU

Sources *The Times* (18 Dec 1944) · private information (1959) · personal knowledge (1959) · Burke, *Gen. GB* (1952) · *Oxford roll of honour*

Archives BL, corresp. and papers, Add. MSS 57296, 57795–57799, 59897, 62743 · McGill University, Montreal, McLennan Library, corresp. and literary MSS · State University of New York, Buffalo, E. H. Butler Library, letters and MSS | BL, letters to Ellen Coleman, Add. MS 59897 · U. Glas. L., letters to D. S. MacColl · U. Leeds, Brotherton L., letters to Sir Edmund Gosse

Likenesses A. John, chalk drawing, 1921, NPG

Nichols, Thomas Low (1815–1901). *See under* Nichols, Mary Sergeant Gove (1810–1884).

Nichols, William. *See* Nicols, William (1655–1716).

Nichols, William Luke (1802–1889), antiquary, born at Gosport, Hampshire, on 10 August 1802, was the eldest son of Luke Nichols, of Gosport, a merchant, who evidently set his son up well. He matriculated at Queen's College, Oxford, on 28 February 1821, graduated BA in 1825, and proceeded MA in 1829. In 1827 he was ordained and was licensed to the curacy of Keynsham, Somerset. During the cholera outbreak of 1832 he bore the responsibility of ministering to the enormous parish of Bedminster, near Bristol. From 1 February 1834 to 31 March 1839 he was minister of the church of St James, Bath; for twelve months he was stationed at Trinity Church, Bath; he was then in charge of a district church near Ottery St Mary, Devon; and from 1846 to 1851 he held the rectory of Buckland Monachorum, near Plymouth, of which he was himself the patron. Nichols then returned to Bath, where he lived in the east wing of Lansdown Crescent, collected a valuable library, and lived the life of a scholar. For several years from 1858 he lived at The Wyke, on Grasmere. For two or three years before 1870 he lived at the old Manor House, Keynsham, but from that date until his death his home was at The Woodlands, near Bridgwater, on the borders of the Quantocks, in Somerset, and midway between Nether Stowey and Alfoxden. Nichols frequently travelled abroad and became well acquainted with the scenery and antiquities of Spain, Italy, Sicily, Greece, and Palestine. He died at The Woodlands on 25 September 1889, and was buried with his parents in the family vault in Gosport churchyard on 2 October. By his will he left the parish the funds for the completion of a bell-tower, which he had begun to erect. It cost, with the bells, £2500.

Nichols had great knowledge of literature, and frequently contributed to periodicals. He was a noted member of the Bath literary set of the time. He published at Bath in 1838 *Horae Romanae, or, A Visit to a Roman Villa*, a pamphlet with a poem prompted by the discovery, during the building of the Great Western Railway, of the site of a

Roman villa at Newton St Loe, near Bath. Nichols edited in 1866 the *Remains of the Rev. Francis Kilvert*, the Bath antiquary. He was elected FSA on 2 February 1865. He printed at Bath for private circulation in 1873 a paper on 'The Quantocks and their associations', which he read to the Bath Literary Club on 11 December 1871 (2nd edn, with illustrations, 1891).

W. P. COURTNEY, *rev.* H. C. G. MATTHEW

Sources Foster, *Alum. Oxon.* · *The Guardian* (2 Oct 1889) · *Bath Chronicle* (3 Oct 1889) · *Bath Chronicle* (10 Oct 1889) · R. E. M. Peach, *Historic houses in Bath and their associations*, 2 vols. (1883–4) · Crockford (1888)
Wealth at death £21,659 13s. 11d.: probate, 2 Nov 1889, *CGPLA Eng. & Wales*

Nicholson. *See also* Nicolson.

Nicholson, Alfred (1788–1833). *See under* Nicholson, Francis (1753–1844).

Nicholson, Asenath Hatch (1792–1855), social observer and philanthropist, was born on 24 February 1792 in Chelsea, Vermont, USA. She was the daughter of the pioneering settlers Michael (*c.*1747–1830) and Martha Hatch (1745–1837). After training as a teacher she taught first in Chelsea, probably in the District 2 schoolhouse, where she was remembered as a remarkable teacher. Like many of her generation Nicholson left rural Vermont for the city; she is listed in the *New York Directory* for 1831 as the schoolteacher wife of merchant Norman Nicholson.

The Nicholsons were disciples of the New England temperance crusader Sylvester Graham, who launched a campaign of diet reform that involved strict vegetarianism and avoidance of stimulants such as those contained in coffee and tea. Asenath Nicholson outlined her version of Graham's regime in *Nature's Own Book* (1835). The Nicholsons operated Grahamite boarding-houses at 79 Cedar Street (1833–4) and at the corner of Wall Street and Broadway (1834). Between 1835 and 1841 she was listed as the proprietor of boarding-houses at 118 Williams Street and at 21 and 26 Beekman Street. She was also active in the causes of temperance and abolition during this period, and worked among the poor of the Five Points section of New York. She later wrote, 'It was in the garrets and cellars of New York that I first became acquainted with the Irish peasantry and it was there I saw that they were a suffering people'. This experience informed her decision 'to personally investigate the condition of the Irish poor' (Nicholson, *Ireland's Welcome to the Stranger*, iii). Widowed in 1841, she left New York in May 1844 for an eight-year stay abroad.

Nicholson went to Ireland first for a stay of fifteen months. With a small grant of Bibles from the Hibernian Society in Dublin, she walked around rural Ireland, distributing Bibles to those who could read and reading the Bible to those who could not. Catholics were suspicious of Bible-reading strangers, while protestant evangelists suspected her broad tolerance and her democratic ideas. Her account of her 1844–5 journey, *Ireland's Welcome to the Stranger* (1847), has left a valuable social history of rural

Ireland on the eve of the great famine. It was also a jeremiad that warned of the dangers of unemployment in the impoverished countryside.

By her own account Nicholson was a remarkable sight. She walked through Ireland wearing india rubber boots, a polka-dot coat, and a bonnet; she carried her Bibles in a large bearskin muff. The Quaker Maria Waring described her as 'repulsive' but fascinating (Harrison, 56). She was a crank and a scold but she had a self-deprecating sense of humour and her concerns for the Irish were generous and genuine.

Nicholson returned to Ireland again in the summer of 1846 to contribute her own effort to famine relief. As she had described the character of the Irish poor in *Ireland's Welcome to the Stranger*, she described their suffering in *Lights and Shades of Ireland* (1850). Nicholson opened her own soup kitchen on Cook Street in Dublin and worked among the poor in the Liberties, with some help from English and American supporters. While some of her funds and provisions were channelled through the central relief committee of the Society of Friends (Dublin), she preferred to work alone. In July 1847 Nicholson closed her Dublin relief operation and went to the west of Ireland, to the area of greatest destitution in western co. Mayo, from Ballina west to the Erris peninsula, where she stayed until April 1848, distributing her supplies of food and clothing, visiting the distressed, and bringing their story to English and American readers.

Nicholson left Ireland in the autumn of 1848, when she felt that her work there was finished. She went to England, where she wrote *Lights and Shades*; the famine section was published in America in 1851 as *Annals of the Famine*. She joined the American pacifist Elihu Burritt's delegation to the international peace conference in Frankfurt and travelled on the continent. She spent the winter of 1851–2 in Bristol before returning to the United States later in 1852. Her last book, *Loose Papers* (1853), describes those travels. She lived in obscurity until her death from typhoid fever in Jersey City, New Jersey, on 15 May 1855, and was buried at Green Wood cemetery, Brooklyn, New York.

MAUREEN O'ROURKE MURPHY

Sources A. H. Nicholson, *Nature's own book* (1835) · A. H. Nicholson, *Ireland's welcome to the stranger* (1847) · A. H. Nicholson, *Lights and shades of Ireland* (1850) · A. H. Nicholson, *Loose papers* (1853) · 'Introduction', A. T. Sheppard, *The Bible in Ireland* (1925) · R. S. Harrison, *Richard Davis Webb: Dublin Quaker printer, 1805–1872* (1993) · A. H. Nicholson, *Annals of the famine in Ireland*, ed. M. Murphy (1998) · C. H. Fitz, 'Asenath Hatch Nicholson', MLS thesis, Southern Connecticut State College · town records, Chelsea, Vermont
Archives PRO NIre., central relief committee papers · Chelsea, Vermont, town records | Boston PL, Richard Davis Webb letters
Likenesses M. Howitt, drawing, repro. in A. T. Sheppard, 'Asenath Nicholson and the Howitt circle', *The Bookman* (Nov 1926), 103

Nicholson, Benjamin Lauder [Ben] (1894–1982), artist, was born at the Eight Bells, Denham, Buckinghamshire, on 10 April 1894, and baptized on 19 May at St Mary's, Denham, the eldest of the four children of Sir William Newzam Prior *Nicholson (1872–1949), painter, and his first wife, Mabel Scott Lauder Pryde (1871–1918); she was

Benjamin Lauder Nicholson (1894–1982), by Humphrey
Spender, *c.*1935

also a painter and the sister of James Ferrier *Pryde (1866–
1941). Ben acknowledged a debt to William's poetic still
lifes and landscapes, though his relationship with his
father was at times difficult. He was deeply attached to his
mother, whom he described as 'the rock on which my
whole existence has been based' (de Sausmarez, 54). He
recalled that 'after a lot of art-talk from our visitors she
always said that it made her want to go downstairs and
scrub the kitchen table … I always remember my
mother's attitude when I came to carve my reliefs'
(ibid., 50). Nicholson's formal education was intermittent:
he was a pupil at Heddon Court, Hampstead, and Gresham's School, Holt, where he excelled at games. He
attended the Slade School of Fine Art, London, in 1910–11,
becoming friendly with fellow pupil Paul Nash, but
claimed that he spent more time playing billiards at the
nearby Gower Hotel. At eighteen he considered becoming
a writer. He spent a year in Tours learning French and a
period learning Italian in Milan. An asthmatic, he was
unfit for military service in the First World War, and in
1917–18 he travelled to the United States for his health. He
produced few paintings in these years.

On 4 November 1920 Nicholson married Winifred
Roberts [see Nicholson, (Rosa) Winifred (1893–1981)], herself a painter, daughter of Charles Roberts, Liberal MP,
and Cecilia Howard, daughter of the ninth earl of Carlisle.
Their working partnership was mutually beneficial. Nicholson later said that he learned a great deal about colour
from Winifred Nicholson and a great deal about form
from Barbara Hepworth, his second wife (J. Rothenstein,
Modern English Painters: Lewis to Moore, 1956, 268). Winifred

led him to lighten his palette. Nicholson described the
early 1920s as a period of 'fast and furious experiment'
(Summerson, 7). He and Winifred spent three successive
winters and springs in Lugano, Switzerland (1920–23);
their visits to Paris *en route* for Lugano enabled Nicholson
to absorb cubist painting at first hand. This was a revelation, and cubism informed his work for the rest of his life.
In 1924 he painted a group of experimental abstract works
but this was an isolated development not taken further
for nearly a decade.

Having returned home from Switzerland in 1923 the
Nicholsons bought Bankshead, a Cumbrian farmhouse on
Hadrian's Wall. For the remainder of the 1920s Nicholson
divided much of his time between there and London. In
August 1928 he made his first visit to St Ives, Cornwall, in
the company of his friend the painter Christopher Wood,
with whom he and Winifred had developed a close collaboration. There they 'discovered' the fisherman-turned-
painter Alfred Wallis, who was an important inspiration
for both men. The encounter encouraged the 'primitive'
streak in Nicholson's painting; primitivizing Cumbrian
and Cornish landscapes and lyrical still lifes dominate his
work of these years. Nicholson had his first one-man
exhibition at the Twenty-One Gallery, London, in 1924,
and in the same year he was invited to join the Seven and
Five Society; he was a leading member of the group and he
took it into increasingly radical territory.

In 1931 Nicholson met the sculptor (Jocelyn) Barbara
*Hepworth (1903–1975), the daughter of Herbert Raikes
Hepworth, civil engineer. They married on 17 November
1938, following Nicholson's divorce from Winifred in that
year. Ben and Barbara began to share a studio in Hampstead in 1932 and a community of style was evident in
their joint exhibition at Tooth's Gallery, London, at the
end of the year. They were both members of Unit One, an
avant-garde alliance of painters, sculptors, and architects
formed in 1933 that also included Paul Nash and Henry
Moore. Nicholson's work evolved rapidly towards an
uncompromising abstraction. The experience of working
alongside Hepworth and the presence of her tools in the
studio encouraged Nicholson's first abstract reliefs at the
end of 1933. At the beginning of the following year he
made the first white reliefs, hand-carved and painted all-
white, on which his international reputation was
founded. The white reliefs, for example those of 1935 in
the Tate and British Council collections, represent a major
contribution to twentieth-century English and European
modernism.

Winifred had moved to Paris in 1932 and Nicholson
made regular visits to see her and their three children,
Jake, Kate, and Andrew, between 1932 and 1936. During
these trips—on which Hepworth would often join him—
he established close friendly contacts with Paris-based artists, as well as dealers and critics. Picasso and Braque were
most important to Nicholson at first, to be succeeded by
Miró, Arp, Calder, and Mondrian. Nicholson drew on these
diverse influences in making his own quite distinctive and
independent contribution. He and Hepworth were invited

to join the group Abstraction-Création in 1933 and exhibited alongside their continental counterparts both abroad and in England. Following Nicholson's first visit to Mondrian's studio in Paris in 1934 a warm relationship developed between the two, and Nicholson's work rapidly grew close to that of Mondrian. Nicholson memorably described the visit in a letter of 1948: 'The feeling in his studio must have been very like the feeling in one of those hermits' caves where lions used to go to have thorns taken out of their paws' (de Sausmarez, 57). Nicholson was instrumental in Mondrian's move to London in 1938, where he joined the 'Nest of Gentle Artists' in Hampstead that Herbert Read described in his memoir of that title (*Apollo*, September 1962, 537–9). Nicholson was a vital link between Paris and London, and his advocacy of abstract art was crucial in establishing London as a centre of the international avant-garde in the 1930s. This was commemorated by the publication in London in 1937 of *Circle: International Survey of Constructive Art*, edited by Nicholson, the architect Leslie Martin, and the sculptor Naum Gabo.

Shortly before the outbreak of war in 1939 Nicholson and Hepworth left London for Carbis Bay, near St Ives, with their triplets, Simon, Rachel, and Sarah, who had been born in 1934. St Ives and the landscape of the Penwith peninsula entered his work immediately, often in conjunction with still lifes set before open windows. A vivid sense of place is present in these works. Nicholson was a significant player in the rise to international prominence of St Ives. Following his move into one of the large Porthmeor studios in the town in 1949 he began to work on a series of monumental still-life paintings. These are architectural in feeling and often contain allusions to landscape. In them he explored the interplay between abstraction and representation. As he wrote in his 'Notes on abstract art' (1941; rev. 1948): 'the kind of painting which I find exciting is not necessarily representational or non-representational, but it is both musical and architectural' (de Sausmarez, 34). Nicholson's growing international reputation after the war owed much to these magisterial still lifes, and he was awarded a series of major prizes in the 1950s. These included the first prize at the 39th Pittsburgh International Exhibition, held at the Carnegie Institute in 1952; the Ulisse prize at the 1954 Venice Biennale (for which he was selected as British representative together with Francis Bacon and Lucian Freud); the governor of Tokyo award in 1955; the first Guggenheim international painting prize in 1956, for *August 1956* (*Val d'Orcia*) (Tate collection); and the international prize for painting at the 1957 São Paulo Bienal.

Following his move to Switzerland in 1958 Nicholson focused upon renewed exploration of the abstract carved relief. His interest in the architectural possibilities of the relief in relation to landscape led to the realization of two large-scale outdoor projects: for Documenta III in Kassel in 1964 he designed a free-standing wall relief and, at the end of his life, he created a second one in the garden of Sutton Place, near Guildford, Surrey, in collaboration with the landscape architect Geoffrey Jellicoe.

Throughout his life drawing was an integral part of Nicholson's practice, not as preparatory studies but as autonomous works in themselves. His drawings are characterized by an incisive linear clarity. He especially enjoyed making drawings of still life, architecture, and landscape. He drew extensively abroad, particularly in Italy and Greece, as well as in England:

> I have favourite places—Mycenae and Pisa, and Siena, for instance—and I feel that in a previous life I must have laid two or three of the stones in Siena Cathedral, and even perhaps one or two of those at Mycenae! (de Sausmarez, 51)

Print-making was also important to Nicholson—from the early linocuts of the late 1920s to the etchings of the 1960s made with the Swiss printer François Lafranca—as was textile design.

Nicholson and Hepworth were divorced in 1951, and on 13 July 1957 Nicholson married Felicitas Maria (*b*. 1922), a German journalist and photographer, born in Berlin, the daughter of a banker, Kurt Vogler. They moved from St Ives to Lake Maggiore, near Ascona, in the Ticino region of Switzerland where Nicholson had lived in his twenties. They divorced in 1977. Nicholson returned to England alone in 1971, first to Great Shelford, near Cambridge, then in 1974 to London. He died on 6 February 1982 at his home in Pilgrim's Lane, Hampstead, and was cremated at Golders Green on 12 February.

In his later years Nicholson was recognized as the foremost modernist painter of his generation in Britain, and an important figure in the history of twentieth-century art. He was appointed OM in 1968 and received the Rembrandt prize in 1974. He exhibited extensively around the world, including two major retrospectives in his lifetime at the Tate Gallery (1955 and 1969), a rare distinction. Examples of his work are in museum collections throughout the world, with the largest group held by the Tate collection. He brought to British art a very valuable internationalist outlook. He took up and made his own the innovations of the pioneers of cubism and abstraction. Two groups of works stand out among his most original achievements—the white reliefs of the 1930s and the grand still-life compositions of the 1950s. In his work poetry and discipline, sensuous lyricism and geometric order, are held in creative tension.

Nicholson took a special pleasure in working with his hands and had a profound respect for craftsmanship. He gave particular attention to his materials and to the preparation of the surfaces of his paintings and reliefs. He had a great flair for ball games of all sorts (tennis, golf, table-tennis) and often drew an analogy between the perfect poise needed for both drawing a tree and playing a ball game well. Small in height, Nicholson dressed immaculately in an informal style of his own devising. He shared with his father, William, a love of puns and practical jokes. He was a determined avoider of formality and convention, and disliked personal publicity. His singleness of purpose and dedication to his work were absolute. Nicholson was critical of intellectual approaches to art that lacked intuitive feeling and poetry. He was a very perceptive writer on art and a marvellous letter-writer.

SOPHIE BOWNESS

Sources M. de Sausmarez, ed., *Ben Nicholson, a 'Studio International' special* (1969) · H. Read, introduction, in *Ben Nicholson: paintings, reliefs, drawings* (1948) · H. Read, introduction, *Ben Nicholson: paintings, reliefs, drawings*, rev. edn (1955) · H. Read, introduction, in *Ben Nicholson: work since 1947*, [2] (1956) · J. Lewison, *Ben Nicholson* (1993) [exhibition catalogue, Tate Gallery, London, 13 Oct – 9 Jan 1994] · S. A. Nash, *Ben Nicholson: fifty years of his art* (1978) [exhibition catalogue, Albright-Knox Art Gallery, Buffalo, 21 Oct – 26 Nov 1978] · J. Summerson, *Ben Nicholson* (1948) · J. Russell, *Ben Nicholson* (1969) · N. Lynton, *Ben Nicholson* (1993) · C. Harrison, *Ben Nicholson* (1969) [exhibition catalogue, Tate Gallery, London, 19 June – 27 July 1969] · J. Lewison, *Ben Nicholson: the years of experiment 1919–39* (1983) [exhibition catalogue, Kettle's Yard Gallery, Cambridge, 9 July – 29 August 1983] · S. J. Checkland, *Ben Nicholson: the vicious circles of his life and art* (2000) · Tate collection, Ben Nicholson archive · *DNB* · personal knowledge (2004) · private information (2004) · *CGPLA Eng. & Wales* (1982) · b. cert. · A. Nicholson, ed., *William Nicholson: painter* (1996) · m. certs. [Rosa Winifred Roberts; Jocelyn Barbara Hepworth; Felicitas Maria Vogler] · d. cert. · divorce certs.

Archives Tate collection, archive, corresp. and papers | Smithsonian Institution, Washington, DC, Archives of American Art, A. E. Gallatin archive; G. L. K. Morris archive · Tate collection, Barbara Hepworth archive · Tate collection, Christopher Wood archive · University of British Columbia, Victoria, Herbert Read archive | FILM 'Ben Nicholson', John Read (director), for the Arts Council (1985) | SOUND BBC Sound Archive, 'Frances Hodgkins: portrait of an artist', Third Programme (11 Feb 1970), interview, BBC tape number 32877

Likenesses W. Nicholson, pen-and-pencil drawing, 1894; sold Bonham's, London, 11 Nov 1999, lot 226, repro. in sale catalogue · W. Nicholson, oils, *c*.1901 (*The Boy with the Caroline Mug*), U. Nott. · W. Nicholson, oils, *c*.1902 (*Portrait of Ben Nicholson as a Boy*, unfinished), priv. coll.; repro. in Lewison, *Ben Nicholson* (1993), 238 · W. Nicholson, oils, *c*.1902 (*Hawking*); on loan to Fenton House, Hampstead · W. Nicholson, oils, *c*.1906 (*The Paper Cap*); on loan to Nottingham Castle Museum and Art Gallery · W. Orpen, group portrait, oils, 1908 (*A Bloomsbury family*), Scottish National Gallery of Modern Art, Edinburgh · M. Nicholson, oils, *c*.1910–1914, NPG; repro. in Lewison, *Ben Nicholson* (1993), 18 · J. W. B., ink and wash caricature, *c*.1916, NPG · M. Beerbohm, caricature, 1918 · F. Dobson, conté and gouache drawing, 1919, priv. coll.; repro. in N. Jason and L. Thompson-Pharoah, *The sculpture of Frank Dobson* (1994), 37 · F. Dobson, plaster bust, 1920 · W. Nicholson, oils, 1927 (*Ben with Jake*), priv. coll.; repro. in A. Nicholson, ed., *Unknown colour: paintings, letters, writings by Winifred Nicholson* (1987), 52 · W. Nicholson, oils, 1927 (*Starry-Eyed*), priv. coll.; repro. in J. Collins, *Winifred Nicholson* (1987), 46 [exhibition catalogue, Tate Gallery, London, 3 June – 2 Aug 1987] · B. Nicholson, double portrait, pencil drawing, 1932 (*Two heads, with Barbara Hepworth*; 1933 (*St Rémy, Provence*), priv. coll.; repro. in *Ben Nicholson: paintings, reliefs, drawings*, 2nd edn (1955), pl. 63b · photographs, 1932 (with B. Hepworth), Hult. Arch. · B. Nicholson, double portrait, oil and pencil on board, 1933 (with Barbara Hepworth), priv. coll.; repro. in Lewison, *Ben Nicholson* (1993), 128 · B. Nicholson, double portrait, oil and pencil on canvas, 1933 (with Barbara Hepworth; 1933 (*St Rémy, Provence*), NPG · H. Spender, photograph, *c*.1935, NPG [*see illus.*] · B. Nicholson, self-portrait, pencil and coloured wash on paper, *c*.1954, priv. coll.; repro. in *Art News and Review* (24 July 1954), 1 · B. Brandt, photographs, 1956, Museum of Modern Art, New York · F. Vogler, photographs, *c*.1957–1970, priv. colls.

Wealth at death £2,122,555: probate, 25 Oct 1982, *CGPLA Eng. & Wales*

Nicholson, Brinsley (1824–1892), military surgeon and literary scholar, born at Fort George, Scotland, was the eldest son of Brinsley W. Hewittson Nicholson (*d.* 1857x9?), who was on the army medical staff. After passing his boyhood at Gibraltar, Malta, and the Cape, where his father was stationed, Nicholson entered Edinburgh University in 1841, took his MD in 1845 (becoming LRCS in 1845), and finished his medical studies in Paris. He became an army surgeon, spent some years in South Africa, and served in the Cape Frontier War in 1853 and 1854. His careful observation and knowledge of the native tribes were displayed in the genealogical tables of Kaffir chiefs contributed by him to a *Compendium of Kaffir Laws and Customs*, printed by the government of British Kaffraria at Mount Coke in 1858. During his long rides and lonely hours in those years the study of Shakespeare proved a constant solace. He was in China during the war of 1860, and present at the famous loot of the Summer Palace at Peking (Beijing); and he took part in the New Zealand wars between 1860 and 1864. He then served as surgeon-major at Cork from 1866 until 18 November 1871, when he retired from the army with the honorary rank of deputy inspector general: he settled near London and devoted himself seriously to Elizabethan literature.

In 1875 Nicholson edited, for the recently formed New Shakspere Society, the first folio and the first quarto of *Henry V*, and began the preparation of the parallel texts of the same play, issued in 1877, but he was prevented from completing this by severe illness. He afterwards read several papers at meetings of the New Shakspere Society, and, encouraged by his friend and fellow student, Professor W. T. Gairdner of Glasgow, he brought out in 1886 an excellent reprint of Reginald Scot's *Discoverie of Witchcraft* (1584). He subsequently worked on editions of Jonson, Chapman, and Donne; but he succeeded in bringing near completion only his edition of *The Best Plays of Ben Jonson*, which was published posthumously in 1893, with an introduction by Professor C. H. Herford, in the Mermaid Series (2 vols.). His edition of Donne's poems was completed for the Muses' Library in 1895. He was an occasional contributor to *Notes and Queries*, *The Athenaeum*, *Antiquary*, and *Shakespeariana*. His habits of accuracy and his full acquaintance with the literature of the period made his criticism valuable, if not brilliant, and he was always ready to help a fellow scholar. He died on 14 September 1892, at his home, Surrender Lodge, Queen's Road, South Norwood, London. He had married in 1875, and his wife, Mary Ann Lucy Nicholson, survived him.

L. T. SMITH, rev. NILANJANA BANERJI

Sources private information (1894) · Boase, *Mod. Eng. biog.* · *CGPLA Eng. & Wales* (1895)

Archives U. Edin. L., corresp. with James Halliwell-Phillipps

Wealth at death £486 13s. 11d.: administration, 18 Oct 1892, *CGPLA Eng. & Wales*

Nicholson, Charles (1795–1837), flautist, son of the flautist Charles Nicholson, was born at Liverpool. He was taught by his father and went to London when quite young. He became principal flute at Drury Lane and then at Covent Garden, and from about 1832 he was principal flute to the Royal Italian Opera. He also played at the Philharmonic Society's concerts, where several of his compositions for the flute were performed between 1823 and 1842. On the foundation of the Royal Academy of Music in 1822 he was appointed professor of the flute.

Nicholson was the most celebrated flautist of his day.

Charles Nicholson (1795–1837), by T. Bart, 1834

His father was probably the first to enlarge the finger- and mouth-holes on the instrument in order to increase its tone, and Nicholson had his flutes built this way. He was noted for his powerful sound and his technical brilliance, although his hard tone was not universally admired. He experimented with new types of vibrato and advocated the use of alternative fingerings, and he was the first to introduce glissando, hitherto thought to be impossible on the flute. Many large-holed flutes were made, and the makers stamped their instruments 'C. Nicholson's Improved' and paid royalties, which provided him with a good income. Nevertheless, Nicholson died in London, on 26 March 1837, in poverty.

Nicholson's Complete Preceptor for the German Flute (1816) was the first of several instruction books published by him, and it was still in use in 1875 when Harrington Young issued *Charles Nicholson's School for the Flute*, based on the original *Preceptor* and his own *Preceptive Lessons*. His compositions included thirteen fantasias for flute and piano and fifteen airs with variations for flute and piano. *Pot Pourri* was frequently performed in public to demonstrate the power of the instrument.

J. C. HADDEN, rev. ANNE PIMLOTT BAKER

Sources *Quarterly Musical Magazine and Review*, 5 (1823), 82–8 · P. Bate, *The Flute* (1969), 111–12 · *New Grove* · G. Hogarth, *The Philharmonic Society of London* (1862) · R. S. Rockstro, *Treatise on the flute* (1890)
Likenesses T. Bart, oils, 1834, NPG [*see illus.*] · M. Gauci, lithograph, BM; repro. in *Flutists' Magazine* · T. Wageman, stipple (after G. Hargreaves), BM

Nicholson, Sir Charles, first baronet (1808–1903), educationist and politician, was born in Cockermouth, Cumberland, on 23 November 1808. He was the only surviving child of Charles Nicholson of London, merchant and agent to Lord Egremont, and Barbara, youngest daughter of John Ascough of Bedale.

After graduating MD at Edinburgh University in 1833, Nicholson emigrated to Australia, and settled on some property belonging to his uncle near Sydney in May 1834. Here for some time he practised as a physician. He was also a successful businessman, buying land and stock and forming sheep stations. A good classical scholar, well read in history and science, an able writer, and a lucid speaker, he soon became prominently identified with the social and political interests of the colony. In June 1843 he was returned to the first legislative council of New South Wales as one of the five members for the Port Phillip district (later the state of Victoria). In July 1848, and again in September 1851, he was elected member for the county of Argyle. From 2 May 1844 to 19 May 1846 he was chairman of committees of the legislative council. In 1846 he was chosen speaker. He was twice re-elected and retained the office until the grant to the colony of responsible government in 1855–6, when he became for a short time a member of the executive council. When in 1859 the district of Moreton Bay was separated from New South Wales and formed into the colony of Queensland, Nicholson was nominated on 1 May 1860 a member of the legislative council of the new colony, and was president during the first session, resigning the office on 28 August 1860.

Nicholson was from the first a powerful advocate of popular education in New South Wales. He was a member of the select committee to inquire into the state of education in the colony moved for by Robert Lowe and appointed in June 1844. His name, however, is more closely associated with the foundation of the University of Sydney. In December 1850 he was nominated to the original senate of the university. He was a generous donor to its funds, and endowed it with many valuable gifts, including the museum of Egyptian, Etruscan, Greek, and Roman antiquities, which he collected with much personal exertion and at considerable cost. Between 1856 and 1859 he visited England to raise funds for the university. He was instrumental in obtaining a grant of arms from the Heralds' College in 1857, and the royal charter from Queen Victoria in 1858. On 3 March 1851 he was unanimously elected vice-provost, and delivered an inaugural address at the opening of the university on 11 October 1852. He was chancellor from 13 March 1854 until 1862, when he left Australia permanently for England.

Nicholson was knighted by patent on 1 March 1852, and was the first Australian to be created a baronet (of Luddenham, NSW, on 8 April 1859). He was made honorary DCL of Oxford in 1857, honorary LLD of Cambridge in 1868, and honorary LLD of Edinburgh in 1886. He married, on 8 August 1865, Sarah Elizabeth, eldest daughter of Archibald Keightley, registrar of the Charterhouse, London. They had three sons of whom the eldest, Charles Archibald *Nicholson, succeeded to the baronetcy and the youngest, Sir Sydney Hugo *Nicholson, founded the Royal School of Church Music. After his return to England, Nicholson chiefly resided in Hadleigh, Essex, actively occupied as a magistrate, as chairman of the Liverpool, London, and Globe Insurance Company, and as director of other undertakings. He was a leading member of the Royal Colonial Institute, the Royal Society of Arts, and the British Association. He continued to pursue Egyptian, classical, and Hebrew scholarship. Preserving his vigour until the end, he died on 8 November 1903 at his residence, The Grange, Totteridge, near Barnet, Hertfordshire, and was buried in Totteridge churchyard.

CHEWTON ATCHLEY, rev. C. A. CREFFIELD

Sources AusDB · The Times (10 Nov 1903) · The Lancet (21 Nov 1903) · H. E. Barff, Short historical account of Sydney University (1902) · G. Bowen, Thirty years of colonial government (1889) · B. Burke, A genealogical and heraldic history of the colonial gentry, 1 (1891), 289

Archives University of Sydney | CUL, letters to Joseph Bonomi · CUL, letters to Sir George Stokes

Likenesses J. R. Jackson, mezzotint (after H. W. Phillips), BM · H. W. Phillips, oils, University of Sydney · T. Woolner, medallion, University of Sydney, archives · wood-engraving, NPG; repro. in ILN (3 Sept 1859)

Wealth at death £87,810 7s. 5d.: probate, 15 Dec 1903, CGPLA Eng. & Wales

Nicholson, Sir Charles Archibald, second baronet (1867–1949), architect, was born at 26 Devonshire Place, London, on 27 April 1867, the eldest son of Sir Charles *Nicholson, first baronet (1808–1903), educationist and politician, and his wife, Sarah Elizabeth Keightley (d. 1923). Sir Sydney Hugo *Nicholson (1875–1947), the organist and church musician, was a younger brother. Charles was educated at Rugby School and at New College, Oxford, where he graduated in 1889 with a third class in modern history. He entered the architectural profession as a pupil in the office of J. D. Sedding, and to his training under this master of the Victorian Gothic style he owed much of his skill and enthusiasm for church design in structure as well as fittings and adornment. Subsequently he worked with Henry Wilson, another of Sedding's pupils, and in 1893 set up in practice for himself. In that year he won the Tite prize given for architectural design by the Royal Institute of British Architects, of which he was elected a fellow in 1905.

From 1895 until 1916 Nicholson was in partnership with Major Hubert Christian Corlette (d. 1956). In 1927, when the see of Portsmouth was founded, Thomas Johnson Rushton joined him in the adaptation and enlargement of the parish church of St Thomas à Becket, to form the new cathedral. This association continued until Nicholson's death. In the course of his career Nicholson was appointed consulting architect to seven cathedrals—Lincoln, Wells, Lichfield, Llandaff, Sheffield, Portsmouth, and Belfast—and diocesan architect to the sees of Wakefield, Winchester, Portsmouth, and Chelmsford.

Nicholson's skill and ingenuity were nowhere better shown than in the very large number of new parish churches which he designed and built. Besides these he refashioned, augmented, or furnished a much larger number of existing churches. The close of the Second World War brought him memorial work from many quarters, and one of the first memorial chapels was that built for his own school at Rugby. Another school chapel, at Clifton

College, is much admired for its handling of the hexagonal lantern. Nicholson's Anglican cathedral work included the new east chapel at Norwich, the west front of Belfast (with memorial western porches, a new chapel of the Holy Spirit, and baptistery), various additions to Chelmsford, and the reconstruction of Portsmouth. Internal work and restoration were carried out at Brecon, Carlisle, Exeter, Leicester, Lichfield, Lincoln, Llandaff, Manchester, Salisbury, Wakefield, Wells, and Winchester. Nicholson used the English Gothic style with complete freedom, conceiving, in common with his contemporaries, that his work was not the less original in employing its idiom. Resourceful and creative, he delighted in the constructional problems which each task offered. Although practical and realistic, he was always an artist: a finished draughtsman, he had a delight in colour and used it frequently and with great effect in his decorative design. For secular buildings Nicholson could lay aside his Gothic style: Burton Manor, in the Wirral, is a distinguished classical house, and at Kingston, Jamaica, he produced a striking design for the government buildings in reinforced concrete, anticipating the later development of this material. Both these undertakings were carried out in partnership with Corlette.

Nicholson, who succeeded to the baronetcy in 1903, shunned publicity and found his chief recreation in travel. He was twice married: first, on 1 October 1895 to Evelyn Louise (d. 1927), daughter of the Revd Henry Arnold Olivier, and sister of Sydney Haldane Olivier (1859–1943). They had one son, John Charles (b. 1904), who succeeded his father as third baronet, and two daughters. Nicholson married second, on 10 June 1931, Catherine Maud, daughter of Luckham Warren, of Winchfield, Hampshire. He died on 4 March 1949 at Headington, Oxford, and was buried at South Benfleet, Essex. His second wife survived him.

W. H. GODFREY, rev. CATHERINE GORDON

Sources A. S. Gray, Edwardian architecture: a biographical dictionary (1985), 273–4 · The Builder, 176 (1949), 300 · Architect and Building News (11 March 1949), 220 · RIBA Journal, 56 (1948–9), 290 · personal knowledge (1959) · Burke, Peerage (1959) · CGPLA Eng. & Wales (1949)

Archives Hants. RO, corresp. · RIBA BAL, corresp. with William Begley · RIBA BAL, correspondence with Harry Goodhart-Rendel · RIBA BAL, RIBA nomination MSS

Likenesses portrait, repro. in Architect and Building News, 220

Wealth at death £19,912 9s.: probate, 13 July 1949, CGPLA Eng. & Wales

Nicholson, Charles Ernest (1868–1954), yacht designer, was born at Gosport on 12 May 1868, the second son in the family of three boys and five girls of Benjamin Nicholson, naval architect, and his wife, Sarah Watson. Educated at Mill Hill School, he joined the family firm of Camper and Nicholsons Ltd in 1886 and at the age of twenty-one became the firm's chief designer, a post which he filled until his death. Later, he was chairman and managing director, to the age of seventy-two. In 1895 he married Lucy Ella (d. 1937), daughter of William Edmonds, a solicitor. They had two daughters and three sons, the second of whom, John, followed his father in the firm and became chairman in 1940.

Nicholson rapidly made his presence felt in the firm and soon sailing yachts of all kinds from his board were challenging those of G. L. Watson, the acknowledged master of the time. Nicholson, a rare combination of artist, technical genius, and businessman, was undoubtedly one of the greatest and most versatile yacht architects of all time. His skill as a helmsman contributed in no small measure to his success. He built up the greatest yacht yard in this country at Gosport and later a second at Southampton. Both had difficulty in keeping pace with the designs of yachts of all conceivable kinds which flowed in a steady torrent from his imaginative brain.

Nicholson designed sailing craft of all sizes from a 12 foot dinghy for his grandchildren to J-class America's Cup challengers of which he built four, notably *Shamrock IV* in 1914 and *Endeavour* in 1934, both potential winners; that they failed to win the cup was due to extraneous circumstances and no fault of Nicholson's. In 1939, which marked the end of the pageant of big-class yacht racing, the 12 metre fleet was almost entirely of Nicholson's design and construction. By the mid-thirties ocean racing was becoming popular and inevitably Nicholson was commissioned to design and build a suitable vessel. Not limited by cost, he produced the cutter *Foxhound* in 1935, 45 feet on the waterline, about the same size as a 12 metre. Nothing comparable had been built in this country. She was followed by the yawl *Bloodhound* and *Stiarna*, a cutter, of similar design. These yachts were highly successful and throughout long careers stood up to the hard punishment of offshore racing; and, in the 1960s, were still in commission, *Bloodhound* being then owned until 1969 by Elizabeth II and the duke of Edinburgh. Nicholson designed cruising yachts of all kinds from 5 tons up to such vessels as the 699 ton schooner *Creole* (1927).

Nicholson was always a jump ahead. He was the first yacht designer to see the possibilities of Bermuda rig and in 1921 re-rigged the 23 metre *Nyria*, which he had designed and built in 1906, with a jib-headed mainsail. This brought a storm of derision characteristically and rightly ignored by Nicholson. She proved a great success and revolutionized the rig of all modern yachts.

In between the sailing vessels came steam and motor yachts, enough of them alone to constitute a man's lifework. About 1911 Nicholson produced two beautiful traditional clipper-stem steam yachts, *Marynthea* (900 tons) and *Miranda*. He then turned his attention to diesel yachts, the first being *Pioneer* (400 tons), and, in 1937, *Philante* (1612 tons), the largest motor yacht until then built in Britain. She later became the Norwegian royal yacht. These fine vessels were of a type quite different from the traditional steam yacht. Entirely 'Nicholson' in conception, they were excellent sea boats, with fine accommodation and a wide radius of action.

In the First World War, as a separate venture, Nicholson designed and built flying-boat hulls in wood. In the same period he formed, as a separate firm, the Laminated Wood Ship Company, to design and build wooden cargo vessels of 1000 tons dead weight to help the urgent need for tonnage to replace losses due to enemy submarine action. The method of construction was original, based on a longitudinal system of framing with multi-skin planking and deck, and planned to use home-grown timbers such as oak, fir, and larch. Some of these ships were still in commission many years after the war. As a further example of his versatility, Nicholson designed a training ship, *Sebastian de Elcano* (3000 tons), for the Spanish government. She was a fore-and-aft four-masted schooner. The drawings included the minutest detail so that she could be built in Spain.

Nicholson's vast output was due not only to his tremendous capacity for concentrated thought and work but also to his ability and judgement in gathering to work under him a team of men each an expert in his own sphere. Unfortunately for students of Nicholson's work most of his drawings and plans were burned in a fire at the works in 1910 and again in 1941 when the yard at Gosport was virtually destroyed by enemy action. Fortunately Beken's matchless photographs are still available.

Nicholson was the technical brain of the Yacht Racing Association from 1910 until the outbreak of war in 1939. He was also a member of the Royal Institution of Naval Architects. In 1944 he was awarded the diploma of royal designer for industry and in 1949 he was appointed OBE. Throughout his life he devoted much time to the Gosport War Memorial Hospital of which he became chairman in 1934; in that year he was made the first honorary freeman of the borough of Gosport. Nicholson died at his home at Faringdon, Hill Head, Hampshire, on 27 February 1954.   E. F. HAYLOCK, *rev.*

Sources *Yachting World* (April–July 1954) · private information (1971) · personal knowledge (1971) · *The Times* (1 March 1954) · *CGPLA Eng. & Wales* (1954)
Likenesses P. Beer, portrait, priv. coll. · Owl, caricature, mechanical reproduction, NPG; repro. in *VF* (13 Aug 1913)
Wealth at death £92,725 6s. 7d.: probate, 6 July 1954, *CGPLA Eng. & Wales*

Nicholson, Edward Chambers (1827–1890), chemist and dye manufacturer, was born in January 1827 at Lincoln, the seventh son of Robert Nicholson. His mother died the following year and he was brought up by an aunt and, when he was ten, sent away to school in Uxbridge. He started work assisting a chemist and druggist at Andover and then went to work in a London laboratory before entering as one of the first students at the Royal College of Chemistry in 1845. Here he came under the influence of Dr A. W. Hofmann (1818–1888), who was particularly interested in the coal tar derivatives. Through teaching and supervising research, Hofmann inspired many eminent research chemists, including William Perkin.

Nicholson, after working for a couple of years as Hofmann's research assistant, left to investigate the chemistry of iron making with a south Wales company. He was obliged to abandon this work because of an attack of typhoid fever, and returned to London. In 1853 he joined in partnership with two fellow students at the Royal College of Chemistry, as Simpson, Maule, and Nicholson, to manufacture fine chemicals. Nicholson took the lead in meticulous chemical research which he had the ability to transform into viable manufacturing processes. For example, he was credited with the first use of iron stills with mechanical stirring gear. In Hofmann's words: 'in him was united the genius of the manufacturer and the habits of a scientific investigator' (Fox, 104).

Nicholson became very interested in the discovery in 1857 of a mauve coal tar dye by another of Hofmann's students, William Perkin. The partners were refused a licence to use Perkin's process but supplied the latter with raw materials, and soon discovered their own magenta dye process; by 1865 they were the largest producers of coal tar colours in Great Britain. The original premises in Walworth, south London, became too small for their business and in 1865 they moved to the newly built Atlas Dye Works at Hackney Wick, London.

Nicholson's process for making magenta dye, though subject to a provisional patent, was copied and the firm sought injunctions against other makers, including Read Holliday. After long and costly proceedings, the House of Lords ruled in 1866 that, because of careless drafting, the patents on which the firm relied were invalid; they had no legal protection against imitators. Competition brought a collapse in dye prices, from £12 per gallon in 1860 to 12s. in 1866, a 95 per cent fall. As the firm was innovative and efficient, this was not calamitous; within a few years of developing magenta aniline dyes it was offering sulphonated, alkylated, and azo dyes in a wide range of colours and for various uses.

In 1868, when he was only forty-one, Edward Nicholson decided to retire from the business to which he had made such an enormous contribution. There are various possible reasons: his partner George Simpson had retired a couple of years earlier; Hofmann, his mentor and friend, had returned to Germany as professor at the University of Berlin and his inspiration was no doubt sorely missed; and Nicholson had already made a substantial fortune (his will was proved at £147,710). Possibly he wished to withdraw from the pressures of competitive business and, a gentle research chemist, devote himself to his interest in rosaniline dyes. The retirement of the leading British researchers coincided with a great strengthening of the German chemical industry, many of whose chemists had worked in British factories and laboratories. Despite the onset of German competition from about 1870, the firm re-formed as Brooke, Simpson, and Spiller and continued to prosper until the mid-1880s.

Nicholson was an original member of the Society of the Chemical Industry and a fellow of the Institute of Chemistry. Little is known of his private life. His wife, Louisa, survived him and a son, John, joined him in the business in 1866. He died on 23 October 1890 from cancer at his home, Carlton House, Herne Hill, London.

FRANCIS GOODALL

Sources M. R. Fox, *Dye-makers of Great Britain, 1856–1976: a history of chemists, companies, products, and changes* (1987) • P. J. T. Morris and C. A. Russell, *Archives of the British chemical industry, 1750–1914: a handlist* (1988) • L. F. Haber, *The chemical industry during the nineteenth century* (1958) • D. W. F. Hardie and J. D. Pratt, *A history of the modern British chemical industry* (1966) • W. A. Campbell, *The chemical industry* (1971) • *CGPLA Eng. & Wales* (1890)

Likenesses portrait, repro. in Fox, *Dye-makers of Great Britain*
Wealth at death £147,710 12s. 6d.: resworn probate, Dec 1892, *CGPLA Eng. & Wales* (1890)

Nicholson, Edward Williams Byron (1849–1912), librarian, was born on 16 March 1849 in Green Street, St Helier, Jersey, the only child of Edward Nicholson RN (1821–1850) and Emily Hamilton Wall (1821–1890), an actress. His father had left the navy in 1847 and died in California, a casualty of the gold rush, leaving his widow almost destitute. She moved with her son to Portsea, then to live with her mother at Llanrwst in north Wales, where Edward attended the grammar school from 1857 to 1859. After a term at Liverpool College, Nicholson was, from 1860, educated at Tonbridge School, Kent. In 1867 he went to Trinity College, Oxford, as a classical scholar; he gained a first in classical moderations in 1869 and a third in law and history in 1871. He won the Gaisford prize for Greek verse the same year and the Hall Houghton junior Greek Testament prize in 1872. He was school librarian at Tonbridge and librarian of the Oxford Union, demonstrating at an early age a laudable application to cataloguing by producing published catalogues of each library. After a brief spell of teaching at the Rookery School in Headington, Oxford, Nicholson was appointed librarian of the London Institution in January 1873.

The institution, founded in 1805 for the diffusion of knowledge by means of lectures and a circulating library, was by then almost moribund. With the support of its honorary secretary, the Revd William Rogers of St Botolph without Bishopsgate, Nicholson reorganized the society, increasing its membership and revenue, revitalizing its lectures, and greatly improving both the contents and the use of its library. In 1877, inspired by press accounts of a conference of American librarians, he was the prime mover in the organization of an international conference of librarians in London, at which, largely on his initiative, the Library Association of the United Kingdom and the Metropolitan Free Libraries Committee were formed. Nicholson was active in both associations, but resigned from the Library Association council in 1881, impatient with its reluctance to take a stand on major issues and its failure to instigate 'one single improvement however trifling in library-management or library-appliances' (Manley, 19–20).

Nicholson had married on 1 February 1876 Helen Grant (1850–1938), daughter of the Revd Sir Charles Macgregor, third baronet. They had three daughters, Violet (*b.* 1877), Myrtle (*b.* 1881), and May (*b.* 1885). Keen to make his mark on the world and to improve his income, Nicholson contemplated literary work. Then in 1881 Bodley's librarian died and Nicholson put his name forward hesitantly, aware of his shortcomings as palaeographer, bibliographer, and linguist, but confident of the relevance of his practical experience and his proven capacity for hard work and organization. Departing from a long tradition of scholar–librarians, the library's governing body of curators, to the surprise of the university, elected him. He owed his election to the support of Benjamin Jowett and to a general feeling that the time had come to modernize

Edward Williams Byron Nicholson (1849–1912), by unknown engraver

the Bodleian. Under the benign direction of H. O. Coxe, librarian since 1860, it had on the strength of its collections maintained its reputation as one of the world's great libraries, despite its cramped accommodation, minimal staff, and inadequate catalogues. In a prescient leader on 6 February 1882 *The Times*, while recognizing Nicholson's technical qualifications and thorough experience in the mechanics of librarianship, warned of the ordeal facing anyone chosen to succeed the courtly and scholarly Coxe. This view was echoed thirty years later in the *Times* obituary: 'it was a difficult post to fill and a difficult time' (*The Times*, 18 March 1912, 11).

In 1888 Nicholson published a report on his first five years in office, describing them as 'a time of transition and reorganization' ('The Bodleian Library 1882', Bodl. Oxf., Library Records, d.34). It records many changes: the extension of the library into the remaining ground-floor rooms of the Old Schools quadrangle and into the basement of the Sheldonian Theatre; the introduction of new cataloguing rules and a classification scheme for current accessions; a great increase in the numbers of books acquired and of catalogue slips produced; the provision of open access to reference works in the Radcliffe Camera; and the enlargement of the staff by the employment of boys to undertake the more routine library tasks.

The report glossed over the opposition provoked by the rapid introduction of so many changes. Several curators mistrusted such wholesale reorganization and sought to curb the excessive zeal of the brash young professional.

Falconer Madan, the senior sub-librarian, who despised Nicholson's deficiencies of scholarship and venerated the memory of Coxe's antiquated administration, fuelled their opposition with secret reports on the librarian's shortcomings and with anonymous criticism of the new regime in *The Library*. Nicholson, autocratic by nature, jealous of the dignity of his office, and impatient of criticism, went into battle on every issue. The result was a series of bitter conflicts which dogged his long term in office, broke his health, and masked the extent of his achievements, which were considerable.

It was Nicholson's constant refrain that the Bodleian was 'underroomed, undermonied and undermanned' ('The curatorial election of February 1899', Bodl. Oxf., Library Records, d.43). Shortage of funds precluded new building or the enlargement of the established staff, but judicious recruitment, careful training, and meticulous organization—at which Nicholson excelled—made the most of limited resources. His staff were rigorously supervised, and their duties minutely detailed in the *Staff Kalendar* which was published annually from 1902. The employment of boys freed library assistants to work on cataloguing, while training and incentives for promotion produced a steady supply of better-qualified staff. Unfortunately Nicholson's insistence on very detailed cataloguing and on the continuation of Coxe's subject-catalogue slowed down progress on the essential author-catalogue. His vigorous defence of the copyright privilege and enthusiasm for the preservation of ephemeral printing increased accessions but exacerbated the shortage of storage space. It was only in 1907 that, thanks to Thomas Brassey, funds became available to remedy some of the underlying problems. Extra staff were recruited to revise the old author-catalogue. The north range of the picture gallery was converted into an additional reading room. Work began on what was to be Nicholson's most lasting monument, the first specially constructed underground book store ever made, equipped with rolling bookcases, to a plan first mooted by him in 1899.

By 1907 long years of overwork and of controversy had taken their toll on Nicholson's constitution. Heart disease was diagnosed as early as 1890. He suffered a breakdown in 1901 and twice collapsed in the street in 1907. His absences from work increased and he suffered a further relapse in 1909. Suspicious of the curators' motives, he resisted all their suggestions that he should take leave of absence until forced to do so late in February 1912. He died on 17 March 1912 at his home, 2 Canterbury Road, Oxford, and was buried on 20 March at Holywell cemetery.

Nicholson's interests outside the Bodleian were varied. He was a devoted husband and father, an enthusiastic cyclist and swimmer, a chess player and composer of limericks. He published on a wide range of subjects including classical literature, comparative philology, and Celtic antiquities. He was a strong opponent of vivisection and supporter of the cause of women—his last battle with his senior colleagues and curators was over the appointment of a woman to the permanent staff. In a memorial address to the annual meeting of the Library Association in 1913,

Henry Tedder gave a graphic description of Nicholson, who was 5 feet 10 inches tall and of athletic build, with 'drooping moustache, small side whiskers, an ever-tumbling monocle, a straw hat worn summer and winter, a certain defect in one eye, a hurried and eager walk, and a general disregard for outward show' (Tedder, 108). His kindliness, consideration for their welfare, and total lack of malice towards his opponents were frequently recorded by his junior staff. G. W. Wheeler, who had known the Bodleian before 1882, summarized Nicholson's achievement in 1940 in a letter to R. H. Hill: 'I have always regarded him as almost the refounder of the Library' (Bodl. Oxf., Library Records, d.142).

MARY CLAPINSON

Sources K. A. Manley, 'E. W. B. Nicholson (1849–1912) and his importance to librarianship', DPhil diss., U. Oxf., 1977 · H. H. E. Craster, *History of the Bodleian Library, 1845–1945* (1952); repr. (1981) · Bodl. Oxf., MSS Nicholson · Library records, Bodl. Oxf. · S. Gibson, 'E. W. B. Nicholson, 1849–1912: some impressions', *Library Association Record*, 51 (1949), 137–43 · H. Tedder, 'E. W. B. Nicholson … in memoriam', *Library Association Record*, 16 (1914), 95–108 · R. H. Hill, 'The Bodleian since 1882: some records and reminiscences', *Library Association Record*, 42 (1940), 76–85 · C. J. Purnell, 'Edward Williams Byron Nicholson', *Library Assistant*, 9 (1912), 70–72

Archives Bodl. Oxf., corresp. and papers · Bodl. Oxf., handbook of library management · Bodl. Oxf., library records | Bodl. Oxf., corresp. with H. M. Bannister

Likenesses photograph, 1855, Bodl. Oxf., library records, d. 1781, pl. 15 · Stilliard & Banbury, photographs, 1883, Bodl. Oxf., library records, d. 137 · Hill & Saunders, photographs, 1892–1906, Bodl. Oxf., library records, d. 137 · D. Hardie, portrait, 1927 (after photograph), Bodl. Oxf. · engraving, AM Oxf. [*see illus.*]

Wealth at death £3880 11s.; deficiency in free assets of £384 5s.: Bodl. Oxf., library records, d.142, fols. 92–3, solicitor's letter, 23 Oct 1912

Nicholson, Francis (*bap.* 1650, *d.* 1731), Roman Catholic convert, was the son of Thomas Nicholson, and was baptized on 27 October 1650 at the collegiate church at Manchester. He was admitted to University College, Oxford, early in 1666, and graduated BA on 18 January 1669 and MA on 4 June 1673. After his ordination he preached at Oxford and near Canterbury. Obadiah Walker was his tutor at Oxford, and from him he appears to have acquired his high-church and Roman Catholic views. A sermon in favour of penance, which he preached at St Mary's Church, Oxford, on 20 June 1680, caused him to be charged before the vice-chancellor with spreading false doctrine, and he was ordered to recant. This, however, he declined to do, and his name was reported to the bishop in order to stop his preferment.

On the accession of James II, Nicholson declared himself a Roman Catholic and became an ardent champion of his adopted church. He attempted in vain to persuade John Hudson of University College to become an adherent of the king. With Walker he was engaged in retrieving for publication at Oxford some of the works of the Catholic convert, the late Abraham Woodhead, and in 1688 he wrote an appendix to Woodhead's 'Discourse on the eucharist', entitled 'The doctrine of the Church of England concerning the substantial presence and adoration of our blessed saviour in the eucharist asserted'.

On the deposition of James II in 1688 Nicholson joined the English Carthusians at Nieuwpoort in the Spanish Netherlands, but the austerities of their rule obliged him about four years afterwards to leave the order, and he returned to England. He then proceeded to Portugal, where he served at the court of Queen Catherine, the widow of Charles II, now living in Lisbon. He became friendly with the superiors of the English college in that city. It is recorded that he spent his retirement in devotion, study, and agricultural pursuits.

In 1706 Nicholson bought a country house, vineyard, and other lands at Pera on the southern bank of the Tagus opposite Lisbon. In 1721 he conveyed the whole of this property to the English college on the understanding that his debts should be paid and that a sum of £12 per annum together with board and lodging should be allowed him for life. He died at Lisbon on 13 August 1731 and was given a splendid funeral at the college, where he was buried. In his will he stipulated that if it were ever necessary for the college to sell or alienate Pera the proceeds were to be employed in the purchase of another country residence. Moreover a portion of the income which might be derived from the property thus bestowed was to be spent on the education of two students from Lancashire. The excellent situation of the property and its accessibility to the coast made it a popular resort for the students up to the time of the closure of the college in 1971.

C. W. SUTTON, *rev.* MICHAEL E. WILLIAMS

Sources W. Croft and [J. Kirk], *Historical account of Lisbon College* (1902), 60–69 · Gillow, *Lit. biog. hist.*, 5.178–80 · *Catholic Magazine* (1835), 208–10 · Wood, *Ath. Oxon.*, new edn, 4.449 · T. Jones, ed., *A catalogue of the collection of tracts for and against popery*, 2, Chetham Society, 64 (1865), 358–9 · *Hist. U. Oxf.* 4: *17th-cent. Oxf.*

Archives W. Yorks. AS, Leeds, Yorkshire Archaeological Society, letters, MS 46 | Ushaw College, Durham, Lisbon collection · W. Yorks. AS, Leeds, Yorkshire Archaeological Society, letters to Cuthbert Constable

Nicholson, Sir Francis (1655–1728), army officer and colonial governor, was born at Downholme Park, in the North Riding of Yorkshire, on 12 November 1655. He was probably the son of a local gentleman, Thomas Nicholson. He may, however, have been an illegitimate son of Charles *Paulet, Lord St John of Basing (1630/31–1699) (later sixth marquess of Winchester and first duke of Bolton), in whose household he served as a youth. Regardless of his parentage, Nicholson enjoyed the patronage of Paulet, as well as of Paulet's son-in-law, John Egerton, third earl of Bridgewater, throughout much of his subsequent career. Nicholson acquired at least some formal education, possibly at the free school at Richmond, or at Bolton Hall, Paulet's Yorkshire mansion.

Nicholson entered the army as an ensign in the King's Holland regiment in 1678. He served briefly in Flanders, and then, in July 1680, joined as a lieutenant a regiment formed to reinforce the British garrison in Tangier. By the autumn of 1682 Nicholson was acting as a courier for the garrison commander, Colonel Percy Kirke, embarking on a series of remarkable journeys in Morocco and across

Spain and France. Nicholson served in the Tangier garrison until its evacuation in February 1684. In May 1684 he joined the garrison of Portsmouth, where he was stationed until 1686. It is not clear that Nicholson was among the companies from his regiment which fought at the battle of Sedgemoor in 1685, but he certainly was present with his regiment at the last of Lord Chief Justice George Jeffries' 'bloody assizes' afterwards, when survivors of Monmouth's rebellion were tried and sentenced.

In July 1686 Nicholson was appointed captain of a company of soldiers to accompany Colonel Sir Edmund Andros, governor of the newly formed dominion of New England. On arrival in Boston, Nicholson assisted Andros in overseeing construction of a fort to command the city, travelled to Connecticut to secure surrender of that colony's charter, conducted diplomatic and espionage work against the French, and otherwise helped consolidate royal authority in New England. Andros nominated him to the council of the dominion, and in 1688 Nicholson was appointed lieutenant-governor of the dominion, when the colony's jurisdiction was extended south to incorporate New York.

News of the revolution of 1688 reached New England in May 1689, and led to the imprisonment of Governor Andros in Boston and to a revolt against Nicholson in New York. A militia commanded by Jacob Leisler occupied Fort James on 31 May, and shortly thereafter Nicholson returned to England, abandoning both his New York post and his beleaguered superior officer. There he discovered Charles Paulet, now marquess of Winchester, was a prominent supporter of William III. Paulet secured Nicholson's appointment as lieutenant-governor of Virginia, and Nicholson promptly departed for the colony, and arrived in Virginia in May 1690.

As he had in New England and New York, and with considerably more success, Nicholson worked to bolster royal authority. He toured the frontiers to assess personally the threat of American Indian attack, strengthened the governor's authority over colonial defence, reorganized and revitalized the colonial militia, worked to enforce the Acts of Trade and payment of quitrents, and fired off several detailed reports recommending the dissolution of charter and proprietary governments in favour of royal governments in the colonies. Perhaps most important, Nicholson lent his energy and authority to efforts to found a Church of England college, which became the College of William and Mary. All in all, as he noted in September of 1692, he had successfully promoted 'the service of God Almighty', and had asserted 'the Royal prerogative upon all occasions'.

Colonel Edmund Andros replaced Nicholson in Virginia in 1692. Early the next year, while in London lobbying for a royal charter for the College of William and Mary, Nicholson was appointed governor of Maryland. Nicholson went to that colony in the summer of 1694, and served as governor until December 1698. He energetically promoted the Church of England, and laid out new parishes, worked to find priests to staff them, and donated £5 to each new parish. He promptly set in motion plans to relocate the colony's capital, Annapolis. Laid out to Nicholson's design, the new town utilized a baroque plan which gave prominent emphasis to the authority of church and state. In October of 1694 he wrote to Thomas Tenison, archbishop of Canterbury, requesting support to establish 'a system of free schools to provide instruction in Latin, Greek, [and] writing', and contributed £25 to each county for the project. One of these schools, the King William School of Annapolis, eventually became St John's College. As would continue to happen throughout his career, Nicholson's years in Maryland were tarnished by bitter personal animosity, but all in all he demonstrated substantial executive ability. His efforts on behalf of the church brought him to the attention of the archbishop of Canterbury and Lord Chancellor Somers, and led to his reappointment as governor of Virginia in 1698.

Nicholson arrived in Virginia charged with instructions drafted by John Locke, a client of Somers and by 1698 an influential figure on the Board of Trade. Nicholson's efforts to follow these instructions, curtailing plural office-holding and attempting to reform land distribution, caused him eventually to alienate a group of influential Virginians, led by the Harrison family and the powerful Church of England commissary James Blair. As in Maryland, Nicholson devoted considerable attention to the church, meeting the clergy in April 1700 and proposing revisions to Virginia law to strengthen religion in the colony. He joined the Society for the Propagation of the Gospel in Foreign Parts in 1701, and remained a lifelong supporter. He also spearheaded the removal of the capital from Jamestown to Williamsburg, the site of the College of William and Mary. When Queen Anne ascended the throne in 1702, Nicholson sponsored an elaborate celebration in Williamsburg, replete with fireworks, parades, and a muster of the colonial militia, for which he donated £500. His greatest accomplishment was financial, increasing royal revenues substantially and building up the colony's monetary reserves, which totalled more than £5700 by the end of his administration. By 1702, however, the Harrison/Blair faction was agitating for Nicholson's removal. Commissary Blair orchestrated a vicious assault on the governor's character in letters to his clerical patrons in England, and in May 1703 six members of the governor's council petitioned the queen asking for Nicholson's removal. Protests against Nicholson's administration coincided with a shift in imperial patronage in London, and led, in April 1705, to Nicholson's replacement in Virginia by a protégé of the duke of Marlborough.

Nicholson returned to England, where he remained for the next four years. He was elected a fellow of the Royal Society in 1706, and continued his support of colonial churches, providing donations for Church of England churches in New Jersey and South Carolina in 1706 and 1707. By 1709 Nicholson was back in America, having volunteered to accompany an expedition for a proposed attack on French Canada. Plans for invasion, however, foundered ignominiously when the ministry cancelled the naval orders supporting the attack, and Nicholson then returned to England. In 1710 he was promoted brigadier-general in command of the expedition which conquered Nova Scotia, and the following year was promoted lieutenant-general. Nicholson received a commission from the Society for the Propagation of the Gospel in 1712, and became a prominent advocate for the creation of a Church of England bishop in the North American colonies. In the same year he was appointed royal commissioner to audit colonial accounts, which ultimately resulted in bitter conflict with the governors of Massachusetts and New York. He served as lieutenant-governor of Nova Scotia from 1712 until 1715, when the accession of George I and the ascendancy of the whigs led to his dismissal.

Royal officials called upon Nicholson's extensive experience one last time when South Carolina changed from a proprietary to a royal colony in 1719. Nicholson arrived in that colony in 1720, having been knighted that year, and served as governor there until 1725. His tenure in office was relatively uneventful, though he did manage to earn the hostility of the Charlestown merchants by failing to support paper-currency laws. In 1725, with the merchants calling for his reassignment and in declining health, Nicholson asked for leave to return to England.

Nicholson died on 5 March 1728, leaving an estate ultimately valued at £545 to the Society for the Propagation of the Gospel. This represented only a fraction of his philanthropy, for he donated almost £5000 over his lifetime, including funds for the construction or repair of at least seventy-one churches, schools, court houses, and royal government buildings in eleven colonies. He was an ardent lifelong sponsor of the Church of England, supporting churches, clergymen, and educational institutions in every mainland colony. He championed the Church of England revival in New England, sending funds to reverends Timothy Cutler, Daniel Browne, and Samuel Johnson, who held teaching positions at Yale, and whose conversion to the Church of England created, as Nicholson wryly put it, such 'a great bustle in New England'. While his irascible demeanour and ferocious temper produced more than his share of enemies and led to several official investigations into his conduct, Nicholson's energy, patronage of education and religion, imperial vision, and faithful advocacy of royal authority made him one of the crown's more effective colonial servants.

KEVIN R. HARDWICK

Sources F. Nicholson, 'Journal of an expedition … for the reduction of Port Royal', *Boston News Letter* (30 Oct–6 Nov 1710) [reprinted in *Reports and Collections of the Nova Scotia Historical Society*, 1 (1879)] · *An apology or vindication of Francis Nicholson, esq., his majesty's governor of South Carolina, from the unjust aspersions cast on him by some of the members of the Bahama-Company* (1724) · F. Nicholson, *Papers relating to an affidavit made by His Reverence James Blair, clerk, pretended president of William and Mary College, and supposed commissary to the bishop of London in Virginia, against Francis Nicholson, esq; governor of the said province. Wherein his Reverence's great respect to government, and obedience to the ninth commandment, Thou shalt bear no false witness, etc., will plainly appear; as will also his gratitude to the said governor, from whom he had received so many favors, and to whom he was himself so highly obliged, in several original letters under his own hand, some whereof are here published, and more (God willing) shall hereafter* (1727) · *CSP col.*, vols. 12–

32 · 'Documents relating to the early history of the College of William and Mary and the history of the church in Virginia', *William and Mary Quarterly*, 2nd ser., 19 (1939), 355–61 · 'Instructions to Francis Nicholson', *Virginia Magazine of History and Biography*, 4 (1896–7), 49–54 · 'Papers relating to the administration of Francis Nicholson and to the founding of William and Mary College', *Virginia Magazine of History and Biography*, 7 (1899–1900), 153–72, 275–86, 386–401; 8 (1900–01), 46–58, 126–46, 260–73, 366–85; 9 (1901–2), 18–33, 152–62, 251–62 · 'William and Mary College: recently discovered documents', *William and Mary Quarterly*, 2nd ser., 10 (1930), 239–53 · W. J. Hinke, ed., 'Report of the journey of Francis Louis Michel, from Berne, Switzerland, to Virginia, October 2, 1702 – December 1, 1702', *Virginia Magazine of History and Biography*, 24 (1916), 125–9 · P. C. Legg, ed., 'The governor's "extacy of trouble"', *William and Mary College Quarterly Historical Magazine*, 2nd ser., 22 (1942), 389–98 · S. C. McCulloch, ed., 'The fight to depose Governor Francis Nicholson: James Blair's affidavit of June 7, 1704', *Journal of Southern History*, 12 (1946), 403–22 · H. R. McIlwaine and others, eds., *Executive journals of the council of colonial Virginia*, 6 vols. (1925–66), vols. 1–3 · W. S. Perry, *Papers relating to the history of the church in Virginia* (1870) · L. B. Wright, 'William Byrd's opposition to Governor Francis Nicholson', *Journal of Southern History*, 11 (1945), 68–79 · G. T. Christopher, 'The feuding governors: Andros and Nicholson at odds in colonial Maryland', *Maryland Historical Magazine*, 90 (1995), 334–48 · F. Downey, 'The governor goes a-wooing: the swashbuckling courtship of Nicholson of Virginia, 1699–1705', *Virginia Magazine of History and Biography*, 55 (1947), 6–19, 180 · J. D. Kornwolf, 'Doing good to posterity: Francis Nicholson, first patron of architecture, landscape design, and town planning in Virginia, Maryland, and South Carolina, 1688–1725', *Virginia Magazine of History and Biography*, 101 (1993), 333–74 · L. Labaree, 'Nicholson, Francis', *DAB* · B. T. McCully, 'From the North Riding to Morocco: the early years of Governor Francis Nicholson, 1655–1686', *William and Mary Quarterly*, 3rd ser., 19 (1962), 534–56 · B. T. McCully, 'Nicholson, Francis', *DCB* · B. T. McCully, 'Governor Francis Nicholson, patron *par excellence* of religion and learning in colonial America', *William and Mary Quarterly*, 3rd ser., 39 (1982), 310–33 · S. S. Webb, 'The strange career of Francis Nicholson', *William and Mary Quarterly*, 3rd ser., 23 (1966), 513–48 · R. B. Winton, 'Governor Francis Nicholson's relations with the Society for the Propagation of the Gospel in Foreign Parts, 1701–1727', *Historical Magazine of the Protestant Episcopal Church*, 17 (1948), 274–96

Archives Colonial Williamsburg Foundation, Williamsburg, Virginia, corresp. and papers · Harvard U., papers on South Carolina · Harvard U., Houghton L., corresp. and petitions · L. Cong., papers relating to expedition against Annapolis Royal · LPL, corresp. · Public Archives of Nova Scotia, Halifax, journal [copy] · RS, 'Letters and communications from Americans' · United Society for the Propagation of the Gospel, London, journals · Yale U., letters to David Humphreys | College of William and Mary, Williamsburg, Virginia, Earl Gregg Swem Library, George Keith, 'Benefactions of Francis Nicholson, Esqr., to the church and clergy in North America' · College of William and Mary, Williamsburg, Virginia, Fairfax-Harrison papers · Colonial Williamsburg Foundation, Williamsburg, Virginia, William Blathwayt papers · Hunt. L., letters to Lord Bridgewater · Hunt. L., Cadwallader Jones papers · L. Cong., William Blathwayt papers · LPL, Fulham MSS · Museum of the City of New York, Samuel Vetch papers · Newberry Library, Chicago, Edward E. Ayer MS collection

Wealth at death £545—donated to the United Society for the Propagation of the Gospel, London

Nicholson, Francis (1753–1844), watercolour painter, was born on 14 November 1753 at Pickering in Yorkshire, the son of Francis Nicholson (d. c.1788), a weaver; his mother, whose name was Jackson, was a Quaker. Nicholson dated his determination to be an artist from seeing a portrait at the age of seven but his father discouraged such 'precarious fancy employment' (Royal Watercolour Society, J

69/2). Eventually he was allowed to go to Scarborough for instruction by a copyist of old masters. On his return to Pickering he found work drawing horses, dogs, and game for the local gentry. After two more years Nicholson went to London and 'was delighted to find hundreds of people like myself who neither knew nor cared about agriculture, cattle, manure and tillage' (Davies, 8). He received lessons from a German artist, Conrad Martin Metz, until lack of funds forced him to return home; there he spent several months painting the ceiling of a large summer house with mythological creatures for Mr Hayes, a local magistrate.

In 1783 Nicholson settled in Whitby, where he met his wife, Sally Blanchard; they married in Malton about 1787. Nicholson's first inclination was to be a portrait painter but he found it impossible to flatter; after Lord Mulgrave employed him to make watercolour sketches of his estates, Nicholson turned entirely to landscape drawing, a genre which he had hitherto despised. In 1789 he first exhibited at the Royal Academy with *A View of Castle Howard*. He worked up to sixteen hours a day, and he could finish six drawings in that time, etching outlines of views, copying, and then colouring them; his pictures were sent for sale in London and Scarborough. After nine years Nicholson moved to Knaresborough. In 1794 John Stuart, first marquess of Bute, engaged Nicholson to do sketches around the Isle of Bute. Nicholson then moved to Ripon and found another patron in Walter Fawkes of Farnley Hall. He also became acquainted with an Irish couple, Sir Henry Tuite and his wife, with whom he spent some years working and travelling before moving to Weybridge in Surrey to live near them; this relationship seems to have ended unsatisfactorily. By 1803 Nicholson was living in London in Somerstown and then at 10 Titchfield Street; in 1806 he moved to 1 Great Chesterfield Street and finally in 1810 to 52 Charlotte Street, Portland Place. By now Nicholson had a considerable teaching practice which included ladies of fashion who came merely to watch him work (including one who used to arrive at eight in the morning still in her nightcap and curl papers); Nicholson called such pupils his 'guinea fowl'. His contemporary reputation was such that drawings were fraudulently sold as being by Nicholson within his own lifetime.

In 1804 Nicholson was a founder member of the Society of Painters in Water Colours. He was elected president in December 1812 when the society was reconstituted to accept oil paintings, but resigned the following year. In all he exhibited 277 pictures with the society, the last in 1815; he also showed at the Royal Academy and the Society of Artists. His drawings, which were invariably unsigned, sold for up to 15 guineas. His style progressed from early tinted sketches to fully developed exhibition watercolours; the subject matter is romantic—including mountains, lakes, waterfalls, and ruins—but his work lacks distinction. J. L. Roget commented that perhaps 'his art would have been better for more sketching from nature, and less of midnight oil' (Roget, 1.154). Although Nicholson's obituarist in *Art Union* called him the 'Father of the English watercolour' this was perhaps more a tribute to his longevity and his productivity than to his art; Martin Hardie assessed Nicholson as 'a man of ideas and probably an excellent teacher' but 'on the whole a mediocre artist' (Hardie, 3.235) and none of his work was included in the 'Great Age of British Watercolours' exhibition held at the Royal Academy in 1993. The Victoria and Albert Museum, the British Museum, and the Whitworth Gallery, Manchester, are among the public galleries which have examples of his work.

Nicholson had many interests. In 1820 he published *The Practice of Drawing and Painting Landscapes from Nature in Water-Colours*; his eight hundred lithographs included eighty-one *Sketches of British Scenery* (1821) and *Six Views of Scarborough* (1822). Throughout his career Nicholson made trials with pigment and technique: in 1799 the Society of Arts paid him £20 for experimental work but some drawings have suffered as a result of his experiments. He also built organs and even after he had lost his hearing he continued to attend concerts 'where his face became as familiar as that of the doorkeeper' (Davies, 12). Another love was fishing: he would stand for hours in trout streams despite having been told when he was thirty that he was consumptive. In old age Nicholson wrote an autobiographical memoir, a copy of which is in the Royal Watercolour Society archives. Likenesses show him with a long, aquiline face and strong features; there is a self-portrait in oils at Killerton House in Devon, the home of his pupil Henrietta Anne Fortescue. Francis Nicholson died at the age of ninety on 6 March 1844 at 52 Charlotte Street; his wife predeceased him. A sale of his remaining works by Christie and Manson on 24 April 1844 included more than 100 drawings, 1400 sketches, and 44 oil paintings.

Nicholson had two daughters, both of whom painted: Sophia who married William Ayrton and Marianne (1792–1854) who married Thomas Crofton Croker, the Irish writer and antiquary. He also had two sons, Alfred and Francis. **Alfred Nicholson** (1788–1833) served in the Royal Navy for some years before becoming a professional artist and drawing-master. He lived in Ireland before settling about 1818 in London, where he died on 23 November 1833. Redgrave described his drawings as a combination of 'much graceful finish with force and general effect'. Nicholson's nephew **George Nicholson** (1787–1878), was also a watercolour painter and probably the son of Nicholson's brother, George, a house painter. York Art Gallery has examples of his work. He published two series of lithographs in 1821 and 1822 and also worked on the restoration of the pictures at Castle Howard. He died in Filey on 7 June 1878, and was buried at Old Malton.

SIMON FENWICK

Sources J. L. Roget, *A history of the 'Old Water-Colour' Society*, 2 vols. (1891) · R. Davies, 'Francis Nicholson: some family letters and papers', *OWCS*, 8 (1931), 1–39 · B. S. Long, 'Francis Nicholson', *Walker's Quarterly* [whole issue], 14 (1924) · Royal Watercolour Society archives, London [incl. autobiographical memoir] · M. Hardie, *Water-colour painting in Britain*, ed. D. Snelgrove, J. Mayne, and B. Taylor, 3: *The Victorian period* (1968), 234–7 · H. Mallalieu, 'Francis Nicholson: a doughty biter of feeding hands', *Water-Colours and*

Drawings, 4/3 (1989), 15–18 • Redgrave, *Artists*, 2nd edn, 309 • *DNB* • *Art Union*, 6 (1844)

Archives priv. coll., MSS | Royal Watercolour Society, Bankside Gallery, London, MSS

Likenesses H. Kirchoffer, watercolour, 1814, repro. in Mallalieu, 'Francis Nicholson' • F. Nicholson, self-portrait, oils, *c*.1837, NPG • M. Gauci, lithograph (after J. Green, 1818), BM, NPG; repro. in Long, 'Francis Nicholson' • F. Nicholson, self-portrait, oils, Killerton, Devon • F. Nicholson, self-portrait, pencil, repro. in Davies, 'Francis Nicholson'

Nicholson, George (1760–1825), printer, was born in Keighley, Yorkshire, the son of John Nicholson, one of a family of printers, who in 1781 started a business in Bradford. By 1784 George and a brother had set up independently, producing mainly chapbooks and popular penny cards, but some time before 1797, having moved to Manchester, he was printing books to a high standard, educational or didactic titles of some range and importance. One such, *Pious Reflections for Every Day of the Month; Translated from the French of Fénelon* (1797), was the work of an eminent Manchester cleric, John Clowes, and went into several editions. Another, with Nicholson himself as author, *The Conduct of Man to Inferior Animals* (1797), reached a fourth edition in 1819, combined with his *Primeval State of Man* (1801), and *Arguments … in Favour of a Vegetable Diet* (1801).

From 1799 to 1800 Nicholson was in Ludlow, Shropshire; a number of printers already operated there, so after less than two years he moved to Poughnill, a small isolated area nearby, his base until 1807, from which he produced widely varying titles. Here he started a celebrated and innovatory collection of pocket books, issued in a tiny 32mo format; these sold at from 9*d*. to 1*s*. 6*d*. His ongoing *Literary miscellany: a selection and extracts, classical and scientific, with originals in prose and verse*, in duodecimo, eventually comprised over 80 parts in 20 volumes. Many of the titles had already appeared in larger-format editions. *The Advocate and Friend of Woman* (1805), *On Education* (1805), and an edition of Milton's poems (1800) represent just a few of the incredible range from Poughnill.

Finally Nicholson set up in Stourport, Worcestershire, remaining in Bridge Street premises there for the rest of his life, from 1807 to 1825. From Stourport merchandise could be dispatched easily by the new canal network to London and much of England. For some time, with an established reputation, his imprints had named well-known London booksellers as agents. For all his books, even the pocket series, he commissioned work from the finest illustrators and engravers of the day: Bewick, Craig, Chapman, Austin, or Bromley. Other titles indicative of his range include, as author, *Stenography, or, A New System of Shorthand* (1806); as compiler or editor, *The British Orpheus, with Music* (1819), *Songs and Ballads* (1810), *The Juvenile Preceptor, or, A Course of Moral and Scientific Instruction* (4 vols., 1805), and *A Spelling and Pronouncing Dictionary* (1814). There were selected editions of such major authors as Milton (1800), Pope (1811), Goldsmith (1801), Benjamin Franklin (1801), Marcus Aurelius (1811), and lesser-known writers

such as Nathaniel Cotton (1800) and Soames Jenyns (1801). Miscellanies included the popular *Gothic Stories* (1799) and *Moral Tales* (1802). One widely reviewed title, *The Cambrian Traveller's Guide and Pocket Companion* (1808, 2nd enlarged edn, 1813), covered Wales and the marches, with useful indexes, one to plant species. (A third 'corrected' edition, of 1840, by his son Emilius Nicholson, is inferior in typography and content.) Later he printed the work of local authors and poets, such as Mary Southall's *Description of Malvern* in 1822.

An obituarist in the *Gentleman's Magazine* wrote of Nicholson as 'a man we hesitate not to place with the names of Dodsley and Baskerville' (*GM*, 1st ser., 95/2, 1825, 642). An MP for Worcester, Thomas Rowley Hill, who as a boy had known Nicholson, 'distinctly remembered him as a tall, gaunt man. He was an author, and printed chiefly by his own hands' (Burton, 198). He did not neglect the jobbing demands on a local printer, and was involved in the civic affairs of Stourport. His monument in the churchyard there was inscribed: 'The subject of this memorial was a man of strict integrity, expansive mind, devoted to the interests of literature, and a warm advocate of humanity'. He died at Stourport on 1 November 1825. His widow, Mary Nicholson, carried on the printing business after his death.

A. L. COOPER

Sources J. R. Burton, 'Early Worcestershire printers and books', *Transactions of the Worcestershire Architectural and Archaeological Society*, 24 (1897–8), 197–213 • A. Cooper, 'Printed and sold by G. Nicholson', *Quadrat*, 2 (1995), 3–8 • Ll. C. Lloyd, 'The book-trade in Shropshire', *Transactions of the Shropshire Archaeological Society*, 48 (1934–5), 65–142, 145–200 • *GM*, 1st ser., 95/2 (1825), 642 • C. H. Timperley, *A dictionary of printers and printing* (1839), 696 • I. L. Wedley, *Old Stourport* (1912) • I. L. Wedley, *The passing of Mitton* (1921) • letters from George Nicholson to Thomas Bewick, priv. coll. • *Nineteenth century short title catalogue* (1984–95) • *DNB* • memorial stone, Stourport churchyard • *Literary Miscellany*, BL • *Literary Miscellany*, Shropshire County Libraries

Archives priv. coll., letters to Thomas Bewick

Nicholson, George (1787–1878). *See under* Nicholson, Francis (1753–1844).

Nicholson, George (1795?–1838), artist, was the son of Mrs Isabella Nicholson, *née* Wilkinson, and brother of Samuel and Isabella Nicholson. Following the death in 1814 of their father, a former school proprietor in Manchester and subsequently typographer in Liverpool, the whole family engaged in artistic work. Mrs Nicholson executed remarkable copies in needlework of well-known pictures. These were finely wrought in silk; in some cases of landscapes the sky was painted on a background of silk velvet. These included a copy of *The Grecian Votary*, by Nicolas Poussin, in the National Gallery, London. A similar copy of Rembrandt's *Belshazzar's Feast* and a portrait of George III were, with many other examples of Mrs Nicholson's handicraft, exhibited in Liverpool, and disposed of there about 1847.

Prior to his early death, hastened by anxieties over debts incurred through signing a bond in favour of a friend, Mr

Nicholson, also a self-taught engraver on wood, taught both his sons to draw and to engrave. Between 1827 and 1838 George Nicholson exhibited at the Liverpool Academy exhibitions some fifty drawings, mostly landscapes in watercolour or in pencil. In 1821 he was awarded the silver Isis medal of the Society of Arts for a drawing of Stirling Castle, afterwards bought by the sculptor Sir Francis Chantrey. With his elder brother Samuel (who drew with great skill with the lead pencil, winning in 1821 the silver medal of the Society of Arts for a large drawing; painted in watercolours; and taught drawing), he published: *Twenty-Six Lithographic Drawings in the Vicinity of Liverpool* (Liverpool, 1821); and *Plas Newydd and Valle Crucis Abbey* (1824). The illustrations were drawn in a fine line, and more resemble woodcuts than was usual in early lithographs. A second series of 'Eight select views, in the county of Caernarvon, drawn from nature and on stone, by George Nicholson, and printed by Charles Hullmandel' (Marples, 223), without date, was published under the patronage of Lady Eleanor Butler and the Hon. Miss Ponsonby, the 'Ladies of Llangollen', about 1827.

Having honoured his father's debts, and with the prospect of discharging those of his own that remained, George Nicholson died in 1838 of the effects of an attack of cholera and influenza which led to tuberculosis. He never married. His brother Samuel Nicholson had died after being bitten by a mad dog about 1825. Their youngest sister, Isabella Nicholson, exhibited drawings in watercolour and pencil of flowers, birds, and occasionally landscapes at the Liverpool Academy between 1829 and 1845.

ALBERT NICHOLSON, *rev.* ANNETTE PEACH

Sources exhibition catalogues, Liverpool Academy (1827–38) · private information (1894) · D. Marples, 'On picture-printing—chromo-lithography', *Proceedings of the Literary and Philosophical Society of Liverpool*, 22 (1867–8), 193–224 · E. Morris and E. Roberts, *The Liverpool Academy and other exhibitions of contemporary art in Liverpool, 1774–1867* (1998), 450

Nicholson, George (1847–1908), gardener and botanist, was born at Ripon, Yorkshire, on 7 December 1847, the son of James Nicholson, gardener, and his wife, Hannah, *née* Burr. Initially trained under his father, he then worked for some time in the gardens of Messrs Fisher and Holmes at Sheffield, before spending two years at the municipal nurseries of La Muette, Paris. On his return to England he worked at the nurseries of Messrs Low at Clapton. In 1873 he was appointed clerk to John Smith, the curator at Kew; in 1886 he succeeded Smith as curator. In 1875 he married Elizabeth Naylor Bell; she died soon after, leaving him a son who become an engineer in the Royal Navy. Nicholson retired owing to ill health in July 1901, but continued his botanical researches at Kew as far as his strength allowed.

A fluent speaker in French and German, Nicholson paid holiday visits to France and Switzerland, and travelled in Germany, northern Italy, and Spain. He was impressed with the value of a knowledge of foreign languages to young gardeners, and devoted much of his leisure to teaching some of them French. In 1893 he went to the Chicago Exhibition as one of the judges in the horticultural section; there he took the opportunity to study the forest trees of the United States. In 1902, the year after his retirement, he visited New York as delegate of the Royal Horticultural Society to the plant-breeding conference.

Until 1886 Nicholson devoted much attention to the critical study of British flowering plants. His first published work, 'Wild flora of Kew gardens and pleasure grounds', appeared in the *Journal of Botany, British and Foreign*, for 1875. In the same year he joined the Botanical Exchange Club, and to its reports and to the *Journal of Botany* he contributed notes on such segregates as those of *Rosa* and of *Cardamine pratensis*. The 'Wild fauna and flora of Kew Gardens', issued in the *Kew Bulletin* (additional ser. 5) in 1906 was largely his work. Out of 2000 fungi enumerated, 500 were found by Nicholson. His herbarium of British plants was presented, towards the end of his life, to the University of Aberdeen, through his friend James Trail, professor of botany there.

When Sir Joseph Hooker was reorganizing and extending the arboretum at Kew he found an able assistant in Nicholson, who wrote on the genera *Acer* and *Quercus* and twenty articles on the Kew arboretum in the *Gardeners' Chronicle*, during 1881–3. A valuable herbarium which he formed of trees and shrubs was purchased by the Bentham Trust in 1889 and presented to Kew. His *Hand-List of Trees and Shrubs Grown at Kew* (1894–6) demonstrated his knowledge of this class of plants. Nicholson's *magnum opus* was *The Illustrated Dictionary of Gardening* (4 vols., 1884–7; French edn, 1892–9; two supp. vols., 1900–01). This standard work of reference, most of which was not only edited but also written by Nicholson, became the forerunner of the Royal Horticultural Society's *Dictionary of Gardening*. Although an expert on oaks and maples he never realized his ambition to write a standard work on hardy trees and shrubs.

Nicholson's gentle, unselfish character, together with his reputation as a horticulturist, made him the obvious choice for first president of the Kew Guild, which was founded in 1893. He was elected an associate of the Linnean Society in 1886, became a fellow in 1898, and was awarded the Veitch memorial medal of the Royal Horticultural Society in 1894, and the Victoria medal of honour in 1897. In 1901 Udo Dammer named a Central American palm *Neonicholsonia georgei* and C. E. Salmon named a moss, found on a tree-fern at Kew, *Fissideus nicholsoni*. An athletic man, and a keen mountaineer, Nicholson died of heart trouble at his home, 37 Larkfield Road, Richmond, on 20 September 1908. His remains were cremated. The Royal Horticultural Society founded the Nicholson prize, awarded to students sitting the Wisley diploma examination, in his honour.

G. S. BOULGER, *rev.* RAY DESMOND

Sources *Bulletin of Miscellaneous Information* [RBG Kew] (1908), 422–7 · *Journal of Botany, British and Foreign*, 46 (1908), 337–9 · *Gardeners' Chronicle*, 3rd ser., 44 (1908), 239 · F. A. Stafleu and R. S. Cowan, *Taxonomic literature: a selective guide*, 2nd edn, 3, Regnum Vegetabile, 105 (1981), 740–42 · *CGPLA Eng. & Wales* (1908)

Archives RBG Kew | U. Aberdeen, plant specimens · U. Glas., plant specimens
Likenesses drawing, repro. in *Garden*, 48 (1895), frontispiece · photograph, repro. in E. Nelmes and W. Cuthbertson, *Curtis's Botanical Magazine dedications, 1827–1927* (1931), 302
Wealth at death £2020 5*s.* 10*d.*: probate, 29 Oct 1908, *CGPLA Eng. & Wales*

Nicholson, Henry Alleyne (1844–1899), biologist and geologist, was born on 11 September 1844 at Penrith, Cumberland, the son of John Nicholson, a distinguished biblical scholar, and his wife, Annie Elizabeth, daughter of the naval captain Henry Waring, of Lyme Regis, Dorset. His paternal grandfather, the Revd Mark Nicholson, was president of Codrington College, Barbados.

Nicholson received his early education under Francis Newman, and at Appleby grammar school, then went on to the University of Göttingen in Germany. There he became a student in zoology and took the degree of PhD. On returning to Britain he studied medicine and natural science at the University of Edinburgh from 1862 to 1867; he took the degree of bachelor of science in 1866, and in the same year was awarded the Baxter scholarship in natural science. The following year he proceeded to the degrees of bachelor of medicine, master of surgery, and doctor of science; his doctoral thesis, 'On the geology of Cumberland', gained him the gold medal of the university for that year. In all the subjects of examination he gained a first class; and when, in 1869, he took the MD degree, he was awarded the Ettles medical scholarship for attaining the highest position among the graduates.

Even in his schooldays Nicholson had devoted much attention to the geology of his native county and Westmorland; and while a student at Edinburgh he learned anatomy under John Goodsir (1814–1867), zoology under George James Allman (1812–1898), and botany under John Hutton Balfour (1808–1884), thus laying the foundation of that wide zoological knowledge which subsequently stood him in good stead.

From 1869 to 1871 Nicholson was lecturer in natural history at the extra-mural school of medicine at Edinburgh, and for a short period also practised medicine. In 1871 he became professor of natural history and botany at the University of Toronto. He retained the position for three years, exchanging it in 1874 for the professorship of comparative anatomy and zoology at the Royal College of Science, Dublin. However, soon after accepting the Dublin post, he was offered the professorship of biology at Durham College of Physical Science, which he accepted and filled until 1875. Subsequently, he lectured at Newcastle upon Tyne for two sessions, and then accepted the offer of the chair of natural history at the University of St Andrews. There he was instrumental in founding a zoological school, and helped extend university teaching to Dundee; he also delivered lectures to the Ladies' Educational Association of St Andrews, Dundee, and Cupar. Nicholson remained at St Andrews until 1882, when he was appointed regius professor of natural history at the University of Aberdeen—a post he held until his death. When he first succeeded to this chair, zoology was the chief science on

which he had to lecture. However, a change in the curriculum elevated geology to a more important status, and it was to this subject that Nicholson devoted his energies.

Nicholson was the Swiney lecturer in geology at the British Museum (Natural History) from 1878 to 1882, and from 1890 to 1894. During the illness of Sir Charles Wyville Thompson, then professor of natural history at Edinburgh, Nicholson took over his duties during 1878 and the two following years. In 1880 Nicholson was appointed examiner in natural history and the cognate branches of science to the University of New Zealand. In 1867 he was elected a fellow of the Geological Society of London, in 1879 he received the Lyell Fund, and in 1888 was awarded the Lyell medal by the council of that society. He was also elected a fellow of the Linnean Society in 1876, and on 3 June 1897 was admitted FRS.

Nicholson's interests focused on the palaeontological aspect of zoology. His most important investigations were considered to be those concerning field geology and Palaeozoic invertebrates such as graptolites, stromatoporoids, corals, and polyzoa. He also worked towards understanding the geological succession of the Palaeozoic rocks of the Lake District. On this last task he collaborated with John Edward Marr (1857–1933). Nicholson also played a role in the 'highlands controversy'. He was one of a few people who agreed with the theory of his predecessor at Aberdeen, James Nichols (1810–1879), regarding the geology of the north-west highlands of Scotland. Nicholson also gave much help and encouragement to Charles Lapworth (1842–1920), who later revived the 'highland controversy' and revealed the true nature of the geology in that region.

Nicholson was author of the following works: *Essay on the Geology of Cumberland and Westmoreland* (1868); *A Manual of Zoology for the Use of Students* (2 vols., 1870; 7th edn, 1 vol., 1887); *A Monograph of the British Graptolitidae: Introduction* (1872), issued by the Palaeontographical Society; and *A Manual of Palaeontology for the Use of Students* (1872; 2 vols., 1879). A third and enlarged edition of this last work, co-written with Richard Lydekker, was published in 1889. Other works of a similar nature included *Introduction to the Study of Biology* (1872), *The Ancient Life-History of the Earth* (1877), *Synopsis of the Classification of the Animal Kingdom* (1882), and *A Monograph of the British Stromatoporoids* (1886–92), published by the Palaeontographical Society. He contributed more than 150 papers and memoirs to the publications of various scientific societies and periodicals. Furthermore, he also produced articles—'Buffon', 'Corals', 'Cuttle-fishes', and 'Cuvier'—to the ninth edition of *Encyclopaedia Britannica*. Nicholson died at Aberdeen University on 19 January 1899. He was survived by his wife, Isabella (*née* Hutchison), with whom he had five children including the orientalist Reynold Alleyne *Nicholson (1868–1945).

RICHARD LYDEKKER, *rev.* YOLANDA FOOTE

Sources *Alma Mater* [Aberdeen University] (25 Jan 1899), 115–21 · *Alma Mater* [Aberdeen University] (8 March 1899), 176–8 · *Nature*, 59 (1898–9), 298–9 · *Natural Science* (March 1899), 247–8 · G. J. Hinde,

Geological Magazine, new ser., 4th decade, 6 (1899), 138–44 · W. Whitaker, *Quarterly Journal of the Geological Society*, 55 (1899), lxiv–lxvi · *Yearbook of the Royal Society* (1899), 189 · *WWW* · Venn, *Alum. Cant.* · D. R. Oldroyd, *The highlands controversy: constructing geological knowledge through fieldwork in nineteenth-century Britain* (1990) · *CCI* (1899)

Archives BL, lecture notes, Add. MS 31205 | NL Scot., corresp. with Blackwoods

Likenesses photograph, repro. in *Alma Mater* (25 Jan 1899) · portrait, repro. in *Geological Magazine*

Wealth at death £7878 7s. 5d.: confirmation, 27 March 1899, *CCI*

Nicholson, Isaac (1789–1848). *See under* Bewick, Thomas, apprentices (*act.* 1777–1828).

Nicholson, John (1729/30–1796), bookseller, was born at Mountsorrel, Leicestershire, the son of a farmer; he was perhaps John, the son of Edward and Mary Nickols (or Nichols), who was baptized at Mountsorrel on 19 April 1730. Nicholson was said originally to have been a staymaker. On 28 May 1752 he married Mary Anne (*c.*1730–1814), daughter of the Cambridge bookseller, circulating-library keeper, and printseller Robert Watts (*c.*1696–1752).

Nicholson began as a bookseller in Cambridge with a street stall, but with his marriage he became established in his wife's father's old shop in King's Parade, by the old provost's lodge of King's College. The premises included a circulating library, and Nicholson developed the business, specializing in lending out undergraduate textbooks as well as lighter reading—'the most choice collection of Lounging Books that the genius of Indolence could desire' (*Gradus ad Cantabrigiam*, 59). He was celebrated for hawking his stock and ready-made undergraduate themes (essays) round the colleges, and inherited from Watts the nickname 'Maps', after his familiar call. For suitable fees (some thought them expensive), he was able to provide both themes and sermons in manuscript. This necessarily discreet business won him many friends.

As a complement to this Nicholson developed a small publishing business, beginning with *The History of Israel Jobson, the Wandering Jew* (1757). It was atrociously printed, but his subsequent choice of books, including annotated classical texts and undergraduate guides to the work of John Locke and Roger Cotes, did not require high typographical standards. He also developed a bookbinding business, repairing many of the early books in the university library. As a sideline, he sold plaster figures.

Nicholson's trade, and perhaps his Leicestershire background, brought him the friendship of Richard Farmer, the university librarian, and with Farmer's encouragement in 1788 he presented his own full-length portrait, by Philip Reinagle, to be hung in the university library—still a unique distinction for any member of the Cambridge book trade.

Nicholson and his wife had three children (John, baptized on 11 October 1754; Sarah, baptized on 23 May 1756; Joseph, baptized on 20 July 1760). William Nicholson, a printer at Wisbech (*d.* 1792), was a brother of Nicholson. John Nicholson died in Cambridge on 8 August 1796 of a

John Nicholson (1729/30–1796), by Philip Reinagle, 1788

'lingering complaint of strangury and stone' (*GM*), aged sixty-six, having made his will many years earlier, on 13 July 1782. He was buried in St Edward's churchyard on 13 August 1796 and was succeeded in his business by his son John (1754–1825), who continued in the old premises until they were demolished to make way for the new screen in front of King's College. John Nicholson the younger retired about 1821, and was briefly succeeded by his son, **John Nicholson** (1781–1822), who wrote two anonymously published plays: *Paetus and Arria* (1809), and *Right and Wrong* (1812), the latter described by Genest as 'insipid to the last degree' (Genest, 8.275). Nicholson died in 1822, at some point after 5 August, the date on which he drew up his will; he left most of his estate to his three sisters and his mother, Mary.   DAVID MCKITTERICK

Sources C. Wordsworth, *Social life at the English universities in the eighteenth century* (1874), 378–85 · H. Gunning, *Reminiscences of the university, town, and county of Cambridge, from the year 1780*, 1 (1854), 198–200 · D. McKitterick, *Cambridge University Library, a history: the eighteenth and nineteenth centuries* (1986) · D. McKitterick, *A history of Cambridge University Press*, 2 (1998) · *GM*, 1st ser., 66 (1796), 708 · *Cambridge University Calendar* (1802), l–lii [tripos verses about Nicholson, 1781] · Genest, *Eng. stage*, 8.274–5; 10.230 · parish register, Mountsorrel, Leics. RO · parish register, Cambridge, St Edward's, Cambs. AS · Downing College, Cambridge, Bowtell papers · *DNB* ·

Gradus ad Cantabrigiam (1803) • will, PRO, PROB 11/1668, sig. 161 [J. Nicholson (1781–1822)]

Likenesses P. Reinagle, oils, 1788, CUL [*see illus.*] • J. Caldwell, engraving, 1790 (after oils by P. Reinagle), repro. in J. W. Goodison, *Catalogue of Cambridge portraits* (1955) • J. K. Baldrey, engraving, 1791

Nicholson, John (*c.*1777/8–1866). *See under* Nicholson, William (*bap.* 1782, *d.* 1849).

Nicholson, John (1781–1822). *See under* Nicholson, John (1729/30–1796).

Nicholson, John (1790–1843), poet, known as the Airedale Poet, was born on 29 November 1790 at Weardley, near Harewood, in Wharfedale, the eldest son of Thomas Nicholson (*fl. c.*1765–1835), a wool-sorter, and Martha Whitley (*c.*1770–1853), a farmer's daughter. Soon after his birth his father was employed by his wife's brother in a mill at Eldwick, near Bingley, in Airedale. Nicholson was educated at home, and recalled his father reading to his family the Bible, Milton, Pope's Homer, Blair's *Grave*, Young's *Night Thoughts*, 'and the rest of the poets of the old school' (Ogden, 'Unpublished documents', 3). He completed his education at Bingley grammar school, under the Revd Dr Richard Hartley, and was then apprenticed as a wool-sorter in the mill at Eldwick. On 11 July 1810 he married Mary Driver, a local girl of about his own age, who died in childbirth later that year. Following this traumatic experience he became for a while a Wesleyan preacher. On 13 February 1813 he married Martha Wild (*c.*1792–1874), of Bingley, who remained devoted to him and with whom he had nine children. In 1818 he got a good job as a wool-sorter at Shipley Fields Mill, and went to live in a cottage at Red Beck; in 1822 he had similar work at Harden Beck, near Bingley.

While living at Red Beck, Nicholson became well known locally as a poet and impromptu versifier. His first substantial works were two plays, *The Robber of the Alps* and *The Siege of Bradford* (1821), which were performed successfully in Bradford, at Thompson's Theatre. *The Siege* told the story of Bradford's part in the civil war, and according to the author was intended 'to show, that even in the lowest station of life, there are persons who remain steadfast to their king, and unmoved by all the insinuations of disaffected men' (Ogden, 'Unpublished documents', 5). During the period of working-class agitation in the 1820s and 1830s Nicholson's views were conservative; he wrote in favour of the improved conditions for working people proposed by Richard Oastler and John Fielden, but against Catholic emancipation and Owenism. His best-known long poem, *Airedale in Ancient Times*, though chiefly concerned with scenery and history, is also royalist in spirit. It was published in 1825, sold very well, and gave Nicholson the idea of earning his living by writing poetry, publishing it in pamphlets, and travelling about, hawking them to the nobility and gentry. This source of income almost dried up in 1833, with the bankruptcy of his cousins G. and E. Nicholson, who had printed much of his work and whose stock was auctioned to pay their debts. From 1833

Nicholson was employed in the warehouse of Titus Salt at Bradford, where he lived in Mill Street.

Most of Nicholson's earnings from poetry, however, had been spent on drink, which had become the curse of his life, as he was well aware. In 1835 he signed the pledge and wrote 'The Wish of the Drunkard's Family', published by the Wilsden Temperance Association, but his reformation lasted only seventeen weeks. The manner of his death was sadly predictable. Like most Bradfordians he liked to get away from the smoky town when he could. On the eve of Good Friday 1843 (14 April) he left home to visit an aunt in Eldwick. On the way he called at several public houses before attempting, on a dark and stormy night, to cross the River Aire by the stepping stones above Shipley. He apparently fell in and struggled to the opposite bank, but was too weak to move further, and died of exposure. More than 1000 people attended his funeral at Bingley parish church on 18 April. His widow and family were assisted by Salt, W. E. Forster, and the profits from a collected edition of Nicholson's poems, published in 1844 with a life by John James; a more complete collection appeared in 1876, with a life by W. G. Hird.

Nicholson's fragmentary education, and the patronage of the nobility and gentry, were enough to ruin him as a poet and as a man; they encouraged a rhapsodical mode of writing and an undisciplined manner of living, such that after his death many saw him as a tragic hero. He composed amusing impromptus in dialect, but most of his serious poetry imitates 'the poets of the old school'. Some of his lyrics, however, are more original, especially 'On a calm summer's night'.   JAMES OGDEN

Sources J. Nicholson, *Poems*, ed. J. James (1844) • J. Nicholson, *Poetical works*, ed. W. G. Hird (1876) • J. Ogden, 'John Nicholson: unpublished documents', *Bradford Antiquary*, pt 45 (1971), 1–15 • J. Ogden, 'John Nicholson: unpublished poems', *Bradford Antiquary*, pt 47 (1982), 37–44 • C. Forshaw, ed., *The poets of Keighley, Bingley, Haworth and district* (1891) [includes bibliography of Nicholson by C. Federer] • IGI • d. cert.

Archives Bradford Central Library, local history department, MSS • Keighley Public Library, MSS • Saltaire Public Library, MSS

Likenesses W. O. Geller, oils, *c.*1830, Bolling Hall Museum, Bradford • W. O. Geller, mezzotint (after his oil painting), BM, NPG; repro. in Nicholson, *Poems*

Nicholson, John (1821–1857), army officer in the East India Company, eldest son of Dr Alexander Nicholson, a successful Dublin physician, was born in Dublin on 11 December 1821.

Education and early army career Dr Nicholson died in 1830, leaving a widow, two daughters, and five sons. The family moved to Lisburn, co. Wicklow, where Mrs Nicholson's mother, Mrs Hogg, resided, and from there to Delgany, where good private tuition was obtained for the children. Nicholson afterwards went to Dungannon College. His uncle, James Weir Hogg, obtained a cadetship for him in the Bengal infantry. He was commissioned ensign on 24 February 1839 and embarked for India, arriving in Calcutta in July. He joined for duty at Benares and was attached to the 41st native infantry. In December 1839 he was posted to the 27th native infantry at Ferozepore.

John Nicholson (1821–1857), by Kilburn

Afghanistan, 1840–1842 In October 1840 Nicholson accompanied the regiment to Jalalabad in Afghanistan. In July 1841 he went with it to Peshawar to bring up a convoy under Major Broadfoot, and on the return of the regiment to Jalalabad it was sent on to Kabul, and from there to Ghazni, to join the garrison there under Colonel Palmer. When Ghazni was attacked in December 1841 by the Afghans, young Nicholson took a prominent part in the defence. The garrison was greatly outnumbered, and eventually had to withdraw to the citadel; there it held out until the middle of March, when Palmer felt compelled to make terms, and an agreement was signed with the Afghan leaders by which a safe conduct to the Punjab frontier was secured for the British troops. The British force was then placed in quarters in a part of the town just below the citadel. The Afghan leaders, however, then attacked the British troops on 7 April. Lieutenants Crawford and Nicholson, with two companies of the 27th native infantry, were in a house on the left of those occupied by the British, and received the first and sharpest attack. They were cut off from the rest; their house was fired by the enemy and they were driven from room to room, fighting against odds for their lives, until at midnight of 9 April they found themselves exhausted with fatigue, hunger, and thirst, the house nearly burnt down, the ammunition expended, the place full of dead and dying men, and the position no longer tenable. The front was in the hands of the Afghans, but Nicholson and Crawford did not lose heart. A hole was dug with bayonets with

much labour through the wall of the back of the house, and those who were left of the party managed to join Colonel Palmer. The British troops, however, were ultimately made prisoners, the sepoys enslaved, and the Europeans confined in dungeons. In August they were moved to Kabul, where they joined the other British captives, were kindly treated, and after a few days moved to Bamian. In the meantime major-generals George Pollock and William Nott were advancing on Kabul from Jalalabad and from Kandahar, and the prisoners, having opened communication with Pollock and bribed their gaolers, on 17 September met the force which Pollock had sent to rescue them.

The Punjab, 1843–1857 On the return of the army to India, Nicholson was made adjutant of his regiment on 31 May 1843. In 1845 he passed the interpreters' examination, and was given an appointment in the commissariat. In this capacity he served in the campaign in the Sutlej, during the war with the Sikhs, and was present at the battle of Ferozeshahr. At the end of the war Nicholson was selected, with Captain Broome of the artillery, to instruct the troops of the maharaja of Kashmir. The appointment was made by the governor-general, Lord Hardinge, at the request of Sir Henry Montgomery Lawrence. Nicholson had made the acquaintance of both Henry and George Lawrence in Afghanistan; the latter had been a fellow captive, and the former, now at the head of the council of regency of the Punjab, had not forgotten Nicholson.

Nicholson reached Jammu on 2 April 1846, and remained there with Maharaja Gulab Singh until the end of July, when he accompanied him to Kashmir. The Sikh governor, however, refused to recognize the new maharaja, and Nicholson avoided capture only by hastily escaping by one of the southern passes. Lawrence himself put down the insurrection, and in November Nicholson was again settled at Kashmir, officiating in the north-west frontier agency. In December Nicholson was appointed an assistant to the resident at Lahore. He left Kashmir on 7 February 1847, and went to Multan on the right bank of the Indus. Later he spent a few weeks with his chief, Henry Lawrence, at Lahore, and in June was sent on a special mission to Amritsar, to report on the general management of that district. In July he was appointed to the charge of the Sind Sagar Doab, a country lying between the Jhelum and the Indus. His first duty was the protection of the people from the chiefs; his next was the care of the army, with attention to discipline and drill.

In August Nicholson was called upon by Captain James Abbott to move a force upon Simalkand, whose chief had in vain been cited to answer for the murder of women and children at Bukkur. Nicholson arrived on 3 August and took possession. He was promoted captain on 20 March 1848. In the spring of 1848 Mulraj rebelled and seized Multan. As the summer advanced the rebellion spread, and Nicholson, who at the time was down with fever at Peshawar, hurried from his sick bed to secure Attock. He made a forced march with sixty Peshawar horse and 150 newly raised Muslim levies, and arrived at Attock just in time to save the place. From Attock he scoured the country, putting down rebellion and bringing mutinous troops to reason. But he felt uneasy at leaving Attock and, at his request, Lawrence sent Lieutenant Herbert to him to act as governor of the Attock Fort. On Herbert's arrival on 1 September Nicholson at once started off for the Margala Pass to stop Sirdar Chattar Singh and his force and turn them back. The defile was commanded by a tower, which Nicholson endeavoured to storm, leading the assault; but he was wounded, and his men fell back. The garrison were, however, sufficiently frightened to evacuate the place during the night.

When the Second Anglo-Sikh War began Nicholson's services were invaluable. He provided boats for Sir Joseph Thackwell to cross the Chenab and supplies for his troops, and kept him informed of the movements of the enemy. At Chilianwala he was with Lord Gough, to whom he rendered services which were cordially acknowledged in the dispatch of the commander-in-chief. Again, at the crowning victory of Gujrat, he earned the thanks of his chief. With a party of irregulars on 23 February 1849 he secured nine guns of the enemy. He accompanied Sir Walter Raleigh Gilbert in his pursuit of the Sikhs, and day by day kept Lawrence informed of the movements of the force. For his services he was promoted brevet major on 7 June 1849. On the annexation of the Punjab, Nicholson was appointed a deputy commissioner under the Lahore board, of which Sir Henry Lawrence was president. In December 1849 he obtained furlough to Europe, and left Bombay in January 1850, visiting Constantinople and Vienna, and arriving in England at the end of April. During his furlough he visited the chief cities of continental Europe and studied the military systems of the different powers.

Nicholson returned to India at the end of 1851, and for the next five years worked as an administrative officer at Bannu, being promoted brevet lieutenant-colonel on 28 November 1854. The character of his frontier administration was remarkable. He reduced those regarded as the most ungovernable people in the Punjab to such a state of order and respect for law that in the last year of his charge there was no crime of murder or highway robbery committed or even attempted. Lord Dalhousie spoke of him at this time as 'a tower of strength'. Sir Herbert Benjamin Edwardes thought him as fit to be commissioner of a civil division as general of an army. A story dating from this period, that appears in many accounts of Nicholson's life, is that his courage and his fairness in administering justice so impressed the Punjabi villagers that they began to worship him as a god, known as Nikkul Seyn. The truth seems to be that in 1848 a mendicant holy man, impressed by Nicholson's ruthless, and often cruel, use of power, tried to get in his good graces by erecting a shrine to him. He succeeded in getting others who feared the strange officer to join in making offerings both at the shrine and to Nicholson in person in order to gain favour and to protect themselves from his wrath. Growing weary of this attention the young Nicholson responded in a characteristic fashion: he flogged and imprisoned his devotees. It was

this attitude that led his superior, Sir John Lawrence, to warn him not to hang people without evidence, and to use the courts.

The mutiny and Nicholson's death, 1857 When the Indian mutiny broke out and the news of the outbreak at Meerut and the seizure of Delhi reached the Punjab in May 1857 Nicholson was deputy commissioner at Peshawar. At once movable columns under Chamberlain and Reed were formed, while Cotton, Edwardes, and Nicholson watched the frontier. In May the news of the outbreak of two sepoy regiments at Naushahra reached Peshawar. The sepoy regiment at Peshawar was at once disarmed, and Nicholson accompanied a column to Mardan to deal with the mutinous 55th native infantry from Naushahra. No sooner did the force appear near Mardan than the mutineers fled towards the hills of Swat. Nicholson, with a handful of horsemen, pursued and charged them. They broke and dispersed, but the detached parties were followed to the borders of Swat, where a remnant escaped.

On the appointment of Brigadier-General Chamberlain to the post of adjutant-general, Nicholson was selected to succeed him, on 22 June 1857, in the command of the Punjab movable column, with the rank of brigadier-general. He joined the column at Phillaur. There were two suspected sepoy regiments in the force whom it was necessary to disarm without giving them a chance to mutiny and massacre, or to break away beforehand with their arms. Nicholson ordered the whole column to march on Delhi, and so arranged the order of march that the suspected regiments believed themselves to be trusted, but, on arriving at the camping ground, found themselves in front of the guns and surrounded by the rest of the force. They were at once ordered to pile arms, and only eight men even tried to escape.

On 28 June Nicholson, with the movable column, left Phillaur and returned to Amritsar, arriving on 5 July. Here Nicholson heard that a regiment had risen at Jhelum, and that there had been a revolt at Sialkot, in which many Europeans had been murdered. These mutineers, having cast off their allegiance to the British government, were hastening to join the rebels at Delhi. Nicholson determined to intercept them. He made a rapid march with European troops under a July sun to Gurdaspur. At noon on 12 July he found the mutineers at Trimmu Ghat. In less than half an hour they were in full retreat towards the Ravi River, leaving over 300 killed and wounded. Nicholson had no cavalry, and was unable to pursue. He therefore withdrew to Gurdaspur. The rebels re-formed on the other side of the river. Nicholson found on the 14th that the mutineers had taken up a position on an island in the Ravi River, and had run up a battery at the water's edge. By the 16th Nicholson had prepared boats in which to cross to the island. He advanced his guns to the riverbank and opened a heavy fire, drawing the attention of the enemy, while he got his infantry across to one extremity of the island, and, placing himself at their head, advanced upon the enemy. The battery was carried and the gunners bayoneted. Soon the mutineers were all either killed or driven into the water.

Nicholson returned to Amritsar with the column, and then went on to Lahore. He arrived at Lahore on 21 July and received orders to march his force on Delhi without delay. On 24 July he rejoined the movable column. The following day he crossed the Bias River, and pushed on rapidly. When the column approached Karnal he posted on ahead, by desire of General Wilson, who was commanding at Delhi, in order that he might consult with him. After examining all the posts and batteries round Delhi he rejoined his column, and marched with it into the camp at Delhi on 14 August.

Realizing that the enemy were manoeuvring to get behind the British, Nicholson was directed to attack them. He marched out in very wet weather; the way was difficult, and he had to cross two swamps and a deep, broad ford over a branch of the Najafgarh. In the afternoon of 25 August he found the enemy in position on his front and left, extending some 2 miles from the canal to the town of Najafgarh. Nicholson attacked the left centre, forced the position, and swept down the enemy's line of guns towards the bridge, putting the enemy (6000 strong) to flight, and capturing thirteen guns and the enemy's camp equipment. Congratulations poured in. General Wilson wrote to thank him. Sir John Lawrence telegraphed from Lahore: 'I wish I had the power of knighting you on the spot. It should be done.' In further proof of his appreciation of Nicholson's services, the chief commissioner wrote to him on 9 September that he had recommended him for the appointment of commissioner of Leia.

On the morning of 14 September the assault of Delhi took place, and Nicholson commanded the main storming-party. The breach was carried, and the column, headed by Nicholson, forced its way over the ramparts into the city and pushed on. Conspicuous at the head of his men, Nicholson was shot through the chest. In agony, he was placed on a litter and carried to a hospital tent; he lingered until 23 September. He was buried in the new burial-ground in front of the Kashmir Gate in Delhi, and near Ludlow Castle. He had never married.

Following his death Nicholson was much praised by soldiers and civilians. The queen announced that if Nicholson had survived he would have been made a KCB. The East India Company, in recognition of his services, voted his mother a pension of £500 a year. A committed evangelical and a courageous soldier, Nicholson became a Victorian imperial hero, 'the saviour of Delhi'.

Some later writers have not been sympathetic to Nicholson. His ferocious hatred of the mutineers and the civilian population of Delhi has often been cited, sometimes unfairly, as representative of British opinion. He reminded his piously approving mother that the Bible states that 'stripes shall be meted out according to faults'. In his accounts of the killing of hundreds of fleeing Indian soldiers, mixed with reference to the just vengeance of the God of Battles, some have perceived a tortured sadism. If he had his way, he wrote, the rebels would get 'flaying alive, impalement or burning'; 'I would inflict the most excruciating tortures I could think of.' Yet such views were repellent to many Punjab officials. Some of his fellow officers, while extolling his handsome, commanding figure, his courage and endurance, found him arrogant and self-righteous but shy and reticent.

R. H. VETCH, rev. AINSLIE T. EMBREE

Sources L. J. Trotter, *The life of John Nicholson, soldier and administrator* (1898) · R. H. Haigh and P. W. Turner, *Nickalsain: the life and times of John Nicholson* (1980) · H. Pearson, *The hero of Delhi: a life of John Nicholson* (1939) · E. J. Thompson, *The other side of the medal* (1926) · C. Hibbert, *The great mutiny, India, 1857* (1978) · J. W. Kaye and G. B. Malleson, *Kaye's and Malleson's History of the Indian mutiny of 1857–8*, new edn, 6 vols. (1909) · C. Raikes, *Notes on the revolt in the north-west provinces of India* (1858) · East-India Register and Army List (1858)

Archives BL OIOC, corresp., MS Eur. F 171 · BL OIOC, corresp. and papers, MS Eur. E 211

Likenesses W. Carpenter, chalk drawing, 1854, NPG · J. H. Foley, monument, 1862, Lisburn church, co. Wicklow · T. Brock, bronze statue, *c*.1904, Nicholson Garden, Delhi · J. R. Dicksee, oils (posthumous), County Museum, Armagh; copy by C. Vivian, East India and Sports Club, London · T. Farrell, bust (after J. H. Foley), East India and Sports Club · Kilburn, daguerreotype, NPG [*see illus.*] · J. W. Knight, stipple (after daguerreotype by Kilburn), NPG · eight portraits, BL OIOC · wood-engraving (after photograph by Savory), NPG; repro. in *ILN* (31 Oct 1857)

Nicholson, John Miller (1840–1913), artist and photographer, was born on 29 January 1840 at Church Street, Douglas, Isle of Man, the eldest of the three sons of William Nicholson (*c*.1818–1878), house painter and decorator, and his first wife, Christian (*c*.1812–1844), daughter of John Bell, a shipwright, of Douglas and his wife, Isabella. His father was Cumbrian and his mother was Manx. Nicholson was educated at the Douglas diocesan grammar school where the principal, Mr Pearson, soon discovered the boy's artistic talents and encouraged him. A natural draughtsman, Nicholson spent much of his spare time copying pictures, or engravings, from books and magazines, and this early training was to serve him well as an artist in later life. On leaving school he joined his father's painting and decorating business in Well Road Hill, Douglas, as an apprentice painter, but he also continued to develop his artistic talents.

With a passion for the sea inherited from his grandfather, a mariner and owner of three brigs in Whitehaven, Nicholson could be seen every morning before starting work on Douglas shore sketching in pencil the sunrise and the effect of the light on the sea and the land. At other times he would be on the bustling Douglas quayside sketching the people, the buildings, or the vessels in the harbour. Nicholson's pencil sketches are meticulously drawn and works of art in themselves with minute notes written in the margins recording the time, date, weather conditions, and colours. He became so adept that he could complete a sketch within thirty minutes. Years later he would return to these sketchbooks for reference and paint an oil painting, or watercolour, from one of the drawings. John Ruskin purchased a number of Nicholson's pencil sketches at £5 each, so highly did he regard them, and distributed them to art galleries throughout Britain to be kept in their permanent collections. Nicholson regularly corresponded with Ruskin, sending him sketches and pictures for assessment, to which Ruskin replied with constructive criticism. On 1 November 1870 he married Ann Jane Coole (c.1841–1931); they had a son and a daughter.

From 1873 Nicholson exhibited frequently at Liverpool, Manchester, Birmingham, and at the Grosvenor Gallery, London, where his pictures were often purchased on the day the exhibition opened. At one such exhibition he was offered 1 guinea per square inch for as many pictures as he could supply, but Nicholson bluntly refused the offer.

In 1880 John Ruskin wrote to Nicholson, telling him 'but you are cramped and chilled by Isle of Mansiness—you ought to take knapsack on shoulder—a grey paper book—half a dozen colours and a bit of chalk—and so walk to Naples and back' (Kelly, 6). Eventually, in the spring of 1882 Nicholson travelled to Italy, where he planned to spend three months studying the architecture and the old masters, but he returned after only six weeks, denouncing southern Italy as ugly and dirty. However, he had drawn sketches on his travels and on his return he painted a number of large oil paintings of Venice and Verona. These paintings were much more impressionistic, in the style of Turner, with the detail suppressed, but definite values given to colour, light, shade, composition, and atmosphere. When he exhibited two of the oil paintings of Venice in London they were highly praised by the art critics and demand for his pictures grew. This adulation so embarrassed Nicholson, whose shyness had increased rather than diminished, that he stopped exhibiting anywhere other than the Isle of Man. But for his aversion to public acclaim, and his non-commercial attitude, Nicholson would have ranked with the best of the Victorian painters.

In August 1918 the Baume trustees purchased for £1000 the whole of the 'Studio Collection of 57 Pictures' of the late John Miller Nicholson, which had been advertised for public auction on 8 August in the Masonic Hall, Douglas. In 1927 the trustees entered into an agreement with the Manx Museum that the collection be kept and displayed there, and following further bequests and purchases over 100 examples of his work are now held.

Nicholson's artistic talents were not confined to oil paintings and watercolours. Also an accomplished photographer, he recorded scenes around Douglas, particularly depicting the promenade, harbour, and quayside, and in 1891 he won three medals, at the Liverpool international exhibition, the Leeds international exhibition and the Gloucestershire Photographic Society exhibition. Locally, his illuminated addresses were in great demand, which incorporated a watercolour of a Manx scene, together with carefully executed lettering, at which Nicholson excelled. When *The Manx Note Book* magazine was published in January 1885 the editor, A. W. Moore, asked Nicholson to produce the sketches, initial letters, and tail pieces. In the twelve issues that were printed between 1885 and 1887 there are over 150 illustrations drawn by Nicholson.

The painting and decorating business, in partnership with his brother, James Bell Nicholson, also produced some artistic work of great merit, especially in ecclesiastical decoration. In St German's Cathedral at Peel there are paintings of the four evangelists and six Old Testament figures executed upon oak panels by Nicholson in May 1885, but the finest examples of his work are the murals in St Thomas's Church, Douglas. These were painted by Nicholson between 1896 and 1910, with James undertaking all the lettering to the texts. Now recognized as being 'of world importance', the murals were restored in 1998 at a cost of over £250,000.

When Joseph E. Douglas wrote his biography of John Miller Nicholson in 1931 the printers unfortunately misspelt Nicholson's middle name as 'Millar' throughout the book. This led to some confusion in later literature and exhibitions, but was finally corrected in the 1990s. Nicholson died on 24 March 1913 at 1 Laureston Terrace, Douglas, Isle of Man, and was buried in Douglas cemetery on 27 March.   ALAN E. KELLY

Sources J. E. Douglas, *John Millar Nicholson, 1840–1913* (1931) · M. Ingram and others, eds., *Art of Mann* (1996) · A. Knox, 'John Miller Nicholson', *Mannin*, 1/1 (May 1913), 25–7 · *Special exhibition of the work of John Millar Nicholson*, Manx Museum (1965), 11 · M. Douglas, 'Pathfinders in painting', *This is Ellan Vannin* (1968), 112–15 · V. Roach, *Douglas in the 1890s: the photographs of John Millar Nicholson* (1985) · P. Kelly, *The Nicholson murals in St Thomas's Church* (1985) · J. E. Douglas, 'John M. Nicholson', *Manx Quarterly*, 12 (June 1913), 1212–15 · *Index of monumental inscriptions, Douglas borough cemetery*, Isle of Man Family History Society [n.d.] · *Monumental inscriptions, Douglas borough cemetery, blocks E to K*, Isle of Man Family History Society [n.d.] · *Douglas borough burial register, 1889–1989, book 2, K–Z*, Isle of Man Family History Society [n.d.] · S. Harrison, 'John Miller Nicholson, 1840–1913', *100 years of heritage* (1986), 102–5

Archives Manx National Heritage, Douglas, Isle of Man, collection | Manx National Heritage, Douglas, Isle of Man, Baume collection of Nicholson pictures

Likenesses J. M. Nicholson, self-portrait, oils, 1870, Manx National Heritage, Douglas · J. M. Nicholson, self-portrait, pen and ink, 1879, Manx National Heritage, Douglas · photograph, c.1900, Manx National Heritage, Douglas

Nicholson, John William (1881–1955), mathematical physicist, was born on 1 November 1881 at 7 High Terrace, Darlington, first child of John William Nicholson (b. c.1853), ironworks clerk (afterwards a works manager, of Redcar), and his wife, Alice Emily (b. c.1860), daughter of John Kirton, painter. Nicholson had a brother and two sisters. From Middlesbrough high school he went to the University of Manchester where he graduated BSc in physics in 1902 and MSc in 1905. He went to Trinity College, Cambridge, in 1902 and was equal tenth wrangler in part one of the mathematical tripos of 1904 and gained a 1:2 in part two in 1905. He won the Isaac Newton studentship in 1906 and numerous other awards and prizes. He also took a London BSc (second class in mathematics, first class in experimental physics, 1903) and DSc (1906).

In 1912 Nicholson was appointed (controversially, as there was an established internal candidate) professor of mathematics in the University of London at King's College. He collaborated there with T. R. Merton on the measurement and interpretation of spectral line intensities. Balliol College, Oxford, recruited him as fellow and tutor in mathematics and physics in 1921, and he became a university lecturer in mathematics at Oxford in 1927. He was elected to the Royal Society in 1917 (council member 1920–21), and was an influential member of many scientific bodies, including the Royal Astronomical Society (a fellow from 1911), the Röntgen Society (president 1921–2), and the British Association committee on mathematical tables (chairman 1920–30).

Nicholson assisted Arthur Schuster with the third edition of *An Introduction to the Theory of Optics* (1924), and made some ninety journal contributions on diverse topics. His most significant work was on an atomic structure model he derived from a study of unassigned lines in the spectra of stellar nebulae and the solar corona. This he unveiled at the Portsmouth British Association meeting of August 1911, and developed in *Monthly Notices of the Royal Astronomical Society* during 1912. In his first note (dated from Trinity College, 25 October 1911), he described an atomic model comprising a tiny heavy positively charged nucleus around which electrons rotated in a circular orbit equidistant from each other. A four-electron element which he called 'nebulium' was identified as the origin of the mysterious nebular lines, which he was able to account for quantitatively using the model. Turning to the coronal spectra, a further protoelement, 'protofluorine', was proposed. In his second note about it (dated again from Trinity, 28 April 1912) he introduced Planck's constant into his analysis, suggesting that 'the angular momentum of an atom can only rise or fall by discrete amounts'. He appears to have been the first to relate quantum theory to atomic spectra. Niels Bohr knew of Nicholson's work and discussed it in the first of his 1913 trilogy on atomic structure (*Philosophical Magazine*, July 1913), tactfully objecting (*inter alia*) that Nicholson's model was inherently unstable. In his old age, Bohr was more dismissive: 'It was a play with numbers', he said (Bohr).

In 1922, with the Astronomer Royal and the mistress of Girton among the witnesses, Nicholson married Dorothy Maud *Wrinch (1894–1976), feminist and mathematician. In 1930, as Jean Ayling, she published a polemic on marriage and parenthood, *Retreat from Parenthood*. The couple had one child, Pamela (1927–1975). In the later twenties Nicholson published little and his teaching deteriorated. In May 1930 he was treated in Norwood Sanatorium for alcoholism. Shortly afterwards a conjugal separation was agreed. On 12 October 1930 he was removed from Balliol to the Warneford Hospital in Oxford, where he was confined as a certified lunatic. Incurable insanity became a ground for divorce by the Matrimonial Causes Act of 1937; Nicholson and Wrinch were divorced in 1938. He died at the Warneford from heart disease on 10 October 1955. His funeral was held at Redcar four days later. Nicholson had made a will in favour of Wrinch on their wedding day; it was proved on her behalf despite their divorce and her remarriage.   JOHN JONES

Sources R. McCormmach, 'The atomic theory of John William Nicholson', *Archive for History of Exact Sciences*, 3 (1966–7), 160–84 · W. Wilson, *Memoirs FRS*, 2 (1956), 209–14 · P. G. Abir-Am, 'Synergy or clash: disciplinary and marital strategies in the career of mathematical biologist Dorothy Wrinch', *Uneasy careers and intimate lives: women in science, 1789–1979*, ed. P. G. Abir-Am and D. Outram (1987), 239–80 · Balliol Oxf., archives, MBP 49 and 49* · King's Lond., J. W. Nicholson MSS, KA/FPA/1921 · J. I. Heilbron and T. S. Kuhn, 'The genesis of the Bohr atom', *Historical Studies in the Physical Sciences*, 1 (1969), 211–90 · editorial, *Engineering* (29 Sept 1911), 417–18 [summary of J. W. Nicholson's paper, 'The atomic structure of the elements, with theoretical determinations of the atomic weight', read at the British Association meeting, 1911] · N. Bohr, transcript of an interview with T. S. Kuhn, L. Rosenfeld, E. Rüdinger, and A. Petersen, 7 Nov 1962, American Institute of Physics, College Park, Maryland, Niels Bohr Library · b. cert. · d. cert.

Archives Balliol Oxf., financial matters relating to Nicholson's lunacy · Balliol Oxf., MSS and corresp. · King's Lond., personal file

Likenesses Maull & Fox, photograph, c.1922, repro. in *Journal of the Röntgen Society*, 18 (1922) · photograph, c.1925, repro. in Wilson, *Memoirs FRS*, facing p. 209

Wealth at death £1911 2s. 1d.: administration, 28 Dec 1955, *CGPLA Eng. & Wales*

Nicholson, Joseph Shield (1850–1927), economist, the only son of the Revd Thomas Nicholson, Independent minister at Banbury, and his wife, Mary Anne Grant, was born at Wrawby, Lincolnshire, on 9 November 1850. His education began at a preparatory school at Lewisham. After attending classes at King's College, London, he matriculated there in 1867, and gained his BA with high honours in 1870. From 1872 to 1873 he studied at Edinburgh University. In 1873 he went to Trinity College, Cambridge, where he graduated with a first class in the moral sciences tripos in 1876. In 1877, the year of its institution, and again in 1880, Nicholson was awarded the Cobden (triennial) prize. The earlier of his prize essays, published in 1878 under the title of *The Effects of Machinery on Wages*, gained for him the Cambridge degree of ScD. In 1877 he was placed first in the London MA examination (philosophy branch) and obtained the Gerstenberg prize for special distinction in political economy. Subsequently, accompanied by his friend James George Frazer, he went to Heidelberg, where he attended lectures, chiefly on law, at the university.

From 1876 to 1880 Nicholson was a private tutor at Cambridge; he lectured on English history at Trinity College, and took an active part in the extra-mural teaching of the university. For two years (1878–80) he lectured on political economy for the Association for the Higher Education of Women in Cambridge. In the early days of the Cambridge chess club (founded 1871) Nicholson was an outstanding player, and a member of the team which, in 1874, defeated Oxford for the first time. In later years he became widely known through the chess column of *The Times* as a subtle composer and solver of chess problems. Nicholson was also devoted to boating and fishing, and he was an accomplished swimmer. His vacations at this period were usually spent in the north of Scotland, and his daring exploits in the seas around Cape Wrath and in the lochs of Sutherland became a tradition of the district.

In 1880, before he was thirty, Nicholson was elected to the chair of political economy and mercantile law at the University of Edinburgh. He arrived in Edinburgh from

Joseph Shield Nicholson (1850–1927), by Henry Lintott, 1926

Cambridge with a reputation as a hard worker and as a teacher of great ability, who could expound economic principles with lucidity and bring them into close and intelligible relation with the problems of the day. This reputation he fully justified throughout the whole period of forty-five years during which he held the chair. As professor he maintained the highest Scottish traditions. His teachings and his writings played a definite and important part in the formation of public opinion. On questions of imperial economic policy and of currency and banking he attained a position of exceptional authority. In the difficult period of war finance his counsel and consistent teaching did much to keep depreciation of currency within remediable limits. There were few teachers of his time in Scotland who did more to bring academic life into touch with that of the community. He was the pioneer of economic history in Scotland, and during his professorship his department grew until it included nearly half as many teachers as there had originally been students.

Nicholson was fourteen years in writing his main work, *Principles of Economics*. Even when he started, the subject's growing complexity and specialization were making the general treatise a difficult achievement. P. H. Wicksteed's *Common Sense of Political Economy* (1910) excepted, Nicholson's was the last successful attempt to bring it off. The book also seemed old-fashioned by its omission of the marginal principle, which by then had come to dominate economics, at any rate at its academic leading edge. But its merits—vitality, lucid style, and skilful interweaving of theory and historical evidence—were immediately appreciated. To Nicholson himself, it was his political views,

rather than his approach to economics, that were becoming obsolete. 'It is not pleasant', he told the Edinburgh chamber of commerce in 1893, 'for a man at my time of life to be accused of being reactionary, old-fashioned and fossilised.' Nicholson was referring to his hostility to trade unions, which he considered just another form of monopoly: but his economic liberalism in general had faded from fashion as reformers devised ever more tasks for the state to perform. But, however uncomplicated his ideology and aggressive his defence of it, he was never an inflexible doctrinaire on practical questions of economic policy. Indeed his ability to present with equal pungency, if not equal conviction, both sides of a question make his *The Effect of Machinery on Wages* (1879), *Essays on Present Monetary Problems* (1888), *The Tariff Problem* (1903), and the policy-oriented sections of the *Principles* among the most worthwhile economic writing of the age. Only the later work, *Inflation* (1919), lapses into the empty rhetoric which disfigures much of his directly political writing. For the most part he was a conciliatory bimetallist, a moderate under-consumptionist, a pragmatic free-trader, and a subtle defender of the quantity theory of money.

No estimate of Nicholson's personality would be complete without a reference to his literary activities of a lighter kind. His romance *A Dreamer of Dreams* (1889) is very revealing as a human document, while the other two—*Thoth* (1888) and *Toxar* (1890)—in their allegorical undertones give many of his views on life and its problems. The link between these and his books on Ariosto—*Tales from Ariosto* (1913) and *Life and Genius of Ariosto* (1914)—is to be found in the position assigned to Ariosto as 'the father of modern romance'.

Nicholson was an honorary LLD of the universities of St Andrews (1911) and Edinburgh (1916), FRSE (1884), FBA (1903), and medallist of the Statistical Society (1918). In 1885 he married Jeanie, daughter of William Ballantyne *Hodgson, his predecessor in the chair of political economy at Edinburgh. They had one son (who died of wounds in the First World War) and two daughters. In 1925 Nicholson resigned his chair owing to an illness. He died at Edinburgh on 12 May 1927, following an operation.

Nicholson's likes and dislikes were never anything but transparent. A clear mind, a warm temperament, and a forceful style make him the most readable of the economists of his day. Even his devotion to Adam Smith is attractive, loyal but not uncritical, admiring but not unctuous. When Nicholson died, *The Times* wrote that 'he knew his *Wealth of Nations* as thoroughly as the Scottish peasant knows his Bible, and believed in it almost as thoroughly'. Certainly, it would involve a long search to find a truer disciple of Adam Smith.

W. R. SCOTT, *rev.* JOHN MALONEY

Sources *The Times* (13 May 1927) · *University of Edinburgh Journal*, 2 (1927–8) · W. R. Scott, 'Joseph Shield Nicholson, 1850–1927', *PBA*, 13 (1927), 346–67 · J. Maloney, *The professionalisation of economics* (1991) · private information (1937) · personal knowledge (1937)
Archives U. Edin. L., lecture notes | BL, corresp. with Macmillans, Add. MS 55209 · BLPES, letters to Edwin Cannan · NL Scot., corresp. with Blackwoods · SOAS, letters to Sir Charles

Addis · U. Cam., Marshall Library of Economics, letters to John Neville Keynes
Likenesses W. Stoneman, photograph, 1919, NPG · H. Lintott, portrait, 1926, U. Edin. [*see illus.*] · W. Hole, etching, NPG; repro. in *Quasi cursores* (1884)
Wealth at death £3787 18s. 7d.: probate, 1927, *CGPLA Eng. & Wales*

Nicholson, Joshua (1812–1885), silk manufacturer, was born on 26 October 1812 at Luddendenfoot near Halifax, Yorkshire, the youngest son of Joshua Nicholson, a builder, and his wife, Rachel (*née* Kitchen), and baptized at Warley Congregational Church on 25 July 1813. He was apprenticed to a well-known Bradford silk mercer named Turner. His childhood was hard but he set about educating himself while at Bradford and first became interested in liberalism. After a short stay in Huddersfield he went to Leek in January 1837 working as a traveller for the silk manufacturing firm of J. and J. Brough & Co. The same year, on 13 September, he married Ellen Oldfield, the daughter of John Oldfield, a saddler of Wakefield, at St John's Church, Wakefield; they had four children. The eldest son, Joshua Oldfield, became a silk warehouseman in Macclesfield, Arthur became a partner in his father's firm and later received a knighthood, and Harry Edwin, the youngest son, died as a result of a railway accident aged twenty-two years. The daughter, Mary Elizabeth, married Frederick Eastwood, a woollen manufacturer in Huddersfield.

Nicholson became a partner in the firm of J. and J. Brough in 1856, and when the Brough brothers retired in 1869 he became head of the firm, which then consisted of himself, B. B. Nixon, W. S. Brough, Arthur Nicholson, Edwin Brough, and John Hall. From the early 1860s he acquired considerable wealth as the firm over the next two decades made increasing profits, some of which were invested in the construction of large mills in the Fountain Street area. Leek's position as the only town in England primarily engaged in producing sewing threads meant that it was relatively unaffected by the increased foreign competition after 1860 (unlike Spitalfields, Coventry, and Macclesfield). The Leek Embroidery Society, which was established in 1868, probably encouraged the sale of silk thread. In the 1880s braids were also extensively made.

On arrival in Leek, Nicholson helped to establish a mechanics' institute. Like many silk manufacturers he was a staunch admirer of Richard Cobden and hoped to form a Cobden Club. However, his enlarging wealth encouraged him to attempt to provide general cultural facilities: his plans were announced in autumn 1881, when his health was already declining, and work on the Nicholson Institute began in January 1882.

The institute, which finally cost about £30,000, was opened in October 1884 with considerable ceremony. The library and reading rooms contained about 6000 books of great variety chosen by Nicholson's son Joshua. An inaugural exhibition was held in the art gallery, which included works by Titian, Canaletto, Rubens, Reynolds, and Rossetti. Both the news room and the art gallery were to be open until 10 p.m., but the art classes were held during the day. Lectures were given by prominent persons both national and local, including William Morris. However, the entry charge of 5s. was too much for the average silk operative.

Nicholson became a trustee of the newly erected Derby Street Congregational Church in 1861, and funded the independent churches generously. He was also a prominent Liberal in the county, serving as president of the North Staffordshire Liberal Association, and giving financial support to the Liberal cause and its free trade policies.

Nicholson died on 24 August 1885, of 'general decay' after a prolonged illness, at his home, Stockwell House, Stockwell Street; he was buried in Leek cemetery. Unlike his son Arthur, who moved to a country estate, he never left Leek, always living close to his mills. After his death the Congregationalist minister, Josiah Hankinson, spoke of his 'imperious will, force and individuality of character', remarking that he was 'outspoken to a degree' and had 'fearless, unswerving loyalty to his religious convictions'. SARAH BUSH

Sources *Leek Times* (19 Nov 1881) · *Leek Times* (18 Oct 1884) · *Leek Times* (29 Aug 1885) · *Leek Times* (5 Sept 1885) · Brough, Nicholson and Hall Ltd records, D 4241/5/1, D4241/4/27, D4241/4/28 · P. Smith, *The Nicholson Institute, Leek* (1984), 8, 27 · Staffs. RO, Dartmouth MSS · H. Woodhead, *The story of a Leek church* (1988), 67 · G. A. Lovenbury, *A certain group of men* (1989) · *CGPLA Eng. & Wales* (1885)
Archives Staffs. RO, records of Brough, Nicholson and Hall Ltd | Staffs. RO, Brough MSS, letters relating to Davenport, Brough, and Brindley, Leek
Likenesses Sandeman & Hodgson, photograph · engravings (after photograph by Sandeman & Hodgson), repro. in H. Warrington, *About Leek*, 3
Wealth at death £48,013 11s. 9d.: probate, 28 Oct 1885, *CGPLA Eng. & Wales*

Nicholson, Sir Lothian (1827–1893), army officer, third son of George Thomas Nicholson of Waverley Abbey, near Farnham, Surrey, and Anne Elizabeth, daughter of William Smith, MP for Norwich, was born at Ham Common, Surrey, on 19 January 1827. He was educated at Mr Malleson's school at Hove, and in 1844 entered the Royal Military Academy, Woolwich. On 6 August 1846 he was commissioned second lieutenant, Royal Engineers (first lieutenant on 26 January 1847). After the usual Chatham course he was sent, in January 1849, to North America, and spent two years between Halifax, Nova Scotia, and New Brunswick. On his return to England he was stationed at Portsmouth, and on 1 April 1855 was promoted second captain. In July he was sent to the Crimea. He served in the trenches during the last month of the siege of Sevastopol, in command of the 4th company, Royal Engineers, which he also commanded in the expedition to Kinburn. He helped demolish the Sevastopol docks, was mentioned in dispatches, received the Mejidiye (5th class), and was promoted brevet major on 2 November 1855.

Nicholson returned home in June 1856 and was stationed at Aldershot, where he was employed in laying out the new camp. On 6 October 1857 he embarked with the 4th company, Royal Engineers, for Calcutta to take part in the suppression of the Indian mutiny. On arrival in India he joined Lord Clyde and served for some time on his staff. He repaired the suspension bridge over the Kali Nadi, on the road to Fatehgarh, and so enabled a rapid march to be made to Fatehgarh and many stores and other government property to be secured. He was at the action of the Alambagh and at the siege and final capture of Lucknow, when he commanded the Royal Engineers on the left bank of the river and constructed the bridges over the Gumti. Nicholson remained at Lucknow as chief engineer to Sir Hope Grant. He served in the operations in Oudh, was at the action of Bari, and took an active part in the subjugation of the *terai*. He was superintending the construction of bridges and roads when, while out shooting, his gun exploded and he permanently injured his hand. Mentioned in dispatches, for his services he was promoted brevet lieutenant-colonel on 20 July 1858. He was made a CB in May 1859 and given the distinguished service reward.

Nicholson returned to England in May 1859, and on 20 June became a first captain in the corps. He was stationed in the Isle of Wight and was employed in the construction of the Solent defences. In 1861 he was appointed commanding royal engineer of the London or home district. On 20 July 1866 he was promoted brevet colonel, and from October 1866 to 1868 commanded the Royal Engineers at Gibraltar. From 1868 to 1872 he was assistant adjutant-general of Royal Engineers in Ireland. On 27 January 1872 he was promoted regimental lieutenant-colonel, and from then until October 1878 commanded the Royal Engineers at Shorncliffe. On 1 October 1877 he was promoted major-general and on 1 October 1878 was appointed lieutenant-governor of Jersey, and to command the troops there. He held the appointment for five years. On 19 October 1881 he was promoted lieutenant-general.

After leaving Jersey in 1883 he was unemployed until 8 July 1886, when he was appointed inspector-general of fortifications and of Royal Engineers in succession to Lieutenant-General Sir Andrew Clarke. During the time Nicholson held this important office the defence of the coaling stations abroad was in progress, and he initiated the works for revising and improving the defences of the United Kingdom under the Imperial Defence Act and for the reconstruction of barracks under the Barracks Act. In June 1887 he was made a KCB, and was colonel-commandant, Royal Engineers, from June 1890 until his death.

Nicholson married in London, on 21 November 1864, Mary (1841–1921), daughter of John Romilly, first Baron Romilly. They had seven sons and three daughters, who, with their mother, survived him. With a good constitution and energetic, Nicholson enjoyed an active life and delighted in field sports. With an intense *esprit de corps* he combined a wide sympathy with the other branches of the army and supported many philanthropic efforts. He contributed several papers to *The Professional Papers of the Corps of Royal Engineers*.

On 26 March 1891 Nicholson was appointed governor and commander-in-chief of Gibraltar. He died there on 27 June 1893, after a short attack of fever, and was buried in the cemetery at Gibraltar.

R. H. VETCH, *rev.* ROGER T. STEARN

Sources War Office MSS, PRO · *Royal Engineers Journal*, 23 (1893) · A. D. Lambert, *The Crimean War: British grand strategy, 1853–56* (1990) · G. B. Malleson, *History of the Indian mutiny, 1857–1858: commencing from the close of the second volume of Sir John Kaye's History of the Sepoy War*, 2 (1879) · C. Hibbert, *The great mutiny, India, 1857* (1978) · Boase, *Mod. Eng. biog.* · Kelly, *Handbk* · Burke, *Peerage* · E. W. C. Sandes, *The military engineer in India*, 1 (1933)
Archives NAM, Indian revolt diary · Royal Engineers Museum, Gillingham, Crimea notebook, incl. charts, maps, and plans | BL, letters to Florence Nightingale, Add. MS 45810
Likenesses oils, Royal Engineers, Chatham, Kent · wood-engraving (after photograph by Fry & Son), NPG; repro. in *ILN* (8 July 1893)
Wealth at death £8695 3s. 5d.: probate, 11 Aug 1893, *CGPLA Eng. & Wales*

Nicholson, Margaret (1750?–1828), assailant of George III, was born in Stockton-on-Tees, co. Durham, the daughter of George Nicholson, a barber of that town. She was a housemaid to several families, one of her places being in the service of Sir John Sebright. After leaving her last position she lodged for three years in the house of a stationer named Fisk, at the corner of Wigmore Street, London, supporting herself by taking in plain needlework. Although Fisk afterwards stated that 'she was very odd at times', neither he nor any of her acquaintances suspected her of insanity.

In July 1786 Nicholson sent a petition to the privy council containing delusory ramblings concerning usurpers and pretenders to the throne. On the morning of 2 August she stood with the crowd that waited at the garden entrance of St James's Palace to see the king arrive from Windsor. As he alighted from his carriage she approached him with a blank piece of paper resembling a petition, which he received. At the same moment, she attempted to stab him with an old ivory-handled dessert knife. The king evaded the first blow, but a second thrust fell closer to the mark. The king was not injured in what appeared to be a half-hearted, poorly prepared assault. After Nicholson was disarmed, the king sensed the danger she faced from outraged bystanders and cried out, 'The poor creature is mad; do not hurt her, she has not hurt me.'

Nicholson was examined by Thomas Monro (J. B.) of Bethlem Hospital (who was later to be summoned to attend the king), and brought immediately before the privy council because her crime was treason. In attendance at this hearing were the archbishop of Canterbury, Lord Sydney, the newly elected home secretary, three dukes, two earls, and three other peers. A search of Nicholson's lodgings yielded a cache of letters to public figures, replete with the delusion concerning her rightful claim to the throne, warning that 'England would be discharged with blood for a thousand years if her claims were not publicly acknowledged' (Jones, 204). Based on this discovery and the testimony of two physicians, Nicholson was declared insane and, on the order of the home secretary, committed to Bethlem for life. Non-penal placements were not unheard of in the 1700s and persons could be sent to Bethlem on the order of the sovereign or a branch of central administrative government. However, as a state prisoner, the more appropriate disposition would have been gaol. Even the formal introduction of the verdict, 'not guilty by reason of insanity', and the subsequent Criminal Lunatics Act of 1800, mandating secure confinement 'until His Majesty's pleasure be known', were silent on the precise nature of the incarceration. Persons so acquitted were routinely housed either in gaols or madhouses until the establishment, exactly 100 years after Nicholson's disposition, of Broadmoor Asylum for Criminal Lunatics. She remained in Bethlem for forty-two years until her death on 14 May 1828. Early in 1811 Percy Bysshe Shelley and Thomas Jefferson Hogg, then undergraduates at Oxford, published a thin volume of burlesque verses entitled *Posthumous Fragments of Margaret Nicholson, Edited by her Nephew, John Fitz Victor.*

Margaret Nicholson's place in the history of criminal insanity was apparently obscured by George III's kindness in interceding on her behalf and thereby substituting the privy council for an Old Bailey jury. Only the latter would have insisted on a fully articulated defence—complete with defence counsel—as witnessed in the trial of the king's subsequent assailant, James Hadfield. Both attempts at regicide sprang from political delusions, but only Hadfield's have become part of legal lore, doubtless owing to his skilful advocate, Thomas Erskine. Accordingly, Nicholson's 'trial' involved only the manifest features of her derangement. With a lifelong commitment to Bethlem the likely initial disposition, no principle of law and no standard of madness reached a level of scrutiny and debate sufficiently critical to effect a change in jurisprudence regarding insanity. Margaret Nicholson's prosecution and disposition serve instead as an exemplar of the extra-judicial manner in which one could enter Bethlem, and as further evidence of the early use of testimony by asylum superintendents in matters criminal and mental.

JOEL PETER EIGEN

Sources N. Walker, *Crime and insanity in England*, 1 (1968) · P. H. Allderidge, 'Criminal insanity: Bethlem to Broadmoor', *Proceedings of the Royal Society of Medicine*, 67 (1974), 897–904 · K. Jones, *Lunacy, law and conscience, 1744–1845: the social history of the care of the insane* (1955) · *Annual Register* (1786)

Likenesses line engraving, pubd 1786, BM, NPG · J. T. Smith, etching (in old age), BM · T. Taylor, line engraving, BM, NPG; repro. in *New Lady's Magazine* (1786) · prints, NPG

Nicholson, Marjorie (1914–1997), socialist and trade unionist, was born at 22 Cherryburn Gardens, Benwell, Newcastle upon Tyne, on 22 December 1914, the daughter of Edward Nicholson, manager of a hat factory, and his wife, Edith Emma, *née* Bone. Later the family moved to Kenton, Middlesex, and she was sent to Harrow high school. There she had an exemplary record, with high academic ratings leading to an open scholarship to read history at St Hilda's College, Oxford, the George Heelum scholarship, a Middlesex education committee senior county award, and another award from the Stapley Trust.

As an undergraduate she was thus comfortably self-supporting and obtained second-class honours in modern history in 1936. By that time she had converted from the family tradition of Conservatism to socialism, and through the Oxford University Labour Club had met G. D. H. Cole and some of the leading young socialists such as Richard Crossman and Patrick Gordon Walker, then a don at Christ Church. She became committed to Indian independence and ultimately to self-government in the British colonial empire. On leaving Oxford she taught history at East Ham Grammar School for Girls and lectured for the Workers' Educational Association. By 1941 she had returned to Oxford as the organizing tutor in history for the Oxford delegacy in extra-mural studies in Berkshire, Buckinghamshire, and Oxfordshire. Her political ambition increasing, she stood as a Labour candidate in the strongly Conservative constituency of Windsor in the first three general elections after the Second World War.

In 1945 Nicholson joined the Fabian Colonial Bureau as assistant secretary. There she forged close, enduring friendships with Rita Hinden, the secretary, and Arthur Creech Jones, the former chairman, who was then undersecretary and within a year secretary of state for the colonies. Her talents for negotiation and for writing succinct articles on colonial political and economic issues emerged at this time. This was an exhilarating period to be at the hub of Labour's interest in colonial development. The government was funding research into constitutional and economic progress, the Colonial Office and other ministries were issuing much more information about colonial issues, and interchange of ideas with emergent political leaders in the colonies had been well established. In the office of the bureau she met many of those leaders, and over the years she conducted a considerable correspondence with them. In 1950, when Rita Hinden resigned to become editor of *Socialist Commentary* and Creech Jones, out of parliament, resumed his chairmanship of the bureau, Nicholson became its secretary. The bureau then was facing financial and organizational difficulties. To widen its outlook she introduced into its journal, *Venture*, more frequent signed articles and, following discussion there of the moral issues of trusteeship, issued a questionnaire on whether the prime aim of the Labour Party's colonial policy should be political, economic, or social development. On the basis of the responses to this questionnaire she submitted for further consideration a memorandum on long-term aims for Labour. Her own view was that the colonial governments should collaborate with nationalist leaders in breaking the dependence of colonial peoples on the ruling power.

After five years Nicholson, recognizing that the bureau no longer exercised its original influence in the Labour Party, transferred to the Trades Union Congress (TUC) Commonwealth section to work on policy development. She maintained her relations with the bureau, attending its periodic conferences and writing for *Venture*. Nevertheless, direct contact with the politically active trade union leaders in the British dependencies, and the continuity of the TUC's work, distanced from the ebb and flow of parties in the British government, suited her better.

A love of fieldwork had been born in 1949, when the Fabians gave Nicholson three months' leave to conduct classes for adults in the Eastern Provinces of Nigeria. That course, on the making of modern nations, organized by the Oxford extra-mural studies delegacy, covered most of the problems facing colonies aspiring to independence, many of which were being explored in bureau pamphlets and all of them by colonial officials and academics. Every opportunity offered later by the TUC to observe and report on the relations between local governments overseas and the trade unions was welcomed. On further visits to Tanganyika in 1954 and to Nigeria in 1960 and 1970 the advice she gave to the unions, based on considered TUC policy, was not always what they had hoped to hear. Nevertheless, she respected their members' dignity and ability to decide what they wanted, and her aim was always to help them attain it through the constitutional methods provided by their union structure rather than through the oratory of unstable political pressure groups. In *New Fabian Colonial Essays* she argued that the initiative for political development lay with the colonial peoples, with Britain merely assisting, and that accepting the goal of self-government precluded the imposition of a specifically socialist policy. Her practical recommendations to the Commonwealth section committees on her return were based on stringent observation, experience, wide reading, and recognition of the colonial peoples' ultimate goals.

On retirement in 1972 Nicholson settled in St Albans and embarked on a scholarly study of the influence of the TUC overseas from 1916 to 1965. Unfortunately she died before the second volume was completed. Research for this work took her to India in 1973, thus fulfilling a lifelong ambition, and to the West Indies in 1976, where she met many old friends in positions of authority. While not allowing it to cloud her judgement, her appreciation of the scholarship and diverse talents of others was generous.

On 14 September 1946 Nicholson married Lionel Victor Van der Meulen Fowler (*b.* 1900/01), journalist, son of Henry Walter Willson Fowler, company secretary, and former husband of Constance Marjorie, *née* Phillips, from whom he was divorced; they themselves were later divorced. She was appointed MBE in 1969. She died of a subarachnoid haemorrhage at Hemel Hempstead General Hospital on 22 July 1997. A memorial service was held on 1 August in the parish church of St Michael, St Albans.

PATRICIA M. PUGH

Sources London Metropolitan University, Trade Union Congress collections · Bodl. RH, Fabian Colonial Bureau MSS · Bodl. RH, Creech Jones MSS · Bodl. RH, Perham MSS · London School of Economics, Fabian Society MSS · register of St Hilda's College, Oxford, St Hilda's College, Oxford · *The Guardian* (11 Aug 1997) · b. cert. · m. cert. · d. cert.
Archives London Metropolitan University, TUC collections, research notes and personal papers | Bodl. RH, Fabian Colonial Bureau MSS, MS Brit. Emp. s.365 · Bodl. RH, Arthur Creech Jones MSS, MS Brit. Emp. s. 332 · London School of Economics, Fabian Society MSS

Likenesses photographs, London Metropolitan University, TUC collections, Marjorie Nicholson Archive
Wealth at death £320,008: probate, 29 Sept 1997, *CGPLA Eng. & Wales*

Nicholson, Michael Angelo (1794–1841). *See under* Nicholson, Peter (1765–1844).

Nicholson [*née* Jackson], **Nancy** (1788–1854), miser and eccentric, was born on 3 May 1788 at Drax, Yorkshire, the only child of John Jackson (*d.* 1810), vicar of Drax, and his second wife (*d.* 1842). Her father was the master of Drax grammar school, and it was probably the prospect of succeeding to this position and other financial rewards which induced the Revd John Nicholson (*d.* 1850) to marry her in October 1811. Although Nicholson became not only master of the school but also vicar of Drax, the couple had a miserable marriage. While Nancy Nicholson's miserliness was of a legendary order, her husband was not faultless: periodically he got very drunk, and was known to beat her. As mistress of the school she exercised her economizing talents to the full, serving the boys tiny meals and making them perform many household chores, which apparently included pilfering fruit from neighbours' gardens. After the Nicholsons were relieved of the charge of the school, she turned to the keeping and marketing of livestock, especially pigs, at which she proved herself very successful. Her business sense was further evidenced by the care she took to ensure that her own name as well as her husband's appeared on the deeds for the considerable amount of land which they purchased. After they separated in 1845 Nicholson consoled himself with an accordion, while his wife passed through a period of unusual extravagance, subscribing to a weekly newspaper and having her portrait painted. This was perhaps unwise in a woman of some 17 stone, who always refused to purchase new clothes. After her husband's death on 8 February 1850, Nancy Nicholson energetically sought for a post as a housekeeper, finding her leisured existence as a woman of property a dull one. In 1850 she joined the Roman Catholic church, but left it when a priest asked for a small donation towards the building of a church at Howden. She died on 6 August 1854 at her house in Asselby, leaving several expectant relatives out of her will. A distant cousin received £1500 but the bulk of her property was bequeathed to a half-nephew. Much of her apparent oddity could be more fairly viewed as the result of frustrated intelligence and energy, coupled with a total disregard for the conventions of her sex and class.

ROSEMARY MITCHELL

Sources *The life of Mrs Nancy Nicholson of Drax* (1855) · S. Baring-Gould, *Yorkshire oddities, incidents and strange events*, 2 vols. (1874), 2. 25–95 · Boase, *Mod. Eng. biog.*
Likenesses portrait, *c.*1845

Nicholson, Norman Cornthwaite (1914–1987), poet, was born on 8 January 1914 at 14 St George's Terrace, Millom, Cumberland, the only child of Joseph Nicholson, tailor and draper, of Millom, and his wife, Edith Cornthwaite, the daughter of a butcher. His mother died when he was five, and his father remarried three years later. He was educated at Millom secondary school, but in his adolescence he developed tuberculosis and from 1930 to 1932 was confined to hospital in Hampshire. One of his lungs was removed. This was the only period in his life when he spent any considerable time away from his native and ancestral Millom, the source of much of his inspiration both in verse and prose.

Nicholson began writing at an early age. He was encouraged in this by a local clergyman, the Revd Samuel Taylor, who put him in touch with Brother George Every, a poet, literary critic, and theologian, and a contributor to *The Criterion*; through Every, Nicholson was introduced in 1938 to the editor of that journal, T. S. Eliot, who showed an interest in his poems. In the same year, Nicholson began to give lectures on literature to local Workers' Educational Association classes, material from which he used in his first critical book, *Man and Literature* (1943); but already, in 1942, he had edited a Penguin *Anthology of Religious Verse*, and before that had started to publish poems in periodicals, including some in the United States.

Nicholson's upbringing was in the Methodist church, to which his stepmother belonged, but in 1940 he was confirmed in the Church of England. His Christian faith was central to him throughout his life. Much of his poetry and his verse-plays drew on this faith, nourished by his devotion to the landscapes, history, people, and stories of Cumberland. All are abundantly present in his first individual volume of poems, *Five Rivers*, which Eliot accepted for Faber and Faber and which was published in 1944. This had been preceded in 1943 by a selection of his work published in one volume alongside selections from Keith Douglas and J. C. Hall. Nicholson went on to publish another ten books and pamphlets of poems, including *Selected Poems* in 1966, augmented in 1982. All were well received, as authentic and sometimes gently quirky products of a life which, though restricted by Nicholson's fragile health ('My ways are circumscribed', he wrote in the poem 'The Pot Geranium'), had broader visions of a universe of rock, rivers, hills, and the sea.

In appearance Nicholson was craggy, and he became increasingly bewhiskered with impressive sideburns. He had a fine head, brightly flashing and mischievous eyes, and an engaging and often roguish smile. His voice, as a result of lung operations, was hoarse but also strikingly vigorous: he was a splendid reader not only of his own poems but of other poets too, especially his beloved Wordsworth, parts of whose *Prelude* he read in a memorable series of BBC Third Programme broadcasts in the early 1960s. He was a much sought-after reader at literary gatherings up and down the country and, though these expeditions often exhausted him, he enjoyed them.

In 1956 Nicholson married a teacher, Yvonne Edith, daughter of John Oswald Gardner, engineering draughtsman. The partnership was a very happy one until her death in 1982. Her loss left him desolate; and, much though he enjoyed the literary recognition and honours which increasingly came to him in his later years, they could not compensate for her absence. They had lived cheerfully in the small terraced house in Millom which

had always been Nicholson's home (indeed, he had been born there, when it was also his father's shop), and he continued to live there after Yvonne's death. They had no children.

Nicholson was elected a fellow of the Royal Society of Literature in 1945, and that year was given the Heinemann award. In 1967 he shared the Cholmondeley award for poetry with Seamus Heaney and Brian Jones. He received a Society of Authors travelling bursary in 1973 (spent visiting Scandinavia) and an Arts Council bursary in 1977, which was also the year he was awarded the queen's medal for poetry. He received the honorary degree of MA from the University of Manchester in 1959 and another from the Open University in 1975. Manchester Polytechnic conferred on him an honorary fellowship in 1979, and he received a LittD from the universities of Liverpool (1980) and Manchester (1984). One of his most treasured honours, which he delighted in showing to visitors, was the OBE, conferred in 1981. Perhaps even more, he was deeply moved by a volume of poems and prose pieces by many distinguished writers, *Between Comets* (edited by William Scammell), published and presented to him on his seventieth birthday in 1984.

Among Nicholson's many other publications were books and anthologies concerned with the history and topography of the Lake District, four verse-plays, two early novels, and a life of William Cowper (1951). The most individual and revealing of all is *Wednesday Early Closing* (1975), a memoir of his early years, full of the characters, anecdotes, sights, sounds, and smells of his Millom boyhood. He died on 30 May 1987 at Whitehaven, Cumberland.   ANTHONY THWAITE, *rev.*

Sources N. Nicholson, *Wednesday early closing* (1975) · P. Gardner, *Norman Nicholson* (1973) · *The Independent* (2 June 1987) · personal knowledge (1996)
Archives JRL, corresp. and literary papers · Literary and Philosophical Society of Newcastle upon Tyne, corresp. and literary papers | U. Hull, Brynmor Jones L., letters to Harry Chambers
Likenesses J. D. Palmer, bust, Carlisle Cathedral
Wealth at death £215,936: probate, 29 Sept 1987, *CGPLA Eng. & Wales*

Nicholson, Peter (1765–1844), architectural writer and mathematician, was born at Prestonkirk, Haddingtonshire, close to Edinburgh, on 20 July 1765, the third of nine children. His parents were George Nicholson (1733–1832), a stonemason, and Margaret Hastie.

Early years Nicholson had no formal education beyond his village school, where he showed considerable talent in mathematics, even studying, by himself, geometry that was far in advance of what was taught at the school. At the age of twelve he began helping his father, but it was work that proved not to his liking. He was then apprenticed for four years to a cabinet-maker in Linton, Haddingtonshire. On finishing his apprenticeship he went to Edinburgh to find work as a journeyman cabinet-maker, while continuing his own studies in mathematics. In 1788, aged twenty-four, he went to London. His workshop colleagues there, seeing his skill in drawing and calculating, asked him for advice, and in consequence he opened an evening school

Peter Nicholson (1765–1844), by James Green, c.1816

in Berwick Street, Soho. Encouraged by the success of the school and its profits, he was able to produce his first book, *The Carpenter's New Guide* (1792), for which he engraved his own plates. In the *New Guide* he published for the first time a method of constructing complex groins and niches. Then between 1795 and 1798 he published *The Principles of Architecture* and in 1797 *The Carpenter's and Joiner's Assistant*. He had meanwhile overstretched his finances and was imprisoned for debt. It was in return for the repayment of these debts to obtain his release that he wrote *The Carpenter's Assistant* for the publisher Taylor.

Architectural commissions Nicholson was married twice, first to Mary Perry (1766–c.1798) on 17 December 1791 at Marylebone. With her he had one son, Michael Angelo [*see below*]. There was a second child but Mary died before Nicholson left for Glasgow in 1799. With his two young children Nicholson led a peripatetic life in Glasgow, changing address at least once a year. At the age of thirty-four Nicholson had returned to Scotland, at the request of a wealthy merchant, James Laurie, and for the next eight years he practised as an architect in Glasgow. On 27 August 1804 he married Jane Jamieson (d. 1832) in Anderston church, Glasgow. She was from a well-to-do north country family and had a brother, Thomas Jamieson, who was a draper in Gateshead. Together they had a son, Jamieson Thomas, and a daughter. These were busy years for Nicholson: in 1802 and 1805 he built two elegant timber bridges over the Clyde in Glasgow, and he designed Yorkhill House in the Greek manner for Fulton Alexander at Patrick, Renfrewshire (illustrated as the frontispiece to his *Practical Builder*, 1825). Most notable, though, was his Carlton Place, Lauriston, Glasgow, for his patron James

Laurie, which he designed in 1802, again using Greek Doric detailing. He also laid out the town of Ardrossan, Renfrewshire; the harbour was constructed under the direction of Thomas Telford.

In 1808 Nicholson was appointed surveyor to the county of Cumberland, on the recommendation of Telford, and went to live in Carlisle. He oversaw the building of the new courts of justice to Telford's designs, work that he left to be finished by Robert Smirke when he returned to London in 1810. Nicholson also carried on publishing, and put out a second edition of his *Principles of Architecture* in 1809. While living in Carlisle he also built a number of houses in the county of Cumberland, including Castletown House, Rockliffe, in 1809 for a wealthy solicitor, Robert Mounsey, and, in 1810, Houghton House, Houghton, for William Hodgeson, clerk of the peace. Both these commissions surely derived from his work on the court house. In 1812, having returned to London, he drew up the designs for a major remodelling of Corby Castle under the direction of the owner, Henry Howard. The work on these houses kept him in contact with the Cumberland area until the last was finished in 1814.

Further publications It is not known why Nicholson left what seemed a promising career in the provinces to return to London. It may have been to pursue his writing, for he had been commissioned to draw some plates for Rees's *Cyclopaedia* and to prepare a manuscript for a proposed architectural dictionary; his friend and occasional assistant Richard Brown noted in his memoir of 1849 in *The Builder* that Nicholson was inspired to write his architectural dictionary by *The Cabinet Dictionary*, published in two volumes by Thomas Sheraton in 1803. Once back in London he began again to give private tuition in the various aspects of his profession, and in mathematics, land surveying, mechanical drawing, and fortification, as well as geography and navigation; to this end he set up a school in Oxford Street. With the assistance of his son Michael Angelo, Nicholson embarked on his most prolific period of writing. The most important books of this period, from 1812 until 1827, are *The Architectural Dictionary* (1812–19), which contained plates of many of his executed buildings, and *The New Practical Builder and Workman's Companion* (1823), possibly the best of his publications. He was particularly interested in the construction of staircases, and in 1814 he was awarded the gold medal of the Society of Arts in recognition of his contributions towards improvements in the manufacture of staircases and the shaping of handrails. In the same year the society also awarded him £20 for his invention of the 'centrolinead', an instrument for drawing lines that converge towards an inaccessible point, off the draughtsman's drawing-board, and this was followed by a silver medal the next year for improvements to the instrument. This instrument was an invaluable aid in drawing up complex structures, such as staircases, and was still in some use until the mid-twentieth century. In 1826 he and his son published *The Practical Cabinet Maker, Upholsterer, and Complete Decorator*, which contained many plates on the latest fashions in furniture and details, including room settings, curtains, and polishes. He also wrote a number of small books on mathematical subjects and published new editions of books that he had written earlier. In 1827 he began to publish a part-work in twelve sections, *The School of Architecture and Engineering*. The work was abandoned after section 5, owing to the bankruptcy of the publisher, and Nicholson lost heavily as a result.

Later years In 1829, aged sixty-four, Nicholson left London for the last time and went to live in Morpeth, Northumberland, in a small house bequeathed to him by a relative, saying that he was going to develop some land bought with his brother-in-law. Nicholson's father came to live with them and died, aged ninety-nine, in 1832. On the death of his wife, Jane, also in 1832 he moved again, to Newcastle upon Tyne, where he once more opened a school, but it did not make money, and in July 1834 a subscription was raised in the town and £320 presented to him. His professional abilities were greatly appreciated in Newcastle and, among other honours, he was elected president of the Northumberland Institution for the Promotion of the Fine Arts in 1835. He still carried on writing in his declining years but was generously supported by Thomas Jamieson of Newton, Northumberland. He died at Carlisle on 18 June 1844, and was buried in the now demolished Christ Church graveyard, Carlisle, where a plain headstone marked the site. A monument to him, by R. W. Billings, was set up in Carlisle cemetery, Dalston Road, in 1856.

Nicholson was probably the most prolific communicator on the technical aspects of architecture in the first half of the nineteenth century and his influence should not be underestimated. He wrote at least twenty-seven books and two collaborations, which all went into many reprints and which were still being republished and updated by others well after his death. He also wrote articles and entries for Rees's *Cyclopaedia* and Brewster's *Edinburgh Encyclopaedia*. Furthermore his was one of the leading intellects concerning technical architectural matters and remains to this day essential reading on the period.

Nicholson was, as Richard Brown commented (*The Builder*), a large man 'and strong made, well calculated for enduring fatigue', a figure seen in at least two of his portraits, one by James Green (1771–1834) in the National Portrait Gallery, and J. Cochran's engraving used as the frontispiece of the 1848 edition of *The Practical Builder*. Brown also said that 'Sundays and Weekdays were alike to him' (ibid.) and that 'he had always gone to work in his studies like a blacksmith on his anvil' (ibid.). This seems a particularly accurate observation in consideration of his prolific publishing and Nicholson's keen desire to understand how things were made, especially staircases, and to try to improve on existing methods, writing them up in such a way that ordinary tradesmen could understand and profit from them. Financially he was not so astute, and often used, without permission, plates that had been used in other publications such as in his *Architectural Dictionary*; Nicholson had sold the copyright to his publisher Barfield, and then used the same plates, without permission, in *Practical Builder* for another publisher, Kelly. A chancery suit was the outcome, and this was not the only time that

he reused plates in this way. Thus, despite his prolific output, he was in constant financial insecurity.

Nicholson's great gift as a mathematician was his ability to simplify and generalize traditional methods as well as inventing new ones. The rules that he formulated for finding sections of prisms, cylinders, or cylindroids enabled joiners to construct the great sweeping, curved staircases that were so fashionable in the early nineteenth century with much greater ease, speed, and economy of timber. Nicholson was the first author to write about the practical creation of joints, and the hinging and hanging of doors and shutters. He was also the first to note that Grecian mouldings were conic in section and that the volutes of Ionic capitals should be composed of logarithmic spirals. The complexity of the geometry involved in setting out fine woodwork meant that Nicholson was writing for an informed audience rather than the novice, as he sometimes thought. It was, perhaps, for this reason that he wrote so many books on mathematics really to help the enthusiastic tradesman. Nicholson's books were also sold in America but despite, or perhaps because of, his use of Greek revival ornament, then so popular there, he became the subject of much plagiarism. As a result, he is perhaps not as well known in America as he should be.

As an architect Nicholson may not have been outstanding but he was one of the early British proponents of the Greek revival style, perhaps reflecting something of his political leanings. Greek detailing may be seen, for example, in Corby Castle, Cumberland (1812–17), both in the Doric portico and in the internal plasterwork. Less obviously, the influence can be seen in the pedimented terrace houses of 51–2 (formerly 7 and 8) Carlton Place, Glasgow, built for James Laurie and his brother. His reputation then and now lies chiefly, however, in the great value of his architectural writing rather than his buildings.

Michael Angelo Nicholson (1794–1841), architectural draughtsman, was born on 14 February 1794, the son of Peter Nicholson and his first wife, Mary Perry. About 1810 he studied under Richard Brown at his architectural drawing school in Wells Street, London. He then studied with John Foulston, like Brown a west countryman and a minor architect. In 1814 he enrolled as a student at the Royal Academy Schools. He had first exhibited at the Royal Academy in 1812 and continued to show until 1828. He married Agnes (Nancy) Gibson in the Gorbals, Lanarkshire, on 27 April 1822; she was the daughter of a Glasgow bleacher, another example of the long but irregular relationship of the whole Nicholson family with the Glasgow region of Scotland. Their first child was a daughter, Marrion, born in 1824 in London and named after her mother's sister. A second daughter, Jane, was born in 1825, a third daughter, Jessie, in 1827, and a son, Peter, in 1829. In all they had ten children. Jane married the architect Alexander 'Greek' Thomson and her sister Jessie married Thomson's partner John Baird in a double ceremony in 1847.

Michael Angelo Nicholson drew the frontispiece for Richard Elsam's *Practical Builder's Perpetual Price Book* (1825), and provided the lithograph plates for Henry William Inwood's *Erechtheion* (1826). He described himself as an architect on the title-page of his *The Five Orders, Geometrical and in Perspective* (1834). He claimed responsibility for the design of Carstairs House, Lanarkshire (1823), and illustrated the building in his father's *New Practical Builder* of the same year. Michael Angelo Nicholson had also, by this date, set up a drawing school in Melton Place, Euston Square, London, and embarked on a major collaboration with his father to produce *The Practical Cabinet Maker, Upholsterer, and Complete Decorator* (1826). This was, and remains, an important book in the manner of the early nineteenth-century books on furniture and interior design by such as George Smith and Thomas Hope; their book was grounded in Peter Nicholson's training as a cabinet-maker and his son's awareness of contemporary design.

Nicholson also claimed to have improved his father's invention of the centrolinead, and to have invented the inverted trammel, an instrument for drawing ellipses. It is sometimes hard to appreciate the difficulties experienced by draughtsmen before the arrival of computer-aided design.

Michael Angelo Nicholson's tenth child, Margaret, was born shortly after he died, aged forty-seven, on 11 November 1841 at Melton Place. His wife, Nancy, survived him, but in 1845 their eldest daughter, Marrion, died in March, the youngest daughter died in May, and Nancy herself died in December that year. This left four daughters and one son, who went to live in Glasgow with relatives, while their brother Peter emigrated to the United States, where he became an architect in Philadelphia and died in 1902. It is likely that this Peter Nicholson went to America to try not only to better himself but also to do something about the reputation of his grandfather and stop the plagiarism of his books. Peter Nicholson and his brother-in-law Alexander Thomson frequently corresponded across the Atlantic.

The whole Nicholson family reveals the complex interdependence of professional and family links common to nineteenth-century architects and the career of Peter Nicholson senior admirably displays the growth of the practice of architecture itself, as he came from quite humble artisan origins, taught himself, and passed that knowledge on to others through his writing.

TREVE ROSOMAN

Sources Colvin, *Archs.* · R. Brown, 'Recollections of Peter Nicholson', *The Builder*, 7/360 (29 Dec 1849), 615–16 · *DNB* · R. McFadzean, *Alexander Thomson* (1979), 16–18 · A. L. Macdonald, 'The ingenious Mr Nicholson', *The Alexander Thomson Society Newletter*, 19 (Aug 1997) · D. Cruickshank, 'A merchant's palace', *Architects' Journal*, 192 (Nov 1991), 40–43 · M. Hambly, *Drawing instruments, 1580–1980* (1988) · bap. reg. Scot. · S. C. Hutchison, 'The Royal Academy Schools, 1768–1830', *Walpole Society*, 38 (1960–62), 123–91, esp. 167 · *IGI* · d. cert. [Michael Angelo Nicholson] · manuscript family history of Alexander Thomson, priv. coll.

Likenesses J. Green, oils, *c.*1816, NPG [see illus.] · C. Armstrong, line engraving, 1824 (after T. Heaphy), BM, NPG · H. Adlard, stipple, 1825, BM, NPG · J. Cochran, stipple, 1825 (after W. Derby), BM, NPG · J. Cochrane, engraving, repro. in P. Nicholson, *The practical builder* (1848), frontispiece · pen-and-ink drawing, NPG

Nicholson, Renton [*called* the Lord Chief Baron] (1809–1861), impresario, was born in a house opposite to the Old Nag's Head tavern in the Hackney Road, London, on 4 April 1809; he was brought up by his sisters and educated under Henry Butter, the author of the *Etymological Spelling Book*. At the age of twelve he was apprenticed to a pawnbroker, and in 1830 he started in business as a jeweller at 99 Quadrant, Regent Street, London. On 1 December 1831 he went bankrupt, and paid the first of many visits to the King's Bench and Whitecross Street prisons. He afterwards picked up a living by frequenting gambling rooms or billiard rooms, and in the summer months went speeling, that is, playing roulette in a tent on racecourses. He afterwards kept a cigar shop in Warwick Street, to which a gambling and drinking room was attached, and subsequently became a wine merchant. He again went bankrupt in 1836, in which year he married, although his wife's name is not known. Finally, a printer, Joseph Last of Edward Street, Hampstead Road, employed him to edit *The Town*, a weekly paper, the first number of which appeared on Saturday 3 June 1837. A sensationalist, semi-pornographic paper, concentrating on scandal in high life, it described itself as 'a popular representative of the people, returned to serve them weekly, and elected upon the glorious system of universal suffrage' (McCalman, 225). The last issue, numbered 156, appeared on Saturday 23 May 1840. In the meantime, in conjunction with Last and Charles Pitcher, a sporting character, he had started *The Crown*, a weekly paper supporting the beer sellers, which folded in 1839.

In partnership with Thomas Bartlett Simpson, in 1841 Nicholson opened the Garrick's Head and Town Hotel, 27 Bow Street, Covent Garden, and in a large room in this house, on Monday 8 March 1841, established the well-known Judge and Jury Society, where he himself soon presided, under the title of 'the Lord Chief Baron'. Members of both houses of parliament, statesmen, poets, actors, and others visited the Garrick's Head to witness the mock trials. These were humorous, and gave occasion for much real eloquence, brilliant repartee, fluent satire, and *double entendre*. The cases frequently revolved around divorce or seduction, giving occasion for lewd jokes and cross-dressing. On 31 July and 1 and 2 August 1843 he gave a three days' fête at Cremorne Gardens which attracted large crowds, and was repeated at Easter the following year, and on Sundays. In October, Nicholson was again in the Queen's Bench, although Cremorne Gardens proved financially viable under his successor, T. B. Simpson.

In 1844 the Judge and Jury Society was removed to the Coal Hole, Fountain Court, 103 Strand (opposite the Evangelical Exeter Hall), and the entertainment was varied by the introduction of mock elections and mock parliamentary debates. At various times Nicholson 'went circuit', and held his court in provincial towns. During the summer months he attended the races with a large tent, in which he dispensed refreshments. He was also a caterer at Camberwell and other fairs, where he had dancing booths.

In 1846 Nicholson was back at the Garrick's Head, where

he added to his usual attractions *poses plastiques* and *tableaux vivants*. His wife died at Boulogne on 15 September 1849, and shortly afterwards he rented the Justice tavern in Bow Street. Again in difficulties, he accepted an annual salary to preside at the Garrick's Head, until July 1851, when he became landlord of the Coal Hole, and held his court three times a night. His last remove was on 16 January 1858, to the Cider Cellar, 20 Maiden Lane, where he opened his court and his exhibition of *poses plastiques* on 22 January. He took advantage of public discussion of prostitution to produce a case on that topic, which attracted crowded audiences.

Nicholson died of dropsy and heart disease at the house of his daughter, Eliza Nicholson, proprietor of the Gordon tavern, 3 Piazza, Covent Garden, on 18 May 1861 and was buried in Brompton cemetery. He published a number of works, including his autobiography (1860) and two works on boxing. In 1843 he owned and edited the *Illustrated London Life*, which ran to twenty-five issues.

G. C. BOASE, *rev.* K. D. REYNOLDS

Sources R. Nicholson, *The Lord Chief Baron Nicholson: an autobiography* (1860) • *N&Q*, 4th ser., 6 (1870), 477 • *N&Q*, 4th ser., 7 (1871), 286, 327 • I. McCalman, *Radical underworld: prophets, revolutionaries, and pornographers in London, 1795–1840* (1988) • M. Mason, *The making of Victorian sexual attitudes* (1994)
Likenesses A. Henning, oils, *c*.1841–1861, Museum of London • group portrait, repro. in Mason, *Making of Victorian sexual attitudes* • lithograph, BM
Wealth at death frequently bankrupt

Nicholson, Reynold Alleyne (1868–1945), orientalist, was born at Keighley, Yorkshire, on 19 August 1868, the eldest of the five children of Henry Alleyne *Nicholson (1844–1899) and his wife, Isabella Hutchison, from Kirkcaldy in Fife. His father, then a practising surgeon, later became professor of natural history at the universities of St Andrews and Aberdeen. Nicholson went to school in these two cities and from Aberdeen University entered Trinity College, Cambridge, as a pensioner in 1887. After being awarded the Porson prize for Greek verse in his first year he became a scholar of his college, and in 1890 obtained a first class in part one of the classical tripos and again won the Porson prize. Although he dropped to a third class in part two (1891) he gained a first in the Indian languages tripos in 1892.

Nicholson's interest in oriental languages was first stimulated in the library of his grandfather, the biblical scholar John Nicholson, from whom he inherited a collection of Arabic and Persian manuscripts. It was fostered by E. G. Browne, with whom he read Persian, and by short periods of study at Leiden and Strasbourg, where he read Arabic with Michael Jan de Goeje and Theodor Nöldeke. His election to a fellowship at Trinity in 1893 opened the partnership with Browne which lasted until the latter's death in 1926. Except for one year's tenure of the chair of Persian at University College, London, in 1901–2, the whole of Nicholson's academic career was spent in Cambridge. He returned there to succeed Browne first as lecturer in Persian (1902–26), then in 1926 (when he was also re-elected fellow of Trinity) as Sir Thomas Adams's professor of Arabic.

From the first, Nicholson was strongly attracted to the literature of Sufism. For his fellowship thesis he made a selection from the mystical odes of Rumi called *Dīvāni Shamsi Tabrīz*, the publication of which, with translation and annotation, in 1898 placed him at once in the front rank of oriental scholarship. Between 1905 and 1914 he published editions or translations of four major works on Sufism, two in Persian ('Attar's *Tadhkiratu 'l-awliyá*, 2 vols., 1905–7, and *Kashf al-mahjúb* of Hujwiri, 1911) and two in Arabic (Ibn al-'Arabi's odes, *Tarjumán al-ashwáq*, 1911, and *Kitáb al-lum* of al-Sarraj, 1914), besides various collaborations with Browne. In 1914 he summed up his studies in a manual for the general reader, *The Mystics of Islam*. Meanwhile he had written his *Literary History of the Arabs* (1907), a personal appreciation of Arabic literature, which became a standard text. He also issued an annotated series of Arabic readers (1907–11).

Nicholson's publications resumed after the war with two important volumes, *Studies in Islamic Poetry* and *Studies in Islamic Mysticism* (both 1921), supplemented in 1923 by a small but significant work entitled *The Idea of Personality in Sufism*. His major project in this period was a complete critical edition with translation and annotation of the *Mathnawí* of Rumi, the greatest literary achievement of Persian mysticism. Eighteen years of sustained industry enabled him to issue between 1925 and 1940 the eight volumes he had planned; a final volume, intended to sum up Rumi's life and work and his place in the history of Sufism, remained unwritten.

Nicholson's work on Sufism was considered the greatest single contribution made by a European scholar to the subject. He was responsible for opening up one of the major developments of human thought for both specialists and the lay reader, transforming the understanding of it by presenting its major products with rare imagination and literary taste, as well as with careful scholarship. He himself was gifted with poetic sensibility and talent. In earlier years he wrote light verse, some of which he reprinted in *The Don and the Dervish* (1911), and in 1922 he published a volume of *Translations of Eastern Poetry and Prose*.

Nicholson was an honorary LLD of Aberdeen (1913), a fellow of the British Academy (1922), gold medallist of the Royal Asiatic Society (1938), and an associate member of the Persian Academy. In outward manner he was reserved and in public speech he was diffident, but as a teacher he was kind and sympathetic, and regarded with affection. His chief recreation was golf, and as an undergraduate he played in the Cambridge team against Oxford. In 1903 he married his first cousin, Cecilia, daughter of Thomas Varty, of Penrith; there were no children. After retiring in 1933 he continued to take an interest in the oriental school until in 1940 failing health and eyesight forced him into retreat in north Wales. He died at Fairholme Nursing Home, Woodlands Road, Saltney, Chester, on 27 August 1945. He was survived by his wife.

H. A. R. GIBB, *rev.* CHRISTINE WOODHEAD

Sources *The Times* (31 Aug 1945) · R. Levy, 'R. A. Nicholson', *PBA*, 31 (1945), 399–406 · personal knowledge (1959) · private information (1959) · *CGPLA Eng. & Wales* (1946)
Likenesses W. Stoneman, two photographs, 1922–30, NPG
Wealth at death £10,579 1s.: probate, 13 March 1946, *CGPLA Eng. & Wales*

Nicholson, Richard (*bap.* 1563, *d.* 1638/9), organist and composer, was baptized on 26 September 1563 in the church of St Oswald, Durham; a younger son, he had at least two brothers—Thomas (later of Growton) and Christopher (later of Stratford)—and two sisters—Elizabeth (who married one Botcher) and Margaret (who married one Sugden). He was a boy chorister in the choir of Durham Cathedral from 1576 to 1580. On 23 January 1596 he was appointed *informator choristarum* at Magdalen College, Oxford, although he was in receipt of payments from the college for several months prior to that date. He probably combined his mastership of the choristers with the post of college organist. Nicholson received the Oxford BMus degree in the same year, possibly a result of his composition of his five-part Latin motet *Cantate domino*, which survives in manuscript. In 1626 he was appointed the first master of the music praxis under the foundation which had been established by William Heather.

With the exception of a small quantity of instrumental consort music, all the music that can be reliably attributed to Nicholson is for voices. Only two sacred works have survived, one of which (his fine full anthem, 'O pray for the peace of Jerusalem') is clearly inspired by the setting of the same text by his contemporary Thomas Tomkins, with which it has overt musical similarities. Nicholson's consort anthem, 'When Jesus sat at meat', for voices and viols (with vocal solos for two boys), was probably composed for the meetings at which Nicholson was required to perform in the Oxford music school on Thursday afternoons under the terms of the Oxford music praxis. Nicholson was invited to contribute to Thomas Morley's *The Triumphs of Oriana* (1601), which suggests that even at a relatively early age he was already held in high esteem by his contemporaries. His most unusual composition is a three-voice madrigal cycle in eleven sections chronicling the courtship of Joan and John.

The last reference to Nicholson in the college accounts is in 1638. He had died by 18 November 1639, when Arthur Philipps was elected as his successor. His will, drawn up on 8 November 1625 and proved by his nephew and remaining executor, Thomas Nicholson of Stapleford Tawnie, Essex, on 7 May 1642, reveals that he was probably unmarried, but had a wide circle of kin, godchildren, and friends.   JOHN MOREHEN

Sources P. Brett, ed., *Consort songs*, Musica Britannica, 22 (1967) · *Richard Nicholson: Collected madrigals*, ed. J. Morehen (1976), vol. 37 of *The English madrigalists* · J. Morehen, 'Nicolson, Richard', *New Grove* · C. Monson, 'Richard Nicolson: madrigals from Jacobean Oxford', *Early Music*, 6 (1978), 429–35 · G. Spearitt, 'Richard Nicholson and the "Joane, Quoth John" songs', *Studies in Music* [Australia], 2 (1968), 33–42 · will, PRO, PROB 11/189, fols. 88r–88v · G. Spearitt, 'The consort songs and madrigals of Richard Nicholson', *Musicology*, 2 (1965–7), 42–52 · N. C. Carpenter, *Music in the medieval and Renaissance universities* (1958), 158, 161, 171 · parish register, Durham, St Oswald, 26 Sept 1563 [baptism]

Nicholson, Samuel (*fl.* 1597?–1602), poet and divine, was most likely the Samuel Nicholson of St Catharine's College, Cambridge, who graduated BA in 1597–8. He took orders, and described himself on the title-page of his 1602 devotional treatise, *Gods New-Yeeres Gift Sent unto England*, as 'M. of Artes'. In addition to this religious tract Nicholson also was the author of *Acolastus his After-Witte* (1600). Copies of this work—a poem of 446 stanzas, each containing 6 decasyllabic or hendecasyllabic lines—are extremely rare. Although it is largely forgotten today *Acolastus* occasioned considerable comment in the middle years of the nineteenth century. Facsimile editions were produced in 1866 and 1876 by J. O. Halliwell and Alexander B. Grosart respectively. The work's primary source of fascination for nineteenth-century readers seems to have been its blatant plagiarism: sizeable passages in the work have been borrowed from Shakespeare's *Rape of Lucrece* and from *Venus and Adonis*, as well as from numerous of the history plays. To a lesser extent Nicholson also lifted passages from Thomas Nash's *Pierce Penniless*. Nineteenth-century men of letters were divided over the significance of these borrowings. J. Payne Collier accused Nicholson of 'the most scandalous literary thefts, and unacknowledged appropriations' (Collier, 2.46), while Halliwell argued that Nicholson must have considered these appropriations 'so well known that a special acknowledgment was unnecessary' (Nicholson, *Acolastus*, ed. Halliwell, 'Preface', vi). Grosart praised Nicholson's 'prescient discernment of the genius of Shakespeare', and even went so far as to suggest that *Acolastus* occupied a pivotal place in English literary history for 'the witness it bears to the popularity of Shakespeare thus (comparatively) early' (Nicholson, *Acolastus*, ed. Grosart, 'Preface', v). Nicholson dedicated *Acolastus* to 'his deare Achates, Master Richard Warburton', describing the work as 'the first borne of my barren invention … begotten in my anticke age'. It seems likely that 'anticke' was meant to signify not 'antique', but rather 'antic' in the sense of youthful, or sportive (Nicholson, *Acolastus*, ed. Grosart, 'Introduction', ix).   ELIZABETH GOLDRING

Sources S. Nicholson, *Acolastus, his after-witte*, ed. J. O. Halliwell (privately printed, London, 1866) · S. Nicholson, *Acolastus his after-witte: a poem*, ed. A. B. Grosart (1876) · J. P. Collier, ed., *A bibliographical and critical account of the rarest books in the English language*, 2 vols. (1865) · S. Nicholson, *Gods new-yeeres gift sent unto England* (1602) · Venn, *Alum. Cant.* · Cooper, *Ath. Cantab.*, vols. 1–2 · W. T. Lowndes, *The bibliographer's manual of English literature*, ed. H. G. Bohn, [new edn], 6 vols. (1864) · *DNB*

Nicholson, Sir Sydney Hugo (1875–1947), founder of the Royal School of Church Music and choral director, was born on 9 February 1875 at 26 Devonshire Place, London, the third and youngest son of Sir Charles *Nicholson, first baronet (1808–1903), of Luddenham, and Sarah Elizabeth Keightley. His first name recalled his father's residence in Australia (1834–62). His brothers were the architect Sir Charles A. *Nicholson, and the stained glass artist Archibald Keightley Nicholson. He was educated at Rugby School and New College, Oxford, taking a third-class degree in English in 1897. He studied organ and composition for three years at the Royal College of Music, London, under Walter Parratt and Charles Villiers Stanford, took the Oxford BMus in 1902, and studied at the conservatory in Frankfurt am Main (1903–4). He was organist of Chipping Barnet parish church, Hertfordshire (1897–1903), briefly of the lower chapel of Eton College (1903), and acting organist of Carlisle Cathedral from 1904. Offered a post as organist of Canterbury Cathedral in 1908, he withdrew in favour of a similar post at Manchester Cathedral, and in 1919 became organist of Westminster Abbey. As well as officiating at many royal services he and the choir made the first broadcast of choral evensong on the BBC on 6 October 1926. By his own admission he was not an organist of the first rank, and this may have contributed to his decision to resign from the abbey in 1928. In 1927 he founded the School of English Church Music, and was its first director. He was appointed MVO in 1926, was awarded a Lambeth doctorate in 1928, and was knighted for his services to church music in 1938.

An able organizer and administrator, not afraid of change and innovation, Nicholson made an impact at Carlisle, Manchester, and Westminster, though his musical taste was conservative. At Westminster Abbey he moved on most of the old lay clerks, introduced regular rehearsal, and doubled the number of boys to share the load of singing daily services. He also founded the large special choir with annual performances of Bach's St Matthew passion. Earlier he had instituted a church choral union (Barnet) and diocesan music societies (Carlisle and Manchester) to bring parish church choirs together. Through the Church Music Society and the archbishops' committee on church music (1922) he became engaged with questions of musical standards in Church of England parish churches. Much of this background influenced the two parts of his new foundation: the residential College of St Nicolas to train church musicians and the School of English Church Music, a network of affiliated Anglican churches committed to raising standards of music in worship.

Nicholson had considered turning his attention to these matters since at least 1925 or 1926. On 6 December 1927, at a meeting at Westminster Abbey, he founded the School of English Church Music, bought the first premises, Buller's Wood, Chislehurst, in October 1928, and became warden of the small College of St Nicolas in January 1929. Membership of the school expanded from 105 in 1928 to more than 2000 affiliates in Britain and overseas by the time of his death. The initial success of this ambitious enterprise depended almost entirely on Nicholson's enthusiasm and vigour, with financial support from *Hymns Ancient and Modern*. He toured widely in Britain and throughout the empire. Early achievements included four enormous choral festivals (one of which involved 4000 voices at Crystal Palace in 1933), residential courses for boys, day courses, and a summer school for choirmasters and clergy.

At the beginning of the Second World War the College of St Nicolas was closed and the school was relocated to St Michael's College, Tenbury, where Nicholson became acting organist and choirmaster until 1943, when he set up temporary quarters in Leamington Spa. In 1945 it was granted a royal charter and became the Royal School of Church Music. Both school and college were then re-established in Canterbury, and he continued as director of the school. Nicholson died at Ashford Hospital, Kent, on 30 May 1947 after several strokes; his ashes were interred in the cloisters of Westminster Abbey on 6 June.

Nicholson's ideas were reflected in *Church Music: a Practical Handbook* (1920), *Quires and Places where they Sing* (1932), and, with G. L. H. Garner, *A Manual of English Church Music* (1923). He wrote three musical dramatic pieces, including *The Children of the Chapel*, and a novel, *Peter*, which tells the story of a boy chorister through the ages. He guided much of the musical editing of *Hymns Ancient and Modern* from the supplement of 1916 to the revised edition, which appeared in 1950. A small number of organ and choral works were published.

An enthusiastic early motorist, Nicholson enjoyed sketching, carpentry, printing, and photography. His overall concern for the well-being of his boy choristers resulted in the establishment of a choir club and holidays at Carlisle and scout troops at Manchester and Westminster Abbey. His obituary in the *Musical Times* (July 1947) reported 'a man of excellent presence' and 'courteous manner', 'a confirmed bachelor' who 'lived comfortably, though simply'.   JOHN HARPER

Sources S. H. Nicholson, 'Musings of a musician', typescript, 1939, Royal School of Church Music, Dorking, Nicholson Archive [autobiography] · Royal School of Church Music, Dorking, Nicholson MSS, Nicholson Archive · W. Shaw, *Vocation and endeavour: Sir Sydney Nicholson and the early years of the Royal School of Church Music* (1997) · 'Mr Sydney Nicholson', *Musical Herald* (Nov 1916), 367–70 · D. G., 'Sir Sydney Nicholson, 1875–1947', *MT*, 88 (1947), 235–6 · B. N. Sampson, 'The Royal School of Church Music: a study of its history, its organization, and its influence', MA diss., 2 vols., University of Sheffield, 1971 · *English Church Music* (1928–47), esp. July 1947 · *CGPLA Eng. & Wales* (1947) · b. cert.

Archives Royal School of Church Music, Dorking, Surrey, archive | BL, corresp. with Macmillans, Add. MS 55240 | SOUND BL NSA, performance recordings

Likenesses G. C. Beresford, photograph, 1922, NPG · W. Stoneman, photograph, 1940, NPG · photograph, Royal School of Church Music · plaster plaque (as child), Royal School of Church Music, Dorking, Surrey

Wealth at death £32,337 10s. 3d.: probate, 14 Oct 1947, *CGPLA Eng. & Wales*

Nicholson, Thomas Joseph. *See* Nicolson, Thomas (1644x6–1718).

Nicholson, Wilfred (1821–1921), paint manufacturer, was born in London on 13 September 1821, the third surviving child of Thomas Nicholson and his wife, Elizabeth, *née* Coulson (d. 1859). In 1810 his father had moved from co. Durham to London to find work and after various jobs joined Henry Grace, white lead manufacturer of Bethnal Green, where he later became manager.

Nicholson left school at thirteen and started work at Graces, gaining practical knowledge of paint ingredients and colours; most decorators of the day mixed their own paints and varnishes rather than buying ready-made products. Nicholson's interests were in selling rather than manufacture, and he became the firm's commercial traveller when he was twenty-six. He was popular and within ten years had been elected to the Commercial Travellers' Association Council; there he was a strong supporter of the association's charitable work, especially with its schools.

Nicholson met his future wife, Ann Clements (d. 1892), through his work with the Sunday school and social work at St Matthew's Church, Bethnal Green, and they were married on 23 July 1843. They had ten children; the two surviving boys attended the City of London School and the two youngest girls were taught at the school newly established by Frances Mary Buss at Camden Town. Henry Grace died in 1858 but Nicholson was not offered a partnership in the firm. Instead, three years later he was invited into partnership by John Jenson, whose high class varnish business at that time was much smaller than Grace's. Jenson and Nicholson developed a range of ready-to-use paints to supplement the business in oils, colours, and varnishes. Nicholson concentrated on marketing the firm's products. He travelled widely in the United Kingdom and on the continent, exhibiting in Paris in 1869/70 and Moscow in 1872. Agencies were set up to serve the major export markets in France and Belgium; sales to Australia and New Zealand were supplied through merchant houses.

Jenson retired from the partnership in 1874. Within a few years Nicholson was joined by two of his sons, one of whom stayed only for a short time while the other, John (b. 1860), became a partner in 1893. They had been sent to George Mence Smith, who had a chain of hardware and oil shops, to learn about the paint business, and to Paris to learn some French and about continental business methods, before they joined their father. After John became a partner, Nicholson gradually reduced his involvement in active management although he never formally relinquished his partnership. Instead he spent more time on outside charitable activities. He had become a liveryman in the Painter–Stainers' Company in 1860 and master in 1881–2, and was closely involved in the company's charitable work for almost fifty years.

Nicholson was brought up in a Christian home and throughout his life was a regular worshipper, latterly in the local Congregational church. His connection with the Sunday school movement was lifelong and he first visited the continent in 1864 as a representative of the Sunday School Union. He supported the 1870 Education Act, even though it prohibited denominational teaching in board schools. As well as his work on the management committee of the Royal Commercial Travellers' Schools, he was interested in the Reedham Orphanage and many other charities. The Nicholson family moved a number of times but their homes were close to the business in north London. In 1894 Nicholson and his old friend Smith went on a cruise through the Norwegian fjords. Nicholson remained active in his charitable work until his mid-nineties and died on 9 January 1921, a few months short of his hundredth birthday.   FRANCIS GOODALL

Sources *The story of an English firm; Jenson and Nicholson Ltd, founded 1861* (1948) • H. Kimber, *Wilfred Nicholson, 1821–1921; a brief record of his life and work* (1960) • Painter–Stainers' Company, court minutes, GL, 5667/8
Archives Hackney Archives, London, Berger MSS • Hackney Archives, London, Jenson MSS • Hackney Archives, London, Nicholson MSS
Likenesses portraits, repro. in Kimber, *Wilfred Nicholson*
Wealth at death £23,636 8s. 5d.: probate, 5 April 1921, CGPLA Eng. & Wales

Nicholson, William (1591–1672), bishop of Gloucester, was born at Stratford St Mary, near Hadleigh, Suffolk, on 1 November 1591, the son of Christopher Nicholson, a wealthy clothier, and his wife, perhaps called Prisila. In 1598 he became a chorister at Magdalen College, Oxford, and was educated at the grammar school adjoining the college. He matriculated on 16 June 1610, graduated BA on 4 November 1611, and proceeded MA on 20 June 1615. He became one of the clerks of the college. In 1614 he was appointed to the college living of New Shoreham, Sussex, but he remained at Magdalen, serving as chaplain from 1616 to 1618. He found a patron in Henry Percy, earl of Northumberland, who had been tried and sentenced for complicity in the Gunpowder Plot of 1605 and was imprisoned in the Tower of London until 1621. Nicholson was appointed as tutor for his son, Algernon Percy, and as chaplain to the earl. Algernon became in due course a responsible and influential figure at the court of Charles I and apparently maintained an interest in his former tutor.

Nicholson's métier was clearly in education. On 3 July 1616 he was appointed master of the free school at Croydon, Surrey, 'for which he was well qualified being excellently skilled in the critical part of grammar' (Yardley, 200). There he could share with his pupils his delight in grammar, and 'his discipline and powers of instruction were much celebrated' (Heber, 2.197). On 24 February 1619 (or perhaps 1620) he married, at St Mary Mounthaw, Fish Street Hill, London, Elizabeth, widow of Robert Brigstocke of Croydon (buried on 10 January 1619) and daughter of Edward Heighton, also of Croydon; she already had a son, John. In 1626 Nicholson was instituted as rector of Llandeilo Fawr, Carmarthenshire. William Laud, as bishop of St David's, was patron of the living and Nicholson's gifts as a teacher were recorded in the bishop's register. Three years later 'quitting the school he retired to Wales' (Heber, 2.198; Yardley, 200), to live in his parish. He learned some Welsh, which he used when he preached. A lasting memorial of his work there was to be found in the books which he later published. *A Plain Exposition of the Church Catechism* (1655) and *Ekthesis pisteos, or, An Exposition of the Apostles' Creed* (1661) were based on the regular teaching which he gave to the children and the sermons which he preached there.

In 1643 Nicholson was nominated to serve in the Westminster assembly. Reginald Heber believed that he never took his place there (Heber, 2.197). He was appointed, though not immediately installed, as a canon residentiary at St David's Cathedral, and in 1644 he became archdeacon of Brecon. Deprived of these preferments by parliament he joined Jeremy Taylor and William Wyatt and set up a school near Llandeilo in Llanfihangel Aberbythych, their 'Collegium Newtoniense'. Wood knew of 'several youths most loyally educated there, and afterwards sent to the universities' (Wood, *Ath. Oxon.*). Heber considered that 'their success, considering their remote situation and the distresses of the times, appears to have been not inconsiderable' (Heber, 1.42). Throughout, Nicholson remained unswervingly loyal to the Anglican church, publishing in 1658 *An Apology for the Discipline of the Ancient Church*. Bishop Thomas Ken praised him as 'honest Nicholson', who 'didst answer satisfactorily' (Ken, 29).

At the Restoration Nicholson regained his parish and archdeaconry and was installed in his canonry. With his elevation to the bench of bishops imminent he took the degree of DD by diploma. On 6 January 1661 he was consecrated bishop of Gloucester by Gilbert Sheldon, bishop of London, whom he regarded as his patron, and Accepted Frewen, archbishop of York, and was given the parish of Bishop's Cleeve to augment a poor bishopric. Heber considered that 'his unshaken loyalty and bold and pertinacious defence of the church during its most helpless and hopeless depression had given him strong and legitimate claims on the patronage of the government' (Heber, 2.198). Heber would not follow Wood, who recorded the rumour that Nicholson had bribed Lord Clarendon to secure his own advancement. His primary task was, as his visitation articles of 1664 indicate, to secure uniformity in the diocese. Twenty-six ministers ejected in 1662 because they could not accept the Act of Uniformity had to be replaced. To hold two benefices was one solution. He thought highly of George Bull, rector of Suddington St Peter in his new diocese, and in 1662 Clarendon appointed him 'at the request and application of his constant Patron and worthy Diocesan Dr Nicholson' (Nelson, 52) to the neighbouring parish of Suddington St Mary. Nicholson showed himself sympathetic to nonconformists. To William Tracy, of Oddington, he 'offered as good a living as any in the diocese if he would conform' (*VCH Gloucestershire*, 2.39). His registers suggest a slow start to this process of recruitment, but a consistent record of institution can be traced from 1664 until 1671. He could persevere with laymen. Walter Bishop, a Quaker from Elmstone, was excommunicated and spent two years in Gloucester gaol, 'the bishop often sending for him and sometimes keeping him to dinner reasoning the case with him' (*CSP dom.*, 1667–8, 301). Thanks to his persuasion Walter conformed.

Clergymen were urged to restore the fabric of their churches, and Nicholson set an example at the cathedral. He provided a new font which occasioned sharp criticism from the writer of a scandalous pamphlet, *Magna Charta, or, More News from Rome*, one Wallis, 'a cobbler of scurrilous wit', whose 'scoffs are read with much applause by the people' (Wood, *Ath. Oxon.*, 3.950n.; *CSP dom.*, 1664–5, 309). Altar candlesticks were commissioned in 1661, and a splendid organ case was built by Thomas Harris in 1665.

One pleasurable task was to write a certificate of the orthodoxy, conformity, and good conduct of Abraham Gregory, the master of the free school at Gloucester, who was asking Cambridge to grant him his MA degree 'which he was unable to take during the late rebellion on account of his loyalty' (*CSP dom.*, 1664–5, 186). Another obligation was to support Henry Fowler, a firm royalist, whose election as mayor of Gloucester for 1671 was being challenged by a seditious faction in the city.

As bishop, Nicholson retained the archdeaconry of Brecon, and he engaged in a long and unsuccessful legal battle with William Lucy, bishop of St David's, to secure his right to hold archidiaconal visitations. Gloucester was not a wealthy bishopric and the income from his archdeaconry, his canonry, Llandeilo Fawr, and Bishop's Cleeve was a valuable resource. In 1663 he acquired the rectory of Llansanffraid-ym-Mechain, Montgomeryshire. He resigned Llandeilo Fawr on 6 October 1665, and his canonry on 12 September 1668. The archdeaconry he retained until the last months, perhaps the last weeks, of his life. His successor was collated three days after his death. He died at the bishop's palace on 5 February 1672 at the age of eighty, and was buried with his wife, who had died on 20 April 1663, in a side chantry of the lady chapel in Gloucester Cathedral. A monument was erected by her grandson and executor, Owen Brigstocke, gentleman, of Llechdwnni, sheriff of Carmarthenshire in 1657 and 1669. The graceful and affectionate inscription was written by Nicholson's protégé, Dr George Bell. Nicholson's will dated 18 November 1671 and 29 January 1671 divided land in Carmarthenshire and other property among his kin, especially his cousin and chancellor, John Nicholson (also his executor), and his wife's descendants, including Bridget Langley, latterly in charge of his household. He seems to have been childless.   DAVID WALKER

Sources Foster, *Alum. Oxon.* · Wood, *Ath. Oxon.*, 1st edn · R. Nelson, *The life of Dr George Bull* (1713) · R. Heber, *The life of the Right Rev. Jeremy Taylor D.D., lord bishop of Down Connor and Dromore* (1824) · E. Yardley, *Menevia sacra*, ed. F. Green (1927) · *CSP dom.*, 1664–5; 1667–8; 1670 · Carmarthen RO, MS 330.1 · *Calendar of the Clarendon state papers preserved in the Bodleian Library*, 5: 1660–1726, ed. F. J. Routledge (1970) · *VCH Gloucestershire*, vol. 2 · J. Buckley, *Genealogies of Carmarthenshire sheriffs*, 1: 1539–1759 (1910) · T. Ken, *Ichabod, or, The five groans of the church* (1663) · IGI [parish registers, London, St Mary Mounthaw, Fish Street Hill; Suffolk, Stratton St Mary] · PRO, PROB 11/338, fols. 366r–367r

Nicholson, William (1753–1815), chemist and inventor, was born in December 1753 in the City of London, the son of George Nicholson, a solicitor in the Inner Temple, and his wife, Hannah. He was baptized on 20 January 1754 at St Pancras Old Church, Middlesex. He was educated at a boarding-school near Richmond in Yorkshire, where he showed ability in languages and in making mathematical and optical instruments. At about the age of fifteen he joined the East India Company and made at least two voyages to China before 1773. In the late 1770s he worked as a commercial agent in Rotterdam for Josiah Wedgwood, the pottery manufacturer. By 1780 he had settled in London, and about this time he married Catherine, the daughter of Peter Boullie of London. They had twelve children, of

William Nicholson (1753–1815), by T. Blood, pubd 1812 (after Samuel Drummond)

whom eight survived to maturity. The eldest son, William, wrote a memoir of his father (now in the Bodleian Library, Oxford).

In London Nicholson embarked on a dual career as a mathematics teacher and author. It was probably an association with the dramatist Thomas Holcroft that introduced him to literary work. An anonymous publication critical of established religion, *The Doubts of the Infidels* (1781), was ascribed to him. So, later, were an enlarged edition of James Ralph's *Critical review of the public buildings, statues and ornaments in and around London and Westminster* (1783) and a translation from the French of Maistre de La Tour's *History of Ayder Ali Khan* (1784). Nicholson's first work under his own name was his *Introduction to Natural Philosophy* (2 vols., 1782), in which he extended the traditional natural philosophy curriculum into the fields of chemistry and the practical arts. The book became popular as an introductory text for students, reaching a fifth edition in 1805. With *The Navigator's Assistant* (1784), however, Nicholson was less successful in finding student readers.

In 1784, at Wedgwood's suggestion, Nicholson was appointed secretary of the General Chamber of Manufacturers of Great Britain, and it was in this capacity that he published *An abstract of such acts of parliament as are now in force for preventing the exportation of wool* (1786). In November 1784 he became one of the secretaries of the Coffee House Philosophical Society. This body, founded in 1780, convened for its first three years at the Chapter Coffee House, and then mostly at the Baptist Head Coffee House; its minutes, compiled by Nicholson, survive for the period 1780–87. In this group Nicholson associated with some of the leading members of the London scientific community, including J. H. de Magellan (who proposed him for

membership), Wedgwood, Richard Kirwan, Tiberius Cavallo, and Adair Crawford. The provincial honorary members included Joseph Priestley, James Watt, and James Keir from the Birmingham Lunar Society. Many of the discussions touched upon chemistry, particularly that of the new gases, or 'airs', recently discovered by Priestley and others.

In the late 1780s Nicholson turned his attention to the production of chemical texts. A series of translations of the works of Antoine François de Fourcroy began with the *Elements of Natural History and Chemistry* (4 vols., 1788), and the supplement to the same work (1789). Nicholson subsequently brought out *Synoptic Tables of Chemistry* (1801) and *A General System of Chemical Knowledge* (11 vols., 1807), also translated from Fourcroy.

Notwithstanding his interest in French contributions to chemistry, however, Nicholson was reluctant to embrace the oxygen theory of A. L. Lavoisier and his collaborators, or to renounce the traditional belief in phlogiston. In 1789 he published a second edition of Kirwan's *Essay on Phlogiston and the Composition of Acids*, which had originally appeared in 1787 and had been translated into French the following year with comments by the leading opponents of the phlogiston theory. Nicholson translated the French remarks into English and added a concluding response by Kirwan and an introduction of his own, in which he made influential criticisms of what seemed to be excessive claims to accuracy of weight measurement by Lavoisier. In his own chemistry textbook, *The First Principles of Chemistry* (1790; 3rd edn, 1796), Nicholson declined to commit himself to either side in 'the controversy for and against phlogiston', a position that he asserted was the proper one for a teacher of beginning students.

Chemical writings continued to comprise a large proportion of Nicholson's output in the 1790s. He produced his own *Dictionary of Chemistry* (2 vols.) in 1795, a work that was later revised as *A Dictionary of Practical and Theoretical Chemistry* (1808) and subsequently became the basis for Andrew Ure's *Dictionary of Chemistry* (1821). He also translated from J. A. C. Chaptal *Elements of Chemistry* (3 vols., 1791) and later *Chemistry Applied to the Arts and Manufactures* (4 vols., 1807). Another translation, which brought the method of chlorine bleaching to the attention of English readers, was *The Art of Bleaching Piece-Goods* (1799) from the work by Pajot de Charmes.

Chemistry was not the only field in which Nicholson was active in this period, however. He was engaged by Magellan to make the translation *Memoirs and Travels of Mauritius Augustus Count de Benyowsky* (2 vols., 1789), and he contributed a substantial introduction to the autobiography of this Hungarian adventurer. In 1787 he published a paper in the Royal Society's *Philosophical Transactions*, describing designs of slide-rules for calculations in various fields of applied mathematics. Two subsequent papers in the same journal (in 1788 and 1789) described an electrical induction apparatus, and a paper in the *Memoirs of the Literary and Philosophical Society of Manchester* (in 1789) detailed a new design of hydrometer. In 1790 Nicholson was granted a patent (no. 1748) for the plan of a machine for printing on paper and fabrics by means of rotating cylinders. The proposal remained, as Samuel Smiles put it, 'merely the register of an idea' (Smiles, 164), and was never put into practice. Nicholson was subsequently consulted by Friedrich König, the inventor of a machine for the same purpose constructed on different principles, but never asserted a prior claim. His next patents were for a device for manufacturing files by cutting grooves in metal (no. 2641, 1802), for a steam blasting apparatus (no. 2990, 1806), and for a suspension system for carriages (no. 3514, 1812).

At the beginning of the 1790s Nicholson was living in Red Lion Square, London; by the end of the decade, after moving several times, he had settled in Soho Square. In 1799 he is reported to have given a series of public lectures on natural philosophy and chemistry, and about the same time he opened a mathematics school in Soho, which initially attracted twenty students. The school gradually declined, though Nicholson continued it for several years with the help of hired teachers. Meanwhile, in March 1797, he had begun publication of his *Journal of Natural Philosophy, Chemistry, and the Arts*. 'Nicholson's journal', as it was known, offered its readers a novel combination of original research papers, reviews, and summaries of the contents of provincial and foreign journals. As editor, Nicholson inevitably shouldered most of the burden of producing translations, reports, and reviews. Sixty-two research papers in the journal are also ascribed to his authorship in the Royal Society's *Catalogue of Scientific Papers*.

Nicholson's most significant accomplishment, performed with the surgeon Anthony Carlisle in May 1800, was the use of current from a voltaic cell to decompose water into its constituent gases, hydrogen and oxygen. The following year both men were appointed to the committee for chemical investigation at the new Royal Institution, though Nicholson never had the honour of a fellowship of the Royal Society, as conferred on his collaborator.

In the first decade of the nineteenth century Nicholson became involved in various water-supply projects, an interest already signalled by his translation from J. B. Venturi, *Experimental Enquiries Concerning the Lateral Communication of Motion in Fluids* (1799). In December 1806 he was appointed engineer to the West Middlesex Water Works Company, but was dismissed the following year for neglecting his duties. He was subsequently involved with planning the water supply of Portsmouth by the Portsea Island Company, though his *Letter to the Proprietors of the Portsea Island Waterworks* (1810) reveals a falling-out there also. Towards the end of his life Nicholson was said to have been involved with a scheme for water supply to Southwark.

The author of some important scientific writings who could claim some notable discoveries, Nicholson also earned the respect of his contemporaries for his tireless work as a scientific journalist. But he never prospered financially, suffering, as one of his obituaries records, 'the common fate of projectors' (*New Monthly Magazine*, 77):

continual labour without material reward. His final decade was one of increasing financial difficulties. Apparently to relieve debts, he lent his name to the publishers of *The British Encyclopaedia* (6 vols., 1809). His journal faced strenuous competition from Alexander Tilloch's *Philosophical Magazine*, which had entered the market one year after his own. In 1813 Nicholson's journal was absorbed by Tilloch's, in what was ostensibly a merger but actually a take-over. About the same time Nicholson's health gave out. He died on 21 May 1815, at his home in Charlotte Street, London, after a lengthy illness.   JAN GOLINSKI

Sources W. Nicholson, memoir, Bodl. Oxf., MS Don. e.125 · R. S. Woolner, 'Life and scientific work of William Nicholson, 1753–1815', MSc diss., U. Lond., 1959 · *New Monthly Magazine*, 4 (1815), 76–7; repr. in *GM*, 1st ser., 86 (1816), 70–71 · 'Memoir of William Nicholson', *European Magazine and London Review*, 62 (1812), 83–7 · A. Thackray, 'Nicholson, William', *DSB* · *ESTC* · *Catalogue of scientific papers*, Royal Society, 1–6 (1867–72) · R. W. Corlass, 'A philosophical society of a century ago', *The Reliquary*, 18 (1877), 209–11 · T. H. Levene and G. L'E. Turner, eds., *Discussing chemistry and steam: the minutes of a Coffee House Philosophical Society 1780–1787* (2002) · S. Lilley, 'Nicholson's Journal', *Annals of Science*, 6 (1948–50), 78–101 · parish register (baptism), 20 Jan 1754, London, St Pancras Old Church · S. Smiles, *Men of invention and industry* (1884) · Nichols, *Lit. anecdotes*, 5.376

Archives MHS Oxf., Minutes of the Coffee House Philosophical Society, MS Gunther 4

Likenesses T. Blood, stipple (after portrait by S. Drummond), BM, NPG; repro. in *European Magazine and London Review*, facing p. 83 [*see illus.*]

Nicholson, William (1781–1844), portrait painter and etcher, was born at Ovingham, Northumberland, on 25 December 1781, and baptized there on 20 January 1782, the second of the four sons of James Nicholson, schoolmaster, of Ovingham, and his wife, Elizabeth Orton. His father was shortly afterwards appointed master of the grammar school in Newcastle, where Nicholson probably received his education. On leaving school he went to work for a stationer in the town, but showing a marked talent for drawing was allowed to become a pupil of Boniface Muss at Newcastle. Here he made rapid progress, and perhaps encouraged by his master's son Charles, began painting miniatures. He soon attracted commissions, but feeling that his prospects as a miniature painter might be better advanced at Hull, he moved there to join his engraver brother, and soon gained work painting miniatures of local army officers. He later began to work on a larger scale, and returning to Newcastle set up as a portrait painter, and in 1808 began to exhibit at the Royal Academy with *A Group of Portraits, &c., Servants of C. J. Brandling, M. P. Gosforth House, Northumberland*. In 1814, and having meanwhile exhibited a further two portraits at the Royal Academy, Nicholson decided to seek his fortune in Edinburgh. Here his first task, as he communicated in a letter to his friend the Revd John Hodgson, sent from Edinburgh on 3 July 1814, was to accumulate portraits of 'public characters', also expressing the opinion: 'If I once get connected here, which I flatter myself I shall be able to do, there is a much greater field here than in Newcastle' (MS letter, 3 July 1814, Newcastle Central Library). His faith in his ability to succeed as a painter in Edinburgh was justified shortly after his arrival there by the acceptance of eight of

William Nicholson (1781–1844), by William Smellie Watson

his works for the seventh exhibition of the Edinburgh Exhibition Society, organized by the Associated Artists in 1814. These comprised genre, architectural, animal, landscape, and portrait works; among the portraits was one of the wood-engraver Thomas Bewick (1812; Laing Art Gallery, Newcastle), which was later engraved by Thomas Ranson, and in 1816 shown at the Royal Academy. In the following year he was represented by twenty works, including portraits of James Hogg, the Ettrick Shepherd, and Tennant the poet, and his name appears in the catalogue as a member of the Edinburgh Exhibition Society; and in 1816 he exhibited portraits of Daniel Terry the actor, the earl of Buchan, and a second portrait of Hogg, along with twenty other works. In April 1818 he began to publish, from 36 George Street, a series entitled Portraits of distinguished living characters of Scotland, drawn and etched by William Nicholson from his portraits and those by other painters. Two parts only, with text, of three plates each were issued; but further publication in that form was discontinued, though the artist continued to produce in the immediately succeeding years a few other etchings from his portraits, and in 1886 an edition of seven subjects was printed in America by his son, W. L. Nicholson, of Washington City, who possessed the original plates. Nicholson's etchings include portraits of Sir Walter Scott, James Hogg, Lord Jeffrey, George Thomson, Professor Playfair, Professor John Wilson, Sir William Allan, president of the Royal Scottish Academy, James Watt the engineer (in his eighty-second year, 1817); and among them was a reduced copy of Alexander Nasmyth's original portrait of Robert Burns, and a very striking reproduction of one of Sir Henry Raeburn's self-portraits. In his prospectus the artist stated that:

in the mode of execution, he has endeavoured to follow a middle style, combining, to the utmost of his power, the freedom of the painter's etching (and in this respect, of course, holding up Vandyke and Rembrandt to himself as his models), with the finish of a regular engraving.

The heads are carefully modelled, and they were considered successful as likenesses. In 1821 Nicholson married Maria, daughter of Walter Lamb, of Edinburgh, and in this year sent to the first modern exhibition of the Institution for the Encouragement of the Fine Arts in Scotland portraits of William Allan in Tartar costume, Sir Thomas Dick Lauder and his wife, and Sir Adam Ferguson; and in 1825 he exhibited ten works, including portraits of George Thomson and the Revd Dr Jamieson. His name first appears as an associate of the institution in the catalogue of their exhibition (of ancient pictures) in 1826.

Early in that year, together with the architect Thomas Hamilton, Nicholson was active in the foundation of a Scottish academy, and at the first general meeting of the Scottish Academy of Painting, Sculpture, and Architecture, held on 27 May 1826, he was elected secretary. Although he resigned on 26 April 1830 in order to pursue his professional commitments, he remained a valued member of the academy. He had sent twenty-six works to its first exhibition in 1827, and he contributed liberally to every one of its succeeding exhibitions, many of his later works being genre pictures and landscape and coast subjects in oils, until his death by fever, after a few days' illness, in Edinburgh, on 16 August 1844. He left two sons and two daughters.

Among the eminent men whose portraits were painted by Nicholson was Sir Walter Scott, of whom he executed at least four watercolours, the earliest of which is dated 1815, and was etched by the artist in 1817. Together with several other portraits by Nicholson, including those in oil of William Allan and James Hogg, and his own self-portrait, some of his portraits of Scott are in the Scottish National Portrait Gallery, Edinburgh. Others are at Abbotsford, where also are his watercolours of Scott's daughters, Sophia and Anne. The National Gallery of Scotland holds his watercolours of the poet Helen D'Arcy Cranstoun, and a sketchbook of Nicholson's early chalk studies. Nicholson's reputation as a portraitist has tended to obscure the fact that he was also an able painter of landscapes. Some of his earliest known work was in the latter genre, for example, his *North East View of St Nicholas Church, Newcastle, 1799* (Pease collection, Newcastle Central Library). At the Royal Scottish Academy from its foundation in 1839 until his death, Nicholson mainly showed landscapes.   J. M. GRAY, rev. MARSHALL HALL

Sources E. Mackenzie, *A descriptive and historical account of the town and county of Newcastle upon Tyne*, 2 vols. (1827) · G. Harvey, *Notes of the early history of the Royal Scottish Academy* (1870) · W. D. McKay and F. Rinder, *The Royal Scottish Academy, 1826–1916* (1917) · M. Hall, *The artists of Northumbria*, 2nd edn (1982) · H. Smailes, *The concise catalogue of the Scottish National Portrait Gallery* (1990) · K. Andrews and J. R. Brotchie, *Catalogue of Scottish drawings* (1960) · MS letter from W. Nicholson to Revd John Hodgson, 3 July 1814, cited in undated press cutting inserted in *Baptismal register, Ovingham parish church, volume one, 1679–1812*, Newcastle Central Library · 'Catalogue of Pease collection', Newcastle Central Library

Likenesses W. Nicholson, self-portrait, oils, Scot. NPG · W. Nicholson, self-portrait, oils, Royal Scot. Acad. · W. S. Watson, portrait, Royal Scot. Acad. [*see illus.*]

Nicholson, William (*bap.* 1782, *d.* 1849), poet, was born at Tannimaus, Borgue, Kirkcudbrightshire, and baptized on 15 August 1782, the youngest among seven or eight children of a carrier and publican, James Nicholson (*c*.1722–1802), and his wife, Barbara Houston (*c*.1741–1802), member of a notable family in close-knit Borgue. From his mother William learned traditional lore, the metrical psalms, and poems by Ramsay and Burns, while his father knew local characters, like the gypsy Billy Marshall, and loved music. He received a scanty education at Ringford, Kirkcudbrightshire, being ridiculed at school for his extreme short-sightedness (which afterwards limited his choice of occupation). His writing and spelling were not adequate to prepare his poetry for print, and it was thus primarily performance art; in its surviving written form his verse was inevitably influenced by the person transcribing it. At fourteen he became a pedlar, and at twenty he purchased a set of pipes; his music and poetry made him a welcome guest to customers in rural Galloway, Dumfriesshire, and Ayrshire.

The combination of outdoor solitude and intermittent conviviality suited Nicholson, and (though often criticized for preferring these to commerce) he appears to have been very successful as a pedlar until 1812, when he lost his capital in trying to set up a horse to carry his goods. By the winter of 1813 he was unemployed and, wishing to publish his poetry by subscription, he went to Edinburgh. The advertisement to his *Tales, in Verse, and Miscellaneous Poems: Descriptive of Rural Life and Manners* (1814) acknowledges the help of James Hogg: his 'generous and unwearied attention, since the Author came to Edinburgh, where he was almost friendless, and unknown'. Nicholson then set out on his rounds, bearing poems for his 1500 subscribers instead of muslins and tobacco pipes, and realized about £100. The collection mixes songs like 'Dark Rolling Dee' with more ambitious poems like 'The Country Lass', in which the subject's choice of Sandy the shepherd among her various wooers (a farmer's son, a kirkless minister, a shepherd, and a merchant) represents a sound preference for honest worth. Nicholson's failure in re-establishing himself in his trade was due to a fall in the price of muslins as well as to his increasing fondness for drink and preoccupation with unorthodox ideas.

In November 1825 Nicholson sold his goods and visited Glasgow to republish works advocating universal redemption: he heard voices, which urged him to travel to London on foot in 1826 to see George IV about Catholic emancipation and Greek independence. General Dirom helped with the expenses of his journey, and Allan Cunningham relieved his destitute state when he was robbed on arrival in London. John M'Diarmid wrote a memoir for a second edition of his poems of 1828, which includes his masterpiece of the supernatural, 'The Brownie of Blednoch'. His many friends included Alexander Murray and Henry Duncan of Ruthwell, while Mactaggart wrote in his *Scottish Gallovidian Encyclopedia* 'If I have a *saxpence* in the world, a

part of it be his, and a word to spare, let that be said in his favour' (Mactaggart, 487). Except for some temporary work as a drover Nicholson appears to have lived for the rest of his life as an itinerant bard and musician, maintained by his hearers and friends. He died in his native parish of Borgue on 16 May 1849, and was buried there, in Kirkandrews churchyard.

John Nicholson (*c*.1777/8–1866), publisher and antiquary, was the reputed elder brother of William. He married Mary Smith, daughter of a Russia merchant, on 2 November 1827 in Kirkcudbright, where he settled after being a handloom weaver and a soldier. He was a significant contributor to, as well as the printer of, works such as *The History of Galloway* (1841) and *Historical and Traditional Tales … Connected with the South of Scotland* (*c*.1843), and ran a short-lived newspaper, the *Stewartry Times*. He died of bronchitis, aged eighty-eight, on 11 September 1866 at Kirkcudbright. His wife predeceased him.

T. W. BAYNE, *rev.* GILLIAN HUGHES

Sources census returns for Kirkcudbright, 1841, 1851, 1861 · J. M'Diarmid, 'Life of the author', in W. Nicholson, *Tales in verse and miscellaneous poems: descriptions of rural life and manners* (1828) · C. Rogers, *The modern Scottish minstrel*, vol. 3 (1856) · A. Trotter, *East Galloway sketches, or, Biographical, historical and descriptive notices of Kirkcudbrightshire, chiefly in the nineteenth century* (1901) · J. Mactaggart, *The Scottish Gallovidian encyclopedia* (1824); new edn, ed. L. L. Andern (1981) · M. M'L. Harper, *Rambles in Galloway* (1876) · M. M'L. Harper, *The bards of Galloway* (1889) · J. Nicholson and W. Mackenzie, *The history of Galloway from the earliest period to the present times* (1841) · J. Nicholson, *Historical and traditional tales, sketches, poems, etc. connected with the south of Scotland* (*c*.1843) · M. M'L. Harper, memoir, in W. Nicholson, *Poetical works*, 3rd edn (1878) · J. Cameron, 'William Nicholson: the pedlar, piper, and poet of Galloway', Mitchell L., Glas. · *IGI* · d. cert.
Archives Hornel Library, Kirkcudbright, MS transcriptions of poems
Likenesses J. Faed, portrait, 1836 · engraving (after Faed portrait), repro. in W. Nicholson, *Poetical works*, 3rd edn (1878), frontispiece

Nicholson, William (1816–1865), politician in Australia, the son of Miles Nicholson, a farmer, and his wife, Hannah, *née* Dalziel, was born at Tretting Mill, Lamplugh, Cumberland, on 27 February 1816. Educated at Hensingham and Whitehaven, he became a clerk in Liverpool to the firm of McAndrew and Pilchard, fruit merchants, about 1836. In 1841 he married Susan Burkitt, *née* Fairclough, in Liverpool, and the couple emigrated to Melbourne, Australia, where Nicholson set up in business as a grocer. 'By the sheer force of intellect, energy, and character' (Kelly, 2.263) he rose to fortune, developing his business into the mercantile firm of W. Nicholson & Co.

In November 1848 Nicholson was elected to the city council of Melbourne for Latrobe ward. Early in 1850 he was created alderman, and on 9 November 1850 he became mayor of Melbourne. His year of office was one of the most eventful in the history of the colony, being that of the gold discoveries and the erection of Victoria into a separate government. He contested a city seat unsuccessfully in the first election (1851) for the partly elected legislative council but in November the following year, after resigning from the city council, was elected for North

Bourke in the legislative council, where he quickly came to the fore. In December he seconded an unsuccessful vote of censure on the government. During the same session he was elected a member of the committee to inquire into the state of the goldfields, the first of more than a score of select committees, including that on the constitution, on which he served; the following session he was on another committee for revising the constitution.

As mayor of Melbourne, Nicholson had consistently opposed a system of voting by ballot—a position he repeated in his first address to the electors of the legislative council in 1851. But he completely changed his views, and on 18 December 1855, after unsuccessful suggestions to the ministers to adopt the ballot, he moved a resolution to the effect that any electoral act should be based upon the principle of voting by ballot. The ministry made this a test question, and, being defeated by thirty-three votes to twenty-five, resigned office. Nicholson abandoned arrangements to visit England on being unexpectedly sent for by the governor, Sir Charles Hotham, but his attempt to construct a cabinet was ultimately unsuccessful. In spite of this failure, victory for the ballot was won: Nicholson forced the recalled ministry to accept it as part of their electoral act, his own project being superseded by the method drafted by the lawyer and politician Henry Samuel Chapman.

Shortly afterwards (1856) Nicholson returned to England, where he was welcomed as the 'father of the ballot'—not yet adopted in the old country—and spoke in public on the subject on several occasions. On 14 April 1858, at the Freemasons' Hall, he was presented by the council of the Society for Promoting the Adoption of the Ballot with an address, signed by Richard Cobden, John Bright, and others, recognizing his services in the cause. John Stuart Mill, writing to Chapman in the same year, refers to Nicholson's fame, and the interest aroused in England by the adoption of the ballot in Victoria.

After returning in July 1858 to Melbourne, Nicholson unsuccessfully contested one of its districts, but was elected to the assembly for Murray in January 1859, and for Sandridge at the general election in August of the same year. The Constitutional Association, formed to overthrow the existing O'Shanassy government, did handsomely at the election, and in November 1859, at the opening of parliament, Nicholson defeated the government on an amendment to the address.

Nicholson now became premier, and formed a strong ministry, with James McCulloch in charge of finance. His attempt to settle the land question in November 1859 on the basis of throwing open the colony's lands in blocks to free selection, and of payment by instalments, led to a nine-month battle between assembly and council. The upper chamber emasculated his bill, and Nicholson offered to resign, but the governor, Sir Henry Barkly, declined to accept his resignation on public grounds. Nicholson continued in office, reinstating the more important clauses and sending the bill back to the council. That chamber cut out the amendments a second time, and

Nicholson resigned; but after the failure of three others to form a ministry he returned to office, with his cabinet impaired by the loss of two leading ministers. Ultimately, after the storming of parliament house (28 May) and compromise on both sides, the bill, considerably changed and weakened, became the Land Act of 1860. After a short recess in November 1860, Nicholson was defeated on an amendment to the address and resigned office. In 1862 he joined O'Shanassy's third administration, without portfolio.

Nicholson was a great promoter of the benefit building society systems, a founder of the Bank of Victoria, and chairman of the Australian Fire and Life Insurance Company, the Hobson's Bay (Railway) Company, and the Melbourne chamber of commerce. The Early Closing Association enjoyed some success under his presidency (1851), and he held a very high reputation as a magistrate.

Nicholson's health deteriorated in 1863, and the onset of paralysis in January 1864 led to his death, at Barham House, St Kilda, Melbourne, on 10 March 1865. He was buried according to Anglican rites at the Melbourne general cemetery on 13 March. He was survived by his wife and their four sons. In an obituary in the Melbourne *Argus* he was described as 'a straightforward, well-meaning, honest, and upright man', and as 'the father of the ballot'. While Chapman had drafted the ballot legislation, Nicholson had moved the adoption of the principle and persisted with the issue. The introduction of the ballot constitutes his enduring claim to our attention.

C. A. HARRIS, rev. JOHN LACK

Sources *The Argus* [Melbourne] (9 July 1851) · *The Argus* [Melbourne] (28 July 1851) · *The Argus* [Melbourne] (23 Aug 1851) · *The Argus* [Melbourne] (19 Dec 1855) · *The Argus* [Melbourne] (20 Dec 1855) · *The Argus* [Melbourne] (10 March 1865) · W. Kelly, *Life in Victoria, or, Victoria in 1853 and Victoria in 1859, showing the march of improvement*, 2 (1859), 262–72 · T. McCombie, *The history of the colony of Victoria from its settlement to the death of Sir Charles Hotham* (1858) · P. Mennell, *The dictionary of Australasian biography* (1892) · G. Serle, *The golden age: a history of the colony of Victoria, 1851–1861* (1963) · P. Cook, 'Nicholson, William', *AusDB*, vol. 5 · B. Barrett, *The civic frontier: the origin of local communities and local government in Victoria* (1979) · D. Dunstan, *Governing the metropolis: politics, technology and social change in a Victorian city: Melbourne, 1850–1891* (1984) · R. Wright, *A people's counsel: a history of the parliament of Victoria, 1856–1990* (1992) · E. Scott, 'The history of the Victorian ballot', *Victorian Historical Magazine*, 8 (1920–21), 1.1–13; 2.49–62 · R. S. Neale, 'H. S. Chapman and the "Victorian" Ballot', *Historical Studies: Australia and New Zealand*, 12 (1965–7), 506–21

Likenesses portrait, *c*.1855, Melbourne town hall, Australia; destroyed by fire, 1920s · photograph (after portrait), repro. in Scott, 'History of the Victorian ballot', 8/1 (Nov 1920), facing p.1

Nicholson, William Adams (1803–1853), architect, was born on 8 August 1803 at Southwell, Nottinghamshire, the son of James Nicholson, carpenter and joiner, later sub-agent to Sir Richard Sutton's estates in Nottinghamshire and Norfolk, and his wife, Sarah, *née* Adams. From 1821 to 1824 Nicholson was articled to the London architect John Buonarotti Papworth. He was twice married. In 1824 he married Leonora, youngest daughter of William *Say, mezzotint engraver, of Norton Street, London, and

Papworth's sister-in-law. His second wife was Anne Tallant, who survived him. There were no children from either marriage.

In 1828 Nicholson moved to Lincoln, and built up an extensive practice. His designs included churches at Glandford-Brigg, Wragby, and Kirmond, and he supervised the restoration of many other churches, including St Peter's at Gowts in Lincoln, which was not quite completed at his death. He also designed the Wesleyan chapel in Lincoln in 1837. As well as churches, he designed country houses, including Worsborough Hall, Yorkshire, the castle of Bayons Manor, and Elkington Hall, near Louth, Lincolnshire. He superintended the rebuilding of the village of Blankney, near Lincoln, and built farm buildings for several landowners, including Sir J. Wyldbore Smith and Charles Turnor. His public buildings included Mansfield town hall, Nottinghamshire, and the union workhouse and the corn exchange in Lincoln. From 1839 to 1846, as Nicholson and Goddard, the firm carried out many works.

Nicholson was elected a fellow of the Institute of British Architects in 1835. His 'Report on the construction of the stone arch between the west towers of Lincoln Cathedral' was printed in the *Transactions of the Institute of British Architects* (1842). He was also a member of the Lincolnshire Literary Society, and of the Lincolnshire Topographical Society, to whose *Selection of Papers Relative to the County of Lincoln* (1843) he contributed.

Nicholson died in Boston, Lincolnshire, on 8 April 1853 and was buried in the churchyard of St Swithin, Lincoln.

W. A. VAN S. PAPWORTH, rev. ANNE PIMLOTT BAKER

Sources Dir. Brit. archs. · Boase, Mod. Eng. biog. · The Builder, 11 (1853), 262 · IGI
Archives Lincs. Arch., estimate of alterations at Brattleby Hall; notebook of reports on churches, incl. contributions from others · RIBA, nomination papers
Likenesses portrait, RIBA BAL, photographic collection

Nicholson, William Gustavus, Baron Nicholson (1845–1918), army officer, the youngest son of William Nicholson Nicholson (born Phillips, in 1827 he assumed the surname and arms of Nicholson), deputy lieutenant and JP, and his wife, Martha, daughter of Abram Rhodes of Wold, Newton Hall, Yorkshire, was born on 2 March 1845 at Mansion House, Roundhay Park, Leeds. He was educated at Leeds grammar school and the Royal Military Academy, Woolwich, where he passed out first in his term and was awarded the Pollock medal. In March 1865 he was commissioned into the Royal Engineers, and from 1868 to 1871 served on Barbados. He volunteered for service in India and worked in the public works department at Hyderabad and as assistant engineer in the Punjab irrigation branch. In 1873 he transferred to the military works department. He married in 1871 Victoria, daughter of D. Dillon. They had no children, and she survived her husband.

Nicholson accompanied the Kandahar field force in 1878 and the Kurram field force in 1879 during the Second Anglo-Afghan War. He served as a field engineer in Afghanistan, fighting in the engagements at the Shutar

William Gustavus Nicholson, Baron Nicholson (1845–1918), by Bassano, c.1898

Gardan Pass, Charasia, and distinguished himself during the defence at Lataband. In 1880 he accompanied Sir Frederick Roberts from Kabul to Kandahar, fighting in the battle on 1 September outside the city. He was awarded a brevet majority for his services in Afghanistan, where he established a reputation as a skilled staff officer. Perhaps more importantly he attracted Roberts's attention. In 1880 he was appointed secretary to the defence committee responsible for examining coast and frontier defences in India.

In 1882 Nicholson served with the Indian contingent during the Egyptian campaign, taking part in the battle of Tell al-Kebir. In 1884 he accompanied Sir Robert Sandeman and Sir Charles Metcalfe MacGregor on a reconnaissance mission in Baluchistan. From 1885 to 1890 he was assistant adjutant-general, Royal Engineers, in India, working with the defence committee. In 1886–7 he served in Burma as assistant adjutant-general, being mentioned in dispatches and awarded the brevet of lieutenant-colonel. He acted as military secretary to Roberts, the commander-in-chief, from 1890 to 1893, after which he worked for two years in the military works department as chief engineer on the north-west frontier. In 1895 he was appointed deputy adjutant-general of the Punjab command. He served as chief of staff with the Tirah expeditionary force in 1897–8, under Sir William Lockhart, carrying out punitive operations against the Afridis in Tirah. In 1898 he was created KCB for his services, and appointed adjutant-general in India.

Roberts requested that Nicholson join him as military secretary following the initial disasters of the Second South African War. In February 1900 Nicholson was appointed director of transport, in which capacity he exerted an important influence on the campaign. He also participated in operations in the Orange Free State—including Paardeberg, Poplar Grove, Driefontein, and the Vet and Zand rivers. He also took part in the fighting near Johannesburg, Pretoria, and Diamond Hill in the Transvaal. In November 1900 he returned to England, and for his services was twice mentioned in dispatches; in October 1900 he was promoted major-general.

Following the appointment of Roberts as commander-in-chief, Nicholson was promoted lieutenant-general and offered in November 1901 the post of director-general of mobilization and intelligence at the War Office. He proved a great success, overseeing the preparation of detailed defence plans and the collection of intelligence, laying the foundations for a modern general staff despite strong opposition. Following the reorganization of the War Office in 1904, Nicholson was eventually appointed as chief British military attaché with the Japanese army in Manchuria. In July 1904 he joined the Second Army, which he accompanied during the battle of Liaoyang and its later capture. Despite bad health he remained in the Far East until January 1905 before returning to England.

Nicholson succeeded Sir Hubert Plumer as quartermaster-general in December 1905 and the following year was promoted general. In 1908 he succeeded Sir Neville Lyttelton as chief of the Imperial General Staff and the same year was made a GCB. During his tenure of office Nicholson played a crucial part in devising new strategic plans, in the reorganization of the British army, and in the consolidation of the Territorial Force and of a modern general staff. He was made an aide-de-camp general to George V in 1910, promoted field marshal in 1911, and raised to the peerage on retiring from the army council in 1912. Later the same year he was appointed chairman of the army in India committee, created to inquire into the role and cost of the Indian army. After a year in India examining evidence he returned home when its report was submitted in 1913. The outbreak of the war, however, prevented its controversial recommendations being implemented.

Nicholson served on the committee of imperial defence during the war, participating in the commissions of inquiry into the Dardanelles and Mesopotamia campaigns. He also acted as chairman of the London Territorial Force Association and in October 1916 was made colonel-commandant of the Royal Engineers. He died on 13 September 1918 at his home at 51 Pont Street, Chelsea, London, and his body was interred four days later at Brompton cemetery. At his death the peerage became extinct.

Nicholson enjoyed a brilliant yet rather unusual military career, mostly in India. He was a gifted staff officer and military administrator, but his career was dogged by a reputation for being difficult to handle: he was known as Old Nick. Despite never having personally commanded a unit or passed Staff College, exceptionally he rose to field marshal and held the office of chief of the Imperial General Staff through sheer hard work, personal intelligence, and ability.

T. R. MOREMAN

Sources G. K. Scott-Moncrieff, 'Memoir: Field-Marshal Lord Nicholson GCB, Colonel Commandant, RE', *Royal Engineers Journal*, new ser., 28 (1918), 237–49 · *The Times* (17 Sept 1918) · 'Death of Lord Nicholson, soldier and administrator', *The Times* (15 Sept 1918) · J. Gooch, *The plans of war: the general staff and British military strategy, c.1900–1916* (1974) · 1892–1914 letters (72) to Spencer Wilkinson, NAM, NAM 9011-42 · C. E. Callwell, *Tirah 1897* (1911) · Lord Roberts [F. S. Roberts], *Forty-one years in India*, 2 vols. (1897) · *Army List* · DNB · *Proceedings of the committee on the obligations devolving on the army of India, its strengths and cost (Army of India Committee, 1912)* (1913) · T. A. Heathcote, *The military in British India: the development of British land forces in south Asia, 1600–1947* (1995) · T. Pakenham, *The Boer War*, another edn (1982) · Burke, *Peerage* · WWW

Archives CUL, corresp. with Lord Hardinge · NAM, letters to Lord Roberts · NAM, letters to Spencer Wilkinson · NRA, priv. coll., letters to General Sir J. S. Ewart

Likenesses Bassano, photographs, c.1898, NPG [*see illus.*] · G. H. Neale, oils, Royal Engineers, Chatham, Kent · portrait (as Colonel Commandant RE), repro. in Scott-Moncrieff, 'Memoir' · portrait, Royal Engineers; destroyed by fire, c.1996

Wealth at death £91,151 10s.: probate, 7 Nov 1918, CGPLA Eng. & Wales

Nicholson, Sir William Newzam Prior (1872–1949), artist, was born at 12 London Road, Newark-on-Trent, on 5 February 1872, the youngest child of William Newzam Nicholson (1816–1899), engineer, of the Trent ironworks, and later MP for Newark, and his second wife, Ann Elizabeth Prior (1839–1899), of Woodstock, Oxfordshire. Nicholson's disinclination, at an early age, for the normal routine of studies at Magnus Grammar School, Newark (1881–8), where he was at first a boarder, and the lively interest that he took in the lessons of the school's drawing master, W. H. Cubley, finally convinced his parents that it would be foolish to oppose his determination to become an artist.

At the age of sixteen Nicholson passed the entrance examination to the school of art at Bushey run by Hubert von Herkomer. Here he met fellow student Mabel Scott Lauder Pryde (1871–1918), who was to become his first wife. She introduced him to her brother, the artist James Ferrier *Pryde. Nicholson left Herkomer's in 1891 following what Herkomer termed 'a piece of Whistlerian impudence' (William had posed a nude model with an open umbrella) (Steen, *William Nicholson*, 44). In the autumn of that year Nicholson visited Paris and enrolled for a short time at the Académie Julian. After his marriage on 25 April 1893, he settled first at the Eight Bells, Denham, Buckinghamshire, where he and his wife were almost immediately joined by her brother, James Pryde.

In 1894 Pryde and Nicholson, as J. & W. Beggarstaff, began to collaborate on a series of posters which were revolutionary in style with their boldness of outline, simplicity of treatment, and striking silhouettes, and their flat, pure colours. These included designs for *Don Quixote* (made for the 1895 production of Sir Henry Irving but not

Sir William Newzam Prior Nicholson (1872–1949), by Augustus John, 1909

finest portraits are those of Max Beerbohm (*c*.1903) and Gertrude Jekyll (1920), both in the National Portrait Gallery, London; of his friend Walter Greaves (1917) in Manchester City Galleries; and of George Saintsbury (1923) at Merton College, Oxford. Nicholson's real love, however, was landscape and still-life painting, and it is these works that are especially highly regarded today. His son Ben *Nicholson admired—and acknowledged a debt to—their 'poetic spirit' (B. Nicholson, 73). Modest in scale, they have a tonal mastery, economy of means, sensitivity of touch, and acuteness of perception which is very distinctive. Nicholson had a special feeling for the English downlands, whether the Sussex downs around Rottingdean where he moved in 1909 or, later, the Wiltshire downs. Between the wars he also painted in France and Spain. His still-life compositions took as their subjects the silver, lustreware, jugs and mugs, vases, goblets, glass, flowers, fruit, mushrooms, and fish of his domestic surroundings. His repertory of still-life objects was a heritage Ben Nicholson prized.

William Nicholson's painting has affinities with Whistler and Manet: he did not respond to later French painting. He had a great admiration for the work of Velázquez. In the 1920s his palette lightened and his handling became freer: these later paintings are more experimental and he learned from the younger artists of his own family—his second wife, Edith (Edie) Stuart Wortley (1890–1958), daughter of Sir Lionel Phillips, first baronet, and widow of Lieutenant-Colonel John Stuart Wortley, whom he had married in 1919 after his first wife died of influenza, his son Ben, and Ben's wife, Winifred Nicholson [see Nicholson, (Rosa) Winifred]. William was independent of any school of painting and refused election to the Royal Academy, at which he never exhibited. He was knighted in 1936 and had an important retrospective at the National Gallery, London, in 1942.

Nicholson had a strong interest in the theatre and made designs for a number of productions. In 1904, for example, J. M. Barrie invited him to design costumes and scenery for the first production of *Peter Pan* and in 1922 he contributed sets and costumes to Nigel Playfair's production of John Gay's opera *Polly*. In 1925 he designed the décor and costumes for Léonide Massine's ballet *The Rake* in the revue *On with the Dance* mounted by C. B. Cochran and Noël Coward at the London Pavilion. Nicholson loved poetry and illustrated the works of his writer friends (such as W. H. Davies and Siegfried Sassoon) and others. Together with the writer and poet Robert Graves, who married Nicholson's daughter Nancy in 1918, he edited the review *The Owl*. His natural sympathy with children produced work of great charm such as *The Pirate Twins* (1929), written and illustrated by Nicholson, and his illustrations for Margery Williams's *The Velveteen Rabbit* (1922).

In figure Nicholson was slight and graceful and very agile. His friend Gordon Craig described him as 'skilful beyond words in handling anything where eye and hand and brain have to be under perfect control, and in absolute harmony' (G. Craig, *Woodcuts and some Words*, 1924, 8).

used on the hoardings), *Harper's Magazine* (1895), and *Rowntree's Elect Cocoa* (1896).

The Beggarstaff partnership was short-lived but the originality of their posters was widely recognized. In the following years Nicholson evolved out of the posters a personal style which he began to exploit through the medium of the woodcut. In this venture he had the good fortune to be encouraged by J. A. McNeill Whistler who recommended him to the publisher William Heinemann. The publications that followed established Nicholson's solo reputation. *An Alphabet* and *An Almanac of Twelve Sports*, with verses by Rudyard Kipling, both appeared in 1897 (title-pages post-dated 1898), *London Types*, with verses by W. E. Henley, in 1898, and *The Square Book of Animals* in 1899. Nicholson also made a series of portrait woodcuts, the first of which was the irreverent, affectionate jubilee portrait of Queen Victoria (originally published in Henley's *New Review* in June 1897), which brought him great success. These were collected in the two series of *Twelve Portraits* (1899 and 1902), the first of which was awarded a gold medal at the 1900 Paris Exhibition. The Heinemann windmill colophon still used today was designed by Nicholson at this time.

After the turn of the century Nicholson concentrated on painting, and portrait commissions were his main means of support. His subjects included many of the prominent figures of the period, and in 1909 he wrote of 'relays of sitters every twenty minutes' (Nicholson to T. W. Bacon, 26 May 1909, Whitworth Art Gallery, Manchester). He was best-known in his lifetime as a portrait painter. Among his

He dressed with meticulous but unconventional fastidiousness. His wardrobe was famous for its delicately spotted shirts and dressing gowns, canary-yellow waistcoats, and immaculate white trousers—worn also for painting. His distinctive taste was evident in his homes, for example The Grange at Rottingdean and his London studio-residence at Apple Tree Yard. He had a very particular sense of humour and a fondness for puns. He was companionable and would paint unperturbed while a stream of visitors passed through his studio. Ben Nicholson observed: 'Behind his personality lay a very simple direct painterly approach' (B. Nicholson, 71). He did not like to talk about art and eschewed art theory.

Nicholson's singular achievement rests on three diverse strands of work: the pioneering and influential posters and woodcuts made when he was still in his twenties, the portraits of distinguished contemporaries, and the poetic landscapes and still-lifes. His best work has a subtlety, virtuosity, and individual voice that places it with the finest of its period.

With his first wife, Mabel, Nicholson had four children, Ben, Tony, Nancy, later a fabric designer, and the architect Christopher (Kit). Tony was killed on active service in France in 1918 a few months after his mother's death. With his second wife, Edie, Nicholson had a daughter, Liza, who was born in 1920. The writer Marguerite Elena May Steen (1894–1975) was Nicholson's companion from 1935 until his death. Nicholson died at his home, Little Triton, Blewbury, Berkshire, on 16 May 1949. He was cremated on 19 May and his ashes were buried at Newark on 22 July. SOPHIE BOWNESS

Sources DNB · A. Nicholson, ed., *William Nicholson: painter* (1996) · C. Campbell, *William Nicholson: the graphic work* (1992) · M. Steen, *William Nicholson* (1943) · L. Browse, *William Nicholson* (1956) [with a catalogue of the oil paintings] · B. Nicholson, 'William Nicholson', *London Magazine, a Monthly Review of Literature*, new ser., 7/3 (1967), 69–73 · C. Campbell, *The Beggarstaff posters: the work of James Pryde and William Nicholson* (1990) · P. Reed, *catalogue raisonné* of William Nicholson's oil paintings [forthcoming] · *William Nicholson, painter: landscape and still life* (1995) [exhibition catalogue, Towner Art Gallery, Eastbourne, 4 Nov – 31 Dec 1995] · *William Nicholson: paintings, drawings, and prints* (1980) [exhibition catalogue, FM Cam., 15 July – 25 Aug 1980] · R. Nichols, *William Nicholson* (1948) · S. Kennedy North, *William Nicholson* (1923) · *William Nicholson, 1872–1949* (1990) [exhibition catalogue, Browse and Darby, London, 22 March – 21 April 1990] · private information (2004) · *CGPLA Eng. & Wales* (1950) · b. cert. · m. certs. · M. Steen, *Pier glass: more autobiography* (1968) · University of Manchester, Whitworth Art Gallery, T. W. Bacon archive

Archives Tate collection, letters · V&A, department of prints and drawings · William Nicholson Trust Archive, London | Tate collection, letters to Ben Nicholson · University of Manchester, Whitworth Art Gallery, T. W. Bacon archive

Likenesses P. May, drawing, 1895 (*The Beggarstaffs*), repro. in *The Studio*, 5 (1895), 214 · W. Nicholson, woodcut, 1897 ('A was an Artist'), repro. in Nicholson, *An Alphabet* (1898) · J. Pryde, lithograph, c.1897, repro. in *The Studio*, 12 (1898), 179 · P. May, drawing, 1898 (*Brother Brushes*), priv. coll. · M. Beerbohm, pen and wash caricature, c.1900, priv. coll.; repro. in *Sir William Nicholson* (1967) [exhibition catalogue, Marlborough Gallery, London, March 1967] · M. Beerbohm, caricature, watercolour, 1903, Castle Museum, Nottingham · A. L. Coburn, photogravure, 1908, NPG · W. Orpen, group portrait, oils, 1908 (*A Bloomsbury Family*), Scottish National Gallery of Modern Art, Edinburgh; repro. in A. Nicholson, ed., *William Nicholson, painter*, 93 · A. John, oils, 1909, FM Cam. [*see illus.*] · M. Arbuthnot, photographs, 1912 · W. Orpen, group portrait, oils, 1912 (*The Café Royal*), Musée d'Orsay, Paris · D. Morris, chalk and pencil drawing, 1914, Whitworth Art Gallery, Manchester · E. Nicholson [Elizabeth Drury], oils, c.1919, priv. coll.; repro. in Nicholson, ed., *William Nicholson*, 178 · M. Beerbohm, caricature, drawing, 1924, priv. coll.; repro. in M. Beerbohm, *Observations* (1925) · Winifred Nicholson, oils, c.1926–1927, priv. coll.; repro. in Nicholson, ed., *William Nicholson*, 220 · D. Low, oils, c.1934, Wolverhampton Art Gallery · A. C. Cooper, two photographs, 1943, NPG

Wealth at death £7558 15s. 3d.: probate, 6 May 1950, *CGPLA Eng. & Wales*

Nicholson, William Patteson (1876–1959), Presbyterian minister and evangelist, was born on 3 April 1876 at Cottown, Bangor, co. Down, one of seven children of sea captain John G. Nicholson and his wife, Ellen Campbell (*d.* 1931). The Nicholsons were devout Presbyterians; William Patteson was the name of their minister in Bangor and three of their children became foreign missionaries. William, however, originally chose a different path, going to sea at sixteen, following education at Fisherwick Presbyterian church school and the Model School in Belfast, to where the family had moved. After a spell as a hard-drinking railway construction worker in South Africa he returned home and experienced a sudden conversion on 23 May 1899. He entered the Glasgow Bible Training Institute in 1901 and among his lecturers were James Orr and James Denney of the Glasgow United Free Church College and the famous Edinburgh preacher Alexander Whyte. In his vacations he assisted his former Belfast minister, Dr Henry Montgomery, in his Shankill Road mission, gaining experience of open-air evangelism.

In 1903 Nicholson began his apprenticeship as an evangelist, employed by the Lanarkshire Christian Union, preaching with some success in a community of coalminers and steelworkers. He married Ellison D. Marshall (*d.* 1926) of Bellshill, Lanarkshire, in 1907 and the following year he joined the team of American evangelists Chapman and Alexander, with whom he worked in Australia and America. His growing reputation as a preacher led to his ordination in 1914 as an evangelist in the Presbyterian church in the USA and to his appointment in 1918 to the staff of the Los Angeles Bible Institute under its dean, the prominent American fundamentalist R. A. Torrey.

On a visit to his native Ulster in 1920 he was persuaded to undertake a mission in Bangor; this led to a series of missions in Portadown, Lurgan, Newtownards, Lisburn, Belfast, Londonderry, Ballymena, and Carrickfergus, which had a tremendous impact in the province, making his name a household word. The political situation was explosive in the context of the partition of Ireland, accompanied by widespread sectarian violence. Gunfire could be heard during mission services in Belfast and in the first week of the mission in the Albert Hall in February 1922 more than thirty people were killed and almost one hundred wounded in Belfast, yet thousands attended. Nicholson's populist presentation of the gospel attracted large numbers of working men, particularly shipyard workers, normally beyond the ministrations of the churches. His message was simple and stark: turn or burn, Christ or hell, reject the 'world'—alcohol, tobacco, dancing, the theatre, and the cinema. Thousands responded—and more than 20,000 in the province professed conversion.

Nicholson has been credited with saving Ulster from civil war, and a republican commented that the men who had been trying to shoot him were now trying to convert him. It has also been suggested, however, that, as in the revival of 1859, the Nicholson 'revival' confirmed Ulster protestant consciousness of being different from Catholic Ireland, thereby justifying partition. Nicholson returned to Los Angeles in 1923 but a year later he was back in Ulster to lead a new series of missions, including one in Dublin. His ministry had always been divisive, but now the divisions were sharper. A militant fundamentalist, coming from the conflict between fundamentalists and modernists in America, he attacked alleged modernism in Irish Presbyterianism, contributing significantly to a campaign which culminated in the trial for heresy before the Presbyterian general assembly of a theological professor, Ernest Davey. Davey's acquittal led to a small schism in Irish Presbyterianism but many of Nicholson's converts became ministers and elders in the mainstream Presbyterian church, undoubtedly strengthening its conservative puritan and pietist traditions.

It was not only in Ulster that Nicholson was effective as an evangelist: he held successful missions in Australia, New Zealand, South Africa, and the United States. Perhaps his most improbable evangelistic success was in Cambridge University in 1926. His irreverent populism attracted some undergraduates who affectionately called him 'Willie Nick', though others, including the future archbishop of Canterbury, Michael Ramsay, were permanently prejudiced against evangelicalism by Nicholson's buffoonery and vulgarity. The Cambridge Inter-Collegiate Christian Union, which had invited him, was greatly strengthened both by the large number of converts and by the impact of Nicholson's ministry.

Later in 1926, while Nicholson was leading a mission in Australia, his wife died suddenly. Subsequently he himself suffered a heart attack and in 1927 he married the matron of the Australian hospital in which he had been treated, Fanny Elizabeth Collett (d. 1979). She returned with him to his home in Glendale, Los Angeles. He had resigned from the Los Angeles Bible Institute in 1924 but had retained his home there and his son worked for the Bible Institute. There were also two daughters of his first marriage.

Nicholson's cardiac problems handicapped his later life and ministry, though he made frequent visits to Ulster and conducted a number of missions without making the impact of earlier years. The Revd Ian Paisley claims that at the beginning of his ministry in what was then a mission hall on the Ravenhill Road in Belfast, Nicholson gave him his blessing, praying that God would give him a tongue as sharp as a cow's in the service of the gospel. Returning to Ireland in 1959, Nicholson suffered a final heart attack and died on 29 October in the Victoria Hospital, Cork. He was buried in Clandeboye cemetery in his native Bangor on 2 November 1959 after a service in Hamilton Road Presbyterian Church. FINLAY HOLMES

Sources S. W. Murray, *W. P. Nicholson: flame for God in Ulster* (1973) · *From civil war to revival victory* (Faith Mission, Belfast, 1926) · I. R. K. Paisley, *The man God used to deliver Ulster* (1976) · S. E. Long, *W. P. Nicholson: the rude evangelist* (1983) · S. Barnes, *All for Jesus: the life of W. P. Nicholson* (1996) · D. N. Livingstone and R. A. Wells, *Ulster–American religion* (1999) · O. Chadwick, *Michael Ramsay: a life* (1990) · F. D. Coggan, *Christ and the colleges* (1934) · b. cert.
Likenesses photograph, repro. in Murray, *W. P. Nicholson*

Nicholson [née Roberts], **(Rosa) Winifred** (1893–1981), painter and writer, was born on 21 December 1893 in Oxford, the eldest child in the family of two daughters and one son of Charles Henry Roberts MP, of Oxford, and his wife, Lady Cecilia Maude (d. 1947), daughter of George James Howard, ninth earl of Carlisle. She studied art formally at the Byam Shaw School of Art in London c.1910–1914 and 1918–1919, but as a teenager learned much from her grandfather George Howard, a self-taught painter who befriended the artists Edward Burne-Jones, William Morris, and Giovanni Costa. In 1920 she married the painter Ben (Benjamin Lauder) *Nicholson (1894–1982), son of the painter Sir William Newzam Prior *Nicholson and his wife, Mabel Pryde, also a painter. They had two sons and a daughter. Their marriage was dissolved in 1938 and Ben Nicholson married the sculptor Barbara Hepworth, but the eighteen-year working partnership that Winifred and Ben Nicholson shared was most fruitful for the development of their artistic careers.

In 1924 Winifred Nicholson purchased Bankshead, a stone farmhouse built over the remains of a Roman milecastle on Hadrian's wall, near Brampton, Cumberland, and this unusual residence remained her home all her life. Although it was high up and windswept, she created at Bankshead a garden full of her favourite wild flowers, which helped to inspire both her painting and her writing.

In 1925, at the Mayor Gallery, London, Nicholson had the first of her eighteen one-woman exhibitions, which was well received critically. There was a major retrospective at the Tate Gallery in 1987. Between 1926 and 1935 when, with her husband, she was a leading member of and exhibitor with the Seven and Five Society, her work was consistently praised for its idiosyncratic approach to light and colour. This was her most important artistic legacy. From 1926 to 1930 she shared her ideas about colour with the painter Christopher Wood and for those few years their work looked similar. She kept to a narrow range of subject matter, the most prominent being a composition of flowers on a window-ledge with a panoramic landscape beyond.

Winifred Nicholson's ideas on colour theory appeared in an essay entitled 'Unknown colour', published in *Circle: an International Survey of Constructive Art* (ed. J. L. Martin, B. Nicholson, and N. Gabo) in 1937. In this she stated her belief that colour was not tied down to form but instead floated free, and that research into the nature of colour would lead to questions 'about being itself'. Her mind was

(Rosa) **Winifred Nicholson** (1893–1981), by Pamela Chandler, 1969

of an imaginative and spiritual bent, and from the 1930s until her death she was an ardent Christian Scientist. This led her to shun alcohol and medical establishments and to follow a practical, independent, and disciplined life. She designed and made her own clothes, sometimes colouring the fabric with home-made dyes; this gave the articles a most individual style and character. Her pea-pod soup and her manner of driving were legendary. Winifred Nicholson died at Bankshead on 5 March 1981, three weeks before an exhibition of her new paintings opened in London.   JUDITH COLLINS, rev.

Sources W. Nicholson, *Flower tales* (1976) · J. Collins, *Winifred Nicholson* (1987) [exhibition catalogue, Tate Gallery] · *Unknown colour: paintings, letters, writings by Winifred Nicholson*, ed. A. Nicholson (1987) · private information (1993) · *CGPLA Eng. & Wales* (1981)
Archives Tate collection, Tate Gallery archive, letters from her and her family to Edith Jenkinson · Tate collection, Tate Gallery archive, corresp., mainly letters from Christopher Wood
Likenesses P. Chandler, photograph, 1969, NPG [*see illus.*]
Wealth at death £186,402: probate, 14 April 1981, *CGPLA Eng. & Wales*

Ní Chonaill [*married names* O'Connor, Ó Laoghaire], **Eibhlín Dhubh** [Eileen O'Connell; *known as* Eibhlín Dubh] (*b. c.*1743, *d.* in or after 1791), poet, was one of the twelve surviving children of the twenty-two children of Domhnall Mór Ó Conaill (*d.* 1770) and his wife, Máire Ní Dhuibh (*c.*1705–1795), of Derrynane, co. Kerry.

The Uí Chonaill (O'Connells or Connells) of Derrynane were a noted and prosperous Catholic family. Among Eibhlín's brothers were Count Daniel *O'Connell (1745–1833) and Morgan (father of Daniel O'Connell (1775–1847),

the Liberator). The women of the family were noted as poets. Eibhlín's mother, Máire Ní Dhuibh, may have been a descendant of the seventeenth-century poet Piaras Feiritéar; she and her sister Siobhán are credited with a number of poems, in particular with laments.

In Gaelic tradition, both scholarly and popular, Eibhlín retains her maiden name and the adjective Dubh (feminine form of *dhubh*, 'dark'). She was married at 'under 15' to an O'Connor of Firies, co. Kerry, who died six months later. In 1767 she married, against the wishes of her family, Art Ó Laoghaire (Art O'Leary; 1746?–1773) of Rath Laoich near Macroom, co. Cork, who had been an officer in the Austrian army. He died on 4 May 1773, in a quarrel with a protestant neighbour. Folklore ascribes the cause of the quarrel between Art Ó Laoghaire and Abraham Morris, high sheriff of Cork, to sexual jealousy or to Morris's demand to buy Ó Laoghaire's horse for £5 which as a protestant he was entitled to do. Morris and the soldiers who fired the fatal shots after a failed ambush by Ó Laoghaire were declared guilty of murder by coroner's inquest in June, but Morris was acquitted by a grand jury in September 1773. The quarrel is the subject of the very celebrated poem *Caoineadh Airt Uí Laoghaire*.

Caoineadh Airt Uí Laoghaire survived in folk memory, with Eibhlín Dhubh's name attached as the author, until it was written down in the nineteenth century. The earliest surviving manuscripts date from the 1840s. The poem has been much studied, praised, and translated and remains a controversial text in modern Gaelic scholarship. The manuscript versions show great variation and also include lines which occur in earlier *Caoineadh* (poems of lamentation); the poem exhibits several conventions of the genre, including praise of the dead man's house and family, exclamations of love, apparent reproaches addressed to other mourners.

Several academic writers have suggested that the *Caoineadh* was composed or rather performed extempore as part of the ceremony of lamentation or keening which is well attested as an essential part of the traditional response to death in Gaelic society. Others have pointed to the anomaly of seeing a woman of Eibhlín Dhubh's class as a keener, and drawn a distinction between the folk custom and the lament as literary artefact, attaching Eibhlín Dhubh's poem to the literary tradition while conceding its wide oral diffusion.

Some doubt has also been cast on Eibhlín Dhubh's authorship of the poem. This seems impossible to determine from the evidence now available. The instability of the text adds to the problem; however, all versions are, to different degrees, remarkable for the speaker's energy in depicting herself, her own actions, and emotions. The speaker describes her sudden falling in love, her pleasure in marriage, leaping on the horse which came to her door with bloody saddle, her discovery of Art's murdered body, and in one version (possible tampered with by a scholarly transmitter) her drinking his blood. It expresses pride in her own and her husband's family connections and threatens Morris with an appeal to the king in London.

The poem also mentions two children of the marriage

and a third yet unborn. One of the two who are named, Conchubhar Ó Laoghaire (1768–1846), was partly educated in France, became a captain in the *gardes françaises*, later a barrister, married three times, and had a son who also died in 1846. Letters from her brother Daniel refer to Eibhlín's son and grandson and record that 'it is however no small comfort to be assured there remains some livelihood for his orphans and widow' (Collins, 'Arthur O'Leary', 1949, 2; O'Connell, 2.94). The date of Eibhlín Dhubh's death is unknown but she was alive in 1791.

While the mutations of the texts and the many political agendas that have surrounded its transmission make the question of authorship, and the relation to the keening tradition, a complex one, it seems on balance sensible to accept that the poem belongs in essence to its traditional author.   EILÉAN NÍ CHUILLEANÁIN

Sources S. Ó Tuama, *Caoineadh Airt Uí Laoghaire* (1961) · Mrs M. J. O'Connell, *The last colonel of the Irish brigade*, 2 vols. (1892) · B. Ó Buachalla, *An Caoine agus an Chaointeoireacht* (1998) · J. T. Collins, 'Arthur O'Leary, the outlaw', *Journal of the Cork Historical and Archaeological Society*, 2nd ser., 54 (1949), 1–7; 55 (1950), 21–4 [suppl.]; 61 (1956), 1–6 [suppl., no. 2] · S. Ní Chinnéide, 'A new view of eighteenth-century life in Kerry', *Journal of the Kerry Archaeological and Historical Society*, 6 (1973), 83–100 · L. M. Cullen, 'The contemporary and later politics of *Caoineadh Airt Uí Laoghaire*', *Eighteenth-Century Ireland*, 8 (1993), 7–38

Nickalls, Guy (1866–1935), oarsman, was born at Horton Kirby, Kent, on 12 November 1866, the third son of Tom *Nickalls (1828–1899) of Horton Kirby and afterwards of Patteson Court, Nutfield, Surrey, and his wife, Emily Quihampton. His father, a stockbroker, was an original member of the London Rowing Club. Like his younger brother Vivian, also a prominent oarsman, he was educated at Eton College (1877–87) and Magdalen College, Oxford (1887–90), where he took a pass degree in 1890. In early youth he was considered to be of delicate constitution, but after he had been at Eton a short time he began to develop the physique and stamina that eventually made him an outstanding oarsman. He took the advice he later gave both his sons, which was 'not to sit back on the sidelines' (G. O. Nickalls, *Rainbow in the Sky*, 40), and had many other interests in life, especially in connection with sport.

It was on account of his remarkable successes in boat-racing that Nickalls was best known. He rowed for Eton two years, winning the ladies' plate in 1885, and five years for Oxford (1887–91), being a member of the winning crew the last two years. Over the Henley course he rowed in all 81 races, of which he won 67 and lost 13, one being a dead heat. This extraordinary achievement included the following victories: five diamond sculls, six goblets or pair-oared races, seven stewards' or four-oared races, four grand challenge cups, one Olympic eights, and one ladies' plate. Probably the most notable of all these achievements was his rowing, at the age of forty-one years and eight months, at number 4 in the Leander eight which won a gold medal at the 1908 Olympic games. In writing of them in his autobiography he commented:

I do not wish for a moment to take any credit to myself. … Nature has endowed me with a fairly strong body, a

constitution of iron, and a will power or stubbornness above the average. These I have tried my best not to abuse, and any man so built and constituted, given my opportunities, could no doubt have done the same.   (G. Nickalls, *Life's a Pudding*, 205)

From 1891 to 1922 Nickalls was a member of the stock exchange. He married in 1898 Ellen Gilbey (*d*. 1935), daughter of Henry Gold JP of Hedsor, Buckinghamshire, and sister of Sir Harcourt Gilbey Gold, also a notable oarsman. An enthusiast in all things, Nickalls forced his way into the army at the age of forty-seven without previous military experience. He went to France in 1917 as superintendent of the physical and bayonet training of a division (afterwards increased to three divisions), and remained abroad until the end of hostilities. Later in life he devoted a considerable amount of his time to work on behalf of the Worcester College for the Blind, and was successful in collecting a considerable sum as the foundation of a permanent endowment fund.

On 7 July 1935, while travelling north for his annual fishing holiday in Scotland, Nickalls was involved in a car accident, and died from his injuries, on 8 July 1935, at Leeds General Infirmary. His widow died in the following month. Of their two sons, the elder, Guy Oliver Nickalls (1899–1974), was chairman of the Amateur Rowing Association and senior steward of Henley royal regatta.

HARCOURT GOLD, *rev.* NEIL WIGGLESWORTH

Sources *The Times* (9 July 1935) · G. Nickalls, *Life's a pudding: an autobiography* (1939) · private information (2004) · G. O. Nickalls, *A rainbow in the sky: reminiscences* (1974) · CGPLA Eng. & Wales (1935)
Archives FILM BFI NFTVA, news footage
Likenesses photograph, repro. in Nickalls, *Life's a pudding*, frontispiece
Wealth at death £7701 18s. 9d.: administration with will, 28 Nov 1935, CGPLA Eng. & Wales

Nickalls, Thomas [Tom] (1828–1899), stock jobber, was the elder son of Patteson Nickalls (*d*. 1868). His younger brother was Sir Patteson Nickalls (1836–1910), a renowned pro-Boer Liberal and fellow stock jobber. Almost nothing is known about his early life, except that aged five he accompanied his father, a corn dealer, to Chicago. There, according to one source, Tom (as he was always known) 'hunted wolves in the forest' (Boase, *Mod. Eng. biog.*, 6.294). Nickalls returned to England in 1845. He married Emily, daughter of Henry Quihampton, a farmer, on 3 July 1860. She was to become the first woman to climb Mont Blanc and Mont Rosa in the same week. The couple first settled at Cheriton Villa in Bromley, Kent. Their eldest child, Guy *Nickalls, was born on 12 November 1866 (*d*. 1935), and eleven others followed. All, except one, survived infancy—a rare achievement for a Victorian family.

From 1864 up until his death Nickalls worked as a stock jobber in the City of London, concerned with the business of selling securities to stockbrokers, and playing a key role in setting prices on the exchange. He was to become highly successful in his chosen career and one of the leading jobbers on the American market. Yet in 1868 he suffered a severe setback. At the suggestion of some of its more senior members, who promised to pay his costs, he (according to his son's account) agreed to fight a stock exchange law case. Unfortunately for Nickalls, Lord Chief Justice Bovill later ruled against such a payment, and he was told to foot the bill of £18,000. This, however, seems to have had little real effect on the enterprising Tom, as he subsequently embarked on a European tour with his wife and children. From 1868 they lived at Holmesdale House, Horton Kirby, Kent.

Nickalls became active in the vigorously competitive (and in contemporary stock exchange terms, most largely dealt-in) world of American railroad financing. In 1872 his prominence and success in the American markets earned him the accolade the 'Erie King'. A clerk of the 1870s remembers Nickalls as a great, burly man whose habit was 'to come into the market and bellow, "I buy Eries."' (Kynaston, *The City of London*, 38). Despite the dubious ethical standards applied in railroad financing, Nickalls always displayed integrity and independence of mind. Not only was he the most significant jobber in the American market, but he was also a well-liked figure on the stock exchange. He must also have exerted a deal of influence over his sons Guy and Vivian, who both chose to follow him onto the exchange.

Nickalls was a keen sportsman. He had been an original member of the London Rowing Club (founded in 1856), and in 1879 he became master of the Surrey stag hounds. In 1887 he bought a large sporting estate in Sweden and then another adjoining it in Norway. He also ensured that his children were taught shooting, horse and hound riding, cricket, boxing, and billiards during their holidays.

Despite his early rowing accomplishments, Tom's great ambition was for his sons to become cricketers; Guy remembered his saying: 'Cricket, my boy, will take you round the world, and rowing, up and down the Thames' (G. O. Nickalls, 38). However, he did not seem too disappointed when Guy took to rowing at Eton and Oxford, culminating in his captaincy of the university boat club. On one famous occasion in 1890 Nickalls senior treated his son's crew to a long weekend at Brighton's Grand Hotel to prepare themselves for the boat race. When Oxford won Guy recalled that his father slipped him a cheque for £100, and joined in the post-race festivities. As he had just won £7000 from a colleague on the stock exchange, by betting against Cambridge, Nickalls too had something to celebrate. Guy and Vivian dominated the Henley Diamond Sculls competition from 1888 to 1896.

Tom Nickalls died on 10 May 1899 at Patteson Court, near Redhill, Surrey, where he and his family had lived since 1872, and was buried at Nutfield; his wife survived him. A brief obituary in *The Times* read: 'He prospered in business, and while not neglecting the Stock Exchange, gave up much time to sport … Mr Nickalls was perhaps best known to the general public as the father of the famous scullers, Mr Guy and Mr Vivian Nickalls' (12 May 1899). JUDY SLINN

Sources D. T. A. Kynaston, 'Nickalls, Thomas', *DBB* · D. Kynaston, *The City of London*, 4 vols. (1994–2001) · Boase, *Mod. Eng. biog.* · G. O. Nickalls, *Life's a pudding* (1939) · V. Nickalls, *Oars, wars and horses* (1932) · J. H. Richardson, *From the City to Fleet Street* (1927) · C. Duguid, *The story of the stock exchange* (1901) · *Financial Times* (20

July 1891) · *Citizen* (18 July 1896) · *Citizen* (13 May 1899) · *WWW* · *CGPLA Eng. & Wales* (1899) · *The Times* (12 May 1899) · *The Times* (5 Oct 1910) [Sir Patteson Nickalls] · m. cert. · d. cert.

Likenesses portrait, repro. in *British sports and sportsmen*, 2 (1908), 184 · portrait, repro. in *Bailey's Magazine* (Feb 1884), 1–2 · portrait, repro. in *VF* (21 Nov 1885) · portrait, repro. in *ILN* (20 May 1899), 209

Wealth at death £135,815—gross: Kynaston, 'Nickalls, Thomas' · £141,219 4s. 9d.: probate, 20 June 1899, *CGPLA Eng. & Wales*

Nickle, Sir Robert (1786–1855), army officer, was the son of Robert Nicholl of the 17th light dragoons, who changed the spelling of his name to Nickle. Nickle was born at sea on 12 August 1786, and appears to have been educated at Edinburgh. He entered the army when under thirteen years of age as an ensign in the Royal Durham fencibles, serving in the Irish rising of 1798–9. In January 1801 he was gazetted as ensign to the 60th regiment, and on 19 May was transferred to the 15th regiment, becoming a lieutenant on 6 January 1802. He was transferred to the 8th garrison brigade on 25 October 1803, and to the 88th regiment (Connaught Rangers) on 4 August 1804. With this regiment he was ordered to South America in 1806, and was present at Buenos Aires by 2 July 1807. On 5 July he volunteered to lead the forlorn hope, and in the hard-fought advance into the city was severely wounded, the rest of his party being either wounded or killed; he showed great coolness and daring.

After returning for a few months to England, Nickle's regiment embarked for the Peninsula, arriving at Lisbon on 13 March 1809. He was promoted captain on 1 June 1809, and served through the Peninsular War, except for five months, being present at many general actions—Talavera, Busaco, Torres Vedras, Vitoria, Pyrenees, Nivelle, Nive, Orthez, and Toulouse; in the last he was severely wounded. For Nivelle he received a gold medal, and for the others a silver medal. He usually commanded the light company of the 88th, and was distinguished for generosity and bravery. His conduct towards a fallen enemy at Pamplona was a conspicuous instance of chivalry. On another occasion he carried off a wounded comrade in the face of the French, who ceased firing to applaud his bravery. On 15 June 1814 he sailed from the Gironde with his regiment for America, and was present at the battle of Plattsburg and at the crossing of the Savannah River, where he was wounded. In 1815 he was present in Paris with the army of occupation.

During the following years Nickle's regiment was in Great Britain. On 21 January 1819 he became brevet major, and on 28 November 1822 major. On 30 June 1825, when he became lieutenant-colonel, he parted with his regiment, and was unattached until, on 15 June 1830, he took command of the 36th regiment, with which he went to the West Indies. From 14 July 1832 to March 1833 he administered St Kitts in the governor's absence. In 1833 he returned to London, and for a time was again unattached. On the outbreak of the French Canadian uprising in 1838 he volunteered for service in Canada, was detached for 'particular duty', and did good work in raising several volunteer forces in the colony and restoring calm. He was made KH in 1832 and knighted on 13 March 1844. On 28 June 1848 he became brevet colonel and on 11 November 1851 a major-general.

Nickle was twice married. His first wife, whom he married on 15 November 1818, was Elizabeth, daughter of William Dallas, writer to the signet; a son (who served in the Indian army) and two daughters (one of whom married Sir Charles M'Grigor) from this marriage survived their father. Nickle's second wife was the widow of Major-General Nesbitt; she survived him.

In 1853 Nickle was appointed commander of the military forces in Australia, where, after adventures and shipwreck, he arrived early in 1854. Stationed first at Sydney and later at Melbourne, he had to deal with serious disturbances in 1854 in the gold-mining districts. He reached Ballarat in December, three days after the storming of the Eureka stockade. He won the respect of the diggers, and rapidly restored order. The strain on him proved too severe; early in 1855 he applied for leave to return home on account of his health, but died at his residence, Upper Jolimont House, Melbourne, before his relief could reach him, on 26 May 1855. He was buried with military honours at the Carlton cemetery, Melbourne. Nickle was a thoroughly professional soldier, a man of calm judgement, notably humane and courteous.

C. A. HARRIS, rev. JAMES FALKNER

Sources Army List · Annual Register (1855) · Hart's Army List · Melbourne Morning Herald (28 May 1855) · H. Jourdain, History of the Connaught rangers (1924) · Boase, Mod. Eng. biog. · AusDB

Nickolls, John (1710/11–1745), antiquary, was born in Ware, Hertfordshire, the son of John Nickolls, a Quaker miller and grain merchant in the town. He was apprenticed to another Quaker merchant, Joseph Wyeth, of London and after serving his time became a partner with his father but continued to reside in London, in Trinity parish, Queenhithe. His home there housed his extensive collection of prints and books. He was a voracious collector of prints of head and shoulders portraits, most of which he obtained from stalls in Moorfields. By the time of his death his collection numbered about 2000 and was bound in ten volumes. These afterwards furnished Joseph Ames with material for his Catalogue of English Heads (1748). After Nickolls's death they were purchased for 80 guineas by Dr John Fothergill for his library, and on Fothergill's death in 1780 the entire collection was sold for £150 to John Thane, printseller of Rupert Street, Soho, who cut up the volumes and disposed of the portraits to the principal collectors of the time.

Nickolls also assembled an extensive collection of books and tracts, many written by fellow Quakers. The most valuable item in this library was a collection of about 130 manuscript letters addressed to Oliver Cromwell, written mainly between 1650 and 1654, though some date from as late as 1658. Among them were letters from Sir Harry Vane, John Bradshaw, and Andrew Marvel, together with numerous addresses from nonconformist ministers and army colonels. The letters had at one time been owned by John Milton, upon whose death they were acquired by his secretary, Thomas Ellwood. From Ellwood

they had passed to Joseph Wyeth. Nickolls obtained the original letters from Wyeth's widow and published them in 1743 under the title Original Letters and Papers of State Addressed to Oliver Cromwell Concerning the Affairs of Great Britain from 1649 to 1658. Several of these letters Nickolls allowed Thomas Birch to use for his entry on Cromwell in the General Dictionary, Historical and Critical (1731–41). After Nickolls's death they were presented by his father to the Society of Antiquaries of which Nickolls had been elected a fellow in January 1740.

Nickolls died of a fever in London on 11 January 1745, aged thirty-four, and was buried in Bunhill Fields, London, on 16 January.

CHARLOTTE FELL-SMITH, rev. M. J. MERCER

Sources Nichols, Lit. anecdotes, 2.156–61 · N&Q, 2nd ser., 11 (1861), 123

Nicks [née Barker], **Catherine** (d. 1709), merchant, arrived in India in 1678 as Catherine Barker, 'a participant in one of the early nuptial sweepstakes sponsored by the company' (Saxe, 136). In England Catherine had at least one sister, Dionysia, and one brother, Ted. Nothing is known of Catherine's life prior to her arrival in India, though on the evidence of her autograph letters she does not appear to have had an especially good education. On 4 November 1680 she married John Nicks (d. 1711), secretary to the Fort St George (Madras) council, who had arrived in India in 1668.

Both Catherine and John developed extensive private trading interests during the 1680s and prospered thereby. In 1688 John was made chief of the new 'Conimeer' factory situated north of Pondicherry, an appointment only confirmed by the court on the condition that the company's position was not prejudiced 'by his Wife's crafty trading … [who] makes her gains of our loss' (Diary of William Hedges, 2.cclviii). Indeed, Catherine was certainly notorious, and possibly unique at the time, for trading under her own name rather than that of her husband. In 1691 John was dismissed his position because of a debt he owed the company, and in May 1692 was imprisoned at Fort St George. In that same year Catherine and Elihu Yale (1649–1721), president of Fort St George, allegedly conspired to steal a quantity of fine cloth from the company's Conimeer warehouse. A warrant was issued for Catherine's arrest but she appears not to have been imprisoned.

Catherine also attained notoriety as a result of her alleged romance with Yale. Rumours of an affair, the veracity of which has since been disproved by Yale's biographer Hiram Bingham, were circulated by Yale's critics who claimed the relationship had begun by the time of their collusion in the Conimeer theft, when Catherine lived with Yale and a second woman, Hieronima de Paiva, during several visits to Madras. Yale's opponents also maintained that he was father to three of Catherine's children, an allegation likewise since discredited. Catherine had ten children in total. These included eight daughters (Anne, Isabella, Jane, Katherine (or Catherine), Mary, Sibella, Betty, and Ursa) and two sons (John, who died at

Madras on 6 December 1686, and Elihu, who went to England). In 1699 John Nicks went to England with Betty and Ursa, where he was able to clear his name with the company. He returned to Madras as a free merchant but lived estranged from Catherine until his death on 14 March 1711.

During this time Catherine expanded her trading interests, many of which were clearly illicit. She owned two country ships and had shares in various others, and traded extensively in a variety of English and East Indian goods including diamonds. She appears to have been highly motivated in her trading to provide for the education and social advancement of her children in England, where they were under the supervision of Yale, their godfather, and Dionysia and Henry Toombs, Catherine's sister and brother-in-law. Periodically Catherine remitted portions of her estate to Yale, who, however, proved to be an unreliable agent.

Catherine died in Madras on 9 December 1709 and was buried in the compound of St Mary's Church, Fort St George. Her son-in-law William Warre acted as executor of her modest estate of about 20,000 pagodas (about £7000), over which there was some wrangling. A substantial portion of Catherine's funds in England, designed for the use of her children, was lost in 1711 following the bankruptcy of Sir Steven Evance, with whom Yale had deposited the money. As a summary, Colonel Henry Yule's assessment of Catherine as a 'crafty and ill-conducted … but warm-hearted woman' (*Diary of William Hedges*, 2.cclx) seems fair.   ANDREW GROUT

Sources E. L. Saxe, 'Fortune's tangled web: trading networks of English entrepreneurs in Eastern India, 1657–1717', PhD diss., Yale U., 1979, 135–47 • *The diary of William Hedges … during his agency in Bengal; as well as on his voyage out and return overland (1681–1687)*, ed. R. Barlow and H. Yule, 2, Hakluyt Society, 75 (1888) • *Diaries of Streynsham Master*, ed. R. C. Temple, 2 vols. (1911) • J. J. Cotton, *List of inscriptions on tombs or monuments in Madras* (1905) • H. D. Love, *Vestiges of old Madras, 1640–1800*, 4 vols. (1913) • S. A. Khan, *Sources for the history of British India in the seventeenth century* (1926) • I. B. Watson, *Foundation for empire: English private trade in India, 1659–1760* (1980) • biographical file, BL OIOC • H. Bingham, *Elihu Yale: the American nabob of Queen Square* (1939)
Archives Berks. RO, Benyon Business Papers • PRO, MSS, CME, C.108/299
Wealth at death approximately 20,000 pagodas [about £7000]; may have left additional funds in England: Saxe, 'Fortune's tangled web', 147

Niclaes, Hendrik [Henry Nicholas] (**1502–c.1580**), founder of the Family of Love, was born on 10 January 1502. His birthplace cannot be identified, but the language in which he wrote, Western Low German, indicates the area of the present German–Dutch border extending from Westphalia to East Friesland. His father, Nicolaus (*fl.* 1480–1525)—his patronymic is not known—was a merchant, and Hendrik had at least one brother.

Early life Hendrik's elementary education was entrusted to a local priest when he was five. He showed signs of piety at an early age and, when he was just under eight, he began to have doubts about the satisfaction of sin achieved by Christ. Unable to answer his son's questions convincingly, Nicolaus took him to a nearby Franciscan convent where Hendrik baffled the friars with his insistent queries. Their replies were no more satisfactory than his father's. Shortly afterwards he started to have the first visions from which he would derive his mission as a prophet and a religious leader.

At about the age of nine Niclaes advanced to a Latin school, where he soon acquired some proficiency, and three years later started to work as an apprentice in the family business. In 1521, the year of the Diet of Worms, he came under the influence of Luther's ideas, above all his criticism of Catholic abuses and his emphasis on the Bible, although he never approved of Luther's break with the church of Rome or with the teaching of justification by faith. He started to study the scriptures himself and to discuss them with a group of like-minded acquaintants. In 1529, after the second Diet of Speyer and the imperial attempt to enforce the 1521 edict against Luther, Niclaes was arrested on suspicion of heresy, questioned, and acquitted.

Holland and the Anabaptists Niclaes continued to be attracted by the evangelical movement of sympathizers with the early Reformation. This was one reason for his decision to settle in Amsterdam about 1532 together with his wife, whom he had married in 1522 and with whom he would have at least five children, and his brother Johan, a brewer. Another reason was the commercial importance of the city, and the possibilities which it offered an enterprising merchant. He arrived at a time when the evangelical sympathizers, tolerated, protected, and sometimes even encouraged by the magistracy, were being drawn by the new brand of Anabaptism which was introduced into Emden by the Swabian preacher Melchior Hoffmann and then propagated in Holland by his disciples. The emphasis of this new movement lay far more on millenarianism and the role of prophets who would usher in Christ's kingdom on earth than on adult baptism and other tenets so prominent among the early Anabaptists in Switzerland and southern Germany. The exact nature of Hendrik Niclaes's dealings with the Dutch Anabaptists is not clear. He was certainly in touch with them, and in 1532 was again arrested on suspicion of heresy, but he was cleared of the charge by the court of Holland in The Hague.

In 1534 the attitude of the Dutch Anabaptists began to change as a wave of eschatological excitement spread, and the belief arose that the new Jerusalem was about to dawn in the city of Münster in Westphalia. Numerous Dutch Anabaptists set out for Germany, but there was also a belief in the apocalyptic role of Amsterdam. As the fanaticism of the Anabaptists in Münster grew, episodes occurred in Amsterdam which suggested that the Dutch Anabaptists were about to abandon the peaceful piety which had made them so acceptable to the magistrates. In May 1535 they stormed the town hall, killing certain members of the town council. The authorities responded with persecution, and Amsterdam, after being one of the most tolerant cities in the northern Netherlands, became the most intolerant, with a new council renowned for its Catholic orthodoxy. A month later, in June 1535, Münster was recaptured by its Catholic bishop and many of the surviving Anabaptist leaders were tortured and executed.

Niclaes was always opposed to violence, and the town council of Amsterdam seems to have used him as an intermediary to persuade the Anabaptists to abandon their revolutionary objectives. Despite his earlier arrest Niclaes, who was typical of the rich tradesmen to whom Amsterdam owed its prosperity, enjoyed the trust of the authorities and was not implicated in any of the trials of Anabaptists of the second half of the decade. Nevertheless, he retained an interest in the movement's members, now disbanded, leaderless, and persecuted. It was mainly to them that he referred the visions and revelations which he received in 1540 and which inspired him to found a sect of his own, the Family or House of Love (Huis der Liefde, Familia Charitatis).

The Family of Love The name of Hendrik Niclaes's sect was derived from the third and last of the divisions of history before the millennium, originally propounded by Joachim da Fiore, corresponding to the spirit and the theological virtue of charity. The Family of Love was to be a strictly hierarchical organization, with Niclaes at its head attended by his elders, and six inferior priestly orders beneath him. It was open to all confessions, but members had to accept the supremacy and the message of the founder. Hendrik Niclaes signed himself with the initials HN (which could be interpreted as *Homo Novus*) and made the highest claims for his own status. Living in the last age of time, he was to repair the imperfection brought about by original sin and thus to succeed where even Christ had failed. He was to cleanse Christianity of the distortions introduced by the churches. Rejecting the literal approach to the Bible of the Lutherans, he allegorized the scriptures and held that the sacraments and ecclesiastical ceremonies were of purely symbolical (and provisional) significance. He disapproved of protestant condemnation of Rome, denied that the pope was Antichrist, and encouraged his members to attend Catholic religious services—or protestant ones, according to the territory in which they lived—provided they had in their hearts the true faith that was about to be revealed. In his eagerness to avoid any form of violence he advocated conformity to the religion of the state. He taught, as many Anabaptists did, that perfection could be attained through the assiduous imitation of the suffering and life of Christ. This—and here he revealed the influence of the northern European mystics—would lead to a return to the purity preceding the fall and a state of being 'godded with God', an idea which his enemies interpreted as a licence to sin.

The foundation of the Family of Love coincided with Niclaes's decision to leave Amsterdam for another important commercial centre, Emden in East Friesland. There, where he was also known as Hendrik van Amsterdam and, like his brother Johan, was accorded citizenship shortly after his arrival, he gathered round him his first followers. Described by a contemporary as 'a man of a reasonable tall stature, somewhat grosse in bodie … verie brave in his apparell' (Rogers, fol. B5v), Hendrik Niclaes undoubtedly had a considerable personal appeal, even if he was inclined to exaggerate the extent of his suffering and his ill treatment by others in order to demonstrate his sanctity. When judging his success on the European continent it is not always easy to distinguish between his own charisma, his message, and his money. His early adherents included indigent former Anabaptists—Hendrik Jansen van Barrefelt and Augustijn van Hasselt—whom he assisted financially and whose ingratitude he would later deplore. But there were also far richer men, members of the East Frisian nobility and scholars like Lambertus Hortensius in Holland, who translated some of his works into Latin, attracted, at a time of confessional strife, by a movement which rose above the conflicting churches. Finally there were Niclaes's own relatives. By marrying into well-connected families in Emden and the Netherlands his two sons and three daughters helped him create a wide network extending throughout the Low Countries.

Spreading the word In order to spread his doctrine Niclaes needed printers. Using as his intermediary Hendrik Jansen van Barrefelt, he chose as his first printer Dirk van den Borne, who had once worked for the Anabaptist David Joris, and who lived conveniently beyond the East Frisian borders in the Netherlands, in Deventer in Overijssel. Van den Borne produced some five works by Niclaes between 1553 and 1555. These included the first version of one of his most successful books, *Terra pacis, or, The Land of Peace*, an allegorical description of the pilgrimage to heaven which has sometimes been regarded as a source of Bunyan's *Pilgrim's Progress*, and was described by the Cambridge Platonist Henry More as 'the very best of his writings that I have mett with' (Nicolson and Hutton, 297). For his main work, however, *Den speghel der gherechticheit* (1556/7), or, *The Glasse of Righteousness*, Hendrik Niclaes applied to a young French printer, Christopher Plantin, who had just established himself in Antwerp (the residence of Hendrik Niclaes's eldest son, Frans Hendricks, who had married into a family of local cloth merchants and looked after his father's business interests). Although Plantin placed his press at Niclaes's disposal, he was barely involved in the publication of his great work. Niclaes himself supplied the types, the woodcuts, and the paper, and the production was supervised by Augustijn van Hasselt. Nevertheless this was the beginning of both a business partnership and a friendship. Plantin published other writings by Niclaes; the two men participated in a number of commercial enterprises, such as the production and marketing of Hebrew bibles in 1566–7; and through Plantin, Niclaes encountered the circle of humanists which gathered round the printer's firm and included the cartographer Abraham Ortelius.

The Familists' habit of conforming to the official faith meant that they were hardly considered a danger to the state in the Low Countries and do not appear to have been prosecuted. Yet Niclaes had many enemies. The Roman Catholics regarded him as a heretic. The authorities placed his works on the Antwerp Index in 1570 and on later Roman indexes. Fellow sectaries, such as David Joris, resented him as a rival and attacked him. But his main opponents were the Reformed ministers he encountered in Emden: Adriaen de Kuiper, Martin Micron, Nicolas Carinaeus, and Gellius Faber. Although he had long led a respectable life in Emden, hostility to him erupted with the publication of his writings in the 1550s. In 1561, after being publicly criticized by local preachers, he departed for the Netherlands, making for the port of Kampen in Overijssel where Augustijn van Hasselt would print for him. His wife had died in Emden about this time.

Niclaes remained in Kampen until about 1565 and then moved to Rotterdam. There his youngest son, Nicolas Hendricks, married to the daughter of a Brabantine nobleman, had arranged for his accommodation. In 1567, however, after further visions had coincided with the strengthening of the Spanish hold on the Netherlands, Hendrik Niclaes left Rotterdam for another trading centre, Cologne. By this time he could claim to be at the head of a movement which had ramifications in many parts of Europe. His works were widely circulated in Low German in the Low Countries and Germany. Some were translated into Latin and French, and were read in Paris in circles close to the court.

The English Familists There is no evidence that Niclaes came to England, and yet it was there that his sect seems to have been most successful. The Family of Love was introduced into England by Christopher Vittels. Vittels, who was said to have originated as a joiner from Delft, was at one point resident in Southwark, and became a successful merchant importing textiles from the continent. He may at first have been close to Anabaptism, but in the mid-1550s he had already started to proselytize a hybrid form of Familism and was charged with being an Arian in 1558–9. It is not known when, or indeed whether, he actually met Niclaes, and it was not until the 1570s that, having translated the latter's works into English, he started to import the printed editions from Cologne. Niclaes thus became one of the first exponents of the mystical tradition of northern Europe to have his works circulated in England, and to this he owed much of his success.

The English Familists tended to have a mystical inclination. They came from circles of religious dissent which were usually moderate in character, whether protestant or Catholic, but which might even include Anabaptists, like the Surrey sectarians detected in 1561. The largest groups were concentrated in London and in Cambridgeshire and the Isle of Ely (with enclaves in western Suffolk, eastern Huntingdonshire, and northern Essex) but Familists could also be found elsewhere in the south. They ranged from craftsmen to squires and yeomen of the queen's guard, many of them highly respectable citizens serving as churchwardens, bailiffs, constables, and parish officers. Their practice of Familism was limited to intermarriage, reciprocal bequests, and the reading and discussion of Niclaes's works in closed circles.

By the late 1570s the English movement had become so numerous that a campaign against it was mounted by a group of puritan theologians led by John Knewstub and eager to deflect official hostility from themselves. Sermons were preached against the Family of Love from 1576 onwards; attacks were published by Stephen Batman (1577), John Rogers (1578–9), Knewstub (1579), and William Wilkinson (1579); and a number of Familists were arrested and imprisoned, albeit briefly, between 1578 and 1581. Niclaes himself remonstrated against these activities in a letter to the English bishops.

Death and influence In Cologne, Niclaes revised all his earlier writings and added others which were printed by the mysterious Niclas Bohmbargen. He drew up the text on which the chronicles of the sect, *Cronica* and *Acta HN*, are based, as well as the elaborate description of the Familist hierarchy, *Ordo sacerdotis*. He was joined by one of his most distinguished followers, the preacher Huibert Duifhuis, who was to play a significant part in the reformation of Utrecht where he tried to compromise between Catholicism and Calvinism. But the Cologne period was also one of quarrels which account for the increasingly cantankerous tone of Niclaes's writings. He was now attacked by men who had once admired him. In 1574–5 he broke with some of his main followers, critical of his autocratic claims—Duifhuis, Augustijn van Hasselt, Hendrik Jansen van Barrefelt (who started to write his own works under the pseudonym Hiël), and Plantin and his circle.

Hendrik Niclaes died in Cologne in or shortly after 1580, the date of his last publication. By the time of his death he had lost a sizeable part of his following on the continent, even if there are signs that belief in him persisted at least until 1606, when a group of German Familists addressed a petition to James I. Yet his sect continued to flourish in England well into the seventeenth century. There his future lay, but more as a mystical writer than as a sectarian leader. The English translations of his works were reissued during the Commonwealth and were acquired by Quakers, devotees of Jakob Boehme, and those fascinated by mystical experience. ALASTAIR HAMILTON

Sources A. Hamilton, ed., *Cronica, Ordo sacerdotis, Acta HN: three texts on the Family of Love* (1988) · H. de la F. Verwey, 'De geschriften van Hendrik Niclaes: prolegomena eener bibliographie', *Het Boek*, 26 (1940–42), 161–211 · C. W. Marsh, *The Family of Love in English society, 1550–1630*, another edn (1994) · P. V. Blouw, 'Printers to Hendrik Niclaes: Plantin and Augustijn van Hasselt', *Quaerendo*, 14 (1984), 247–72 · A. Hamilton, *The Family of Love* (1981) · H. Nippold, 'Heinrich Niclaes und das Haus der Liebe', *Zeitschrift für die historische Theologie*, 32 (1862), 323–402, 473–563 · *The displaying of an horrible secte of … heretiques … the familie of love, with the lives of their authours [i.e. D. Joris and H. Niclas] … newely set foorth by J. R[ogers]: whereunto is added certeine letters sent from the same family*, ed. J. Rogers and S. Bateman, another edn (1579) · I. Simon, 'Hendrik Niclaes: Biographische und bibliographische Notizen, Emden (1540–60)', *Niederdeutsches Wort*, 13 (1973), 63–77 · A. Hamilton, 'Three epistles by Hendrik Niclaes', *Quaerendo*, 10 (1980), 47–69 · P. V. Blouw, 'Was Plantin a member of the Family of Love? Notes on his dealings with Hendrik Niclaes', *Quaerendo*, 23 (1993), 3–23 · J. D. Moss, 'Godded with God': Hendrik Niclaes and his Family of Love (1981) · N. Smith, *Perfection proclaimed: language and literature in English radical religion, 1640–1660* (1989) · *The Conway letters: the correspondence of Anne, Viscountess Conway, Henry More, and their friends, 1642–1684*, ed. M. H. Nicolson, rev. edn, ed. S. Hutton (1992)

Archives LPL, MSS 871, 937 · University of Leiden, MSS Lk 620–621

Likenesses C. van Sichem, engraving, repro. in J. Davies, *Apocalypsis* (1655)

NicLeòid, Ceit. *See* MacLeod, Catherine (1914–2000).

Nicol, Alexander (*bap.* 1703), poet and schoolmaster, was baptized on 10 December 1703 in the eastern end of Kettins parish, Forfarshire, the son of Alexander Nicol (*d.* 1711) packman, and Margaret Mitchell. Very little is known about Alexander Nicol's parents. From the scant genealogical information available it seems likely that both his mother and father came from unprivileged households in Forfarshire and that his father was an itinerant packman or 'poor mechanic' ('An account of the author' in Nicol, *Poems*) who died when Alexander was seven years old. The family seemed to live on the Pitcur estate, Kettins parish, Forfarshire, for much of the time of Alexander's upbringing, and his own rendition of his circumstances as 'my vulgar life and education' were compounded by what the poet himself records as harsh treatment from a childhood nurse who 'brack my back' and 'did me almost smother' and, warming to his theme, 'it made me stark stane blind … for a whole years space' (ibid.). Teenage efforts to support himself in his father's trade as a pedlar are related by the poet as foundering on the physical frailty occasioned by his childhood and his increasing interest and enthusiasm for the songs and ballads he dealt in. Obtaining instruction from 'good people where I past' (ibid.) he developed his literacy and, encouraged by the kindly patronage of local landowners, by 1739 he had become teacher of English in Abernyte parish, Perthshire.

In March 1737 Nicol married Margaret Thain in Alyth, Forfarshire. The couple had at least two children: George, baptized in Abernyte in 1738, and Patrick, who appears in the same baptismal roll for March 1740.

Nicol's improved circumstances and new parental and scholastic responsibilities evidently inspired him because in 1739 his first miscellany of poems, *Nature without Art, or, Nature's Progress in Poetry* was published. Following his move to teach at Collace parish, Perthshire, during the 1740s, he obtained subscriptions for a further volume *The Rural Muse, or, A Collection of Miscellany Poems both Comical and Serious* which duly appeared in 1753. Although he was evidently a long serving parish schoolmaster in Collace, and, like Robert Burns, inducted as a freemason with subscribers for his poetry from Dundee to Edinburgh, regrettably little is known of Nicol's life or character from this point onwards. After the 1766 publication of his final work *Poems on Several Subjects both Comical and Serious in Two Parts*, Alexander Nicol fades from view, to the extent that in the succeeding centuries the number of references to the man or his work may be numbered on one hand. At present neither his date of death nor his resting place has been positively identified.   RICHARD IAN HUNTER

Sources A. Nicol, *The rural muse, or, A collection of miscellany poems both comical and serious* (1753) · A. Nicol, *Poems on several subjects both comical and serious in two parts* (1766) [incl. 'An account of the author being an epistle to the right honourable Susanna countess of Strathmore, in the year 1727' 1.1–4] · R. Ford, *The harp of Perthshire* (1893) · *DNB* · C. Craig, ed., *The history of Scottish literature*, 2: *1660–1800*, ed. A. Hook (1987) · bap. reg. Scot. · m. reg. Scot.

Nicol, Davidson Sylvester Hector Willoughby (1924–1994), university administrator and diplomatist, was born on 14 September 1924, the son of Jonathan Josibiah Nicol,

civil servant, in Bathurst Village, outside Freetown, Sierra Leone. He spent part of his boyhood in Nigeria (where he is said to have learnt five Nigerian languages), then returned to Sierra Leone to the Prince of Wales School in Freetown. There, having passed the London matriculation examination at fourteen, and taken a London external intermediate BSc at seventeen, he taught science. Then, in 1943, he won a government scholarship to read natural sciences at Christ's College, Cambridge. In 1947 he graduated BA with first-class honours, the first black African to do so. With a medical degree from the London Hospital Medical College, London University, he was appointed in 1952 a lecturer at Ibadan (Nigeria) University medical school where he did research into tropical malnutrition. In 1957 he returned to Cambridge as a fellow of Christ's College (the first black African with a Cambridge fellowship) and did important work on the structure of insulin, published in *The Mechanism of Action of Insulin* (1960) and *The Structure of Human Insulin* (1960). On 11 August 1950 he married Marjorie Esmé (*b.* 1919/20), daughter of Arthur Johnston, assistant police superintendent. Like her husband she was a doctor, from Trinidad. They had three sons and two daughters (the marriage was dissolved in 1987).

In 1958 Nicol gave up his Cambridge fellowship and returned to Freetown where, after a brief spell as senior government pathologist, he became in 1960 principal of Fourah Bay College. Affiliated in 1876 to Durham University, which had left it a somnolent backwater, the college was now, in the period of African decolonization, receiving generous financial support from the British government. Nicol was determined to make it a university institution of distinction, worthy of a new independent nation (as Sierra Leone became in 1961). Under his dynamic principalship it blossomed with new teaching and research departments, high-calibre staff appointments and impressive buildings. In 1966 it became a constituent college of the newly founded University of Sierra Leone. Nicol was first vice-chancellor. His outstanding leadership was recognized by the British government in 1964 with his appointment as CMG.

In 1968 Nicol resigned and began a new career as a diplomatist. In 1969 he was appointed Sierra Leone ambassador to the United Nations, and served in 1970–71 as chairman of the Security Council, an unfamilar task which he fulfilled skilfully, dealing efficiently with crises in the Middle East, Cambodia, and South Africa. He published an account of his experiences in 1981 in *Paths of Peace*. In 1971 he was moved to London as high commissioner for Sierra Leone. But in 1972 he left Sierra Leone government service and returned to the United Nations as under-secretary-general and as director of the United Nations Institute for Training and Research (UNITAR), which he built up as a centre of educational excellence. He was also involved in founding the United Nations University. In 1983 he retired and settled in his beloved Cambridge, at Girton. Already in 1972 he had been elected, to his intense pleasure, an honorary fellow of Christ's College, which he rewarded with benefactions and enlivened by his regular visits (he was a great raconteur).

At least as important to Nicol was his career in literature and scholarship. Under the name Abioseh Nicol he published two collections of short stories in 1965 (*The Truly Married Woman* and *Two African Tales*), and contributed poems to the anthology *Modern African Poetry* (1982). One of them has often been quoted:

> You are not a country
> Africa
> You are a concept
> Fashioned in our minds each to each
> To hide our separate fears
> To dream our separate dreams.

His was the dream, which inspired so many Africans during the early years of independence, of a newly regenerated Africa, outlined in a series of lectures delivered at the University of Ghana, and published as *Africa: a Subjective View* (1964). It concluded by saying that 'Africa … now belongs to us again, and we should see to it that we are always worthy of it' (p. 80). During his years at UNITAR he edited and contributed to several volumes on international issues, drawing on his own experience.

Nicol was also a historian. In 1960 he published a pathbreaking article, 'West Indians in west Africa', and in 1969 a perceptive study of the nineteenth-century Sierra Leone doctor Africanus Horton, who was like himself a talented polymath. During his retirement he held visiting fellowships and professorships at various North American universities where he continued with his historical research. Honours were showered on him—ten honorary degrees, decorations from the governments of Sierra Leone and Liberia—and wherever he went his tall, handsome presence and his blend of great personal dignity with genial affability made him an unforgettable figure of charm and distinction. He died of cancer at Addenbrooke's Hospital, Cambridge, on 20 September 1994.

CHRISTOPHER FYFE

Sources 'Address by the master [Sir Hans Kornberg] at the memorial service for Dr D. S. H. W. Nicol, Saturday, 25 November 1994', typescript from the records of Christ's College, Cambridge · *The Guardian* (7 Oct 1994) · *The Independent* (7 Oct 1994) · *West Africa* (7 Oct 1994) · *The Times* (19 Oct 1994) · D. Nicol, *Africa: a subjective view* (1964) · WWW, 1991–5 · m. cert. · d. cert. · CGPLA Eng. & Wales (1995) · private information (2004)
Archives Bodl. Oxf., papers relating to service with the United Nations · CAC Cam., papers
Likenesses photograph, repro. in *The Guardian*
Wealth at death £178,748: probate, 26 Jan 1995, CGPLA Eng. & Wales

Nicol, Emma (1800–1877), actress, was the eldest daughter of the actress Sarah Bezra *Nicol (d. in or after 1834); she was possibly the daughter of Henry and Sarah Nicoll baptized at St Andrew's, Holborn, London, on 20 September 1800. She first appeared in Edinburgh aged seven on the occasion of her mother's benefit on 2 May 1808 and danced 'a new pas seul'. The next month she was Gossamer in *The Forty Thieves* and thereafter played for many years in Edinburgh, either in the Royal or in the Minor Theatre. By 15 February 1819 she was playing adult parts and was Martha in *Rob Roy*. When George IV visited the Theatre Royal in 1822 she was Mattie in *Rob Roy*. In the

same year she was Madge Wildfire in *The Heart of Midlothian* and had other good parts. She left Edinburgh in 1823 or 1824 and reached Drury Lane by November 1824, when she played Flora in *The Wonder*; she continued in a variety of parts at Drury Lane, where she was also a chorister, until 1829. She then joined the Surrey company run by R. W. Elliston for two seasons, confining herself to portraying old women.

A tour of Scottish theatres followed, after which Emma Nicol concentrated on portraying elderly women, the kind of part in which her mother had made her reputation. In 1834 she was re-engaged for the Edinburgh Theatre Royal by W. H. Murray and on 8 November played Mrs Gloomly in *Laugh when you can*. She remained in Edinburgh playing a large assortment of parts at the Theatre Royal, which came under the management of Lloyd by 1851. In 1852 she acted under the Rollison and Leslie management in roles based on Scott's Waverley novels, and she was retained by Wyndham when he opened on 11 June 1853. She was the original Hon. Mrs Falconer in Ebsworth's comedy £150,000 on 1 September 1854 and she played with J. L. Toole in *Henry VIII*. On 7 June 1858 she was the original Mattie Hepburn in Ballantine's *Gaberlunzie Man*. She moved with Wyndham to the New Queen's Theatre when the Royal closed on 25 May 1859, and appeared with Irving as Queen Elizabeth to his Wayland Smith in the burlesque of *Kenilworth*. She was associated with Irving in nearly every piece in which he appeared during the next two and a half years as a member of the stock company. In May 1862 the last nights of her public appearances were specially announced and on 23 May she took her farewell benefit, playing Widow Warren in *Road to Ruin* and Miss Durable in *Raising the Wind*. She played again on 31 May for the benefit of Wyndham and his wife as the Hostess in *The Honeymoon* and spoke a farewell address to the audience.

Emma Nicol never aspired to metropolitan fame and was content with the respect of managers and audiences in Scotland, but after her retirement she moved to London, where she died, aged seventy-seven, at her home at 52 Thornhill Road, Islington, on 2 November 1877.

[ANON.], rev. J. GILLILAND

Sources J. C. Dibdin, *The annals of the Edinburgh stage* (1888) · Boase, *Mod. Eng. biog.* · private information (1894) · CGPLA Eng. & Wales (1877) · d. cert. · IGI
Wealth at death under £3000: administration with will, 30 Nov 1877, CGPLA Eng. & Wales

Nicol, Erskine (1825–1904), genre painter, son of James Main Nicol, assistant to a wine merchant, and Margaret Alexander, was born in South Leith on 25 July 1825, the eldest of a family of five sons and one daughter. At an early age he was employed as a house painter in Leith but an interest in fine art led him also to enter the Trustees' Academy in Edinburgh in 1838. He studied there under Sir William Allan and Thomas Duncan, and in 1843 he progressed to the recently formed Royal Scottish Academy life school. While still a student he had his first painting, *Fruit*, accepted for a Royal Scottish Academy annual exhibition in 1841. Later, during the early 1840s (probably while he was attending the evening classes in the academy) he was appointed drawing master at Leith high school.

In 1846, having resigned from his teaching post, Nicol travelled to Dublin where he remained until about 1850. He found employment there both as a teacher and as a portrait painter. However, it was Nicol's keen observation of Irish everyday life and humour that fed his imagination and supplied the material for most of his painting for the rest of his career. While in Ireland he had the good fortune to find a patron in a Mr Armstrong of Rathmines; this enabled him to send two paintings back to Edinburgh for the 1849 and 1850 Royal Scottish Academy annual exhibitions, both of Irish subjects.

Nicol settled back in Edinburgh in 1850 and very quickly established his reputation. On 10 June 1851 he married Janet Watson; they had one son and a daughter before she died in 1863. In 1855 Nicol was elected an associate of the Royal Scottish Academy and only four years later, in 1859, he became an academician. As well as being a successful exhibitor at the Royal Scottish Academy until 1885 Nicol also exhibited at the Royal Academy on a regular basis between 1851 and 1893. He was elected an associate of the Royal Academy in 1866. In common with many of his Scottish contemporaries with ambition, Nicol turned his attention from Scotland to London. In 1862 he first rented a studio in St John's Wood and from 1864 he lived at Clonave Villa, 24 Dawson Place, Pembridge Square, in Bayswater. On 20 April 1865 he married Margaret Mary (1831/2–1919), daughter of Thomas Wood, a merchant; they had two sons and a daughter. In addition to his London base, Nicol also built himself a studio in Ireland, at Clonave, Deravaragh, in co. Westmeath. This enabled him to continue working closely with his preferred subject matter until ill health forced him to stop travelling over to Ireland. Instead, Nicol found an alternative studio in a disused church in Pitlochry in Perthshire: thus Scottish rural life became the focus of his attention, although by this time he was producing little actual work.

Erskine Nicol's art education in Edinburgh links him firmly to the tradition of David Wilkie and Scottish narrative painting. Rather than assimilating any artistic influences during his stay in Dublin, the importance of these years lay in his collection of subject matter. On his return to Scotland he immediately settled down to producing large numbers of Irish cottage scenes, many full of wit and even caricature. From *Paddy's Toilet* (exh. Royal Scottish Academy 1851) to *The Day after the Fair* (1860; Royal Scottish Academy) even the titles demonstrate his comic presentation of the rural poor, ironically just a few years after the devastating effects of the Irish potato famine. Nicol's Royal Scottish Academy diploma work, for example—*The Day after the Fair*—presents a cottage interior in which the head of the household sits bandaged and suffering from a hangover while his less than stoical wife prepares him a cup of tea. This painting combines the delicate qualities of light and shadow with the sharply drawn characters in the subject; extraneous detail is kept to a minimum. A slightly later work, *The Rent Day: Signing the New Lease* (1868; Leicester City Museums), recalls very

closely Wilkie's *The Letter of Introduction* (1813; National Gallery of Scotland) both in the arrangement of the figures and their setting. Nicol's work may also be compared with that of Thomas Faed, but whereas Faed's painting tends to be highly finished and somewhat sentimental, Nicol's brushwork remains direct and although he treats his subject with gentle humour he does not idealize it. In his later paintings, Nicol turned to more serious subjects and, in common with many of his Scottish contemporaries such as Thomas Faed and William McTaggart, explored such themes as immigration, emigration, and shipwreck as for example in *The Missing Boat* (1876; Royal Holloway College).

Despite the humour of many of Nicol's paintings he was a serious, shy, and reserved man. A photograph of about 1859 (Royal Scottish Academy) presents him in a thoughtful pose, his face partially hidden behind a thick, black beard. In 1885, after a serious illness, Nicol officially retired; he moved out of London to The Dell in Feltham, Middlesex. He also had a Scottish home, Torduff House in Colinton, then a village on the outskirts of Edinburgh. On 8 March 1904 Erskine Nicol died at The Dell; he was buried at Rottingdean in Sussex. JOANNA SODEN

Sources *Annual Report of the Council of the Royal Scottish Academy of Painting, Sculpture, and Architecture*, 77 (1904), 9–10 · J. Dafforne, 'British artists, their style and character: no. XCI Erskine Nicol', *Art Journal*, 32 (1870), 65–7 · C. B. de Laperriere, ed., *The Royal Scottish Academy exhibitors, 1826–1990*, 4 vols. (1991), vol. 3, pp. 367–71 · Graves, *RA exhibitors*, 5.367–8 · W. D. McKay, *The Scottish school of painting* (1906), 347–51 · D. Irwin and F. Irwin, *Scottish painters at home and abroad, 1700–1900* (1975), 304–5 · J. L. Caw, *Scottish painting past and present, 1620–1908* (1908), 163–4 · P. J. M. McEwan, *Dictionary of Scottish art and architecture* (1994), 436 · J. M. Wallace, *Further traditions of Trinity and Leith* (1990), 65–70 · *DNB* · b. reg. Scot. · Royal Scot. Acad. · m. reg. Scot. · m. cert.

Archives Royal Scot. Acad., letter collection, corresp. · Royal Scot. Acad., life school records

Likenesses photograph, *c.*1859, Royal Scot. Acad. · W. F. Douglas, oils, exh. 1862, Royal Scot. Acad. · E. Nicol, self-portrait, pencil drawing, 1892, Scot. NPG · T. Faed, wash drawing, Scot. NPG · Lock & Whitfield, woodburytype photograph, NPG; repro. in T. Cooper and others, *Men of mark: a gallery of contemporary portraits* (1880) · E. Nicol, self-portrait, charcoal drawing, Scot. NPG · C. Stanton, plaster bust, Scot. NPG · J. G. Tunny, carte-de-visite, NPG · wood-engraving, NPG; repro. in *ILN* (30 June 1866)

Nicol, George (1740?–1828), bookseller and publisher, was probably born in May 1740 in Scotland. Little is known of his family and early life. By 1769 he was living in London, where he was employed as an assistant and subsequently as a partner to his uncle David Wilson, a bookseller on the Strand: their joint names appear in the imprint to Stephen Hales's *Statical Essays* (first published 1733) and Robert Wallace Johnson's *New System of Midwifery* (1769). On his uncle's death, Nicol inherited a share in *The Gazetteer*, in which he took a close interest.

In 1773, at James West's sale, Nicol purchased the majority of the Caxtonian volumes for George III, an act which upset rival booksellers, such as John Almon, but might have helped Nicol gain the position of bookseller to the king in 1781 (which he held until relinquishing it in 1820). Four years later (on the request of George III and under the guidance of Sir Joseph Banks) Nicol was responsible for republishing a second, superior edition of Captain James Cook's account of his third and last voyage (3 vols., 1785). Nicol also became involved with John Boydell's Shakspeare Gallery and its attendant publications, and probably initiated plans to publish Boydell's edition of Shakespeare from his own press at his home in Pall Mall. Although the task was eventually carried out by William Bulmer, Nicol remained involved in the project with responsibility for supervision of the letterpress. Together with Bulmer, Boydell, and the typefounder William Martin, Nicol wished to create a type that combined utility with beauty to rival continental designs. Their aim was achieved with a typeface—later named the 'Bodoni Hum'—produced in a hoax experiment by the Shakespeare printing office, which experts took to be the work of the continental master Bodoni. The output from this printing office contributed largely to the growing reputation and popularity enjoyed by British produced books at the turn of the century.

Throughout his career Nicol gained a reputation for arranging and cataloguing the libraries of members of the aristocracy. In 1812 he organized the sale of books owned by the late third duke of Roxburghe, for which he wrote the catalogue and oversaw a highly successful auction, prompting what Thomas Frognall Dibdin termed 'bibliomania' and the establishment of the Roxburgh Club: the collection, assembled by Nicol for £5000, sold for £23,341 during the forty-two-day sale.

On 8 September 1787 Nicol married Mary Boydell at St Olave Jewry in the City of London. **Mary Nicol** (*bap.* 1747, *d.* 1820), print collector and writer, was Nicol's second wife; no detail is known of his first marriage, from which he had a son, William. Mary Boydell, one of the nine children of Samuel Boydell (1727–1783), farmer, and his wife, Ann, *née* Turner (1725–1764), was born at Broad Lane, Hawarden, Flintshire, and was baptized on 10 December 1747 at Hawarden. Her younger brother Josiah *Boydell later achieved fame as an artist and publisher. Prior to her marriage she travelled on the continent with her uncle, the publisher and owner of the Shakspeare Gallery, John Boydell. Her manuscript memoirs of the tour were illustrated by a collection of drawings. A noted beauty with 'a countenance [which] beamed with the benevolence which formed the distinguishing feature of her character' (*GM*, 1824), she attracted many admirers, including the miniature and portrait painter Ozias Humphry. In 1786 she survived an attempt on her life by shooting, near Leicester Square, London. From 1790 to 1791 she acted as lady mayoress of London when her uncle served as lord mayor. Mary died at Pall Mall on 21 December 1820 and was buried in St Olave Jewry. Following her death her collection of prints was sold, with the duke of Buckingham the principal purchaser.

Towards the end of his life George Nicol described himself, though poor, as having credit 'without end', owed in part by his confidante and friend Lady Essex Ker, sister of the duke of Roxburghe, from whose estate Nicol and later his son attempted to regain their moneys after her death.

Courteous and tactful in business, Nicol was said to be 'not a bookseller but a gentleman dealing in books' (*GM*, 98/2, 279). He retired from business in 1825 and died at his house in Pall Mall, London, on 25 June 1828, after a long illness. He too was buried at St Olave Jewry.

VIVIENNE W. PAINTING

Sources *GM*, 1st ser., 90/2 (1820), 574 · *GM*, 1st ser., 94/1 (1824), 236 · *GM*, 1st ser., 98/2 (1828), 279–81 · R. L. Haig, *The Gazetteer, 1735–1797* (1960) · FM Cam., Perceval and Hayley MSS · letters, NL Scot., reg. 968, fol. 281 · *Annual Register* (1828), 243–4 · *The parish of St James, Westminster*, 1/1, Survey of London, 29 (1960) · *N&Q*, 8th ser., 2 (1892), 422 · *N&Q*, 11th ser., 8 (1913), 223–4 · W. B. Todd, *Dictionary of printers, London and vicinity, 1800–1840* (1972) · H. R. Plomer and others, *A dictionary of the printers and booksellers who were at work in England, Scotland, and Ireland from 1726 to 1775* (1932); repr. (1968) · G. Nicol, 'Paper on the Shakespeare Gallery', St Bride Printing Library, London, 39802 · G. C. Williamson, *Life and works of Ozias Humphry* (1918) · parish register, Hawarden, Flintshire RO [baptism], 10 Dec 1747 · IGI

Archives NL Scot., letters · St Bride Institute, London, St Bride Printing Library, papers | BL, letters to Sir Joseph Banks, Add. MSS 33977–33981 · FM Cam., Hayley MSS · FM Cam., H. Perceval MSS · RA, letters, RA III/26/28/32/53/56

Likenesses W. Beechey, oils (Mary Nicol) · engraving, BM · portrait, repro. in T. F. Dibdin, *Bibliographical decameron*, 2 (1817) · portrait, NL Scot.

Wealth at death left substantial collection of prints; Mary Nicol: will, 1820, PRO, PROB 11/1638

Nicol, James (1769–1819), Church of Scotland minister and poet, was born on 30 September 1769 at Innerleithen, Peeblesshire, the son of Michael Nicol, and his wife, Marrion Hope. He was educated at the parish school before going on to Edinburgh University to study for the ministry of the Church of Scotland. After acting as a tutor to several families, he was licensed to preach by the presbytery of Peebles in March 1801. In May of the following year he became assistant to John Walker, minister of Traquair, near Innerleithen. Nicol succeeded him in that charge following Walker's death, in November 1802. On the 25th of that month he married Agnes Walker, his predecessor's sister, who had provided much of the inspiration for his poetry. They had three daughters and three sons, one of whom, James *Nicol, later distinguished himself as a geologist. The elder James's reputation as a poet was established by the publication of *Poems, Chiefly in the Scottish Dialect* (1805). In the opinion of Charles Rogers this entitled him to a reputable position among the nation's poets, although he was critical of what he considered to be an excessive imitation of Robert Burns. Nicol also contributed poems to the *Edinburgh Magazine*, as well as a number of articles to the *Edinburgh Encyclopaedia*.

Nicol was diligent in his parochial duties and much of his assistance to parishioners was of a practical nature, stemming from his knowledge of medicine. In 1808 he founded the first friendly society at Innerleithen. Although he was described as 'a stranger to the house of mirth' (Nicol, xi), Alexander Whitelaw commented on a kind and amiable disposition which made him universally appreciated. There was, however, a distinct change in his religious views. In the biographical introduction to his posthumously published *An Essay on the Nature and*

Design of Scripture Sacrifices (1823) there is ample evidence of his increasing unorthodoxy. He himself acknowledged that his thinking had taken him to conclusions very different from those in which he was educated. His colleague James Brewster was one of those dismayed by the trend of his friend's speculations. His position as a minister might have been in question had he not died, after a short illness, on 5 November 1819 at Traquair.

LIONEL ALEXANDER RITCHIE

Sources J. Nicol, 'Memoir', *An essay on the nature and design of scripture sacrifices, in which the theory of Archbishop Magee is controverted*, ed. B. Mardon (1823) · *Fasti Scot.* · C. Rogers, *The Scottish minstrel*, 2nd edn (1870) · A. Whitelaw, ed., *The book of Scottish song* (1844) · bap. reg. Scot.

Nicol, James (1810–1879), geologist, was born on 12 August 1810, at Traquair manse, near Innerleithen, Peeblesshire, son of the local minister, James *Nicol (1769–1819) and his wife, Agnes (née Walker). He entered Edinburgh University in 1825; he studied arts and divinity with holy orders in view, but also attended the mineralogical/geological lectures of Robert Jameson. In 1840–41 Nicol studied theology, philosophy, and geological subjects at Bonn and Berlin. His principal academic contact in Berlin was the palaeontologist and zoologist Christian Gottfried Ehrenberg, but he also attended the lectures of the geologist Heinrich von Dechen.

On returning to Britain, Nicol began extensive reconnaissance survey work in Scotland. In 1844 he published his *Guide to the Geology of Scotland* with accompanying geological map—a work which showed considerable knowledge of Scottish geology. In 1847–8 he was assistant secretary of the Geological Society of London and edited its *Journal*. In London he met leading geologists such as Charles Lyell, Henry De la Beche, and Roderick Murchison. With such support, in 1849, he gained the chair of geology and mineralogy at Queen's College, Cork. The same year, in Ireland, he married Alexandrina Anne Macleay Downie.

In 1848 Nicol published an important paper on the geology of the southern uplands of Scotland, arguing that they were of Silurian age. The following year he published the first figures of graptolites from this region. Some results from fieldwork with Murchison in the Girvan area and the southern uplands were utilized in Murchison's *Siluria* (1854), and when Murchison suggested that highland rocks might be metamorphosed equivalents of the Silurians of the southern uplands the idea was endorsed by Nicol. He also supported Murchison in his debate with Adam Sedgwick about the placement of the Cambrian–Silurian border in Wales. Murchison and Nicol worked in the southern uplands in the seasons 1850–52, and they jointly published a geological map of Europe (1856). In 1853, with Murchison's support, Nicol obtained the Aberdeen chair of civil and natural history.

In 1855 Nicol accompanied Murchison to the north-west highlands of Scotland, but a difference of opinion began to develop between them. Murchison thought he could discern a regularly ascending stratigraphic sequence from the 'Fundamental Gneiss' of the west coast, through the Torridon Sandstone, then a sequence of quartzites, shales, and limestones, next a large area of unfossiliferous schistose rocks (the 'Moine Schists'), and finally the Old Red Sandstone of the east coast. With Charles Peach's discovery in 1854 of fossils (thought to be Silurian by the survey palaeontologist) in limestones near Durness, Murchison thought that the Moine Schists might also be Silurian, given that they lay between the Durness Limestone and the Old Red Sandstone (Devonian). However, Nicol contested this interpretation in a series of papers published between 1857 and 1861, and in a book, *The Geology and Scenery of the North of Scotland* (1866). He envisaged a 'zone of complication' running from Durness to Skye, and that there was a repetition in the stratigraphic sequence due to faulting along this line, igneous rock being intruded along the line of fault. Thus he proposed that metamorphic rocks to the east of the zone of complication were essentially the same as the western gneisses, having been brought to the surface by faulting. This idea, if true, would deny Murchison territory that he was depicting in 'his' Silurian colours to the east of the zone of complication.

There thus arose a bitter contest between Nicol and Murchison (supported by his young 'lieutenant', Archibald Geikie). Murchison emerged victorious, with Nicol finding little support, apart from his colleague at Aberdeen, H. A. Nicholson. Nicol's geological reputation suffered, and the views of Murchison and Geikie became paradigmatic in the 1870s. However, the structure favoured by Murchison and Geikie was challenged in 1878 by Henry Hicks, and, with further work by Charles Callaway and Charles Lapworth, a new theory was proposed, according to which the zone of complication was due to low-angle thrust faulting. There was indeed some repetition of the Fundamental (Lewisian) Gneiss; but the Moine Schists were supposedly formed during the earth movements associated with the thrusting process. The debate has been called the 'highlands controversy' and when it was over, with the survey field staff accepting the views of Lapworth rather than their chief, Geikie, the deceased Nicol was hailed by John Judd at the meeting of the British Association in Aberdeen (1885) as having been 'right all along'. This claim was not strictly correct, as Nicol did not have the idea of low-angle thrust faulting, and did not contemplate the idea of the Moine Schists being metamorphosed during their emplacement. Even so, Nicol changed from being a somewhat discredited geologist in his own day—accorded only four lines in his obituary in the *Geological Magazine* (1879)—to become one of the great folk heroes of Scottish geology. A memorial tablet was erected in his honour at Aberdeen University in 1920, unveiled by John Horne, one of the surveyors who had vindicated Nicol's work.

Nicol published several useful elementary scientific texts (including *A Catechism of Geology*, 1842, *Introductory Book of the Sciences*, 1844, and *Elements of Mineralogy*, 1858), the last of these based on an *Encyclopaedia Britannica* article. He taught zoological anatomy at Aberdeen as well as geology, but apparently with less success and enthusiasm. Nicol was described by Geikie as tall, of abundant sandy hair, and with a pronounced south-Scottish accent. A student said of him that he was 'somewhat large of bone, spare of flesh yet not lean, erect in figure and firm in gait, … a man in hard condition, unused to luxury and capable of physical endurance'. He was a 'kindly man … but something in the firm straight mouth told of a possible dourness it were better not to provoke' (Anderson, 89). Nicol retired in 1878. He died the following year in London, on 8 April 1879, at 6 Beaumont Street, Portland Place; he was survived by his wife.   DAVID OLDROYD

Sources H. C. Sorby, *Quarterly Journal of the Geological Society*, 36 (1880), 33–6 · P. J. A. [P. J. Anderson], ed., *Aurora borealis academica: Aberdeen University appreciations, 1860–1889* (1899), 83–94 · J. W. Judd, 'Presidential address to the geology section of the British Association', *Report of the British Association for the Advancement of Science*, 55 (1886), 994–1013 · D. R. Oldroyd, *The highlands controversy: constructing geological knowledge through fieldwork in nineteenth-century Britain* (1990) · [J. Horne], 'The Nicol memorial', *Geological Magazine*, 57 (1920), 387–92 · *DNB* · *CGPLA Eng. & Wales* (1879)

Archives GS Lond., map of Cantyre · U. Aberdeen L., special libraries and archives, lecture notes · U. Edin. L., special collections division, diary | BGS, letters to C. W. Reach and Roderick Impey Murchison · Elgin Museum, Elgin, letters to George Gordon · GS Lond., letters to Roderick Impey Murchison

Likenesses A. B. Woodward, memorial tablet, U. Aberdeen · photograph, U. Aberdeen, archives; repro. in Oldroyd, *Highlands controversy*, 149

Wealth at death £7190 4s. 9d.: confirmation, 11 Sept 1879, *CCI*

Nicol, John. *See* Nicoll, John (c.1590–1668).

Nicol, John (1755–1825), sailor, was born at Currie, near Edinburgh, the third of five children. His father was a cooper who died about 1780, and his mother died in childbirth when he was very young. Both his parents were Scottish. His father appears to have tried to give all his children a good education but John, on his own admission, did not make the most of it. From reading Defoe's *Robinson Crusoe* many times over he longed to be at sea. His father, however, insisted that he learned a trade and he was apprenticed to a cooper. When in 1776 his period of 'bondage' expired, after a few months as a journeyman to become proficient at his trade, he volunteered for the Royal Navy. 'Now I was Happy, for I was at Sea' (*Life and Adventures*, 1937, 2.38).

Nicol was first sent on board the *Proteus* and was appointed cooper. He spent the next seven years on the eastern seaboard of North America. When the *Proteus* became a prison ship, he served ashore at St John's, Newfoundland, brewing spruce for the fleet. He then joined the *Surprise* and she captured several American privateers. After escorting a series of convoys the *Surprise* was paid off in 1783 and Nicol returned to Scotland.

During the next ten years Nicol served in six different merchant ships. These included a whaler off Greenland. However, the 'cold was so intense and the weather often so thick, I felt so cheerless that I resolved to bid adieu to the coast of Greenland for ever, and seek to gratify my curiosity in more genial climes' (*Life and Adventures*, 1937, 2.74). He subsequently spent time in the West Indies where 'I wrought a good deal on shore and had a number of blacks under me' (ibid., 2.78). He then circumnavigated

John Nicol (1755–1825), by William Home Lizars, pubd 1822

the world on a voyage of discovery and trade, rounding Cape Horn and visiting China. However, his most memorable voyage was probably taking female convicts to New South Wales. There was a close intimacy between many of the women and the crew. 'Every man on board took a wife from among the convicts, they nothing loath' (ibid., 2.134). Nicol's 'wife' was named Sarah Whitelam. She had a son by him during the voyage but they were separated on arrival at Port Jackson on 15 July 1791 and though he sought for her later, he never again saw either her or his son.

After a whaling voyage and further visits to China, on returning to England in 1794 he was impressed into the king's service. It was 'a bondage that had been imposed upon me against my will … not that I disliked it, but I had now become weary of wandering for a time, and longed to see Scotland again' (*Life and Adventures*, 1937, 2.179). He saw much action including the battles of Cape St Vincent (1797) and the Nile (1798). 'We gave them three such cheers as are only to be heard in a British man-of-war' (ibid., 2.188). He also spent many months blockading Cadiz and was finally discharged following the peace of Amiens (1802). Nicol now returned to Scotland, married his cousin, Margaret (d. 1818), and settled down as a cooper in Edinburgh. However, when war broke out again, he was fearful of the press gang and, as he had promised his wife not to go to sea again, left his business and retired to Cousland, near Edinburgh, where he lived a hand-to-mouth existence, frightened all the time of being impressed. After the war he returned to Edinburgh but was unable to obtain regular employment. His last years were spent in poverty and he died in Edinburgh in October 1825, his wife having predeceased him in 1818.

Nicol's career was therefore little different from that of many other mariners of his time, but in 1822 he had been fortunate to meet a 'polyartist', John Howell, who recorded his experiences. The result was a remarkable account written apparently in Nicol's own words and is an important example of the lives of so many otherwise anonymous late-eighteenth- and early nineteenth-century sailors. It concludes 'I have been a wanderer and the child of chance all my days; and now I only look for the time when I shall enter my last ship, and be anchored with a green turf upon my breast; and I care not how soon the command is given' (*Life and Adventures*, 1937, 2.213).

HENRY BAYNHAM

Sources *The life and adventures of John Nicol, mariner*, ed. J. H. [J. Howell] (1822) · *The life and adventures of John Nicol, mariner*, ed. J. H. [J. Howell], ed. A. K. Laing (1937) · *GM*, 1st ser., 95/2 (1825), 472–3 · *Annual Biography and Obituary*, 10 (1826), 454–5
Likenesses W. H. Lizars, drawing, repro. in Nicol, *Life and adventures of John Nicol* (1822) [*see illus.*]

Nicol, Mary (*bap.* 1747, *d.* 1820). *See under* Nicol, George (1740?–1828).

Nicol, Robert Bell (1905–1978), player and teacher of the highland bagpipe, was born on 26 December 1905 at West Lodge, Durris, Kincardineshire, the youngest of the three children of David Nicol (1861–1934), a salmon fisher from Banchory, and his wife, Mary McDonald (1862–1956). On leaving school, he was employed as a stalker and fisherman on the Cowdray estate and, from 1924 onwards, at Balmoral. He never married and lived latterly with his sister Jean (*c.*1904–1972) at their cottage near Ballater.

Having been taught the pipes by local players as a boy, from the mid-1920s Nicol, together with his friend and colleague Robert Urquhart Brown (1906–1972)—the two being known collectively as 'the Bobs of Balmoral'—received master-class instruction from John MacDonald of Inverness (1865–1953). Nicol went on to win most of the top piping awards, including the gold medals at Oban and Inverness (1930), the Clasp (1932), and the Bratach Gorm (1939). From 1942 to 1945 he saw active service as pipe major, 2nd battalion Gordon Highlanders. He was also a skilled reed maker.

Although raised on Deeside, Nicol had strong west highland connections. His mother was a Gaelic speaker, and he set many of her songs for the pipes. He recounted his grandmother's stories of the clearances in Moidart, and of living under tarpaulins on the shore, saying:

> It never struck me until I was a grown up man that it was true; it had actually happened to us; I thought that they were just fairy stories from long ago … I think it was the poverty—it must have been—the terrible grinding poverty—that gave such sadness to the music. (private information)

Nicol taught orally transmitted texts by the canntaireachd, or singing method, and before beginning a tune would raise his hand in a characteristic gesture and say, 'This is the way that ever I had it from Old John', and he followed scrupulously what he had himself been taught. He was not opposed to printed scores as such, and warmly recommended the collections of C. S. Thomason, Donald MacDonald, William Ross, and Donald MacPhee for reprinting shortly before his death. Yet, like his teacher John MacDonald, he was obliged to work in an ethos where success in competition required a degree of conformity with the published scores of the Piobaireachd

Society which dominated competitive bagpipe playing in Scotland throughout the twentieth century. Like MacDonald, he privately condemned these for distorting and coarsening the music, declaring: 'The timing of the tunes has been altered, they drew lines, and so many notes have to go in there, and so many in here …', and described the society's editor, Archibald Campbell (1877–1963), as 'no musician' (Donaldson, 459–60). Yet he and Brown had been taught by John MacDonald on the recommendation of the society, and he acted as its instructor in the Uists between 1953 and 1957.

By the middle of the twentieth century Nicol and Brown had become the leading piobaireachd teachers of their generation and they attracted pupils from all over the world. In 1978 the Balmoral Schools of Piping were founded in the United States to commemorate their memory.

Although piping and piobaireachd formed the central focus of Robert Nicol's life, he refused to charge for instruction. The only recordings commercially distributed which show him as a player, *Pibroch: Pipe-Major Robert Nicol* (Tangent TGMMC 503), were made under atrocious conditions in Braemar in the winter of 1953–4, and he was anxious to redo them. But after a severe illness in 1958 he lost control of his right hand and did not completely recover his technical mastery. He continued his teaching activities with overseas tours, however, and with the introduction of cassette tapes his lessons were eagerly copied and circulated throughout the world. Nicol saw in this a danger that fixed printed texts could simply be replaced by fixed audio ones. He insisted that his pupils should cultivate an individual style, and that his recordings must not be parroted. Yet within twenty years of his death they were circulating commercially, promoted by leading figures in the piping establishment as a prescriptive hotline to 'tradition'.

Nicol was of medium height and stocky build, habitually clad in comfortable tweed plus fours. His alert, slightly quizzical countenance was given additional interest (at least to his younger pupils) by his glass eye, the result of a shooting accident in 1926. When he played his practice chanter, he would close the good eye, turn a startling magenta colour, and transfix the pupil with the blazing, sightless orb. A complex and sensitive man of immense personal probity, he concealed behind a reserved façade a rare kindliness, humour, and generosity of spirit.

Robert Nicol died at his home, 3 Blacksmith's Cottages, Birkhall, near Ballater, on 4 April 1978. After a requiem mass at St Nathalan's Church, Ballater, which was attended by hundreds of pipers, he was buried at Durris parish church, Kirkton of Durris, on 8 April 1978.

WILLIAM DONALDSON

Sources W. Donaldson, *The highland pipe and Scottish society, 1750–1950* (2000) · N. Matheson, 'Robert Nicol', *Masters of piobaireachd, volume 1*, Greentrax Recordings, CDTRAX153 (1997) [disc notes] · 'Pipe Major Bob Nicol', *The Gordon highlanders pipe music collection*, ed. [P. Graham and B. MacRae], 2 (1985), xx–xxiii · NL Scot., Piobaireachd Society MS Acc. 9103 · P. Mollard, 'Robert B. Nicol in Brittany', *Piping Times*, 25/1 (1972–3), 29–30 · 'Piping Society of London',

Oban Times (4 March 1939), 5 · G. Balderose, 'The Balmoral schools', *The Voice* (spring 1995), 43–5 · private information (2004) · personal knowledge (2004) · b. cert. · d. cert.

Archives SOUND U. Edin., School of Scottish Studies

Likenesses photographs, repro. in 'Pipe Major Bob Nicol', ed. Graham and MacRae

Wealth at death £26,451.80: confirmation, 1978, *CCI*

Nicol, Sarah Bezra (*d.* in or after **1834**), actress, was housekeeper to Colonel and the Hon. Mrs Milner about 1800 and became a member of the Shakespearean Society of London, the members of which used to act in a little theatre in Tottenham Court Road. She played Belvidera in *Venice Preserv'd* for a charitable benefit at the old Lyceum and was encouraged by her employers to gain experience and go on the stage professionally. This she did in the provinces. She married soon after, and a daughter, Emma *Nicol, was born in 1800. Neither Mrs Nicol's maiden name nor the venue for her début has been recorded. Her husband, a printer, obtained a position in Edinburgh, and she appeared there on 15 December 1806 as Cicely in *Valentine and Orson*. She continued there, and by 1807 had succeeded Mrs Charteris in old women's roles at the Theatre Royal. On 2 May 1808 she had her first benefit, in which her daughter Emma also appeared. She accompanied Henry Siddons to the New Theatre Royal in Leith Walk and played Monica in W. W. Dimond's *The Flowers of the Forest*. By 1817 she was acting such parts as Mrs McCandlish in Daniel Terry's adaptation of Scott's *Guy Mannering* and Mrs Malaprop in *The Rivals*. At the first production in Edinburgh of *Rob Roy* on 15 February 1819 she played Jean McAlpine. In December 1819 she was Mrs Hardcastle in *She Stoops to Conquer* when gas was used in the theatre for the first time. On the occasion of George IV's visit to the theatre, on 27 August 1822, she again played Jean McAlpine. A variety of parts followed, and in 1822 she was receiving £2 a week and filling all the first old-woman parts, modelling herself, it was said, on Mary Ann Davenport's performances in such parts in London. On 27 December 1828 she was Audrey in *As You Like It* on the occasion of a special production, with costumes designed by J. R. Planché. She was replaced in the 1833 season, and in the following season, by now being elderly and unfit, she appeared only occasionally. At her farewell benefit on 10 April 1834 she played three parts—Mrs Malaprop, Miss Durable, and Mrs Deborah Doublelock. She died soon after her retirement in 1834. Four of her daughters were also actresses.

J. GILLILAND

Sources J. C. Dibdin, *The annals of the Edinburgh stage* (1888) · Hall, *Dramatic ports.* · *DNB*

Likenesses portrait (as Mrs Malaprop), Edinburgh Theatre Royal; repro. in *National Drama* · print, Harvard TC

Nicol, William (**1744–1797**), schoolmaster, was born in Dumbrelton, in the parish of Annan, the only child of a Dumfriesshire tailor, who died young. After receiving elementary education in his parish school and from John Orr, a travelling teacher, he earned some money by teaching, and was able to pursue a university career at Edinburgh, where he studied both theology and medicine. Allusions in Burns's 'Elegy on Willie Nicol's Mare' seem to indicate that he was a licentiate of the church (*Works*, ed. Dcouglas, 2.291). Throughout his college course he was constantly employed in tuition, and on 2 February 1774 was appointed a classical master at the Edinburgh high school, having won the post in open competition. The rector was Alexander Adam, and Walter Scott was a pupil. Scott condemned Nicol as 'worthless, drunken, and inhumanly cruel to the boys under his charge', and describes him physically assaulting Adam (Lockhart, *Life of Scott*, 1.33). To avenge an insult against the rector, Scott once pinned to Nicol's coat-tail a paper inscribed with *Aeneid*, iv.10—part of the day's lesson—substituting 'vanus' for 'novus': 'Quis vanus hic nostris successit sedibus hospes?' ('Who is this worthless stranger who has approached our abode?'; ibid., 110).

Burns early made Nicol's acquaintance—their first meeting is not recorded—and his various letters to his 'worthy friend', and the fact that he named his third son after him, prove that the poet found in him more than the drunken tyrant described by Scott, or the pedantic boor ridiculed by Lockhart (Lockhart, *Life of Burns*, 1.193). Nicol, according to Steven, 'would go any length to serve and promote the views and wishes of a friend', and was instantly stirred to hot wrath 'whenever low jealousy, trick, or selfish cunning appeared' (Steven, 95). Alexander Young, the Edinburgh lawyer, spoke of him as 'one of the greatest Latin scholars of the age' (in Lindsay, 143) and was employed by Nicol to recover his claims for payment for his work in translating the medical law theses of the graduates at the university.

Burns was Nicol's guest from 7 to 25 August 1787 in the house over Buccleuch Pend, from which he visited the literary 'howffs' or brewhouses of the city. Nicol accompanied him in his three weeks' tour through the highlands, Burns anticipating much entertainment from his friend's 'originality of humour' (Lockhart, *Life of Burns*, 1.222). Knowing Nicol's fiery temper, he likened himself to 'a man travelling with a loaded blunderbuss at full cock' (Chambers, 2.107). The harmony of the trip was rudely broken at Fochabers, when Burns visited and dined at Gordon Castle, leaving Nicol at the village inn. Incensed at this apparent neglect, Nicol resolved on proceeding alone, and Burns surrendered the pleasure of a short sojourn at Gordon Castle, and the opportunity to make important contacts, in order to join his irate friend. He made reparation with 'Streams that glide in orient plains', and in his letter to the castle librarian did not spare the 'obstinate son of Latin prose' (*Works*, ed. Dcouglas, 4.279).

In 1789 Burns and Allan Masterton, an Edinburgh writing master and musical composer, visited Nicol while he spent his autumn recess at Moffat, and made him the protagonist of the bacchanalian song, 'Willie brewed a peck o' maut'. Burns wrote, 'we had such a joyous meeting that Mr. Masterton and I agreed, each in our own way, that we should celebrate the business' (*Works*, ed. Douglas, 2.246). The following year Nicol bought the small estate of Laggan, Dumfriesshire, and became in Burns's words 'the illustrious lord of Laggan's many hills' (ibid., 6.55). He left the high school in 1796, opening his own school. Nicol died on 21 April 1797, and was buried at Calton. He was married, and had seven children, of whom three survived him.　　　T. W. BAYNE, rev. SARAH COUPER

Sources J. G. Lockhart, *Memoirs of the life of Sir Walter Scott*, 1 (1837) · J. G. Lockhart, *The life of Robert Burns*, 2 vols. (1914) · W. Steven, *The history of the high school of Edinburgh* (1849) · *The works of Robert Burns*, another edn, ed. W. S. Douglas, 6 vols. (1877–9) · *The life and works of Robert Burns*, ed. R. Chambers, 4 vols. (1851–2) · *The works of Robert Burns*, another edn, ed. J. Currie, 4 vols. (1815) · Irving, *Scots.* · J. D. Ross, *Who's who in Burns* (1927) · T. Royle, *The mainstream companion to Scottish literature* (1993) · *N&Q*, 2 (1850), 493 · M. Lindsay, *The Burns encyclopedia*, 3rd edn (1980)

Nicol, William (*c*.1771–1851), geologist and scientific lecturer, was probably born at Humbie in Haddingtonshire, though no record of his birth or baptism has been found. His parents were Marion Fowler and Walter Nickol or Nicoll, who were married in Humbie in August 1768, and they had at least one other child, Marion, born in May 1772 at Humbie. Nothing is known of Nicol's childhood or education, but it appears that at about the age of fifteen, in 1786, he became assistant to Henry Moyes (1749–1807), the renowned blind public lecturer on science. After Moyes's death, in the middle of a lecture course in Doncaster in 1807, Nicol bought his apparatus and manuscripts and continued his master's lecturing circuit of English provincial centres in his own right well into the 1830s. He never married, but spent more and more time in Edinburgh, where he was involved on the periphery of intellectual and university circles.

Nicol is associated with two inventions of considerable significance, both of which helped to lay the foundations of the modern sciences of mineralogy and petrology. The first was the prism which bears his name, a sophisticated optical filter designed to polarize light. Used in pairs as polarizer and analyser, the Nicol prism was a pioneering device which enabled minerals to be identified through optical characteristics which derive from their crystal structures. This was published in 1829, in a journal edited by one of Nicol's most influential friends, Robert Jameson (1774–1854), professor of natural history at the University of Edinburgh (W. Nicol, 'On a method of so far increasing the divergence of the two rays in a calcareous spar that only one image may be seen at a time', *Edinburgh New Philosophical Journal*, 6, 1829, 83–4). However, the theory and usefulness of this device was not immediately appreciated, and it was not until five years later that William Henry Fox Talbot (1800–1879), the pioneer of photography, announced that he had read about the device in a German journal and realized that the Nicol prism could be effectively applied to the microscope. Even more mysteriously, a paper explaining the mathematics of the Nicol prism written in 1837 by Edward Sang (1805–1890), whose mother was a distant relation of William Nicol, was inexplicably 'neglected and left lying in a drawer till rescued from oblivion by Tait fifty-four years later' (Knott, 17).

The second device, which involved Nicol in some fierce controversy, was that of the preparation of thin slices or 'sections' of fossils or minerals for viewing through the microscope. In this, the specimen was cemented to a glass plate and then ground down so thinly that its structure became visible: this was first discussed in *Observations on Fossil Vegetables*, a volume published in 1831 about the microscopic structure of fossil plants, dedicated to William Nicol by his friend Henry Witham (1779–1844) of Lartington Hall. Witham disputed Nicol's priority in this invention, and the second edition of his book (*The Internal Structure of Fossil Vegetables*, 1833) deleted all but one references to his former friend. Nicol for his part claimed that his technique improved upon that used by an Edinburgh lapidary named George Sanderson. However, it was not until the method was taken up during the late 1850s by the Sheffield geologist Henry Clifton Sorby (1826–1908) that its potential began to be realized.

Besides his collections of fossils and minerals—Nicol on occasion lent Sir David Brewster (1781–1868) specimens for examination—he also built up a fine collection of shells. This included the type specimen of a shell known as 'Nicol's cone'. As with his geological material, he was prepared to lend specimens to like-minded acquaintances for study and publication, and at his death he left his entire house and its contents to Alexander Bryson (1816–1866), a younger man who had had similar interests to his own. Despite having been elected an associate of the Edinburgh-based Society of Arts, later the Royal Scottish Society of Arts, in December 1826, and subsequently being elected a fellow of the Royal Society of Edinburgh in 1838, Nicol appears to have lived a quiet life in Edinburgh after effectively retiring from his peripatetic lecturing in the early 1830s; he was cared for by his sister, Marion, who was unmarried and acted as his housekeeper, and two female servants. He died at his home, 4 Inverleith Terrace, Edinburgh, on 2 September 1851, and was buried at Warriston cemetery.　　　A. D. MORRISON-LOW

Sources A. D. Morrison-Low, 'Edinburgh portraits: William Nicol, FRSE, c.1771–1851, lecturer, scientist and collector', *Book of the Old Edinburgh Club*, new ser., 2 (1992), 123–31 · will, testament of William Nicol, NA Scot., SC 70/4/17 · *The Scotsman* (6 Sept 1851) · J. A. Harrison, 'Blind Henry Moyes, "an excellent lecturer in philosophy"', *Annals of Science*, 13 (1957), 109–25 · A. Geikie, *The founders of geology* (1897), 276–8 · C. G. Knott, 'Mathematics and natural philosophy', *Edinburgh's place in scientific progress* (1921), 1–30, esp. 17–18 · E. Sang, 'Investigation of the action of Nicol's polarizing eyepiece', *Proceedings of the Royal Society of Edinburgh*, 18 (1890–91), 323–36 · P. G. Tait, 'Note on Dr Sang's paper', *Proceedings of the Royal Society of Edinburgh*, 18 (1890–91), 337–40 · H. Witham, *Observations on fossil vegetables* (1831) · H. T. M. Witham, *The internal structure of fossil vegetables* (1833) · W. Nicol, 'On a method of so far increasing the divergence of the two rays in calcareous spar that only one image may be seen at a time', *Edinburgh New Philosophical Journal*, 6 (1829), 83–4 · W. Nicol, 'Observations on the structure of recent and fossil coniferae', *Edinburgh New Philosophical Journal*, 16 (1834), 137–58 · H. F. Talbot, 'Facts relating to optical science, no. II: on Mr Nicol's polarizing eye-piece', *London and Edinburgh Philosophical Magazine*, 3rd ser., 4 (1834), 289–90 · J. M. Eyles, 'An Edinburgh scientist: William Nicol of prism fame', *The Scotsman* (1 Sept 1951) · bur. reg. Scot.

Likenesses W. Ward, engraving (after portrait by J. R. Smith, 1806), BM; repro. in Morrison-Low, 'Edinburgh portraits'

Wealth at death approx. £3000–£4000; also government annuity of £120 1s. 0d.: inventory, NA Scot., SC 70/1/73, fols. 959–60

Nicolas, Dafydd (*bap.* 1705?, *d.* 1774), poet and schoolmaster, was born in Llangynwyd, Glamorgan, and was probably the Dafydd Nicolas who was baptized there on 1 July 1705, and who later kept a school in the parish. He was the son, it was claimed, of Robert Nicolas and Anne Rees, both of Llangynwyd, whose marriage is recorded in the parish registers on 12 February 1699. The identification was made by the antiquary and folklorist Thomas Christopher Evans (Cadrawd; 1846–1918). It is very likely, however, that the poet lived for a while in the parish of Ystradyfodwg and, possibly, in Glyncorrwg and Cwm-gwrach. In his younger days Nicolas was probably an itinerant schoolmaster in various parts of Upper Glamorgan.

Towards the middle of the eighteenth century, or possibly a little earlier, Nicolas's marked ability attracted the attention of the Williams family of Aberpergwm, a mansion in the parish of Nedd Uchaf, Glamorgan, once renowned for its bardic patronage and its valuable collection of manuscripts, and he lived there from then until his death. It was frequently maintained in the nineteenth century that he was retained and supported there as a sort of family bard, the last, it was claimed, to fulfil this ancient function in any part of Wales. But if that really was his status, it is very strange that no panegyric or elegy addressed by him to any member of the Williams family of Aberpergwm is now extant. Much weight must therefore be given to the statement made in 1795–6 by William Davies (1756–1823) of Cringell, Llantwit-juxta-Neath, a responsible and well-informed antiquary, that Nicolas was engaged as a 'Private Tutor at Aberpergwm'.

Although, according to Edward Williams (Iolo Morganwg; 1747–1826), he was 'self-educated' and 'self-taught', Nicolas won considerable renown as a gifted classical scholar. William Davies of Cringell was convinced that he fully merited the reputation he had acquired 'as a poet, as well as a classic scholar' and, in his view, the well-known composition 'Ffanni blodau'r ffair'—or 'Fanny Blooming Fair', as Nicolas himself had written—was a worthy imitation of Horace. According to a tradition that was current in the Neath valley towards the end of the eighteenth century, he had translated the *Iliad* into Welsh. Iolo Morganwg maintained that Dafydd Nicolas, whom he considered to be the most talented of all the Welsh poets he had known, had acquired a firm grasp of Latin, Greek, and French.

Although there is little artistic merit in the few poems Nicolas composed in the strict metres, his free-metre verses have rightly won for him a secure place in the literary history of Glamorgan. Two delightful lyrics, entitled 'Callyn serchus' and 'Ffanni blodau'r ffair', were attributed to him by Maria Jane Williams (1795?–1873) in *Ancient National Airs of Gwent and Morganwg* (1844), and his name has often been connected with the words of the equally enchanting 'Y deryn pur'. These three beautiful love lyrics were designed to be sung to the accompaniment of various airs, both old and modern. They provide conclusive evidence that their author was sensitively responsive to the music of words and that he took a great delight in the rhythmical cadences and spontaneity of his metres. Some critics are convinced that his free-metre verse was the best work produced by a Glamorgan bard in the first half of the eighteenth century.

The authorship of a long letter, which attempts to analyse the technique of free-metre composition, is attributed to Nicolas in one of Iolo Morganwg's manuscripts. This is the only extant copy of the letter, which is in Iolo's autograph, and both the style and diction suggest that it is one of the latter's many forgeries. It was Nicolas's renown in Glamorgan as a classical scholar and as a free-metre poet that probably prompted Iolo to attribute the forgery to him. Nicolas died at Aberpergwm on 8 February 1774, and was buried there.   C. W. LEWIS

Sources G. J. Williams, *Traddodiad llenyddol Morgannwg* (1948), 241–3, 290–300 [also the index] · C. W. Lewis, 'The literary history of Glamorgan from 1550 to 1770', *Glamorgan county history*, ed. G. Williams, 4: *Early modern Glamorgan* (1974), 535–639, esp. 616–17 · D. Rhys Phillips, *The history of the Vale of Neath* (1925), 546–53, 738–9 · Cadrawd [T. C. Evans], *History of Llangynwyd parish* (1887), 186–8 · M. J. Williams, *Ancient national airs of Gwent and Morganwg* (1844), 10–11, 14–15, 32–3, 77–8, 81 · W. O. Pughe, ed., *The Cambrian register*, 2 (1799–1818), 564–6 · NL Wales, Llanover MS. C35, 165–74 · J. Williams (ab Ithel), *Taliesin*, 1 (1859–60), 92–5 · W. Williams, letter to J. M. Traherne, Sept 1833, NL Wales, MS 6598, no. 81 · W. Davies, *The Cambrian* (Aug 1805) · W. Young, *Guide to the beauties of Glyn Neath* (1835), 83 · L. Hopkins, *Y fel gafod* (1813), 98, 100–01 · NL Wales, Llanover MSS C12, 121–8, 198–9; C40, 473–5, 511; C54, 133, 380–82; C59, 180, 321–3, 386 · NL Wales, MS 112, 198 · NL Wales, MS 166, 107

Nicolas, Granville Toup (1832–1894). *See under* Nicolas, Sir John Toup (1788–1851).

Nicolas, Sir John Toup (1788–1851), naval officer, the eldest son of Lieutenant John Harris Nicolas RN (1758–1844) of East Looe, Cornwall, and his wife, Margaret (*d.* after 1851), the daughter and coheir of John Blake, was born at Withen, near Helston, Cornwall, on 22 February 1788. Sir Nicholas Harris *Nicolas (1799–1848) was his brother. As early as 1797 he was on the books of one or other of the gun-vessels stationed on the coast of Devon and Cornwall, but seems to have first gone to sea in 1799, in the *Edgar* with Captain Edward Buller, whom he followed in 1801 to the *Achille*. He was afterwards in the frigate *Naiad*, but in 1803 was again with Buller in the *Malta* (80 guns). He was made lieutenant on 1 May 1805, and, remaining in the *Malta*, was present in the action off Cape Finisterre on 22 July 1805. From 1807 he was flag lieutenant to Rear-Admiral George Martin in the Mediterranean, and in October 1809 was appointed acting commander of the *Redwing*. He had been previously promoted from home on 26 August and appointed to the brig *Pilot*, which he joined at Portsmouth in April 1810.

In the *Pilot* Nicolas went out again to the Mediterranean, and for the next four years was employed in most active and harassing service on the coast of Italy, capturing or destroying many coastal vessels and vessels laden with stores for the Neapolitan government. Alone, or with the sloop *Weasel* or the frigate *Thames*, he is said to have captured or destroyed no fewer than 130 of the enemy's vessels between his first coming on the coast and July 1812. He afterwards went to the Adriatic, and continued there with the same activity and good fortune. He returned to England towards the end of 1814, but on the escape of Napoleon from Elba was again sent out to the Mediterranean, where, on 17 June, off Cape Corse, he engaged the French sloop *Egérie*. After several hours both vessels had suffered severely and the *Egérie* had lost many men, killed and wounded. The *Pilot*'s loss in men had been slight, but her rigging was cut to pieces, and the *Egérie* escaped. The *Pilot*'s first lieutenant, Keigwin Nicolas, a brother of the commander, was among the wounded. On 4 June 1815 Nicolas was made a CB; on 26 August he was promoted post captain, in October he received from the king of Naples the cross of St Ferdinand and Merit, and in the following April he was made a knight commander of the order. He returned to England in July 1816, when the *Pilot* was paid off. On 1 August 1818 he married Frances Anna, the daughter of Nicholas Were, of Landcox, near Wellington in Somerset; they had four sons and two daughters.

From 1820 to 1822 Nicolas commanded the frigate *Egeria* on the Newfoundland station, and on his return to England was sent to Newcastle, where a dispute between the keelmen and shipowners threatened to cause a disturbance. The mere presence of the frigate in the Tyne led to a quick agreement, and the *Egeria* went to Sheerness and was paid off. Nicolas's conduct and tact on this occasion were highly approved. He was made a KH on 1 January 1834. From 1837 to 1839 he commanded the *Hercules* (74 guns) on the Lisbon station; from 1839 to 1841 the *Belle-Isle* in the channel and the Mediterranean; and from 1841 to 1844 the *Vindictive* on the East India station. He returned to England via Tahiti, where he was sent to protect British interests during the arbitrary proceedings of the French in dealing with Mr Pritchard.

Nicolas invented 'several highly valuable appliances for the service' and, in improving and embellishing his ship, 'he appears to have been utterly regardless of his own finances' (*GM*, 666). He was superintendent of Royal William Victualling Yard, Plymouth, from September 1847 to February 1850. In December that year he was promoted rear-admiral. He died at Plymouth on 1 April 1851, survived by his wife, and was buried on 4 April in St Martin's Church by Looe, Cornwall. He was the author of *An Inquiry into the Causes which have Led to our Late Naval Disasters* (1814) and *A Letter to Rear-Admiral Du Petit Thouars on Late Events at Otaheite* (1843).

His son, **Granville Toup Nicolas** (1832–1894), born on 15 August 1832, entered the navy in 1848, was promoted lieutenant in 1856 after service in the Black Sea, and in the following year was appointed to the *Leopard*, the flagship of Sir Stephen Lushington, on the south-east coast of America. Thence he was appointed to Sir James Hope's flagship, the *Impérieuse*, on the China station. He was later left in command of the gunboat *Insolent*, and was repeatedly engaged in the operations for the suppression of the Taiping uprising. He was promoted commander in 1867, retired as captain in April 1882, and died at Edinburgh on 21 April 1894.   J. K. LAUGHTON, *rev.* ANDREW LAMBERT

Sources E. D. H. E. Napier, *The life and correspondence of Admiral Sir Charles Napier*, 2 vols. (1862) · J. Marshall, *Royal naval biography*, suppl. 4 (1830), 53 · 'Biographical memoir of Captain John Toup Nicolas of the Royal Navy', *Naval Chronicle*, 40 (1818), 333–55 · O'Byrne, *Naval biog. dict.* · *GM*, 2nd ser., 35 (1851), 665 · W. James, *The naval history of Great Britain, from the declaration of war by France, in February 1793, to the accession of George IV in January 1820*, 5 vols. (1822–4) · P. Mackesy, *The war in the Mediterranean, 1803–1810* (1957) · G. S. Graham, *The China station: war and diplomacy, 1830–1860* (1978) · Boase, *Mod. Eng. biog.*
Archives BL, corresp. with Lord Aberdeen, Add. MSS 43241–43244
Likenesses Blood, stipple, pubd 1818, BM, NPG

Nicolas, Sir Nicholas Harris (1799–1848), antiquary and author, was born at Dartmouth on 10 March 1799 and privately baptized by the minister at St Petrox, Dartmouth, on 1 April that year. He was the fourth and youngest son of John Harris Nicolas RN (1758–1844) and Margaret, daughter and coheir of John Blake. His eldest brother was Sir John Toup *Nicolas. His great-grandfather came to Britain after the revocation of the edict of Nantes (1685) and settled at Looe in Cornwall. On his mother's side he was related to the Revd Jonathan *Toup. Nicolas entered the Royal Navy as a first-class volunteer on 27 October 1808; in April 1812 he went out to the Mediterranean as a midshipman and joined the sloop *Pilot*, commanded by his eldest brother, John Toup Nicolas. He was promoted lieutenant on 20 September 1815 but went on half pay early in the following year. After a period living at his home in Looe and spending some months in France, he read for the bar and was called to the Inner Temple on 6 May 1825. He did not enter into general practice, a decision later regretted by his widow, and, apart from some peerage claims before the House of Lords, he spent the rest of his life on antiquarian research and writing; his literary output was considerable and of high quality.

On 28 March 1822 Nicolas married Sarah (1800–1867), the youngest daughter of John Davison of the East India Company and of Loughton in Essex. They had two sons and six daughters; two others died young. The Davisons claimed descent from William Davison, secretary of state to Elizabeth I. Nicolas's investigations into the life of his wife's forebears led to the publication in 1823 of the *Life of William Davison, Secretary of State to Queen Elizabeth*; that year he also published, anonymously, *Index to the Heralds' Visitations in the British Museum*; a second edition followed in 1825. In 1821 he had presented to George IV a manuscript entitled *An heraldic arrangement by which armorial distinctions are assigned to the ensigns of noblemen and gentlemen having the most elevated civil and military offices, etc*; he also sent a copy to Henry Ellis at the British Museum (BL, Add. MS 6525). The year 1824 saw the publication of *Notitia historica*, a historical miscellany, later revised as *The Chronology of History* (1833, 1838).

In the following year Nicolas's *Synopsis of the Peerage of England* went to press—'his greatest work in the sense of labour', according to his wife (Haynes, 239); it was later praised by G. E. Cokayne, on whose *Complete Peerage* the *Synopsis* has been cited as an influence, and J. H. Round. A revised and corrected edition of the *Synopsis*, entitled *The*

Historic Peerage of England, was produced in 1857 by William Courthope, Somerset herald. By the time he was called to the bar in 1825 Nicolas was already well launched on an antiquarian career. On 10 February 1825 he was elected a fellow of the Society of Antiquaries and, when a vacancy occurred the following year, he joined the council. However, his name was omitted from the list for re-election in April 1827; John Caley said that Nicolas 'made himself troublesome in the Council by looking too closely after things' (BL, Add. MS 36527, fol. 183); he had requested but was refused access to the accounts and records. Nicolas proposed his own list in opposition to the house list in 1828; he 'conducted his case with presence of mind, skill and ability' (BL, Add. MS 36527, fol. 183), but was decisively beaten; he received only 22 votes, with over 100 against, and he resigned in disgust. He continued his criticism of the council in the *Westminster Review* and in an article in the *Retrospective Review*, which he edited with Henry Southern in 1827 and 1828. At about this time he began an association with William Pickering who published many of his works; 'this combination was responsible for a number of well-produced books remarkable for their handsome title-pages' (G. Keynes, *William Pickering, Publisher*, 1969, 18). For Pickering's Aldine edition of the poets Nicolas contributed lives of eight poets, of which that on Chaucer is notable for being based on research in the public records. During the years 1826 to 1829 a number of works were published, including *Testamenta vetusta*, *Remains of Lady Jane Grey*, *History of the Battle of Agincourt*, *Private Memoirs of Sir Kenelm Digby*, and a *Memoir of Augustine Vincent, Windsor Herald*. Vincent (1584?–1626) was a pioneer in the use of the public records for genealogical research. In 1828 Nicolas edited *The Siege of Carlaverock, 1300* and *The Roll of Arms of Peers and Knights in the Reign of Edward II*; in the following year a further two rolls were published in the single volume *Rolls of Arms of the Reigns of Henry III and Edward III*. The rolls were 'accompanied by some excellent notes and introductory remarks' (J. A. Montague, *A Guide to the Study of Heraldry*, 1840).

In 1830 Nicolas turned his attention to the record commission; in *Observations on the State of Historical Literature* (1830), addressed to the home secretary, Lord Melbourne, he was critical of the composition of the commission, and of the selection, quality, and cost of its publications, the condition of some public records, and the fees charged to examine them. Sir Francis Palgrave responded to some of the criticisms with *Remarks Submitted to Viscount Melbourne* (1831), to which Nicolas replied with *Refutation of Palgrave's Remarks*, which was appended to a reissue of the *Observations*. In 1831 Nicolas published, anonymously, *Public records: a description of the contents, objects, and uses of the various works printed by authority of the record commission*; it is a lucid and concise account, giving no hint of its author's views on the need for reform. When, eighteen months after the appointment of a new commission following the accession of William IV, there were no signs of change, Nicolas wrote *A letter to … Lord Brougham …, lord high chancellor, on the constitution and proceedings of the present commission etc.* (1832), complaining that the new commission

sought to perpetuate the habits of its predecessor. It was mainly owing to his exertions that the select committee of 1836, under the chairmanship of Charles Buller, was appointed to enquire into the public records; the Public Records Act, as it became known, followed in 1838.

Nicolas gave evidence to the parliamentary inquiry of 1835 into the British Museum. In 1837 he enthusiastically endorsed changes introduced by Panizzi which included printed application forms for books; he congratulated Panizzi on the 'great improvements … you have done wonders in a few weeks' (Miller, 135–6). But Nicolas had clearly forgotten this by 1846, when he complained about poor service; Panizzi responded with a pamphlet quoting Nicolas's earlier remarks on the title-page.

On 12 October 1831 Nicolas was created a knight of the Royal Guelphic Order of Hanover, and on 16 August the following year he was appointed chancellor and senior knight commander in the Order of St Michael and St George; these offices were without remuneration. He was promoted GCMG on 6 October 1840. During the 1830s he was critical of anomalies in the Order of the Bath, including the lack of men of literary merit appointed to the order, and he proposed its reorganization, including a new office of chancellor, which he himself aspired to fill. However, he was unable to repeat his success with the record commission; it appears that he irritated William IV with the manner of his advocacy (Risk, chap. 5), but most of his proposals were adopted early in Victoria's reign. In 1842 Pickering, in conjunction with John Rodwell, published Nicolas's *History of the Orders of Knighthood of the British Empire etc.* (4 vols., originally issued in parts) at a cost of between £3000 and £4000. In Muir's view, 'it is doubtful whether the technical quality of these prints could be surpassed today'; the plates 'using gold leaf … are truly magnificent' (Muir, 152). This work continues to be a valuable source for historians of the subject.

Nicolas's other noteworthy publications included *The Scrope and Grosvenor Controversy* (2 vols., 1832), 'a magnificent work of 150 copies only' (DNB), and from 1834 seven volumes of the *Proceedings and Ordinances of the Privy Council of England, 1386–1542*, for which he received £150 per volume, but after 1837 this project was halted. His two-volume edition of 'The Compleat Angler' of Izaak Walton and Charles Cotton (1836) was 'one of the best, possibly the very best' of over 100 editions published during the nineteenth century (Muir, 21). Throughout his career Nicholas contributed to the *Gentleman's Magazine*, sometimes under the pseudonym of Clionas, an anagram of Nicolas. Other articles appeared in *Archaeologia*, the *Westminster Review*, *Quarterly Review*, *The Spectator*, and *The Athenaeum*. He was also generous in assisting others, such as Dallaway and Cartwryht (*History of Sussex*) and Emma Roberts (*Rival Houses of York and Lancaster*, 2 vols., 1827), and did much spadework on William Forsyth's *History of the Captivity of Napoleon* (3 vols., 1853). In 1859 the College of Arms purchased eighteen volumes of manuscripts from his widow; others are in the British Library.

Nicolas achieved a measure of success assisting or conducting peerage claims in the House of Lords; it is thought that Hatton, the venal peerage lawyer in Disraeli's *Sybil* (1845), was based on him. However, he was unable to consolidate his position owing in part, according to his widow, to lack of support from more senior advocates; furthermore, his successes resulted in only limited pecuniary reward. Earlier Nicolas had published anonymously, and for private circulation, *A letter to the duke of Wellington on the propriety and legality of the creation of peers for life* (1830); there was a second edition in the same year and a third, over his name, in 1834. It was an interest that he shared with his friend Charles Babbage.

The navy was a continuing interest for Nicolas; he wrote articles for the *Naval and Military Magazine*. Two volumes of his incomplete *History of the Navy*, first mooted in 1825, were published in 1847. In 1844–6 Nicolas published seven volumes of *Despatches and Letters of Lord Nelson*. A reprint in paperback was issued in 1997–8; in its foreword, Michael Nash noted that 'The "Nicolas", as it is generally known, has never been superseded'.

'In person', wrote the Revd Joseph Hunter of Nicolas, 'he is rather below middle size, stoops a little, has a keen eye, nose rather hooked: fine skin, delicate form' (BL, Add. MS 36527, fol. 184). In personality he was a man of contrasts: a warm, convivial, and sensitive family man and friend, but a stubborn and passionate advocate, in whom some detected bitterness. He could be direct, even brusque to old friends; he chided J. B. Nichols, publisher of the *Synopsis*, for not ensuring that it was reviewed, and in 1841 there was 'a bruising encounter' with Hunter when Nicolas considered him tardy in producing records (Cantwell, 70). Although not interested in politics, he was a radical in outlook and unrelenting in seeking to right shortcomings and abuses in institutions which impinged on his interests. He was, wrote Risk, 'a curious amalgam of a medieval Crusader with the conscience of a late Victorian Nonconformist' (Risk, 45).

For Nicolas lack of money was a constant problem and the need to provide for a large family led to a life described as one of 'perpetual drudgery' (*DNB*): yet the nature of his considerable literary output suggests that of a financially independent and industrious scholar—some of his works were in editions limited to 50 or 150 copies, others were unremunerative. When his income from peerage claims ceased from the early 1840s he became wholly dependent on his writing and his financial position worsened. In the spring of 1848 he was forced to move to Capécure, a suburb of Boulogne, where, on 3 August 1848, he died at Château Bertrand, rue Amrémont, from a gastric fever which led to 'congestion of the brain'. He was buried in Boulogne cemetery on 8 August. His wife and eight children survived him. On 31 October 1853 Lady Nicolas was granted a civil-list pension of £100; she died at Richmond, Surrey, on 12 November 1867. Four of his children are buried in Kew churchyard.   COLIN LEE

Sources *DNB* · J. Hunter, notices of contemporaries, 1827–36, BL, Add. MS 36527, fols. 182–6 · E. S. P. Haynes, *Life, law and letters* (1936), 226–74 · J. C. Risk, *The history of the order of the Bath* (1972), chap. 5 · Burke, *Gen. GB* (1883) · J. Evans, *A history of the Society of Antiquaries* (1956), 247–50 · J. D. Cantwell, *The Public Record Office, 1838–1958*

(1991), 2–4, 70, 90–91 · E. Miller, *Prince of librarians: the life and times of Antonio Panizzi of the British Museum* (1967), 135–6, 170–71 · *GM*, 1st ser., 92/1 (1822), 369 · *GM*, 2nd ser., 30 (1848), 425–9 · P. H. Muir, *Victorian illustrated books* (1989), 21, 152 · A. R. Wagner, *The records and collections of the College of Arms* (1952), 45

Archives BL, papers, Add. MSS 28847, 28849, 41492 · Coll. Arms, genealogical and other collections · Hunt. L., letters | BL, letters to Charles Babbage, Add. MSS 37184–37201, *passim* · BL, letters to Sir Henry Ellis, Add. MS 6525 · BL, letters to S. Grimaldi, Add. MSS 34188–34189 · BL, letters to J. Hunter, Add. MS 24872 · BL, letters to J. G. Nichols and J. B. Nichols, Add. MS 36987 · BL, Add. MSS 19704–19708, 28847 · Bodl. Oxf., corresp. with Sir Thomas Phillipps · U. Nott. L., letters to duke of Newcastle

Likenesses H. Weigall, bust, exh. RA 1837 (after unknown artist) · portrait, NPG, Heinz archive

Wealth at death negligible; moved to France because of his debts: *DNB*

Nicolaus à Santa Cruce. *See* Cross, Nicholas (1614/15–1698).

Nicolay, Sir William (1771–1842), army officer and colonial governor, was born into an old Saxe-Gotha family settled in England. He entered the Royal Military Academy, Woolwich, as a cadet on 1 November 1785, but did not obtain a commission as second lieutenant in the Royal Artillery until 28 May 1790. In April 1791 he embarked for India with two newly formed companies of Royal Artillery, known as the east India detachment, which later formed the nucleus of the old sixth battalion. He served under Lord Cornwallis at the siege of Seringapatam in 1792, and was an assistant engineer at the reduction of Pondicherry in 1793. Meanwhile, with some other artillery subalterns, he had been transferred in November 1792 to the Royal Engineers, in which he became first lieutenant on 15 August 1793 and captain on 29 August 1798. He was present at the capture of St Lucia, where he was left by Sir John Moore as commanding engineer. He afterwards served under Sir Ralph Abercromby at Trinidad and Tobago until a broken thigh compelled him to return home, leaving him incapacitated for two years.

When the Royal Staff Corps was formed, to provide a corps for quartermaster-general's and engineer duties under the Horse Guards instead of under the Ordnance, Nicolay was appointed major of the new corps from 26 June 1801, and on 4 April 1805 he became lieutenant-colonel. In 1806 he married the second daughter of the Revd Edmund Law of Whittingham, Northumberland. He was employed on the defences of the Kent and Sussex coasts during the invasion alarms of 1804–5 and on intelligence duties under Sir John Moore in Spain in 1808; he was present the following year at Corunna. He became a brevet-colonel on 4 June 1813. In 1815 he proceeded to Belgium in command of five companies of the Royal Staff Corps, and took part in the battle of Waterloo (for which he received CB and medal) and the occupation of Paris. There he remained until the division destined to occupy the frontier, and of which the staff corps formed part, moved to Cambrai. He became a major-general on 12 August 1819.

Nicolay was governor of Dominica from April 1824 to July 1831, of St Kitts from 1832 to 1833, and of Mauritius from 1833 to February 1840, an anxious time, when, owing to the recent abolition of slavery and other causes, there was much ill feeling in the island towards the British.

Nicolay, who had been made KCH, was promoted to lieutenant-general on 10 January 1837, and was appointed colonel, 1st West India regiment, on 30 November 1839. He died at his residence, Oriel Lodge, Cheltenham, Gloucestershire, on 3 May 1842.

H. M. CHICHESTER, *rev.* LYNN MILNE

Sources D. P. Henige, *Colonial governors from the fifteenth century to the present* (1970) · H. M. Vibart, *The military history of the Madras engineers and pioneers*, 2 vols. (1881–3) · J. Philippart, ed., *The royal military calendar*, 3rd edn, 5 vols. (1820) · *GM*, 2nd ser., 18 (1842), 205 · F. Duncan, ed., *History of the royal regiment of artillery*, 2 (1873)

Nicoll, Alexander (1793–1828), orientalist, was born on 3 April 1793 in Monymusk, Aberdeenshire, the youngest son of John Nicoll, maker of noggins (wooden dishes). His elder brother Lewis Nicoll was an advocate in Aberdeen. He was educated successively at a private school (1797–9), the parish school in Monymusk (1799–1805), Aberdeen grammar school (July–November 1805), and the Marischal College, Aberdeen (1805–7), which he entered on a bursary; he was awarded the silver pen as the best new Greek scholar in 1806. In December 1807 he moved to Balliol College, Oxford, after gaining a Snell exhibition, partly on the recommendation of John Skinner (1744–1816), bishop of Aberdeen (the Nicolls were devout Episcopalians). He studied diligently, as always, and graduated BA in 1811.

By 1813 Nicoll had turned his attention to oriental languages, chiefly Hebrew, Arabic, and Persian. In April 1814 he was appointed a sub-librarian in the Bodleian Library, mainly on the strength of his linguistic ability. He made it his task to complete the cataloguing of the oriental manuscripts and began on those purchased from Edward Daniel Clarke in 1808, publishing the catalogue of the oriental items of that collection in 1815.

In July 1816 Nicoll married Johanna, youngest daughter of Alexander Anderson Felborg, of Copenhagen, but the union was cut short by her death only eight days later. In June the following year he was ordained deacon in the Church of England, serving as curate at St Martin's, Carfax, Oxford, and in 1818 he was made priest. Meanwhile he started work on the main Bodleian catalogue of oriental manuscripts, begun by Joannes Uri but left unfinished after the first volume (1787). This was a considerable undertaking, since the manuscripts numbered over 30,000, and when the first part of Nicoll's volume appeared in 1821, describing documents of a dozen languages, his reputation quickly spread throughout Europe. In June 1822 he was appointed regius professor of Hebrew on the recommendation of the outgoing professor, Richard Laurence; this raised Nicoll's annual income from £200 to £2000. Later the same year he received the DCL degree. Nevertheless, he continued work on the catalogue in addition to fulfilling both his pastoral and his professorial obligations, reorganizing the Hebrew course and increasing the number of pupils. On 28 May 1823 Nicoll married his second wife, Sophia, eldest daughter of James

*Parsons (1762–1847), vice-principal of St Alban's Hall; they had three daughters.

Nicoll's linguistic abilities became proverbial, and it was said of him that he could travel to the Great Wall of China without needing an interpreter. He had a wide acquaintance among foreign scholars by correspondence and from their visits to the Bodleian as well as his own visits to the great manuscript collections of France, Germany, and Denmark. In April 1828 he developed a disorder of the trachea, from which he died on 24 September, at the early age of thirty-five; his wife survived him. The second part of his Bodleian catalogue was almost complete, and was published in 1835 by his successor in the regius chair, Edward Bouverie Pusey. His father-in-law published a selection of his sermons with a memoir of his life in 1830.

R. S. SIMPSON

Sources J. Parsons, 'Some particulars of the life of Alexander Nicoll', *Sermons by the late Rev. Alexander Nicoll*, ed. J. Parsons (1830), ix–xliv · Chambers, *Scots.*, rev. T. Thomson (1875) · Anderson, *Scot. nat.* · W. D. Macray, *Annals of the Bodleian Library, Oxford*, 2nd edn (1890), 290, 296–7, 309 · Foster, *Alum. Oxon.* · *DNB*
Archives Bodl. Oxf., notebooks · Bodl. Oxf., corresp. and memoir
Likenesses relief medallion, Christ Church Oxf.
Wealth at death income of *c.*£2000 p.a. as regius professor

Nicoll, (John Ramsay) Allardyce (1894–1976), literary scholar and university teacher, was born on 28 June 1894 at 9 Hillside Gardens, Partick, Glasgow, the younger child and only son of David Binny Nicoll, law clerk (afterwards stationer), and his wife, Elsie Jane Allardyce. Educated at Stirling high school (from 1908), he matriculated in 1911 at Glasgow University, where he was G. A. Clark scholar in English, graduating MA in 1915. In the general council rolls of the university (1920) Nicoll is listed as a journalist, but in August 1920 he was appointed lecturer in English at King's College, University of London. He was promoted quickly and on 1 September 1924, aged only thirty, took the chair of English at East London College (later Queen Mary and Westfield), University of London, where he remained until September 1933. Theatre was his passion and he made it his mission throughout his long career to demonstrate what he believed was then imperfectly acknowledged—that drama could be properly understood only through study of theatrical context and performance.

In 1933 Nicoll secured a post at Yale which might have been tailor-made, as professor of the history of drama and dramatic criticism and chair of the drama department. This appointment he held until 1945, though from late 1942 or early 1943 he was seconded on war work at the British embassy, Washington. He established a strong graduate school in theatre history; and with funding from the Rockefeller Foundation, Nicoll and his doctoral students travelled to Europe in the mid-1930s photographing materials to form the Rockefeller Theatrical Prints collection. The project yielded, among much else, 'a complete photographic record of the Inigo Jones [masque] designs' at Chatsworth and 'the exceedingly informative drawings of the contemporary Turin ballet'—which Nicoll put to good use in his *Stuart Masques and the Renaissance Stage* (1937) (preface, 9). Nicoll returned to Britain in 1945 to head the English department at the University of Birmingham, a post he held until his retirement in 1961, when he became professor emeritus. From 1951 to 1961 he was also founding director of the associated Shakespeare Institute.

Nicoll published a short book on Blake in 1922 and an edition of Chapman's Homer in 1927, but his main academic reputation was built on drama and theatre history. Early work included *An Introduction to Dramatic Theory* ([1923])—revised as *The Theory of Drama* (1931)—and contributions to Restoration studies. He succeeded Montague Summers in this field to contribute annually to *The Year's Work in English Studies* for the years 1923–31; and *Restoration Drama* (1923) inaugurated Nicoll's magisterial series on the history of British drama after 1660, successive volumes of which appeared at regular intervals (1925, 1927, 1930), in the first instance extending the period covered down to 1850.

In addition to historical–critical commentary and analysis, these surveys contained indispensable handlists registering all recorded plays from each period by title, licensing date by the lord chamberlain (where applicable), and, if any, first performance and publication, a task which Nicoll carried out virtually single-handed. The final volumes of the survey (which took the work on to 1900) were in proof by 1938–9, but publication was delayed until 1946. The work of listing demanded 'a great deal of laborious effort' and its completion to 1900, Nicoll reported later, 'was accompanied, not surprisingly, by a very real feeling of relief' (preface, *English Drama, 1900–1930*, vii). Whereas the period 1660–1700 contained only 600 plays, for 1850–1900 there were 20,000 items in a field where the bibliographical groundwork was almost non-existent. A reviewer commented on Nicoll's having 'brought to a triumphant conclusion a work destined for enduring use in research' (*TLS*, 21 Sept 1946, 446). Over time, the handlists, never claimed as exhaustive or definitive, were continually added to and corrected by Nicoll (and other scholars working independently). Between 1952 and 1959 Cambridge reissued the entire work as *A History of English Drama, 1660–1900* (6 vols.), with a new index volume that also stood as a substantive record of authors and play titles between 1660 and 1900.

In 1919 Nicoll married Josephine Calina (1890–1962), a Polish refugee whose pamphlet *Shakespeare in Poland* (1923) was an early publication of the Shakespeare Association, for which Nicoll compiled a bibliography of Dryden's Shakespearian adaptations (1922) and a piece on Shakespeare's editors (1924). With his wife he also edited Holinshed's *Chronicles as used in Shakespeare's Plays* (1927). Nicoll then inherited from Sir Edmund Chambers responsibility for Shakespeare in the 1930 volume of *The Year's Work in English Studies* and, apart from a break during the war (with the volumes for 1941–3), he compiled this section annually until 1950.

In 1948 Nicoll became founding editor of *Shakespeare Survey*, the first journal devoted exclusively to Shakespeare.

Published annually and sponsored by Birmingham University, the Shakespeare Memorial Theatre, and the Shakespeare Birthplace Trust, it was begun at mid-century when, as Nicoll wrote in the first issue, 'it was time to take stock, to inquire what in fact we have accomplished in study and on the stage, and by considering what yet remains to be done, to direct our path for the future' (1, v). The climate was right for Shakespearian initiatives and, despite some university opposition to the idea of a remote, exclusively postgraduate, outpost, Nicoll won support to establish the Shakespeare Institute at Stratford upon Avon. Suitable premises became available at Mason's Croft and under his directorship he created a thriving research school for Elizabethan life and literature.

Many of the titles of Nicoll's works suggest a broad-brush approach—*British Drama* (1925 etc.), *The Development of the Theatre* (1927), *Masks, Mimes and Miracles* (1931), *Film and Theatre* (1936), *World Drama* (1949)—but they are underpinned by a prodigious, wide-ranging knowledge of the theatre, including Greek, Italian, and French. He sought to make drama appeal beyond the purely academic, as in *The English Stage* (1928), for Benn's Sixpenny Library, and *Shakespeare* (1952), his slim but informative contribution to Methuen's Home Study series.

Nicoll believed in the theatre as a deeply humanizing activity. He deplored certain modern trends which prioritized gesture over language and questioned the function of the audience, the life-blood of drama. A lecture read at Edinburgh (1962) attacked 'the current cult of Brechtian alienation'; and in *British Drama* (5th edn, 1962) Nicoll showed his general discomfiture with dramatists like Osborne, Pinter, and Beckett, whose *Waiting for Godot* he described as 'somewhat repetitively boring' (334). For the posthumous sixth and last edition (1978), the chapter on twentieth-century drama was replaced with a more sensitive version by J. C. Trewin.

After the death of his first wife, Nicoll married, on 21 December 1963, Maria Dubno, a librarian, who assisted him with some of his later publications. He was exceptionally active in retirement. His editorship of *Shakespeare Survey* was not relinquished until 1965; and he was Andrew Mellon visiting professor of English at the University of Pittsburgh, in 1963–4, 1965, 1967, and 1969. His main works after 1961 include *The Theatre and Dramatic Theory* (1962), *The World of Harlequin* (1963), *English Theatre: a Modern Viewpoint* (1968), which softened some earlier criticisms of contemporary drama, and *English Drama, 1900–1930* (1973), an unexpected extension of Nicoll's earlier survey, with a handlist of 1500 plays based on the MS 'day books' of the lord chamberlain's office. At his death he was at work on *The Garrick Stage: Theatres and Audience in the Eighteenth Century*. This was published posthumously (1980), with Sybil Rosenfeld of the Society for Theatre Research (a pupil of his at King's in the early 1920s) as editor, and Maria Dubno assisting with the illustrations.

For all his academic renown and international acquaintance in the world of Shakespeare and theatre history, Nicoll was a relatively shy man who sometimes seemed aloof to those who did not know him. Professor Stanley Wells, a later successor to the directorship of the Shakespeare Institute, who knew him personally, described him as a 'tall, slim, elegant figure, with a twinkle in his eye' and 'a courteous, slightly diffident grace' (*DNB*). His dry humour was rarely allowed to penetrate his lectures or published work; however, his ability as a mimic suggested he had the makings of an actor, and, if pressed, could be an excellent raconteur. He was a fair-minded, democratically inclined head of department and intensely loyal to all his staff. A Festschrift on masque, written by former colleagues and pupils, was published by Cambridge in 1967. Nicoll was honoured by the universities of Toulouse and Montpelier (DèsL), Durham and Glasgow (DLitt), and Brandeis (DHL). He was president of the Society for Theatre Research (1958–76) and a life trustee of the Shakespeare Birthplace Trust.

Allardyce Nicoll's favourite recreation was walking in the Malvern hills. He died at his home, Wind's Acre, Colwall, Herefordshire, near Malvern, on 17 April 1976 and was cremated at Worcester on 23 April. There were no children from either marriage.

JOHN RUSSELL STEPHENS

Sources *The Times* (22 April 1976) · *The Times* (29 April 1976) · *Theatre Notebook*, 30 (1976), 50–51 · *TLS* (1 Jan 1931) · *TLS* (21 Sept 1946) · *TLS* (29 June 1973) · *TLS* (2 May 1980) · *The Times* (15 Aug 1962) · 'Preface', *Stuart masques and the Renaissance stage* (1937) · *Shakespeare Survey*, 1 (1948) · A. Nicoll, *British drama*, 5th edn (1962) · A. Nicoll, preface, *English drama, 1900–1930* (1973) · 'Preface', *The Garrick stage* (1980) · *DNB* · records of Stirling high school · records, U. Glas., Archives and Business Records Centre · records, U. Lond. · 'Bulletins', Yale U., school of drama · private information (2004) · m. cert. [Maria Dubno] · b. cert.

Archives U. Birm. L., corresp.

Likenesses L. Knight, drawing (walking in Malvern hills)

Wealth at death £28,013: probate, 2 Feb 1977, *CGPLA Eng. & Wales*

Nicoll, Anthony (1611–1659), politician, was born on 14 November 1611 at St Tudy, Cornwall, and baptized there on 24 November. He was the first son and heir of Humphry Nicoll (1577–1642) of Penvose in St Tudy and his wife, Philip (*d.* 1668), daughter of Sir Anthony Rous of Halton in St Dominick, Cornwall. His father sat in parliament for the borough of Bodmin, Cornwall, in 1628–9; he was a friend of Sir John Eliot and a forced loan refuser. His mother was the sister of Francis Rous and half-sister of John Pym. At an unknown date he married Amey (*d.* 1681×1685), daughter and coheir of Peter Speccott of Speccott, Thornbury, Devon; they had five sons and two daughters.

Nicoll entered parliament for the first time in spring 1640, representing the Cornish borough of Bossiney, where his family had property interests. He sat for Bodmin in the Long Parliament later that year, taking the place of John Bramston of the Middle Temple who was initially returned for the borough. Nicoll challenged Bramston's election and, although a majority on the Commons committee of privileges upheld it, publication of the committee's report was obstructed by John Pym, allowing Nicoll to sit in Bramston's place. In March 1641 Pym nominated Nicoll to be present at the earl of Strafford's trial, and in August Nicoll was sent by both houses to the king in Scotland to notify him of their intention to send parliamentary commissioners to join him.

With the approach of civil war Nicoll responded to the ordinance of 9 June 1642—appealing for plate, money, and horses for parliament—by offering two horses. He continued to sit in the Commons during the conflict and was very active, working mainly with Denzil Holles and the presbyterian members. On 11 March 1643 he was sent by the house to Exeter, warning the Devon and Cornwall parliamentary committees that their local cessation negotiations were highly 'derogatory to the power and authority of Parliament' (*JHC*, 3, 1642–4, 999) and that no further action was to be taken without its consent. In May Nicoll fought for parliament at the battle of Stratton in north Cornwall, but his commander, the earl of Stamford, complained that Nicoll's action in withdrawing the cavalry had contributed to parliament's defeat. In the same year Nicoll was appointed to the Devon sequestration committee; in 1644 he was named to the Cornish committees for executing parliamentary ordinances and for levying assessments, and was appointed receiver-general for the duchy of Cornwall.

In June 1647 Nicoll was one of eleven presbyterian MPs who withdrew from the house in response to the army's accusation that they were endeavouring 'to overthrow the rights and liberties of the subjects of this nation, in arbitrary violent or oppressive ways' (Rushworth, 4.570). Four specific allegations were made against Nicoll: that he had unlawfully retained his seat for Bodmin after the committee of privileges had declared his election void; that he had tried by undue influence to make a faction in the house by securing the return of twenty-eight members; that he had taken bribes from disabled members to secure their readmission; and that he enjoyed too many offices. He acknowledged the unfavourable decision of the committee of privileges, requesting that the matter be re-examined, but denied taking bribes. On the question of offices, he admitted continuing as master of the armoury in the Tower, but claimed that since the self-denying ordinance of 1645 he had not received an income; that he had held the position of receiver of the duchy of Cornwall only temporarily, after the occupation of Cornwall by the royalists had rendered it unprofitable; and that he had surrendered the more lucrative post of 'customer' of Plymouth and the Cornish ports. Concluding that his total receipts from offices had been £500, he claimed to have spent more than this in service to parliament.

On 6 August 1647 the army entered London. Nicoll promptly set out for Cornwall with a pass from the speaker, but was stopped at Salisbury and taken to Sir Thomas Fairfax's quarters at Kingston because he did not have a pass from the general. On 21 August he was handed over to the custody of parliament, but escaped. The vote impeaching him was not revoked until 8 June 1648, when his help was needed to suppress royalist disturbances in Cornwall and he was reinstated as MP for Bodmin. In July he was added to the powerful sub-committee of the Cornwall county committee; on 12 October he sat on the Cornish committee of sequestration; on 1 November he received a grant for life of the office of master of the armouries in the Tower and at Greenwich; and on 2 December he was one of the county commissioners of militia in Cornwall. However, his parliamentary career was again interrupted towards the end of 1648: on 6 December he was among the 100 presbyterian MPs excluded in Pride's Purge. On 12 December the revocation of the vote against him was cancelled.

Nicoll's political fortunes were again restored in 1654, when he was returned for Cornwall in the first protectorate parliament and was appointed a Cornish commissioner for removing scandalous clergy. On 13 March 1655, when a rising was feared in Cornwall, he told John Thurloe that 'Cornwall was cavalierish enough … divers cavaliers are committed, and truly tis not more than need, for I think some of them very dangerous and would engage in any design' (*Thurloe*, 3.227). Between March 1655 and January 1656 Nicoll was one of twelve commissioners appointed to assist Major-General John Desborough in Cornwall, the latter reporting to Thurloe that Nicoll was among the most 'harty and cordial' Cornish parliamentarians. Nicoll was returned for Cornwall to the second protectorate parliament in 1656, and was appointed sheriff of the county in the following year. He died of a fever on 20 February 1659, and was buried at the Savoy, London, two days later. He was survived by his wife and at least three of their sons, Humphrey, Peter, and Anthony. An elaborate monument commemorating his life and containing effigies of himself, his wife, and their five sons was erected at St Tudy church in 1681 by his wife. ANNE DUFFIN

Sources M. Coate, *Cornwall in the great civil war and interregnum, 1642–1660* (1933) · A. Duffin, *Faction and faith: politics and religion of the Cornish gentry before the civil war* (1996) · J. L. Vivian, ed., *The visitations of Cornwall, comprising the herald's visitations of 1530, 1573, and 1620* (1887) · Keeler, *Long Parliament* · *DNB* · *IGI* · D. Underdown, *Pride's Purge: politics in the puritan revolution* (1971) · J. Rushworth, *Historical collections*, new edn, 8 vols. (1721–2) · Thurloe, *State papers* · will, PRO, PROB 11/309, fols. 169v–170r
Archives HLRO, letters, MSS | Bodl. Oxf., MSS Rawl., letters · Bodl. Oxf., Tanner MSS · Bodl. Oxf., Thurloe papers
Likenesses effigy on monument, 1681, St Tudy church, Cornwall
Wealth at death 40s. to mother; £500 to son within seven years of mother's death; residue to son and heir: will, PRO, PROB 11/309, fols. 169v–170r

Nicoll, Francis (1771–1835), Church of Scotland minister, was born at Lossiemouth, third son of John Nicoll, merchant. He graduated MA from King's College, Aberdeen, in 1789 and was licensed by the presbytery of Elgin in September 1793. He spent several years as a tutor with Sir James Grant of Grant before he was presented to the parish of Auchtertool in Fife by the earl of Moray. He was ordained there in September 1797. Two years later he was translated to the recently united parish of Mains and Strathmartine, Forfarshire. In 1807 he was honoured with the degree of DD from St Andrews University. By this time

he had established himself as one of the group of moderate clergy who dominated the church's counsels and he served as moderator of the general assembly in 1809.

Nicoll married, on 25 October 1814, Anne Ramsay (d. 1842) from Edinburgh, with whom he had two daughters and a son. In 1820 he moved to St Andrews, where he was appointed principal of the United College of St Leonard and St Salvator, a position tenable jointly with the parish of St Leonard. In 1822 he was chosen rector of St Andrews University, and he was responsible for drafting the address from the university which was presented to George IV during his visit to Scotland in August of that year. It was Nicoll's initiative that brought Thomas Chalmers to St Andrews to occupy the chair of moral philosophy in 1823. The move caused considerable surprise at the time, given Chalmers's position as a leading evangelical, and the reputation St Andrews enjoyed as a moderate stronghold. Chalmers was also apparently absorbed with the social experiment he was conducting in St John's parish, Glasgow, at this time and his translation to the chair was an unexpected change of direction. Any misgivings Nicoll may have entertained were quickly given substance when there was friction between the two men over the issue of pluralities. This induced Nicoll to resign as minister of St Leonard's in September 1824.

Nicoll was a popular and influential figure in the church and was described by Lord Cockburn as 'a plain, good-natured man, with the appearance and manner of a jolly farmer, and an attractive air of candour and simplicity' (*Memorials*, 232). He died on 8 October 1835 at St Andrews.
LIONEL ALEXANDER RITCHIE

Sources *Fasti Scot.* · S. J. Brown, *Thomas Chalmers and the godly commonwealth in Scotland* (1982), 164–71 · A. H. Millar, *Roll of eminent burgesses of Dundee* (1887), 256 · J. Grierson, *Delineations of St Andrews* (1833) · *Memorials of his time, by Henry Cockburn* (1856), 232
Archives NL Scot., letters | U. Edin., New Coll. L., letters to Thomas Chalmers
Likenesses Raeburn, oils, U. St Andr.
Wealth at death £3526 7s. 9d.: inventory, 1838, Scotland

Nicoll, John (*c*.1590–1668), chronicler, 'wes borne and bred' in Glasgow, as he repeatedly records, but nothing is known of his parentage (Nicoll, 162, 184). On 21 October 1606 he married Bessie (d. 1627), the daughter of James Thomson, an Edinburgh merchant, and on 19 October 1609 he became a member of the Society of Writers to the Signet. He maintained a link with his birthplace by becoming a burgess of Glasgow in 1615, and added a burgess-ship of Edinburgh in 1619. His first wife died in August 1627, and a few months later, on 12 December 1627, he married Magdalene, daughter of another Edinburgh merchant, Andrew Hutchison.

Nicoll began to write his observations of events or remarkable occurrences (the word 'diary' is a nineteenth-century editorial imposition), the work for which he is remembered, in 1637. His volume covering 1637–50 is lost, but that dealing with 1650–67 survives and provides a very useful, though rambling and scrappy, source of information, gossip, and opinions on public affairs under successive regimes. The judgement that he was of a 'peaceable but somewhat time-serving disposition' (*DNB*) is charitable, for he was always anxious to conform to the interpretations of those in power, and this meant that he frequently revised his writings to update his comments. Thus in relating the marquess of Montrose's execution in 1650 Nicoll, employing the official epithets of the day, called James Graham an excommunicate rebel and bloody traitor, but later crossed such terms out and substituted references to 'that noble Marquis'. In addition to such self-censorship he added a general disclaimer: what he had written had reflected not his own opinions but the 'reall wordis' of those in power (Nicoll, x). Though this leads to inconsistency, the malleable chronicler provides an interesting barometer of popular acceptance of official opinion.

The general impression the observations give of Nicoll is that of a man carefully avoiding active involvement in events, shocked by the violence of the time, and concentrating his life on his profession—he served as clerk to the Society of Writers to the Signet from 1647 to 1654. He ventured to be a candidate for the post of clerk to the Church of Scotland, at an election held in the highly contentious Glasgow assembly of 1638, though as it had been decided in advance that Archibald Johnston of Wariston would be elected this was hardly a serious attempt to take part in public life, and he received no votes. Perhaps it was his Glasgow connection that moved him to put his name forward for he retained a sentimental attachment to his birthplace all his life. Two of his sons and two grandsons, all Edinburgh writers, also became Glasgow burgesses, and his son John became in addition an Edinburgh burgess and writer to the signet. As well as his observations of events from 1637 Nicoll compiled an account of Scotland's kings up to the Reformation, and an outline of events from then to 1637. His observations thin notably before ending in 1667, no doubt as the result of advancing age. He was buried in the churchyard of Greyfriars, Edinburgh, on 26 February 1668.　　　　　　　　　　DAVID STEVENSON

Sources J. Nicoll, *A diary of public transactions and other occurrences, chiefly in Scotland, from January 1650 to June 1667*, ed. D. Laing, Bannatyne Club, 52 (1836) · *DNB* · *The Society of Writers to His Majesty's Signet with a list of the members* (1936) · J. R. Anderson, ed., *The burgesses and guild brethren of Glasgow, 1573–1750*, Scottish RS, 56 (1925) · C. B. B. Watson, ed., *Roll of Edinburgh burgesses and guild-brethren, 1406–1700*, Scottish RS, 59 (1929) · H. Paton, ed., *The register of marriages for the parish of Edinburgh, 1595–1700*, Scottish RS, old ser., 27 (1905) · H. Paton, ed., *Register of interments in the Greyfriars burying-ground, Edinburgh, 1658–1700*, Scottish RS, 26 (1902)
Archives NL Scot., diary

Nicoll, Robert (*bap.* 1814, *d.* 1837), poet, was baptized on 7 January 1814 at Tullybelton in the parish of Auchtergaven, Perthshire, the second son of the nine children of Robert Nicoll, farmer, and his wife, Grace, *née* Fenwick, a saleswoman. When he was only five years old his father lost his farm through providing security for a relative's loan, and became a day labourer at Orde Braes. At an early age Robert worked as a herd in the summer, attending school during the winter, and reading when and where he could. At the age of sixteen he was apprenticed to Mrs J. Hay Robertson, a grocer and wine merchant in Perth, where he

remained until 1832, studying in his free time, taking advantage of a friend's loan of a ticket for the Perth Library, and joining the Young Men's Debating Society.

Nicoll contemplated emigrating to the United States after he finished his apprenticeship, but instead visited Edinburgh, where Christian Isobel Johnstone introduced him to Robert Gilfillan and Robert Chambers. His first published tale, entitled 'Il Zingaro', appeared in *Johnstone's Magazine* in 1833, but finding no employment in Edinburgh beyond that of an occasional contribution to that magazine, he went to Dundee, where friends including P. R. Drummond helped him to open a circulating library in Castle Street. He published *Poems and Lyrics* in 1835, with some success; the poems written in his native dialect were superior to those written in English, and he was consequently described by Ebenezer Elliott, the anti-corn law agitator, as 'Scotland's second Burns' (Irving, *Scots.*, 390). He was also active as a writer and lecturer in liberal politics. In 1836 he gave up the circulating library, and returned to Edinburgh until his friend William Tait obtained for him the editorship of the *Leeds Times*. Soon after this, on 9 December 1836, he married Alice Suter (or Souter), niece of Peter Brown, editor of the *Dundee Advertiser*. Nicoll brought a radical political vigour to the newspaper, which greatly increased its circulation, and helped Sir William Molesworth to win the general election of 1837. The salary was only £100 per year, so Nicoll supplemented his income by writing for a Sheffield journal. His health worsened under the strain and Tait encouraged him to travel by steamer to Edinburgh. He arrived in October and went to stay with the Johnstones at Laverock Bank, where he was visited by his parents and friends, and was sent £50 by Molesworth. He died there of consumption on 7 December 1837, and was buried at North Leith churchyard. He was survived by his wife. His brother William wrote a touching inscription for his tombstone, and was himself buried in the same grave a few years later. Although he was all but forgotten by the twentieth century, Nicolls's reputation increased for some time after his death, and in 1857 a 50 foot-high obelisk was funded by public subscription and erected to his memory near his birthplace.　　　　　　　　　　SARAH COUPER

Sources C. I. Johnstone, 'Preface', in R. Nicoll, *Poems and lyrics*, 4th edn (1852), 1–64 · J. G. Wilson, ed., *The poets and poetry of Scotland*, 2 (1877), 370–71 · C. Rogers, *The modern Scottish minstrel, or, The songs of Scotland of the past half-century*, 4 (1857), 225–7 · P. R. Drummond, *The life of Robert Nicoll* (1884) · Anderson, *Scot. nat.* · 'Samuel Smiles', 'The story of Robert Nicoll's life', *Good Words*, 16 (1875), 313–18; 414–19 · Chambers, *Scots.* (1855) · *North British Review*, 16 (1851–2), 168–73 · W. Walker, *The bards of Bon-Accord, 1375–1860* (1887), 438 · Irving, *Scots.* · J. F. Waller, ed., *The imperial dictionary of universal biography*, 3 vols. (1857–63) · P. R. Drummond, *Perthshire in bygone days* (1879) · *IGI*

Nicoll, Whitlock (1786–1838), physician, son of Iltyd Nicoll (c.1744–1787), rector of Tredington, Worcestershire, and Anne, daughter of George Hatch of Windsor, was born at Tredington, on 1 September 1786. Fatherless before he was two years old, he was educated by the Revd John Nicoll, his uncle, and placed in 1802 to live with John Bevan, a surgeon at Cowbridge, Glamorgan. In 1806 he went to London to become a student at St George's Hospital, and in 1808 he was appointed house surgeon at the Lock Hospital; he received the diploma of membership of the Royal College of Surgeons in 1809.

Nicoll then became the partner of John Bevan and engaged in general practice. He went to live in Ludlow, Shropshire, where he worked as a physician, establishing a very successful practice. He took an MD degree on 17 May 1816 at Marischal College, Aberdeen, and was admitted an extra-licentiate of the Royal College of Physicians on 8 June 1816. Through the influence of his cousin Sir John Nicoll he received in 1817 the degree of MD from the archbishop of Canterbury. He began to write as an authority on medicine in the *London Medical Repository* in 1819 and his *Sketch of the Oeconomy of Man* appeared in the same year.

Nicoll's first publication, 'Tentamen nosologicum', appeared in the *Repository* (vol. 7, no. 39), and comprised a general classification of diseases based upon their symptoms; the three main divisions included 'febres', of which he described three orders; neuroses, with seven orders; and cachexiae, with eleven orders. However, the arrangement shows nothing more than the ingenuity of a student. Nicoll also published *The History of the Human Oeconomy* (1819), suggesting a general physiological method of inquiry in clinical medicine; *Primary Elements of Disordered Circulation of the Blood* (1819), which contained one hundred obvious remarks on the circulation; *General Elements of Pathology* (1820); and *Practical Remarks on the Disordered States of the Cerebral Structures in Infants* (1821), which was first read before an audience at the King and Queen's College of Physicians in Ireland on 6 December 1819 and which is the most interesting of his medical writings. In this last work Nicoll seems to have noticed some of the phenomena of the reflection of irritation from one part of the nervous system to another, though his argument is confused. At this time he became a member of the Royal Irish Academy.

On 17 March 1826 Nicoll graduated MD at Glasgow, after which he moved to London, where he was admitted a licentiate of the Royal College of Physicians, on 26 June 1826. He attained some success in practice in the capital and was elected FRS on 18 February 1830. He published two ophthalmic cases of some interest in the *Medico-Chirurgical Transactions*.

Nicoll had acquired in boyhood from the Revd John Nicoll a taste for Hebrew and for theology which remained throughout his life. He left several theological works in manuscript, which were published in 1841 along with a short sketch of his life. Five theological treatises were published during his lifetime: *An Analytical View of Christianity* (1822); *Nugae Hebraicae* (1825); *Nature the Preacher* (1837); *Remarks on the breaking and eating of bread and drinking of wine in commemoration of the passion of Christ* (1837); and *An Inquiry into the Nature and Prospects of the Adamite Race* (1838).

Nicoll was twice married: first on 12 July 1812 to Margaret (*d.* 1831), daughter of the Revd Robert Rickards, the wedding taking place at Llantrisant church. Margaret Nicoll suffered several miscarriages, and her one full-term pregnancy ended with the sacrifice of the child to save the mother. In 1832 Nicoll married Charlotte, daughter of James Deacon *Hume (1774–1842), secretary to the Board of Trade. The marriage produced a son and a daughter. However, Charlotte died from puerperal fever soon after the birth of her daughter. A distraught Nicoll gave up medical practice and moved to Southampton before settling at Wimbledon Common, Surrey, where he died on 3 December 1838.

NORMAN MOORE, rev. PATRICK WALLIS

Sources Munk, *Roll* · *GM*, 2nd ser., 11 (1839), 109 · Foster, *Alum. Oxon.* · W. I. Addison, *A roll of graduates of the University of Glasgow from 31st December 1727 to 31st December 1897* (1898) · P. H. Thomas, 'Whitlock Nicoll (1786–1838) and paediatrics', *Child care through the centuries*, ed. J. Cule and T. Turner (*c*.1986), 48–59 · IGI

Nicoll, Sir William Robertson (1851–1923), journalist, was born on 10 October 1851 at Lumsden, Aberdeenshire, the elder son of the Revd Harry Nicoll (*d.* 1891), Free Church of Scotland minister of Auchindoir, Aberdeenshire, and his wife, Jane Robertson. Nicoll acquired his lifelong love of books in his father's copious library of 17,000 books, to which much of his salary was devoted. He attended the parish school of Auchindoir and Aberdeen grammar school. At fifteen, he entered Aberdeen University, graduating MA in 1870. After four years' training at the Free Church Divinity Hall, he was ordained to his first charge at Dufftown, Banffshire, in 1874. He was already writing regularly for the *Aberdeen Journal*, by the age of twenty earning £100 p.a. from journalism. In September 1877 he was inducted minister of the Free Church, Kelso, and the next year, on 21 August in Edinburgh, he married Isa, only child of Peter Dunlop, a prosperous Berwickshire farmer; their son and daughter were born in the manse at Kelso. Witnessing Gladstone's first Midlothian campaign captured Nicoll for the Liberal cause. While in Kelso, he began to edit *The Contemporary Pulpit* for Swan, Sonnenschein, and *The Expositor*, which he directed until his death, for Hodder and Stoughton. Nicoll visited Germany and Norway, where he caught typhoid in 1885. Pleurisy and the fear of tuberculosis, which had killed his father, brother, and sister, ended his promising preaching career, and he moved to Glenroy, Highland Road, Upper Norwood, London, to devote himself to journalism. With his wide intellectual base, his liberal political and theological enthusiasms, and his clerical experience, Nicoll was ideally positioned to write for the huge nonconformist constituency, hitherto rather narrowly served by journalists. Hodder and Stoughton began publication on 5 November 1886 of the *British Weekly: a Journal of Social Progress*, a penny weekly with Nicoll as editor. It quickly became a success, with J. M. Barrie, S. R. Crockett, and John *Watson ('Ian Maclaren') as regular contributors; for thirty years he was assisted on it by Jane T. *Stoddart. Nicoll often wrote as 'Claudius Clear', his letters under that name being later republished (1901, 1905, 1913). He portrayed his abandoned, rural Scotland in a number of rather sentimental pieces, and may be said to have founded the 'kailyard school' of Scottish writing by discovering Barrie, who initially wrote Scottish character sketches for the *British Weekly* (from 1887), and encouraging Watson to write *The Bonnie Briar Bush* for it in 1893. In 1891 Nicoll founded the successful literary monthly *The Bookman*, and in 1893 *Woman at Home*, an illustrated magazine intended as a *Strand Magazine* for women, and subtitled 'Annie S. Swan's Magazine', the Scottish novelist (Anne Burnett Smith) being its chief contributor.

Nicoll and his wife were often unwell. In 1892 they moved to Bay Tree Lodge, Hampstead, with room for 24,000 books. In 1894 Isa Nicoll died, following an operation, and Nicoll was left to rear their children. If anything, he increased his literary output, with *Literary Anecdotes of the Nineteenth Century* (2 vols., 1894–6), edited with T. J. Wise. In 1896 he visited the USA with J. M. Barrie and on 1 May 1897 he married Catherine, daughter of Joseph Pollard, of Highdown, Hitchin, Hertfordshire; they had one daughter. Catherine Nicoll was the model for Percy Bigland's painting *A Quaker Wedding*, and was herself a competent water-colourist. His second marriage rejuvenated Nicoll: the years from 1897 to 1914 were the most energetic and fruitful of his always productive career. In addition to his usual journalism, he began again to preach and lecture widely. He played a prominent role in the 'passive resistance' movement against the 1902 Education Act, and campaigned for a fair settlement between the United Free Church of Scotland and the 'Wee Frees', which was achieved in 1905. Nicoll supported the Lloyd George group in the Liberal governments of 1905–16, though he was lukewarm about home rule. His knighthood in 1909 recognized his position as 'the intellectual leader of nonconformity—the chief exponent of its thought, and the most effective advocate of its cause in the press' (*Daily Chronicle*, cited in Darlow, 210). He was a strong supporter of war with Germany and his 'War notes' in the *British Weekly* often reflected Lloyd George's thinking and supported him as he rose to the premiership.

Nicoll's health began to fail in 1920, though he wrote until his death. He was made CH in 1921. He died, from an abscess, on 4 May 1923 at his home in Hampstead, and was buried in Highgate cemetery. He was a tubby man, with a scrappy moustache, who smoked heavily. He disliked fresh air, and always had a fire blazing in his study. Much of his literary output was dictated from his bed. He was fascinated by palmistry and was notorious for absent-mindedness, often returning from house parties with other men's clothes. H. A. Vachell recalled:'he had a dry, pawky wit. He was well-named "Sense and Sensibility"' (Darlow, 415). Nicoll was among the most prolific of British journalists and succeeded in being both popular and erudite; it was said of him that he had 'the keenest nose for a book that will sell of any man in the book business' (Clement Shorter, in Price, 73). His nonconformist readership declined after the war and from that point of view his death was well timed.   H. C. G. MATTHEW

Sources T. H. Darlow, *William Robertson Nicoll* (1925) · A. Whigham Price, 'W. Robertson Nicoll and the genesis of the Kailyard school', *Durham Journal*, 86 (Jan 1994), 73–82

Archives U. Aberdeen L., corresp., news-cuttings, incl. letters of sympathy to Lady Robertson Nicoll · U. Edin. L., corresp. with Charles Sarolea
Likenesses E. O. Hoppé, photograph, NPG

Nicolls, Sir Augustine (1559–1616), judge, was born in April 1559 at Ecton, Northamptonshire, the second son of Thomas Nicolls and his wife, Ann, daughter of John Pell of Ellington, Huntingdonshire. Augustine's paternal grandfather, George, a double reader of the Middle Temple, died in 1575 at the age of ninety-six, thereby comfortably outliving his own son Thomas, Augustine's father, who also practised as a common lawyer and whose call to read at the Middle Temple came two years before his death on 29 June 1568. Nothing is known of Augustine's early education, but he was admitted to membership of the Middle Temple gratis in the year of his grandfather's death, and to a house chamber shortly afterwards. Called to the bar in February 1584, Nicolls delivered his reading in August 1602; a brief note of these lectures on the Henrician Statutes of Wills (1540 and 1543) survives in manuscript.

Inclusion in the group call of serjeants announced early next year meant that Nicolls almost immediately faced the burden of reading for a second time, although the task was somewhat lessened by pairing his serjeant's reading in March 1603 with the single reading of John Dodderidge. When the call eventually took place in May, following James I's accession, Nicolls named as his patrons three men with strong Northamptonshire connections: William, second Lord Compton, Henry, fourth Lord Mordaunt, and the judge Sir Christopher Yelverton. His next preferment, to the recordership of Leicester in December 1603, was the result of a contested election; although Nicolls had defeated the candidate recommended to the corporation by the earl of Huntingdon, the latter shortly afterwards described him as 'for Learning wisdome and integritie ... to[o] good to continue with them' (Stocks, 1.14). Made serjeant-at-law to Queen Anne in 1607, Nicolls was next year mentioned by Chief Justice Coke and Attorney-General Hobart as a possible candidate for the vacant place of attorney in the court of wards. In 1610 he became serjeant to Prince Henry; two years later he was knighted on being raised to the bench as justice of common pleas, and in 1615 he was appointed chancellor to Prince Charles.

Nicolls's sudden death at Kendal on 3 August 1616 while following the northern assize circuit aroused suspicions, not least because his last meal had been taken with the recusant Lord William Howard. However a judicial colleague described him as dying of a 'surfeit', before going on to praise Nicolls's integrity, scholarship, and piety (*Diary of Sir Richard Hutton*, 13). James Whitelocke, a younger Middle Templar, echoed these commendations, and also characterized Nicolls as 'a cumly man' of 'exceeding pleasant and affable behavior' (*Liber famelicus*, 52). In an expansive funeral eulogy Robert Bolton, who had been presented by Nicolls in 1610 to the living attached to his then recently acquired manor of Broughton, depicted his former patron as calm, careful, and compassionate,

Sir Augustine Nicolls (1559–1616), by unknown sculptor, c.1616 [detail]

unusually punctilious and upright in his judicial role, as well as a committed and effective anti-papist, sabbatarian, and favourer of godly preachers.

Nicolls had married Mary Bagshaw, *née* Henning, the widow of a London vintner; she predeceased him and the couple had no children. In his will Nicolls expressed affection for his 'most deare and welbeloved wife a parte of my selfe', asking to be buried at her side at Faxton 'with a representation of my selfe kneelinge thereby in my Judges Robes of scarlett furred' (PRO, PROB 11/128, fol. 133r); this alabaster sculpture is now in the Victoria and Albert Museum. After an orthodox Calvinist preamble affirming his hope and trust in salvation through Christ's merits alone, Nicolls emphasized his concern to ensure the discharge of all his worldly debts 'to the uttermost Farthing' (ibid., fol. 134v). To this end, and as befitted an expert in testamentary law not enamoured of the ecclesiastical probate jurisdiction, the judge noted that he had so conveyed all his lands 'that I may by my will limitt and declare the use of them to such person and persons and for such estate and estates as I shoulde thinke fitt' (ibid.).

Together with colleagues and neighbours from the Middle Temple and Northamptonshire, his brother William, and his stepson Edward *Bagshaw, Nicolls's trustees included his nephew and designated heir **Sir Francis Nicolls**, first baronet (*bap.* 1586, *d.* 1642), the elder son of Augustine's soldier brother Francis Nicolls (*d.* 1604) and Anne Seymour. Francis Nicolls was baptized at Hardwick, Northamptonshire, on 20 February 1586, and attended Brasenose College, Oxford, where his tutor was probably

Robert Bolton. He gained a special admission to the Middle Temple without fee during his uncle's reading, and by 1616 had married his uncle's stepdaughter Mary Bagshaw (*d.* 1634). He inherited a substantial west midlands estate and was prominent in local government and politics, serving as JP from 1620 and representing Northamptonshire in Charles I's third parliament. Although his previous resistance to the forced loan may have helped his candidacy, as MP he remained largely inactive. In 1635 he was accused before the high commission of keeping a conventicle in his house; with Bagshaw's assistance the case dragged out inconclusively over five years. The baronetcy Francis Nicolls received in 1641, less than a year before his death, doubtless reflected his service as secretary to the elector palatine in 1640, as well as the crown's severe financial plight. He died on 4 March 1642, probably at Hardwick, where he was buried.   WILFRID PREST

Sources DNB · W. R. Prest, *The rise of the barristers: a social history of the English bar, 1590–1640*, 2nd edn (1991) · V. C. D. Moseley, 'Nicolls, Francis', HoP, *Commons* [draft] · W. C. Metcalfe, ed., *The visitations of Northamptonshire made in 1564 and 1618–19* (1887), 119 · C. T. Martin, ed., *Minutes of parliament of the Middle Temple*, 4 vols. (1904–5), vols.1–2 · Baker, *Serjeants* · *Liber famelicus of Sir James Whitelocke, a judge of the court of king's bench in the reigns of James I and Charles I*, ed. J. Bruce, CS, old ser., 70 (1858) · *The diary of Sir Richard Hutton, 1614–1639*, ed. W. R. Prest, SeldS, suppl. ser., 9 (1991) · *Records of the borough of Leicester*, 4: *1603–1688*, ed. H. Stocks (1923) · PRO, PROB 11/128, fols.133r–134v; DCO rolls ser., box 122A, 1607–8 · *The letters of John Chamberlain*, ed. N. E. McClure, 2 vols. (1939) · M. C. Mirow, 'The ascent of the readings', *Learning the law*, ed. J. A. Bush and A. Wijffels (1999), 227–54 · GEC, *Baronetage*, 2.114
Archives Lincoln's Inn, London, Maynard MSS
Likenesses alabaster effigy, c.1616, V&A [*see illus.*]
Wealth at death substantial; manors of Faxton, Broughton, Northamptonshire, and Kibworth-Beauchamp, Leicestershire; rectory and parsonage of Daston; lands in Broughton valued at £2860; other lands in Warwickshire, Northamptonshire, Leicestershire: DNB; will, PRO, PROB 11/128, fols. 133r–134v

Nicolls, Benedict (*d.* 1433), bishop of St David's, is described by Francis Godwin as a bachelor of laws. He was rector of 'Staplebridge in the diocese of Salisbury' (perhaps Stapleford, Wiltshire) and Conington, Huntingdonshire, in 1408, when, following the confusion caused in the diocese of Bangor by the schism and the Glyn Dŵr rebellion, he was made bishop there by papal bull dated 18 April, in succession to Lewis Byford. He received the temporalities on 22 July and the spiritualities on 10 August. In 1410 he was one of those who tried and condemned the Lollard John Badby, and in 1413 he acted as assessor to Archbishop Henry Chichele when Sir John Oldcastle was tried and excommunicated for heresy. In 1414, and again in 1429, he appeared as a trier of petitions. His register is the earliest to survive for Bangor, and it has been published.

On 17 December 1417 Nicolls was translated to St David's in succession to Stephen Patrington. He made his profession of obedience to the archbishop of Canterbury on 12 February 1418 and had the temporalities on 11 June. On 17 May 1418 he made Thomas Wollaston, precentor of St David's, his vicar-general while he himself was abroad, and again from 26 January 1428 to November 1430. In 1419 he was guarantor for a loan to the king. He was one of those appointed in 1425 to determine the claim of precedence between the earls marshal and Warwick. In 1427 he was present at the opening of parliament, when Chichele preached against the Statute of Provisors, and in the following year subscribed to the answer which parliament returned to Gloucester defining his position as protector. On 4 March 1433 he appropriated the rectory of Lampeter, Cardiganshire, to the precentor of St David's. He died on 25 June 1433 and was buried at St David's Cathedral, where he had founded a chantry. His will, drawn up on 14 June 1433, was proved on 14 August.   GLANMOR WILLIAMS

Sources W. Hughes, *Bangor* (1911) · B. Willis, *A survey of the cathedral church of Bangor* (1721) · A. I. Pryce, 'The register of Benedict, bishop of Bangor, 1408–17', *Archaeologia Cambrensis*, 7th ser., 2 (1922), 85–107 · B. Willis, *A survey of the cathedral church of St David's* (1717) · E. Yardley, *Menevia sacra*, ed. F. Green (1927) · W. B. Jones and E. A. Freeman, *The history and antiquities of St David's* (1856) · W. L. Bevan, *St David's* (1888) · G. Williams, *The Welsh church from conquest to Reformation*, rev. edn (1976) · F. Godwin, *De praesulibus Angliae commentarius* (1616) · Bangor diocesan register, 1408–17, NL Wales

Nicolls, Ferdinando. *See* Nicholls, Ferdinando (1597/8–1662).

Nicolls, Sir Francis, first baronet (*bap.* **1586**, *d.* **1642**). *See under* Nicolls, Sir Augustine (1559–1616).

Nicolls, Sir Jasper (1778–1849), army officer, was born at East Farleigh, Kent, on 15 July 1778. His father was a captain in the 1st foot (Royal Scots), and subsequently became colonel of his regiment and mayor of Dublin. His mother was daughter and coheir of William Dan of Gillingham, Kent. Jasper was educated at a private school kept by the Revd A. Derby at Ballygall, co. Dublin, and afterwards at Trinity College, Dublin. Gazetted ensign in the 45th regiment on 24 May 1793, when only fourteen, he continued at college until September 1794, when he joined his regiment, becoming lieutenant on 25 November. He spent five or six years in the West Indies, and became captain on 12 September 1799. In 1802 he went to India as military secretary and aide-de-camp to his uncle, Major-General Oliver Nicolls, commander-in-chief in the Bombay presidency; in 1803, after the battle of Assaye, he joined the army commanded by Sir Arthur Wellesley; according to Stocqueler, he was employed in the quartermaster-general's department. Present at the battle of Argaon and the siege and capture of Gawilgarh, he returned home soon after the campaign, becoming major on 6 July 1804. In the following year he served with the 45th in Lord Cathcart's expedition to Hanover. In 1806 he sailed with his regiment to take part in the unfortunate campaign under Lieutenant-General Whitelocke which ended so disastrously at Buenos Aires in July 1807. In the ill-organized assault of that town Nicolls found himself isolated with seven companies of his regiment. In this difficult position he displayed conspicuous resolution, and held his ground. Next day, following a disgraceful agreement between Whitelocke and the Spanish general Linares, Nicolls, together with the other isolated troops, evacuated the town. The 45th did not surrender, and it is the legitimate boast of his family that Nicolls refused to give up the colours of his regiment. So conspicuous was his conduct on this occasion that Whitelocke particularly mentioned Nicolls in his dispatches; he was the only regimental officer mentioned. Nicolls was a witness at the subsequent court martial of Whitelocke.

On 29 October 1807 Nicolls was appointed lieutenant-colonel of the York rangers. Almost immediately afterwards he was transferred to the command of the 2nd battalion 14th regiment, which he himself was chiefly instrumental in raising from volunteers in the Buckinghamshire militia. In 1808 he embarked at Cork with his battalion as part of the reinforcements taken to the Peninsula by Sir David Baird. At Corunna he was in the brigade of Major-General Rowland Hill, and well deserved the gold medal he received for that action. He was again mentioned in dispatches. In the summer of 1809 he took part in the disastrous Walcheren expedition, and on 12 August led his battalion in the successful assault on an entrenchment close to the walls of Flushing. In September, after the fall of Flushing, Nicolls returned to England and married, on 21 September, Anne, eldest daughter of Thomas Stanhope Badcock of Little Missenden Abbey, Buckinghamshire. They had one son and eight daughters.

In April 1811 Nicolls was appointed assistant adjutant-general at the Horse Guards. He was promoted deputy adjutant-general in Ireland in February 1812, and a few months later went to India to be quartermaster-general of king's troops. During the Anglo-Nepal War of 1814–16 Nicolls—who was gazetted colonel on 4 June 1814—was selected to command a column for the invasion of Kumaon and in a few days captured Almora and reduced Kumaon. The commander-in-chief in India publicly referred to 'the rapid and glorious conquest of Camoan by Colonel Nicolls'. In the Pindari and Anglo-Maratha wars of 1817–18 Nicolls commanded a brigade. Promoted major-general on 9 July 1821, he vacated his appointment as quartermaster-general of king's troops. In April 1825 he was appointed to command a division in the Madras presidency, and soon after his arrival was selected to command a division of the army which, under Lord Combermere, captured the strong fortress of Bharatpur (18 January 1826). He commanded one of the assaulting columns which was headed by the grenadiers of the 59th, who advanced to the strains of the 'British Grenadiers', played by the general's orders. As Napier said of another officer who encouraged his highlanders in the peninsula with the bagpipes, 'he understood war'. Although the 59th had been carefully trained in the use of hand grenades, the general ordered that no powder should be used, for, as he remarked, the lighted match of a grenade causes a moral effect on the enemy as great as if it were loaded, while if it is loaded the throwers are almost as likely to be injured as the enemy. For his services at Bharatpur, Nicolls was made a KCB (1826). After the fall of Bharatpur he returned to Madras, where he remained until April 1829, when he was transferred to Meerut. In 1833 he was appointed colonel of the 93rd highlanders.

On 10 January 1837 Nicolls became lieutenant-general,

and in 1838 once more went to India as commander-in-chief in Madras. In 1839 he was transferred to Bengal as commander-in-chief in India, but his part was not very important. He was opposed to Lord Auckland's invasion of Afghanistan, and wanted later to substitute General Nott for General Elphinstone as commander in Kabul, but was overruled by Auckland's successor, Lord Ellenborough, who was described as being 'violently enthusiastic on all military subjects' (Macrory, 266), and who as often as not bypassed Nicolls, to the latter's intense exasperation. Nicolls was opposed to the annexation of Sind which led to a quarrel with Sir Charles Napier, and in March 1843 he resigned his appointment and returned to England. In 1840 he was transferred from the colonelcy of the 93rd highlanders to that of the 38th regiment, and four years later again transferred to that of the 5th fusiliers. Nicolls died on 4 May 1849, at his residence near Reading in Berkshire.   W. W. KNOLLYS, *rev.* JAMES LUNT

Sources *Army List* · *East-India Register* · diary of Sir Jasper Nicolls, BL OIOC, MS Eur. F 175 · proceedings of the general court martial of Lieutenant-General Whitelocke, PRO · *Memoirs and correspondence of Field Marshal Viscount Combermere, from his family papers*, ed. M. W. S. Cotton [Viscountess Combermere] and W. Knollys, 2 vols. (1866) · regimental records of 14th regiment — later West Yorkshire regiment — late prince of Wales's regiment of Yorkshire · J. W. Kaye, *History of the war in Afghanistan*, 3rd edn, 3 vols. (1874) · W. F. P. Napier, *History of the war in the Peninsula and in the south of France*, new edn, 6 vols. (1886) · L. J. Trotter, *Lord Auckland* (1893) · Fortescue, *Brit. army*, vols. 5–12 · J. H. Stocqueler, *Memorials of Afghanistan: being state papers, official documents, dispatches, authentic narratives, etc.* (Calcutta, 1843) · P. Macrory, *Signal catastrophe: the story of a disastrous retreat from Kabul, 1842* (1966) · *GM*, 2nd ser., 32 (1849), 315–16

Archives Argyll and Sutherland Highlanders Regimental Museum, Stirling Castle, letter-book · BL OIOC, corresp. and diaries, MS Eur. F 175 · BL OIOC, corresp. relating to India · NAM, corresp. and memoranda | BL OIOC, letters to J. Macnabb, MS Eur. F 206 · PRO, Law MSS, corresp. with Lord Ellenborough, PRO 30/12 · W. Sussex RO, letters to W. S. Badcock

Likenesses oils, NAM

Nicolls, Mathias (*bap.* 1626, *d.* 1692/3), jurist and colonial administrator, was baptized on 29 March 1626, the son of Mathias Nicolls (*d.* 1631), Church of England clergyman, and Martha Oakes (*d.* in or after 1631). After the death of his father he and his mother moved to Plympton in Devon. Mathias went on to study law at both the Inner Temple and Lincoln's Inn, and was admitted to the bar in 1649. A London barrister for the next fifteen years, it was during this period that he married Abigail Jones (*d.* in or after 1693).

Created a captain and the secretary to the royal commission sent to conquer New Netherland in 1663, Nicolls and his family arrived in North America in the following year with the English force sent to seize control of the colony from the Dutch. After the successful conquest Nicolls was appointed provincial secretary of the new English colony. He held a variety of public offices in each of the eight English colonial administrations in New York from 1664 to 1687, including president of the court of assizes and member of the provincial council. Exercising considerable influence on the political and legal affairs of the colony,

he was responsible for much of the early administrative continuity. As provincial secretary, he transcribed, annotated, or endorsed thousands of pages of documents from 1664 to 1680, and he probably was the principal author of many of them. These records preserved details of England's efforts to replace Dutch culture, law, and commercial networks with English law and institutions, as well as to bring English colonists firmly under the authority of the duke of York and the British crown.

Nicolls used his legal expertise to shape many of New York's colonial laws. He is widely credited as the author of the 'Duke's Laws', a civil and criminal code instituted in 1665, which provided the first English laws in the colony. In creating the new legal code, Nicolls drew on the laws of other colonies; however, unlike the provisions for other English American colonies, the Duke's Laws did not provide for a colonial assembly. When in 1673 the Dutch recaptured New York for a period of fifteen months, he and his family fled to Connecticut. During their exile three of the Nicollses' children drowned.

During the 1674–80 Andros administration Nicolls held a number of important offices, serving as provincial secretary and as secretary of the governor's council. He continued to exercise influence in the colony's judicial affairs in his positions as judge and secretary of virtually every type of colonial court. Nicolls also served as captain of the Long Island volunteer troop of horse. In addition, he was mayor of New York city, and in the years when he was not mayor, he served as alderman. He returned to England in 1681 when Governor Andros was recalled to face charges of misconduct. He was present at the hearing and helped Andros to refute the charges.

Nicolls returned to New York in 1682 and was prominent during the administration of Governor Thomas Dongan. When colonists finally prevailed upon the duke of York to allow a colonial assembly, Nicolls again played a decisive role. He was speaker of New York's first assembly in 1683, which modified the Duke's Laws, including imposing an English land system and county structure on the province. In addition, the 1683 assembly approved a charter of liberties and privileges, which set forth colonists' traditional English liberties within a representative government. Many historians credit Nicolls with authorship of the charter. With the collapse of New York's government in 1689 following news of James II's deposition, Nicolls temporarily retired to an estate at Cow Neck, Long Island. He was granted the position of provincial vendue master on 28 November 1692 and died sometime between that date and 22 July 1693, when his widow received letters of administration.

His son, **William Nicolls** (1657–1723), lawyer and colonial administrator, was also trained in the law in England. However, his legal studies were probably interrupted by his service as an officer in the British army in France in the late 1670s. At an unknown date he married Anne, daughter of Jeremias van Rensselaer and widow of Kilian van Rensselaer. They had three daughters and three sons. Nicolls held a number of public offices in colonial New York, having returned to the colony in 1681. He served as prosecutor in various courts and was appointed attorney-general in 1687. Imprisoned by Jacob Leisler during the overthrow of New York's government in 1689, after Leisler's arrest in 1691 Nicolls served as prosecutor in the latter's felony and treason trial.

By 1710 Nicolls was a prominent tory and served as speaker of the New York assembly. In that capacity he was frequently at odds with whig governor Robert Hunter. After several years of political struggles Governor Hunter successfully used the press to outmanoeuvre Nicolls and his other opponents, mocking them in a satirical play called *Androboros* (1714). *Androboros* successfully undermined voters' confidence in many tory candidates, and after its publication most of Hunter's candidates for the 1716 assembly won their elections. The whigs then claimed a majority in the assembly, and Nicolls resigned as speaker. He died in Long Island, New York, in May 1723.

CYNTHIA J. VAN ZANDT

Sources P. R. Christoph, ed., *New York historical manuscripts: English, volume 22*, 3 vols. (Baltimore, 1980) • P. R. Christoph and F. A. Christoph, eds., *The Andros papers: files of the provincial secretary of New York during the administration of Governor Sir Edmund Andros, 1674–1680*, 3 vols. (1989–91) • P. R. Christoph, *The Dongan papers, 1683–1688* (Syracuse, 1989–91) • R. C. Ritchie, *The duke's province: a study of New York politics and society, 1664–1691* (1977) • J. M. Murrin, 'English rights as ethnic aggression: the English conquest, the charter of liberties of 1683, and Leisler's rebellion in New York', *Authority and resistance in early New York*, ed. W. Pencak and C. E. Wright (1988), 56–94 • M. L. Lustig, *Privilege and prerogative: New York's provincial elite, 1710–1776* (Fairleigh Dickinson University Press, Madison and Teaneck, 1995) • C. A. Kierner, *Traders and gentlefolk: the Livingstons of New York, 1675–1790* (Ithaca, NY, 1992) • P. U. Bonomi, *A factious people: politics and society in colonial New York* (1971) • P. U. Bonomi, *The Lord Cornbury scandal: the politics of reputation in British America* (1998) • J. Butler, *Becoming America: the revolution before 1776* (2000) • P. R. Christoph, 'Nicholls, Matthias', *ANB* • *DNB*
Archives New York State Library, New York State Archives, New York colonial manuscripts series | Mass. Hist. Soc., Winthrop papers

Nicolls [Nichols], **Philip** (*fl.* 1547–1564), Church of England clergyman and protestant religious controversialist, was born at Ilfracombe in north Devon. Garrett states that he was probably the son of John Nycholl, rector of Landewednack in Cornwall between 1536 and 1549. Very little is known about Philip Nicolls's earliest years. His written works suggest that between 1547 and 1549 he was living in south Devon, probably at Totnes, from where he travelled to attend sermons in the nearby parishes of Marldon and Harberton. On 24 March 1547 he was at Marldon, where he heard Richard Crispyne, canon of Exeter and rector of Woodleigh, preach a sermon against Luther and the doctrine that scripture was a touchstone against which all religious doctrines should be tested. After the sermon Nicolls wrote Crispyne a letter of remonstrance, which he sent to him on 30 April. A private disputation between the two men followed: 'the Sunday after Corpus Christi day' (Nicolls, sig. C1r–v) at Harberton, where Crispyne was beneficed, and subsequently Nicolls published *The Copie of a Letter Sente to one Maister Chrispyne* (7 November 1547). He

dedicated the work to his patron and 'syngular good maister Syr Peter Carew', a prominent local protestant who had urged him to print it (Nicolls, sig. A2r–A3v). Strongly protestant, the tract rejects the role played by church tradition in the historical transmission of religious truth: scripture alone, Nicolls argues, is a valid foundation for Christian doctrines and church practice. The same evangelical zeal is evident in his second publication, *Here Begynneth a Godly Newe Story* (10 May 1548) in which he asserts that political considerations should never be allowed to restrain the pace of Reformation in England, or to compromise its doctrinal principles.

Nicolls's convictions led to his support of the protestant reform programme pursued by Edward VI's government. During the western rebellion of June to August 1549 he wrote in the government's favour against the rebels. 'An answer to the articles' (BL, Royal MS 18 B.xi) was written by Nicolls, possibly at the request of Sir Peter Carew, during July and August 1549. It refutes in detail the rebels' demand that abrogated Catholic rites must be restored, and defends the new protestant religious settlement as represented by Thomas Cranmer's 1549 prayer book.

Nicolls's precise whereabouts between 1549 and 1557 are open to speculation. His flight into exile, presumably made to escape religious persecution by Queen Mary's regime, probably first took him to Wesel in Germany, from where he later travelled to Aarau in Switzerland. He is listed in the Aarau city records as a member of the colony of English exiles that had arrived there on 11 August 1557, a community that had fled from Wesel that spring. These records also furnish the only known references to Nicolls's wife (her name is unknown) and to his formal education: they describe him as a student living with his wife in the house of Laurence Wyerman. Despite conjectures that Nicolls was possibly the father of the Philip Nicolls (*d.* 1601) who was later a canon of Exeter, no direct evidence remains that the marriage produced any children. The claim that the nonconformist Josias Nicholls (*d.* 1639/40) may have been his son has proved to have been mistaken.

Upon the accession of Elizabeth I, Nicolls left Aarau, shortly after 19 January 1559, and by 1560 he was back in England. In the same year he wrote Sir William Cecil a letter in which he urged him to use his influence: 'against the enormities of idolatry that were allowed in the court and even in the Queen's chapel' (*Salisbury MSS*, 1, 254). He concludes, somewhat optimistically, by asking Cecil to read this letter to Elizabeth. On 23 November 1562, on the presentment of Sir Francis Knollys, he was appointed to the living of Rimpton in the diocese of Wells. However, on 22 June 1564 Nicolls was succeeded in this living by a new incumbent, having resigned his post, after which no more is heard of him. His place and date of death are unknown and no will made by him has ever been found.

C. BRADSHAW

Sources P. Nicolls, *The copie of a letter sente to one Maister Chrispyne* [1547] • C. H. Garrett, *The Marian exiles: a study in the origins of Elizabethan puritanism* (1938); repr. (1966) • *Calendar of the manuscripts of the most hon. the marquis of Salisbury*, 1, HMC, 9 (1883) • R. Whiting,

The blind devotion of the people: popular religion and the English Reforma-tion (1989) · F. W. Weaver, ed., *Somerset incumbents* (privately printed, Bristol, 1889) · G. Scheurweghs, 'On an answer to the art-icles of the rebels of Cornwall and Devonshire', *British Museum Quarterly*, 8 (1933–4), 24–5 · *DNB* · Foster, *Alum. Oxon.*, 1500–1714 [John Nicols] · J. Polsue, *A complete parochial history of the county of Cornwall*, 2 (1868); repr. (1974), 390

Archives BL, Royal MS 18 B.xi

Nicolls, Richard (1624–1672), army officer and colonial governor, was born in Ampthill, Bedfordshire, the fourth son of Francis Nicolls (*d.* 1624), lawyer and keeper of Ampthill Park, and Margaret, daughter of Sir George Bruce of Carnock. The family was royalist, and at the out-break of the civil war Nicolls assumed the command of a troop of horse while his two brothers commanded infan-try companies. All three went into exile with the Stuarts. While in exile in France, Nicolls joined the household of James, duke of York and future James II, and served with him in the forces of Marshal Turenne during the war of the Fronde. It may have been from this experience that he acquired the title of colonel. At the restoration of Charles II he remained in the household of James, where he became a groom of the bedchamber. In 1663 he was awarded the degree of doctor of civil law from the Univer-sity of Oxford.

The government of Charles II was intent on a more for-ward policy in regard to the North American colonies, sending a commission to investigate the New England col-onies, which had sided with parliament during the inter-regnum. At the same time the government decided to con-quer the Dutch colony of New Netherland in order to give England an unbroken chain of colonies from Virginia to Maine. A new colony, which included present-day Maine, part of Connecticut, New York, New Jersey, and Pennsyl-vania, was also created, and James was granted the propri-etorship of the colony. Nicolls was given the task of enfor-cing royal authority and carrying out these policies. He was given leadership of the commission, whose other members were Sir Robert Carr, George Cartwright, and Samuel Maverick. The last was a well-known adversary of the government of Massachusetts Bay, giving the commis-sion a clear bias.

In June 1664 Nicolls sailed with 300 soldiers, three naval vessels, and a freighter to conquer New Netherland and create the new colonies. The ships parted during the voy-age and he had to assemble them again, meanwhile ask-ing Massachusetts for help. The colony's refusal foretold a troubled future for the commission, but the militia from the English towns of eastern Long Island did join him as they disliked the Dutch government in New Amsterdam. On 18 August 1664 he arrived before New Amsterdam. Peter Stuyvesant, the Dutch governor, was forewarned of the invasion but did not have the resources to make the town defensible. Moreover, although he and his soldiers wanted to fight, the townspeople wanted none of it. On 27 August the Dutch garrison surrendered with the honours of war and were given terms that allowed them to sail for home, and that allowed the Dutch colonists permission for continued immigration, and allowed them to keep their church and many of their customs. Indeed fairness

characterized Nicolls's dealings with the Dutch. This was a sensible policy, since the Dutch vastly outnumbered the English there and were a relatively prosperous people.

Having pacified the Dutch, Nicolls had to create a gov-ernment for the new proprietary colony. In doing so he had three considerations. James had given him authority to create a government but he did not want a representa-tive assembly, such bodies already being noted for their contrariness. Another group to be considered were the English towns on the east end of Long Island, which had been settled from New England and had strong ideas about popular government. Finally, there were the Dutch, who needed a new institutional framework. Nicolls called a conference at Hempstead for 28 February 1665 to con-sider the nature of the new government. The only dele-gates were from the English settlements who arrived hop-ing to negotiate. They were soon disappointed, as Nicolls essentially informed the delegates that a governor and the council would rule the colony with the aid of sheriffs and justices of the peace appointed by the governor. The coun-cil and the officers would also sit as the court of assize, the highest court in the colony. He also imposed a code of laws, to be known as the Duke's Laws, based upon existing colonial codes, compiled by his secretary Mathias Nicolls (unrelated), that would provide the legal framework for the colony. One new county, Yorkshire, was created at this time, and it took in all the English settlements. Local gov-ernments were left in place with a good deal of local con-trol. The Dutch were left with their institutions, but over time the new form of English government was ultimately extended throughout the colony. On 13 June 1665 Nicolls appeared before the city magistrates of New York and informed them that the old Dutch city government was to be replaced with a new city council format with an appointed mayor and aldermen. While the Dutch pro-tested, they were simply overruled. Albany was given a similar government with the addition of a strong voice from the commander of the English garrison.

Having settled the government of the new colony, New York, Nicolls set about completing his work as a commis-sioner. By the time he joined his fellow commissioners, they had thoroughly alarmed the governments of New England, especially Massachusetts Bay. While the com-mission worked to complete its investigations, the colon-ists, who feared claims of disloyalty and royal destruction of their quasi-republican institutions, sought to under-mine their work. Not much would come of the commis-sion's report, but it further agitated relations between the new government and the colonies, setting them on the road that would lead in the end to the consolidation of the New England colonies into the dominion of New England. Nicolls showed a willingness to keep the peace in the con-flicts that came about during his administration. Through negotiation and diplomacy he settled taxes upon the Eng-lish and Dutch, persuaded the Dutch in America to sign an oath of loyalty, melded the disparate parts of the local economy, and placated if not pleased the English of east-ern Long Island. By the time he returned to England in 1668, he left a peaceful and prosperous colony which wished him well. On his return to England he rejoined James's household, and in the Third Anglo-Dutch War he went to sea as a volunteer serving James, who was then acting in his capacity as lord high admiral. Nicolls, who never married, was killed at the battle of Solebay on 28 May 1672 and buried in Ampthill church, where the cannon-ball which killed him became a part of his funeral monument.　　　　　　　　　　　　ROBERT C. RITCHIE

Sources R. C. Ritchie, *The duke's province: a study of politics and society, 1664–1891* (Chapel Hill, 1977) · J. R. Brodhead, *The history of the state of New York, 1609–91*, 2 vols. (New York, 1853) · E. B. O'Callaghan, *Documents relating to the colonial history of the state of New York*, 15 vols. (Albany, 1856–7), vol. 3 · E. B. O'Callaghan, *Documentary history of the state of New York*, 4 vols. (Albany, 1850–51) · C. W. [C. Wooley], *A two years journal in New York* (1701) · *CSP col.*, vol. 5 · L. H. Leder, *Robert Livingston, 1654–1728, and the politics of colonial New York* [1961] · O. Rink, *Holland on the Hudson: an economic and social history of Dutch New York* (1986)
Archives Longleat House, Wiltshire | BL, Add. MSS; Egerton MSS · PRO, Colonial Office papers, 1, 5

Nicolls, William (1657–1723). *See under* Nicolls, Mathias (*bap.* 1626, *d.* 1692/3).

Nicols, Thomas (*fl.* 1652), writer on gemstones, was the son of John Nichols, who practised as a physician in Cambridge. He may possibly be identified with the fifth son of Dr Nicholls, born at Cambridge, who was entered at Trinity College, Dublin, on 10 June 1640, aged eighteen. He was admitted as a sizar at Jesus College, Cambridge, on 13 July 1640. Nicols wrote what is generally considered to be the first independent gemmological book by a British author. It was first published in 1652 as *A lapidary, or, The history of pretious stones: with cautions for the undeceiving of all those who deal with pretious stones*, 'by Thomas Nicols, sometimes of Jesus-Colledge in Cambridge'. The book is separated into two distinct parts. The first part is a general treatise on gemstones, while the second describes the individual characteristics of particular gemstones and decorative materials. Nicols states in his preface that he has used much material from Boetius de Boot's *Gemmarum et lapidum* (1st edn, 1609) and from other authors such as Pliny. His classification of gemstones by their properties is, like de Boot's, presented on a folding table. The book describes methods of falsifications and enhancements of gemstones, including their dyeing and foiling when set in jewellery. This information is presented in a style that suggests that Nicols may have had personal experience of the subject, as well as his demonstrable skill in compiling a comprehensive treatise from the works of earlier authors. The book was reissued in 1653 as *Arcula gemmae* and in 1659 as *Gemmarius fidelius*; these reissues are often referred to as the second and third editions but appear to be the original printing with new title-pages. Indeed a copy in the Natural History Museum (Mineralogy Library) has the 1659 title-page pasted over the original 1652 title-page. There were also German editions in 1675 and 1734. Nothing else is known of Nicols's life or work.

　　　　　　　　THOMPSON COOPER, *rev.* NIGEL ISRAEL

Sources T. Nicols, *A lapidary, or, The history of pretious stones* (1652) · J. Sinkankas, *Gemology: an annotated bibliography* (1993) · *Goldsmiths*

Journal (Jan–Sept 1929) · C. H. Cooper, *Annals of Cambridge*, 3 (1845), 475 · *GM*, 2nd ser., 17 (1842), 430, 594 · Venn, *Alum. Cant.*

Nicols, William (1655–1716), Latin poet and Church of England clergyman, was the son of the Revd Henry Nicholls (Nicols) of Hilton, near Cowbridge, Glamorgan. He matriculated at Oxford from Christ Church as a 'poor scholar' on 14 April 1671 and graduated BA on 24 March 1675 and MA on 14 December 1677. Here he found favour with John Fell, dean of Christ Church and bishop of Oxford, and worked as his amanuensis, collecting manuscripts of St Cyprian, used in the bishop's edition, and of St Augustine, which were later sent to Paris for the Benedictines' edition.

On 4 June 1690 Nicols was presented to the rectory of Cheadle, Cheshire, but resigned it on his appointment to the rectory of Stockport, in the same county, on 24 March 1694. On 9 June 1692 he married, at Flixton, near Manchester, Elizabeth, daughter of Peter Egerton of Shawe, Lancashire, and they had several children. She died on 1 October 1708, aged forty-three, and was buried at Chester Cathedral, where her husband set up a monument to her memory in Latin.

By 1709 Nicols had written *De literis inventis libri sex* (1711), a hefty, six-book treatise on the invention of writing, composed wholly in Latin elegiacs. The volume is warmly dedicated to Thomas Herbert, eighth earl of Pembroke, a contemporary at Christ Church who later supported Nicols's son at Charterhouse. It displays Nicols's compendious classical knowledge; the antiquary Thomas Hearne called him 'a man of some learning' (*Remarks*, 2.299). In the first book, Nicols is somewhat shackled by too literal an interpretation of his title: he does little more than list such subjects as the inventor of writing, types of alphabet, and writing materials, and his verse struggles to rise above the prosaic. In the second, however, he acknowledges this and declares an intention to loosen his style. Nicols's aetiology is a curious mixture, supplemented by copious footnotes, of allusions to biblical and classical sources, although his reconciliation of the classical pantheon with Christian theology is happier than that of many other writers who attempt the same *mélange*. His discussion of the Bible (in book 4) becomes a vehicle for lengthy attacks on Catholicism. Reasoned at first, his invective against Rome increases until his impassioned desire for her defeat by protestantism climaxes in the vitriolic 'Et gelida meretrix nuda jacebis humo' ('you will lie cast down on the freezing earth, a naked harlot').

Marriott, in his *Antiquities of Lyme*, refers to Nicols as the 'Stockport bard' and quotes lines from the sixth book in which he records his rebuilding of the Stockport rectory:

> Mersaeae ad ripam tumet undique collis amoenus,
> Quem super impensis jam prope structa meis
> Stat domus.

Marriott translates:

> A hill from Mersey swells, of circuit large,
> Most sweet to view; – built nigh at my sole charge,
> Here high its form a stately dwelling rears.
> (Marriott, 282)

Nicols is most quoted for this passage and others from the

same book which describe Manchester and Derbyshire; they are the most satisfactory parts of this volume and truly picturesque examples of topographical poetry.

Nicols's *Peri Archōn, sive, De principiis religionis Christianae libri septem* appeared posthumously in 1717. The work is dedicated to the archbishop of Canterbury, and comprises seven books of hexameters on Christianity. It makes enquiry into the principles of Christian living, and deals with diverse aspects of the faith such as the doctrine of original sin, baptism, discussion of the sacrament, and the morality of lying. Appended to this, with a separate title-page and dedication to the archbishop of York, is his *Liturgica*, which contains translations into Latin hexameters and elegiacs of the Lord's prayer and some psalms and canticles, as well as paraphrases of these and some passages of scripture. Such an exercise was not uncommon among neo-Latin poets, and can be found in many volumes of similar date, but Nicols's is more ambitious in scope and successful in execution than many other examples.

A speech delivered by Nicols to the Society for Promoting Christian Knowledge on 29 December 1715, presenting to it a certain Bartholomew Ziegenbalg, one of the first Danish missionaries to the East Indies, was published in Latin and English as *Orationes duae* in 1716. Although his work can lack moderation of tone, Nicols's Latin flows throughout with an ease and elegance that bears witness to a thorough knowledge of classical literature and great facility in versification, as well as an enthusiasm undaunted by the scale of his undertakings. Nicols died towards the end of 1716 in the parish of St Martin-in-the-Fields, Middlesex, still incumbent of the rectorship of Stockport.   Ross Kennedy

Sources Foster, *Alum. Oxon., 1500–1714* [William Nicholls] · J. P. Earwaker, *East Cheshire: past and present, or, A history of the hundred of Macclesfield*, 1 (1877), 394; 2 (1880), 655 · *Remarks and collections of Thomas Hearne*, ed. C. E. Doble and others, 2, OHS, 7 (1886), 299–300 · W. Marriott, *The antiquities of Lyme* (1810), 255, 258, 281, 299 · *DNB*

Nicolson [*née* Cory], **Adela Florence** [*pseud.* Laurence Hope] (1865–1904), poet, was born at Stoke House, Stoke Bishop, Gloucestershire, on 9 April 1865. She was the daughter of Arthur Cory (*d.* 1903), colonel in the Indian army, and his wife, Elizabeth Fanny Griffin (1834–1916). Her sister was the novelist Victoria Cross [see Cory, Annie Sophie]. She was educated with her elder sister Isabel, at a boarding-school in Montague Road, Richmond, run by a Belgian, Jacques Philippart, and at the age of sixteen joined her parents in Lahore, India. Here she worked with her father on the *Civil and Military Gazette*, later to be associated with the Kiplings. In 1889 she married Colonel Malcolm Hassels Nicolson of the Bengal army and settled at Madras. Her poetry was published under the pseudonym Laurence Hope, and it was not until after her death that the poems were published in her name. Her first volume of poetry, *The Garden of Kama and other Love Lyrics from India*, was published in 1901. Generally reviewed as the work of a man, it attracted enormous attention and was repeatedly reissued every year for the next fourteen years. While the substance of the poems is not drawn from any identifiable Indian source, the exotic settings emphasized a passionate intensity which was seen as oriental. The influence of Swinburne and the Pre-Raphaelites can also be discerned in this and later works.

After spending some time in north Africa Adela Nicolson published *Stars of the Desert* (1903); in that year she met Thomas Hardy, who greatly admired her work, and with whom she corresponded until her death. He wrote a preface for *Indian Love*, a volume of her poetry; it was published posthumously in 1905, but Hardy's preface was not included. Some of her shorter poems, such as 'Four Indian Love Lyrics' in the musical setting of Amy Woodforde Finden (1860–1919), continued to be very popular into the 1930s and were recorded by, among others, John MacCormack, Dame Clara Butt, and Rudolph Valentino. After her husband's death in August 1904 Nicolson suffered from depression and committed suicide by consuming perchloride of mercury on 4 October 1904 at Dunmore House, Teynampet, Madras. She was buried, like her husband, in St Mary's cemetery, Madras. Her only son, Malcolm Josceline Nicolson, subsequently edited her poems.

Malcolm Hassels Nicolson (1843–1904), the son of Major Malcolm Nicolson (1792–1850), 30th Bengal lancers, and his second wife, Caroline Yates (*d.* 1906), daughter of Major-General Richard Hassells Yates, Madras army, was born on 11 June 1843. He joined the army in 1859 as ensign in the Bombay infantry and was promoted lieutenant in 1862. His first active service was in the Abyssinian expedition of 1867–8; he was present at the action at Azogel and at the capture of Magdala, and received the Abyssinian medal. He attained the rank of captain in 1869. During the Anglo-Afghan War of 1878–80 he took part in the occupation of Kandahar and fought at Ahmed Khel and Ursu. He was mentioned in dispatches, and in 1879 was promoted to the rank of major. After the war he received the Afghan medal with one clasp, and in March 1881 the brevet rank of lieutenant-colonel; he became army-colonel in 1885 and substantive colonel in 1894. For his services in the Zhob valley campaign of 1890 he was again mentioned in dispatches, and was made CB in 1891. From 1891 to 1894 he was aide-de-camp to Queen Victoria, being promoted major-general in the latter year and lieutenant-general in 1899. He died on 7 August 1904 at Mackay's Gardens Nursing Home, Madras, and was buried in St Mary's cemetery. General Nicolson was an expert linguist, having passed the interpreter's test in Baluchi, Brahui, and Persian, and the higher standard in Pushtu.

F. L. Bickley, rev. Sayoni Basu

Sources Blain, Clements & Grundy, *Feminist comp.* · L. Hope [A. F. Nicolson], introduction, *The garden of Kama, and other love lyrics from India* (1908) · *The Times* (11 Aug 1904) · M. J. Nicholson, introduction, in *Selected poems from the Indian love lyrics* (1922) · J. Jealous, 'Hope, Laurence', *The 1890s: an encyclopedia of British literature, art, and culture*, ed. G. A. Cevasco (1993) · *Madras Mail* (5 Oct 1904) · [T. Hardy], 'Laurence Hope', *The Athenaeum* (29 Oct 1904), 591 · *GM*, 8th ser. (1904), 634 · private information (2004) [C. Mitchell]
Likenesses G. C. Beresford, photograph, repro. in *Selected poems*, frontispiece · portrait, repro. in L. Hope [A. F. Nicolson], *Songs from the garden of Kama: illustrated* (1909), frontispiece

Wealth at death £101 10s. 11d.: administration with will, 17 May 1905, *CGPLA Eng. & Wales*

Nicolson, Alexander (1827–1893), sheriff-substitute and Gaelic scholar, son of Malcolm Nicolson (d. c.1846), was born at Usabost in Skye on 27 September 1827. His early education was obtained from tutors. After the death of his father he entered Edinburgh University, intending to study for the Free Church of Scotland. He graduated BA in 1850, and in 1859 received the honorary degree of MA 'in respect of services rendered as assistant to several of the professors'. At college Nicolson had a distinguished career. He was assistant to Sir William Hamilton and lectured to the class of logic in his stead when he fell ill, and similarly took over from Professor Macdougall in the class of moral philosophy for two years. Abandoning the study of theology at the Free Church college, he took to literature, and for some time acted as one of the sub-editors of the eighth edition of the *Encyclopaedia Britannica*. Shortly afterwards he became one of the staff of the *Edinburgh Guardian*, a short-lived paper of high literary quality. For a year he edited an advanced Liberal paper called the *Daily Express*, which afterwards merged in the *Caledonian Mercury*. He edited *Edinburgh Essays* (1857) and wrote for *Blackwood's*, *Good Words*, *Macmillan's Magazine*, and other periodicals and newspapers. But Nicolson was not fitted for the career of a journalist, and, turning to law, was called in 1860 to the Scottish bar. He had little practice, however, and for ten years reported law cases for the *Scottish Jurist*, of which he was latterly editor. He acted as examiner in philosophy in the university, and examiner of births in Edinburgh and the neighbouring counties. In 1865 he was appointed assistant commissioner by Argyll's Scottish education commission, and in this capacity visited nearly all the inhabited Western Isles and inspected their schools. His report, published in 1867 as a blue book ('Schools in Scotland: Hebrides', *Parl. papers*, 1867, 25), contained a vast amount of information regarding the condition of the people in the various islands. In 1872 Nicolson, despairing of a practice at the bar, accepted the office of sheriff-substitute of Kirkcudbright, and declined an offer of the Celtic chair in Edinburgh University, which Professor J. S. Blackie and he had been mainly instrumental in founding. In 1880 he received the degree of LLD from Edinburgh University. In 1883 he was one of the members of the Napier commission on the condition of the crofters. When the gunboat *Lively*, with the commissioners on board, sank off Stornoway, Nicolson had great difficulty in saving the manuscript of his *Memoirs of Adam Black*, on which he was engaged at the time and which was published in two volumes in 1885.

That year Nicolson became sheriff-substitute of Greenock; but he retired in 1889, with a pension, on the ground of ill health. He returned to Edinburgh, where he occupied himself in literary work of no great importance. He died suddenly at the breakfast table on 13 January 1893, and was buried in Warriston cemetery, Edinburgh.

It is as a Gaelic scholar that Nicolson is chiefly remembered, especially for his articles in *The Gael*, a Celtic periodical, his collection of Gaelic proverbs (1881, reprinted with a biographical note by M. MacInnes, 1951), and his revised version of the Gaelic Bible, which he undertook at the request of the Society for the Propagation of Christian Knowledge. He was also an excellent Greek scholar. He was popular in society, and his stories and songs, such as 'The British Ass' and 'Highland Regiments' Ditty', were long remembered in Scotland. His verses were published posthumously (1893). Nicolson was a keen lover of athletic sports and an enthusiastic volunteer.

GEORGE STRONACH, rev. H. C. G. MATTHEW

Sources *The Scotsman* (14 Jan 1893) · *The Times* (14 Jan 1893) · W. Smith, 'Memoir', in A. Nicolson, *Verses* (1893) [preface] · M. MacInnes, 'Memoir', in A. Nicolson, *Gaelic proverbs* (1951) [preface] · H. Whyte, 'Sheriff Nicolson', *Celtic Monthly*, 16 (1908) · CCI (1893)
Likenesses portrait, repro. in A. Nicolson, *Verses* (1893)
Wealth at death £762 11s. 9d.: confirmation, 24 March 1893, CCI

Nicolson, Arthur, first Baron Carnock (1849–1928), diplomatist, was born on 19 September 1849 in London, the second son of Admiral Sir Frederick Nicolson, tenth baronet (1815–1899), and the first of his three wives, Mary Clementina Marian (d. 1851), daughter of James Loch of Drylaw. Nicolson was intended by his family for the Royal Navy, and entered HMS *Britannia* at the age of twelve, after private schooling in Wimbledon. He passed third out of *Britannia*, but did not join the navy. Instead, he went in 1863 to Rugby School, and then in 1867 to Brasenose College, Oxford, where he did not take a degree. During 1869 and 1870 he prepared for the Foreign Office examinations by studying French in Switzerland and German in Dresden. He passed first into the Foreign Office, and joined that institution on 23 August 1870.

Nicolson acted as assistant secretary to the foreign secretary, Lord Granville, from July 1872 to February 1874. He became acting third secretary at Berlin in that month, and, in November 1874, transferred to the diplomatic service. He did not return to the Foreign Office until 1910. From Berlin he was posted to Peking (Beijing) as second secretary in 1876 and back to Berlin in 1878. A year later he was sent to Constantinople, where he remained until late 1882. At this post he met a number of people, including Charles Hardinge (a future permanent under-secretary at the Foreign Office) and Donald Mackenzie Wallace (journalist and expert on Russia), who later would be important for his career. Further, he met, became engaged to, and married, on 20 April 1882, (Mary) Katharine Rowan Hamilton (d. 1951), the youngest daughter of Archibald Rowan Hamilton of Killyleagh Castle, co. Down, and the sister-in-law of Lord Dufferin, the British ambassador to Constantinople. Nicolson's marriage was a mixed blessing. He and his wife enjoyed a very happy private life; however, her social connections aside, Lady Nicolson (as she later became) was an impediment to his career, for she 'shuns society and dresses like a housemaid' (Hardinge to Bertie, 4 Dec 1903, PRO, Bertie MSS, FO 800/163).

After Constantinople, Nicolson served successively in Athens, where he was chargé d'affaires from 1884 to 1885; in Tehran, as secretary of legation, from 1885 to 1888; and, for the next four years, in Budapest, as consul-general. He spent 1893 as secretary of embassy in Constantinople, and

Arthur Nicolson, first Baron Carnock (1849–1928), by unknown photographer, c.1888

in mid-1894 became British agent and consul-general at Sofia. A year later he became minister at Tangier, where he spent almost ten years. At Tangier, Nicolson's career accelerated. While he had done well at his earlier posts (he was created CMG in 1886 and KCIE in 1888 as rewards for his services), his progress in the diplomatic service had been unexceptional. However, the Anglo-French discussions concerning Morocco (which were part of the negotiations leading to the *entente cordiale* of 1904) and the Franco-German rivalry over Morocco put Nicolson at one of the centres of British diplomacy and gave him an opportunity to display his abilities. He was made a KCB and KCVO as a result of his efforts, and was appointed ambassador to Madrid on 1 January 1905. His time in Spain was brief. At the end of 1905, owing in part to the intervention of Charles Hardinge, Nicolson was offered and accepted the embassy at St Petersburg (although his formal appointment to that post did not take place until February 1906). But before he took up his position in Russia, Nicolson served as the British representative to the Algeciras conference, which ran from January to April 1906. His performance at the conference was seen as exceptional. Sir William Tyrrell, the influential précis writer to the British foreign secretary, Sir Edward Grey, wrote to Nicolson on 3 April 1906 that 'you easily carry off the lion's share of the success of this most tiresome negotiation [Algeciras], and we don't mind basking in your reflected sunshine' (PRO, Nicholson MSS, FO 800/338).

Nicolson served in St Petersburg for the next four years. During this time, his views of Russia shaped by Mackenzie Wallace, he was instrumental in the negotiation of the Anglo-Russian convention, signed 31 August 1907. His performance during the talks was impressive: so much so that Lord Morley, the secretary of state for India, wrote

that Nicolson 'deserves his reputation as the best man of his day in his own trade. He is quiet, steady, full of ready resource, not making difficulties, nor delighting to put the other man into a hole' (Morley to Minto, 2 Aug 1907, BL OIOC, MS Eur. D/573/2). More tangible praise came from Grey, who ensured that Nicolson received the GCB for his efforts.

In part owing to further determined lobbying by Hardinge, Nicolson became permanent under-secretary in 1910. For the next six years Nicolson was at the centre of British foreign policy. Before the war he advised Grey that Britain should turn her loose entente with France and Russia into a formal alliance designed to check Germany's aggressive policy. Nicolson was convinced that the security of Britain and her empire depended on such a policy. He believed that otherwise France and Russia would view Britain as an unreliable partner and instead try to reach an accommodation with Germany. In particular, Nicolson advocated maintaining the close relationship with Russia that he had helped to bring about. Such an approach was unacceptable to Grey. Within his own party there were many who felt that autocratic Russia was an inappropriate partner for Liberal Britain. Others insisted on attempting to achieve better relations with Germany. And a substantial number objected to Britain's joining any alliance system whatsoever. This, combined with Lady Nicolson's outspoken support for Ulster, diminished his influence with Grey. Nicolson did not enjoy the routine bureaucratic work at the Foreign Office and, with his health poor owing to arthritis, pressed Grey for an opportunity to return to diplomacy. Nicolson was scheduled to become ambassador to Paris in the autumn of 1914, but this move was placed in abeyance by the outbreak of war.

During the July crisis Nicolson urged Grey to make Britain's support for France and Russia clear to Germany and, if war broke out, to join the former pair. 'Should we waver now', he wrote to the foreign secretary as the guns began to fire on 1 August, 'we shall rue the day later' (Nicolson to Grey, 1 Aug 1914, PRO, Grey MSS, FO 800/94). Whether his advice had an influence on Grey's decision to take Britain into the conflict is uncertain, but Britain's wartime alliance with France and Russia was clearly what Nicolson had long believed was necessary to check Germany's belligerence. Throughout the war, and despite his increasing physical difficulties, Nicolson played an active role in British policy. In particular, he continued to advocate maintaining close relations with Russia, despite the latter country's drift to the political right and threat of internal collapse. However, by mid-1916 his health had deteriorated to such an extent that he asked Grey to be relieved of his post. On 20 June he was succeeded as permanent under-secretary by Lord Hardinge. That year he was created Baron Carnock of Carnock, having succeeded as eleventh baronet on 29 December 1899.

In retirement Carnock briefly acted as an assistant private secretary to George V, and later served as a director of the London City and Midland Bank. He devoted himself to family life, and remained close to his three sons and daughter. His third son, Sir Harold *Nicolson, followed him into the diplomatic service; he was also his father's biographer. After a lingering illness Nicolson died on 5 November 1928 at his Chelsea home, 53 Cadogan Gardens.

Nicolson was one of the greatest diplomatists of his day. He was particularly sympathetic to the point of view of foreigners and was able to convey their feelings to his political masters. This was particularly evident in his dealings with Russia, the country that was the centrepiece of his career. At the same time, however, Nicolson never became an advocate for the country to which he was accredited; he was a firm believer in the maintenance of Britain's own interests and he pursued them tenaciously. By reason of his position as ambassador to Russia, his friendship with Hardinge, and his own tenure at the Foreign Office, Nicolson must be considered as one of those civil servants most influential in the formulation of British foreign policy in the decade before the First World War. KEITH NEILSON

Sources H. Nicolson, *Sir Arthur Nicolson, Bart., first Lord Carnock: a study in the old diplomacy* (1930) · Z. S. Steiner, *The foreign office and foreign policy, 1898–1914* (1969) · K. Neilson, '"My beloved Russians": Sir Arthur Nicolson and Russia, 1906–1916', *International History Review*, 9 (1987), 521–4 · K. Neilson, *Britain and the last tsar: British policy and Russia, 1894–1917* (1995) · PRO, Nicolson MSS · Burke, *Peerage* · Burke, *Gen. GB* · *DNB* · BL OIOC, Morley MSS · Grey MSS, PRO · Bertie MSS, PRO
Archives PRO, corresp., journals, and papers, PRO 30/81 · PRO, corresp. and papers, FO 800/336–81 | Balliol Oxf., corresp. with Sir Louis Mallet · BL, letters to Sir Austen Layard, Add. MSS 39034–39036, 39098 · Bodl. Oxf., letters to Herbert Asquith · CUL, corresp. with Lord Hardinge · HLRO, corresp. with John St Loe Strachey · PRO, letters to Odo Russell, FO 918 · PRO, corresp. with Sir Henry Hyde Villiers, FO 800 · Trinity Cam., corresp. with Sir Henry Babington Smith
Likenesses sepia cabinet photograph, c.1888, NPG [see illus.] · Russell, photograph, 1916, repro. in Nicolson, *Sir Arthur Nicolson* · P. A. de Laszlo, oils, priv. coll.
Wealth at death £9131 1s. 0d.: probate, 19 Dec 1928, CGPLA Eng. & Wales

Nicolson, (Lionel) Benedict (1914–1978), art historian, was born on 6 August 1914 in his grandfather's house, Knole, near Sevenoaks, Kent, the elder son and elder child of Sir Harold George *Nicolson (1886–1968), diplomatist, author, and MP, and his wife, Victoria Mary (Vita) Sackville-*West (1892–1962), poet, novelist, biographer, and gardener. He was educated at Eton College and at Balliol College, Oxford, where he made lifelong friends such as Isaiah Berlin, John Pope-Hennessy, and Philip Toynbee. With his deep interest in the arts, acquired during school holidays on visits to Italy, he helped to found the Florentine Club, an undergraduate society which enticed to Oxford speakers of the calibre of Kenneth Clark, Duncan Grant, and Clive Bell.

Nicolson had no formal education in art history, but on leaving Oxford in 1936 with a second-class degree in modern history he travelled widely, visiting the art galleries and private collections of Europe and America, and spent several months at I Tatti, Florence, as the pupil of Bernard Berenson. In 1937 he was invited by Kenneth Clark (then director) to fill an unpaid post in the National Gallery, and

worked there for some months before pursuing his studies at the Fog Art Museum, Boston. On Nicolson's return to London, Clark appointed him deputy surveyor of the king's pictures (Clark himself was surveyor until 1944) and he helped to catalogue the Royal Collection and find wartime refuges for its major works of art until he was called up. After serving in an anti-aircraft battery at Chatham he obtained a commission in the intelligence corps. Posted as an interpreter to camps for Italian prisoners of war, he was found too sympathetic to the young Italians to make a good gaoler, and was transferred to the Middle East in 1942 as an instructor in interpreting military air photographs. He was invalided home from Italy in March 1945 after a road accident which broke two bones in his spine.

Nicolson resumed his work as deputy surveyor, now under Anthony Blunt, organizing at Burlington House an exhibition of the paintings of Sir Thomas Lawrence, and began to publish articles and introductions on a wide variety of artists, including Modigliani, Vermeer, Cézanne, Seurat, and the painters of Ferrara. Never a natural courtier, he was perhaps relieved to resign his official functions in 1947 when he was invited—largely at the instigation of Herbert Read and Ellis Waterhouse—to edit the *Burlington Magazine*, which from then onwards became the central interest of his life. He remained its editor until his death thirty-one years later.

The *Burlington Magazine* already had an international reputation as a scholarly journal of the history of the fine arts, but during the war years it had suffered in quality, esteem, financial viability, and bulk, and having no full-time editor, lacked an editorial policy. Nicolson soon changed all that. He was not a man who imposed his authority, being more diffident and slower-witted than many of the formidable scholars whom he attracted to write for him or the museum administrators whose decisions he often challenged in his editorials. His strength lay in his gentleness. He was totally without guile. In a profession reputed to be malevolent, he appeared an innocent, and looked increasingly like an El Greco. His integrity was unquestioned. As an editor he was meticulous, setting a standard of accuracy by his own frequent contributions, and he attracted writers of distinction by his own distinction. Slowly he developed qualities of tact, humour, and self-confidence. He made the *Burlington* something entirely his own, in defiance of advice and sometimes of instruction from his editorial board, even cooking its minutes, it was said, to get his own way. Under his long editorship the *Burlington* became the most respected art journal in the English language, and probably in the world.

Nicolson's interests ranged over the whole field of Western painting except the most modern, for he preferred realist to abstract art, but he did not pretend to an equivalent knowledge of other visual arts such as architecture and furniture, which were allowed only a subordinate place in the magazine and on which he took careful advice. His major books indicate a sustained interest in paintings which made dramatic use of light, particularly candle-light, in the Caravaggiesque tradition. The first (1958) was on the Dutch painter Hendrick Terbrugghen, the second (1968) on Joseph Wright of Derby, and the third (1974) on Georges de La Tour, which he wrote in collaboration with Christopher Wright. In between, he wrote two minor books, *The Treasures of the Foundling Hospital* (1972), and *Courbet: the Studio of the Painter* (1973). For many years before his death he had been working on lists of paintings by followers of Caravaggio, and the book was published posthumously (1979) under the title *The International Caravaggesque Movement*, with an introduction by Anthony Blunt.

Nicolson's style of writing, in which one could trace the influence of both his parents, was elegant and clear, and his research profound, but what distinguished his books and articles was his gift for evoking the social and historical background of the artists whom he admired, for example the early industrial revolution in *Joseph Wright of Derby*. 'The enemies of scholarship', he wrote in the foreword to his *Terbrugghen*, 'are tact and urbanity'; the gentleness of his nature was stiffened, when his professional talents were engaged, by a steely determination to discover and express the truth. His friends were often startled by the candour with which he exposed a fake, whether a painting or a person. But seldom can a scholar who knew so much have confessed his ignorance so often.

On 8 August 1955 Nicolson married Luisa, daughter of Professor Giacomo Vertova of Florence, herself a distinguished art historian and a previous assistant to Berenson. There was a daughter of the marriage, which was dissolved in 1962. He was appointed MVO in 1947 and CBE in 1971, and in 1977 was elected a fellow of the British Academy. Nicolson's death on 22 May 1978 was very sudden. He collapsed with a massive stroke in a London underground station as he was returning from dining at his club, and died in Middlesex Hospital, Westminster. He was sixty-three. Following cremation at Golders Green, his ashes were buried at Sissinghurst parish cemetery.

NIGEL NICOLSON, rev.

Sources F. Haskell, 'Benedict Nicolson and the *Burlington Magazine*', *Burlington Magazine*, 119 (1977), 229–30 · F. Haskell, *Burlington Magazine*, 120 (1978), 428–31 · G. Robertson, 'Lionel Benedict Nicolson, 1914–1978', *PBA*, 68 (1982), 606–16 · J. Lees-Milne, *Harold Nicolson: a biography*, 2 vols. (1980–81) · V. Glendinning, *Vita Sackville-West* (1983) · H. Nicolson, *Diaries and letters*, ed. N. Nicolson, 3 vols. (1966–8) · N. Nicolson, *Long life* (1997) · personal knowledge (1986) · private information (1986) · L. Vertova, *Ben Nicolson* (1991) · D. Sutton, *Apollo*, 108 (1978), 69 · *The Times* (26 May 1978) · b. cert. · d. cert.

Archives *Burlington Magazine*, London, files · Bodl. Oxf., corresp. with Sibyl Colefax · Harvard University, near Florence, Italy, Center for Italian Renaissance Studies, letters to Bernard Berenson · Sissinghurst Castle, Kent, letters to brother and parents · Tate collection, Tate Gallery archive, corresp. with Kenneth Clark

Likenesses R. Moynihan, oils, 1977–8, NPG · B. Schwarz, photograph, repro. in Haskell, *Burlington Magazine*

Wealth at death £329,827: letter to Nigel Nicolson from Rubinstein Callingham, solicitors, 2 Oct 1978

Nicolson, Eric James Brindley (1917–1945), air force officer, was born on 29 April 1917 at 38 Crediton Hill, Hampstead, the son of Leslie Gibson Nicolson, of independent means, and his wife, Dorathea Hilda Ellen, *née*

Brindley. Educated at Tonbridge School, he began work in 1935 as an experimental engineer in Shoreham. On 21 December 1936 he joined the Royal Air Force as an acting pilot officer on a four-year short-service commission, having begun his flying training that October at the White Waltham civil flying school. He completed his service training at Ternhill, Shropshire, and on 7 August 1937 joined 72 squadron at Church Fenton. The squadron was then flying Gloster Gladiator fighters but in April 1939 it began re-equipping with Spitfires and soon afterwards, on 12 May, Nicolson was promoted flying officer. On 29 July 1939 he married Muriel Caroline Kendall, daughter of Arthur Kendall, a farmer, of Kirkby Wharfe; they had one son, born in the late summer of 1940.

Nicolson, generally known as Nick, was an extrovert character, gregarious, talkative, and high-spirited. He was also a first-rate pilot and air-to-air marksman, displaying 'at all times the characteristics which epitomised the RAF's esoterically-termed "press-on" type of pilot' (Bowyer, 227). After the outbreak of war 72 squadron moved to Leconfield, from where it flew its first operational sorties, without engaging the enemy. After further moves with the squadron Nicolson was posted, on 15 May 1940, to the newly formed 249 fighter squadron as acting flight commander. Soon afterwards 249 squadron was moved to Leconfield, where in June it was re-equipped with Hawker Hurricanes. Fully operational from 3 July, the squadron was sent on 14 August to Boscombe Down, Wiltshire, to reinforce the defence of southern England against the massed attacks of the *Luftwaffe*.

On 16 August 1940 soon after midday 249 squadron was scrambled to patrol the airspace between Poole and Romsey, Nicolson leading the three Hurricanes of 'red section'. After a diversion towards enemy planes over Gosport, which were soon engaged by Spitfires, red section climbed to join the main formation. At this point they were caught in the 'fatal fighter trap' by an enemy attacking quickly out of the sun (Saunders, 'Battle of Britain VC', 306). All three Hurricanes of red section were hit. One of Nicolson's colleagues managed to return to base, but the other was forced to bale out and fell to his death after his parachute collapsed at 1500 ft. Nicolson's own plane was struck by cannon in the cockpit and the fuselage fuel tank, and he was wounded in the foot and the face. With his cockpit ablaze he prepared to bale out, but at this moment a Messerschmitt Bf110 dived in front of him. Nicolson attacked, forcing the enemy plane to take evasive action. According to his terse combat report he continued firing 'till I could bear heat no more' (ibid., 311). When he baled out, at 12,000 ft, the skin on his burned hands was 'hanging down like a little boy's trousers' (ibid., 309). A circling enemy fighter compelled him to 'play dead' on his parachute and as he floated down he was given additional shotgun wounds by an overzealous sergeant in the Local Defence Volunteers. His inaugural experience of aerial combat had lasted less than fifty minutes.

Badly wounded, Nicolson was taken to the Royal Southampton Hospital and later sent to the RAF hospital at

Halton. After recovery he was posted to the RAF convalescent facility at Torquay where, on 15 November 1940, he learned that he had been awarded the Victoria Cross. He received the medal from the king at Buckingham Palace, on 25 November, at a ceremony watched by his wife, mother, and two sisters. Nicolson was the only pilot of RAF Fighter Command to win the Victoria Cross during the battle of Britain—and, it would prove, during the whole war, as he was the only one with the required two witnesses—and he was acutely aware of the signal honour that had been bestowed upon him. This inevitably brought its pressures. A criterion for several such awards during the 1914–18 war had been a high tally of victories, whereas Nicolson was decorated after his first combat. He felt that others were more deserving and was particularly conscious of having survived where they had not.

With typical resolve Nicolson sought the earliest possible return to flying duties, in spite of his injuries, and on 24 February 1941 he joined the instructional staff of 54 operational training unit. He returned to flying that April with familiarization flights in a Miles Master and on 22 September he was given command of 1459 flight (later 538 squadron) at Hibaldstow, an experimental night-fighter unit equipped with the twin-engined Douglas Havoc Turbinlite. Six months later, on 17 March 1942, he was posted to Alipore, India, becoming staff officer at the headquarters of 293 wing. Another desk job followed, with an attachment to air headquarters at Bengal in mid-December. His continued wish for a more active role was granted on 4 August 1943 when he was given command of 27 squadron at Agartala, Burma. The squadron's De Havilland Mosquito fighter-bombers were to be deployed in support of the jungle campaign and Nicolson set about improving an already high reputation for operational efficiency. While in this command he was awarded the DFC 'for consistently showing himself to be a courageous and enterprising leader' (Saunders, 'The last flight', 21).

Nicolson left 27 squadron on 11 August 1944 to become wing commander (training) at the 3rd Tactical Air Force headquarters at Comilla, Bengal. While there he spent time with 355 squadron at Salboni, assessing the results of aircrew training. The squadron's Liberator bombers were then engaged in long-range bombing missions on Japanese targets in Burma and on 1 May 1945 Nicolson joined the crew of KH210 as an observer for a raid on Rangoon. Two hours after take-off the plane's starboard engines caught fire and at 2.50 a.m. on 2 May 1945 the plane ditched in the Bay of Bengal. There were only two survivors from the crew of eleven: one of them reported seeing Nicolson give a cheery thumbs-up sign just before taking his ditching station. It was probably the last time that he was seen alive. His body was never found, and he is commemorated on column 445 of the Singapore memorial, alongside his companions.

While on active service abroad Nicolson had been chosen as the Conservative parliamentary candidate for York. On 29 October 1946 his widow, with their young son, received his DFC at a ceremony at Buckingham Palace,

and on 16 August 1970 she unveiled a memorial to him at Millbrook in Hampshire, near the site of his parachute landing thirty years earlier.　　　　ROBIN HIGHAM

Sources A. Saunders, 'The battle of Britain VC', *The battle of Britain, then and now*, ed. W. G. Ramsey (1982) · C. Bowyer, *For valour: the air VCs* (1978) · A. Saunders, 'The last flight of the only battle of Britain VC', *After the Battle*, 30 (1980) · J. Laffin, *British VCs of World War 2: a study in heroism* (1997) · T. F. Neil, *Onward to Malta: memoirs of a Hurricane pilot in Malta, 1941* (1992) · *The Aeroplane* (20 July 1945), 61 · *The register of the Victoria cross*, 3rd edn (1997) · F. K. Mason, *Battle over Britain* (1969) · b. cert. · m. cert.
Likenesses photograph, repro. in *Register of the Victoria cross*, p. 240 · photograph, repro. in Ramsey, ed., *Battle of Britain*, p. 309
Wealth at death £212 19s. 7d.: probate, 4 Dec 1945, *CGPLA Eng. & Wales*

Nicolson, Sir Harold George (1886–1968), diplomatist and politician, was born at the British legation, Tehran, on 21 November 1886, the third son of Arthur *Nicolson, first Baron Carnock (1849–1928), and his wife, (Mary) Katharine Rowan (d. 1951), the youngest daughter of Captain Archibald Rowan Hamilton of Killyleagh Castle, co. Down. He was born into a minor patrician family with a well-established tradition of public service. His father was a distinguished diplomatist himself, becoming permanent under-secretary at the Foreign Office in 1910. Through his maternal aunt he was related to the imperial statesman-cum-diplomat Frederick Temple Hamilton-Temple-Blackwood, the marquess of Dufferin. Not surprisingly, in light of his lineage, the young Nicolson turned to diplomacy as a career.

Youth and education Much of Nicolson's early youth was spent either abroad, wherever his father was posted, or at the Irish estates of his mother's relatives. It was in these great Irish houses, he would reflect in later life, that he found 'anchors in a drifting life, … the only places where I ceased to be a pot-plant for ever being bedded out in alien soil' (Nicolson, *Desire to Please*, 5). Only Tangier, where his father was Britain's minister from 1894 to 1904, held a similar spell over him throughout his life. At the age of nearly nine, in 1895, he was sent away from his beloved Morocco to attend The Grange, a preparatory school near Folkestone. He hated the regimented life at The Grange as much as he loathed Wellington College, where he was sent in 1900, although under the spell of its master, the Revd Bertram Pollock, later bishop of Norwich, he learned to love literature and the classics. Nicolson moved on to Balliol College, Oxford, in 1904, having spent the intervening year after leaving Wellington at Weimar to learn German. After the conventional dullness of Wellington, Nicolson flourished in Balliol's liberal and cerebrally stimulating climate, but left Oxford in 1907 with only a pass degree, having obtained a third in classical honour moderations the previous year.

Early years as a diplomatist While still at Balliol Nicolson decided to try for diplomacy. On leaving Oxford he went to Paris and Hanover to complete his language studies—he later described his experiences in his delightful, semi-autobiographical *Some People* (1927)—and in October 1909, much to everyone's (especially his father's) surprise, he passed second in the competitive entrance examination

Sir Harold George Nicolson (1886–1968), by Howard Coster, 1935

for the diplomatic service. He spent his early years in the service as an attaché at Madrid (from February to September 1911) and then as third secretary at Constantinople (from January 1912 to October 1914). On 1 October 1913 he married the Hon. Victoria Mary (Vita) Sackville-*West (1892–1962), only child of Lionel Edward Sackville-West, third Baron Sackville, and his wife and first cousin, Victoria Josefa Sackville-West, daughter of Lionel Sackville-West, second Lord Sackville, and his mistress, Josefa de la Oliva (known as Pepita), a Spanish dancer. Redoubtable as she was eccentric and irascible, Lady Sackville was to cause the Nicolsons great anxiety in future years. Nicolson's marriage to Vita, too, was the source of much despair. None the less this unconventional union, and its bond of mutual and deep understanding and affection, remained the bedrock of his life. There were two sons of the marriage: Lionel Benedict *Nicolson (1914–1978) and Nigel (b. 1917).

Nicolson was recalled to the Foreign Office in the spring of 1914. During his home leave the First World War broke out. He was drafted back into duty, and it was left to him, as the youngest member of staff, to recover on 3 August Britain's declaration of war on Germany from the German embassy, which had been erroneously delivered after intercepted German wireless traffic suggested that Germany had already declared war (Nicolson, Lord Carnock, 424–6). Nicolson was exempted from military duty on account of his position at the Foreign Office. His war work earned him his first professional spurs. Much of it involved relations with the neutral powers; but he was also, with Sir Mark Sykes and Leo Amery, one of the chief draftsmen of the Balfour declaration, which committed Britain to supporting a Jewish homeland in Palestine. More importantly perhaps for the future course of his diplomatic career, he was brought in closer contact with the

problems of south-eastern Europe. His war work allowed him to forge closer ties with the supporters of the pro-entente Hellenist leader Eleftherios Venizelos, ties which would stand him in good stead at the Paris peace conference and the later Near Eastern conferences of the early post-war years.

At the end of hostilities Nicolson was attached to the British delegation at the Paris peace conference, where he served under his beloved chief Sir Eyre Crowe on a number of Balkan committees. Officially, Nicolson was only a junior adviser, but he soon established for himself a reputation for penetrating analyses and sound political judgement. He had travelled to Paris with high hopes, yet before long concluded that the conference was doomed to fail to deliver the lasting peace he had hoped for. In 1919 he accompanied General Smuts on a mission to Belá Kun's Soviet-style government at Budapest. For his services during the war and at the conference Nicolson was appointed CMG in 1919 and promoted to first secretary. After the conference he was appointed private secretary to Sir (James) Eric Drummond, the first secretary-general of the infant League of Nations. This appointment was perhaps as much a reward for the notable success of his conference work as it was a reflection of his strong pro-league sentiments. At Paris he had become strongly imbued with Wilsonian ideals and regarded the league as the panacea for the ills of international politics rather than the 'separatist alliances and combinations' of the old pre-war diplomacy (Nicolson to Viorel Tilea, 9 Dec 1919, Tilea MSS, box 67).

Marital complications and further diplomatic career Nicolson's professional success in these years, however, was marred by considerable conjugal disquiet. In 1915 the Nicolsons had bought Long Barn, a semi-derelict medieval farmstead in the Kentish weald not far from Sevenoaks, near Vita's ancestral home, Knole. At Long Barn the Nicolsons laid the foundations of their reputations as successful gardeners and writers. There Vita launched upon poetry and Nicolson wrote the first of his six literary biographies, Paul Verlaine, and also Sweet Waters, his first novel (both 1921). Yet their marriage was strained very nearly to breaking-point because of Vita's love affair with Violet Trefusis. The Nicolsons' marital crisis reached its near-farcical climax in the abortive elopement of the two women to northern France with Nicolson in hot pursuit in a two-seater aeroplane. Nicolson was himself by no means a stranger to homosexual affairs; but his forbearance and patience enabled the Nicolsons to continue their marriage.

In June 1920 Nicolson was recalled to the Foreign Office. By this time his enthusiasm for the league had already begun to wane. Possibly under the strong influence of Crowe, now permanent under-secretary, he became more sceptical of the league and reverted to a more traditional concept of diplomacy. His duties at the Foreign Office were mostly concerned with Near and Middle Eastern affairs. Stirred by Venizelos's fall in November 1920 and the reverses suffered by Greece in the conflict with Turkey, the philhellene Nicolson challenged received Foreign

Office opinion by arguing against any compromise with the Kemalist forces. It was the first time that he stood up to his masters on a major policy issue. Ultimately the course of the campaign in Asia Minor rendered his recommendations impracticable. Nicolson, however, remained the Foreign Office's chief expert on the remnants of the Eastern question. His notable 'Memorandum … respecting the Freedom of the Straits', of 15 November 1922, formed the basis of British policy at the Lausanne conference of 1922–3 (Medlicott and others, *Documents on British Foreign Policy*, 1st ser., 18, appx 1). At Lausanne he acted as Lord Curzon's private secretary and was Britain's representative on a number of subcommittees. Nicolson later rendered his account of the proceedings at Lausanne in *Curzon: the Last Phase* (1934). Although busy with diplomatic work he still found time to write three further literary biographies: *Tennyson* (1923), *Byron: the Last Journey* (1924), and *Swinburne* (1926).

In 1925 the new head of the Foreign Office, Sir William Tyrrell, transferred Nicolson to Tehran as counsellor of legation. Relations between the two men had been strained, and Nicolson always suspected an element of personal spite in Tyrrell's decision to transfer him. A posting to Persia in the 1920s involved an arduous journey by sea to Haifa or via Russia and the Caspian Sea to Resht and thence across the desert in a motor car to Tehran. (His wife's *Passenger to Tehran*, 1926, offered a glimpse into this unglamorous aspect of diplomatic life.) Nicolson's two years in the city of his birth marked the nadir of his diplomatic career. Separated from his wife and sons, he suffered from the geographical, intellectual, and social isolation Persia imposed upon him. Worse still, his relations with his chief, Sir Percy Loraine, were rather reserved. Unlike Ponderous Percy, Nicolson was too much of an individualist ever to take seriously the representative side of diplomacy. 'I loathe processions & gholams & sowars & uniforms & tail coats & all that …—I can't hide my loathing & P[ercy] … gets rather distressed' (Nicolson to Lancelot Oliphant, 12 March 1926, Sissinghurst, Nicolson MSS). Nicolson's lack of diplomatic decorum, his indulgence for intellectual frivolity, and his tendency to tease ('my jokes … are greeted with a "two minute silence"'; ibid., Nicolson to Oliphant, 28 May 1926) only added to the strain. Loraine, moreover, took umbrage when he suspected Nicolson of lampooning him in his essays 'on real people in imaginary situations and imaginary people in real situations', *Some People* (1927), which he wrote at Tehran. 'A cad's book', Loraine called it (Waterfield, 116). Nicolson's differences with his chief, however, were not merely questions of style but also of policy. In September 1926, when in charge of the legation, he sent a long dispatch in which he criticized 'certain inherited maxims' of Britain's 'buffer state' policy towards Persia and Loraine's 'too rosy picture' of the situation (Nicolson to Sir Austen Chamberlain, (no. 486), 30 Sept 1926, *Documents on British Foreign Policy*, ser. 1a, 2, no. 447; and to parents, 28 Aug 1926, Sissinghurst, Nicolson MSS). It was the second time that Nicolson had taken it upon himself to challenge received Foreign Office wisdom. This time, however, his Foreign Office colleagues were incensed at his breach of protocol in criticizing his highly regarded former chief. The foreign secretary minuted:

> if Mr Nicolson were a fool, I should remove him. As he is certainly not a fool, I infer that, away from daily contact with us, our intentions are not as clear to him as to us. Let us make them clear.   (Min. Chamberlain, 9 Nov 1926, FO 371/11481/E5994/92/34)

On his recall to London in the following summer he was demoted to first secretary.

Nicolson was depressed at the lack of progress in his career. Instead of shaping policy, he found himself 'strand[ed] in this bog in which I have wasted the best years of my life', having to execute policies in which he did not believe (Nicolson to Owen O'Malley, 23 Aug 1927, Sissinghurst, Nicholson MSS). For the first time he considered leaving the service, but stayed 'an ageing limpet stuck to the hulk of British diplomacy' (ibid., Nicolson to Lancelot Oliphant, 28 Dec 1926). His next post was Berlin. What ground he had lost as chargé d'affaires at Tehran he regained when in charge of the Berlin embassy in 1928. His dispatches from there re-established his high reputation and he was promoted to counsellor again. Nevertheless, in September 1929 Nicolson resigned from the diplomatic service, when he accepted an offer to join the Beaverbrook press. He was then halfway up the diplomatic career ladder with the distinct prospect of a legation or minor embassy in the near future. His colleagues were mystified by his decision. It was, however, a step which he did not take lightly. He remained attached to his old profession and occasionally longed 'to creep back into the F. O.' (ibid., Nicolson to Lancelot Oliphant, 24 Aug 1935). The unbearable absences from his wife and sons and their financial dependence upon the increasingly quarrelsome Lady Sackville induced him to take this decision. But his disillusionment with the policy-makers and his own nascent political ambitions were equally potent factors.

Sissinghurst, politics, and writing With his resignation began Nicolson's public life. The year 1930 marked a major turning point. From January 1930, and for the next eighteen months, he wrote the 'Londoner's diary' in the *Evening Standard*, an occupation which the fastidious Nicolson found increasingly irksome. From new year 1930 he also kept the daily diary for which he would perhaps primarily be remembered. In the spring of 1930 the Nicolsons moved from Long Barn when a neighbouring poultry farmer threatened to invade their rural isolation. At Sissinghurst Castle, the remnants of an Elizabethan manor house near Cranbrook, they found a new home. There Vita Sackville-West's poetic temperament and gardening expertise combined with Nicolson's classically trained sense of architectural form and order to create one of the most celebrated gardens in England (now one of the most visited of National Trust properties).

The political and economic crisis of 1931 convinced Nicolson of the inadequacy of the existing parliamentary machinery to solve contemporary problems. Having declined to stand as a Liberal for Falmouth, he joined the New Party under Sir Oswald Mosley, the son-in-law of his old mentor, Lord Curzon, with whom he had formed a friendship at Berlin in 1929. At the 1931 general election he unsuccessfully contested the Combined Universities seat. He also became editor of *Action*, the Mosley party's weekly organ. However, when Mosley embraced fascism, in 1932, Nicolson severed his links with him.

Out of a job, Nicolson was once more thrown upon his resources as a writer. In 1932 he published his second novel, *Public Faces*, a benign satire about an international crisis into which he worked his own league and Persian experiences, and which characteristically ended on the notion that honesty is the best policy. Already in 1930 he had published the biography of his father, *Lord Carnock*. His 'Studies in modern diplomacy' trilogy was now completed by his insightful account of the Paris peace conference, *Peacemaking 1919* (1933), followed in 1934 by his book on Lord Curzon's foreign secretaryship. A well-paid lecture tour of America with his wife resulted in the commission to write the biography of the American financier turned diplomat Dwight Morrow, which was published in 1935. It was followed two years later by *Helen's Tower*, an account of the career of his uncle, the marquess of Dufferin. During these years Nicolson rose to prominence as a regular and popular broadcaster on the wireless.

At the general election of 1935 Nicolson finally realized his political ambitions by being elected by a narrow margin as the National Labour candidate for Leicester West, a nomination which had been fixed by his wife's relative Herbrand Edward Dundonald Brassey Sackville, the ninth Earl De La Warr. Nicolson never climbed to the 'top of the greasy pole'. Like many of his class and generation, he felt politically uprooted, defining himself in terms of family ties and friendships rather than party labels. By choosing National Labour his political fortunes were bound up with those of Ramsay MacDonald. While his Leicester election was made possible only with Conservative support, he was fiercely anti-tory in his private sentiments, yet at the same time unable to understand the aspirations of the middle and working classes in his industrial constituency. But although he was perhaps not made for the cut and thrust of party politics, Nicolson was one of the best-informed speakers on foreign affairs in the long parliament of 1935, warning early and consistently of the dangers of appeasement. His expertise in foreign affairs was also very much in evidence in his slim, but elegant and instructive *Diplomacy* (1939). His support for Churchill, however, never yielded the desired results. He held junior office at the Ministry of Information from 1940, but to his dismay was returned to the back-benches in 1941. Perhaps his most effective contributions to the war effort were his weekly column 'Marginal comment' in *The Spectator* (1939–40, 1941–52), and the Penguin paperback *Why Britain is at War* (1939). From 1941 to 1946 he served on the board of governors of the BBC. His political career came to an end in 1945 when, standing as an independent but with Conservative backing, he lost his seat in the Labour landslide.

Last years Nicolson retained his hopes of re-entering politics. Having unsuccessfully sought a peerage as a cross-bencher from Prime Minister Attlee, he joined the Labour Party in 1947 and in the following year contested the North Croydon by-election. Both steps were half-hearted at best. His bid for election—'this nightmare'—ended in defeat (Nicolson to Sibyl Colefax, 28 Feb 1948, Colefax MSS, MS.Eng.c.3166); his socialism was 'purely cerebral' (Nicolson to Vita Sackville-West, 7 May 1948, N. Nicolson, *Diaries*, 3.148-9). An incautiously disdainful 'Marginal comment' on his electioneering experience (published in *The Spectator* of 19 March 1948) put paid to all further hopes of re-entering politics and the much-coveted peerage eluded him forever. His only link with the world of politics and diplomacy were his regular broadcasts. In 1946 he covered the abortive Paris peace conference for the BBC. Apart from broadcasting, he channelled his prodigious energies into writing. The decade and a half after the end of the war saw a series of very different books from his pen. In 1945 he edited with his wife *Another World than This*, a poetry anthology. His next books were *The Congress of Vienna* (1946), *The English Sense of Humour* (1947), and *Benjamin Constant* (1949). In 1948 he was commissioned to write the official biography of George V—an awkward assignment skilfully executed; it was published four years later and confirmed his high reputation as a writer. It also earned him a knighthood as KCVO and an honorary fellowship of Balliol (both 1953). His Chichele lectures during 1953 at Oxford were published in the following year as *The Evolution of Diplomatic Method*. His last productive years saw another spate of books: *Good Behaviour* (1955), *Sainte-Beuve* (1957), *Journey to Java* (1957), *The Age of Reason* (1960), and *Monarchy* (1962). From 1949 to 1963 he also contributed weekly book reviews to *The Observer*.

Nicolson's last book, on kingship, was his perhaps least satisfactory. He himself took it as a sign of his waning powers. His wife's death, in 1962, dealt a violent blow to him from which he never recovered. Her death marked the end of a unique marriage and of his life as a writer. He had always been a glutton for work. Besides his writing he had found time to serve on the National Trust executive committee (1947–68) and the London Library committee (1952–7). He was also a trustee of the National Portrait Gallery (1948–64), and president of the Classical Association (1950–51). His last years, however, were spent in melancholy decline at Sissinghurst. He died there on 1 May 1968, following a stroke, and was buried at Sissinghurst church. He was survived by his two sons.

Nicolson was in many ways 'a nineteenth-century character … living an eighteenth century life in the midst of the twentieth century' (J. Sparrow, *Harold Nicolson and Vita Sackville-West*, 6). His background and his strong intellectual tastes made him an élitist. But he was no snob, and disliked pomp and formality. He was known to a wide circle as a responsive and entertaining companion, but his diaries, edited by his son Nigel in three volumes (1966–8), quickly became a standard source for the period and revealed his capacity for self-scrutiny. He brought to politics shrewd practical wisdom combined with humanistic values, and to literature an easy, slightly ironic, classical style. 'His life tended to zigzag, but he extracted from it much pleasure' (N. Nicolson, 'Introduction', *Diaries*, 9). James Lees-Milne described him as 'stocky in build and cheerful in countenance; jaunty in movement; mischievous and benignant in manner' (*DNB*).

T. G. OTTE

Sources Sissinghurst Castle, near Cranbrook, Kent, Nicolson MSS · N. Nicolson, ed., *Diaries and letters of Harold Nicolson*, 3 vols. (1966–8) · S. Olson, ed., *Harold Nicolson: diaries and letters, 1930–64* (1980) · J. Lees-Milne, *Harold Nicolson: a biography*, 2 vols. (1980–83) · N. Nicolson, ed., *Vita and Harold: the letters of Vita Sackville-West and Harold Nicolson, 1910–1962* (1992) · N. Nicolson, *Portrait of a marriage*, new edn (1992) · Bodl. Oxf., MSS Rumbold · Bodl. Oxf., MSS Colefax · Ratiu Family Charitable Foundation, London, Tilea MSS · W. N. Medlicott and others, eds., *Documents on British foreign policy, 1919–1939*, 1st ser., vol. 17; ser. 1a, vol. 2 · PRO, Foreign Office archives, FO 371/11481 · HLRO, Beaverbrook papers · H. Nicolson, *Sir Arthur Nicolson, Bart: Lord Carnock* (1930) · H. Nicolson, *The desire to please* (1943) · H. Nicolson, *Curzon, the last phase, 1919–1925* (1934) · H. Nicolson, *Peacemaking 1919* (1933) · H. Nicolson, *Some people* (1927) · H. Nicolson, 'Marginal comment', *The Spectator* [various issues] · G. Waterfield, *Professional diplomat: Sir Percy Loraine* (1973) · L. Wolff, 'The public faces of Harold Nicolson: the thirties', *Biography*, 5 (1982), 240–52 · A. Scott-James, *Sissinghurst: the making of a garden* (1973) · V. Glendinning, *Vita: the life of Vita Sackville-West* (1983) · D. Cannadine, *Aspects of aristocracy: grandeur and decline in modern Britain* (1995) · T. G. Otte, *Harold Nicolson and diplomatic theory: between old diplomacy and new* (1998) · *DNB* · *WWW, 1961–70* · T. G. Otte, 'Nicolson', in G. R. Berridge, M. Keens-Soper, and T. G. Otte, *Diplomatic theory from Machiavelli to Kissinger* (2001), 125–50 · D. Drinkwater, 'Sir Harold Nicholson as international theorist', PhD diss., Australian National University, 2002

Archives Balliol Oxf., diaries · Sissinghurst Castle, near Cranbrook, Kent, corresp. | Bodl. Oxf., corresp. with Sibyl Colefax · Bodl. Oxf., corresp. with Lionel Curtis · Bodl. Oxf., corresp. with Sir Horace Rumbold · CAC Cam., corresp. with Sir E. L. Spears · Georgetown University, Washington, DC, letters to Christopher Sykes · Harvard University, near Florence, Italy, Center for Italian Renaissance Studies, letters to Bernard Berenson · HLRO, corresp. with Lord Beaverbrook · King's AC Cam., letters to Clive Bell · King's Lond., Liddell Hart C., corresp. with Sir B. H. Liddell Hart · PRO, Foreign Office archives, FO 371 · Rice University, Houston, Texas, Woodson Research Center, corresp. with Julian S. Huxley · Royal Society of Literature, London, letters to Royal Society of Literature · U. Durham, letters to William Plomer | SOUND BL NSA

Likenesses W. Rothenstein, red chalk drawing, 1925 · H. Coster, photographs, 1930–39, NPG [*see illus.*] · Y. Karsh, photograph, 1949, NPG · W. Stoneman, photograph, 1955, NPG · W. Suschitzky, photograph, 1957, NPG · photograph, repro. in Nicolson, ed., *Vita and Harold* (1992), facing p. 310 · photograph, repro. in M. Jebb, ed., *The diaries of Cynthia Gladwyn* (1995), following p. 96 · photographs, repro. in Nicolson, ed., *Diaries and letters* · photographs, repro. in Lees-Milne, *Harold Nicolson*

Wealth at death £22,748: probate, 12 Nov 1968, *CGPLA Eng. & Wales*

Nicolson, Malcolm Hassels (1843–1904). *See under* Nicolson, Adela Florence (1865–1904).

Nicolson, Thomas [Thomas Joseph Nicholson] (1644×6–1718), vicar apostolic of Scotland, son of Thomas Nicolson of Cluny, later of Kemnay, Aberdeenshire, or of Pitmedden, and his wife, Elizabeth Abercromby of Birkenbog, Banffshire, was born at Birkenbog. He matriculated at Aberdeen University in 1660 and in November 1666 was made a regent (professor) in Glasgow University and taught Greek, mathematics, and philosophy. In autumn 1681 he refused to take the Test Act oath and resigned his regency. He entered the Scots College, Douai, in July 1682,

having become a Catholic a few months before, went on to Padua, where he taught in the episcopal seminary, and in October 1685 was made prefect of studies.

Ordained priest on 9 March 1686 Nicolson returned to Scotland in December 1687 and worked in Edinburgh and Glasgow. At the revolution he was imprisoned, in December 1688, then in summer 1689 was banished, his brother being cautioner against his return. From 1689 to 1694 he was chaplain to the English nuns at Dunkirk and in poor health. Giving Scotland a bishop had long been mooted and on 7 September 1694 he was appointed vicar apostolic of Scotland with the titular see of Peristachium. He received episcopal ordination on 27 February 1695 in secret at Paris but could not go to Scotland until his brother's bond was cancelled. Eventually, having travelled to England in November 1696 and been imprisoned there for six months, he arrived in Edinburgh in July 1697.

Thereafter, living at Preshome, Banffshire, Nicolson acted with authority and vigour. Boundaries for priests to work within were fixed and in 1701 the Jesuits submitted to his authority. He united lowlands and highlands by making an extensive journey to the west highlands and islands to administer confirmation. In 1704 he ordained a priest, the first ordination in Scotland since the Reformation, and in 1714 set up a small seminary at Loch Morar. The statutes which he laid down remained in force until 1780.

After the Jacobite rising of 1715 Nicolson was imprisoned for a time. He died at Preshome on 12 October 1718 and was buried in St Ninian's churchyard, Tynet, Banffshire. To the end he retained a great love for books and study. Already in 1706 James Gordon had been made his coadjutor and successor. The Roman Catholic church in Scotland was fortunate in its first bishop.

MARK DILWORTH

Sources J. Darragh, *The Catholic hierarchy of Scotland: a biographical list, 1653–1985* (1986) · W. Doran, 'Bishop Thomas Nicolson: first vicar-apostolic, 1695–1718', *Innes Review*, 39 (1988), 109–32 · A. Bellesheim, *History of the Catholic Church in Scotland*, ed. and trans. D. O. H. Blair, 4 (1890) · W. Forbes-Leith, ed., *Memoirs of Scottish Catholics*, 2 vols. (1909), vol. 2 · J. F. S. Gordon, ed., *The Catholic church in Scotland* (1874), 1–2 · M. Dilworth, *The Scots in Franconia* (1974) · *Fasti academiae Mariscallanae Aberdonensis: selections from the records of the Marischal College and University, MDXCIII–MDCCCLX*, 2, ed. P. J. Anderson, New Spalding Club, 18 (1898), 227 · P. J. Anderson, ed., *Records of the Scots colleges at Douai, Rome, Madrid, Valladolid and Ratisbon*, New Spalding Club, 30 (1906)

Archives Sacra Congregazione di Propaganda Fide, Rome, reports · Scottish Catholic Archives, Edinburgh, letters

Likenesses portrait, Brockloch, Kirkpatrick Durham, Kirkcudbrightshire; repro. in Darragh, *Catholic hierarchy*, frontispiece; copy, Blairs College, Aberdeen

Nicolson, Thomas Rae (1879–1951), athlete, was born on 3 October 1879 at Auchgoyle Farm, Millhouse, Tighnabruaich, on the Kyles of Bute, Argyll, the third son in the family of ten sons and one daughter of Neil Nicolson, a farmer, and his wife, Anne McAlpine. He attended Millhouse School, farmed at Corra Farm, Tighnabruaich, and married Isabella Kerr Hutton, with whom he had three sons and one daughter.

Nicolson was arguably the finest Scottish athlete of his generation. At the turn of the twentieth century he became captain of the famous Kyles Athletic camanachd (shinty) team, of which his father was one of the founders in 1896; together with six of his brothers, who also played for the club, he won many honours. He was also an accomplished wrestler, golfer, and footballer and had trials with Queen's Park Football Club. Willie Maley, the Celtic Football Club manager, was a long-standing friend.

It was as an outstanding amateur in throwing events that Nicolson made his name. He excelled at the shot and hammer to the extent of being one of the few who could challenge the Irish-American throwers of his day, and was reckoned one of the few Scottish amateurs able to match the professionals who competed at the highland games; he never followed his brothers into the professional ranks on the highland games circuit. Standing 6 feet tall, and weighing 175 pounds, he achieved a series of record-breaking performances based on his inherited natural strength (his father was 6 feet 3 inches tall) and diligent practice on his Argyll farm.

Nicolson began competing at the Scottish Amateur Athletic Association (SAAA) championships in 1901, the first of twenty-eight appearances. In 1903 he won his first Scottish hammer-throwing title, achieving an unsurpassed nineteen consecutive titles in the years up until 1924; he won the SAAA title again in 1926 and 1927 and was placed second in 1929, aged fifty. His best performance was a hammer throw of 50.84 metres in a Scotland v. America contest at Edinburgh in 1908. This stood as a Scottish record for thirty-nine years and was a British record for fifteen. He was also Scottish amateur shot champion on fourteen occasions. At the Olympic games in London in 1908 he was placed fourth in both the hammer and the shot; at the Antwerp Olympics in 1920, he was sixth in the hammer, despite arriving late owing to his farming commitments. Throughout his long career he was known for his geniality, modesty, durability, and awesome strength. He died at the Western Infirmary, Glasgow, on 18 April 1951, and was buried in the Kilbride churchyard, Ardlamont, Argyll. His wife predeceased him.　　　　　HUGH D. MacLENNAN

Sources J. W. Keddie, *Scottish athletics, 1883–1983* (1982) · I. Thorburn, ed., *The Kyles: a celebration of 100 years* (1996) · J. W. Keddie, 'The Nicolsons of Kyles', *Athletics Weekly* (6 Feb 1982) · R. Hutchinson, *West Highland Free Press* (2 Feb 1996) · C. Paterson, 'The Kyles', *Shinty yearbook* (1977–8), 35–7 · W. L. Inglis, *A history of Cowal highland gathering* (1960) · b. cert. · d. cert. · private information (2004)
Archives priv. coll.
Likenesses photograph, repro. in Keddie, *Scottish athletics* · photograph, repro. in Thorburn, ed., *The Kyles*, 1 · photograph, repro. in Keddie, 'The Nicolsons of Kyles', 1
Wealth at death £10,701 5s. 3d.: confirmation, 10 Oct 1951, *CCI* · £764 6s.: eik, 7 March 1952, *CCI*

Nicolson, William (1655–1727), Church of Ireland bishop of Derry and antiquary, was born on Whitsunday, 3 June 1655—according to local tradition, in the porch of the parish church of Great Orton, Cumberland. His father, Joseph Nicolson (1622/3–1686), was a time-serving clergyman of varied intellectual interests, who had been installed in the

William Nicolson (1655–1727), by W. Miln, 1891 (after unknown artist, *c.*1715–20)

living of Plumbland, in the same county, by the parliamentarian regime in 1647; his mother, Mary (*d.* 1689), was the daughter of a local puritan gentleman, John Briscoe of Crofton Hall, among whose properties was an estate at Great Orton. Joseph Nicolson transferred to the rectory of Great Orton in 1657, and accumulated several more Cumberland livings by 1660. A rapid readjustment ensured that he retained this sheaf of preferments after the Restoration, but the sum total of his income was not large, and his hopes of further advancement dim. Thus William, the eldest of three sons, enjoyed only limited material advantages in his youth. He attended a local school at Dovenby, and was able to enter Queen's, Oxford (his father's old college), in 1670 as a 'batteller'.

Clergyman and scholar, 1670–1702 Thomas Hearne, a hostile witness, recalled that at Oxford Nicolson was observed to possess 'good, strong parts but was a very drunken, idle fellow' (*Remarks*, 2.62). Conviviality cannot have preoccupied him, however, for he was elected taberdar of the college after graduating BA in 1676 (he took his MA three years later), and a fellow in 1679. His talents also attracted the attention of a fellow Cumbrian, Secretary of State Sir Joseph Williamson, who paid for him to travel to Germany in 1678, possibly in order to prepare him for the diplomatic service. Nicolson spent five months in Saxony attending Leipzig University. His flair for languages enabled him to master German, as Williamson had presumably intended, but his principal interests were of a scholarly kind. While in Leipzig, at the instigation of the Lutheran theologian Johann Schertzer, he translated into Latin an essay by Robert Hooke on the motion of the earth, which he published in 1679. On his return to Oxford he continued to receive financial assistance from Williamson, and was the first holder of a lectureship in Anglo-Saxon studies established by Williamson at Queen's. Nicolson became acquainted with the Dutch Anglo-Saxonist Francis Junius, and was appointed by Bishop Fell to edit Junius's unfinished dictionary of the 'Northern languages', a mammoth task of which he accomplished only the transcription. He also contributed to the multi-volume *English Atlas* projected by the London publisher Moses Pitt: Nicolson was responsible for chapters on Poland and Denmark in the first volume (1680) and produced the second and third volumes (1681–2), covering the German empire, entirely by himself.

In December 1679 Nicolson was ordained a deacon, and in 1681 received from Bishop Rainbow of Carlisle a cathedral prebend and a small living as vicar of Torpenhow. At first he hoped his college would allow him to retain his fellowship, but there were difficulties, and during a prolonged negotiation Rainbow offered him, in addition, the newly vacant archdeaconry of Carlisle. In these circumstances Nicolson left Queen's, and in October 1682 became archdeacon and rector of the attached parish of Great Salkeld, which he made his residence. In 1699 he added another vicarage to his quiver. Yet he was still by no means well-to-do, and his first attempt at finding a wife, in 1684, foundered on the unwillingness of the prospective bride and her family to contemplate an alliance with a clergyman of slender means. Two years later, however, he married on 3 June Elizabeth (1656–1712), daughter of Dr John Archer of Oxenholme, near Kendal, a 'modest' woman (*Diary of Ralph Thoresby*, 1.276) with whom he was very happy. They had eight children.

The day after the proclamation of James II, Nicolson preached a sermon at Carlisle Cathedral welcoming the new king and promulgating a doctrine of passive obedience to a divinely ordained ruler. Kings, he declared, were 'God's vicegerents on earth' (Nicolson, *Sermon Preached in the Cathedral Church of Carlisle*, 7). He also praised the deceased Charles II for enforcing uniformity of religious observance. In an act of political opportunism, the sermon was dedicated to the clerk of the privy council, Philip Musgrave, son of Sir Christopher Musgrave, the most powerful political figure in the locality. Despite the exalted view of monarchy presented in this sermon Nicolson evidently found little difficulty in accepting the revolution, and in May 1689 urged the diocesan clergy to swear allegiance to the new regime; any wavering would only serve the interests of the enemies of the established church. It seems most appropriate to characterize him at this point as a tory: certainly, his attitude to nonconformists was one of hostility, as manifested, for example, in his unwillingness to support the establishment in Carlisle of a society for the reformation of manners because of the involvement of local dissenters (although he later came round to supporting the movement in general, and published a sermon he had preached in 1706 to the London societies). Throughout his ecclesiastical career Nicolson

displayed a devotion to duty and a determination to maintain the material resources and corporate privileges of the church, even if his own religious faith was practical rather than mystical.

Although far removed from the university, Nicolson did not lack intellectual stimulation or companionship. He amassed a substantial library and antiquarian collection. Ralph Thoresby, visiting in 1694, was highly impressed by his 'museum' of coins and 'natural curiosities' (*Diary of Ralph Thoresby*, 1.275). Thoresby was one of a number of friends of a similar inquiring disposition with whom Nicolson corresponded. Through their recommendation he was (somewhat belatedly) elected FRS in 1705. In the early 1690s he began work on a history of Northumbria: it was never completed, though the research proved useful to other writers, including Edward Lhuyd and the philologist John Ray, whose *Collection of English Words* (1691) drew heavily on Nicolson's Northumbrian compilations. Nicolson also contributed to the *Linguarum veterum septentrionalium thesaurus* produced by George Hickes in 1703. But his most important work was his *English Historical Library*, published in 1696–9, a comprehensive bibliography of printed and manuscript materials on English history, compiled with a patriotic as well as a scholarly purpose. The work was also infused with a vigorous wit, which made austere commentators suspicious, and there were inevitably errors, which exposed Nicolson to the criticism that he was hasty and sometimes slapdash in his scholarship. He then turned his attention northwards, and in 1702 produced a *Scottish Historical Library* (1702). Much later, when he was domiciled in Ireland, there followed an *Irish Historical Library* (1724), though this was seriously marred by his manifest ignorance of the Irish language. The three works were reprinted together in a compendium volume in 1736.

Bishop of Carlisle, 1702–1718 Until 1702 Nicolson maintained a moderate tory outlook in secular politics. A sermon he preached before the House of Lords in 1702 on the anniversary of the execution of Charles I, while by no means high-flying in its political doctrine, was still distinctively tory in tone: the definition of royal authority was repeated verbatim from his sermon of 1685; he reprimanded those who denounced James II in order to prove loyalty to King William; and he developed a providential interpretation of the revolution which, he argued, was not enough to justify abandoning traditional beliefs in divine right and passive obedience. Locally, his main friendships were with such supporters of the 'church' interest as the Musgraves and Grahmes, and as late as 1702 he was active on behalf of tory candidates in parliamentary elections. When, to his surprise, he was advanced to the vacant bishopric of Carlisle in 1702 it was with the endorsement of Sir Christopher Musgrave and the tory Archbishop Sharp of York. In his new incarnation he had an entrée into national politics and characteristically attended to his duties in the House of Lords with great conscientiousness. He then began to change his political complexion. In part this may have been the manifestation of a pragmatism inherited from his father; but it was also a reaction against the increasing stridency of the high-church faction, and in particular a result of personal clashes with prominent high-churchmen, most notably Francis Atterbury. During the 'convocation controversy' of the late 1690s Nicolson had opposed Atterbury's arguments from a historical point of view. In return Atterbury had offered gratuitous offence to Nicolson, deriding his scholarship, and Nicolson, who privately referred to Atterbury as a 'foul-mouthed preacher' (Nichols, 1.220), had been moved to reply in print. Thus when Atterbury, of all people, was nominated in 1704 to the deanery of Carlisle, the consequences were predictable. The two men, both strong characters and with a history of mutual animosity, inevitably quarrelled. Nicolson, having at first refused to institute Atterbury, was then drawn into factional disputes within the cathedral chapter, which called into question the authority of both dean and bishop. In attempting to assert his rights of visitation over the chapter, Nicolson became embroiled in a protracted legal struggle which was resolved only by the passage of a parliamentary statute in 1708 in favour of episcopal authority. This dispute confirmed Nicolson's change of party allegiance, as he found himself relying for support within the ecclesiastical establishment on the low-church party, and in parliament on the whigs, especially Sir James Montagu, MP for Carlisle, the attorney-general and brother of the junto lord, Halifax.

This shift towards the whigs had been foreshadowed in 1704 when, having supported previous bills against occasional conformity to the Church of England, Nicolson opposed the 'tack' of the third Occasional Conformity Bill to the land tax. He distanced himself from the tories' 'church in danger' electoral campaign in the following year, and by 1708 was backing whig candidates in elections rather than his old friends. He found some difficulty over the union with Scotland in 1707. Certainly he favoured the measure on political grounds: he had advocated it strongly in the introduction to a historical collection of Anglo-Scottish treaties he had published in 1705, entitled *Leges marchiarum*, and in a sermon before the queen in 1707 he described the union itself as 'a most glorious deliverance' (Nicolson, *The Blessings of the Sixth Year*, 26). But he was concerned for the security of the Church of England and assisted Archbishop Tenison of Canterbury in drafting a saving act, though its provisions did not go so far as high-churchmen would have wished. On the other hand, he had no compunction in condemning the high-church Dr Sacheverell 'and his rabble' in 1710 (James, 201), even though for once he was not present in parliament for the crucial vote on Sacheverell's impeachment. In the ensuing general election of 1710 Nicolson intervened at Carlisle in support of Sir James Montagu to an unprecedented degree. Afterwards he found himself named in an election petition from the defeated tory candidate, one of whose charges was that Nicolson had publicized a private letter from Montagu, with the news that the former attorney-general had been granted a pension, in an effort to persuade undecided voters that Montagu still enjoyed royal favour. Tories in the Commons passed a resolution denouncing this interference as an infringement on the liberties and privileges of their house.

Nicolson enjoyed some share in the political triumph of the whigs in 1714 to the extent that he was made lord almoner to the new king, but for some time this proved to be the limit of his advancement. He may have been held back because, to the more advanced whigs, he still appeared too much of a 'church tory'. Certainly he had been sufficiently firm in support of the interests of the established church to have given his backing to the Occasional Conformity Act of 1711 (which, for tactical reasons, the whig junto had also endorsed) and, more significantly perhaps, the Schism Act of 1714, against nonconformist education, which had been a pet project of high tories. Subsequently, he gave further evidence of traditional churchmanship. In 1717 he protested in person to George I against proposals to repeal the Occasional Conformity Act and rallied episcopal opposition. The following year he was drawn into the controversy that followed Bishop Hoadly's notoriously Erastian sermon at the Chapel Royal. Nicolson was invoked by one anti-Hoadleian writer as a witness to the fact that the original sermon had been more extreme than the printed version; then he himself claimed in a pamphlet, *A Collection of Papers Scattered Lately about the Town … with some Remarks upon them* (1717), that Hoadly had modified his text on the advice of Bishop White Kennett. The episode damaged not only Nicolson's friendship with Kennett but his entire reputation. It was a low point in his career. His wife had died in 1712, and he had a large family to support from what was still only a moderate income. For once in his life this usually robust character fell prey to depression.

Bishop of Derry, 1718–1727 Thus when Nicolson was offered in March 1718 translation to the more lucrative Irish diocese of Derry, he was willing to accept, even though it cost him his almoner's place and removed him from the centre of the political stage. As far as the ministry was concerned, this move marginalized one of the most trenchant critics of its ecclesiastical policy, who even after receiving notification of his appointment was willing to vote against the administration on an issue (the Bristol Workhouse Bill) with implications for the maintenance of the Anglican monopoly of public office. Archbishop Wake of Canterbury, who had worked alongside him since 1714 in seeking to restrain the anti-clerical elements in the whig party, lamented that he had, in a manner of speaking, lost his right hand with Nicolson's departure. The new bishop of Derry visited his diocese for the first time in the summer of 1718 before returning to Carlisle to wind up his affairs. In May 1719 he arrived in Ireland to settle permanently, one of the conditions of his appointment having been that he reside.

Nicolson threw himself into his new role, putting aside any bitterness he might have felt at suffering a form of political and intellectual exile. The diocese contained a large and assertive body of protestant dissenters: Presbyterians of Scottish extraction, whose ethnic and religious cohesion made them far more formidable than English nonconformists. The Church of Ireland itself was also poorly endowed. Nicolson, as ever, proved himself an active and energetic prelate, despite age and increasing infirmity. He continued his determined opposition to dissent, and in the Irish parliament was loud in defence of the sacramental test and in denunciation of any proposed toleration for Presbyterians. At the same time he was a keen advocate of the implementation, and indeed the reinforcement, of the penal code against Catholics. But for all these iron convictions and for all his bluster, Nicolson showed himself to be, in his private correspondence, capable of sympathy for the economic deprivation of Irish people, Presbyterian and Catholic no less than Anglican. On 'national' questions he was always a prominent defender of English interests against the demands of 'patriot' politicians. In the celebrated case of *Annesley* v. *Sherlock* (1717–19), which raised the issue of the jurisdictional autonomy of the Irish upper house, he argued against maintaining the rights of the Dublin parliament against Westminster. He thus became a principal object of attacks from the 'Irish party' among the bishops, and in particular was accused by his political enemies of nepotism. But, unlike other English appointees to Irish sees, he could never be denounced as an absentee, and as years passed he grew fond of his adopted country and appreciated more clearly the difficulties under which the Irish economy laboured.

On the death of Archbishop Lindsay of Armagh in 1724 Nicolson was considered a possible successor, while he himself recommended his friend Henry Downes, bishop of Killala. Neither was appointed, but in January 1727 Nicolson did find himself nominated to the vacant archbishopric of Cashel. Although to accept the offer would have meant a financial loss, he agreed to go in order that Downes (who himself had a large family to provide for) might succeed him in Derry. Fate intervened, however, and on 14 February Nicolson suffered a fatal apoplectic fit 'as he sat in his chair in his study' (*Remarks*, 9.281). He was buried in the cathedral at Derry. His eldest son, Joseph, chancellor of the diocese of Lincoln, followed him to the grave in the same year. The other surviving son, John, whom he had previously provided with a living in Ireland, inherited his library and 'museum'. As well as his multifarious published works, Nicolson left a large collection of diaries, notebooks, and private papers. The diaries, which cover the periods 1684–5, 1690, and 1700–25, include the best surviving record of debates and proceedings in the House of Lords in the reign of Queen Anne, and from a historical point of view probably constitute his most valuable legacy.   D. W. HAYTON

Sources F. G. James, *North country bishop: a biography of William Nicolson* (1956) · *The London diaries of William Nicolson, bishop of Carlisle, 1702–1718*, ed. C. Jones and G. Holmes (1985) · P. J. Dunn, 'The political and ecclesiastical activities of William Nicolson, bishop of Carlisle, 1702–1718', MA diss., U. Lond., 1931 · 'Bishop Nicolson's diaries', ed. Bishop of Barrow-in-Furness and others, *Transactions of the Cumberland and Westmorland Antiquarian and Archaeological Society*, new ser., 1 (1901), 6–48; 2 (1902), 156–230; 3 (1903), 1–58; 4 (1904), 1–70; 5 (1905), 1–31; 35 (1935), 80–145; 46 (1946), 192–222; 50 (1950), 114–29 · BL, Add. MS 34265 · J. Nichols, ed., *Letters on various subjects … to and from William Nicolson*, 2 vols. (1809) · W. Nicolson, *A sermon preached in the cathedral church of Carlisle, on Sunday Feb. 15 1684/5* (1685) · W. Nicolson, *A sermon preached before the Rt. Honble the lords spiritual and temporal in the collegiate church of Westminster … 31 Jan. 1702* (1702) · W. Nicolson, *The blessings of the sixth year* (1707) [sermon preached before the queen at St James's Chapel, 8 March 1706/7] · J. Nicolson and R. Burn, *History and antiquities of Westmorland and Cumberland*, 2 vols. (1777) · C. R. Hudleston and R. S. Boumphrey, *Cumberland families and heraldry*, Cumberland and Westmorland Antiquarian and Archaeological Society, extra ser., 23 (1978) · Christ Church Oxf., Wake MSS · *The diary of Ralph Thoresby*, ed. J. Hunter, 2 vols. (1830) · *Walker rev.* · G. V. Bennett, *The tory crisis in church and state, 1688–1730: the career of Francis Atterbury, bishop of Rochester* (1975) · G. V. Bennett, *White Kennett, 1660–1728, bishop of Peterborough* (1957) · R. Mant, *History of the Church of Ireland* (1840) · P. McNally, '"Irish and English interests": national conflict within the Church of Ireland episcopate in the reign of George I', *Irish Historical Studies*, 29 (1994–5), 295–314 · Foster, *Alum. Oxon.* · *Remarks and collections of Thomas Hearne*, ed. C. E. Doble and others, 11 vols., OHS, 2, 7, 13, 34, 42–3, 48, 50, 65, 67, 72 (1885–1921)

Archives BL, corresp., Add. MS 34265 · Bodl. Oxf., collections and notes, incl. plan for his book on Northumbria · Bodl. Oxf., collections relating to his *English Historical Library* · Bodl. Oxf., corresp. · Chapter House Library, Carlisle · HLRO, diaries [photocopies] · priv. coll., diary · PRO NIre., diaries, almanacs, and accounts [copies] · Queen's College, Oxford, travel journal · TCD, commonplace book, MS. 716 · Tullie House Library, Carlisle, diaries and papers · U. Edin. L., adversaria for his *Scottish Historical Library* | Bodl. Oxf., letters to Arthur Charlett · Bodl. Oxf., MSS Rawl. · Bodl. Oxf., MSS Tanner · Christ Church Oxf., letters to William Wake [copies in BL, Add. MS 6116 and V&A NAL] · LPL, corresp. with David Wilkins · TCD, corresp. with William King · W. Yorks. AS, Leeds, Yorkshire Archaeological Society, letters to Ralph Thoresby

Likenesses W. Miln, portrait, 1891 (after unknown artist, *c.*1715–1720), Queen's College, Oxford [*see illus.*] · portrait (after oils, Queen's College, Oxford), repro. in James, *North country bishop*, frontispiece

Wealth at death property in Cumberland, books, and collection of 'antiquities' to second son, John, and £1000 to each of surviving six children: James, *North country bishop*, 278–9; copy of will at NL Ire., MS D/27164

Nield, Sir William Alan (1913–1994), civil servant, was born on 21 September 1913 at 5 Lorland Road, Stockport, Cheshire, the third and youngest son of William Herbert Nield (d. 1946), rope coupling manufacturer and cotton mill manager, and his wife, Ada, *née* Byram (d. 1946/7). He was educated at Stockport grammar school (1926–32) and St Edmund Hall, Oxford (1932–6). After a year reading modern languages, notably German, he switched to philosophy, politics, and economics (PPE), and took a first-class degree. He had been influenced by seeing at first hand the effects of the great depression in Lancashire, where the cotton industry collapsed, and at Oxford he became chairman of the Labour Club and secretary of the union. He played lacrosse for the university. He also met Gwyneth Marion Davies (1913–1994), the daughter of William Henry Davies, a Welsh Baptist minister. She was also reading PPE, at St Hilda's College. They married on 6 March 1937 and after the war had four children.

In 1936 Nield visited Germany, where he saw Hitler's war machine. In 1937 he joined the Labour Party's research and policy department, concentrating on finance, trade, and defence. He left in June 1939, believing in a more activist foreign policy, and became editor of the independent *K-H Newsletter* service. Before war was declared, he joined the Royal Air Force to train as a pilot. In September 1940 he was sent to Canada to serve with the Royal Canadian Air Force. When he returned to Britain he worked in intelligence (he was mentioned in dispatches in 1944) and served with the Allied Control Commission for Germany. There the sight of a concentration camp and other atrocities intensified his belief in the need for vigilance to preserve human values.

In 1946 Nield was demobilized as a wing commander and joined the civil service. Except for a brief period in the Treasury, from 1947 to 1949, he served in the Ministry of Food and its successor the Ministry of Agriculture, Fisheries and Food until 1964, becoming an under-secretary in 1959. In 1963 he worked on the unsuccessful application for UK entry to the European Community. In the following year he was dismayed to see the UK left outside the door while the European Community and the United States made the final decisions in the Kennedy round of negotiations on the General Agreement on Tariffs and Trade.

It was between 1964 and 1976 that Nield served the state most conspicuously. He was a key figure as under-secretary (1964–5) and deputy under-secretary of state (1965–6) in the Department of Economic Affairs (DEA) under George Brown and then a deputy secretary at the Cabinet Office (1966–8). This was the period when the DEA was set up to be in 'creative tension' with the Treasury. Nield was well suited to sustain such a role. He had passionate views about the integrity of the public service, the importance of manufacturing industry, and the need for Britain to join the European Community. He believed in telling ministers what they needed to know, not what they wanted to know. He lived his official life on the edge. But by the time he became the permanent under-secretary of state of the DEA in 1968 the battle with the Treasury had been lost and the DEA was disbanded in 1969. He was made CB in 1966 and KCB in 1968.

Nield returned to the Cabinet Office in 1969 as permanent secretary in charge of economic affairs, in particular the reopening of negotiations to join Europe. From October 1969 he was the senior official briefing the negotiating team in Brussels and he led the preparation of the 1971 white paper which set out the choice facing the country and the case for membership. A national referendum in 1975 accepted the conclusion. For his work he was made GCMG in 1972.

In 1971 Rolls Royce went into receivership, ruined by the expense of developing the RB211 aero engine for the Lockheed airbus. Nield fought to persuade Whitehall to save the country's aero-engine business. He led the delegation which went to the United States and renegotiated the contract with Lockheed. The government established Rolls-Royce (1971) Ltd to take over the RB211 and the UK continued to build aero-engines.

In 1972 there was constitutional crisis and disorder in Northern Ireland and the government assumed direct rule. Nield was sent as permanent secretary to construct a new department, the Northern Ireland Office, under William Whitelaw as secretary of state, and to remodel civil government and establish working relations with local officials and community leaders. He was the government's adviser while it laid down the main themes of direct rule, notably a certain neutrality about the future of Northern Ireland, and an insistence on a more widely acceptable form of devolution.

Nield retired from the civil service in 1973. At the government's request he served as deputy chairman of Rolls-Royce (1971) Ltd from then until 1976. He and his wife devoted much energy to their large garden in Chesham Bois, Buckinghamshire, and to the affairs of their Oxford colleges. He was the president of the St Edmund Hall Association from 1981 to 1983 and was the driving force behind a major appeal for funds. He was elected an honorary fellow in 1989. Lady Nield was similarly concerned with St Hilda's. She died on 24 August 1994, and he died twenty days later, on 13 September, at Stoke Mandeville Hospital, near Aylesbury, Buckinghamshire, of cancer of the stomach. He was cremated at the Chilterns crematorium, Amersham, on 21 September. He was survived by his two sons and two daughters. A service of thanksgiving was held in memory of him and Lady Nield in the chapel of St Faith, St Paul's Cathedral, London, on 8 November 1994, and a garden was established at St Hilda's College, Oxford, in their memory.   ARTHUR GREEN

Sources *The Times* (20 Sept 1994) · *WWW* · *St Edmund Hall Magazine* (1994–5) · private information (2004) [Lady Andrews; Michael Nield] · b. cert. · m. cert. · d. cert.
Likenesses photograph, repro. in *The Times*
Wealth at death £395,559: probate, 8 June 1995, *CGPLA Eng. & Wales*

Niemann, Edmund John (1813–1876), landscape painter, was born at Islington, London. His father, John Diederich Niemann, a native of Minden in Westphalia, was a member of Lloyd's, and the young Niemann entered that establishment as a clerk at the age of thirteen. In 1839, however, a love of painting induced him to adopt art as a profession. He took up residence at High Wycombe in Buckinghamshire, and remained there until 1848, when he returned to London to be secretary of the Free Exhibition (later the Portland Gallery) held in the Chinese Gallery at Hyde Park Corner. He began to exhibit at the Royal Academy in 1844, when he sent an oil painting, *On the Thames, Near Great Marlow*, and a drawing, *The Lime Kiln at Cove's End, Wooburn, Bucks*. He continued to exhibit at the Royal Academy until 1872; but more often his works appeared at the British Institution and the Society of British Artists, as well as at Manchester, Liverpool, and other provincial exhibitions.

Niemann's pictures, some of which are large, illustrate every phase of nature. They show great versatility, but have been described as at once dextrous and depressing. The scenery of the Thames and of the Swale, near Richmond in Yorkshire, often furnished him with subject matter. One of his best and largest works was *A Quiet Shot*, afterwards called *Deer Stalking in the Highlands*, exhibited at the British Institution in 1861. Among others may be named *Clifton*, 1847; *The Thames at Maidenhead* and *The*

Thames Near Marlow, 1848; *Kilns in Derbyshire*, 1849; *Troopers Crossing a Moss*, 1852; *Norwich*, 1853; *The High Level Bridge, Newcastle*, 1863; *Bristol Floating Harbour*, 1864; *Hampstead Heath*, 1865; and *Scarborough*, 1872. Niemann also painted occasional marine pictures, executed in a rather solid style, such as *A Paddle Frigate and Ships of the Line at Spithead* (1855). He suffered much from ill health during the last few years of his life, and there is a consequent falling off in his later works.

Niemann married Caroline Matilda with whom he had at least six children, five of whom were baptized at St Pancras on 30 October 1861. His son Edward H. Niemann, also an exhibiting landscape painter, worked in a similar style and his paintings are sometimes mistaken for those of his father. Niemann died of apoplexy, at his home, The Glebe, Brixton Hill, London, on 15 April 1876. Many of his works were exhibited at the opening of the Nottingham Museum and Art Galleries in 1878. The Victoria and Albert Museum has a landscape by him, *Amongst the Rushes*, and four drawings in watercolours. *A View on the Thames Near Maidenhead* is in the Walker Art Gallery, Liverpool.

R. E. Graves, rev. Mark Pottle

Sources *Art Journal*, 38 (1876), 203 · *The Times* (18 April 1876) · Mallalieu, *Watercolour artists*, vol. 1 · Wood, *Vic. painters*, 2nd edn · S. H. Pavière, *A dictionary of British sporting painters* (1965) · R. Parkinson, ed., *Catalogue of British oil paintings, 1820–1860* (1990) [catalogue of V&A] · Bryan, *Painters* (1903–5) · *The exhibition of the Royal Academy* (1844–72) [exhibition catalogues] · *Catalogue of the works of British artists in the gallery of the British Institution* (1848–63) [exhibition catalogues] · exhibition catalogues (1844–63) [Society of British Artists] · G. H. Shepherd, *Critical catalogue of some of the principal pictures painted by the late Edmund J. Niemann* (1890) · IGI
Likenesses E. H. Corbould, oils, Castle Museum, Nottingham

Niemeyer, Sir Otto Ernst (1883–1971), civil servant and banker, was born in Streatham, London, on 23 November 1883, the eldest of three children and only surviving son of Ernst August Wilhelm Niemeyer, a merchant of Hanover who emigrated to Liverpool in 1870, moved to London in 1882, and became a naturalized British subject, and his wife, Ethel, daughter of Roderick Rayner of J. H. Rayner & Co., Liverpool, west African merchants. He was educated at St Paul's School and Balliol College, Oxford, where he obtained first-class honours in both classical honour moderations (1904) and *literae humaniores* (1906). In 1906 he won first place in the civil service examination, beating J. M. Keynes, and was immediately posted to the Treasury. In 1910 he married a distant cousin, Sophie Charlotte Benedicte, daughter of Dr Theodor Niemeyer, of Hildesheim. They had a daughter and three sons, one of whom was killed on active service in 1943.

Niemeyer's progress in the Treasury was rapid. After the major reorganization which divided the Treasury into finance, supply, and establishments departments in 1919, he became deputy controller of finance in 1920, succeeding Basil Blackett as controller two years later. As controller he was the principal adviser to the chancellor of the exchequer on all financial matters, including taxation and debt management and domestic and international

Sir Otto Ernst Niemeyer (1883–1971), by Lafayette, 1927

monetary policy. According to his deputy controller, he was, with John Bradbury,

> the outstanding Treasury official of the post-war years. Whereas Bradbury had a more ingenious mind, and could always be relied upon to prepare three alternative methods of dealing with a problem, Niemeyer would have only one solution but that one which would go straight to the heart of the problem. (Leith-Ross, 106)

Taking Blackett's place on the financial committee of the League of Nations, he immediately played a vital role in Vienna in implementing the league's reconstruction plan for Austria; even as a Treasury official he became 'internationally important' for his work for the league, in which he worked closely with the governor of the Bank of England, Montagu Norman (Sayers, 162–70). Norman 'liked the straightforward, the downright', and that 'he found and liked in Niemeyer' (Jacobsson, 120).

In the controversial decision to return the pound sterling to gold at the pre-war parity in April 1925, it is 'clear that the decision was taken by the Chancellor (Churchill) … and that the most decisive advice was that of a Treasury official (Niemeyer)' (Sayers, 134). Niemeyer had no doubt that Britain should return to the gold standard, as a safeguard against inflation and as the best means to British prosperity. 'No one would advocate such a return', he told Churchill, 'if he believed that in the long run the effect on trade would be adverse' (Moggridge, 68). Churchill used Niemeyer's arguments to defend his decision, though he came to regret it and resented what Niemeyer and Norman had persuaded him to do. Niemeyer, on the other hand, objected to the abandonment of the gold standard in September 1931.

In 1927 Niemeyer unexpectedly resigned from the Treasury, aged only forty-four and near the top of the tree. He may have felt at a dead end in the Treasury, where he was unlikely to succeed the permanent secretary, Warren Fisher, only four years his senior. Although he found his job 'as interesting … as any in Europe' he told Blackett he 'could not refuse' an offer from Norman to join the Bank of England (O'Halpin, 36). There he could continue the work on European reconstruction which he had begun in 1922 and help to build up the international side of the bank. His first overseas assignment was to New York to discuss the international financial situation early in 1928. In 1930 he was sent on a mission to Australia. Preaching the virtues of balanced budgets and central banks independent of government he was not warmly received, but he was invited to go on to New Zealand before he returned to London. Later missions to Brazil (1931), Argentina (1933), India (1936), and China (1941) were more successful. In Europe, as well as chairing the financial committee of the League of Nations until 1937 and representing the bank on the Council of Foreign Bondholders from 1935 until 1966, he became a director of the Bank for International Settlements (BIS) in 1932, chairman (1937–40), and vice-chairman until 1964. Throughout this long period he regularly accompanied the governor to the monthly board meetings in Basel, providing continuity and helping to ensure the survival of the BIS.

Niemeyer was also active in the bank's efforts in the 1930s to assist various depressed industries in Britain, notably in forming the Agricultural Mortgage Corporation and the Lancashire Cotton Corporation. In 1938 Norman took extraordinary steps to have Niemeyer and Cameron Cobbold elected to the court of the bank as the first two executive directors. During the Second World War Niemeyer's service for the bank was as varied as it had been before the war: on the outbreak of war he was sent to Washington, and in July 1940 he was transferred to Ottawa in case the bank and the government should have to leave Britain. In 1943, when Norman set up a committee on post-war domestic finance, he appointed Niemeyer chairman. When Norman had to retire in 1944, 'Only one name within the Bank was half-heartedly considered—Niemeyer—but only to be rejected because of unacceptability to the Prime Minister', Winston Churchill (Sayers, 653–4).

According to Cobbold:

> Niemeyer combined to an unusual degree a first-class intellect with practical common sense and judgment. He had complete integrity, held strong views, particularly about sound money, and was not easily shaken. He could be an outspoken critic, but his criticisms were always softened by personal charm and an innate simplicity. His rare compliments were the more appreciated for their rarity. Montagu Norman, himself fastidious in dress and appearance, and a great admirer of Niemeyer, always teased him about his untidiness and unwillingness to 'smarten himself up'. (*DNB*)

When Cobbold became governor in March 1949, Niemeyer retired as executive director, though staying on the court until 1952, and concentrated on his directorship of the BIS. He 'remained available as an active adviser' on monetary policy (Fforde, 372). Cobbold, like Norman, frequently assigned him to chair special committees—almost immediately one on the sterling-dollar exchange rate. Still a staunch supporter of fixed exchange rates, Niemeyer was strongly opposed to a devaluation of the pound. He was one of the group of senior colleagues Cobbold always consulted on interest rate policy.

Outside the bank Niemeyer had helped to set up the National Council for Mental Health, chairing the Provisional National Council (1943–6). He was one of the long-serving lay leaders of the London School of Economics, as chairman of its court of governors (1941–57) and a governor until 1965. He was also a governor of his old school and of Marlborough College. He had been appointed CB in 1921, KCB in 1924, and GBE in 1927. He died at his home, Nash House, Lindfield, Sussex, on 6 February 1971.

SUSAN HOWSON

Sources DNB · H. Clay, *Lord Norman* (1957) · R. Dahrendorf, *LSE: a history of the London School of Economics and Political Science, 1895–1995* (1995) · J. Fforde, *The Bank of England and public policy, 1941–1958* (1992) · P. J. Grigg, *Prejudice and judgment* (1948) · S. Howson, *Domestic monetary management in Britain, 1919–38* (1975) · S. Howson, *British monetary policy, 1945–51* (1993) · E. E. Jacobsson, *A life for sound money: Per Jacobsson, his biography* (1979) · F. Leith-Ross, *Money talks* (1968) · D. E. Moggridge, *British monetary policy, 1924–1931: the Norman conquest of $4.86* (1972) · E. O'Halpin, *Head of the civil service: a study of Sir Warren Fisher* (1989) · G. C. Peden, *The treasury and British public policy, 1906–1959* (2000) · R. S. Sayers, *The Bank of England, 1891–1944* (1976)
Archives Bank of England, London, archive, papers, mainly as adviser and director of Bank of England, OV9 · PRO, papers, T 176 | Bank of England, London, archive, chief cashier's files, C40 · Bank of England, London, archive, governor's files, G1 · BL OIOC, letters to Sir Basil Blackett, MS Eur. E 397 · PRO, chancellor of exchequer's files, T 171–172 · PRO, Hopkins MSS, T 175 · PRO, Leith-Ross MSS, T 188
Likenesses Lafayette, photograph, 1927, NPG [*see illus.*] · W. Stoneman, photograph, 1937, NPG; repro. in Fforde, *Bank of England*, 337
Wealth at death £28,686: probate, 5 May 1971, *CGPLA Eng. & Wales*

Nieto, David (1654–1728), rabbi and scholar, was born in Venice on 18 January 1654, the son of Phineas or Pinchas Nieto. He studied medicine in Padua, and then functioned as a *dayan* (religious judge), preacher, and physician in Leghorn. By 1687 he had married Sara (1653–1741). They had three sons, including Isaac, who was born in Leghorn on 15 September 1687, and Moses.

In 1701 Nieto was called to London as *haham* of the Spanish and Portuguese Jewish congregation which that year moved to the newly built Bevis Marks Synagogue. Here he not only assumed leadership of the Sephardi community, with whom he founded an orphan asylum, Shaar Or ve-Avi Hayettomim ('gate of light and father of orphans'), in 1703 and Bikur Holim ('society for visiting the sick') in 1709, but also wrote numerous scholarly works and achieved general celebrity through his engagement in philosophical controversy of the day. On arrival Nieto lacked proper

English and an intellectual understanding of English society, but he quickly entered into discussions of the relationship of science and religion which had been stimulated by the work of Isaac Newton. Like Christian advocates of Newtonian science, he rejected both Aristotelianism and the mechanistic and potentially atheistic worldviews of Thomas Hobbes and René Descartes. Like Samuel Clarke, he believed that there could be no separation between God and his creation. The recent inventions of the barometer, thermometer, and telescope could not be explained merely as scientific discovery and required theological explanations of divine providence, while Judaism had to be justified in the language of science.

Nieto's first work, *Pascalogia*, written in his native Italian, demonstrated his preoccupation with astronomy and calendration, and elaborated on the discrepancies between the Jewish calendar for passover and that of the Greek and Latin churches for Easter. Written in 1693, it was printed in London in 1702, but published that year in Colonia with a dedication to Cardinal Francesco Maria de' Medici, so that Christians in Italy would not be prevented from reading a work by an author whose true location would instantly brand him a heretic.

In the following year Nieto became embroiled in controversy as a result of a sabbath sermon on 20 November in which he castigated the deists who regarded nature as separate from God, and explained that what deists termed as nature was really God functioning through his divine providence. Several members of his congregation apparently misunderstood his meaning. Joshua Zarfati petitioned against him, accusing him of having heretical ideas similar to Spinoza's and interpreting him as implying that nature and God were separate forces. The Bevis Marks *mahamad*, or ruling committee, rather surprisingly appealed to the attorney-general Sir Edward Northey for an opinion as to whether Zarfati might be excommunicated and whether related cases might be brought in the secular courts. When Northey replied that this was a matter of internal Jewish jurisdiction, they appealed to the rabbinical court of the Amsterdam Portuguese congregation, but this brought no decision. Annoyed that individual members could hold back the entire congregation, the *mahamad* ruled that in future no decision could be referred to Amsterdam, thus establishing their independence. Meanwhile Nieto explained his viewpoint in *De la divina providencia* (1704), and was also defended by the revered religious leader of the Portuguese Sephardic Altona congregation, the Haham Zvi, and by two other religious judges, who noted that he identified nature with God and that although he was acquainted with the mischievous theories of naturalistic philosophers he rejected them. In 1705, after mediation from members of the London Ashkenazi community, Nieto was finally exonerated from all the charges.

Nieto continued to publish. In 1705 and 1706 there appeared *Bakasoth*, or supplications for particular occasions. His most noted work, *Matteh Dan veKuzari helek sheni* ('Rod of Dan and the second Kuzari'), published in London

in 1714, was a defence of oral law, written in Hebrew and Spanish for the benefit of crypto-Jews newly arrived from the Iberian peninsula who were returning to open Judaism. Later the book was published in Italian and Yiddish. He also wrote *Sha'ar Dan*, an unfinished anthology of sayings from the Babylonian Talmud. His *Esh daat* ('Fire of the law') published in 1715, was an attack on the popular rabbi Nehemiah Hayoun, the suspected follower of the false messiah Shabetai Zvi; like his other works it was in the form of dialogues.

Nieto befriended the Portuguese crypto-Jew, physician, and philosopher Jacob de Castro Sarmento and the poet Daniel Lopez Laguna. He became well versed in Greek and Roman classics and in secular intellectual subjects, and although he did not learn English sufficiently well to write scholarly texts in the language he corresponded with numerous gentile theologians, philosophers, and intellectuals. He died on his seventy-fourth birthday according to the Hebrew calendar, 10 January 1728, and was buried in the Beth Holim burial-ground, London. He was eulogized by his son Isaac and by the eminent physician Isaac de Sequeyra Samuda, who composed the epitaph on his tombstone which celebrated him as theologian, sage, physician, astronomer, poet, preacher, logician, physicist, rhetorician, linguist, and historian. Isaac Nieto succeeded his father as *haham* of Bevis Marks. YITZCHAK KEREM

Sources M. Bensabat Amzalak, *David Nieto, noticia biobibliografica* (Lisbon, 1923), 9–14 · Z. H. Aschkenasi, *Rechtfertigung des Rabbi David Nieto gegen den Vorwurf in seiner Predigt Spinozas Lehre zu verbreiten* (Berlin, 1930) · D. Nieto, *Matteh Dan veKuzari helek sheni: the rod of judgment, being a supplement to the book Kuzari*, ed. L. Loewe (1845) · I. Nieto, *Sermones funebres a las deplorables memorias del muy reverendo, y doctissimo H. H. y Doctor R. David Nieto* (1728) · J. Petuchowski, *An eighteenth century defence of Jewish tradition* (New York, 1954), 14–31 · I. de Sequeyra Samuda, *Sermam funebre para as exequias dos trinta dias* (London, 1728) · I. Solomons, *David Nieto, haham of the Spanish and Portuguese Jews' congregation* (1931), 24 · D. Ruderman, *Jewish thought and scientific discovery in early modern Europe* (1995) · D. B. Ruderman, *Jewish enlightenment in an English key: Anglo-Jewry's construction of modern Jewish thought* (2000) · D. S. Katz, *The Jews in the history of England, 1485–1850* (1994)
Archives Hebrew University, Jerusalem, Jewish National and University Library, scholarly MS, 92 F 134(9)
Likenesses portrait, 1705, repro. in Solomons, *David Nieto*, 61 · portrait, 1705, repro. in Amzalak, *David Nieto*, 8 · portrait, 1726, repro. in Amzalak, *David Nieto*, following p. 12

Ní Fhoghludha, Áine (1880–1932), Irish language writer, was born in Ring, co. Waterford, on 10 November 1880, the daughter of Mícheál Ó Fhoghludha (1846–1905), headmaster in Ring school, and Eibhlín de Brún, schoolteacher. Her father was renowned for his work for the Irish language. Áine (baptized Anna Gertrude) was educated first in Ring and then at the Mercy Convent in Dungarvan. She was awarded a BA in Irish from University College, Cork. She taught initially in the Convent of Mercy secondary school in Dungarvan but also in primary schools in co. Waterford. She was a staunch supporter of Irish nationalism and it was claimed her advocacy of Irish republicanism cost her her teaching post after the Easter rising of

1916. She married Séamus Ó Néill (1892–1974), a school-teacher and member of the Irish Republican Brotherhood, on 21 June 1917 and the couple moved to Cashel in co. Tipperary. They remained childless. Séamus was interned in England after the rising and was also involved with the Irish Republican Army in Tipperary during the War of Independence. However, he did not partake in the civil war and was among the first men to join the new police force of the Irish Free State, the Garda Síochána.

Áine took occasional teaching posts after 1916 and was active in the militant nationalist organization Cumann na mBan (the Women's Council). She acted as a messenger for the IRA during the War of Independence. Her fame rests with the publication of a collection of poetry, *Idir na Fleadhanna*, first published in 1922 and reprinted in 1930, and a collection of stories for children, *Brosna*, which appeared in 1925. The book was widely used in Irish secondary schools.

Áine Ní Fhoghludha's health had not been good throughout the 1920s and she died of pneumonia in Cahirciveen in co. Kerry on 14 April 1932. She was buried in Ring, co. Waterford.   MARIA LUDDY

Sources D. Breathnach and M. Ní Mhurchú, *Beathaisnéis A Dó, 1882–1982* (1990), 105–7

Nigel (*d.* 919) is an alternative name first coined by Henry of Huntingdon for Niel, mentioned in the E text of the Anglo-Saxon Chronicle as having been slain by his brother Sihtric in 921 and therefore once thought to have been a viking king in Northumbria. However, modern writers believe that the Anglo-Saxon chronicler confused two entries in the Irish annals. The annals of Ulster for 888 record that a Sihtric, son of *Ívarr, slew his own brother. Under the year 919, the same annals state that another Sihtric, Ívarr's grandson, defeated and killed the Irish king Niáll Glúndub at the battle of Kilmashogue. Nigel is to be identified with the latter [*see* Niáll mac Áeda (*c.*869–919)].   MARIOS COSTAMBEYS

Sources *ASC*, s.a. 921 [text E] · W. M. Hennessy and B. MacCarthy, eds., *Annals of Ulster, otherwise, annals of Senat*, 4 vols. (1887–1901) · Henry, archdeacon of Huntingdon, *Historia Anglorum*, ed. D. E. Greenway, OMT (1996) · *The chronicle of Henry of Huntingdon*, ed. and trans. T. Forester (1853); facs. edn (1991)

Nigel (*c.*1100–1169), administrator and bishop of Ely, was a nephew of Roger, bishop of Salisbury. His date of birth is uncertain, but must have been about 1100. He was possibly, but not certainly, the brother of *Alexander who became bishop of Lincoln. Nigel himself had at least two sons, one obscure, called William the Englishman, the other very prominent in Henry II's regime, *Richard fitz Nigel, born *c.*1130. Like Alexander, Nigel was a pupil of Anselm of Laon. He attended the consecration of Bishop Bernard of St David's (*d.* 1148) at Westminster in September 1115. It is uncertain when he took clerical orders, but he held a prebend of St Paul's Cathedral at Chiswick, and was also an archdeacon in his uncle's diocese of Salisbury. Nigel first appears as a witness to a royal charter in 1126, and in total witnessed over thirty of Henry I's surviving charters. The importance of his link to Roger of Salisbury

is emphasized by the fact that until 1133 such charters always referred to him as 'nephew of the bishop'. However, Nigel was reaching an administrative prominence of his own, and it is likely that from the mid-1120s he was Henry I's treasurer. The pipe roll of 1130 records Nigel receiving treasure in Normandy with Osbert de Pont de l'Arche, and in May 1131 at Rouen he witnessed a papal letter as 'Nigel the treasurer' (*Reg. RAN*, 2, no. 1691 n.). The same pipe roll also gives some indication of the extent and distribution of his lands: he was pardoned a total of 66s. in Wiltshire, 30s. in Huntingdonshire, 22s. in Hampshire, 10s. in Berkshire, 6s. 8d. in Essex, and 6s. in Middlesex. A document from the second half of the 1130s concerning the king's household, the *Constitutio domus regis*, was quite possibly written for, or even by, Nigel.

Like many of Henry I's 'new' men, Nigel was well rewarded, and in accordance with Henry's wishes he was elected bishop of Ely in 1133, and consecrated at Lambeth by the archbishop of Canterbury on 1 October. Secular business took him back to London almost immediately, but his early years as bishop were not without their benefits for Ely. As a first step to the resumption of any lands that had previously been wrongfully alienated he ordered a description to be made of the possessions of the church. With backing from the pope, Henry I, and Stephen he succeeded in regaining certain lands. In general, however, the entrusting of the administration of the bishopric to a former monk of Glastonbury called Ranulf was not successful. He reputedly dispersed rather than reassembled the church's possessions and quarrelled heatedly with the monks for two years up to 1137. Ranulf's fall, however, came not through the internal affairs of the monastery, but rather through a plot of potentially national consequence. Its details are somewhat uncertain, but according to Orderic Vitalis, Ranulf and his collaborators planned that all Normans should be killed and the government of the realm handed over to the Scots. Nigel learnt of the conspiracy, and passed on the information to other prelates and nobles, and to royal officials. Ranulf fled and Nigel was reconciled with his monks.

As his behaviour in relation to the conspiracy shows, Nigel was loyal to Stephen early in his reign. Like his uncle Roger he had accepted the king's succession, and, according to William of Malmesbury, Roger obtained the chancellorship for Alexander and the treasurership for Nigel. In February 1136 Nigel was with Stephen in the north, where he witnessed charters at York and Durham, and on his return south he witnessed the king's Oxford charter in April. During 1137 he was in Normandy with the king, and witnessed a charter at Rouen. However, the power of Nigel and his kinsmen made them feared by Stephen and unpopular for their influence over the king, with rivals, notably the Beaumont family, who accused them of plotting in favour of Henry I's daughter, the Empress Matilda. The *Gesta Stephani* described Nigel, together with Alexander, bishop of Lincoln, as:

> men who loved display and were rash in their reckless presumption … disregarding the holy and simple manner of life that befits a Christian priest they devoted themselves so

utterly to warfare and the vanities of this world that whenever they attended court by appointment they … aroused general astonishment on account of the extraordinary concourse of knights by which they were surrounded on every side. (*Gesta Stephani*, 72)

At the king's court in Oxford on 24 June 1139 Roger and Alexander were arrested, but Nigel, who had not yet reached court, succeeded in fleeing to his uncle's castle at Devizes. Through ostentatiously harsh treatment of his kinsmen the king forced Nigel to surrender. He left for Ely, having, according to Orderic, been declared a public enemy of the whole country. Nigel fortified his position, but was attacked first by a royal force and then, at the end of 1139, by the king in person. The assault, using boats and a specially constructed bridge, proved successful. Nigel fled by night with only three companions and succeeded in reaching the empress, who was then at Gloucester. He may at this stage have sent a delegation to Rome to complain of his expulsion, and on 5 October 1140 Innocent II issued a bull ordering his restoration. Meanwhile the see was in the custody possibly first of Aubrey de Vere, and then from May 1140 of Geoffrey de Mandeville and perhaps of the earl of Pembroke.

Nigel's position was strengthened by Stephen's capture at Lincoln on 2 February 1141. On 3 March he was one of the people present at the empress's ceremonial procession in Winchester Cathedral. He witnessed her charters at Oxford in late March, at St Albans probably in June, at Westminster at midsummer, at Oxford again in late July or early August, and at Reading. The empress, moreover, restored him to his see, but Stephen's release from captivity in November 1141 marked another shift in fortunes. The king struck back by sending against Nigel the earl of Pembroke and Geoffrey de Mandeville, now earl of Essex. Afraid, Nigel sent to the king and was received into his peace. This, however, did not mark the end of his difficulties. The events of 1143 are confused, but in March of that year he attended the king's council at London, perhaps in order to answer an appeal by a clerk named Vitalis whom Nigel had expelled from his church for simony. Soon afterwards he may have gone to join the empress, but was surprised and plundered by the king's men at Wareham. Geoffrey de Mandeville, possibly with the absent bishop's knowledge, and certainly at the request of his knights, took over the Isle of Ely as one of the centres of his rebellion against the king. Perhaps at the council in March, or perhaps at another later in the year, Nigel was also charged with alienating church lands to knights and with encouraging sedition in the realm. As a result, he appealed to Rome, but first had to take various precious treasures from his church, in return for which he gave back to the monks the vill of Hadstock, which they had long claimed. Having reached Rome, and helped by his treasure, by the archbishop of Canterbury, and by a letter of commendation from Gilbert Foliot, abbot of Gloucester, in May 1144 Nigel obtained several bulls from Pope Lucius II, which reinforced his position. Nigel then returned from Rome to Ely, and soon afterwards Geoffrey de Mandeville died. Only slowly, however, did the king and Nigel come to terms, and Stephen required a payment of £200 and the giving of Nigel's son Richard as a hostage before he restored him, through an agreement made at Ipswich. Again the raising of the money afflicted the church and again, apparently, the vill of Hadstock was in return confirmed to the monks. Nigel's part in the later stages of the reign was rather quieter. In 1147–8 he resumed his witnessing of royal charters. In 1150 he was present at a meeting of the Norfolk and Suffolk shire court specially ordered by the king, and in 1153–4 he was addressed in a royal charter concerning a grant to St Radegund's priory, Cambridge. Late in 1153 he was one of the witnesses of Stephen's charter granting the kingdom to Henry II after his death, according to the terms of the treaty of Winchester.

On 19 December 1154 Nigel attended the coronation of Henry II, and with the new reign his former prominence was restored. Even though the exchequer had not completely collapsed during Stephen's reign, it remains likely that considerable renewal was necessary. According to the *Liber Eliensis* Nigel bought the treasurership for his son, Richard, for the sum of £400, and Richard gives a highly laudatory account of Nigel in the *Dialogus de Scaccario*, written at the end of the 1170s. Richard treats him as a repository of opinion on various matters, notably the privileges of the barons of the exchequer. Nigel may indeed have had a hand in a significant element of policy making, with an insistence that previously alienated royal demesnes be restored to the king. In 1159–63 he was present at the king's court for a judicial hearing, and on 29 September 1165 he was the first named of the royal justices in whose presence a quitclaim was made at the exchequer. For his service he duly received rewards, for example enjoying *terrae datae* in Gloucestershire early in Henry II's reign.

Nigel's relations with the monks of Ely, however, remained difficult. Their disputes focused on the issue of the church's dispersed lands, and on 22 February 1156 Pope Adrian IV (*r.* 1154–9) issued a bull threatening Nigel with suspension unless within three months he restored the church's possessions to their state when he became bishop of Ely. The king's absence in France prevented full restitution, but further bulls concerning Ely's unjust losses were issued by Adrian, and related orders by the archbishop of Canterbury. Finally, at the petition of the king, archbishops, and bishops, and of John of Salisbury, Adrian lifted the threat of suspension on the condition that Nigel swear in the presence of Archbishop Theobald (*d.* 1161) that he would strive for the restoration of Ely's lands and would alienate no others. Even then, a further scandal arose because Nigel made a married clerk sacrist of Ely, drawing upon the bishop admonition from Archbishop Thomas Becket.

On 3 June 1162 Nigel was present at Becket's consecration, and he also attended the council at Clarendon in January 1164. However, Nigel's active life was ended by paralysis, by which he was struck in either or both of autumn 1164 or spring 1166. He seems to have taken little part in the Becket dispute. A letter of Becket in 1166 names him and the bishop of Norwich as responsible for giving force to the excommunication of the earl of Norfolk, while a letter of Gilbert Foliot, probably from June of the same year, demands that Nigel seal a letter of appeal directed to the pope against Becket. The pipe roll of 1165/6 records him rendering account of £59 3s. 4d. in the matter of his promise of service concerning Wales, and that of 1167/8 payments for the aid for the marriage of the king's daughter. Nigel's last years seem to have been spent quietly at Ely, and he died on 30 May 1169. In the north chancel aisle of Ely Cathedral, an impressive mid- or late twelfth-century marble slab, depicting a large angel holding a small naked figure, may be a memorial to Nigel, although it does not bear his name and the imprecise dating cannot associate it with him for certain.

JOHN HUDSON

Sources E. O. Blake, ed., *Liber Eliensis*, CS, 3rd ser., 92 (1962) · *Pipe rolls* · R. Fitz Nigel [R. Fitzneale], *Dialogus de scaccario / The course of the exchequer*, ed. and trans. C. Johnson (1950) · Ordericus Vitalis, *Eccl. hist.* · William of Malmesbury, *The Historia novella*, ed. and trans. K. R. Potter (1955) · *Reg. RAN*, vols. 2–3 · K. R. Potter and R. H. C. Davis, eds., *Gesta Stephani*, OMT (1976) · R. C. van Caenegem, ed., *English lawsuits from William I to Richard I*, 2 vols., SeldS, 106–7 (1990–91) · *The letters of John of Salisbury*, ed. and trans. H. E. Butler and W. J. Millor, rev. C. N. L. Brooke, 2 vols., OMT (1979–86) [Lat. orig. with parallel Eng. text] · J. C. Robertson and J. B. Sheppard, eds., *Materials for the history of Thomas Becket, archbishop of Canterbury*, 7 vols., Rolls Series, 67 (1875–85) · F. Liebermann, *Einleitung in den Dialogus de scaccario* (Göttingen, 1875) · *The historical works of Gervase of Canterbury*, ed. W. Stubbs, 1: *The chronicle of the reigns of Stephen, Henry II, and Richard I*, Rolls Series, 73 (1879) · *Letters and charters of Gilbert Foliot*, ed. A. Morey and others (1967) · R. H. C. Davis, *King Stephen*, 3rd edn (1990) · H. G. Richardson and G. O. Sayles, *The governance of medieval England* (1963)
Likenesses statue, probably Ely Cathedral

Niger, Ralph (b. c.1140, d. in or before 1199?), theologian and chronicler, is of unknown origins. He became a friend of John of Salisbury, and was educated, like him, in the Parisian schools. Unlike his more distinguished compatriot, however, he did not acquire significant office or benefice, although his writings, still for the most part unpublished, reveal a man of considerable erudition in canon and civil law, biblical exegesis, and history. The details of his career can be glimpsed only intermittently from chance references. He was a pupil of Gerard Pucelle at Paris before 1165; he introduced Konrad von Wittelsbach (then archbishop-elect of Mainz) to the exiled Thomas Becket in 1164 or 1165; and he corresponded with John of Salisbury in late 1166, when he seems to have spent some time in the schools at Poitiers. By then he was a master of arts. To his later regret he held some position in Henry II's court in the late 1160s, and Gervase of Tilbury describes him as a fellow member of the court of the young King Henry (son of Henry II, crowned 14 June 1170). He was a firm supporter of Thomas Becket, and the alienation from Henry II, which prevented his return to England until after that king's death in 1189, may have been occasioned by his association with Becket's cause. He may have refused to take the anti-papal oath which Henry imposed in late 1169; or he may have supported the Young King's

rebellion in 1173–4. For whatever reason, Henry II's displeasure denied him return to England and the advancement in the English church which his talents deserved. He devoted himself to biblical scholarship, and probably taught in Paris, producing a stream of commentaries on the Old Testament, for which he sought approval from the highest authorities in the church. In 1191 collections of his works were submitted to the archbishops of Sens and Rheims, who informed the pope a year later that nothing contrary to the faith or dangerous to Christian teaching had been found in the works submitted to them.

Ralph Niger's proscription was ended by Henry II's death, and his two chronicles were probably written in England in the 1190s. His residence in England is corroborated by legal records from 1194–5, one of which concerns a prebend at Lincoln, and by a charter of King John (31 August 1199) confirming to Roger Crispus a house in London which he had formerly, as count of Mortain, granted to Master Ralph Niger. The latter document probably establishes the *terminus ante quem* for his death, despite a reference in his longer chronicle which speaks of Archbishop Hubert Walter (d. 1205) in the past tense. Although he praised the Cistercians highly there is no evidence that he was a member of the order. He was and always remained a secular clerk. What survives of his large theological output consists mainly of works of biblical commentary, but also includes a book on the four liturgical feasts dedicated to the Virgin, while his *De re militari*, written in 1187–8, provides a significant critique of the crusading movement. But only two copies of these writings are known: an eight-volume set in Lincoln Cathedral Library, from which one book was lent out (and lost) in the middle ages, and an incomplete set in the monastic library at Bury St Edmunds, from which only the *De re militari* survives, now in Pembroke College, Cambridge. These English copies lend further support to the view that he spent his final days in England; but the paucity of the survival suggests limited circulation. Knowledge of his historical works would have been equally small, had it not been for the fact that the Cistercian chronicler Ralph of Coggeshall used Niger's shorter chronicle as the starting point of his own composition. In some ways his career is similar to that of Herbert of Bosham: he was an independently minded Paris-trained clerk, shipwrecked by fortune and compelled to spend the greater part of his productive years in uncongenial exile. His bitter comments on Henry II, whom he usually could not bring himself even to name (calling him 'the king under whom St Thomas, the English martyr suffered'; *De re militari*, 206), are explained at least in part by his own experiences. Like Herbert he expressed unpopular opinions about people and events, with praise for the young King Henry and criticism of the crusading movement.

A. J. DUGGAN

Sources *Radulfi Nigri chronica: the chronicles of Ralph Niger*, ed. R. Anstruther, Caxton Society, 13 (1851) · *Radulfus Niger, De re militari et triplici via peregrinationis Ierosolimitane, 1187/1188*, ed. L. Schmugge, Beiträge zur Geschichte und Quellenkunde des Mittelalters, 6 (1977) · G. B. Flahiff, 'Deus non vult': a critic of the third crusade', *Mediaeval Studies*, 9 (1947), 162–88 · R. Pauli, 'Die chronicon des Radulphus Niger', *Nachrichten der Gesellschaft der Wissenschaften zu*

Göttingen (1880), 569–89 • 'Ex Radulfi Nigri et Radulfi Coggeshalensis chronicis', [*Ex rerum Anglicarum scriptoribus*], ed. R. Pauli and F. Liebermann, MGH Scriptores [folio], 27 (Hanover, 1885); repr. (Stuttgart, 1975), 327–43 [repr. 1975] • M. Priess, *Die politische Tätigkeit und Stellung der Cisterzienzer im Schisma von 1159–1177*, Eberings Historische Studien, 248 (1934), appx 2, 260–65, esp. 261 • G. B. Flahiff, 'Ralph Niger: an introduction to his life and works', *Mediaeval Studies*, 2 (1940), 104–26 • G. B. Flahiff, 'Ecclesiastical censorship of books in the twelfth century', *Mediaeval Studies*, 4 (1942), 1–22, esp. 1–2 • L. Schmugge, 'Thomas Becket und König Heinrich II. in der Sicht des Radulfus Niger', *Deutsches Archiv*, 32 (1976), 572–9 • *The letters of John of Salisbury*, ed. and trans. H. E. Butler and W. J. Millor, rev. C. N. L. Brooke, OMT, 2: *The later letters, 1163–1180* (1979), 198–209 [Lat. orig. with parallel Eng. text] • 'E Gervasii Tileburiensis Otiis imperialibus', [*Ex rerum Anglicarum scriptoribus*], ed. R. Pauli and F. Liebermann, MGH Scriptores [folio], 27 (Hanover, 1885), 370 • W. Holtzmann, ed., *Papsturkunden in England*, 2 (Berlin), Abhandlung der Gesellschaft der Wissenschaften zu Göttingen, 3rd ser., 14–15 (1935–6), 453–5 • F. W. Maitland, ed., *The rolls of the king's court in the reign of King Richard the First, AD 1194–1195*, PRSoc., 14 (1891), 88 • H. Kantorowicz and B. Smalley, 'An English theologian's view of Roman law: Pepo, Irnerius, Ralph Niger', *Mediaeval and Renaissance Studies*, 1 (1941), 237–52, esp. 244–52 • A. L. Gabriel, *Garlandia—studies in the history of the medieval university* (1969), 1–37, esp. 24 • F. Palgrave, ed., *Rotuli curiae regis: rolls and records of the court held before the king's justiciars or justices*, 2 vols., RC, 27 (1835), i, 87

Archives Bibliothèque Nationale, Paris, MS Lat. 15076 • BL, Cotton MS Cleopatra C.x • BL, Cotton MSS Vespasian D.x, Royal 13.A.xii • CCC Cam., MS 343, fols. 1v–18v • College of Heralds, London, MS 11 • Lincoln Cathedral, dean and chapter library, MSS 15, 23–7 • Pembroke Cam., MS 27 • TCD, MS E.iv.24

Niger, Roger [Roger le Noir, Roger de Bileye] (*d.* 1241), bishop of London, is occasionally called 'de Bileye', suggesting that he came from Beeleigh in Essex. The son of parents named Ralph and Margery (for whom he founded a chantry in St Paul's Cathedral), he was undoubtedly university-educated, a *magister* with a reputation as a theologian. But although his friendship with Edmund of Abingdon (*d.* 1240) might suggest that he was a graduate of Oxford, it seems more likely that he attended Paris University. He became prebendary of Ealdland *c.*1212, and archdeacon of Colchester certainly by 27 November 1218, possibly as early as 1216. He was elected bishop of London in 1228, his election received the royal assent on 27 April 1229, when the temporalities were restored, and he was consecrated on 10 June 1229. His election to the bishopric was one of a group of similar elections at this stage of Henry III's reign, in which bishops were elected from within the chapters over which they were to preside, and in which there are few signs of royal or other outside pressure being applied.

In his career as bishop, Roger Niger certainly showed decided independence of the crown, and a preparedness to uphold the rights of the church against Henry III. He twice, in September 1232 and October 1233, forced the king to restore Hubert de Burgh (*d.* 1243) to sanctuary, after de Burgh had been dragged out by royal agents. In 1233, when he was returning from the continent, he coincided at the port of Dover with Walter Mauclerk, bishop of Carlisle (*d.* 1248), who had just been taken off the ship in which he was about to cross the channel, on the grounds that he lacked royal licence to depart. Niger promptly

excommunicated those responsible, sought out the king at Hereford, and renewed the sentence in Henry's presence, ignoring the king's grumbles and prohibitions. However, it would be wrong to imply that his relationship with the crown was consistently bad. In 1231 he was summoned to Oxford, together with the other bishops of the province of Canterbury, to discuss the revolt in Wales. In 1235 he was involved in the settlement of the dispute between Earl Warenne and the prior of Cluny over the nomination and institution of the prior of Lewes. In 1236 Walter de Burgh was ordered not to allow a plea about the burial place of the chapel of Romford, Essex, to proceed 'before the king has had a discussion about it with the bishop of London' (*Close Rolls*, 3.314).

On occasion Henry III took care to preserve Niger's rights. In 1234 he ordered that a suspected killer should be handed over to the bishop or his official if they so requested, and in 1237 the constable of the Tower of London was instructed to hand over to the bishops of London and Lincoln all the clergy involved in a riot against the papal legate Otto at Osney, but to make the Tower's prison available to the bishops for their continued incarceration if convenient. Henry also made a number of grants to Niger and did him favours. For instance, in 1232 the bishop received a grant of a Monday market at Acton, in 1235 he was pardoned 40 marks owing from the aid for the war against Richard Marshal, and in 1240 he received a gift of fifteen royal deer, which he was to be permitted to take with his own hounds. The royal bounty even continued posthumously, for in 1242 his executors were pardoned an outstanding fine of 10 marks, imposed by justices itinerant in Essex, and instructed to apply the money to keeping a lamp or candle burning at the bishop's tomb in St Paul's.

Bishop Niger did not show his concern for church rights and reform only in opposition to the claims of the crown. Although he was a devoted friend of the Franciscans, he nevertheless aspired to exercise jurisdiction over them, and demanded oaths of canonical obedience. However, the response of the friars was to apply to Rome for protection, and the bull *Nimis iniqua*, of 21 August 1231, gave them exemption from episcopal control not just in London but throughout Christendom. In the following year Niger was forced to go to Rome himself, to answer charges of collusion in attacks on Italian clergy in England (even though he had excommunicated the malefactors responsible). He succeeded in proving his innocence, though only after a heavy outlay. On his way there he was robbed by citizens of Parma, but this was later to prove advantageous for St Paul's, for the Parmesans, attributing their tribulations in their war against Frederick II (*r.* 1220–50) to the curse which the bishop of London had laid upon them after the theft, in 1247–8 vowed to contribute a sum equivalent to the proceeds of the robbery to the cathedral building fund. Niger was also occasionally employed as a papal agent. In 1229 he was one of those commissioned to select an archbishop for Dublin, and in 1235 was charged with the examination of John of Hertford, newly elected abbot of St Albans, whom he subsequently blessed.

An active diocesan administrator, Roger Niger issued a

set of statutes for the London archdeaconry, which, as his own introductory letter makes clear, were principally designed to deal with the distinctive problems created by the size and density of population of the city. Additionally, the statutes attempted to encourage the communal life of the London clergy, by provisions for regular business meetings between them, and administration of funds for the common good. It is perhaps possible to detect a collegiate atmosphere in the instruction that fines for non-attendance at meetings should be paid in wine. Niger was also an enthusiastic defender of the rights and privileges of his diocese. In 1225, while still archdeacon of Colchester, he clashed with Henry III over the exemptions claimed by the collegiate church of St Martin's-le-Grand, a royal peculiar, and demanded procurations from its dean, in spite of being repeatedly urged by the king not to do so. As a result Henry forbade the judges in court Christian to proceed with the ensuing litigation, and appealed to the pope. It is clear that St Martin's did eventually succeed in establishing its exempt status. But Niger was more successful in the case of St Leonard's, a dependent chapel of St Martin's, and secured the subjection of the church, its priest, and its parishioners to the archdeacon and bishop of London.

Niger also reinforced the rights of the dean and chapter of St Paul's, not only confirming the grants of preceding bishops of London, but granting the right to issue sentences of interdict and excommunication against any who should improperly withhold their property and rents, and endorsing the validity of such sentences within his diocese. He set up commissions to decide disputes between St Paul's and the Essex abbeys of Walden and Colchester; their findings were generally favourable to St Paul's. At the very end of his tenure of the archdeaconry of Colchester, he left his houses on the south side of St Paul's Churchyard to his successors in the post of archdeacon, and then, as bishop, himself confirmed the grant. Very shortly afterwards he confirmed a grant for a similar purpose by Henry of Cornhill, the chancellor of the diocese. He was also a contributor to the fabric of the cathedral, and dedicated the choir on 1 October 1240.

Roger Niger died at his manor of Stepney on either 29 September or 2 October 1241. Buried in St Paul's Cathedral, he was widely revered as a saint. His heart appears to have been interred at Beeleigh, where the 'heart of St Roger' is referred to in 1249, and his tomb in the cathedral became a place of pilgrimage. One anecdote about him certainly suggests fortitude. On 6 January 1230 he was celebrating mass in the cathedral when a violent thunderstorm threw the congregation into panic and caused a mass exodus. The bishop remained steadfastly at the high altar, accompanied by a single deacon, and when those who had fled recovered their nerve and returned, calmly continued the mass. Matthew Paris describes him as a man of profound knowledge of literature, honourable and praiseworthy in every way, a devoted defender of religion, and free from every kind of pride. Furthermore, he exhibited remarkable sanctity, was a perceptive preacher and an eloquent talker, a good trencherman, and handsome. Inflated as these eulogies may be, they clearly reflect the high regard in which Roger was held.

R. M. FRANKLIN

Sources Paris, *Chron.*, vols. 3–5 · Chancery records · M. Gibbs, ed., *Early charters of the cathedral church of St Paul, London*, CS, 3rd ser., 58 (1939) · *VCH London* · F. M. Powicke and C. R. Cheney, eds., *Councils and synods with other documents relating to the English church, 1205–1313*, 1 (1964), 325–37 · M. Gibbs and J. Lang, *Bishops and reform, 1215–1272* (1934) · *Hist. U. Oxf. 1: Early Oxf. schools* · *Fasti Angl., 1066–1300*, [St Paul's, London] · *Rogeri de Wendover liber qui dicitur flores historiarum*, ed. H. G. Hewlett, 3 vols., Rolls Series, [84] (1886–9) · H. R. Luard, ed., *Flores historiarum*, 3 vols., Rolls Series, 95 (1890) · C. R. Cheney, *English bishops' chanceries, 1100–1250* (1950) · W. S. Simpson, ed., *Documents illustrating the history of St Paul's Cathedral*, CS, new ser., 26 (1880) · F. M. Powicke, *King Henry III and the Lord Edward: the community of the realm in the thirteenth century*, 2 vols. (1947) · D. Knowles [M. C. Knowles], *The religious orders in England*, 1 (1948) · *Close rolls of the reign of Henry III*, 3, PRO (1908)

Nightingale, Florence (1820–1910), reformer of Army Medical Services and of nursing organization, was born on 12 May 1820 at Villa Columbia, Florence, where her parents were on a European tour. Their other daughter, Frances Parthenope Nightingale (1819–1890) [*see* Verney, Frances Parthenope], born in Naples, had been given the classical name of her birthplace. Their father, William Edward Nightingale (1794–1874), son of William Shore, a Sheffield banker, had inherited Derbyshire estates from his uncle, Peter Nightingale, and had changed his name by royal warrant. W. E. N., as he was known to friends, was handsome and cultivated, with a reputation for wit. In 1818 he married Frances Smith (1789–1880), daughter of William Smith, a Unitarian and supporter of dissenters. Frances was the beauty of this distinguished family of five brothers and five sisters, most of whom married into prosperous, intellectual families, thus supplying the Nightingale girls with numerous relatives who were an important factor in their lives; several were later associated with Florence in her work.

Early life In 1826 William Nightingale bought Embley Park in Hampshire, and the family routine was to spend summer at Lea Hurst in Derbyshire, and winter at Embley with visits to London interspersed with visits to and from relatives. Although in private notes as an adolescent Florence railed against the empty life of her parents, and though biographers have represented Mr Nightingale as an 'amiable dilettante', he took his squirearchical duties seriously. As a dedicated educationist he supported schools on his estates at personal expense; in 1834 he stood as a whig for Andover on a distinctly radical manifesto; he was high sheriff in 1829; and he supervised the education of his daughters. Finding Florence an apt pupil he gave her a sound education in classics, philosophy, and modern and classical languages. Biographers, particularly feminists, anxious to portray Florence as the frustrated Victorian daughter, have tended to depict her mother, known as Fanny, as merely a pleasure-seeking hostess, but she attracted some of the best intellects of the day, including Lord Ashley, the editor of *The Times* John Delane, the eminent theologian Chevalier Christian Bunsen, the

Florence Nightingale (1820–1910), by Goodman, c.1857

prison architect Sir Joshua Jebb, the historian Leopold von Ranke, and many others. Florence met and enjoyed the company. In private notes she wrote 'I must overcome my desire to shine in company', but she undoubtedly did shine and enjoy it.

Although she did not inherit her mother's beauty Florence was described by Mrs Gaskell as 'tall, willowy in figure, [with] thick shortish rich brown hair, a delicate complexion, and grey eyes that are generally pensive but could be the merriest' (Cook, 1.39). Florence was a good mimic, attractive to men, and had a number of suitors; many of the men she met through her parents remained lifelong friends. Half the Nightingale Fund council was originally known to her through her parents.

In spite of these advantages Florence Nightingale was an unhappy young woman. She suffered from bouts of depression and feelings of unworthiness, and she questioned the purpose of life for the upper classes. Unlike her mother and sister, who were content to do good works on the estates, she pondered on the need for charity and the causes of poverty and unemployment. At the age of sixteen she recorded that on 7 February 1837 'God had called her to His service', though what God wanted her to do was unclear. She became interested in the mystics and studied the lives of people such as St Teresa of Avila and St John of

the Cross, and with the help of Bunsen she studied Schopenhauer and the new biblical criticism. At the same time Julius Mohl, who had married Mary Clarke, a friend of the Nightingales, interested her in comparative religion. Looking for scope to give service she found none in the Church of England, and in 1845 she tried to persuade her parents to let her go to Salisbury Infirmary to nurse. Not surprisingly they refused. Her private notes became more despairing and dramatic, seeing 'nothing in life but death'. From these depths she was rescued by Charles and Selina Bracebridge, to whom she became strongly attached, and who persuaded her parents to let her travel with them to Rome for the winter of 1847–8. There she met Sidney Herbert and his wife, (Mary) Elizabeth Herbert, whose social concerns she shared and with whom she became friends. Her contacts with Sidney Herbert were to be of central importance to her later national prominence. During this visit she also met Madre Santa Columba, who became her spiritual mentor, at the convent of the Trinità dei Monti, where she became convinced that she had a mission from God to the sick.

In 1850, during travels with the Bracebridges and on the advice of Bunsen, Florence contrived a visit to the religious community at Kaiserwerth-am-Rhein. This was a turning point in her life: she felt that Pastor Theodor Fliedner and the deaconesses were doing God's work, with women of humble birth devoting their lives to the sick and the deprived. Later she denied that she had 'trained' at Kaiserwerth, saying that 'The nursing was nil and the hygiene horrible' (As Miss Nightingale Said, 11), but that she had never seen purer devotion. Here she saw a possibility of changing nursing, not on the lines of the sisterhoods, where the 'ladies' supervised and nurses did the menial work, but by training suitably motivated women of any class. Her anonymous account of the community, The Institution of Kaiserwerth on the Rhine, for the Practical Training of Deaconesses, etc. (1851), printed 'by the inmates of the London Ragged Colonial Training School', was her first publication.

Florence returned to England and was again at odds with her parents. She finally refused marriage with Richard Monckton Milnes, later Baron Houghton, who had wooed her for nine years, a union that would have delighted her parents. The rejection came hard, for Monckton Milnes seems to have understood her more than most. He was to remain a valued member of the Nightingale council until his death in 1885. Florence was not the only thwarted daughter: Parthe, with her own peculiar gifts, still unmarried, became ill and obsessive about her sister (Woodham-Smith, 84–8). Sir James Clark, the family physician, with considerable perspicacity advised that Florence leave home, and the Herberts suggested that she should accept the post of unpaid superintendent to the Institute for Sick Governesses in Distressed Circumstances in Harley Street, London, of which a friend, Lady Canning, was the chairman. Before taking up the post Nightingale paid another visit to the Sisters of Charity in Paris (after taking the advice of H. E. Manning), visited other hospitals, and continued studying the blue books, making herself an expert on hospital administration. Once installed at the institute in August 1853 she impressed all who came into contact with her, including Dr Bence Jones, who was considering starting a training school for nurses at St George's Hospital, and William Bowman, with her skill both as a nurse and as an organizer. She demanded improvements in the facilities and threatened resignation unless Roman Catholics and Jews could be admitted as patients (Smith, 11). In August 1854, while she was at Harley Street, there was a devastating epidemic of cholera in Soho, and Nightingale went to help with the flood of patients overwhelming the Middlesex Hospital. These early experiences showed her to have a remarkable flair for imposing her will on institutions, as well as 'an extraordinarily rich and firm imaginative grasp of the relations between individuals and the siting and working of things and of human beings' relations to them' (ibid., 12).

The Crimean War The Crimean War broke out in March 1854, and in September British and French troops disembarked for the invasion of the Crimea. In October William Howard Russell sent dispatches to *The Times* in which he described the neglect of the wounded and the lack of nurses (*The Times*, 9, 12, 15, and 29 Oct 1854). Much of the public indignation fell on the head of Sidney Herbert, now secretary of state at war, who on 15 October wrote to Nightingale, asking her to take a party of nurses, at the government's expense, to Scutari. The letter crossed with one from Nightingale herself to Elizabeth Herbert offering to take a small private expedition, evidently the consolidation of an emerging plan (Smith, 26). On 16 October Nightingale met Sidney Herbert and the matter was arranged. 'Florence is sole leader', her sister recorded (ibid., 27). With the aid of Lady Canning and Elizabeth Herbert, within five days a party of thirty-eight nurses was assembled, consisting of fourteen professionals and twenty-four from religious sisterhoods, including five Catholic nuns from Bermondsey, five from Norwood, and fourteen from Anglican sisterhoods. The party, accompanied by Mr and Mrs Bracebridge, arrived at Scutari on 5 November and climbed the slopes to the enormous dilapidated Turkish barracks, over which Florence Nightingale said should have been inscribed Dante's words 'All hope abandon, ye who enter here.'

At Scutari, on the Asiatic side of the Bosphorus, opposite Constantinople, were four hospitals to house wounded troops brought by ship across the Black Sea from the battleground. The nursing party was received with sullen opposition by doctors and officials (Cook, 1.182). Nightingale at once began to assert her authority and to use her influence in London (which she was careful to see was apparent to those at Scutari) to improve the conditions in the hospitals, especially with respect to hygiene. She used money from the *Times* fund to buy needed equipment locally and to make up palliasses. When 125 Turkish workers struck for more money, she dismissed them and hired

Greeks (Smith, 37). She organized and improved the quality of the male nursing orderlies, who did the bulk of the nursing. Professor Smith calculates that Nightingale had dismissed thirteen of her original female nursing contingent by Christmas 1854.

The battle of Balaklava dramatized the need for good nursing, and as the sick and wounded were brought across the Black Sea the doctors turned to the Nightingale party for help on 9 November 1855 (Woodham-Smith, 168–70). For the next six months the doctors and nurses battled against overwhelming odds. Not only were they nursing 4 miles of patients but, because of the breakdown in purveying, Nightingale was acting as quartermaster. In January 1855 she wrote to Sidney Herbert 'Nursing is the least of the functions into which I have been forced' (*As Miss Nightingale Said*, 34). Appalled by the inadequate feeding arrangements she persuaded Lord Panmure, secretary of state for war, to arrange for Alexis Soyer, chef at the Reform Club, to come out and reorganize the cooking, though it was standard practice for male nursing orderlies to be responsible for providing their patients' meals.

While Nightingale was coping with the nursing, welfare, and rehabilitation of the sick, her task was complicated by the arrival of parties of nuns and 'lady ecclesiastics', sent as reinforcements by Herbert and led by Mary Stanley and Mother Mary Frances Bridgeman. Nightingale was furious at the absence of consultation and threatened resignation. She rightly saw that the new party affected her position as 'sole leader'. She was also alarmed both by the high proportion of Roman Catholics, a sensitive issue because of defections to Rome at the time, and, more important, because she regarded her experiment as the opportunity to prove the value of female nursing in wartime: to achieve this there had to be discipline, and she had to be in control. That she was autocratic there is no doubt, and her dealings with Mary Stanley seem harsh; she thought Sidney Herbert had betrayed her by allowing these missions, and on 3 April 1856 she reminded him: 'Your letter is written from Belgrave Square, I write from a hut in the Crimea. The point of site is different' (*As Miss Nightingale Said*, 40). This determination to remain in control and the acerbic way she dealt with would-be helpers gave fodder to later biographers counteracting the 'ministering angel' legend (Smith, chap. 2).

Nightingale proved a formidable administrator and organizer, and her role at Scutari was, like that of her male colleagues and predecessors, as much that of a 'General Purveyor', as she described herself, as of a medical nurse. The acquisition of clothing and equipment, given the priorities of war and the disorganization of the suppliers in Britain, was in itself a striking achievement. Although her duties were chiefly administrative, she made a point of visiting the wards: a Chelsea pensioner later recalled, perhaps with some exaggeration: 'Miss Nightingale was always coming in and out. She used to attend to all the worst cases herself' (Cook, 1.235). Her insistence on uniform, discipline, and orderly procedures in the midst of considerable squalor set a standard that permanently affected the self-esteem of what became the British nursing profession. Mary Stanley thus described her in December 1854:

> there sat dear Flo writing on a small unpainted deal table. I never saw her looking better. She had on her black merino, trimmed with black velvet, clean linen collar and cuffs, apron, white cap with a black handkerchief tied over it. (ibid., 1.234)

In May 1855 Florence Nightingale crossed to the Crimea to inspect the war hospitals, and while there collapsed and was dangerously ill with 'Crimean fever', which she referred to as 'typhus' but which was probably *Brucella melinites*, or perhaps *Brucella melitensis* (D. A. B. Young, *BMJ*, 23 Dec 1995, vol. 311). Nursed by the devoted Selina Bracebridge, Nightingale made a slow and painful recovery. She resisted efforts by officials to ship her home and returned to Scutari to continue working; in all she made three inspections of the Crimea, and on Good Friday 1856 she was given full jurisdiction over 'the East' (Smith, 63).

When the news of her illness reached Britain there were prayers for her recovery, the queen asked to be kept informed, poems were addressed to her, and *The Times* referred to her as 'The Lady of the Lamp'. A description of her midnight vigils by Mr Macdonald, the *Times* almoner in the Crimea, defined what quickly became her iconic stature and anticipated the depiction, not only of Florence Nightingale but of nurses generally, in a thousand novels and films:

> She is a 'ministering angel' without any exaggeration in these hospitals, and as her slender form glides quietly along each corridor, every poor fellow's face softens with gratitude at the sight of her. When all the medical officers have retired for the night and silence and darkness have settled down upon those miles of prostrate sick, she may be observed alone, with a little lamp in her hand, making her solitary rounds.   (Cook, 1.237)

Henry Longfellow's poem of 1856 became one of the best-known of Victorian verses:

> Lo! in that hour of misery
> A lady with a lamp I see
> Pass through the glimmering gloom,
> And flit from room to room.

Sidney Herbert wrote 'There broke out in different parts of the country a feeling of immediate and spontaneous expression of public gratitude and isolated portions of the country were preparing to make gifts to her.' With the advice of the Nightingale family it was decided to co-ordinate this response into a national appeal to 'enable Miss Nightingale to carry out a service close to her heart'. In November 1855 a public meeting was held in Willis Rooms, St James, London, with the duke of Cambridge in the chair. A report was sent to Nightingale in Scutari, who was asked by the trustees of the fund for her plans for its use. Beset by the problems of giving evidence to the sanitary commission sent out by Lord Panmure, the internecine squabbling, and the organization of the hospital, she replied with logic, if asperity, 'If I had asked for a Fund you might have asked me for a plan': she had not asked and she had no plan. The fund, which raised £45,000, she came to see as a millstone.

The war ended in June 1856 with little cause for rejoicing. Out of 94,000 men sent to the war area, 1760 died of wounds but 16,300 died of disease, and 13,000 were invalided (Smith, 73). As she had questioned the causes of poverty, Nightingale now questioned the reasons behind this preventable death-rate. She recognized, as few people did, the grievances of the ordinary soldier and she wrote, time and again, 'I stand at the altar of murdered men and while I live I will fight their cause'.

Return to England: royal commission Florence Nightingale returned to England in July 1856 a changed woman. Emaciated and tense, and weighed down with the burden she felt had been placed on her, she realized that if such suffering were never to happen again the Army Medical Service, and, if necessary, the army itself, must be reformed. To this end she set about asking for a royal commission. She set up what became known as her 'reform cabinet', a group of well-placed male advisers. In September 1856 she was invited to Balmoral and established what was to be a highly effective relationship with the queen and Albert. On 16 November 1856 it was agreed at an interview she had with Lord Panmure that a commission would be established, but nothing followed. Having used influential allies, royal approbation, and the threat to publish her own report, eventually in April 1857 Nightingale saw a commission established with four subcommittees and Sidney Herbert as chairman. *Notes on matters affecting the health, efficiency, and hospital administration of the British army* (1858), her own report of 830 pages, printed and privately circulated but never published, was backed by statistical evidence that showed how much of mortality was due to the state of the hospitals. The causes of the Crimean disaster were examined and a comparison made between the death-rate of the army in peacetime and the civilian rate, Nightingale's conclusion being 'Our soldiers are enlisted to die in barracks'. Her report constitutes 'an astonishing example of her gift for imagining palpable needs and assembling workable remedies' (Smith, 81). The reforms set in train as a result of the commission marked a turning point in the Army Medical Service. With respect to the commission, Nightingale was, as E. T. Cook put it, 'an unremitting task-master' (Cook, 1.356); but F. B. Smith argues that she was lax about preparing her witnesses and gave the impression 'that she did the work while Herbert played the dilettante figure-head', when the opposite was in fact the case; moreover, 'behind Herbert's back she was envious and disparaging' (Smith, 83). Her own evidence was given in written form. In 1858 she was elected a member of the Statistical Society, and at the Statistical Congress of 1860 'Miss Nightingale's scheme for uniform hospital statistics' was the principal subject for discussion. Breaking her social isolation, Nightingale gave a series of breakfast parties at the Burlington Hotel during the conference. Her model statistical forms were well received and were soon adopted by the major London hospitals.

While working on the report with frenetic urgency at the Burlington, Nightingale collapsed manifesting cardiac symptoms (probably sequelae of the Crimean fever) so severe that it was thought she would die. She recovered, but remained depressed and continued to suffer from nausea, insomnia, and palpitations. The accepted medical wisdom was that excessive mental exertion on the part of a woman was unnatural and would lead to breakdown: the standard treatment was complete rest and quiet. Florence Nightingale took to her bed or couch because the doctors ordered it, but she continued to work feverishly and was hostile to anyone, including her family, who she thought did not understand her mission. This was the beginning of her twenty years of invalidism. In 1861 she had a further severe episode when she was unable to walk and suffered from alarming spondylitis.

Determined to work come what may Nightingale used her illness to free herself from family commitments, though she often used relatives ruthlessly to help with her various projects; several were coerced into acting as secretaries or guardians in the house that her father purchased for her in South Street in London's Mayfair. Here she lived with five servants, with Dr Sutherland, whom she had met in the Crimea, installed downstairs as her amanuensis to whom she fired off notes and instructions. She now astutely exploited the isolation provided by her illness to further—mostly by remorseless use of correspondence—reforms in the army, the promotion of sanitary science, the collection of statistics, the design of hospitals, and the reform of nursing and midwifery services: no Victorian, except perhaps the queen, made more effective use of attrition by letter! Not for her were the waiting in the corridors of power and the attending of committees; people came to her and by appointment.

By March 1858 Nightingale wrote a 'last letter' to Sidney Herbert excusing herself from the responsibility of the Nightingale Fund. The council, concerned that the money had been collected from the public for a specific purpose, made tentative approaches to London hospitals, but they were all wary of what they thought would be an *imperium in imperio*. In November Nightingale became involved in correspondence in *The Builder* (26 February 1859, no. 99) concerning the rebuilding of St Thomas's Hospital. The faction advocating a move to the suburbs welcomed her as an ally, and as a quid pro quo offered accommodation for a school of nursing bearing her name. Anxious about the unrest concerning the fund, Nightingale put forward a plan which was rejected by the hospital authorities, who countered with a much less ambitious plan, which, in spite of reservations by the council, she accepted as 'not the best possible but the best conceivable'. The chairman of the council, Sidney Herbert, and the secretary, Arthur Hugh Clough, Nightingale's cousin by marriage, both sick men, began negotiations, and a scheme was drawn up on scraps of paper. In June 1860 the school was opened, with fifteen probationers working as assistant nurses, six of whom were dismissed or left and one of whom died of typhus within a year. The following year both Sidney Herbert and Arthur Clough were dead: Florence Nightingale, herself ill, was devastated, and left the organization of the school to the council, with another cousin, Henry Bonham-Carter, as secretary, soon to be joined by her brother-in-law, Sir Harry Verney, as chairman.

Herbert's death robbed Nightingale of her chief contact with cabinet-level politics, and she never overcame this loss. However, another very different confidant was found in the person of Benjamin Jowett, later master of Balliol College, Oxford, with whom she came in contact through his having been given by Clough a copy of a draft of her 'Suggestions for thought to the searchers after truth among the artizans of England'. Jowett (differing from J. S. Mill) advised against publication, and the book, though set in type and bound in three volumes in 1863, was never publicly issued. He and Nightingale corresponded regularly, and met from time to time, until Jowett's death in 1893. Their first meeting occurred in 1862 when Nightingale asked Jowett to come to London to give her the sacrament, which he did (*Dear Miss Nightingale*, xvii). Their relationship was thus centred on religion and the discussion of religion, and was essentially epistolatory. Jowett was a bachelor, and it is not impossible that he proposed marriage to Florence Nightingale, as Cordelia Sorabji much later recalled being told by him (ibid., xxxii), but it is not probable. A marriage between two of the great Victorian manipulators-by-correspondence would certainly have been exotic; it would also have probably been unhappy. There was no need for Jowett and Nightingale to marry, for their preferred means of intercourse was already available and employed. Jowett's letters to Nightingale were edited by E. V. Quinn and John Prest (1987); her letters to him were mostly destroyed by their recipient shortly before his death.

In office As Florence Nightingale recovered from her acute attack in 1861 she was roused to a new challenge. She had pressed Lord Palmerston, a family friend, to appoint Lord De Grey, a known reformer, as viceroy of India, and Captain Douglas Galton, a cousin by marriage, as under-secretary in charge of health and sanitation. The sanitary commission on India, which was to have been chaired by Herbert, began sitting; it reported in 1863. Nightingale gathered material for it by sending out a questionnaire to 200 stations in India (Smith, 115). Her knowledge of India became so encyclopaedic that every viceroy visited her before leaving Britain. Although she made mistakes onto which detractors fastened (ibid., 114–25), she was right about the fundamental importance of irrigation and the need for a pure water supply, and her views on famine, poverty, and debt were eminently sensible. Before the official report was completed she sent 'Instructions' about improvements to Indian barracks, but these were blocked by the India Office (ibid., 118). Her paper for the National Association for the Promotion of Social Science, 'How people may live and not die in India' (1863), was read to its meeting in Edinburgh to great acclaim. One of her advisers on India, Sir John Lawrence, became governor-general in 1863, and a new channel of influence opened, especially with respect to sanitary reform there.

During this period Nightingale was involved with the training of midwives, a subject on which she felt strongly. Part of the Nightingale Fund was used to finance an experimental training scheme at King's College Hospital, where her friend Mary Jones, under the aegis of the sisterhood of St John the Divine, was the sister superior. The scheme had only limited success and folded in 1867, not because of puerperal fever and 'her cavalier attitude to infection' (Smith, 112) but because of an acrimonious dispute between the sisterhood, the hospital authorities, and the bishop, which even Nightingale's eirenic intervention could not quell. Nevertheless, the experiment and Nightingale's 'Introductory notes on lying-in hospitals and proposals for training of midwives' laid the foundation for further schemes (Donnison, 73). Nightingale maintained that efficient nursing depended on well-designed hospitals, and, having studied hospital design all over Europe, she was quick to condemn the proposals for Netley on Southampton Water. In spite of her insistence that female nurses should be the backbone of military hospitals, and massive correspondence on the subject, the War Office remained unenthusiastic. It took another war to change this attitude.

In 1861 Nightingale was approached by William Rathbone, a philanthropist, about the possibility of supplying trained nurses for a poor-law institution in Liverpool. Few trained nurses were available at that time, but, much concerned about the fate of the sick in these institutions, in 1864 she sent Agnes Jones, who had trained at Kaiserwerth, and eight Nightingale nurses. They battled against appalling conditions and prejudice, until in 1868 Agnes Jones died of exhaustion and typhus, and this scheme came to an end. However, fired by accounts of neglect in workhouses in London, Nightingale now threw her influence behind the Association for Improving Workhouse Infirmaries, with co-workers such as J. S. Mill, Charles Dickens, and Louisa Twining, which eventually resulted in the Metropolitan Poor Law Act (1867). At the same time she persuaded the fund council to divert money for a training scheme for nurses based at the Highgate Poor Law Infirmary, and later, in 1881, more successfully, for a team of Nightingale nurses at the St Marylebone Institute, thus laying the foundation for trained nursing in the new municipal hospitals after the Local Government Act (1888).

In 1867 Nightingale wrote 'never think you have done anything effective in nursing until you have nursed, not only the poor sick in workhouses but those at home'. Again working in co-operation with William Rathbone, with whom she did not always agree, she gave urgent consideration to the need for a home-nursing scheme in London. She arranged for Florence Lees to conduct a survey to ascertain the need, which resulted in *The Report of the National Association for Providing Trained Nurses for the Sick Poor*. The following year, 1875, the Metropolitan and National Nursing Home was opened in Bloomsbury with Florence Lees as superintendent. Later Nightingale used her influence to ensure that the greater part of the women's jubilee offering to Queen Victoria was used to provide nursing for the sick poor at home, and the Bloomsbury Training Home became the model for the training scheme for the Queen's Institute for District Nursing.

'Out of office', 1870–1880 Florence Nightingale's influence on the army and India was declining, and in 1872, when the new viceroy did not come to see her and ignored her advice, she wrote 'this year I go out of office' (Cook, 2.240). Gladstone was one of those canny enough not to be drawn into the Nightingale web, though they corresponded from time to time. Nightingale was unsympathetic to his policies, and when he did call, without an appointment, she declined to receive him. The death of her father in 1874, quickly followed by that of Mrs Bracebridge, depressed her. She returned to her youthful interest in the mystics and prepared a never-completed book on those of the middle ages. Increasingly she felt isolated and despondent. Lying in bed she wrote vast quantities of spiritual meditation. E. T. Cook, who collected these for his biography, commented on them: 'The notes are often heart-rending in their impression of loneliness, of craving for sympathy which she could not find, of bitter self-reproach' (ibid.). She was not, however, wholly inactive, and she turned her attention to the school that bore her name, the Nightingale School attached to St Thomas's Hospital in London. In spite of publicity there had been few suitable candidates, and the attrition rate was 40 per cent. She now realized that the agreement with St Thomas's had been one-sided, and she complained that the Nightingale probationers were doing half the hospital's work. After legal advice, consideration was given to spending capital and starting elsewhere. Eventually the council settled for a series of compromises, which never satisfied Nightingale and which failed to answer the fundamental questions: how should nurses be prepared to meet the health needs of the population, who should train and educate them, and how should they be tested (Baly, preface)? It is a paradox that Florence Nightingale should be best known for what she failed to achieve: a credible training for nurses in the school to which her name was given (*As Miss Nightingale Said*, preface).

Old age, 1880–1910 At the age of sixty Florence Nightingale considered herself old. Her friends and collaborators were dead, but her health improved. The thin, waspish woman who sent mordant, aphoristic letters to ministers now metamorphosed into a stout, benevolent old lady. She tried to keep up with public-health matters but she was increasingly out of touch. In 1888 St Thomas's appointed a matron without consulting her or the council. She continued to write sentimental addresses to probationers until 1889, but by now her eyesight was failing. After the death of her sister in 1890 she found something of a new life at Claydon House, near Bicester, where she cared for the estate and her brother-in-law (Claydon, now owned by the National Trust, houses her large bed and various memorabilia), but her last visit there was in 1894–5. She spent almost the whole of her final fifteen years in her room in South Street, London. Although from 1902 she could write only with great difficulty and her memory was failing, it was only in 1906 that the India Office was asked to stop sending her relevant papers on sanitation. She was the recipient of many honours, including membership of the German order of the cross of merit and the French *Secours* *aux blessés militaires*. In 1907 the king made her a member of the Order of Merit, the first woman to be so honoured, and this encouraged something of a revival of interest. In 1908 she received the freedom of the City of London.

Portraits are of particular importance in the life of a publicly well-known recluse. They are listed as appendix C in Cook's biography. Nightingale generally refused to sit, and disliked being photographed. Even so, Cook lists twenty-four likenesses that are 'authentic', and the National Portrait Gallery has a useful collection of photographs of her. Especially important among her images is Jerry Barrett's oil, now in the National Portrait Gallery; it was engraved by S. Bellin as *Florence Nightingale at Scutari, a Mission of Mercy* (1856). Barrett travelled to Scutari to paint her; she refused to sit, but gave ample opportunity for him to observe her (Smith, 85). In the 1980s the portrait was reproduced on British £10 notes. The *Illustrated London News* published a woodcut of Nightingale with a lamp in the Scutari hospital (24 February 1855). A photograph by the London Stereoscopic Company, taken at the request of the queen in 1856, was much reproduced. A fine bust by Sir John Steell (1859) was made for the Royal United Service Institution (now in the National Army Museum). G. F. Watts began a portrait in 1864 that he was unable to finish; Sir William Blake Richmond's oil portrait (1887, but begun earlier) established the icon of the later Nightingale, uncannily like that of Queen Victoria.

Florence Nightingale outlasted her early Victorian colleagues, and was the chief living link with those days of sanitary reform and the start of the assertion by women of a claim to a recognized, official, professional role in the central actions of national life. She died in her sleep in her room at 10 South Street, Park Lane, London, on 13 August 1910. An offer of burial in Westminster Abbey was declined by her relatives, and she was buried next to her father and mother in the churchyard of East Wellow, Hampshire, the coffin borne to the grave by sergeants drawn from the regiments of the guards. Memorial services were held in St Paul's Cathedral on 20 August, in Liverpool Cathedral, and in many other places of worship.

Religion and attitude to women   Florence Nightingale's attitude to health and the deprived must be seen in the light of her own idiosyncratic theology. Brought up by parents basically Unitarian, exposed to the philosophy of the Enlightenment, biblical criticism, and new scientific theories, like a number of her contemporaries she heard Matthew Arnold's 'melancholy, long, withdrawing roar' (M. Arnold, 'Dover Beach') of the sea of faith. Aware of her own spiritual need she sought guidance from different mentors, and at the age of thirty-two tried to set out her own philosophy in 'Suggestions for thought', dedicated to 'The Artizans of England—Seekers after Truth', whom she thought had been led astray by the teachings of the positivists. Volumes 1 and 3 are devoted to explaining God's will and God's law, and have Unitarian undertones. A disciple of the teaching of Jacques Quetelet, she believed there was a causal explanation for all human behaviour, and if the cause was corrected behaviour would improve; this argument, she thought, could be applied to health. If the factors causing ill health were removed mankind would become healthy, and the key to this lay in sanitary science. In an involved exegesis she linked this with God's will, which was that mankind must help mankind: as an example men should not pray to be delivered from cholera but bend their efforts to supplying clean water and proper sanitation. She looked to the day when sanitary science would overcome ill health and when hospitals, which she regarded as an 'intermediate state of civilization', would be abolished. It was for this reason that she continued to disregard the germ theory of infection: she thought it would lead people into ignoring the need for hygiene and sanitation. Influenced by Spinoza, she argued that God's laws were unalterable and therefore miracles were impossible. God's law was manifest in nature, and it is noticeable that in her best-selling book *Notes on Nursing* (1860) she referred to disease as being 'a reparative process which Nature has instituted'. It was the duty of the nurse to put the patient in a position for nature to act on him; the nurse was thus aiding God's law, hence the emphasis on fresh air and the design of the Nightingale wards.

Volume 2 of Nightingale's 'Suggestions' is a diatribe about the wrongs suffered by women and is out of place in a metaphysical disquisition. Virginia Woolf in *A Room of One's Own* (1929) referred to it as 'Shrieking aloud in agony' (p. 47). Florence Nightingale's attitude to women was contradictory. She considered them selfish, and, though she adulated a chosen few, she preferred working with men. She was an early campaigner for women's rights, particularly their right to property, and she inveighed against the limitations imposed on educated women undertaking worthwhile and paid work. However, in her later years she was irritated by women clamouring to enter male preserves like medicine, maintaining that there was plenty to be done in women's work like midwifery, teaching, and nursing. She made no common cause with women claiming the right to train as physicians. She argued against J. S. Mill that the lack of a vote was the least of women's disabilities. Her attitude to women was patrician, though at the end of her life she accepted that she had not taken sufficient account of 'ordinary women'. In fact she was a child of her time, and she lived for ninety years: the enthusiasms of radical youth were replaced by a more reactionary old age.

Historiography   At her death Nightingale's papers passed to her executor, Henry Bonham-Carter, who authorized Sir Edward Tyas Cook to write an official biography. Cook's two-volume *Life of Florence Nightingale* was published in 1913, and is an exceptionally well-researched example of its genre; it is also both sympathetic and critical, and remains a valuable biography as well as being an archival quarry. In 1918 Lytton Strachey included a short memoir of Nightingale in his *Eminent Victorians*. Influenced by Freud he moved away from investigation into the realms of psychotherapy and fictionalization, claiming that the real Florence Nightingale was 'more interesting than the legendary one though less agreeable'. While highlighting the harsh aspects of her life Strachey did not deny her achievements.

Early nursing historians were the most ardent keepers of the Nightingale flame (for example, M. A. Nutting and L. L. Dock, *A History of Nursing*, 1907). Anxious to portray nursing as an educated and homogeneous profession they overstated the failures of nursing pre-1860 and exaggerated the transformation. Nightingale was the ideal icon for publicity—educated, impeccably respectable, and a national heroine; her lamp became the symbol of nursing. Anna Neagle thus portrayed her in Herbert Wilcox's film *The Lady with a Lamp* (1951), though with a few Stracheyesque additions. Because Cook's biography was so monumental, and because of the sheer volume of material scattered in collections and libraries, most subsequent biographies were a recension of it. In 1950 Cecil Woodham-Smith produced a popular biography in which she claimed to have had access to new material. However, it added little to the life by Cook and errors and misconceptions remained.

Since 1950 there has been an upsurge of interest in this enigmatic woman who is a Victorian figure but, on the other hand, strangely contemporary. The medical profession has attempted to explain her invalidism and various diagnoses have been expounded, including the theory that it was psychosomatic (Pickering), and theologians have examined her spirituality and its effect on her work. Research on the Nightingale Fund papers shows there was no sudden reform in nursing: it was a slow, inevitable process due to a multiplicity of factors, and, as Monica Baly has argued, the so-called Nightingale legacy was a mixed blessing. Other historians have taken an iconoclastic approach. Barry Smith's striking study (1982) stripped away the iconic aspects of the Nightingale legend to examine the remarkable network of manipulation (mostly by letter) by which she sought to impose her will and achieve her objectives.

Florence Nightingale remains an enigmatic figure. Her sense of being 'in office' and 'out of office' reflects the frustration of a woman who sensed power but who, in the circumstances of the time, could use it only obliquely, and then chiefly by persuading men to act for her. Her remarkable practical ability, her intense religiosity, her illnesses, and her image of herself as a medieval recluse in a modern age reflect a complex character whose complexity grows with time and with the changing role of women in public life.   MONICA E. BALY and H. C. G. MATTHEW

Sources E. T. Cook, *The life of Florence Nightingale*, 2 vols. (1913) · C. Woodham-Smith, *Florence Nightingale, 1820–1910* (1950) · M. A. Nutting and L. L. Dock, *A history of nursing: the evolution of nursing systems from the earliest times to the foundation of the first English and American training schools for nurses* (1907) · L. Strachey, *Eminent Victorians* (1948) · *'Ever yours, Florence Nightingale'*, ed. M. Vicinus and B. Negaard (1989) · R. Van der Peet, *The Nightingale model of nursing* (1995) · A. Summers, *Citizens and angels* (1988) · J. Donnison, *Midwives and medical men: a history of inter-professional rivalries and women's rights* (1977) · R. S. Hodgkinson, *The origins of the national health service: the medical services of the new poor law, 1834–1871* (1967) · G. Pickering, *The creative malady* (1974) · F. B. Smith, *Florence Nightingale: reputation and power* (1982) · M. E. Baly, *Florence Nightingale and*

the nursing legacy (1986); 2nd edn (1997) · *As Miss Nightingale said …: Florence Nightingale through her sayings*, ed. M. E. Baly, 2nd edn (1997) · W. J. Bishop and S. Goldie, *A bio-bibliography of Florence Nightingale* (1962) · *A calendar of the letters of Florence Nightingale*, ed. S. Goldie (1983) [microfiche; with introduction by S. Goldie] · b. cert. · *CGPLA Eng. & Wales* (1910) · *Dear Miss Nightingale: a selection of Benjamin Jowett's letters to Florence Nightingale, 1860–1893*, ed. E. V. Quinn and J. Prest (1987) · *BMJ*

Archives Anglesey County RO, Llangefni, letters · BL, corresp. and papers, Add. MSS 43393–43403, 45750–45859, 46123, 46176, 46385, 47714–47767, 49623, 52427, 59786, 68882–68890 · BL, letters, RP 2027–2028 [copies] · Bucks. RLSS, letters relating to Royal Buckinghamshire Hospital · Claydon House, Buckinghamshire, corresp. and papers; diary · LMA, corresp. and papers · University of British Columbia, Woodward Biomedical Library, corresp. · University of Kansas Medical Center, Kansas City, Clendening History of Medicine Library and Museum, letters · Wellcome L., corresp. relating to Crimea, etc. · Wellcome L., letters · Women's Library, London, papers | Balliol Oxf., letters to Sir Louis Mallet · BL, letters to T. G. Balfour, Add. MS 50134 · BL, corresp. with W. E. Gladstone, Add. MSS 44397–44488, *passim* · BL, corresp. with Sir J. Hall, Add. MS 39867 · BL, corresp. with Lord Ripon, Add. MS 43456 · BL, corresp. with Verney family, Add. MSS 68882–68890 · BL OIOC, letters to Sir Mountstuart Grant-Duff, MS Eur. F 234 · BL OIOC, letters to William Rowntrie Robertson · Bodl. Oxf., corresp. with H. W. Acland · Bodl. Oxf., corresp. with Doyle family · British Red Cross Museum and Archives, London, corresp. with Sir Robert Loyd-Lindsay · CUL, corresp. with Lord Mayo · Derbys. RO, letters to C. B. N. Dunn · Emory University, Atlanta, Georgia, Pitts Theology Library, corresp. with H. E. Manning · Hants. RO, letters to Bonham-Carter family · Leics. RO, corresp. with Martin family · LMA, corresp. with Henry Bonham-Carter and others on business of Nightingale Fund, with papers · Lpool RO, corresp. with William Rathbone · NA Scot., letters to Lord Panmure · NAM, corresp. with Lord Raglan · NL Ire., letters to Sir Ranald Martin · NRA, priv. coll., letters to Lord Wemyss · Royal British Nurses' Association, London, corresp. with William Clark [copies] · Royal London Hospital Archives and Museum, corresp. with Eva Luckes · St Thomas's Hospital, London, corresp. with William Smith · Trinity Cam., letters to Lord Houghton · U. Newcastle, Robinson L., letters to Sir Charles Trevelyan · U. Nott. L., letters to duke of Newcastle · U. Wales, Bangor, letters to William Rathbone relating to Bangor typhoid epidemic of 1882 · UCL, corresp. with Sir Edwin Chadwick · UCL, corresp. with Karl Pearson · W. Yorks. AS, Leeds, letters to Lady Canning · Wellcome L., letters to Sir William Aitken · Wellcome L., letters to G. H. De'ath · Wellcome L., letters to William Farr · Wellcome L., letters to Louisa Gordon · Wellcome L., letters to Mrs T. H. Green · Wellcome L., letters to Amy Hughes · Wellcome L., letters to Sir John Lefroy · Wellcome L., corresp. with Sir Thomas Longmore · Wellcome L., letters to Charles Plowden · Wilts. & Swindon RO, corresp. with Lord Pembroke |SOUND BL NSA, recorded talks

Likenesses W. White, watercolour drawing, c.1836 (with her sister), NPG · J. Barrett, watercolour study, 1846, NPG · Elizabeth, Lady Eastlake, pencil drawing, 1846, NPG · R. J. Lane, chromolithograph, pubd 1854 (after H. Bonham-Carter), BM, NPG · F. Holl, lithograph, pubd 1855 (after P. N.), NPG · J. Barrett, group portrait, oils, 1856?, NPG; study, NPG · H. Bonham-Carter, plaster statuette, c.1856, St Thomas's Hospital, London · Goodman, albumen print, c.1857, NPG [see illus.] · Scharf, pencil drawing, 1857, NPG · Goodman, photograph, 1858, Claydon House, Buckinghamshire · H. Hering, photograph, c.1858, repro. in Cook, *Life* · J. Steell, marble bust, 1859, NAM; repro. in Cook, *Life* · J. Steell, bust, 1862, Derby Art Gallery; bronze cast, NPG · W. B. Richmond, oils, 1887, Claydon House, Buckinghamshire · S. G. Payne & Son, photograph, 1891, repro. in Cook, *Life* · E. Bosanquet, photograph, 1906, repro. in Cook, *Life* · F. A. de Biden Footner, watercolour, 1907, repro. in Cook, *Life* · Feodora, Countess von Gleichen, chalks, 1908, Royal

Collection · A. G. Walker, statue, 1915, Waterloo Place, London · J. Barrett, oils, NPG · probably J. Barrett, three pencil and watercolour sketches, NPG · F. A. de Biden Footner, pencil with watercolour drawing, repro. in Cook, *Life* · H. Bonham-Carter, pencil drawing (aged about twenty-five), repro. in Cook, *Life* · A. E. Chalon, drawing (as child), Claydon House, Buckinghamshire · Feodora, Countess von Gleichen, statue, London Road, Derby · C. H. Jeens, stipple (after statue by H. Bonham-Carter), BM; vignette on title to C. Yonge's *Book of golden deeds* (1864) · Pinches, medal, NPG · W. Simpson, drawing, repro. in W. Simpson, *The seat of war in the East*, 2nd ser. (1856) · cartes-de-visite, NPG · photogravure, NPG; repro. in *The Sphere* (20 Aug 1910) · relief tablet, St Paul's Cathedral, London · wood-engraving, NPG; repro. in *ILN* (24 Feb 1855)

Wealth at death £36,127 16s. 8d.: probate, 31 Oct 1910, *CGPLA Eng. & Wales*

Nightingale, Joseph (1775–1824), writer, was born at Chowbent, in the chapelry of Atherton, parish of Leigh, Lancashire, on 26 October 1775. He became a Wesleyan Methodist in 1796, acting occasionally as a local preacher, but never entered the Methodist ministry and ceased to be a member in 1804. On 17 November 1799 he married Margaret Goostry; they had four children. His son Joseph Sargent Nightingale (1809–1895) became an independent minister.

For some time Nightingale was master of a school at Macclesfield, Cheshire, but went to London in 1805, at the suggestion of William Smyth (1765–1849), later professor of modern history at Cambridge. By this time he was a Unitarian; he became a minister of that denomination, preaching his first sermon on 8 June 1806 at Parliament Court Chapel, Bishopsgate, but he never held a pastoral charge and supported himself chiefly by his pen.

After the publication of his *Portraiture of Methodism* (1807) Nightingale was exposed to much criticism. When an article in the *New Annual Register* for 1807 characterized him as 'a knave' he brought an action for libel against John Stockdale (1749?–1814), the publisher, and recovered £200 in damages on 11 March 1809. In 1824 he was again received into membership by the Methodists. In private life 'he was of a kind disposition, lively imagination, and possessed a cheerfulness that never deserted him' (*GM*, 568).

Nightingale's works, extending to almost fifty volumes, cover a wide range of subject matter. To his contested work on Methodism he added the highly sympathetic *A Portraiture of the Roman Catholic Religion* (1812) and a careful compilation, *The Religions and Religious Ceremonies of All Nations Faithfully and Impartially Described* (1821). His highly successful memoirs of Queen Caroline, which appeared in 1820–22 (reprinted 1978), was only one of his publications on that subject, including a set of verses (1821). The largest part of his output, with perhaps the most lasting value, dealt with topographical subjects. They include a guide to watering places (1811); accounts of Staffordshire, Somerset, and Shropshire, three volumes (1813) continuing *The Beauties of England and Wales* by E. W. Brayley (1773–1854); surveys of London and Westminster (1814–15); and *The History and Antiquities of the Parochial Church of St. Saviour, Southwark* (1818). He was also a regular contributor to early

volumes of the Unitarian periodical the *Monthly Repository*. He died in London on 9 August 1824 and was buried at Bunhill Fields.   C. W. SUTTON, *rev.* R. K. WEBB

Sources *GM*, 1st ser., 94/2 (1824), 568–9 · private information (1894) · [J. Watkins and F. Shoberl], *A biographical dictionary of the living authors of Great Britain and Ireland* (1816)

Likenesses R. Roffe, engraving (after portrait by Shoesmith), repro. in J. Nightingale, *Rational stenography, or, Short-hand made easy* (1823)

Nightingall, Sir Miles (1768–1829), army officer, born on 25 December 1768, entered the army on 4 April 1787 as ensign, 52nd foot, and joined that regiment at Madras, from Chatham, in July 1788. He served with the grenadier company at the capture of Dindigul and the siege of Palicatcherry in 1790, and afterwards was brigade major of the 1st brigade of Lord Cornwallis's army at the siege of Bangalore, the capture of the hill forts of Savanadrug and Ostradroog, and the operations before Seringapatam. In August 1793 he was at the taking of Pondicherry, where his knowledge of French led to his appointment as brigade major. Having been promoted to a company in the 125th foot in September 1794 he returned home and was aide-de-camp to Lord Cornwallis, then commanding the eastern district. He obtained a majority in the 121st, was appointed brigade major in the eastern district, and purchased a lieutenant-colonelcy in the 38th foot in 1795.

Nightingall volunteered for the West Indies and was placed in command of the old 92nd, with which he was present at the capture of Trinidad in 1797. He was extra-aide-de-camp to Sir Ralph Abercromby at Puerto Rico, and was afterwards made inspector of foreign corps, which appointment he resigned on account of ill health. He returned home in October 1797. He subsequently went to San Domingo in December as adjutant-general with Brigadier-General Thomas Maitland, arranged the evacuation of Port-au-Prince with M. Herier, the agent of Toussaint l'Ouverture, and was sent home with dispatches.

Cornwallis, then lord lieutenant of Ireland, asked for Nightingall to be sent over to command one of the battalions of light companies under Major-General John Moore. He became aide-de-camp to Cornwallis and commanded the 4th battalion of light infantry. He again accompanied Major-General Maitland to the West Indies and America, and on his return was appointed assistant adjutant-general of the forces encamped on Barham Down, near Canterbury, which he subsequently accompanied to The Helder. He was present in the actions of 2 September and 19 October 1799, but had to return home through ill health. He was deputy adjutant-general to Maitland in the expedition to Quiberon in 1800, brought home the dispatches from Isle Houat, and was assistant quartermaster-general of the eastern district in June to October 1801. He was on the staff of Lord Cornwallis when the latter went to France as ambassador-extraordinary to conclude the peace of Amiens in 1802, and was afterwards transferred to the 51st regiment and appointed quartermaster-general of the king's troops in Bengal.

Nightingall arrived in Calcutta in August, and became brevet colonel on 25 September 1803. He was with the army under Lord Lake at Agra and Laswari, and afterwards returned to Calcutta. He was military secretary to Lord Cornwallis from his arrival until his death at Ghazipur on 17 October 1805, after which Nightingall reverted to the duties of quartermaster-general. In February 1807 he returned home and was appointed to a brigade in the secret expedition under Major-General Brent Spencer which went to Cadiz and afterwards joined Sir Arthur Wellesley's force in Portugal. He commanded a brigade, consisting of the 29th and 82nd regiments, at Roliça and Vimeiro. In December 1808 he was appointed governor and commander-in-chief in New South Wales, but illness obliged him to give up the appointment. He held brigade commands at Hythe and Dover in 1809–10. He became a major-general on 25 July 1810, joined the army in the Peninsula in January 1811, and was appointed to a brigade, consisting of the 24th, 42nd, and 79th regiments, in the 1st division. It was known as the Highland brigade or the brigade of the line, the rest of the division consisting of guards and Germans. He commanded the 1st division at the battle of Fuentes d'Oñoro on 6 May 1811, where he was wounded in the head.

Nightingall left the Peninsular army at Elvas in July that year, having been appointed to a division in India, but before he could take up that post he was nominated by Lord Minto to be commander-in-chief in Java, where he arrived in October 1813. He organized and commanded a number of small expeditions against the pirate states of Bali and Boni in Macassar in April and May 1814. Having established British authority in the Celebes, he returned to Java in June 1814, and remained there until November 1815, when he proceeded to Bombay. He became a lieutenant-general on 4 June 1814. He commanded the forces in Bombay, with a seat in council, from 6 February 1816 until 1819, when he returned home overland.

Nightingall married, at Richmond, Surrey, on 13 August 1800, Florentia, daughter of Sir Lionel Darell, first baronet and chairman of the East India Company. He was made a KCB on 4 January 1815. He had gold medals for Roliça, Vimeiro, and Fuentes d'Oñoro, and was colonel successively of the 6th West India regiment and the 69th foot. He was returned to parliament for Eye, a pocket borough of the Cornwallis family, in 1820 and again in 1826. He died at Gloucester on 12 September 1829, aged sixty-one.

H. M. CHICHESTER, rev. JAMES FALKNER

Sources Army List · J. Philippart, ed., The royal military calendar, 1 (1815), 286–9 · GM, 1st ser., 99/2 (1829), 463–5 · United Service Journal (1829)

Archives BL OIOC, papers, MS Eur. E 227 · NAM, department of archives, letter-books

Nihell, Elizabeth (b. 1723), midwife, was born in London. She studied midwifery at the Hôtel-Dieu in Paris under Marie-Claude Pour for two years during the late 1740s. As a foreigner she had great difficulty getting admitted there as an apprentice, but eventually succeeded with assistance from the duke of Orléans. It was an impressive practical training, for a handful of apprentice midwives delivered about 1300 women every year. By 1754 she was back in London, living in Panton Square near the Haymarket with her husband, James Nihell (c.1708–1759), who practised surgery.

Elizabeth Nihell deplored the growing fashion for men-midwives. In A Treatise on the Art of Midwifery (1760) she argued that male practitioners lacked patience and sensitivity and were too quick to resort to metal instruments, causing needless infant deaths. She also condemned the practice of paying men-midwives higher fees than women. She vigorously criticized William Smellie, who taught midwifery to surgeons using a leather mannequin, but she also considered it unethical to oblige poor women in charitable institutions to give birth in the presence of male students. Her arguments were ridiculed by Tobias Smollett (a former pupil of Smellie's) in an essay in the Critical Review (1760), which nevertheless paid her the compliment of insinuating that her husband must have written the book. Elizabeth Nihell's defence of her profession helped to raise public awareness of an important problem. A French translation of her book, updated, was published in 1771.

Elizabeth Nihell had at least one child. That she was still in practice near the Haymarket in 1772 is indicated by a list of London midwives published that year.

CATHERINE CRAWFORD, rev.

Sources London Evening-Post (21–3 Feb 1754), 3 · The danger and immodesty of the present too general custom of unnecessarily employing men-midwives (1772) · J. H. Aveling, English midwives: their history and prospects (1872) · H. Carrier, Origines de la maternité de Paris: les maîtresses sages-femmes et l'office des accouchées de l'ancien Hôtel-Dieu (1378–1796) (Paris, 1888) · P. J. Klukoff, 'Smollett's defence of Dr Smellie in The Critical Review', Medical History, 14 (1970), 31–41 · J. Donnison, Midwives and medical men: a history of inter-professional rivalries and women's rights (1977) · A. Wilson, The making of man-midwifery: childbirth in England, 1660–1770 (1995) · P. J. Wallis and R. V. Wallis, Eighteenth century medics, 2nd edn (1988)

Nimham, Daniel (c.1726–1778), leader of the Mohican Indians, was born into the Wappinger branch of the Mohican Indians, the son of one Nimham, a headman. Nimham first appears in the historical record in 1756, when 225 Wappingers moved from the New York highlands to the western Massachusetts mission town of Stockbridge for protection from the French and their native allies during the French and Indian War. There they joined fellow Mohicans and mingled with other American Indian refugees.

During the French and Indian War, the American Indians of Stockbridge fought alongside the British, playing key roles in the northern campaigns and defence of the frontier. They were also some of the few American Indians who remained loyal to the British during the pan-Amerindian uprising against British rule commonly referred to as the Pontiac War (1763–6). Nimham held the rank of captain, a rank often given to American Indian leaders, indicating his prominence within the Stockbridge community.

Nimham gained national prominence when he led a campaign to reassert claim over 204,800 acres of the New York lands the Wappingers had vacated for the safety of Stockbridge. Whether or not they intended the move to Stockbridge to be permanent or merely a safety precaution until the war's conclusion is uncertain, but Nimham and his supporters certainly felt their land had been stolen by New York land barons during the war and leased illegally. Nimham found support from Massachusetts speculators who hoped to get pieces of Mohican land in exchange and farming squatters on the tribal lands who did not want to pay the land barons rent. He lodged a formal complaint in 1762 for the return of the land and had his case heard before the lieutenant-governor and the governor's council in 1765. Without a lawyer willing to represent him, and the council influenced by the white claimants which included the powerful Philipse family, Nimham stood no chance of success.

When the case was rejected Nimham led a group of seven Stockbridge Mohicans to Britain to plead their case. After arriving in London in summer 1766, the four men and three women met with a mixed reaction. As with other visits by American Indians, the crowd was always beguiled by the spectacle of these strangers. However, George III initially expressed annoyance because 'these Indians have been brought over without any Authority of His Majesty' (second earl of Shelburne to Board of Trade, 16 Aug 1766, Shelburne papers, vol. 53, fols. 13–14). Because Nimham and his companions were the leaders of their people, the king was by tradition obliged to treat them as fellow heads of state, and as his personal guests at a cost of £555 12s. 2½d. Nevertheless, Nimham and his companions also met with a sympathetic response, not least in time from George III. Writing to Sir Henry Moore, governor of New York, Lord Shelburne, secretary of state for the southern department (who oversaw American affairs), declared that the king has 'tender compassion for those Unhappy People, whose Distresses have driven them so far, to seek His Royal Protection'. The Board of Trade, to which Nimham's land claim had been referred, found 'the colour of great prejudice and partiality [in the New York hearing], and of an Intention to intimidate these Indians from prosecuting their Claims'. Shelburne himself was outraged:

> It appears extraordinary that these Indians having continued in the uninterrupted Possession of this Land, and the actual Improvement and settlement of a great part of it, should, whilst they were Fighting under His Majesty's Banners, be deprived of the Possession of it. (Shelburne to Moore, 11 Oct 1766, Shelburne papers, vol. 53)

Sir Henry Moore was ordered to convene a new hearing with the expectation that the land would be restored to the Wappingers. But little had changed in New York, where local land barons held more sway than an imperial government whose authority was diminishing in the wake of recent colonial riots against taxation. Nimham and his supporters lost their case once again in March 1767. Moreover, they lost further lands in paying their debts incurred in prosecuting the case.

The Stockbridge Indians were perhaps the most avid supporters of the American patriot cause. Many joined the Massachusetts militia before the outbreak of fighting, and more enlisted in the American army once hostilities erupted. Nimham arrived in Cambridge, Massachusetts,

in June 1775 to join George Washington's army, which was laying siege to Boston. Nimham and his tribesmen were especially active in New York, where they fought British forces of regulars, American loyalists, and allied American Indians. On 31 August 1778 a band of Stockbridge Indians led by Nimham were ambushed in a trap at Kingsbridge, New York, laid by the Queen's rangers under the command of Lieutenant-Colonel John Simcoe. Nimham, his son, Abraham, and about forty others were killed by British forces, but not before Nimham was able to wound Simcoe, who later remarked that 'the Indians fought most gallantly' (Simcoe, 86).

TROY O. BICKHAM

Sources P. Frazier, *The Mohicans of Stockbridge* (1992) • C. G. Calloway, *The American Revolution in Indian country: crisis and diversity in Native American communities* (1995) • P. Frazier, 'Nimham, Daniel', *ANB* • J. G. Simcoe, *Simcoe's military journal: a history of the operations of a partisan corps, called the queen's rangers, commanded by Lieut. Col. J. G. Simcoe* (1844) • J. M. Sosin, *Whitehall and the wilderness: the middle west in British colonial policy, 1760–1775* (1961) • colonial office papers, PRO, ser. 5, vols. 65–82 • U. Mich., Clements L., Shelburne papers

Nimmo, Alexander (1783–1832), civil engineer, was born at Kirkcaldy, Fife, the son of a watchmaker who afterwards kept a hardware shop. He was educated at Kirkcaldy grammar school, where he is said to have been brilliant. In 1796–9 he attended Latin, Greek, mathematics, logic, ethics, and natural philosophy classes at St Andrews University and in 1799–1800, physics, ethics, and mathematics classes at Edinburgh University. He then went north to be second master of Fortrose Academy where it is recorded that he taught 'arithmetic, bookkeeping and drawing; the elements of Euclid, navigation, land surveying and other mensurations; architecture, fortification and gunnery; also the elements of chemistry and natural philosophy' (Ruddock, 197). He is said to have read seven languages. At the age of twenty-two, against severe competition, he became rector of Inverness Academy where, according to Joseph Mitchell, he was considered 'a gentleman of great scientific acquirements' (Mitchell, 44). About 1810 Nimmo resigned his post because the governors had censured him for failing to attend church. He was then employed on the recommendation of Thomas Telford by the commission on the practicability of draining and cultivating the bogs in Ireland.

Nimmo was a protégé of Telford, coming to his notice as a competent person to accurately determine the boundaries of the northern counties of Scotland for the commissioners for highland roads and bridges. They recorded that he performed this task during his summer vacation of 1806 with 'a zeal and intelligence surpassing their expectations' (Arrowsmith, 20), and published his 'Historical statement of the erection and boundaries of the shires of Inverness, Ross, Cromarty, Sutherland, and Caithness' in their third report (1807). On another occasion while rector, he surveyed and estimated the cost of a drove road along Loch Treig crossing Rannoch Moor to Glen Lyon and Killin, work which formed the basis for a Telford report of 1810.

About this time, almost certainly at Telford's instigation, Nimmo wrote valuable original articles for *The Edinburgh Encyclopaedia* on 'Boscovitch's theory', the theory of bridges, the theory of carpentry, and 'Draining', all first published in 1812–13 and later, part of 'Navigation, inland', published in 1821. Throughout 1811, 1812, and 1813 Nimmo worked intensively for the Irish bogs commission and his admirable series of maps and reports on draining and cultivating bogs in Roscommon, co. Kerry, Cork, and Galway, covering close on 2000 square miles, were published in 1814 in the commissioners' fourth report. His proposals included canals, river navigation improvements, and roads. In 1814–15 Nimmo made proposals for a harbour near Dunmore, Waterford, and for improving the river and harbour of Cork. About this time he embarked on a study tour of public works in France, Germany, and the Netherlands. On his return he became engineer for extensive works at Dunmore harbour for which he prepared a plan in 1818. From 1820 onwards Nimmo was employed by the Irish fisheries board to make surveys of the coast and harbours of Ireland and their internal communication, and to build various harbours and piers. Several of his charts were published in 1821–2, his work culminating in 1832 with *New Piloting Directions for St George's Channel and the Coast of Ireland*.

In 1822 Nimmo was also appointed engineer for improving the western district of Ireland, mainly Connemara, where he built Corrib Lodge in the Maam valley as his residence. By 1830, £167,000 had been spent in reclaiming waste land and opening up the country, at the same time making a major contribution to the alleviation of poverty and famine. During Nimmo's lifetime upwards of thirty piers or harbours were built under his direction on the Irish coast, and a harbour at Porth-cawl in Glamorgan; the Wellesley Bridge and docks at Limerick were also designed by him. He built many bridges and is notable for a flamboyant Gothic-influenced design style, good examples of which can still be seen on the former turnpike road at Poulaphouca between Dublin and Baltinglass. His most important bridge was the elliptical five-arch masonry Wellesley (now Sarsfield) Bridge over the Shannon at Limerick, constructed in 1824–35 for £89,000. This skilfully designed bridge, with its whole soffit curved in cross-section into a double bell-mouth shape, is described by Ruddock as 'in everything except size the equal of Perronet's and in its basic form at least a little nearer perfection' (Ruddock, 200). In 1825 Nimmo became interested in railways and reported on a proposed Limerick to Waterford line.

From about 1823 Nimmo practised increasingly in north-west England as a consulting engineer to, for example, the Mersey and Irwell Navigation and the duchy of Lancaster, and jointly with Telford and Robert Stevenson on the abortive Wallasey trans-Wirral ship canal in 1828. In 1826 he gave evidence to parliamentary committees on the Liverpool and Manchester Railway and Norwich Navigation. Later work included the St Helens and Runcorn Gap Railway, the Preston and Wigan Railway, and the Birkenhead and Chester Railway. He was engineer for the Liverpool and Leeds Railway and the Manchester, Bolton, and Bury Railway. In 1827 Nimmo won great distinction for the brilliance of his evidence under cross-examination in the trial between Liverpool corporation and the Mersey Navigation Company regarding the effect on the Mersey river-bed of abstracting water at Woolston. It has been said that he was 'the only engineer of the age who could at all have competed with [Henry] Brougham, the examining counsel, in his knowledge of the higher mathematics and natural philosophy, on which the whole subject in dispute depended' (*DNB*).

Although business occupied much of his time, Nimmo also made contributions to practical astronomy, chemistry, and geology. He was elected a fellow of the Royal Society of Edinburgh in 1811, a member of the Royal Irish Academy (to whom he contributed a paper relating geology and navigation) in 1818, and a member of the Institution of Civil Engineers in 1828. He is not known to have received any formal practical training and was one of the earliest British engineers with an academic approach to his work: as Stevenson commented to Telford, 'there is no bringing him to rule-of-thumb-work' (Stevenson to Telford, 18 Nov 1828, NL Scot., Acc 10706.14). Nimmo died at his home, 78 Marlborough Street, Dublin, on 20 January 1832, aged forty-nine; his obituarist in the *Galway Independent* justly commented on his immensely useful life and that 'as a theorist and scientific member of his profession, he has left no equal'.   ROLAND PAXTON

Sources Anderson, *Scot. nat.* · M. F. Conolly, *Biographical dictionary of eminent men of Fife* (1866) · J. W. de Courcy, 'Alexander Nimmo, engineer: some tentative notes', 1981, University College, Dublin, department of civil engineering [typed MS; paper for National Library of Ireland Society] · T. Ruddock, *Arch bridges and their builders, 1735–1835* (1979), 196–200 · A. W. Skempton, *British civil engineering, 1640–1840: a bibliography of contemporary printed reports, plans, and books* (1987), 148–9 · 'Commissioners of highland roads and bridges: third report', *Parl. papers* (1807), 3.231, no. 100 [incl. A. Nimmo, 'Historical statement of the erection and boundaries of the shires of Inverness, Ross, Cromarty, Sutherland, and Caithness', pp. 75–91] · A. Arrowsmith, *Memoir relative to a map of Scotland* (1809), 20–1 · A. Nimmo, *The King…against Samuel Grimshaw…for a nuisance in diverting the water from the river Mersey, at Woolston…Lancaster Castle*, evidence to Lancashire Summer Assizes in the King's Bench, 10 Sept 1827, 162–78 · *Manchester Courier* (13 Nov 1830) · *Manchester Courier* (6 Aug 1831) · *Manchester Courier* (8 Oct 1831) · private information (2004) · J. Mitchell, *Reminiscences of my life in the highlands*, 1 (1883); facs. edn with introduction by I. Robertson (1971) · R. Stevenson to T. Telford, 18/11/1828, NL Scot., Acc. 10706. 14 · *Galway Independent* (28 Jan 1832) · D. Brewster and others, eds., *The Edinburgh encyclopaedia*, 18 vols. (1808–30)

Archives NL Scot., journal of survey of Inverness-shire | NL Scot., letters, incl. the Robert Stevenson to Telford letter of 18/11/1828 · NRA, priv. coll., letters to Maurice Fitzgerald · PRO NIre., letters to M. Fitzgerald

Likenesses J. E. Jones, bust, Royal Dublin Society

Nimmo, Derek Robert (1930–1999), actor, was born at 26 Springbourne Road, Liverpool, on 19 September 1930, the son of an insurance clerk, Henry Nimmo, and his wife, Marjorie Sudbury Hardy. He was educated at Quarry Bank School, Liverpool, where the enlightened headmaster, R. F. Bailey, prided himself on developing his pupils' imaginations: the vigorous theatre society recruited

Derek Robert Nimmo (1930–1999), by A. Harris, 1973

Nimmo for a number of female roles (and the part of a toadstool) before he distinguished himself as Cassius in *Julius Caesar*. His early flair for comedy (and self-parody) was illustrated by his riding to school on an old sit-up-and-beg bicycle, turning his toes out and beaming on all those he passed with ineffectual benevolence.

He left school at seventeen, and briefly and reluctantly followed his father into the insurance business. He later said, 'You just have to prove yourself to your father. So I went into his business and passed all my exams. Then I was free to be myself' (*The Independent*). After national service (as a corporal in intelligence in Cyprus) he briefly considered the priesthood as a career but instead took a job with a paint company at £12 a week. In his spare time he organized dances and popular music concerts, at one of which he met his future wife, Patricia Sybil Anne Brown (b. 1929/30), who introduced him to an amateur dramatic society. In 1952 he turned professional when he got his first part at the Hippodrome, Bolton, as Ensign Blades in J. M. Barrie's *Quality Street*. He spent four years in repertory—at Clacton-on-Sea, New Brighton, Nottingham, Oldham, and Worcester. On 9 April 1955 he married Patricia Brown; they had two sons and a daughter. Between acting jobs Nimmo took a number of theatre-related jobs: as an assistant to Lew Grade, as a road manager for singer Al Martinez, as a theatrical publicist, and as an impresario, running an agency that put on jazz concerts. With his wife and growing family he sometimes lived in a caravan that he towed from venue to venue.

Nimmo made his first London appearance in Jean Anouilh's *Waltz of the Toreadors* at the Criterion Theatre in 1957 but his career was made in the lighter sort of plays that gave scope to his individuality: *The Amorous Prawn* (Saville Theatre, 1959), *The Irregular Verb to Love* (Criterion, 1961), and the farce *See How They Run* (Vaudeville Theatre, 1964), in which he played the first of the series of clergymen that were to be his speciality. He later admitted to feeling slightly uncomfortable playing bishops, headmasters, and other authority figures for laughs when in real life such people were his friends. He had a great popular success in the musical *Charlie Girl* at the Adelphi, which ran for over 2000 performances between 1965 and 1971. He was in a number of films, including the Beatles' *A Hard Day's Night* (1964) and *Casino Royale* (1969), but his style of buffoonery did not really suit the big screen in the 1960s.

In 1966 Nimmo's comedy career was boosted by a number of television appearances. He was the new neighbour and boyfriend of comedian Sheila Hancock in *The Bed-Sit Girl* and a P. G. Wodehouse 'silly ass' in *The World of Wooster* before taking the role of the Revd Mervyn Noote, a scatty chaplain, in *The Bishop Rides Again*, a single play for the BBC Comedy Playhouse slot. The play was so successful that its writers, Edwin Apps and Pauline Daveney, expanded it into a series, *All Gas and Gaiters*, in the following year. Nimmo was the self-effacing curate opposite William Mervyn's bishop and Robertson Hare's archdeacon. The show ran for five series. The clerical theme was continued in *Oh Brother!*, in which Nimmo played an accident-prone monk, Brother Dominic, for three series (1968–70). A sequel, *Oh Father!* (1973), followed. Nimmo won the Royal Television Society's silver medal in 1970 and the Variety Club of Great Britain's showbusiness personality of the year award in 1971. Throughout the 1970s and 1980s he was a regular in television situation comedies, notably *Life Begins at Forty* (1978 and 1980), with Rosemary Leach, and *Hell's Bells* (1986), in which he once more donned clerical attire to play Dean Selwyn Makepeace, whose life between a touchy sister and a young fiancée is further complicated by the arrival of a new bishop.

Nimmo's great television popularity lasted some twenty years, after which he mainly did stage work, both as a performer and as an impresario, running Intercontinental Entertainment, which toured productions around the world. Nimmo was particular about the plays he would produce; he hated the contemporary tendency to crudity and explicit sex. The tours took him principally to Africa, America, Australia, and the Middle and Far East, and proved highly profitable. He used to joke with friends in Britain that if they wanted to see him they would have to buy a long-haul air ticket. But he maintained his profile as an entertainer in Britain through his long-running connection with the radio show *Just a Minute*. He had taken part in the first recording of the show in July 1967, a panel game in which contestants had to talk for a minute on a given subject without hesitation, repetition, or deviation. Nimmo's ability to gain time for thought by drawling and stuttering drew from his clergyman persona, and his calculated rudeness to the game's chairman, Nicholas Parsons, added to the humour. He continued to appear on the programme until his death. He was a connoisseur of food and wine and a popular after-dinner speaker, and wrote a number of books, including *Derek Nimmo's Drinking Companion* (1979), *Table Talk* (1990), and *Memorable Dinners* (1991); he also edited *O Come on All ye Faithful: a Humorous Church Collection* (1986). Derek Nimmo died on 24 February 1999 in the Chelsea and Westminster Hospital. He had fallen down a flight of steps on 3 December, and spent some time in a coma before eventually succumbing to pneumonia.

Blessed with imposing height, a plummy voice, and distinctive looks, Nimmo could stutter, bumble, and wriggle without losing the respect of his audience. His clerical incompetents poked fun at the Anglican establishment without satirical or destructive intent. Nimmo himself was a convinced Christian and was deeply offended by the controversial theological pronouncements of the bishop of Durham: when lightning struck York Minster shortly after the bishop's consecration there, Nimmo said it showed that God had a sense of humour (*The Times*).

DENNIS BARKER

Sources personal knowledge (2004) · *Daily Telegraph* (25 Feb 1999) · *The Times* (25 Feb 1999) · *The Scotsman* (25 Feb 1999) · *The Independent* (26 Feb 1999) · *The Guardian* (25 Feb 1999) · b. cert. · m. cert. · d. cert. · *WW*
Likenesses A. Harris, photograph, 1973, News International Syndication, London [*see illus.*] · group portrait, photograph, 1974, Hult. Arch. · group portrait, photograph, 1982, Hult. Arch. · photograph, repro. in *The Independent* · photograph, repro. in *The Guardian* · photograph, repro. in *Daily Telegraph*
Wealth at death £561,717: probate, 2001, *CGPLA Eng. & Wales*

Nimmo, James (1654–1709), covenanter, was born in July 1654, the third child, and only son, of John Nimmo (*b.* 1622, *d.* after 1712), factor and baillie on the estate of Boghall, Linlithgowshire, and his wife, Janet Muire (*d.* in or before 1689). He attended the school at Bathgate but owing to a disagreement between his father and the schoolmaster was transferred to the school in Stirling. Nimmo joined the covenanter insurgents after Drumclog, and was among those defeated at Bothwell Bridge on 22 June 1679. Outlawed as a result, he intended to flee to the Netherlands, but went instead to the north of Scotland and was taken into the service of the laird of Park, in Moray. Fear of discovery led him to take service with the laird of Lethen. There, on 14 December 1682, he married Elizabeth Brodie (*d.* in or after 1711), granddaughter of John Brodie of Windyhills. The marriage was conducted by the nonconformist minister Thomas Hog. With the arrival of a party of soldiers under Mackenzie of Siddie he fled to Pluscarden and eventually went south to Edinburgh, arriving on 23 March 1683. His wife joined him on 30 April. They went to Berwick and it was there, on 5 November 1684, that he heard that his father had been imprisoned for communicating with him; he was released in or before February 1685.

In November 1685 Nimmo sailed to the Netherlands, arriving in Rotterdam on 4 December. He returned to Scotland in April 1688 and obtained a post in customs in Prestonpans (1690–91). Soon he turned his hand, successfully, to trading. He was chosen to sit on Edinburgh town council in 1700 and was appointed town treasurer in 1702. He

had four sons and a daughter: John, born in Berwick in 1684, James (1686–1758), born in Rotterdam, and like his elder brother baptized by Mr Hog, Grizel (*b.* 1688), Thomas (1690–1691), and Alexander (1693–1695). He died in Edinburgh on 6 August 1709, after a period of illness, leaving a work entitled *Narrative … written for his own satisfaction, to keep in some remembrance the Lord's ways, dealings, and kindness towards him, 1654–1709*, printed in 1889.

T. F. HENDERSON, *rev.* ALISON G. MUIR

Sources J. Nimmo, *Narrative of Mr James Nimmo: written for his own satisfaction, to keep in some remembrance the Lord's ways, dealings, and kindness towards him, 1654–1709*, ed. W. G. Scott-Moncrieff, Scottish History Society, 6 (1889) · *Reg. PCS*, 3rd ser., 10.352–4, 407, 418–39, 444–50, 460–87 · G. Bain, *Lord Brodie: his life and times, 1617–80* (1904), 187–93

Nimmo, Margaret Jane (1850–1938), headmistress, was born on 20 October 1850 at 9 Ash Grove, South Hackney, Middlesex, the daughter of David Nimmo, an Independent minister, and his wife, Mary (*née* Hutton). Until 1865 she was educated at home, but thereafter she took advantage of the new educational opportunities opening up for women. From 1865 to 1869 she attended Bedford College, London, one of the only two colleges then open to women in England, extending her studies both there and in France and Germany between 1869 and 1873. Having taken the University of London general examination for women in 1870, she became in 1875 a teacher at the fledgeling Notting Hill High School for Girls, one of the first Girls' Public Day School Company (GPDSC) schools and almost a training school for future headmistresses. After the University of London amended its charter to allow women to take degrees in 1878, she left Notting Hill and enrolled herself at University College, London, gaining her BA in 1881.

When the Blackheath GPDSC High School for Girls opened in 1880, Miss Nimmo became its second mistress and its first graduate teacher. Here she established high standards in mathematics and classics and taught 'interesting and instructive' experimental chemistry despite little support as yet for science. She transplanted the new disciplined ethos of girls' public secondary education when appointed first headmistress of King Edward VI Grammar School for Girls, Birmingham, in 1883. This school was a prime example of the post-1869 extension of educational endowments to girls; it was founded in 1880 at the insistence of the charity commissioners for girls up to the age of seventeen. One half of the scholarships were held by girls who had attended public elementary schools. Paid a professional salary, Miss Nimmo created a working atmosphere in a school which ran like clockwork. She put considerable stress upon information, rote learning, and competition, and developed high academic standards with increasing numbers going on to university, although, until 1910, subjects like science and gymnastics suffered from a lack of facilities.

Remembered for her severe, Savonarola-like features and black, rustling silk gowns, Miss Nimmo was regarded as an all-seeing, authoritative figure. She took great care to keep her girls segregated from boys. A teacher was on one occasion reprimanded for playing tennis without a hat on. Yet Miss Nimmo was also affectionately recalled as sympathetic and always concerned for the welfare of the girls. She oversaw the grammar school's move from Aston to Handsworth in 1911 and amalgamations which, by 1915, increased the pupils under her to about 460, some 300 more than when the school opened in 1883. Although not a radical, Miss Nimmo therefore did much to extend educational opportunities for girls in Birmingham. She retired in 1915 but frequently attended school functions and, in fact, used the speech day of 1920 to lead a successful protest against the local authority taking over the King Edward schools.

Known as a 'puritan liberal' who doubted whether a Conservative could be honest, and a determined upholder of free trade, Miss Nimmo suited well the dominant Birmingham nonconformist bourgeoisie. Although not supportive of militant suffragism on her staff, she was said to have mellowed in later years. She retired to Gerrards Cross, Buckinghamshire, where she died at her niece's house at Hethersett North Park on 7 April 1938; she was buried at Brookwood cemetery. RUTH WATTS

Sources A. Thorne, *King Edward's Grammar School for Girls, Handsworth, 1883–1983* (1983) · private information · R. Waterhouse, *Six King Edward grammar schools, 1883–1983* (1983) · M. C. Malim and H. C. Escreet, eds., *The book of the Blackheath High School* (1927) · *A catalogue of the archives of Bedford College, 1849–1985*, Bedford College [1987] · J. E. Sayers, *The fountain unsealed: a history of the Notting Hill and Ealing high school* (privately printed, Broadwater Press, 1973) · Birmingham biography newspaper cuttings, 1937–8, Birm. CL, 28 · Birmingham biography newspaper cuttings, 1941–2, Birm. CL, 33 · J. Sondheimer and P. R. Bodington, eds., *The Girl's Public Day School Trust, 1872–1972: a centenary review* (1972) · J. S. Pederson, *The reform of girls' secondary and higher education in Victorian England* (1987) · K. E. McCrone, '"Playing the Game" and "Playing the Piano": physical culture and culture at girls' public schools c.1850–1914', *The private schooling of girls past and present*, ed. G. Walford (1993), 33–55 · C. Monthorpe, 'Science education in the public schools for girls in the late nineteenth century', *The private schooling of girls: past and present*, ed. G. Walford (1993), 56–78 · *The historical record, 1836–1912: being a supplement to the calendar completed to September 1912*, University of London (1912) · 'Royal commission on secondary education: minutes of evidence', *Parl. papers* (1895), vol. 44, C. 7862-I · b. cert. · *CGPLA Eng. & Wales* (1938)

Archives King Edward Resources Centre, Edgbaston Park Road, Birmingham, King Edward VI Foundation Archives

Likenesses photograph, King Edward VI Grammar School for Girls, Handsworth, Birmingham · photographs, repro. in Sayers, *Fountain unsealed*

Wealth at death £3,112 0s. 3d.: probate, 10 June 1938, *CGPLA Eng. & Wales*

Nimptsch, Julius [Uli] (1897–1977), sculptor, was born in Berlin on 22 May 1897, the younger son and second of the four children of Siegfried Nimptsch, a broker on the Berlin stock exchange. He was a descendant of the distinguished German poet Nikolaus Niembsch von Lenau (1802–1850). He studied sculpture at the Akademie der Künste in Berlin from 1919 to 1926 under Wilhelm Gerstel and Hugo Lederer and was awarded a Rome prize in 1928. Rome was his base throughout the 1930s, though he lived in Paris for a year and returned to Germany in 1936–7. He lived in Bavaria but left Germany for the sake of his Jewish wife Ruth Berthe Steinthal (d. 1974), daughter of Max Steinthal of Berlin, whom he married in 1925, and with whom he had one son. He went to Paris and Rome again before settling in London in 1939. He arrived with no knowledge of English, but took British nationality after the war and lived in Fulham Road, London.

In Italy Nimptsch had worked privately and there is no record of public exhibition. He is reported to have said that he studied his 'masters the Greeks and Romans'. He was always a modeller and not a carver, and several studies of the female nude survive from this period. The life model—usually young—was his preferred subject, and, despite working in Rome, it was the naturalistic style of Jules Dalou and Charles Despiau that was his example. His masterpiece from the 1930s was *Marietta* (1936–8), a full-length standing nude with her hands over her head, a cast of which was acquired by Leeds City Art Gallery in 1944 at the time of the exhibition arranged by Philip Hendy. This life study of a young girl, in a restrained and self-contained pose, is typical of his work, except that it is life-size and not a small-scale study.

Wartime sculptures made in London by Nimptsch were different, being small-scale high reliefs in bronze or lead of narratives from the Bible or classical mythology. He returned, however, to life studies and was not influenced by British sculpture. He exhibited comparatively rarely, having one-man exhibitions at the Redfern Gallery, London (1942), and at Leeds (1944), then at the Walker Art Gallery, Liverpool (1957), the Stone Gallery, Newcastle upon Tyne (1965), and finally at the Diploma Gallery of the Royal Academy of Arts, London (1973). His work was included in some of the Arts Council's outdoor sculpture exhibitions in the 1950s and 1960s. In 1951 *Girl Sitting on a Stone Plinth* was acquired for the Arts Council's collection, and his best-known work, *Olympia* (1956), a reclining nude lying full length, supported on an elbow and an arm, was acquired by the Tate Gallery, London (Chantrey bequest).

Portrait busts were commissioned of Paul Oppé (1949, print room, British Museum, London), Sir Caspar John (1959), Sir Mortimer Wheeler (1969, British Academy, London), and Brendan, Viscount Bracken (Bracken House, London). The over life-size sculpture of Lloyd George (1961–3) for the House of Commons had been originally commissioned from Sir Jacob Epstein, but after his death in 1959 it was awarded to Nimptsch. A group, *The Good Samaritan* (1961), was commissioned by Selly Oak Hospital, Birmingham, and *Neighbourly Encounter* (1961) by the London county council for Silwood housing estate.

Nimptsch exhibited at the Royal Academy almost annually from 1957 to 1969 and was elected an ARA in 1958 and an RA in 1967. He bequeathed ten of his sculptures to the academy, along with the portrait of himself by Oskar Kokoschka, who had been a friend in London. In Britain after the war his work as a life sculptor was unfashionable, but he persevered with the subject he most admired in work that is consistent over forty years. He has had no exhibition since 1973, and there are few sculptures on the market. His best nude studies possess an admirable sense of the conflict between liveliness and restraint, and few other sculptors in Britain took on this subject with such seriousness or such a sense of decorum. Uli Nimptsch died on 2 January 1977 in London.   DAVID FRASER JENKINS

Sources catalogue file, Tate collection · *Uli Nimptsch RA, sculptor* (1973) [exhibition catalogue, Royal Academy of Arts] · *CGPLA Eng. & Wales* (1977) · *DNB*
Wealth at death £22,049: probate, 13 May 1977, *CGPLA Eng. & Wales*

Ninian [St Ninian] (*supp. fl.* **5th–6th cent.**), missionary and bishop, is credited with building Candida Casa at Whithorn, in south-west Scotland, where he was buried. It is symptomatic of the paucity of firm information about his life that there should be entrenched scholarly disagreement even about when he lived. It was generally assumed, on inadequate evidence, that he flourished in the fifth century; but more recently it has been argued, from the same inadequate evidence, that he was active as late as the mid-sixth century. Another suggestion is that there were, in fact, two Ninians, who flourished in the fifth and sixth centuries respectively. The only certainty is that the life and career of the real St Ninian is impenetrably obscure.

The chief medieval account of Ninian's career is a life written in the twelfth century, which, because of both its hagiographical nature and its late date, is an unconvincing source for any genuine information about the saint. There are, however, much earlier works, the eighth-century *Miracula Nynie episcopi* and Bede's *Historia ecclesiastica* (completed in 731), which give details about the saint's career. Both claim that he travelled to Rome (either for training or for consecration as bishop); that he converted some Picts (the Picts south of the Mounth, according to Bede); and that he built the church known as Candida Casa ('white house') at Whithorn, which he dedicated to St Martin of Tours. The *Miracula* add that he restored the sight of a King Tudwal who had become blind after harassing the saint.

Unfortunately it is impossible to give unqualified credence to any of this material. None of it can be traced earlier than the Anglian bishopric at Whithorn established in Bede's time. Ninian's trip to Rome could too easily be an eighth-century hagiographical fiction, and the blinding of Tudwal a stock attempt by Whithorn to arm itself against secular interference through this salutary tale (possibly aimed originally at seventh-century kings of Man who descended from a King Tudwal). The statement that Ninian converted some Picts may have a kernel of truth, but it could also reflect Anglian claims of overlordship over the southern Picts (which they exercised in the decades prior to the catastrophic battle of 'Dunnichen' or 'Nechtansmere' in 685), or equally an attempt to find a figure to counter Iona's St Columba. The seed of reality may simply be that Ninian converted the people called Cruithnig, who may have migrated from Ulster to the Rhinns of Galloway in the fifth century, and that the coincidence that Cruithnig was also the Gaelic name for the Picts was later exploited (perhaps by the Gaelic monastery which, it has been suggested, was established at Whithorn in the sixth century). Attempts have been made to link St Ninian with place-name evidence for Brittonic influence over the southern Picts, but the most that this evidence can show is that the southern Picts adopted Christianity from their southern neighbours, the Britons. The Britons they came into contact with are likely to have been their neighbours the Votadini (Gododdin), rather than a bishop from Scotland's south-west extremity. Finally, there is doubt about whether St Ninian should in any sense be regarded as the founder of Whithorn, or about what kind of Christian settlement Whithorn may have originally been. No archaeological evidence for a church site of fifth-century date has been forthcoming, and it has been suggested that it was an Irish monastic foundation of the sixth century.

The obscurity of the real St Ninian may, in part, be a consequence of the belief that he was the first evangelist of the Picts, which must have made it even more likely that what was recorded about his life was too important to be determined simply by the random chance of prosaic reality. His cult spread throughout Scotland and into the northern isles, and was carried by medieval Scottish merchants to their places of worship overseas. Whithorn became a major Scottish pilgrimage centre, visited by Robert I (*r.* 1306–29) during his last illness and regularly by James IV (*r.* 1488–1513). In more modern times Ninian has vied with Columba for the symbolic role of 'Scotland's apostle', which has made it even more difficult to arrive at a dispassionate assessment of the evidence for his alleged conversion of the southern Picts and the dating of his career.   DAUVIT BROUN

Sources A. Macquarrie, 'The date of Saint Ninian's mission: a reappraisal', *Records of the Scottish Church History Society*, 23 (1987–9), 1–25 · J. MacQueen, *St Nynia: with a translation of the Miracula Nynie Episcopi and the Vita Niniani by Winifred MacQueen* (1990) · D. Broun, 'The literary record of St Nynia: fact and fiction?', *Innes Review*, 42 (1991), 143–50 · C. Thomas, *Whithorn's Christian beginnings* (1992) · A. C. Thomas, 'The evidence of north Britain', *Christianity in Britain, 300–700*, ed. M. W. Barley and R. P. C. Hanson (1968), 93–122 · A. A. M. Duncan, 'Bede, Iona and the Picts', *The writing of history in the middle ages: essays presented to Richard William Southern*, ed. R. H. C. Davis and J. M. Wallace-Hadrill (1981), 1–42 · D. Fahey, 'The historical reality of St Ninian', *Innes Review*, 15 (1964), 35–46 · P. A. Wilson, 'St Ninian and Candida Casa: literary evidence from Ireland', *Transactions of the Dumfries and Galloway Natural History and Antiquarian Society*, 41 (1962–3), 156–85 · P. A. Wilson, 'St Ninian: Irish evidence further examined', *Transactions of the Dumfries and Galloway Natural History and Antiquarian Society*, 46 (1969), 140–59 · P. Grosjean, 'Les Pictes apostats dans l'épître de S. Patrice', *Analecta Bollandiana*, 76 (1958), 354–78 · P. Hill, *Whithorn and St Ninian: the excavation of a monastic town, 1984–91* (1997)

Nisbet, Alexander (1657–1725), heraldic writer, was born in Edinburgh in April 1657 and was baptized on the 23rd, the eldest son and the third of the ten children of Adam Nisbet (*d.* 1674), writer to the signet in Edinburgh, and his wife, Janet, only daughter of Alexander Aikenhead, writer to the signet. He matriculated at Edinburgh University in 1675, graduating in arts in 1682.

Like his father and maternal grandfather, Nisbet embarked upon a legal career but, by his own account, 'stole as many hours as possible from business' (Nesbitt, 139) to study heraldry. Many interesting Scottish heraldic manuscripts, like the sixteenth-century book of blazon of

Sir David Lyndsay of the Mount (now in the National Library of Scotland), had survived, but only one Scottish reference work on the subject was available and that was *The Science of Heraldry* (1680) by the lord advocate, Sir George Mackenzie of Rosehaugh. By 1687 Nisbet had given up his legal work entirely and was resolved to write a complete and scientific system of heraldry.

Unmarried and living at his family home, the old mansion house of Dean, Edinburgh, Nisbet toiled devotedly at his task for many years. He did not at first realize the high cost of producing an illustrated work and, by the end of the century, was despairingly convinced that he would have to abandon his project for lack of funds. However, his friends persuaded him to apply to parliament for an allowance, and as proof of his capabilities he published in 1703, at his own expense, his *Essay on Additional Figures and Marks of Cadency*, commenting, 'I may say without vanity that nothing of this nature so perfect has hitherto been published' (Nesbitt, 144). Parliament duly granted him £248 6s. 8d. per year, but the financial arrangements for the union of parliaments of 1707 resulted in the disappearance of the fund from which he was paid, and he received no more.

Nisbet was present in the crown room of Edinburgh Castle on 26 March 1707 when the Scottish regalia was solemnly deposited there, but soon afterwards he retired to the country to continue his writing. Although finance remained a problem, his major *System of Heraldry, Speculative and Practical* finally appeared in 1722, earning him an enduring reputation as Scotland's greatest heraldic writer. Three years later, on 5 December 1725, Nisbet died at Dirleton, Haddingtonshire, where he was then living, and was buried on 7 December in Greyfriars churchyard, Edinburgh, beside his father. No portrait of him seems to exist, but George Crawford, author of *The Peerage of Scotland*, commented, 'He was a courtly, modest gentleman, who had as many friends and as few enemies as any man I have known' (Nesbitt, 147-8).

ROSALIND K. MARSHALL

Sources R. C. Nesbitt, *Nisbet of that ilk*, reprint (1994) · *Alexander Nisbet the herald, 1657-1725* (1934) · *DNB* · 'Part of the science of herauldrie and the exterior ornaments of the shield', Lyon Office, Edinburgh, MS 39 · 'Blazon of the arms of Scottish families', U. Edin. L., MS La.111.284 · 'Genealogical collections with some heraldic plates', NL Scot., Adv. MS 34.3.5
Archives Lyon Office Library, draft MS with additions and corrections from *System of heraldry* · U. Edin. L., special collections division, ordinary of Scottish arms | NL Scot., genealogical collections
Wealth at death died in poverty: Nesbitt, *Nisbet*, 147

Nisbet, Charles (1736–1804), Church of Scotland minister and college head, was born on 21 January 1736 in Long Yester, Haddingtonshire, Scotland, the second of four children of schoolmaster William Nisbet and his wife, Alison Hepburn. Prepared by his father he entered Edinburgh University in 1752 and later attended Divinity Hall, completing his studies in 1760. Licensed to preach by the Edinburgh presbytery of the Church of Scotland in 1760, Nisbet first presided at Gorbals Chapel of Ease. In 1764 he was called to Montrose, on the north-east coast, and was ordained by the presbytery of Brechin on 17 May of that year.

During ten years as second, and eleven as first minister at Montrose, Nisbet became a well-known, if somewhat controversial, figure in the Scottish church. He gradually emerged as a leader within the evangelical or popular party of the church, frequently expressing opposition to the moderate party's control over the general assembly, and to moderates' practices, including patronage appointments to church livings and the tendency to emphasize morality rather than piety in sermons and writings. During these years his pastoral performance evidently satisfied his congregation, but he squabbled with his church session over the glebe, which was retained by the man whom Nisbet succeeded as first minister, over his salary, and over the need for a new church building. A short, stout man with piercing eyes, given to formal dress, Nisbet possessed a combination of inordinate intelligence and acerbic wit which enhanced both his effectiveness in debate and his prickly relations with his board.

Nisbet's notoriety increased during the American revolutionary era. His dismay at agricultural hard times and at what he believed to be commercial discrimination by England against Scotland prompted a desire for political reform along the lines advanced by the Scottish commonwealth whigs. He consequently developed a sympathy for the American protests against British efforts to interfere in the internal affairs of the colonies, and outspokenly defended the revolutionaries from his pulpit and in the general assembly, which earned the opprobrium of moderates in general and his own congregation in particular. Additionally, his long held suspicion of Roman Catholic intentions, especially in the highlands, made him an activist in the protests against the employment of Scottish Catholics in the British military, and he became linked with Lord George Gordon's parliamentary campaign against the practice. After the Gordon riots of 1780 Nisbet was questioned as a suspected agent, but was released without charge.

Dismay at Scotland's economic and political prospects, the rift with his church board, and criticism of his pro-American stance combined to make Nisbet uncomfortable in Scotland by the early 1780s. His American sympathies led to an honorary doctorate of divinity, presented in 1783 by the College of New Jersey, in Princeton, under the charge of Nisbet's old friend and fellow Scottish cleric, John Witherspoon. It also led to a call in 1784 from the trustees of the newly founded Dickinson College in Carlisle, Pennsylvania, to become its first principal. Sensing an opportunity to serve God in a new way, to better his economic circumstances, and to bring the Scottish Enlightenment to a country that had just thrown off the shackles of British domination, Nisbet set sail for America in early 1785.

The Nisbet family that arrived in Carlisle on 4 July 1785 consisted of the minister, his wife, Anne Tweedie (d. 1807), the daughter of Thomas Tweedie of Quarter, whom he had married in June 1766, and four surviving children of the eight who had been born to the couple in Montrose.

The eldest, Thomas (1767–1804), became an alcoholic shortly after arrival in America and was the bane of his parents' lives until his death, while two girls grew up to marry well, and the younger boy became a judge in Maryland.

Nisbet's American career was largely unsuccessful. Despite his reformist bent in Scotland the degree of social and political democracy in post-revolutionary Pennsylvania shocked him. He deplored Americans' self-interestedness and bridled at their refusal to bow to his learning and experience. He quarrelled with the college trustees over their refusal to let him govern. He felt his students were solely set on preparing for careers, not on absorbing Enlightenment arts and sciences. As co-pastor of Carlisle's Presbyterian church, he criticized the congregation for non-support and for lack of sincere religious convictions. Pennsylvania and national politics dismayed him. He labelled American political leaders as either demagogues or weaklings, but at the same time lamented the unwillingness of the masses to put aside their self-interest for the common good. For Nisbet the proof of these convictions came in Carlisle's riotous opposition in 1787 to the ratification of the United States constitution, which most townspeople considered anti-democratic, and in the enthusiasm so many Americans demonstrated for the French Revolution, which Nisbet deplored as an attack on social order and godliness.

Nisbet's alienation from America prevented him from continuing the involvement with the church that he had maintained in Scotland. Instead, he assumed the role of caustic critic of American affairs in private correspondence with like-minded friends in America and in Scotland, and exercised little influence on college, church, or state. The reform-minded Scottish cleric became the conservative critic of America because his concept of the social order could not adjust to the democratic individualism characteristic of the post-revolutionary United States. Disillusioned, Nisbet died in Carlisle after a short illness, probably pneumonia, on 18 January 1804, and was buried there two days later.   DAVID W. ROBSON

Sources S. Miller, *Memoir of the Rev. Charles Nisbet D.D.* (1840) · C. C. Sellers, *Dickinson College: a history* (1973) · D. W. Robson, 'Anticipating the brethren: the Reverend Charles Nisbet critiques the French Revolution', *Pennsylvania Magazine of History and Biography*, 121 (1997), 303–28 · D. W. Robson, 'Enlightening the wilderness: Charles Nisbet's failure at higher education in post-revolutionary Pennsylvania', *History of Education Quarterly*, 37 (1997), 271–90 · *Fasti Scot.*, new edn, vol. 5 · R. W. White, *A family chronicle, Charles Nisbet, book one* (1980) · *Carlisle Gazette* [Carlisle, PA] (1 Feb 1804)

Archives Dickinson College Library, Carlisle, Pennsylvania, letters, papers, lectures | NA Scot., Church of synod general assembly, synod and presbytery records · University of Pittsburgh, Pennsylvania, Darlington Library, Addison corresp.

Likenesses portrait, 1922 (after H. T. Carpenter) · H. T. Carpenter, oils, Dickinson College, Carlisle, Pennsylvania

Wealth at death $990 plus $9954 in debts owed to him; also library valued at $356: inventory of goods and chattels belonging to the estate of the late Dr Charles Nisbet, 25 Sept 1804, Dickinson College Archive, Carlisle, Pennsylvania

Nisbet, Sir John, Lord Dirleton (1610–1688), judge and politician, was born at Edinburgh on 1 July 1610, son to Sir

Sir John Nisbet, Lord Dirleton (1610–1688), by Robert White (after David Paton)

Patrick Nisbet, Lord Eastbank, and Jean Arthur, who is sometimes confused as wife to Patrick Nisbet of Drydene. His father, who was third son of James Nisbet, merchant of Edinburgh, and Margaret, sister of Thomas Craig of Riccarton, Edinburghshire, became an ordinary lord of session in 1635, at which time he took his title. He was subsequently knighted (1638), but on 13 November 1641 he and three other judges were replaced by the estates for certain 'crimes libelled against them' (*Historical Works of Balfour*, 3.152). John Nisbet graduated at Edinburgh in 1629, was admitted advocate on 20 November 1633, and distinguished himself as council for Lord Balmerino in 1634. He was appointed sheriff-depute and commissary of Edinburgh in 1639.

Nisbet's career during the years of the covenanting and Cromwellian governments was characterized by little effective political involvement on the one hand and an expanding legal practice on the other. Royal favour did come his way in the 1640s when he was appointed advocate to Prince Charles warranted under the sign manual of Charles I. The fact that the marquess of Montrose, facing the charge of treason in 1641, petitioned parliament to include Nisbet in his defence team is no doubt testament to Nisbet's instinctive crown loyalty but also, more importantly, to his reputation as a formidable advocate. Along with senators of the college of justice and the senior lawyers of Edinburgh he declared his support for the royalist engagement in 1648, yet seems not to have particularly suffered from its failure. He continued as commissary of Edinburgh throughout the 1650s and accumulated his fortune when political prospects were limited.

By the early 1660s Nisbet was a wealthy advocate and in 1663 purchased the lands of Dirleton from James Maxwell, Viscount Cranborne, heir to the earl of Dirleton. On 14 October 1664 he was appointed lord advocate after Sir John Fletcher, lord advocate 1661–4, was forced to demit the office, and took the title Lord Dirleton. As lord advocate he was a severe prosecutor of the covenanters, although it would have been impossible to remain in office without a rigorous policy. Knowledge of his role in these repressions depends too much on the testimony of presbyterian historians such as Robert Wodrow. None the less, the repression was real enough. After the Pentland rising of 1666, on 15 August 1667 Nisbet arranged that fifty persons accused of being rebels and part of the rising were tried in their absence and sentenced to death. The scale rather than the nature of this extreme procedure was unusual, and the precaution was taken to indemnify the judges by act of parliament.

Ironically, George Hickes, chaplain to secretary of state John Maitland, earl of Lauderdale, suggested that Nisbet fell from office because he was a presbyterian 'fanatic' (BL, Lansdowne MS 988, fol. 154). However, Nisbet's real difficulties resulted from party politics, not from his views on religion. In 1670 he was one of the commissioners sent to London to confer over Charles II's proposal for a union of the kingdoms. Lauderdale was directed by his king to procure the agreement of the Scottish parliament, but Nisbet expressed personal opposition to its abolition. While not alone in this view, he was now out of favour with Lauderdale and his party, nor could he rely on the parliamentary opposition when led by the duke of Hamilton. Hamilton was lukewarm towards Nisbet's repressive measures against extreme presbyterians, his estates being in the disaffected areas. When Nisbet's cousin Sir Patrick Nisbet of Dean was accused of perjury before the privy council, the word spread that the lord advocate was suspected of arranging a bribe to settle the case. Although nothing could be proved Nisbet was subsequently accused by Lord Halton (Hatton), Lauderdale's brother, of taking fees from both sides in a case relating to the entail of the Leven estates. The judges of the court of session were directed to investigate the case and while again nothing was actually proved Nisbet, short of allies, resigned in 1677, even though his successor, Mackenzie of Rosehaugh, advised a legal defence. It was possible to be a royalist presbyterian and to prosecute presbyterian extremists but impossible to remain lord advocate without political support.

Gilbert Burnet described Nisbet as 'one of the worthiest and learnedest men of his age', though he 'loved money too much' (Burnet, 1.279, 2.129–30). He was clearly a man of letters as well as an effective lawyer. At the burning of his house he is said to have lost a curious Greek manuscript, for the recovery of which he offered £1000 sterling. A catalogue of his library was printed in 1690, and a copy is in the National Library of Scotland, Edinburgh. His *Some Doubts and Questions, in the Law*, edited by Sir William Hamilton of Whitelaw, advocate, and his collections, and comments on, the decisions of the lords of council and session from 7 December 1665 to 26 June 1677, were published together, posthumously, in 1698 by the printer George Mosman, the privy council granting Mosman a nineteen-year licence. Nisbet was also commercially active and, as well as extending his Dirleton estate, invested in coalmining and merchant shipping.

Nisbet married four times: his first wife was Margaret Fletcher; on 16 June 1653 he married Helen, daughter to Alexander Hay, clerk of session, whose mother Jean Winerame he supported; his third marriage was to Susanne, second daughter of Sir James Monypenny of Pitmilly; last, on 30 January 1670, he married Jean, daughter of Sir Alexander Morrison of Prestongrange. Nevertheless, he died in 1688 without male heirs and his kinsman William Nisbet, a future shire commissioner, succeeded to the estate of Dirleton. Nisbet's will and testament survive and show him to have been financially comfortable at his death, his inventory of goods and money amounting to over £19,000 Scots. He was buried at Greyfriars, Edinburgh, on 13 April 1688.   A. J. MANN

Sources DNB · NA Scot., Biel MSS, ED.6. ED.6–464; 988 · G. Mackenzie, *Memoirs of the affairs of Scotland* (1821), 324–6 · commissary court records, register of testaments (Edinburgh), NA Scot., CC 8/8/79 · J. Nicoll, *A diary of public transactions and other occurrences, chiefly in Scotland, from January 1650 to June 1667*, ed. D. Laing, Bannatyne Club, 52 (1836), 421 · R. Wodrow, *The history of the sufferings of the Church of Scotland from the Restauration to the revolution*, 2 vols. (1721–2) · *Bishop Burnet's History* · Register House, old parish registers, NA Scot., RH. OPR. 705.1 · M. D. Young, ed., *The parliaments of Scotland: burgh and shire commissioners*, 2 (1993), 543 · APS, 1661–9, 562–3 · F. J. Grant, ed., *The Faculty of Advocates in Scotland, 1532–1943*, Scottish RS, 145 (1944), 165 · D. Laing, ed., *A catalogue of the graduates … of the University of Edinburgh*, Bannatyne Club, 106 (1858), 43 · *The historical works of Sir James Balfour*, ed. J. Haig, 3 (1824), 152, 222 · privy council registers, NA Scot., PC.2.27.7v · BL, Lansdowne MS 988, fol. 154

Archives NA Scot., corresp. and MSS, GD 205/60440 · NA Scot., papers as lord advocate, corresp. · Yale U., 'Sir John Nisbet's observations' | BL, letters to duke of Lauderdale and Charles II, Add. MSS 23123–23138, *passim* · NA Scot., Biel muniments, ED.6 403–2152

Likenesses J. Brand, ink drawing, 1791 (after R. White), Scot. NPG · G. P. Harding, pen and ink, and wash drawing (after D. Paton), NPG · R. White, line engraving (after D. Paton), BM, NPG [*see illus.*] · watercolour on ivory, Scot. NPG; on loan from National Museum of Scotland

Wealth at death £19,523 Scots: testament and will registers with commissary court records of Edinburgh, 21 Aug 1688, NA Scot., CC 8/8/79

Nisbet, John (1627–1685), covenanter activist, was the son of James Nisbet, a tenant farmer of Hardhill, near Loudoun, Ayrshire. As a youth he entered military service on the continent, but was present at the coronation of Charles II at Scone in 1650. In the company of the king he subscribed the covenant, swearing his allegiance to 'all the acts of reformation attained to in Scotland from 1638 to 1649' (Howie, 504). Thereafter he returned to the family home at Hardhill, where he married Margaret Law. The couple had at least three sons, including Alexander, James, and John.

A man of strict presbyterian principles, Nisbet soon found himself in opposition to the episcopal regime imposed by the crown at the Restoration. He appeared regularly at illegal field conventicles throughout the 1660s, and in November 1666 took an active part in the ill-fated Pentland rising in which he was seriously wounded. His exploits at Pentland earned him the rank of captain in the covenanting movement, and in that capacity he was present at the battles of Drumclog and Bothwell Brig in June 1679. In the wake of the latter, Nisbet was denounced an outlaw and a reward of £2000 (Scots) offered for his capture. As a result his family suffered brutal treatment at the hands of dragoons eager to secure the bounty, who—on one such occasion—seized the youngest son and kicked 'him several times to the ground … and left him in his blood' (Hewison, 2.368). During such occurrences Nisbet spent his time hiding in a cave 'near or about his own house', where he passed the time '[writing] out all the new testament' (Howie, 505).

Undoubtedly, Nisbet's 'courage … hardiness and considerable warmth of spirit' gained the admiration of many contemporaries (Wodrow, 4.236), as did the privations suffered by his family. His wife, Margaret, fell ill in December 1683, and died 'on the eighth day of her sickness' (Howie, 494). In November 1685 Nisbet was captured at Fenwick, Ayrshire. His companions were shot in the ensuing scuffle, but for the sake of the reward Nisbet was spared, and imprisoned in the Tolbooth at Edinburgh. He was executed at the Grassmarket on 4 December 1685, 'in the fifty-eighth year of his age' (Howie, 505). Nisbet wrote a brief 'Relation' of his trial before the privy council (at which he denounced the king as a papist), which is reproduced in Robert Wodrow's *History of the Sufferings of the Church of Scotland*. His son James kept a diary of his own religious experiences (but containing some incidental references to his parents), which was published as the *Private life of the persecuted, or, Memoirs of the first years of one of the Scottish covenanters* at Edinburgh in 1827.   VAUGHAN T. WELLS

Sources J. Howie, *The Scots worthies*, ed. W. H. Carlaw, [new edn] (1870) · *Reg. PCS*, 3rd ser., vols. 9, 12 · J. K. Hewison, *The covenanters: a history of the church in Scotland from the Reformation to the revolution*, 2nd edn, 2 (1913) · *Historical notices of Scotish affairs, selected from the manuscripts of Sir John Lauder of Fountainhall*, ed. D. Laing, 2, Bannatyne Club, 87 (1848) · R. Wodrow, *The history of the sufferings of the Church of Scotland from the Restauration to the revolution*, 2 vols. (1721–2) · Anderson, *Scot. nat.*, vol. 3 · *DNB*
Wealth at death estate forfeited *c*.1680

Nisbet, Murdoch (*fl.* 1531–*c*.1559), biblical translator, was a notary public in the diocese of Glasgow. A resident of Hardhill in the parish of Loudoun, Ayrshire, Nisbet's notarial work associated him with known religious dissidents in the area around Kyle and Cunninghame, and particularly with the Campbells of Cessnock and Lockharts of Bar. He took part in Bible reading in a conventicle, an activity which was prosecuted elsewhere in the diocese as early as 1531. The group read from a manuscript New Testament translated by Nisbet into Scots from the revised version of the Lollard New Testament. Nisbet's manuscript New Testament survived for some time as a family heirloom, but it was eventually sold and is now in the British Library (Egerton MS 2880). Although the manuscript does not bear Nisbet's name, it does bear an embellishment on several verso leaves which resembles Nisbet's notarial instrument; this, in addition to his family's ownership of the text, suggests that he was in fact the copyist. The biblical text, along with some of the Old Testament epistles, was copied with slightly elaborated initials in red and green, and such other features as running book and chapter headings.

The date of transcription is impossible to determine; a later family memoir claims that Nisbet had to flee abroad some time during the reign of James V because of his beliefs, during which time he 'took a Copy of the New Testament in Writ' (Nisbet, 3). At a later date, the manuscript was augmented with additions drawn from Miles Coverdale's New Testament, published by James Nycolson at Southwark in late 1537 or early 1538 (STC 2838). These include a preface to the New Testament, Tyndale's revised preface to Romans, book summaries divided by chapter, marginal glosses and cross-references, and liturgical reading markers; all of them, like the text, were transcribed into Scots. A few changes to the text were also made, most significantly the altering of 'sacrament' to 'secret' in nine places. This second stage of textual composition was produced with a less careful, perhaps more rushed hand than that of the New Testament text, though it is possible that it was still Nisbet's work. The additional material presents throughout a developed solafideist theology, with occasional anti-papal or anti-monastic glosses. In the preface to Romans, Tyndale's later position on law and gospel is set out along with much basic Lutheran theological material.

The only significant alteration made by the copyist in this second stage was the omission of a gloss on Matthew 5: 34 which mitigated Christ's prohibition on swearing, which suggests that although Nisbet's circle readily accepted much of protestant theology it was unwilling to depart from its typically Lollard aversion to swearing. That this should be so after 1538 shows that Lollardy had a lasting, if limited, influence in the south-west of Scotland. The family memoir reports that in 1539 Nisbet 'digged and built a Vault in the Bottom of his own House' to avoid detection of his conventicle's Bible reading; he emerged during the regency of Mary of Guise, that is, some time between 1554 and 1559, to take part in iconoclastic activity 'tho' then an old Man' (Nisbet, 3). The date of his death is not recorded. Knox and his historiographical successors do not mention Nisbet, but this may reflect the limitations of their researches rather than the true extent of his importance. Among Nisbet's descendants was a martyr of the covenanter cause, John Nisbet, who was executed in 1685.   MARTIN HOLT DOTTERWEICH

Sources J. Nisbet, *A true relation of the life and sufferings of John Nisbet in Hardhill*, 2nd edn (1719) · T. G. Law, ed., *The New Testament in Scots*

... c. 1520, 3 vols., STS, 46, 49, 52 (1901–5) • J. Anderson, ed., *Calendar of the Laing charters, AD 854–1837, belonging to the University of Edinburgh* (1899), 102 • G. S. Pryde, ed., *Ayr burgh accounts, 1534–1624* (1937), 74 • M. H. B. Sanderson, *Ayrshire and the Reformation* (1997), 42–3 • T. M. A. Macnab, 'The New Testament in Scots', *Records of the Scottish Church History Society*, 11 (1951–3), 82–103 • D. F. Wright, '"The commoun buke of the kirke": the Bible in the Scottish Reformation', *The Bible in Scottish life and literature*, ed. D. F. Wright (1988), 155–78 • W. I. P. Hazlett, 'Nisbet, Murdoch', *DSCHT* • G. Tulloch, *A history of the Scots Bible* (1989) • T. M. Lindsay, 'A literary relic of Scottish Lollardy', *SHR*, 1 (1903–4), 260–73 • P. Wiechert, 'Über die Sprache der einzigen schottischen Bibelübersetzung von Murdoch Nisbet', PhD diss., University of Königsberg, 1908 • L. J. Trinterud, 'A reappraisal of William Tyndale's debt to Martin Luther', *Church History*, 31 (1962), 24–45

Archives NA Scot., charter, MS GD 163 (Portland muniments) 10/2 • NL Scot., charter, Laing Charters no. 390

Nisbet, William (1759–1822), physician and writer, gained his MD at Aberdeen in 1785 and became MRCS at Edinburgh in 1786. After 1801, he practised in Fitzroy Square, London. Despite his prolific publications, little else is known of his life. The most famous of his numerous medical books was *The Clinical Guide* (pt 1, 1793–9; pts 2 and 3, 1800). Unlike other contemporary medical guidebooks, which were often unwieldy in size and verbose in language, Nisbet promised a work that was factual, lucid, and atheoretical. All parts included a practical pharmacopoeia. The title pages stated that the work was to be used as 'a memorandum-book for young practitioners', and it was explicitly marketed at young hospital-based doctors, in whose coat pockets the octavo-sized *Clinical Guide* would easily sit.

Among Nisbet's other medical books were *First Lines of the Theory and Practice in Venereal Diseases* (1787), *An Inquiry into ... the Cure of Scrophula and Cancer* (1795), *On the Diseases of Infancy and Childhood* (1800), *A Practical Treatise on Diet* (1801), and *A Medical Guide for the Invalid to the Principal Watering Places of Great Britain* (1804).

Nisbet was also almost certainly the author of the anonymous *Picture of the present state of the Royal College of Physicians of London; containing memoirs, biographical, critical, and literary* (1817), later published as *Authentic memoirs, biographical, critical, and literary, of the most eminent physicians and surgeons of Great Britain* (1822). This work is important in nineteenth-century medical biographical writing. Unlike any previous collection of medical biographies, *Authentic Memoirs* included details not only of living subjects, but also of a wide variety of medical practitioners. Its polemical and cynical tone was also unusual in contemporary medical biography. The book strongly criticized the fellows of the Royal College of Physicians of London for failing to relax their fellowship requirements, particularly for medical practitioners with Scottish or continental qualifications. While the colourful and pithy biographical sketches were often scathing of fellows, for their lack of science and love of society, they also praised reformist licentiates of the college for their scientific attainments and moral characters.

Although few details of Nisbet's life have survived, he is noteworthy as an early popularizer of medical guidebooks, aimed at a professional and lay audience, that were as easy to read as they were to hold. MARTEN HUTT

Sources M. Hutt, 'Medical biography and autobiography in Britain, c.1780–1920', DPhil diss., U. Oxf., 1995, 63–70 • Watt, *Bibl. Brit.* • [J. Watkins and F. Shoberl], *A biographical dictionary of the living authors of Great Britain and Ireland* (1816) • *DNB* • R. Hunter and I. Macalpine, 'Manuscript evidence for William Nisbet's authorship', *Medical History*, 6 (1962), 187–9

Nisbett [*née* Macnamara; *other married name* Boothby], **Louisa Cranstoun** (1812–1858), actress, was born on 1 April 1812 in Balls Pond, Hackney, Middlesex, one of the three daughters of Frederick Hayes Macnamara and his wife, Jane Elizabeth, *née* Williams. Her aunt was Lady Cranstoun and her paternal grandfather was a merchant in St Kitts, West Indies, who spent three fortunes. On his marriage her father quit the 52nd foot and tried work as a merchant, but soon decided for the stage under the name of Mordaunt. He played in private theatres, such as those in Wilmington Square and Berwick Street, where his daughter is said to have joined him, as Miss Mordaunt, at an early age. Before she was ten she appeared at the Lyceum (then the English Opera House) for her father's benefit, and then undertook parts beyond her years, such as that of Edward IV's mistress Jane Shore, which was considered unsuitable. In 1826 she played Lady Teazle at Greenwich, then joined the elder Macready's company at Bristol, and afterwards moved to Cardiff and Stratford upon Avon, where her parts included Portia, Lady Macbeth, Young Norval, and Edmund in *The Blind Boy*. Plays in Northampton, Southampton, and Portsmouth followed, and on 26 October 1829 she was at Drury Lane as Widow Cheerly in Andrew Cherry's *The Soldier's Daughter*, where her aunt visited her in the green room and her success was assured. During the next two years she played a large variety of parts, some original, at Drury Lane and the Haymarket. In 1831 she left the stage, costing her father £1500 for breach of contract at those two theatres, to marry John Alexander Nisbett of Brettenham Hall, Suffolk, a captain in the first Life Guards, whom she described as 'never a husband, always a lover'. He was killed on 2 October of that year falling from his horse. His affairs were thrown into chancery, and some years elapsed before Mrs Nisbett obtained any provision under his will. Consequently she returned to Drury Lane to play comedy parts, and went on to act in various provincial towns.

In December 1834, at a salary of £20 a week, Mrs Nisbett became the nominal manager of the little Queen's Theatre in Tottenham Street, London, where it was difficult to see the stage owing to the large fashionable bonnets of the women in the audience. In February 1835 she played Esther in Douglas Jerrold's *Schoolfellows*, supported by her two sisters. The same year she took some time out at other theatres, the Strand and the Adelphi, where on 21 December she was the original Mabellah in Jerrold's *Doves in a Cage*. She also played at the Queen's, where she reopened with five light pieces, in three of which she herself appeared. Her greatest triumph was at the Haymarket,

Louisa Cranstoun Nisbett (1812–1858), by James Godsell Middleton, exh. RA 1838 [as Neighbour Constance in *The Love Chase* by Sheridan Knowles]

where Webster engaged her to play a part written especially for her, that of Constance in *The Love Chase* by Sheridan Knowles, at a very liberal salary. This play ran for nearly a hundred nights and evoked verses about her from a member of the audience. After the close of the season Mrs Nisbett visited Dublin's Hawkins Street Theatre, and on 30 September 1839 she was at Covent Garden with Madame Vestris in *Love's Labours Lost*. On 4 March 1841 she gave an unequalled performance as the original Lady Gay Spanker in Boucicault's *London Assurance*. On the collapse of the Covent Garden management in 1842 she returned to the Haymarket, but was back at the Garden later in the year. On 1 October she was Rosalind to W. C. Macready's Jaques at Drury Lane, where her playing was said by Macready to be inadequate. By this time her financial affairs were settled and she owned a chariot and pair and an elegant little suburban villa. On 15 October 1844 she married Sir William Boothby, bt, of Ashbourne Hall, Derbyshire, at the Episcopal Chapel, Fulham; he died on 21 April 1846. During her short time in Derbyshire she was reputed to have gained the affection of all classes, particularly the poor.

Lady Boothby returned to the stage again as Constance in *The Love Chase* at the Haymarket on 12 April 1847, and in December of that year she took part in a Shakespearian night at Covent Garden with other well-regarded actors, when £800 was raised for the purchase of Shakespeare's birthplace. In 1849 she was included in the company about to start at the Olympic when it was burnt down on

29 March. She then moved to Drury Lane, which was opened by James R. Anderson on 26 December. With her sister Jane Mordaunt she played at the Marylebone on 21 November 1850, and remained there until transferring back to Drury Lane, where she made her last appearance on the stage, as Lady Teazle, on 8 May 1851. Her health had broken down and she retired to St Leonards, Sussex. She was, however, able to take drives in the surrounding countryside, and J. R. Planché met her with her mother, brother, and a sister with two children at a picnic at Bodiam Castle in 1857. All these relatives died within six months and were not long survived by Lady Boothby, who died, at Rosemount, St Leonards, of a stroke on 16 January 1858. She was tall, with a long neck, a lithe figure, an oval face, lustrous eyes, and dark hair. Many writers especially mention her magical laugh, and she was called one of the most entertaining, spirited actresses ever seen on the London stage.   JOSEPH KNIGHT, *rev.* J. GILLILAND

Sources Mrs C. Baron-Wilson, *Our actresses*, 2 vols. (1844) • J. R. Planché, *The recollections and reflections of J. R. Planché*, 2 vols. (1872) • J. W. Marston, *Our recent actors*, 2 vols. (1888) • Boase, *Mod. Eng. biog.* • Ward, *Men of the reign* • E. Stirling, *Old Drury Lane*, 2 vols. (1881) • Genest, *Eng. stage* • H. B. Baker, *The London stage: its history and traditions from 1576 to 1888*, 2 vols. (1889) • *The life and reminiscences of E. L. Blanchard, with notes from the diary of Wm. Blanchard*, ed. C. W. Scott and C. Howard, 2 vols. (1891) • *The Era* (24 Jan 1858) • Hall, *Dramatic ports.* • A. Davies and E. Kilmurray, *Dictionary of British portraiture*, 4 vols. (1979–81)

Archives Theatre Museum, London

Likenesses J. G. Middleton, oils, exh. RA 1838, Worthing Museum and Art Gallery, West Sussex [*see illus.*] • engraving, repro. in Wilson, *Our actresses* • portrait, repro. in *ILN*, 10 (1847), 256 • portrait, repro. in R. Mander and J. Mitchenson, *A picture history of the British theatre* (1957) • portraits, repro. in *Theatrical Times*, 2 (1847), 121, 130 • portraits, repro. in *Dramatic and Musical Review*, 3 (1844), 498, 527 • prints, NPG • prints, BM • twelve portraits, Harvard TC

Wealth at death under £3000: administration, 13 Feb 1858, *CGPLA Eng. & Wales*

Nissen, Peter Norman (1871–1930), mining engineer and inventor of the Nissen hut, was born on 6 August 1871 in New York, the second of the three children of Georg Hermann Nissen (1832–1913), a Norwegian mining engineer, and his wife, Annie Lavinia (1842–*c*.1930), daughter of Elisha Fitch of Nova Scotia. His education at Trinity College, Trinity, North Carolina (1887–8 and 1890–91), and at Queen's University, Kingston, Ontario (1896–7), both of which he left without taking a degree, was interrupted by long periods working at goldmines in the USA and Canada where crushed ore was fed to stamp mills for finer crushing. Georg Nissen suggested improvements in which heavier stamps would be used and each stamp would have its own mortar, unlike the conventional mill where five stamps crushed ore in one mortar. Peter Nissen, having failed to sell the Nissen stamp mill in the United States, redesigned it and introduced it to the Witwatersrand of Transvaal. The Nissen stamp mill proved its superiority over the conventional mill during the period June to September 1911 in Johannesburg. Sales continued until 1926 when it was superseded by the tube mill.

In 1915 Nissen was in France as a temporary lieutenant in the Royal Engineers. In reply to a pressing need for behind the lines accommodation he submitted a design for a semicircular hut similar in principle to the indoor ice hockey sheds of Ontario. For the remainder of the First World War he was settled at Hesdin, in the Pas-de-Calais, where he organized the production of Nissen huts from components made in England which were then shipped to France and Belgium. About 100,000 of the smaller bow huts were assembled, each housing twenty-four men; also 10,000 of the larger hospital huts, each accommodating twenty-four patients. Nissen was awarded the DSO and the order of St Sava of Serbia. He left the British army with the rank of lieutenant-colonel. Immediately after the war he established Nissen Buildings Ltd, which produced Nissen hut type buildings for industry and housing on a site at Rye House, Hoddesdon, Hertfordshire. A Nissen house in Yeovil, Somerset, was listed by the Department of the Environment as an important example of a cost-cutting design for cheap housing. Nissen was thus a pioneer of the mass production of prefabricated huts and houses.

Naturalized as a British subject in 1921, Nissen moved to Deepdale, Westerham Hill, Westerham, Kent, in 1922. On 2 January 1900 he had married Louisa Mair Richmond (1873–1923); they had one daughter. He married Lauretta Maitland (1882–1954) on 4 May 1924; there were two sons. Nissen died of pneumonia at his home on 2 March 1930 and was buried three days later at St Mary the Virgin, Westerham.   F. W. J. MᶜCOSH

Sources private information (2004) · G. Nissen and H. Nissen, *Slekten Nissen fra Bov Sogn i Sønderjylland* (Trondheim, 1978), 738 · *Journal of the Chemical, Metallurgical and Mining Society of South Africa* (Oct–Dec 1911) · *Journal of the Chemical, Metallurgical and Mining Society of South Africa* (Jan 1912) · *Journal of the Chemical, Metallurgical and Mining Society of South Africa* (March 1912) · 'Lt. Col. Nissen speaks to Engineering Society, Queen's University, Kingston', *Queen's Journal* (3 Feb 1920) · model of Nissen bow hut (scale 1 inch to 1 foot, with statistics), IWM, general catalogue 12404 · 'Nissen steel buildings for industrial purposes', *British Engineers' Export Journal* (Aug 1924) · J. Sweet, 'Nissen council homes are now listed buildings', *South Somerset News and Views* (Jan 1988) · F. W. J. MᶜCosh, *Nissen of the huts* (1997) · d. cert. · parish register, St Mary the Virgin, Westerham, Kent, 5 March 1930 [burial]

Likenesses photograph, *c*.1916, priv. coll.

Wealth at death £2040 5s. 7d.: probate, 24 May 1930, *CGPLA Eng. & Wales*

Nithsdale. For this title name *see* Douglas, Sir William, lord of Nithsdale (*c*.1360–1391); Maxwell, Robert, first earl of Nithsdale (*b*. after 1586, *d*. 1646); Maxwell, Winifred, countess of Nithsdale (1672–1749); Maxwell, William, fifth earl of Nithsdale (1676–1744).

Niven, (James) David Graham (1910–1983), actor and author, was born on 1 March 1910 in Belgrave Mansions, London, though in his best-selling autobiographies he later followed the example of his own Hollywood studio publicists by listing the more romantic and picturesque birthplace of Kirriemuir in Scotland. He was the youngest of the four children (two sons and two daughters) born to William Edward Graham Niven (*d*. 1915), a landowner, and his wife, Henrietta Julia Degacher (*d*. 1932), daughter of Captain William Degacher of the South Wales Borderers. At the outbreak of the First World War his father enlisted

(James) David Graham Niven (1910–1983), by Cornel Lucas, 1954

in the Berkshire yeomanry and was killed in action at Gallipoli on 21 August 1915, leaving a widow to bring up their children in somewhat reduced circumstances until in 1917 she married Thomas Platt (from 1922 Comyn-Platt), a former diplomat and three times an unsuccessful Conservative Party parliamentary candidate.

Niven neither knew his father well nor cared for his stepfather at all, his childhood being largely spent at a succession of preparatory boarding-schools (from one of which, Heatherdown in Ascot, he was summarily expelled for stealing); at Stowe School he at last found in the pioneering headmaster J. F. Roxburgh the father figure he so lacked at home. It was at Roxburgh's urging that he was taken into the Royal Military College at Sandhurst in 1928, and his final school report on Niven was unusually prescient: 'Not clever, but useful to have around. He will be popular wherever he goes unless he gets into bad company, which ought to be avoided because he does get on with everybody'.

It was while at Sandhurst that, in a college production of *The Speckled Band*, Niven made his first notable stage appearance, though there was as yet little indication of any desire to enter the acting profession. Instead he was dispatched from Sandhurst in 1929 into the Highland light infantry as a junior officer and stationed on Malta, which conspicuously lacked the social and night life to which he had now become accustomed as a young man about London. After several military pranks born of tedium had misfired, and his army future looked extremely bleak, he sent a telegram to his commanding officer in the summer of 1933 reading simply 'Request Permission Resign Commission', a request which was met with evident relief and almost indecent haste.

With no immediate job prospects in England, his mother recently deceased, and only a vague idea that he might perhaps quite like to be an actor, Niven set sail for Canada: he was just twenty-three and it seemed as good a place as any to start a new life. Within a matter of weeks he had travelled south to New York and found work as a whisky salesman before joining a dubious pony-racing syndicate in Atlantic City, New Jersey. From there he travelled to Los Angeles and began to seek employment as an extra in minor westerns. His Hollywood fortunes distinctly improved when he formed a romantic attachment to the actress Merle Oberon however, and by 1939 as a contract artist at the Goldwyn Studios he had made starring appearances in *The Charge of the Light Brigade* (1936), *The Prisoner of Zenda* (1937), *The Dawn Patrol* (1938), *Raffles* (1939), and *Wuthering Heights* (1939), among a dozen other and lesser films. His Hollywood image was that of the 'grin and tonic' man, a veneer actor who traded in a kind of jovial good fortune, that of the happy-go-lucky adventurer who once shared, with Errol Flynn, a beach house known locally as Cirrhosis-by-the-Sea on account of its constant stock of alcohol.

In truth Niven was a considerably more serious, astute, and talented man, one whose behaviour at the declaration of the Second World War showed characteristic courage: he abandoned a lucrative studio contract and a career which was at last successful and was the first of the few British actors to return from California to enlist. He rejoined the army as a subaltern in the rifle brigade, was released to make three of his best films (*The First of the Few*, 1942; *The Way Ahead*, 1944; and *A Matter of Life and Death*, 1945), and returned to Hollywood in 1946 accompanied by his beloved first wife, Primula Susan (Primmie) Rollo (1918–1946), whom he had married in 1940, and their two young sons, David and James. Primula was the daughter of Flight Lieutenant William Hereward Charles Rollo, solicitor, grandson of the tenth Baron Rollo. Within a few weeks of the Nivens' arrival in California however, Primmie was killed in a fall down a flight of cellar stairs, and though Niven was to marry again in 1948 (the Swedish model Hjördis Paulina Tersmeden, with whom he adopted two daughters, Kristina and Fiona) a certain sadness was now discernible behind the clenched grin of the gentleman player.

Niven's post-war career as an actor was generally undistinguished, coinciding as it did with the collapse of the Hollywood raj of expatriate British officers and gentlemen on screen. By 1951 however, with the publication of his first novel (*Round the Rugged Rocks*), he had discovered a second career as a writer, and in the 1970s he published two anecdotal volumes of memoirs (*The Moon's a Balloon*, 1971; *Bring on the Empty Horses*, 1975) which were the most successful ever written by an actor and ran into many millions of paperback reprints. Shortly before his death he also published a second novel (*Go Slowly, Come back Quickly*, 1981) and had become a regular guest on British and American television chat shows where, as himself, he gave some of his best performances.

In 1958 Niven deservedly won an Oscar for *Separate Tables*, in which he played an army officer who invented a private life when his own proved unsatisfactory, a habit often endorsed by Niven himself in his autobiographies. His later films of note included *The Guns of Navarone* (1961), *Paper Tiger* (1974), and *Murder by Death* (1976). *The Pink Panther* (1963), in which his eternally suave jewel thief contrasted with the bungling, incompetent Inspector Clouseau of Peter Sellers, was his last big commercial success. During an author tour for his last novel in 1981 he was stricken with motor neurone disease which condemned him to a lingering and painful death, one he approached with all the courage and good humour which were the hallmarks of his life. Niven died on 27 July 1983 at his home in the Swiss village of Château d'Oex where he spent many of his later years skiing. He was buried there. A memorial service was held at St Martin-in-the-Fields in London, attended by more than 5000 people.

SHERIDAN MORLEY, *rev.*

Sources D. Niven, *The moon's a balloon* (1971) · D. Niven, *Bring on the empty horses* (1975) · S. Morley, *The other side of the moon* (1985) · *The Times* (30 July 1983) · personal knowledge (1990) · private information (1990)

Archives FILM BFI NFTVA, *Parkinson: the interviews*, BBC 1, 22 Aug 1995 · BFI NFTVA, performance footage | SOUND BL NSA, 'David Niven: Anglo-Saxon type 2008', T6018BW BD1 · BL NSA, documentary recording · BL NSA, oral history interview · BL NSA, performance recordings

Likenesses C. Lucas, photograph, 1954, NPG [*see illus.*]

Niven, Frederick John (1878–1944), novelist, was born on 31 March 1878 in Valparaiso, Chile, the youngest of the three children of John Niven, originally a sewed muslin manufacturer in Glasgow though temporarily in the British consular service, and his wife, Jane, daughter of George Barclay, a Baptist preacher. When Niven was five years old the family returned to Glasgow, where he was educated at Hutcheson's Grammar School.

His parents opposed Niven's wish to become a painter, and as a compromise he enrolled for evening classes in Glasgow School of Art while beginning an apprenticeship in a soft goods manufacturing warehouse. He later wrote in his autobiography: 'I was not enthusiastic about manufacturing … it was Charlie Maclean, head of the wincey department, who informed me, gazing at me solemnly one day, "Freddy, the plain fact is that ye dinna gie a spittle for your work" ' (Niven, 26–7). He left for more congenial employment with MacLehose & Son, librarians and booksellers in Glasgow.

In 1899, because of lung trouble, Niven travelled to British Columbia, Canada, where he regained his health and led an energetic outdoor life. On his return to Glasgow he began a career in journalism. He moved to England and his first novel, *The Lost Cabin Mine*, appeared in 1908. In 1911 he married Mary Pauline Thorne-Quelch (*d.* 1968), who, as his editor's daughter, had typed his manuscripts. *Justice of the Peace*, his best-known novel, was published in 1914 and attracted critical praise, not least for its affectionate and detailed picture of Glasgow.

Found unfit for military service, Niven spent the First World War in London, working for a time in the War Office under the novelist John Buchan. In 1920 he returned to Canada with his wife to settle on the shores of Kootenay Lake, near Nelson, British Columbia, and became a full-time novelist. He produced a number of 'potboiler' westerns and historical novels set in North America, but became respected as a Canadian novelist with the publication of his 'prairie trilogy', *The Flying Years* (1935), *Mine Inheritance* (1940), and *The Transplanted* (1944), which describe the opening up of the Canadian west through the eyes of expatriate Scots.

However, Niven also continued to write the realistic novels of Scottish urban life for which he is better known in Britain. Autobiographical elements can be traced in many of these, with their recurrent themes of Calvinism and maternal influence. *Justice of the Peace* is the story of a young man apprenticed in his father's textile warehouse but determined to become a painter. The father–son relationship is well handled, though the portrait of the forbidding, neurotic mother has elements of melodrama. The eponymous mother in *Mrs Barry* (1933), in contrast, is perhaps implausibly good and heroic. Niven retained clear memories of his youth in Glasgow and returned to a warehouse setting for *The Staff at Simson's* (1937), a near-documentary novel which follows characters over twenty years.

Although he expressed great affection for Scotland, Niven remained in Canada for the rest of his life. After a series of heart attacks he died in hospital in Vancouver on 30 January 1944. His wife survived him.

MOIRA BURGESS

Sources F. Niven, *Coloured spectacles* (1938) · W. H. New, 'Frederick John Niven', *Canadian writers, 1890–1920*, ed. W. H. New, DLitB, 92 (1990), 271–5 · A. St John Adcock, 'Frederick Niven', *The glory that was Grub Street* [1928], 247–57
Archives University of British Columbia
Likenesses photograph, University of British Columbia Library, Vancouver, special collections division; repro. in W. H. New, 'Frederick John Niven', 272 · photograph, repro. in *Scotland's Magazine* (March 1962), 45

Niven, James (1851–1925), public health administrator, was born on 12 March 1851 in Peterhead, Aberdeenshire, the son of Charles Niven (*b.* 1802?), ginger beer brewer and spirit dealer, and his wife, Barbara Davidson (*b.* 1810/11) of Monouhitter, Aberdeenshire. He attended Aberdeen University, graduated MA in 1870, and then went to Queens' College, Cambridge, where he was eighth wrangler in the mathematical tripos in 1874 (three of his brothers were also wranglers). He was elected a fellow of his college and originally planned to study engineering, but after graduating MA in 1877 he went on to study medicine at St Thomas's Hospital, London; he graduated MB in 1880.

Niven's first appointment was in London, as assistant medical officer to the Deptford fever and smallpox hospitals. This was followed by four years' general practice in Manchester, during which he began to publish on infectious diseases. In 1884, with William Sinclair (1846–1912), gynaecologist at Manchester Southern Hospital and a fellow Scot, Niven co-founded the Manchester-based *Medical Chronicle*, which he later edited alone and which gained a worldwide circulation. In 1886 he became medical officer

of health (MOH) for the borough of Oldham, and medical superintendent of its Westhulme Fever Hospital. Over the next eight years he made a reputation as an active MOH with considerable scientific ability. His work on tuberculosis so impressed members of Oldham Medical Society that they raised funds for him to study Robert Koch's treatment in Berlin. Niven graduated BCh in 1889.

On 7 September 1894 Niven married Margaret (*d.* 1912), second daughter of John Adams of Collow Grange, Wragby, Lincolnshire. Earlier that year he had been appointed MOH for the city of Manchester, a post he retained for the rest of his career. Initially he had responsibility for two clerks and some juniors; at his departure, after twenty-eight years, he had charge of 860 staff, two sanatoriums, an isolation hospital acquired from Manchester Royal Infirmary, and twelve maternity and child welfare centres. That the city's death rate fell from 24.2 per thousand in 1893 to 13.8 per thousand in 1921 can be attributed in part to improvements in sanitation, maternity services, health visiting, infant welfare, smoke abatement, and preventive measures against TB—for all of which Niven gained Manchester an international reputation. He pioneered health visiting and was one of the first medical officers in any country to propose the notification of tuberculosis. He also formed a unique collaboration with Professor Sheridan Delépine of Manchester University's public health laboratory to clean up the city's milk supply.

Niven was lecturer in public health at Manchester University, an examiner in sanitary science at Cambridge, president of the epidemiological section of the Royal Society of Medicine, and president of Manchester Statistical Society (1907–9). Aberdeen University awarded him the honorary degree of doctor of letters in 1910, and he received medals from the Royal Institute of Public Health and other bodies.

Six feet tall and of spare build, Niven was an exceptionally shy, kind man, with simple tastes. He found it difficult to form friendships, yet inspired deep affection in those who worked closely with him. His department became the training ground for many public health workers, and his advice was constantly sought by the Local Government Board and the Ministry of Health. According to Sir George Newman, he was 'one of the deepest and most original thinkers that the public service ever had. Again and again those who believed they had broken fresh ground found the problems stated and their solution proclaimed in Niven's writings of years before' (*BMJ*, 17 Oct 1925, 710).

On his retirement in 1922 Niven was publicly thanked by Manchester city council. His *Observations on the History of Public Health Effort in Manchester* (1923) provided a valuable account of the work accomplished by his department, with recommendations for the future. But about his own future he became increasingly despondent; his wife had died in 1912, and his two daughters had left home. Niven eventually moved into lodgings, frustrated by the slowing of his physical and mental powers. Then, finally, he visited the Isle of Man, on 28 September 1925. He stayed at a hotel that night, and on Tuesday 29 September he disappeared after paying his hotel bill and leaving his bag there with a note and money. His body was found in Onchan harbour the following morning, on 30 September. The note asked that he should be buried at sea near Douglas. An inquest at Douglas on 2 October found that he had taken poison and then drowned himself while temporarily insane. Niven's body was cremated at Manchester crematorium on 7 October 1925.   JOAN MOTTRAM

Sources *Manchester Guardian* (1 Oct 1925) · *Manchester Guardian* (3 Oct 1925) · *The Examiner* (2 Oct 1925) · *Medical Officer* (10 Oct 1925), 160 · *The Lancet* (10 Oct 1925), 783 · *BMJ* (17 Oct 1925), 710–11 · *Oldham Chronicle* (3 Oct 1925) · *BMJ* (10 Oct 1925), 673 · *The Times* (2 Oct 1925) · 'Funeral of the late Dr Niven', *Manchester Guardian* (7 Oct 1925) · M. Armitstead, 'The life and work of James Niven', DPH diss., Manchester University, 1958 · W. P. Povey, 'James Niven … 1851–1925', *Some Manchester doctors: a biographical collection to mark the 150th anniversary of the Manchester Medical Society, 1834–1984*, ed. W. J. Elwood and A. F. Tuxford (1984), 98–100 · census returns for Peterhead, 1851 · census returns for Mumps ward, Oldham, 1891, PRO, RG 12/3308 · *Medical Directory* (1882–96) · *Manchester, Salford and Suburbs Directory* (1894–1925) · *Manchester Guardian* (8 Sept 1894) · *Roll of graduates of the University of Aberdeen, 1860–1900*, 405–6 · parish register, Peterhead, 12 March 1851 [birth] · Venn, *Alum. Cant.* · *CGPLA Eng. & Wales* (1925)

Likenesses Lafayette, photograph, repro. in *BMJ* (10 Oct 1925), 673

Wealth at death £5832 19s. 6d.: probate, 10 Nov 1925, *CGPLA Eng. & Wales*

Niven, Sir (Cecil) Rex (1898–1993), colonial official and author, was born on 20 November 1898 in Torquay, the only son of the Revd Dr George Cecil Niven, missionary, and his wife, Jeanne, *née* Rawlings. Educated at Blundell's School, Tiverton, Devon, he went up to Balliol College, Oxford, in 1916. Three defining memories of his youth never faded: his childhood travels with his mother from Japan and a lengthy visit to Egypt; the wartime interruption to his undergraduate studies at his beloved Balliol College, leading to service as a lieutenant with the Royal Field Artillery in France in 1917, where he won the MC in the last battle of the war before returning to graduate in 1920 in modern history on the unclassified shortened honours course; and his commitment to the Church of England, in which he had been reared. Like so many of his ex-officer generation, Niven saw in his wartime leadership and responsibilities the making of a likely career in the colonial service, then actively recruiting to make up its manpower losses. After three months' training, he was posted to Nigeria in 1921, at £500 p.a.

During his forty years' service, all of it spent in Nigeria, Niven moved steadily, even rapidly, up the slow post-war promotional ladder, his reputation for being something of an intellectual as well as an extremely keen administrator growing all the time. In Maiduguri, bordering on the Sahara, he planted a million seedlings of the handy Indian shade tree the neem, for which amenity he was long gratefully remembered. His deep experience of field administration and the native authority system (that bedrock of the Lugardian policy of indirect rule), which earned him the residentship of the major emirate provinces of Kano and then Bornu, was matched by Whitehall-style experience of secretariat work not only in the regional headquarters of Kaduna but also in the central government in Lagos. Here, during the sensitive war years, the governor, Sir Bernard Bourdillon, assigned Niven the job of establishing a public relations office, the first of its kind in Nigeria. This Niven accomplished with characteristic flair, earning the bonus (which was to stand him in such good stead in the coming years) of getting to know personally many of the nascent nationalist leaders. He was appointed senior resident in 1947. Yet, to his chagrin rather than to the surprise of some of his colleagues, when the ultimate chance of gubernatorial office came within his reach in 1952, the hoped-for prize eluded him. Despite having twice acted as lieutenant-governor, Niven was not appointed to Kaduna.

Though Niven retired from the colonial service in 1954, he continued his Nigerian career for another decade. For a while he represented one of the country's large commercial firms, persuading local authorities and the government to buy Land Rovers and Bailey bridges. Already appointed president of the Northern house of assembly (of which he had been a member since 1947) in 1952, he held the post until 1958, when he became its first speaker. Here was an office whose dignity Niven at once enjoyed and enhanced: 'he loved ceremony and was not against pageant' (*The Times*, 27 Feb 1993). He personally chose the robes with Messrs Ede and Ravenscroft and was influential in the selection of the 'Northern knot' as the legislature's device. Succeeded by a Northern Nigerian at self-government, he accepted the invitation of the independent government to serve as commissioner on special duties, from 1959 to 1962.

Niven finally retired in 1962. He spent the next six years serving Mervyn Stockwood as deputy secretary of the Southwark diocesan board of finance. In 1968 he was back in Nigeria, at the invitation of the federal government of General Yakubu Gowon, to advise them on how to present their case against the secession of Biafra, a public relations campaign which they seemed to be losing in the outside world. Back in Britain he settled in Kent, first at Deal and then at Walmer. From 1976 to 1980 he was a member of the general synod for the Canterbury diocese. He also served on a number of councils, including the Royal Society of Arts, and was a life member of the British Red Cross Society as well as a member of the Britain–Nigeria Association. His wife, Dorothy Marshall, the daughter of David Marshall Mason, MP and banker, whom he had married on 9 June 1925 and who had shared all his Nigerian years, died in 1977, a few years after the death of their younger daughter in a sailing accident off Ramsgate. In 1980 Niven married Pamela, widow of Dr O. H. B. Beerbohm and daughter of G. C. Leach of the Indian Civil Service. A staunch Oxonian, at the age of ninety he 'mischievously', as he related the episode, put his name forward for the vacant mastership of Balliol.

Everything Niven did was 'full of that zest, which was the touchstone of his personality' (*Balliol College Annual Record*, 97). He had a lively sense of humour, sometimes bordering on the malicious and shading into the sarcastic when he told tales of his seniors in the service. 'No-one', he wrote of one governor under whom he served, 'could describe him as cosy or approachable' (Niven, 193). A prolific writer with a dozen books to his name, at one time his *A Short History of Nigeria* (1937) and *How Nigeria is Governed* (1950) were widely read in Nigerian schools. His long-concealed ghosting of the autobiography of Sir Ahmadu Bello, the sardauna of Sokoto and first premier of Northern Nigeria, *My Life* (1960), resulted in an important and finely crafted book. While Niven's *The War of Nigerian Unity* (1970) was too *parti pris* to constitute a lasting contribution to the literature on the Biafran war, his memoir (in no sense an autobiography, for it opens with his departure for Lagos in 1921) *Nigerian Kaleidoscope* (1982) remains in the front rank of colonial service reminiscences.

Niven was appointed CMG in 1952 and knighted in 1960. He died at Buckland Hospital, Dover, on 22 February 1993. He was survived by his second wife and the elder of his two daughters by his first marriage.

A. H. M. KIRK-GREENE

Sources R. Niven, *Nigerian kaleidoscope* (1982) • *Daily Telegraph* (25 Feb 1993) • *The Times* (27 Feb 1993) • personal knowledge (2004) • interview (transcript), Bodl. RH • *Colonial Office List* • *WWW* • Balliol College Annual Record (1993) • Burke, *Peerage*
Archives Bodl. RH, transcript of interview, MS Afr. s.1832
Likenesses M. Boxer, ink drawing, c.1970–1979, NPG • double portrait, photograph (with Barbara Stanwyck), Hult. Arch. • photograph, repro. in Niven, *Nigerian kaleidoscope* • photograph, repro. in *Daily Telegraph* • photograph, repro. in *The Times* • photograph, priv. coll.
Wealth at death under £125,000: probate, 19 April 1993, CGPLA Eng. & Wales

Nivison, Robert, first Baron Glendyne (1849–1930), stockbroker, was born on 3 July 1849 at Sanquhar, Dumfriesshire, the eldest of five sons of John Nivison (1824–1898), a colliery manager, and Janet, daughter of James Hair, of Sanquhar. His two sisters never married. He was educated at a private school in his home town, and at the age of fifteen became a junior at the Sanquhar branch of the British Linen Bank. From 1869 until 1881 he was an employee of the London and Westminster Bank, latterly working as a senior clerk in the securities department of the bank's London head office.

In 1881 Nivison became a junior partner in the stockbroking firm of T. P. Baptie and he was admitted as a full member of the stock exchange in 1883. He retained a working alliance with the Westminster Bank, with whose support in 1886 he established his own stockbroking firm of R. Nivison. It immediately prospered, and after 1891 achieved a special ascendancy as financial adviser to self-governing overseas dominions.

Nivison married on 11 May 1877 Jane (d. 1918), daughter of John Wightman, of Sanquhar. They had three sons (of whom the youngest was killed in action in 1916) and five daughters. Nivison had few interests outside his family, and his brother Samuel (1860–1925), his eldest son John (1878–1967), cousin Walter Hair, sons-in-law, and grandsons were all partners in Nivisons at different times. The partners continued to work together in one room until

the dissolution of the firm in 1986. It enjoyed an exceptional reputation for probity throughout its century of existence.

Nivisons was entrusted with placing all Australian state government loans on the London market from 1891, and was also responsible for floating government or state loans for South Africa (beginning with Natal in 1901), Canada (starting with the Newfoundland loan of 1902), and India (from 1906). The firm was later appointed broker to the Indian government, but did not undertake business for the younger African colonies and had no contacts with the Colonial Office. It also handled many colonial municipal loans, beginning with Melbourne in 1892 and Toronto in 1894, and shared much of the business in British municipal loans with the firm of Scrimgeour. Although Nivison was most closely identified with Australia (which he never visited), his firm was interested in various Canadian industrial enterprises, and his family became large private shareholders in the Algoma Steel Corporation.

In the early 1890s Nivison devised his own rules for issuing Australian and other colonial loans in London. He introduced underwriting syndicates instead of abandoning loan issues to the uncertainties of a public tender system. He discussed terms with prospective borrowers, judged what the market would take, and on the day of issue walked round City institutions offering them an opportunity to participate. His terms favoured the borrowers at time of issue, and reflected his determination to enforce an orderly market. If any institution declined sub-underwriting at the price offered, it was deleted from Nivison's list, and never again given an opportunity to participate in a Nivison issue. He thus personally disciplined the market. Nivison was always firm in his judgement and a byword for reliability; using this reputation, he built up an exceptional network of brokers and jobbers, who drew trustees into investing their clients' funds in dominion securities. His successes increased his authority greatly.

In character, Nivison was outwardly modest, loyal, and kindly, with a masterful self-reliance in all his activities. He was decisive in business, though his autocratic tendencies were tempered by a stubborn fair-mindedness. He was a generous donor to hospital charities, but his private acts of benevolence to individuals were greater. He received a baronetcy in 1914, and was created Baron Glendyne of Sanquhar in 1922. He was the only businessman who received a peerage in that notorious new year's honours list on whom there was no blemish or tincture of scandal. He seldom attended, and never spoke in, the House of Lords. He died of heart failure on 14 June 1930 at his residence, Branch Hill Lodge, Hampstead, and was buried in Hampstead cemetery.

RICHARD DAVENPORT-HINES

Sources private information (2004) • R. T. Appleyard and C. B. Schedvin, eds., *Australian financiers: biographical essays* (1988) • GEC, *Peerage* • *The Times* (16 June 1930)
Archives priv. coll., business papers

Nix [Nykke], **Richard** (c.1447–1535), bishop of Norwich, is usually described as the son of Richard Nix of Somerset and his wife, Joan (or Alice) Stillington, who was probably a relative of Robert Stillington, bishop of Bath and Wells (d. 1491); he is sometimes called the son of Thomas Nykke, who may have been the prominent London mercer of that name, since Richard is on one occasion described as 'of the diocese of London' (Mitchell, 278). The date of his birth was about 1447, if subsequent estimates of his age are to be accepted. He studied at Oxford University, 'but in what house … he was educated it appears not' (Wood, 2.744), and also at Cambridge, probably before 1473, as a member of Trinity Hall. He was a student, together with his brother William, at Ferrara in 1479 and later at Bologna, where he was admitted as doctor of both civil and canon law in March 1483.

Nix was a considerable pluralist before he became a bishop, although he was careful to obtain papal dispensations for his benefices. Beginning with Ashbury, Berkshire, in 1473, these also came to include rectories and vicarages in Somerset, Devon, and co. Durham, and canonries and prebends at Wells, Exeter, Southwell, York, and St George's Chapel, Windsor. During the 1490s he was archdeacon of Exeter and Wells, holding these offices simultaneously for at least five years, and he became dean of the Chapel Royal and registrar of the Order of the Garter. The distribution of his various livings and offices reflects primarily the interests of his principal patron, Richard Fox (d. 1528), who was successively bishop of Exeter (1487–92), of Bath and Wells (1492–4), of Durham (1494–1501), and finally of Winchester. Fox appointed Nix to be his official and vicar-general at Bath and Wells in 1492, and at Durham in 1495, and no doubt it was through Foxe, who was keeper of the privy seal between 1487 and 1516, that Nix came to be quite an active attender of Henry VII's council from 1498 onwards.

Nix became bishop of Norwich by papal provision of 26 February 1501 and held the see until his death in 1535. He appears to have been a conscientious and energetic bishop, largely resident in his diocese, who devoted himself to its administration, until old age and partial blindness eventually hampered his activity. He also became an influential member of the episcopal bench. Aspersions about his moral character date from later in the sixteenth century and lack any clear foundation. A prickly personality, he nevertheless appears to have instilled a good measure of loyalty, even of affection, both in many of the diocesan officials who served under him and in a variety of lay people, notably among the East Anglian gentry and aristocracy. His fair-mindedness and efficiency are well illustrated by the records of his visitations of religious houses in the diocese, which survive for a number of years during his episcopate. His relations with Cardinal Thomas Wolsey (d. 1530) were tense. In 1514 Nix was appointed by papal bull to receive Wolsey's oath on his translation from Lincoln to be archbishop of York and, together with the bishop of Winchester, to invest him with the pallium. In the following year he took part in the ceremony attending the reception of the cardinal's hat for Wolsey, whose frequent interventions in his diocese thereafter irked Nix considerably. Wolsey's triumphal progress in 1517

through Norfolk and Suffolk, the cardinal's native county, brought involvement in a number of cases that touched on interests of Nix, including the dispute between the cathedral priory and the city of Norwich, which Wolsey pursued through to a settlement in 1520. Nix opposed, unsuccessfully, the appointment of Wolsey's natural son, Thomas Winter, as archdeacon of Suffolk in 1526, and as archdeacon of Norwich in 1529.

Nix was a consistent opponent of Lollardy and the early manifestations of the Reformation. In the first two decades of his reign some half a dozen people were burnt for heresy in his diocese, and a number of other suspects abjured or performed penance. Thereafter the greatest challenges came from Cambridge University, especially in the person of Thomas Bilney, and through literature from abroad. Bilney made at least two preaching tours in the diocese in the 1520s, and when he returned there in 1531, subsequent to his conviction in 1529 before Bishop Cuthbert Tunstall of London (d. 1559), Nix sanctioned his execution as a relapsed heretic in Norwich in August 1531. Writing to Archbishop William Warham of Canterbury (d. 1532) in May 1530, Nix regretted the influx of printed books containing 'arronious opinions' from overseas, 'for if they continue any time I think they shall undoe us all'. In the same letter he records his attempts to prevent the spread of vernacular New testaments; his belief that the people in the diocese who were infected with heresy were merchants and those living near the sea, rather than gentlemen and the commonalty; and his disappointment that many of those spreading the new ideas came from a Cambridge college that had been founded by a previous bishop of Norwich, and had strong East Anglian links, namely Gonville Hall, established by Bishop William Bateman (d. 1355): 'No clerk who had lately come out of it [Gonville Hall] but savoureth of the frying pan, although he speak never so holily' (Strype, 2.694–6, letter 12; LP Henry VIII, 4, pt 3, no. 6385). That Thomas Bilney had been a fellow of Nix's own college, Trinity Hall, must also have been poignant.

An English ambassador in Rome in 1528 told the pope a 'merry tale' about Nix, showing that his age had not affected his spirits. Nevertheless his final years were marked with sadness and frustration, as he came to be increasingly out of sympathy with developments in the country. He became a leader of the conservative opposition. But though he had been a supporter of papal authority, and opposed Henry VIII's divorce, he complied grudgingly with the statutory measures taken to sever ties with Rome.

In 1530 Nix was arraigned in the court of king's bench, along with Abbot Reve of Bury St Edmunds and some other ecclesiastics, on a *praemunire* charge of having abetted Cardinal Wolsey in the exercise of his legatine powers; the irony is unlikely to have amused Nix. Then in February 1534 he was prosecuted in the same court on another charge of *praemunire*, this time allegedly for breaching the privileges of the people of Thetford while exercising his episcopal jurisdiction there—in reality, according to the imperial ambassador, because of Archbishop Cranmer's anger at the burning of Bilney three years earlier. He was convicted and condemned to the confiscation of all his property, while his body was to be at the king's mercy; confined to the Marshalsea prison, he agreed to pay a huge fine of £10,000, and was later pardoned by act of parliament.

Beginning in July 1534 the diocese of Norwich was subjected to a visitation by William May on behalf of Archbishop Cranmer, but Nix refused to acknowledge Cranmer's authority to visit and the visitation ground to a halt. He was summoned before the council in the Star Chamber in January 1535 but excused himself from attending on the grounds of infirmity. In June he was dispatching prayers for Henry VIII and Anne Boleyn through his diocese, while in November, according to reports from the duke of Norfolk and Thomas Legh to Thomas Cromwell, he was distributing his wealth lavishly among his dependants. Nix died between 15 and 29 December 1535, and was buried under an altar tomb in his cathedral church, towards the east end of the south side of the nave.

As bishop of Norwich, Nix was deeply interested in the management of property and in the accumulation of wealth that derived from it, though not particularly interested in improving his dwellings. He appears to have acquired his wealth by careful husbanding of resources and good fortune, Norwich not being an especially rich see. Even though burdened with large fines in his last years, he still had 1634¾ ounces of plate at his death. He also acted as moneylender and at his death he was owed £3067 from various clerics and lay people.

Nix rebuilt with stone vaulting the roof of the north and south transepts of Norwich Cathedral, which had been destroyed by fire in 1509. At Trinity Hall, Cambridge, he founded three fellowships—two for canonists and one for a civilian—and one scholarship. Books known to have been owned by him included a Latin translation of Plato's *Republic*, a Latin Bible, and a Sarum breviary, Thomas Aquinas's commentary on the letters of St Paul, Barthelemy Montagnana's *Consilia medica*, John Arderne's *Chirurgia*, a work entitled *Speculum fleobothomie*, a book of medical recipes in English, various works of canon law by Giovanni d'Andreae, Louis Pontano, and Baldus de Perusio, and other works by Peter de Alliaco, John Campanus, and F. Cumanus. In 1493 he had been bequeathed three works of Cicero by John Lascy, a canon of Wells, namely *Epistolae*, *De officiis*, and *De amicitia*.

NORMAN P. TANNER

Sources DNB · Emden, *Cam.* · Emden, *Oxf.* · D. MacCulloch, 'Richard Nix and the old world, 1501–1535', *Suffolk and the Tudors: politics and religion in an English county, 1500–1600* (1986), 130–57 · R. Houlbrooke, *Church courts and the people during the English Reformation, 1520–1570* (1979) · A. Jessopp, ed., *Visitations of the diocese of Norwich, A.D.1492–1532*, CS, new ser., 43 (1888) · R. Houlbrooke, 'Persecution of heresy and protestantism in the diocese of Norwich under Henry VIII', *Norfolk Archaeology*, 35 (1970–73), 308–26 · LP Henry VIII · R. Houlbrooke, 'Bishop Nikke's last visitation, 1532', *Medieval ecclesiastical studies in honour of Dorothy M. Owen*, ed. M. J. Franklin and C. Harper-Bill (1995), 113–29 · D. MacCulloch, 'A Reformation in balance: power struggles in the diocese of Norwich, 1533–53', *Counties and communities: essays on East Anglian history presented to Hassell Smith*, ed. C. Rawcliffe, R. Virgoe, and R. Wilson, Centre of East Anglian Studies, Norwich (1996), 97–114 · Wood, *Ath. Oxon.* · R. J. Mitchell, 'English law students at Bologna in the fifteenth century', *EngHR*, 51 (1936), 270–87 · J. Strype, *Memorials of the most reverend father in God, Thomas Cranmer*, ed. P. E. Barnes, new edn, 2 vols. (1853), vol. 2, pp. 694–6 · CSP Spain, vol. 10, p. 36 · F. Heal, *Of prelates and princes: a study of the economic and social position of the Tudor episcopate* (1980)

Archives Norfolk RO

Wealth at death abundant wealth; incl. 1634¾ ounces of plate, and £3067 owed to him: MacCulloch, 'Richard Nix'; MacCulloch, 'A Reformation'

Nixon, Anthony (*fl.* 1592–1616), pamphleteer, claims in his pamphlet *Oxfords Triumph* to have 'bene a member of that famous Universitie' (sig. A3v), and his writings suggest some training in theology. They also consistently exemplify the adaptability of the freelance Jacobean hack, ready to turn his hand to any subject and to plagiarize his fellow writers in the process.

He is probably the Anthony Nixon who in 1592, together with two accomplices, was committed to Newgate prison for 'taking upon them to be purcevants', arresting a suspected papist on the authority of a forged warrant, and extracting money from him (Lansdowne MS 99, no. 88). Nixon, who is identified in testimony as being 'of Northampton, and sojourneth at one Hudsons', was for some reason detained much longer than his fellows and wrote a personal appeal to Lord Burghley in 1593, claiming that he had suffered two bouts of the plague while in prison. We may catch an echo of this experience in the pamphlet *Londons Dove* (1612), where Nixon declares:

> Let no man speake of extremitie, that hath not known Captivitie … There dwelles the melancholy Muses of sad petitions … the poore mans thoughts which runne as swift as *Pegasus*, expecting an answere, doe in vaine make a thousand long lookes out of the yron grate. (sig. C2r)

The young Nixon's petition for release is elaborately phrased and composed in an elegant hand, clearly the product of an aspiring writer.

The Rome-baiting impulse behind this youthful escapade reappears in several of the pamphlets Nixon produced to commemorate important events in the new reign, such as *Elizaes Memoriall: King James his Arrivall, and Romes Downefall* (1603), *The Blacke Yeare* (1606), a mock-prognostication marking delivery from the Gunpowder Plot the year before, and his hymn to protestant unity in *Great Brittaines Generall Joyes* (1613), celebrating the marriage of Princess Elizabeth and the elector palatine, and still castigating the 'rabble of unnaturall Englishmen' (sig. B4r) that had tried to blow up parliament in 1605. Nixon was careful not to criticize the king's cautious foreign policy—in *Oxfords Triumph* (sig. C4v) he describes James I as a scrupulous arbiter in a debate about 'Whether it be more to defend, or enlarge the boundes of an Empire or Kingdome'—but he was not unresponsive to the more assertive voices in Jacobean public life. *The Warres of Swethland* (1609) is dedicated to Philip Herbert, earl of Montgomery (an enthusiastic patron of colonial ventures), and salutes the bellicose forays of English mercenaries in Sweden's hostilities with Poland in 1608. English intervention in this war was on behalf of the Polish king, however, and Nixon rather spoils the recruiting potential of his pamphlet by editorializing on behalf of Swedish fears that 'their Religion and government would now be forced and adulterated by the tyrannous command, and superstitious customes of *Poland*' (sig. F4v).

Nixon's previous pamphlet *The Travels of M. Bush* (1608) records perhaps the most remarkable of the journeying stunts undertaken in a period when such things were fashionable in England. One of its backers was Robert Harcourt, leader of an ill-fated mission to colonize Guiana in 1609. The same interest in unorthodox enterprise is evident in Nixon's pamphlet about the adventures of the Sherley brothers, *The Three English Brothers* (1607). This particular clan was out of favour with the English government because of their piratical exploits and their activities in the Middle East but fetched their inspiration from men like the earl of Essex and the militant ethos associated with Prince Henry's circle. While it is unlikely that Nixon enjoyed access to such a group he may well have been regarded by them as a reliable chronicler of English deeds abroad. At any rate there are reasons to believe that he was commissioned by Thomas Sherley, the only one of the brothers to return permanently to England, to relate his colourful adventures and to publicize the current plight of his kinsmen.

Thirteen pamphlets published between 1602 and 1616 can be confidently ascribed to Nixon's hand, and his distinctive style has been found in a number of others, including the anonymous *Newes from Sea* (STC 25022). He is much given to sententious digression and euphuistic rhetorical patterns, and is expert at padding out a topic with generalized moral commentary, personified abstractions, and extended simile. These were Nixon's means of edifying the rough news stories that he was furnished with by stationers like Nathaniel Butter, with whom he was associated for several years from 1608. But he is not simply the earnest scribe; he also cultivates the mixed tone that he found in urban popular writing in the 1590s, and several of his pamphlets are a gallimaufry of jest book, allegorical homily, and verse both invented and borrowed. In *The Christian Navy* (1602) his sententious verse treatment of a conventional theme is enlivened with chunks of Chaucer; *The Scourge of Corruption* (1615) is a hybrid of moral tract and jest book—his summary of one anecdote as 'A fine peece of knavery done … in shew of piety and religion' (p. 20) makes an apt comment on the youthful exploit that landed him in gaol; and *A Strange Foot-Post* (1613) shows him trying his hand at the kind of fantastic satire made popular by Joseph Hall and others. ANTHONY PARR

Sources examination of John Norbury, Henry Mumford, and Anthony Nixon in 1592, BL, Lansdowne MS 99, no. 88 · J. Hunter, 'Chorus vatum Anglicanorum', 1843, BL, Add. MS 24488 · L. Ennis, 'Anthony Nixon: Jacobean plagiarist and hack', *Huntington Library Quarterly*, 3 (1939–40), 377–401

Nixon, Francis Russell (1803–1879), bishop of Tasmania, son of the Revd Robert *Nixon (1759–1837) [*see under* Nixon, John Colley] and his wife, Ann Russell, was born on 1 August 1803 and admitted into Merchant Taylors' School, London, in March 1810. In 1822 he was elected a probationary fellow of St John's College, Oxford, whence he graduated BA (third class in classics) in 1827, MA in 1841, and DD in 1842. He was ordained deacon in 1827 and priest in 1828. Nixon held several minor charges and acted as chaplain to the embassy at Naples, and was then made, in January 1836, incumbent of Sandgate, Kent. In November 1838 he was preferred to the vicarage of Ash, near Wingham, Kent, by Archbishop William Howley, who also appointed him one of the six preachers in Canterbury Cathedral.

Nixon was married three times: in 1829 to Frances Maria, second daughter of the Revd Thomas *Streatfeild of Chart's Edge; they had two daughters and a son before she died on 22 September 1834. His second wife was Anna Maria (*d*. 26 Nov 1868), daughter of Charles Woodcock, a judge in the civil court at Madras; married in 1836, they had a further eight children. Thirdly he married Flora Elizabeth Agnes, elder daughter of E. Müller of Switzerland, in 1870; they had two sons.

On 24 August 1842 Nixon was consecrated in Westminster Abbey as bishop of the newly constituted see of Tasmania. Both the appointment and its acceptance appear mistaken. Van Diemen's Land (as the colony, though not the see, was called until 1856) was a strange place, receiving thousands of transported convicts annually until 1853, with economic troubles and political dissent adding more stresses. Not only secularist liberals but also Catholics, Presbyterians, and dissenters asserted their views, while Anglicans had learned to do without episcopacy. Nixon lacked the zeal, toughness, and spirituality which might have transcended these problems. Laudian in belief, ornate and supercilious in manner, he clashed on various fronts: with civil authority, especially that of Sir John Eardley Eardley-Wilmot, lieutenant-governor from 1843 to 1846; with other religionists, most remarkably in protesting against the appointment of a Catholic bishop of Hobart Town; and with his own flock, both individual clergy and a vehement low-church movement.

The alienation between Nixon and his contemporaries in Tasmania was for both sides a disaster, even a tragedy, but in time the bishop mellowed—or surrendered: reversing earlier stances he accepted a non-denominational form of state education and synodical government of the church. Nixon eventually returned to England in 1862, and was presented in the following year to the valuable rectory of Bolton-Percy, York. He resigned this charge in 1865, and retired at Vignolo, Stresa, on Lake Maggiore, Italy, where he died on 7 April 1879, survived by his wife.

Nixon appears to have been happier in his personal than in his professional life, and was an accomplished musician and artist. Besides charges and pamphlets issued in Tasmania between 1846 and 1856, he published: *The History of Merchant Taylors' School* (1823) with five lithographic views, which constitute its only interest; *Lectures, Historical, Doctrinal, and Practical, on the Catechism of the Church of England* (1843); and *The Cruise of the Beacon: a Narrative of a Visit to the Islands in Bass's Straits* (1857).

C. J. ROBINSON, *rev.* MICHAEL ROE

Sources *The pioneer bishop in Van Diemen's Land, 1843–1863: letters and memories of Francis Russell Nixon*, ed. N. Nixon [1953] · W. R. Barrett, 'Nixon, Francis Russell', *AusDB*, vol. 2 · P. A. Howell, 'Bishop Nixon and public education in Tasmania', *Melbourne studies in education* (1967), 168–209 · H. Condon, *Francis Russell Nixon* (1981) · T. Brown, 'Francis Russell Nixon', *Dictionary of Australian artists*, ed. J. Kerr (1992), 579–80 · Burke, *Gen. GB* · Kelly, *Handbk* · *CGPLA Eng. & Wales* (1879)

Archives State Library of Tasmania, Hobart, corresp. and papers | Lpool RO, letters to Lord Stanley

Likenesses G. Brown, engraving, 1845? (after G. Richmond, c.1842) · J. S. Prout, engraving, 1846? (after G. Richmond, c.1842) · H. Robinson, stipple, pubd 1850 (after G. Richmond, c.1842), BM, NPG · carte-de-visite, NPG

Wealth at death under £800: probate, 13 June 1879, *CGPLA Eng. & Wales*

Nixon, James (c.1741–1812), miniature painter, was the son of Robert Nixon, a successful Irish merchant working in Uphall and Tokenhouse, London. He entered the Royal Academy Schools on 17 March 1769. According to Farington he was fifty-one in 1793, but he was said to be seventy-one at his death in 1812. Little is known of his early life or education. A fellow pupil, Joseph Farington, refers in his diaries to a brother, the Revd Robert *Nixon (1759–1837) [see under Nixon, John Colley], and two sisters, one of whom married Sir James Colleton. Nixon was a member of the Society of Artists, and exhibited with them from 1765 until 1771. His *Portrait in Water Colours* was probably a miniature portrait of Joseph Farington (1765; NPG). The two young men seem to have formed a close enough friendship for Farington, in later years, to interest himself in Nixon's troublesome financial situation; he canvassed for donations among friends and colleagues, petitioned the council of the Royal Academy both on Nixon's behalf and later in support of his widow, and counselled Nixon on a fairly regular basis between 1799 and 1807. The two men met at dinners, the Academy Club, the British Institution, and various exhibitions, and were members of the club of Old Slaughter's Coffee House, St Martin's Lane; often Farington's diary entries read simply: 'Nixon called'. He may have found Nixon tiresome at times, but he remained a loyal friend and was touched when Nixon presented him with 'a *Miniature of me* which he painted & exhibited in 1765' on 19 January 1807, and six days later showed it to his company at dinner: 'they thought it a picture painted with breadth—much upon Sir Joshua's principle—& well coloured' (Farington, *Diary*, 25 Jan 1807).

Nixon's work was also admired by Horace Walpole, who wrote of a miniature of a lady in the character of Diana exhibited at the Society of Artists in 1770: 'A very fine picture, and, I believe, the best he ever painted' (Graves, *Artists*, 182). From 1772 to 1807 he was an annual contributor to the Royal Academy's exhibitions, and was elected associate in 1778. He was greatly attached to the academy, and was strongly influenced by Sir Joshua Reynolds; he exhibited a portrait of Reynolds there in 1779. He is best known as a painter of miniatures, but he also painted portraits in oil and watercolour, historical subjects, and book illustrations; the latter included a series of ten designs illustrating *Tristram Shandy*, which he exhibited at the academy in

1786. From 1792 he was miniature painter to the duchess of York, and he held the appointment of limner to the prince of Wales from 1803. He was appointed deputy secretary to the British Institution in March 1806, but was given notice that his services were no longer required on 24 November 1806; he exhibited works there in 1806 and 1807. Augustus Toussaint was a pupil.

Nixon painted Elizabeth Farren as Thalia (exh. RA, 1787) and other theatrical celebrities, as well as scenes from literature, particularly Shakespeare. His portraits of Dr Francis Willis (exh. RA, 1789; engraved by F. Bartolozzi), the duchess of Devonshire (exh. RA, 1782; engraved by F. Bartolozzi, 1783), and Elizabeth Hartley as Elfrida (exh. Burlington Fine Arts Club, 1889; engraved by W. Dickinson, 1780) are among his works to have been engraved (impressions, BM). A small collection of his miniatures is in the Victoria and Albert Museum, London. A miniature of Mary Bowles (*née* Elton) as Ophelia at the Elton family seat, Clevedon Court, Somerset, is possibly the *Ophelia* exhibited at the Royal Academy in 1782. When Nixon signed his work it was often simply with an N.

Nixon spent much of his professional life in London, but was living in Newcastle upon Tyne in 1794 and early 1798, and in Edinburgh (1795–1797?), where he met Raeburn and painted a miniature of the count of Artois in 1797. Farington first mentions Mrs Nixon in 1797. Nixon took lodgings in London, but 'she is settled at Twickenham having the care of two daughters of Mr. Mackenzie who with his wife resides there.—A sister of Mr. Mackenzie married a brother of Mrs. Nixon' (Farington, *Diary*, 16 Aug 1799). She left that situation in 1804, after one of the daughters married.

Nixon's last years were fraught with financial troubles and the thwarted ambition to become an academician. In 1800 he received £150 in assistance from the Royal Academy. On 18 April 1802 Farington wrote that Nixon 'has not got a shilling by his profession in the last 7 months' (Farington, *Diary*). After his death Farington calculated that over the years the academy gave him 'towards £500, mostly in donations and a pension' (ibid., 1 Aug 1808). There were difficulties in April 1806 with Philips the auctioneer over advances that had not been recovered through sales of work, and he was 'arrested at the Gallery for £30 for a debt which He said He did not owe but should be obliged to pay' (ibid., 3 Dec 1806).

On 11 January 1805 Farington reported: 'He has lately been subject to a complaint called *nervous*, viz: a numbness in his left arm and Hand' (Farington, *Diary*). On 5 April 1807: 'Poor Nixon had a *Paralytic stroke* … [Mrs Nixon] thought this a *second attack* of the kind, for sometime since He suddenly fell down at Knightsbridge but recovered immediately' (ibid., 11 April 1807). He lost the full use of his limbs and could move only with difficulty. Mrs Nixon settled her husband in Tiverton, Devon, probably in August 1808, after receipt of a legacy of £135 from the painter and engraver Giuseppe Marchi. Nixon died in Tiverton on Saturday 9 May 1812, at five o'clock.

ARIANNE BURNETTE

Sources Farington, *Diary* · Graves, *Artists* · *Engraved Brit. ports.* · *GM*, 1st ser., 82/1 (1812), 499 · B. S. Long, *British miniaturists* (1929) · *Summary catalogue of miniatures in the Victoria and Albert Museum* (1981) · Graves, *RA exhibitors* · Graves, *Brit. Inst.* · R. Walker, *National Portrait Gallery: Regency portraits*, 2 vols. (1985) · D. Foskett, *Miniatures: dictionary and guide* (1987) · G. Reynolds, *English portrait miniatures* (1952); rev. edn (1988) · Waterhouse, *18c painters* · R. Walker, *The eighteenth and early nineteenth century miniatures in the collection of her majesty the queen* (1992) · DNB

Nixon, John (1815–1899), coal owner, was born at Barlow, Durham, on 10 May 1815, the only son of a tenant farmer. He was educated at the village school and then at Dr Bruce's academy, Newcastle. At fourteen he returned to the family farm for two years before being apprenticed to Joseph Gray, mining agent for the north of England estates of the marquess of Bute. From 1837 to 1839 he worked as an overman (minor official) at Garesfield colliery. A newspaper advertisement took him to Crawshay Bailey's Nant-y-glo ironworks but the post proved to be unsuitable. On the recommendation of Joseph Gray, he then carried out a survey of the Dowlais coal workings for Lord Bute. Having made his report, he accepted a post with an English company interested in building an ironworks near Nantes in France. This, too, was short-lived as he found himself in the uncomfortable position of reporting to his employers that their coal takings were inadequate to support the enterprise.

Nixon's first major business achievement was to create a new market for Welsh steam coal in France. There were two large obstacles: good Newcastle coal was already well established in France, and Welsh coal was more expensive. To overcome these, Nixon took a cargo of Welsh steam coal to give to those willing to conduct trials under his supervision. Having demonstrated an efficiency gain greater than the price difference, he not only secured orders from French sugar refiners and steamboat owners, but he also persuaded the French navy, well ahead of the Royal Navy, to adopt Welsh coal (*Merthyr Guardian*, 12 May 1860). Initially the coal for this entirely new market was supplied by Thomas Powell, the south Wales steam-coal producer, on a commission basis, but by 1845 Nixon had opened, with two partners, his own pit at Werfa in the Aberdâr (Cynon) valley.

By the time he was thirty the pattern of Nixon's career was set, and he concentrated his energies on the coal industry of south Wales. With William Cory, the London coal merchant, and Hugh Taylor MP, the Durham colliery owner, as his major active partners, Nixon in 1855 formed the firm of Nixon, Taylor, and Cory. They sank the Navigation colliery between 1855 and 1863; bought the Deep Duffryn colliery in 1856; sank (in the adjoining Taff valley) the Merthyr Vale colliery between 1867 and 1878; and returned to the Cynon valley to sink the collieries of Glyn Gwyn Level (1889) and Cwm Cynon (1896). By the time of Nixon's death the annual output from his pits was 1.25 million tons. However, exploration at the Navigation and Merthyr Vale collieries had involved searching for seams well below those already proved: the time, difficulty, and expense (£255,000 at Merthyr Vale) demonstrated the real

risks of doing so. A limited company, Nixon's Navigation, was therefore created in 1882. Nixon himself held nearly one-third (2340) of the £100 shares in a total capital of £780,000; and there were only five other major shareholders, a position still unchanged at his death. If not financially pioneering, the firm was for a time a financial curiosity in south Wales, being run on the cost-book system, common in Cornish tin mines. The advantage over an ordinary partnership was that the shares could be transferable, but the partners were obliged to provide capital as needed.

Nixon made two other personal contributions to the south Wales coal industry. He was one of the promoters of the 1856 act to develop harbour facilities at the mouth of the Ely River, which led to the opening of the Penarth docks in 1865. More important was his intervention at the neighbouring Bute docks in Cardiff. In the early 1850s the Bute trustees had decided to build a second (east) dock to accommodate the burgeoning coal trade. General satisfaction gave way to dismay as details emerged during construction; in particular the sill of the new dock was to be at the same depth as the original 1839 west dock, and it was to be just 200 feet wide. Thus neither the increased size of ships nor the growing volume of shipping could be accommodated. Nixon tenaciously led the campaign to change the plans; although construction was already under way, and the distinguished engineer in charge, Sir John Rennie, asserted that it was technically unfeasible to alter the depth of the sill, substantial changes were made.

Nixon made an important contribution to the introduction of innovative mining methods in south Wales. In the early 1860s he pressed through the application of the longwall mining system to replace the traditional Welsh pillar-and-stall method of working. Whether he was the first to make this change in south Wales has been challenged and would be difficult to establish. Some doubts also surround his claim to have first substituted double-shift for single-shift working. There is an element of inevitability about both changes, as the increasing scale and expense of coal mining put a premium on the efficiency and intensity of working. There is no doubt, however, that John Nixon was a leading figure in these developments, which involved a readiness to confront miners' opposition head on.

Nixon also made some specific inventions, the most influential of which was the 'Billy playfair' machine. Welsh miners were paid only for large coal, and the assessment by colliery officials (croppers) of the amount of small coal sent up in the trams was always a contentious issue. Nixon's machine, the use of which spread rapidly, made it possible objectively to weigh the small coal. In the early 1860s Nixon also invented and installed at the deepest pit in south Wales (Navigation, 425 yards) his ventilation machine and winding equipment, but despite the remarkably good safety record at Navigation, his ventilation machine was not used elsewhere.

Nixon also participated in the development of joint

activity by owners in south Wales, especially over industrial relations. He chaired the meeting held at the Windsor Hotel, Cardiff, on 14 March 1864, which led to the formation of the Aberdare Steam Coal Association, the forerunner of the more general Coalowners' Association initiated in 1873. Although not a major participant, he served on the central sliding scale committee from 1880 to the early 1890s, and in negotiations he was an increasingly firm supporter of the hard-line W. T. Lewis, first Baron Merthyr, who was one of his executors.

Nixon was a genuine entrepreneur who showed great tenacity and application in business. His private life was obscure, but he is known to have been married by 1872 to a wife named Elizabeth. They had no children but his nephew, C. J. Gray, and great-nephew, H. E. Gray, were managing Nixon's main collieries from the 1880s. He was a keen grouse sportsman, and owned houses in Brighton and at 117 Westbourne Terrace, London, where he died on 3 June 1899. He was buried at Aber-ffrwd cemetery, Mountain Ash, on 8 June, and the residue of his estate of nearly £1.2 million went to his great-nephews.

JOHN WILLIAMS

Sources J. E. Vincent, John Nixon: pioneer of the steam coal trade in south Wales (1900) · J. H. Morris and L. J. Williams, The south Wales coal industry, 1841–1875 (1958) · L. J. Williams, 'Nixon, John', DBB · [J. Nixon], Ferndale colliery explosion: the 'single shift' system of working collieries as practised in Wales (1867) · The single-shift system of working collieries as practised in Wales: the cause of nearly double the loss of life (1867) [repr. of letters from J. Nixon to The Mining Journal etc.] · J. Davies, Cardiff and the marquesses of Bute (1981) · L. J. Williams, 'The Monmouthshire and South Wales Coalowners Association', MA diss., 1955 · Colliery Guardian (8 Nov 1862) · Cardiff and Merthyr Guardian (12 May 1860) · R. H. Walters, The economic and business history of the south Wales steam coal industry, 1840–1914 (1977) · E. L. Chappell, History of the port of Cardiff (1939) · W. G. Dalziel, Monmouthshire and South Wales Coal Owners Association (1896) · obituaries
Likenesses photogravure photograph, NMG Wales
Wealth at death £1,155,069 17s. 1d. (in UK): probate, 26 July 1899, CGPLA Eng. & Wales

Nixon, John Colley (b. before 1759, d. 1818), merchant and artist, was the son of Robert Nixon, a successful Irish merchant working in Uphall and Tokenhouse, London. The date of John Nixon's birth as well as details from his childhood remain obscure. In his memoirs Henry Angelo mentions John as a young man who 'resided for many years in Basinghall street, where, over his dark warehouses, he, and his brother Richard, kept "Batchelor's court"' (Reminiscences, 208). James *Nixon, miniature painter, was also his brother. Another brother, **Robert Nixon** (1759–1837), served as the curate of Foot's Cray in Kent from 1784 to 1804, and like John was an artist and 'honorary exhibitor' at the Royal Academy. It was the Revd Robert Nixon who recognized William Turner's early artistic talent, and introduced him to J. F. Rigaud, who facilitated Turner's entrance into the Royal Academy Schools. He married Ann Russell, with whom he had at least two sons; the second son, Francis Russell *Nixon, became the first bishop of Tasmania. Robert Nixon died at Kenmure Castle, New Galloway, on 5 November 1837.

John Nixon was a wealthy merchant who served as the secretary to the Beefsteak Club, was an accomplished amateur actor, and had a remarkable visual memory which he employed in his caricatures of Georgian life. It is the latter recreation for which he is best-known, and a large number of Nixon's sketches exist in public collections, including the Victoria and Albert Museum and the National Portrait Gallery, London. Nixon made numerous satirical drawings of his visit to Paris from 1802 to 1804, and the social eclecticism of Bath, where he accompanied his friend the caricaturist Thomas Rowlandson in 1792. Nixon exhibited thirty-nine genre and landscape paintings between 1781 and 1815 as an honorary exhibitor at the Royal Academy. In the 1790 exhibition catalogue Nixon's London address is given as 4 Cateaton Street. John Nixon died at Ryde, Isle of Wight, in 1818.

L. H. CUST, rev. DOUGLAS FORDHAM

Sources A Georgian comedy of manners: humorous watercolours of life in Bath, the west country and London by John Nixon (1750–1818) (1994) [exhibition catalogue, Holburne Museum, Bath, 1994] · The reminiscences of Henry Angelo, ed. H. Lavers Smith, 2 vols. (1904) · S. F. D. Rigaud, 'Facts and recollections of the XVIIIth century in a memoir of John Francis Rigaud', ed. W. L. Pressly, Walpole Society, 50 (1984), 1–164, esp. 105–6 · Waterhouse, 18c painters · A. Bailey, Standing in the sun: a life of J. M. W. Turner (1997) · GM, 1st ser., 88/1 (1818), 644 · GM, 2nd ser., 9 (1838), 104 · Graves, RA exhibitors, 5 (1906), 374 · will, PRO, PROB 11/1602, sig. 137, fols. 251v–252r

Nixon, Sir John Eccles (1857–1921), army officer, was born at Brentford, Middlesex, on 16 August 1857, the youngest son of Captain John Piggott Nixon of the 25th Bombay native infantry and later the Indian political service and his wife, Ellen, daughter of G. Cooper of Brentford. He was educated at Wellington College and the Royal Military College, Sandhurst. Nixon was commissioned as a sublieutenant in the 75th foot in September 1875. In May 1878 he entered the Bengal staff corps and joined the 18th Bengal cavalry. For ten years he served with his regiment, fighting in the Second Anglo-Afghan War (1879–80) and the Zaimukht punitive expedition, for which he was mentioned in dispatches. In 1881 he participated in the Mahsud Waziri expedition on the north-west frontier. Nixon joined the garrison instruction staff in April 1888 as a captain, beginning a fifteen-year period of continuous staff employment during which he served with the Chitral relief force (1895) and the Tochi field force (1897–8). For the former he was promoted brevet lieutenant-colonel in January 1896, and was mentioned in dispatches on both occasions. With the rank of colonel Nixon was appointed an assistant quartermaster-general in March 1899, and at the end of 1901 he was sent to South Africa where he remained until the end of the Second South African War, commanding a cavalry column operating in the Transvaal and the Orange Free State. Nixon was awarded the campaign medal with four clasps, was mentioned in dispatches, and was created CB in 1902.

Following his return to India, Nixon held a succession of command and staff appointments. In 1902 he resumed his job as assistant quartermaster-general for intelligence. In May 1903 he was made commander of a second-class district, in August 1906 inspector-general of cavalry, and in May 1908 a divisional commander. Nixon was then given

Sir John Eccles Nixon (1857–1921), by Vandyk, pubd 1915

the prestigious appointment of general officer commanding the southern army in October 1912, which he held until February 1915, when he assumed command of the northern army. During this period he rose steadily through the ranks: major-general in March 1904, lieutenant-general in February 1909, and finally general in May 1914, establishing a reputation as an energetic and capable staff officer and commander. For his services he was created KCB in 1911.

In April 1915 Nixon took command of Indian expeditionary force D deployed in Mesopotamia, which had originally landed in November 1914 following the entry of Turkey into the war to protect Basrah and oilfields near the Shatt al-ʿArab. Shortly after he arrived the Turkish army attacked an entrenched British position at Shaybah, but they were repulsed after heavy fighting. General Sir Beauchamp Duff, commander-in-chief in India, ordered Nixon to retain control of the Basrah vilayet, the mouth of the Tigris River, and as much of the surrounding area as deemed necessary to protect a pipeline and local oilfields. Although the secretary of state for India had expressly ordered that no further advances should be undertaken, Nixon was also instructed by Duff, after acquainting himself with the local position, to submit plans to secure the Basrah vilayet and for a subsequent advance on Baghdad. He was also specifically ordered to report on the military requirements of such an expedition, particularly about the adequacy and suitability of the river transport expected to arrive from India, Burma, and Egypt.

A series of operations was undertaken under Nixon's command, with the approval of the government of India, to control the Basrah vilayet. On 31 May troops led by Sir Charles Townshend captured a strong Turkish position at Kurna, despite severe flooding of the surrounding area. This difficult feat of arms was followed by the capture of Amara, 90 miles upriver, and then Nasiriyyah on 25 July, which was defended by a large Turkish force. Following these successful operations an elated and over-optimistic Nixon proposed, in order to consolidate control of the Basrah vilayet, the capture of Kut al-Amara, located 150 miles upriver, which was eventually sanctioned by the government of India and the cabinet. The enemy defensive positions on either side of the river were skilfully captured by Sir Charles Townshend, who entered Kut on 29 September. The defeated Turks were pursued 60 miles further northwards to Aziziyyah, which was occupied on 3 October and fortified as the northernmost British defensive outpost.

Nixon was not content with his recent successes, however, and proposed further offensive operations to offset the effects of recent Turkish victories at the Dardanelles. On 3 October he telegraphed the secretary of state for India, 'I consider I am strong enough to open the road to Baghdad, and with this intention I propose to concentrate at ʿAziziyyah'. Nixon's force was still badly short despite repeated earlier requests for tugs, barges, and other shipping, however, on which he was completely dependent for transport and supply along the narrow, winding Tigris River. Moreover, reserves of medical personnel and stores available in Mesopotamia and India were insufficient to support a major operation. The deadlock at the Dardanelles finally convinced the cabinet of the merits of advancing on Baghdad. Two Indian divisions were dispatched from France as reinforcements, but no serious endeavour was made to increase the amount of water transport. Despite continued doubts expressed by Sir Beauchamp Duff that insufficient troops and transport were available, on 23 October 1915 the secretary of state authorized Nixon to advance if he judged sufficient forces were at his disposal for the operation.

On 22 November Townshend attacked a superior number of Turkish troops entrenched in a strong position astride the Tigris at Ctesiphon. By nightfall the battle was lost, and several days later Townshend conducted a fighting retreat to Kut, where he was besieged on 6 December by several Turkish divisions. A series of unsuccessful attempts was made to relieve the beleaguered division by the remaining British and Indian troops in Mesopotamia and further reinforcements. Sir John Nixon relinquished his command on 19 January 1916 through ill health, leaving behind for his successor an administrative nightmare. A chronic shortage of river transport meant it was impossible to evacuate large numbers of sick and wounded from either Kut or the relieving force, which suffered hardships owing to a lack of doctors and medical supplies. Despite further attempts during the spring to relieve the town, imminent starvation compelled Townshend to unconditionally surrender Kut on 29 April 1916.

Nixon was summoned to England to appear before the Mesopotamia commission of inquiry appointed in August 1916 to investigate the underlying causes of the débâcle in Mesopotamia. 'The weightiest share of responsibility', the commission's final report noted, 'lies with Sir John Nixon, whose confident optimism was the main cause of the decision to advance' ('War in Mesopotamia', 111). The army council also ordered that Nixon submit a written explanation of his conduct during the campaign, depending on which further action might be taken. An announcement was finally made in the House of Commons on 28 October 1918, however, that the army council considered Nixon's description of events satisfactory. In recognition of his services, in 1919 a GCMG was conferred on Nixon, and he was also posthumously made a grand officer of the Légion d'honneur in 1922. The nine months of command in Mesopotamia were Nixon's last active service. He had married in 1884 Amy Louisa, daughter of James Wilson, of Gratwicke, Billingshurst, and Felpham Manor, Sussex, and they had one son. His health gradually deteriorated and on 15 December 1921 he died at St Raphael, Var, France, survived by his wife.   T. R. MOREMAN

Sources DNB · Indian Army List · 'Commission ... to enquire into the operations of war in Mesopotamia', Parl. papers (1917), 16.773, Cd 8610 · F. J. Moberly, ed., The campaign in Mesopotamia, 1914–1918, 4 vols. (1923–7) · A. J. Barker, The neglected war: Mesopotamia, 1914–1918 (1967) · P. K. Davis, 'British and Indian strategy and policy in Mesopotamia', PhD diss., U. Lond., 1981 · C. V. F. Townshend, My campaign in Mesopotamia (1920) · Report by Gen. Sir John Eccles Nixon on the operations in Mesopotamia for the period from the beginning of October 1915, to the date he relinquished command of the force, 19 January 1916 (1916)
Archives CUL, corresp. with Lord Hardinge
Likenesses Vandyk, photograph, pubd 1915, NPG [see illus.]
Wealth at death £2255 8s. 9d.: probate, 11 April 1922, CGPLA Eng. & Wales

Nixon, Robert [called the Cheshire Prophet] (supp. fl. **late 15th–early 17th cent.**), supposed prophet, was variously given as having been born in 1467 in Delamere, Cheshire, and as having lived in the reign of James VI and I. He did not in fact exist in either of those periods, but was invented, or rather assembled, in 1701, from components chiefly originating in Scotland and medieval and Reformation England. Of these, the two most important were the thirteenth-century legend Thomas the Rhymer of Erceldoune, and William Nixon, the man of Delamere, who did exist and who is the likely origin of the name of his 'descendant'. It cannot be excluded that a real Robert Nixon had a hand in the compilation of the much older prophecies disseminated under his name. For these, the compilers may have used as a convenient source The Whole Prophecies of Scotland, England France ..., published in Edinburgh in 1603 and many times reissued. For many eighteenth-century readers the vital element of the prophecy was contained in the last stanza, a call for the return of the deposed Richard III:

Then rise up Richard, son of Richard,
And bless the happy reign,

Thrice happy he who sees this to come,
When England shall know rest and peace again.
(Axon, 56)

The call, of course, was understood to refer to another and more recent usurpation. The compilers' manuscripts survive in the Cheshire record office (Ches. & Chester ALSS) and contain references to Vale Royal, the Cheshire estate of the Cholmondeley family. Francis and Thomas Cholmondeley both represented Cheshire in parliament and both suffered imprisonment in 1689 for refusing the oath of allegiance to William and Mary. Francis was highly intransigent in the matter, and Thomas accepted a commission from the exiled James Stuart. The prophecies of Robert Nixon are now believed to have been compiled and issued, probably under the auspices of this family, in 1701: Dickens's The Pickwick Papers refers to an edition of that year. The period 1700–02 was one of high tension. The high-church tories led by Atterbury were becoming increasingly militant, the deaths of King William and of his successor, Anne's only son, gave rise to great anxiety over the future of the monarchy, and led to the Act of Settlement in 1701; in that year rumours circulated that Louis XIV had decided to sponsor a Jacobite invasion. Such factors may help explain Nixon's 'birth' at this, rather than any other, time. It was for long thought that the prophecies were first published in 1714, by the whig and Hanoverian John Oldmixon. But Oldmixon clearly implied in his introduction that his edition was a response to an earlier, Jacobite version; in any case, the Nixon now resurrected by him had evidently seen a new name in the runes, for the Oldmixon edition printed a different couplet:

Nixon from 'mongst the dark decrees of fate, Says
'George the son of George shall make us great'.

The prophet Robert Nixon, then, was brought into the world by the dark decrees of politics—but a real Robert Nixon was in existence in 1737, the leader of a Jacobite group which had planted a bomb in Westminster Hall, and produced a paper proclaiming the legitimacy of James Francis Stuart. There is no known connection between myth and man.   STEPHEN WRIGHT

Sources W. E. A. Axon, Nixon's Cheshire prophecies (1878) · J. Easton, ed., Robert Nixon, the Cheshire Prophet, an 18th c. propaganda (1999) · K. Thomas, Religion and the decline of magic (1991) · P. K. Monod, Jacobitism and the English people, 1688–1788 (1989) · L. Coote and T. Thornton, 'Richard, son of Richard: Richard III and political prophecy', Historical Research, 73 (2000), 321–40 · T. Thornton, 'Reshaping the local future: the development and uses of provincial political prophecies, 1300–1900', Prophecy: the power of inspired language in history, 1300–2000, ed. B. Taithe and T. Thornton (1997), 51–67
Archives Ches. & Chester ALSS, DDX 123, DCC 37/1

Nixon, Robert (1759–1837). See under Nixon, John Colley (b. before 1759, d. 1818).

Nixon, Samuel (1803–1854), sculptor, lived his early years in obscurity (nothing is known of his parents), but his obituary in the Art Journal suggests that he had been born and brought up in London. A 'Mr Nixon, Jnr', his nephew, is known to have carved the column capitals of St Barnabas, Homerton, Hackney, Middlesex, in 1845, while a glass painter of some contemporary repute known only as 'Mr Nixon' may have been his brother. It is not known who Samuel Nixon's masters were and there is no record of his attendance at the Royal Academy Schools. Neither is it known whether he was related to James Nixon (1741–1812), a miniature painter who entered the Royal Academy Schools in 1769. Samuel Nixon exhibited at the Royal Academy summer exhibitions from 1826 to 1846, his early pieces—*The Shepherd* (1826), *The Reconciliation of Adam and Eve after the Fall* (1828), *The Birth of Venus* (1830), and *The Infant Moses* (1831)—suggesting an ambition to be a sculptor of idealized works. He was, nevertheless, principally employed during the next few years on commissions for portrait and sepulchral sculpture. When the architect Philip Hardwick was engaged with the building of Goldsmiths' Hall in Foster Lane, Cheapside, he employed Nixon to do the sculptural decorations in Roche Abbey stone. Nixon's group of children representing *The Four Seasons* (1840) for the grand staircase of the building was described in the artist's obituary in the *Gentleman's Magazine* as 'a work of the highest merit'. He also executed a statue of the company's founder, John Carpenter (1844), for the City of London School, and one of Sir John Crosby (1845) to be placed in Crosby Hall in Bishopsgate.

Nixon's principal work was the statue of William IV, erected on 18–19 December 1844 at the end of King William Street in the City, on the exact site of the famous Boar's Head tavern in Eastcheap. The statue, 15 feet 3 inches high, was constructed of two blocks of Foggin Tor Devon granite, together weighing 20 tons. Although the commission was prestigious, both Nixon and his friends considered the fee, £2200, incommensurate with the difficulties involved in carving such an intractable material as granite. In addition, his expenses seem not to have been paid by his patrons, the corporation of the City of London, and the commission nearly ruined him financially (*GM*, 1854). In 1935 the statue was taken down and the following year re-erected on a new, smaller, pedestal in a public garden in King William Walk, Greenwich. Nixon's workshop was at 2 White Hart Court, Bishopsgate, and he died at his home, Kennington Place, Kennington Common, London, on 2 August 1854, aged fifty-one.

L. H. CUST, rev. TERRY CAVANAGH

Sources *GM*, 2nd ser., 21 (1844), 179 • *GM*, 2nd ser., 42 (1854), 405–6 • *Art Journal*, 16 (1854), 280 • R. Gunnis, *Dictionary of British sculptors, 1660–1851* (1953) • J. Blackwood, *London's immortals: the complete outdoor commemorative statues* (1989), 54 • Graves, *RA exhibitors* • Redgrave, *Artists*

Nkomo, Joshua Mqabuko Nyongolo (1917–1999), politician in Zimbabwe, was born on 19 June 1917 at Tshimale, a mission station in the Semokwe 'native reserve', Malobo district, south of Bulawayo, Southern Rhodesia, the third among the eight children of parents who worked for the Congregationalist London Missionary Society, his father as a driver and his mother as a cook. He received his early education from the society, completing standard six before becoming a schoolteacher. In 1942 he travelled to South Africa, where he enrolled at Adams College, Natal,

Joshua Mqabuko Nyongolo Nkomo (1917–1999), by Andrew Wilson, *c.*1962

for three years before attending the Jan Hofmeyr School of Social Work in Johannesburg, graduating with a diploma in social science. After his return to Southern Rhodesia he continued his studies through correspondence school, and earned a bachelor of arts degree in economics and social science from the University of South Africa, Johannesburg. Meanwhile he worked first as a social worker for Rhodesia Railways in Bulawayo (the first African to hold such a post) and then as organizing secretary of the Rhodesian African Railway Workers' Union. In 1949 he married Johanna Fuyane Magwegwe; they had two sons and two daughters.

In his youth Nkomo searched for a serviceable ideology, but it was not in his temperament to drop one faith when he adopted another. He was brought up a Congregationalist. Later he became a Methodist lay preacher, and shortly before his death he was baptized as a Roman Catholic. Yet at least from 1953 to the end of his life he was an adherent to Zimbabwean traditional religion. In 1953 he visited the High God shrine at Dula and was given power to fight the nationalist war. Right to the end of his days he would visit his favourite shrine, to recover under its sacred trees. His Marxism, symbolized by photographs of him, massive in a Soviet field marshal's uniform, was never more than an additional serviceable set of ideas and alliances. He was similarly capable of combining many 'ethnic' identities. He came to be seen as leader of the Ndebele (Matabele). In fact, he was a Kalanga, descendant of the pre-Ndebele peoples of the Zimbabwean south-west. In his youth he was a member of the Kalanga Cultural Promotion Society. But simultaneously he was a supporter of the Matabele Home Society and an avid collector of Ndebele traditions. He was a pan-Africanist, a Zimbabwean nationalist, an Ndebele cultural patriot, and a Kalanga. He never saw these identities as conflicting any more than he saw an inconsistency in being a Christian and a traditionalist. One of Nkomo's gifts to Zimbabwe was the idea—and practice—of a hierarchy of identities.

But the identity of Zimbabwean nationalist was the most important. During his time in South Africa in the 1940s Nkomo was influenced by the ideas of the African National Congress (ANC), and on his return he headed the Bulawayo branch of the Southern Rhodesian ANC. In 1952 he was invited by Sir Godfrey Huggins to be one of the African representatives in the Southern Rhodesian delegation to a conference in London to mark the formation of the Federation of Rhodesia and Nyasaland. Huggins's hopes of compliance were disappointed, and at the conference Nkomo attracted considerable attention for his advocacy of African rights. When the Southern Rhodesian ANC was reformed in 1957, Nkomo became its president. He was president also of the two successor movements, the National Democratic Party, formed in 1960, and the Zimbabwe African People's Union (ZAPU), formed in 1961. In 1963 the nationalist movement split. There was a revolt against Nkomo's leadership by a group of ZAPU officials who included Robert Mugabe, Ndabaningi Sithole, and Herbert Chitepo. The rebels eventually formed the Zimbabwe African National Union (ZANU). But Nkomo's ZAPU remained a national party, and in the mid-1960s enjoyed political dominance in most Shona-speaking areas as well as in the Ndebele-speaking west. Right up to the Zimbabwean independence election of 1980 Nkomo (who spent most of the intervening period restricted to Gonakudzingwa on the south-eastern border and then, following the failure of constitutional talks in Geneva in 1976, in exile) remained confident that ZAPU commanded a national majority.

Whenever he could during the 1970s, Nkomo tried to go for a political rather than a military solution, and he was dumbfounded by ZAPU's overwhelming defeat in the independence election of 1980. This was the result of the geographical imbalance of the 1970s guerrilla war. Nkomo's guerrilla army, ZIPRA, operated out of Zambia; Mugabe's rival guerrilla army, ZANLA, operated along the eastern frontier with Mozambique. ZIPRA was armed by the Soviet Union, ZANLA by China. Nkomo's army was effective throughout western Zimbabwe, and in the late 1970s the high command was planning a conventional war, whereby tanks and war planes would advance on Bulawayo and Salisbury. Meanwhile Mugabe's ZANLA was employing a quite different strategy of mass deployment of guerrillas throughout east and central Zimbabwe. These young men 'politically educated' the peasantries and told them that they must vote for Robert Mugabe. The Lancaster House conference of 1979 was crucial. Nkomo's

military commanders urged him to wait until they could launch an attack on the towns. But as always he wanted to go to the electorate. Even then a disastrous regional split could have been avoided had Nkomo and Mugabe fought the 1980 election together as the combined Patriotic Front (formed in 1976), which would have won every constituency. Nevertheless, Mugabe insisted that ZANU and ZAPU fight the election as competing parties. ZANU won fifty-seven seats and ZAPU only twelve. Worse still, all twelve were in the west of Zimbabwe.

The newly independent country now faced the impossible situation of two parties equally committed to a one-party state. For a while Nkomo managed to persuade his followers to accept the result, and from 1980 to 1982 he served in the government, as minister of home affairs and then minister without portfolio. But Mugabe and his party feared that ZAPU, supported by the Soviet Union and the South African ANC, would launch a coup—and they were being fed lies by white intelligence officers secretly working for the South African government. Tensions between former ZANLA and former ZIPRA guerrillas who were being integrated into the new national army exploded in fire-fights. In any case Mugabe could not accept anything less than total national support for his government. A campaign began to hunt down ex-ZIPRA guerrillas and to arrest ZAPU political leaders. Armed men took to the bush in Matabeleland; South Africa meddled; Nkomo was unfairly blamed for the violence; Mugabe sent in the fearsome fifth brigade to 'subdue' the population, resulting in the deaths of some 10,000 Ndebele citizens. Nkomo had reason to fear for his life, especially after soldiers shot dead three of his employees at his home in Bulawayo. On 8 March 1983 he fled to Botswana. It was the low point of his life. His supporters in Zimbabwe felt abandoned. His past patrons now gave him no support. The most significant product of his exile was his autobiography, *Nkomo: the Story of my Life*, which was published in London in 1984. With its denunciation of Mugabe's government as genocidal and with its call for pluralist democracy, the book was not published inside Zimbabwe.

Nkomo returned to Zimbabwe in 1985 to contest the national elections, in which ZAPU held most of its seats despite the violence of state repression. The terrible stalemate seemed doomed to continue; attempt after attempt to unite the parties broke down. Then in December 1987 Nkomo made the final concessions, accepting a united party that would bear the name ZANU. Many people in Matabeleland felt that this was a surrender. But it ended the violence. Nkomo became senior minister and then (from August 1990) vice-president. The old leaders of ZAPU, under the cover of unity, were allowed to control local government in western Zimbabwe.

In the last twelve years of his life Nkomo concentrated on patronage politics in Matabeleland and on building a family fortune in land and business assets. He became 'too fat', as the shrine priests say, both physically and metaphysically. Many people became disillusioned with him. Nevertheless, his death at the Parirenyatwa Hospital in Harare on 1 July 1999, of prostate cancer, was the occasion for huge demonstrations of memory and mourning: perhaps the last old-style Zimbabwean nationalist event. He was buried at Heroes' Acre, Harare, on 5 July, and was survived by his wife and three children, one son having predeceased him. His absence contributed to the election results of June 2000, when old ZAPU men were swept away all over Matabeleland by candidates of the Movement for Democratic Change. Mugabe desperately tried to capture Nkomo's image, and his damning autobiography was at last made available to Zimbabweans in the government press. 'Father Zimbabwe' had become the last hope for the survivors of nationalism.   TERENCE O. RANGER

Sources J. Nkomo, *Nkomo: the story of my life* (1984) · *The Times* (2 July 1999) · *Daily Telegraph* (2 July 1999) · *The Independent* (2 July 1999) · *The Guardian* (2 July 1999) · *International who's who*
Likenesses A. Wilson, photograph, *c.*1962, Hult. Arch. [*see illus.*] · photograph, repro. in *The Times* · photograph, repro. in *The Guardian* · photograph, repro. in *The Independent*

Nkrumah, Kwame (1909?–1972), president of Ghana, was born at Nkroful, Nzima, a village in the south-west of Gold Coast Colony. As birth certificates were not then mandatory, the exact date of his birth is uncertain. He was probably born on 18 September 1909 and baptized in the local Roman Catholic church three days later. On occasions in later life he was to give his year of birth as 1912, almost certainly erroneously. His father, a goldsmith from a town on the border with the Ivory Coast, named him Nwia Kofi but his baptismal name was Francis. In addition, like all Akan, he had a day name, Kwame (Saturday), and at various stages of his career used each of these as a forename. One of several children of his father, he was the only child of his mother, Nyaniba, a trader. He attended the Roman Catholic elementary school at his father's town, Half Assini, living for some of the time in the house of the local priest, a German, Father George Fischer. At the age of fourteen or fifteen he became a pupil teacher at the same school. A year later, in 1926, he was spotted during a school inspection by the principal of the government training college in Accra who recommended that he should be formally trained at the college. The year in which he began his studies there the training college was merged with the newly founded Prince of Wales College at Achimota and Nkrumah was thus to become one of the first graduates of this colonial educational showpiece.

Studies abroad On graduation Nkrumah was employed as the teacher of lower class one at the Roman Catholic junior school at Elmina but stayed there only a year as he was appointed headmaster of the Catholic junior school in Axim, about 8 miles from his birthplace. He remained there for two years before taking up a teaching post in the Catholic seminary at Amissano. It is clear that at this stage of his career he was seriously considering the priesthood. But his commitment to furthering his education in Britain was also apparent. He sat and failed the London matriculation examinations and enrolled with Wolsley Hall. The alternative to British higher education, studying in America, was apparently inspired by the legendary African vice-principal of Achimota, the American-educated Kwegyir Aggrey, and the charismatic Nigerian editor of the *West*

Kwame Nkrumah (1909?–1972), by unknown photographer, 1964

African Pilot, Nnamdi Azikiwe, who was also American trained and with whom the young Nkrumah was in touch. He was accepted at Lincoln University, near Philadelphia, Pennsylvania, which also offered him a small scholarship.

Nkrumah's undergraduate years at Lincoln, a small university for black men, supported by the Presbyterian church, lasted from 1935 to 1939. His reports suggest that he was a good if reserved student who was forced to take a succession of jobs, some of them menial, to supplement his inadequate grant. His increasingly radical political engagement is apparent in his choice of term papers and prize essays. He was awarded his BA degree in economics and sociology in 1939. In the same year he enrolled at the University of Pennsylvania where his successful studies for an MSc degree in education were supported by a heavy teaching load at his alma mater, Lincoln. At the same time he was keeping his options open by completing another bachelor's degree in sacred theology at Lincoln. In 1942 he embarked upon a research degree in philosophy at Pennsylvania which he never successfully completed. From now onwards his interests became focused upon anti-imperialism. It is very likely that his first major publication, *Towards Colonial Freedom*, not published until 1947, was drafted between 1942 and 1945. During this period it is clear that he was becoming more involved in radical black political circles, including organizations of anti-colonial African students studying in the USA. By the end of his period in the USA he was a committed, radical nationalist.

The reasons for Nkrumah's departure to Britain in May 1945 to pursue his studies are unclear. In rapid succession he registered for a PhD degree in anthropology at the London School of Economics, for another in philosophy at University College, London (where he was supervised by A. J. Ayer), and was admitted as a student by Gray's Inn. But politics now dominated his life. He became deeply involved in the increasingly radical African student political groupings, some of which had links with communist organizations in Britain and eastern Europe. He assisted George Padmore, the veteran West Indian journalist and activist, in the convening of the celebrated Pan-African Congress which met in Manchester in October 1945.

Nationalist leader In August 1947 a new nationalist party, the United Gold Coast Convention (UGCC), was formed in the Gold Coast. It invited Nkrumah, who was well known to Ako Adjei, one of its leading members, to become its general secretary. Nkrumah arrived in the Gold Coast in November 1947 and in a remarkably short time turned a moderate protest movement into an extensive mass party by linking it with numerous local voluntary associations which, in one way or another, expressed discontent with the colonial government. Although the UGCC had played no part in inciting the urban rioting which rocked the country from the end of February 1948, the humiliation of an unprepared government ensured that the Gold Coast's only nationalist movement now enjoyed considerable power. The report of the Watson commission of inquiry into the riots forced the British to alter their timetable of devolution. A new constitution was hammered out by an all-African committee, and elections, based upon universal suffrage, were to be held.

Although the UGCC dominated the centre stage, Nkrumah wearied of its leadership's gradualism. While still formally its general secretary he formed a 'vanguard party' within the UGCC, the committee on youth organization, based upon his and his most immediate lieutenants' personal links with leaders of organized labour and local associations throughout the country. Affronted by his radicalism and his lack of deference, the UGCC leadership sought to control its general secretary. By June 1949 a final break had occurred, and Nkrumah established his own party, the Convention People's Party (CPP), well to the left of the UGCC. Nkrumah denounced the UGCC's modest ambition of 'self government in the shortest possible time' and demanded 'self government NOW'. To bring this about he organized a positive action campaign which included a partially successful general strike. On the grounds of inciting an illegal strike—for some of the strikers were civil servants whose contracts expressly forbade strike action—Nkrumah and many other party leaders were tried and imprisoned.

Independence In the meantime the country's first general election was being planned. The UGCC, its task lightened by the imprisonment of its radical opponents, nevertheless failed to capitalize on the situation. The CPP swept the polls in February 1951 and Nkrumah was returned for Accra Central (winning 22,780 of the 23,122 votes cast in the constituency). Nkrumah was released from prison, initiating a remarkably close relationship between himself and the last colonial governor, Sir Charles Arden-Clarke. From 1951 to 1954 the CPP dominated the cabinet in an unforeseen harmonious period of diarchy with the British. In 1954 further elections ushered in a transitional period of internal self-government and saw the CPP taking 72 of the 104 seats. Prime minister from March 1952, Nkrumah was suddenly confronted by a serious threat in the form of the National Liberation Movement (NLM), a coalition of regional, anti-socialist opponents led by an especially powerful movement among the Asante people, the relict of a great pre-colonial empire. Nkrumah's sincere wish for a unitary, socialist state was challenged by a largely extra-parliamentary campaign. His inability to control this allowed the opposition to force a further pre-independence election upon an unwilling CPP government in which the CPP again took close to 75 per cent of the seats. His frustration with what he was to denounce as 'tribalism' and, because the NLM enjoyed support from many of the traditional chiefs whose authority the CPP was trying to supplant, what he decried as 'feudalism' almost certainly fuelled his distaste for opposition. Following the grant of independence in March 1957, he was swift to illegalize parties based upon regional, ethnic, or confessional principles. He was also to use authoritarian measures, including detention without trial, against those politicians who had threatened the smooth transfer of power from the British.

In less than a decade Nkrumah had led the first sub-Saharan colony to independence and in the process had achieved a pre-eminence among political leaders in the developing world despite the smallness of his country. His achievements were considerable. At the material level Ghana had largely Africanized its civil service, and had vastly expanded its infrastructure, education, and health services. A new university had been built, as had a fine deep water port, and the plans for the great hydroelectric scheme, the Volta River project, were well advanced. Much of this was facilitated by the huge increases in revenue from Ghana's major export crop, cocoa, but it owed a great deal to the prime minister's own exuberant enthusiasm for development. Less tangibly, Nkrumah had established himself permanently as an almost iconic figure, especially for Africans and people of African descent, but more widely for many in the colonial world. He symbolized pride and achievement and did so with considerable *élan*. This enabled him to host the All African People's Convention in April 1958, the precursor of the Organization of African Unity, thus establishing himself as the leading voice in the pan-African movement.

Erosion of support Domestically things were less propitious. The world price for cocoa was falling by the late 1950s, ensuring that the ambitious development plans could only be advanced by debt. Internal dissent—which included conspiracies against the government, bombings, and at least two serious assassination attempts—was increasingly harshly dealt with. Many elements of civil society, including trade unions, lost their autonomy as they were forcibly brought within the fold of the government party. In 1960 Nkrumah fulfilled an early ambition by declaring Ghana a republic and by winning the presidential election; many opposition figures doubted the fairness of both the process and the voting figures. In a brief time the country was formally declared a one-party state.

In power since 1951 and ineffectively opposed for much of this time, the party became arrogant, increasingly insensitive to its roots, and certainly corrupt. At the same time the country, increasingly indebted, its reserves run down, lost much of its developmental verve. Nkrumah's dominant position as a world statesman was eroded by widespread awareness of conditions in Ghana every bit as much as it was by the advent of a new generation of successful African politicians on the world stage. On 24 February 1966, while absent on a peacemaking mission in Vietnam, he was ousted by Ghana's first military coup. The military regime and its civilian advisers now undertook a campaign to vilify Nkrumah and his party. This was only temporarily successful as many Ghanaians and many outside Ghana have never forgotten the almost legendary role of this pioneer of African liberation. He went into exile in Guinea, whose president, Sekou Toure, provided him with sanctuary and a symbolic co-presidency. Nkrumah died on 27 April 1972 in a hospital in Bucharest, Romania, while undergoing therapy for skin cancer.

Significance Nkrumah's personal life is something of a mystery. A somewhat private, even lonely man, his only fully acknowledged relationship was his marriage, in 1957, to Fathia Halen Ritz, an Egyptian, with whom he had a son and two daughters; she survived him. He was an unflamboyant teetotaller and almost certainly did not salt away funds in private accounts. Ideologically it seems very likely that he had great faith in socialism from at least the early 1940s and had pragmatically suppressed this during the period from 1951 to 1957 when he worked in harness with an outgoing colonial regime. After independence his belief in central planning, state ownership, and centralism came to the fore, but his policies were never radical enough to include land reform or the nationalization of property. He was eventually reburied in Ghana, twenty years after his death, and formally commemorated by a memorial garden on the seafront of central Accra.

RICHARD RATHBONE

Sources *The autobiography of Kwame Nkrumah* (1957) · M. Sherwood, *Kwame Nkrumah: the years abroad* (1996) · R. Rathbone, ed., *Ghana*, 2 vols. (1992), ser. B/1 of *British documents on the end of empire* · C. L. R. James, *Nkrumah and the Ghana revolution* (1977) · B. Davidson, *Black star* (1973) · *CGPLA Eng. & Wales* (1972) · *Daily Graphic* (2 July 1992)
Archives George Padmore Library, Accra · Institute of African Studies, Legon, Ghana · National Archives of Ghana, Accra, papers · University of Ghana, Legon, Balme Library | FILM BFI NFTVA, documentary footage · BFI NFTVA, news footage | SOUND BBC WAC · BL NSA, current affairs recordings · BL NSA, 'Memoirs of Nkrumah Kwame', 25 March 1982, C48/11 · BL NSA, oral history interview · IWM SA, oral history interview
Likenesses photographs, 1956–66, Hult. Arch. [*see illus.*]
Wealth at death £6250 in England and Wales: probate, 19 Dec 1972, *CGPLA Eng. & Wales*

Nkumbula, Harry Mwaanga (1917?–1983), African nationalist leader in Northern Rhodesia, was born in the village of Maala, in the Namwala district, an Ila-speaking area of the southern province of Northern Rhodesia. He came to believe that he was born in March 1917, but acknowledged that the actual date was likely to remain a mystery. He was the son of Longwani Nkumbula (*c.*1873–1963), who had worked in South Africa before his marriage. Harry was the youngest of three children and the only son. His mother died at his birth. He was educated at Methodist mission schools and completed standard VI at the Kafue Training Institute in 1934. He then taught for several years in Namwala district. He married Cecily Shimangalu, the daughter of a schoolteacher, in 1935; they had four children before divorcing in 1952.

Nkumbula joined the government teaching service in 1938 and later worked on the copperbelt in Mufulira and Kitwe. During the Second World War he became involved in the emerging African nationalist movement. He was secretary of the Mufulira Welfare Association and was a co-founder of the Kitwe African Society. After some time at the Chalimbana Teacher Training School, he was sent in 1946, with the support of Sir Stewart Gore-Browne, to Makerere University College, Kampala. He moved from there to the Institute of Education, University of London, where he completed a diploma. He then enrolled at the London School of Economics to study economics. While in London in 1949 he helped Dr Hastings Banda draft an important pamphlet against the proposed central African federation. After failing his examinations he was, however, compelled to return home early in 1950 without a degree.

In 1951 Nkumbula was elected president of the Northern Rhodesian African Congress, which was soon renamed the African National Congress (ANC). He was chosen as a militant, articulate, and uncompromising opponent of the federation. Nkumbula's call for a national day of prayer—a national strike under another name—against federation was largely unsuccessful as a result of the opposition of Lawrence Katilungu, president of the African Mine Workers' Union, who campaigned against it on the copperbelt. The Federation of Rhodesia and Nyasaland was established in October 1953 despite African opposition. Although a boycott of European-owned butcheries in Lusaka in the early months of 1954 had some success, Nkumbula and the ANC continued to find it difficult to mobilize the people against federation.

Nkumbula and the ANC's secretary-general, Kenneth Kaunda, were imprisoned for two months early in 1955 for distributing subversive literature. While the experience of imprisonment, with hard labour, had a radicalizing influence on Kaunda, it had a moderating impact on

Nkumbula. He was increasingly influenced by white liberals such as Harry Franklin, and came to be seen as willing to compromise on the fundamental issue of majority rule. Opposition to what was seen as his autocratic leadership of the ANC eventually resulted in a split and the establishment of the Zambia African National Congress (ZANC) under the leadership of Kaunda in October 1958. ZANC was banned in March 1959, but its leaders took over the United National Independence Party (UNIP) in the later months of that year. UNIP, under Kaunda's leadership, was both better organized and more militant than Nkumbula's ANC and took the leading position in the movement towards independence.

Nkumbula played a secondary role in constitutional talks in London in 1960–61 and was removed from the political scene between April 1961 and January 1962, while serving a nine-month prison sentence for causing death by dangerous driving. In the build-up to elections under the complex Macleod constitution in October 1962, Nkumbula accepted substantial funding from Moise Tshombe's regime in Katanga, and made a secret electoral pact with Sir Roy Welensky's United Federal Party. In the elections the ANC won seven seats and held the balance between UNIP and the United Federal Party. Nkumbula eventually chose to join in a coalition with UNIP and became minister of African education. The alliance lasted until the pre-independence elections of January 1964 which were won by UNIP. Nkumbula, whose party had been troubled during 1963 by a split over the alliance with UNIP, and over co-operation with the United Federal Party and Tshombe, became leader of the opposition with ten seats to UNIP's fifty-five.

The ANC had been largely confined to Nkumbula's regional base in the southern province. The party won seats in the western province in the general elections of 1968, but Nkumbula offered little resistance to Kaunda's moves towards the formation of a one-party state. On 27 June 1973 Nkumbula announced in the Choma declaration that he was joining UNIP. The ANC was wound up following the dissolution of parliament in October 1973. Critics alleged that he was bought off with an emerald mine. Nkumbula's last significant political intervention was an ill-starred attempt, together with Simon Kapwepwe, to stand against Kaunda for the presidential nomination in 1978.

In his last years Nkumbula received some recognition as the father of Zambian politics. He was a man who was almost universally liked. He had few personal enemies and some improbable admirers, including the novelist Doris Lessing, who wrote about him warmly in her autobiography. He was, however, one of a number of African nationalist leaders whose essential moderation—critics would say laziness, lack of ruthlessness, or fondness for the good life—led them to lose out in the race for power which was an unavoidable part of the decolonization process. He died on 8 October 1983.   HUGH MACMILLAN

Sources D. Mulford, *Zambia: the politics of independence* (1967) · G. Mwangilwa, *Harry Mwaanga Nkumbula: a biography of the 'old lion' of Zambia* (Lusaka, Zambia, 1982) · K. Macpherson, *Kenneth Kaunda of Zambia: the times and the man* (1974) · J. J. Grotpeter, B. V. Siegel, and J. R. Pletcher, *Historical dictionary of Zambia*, 2nd edn (1998) · private information (2004)
Archives Bodl. RH, Welensky papers, letters · United National Independence Party, Lusaka, Zambia, African National Congress papers
Likenesses photographs, repro. in Mwangilwa, *Harry Mwaanga Nkumbula*

Noad, Henry Minchin (1815–1877), electrician, was born at Shawford, near Frome, Somerset, on 22 June 1815, the oldest of three sons of Humphrey Noad (d. 1845) and his wife, Maria Hunn (d. 1860), a half-sister of George Canning. He was educated at Frome grammar school, and was intended for the civil service in India, but the untimely death of his patron, William Huskisson, caused a change in his career, and he commenced the study of chemistry and electricity. About 1836 he delivered lectures on these subjects at the literary and scientific institutions of Bath and Bristol. He next examined the peculiar voltaic conditions of iron and bismuth, described some properties of the water battery, and elucidated that curious phenomenon, the passive state of iron. He joined the London Electrical Society shortly after its foundation in 1837.

In 1839 Noad published *A Course of Eight Lectures on Electricity, Galvanism, Magnetism, and Electro-Magnetism*, which became a recognized textbook, passing through four editions. In 1857 it was replaced by the two-volume *Manual of Electricity*. He also contributed a number of other popular and introductory works on electricity. These texts became crucial resources for budding electricians and telegraph engineers for much of the rest of the century. In 1845 he went to London and studied chemistry under August Wilhelm Hofmann in the newly founded Royal College of Chemistry. While with Hofmann he researched the oxidation of cymol or cymene, the hydrocarbon which Gerhardt and Cahours discovered in 1840 in the volatile oil of Roman cumin. The results were in part communicated to the Chemical Society (*Memoirs*, 3, 1845–8, 421–40) at the time, and more fully afterwards to the *Philosophical Magazine*, 32, 1848, 15–35. Among other organic products legumine and vitelline also formed materials for his investigations. In 1847 he was appointed to the chair of chemistry in the medical school of St George's Hospital, which he held until his death. In 1848 he contributed a treatise, *Chemical Manipulation and Analysis, Qualitative and Quantitative*, to the Library of Useful Knowledge. This work was widely regarded as a reworking of and a successor to Michael Faraday's book of the same title published in 1827. Like Noad's *Lectures on Electricity* it proved an influential student textbook during the second half of the century. About 1849 he obtained the degree of doctor of physics from the University of Giessen. In 1850–51 he conducted, jointly with Henry Gray (the author of Gray's *Anatomy*) an inquiry into the composition and functions of the spleen. Interest in such research in medical chemistry was burgeoning during this period, building on the work of Justus von Liebig, professor of chemistry at Giessen. The essay resulting from this investigation gained the Astley Cooper prize of 1852. When the Panopticon of Science and Arts in Leicester Square was opened in 1854, under the proprietorship of the former electrical instrument maker G. M. Clarke, Noad was appointed instructor in chemistry there. On 5 June 1856 he was elected a fellow of the Royal Society.

Noad next experimented on the chemistry of iron, and in 1860 contributed the article 'Iron' to Robert Hunt's edition of *Ure's Dictionary*. This led to his appointment as consulting chemist to the Ebbw Vale Iron Company, the Cwm Celyn, and Blaenau, the Aberdâr and Plymouth, and other ironworks in south Wales. In 1866 he became examiner of malt liquors to the India Office, and in 1872 an examiner in chemistry and physics at the Royal Military Academy, Woolwich.

Noad died at his home, East Cowes Villa, Lower Norwood, London, on 23 July 1877. Charlotte Jane (*b*. 1814/15), his widow, died on 25 March 1882. He was remembered as 'a man of cheerful, happy nature, of ripe experience, and varied knowledge, of perfect sincerity and generous sympathy with younger men of his craft, and with a fearless outspokenness against everything which bore the semblance of baseness and wrongdoing' (*The Engineer*, 76–7).

G. C. BOASE, *rev.* IWAN RHYS MORUS

Sources I. R. Morus, 'Currents from the underworld: electricity and the technology of display in early Victorian England', *Isis*, 84 (1993), 50–69 · *JCS* (1870) · *The Engineer*, 44 (1877), 76–7 · *CGPLA Eng. & Wales* (1877)
Wealth at death under £800: probate, 8 Aug 1877, *CGPLA Eng. & Wales*

Noailles, Antoine de (1504–1563), soldier and diplomat, was born on 4 September 1504 at the Château de la Fage, Noailles, the eldest son of Louis (1485–1540), seigneur de Noailles, of a modest family of the ancient provincial nobility of the sword of Limousin, which had served the kings of France as soldiers during the previous century. His mother was Catherine de Pierrebuffière (*d*. 1527), and his brothers François and Gilles (both, like Antoine himself, envoys to England) entered the church and became in succession bishops of Dax (1556–85 and 1585–97, respectively) and important state servants.

Antoine de Noailles began his military apprenticeship in Italy in 1521, in the company of Germain de Bonneval, and after the latter's death at Pavia in 1525 entered the service of a major local patron and distant kinsman, François de la Tour, vicomte de Turenne, son-in-law of the rising court favourite Anne de Montmorency, who later claimed Noailles was 'of his own bringing up' (Tytler, 2.356). He accompanied Turenne on a diplomatic mission to Rome and Venice in 1528 and then to Spain to conclude the marriage treaty in March 1530. It may have been through the patronage of Turenne, then captain of the royal guard, that he obtained a post in the military household of François I in 1529. He was commissioned to help organize the defence of Provence in 1536, was with the king's army in Artois in 1537, and was also active in Piedmont. It was the king's intervention in 1537–40 which in May 1540 secured him the hand of a local heiress, Jeanne de Gontaut, whose father, the vicomte de Gramat, opposed the match. He served in the victory at Ceresole in Italy in April 1544 and, as lieutenant of the Italian infantry under Nemours, was involved in the disastrous defeat of the French attempt to recapture Boulogne from the English of October 1544.

With the accession of Henri II and the return of Montmorency to favour, Noailles was on 20 September 1547 appointed *conseiller du roi* and *maître d'hôtel*, a post often held by ambassadors. On 4 April 1548 he was commissioned to fit out at Brest the fleet necessary for the transport of French troops under d'Essé to Scotland and on 31 January 1549 for the expedition under Termes; he spent much of 1548–50 on this work. In the words of Jean Beaugué, the king had chosen him as a 'person of great ability and virtue' (Beaugué, 8). As a reward he was made governor of the Château du Ha at Bordeaux in January 1550, then (in 1551) lieutenant-général du roi in Guyenne and governor of Bordeaux in January 1552. In 1551 he returned briefly to Italy to participate in the defence of Parma. He therefore came in April 1553 to his appointment as ambassador to England, his first major diplomatic post, equipped with military experience, knowledge of court politics, and close ties of clientage with the constable, Montmorency, but above all with experience in military administration. His education and career had equipped him with Latin, Italian, and Spanish.

Antoine de Noailles is one of the best-known French ambassadors in Tudor England as a result of the dramatic events through which he served his term and the fairly complete survival of his papers as ambassador. He faced formidable problems. His geographical knowledge of the country outside the south-east was limited ('Yorck qui n'est pas loing de Bristo'; Vertot, 3.96) and he did not speak the language. Yet, he rapidly formed an effective information network, with contacts who included Mary's household servant Sir John Leigh. His main assistants were M. de la Marque and his brother Gilles; a secretary was Philibert du Cros, who later served Mary Stuart. Almost as soon as he arrived, he was drawn into attempts to bolster up Northumberland's plans to exclude Mary Tudor from the throne and then, after Mary's triumph in July, to ensure that her marriage with Philip did not go ahead. At the coronation of Mary on 1 October 1553 he was reported by Simon Renard, the imperial ambassador, as whispering to Princess Elizabeth, when she complained to him of the weight of her coronet, 'that she should have patience and that once the crown were on her head it would seem lighter' (Griffet, 60).

As a diplomat Noailles was required to keep England out of an alliance with the Habsburgs, but as a man of action he felt drawn into plans to prevent the marriage by force at a time when French interests did not coincide exactly with those of the potential opposition. In all this he was faced by the determined opposition of Simon Renard (a former ambassador to France). Noailles could do little to stop Mary's marriage, but sought, cautiously at first (in France, Montmorency was more inclined to caution than his Guise rivals), to foster opposition without direct promises of aid until he became aware of the full scope of the plot against Mary in December 1553. The Wyatt rebellion broke out prematurely in mid-January and elicited a decision to give aid on the part of France. However, when the rebellion collapsed on 7 February, Noailles was compromised by the arrest of his dispatches. Far from discouraging him, this spurred him to further activity, though at first he could do little, closely supervised as he was by the council and threatened with demands for his recall. He had only expected to be in England for a year and several times asked for his recall. However, he was an inveterate man of action and from the summer of 1555 became deeply involved in another conspiracy, that of the exile Sir Henry Dudley. In April 1556 Dudley's friends in England started to be arrested and Noailles's part in the conspiracy was revealed. The situation became so threatening that he asked for his recall on grounds of ill health (to be replaced temporarily by his brother Gilles until his other brother, François, was ready to become ambassador). He took his leave on 25 May 1556 and left on 4 June. His experiences left him with a lasting dislike of England. By 1555, like many of his fellow ambassadors, he had formed the opinion that the English were to be criticized for 'triviality and inconstancy but above all … for all kinds of lying' (Harbison, *Rival Ambassadors*, 64) and 'so little trustworthiness' (Vertot, 2.242).

Noailles had been created a *gentilhomme de la chambre du roi* in January 1555, and in August 1557 was chosen as one of the superintendents of the education of the royal children. After the start of war with England in June 1557 and the defeat of St Quentin on 10 August, he was briefly sent to Coucy-le-Château to see to its defence but three weeks later was recalled and sent to Guyenne to resume his post as governor of Bordeaux. Following the death of Henri II there is reason to believe he was out of favour with the Guise regime of 1559–60, for in those years he spent little time at Bordeaux and did not find a place in the new royal household, though he was assigned 800 livres tournois in July 1559 as a reward for forty years' service and the loss of his household posts. He was back from November 1561, when he received the royal appointment of mayor of Bordeaux and helped to prevent the city falling into protestant hands. In January 1563 he was promoted chevalier of the order of St Michel, but he died at Bordeaux on 11 March, following a sudden illness, which it was suspected resulted from poisoning. He was described by Monluc as 'a good, wise gentleman and the king's good servant' (Monluc, 3.61, 65–6) and by his own brother Gilles as 'this great worthy man our brother whom we can justly call a father' (Tamizey, 86). His heart was buried in Bordeaux Cathedral, his body at Noailles. His only surviving son, Henri, born at London in 1554, was the ancestor of the ducs de Noailles (peerage created in 1663).

DAVID POTTER

Sources Père Anselme, *Histoire généalogique de la maison royale de France, des grands officiers de la couronne*, 9 vols. (1733) · J. de Beaugué, *Histoire de la guerre d'Écosse*, ed. J. Bain, Maitland Club, 2 (1830) · *Catalogue des actes de François 1er*, 10 vols. (Paris, 1887–1908) · M.-T. de Martel, *Catalogue des actes de François II*, 2 vols. (Paris, 1991) · *Catalogue des actes de Henri II*, [6 vols.] (1979–) · *Mémoires de Martin et Guillaume du Bellay*, ed. V. L. Bourrilly and F. Vindry, 4 vols. (Paris, 1908–19) · H. Griffet, *Nouveaux éclaircissements sur l'histoire de Marie reine d'Angleterre … adressées à M. David Hume* (1766) · E. H. Harbison, *Rival ambassadors at the court of Queen Mary* (1940) · E. H. Harbison, 'French intrigue at the court of Queen Mary', *American Historical Review*, 45 (1939–40), 533–51 · R. J. Kalas, 'Marriage, clientage, office holding and the advancement of the early modern French nobility: the Noailles family of Limousin', *Sixteenth-Century Journal*, 27 (1996), 365–83 · R. J. Kalas, 'The noble widow's place in the patriarchal household: the life and career of Jeanne de Gontaut', *Sixteenth-Century Journal*, 24 (1993), 515–39 · H. de la Ferrière and [C. de Médicis], *Lettres de Catherine de Médicis*, 11 vols. (Paris, 1880–1943) · B. de Monluc, *Commentaires*, ed. A. de Ruble, 5 vols. (1864–72) · L. Paris, *Les papiers de Noailles de la bibliothèque du Louvre* (1875) · J. P. Tamizey de Larroque, 'Antoine de Noailles à Bordeaux, d'après des documents inédits', *Actes de l'Académie des Sciences, Belles-lettres et Arts de Bordeaux*, 4 (1876) · P. F. Tytler, *England under the reigns of Edward VI and Mary*, 2 vols. (1839) · L'Abbé de Vertot, *Ambassades de messieurs de Noailles en Angleterre*, ed. C. Villaret, 5 vols. (Paris, 1763)
Archives Bibliothèque Nationale, Paris, fonds français 6908, 6948 · Quai d'Orsay, Paris, Archives du Ministère des Relations Extérieurs, Angleterre correspondance politique, X–XX
Likenesses P. L. van Schuppen, engraving (after a lost contemporary portrait), Bibliothèque Nationale, Paris, Collection Clairambault, No. 1139, vol. 29, no. 1651

Noake, John (1816–1894), antiquary and journalist, son of Thomas Noake, a builder and surveyor, and his wife, Ann, was born in Sherborne, Dorset, on 29 November 1816. He moved to Worcester in 1838 to work on *Berrow's Worcester Journal*, and lived there until his death. He subsequently worked on the *Worcestershire Chronicle* and then the *Worcestershire Herald*. In 1874 he retired from active journalism and in 1875 he entered public life as a city councillor. He held the offices of sheriff and alderman, and was mayor in 1880, when he had the satisfaction of reopening the city's old guildhall, originally erected in 1721–3. Noake had strenuously opposed all plans for its replacement by a new building, and supported its enlargement and restoration.

Noake gave further evidence of his long-standing interest in local history in his publications. His eight works on the history of his adopted county were mainly compilations of facts gathered from various sources, reflected in such titles as *Notes and Queries for Worcestershire* (1856) and *Worcestershire Nuggets* (1889), the latter based on a detailed examination of uncatalogued papers in the city library. He also published *The Monastery and Cathedral of Worcester* (1866) and *Worcester Sects: a History of its Roman Catholics and Dissenters* (1861), and contributed regularly to local newspapers and the *Transactions* of the Worcester Diocesan Architectural and Archaeological Society, published in the *Papers of the Associated Architectural Societies*. For many years he served as one of the honorary secretaries of the Worcester Diocesan Architectural and Archaeological Society. On his resignation in July 1892 his long service was recognized with a handsome testimonial.

Noake was married three times. His first wife was Miss Mary Woodyatt of Ashperton; they had a son, Charles, and a daughter. He subsequently married Miss Sarah Brown of Shrewsbury and then, on 13 August 1873, Mary Jane Stephens, *née* Glover (d. 1893), the widow of a Worcester merchant. Noake died at his home, 2 St Mary's Terrace, London Road, Worcester, on 12 September 1894, and was buried at the cemetery in Astwood Road, Worcester, on 15 September. W. P. COURTNEY, rev. ROBIN WHITTAKER

Sources *Berrow's Worcester Journal* (15 Sept 1894) · E. O. Browne and J. R. Burton, eds., *Short biographies of the worthies of Worcestershire*

(1916) · private information (1894) · *CGPLA Eng. & Wales* (1894) · m. cert.

Archives Herefs. RO · Worcs. RO, MS autobiography | Bodl. Oxf., corresp. with Sir T. Phillipps · U. Edin. L., letters to James Halliwell-Phillipps

Likenesses photograph, repro. in J. Noake, *Worcestershire nuggets* (1889)

Wealth at death £5256 13s.: probate, 9 Oct 1894, *CGPLA Eng. & Wales*

Nobbes, Robert (1652–1706?), Church of England clergyman and writer on angling, was born at Bulwick, Northamptonshire, on 21 July 1652 and baptized on 17 August, the son of John Nobbes, the rector there, and his wife, Rachel. He was sent to Uppingham School, then admitted on 24 June 1668 as a pensioner to Sidney Sussex College, Cambridge, from where he graduated BA in 1671 and proceeded MA in 1675. He was ordained deacon at Peterborough on 16 June 1671 and priest on 24 September 1676. In the latter year he became vicar of Apethorpe and Wood Newton in Northamptonshire.

In 1682 Nobbes published the earliest major work devoted to pike fishing, *The Art of Trolling*. It offers advice, obviously drawn from his own considerable experience of the sport, on tackle and seasons. Allowing for changes in technology, the modern reader would recognize much of it as still valid, with the exception of using live ducks as bait. He seems to have taken part of his introduction, 'To the ingenious reader', from the dedication of Robert Venables's *The Experienc'd Angler* (1662), while the rest comprised his own verses, 'On the Antiquity and Invention of Fishing, and its Praise in General' and 'The Fishermen's Wish', together with poems by other Cambridge men. Nobbes's work was republished in facsimile in 1790 and is included in a number of later publications, such as *The Angler's Pocket Book* (1800?) and in another work with the same title published in London (1814). Thomas Best incorporated the whole text in the tenth edition of his own *Art of Angling* (1814) and retained chapters four to thirteen in the eleventh edition in 1822.

Apparently Nobbes compiled a manuscript volume which included an article on fishing, records of his children's baptisms up to 1701, and various other material, but this has disappeared. Nothing is known of his wife and family. In 1690 Nobbes ceased to be vicar of Apethorpe and Wood Newton. After an unexplained gap he became on 4 August 1702 rector of Sausthorpe, Lincolnshire, which post he held until 1706, when he is assumed to have died.

J. R. LOWERSON

Sources DNB · H. I. Longden, *Northamptonshire and Rutland clergy from 1500*, ed. P. I. King and others, 16 vols. in 6, Northamptonshire RS (1938–52), vol. 10, p. 87 · Venn, *Alum. Cant.* · [R. Nobbes], *The compleat troller, or, The art of trolling, by a lover of the sport* (1682) · T. Westwood and T. Satchell, *Bibliotheca piscatoria* (1883), 136 · N&Q, 2nd ser., 3 (1857), 288

Nobbs, George Hunn (1799–1884), missionary, was born on 16 October 1799 in Ireland. His parentage is unknown, but he claimed to be the unacknowledged son of Francis Rawdon Hastings, first marquess of Hastings and second earl of Moira, and Jemima ffrench, the daughter of an

George Hunn Nobbs (1799–1884), by Henry Adlard (after William Edward Kilburn)

Irish baronet implicated in the Irish rising, whom Hastings had married in Ostend in 1798. These details cannot be verified and probably provide nothing more than a romantic cover for Nobbs's illegitimacy. Nothing certain is known of his childhood and education. By his own account he was in the care of a childless couple named Nobbs who lived near Yarmouth and whose surname he assumed. Raymond Nobbs, his descendant, puts forward the possibility that Nobbs's foster-father may have been Isaac Nobbs, a Norfolk hatter, who had served as a missionary for the London Missionary Society on Tongatapu in 1797. In November 1811 at the age of twelve Nobbs entered the Royal Navy through the influence of his mother's friend Admiral Robert Murray and set sail for Australia. In 1816 he joined a ship belonging to South American insurgents and served with them for six years, suffering capture and imprisonment by the Spanish forces on three occasions. Following his part in the capture of the Spanish frigate *Esmeraldas* at Callao in 1820 he was commissioned a lieutenant in the Chilean navy. Like the account of his parentage the details of his early life cannot be verified.

Nobbs was in England in 1822 when his foster-mother died. About this time he relinquished his commission; he next made several journeys to west Africa as chief mate and captain of the *Gambia*, a merchant vessel, and returned to England in 1824. His motives for going to Pitcairn are unclear and Nobbs himself gave two different versions to his patron, Admiral Fairfax Moresby. In 1828 he was again in Callao where he joined forces with an American, Noah Bunker, with whom he set off on a sealing expedition. It seems that they lost their crew and cargo by misadventure, and fearful of their creditors they made for Pitcairn, where they landed on 28 October 1828.

Nobbs arrived in Pitcairn a few months before the death of John Adams, the sole survivor of the mutineers of HMS *Bounty*, and he soon acquired a position of authority in the island community, acting as teacher, pastor, and doctor. On 18 October 1829 he married Sarah (1810–1899), daughter of Charles Fletcher Christian and granddaughter of Fletcher Christian; her mother was Tahitian. They were to have seven sons and five daughters.

In 1831 Nobbs and the Pitcairn community of eighty-seven people moved to Tahiti, but they returned to Pitcairn in the same year, about a fifth of them having died. An unsettled period followed and Nobbs was supplanted as leader by Joshua Hill, who arrived on the island in 1832 claiming to be a representative of the British government. In March 1834 Nobbs and his family were forced to leave the island and took refuge on Mangareva. They returned to Pitcairn in the following October after Hill's pretensions had been unmasked. Despite Pitcairn's acquisition in 1838 of a constitution, legal code, and elected magistrate, Nobbs remained the true leader of the community.

From 1850 the Society for the Propagation of the Gospel (SPG) had been active in promoting the interests of the islanders, and in August 1852 Nobbs's authority was radically confirmed with the arrival of Admiral Fairfax Moresby. At the request of the islanders he arranged for Nobbs to return to England to receive ordination. Nobbs was made deacon on 24 October and priest on 20 November by Dr Blomfield, the bishop of London, and placed on the list of SPG missionaries with a salary of £50 a year. During his visit to Britain, Nobbs had an audience with Queen Victoria and was entertained by members of London society, including the duke and duchess of Northumberland. The Pitcairn Fund Committee raised several hundred pounds, which Nobbs took with him on his return to Pitcairn in May 1853, to ameliorate the conditions of the islanders.

In 1856, on the advice of the Pitcairn Fund Committee, Admiral Moresby, and Nobbs himself, the community members agreed that it would be in their interests to leave Pitcairn and settle on Norfolk Island, a former convict settlement, which was larger and better endowed with natural resources. This was accomplished with the help of the Royal Navy and they landed on 8 June 1856. Norfolk Island was provided with a constitution by Sir William Denison, governor-general of Australia, who also gave Nobbs an increase in salary of £50 a year and provided another teacher to enable him to concentrate on his duties as chaplain.

With increasing age Nobbs became less active, but he remained a focus of authority. Whatever his background or original motives in settling on Pitcairn, his strong leadership, longevity, and devotion to the islanders over fifty-six years had enabled the community to survive and develop. He died on Norfolk Island on 5 November 1884 surrounded by his large family, and was buried there two days later.　　　　G. C. BOASE, *rev.* CLARE BROWN

Sources R. Nobbs, *George Hunn Nobbs, 1799–1884* (1984) · *AusDB* · D. Belcher, *The mutineers of the Bounty and their descendants* (1870) · C. Lucas, *The Pitcairn Island register book* (1929) · *Bath Chronicle* (22 Jan 1885) · C. F. Pascoe, *Two hundred years of the SPG*, rev. edn, 2 vols. (1901) · *DNB*
Archives Mitchell L., NSW, MSS | Bodl. RH, Society for Propagating the Gospel in Foreign Parts archives · SPCK Archives, London
Likenesses H. Adlard, stipple (after daguerreotype by W. E. Kilburn), NPG [*see illus.*]

Nobkissen. *See* Nabakrishna, maharaja (*c.*1718–1797).

Noble, Sir Andrew, **first baronet** (1831–1915), industrialist and expert in artillery, the third son of the twelve children of George Noble (*d.* 1847), a retired naval captain of Greenock, Renfrewshire, and his wife, Georgiana, only daughter of Andrew Donald Moore of Ottercaps, Virginia, USA (formerly of Ayrshire), was born at 65 Union Street, Greenock, on 13 September 1831. His father came of a landed Dunbartonshire family. Andrew was first educated in Greenock and later at Edinburgh Academy, and entered Woolwich as a cadet in the spring of 1847. In June 1849 he joined the Royal Artillery, served for eleven years, being made captain in 1855. Most of his uneventful military career was abroad. While in Canada he met, and in 1854 married, Margery Durham (*d.* 1929), daughter of Archibald Campbell, a notary in Quebec; they had four sons and two daughters.

Always interested in mathematics and chemistry, Noble embraced several scientific pursuits before concentrating on the branch of inquiry in which he was to gain distinction. He returned to England from the Cape in January 1858, and, on being made secretary to the Royal Artillery Institution at Woolwich, found the naval and military authorities in controversy over superseding the old muzzle-loaded, smooth-bore guns by a new system of breech-loaded, rifled artillery. Remarkably, no advance in gunnery had been made between the Napoleonic and the Crimean wars. It was soon after the battle of Inkermann that William George Armstrong submitted to the War Office for trial his rifled breech-loading field gun, and began a controversy which agitated military minds for several years. The subject exactly suited Noble's aptitude for patient, scientific experiment and accurate observation, and he lost no time in taking part in it. In September 1858 he was appointed secretary to the special committee on rifled cannon, and the new system of artillery was adopted officially by the services towards the end of 1858, a step which polarized opposition by the more conservative military men.

Noble was increasingly recognized as an artillery specialist, and in August 1860 resigned from the army to join Armstrong's Elswick Ordnance Company, Newcastle upon Tyne, where the government orders for rearmament were then being carried out. Armstrong valued the specialist military technical knowledge which Noble would bring to the firm, and offered him a partnership in the business and joint management, with George W. Rendel, of the works. In 1863 the Elswick Ordnance Company was amalgamated with the adjacent Hydraulic Engineering

Works as Sir W. G. Armstrong & Co., with Noble as an original partner. Noble was now free to pursue his scientific inquiries, and he made full use of the resources for his experiments in ballistics and explosives. His experiments and observations followed the lines of those of T. J. Rodman, Sir Benjamin Thompson (Count Rumford), and earlier investigators, in ascertaining the conditions which follow an explosion, but he carried the examination of fired gunpowder further than any of his predecessors. Confining the charge in a closed steel vessel, he determined the temperatures and pressures created, and analysed the gases and residues. Based on these experiments he developed methods for recording the pressures in the chamber of a gun, and the velocity of the projectile in its passage through the bore. His techniques were entirely new, and the exact science of ballistics is due to his work. The practical result of his experiments and conclusions was a complete alteration in the composition of gunpowder and in the design of guns. The use of hand rammed black powder was superseded by slow-burning explosive charges of regular size and shape, which gave more controlled explosion pressures. Improvements in the manufacture of gun steel assisted progress, allowing larger chambers capable of withstanding larger charges. Still faced with military hostility Noble argued that Elswick breech-loaders were best for the broadside armament of ships. The services eventually conceded, and about 1881 the new guns and explosive charges were introduced into the navy.

From 1868 the Elswick works had entered an arrangement with Charles Mitchell & Co., shipbuilders, of Walker-on-Tyne, for the building of warships, Rendel's speciality, which left Noble in charge of ordnance and acting head when Rendel became a civil lord of the Admiralty in 1881. Armstrong and Mitchell amalgamated in 1882 with Noble, the largest shareholder, as vice-chairman. The company became Sir W. G. Armstrong, Whitworth & Co. Ltd, and Noble, then aged seventy, became chairman on Armstrong's death in December 1900.

The Elswick company had been exceedingly profitable under Noble's influence from the 1880s. Noble combined scientific ability with administrative powers. He had controlled a large business, was in daily attendance at his office or workshops, and actively supervised every detail. Despite opposing the Nine Hours League and the 1871 engineers' strike, he had achieved great success. After his day's work he had continued his technical studies in his library or laboratory, often far into the night. Nevertheless, he thoroughly enjoyed many recreations, including real tennis, fishing, and shooting. His hospitality was unbounded. He had a happy home life and his houses were the centre of large gatherings of relations and friends. However, the company went into relative decline early in the twentieth century. Noble had become unimaginative and conservative in engineering design, autocratic in dealing with his managers, and dynastic in his approach to his succession—two of his four sons, Saxton and John, became directors of the company.

Recognized as the leading authority, Noble acted on numerous committees dealing with guns and gunpowder. He took little share in public life; he published his researches through the learned societies. In many experiments he collaborated with Sir Frederick Augustus Abel, and two of his most important papers (in 1875 and 1879) were published in their joint names in *Philosophical Transactions*. In 1906 he reprinted his papers and lectures in the volume *Artillery and Explosives*.

Noble was elected a fellow of the Royal Society in 1870, was made a CB in 1881, created a KCB in 1893, and a baronet in 1902. He was a vice-president of the Institution of Naval Architects in 1900, and its honorary vice-president from 1905. He was also the recipient of many scientific honours and foreign decorations including the royal medal of the Royal Society (1880) and the Albert medal of the Royal Society of Arts (1909). At the end of 1911 he ceased active management of the business, but remained chairman. About 1905 he bought the Callendar estate of Ardkinglas by Loch Fyne, Argyll, Scotland, and in the house which Sir Robert Lorimer designed for him there he died on 22 October 1915, and was buried at Cairndow on the estate.   STAFFORD M. LINSLEY

Sources DNB · P. W., *PRS*, 94A (1917–18), i–xvi · 'A great Victorian: Sir Andrew Noble …', *Armstrong Whitworth Record* (spring 1932), 3–13 · R. J. Irving, 'Noble, Sir Andrew', *DBB* · E. Allen and others, *The north-east engineers' strikes of 1871: the Nine Hours' League* (1971) · J. D. Scott, *Vickers: a history* (1962) · Burke, *Peerage* · *CGPLA Eng. & Wales* (1915)
Archives CUL, letters and MSS · NRA Scotland, priv. coll., papers · Tyne and Wear Archives Service, Newcastle upon Tyne, corresp. | CUL, letters to Sir George Stokes · Tyne and Wear Archives Service, Newcastle upon Tyne, Armstrong MSS; corresp. with Lord Rendel
Likenesses engraving (after portrait by H. H. Browne), repro. in *PRS* · four photographs, repro. in 'A great Victorian'
Wealth at death £734,418 5s. 11d.: probate, 31 Dec 1915, *CGPLA Eng. & Wales*

Noble, Francis (d. 1792), publisher and proprietor of a circulating library, and his brother **John Noble** (d. 1797), publisher and proprietor of a circulating library, are of uncertain origins. They may have been of French descent, and related to William Noble (apprentice to the London bookseller Benjamin Walford in 1709) and the bookseller S. Noble (fl. 1713–1717), of Long Walk, Cheapside. They were certainly either the siblings or close relations of the bookseller and library proprietor Samuel Noble (fl. 1760–1779) of Carnaby Street, of the journeyman bookseller Edward Noble (d. 1786), who was foreman of John Nichols, and of Drusilla, the wife of the engraver Jacob Bonneau (d. 1786). There is no record of their having served apprenticeships with members of the Stationers' Company. Although the Noble brothers operated on the fringe of the established book trade throughout their careers, they are noteworthy for their role in popularizing the commercial circulating library in England, and for developing an active and popular publishing programme which supplied their own and other such libraries with appropriate publications.

Francis opened a bookshop at the Otway's Head, St Martin's Court, Leicester Fields, London, in the autumn of

1737, and began collaborating in minor publishing ventures. He moved to larger premises in the same street about 1743, and in the same year John opened his own bookshop at Dryden's Head, also in St Martin's Court. In the winter of 1744–5 the two brothers went into partnership at the new Otway's Head, where they began to advertise one of the earliest circulating libraries in London. A catalogue, *The Yearly and Quarterly Subscriber*, was produced soon afterwards, listing about 1400 titles and with an engraved frontispiece by Bonneau, depicting a library. In 1749 the partnership was ended and the brothers maintained separate businesses, though frequently collaborating with one another. Having moved to yet further premises in St Martin's Court, John resurrected his earlier trade sign and established his own bookshop and library, where he remained throughout his career. Francis stayed in their previous shop until 1752, but moved to larger premises in nearby King Street, Covent Garden. His new library was illustrated on a trade card engraved by Simon Ravenet. In 1759 he moved once again to larger premises on the south side of High Holborn, where he remained until his retirement.

In the years prior to his partnership Francis Noble had published more than fifty titles, usually in collaboration with other booksellers. These were mainly works of a popular nature, such as collections of tales, reprints of existing imaginative works, or else books designed for children. John began publishing similar works on his own account in 1744, but from the following year the imprint F. & J. Noble begins to appear. During the five years of their partnership the rate of publishing declined, and the brothers appear to have rather concentrated upon developing their circulating library business. However, from about 1750 the brothers began once more to develop a programme of publishing popular imaginative literature, both individually and in collaboration, including authors such as Defoe, as well as a host of anonymous and pseudonymous works. Although many of their books are difficult to date accurately, there appears to have been two main periods of publishing activity: between 1754 and 1757, and between 1766 and 1773. A survey by James Raven indicates that the Noble brothers may have been 'responsible for a tenth of all prose fiction titles published in the 1750s and 1760s', and that 'over one hundred and seventy novels and fiction miscellanies (and further editions) were issued jointly for F. and J. Noble between 1744 and 1778' (Raven, 303).

The brothers also occasionally reissued remaindered works by other publishers and library suppliers under their own imprints. These publications were supplied in large numbers to satisfy a growing demand for such works from their own and also from other circulating libraries in London and the provinces. By the mid-1760s Francis alone claimed to hold a library stock of 20,000 volumes (although only a third as many titles), which had grown to 30,000 by 1787. Subscribers were charged half a guinea (10s. 6d.) a year and were allowed to borrow two books at a time for six days.

The mediocre literary quality of the Nobles' productions, combined with the undoubted success of their publishing enterprises, led to criticisms in the literary journals and among other members of the book trade. According to the *Critical Review*, they 'never paid to any author for his labour a sum equal to the wages of a journeyman taylor', and others regarded their works as formulaic and likely to debauch the young female customers of their libraries. The brothers responded to their critics in a series of advertisements appearing in their volumes, and in their *Appeal to the Public*, which accused the *London Magazine* of having traduced 'every novel we publish, … frequently without reading them'. These disputes did not damage the reputations of the brothers or the growing popularity of circulating libraries, and served rather to publicize their activities.

At some point Francis Noble married Ann, and the couple moved to Kentish Town, Middlesex. They had two sons, both of whom died young, and two daughters: Elizabeth married Henry Mann, and Clarissa remained unmarried. Francis retired from business in 1789–90 after his daughter won a share in a £30,000 state lottery prize. He died in Kentish Town in June 1792; probate of his estate was granted to his daughters on 28 June 1792, his wife having died. John Noble had retired from business in 1778, and likewise lived in Kentish Town. He died there in September 1797, apparently unmarried and without any surviving children.

DAVID STOKER

Sources J. Raven, 'The Noble brothers and popular publishing', *The Library*, 6th ser., 12 (1990), 291–345 • H. M. Hamlyn, 'Eighteenth-century circulating libraries in England', *The Library*, 5th ser., 1 (1946–7), 197–222 • K. A. Manley, 'London circulating library catalogues of the 1740s', *Library History*, 8 (1989), 74–9 • Nichols, *Lit. anecdotes*, 3.648 • I. Maxted, *The London book trades*, 6.284 • A. D. McKillop, 'English circulating libraries, 1725–50', *The Library*, 4th ser., 14 (1933–4), 477–85 • H. R. Plomer and others, *A dictionary of the printers and booksellers who were at work in England, Scotland, and Ireland from 1726 to 1775* (1932); repr. (1968), 182 • will, PRO, PROB 11/1220, sig. 347 • will, PRO, PROB 11/1296, sig. 193 [John Noble] • *Critical Review*, 3 (1757), 384 • F. Noble and J. Noble, *An appeal to the public (by F. & J. Noble, booksellers), from the aspersions cast on them by the anonymous editor of the London Magazine* (1773) • F. Noble and J. Noble, *A second appeal to the public from F. & J. Noble* (1773)

Wealth at death died fairly wealthy: will, PRO, PROB 11/1220, sig. 347 • John Noble: died fairly wealthy: will, PRO, PROB 11/1296, sig. 193

Noble, Frank (1927–1980), schoolteacher and historian, was born on 19 January 1927 at 1 Station Road, Ryhill, near Wakefield, Yorkshire, the youngest of three children of Stanley Noble (1888–1976), a coalminer and later a market gardener, and his wife, Bertha Cutts (1894–1973). After attending Hemsworth grammar school (1937–46), he gained a second-class honours degree in geography (1949) and a diploma in education (1950) at Sheffield University, to which he added in 1960 a rural education diploma from Reading University.

In July 1950 Noble was appointed assistant in charge of geography and history at Knighton county secondary school, Radnor, in the Welsh border market town which became his permanent home. He married the local girl (Rosemary) June Roberts (b. 1929), daughter of John

Thomas Roberts, a farmer, on 5 April 1953; Susan, their only child (b. 1954) became a chartered librarian. Children remember Frank Noble as a charismatic teacher, who achieved national headlines in 1955, when a pupil's uncle discovered three Celtic gold torques of 800 BC, later deposited in the National Museum of Wales.

Part-time tutoring locally for the Workers' Educational Association from 1954 was followed by a full-time post as its tutor-organizer for Herefordshire and Shropshire from 1961. Noble's interest in border history, especially Offa's Dyke, was deepened through his day schools, projects, and courses. He explored the dyke's origins and purpose, and also developed its popular appeal, campaigning from the mid-1960s for the opening of the Offa's Dyke long-distance footpath, centred on his home town of Knighton (or Tref-y-Clawdd, 'the town on the dyke'). Seeing benefits for the marginal economies of the marches as well as for walkers' health and enjoyment, he investigated routes, led waymarking parties and study tours, and in 1969 set up the Offa's Dyke Association to front the campaign and provide information for walkers. The path was opened in 1971 and both association and route continue to flourish. He wrote the first popular guide to the path, *The Shell Book of Offa's Dyke Path* (1969), revised as *The ODA Book of Offa's Dyke Path* (1975). He was made MBE for services to the Offa's Dyke Association (1979) and received the Knighton civic award (1980).

Not satisfied that Sir Cyril Fox's monumental survey of Offa's Dyke (1925–32) gave its definitive story, Noble sought, principally by documentary research into land use and treaties, to people the landscape so meticulously described by Fox. Working for the Open University (OU) from 1971 as a part-time senior counsellor (full-time from 1975), he also enrolled as a student from 1973 to pursue research into the dyke's origins. He pioneered telephone tutorials for OU rural students and, when multiple sclerosis reduced his own powers, investigated ways of helping disabled students. Seriously incapacitated by the time he received his MPhil degree in 1978, he could do little more before his death, aged fifty-three, two years later. In 1983 significant parts of his thesis were published as *Offa's Dyke Reviewed* (British Archaeological Reports 114), edited by his tutor, Margaret Gelling. Manchester University and others subsequently continued his Offa's Dyke researches.

A champion of causes, Noble led by example: a march to prevent a local beauty spot being despoiled, and—in Hereford—campaigns to save a half-timbered building and to secure excavation in advance of road building. President (1965) of Herefordshire's Woolhope Club and an active Radnorshire Society committee member, he wrote many articles for historical journals. His enthusiasm was infectious, whether on a formal occasion or a field trip: he encouraged active participation, inspiring lifelong interests for many students. He taught townsfolk to appreciate the countryside and its origins, and country people to value the living history of their environment. His deep bass voice, Yorkshire with a Welsh overlay, was unmistakable, especially when arguing a point: though strong in his beliefs, he was always respected. He died on 30 December 1980 at his home, Beechwood, Presteigne Road, Knighton, close to Offa's Dyke path, his lasting memorial. He was cremated at Hereford crematorium on 5 January 1981 and his ashes were buried in Ryhill cemetery. His wife survived him. ERNIE KAY

Sources personal knowledge (2004) · private information (2004) · *Offa's Dyke Association Newsletter*, 26 (spring 1981), 1, 10–24 · *Offa's Dyke Association Newsletter*, 28 (winter 1981–2), 12–13 [bibliography] · A. McConnell, 'Frank Noble and Offa's Dyke', *Current Archaeology*, 94 (Oct 1984), 340
Archives Offa's Dyke Association, Knighton, Radnorshire · Open University, Milton Keynes · Radnorshire Society, Llandrindod Wells, Radnorshire · Woolhope Club, Hereford, Herefordshire
Likenesses J. O'Donnell, crayon sketch, c.1963–1967, Offa's Dyke Centre, Knighton, Radnorshire; repro. in *Offa's Dyke Association Newsletter*, 26 (spring 1981)
Wealth at death £21,822: probate, 24 June 1981, CGPLA Eng. & Wales

Noble, George (fl. 1795–1828), engraver, was a son of Edward Noble (1740/41–1784), a bookseller and the author of a book entitled *Elements of Linear Perspective*, and the brother of Samuel *Noble (1779–1853) and William Bonneau *Noble (1780–1831). The maiden name of his mother (c.1746–1829) was also Noble. The dates of his birth and death are not recorded, though it is probable that he was born in London in the late 1770s. All three brothers took up careers connected with the arts, possibly following the tradition of their maternal relatives, who were artists and drawing-masters. George worked in London as a historical engraver and engraved illustrations for many of the fine publications of the day. He produced work for the print publisher John Boydell and was responsible for several in the important series of prints illustrating Shakespeare's plays after paintings by British artists, published in 1802. These plates include the scene *Bassanio, Portia, and Attendants*, after Richard Westall, from *The Merchant of Venice*, and *Cleopatra, Guards, etc*, after Henry Tresham, from *Antony and Cleopatra*. Noble also produced several of the illustrations for one of the sumptuous illustrated British histories issued in that period, Robert Bowyer's publication of David Hume's *History of England* (1806). In addition he provided illustrations of Elizabeth Inchbald's *The British Theatre* (1808). In 1803 Bowyer published a *Commemoration of the Four Great Naval Victories Obtained by the English during the Late War*, for which Noble engraved oval portraits of Admiral Lord Duncan and other naval officers from miniatures by John Smart which form part of a large plate designed by Robert Smirke and engraved by James Parker, in commemoration of the battle of Camperdown (11 October 1797), one of the naval engagements of the Napoleonic wars. Although the last publication on which he is known to have worked was issued in 1808, Noble is listed in directories as a historical engraver at the address 5 Goodge Street, Tottenham Court Road, London, until 1828, so it is possible he was working until this date. The date of his death is unknown. R. E. GRAVES, rev. RUTH COHEN

Sources Redgrave, *Artists*, 311 · T. Dodd, 'Memorials of engravers in Gt. Britain', vol. 10, BL, Add. MS 33403 · *Pigot and Co.'s London and Provincial New Commercial Directory* (1823), 148, 338 · *Pigot and Co.'s*

London and Provincial New Commercial Directory (1828–9), 98, 218 · *Engraved Brit. ports.*, 6.658 · Thieme & Becker, *Allgemeines Lexikon*, 25.494 · G. K. Nagler, *Neues allgemeines Künstler-Lexikon*, 10 (Leipzig, 1847), 249 · W. H. Friedman, *Boydell's Shakespeare Gallery* (1976), 220–45

Noble, James (1774–1851), naval officer, was the second of the three surviving sons of Isaac Noble and his wife, Rachel de Joncourt, the daughter of a French protestant. His paternal grandfather, Thomas Noble, emigrated from Devon to North America, joined the Moravians, and placed his whole property, £4000, in their funds. Isaac Noble left the sect, but could only recover £1400, with which he bought an estate of 1400 acres in East Jersey. When the American War of Independence broke out he served in the royal army, and was killed in 1778. The estate was forfeited at the peace, and the widow travelled to England, where she was granted a pension of £100 a year. Her eldest son, Richard, a midshipman of the frigate *Clyde*, was lost in the prize-ship *La Dorade* in 1797; the youngest, De Joncourt, also a midshipman, died of yellow fever in the West Indies.

James Noble entered the navy in 1787, and, having served in several different ships on the home station, was in January 1793 appointed to the *Bedford* (74 guns), in which he went to the Mediterranean, was landed at Toulon with the small-arms men, and was present in the actions of 14 March and 13 July 1795. He was then moved to the *Britannia*, Hotham's flagship, and on 5 October was appointed to the *Agamemnon*, as acting lieutenant with Commodore Nelson. The promotion was confirmed by the Admiralty, to date from 9 March 1796.

The service of the *Agamemnon* at this time was particularly active and dangerous, and Noble's part in it was very distinguished. On 29 November 1795 he was landed to carry dispatches to De Vens, the Austrian general, then encamped above Savona. He was taken prisoner on the way and detained for some months before being exchanged. He rejoined the *Agamemnon* at Genoa about the middle of April 1796. A few days later, on 25 April, he was in command of one of the boats sent in to cut out a number of the enemy's store ships from under the batteries at Loano. While cutting the cable of one of these vessels Noble was struck in the throat by a musket ball. 'It is with the greatest grief', Nelson reported, 'I have to mention that Lieutenant James Noble, a most worthy and gallant officer, is, I fear, mortally wounded' (O'Byrne, 2.818). Noble wrote:

> I was completely paralysed, and my coxswain nearly finished me by clapping a 'tarnaket', in the shape of a black silk handkerchief, on my throat to stop the loss of blood. Luckily a mate stopped me from strangulation by cutting it with his knife, to the great dismay of the coxswain, who assured him I should bleed to death. The ball was afterwards extracted on the opposite side.

In June Noble followed Nelson to the *Captain*, and in July was placed in temporary command of a prize-brig fitted out as the gunboat *Vernon*. In October he rejoined the *Captain* as Nelson's flag lieutenant. He went with Nelson to the *Minerve*, was severely wounded in the action with the *Sabina* on 20 December 1796, and on the eve of the battle of St Vincent returned with Nelson to the *Captain*. In the battle he commanded a division of boarders, and, assisted by the boatswain, boarded the *San Nicolas* by the spritsail yard. For this service he was promoted commander (27 February 1797). On his return to England he was examined at Surgeons' Hall, and obtained a certificate that 'his wounds from their singularity and the consequences which have attended them are equal in prejudice to the health to loss of limb'. The report was lodged with the privy council, but, 'as a voluntary contribution to the exigencies of the State', he did not then apply for a pension. Some years later, when he did apply, he was told that 'their lordships could not reopen claims so long passed where promotion had been received during the interval.'

In March 1798 Noble was appointed to the command of the sea fencibles on the coast of Sussex, and on 29 April 1802 was advanced to post rank. He had no further service, and on 10 January 1837 was promoted rear-admiral on the retired list. On 17 August 1840 he was moved on to the active list, and on 9 November 1846 he became vice-admiral.

Noble married three times. In 1801 he married Sarah (d. 1818), the daughter of James Lamb of Rye, Sussex; they had seven sons and three daughters. In 1820 he married Dorothy (d. August 1840), the daughter of Dr Halliday, and on 2 February 1842 Jane Anne, the widow of Edmund Spettigue. Three of his sons became naval officers. He died in London on 24 October 1851. His autobiography, apparently written from memory about 1830, and not entirely accurate, was privately printed.

J. K. Laughton, *rev.* Andrew Lambert

Sources D. Syrett and R. L. DiNardo, *The commissioned sea officers of the Royal Navy, 1660–1815*, rev. edn, Occasional Publications of the Navy RS, 1 (1994) · O'Byrne, *Naval biog. dict.* · *GM*, 2nd ser., 37 (1852), 92 · *The dispatches and letters of Vice-Admiral Lord Viscount Nelson*, ed. N. H. Nicolas, 7 vols. (1844–6) · J. S. Tucker, *Memoirs of Admiral the Rt Hon. the earl of St Vincent*, 2 vols. (1844), vol. 1 · *Autobiography of James Noble* (privately printed, c.1830) · Boase, *Mod. Eng. biog.*

Noble, John (d. 1797). *See under* Noble, Francis (d. 1792).

Noble, John (1827–1892), politician and financial writer, was born at Boston, Lincolnshire, on 2 May 1827, the only son of John Noble of Brighton. For seventeen years he was known in east Lincolnshire as an energetic supporter of the Anti-Corn Law League. He moved to London in 1859 and was admitted to the Middle Temple on 2 May 1861 but was never called to the bar.

Noble was an active campaigner, engaged in social and political agitation across a broad range of issues. He was one of the founders of the Alliance National Land and Building Society, and joined Washington Wilks and others in establishing the London Political Union for the advocacy of manhood suffrage. In 1861 he was active in lecturing on the free breakfast-table programme. In 1864 he was in partnership with C. F. Macdonald as financial and parliamentary agents promoting street railways in London, Liverpool, and Dublin. He actively promoted the election of John Stuart Mill for Westminster in 1865, and advocated municipal reform in London. In 1870 he became parliamentary secretary to Alexander Brogden, MP for Wednesbury. On the formation of the County Council Union in 1889 he became its secretary. He delivered in his day many hundreds of lectures on political, social, and financial subjects, habitually took part in the proceedings of the Social Science Congress, and was lecturer to the Financial Reform Association. He died at his home at 39 Lady Margaret Road, Kentish Town, London, on 17 January 1892, and was buried four days later at Highgate cemetery.

An ardent peace campaigner, Noble wrote *Arbitration and a congress of nations as a substitute for war in the settlement of international disputes* (1862). The bulk of his published work, however, was in the field of economics and mostly concerned the areas of taxation and fiscal reform. He published a number of works on these topics in the 1860s and 1870s. However, his lifelong support of free trade led to his writing *Free trade, reciprocity, and the revivers: an enquiry into the effects of the free trade policy upon trade, manufacturers and employment* (1869). Drawing on his experiences as an active political agent for the Liberal Party, Noble compiled his *Facts for Liberal Politicians* (1880), which was revised in 1892 as *Facts for Politicians*.

G. J. HOLYOAKE, rev. MATTHEW LEE

Sources H. Perris, 'Memoir', in J. Noble, *Facts for politicians* (1892) · Boase, *Mod. Eng. biog.* · J. Hutchinson, ed., *A catalogue of notable Middle Templars: with brief biographical notices* (1902) · *CGPLA Eng. & Wales* (1892)
Likenesses portrait, repro. in Noble, *Facts for politicians*
Wealth at death £1312 13s. 4d.: administration, 9 Feb 1892, *CGPLA Eng. & Wales*

Noble, Mark (1754–1827), biographer and antiquary, was born in Digbeth, Birmingham, the third surviving son of William Heatley Noble. His father was a businessman much of whose fortune came from selling consumer goods to traders who would use them to barter for slaves in west Africa. He had also a large mill for rolling silver and for plating purposes. Mark was educated at schools at Yardley, Worcestershire, and Ashbourne, Derbyshire. When his father died he inherited a modest fortune and began a short-lived career as a lawyer. He was articled to a Birmingham solicitor called Barber and about 1778 he established his own law firm. But literature and history proved more attractive to him than law, and in 1781 he was ordained to the curacies of Baddesley Clinton and Packwood, Warwickshire. On the sudden death, a few weeks afterwards, of the incumbent, Noble was himself presented to the two livings ('starvations', he called them). Noble was now a married man; details of his wife are unknown. The couple took a house at Knowle, Warwickshire, conveniently situated for both his parishes. Here he divided his interests among his congregation, his books, and a farm.

In 1784 Noble produced his best-known work, *Memoirs of the Protectorate-House of Cromwell*. This curious history, full of value judgements and personal attacks, received poor

reviews at the time (for instance in the *Gentleman's Magazine*, June 1787) and has not been of enduring value to historians. It is confusingly structured and contains a number of factual errors. Nevertheless, Thomas Carlyle made use of the work in his edition of *Oliver Cromwell's Letters and Speeches*. Furthermore, the earl of Sandwich was enthusiastic about it and he and Noble became regular correspondents. Lord Leicester, afterwards Marquess Townshend, likewise became a warm patron, and appointed Noble his chaplain. Noble also published half a dozen other works of history, including *The Lives of the English Regicides* (1798) and a three-volume *Continuation* (1806) of James Granger's *Biographical History of England*. He also wrote a number of unpublished pamphlets, the product of years of sometimes flawed, but apparently laborious, antiquarian research. Titles included *History of the Records in the Tower of London, with the Lives of the Keepers, especially since the Reign of Henry VIII*, *Catalogue of the Lord Chancellors, Keepers, and Commissioners of the Great Seal*, and a *History of the Masters of the Rolls*. On the recommendation of Sandwich and Leicester, Lord Chancellor Thurlow presented Noble to the valuable rectory of Barming, Kent, in 1786, where he lived for forty-two years. On 1 March 1781 he was elected a fellow of the Society of Antiquaries, and contributed five papers to the *Archaeologia*. He was also a fellow of the Society of Antiquaries of Edinburgh. He died at Barming on 26 May 1827, and was buried in the church, where a monument was erected to his memory.

GORDON GOODWIN, rev. ADAM I. P. SMITH

Sources F. L. Colvile, *The worthies of Warwickshire who lived between 1500 and 1800* [1870] · *GM*, 1st ser., 97/2 (1827), 278–9 · W. Richards, *A review of the Memoirs of the protectoral-house of Cromwell by the Rev. Mark Noble* (1787)
Archives Bodl. Oxf., corresp. and papers · Yale U., Farmington, Lewis Walpole Library, papers | Bodl. Oxf., letters to James Gomme · NMM, letters to Lord Sandwich
Likenesses J. Hancock, print, BM; repro. in M. Noble, *Memoirs of the protectorate-house of Cromwell*, 2 vols. (1784) · J. K. Sherwin, stipple, NPG

Noble, Matthew (bap. 1817, d. 1876), sculptor, was baptized on 23 March 1817 at Hackness, North Riding of Yorkshire, the third child of five sons and four daughters of Robert Noble (b. c.1790), a stonemason, and his wife, Elizabeth (b. c.1786). He was apprenticed to his father and as a young man attracted the attention of a local landowner, Sir John Johnstone of Hackness Hall, who arranged for him to study in London. He was a pupil of the sculptor John Francis in London, and lived in the latter's home at 56 Albany Street. In 1845 he began exhibiting at the Royal Academy. His early works included busts of the countess of Galloway (exh. RA, 1848) and the painter William Etty (marble, 1850; NPG), a statuette of the Hon. E. V. Vernon, archbishop of York (exh. RA, 1849), and, his first important public work, the statue of Sir Robert Peel (marble; 1853) for St George's Hall, Liverpool. He married Frances Mary Claxton (b. 1827), who lived in the household of his master John Francis (she was described as his grand-daughter in the 1851 census), on 29 December 1855 at the Old Church, St Pancras, London.

Matthew Noble (*bap.* 1817, *d.* 1876), by William Walker & Sons

In 1853 Noble was commissioned to execute the monument to Arthur Wellesley, first duke of Wellington (bronze; 1856) in Piccadilly, Manchester. This was awarded following an open competition; however, the choice of Noble, who was still a comparatively young and unknown sculptor, was said to have aroused some controversy. The design of the monument, consisting of a statue with four allegorical supporting figures and four reliefs, bears similarities to Noble's entry in the national competition for the Wellington monument in St Paul's Cathedral, held in 1856 and for which he was awarded fifth (equal) prize. Despite the earlier controversy, Noble was to become a leading provider of statuary for Manchester and surrounding areas during the mid-nineteenth century. His statues included those of Queen Victoria (marble; 1857) and Prince Albert (marble; 1864) for Peel Park, Salford (both now art gallery forecourt, Salford), Joseph Brotherton (bronze, 1858; Irwell Embankment, Manchester), and Oliver Cromwell (bronze, 1875; Wythenshawe Park, Cheshire). His most important public work, also for Manchester, was the Albert memorial (1862–7) in Albert Square. Noble's 9 foot high marble statue of the prince was commissioned by the mayor, Thomas Goadsby, and stands within an elaborate Gothic canopy designed by the architect Thomas Worthington.

Noble made many notable public monuments in other parts of the country. In London his best-known works are the statue of the explorer Sir John Franklin (bronze, 1856;

Waterloo Place), with pictorial reliefs representing Franklin's voyage to the north-west passage and burial in the ice; *Sir James Outram* (bronze, 1871; Victoria Embankment); and *Edward Stanley, Fourteenth Earl of Derby* (bronze, 1874; Parliament Square). Elsewhere, his works include *Dr Isaac Barrow* (marble, 1858) at Trinity College, Cambridge, the *Second Duke of Sutherland* (bronze; 1866) at Dunrobin Castle, Sutherland, and *Queen Victoria* (marble, 1872) for Bombay.

Noble also executed a large number of portrait busts, for example *Michael Faraday* (marble, 1854; RS), *Giuseppe Garibaldi* (marble, exh. RA, 1867; V&A), and several repetitions of his busts of Queen Victoria and Prince Albert, as well as about thirty funerary monuments, including *Earl de Grey* (marble, 1864; St John Baptist, Flitton, Bedfordshire) and the *Revd Henry Venn* (marble, 1875; St Paul's Cathedral). Rare 'ideal' works by the sculptor are *Purity* (*c.*1859) and *Amy and her Pet Fawn* (exh. RA, 1869), which were engraved in the *Art Journal* in 1859 and 1872, and two bronze reliefs illustrating Thomas Hood's poems 'The Bridge of Sighs' and 'The Dream of Eugene Aram', which were incorporated on the sculptor's monument to Hood (1854) in Kensal Green cemetery, Middlesex (the reliefs were later removed).

Noble was a remarkably prolific sculptor, even by nineteenth-century standards when the production of commemorative statues to political and military figures was at its most accelerated. Indeed his friends were surprised that he should have been able to produce the amount of work that he did as he was said to have been a man of delicate constitution. That Noble indulged more than his contemporaries in the common practice of delegating work to assistants is suggested by Thomas Woolner's remark that he 'never touches the work that goes under his name' (letter to Lady Trevelyan, 23 Dec 1860; Read, 24). His works typify modern realism in mid-nineteenth-century portraiture, in the manner of Sir Francis Chantrey, and are characterized by an assured though somewhat standardized naturalism—particularly in the representation of modern dress—adapted to large-scale production methods. According to the *Art Journal*, Noble was esteemed not only for his abilities but for 'rare kindly qualities of mind and heart. Generous in his acts and in his sympathies, amiable in his disposition, his nature was essentially kind and good' (*Art Journal*, 1876, 276). Of his four sons, Charles died in 1874 at the age of sixteen; another, Herbert, who had shown promise as a sculptor, died tragically in a railway accident at Abbots Ripton in January 1876 at the age of nineteen. These events were said to have hastened Matthew Noble's own death. He died of pleuropneumonia on 23 June 1876 at his home, 43 Abingdon Villas, Kensington, and was buried at Brompton cemetery, London. The unfinished works in his studio were completed by his assistant Joseph Edwards. In 1876 Noble's widow presented his plaster models to the corporation of Newcastle upon Tyne where they were displayed in Elswick Hall but most of them were later destroyed. MARTIN GREENWOOD

Sources *Art Journal*, 38 (1876), 275–6 · R. Gunnis, *Dictionary of British sculptors, 1660–1851* (1953); new edn (1968) · J. Robinson,

Descriptive catalogue of the Lough and Noble models of statues, bas-reliefs and busts in Elswick Hall, Newcastle upon Tyne, 6th edn (1914) · B. Read, Victorian sculpture (1982) · Graves, RA exhibitors · DNB · M. Stocker, 'Noble, Matthew', The dictionary of art, ed. J. Turner (1996) · Scarborough Mercury (14 April 1979), 3 · The Builder, 34 (1876), 645 · Thieme & Becker, Allgemeines Lexikon · R. Ormond, Early Victorian portraits, 2 vols. (1973) · J. Blackwood, London's immortals: the complete outdoor commemorative statues (1989) · D. Brumhead and T. Wyke, A walk round Manchester statues (1990) · CGPLA Eng. & Wales (1876) · d. cert. · IGI · census returns, 1851

Likenesses W. Walker & Sons, photograph, NPG [see illus.] · J. & C. Watkins, carte-de-visite, NPG · portrait, Tate collection · wood-engraving (after photograph by C. Watkins), BM, NPG; repro. in ILN (8 July 1876)

Wealth at death under £2000: probate, 17 July 1876, CGPLA Eng. & Wales

Noble, Michael Antony Cristobal, Baron Glenkinglas (1913–1984), politician, was born on 19 March 1913 at Las Palmas, Canary Islands, the third son and youngest among the five children of Sir John Henry Brunel Noble, first baronet of Ardkinglas (1865–1938), barrister, and his wife, Amie Grogan, née Walker-Waters (1878/9–1973), a widow. His grandfather Sir Andrew Noble, first baronet of Ardmore, was a founder of the engineering and armaments firm Armstrong, Whitworth & Co., of which his father was a director.

Michael Noble was educated at Eton College and Magdalen College, Oxford, where he took a third in *literae humaniores* in 1935. He played bridge for the university at the first varsity match, held in London in February 1935, a fixture initiated on the Cambridge side by his later ministerial colleague Iain Macleod. He married, on 11 September 1940, Anne (b. 1923), daughter of Sir Neville Arthur Pearson, second baronet, of St Dunstan's, London. They had four daughters. From 1941 to 1945 he served in the Royal Air Force Volunteer Reserve, reaching the rank of squadron leader in 1943. During the post-war years he concentrated on farming the family's Argyllshire estate. He was president of the Black Face Sheep Breeders' Association and of the Highland Cattle Society. From 1949 until 1951 he was a member of Argyll county council.

In June 1958 Noble was elected Unionist MP for Argyllshire at a by-election. His rise thereafter was swift. In 1959 he was made parliamentary private secretary to John Maclay, secretary of state for Scotland. In 1960 he was appointed an unpaid assistant government whip, and from November 1960 Scottish whip. From November 1961 until July 1962 he was a government whip and lord commissioner of the Treasury. After only four years in the Commons Noble was promoted to succeed John Maclay as secretary of state for Scotland in Harold Macmillan's 'night of the long knives' reshuffle of July 1962. His comparative youth and enthusiasm outweighed his ministerial inexperience, and his appointment was seen as an attempt to revitalize a government in the doldrums.

Noble is not judged to have disappointed. His achievement was the more remarkable given the high reputation of his predecessor and the fact that most of his own tenure was seen as a run-up to the general election of 1964 following a long period of Conservative government. His personal intervention in cabinet is credited with securing the transfer of the Post Office Savings Bank to Glasgow. He also fought for roll-on-roll-off ferries for the Western Isles. In the face of Treasury reluctance a £10 million loan was secured for Wiggins Teape, which persuaded the company to build a pulp mill at Fort William. Probably Noble's most significant achievement lay in the Scottish Office's reaction to the Toothill report on the Scottish economy, published in late 1961. Although the report's conclusions, including the need for economic planning and an emphasis on new instead of old, heavy industries, have been criticized, Noble's white paper on central Scotland was broadly welcomed, despite its late appearance. It identified growth areas and new towns, and showed a commitment to regional economic planning which like-minded Conservatives claimed 'brought about a complete change of attitude' (Heath, 265) in Scotland.

Noble was fortunate in having a Scottish Office which contained considerable civil-service talent, to which he is credited with having given free rein. Less fortunate were the economic and political circumstances with which Noble had to contend. Unemployment was high compared with the rest of the UK. The Scottish railway system was under threat as a result of the Beeching report of March 1963, which outraged local opinion. The recommendations of the Mackenzie committee, favouring amalgamation of the South of Scotland Electricity Board with the North of Scotland Hydro-Electric Board, also prompted activity by pressure groups. There were examples of interested parties, such as the trade unions and the Scottish Council (Development and Industry), bypassing the secretary of state and going directly to the relevant UK ministry. From March 1963 he faced a Labour opposition well co-ordinated by William Ross. Until the emergence of Sir Alec Douglas-Home as Conservative Party leader and prime minister from October 1963, he also encountered indiscipline in his own ranks, especially among the rural representatives under pressure from a Liberal revival. To these difficulties should be added the very poor state of Conservative Party organization in Scotland.

Noble's record in these areas was mixed, and bore signs of frenetic activity. As chairman of the Unionist Party in Scotland in 1962–3 he attempted to do something about Scottish Conservative organizational problems by, for example, appointing a public relations officer, but was able to do little about the need for more central control. He resisted the full implementation of the Beeching cuts, which would have closed all railways north of Inverness, and attempted to market Scotland as a business location to United States companies with an official trip to America in autumn 1963. He blocked proposals to merge the North of Scotland Hydro-Electric Board, which was in tune with a wave of opinion in the highlands, but ran contrary to those who claimed that, with its construction phase over, there was no need for its separate existence. The Countryside and Tourism Amenities Bill, which proposed a tourism tax to finance non-commercial facilities, ran into opposition from bodies such as the Scottish Tourist Board and was dropped. Of more lasting influence were, perhaps, the plans put forward by Noble and his minister of state, Jack Nixon Browne, Lord Craigton, for the reorganization of local government on a two-tier model. These were still incomplete when Noble left office in October 1964.

From 1964 until January 1969 Noble was a member of the Conservative leader's consultative committee, or shadow cabinet, and a spokesman on Scotland. On the Conservatives' return to power in June 1970, Edward Heath appointed him president of the Board of Trade with a seat in the cabinet. From October 1970 until November 1972 he was minister for trade, outside the cabinet, in a reorganized trade and industry department. In this position he was part of a ministerial group that was closely involved with the crisis over Upper Clyde Shipbuilders in the second half of 1971, and which argued for the Civil Aviation Act to open up opportunities for the private sector in air transport. Noble regretted the time away from Scotland which the extensive travelling attached to this position involved.

At the general election of February 1974 Noble stood down from his Argyllshire seat, which he had held since 1958, and was given a life peerage as Lord Glenkinglas of Cairndow. From 1966 to 1970 he was chairman of Associated Fisheries, and from 1969 to 1970 of Glendevon Farms. After retiring from government Lord Glenkinglas again accepted appointments in industry. He was chairman of the British Agricultural Export Council from 1973 to 1977, and of the Hannover Housing (Scotland) Association from 1978 to 1980. He was also a director of John Brown Engineering, a survivor of Upper Clyde Shipbuilders, from 1973 to 1977, and of Monteith Holdings from 1974. Noble's patrician, bland air, that of the likeable Anglo-Scots grandee, was complemented by his reputation as 'an excellent, slow-paced, chain-smoking raconteur' (Glasgow Herald, 17 May 1984). His was the moderate, progressive Conservatism of the Macmillan–Home–Heath era. He was never a forceful orator and did not make a reputation at the dispatch box, but was regarded as effective in dealing with delegations. Noble was made a privy councillor in 1962. He died at his home, Strone House, Cairndow, on his Argyllshire estate, of cardiac failure and emphysema on 15 May 1984. His funeral service was held at Cairndow church, Argyllshire, on 19 May 1984.   GORDON F. MILLAR

Sources The Times (17 May 1984) · Glasgow Herald (17 May 1984) · The Scotsman (17 May 1984) · G. Pottinger, The secretaries of state for Scotland, 1926–1976 (1979), 156–65 · Burke, Peerage (1978) · Burke, Peerage (1999) · WWW, 1981–90 · WWBMP · C. Harvie, No gods and precious few heroes—Scotland, 1914–1980 (1981), 110–11 · C. Harvie, Scotland and nationalism (1994), 130, 192 · W. Ferguson, Scotland, 1689 to the present (1978), 394–7 · m. cert. · d. cert. · matriculation records, Oxf. UA · W. D. Rubenstein, The biographical dictionary of life peers, 172 · J. Ramsden, The winds of change: Macmillan to Heath, 1957–1975 (1996), 135–6 · E. Heath, The course of my life (1998), 264 · F. W. S. Craig, British parliamentary election results, 1950–1973, 2nd edn (1983), 633 · F. W. S. Craig, British parliamentary election results, 1974–1983 (1984), 294 · R. Shepherd, Iain Macleod (1994), 20 · Debrett's Peerage (2000), B798 · www.macdonald60.fsnet.co.uk [Clan Donald Magazine online, 5 (1971)] · J. T. Ward, The first century: a history of Scottish tory organisation, 1882–1982 (1982), 38 · CCI (1986)

Likenesses G. Hales, photograph, 1971, Hult. Arch. · photograph, repro. in Glasgow Herald · photograph, repro. in The Scotsman

Wealth at death £238,360.70: corrected gross estate (£216,707.01 in UK): eik to confirmation, 26 March 1986, CCI

Noble, Montague Alfred (1873–1940), cricketer and dentist, was born on 28 January 1873 at Dixon Street, Sydney, New South Wales, Australia, the eighth son of Joseph Noble, grocer and later builder, and his wife, Maria Collins. His parents had emigrated from Egham, Surrey, earlier in the nineteenth century. After leaving school he was briefly a bank clerk before qualifying as a dentist in 1901, setting up in practice, and becoming in 1902 a dental surgeon at the dental hospital in Sydney.

Throughout his cricketing life, Noble was associated with the Paddington club, and first played for New South Wales on their New Zealand tour in 1894. Later in the year he made 152 not out for a Sydney colts eighteen against A. E. Stoddart's English tourists. He made his début in test cricket against England at Melbourne in 1898, taking 6 wickets for 49, appearing 'in the colonial team with the happiest results' (Wisden, 1899, 393). It was as an all-rounder—one of Australia's greatest—that he played in a further forty-one consecutive matches for Australia up to 1909, including four tours to England and one to South Africa.

Although Noble's only test century was against England at Sydney in 1903, he had the ability to bat defensively for long spells, never more so than at Manchester in 1899 when—in two innings of 60 not out and 89—he was at the wicket for eight and a half hours to save the match. He bowled his off-breaks at a brisk pace, relying on swerve rather than spin. At Melbourne, against England in 1902, he had a match analysis of 13 for 77. Six months later, in the only test ever played at Sheffield, he took 11 for 103, 'breaking back again and again in an unplayable way' (Wisden, 1903, 269). In test cricket he made 1997 runs (30.25) and took 121 wickets (25.00).

In 1903 Noble was appointed captain of Australia, and, apart from the tour to England in 1905, he remained so for six years. 'Mary Ann', as he was nicknamed from his initials, was an authoritarian figure and a disciplinarian who later trenchantly expressed his views on captaincy in his book The Game's the Thing (1926). Of him C. A. Macartney wrote: 'a strong character, hard but just. His judgement of other players' capabilities was astonishing. He was a rare personality and I know of none greater' (Pollard, 214).

Noble was an equally dominant figure in the controversies of the day between players and administrators, being briefly suspended (with nine other players) by the New South Wales Cricket Association in 1906 when he led the opposition on behalf of players' rights. Later he wrote in the press that the Australian board of control in the six years of its existence had 'not been credited with one single act of conciliation or forbearance' (Sydney Morning Herald, 29 Feb 1912). The upshot of these conflicts was the refusal of many leading players to travel to England in

1912, though by now Noble (almost forty years of age) had virtually retired from first-class cricket.

Noble married on 14 January 1914 Elizabeth Ellen Ferguson (d. 1963); her brother, William Ferguson (1880–1958), was a scorer and baggage-man for forty-three overseas tours. They had three sons and a daughter.

Test cricket apart, Noble's record as a batsman in the Sheffield shield competition was unmatched until the era of W. H. Ponsford and Don Bradman. Two of his highest scores in first-class cricket were both made against Sussex (284 in 1902 and 267 in 1905), while for New South Wales against Victoria in 1905 he made 281. When he retired in 1919 he had made 13,975 runs (40.74) and taken 625 wickets (23.11). He continued to play first-grade cricket for Paddington until 1925 and, as he had done thirty-one years earlier, played that year for a colts eleven (as their mentor) against an England eleven led by A. E. R. Gilligan, on whose tour he wrote *Gilligan's Men* (1925), one of four major contributions he made to the literature of cricket.

Noble's commanding personality must have contributed to his election as president of the Dental Association of New South Wales in 1915. He briefly relinquished his career in dentistry but returned to it in the 1930s. In a full life, he was variously a New South Wales selector, a cricket journalist, a pioneer of test match broadcasting, and the president of the New South Wales Baseball Association. He died in Sydney on 22 June 1940, and was buried at Waverley cemetery, Sydney. A stand at the Sydney cricket ground is named after him.　　GERALD M. D. HOWAT

Sources AusDB, vol. 11 · DNB · Wisden (1894–1926) · Wisden (1941) · *The Times* (24 June 1940) · *Oxford companion to Australian cricket* (1996) · J. Pollard, *The turbulent years of Australian cricket* (1987) · C. Harte, *A history of Australian cricket* (1993) · M. A. Noble, *The game's the thing* (1926) · M. A. Noble, *Gilligan's men* (1925) · H. S. Altham, *A history of cricket* (1926) · *Sydney Morning Herald* (Feb 1912) · *Sydney Morning Herald* (24 June 1940) · M. Fiddian, *Australian all-rounders* (1992) · P. Bailey, P. Thorn, and P. Wynne-Thomas, *Who's who of cricketers* (1984)
Archives FILM BFI NFTVA, sports footage
Likenesses E. Hawkins, photograph, 1899, repro. in *Wisden* (1900) · photograph, c.1902, repro. in *Wisden* (1941) · photograph, c.1905, repro. in D. Frith, *Pageant of cricket* (1987) · photograph, c.1920, repro. in Pollard, *Turbulent years* · G. W. Beldham, photograph, repro. in D. Batchelor, ed., *Great cricketers* (2000) · C. Tayler, portrait (after photograph), repro. in G. Batchelor, ed., *Great cricketers* (2000)

Noble, Sir Percy Lockhart Harnam (1880–1955), naval officer, son of Charles Simeon Noble and his wife, Annie Georgina Noble, was born on 16 January 1880 in India where his father was a major in the Bengal staff corps. He entered the *Britannia* as a naval cadet in 1894 and spent his midshipman's time in the *Immortalité* on the China station. In view of his subsequent career it seems strange that his captain should notice him in his report as lazy and dull. During his sub-lieutenant's courses Noble was detailed for the naval guard of honour mounted at Windsor for the funeral of Queen Victoria. When the horses which were to draw the gun-carriage bearing the coffin became restive, and later unmanageable, Noble suggested that they be unhitched and the gun carriage drawn by the

naval guard of honour, a precedent followed in every subsequent royal funeral. He was appointed MVO.

After service in the battleships *Hannibal* in the channel squadron and *Russell* in the Mediterranean, Noble was appointed flag lieutenant to A. L. Winsloe, commanding destroyer flotillas at home. He commanded the destroyer *Ribble* from 1907 to 1908, when he joined the signal school at Portsmouth and qualified as a signal specialist. A brief appointment to the royal yacht *Victoria and Albert* for Edward VII's visit to Copenhagen was followed by a commission in China as flag lieutenant to Winsloe, and on completion of that duty he returned to the royal yacht as first lieutenant, being promoted commander when he completed the appointment in 1913. In December he joined the *Achilles*, in the 2nd cruiser squadron, Home Fleet, as executive officer, and three years later was transferred, still as executive officer, to the large cruiser *Courageous*, flagship of the light cruiser force, Grand Fleet. His promotion to captain came in June 1918 and in October of that year he was made flag captain to Sir Allan Everett in the *Calliope*, transferring to the *Calcutta* in 1919. In 1922 he was appointed to the *Barham* in command and as flag captain to Sir Edwyn Alexander-Sinclair, then commanding 1st battle squadron, Atlantic Fleet. He was promoted CVO in 1920.

Noble's next command (1925) was the *Ganges*, the boys' training establishment at Shotley, and his experience in this post led to his selection two years later (1927) as the first commanding officer of the *St Vincent*, a new boys' training establishment being set up at Gosport. This was followed by an appointment as director of the operations division on the naval staff, 1928–9, and his promotion to rear-admiral (1929).

In 1931 Noble became director of naval equipment in the Admiralty and at the end of the following year was selected to command the 2nd cruiser squadron in the Home Fleet, flying his flag in the *Dorsetshire*, then in the *Leander*. In 1935 he was brought back to the Admiralty as fourth sea lord where he was successful in obtaining marriage allowances for naval officers. He was promoted vice-admiral while holding this appointment and in 1937 was chosen to command the China station. He was appointed CB in 1932 and KCB in 1936.

Noble's qualities of tact and restraint were continuously called into play during this difficult period in the Far East. The Japanese were engaged in their war with China and frequently made threatening advances to the borders of the British settlements at Hong Kong and Shanghai. Noble managed to prevent any of these threats from developing into outright hostilities, and the skill with which he handled all such incidents brought him many expressions of the Admiralty's appreciation.

In 1939 Noble was promoted admiral, relinquished his command in July 1940, and in February 1941 was appointed commander-in-chief western approaches. It was this command which bore the responsibility for the war against German U-boats, which by that time had established a definite ascendancy in the Atlantic. Setting up his headquarters in Liverpool, Noble set about his task with his usual thoroughness. He realized that special training in anti-submarine warfare was the key to ultimate victory in this campaign, and although he was continuously hampered by a shortage of anti-submarine forces, he laid down the principles of training and also established the group organization of escort forces which was later to pay a high dividend in the Atlantic war. He himself went to sea and flew with Coastal Command so that the crews knew that he understood their problems and there were forged 'links of mutual confidence of inestimable value'. By the time he left the command, the British anti-submarine forces had reached a degree of organization and training which left his successor, Sir Max Horton, a firm and lasting foundation on which to wage successful warfare.

On leaving Liverpool in the autumn of 1942 Noble was sent to Washington as head of the British Admiralty delegation. He saw the switch from the defensive to the offensive in the naval war, and much of the credit for the smooth co-operation both in planning and in operations between the British and American navies was owed to Noble for the qualities of firmness, tact, and sound sense which he brought to the deliberations of the combined chiefs of staff. For his services in Washington he was appointed GBE in 1944 and was made a commander of the American Legion of Merit in 1946.

Noble was twice married: first, in 1907, to Diamantina Isabella (d. 1909), daughter of Allan Campbell. Their son, Commander Sir Allan Noble, on retiring from the navy entered parliament and was minister of state for foreign affairs in 1956–9. In 1913 Noble married, secondly, Celia Emily (d. 1967), daughter of Robert Kirkman Hodgson; they had a son.

In 1943 Noble was appointed first and principal naval aide-de-camp to George VI. He retired from the navy on 16 January 1945 and was made rear-admiral of the United Kingdom. He received the grand cross of the royal order of St Olaf for his services to the Royal Norwegian Navy. He died at his home, 66 Ashley Gardens, London, on 25 July 1955.   PETER KEMP, rev.

Sources *The Times* (26 July 1955) · *WWW* · S. W. Roskill, *The war at sea, 1939–1945*, 3 vols. in 4 (1954–61) · personal knowledge (1971) · *CGPLA Eng. & Wales* (1955)

Archives CAC Cam., MSS · CAC Cam., midshipman's journals, etc.

Likenesses W. Stoneman, photograph, 1942, NPG · O. Birley, oils, c.1945–1948, Royal Naval College, Greenwich · J. Rosciwewski, pen-and-ink drawing, IWM

Wealth at death £10,631 3s. 5d.: probate, 28 Sept 1955, *CGPLA Eng. & Wales*

Noble, Raymond Stanley [Ray] (1903–1978), band leader and composer, was born on 17 December 1903 at 1 Montpelier Terrace, Brighton, the son of Frank Stanley Noble, a London neurologist, and his wife, Maude Edith Poole. He began to play the piano when he was ten, and subsequently studied with Brigain Dale at the Royal Academy of Music for five years, becoming an accomplished player at the age of fifteen and an LRAM at sixteen. Noble already had his sights set on a career in the dance-band world, but

Raymond Stanley Noble (1903–1978), by unknown photographer, 1935?

for a while worked in a bank at Streatham and led a local band.

Noble learned his skill as an arranger through listening to and analysing recordings and achieved a remarkable facility in the art. His name first came to light in *Melody Maker* for July 1926 when he won a competition to find a British arranger who could compete with the Americans dominant at the time. His arrangement of 'There'll come a sometime' was printed in the magazine with a promise of a recording by the Bert Ralton band. Unfortunately Ralton was killed in 1926 while touring South Africa and the session never happened; eventually it was recorded by Bert Firman. Noble settled in Streatham and embarked on a brilliant career of composing and arranging. By 1927 he had done some work for Debroy Somers, the founder and first director of the Savoy Orpheans, and during that year he was on the staff of Lawrence Wright, the publisher. When Jack Payne started broadcasting with the BBC Dance Orchestra in 1928, Noble became staff arranger and a number of his arrangements were featured on the radio; he achieved a successful hit in 1929 with 'Nobody's fault but your own'.

In the summer of 1929 Ray Noble took over from Carroll Gibbons as director of light and dance music with the Gramophone Company, and from 1929 to 1934 all dance records by the 'house' band of HMV, mostly made in Queen's Hall or at the Abbey Road studios, were directed by him under the name of the New Mayfair Dance Orchestra; by 1933 this was usually billed as Ray Noble and his Orchestra. Notable members of the band in this period included Freddy Gardner, Nat Gonella, Lew Davis, and

Max Goldberg, and with such musicians available it was not surprising that an occasional jazz item was recorded—such as 'Tiger Rag' (1933) and 'The Japanese Sandman'. From 1930 to 1936 Noble used Al Bowlly as vocalist and produced a number of inspired recordings, notably 'Goodnight, sweetheart' (1931), which became Noble's best-known song and his signature tune, the original recording remaining in the catalogue until 1943. Another big hit of that year was the recording of Tolchard Evans's 'Lady of Spain'. His work was aimed at the dance-music world, and most of his recordings leaned towards the 'sweet' category. He kept up an output of highly successful ballads that included 'Love is the sweetest thing', used in the film *Say it with Music* (1932); 'What more can I ask?' in *Little Damozel* (1933); 'Pull down the blind' in *Brewster's Millions* (1934); 'Kick over the traces' in *Girls Please* (1934); 'Love is a song' in *Princess Charming* (1935); and 'For only you' in *Let's Make a Night of It* (1936). Others from the 1930s included 'Love locked out' (1933), 'The very thought of you' (1934), 'The touch of your lips' (1936), and 'I hadn't anyone but you' (1938).

Ray Noble went to the USA in 1934 with Al Bowlly, and in 1935 he settled in America, where he directed his own band at the Rainbow Room in New York until 1937. The band, which had been assembled by Glenn Miller, included a number of leading American jazz musicians. Noble's own writing took on a more robust jazz element, and his instrumental 'Cherokee' (1938) became the theme tune of the Charlie Barnet band. Its unusual harmonic structure, so different from the general Tin Pan Alley material of the day, caused it to be of great interest to the modern American jazz fraternity, and it became the basis of the Charlie Parker classic 'Koko'. Noble stylishly directed his band from a white piano, and socialized with the guests. He became popular on the radio, appearing in the *Lanny Ross Show* (1936), *Refreshment Time* (1936), and the *Burns and Allen Show* (1937–8). He moved to California in 1937 and appeared in a number of films, generally playing an upper-class 'silly ass' kind of Englishman, a role he developed in the Edgar Bergen–Charlie McCarthy show as stooge and music director over a period of fourteen years. He was featured with one or other of his bands in such films as *The Big Broadcast of 1936* (1935), *A Damsel in Distress* (1937), *Here We Go Again* (1942), *Lake Placid Serenade* (1942), and *Out of this World* (1945).

At various times in the 1930s and 1940s Noble returned to England to organize and run orchestras; he alternated this work with further film and broadcast commitments in the USA until he retired in 1958 and lived for ten years in the Channel Islands. In 1968 he returned to America to pass the rest of his retirement in Santa Barbara, California. In 1978, suffering from cancer, he made a final visit to England and died in University College Hospital, London, on 3 April. In spite of so much time in America he remained very English and retained his native accents. The Ray Noble Orchestra is now remembered and admired for its polished sound, rich ensembles, firm beat, and tasteful arrangements, and its recordings, especially those made in conjunction with the legendary Al Bowlly, have come to be among the most collectable in the dance-band field.

PETER GAMMOND

Sources P. Gammond, *The Oxford companion to popular music* (1991) · J. Chilton, *Who's who of British jazz* (1997) · J. Godbolt, *A history of jazz in Britain, 1919–1950* (1984) · I. Carr and B. Priestley, *Jazz: the essential companion* (1987) · *New Grove* · b. cert. · d. cert. · B. Rust, notes to *The Ray Noble Orchestra*, World Record Club boxed set [14 LPs], limited edition

Likenesses photograph, 1935?, NPG [*see illus.*]

Noble, Richard (1684–1713), murderer, was the eldest of three sons of Benjamin Noble, a coffee-house keeper at Bath. He received a good education, was articled as a clerk to an attorney, and entered the profession on reaching adulthood. Apparently he soon began to use his professional position to cheat his clients. About 1708 Noble was applied to for legal assistance by John Sayer of Biddlesden in Buckinghamshire, to whom he had been introduced by Sayer's father-in-law, Colonel Salisbury. Sayer was the owner of various properties worth £1800 a year. He had married Mary Nevil (or Nevell), daughter of Admiral John Nevell, in January 1699 (Colonel Salisbury was her mother's second husband). A marriage settlement was drawn up resting a considerable sum on Sayer's wife, including £50 a year pin money and £100 a year for every £1000 of the residue of her estate, which amounted to £3000 besides jewels. However, Sayer was on very bad terms with his wife. It seems that the marriage had been poorly conducted on both sides with Mrs Sayer's apparently refusing her husband admittance to her bed and Mr Sayer's seeking pleasure elsewhere: 'upon this he took to other women, and as Town Gallantry is always fatal, poor Mr Sayer met the punishment in the Sin' (*A Full Account of the Case of John Sayer*, 4).

Noble himself had become close to Mary Sayer and in 1709 he was empowered to draw up a deed of separation between her and her husband. Noble harassed Sayer by various suits in chancery connected with his wife's separate estate. He was now living with Mrs Sayer, who on 5 March 1712 bore him a son in Somerset. Upon her elopement Sayer put an advertisement in *The Post Boy* of 1 March 1712. He then brought an action for criminal conversation against Noble and in January 1713 procured a warrant empowering him to arrest Mrs Sayer, 'she being gone from him, and living in a loose and disorderly manner' (*A Full Account of the Case of John Sayer*, 13). On 29 January Sayer, accompanied by two constables, proceeded to the house of Joseph Twyford in George Street, The Mint, London, where Mrs Sayer was then living with Noble and her mother, Mrs Salisbury. The visitors were admitted but Noble no sooner saw Sayer than he drew his sword and thrust it through his heart. Noble and the two women were arrested, the coroner having made a formal warrant against the women as aiding and abetting the murder. They were committed to the Marshalsea and arraigned at Kingston assizes in Surrey. The two women were acquitted and went on to invest a considerable sum of money in Noble's defence. According to one account he had no fewer than twenty lawyers and thirty solicitors acting for him (*A Full and Faithful Account of the Intrigue between Mr. Noble and Mrs. Sayer*, 2). The cost of the defence was said to have been above £2000. It was also suggested that witnesses and the coroner had been suborned: apparently Noble provided a good dinner in the Marshalsea during the adjournment.

Noble pleaded self-defence but was condemned to death and was executed at Kingston on 28 March 1713; he was buried the following day, accompanied by a funeral procession. It seems clear that Noble had expected to be reprieved: at his execution he delivered a note to the clergy attending him, forgiving the lord chief justice Parker for not granting him a reprieve. This case seems to have become something of a *cause célèbre* because of the elements of romance and drama. Popular opinion was sympathetic to Noble, an attitude that angered some commentators: 'Here's a Man who stole the estate, the wife, the life of his benefactor; and when justice overtook him, you say, "Tis Pity"' (*A Full and Faithful Account of the Intrigue between Mr. Noble and Mrs. Sayer*, preface).

HEATHER SHORE

Sources *A full account of the case of John Sayer … from his … marriage with his wife to his death: including the whole intrigue between Mrs Sayer and Mr Noble* [1713] · *A full and faithful account of the intrigue between Mr. Noble and Mrs. Sayer; their ill usage of Mr. Sayer and his family …* (1713) · Student of the Inner Temple, *The case of Mr. Richard Noble impartially considered* (1713) · *The whole and true tryals and condemnation of all the prisoners who were try'd at Kingston in the county of Surry … with a full and particular account of the whole tryal of Mr. Noble, Mrs. Sayer, and Mrs. Salisbury, for the murder of Squire Sayer* [1712] · *Post Boy* (1 March 1712) · *British Mercury* (1 April 1713) · DNB

Noble, Samuel (1779–1853), engraver and Swedenborgian minister, was born in London on 4 March 1779. His father, Edward Noble (1740/41–1784), was a bookseller and mathematician, the author of *Elements of Linear Perspective* (1772). His brothers were George *Noble and William Bonneau *Noble. His mother (c.1745–1829), a sister of the drawing-master William Noble, provided him with a good education, including Latin, and he was apprenticed to an engraver. He acquired great skill as an architectural engraver and made a good income. His religious convictions were the result of a reaction, in his seventeenth year (1796), against Thomas Paine's *Age of Reason*; he appears to have anticipated, as a natural deduction from Paine's premises, that denial of the real existence of Jesus Christ which Paine did not publish until 1807. About 1798 he came across Swedenborg's *Heaven and Hell*, as translated (1778) by William Cookworthy. At first repelled, he afterwards became fascinated by Swedenborg's doctrines, and attached himself to the preacher Joseph Proud at Cross Street, Hatton Garden.

Proud urged Noble to the ministry of the New Church as early as 1801, and he occasionally preached, but in 1805 felt that he was too young to take charge of the Cross Street congregation. He was one of the founders (1810) of the society for printing and publishing the writings of Emanuel Swedenborg, and assisted in establishing (1812) a quarterly organ, the *Intellectual Repository and New Jerusalem*

Magazine, of which until 1830 he was the chief editor and principal writer. In 1819 he resigned good prospects in his profession to become the successor of Thomas F. Churchill as minister of the Cross Street congregation (then worshipping in Lisle Street, Leicester Square). He was ordained on Whitsunday 1820. His ministry was able and effective, despite a speech defect. The congregation, which had been overflowing under Proud and had since declined, was raised by Noble to a more solid prosperity, and repurchased (in 1827) the chapel in Cross Street, then vacated by Edward Irving. In addition to his regular duties he engaged in mission work as a lecturer both in London and the provinces. Of his few published works his *Appeal in Behalf of the … Doctrines … Held by the … New Church* was said to hold among Swedenborgians 'the same place that Barclay's "Apology" does among the quakers' (White). It originated in lectures at Norwich in reply to the *Anti-Swedenborg* (1824) by George Beaumont, an independent Methodist minister at Ebenezer Chapel in that city. The *Appeal*, which appeared in 1826 and went through many editions, was characterized by Coleridge as 'a work of great merit' and one in which 'as far as Mr. Beaumont is concerned, [Noble's] victory is complete.'

Noble's leadership of his denomination was not undisputed. His first controversy was with Charles Augustus Tulk (1786–1849), a rationalizer of Swedenborg's theology, who was excluded from the society. Noble was the first to develop a doctrine which, by many of his co-religionists, was viewed as a heresy. He held that the body of Christ was not resuscitated, but dissipated in the grave, and replaced at the resurrection by a new and divine frame. Hence the controversy between 'resuscitationists' and 'dissipationists'; John Clowes and Robert Hindmarsh rejected Noble's view, but his chief antagonist was William Mason (1790–1863). In support of Noble's position a Noble Society was formed.

In 1848 Noble suffered from cataract, and, in spite of several operations, became permanently blind. He revised, by the help of amanuenses, the translation of Swedenborg's *Heaven and Hell*, giving it the title *The Future Life* (1851). He died in London on 27 August 1853, and was buried at Highgate cemetery.

ALEXANDER GORDON, rev. TIMOTHY C. F. STUNT

Sources W. Bruce, 'Memoir', in S. Noble, *An appeal in behalf of the views of the eternal world and state … held by the body of Christians who believe that a new church is signified*, 3rd edn (1855) · W. White, *Swedenborg, his life and writings*, 1 (1867), 230; 2 (1867), 613 ff. · J. Hair, *Regent Square: eighty years of a London congregation* (1898), 11–14 · private information (1894)

Noble, William (1828–1904), astronomer, was born on 27 November 1828 in Islington, north London, the eldest son of William Noble of Berwick, later a merchant in London. After a private education he served in India, and on 22 August 1851 married Emily Charlotte (d. 1899), the only child of Edward Irving, an officer in the 61st regiment. They had four sons, three of whom died on service, and two daughters who survived him. On retiring from army service in 1858, he settled down to life as a country gentleman in Sussex. There he devoted his time to astronomy and local government, and served for many years on the Uckfield bench as a magistrate and poor-law guardian. Like many gentlemen who were masters of their own time, he became renowned for what might be termed his eccentricities.

Noble was found genial and popular by many, but he was 'fearlessly outspoken' (Hollis, 298), to the point of blind prejudice, in condemning place-seeking and self-advancement in public life. He led the 'Mechanics', a faction of younger members of the Royal Astronomical Society (RAS), who by 1877 numbered at least forty-seven and tried to provoke reform of their society via outspoken critiques published in the journal *English Mechanic*. Noble despised J. Norman Lockyer's cultivation of the Devonshire commission to obtain government funds for pure research at a new solar physics observatory. Hence about 1879 he organized and was secretary of the Society for Opposing the Endowment of Research, and continued attacks long after that observatory was founded. He was elected a fellow of the RAS in 1855 and served on its council from 1866 to 1880. In 1879 he led a clique on the council which refused to endorse the medal for 'Airy's indicated choice' Huggins in order only, as Richard Proctor wrote, to give 'a severe rebuke' to G. B. Airy, the astronomer royal. Revd Charles Pritchard, Savilian professor at Oxford, sprang to Airy's defence by issuing an alternative ballot list that would remove 'the insane Captain' Noble whose 'aggressiveness amounts to a disease'. It succeeded: Noble was not re-elected, while Airy remained on the council until 1886, when he was aged eighty-five. Pritchard exulted: 'The Sewerage is stopped, and the big rat gone' (Pritchard to Airy, 13 and 14 Feb 1880, RGO 6 244, 509 and 510). But Proctor made such threats against the 72-year-old professor that he became so ill that friends feared for his life. Noble served the RAS council again for all but two years from 1886 until his death.

Noble's observatory held a 4 inch equatorial telescope. He did not confine himself to a single field of study, such as double stars or the planets, but was content to observe whatever was of interest in the sky. His public-spiritedness also found expression in his astronomy. For nearly forty years from the mid-1860s he wrote a fortnightly column on astronomy in the *English Mechanic* under the pen-name 'A fellow of the Royal Astronomical Society'. This was probably the earliest regular astronomical feature intended for the lay or amateur reader to appear in any British periodical. In his hundreds of articles Noble provided a wealth of factual information and informed opinion on most branches of contemporary astronomy. His *Hours with a Three-Inch Telescope* (1886) provided a concise and readable guide for beginners. He was a tireless correspondent, advising numerous amateurs on how to set up observatories and perform useful work. By the 1880s he realized that the growing popularity of serious amateur astronomy required organizational structures of a different type from those provided by the RAS,

which by that date was increasingly catering for professionals. He became a member of the Liverpool Astronomical Society, founded in 1881 to meet the needs of observing amateurs, and was a moving force behind the founding of the British Astronomical Association in 1890, which he served as first president from 1890 to 1892.

Noble was a striking and colourful personality. Famed for his racy speech and unvarnished opinions, he epitomized the retired army officer and country squire of the late Victorian age. A photograph showing him resplendent in boots and nursing a shotgun on the doorstep of his residence, Forest Lodge, Maresfield, Sussex, captures some of the spirit of the man. He was a major force in the advancement of the popular understanding of astronomy and in creating the organizational structures of modern amateur astronomy. He died at his home on 9 July 1904, and was buried on 13 July at the church in Nutley, Sussex.

ALLAN CHAPMAN

Sources *Monthly Notices of the Royal Astronomical Society*, 65 (1904–5), 342–3 · *Journal of the British Astronomical Association*, 14 (1903–4), 351–2 · *The British Astronomical Association, the first fifty years (1890–1940)* (1949) · H. P. Hollis, 'Captain Noble', *The Observatory*, 27 (1904), 298–300 · *Journal of the British Astronomical Association*, 15 (1904–5), 228–9 · R. Proctor, 'The RAS medal', *Newcastle Weekly Chronicle* (28 Feb 1880) · C. Pritchard, letters to G. B. Airy, 13–14 Feb 1880, CUL, RGO 6, 244, 509 and 510 · m. cert. · d. cert.

Archives RAS, RAS letters

Likenesses photograph, repro. in *British Astronomical Association* · portrait, repro. in *Journal of the British Astronomical Association*

Wealth at death £9063 9s. 6d.: probate, 6 Aug 1904, CGPLA Eng. & Wales

Noble, William Bonneau (1780–1831), landscape painter, was born on 13 September 1780 in London, the youngest son of Edward Noble (1740/41–1784), bookseller and mathematician, author of *Elements of Linear Perspective* (1771), and brother of Samuel *Noble (1779–1853) and George *Noble (*fl.* 1795–1828). His mother (*c.*1745–1829) was the sister of the drawing-master William Noble (from a different family). He himself became a successful drawing-master but, hoping to succeed as a painter, spent two summers in Wales sketching the scenery. Three watercolours worked from these sketches, *View of Machynlleth, North Wales*, *Montgomery Castle*, and *View near Dolgelly*, were exhibited at the Royal Academy in 1809. But in 1810 his drawings were rejected, and although he had two views of Charlton and Bexley, in Kent, in the exhibition of 1811, he never recovered from this setback. Disappointed in love at the same time, he became depressed and soon had very little work. In 1825 he attempted suicide, and he died in poverty on 14 September 1831 in Somers Town, London. He left a long poem, 'The Artist', in manuscript.

R. E. GRAVES, *rev.* ANNE PIMLOTT BAKER

Sources S. Noble, *GM*, 1st ser., 101/2 (1831), 374–5 · Mallalieu, *Watercolour artists*, vols. 1–2 · Graves, *RA exhibitors* · Bryan, *Painters* (1903–5)

Noble, William Henry (1834–1892), army officer, eldest son of Robert Noble, rector of Athboy, co. Meath, and grandson of Dr William Newcome, archbishop of Armagh, was born at Laniskea, co. Fermanagh, on 14 October 1834. He studied at Trinity College, Dublin, where in

1856 he graduated BA with honours in experimental science (MA 1859). At the end of the Crimean War, just before taking his BA, he passed for a direct commission in the Royal Artillery (lieutenant 6 March 1856). He became captain in 1866, major in 1875, lieutenant-colonel in 1882, and brevet colonel in 1886. From 1861 to 1868 he served as associate member of the ordnance select committee for carrying out ballistic and other experiments in scientific gunnery. He was then appointed to the staff of the director-general of ordnance, and subsequently acted until 1876 as a member of its experimental branch at Woolwich, serving as member or secretary of numerous artillery committees, including those on explosives, on rangefinders, and on iron armour and equipment.

Promoted major in 1875, Noble returned to regimental duty. He was posted to a field battery, but immediately after was sent to the United States as one of the British judges of weapons at the Centennial Exhibition at Philadelphia. He was member and secretary of the group of judges of the war section, and by special permission of the commander-in-chief of the United States army visited all the arsenals, depots, and manufacturing establishments of war material. In June 1877 he was sent to India as member and acting secretary of a special committee appointed by Lord Salisbury to report on the reorganization of the ordnance department of the Indian army and its manufacturing establishments in the three presidencies. He was so employed from February 1876 to November 1878, when, on the outbreak of the Second Anglo-Afghan War, he was appointed staff officer of the field train of the Kandahar field force. He organized the field train at Sukkur, and commanded it on its march through the Bolan Pass.

In 1880 Noble was posted to a field battery at Woolwich; in April 1881 became a member of the ordnance committee, and in July 1885 was appointed superintendent of Waltham Abbey royal gunpowder factory, Essex. On reaching his fifty-fifth birthday in October 1889 he was retired under the age clause with the rank of major-general, but as it was found he could not be spared he was restored to the active list in 1890 and continued at Waltham. Very large quantities of prismatic gunpowder (EXE and SBC) were manufactured at Waltham Abbey or by private contract from his discoveries, which, by permission of the War Office, were protected by a patent granted to him in 1886. The manufacture of cordite was largely due to his researches.

Noble married in 1861 Emily, daughter of Frederick Marriott, one of the founders of the *Illustrated London News*, and they had two sons and four daughters; his wife survived him. Noble, a fellow of the Royal Society and member of other learned societies, was author of *Report of various experiments carried out under the direction of the ordnance select committee relative to the penetration of iron armour-plates by steel shot* (1886), *Useful Tables (for Artillerymen)* (1874), and *Descent of W. H. Noble from the Blood Royal of England* (1889). He died at his home, Thrift Hall, Waltham Abbey, Essex, on 17 May 1892, aged fifty-seven.

H. M. CHICHESTER, rev. ROGER T. STEARN

Sources *Army List* · *The Times* (21 May 1892) · B. Robson, *The road to Kabul: the Second Afghan War, 1878–1881* (1986) · E. M. Spiers, *The late Victorian army, 1868–1902* (1992) · Boase, *Mod. Eng. biog.*
Archives BL OIOC, journals, MS Eur. A 107
Likenesses R. T. & Co., wood-engraving, NPG; repro. in *ILN* (28 May 1892)
Wealth at death £3117 3s. 7d.: resworn probate, Jan 1895, *CGPLA Eng. & Wales* (1892)

Nobys, Peter (*b. c.*1480, *d.* in or after **1525**), college head, son of John and Rose Nobys of Norwich diocese, is first recorded at Cambridge, graduating as BA on 27 January 1501. In 1503 he was admitted as a junior fellow at Corpus Christi College and on his attaining the degree of MA and priest's orders in 1504 he was statutorily qualified for a full college fellowship, which he held until 1509. The rectory of West Halton, Lincolnshire, which he held from 20 June 1508 to February 1515, subsidized his further theological studies for the degree of BTh, to which, having been a university preacher in 1514, he was admitted early in 1516. Shortly after, he was unexpectedly elected master of his college following the sudden death of Thomas Edyman, recently appointed successor to the aged master, Thomas Cosyn, who had died in July 1515. Then in October 1516 the president, John Seyntwary, died, leaving Nobys his principal executor and his successor in the college's rectory of Landbeach from February 1517. About May 1519 Nobys set out for Rome, having obtained leave of absence from his diocesan and, from the university, admission to the degree of DTh and sealed letters testimonial. In Rome he obtained a papal privilege, of 14 January 1520, granting indulgences of twenty-five years to all participants in the Corpus Christi ceremonies conducted by the college.

Under Nobys college administration was efficient, long-running legal disputes were settled, and the east range of the court retiled. The room under the gallery next to St Benet's Church was adapted, in accordance with Seyntwary's will, 'for the makying and orderying of the howse for there Munymentes and other vtensylys'. The 'ordering' was mainly carried out by the master, as numerous endorsements in his hand testify, though the register of donations he compiled, his 'white book', soon disappeared; its loss was later deplored by Matthew Parker. Nobys' greatest and lasting service to the college was the assembling of an up-to-date library, largely of printed books, strong in theology, to supersede the obsolescent fellows' lending library of Thomas Markaunt. Its impressive list of contents forms a schedule to the agreement with the college, of 30 June 1523, for annual commemorations in St Benet's Church for himself and his parents. These were attached to an earlier undertaking of 14 March 1521, binding the fellowship to observe all existing commemorations in perpetuity.

Nobys vainly attempted to erect legal barriers against impending change. The widening ideological rift between himself and the rising generation of progressive fellows probably forced his retirement in the summer of 1523. From 26 November 1521, by an agreement with Thetford Priory, Norfolk, he had the use of 'two lofte chambers' and a stable for life, with an annuity of 5 marks, as the result of a prearrangement with Sir Thomas Wyndham, under whose will of 22 October 1521 he was a legatee. In 1523 he resigned Landbeach rectory in favour of Mr Cuttyng, a senior fellow, in return for an annual pension of 50 marks. Thereafter, apart from a brief emergence in July 1525 to conclude Seyntwary's affairs, he faded into obscurity, leaving no known will. For him 'the times were out of joint'. Historians, other than Masters, have tended to do Nobys less than justice. Until recently even his library, subsumed into Parker's greater bequest, was scarcely appreciated or credited to him.   CATHERINE HALL

Sources R. Masters, *The history of the College of Corpus Christi and the B. Virgin Mary … in the University of Cambridge* (1753), 61–3; appx, 31–2 · J. Josselin, *Historiola Collegii Corporis Christi*, ed. J. W. Clark, Cambridge Antiquarian RS, 17 (1880), 26, 35, 38 · Emden, *Cam.*, 425–6 · M. Bateson, ed., *Grace book B*, 2 vols. (1903–5) · W. G. Searle, ed., *Grace book Γ* (1908) · muniments, CCC Cam., xxxi–105, 128; documents, CCC Cam., Misc. 14–15, 17; accounts, 1517–23, CCC Cam. · Cambs. AS, Antrobus no. 49 · J. M. Fletcher and J. K. McConica, 'A sixteenth-century inventory of the library of Corpus Christi College, Cambridge', *Transactions of the Cambridge Bibliographical Society*, 3 (1959–63), 187–99

Archives Cambs. AS, Antrobus · CCC Cam., muniments

Wealth at death see CCC Cam. muniments, xxxi–128 of 1523 and 1525

Nock, Oswald Stevens (1905–1994), engineer and railway historian, was born on 21 January 1905 at Grasmere, Holland Road, Sutton Coldfield, Warwickshire. He was the first son of Samuel James Nock (1870?–1955?), a securities clerk at the Midland Bank, Birmingham, and his wife, Rose Amy, *née* Stevens (1869?–1958?), a schoolteacher before her marriage. Shortly after Nock's birth, his father became manager of a bank in Reading and his young son found himself playing trains in the nursery of a very comfortable middle-class household with servants. Real trains were only a pushchair ride away from home, with the main line of the Great Western Railway and the branch line of the South Eastern and Chatham Railway both passing through the town. It was here that 'Ossie' Nock's fascination with railways began.

Between 1913 and 1916 Nock attended first Marlborough House then Reading School, finally becoming a boarder at Giggleswick School in 1916 when the family moved to Barrow in Furness. His understanding of railway history and operation and a love of the countryside evolved in Cumbria. His lifelong interest in photography also started when he was a teenager, having been given his first camera in 1919. Despite Giggleswick School's concentration on the classics, and his mediocre performance in maths and science, he began to aim for a career in locomotive engineering. In 1920 he passed his school certificate and then London matriculation examinations, entering the City and Guilds Engineering College, London, in the following year.

In London, Nock was able to explore the capital's railway stations and become acquainted with the huge variety of locomotives and rolling-stock of the many independent companies soon to be 'grouped' by act of parliament into four larger organizations. In 1924 he obtained both a BSc and an ACGI (Associate of the City and Guilds of London Institution), and after unsuccessful applications

Oswald Stevens Nock (1905–1994), by unknown photographer

to the Great Western Railway, Vickers of Barrow, and Armstrong Whitworth & Co., Newcastle, he became a graduate trainee at the Westinghouse, Brake, and Saxby Signal Co. Ltd in 1925.

Nock's entry into this side of railway engineering came at an exciting time, when Westinghouse was working with a number of progressive signal engineers of the newly formed 'big four' railway companies on innovative electrical rather than traditional mechanical signalling schemes. Unfortunately the economic depression soon led to redundancies at Westinghouse and, although he stayed with the company, he decided at the beginning of the 1930s to turn his interest in writing into a commercial activity. His first successful piece, entitled 'Hyde Park's ghost trains', was published in the *Evening News* in 1932. Two years later, in April 1934, a suggestion to *The Star* newspaper gave him the opportunity officially to ride on the footplate of the London, Midland, and Scottish Railway's newest express steam locomotive. He had first started to systematically record and analyse locomotive performance while at the City and Guilds College. His interest had been stimulated by the monthly 'British locomotive practice and performance' reports of Cecil J. Allen published in the *Railway Magazine*, and from 1934 onwards he regularly sent information for inclusion in these reports. He eventually inherited this series from Allen in January 1959 and contributed 264 articles before relinquishing the task in December 1980, having travelled by train in Britain and abroad many thousands of miles.

On 15 May 1937 Nock married Olivia Hattie (1913/14–1987), daughter of William George Ravenall, at Bushey parish church; they had met in the buffet of King's Cross Station and took their honeymoon on the *Flying Scotsman*. They had a daughter and a son, settling in a large house on Sion Hill, Bath, where Nock created an 'O' gauge model railway with twenty-three hand-built locomotives. By the outbreak of war in 1939, he had achieved considerable literary success in both the popular and the technical press. At the start of hostilities *The Engineer* commissioned from him a series on railway signalling followed by another on locomotive performance in wartime conditions which was published in 1944–5. In 1942 he became a member of the Institution of Civil Engineers. His loyalty to Westinghouse was finally rewarded in 1945 when he was made chief draughtsman of the brake section, followed four years later by his promotion to chief draughtsman.

For Nock the succeeding twenty-five years until his retirement in 1970 were remarkably productive. Following British Rail's ambitious modernization plan of 1955 and the sudden demand for new signalling equipment, he supervised the considerable expansion of Westinghouse's drawing office. In 1957 he was made chief mechanical engineer, and as the job required him to visit a number of foreign railways, he was able to add to his portfolio of overseas locomotive performances. As if his work at Westinghouse during this period was not enough, his tally of articles increased, and he also found time to write fifty-eight railway books—an average of two a year. The first of these appeared in 1945—*The Locomotives of Sir Nigel Gresley*. Thereafter, subjects ranged from the general—for example, *The Boys' Book of British Railways* (1951)—to the particular—including works such as *The Midland Compounds* (1964). He benefited from a post-war boom in specialist railway publishing spearheaded by the new firms of Ian Allan, and David and Charles.

On 9 April 1969 Nock was made president of the Institution of Railway Signal Engineers (IRSE), having been a member since the 1920s. Already commissioned by the publishers A. and C. Black to write a series of books on world railways, he took the opportunity during his presidential year to lead the IRSE summer convention to Belgium and then went on with his wife to Australia to address the IRSE branch there. His retirement allowed the couple to travel all over the world, visiting among other places New Zealand, India, Canada, and Fiji. He continued to produce regular articles for the railway press, and his output of books escalated to almost five a year, Black's series on world railways eventually running to seven volumes and culminating in 1979 with *Railways of the USA*.

By the time of his death, at St Martins Hospital, Bath, on 21 September 1994, from cardiac failure, Nock had written over 140 books, a remarkable achievement considering that the first did not appear until he was forty. Although he was no academic when compared to the railway author Jack Simmons, his books were nevertheless based on sound research and on knowledge acquired from inside the industry. If they had faults—repetition and a bias towards locomotive performance were two which later critics seized upon—they arose because the author was an enthusiast who infused all his texts with his own experience. His work was always accessible and engaging. He was never a controversial writer but his strong views sometimes surfaced in his work. He was critical of the way in which Britain's railways had been nationalized in 1948, for example, and in his autobiography *Line Clear Ahead* (1982) he was not afraid to make some pointed comments about former managers at Westinghouse. He did, however, manage to avoid the hazard of nostalgia and as a true supporter of railway travel he delighted in genuine improvements to railway services. In 1974 his book *Electric Euston to Glasgow* celebrated British Rail's achievements on the old London and North Western Railway main line, and in 1980 he chronicled the success of the high speed diesel trains in *Two Miles a Minute*. His books and articles inspired a generation of railway enthusiasts. M. A. VANNS

Sources *The Times* (8 Oct 1994) · *The Independent* (7 Oct 1994) · O. S. Nock, *Line clear ahead: 75 years of ups and downs* (1982) · b. cert. · m. cert. · d. cert.
Likenesses photograph, News International Syndication, London [*see illus.*]
Wealth at death £116,072: probate, 28 Nov 1994, *CGPLA Eng. & Wales*

Nodal, John Howard (1831–1909), journalist and dialectologist, was born on 19 September 1831 in Downing Street, Ardwick, Manchester, the son of Aaron Nodal (1798–1855), a Quaker grocer and town councillor. He was a member of the Society of Friends and was educated at Ackworth School, Yorkshire (1841–5), a Quaker school. His first employment, aged seventeen, was as a clerk at the Electric Telegraph Company in Manchester, where he later became manager of the news department. From 1850 to 1853 he also acted as secretary of the Manchester Working Men's College. On 14 June 1859 he married Helen, daughter of Lawrence Wilkinson; the couple had two sons and three daughters.

Nodal began early to contribute to the local press and he edited the *Volunteer Journal* during the volunteer movement of 1860–62. His career as a full-time journalist began in January 1864, when he was appointed sub-editor of the daily *Manchester Courier*. From 1867 to 1870 he occupied a similar position on the *Manchester Examiner and Times* while also editing (1866–8) the *Free Lance*, a humorous and satirical Manchester weekly, and founding and editing (1868–71) *The Sphinx*, a weekly periodical of art and literature. In 1871 he became editor of the ailing *Manchester City News*, remaining there until 1904 and transforming it into a popular and financially successful journal. He was instrumental in moulding its policy and ideals, and it quickly came to reflect his wide-ranging interests not only in the public life of Manchester but also in local work on science, literature, and language. On the model of *Notes and Queries*, to which he was a regular contributor, Nodal established 'City News notes and queries' within the main newspaper. This developed into an independent periodical (8 vols., 1878–89) which he edited. *Country Notes: a Journal of Natural History and Out-Door Observation* (2 vols., 1882–3), which he also edited, similarly originated in articles in the *Manchester City News*. From 1875 to 1885 he was on the staff of the *Saturday Review*.

Nodal played a prominent role in the Manchester Literary Club, editing volumes 1 to 6 of its *Papers* (1874–80) and serving as president (1873–9) and vice-president (1879–86). A founder member of the club's glossary committee (1872), which aimed to compile a Lancashire glossary, he published his *Dialect and Archaisms of Lancashire* (1873) as part of its first report. Upon the relocation of the English Dialect Society from Cambridge to Manchester, he took over as honorary secretary (1876–94) from its founder, W. Skeat, with whom he worked on the *Bibliographical List of … the Various Dialects of English* (vols. 1–3, 1873–7), editing the third volume (1877). He published (with George Milner) *The New Glossary of the Lancashire Dialect* (pt 1, 'A–E', 1875), which was widely and favourably reviewed; part 2 appeared in 1882. Nodal was actively involved in the collection of local material for the *English Dialect Dictionary* (6 vols., 1896–1905), edited by Joseph Wright. In 1878 he established the English Dialect Library in the Central Free Library in Manchester. He also played a major part in founding the Manchester Arts Club (1879). He published a variety of other works on local artistic, literary, and bibliographical matters, including *Special Collections of Books in Lancashire and Cheshire* (1880) and *The Bibliography, Biographical and Topographical, of Ackworth School* (1889).

After his first wife's death Nodal married Edith, daughter of Edmund and Anne Robinson of Warrington, Lancashire. He died, aged seventy-eight, on 13 November 1909 at his home, The Grange, 6 Clifton Road, Heaton Moor, near Stockport, and was interred at the Society of Friends' burial-ground at Ashton upon Mersey, near Salford.

L. C. MUGGLESTONE

Sources DNB · *Manchester City News* (20 Nov 1909) · *Manchester Guardian* (15 Nov 1909) · Manchester Literary Club MSS, 1882, 1910 · J. H. Nodal, *The bibliography, biographical and topographical, of Ackworth School* (1889) · reports, English Dialect Society, 1874; 1876; 1878 · E. M. Wright, *The life of Joseph Wright*, 2 vols. (1936) · IGI · d. cert.
Archives JRL, corresp. and papers, incl. letters relating to the English Dialect Society · Man. CL, Manchester Archives and Local Studies, corresp.
Wealth at death £4129 19s. 6d.: probate, 24 Dec 1909, CGPLA Eng. & Wales

Nodder, Frederick Polydore (*fl.* 1773–1800), botanical artist and publisher, is said to have been of German extraction, but nothing certain is known of his birth or early life. He is first recorded, together with his wife, Elizabeth, on 5 September 1773, when his son Frederick William Nodder was baptized at St Martin-in-the-Fields, London. In 1774 a Mr Nodder of Panton Street submitted several novelty paintings on silk, or works in human hair, to the Society of Artists. It is likely that this artist can be identified with Frederick Polydore Nodder, since it was from this address that he exhibited five flower paintings at the Royal Academy between 1786 and 1788. In the exhibition catalogue he was described as 'Draughtsman in Natural History' and as 'Botanic Painter to her Majesty', under the protection of Queen Caroline.

Obviously sensitive to the nuances of the market,

Nodder occasionally called on this title to promote various publications, for example Thomas Martyn's *Flora rustica* (1792). However, the mainstay of his career was not his work for the royal family but the many diagrams he etched, after his own technical drawings, to illustrate various botanical volumes. The first of these was Martyn's *Thirty-Eight Plates with Explanations* (1788), where the illustrations actually underpinned the whole project to illustrate Linnaeus's system of vegetables. This was followed with a number of designs and engravings for Erasmus Darwin's *Botanic Garden* (1789). In 1792 Nodder was entirely responsible for designing and publishing the etchings in *Flora rustica*. Each of the finely etched and carefully hand-coloured plates in this publication follows the same compositional format by focusing on a single example of the named flower. Additionally each is signed 'Drawn, Engraved & Publish'd by F. P. Nodder, No. 15 Brewer Street, Golden Square London', and the volume and its plates were all published by Nodder himself. These obviously met with approval. In Thomas Dodd's estimation Nodder's 'singular productions … are accurately represented, being neatly etch'd and coloured corresponding to nature' (Dodd, fol. 134). Interestingly, however, a number of the plates in George Shaw's *Vivarium naturae, or, The Naturalist's Miscellany* (1789–1813) display a variety of initialized signatures, including S. N., D. N., R. N., and S. R. N., and this has been taken as evidence that the whole of the Nodder family was involved in producing these plates, published by 'Nodder & Co.' It is certainly known that Frederick Nodder's wife, Elizabeth, and their son Richard P. Nodder (*fl.* 1793–1820), a gifted painter who exhibited a number of animal subjects at the Royal Academy and won the title botanic painter to George III, continued producing botanic plates after references to Frederick Nodder ceased about 1800.

LUCY PELTZ

Sources Desmond, *Botanists*, rev. edn · T. Dodd, Memoirs of English engravers, 1550–1800, BL, Add. MS 33403, fol. 134 · Graves, *RA exhibitors* · Graves, *Soc. Artists* · T. Martyn, *Thirty-eight plates with explanations: intended to illustrate Linnaeus's system of vegetables* (1788) · T. Martyn, *Flora rustica* (1792) · DNB · IGI
Archives NHM

Noel, Sir Andrew (*c.*1552–1607), administrator, was born at Dalby, Leicestershire, the second son of Andrew Noel (*b.* in or before 1512, *d.* 1563) but the first son of his mother, Elizabeth Hopton, his father's second wife and the heir of John Hopton of Hopton, Staffordshire, and widow of Sir John Peryent (*d.* 1551). The elder Andrew established his family's fortune through his office as the feodary for the counties of Northampton, Rutland, Leicester, and Lincoln. He also served as the sheriff of Lincoln and of Rutland and as a knight of the shire for Rutland in 1553. When he died on 31 January 1563 he left the bulk of his estate to the minor Andrew Noel instead of his eldest son, John. The young Andrew attended Cambridge University and matriculated at Peterhouse in Michaelmas term 1565. By 1581 he had married Mabel (*d.* 1603), the daughter of Sir James Harington of Exton, Rutland. The couple produced four sons: Edward *Noel, second Viscount Campden (*bap.* 1582, *d.* 1643), Charles, Arthur, and Alexander; they also had three daughters, all of whom married well: Lucy, Theodosia, and Elizabeth.

Because of his inheritance, Noel owned lands in several counties, including the rich manors of Dalby in Leicestershire and Brooke in Rutland. His career in local government began in 1579 when he first appeared as a justice of the peace for Leicestershire where he later served as sheriff in 1583–5. Thanks to his marital alliance with the Haringtons, one of the two leading families of Rutland, Noel began to play a more prominent role in Rutland and appears to have made Brooke his principal residence. First appearing as a justice of the peace about 1582, in 1584 he served as one of Rutland's knights of the shire. Queen Elizabeth knighted him at Greenwich on 2 March 1586 and picked him as sheriff for Rutland in 1587–8, in 1595–6, and, fatefully, in 1600–01. Meanwhile he continued to sit as a knight of the shire for Rutland in 1586, 1589, and 1593, along with his Harington in-laws. From 1587 onward he held positions as deputy lieutenant and commissioner for musters in both Leicestershire and Rutland. That same year his wife appeared as a mourner at the funeral of Mary, queen of Scots, at Peterborough.

When Queen Elizabeth called a parliament on 11 September 1601 Noel was sheriff and prohibited from electing himself to parliament. When he attempted to promote the candidacy of his nineteen-year-old son, Edward, his brother-in-law Sir John *Harington opposed it. At strong local urging, Noel illegally returned himself, only to have the Commons void his election. Narrowly avoiding imprisonment and a fine, he conducted a by-election, hotly contested by the Haringtons, that selected his son Edward as Rutland's second knight of the shire. Sir John Harington sued his brother-in-law over the election in Star Chamber and harassed him locally in Rutland. Apparently their rift healed because in his will, written on 11 December 1605, Noel made Harington one of his overseers. Codicils added on 9 August and 15 October 1607 did not alter that arrangement. Noel made his eldest son, Edward, his heir, while still making generous provisions for his other sons and unmarried daughters. His wife, Mabel, had predeceased him on 21 January 1603. Noel died at Brooke on 19 October 1607 but was buried at the original family seat of Dalby on 8 December.

RONALD H. FRITZE

Sources DNB · J. E. Neale, *The Elizabethan House of Commons* (1949) · HoP, *Commons, 1558–1603* · HoP, *Commons, 1509–58* · Venn, *Alum. Cant.* · W. Camden, *The visitation of the county of Leicester in the year 1619*, ed. J. Fetherston, Harleian Society, 2 (1870) · G. J. Armytage, ed., *The visitation of the county of Rutland in the year 1618–19*, Harleian Society, 3 (1870) · J. E. Neale, 'More Elizabethan elections', *EngHR*, 61 (1946), 18–44, esp. 32–44 · M. A. Kishlansky, *Parliamentary selection: social and political choice in early modern England* (1986) · W. A. Shaw, *The knights of England*, 2 vols. (1906)

Noel [*née* Milbanke], **Anne Isabella** [Annabella], *suo jure* **Baroness Wentworth, and Lady Byron (1792–1860),** philanthropist and wife of the poet Lord Byron, was born at Elemore Hall, Pittington, Durham, on 17 May 1792, the only child of Sir Ralph Milbanke (afterwards Noel), sixth baronet (1747–1825), and his wife, Judith Noel (1751–1822),

Anne Isabella Noel, *suo jure* **Baroness Wentworth, and Lady Byron (1792–1860),** by unknown photographer

eldest daughter of the first Viscount Wentworth. Her father, the eldest son of Sir Ralph Milbanke of Halnaby Hall, Yorkshire, was the whig MP for Co. Durham and was renowned for his work for the poor and his support for the abolition of slavery. Both parents were enlightened, and Annabella and her adopted sister, Sophie Curzon, were among the first to be inoculated. She was brought up to be concerned for the workers and tenants of the estate and helped establish a school in Seaham. An early reader, Annabella Milbanke was especially interested in mathematics and astronomy, which she studied with a Cambridge tutor; new ideas on magnetism and phrenology fascinated her.

In 1810 Annabella Milbanke attended her first London season: she loved dancing and attracted many eligible suitors. She met George Gordon Noel *Byron, sixth Baron Byron (1788–1824), in 1812, the year he became famous, and soon after rejected his first marriage proposal. They communicated during 1813, often discussing literature in their letters, and he visited her at Seaham. She accepted Byron's second proposal in 1814 and they were married on 2 January 1815, spending their honeymoon at Halnaby Hall. On the first day Byron received a love letter from his half-sister Augusta Leigh, which he showed to his wife, saying he had married her out of revenge for her previous refusal.

Augusta came to stay with them in London. Both women were concerned about Byron's mental condition, and his aunt and a cousin came to protect the pregnant Lady

Byron from his threats. The baby, (Augusta) Ada, [*see* Byron, (Augusta) Ada, countess of Lovelace], was born on 10 December. On 15 January 1816 Lady Byron, at Byron's request, took the baby to her parents' home in Leicestershire, promising to return if his doctor advised it. Byron did not accept her parents' invitation to join his wife and they never met again.

Eventually Lady Byron's parents discovered the cause of their daughter's distress and consulted an eminent lawyer. Rumours about Byron and his half-sister, prevalent before his marriage, resurfaced and they were ostracized from society. Byron decided to leave the country; he departed on 25 April 1816 and never returned. In 1824 he died helping in the Greek War of Independence. On his deathbed he talked urgently to his faithful servant Fletcher, telling him to go to Lady Byron and say he was 'friends with her'. There was much more but Fletcher could not understand him. Lady Byron was devastated when Fletcher visited her and could impart little of Byron's last words to her.

Lady Byron supervised the education of her daughter, Ada, who proved to be a very intelligent child. She persuaded the mathematician Augustus de Morgan that her daughter should not give up mathematics on her marriage in 1835 to Lord King (later earl of Lovelace). Letters from her daughter to Lady Byron suggest that their relationship was a close one, until Ada fell into the hands of bookmakers, shortly before her premature death from cancer in November 1852. Lady Byron found it impossible to forgive her son-in-law for failing to prevent Ada's association with gamblers; she was similarly disillusioned with her close friend Anna Jameson, who had secretly lent her daughter money.

Meanwhile, Lady Byron had returned to her early ambitions to help the poor and ignorant. She tried to investigate and understand problems and offered not only money but practical suggestions. A supporter of the Brighton Co-operative Society, she helped pioneer a branch in Hastings. She also lent the ground floor of her house in Brighton to the mechanics' institute for educational purposes.

However Lady Byron's main interest was developing education for the underprivileged, and her greatest achievement was to establish Ealing Grove School. She had visited and written about Emanuel de Fellenberg's school at Hofwyl in Switzerland and used his principles in establishing the Ealing School. Its aim was practical as well as idealistic, and lessons included allotment schemes, carpentry, masonry, and the commercial principles of marketing garden produce, and Ada regularly helped by giving lessons. An agricultural school was also set up on the Leicestershire estate. Many notable people visited Ealing Grove, including the writer Joanna Baillie, Seymour Tremenheere of the council of education in London, and her son-in-law, the earl of Lovelace, who started a school with similar aims at Ockham in Surrey.

In 1840 Lady Byron attended the British and Foreign Anti-Slavery Convention and became involved in improving slum conditions and discussing rights for women. She shared with Mary Carpenter (1807–1877), the pioneer worker in reformatories for girls, the belief that society should undertake the education and care of orphans. In 1852 she bought Red Lodge in Bristol, which Mary Carpenter administered as a reformatory for girls.

On the death of her mother in 1822 Lady Byron took the name Noel but continued to be known as Lady Byron. By the death of her cousin, Nathaniel Curzon, Baron Scarsdale, in 1856, the abeyance of the barony of Wentworth terminated, and she became Baroness Wentworth. She died on 16 May 1860 at home in 11 St George's Terrace, Regent's Park, London. She was buried in Kensal Green cemetery, London.

Many people who knew Lady Byron well would have been surprised to read the hostile judgements made about her by notable twentieth-century writers; none more so than Lord Byron, who wrote as early as March 1816: 'I do not believe—that there ever was a better, or even a brighter, a kinder or a more amiable and agreeable being than Lady B' (*Byron's Letters and Journals*, 5.44). He told William Parry eight years later that 'The prospect of retirement in England with my wife and Ada gives me an idea of happiness I have never experienced before' (Parry, 122). Amelia Matilda Murray said that she was 'one of those pure spirits, little valued by the world, though worshipped by those who knew her well' (A. M. Murray, *Recollections of Amelia Matilda Murray*, 1868, 72).

JOAN PIERSON

Sources R. G. King-Milbanke, second earl of Lovelace, *Lady Noel Byron and the Leighs* (1887) · R. G. N. Milbanke, second earl of Lovelace, *Astarte, a fragment of truth concerning George Gordon Byron* (1905) · Lovelace MSS, Bodl. Oxf. · *Byron's letters and journals*, ed. L. A. Marchand, 12 vols. (1973–82) · *The life and letters of Anne Isabella, Lady Noel Byron*, ed. E. C. Mayne (1929) · D. L. Moore, *Ada, countess of Lovelace* (1977) · W. Parry, *The last days of Lord Byron* (1825) · M. Elwin, *Lord Byron's wife* (1962) · M. Strickland, *The Byron women* (1974) · P. Gunn, *My dearest Augusta* (1968) · H. B. Stowe, *History of the Byron controversy* (1870) · M. Gardiner, countess of Blessington, *A journal of conversations of Lord Byron*, new edn (1893) · J. Pierson, *The real Lady Byron* (1992) · d. cert.
Archives BL, family corresp., Add. MS 31037 · Bodl. Oxf., corresp. and papers · Boston PL, letters and papers · Ransom HRC, corresp. and papers | BL, corresp. with Lord Holland, Add. MS 51639 · BL, corresp. with Lady Melbourne, Add. MS 45547 · Bodl. Oxf., letters to Mary Somerville and her family · CKS, letters to Mary Duppa (later Faunce) · U. Birm. L., corresp. with Harriet Martineau · University of Kansas, Lawrence, Kenneth Spencer Research Library, corresp. with George Macdonald
Likenesses C. Hayter, portrait, 1812 · M. A. Knight, portrait, c.1820, Castle Museum, Nottingham · Freeman, steel engraving, 1833 · J. Hoppner, portrait (aged about 8), Hull City Museum, Ferens Art Gallery · photograph, NPG [*see illus.*]
Wealth at death under £70,000: resworn probate, July 1861, *CGPLA Eng. & Wales* (1860)

Noel, Baptist, third Viscount Campden (*bap.* **1611**, *d.* **1682**), royalist army officer, was baptized at Brooke, Rutland, on 13 October 1611. He was the eldest son and heir of Sir Edward *Noel (*bap.* 1582, *d.* 1643) and his wife, Juliana (*d.* 1680), eldest daughter and coheir of Sir Baptist *Hicks. In 1617 Sir Edward was created Baron Noel of Ridlington; in 1629 he inherited from his father-in-law the titles Baron Hicks of Ilmington and Viscount Campden.

In 1628 Baptist Noel was created MA at Cambridge University. On Christmas day 1632 he married Lady Anne Feilding (d. 1636), the second daughter of William *Feilding, first earl of Denbigh, and his wife, Susan, daughter of Sir George *Villiers [see under Villiers, Sir Edward]. According to one report Noel lost £2500 of the £3000 dowry provided by the king in one day at tennis with court gallants. On 9 November 1635 he became royal gamekeeper for Oakham, Rutland. His wife, Anne, died on 24 March 1636 and was buried at Campden. Their three children all died young. On 2 June 1638 he married his second wife, Anne (d. 1639), daughter of Sir Robert Lovet of Liscombe, Buckinghamshire, and his wife, Anne, daughter of Richard Saunders of Dinton in the same county. She was also recently widowed: her first husband, Edward Bourchier, fourth earl of Bath, had died in March 1637. Her marriage to Noel lasted barely six months, and she was dead by 25 January 1639 when the administration of her estate was granted. Within the year, on 21 December, Noel had married again, his third wife being Hester (bap. 1616, d. 1649), daughter and coheir of Thomas Wotton, second Baron Wotton, and his wife, Mary Throckmorton. They had four daughters and two sons; the eldest son, Edward, who was to succeed to his father's titles in due course, was baptized at Boughton Malherbe, Kent.

In 1639 Noel and his father accompanied Charles I north against the Scots. In 1640 Noel was elected MP for Rutland to both the Short and Long parliaments. He offered £1000 for the loan of November 1640 and was appointed to the committees for the army and for dealing with the patentee Sir Henry Spiller, but voted against the earl of Strafford's attainder and in March 1642 received permission to leave London. The king appointed him a commissioner of array for Rutland, though the commission was not implemented in the county. Like his father, Noel became a troop commander. Parliament ordered his arrest on 17 December 1642. Noel was based around the powerful garrison at Newark when he succeeded as third Viscount Campden upon the death of his father at Oxford on 8 March 1643. Seven days later he was made a colonel of horse. On 22 March Lord Grey of Groby, commander of parliament's east midlands association, suggested to the House of Lords that Campden, who was at Belvoir Castle, having raised 'a brave troop of horse', should forfeit his rents (Eighth Report, HMC, 2.59). Campden was still busy plundering and imprisoning local opponents in June. In 1643 his men looted the house of Sir William Armine at Osgodby, Lincolnshire. In July it was reported that 'Lord Camden intends to set before Peterborough, and hath a far greater force come into Stamford [which is] fortifying there' (ibid., 7th Report, 555). On 24 July he was commissioned brigadier of horse and foot.

Campden was assessed by the parliamentarian committee for the advance of money at £4000 on 14 June 1644 and his estates were sequestrated two months later on 24 August. In May 1645 his Gloucestershire mansion, Campden House, was burnt down when it was abandoned by its royalist garrison. Campden resigned his field command at the Oxford parliament and by October 1645 was a prisoner

in London, where he began compounding for his delinquency. He was released in August 1646 on recognizances, and in September he gained a pass to return to Rutland. His fine of £19,558, set on 9 July 1646, demonstrated the measure of his perceived delinquency. Persistent petitioning reduced the fine by stages and after he had paid a moiety and entered into possession of his estates, the figure rested at £9000 in November 1647. On 19 May 1648, after long negotiation and with Campden severely in debt, his assessment was discharged on payment of £100. His wife, Hester, is said to have died the following year and been buried at Exton on 17 December 1649.

The manuscripts of Mildmay Fane, earl of Westmorland contain a poem, 'A pepper Corn, or small cent sente to my Lord Camden for the loan of his house at Kensington, 9 Feb. 1651'. That year Campden was summoned before the committee of examinations. On 8 March he was dismissed, having given a bond of £10,000 for himself with sureties of £5000 each to do nothing prejudicial to the Commonwealth and the government, and to appear before the council upon summons. Campden married his fourth wife, Lady Elizabeth Bertie (d. 1683), eldest daughter of Montague *Bertie, second earl of Lindsey, and his wife, Martha, née Cokayne, on 7 July 1655. They had nine children.

At the Restoration Campden was made captain of a troop of horse, lord lieutenant of Rutland (August 1660), and JP for Middlesex (1661): the lord lieutenancy was one of several such appointments made in partial recompense of debts owed by the crown to loyal peers. In his last years Campden was most significant in local affairs. His influence succeeded in getting his eldest son elected MP for Rutland in 1661 and his second son, Henry, for Stamford in 1677, the latter in a contested election where Campden, who was recorder of the town, spent over £1000. In the Lords, Campden was a loyal supporter of the court and in due course a tory. His royalist experience, reinforced by family connections to the earl of Danby, who was married to his fourth wife's sister, ensured that Campden's proxy vote was safely in the hands of the Danby camp. Campden died at his seat at Exton on 29 October 1682, aged seventy, and he was later buried at Exton. His monument, by Grinling Gibbons, dominates the east wall in the north transept of the church. In his will, proved on 5 November 1682, Campden made bequests to his wife, children, sons-in-law and servants. His wife survived him by only a few months, dying about 20 July 1683.

S. L. SADLER

Sources GEC, Peerage, new edn, vol. 2 · J. E. Doyle, The official baronage of England, 3 vols. (1886), vol. 1, pp. 308–9 · will, PRO, PROB 11/371, sig. 127 · JHL, 7 (1644–5), 660 · JHL, 8 (1645–6), 457, 477 · JHC, 2 (1640–42), 48, 469, 894 · JHC, 3 (1642–4), 605 · CSP dom., 1635, 470 · Fifth report, HMC, 4 (1876), 403 · Sixth report, HMC, 5 (1877–8), 130 · Seventh report, HMC, 6 (1879), 493, 555 · Eighth report, 2, HMC, 7 (1910), 59 · The manuscripts of his grace the duke of Portland, 10 vols., HMC, 29 (1891–1931), vol. 1, p. 99 · M. A. E. Green, ed., Calendar of the proceedings of the committee for compounding ... 1643–1660, 5 vols., PRO (1889–92), vol. 1, pp. 20, 63, 88, 773; vol. 2, pp. 939–40; vol. 3, p. 2309 · M. A. E. Green, ed., Calendar of the proceedings of the committee for advance of money, 1642–1656, 1, PRO (1888), 81, 401 · E. Walker, Historical discourses (1705), 126 · J. Bruce, ed., Letters and papers of the Verney family down to the end of the year 1639, CS, 56 (1853), 58 · The *journal of Sir Simonds D'Ewes from the beginning of the Long Parliament to the opening of the trial of the earl of Strafford*, ed. W. Notestein (1923), 52 · Keeler, *Long Parliament*, 286 · P. R. Newman, *Royalist officers in England and Wales, 1642–1660: a biographical dictionary* (1981), 274 · P. R. Newman, *The old service: royalist regimental colonels and the civil war, 1642–1646* (1993), 87, 189 · Clarendon, *Hist. rebellion* · S. R. Gardiner, *History of the great civil war, 1642–1649*, new edn, 4 vols. (1901–5), vol. 2, p. 210 · Venn, *Alum. Cant.* · [T. Birch and R. F. Williams], eds., *The court and times of Charles the First*, 2 (1848), 219 · E. Cruickshanks and B. D. Henning, 'Noel, Edward', HoP, *Commons, 1660–90* · E. Cruickshanks and B. D. Henning, 'Noel, Henry', HoP, *Commons, 1660–90* · E. Cruickshanks and B. D. Henning, 'Rutland', HoP, *Commons, 1660–90*, 1.362 · A. Fletcher, *The outbreak of the English civil war*, rev. edn (1985), 367 · B. Matthews, *The book of Rutland* (1978), 77 · J. Wright, *The history and antiquities of the county of Rutland* (1973), 48, 49, 60, 108 · *VCH Rutland*, 1.187–8, 190; 2.xxxiv, 30, 40, 133 · A. Swatland, *The House of Lords in the reign of Charles II* (1996), 11, 44, 251, 266 · V. L. Stater, *Noble government: the Stuart lord lieutenancy and the transformation of English politics* (1994), 74

Likenesses G. Gibbons, marble funeral monument, 1686 (with his fourth wife), Exton church, Rutland; repro. in *VCH Rutland*, 2, facing p. 40

Wealth at death see will, PRO, PROB 11/371, sig. 127

Noel, Baptist Wriothesley (1799–1873), Church of England clergyman and Baptist minister, was born at Leightmount, Scotland, on 10 July 1799 into a household which combined whig politics, evangelical devotion, aristocratic unconventionality, and strong-mindedness in a potent blend. He was the tenth son among the sixteen children of Sir Gerard Noel Noel, second baronet (1759–1838), of Exton Park, Rutland, an eccentric whig politician and landowner, and his first wife, Diana *Noel (1762–1823), only child of the evangelical Admiral Charles *Middleton, first Baron Barham, to whose barony she succeeded in 1813. Baptist Noel was the younger brother of Charles Noel, who in 1841 was created earl of Gainsborough, and of Gerard Thomas *Noel, the well-known evangelical vicar of Romsey Abbey, Hampshire; he was the uncle of Caroline Noel, the hymn writer. Tall and handsome, Noel's most striking feature was his voice: its silvery tones and melodious cadences proved highly effective in leading many to 'serious religion'.

Noel was educated at Westminster School (1810–17) and Trinity College, Cambridge, where he proceeded MA in 1821. In the same year, after touring the continent, he enrolled at Lincoln's Inn; two years later, however, and against the wishes of his family, he abandoned the law and was ordained in the Church of England, serving initially as assistant curate at Cossington, Leicester. In January 1827 he acquired the lease of St John's Chapel, Bedford Row, Holborn, a proprietary chapel of some prominence within the evangelical party which had previously served as the pulpit of Richard Cecil and Daniel Wilson, where he attracted sizeable and influential congregations. He married, on 17 October 1826, Jane (*d.* 1889), the eldest daughter of Peter Baillie of Dochfour, Inverness-shire, with whom he had four sons and four daughters. They resided first at Walthamstow and later at Crouch Hill, Hornsey.

Though a powerful and respected preacher, Noel's reputation as a giant of the Victorian era is due largely to his

Baptist Wriothesley Noel (1799–1873), by Henry Cousins (after George Patten)

emergence as a prolific religious writer, whose publications put forward strong views on contemporary religious and political issues. A vigorously reformist whig, the principal concern of his writings was the evangelization of the urban poor and the perceived inability of the Church of England fully to meet the rapidly changing spiritual needs of the nation. His *State of the Metropolis Considered* (1835) is a classic—and much neglected—early statement of that view of 'spiritual destitution' in the great cities which was to electrify many Anglicans in the turbulent 1840s. In 1840 he conducted a public inquiry into the condition of elementary schools in several major cities. He was one of the comparatively few churchmen publicly to attack the corn laws, his *Plea for the Poor* (1841) running through at least twenty-nine editions. Such reformist views delighted his whig friends and won him a chaplaincy to Queen Victoria from the outgoing Melbourne administration. In becoming an outspoken advocate of Christian unity, however, and especially in offering unqualified support for the pan-evangelical London City Mission and the Evangelical Alliance (in both of which he played a leading role) he provoked considerable personal criticism from strict churchmen.

Despite his reforming tendencies Noel was dismissive of both catholic and liberal innovations. He denounced Tractarianism as 'a serious offence against Christ' (B. Noel, *A Defence of a Tract Entitled 'Unity of the Church'*, 1837, 6) and the doctrine of baptismal regeneration as a popish survival from medieval times. He rejected both ecclesiastical voluntarism and disestablishment, arguing instead for the concurrent endowment of evangelical dissent. He became highly critical of state intrusion, describing the Disruption of the Church of Scotland as 'the great religious event of our day' (B. Noel, *The Case of the Free Church of Scotland*, 1844, 94), and of the proposed Maynooth grant, which he perceived as inconsistent given the state's refusal financially to support orthodox dissent in Britain. He was also critical of the circumstances leading to the legal entanglements surrounding James Shore and J. C. Gorham, both evangelical opponents of the high-church martinet Bishop Phillpotts of Exeter.

These various church–state tensions eventually compelled Noel to abandon the established church. In November 1848 he announced his secession to a stunned congregation at St John's, publishing, in the following month, his celebrated *Essay on the Union of Church and State*—a detailed and impassioned attack on the Church of England and its civil connection. The work was not only highly popular but also provoked a lively response from both churchmen and dissenters. Noel then withdrew from public life, albeit temporarily. On 25 March 1849 he preached at the Scottish Church in Regent's Square, his first appearance in a nonconformist pulpit. Shortly thereafter, and perhaps fearing prosecution for preaching outside the church in violation of Anglican canon law, he took the oaths prescribed by 52 Geo. III, thus gaining legal protection as a dissenting minister. In May 1849 he preached for Thomas Binney at the Weigh House Chapel, and on 9 August he was baptized by immersion at John Street Baptist Chapel, Holborn, where, in the following September, he became minister. Here he enjoyed continued success as a preacher and pastor. Despite his own secession and vigorous attack on the church, during the 1850s and 1860s he declined invitations to become involved in the campaign to bring about disestablishment. However, he did champion the cause of the North in the American Civil War, particularly at the great meeting in the Free Trade Hall, Manchester, in June 1863, as well as that of the Baptist minister G. W. Gordon, who in 1865 was executed for participating in the Jamaica outbreak. Noel was also active in the Baptist Union, twice serving as chairman (1855 and 1867). In 1864 he publicly defended the evangelical Anglican clergy from an attack by C. H. Spurgeon.

Noel remained as minister at John Street Chapel until 1869. In retirement he resided in Stanmore, Middlesex, preaching on Sunday mornings at the small nonconformist chapel at Edgware; on Sunday evenings, however, he attended services at the local parish church, and on Wednesdays assisted the rector at lectures held at the local memorial institute. He remained healthy and active until shortly before his death on 19 January 1873 at Stanmore, Middlesex, where he was buried.

Noel was one of the most influential evangelical clergymen of early Victorian England. His secession, which caused almost as much sensation as that of Newman three years earlier, was a great blow to the church and the evangelical party, and his subsequent reluctance to associate with 'political dissent' severely diminished the Liberationist campaign for the disestablishment of the Church of England. On the other hand, the acquisition of a leading evangelical aristocrat by the Baptists added considerable social lustre to their movement, and Noel bolstered their intellectual vigour during a critical period of English religious history. So numerous and energetic were his spiritual activities, and so popular and influential his writings, that few accomplished more on behalf of 'serious religion' in his time.　　　　　GRAYSON CARTER

Sources G. Carter, 'Evangelical seceders from the Church of England, *c*.1800–1850', DPhil diss., U. Oxf., 1990 · D. W. Bebbington, 'The life of Baptist Noel', *Baptist Quarterly*, 24 (1971–2), 389–411 · K. R. M. Short, 'Baptist Wriothesley Noel', *Baptist Quarterly*, 20 (1963–4), 51–61 · D. M. Lewis, ed., *The Blackwell dictionary of evangelical biography, 1730–1860*, 2 vols. (1995) · J. Julian, ed., *A dictionary of hymnology* (1892), 809 · J. Dix, *Pen and ink sketches of poets, preachers, and politicians* (1846), 245 · Boase, *Mod. Eng. biog.* · S. Noel, *Ernest Noel* (1932) · E. F. Noel, ed., *Some letters and records of the Noel family* (1910) · Venn, *Alum. Cant.* · *Old Westminsters*, 2.693 · W. P. Baildon, ed., *The records of the Honorable Society of Lincoln's Inn: admissions*, 2 (1896), 93 · Burke, *Peerage*

Archives Leics. RO, family MSS · NRA, priv. coll., family MSS | CUL, British and Foreign Bible Society MSS

Likenesses W. Harland, stipple, pubd 1842 (after A. Wivell), NPG · W. J. Edwards, stipple, pubd 1851 (after drawing by G. Richmond), NPG · H. Cousins, engraving (after G. Patten), NPG [*see illus.*] · Maull & Polyblank, carte-de-visite, NPG · D. J. Pound, stipple and line engraving (after unknown photograph), BM, NPG; repro. in D. J. Pound, *Drawing room portrait gallery of eminent personages* (1859–60) · G. B. Shaw, stipple (after drawing by H. Anelay), BM, NPG · portrait, Exton Park, Rutland · portrait, Regent's Park College, Oxford

Wealth at death under £3000: probate, 12 Feb 1873, *CGPLA Eng. & Wales*

Noel, Conrad Le Despenser Roden (1869–1942), Church of England clergyman and Christian socialist, was born on 12 July 1869 in Kew, London, the eldest son of the Hon. Roden Berkeley Wriothesley *Noel (1834–1894), poet and essayist, and then groom of the privy chamber in the court of Queen Victoria, and his wife, Alice Maria Caroline de Broë (*d.* 1919). His grandfather was Charles Noel, first earl of Gainsborough (1781–1866). After an unhappy time at Wellington School and Cheltenham College, he studied at Corpus Christi College, Cambridge, but was rusticated for one year and never returned to take his degree. After a period at Chichester Theological College, he was offered a curacy at All Saints, Plymouth, but the bishop of Exeter refused to ordain him on the grounds that his theology was both pantheist and Romanist.

Noel was ordained deacon in 1894 in the diocese of Chester, and in that year married Miriam Greenwood. He was curate in Flowery Field, Hyde, Cheshire, but resigned after church members objected to his socialism. After several curacies, in 1910 he became vicar of the Essex village of Thaxted, the patron of which was the socialist countess of Warwick, and he remained there until his death on 22 July 1942. He and his wife had one daughter, Barbara, whose husband, Jack Putterill, succeeded him as vicar of Thaxted in 1942.

Theologically, Noel, like many Christian socialists, was deeply influenced by F. D. Maurice. He believed that all

Conrad Le Despenser Roden Noel (1869–1942), by Gertrude Hermes, 1938

humanity was rooted and grounded in God, and some critics believed that he was close to pantheism. He saw the whole world as a universal sacrament, and the church as the foretaste of God's kingdom. One of Noel's most frequently used terms for the kingdom was 'the Commonwealth of God'. His language was both poetic and polemical, often marked by a desire to shock. Jesus was often described as the 'Divine Outlaw', and the church as a 'Red Army'.

Noel was impatient with vagueness in religion and politics, and was highly critical of Christian social thinkers who spoke only of 'general principles'. As he said in 1935, 'The man who is content with laying down general principles will never be compelled to lay down his life. He will found an ethical society and die comfortably in his bed' (Noel, 'City of God', 3). Though he was a strong supporter of the Soviet Union and of the Communist Party, his socialism owed more to William Morris and the romantic and utopian traditions than to Marx. He was a member of the Independent Labour Party, but resigned in 1911 and joined the British Socialist Party which later became the Communist Party of Great Britain.

Thaxted church was a source of inspiration to thousands of people. Here they found the music of Gustav Holst (1874–1934), often played by the composer himself, the Morris dances and summer festivals, brilliantly coloured banners and tapestries, and a liturgical space which encouraged expansion, freedom, and festivity. The atmosphere reflected Noel's view that God was 'the maker of the sense of wonder, justice, love and worship; of the sense of colour which delights in the flowers, pictures, sunrises and gay fabrics; of the sense of justice which drives men to rebellion against tyrants who rob men's souls of vigour, their minds of leisure, and their bodies of nourishment; of the sense of smell which rejoices in roses and frankincense; of the sense of hearing which responds to poetry and music' (Noel, 'Some articles of the faith').

Noel was a key figure in the revival of corporate and democratic liturgy in the Church of England. In worship and in life, he was attracted to the middle ages, though not uncritically. He was strongly opposed to puritanism and sabbatarianism which he attacked in his first published work, *The Day of the Sun* (1901). Liturgically and theologically, Noel was strongly anti-Roman-Catholic, regarding the Roman Church as decadent in ceremonial, and fascistic in its politics. He was opposed to those Anglo-Catholics who copied Rome, and preferred to call himself a 'Catholic socialist'.

Noel saw liturgy as an expression in historical time of 'the life of the world to come'. The Thaxted movement was a deeply sacramental movement, rooted in splendid and colourful worship, as well as a prophetic movement, committed to a revolutionary vision of a new world. The eucharistic celebration was central to Noel's vision of the world. The mass was a prelude to the new world order in which goods would be justly produced and equally distributed.

Noel's life was filled with controversy. He fostered a devotion to Thomas Becket and to John Ball, leader of the peasants' revolt of 1381. He hung the red flag, the Sinn Féin flag, and the flag of St George in Thaxted church, and there were violent scenes when right-wing visitors pulled them down. The red flag, contrary to popular belief, was not emblazoned with the hammer and sickle but with the words 'He hath made of one blood all nations', and it hung inside, not outside, the church. Noel's pamphlet *The Battle of the Flags* (1922) described the meaning of the flags and the controversy about them.

Noel founded the Catholic Crusade, a group of Anglican socialists, differing from other Christian socialist organizations by its tight discipline and its commitment to revolution. Behind it was a coherent holistic philosophy. This philosophy was, according to Noel, 'all of a piece'. 'It will change your views on music, on decoration, on the colour of a piece of material, equally with your view of man's end, the reading of history, and the revolution' (Noel, 'Anglo-Catholics and the Catholic crusade').

Some members of the Catholic Crusade were among the founders of British Trotskyism, and one of the reasons given for the expulsion of Trotskyists from the Communist Party in 1932 was their association with Noel (Gallacher). The crusade finally split, partly over the Stalin–Trotsky dispute, though a section of it, the Order of the Church Militant, survived Noel's death by a few years.

While he was unbalanced and outrageous in the expression of his views, Noel was a visionary and prophetic figure who anticipated much that was to come later in politics, liturgy, and biblical interpretation. He died on 22 July 1942 at the vicarage, Thaxted, Essex, and was survived by his wife.

KENNETH LEECH

Sources R. Groves, *Conrad Noel and the Thaxted movement* (1967) · K. Leech, ed., *Conrad Noel and the Catholic Crusade: a critical evaluation* (1993) · R. Woodifield, *Catholicism, humanist and democratic* (1954) · R. Woodifield, 'Conrad Noel', *For Christ and the people*, ed. M. B. Reckitt (1968), 135–79 · C. Noel, *Socialism in church history* (1910) · C. Noel, *The battle of the flags* (1922) · *Conrad Noel: an autobiography*, ed. S. Dark (1945) · C. Noel, *The life of Jesus* (1937) · W. Gallacher, 'We have no room for Trotskyists', *Daily Worker* (23 Aug 1932) · C. Noel, 'Anglo-Catholics and the Catholic Crusade - 1', *Catholic Crusader*, 23

(16 Jan 1933), 2–3 · C. Noel, 'Some articles of the faith', *The New World*, 8 (Nov 1928) · C. Noel, 'The city of God', *The Challenge*, 8 (Oct 1935), 3 · *DNB* · d. cert. · *CGPLA Eng. & Wales* (1942)

Archives U. Hull, Brynmor Jones L., corresp., MSS, sermons and 'Memories' (MS version of autobiography) | BL, corresp. with Society of Authors, Add. MS 63311 · U. Edin. L., corresp. with Charles Sarolea · University of Warwick, Reg Groves Archives **Likenesses** G. Hermes, bronze, 1938, unknown collection; copyprint, NPG [*see illus.*]
Wealth at death £942 18s. 4d.: probate, 3 Nov 1942, *CGPLA Eng. & Wales*

Noel [*formerly* Edwardes; *née* Middleton], **Diana**, *suo jure* **Baroness Barham** (1762–1823), evangelical patron, was born on 18 September 1762 at Barham Court, Teston, Kent, the only child of Sir Charles *Middleton (1726–1813), first lord of the Admiralty, tory MP for Rochester, and one of the nation's leading agriculturists, who was created Baron Barham in 1805, and his wife, Margaret (d. 1792), daughter of James Gambier, warden of the Fleet Prison, and aunt of Lord Gambier, the evangelical admiral of the fleet.

For many years, Diana Middleton's family resided with her mother's childhood friend, Lady Elizabeth Bouverie, either at the Middletons' London home at 36 Hertford Street, Hanover Square, or at Bouverie's attractive estate, Barham Court. At her death Barham Court passed to Sir Charles Middleton; at his death it passed to Diana. It was at Teston during the 1780s (and through the influence of the clergyman James Ramsay, a former navy surgeon, who had been appointed rector of Teston by Lady Elizabeth Bouverie) that the Middletons assumed a position of leadership in the abolitionist movement, recruiting, bringing together, and encouraging the campaign's leading adherents, including Thomas Clarkson and William Wilberforce. Outside Clapham, Barham Court served as the pre-eminent centre of the crusade against the slave trade.

In light of the Middletons' evangelical convictions (which their daughter shared from an early age) it is not easy to explain how or why she became engaged to a man of quite different tastes and outlook. On 21 December 1780, however, she married, at St George's Church, Hanover Square, Gerard Noel Edwardes (1759–1838) (after 1798 Gerard Noel Noel) of Exton Park, Rutland, a wealthy—and highly eccentric—landowner and whig MP for Rutland, with whom she had eighteen children, including Gerard Thomas *Noel and Baptist Wriothesley *Noel.

Throughout much of her life Diana maintained a wide and influential circle of evangelical friends and relations. Despite her husband's considerable wealth and family connections in the midlands, her life continued to revolve around Teston, where her children were exposed to many of the leading politicians and religious figures of the day. They were also exposed, through Gerard Noel's interest in the game of cricket, to the prince of Wales' fashionable circle at Brighton.

In 1813, upon the death of her father, Diana succeeded to the barony under a special remainder. She then separated from her profligate and eccentric husband (who exhibited little interest in spiritual matters), setting up house at Fairy Hill on the Gower peninsula of south Wales, where she established Lady Barham's Connexion, a body

of six chapels (and a number of free schools) connected with the Welsh Calvinistic Methodists: Bethesda, Burry Green (1814); Bethel, Pen-clawdd (1816); Trinity, Cheriton (1816); Paraclete, Newton (1818); Immanuel, Pilton Green (1821); and Mount Pisgah, Parkmill (1822). On Sundays, after being carried across the fields by two flunkeys in a sedan chair, she occupied a separate room behind the pulpit at Bethesda Chapel; warmed by an open fire, it contained an elevated box pew which was entered by a flight of steps and was reserved exclusively for the Fairy Hill household. When her ladyship grew tired of the sermon, the door of the room was closed and she departed for home.

Initially Lady Barham engaged ministers from England to fill her pulpits; over time, however, she began to employ Welsh ministers, the most prominent being William Griffiths (d. 1849), the so-called Apostle of Gower. Shortly before her death a disagreement over a minor point of church order produced an unfortunate rupture between the Connexion and the Welsh Calvinistic Methodists, which was slow to heal.

Lady Barham, who had been in poor health for some years, died at Fairy Hill on 12 April 1823, and was buried at Teston. Her elaborate cortège from Wales to Teston produced considerable public interest. The Connexion then passed briefly to the care of her eldest son, Charles, but was eventually conveyed to the Welsh Calvinistic Methodists. Although deeply religious and often generous to a fault, she was also an autocrat who expected her ministers and congregations to toe the line. GRAYSON CARTER

Sources J. Barfett, *Funeral sermon of Lady Barham* (1823) · I. H. Jones, 'Lady Barham in Gower', *Journal of the Gower Society*, 9 (1956) · *Evangelical Magazine and Missionary Chronicle*, new ser., 1 (1823), 236–7 · A. N. Jones, *Gower memories of William Griffiths* (1957) · 'Memoir of the late Rev. William Hammerton, of Newton', *Evangelical Magazine and Missionary Chronicle*, new ser., 13 (1835), 45–8 · *Collin's peerages of England*, 9 vols. (1812), 9.246–9 · W. Williams, *A memoir of the life and labours of the Rev. Wm. Griffiths* (1863) · GEC, *Peerage* · D. W. Bebbington, 'Barham, Baroness', *The Blackwell dictionary of evangelical biography, 1730–1860*, ed. D. M. Lewis (1995) · E. F. Noel, *Some letters and records of the Noel family* (1910) · R. Lucas, *A Gower family* (1986), 45–6 · R. Jones, *Gower fact and fable* (1975), 13 · I. H. Jones, 'Life and death at Fairy Hill', *Journal of the Gower Society*, 13 (1960) · M. E. Moody, 'Religion in the life of Charles Middleton, first Baron Barham', *The dissenting tradition: essays for Leland H. Carlson*, ed. C. R. Cole and M. E. Moody (1975), 140–63
Archives Glamorgan RO, Cardiff · Leics. RO, corresp. · Leics. RO, family MSS · priv. coll., family MSS
Likenesses Rayburn, oils, priv. coll.

Noel, Edward, second Viscount Campden (*bap.* **1582**, *d.* **1643**), royalist nobleman, was the eldest son and heir of Sir Andrew *Noel (c.1552–1607) of Dalby, Leicestershire, and of Brooke, Rutland, and his wife, Mabel (d. 1603), daughter of Sir James Harington. He was born at Brooke and baptized there on 2 July 1582. Educated at Sidney Sussex College, Cambridge, he entered the Inner Temple in 1600. He was returned for Rutland at a by-election to the 1601 parliament after his father's election had been declared void. He served in Ireland under Mountjoy in the latter stages of the campaign against the earl of Tyrone and was knighted by the lord deputy on 13 May 1602. On 20

Edward Noel, second Viscount Campden (*bap.* 1582, *d.* 1643), by Joshua Marshall, 1664 [with his wife, Juliana (*née* Hicks), Viscountess Campden]

December 1605 he married Juliana (*d.* 1680), eldest daughter and coheir of Sir Baptist Hicks. He acted as sheriff of Rutland in 1608–9 and 1615–16. In 1611 he purchased the thirty-fourth baronetcy (dated 29 June) and in 1617, while at Burley on the Hill, James VI and I created him Baron Noel of Ridlington by patent dated 23 March.

Noel had inherited Ridlington, Rutland, from his mother and in 1609 was granted the fee farm of the manor of Claxton in Leicestershire along with Thomas Philipps, though it soon passed to the earl of Rutland. He also held land in Lyfield Forest in Rutland, of which he had been master of the game by 1614 when the king ordered him to prevent hunting there for three years. He was bailiff of the forest in 1623 and a year later was asked to ensure the preservation of game within 6 miles of Burley on the Hill. About the time of his ennoblement he sold his Dalby estates to the earl of Buckingham and moved wholly to Rutland, hoping in turn to buy Burley on the Hill from the countess of Bedford but instead seeing Buckingham subsequently buy that too.

Though regularly present at court, Noel did not always support royal policy. In 1621 he was one of thirty-three lords who signed a petition objecting to James's awarding of precedence to English holders of Scottish and Irish titles. In 1624 he was appointed to the county subsidy commissioners for the three subsidies voted by parliament in that year. On 5 November 1628 the duchess of Lennox and others petitioned the privy council to give him custody of his sister, the countess of Castlehaven, who was judged incapable of looking after herself, and who had set fire to her Drury Lane residence, endangering the duchess's property. Noel's father-in-law had been given the titles Baron Hicks of Ilmington (Warwickshire) and Viscount Campden (Gloucestershire) with reversion to Noel if, as expected, he died without a male heir. Hicks died on 18 October 1629 and the titles duly passed to Noel.

Campden lent £2500 to the exchequer in 1631, during the years of Charles I's personal rule. Even before this was repaid he was helping with Charles's extra-parliamentary financial exactions, assisting in the collection of ship money in Rutland, ensuring a surplus of £800 over the assessed amount in 1637. In 1639 he accompanied Charles to York during the first bishops' war. At the end of the second bishops' war he was part of the council of peers at York and was instrumental in trying to obtain a loan of £250,000 from London to pay the army wages in the interim before parliament could vote through supply. He was sent to London as part of the six-man negotiating team. After the loan was agreed he sought to guarantee that the burden of the loan would not be borne by the lesser peers as against the privy councillors.

At the outbreak of the first civil war Campden was commissioned by the king to raise first a regiment of horse and later three regiments of horse and three of foot, his military commands bringing him within the regional command given to Henry Hastings (later Baron Loughborough). Four of Campden's five children were associated with the royalist war effort. Elizabeth was married to John, Baron Chaworth of Armagh, and Mary to Sir Erasmus de la Fontaine of Kirkby Bellars, commissioners of array for Nottinghamshire and Leicestershire respectively. Campden and both his sons, Sir Baptist *Noel (*bap.* 1611, *d.* 1682) and Henry (*d.* 1643), were by 1643 amassing arms for the royalist cause, probably for the regiments Campden had been commissioned to raise. (A fifth child, Penelope, had been born in April 1610 and died in 1633 at Brooke.)

Nevertheless, as with other leading figures in midlands society, parliament still hoped as late as early 1643 to persuade Campden to contribute towards its cause, and on 18 February he was ordered to contribute to parliament's assessments. He persuaded the House of Lords to forbear and so Lord Grey of Groby, commander of parliament's east midland association, was instructed not to levy the assessment. This stung Grey into a letter to parliament in which he reported that Campden had tried on two occasions to bribe him with £50 to leave him and his sons unmolested. Grey was well aware of their collecting of arms and had already made attempts to prevent the militarization of Rutland. Henry Noel was captured as he attempted to create a garrison at his own house at Langar (North Luffenham) in February 1643 and died in captivity in the following July; he was later buried at Campden. In the meantime his father used the hiatus caused by his appeal to parliament to abandon his house, taking with him the weapons Grey suspected him to have stockpiled.

He went to Oxford where just over a week later, on 8 March, he died.

Campden's body was returned to Campden, where his wife erected a monument with an epitaph by Joshua Marshall. His heir, Baptist Noel, third Viscount Campden, served as a commissioner of array for Rutland and as a colonel of horse, working on behalf of the royalist cause until he was captured in 1645. He compounded in 1646 and his initial fine was set at £19,558, later reduced to £11,078. The second viscount's widow, Juliana, went to live at Brooke after his death and petitioned parliament for an allowance out of the sequestered estates. She was charged £4000 for her composition and by 7 November 1649 had paid £1100. She then petitioned for relief but was ordered to pay another £900, making a total of £2000 or half the original assessment, the rest being suspended in April 1650. She remained at Brooke where she apparently 'maintained great state and dispensed much hospitality' (DNB) and died there on 25 November 1680. She was buried at Campden on 12 January 1681.   MARTYN BENNETT

Sources DNB · J. Nichols, *The history and antiquities of the county of Leicester*, 2/1 (1795) · *Fifth report*, HMC, 4 (1876) · *JHL*, 5–6 (1642–4) · M. A. E. Green, ed., *Calendar of the proceedings of the committee for advance of money, 1642–1656*, 1, PRO (1888), 677 · M. Bennett, 'The royalist war effort in the north midlands, 1642–1646', PhD diss., Loughborough, 1986 · *Report on the manuscripts of the late Reginald Rawdon Hastings*, 4 vols., HMC, 78 (1928–47), vol. 2 · J. Wright, *The history and antiquities of the county of Rutland* (1684); repr. (1973) · GEC, *Peerage* · S. M. Thorpe, 'Noel (Nowell), Andrew', HoP, *Commons, 1558–1603* · S. M. Thorpe, 'Noel, Edward', HoP, *Commons, 1558–1603* · Foster, *Alum. Oxon.*

Likenesses J. Marshall, sculpture, 1664, Chipping Camden church, Glos. [see illus.]

Noel, Gerard Thomas (1782–1851), Church of England clergyman, was born on 2 December 1782 at Ketton, Rutland, the second son of Sir Gerard Noel Edwardes of Exton Park, Rutland (1759–1838), who adopted the surname Noel in 1798 and inherited a baronetcy in 1813, and his first wife, Diana *Noel (1762–1823), only child of Charles *Middleton, first Baron Barham, who became Baroness Barham in 1813. His elder brother, Charles Noel Noel (1781–1866), became whig MP for Rutland and was created earl of Gainsborough in 1841. His younger brother was Baptist Wriothesley *Noel, the celebrated London evangelical. Gerard was educated at Langley, Kent, before he matriculated at Trinity College, Cambridge, in 1804, graduating BA in 1805 and MA in 1808. He was admitted to Lincoln's Inn on 14 July 1798, and was ordained deacon on 2 March 1806 (priest on 28 June 1807) by George Pretyman Tomline, bishop of Lincoln. He served as curate of Radwell, Hertfordshire (1806–7); vicar of Rainham, Kent (1807–26); and curate of Richmond, Surrey (1826–34). He was prebendary of Winchester from 13 March 1834 until his death. On the presentation of the dean and chapter of Winchester he became vicar of Romsey, Hampshire, a living he held from 30 November 1840 until his death, where he restored the abbey church from his own private fortune. He was married, firstly, in February 1806, to Charlotte Sophia (d. 31 Aug 1838), daughter of Sir Lucius

O'Brien, bt, with whom he had six daughters, and, secondly, on 15 May 1841, to Susan (d. 14 Feb 1890), daughter of Sir John Kennaway.

Noel was well-connected in the clerical world, not only through his influential family but also through his close friendships with William and (later) Samuel Wilberforce. His theology was Calvinistic and premillennialist. In 1828 he published his most influential work, *A Brief Enquiry into the Prospects of the Church of Christ*. Anxious, tormented even, by the rising tide of liberalism and secularism within contemporary society, Noel attempted to present Christianity in a manner which would enable it to contend against the new thinking. His response was somewhat pessimistic in nature, arguing that 'the ages which have unfolded their successive eras since the first advent of our Lord, have been ages of night and woe'. He then invited his fellow Christians 'to a more distinct recognition of the authority of Christ as the constituted Governor of *this world*' (Noel, *A Brief Enquiry*, 8–9), an authority which is not to be manifested until his second advent. Moreover, he claimed, every man should be diligent in doing his duty in his appointed place, until that time comes. Perhaps ironically, as the millennialist movement began to gain momentum, Noel became a critic of the Albury circle, founders of the Catholic Apostolic church, with its separatist ecclesiology and deeply pessimistic pronouncements, especially after the appearance of the 'gifts' among Edward Irving's congregation at Regent Square.

Like his celebrated brother, Noel achieved a certain prominence as an evangelical preacher. His other publications included *A Selection of Psalms and Hymns for Public Worship* (1810), *Arvendel; or, Sketches in Italy and Switzerland* (1826), *Fifty Sermons for the Use of Families* (2 vols., 1826–7), and *Sermons, Preached at Romsey*, with a preface by Samuel Wilberforce (1853). He died at Romsey vicarage on 24 February 1851, and was buried at Romsey. Noel was a kind, generous, and popular man. As Bishop Wilberforce enquired in his preface to Noel's Romsey sermons, 'And where in the English Church was he not known? And where was he known without being beloved?'   GRAYSON CARTER

Sources Boase, *Mod. Eng. biog.* · Venn, *Alum. Cant.* · *GM*, 2nd ser., 35 (1851), 446 · J. Julian, ed., *A dictionary of hymnology* (1892), 809 · archbishop's act book, LPL, MS VB 1/13, 304 · J. Foster, ed., *Index ecclesiasticus; or, Alphabetical lists of all ecclesiastical dignitaries in England and Wales since the Reformation* (1890), 130 · W. H. Oliver, *Prophets and millennialists: the use of biblical prophecy in England from the 1790s to the 1840s* (1978), 74–8, 95–6, 126

Archives Exton Park, Rutland, Noel family MSS · Leics. RO, Noel family MSS · priv. coll., Noel family MSS

Likenesses J. Cooper, mezzotint (after W. Say), BM, NPG · W. Say, mezzotint (after J. Cooper), BM, NPG

Noel, Henry (d. 1597), courtier, was the second son of Sir Andrew Noel (d. 1562) of Dalby on the Wolds, Leicestershire, and his second wife, Elizabeth (fl. 1550), daughter of John Hopton and widow of Sir John Perient. He matriculated as a pensioner at Peterhouse, Cambridge, at Michaelmas 1568, but did not take a degree. He sailed, as did Walter Ralegh, on Sir Humphrey Gilbert's voyage of exploration in 1578, aboard the ship commanded by Ralegh's brother, Carew. By May of the following year

Noel resided in London, where a warrant for his arrest charged him and John Wotton with an assault on John Parker, gentleman. Noel suffered no lasting inconvenience from this affair, despite the fact that one of Parker's servants was killed in the fray. He participated in the 'Fortress of perfect beauty' tiltyard show held to honour the Anjou marriage negotiations in May 1581, and joined the scores of courtiers who accompanied Anjou to Rochester on his departure from England in February 1582. Noel was again in trouble with the authorities in July 1583, when William Fleetwood, recorder of London, complained to Burghley that a servant of 'M. Nowell of the Court' had killed a carman, whereupon Noel had pleaded his status at court to block Fleetwood's efforts to indict him and his servant for the crime.

Noel was an established courtier by June 1584 when a royal warrant described him as 'our trustie and welbeloued seruante Henry Noell' (Hunt. L., EL 1328) in the course of granting him the right to search out and hold in fee farm lands concealed from the crown to the value of 100 marks per annum. No Elizabethan document records his alleged membership in the band of gentleman pensioners, nor his tenure of any office at court. His name does appear, however, on the lists of new year's gift exchanges with the queen in 1584 and 1586. He jousted in every accession day tilt from 1583 to 1595 except for the 1592 running. George Peele described his participation on two of these occasions, in his *Polyhymnia* (1590) and in *Anglorum feriae* (1595). Noel was created MA during the queen's progress to Oxford on 27 September 1592. Sir John Harington termed him 'one of the great gallants' of his time (Harington, 141). In his *Apophthegms*, Sir Francis Bacon recalled Noel's quip 'That courtiers were like fasting-days; They were next the holydays, but in themselves they were the most meagre days of the week' (Spedding, 13.379). In spite of this complaint, Noel's rewards as a courtier were far from meagre. In addition to the patent to obtain concealed lands, he was granted a lease in reversion worth 100 marks yearly in 1589, a free gift of more than £668 in 1592, and in the following year a monopoly to import stone and earthen pots, bottles, and heath for brushes.

Noel apparently owed his seats in the parliaments of 1589 (Morpeth) and 1593 (Cricklade) to the favour, respectively, of Henry, first Lord Hunsdon, and of Giles Chandos, third Lord Chandos. His circle at court also included Ralegh and Henry Percy, ninth earl of Northumberland. To Ralegh's poetic rebus on his name:

> The word of denial and the letter of fifty
> Makes the gent. name that will never be thrifty

Noel is said to have replied with:

> The foe to the stommacke, and the word of disgrace
> Shewes the gent. name with the bold face.
> (*Diary of John Manningham*, 162)

Noel is also credited with one other poem, the pastoral lament 'Of Disdainfull Daphne' subscribed 'M. H. Nowell' in *Englands Helicon* (1600). It is possible that he collaborated with Sir Christopher Hatton and three others on the Inner Temple play *Gismond of Salern*. A 'Hen No' was connected

with this play, but its production at court about 1567 seems too early for Noel, who matriculated at Cambridge in the following year.

Noel's other intellectual interests gained him a modest reputation as a patron. In 1585 he received the dedication of Thomas Watson's *Amyntas* in Latin verse, and at about the same time the dedication of Watson's *Compendium memoriae localis*. In the same year, Charles Turnbull dedicated to Noel his *Treatise … of the Use of the Celestiall Globe*, a book on astronomical and geographical measurements. Turnbull's brother, Richard, dedicated his *Exposition upon the XV. Psalme* to Noel in 1592, noting that Charles had been 'reading vnto your worship the Mathematiques' at the time of his earlier dedication (sig. A3). Noel signed a letter to the musician John Dowland, 'your olde Master and Frend' (Doughtie, 612), and both Thomas Morley and Thomas Weelkes published elegiac songs in his honour after his death.

Noel never married. In a letter to Sir Robert Cecil of 3 August 1593 he complained of illness and begged permission to leave the court for a journey to Spa. Whether or not this was a sign of failing health, he died in London on 26 February 1597, as a result, according to Fuller's *Worthies*, of over-exerting himself in a game of balloon. At the queen's direction he was buried in St Andrew's Chapel, Westminster.   STEVEN W. MAY

Sources Venn, *Alum. Cant.* · APC, *1578–80*, 121, 128 · S. W. May, *The Elizabethan courtier poets* (1991) · HoP, *Commons, 1558–1603* · H. Ellis, ed., *Original letters illustrative of English history*, 3rd ser., 4 (1846); facs. edn (1969) · J. Harington, *A supplie or addicion to the catalogue of bishops to the yeare 1608*, ed. R. H. Miller (1979) · *The letters and life of Francis Bacon*, ed. J. Spedding, 7 vols. (1861–74) · *The diary of John Manningham of the Middle Temple, 1602–1603*, ed. R. P. Sorlien (Hanover, NH, 1976) · E. Doughtie, *Lyrics from English airs* (1970) · *The household papers of Henry Percy, ninth earl of Northumberland, 1564–1632*, ed. G. R. Batho, CS, 3rd ser., 93 (1962) · Hunt. L., MS EL 1328 · *DNB*

Noel, John Baptist Lucius (1890–1989), mountaineer and photographer, was born on 26 February 1890 at Newton Abbot, Devon, the third and youngest son of Colonel the Hon. Edward Noel (1852–1917) and his wife, Ruth Lucas (d. 1926), daughter of W. H. Lucas of Trenif?e, Cornwall. He was baptized Baptist Lucius and added the name John by deed poll in 1908. His father, the younger son of the second earl of Gainsborough, was a prominent soldier and military historian. Noel was educated at Lausanne, Switzerland, but often skipped classes to visit the mountains. His mother was an artist and encouraged him to study painting in Florence. His father's influence prevailed and he attended Sandhurst, though he passed into the regular army, not the Indian army, to his father's disappointment. In 1909 he was commissioned as second lieutenant, and applied to join the East Yorkshire regiment since it was stationed in northern India.

Noel's regiment spent summers in the hills of the Himalayas and he spent his leave plotting routes through the forests of Sikkim towards Tibet. After being promoted lieutenant in 1912, he took his leave in 1913 and travelled in disguise and without permission across an unguarded pass into Tibet with three Himalayan guides. Tibetan authorities forced Noel to turn back when he got within

40 miles of Mount Everest, 'nearer at that time than any white man had been' (Noel, 62). When war started in 1914, Noel was on leave in Britain and joined the King's Own Yorkshire light infantry, as his own regiment was still in India. During the retreat from Mons he was taken prisoner by the Germans. He escaped and made his way through enemy lines, travelling at night by the stars. He rejoined his regiment at Ypres and was promoted captain in 1915, the year of his marriage to Sybil Graham (d. 1939), an actress whom he had met in Kashmir. He was decorated with the 1914–15 star, the British war medal, and a victory medal. In 1917 he became an instructor in the machine-gun corps and was temporary major from 1918 to 1920. From 1920 he served as revolver instructor at the small arms school at Hythe, Kent, and wrote several pamphlets on revolvers and automatic pistols, as well as publishing, jointly with his wife, a collection of cooking recipes for soldiers.

In 1919 Noel gave a lecture on his pre-war travels in Tibet at the Royal Geographical Society. Sir Francis Younghusband orchestrated the press coverage of Noel's paper to generate interest in a British expedition to climb Everest, an effort that bore fruit in 1921, when Tibet gave permission for the ascent. Noel joined the second Everest expedition in 1922 as photographer and film-maker. He had been interested in cinematography since the age of fourteen, when he saw Herbert Ponting's Antarctic film sixteen times. After the war, when he was stationed in northern Persia guarding oilfields, he made a short film about the caviar industry on the Caspian Sea. Since the army would not grant him leave for Everest in 1922, Noel retired and was granted the rank of major.

Noel's silent film *Climbing Mt. Everest* (1922) combines elements of adventure film and ethnographic travelogue. Extended sequences depict the manners and customs of Tibet, 'devil dances' at the Rongbuk monastery at the foot of Everest, as well as the ascent of the mountain. Noel's technical achievements—filming with a Newman Sinclair camera at 23,000 feet and developing film under harsh conditions in a tent at 16,000 feet—were overshadowed by the expedition's failure to reach the summit.

In 1924 Noel formed Explorer Films Ltd, with Younghusband as chairman, and paid £8000 for the film and photographic rights to Everest. He posted letters from Tibet with his own Everest stamp, and sent his film to Darjeeling for developing by Arthur Pereira, who in turn sent extracts to Pathé news. Noel also made innovative use of telephoto lenses and time-lapse film techniques. His silent film *The Epic of Everest* (1924) contrasted the masculine climbers with the mystical Tibetans, and suggested that spiritual forces on Mount Everest might be responsible for the disappearance of George Mallory and Andrew Irvine. Noel exhibited his film in London with dances by a group of monks from the Tibetan Buddhist monastery at Gyantse. Officials in Tibet, Sikkim, and Bhutan were offended by certain scenes in the film and by the performances of the monks, who had not been given permission to leave Tibet. The Dalai Lama saw pictures of the monks in newspapers and said he considered 'the whole affair as a direct affront to the religion of which he is the head' (Hansen, 737). The controversy over the 'dancing lamas' led to the cancellation of future Everest expeditions and a chill in Anglo-Tibetan relations, and Noel became *persona non grata* among British diplomats, geographers, and mountaineers for almost thirty years.

Noel's American lecture tour without the monks enjoyed great success, as did the American edition of his book *Through Tibet to Everest* (1927; repr., 1931, 1989), which was not as well promoted in Britain. His wife also published *Magic Bird of Chomolungma* (1931), about Tibetan folk-tales she had collected in Tibet in 1924. British diplomats curtly rebuffed Noel's attempts to organize Himalayan

John Baptist Lucius Noel (1890–1989), self-portrait, 1924

expeditions in the 1930s. He filled out an application to become a naturalized American citizen, but the paperwork was misplaced.

Noel was Roman Catholic, and one of his uncles was private secretary to several popes. Pope Pius XI, who was also a climber, sent his blessings to Noel's Everest endeavours and invited him to the canonization of St Bernadette at St Peter's in Rome in 1933. Noel surreptitiously shot the only photographs of the ceremony, with a camera disguised as a prayer book. He occasionally lectured on St Bernadette's story, and his photographs of the canonization were later given to the Society of Our Lady of Lourdes.

After his first wife died in 1939, Noel married Mary Sullivan (d. 1984), daughter of John Sullivan, clerk, on 17 November 1941 at the church of the Immaculate Conception, Barnstaple, Devon. They had one daughter, Sandra, in 1943. During 1941-3 he joined the intelligence corps and was restored to the rank of captain. He worked out the best supply-route from India to Burma, and it was briefly known as the Noel Road before being renamed the Stilwell Road. In 1944 he moved to Smarden, Kent, and restored several old homes.

After the first ascent of Everest in 1953, Noel began to give mountaineering lectures again with his films and hand-coloured photographs. Younger climbers and filmmakers often visited him at Romney Marsh, Kent, to hear his eyewitness account of the disappearance of Mallory and Irvine, and he became something of an elderly sage from the 1960s to the 1980s. Footage from his Everest films appeared in many subsequent mountaineering films and television programmes. Noel's version of events also strongly influenced histories of the Everest expeditions written during this period.

Noel stood 6 feet 2 inches in his prime, and was known for his showmanship, mischievous humour, and an imperious demeanour that mellowed with age into an Edwardian charm. He died of pneumonia and great old age on 12 March 1989 at Ashford Nursing Home, 407 Hythe Road, Ashford, Kent. He was cremated at Charing and a memorial service was held on 24 April at St Mary's, Cadogan Street, London. No diaries or papers survived, but his films and photographs remain a vivid and lasting legacy.

PETER H. HANSEN

Sources J. B. L. Noel, *Through Tibet to Everest* (1927) · P. H. Hansen, 'The dancing lamas of Everest: cinema, orientalism and Anglo-Tibetan relations in the 1920s', *American Historical Review*, 101 (1996), 712-47 · W. Unsworth, *Everest* (1981) · K. Brownlow, *The war, the west and the wilderness* (1979), 452-64 · D. Clark, 'Capt. Noel's 1922 conquest of Everest', *American Cinematographer*, 71/8 (Aug 1990), 36-40 · private information (2004) [Sandra Noel] · *The Independent* (16 March 1989) · *The Guardian* (17 March 1989) · *The Times* (13 March 1989) · *Daily Telegraph* (13 March 1989) · *GJ*, 155 (1989), 445-6 · *Mountain*, 128 (1989), 42-3 · *Sunday Times* (28 Sept 1969) · Burke, *Peerage* (1999) [Gainsborough] · file, Sci. Mus., ScM 1008/18/06 · private information [G. Hattersley-Smith] [typescript] · ministry of defence records · m. cert. [Mary Sullivan] · d. cert. · *Debrett's Peerage*

Archives priv. coll., photographs | RGS, Everest expedition archives · RGS, photographic library | FILM BFI NFTVA · British Pathé, London, newsreel collection | SOUND BL NSA

Likenesses J. B. L. Noel, self-portrait, photograph, 1924, RGS [*see illus.*] · photographs, repro. in Clark, 'Capt. Noel's 1922 conquest of Everest'

Wealth at death £95,976: probate, 21 Aug 1989, *CGPLA Eng. & Wales* · £50,178: *The Independent*, 19 Sept 1989

Noel, Roden Berkeley Wriothesley (1834-1894), poet and essayist, was born in London on 27 August 1834, the fourth son of Charles Noel, Lord Barham (1781-1866), who was created earl of Gainsborough in 1841. His mother, Frances Jocelyn (d. 1897), second daughter of Robert Jocelyn, third earl of Roden, was his father's fourth wife. Noel considered himself an Irishman through her influence. He grew up at his family seat, Exton Park in Rutland, but spent a lot of time with his maternal grandfather at Tolleymore.

Noel was sent to Harrow School for two years (1847-9), and then spent five years under private tuition in Wiltshire (1849-54) before entering Trinity College, Cambridge, in 1854 with a view to studying for the church. He graduated MA in 1858 but decided that the church was not his vocation. During the next two years he travelled in the East, and he met the de Broë family while ill in Beirut. On 21 March 1863 he married the eldest daughter, Alice Maria Caroline de Broë (d. 1919). They had three children—Frances (b. 1864), Conrad le Despenser Roden *Noel (b. 1869), and Eric (b. 1871)—and lived in Kew, London.

The year he married, Noel published his first work, *Behind the Veil, and other Poems*. He became a groom of the privy chamber to Queen Victoria in 1867, a post he was to hold until 1871. In 1868 he published *Beatrice, and other Poems*, in which he was markedly influenced by Shelley. However, the work which was best received and which remained most popular with his contemporaries was *A Little Child's Monument* (1881), inspired by Eric's death in 1877 at the age of five. E. C. Stedman compared it favourably with his more 'laboured' volumes *The Red Flag and other Poems* (1872) and *The House of Ravensburg*, a five-act verse drama (1877).

Besides poetry, Noel's works included *A Life of Lord Byron* (1890), and he edited a selection of Edmund Spenser's poems (1887) and the plays of Thomas Otway (1888). His critical essays included papers on Thomas Chatterton, Byron, Shelley, Wordsworth, Keats, Victor Hugo, Tennyson, and Walt Whitman, and these were issued as *Essays upon Poetry and Poets* in 1886. A selection from his poems, with a prefatory notice by his friend Robert Buchanan, was issued in the Canterbury Poets series in 1892. Noel died very suddenly of a heart attack on 26 May 1894 while in a taxi in the city of Mainz, Germany. His wife survived him.

JESSICA HININGS

Sources J. A. Symonds, 'The Hon. Roden Noel, 1834-1894', *The poets and the poetry of the nineteenth century*, ed. A. H. Miles, 6 (1905), 81-8 · *The Athenaeum* (2 June 1894), 711-12 · Venn, *Alum. Cant.* · Burke, *Peerage* · *GM*, 4th ser., 5 (1868), 531 · *GM*, 3rd ser., 19 (1865) · *The Times* (28 May 1894) · E. C. Stedman, *Victorian poets*, 13th edn (1887) · D. J. O'Donoghue, *The poets of Ireland: a biographical and bibliographical dictionary* (1912)

Archives Ransom HRC, papers | BL, corresp. with Macmillans, Add. MS 55007 · BL, letters to W. E. Gladstone, Add. MSS 44444-44517 · Bodl. Oxf., letters to Bertram Dobell · NL Scot., letters to

Blackwoods • TCD, letters to Edward Dowden • U. Reading L., letters to C. E. Mathews • UCL, corresp. with G. C. Robertson
Wealth at death £11,676 9s. 10d.: probate, 9 July 1894, CGPLA Eng. & Wales

Noel, Thomas (1799–1861), poet, was born at Kirkby Mallory on 11 May 1799, the eldest son of the Revd Thomas Noel (1774/5–1854), who had been presented to the livings of Kirkby Mallory and Elmsthorpe, both in Leicestershire, by his kinsman Thomas Noel, Viscount Wentworth, in 1798, and held them until his death. Thomas Noel graduated BA from Merton College, Oxford, in 1824. On 29 January 1831 he married Emily Anne, the youngest daughter of Captain Halliday of Ham Lodge, Twickenham; they had two children.

In 1833 Noel issued a series of stanzas on proverbs and scriptural texts, entitled *The Cottage Muse* and in 1841 *Village Verse* and *Rymes and Roundelayes*. The latter volume includes verses focusing on the scenery of the Thames, a version of the 'Rat-Tower Legend', the 'Poor Voter's Song', and the 'Pauper's Drive', often wrongly attributed to Thomas Hood. The 'Pauper's Drive' was set to music by Henry Russell in 1839. Noel also wrote the words of the familiar song 'Rocked in the Cradle of the Deep'. Among other friends he counted Thomas Vardon, the librarian of the House of Commons, and Lady Byron, the wife of the poet, who was a distant connection. In 1858 Noel and his family went to live at Brighton, where he died, at 5 Landsdown Street, on 22 May 1861. His wife survived him.

THOMAS SECCOMBE, rev. MEGAN A. STEPHAN

Sources N&Q, 10 (1854), 285, 350, 453 • N&Q, 7th ser., 12 (1891), 486 • N&Q, 8th ser., 1 (1892), 153 • N&Q, 8th ser., 6 (1894), 52 • Allibone, Dict. • Boase, Mod. Eng. biog., 2.1160 • J. Payn, Some literary recollections (1884), 87–92 • M. R. Mitford, Recollections of a literary life, new edn, 1 (1857), 41, 51–5 • GM, 2nd ser., 41 (1854), 214–15 • Daily Telegraph (30 June 1894) • Foster, Alum. Oxon. • IGI
Archives Bodl. Oxf., letters and poems to Lady Byron
Wealth at death £5000: probate, 17 June 1861, CGPLA Eng. & Wales

Noel, William (1695–1762), judge, was born on 19 March 1695, the second son of Sir John Noel, fourth baronet (c.1668–1697), of Kirkby Mallory, Leicestershire, and his wife, Mary (d. 1751), youngest daughter and coheir of Sir John Clobery of Winchester, Hampshire, and Bradstone, Devon. He was educated at Lichfield grammar school and in 1713 matriculated at Pembroke College, Cambridge. His training as a lawyer began in 1717 when he was admitted a student at the Inner Temple, and he was called to the bar in 1721. He had already married Elizabeth, a younger daughter of Sir Thomas Trollope, third baronet, of Casewick, Lincolnshire; they had four daughters.

The opportunity to enter parliament came very shortly after the 1722 general election when a client, the Hon. Brownlow Cecil, succeeding his father as earl of Exeter, vacated his borough seat for Stamford, Lincolnshire, in Noel's favour, whereafter Noel retained the seat until the 1747 election. The town's corporation also chose Noel as its deputy recorder. A tory, he acted in opposition to Sir Robert Walpole's ministry, as did his elder brother, Sir Clobery Noel, fifth baronet, who was elected knight of the shire for Leicestershire in 1727. It was consequently some time before he began to make progress on the ladder of legal preferment. In December 1731 he was one of the counsel defending Richard Franklyn, who had been put on trial for libelling the government in *The Craftsman*, the principal mouthpiece of the 'country' opposition, but in the opinion of the tory leader in the Commons, Sir William Wyndham, only Noel, 'who spoke extremely well' (Colley), made any impression in an otherwise poorly presented case. He became a king's counsel in February 1738 and in April a bencher at his inn of court, the Inner Temple.

The early 1740s saw a degree of moderation enter his political behaviour; in February 1741, for instance, he declined to support the motion calling for Walpole's removal from office, and after Walpole's fall early in 1742 was nominated by both the court and the opposition to serve on the 'secret committee' to inquire into the former premier's conduct in office. Though initially a supporter of the incoming Wilmington ministry, he subsequently tended to steer an independent line in the house, committing himself to neither government nor opposition. By the mid-1740s he had all but lost his tory identity and was now seen as an 'old whig'. At Carlisle in September 1746 he acted as leading counsel for the crown against several Jacobite rebels, and in December was appointed one of the Commons managers of the impeachment of the Jacobite Lord Lovat, during the course of which in March 1747 he responded to technical objections raised by Lovat in his defence.

Noel's political alignment with Henry Pelham's ministry by the time of the 1747 election was most clearly witnessed in his being elected for the Cornish borough of West Looe on the government interest. In October 1749 he was appointed chief justice of Chester. He unsuccessfully sought the office of master of the rolls from Lord Chancellor Hardwicke; but on 3 May 1757, through Hardwicke's influence, he was finally raised to the judicial bench as justice of the common pleas, relinquishing his seat in parliament but retaining his post as Chester judge. He was not, however, given the customary knighthood. Horace Walpole thought him 'a pompous man of little solidity', though when once observing him give opinion before the House of Lords, Walpole conceded that his manner was 'like Lord Mansfield's, and very rapid and full of fire' (Walpole). Noel died on 8 December 1762.   A. A. HANHAM

Sources HoP, Commons, 1715–54, 1.214; 2.297 • HoP, Commons, 1754–90, 3.203 • J. Nichols, The history and antiquities of the county of Leicester, 4/2 (1811), 767, 770 • Foss, Judges, 8.349–51 • L. Colley, In defiance of oligarchy: the tory party, 1714–60 (1982), 225 • Sainty, Judges, 81 • Sainty, King's counsel, 92 • W. R. Williams, The history of the great sessions in Wales, 1542–1830 (privately printed, Brecon, 1899), 47 • State trials, 17.662–3 • will, PRO, PROB 11/882 • H. Walpole, Memoirs of King George II, ed. J. Brooke, 3 (1985), 20 • GM, 1st ser., 32 (1762), 600
Likenesses W. Gauci, lithograph (after portrait), BM, NPG
Wealth at death Bloomsbury Square residence; estates in Leicestershire and Lincolnshire: will, PRO, PROB 11/882

Noel-Baker. For this title name see Baker, Philip John Noel-, Baron Noel-Baker (1889–1982).

Noel-Buxton. For this title name *see* Buxton, Noel Edward Noel-, first Baron Noel-Buxton (1869–1948); Buxton, Lucy Edith Noel-, Lady Noel-Buxton (1888–1960).

Noell, Sir Martin (*bap.* **1614**, *d.* **1665**), financier and merchant, was baptized in Stafford on 11 March 1614, the son of Edward Noell and his wife, and cousin, Grace, also born Noell. He had at least two brothers and a sister. He was probably apprenticed as a London scrivener and continued to be an active member of the Scriveners' Company throughout his life. In 1648 he was serving as a commissioner for the militia and for the collection of tax arrears in London, by which time he had also already branched out into commerce, being recorded as a ship-owner.

Noell's true métier appeared in 1651 with his appointment as co-farmer of the excise on salt; he combined this with actually managing the salt works in North and South Shields, buttressing his position by obtaining quasi-monopoly rights in that commodity. During the course of the decade, with or without partners, he took on the farming of more revenues, and in 1657–9 he was co-postmaster-general with John Thurloe who may have been a relative by marriage. Associated with Thomas Povey in trying to promote a West India company, Noell was also active in the Levant and East India companies.

Noell sat for his home town of Stafford in the second protectorate parliament of 1656–8, but is recorded as a more active speaker in the 1659 parliament of Richard Cromwell. He spoke vigorously in support of the protector's Baltic policy, arguing that England's commercial interests required a strong anti-Dutch and so pro-Swedish stance, even at the risk of war. Later in the session he had to defend himself against accusations of having made an illicit profit out of transporting captured Irish, Scottish, and English royalist soldiers, political prisoners, and convicted criminals to Barbados; he denied not the facts of such transportation but the allegations of cruelty and profiteering arising therefrom. He also came under attack in his capacity as a revenue farmer and would-be monopolist. A small pointer to Noell's wealth is his having paid £520 at the end of 1657 to avoid becoming an alderman of the City.

It was through his West Indian interests that Noell's career most obviously spanned the Restoration. None the less, his fall from favour and loss of revenue farms and offices under the restored Commonwealth of 1659 may have been what stood him in best stead in the following year, rather than secret payments to the royalist cause before May 1660, for which there is no evidence beyond inference. Samuel Pepys was a little surprised at Noell's knighthood in 1662; whether it is sufficiently explained by the resumption of his dual role as West India lobbyist and as revenue farmer and government creditor remains an open question. Noell also had Irish interests, for the better protection of which he became a member of the Irish parliament from 1661 to his death from the plague on 29 September 1665 at his home in the parish of St Olave Jewry, London. His wife, Elizabeth, survived him by only two

weeks, dying on 13 October. Noell was survived by five sons and two daughters. That his eldest son was knighted within a month of Noell's death suggests continuing royal favour, although his executors did not escape unwelcome attention from royal revenue officials, notably in connection with allegations of his having profited improperly from the gains of privateering—England and Spain remaining technically at war until some little time after the Restoration.

Historians have differed in their judgements of Noell's importance. In the story of relations between government and City, the worlds of high politics and high finance, his career helps to fill the gap after the revenue farmers and disbursing officials of early Stuart times and before the goldsmiths, proto-bankers, and other financial fixers of the later seventeenth century. He died a rich but not fabulously wealthy man, having already settled much of his property and set up a substantial charity in his native town.

G. E. AYLMER, *rev.*

Sources G. E. Aylmer, *The state's servants: the civil service of the English republic, 1649–1660* (1973) • Pepys, *Diary* • *APC* • *CSP col.* • W. A. Shaw, ed., *Calendar of treasury books*, 1, PRO (1904) • A. B. Beaven, ed., *The aldermen of the City of London, temp. Henry III–[1912]*, 2 vols. (1908–13) • BL, Add. MS 11411 • BL, Egerton MS 2345

Nokes [Noke], **James** (*c.*1642–1696), actor, was born, probably in London, of obscure parents; one report says his father kept a toyshop in Cornhill, a district in which Nokes lived for a number of years. The family name is often spelt Noke (his will uses this spelling both for James Nokes and several nephews and cousins), though theatrical records and other contemporary accounts usually call him Nokes or Noakes.

Nokes began his career as a boy actor, playing women's parts, in the company of John Rhodes at the Cockpit in Drury Lane, London (1659–60). Other members of this company included his older brother Robert Nokes (*d.* 1673), Thomas Betterton, and, among others who 'commonly Acted Womens Parts', Edward Kynaston and Edward Angel (Downes, 43–6). In November 1660 he became one of the original members and shareholders of the Duke's Company, under the management of Sir William Davenant, along with Betterton and Robert Nokes, and in spite of his youth was considered responsible enough to act as one of Davenant's three deputies in overseeing the accounts. Though he was not formally sworn as member of the company and servant of the duke of York until 1668 (possibly because he was under age at the time of the opening of the new theatre at Lincoln's Inn Fields in 1662), he was acting adult male roles in 1664, the year of his first comic part, as Sir Nicholas Cully in Sir George Etherege's *The Comical Revenge*, a play which 'got the Company more Reputation and Profit than any preceding Comedy' (ibid., 57). He soon became the leading comic actor of his time.

Nokes's career as comic actor in the Duke's Company (and later the United Company) lasted nearly thirty years. According to the *Oxford English Dictionary* and dictionaries of slang the word 'nokes' during this time came to mean a fool, a ninny, a dullard. One of his most celebrated roles was the bumbling Sir Martin in John Dryden's *Sir Martin Mar-All* (1667), a part which Dryden 'Adapted ... purposely for the Mouth of Mr. *Nokes*': 'All the Parts being very Just and Exactly perform'd, especially Sir Martin and his Man ... several others have come very near him, but none Equall'd Mr. *Nokes* in *Sir Martin*' (Downes, 62). The play proved extraordinarily popular: Samuel Pepys, who found it 'the most entire piece of Mirth ... that certainly was ever writ', saw it eight times and Charles II at least nine times (Edmond, 198). Cibber describes his performance and the reaction of the audience, commenting that Nokes was able to produce 'General Laughter' by his 'silent Eloquence', without speaking.

> In the Character of Sir *Martin Marrall*, who is always committing Blunders to the Prejudice of his own Interest ... and was, afterwards afraid to look his governing Servant, and Counsellor in the Face; what a copious, and distressful Harangue have I seen him make, with his Looks (while the House has been in one continued Roar, for several Minutes) before he could prevail with his Courage to speak a Word to him! ... What Tragedy ever shew'd us such a Tumult of Passions, rising, at once in one Bosom! (Cibber, 83–4)

Another comic part in which Nokes excelled was Old Jorden in Edward Ravenscroft's *The Citizen Turn'd Gentleman, or, Mamamouchi* (1671), performed at the company's new theatre at Dorset Garden. According to Downes, 'this Comedy was looked upon by the Cricticks for a Foolish Play; yet it continued Acting 9 Days with a full House'. Dryden objected to the character Nokes played as an

> unnatural strain'd Buffoon ... such a Fop
> As would appear a Monster in a shop.
> (Hume, 276)

Nevertheless Ravenscroft's farce, largely because of Nokes's performance in the principal role, was a great success: 'Mr. *Nokes* in performing the *Mamamouchi* pleas'd the King and Court, next *Sir Martin*, above all Plays' (Downes, 70). An extended passage in William Wycherley's *The Gentleman Dancing-Master* (1672) compares the comic actors Nokes and Angel, concluding that Nokes is 'a better Fool' who can serve as a model for fops in 'all the beaux monde' (III.i.39–71); as Holland says, the lines gain additional ironic point by being spoken on stage by Nokes himself as the affected Monsieur de Paris (Holland, 63–4).

After Angel's death in 1673 Nokes regularly played opposite Anthony Leigh. Many plays, according to Cibber, 'liv'd only by the extraordinary Performance of *Nokes* and *Leigh*': 'when *Nokes* acted with [Leigh] in the same Play, they return'd the Ball so dexterously upon one another that every Scene between them, seem'd but one continu'd Rest of Excellence' (Cibber, 86–7). Among the roles played by Nokes, mostly opposite Leigh, between the mid-1670s and his retirement from the stage in 1692, were Sir Davy Dunce in Thomas Otway's *The Soldier's Fortune*, Vinditius (based on Titus Oates) in Nathaniel Lee's *Lucius Junius Brutus*, Gomez in Dryden's *The Spanish Fryar* (three of the six parts Nokes played in the year 1681), Sir Cautious Fulbank in Behn's *The Lucky Chance* (1687), and the title role in Shadwell's *The Squire of Alsatia* (1688). He was especially known for comic transvestite roles, such as the Nurse in Otway's *Caius Marius*, an adaptation of *Romeo and Juliet* (1680), the

Nurse in Henry Nevil Payne's *The Fatal Jealousy* (1672), and Lady Beardly in Thomas D'Urfey's *Virtuous Wife* (1680), parts for which he gained the nickname Nurse Nokes.

Cibber describes Nokes as 'an Actor of a quite different Genius from any I have ever read, heard of, or seen, since or before his Time', one characterized by 'a plain and palpable Simplicity of Nature, which was so utterly his own, that he was often as unaccountably diverting in his common Speech, as on the Stage'. His acting style was essentially naturalistic, that of a 'strict ... Observer of Nature', giving the impression that it did not 'cost him an Hour's Labour to arrive at that high Reputation he had, and deserved':

> I saw him once, giving an Account of some Table-talk, to another Actor behind the Scenes, which, a Man of Quality accidentally listening to, was so deceiv'd by his Manner, that he ask'd him, if that was a new Play, he was rehearsing? (Cibber, 82–3, 85)

Cibber speaks of 'the ridiculous Solemnity of Nokes's Features' which prompted laughter and 'involuntary Applause' even 'at his first Entrance in a Play', and suggested that, like many clowns, he had the gift of pathos:

> In the ludicrous Distresses, which by the Laws of Comedy, Folly is often involv'd in; he sunk into such a mixture of piteous Pusillanimity, and a Consternation so rufully ridiculous and inconsolable, that when he had shook you, to a Fatigue of Laughter, it became a moot point, whether you ought not to have pity'd him. When he debated any matter by himself, he would shut up his Mouth with a dumb studious Powt, and roll his full Eye, into such a vacant Amazement, such a palpable Ignorance of what to think of it, that his silent Perplexity (which would sometimes hold him several Minutes) gave your Imagination as full Content, as the most absurd thing he could say upon it. (ibid., 83–4)

Nokes continued as a shareholder in the Duke's Company, and in 1674 held one and a half shares (of twenty). When he retired from acting, he had accumulated considerable wealth, investing some of it in the purchase of a country house in Totteridge, near Barnet, Hertfordshire (he also had lodgings in Cornhill, London, and a house in 'Essex buildings', which he left to his two nephews). At his death in September 1696 at Totteridge, his estate was valued at over £1500 a year, and included a thirty-sixth share in the New River Waterworks company, bringing water from the countryside to London. His principal legatee was his cousin Frances Noke, who was to receive an annual payment of £100 from his shares in the water company and inherited his remaining 'goods and chattels', including the house at Totteridge. There were also generous legacies to his nephews Charles and William Noke (possibly the sons of Robert Nokes) and their six children, as well as to the two trustees, Benjamin Huxley and Geoffrey Richards, to whom the New River company shares were bequeathed. According to Cibber, Nokes as comic actor 'never was tolerably touch'd by any of his successors', and when later actors performed the roles of Nokes and Leigh, 'the Characters were quite sunk, and alter'd' (Cibber, 86).

WARREN CHERNAIK

Sources C. Cibber, *An apology for the life of Colley Cibber*, new edn, ed. B. R. S. Fone (1968) · J. Downes, *Roscius Anglicanus*, ed. J. Milhous and R. D. Hume, new edn (1987) · Highfill, Burnim & Langhans,

BDA • Genest, *Eng. stage* • W. Van Lennep and others, eds., *The London stage, 1660–1800*, pt 1: *1660–1700* (1965) • L. Hotson, *The Commonwealth and Restoration stage* (1928) • P. Holland, *The ornament of action: text and performance in Restoration comedy* (1979) • M. Edmond, *Rare Sir William Davenant* (1987) • R. D. Hume, *The development of English drama in the late seventeenth century* (1976) • T. Betterton, [W. Oldys and others], *The history of the English stage* (1741) • T. Davies, *Dramatic miscellanies*, 3 vols. (1784) • T. Brown, *Letters from the dead to the living* (1702) • J. Milhous and R. D. Hume, eds., *A register of English theatrical documents, 1660–1737*, 2 vols. (1991) • W. Wycherley, *Plays*, ed. A. Friedman (1979) • J. L. Chester, ed., *The parish registers of St Michael, Cornhill, London*, Harleian Society, register section, 7 (1882) • J. Doran and R. W. Lowe, 'Their majesties' servants': annals of the English stage, rev. edn, 3 vols. (1888) • C. Leech, T. W. Craik, L. Potter, and others, eds., *The Revels history of drama in English*, 8 vols. (1975–83) • A. Nicoll, *A history of English drama, 1660–1900*, 1 (1952) • *DNB*

Wealth at death £1500 p.a.; at least two houses; shares in New River Wwaterworks company; generous legacies: will, PRO, PROB 11/434 sig. 209; Hotson, *The Commonwealth*, 290

Nolan, Anthony (1971–1979), inspiration of a medical research charity, was born in Australia on 2 December 1971, the son of James Gerald Nolan, haulage company subcontractor, and his wife, Shirley (1942–2002). Anthony was found to be suffering from Wiscott Aldrich syndrome, a rare bone marrow disease which incapacitated his immune system. He required constant medical attention: prone to haemorrhaging, he was anaemic and was so vulnerable to infection that he could not play with children or animals. No suitable donor of bone marrow could be found for Anthony among blood relatives, and his disease was diagnosed as incurable. In 1973 a bone marrow transplant was successfully performed using marrow from a non-relative and Anthony's case seemed more hopeful. His mother took him to London that year hoping to find a donor, but discovered that there was no register of tissue-typed potential donors. She decided to found one, and in 1974 established the Anthony Nolan register at Westminster Children's Hospital, supported by pathologist Dr David James. Financial backing from the Round Table charity enabled the expensive and complex tissue-typing to proceed. In 1978 the register moved to St Mary Abbots Hospital, where the Anthony Nolan Laboratory was opened. Despite its successes no suitable donor could be found for Anthony and on 21 October 1979 at the Westminster Children's Hospital, London, he died aged seven. His mother, however, continued the work in his name. In 1988 the Anthony Nolan Bone Marrow Trust was established and since 1996 the Anthony Nolan Research Institute has undertaken research on bone marrow transplants from two well-equipped laboratories funded by the trust. This work complements the establishment of the register as its aim is to improve the rather low success rate (about 50 per cent) for bone marrow transplants.

By 2000, 2500 donors had been found for transplants through the work of the trust, which maintained a register of more than 300,000 tissue-typed volunteers. It became one of the largest such databases in the world and some fifty registers around the world were modelled on it. International co-operation among trusts further increased the possibility of finding an appropriate unrelated donor for each patient. In 2000 Shirley Nolan was appointed OBE in recognition of her work, which she started for her son but continued to prevent others from sharing his fate. Tragically she began to suffer from Parkinson's disease at the age of only thirty-nine and on 14 July 2002 took her own life, using the manner of her death to campaign for the legislation of euthanasia in Australia, where she had spent her final years.

ELIZABETH BAIGENT

Sources d. cert. • www.anthonynolan.org.uk • private information (2004) [Anthony Nolan Trust] • *The Guardian* (17 July 2002) [obit. Shirley Nolan] • *The Independent* (17 July 2002) [obit. Shirley Nolan] • *The Times* (17 July 2002) [obit. Shirley Nolan]

Nolan, Frederick (1784–1864), theologian, was born at Old Rathmines Castle, co. Dublin, the seat of his grandfather, on 9 February 1784, the third son of Edward Nolan of St Peter's, Dublin, and his wife, Florinda. In 1796 he entered Trinity College, Dublin, but did not graduate, and on 19 November 1803 matriculated at Oxford as a gentleman commoner of Exeter College, chiefly in order to study at the Bodleian and other libraries. He passed his examination for the degree of BCL in 1805, but he did not take it until 1828, when he proceeded DCL at the same time. He opposed plans to reform teaching in the university, attacked new textbooks and also deplored any compromise with dissenters. He was ordained in August 1806, and after serving curacies at Woodford, at Hackney, and at St Benet Fink, London, he was presented, on 25 October 1822, to the vicarage of Prittlewell, Essex. In 1814 he was appointed to preach the Boyle lectures, in 1833 the Bampton lectures at Oxford, and from 1833 to 1836 the Warburtonian lectures; he was the first clergyman to be chosen to deliver these three lecture series in immediate succession.

Nolan was an extreme theological conservative, and strongly opposed to the Oxford Movement (publishing in 1839 *The Catholic Character of Christianity as Recognised by the Reformed Church*, as a reply to Tracts for the Times). His outspoken, reactionary views appealed alike to high-churchmen and evangelicals. His Boyle lectures were published as *The expectations formed by the Assyrians that a great deliverer would appear about the time of Our Lord's advent demonstrated* (1826) and *The Time of the Millennium Investigated* (1831), the latter privately printed at his own press at Prittlewell. He published his Bampton lectures as *The Analogy of Revelation and Science Established* (1833). The lectures attempted to demonstrate the unreliability of science. He published other works of a similar sort, showing an eclectic if outdated knowledge, but failed significantly to influence contemporary thought. For some of his pamphlets he used the pseudonym Sarah Search.

Nolan was elected a fellow of the Royal Society in 1832. He died at his home, Geraldstown House, Navan, co. Meath, on 16 September 1864, and was buried in the ancestral vault in Navan churchyard. He was married, and his wife Angelina survived him. They had no children.

GORDON GOODWIN, rev. H. C. G. MATTHEW

Sources *GM*, 3rd ser., 17 (1864), 788–9 • Boase, *Mod. Eng. biog.* • P. Corsi, *Science and religion: Baden Powell and the Anglican debate, 1800–1860* (1988) • Foster, *Alum. Oxon.* • Allibone, *Dict.* • *CGPLA Eng. & Wales* (1864)

Wealth at death under £6000 in England: probate, 8 Oct 1864, *CGPLA Eng. & Wales* · £8000 in Ireland: probate, 8 Oct 1864, *CGPLA Ire.*

Nolan, Lewis Edward [Louis, Ludwig] (1818–1854), army officer and writer on cavalry, was born on 4 January 1818 in York county, Upper Canada, the second son of John Babington Nolan (1786?–1850), captain 70th foot, and his second wife, Elizabeth (1779–1870), daughter of George Harland Hartley and already twice widowed. Lewis had two stepbrothers and two brothers, all of whom held commissions in either the Austrian or British armies. His grandfather, Babington Nolan, died in 1796 on the West Indian island of St Domingo, serving with the 13th light dragoons.

Shortly after Nolan's birth, the family moved to Scotland and subsequently to Italy, where on half pay his father became British vice-consul in Milan, then Austrian-ruled. Educated at the military college in Milan, on 15 March 1832 Nolan joined the 10th Imperial and Royal Hussars, a Hungarian unit of the Austrian army. Tutored by the famous riding instructor Colonel Haas and later serving with his regiment in Austria's Hungarian and Polish provinces, Nolan's 'great zeal and application' and his skills as a daring horseman and expert swordsman were officially praised. Visiting England in 1838, Lieutenant Nolan attended a royal levée and saw Queen Victoria crowned. Pleading ill health the following year, Nolan returned to his family in Scotland. While nominally in the Austrian army until October, on 15 March 1839 Nolan's name appeared as a cornet through purchase in the 15th (the King's) light dragoons, and he sailed with the regiment to Madras. Nolan's first spell in India was short: on 26 March 1840 he obtained two years' sick leave. On 19 June 1841 Nolan purchased advancement to lieutenant, and on 8 March 1842 was posted to the cavalry depot at Maidstone for a riding master's course. There an instructor noted his 'thoroughly amiable temper, kindness of disposition and really fascinating manner … [he] lived only to be a soldier' (Henderson, 193–4).

Nolan went back to India in May 1843 and was appointed riding master of the 15th light dragoons in August 1844. The following year Major-General Clement Hill commented on his 'active and zealous' work. Socially, Nolan was making his name as an accomplished rider at military race meetings and attending levées, balls, and reviews. In January 1849 he became aide-de-camp to Lieutenant-General Sir George Berkeley, commander-in-chief Madras, and later extra aide-de-camp to the governor, Sir Henry Pottinger. On 8 March 1850, two months after his father's death, Nolan purchased his captaincy, and in January 1851 yet once more secured two years' sick leave. After a short stay in England, in summer 1852 Nolan observed cavalry manoeuvres in Russia, Sweden, and Prussia, before taking command of the 15th light dragoons' depot troop at Maidstone. He led the regiment's detachment at Wellington's funeral.

A slim, dark-haired figure with trim moustache, known as Louis to his family and Ludwig in the Austrian army, Nolan spoke five European languages and several Indian dialects. There is no evidence that his three lengthy spells of sick leave were due to ill health. Acting as a model for its illustrations, he published *The Training of Cavalry Remount Horses: a New System* (1852) and *Cavalry: its History and Tactics* (1853). He advocated a major role for *arme blanche* cavalry in war, and claimed they could successfully charge artillery. Nolan also designed a cavalry saddle which 'much pleased' the duke of Cambridge (*Maidstone Journal*, 3 May 1853).

In March 1854 Britain declared war on Russia, and Nolan went to Turkey in advance of Lord Raglan's expeditionary force to buy cavalry horses, but was let down by local contractors. Nevertheless, Raglan recorded Nolan's 'zeal and intelligence' and sent him on another purchasing mission to Syria. On his return, Nolan actively assumed the duties of aide-de-camp to Brigadier-General Richard Airey, commanding the 1st brigade of the light division, and went with Airey when he became quartermaster-general at Raglan's headquarters. Having landed with the combined British, French, and Turkish force on the Crimean peninsula, 'the brave and daring Captain Nolan' (Powell, 14) came under fire at the first skirmish on the Bulganek River and carried executive orders during the battle of the Alma on 20 September 1854. Angry that the cavalry had not pursued the retreating enemy, Nolan then rode with the allies to besiege Sevastopol from uplands to the south.

On 25 October 1854 Nolan carried the fateful order to Lord Lucan (commanding the cavalry division) before the celebrated charge of the light brigade. Overlooking the plain of Balaklava from the heights, Raglan saw Russian troops preparing to withdraw British guns captured earlier that day from redoubts on a low ridge, which divided the plain into two valleys. Before he descended with the message, ordering Lucan 'to prevent the enemy taking away the guns', Nolan received 'careful instructions' from Airey and Raglan (Calthorpe, 1.314). However, situated between his two cavalry brigades, Lucan could see no guns owing to the lie of the land. Later, he claimed that on asking which guns he was to 'attack' Nolan pointed towards the end of the north valley where massed Russian cavalry were protected by artillery drawn up in front of them and on flanking high ground.

Having delivered the order, Nolan joined the 17th lancers and rode with them behind Lord Cardigan, the brigade commander. Before the advance had progressed far, Nolan galloped beyond Cardigan, shouting and waving his sword as he looked back towards the moving brigade. In the confusion of battle, his intentions were unclear, and almost immediately he was killed by a shell bursting to Cardigan's right. Raglan reproached Lucan for the subsequent débâcle, and he in turn blamed Nolan. Whether Nolan sought to speed up the advance, divert it towards the captured redoubts, or stop the attack altogether remains moot. So must the precise nature of his last conversation with Lucan. A memorial erected in Holy Trinity Church, Maidstone, recorded that he 'fell at the head of the light cavalry brigade in the charge at Balaklava'. Unmarried, and survived by his mother, Nolan bequeathed his possessions to Colonel George William Key and the copyright of his first book to Captain Lennox Berkeley.　　　　　　　　　　　　　　　JOHN SWEETMAN

Sources *Army List* · A. W. Kinglake, *The invasion of the Crimea*, 8 vols. (1863–87) · H. Moyse-Bartlett, *Louis Edward Nolan and his influence on the British cavalry* (1971) · R. Henderson, *The soldier of three queens* (1866) · H. Powell, *Recollections of a young soldier during the Crimean War* (1876) · S. J. G. Calthorpe, *Letters from headquarters, or, The realities of the war in the Crimea*, 2nd edn, 2 vols. (1857) · G. Paget, *The light brigade in the Crimea* (1881) · C. Hibbert, *The destruction of Lord Raglan* [1961] · C. Woodham-Smith, *The reason why* (1957) · J. Sweetman, *Raglan: from the Peninsula to the Crimea* (1993) · Boase, *Mod. Eng. biog.*
Archives NAM, department of archives, journal, 8906/41
Likenesses memorial tablet, Holy Trinity Church, Maidstone · portrait, repro. in *ILN* (24 Nov 1854)

Nolan [Nowlan], **Michael** (1763?–1827), legal writer, was born in co. Meath, Ireland, the son of Edward Nowlan, a lawyer. He matriculated as Michael Nowlan, at Trinity College, Dublin, in 1780, having been taught by the Revd John Buck; he graduated BA in 1784 and LLB in 1787. He was admitted an attorney of the court of exchequer in Ireland about 1787. Admitted at Lincoln's Inn in 1784, as Michael Nolan, he was called to the English bar on 3 February 1790. In 1793 he published *Reports of Cases Relative to the Duty and Office of a Justice of Peace from 1791 to 1793*; he edited the *Reports* of Sir John Strange (2 vols., 1795); and he was one of the joint editors of the supplement to Charles Viner's *General Abridgment* (6 vols., 1799–1806). He also practised as a special pleader on the home circuit and at the Surrey sessions.

In 1805 Nolan came to prominence with the publication, in two volumes, of *A Treatise of the Laws for the Relief and Settlement of the Poor*. This work, which gave a clear account of the law, with full references to authorities, reached a fourth edition in 1825, and established Nolan as an authority on the law of relief.

As member for Barnstaple in the parliament of 1820–26 Nolan introduced the poor law reform bills of 1822–4. He retired from parliament in March 1824 on being appointed justice of the counties of Brecon, Glamorgan, and Radnor. He died in 1827.

J. M. RIGG, *rev.* JONATHAN HARRIS

Sources W. P. Baildon, ed., *The records of the Honorable Society of Lincoln's Inn: the black books*, 4 (1902), 240 · Burtchaell & Sadleir, *Alum. Dubl.* · A. J. Webb, *A compendium of Irish biography* (1878) · *Hansard 2* (1822), 7.1560–96; (1824), 10.450 · J. G. Marvin, *Legal bibliography, or, A thesaurus of American, English, Irish and Scotch law books* (1847), 539–40 · *Wilson's Dublin directory* (1788), 113 · J. R. Poynter, *Society and pauperism: English ideas on poor relief, 1795–1834* (1969), 297–8 · Holdsworth, *Eng. law*, 13.448 · H. J. Rose, *A new general biographical dictionary*, ed. H. J. Rose and T. Wright, 12 vols. (1848), vol. 10, p. 348

Nolan, **Sir Sidney Robert** (1917–1992), artist, was born on 22 April 1917 in Carlton, an inner suburb of Melbourne, Australia, the eldest of four children of Sidney Henry Nolan, a fifth-generation Irish-Australian who worked as a tram driver and part-time publican and bookmaker, and his wife, Dora Irene, *née* Sutherland. The ethos of the family was typical of the Australian working class of that

Sir Sidney Robert Nolan (1917–1992), by Ida Kar, 1958

period, with little emphasis on education but great passion for sport. Nolan devoted much of his energy to physical activity as a swimmer, a daring diver, and a racing cyclist, and until his death maintained a spare, muscular frame. Much of his swimming and diving took place at the beachfront Melbourne suburb of St Kilda, to which the family moved soon after his birth, and which figured largely in his early paintings.

Apprenticeship and early career Nolan attended Brighton Road state school and Brighton Technical School, Melbourne, until 1932, when he went to Prahran Technical College, Melbourne, to study design and crafts. He began there to use some of the diverse media that were to be exploited by him for the rest of his life, including the making of commercial illuminated signs with such materials as tin foil, glass, and transparent enamels. In 1933 he went to work for Fayrefield Hats at Abbotsford, Victoria, where he stayed for over five years. While working on display stands, he became acquainted with spray paints, another medium which was to fascinate him for life and to which he returned in his final years. He designed posters featuring page-boys in the company's hats which, as a handsome young man, he occasionally modelled himself.

In 1934 Nolan became a not very diligent attender of evening classes at the National Gallery of Victoria Art School, studying intermittently under Charles Wheeler and William Beckwith McInnes. He spent more hours at the nearby public library, read voraciously, and became particularly fascinated by the books of James Joyce, D. H. Lawrence, Marcel Proust, Kierkegaard, Nietzsche, Marx, and Dostoyevsky. During his heroic cycling activities (200 miles a day was not uncommon) he met a fellow art student who suggested that he should take his studies more seriously. In 1936 he left the family home to move into a ramshackle condemned building where he used as painting surfaces any material that came to hand, including loosened slates from the building's roof. It was in this derelict building that he held his first exhibition. At this time he also began to write poetry. Thereafter he wrote poetry intermittently—and with considerable skill—throughout his life.

During his apprentice years Nolan led the classic life of the impoverished student. He stowed away (abortively) on a Europe-bound ship, worked on a hamburger stand, and spent his wages on eating oysters. In 1938 he showed his portfolio to Sir Keith Murdoch, the press magnate and an influential trustee of the National Gallery of Victoria, who passed him on to the art critic of *The Herald* (Melbourne), Basil Burdett, who did not much like what he saw but recommended him to an art-obsessed solicitor, John Reed. Nolan's meeting with Reed was one of the two catalytic encounters of his life. In that same year, at Reed's bidding, he joined the new Contemporary Art Society (CAS) in Melbourne. He also married Elizabeth Paterson, granddaughter of the 'Heidelberg school' painter John Ford Paterson. They moved to Ocean Grove, by the sea, and Nolan laboured in asparagus fields as well as, with his wife, taking on a pie shop.

In 1939 Nolan exhibited at the CAS inaugural exhibition at the National Gallery of Victoria a painting entitled *Head of Rimbaud* (Rimbaud being a writer he obsessively admired for his entire adult life). The painting was largely abstract and met with some ridicule. A fellow painter, Adrian Lawlor, asked him, 'What exactly is a rimbaud? A French cheese?' In 1940 Serge Lifar commissioned him to do the décor for his ballet *Icare* in Sydney. Nolan also held his first exhibition at his studio. It was opened by John Reed who, with his wife, Sunday, had taken up Nolan as their major protégé. Nolan's daughter, his only child, was born in that year, after he and Elizabeth had already separated, partly because she resented the influence of the Reeds and the amount of time Nolan spent at the Reeds' house, Heide.

During this period Nolan produced his first important sequence of paintings, brightly coloured pictures of the beach at St Kilda, with vigorous studies, tinged by his early love of abstraction, of divers, swimmers, sun-bathers, and so on. These paintings were much influenced by his early enthusiasm for the work of the Douanier Rousseau, although they were far from being naïve. He also produced inventive visions of the permanent St Kilda fun fair, Luna Park. He continued to paint St Kilda pictures until about 1946 but, from 1942 onwards, simultaneously worked on a series of largely landscape paintings of the Wimmera, the partly desolate, partly beautiful, wheat growing area in western Victoria.

Nolan had been conscripted into the army in 1942 and, after initial basic training, was posted to the Wimmera, spending his time guarding stores against the risks of Japanese invasion. He was promoted to corporal. His military duties were not sufficiently onerous to prevent a prolific output of paintings for which the Reeds provided the essential art supplies. He suffered the loss of two finger joints in an accident but their absence did not affect his capacities as a painter. At this time he embarked on a relationship with Sunday Reed. Nolan and the Reeds, apart from his absence in barracks, maintained a *ménage à trois* which lasted until 1947 and survived the complexities of his desertion from the army in 1944.

Nolan worked closely with John Reed and the writer Max Harris on an intellectual monthly magazine called *Angry Penguins*, which in 1944 published, illustrated by Nolan, a group of poems by Ern Malley. This constituted Australia's most significant literary scandal, since Ern Malley did not exist, having been invented by two soldier poets, James McAuley and Harold Stewart, to prove that 'modern poetry' was a sham. The hoax was rapidly exposed but, not least because Malley's verse was never less than interesting, Nolan's involvement did him no harm and sparked off several interesting paintings.

Ned Kelly and other Australian legends At the end of 1945 Nolan became interested in the life and times of the notorious, but in Australia much worshipped, nineteenth-century bushranger Ned Kelly. Nolan's paternal grandfather had been one of the Victoria policemen who had pursued Kelly. Nolan and Harris toured Kelly's territory, around Ballarat and Glenrowan, and spoke to Kelly's surviving relatives before Nolan settled down at Heide to paint the first Ned Kelly series, on which his lasting public fame was based.

Nolan once said that 'Kelly is the millstone round my neck' (personal knowledge). By this he meant many things: that Kelly was associated with him often to the overshadowing of and even to the exclusion of other meritorious work; that Kelly was, after the initial exhibition at the Velázquez Gallery in Melbourne in 1948, a kind of incubus he could not shake off; that Kelly images by themselves, or intruding into paintings on totally different subjects, were painted not just for a few years but were a lifetime's work. Through his paintings Nolan immortalized the square black Kelly mask and armour, which in fact owed more to an abstract black rectangle by the Russian artist Kazimir Malevich than the contemporary engravings and penny-dreadful illustrations of Kelly. (Nolan used to say that 'the black square is the most powerful device in twentieth-century painting'; personal knowledge.) Nolan's Kelly became as Australian an icon as Ayer's Rock (Uluru) and the Sydney Opera House and, partly at least because of those unmistakable images, Ned Kelly himself became, alongside Sir Donald Bradman and the racehorse Phar Lap, an archetypal Australian hero.

In 1947 Nolan left Heide and went to Queensland, spending time in Brisbane and on Fraser Island, the scene of his next major series, about the shipwrecked Mrs Fraser and the convict Bracefell. Nolan, so many of whose paintings were inspired by books, proved in the Mrs Fraser paintings to be the inspirer of Patrick White's novel *A Fringe of Leaves* (1976). In 1948 he moved to Sydney and married, on 25 March, Cynthia Hansen, *née* Reed (*d.* 1976), John Reed's sister. After this the close relationship between Nolan and John and Sunday Reed came to an end.

The next few years were intensely productive. The year 1948 saw Nolan's first engagement with the paintings of disused mines and his reconstruction of that central episode of Australian history, the gold rush of the 1850s and the battle of the Eureka Stockade—a subject which formed the basis of one of his major public commissions, the gigantic enamel mural in 1965 for the Reserve Bank of Australia in Melbourne. He had his first critical and commercial success with his paintings of the central Australian desert in 1950. These were followed by his remarkable paintings of the outback and his exploration of the calamitous drought areas in Queensland in 1952. After Kelly and Mrs Fraser, his next major series was devoted to the explorers Burke and Wills, whose epic, tragic, and fatal south to north crossing of the continent to find the Gulf of Carpentaria was one of the several heroic failures of Australian life that so engaged his sympathies. Burke and Wills, like Kelly, remained fixed in Nolan's mind and he continued to paint them for nearly three decades in different styles. Once he got an idea for a series into his head he rarely let it go.

Wider horizons Early in 1949 the second catalytic encounter of Nolan's artistic life occurred. Sir Kenneth Clark, visiting Sydney, was struck by a Nolan painting in an otherwise humdrum exhibition, and sought him out. A firm friendship and intellectual rapport ensued, so that once Nolan settled in London, Clark was able to open every important door for him, whether socially, artistically, or commercially. Clark's patronage through the 1950s and 1960s was crucial, as was the support of the director of the influential Whitechapel Art Gallery in London, Bryan Robertson, who gave Nolan a major retrospective exhibition there in June 1957. Before that, however, Nolan had gone to England with his wife, Cynthia, and her daughter Jinx (whom Nolan later adopted). They spent 1951 in Cambridge but already his restless need for travel was manifesting itself. His Australian travelling never ceased, but he also moved around extensively in Europe, producing notable work particularly in Italy in 1952.

In 1955 Nolan, with Cynthia and Jinx, rented a small flat near Paddington Station in London, and had a substantial one-man show at the Redfern Gallery. In 1956 he moved to the Greek island of Hydra, where he and his wife formed a close relationship with the Australian novelist George Johnston and his wife, the writer Charmian Clift. Johnston incorporated Nolan, as Tom Kiernan, into his novel *Clean Straw for Nothing* (1969). He also introduced him to the work of his fellow Australian Alan Moorehead, notably his book on Gallipoli. Nolan became obsessed with Troy and Gallipoli more or less simultaneously, but first painted the sequence he called *Leda and the Swan*, influenced by the work of Robert Graves and by W. B. Yeats's sonnet. He saw the Leda paintings as a kind of dry run for the Gallipoli series, not least because it was Leda who had given birth to Helen of Troy. He was particularly fascinated by the idea that Troy (with its epic, Homeric deeds) should be the site of the First World War débâcle of Gallipoli, which took so many Australian lives and left such a permanent scar on—and created such an enduring myth in—the Australian national character. The Gallipoli paintings, the best of which were done on Hydra and in Nolan's riverside studio in Putney, London, to which he moved in 1957, were notable not only for their quality but for their fusion of ancient and contemporary mythology. Nolan later, in 1978, presented hundreds of his Gallipoli paintings and drawings to the Australian War Memorial in Canberra, in memory of his brother Raymond John Nolan, who had died in a drowning accident in 1945.

In 1958 Nolan was awarded a Commonwealth Fund Harkness fellowship to travel, study, and work in the United States. By 1960 he had established close personal and intellectual friendships with the writers Patrick White and C. P. Snow, and subsequently did most of their book jacket paintings. While never slowing the relentless pace of his studio work, he accepted commissions for magazines, travel paintings, and drawings, and for stage designs which ranged from straight plays to ballet and opera sets for the Royal Opera House in Covent Garden, London, and the Australian Opera in Melbourne. He also formed a close collaboration with the American poet Robert Lowell and illustrated several books for him, including, notably, his very free translation of Baudelaire's *The Voyage* (1968). He also illustrated books of verse by the Australian writers Randolph Stow and Charles Osborne.

In the 1963 new year's honours list Nolan was created CBE. The following year he travelled to the Antarctic with Alan Moorehead (whom he had inspired with his Burke and Wills paintings to write his magisterial account of the explorers' disastrous journey, in *Cooper's Creek*, 1963). The Antarctic journey—a US Navy expedition to McMurdo Sound—produced some singularly successful paintings which he soon followed up with a series of illustrations of Shakespeare's sonnets shown in several English venues, including the Aldeburgh Festival. He had already developed a fruitful relationship with the creators of the Aldeburgh Festival, Benjamin Britten and Peter Pears, was a frequent festival visitor and exhibitor, and did some fine paintings inspired by Britten's works, such as his settings of Thomas Hardy's *Winter Words* and Bertolt Brecht's *Children's Crusade*.

In 1965 Nolan took up a creative arts fellowship at the Australian National University in Canberra and in 1966 moved temporarily to New York, where he rented a penthouse and a ground floor studio at the Chelsea Hotel. It was during this period that he collaborated particularly closely with Robert Lowell, doing some powerful paintings based on his translation of *Prometheus Bound* (1969). He also did several rather undistinguished covers for *Time* magazine. He then embarked on a series of massive polyptyches such as *Desert Storm* (Australian landscape), *Inferno* (based on Dante and Lowell), and *Riverbend I*, *Riverbend II*, and *Glenrowan*, all based on Ned Kelly but emphasizing the landscape rather than the human figures.

Nolan also travelled widely in Africa, producing some fine animal paintings, particularly of zebras, gorillas, and gazelles. He became much enamoured of China, first gaining entry, via Pakistan, in 1965, and returning in 1972, 1978, and 1983. He produced probably his most significant Chinese painting in 1984, in the form of the fourteen large canvases commissioned for the lobbies of the headquarters buildings of Hong Kong Land in Hong Kong.

Among the most copious of Nolan's works were a series of small mixed media on paper paintings, each about 30 cm high by about 24 cm wide. He painted literally thousands of these in the late 1960s and early 1970s and enclosed them in a series of glass-framed panels in groups of six or eight or nine, always with a grand design in mind. One sequence, the *Wildflowers*, was presented to the Reid Library of the University of Western Australia in Perth. The remaining three sequences were *Shark*, housed in the lobby of the Studio Theatre at the Sydney Opera House, *Paradise Garden*, comprising over 1000 individual paintings, in the lobby of the State Theatre of Victoria in Melbourne, and *Snake*, the largest of them (some 20 feet high and 150 feet wide), with some 1620 separate paintings displaying the undulating body of a giant snake in a mosaic created out of the individual paintings, which at the time of his death was still held in store. These three were known collectively as *Oceania*, and together they were an extraordinary tribute to the flora and wildlife of Australia and New Guinea. Taken all together they display not only Nolan's astonishing fecundity but also his breathtaking confidence in his architectonic vision. At the other end of the scale, he also experimented with sculpture, producing, in collaboration with the goldsmithing foundry of Jean-François Victor Hugo in the south of France, some beautiful gold sculptures only a few inches high but immensely strong in their sculptural impact.

Later life In 1971 Nolan took part in the Adelaide Festival and travelled in Australia with Benjamin Britten and Peter Pears. In June 1973 he had a major retrospective exhibition at the Royal Dublin Society in Éire, the most important show since the Whitechapel one in 1957 and before the National Gallery of Victoria one in 1987. It cemented his long and deep love of Ireland and its culture. (He long contemplated the acquisition of some land in co. Clare, from which his ancestors had migrated to Australia.) In 1974 he joined in a cultural exchange exhibition in Beijing (Peking) and Nanjing (Nanking) under the aegis of the Australian department of foreign affairs. In 1975 he produced his sequence of Oedipus paintings, involving Oedipus, the Sphinx, and a monstrous chicken.

On 23 November 1976 Cynthia Nolan committed suicide in London. Nolan was given great support at this time by Mary Elizabeth à Beckett Perceval, painter, daughter of (William) Merric Boyd, potter, sister of Nolan's great friend and rival Arthur Boyd, and former wife of the painter John Perceval. Nolan had known her as a close friend for all their adult lives. They married in London on 20 January 1978. They then lived for the next seven years at The Ruthland in Herefordshire. Nolan's remarriage provoked an intemperate attack from Patrick White in his memoir *Flaws in the Glass* (1981), thus ending one of Nolan's

(and White's) most enduring and intellectually productive friendships. Nolan responded to White's attack by producing a large, scatological painting called *Nightmare*, containing a devastating caricature of White.

In March 1980 Nolan went to Canberra for the opening of the Nolan Gallery at Lanyon, to which he presented several major works, including some classics from the Kelly and Burke and Wills series. In 1981 he exhibited at Lanyon a magnificent series of large crayon drawings based on Marcus Clarke's great nineteenth-century novel of Australian convict life, *For the Term of his Natural Life*. He was knighted in the queen's birthday honours list the same year, and received many other honours, including life membership of the National Gallery of Victoria and honorary membership of the American Academy of Arts and Letters. In 1983 the queen appointed him a member of the Order of Merit. He was elected an associate member of the Royal Academy of Arts in 1987, a full Royal Academician in 1991, and a senior academician in 1992. In 1987 the National Gallery of Victoria staged a massive seventieth birthday retrospective exhibition, which travelled on to Sydney, Perth, and Adelaide.

In 1983, while maintaining a flat in Whitehall Court in London, with a studio with a view over the Thames and the Royal Festival Hall, Nolan and his wife, Mary, bought a beautiful house, The Rodd, Presteigne, Radnorshire, on the border with Herefordshire. It was built mostly in the sixteenth and seventeenth centuries, and there they established both a herd of Welsh black cattle and the Sidney Nolan Trust (to benefit the arts and artists), and staged many successful concerts and exhibitions. It was in his last years at The Rodd that Nolan came full circle with his early years in the hat factory. He returned to the abstract art that had always fascinated him, but which he had never previously fully practised. He developed a highly sophisticated technique of painting with cans of spray paint. He rightly resented the accusation that he was merely imitating American painters of the New York school, such as Frank Stella, pointing out that he had first used this technique in the 1930s and 1940s. One of his last works was a spray-painted, entirely representational self-portrait, with his face encased in a Kelly mask.

Nolan's standing as one of two dominant figures in Australian art of the second half of the twentieth century, always in amicable contention with his close friend and eventual brother-in-law, Arthur Boyd, is assured. He also enjoyed a considerable reputation in Britain, the United States, and Europe. Even in old age he retained his athletic figure and bearing, and possessed, like other autodidacts before him, a formidably wide reading and knowledge of literature, art, and philosophy. He made friends easily but was cruelly misled by those who looked after his financial affairs. He was, despite this, a notably generous benefactor, giving substantial quantities of valuable paintings to state and national galleries and other public institutions. He was, above all, a cultivated, elegant man, with a dry, occasionally sharp wit, and a brilliant conversationalist, who had considerable charm.

Nolan died at the Westminster Hospital, London, on 27

November 1992, of heart failure and pneumonia. He was survived by his wife, Mary. A memorial service was held at the National Gallery of Australia in 1993, at which the prime minister of Australia, Paul Keating, was among the speakers. T. G. ROSENTHAL

Sources K. Clark, C. McInnes, and B. Robertson, *Sidney Nolan* (1961) • J. Clark, *Sidney Nolan: landscapes and legends* (1987) • T. G. Rosenthal, *Sidney Nolan* (2002) • *WWW*, 1991–5 • personal knowledge (2004) • private information (2004) • m. cert. [Mary Perceval] • d. cert.
Archives FILM BFI NFTVA, 'Sidney Nolan: such is love', Channel 4, 19 April 1987 • BFI NFTVA, 'Jancis Robinson meets Sir Sidney Nolan', ITV, 15 Dec 1987 | SOUND BL NSA, performance recordings
Likenesses I. Kar, photograph, 1958, NPG [*see illus.*] • photographs, repro. in Clark, McInnes, and Robertson, *Sidney Nolan*
Wealth at death £2,324,118: probate, 20 July 1993, *CGPLA Eng. & Wales*

Nollekens, Joseph (1737–1823), sculptor, second son of the painter Joseph Francis *Nollekens (1702–1748) and Mary Ann Lesack, was born on 11 August 1737 at 28 Dean Street in Soho, London, and baptized the next day at the Roman Catholic chapel in Duke Street, Lincoln's Inn Fields. After the death of Old Nollekens in 1748, his widow married Joseph Willems or Williams, and later settled with her husband in his native Wales.

Early life and Rome, 1737–1770 The young Joseph Nollekens was placed in 1750 with the sculptor Peter Scheemakers, who worked in Vine Street, Piccadilly, and who, like Old Nollekens, was a native of Antwerp. He served seven years as apprentice and five as journeyman. Little Joe (as he was then known) was considered 'a civil, inoffensive lad, not particularly bright' and so honest that Mrs Scheemakers 'could always trust him to stone the raisins' (Smith, 1.4). His favourite occupation at this time was bell-ringing at St James's Church. As ambition overtook him, he attended William Shipley's drawing school in the Strand; Smith says that he took lessons in drawing from the Danish sculptor William Henry Spang. He also drew and modelled from the plaster casts in the Duke of Richmond's Gallery, which opened in Whitehall in March 1758.

Nollekens came into public notice by winning prizes at the Society of Arts. In 1759 he was awarded 3 guineas for a drawing of a faun (RSA) and 15 guineas for a model in clay; in 1760 30 guineas for an original bas-relief of *Jeptha's Rash Vow*, and a gratuity of 10 guineas for another model; the next year he won 10 guineas, and in 1762 50 guineas for a bas-relief in marble of *Timocles and Alexander*, regarding which the judges were 'of the opinion that he has eminently distinguished himself' (RSA, minutes, committee of polite arts, 6 April 1762). After receiving his last premium on 21 May, he was able to satisfy an old ambition of travelling to Rome 'to see the works of Michelangelo and other great men' (Smith, 1.5). He passed through Paris, Lyons, Turin, Venice, Bologna, and Florence, and arrived in Rome on his twenty-fifth birthday, 11 August 1762.

For employment Nollekens entered the studio of Bartolommeo Cavaceppi, for whom he restored, copied, and no doubt counterfeited the antique. He worked also for

Joseph Nollekens (1737–1823), by Lemuel Francis Abbott, *c*.1797 [with his bust of Charles James Fox]

Thomas Jenkins, banker and dealer of dubious honesty, sometimes in partnership. A headless statue of Minerva, for instance, acquired cheaply by Nollekens and fitted with an alien head, was sold by Jenkins to William Weddell of Newby Hall, Yorkshire, for £1000. For Thomas Anson of Shugborough he made a fine marble copy of the Ildefonso *Castor and Pollux* (1767; V&A). Through the painter and dealer Gavin Hamilton he had orders in 1764 from several Englishmen who were at Rome together, for marble copies of Bartolommeo Cavaceppi's *Boy on a Dolphin*. The finest was for Cecil Brownlow, ninth earl of Exeter, while others he made half-size for Lord Palmerston, Viscount Spencer of Althorp, and probably the earl-bishop of Derry (Ickworth, Suffolk). Many of Nollekens's contacts at Rome probably came through the painter and architect James 'Athenian' Stuart, and evidently he joined the progressive artistic circle that centred at the Villa Albani. The patronage of Cardinal Albani protected him from censure when he neglected his religious duties.

Nollekens's first portrait head was of the actor David Garrick (1764; priv. coll.), who recognized the sculptor when drawing in the Vatican and gave him 12 guineas. Other portraits of English tourists followed, including those of Laurence Sterne (1767, marble version, NPG), Frederick Howard, eighth earl of Carlisle, and the engraver and designer G. B. Piranesi (Accademia, Rome). They convey a subtle, intimate quality not to be found later in his London portraits. Nollekens sent some works, including the bust of Sterne, to Stuart in London, to be exhibited at the Free Society of Artists.

The works made by Nollekens in Rome showed that

already he was a highly accomplished modeller, and cutter of marble. By 1765 he lived and had his studio off the via del Babuino. In 1768 he won the gold medal at the concorso Balestra with a terracotta group of *Jupiter, Juno, and Ino* (lost) and in June 1770 he was made a member of the academy at Florence. At Rome, and whenever travelling, he carried sketchbooks in which he drew the paintings and statues, ancient and modern, that caught his attention. By this means he made his own repertory of examples, and absorbed the principles of antique and classical style. Two complete sketchbooks survive at the Ashmolean Museum, Oxford, and loose sheets are in other collections.

In October 1770 Nollekens began his journey home and, as a sketchbook shows, travelled by Genoa, Vienne, and Paris, reaching London at Christmas. He was already well known in England through the many tourists he had met on their grand tour, including future patrons such as Lord Holland, Lord Yarborough, and Charles Townley; through portraits and other works he had sent home for exhibition; and for a small fortune already invested in the City.

London, 1771–1810 Nollekens lost no time in London. Before 25 March 1771 he had taken the house, 9 Mortimer Street, Marylebone, where more than fifty years later he was to die. It was a corner property with a yard and adequate outbuildings, previously occupied by the portrait painter Francis Newton RA, secretary to the Royal Academy. Nollekens visited Holland House, and completed in marble a bust of Lord Holland. This he exhibited at the Royal Academy in May along with two models which probably had been made in Rome. He was elected an associate of the Royal Academy on 15 October 1771, and Royal Academician on 9 February 1772, and was included in Johan Zoffany's group portrait *The Academicians of the Royal Academy* (Royal Collection) which was exhibited that May.

On 5 February 1774 Nollekens married Mary (1742/3–1817), younger daughter of Saunders Welch, justice of the peace for Westminster. Mary Nollekens was already past thirty years of age and, as Nollekens's biographer J. T. Smith described, liked to show her superiority when she was impatient with her husband's ignorance, low tastes, or vulgar manners. Her sister Anne attempted, in vain, to improve Nollekens's spelling. Samuel Johnson, a close friend of Saunders Welch, said (perhaps half in joke), 'Yes, I think Mary would have been mine if little Joe had not stepped in' (Smith, 1.126). They made a curious pair: Nollekens was short and bandy-legged, with a large head and aquiline nose, while she was tall and graceful with attractive features. There were no children, but the marriage was not unhappy. They shared a passion for economy which, if Smith's accounts are accurate, increased with the years and was not just mean but squalid. He describes, for instance, Mrs Nollekens taking her dog round Oxford Market where he could feed himself on discarded scraps, and joining the paupers' queue at the doctor's to avoid paying a fee; and Nollekens taking home the nutmegs he pocketed at Royal Academy dinners, and, when being shaved, keeping the used lather for washing himself at home.

Nollekens was often at the houses of Charles Townley and Dr Burney, though he hardly appreciated music or conversation, taking more pleasure (according to Smith) in London street cries, the milkmaids' dance on May day, Punch, and the changing of the guard.

At Rome, Nollekens had acquired cheaply a fine collection of ancient terracottas, found down a well near the porta Latina, and in 1783 he sold them, not expensively, to Charles Townley (BM). Otherwise we do not hear of his continuing to trade in antiquities, though he would buy marbles, models, and engravings at the London salerooms.

Nollekens's considerable output during these first ten years in London proves not merely artistic ability, but the efficient organization of his studio. Early assistants included Giuseppe Angelini, whom he had known in Rome, and Nathaniel Smith, his former schoolfriend and the father of John Thomas Smith. In portrait busts Nollekens scarcely had a rival, and it was largely through his facility to capture and animate a likeness that they became very popular in England. For forty-five years the great and the fashionable of both sexes came to the modelling room in Mortimer Street. The taste of the day was for a style which passed for antique, with close-cropped hair and conventional cloak thrown over the shoulders. Occasionally he copied contemporary or academic dress and wig, but to work it was more troublesome. He was commissioned for a bust of George III (1773; Royal Society, London), but the king seems not greatly to have liked this forceful portrait, preferring the anodyne bust by John Bacon (1774; Society of Antiquaries, London). The bust of Dr Samuel Johnson, made not in marble but in plaster (1777; Johnson Birthplace Museum, Lichfield), did not please the doctor or his women friends, who objected to the copious locks of natural hair. However, Chantrey considered it to be 'by far the finest bust our friend ever produced' (Smith, 2.73n.).

As to Nollekens's funeral monuments, the most notable were to Lady Henrietta Williams Wynn (d. 1771, Ruabon, Denbighshire), with its baroque-style statue of Hope, Bishop Richard Trevor (d. 1771, Auckland Castle, co. Durham), and Sir Thomas Salusbury (d. 1774, Great Offley, Hertfordshire); the latter two have full-size statues of the deceased, sitting and standing respectively. On smaller monuments he liked to include a mourning lady, whom he made slim and scantily dressed, or sentimental putti. He kept coloured drawings of his stock types of monument ready to show to clients.

In 1782, through the Royal Academy, Nollekens was awarded a government commission for the monument to three naval captains—William Bayne, William Blair, and Lord Robert Manners. His first design, free-standing and baroque in composition, was altered, in effect by a committee headed by Sir Joshua Reynolds, into an elaborate but frozen allegory. The monument was erected in Westminster Abbey but hidden for years beneath scaffolding because William Pitt would not supply a text for the inscription. When at last Nollekens applied directly to the king, Pitt was greatly vexed, and he would never sit for a bust. After this Nollekens lost interest in public monuments. The monument to Mrs Howard of Corby, who died in childbirth in 1789 (Wetheral, Cumbria), occupied him for ten years; when it was finally complete, Benjamin West thought it superior to the works of Canova (Farington, *Diary*, 25 June 1806).

Like every artist with academic ambitions, Nollekens attempted mythological or 'poetical' works, and from two generous patrons he obtained more commissions than any of his contemporaries. Charles Watson-Wentworth, marquess of Rockingham, ordered a *Venus* (1773), a *Minerva* (1775), and a *Juno* (1776). These, together with a restored antique statue of Paris bought earlier from the collector William Lock, made up a group of *The Judgment of Paris* (the four statues are now at J. Paul Getty Museum, Malibu). Lord Rockingham later ordered a statue of Diana (V&A). Lord Yarborough commissioned *Venus Chiding Cupid* (1778) and *Seated Mercury* (1783; both Usher Art Gallery, Lincoln). Nollekens considered these ideal statues as having been modelled in the antique style, but they resemble more the sixteenth-century works of Giovanni Bologna, who was much admired by this sculptor. It was generally understood by his fellow artists that, while Nollekens was greatly experienced, and the best practical sculptor in London, he lacked the classical knowledge and intellect necessary for poetical sculpture. Flaxman, while admitting that Nollekens was the first English sculptor who had 'formed his taste on the antique and introduced a purer style of art' (J. Flaxman, *Lectures on Sculpture*, 2nd edn, 292), compared him unfavourably with Thomas Banks, saying that he 'wanted Mind' (Farington, *Diary*, 5 Feb 1805).

Nollekens's portrait busts were in great demand, and their prices rose from 50 guineas in 1771 to 150 guineas. He was always available at a moment's notice to take the cast of a newly deceased person's face. Two busts of whig statesmen, the marquess of Rockingham (*d.* 1782, priv. coll.; copy in City Museum and Art Gallery, Birmingham) and Sir George Savile (*d.* 1784; V&A), both made from death masks, were repeated several times for members of the family and political associates. The spirited bust of Charles James Fox (1791; State Hermitage, St Petersburg) attracted great attention, and nine copies of it are known. However the radical Francis Russell, fifth duke of Bedford, clearly thought the 1791 bust inappropriate, with its curled hair and pigtail, and in 1802 Nollekens made for this duke a second bust of Fox, more classical in style, which was placed in the Temple of Liberty at Woburn Abbey, Bedfordshire, together with the heads of six Foxite friends. Over thirty copies of the Fox busts were made. Nollekens became a kind of unofficial sculptor to the whigs, analogous to the architect Henry Holland, and several great houses could boast a series of his busts, the best collection being at Windsor Castle. Busts in popular demand included the duke of Bedford (1801; formerly Holland House, Kensington), William Pitt (1806; priv. coll.), and Spencer Perceval (1813); the last two were made from death masks. The busts of Fox and Pitt were referred to as his 'stock pieces' (Smith, 2.74). From the death mask of

Pitt, who would not sit when alive, Nollekens is said to have made seventy-four marble busts, as well as six hundred casts in plaster at 6 guineas, and a statue of Pitt for the Senate House, Cambridge, at £3000 (plus £1000 for the pedestal). In 1812 the statue was erected, and Nollekens went to Cambridge for a week, to be 'much feasted and caressed by Heads of Colleges' (Farington, *Diary*, 12 July 1812).

Last years, 1810–1823 Nollekens's portrait busts became even more popular as he grew older; he made thirty of them between 1810 and 1816. As late at 1815, when the banker Thomas Coutts asked to whom he should go for a bust, he was told by the painter Henry Fuseli, 'although Nollekens is superannuated in many particulars, yet in a bust he is unrivalled … [for] a group of figures, I should have recommended Flaxman; but for a bust, give me Nollekens' (Smith, 2.50). Busts of the late period include the prince of Wales (1808; BM), the duke of Wellington (1813; Apsley House, London), and the Revd Charles Burney (1815; BM). After 1800 his modelling became more generalized, the features rather broader. The busts of women, of which he had done few before 1800, became more numerous and, curiously, the later ones show more of the character of the sitter. Benjamin West told the diarist Joseph Farington that, at seventy-four years old, Nollekens rose at six, breakfasted soon after seven, and received his first sitter before eight (Farington, *Diary*, 21 Nov 1811). The studio continued to work efficiently, and his late assistants included the sculptors Sebastian Gahagan and Lawrence Goblet. Joseph Bonomi (1796–1878), the son of the more famous architect, was a favoured pupil, but went on to become an Egyptologist.

In 1811 Nollekens saw a bust in plaster of Horne Tooke which had been sent to the Royal Academy by the then young and unknown Francis Chantrey, and he told the hanging committee, 'There's a very fine work—let the man who made it be known. Remove one of my busts and put this one in its place, for well it deserves it' (Cunningham, 3.190). Chantrey always honoured him for this.

After 1800, for recreation, Nollekens took to modelling small figures or groups, usually based on classical or biblical themes; a number were included in the Royal Academy exhibitions. A hundred or so in terracotta were in the studio sale, and although some thought these sketches to be works of genius, superior to the marbles, Cunningham found them somewhat commonplace: 'common postures and hackneyed meanings abound' (Cunningham, 3.199).

In later years Mrs Nollekens put on weight and could hardly move without assistance. She sat in her chair with a sadly crooked spine, of which her husband in her presence would show drawings to visitors. She died on 17 August 1817, and Nollekens, without much change in his frugal habits, was now given to moderate but unexpected acts of generosity, though he became ever less observant of his religious duties. He too had bouts of illness. In 1780, suffering from a diseased mouth, he had spent some weeks at Harrogate; he was unwell again in 1807. Age showed after an accident in 1812, and in 1814 Farington found him looking old and infirm; by 1816 he was 'nearly as deaf as a post' (Smith, 2.52). That year, when he exhibited four busts including those of Thomas Coutts, Charles Jenkinson, first earl of Liverpool, and Henry Pelham Clinton, fourth duke of Newcastle, he gave up working. By 1819, after three paralytic seizures, he was almost immobile, but he was cared for by devoted servants of long standing, and by his assistant Goblet, who left his own family and lived at Mortimer Street for some years. He died on 23 April 1823 and was buried on 1 May at St Mary's Church, Paddington.

Posthumous reputation After his wife's death, Nollekens made a new will, to which he added fourteen codicils. After minor bequests and annuities, the residue of the fortune of nearly £200,000 was left to three 'outsiders': the Revd Thomas Kerrich, librarian at Cambridge; Francis Douce, an antiquary; and Francis Russell Palmer, natural son of the fifth duke of Bedford, whose mother was one of Nollekens's close friends. The ensuing law case was settled in the legatees' favour in 1827 (*GM*, 2nd ser., 2, August 1834, 215). John Thomas Smith, who had grown up as one of the family and was repeatedly promised a legacy, had nothing but £100 as fee for being an executor. His response was to write the entertaining and venomous biography *Nollekens and his Times*, which occupied him for five years. It contains little information about Nollekens's professional life; mostly anecdotal, much of its malicious gossip was supplied by Nollekens's servants.

Two years later Allan Cunningham, secretary and assistant to Chantrey, though not denying the truth of Smith's book, wrote a kinder account. Contrary to Smith's assertions of meanness, the studio assistants had been generously paid; and he indicated Nollekens's invariable honesty and his genial good humour. In Farington's *Diary*, where there is no mention of disrespect from colleagues (except Flaxman), it is clear that Nollekens's views were valued on many subjects, particularly on antique sculpture. The council minutes of the Royal Academy show that he was more conscientious than most academicians in his attendance.

Nollekens made over a hundred funeral monuments but, apart from the allegories on the monuments, never a religious work. His fame lies chiefly in his portrait busts of which he made over 170; not unlike the paintings of Reynolds, they make up a visual record of the personalities of the times. If he lacked the genius of Chantrey, the busts of Nollekens are lifelike and animated, elegant and unaffected, though perhaps not always conveying character. Nollekens was not appreciated by his immediate successors, the circle of Flaxman, George Romney, and Thomas Hayley, but he was esteemed by sculptors of the next generation—Chantrey, Cunningham, and John Gibson.   JOHN KENWORTHY-BROWNE

Sources J. T. Smith, *Nollekens and his times*, ed. W. Whitten, new edn, 2 vols. (1920) · A. Cunningham, *The lives of British painters etc.* [1830], 3.122–99 [partly an eyewitness account by Chantrey's assistant] · Farington, *Diary* · M. Whinney, *Sculpture in England,*

1530–1830 (1964); J. Physick, rev., rev. edn (1988), 287–302 · J. Ingamells, ed., *A dictionary of British and Irish travellers in Italy, 1701–1800* (1997), 709–11 · S. Howard, 'Boy on a dolphin': Nollekens and Cavaceppi', *Art Bulletin*, 46 (1964), 177–89 · J. Wilton-Ely, 'A bust of Piranesi by Nollekens', *Burlington Magazine*, 118 (May 1976), 593–5 · J. Kenworthy-Browne, 'Nollekens in Rome: 1, establishing a reputation', *Country Life*, 165 (7 June 1979), 1844–8 · J. Kenworthy-Browne, 'Nollekens in Rome: 2, genius recognised', *Country Life*, 165 (14 June 1979), 1930–31 · J. Kenworthy-Browne, 'A monument to three Captains', *Country Life*, 141 (27 Jan 1977), 180–82 · J. Kenworthy-Browne, 'The Temple of Liberty at Woburn Abbey', *Apollo*, 130 (July 1989), 27–32 · J. Kenworthy-Browne, 'Terracotta models by Joseph Nollekens R.A.', *Sculpture Journal*, 2 (1998), 72–4 · N. Penny, 'Lord Rockingham's sculpture collection and *The judgment of Paris*', *J. Paul Getty Museum Journal*, 19 (1991), 5–34 · N. Penny, 'To honour Pitt the younger', *Country Life*, 156 (19 May 1977), 1336–7 · J. Lord, 'Joseph Nollekens and Lord Yarborough: documents and drawings', *Burlington Magazine*, 130 (1988), 915–19 · R. Gunnis, *Dictionary of British sculptors, 1660–1851*, new edn ([forthcoming, 2005])

Archives PRO, family papers, C 112/183

Likenesses attrib. (separately) J. Barry, M. Mosser, oils, *c*.1769, Yale U. CBA · J. F. Rigaud, oils, exh. RA 1772; Christies 23 March 1979, lot 113 · C. Grignon, chalk and bodycolour, *c*.1780, Hunt. L. · L. F. Abbott, oils, *c*.1797, NPG [*see illus.*] · H. Edridge, pencil and watercolour drawing, 1807, BM · G. Dance, black chalk drawing, Feb 1810, RA · W. Beechey, oils, exh. 1812, Tate collection · G. H. Harlow, oils, *c*.1815 (unfinished), priv. coll. · L. A. Goblet, herm bust, plaster, exh. 1816, AM Oxf. · J. Lonsdale, oils, *c*.1816, NPG · F. Chantrey, marble bust, 1818, Woburn Abbey, Bedfordshire · J. Jackson, pencil and watercolour drawing, *c*.1818, BM · F. Chantrey, marble bust, 1819–20, BM · J. Northcote, oils, *c*.1820, FM Cam. · L. A. Goblet, marble bust, exh. 1821, V&A · W. Behnes, marble bas-relief on monumental tablet, St Mary's parish church, Paddington, London · A. Chalon, ink drawing, V&A · F. Chantrey, busts, AM Oxf. · F. Chantrey, pencil drawing (preliminary to his bust of 1818), Hunt. L. · H. Singleton, group portrait, oils (*The Royal Academicians in General Assembly, 1793*), RA · J. Zoffany, group portrait, oils (*The Royal Academicians, 1772*), Royal Collection

Wealth at death £200,000 incl. several London houses: Cunningham, *The lives of British painters*, 3.193

Nollekens [Nollikins], **Joseph Francis** (1702–1748), painter, commonly called Old Nollekens, the second son of Jan Baptiste Nollekens (*bap.* 1665, *d.* 1740×49) and Anne-Angélique Le Roux was born in Antwerp, Southern Netherlands, on 10 June 1702 (which instead may have been his date of baptism) and baptized there as Corneille François Nollekens. Jan Nollekens (1695–1783), who worked in Paris but from whose hand no paintings have been identified, was his elder brother. Joseph Francis's father was a minor painter of landscape and genre who about 1708 brought him to England, where he later studied under Peter Tillemans. The scanty records of his life are generally inconsistent, but his father, finding insufficient work in England, went to France and later died at Roanne. Joseph Francis also went to France, where he was said to have studied under Antoine Watteau. He returned to England in 1733, married Mary Ann Lesack who was of French descent but was born in England, and lived in Soho, London. Of their five children, only the second, the sculptor Joseph *Nollekens (1737–1823), settled in England.

In 1726 a 'Conversation by Nollikins' (described thus in the sale catalogue) was sold by the earl of Peterborough; it was doubtless by Joseph Francis Nollekens's father, as are various village scenes in the style of David Teniers, one signed 'J. B. Nollekens'. At Stowe, Buckinghamshire, there were originally, in the lake pavilions, decorative paintings from the *Pastor fido* of Battista Guarini (1538–1612), and scenes of Bacchic revels in the temple of Bacchus, all by 'Nollikins' but all destroyed without record. The Stowe archives show that in 1729 'Mr Knollekyns' was paid £30 13s. 7d. 'for Oyle and Colour'.

Paintings by Joseph Francis Nollekens from 1733, which are sometimes signed and dated, show development from the French style to a more English taste. From France no doubt came his lively use of paint and ease of composition. There are *fêtes-champêtres* in the style of Watteau, some of them set among ruins copied from Giovanni Paolo Panini, and musical parties of elegant society set in front of country houses. By about 1740 he painted interiors and conversation pieces much in the style of Hogarth and Francis Hayman. His last paintings, which George Vertue thought 'the best of his works' (Vertue, *Note books*), were of his own children at play or study. The figures, probably inspired by Philip Mercier and on a larger scale than the conversation pieces, are shown with realism and charm. Two of these are in the Yale Center for British Art, New Haven, Connecticut. Nollekens attracted a fashionable clientele which included the marquess of Stafford. His chief patron was Richard Child, first Earl Tylney, the builder of Wanstead, Essex, where in 1822 seventeen of his works were sold. One, *Interior of the Saloon at Wanstead, with an Assemblage of Ladies and Gentlemen*, fetched the high price of £127 1s. His paintings are to be found in country houses, for instance at Badminton House, Gloucestershire, Petworth, Sussex, Longleat, Wiltshire, and Belton House, Lincolnshire (a bird's eye view of the house, signed and dated 1736), and at Windsor Castle; four are in the Yale Center for British Art in New Haven.

J. T. Smith relates an anecdote from James Northcote RA, who had it from the sculptor Thomas Banks, that Old Nollekens owed his death to his nervous terrors for his property (Smith, 1.2). He was a Roman Catholic, which, with his reputation as a miser, gave him great anxiety during the Jacobite rising of 1745. Dread of robbery finally threw the artist into a nervous illness; he lingered until January 1748, when he died, possibly on the 21st, at his home, 28 Dean Street, Soho, London. He was buried at Paddington, Middlesex, and it seems that he had provided sufficiently for his family.　　JOHN KENWORTHY-BROWNE

Sources M. J. H. Liversidge, 'An elusive minor master: J. F. Nollekens and the conversation piece', *Apollo*, 95 (1972), 34–41 · Vertue, *Note books*, 3.137–8 · J. T. Smith, *Nollekens and his times*, ed. W. Whitten, new edn, 2 vols. (1920), vol. 1, pp. 2–5; vol. 2, p. 41 · *A catalogue of the magnificent and costly furniture of the princely mansion, Wanstead House* [1822] [sale catalogue, Mr Robins, 10 June – 11 July 1822, esp. 19–21 June] · H. Hymans, 'Nollekens (Nollikins), Joseph', *Biographie nationale*, 15/2 (Brussels, 1899), 814–15 · Farington, *Diary*, 5.1968; 6.2109 · M. J. Gibbon, 'The history of Stowe' pt 15, *The Stoic*, 25/2 (1972), 65
Archives PRO, family papers, C 112/183

Non (*fl.* 6th cent.). *See under* David (*d.* 589/601).

Nonant, Hugh de (*d.* 1198), administrator and bishop of Coventry, was a scion of an important Norman ecclesiastical family with strong connections in the diocese of Lisieux.

Background and early career Nonant's maternal uncle was Arnulf, bishop of Lisieux (*d.* 1184), who was responsible for his upbringing and first advancement. Initially Nonant was given the prebend of Chapelle Hareng, near Thibouville (Eure). Later his uncle apparently set him up in a number of jurisdictions around Gacé (Orne), close to the place from which Hugh took his toponym: these included the deanery of Gacé, the prebend of Croisilles at Lisieux, and also the archdeaconry of the same. It would seem that Nonant was sent to Canterbury for his education. Presumably it was here that he acquired the forensic and linguistic skills that were to serve him so well in his political career. He is first recorded in Becket's entourage in 1164, and went into exile with the archbishop, but was reconciled to the king in 1170, entering his service and becoming a close friend and confidant. There is a tradition that Hugh de Nonant was made archdeacon of Oxford in succession to Walter de Coutances (*d.* 1207), on the latter's appointment as bishop. But even though Arnulf of Lisieux implies that Nonant had indeed given up the archdeaconry of Lisieux before 1181, there is no direct evidence for the Oxford tradition, and it is probable that the confusion arises from Bishop Walter's appointment, between 1183 and December 1184, of his nephew, Master John de Coutances, who was treasurer of Lisieux at the time, to the archdeaconry. In 1184 Nonant was sent by the king on an important diplomatic mission to the pope, Lucius III (*r.* 1181–5), to intercede for Henry the Lion, duke of Saxony. His success in this was probably the reason for his appointment in January 1185 to the see of Coventry, which had been vacant since the death, possibly by poison, of his predecessor, the celebrated canonist Gerard Pucelle, in the previous year.

Hugh de Nonant was not consecrated for a long time, nearly three years, an unusual occurrence explained by his continued involvement with Henry II's diplomatic business. Nonant was again sent to Rome in 1186, this time to seek permission for the crowning of John as king of Ireland. He arrived back at Dover as papal legate, along with the cardinal-deacon Octavian, on Christmas eve 1186. Christmas was kept at Canterbury and the new year in London, but although Nonant and Octavian were apparently equipped with the appropriate authority, there is no evidence that any such consecration actually took place. Almost immediately Archbishop Baldwin of Canterbury (*d.* 1190), by then already embroiled in a long dispute with his monks concerning his plan to found a collegiate church at Hackington, took exception to the potential encroachment upon his authority by their legatine position and persuaded the king to delay proceedings. Nonant went abroad with the king in February, having first been sent fruitlessly, along with the bishops of Norwich and Worcester, to intercede between Baldwin and his monks. He is last recorded on the continent on 1 January 1188. Nonant returned to England with the archbishop, three days before the king, on 30 January 1188, and was finally consecrated on 31 January, by Archbishop Baldwin at his manor of Lambeth.

Bishop of Coventry Bishop Hugh only remained in England until March, although he was present at the Council of Geddington on 11 February 1188, when he inveighed against the monks of Canterbury. After Henry II left England for the last time on 10 July 1188, Bishop Hugh almost certainly joined him and remained with him until the end of the king's life—he is recorded with Henry II at La Ferté in June 1189, and Henry died on 6 July 1189. He returned to England on Richard I's instructions in August of that year and was present at the coronation and the Council of Pipewell (15 September 1189).

The celebrated dispute between Nonant and the monks of his cathedral priory in Coventry took place in the short period between the coronation of Richard I and the king's departure on crusade on 12 December 1189. Nonant's views on that English anachronism, the monastic cathedral chapter, were entirely in sympathy with those of Archbishop Baldwin and most of his contemporaries as bishops. However, they were most vehemently expressed in the armed fracas in Coventry Cathedral priory that seems to have taken place on 9 October 1189. It would appear that blood was spilt, including that of the bishop himself, during the confrontation. Gervase of Canterbury records the bishop's invasion of the claustral buildings, his causing of the prior to flee and the expulsion of the monks. Parts of the priory seem to have been destroyed, and the community's muniment chests were broken into and its privileges destroyed. When Bishop Hugh complained formally about this incident to his fellow bishops assembled at Westminster on 22 October 1189, he is said then to have uttered to the king the famous prophecy that within two months there would not be a single monk left in any English cathedral, adding the imprecation 'monachi ad diabolos' ('to the devil with monks'; *Works of Gervase of Canterbury*, 1.470). A short-lived community of secular canons, on whose worth opinions were divided, was set up in place of the monks in Coventry. They survived until January 1197, though the corporate existence of their predecessors also seems to have been somehow preserved, since the latter are recorded as suing for novel disseisin in the royal court in 1194.

In the early stages of Richard I's financing of his crusade, Bishop Hugh purchased the shrievalties of Warwickshire, Leicestershire, and Staffordshire for 200 marks. For a bishop to hold secular office of this subordinate, but none the less highly lucrative, kind was clearly against the canons of the Third Lateran Council, and chapter 12 in particular. It was probably this that caused Nonant to fall out with Archbishop Baldwin, with whom he had been of one mind in their attitude to black monk cathedrals. It may also be significant, however, that according to Gervase he also had to promise the king another 300 marks to buy his support for the attack on his cathedral priory. Once King Richard himself had left England, at the very end of 1189, William de Longchamp, chancellor of England and bishop-elect of Ely (*d.* 1197), and Hugh du Puiset, bishop of Durham (*d.* 1195), the designated justiciars, rapidly fell

out. Richard I, still at this time in Normandy, summoned a council for Candlemas (2 February 1190): Bishop Hugh was one of the large group of bishops who escorted the justiciars on their way to the king. Archbishop Baldwin, on the other hand, who was busy with his own crusading preparations in England, called an ecclesiastical council to be held in Westminster on 19 February, and then himself left for Normandy on 6 March. Soon afterwards, while at Rouen, he suspended Bishop Hugh, who, when challenged about his continued holding of the shrievalty, promised, in letters patent addressed to the king, to resign such offices as were degrading to his episcopal status within a fortnight of Easter (25 March), and, in similar letters to the archbishop, renounced his right of appeal. Or, at any rate, such were the terms in which Archbishop Baldwin described this in a letter to his deputy, Richard fitz Nigel (*d.* 1198), bishop of London. It would seem that Bishop Hugh did not observe them, for later in June that year at court at Montrichard, he struck a new bargain with the king for his shires.

The quarrel with Longchamp Bishop Hugh was on good terms with Longchamp at this time, the period of the latter's coup destroying du Puiset. At the Council of Westminster called on 13 October 1190, doubtless at Longchamp's behest, Bishop Hugh's moves against his cathedral priory were endorsed—the monks were ejected on Christmas eve of that year. But by the autumn of 1191 the complexion of politics in England had changed, with the increasing efforts of the king's brother, Count John of Mortain, to extend his power in England and establish his position as Richard I's successor, together with the arrival on the scene of Walter de Coutances, archbishop of Rouen, the king's representative and aspirant to Canterbury, and Geoffrey Plantagenet (*d.* 1212), the king's half-brother, by now, finally, archbishop of York. All three men were anxious for influence and power. When Longchamp laid violent hands on Geoffrey at Dover, in a series of events that came to be presented as a parallel to the martyrdom of Thomas Becket, with the chancellor in the role of Henry II, it was Bishop Hugh, now firmly in John's camp, who conveyed the news to the count at Lancaster in late September and urged him to take action. In the circumstances as King Richard had left them, Longchamp's refusal to play anything by the rules of accepted behaviour was ultimately folly. He could not survive a concerted coalition of churchmen and the remaining great men of the realm against him. Clearly Bishop Hugh was astute enough to realize this and to shift his support to John, as the only realistic heir to the throne should Richard never return. He seems to have been John's principal adviser, and played a leading role in the ensuing confrontation with Longchamp. He was present at the assembly of notables held near Reading on 5 October, which Longchamp was too craven to attend, and there translated into French King Richard's Latin letters to Archbishop Walter, for the benefit of laymen. The following day, a Sunday, he was one of the three bishops sent unsuccessfully to fetch Longchamp from Windsor. At noon, during mass, the bishops laid a curse upon all those who had laid hands on Archbishop Geoffrey: it was Bishop Hugh who explained the proceedings and the meaning of the sentence to the people present. The following day, after Longchamp's flight from Windsor to London became apparent, Bishop Hugh made a celebrated quip about the need to go to London, 'to buy some winter clothes' (*Gir. Camb. opera*, 4.403): on his advice Count John and the bishops took the road to Staines, where there was a minor but important skirmish. On Thursday 10 October he spoke first in the settlement negotiations, and was subsequently present at Canterbury for the election of a new archbishop (the short-lived Reginald Fitzjocelin) on 27 November 1191.

The destruction of Longchamp's power was complete, and Bishop Hugh then conducted a hate campaign against his former friend: his hilarious, and justly famous, open letter, which described the former justiciar's trials and tribulations on leaving the country, was copied almost verbatim into virtually all the chronicles of the period. The story of the hapless bishop, dressed as a whore, 'touched up' by a coarse sailor on the waterfront at Dover, eventually mobbed and stoned by the local populace, is a masterpiece of sheer spite. Although Longchamp attempted to riposte when he eventually escaped to Rome, having Bishop Hugh, among others, excommunicated, all these sentences were ignored in England. On hearing of the captivity of Richard I in 1193 Bishop Hugh is said to have started immediately for Germany with funds, but to have been robbed *en route*. And although he reached Richard in Germany, he found it prudent to return almost immediately to France, since his relations with the king appear to have become strained, a situation almost certainly exacerbated by the treasonable behaviour of the bishop's brother Robert.

Withdrawal and death After Richard had returned to England he issued instructions, on 31 March 1194, that Hugh de Nonant should answer for his crimes both as bishop and sheriff. Bishop Hugh was able to obtain pardon by paying the immense sum of 5000 marks, but his brother Robert remained in prison in Dover, where he later died. It has been said that the bishop never returned to England, but there is a note in the Chester cartulary that says he instituted clerks to three churches owned by St Werburgh's Abbey on the presentation of Abbot Geoffrey. The latter was certainly elected only in 1194, the year in which his predecessor Abbot Robert (III) resigned, possibly before 29 June, but definitely before 25 September. Given this fourteenth-century reference to a lost charter or charters, Bishop Hugh must have returned to England between 1193 and 1196. Nonant witnessed fines made at Westminster in the winter of 1196–7 and his seal (the only surviving impression) is attached, along with many others, to the corroboration of the agreement between Archbishop Hubert Walter and his monks concerning Lambeth (Surrey) issued between 25 March and 31 May 1197. By mid-July Nonant was again in Normandy, never to return.

The other surviving records of Bishop Hugh's episcopate are entirely what would be expected for a bishop of the period: indeed, it might be said that they are extremely numerous for one who may perhaps have had no more than three years of active episcopacy. There is certainly no obvious anti-monastic bias in their content. The ascription to him of constitutions for his cathedral in Lichfield is, however, now known to be false. In January 1198, when the monks of Coventry were finally restored to their cathedral, Bishop Hugh was lying terminally ill at Bec, repentant and clad in the Benedictine habit, like an old-fashioned Norman aristocrat. He finally died on Good Friday (27 March) 1198—in the admittedly biased words of the Winchester annalist, 'after a long illness and unbearable suffering, followed by a well-deserved death' (*Ann. mon.*, 2.67).

M. J. FRANKLIN

Sources M. J. Franklin, 'The bishops of Coventry and Lichfield, c.1072–1208', *Coventry's first cathedral: the cathedral and priory of St Mary* [Coventry 1993], ed. G. Demidowicz (1994), 118–38 · *Chronica magistri Rogeri de Hovedene*, ed. W. Stubbs, 4 vols., Rolls Series, 51 (1868–71) · *Radulfi de Diceto … opera historica*, ed. W. Stubbs, 2 vols., Rolls Series, 68 (1876) · *The historical works of Gervase of Canterbury*, ed. W. Stubbs, 2 vols., Rolls Series, 73 (1879–80) · W. Stubbs, ed., *Chronicles and memorials of the reign of Richard I*, 2: *Epistolae Cantuarienses*, Rolls Series, 38 (1865) · *Chronicon Richardi Divisensis / The Chronicle of Richard of Devizes*, ed. J. T. Appleby (1963) · J. C. Robertson and J. B. Sheppard, eds., *Materials for the history of Thomas Becket, archbishop of Canterbury*, 7 vols., Rolls Series, 67 (1875–85) · *Gir. Camb. opera* · W. Stubbs, ed., *Gesta regis Henrici secundi Benedicti abbatis: the chronicle of the reigns of Henry II and Richard I, AD 1169–1192*, 2 vols., Rolls Series, 49 (1867) · *The letters of Arnulf of Lisieux*, ed. F. Barlow, CS, 3rd ser., 61 (1939) · *Ann. mon.* · J. T. Appleby, *England without Richard, 1189–1199* (1965) · J. Gillingham, *Richard the Lionheart*, 2nd edn (1989) · *Fasti Angl., 1066–1300*, [Lincoln] · M. Richter, ed., *Canterbury professions*, CYS, 67 (1973) · D. Wilkins, ed., *Concilia Magnae Britanniae et Hiberniae*, 4 vols. (1737) · J. Tait, ed., *The chartulary or register of the abbey of St Werburgh, Chester*, 2 vols., Chetham Society, new ser., 79, 82 (1920–23) · D. Knowles, C. N. L. Brooke, and V. C. M. London, eds., *The heads of religious houses, England and Wales, 1: 940–1216* (1972) · M. J. Franklin, ed., *Coventry and Lichfield, 1183–1208*, English Episcopal Acta, 17 (1998)

Nongqawuse [Nonquase] (*b. c.*1840, *d.* in or after 1905), prophet, was orphaned at an early age, possibly during the 1850–53 Cape Frontier War between the Xhosa and the British, and went to live with her uncle, Mhlakaza, at the Gxarha River in independent Xhosa. Reliable documentation on her life and character is very thin, and although her prophecies and their consequences have been extensively recorded, the details of her motivations and her personal life must remain forever obscure.

In April 1856 Nongqawuse and a younger cousin, Nombanda, went out into the fields to scare the birds away from the standing corn. When they returned home Nongqawuse reported that they had met two strangers who introduced themselves as persons long dead, and, according to the reliable account of W. W. Gqoba, continued as follows:

> You are to tell the people that the whole community is about to rise again from the dead … all the cattle living now must be slaughtered, for they are reared with defiled hands as the people handle witchcraft. Say to them that there must be no ploughing of lands, rather must the people dig deep pits (granaries), erect new huts, set up wide, strongly built cattlefolds. (Peires, 79)

These prophecies were accepted by Nongqawuse's

uncle Mhlakaza, a Christian convert who had been dismissed by his former employer, an Anglican clergyman, on account of his increasingly visionary religious experiences. Such prophecies were not entirely new. They had multiplied in the climate of despair which had been generated by continual Xhosa military defeats, and they had lately been boosted by exaggerated reports of Russian successes against the British in the Crimea. The notion that existing cattle had somehow become contaminated was a reaction to the recent outbreak of lung sickness, a hitherto unknown and deadly cattle disease newly arrived from Europe. Enquirers who visited Nongqawuse's place were shown black shapes bobbing up and down in the misty sea and told that these were the dead, waiting to rise as soon as all the cattle had been slaughtered. On other occasions Nongqawuse entered a particular bush, and conversed with spirits audible only to herself.

A turning point was reached in July 1856 when Sarhili, king of all the Xhosa, visited Nongqawuse and became convinced of the truth of her prophecies. He ordered his subjects to kill all their cattle and destroy their entire stock of corn. Disappointment followed disappointment as the dead failed to rise, but the movement was kept going by the desperation of the committed believers, who had slaughtered all their cattle and could no longer retreat from the path they had chosen. The fact that many Xhosa remained sceptical and refused to kill their cattle only incensed the believers and provided an excuse for the continued non-fulfilment of the prophecies. The situation was further exacerbated by the actions of Governor Sir George Grey, who took advantage of the catastrophe to break the power of the Xhosa chiefs and to free their land for colonial settlement.

The relationship between the two figures at the centre of the prophecies, Nongqawuse and Mhlakaza, remains unclear, but it would seem that Nongqawuse alone had visions which were subsequently interpreted by Mhlakaza. The only contemporary description of Nongqawuse, provided by a colonial spy, depicts her as 'a girl of about 16 years of age, has a silly look, and appeared to me as if she was not right in her mind' (Peires, 87). As the movement approached its climax, Nongqawuse seems to have become increasingly unable to cope with the consequences of her prophecies; she became sick, and her role as prophetess was taken over by her cousin Nombanda.

The prophecies peaked with the 'great disappointment' of February 1857 but the flames of despair kept it going until June 1857, when all hope was finally extinguished. By that time, more than 400,000 cattle had been killed and approximately 40,000 Xhosa had starved to death. Among these was Mhlakaza. Nongqawuse herself did not die, but fled across the Mbashe River into Bomvanaland. In March 1858 the chief of the Bomvana handed her over to Major John Gawler, a British magistrate responsible for implementing the policies of Governor Grey. Grey had set up a military tribunal with the purpose of convicting the Xhosa chiefs of levying war against the British crown. Gawler was charged with the task of preparing Nongqawuse as a witness in this dubious case. He brought her to

King William's Town, dressed her up, and had her photograph taken, but he was unable to get a coherent statement out of her, and the fragments that survive have clearly been doctored by colonial officials.

Nongqawuse and another prophet were taken by Major Gawler to Cape Town in October 1858, for purposes unknown. The two women were accommodated with other female Xhosa prisoners in the Paupers' Lodge, but after that Nongqawuse disappears from the official records. A colonial administrator mentioned in a passing reminiscence that she had married, and that she was living with her husband in the Alexandria district as late as 1905. Her reputed grave is located on the farm Glenthorn, and there is a plaque erected by local residents. But her journey to Alexandria and the exact nature of her relationship with the colonial officials remain, like so many other aspects of her life, a complete mystery.

J. B. PEIRES

Sources J. B. Peires, *The dead will arise: Nongqawuse and the great Xhosa cattle-killing movement of 1856–7* (1989) • W. W. Gqoba, 'The cause of the cattle-killing of the Nongqawuse period', in A. C. Jordan, *Towards an African literature* (1973), 70–75 • Examination of the kaffir prophetess Nonqause before Major Gawler, 27 April 1858, Cape archives, file Bk 14
Likenesses photograph, 1858, repro. in Peires, *Dead will arise*, facing p. 160

Noonan [*formerly* Croker], **Robert Philippe** [*pseud.* Robert Philippe Tressell] (**1870–1911**), author, was born Robert Philippe Croker on 18 April 1870 at 37 Wexford Street, Dublin. But the vastly influential novel for which he is known—*The Ragged Trousered Philanthropists*—was published posthumously and his true identity remained hidden until forty years after his death. He was the illegitimate son of Samuel Croker, a substantial man of property, resident magistrate, and retired inspector in the Royal Irish Constabulary, and Mary Noonan. Two other children were born from this union. Robert's father died when he was a boy, and his education, though good, was incomplete. By all accounts he was an exceptional linguist and skilful artist, but he served no apprenticeship despite working as a signwriter and housepainter from leaving school at sixteen until his death. In 1890 he emigrated to South Africa, where he lived comfortably and bought a plot of land. On 17 October 1891 in Cape Town he married Elizabeth Hartel (*b.* 1872/3); they had a daughter, Kathleen, the following year, but Elizabeth died shortly thereafter.

Noonan, as he now called himself, raised Kathleen alone, supplementing his artisan's income through journalism. In 1896 he moved to Johannesburg in the Transvaal, where with John (Sean) MacBride (executed in 1916 for his part in the Dublin Easter rising) and Arthur Griffiths, later president of the Irish republic, he helped form the Irish brigade, which fought against the British in the Second South African War. Before hostilities began in 1899, Noonan had returned to Cape Town and thence to Britain, where he settled in Hastings in 1901. Working in the building trade at subsistence wages, he contracted tuberculosis, was influenced by socialist writers such as Robert Blatchford, and became an active member of the unusually large Hastings branch of the Social Democratic Federation, whose banner he painted. He spent his spare time during the last ten years of his life writing by hand the 1800-page manuscript of *The Ragged Trousered Philanthropists*, which brought posthumous fame. In 1910, when his daughter was eighteen, Noonan determined to make a new start in Canada, but *en route* he was taken seriously ill in Liverpool, where, after living for a while in a workhouse, he died in the Royal Infirmary on 3 February 1911; he was buried in a pauper's grave in the city's Walton Park cemetery. In 1913 his daughter, Kathleen, sold his manuscript outright for £25 to the publisher Grant Richards, whose editor Jessie Pope cut the text to about 100,000 words; and this 'damnably subversive, but … extraordinarily real' novel (as Richards described it) was published in April 1914.

Although the title page of the manuscript is clearly signed Tressell (which was how Noonan wrote the word for a painter's trestle in his manuscript), for some unknown reason the author's name was printed as Tressall in the first edition and in the Grant Richards abridged cheap edition of 1918. Sardonic and satirical in tone, the novel's great strength is its minute and convincing observation of the hero's workmates, whose 'philanthropy' consists of letting employers reap the surplus value their labour produces. Its political argument, though crude, is powerful, and the use of names—Crass, Didlum, Graball, Slyme, and Sweater all live in Mugsborough—redolent of John Bunyan and Charles Dickens. The story covers a year in the life of Frank Owen, who tries to arouse his workmates to the evils of the system which exploits them, helped by the mysterious Barrington, an educated, middle-class man, who is another *alter ego* for the author. A clear, convincing, and often poignant narrative emerges; but Tressell was not a great creative writer and his development of plot and character is much weaker. Moreover, the inability (implied in the title) of the working class ever to see beyond their immediate circumstances makes their acceptance of socialism seem unlikely and gives the novel a pessimistic context. Nevertheless, it presents a unique view of early twentieth-century working-class life through the eyes of an articulate proletarian.

Reissued many times between the wars, *Philanthropists* was published in Canada, Germany, and the United States, with pirated translations appearing in Romania and the Soviet Union. Penguin Books published the abridged version in April 1940. By then it had sold, at a conservative estimate, more than 100,000 copies. Penguin reprinted it in May 1940, January 1941, and May 1942, with an Australian edition in October 1942, all widely read and lent on by soldiers during the Second World War, while the Richards Press printed eight abridged editions between 1944 and 1951, with a final Richards original version in 1954. By then F. C. Ball, who had spent his life researching Tressell, had fixed beyond reasonable doubt his Croker–Noonan identity and, equally important, located his manuscript. This was finally published in full (with his pseudonym spelt properly at last) in 1955 by Lawrence and Wishart, who subsequently reprinted it many times. This full text

has been published in the Soviet Union and translated into Bulgarian, Czech, French, German, Japanese, and Swahili. Stage adaptations have been frequent since the 1920s. BBC television broadcast one in 1967, the year in which Tressell's daughter, Kathleen, who was believed to have died in 1918, returned from years spent in Canada and was interviewed by a reporter from *The Times*; she later confirmed most of the facts of Tressell's life which F. C. Ball had established by years of tireless work.

PATRICK RENSHAW

Sources F. C. Ball, *One of the damned* (1973) · F. C. Ball, introduction, in *The Robert Tressell papers: exploring 'The ragged trousered philanthropists'*, Robert Tressell workshop (1982) · A. Sillitoe, introduction, in R. Tressell, *The ragged trousered philanthropists* (1965) · J. Mitchell, *Robert Tressell and 'The ragged trousered philanthropists'* (1969)
Likenesses three photographs, repro. in Ball, *One of the damned*, 42–3

Noorthouck, John (1732–1816), author, was born at his father's shop at the east corner of Milford Lane, the Strand, London, on 12 June 1732, the son of Harman Noorthouck (*c*.1704–1772), a bookseller. He left school at fourteen, having learned only 'plain reading, writing, and common arithmetic' (autobiography, fol. 4), and worked as his father's shop assistant. The family moved to Watford in 1746. Noorthouck was bound apprentice to his father at Stationers' Hall on 5 September 1749, the same day as his sister Sarah. Neither was freed until 5 December 1769. Noorthouck was admitted to the livery on 6 February 1770.

Noorthouck left Watford for London in 1757, and lived for many years in Barnard's Inn, Holborn, working as an indexer, press corrector, and miscellaneous writer. His first point of contact in London was Ralph Griffiths, publisher of the *Monthly Review* to which Noorthouck contributed until he resigned on 3 October 1793. 'The weakness of my eyes', he explained, 'will not go through what used to be moderate work; for candlelight, the principal light of a winter's day I dare not now use' (Noorthouck to R. Griffiths, Bodl. Oxf., MS Add. C.89).

Noorthouck is remembered for *A new history of London, including Westminster and Southwark, describing the public buildings, late improvements etc illustrated with copper-plates* (1773). In a *Proposal for a History of London* of February 1772 he explained that it was his intention 'to give … an account of the metropolis in a convenient size, and at a handy price'. He admitted that the work owed much to Stow, Strype, and Maitland, but its emphasis on the City and the livery halls gives it a value in its own right. The work shows Noorthouck's strong personal allegiance to the corporation and the Stationers' Company. He also compiled *An historical and classical dictionary, containing the lives and characters of the most eminent and learned persons in every age and nation* (2 vols., 1776), and an abstract calendar of the Stationers' Company court books, 1640–1779, which is still in regular use as a finding aid for scholars in the field.

Noorthouck's chambers in Barnard's Inn were destroyed by fire during the Gordon riots in June 1780. He remained in London until 1785, when an annuity of £20 bequeathed him by William Strahan, printer of the *Monthly Review*, allowed Noorthouck and his unmarried sister Sarah to move first to Peterborough and then to Oundle, Northamptonshire, where he died in July 1816. He was a bachelor. His sister Sarah was granted letters of administration of his goods on 16 August 1816. He left an unpublished autobiography which was offered for sale by the bookseller John Russell Smith in April 1852, and is now at Yale University. ROBIN MYERS

Sources J. Noorthouck, autobiography, Yale U., Beinecke L. • private information (2004) [L. F. Blitzer] • *DNB* • D. F. McKenzie, ed., *Stationers' Company apprentices*, [3]: *1701–1800* (1978) • apprenticeship, freedom, and livery registers and court books, Stationers' Hall, London, Stationers' Company Archives • letters, Bodl. Oxf., MS Add. C. 89 • J. Noorthouck, *Proposal for a history of London* (1772) • *GM*, 1st ser., 86/2 (1816), 188–9 • Nichols, *Illustrations*, 8.488–9

Archives Bodl. Oxf., letters to Ralph Griffiths • Stationers' Hall, London, Stationers' Company Archives, apprenticeship and freedom registers • Yale U., Beinecke L., autobiography

Wealth at death see administration, PRO, PROB 6/192/236

Nooth, John Mervin (1737–1828), physician and army officer, was born on 5 September 1737 at Sturminster Newton, Dorset, the son of Henry Nooth, apothecary, and his wife, Bridget, daughter of John Mervin, apothecary. He studied medicine at Edinburgh, graduating MD in 1766, and subsequently spent some time on the continent. In 1773 he was living in London and acquainted with some members of the Royal Society. Part of a letter he had written to Benjamin Franklin suggesting improvements to an electrical machine was read to the society in June 1773, and in the following March he was elected a fellow, Franklin being one of his sponsors.

The paper for which Nooth is chiefly remembered was read on 15 December 1774: 'The description of an apparatus for impregnating water with fixed air' (*PTRS*, 65, 1775, 59–66). 'Fixed air' was the name given to carbon dioxide in 1756 by Joseph Black, and the treatment of diseases, particularly those of a 'putrid' nature such as scurvy, by imbibing water impregnated with fixed air, had been advocated by Joseph Priestley. Nooth's apparatus for absorbing fixed air in water consisted of three glass vessels fitted together with airtight joints. Fixed air generated in the lowest vessel passed through a valve into water contained in the middle vessel. Any water displaced upwards by the gas entered the top vessel. The apparatus, which made possible the domestic production of 'spa water', was commercially successful, and large numbers were manufactured. A modified form of Nooth's apparatus was used in December 1846 to administer the ether in the first-known employment of a general anaesthetic in a surgical operation.

Probably shortly before Nooth's departure to New York in 1775, to take up an appointment as physician-extraordinary and purveyor to the forces, North America, he married Sarah Williams, a young widow. They had three children. Their two sons, John Mervin (1778–1821) and Henry (1781–1861), were born in New York and both had military careers. A third child, Mary, was born in Quebec in 1791 and died unmarried in 1846.

In 1779 Nooth became superintendent-general of hospitals for the British forces in North America. He returned to England in 1784, after the War of Independence was over, but was recalled to serve in Quebec in 1788. He took a great interest in the political and economic situation in Lower Canada, and corresponded on the subject, at great length, with Sir Joseph Banks. He left Canada in 1799, subsequently serving in Gibraltar, where his wife died in 1804, from 1804 to 1807. He retired to Bath in 1807 and on 19 August that year married a widow, Elizabeth Willford (1761–1850). He had acquired a high reputation, and in 1800 Edward, duke of Kent (the father of Queen Victoria), whom he had attended in Canada in 1798 after a riding accident, had appointed him physician to his household. Nooth died at his home, 12 Great Pulteney Street, Bath, on 3 May 1828, and was buried at St Nicholas, Bathampton.

E. L. SCOTT

Sources D. Zuck, 'Dr Nooth and his apparatus', *British Journal of Anaesthesia*, 50 (1978), 393–405 • D. Zuck, 'John Mervyn Nooth: an update', *Anaesthesia*, 48 (1993), 712–14 • private information (2004) • J. Priestley, *Directions for impregnating water with fixed air; in order to communicate to it the peculiar spirit and virtues of Pyrmont Water, and other mineral waters of a similar nature* (1772) • correspondence, J. Banks–J. M. Nooth, *Le Naturaliste Canadien*, 58 (1931), 139–47, 170–77 • W. Johnston, *Roll of commissioned officers in the medical services of the British army … 20 June 1727 to 23 June 1898*, ed. H. A. L. Howell (1917) • C. G. Roland, 'Nooth, John Mervin', *DCB*, vol. 6 • will, PRO, PROB 11/1742, sig. 371

Archives PRO, letters, 30/55

Wealth at death see will, PRO, PROB 11/1742, sig. 371

PICTURE CREDITS

Oxford dictionary of
national biography